Nov. 28–Dec. 1, 2011
Scottsdale, AZ, USA

Association for
Computing Machinery

Advancing Computing as a Science & Profession

MM'11

Proceedings of the 2011 ACM Multimedia Conference

Sponsored by:

ACM SIGMultimedia

Volume 1

Association for
Computing Machinery

Advancing Computing as a Science & Profession

The Association for Computing Machinery
2 Penn Plaza, Suite 701
New York, New York 10121-0701

Notice to Past Authors of ACM-Published Articles
ACM intends to create a complete electronic archive of all articles and/or other material previously published by ACM. If you have written a work that has been previously published by ACM in any journal or conference proceedings prior to 1978, or any SIG Newsletter at any time, and you do NOT want this work to appear in the ACM Digital Library, please inform permissions@acm.org, stating the title of the work, the author(s), and where and when published.

ISBN: 978-1-4503-0616-4 (Digital)

ISBN: 978-1-4503-1358-2 (Print)

Additional copies may be ordered prepaid from:

ACM Order Department
PO Box 30777
New York, NY 10087-0777, USA

Phone: 1-800-342-6626 (USA and Canada)
+1-212-626-0500 (Global)
Fax: +1-212-944-1318
E-mail: acmhelp@acm.org
Hours of Operation: 8:30 am – 4:30 pm ET

ACM Order Number: 433117

Printed in the USA

Message from the General Chairs

We are delighted to welcome you, on behalf of the entire organizing committee, to the 19th ACM International Conference on Multimedia ACM Multimedia 2011 (MM'11), held between November 28th and December 1st, 2011, in Scottsdale, Arizona, USA.

ACM Multimedia (MM) is the flagship conference of the Special Interest Group on Multimedia (SIGMM), which profiles cutting-edge scientific developments and showcases innovative industrial multimedia technologies and applications. The conference aims to promote intellectual exchanges and interactions among scientists, engineers, students, multimedia users, and artists through various events, including keynote talks from leaders in the area, oral and poster sessions focused on research challenges and solutions, workshops in up-and-coming key areas of research, technical and industrial demonstrations of prototypes and commercial products, tutorials, research and industrial panels, doctoral symposium, mentoring events, scientific competitions (including an open source software and a multimedia grand challenge competition), and interactive art exhibits.

Our key motivation while organizing the MM'11 conference was to find innovative ways to design an "inclusive" conference program: lowering the barriers between various MM sub-communities, boosting the cross-fertilization of ideas among the contributors and attendees across the various MM events, and maximizing the return-on-investment for the MM'11 participants. Examples of this new approach include the following:

- New plenary poster sessions, where *all* contributors (i.e., authors of long and short research papers, of workshop papers, and contributors to all other MM'11 events) are invited to share poster versions of their contributions with the rest of the MM'11 community. These plenary poster sessions allow conference participants to get a quick idea of interesting things happening in the multiple parallel sessions they cannot clone themselves to attend!
- Workshops were aligned with the other MM'11 events, instead of being held on a separate "workshops day" where many workshop participants never got to know the main conference and vice-versa. Our aim was to integrate workshops (which were chosen, in the first place, to represent emerging topics that complement the areas covered by the main technical program) organically with the other conference events and encourage broader participation by registrants in all conference and workshop programs.
- These innovations aimed to eliminate barriers in the program had to be supported by corresponding innovations in the MM'11 registration policies. Thus, we have instituted an "all-in-one" registration fee structure, which covers attendance to all MM'11 events, including presentation and poster sessions, panels, demonstrations, tutorials, and workshops.
- By keeping the overall registration fee lower than recent years and by shaving one day off from the conference program, we also reduced the overall participation cost for most of the MM'11 attendees.

A travel grants program, generously supported by the National Science Foundation (NSF) and SIGMM, also helped us lower the barrier for participation for many students and, as of this writing, a full 30% of the registrants to MM'11 are students. We also have a number of mentorship activities, including women mentoring event, organized and sponsored by SIGMM, a Doctoral Symposium program, which (in addition to having regular panels and presentations as before) this year opened up its doors to all student authors who want to present posters at the event, a panel on "*Job Opportunities and Career Perspective for Fresh Graduates of the Multimedia Community*", and a new "*vis-a-vis meeting with researchers*" social event where graduate students will meet and exchange ideas and receive guidance with internationally recognized researchers in their research area.

Of course, apart from the above, MM'11 also continued with programs that proved to be extremely successful in the past. We have continued with the well-established and highly successful Open Source Software Competition, with special emphasis this year on instructional open source software designed for educational use in teaching multimedia-related courses at undergraduate or graduate level. Like the previous years, the Multimedia Grand Challenges competition attracted challenges from many leaders of the multimedia industry, including HP, Technicolor, Nokia, Yahoo, Huwei, and 3D Life, and proposals from all over the world. Similarly, this year's industrial exhibits program, which complements the MM technical demonstrations program, will focus on cutting-edge research prototypes, including system and product demonstrations from many industrial leaders, such as IBM, FX Palo Alto Labs, Microsoft Research, Exalead, and Yacast. The panels program emphasizes opportunities and challenges faced by researchers, industry, and open-source communities in multimedia and thus covers timely topics, such as "*Smart Games*", "*Towards Synergy Between the Open Source and the Research Multimedia Communities*", and "*Innovating the Multimedia Experience*".

We are enthused to report that MM'11 includes three exciting keynote talks by three industry and academic leaders in multimedia research: Alex Pentland, Head of the MIT Human Dynamics Lab, Genevieve Bell, Director of the Interaction and Experience Research at the Intel Labs, and Arnaud Robert, Senior Vice President of Technology at The Walt Disney Studios. Last, but certainly not the least, we are proud that MM'11 hosts the prestigious SIGMM Technical Achievement Award presentation to Prof Shih-Fu Chang (Columbia University) and his award acceptance speech.

We would like to acknowledge those who have contributed to the success of MM'11. First of all, we would like to thank all authors who submitted papers to the technical program, various workshops, and other events of MM'11. We also thank the authors of the accepted papers who will present their work in MM'11 and the panelists and keynote speakers who have accepted to participate in the conference to discuss current and future challenges in the field of multimedia and to propose innovative solutions. We are grateful to the members of the various program committees and external reviewers who have helped put together a high-quality program and would like acknowledge members of the various MM'11 organizing committees and many student volunteers for their invaluable help at every step of the process. We would like to thank the staff of ACM and Sheridan for their continuous support and the Conference Management Toolkit Team (CMT) at Microsoft for letting us use CMT for handling the submission and review workflows of MM'11. Finally, we would like to thank our sponsors (as of this writing), Google, IBM, Microsoft, FxPal, Technicolor, Qualcomm, Springer, Yahoo!, Arizona State University, and the University of Texas at Dallas, who have extended their generous support to MM'11. We would also like to thank the National Science Foundation (NSF) and SIGMM for their generous support for the MM'11 student travel award program

We hope that you will enjoy the ACM MM'11 conference.

K. Selçuk Candan
Sethuraman (Panch) Panchanthan
Balakrishnan (Prabha) Prabhakaran
ACM MM'11 General Chairs

Message from the Technical Program Chairs

We have an exciting technical program at ACM Multimedia 2011. The process to select the technical program included several innovations. These innovations — guided by the recent report by a select SIG Multimedia committee — include the following: move to technical areas instead of tracks, each submitted paper had a primary area and an optional secondary area set by the authors at the time of submission, and an author rebuttal phase.

The ten areas were as follows:

- Multi-modal Integration and Understanding in the Imperfect World
- Media Analysis and Search
- Scalability in Media Processing, Analysis, and Applications
- Multimedia Systems and Middleware
- Media Transport and Sharing
- Multimedia Security
- Media Authoring and Production
- Location-based and Mobile Multimedia
- Human, Social, and Educational Aspects of Multimedia
- Arts and Contemporary Digital Culture

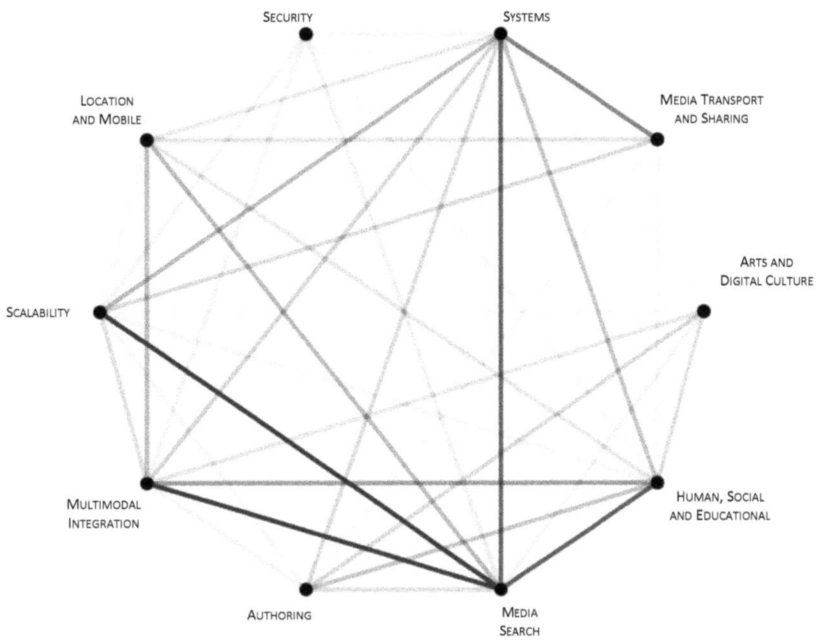

CROSS-LINKAGES BETWEEN PRIMARY AND SECONDARY AREAS

The areas — chosen in consultation with the broad SIG Multimedia community — reflect core research areas (e.g. multimedia systems and middleware), as well as different multimedia research contexts (e.g. location-based mobile multimedia). Typically, each area had two area chairs managing the review process; media analysis and search was an exception: due to the large number of submissions (39%), we assigned six area chairs to manage this area. The figure above shows the relationship between areas in the papers submitted for review— there is an edge between two areas when a paper has both areas specified in the paper. In the figure, edges with higher strength are more opaque.

Many authors specified both primary and secondary areas, resulting in the assignment of two reviewers from the primary area and one reviewer from the secondary area. In the minority of cases when there was no secondary area, we assigned all three reviewers from the primary area. The selection of reviewers from two different areas, allowed for a cross-disciplinary evaluation of the submitted paper. In past conferences a paper submitted to one of the four tracks was exclusively evaluated by reviewers from that track. Additionally, to increase the responsibility of the chairs as well as to give more credit to their work on their accepted paper, we have indicated the name of the AC that was supervising the reviewing process and which recommended the paper for acceptance.

The conference was highly competitive with low acceptance rates. We received a total of 666 submissions which included 335 long papers and 331 short papers. Subsequent to the initial notification, authors had one week to rebut the criticisms of the papers. After the rebuttal phase, the area chairs led a discussion with the reviewers on the merits of each paper, which included the author rebuttals. In the end, we accepted 58 long papers, with an acceptance rate of 17.3%, and 120 short papers with an acceptance rate of 36.3%. We additionally recommended 52 long papers to appear as short papers. The figure below shows the distribution of primary areas for all papers. We selected three papers were selected for the best paper and best student paper session. We solicited nominations from each area, for best student paper and best paper competition. The technical program chairs selected three from the nominations.

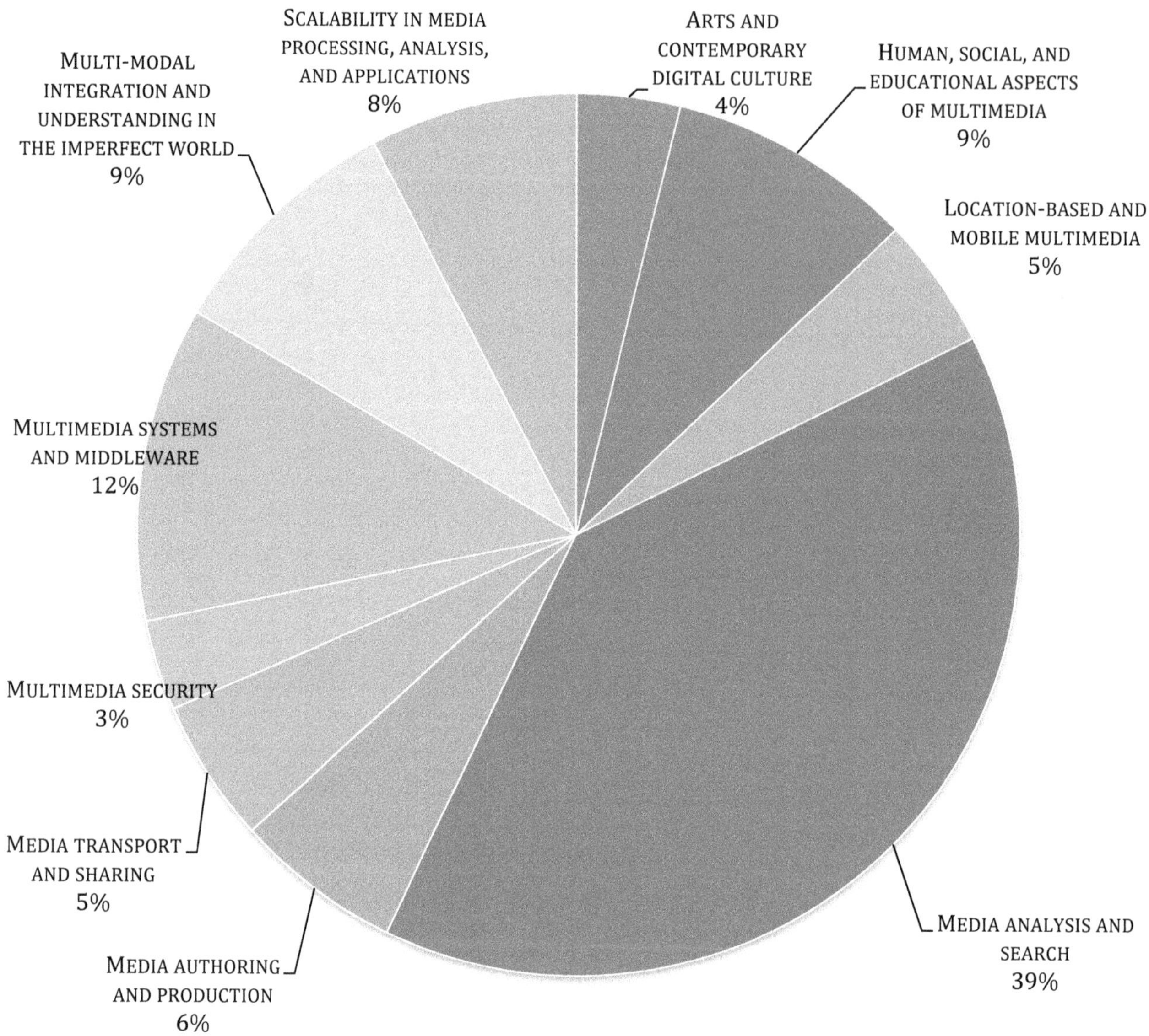

We would like to thank all of our area chairs and reviewers who volunteered a significant amount of their time to ensure a high quality program.

Hari Sundaram,
ACM MM'11,
Technical Program Chair
Arizona State University, USA

Wu-Chi Feng,
ACM MM'11,
Technical Program Chair
Portland State University, USA

Nicu Sebe,
ACM MM'11,
Technical Program Chair
University of Trento, Italy

Table of Contents

Session 3: Multi-modal Integration and Understanding in the Imperfect World

Session 4: Arts and Contemporary Digital Culture

Session 5: Media Transport and Sharing

Session 6: Media Authoring and Production 1

Session 7: Media Analysis and Search 1

Session 8: Media Authoring and Production 2

Session 9: Media Analysis and Search 2

Session 13: Media Analysis and Search 4

Session 14: Applications

Plenary Talk Sessions

Session Events

Panels

Workshop Overviews

Tutorial Overviews

Grand Challenge Session

Open Source Software Competition

Industrial Exhibits 1

Technical Demos 1

Industrial Exhibits 2

Technical Demos 2

Oral Presentation Session

Posters Session

ACM Multimedia 2011 Conference

General Chairs:	K. Selçuk Candan *(Arizona State University, USA)* Sethuraman Panchanathan *(Arizona State University, USA)* Balakrishnan Prabhakaran *(University of Texas at Dallas, USA)*
Local Arrangement Chairs:	Vineeth Nallure Balasubramanian *(Arizona State University, USA)* Baoxin Li *(Arizona State University, USA)*
Technical Program Committee Chairs:	Wu-Chi Feng *(Portland State University, USA)* Nicu Sebe *(University of Trento, Italy)* Hari Sundaram *(Arizona State University, USA)*
High-Risk High-Return Papers Chairs:	Ramesh Jain *(Portland State University, USA)* Ralf Steinmetz *(TU Darmstadt, Germany)* Svetha Venkatesh *(Curtin University, Australia)* Michelle Zhou *(IBM Research, USA)*
Multimedia Grand Challenge Chairs:	Gerald Friedland *(ICSI, University of California at Berkeley, USA)* Yohan Jin *(MySpace, Inc., USA)*
Tutorials Chairs:	Jiebo Luo *(University of Rochester, USA)* Thomas Plagemann *(University of Oslo, Norway)* Zhongfei Zhang *(Binghamton University, USA)*
Panels Chairs:	Shahram Ghandeharizadeh *(University of Southern California, USA)* Forouzan Golshani *(California State University Long Beach, USA)* Stefan Gobel *(TU Darmstadt, Germany)*
Technical Demo Chairs:	Vincent Charvillat *(University of Toulouse, France)* Shervin Shirmohammadi *(University of Ottawa, Canada)* Roger Zimmerman *(National University of Singapore, Singapore)*
Industrial Exhibit Chairs:	Deepak Turaga *(IBM T. J. Watson Research Center, USA)* Dulce Ponceleon *(IBM Almaden, USA)* Ajay Divakaran *(Sarnoff Corporation, USA)*
Workshop Chairs:	Jin Li *(Microsoft Research, USA)* Maria Luisa Sapino *(University of Turin, Italy)* Borko Furht *(Florida Atlantic University, USA)*
History Preservation Chairs:	Alberto Del Bimbo *(University of Florence, Italy)* Chabane Djeraba *(University of Lille, France)* Carsten Griwodz *(University of Oslo, Norway)*
Web Chairs:	Xiaohu Guo *(University of Texas at Dallas, USA)* Daragh Byrne *(Dublin City University, Ireland)*

Sponsorship Chairs:	Abdulmotaleb El Saddik *(University of Ottawa, Canada)* John R. Smith *(IBM T. J. Watson Research Center, USA)* Wolfgang Klas *(University of Vienna, Austria)* Yong Rui *(Microsoft Research Asia, China)*
Publicity and Social Media Chairs:	Romulus Grigoras *(University of Toulouse, France)* Marcel Worring *(University of Amsterdam, The Netherlands)* Laurent Amsaleg *(CNRS-IRISA, France)*
Doctoral Symposium Chairs:	Yu-Ru Lin *(Arizona State University, USA)* Vincent Oria *(NJIT, USA)*
Travel Grant Chairs:	Jong Wook Kim *(Teradata, USA)* Tao Mei *(Microsoft Research Asia, China)* Antonio Picariello *(University of Naples, Italy)*
Proceedings Chairs:	Marco Patella *(University of Bologna, Italy)* Xavier Anguera *(Telefonica R&D, Spain)*
Interactive Art Exhibit Chairs:	Todd Ingalls *(Arizona State University, USA)* David Tinapple *(Arizona State University, USA)*
Open Source Software Competition Chairs:	Wei-Tsang Ooi *(National University of Singapore, Singapore)* Pablo Cesar *(CWI, The Netherlands)*
Finance and Registration Chairs:	Ming Li *(California State University Fresno, USA)* Shu-Ching Chen *(Florida International University, USA)*
Industrial Panels Chairs:	Khaled El-Maleh *(Qualcomm, USA)* Haohong Wang *(TCL Research America, USA)*

ACM Multimedia 2011 Program Committees

Location-Based and Mobile Multimedia Chairs:
Gang Hua *(IBM Research, USA)*
Daniel Gatica-Perez *(Idiap Research Institute, Switzerland)*

Location-Based and Mobile Multimedia:
Jianfei Cai *(Nanyang Technical University, Singapore)*
Roberto Cesar *(University of San Paulo, Brazil)*
Tim Cheng *(University of California Santa Barbara, USA)*
Radek Grzeszczuk *(Nokia Research Center Palo Alto, USA)*
Ton Kalker *(Huawei Technologies, USA)*
Stephan Kopf *(University of Mannheim, Germany)*
Thommen Korah *(Nokia Research Center Hollywood, USA)*
Paisarn Muneesawang *(Naresuan University, Thailand)*
Timo Ojala *(University of Oulu, Finland)*
Nuria Oliver *(Telefonica, Spain)*
Michael Rohs *(University of Munich, Germany)*
Enrico Rukzio *(University of Duisburg-Essen, Germany)*
Eckehard Steinbach *(Munich University of Technology, Germany)*
Ye-Kui Wang *(Huawei Technologies, USA)*
Hongkai Xiong *(Shanghai Jiao Tong University, China)*
Yu Zheng *(Microsoft Research Asia, China)*

Scalability in Media Processing, Analysis, and Applications Chairs:
Xian-Sheng Hua *(Microsoft Research Asia, China)*
Lei Chen *(Hong Kong University of Science & Technology, China)*

Scalability in Media Processing, Analysis, and Applications:
Edward Chang *(Google Inc., USA)*
Michel Crucianu *(CNAM, France)*
Bin Cui *(Peking University, China)*
Alan Hanjalic *(TU Delft, The Netherlands)*
Ichiro Ide *(Nagoya University, Japan)*
Vincent Oria *(NJIT, USA)*
Malcolm Slaney *(Yahoo, USA)*
Jingdong Wang *(Microsoft Research Asia, China)*
Shuicheng Yan *(National University of Singapore, Singapore)*
Jun Yang *(Carnegie Mellon University, USA)*
Xiangmin Zhou *(CSIRO, Australia)*
Xiaofang Zhou *(University of Queensland, Australia)*

Multi-Modal Integration and Understanding in the Imperfect World Chairs:

Cees Snoek *(University of Amsterdam, The Netherlands)*
Marco Bertini *(University of Florence, Italy)*
Alexander Hauptmann *(Carnegie Mellon University, USA)*

Multi-Modal Integration and Understanding in the Imperfect World:

Andrea Cavallaro *(Queen Mary University of London, UK)*
Yinpeng Chen *(Arizona State University, USA)*
Stefanie Nowak *(Fraunhofer IDMT, Germany)*
Tamara Berg *(Stony Brook University, USA)*
Daragh Byrne *(Dublin City University, Ireland)*
Josep Casas *(Technical University of Catalonia, Spain)*
Rita Cucchiara *(University of Modena, Italy)*
Fernando de la Torre *(Carnegie Mellon University, USA)*
Abdulmotaleb El Saddik *(University of Ottawa, Canada)*
Benoit Huet *(Eurecom, France)*
Yu-Gang Jiang *(Columbia University, USA)*
Michael Lew *(Leiden University, The Netherlands)*
Rainer Lienhart *(Augsburg University, Germany)*
Wei-Hao Lin *(Google Inc., USA)*
Suzanne Little *(Open University, UK)*
Joao Magalhaes *(NOVA University of Lisbon, Portugal)*
Vasileios Mezaris *(ITI-CERTH, Greece)*
Adrian Ulges *(DFKI, Germany)*
Remco Veltkamp *(Utrecht University, The Netherlands)*
Rong Yan *(Facebook, USA)*
Ichiro Ide *(Nagoya University, Japan)*

Media Analysis and Search Chairs: Tat-Seng Chua *(National University of Singapore, Singapore)*
Lexing Xie *(Australian National University, Australia)*
Bernard Merialdo *(Eurecom, France)*
Marcel Worring *(University of Amsterdam, The Netherlands)*
Qi Tian *(University of Texas at San Antonio, USA)*
Kiyoharu Aizawa *(University of Tokyo, Japan)*

Media Analysis and Search: Laurent Amsaleg *(CNRS-IRISA, France)*
Xavier Anguera *(Telefonica R&D, Spain)*
Yiannis Avrithis *(NTUA, Greece)*
Noboru Babaguchi *(Osaka University, Japan)*
Juan Cao *(Chinese Academy of Sciences, China)*
Liangliang Cao *(University of Illinois at Urbana-Champaign, USA)*
Shih-Fu Chang *(Columbia University, USA)*
Xinyi Cui *(Rutgers University, USA)*
Mohamed Daoudi *(LIFL, France)*
Tri Do *(Idiap Research Institute, Switzerland)*
Dan Ellis *(Columbia University, USA)*
Ed Fox *(Virginia Tech, USA)*
Yuli Gao *(Google, Inc., USA)*
Zan Gao *(Beijing Univ. of Posts and Telecommunications, China)*
Mei Han *(Google, Inc., USA)*
Allan Hanbury *(Vienna University of Technology, Austria)*
Richard Hong *(Hefei University of Technology, China)*
Winston Hsu *(National Taiwan University, Taiwan)*
Hayley Hung *(University of Amsterdam, The Netherlands)*
Rongrong Ji *(Columbia University, USA)*
Qifa Ke *(Microsoft Research, USA)*
Lyndon Kennedy *(Yahoo! Research, USA)*
Yannis Kompatsiaris *(CERT-IT, Greece)*
Jiebo Luo *(University of Rochester, USA)*
R Manmatha *(University of Massachusetts Amherst, USA)*
Stéphane Marchand-Maillet *(University of Geneva, Switzerland)*
Tao Mei *(Microsoft Research, USA)*
Frank Nack *(University of Amsterdam, The Netherlands)*
Paul Natsev *(IBM Research, USA)*
Chong Wah Ngo *(City University of Hong Kong, China)*
Noel O'Connor *(CLARITY, Ireland)*
Bo Qiu *(Institute for Infocomm Research, Singapore)*
Shinichi Satoh *(NII, Japan)*
Behzad Shahraray *(AT&T Labs Research, USA)*
Heng Tao Shen *(University of Queensland, Australia)*

Media Analysis and Search (continued):

Jialie Shen *(Singapore Management University, Singapore)*
Alan Smeaton *(Dublin City University, Ireland)*
Julian Stottinger *(Vienna University of Technology, Austria)*
Hao Tang *(HP Labs, USA)*
Jinhui Tang *(Nanjing University of Science and Technology, China)*
Jasper Uijlings *(University of Trento, Italy)*
Koen Van de Sande *(University of Amsterdam, The Netherlands)*
Roelof van Zwol *(Yahoo! Research, USA)*
Jun Wang *(IBM Research, USA)*
Meng Wang *(National University of Singapore, Singapore)*
Ye Wang *(National University of Singapore, Singapore)*
Lynn Wilcox *(FX PAL, USA)*
Xiao Wu *(Southwest Jiaotong University, China)*
Zhipeng Wu *(University of Tokyo, Japan)*
Dong Xu *(Nanyang Technical University, Singapore)*
Eric Zavesky *(AT&T Labs Research, USA)*
Zheng-Jun Zha *(National University of Singapore, Singapore)*
Cha Zhang *(Microsoft Research, USA)*
Lei Zhang *(Microsoft Research Asia, China)*

Media Authoring and Production Chairs:

Susanne Boll *(University of Oldenburg, Germany)*
Dick Bulterman *(CWI, The Netherlands)*

Media Authoring and Production:

Cyril Concolato *(Telecom ParisTech , France)*
Ritendra Datta *(Google Inc., USA)*
Andreas Girgensohn *(FX PAL, USA)*
Luiz Fernando Gomes Soares *(PUC-RIO, Brasil)*
Fons Kuijk *(CWI, The Netherlands)*
Rodrigo Laiola Guimaraes *(CWI, The Netherlands)*
Qian Lin *(HP Labs, USA)*
Wei-Hao Lin *(Google Inc., USA)*
Feng Liu *(Portland State University, USA)*
Frank Nack *(University of Amsterdam, The Netherlands)*
Maria Pimentel *(ICMC-USP, Brasil)*
Cecile Roisin *(Grenoble University – INRIA, France)*
Lloyd Rutledge *(Open University, The Netherlands)*
Ansgar Scherp *(University of Koblenz-Landau, Germany)*
Jacco van Ossenbruggen *(VU University, The Netherlands)*

Multimedia Systems and Middleware

Chairs: Pål Halvorsen *(University of Oslo, Norway)*
Wei-Tsang Ooi *(National University of Singapore, Singapore)*

Multimedia Systems and Middleware: Dewan Tanvir Ahmed *(University of Ottawa, Canada)*
Laszlo Boszormenyi *(Klagenfurt University, Austria)*
Vincent Charvillat *(IRIT - University of Toulouse, France)*
Sheng-Wei Chen *(Academia Sinica, Taiwan)*
Yen-Kuang Chen *(Intel, USA)*
Touradj Ebrahimi *(EPFL, Switzerland)*
Alexander Eichhorn *(Simula Research Lab, Norway)*
Romulus Grigoras *(University of Toulouse, France)*
Ravindra Guntur *(National University of Singapore, Singapore)*
Hermann Hellwagner *(Klagenfurt University, Austria)*
Andreas Mauthe *(Lancaster University, UK)*
Ketan Mayer-Patel *(UNC-Chapel Hill, USA)*
Sebastien Mondet *(University of Oslo, Norway)*
Klara Nahrstedt *(University of Illinois at Urbana-Champaign, USA)*
Nabil Sarhan *(Wayne State University, USA)*
Karsten Schwan *(Georgia Institute of Technology, USA)*
Timothy Shih *(National Central University, Taiwan)*
Ralph Steinmetz *(TU Darmstadt, Germany)*
Jingtao Wen *(Tsinghua University, China)*
Chuan Wu *(University of Hong Kong, China)*
Ja-Ling Wu *(National Taiwan University, Taiwan)*
Michael Zink *(University of Massachusetts Amherst, USA)*

Human, Social, and Educational Aspects of Multimedia Chairs:

Massimo Zancanaro *(Fondazione Bruno Kessler, Italy)*
Mor Naaman *(Rutgers University, USA)*

Human, Social, and Educational Aspects of Multimedia:

Elisabeth Andre *(University of Augsburg, Germany)*
Tico Ballagas *(Nokia Research Palo Alto, USA)*
Frank Bentley *(Motorola Mobility Applied Research Center, USA)*
K. Selçuk Candan *(Arizona State University, USA)*
Marc Cavazza *(University of Teesside, UK)*
Pablo Cesar *(CWI, The Netherlands)*
Keith Cheverst *(Lancaster University, UK)*
Gregorio Convertino *(Palo Alto Research Center, USA)*
Matthew Cooper *(FX PAL, USA)*
Aiden Doherty *(University of Oxford, UK)*
Berna Erol *(Ricoh California Research Center, USA)*
Leonardo Giusti *(MIT, USA)*
Erik Grönvall *(Aarhus University, Denmark)*
Alex Jaimes *(Yahoo! Research, USA)*
Ramesh Jain *(University of California Irvine, USA)*
Antonio Krueger *(DFKI, Germany)*
Oswald Lanz *(Fondazione Bruno Kessler, Italy)*
Bruno Lepri *(Fondazione Bruno Kessler, Italy)*
Venet Osmani *(CREATE-NET, Italy)*
Matthias Rehm *(University of Aalborg, Denmark)*
Nicu Sebe *(University of Trento, Italy)*
Börkur Sigurbjörnsson *(Yahoo! Research, USA)*
Ramanathan Subramanian *(University of Trento, Italy)*
Hari Sundaram *(Arizona State University, USA)*
Raphael Troncy *(Eurecom, France)*
Svetha Venkatesh *(Curtin University, Australia)*
Justin Weisz *(IBM T.J. Watson Research, USA)*
Michelle Zhou *(IBM Research, USA)*

Arts and Contemporary Digital Culture Chairs: Aisling Kelliher *(Arizona State University, USA)*
David A. Shamma *(Yahoo! Research, USA)*

Arts and Contemporary Digital Culture: Barbara Barry *(One Laptop Per Child, USA)*
Joanna Berzowska *(Concordia University, Canada)*
Elizabeth Churchill *(Yahoo! Research, USA)*
Luca Farulli *(Academy of Fine Arts of Venice, Italy)*
Karrie Karahalios *(Univ. of Illinois at Urbana-Champaign, USA)*
Jofish Kaye*(Nokia Research Palo Alto, USA)*
Andruid Kerne *(Texas A&M, USA)*
Ann Morrison *(HIIT, Finland)*
Edgar Roman-Rangel *(Idiap Research Institute, Switzerland)*
Jurgen Scheible *(Aalto University, Finland)*
Sha Xin Wei *(Concordia University, Canada)*

Open Source Software Competition Chairs: Wei-Tsang Ooi *(National University of Singapore, Singapore)*
Pablo Cesar *(CWI, The Netherlands)*

Open Source Software Competition Evaluation Members: John Adcock *(FX PAL, USA)*
Xavier Amatriain Rubio *(Netflix, USA)*
Marco Bertini *(University of Florence, Italy)*
Andrea Vedaldi *(Oxford University, UK)*
Mathias Lux *(Klagenfurt University, Austria)*
Ye Wang *(National University of Singapore, Singapore)*
Ketan Mayer-Patel *(UNC-Chapel Hill, USA)*
Sebastien Mondet *(University of Oslo, Norway)*
Hendrik Knoche *(EPFL, Switzerland)*
Pavel Korshunov *(EPFL, Switzerland)*
Cyril Concolato *(Telecom ParisTech , France)*

Multimedia Grand Challenge Chairs: Gerald Friedland *(ICSI, University of California at Berkeley, USA)*
Yohan Jin *(MySPace, Inc., USA)*

Multimedia Grand Challenge: Patrick Perez *(Technicolor, France)*
Qian Lin *(HP Labs, USA)*
Kaushal Kurapati *(Yahoo! Research, USA)*
Timo Pekka Pylvanainen *(Nokia Research Center Tampere, Finland)*

Doctoral Symposium Chairs: Yu-Ru Lin *(Arizona State University, USA)*
Vincent Oria *(NJIT, USA)*

Doctoral Symposium: Cristian Borcea, *(NJIT, USA)*
K. Selçuk Candan *(Arizona State University, USA)*
Cees Snoek *(University of Amsterdam, The Netherlands)*
Michelle Zhou *(IBM Research, USA)*
Michel Crucianu *(CNAM, France)*
Surendar Chandra *(FX PAL, USA)*
Valerie Gouet-Brunet *(CNAM, France)*
Maria Luisa Sapino *(University of Turin, Italy)*
Ichiro Ide *(Nagoya University, Japan)*
Shinichi Satoh *(NII, Japan)*

ACM Multimedia 2011 Additional Reviewers

Parag Agarwal *(Microsoft, USA)*
Nikolaus Bee *(Augsburg University, Germany)*
Joan-Isaac Biel *(Idiap Research Institute, Switzerland)*
Damian Borth *(DFKI, Germany)*
Liangliang Cao *(IBM Research, USA)*
Axel Carlier *(National University of Singapore, Singapore)*
Robert Ming-Yu Chen *(Carnegie Mellon University, USA)*
Shu-Ching Chen *(Florida International University, USA)*
Yan-Ying Chen *(National Taiwan University, Taiwan)*
Wen-Huang Cheng *(Academia Sinica, Taiwan)*
Zhiyong Cheng *(Singapore Management University, Singapore)*
Tzu-Hsuan Chiu *(National Taiwan University, Taiwan)*
Wei-Ta Chu *(Nanyang Technical University, Singapore)*
Sashikanth Damaraju *(Texas A&M University, USA)*
Chi Tai Dang *(Augsburg University, Germany)*
Daisuke Deguchi *(Nagoya University, Japan)*
Lei Ding *(Ohio State University, USA)*
Cem Direkoglu *(Dublin City University, Ireland)*
Lixin Duan *(Nanyang Technical University, Singapore)*
Abdallah El Ali *(University of Amsterdam, The Netherlands)*
Gwenn Englebienne *(University of Amsterdam, The Netherlands)*
Marin Ferecatu *(CNAM, France)*
Rogerio Feris *(IBM Research, USA)*
Mingchen Gao *(Rutgers University, USA)*
Thomas Gloe *(Dresden University of Technology, Germany)*
Luke Gottlieb *(International Computer Science Institute, USA)*
Benjamin Guthier *(University of Mannheim, Germany)*
William Hamilton *(Texas A&M University, USA)*
Matthew Hill *(IBM Research, USA)*
Steven Hoi *(Nanyang Technical University, Singapore)*
Liang-Chi Hsieh *(National Taiwan University, Taiwan)*
Min-Chun Hu *(Nanyang Technical University, Singapore)*
Minqing Hu *(Teradata, USA)*
Chun-Hsiang Huang *(Nanyang Technical University, Singapore)*
Adam Janin *(International Computer Science Institute, USA)*
Matthias Kirchner *(Dresden University of Technology, Germany)*
Felix Kistler *(Augsburg University, Germany)*
Yin-Hsi Kuo *(National Taiwan University, Taiwan)*
Namhee Kwon *(Incentica Lab, USA)*
Wen-Yu Lee *(National Taiwan University, Taiwan)*
Tayeb Lemlouma *(IRISA, France)*
Chuanjun Li *(PROS Pricing, USA)*
Xirong Li *(University of Amsterdam, The Netherlands)*
Yen-Liang Lin *(National Taiwan University, Taiwan)*
Dong Liu *(Columbia University, USA)*
Tinglin Liu *(Rutgers University, USA)*
Wei Liu *(Columbia University, USA)*
Zhiyuan Liu *(Google Inc., USA)*
Zhu Liu *(AT&T Labs, USA)*
Wenjun Lu *(University of Maryland, USA)*
Mathias Lux *(Klagenfurt University, Austria)*
Zhigang Ma *(University of Trento, Italy)*
Kevin McGuinness *(Dublin City University, Ireland)*
Michele Merler *(Columbia University, USA)*
Robert Mertens *(International Computer Science Institute, USA)*
David Monaghan *(Dublin City University, Ireland)*
Joe Munoz *(Hatch Labs, USA)*
Spiros Nikolopoulos *(CERTH, Greece)*
Naoko Nitta *(Osaka University, Japan)*
Yin Qu *(Texas A&M University, USA)*
Giuseppe Rizzo *(Eurecom, France)*
Daniel Rule *(MySpace, USA)*
Philipp Schaber *(University of Mannheim, Germany)*
Klaus Schöffmann *(Klagenfurt University, Austria)*
Christian Schulze *(DFKI, Germany)*
Sancho Sebastine *(Datran Media,USA)*
Xiance Si *(Google Inc., USA)*
Jacopo Staiano *(University of Trento, Italy)*
Junwoon Suh *(Sarnoff Corporation, USA)*

Myunghoon Suk *(University of Texas at Dallas, USA)*
Jichao Sun *(NJIT, USA)*
Tomokazu Takahashi *(Gifu Shotoku Gakuen University, Japan)*
Yan Tang *(AMD, USA)*
Giorgos Tolias *(NTUA, Greece)*
Avinash Varna *(Intel, USA)*
Johannes Wagner *(Augsburg University, Germany)*
Yichu Wang *(University of California, Santa Barbara, USA)*
Zhiyu Wang *(Google Inc., USA)*
Hazem Wannous *(Telecom Lille, France)*
Andrew Webb *(Texas A&M University, USA)*
Kenji Yamada *(AT&T Interactive, USA)*
Keiji Yanai *(University of Electro-Communications, Japan)*
Xin Yang *(University of California Santa Barbara, USA)*
Victoria Yanulevskaya *(University of Trento, Italy)*
Xiangqian Yu *(NJIT, USA)*
Gloria Zen *(University of Trento, Italy)*
Shaoting Zhang *(Rutgers University, USA)*
Lin Zhong *(Rutgers University, USA)*

ACM Multimedia 2011 Sponsors & Supporters

Financial Support Provided by the Following Sponsors:

Gold:

Silver:

Bronze:

Contributor:

Student Travel Award Provided by the Following Federal Agency:

Keynote Talk

Content Based Multimedia Retrieval: Lessons Learned from Two Decades of Research

Shih-Fu Chang
Columbia University, New York, NY, USA
sc250@columbia.edu

Abstract

In the past two decades, we have witnessed bourgeoning research on content based multimedia information retrieval, covering a wide range of topics such as feature extraction, content matching, structure parsing, semantic annotation, multimodal analysis, 3D content retrieval, and user-in-the-loop interaction. More than ten years have also passed since the publication of the influential survey paper by Smeulders *et al* on content based image retrieval. Recently, exciting solutions are emerging in several practical contexts such as mobile media search, augmented reality, and Web-scale copy detection. However, many fundamental problems remain open, including but not limited to large-scale semantic annotation, multimedia ontological organization, and human-machine interaction for searching complex events. In this talk, I will discuss lessons learned from our past research, drawing from successes and failures in developing and deploying a few image/video search systems in different domains, and then share views about promising future directions.

Categories & Subject Descriptors: Information Systems, Information Storage and Retrieval

General Terms: Algorithms, Experimentation, Human Factors

Bio

Shih-Fu Chang is the Richard Dicker Professor in the Departments of Electrical Engineering and Computer Science, and Director of Digital Video and Multimedia Lab at Columbia University, where he has also co-led the ADVENT research consortium sponsored by more than 25 industrial partners. With more than 400 published papers and 25 patents, he has made influential contributions to multimedia retrieval, communication, and security. He has received ACM SIGMM Technical Achievement Award in 2011, IEEE Kiyo Tomiyasu Award in 2009 (for pioneer contributions to image classification and search), IBM Faculty Award, ACM Recognition of Service Award, Navy ONR Young Investigator Award, and NSF CAREER Award. Work by him and his collaborators has been recognized with many Paper Awards, including the Most Cited Paper of the Decade Award from JVCIR. He is a Fellow of IEEE and the American Association for the Advancement of Science (AAAS). He served as General Co-Chair of ACM MM (2000 and 2010), Editor-in-Chief for IEEE Signal Processing Magazine (2006-8), and Chair of Columbia's Electrical Engineering Department (2007-2010).

MM'11, November 28–December 1, 2011, Scottsdale, Arizona, USA.
ACM 978-1-4503-0616-4/11/11.

Active Query Sensing for Mobile Location Search

Felix X. Yu
Dept. of Electrical Engineering
Columbia University
New York, NY 10027
yuxinnan@ee.columbia.edu

Rongrong Ji
Dept. of Electrical Engineering
Columbia University
New York, NY 10027
rrji@ee.columbia.edu

Shih-Fu Chang
Dept. of Electrical Engineering
Columbia University
New York, NY 10027
sfchang@ee.columbia.edu

ABSTRACT

While much exciting progress is being made in mobile visual search, one important question has been left unexplored in all current systems. When the first query fails to find the right target (up to 50% likelihood), how should the user form his/her search strategy in the subsequent interaction? In this paper, we propose a novel *Active Query Sensing* system to suggest the best way for sensing the surrounding scenes while forming the second query for location search. We accomplish the goal by developing several unique components – an offline process for analyzing the saliency of the views associated with each geographical location based on score distribution modeling, predicting the visual search precision of individual views and locations, estimating the view of an unseen query, and suggesting the best subsequent view change. Using a scalable visual search system implemented over a NYC street view data set (0.3 million images), we show a performance gain as high as two folds, reducing the failure rate of mobile location search to only 12% after the second query. This work may open up an exciting new direction for developing interactive mobile media applications through innovative exploitation of active sensing and query formulation.

Categories and Subject Descriptors

H.4 [**Information Systems Applications**]: Miscellaneous; I.4 [**Image Processing and Computer Vision**]: [Scene Analysis, Object recognition]

General Terms

Algorithms, System, Measurement

Keywords

Mobile Visual Search, Mobile Location Recognition, Active Query Sensing, Content-based Image Retrieval

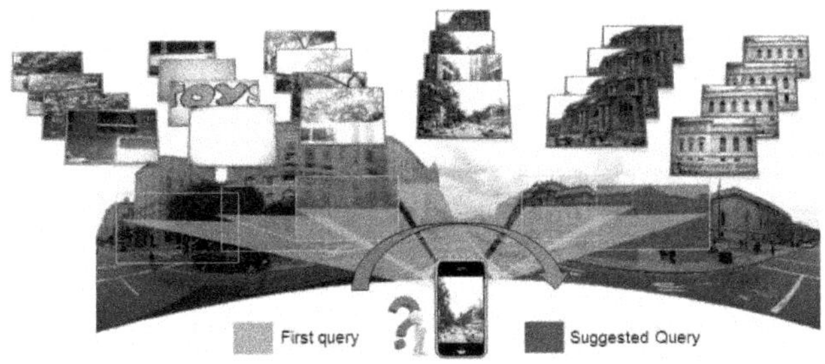

Figure 1: In mobile location search, the initial query often fails, as indicated by the incorrect matching results (in red). We propose Active Query Sensing to suggest the best view for subsequent queries (shown in blue) without leaving users to trials and errors.

1. INTRODUCTION

As mobile handheld devices become pervasive, new applications like mobile media search emerge. One promising example is searching information about products, locations, or landmarks, by taking a photograph of the target of interest using the mobile device. The captured image is used as a query, sent over the mobile network to the server in which reference images of the candidate objects or locations are matched in order to recognize the true target. Such mobile visual search functionalities have been shown recently in commercial systems, such as snaptell [1], Nokia point and find [2], kooaba [3], and a few research prototypes [4][5][6]. One of the most interesting topics with wide applications is the mobile location search [6][7]. Mobile location search offers a service complementary to GPS or network based localization, because the recognized location may be more precise and no satellite or cellular network infrastructures are needed.

Mobile location search systems mentioned above are built based on image matching, whose success depends on the separability of image content associated with different targets (inter-class distance), divergence of content among reference images of the same target (within-class variation), and distortion added to the query image during the mobile imaging process. Ideally, every view of a target location can be used as a query to successfully recognize the true target, correctly rejecting others.

However, not every view[1] of a location is distinctive enough to be used as a successful query, as illustrated in Figure 1.

[1]We use a generic term "view" to refer to the orientation, scale, and location for taking the image as the mobile visual query input.

Figure 2: The geographical distribution of the five routes in the NAVTEQ New York City data set, which covers 0.3 million street view images taken from 50,000 locations.

Figure 3: (a) The visual coverage of six cameras in the NAVTEQ NYC data set. (b) Typical example of six photos in one location (the Metropolitan Museum of Art) of the NYC street view data set.

In an experiment to be described later in the paper, only 47% of locations are successfully recognized when the online mobile query is taken from an arbitrary view. When it fails, incorrect locations with visually similar appearances are returned as the top match. Such performance appears to be consistent with the modest accuracy (0.4-0.7 average precision) reported in the state-of-the-art systems [8][4][6][9] for mobile location search. Several exciting research directions are being pursued to advance the state of the art and reduce the recognition errors. Discussion of the related works will be presented in Section 5.

Different from prior works, in this paper we focus on a novel aspect of improving the mobile visual search experience. We hypothesize that there exist unique preferred views for successful recognition of each target location. For example, some views of a location consist of unique "signature" attributes that are distinctively different from others. Other views may contain common objects (trees, walls, *etc.*) that are much less distinctive. When searching for specific targets, queries using such unique preferred views will lead to much better recognition results. To this end, we propose an automated **A**ctive **Q**uery **S**ensing (**AQS**) system to automatically determine the best view for visual sensing to take the visual query.

Fully automatic AQS is difficult to achieve for the initial query because the user location is unknown to the system a priori. Thus location-specific information is missing for determining the best view for query. Although some prior information (like GPS or previously seen locations plus trajectories) may be available for predicting the likely current locations, it is not always reliable. As a result, we adopt a more pragmatic goal, aiming at significantly improving the success rate of the second query if and after the first query fails. This will bring major improvements over today's systems, in which users are often left helpless and have to appeal to repetitive trials and errors after the first query fails.

Specifically, we present an innovative AQS system that includes two major components of both offline salient view learning and online active query sensing:

- First, we have developed automatic methods for assessing the "saliency" of views associated with a location. Such saliency measures are derived from offline analysis of the matching scores between a given view and other images (including those of the same location and different locations), unique image features contained in the view, or combinations of these two. We found the proposed saliency measure can provide much more reliable predictions about the best query views, compared with alternatives using random selection or the dominant view.
- Second, we use the first query as a "probe" to narrow down the search space and form a small set of candidate locations, from each of which the first query is aligned, then the optimal view change (*e.g.*, turn to the right of the first query view) is predicted[2] in order to sense the discriminative view for the next query.

The proposed AQS system is general, without requiring special hardware on mobile devices. It is applicable to any visual location search system in which each location is associated with multiple reference views. Using a large database of about 50,000 locations (300,000 street view images), we will demonstrate the power of the proposed AQS system in significantly reducing the location search error.

The rest of the paper is organized as follows. In Section 2, we present a case study over the NAVTEQ street view data set as further justification of the proposed Active Query Sensing idea. Section 3 includes an overview of the AQS system and constituent components, including the basic visual matching component suitable for large scale data sets, the offline salient view analysis, the online query alignment, and the best query view suggestion. Section 4 shows the quantitative evaluation and in-depth analysis of the results. We discuss related works and summarize novel contributions of this work in Section 5. Finally, in Section 6, we present conclusions and open research problems.

2. CASE STUDY AND PROBLEM JUSTIFICATION

To further motivate the problem, we present a brief summary of a case study of mobile location search using a NAVTEQ data set captured in Manhattan of New York City. Details about implementations of the visual search system will be described in Section 3 of the paper.

2.1 NAVTEQ 0.3M NYC Data Set

The data set consists of close to 300,000 images of about 50,000 locations in Manhattan collected by the NAVTEQ street view imaging system during September and October of 2009 over 5 routes, as shown in Figure 2. Each geographical location contains six surrounding views separated by 45 degrees. Note the right rear view and the rear view are

[2]For each location in the database, we have multiple image samples with parametric viewing angles.

Figure 4: Location dependent visual distinctiveness. (a) Percentage of locations in the test query set (cropped from Google Street View) with different numbers of searchable views. About 87% of locations have a partial set of views (1 to 5) that can be used to successfully recognize the right locations, confirming the need of prudent query view selection. (b) Distribution of the test query locations with different degrees of searchability over the NYC Manhattan map.

Figure 5: Two exemplar image panoramas in the NAVTEQ NYC data set.

not covered in this setup. The locations are imaged at a four meter interval on average. The view orientations are shown in Figure 3 (a) and a typical example of six photos of a location is shown in Figure 3 (b). In addition, for each location there is also a panorama image captured by the panoramic camera (Ladybug 3), as shown in Figure 5. Both reference images and panoramas are geo-tagged based on the GPS system plus the Inertial Measurement Unit (IMU) and Distance Measurement Instrument (DMI) on the mobile imaging vehicle.

In this preliminary case study, we simulate the mobile location search scenarios by creating a test set using the Google Street View interface. We manually cropped queries from Google Street View (Figure 7) in 226 randomly chosen locations covered by the above mentioned routes in NYC. Although such test images are less ideal compared to real photos captured by mobile phones, we use them for initial testing since they are quite different from the reference images in the NAVTEQ data set and many challenging conditions (like occlusion and time change) are presented.

For each location, six query images are cropped from viewing angles similar to the view orientations used in the database (as shown in Figure 3 (a)). This results in 1,356 images with angles and ground truth locations tags. For each query image, we consider a returned reference image as relevant if it has visual overlap with the query image, as shown in Figure 3. Due to the fixed geometry and interval used in image acquisition, the ground truths of each query result set can be computed without the laborious manual annotation. Depending on the viewing angle of a reference image, the number of relevant images in the database varies, *e.g.* the front view has more relevant images as its field of view overlaps with more images. Note this is different from the ground truth definition for locations that based on a certain distance threshold.

2.2 Location Dependence and Need of Active Query Sensing

For each simulated query image from each of the random locations, we find the most likely location (among the 50,000 locations in the database) that has the highest aggregated matching scores between the query image and the multiple views associated with the location. Details of the matching process will be described in Section 3.1. A returned location is considered correct if it is within a distance threshold from the query location. Setting the appropriate threshold needs to consider several factors, such as the application requirements and the visual overlap of reference images. We set it to 200 meters in this initial study since two locations may still share overlapped views at this distance in our data set. Figure 4 (a) shows the proportions of the test locations that can be correctly recognized, broken to groups that can be recognized by a different number of searchable views (0 to 6). 11.1% of the locations cannot be recognized using any of the views cropped from the same location on Google Street View. This appears to validate our assumption that there is sufficient content difference between the reference images in the NAVTEQ database and the simulated test images cropped from Google Street View. Only 3.5% of the locations can be correctly recognized by all of their six constituent views. The rest of locations (85.4%) are recognizable only with a subset of the views, with most locations being searchable by 3 of the 6 views. This supports our hypothesis presented in Section 1 - each location has a unique subset of preferred views for recognition and the problem of automatically determining such preferred views are interesting and practical. In addition, only 42.1% of the test query images from Google Street View were successful. This indicates that if a mobile user randomly selects views for location search, more than half of the times he/she will not get correct results (even though the distance threshold was set to be quite generous, say 200m). This again validates the motivation of AQS.

Another important finding is *Location Dependence.* Figure 4 (b) shows the distribution of the locations with different numbers of searchable views. It's clear that different locations have different degrees of "difficulty" - some have more searchable angles than others. Additionally, locations of the same search difficulty do not significantly cluster together. This implies that any active query suggestion solution needs to be location adaptive and take into account the unique characteristics of the query in an online fashion. Finally, we also find there is no single dominant view that can successfully recognize all locations, though some views (*e.g.*, the front view) are more effective than others.

In addition, this Location Dependence assumption forms another basis of our Active Query Sensing: Only in the case

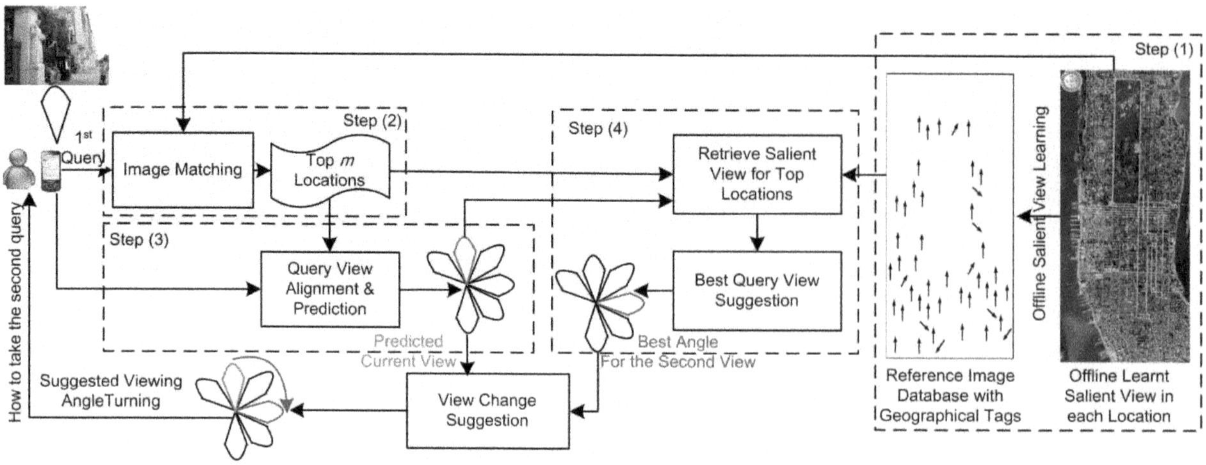

Figure 6: The architecture and process flow of the proposed Active Query Sensing system.

Figure 7: The Google Street View interface is used to crop images to simulate online mobile queries.

that the mobile visual search results are "Location Dependent", we need Active Query Sensing. Otherwise we can always suggest the mobile user a "dominant" view, say pointing at the middle of the street (the front view) *etc.* We also find that only 3.5% of locations can be correctly searched when using a random query viewing angle. It means random selection of query view has a big gap from this "search bound", which is the ultimate goal of our active query sensing.

3. ACTIVE QUERY SENSING

Two fundamental components are needed in developing a mobile AQS system to actively suggest the best query view for searching each location that user might be interested in. First, an offline analysis is needed to discover the best query view(s) for each location indexed by the system. Second, an online mapping process is needed to estimate the most likely view of the first query (which has failed). Afterwards, an online step based on the majority voting principle is used to suggest the most beneficial view change to the user in order to form the next query.

Figure 6 shows the overall architecture and the process flow of the proposed AQS system. Given the first query submitted by the user, the image matching component (Section 3.1) computes the scores for the reference images and returns the top candidate locations. Assuming the top returned location is incorrect[3], the active view suggestion process kicks in. First, the most likely view of the current query image is estimated through coarse classification of the query image to some of the predefined views (*e.g.*, side, front-back, *etc.*) and then refined by aligning the query image to the panorama or the multi-view image set associated with each of the top candidate locations (Section 3.3). Such alignment process can also be used to filter out outlier locations that are inconsistent with the majority of the candidate locations in terms of predicting the current query view. The filtered candidate location set is then used to retrieve the salient view associated with each possible location, which has been pre-computed offline (Section 3.2). A majority voting process is used to determine the best query view for the next query (Section 3.3). The difference between the best query view and the predicted current view is then used to come up with the view change suggestion to the user, who may then turn the camera phone by following the suggested change.

We go through each of the components described above in the following subsections.

3.1 Million Scale Image Matching

We achieve approximate image matching in a million scale image database using Bag of visual Words (BoW) with inverted indexing technique. Our implementation basically follows the algorithm described in [11], which uses a hierarchical tree based structure for efficient codebook construction and visual local feature quantization. In addition, we also test the incorporation of multi-path search [7] and spatial verification [10] to improve the accuracy. The experimental result over a validation set is shown in Figure 8. Our current system uses the six high-resolution views captured by individual cameras, though image crops from panoramas can be incorporated as well. We summarize below some of the specific findings about implementations over the NAVTEQ NYC data set.

Local Feature Extraction: Both interest point detection and dense sampling are tested in building our search

[3]We assume only the top location is returned to the mobile user and the user is able to realize the response is actually wrong by inspecting the scenes of the predicted location or verifying the associated information (*e.g.*, recommended stores missing in the neighborhood)

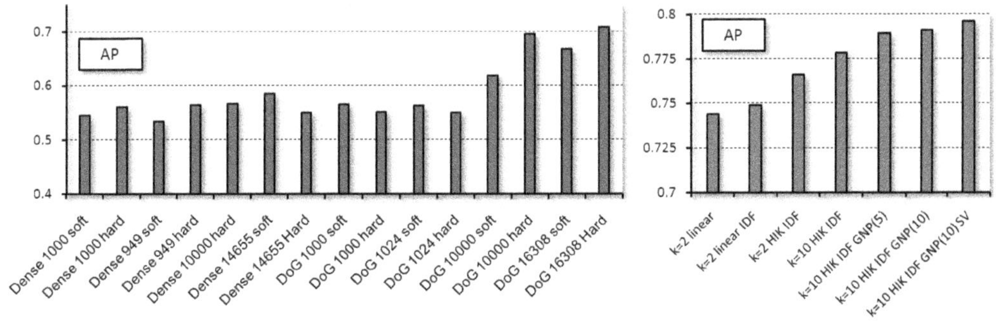

Figure 8: Comparison of image matching performance with different configurations. (a) Small codebook configurations with varying local detector, codebook size, hierarchical clustering, and quantization; (b) Million sized codebook configuration with varying branching factor, histogram intersection kernel, GNP search [7], IDF, and spatial verification [10].

system. The former is based on Difference of Gaussian [12], while the latter is based on multi-scale sliding window with 3 scales and fixed steps, producing approximately equal numbers of local features. As shown in Figure 8 (a), DoG outperforms dense sampling under different configurations of codebook sizes and quantization methods.

Local Feature Clustering: We use the Hierarchical K Means Clustering to build a million scale Vocabulary Tree [11]. There are two basic settings in building the Vocabulary Tree: (1) Branching Factor B controls how many clusters are built to partition a given set of local features into its lower hierarchy; (2) Hierarchical Layer H controls the number of hierarchical layers in the tree. There is a tradeoff between speed and quantization accuracy in choosing different B and H values. With empirical validation, we set $B = 10$, and $H = 6$ to construct our final codebook of approximately one million codewords.

Quantization: Soft quantization has been found in [13] to improve the retrieval precision. In our case, soft quantization performs better when the codebook size is small. But as the codebook size increases, the performance of soft quantization degrades, and is outperformed by hard quantization in our million-scale codebook configuration. Greedy N-Best Path (GNP) [7] is used to rectify the quantization errors by searching multiple paths over the quantization tree. We found that by using GNP of 10 paths we achieved a slight gain in average precision (2%).

Spatial Verification: We further incorporate the spatial matching proposed in [10], which considers a point in one image matches a point in another image only if a sufficient number of nearby local features are also matched. This process is easy to be implemented, but the performance improvement is minor (only 0.5%), perhaps due to the precise matching capability of the large codebook (one million).

Inverted Indexing: Finally, we implement Histogram Intersection Kernel (HIK) [14] matching with inverted indexing in our search system to ensure the scalability to the million scale database. Once a certain amount of local descriptors from one query are assigned into a given visual word, we assign all images indexed by this visual word a certain score.

The final million-scale codebook configuration is shown in Table 1. The performance of the final baseline system is satisfactory and comparable with the state of the art. It achieves an average precision at 0.79 over a validation subset from the NAVTEQ data set. Over the widely used UKbench

Table 1: The final one million codebook configuration

Component	Choice
Local Feature	DoG + SIFT [12]
Clustering	Hierarchical K Means ($B = 10, H = 6$)
Quantization	Hard Quantization with GNP [7] $N = 10$
Inverted Indexing	HIK kernel based
Spatial Verification	Neighborhood Voting [10]
Word Frequency	TF-IDF

benchmark [11], it even slightly outperforms the results in [11] by a large-scale vocabulary tree.

It is important to note that image matching is not the focus of the paper. Our proposed AQS approach is general, independent of the image matching subsystem used as long as the assumption about the location-dependent preferred query view holds. In addition, it can be applied to any visual location search system without requiring any additional hardware on mobile devices.

3.2 Offline Salient View Learning

Given a location of interest, which view is the best candidate for matching the reference images in the database and recognizing the true location? As discussed earlier, each location has certain views that are more salient and can be used for successful retrieval. Figure 9 shows another example to illustrate the concept. Intuitively, two approaches can be considered - *content-based* and *training performance based*. The former explores the unique attributes contained in each view such as distinct objects, local features, *etc.*, while the latter predicts the test performance by assessing the query effectiveness over a training data set. We have developed methods based on both ideas. Note in the discussion below, we assume the continuous space of view can be appropriately discretized, for example, to a finite set of choices (*e.g.*, six angles used in the NAVTEQ data set).

Content based View Saliency Prediction: With the BoW representation, distinctive visual words have a better discriminating power than words that appear in most locations in the databases. This concept has been well explored in the information retrieval and image classification literatures, following the concept of TF-IDF (Term Frequency - Inverse Document Frequency). A word is considered more distinctive if its frequency of occurrence in the database images (documents) is low. Extending this concept, we define

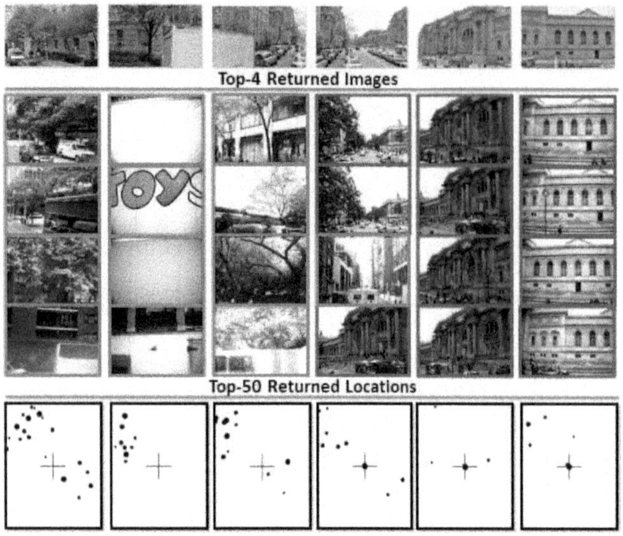

Figure 9: Top: the six views of the Metropolitan Museum of Art in New York City; Middle: The top 4 returned images for each view (blue: correct, red: incorrect); Bottom: the geographical distribution of returned locations of different views. Cross indicates the actual query location while locations of the matched images are shown in different sizes according to the rank orders.

a TF-IDF related content-based feature as follows:

$$F(k) = count(word_i | IDF(word_i) > k/K \times IDF_{max}), \quad (1)$$

where $k = 1, 2, ..., K-1$. If we set K to be 10, then the above feature accounts for the number of visual words whose IDF exceed certain thresholds (up to 90% with 10% increment). Intuitively, images of salient views will have more words with high IDF than images of non-salient views.

We train a Support Vector Machine (SVM) based classifier and use its classification score to predict the saliency of an image. A subset of geo-tagged locations sampled from Google Street View (described in Section 2.1) was used as a labeled training set to train the SVM classifier. Since the feature dimension is kept low (10 if $K = 10$), a training set of such a size is adequate.

Training Performance based View Saliency Prediction: As described in Section 2, each location is associated with a finite set of reference images captured in different views. Each of the reference images can be used to query the database and evaluate its capability in retrieving related images of the same location, or other locations sharing overlapped scenes. Although there is always a gap between such training performance and the real test performance when querying by new images that have not been seen before, the score distributions of relevant (positive) images and irrelevant (negative) images can serve as an approximate measure.

An ideal score distribution is the one that has maximal separation between the scores of the positive results and those of the negative ones, like the first score distribution shown in Figure 10. Scores that have very small separation (second distribution in Figure 10) or mixed results (third and fourth distributions in Figure 10) do not generalize well. To approximate the robustness of such query results, we develop two simple methods. The first one is based on the

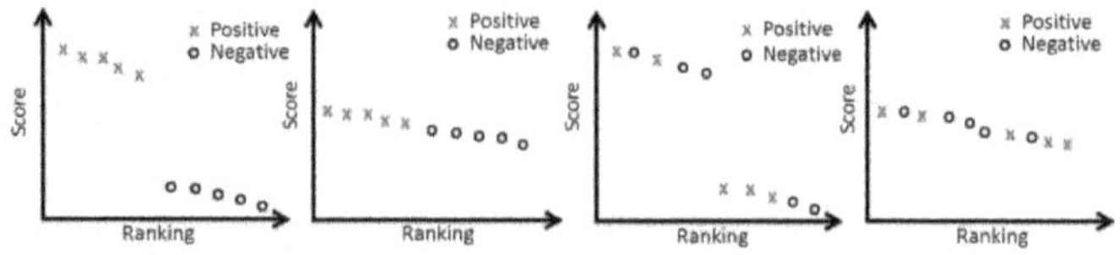

Figure 10: A good score distribution is the one that can maximally distinguish the positive results (red) from the negative (black). Several examples of score-rank distributions are shown, with the first one being the most reliable one and the last being the least (second one with the identical AP to the first).

commonly used metrics, Average Precision (AP), as below:

$$AP = \frac{\sum_{r=1}^{N_{relevant}} P(r)}{N_{relevant}}. \quad (2)$$

$N_{relevant}$ is the number of relevant documents to the current query; r is the the rth relevant document; $P(r)$ is the precision at the cut-off rank of document r. In the literature, there are some subtle variations in definition of AP. The one used above sometimes is also called full-length AP.

The other measurement, called *Saliency* as defined below, is similar to AP with several important modifications. First, we compute the ratio of the positive score statistics to that of the negative scores. Second, we incorporate the actual score values in the measure. Both modifications are important, as we are interested in the score separation between the positive and negative classes:

$$Saliency = \frac{\sum_{i=1}^{N}\sum_{j=1}^{i} score(j)rel(j)/i}{\sum_{i=1}^{N}\sum_{j=1}^{i} score(j)\overline{rel}(j)/i}, \quad (3)$$

where N is the number of returned locations, which can be a fixed size or adjusted based on the number of positive samples[4]. $score(j)$ is the location matching score, which is the maximal score of its six views. $rel(j)$ is the relevance judgement of the jth returned location, which gives 1 for correct locations and 0 for incorrect. Conceptually, other statistical measures, such as KL Divergence, can also be used.

Note the numerator in Equation 3 is very similar to that of AP, except the score values are used instead of binary values (1 for positive and 0 for negative) and the inner average is repeated for every sample, not just for the positive points. Despite the simplicity of the above saliency measure, surprisingly it has a significantly superior prediction accuracy to all other measures (Section 4).

The offline measures of saliency for each view can also be used to "grade" the searchability of each location, as discussed in Section 2. Based on the search results of the associated views, a location can be categorized into one of the following groups.

- *View-Independent Confident Location:* Users can take photos in any arbitrary view to find this location.

[4]In our experiments to be reported later, we use 3 times of the number of positive points so that we can compute the statistics from the top result set covering both sufficient positive and negative results.

Algorithm 1: Online view estimation and Active Query Sensing procedure

```
Given query q, get the top N most likely locations (Section 3.1).
if the first location is incorrect then
    Obtaining candidate location set L̂ {
        Remove locations in the top-N set that are geographically close to the first location;
        Predict the viewing angle of the first query using GIST + SVM with the voting refinement (Equation 4);
        Discard the outlier locations with predicted viewing angles inconsistent with the one obtained before;
    }
    Majority voting within L̂ {
    for l ∈ L̂ do
        Retrieve the saliency of the remaining views Θ;
        Estimate the camera movement to the most salient view in l;
    end
        Majority voting to determine the best view for the second query.
    }
end
```

- *View-Dependent Searchable Location:* Users can take photos in certain views to find this location.
- *Difficult Location:* Users cannot find this location no matter which view he/she use to form the visual query.

There is room for improvement with the above analysis. First, the offline analysis is only limited to the discrete views that have been indexed in the database. In practice, users can sample the view space in a much more flexible manner. Second, there is likely to be generalization gap between offline analysis based on training performance and the real-world online testing. Nonetheless, the offline analysis offers an approximate yet systematic process of discovering the preferred query views for all of the searchable locations.

3.3 Online View Estimation and Active Query Sensing

We describe the modules for online view estimation and active query view suggestion in this section. The main process is summarized in Algorithm 1. Given the first query that fails to recognize the correct location, the objective is to develop automatic methods that can estimate the likely view captured by the first query, and from the candidate location set, discover the best view for the next query.

Using the image matching subsystem, we first find a small set of top-N most likely locations. Locations close to the first location are removed as the first location has been judged as incorrect by the user. Next, we employ a SVM classifier to assign the first query image to one of few rough orientations, followed by refinement based on image matching. Algorithm 1 shows the working pipeline of our online active query sensing. Some key components of Algorithm 1 are explained in detail below.

Viewing Angle Estimation: Although the visual content in different views of the location database could be very diverse, there exist general patterns differentiating each other. For example, the side views tend to contain more features related to buildings, trees, and sides of parked vehicles, while other views (*e.g.*, front) has more attributes like sky lines, streets, and front/back views of vehicles. Such differences tend to be holistic reflecting the overall characteristics of the scenes, thus motivating the choice of GIST descriptor [15] for view classification.

We train the SVM classifiers offline based on GIST features extracted from 3000 images (500 for each view) randomly chosen from our database. Given an online query, we use the classifier to predict the current viewing angle in one-vs-all manner. GIST feature is efficient in describing the global configuration of images. However, in our case, as shown in Figure 3, View 1 and View 5, as well as View 2 and View 6 have very similar visual appearance. To address this problem, we further use a refinement step based on the image matching results:

$$\arg\max_{\theta_i} \sum_{l} P(\theta_i|l,q)P(l|q), \tag{4}$$

where θ_i is a candidate view under consideration, $P(\theta_i|l,q)$ is the matching score between query q and view i of location l. $P(l|q)$ can be modeled by location score distribution based on query q, combined with additional metadata such as GPS or the history data about the user locations. The default $P(l|q)$ is a positive constant for top matching locations (candidates), and zero for others.

This refinement works because similar views, even from different locations, typically have similar visual contents *e.g.*, skylines, side of a truck *etc.*, which are more likely to be included in the top image match results. This phenomenon is also observed in the recent work of [5] for street view image search. So the final angle estimation method is based on the combination of both local feature (SIFT for image matching) and global feature (GIST for SVM classification). This approach is fairly robust in our application scenarios, which will be shown experimentally later. It should be noted that when the solution space for view prediction (and alignment) is large, a more sophisticated correspondence matching method, such as RANSAC, may be needed to reliably align the query image to the panorama associated with each location. However, the impact on the speed will need to be carefully investigated as a fast response is needed for such online applications.

Once the current query view is estimated, we further use it to filter out the outlier locations that produce inconsistent view estimation. Empirically, we found that this step is very useful.

Majority Voting for View Suggestion: Given the filtered candidate set of the locations, we use a majority voting scheme to predict the most beneficial view to be used as the next query. It can be expressed as:

$$\arg\max_{\theta_i \in \Theta} \sum_{l \in \hat{L}} H_{saliency}(\theta_i|l)P(l|q), \tag{5}$$

where $H_{saliency}(\theta_i|l)$ outputs 1 if the saliency of view θ_i and location l is greater than a threshold. $P(l|q)$ is modeled by the location score distribution after removing outlier locations with inconsistent view estimations. Setting $P(l|q)$ as a positive constant for all top-N locations and zero for others leads the above equation to a majority voting.

The scheme takes into account the saliency of each view with respect to each remaining candidate location. With the predicted best query view and the estimated viewing angle of the current query, we can then make suggestions to the

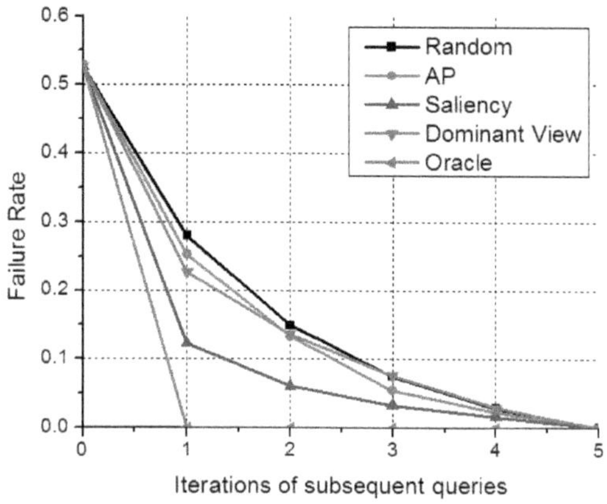

Figure 11: Failure rates over successive query iterations based on different active query sensing strategies: (1) Random view suggestion, (2) AP-based view suggestion, (3) Saliency based view suggestion, (4) Dominant view suggestion, and (5) Oracle view suggestion.

Table 2: Percentages of successful location search using query images from different views

$View_1$	$View_2$	$View_3$	$View_4$	$View_5$	$View_6$
0.45	0.26	0.58	0.65	0.53	0.35

user to inform him/her of the best way of turning or moving the camera phone for the subsequent visual search.

4. EVALUATIONS

We evaluate the performance of the components and overall system of the proposed active query sensing approaches for mobile location search, using the NAVTEQ NYC data set (about 300,000 images, 50,000 locations). The test queries are the 1,356 images over 226 locations randomly cropped from the Google Street View interface as described in Section 2.1. Out of the 226 locations, 11.1% were found to be unsearchable by any of the views and thus were discarded. The remaining 201 locations are searchable by at least one viewing angle. The proportions of searchable locations by various numbers of views are shown in Figure 4.

We first analyze the "dominance" of each view of the query set. Table 2 shows the percentages of successful searches over the 201 test locations by each of the six views. It is interesting to see each view has a reasonable chance of success (between 35% and 65%) while View 2 has the lowest rate. This is due to the relatively low quality of the camera used for View 2 in the database. View 4, the one pointing to the front of the imaging vehicle, has the highest success rate as it appears to cover the most visual objects (*e.g.*, buildings on both sides), as well as the most distinctive features such as sky lines.

Salient View Prediction: Next, we evaluate the performance of predicting search robustness using offline saliency analysis, described in Section 3.2. Table 3 shows the percentages of successful search over 201 test locations by using different methods to predict the best view for each test location. We compared two types of proposed methods - training performance based: AP and Saliency, and content based: IDF SVM[5] classifier, as described in Section 3.3, against

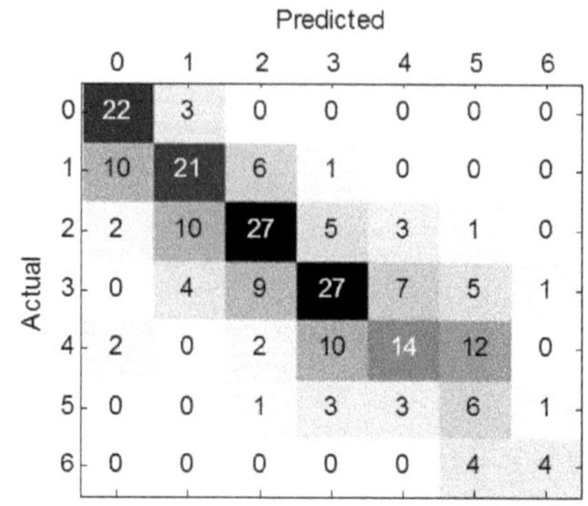

Figure 13: Confusion matrix for location search difficulty prediction (the predicted number of successful views vs. the ground truths)

the random view selection and the one that always chooses the most dominant view (View 4). Surprisingly, the content-based classifier did not perform as well as expected, possibly due to the large content confusion among different locations in the NYC data set. Among all the competing approaches, the saliency measure (as defined in Equation 3) incorporating the score statistics ratio between the positive and the negative groups turned out to achieve the highest performance (84%) with a large margin over other approaches (the next best one is 68% by AP).

Table 3 shows the robustness comparison of different approaches. The experiment is performed on all the 201 searchable locations. For each location, we pick up the external mobile query with the most salient angle predicted offline. Then, we test whether or not we can correctly find the true location using this query. This table shows the robustness validation of different view discrimination measurements. For content based approach (SVM based on statistics of distinctive visual words), we set $K = 10$ in Equation 1. For each testing location, we use an SVM classifier to get the probability based classification results, and the viewing angle with largest probability to be discriminative is predicted to be the most salient viewing angle. The result is based on a five-fold cross validation on the test set. As shown in Table 3, our saliency measurement obtains the highest score.

Query View Estimation: For the module of view estimation of test queries, we found the GIST based SVM classifier was able to achieve 86.5% classification accuracy over the 1,356 test image queries if we are only concerned with View 1-4. When Views 5 and 6 are added, they cause confusion with views of highly similar content (View 1 with View 5, and View 2 with View 6). This is reasonable due to symmetrical nature (180 degrees opposite direction) and thus similar visual content between the two views in each of the symmetrical pairs. To resolve this, we applied the maximal voting scheme based on image matching scores (as described in Equation 4). It helps to keep the view estimation accuracy as high as 82.1% among all six viewing angles.

Active Query View Sensing: Finally, we evaluate the effectiveness of the proposed AQS system in helping users choose the best view for subsequent queries after the first query fails. We initialized the simulated system with a randomly chosen viewing angle in the first visual search. As

[5]Since the content-based SVM classifier requires supervised training, we adopted a five-fold cross validation process to partition the test query set for separate training and testing.

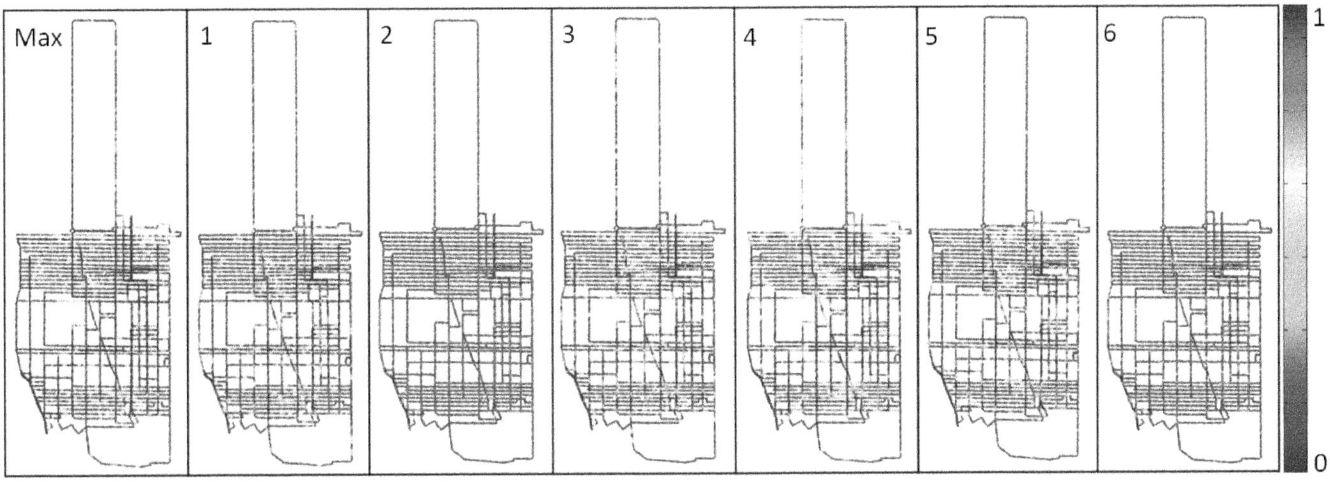

Figure 12: Geographical location confidence (measured by saliency) distribution in New York City with respect to different views, where "Max" denotes assigning the maximal confidence among six views to each location.

Table 3: Location search accuracy using different methods in predicting the best query view for each location

Method	Random	Dominant Angle	Content Based	AP	Saliency
Percentage correct prediction	0.4735	0.6517	0.5521	0.6816	0.8458

discussed earlier, only 47% of the random query images succeeded, resulting in a 53% failure rate after the first query (as shown in Figure 11). We then evaluated the performance of reducing the failure rates in subsequent queries by using different active query strategies, including the proposed AQS method based on view saliency measure, other methods based on AP, dominant view, random selection, and the oracle scheme which knows the correct answers and always chooses a successful view after the first query. The performance gain achieved by the saliency based AQS scheme is quite impressive – 12% error rate after only one additional query compared to the next best one 23% by the dominant view. As the number of query iterations increases, the proposed AQS solution consistently maintains significant edge over all other methods. Eventually, the error rate drops to zero for all methods since this test set consists of searchable locations only (*i.e.*, at least one view can be used to recognize the location).

Location Difficulty Level Prediction: We further evaluate how well the proposed saliency measure (described in Section 3.2) can be used to predict the difficulty level of each location in terms of location recognition. Ideally, we would like to be able to generate the confidence distribution map similar to the one shown in Figure 4. Accurate prediction of such a confidence distribution map can facilitate development of very interesting applications. For example, users may use such information to determine how much to trust the visual search based location information when he/she has additional information (like GPS) to roughly know the geographical region he/she is located in. Figure 12 shows the distributions of saliency for each viewing angle as well as their maximum among all views of each location computed from the NYC data set. To avoid outliers caused by poor image quality or missing data, a simple Gaussian smoothing was also used. The resulting distribution maps confirm the location dependence assumption we have made in the paper. By thresholding the saliency values in each view, we further predicted the number of views that can be used to successfully search each location. We compared the estimated number of successful views against the ground truths associated with the 1,356 test query images cropped from Google Street View. The confusion matrix, shown in Figure 13, confirms the effectiveness of the proposed saliency based estimation.

5. RELATED WORK

Many exciting research directions are being pursued to advance the field of mobile visual search. For mobile location recognition, [16] adopted sequential matching of more than one reference views to estimate the pose and motion direction. [7] presented a method for large-scale location recognition based on geo-tagged video streams with multi-path search over a vocabulary tree. [17] also adopted a vocabulary tree based approach for real-time loop closing. [18] described an approach to recognize locations by mobile image search, which utilized a hybrid color histogram to compensate its original ranking results. [19] presented a system to identify landmark buildings based on image data, metadata, and other photos taken within a consecutive 15-minute window. [20] adopted a structure-from-motion technique to build 3D scene models for vision-based city scene localization. Compact descriptors were proposed in [6] to greatly reduce the delay in computation and communication. Discovery of vanishing points and identification of facades were proposed in [9]. Confusing features such as trees and road markings were removed based on geo-tag supervision [5]. Fusion of multiple image representations (facade-aligned and viewpoint-aligned) was used to improve the search accuracy [8]. Despite the impressive progress shown, none of these works address the active sensing problem to help users take a better second query in the subsequent location search.

In image search, there have been long standing works in relevance feedback [21]. The basic idea is to use iterative labeling of the top returned results to learn a refined ranking function [21][22]. By dealing with the user gap [23], there are related works in helping and suggesting users to better formulate their queries. For instance, [23] presented a work for visual query suggestion, which provides images to help users express their search intent despite the ambiguity in the textual queries. One closely related topic is active learning [24], in which the system tries to find the most informative sample to collect user feedbacks in order to learn an improved decision function. Our problem is different in actively determining the best view to sense in the real-world scene (rather than the sample space in the database) and in trying to recognize the correct target (instead of a decision).

Our work is also related to a few topics in information retrieval. For instance, [25] proposed a learning scheme to predict the query difficulty, which measures the contribution of each query term to the final result set. [26] learnt a support vector machine to predict the query success based on TF and IDF of query keywords. [27] studied several predictors of the query performance based on the IDF statistics of the query terms. The suggestion models mentioned above are typically learnt from the statistical distributions of the document corpus and query logs. On the contrary, our paper focuses on strategies for visually searching the physical surroundings of real world geographical locations.

6. CONCLUSIONS AND FUTURE WORKS

Active Query Sensing aims to help the mobile user take a successful second query once the first query fails (more than 50% of chance as discussed in the paper). It informs the mobile user how to sense his/her surrounding environment so that the captured image is most distinctive and can be used to recognize the location. To achieve this goal, we develop a novel Active Query Sensing system that actively discovers the best query strategy and suggests the best sensing view after the first visual query fails. To the best of our knowledge, this is the first effort in addressing the user needs by iterative refinements of mobile visual search. We develop several saliency measures based on score distributions to predict the robustness of each query view and the search difficulty of each location. In addition, we develop an online process for estimating the viewing angle of an unseen novel query and suggesting the best view change prior to forming the next query. Using a large street view image data set (0.3 million images over 50,000 locations) of the New York City, our system shows a performance gain as high as two-fold: Our sensing strategy can reduce the failure rate of mobile location search to only 12% after the second query. Our statistical saliency measure can also be used to robustly predict the difficulty of visually recognizing individual locations, allowing users to decide where the mobile search service can be best trusted.

The future work includes incorporation of other image representations *e.g.*, panorama and range data, to provide more flexibility in view suggestion (translation, zoom *etc*). The proposed system also has great potential for applications beyond location search, such as products and landmarks.

Another future work is to provide intuitive user interfaces to maximize the utility of the proposed AQS search system. For example, when the user is not sure about the correctness of the search result, we may provide extra information (besides just the images of the predicted location) such as street names, landmarks in the vicinity, *etc.*

7. ACKNOWLEDGEMENTS

We would like to thank NAVTEQ for providing the NYC image data set, Dr. Xin Chen and Dr. Jeff Bach for their generous help. This work has been supported in part by NSF awards #CNS-07-51078 and #CNS-07-16203.

8. REFERENCES

[1] http://www.snaptell.com/.
[2] http://www.pointandfind.nokia.com/.
[3] http://www.kooaba.com/.
[4] J. Knopp, J. Sivic, and T. Pajdla. Avoiding confusing features place recognition. *ECCV*, 2010.
[5] B. Kaneva, J. Sivic, A. Torralba, S Avidan, and W. Freeman. Matching and predicting street level images. *Workshop on Vision for Cognitive Tasks, ECCV*, 2010.
[6] B. Girod, V. Chandrasekhar, D. Chen, N.-M. Cheung, R. Grzeszczuk, Y. Reznik, G. Takacs, S. Tsai, and R. Vedantham. Mobile visual search. *IEEE Signal Processing Magazine*, July, 2011.
[7] G. Schindler and M. Brown. City-scale location recognition. *CVPR*, 2007.
[8] D. Chen, G. Baatz, K. Koser, S. Tsai, R. Vedantham, T. Pylvanainen, K. Roimela, X. Chen, J. Bach, M. Pollefeys, B. Girod, and R. Grzeszczuk. City-scale landmark identification on mobile devices. *CVPR*, 2011.
[9] G. Baatz, K. Koser, D. Chen, R. Grzeszczuk, and M. Pollefeys. Handling urban location recognition as a 2d homothetic problem. *ECCV*, 2010.
[10] J. Sivic and A. Zisserman. Video google a text retrieval approach to object matching videos. *ICCV*, 2003.
[11] D. Nister and H. Stewenius. Scalable recognition with a vocabulary tree. *CVPR*, 2006.
[12] D. Lowe. Distinctive image features from scale-invariant keypoints. *IJCV*, 2004.
[13] J. Philbin, O. Chum, M. Isard, J. Sivic, and A. Zisserman. Lost quantization: Improving particular object retrieval large scale image databases. *CVPR*, 2008.
[14] J. Wu and J. Rehg. Beyond the euclidean distance: Creating effective visual codebooks using the histogram intersection kernel. *ICCV*, 2009.
[15] A. Oliva and A. Torralba. Modeling the shape of the scene a holistic representation of the spatial envelope. *IJCV*, 2001.
[16] W. Zhang and J. Kosecka. Image based localization urban environments. *3DPVT*, 2006.
[17] E. Eade and T.Drummond. Unified loop closing and recovery for real time monocular slam. *BMVC*, 2008.
[18] T. Yeh, K. Tollmar, and T. Darrell. Searching the web with mobile images for location recognition. *CVPR*, 2004.
[19] D. Crandall, L. Backstrom, and D. Huttenlocher. Mapping the world's photos. *WWW*, 2009.
[20] A. Irschara, C. Zach, J. Frahm, and H. Bischof. From structure-from-motion point clouds to fast location recognition. *CVPR*, 2009.
[21] Y. Rui, T. Huang, and S. Chang. Image retrieval current techniques, promising directions, and open issues. *Journal of Visual Communication and Image Representation*, 1999.
[22] R. Datta, D. Joshi, J. Li, and J. Wang. Image retrieval ideas, influences, and trends of the new age. *ACM Computing Surveys*, 2008.
[23] Z.-J. Zha, L. Yang, T. Mei, M. Wang, and Z. Wang. Visual query suggestion. *ACM Multimedia*, 2009.
[24] S. Tong and E. Chang. Support vector machine active learning for image retrieval. *ACM Multimedia*, 2001.
[25] E. YomTov, S. Fine, D. Carmel, and A. Darlow. Learning to estimate query difficulty. *SIGIR*, 2005.
[26] K. Kwok, L. Grunfeld, H. Sun, P. Deng, and N. Dinstl. Robust track experiments using pircs. *TREC*, 2004.
[27] B. He and I. Ounis. Inferring query performance using pre-retrieval predictors. *String Processing and Information Retrieval*, 2004.

Color-plus-Depth Level-of-Detail in 3D Tele-immersive Video: A Psychophysical Approach*

Wanmin Wu, Ahsan Arefin, Gregorij Kurillo†, Pooja Agarwal, Klara Nahrstedt, Ruzena Bajcsy†
Department of Computer Science, University of Illinois at Urbana-Champaign, Urbana, IL, USA.
†Department of EECS, University of California at Berkeley, Berkeley, CA, USA.
{wwu23, marefin2, pagarwl, klara}@illinois.edu, †{gregorij, bajcsy}@eecs.berkeley.edu

ABSTRACT

This paper presents a psychophysical study that measures the perceptual thresholds of a new factor called Color-plus-Depth Level-of-Detail peculiar to polygon-based 3D tele-immersive video. The results demonstrate the existence of Just Noticeable Degradation and Just Unacceptable Degradation thresholds on the factor. In light of the results, we describe the design and implementation of a real-time perception-based quality adaptor for 3D tele-immersive video. Our experimental results show that the adaptation scheme can reduce resource usage while considerably enhancing the overall perceived visual quality.

Categories and Subject Descriptors

H.1.2 [**Information Systems**]: Models and Principles—*human factors*; H.4.3 [**Information Systems Applications**]: Communications Applications—*Computer conferencing, teleconferencing, and videoconferencing*

General Terms

Design, Experiment, Human Factors, Measurement

Keywords

Tele-immersive Video, Perception, Psychophysics, Color-plus-Depth, Level-of-Detail, Adaptation

1. INTRODUCTION

The past few years have witnessed a surge of interest in telepresence video collaboration technologies. Several industrial systems have arisen [1][2], yet with a limited application domain as most are still concentrated solely on desktop video-conferencing scenarios. Emerging is the 3D tele-immersion technology that expands the horizon by supporting full-body interaction of physical activities in virtual reality environments. Applications have been found in cyber-archeology, rehabilitation, collaborative dancing, and gaming (e.g., [28][29]).

Despite great potential, today's tele-immersive systems still face significant challenges due to the high interactivity requirement and resource demand. Great research efforts have been devoted to making the systems more efficient [5][21][28], with notable improvement, but the focus has been primarily on system-centric, algorithmic optimizations. The systems still struggle with heavy temporal and spatial overheads and complexities, limiting their broader deployment.

Since the ultimate goal of tele-immersion is to deliver a satisfying experience to end users, we believe that taking a more human-centric perspective would be beneficial. It is known that the Human Visual System (HVS) has perceptual limitations, so the research question is whether it is possible to exploit these limitations and reduce data load and/or rate without impairing much perceived quality. Similar questions have been studied in traditional video-conferencing systems for factors such as jitter [7], audio-visual sync [27], latency [11], and frame rate [3][16]. However, 3D tele-immersive video possesses unique characteristics whose perceptual impact is little understood.

Perhaps the most important trait that distinguishes 3D tele-immersion from the traditional video-conferencing is its color-plus-depth video format as the visual representations of users. Therefore, the density and accuracy of the texture and depth maps is a new and critical factor in tele-immersive video, which we combine and refer to as the *Color-Plus-Depth Level-of-Detail (CZLoD)*. In this work, we make the first attempt to psychophysically study this factor in *polygon-based* 3D tele-immersive video. We employ the method of limits from psychophysics [8] to examine two perceptual thresholds - Just Noticeable Degradation (JNDG) and Just Unacceptable Degradation (JUADG). We evaluate forty stimuli in four varied conditions with different contents and pixel resolution settings. The results indicate that the threshold levels are actually fairly generous (i.e., a fair amount of degradation can be suffered) and are related to both activity type and resolution. In general, fine motor activity exhibits lower threshold levels than gross motor activity, and lower resolution video exhibits lower threshold levels than higher resolution levels.

In light of the results, we design and implement a perception-

*Area chair: Pål Halvorsen. This material is based upon work supported by the National Science Foundation under Grant No. CNS 0834480. Any opinions, findings, and conclusions or recommendations expressed in this material are those of the author(s) and do not necessarily reflect the views of the National Science Foundation.

MM'11, November 28–December 1, 2011, Scottsdale, Arizona, USA.
Copyright 2011 ACM 978-1-4503-0616-4/11/11 ...$5.00.

based real-time adaptation scheme for CZLoD in 3D tele-immersion. Implemented as a closed feedback loop, the adaptor monitors various interdependent Quality-of-Service (QoS) parameters to determine the appropriate degradation ratio for CZLoD. The actual degradation, nevertheless, is achieved by controlling a *detailing parameter*, whose mapping to the degradation ratio is unpredictable as it varies with environments and activities. Thus a learning algorithm is used to learn the quantitative model of the relationship between the detailing parameter and the CZLoD degradation ratios. We evaluate the adaptation scheme in a real-world 3D tele-immersive testbed, and the experimental results demonstrate that the proposed scheme can achieve considerable improvement in frame rate without impairing perceived detailing quality. We also record the generated tele-immersive video with and without adaptation respectively and conduct a crowdsourcing subjective study to compare their overall quality. The collected responses show that over 90% of users thought the video with adaptation was better than the unimpaired video.

Our work is partly inspired by the level-of-detail concept in 3D graphics [18]. Nevertheless, we believe there are four main factors that distinguish our work: (1) we are the first to psychophysically measure perception thresholds of level-of-detail in 3D video. (2) Tele-immersion is a distributed, highly interactive pipeline, so almost all of our design choices are made carefully for the interactive timing bounds (Section 5). (3) Since tele-immersion is about real-time video where scene complexity is unpredictable, the relationship between the detailing parameter and the resulting CZLoD is unpredictable too; therefore, we learn a predictive model about their relations at run-time (Section 5.2.3). We also show that the predictor can produce very high accuracy in real time (Section 5.3). (4) We demonstrate how the perceptual thresholds obtained psychophysically can be applied to practice for real-time resource management.

In this work, we develop an intra-stream data adaptation scheme that reduces level-of-detail within each stream at the sending side without users being aware of it. This human-centric approach effectively alleviates the data load for computation-intensive operations, thus improving the temporal efficiency of the systems. Yet even with intra-stream data reduced, spatial (bandwidth) efficiency is still a problem due to the multi-stream/multi-site nature of tele-immersive collaboration. In our other work [33], we have actually addressed the spatial challenge with an inter-stream data adaptation scheme at the networking phase that reduces the number of streams with minimal disruption to visual quality.

We begin by reviewing related work (Section 2), and then discuss tele-immersive video in greater depth (Section 3). A psychophysical study of perceptual limitation and acceptability on the detailing factor is then described (Section 4). We present the construction of our perception-based quality adaptation scheme (Section 5). The paper concludes by discussing the limitations of the study and implications of our research (Section 6).

2. RELATED WORK

The ultimate goal of 3D tele-immersion is to enable people to interact across distance just as if they were co-located physically. This is achieved by fusing the 3D representations of geographically distributed users into a virtual reality environment in real time. The history of 3D tele-immersion can be traced back to about a decade ago, when researchers demonstrated the first networked tele-immersive application that could run at 2 to 3 frames per second (fps) [28]. Various efforts have been made to improve the efficiency of the systems in diverse components such as depth reconstruction [15][34], coordinated data transport protocol [21], rendering [28], as well as real-time 3D video compression [35]. Despite the notable improvement, tele-immersive systems are still far from becoming a commodity due to the high interactivity demand and heavy computational complexities. In this paper, we tackle the challenge from a different perspective by examining data redundancy in terms of psychophysical principles. We believe our approaches are orthogonal to the system-centric algorithmic improvements, and thus can be combined to provide greater performance benefits.

Psychophysics is not new to the multimedia community. The JPEG codecs [12], for example, compress images by eliminating high frequency details that are invisible to human eyes. Audio compression algorithms, such as MP3, exploit psychoacoustic principles to reduce information that is less audible to human ears [9]. Recently, psychophysics is also being applied to haptic feedback where the samples with imperceptible changes are removed from network transmission [26]. Perhaps the most relevant to our work is the recent psychophysical study conducted by De Silva *et al.* that considered the Just Noticeable Difference in Depth (JNDD) in 3D video [24]. However, the context is very different from this work in that the video content therein is for offline-generated 3D-TV. The real-time requirement of polygon-based tele-immersive video leads to the emergence of a new definition of CZLoD that is not applicable in 3D-TV video (this will become more apparent in Section 3). We also develop (to our knowledge) the first perception-based adaptation scheme for polygon-based 3D tele-immersion.

3. TELE-IMMERSIVE VIDEO

To avoid any confusion, we have to first point out that tele-immersive video is different from the commonly known stereoscopic video (as in 3D movies) which creates depth illusion with two offset imaging sequences for the two eyes of viewers respectively. Unlike such stereoscopic video, tele-immersive video refers to the *color-plus-depth* video, created and visualized *in real time*.

3.1 Real-time Acquisition

The acquisition pipeline in 3D tele-immersion mainly consists of three stages: capture, transmission, and visualization. Tele-immersive video is often captured by an array of synchronized cameras surrounding the physical environment. Unlike conventional multi-view video conferencing/lecturing systems, each camera here is a stereo unit, typically equipped with binocular or trinocular lenses, and connected to a host computer via IEEE 1394 (FireWire) interface. At interactive rates, the host computer grabs image frames synchronously from all lenses and produces *color-plus-depth* frames. A more detailed description of this 3D reconstruction process is deferred to Section 3.2. After the 3D reconstruction is completed with some post-processing (filtering, smoothing, regularity enforcement), the 3D frame is sent to the collaborating site(s) for visualization in a virtual-reality environment where all participants can seamlessly interact.

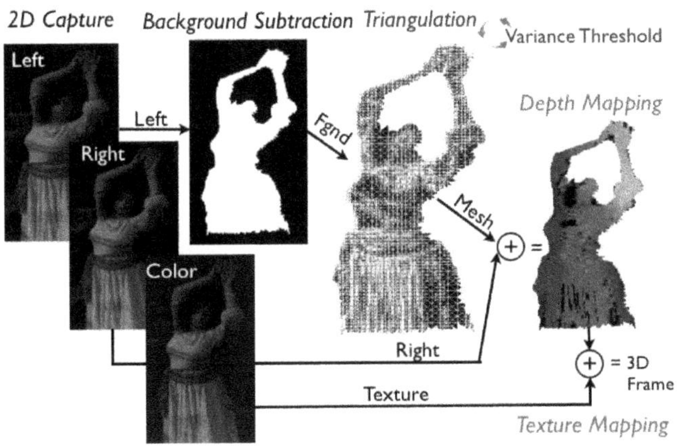

Figure 1: Hybrid depth and texture mapping process: expensive depth cross-correlation is only performed on vertices after meshing, and depths for the other pixels are linearly interpolated (adapted from [29]).

3.2 Color-Plus-Depth Level-of-Detail

In this section, we describe the generation of color-plus-depth frames in greater detail. As Figure 1 illustrates, after the raw frames are fetched from the stereo camera, they are first preprocessed (e.g., resizing, rectification). Then one of the images is used as the "reference frame" (e.g., the image from the left eye of the camera as shown in Figure 1), where background subtraction is performed. The next major step normally would be to reconstruct the 3D information of the frame for each foreground pixel. However, obtaining an accurate, dense (per pixel) depth map on commodity hardware turns out to be very time-consuming. In addition, transmitting the full-sized texture information would be quite costly in network bandwidth as well as in visualization latency, given the multi-site, multi-stream nature of tele-immersion. For these reasons, several tele-immersive systems use the polygonal modeling approach [15][20][30], to alleviate both temporal and spatial overheads.

In this approach, after background subtraction the reference frame is decomposed into polygons (e.g., triangles) based on texture homogeneity. This is done by recursively refining bisection until the variance within every polygon is less than a threshold TH_{var}. Importantly, afterwards the expensive depth-correlation operation is only performed on mesh vertices [29]. The depth calculation for the other pixels can thus be largely simplified by linear interpolation. Similar subdivision can be applied for textures as well. Since now only the coordinates and textures of vertices need to be transmitted (and those of the remaining pixels to be approximated at the receiving/rendering side), such region-based representations (and the accompanying hybrid depth and texture mapping algorithms) lead to a reduction of frame size as well as data manipulation time in all stages of the tele-immersion pipeline, making them favorable for resource-intensive tele-immersion applications. Due to its clear benefits compared to the conventional point cloud approach (with substantially less data to process and transmit), this polygon modeling approach is very likely to become more widely adopted in the future.

We can observe that the number of foreground vertices after meshing regulates the color-plus-depth granularity of the mesh. It also determines the density/accuracy of tele-immersive video due to the disparate treatment of vertices and non-vertices in 3D reconstruction and texture mapping. Hence, we refer to this metric as the *Color-plus-Depth Level-of-Detail (CZLoD)* metric, which characterizes the spatial (including z-axial) and textural richness and accuracy of polygon-based tele-immersive video. Clearly, it is largely impacted by the setting of the *variance threshold* $TH_{var}(\in \mathbb{Z})$. The smaller the variance threshold is, the finer the meshing is, and the more dense/accurate the depth and texture maps will be. Therefore, the variance threshold TH_{var} is a *detailing parameter* for the CZLoD of tele-immersive video.

Notations	Descriptions
$JNDG$	Just Noticeable Degradation Ratio
$JUADG$	Just Unacceptable Degradation Ratio
p	Probability for determining psychophysical thresholds
f_i	2D renfernce frame with frame number i
F_i	Color-plus-depth frame reconstructed from f_i
$CZLoD(F_i)$	Number of foreground vertices in F_i
W	Size of running window for computing frame rate
TH_{var}	Variance threshold (detailing parameter)
TH^h_{fr}, TH^l_{fr}	Upper/lower limit of normal frame rate range
$DR^a(F_i)$	Actual degradation ratio of CZLoD in F_i
$DR^t(F_i)$	Target degradation ratio of CZLoD in F_i
$N_0(F_i)$	CZLoD of F_i when $TH_{var} = 0$
$N_v(F_i)$	CZLoD of F_i when $TH_{var} = v$
$\mathcal{F}$	Mapping function from DR^t to TH_{var}
$err(F_i)$	$= \|DR^a(F_i) - DR^t(F_i)\|$, error of degradation ratio
TH_{err}	Threshold of err to trigger variance learning
Δ_u, Δ_d	Decrease and increase sizes for DR^t adjustment

Table 1: Notations.

We are concerned about whether there are perceptual limits on the *degradation* of CZLoD for the purpose of data reduction. We thus mathematically formulate the metric of *degradation ratio* (DR). Suppose we denote the 2D reference frame as f_i (i is frame number), and the 3D frame generated from it as F_i. Assume $N_0(F_i) \in \mathbb{N}^0$ is the number of foreground vertices computed on f_i if TH_{var} were set to 0, and $N_v(F_i) \in \mathbb{N}^0$ is the number of foreground vertices computed on f_i if TH_{var} were set to v ($v >= 0$), the degradation ratio of CZLoD on the frame F_i can then be expressed as

$$DR(F_i) = 1 - \frac{N_v(F_i)}{N_0(F_i)} \tag{1}$$

where $0 \leq DR(F_i) < 1$. For convenience, Table 7 lists all the notations used throughout the paper.

Obviously, the lower the degradation ratio, the more vertices the frame F_i will contain, resulting in higher definition and accuracy in both texture and depth, and leading to sharper and more stereoscopic images (depending on perceptual mechanisms).

3.3 Stimulus Generation Engine

While 2D video quality studies can utilize a pool of 2D video sequences offered by the Video Quality Expert Group (VQEG) [32], there are no standard test data for tele-immersive video. Since 3D tele-immersion is essentially a live pipeline from cameras to renderers, a naïve way of obtaining test sequences would be to record different test sequences multiple times with different configurations of *treatment factors* (which refer to the sources of variation that are of particular interest to the experimenter [19]). However, this approach not only requires a large amount of effort but also suffers from uncontrollable varying conditions such as captured content and illuminance. Therefore, we propose a stimulus generation engine suitable for general tele-immersive video studies. To ensure the treatment factors are only varied within homogeneous blocks [19], we decouple the capturing from the 3D reconstruction so that different configurations can be applied during each phase, even on the exact image samples if desired.

Figure 2 depicts the three distinct stages of the engine. In Stage 1, a number of frames of the experiment's activities are synchronously captured, preprocessed, and stored. Numerous parameters can be configured at this stage, including the desired pixel resolution, whether to use rectification or background subtraction, the number of frames to take, etc. To generate lower pixel resolution images, the raw frames can be downscaled. In Stage 2, the engine retrieves the specified 2D frames and repeatedly performs 3D reconstruction with varying parameters such as the variance threshold TH_{var}, whether to use trinocular or binocular stereo matching, etc. The host computers then send their reconstructed frames to a renderer that aggregates the frames and writes them to disk storage. In the final stage, the 3D frames are replayed as stimuli with possibly varying parameters such as frame rate. In short, the systematic decomposition allows automatic generation of stimuli with the flexibility of controlling desired treatment factors, while keeping blocking and nuisance factors (e.g., content) fixated [19].

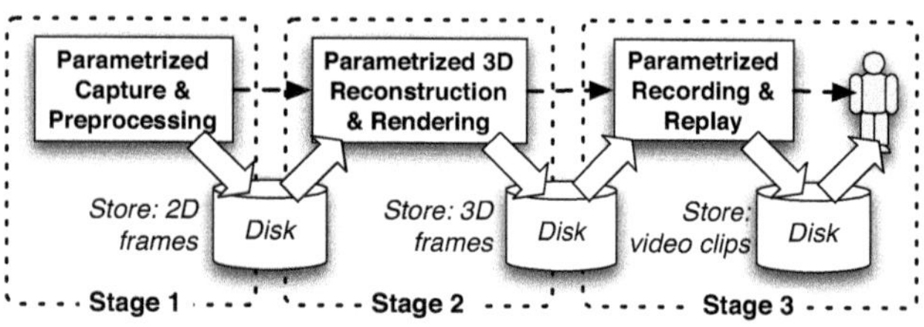

Figure 2: Stimulus generation engine: in Stage 1, 2D frames are taken, preprocessed, and stored; in Stage 2, 3D reconstruction is repeatedly applied with varied parameters; in Stage 3, the stored 3D frames are replayed with parameterization to generate the final stimuli.

4. PSYCHOPHYSICAL EXPERIMENT

The purpose of the psychophysical experiment is to measure two perceptual thresholds of CZLoD degradation: (a) Just Noticeable Degradation (JNDG), and (b) Just Unacceptable Degradation (JUADG). Identification of these thresholds can guide us to develop perception-based CZLoD adaptation mechanism for resource saving without impairing the perceived visual quality. We employed the Ascending Method of Limits [8] as the experimental methodology. It is one of the oldest and most widely used approaches in psychophysics for determining thresholds of sensations. The methodology, originally designed to measure singular intensity such as light luminance and sound frequency, was slightly modified in order to measure degradation level by means of comparison. In our study, CZLoD conditions were presented in sequential pairs, one being an unimpaired reference, and one being the same video impaired. The magnitudes of impairment were presented in an ascending order.

	Gross Motor	Fine Motor
Low Res. 320x240	Exercise-L	Lego-L
High Res. 640x480	Exercise-H	Lego-H

Table 2: Stimulus block codes

4.1 Stimuli

With the experimental methodology in mind, we generated forty stimuli. Below we discuss their conditions, properties, and resource characteristics.

There are two factors that may impact the perception of CZLoD impairment: sequence content and pixel resolution of raw frames (called "blocking factors"). To explore their relationship with the treatment factor CZLoD, we created 2 (contents) $\times$ 2 (pixel resolutions) groups (called "blocks") of stimuli, each having a different configuration of blocking factors. For the first factor (content), we categorized the most frequent tele-immersive activities into two types and recorded a representative video for each type: (a) gross-motor activities such as Tai-Chi training, dancing, and physical rehabilitation that involve large body movement; and (b) fine motor activities such as telemedicine, cyberarcheology, object/tool instructions that involve finer body movement (e.g., on hands), and manipulation of objects. For the former type, we recorded a person (performer) doing an elbow exercise (commonly used in telepresence physical therapies), while for the latter type, we recorded the performer showing a small Lego house where details were not only more demanding for the object but also for the finger movement of the performer. For the second blocking factor (pixel resolution), we chose two levels that had been mostly used in tele-immersive systems [28][31]: (a) high - 640×480, and (b) low - 320×240. The four stimulus blocks were coded as in Table 2.

The stimulus generation engine (Figure 2) was then employed to generate 10 levels of stimuli in each block. In the first stage, the Dragonfly2 stereo camera (Point Grey Inc.) was employed for recording the 2D images for each of the four block conditions. After 2D frames were acquired, 3D frames were generated for each block by repeatedly running binocular stereo matching on the same stored images with varied TH_{var} for obtaining different CZLoD degradation settings. Finally, the 3D color-plus-depth frames were rendered with a fixed frame rate 10 fps (chosen according to [16]) for the subjects. Following the ITU-R BT.500 standard [13], each test sequence was 10 seconds long, so about 100 frames were included.

The 10 stimuli for each block were coded as $S_0, S_1, ...S_9$ with increasing levels of degradation ratio in CZLoD (Figure 3(a)), with an approximate step size of 10% (degradation ratio). Figure 4 shows the snapshots of the lowest and highest stimulus conditions for each block. For each stimulus, the degradation ratio was calculated by averaging across all frames (relative standard deviation measured to be 2.08% - 2.83% for all stimuli). Therein, S_0 was the unimpaired reference stimulus ($TH_{var} = 0$). The TH_{var} values for other

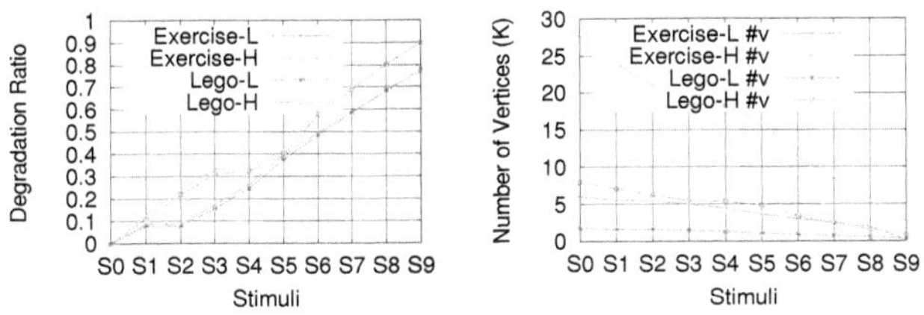

(a) (b)

Figure 3: Stimulus statistics: (a) the degradation ratios gradually increase with the stimulus levels, (b) the actual numbers of vertices (#v).

stimuli were manually chosen to approximately achieve the expected degradation ratio (it was impossible to be exact). Two sets of TH_{var} values were used, one for the lower pixel resolution blocks (Exercise-L/Lego-L), and the other for the higher resolution blocks (Exercise-H/Lego-H). Figure 3(b) presents the actual number of vertices after the meshing process.

4.2 Participants and Procedures

We followed the ITU standard in conducting the experiment [13]. Sixteen adult participants were recruited from University of Illinois at Urbana-Champaign, primarily graduate students and staff in the Department of Computer Science[1]. All had normal or corrected vision. Four participants were Indian, three were American, two were Chinese, two were German, three were Bangladeshi, one was Mexican, and one was South African. The sample consisted of 6 women (37.5%) and 10 men (62.5%). Regarding the level of experience with tele-immersive video, the sample consisted of 5 experts (31.25%) and 11 novices (68.75%).

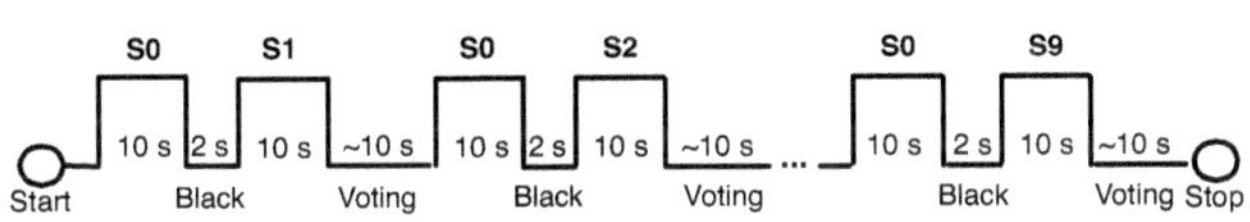

Figure 5: Experimental procedure: sequential {unimpaired, impaired} pairs of stimuli were shown, with ascending degradation ratios. Each stimulus was 10-sec long, the interval showing a black screen was 2-sec long within pair, and the voting period between pairs was about 10-sec long [13].

The sequence of blocks presented was: Exercise-L, Exercise-H, Lego-L, and Lego-H. Figure 5 shows the experimental process (adapted from [13]) within each block. Pairs of stimuli were presented automatically using a script with the ascending levels of degradation. For each pair, the first video was the unimpaired reference video, shown to mitigate memory effect [22], and the second video was the impaired one. In between the pair, there was a 2-second interval with black screen [13]. The voting period after each pair was about 10 seconds long, when the observer was asked if he/she could tell any difference between the two clips, and whether he/she thought any video had unacceptable quality. The subjects were told that they could take a break at any time during the experiment.

[1]The exact age distribution is unknown because some subjects expressed unwillingness to disclose age.

4.3 Apparatus

The experiment was conducted in the MONET (Multimedia Operating and Networking) laboratory at the University of Illinois at Urbana-Champaign. Participants were asked to be seated in front of a LCD monitor during the experiment with a standard viewing distance [13]. The detailed specification of the monitor used is listed in Table 3. 3D displays were available but not used mainly for usability concerns. Despite their rapid growth, today's state-of-the-art 3D displays are not yet ready to be deployed for tele-immersive activities. For example, typical stereoscopic displays require observers to wear goggles to perceive the depth effect, which is intrusive and thus unsuitable for physical activities often conducted in tele-immersive environments. The new autostereoscopic displays eliminate the need for wearing glasses; however our previous experience with them indicates that the technology was far from mature as they caused considerable discomfort for viewers. Lambooij et al. gave a general review of the visual discomfort caused by stereoscopic and autostereoscopic displays [17]. Therefore, in this experiment we resorted to using conventional displays for visualization. However, it is still worth noting that 3D displays are only designed to hypothetically *improve* depth perception [14], not to *enable* it. In fact, depth perception is achieved by a variety of visual cues (such as shading, texture gradient, linear perspective, motion parallax, occlusion, etc.) that are still relevant in tele-immersive video regardless of the type of display used [10]. We chose to trade the possible increase of depth perception for the visual comfort of users, which was believed to be more important.

Table 3: Detailed specification of the monitor used.

LCD Monitor Model	Acer X222W
Dimensions (WxDxH)	51.4 cm x 20.4 cm x 41.8 cm
Resolution	1680 x 1050 / 60 Hz
Dot Pitch	0.282 mm
Response Time	5 ms
Brightness	300 cd/m2

4.4 Evaluation Results

In psychophysics, perceptual thresholds are defined to be the stimulus intensities (in our case, CZLoD degradation ratios) that can be detected/accepted some p portion of the time, with $p = 50\%$ often used [8]. Figure 6(a) shows the measured JNDG and JUADG thresholds in four blocking conditions using probability 50% (equivalent to taking medians in the data). There are several observations:

Existence of perceptual thresholds: There do exist perceptual thresholds on the magnitude of CZLoD degradation that viewers can detect and accept. The average JNDG across all conditions is 61.5%, suggesting that degradation below 61.5% is not noticeable to average users. This implies that we can *transparently* reduce a considerable amount of resource usage by degrading CZLoD without actually impairing the perceived quality. The existence of JUADG (average 81.25%) indicates the degradation should be bounded by this upper limit otherwise it might make the overall quality unacceptable.

Figure 4: Stimulus snapshots: please refer to Figure 3(a) for the stimulus codes and their degradation ratios.

Impact of pixel resolution: JNDGs in both content blocks (Exercise and Lego) are lower for the two 320x240 conditions (Exercise-L/Lego-L) than for the corresponding 640x480 conditions (Exercise-H/Lego-H), indicating that it might be easier for subjects to notice degradation with lower pixel resolution than with higher resolution. This may be possibly because lower resolution already loses much more detail than the higher resolution (in our case, four times); thus any further degradation would become more noticeable. Likewise, JUADGs of Exercise-L/Lego-L are lower than those of Exercise-H/Lego-H.

Impact of content: Within the same pixel resolution condition, the thresholds for the 320x240 resolution (Exercise-L/Lego-L) vary with content, while those for the 640x480 resolution (Exercise-H/Lego-H) do not. Exercise-L has a higher JNDG than Lego-L, meaning that it is harder to notice the degradation in the exercise scene that contains only elbow movement than in the Lego video involving finer granularity object and finger movement. This is partly due to the fact that the arm in elbow exercises requires much less details than the Lego object. Since viewer attention normally focuses on the arms in motion, any changes in other parts of the video tend to go unnoticed (a phenomenon often referred to as "change blindness" in visual perception [25]). Similarly, the tolerance for degradation (JUADG) is higher in Exercise-L than in the Lego-L.

Figure 6(b) presents the cumulative probability distribution of the response data. We have the following observations:

Relationship between noticeability and acceptability thresholds: For every condition, the A curve (for JUADG) is always on the right side of the N curve (for JNDG). This indicates that as degradation increased, at some point subjects started to notice the distortion yet felt it was still acceptable, but after some further degradation, they started to feel the video quality was unacceptable.

Noticeability and acceptability offset: The offsets between the N and A curves in each condition are similar - mostly close to 10%-20%. Considering the step size in our stimuli was about 10%, this means about 0%-20% more degradation than the noticeable region would cause the quality to be perceived as unacceptable. The reason why we consider step size is as follows: Assume for the first six stimulus levels presented (S_0 versus $S_1, S_2, ..., S_6$, Figure 5), the subjects did not notice a difference between the unimpaired and impaired video. Then assume at S_7 they suddenly started to notice the degradation (say, of ratio 70%, meaning JNDG = 70%). It is unclear any ratio between that of S_6 and S_7 is detectable or not due to the discrete stimulus levels we used. Hence it is safer to take the step size into consideration here.

Impact of pixel resolution and content: The observations we have from Figure 6(a) about the impact of the two blocking factors (when p is 50%) are also generally true for other p values (y-axis). For example, Lego-L has lower JNDG and JUADG than Exercise-L. Lego-H and Exercise-H mostly have the same responses. The lower resolution blocks (Exercise-L and Lego-L) generally have lower thresholds than the higher resolution blocks (Exercise-H and Lego-H).

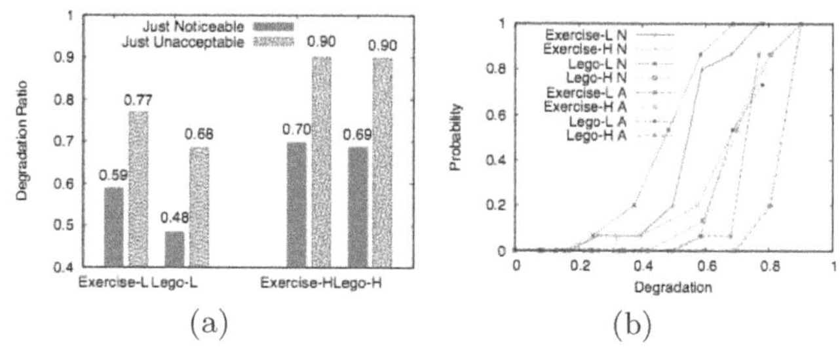

Figure 6: (a) perceptual thresholds on four conditions taken by medians, and (b) psychometric curves of JNDG and JUADG (in the legends, "N" stands for JNDG, and "A" stands for JUADG).

5. ADAPTATION SCHEME

5.1 Overview

QoS parameters are characterized by spatial (intra-frame) and temporal (inter-frame) requirements. For tele-immersive video, the spatial parameter refers to the spatial (including z-axial) resolution, and the temporal parameter corresponds to the frame rate. Naïve tele-immersive applications are often implemented without considering the temporal-spatial balance. The results from our psychophysical study suggest that CZLoD provides tele-immersion developers a powerful tool to control the detail complexity of the video, and in turn control the frame processing time or the frame rate. A major implication of our findings is that transparent degradation on spatial resolution (CZLoD) is possible to achieve "free" saving on resources without users being aware of it, i.e., by degrading CZLoD to a level where the distortion is just unnoticeable. In addition, when frame rate drops to a level that it hurts overall usability, the degradation on CZLoD can further increase (yet within acceptable ranges) to reduce data load and thereby elevate frame rate. Furthermore, past research has implied a curvilinear relationship between spatial quality and frame rate, e.g., improvements in frame rate become less noticeable above approximately 10 frames per second [16]. Therefore, when frame rates are found to be higher than necessary, the CZLoD degradation ratio can be lessened (if possible) to recover or promote the detailing quality thereby reducing frame rate. In short, we can manipulate the CZLoD degradation ratio to achieve a balance between the temporal quality (frame rate) and the spatial quality (CZLoD).

Based on these principles, we propose a novel, human-centric, real-time adaptation scheme (at the sender side) for tele-immersive video. We design the adaptor as a closed feedback loop [4] for the control of detailing quality in tele-immersive video. Figure 7 illustrates the schematic process of the adaptation. It has three major components: QoS Monitor, Decision Engine, and Variance Calculator. QoS Monitor is responsible for collecting and analyzing time series of QoS parameters (e.g., frame processing time, frame size, reconstruction time), and extracting meaningful information online to notify Decision Engine for triggering adaptation. Decision Engine computes an appropriate target CZLoD degradation ratio for the 3D reconstruction process. Since the degradation ratio is actually controlled by manipulating the variance threshold (Section 3.2), a Variance Calculator component is used to compute the correct variance threshold given a target degradation ratio from Decision Engine. Yet a challenge is that the mapping from a desired CZLoD degradation ratio to a variance threshold is unpredictable due to its dependency on scenes (e.g., clothing texture, skin colors, presence of objects, lighting illuminance). Therefore, Variance Calculator dynamically learns a quantitative model between the CZLoD degradation ratio and the appropriate variance threshold. Based on the model, it computes the proper variance threshold given a target degradation ratio, and feeds it into the 3D reconstruction pipeline for video quality adaptation.

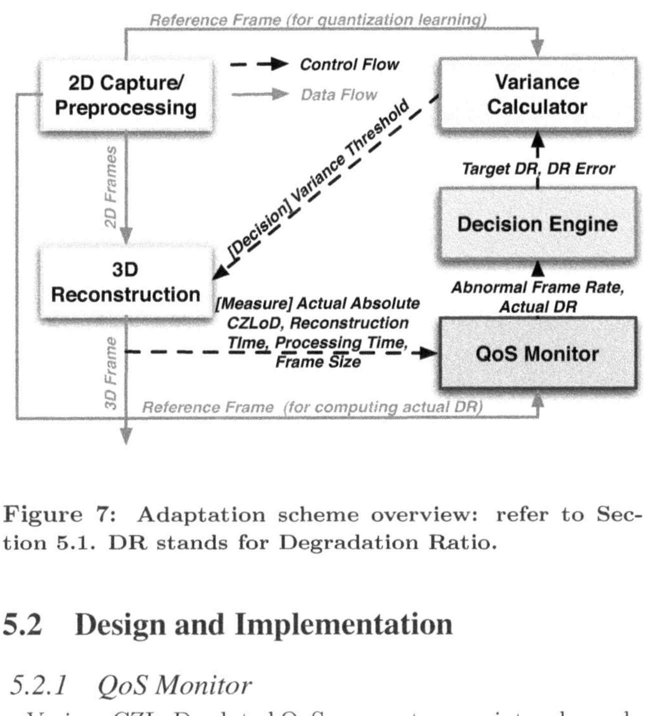

Figure 7: Adaptation scheme overview: refer to Section 5.1. DR stands for Degradation Ratio.

5.2 Design and Implementation

5.2.1 QoS Monitor

Various CZLoD-related QoS parameters are inter-dependent in tele-immersion. Figure 8 depicts the most relevant parameters and their dependencies identified using the Granger-causality graphs [23] over profile data. QoS Monitor continuously collects time-series meta-data of these parameters

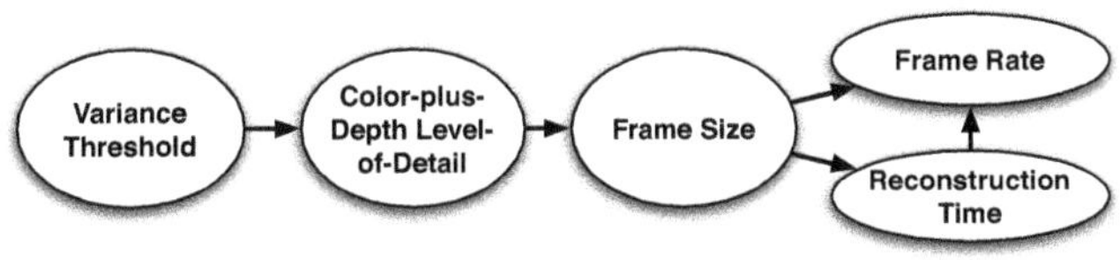

Figure 8: Dependency graph of parameters.

for each frame, and performs online analysis and profiling. It then provides "feedback" to Decision Engine. The feedback includes two types: (a) *frame rate events* (excessively high or low) for triggering increase or decrease of the degradation ratio, and (b) *actual degradation ratio* $DR^a(F_i)$ of every frame F_i.

Since providing real-time feedback in the control loop is key, a simple yet efficient range checking approach is used for evaluating frame rate. Essentially, if the frame rate drops below a lower-limit threshold (TH^l_{fr}), Decision Engine is notified to increase degradation ratio (for lower CZLoD quality); if the frame rate increases beyond an upper-limit threshold (TH^h_{fr}), Decision Engine is notified to decrease degradation ratio (for higher CZLoD quality). The thresholds should be set according to the perceptual characteristics of the frame rate [16]. Compared to the single threshold method where $TH^l_{fr} = TH^h_{fr}$, range thresholding is important for avoiding the flickering effect that can occur when a parameter constantly switches between low and high levels as it hovers near the threshold. For the same reason, the frame rate is not computed on a per frame basis, but averaged over a running window of size W (frames).

Apart from the frame rate reports, QoS Monitor also evaluates the actual degradation ratio of each frame F_i, $DR^a(F_i)$, and reports it to Decision Engine for taking corrective measure. $DR^a(F_i)$ needs to be measured because the sequence complexity and resource condition are constantly changing, meaning it is possible that a target degradation ratio would not be achieved exactly as desired. It is worth pointing out that the precise computation of $DR^a(F_i)$ requires the original 2D frame f_i be reconstructed by setting $TH_{var} = 0$ (refer to Equation 1). To facilitate the computation, the 2D capture/preprocessing component of the live 3D tele-immersion pipeline periodically sends a reference frame f_r to QoS Monitor, on which it applies 3D reconstruction with $TH_{var} = 0$ and computes the reference CZLoD expressed as $N_0(F_r)$ (Section 3). Since this is a relatively expensive operation, it is only periodically performed. We believe this is reasonable considering that performer motion cannot change dramatically within a short period of time; i.e., $N_0(F_r)$ would be very close to $N_0(F_i)$ due to their temporal proximity[2]. Using the latest available $N_0(F_r)$ to approximate $N_0(F_i)$, QoS Monitor can then compute $DR^a(F_i)$ (Equation 1) and report it to Decision Engine.

5.2.2 Decision Engine

The foundation of the adaptation logic in Decision Engine is based on the perceptual thresholds (JNDG and JUADG) on the color-plus-depth spatial resolution of the video. The thresholds decompose the CZLoD quality of tele-immersive

[2]In this approximated computation, an out-of-range result (i.e., $DR^a(F_i) > 1$) is theoretically possible, but very unlikely. If it does occur, $DR^a(F_i)$ is corrected to 1.

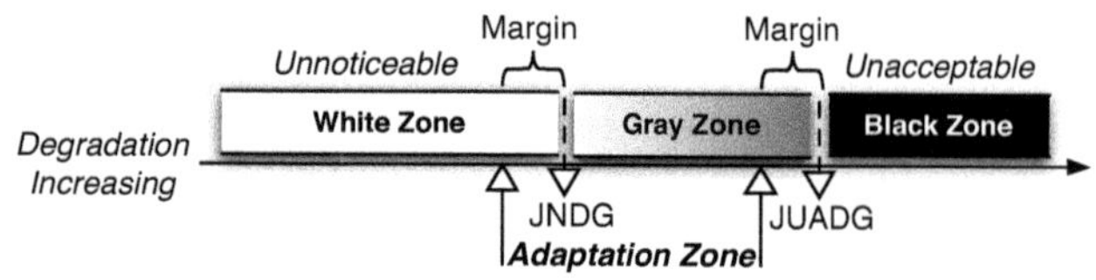

Figure 9: The Just Noticeable (JNDG) and Just Unacceptable (JUADG) thresholds decompose the range of CZLoD degradation to three zones.

video into three zones: *white zone*, where distortion is minimally noticeable; *gray zone*, where the distortion gradually becomes noticeable yet still acceptable; and *black zone*, where the degradation is unacceptable. The basic idea of Decision Engine is to dynamically adjust the target degradation ratio primarily in the gray zone, with some margins (Figure 9). The margins are introduced to account for the step size in our psychophysical experiment (as discussed in Section 4.4) as well as environmental and user dynamics. Hence, if we denote the margin size as B_n and B_a ($0 \leq B_n, B_a \leq 1$) for noticeability and acceptability thresholds respectively, the adaptation zone can be defined as $[JNDG - B_n, JUADG - B_a]$ in terms of degradation ratio.

As mentioned above, Decision Engine receives two types of information from QoS Monitor: (a) abnormal frame rate, and (b) DR^a of every frame. Upon receiving alarms of abnormal frame rate, Decision Engine computes an appropriate target degradation ratio. For this purpose, a linear control mechanism is used. Basically, an abnormally low frame rate ($FR_i < TH^l_{fr}$) means the need for lower CZLoD quality (or higher degradation ratio). Thus the engine computes the target degradation ratio as $DR^t(F_i) = DR^a(F_{i-1}) + \Delta_d$ where $DR^t(F_i)$ denotes the target degradation ratio (greater DR means more degradation), $DR^a(F_{i-1})$ denotes the actual degradation ratio of the last frame F_{i-1} (reported by QoS Monitor), andΔ_d denotes the adjustment size for increasing DR. This ratio is then used for all frames until the next time adaptation is triggered. Similarly, an unnecessarily high frame rate ($FR_i > TH^h_{fr}$) triggers the engine to produce a desired degradation ratio as $DR^t(F_i) = DR^a(F_{i-1}) - \Delta_u$ whereΔ_u is the adjustment size for decreasing DR.

The settings ofΔ_d andΔ_u can follow various protocols, e.g., AIMD (Addictive Increase Multiplicative Decrease), or proportional to frame rate deviation from normal mean. Although much more complicated or aggressive changes may result in faster reaction time, they may also incur more overhead or abrupt changes in the detailing resolution of the video. We find that simple constant small sizes are sufficiently effective in responding to frame rate anomalies while maintaining a gradual and graceful change that is less noticeable. Further, simple models provide superior performance benefits that are critical in such real-time environments. We utilize the measured thresholds from Section 4 to guide the adaptation zone (Figure 9). When the frame rate is excessively low (i.e., to increase DR), if $DR^t(F_i)$ reaches the upper limit of the adaptation zone (close to the black zone in Figure 9),Δ_d is set to 0; i.e., no further degradation is allowed otherwise the quality would become unacceptable. Likewise, when the frame rate is excessively high (i.e., to decrease DR), if $DR^t(F_i)$ reaches the lower limit of the adaptation zone (close to white zone),Δ_u is set to 0; i.e., further improvement on the detailing quality would not be noticeable anyway thus is unnecessary. Besides the calculation of the target degradation ratio, Decision Engine also computes the adaptation error between the actual and target degradation which will be used for Variance Calculator (as explained below).

5.2.3 *Variance Calculator*

Given the target CZLoD degradation ratio DR^t, Variance Calculator is responsible for determining the proper value for the detailing parameter TH_{var} in the 3D reconstruction. However, the mapping $\mathcal{F}$ from DR^t to TH_{var} is nontrivial because it highly depends on external conditions such as scene complexities. Therefore, we dynamically learn a quantitative model in order to predict the correct TH_{var} value for a desired DR^t. The learning process is performed only when Decision Engine finds that the adaptation error $err = |DR^a(F_i) - DR^t(F_i)|$ is larger than some threshold $err > TH_{err}$, meaning that significant changes in scenes might have happened that make the previous model less applicable. To learn a new model, Variance Calculator repeatedly applies 3D reconstruction on the frame f_i with exponentially increasing TH_{var} values, and the resultant $DR^a(F_i)$ values are logged. This process runs in parallel with the actual 3D tele-immersion pipeline and is thus unobtrusive. The TH_{var} values and their resultant $DR^a(F_i)$ values are then fed into a least-square regression module to develop an exponential model as follows [6]:

$$\mathcal{F} : TH_{var} = e^{a \cdot DR^t + b} \tag{2}$$

where e is the Euler number, and a and b are constants. The choice of the above exponential model comes from our extensive curve-fitting experiments with TI video, where their relationships are all a form of Equation 2. With this simple model we are able to achieve a high accuracy (median residual of 0.022%) with as few as 10 training points (refer to Section 5.3). With the model available, Variance Calculator is then able to set a proper variance threshold after 2D preprocessing and before 3D reconstruction for a desired degradation ratio.

5.3 Performance Evaluation

We evaluated the adaptation scheme in a real-world 3D tele-immersive system. The Bumblebee2 stereo camera (Point Grey Inc.) was used. It was connected to a host computer (Intel Xeon quad-core CPU 2.8GHz and 2GB RAM) via an IEEE 1394b card. The pixel resolution used was 320x240. Two professional lamps (Brightline SeriesONE) were employed to produce soft and diffused lighting condition. The rendering machine had an Intel Xeon CPU 2.3GHz, 2GB RAM, and an NVIDIA GeForce 9800 graphics card. The scene was an experimenter performing arm exercises in front of the camera. We compared two conditions — with and without adaptation, using the same experimental setup. Both objective and subjective measurements were collected. The technical metrics such as frame rate, frame size, target and actual degradation ratios were logged, and the rendered video was recorded on the renderer for subjective evaluation. Settings for the algorithmic parameters were: $W = 5, TH^l_{fr} = 8, TH^h_{fr} = 12, B_n =$

-3	-2	-1	0	+1	+2	+3
Much Worse	Worse	Slightly Worse	The Same	Slightly Better	Better	Much Better

Table 4: Rating scale used to compare videos with and without adaptation.

$B_a = 10\%, JNDG = 59\%, JUADG = 77\%, \Delta_u = \Delta_d = 5\%$ (Table 1).

Figure 10(a) shows the frame rate comparison. In this case, the adaptation scheme achieved an average of 27% improvement on frame rate from about 8 fps to 10 fps. According to [16], any improvement below a frame rate of 10 fps is considerably noticeable to users. It is also worth noting that even with the adaptation mechanisms added, the frame rate improves and real-time performance is guaranteed, meaning that the overhead of our algorithms is minimal. We also compared the frame rate with some CPU stress. For this, a process was run together with 3D tele-immersion that took at peak 16% of the CPU load. This simulates conditions where the CPU is less powerful or higher pixel resolution is configured. As Figure 10(b) shows, the frame rates without adaptation dropped to about 6-7 fps with several sudden dips to 3 fps. On the other hand, the frame rates achieved with adaptation (with the same conditions) remained relatively stable around 9 fps (with average improvement being 39.6%). Figure 10(c) shows the actual degradation ratios used with the projected target ratios. The prediction accuracy was high, with a median residual of 0.022%. The average degraded ratio was 22.7%, with a standard deviation of 0.063%. Considering that the JNDG is around 60% (Figure 6), there was still room for much more reduction if the frame rates were below desired thresholds.

We also conducted a user study to compare the visual quality of the recorded video. The crowdsourcing methodology was used due to the simplicity of the experiment. Following the ITU standard for double stimuli video comparison study [13], we made a short video with the following structure (in sequential order): (a) five seconds of text illustrating the purpose of the study, (b) two seconds of text indicating "Video 1" to be shown, (c) ten seconds of Video 1, (d) two seconds of text indicating "Video 2" to be shown, and (e) ten seconds of Video 2, and (f) ten seconds of text asking the rating question: "Compared to Video 1's quality, Video 2's quality is: [the scale shown in Table 4]?" [13]. The video was uploaded to Youtube and was advertised to a mailing list (containing graduate students, staff, and professors in Department of Computer Science). The ranking data were collected anonymously through an online Google Doc Form. A total of 81 responses were collected. Three of them were discarded because respondents notified the experimenter that they submitted by mistake. Figure 10(d) shows the collected ratings. Among the 78 responses, 96.2% of the users thought the video with adaptation turned on was better quality than the video with adaptation turned off, and 3.8% thought they were the same. 12.8% (of total) gave a "(+1) Slightly Better" ranking, 51.3% gave a "(+2) Better" ranking, and 32.1% gave a "(+3) Much Better" ranking. Clearly, our adaptation scheme not only saves system resources (i.e., CPU load), but also improves subjective video quality.

6. CONCLUDING REMARKS

This paper identifies a new critical quality factor called Color-plus-Depth Level-of-Detail (CZLoD) in 3D tele-immersive video. A psychophysical study of the perceptual thresholds of CZLoD is performed and presence of two perceptual thresholds - Just Noticeable Degradation (JNDG) and Just Unacceptable Degradation (JUADG) is demonstrated. Taking CZLoD as a guiding parameter, we design an online human-centric QoS adaptation scheme to dynamically adapt the video quality. Our experiments show that the adaptation scheme considerably reduces the resource demands while enhancing the perceived visual quality.

Future Work. Currently, N_0 is only periodically evaluated in our adaptation scheme (Section 5.2.1); we will investigate real-time statistical approaches for predicting N_0. Also, we employ a simple constant adaptation model for adjusting degradation ratio due to its efficiency (Section 5.2.2), but complex models are worth investigating. As hardware advances, it is possible that the increasing number of cores could run more complex models with demanded time bounds. Further, we measure the perception thresholds on 2D display, and we will perform the study on 3D displays as they mature. Finally, as we have stated previously, we only consider the temporal challenge in this work and address the spatial challenge in our previous work [33]. In future work, we will study their seamless integration.

Discussion. Subjective video quality research suffers from the limitation that the results might vary with the sequence content, and this study is no exception. While we attempt to be representative in choosing the tele-immersive activities for the psychophysical study, we do not intend to draw any general conclusion about the specific values of JNDG and JUADG in all tele-immersive applications. Rather, the main contribution of our study is the identification of the existence of perceptual thresholds on a unique factor that has (to our best knowledge) never been explored in real-time color-plus-depth video. The measurements of the thresholds provide practical guidelines on their estimation in the field. We also demonstrate that by applying these thresholds to practice, we can adapt the detailing quality and achieve considerable resource saving as well as enhancement on the perceived video quality.

7. REFERENCES

[1] Cisco TelePresence, http://www.cisco.com/en/us/products/ps7060/index.html.

[2] Polycom Telepresence, http://www.polycom.com/telepresence.

[3] R. Apteker, J. Fisher, V. Kisimov, and H. Neishlos. Video acceptability and frame rate. *IEEE Multimedia*, 2(3):32–40, 1995.

[4] K. J. Åström and R. M. Murray. *Feedback Systems: An Introduction for Scientists and Engineers.* Princeton University Press, 2008.

[5] H. H. Baker, N. Bhatti, D. Tanguay, I. Sobel, D. Gelb, M. E. Goss, W. B. Culbertson, and T. Malzbender. Understanding performance in Coliseum, an immersive videoconferencing system. *ACM TOMCCAP*, 1(2):190–210, 2005.

[6] A. BjÄorc. *Numerical Methods for Least Squares Problems.* SIAM, 1996.

[7] Y.-C. Chang, T. Carney, S. A. Klein, D. G.

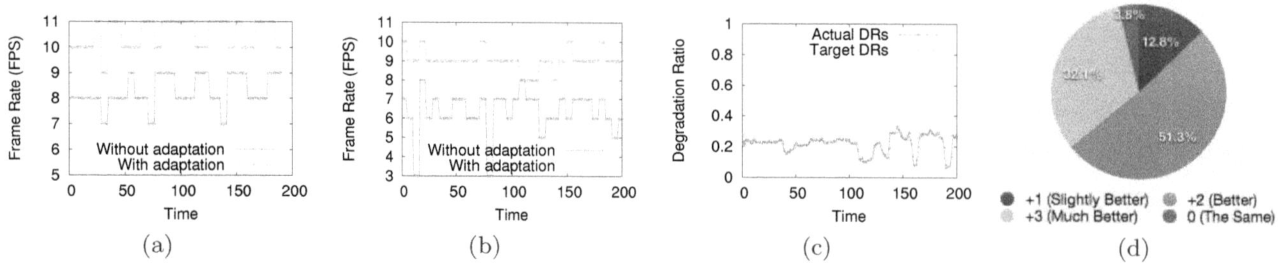

Figure 10: Adaptation performance: (a) the frame rates with and without adaptation where the CPU has no additional load other than tele-immersion, (b) the same comparison with a 16% CPU stress, (c) the degradation ratios (DRs) are well below the just noticeable threshold, with high prediction rate regarding variance threshold, and (d) the subjective evaluation results comparing the quality of the adapted video against the unimpaired video.

Messerschmitt, and A. Zakhor. Effects of temporal jitter on video quality: Assessment using psychophysical methods. In *Proc. of SPIE HVIP'98*, 1998.

[8] G. Gescheider. *Psychophysics: The Fundamentals.* Psychology Press, 3rd edition, 1997.

[9] S. Hacker. *MP3: The Definitive Guide.* O'Reilly, 1st edition, 2000.

[10] I. Howard. *Seeing in Depth. Volume 2: Depth Perception.* I Porteous, 2002.

[11] S. Iai, T. Kurita, and N. Kitawaki. Quality requirements for multimedia communication services and terminals - interaction of speech and video delays. In *Proc. of GLOBECOM '93*, 1993.

[12] ITU. Information technology - digital compression and coding of continuous-tone still images - requirements and guidelines. In *Rec. T.81*, 1992.

[13] ITU. Methodology for the subjective assessment of the quality of television pictures. In *Rec. BT.500*, 2009.

[14] Z. X. Jin, Y. J. Zhang, X. Wang, and T. Plocher. Evaluating the usability of an auto-stereoscopic display. *Proc. of HCI'07*, pages 605–614, 2007.

[15] T. Kanade, P. Rander, and P. Narayanan. Virtualized reality: Constructing virtual worlds from real scenes. *IEEE MultiMedia*, 4(1):43–54, 1997.

[16] J. K. Kies. *Empirical methods for evaluating video-mediated collaborative work.* PhD thesis, Virginia Polytechnic Institute and State University, 1997.

[17] M. Lambooij and W. IJsselsteijn. Visual discomfort and visual fatigue of stereoscopic displays: A review. In *JIST*, volume 53, 2009.

[18] D. Luebke, M. Reddy, J. Cohen, A. Varshney, B. Watson, and R. Huebner. *Level of Detail for 3D Graphics.* Morgan Kaufmann, 2002.

[19] D. C. Montgomery. *Design and Analysis of Experiments.* Wiley, 7 edition, 2008.

[20] P. J. Narayanan, P. W. Rander, and T. Kanade. Constructing virtual worlds using dense stereo. In *Proc. of ICCV'98*, pages 3–10, 1998.

[21] D. E. Ott and K. Mayer-Patel. A mechanism for TCP-friendly transport-level protocol coordination. In *Proc. of USENIX'02*, pages 147–159, 2002.

[22] M. Pinson and S. Wolf. Comparing subjective video quality testing methodologies. In *Proc. of SPIE VCIP'03*, pages 573–582, 2003.

[23] M. E. R. Dahlhaus. *Causality and graphical models for time series.* University Press, Oxford, 2003.

[24] D. D. Silva, W. Fernando, G. Nur, E.Ekmekcioglu, and S. Worrall. 3D video assessment with just noticeable difference in depth evaluation. In *Proc. of ICIP'10*, pages 4013–4016, 2010.

[25] D. J. Simons and R. A. Rensink. Change blindness: Past, present, and future. *Trends in Cognitive Sciences*, 9(1):16–20, 2005.

[26] E. Steinbach, S. Hirche, J. Kammerl, I. Vittorias, and R. Chaudhari. Haptic data compression and communication. *IEEE SPM*, 2011.

[27] R. Steinmetz. Human perception of jitter and media synchronation. *IEEE JSAC*, 14(1):61–72, 1996.

[28] H. Towles, W. chao Chen, R. Yang, S. uok Kum, H. F. N. Kelshikar, J. Mulligan, K. Daniilidis, H. Fuchs, C. C. Hill, N. K. J. Mulligan, L. Holden, B. Zeleznik, A. Sadagic, and J. Lanier. 3D tele-collaboration over Internet2. In *ITP*, 2002.

[29] R. Vasudevan, G. Kurillo, E. Lobaton, T. Bernardin, O. Kreylos, R. Bajcsy, and K. Nahrstedt. High quality visualization for geographically distributed 3d teleimmersive applications. In *IEEE Transactions on Multimedia*, volume 13, pages 573–584, 2011.

[30] R. Vasudevan, G. Kurillo, E. Lobaton, T. Bernardin, O. Kreylos, R. Bajcsy, and K. Nahrstedt. High quality visualization for geographically distributed 3d teleimmersive applications. *IEEE ToM*, 2012.

[31] R. Vasudevan, E. Lobaton, G. Kurillo, R. Bajcsy, T. Bernardin, B. Hamann, and K. Nahrstedt. A methodology for remote virtual interaction in teleimmersive environments. In *Proc. of ACM MMSys'10*, pages 281–292, 2010.

[32] VQEG. http://www.its.bldrdoc.gov/vqeg/.

[33] W. Wu, Z. Yang, I. Gupta, and K. Nahrstedt. Towards multi-site collaboration in 3d tele-immersive environments. In *IEEE ICDCS'08*, 2008.

[34] S. Würmlin, E. Lamboray, and M. Gross. 3D video fragments: Dynamic point samples for real-time free-viewpoint video. Technical report, Institute of Scientific Computing, 2003.

[35] Z. Yang, Y. Cui, Z. Anwar, R. Bocchino, N. Kiyanclar, K. Nahrstedt, R. H. Campbell, and W. Yurcik. Real-time 3D video compression for tele-immersive environments. In *Proc. of MMCN*, 2006.

"Seeing" ENF: Natural Time Stamp for Digital Video via Optical Sensing and Signal Processing *

Ravi Garg
University of Maryland
College Park, USA
ravig@umd.edu

Avinash L. Varna
University of Maryland
College Park, USA
varna@umd.edu

Min Wu
University of Maryland
College Park, USA
minwu@umd.edu

ABSTRACT

Electric Network Frequency (ENF) fluctuates slightly over time from its nominal value of 50 Hz/60 Hz. The fluctuations in the ENF remain consistent across the entire power grid even when measured at physically distant locations. The near-invisible flickering of fluorescent lights connected to the power mains reflect these fluctuations present in the ENF. In this paper, mechanisms using optical sensors and video cameras to record and validate the presence of the ENF fluctuations in fluorescent lighting are presented. Signal processing techniques are applied to demonstrate a high correlation between the fluctuations in the ENF signal captured from fluorescent lighting and the ENF signal captured directly from power mains supply. The proposed technique is then used to demonstrate the presence of the ENF signal in video recordings taken in various geographical areas. Experimental results show that the ENF signal can be used as a natural timestamp for optical sensor recordings and video surveillance recordings from indoor environments under fluorescent lighting. Application of the ENF signal analysis to tampering detection of surveillance video recordings is also demonstrated.

Categories and Subject Descriptors

I.5.4 [**Applications**]: Signal Processing; K.6.5 [**Security and Protection**]: Authentication

General Terms

Security, Algorithms, Experimentation.

Keywords

Video Authentication, Timestamp, Information Forensics, Electric Network Frequency.

*Area chair: Dr. Qibin Sun

MM'11, November 28–December 1, 2011, Scottsdale, Arizona, USA.

1. INTRODUCTION

In the modern era, a huge amount of digital information is available in the form of audio, image, video, and other sensor recordings. Stored on disks and other storage devices, this information has metadata describing the time and place of recording. However, digital tools can be used to modify the stored information. For example, digital editing softwares can be used to cut a clip from an original audio or insert a clip from one audio into another audio, or manipulate the metadata field to alter the recording date. Similar changes can also occur with video surveillance and other recordings. In the absence of any cryptographic protection and watermarking techniques during initial data acquisition, such modifications can be difficult to detect. Developing forensic tools to authenticate data using natural timestamp in the stored digital data presents an attractive direction to complement the existing technologies.

Exploration of Electric Network Frequency (ENF) is an emerging direction to authenticate digital recordings. ENF is the supply frequency of power distribution networks in a power grid. The nominal value of the ENF is 60 Hz in the United States and most parts of the Americas; and in Europe and Asia, 50 Hz is the generally accepted norm except for some parts of Japan and Taiwan. Digital devices, such as audio recorders, CCTV recorders and camcorders that are plugged into the power mains or are located near power sources, pick up the ENF signal because of interference from electromagnetic fields generated by power sources [3]. Battery operated devices are also capable of capturing the ENF signal from electromagnetic fields generated by nearby transmission lines or power equipment.

Importantly, the value of the ENF is not constant, fluctuating from the nominal value because of varying loads on the power grid [3]. For example, in Europe, these fluctuations make the ENF a continuous random variable typically between 49.90 Hz and 50.10 Hz [3]. Similarly, the ENF fluctuations in the United States vary between 59.90 Hz and 60.10 Hz [10]. The fluctuations from the nominal value are consistent across the power grid, and it has been shown that frequency fluctuations measured at locations physically far apart but connected on the same power grid have a similar value [3] [10]. Therefore, the ENF signal recorded at any location in the network of the power grid can serve as a representative signal for the ENF in the area covered by the power grid.

Fluctuations in the ENF have been used successfully to authenticate audio recordings in [3] [10]. These works demonstrate that the ENF signal is captured in audio recordings and exhibit high correlation with the ENF signal recorded from the power mains supply at the corresponding time. It was also shown that the ENF signal can be used as a natural timestamp to authenticate audio recordings, both stand-alone and those associated with videos. All of these works require the active recording of the true ENF signal from the power grid to be used as the ground truth timing to help verify the authenticity of signal content. ENF signal is extracted from the audio in question and compared with the ENF patterns from the power grid stored in a database to determine the time of recording or authenticity of audio. This method also provides rough information about the geographical location in terms of the grid where recording occurred. In contrast to the active recording of the ENF signal, the phase continuity of the ENF signal is used to detect the region of tampering in [9]. Any sudden change in the phase of the ENF signal extracted from audio strongly indicates that the original recording has been modified. This method does not require the use of reference ENF to authenticate a given recording, though the time and the place of recording cannot be determined without matching against a database of reference ENF signals.

Although audio authentication using the ENF signal has been explored in recent years, to the best of our knowledge, no research has investigated the traces of the ENF in visual sensing data such as optical sensor recordings and video recordings, or to bind audio and visual tracks of recordings forensically. An important research question to address in this direction is whether the ENF signal is present and measurable in visual sensing data. Optical sensors and CCD sensors used in video cameras measure the intensity of photons falling on the sensor array and convert them to measurable quantities, such as electric current or further into digital image sequence. The photons generated from indoor fluorescent light sources flickering in accordance to the frequency of the electric current may induce the ENF signal in these recordings. Optical sensors with high temporal bandwidth can potentially measure changes in illumination from fluorescent lightings. On the other hand, CCD sensors used in video cameras capture visual data at the rate of 25/30 frames per second, which is considerably lower than the nominal ENF value of 50 Hz or 60 Hz. So, it is challenging to extract ENF fluctuations from such video recordings due to significant aliasing.

Our research starts with devising experiments to verify the presence of the ENF signal in optical sensor measurements under fluorescent lighting. After establishing the presence of ENF signals, we devise a methodology to extract the ENF signal from video recordings under fluorescent lighting. As will be shown later, the ENF signal in optical sensor and video recordings shows significant correlation with the reference ENF signal extracted from the power mains supply, which can be used to verify or estimate the time of recording. As information about the time of recording can facilitate verification of the integrity of the video recording, we also examine potential applications of the proposed technique to verify the integrity of surveillance videos. Another potential multimedia application of the ENF analysis that we study in this paper determines if the audio and the visual tracks in a video recording are actually captured together, or if the sound track from a different recording has been manually added to the visual track. ENF signals that are extracted

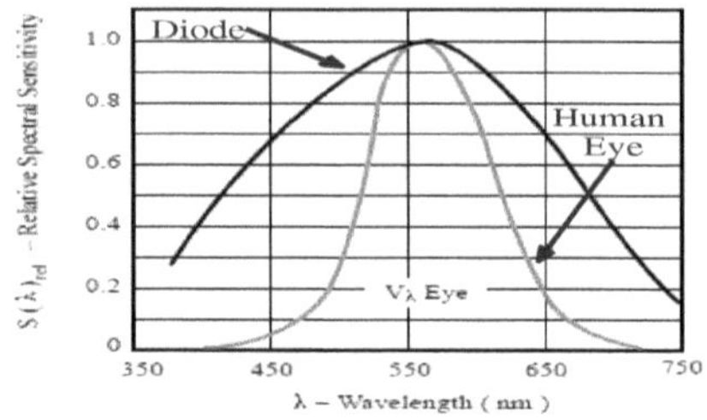

Figure 1: Spectral sensitivity of BPW21 photo diode (From: Vishay Semiconductor Web Catalog).

from both visual and audio tracks can provide natural alignment and binding of audio-visual recordings.

The rest of this paper is organized as follows. In Section 2, a method to detect the presence of the ENF signal from fluorescent lights is developed and validated through several experiments. In Section 3, the presence of ENF signals is established in video recordings in indoor environments illuminated by fluorescent lights, and the use of ENF signal as a natural timestamp for tampering detection of video recordings is demonstrated. Section 4 concludes the paper.

2. ENF MEASUREMENTS USING OPTICAL SENSORS

2.1 Background on Fluorescent Lamps

To understand the mechanism of ENF fluctuations in fluorescent lighting, we present a brief background on the operation of fluorescent lamps. A fluorescent lamp consists of a sealed tube containing a tungsten filament at both ends, an inert gas, and a small amount of mercury vapor. On passing electric current through this tube, electrons traveling in the form of electric current collide against the mercury atoms. If these electrons have enough kinetic energy, electrons in the mercury atoms become temporarily excited to higher energy levels. Unstable high energy levels cause electrons to return to lower energy levels, releasing photons with energy in the ultra-violet(UV) range. Since UV light is invisible to human eyes, the inner wall of the tube is coated with phosphor which absorbs UV light and emits light in the visible light range through another electron excitation process. Applying the electric current at the nominal ENF of 50 Hz/60 Hz to the tube heats the tungsten filament and generates free ions to establish a current path. As the current changes polarity at twice the rate of the nominal ENF, the current path inside the lamp turns on and off at 100/120 times per second. As a result, the lighting fluctuations illuminated by a fluorescent source is expected to be influenced by the ENF signal at a nominal value of 100 Hz/120 Hz.

2.2 Measuring Optical Signal under Fluorescent Light Sources

The first step of our study investigates the presence of the ENF signal in fluorescent lighting fluctuations. The typical wavelength of light emitted by fluorescent lighting occurs in the visible range (400nm-700nm). To record the light intensity, we use photo diodes that produce electric current when light falls on the diodes. We choose BPW21 photo-diodes that have light sensitivity of $9nA/lx$ and high

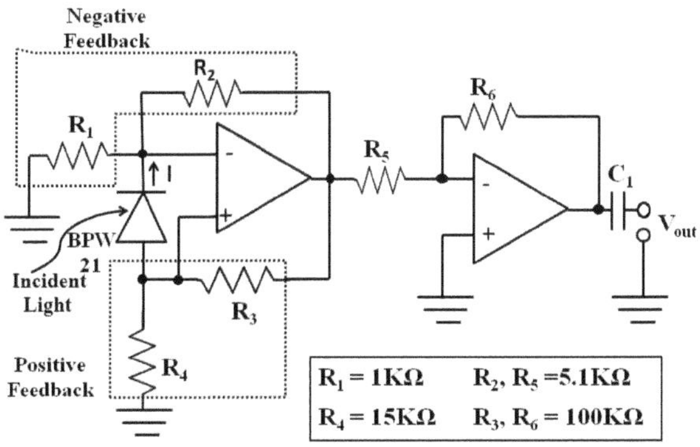

Figure 2: Light sensing circuitry.

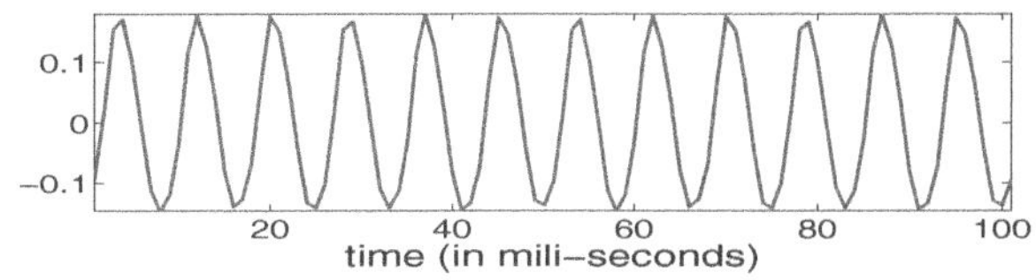

(a) Optical sensor signal from fluorescent lighting

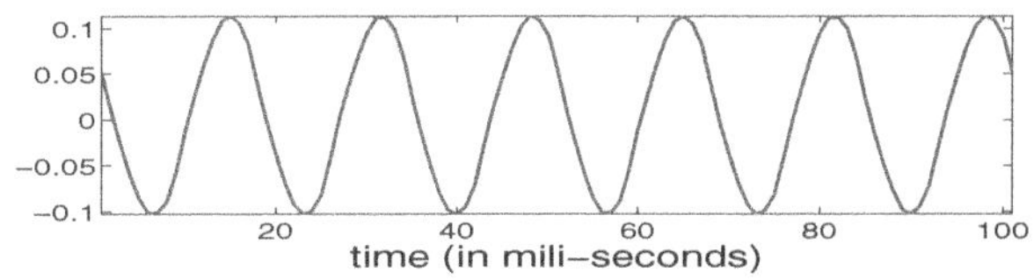

(b) Power mains signal

Figure 3: 100ms segments of ENF signals.

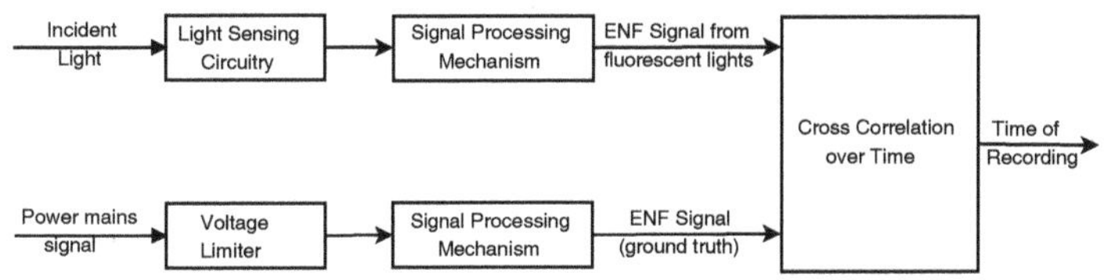

(a) Block diagram for ENF extraction

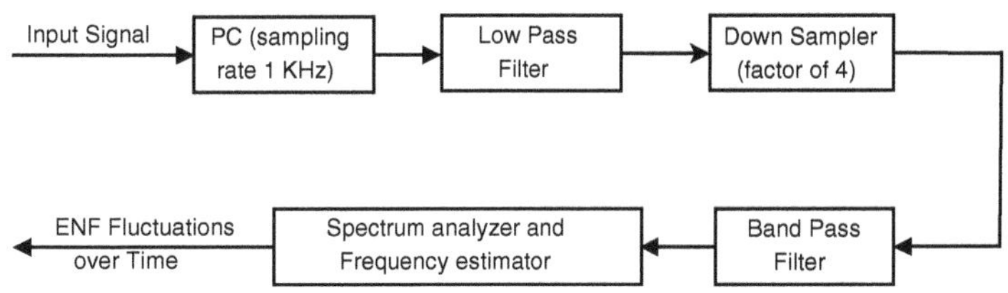

(b) Details of the signal processing module in (a)

Figure 4: Block diagram for estimating the time of recording of sensor signal.

spectral sensitivity in the visible range, as shown in Fig. 1. Using the diode with high spectral sensitivity in the visible range ensures that any infra-red signal generated from nearby heating sources does not interfere with the measurements obtained using the diode. This type of diode has been used in the power engineering literature to verify the presence of inter-harmonic flicker in fluorescent lighting [2]. The BPW21 diodes are extremely sensitive and can capture light shining at an angle or even weak ambient light. As discussed later in Section 2.4, when the fluorescent lamp directly above the sensor is switched off, the ENF signal is still recorded due to the low ambient light present in the corner of the room where recordings happen. The current generated by the photo diodes is on the order of μA, too weak to be directly recorded by common current measuring devices. We use a current-to-voltage amplifier to convert the current to measurable voltage levels. The electric circuit used for this amplification purpose is shown in Fig. 2. In the first stage, a combination of a positive and a negative feedback loop is applied to obtain a robust amplification. Use of the positive feedback loop increases the gain factor and produces less noisy amplification as discussed in [5]. In the second stage, a negative feedback loop is applied to further amplify the output from the first stage. For the given values of circuit parameters in Fig. 2, the overall gain of this circuit from input photo current I induced by incident light to output voltage V_{out} is $8 \times 10^6 \Omega$. The signal obtained after amplification is given as input to a PC sound card and sampled at 1 KHz.

To study the correlation between the ENF signal in fluorescent lighting captured using optical sensors and the ENF signal in power mains supply, we record the ground truth ENF signal directly from the power mains of the electrical supply. We first use a step-down transformer to convert the power supply voltage level to 5V. The transformer output is then given to a voltage divider to limit the current and voltage at safe levels so that it can be given as an input to a PC sound card. A similar mechanism was also used to capture the ENF signal in audio forensics [3]. These experiments are conducted in the state of Maryland (which is part of the eastern power grid of the United States), and the ENF signal captured by optical sensors is expected at around 120 Hz as discussed in Sec. 2.1. To validate the presence of the ENF signal at 120 Hz, Fig. 3(a) shows a time domain plot of a 100ms segment of the optical sensor signal captured under fluorescent lighting and recorded by a PC. The signal can be clearly seen oscillating at a fundamental frequency of about 120 Hz or an equivalent fundamental period of 8.33ms, suggesting that fluorescent lights flicker in accordance with the ENF. The corresponding power mains signal is shown in Fig. 3(b) oscillating at a frequency of about 60 Hz or an equivalent fundamental period of 16.66ms.

To extract the ENF signal, the recorded signals are given as an input to an anti-aliasing low-pass filter with passband of 125 Hz. The resulting signal is downsampled by a factor of 4 to reduce the sampling rate from 1 KHz to 250 Hz, and then passed through an equiripple band-pass filter with a narrow passband centered at 120 Hz for the optical sensor signal and 60 Hz for the power mains signal.

2.3 Correlation between optical sensor signal and power mains signal

In this section, we describe the methods used to compare the ground truth ENF signal captured from the power mains with the ENF signal from fluorescent lighting captured using optical sensors. After pre-processing recorded signals using the method described in Section 2.2, we find the dominant

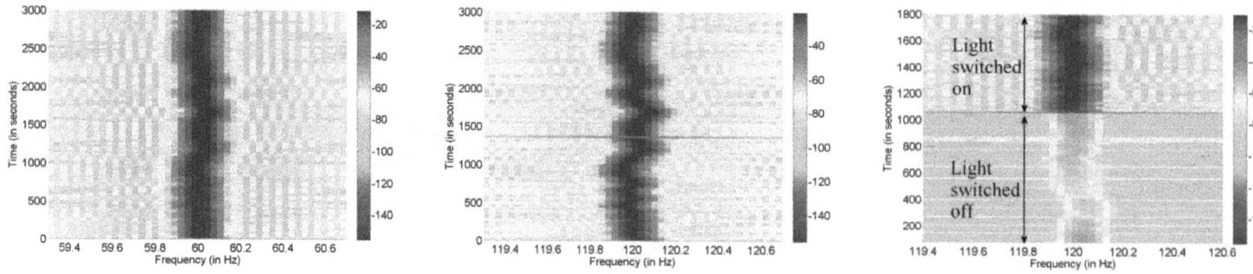

(a) Power mains ENF signal (b) Optical sensor ENF signal (c) Optical sensor ENF signal

Figure 5: (a),(b) ENF fluctuations of signals captured in Experiment 1; (c) ENF for sensor signal in Experiment 2, including a weak signal for first 17 minutes from the ambient light, when the main light is switched off.

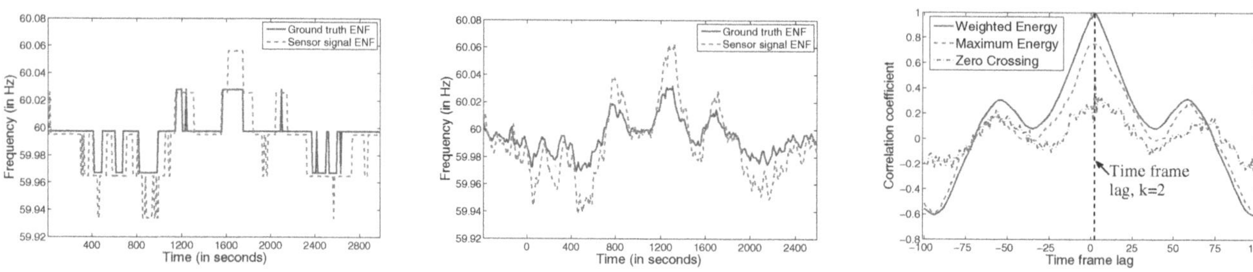

(a) Maximum Energy (b) Weighted Energy (c) NCC Coefficient, $\rho(k)$

Figure 6: (a),(b) ENF fluctuations for Experiment 1 measured using different frequency domain methods; (c) NCC coefficient, $\rho(k)$, as a function of time frame lag k.

instantaneous frequency in each signal to measure the fluctuations in ENF as a function of time. For this purpose, we explore different frequency estimators in time and frequency domains.

Among time domain techniques, we examine the zero-crossing method to estimate the frequency fluctuations in the ENF signal [8]. We divide the signal into overlapping frames of 16 seconds each with an overlap factor of 50%, and count the number of times the signal crosses zero in each frame. The dominant instantaneous frequency in each frame is recorded as one half of the zero-crossing count. This method is easy to compute, but does not give a high estimation accuracy for slowly varying signals. Hence, we also use spectrogram based methods to analyze fluctuations in the ENF signal with higher resolution.

Spectrogram is a common frequency domain analysis tool that can be used to determine the dominant instantaneous frequency of the signal as a function of time [4]. To obtain the spectrogram of the ENF signal, we divide the signal into overlapping frames of 16 seconds each with an overlap factor of 50%. A high resolution FFT of 8192 points is taken for each frame, providing a frequency resolution of approximately 0.03 Hz. After obtaining the spectrogram of the ENF signal, we use the following frequency domain measures to find the dominant instantaneous frequency in the ENF signal:

(a) Maximum energy: In this method, the frequency corresponding to the maximum energy in each time bin of the spectrogram is identified. The resulting one dimensional signal represents the dominant instantaneous frequency as a function of time. This method is susceptible to frequency outliers caused by sudden changes in energy due to factors such as variations in ambient lighting. For example, movement near light sensors can cause transient changes in the maximum energy.

(b) Weighted Energy: The weighted energy method records the weighted average frequency in each time bin of the spectrogram. Average frequency is obtained by weighing frequency bins around the ENF value with the energy present in the corresponding frequency bin as

$$F(n) = \frac{\sum_{l=L1}^{L2} f(n,l)|S(n,l)|}{\sum_{l=L1}^{L2} |S(n,l)|}, \tag{1}$$

where $L1 = \lfloor \frac{(f_{ENF}-0.5)N_F}{fs} \rfloor$ and $L2 = \lceil \frac{(f_{ENF}+0.5)N_F}{fs} \rceil$; fs and N_F are the sampling frequency and the number of FFT points used to compute the spectrogram; $f(n,l)$ and $S(n,l)$ are the frequency and the energy in the lth frequency bin of the nth time frame of the spectrogram of the recorded signal, respectively. Since we are interested in estimating the dominant instantaneous frequency around a known frequency value, i.e., around the nominal value of the ENF; the value of l is chosen to include the band within ± 0.5 Hz of the ENF frequency of interest.Weighting brings robustness against outliers, so this method provides a more accurate estimate of the instantaneous frequencies for a given ENF signal than the maximum energy method.

Compared to the time-domain zero-crossing method, the spectrogram based methods for estimating instantaneous frequency provide significantly higher accuracy. After estimating the frequency fluctuations in ENF signals as a function of time, we find the Normalized Cross-Correlation (NCC) coefficient between the two signals as

$$\rho(k) = \frac{\sum_{n=1}^{N}(F_s(n) - \mu_s)(F_m(n-k) - \mu_m)}{\sqrt{\sum_{n=1}^{N}(F_s(n) - \mu_s)^2 \sum_{n=1}^{N}(F_m(n-k) - \mu_m)^2}}, \quad (2)$$

where $F_s(n)$ and $F_m(n)$ is the dominant instantaneous frequency in nth time frame of the ENF signal in optical sensor recording and power mains recording, respectively; μ_s and μ_m are the mean values of $F_s(n)$ and $F_m(n)$, respectively; and N is the total number of frames in optical sensor signal. The peak in the value of $\rho(k)$ represents the estimated delay of k frames in the time of recording between the optical sensor signal and the power mains signal. The block diagram representation of the overall system used to extract the ENF fluctuations over time and compare them is shown in Fig. 4.

One of the advantage of using a correlation based metric as compared to the Euclidean distance based metrics is that the NCC coefficient depends only on the shape of the ENF signal, whereas distance based metrics rely on the absolute value of the signal. If frequency offset exists between the ground truth ENF signal and sensor ENF signal, then distance based metrics may produce wrong estimates of the time of recording. Frequency offset is generally unknown in advance and it may not be possible to compensate for the offset in the distance metric calculations. Use of a correlation based metric to compare the two ENF signal avoids this limitation of distance based metric [6].

2.4 Results and Discussions

In this section, we describe different experiments conducted to determine the presence of the ENF signal under fluorescent lighting. A light sensing circuitry shown in Fig. 2 is assembled, and its output signal is given as an input to a PC sound card to record it. Power mains signal is also recorded in parallel as the ground truth ENF signal.

Experiment 1: In our first experiment, a fluorescent light is switched on near the light sensing circuitry, and data is recorded for a duration of 50 minutes. Power mains signal recording is started with a delay of 15 seconds from the optical sensor recording in order to determine the accuracy of our method in estimating the time of recording. Spectrograms of the ENF signals obtained from the ground truth signal and the optical sensor signal around the frequencies of interests are shown in Fig 5(a) and Fig. 5(b), respectively. From these figures, we observe that the fluctuations in the ENF signal captured under fluorescent lighting is similar to the fluctuations in the ground truth ENF signal. High correlation between these fluctuations can be seen in the instantaneous frequencies obtained using the maximum energy and the weighted energy frequency estimation methods, as shown in Fig. 6(a) and Fig. 6(b), respectively.

As previously discussed, the fundamental component of the ENF signal from sensors is present at a frequency of 120 Hz. In order to facilitate examination of the ground truth ENF signal and the sensor ENF signal on the same scale, we subtract a DC value of 60 Hz from the sensor ENF signal to obtain the plots shown in Fig. 6(a) and Fig. 6(b). The plot of NCC coefficient, $\rho(k)$, for different frequency estimation methods described in Section 2.3 is shown in Fig. 6(c). The maximum value of the NCC coefficient occurs at the lag of two time frames for all three methods, verifying that the delay between optical sensor signal recording and power mains signal recording is approximately 16 seconds. The NCC coefficient found using the zero-crossing method is miniscule compared to the frequency domain methods because of the low precision of the zero-crossing method for frequency estimation. The NCC coefficient obtained using the maximum energy method is slightly smaller than that obtained using the weighted energy method. This is due to the presence of outlier frequencies affects the maximum energy method.

Experiment 2: In our second experiment, a fluorescent light is switched off for the first 17 minutes and then switched on for the next 13 minutes. In this experiment, the power mains signal is started with a delay of 70 seconds from the sensor signal. The room where the experiment is performed also receives some light from a low ambient light source. The spectrogram of the optical sensor recording for this experiment is shown in Fig. 5(c). From this figure, we observe that the ENF signal is weak for the period when the light is off. However, the fluctuations still show high correlation with the ground truth signal (corresponding power mains signal not shown due to space limit), implying that optical sensors can also capture fluctuations from ambient fluorescent lights. In this case, the NCC coefficient is found to be maximum for the lag of nine time-frames or equivalently 72 seconds, authenticating the approximate timing at which the recording started.

In our experiments, we also find a weak signal around 60 Hz in the optical sensor recordings. The energy in this signal is approximately 20 times less than that of the ENF signal at 120 Hz when fluorescent lights are functioning. This 60 Hz signal component is highly correlated with the ground truth ENF signal, indicating that ENF fluctuations are also captured in the optical sensor signal around the nominal ENF value of 60 Hz. We conjecture that the source of this signal may be from electromagnetic interferences of power supply frequency with the light sensing circuitry.

3. ENF MEASUREMENTS IN VIDEO

The ENF signal measurement in video is not as straightforward compared with the ENF measurements in optical sensors due to the low temporal sampling frequency (frame rate) of video cameras. The ENF signal is present at 50 Hz or 60 Hz, which is considerably higher frequency than the sampling rates in commonly available video cameras. Most of these video cameras are available in three different sampling rates: 24fps, 25fps, and 30fps. Cameras using 24fps are used in movie making, while most amateur hand-held cameras are available in 25fps or 30fps. Cameras with 25fps sampling rates originated from analog TV standard of PAL prevalent in Europe and most of Asia, while 30fps camera originated from NTSC standards prevalent across North America and Japan [1].

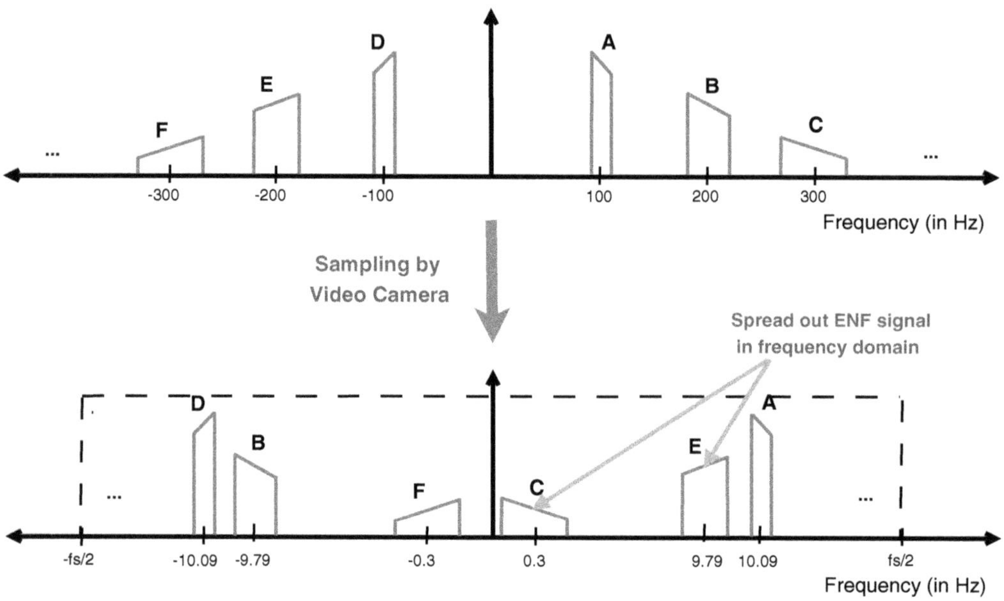

Figure 7: Spectral domain illustration of the aliasing effect in video capturing of ENF signals: (Top) Spectral composition of the original fluorescent light signal powered using 50 Hz supply frequency; (Bottom) Spectral composition of ENF related signals after sampling at 29.97fps by video camera.

The exact frame rates used in most of video cameras may not exactly meet 25fps or 30fps but vary slightly. The PAL standards specify the frame rate to be 24.98fps, and the NTSC standards specify it to be 29.97fps. These slight changes in the recording rates from the nominal values were introduced to make the transmission of color video compatible with black and white television standards and then newly introduced color televisions in 1960s. As different digital video camera manufacturers may not strictly follow the standards, it is common to have NTSC digital cameras with a frame rate of either 29.97fps or 30fps. Similarly, PAL cameras commonly have frame rates of 24.98fps or 25fps. A video recording in an indoor environment using these readily available cameras under fluorescent lighting may lead to significant aliasing of the captured ENF fluctuations depending on the sampling frequency of the camera.

3.1 Aliasing Effect

ENF signals recorded by video cameras under fluorescent lighting undergo significant aliasing due to the lower temporal sampling rate of cameras compared to the 100 Hz/ 120 Hz frequency components present in flickering of fluorescent lights. The ENF signal in the recorded videos appears at different predetermined frequencies, which can be determined from the sampling theorem [7]. As an example, we examine the effect of recording a video under a fluorescent light powered by a 50 Hz source. As current changes polarity at twice the power mains frequency, the fluorescent light flickers at 100 Hz. Additionally, when the power main signal slightly deviates from a perfect sinusoid form, often higher harmonics of decaying energy happen at integer multiples of 100 Hz. The bandwidth of these higher harmonics is also greater than the main component because the practical ENF signal of interest is a narrowband signal and not a perfectly stable sinusoid. So, the bandwidth of the kth harmonic component will be k times the bandwidth of the main ENF component at 100 Hz. Suppose the camera used for capturing video is an NTSC standard camera with a frame rate of 29.97 Hz. Because of the low sampling rate as compared to the required sampling rate to prevent aliasing, the resulting spectra will have periodic tiling of frequency components at $\pm 100 + 29.97k$, $k = 0, \pm 1, \pm 2, \ldots$. Because of the periodic nature of the resulting spectra, it suffices to focus on replicas within one period. Aliasing effect introduced by this video recording example is shown in Fig. 7. From this figure, we observe that multiple copies of the ENF related component will appear in the spectrum of the video signal around different but pre-determined frequencies. These multiple copies arise due to the presence of higher harmonics in the power mains signal, and may be combined strategically to obtain a better estimate of the video ENF signal.

We further recall that the magnitude spectrum of a real valued signal is symmetric about y-axis. Because of this, original spectrum of the ENF signal in fluorescent lights also has symmetric components at -100 Hz and its harmonics, as shown in Fig. 7. After sampling by video camera, the frequency component E, that is at -200 Hz in the spectrum of the original signal, appears at 9.79 Hz in the recorded signal; and the component A present at 100 Hz in the spectrum of the original signal appears at 10.09 Hz. As a result, we obtain replicas of the ENF signal at 9.79 Hz and 10.09 Hz, and they are mirrored versions of each other. Similar analysis can be performed on other combinations of different camera frame rates and power mains frequencies to find the frequencies at which the main component and the first harmonic component of the signal appear. The values of these frequencies are summarized in Table 1.

3.2 Experimental Setup for Video Recordings

In this section, we describe the settings under which experiments are conducted to detect the presence of the ENF signal in videos. We collect video data from three geograph-

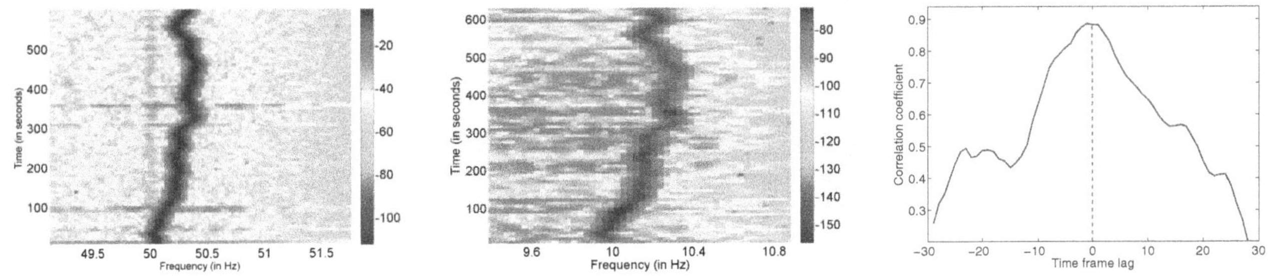

(a) Power mains ENF signal (b) Video ENF signal (c) NCC coefficient, $\rho(k)$

Figure 8: (a),(b) ENF fluctuations measured for the whitewall video experiment in India; (c) NCC coefficient, $\rho(k)$, as a function of time frame lag k.

Table 1: Aliased frequency for different combinations of power mains frequencies and video camera frame rates

Mains (in Hz)	Video (fps)	aliased (in Hz)	2nd harmonic aliased (in Hz)
60	29.97	0.12	0.24
60	30	0	0
50	29.97	10.09	9.79
50	30	10	10

ical regions – India, China, and USA – to demonstrate the capability of the ENF signal to act as a timestamp and authentication signal. To the best of our knowledge, this is the first work reporting the ENF based forensic signal collection and analysis on the Asian continent. For each of these three geographic areas, we collect video data under two settings:

(a) White wall video: In this experiment, we record a constant white wall scene illuminated under fluorescent lights for 10 minutes and examine the video for ENF traces. This experiment can be considered as a first step towards demonstrating the presence of the ENF signal in videos recorded under fluorescent lighting. We find the average intensity of each frame, and pass it through a band pass filter with passband corresponding to the frequencies of interest where aliased components of the ENF signal appear in videos, as listed in Table 1. As the content of the video is mostly the same in each frame, presence of a significant amount of energy in the desired frequency band can be attributed to the ENF signal. A spectrogram is plotted with a window size of 480 video frames ($\approx$ 16 seconds) and an overlap factor of 50%. For all the experiments conducted on video data, a frequency analysis with weighted energy is performed to extract the ENF signal around the aliased frequency bands.

(b) Surveillance video: In this experiment, a camera is placed inside a room for surveillance purposes. A fluorescent light illuminates the room. Occasional movement of people can be seen in the foreground of the video. Recordings performed under this setting can be considered representative of real-life surveillance scenarios in places where few events are expected to occur. In these experiments, because the content in each frame of the video is not constant due to the movement of people, a direct averaging of all frames may not be suitable to perform the frequency analysis. As the ENF signal from fluorescent lights is recorded by each sensor pixel, we can use a part of the video frame to extract the ENF signal. For example, we locate the relatively stationary areas in video frames, where content does not change much. Such areas at the top and bottom areas of each video frame are used to extract the ENF signal based on the spectrogram of average pixel intensity, and the similar settings to those described for white wall video experiments is employed. Alternatively, the process of finding the static regions in frames of the video can be automated using common motion estimation techniques.

3.3 Results and Discussions

(a) ENF Data collected from India: The nominal value of the ENF in India is 50 Hz, hence, the ENF signal reflected in the flickering of light is expected at a fundamental frequency of 100 Hz. In this experiment, we use a 30fps NTSC Sony HDR SR12 camera to record a video. The video camera recording and the power mains recording start simultaneously. From the aliasing discussion in Sec. 3.1, with this sampling frequency, the ENF signal at 100 Hz will appear at an aliased frequency of 10 Hz in video recordings. Spectrogram of the ENF signal for a white wall video recording is shown in Fig. 8(b). From this figure, we can clearly observe a high correlation between the pattern of the ENF signal at 10 Hz and the ground truth ENF signal at 50 Hz obtained directly from power mains supply, as shown in Fig. 8(a). The maximum value of the NCC coefficient, $\rho(k)$, between the video ENF signal and the power mains signal is found to be 0.91 at $k = 0$, as shown in Fig. 8(c). This indicates that the recording starts simultaneously for the power mains signal and the video signal.

For surveillance video recording experiment, the first five minutes of video is recorded with the camera constantly panning, while the remaining part of the video is recorded with a stationary camera. For this duration of the video, all parts of the frames undergo changes. We show the spectrogram of the ENF signal from this video recording in Fig. 9(b). From this figure, we see that the ENF signal is not strong during the first five minutes of the video recording when the camera pans. Nevertheless, the pattern in the ENF signal around 10 Hz for the first five minutes follows a similar pattern to the ground truth ENF signal shown in Fig. 9(a). The NCC coefficient, $\rho(k)$, attains the highest value at $k = 0$ as shown

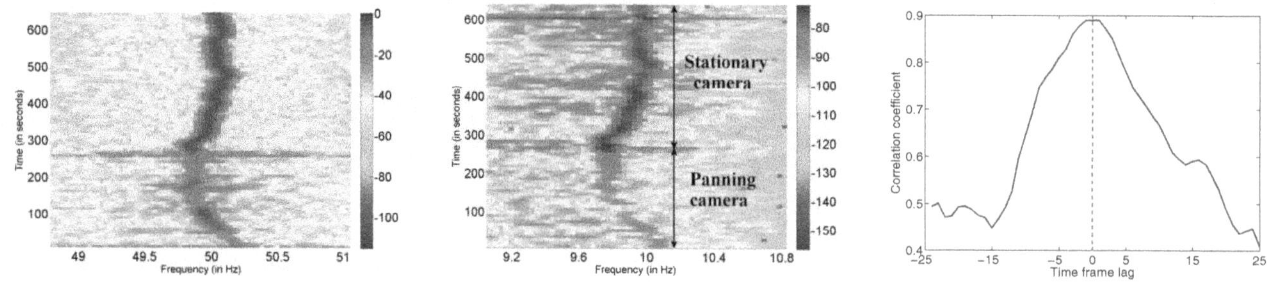

(a) Power mains ENF signal (b) Video ENF signal (c) NCC coefficient, $\rho(k)$

Figure 9: (a),(b) ENF fluctuations measured for surveillance video experiment in India; (c) NCC coefficient, $\rho(k)$, as a function of time frame lag k.

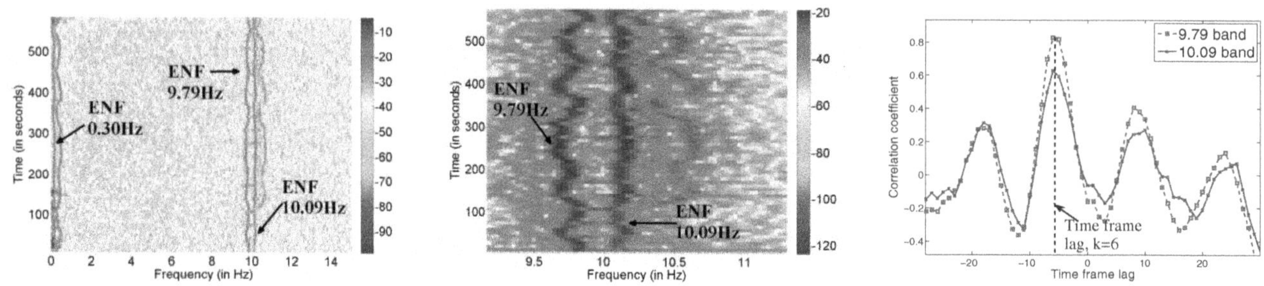

(a) Video ENF signal (b) Video ENF signal (amplified view) (c) NCC coefficient, $\rho(k)$

Figure 10: (a),(b) ENF fluctuations measured for the whitewall video experiment in China; (c) NCC coefficient, $\rho(k)$, as a function of time frame lag k.

in Fig. 9(c). This indicates that the power mains signal and the video signal recording starts at the same time.

For the above mentioned Sony HDR SR12 camera, videos are stored in MPEG-2 format, which involves lossy compression. The bitrate of recorded videos has a range of 700-750 kbps. Our above experiments also suggest that the ENF signal can be extracted from the lossy compressed videos and can be used to find time of recordings of moderately compressed videos.

(b) ENF Data collected from China: In China, 50 Hz supply frequency is used across the power distribution network. As a result, the ENF signal in the fluorescent light flickering can be expected at 100 Hz. We use a NTSC standard Panasonic camera with the frame rate of 29.97fps to record videos in China. For this experiment, video recording is started at a delay of 50 seconds with respect to the power mains signal. As discussed previously in Sec. 3.1 and shown in Fig. 7, we expect the main component of the ENF signal in video recordings to be present in the band around the aliased frequency of 10.09 Hz. Higher harmonics of the ENF signal in video recording are present in the band around 9.79 Hz (from the second harmonic) and 0.30 Hz (from the third harmonic).

The spectrogram of the ENF signal for the white wall video recording is shown in Fig. 10(a). In this figure, we observe that multiple copies of the ENF signal are present near the DC frequencies and 10 Hz frequencies. A magnified version of the figure around 10 Hz band is shown in Fig. 10(b), in which we can see multiple copies of the ENF signal around different frequencies in accordance with our analysis in Sec. 3.1. We also observe from this figure that the bandwidth of the video ENF signal present around 9.79 Hz is double that of the bandwidth of the video ENF signal around the frequency band at 10.09 Hz. This can also be explained from Fig. 7 as the copy of the video ENF signal at 9.79 Hz originates from the second harmonic of the ground truth ENF signal, which is present at 200 Hz from the flickering of fluorescent lights.

As explained in Section 3.1, the 9.79 Hz component of the recorded signal is a mirrored version of the 10.09 Hz component. Therefore, we flip the ENF signal extracted from 9.79 Hz component in NCC coefficient calculation to make the overall correlation positive. The plot of NCC coefficient between the video ENF signal and power mains ENF signal evaluated using the video ENF signal present around 10.09 Hz and 9.79 Hz frequency band is shown in Fig. 10(c). The plot obtained using the video ENF signal from 10.09 Hz band is similar to the plot obtained using the ENF signal from 9.79 Hz frequency band. The maximum value of the NCC coefficient is obtained at a lag of $k = 6$ time frames. This indicates that the video recording was started with a delay of approximately 48 seconds from the power mains signal, which is close to the actual delay of 50 seconds. The small difference is due to the window based signal processing that leads to a limit in the temporal resolution for the ENF based timestamping. It is possible to extract other harmonic copies of ENF traces in the video signal by passing the video ENF signal through bandpass filters with passband frequencies around which each harmonic copy is located. These

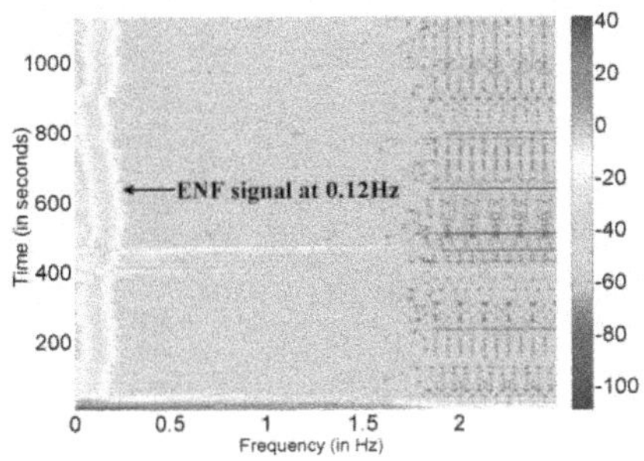

(a) Video ENF signal

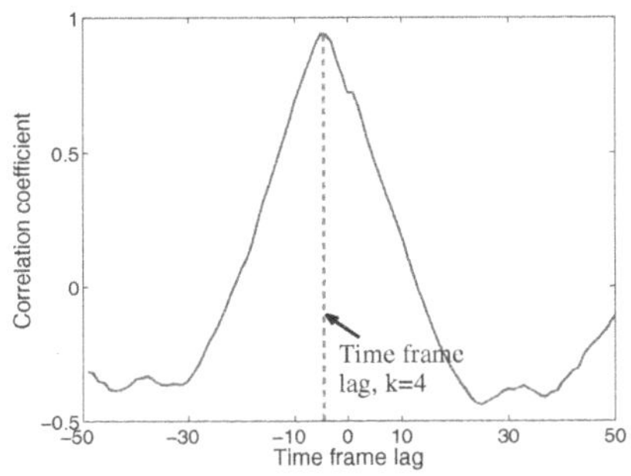

(b) NCC coefficient, $\rho(k)$

Figure 11: (a) ENF fluctuations measured for the whitewall video experiments in US; (b) NCC coefficient, $\rho(k)$, as a function of time frame lag k.

copies of the signal can then be combined to perform correlation analysis to find the time of video recording.

(c) ENF Data collected from USA: The nominal value of the power supply frequency in the United States is 60 Hz. The ENF signal from the flickering of fluorescent lights can be expected at 120 Hz. We use the same 29.97fps Panasonic camera from experiments done in China to conduct video recording in the United States. From Table 1, the ENF signal in the video recordings is expected at aliased frequency of 0.12 Hz. Fig. 11(a) shows the spectrogram of the ENF signal for the white wall video. The presence of a significant energy band at 0.12 Hz confirms the presence of the ENF signal in video recordings. The NCC coefficient between the video ENF signal and the power mains ENF signal is plotted in Fig. 11(b). The maximum value of the NCC coefficient is found to be 0.95 corresponding to a lag of $k = 4$, indicating the video recording was started with a delay of approximately 32 seconds from the power signal. The actual delay in recording time is approximately 38 seconds. This again shows the timestamping capability on the order of approximately 8 seconds.

(d) Tampering detection: We design an experiment to demonstrate an application of the ENF analysis for tampering detection of surveillance videos. For this purpose, we record a video of 980 seconds' long in an indoor environment in India illuminated with fluorescent lights. We perform a simple video clip insertion by cutting the last 160 seconds of video and inserting it in between the remaining clip of the video close to the 340th second. The ENF signal extracted from this tampered video and the ground truth ENF signal extracted from the power mains signal database corresponding to the time of recording is shown in Fig. 12. From this figure, we can locate the regions in the ENF signal from the video, which has similar patterns as the ground truth ENF signal for the given time of recording. We observe that the ENF signal from video recording shows the same pattern as the ground truth ENF signal for 340 seconds in the beginning of the video as shown by the red arrows in the figure. Similarly, video ENF signal from time index 500 second to 980 seconds have the same pattern as the ground truth ENF signal between time index 340th and 820th seconds. The video ENF signal between time index 340th seconds and 500th seconds does not match with the ground truth ENF signal, suggesting that the video recording is likely to be modified in the corresponding region and a video clip insertion operation was performed. More rigorous verification can be performed over visual examination by quantitatively comparing the segments of ENF sequence from video with the reference ENF database.

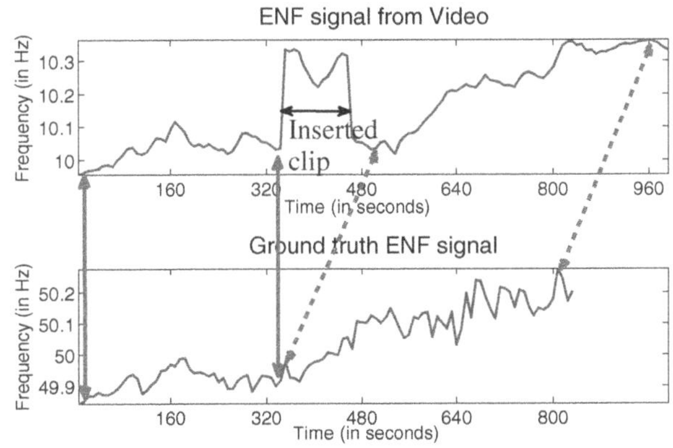

Figure 12: ENF matching result demonstrating the detection of video tampering based on the ENF traces.

(e) Audio-visual authentication and synchronization: We now explore an important application of the ENF analysis for *forensic binding* of audio-visual recording. This determines whether the audio and visual tracks in a video recording are captured together, or if the sound track from a different recording is manually placed with the visual track. ENF signals extracted from both visual and audio tracks can provide natural alignment and binding of audio-visual recordings. As noted above, the ENF signal is captured in the video track due to the flickering of fluorescent lights and in the audio track through electromagnetic interference. When audio and video are recorded simultaneously, we expect that the ENF traces in these two streams should exhibit similar patterns, and the synchronization between the audio and video tracks can be verified by quantitatively comparing these two signals. Discrepancies between the ENF traces in the audio and video would provide a strong indicator of tampering of either the audio or the video. Thus, the synchronization can be authenticated even if the ground truth ENF signal from power mains is not available at the time of recording. Fig.13 shows an example of the ENF traces obtained from the audio and visual tracks of a video record-

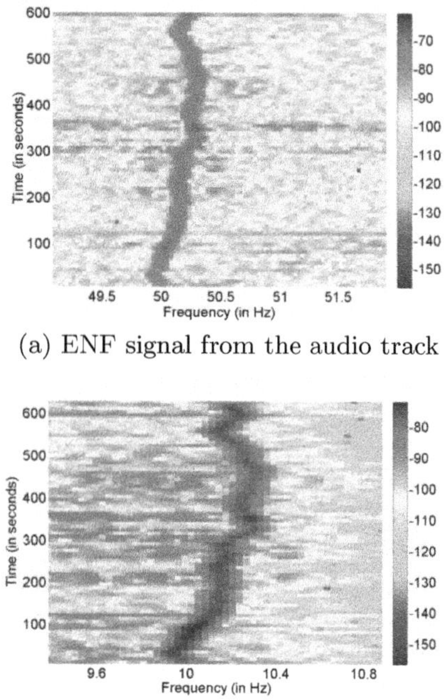

(a) ENF signal from the audio track

(b) ENF signal from the video track

Figure 13: ENF matching between audio and video tracks of a video recording.

ing. From this figure, we see that the ENF signal captured in audio, as shown in Fig.13(a) exhibit similar patterns and have high correlation with the ENF signal captured in visual track, as shown in Fig.13(b). Further quantitative cross correlation analysis can confirm with confidence that the audio-visual tracks in the video are temporally synchronized and authentic.

4. CONCLUSIONS & FUTURE WORKS

In this paper, we have described mechanisms to capture the ENF fluctuations in fluorescent lighting using optical sensors and video camera, and demonstrated the presence of the ENF in indoor video surveillance recordings. Recorded optical and video signals have been shown to have high correlation with the ENF signals captured directly from the power mains supplies. The estimated time of recordings for sensor signals have been shown to be accurate up to 8 seconds. Results from our investigations suggest that the ENF signal can be used as a natural timestamp for optical sensors and video surveillance recordings in an indoor environment. The ENF signal can also be used to facilitate the authentication of sensor and video data, as data modifications by adversaries are likely to cause changes in the ENF signal at the corresponding part of the recordings. Modifications in video recordings can be identified by the discontinuity or alteration in the ENF signal and the ENF traces provides a natural binding of audio and visual tracks to verify their temporal synchronization and integrity. To the best of our knowledge, this is the first work investigating the presence and forensic analysis of the ENF signal in optical and visual recordings, and reporting the ENF based forensic signal collection and analysis in the Asian continent.

In future work, we plan to devise methods to adapt the ENF analysis technique to non-static videos, where the camera itself moves. In such videos, it may be difficult to find any part in the frame that is stationary throughout the video, calling for the need to adapt ENF authentication techniques to non-static video. Furthermore, we are collecting more experimental data to prepare for a larger scale statistical study on tampering detection in video and audio-video synchronization.

5. ACKNOWLEDGEMENTS

The work was supported in part by research grants from U.S. AFOSR #FA9550-09-1-0179 and NSF #0824081, and a University of Maryland Litton Graduate Fellowship. The authors would like to thank Prof. Xianli Wu and Mr. Hui Su for their help in collecting the ENF data in China, and Mr. Daniel Garcia-Romero for recommending references [3] [10]. The authors would also like to thank the anonymous reviewers and the area co-chairs, Dr. Qibin Sun and Dr. Tian-Tsong Ng, for their constructive comments.

6. REFERENCES

[1] A. Bovik. *Handbook of Image and Video Processing.* Academic Press, 2000.

[2] S. Chen, C. Lo, M. Foo, and K. How. Testing of fluorescent lamps for its flickering susceptibility towards interharmonic voltages. In *International Power Engineering Conference*, December 2007.

[3] C. Grigoras. Applications of ENF criterion in forensics: Audio, video, computer and telecommunication analysis. *Forensic Science International*, 167(2-3):136 – 145, April 2007.

[4] S. Haykin. *Advances in Spectrum Analysis and Array Processing*, volume 1. Prentice-Hall, 1991.

[5] W. Hernandez. Input-output transfer function analysis of a photometer circuit based on an operational amplifier. *Sensors*, 8(1):35–50, September 2008.

[6] M. Huijbregtse and Z. Geradts. Using the ENF criterion for determining the time of recording of short digital audio recordings. In *Proceedings of the 3rd International Workshop on Computational Forensics*, IWCF '09, pages 116–124. Springer-Verlag, August 2009.

[7] A. V. Oppenheim, R. W. Schafer, and J. R. Buck. *Discrete-time Signal Processing (2nd ed.).* Prentice-Hall, Inc., 1999.

[8] L. Rabiner and B.-H. Juang. *Fundamentals of Speech Recognition.* Prentice-Hall, Inc., 1993.

[9] D. Rodriguez, J. Apolinario, and L. Biscainho. Audio authenticity: Detecting ENF discontinuity with high precision phase analysis. *IEEE Transactions on Information Forensics and Security*, 5(3):534 –543, September 2010.

[10] R. W. Sanders. Digital authenticity using the electric network frequency. In *33rd AES International Conference on Audio Forensics, Theory and Practice*, June 2008.

Can Computers Learn From Humans to *See Better*? Inferring Scene Semantics From Viewers' Eye Movements *

Ramanathan Subramanian, Victoria Yanulevskaya and Nicu Sebe
Dept. of Information Science and Computer Science
University of Trento
Italy
{subramanian, yanulevskaya, sebe}@disi.unitn.it

ABSTRACT

This paper describes an attempt to bridge the **semantic gap** between computer vision and scene understanding employing eye movements. Even as computer vision algorithms can efficiently detect scene objects, discovering semantic relationships between these objects is as essential for scene understanding. Humans understand complex scenes by rapidly moving their eyes (saccades) to selectively focus on *salient* entities (fixations). For 110 social scenes, we compared verbal descriptions provided by observers against eye movements recorded during a free-viewing task. Data analysis confirms (i) a strong correlation between task-explicit linguistic descriptions and task-implicit eye movements, both of which are influenced by underlying scene semantics and (ii) the ability of eye movements in the form of *fixations* and *saccades* to indicate salient *entities* and *entity relationships* mentioned in scene descriptions.

We demonstrate how eye movements are useful for inferring the meaning of **social** (everyday scenes depicting human activities) and **affective** (emotion-evoking content like *expressive faces*, *nudes*) scenes. While saliency has always been studied through the prism of fixations, we show that saccades are particularly useful for (i) distinguishing mild and high-intensity facial expressions and (ii) discovering interactive actions between scene entities.

Categories and Subject Descriptors

H.1.2 [**User/Machine Systems**]: Human information processing; I.5.4 [**Pattern Recognition Applications**]: Computer vision

General Terms

Algorithms, Measurement, Human Factors

*Area chair: Massimo Zancanaro

MM'11, November 28–December 1, 2011, Scottsdale, Arizona, USA.

Keywords

Eye movements, fixations and saccades, salient entities and interactions, scene semantics

1. INTRODUCTION

The flagship objective of computer vision is to enable computers 'to see what we see', *i.e.*, to endow them with human-like perception so as to extract meaningful descriptions from images [7]. While excellent progress has been achieved in recognizing individual objects [25, 5], analysis of state-of-the-art algorithms in activity and scene understanding [36, 13] indicates the extremely limited use of *context* in scene analysis. This is because the *viewer interprets context* upon discovering salient scene entities and relationships between them. These interpretation rules are based on our understanding of the world and are influenced by many factors which are difficult to model automatically. Therefore, there usually exists a difference between measured scene information and the actual meaning known as **semantic gap**.

Despite the many challenges involved, the need for associating context with content for image description and retrieval applications is strongly advocated in [11]. Also, psychological literature [28] has stressed the importance of object relationships in scene understanding and search. Context is mainly incorporated in multimedia retrieval through user-supplied *metadata*, as typified by ESP game and LabelMe [23], which embellish object-centric information regarding the scene. Tagging images with metadata concerning object relations can be quite tricky though. In everyday scenes comprising many objects, one can come up with multiple descriptions for the each object; the problem becomes intractable when relationships between objects also need to be considered. Nevertheless, studies have shown that human visual attention is limited to *salient* scene objects and their relationships [21, 26], which contribute maximally to scene semantics.

This paper investigates the utility of eye movements as metadata. Eye movements are a reflection of visual attention which is highly contextual- this enables discovery of content central to the scene meaning. Also, eye tracking technology has become inexpensive today, and reliable eye-gaze estimation is achievable using webcams [30]. With time, we believe it should be possible to non-invasively compile large-scale eye gaze data for images browsed on the web. Humans see by making series of saccades and fixations; saccades are rapid eye movements that enable selective attention, while scene content is assimilated during fixations. Fixations and saccades are indicative of salient *entities* and certain forms of *entity relations*. These entities may be individual objects or object parts (*e.g.*, eyes, nose and mouth within a face). While many works on scene understanding have exploited fixations for salient object detection, our experiments confirm that saccades are also highly informative.

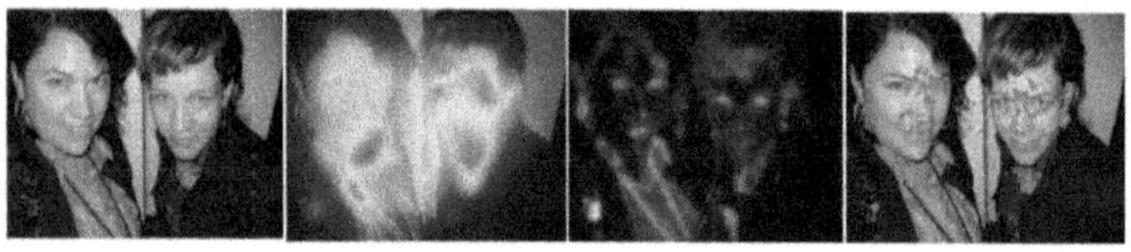

(a) (b) (c) (d)

Figure 1: *'Bottom-up' saliency does not correlate well with eye fixations in meaningful scenes-* For the original image (a), saliency maps predicted by 'bottom-up' models [10],[29] are shown in (b),(c)- parts of the persons' clothing are discovered as salient, while fixations appear on faces (d).

This work makes two main contributions:

1. This is one of the first works to investigate how eye movements are indicative of human perception in social and affective scenes. Social scenes involve humans performing various actions (talking, walking, reading, *etc.*) in real-life, everyday settings while affective stimuli are capable of arousing emotions (emotive faces, erotica, *etc.*) in viewers. A significant proportion of the image content that we see in newspapers and on photo sharing websites constitute social scenes. Also, the multimedia community has acknowledged the need to analyze affective content for retrieval and understanding. This paper demonstrates why eye movements can be regarded as useful metadata for inferring semantics of such scenes.

2. While previous scene understanding works employing eye movements have focused exclusively on fixations, we demonstrate that saccades are also highly informative. Humans instantly perceive interacting entities in social scenes, and such interactions are characterized by vacillating saccades. Moreover, saccades are found to be more effective than fixations for determining the emotional intensity of faces.

The paper is organized as follows. The next section discusses how eye movements have been utilized for scene understanding. In section 3, we describe in detail (a) the methodology we employed to acquire ground truth for social and affective scenes, (b) key observations we made upon analyzing the annotations, and (c) how eye movements are highly indicative of human scene understanding. We demonstrate how understanding scene semantics can benefit a number of contemporary applications in Section 4 and present our conclusions in Section 5.

2. EYE MOVEMENTS FOR SCENE UNDERSTANDING

Interest in studying and predicting human eye movements began decades ago. A majority of saliency prediction approaches [10, 29, 34] employ context-independent low-level features such as intensity, color and orientation to determine regions-of-interest in natural images. These 'bottom-up'/early saliency models imply that our visual attention is independent of scene content. However, many studies [35, 9] have confirmed that besides low-level features, our eye movements are driven by a number of 'top-down' factors such as the task on hand and recognized scene objects. Although some studies [4, 19] argue that interesting image regions are visually salient, early saliency does not correlate well with fixations in meaningful scenes [9, 3, 2] as seen in Fig.1. Recent approaches [12, 37] have achieved higher saliency prediction accuracies upon learning from eye fixations. Even as these efforts have focused on exploiting fixations for understanding scene content, eye movements have rarely been used to infer the scene meaning.

Building on previous work [27, 20] that have examined the use of eye gaze data for scene understanding, we demonstrate how, when combined with scene knowledge (in the form of detected scene objects), fixations and saccades enable semantics inference in *social* and *affective* scenes. In complex social scenes, determining relationships between entities is an extremely challenging task, and has been attempted only recently [5]. Nevertheless, humans can instantly recognize the 'central activity' in the scene with little effort. We asked subjects to provide brief descriptions of social scenes that included important scene objects (nouns) and actions (verbs). Upon manually analyzing those descriptions, regularity in the use of verbs was used to determine whether a scene contained an interaction or not. Most subjects consistently identified and reported scene interactions in the initial part of the descriptions. Also, remaining scene details were not reported as frequently for interactive scenes when compared to non-interactive scenes. In essence, the interacting entities and the interaction mainly constituted the scene gist.

Analysis of the eye-gaze recordings for scenes perceived as *interactive* in the above experiment confirms characteristic saccades vacillating between the interacting entities- these saccades are not observed for scenes without interaction. This is owing to two reasons

- Social interactions are characterized by pose/gaze cues, and being able to determine (and explore details in) the direction of others' attention is an important ability in humans [33, 14]. Therefore, fixations on one interacting entity are almost always succeeded by a fixation on the other.
- Also, short-term memory influences viewers to re-fixate on semantically interesting/informative areas [9]. This is perhaps responsible for saccades vacillating between interacting entities. We generally observe symmetrically vacillating saccades,*i.e.*, the likelihood of a forward/backward saccadic transition between interacting entities is roughly the same. This allows for reliable and automatic detection of interactions in social scenes employing eye movements.

Furthermore, we investigated how eye data are useful for semantics inference in *affective* images. Of late, there has been considerable interest in analyzing multimedia data at the affective (emotional) level, besides the cognitive (content-specific) level [8, 18]. In affective images, viewers are found to attend to those entities which are *emotionally salient* [27]. We demonstrate how this phenomenon can be exploited to distinguish (a) *highly-intense* from *mild/moderately-intense* facial expressions and (b) portraits of *clothed persons* from *nudes*. We believe that being able to automatically recognize these semantic classes is important because

- Even as numerous works have focused on emotion recognition, it is still hard to reliably detect facial expressions from images. While we do not know whether eye movements are characteristic of the facial expression, discovering highly/moderately emotional content from a database can facilitate applications such as content publishing (*e.g.*, advertisements).

- Likewise, while content-based (usually employing skin color) nudity/eroticism detection has generated significant attention over the years, state-of-the-art approaches [16] can only achieve moderate detection rates while maintaining a low number of false positives. However, concepts of nudity and eroticism can be fully comprehended only by humans and psychological literature has already reported the significance of eye movements for nudity detection [17].

We asked observers to rate faces and portraits in order to compile ground truth reflecting human perception. Observers were required to rate intensity of emotion portrayed in face images, whereas for portraits, they were required to rate the degree of nudity/eroticism on a Liekert 7-point scale. Based on the ratings, we noted that observers perceived facial expressions to be 'more intense' when significant facial deformations appeared on the lower half of the face, around the nose and mouth (Fig.7). This is mirrored in the eye movements as well- the eyes are usually the most attended regions in faces. However, visual attention shifts to the lower half of the face when emotions are strongly expressed. Our experiments confirm that saccades are more informative than fixations for distinguishing highly expressive from mildly expressive faces. Also, while faces strongly attract visual attention in normal (clothed) portraits, viewers mostly attend to body parts in nude/erotic stimuli. Fixations are found to be slightly more informative than saccades for clothed/nude portrait classification.

Even as our work is closely related to [26, 19], it is important to note a few significant differences. In [26], the authors ask viewers to name 10 objects they see in each image, while we ask for explicit descriptions comprising nouns and verbs- we therefore, seek to acquire a more natural ground-truth for evaluating scene understanding applications. In [19], significant correlation is observed between what viewers consciously perceive as interesting, eye fixations and low level saliency for 100 images spanning four specific semantic categories. We believe that such an analysis needs to be repeated for a wider class of images including social and affective scenes, as visual attention patterns differ significantly for semantically rich stimuli as compared to simple stimuli used in [26, 19]. Also, while recent efforts [15] have focussed on extracting scene context in terms of spatial relationships between all detected scene objects, some scene objects are more critical to scene understanding as noted in [26]. These *important* objects are consistently named and fixated upon as viewers observe scenes. The following section discusses our ground truth compilation procedure and how, eye movements are highly reflective of scene semantics.

3. CORRELATING EYE MOVEMENTS WITH HUMAN PERCEPTION

We selected 110 social scenes and 160 affective scenes (60 faces, 100 portraits) from the MIT [12] and NUSEF [20] eye tracking data sets for compiling ground truth concerning human perception of semantics. These publicly available databases contain eye movement recordings for a substantial number of semantically rich stimuli compiled under *free-viewing* conditions, where viewers are required to examine images in the absence of any high-level tasks that might bias their viewing patterns. A free-viewing paradigm is most representative of task-agnostic human scene understanding, and facilitates objective measurement of the notion of *saliency*.

The **MIT database** [12] contains eye gaze data for 1003 images including indoor and outdoor scenes, scenes with single or multiple humans and animals captured at mid-resolution, and a few high-resolution face images. Eye-gaze patterns of 15 viewers were recorded as they examined each image for 3 seconds, over two sessions scheduled one week apart. The **NUSEF** database [20] consists of at least 13 gaze patterns per image for 758 gray-scale/color images spanning many semantic categories such as high-resolution human and mammal faces, mid-resolution *portraits* showing face and body of humans/mammals, including *nudes*, and interactive scenes. Eye movements were recorded using a desktop-based eye tracker as viewers observed 350 images for 5 seconds each, over two sessions separated by a 10 minute interval.

3.1 Analyzing linguistic descriptions and eye gaze for social scenes

We asked observers to describe 110 social scenes 'in one or two sentences' for compilation of ground truth reflecting human scene understanding. Viewers were required to include objects (nouns) and object relationships (verbs) that they considered as important in the scene. To minimize noise, we asked viewers to only describe what they saw in the image and not to guess invisible details. All images were described by at least 12 observers; for some images, we collected 20 descriptions. Four exemplar images with five sample descriptions per image are shown in Fig.2.

To analyze the descriptions, we manually listed all the objects named by observers, using the most obvious synonym denoting similar words wherever necessary. Then, we computed a normalized *named frequency* for each scene object, which denotes how frequently the object is named in the descriptions (a named frequency of 1 implies that an object was named in all the descriptions). Furthermore, we represented relationships between objects as an $N \times N$ interaction matrix, where N is the number of named objects for the image. In this work, we are only interested in verbs identifying *interactions* between objects *i.e.*, 'A man *talking* to a woman' or 'A man *carrying* a child' are considered interactive, while 'A man *walking*' does not imply any interaction. We focused on those verbs connecting two or more nouns in the descriptions, taking into account plural noun forms as in 'People are talking'. As for the nouns, we also computed the named frequencies of these interactive verbs. Fig.3 shows an image

Figure 2: Exemplar interactive (top row) and non-interactive (bottom row) scenes along with their descriptions. All nouns are marked in red, while verbs are marked in green.

and the corresponding interaction matrix computed from 20 descriptions.

	Man (1)	Book (1)	Teddy bear (0.75)	Sofa (0.2)
Man (1)		1 (reading)	0.2 (holding)	0.06 (sitting)
Book (1)				
Teddy Bear (0.75)				
Sofa (0.2)				

Figure 3: Interaction matrix for the image on the left containing normalized named frequencies for object and object interactions. Refer to Fig.2 for sample descriptions.

Fig.4 presents the results of ground-truth data analysis. We computed the distribution of the number of named objects per image across all images (Fig.4(a)). On the whole, 484 objects were named for 110 images with a mean of 4.4 ± 1.6 objects per image. This number is much lower than the median object count reported in [26]. This difference is mainly due to the nature of the scene description task involved- in [26], every viewer is asked for a list of 10 objects from which 'important objects' are derived. In an object-centric scene description task, it is highly likely that the viewer starts to look at objects peripheral to the scene meaning. In fact, the authors in [26] employ the 'forgetful urn' model to account for this phenomenon. On the contrary, we ask viewers to perform a more natural scene description task, which results in only the important scene objects being named in the descriptions. This is reflected in the high degree of consistency with which viewers name scene objects (Fig.4(b)). 48% of the objects appear in more than 90% of the descriptions, while only 12% of the objects are named by less than 10% of the viewers. Overall, about 70% of all named objects occur in at least 40% scene descriptions, indicating a high degree of agreement regarding what observers deemed as 'important'.

An equally interesting observation is the consistency with which viewers report object interactions. Fig.4(c) presents the distribution of images according to the degree of interaction between objects, as identified by the viewers. For 45 images, over 80% of the descriptions contained an interaction verb- we assumed these scenes to be interactive. For 37 images, fewer than 30% viewers reported any form of interactions- we assumed these scenes to be non-interactive. Also, when interactions were reported, (i) they mostly represented relationship between two objects; this is probably perhaps because the central activity in most scenes involved only dyadic object interactions. (ii) The interactive verbs appeared in at the beginning of sentences in a vast majority of cases. Table 1 lists the set of interactive verbs most commonly reported by viewers.

We then considered the named frequency of objects in interactive and non-interactive scenes. For scenes involving object interactions, the interacting objects constituted 87% of all named scene objects. For non-interactive scenes, the frequently reported scene objects constituted only 78% of all named objects. The result of a two-sample t-test (assuming equal variances) confirms a significant difference in the proportion of scene content reported by observers in their descriptions (null hypothesis assuming that the proportions are similar is rejected at critical $p = 0.046$). This implies that even though viewers generally succeed in identifying the most important objects, fewer scene details are reported in interactive scenes as compared to non-interactive scenes. In other words, *the interaction along with the interacting entities is perceived as central to the scene meaning and essentially constitute the scene gist.* This observation is reinforced from the analysis of eye movements as well.

For these 110 images, we manually marked out rectangles denoting scene regions containing objects with high named frequency. Overall, the bounding boxes around most frequently named objects covered 38.6% of the total image

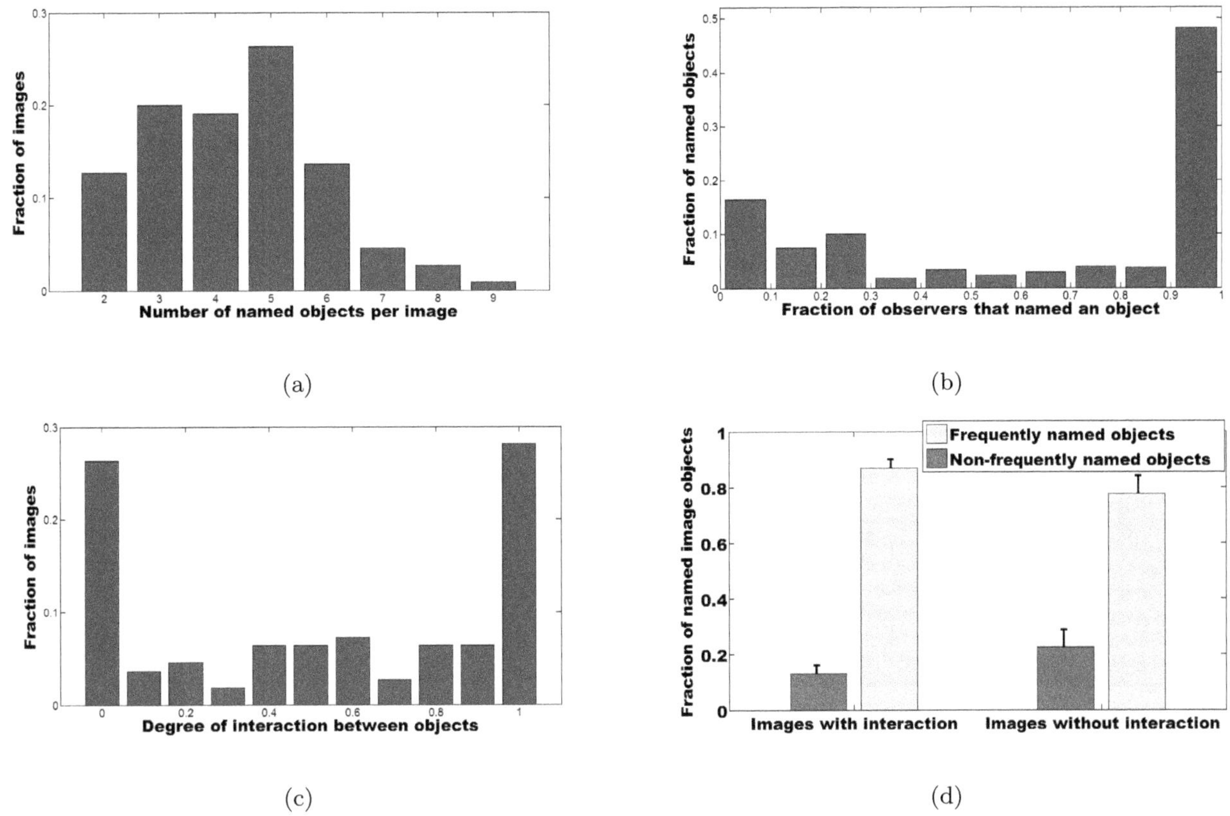

Figure 4: Summary of ground-truth analysis.

Frequently reported verbs	Less frequently reported verbs
feeding	*leaning*
reading	*embracing*
fighting	*wearing*
holding	*waving*
working	*sitting*
pointing	*carrying*

Table 1: More frequently and less frequently reported interactive verbs in descriptions of social scenes.

area. We then computed the proportion of total eye fixations occurring in these regions during the first 0.5, 1.5 and 3 seconds of scene viewing- the proportions were found to be 0.83, 0.82 and 0.8 respectively. This implies that objects frequently reported by viewers are also highly attended to during scene viewing. Also, semantically important objects are fixated at very early by observers, and with time, observers start exploring the remaining scene details.

The *entropy* is used in [12] to measure how much eye fixations are dispersed over the image. We obtained an averaged continuous saliency map for all images by convolving a Gaussian filter with the eye fixation maps of all viewers, in order to measure the variance in user-fixated locations for the different time intervals (Fig.5). It is evident from the figure that viewers choose to explore more and more scene details with time- the entropy increases from 6.37 to 6.94 as we proceed from 500 ms to 3 sec of scene viewing time. However, across all these time intervals, the difference in entropy observed for interactive scenes and non-interactive scenes is significant at $p < 0.05$ ($p_{max} = 0.03$ for 0.5 sec viewing time). This implies that scene details visually processed by viewers during (task-explicit) scene description and (task-implicit) visual exploration are similar- semantically meaningful entities are **attended to** and **named** consistently.

We term this phenomenon of viewers preferentially directing their visual attention towards salient objects and object relationships as *attentional-bias*. In social scenes, we observe an attentional-bias towards interacting objects and the resulting interaction. If we compare saccades for interactive and non-interactive images, a crucial difference is that interactions (such as *read*, *fight*, *point*, *etc.*) are consistently characterized by vacillating saccades between interacting objects. Psychology literature provides support to this phenomenon- such interactions are characterized by pose cues and humans are instantly able to determine and follow the direction of others' attention [14]. Also, short-term or episodic scene memory causes viewers to semantically re-fixate on interesting objects. This influences the occurrence of vacillating saccades between interacting objects. Now, we briefly discuss how we can model this attentional-bias for automated interaction detection.

3.1.1 Automated detection of interactions

Let us represent different scene regions using rectangular regions-of-interest or ROIs. The representative conditional probability $P(m|l)$, which models the likelihood of a saccade to ROI m following a fixation in ROI l is defined as

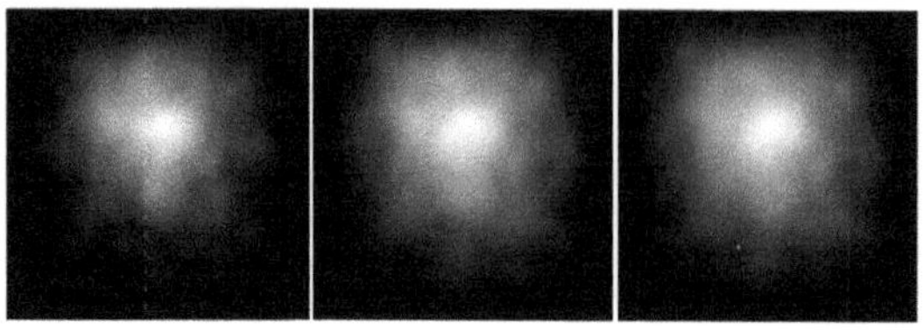

(a) (b) (c)

Figure 5: Continuous Saliency map computed computed for all social scenes from eye fixations over the initial (a) 0.5 sec (Entropy=6.37) (b) 1.5 sec (Entropy=6.76) and (c) 3 sec of scene viewing (Entropy=6.94).

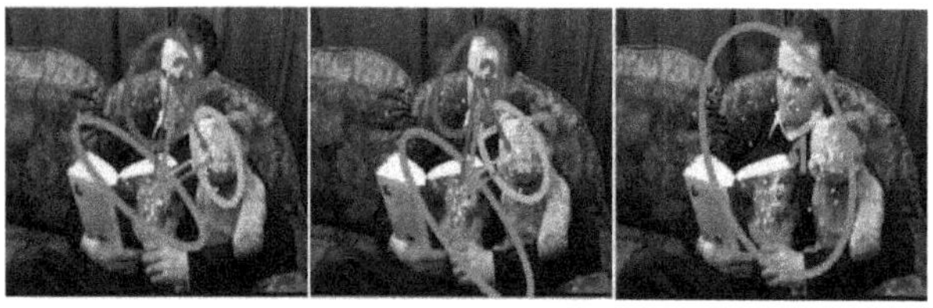

Figure 6: Illustrative example showing how multi-scale fixation clustering and saccadic analysis at scales S1, S2 and S3 enables interaction detection between man and the book.

$$P(m|l) = \frac{|S_{l,m}|}{|F_l|} \quad (1)$$

where $|S_{l,m}|$ denotes the number of saccades from ROI l to m, and $|F_l|$ denotes the number of fixations in region l.

In the absence of algorithms that can achieve 'semantic segmentation' (*i.e.*, reliably identify semantically relevant components of objects), and the error involved in gaze estimation, we employ the property of vacillating fixations to identify interacting clusters, and consequently interacting objects. The top row of Fig.6 presents an illustration of how we identify interaction between the man and the book. We employ the mean-shift based, multi-scale fixation clustering approach proposed in [24] to identify fixation clusters at 3 different scales. At any scale, when multiple clusters are detected, we compute the conditional probability of saccading to a different cluster. We choose that scale where the likelihood of to and from saccades are maximally likely, characterizing vacillating saccades.

$$S = \arg\max_s(\eta_s) \quad (2)$$

where

$$\eta_s = min(\frac{P(m|l)_s}{P(l|m)_s}, \frac{P(l|m)_s}{P(m|l)_s}). \quad (3)$$

To minimize false detections, we consider only cluster-pairs with sufficient membership associated with high saccade probability and η values ($P(m|l) \geq 0.3$ and $\eta \geq 0.5$ for cluster-pair m, l). In the figure, the thickness of the arrows connecting clusters denote the likelihood of a saccade between the two clusters. The strongest and most symmetric interaction occurs between the man and the book at scale $S2$, where $\eta = 0.6$ with $P(book|man) = 0.36$ and $P(man|book) = 0.22$. It is inevitable that some saccades are observed between non-interacting objects as well as viewers explore scene details. However, in most cases, the saccade likelihoods are low (in Fig.6, $P(book|teddy) = 0.2$ and $P(teddy|book) = 0.18$ at scale $S1$) enabling us to discard such cluster-pairs from the analysis.

We attempted saccade-based detection of object interactions at multiple scales to automatically classify the interactive and non-interactive images identified from ground-truth analysis. To determine the effectiveness of saccadic features for discovering the presence or absence of object interactions in social scenes, we employed a leave-pair-out-cross-validation approach (LPOCV). Classification was attempted using linear SVMs and at any time, two samples (one positive and one negative) were used for testing, while the remaining data were used for training. The mean classification accuracy (Acc) and the mean square error (MSE) in accuracies obtained during the different trials are tabulated in Table 2. We obtain an overall accuracy of 77.8%, thereby demonstrating the effectiveness of saccade features for detecting object interactions.

It is also important to note that while vacillating saccades enable discovery of interactions, it is not possible to recognize 'what the interaction is' employing eye movements alone, *i.e.*, we cannot determine whether two persons (discovered employing a person detector) are talking or fighting, employing saccadic cues. However, as contemporary vision algorithms are unable to detect the presence/absence of interactions in images, we believe that detecting interactions, is in itself, a significant step. Further examples of how interactions may be detected in social scenes containing multiple people are shown in the next section.

3.2 Correlating eye movements with viewer ratings for affective scenes

Eye gaze is not only affected by interaction within a scene, but is also strongly influenced by *emotionally salient* content in affective images. We now describe how eye-gaze patterns are useful for distinguishing between (a) high-intensity vs low-intensity facial expressions and (b) portraits of clothed vs nude persons.

3.2.1 Distinguishing highly-expressive from mildly-expressive faces

We asked 12 viewers to rate the intensity of the portrayed facial expressions in 60 images, to understand how humans interpret emotive faces. All images contained an upright and frontal/slightly profile view of a face captured at high resolution. Observers were required to determine whether the portrayed emotion was *positive*, *neutral* or *negative* (termed valence in psychological literature). If they considered the emotional valence to be positive or negative, they were required to rate the intensity of the emotion on a Liekert scale of 1-7. In case an observer perceived a face to be *neutral*, the emotional intensity score was assigned to 0.

At least one observer assigned a non-zero score for every face, implying that viewers perceived some emotion in all the faces. We used the median of the observer scores, M_S, as a threshold to determine whether the face was perceived as mildly or highly expressive- faces with $M_S > 3$ were assumed to be highly emotional. Upon thresholding, 28 faces were found to be highly emotional, while 32 faces belonged to the 'mildly/moderately emotional' category. Faces with extensive deformations around the nose and mouth were perceived to be highly emotional by observers in general. We then studied eye movements on these face images upon automatically determining the ROI rectangles corresponding to the upper and lower face halves employing the Viola-Jones face detector [31] and the neural-network based Rowley eye detector [22]. The top row of Fig.7 presents the valence and median scores for six exemplar faces, along with the automatically determined eye, nose and mouth ROI rectangles.

Upon analyzing eye tracking data for the emotional faces, we made the following observations. Usually, eyes are most salient in the face, and a majority of the fixations appear around the eyes for mildly/moderately expressive faces. However, with increase in the emotional intensity, more and more fixations start appearing in the lower half of the face when significant deformations are observed around the nose and the mouth (Fig.7, middle row). Earlier works [27] have reported classification of expressive faces upon computing the density of eye fixations in the upper and lower face halves. We obtained better results by also employing saccades in addition to fixations, and built our analysis on the following hypotheses.

- Salient entities are fixated for longer times by viewers. Denoting attentional-bias for the ith entity as B_i, we observe that $B_i \propto |F_i|$, where $|F_i|$ denotes total number of fixations (fixation density) in the ith ROI.
- Viewers' eye movements are exploratory in nature as they attend to interesting scene details. Therefore, for a highly salient entity one can expect a large number of intra-saccades (saccades within the same ROI). Conversely, the likelihood of viewers saccading to a less salient entity from a more salient entity is low. Therefore, $B_i \propto |S_{(i,i)}|$ and $B_i \propto \frac{1}{|S_{(i,j)}|}$, where $|S_{(i,j)}|$ denotes number of saccades from the ith to the jth ROI. $B_i \propto \frac{|S_{(i,i)}|}{|S_{(i,j)}|}$, which we term relative saccadic ratio or $SR_{(i,j)}$.

Table 2 shows the results for classification of expressive faces using (a) only fixation density, (b) using only saccades and (c) using the combination of fixations and saccades. We observe that saccade features in the form of saccadic ratios are more effective for classification compared to using fixation densities, and accuracy increases by 5%. The combination of saccades and fixations adds little to using saccades alone.

Fig.7 illustrates why saccades are good features for determining the emotional intensity of faces. There are more intra-saccades within eyes regions in mildly emotive faces ($SR_{(eyes,mouth)} > 1$), while in intensely emotional faces, there are more saccades directed towards the nose and mouth regions ($SR_{(mouth,eyes)} > 1$). We believe that this finding is significant as it means that ***apart from the amount of time we spend on observing salient entities (as captured by fixations), the frequency with which we observe them (as given by the number of intra-saccades) is also important.***

3.2.2 Detection of nude/erotic content

Another area where eye data can be useful for inferring semantics is with respect to the detection of nude/erotic pictures. State-of-the-art pornography detection approaches [16] are only moderately successful, and we believe eye-movement recordings can serve as a useful complement to minimize false detections and verify true positives in the automated analysis of erotic content. Our task was designed to validate the hypothesis that 'Humans understand nude/erotic content best', and based on the on the observation that faces strongly attract visual attention in portraits (images showing face and body), while most fixations occur on the body in nudes.

	Features	Acc	MSE
Social scenes	Saccades	0.778	0.085
Affective scenes (faces)	Fixations	0.675	0.105
	Saccades	0.720	0.096
	All features	0.728	0.097
Affective scenes (nudes)	Saccades	0.835	0.066
	Fixations	0.861	0.058
	All features	0.854	0.063

Table 2: Automatic classification results for social and affective scenes.

As with faces, we asked 12 observers to assign a score concerning the degree of nudity/eroticism for a total of 100 portraits. Each portrait contained a person in a frontal pose such that the face and part of the body (at least up to the chest portion) are visible to viewers. As with the faces, we computed the median score of all viewer ratings as the representative score for a portrait. All portraits that corresponded to median score M_S greater than 3.5 were considered as nudes. 44 of the 100 portraits were rated as nude/erotic.

Using the human upper body [6] and the Viola Jones [31] face detectors, we automatically determined the face and body ROIs in the portraits. The top row in Fig.8 shows the discovered face and body ROIs along with the median user score for each portrait. As evident from the eye fixation patterns shown in the middle row, visual attention is biased towards the face in normal portraits, and heavily skewed towards the body in nudes. Again, we used both saccades and fixations to automatically predict if an image is a nude or not. Table 2 shows the results. In this case, fixations alone predict nudes better than only saccades or a combination of fixations and saccades. This is probably because viewers spend considerable time attending to salient body parts rather than frequently shifting their focus of attention.

4. EXPLOITING INFERRED SEMANTICS FOR INTELLIGENT APPLICATIONS

In the previous section, we showed how classification of certain semantically different scene classes can be achieved using eye movements. This, in itself, is highly useful for applications like image retrieval. In this section, we demonstrate a few more examples where knowledge of semantics can enhance the performance of contemporary applications by considering the paradigms of (a) adaptive scene rendering and (b) automatic scene understanding.

4.1 Adaptive scene rendering

Today, there exist ubiquitous multimedia rendering devices, but they have varying capabilities. Different devices have different display resolutions, and not all devices are endowed the processing power to instantaneously render high

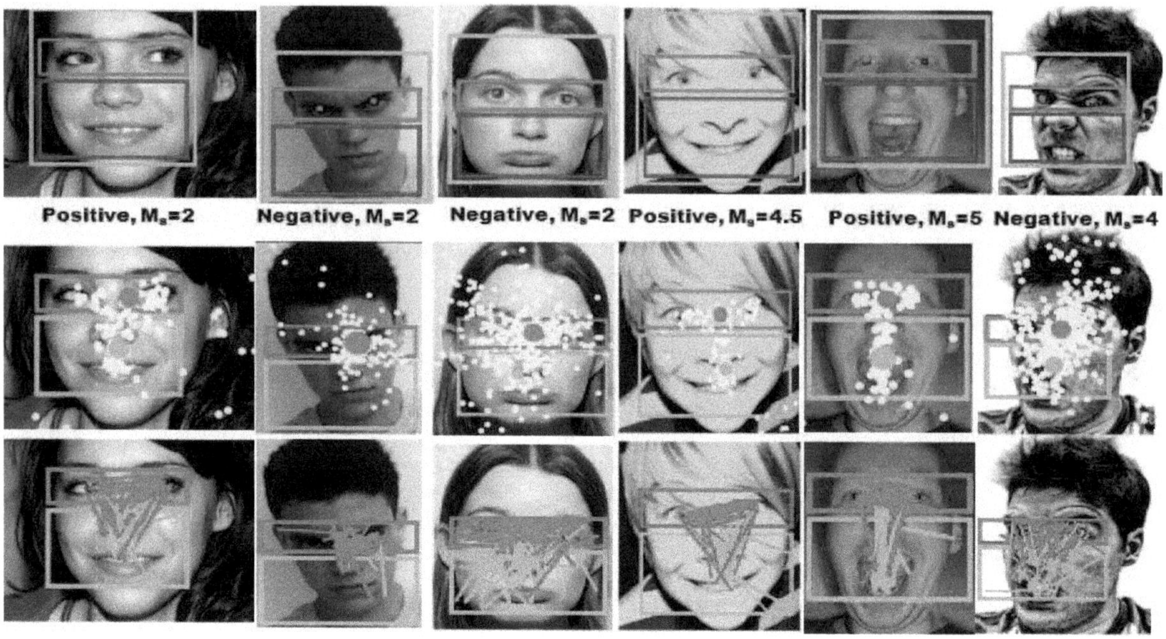

Figure 7: (Top row) Exemplar expressive faces and their median scores. The ROI rectangles for the upper and lower face halves are automatically determined employing face and eye detectors. (Middle row) Distribution of fixations among the two face halves. The red and green circles denote the center of the fixation clusters, and their size denotes cluster membership. Bottom row shows distribution of saccades. More saccades appear on the lower half of the face with increasing emotional intensity.

resolution images. In such cases, it is important to *adaptively* render detail so that the user does not perceive information loss. Techniques such as foveated image rendering [32] and seam carving [1] can be used to preserve regions identified as salient from human fixations. We present how faces can be adaptively rendered so that the user can still perceive can satisfactorily perceive the portrayed facial emotion in Fig.9.

Foveated rendering retains scene details around a foveation point (center of visual attention) while coarsening the rest of the scene. In Fig.9, the foveation point is placed at the center of the *salient* ROI (around the eyes for mildly expressive faces and around the nose and mouth for highly expressive faces). The essence of the facial emotion can be understood in this manner, even if the rendered content is of low resolution. Also, once entities central to the scene meaning can be identified, they can be preserved so that user still understands the scene in re-targeting applications. An example is shown in Fig.10. Once the interacting persons in the scene are identified, they can preserved to perform a more 'semantically correct' image resizing.

4.2 Automated scene understanding- Detection of interacting people

As vacillating saccades enable discovery of interactions in social scenes, combining this information with a person detector allows for identification of interacting people in social scenes. This is a very useful tool to have in tasks like image retrieval. Fig.11 shows two scenes with the same set of objects. However, semantically they are completely different.

We demonstrate some examples for interaction detection in social scenes. We use the state-of-the-art person detector [6] for detecting people in social scenes and also cluster eye fixations at different spacial scales as proposed in section 3.1. Then, we map detected persons to fixation clusters based on two rules: (1) The cluster centroid should be located within a bounding box and (2) the cluster should contain a sufficient number of fixations. If vacillating saccades are observed between clusters corresponding to different people in at least one of the spatial scales, then we consider these two persons to be interacting. Fig.12 illustrates several examples, people enclosed in *red bounding boxes* are identified as *engaged in interactions*, while *no interaction* is detected for those labeled using *white bounding boxes*. The yellow dots depict eye-fixations while arrows denote the direction of strongly directed saccades within the scene.

People appearing in images (a-c) are not found to be interacting with others. Interestingly, scenes (a) and (b) involve interaction between people and objects: two boys are holding a sign, and a person is working on the laptop. Images (d-f) contain interacting persons. Overall, this application demonstrates how information from eye movements can be combined with object detectors for semantic interpretation in complex scenes.

5. CONCLUSION

This paper demonstrates how eye movement recordings are useful data for automated scene understanding when combined with content analysis tools (object detectors). Although impressive progress has been recently achieved in object detection and predicting salient scene content, it is

(a) (b) (c) (d) (e) (f)

Figure 12: Discovering interactions in social scenes.

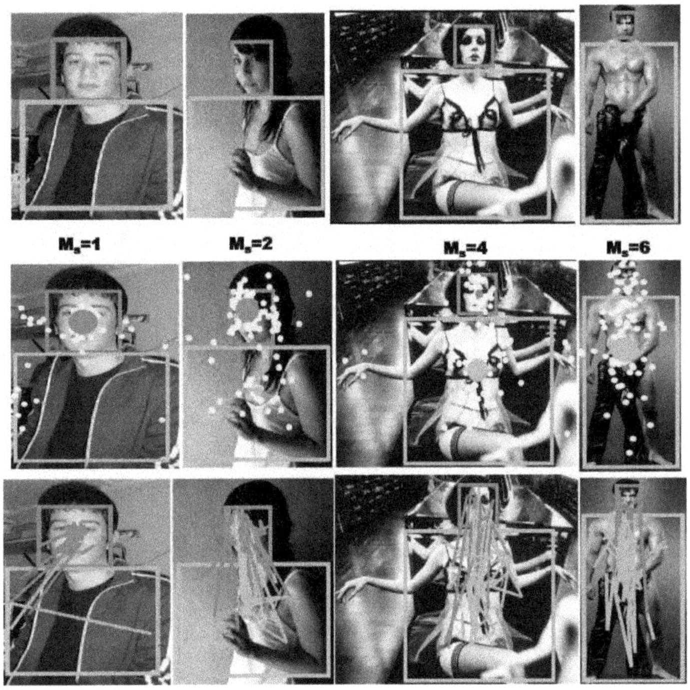

Figure 8: (Top row) Sample portraits with viewer scores for degree of nudity/eroticsm. Outputs of the face and person detectors are used to automatically determine the face and body ROIs. Eye fixation and saccade patterns are shown in the middle and bottom rows respectively. Fixations and saccades are heavily skewed towards the body in nudes.

Figure 9: Foveated rendering of faces. The foveation point is placed at the center of the salient ROI.

currently impossible for purely computational techniques to infer scene semantics such as object interactions from images. Eye movements in the form of fixations and saccades enable discovery of salient entities and entity-relations.

We have shown how eye-movements can be employed for distinguishing interactive and non-interactive social scenes, mild- and high-intensity facial expressions as well as portraits of clothed persons and nudes. With advances in science and technology, it should be possible to non-invasively compile eye movements on a large scale for media browsed on the Internet. In future, we also envision that eye movement recordings will have a critical role to play in automated scene understanding.

(a) (b) (c)

Figure 10: (a) Fixation map overlaid on original 1024x685 image. (b) Seam-carved 800x600 image preserving salient objects (c) Typical seam-carved output.

Figure 11: Exemplar images containing the same set of objects (three persons) but with different semantic meanings ('Three people pose for the camera' vs 'Two women are fighting as the third stands on the side').

6. ACKNOWLEDGEMENTS

This research work was supported by the FP7 GLOCAL and FIRB S-PATTERNS projects.

7. REFERENCES

[1] S. Avidan and A. Shamir. Seam carving for content-aware image resizing. *ACM Transactions on Graphics*, 26(3), 2007.

[2] E. Birmingham, W. F. Bischof, and A. Kingstone. Saliency does not account for fixations to eyes within social scenes. *Vision research*, 49(24):2992–3000, 2009.

[3] W. Einhauser, M. Spain, and P. Perona. Objects predict fixations better than early saliency. *Journal of Vision*, 8(14):1–26, 11 2008.

[4] L. Elazary and L. Itti. Interesting objects are visually salient. *Journal of Vision*, 8(3):1–15, 2008.

[5] M. Everingham, L. Van Gool, C. K. I. Williams, J. Winn, and A. Zisserman. The PASCAL Visual Object Classes Challenge 2010 (VOC2010) Results.

[6] P. F. Felzenszwalb, R. B. Girshick, D. McAllester, and D. Ramanan. Object detection with discriminatively trained part based models. *IEEE Transactions on Pattern Analysis and Machine Intelligence*, 99, 2009.

[7] D. A. Forsyth and J. Ponce. *Computer Vision: A Modern Approach*. Prentice Hall, 2002.

[8] A. Hanjalic and L.-Q. Xu. Affective video content representation and modeling. *IEEE Transactions on Multimedia*, 7(1):143–154, 2005.

[9] J. Henderson. Human gaze control during real-world scene perception. *Trends in Cognitive Sciences*, 7(11):498–504, November 2003.

[10] L. Itti and C. Koch. A saliency-based search mechanism for overt and covert shifts of visual attention. *Vision Research*, 40:1489–1506, 2000.

[11] R. Jain and P. Sinha. Content without context is meaningless. In *ACM International Conference on Multimedia*, 2010.

[12] T. Judd, K. Ehinger, F. Durand, and A. Torralba. Learning to predict where humans look. In *International Conference on Computer Vision*, 2009.

[13] A. Kembhavi, T. Yeh, and L. S. Davis. Why did the person cross the road (there)? scene understanding using probabilistic logic models and common sense reasoning. In *European Conference on Computer Vision*, pages II: 693–706, 2010.

[14] G. Kuhn, B. Tatler, and G. Cole. You look where i look! effect of gaze cues on overt and covert attention in misdirection. *Visual Cognition*, 17(6-7):925–944, 2009.

[15] G. Kulkarni, V. Premraj, S. Dhar, S. Li, Y. Choi, A. C. Berg, and T. L. Berg. Baby talk: Understanding and generating simple image descriptions. In *Computer Vision and Pattern Recognition*, pages 1601–1608, 2011.

[16] J.-S. Lee, Y.-M. Kuo, P.-C. Chung, and E.-L. Chen. Naked image detection based on adaptive and extensible skin color model. *Pattern Recognition*, 40:2261–2270, 2007.

[17] A. D. Lykins, M. Meana, and G. Kambe. Detection of differential viewing patterns to erotic and non-erotic stimuli using eye-tracking methodology. *Archives of sexual behavior*, 35(5):569–575, 2006.

[18] J. Machajdik and A. Hanbury. Affective image classification using features inspired by psychology and art theory. In *Proceedings of the international conference on Multimedia*, ACM International Conference on Multimedia, pages 83–92, 2010.

[19] C. M. M. Masciocchi, S. Mihalas, D. Parkhurst, and E. Niebur. Everyone knows what is interesting: salient locations which should be fixated. *Journal of vision*, 9(11), 2009.

[20] S. Ramanathan, H. Katti, N. Sebe, M. Kankanhalli, and T. Chua. An eye fixation database for saliency detection in images. In *European Conference on Computer Vision*, pages IV: 30–43, 2010.

[21] R. A. Rensink, J. K. O'Regan, and J. J. Clark. To See or not to See: The Need for Attention to Perceive Changes in Scenes. *Psychological Science*, 8(5):368–373, 1997.

[22] H. Rowley, S. Baluja, and T. Kanade. Neural network-based face detection. *IIEEE Transactions on Pattern Analysis and Machine Intelligence*, 20(1):237–28, 1998.

[23] B. C. Russell, A. Torralba, K. P. Murphy, and W. T. Freeman. Labelme: A database and web-based tool for image annotation. Technical report, Tech. Rep. MIT-CSAIL-TR-2005-056, 2005.

[24] A. Santella and D. DeCarlo. Robust clustering of eye movement recordings for quantification of visual interest. In *Proceedings of the symposium on Eye tracking research & applications*, pages 27–34, 2004.

[25] J. Shotton, J. Winn, C. Rother, and A. Criminisi. Textonboost for image understanding: Multi-class object recognition and segmentation by jointly modeling texture, layout, and context. *International Journal of Comput. Vision*, 81(1):2–23, 2009.

[26] M. Spain and P. Perona. Measuring and predicting object importance. *International Journal of Computer Vision*, 2010.

[27] R. Subramanian, H. Katti, R. Huang, T.-S. Chua, and M. Kankanhalli. Automated localization of affective objects and actions in images via caption text-cum-eye gaze analysis. In *ACM International Conference on Multimedia*, 2009.

[28] A. Torralba, A. Oliva, M. S. Castelhano, and J. M. Henderson. Contextual guidance of eye movements and attention in real-world scenes: the role of global features in object search. *Psychological review*, 113(4):766–786, 2006.

[29] R. Valenti, N. Sebe, and T. Gevers. Image saliency by isocentric curvedness and color. In *International Conference on Computer Vision*, 2009.

[30] R. Valenti, J. Staiano, N. Sebe, and T. Gevers. Webcam-based visual gaze estimation. In *International Conference on Image Analysis and Processing*, 2009.

[31] P. Viola and M. J. Jones. Robust real-time face detection. *International Journal of Computer Vision*, 57(2):137–154, May 2004.

[32] Z. Wang, L. Lu, and A. C. Bovik. Foveation scalable video coding with automatic fixation selection. *IEEE Transactions on Image Processing*, 12(2), 2003.

[33] A. Whiten. Evolutionary and developmental origins of the mindreading system. In *Evolution and Development*. Lawrence Erlbaum, 1997.

[34] Y. Yang, M. Song, N. Li, J. Bu, and C. Chen. V: What is the chance of happening: A new way to predict where people look. In *European Conference on Computer Vision*, pages 631–643, 2010.

[35] A. Yarbus. *Eye Movements and Vision*. Plenum Press, 1967.

[36] Z. Zeng and Q. Ji. Knowledge based activity recognition with dynamic bayesian network. In *European Conference on Computer Vision*, pages VI: 532–546, 2010.

[37] Q. Zhao and C. Koch. Learning a saliency map using fixated locations in natural scenes. *Journal of Vision*, 11(3):1–15, 2011.

Combining Content-based Analysis and Crowdsourcing to Improve User Interaction with Zoomable Video*

Axel Carlier
IRIT-ENSEEIHT
University of Toulouse
carlier.axel@gmail.com

Guntur Ravindra
Dept. of Computer Science
National University of Singapore
ravindra@comp.nus.edu.sg

Vincent Charvillat
IRIT-ENSEEIHT
University of Toulouse
vincent.charvillat@enseeiht.fr

Wei Tsang Ooi
Dept. of Computer Science
National University of Singapore
ooiwt@comp.nus.edu.sg

ABSTRACT

This paper introduces a new paradigm for interacting with zoomable video. Our interaction technique reduces the number of zooms and pans required by providing recommended viewports to the users, and replaces multiple zoom and pan actions with a simple click on the recommended viewport. The usefulness of our technique is visible in the quality of the recommended viewport, which needs to match the user intention, track movement in the scene, and properly frame the scene in the video. To this end, we propose a hybrid method where content analysis is complimented by the implicit feedback of a community of users in order to recommend viewports. We first compute preliminary sets of recommended viewports by analyzing the content of the video. These viewports allow tracking of moving objects in the scene, and are framed without violating basic aesthetic rules. To improve the relevance of the recommended viewports, we collect viewing statistics as users view a video, and use the viewports they select to reinforce the importance of certain recommendations and penalize others. New recommendations that are not previously recognized by content analysis may also emerge. The resulting recommended viewports converge towards the regions in the video that are relevant to users. A user study involving 70 participants shows that an user interface incorporating with our paradigm leads to more number of zooms, into more informative regions with fewer interactions.

Categories and Subject Descriptors: H.5.1 [Multimedia Information Systems]: Video

General Terms: Algorithms, Human Factors, Design

Keywords: Interaction Techniques, Zoomable Video, Content-Analysis, Crowdsourcing

*Area chair: Mor Naaman

MM'11, November 28–December 1, 2011, Scotsdale, Arizona, USA.

1. INTRODUCTION

Advances in video compression, video processing algorithms, and video sensors have lead to video cameras that are capable of capturing high resolution videos. Ability to capture HD video (at 1920×1080) is commonly available in mobile phones and hand-held cameras now. Video sequences, of resolution as high as $7,680 \times 4,320$ (UHDTV) have been recorded and transmitted over the Internet[1]. Video playback, however, is still limited in resolution, due to screen constraints (e.g., on mobile devices) or bandwidth constraints (e.g., when streamed over the Internet). As a result, high resolution videos are typically scaled down before transmission or playback, leading to a loss in information.

Zoomable videos have recently been proposed as a new form of media [14] with zooming and panning as two new ways for users to interact with the video. A zoomable video allows an user to zoom into a selected region in the video, leading to a high resolution version of the region to be displayed. The user essentially views the video through a *viewport* that defines a rectangular region in the high resolution video from which the displayed video is cropped. While zooming in, users can pan (i.e., scroll) around by moving the viewport to view different regions in the video. Such zoom and pan ability is useful for many types of videos, including classroom lectures, stage performance and sports video.

Ngo et. al [14] have proposed a user interface to interact with a zoomable video, based on a design similar to commonly used image zooming tools such as Google Maps. To zoom in and out, users can either scroll up and down with the scroll wheel of the mouse, or use the + and − buttons on the interface/keyboard. To pan, users can either drag the video with the mouse, or use the arrow keys on the interface/keyboard. A study of the interfaces [3] has shown that users interact frequently with the video during playback, with 70% of the interactions occurring within 1.6 seconds of each other.

Such user interaction was originally designed for images, where the content is static. Applying it to video, where the content is dynamic, raises several issues. Users typically zoom in to view one or more objects of interest in higher detail. In a video, these objects of interest can move over time. As a result, it is hard for users to position the viewport around an object that is moving. Furthermore, the user can loose track of the object of interest when the object moves out of the viewport. For instance, a user might zoom into a sports video clip to view the activity of a player in more detail.

[1] http://www.bbc.co.uk/news/technology-11436939

If the player moves rapidly, the user would need to quickly pan or zoom out to track the person.

The goal of this research is to propose a new user interaction technique for zooming and panning in a zoomable video, designed with moving content in mind. The new interaction should be simple and intuitive, and users should be able to zoom and pan to view their object of interest easily with few interactions.

Our idea is to recognize the possible objects of interest in the video, and highlight them in a non-intrusive. These highlighted regions are then presented to the users as the *recommended viewports*. When users hover the mouse over any of the recommended viewports, a semi-transparent white overlay will appear, indicating the recommended viewport. Users can click once anywhere in the recommended viewport to zoom and pan into the recommended viewport. Users can still click anywhere outside the recommended viewport to zoom in. At any time, users can drag to move the viewport and right click to zoom out. Note that we replaced mouse wheel scrolling in [14] with clicks, since clicking is a more natural action for selecting a recommended viewport.

The new interaction which we propose is the ability to click on the recommended viewport, there by replacing the action of zooming in and positioning the viewport over the objects of interest (i.e., scrolling and dragging) with a single mouse click.

The recommended viewports serve several purposes. First, it moves along with the detected object of interest, thus making it easy for users to position the viewport over a moving object. If the user's viewport is the recommended viewport, the user's viewport would also move as the recommended viewport moves. As a result, the video pans automatically to track the moving object, further reducing the number of interactions required from the users. Second, the recommended viewport can provide a guide for the user to frame their viewport properly, i.e., in a way that does not violate basic aesthetic principles (e.g., cropping a person's head), leading to more pleasant viewing experience.

The key to the efficacy of our approach is the quality of recommended viewports. Viewports should highlight and track interesting and relevant regions in the video and frame them properly. The research challenge, that we address in this paper, is to automatically compute the recommended viewport given a video. The computer vision research community has studied this domain for many years, and many algorithms exist to detect and track foreground objects, faces, human body, etc, by analyzing the content of the video. While the research community has made significant progress, most of these algorithms work at the "syntax level" of the video content. What the users find interesting, however, depends on the semantic of the video, the purpose of the video, and the intention of the users. It is difficult, therefore, to determine the object of interest just by analyzing the video content using the existing algorithms.

We have recently proposed [2] an approach that relies on implicit feedback of a community of users in order to identify the regions of interest in a video. We refer to the process of collecting user feedback as 'crowdsourcing' as defined by piggyback crowdsourcing systems [6]. By learning from the viewing patterns of the users (which regions of interest are more popular), a re-targeted video highlighting regions of interest is produced. This technique exploits human ability to recognize the semantic of the video and is able to learn the regions of interest from the most common intention of the users. This system, however, collects user traces based on the user interface described by Ngo et al [14] and therefore suffers from the same issues as discussed earlier. In particular, the need for users to pan and track an object of interest introduces delay in identifying a moving object as the region of interest. For instance, in the re-targeted video produced[2], which follows the behavior of most users, an object of interest can move out of frame momentarily, and only moves back into the frame when users react to this event by panning to move the objects back into their viewport. Another drawback of this crowdsourcing system is that, even though the inputs into the crowdsourcing algorithm matches the semantics identified by the users, the process of combining users' intention to produce a region of interest is blind to the content of the video and might violate the basic aesthetic rules.

However, the interface described in this paper adopts a hybrid approach that plays on the strength of both content analysis and crowdsourcing (implicit feedback). Not only semantically important regions of interest are identified, but panning and tracking a region of interest is automated.

We bootstrap the recommended viewports as follows. First, we analyze the content of the video and identify salient regions using motion, faces, and saliency features. These salient regions are recommended to users viewing the video using our interface. Then, we learn which viewports are chosen by the users to view the video, and adapt the recommended viewports to match the intention of most users. By combining both content analysis and crowdsourcing, we are able to recommend properly framed regions of interest that match better with user intention.

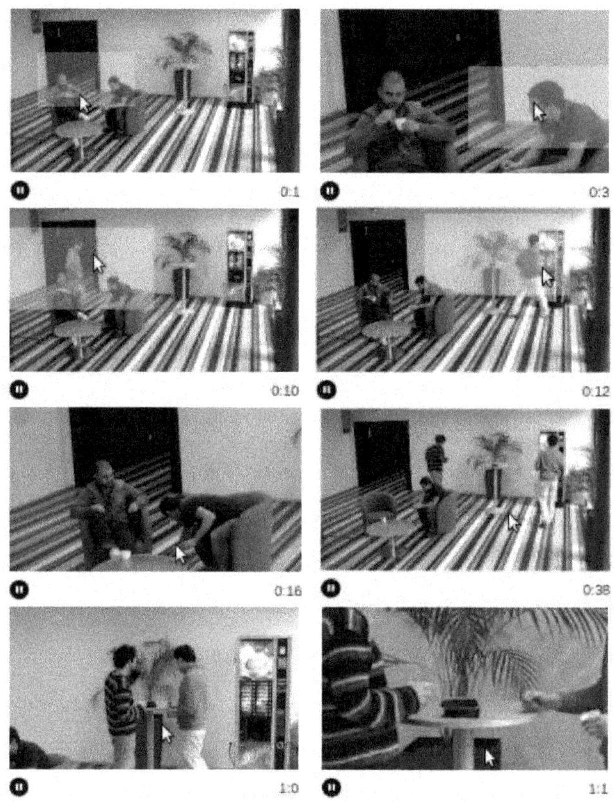

Figure 1: Our Zoomable Interface

In summary, our proposed technique to interact with a zoomable video fuses regions of interest identified from content analysis with regions chosen implicitly by previous users, in order to recommend viewports to new users. These recommended viewports guide user's viewport placement, tracks moving objects of interests, and

[2]http://www.youtube.com/user/autozap

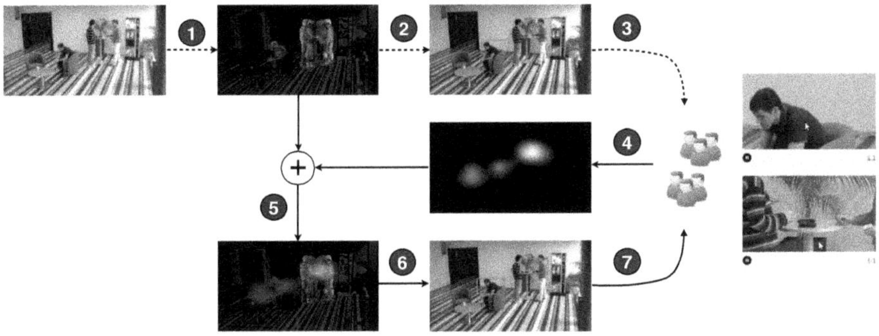

Figure 2: Overview of Approach

thus leads to fewer interactions. Further, the recommended viewports have few violations of basic aesthetic rules and show content that is more relevant to users.

1.1 Example

We illustrate our new interaction technique with an example. Figure 1 shows eight snapshots from our user interface. In the snapshot at time 0:01 (top left), you can see a semi-transparent white rectangle overlayed on the video where the mouse is hovering, indicating the recommended viewport. If the user clicks anywhere within the recommended viewport, the video zooms in, placing the viewport over the recommended ones (time 0:03). Recommendation at further zoom levels becomes available. The user right clicks to zoom out (time 0:10). The new recommended viewport tracks the person in orange sweater as he enters the scene, from time 0:10 to 0:12. The user may also click on the video outside of recommended viewport, as seen in rest of the snapshots.

1.2 Approach Overview

Having briefly described the general idea of recommending viewports, we now give an overview of our approach to compute the recommended viewports.

Figure 2 illustrates the steps taken. We start with a given video. In Step 1, we analyze the content of the video to extract the salient features of each frame. An importance map is built for each frame, indicating the level of saliency in each pixel. The output of Step 1 in Figure 2 shows an example importance map. In Step 2, we cluster the pixels in the importance map. The clusters are analyzed across consecutive frames, and the best viewport trajectory is computed. This viewport trajectory is used as a recommendation, and is integrated into the user interface.

As users use our interface to watch videos (Step 3), we collect information about the viewports chosen by the users. In Step 4, this information is used to generate an interest map, indicating the level of interest users have on each pixel. The interest map is combined with the importance map (Step 5) to generate a new importance map. In Step 6, we repeat what we do in Step 2, with the new importance map. New recommended viewports are shown to the users (Step 7). Steps 4–7 can be repeated by periodically recomputing the new recommended viewports to adapt to new user interests if any.

1.3 Organization

We organize the rest of the paper into six sections. We begin with a review of literature in Section 2, followed by a description of zoomable video in Section 3. In Section 4, we explain how we analyze the content of the video to find the initial recommended viewports (Step 1 and Step 2). Section 5 explains how we crowdsource the interesting regions from users, and combine it to generate new recommended viewports (Step 4 and Step 5). In Section 6, we present our results. Finally, we conclude in Section 7.

2. RELATED WORK

We now discuss related research in the literature and contrast our work with the existing work. We divide existing research into three classes: (i) those that enables new video access and interactions using content analysis, (ii) those that exploit user interactions to learn about the content, and (iii) those that combines both content analysis and user behaviour analysis to learn about content and enable new video access and interactions techniques.

Enabling New Interactions with Content Analysis. Analysis of video content to detect and track objects is highlighted by Goldman et al. [9] as enabler for new interaction paradigms to browse and manipulate video. Examples given include dynamic video annotation and video navigation by direct manipulation. Direct manipulation, also discussed by Dragicevic et al. [7], allows control of video playback and access of nearby frames by directly clicking and dragging on moving objects in the image space. Content nalysis also enables hypervideo links [17], where links associated to moving video objects allows a quick access to additional content.

Many new interactions are made possible by ROI detection, a fundamental problem in content analysis. ROI are commonly detected using visual attention models. The work by Han et al. [10] and Itti et al. [11] are representative in ROI detection on still images. ROI detection can be extended to the temporal dimension: to look for interesting space-time regions within a video. Detection of interesting or important video segment (or shot) enables new video interactions such as those proposed in the *smart player* [4]. The smart player adjusts the video playback speed based on a predicted level of interest for each video shots. Both inter-frame motion estimations and shot boundary detections are used to support automated fast-forwarding during less interesting shots.

Improving the viewing experience is also the ultimate goal of numerous works on image and video retargeting. Rubinstein et al. have identified video cropping as one of the most basic retargeting operator, despite many recent new proposals [15]. El-Alfy et al. uses motion analysis in a video and crops the region with high motion energe for display on a surveillance wall, resulting in zooming and panning effect over time [8]. Liu and Gleicher [12], in their influencial work, linearly combine multiple saliency features to extract prominent regions from an image for video retargeting.

Our work is similar to these previous work. We all rely on video content analysis to identify interesting regions from the video. As mentioned, however, content analysis alone can fail to identify regions relevant to users' intention, since content analysis is often done using low-level information without user context. Existing work that works well often assume a certain context and predetermined user intention (e.g., El-Alfy et al. works in the context of surveillance video where motion is important). In contrast, our work aims to target a wide range of applications.

Enhancing Content Understanding Through Usage Analysis An alternative approach to content-based ROI detection is to observe what the users are looking at and which video object are they clicking on. By collection usage pattern from the users, we can infer the regions in the video that users are most interested in.

In the context of ROI detection in images, Xie et al. [22] found that on small mobile displays, users tend to zoom and scroll more often to view interesting regions in detail. These user actions yield user interest maps, which are used to extract ROIs from the image.

In the context of ROI detection in video, Ukita et. al uses an eye-mark recorder system to track user gaze. Important objects, including moving objects, can be detected and tracked by analyzing the gaze of the users [19]. Shamma et. al proposed a similar approach: to gather information about what is being watched from a user community to understand the content of the video [16]. Syeda-Mahmood and Ponceleon collect implicit feedback from the users by analyzing the playback interaction in the temporal domain (play, fast-forward, pause) and use it to infer the most interesting video segments from the video [18].

Carlier et al. use a zoomable video interface [2] to crowdsource ROIs from users. The detected ROIs are used to create a retargeted version of the video that would automatically pan and zoom.

Our work is similar in spirit with these existing work, especially Syeda-Mahmood and Ponceleon's [18] and Carlier et al.'s [2]. Similar to their approach, we use implicit feedback from users to identify interesting regions. Our work, however, addresses the unique challenge of tracking moving objects using users' feedback, and proper framing of regions around objects.

Combining Content and Usage Analysis Given the strengths and weaknesses of content and usage analysis, it is natural to combine both, as they can complement each other. This technique, however, is not well explored by the research community. Besides our work, presented in this paper, the only other related work we are aware of is the *smart player* [4], which adapts the playback speed from both the visual richness of the scene (estimated from content analysis) and the user preferences (learnt from their video interaction). The player uses implicit feedback and learns how the users change and override automatically recommended fast-forwards.

Unlike the *smart player*, which focuses on interaction in the temporal domain (play and fast forward), our work focuses on interaction in the spatial domain (zoom and pan), detecting of interesting regions to recommend is therefore more challenging.

3. ZOOMABLE VIDEO

This section gives an introduction to zoomable video and the notion of recommended viewport. We describe how a user would interact with the zoomable video using recommended viewport, and defer the discussion of how the recommended viewport is computed to the next section.

Zoomable video is a term coined by Ngo et. al [14] to refer a video that is encoded and stored at multiple resolutions and supports dynamic cropping and random access into the spatial region in the video. Besides normal operation in the temporal dimension such as play, pause, fast forward, a zoomable video supports two new types of operation: zoom and pan. Users view a zoomable video with a display size that is smaller than the maximum resolution of the video. Zooming allows users to magnify a selected region in the video without loss of resolution (up to a maximum zoom level) and panning allows user to move the zoomed in region spatially around the video. Zooming and panning can occur even when the video is playing.

Zoomable videos are very helpful in situations where display devices are computationally constrained by the ability to decode and render high resolution video. Zoomable videos are also useful in cases where devices have access to streamed video over a low bandwidth network interface, resulting in the inability to stream bandwidth intensive high resolution video. Traditionally, computational and bandwidth constraints have been handled by scaling down the video temporally, spatially and in quality. Such an approach would result in loss of information, despite the fact that the capture devices were able to record the video at very high resolution. Zoomable video provides an alternative where users can select regions of interest from a low resolution video and view these regions at higher resolution. Such a scheme can satisfy both bandwidth and computational constraints in a more scalable fashion.

A zoomable video system can be built using a bit-stream switching architecture. The high resolution video is encoded at multiple low resolutions. The lowest resolution video is first accessed and displayed to the user. When a user wishes to view a specific region at a higher resolution, user's intent is represented as a rectangular viewport. This viewport is first mapped to a higher resolution layer. Then a region corresponding to the specified viewport is cropped from the higher resolution layer, and presented to the user. As is evident, the key requirement is the ability for dynamic cropping, which can be a challenge in encoded video. Methods to handle dynamic cropping and other issues related to streaming of zoomable video have been presented in [14].

3.1 Recommended Viewport

A key feature in our proposed interaction is the *recommended viewport*, which corresponds to interesting objects or events in the video, and is a region in the video that the user is likely to zoom into. Hovering the mouse over a recommended viewport reveals a white semi-transparent rectangular box. The user can zoom into the region by left-clicking the recommended viewport with the mouse button. When the mouse cursor hovers over one or more recommended viewports that overlap, only the most important recommended viewport is shown.

Users can left click outside of a recommended viewport to zoom in. In this case, the new viewport of the user is placed such that the center of the viewport is the coordinate of the mouse click. Right-clicking anywhere of the video zooms out.

The recommended viewport automatically moves to track a moving object of interest. If the user's current viewport is one that matches the recommended viewport (by clicking inside a recommended viewport), the user viewport pans automatically along with the recommended viewport.

One design decision we make is to limit the number of recommended viewports per zoom level to three. While using recommended viewport helps users to place their viewport easily with a single mouse click, it also restricts the viewport placement. Presenting too many recommended viewports to the users is not only too inflexible, but can also be confusing. We choose the value of three since we observe that in a typical video there are rarely more than three events of interest at the same time. Of course, this number can be configured to be higher depending on the content.

3.2 Implementation

We implemented our interface on a Web browser using HTML5. The webpage is minimalist in design, and shows only a video can-

(a) Original Frame (b) Saliency Map (c) Motion Map (d) Face Map

Figure 3: Content Analysis

vas of size 320×180 and a play/pause button along with the current playback time. Videos of resolution 1920×1080 are loaded along with a JSON file that contains the recommended viewports. A Javascript crops and scale the video for display in the canvas, as well as highlights the recommended viewport according to the JSON file (when hovered by the mouse).

A critical ingredient to the success of our approach is the quality of the recommended viewports. In the next two sections, we detail how we combine content analysis and crowdsourcing to compute the recommended viewports.

4. CONTENT-BASED ANALYSIS

The recommended viewports are determined based on a sequence of content analysis steps. We use saliency, and motion in the frame as the two main criteria to determine the possible regions of interest (ROI), which then serve as the recommended viewports. In cases where a face can be detected, face position is used as an additional criterion. Saliency is determined using the visual saliency features described in [13]. These features have shown good results for human detection, and hence the saliency is biased towards the presence of human or human-like objects in the video. Figure 3(b) shows an example saliency map.

Motion saliency is based on a moving average of frame differences and is similar to the work in [21]. A single channel disparity image of two successive frames is added to a moving average and used in place of the current frame. As a result the long-term motion pattern is available in a single frame. Figure 3(c) shows what a motion saliency map looks like.

Face detection, for both frontal and profile faces, is done using the Viola-Jones face detector [20]. We track faces across frames using a hue histogram of the detected face, with the CAMShift algorithm. Figure 3(d) shows the result of face detection.

4.1 Importance Maps

Each video frame is now represented by three maps, one for each criteria mentioned above. The pixel values are single channel quantities ranging between 0 and 1. The frames representing the three criteria are linearly combined to give an *importance map I*.

The weights assigned for linear combination may be obtained in many ways. In our experiments, we use empirically derived weights 0.7 for motion, 0.2 for saliency, and 0.1 for faces.

4.2 Clustering of Important Regions

The next step is to cluster pixel elements in the importance map to reveal regions that are candidate ROIs. The pixel elements in the importance map of every image are selected based on a threshold. Selected pixels are clustered using Mean-Shift ([5]) clustering algorithm. We chose a 60 pixels bandwidth in our implementation since it allows to detect significantly different viewports in 1920×1080 videos. Once clustering is performed, the candidate ROIs are determined at each zoom level. All ROIs at a particular zoom level have the same dimensions, i.e., the dimension of the corresponding viewport at that zoom level.

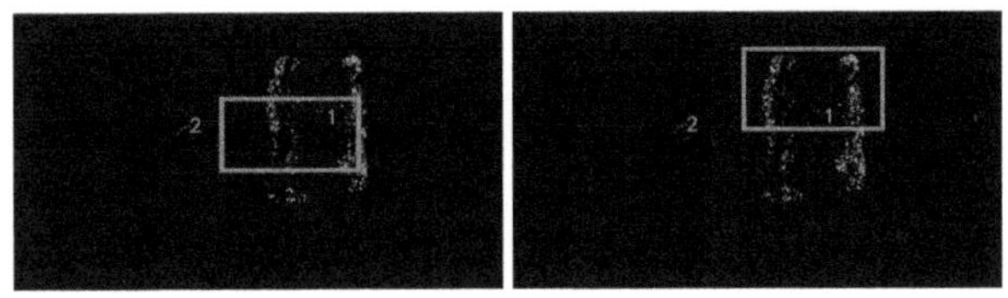

(a) Bad Cut (b) Good Cut

Figure 4: Frames Showing a Bad Cut and a Good Cut

A ROI is a good candidate if it encloses as many cluster points as possible without leaving out cluster points. Hence we need a measure to quantify the extent to which a viewport cuts a cluster into two or more parts. We define a term called the *cut of a viewport*. If a viewport does not cut a cluster, then its cut is very high. The concept of using a cut has been proposed in earlier work [11, 12, 8], but we use the notion of cut in conjunction with clustering to minimize cuts to the top portion of an object. Such an approach is better suited to aesthetically present human-like objects without cutting body parts. Figure 4(a) shows a case where the viewport cuts the clusters into two parts. There is a cluster region enclosed within the viewport, and the remaining cluster points fall outside the viewport. The region within the viewport encloses the lower part of two human subjects whose presence may be identified by the structure of the clusters shown. Hence, this viewport should be penalized. On the other hand figure 4(b) shows a viewport cutting a cluster such that the upper portion of the human subjects is enclosed, and the lower portions are cut out of the scene. This viewport should be treated favourably in comparison to the previous case. Hence the *cut of a viewport* should also account for how the cut is performed.

We now formally define how the cut is computed. For a frame f, let C_f represent all the cluster centroids in f. Let $E(c)$, where $c \in C_f$, be the set of pixels clustered around centroid c. Then $CUT(V_f, f)$, the cut of viewport V_f with top left coordinate (v_x, v_y) and height h (See also Fig 5(a)), is a measure for the extent to which $E(c)$ is fully contained within V_f:

$$CUT(V_f, f) = \frac{\sum_{c \in C_f} \sum_{p \in E(c)} W(p, V_f)}{\sum_{c \in C_f} |E(c)|}$$

where $W(p, V_f)$ with p at coordinate (x, y) is given by

$$W(p, V_f) = \begin{cases} 1 & \text{if} p \in V_f \\ 1 - \varepsilon & \text{if} y > v_y + h \\ \phi & \text{if} y < v_y \\ \rho & \text{otherwise} \end{cases}$$

and $1 > 1 - \varepsilon >> \rho > \phi$ (See also Fig 5(b)). $CUT(V_f, f)$ reaches a maximum value of one when V_f contains all cluster points.

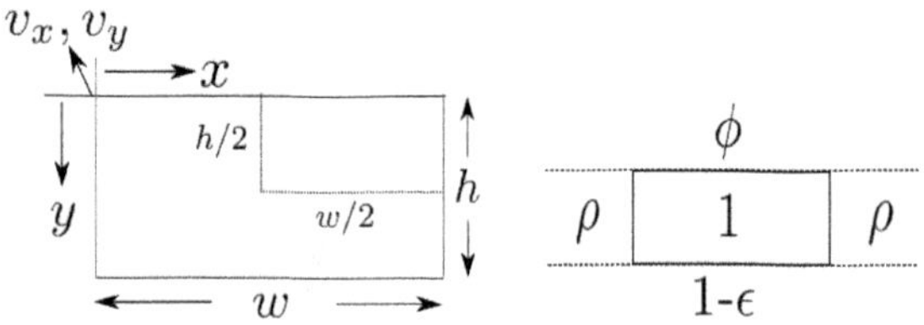

(a) Coordinates (b) Cut Weights

Figure 5: Viewport Coordinate System and Weight Assignment for a Cut

Our goal is to find the best viewports that maximize $CUT(V_f, f)$. This step is achieved by evaluating all candidate viewports and selecting a few that have the highest value of cut.

4.3 Tubing: Finding Recommended Viewports over Time

Viewports change in every frame. When users select a recommended viewport in a frame, the same viewport may not be optimal when recommended in the next frame. The system has to switch to a nearest viewport, causing a virtual camera shake. To minimize the irritation caused by frequent and abrupt change in viewport position, we compute an optimal strategy to switch viewports while maintaining a smooth, linear transition of the viewport position. Such a linear change manifests as a virtual camera pan.

To compute a virtual camera pan, we first designate some frames in the video as key frames. All frames falling between two key frames constitute a *shot*. The viewport is allowed to linearly change position within the shot. We expect the viewport at the beginning of a shot to smoothly change to a viewport at the end of the shot.

In our implementation, we use one key frame every 20 frames. There is a trade off involved in the choice of inter key frame distance. More key frames would lead to less stable viewport (more shaky) and fewer key frames would lead to less optimal recommended viewports (the reason for which will become clear later).

There are multiple candidate viewports at different zoom levels at the beginning and at the end of a shot. We can choose different combination of the starting viewport and ending viewport. Each of these combinations result in a spatial-temporal trajectory of viewports across the frames in between the two key frames. We refer to this trajectory as a *tube*. Since we linearly interpolate the viewports in a tube, a viewport in an intermediate frame may not be the optimal viewport for that frame (as determined by the cut).

Our goal is therefore to find a good tube that gives good overall viewport quality across all frames in the tube. To this end, we define four metrics to evaluate the quality of the tube. Given a tube $\mathcal{T} = < V_f, V_{f+1}, \dots V_{f+N} >$ we first consider the cut metric, which is used to prevent violation of aesthetic rules, especially for human body. We define the *cut of a tube* as the sum of all cuts of viewports in the tube. Second, we consider the importance of the tube, and define the *heat* of a tube as the sum of all importance value in every viewport $V_{i, i\in f \dots f+N}$ in the tube, i.e., the pixel values in the importance map of each frame that falls in the viewport. Third, we consider the *temporal coherence* of a tube. We aim at preserving the motion of foreground objects within a tube. We proceed as in [1] and track our clusters over time by *mode seeking*. A given cluster is tracked across l frames creating a temporal chain of cluster centroids $< c_j, c_{j+1}, \dots c_{j+l} >_{id}$ that starts at frame j. Each chain is assigned an unique id, and every cluster whose centroid is part of this chain is labelled with that same id. With this simple method clusters might split or merge as we track, creating new chains. This is not an issue as it is not required to precisely track and segment objects to ensure temporal consistency [21]. The temporal coherence of a tube can then be computed. For every pair of viewports $V_{f'}$ and $V_{f'+i}$ in the tube, a score proportional to i is added to the tube's coherence value $COH(\mathcal{T})$ every time clusters with the same id can be found in both $V_{f'}$ and $V_{f'+i}$[3] The coherence is then normalized to range into $[0, 1]$. Finally, we consider the spatial displacement of the tube. We define the *regularity* of the tube as the measure for rate of change of the viewport positions within the tube. We compute regularity as

$$e^{-\frac{\|v_f - v_{f+N}\|_2^2}{N^2}},$$

where v_f and v_{f+N} are the initial and final viewport positions respectively, and N is the number of frames in the tube $\mathcal{T}$. This metric penalizes large displacement of viewports with an exponential weighting function.

To find the set of good tubes between two key frames, all possible tubes are computed and assigned a score by simply summing the four metrics. The top k tubes with the highest scores are chosen and form the recommended viewports between the two key frames (we use $k = 3$ in our implementation). An example of the result of creating tubes is shown as viewport sequences in figure 6.

5. COMBINING CONTENT-BASED ANALYSIS AND CROWDSOURCING

Using the approach detailed in the previous section, we have viewports to recommend to users (step 3 of Fig 2). We then start collecting user interaction traces with our zoomable interface. The goal is to find an approach to refine the content based viewport recommendation with the user selected viewports.

While zooming with the interface, each user selects a viewport at a given frame f. This viewport V_f is a rectangle whose top left corner is positioned at (v_x, x_y) and is of size (w, h). The viewport crops the important region the user is interested in. Since the level of interest of each cropped pixel differs with respect to its position within the viewport, as in [2] we assume that users naturally center the viewport on the most interesting area. We then model the interest within a viewport as a gaussian pdf being centered at $\mu = (v_x + w/2, v_y + h/2)$ with a covariance Σ constrained to the dimensions of the viewport: $\Sigma \propto \begin{pmatrix} w^2/4 & 0 \\ 0 & h^2/4 \end{pmatrix}$ and $\int_{V_f} \mathcal{N}(\mu, \Sigma) = 0.99$.

A user interest map UIM_f associated with frame f is then crowdsourced by accumulating the interest levels from multiple users. If we collect K viewport traces from K users who have zoomed on f, a gaussian mixture model can be computed such that $UIM_f^K = 1/K \sum_{k=1}^{K} \mathcal{N}(\mu_k, \Sigma_k)$.

The first image in Figure 7 shows $K = 16$ viewports selected by users while watching a long jump video with our interface. The second image shows the associated user interest map generated using the gaussian mixture model described earlier. In this example, users focus on the sand pit because they were asked to estimate the length of the jump.

With this simple formulation, the user interest map computation stabilizes after only 10 or 15 users. We observed that the KL-divergence $KL(UIM_f^{K+1} || UIM_f^K)$ is negligible for $K \geq 15$. Note

[3] $COH(\mathcal{T}) \propto \sum_{i=f}^{f+N} \sum_{c \in V_i \cap C_i} \sum_{k=i+1}^{f+N} \phi(c,k)$ where $\phi(c,k) = k - f$ if the cluster centroid c has an id that can be found among the ids present in V_k.

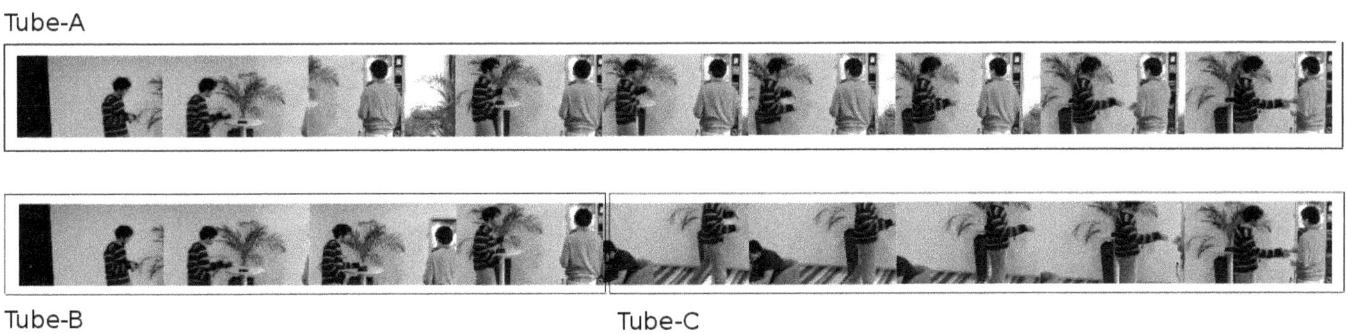

Figure 6: Viewport sequences showing Tubes. Tube-A is a long tube showing a scene where a person in motion is followed. Tube-B and Tube-C are other candidate Tubes rejected by the Tubing algorithm. Tube-B is short and has a low Regularity measure, while Tube-C is not only short but also has a lower cut value that manifests as a not so aesthetic framing

that in this paper we do not consider any sequential estimation of the user interest map where a weight could be used to de-emphasize old traces in a time-varying context.

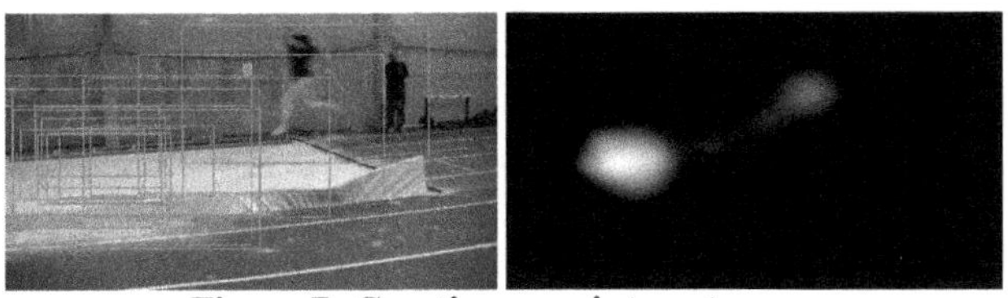

Figure 7: Creating user interest maps

As shown on step 5 of Fig 2, we then use the implicit feedback from users as another modality in the computation of importance map. We merge user interest maps with content-based importance maps by assigning them an equal weight. How to properly weight remains an open question: we plan to study the performances of different (either static or dynamic) weighting strategies in our future work. Yet experiments presented in the next section show that this simple strategy already demonstrates significant success. Indeed by applying the algorithms presented in section 4 to this new importance map, we obtain updated recommended viewports that match intention of the users better.

6. RESULTS

6.1 Experimental Setup

Video Sequences. We use four videos to assess our work. Three of these videos show a long jump, where we can see the end of the runway and the sand pit. The action consists of an athlete running, jumping, and then going back to his coach while the sand is being swept (see Fig 8). We refer to these video clips as longjump0, longjump1 and longjump2, and each last around 30 s.

The fourth video is longer and semantically more complex. Fig 1 summarizes the action taking place in a coffee lounge. At the beginning of the video, two people are sitting in the foreground on blue sofas (times 0:01 and 0:03). A new person in orange sweater is then entering the scene, and loses his keys while removing his wallet from his pocket (time 0:10), before reaching the coffee machine and staying there (time 0:12). At the same time, one of the two seated people picks up the keys (time 0:16) and hands it over to his friend who leaves the scene. After this theft, a fourth person arrives and goes to the coffee machine (time 0:38), after leaving his wallet on the same table as the person in orange (see also Fig 6). At the end of the video, the two people from time 1:00 (Fig 1) take their wallets and leave the scene, leaving the thief alone in the room. We call this 1 minute and 22 seconds video clip coffeelounge.

Figure 8: longjump2 video

Interaction Techniques. We built four variants of user interfaces for zoomable video. The version we proposed in this paper is denoted as RC+U, which stands for *Recommendation based on Content and Usage*.

To study the effect of combining usage analysis with content analysis, we setup a version of the user interface that uses only recommended viewport computed using content analysis, without considering user access pattern. We call this version RC (Recommendation based on Content). This version is equivalent to the output of Step 3, after the process described in Section 4.

The third variant of the user interface we setup is called NR, which stands for No Recommendation. The purpose is to study the effects of presenting recommended viewport to the users. All interaction elements in this user interface remains the same, except that the recommended viewports are removed.

Finally, we setup a variant of the interface which we refer to as NZ, standing for No Zoom. We use NZ in one of our control experiments. NZ does not allow any zooming or panning.

Methodology. We evaluate the three successive versions (NR, RC and RC+U) of our interface by conducting the following user study. In our experiments, the user traces from RC are used to compute the recommended viewports of RC+U.

We assign tasks to users where zooming may be useful. We ask them to estimate the jump length in longjump0, longjump1 and longjump2 and we ask them if there are key thefts and/or wallets thefts in coffeelounge.

First we provide a first group of users with NZ, which plays only the low resolution (320×180 px) version of the video sequences without any interaction. We want to evaluate how well users answer the questions without zooming.

The core of the user study involves comparing the three versions of our interface: NR, RC and RC+U using three independent set of 20 users Users0, Users1 and Users2.

Except for NZ where no interaction is available, we always start our user studies with a learning phase. We first demonstrate the features of the interface, and then observe how users interact with our training video (longjump0). We never continue the study without explicitly reminding the user of interactions he/she did not try.

Then we explain to users what task they have to complete while viewing the next video clips. We always present the clips in the same order: longjump0, longjump1, longjump2 and coffeelounge. We collect a user's answers at the end of each clip. We let users watch the video as many times as they want and we record every interaction into a database. In average the test lasted between 8 and 10 minutes for each participant.

Participants. We collected traces from 16 females and 54 males (total 70 participants), with an age ranging between 19 and 55 years old. Among these users, 10 were presented NZ and 20 each were presented other interfaces.

General Statistics. We collected a total amount of 102,470 events in our database, 34,623 being produced during the training phase on longjump0. All those events are needed to compute user interest maps (see Section 5). However in the following discussion, we only consider a subset of those events that allow us to compute the number of zoom in, zoom out and panning. We got 6,694 of such events from a total number of 434 viewings of our 4 videos (6 viewings per person on an average).

We now present the results of our user studies. We discuss only our data on longjump2 and coffeelounge because of the following reasons. First we used longjump0 to train users. Second longjump1 has been used as a control experiment to check that our results are independant from the set of users. Indeed, we observe that Users2 behave the same as Users1 when viewing longjump1 when they were provided with the same set of recommended viewports using the interface RC (see Table 1). We omit the detailed result of this control experiment here due to space constraint.

Video	Users0	Users1	Users2
longjump1	NR	RC	RC
longjump2 and coffeelounge	NR	RC	RC+U

Table 1: Protocol of the Experiment

6.2 Number of Interactions

We analyze the traces to count the number of user interactions in each of NR, RC, and RC+U. Figure 9 shows the results. We first observed that there is no significant difference in the number of zooms, but the number of pans when using NR is on average almost twice as much as RC+U. Since pans are used mostly to position the viewport correctly, this results show that the recommended viewport is useful in reducing the number of interactions. The number of pans for RC+U is also less than RC, indicating that the quality of recommended viewports for RC+U is better, as users pan less using RC+U. This point will be further elaborated in the next result.

Note that coffeelounge lasts 1 minute 22 seconds while longjump2 is only 35 seconds long, an this explains the difference in the number of panning for each video.

Number of Recommended Viewport Selected To further compare the recommended viewports between RC and RC+U, we analyze the trace at one particular event in the coffeelounge video, to further understand how the recommended viewport are clicked.

When Users1 zoom on the coffeelounge video (with RC), the recommended viewports are clicked 45% of the time. The remaining 55% clicks are outside the recommended viewports (Table 2). The first row of Table 3 gives insights into the distribution of zoom levels of those 45% clicks. It shows that users rarely zoom to the maximum level (i.e. close-ups). This result highlights the importance of the relationship between content semantic and participants' tasks. In this task, automatically detected close-ups are not useful enough to successfully complete the task.

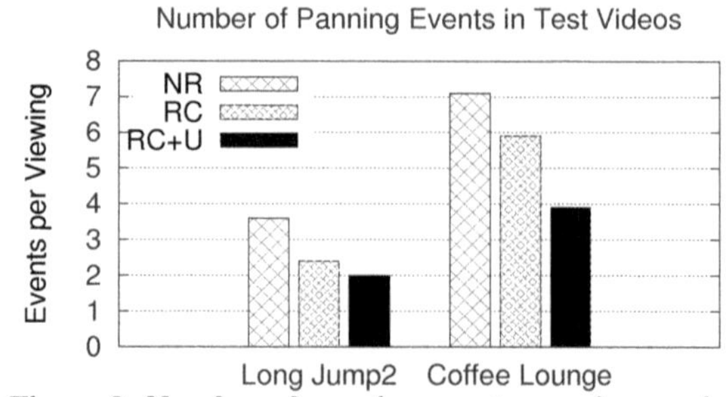

Figure 9: Number of panning events per view session

However, RC+U exhibits better performance regarding the number of recommended viewports clicked like we see on the second row of Table 2. The ratio of clicks on recommended viewports and outside shows that recommended viewports are more relevant. This underlines the interest of combining content analysis with crowdsourcing to learn better ROIs. Moreover, learning better ROIs affects the distribution of zoom levels, summarized by Table 3. As shown below, emergence of task-relevant close-ups encourages users to zoom more when needed.

We observe the same phenomenon on longjump2. Recommended viewports in RC are not really selected by users (only 18%, see first row of Table 2). But once combined with user maps, new recommended viewports are twice as much clicked by users (40%).

Video	longjump2	coffeelounge
RC	18%	45%
RC+U	40%	55%

Table 2: Percentage of clicks in recommended viewports for RC and RC+U

Interface	960 × 540 px	640 × 360 px	320 × 180 px
RC	73.2%	25.6%	1.2%
RC+U	24.6%	42.5%	32.9%

Table 3: Size of the recommended viewports clicked by users on coffeelounge

In summary, we found that integrating user interest maps to improve the relevance of recommended viewports yields a better recommendation. Users more often used the recommended viewports resulting in lower number of panning events.

6.3 Tracking of Moving Objects

We now demonstrate the importance of using content analysis to recommend the initial set of recommended viewports.

Because content analysis includes motion detection and tubing ensures temporal consistency, some recommended viewports track moving objects on the scene. Fig 11 shows one such example, following a character entering the scene and putting his wallet down a table. This recommendation actually helps answering one of the task questions because it makes users identify which wallet belongs to who. This particular region has been selected by 7 users out of 20 using RC.

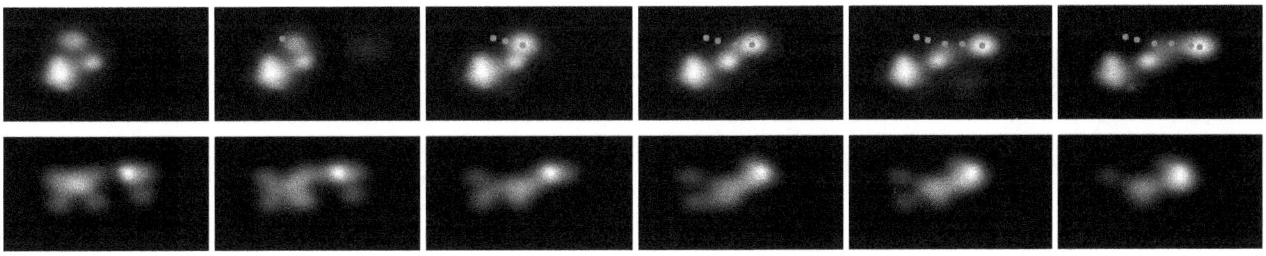

Figure 10: Two sets of user maps during the same time interval: first row comes from use of RC and second row from use of NR

Fig 10 emphasizes the importance of content analysis. The first and second rows show user maps from RC and NR respectively, during the time interval as in Fig 11. We see that the movement of the character clearly emerges as a focused hotspot (materialized by moving red dots) in RC. This hotspot is a result from the previously mentioned 7 viewers who used RC to click on the recommended viewports. With the NR interface, users can not easily follow the moving character even with repeated panning. The user maps from NR (second row of Fig 10) illustrate the absence of a hotspot following the moving person. Therefore, introducing content analysis before explicitly learning from users, reveals more about content semantic than relying only on crowdsourcing.

Figure 11: Example of an object producing a moving recommended viewport.

6.4 Better Framing

The other strength of our approach is that, by integrating content analysis into recommendation of viewport, we can eliminate recommended viewports that violate basic aesthetic rules.

Figure 12 presents the output of our framing optimization on the same frame but with different input. In the left part of the figure, we use user interest maps from NR, resulting in an unsatisfied framing. Users of NR have been watching this region at a higher zoom level centered between the two human subjects in the scene. Hence the user interest maps were produced with a blob at this exact place. The framing optimization placed the recommended viewport in the region maximizing the heat (as per algorithms detailed in the previous section) resulting in a case of bad framing.

The right part of the figure shows the same result but with user interest maps from Users1 as an input. In this case, users were biased with the recommended viewports generated, thanks to content analysis. The corresponding user interest map presents a hotspot slightly shifted to the right compared to the one generated from Users0. As a result, the framing optimization produces a recommended viewport that is aesthetically better as it does not cut body parts of the subjects in the scene.

6.5 Understanding Video Content

Previous results show that recommended viewports from RC+U are selected more often than the ones from RC, but does it mean

Figure 12: Framing with traces from use of NR (left) and use of RC (right)

that it helps them understand the content better? The answer, as shown in this section, is yes.

Table 4 presents users' answers to the questions based on the task specific to coffeelounge. As a reminder, we asked users whether or not a key was stolen (the correct answer is yes), and whether or not a wallet was stolen (the correct answer is no). Whereas it is quite easy to spot the theft of the key even without zooming, there is an ambiguity with regard to the wallets (it may appear as if they were exchanged). Zooming in to the region of the wallets can resolve this ambiguity.

We noticed that 70% users who see the video at a low resolution (NZ) spot the key theft, whereas only 50% identify that no wallets have been stolen. We actually observed during the study that users tried to guess the answer because they could not see accurately, and indeed the answers were equally distributed as yes and no. This result provides us with a lower bound to compare interfaces NR, RC and RC+U.

The percentage of good answers is higher with NR thanks to the zooming functionality, especially for the wallets question (70% of good answers). However results are disappointing for RC. Guiding users with recommendations is potentially double-edged: since they follow the recommendations (Table 2), the quality of their answers is correlated to the relevance of the recommended viewports with respect to the task. About the specific wallets task, it is understandable that content analysis alone fails to detect the region around the wallets as one of the prominent ROIs.

We get the best answers with RC+U, which combines content analysis and crowdsourcing. Indeed we observe in Fig 13 that crowdsourcing complements content analysis to create a new recommended viewport located on the wallets.

Interface	NZ	NR	RC	RC+U
Is there a key stolen ?	70%	75%	70%	**85%**
Is there a wallet stolen ?	50%	70%	50%	**75%**

Table 4: Percentage of right answers to the questions

We do not discuss the answers to the task for longjump2 because the task is not discriminant enough to create differences in

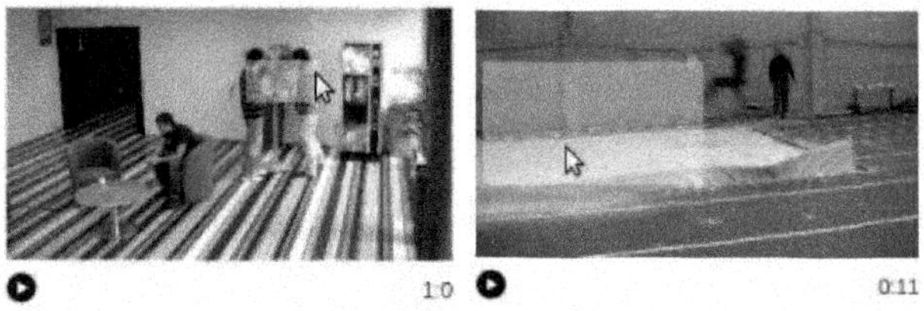

Figure 13: Example of ROIs emerging in RC+U: close-up on the wallets in coffeelounge and sand pit in longjump2.

the quality of answers when different interfaces are used. As the users have a very specific task in the longjump2 video, i.e to identify the length of the jump, the length of the jump is localized to the sand-pit. Hence users directly zoom into the region enclosing the sand-pit irrespective of the interface used. However consistent with coffeelounge task, we observed the emergence of a recommended viewport particularly suited to the task (see Fig 13). Conversely some recommended viewports have a low interest with respect to the assigned task and have not be selected by Users1. As a consequence, they disappeared in RC+U making our video interface adaptive and user-centric.

7. CONCLUSION

The main contributions of the paper are as follows. First, we have proposed the use of recommended viewports as a new way for users to interact with a zoomable video. A recommended viewport highlights interesting and relevant regions in the video and automatically tracks moving objects of interest, making it simple for users to click and zoom on interesting regions. Second, we proposed a hybrid approach to identify suitable recommended viewports automatically, by analyzing the content of the video and the user viewing pattern when watching the video. Our approach plays on the strength of both techniques, using usage analysis to crowdsource user's intention when viewing the video, and using content analysis to help with proper framing of the viewport around objects and with tracking of moving objects. Our approach can be viewed as one that uses implicit feedback from users as another modality to understand the content of the video.

Our work can be extended in many ways. Firstly, more sophisticated content analysis algorithms can be used to identify salient regions, track objects, and frame the viewport aesthetically. Secondly, our current research stops at learning from a set of 20 users. An open question is how to continuously crowdsource from users and adapt the importance map, and thus the recommended viewport. Thirdly, if we have multiple videos of similar types (e.g., multiple lecture videos from the same lecturer), then we can use the user interest map collected on one video to compute proper weights for linear combination of the different saliency features when analyzing the content of other videos. That is, we might be able to perform semi-supervised learning for computer vision algorithms using implicit feedback from users.

Identifying the important and relevance regions in a video has many other applications, beyond improving user interaction with zoomable video. The recommended viewports can be used to produce a retargeted video that automatically zooms and pans, essentially summarizing the content of the video to the users without interaction. Furthermore, we believe that the recommended viewports allows us to better predict what a user would like to watch during a given time in the video. Making such accurate predictions is crucial for prefetching of zoomable video during streaming, and to reduce the response time when users zoom and pan.

Acknowledgement

This research work is supported by National University of Singapore Academic Research Fund under the research grant WBS:R-252-000-368-112, and NExT Search Center, funded by the Singapore National Research Foundation & Interactive Digital Media R&D Program Office, MDA, under the research grant WBS:R-252-300-001-490.

8. REFERENCES

[1] C. Beleznai, B. Fruhstuck, and H. Bischof. Human tracking by fast mean shift mode seeking. *Journal of Multimedia*, 1(1):1–8, 2006.

[2] A. Carlier, V. Charvillat, W. T. Ooi, R. Grigoras, and G. Morin. Crowdsourced automatic zoom and scroll for video retargeting. In *Proceedings of MULTIMEDIA'10*, pages 201–210, Florence, Italy, 2010.

[3] A. Carlier, R. Guntur, and W. T. Ooi. Towards characterizing users' interaction with zoomable video. In *Proceedings of the 2010 ACM workshop on Social, adaptive and personalized multimedia interaction and access*, pages 21–24, Florence, Italy, 2010.

[4] K.-Y. Cheng, S.-J. Luo, B.-Y. Chen, and H.-H. Chu. Smartplayer: User-centric video fast-forwarding. In *Proceedings of CHI'09*, 2009.

[5] D. Comaniciu and P. Meer. Mean shift: A robust approach toward feature space analysis. *IEEE Trans. Pattern Anal. Mach. Intell.*, 24(5):603–619, 2002.

[6] A. Doan, R. Ramakrishnan, and A. Y. Halevy. Crowdsourcing systems on the world-wide web. *Commun. ACM*, 54:86–96, April 2011.

[7] P. Dragicevic, G. Ramos, J. Bibliowitcz, D. Nowrouzezahrai, R. Balakrishnan, and K. Singh. Video browsing by direct manipulation. In *Proceedings of CHI'08*, pages 237–246, Florence, Italy, 2008.

[8] H. El-Alfy, D. Jacobs, and L. Davis. Multi-scale video cropping. In *Proceedings of MULTIMEDIA '07*, pages 97–106, Augsburg, Germany, 2007.

[9] D. B. Goldman, C. Gonterman, B. Curless, D. Salesin, and S. M. Seitz. Video object annotation, navigation, and composition. In *Proceedings of UIST'08*, pages 3–12, 2008.

[10] J. Han, K. N. Ngan, M. Li, and H. Zhang. Unsupervised extraction of visual attention objects in color images. *IEEE Trans. Circuits Syst. Video Techn.*, 16(1):141–145, 2006.

[11] L. Itti, C. Koch, and E. Niebur. A model of saliency-based visual attention for rapid scene analysis. *IEEE Trans. Pattern Anal. Mach. Intell.*, 20(11):1254–1259, 1998.

[12] F. Liu and M. Gleicher. Video retargeting: automating pan and scan. In *Proceedings of MULTIMEDIA '06*, pages 241–250, Santa Barbara, CA, USA, 2006.

[13] S. Montabone and A. Soto. Human detection using a mobile platform and novel features derived from a visual saliency mechanism. *Image and Vision Computing*, 28(3):391–402, 2010.

[14] K. Q. M. Ngo, R. Guntur, A. Carlier, and W. T. Ooi. Supporting zoomable video streams via dynamic region-of-interest cropping. In *Proceedings of MMSys'10*, pages 259–270, Scottsdale, AZ, USA, 2010.

[15] M. Rubinstein, A. Shamir, and S. Avidan. Multi-operator media retargeting. *ACM Trans. Graph.*, 28(3), 2009.

[16] D. A. Shamma, R. Shaw, P. L. Shafton, and Y. Liu. Watch what i watch: using community activity to understand content. In *Multimedia Information Retrieval*, pages 275–284, 2007.

[17] F. Shipman, A. Girgensohn, and L. Wilcox. Authoring, viewing, and generating hypervideo: An overview of hyper-hitchcock. *ACM Trans. Multimedia Comput. Commun. Appl.*, 5(2):1–19, 2008.

[18] T. Syeda-Mahmood and D. Ponceleon. Learning video browsing behavior and its application in the generation of video previews. In *Proceedings of MULTIMEDIA'01*, pages 119–128, Ottawa, Canada, 2001.

[19] N. Ukita, T. Ono, and M. Kidode. Region extraction of a gaze object using the gaze point and view image sequences. In *Proceedings of ICMI'05*, pages 129–136, Torento, Italy, 2005.

[20] P. Viola and M. Jones. Rapid object detection using a boosted cascade of simple features. *CVPR'01*, 1:511–518, 2001.

[21] Y.-S. Wang, H. Fu, O. Sorkine, T.-Y. Lee, and H.-P. Seidel. Motion-aware temporal coherence for video resizing. *ACM Trans. Graph.*, 28:127:1–127:10, December 2009.

[22] X. Xie, H. Liu, S. Goumaz, and W.-Y. Ma. Learning user interest for image browsing on small-form-factor devices. In *Proceedings of CHI'05*, pages 671–680, Portland, Oregon, USA, 2005.

Visual Memes in Social Media

Tracking Real-World News in YouTube Videos

Lexing Xie
Australian National University
lexing.xie@anu.edu.au

Apostol Natsev
IBM Research
natsev@us.ibm.com

John R. Kender
Columbia University
jrk@cs.columbia.edu

Matthew Hill
IBM Research
mh@us.ibm.com

John R. Smith
IBM Research
jsmith@us.ibm.com

ABSTRACT

We propose visual memes, or frequently reposted short video segments, for tracking large-scale video remix in social media. Visual memes are extracted by novel and highly scalable detection algorithms that we develop, with over 96% precision and 80% recall. We monitor real-world events on YouTube, and we model interactions using a graph model over memes, with people and content as nodes and meme postings as links. This allows us to define several measures of influence. These abstractions, using more than two million video shots from several large-scale event datasets, enable us to quantify and efficiently extract several important observations: over half of the videos contain re-mixed content, which appears rapidly; video view counts, particularly high ones, are poorly correlated with the virality of content; the influence of traditional news media versus citizen journalists varies from event to event; iconic single images of an event are easily extracted; and content that will have long lifespan can be predicted within a day after it first appears. Visual memes can be applied to a number of social media scenarios: brand monitoring, social buzz tracking, ranking content and users, among others.

Categories and Subject Descriptors: J.4 [Social and Behavioral Sciences]: Sociology, I.4.9 [Image Processing and Computer Vision]: Applications

General Terms: Algorithms, Measurement, Experimentation.

1. INTRODUCTION

Important happenings from around the world are increasingly captured on video and uploaded to news and social media sites. The ease of publishing and sharing videos has outpaced the progress of modern search engines, collaborative tagging sites, and content aggregation services—leaving users to deal with a deluge of content [2]. This information overload problem is particularly prominent for linear media (such as audio, video, animations), where at-a-glance impressions are hard to develop and are often unreliable. While text-based information networks such as Twitter rely on retweets [5, 18], hashtags, mentions, or trackbacks to identify influence and trending topics [1], similar functions for large video-sharing repository is lacking. A reliable video-based "quote" tracking and popularity analysis system would find immediate practical applications in many domains—e.g., selecting of the "most typical" video for a given topic or collection; measuring influence and ranking people in news events; improving targeted advertising based on page/author influence; and denoising video search and query expansion results, to name a few.

We propose to use visual memes for making sense of video "buzz". A *meme*[1] is defined as a cultural unit (e.g., an idea, value, or pattern of behavior) that is passed from one person to another in social settings. We define a *visual meme* as a short segment of video that is frequently remixed and reposted by more than one author. Video-making requires significant effort and time, so we regard reposting a video meme as a deeper stamp of approval or awareness than simply viewing a video, leaving a comment, giving a rating, or sending a tweet. Example video memes are shown in Figures 1, 2 and 3, represented in a static keyframe format. We can see that each meme instance is semantically consistent, despite many variations in the videos that contain them, such as size, coloring, captions, editing, and so on.

Figure 1 summarizes the approach proposed in this paper. We develop a large-scale event monitoring system for video content, using generic text queries as a pre-filter for content collection on a given topic (Box D). We deploy this system for YouTube, and collect large video datasets over a range of topics. We then perform fast visual meme detection on tens of thousands of videos and millions of video shots (Box A). We showcase the potential applications of visual memes using a network model over the meme videos and authors (Box B). Using this model, we derive graph metrics that capture content influence and user roles. Using such visual meme extraction and exploitation strategies, we have made several observations on real-world news event collections (Box C), such as: over half of the event videos contain remixed content, and about 70% of authors participate in video remixing; video view counts are a poor proxy for the likelihood of a video being reposted; over 50% of memes are discovered and re-posted within 3 hours after their first appearance; meme influence indices can be used to delineate the roles of different user groups, such as *mavens* or *connec-*

*Area chair: Mor Naaman

MM'11, November 28–December 1, 2011, Scottsdale, Arizona, USA.

[1] http://wordnetweb.princeton.edu/perl/webwn?s=meme

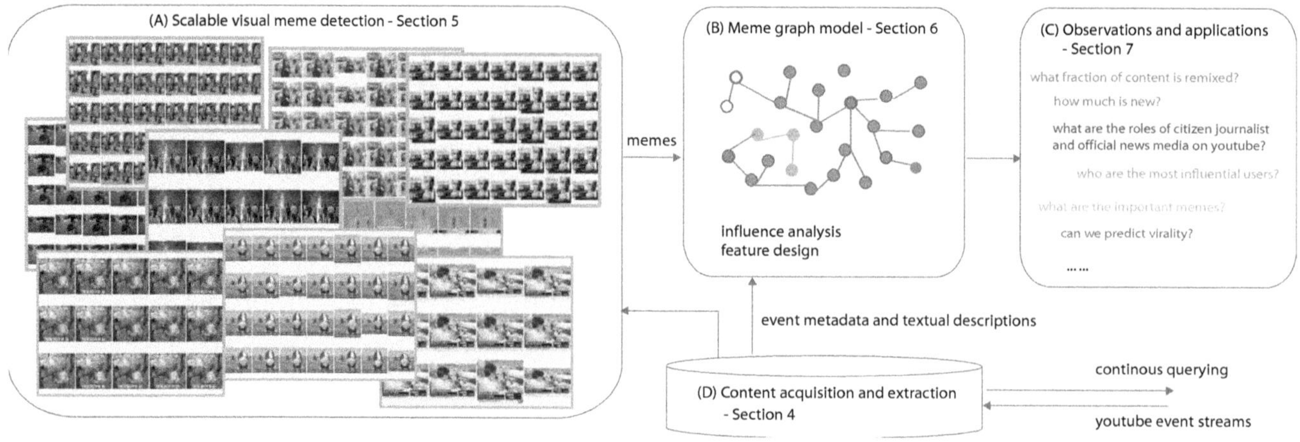

Figure 1: Overview of visual meme tracking and analysis in social event streams. In Box A, the border color of meme clusters denotes the event they are from: green (top): Iran; orange (bottom): SwineFlu.

tors who play notable roles in social changes [14]. We use features derived from the meme network model to predict the lifespan of memes, achieving an area-under-ROC-curve (AUC) measure of 0.78.

The main contributions of this work are as follows:

- We propose *visual memes* as a novel tool to track large-scale video remixing in social media. We implement a scalable system that can extract all memes from over a million video shots, in a few hours on a single CPU.
- We design and implement the first large-scale event-based social video monitoring and visual content analysis system.
- We propose an application for visual memes by building a network model on videos and authors, which can in turn be used to characterize user roles and predict meme lifespan.
- We conduct empirical evaluations with several large event datasets, producing observations about percentage of video remix, user participation, timing of video meme production, meme popularity against traditional metrics, and different user group roles.

2. RELATED WORK

This work relates to active research areas in both multimedia analysis and social media mining.

YouTube has been the focal platform for many social network monitoring studies. The first large-scale YouTube measurement study [6] characterized content category distributions, and tracked exact duplicates of popular videos. Benevenuto et al. studied video response actions on YouTube using metadata [3], and De Choudhury et al. monitored user comments to determine interesting conversations [10]. Recently, early views of YouTube videos have been used to predict ultimate popularity, characterized by view counts [25].

Quoting, duplication, and reposting are popular phenomena in online information networks. One well-known example is retweeting on micro-blogs [5, 18], where users often quote the original text message verbatim, having little freedom for remixing and context changes within the 140 character limit. Another example is MemeTracker [19], which tracks the lifecycles of popular phrases among blogs and news websites. Prior studies have shown that the frequency of video reuse can be used as an implicit video quality indicator [23]. However, none of the prior work has defined the unit for *retweet* or *meme* on a video sharing network.

Tracking near-duplicates in images and video has been a problem of interest since the early years of content-based retrieval. Recent focus of this problem has been on user-dependent definitions of duplicates [8], speeding up detection on image sequence, frame, or local image points [26], and scaling out to web-scale computations using large compute clusters [20]. We note, however, that most prior work in this area is concerned with optimizing retrieval accuracy of detecting near-duplicate frames or sequences, rather than tracking large-scale duplication behavior. Kennedy and Chang [17] tracked editing and provenance of images on the web, with a focus on distinguishing different types of image edits and their ideological perspective. Our work, in comparison, tracks large-scale video remixes using both content and metadata such as authorship and creation time, and focuses on inferring social roles in video propagation.

Several recent works have looked at YouTube phenomena—Biel and Gatica-Perez [4] focused on individual social behavior such as non-verbal cues, while Hong et al. [15] presented content summarization by monitoring a query over time. In comparison, we use visual memes to capture the behavior of large groups and to track information dissemination.

3. VISUAL MEMES AND VIDEO REMIXES

Visual memes are defined as frequently reposted video segments or images. It has been observed that users tend to create "curated selections based on what they liked or thought was important" ([24], page 270). News event collections are particularly suited for studying large-scale user curation, since remixing is more prevalent here than on video genres designed for self-expression, such as video blogs. The unit of interaction appears to be video segments, consisting of one or a few contiguous shots. The remixed shots typically contain minor modifications that include video formatting changes (such as aspect ratio, color, contrast, gamma), and video production edits (such as the superimposition of text, captions, borders, transition effects). Most of these are well-known as the targets of visual copy detection benchmarks [22]. In this paper, *meme* refers both to individual

Figure 2: Visual meme shots and meme clusters. (Left) Two YouTube videos that share multiple different memes. Note that it is impossible to tell from metadata or the YouTube video page that they shared content, and that the appearance of the remixed shots (bottom row) has large variations. (Right) A sample of other meme keyframes corresponding to one of the meme shots, and the number of videos containing this meme over time – 193 videos in total between June 13 and August 11, 2009.

instances, visualized as representative icons (as in Figure 2 Left and Figure 3), and to the entire equivalence class of re-posted near-duplicate video segments, visualized as clusters of keyframes (as in Figure 1 and Figure 2 Right).

Intuitively, re-posting is a stronger endorsement, requiring much more effort than simply viewing, commenting on, or linking to the video content. A re-posted visual meme is an explicit statement of mutual awareness, or a relevance statement on a subject of mutual interest. Hence, memes can be used to study virality, lifetimes and timeliness, influential originators, and (in)equality of reference.

4. MONITORING EVENTS ON YOUTUBE

YouTube has become a virtual worldwide bazaar for video content of almost every type. With more than 48 hours of video being added every minute [2], it is a living marketplace of ideas and a vibrant recorder of current events.

We use text queries to pre-filter content, thus making the scale of monitoring feasible. We use a few generic, time-insensitive text queries as content pre-filters. The queries are manually designed to capture the topic theme, as well as the generally understood cause, phenomena, and consequences of the topic. For example, our queries on the "global warming" topic consist of *global warming, climate change, green house gas, CO_2 emission*, whereas the "swine flu" topic expands into *swine flu, H1N1, H1N1 travel advisory, swine flu vaccination*, and so on. We aim to create queries covering the main invariant aspects of a topic, but automatic time-varying query expansion is open for future work. We use the YouTube API to extract video entries for each query, sorted by relevance and recency. The API will return up to 1000 entries per query, so varying the sorting criteria helps to increase content coverage and diversity. The retrieved video entries are those responding to keyword queries based on YouTube's proprietary algorithm, and often contain entries not directly relevant to the event being monitored. We filter the results to restrict the video database to unique videos, removing redundant entries that responded to multiple queries or whose YouTube identifier matched one that had previously been gathered. Then, for each unique video, we segment it into shots using thresholded color histogram differences. For each shot we randomly select and extract a frame as keyframe, and extract visual features from each keyframe. We process the XML metadata associated with each video, and extract information such as author, publish date, view counts, and free-text title and descriptions.

We use the term *buzz* to refer to all the videos that respond to keyword queries on YouTube, although their content may not be directly related to the target event or topic of interest. We use the term *meme videos* to refer to videos containing one or more memes. The volume of buzz and memes are telling indicators of event evolution in the real world, and we present a few examples in Figure 3.

Figure 3(a) graphs the volume of all unique videos acquired according to their upload date. There are local peaks on the Swine Flu topic during April-May 2009 when new cases were spreading over the globe, and in October-November 2009 when vaccination first became available in the US, following with a steady volume decrease into 2010. For the 21-month period shown for Pakistan politics, there are two notable peaks: in December 2007, at the time of assassination of Benazir Bhutto; and in February-May 2009, during a series of crises, including serial bombings, an attack on the Sri-Lanka cricket team, and nation-wide protests.

Figure 3(b) tracks and illustrates the volume of meme videos for the Iranian Politics topic (dataset Iran3 in Table 1). The number of meme videos is significant—hundreds to thousands per day. There are three prominent peaks in June-August 2009 corresponding to important events in the real world[2]. The first mid-June peak reflects a highly controversial election prompting massive protests and violent clashes. A second mid-June peak captures a viral amateur video on the shooting of Neda Soltan, which became the symbol for the whole event. A third peak in mid-July corresponds to a Friday prayer sermon which drew over two million people, an event described as "the most critical and turbulent Friday prayer in the history of contemporary Iran"[2].

5. SCALABLE VISUAL MEME DETECTION

Detecting visual memes in a large video collection is a non-trivial problem. There are two main challenges. First, remixing online video segments changes their visual appearance, adding noise as the video is edited and re-compressed.

[2]See timeline: http://en.wikipedia.org/wiki/Timeline_of_the_2009_Iranian_election_protests

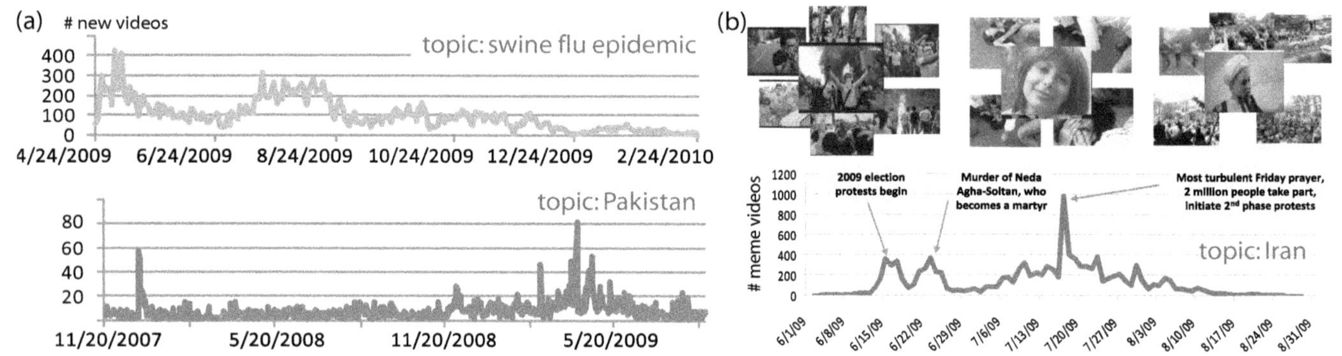

Figure 3: Volume of event buzz and visual memes. (a) Event buzz: number of new videos uploaded daily for two topics. (b) Number of videos containing visual meme on the Iran3 topic, illustrated with the representative memes on a timeline, June-August 2009.

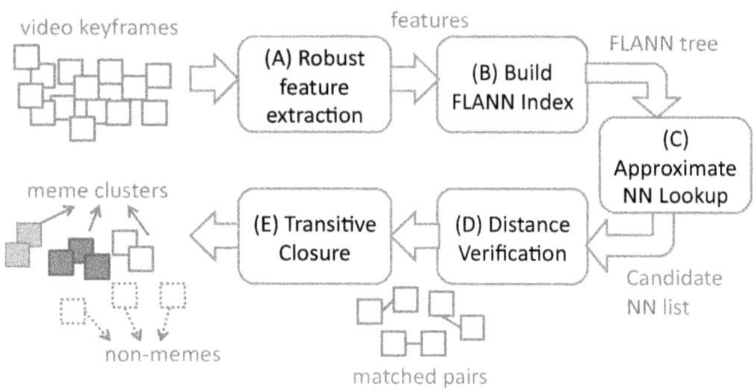

Figure 4: Flow diagram for visual meme detection.

Second, finding all pairs of near-duplicates by matching all N shots against each other has a complexity of $O(N^2)$, which is infeasible for collections containing millions of shots.

Our operational definition of a meme is a reposted video segment that starts and ends at shot boundaries. This definition motivates our processing pipeline of using a single keyframe to represent a video shot (Section 4) without sacrificing matching quality, as the feature-based shot detector is generally robust to intra-shot changes but sensitive to large inter-shot variations in visual appearance.

Our process for detecting video memes is outlined in Figure 4. The input to this system is a set of video frames, and the output splits this set into two parts. The first part consists of a collection of meme clusters, where frames in the same cluster are considered near-duplicates with each other. The second part consists of the rest of the frames, which are not considered near-duplicates with any other frame. Blocks A and D address the robust matching challenge using color correlogram features and query-adaptive thresholding, and blocks B, C and E address the scalability challenge using approximate nearest-neighbor (ANN) indexing and an efficient set transitive closure algorithm.

5.1 Robust keyframe matching

Our solution to the visual appearance challenge is to normalize frames visually, use robust features, and tune the frame matching methods. Before feature extraction, we perform a series of pre-processing steps to normalize the image and reduce noise. These include removing blank or uninformative frames (based on entropy threhsolding); detecting and removing frame borders of uniform colors; normalizing the aspect ratio; performing de-noising; and applying contrast-limited histogram equalization to correct for contrast and gamma differences. We use a frame similarity metric based on the *color correlogram* [16] that captures the local spatial correlation of pairs of colors. The color correlogram is rotation-, scale-, and to some extent, viewpoint-invariant. It was designed to tolerate moderate changes in appearance and shape that are largely color-preserving, e.g., viewpoint changes, camera zoom, noise, compression, and to a smaller degree, shifts, crops, and aspect ratio changes. We also use a "cross"-layout that extracts the descriptor only from horizontal and vertical central image stripes, thereby emphasizing the center portion of the image, while disregarding the corners. This layout improves robustness with respect to text and logo overlay, borders, crops, and shifts. It is also invariant to horizontal or vertical flips, while capturing some spatial layout information. We extract the auto correlogram in a 166-dimensional perceptually quantized HSV color space, and the resulting descriptor with a "cross" layout has 332 dimensions. The result of the above processing (Figure 4 Box A) is a set of features, one per input frame.

Furthermore, we use query-adaptive thresholding on the L_2 distance of the correlogram features to generate a binary judgement for each candidate pair of frames as to whether they are a near-duplicate pair. This corresponds to Figure 4 Box D. The main purpose of this threshold-tuning step is to relax the match threshold for complex query frames and to tighten the threshold for visually simple frames (e.g., blank frames at the extreme). For a given video keyframe q and its correlogram feature $\mathbf{f}_q$, the threshold for determining matches is parameterized as $T_q = \tau \frac{|\mathbf{f}_q|_2}{|\mathbf{f}_{max}|_2}$. Here $|.|_2$ is the L_2 vector norm. $\mathbf{f}_{\max}$ is the collection max feature vector, composed of the largest observed coefficients for each dimension. τ is a global distance threshold tuned on an independent validation dataset. The $|\mathbf{f}_q|_2$ term scales τ based on the information content of q: it lowers the effective threshold for those frames that are visually simple, such as frames with uniform colors or simple charts, which can otherwise lead to false or trivial matches. At the same time, it increases the threshold for highly complex query frames.

5.2 Scaling up

Our solution to the complexity challenge is to use an indexing scheme for fast approximate nearest neighbor (ANN) look-up. Exhaustively finding all pairs of frames that are within a given distance threshold has complexity $O(N^2)$, while ANN indexing can speed this up significantly. We use the Fast Library for Approximate Nearest Neighbor (FLANN) [21] to implement the indexing structure and ANN lookup. FLANN automatically selects the best indexing structure between k-means tree and kd-tree, and chooses the appropriate tree parameters for a given dataset that optimize the trade off between running time and query approximation error. This corresponds to Figure 4 Box B. FLANN allows us to set the maximum number of candidate nodes m to check in a search so that each query runtime is bound to $O(m)$. Executing N queries against the entire set of N keyframes therefore takes $O(Nm)$ time. We have found that values of $m \sim \sqrt{N}$ can approximate k-NN results with over 0.95 precision. Running in $O(N\sqrt{N})$ time, this implementation achieves three decimal orders of magnitude speed-up over exact nearest neighbor search for 1M frames.

We set FLANN to return up to 50 likely neighbors for any query frame q, as the output of Figure 4 Box C. T_q is used to filter out the false neighbors and those that are too far to be declared a match. This filtering results in an incomplete set of matched pairs, depicted as the output of Figure 4 Box D. Therefore, we perform transitive closure on the neighbor relationship to find full equivalence classes of near-duplicate sets. This is done with an efficient set union-find algorithm [12] that runs in amortized time of $O(E)$, where E is the number of matched pairs.

5.3 Discussion

Our design choices for the visual meme detection system aim to find the best combination of accuracy and speed that is feasible to implement in a single PC. Note that using local features such as SIFT can arguably give more accurate near-duplicate detection results but such approaches require larger storage and memory for storing the features, and are less feasible for computing all pairs of near-duplicates in millions of frames on a single node. Most edits are also done at the granularity of entire frames, or even shots, and transformations such as picture-in-picture or significant crops do not not appear to be frequent in casual user remixes. We have found that shot-level matching by keyframes is suitable for capturing community video remixing and provides a good balance of speed and accuracy in public evaluations on video copy detection tasks [22]. Hashing-based techniques [27] are another alternative for speeding up ANN queries but their precision is typically not more than 50%, which is too low for reliably tracking all sets of near-duplicates in large collections. The ANN indexing scheme we adopt scales to several million video shots. On collections consisting of tens of millions to billions of video shots, we expect that the computation infrastructure will need to change—e.g., by implementing a massively distributed tree index [20] and/or hybrid tree-hashing techniques.

A few examples of identified near-duplicate sets are shown in Figures 1 and 2. The performance of the meme detection algorithm is evaluated in Section 7.1.

6. VISUAL MEME NETWORK

Visual memes can be viewed as *links* between videos and also between authors that share the same unit of visual expression. We therefore propose a network model linking visual memes and their authors. This enables us to quantify influence and the importance of visual memes in video-publishing information networks.

Denote a video (or any multimedia document) as d_i in event collection $\mathcal{D}$, with $i = 1, \dots, N$. Each video is authored (i.e., uploaded) by author $a(d_i)$ at time $t(d_i)$, with $a(d_i)$ taking its value from a set of authors $\mathcal{A} = \{a_r, r = 1, \dots, R\}$. Each document d_i can contain a set of memes, $\{v_1, v_2, \dots, v_{K_i}\}$ from a meme dictionary $\mathcal{V}$. In this network model, each meme induces a time-sensitive edge e_{ij} with creation time $t(e_{ij})$, where i, j are over video documents.

6.1 Meme video graph

Let $G = \{\mathcal{D}, \mathcal{E}_G\}$ be a video graph with nodes $d \in \mathcal{D}$. There is a directed edge $e_{ij} \in \mathcal{E}_G$ if documents d_i and d_j share at least one visual meme and if d_i precedes d_j in time: $t(d_i) < t(d_j)$. The presence of e_{ij} represents a possibility that d_j was derived from d_i, even though there is no conclusive evidence within the video collection alone whether or not this is true. We denote the number of shared visual memes as $\nu_{ij} = |\, d_i \cap d_j \,|$, and the time elapsed between the posting time of the two videos as $\triangle t_{ji} = t(d_j) - t(d_i)$.

We use two recipes for computing the edge weight ω_{ij}. Equation 1 uses a weight proportional to the number of common memes ν_{ij}, and Equation 2 scales this weight by a power-law memory factor related to the time difference $\triangle t_{ji}$. The first model is insensitive to $\triangle t_{ji}$, so it can accommodate the resurgence of popular memes, as seen in textual memes [19]. The power law decay comes from known behaviors on YouTube [9], and it also agrees with our observations on the recency of the content returned by the YouTube search API.

$$\omega^*_{ij} = \nu_{ij} \qquad (i,j) \in \mathcal{E}_G \tag{1}$$

$$\omega'_{ij} = \nu_{ij} \triangle t_{ji}^{-\eta} \tag{2}$$

The unit for time t is in days. We estimate the exponent η to be 0.7654, using a process described in Section 7.4. Other edge-weighting factors incorporating the number of views or the rating scores could also be used, although our observations (Figure 6) suggest that the number of views is a poor indicator of the number of memes.

6.2 Meme author graph

Similarly, let us define an author graph $H = \{\mathcal{A}, \mathcal{E}_H\}$, with author nodes $a \in \mathcal{A}$. There is an undirected edge $e_{rs} \in \mathcal{E}_H$ between authors a_r and a_s if they share at least one visual meme in any of their videos.

We compute the edge weights θ_{rs} on edge e_{rs} as the aggregation of the weights on all the edges in the video graph G connecting documents authored by a_r and a_s.

$$\theta_{rs} = \Sigma_{\{i, a(d_i)=a_r\}} \Sigma_{\{j, a(d_j)=a_s\}} \omega_{ij} \tag{3}$$

with $r, s \in \mathcal{A}$, $i, j \in \mathcal{D}$. We adopt two simplifying assumptions in this definition. The set of edges $\mathcal{E}_H$ are bidirectional, as authors often repost memes from each other at different times. The edge weights are cumulative over time, because in our datasets most authors post no more than a handful of videos (Figure 10), and there is rarely enough data to estimate instantaneous activities.

6.3 Meme influence indices

We define three indices based on meme graphs, which capture the influence on information diffusion among memes, and thereby quantify the impact of content and of authors within the video sharing network.

First, for each visual meme v, we extract from the event collection $\mathcal{D}$ the subcollection containing all videos that have at least one shot matching meme v, denoted as $\mathcal{D}_v = \{d_j \in \mathcal{D}, \text{s.t. } v \in d_j\}$. We extract the video document subgraph G_v corresponding to $\mathcal{D}_v$, setting all edge weights $\nu \in G_v$ to 1 since only a single meme is involved. We compute the in-degree and out-degree of every video d_i in $\mathcal{D}_v$ as the number of videos preceding and following d_i in time:

$$\begin{aligned} \zeta_{i,v}^{in} &= \Sigma_j I\{d_i, d_j \in \mathcal{D}_v, \quad t(d_j) < t(d_i)\} \\ \zeta_{i,v}^{out} &= \Sigma_j I\{d_i, d_j \in \mathcal{D}_v, \quad t(d_j) > t(d_i)\} \end{aligned} \tag{4}$$

where $I\{\cdot\}$ is the indicator function that takes a value of 1 when its argument is true, and 0 otherwise. Intuitively, ζ_i^{in} is the number of videos with meme v that precede video d_i (potential sources), and ζ_i^{out} is the number of videos that succeed meme v after video d_i (potential followers).

The video influence index χ_i is defined for each video document d_i as the smoothed ratio of its out-degree over its in-degree, aggregated over all meme subgraphs G_v (Equation 5, where the smoothing factor 1 in the denominator accounts for d_i itself). The author influence index $\hat{\chi}_r$ is obtained by aggregating χ_i over all videos from author a_r (Equation 6). The normalized author influence index $\bar{\chi}_r$ is its un-normalized counterpart $\hat{\chi}_r$ divided by the number of videos an author posted, which can be interpreted as the *average* influence of all videos for this author.

$$\chi_i = \Sigma_v \frac{\zeta_{i,v}^{out}}{1 + \zeta_{i,v}^{in}} \tag{5}$$

$$\hat{\chi}_r = \Sigma_{\{i, a(d_i) = a_r\}} \chi_i, \tag{6}$$

$$\bar{\chi}_r = \frac{\hat{\chi}_r}{\Sigma_i I\{a(d_i) = a_r\}}$$

The above influence indices capture two aspects in meme diffusion: the total volume of memes, as well as how *early* a video or an author is in the diffusion chain. The first aspect is similar to the *reweet* and *mention* measures recently reported for Twitter [5]. The timing aspect in diffusion is new, and it is designed to capture different roles that users play on Youtube, such as information *connectors* and *mavens* [14]. The term *connectors* refers to people who come "...with a special gift for bringing the world together, ...[an] ability to span many different worlds", and *mavens* are "people we rely upon to connect us with new information, ...[those who start] word-of-mouth epidemics".

6.4 Predicting meme importance

We use visual meme network properties to model meme importance. Just as social media influence is commonly understood as multidimensional [1], importance can also be defined in a number of ways: the number of times that a video is viewed [25], the number of times that a video meme is reposted by other YouTube users, or by the lifespan (in days) of all known instances of a meme. Note that neither audience size or the number of views are reliable indicators of influence in social media networks, as shown in Section 7.2. Furthermore, our observations in Section 7.3 show that most memes are re-posted quickly, and our pilot experiments confirm that early meme volumes (on day one or two) are the best predictors of the final meme volume. Therefore, we focus on predicting the lifespan, i.e., the longevity of a message that is kept *alive* by information propagation.

Our meme importance model is derived from three types of features. Each type intends to capture the early trend of meme propagation and author productivity and connectivity, as well as the historical influence of authors. For each visual meme v that first appeared at time $t(v)$ (called *onset* time), we compute features on the meme- and author- subgraphs up to time $t_1 = t(v) + \Delta t$, by including video nodes that appeared before t_1. The parameter Δt is set to one day in this work in order to capture early meme dynamics, as observed in Section 7.3, and similarly to what has been used for view-count prediction [25].

These features we use are as follows:

- The volume of memes up to t_1.
- Static network features of author productivity and connectivity. We use the *total number of videos* that the author has uploaded to capture author productivity. An author's connectivity includes three metrics computed over the author graph of up to time t_1: *degree centrality* is the fraction of other nodes that a node is directly connected to; *closeness centrality* is the inverse of average path length to all other nodes; and *betweenness centrality* is the fraction of all-pairs shortest paths that pass through a node.
- Dynamic features of author diffusion influence. These include the meme influence indices $\hat{\chi}_r$ and $\bar{\chi}_r$ in Equation 6 as well as the aggregate in-degree and out-degree for each author.

To compute author network features, we aggregate the author features for each meme by taking the maximum, average, and standard deviation among the group of authors who have posted or reposted the meme by t_1. We use Support Vector Machines (SVM) [7] to predict meme importance using each of the volume, static, and dynamic network features above as well as their combination.

7. EXPERIMENTS AND OBSERVATIONS

In this section, we present our experimental setup and evaluations on several YouTube event collections. We begin by evaluating the performance of meme detection (Section 7.1), and present several observations on the generation of content buzz and memes in Sections 7.2–7.4. We then build and visualize visual meme graphs (Section 7.5) using the prior observations. We present observations on influence metrics for meme authors (Section 7.6), and these metrics are finally used to predict meme lifespan in Section 7.7.

Using the targeted-querying and collection procedures described in Section 4, we downloaded video entries from about two dozen topics from May 2009 to March 2010. We used four representative sets of large volume, diversity, and change over time, to capture characteristics of events spanning the two extremes of "event urgency": "acute" news stories (Iran election) and "chronic" news stories (swine flu). These datasets are summarized in Table 1. The SwineFlu set is about the H1N1 flu epidemic. The Iran3 set is about Iranian domestic politics and related international events during the 3-month period of summer 2009. The Iran1 set is a 1-month subset of Iran3 focusing on the election in mid-June and the associated political outbreaks. The Housing set is about the housing market collapse in the 2008-09 economic crisis—this hand-annotated set was used as a validation set for tuning the visual meme detection algorithm.

We perform visual meme detection as described in Section 5. We additionally filter the meme clusters identified by the detection system, by removing singletons belonging to a single video or a single author. Moreover, meme reposting analyses are based only on memes posted by at least 10 authors. The prototype system is implemented in C++, Python, and MATLAB, and it was deployed on a single quad-core system with 8GB of memory.

Topic	#Videos	#Authors	#Shots	Upload time
SwineFlu	31,488	10,804	1,202,479	04/09~03/10
Iran3	23,049	4,681	1,255,062	08/07~08/09
Iran1	5,429	2,393	210,259	09/07~07/09
Housing	2,446	654	71,872	08/07~08/09

Table 1: Summary of YouTube event data sets.

7.1 Meme detection performance

We evaluate the visual meme detection method in Section 5 using ground-truth created from the Housing dataset. Specifically, we run multiple versions of k-means clustering with a tight cluster radius threshold; we manually go through a sample of clusters to explicitly mark correct and incorrect near-duplicates. We further augment the detected near-duplicate sets by performing visual content-based queries on the color correlogram feature, and manually mark the top returns. We specifically include many borderline pairs that were confused by the clustering and feature-similarity retrieval steps. The resulting data set contains $\sim 15,000$ near-duplicate keyframe pairs and $\sim 25,000$ non-duplicate keyframe pairs.

We compute the near-duplicate equivalence classes as described in Section 5, and calculate precision (P) and recall (R) on the labeled pairs. The results are shown on Figure 5 for varying values of the threshold parameter τ. We note that the performance is generally quite high with $P > 95\%$. There are several possible operating points, such as $P = 99.7\%$, $R = 73.5\%$ for low false alarm; or $P = 98.2\%$, $R = 80.1\%$ that produces the maximum F1 score of 0.88 (defined as $\frac{2PR}{P+R}$); or $P = 96.6\%$, $R = 80.7\%$ for the highest recall. For the rest of our analysis, we use the last, high-recall, point with $\tau = 11.5$. On the Iran3 set of over 1 million shots, feature extraction takes around 7 hours on a quad-core CPU, and indexing and querying with FLANN takes 5 to 6 CPU hours.

7.2 Content views and re-posting probability

The behavior of remixing and reposting is quite dominant in the video collections we examined. Over 58% of the videos in Iran3, and 70% of the authors, contain visual memes. Likewise, 32% and 45%, respectively, for SwineFlu, as shown in Figure 6(a). These statistics suggest that, for popular topics there is much less original content than re-mixes and reprises of existing sources.

We observe that video popularity is a poor indicator of how likely a video is to be re-posted. In the Iran3 set, for example, the 4 most popular videos have no memes and have nothing to do with Iranian politics, and likewise for 7 of the first 10. One has to get beyond the first 1,600 most popular videos before the likelihood of having near-duplicates passes the average for the dataset, at about 0.58 (see Figure 6(b)). There are several reasons for this mismatch. Among the video entries returned by the YouTube API using various sorting criteria[3] (Section 4), the most viewed are often not related to the query topic—for example, the one with the highest view-count is a popular music video irrelevant to Iranian politics. Moreover, view counts are highly influenced by a "rich-get-richer" effect, fueled by content recommendations, promotions, and over-zealous query expansion schemes, which tend to steer traffic towards popular clips, even if they are not topically relevant. In short, view count is a poor proxy for relevance or importance of video, and therefore is not a good predictor of overall influence.

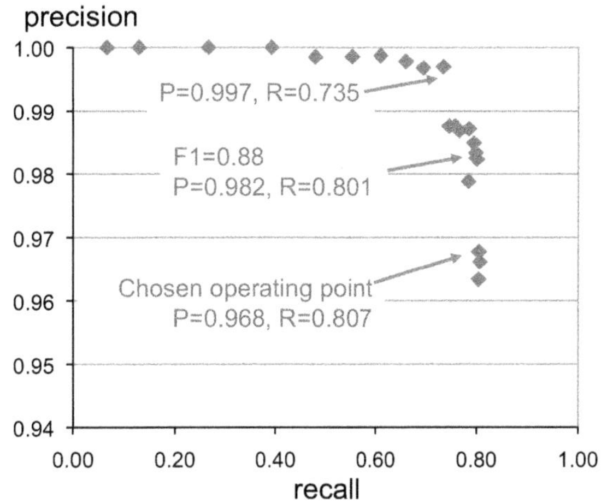

Figure 5: Performance of visual meme detection method on Housing Dataset.

This is an example of the very unequal distribution of views that characterizes this domain. To quantify the inequality of views-counts, we have computed the Gini coefficient [13] of this data set, and find it to have the extreme value of 0.94, both for videos with or without near-duplicates. The Gini coefficient, used in economics, ranges from 0 (each video with an equal number of views) to 1 (one video with all of the views). The value we observed far exceeds the measure of inequality for the distribution of wealth in any known country, which has its maximum at about 0.7.

7.3 Meme onset and reposting interval

We analyze the spread of visual memes by examining the interval between the onset of a meme and when it was re-posted by a second user. Figure 7 contains the histogram and cumulative percentage of these interval distributions. The x-axis quantizes the reposting interval in hourly increments up to 12 hours, and then for one day, week, month, and year. The left y-axis shows the number of meme videos, and the right y-axis shows the cumulative percentage. We can see that over half of the memes are re-posted within 3 hours of initial upload, and over 70% within the same day.

7.4 Content freshness

We conduct an evaluation on the age of the returned videos from YouTube, i.e., content *freshness*. This can be used to determine the extend of influence on video remixing from past entries, and also to guide the parameter settings for meme diffusion network studies. We run the querying

[3] "...titles, keywords, descriptions, authors' usernames, and categories [are used for searching]", from http://code.google.com/apis/youtube/2.0/reference.html

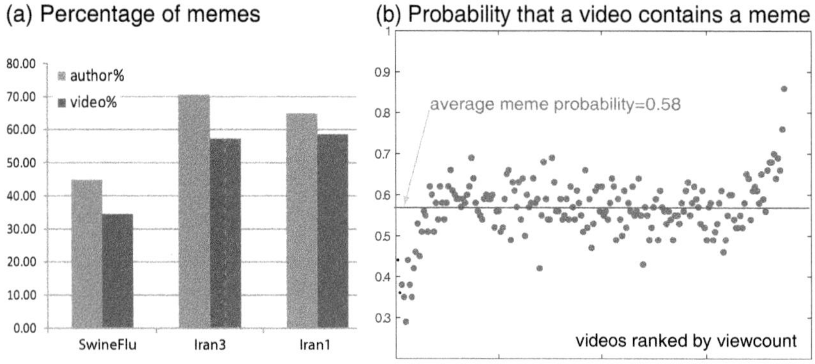

Figure 6: Video reposting probabilities. (a) Fraction of visual memes. (b) Video views vs. meme probability on Iran3 set.

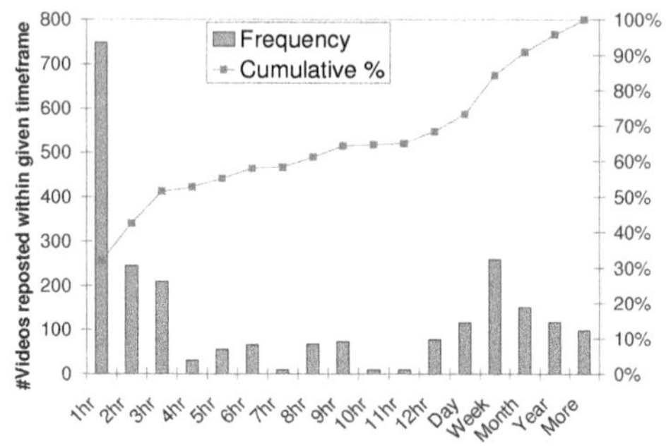

Figure 7: Distribution of meme reposting interval by a second author; see Section 7.3.

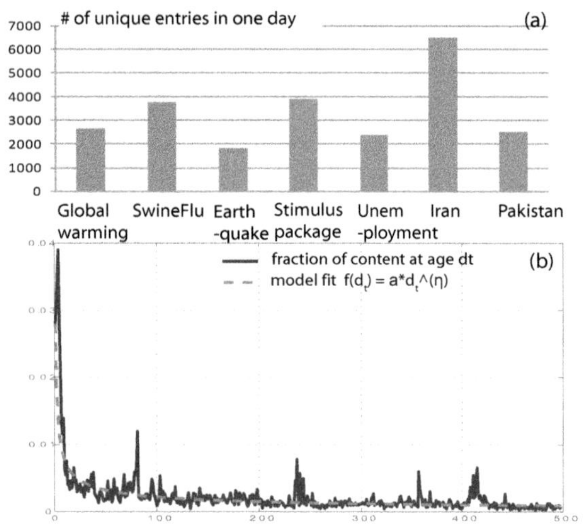

Figure 8: Content freshness experiment. (a) Number of unique entries returned for seven topics. (b) The fraction of unique entries over the age of the video (in days), averaged over the seven topics.

and content extraction during one single day, d_0='2010-04-04', across a set of seven diverse topics spanning environment, health, economics and international politics. Figure 8(a) shows the unique video entries returned for each topic, and Figure 8(b) shows the fraction of videos as a function of its age (the interval between its upload date and d_0, averaged over all seven topics). We note that the video volume is significant for any of these topics (from 1800 to 6500), and that the age distribution is approximately a power law, as observed in related studies [9]. We obtain a power-law regression fit for the content volume versus age: $f(t) = \alpha t^{\eta} \sim 0.0581t^{-0.7654}$. Intuitively, the constant $\eta = -0.7654$ represents a YouTube "memory" factor that affects how much an early video tends to influence meme creation. It is used to scale graph weights in Equation (2).

7.5 Topic hub and content islands

Figure 9 shows an example of the video and author graphs generated over the Iran1 set. Note that each meme induces a diffusion tree in the video graph G, and a clique in the author graph H. The drawing shows all connected video and author nodes, but only the subset of the edges on the minimum spanning tree, in order to avoid cluttering the display. We can easily see that there is one densely connected topic community in each graph, with a number of smaller groups in the periphery. Note that the author graph tends to have fewer isolated components, since aggregating over videos from the same authors lessens the effect of fragmented meme clusters from imperfect detection.

Memes connect content and people that contribute to the same topic in an event. In this dataset, most videos in the central topic hub are shots of post-election street protest activities. Outliers, on the other hand, contain novel views and different perspectives. Meme #052834, for example, appeared in two videos from two different authors who did not post other meme-videos. It turns out that one of the videos (the other no longer available) is an election theme-song in Persian, played over the image of a chimpanzee—a mocking caricature of a known political figure.

We will demonstrate two uses of the meme network model: distinguishing different types of authors via the meme influence index, and predicting meme lifespan.

7.6 Influence index of meme authors

We compute the diffusion index for authors with Equation 6. Figure 10 contains scatter plots of the author influence indices on the y-axis, versus number of videos produced by each author on the x-axis. For both the Iran3 topic and the SwineFlu topic, we plot the total diffusion influence $\hat{\chi}_r$ and the normalized diffusion influence $\bar{\chi}_r$.

In the Iran3 topic we can see two distinct types of contributors. We call the first contributor type *mavens* [14] (marked in red), denoting users who post only a few videos but which tend to be massively remixed and reposted. This particular maven was among the first to post the murder of Neda Soltan, who became the icon of the entire event timeline, We call the second contributor type *connectors* [14] (circled in green), denoting users who tend to produce a large number of videos, and who have high total influence factor but have low average influence per video. They aggregate notable content and serve the role of bringing this content to a broader audience. (A response metric such as view count or number of comments could further confirm this fact.) We examined the YouTube channel pages for a few authors in this group, and they seem to be voluntary political activists with screennames like "iranlover100"—we can also dub them "citizen buzz leaders". Some of their videos are slide shows of iconic images and provide good summaries of the event

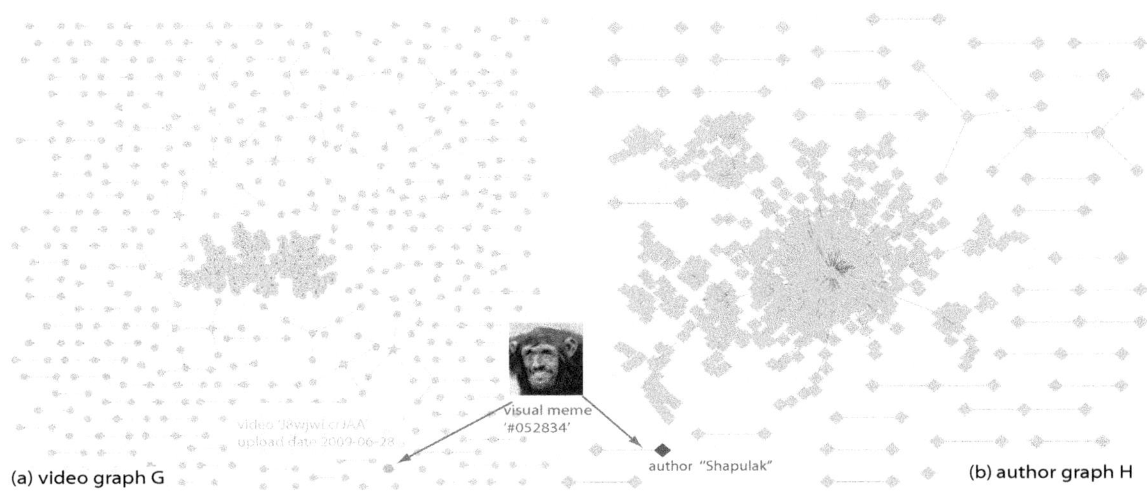

Figure 9: Graphs computed over the Iran1 data set showing (a) the video graph G, (b) the author graph H, and one example outlying meme pair.

timeline. Note that traditional news media, such as AljezeeraEnglish, AssociatedPress, and so on (circled in gray), have rather low influence metric for this topic, partially because the Iran government banned foreign journalists and severely limited international media coverage of the event.

The SwineFlu collection behaves differently in its influence index scatterplots. We can see a number of *connectors* on the upper right hand side of the total diffusion scatter. But it turns out that they are the traditional media (a few marked in gray), most of which have a large number (>40) of videos with memes. The few *mavens* in this topic (marked with green text) are less active than in the Iran topic, and notably they all reposted the identical old video containing government health propaganda for the previous outbreak of swine flu in 1976. These observations suggest that it is the traditional new media who seem to have driven most content on this topic, and, while serendipitous discovery of novel content sill exists, it has less diversity.

These visualizations can serve as a tool to observe different information dissemination patterns in different events, and henceforth characterize influential users. Such tools can identify the key influencers for each event, including both *mavens*, or early "information specialists", and *connectors*, who "bring the rest ... together" [14].

7.7 Meme lifespan prediction results

We predict the lifespan of memes as described in Section 6.4. We prune memes that appear less than 4 times, and use 2,296 memes in Iran1 for training, and 7,583 disjoint memes from Iran3 for testing. We construct the prediction task as a series of binary classification tasks (viral vs. non-viral) over progressive thresholds on meme lifespan (in days). This is because there is no clear-cut criteria about whether a meme's longevity is significant or not. Our pilot experiment also found that using regression directly on meme lifespan does not work well, yielding mean-square errors close to the average lifespan of memes. This is because most of the memes are non-viral, and predicting the lifespan values directly tends to fit the high-volume short-lifespan memes and to produce large errors on the low-volume interesting memes. As a result, we create multiple binary ground-truth by progressively thresholding the meme volume and lifespan between the 60th to 90th percentile on the training set.

The features we use include meme volume (one dimension), centrality measures for authors (three dimensions) and those aggregated over the videos (three dimensions), number of videos produced (one dimension), total and normalized meme influence indices (two dimensions), and the total in- and out- degrees for each author (two dimensions). All except the meme volume features are aggregated by taking the mean, maximum, median, and standard deviation over all authors of a meme. All types of features have a total of 45 dimensions. We train SVM classifiers [7] by searching over hyperparameters and different kernel types—linear, polynomial, and radial basis function. We measure the classification performance using the AUC [11] and plot the results in Figure 11 (top). We can see that author connectivity alone, or fusing all features together, are stronger features than content volume alone. Using all three types of features yields the highest AUC value of 0.779. This performance graph also shows that a suitable threshold of a long-lived meme is about 8 or 9 days (corresponding to the 78-th and 86-th percentile in Iran1), beyond which the performance of all prediction algorithms drop. We show a few top-ranked memes in the bottom half of Figure 11. We note that seven out of the top ten memes are from July 17, 2009, which coincides with the largest activity peak from Figure 3.

8. CONCLUSIONS

We proposed visual memes for tracking and monitoring of real-world events on YouTube, and described a large-scale event-based social video monitoring and analysis system. We proposed a scalable algorithm for extracting visual memes with high accuracy, and applied visual memes for estimating influence and predicting content popularity using network models. Using the proposed system, we have quantified the percentage of remixed content, the relationship between remix popularity and content views, and the timing of the remix. We have also shown that memes can help quantify the roles different users groups play in propagating information. A pilot evaluation showed that meme social graph features can help predict meme lifespan and volume.

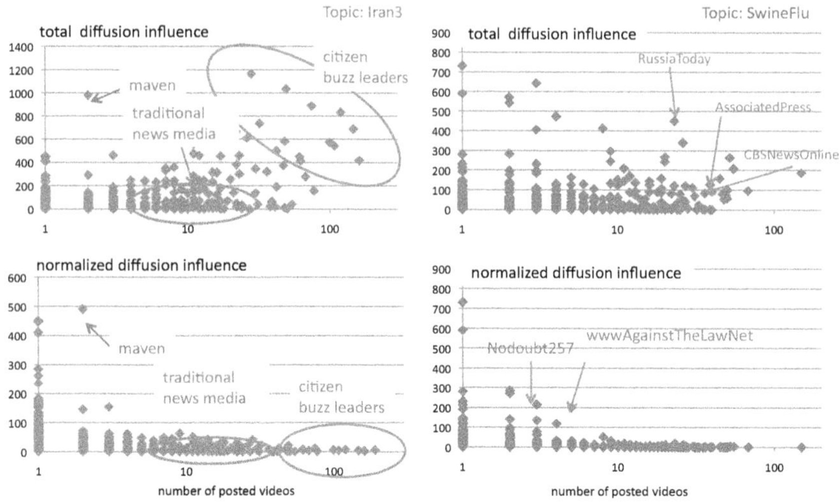

Figure 10: Meme influence indices vs author productivity on topic Iran3 (Left) and SwineFlu (Right); detailed discussions in Sec 7.6.

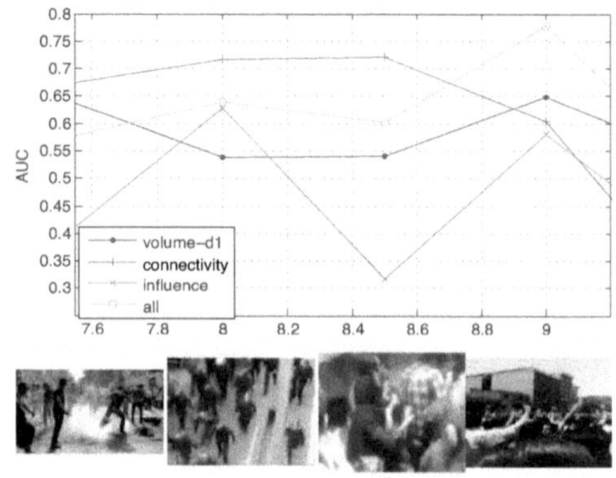

Figure 11: Predicting meme lifespan. Top: Prediction performance (AUC as the y-axis) over varying virality thresholds (as the x-axis, in days). Bottom: Icon example of top-ranked memes.

Future work includes annotating the meanings of visual memes over a course of event, extending the network and content analysis for memes, expanding the number of events and topics for evaluation, and broadening the applications of memes to video genres other than news.

9. REFERENCES

[1] What is the Klout score? Understanding the influence metric. http://klout.com/kscore , retrieved April 2011.

[2] Thanks, YouTube community, for two BIG gifts on our sixth birthday!, May 2011. The official YouTube blog, http://youtube-global.blogspot.com/2011/05/thanks-youtube-community-for-two-big.html .

[3] F. Benevenuto, T. Rodrigues, V. Almeida, J. Almeida, and K. Ross. Video interactions in online video social networks. *ACM Trans. on Multimedia Computing, Communications, and Applications (TOMCCAP)*, 5(4):30, 2009.

[4] J.-I. Biel and D. Gatica-Perez. Voices of vlogging. In *AAAI Int. Conf. on Weblogs and Social Media (ICWSM)*, 5 2010.

[5] M. Cha, H. Haddadi, F. Benevenuto, and K. Gummadi. Measuring user influence in twitter: The million follower fallacy. In *4th Intl. Conf. on Weblogs and Social Media (ICWSM)*, 2010.

[6] M. Cha, H. Kwak, P. Rodriguez, Y.-Y. Ahn, and S. Moon. I tube, you tube, everybody tubes: Analyzing the world's largest user generated content video system. In *Proc. ACM IMC*, pages 1–14, 2007.

[7] C.-C. Chang and C.-J. Lin. *LIBSVM: A library for support vector machines*, 2001. http://www.csie.ntu.edu.tw/~cjlin/libsvm .

[8] M. Cherubini, R. de Oliveira, and N. Oliver. Understanding near-duplicate videos: A user-centric approach. In *Proc. ACM Intl. Conf. on Multimedia*, pages 35–44, 2009.

[9] R. Crane and D. Sornette. Viral, quality, and junk videos on YouTube: Separating content from noise in an information-rich environment. In *Proc. of AAAI symposium on Social Information Processing, Menlo Park, CA*, 2008.

[10] M. De Choudhury, H. Sundaram, A. John, and D. D. Seligmann. What makes conversations interesting?: Themes, participants and consequences of conversations in online social media. In *WWW*, pages 331–340, 2009.

[11] T. Fawcett. ROC graphs: Notes and practical considerations for researchers. *Machine Learning*, 31:1–38, 2004.

[12] B. A. Galler and M. J. Fisher. An improved equivalence algorithm. *Communications of ACM*, 7(5):301–303, 1964.

[13] C. Gini. Measurement of inequality of ncomes. *Economic Journal*, 31:124–126, 1921.

[14] M. Gladwell. *The tipping point: How little things can make a big difference.* Little, Brown and Co., 2000.

[15] R. Hong, J. Tang, H.-K. Tan, S. Yan, C.-W. Ngo, and T.-S. Chua. Beyond search: Event driven summarization for web videos. *ACM Trans. on Multimedia Computing, Communications, and Applications (TOMCCAP)*, 2011.

[16] J. Huang, S. Kumar, M. Mitra, W. Zhu, and R. Zabih. Spatial color indexing and applications. *International Journal of Computer Vision*, 35(3), December 1999.

[17] L. Kennedy and S.-F. Chang. Internet image archaeology: Automatically tracing the manipulation history of photographs on the web. In *Proc. ACM Multimedia*, 2008.

[18] H. Kwak, C. Lee, H. Park, , and S. Moon. What is Twitter, a Social Network or a News Media? . In *Proc. WWW*, 2010.

[19] J. Leskovec, L. Backstrom, and J. Kleinberg. Meme-tracking and the dynamics of the news cycle. In *Proc. KDD*, 2009.

[20] T. Liu, C. Rosenberg, and H. A. Rowley. Clustering billions of images with large scale nearest neighbor search. In *IEEE Workshop on Applications of Computer Vision*, 2007.

[21] M. Muja and D. G. Lowe. Fast approximate nearest neighbors with automatic algorithm configuration. In *Intl. Conf. on Computer Vision Theory and Applications*, 2009.

[22] A. Natsev, M. Hill, and J. Smith. Design and evaluation of an effective and efficient video copy detection system. In *IEEE Intl. Conf. on Multimedia and Expo (ICME)*, 2010.

[23] P. Schmitz, P. Shafton, R. Shaw, S. Tripodi, B. Williams, and J. Yang. International remix: Video editing for the web. In *Proc. ACM Multimedia*, page 798. ACM, 2006.

[24] P. Snickars and P. Vonderau. *The YouTube Reader.* National Library of Sweden, 2010.

[25] G. Szabo and B. A. Huberman. Predicting the popularity of online content. *Commun. ACM*, 53:80–88, August 2010.

[26] H.-K. Tan, X. Wu, C.-W. Ngo, and W.-L. Zhao. Accelerating near-duplicate video matching by combining visual similarity and alignment distortion. In *Proc. ACM Multimedia*, page 861, 2008.

[27] J. Wang, S. Kumar, and S.-F. Chang. Semi-supervised hashing for scalable image retrieval. In *IEEE CVPR*, San Francisco, USA, June 2010.

The Role of Attractiveness in Web Image Search [*]

Bo Geng [†‡]†, Linjun Yang [‡], Chao Xu [†], Xian-Sheng Hua [‡], Shipeng Li [‡]
[†] Key Laboratory of Machine Perception (Ministry of Education), Peking University, Beijing, P.R.China
[‡] Microsoft Research Asia, Beijing, P.R.China
{gengbo, xuchao}@cis.pku.edu.cn, {linjuny, xshua, spli}@microsoft.com

ABSTRACT

Existing web image search engines are mainly designed to optimize *topical relevance*. However, according to our user study, *attractiveness* is becoming a more and more important factor for web image search engines to satisfy users' search intentions. Important as it can be, web image attractiveness from the search users' perspective has not been sufficiently recognized in both the industry and the academia. In this paper, we present a definition of web image attractiveness with three levels according to the end users' feedback, including *perceptual quality*, *aesthetic sensitivity* and *affective tune*. Corresponding to each level of the definition, various visual features are investigated on their applicability to attractiveness estimation of web images. To further deal with the unreliability of visual features induced by the large variations of web images, we propose a contextual approach to integrate the visual features with contextual cues mined from image EXIF information and the associated web pages. We explore the role of attractiveness by applying it to various stages of a web image search engine, including the online ranking and the interactive reranking, as well as the offline index selection. Experimental results on three large-scale web image search datasets demonstrate that the incorporation of attractiveness can bring more satisfaction to 80% of the users for ranking/reranking search results and 30.5% index coverage improvement for index selection, compared to the conventional relevance based approaches.

Categories and Subject Descriptors

H.3.3 [**Information Search and Retrieval**]: Search process

General Terms

Algorithms, Experimentation, Human Factors, Performance.

[†]This work was performed when Bo Geng was visiting Microsoft Research Asia as a research intern.
[*]Area chair: Marcel Worring

MM'11, November 28–December 1, 2011, Scottsdale, Arizona, USA.

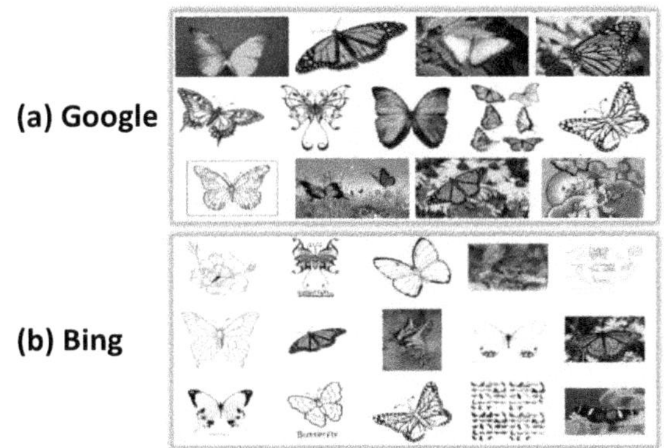

Figure 1: The first page image search results of the query "butterfly" for Google and Bing image search engines, recorded on March 10th, 2011.

Keywords

Web image search, Image attractiveness

1. INTRODUCTION

Existing image search engines are mainly designed to optimize the *topical relevance*, i.e., to what extent the topic of returned images matches that of the text query [13]. However, according to our user study in comparing image search results of Google and Bing, only 8% of the users preferred one to the other due to relevance, which means topical relevance may not be the leading discriminating factor of search engines at the current stage. This may be attributed to the continuous development of information retrieval technologies, with which a carefully designed image search engine can effectively return topically relevant images in most circumstances.

Besides topical relevance, we found that more than 60% of users selected their preferred image search results due to the factors related to the images' attractiveness, e.g. "high quality","sharp", and "beautiful". This indicates that users generally pose a strong demand on the attractiveness of images, even though they may not explicitly state such a need during the search. We call the users' need of getting attractive images the *attractiveness intent*, which is general, implicit in most times, along with the users' image search behavior. It is especially important for those queries for which a large number of relevant images can be returned. In this case, topical relevance is incapable of differentiating these images sufficiently, while attractiveness becomes a more favorable metric to rank the search results so as to satisfy users' attractiveness intent.

Although attractiveness intent is important to the users' satisfaction of a web image search engine, it is insufficiently recognized by both the industry and the academia. As an example shown in Fig. 1, both Google's and Bing's search results contain many unattractive images such as the simple line drawings. While attractiveness has been studied in several literatures, the existing works are more focused on the photographers' perspective [2, 6, 7]. In view of this, it is necessary to investigate what attractiveness implies in the context of web image search from the end users' perspective.

Based on a user study to discover what users expect for attractive images in web image search, we define the attractiveness in three levels, including *perceptual quality, aesthetic sensitivity* and *affective tune*. The perceptual quality is the users' basic requirement on the images' attractiveness, which is used to measure, for an image, whether users can perceive clearly the topics delivered by it. Beyond perceptual quality, aesthetic sensitivity further measures whether an image can be appreciated with an aesthetic experience, instead of a simple knowledge consumption. Finally, affective tune measures to what extent certain emotions can be sensed from the images.

To estimate the web image's attractiveness, we integrate visual features originally designed for photo quality assessment, aesthetics prediction, and affective classification. However, the techniques applied to extracting these visual features are still in its infancy and will usually achieve unstable performance. Moreover, the large variations in web images make the problem more challenging.

Fortunately, web images never appear in isolation but are accompanied with rich contextual information, such as EXIF (Exchangeable Image File Format) information and the associated web pages. Normally, EXIF reflects the camera settings and the environment conditions of the photo when it was taken. It can be used to infer the probability of a photo to be attractive. Besides EXIF, web image attractiveness can also be mined from its host web page. While the page descriptions may indicate the intention of using this image and therefore can be used to infer the image's quality, the page structure that reflects the design expertise or the dominance of the image in the page is also informative. Therefore, we propose a contextual approach to web image attractiveness estimation by integrating the content and the context. The experimental results demonstrate its effectiveness on a large-scale web image database.

Once the attractiveness estimation is finished, we further consider applying it into different stages of a web image search engine and extensively testing its effectiveness. A direct application is to incorporate attractiveness into the relevance based image search ranking model, so that images which are not only relevant but also visually attractive can be promoted in search results. However, attractive images are not always necessarily desirable, e.g., users may hope to browse the product designs instead of searching attractive images for the query "iphone". We consequently propose an interactive reranking approach, which allows users to choose whether to rerank by attractiveness or not. Besides the online ranking/reranking, attractiveness can also be incorporated into the offline process. While hundreds of billions of web images are available in the whole domain, we are only capable of indexing about several billions of them, due to the limitation of data storage and computational cost. The incorporation of attractiveness into index selection can help the search engine filter out the low quality, poorly composed or disgusting images.

The contributions of the paper are summarized as follows:

- To the best of our knowledge, we are the first to give a comprehensive definition of the web image attractiveness based on the feedbacks from end users of a web image search engine, and to perform a comprehensive study on the role of attractiveness in web image search.
- By extensively studying the applicability of attractiveness to different stages of a web image search engine, including online ranking and interactive reranking, as well as offline index selection, we conclude that the attractiveness is an important factor in a user satisfactory image search engine.
- We propose a contextual approach to estimate web image attractiveness, which integrates the images' visual content and the contextual information including image EXIF information and the content and structure of its associated web pages.

The rest of the paper is organized as follows. Section 2 presents some related works. We present the overview of attractiveness in web image search in Section 3. To estimate attractiveness, we introduce the adopted visual and contextual features in Section 4 and Section 5 respectively. Section 6 presents the experimental results on attractiveness estimation. Section 7 reports the performance of applying attractiveness to various stages of the web image search. We finally conclude the paper in Section 8.

2. RELATED WORK

The development of automatic photo attractiveness estimation approaches can be categorized into three stages. In the early stage, researchers focused on photo quality assessment by analyzing the artifacts induced by compression, e.g., JPEG compression[14]. Since the compression artifact is not the only factor to influence photo quality, in the second stage, a large number of methods were proposed to analyze images' visual content according to the professional photography rules, such as *simplicity*, *rule of thirds*, and *visual weight*. Various visual features were designed based on these rules, and then integrated by machine learning algorithms to obtain an attractiveness score [2, 6, 7]. By leveraging the recent developments on social network and media sharing websites, Pedro and Siersdorfer [12] utilized the social information such as tags to improve the prediction of social images' attractiveness.

However, the above features are still not robust enough to precisely predict photo attractiveness, due to the limitation of the adopted techniques which are still not mature enough [2, 6, 7, 12]. In addition, most features are designed for as well as evaluated over photos, and may not work well for paintings, drawings, cliparts, etc. which are pervasive on the web. Different from these works, our work studies the components of attractiveness according to search engine end users' feedback, based on which we analyze the applicability of some existing visual features to the web images' attractiveness estimation, and propose to improve the estimation by using contextual information including image EXIF and the associated web pages.

The research on web image search in the multimedia community has been focusing on developing various content based

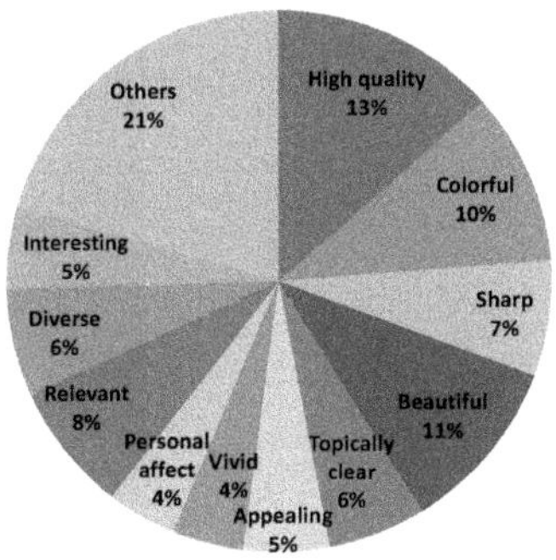

Figure 2: The top ten factors to evaluate the image search results.

methods to improve the relevance of image search results, e.g., concept detection [15] and visual reranking [16, 19]. However, visual attractiveness is seldom considered in these works. In [6, 12], the attractiveness models learned from photo collections were applied to ranking web image search results and social images respectively. However, these works only considered attractiveness as a possible metric to rank images, but did not systematically study the role of attractiveness in the web image search context. Zhang et al. [22] proposed an image search engine specific for high-quality photos. However, the engine only aggregated the photos from community based photo forums instead of the images in the whole web. The photo quality is estimated only based on human ratings which is generally unavailable for web images. As a distinguishing framework, our work treats attractiveness as a first class factor besides topical relevance to impact the general web image search performance. We perform extensive experiments to prove that the incorporation of attractiveness into the conventional online ranking and offline index selection problems can significantly improve user satisfaction.

3. OVERVIEW

In this section, we explore attractiveness in the web image search context, by investigating its components through a user study, and discussing its various applications to an image search engine.

3.1 User study on web image attractiveness

We performed a user study by asking 30 users to compare the search results of 12 queries collected from two well-known image search engines, which are denoted as Engine I and Engine II. The queries were sampled from a query log of Engine I, comprising various categories such as animal ("cat"), celebrity ("Michael Jackson"), scene ("beach"), activity ("hockey"), drawing object ("hearts"), and cartoon ("tinkerbell"). For each query, we downloaded the first-page search results of both engines and presented them to users. Users were asked to judge which search result is better and to give further reasons. They were encouraged to freely describe the reasons for their choice, without being given any suggestions or hints. Asking people to make a comparison is a common approach to evaluating search engines, as has been done in [20, 21]. We eliminated the presentation bias due to different page designs, the trust bias of search engines by hiding the search engine names, and the selection bias by randomly swapping the presentation orders of the two search engines for each query.

From the user provided answers, we summarized the most frequent factors related to users' satisfaction and showed them in Fig. 2. We found that "Relevance" only takes up 8% over all the reasons, which is much less frequent than others like "High quality" (13%), "Beautiful" (11%) and "Colorful" (10%). This is because *topical relevance* for most queries are comparably satisfactory for the results from both the search engines. The factors related to attractiveness can be categorized into three levels according to different users' search intention: (1) perceptual quality, whether users can perceive clearly the meaning conveyed by an image, including "High quality", "Colorful" and "Sharp"; (2) aesthetic sensitivity, whether an image can be appreciated with an aesthetic experience, instead of a simple knowledge consumption, including "Beautiful", "Topically clear" and "Appealing"; (3) affective tune, whether certain emotions can be sensed from an image, including "Vivid" and "Personal affect". Since in this paper, we focus on the estimation of attractiveness and its applications in web image search, the other factors including "Diverse" and "Interesting", will be studied in our future work.

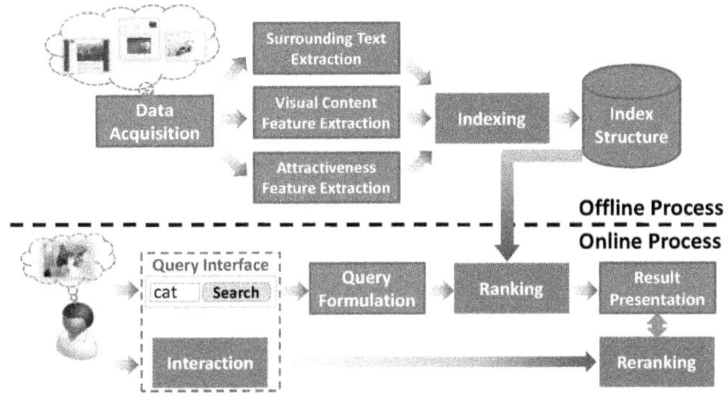

Figure 3: The flowchart of a general web image search engine. The components in which the attractiveness can be applied are highlighted in red.

3.2 Applications

To discuss the applications of attractiveness, we briefly introduce a general flowchart of a web image search engine, as illustrated in Fig. 3. In the offline phase, an image crawler is applied to acquire web images from the World Wide Web. For the crawled images, we extract various features including surrounding text and visual features to represent them. Based on these features, the images are indexed using techniques such as inverted file, in order to speed up the query response. In the online phase, when a user submits a textual query, the search engine applies its ranking model to rank the images according to their ranking features, and return the corresponding images to the user in order. During browsing the search results, users can perform interactions with the search engine to start a second round of search. From this flowchart, it is natural to apply the attractiveness in three components of a web image search engine, namely the ranking, indexing, and user interaction, as highlighted in Fig. 3.

- **Ranking**. For topically relevant images, attractive images are more favorable to users. Therefore, we can incorporate the attractiveness into the relevance based ranking model, by regarding the attractiveness features or scores as additional ranking features, so that not only topically relevant, but also visually appealing images can be promoted in search results.

- **Interactive reranking**. Attractive images may not

Table 1: **Overview of the visual features for web image attractiveness estimation.**

Category	Name	#Dim	Description
Perceptual quality	Lighting	2	The mean (brightness) and variance (contrast) of the pixel intensity in gray [12].
	Color	7	The mean and standard deviation of saturation and hue [2, 12]; Contrast of colors[12]; Colorfulness [12]; Naturalness color attributes[4].
	Sharpness & Blur	3	Sharpness: the mean and standard deviation of Laplacian image normalized by local average luminance [12]; Blur: the frequency distribution of FFT transformed image [6].
	Subject Quality	12	The Lighting, Color, Sharpness of the saliency map reweighted image; The blur detection of the subject region.
Aesthetic sensitivity	Rule of Thirds	1	The composition of the subject estimated by the nearest distance of the subject the region to one of stress points [1].
	Simplicity	4	The edge distribution of the original [6] and the saliency map reweighted image; The distinct hue count of the original image [6] and its subject region.
	Visual Weight	1	The clarity contrast between subject region and the whole image [7].
Affective tune	Dynamics	2	The relative number and length of the static vs. dynamic lines [9].
	Color Emotion	17	Histograms designed to express the emotional impact of image color [18].

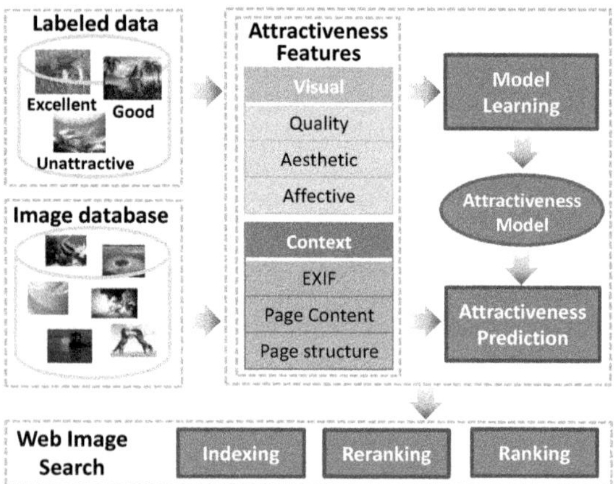

Figure 4: The flowchart of web image attractiveness estimation.

be heavily favored by users for some queries. For example, for the query "iphone", users may desire more the images about its visual designs instead of the attractive images containing an iphone. Therefore, it is more user-friendly to provide an option for users to rerank by attractiveness. With this explicit option, users can decide whether or not to rerank the returned images according to the attractiveness score.

- **Index selection**. There are tens of billions of images in the whole web, but we can only index about a small portion of them due to the storage and computation limitation. The existing approaches for index selection are for web pages, which selects the web pages that users will be interested to search for, based on a learned static rank [10]. We adoped the same framework for image index selection. Furthermore, beyond those features that are designed for web pages in [10], we apply the attractiveness as a new feature indicating whether the images are attractive enough to be searched for, and incorporate it into the learning framework. The incorporation of attractiveness to index selection can help to filter out the low-quality, poorly composed, and disgusting images from an index.

A web image attractiveness estimation system is the core of the above three application. As shown in Fig. 4, the system is based on a learning framework, to combine many carefully designed features. The features include the existing visual features designed mainly for estimating photo attractiveness, as well as the contextual features extracted from image EXIF and associated web pages. We adopted a linear model in this paper to accommodate the large-scale requirement of a practical web image search engine, since a linear model is more efficient to be learned and applied to billions of images. In the following we will mainly introduce the various features.

4. VISUAL FEATURES

In this section, we describe a selected subset of visual features originally designed for photo attractiveness estimation and study their effectiveness when applied to web images.

4.1 Feature Description

A summary of our adopted visual features are presented in Table 1. The visual features are categorized into three levels accordingly to the attractiveness definition: perceptual quality, aesthetic sensitivity, and affective tune.

The perceptual quality features describe the basic qualities of web images, including the brightness, contrast, colorfulness, and sharpness & blur [2, 6, 12]. Some of them are illustrated in Fig. 5 (a)(b)(c). Besides the original implementation which are performed on the whole image, we propose to additionally extract these features on subjects. In this paper, we didn't explicitly detect the subject, but use the saliency map [8] to compute a probability of each pixel to be on the subject. Then, we extract features over the whole image with reweighting by the probability value, or over the subject region detected by the minimal bounding box that contains 90% mass of all probabilities.

The aesthetic sensitivity describes whether an image is visually appealing from the aesthetics perspective. Existing aesthetics visual features are mostly designed based on well-known composition rules, including *Rule of Thirds* which is positioning the subject near the *golden ratio* points, *simplicity*, which is simplifying the subject topic, and *visual weight*, which is balancing the visual weight of the subject and the background. We apply the composition feature [1], the hue count and edge distribution features [6], and the clarity contrast feature [7] to estimate the conformance to each rule respectively. Illustrations of the rules are in Fig. 5(d)(e)(f) respectively.

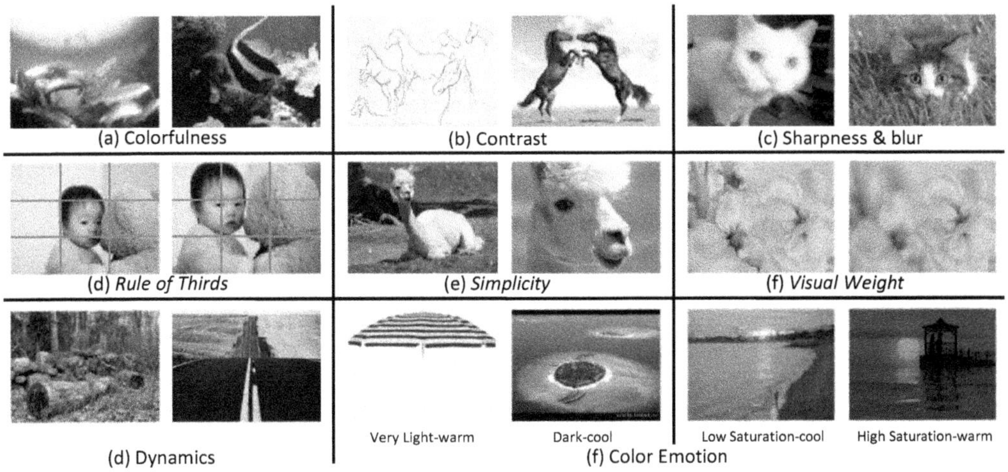

Figure 5: Example images to illustrate the visual features. Left (right) image in each group is unattractive (attractive).

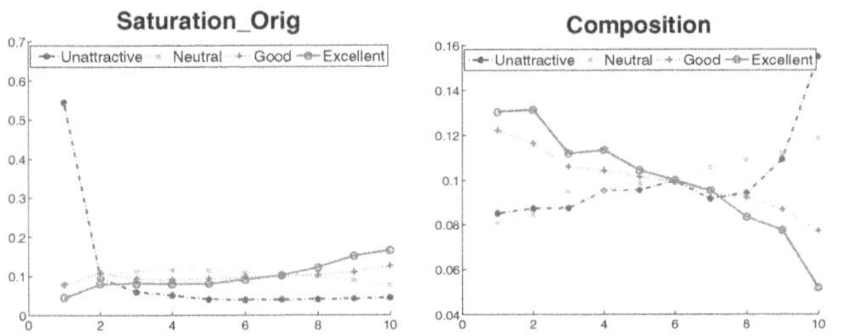

Figure 6: The image distribution of each attractiveness degree over different visual features.

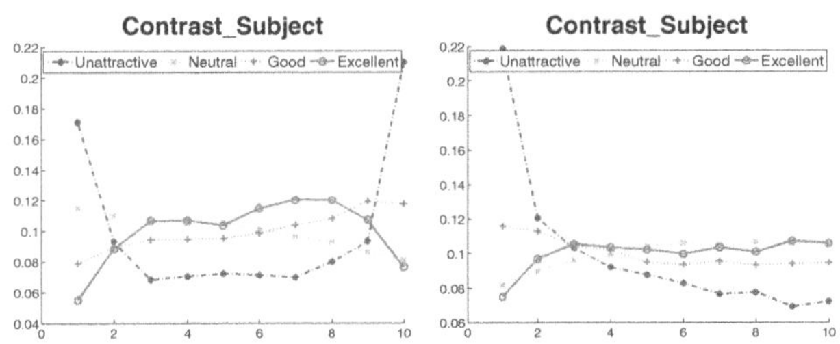

(a) Before Transformation (b) After Transformation

Figure 7: The distribution of images before and after the feature transformation.

The affective tune features model the emotional impact of an image's visual elements to humans. We applied two categories of features to estimate the affective tune, based on the lines and colors respectively. The line-based features are calculated according to the distributions of static and dynamic lines which reflect different emotions [9], as illustrated in Fig. 5(g). The color-based features are represented as a histogram which quantizes the impact of color to emotions, as illustrated in Fig. 5(h)(i).

4.2 Feature Analysis

We analyzed the effectiveness of all above 49-dimensional visual features over the 100Q dataset comprising 95,193 images, which are manually labeled as "Excellent", "Good", "Neutral", or "Unattractive" according to the perceived attractiveness. More details can be found in Section 6.1.

To study the effectiveness of a certain feature, we illustrate the feature distribution, approximated by a 10-bin histogram, for each of the four attractiveness degrees, as shown in Fig. 6. We can observe that for some features, such as "Saturation_Orig"[1] and "Composition", the feature is linearly correlated with the attractiveness degree. For example, an image with a smaller "Composition" value corresponds to an attractive image with a higher probability. However, the correlation for others may be nonlinear. For example, attractive images more probably have a moderate contrast value, as shown in Fig. 7(a). Furthermore, we observe that for these features, attractive (as well as unattractive) images are usually governed by a unimodal distribution. In order to obtain linear features that may perform well for a linear model, we propose to transform these features by the following equation.

$$g(f_i) = \begin{cases} \exp(-\sigma_l(r_i - f_i)) & \text{if } f_i \leq r_i \\ \exp(-\sigma_r(f_i - r_i)) & \text{otherwise} \end{cases} \quad (1)$$

where the parameter r_i is a threshold, σ_l (σ_r) is a parameter to scale the features smaller (larger) than r_i. The transformed feature values of "Contrast_Subject" are shown in Fig. 7(b) as an example, which indicates a linear correlation of the feature value to the attractiveness degree can be obtained. In our implementation, 18 of the 49 features are transformed according to Eqn. (1), including "clarity", "dynamics"; subject "sharpness"; the original and subject-reweighted "lighting", "color contrast", the standard deviation of"sharpness"; the original and subject region's "edge distribution", "blur", and "hue count".

However, the above visual features are still not sufficient for predicting web image attractiveness, due to three-fold reasons. First, the visual features are still not robust enough to predict the rules precisely, since the underlying techniques such as blur detection and saliency extraction are still open research problems that are not well solved. Second, photographers often utilize professional techniques, such as adding special glass filters and post editing, to violate the rules in order to generate special yet attractive effects. Fig. 8(a) shows an attractive image created with the polaroid "old day atmosphere" which is predicted to be unattractive using our visual features. Third, existing visual features are mostly designed for photos, while the source of web images are quite diverse, additionally including paintings, drawings, cliparts, graphics, etc. The attractiveness of these non-photo images is weakly correlated with the photography rules. For

[1]Here, "Orig" denotes the feature extracted over the original whole image, while "Subject" is over the saliency reweighted image or the subject region.

Table 2: The text words with top 10 information gain values.

Words	wallpaper	wallpapers	desktop	gif	coloring	jpg	download	backgrounds	background	printable
IG	0.0213	0.0203	0.0179	0.0114	0.0091	0.0084	0.0069	0.0056	0.0053	0.0050

(a) Photo with Polaroid effect (b) Clipart (c) Painting

Figure 8: Example images to illustrate the limitation of visual features.

example, Fig. 8(b) is an ordinary clipart image predicted as very attractive, while Fig. 8(c) is a beautiful wallpaper painting predicted as unattractive, by using the visual features. Fortunately, a web image never exists in isolation but is accompanied with contextual information other than visual content, which can be utilized to improve the attractiveness estimation.

5. CONTEXTUAL FEATURES

Our contextual features are extracted from three sources, including the image EXIF, as well as the content and structure of the associated web page. We will analyze these information sources and design corresponding features as follows.

5.1 EXIF

EXIF contains rich information on camera settings, which can reflect the photographer's expertise and environment conditions when the photo was taken. Professional photographers often utilize advanced equipments to take photos, such as telephoto and large aperture lens. By manually setting the modes special to their equipments, such as large focal length, they can produce many attractive effects such as shallow depth of field effect (sharpening the foreground and blurring the background). In addition, a nice environment with enough lighting can increase the possibility of producing attractive photos, which often corresponds to a short exposure time and a low ISO. Therefore, we choose the following EXIF metadata to design attractiveness features, including Exposure Program, Focal Length, ISOspeed, Exposure Time, and F-Number. We verified each of these feature by analyzing the feature distributions. Fig. 9 shows two examples, from which we can observe that attractive images are usually taken with "Manual" Exposure Program (value=1) mode instead of "Normal Program" (value=2), as well as telephoto lens with large focal length settings.

It is natural to adopt the values of different EXIF information directly as features. However, in the 100Q dataset, only 11.2% images are accompanied with EXIF. Thus, we need to tackle those images without EXIF. This is achieved by quantizing each feature into four discrete bins, and putting the images without EXIF into a separate bin. Because Exposure Program is categorical information with 10 options, we directly transform it into a binary 10-dimensional vector with proper consideration of missing values. Finally, 30-dimensional EXIF features are extracted for each image.

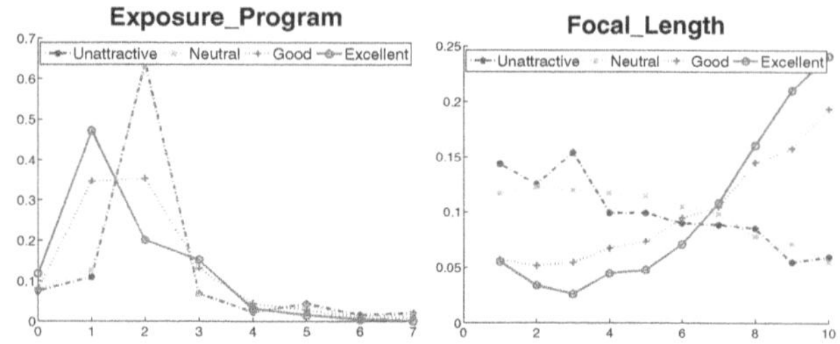

Figure 9: The image distribution of each attractiveness degree over different EXIF features.

5.2 Page Content

Every web image is embedded in at least one web page. The web page authors usually leave rich information in the page content to describe an image, which can be utilized to infer the image's attractiveness. To discover useful information from the pages, we apply information gain (IG) [17] to estimate the correlation between the image attractiveness and the text surrounding it. We select the 10 words with top IG in our 100Q dataset, and show the results in Tabel. 2. It can be observed that the discriminative text words for attractiveness can be categorized into two groups, i.e., image intention ("wallpaper", "desktop", "background" and "download") and image quality ("printable", "coloring", "jpg", and "gif"[2]).

Based on the above analysis, we define a binary feature vector to represent the presence or absence of the eight[3] selected words in seven text sources of a web page, including the text associated with the image such as anchor text, name, surrounding text, and url, as well as the text associated with the page such as title, meta description, and meta keywords. The texts associated with the image and with the page are also aggregated respectively to generate two additional sources.We consider the nine text sources separately since different sources have different confidences to predict attractiveness. Finally, 72-dimensional binary page content features are extracted for each image.

5.3 Page Structure

The page structure can be used to infer the authors' expertise and the the importance of the image w.r.t. the page. Fig. 10 shows three examples, with (a) an attractive image on a professionally designed web page; (b) an amateur image in a personal blog; and (c) an icon in a corner of the page for decoration. We can observe that attractive images are more probably embedded in a professionally/carefully designed web page, e.g., with an appropriate image display size, a structurally long file name to facilitate its identification, and an appropriate length of surrounding text to describe the image content. In addition, attractive images are usually positioned near the center of a page to capture users' attention, while unattractive ones are in the peripheral areas.

[2]Here, "gif" is negatively correlated, while the others are positively correlated.

[3]"wallpaper" and "wallpapers", as well as "background" and "backgrounds", are merged as one word in our implementation.

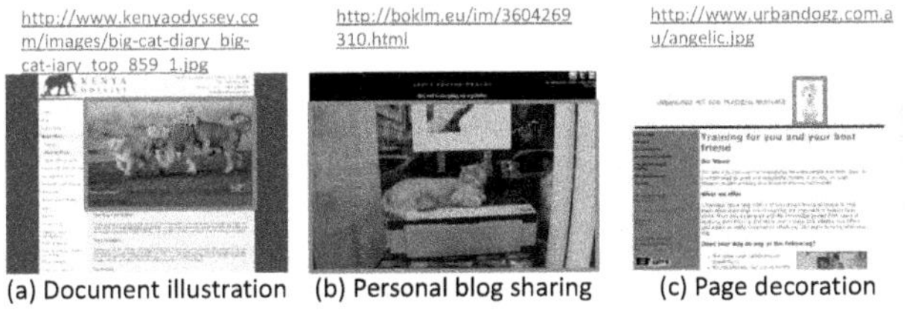

Figure 10: Example images to illustrate the page features related to image attractiveness. The target image is highlighted with a red bounding box.

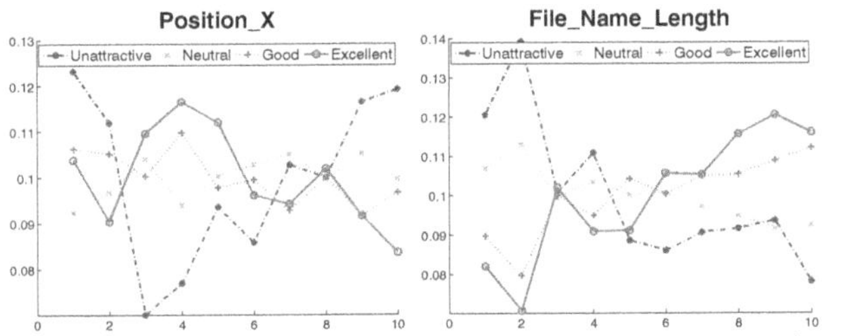

Figure 11: The image distribution of each attractiveness degree for different page structure features.

Based on these properties, we design five features related to page structure, including the image's display size in the page, the length of the image file name, the number of words surrounding the image, and the position of the image in horizontal and vertical dimensions respectively. Fig. 11 presents the distribution of two example features, which illustrates the effectiveness of the proposed features. We utilize the feature transformation in Eqn. (1) to transform the features (except "File_Name_Length"), resulting into a 5-dimensional page structure feature.

6. EXPERIMENTS ON ATTRACTIVENESS ESTIMATION

In this section, we report several experiments on a large-scale web image dataset 100Q to evaluate the effectiveness of the proposed attractiveness estimation approach.

6.1 Dataset and Experiment Setting

The 100Q dataset is collected from a commercial web image search engine (Engine I). We sampled 100 queries according to the query log and crawled the returned images by using them to query Engine I. The selected queries cover many topics that users commonly searched, including celebrity ("michael jackson"), animal ("cat"), cartoon ("tinkerbell"), product ("iphone"), event ("hockey"), and scene ("beach"). For each query, no more than the top 1000 returned images were downloaded, resulting into totally 95,193 images in our dataset. Three labelers were employed to label the attractiveness of each image into four degrees, i.e., "Excellent", "Good", "Neutral", and "Unattractive". The ground truth is determined as the median of the results from the three labelers.

The dataset was evenly split into ten folds, each of which contains the images for ten queries. We chose one fold to tune the parameters of feature transformation in Eqn. 1. Among the remaining nine folds, we selected seven to train the model, one to validate the model parameters, and the rest to evaluate the performance. We switched the fold configuration in a round-robin fashion so that each fold is ensured to be taken as test and validation once. The results

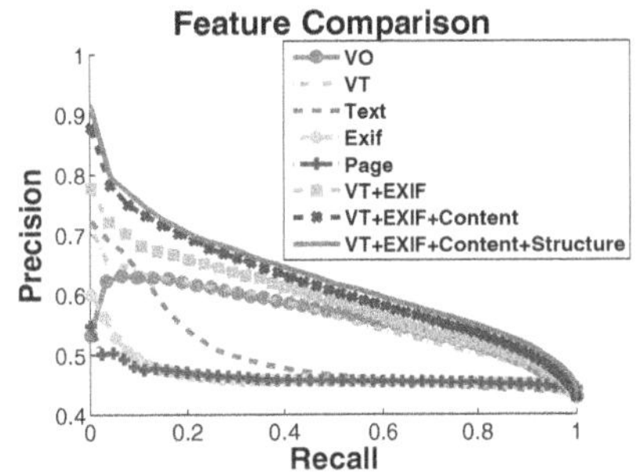

Figure 12: Precision-recall curve of attractiveness prediction using different features.

reported in the paper are the average of the nine results under a specific evaluation metric. RankSVM [5] was applied to train the attractiveness model.

6.2 Results

To evaluate the attractiveness estimation, we present the precision-recall curve in Fig. 12. For computing the precision and recall, we treat "Excellent" and "Good" as positive and the others as negative. It can be observed that due to the limitation of visual features and the diversity of web images, the performance of the original visual features (VO) is quite low, with only 0.62 precision at 0.2 recall. The transformation (VT) can improve the performance a little bit, especially in reducing the false alarm by VO. Among the three categories of contextual features, page content (Content) is comparatively more robust than EXIF and page structure (Structure), even better than VT at low recall. However, Content performs worse at high recall because the feature vector is very sparse and many web pages do not contain the selected eight words. EXIF and Structure are only effective for a limited number of images at low recall, because many images miss EXIF while Structure only is weakly correlated to attractiveness. Even though each independent contextual feature is unable to achieve a high precision, they can complement the visual features. By gradually combining VT with each contextual feature, the performance steadily increases, and finally achieves precision 0.7 at recall 0.2, with totally 12.9% improvements over VO.

7. APPLICATIONS

We applied the proposed attractiveness estimation to three components of web image search, including interactive reranking, ranking and index selection respectively.

7.1 Interactive Reranking

We firstly quantitatively evaluated the performance of reranking by attractiveness over the 100Q dataset. Here, all the returned images are reranked for each query according to their attractiveness scores predicted in Section 6.2. Since images in the first result page (usually containing around 20 images) is more critical to a user's satisfaction to a search result, we evaluated the performance in terms of various measures on the top 20 ranked images, including Precision (Precision@20), Mean Average Precision (MAP@20), and Normalized Discounted Cumulative Gain (NDCG@20). Since the occurrence of an unattractive image in the top ranked results may greatly degrade the user's experience, we propose a new measure called Unattractive Rejection (UR), which is

Table 3: The performance of attractiveness reranking for different features.

	Engine I	VO	VT	EXIF	Content	Structure	VT+EXIF	VT+EXIF +Content	VT+EXIF +Content+Structure
Precision@20	0.559	0.654	0.692	0.563	0.692	0.520	0.721	0.771	**0.782**
MAP@20	0.408	0.485	0.545	0.395	0.544	0.351	0.575	0.652	**0.662**
NDCG@20	0.429	0.481	0.510	0.423	0.503	0.415	0.520	0.559	**0.568**
UR	0.196	0.103	0.072	0.144	0.060	0.119	0.076	0.050	**0.044**

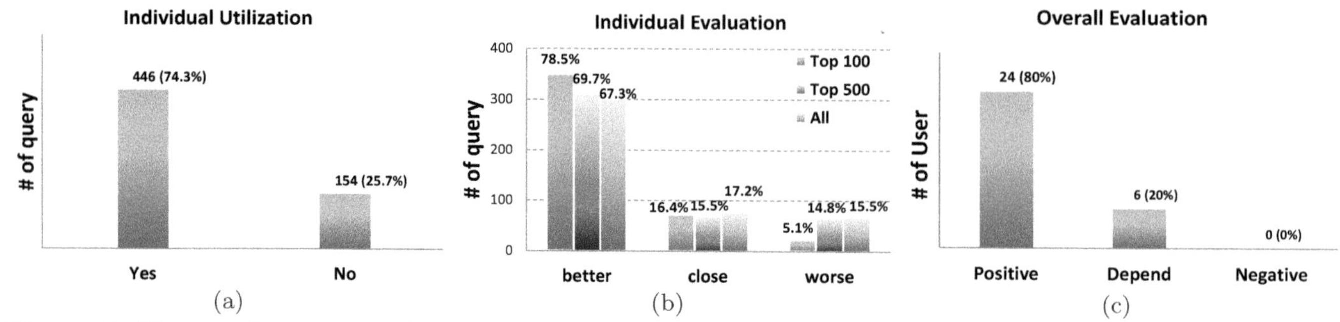

Figure 13: User study on reranking by attractiveness for web image search.

defined as

$$\mathrm{UR} = \frac{1}{|Q|}\sum_{i=1}^{|Q|}\frac{1}{\mathrm{rank}_i}$$

where $|Q|$ denotes the number of queries in test set Q, and rank_i is the rank of the first "unattractive" image in the search results of query i.

The performance comparisons are shown in Table. 3. Similar to the results for attractiveness prediction, utilizing both the transformed visual features and three kinds of contextual features obtains the best performance for all the metrics. In terms of Precision@20, we can conclude that 78% of the top 20 images are above "Neutral", compared to 56% for the search result of Engine I. The 0.044 UR of our final result denotes that the top ranked "Unattractive" image is on average positioned below the 20th, which is much more desirable than the result of Engine I, for which the first unattractive images appear at the 5th position. This result implies that our reranking method can on average eliminate unattractive images in the first page well.

Besides the quantitative results, we also performed a user study of interactive reranking to evaluate whether it is useful for average users. 30 users composed of 13 males and 17 females, with ages ranged from 18 to 29, were invited to perform the study. Among them, 25 users used image search engines frequently, while 5 users seldomly did. We randomly selected 20 queries for each user, and ensured that each query was performed by exactly 6 different users.

For a specific query, a user was firstly presented with the search result from Engine I, and asked whether or not to apply reranking by attractiveness. From the results shown in Fig. 13(a), we found that for 446 out of 600 times users chose to utilize reranking by attractiveness, taking up 74.3% of all. In addition, we observed that for queries such as animal (e.g., cat, dog, butterfly), scene (e.g., beach, sunset, paris), and other queries with attractiveness requirements on images (e.g., wedding dress, rainbow, love), more than five (out of six) users applied reranking. While for queries such as products (e.g., iphone, nike), objects (e.g., shoes, guns, world map), no more than two users chose to rerank. In the latter case, the relevance based results already provide sufficient information related to the queries or attractive counterparts are not their search targets.

For the situations that users chose to apply reranking by attractiveness, we provided them three results in a random order, namely reranking the top 100, top 500 and all images. For each result, users were asked to compare whether the reranked result is better than, close to, or worse than the original result from Engine I, and leave free-style reasons for each comparison. The results are shown in Fig. 13(b). We can observe that for reranking the top 100 search results, it can satisfy the user's search intention for at most 78.5% of the cases, with a degradation for 5.1%. However, as the number of images to be reranked increases, the performance of reranking decreases a little. This is caused by the degradation of topical relevance, since the involvement of more images for reranking may promote the attractive but topically irrelevant images from the bottom of original search results.

We further analyzed the user provided reasons, and found that "Colorfulness", "Visual appeal", "Content richness", "Relevance", and "High quality" were the top five reasons for preferring reranking results, taking up 11.6%, 9.3%, 7.9%, 5.7% and 5.7% of all the factors respectively. Based on this feedback, we can derive that reranking is able to significantly improve the users satisfaction by returning more attractive images. It's also interesting to find that users sometimes thought the reranking result was better because it is more "Relevant", which mostly occurred for queries that favor attractiveness, e.g., butterfly, beach, and wedding dress. Here, the relevance in users' mind, so-called *user relevance*, stands for how "good" a retrieved result is with regard to the user's information need. It is broader than the *topical relevance* by encompassing many other concerns of the user such as attractiveness, interestingness and novelty [13]. On the other hand, the top reasons for reranking being worse is "Irrelevance", "Unwanted color" and "Unusual effects", where "Irrelevance" takes up 46.2% of all reasons. Therefore, a better strategy should be to balance the attractiveness with topical relevance, and treat user relevance as the objective to design web image search engines.

Finally, after all the above studies, users were asked whether or not they would prefer to being provided with the option

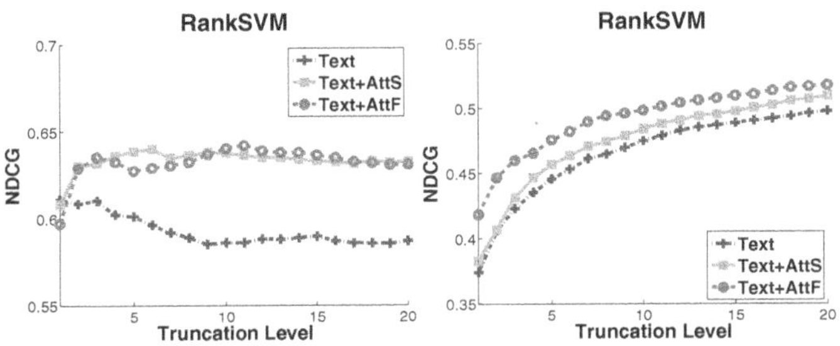

(a) 100Q (b) 594Q

Figure 14: The ranking performance of different feature configurations.

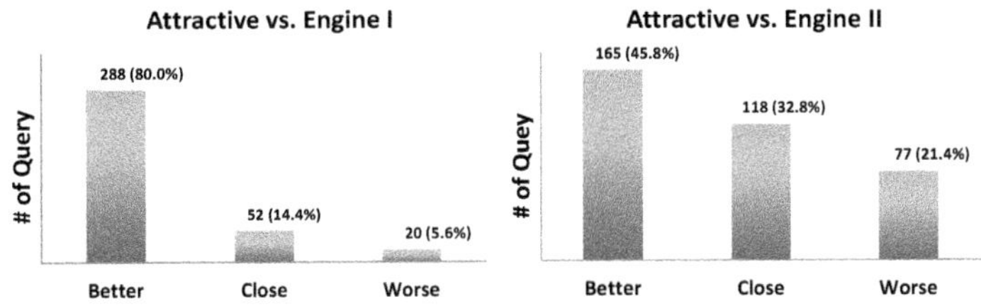

Figure 15: The user study on the ranking performance comparisons.

of attractiveness based interactive reranking for a general web image search. Fig. 13(c) shows that 80% of them supported adding such an option, while 20% thought it would be better to guarantee the relevance, as well as the accuracy of attractiveness estimation before the adoption, and none of them objected the proposal.

7.2 Ranking

We evaluate the ranking with attractiveness through three feature configurations, by comparing the performance of the ranking model trained over text features (Text), text plus the attractiveness score (Text+AttS), and text plus all the proposed attractiveness features (Text+AttF). 154-dimensional textual ranking features were extracted for each query-image pair from the text associated with the images, according to a common text search approach[4]. RankSVM [5] was applied here to learn the ranking model. Note that due to the data split issue, the scores of images from different queries may be predicted by different models while images from the same query are ensured by the same one. This doesn't influence the ranking model learning here, because RankSVM only cares about the pairwise feature differences of images returned for the same query.

We labeled the relevance of each image w.r.t. its query into four degrees including "Excellent", "Good", "Fair" and "Irrelevant". The labeling is not only based on relevance, but also on attractiveness of images. Specifically, images that are topically irrelevant to their associated queries are labeled as "Irrelevant". The remaining ones are labeled as one of "Excellent", "Good", and "Fair" based on whether they are attractive, natural or unattractive respectively. The data split and evaluation setting is the same as in Section 6.1.

From the results in Fig. 14(a), it can be observed that by combining Text with either attractiveness score or features, the performance is significantly improved, by 7.8% and 7.5% w.r.t. Text respectively. This proves that the incorporation of attractiveness features can help the ranking models differentiate topically relevant images with different attractiveness degrees and return more user desired images. We found that Text+AttS and Text+AttF obtained comparable performance. Furthermore, since the 100Q dataset is crawled from the top search results of Engine I, the ranking learning and evaluation may be biased to the search engine's ranking model. To eliminate the bias, we use another large-scale dataset 594Q which contains not only top ranked images but also middle and tail ranked images for each query. It is composed of 594 queries and 137,348 query-image pairs and designed to evaluate the relevance based performance of ranking models [3]. The dataset was split into ten folds and we applied the round-robin setting same as that in Section 6.1 to evaluate the performance. The results are shown in Fig. 14(b). We can derive that Text+AttF and Text+AttS improve 4% and 2.4% over Text for NDCG@20 respectively. Although the improvement is less than that for 100Q, it is statistically significant and the p-values of the t-test of the two approaches over Text in terms of NDCG@20 are 4.24e-9 (Text+AttF) and 3.60e-006 (Text+AttS) respectively.

We also performed a user study to test the whole-page user satisfaction on the search results. The study was performed for the 12 queries over the 100Q dataset under the same setting as in Section 1. Here, the previously employed 30 users were again invited to compare the first page search results of Text+AttF and that of Engine I and Engine II respectively. From the results shown in 15, we can observe that by incorporating the attractiveness into the ranking model, the performance is significantly better than Engine I with 80% voting for "better" while only 5.6% for "worse", and much better than Engine II with 45.5% for "better" while 21.4% for "worse". Actually, as the 100Q dataset was crawled from Engine I, which was shown to perform worse than Engine II for 83% of the cases according to the user study on the same 12 queries, the fact that the incorporation of attractiveness made Engine I outperformed Engine II's results further demonstrates the effectiveness of the proposed method in satisfying end user's search intentions.

7.3 Index selection

To demonstrate the effectiveness of incorporating attractiveness into image index selection, we collected one million images from the whole web, and targeted to select 100,000 among them for indexing. Two baseline approaches including random selection (Random) and static rank based selection (StaticRank) are used to compare with the proposed static rank plus attractiveness based selection (AttracRank). We implemented a modified version of static rank features according to [10], including site-level PageRank, in degree and out degree of each page, the click count of each image, the length and word count of image anchor text, the length of page and image urls, which accounts for totally 8-dimensional features. We utilized RankSVM to train the index selection models for StaticRank and AttracRank approaches over the 100Q dataset respectively, with the relevance label as the ground truth and the model parameters determined by 10-fold cross validation. The selection models were used to predict the scores of one million images, and the top scored 100,000 images were collected for each method.

We evaluated the index selection methods in terms of the ranking performance over the selected subset based on a carefully selected retrieval model. To reduce the uncertainty brought by the setting of different retrieval model parameters, we applied the Okapi-BM25 implemented in

[4]http://research.microsoft.com/en-us/projects/mslr/feature.aspx

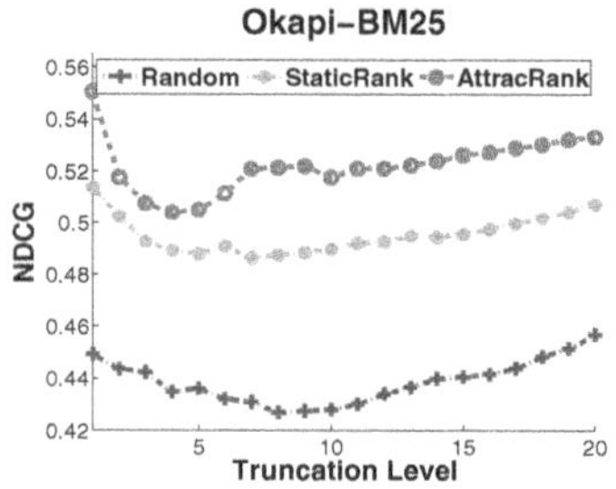

(a) Ranking

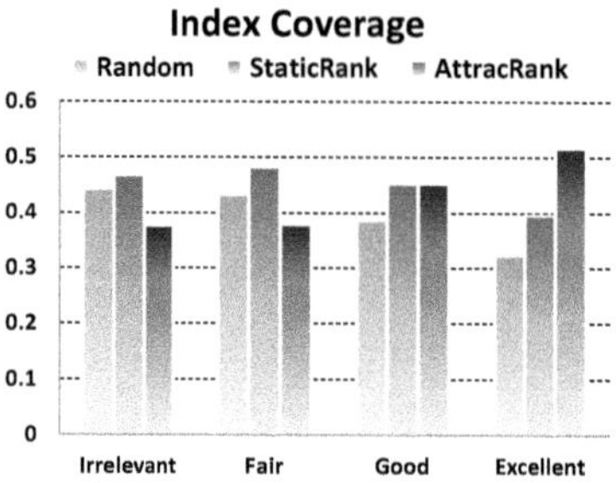

(b) Index Coverage

Figure 16: The performance of three index selection methods in terms of ranking and index coverage.

Lemur[5] with its parameters set to the default value, which was proven as a stable ad-hoc retrieval model [11]. For a specific query, the retrieval model was applied to each index, and all the top 40 ranked images were collected for human labeling. Each query-image pair is labeled into four-degree relevance as for 100Q. We tested the ranking performance of 100 queries over each index, and showed the average NDCG in Fig. 16(a). It can be observed that the ranking performance of Random is rather low, while it is significantly improved for StaticRank by using the features from pages. With the incorporation of attractiveness, the NDCG@20 on AttracRank is improved by 5.14% compared to StaticRank.

Besides the ranking performance, we also evaluated the index coverage of each index, by computing the coverage of all labeled data for each relevance degree. Here, to convert the data from query-dependent to query-independent, the maximum relevance degree is taken as the ground truth of an image if it is returned for more than one query, because the image relevant to at least one query is potentially of interest to search engine users. The results in Fig. 16(b) demonstrate that AttracRank obtained the most "Excellent" images while and the least "Irrelevant" ones. The improvement of AttracRank over StaticRank is 30.5% for indexing "Excellent" and 19.6% for reducing "Irrelevant".

8. CONCLUSIONS

We have witnessed the importance of web image attractiveness to impact users' search experience, especially when the topical relevance has already been effectively satisfied. However, this has not been sufficiently recognized by both the industry and the academia. Therefore, as the first work studying the web image attractiveness from the search engine end users' perspective, we define it according to the users' feedback from three levels, including perceptual quality, aesthetic sensitivity and affective tune. We utilized the existing approaches to extract visual features according to the three levels and investigate their applicability to web image search. To accommodate the unreliability of visual features induced by large variations of web images, we propose a contextual approach to integrate the contextual cues mined from the image EXIF and its associated web pages to complement the visual features, and obtain 12.9% precision improvement on attractiveness estimation. With such a success, we further investigate the role of attractiveness by applying it to various stages of web image search, including online ranking and interactive reranking, as well as offline index selection. The results over three large scale datasets demonstrate that, compared with the conventional relevance based approaches, the incorporation of attractiveness can improve the user experience of online ranking significantly, with nearly 80% of users' preference. Furthermore, it can achieve over 30.5% index coverage improvement for the offline image index selection.

[5]http://www.lemurproject.org/

9. ACKNOWLEDGMENTS

This work is partially supported by NBRPC 2011CB302400, NSFC 60975014 and NSFB 4102024.

10. REFERENCES

[1] S. Bhattacahrya, R. Sukthankar, and M. Shah. A framework for photo-quality assessment and enhancement based on visual aesthetics. In *SIGMM*, 2010.

[2] R. Datta, D. Joshi, J. Li, and J. Z. Wang. Studying aesthetics in photographic images using a computational approach. In *ECCV*, 2006.

[3] B. Geng, L. Yang, C. Xu, and X.-S. Hua. Content-aware ranking for visual search. In *CVPR*, 2010.

[4] K.-Q. Huang, Q. Wang, and Z.-Y. Wu. Natural color image enhancement and evaluation algorithm based on human visual system. *CVIU*, 2006.

[5] T. Joachims. Optimizing search engines using clickthrough data. In *SIGKDD*, 2002.

[6] Y. Ke, X. Tang, and F. Jing. The design of high-level features for photo quality assessment. In *CVPR*, 2006.

[7] Y. Luo and X. Tang. Photo and video quality evaluation: Focusing on the subject. In *ECCV*, 2008.

[8] Y.-F. Ma, X.-S. Hua, L. Lu, and H.-J. Zhang. A generic framework of user attention model and its application in video summarization. *IEEE TMM*, 2005.

[9] J. Machajdik and A. Hanbury. Affective image classification using features inspired by psychology and art theory. In *SIGMM*, 2010.

[10] M. Richardson, A. Prakash, and E. Brill. Beyond pagerank: machine learning for static ranking. In *WWW*, 2006.

[11] S. Robertson and D. A. Hull. The trec-9 filtering track final report. In *TREC*, 2000.

[12] J. San Pedro and S. Siersdorfer. Ranking and classifying attractiveness of photos in folksonomies. In *WWW*, 2009.

[13] T. Saracevic. Relevance: A review of the literature and a framework for thinking on the notion in information science. In *JASIS*, 1976.

[14] H. Sheikh, A. Bovik, and L. Cormack. No-reference quality assessment using natural scene statistics: Jpeg2000. *IEEE TIP*, 2005.

[15] C. G. M. Snoek and A. W. M. Smeulders. Visual-concept search solved? *IEEE Computer*, 2010.

[16] X. Tian, L. Yang, J. Wang, Y. Yang, X. Wu, and X.-S. Hua. Bayesian video search reranking. In *SIGMM*, 2008.

[17] G. Wang and F. H. Lochovsky. Feature selection with conditional mutual information maximin in text categorization. In *CIKM*, 2004.

[18] W. Wei-ning, Y. Ying-lin, and J. Sheng-ming. Image retrieval by emotional semantics: A study of emotional space and feature extraction. In *ICSMC*, 2006.

[19] L. Yang and A. Hanjalic. Supervised reranking for web image search. In *SIGMM*, 2010.

[20] Y. Yue, R. Patel, and H. Roehrig. Beyond position bias: examining result attractiveness as a source of presentation bias in clickthrough data. In *WWW*, 2010.

[21] Z.-J. Zha, L. Yang, T. Mei, M. Wang, and Z. Wang. Visual query suggestion. In *SIGMM*, 2009.

[22] L. Zhang, L. Chen, F. Jing, K. Deng, and W.-Y. Ma. Enjoyphoto: a vertical image search engine for enjoying high-quality photos. In *SIGMM*, 2006.

JIGSAW: Interactive Mobile Visual Search with Multimodal Queries*

Yang Wang †, Tao Mei ‡, Jingdong Wang ‡, Houqiang Li †, Shipeng Li ‡
† University of Science and Technology of China, Hefei 230027, P. R. China
‡ Microsoft Research Asia, Beijing 100080, P. R. China
wyang1@mail.ustc.edu.cn; {tmei, jingdw, spli}@microsoft.com; lihq@ustc.edu.cn

ABSTRACT

The traditional text-based visual search has not been sufficiently improved over the years to accommodate the new emerging demand of mobile users. While on the go, searching on one's phone is becoming pervasive. This paper presents an innovative application for mobile phone users to facilitate their visual search experience. By taking advantage of smart phone functionalities such as *multi-modal* and *multi-touch* interactions, users can more conveniently formulate their search intent, and thus search performance can be significantly improved. The system, called JIGSAW (Joint search with ImaGe, Speech, And Words), represents one of the first attempts to create an interactive and multi-modal mobile visual search application. The key of JIGSAW is the composition of an exemplary image query generated from the raw speech via multi-touch user interaction, as well as the visual search based on the exemplary image. Through JIGSAW, users can formulate their search intent in a natural way like playing a jigsaw puzzle on the phone screen: 1) a user speaks a natural sentence as the query, 2) the speech is recognized and transferred to text which is further decomposed to keywords through entity extraction, 3) the user selects preferred exemplary images that can visually represent his/her intent and composes a query image via multi-touch, and 4) the composite image is then used as a visual query to search similar images. We have deployed JIGSAW on a real-world phone system, evaluated the performance on one million images, and demonstrated that it is an effective complement to existing mobile visual search applications.

Categories and Subject Descriptors

H.3.3 [**Information Storage and Retrieval**]: Information search and retrieval—*Search process*; H.5.2 [**Information Interfaces and Presentation**]: User interface—*User-centered design*

* This work was performed at Microsoft Research Asia.
Area chair: Daniel Gatica-Perez.

MM'11, November 28–December 1, 2011, Scottsdale, Arizona, USA.

General Terms

Algorithms, Experiments, Human Factors

Keywords

Mobile visual search, query formulation, user interface.

1. INTRODUCTION

While on the go, consumers use their phones as a personal Internet-surfing concierge. Searching is becoming pervasive and is one of the most popular applications on mobile phones. People are more and more addicted to conducting searches on their phones. It is reported that one-third of search queries will come from smart phones by 2014 [1]. However, compared with text and location search by phone, visual (image and video) search is still not that popular, mainly because the user's search experience on the phone is not always enjoyable. On one hand, existing forms of queries (i.e., text or voice as queries) are not always user-friendly—typing is a tedious job, and voice cannot express visual intent well. On the other hand, the user's intent in a visual search process is somewhat complex and may not be easily expressed by a piece of text (or text transferred from voice). For example, as shown in Fig. 1(a), the query like "find a picture of a person with a straw hat and a spade" will most likely not result in any relevant search results from existing mobile search engines.

To facilitate visual search on mobile devices, the work described in this paper aims at a more natural way to formulate a visual query, taking full advantage of multi-modal and multi-touch interactions on mobile devices. As shown in Fig. 1(c), users can easily formulate a composite image as their search intent by naturally interacting with the phone through voice and multi-touch. Although similar applications exist, such as Goggles [12], iBing, and SnapTell [26], which support photo shots (using the built-in camera) as a visual query for instant search, as shown in Fig. 1(b), our work represents a complementary mobile visual search by which users can compose an arbitrary visual query (not necessarily an existing image) through natural user interaction.

It is known that visual search on a mobile device is different from that on a desktop. Compared with a desktop PC which predominantly supports text-to-search mode, a mobile phone provides a richer set of user interactions and thus achieves a more natural search experience. For example, beyond the traditional keyboard and mouse inputs, mobile phones are usually enabled to receive multi-modal inputs. The most common interface of this kind combines a

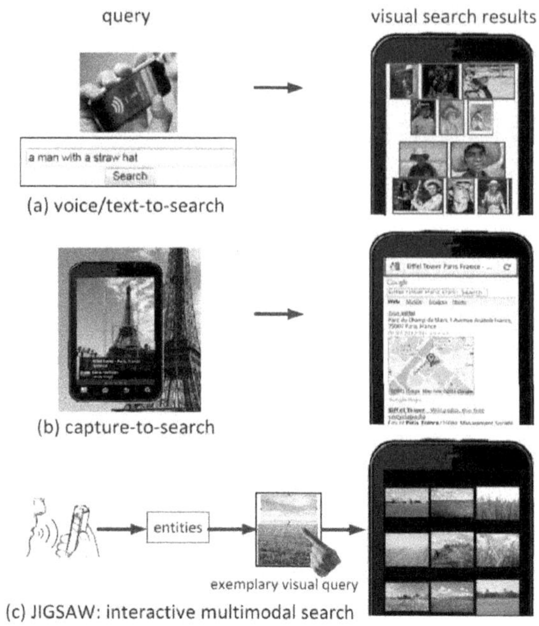

Figure 1: The main modes for mobile visual search: (a) voice/text-to-search, (b) capture-to-search, (c) JIGSAW (this work).

visual modality via the built-in camera with a voice modality via speech recognition. In addition, the multi-touch phone screen, which recognizes multiple simultaneous touch points, provides rich interaction between users and devices. All these advantages provide for a more natural interaction to formulate search intent and thus achieve a better search experience via mobile phone.

There exist some visual search applications for mobile devices. Table 1 is a survey of the recent visual search applications on various mobile platforms. All of them require users to first take a picture and then perform similar image searches in various vertical domains (i.e., capture-to-search mode). However, in many cases, the user's search intent is implicit and cannot be represented through capturing the surroundings. The user, nevertheless, can express his/her intent via a piece of voice description. For example, a user is looking for a restaurant with a red door and two stone lions in front of the door, however s/he forgot the name of the restaurant. Therefore, a client-side tool that can transfer a long textual query into a visual query with user interaction is required to determine the restaurant's name and location.

Although researchers in the computer vision community have proposed various techniques for mobile visual search [4] [5] [27] [32], most of them focus on the problems with capture-to-search mode. For example, Takacs and Yang *et al.* discuss how to represent the captured image with a set of visual descriptors [27] [32]. The transmission of image descriptors between mobile client and server is discussed in [5]. Chandrasekhar *et al.* focus on how to compact visual descriptors using compression techniques [4]. Different from many existing works, this paper studies the problem of visual query formulation on mobile devices, as well as the key techniques in this new search mode. The work is an effective complement to existing mobile visual search systems.

The proposed system, called JIGSAW (Joint search with ImaGe, Speech, And Words), takes advantage of the functionalities on mobile phones, such as multi-modal and multi-touch interactions, to help users formulate their (implicit) search intent more conveniently and thus promote visual search performance. The search procedure consists of the following phases: 1) the user speaks a natural sentence as the query to the phone, 2) the speech is recognized and transferred to text, and the text is further decomposed into keywords by entity extraction, 3) the user selects the preferred exemplary images (given by an image clustering process according to the entities) that can visually represent each keyword and composes a query image through multi-touch, 4) the composed image is then used as a visual query to search similar images. Therefore, the key component of JIGSAW is the composition of an exemplary image query generated from the raw speech via multi-touch user interaction, as well as visual search based on the exemplary image. Through JIGSAW, users can formulate their visual search intent in a natural way like piecing together a jigsaw puzzle on the phone screen. The techniques in JIGSAW include speech recognition, entity extraction, image clustering, large-scale image search, and user interaction.

Table 1: Recent mobile visual search applications.

App	Features
Goggles [12]	product, cover, landmark, namecard
Digimarc Discover [8]	print, article, ads
Point and Find [22]	place, 2D barcode
SnapTell [26]	cover, barcode
SnapNow [16]	MMS, email, print, broadcast
Kooaba [25]	media cover, print

Our contributions are twofold: 1) we propose an interactive and multi-modal visual search system on mobile devices, which takes advantages of natural multi-modal and multi-touch functionalities on the phone, and 2) we propose a context-aware approach to similar image search which takes the spatial relation among exemplary image patches into consideration.

The rest of this paper is organized as follows. Section 2 reviews related work for mobile and desktop visual searching. Sections 3 and 4 describe each component and implementation of JIGSAW. Experiments are presented in Section 5, followed by conclusions in Section 6.

2. RELATED WORK

We review related research on mobile visual search and interactive visual search.

2.1 Visual Search on Mobile

Directly applying keyword-based search to mobile visual search is straightforward yet intrusive. As we have mentioned, typing a long query is not always user-friendly on mobile devices. This is the reason that mobile users type on average 2.6 terms per search [6], which can hardly express their search intent. Compared with text-to-search, capture-to-search is becoming dominant in mobile visual search. It is more convenient for mobile users to take a photo and use it to search on the go. Goggles [12], Point and Find [22], and Snaptell [26], are recent visual search applications in this area.

There exist efforts on mobile visual search in the computer vision community. Most of these efforts have focused on the exploration of different visual descriptors. For example, local features such as Scale-Invariant Feature Transform

(SIFT) feature [18], MPEG-7 image signature, and Speeded Up Robust Feature (SURF) [2] have been devised to handle luminance and geometry variances. In addition to the exploration of visual descriptors, Chandrasekhar *et al.* discuss the issue of compressing these descriptors, so as to reduce the bandwidth and storage costs on mobile devices [4]. They propose to use Compressed Histogram of Gradients (CHoG) to quantize and encode gradient histograms with Huffman and Gagie trees to achieve a very low bit-rate transmission. It demonstrates that SIFT has the advantage over CHoG and MPEG-7 image signature in a system of CD cover search.

The proposed JIGSAW in this paper differs from existing mobile visual search systems in that it represents a new search mode in which mobile users can naturally formulate a visual query on the go.

2.2 Interactive Visual Search on PC

The most related work on generic visual search to JIGSAW is interactive search, in which users specify their search intent interactively. The advanced functionalities in Google and Bing's image search engines enable user to indicate search intent via various filters, e.g., "similar images," color, style, face, and so on. Tineye supports the uploading of an exemplary image as a query example for search [28], while Xcavator even enables users to emphasize certain regions on the query image as the key search components [30]. In a more advanced search engine prototype, such as GazoPa [11] and MindFinder [3], the search is performed by sketching a shape image. The "Concept Map" uses the position and size of a group of tags to filter the top text-based search results [31], while the "Color Map" enables the selection of multiple color hints on a composite canvas as a visual query [29]. However, user interaction on desktop is not as natural as that on mobile device. Therefore, an interactive mobile visual search system which takes advantage of multi-touch and multi-modal functionalities is desirable.

3. JIGSAW

JIGSAW is an interactive mobile visual search application that enables users to naturally formulate their search intent in an interactive way and combines different visual descriptors (e.g., SIFT, color, and edge) for visual search. Figure 2 shows the framework of JIGSAW. On the client-side, a user first speaks a natural sentence to initiate a voice query, e.g., a sentence like "find an iron tower on the grass." On the cloud-side, the system employs speech recognition (SR) to transfer the speech to a piece of text, and then extracts entities from the text. As a result, "tower" and "grass" are recognized as two entities that can be represented by two exemplary images. Directly using those entities as textual queries may not return relevant results, as it only searches the surrounding text and neglects the position and size of these exemplary images on the query canvas. Therefore, we propose to enable users to further specify search intent by touching the screen and dragging their preferred exemplary images, and then formulating a composite visual query. Those exemplary images are automatically generated using a clustering process according to the extracted entities. Finally, we exploit both the text and the composite visual query to search for relevant images, by considering the position and the size of the exemplary images. In the next sections, we will describe the details of each component.

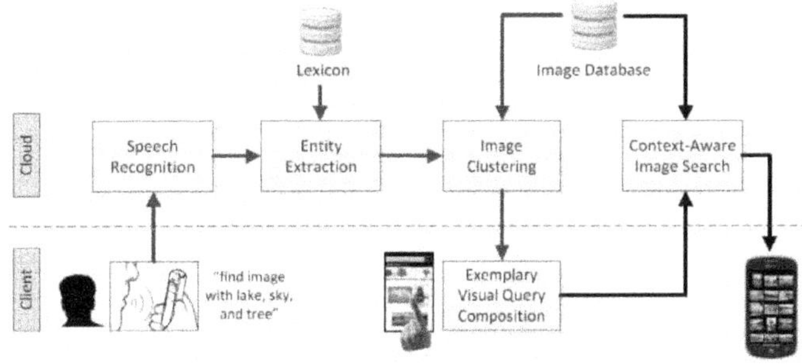

Figure 2: JIGSAW architecture. There are four major components: (1) speech recognition, (2) entity extraction, (3) interactive exemplary visual query composition, and (4) context-aware example-based image search.

3.1 Speech Recognition and Entity Extraction

On the mobile phone, voice is more natural than typing for users. We propose to leverage voice input to help users initiate a query. We employ a Hidden Markov Model (HMM)-based SR engine which is able to handle natural sentences and phrase fragments, and then translate the speech into text [23]. In general, speech recognition engines are usually constructed in a statistical modeling framework, in which the speech utterance will first be transformed into a compact and meaningful representation in the feature space. Then, the decoder takes the feature vectors as input and generates the probability of the hypothesized word sequence based on the acoustic and language models. In JIGSAW, we employed the SR service from a commercial local search engine. However, any state-of-the-art SR engine could be used in this capacity.

The text result from the speech recognition can be directly used as the query for image search. However, it is well-known that existing search engines cannot handle a long query very well. On the other hand, understanding a long sentence is still challenging. For example, issuing a textual query like "find an image with several green trees in front of a white house" may not result in any relevant search. Therefore, we process the original recognized text to extract entities (i.e., keywords like "tree" and "house") for a better visual search. Although general entity extraction is still an open problem despite many efforts [15], the entity extraction in JIGSAW can be reduced to detect the words that can be represented by some exemplary images, so that users can select their preferred images. Therefore, we focus on the detection of meaningful noun words/phrases, such as "building," "car," and "tree," while discarding the vague and general words/phrases like "law" and "holiday." To this end, an entity dictionary is constructed according to WordNet [20] by collecting the noun words which have concrete visual representations (117,798 nouns out of 155,287 words). The judgement on whether an noun has concrete visual representations is based on whether the noun can be represented by the images in the ImageNet [7]. By removing the nouns which have less than 100 images in the ImageNet, 22,117 unique words are kept. In addition, we include other entity names including celebrities, popular products, and landmarks to deal with the names such as "Super man" and "Eiffel." These entity names are obtained by mining the web and the top queries in a commercial search engine [24].

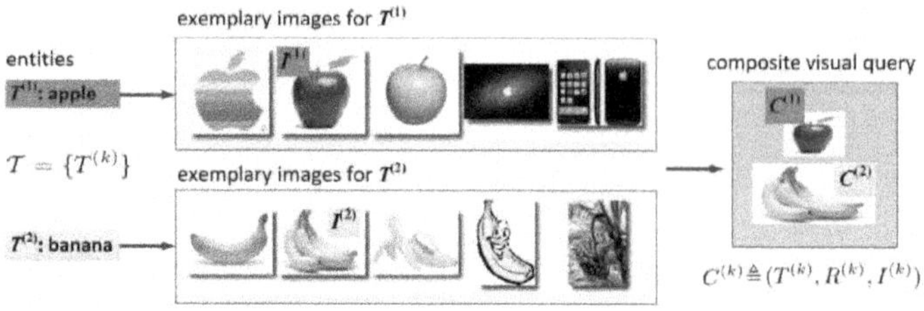

Figure 3: An example for composing a visual query with multiple components $C^{(k)}$ from an initial query $\mathcal{T} = \{T^{(k)}\}_{k=1}^{K}$ with multiple entities $T^{(k)}$. Each entity corresponds to one component in the composite visual query. There are two recognized entities: $T^{(1)}$ = "apple," and $T^{(2)}$ ="banana". For each entity, there is a list of candidate exemplary images to be selected by users. A composite visual query is generated by the selected image $I^{(1)}$ and $I^{(2)}$, where the position and the size ($R^{(1)}$ and $R^{(2)}$) of each component on the canvas are adjusted by the user.

Finally, words in the voice query will be assigned to their longest match. For example, "polar bear" and "Eiffel Tower" are phrases and thus cannot be split. If a user says "find an iron tower under grass," then the extracted keywords would be "tower" and "grass." These keywords are used independently in the following image clustering and search steps.

3.2 Interactive Formulation of Composite Visual Query

Searching for images with a single entity in a text-based search engine can return related results. But it is still challenging for the text-based image search to consider the spatial relation among different entities (i.e., both the position and the size of the entities in the composite visual query). It would be difficult to automatically arrange the entities (i.e., their corresponding exemplary images) on the query image canvas. Therefore, we propose to take advantage of the screen-touch function to enable users to composite a visual query via multi-touch interactions. For each entity, the system returns a set of representative images. Users can select one image per entity and drag onto the composite image canvas, as shown in Fig. 1(c). When users finish selecting the exemplary images, they can formulate their visual queries by adjusting the position and the size of each exemplary image on the composite canvas via multi-touch interactions. JIGSAW is designed for addressing the following ambiguities in the existing text-based image search systems: *polysemy*, *aspect*, *view point*, *position*, and *attributes*.

Polysemy means that a word has multiple meanings, such as apple (fruit or product), football (association football or American football). Aspect indicates that a word may have different concepts, such as apple (company or product), football (ball or game). View point means an object could have various appearances from different angles or perspectives, such as a car (side or front view), or an office (inner or outer). Position indicates in which position the object is expected within the target image. Attribute defines the properties of an entity, such as color, type, and decoration. All these ambiguities lead to difficulties in expressing search intent.

In this paper, we are investigating whether these ambiguities can be solved by introducing some user interactions.

Table 2: Key notations.

I	exemplary image
J	target image to be searched
R	rectangle region for a component on the canvas of the composite visual query
T	entity (i.e., keyword)
C	$C \triangleq (T, I, R)$, component in a composite visual query
K	# of entities
k	index of components ($k = 1, \ldots, K$)
$\boldsymbol{f}$	feature vector of an image
$\boldsymbol{h}$	feature vector of an image grid
$C^{(k)}$	$C^{(k)} \triangleq (T^{(k)}, I^{(k)}, R^{(k)})$, the k-th component
(i,j)	index of a grid in the target image J
$R_J^{(k)}$	$R_J^{(k)} = \bigcup_{i,j \in R^{(k)}} (i,j)$, the union of the grids in J
$e_J^{(k)}(i,j)$	visual similarity between $I^{(k)}$ and image region $R_J^{(k)}$
$d^{(k)}(i,j)$	user intent map for k-th component at (i,j)
$r_J^{(k)}$	relevance between composite query and target image J in terms of k-th component
r_J	overall relevance between composite query and target image J

Based on the above analysis of ambiguities, we introduced the interactive composition of a visual query by manipulating the multiple exemplary images on a given canvas. Specifically, when the user issues a voice query, the system will recognize a set of entities (keywords) $\mathcal{T} = \{T^{(k)}\}_{k=1}^{K}$, and return a list of exemplary images for each entity, as shown in Figure 3, where $T^{(k)}$ indicates one entity and K is the number of entities in the textual query $\mathcal{T}$. By selecting the desired exemplary images, as well as re-positioning and resizing them on the canvas of the composite query image, the user can formulate a visual query. Therefore, the composite visual query can be represented as a set of components $\mathcal{C} = \{C^{(k)}\}_{k=1}^{K}$, where each component $C^{(k)}$ corresponds to one entity $T^{(k)}$, as well as the selected exemplary image $I^{(k)}$ and the position and size $R^{(k)}$ of this image indicated by the user. Thus, $C^{(k)}$ can be further represented by a triplet $(T^{(k)}, I^{(k)}, R^{(k)})$. Table 2 lists the key notations.

3.3 Generation of Exemplary Images

In this section, we present an automatic approach to generating the exemplary images for each entity, by exploiting both ImageNet and image search engines results. It is impractical to allow users to manually select the exemplary images from a number of images (e.g., the top image search results from search engines). It is also not appropriate to directly use the images from ImageNet because of the cross-domain difference between ImageNet and general web images. Thus, we propose a clustering-based approach to generating the exemplary images for a given entity. The next subsections will introduce the visual features and similarity metric for clustering.

3.3.1 Visual descriptors

We adopt three types of visual features, including SIFT [18], color histogram, and gradient histogram, which have been proven to be effective for image retrieval. Since the local descriptor like SIFT may not perform well for some images, such as scene and human, we exploit the discriminative power of color and gradient histogram. For each image, a 128-dimensional SIFT descriptor is extracted at each key

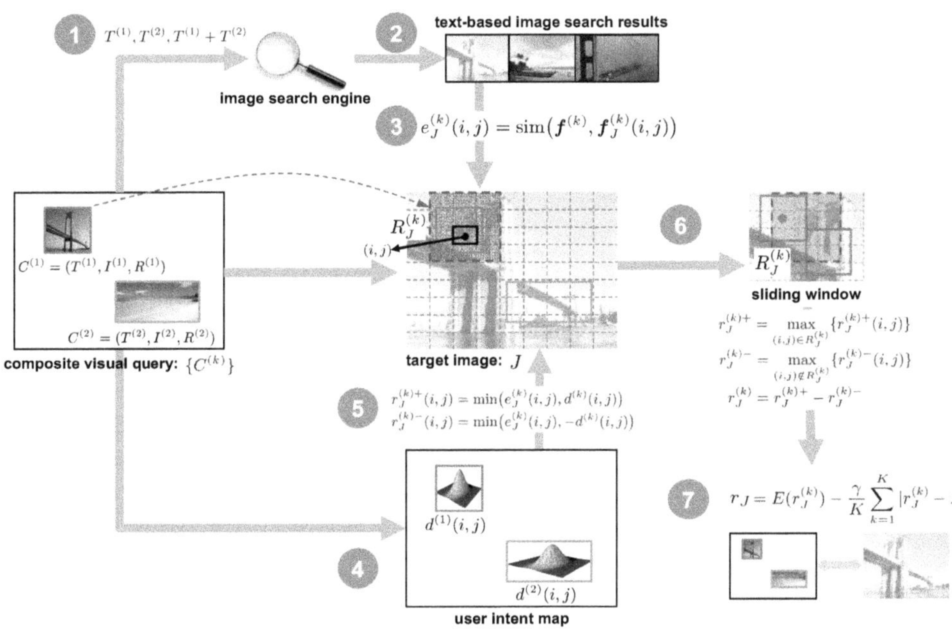

Figure 4: The process for computing the relevance r_J between the composite visual query and a target image.

point. Then, a vocabulary tree is constructed by hierarchical K-means [21], yielding about 6,000 visual words. Each 128-dimensional SIFT descriptor is hashed into a visual word by traversing the tree. Finally, an image is described by the weighted visual words. Color is also quantized to 192 bins in the HSV space, while the gradient is quantized to 8 directions and 8 intensities, yielding a 64-dimensional gradient histogram. As a result, an image is described by the concatenated histogram ($6256 = 6000 + 192 + 64$) of these three kinds of features. It should be noted that these features are normalized individually before the concatenation.

3.3.2 Similarity metric

Let $\boldsymbol{f}_i$ and $\boldsymbol{f}_j$ denote the normalized histograms of image i and j, respectively. The similarity between these two images is given by a weighted intersection kernel between two histograms

$$\mathrm{sim}(\boldsymbol{f}_i, \boldsymbol{f}_j) = \sum_{n=1}^{N} w_n \min(f_{i,n}, f_{j,n}), \qquad (1)$$

where $f_{i,n}$ indicates the n-th element of histogram $\boldsymbol{f}_i$, w_n is the weight for measuring the contribution from the similarity on the n-th element, and N ($N = 6256$) is the dimension of the histogram. Since not all the elements in the histogram are equally important for comparing images, we introduce the weight to differentiate the contributions from different features. We first average features across all the images and obtain an average histogram $\overline{\boldsymbol{f}} = \{\overline{f}_n\}_{n=1}^{N}$, and then define the weight w_n as $w_n = 1/\overline{f}_n$. The more frequent the element across all images, the less important it is. This weighting function is able to not only mine informative elements in the histogram, but also balance different types of descriptors.

3.3.3 Clustering-based exemplary image generation

We employ a clustering-based approach to generating the exemplary images. We first collect the candidate images by selecting images from the ImageNet and the top 1,000 images from a commercial image search engine according to the entity keywords, respectively. Then, we compute a similarity matrix by comparing all pairs of images based on the visual descriptors and similarity metric described in the previous sections. Last, we adopt the affinity propagation (AP) algorithm to find the visual instances [10]. AP is a widely used unsupervised clustering method which can group features into a number of classes. We sort the clusters according to the number of images in descending order. The centers of the top clusters (we used the top 10) are selected as exemplary images for this entity. To avoid background clutter, a salient region detection process is conducted before feature extraction [19]. Only the visual descriptors within the salient regions are considered. Moreover, a Gaussian window is used to weight the descriptors to make the descriptors close to the centers more important.

3.4 Context-aware Exemplar-based Image Search

Given the composite visual query including recognized entities, selected exemplary images, and their intended positions, the task is to search target images which are contextually relevant to the query. By relevance, we mean that the target images are expected to contain both the entity keywords and visually similar objects in the desired positions. The relevance between visual query and target image consists of the visual similarity and the intent consistency based on user indicated position.

Therefore, we design the searching process in Figure 4, which consists of the following steps: 1) generating textual queries by combining the entity keywords $\{T^{(k)}\}$; 2) searching related images according to the textual queries from an image database; 3) computing the visual similarity $\{e_J^{(k)}(i,j)\}$ between each exemplary image and the corresponding region in the target image J, 4) generating user intent map $\{d^{(k)}(i,j)\}$ according to the positions of the exemplary images indicated by users; 5) computing the "positive relevance" $r_J^{(k)+}(i,j)$ and "negative relevance" $r_J^{(k)-}(i,j)$

for each component by considering both visual similarity and the user intent map; 6) computing the combined relevance $r_J^{(k)}$ for each component by considering the surrounding grids in image J (using a sliding window); and 7) computing the overall relevance r_J between the composite query $\mathcal{C}$ and the target image J. In this way, we can rank the related images returned in step 2 according to the overall relevance scores.

3.4.1 Region-based visual similarity $e_J^{(k)}(i,j)$

To compute the region-based visual similarity between an exemplary image in the composite query and the corresponding region in the target image J, we need a visual representation of the region in J. As it is not practical to compute the visual representation of a specific region in J in real-time (as users may frequently change the position and size of this component), we adopt an efficient grid-based search scheme and partition the target image J into small grids $\{(i,j)\}_{i,j=1}^{M}$. Suppose we select the k-th exemplary image (corresponding to the region $R^{(k)}$ in the composite query), and its center position corresponds to the grid (i,j) in J, then the corresponding region $R_J^{(k)}$ in J is given by the union of all the associated grids, i.e., $R_J^{(k)} = \bigcup_{(i,j)\in R^{(k)}}(i,j)$. In each grid, the feature histogram is obtained using the approach described in Section 3.3.1 and saved in advance. Now, the target image J can be represented as $\{\boldsymbol{h}_J(i,j)\}_{i,j=1}^{M}$, where $\boldsymbol{h}_J(i,j)$ is the visual descriptor for the grid (i,j). We choose $M = 9$ in our implementation. Then, the visual representation of $R_J^{(k)}$ can be obtained using the linear fusion of histograms from the related grids:

$$\boldsymbol{f}_J^{(k)}(i,j) = \sum_{(i,j)\in R_J^{(k)}} w_J(i,j)\boldsymbol{h}_J(i,j), \tag{2}$$

where $w_J(i,j)$ is a 2D Gaussian distributed weight centered at the given region, which assigns more importance on the grid close to the center.

Then, the region-based visual similarity between the k-th exemplary image and the region $R_J^{(k)}$ can be given by

$$e_J^{(k)}(i,j) = \mathrm{sim}\big(\boldsymbol{f}^{(k)}, \boldsymbol{f}_J^{(k)}(i,j)\big), \tag{3}$$

where $\boldsymbol{f}^{(k)}$ is the visual descriptor of the k-th exemplary image, while $\mathrm{sim}(\cdot)$ is given in equation (1). Note that in the above equation, we use both the index of (i,j) and k. This is because we will use a sliding window to compute the region-based similarity later to deal with the tolerance of position. Therefore, $e_J^{(k)}(i,j)$ indicates the visual similarity between the k-th exemplary image and the corresponding region centered at (i,j) in the target image J.

3.4.2 Region-based intent relevance $r_J^{(k)}$

The computation of the region-based relevance between the exemplary image $I^{(k)}$ and the corresponding region $R_J^{(k)}$ should take the user intent into account. Intuitively, user intent close to the center of each $R^{(k)}$ is stronger than that which is far away from the center. Moreover, user intent within the exemplary image $R^{(k)}$ is stronger than intent outside of if. We first define the user intent map which is a soft measurement of user intent in the composite query.

Let $(x^{(k)}, y^{(k)})$ denote the center of the k-th exemplary image in the composite visual query. To tolerate the uncertainty of this position specified by the user, we compute the following soft map to represent the user intent:

$$\begin{aligned} d(x,y) &= 2g(x,y) - 1, \\ g(x,y) &= \exp\left\{-\left(\frac{x - x^{(k)}}{\theta \cdot w^{(k)}}\right)^2 - \left(\frac{y - y^{(k)}}{\theta \cdot h^{(k)}}\right)^2\right\}, \end{aligned} \tag{4}$$

where $w^{(k)}$ and $h^{(k)}$ are the width and height of $R^{(k)}$, respectively, and θ is set to a constant $(8\ln 2)^{-1/2}$ to make g degrade to 0.5 at the border of $R^{(k)}$. Then, the intent consistency in terms of k-th component at grid (i,j) is given by

$$r_J^{(k)+}(i,j) = \min\big(e_J^{(k)}(i,j), d^{(k)}(i,j)\big). \tag{5}$$

This is called "positive relevance" as it mainly focuses on the grids within $R_J^{(k)}$. We also present a scheme to penalize the case that an entity exists in an undesired position (i.e., out of the user indicated region). By checking the relevance of each grid outside the region, the penalty score can be obtained by

$$r_J^{(k)-}(i,j) = \min\big(e_J^{(k)}(i,j), -d^{(k)}(i,j)\big) \tag{6}$$

This is called "negative relevance" as it penalties the grids outside $R_J^{(k)}$.

It is not easy for users to indicate their intent very precisely on the composite query canvas (e.g., the exemplary image may be positioned in an approximate position rather than an exact position, and not well resized). Therefore, we need to maintain tolerance to the position and the size of each exemplary image. To deal with the tolerance issue, we use a sliding window for which the size is the same as $R^{(k)}$ and place this window centered at all the grids (i,j) in $R_J^{(k)}$. In other words, the original exemplary image is re-positioned on these sliding windows to introduce some position tolerance. We are always searching for the best match among these sliding windows, as shown in Figure 4. As a result, the "positive relevance" and "negative relevance" between the k-th exemplary image and $R_J^{(k)}$ is computed by

$$\begin{aligned} r_J^{(k)+} &= \max_{(i,j)\in R_J^{(k)}} \{r_J^{(k)+}(i,j)\}, \\ r_J^{(k)-} &= \max_{(i,j)\notin R_J^{(k)}} \{r_J^{(k)-}(i,j)\}. \end{aligned} \tag{7}$$

The combined relevance between the k-th exemplary image and $R_J^{(k)}$ is

$$r_J^{(k)} = r_J^{(k)+} - r_J^{(k)-}. \tag{8}$$

3.4.3 Overall relevance r_J

After we obtained all the region-based relevance $r_J^{(k)}$, the overall relevance between $\mathcal{C}$ and J is computed by combining across all the components. To consider the variance of different components, the overall relevance is given by a fusion function sensitive to both the mean and the variance of each region-based relevance:

$$r_J = E(r_J^{(k)}) - \frac{\gamma}{K}\sum_{k=1}^{K}\left|r_J^{(k)} - E(r_J^{(k)})\right| \tag{9}$$

where $E(r_J^{(k)}) = \frac{1}{K}\sum_k r_J^{(k)}$ is the average relevance, and γ is a positive parameter controlling the penalization degree, which is empirically set to 0.8 in our implementation.

Figure 5: The user interface of JIGSAW on a Windows Phone 7 device. The left is the operation interface, while the right is the search result page.

4. IMPLEMENTATION

We deployed JIGSAW as an application on Windows Phone 7 devices. Figure 5 shows the user interface. On the top of the screen is the text box to accept a textual query. It can also display speech query after tapping the button on the right and record a piece of speech. By tapping the right button, the textual query in the text box will be parsed and the entity keywords will appear in the tag list. Below the tag list, there is an exemplary image list which shows the exemplary images searched according to the selected keyword. The user can drag any exemplary image onto the composite query canvas below, so that the exemplar will be displayed on the canvas. Both lists can slide horizontally by touching and sliding. Double tapping results in the deletion of an item in the list. On the canvas, the user can both reposition the exemplar by dragging or resizing it by two-point touch stretching. Finally, if the user is satisfied with the composite query, s/he can double-tap the canvas to trigger the search. The search results will be displayed in a new page.

5. EVALUATIONS

The dataset includes the images collected by more than 1,000 entities in a commercial image search engine. These entities are collected from some famous datasets, including Caltech-101 [9], Caltech-256 [13], and the 600 most popular entities from ImageNet [7]. To evaluate the usability compared to the capture-to-search mode, we also use a small number of nouns based on their popularity in Flickr (i.e., frequency of tags), including landmark, product, celebrities, and event. For each entity, we searched the top 500 images from the search engine. The combinations of each pair of entities were also issued as the queries to collect more comprehensive data. In order to cover more possible entities, we also included half a million Flickr images into our database. In total, there are about 1.5 million images in the database. It is challenging to index a large number of images by considering the grids in the targeted images. In JIGSAW, we first use the entities extracted from the speech to filter the images and keep about 1,000 images as candidates for the subsequent steps.

Figure 6: Examples of four composite visual queries.

Table 3: Distribution of the number of components.

# of components (entities)	1	2	3	4
# of test queries	40	30	20	10

5.1 Evaluation of Visual Search

To test the performance of image search in JIGSAW, 100 queries were collected as the query set. These queries included 42 concepts used in [31]. Furthermore, we collected some queries from search history in JIGSAW. For queries with more than one component, since not each combination has possible search results, we only selected 58 queries. Figure 6 shows some examples of these queries. As short queries are dominant in the search query logs, we leveraged more short queries in the experiment. Table 3 lists the number of queries with different number of terms.

We compared search performance among text-based image searches, the algorithm in the Concept Map [31], and the proposed JIGSAW. Six people with technical backgrounds were invited to evaluate the system. They tried the system and got familiar with it at first. Then they were asked to label the search results. Images were organized into three levels: 0—not relevant, 1—relevant, 2—very relevant. Each image was labeled by at least three different subjects. The median score was used as the ground truth. The Normalized Discounted Cumulative Gain (NDCG) [17] was used to evaluate the search performance. Limited by the screen size and bandwidth, mobile phones can display much fewer images than a PC, making the top ranked images crucial. NDCG scores are calculated based on the top 20 images.

Figure 7 shows the NDCG for different search methods under different numbers of keywords. Text based image search had the worst performance under all settings because the text-based search was not able to understand the image content only based on text queries, and user intent cannot be well expressed through a piece of text. We also included more common combinations of three keywords, so that the performance of text-based results were a little higher than that of two keywords. JIGSAW is also better than Concept Map because it can consider the spatial representation of the region. In the case of a single keyword, JIGSAW is better

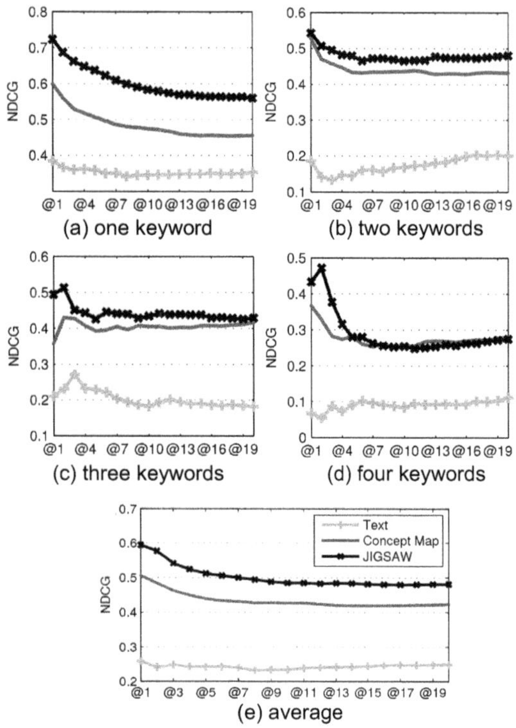

Figure 7: Comparison of the image search performance among three different approaches.

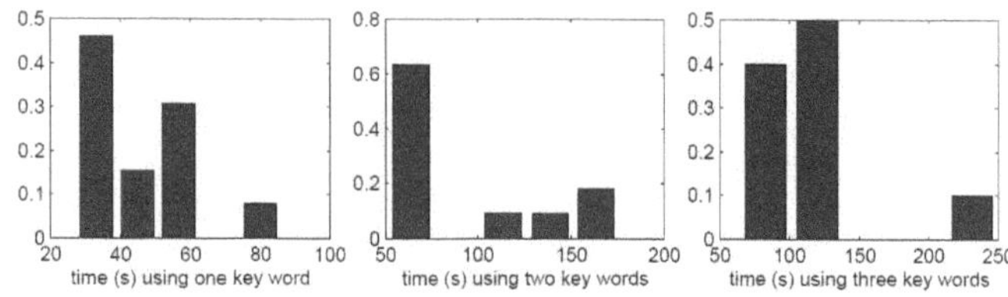

Figure 8: The time distribution for different users to complete a task.

Table 4: A summary of user study by comparing three mobile apps: (a) Google Image, (b) Google's Goggles, and (c) JIGSAW. Each metric is rated from 1 to 5 indicating the worst to the best level.

#Q	Question	(a)	(b)	(c)
1	attractiveness (overall)	2.5	3.5	4.7
2	naturalness (overall)	3.5	3.9	4.1
3	enjoyability (overall)	2.6	3.7	4.5
4	efficiency (overall)	3.0	3.7	3.9
5	input method (overall)	2.5	3.8	4.2
	interaction	2.3	3.7	4.6
6	+ novelty	1.8	3.5	4.6
7	+ naturalness	2.8	3.5	3.8
8	+ user friendly	3.1	3.5	3.8
9	+ efficiency	3.1	3.4	3.9
10	+ clarity of intent	2.8	3.6	4.4
11	effectiveness of search results	2.8	3.5	3.9
12	preference	3.2	4.0	4.1
13	ease to use	2.0	3.3	3.9
14	operation	2.8	3.3	4.2

than Concept Map because JIGSAW uses combined grids instead of separated grids. The performance of JIGSAW and Concept Map get closer as the number of keywords increases because the intended regions become similar.

5.2 Subjective Evaluation of Usability

We invited 12 subjects to use our system on mobile phones. These subjects consist of two female and ten male college students, with the ages ranging from 22 to 27. Half of them already had some experience with multi-touch devices, while three of them had never used smart phones before. Two subjects had experience with visual search on mobile phones and one had experience with speech search on mobile phones. However, after three minutes of orientation and demonstration of JIGSAW, all of them became sufficiently familiar with how to use the system. Three of them felt the interface was very cool when they first saw it. Some of them were even surprised when they found that position and size affected the search results. Most of them were able to get familiar with our system within three to five minutes by completing one or two search trials. It is worth noting that among all subjects, one had difficulty typing on the touch screen, so he felt that speech input greatly helped him. Through the orientation, we found that the JIGSAW is acceptable for most of the subjects.

After learning the system well, they were asked to accomplish some tasks. In each task, one subject randomly choose a keyword from the 1,000 candidates. They first worked on a computer typing the keyword in the text search engine and picked one image within the top 500 results which they found interesting. They were then required to use JIGSAW to find the same image or similar images that satisfied them. We asked them to use a voice query first along with text if necessary, and choose visually similar exemplary image(s) by putting it on the canvas at their intended position. One, two, and three entities were used separately to search images, resulting in 36 tasks in total. In the experiment, only two tasks failed to find the desired images (i.e., the target image did not appear in top 40 results). In 20 tasks, the desired images were in the top 10 results. The time distribution required to successfully complete each task are shown in Figure 8. A questionnaire was also filled out by each user, asking for participants' input on usability, user friendliness, natural experience, and so on. Through these tasks, all of the subjects found JIGSAW successfully facilitates their search intent.

According to our observations, to successfully complete a search task with one keyword usually takes about 30 sec. Each failed trial or extra effort will increase the time by about 20 sec. While according to [14], a typical image search on PC by text query requires about 140 sec. The average response time and number of operations are 1.9 sec. and 9.8 for one entity, 3.6 sec. and 16.6 for two entities, and 7.1 sec. and 26.9 for three, respectively. These show that JIGSAW can play a positive role in accelerating the image search process on mobile phones.

A quantitative evaluation comparing three applications (i.e., Google image search, Goggles, and JIGSAW) are listed in Table 4. This shows the advantage of JIGSAW over traditional text-based image search and the complementary power of capture-to-search applications. All of the subjects thought that JIGSAW is attractive and an effective complement to text-based search modes. 83% thought the composite visual query helped them to find images, and the interface is user friendly, and the process is enjoyable. 75% thought this system is natural and better to use than a text-based

(a) A query includes single entities : accordion

(b) A query includes two entities : bamboo and panda

(c) A query includes three entities: lake, tree, and sky

Figure 9: Some visual examples of JIGSAW results.

search engine. 67% think the voice input is easy to use. Moreover, they are looking forward to new features from JIGSAW, such as color selection or photo capturing. When asked whether they would install this application on their own smartphones, they gave a positive response with 3.9/5.0 on average, indicating that most of them would like to install and use it. Some also hope they would use it on a larger touchscreen. In addition, after an introduction of other visual search systems (e.g., Goggles), all subjects claimed that they would like to use both JIGSAW and other visual search systems to conduct searches for different scenarios.

5.3 Complexity Analysis

We tested the response time with the 100 queries. Figure 10 shows the time consumption with different numbers of keywords. The image search component does not spend much memory. For example, a single keyword with 1,000 candidate images (histograms) needs to be loaded onto the memory. The average number of sift points is 300 per im-

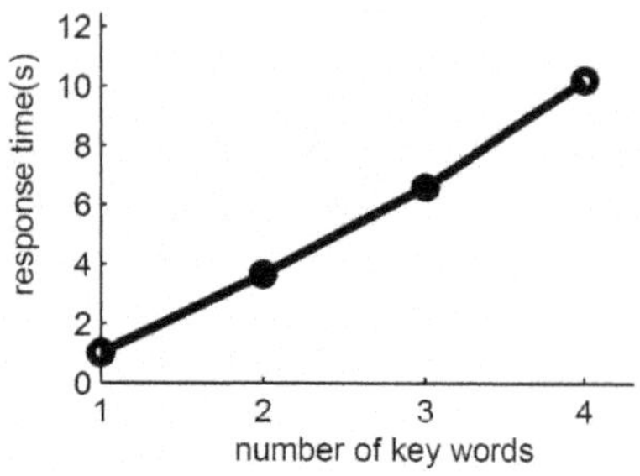

Figure 10: The system response time with different numbers of keywords.

age. Although with the color and edge descriptors, it takes 3.3Kb for each image and 3 Mb for all the 1,000 candidate images in total. This number will increase as the number of keywords increase because of the candidate images. When the number of keywords increases, more components need to be checked, which also multiples the search time. As shown in Figure 10, the time consumption is roughly linear to the number of keywords. Further optimization can be done to reduce the time consumption.

5.4 Visual Examples

In Figure 9, we show some results of JIGSAW, including the user intent which cannot be clearly expressed in the traditional text-based search engine. Such kinds of tasks cannot be accomplished in the capture-to-search mode.

6. CONCLUSIONS

We have proposed an interactive mobile visual search system which enables users to formulate their search intent through natural interaction with mobile devices. The proposed system, called JIGSAW, represents the first study on mobile visual search by taking the advantages of multimodal and multi-touch functionalities on the phone. Our experiments show that JIGSAW is an effective complement to existing mobile search applications, especially in cases where users only have partial visual features in mind for what they want to find. User's search experience on the phone is significantly improved by JIGSAW as it provides a game-like user interface for query formulation. Our future work will include: 1) deploying JIGSAW to tablet systems to create a better user experience, 2) leveraging user behaviors during interaction for better search performance, and 3) expanding entity lexicon to handle more queries.

7. REFERENCES

[1] http://www.pwc.com/gx/en/communications /review/features/mobile-data.jhtml.
[2] H. Bay, T. Tuytelaars, and L. Van Gool. SURF: speeded-up robust features. In *Proc. of ECCV*, pages 346–359, 2008.
[3] Y. Cao, H. Wang, C. Wang, Z. Li, L. Zhang, and L. Zhang. MindFinder: interactive sketch-based image search on millions of images. In *Proc. of ACM International Conference on Multimedia*, pages 1605–1608, 2010.
[4] V. Chandrasekhar, G. Takacs, D. Chen, S. Tsai, R. Grzeszczuk, and B. Girod. CHoG: Compressed histogram of gradients—a low bit-rate feature descriptor. *Proc. of IEEE International Conference on Computer Vision and Pattern Recognition*, pages 2504–2511, 2009.
[5] V. R. Chandrasekhar, S. S. Tsai, G. Takacs, D. M. Chen, N. M. Cheung, Y. Reznik, R. Vedantham, R. Grzeszczuk, and B. Girod. Low latency image retrieval with progressive transmission of CHoG descriptors. In *Proc. of ACM Multimedia Workshop on Mobile Cloud Media Computing*, pages 41–46, 2010.
[6] K. Church, B. Smyth, P. Cotter, and K. Bradley. Mobile information access: A study of emerging search behavior on the mobile internet. *ACM Transactions on the Web*, 1(1), May 2007.
[7] J. Deng, W. Dong, R. Socher, L. Li, K. Li, and L. Fei-Fei. Imagenet: a large-scale hierarchical image database. 2009.
[8] Digimarc Discover. "https://www.digimarc.com/discover/".
[9] L. Fei-Fei, R. Fergus, and P. Perona. Learning generative visual models from few training examples: an incremental bayesian approach tested on 101 object categories. *Computer Vision and Image Understanding*, 106(1):59–70, 2007.
[10] B. Frey and D. Dueck. Clustering by passing messages between data points. *Science*, 315(5814):972–976, 2007.
[11] GazoPa. http://www.gazopa.com/.
[12] Google Goggles. http://www.google.com/mobile/goggles/.
[13] G. Griffin, A. Holub, and P. Perona. Caltech-256 object category dataset. 2007.
[14] M. Jia, X. Fan, X. Xie, M. Li, and W. Ma. Photo-to-Search: Using camera phones to inquire of the surrounding world. In *Proc. of Mobile Data Management*, 2006.
[15] X. Li. Understanding the semantic structure of noun phrase queries. In *Proc. of Annual Meeting of the Association for Computational Linguistics*, pages 1337–1345, 2010.
[16] LinkMe Mobile. http://www.snapnow.co.uk/.
[17] Y. Liu, T. Mei, and X.-S. Hua. CrowdReranking: exploring multiple search engines for visual search reranking. In *Proc. of ACM SIGIR conference on Research and Development in Information Retrieval*, pages 500–507, 2009.
[18] D. Lowe. Distinctive image features from scale-invariant keypoints. *International Journal of Computer Vision*, 60(2):91–110, 2004.
[19] Y.-F. Ma and H.-J. Zhang. Contrast-based image attention analysis by using fuzzy growing. In *Proc. of ACM Multimedia*, pages 374–381, Nov 2003.
[20] G. Miller. WordNet: a lexical database for English. *Communications of the ACM*, 38(11):39–41, 1995.
[21] D. Nister and H. Stewenius. Scalable recognition with a vocabulary tree. In *Proc. of IEEE International Conference on Computer Vision and Pattern Recognition*, pages 2161–2168, 2006.
[22] NOKIA Point and Find. http://pointandfind.nokia.com/.
[23] L. R. Rabiner. A tutorial on hidden markov models and selected applications in speech recognition. *Proc. of the IEEE*, 77(2):257–286, 1989.
[24] S. Sekine, K. Sudo, and C. Nobata. Extended named entity hierarchy. In *Proc. of LREC-2002*, 2002.
[25] Smart VisualTM Kooaba. http://www.kooaba.com/.
[26] SnapTell. http://www.snaptell.com/.
[27] G. Takacs, Y. Xiong, R. Grzeszczuk, and et al. Outdoors augmented reality on mobile phone using loxel-based visual feature organization. In *Proc. of ACM International Conference on Multimedia Information Retrieval*, pages 427–434, 2008.
[28] TinEye. http://www.tineye.com/.
[29] J. Wang and X.-S. Hua. Interactive image search by color map. *ACM Trans. on Intelligent Systems and Technology*, 3(1), 2012.
[30] Xcavator. http://www.xcavator.net/.
[31] H. Xu, J. Wang, X. Hua, and S. Li. Image search by concept map. In *Proc. of ACM SIGIR conference on Research and development in information retrieval*, pages 275–282, 2010.
[32] W.-K. Yang, A. Cho, D.-S. Jeong, and W.-G. Oh. Image description and matching scheme for identical image searching. *Future Computing, Service Computation, Cognitive, Adaptive, Content, Patterns, Computation World*, pages 669–674, 2009.

Personalized Travel Recommendation by Mining People Attributes from Community-Contributed Photos

An-Jung Cheng[†], Yan-Ying Chen[†], Yen-Ta Huang[†], Winston H. Hsu[†] and Hong-Yuan Mark Liao[‡]
[†] Dept. of Computer Science and Information Engineering, National Taiwan University, Taipei, Taiwan
[‡] Institute of Information Science, Academia Sinica, Taipei, Taiwan
{anon,yanying,hyd0916}@cmlab.csie.ntu.edu.tw
winston@csie.ntu.edu.tw, liao@iis.sinica.edu.tw

ABSTRACT

Leveraging community-contributed data (e.g., blogs, GPS logs, and geo-tagged photos) for travel recommendation is one of the active researches since there are rich contexts and trip activities in such explosively growing data. In this work, we focus on personalized travel recommendation by leveraging the freely available community-contributed photos. We propose to conduct personalized travel recommendation by further considering specific user profiles or attributes (e.g., gender, age, race). In stead of mining photo logs only, we argue to leverage the automatically detected people attributes in the photo contents. By information-theoretic measures, we will demonstrate that such people attributes are informative and effective for travel recommendation – especially providing a promising aspect for personalization. We effectively mine the demographics for different locations (or landmarks) and travel paths. A probabilistic Bayesian learning framework which further entails mobile recommendation on the spot is introduced. We experiment on four million photos collected for eight major worldwide cities. The experiments confirm that people attributes are promising and orthogonal to prior works using travel logs only and can further improve prior travel recommendation methods especially in difficult predictions by further leveraging user contexts in mobile devices.

Categories and Subject Descriptors: H.4 [Information Systems Applications]: Miscellaneous; H.2.8 [Database Applications]: Data mining, Spatial databases and GIS

General Terms: Algorithms, Experimentation, Human Factors

Keywords: Personalized tourist recommendation, geo-tagged photos, route planning

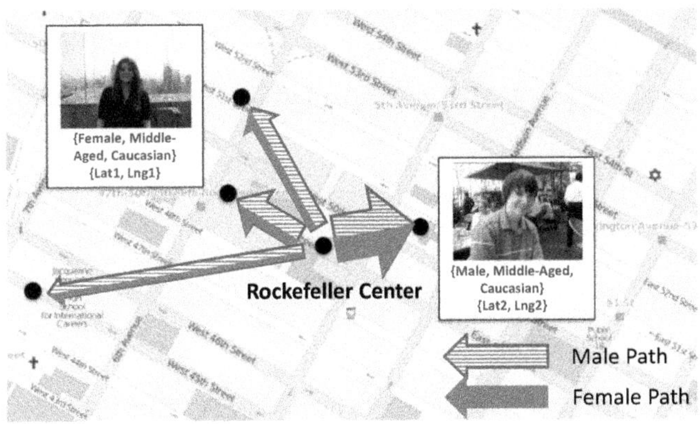

Figure 1: Community-contributed photos are freely available and with rich context information (e.g., geo-tags, time). We can mine the travel patterns for the users by associating their trips with the major landmarks. Meanwhile, we can indirectly mine demographic information (e.g., gender, race, age) from the photos along with the trips by automatically detecting people attributes in the photos. In this example, the width of an arrow denotes the travel frequency between the two locations. The color regions are proportional to the percentages of genders – male (blue) and female (red). Such minded demographic information is promising for personalized travel recommendation and planning; for example, suggesting the best route for Asian travelers in Manhattan or the next location for a family group after visiting Rockefeller Center.

1. INTRODUCTION

With the prosperity of the social media and the success of many photo-sharing websites, like Flickr and Picasa, the volume of community-contributed photos have increased drastically. Such large-scale user-contributed photos contain rich metadata information such as tags, time, and geo-locations (or geo-tags). These overwhelming amounts of context data, though noisy, is tremendously useful for many multimedia applications including annotation, searching, advertising and recommendation [15].

Among all the applications, travel recommendation has been attracted by many researchers because of the importance and the intrinsic relationship between people's everyday lives. In general, a typical travel recommendation system consists of two aspects: generic recommendation and personalized recommendation [19]. For the generic recommendation, it contains the suggested travel information for the destination given by user when he/she is planning a trip,

MM'11, November 28–December 1, 2011, Scottsdale, Arizona, USA.

which answers the question like *"I want to go to New York, what are the must-see attractions?"*. The personalized recommendation, on the other hand, takes user's profile into account such that it can provide a more appropriate recommendation result matching user preferences. Both aspects are to support route planning before the journey.

Millions of human-sensors [16] capture different aspects of the spatio-temporal information. In order to mine the travel knowledge automatically, a focus of recent interest is the use of user-contributed resources, including the textual travelogues (i.e., blogs or logs) ([10, 9, 8]) and photos taken during the trips ([2, 14]). Discovering and summarizing knowledge from these huge amount of user-contributed multimedia resources provide us useful tourist information.

However, the previous works solely consider the travel logs and ignore the rich people attributes in the photo contents. Such rich people attributes can be automatically detected and provide another important aspect regarding travel demographics (e.g., gender, race, age). Figure 1 illustrates the real attribute-oriented travel movements in our dataset in Manhattan[1]. Rather than the plain travel frequencies between certain locations, we can further investigate their demographic distributions for the people attributes, which are promising for personalized travel recommendation and planning. Meanwhile, we had observed that such (detected) people attributes are correlated with traveling between locations (cf. Section 3.2).

Additionally, based on the mined people attributes and preferred travel patterns between locations, it is able to adopt the mobile devices where the user profile and context information (e.g., geo-locations) can be easily detected from mobile sensors and further entails the "location-aware" – recommending next travel location from his/her current location or even delivering context-related advertisements or services ([4, 13]).

In this work, we focus on the personalized recommendation framework to provide not only a context-aware recommendation system (i.e., *mobile travel recommendation*) but also a *route planning* application before the journey. The personalization is achieved by adopting specific user profiles with the automatically detected people attributes (e.g., gender, age and race) along with the trips. That is, the question we want to answer is, for example, *"For a male, what is the suggested travel sequence in Rome?"* (route planning), *"I am a female, I am now at Central Park in Manhattan, what is the next suggested destination?"* (mobile travel recommendation). Although users are reluctant to reveal their true identities or profiles in the community-contributed photos, we can actually indirectly mine the demographic information about these trips from their associated photos.

In this sense, we crawl 4 millions geo-tagged photos belonging to eight major worldwide cities, adopt the people attribute detectors on the generated photo trips and then provide a probabilistic recommendation model based on the user's profiles and the travel logs information. Experiments show that the people attributes are very informative and helpful for both mobile travel recommendation and route planning. To summarize, the contributions of this paper are:

- To our best knowledge, this is the first research work that uses the additional context in the photo, i.e., people attributes, to support the personalized recommendation framework. We leverage these automatically detected people attributes in the large-scale photos for social media mining and uncover the differences in travel behaviors across demographic groups.
- We propose a probability-based personalized travel recommendation model based on user's attributes and the knowledge mined from travel logs. Such scheme is promising to apply in mobile environment. (Section 7)
- We conduct the experiments on eight major cities in the world and show that using people's attributes has the potential to improve the personalized travel recommendation, especially in the location where people have diverse choices of the next stops. (Section 9)

[1]Note that the photos in the paper are courtesy of Flickr users under the Creative Commons License.

The remainder of this paper is structured as follows. In the next section, we discuss the related work. Section 3 are some attribute-related characteristics on photo trips and our system overview is described in Section 4. Section 5 introduces people attribute detection scheme. The proposed recommendation algorithms and the application are mainly in Section 6, Section 7 and Section 8. The experimental results and discussions are reported in Section 9, followed by the conclusion in Section 10.

2. RELATED WORK

Trip mining and recommendation has been shown important in recent years. Generally, the data sources for learning to recommend can be roughly classified into three categories: GPS trajectory data, travelogues (i.e., blogs), and geo-tagged photos.

GPS trajectory data which obtained by GPS receivers are mainly used at the early stage. Zheng et al. [18, 19, 20] utilize GPS trajectory data to extract the interesting locations, classical travel sequences and provide a personalized friend and location recommender using the similarity of users in terms of their location histories. The main obstacle for trajectories-based method is that the data resources is not easy to obtain from a large number of people.

[10, 9, 8] provide location-based travel recommendation which analyzes the blogs to obtain trip-related knowledge. [10] emphasizes on the mining of city landmarks by a graph-based method. [9] proposes a probabilistic topic model which discovers topics from travelogues and then represents locations with appropriate topics for further destination recommendation and summarization. The goal of [8] is to automatically recognize and rank the landmarks for travelers. They use geo-tag information, metadata of photos and user knowledge in Yahoo! Travel Guide to identify and rank landmarks for any location specified by the travelers. The travelogue-based method has the difficulty in determining the certain location of travelogues which are usually unstructured and contain much noisy metadata. They only play a role of destination recommendation which merely shows the information about a location.

Recently, there is an increasing tendency to adopt the information from geo-tagged photos. Crandall et al. [7] systematically adopt large-scale photos to discover important landmarks. They evaluate on many cities and indicate that the time-stamped and geo-tagged photos will construct the typical pathways of people movements. Arase et

Table 1: Relationship of people attribute and travel patterns measured by entropy and mutual information in 5 locations sampled from 5 major worldwide cities. Taking the nearest five locations (indexed by j) into considerations, as starting from location i, the entropy for the uniform choice is $H(L_{i \to j}) = 2.3219$. We show how the entropy (uncertainties in choosing next visiting location) will be reduced as introducing mined (from community-contributed photos) knowledges. Here F denotes the calculated visiting frequencies between location i and j from the photo trips (cf. Figure 4(d)); A denotes the (detected) people attributes along with the photo trips. We can see that the people attributes (A) are promising to predict travel locations $L_{i \to j}$. See more explanations in Section 3.2.

City	Location i	$H(L_{i \to j})$	$H(L_{i \to j}\|F)$	$H(L_{i \to j}\|A, F)$	$I(L_{i \to j}; A\|F)$
Manhattan	Madison Square	2.3219	1.9911	1.4582	0.5329
Rome	Castel Sant'Angelo	2.3219	1.8909	1.0068	0.8841
Berlin	Marx-Engels Forum	2.3219	0.8281	0.1883	0.6397
Barcelona	Casa de la Caritat	2.3219	0.9751	0.3907	0.5844
Taipei	Xinyi Square	2.3219	1.9796	0.8566	1.1229

al. [2] define the problem of photo trip pattern mining and show an application with which users can search frequent trip patterns given some preferences (e.g., destination, visit duration, trip theme). Although they also provide a similar route planning framework, the recommendation level is inter-cities, while our work is based on the intra-cities level for a one-day trip recommendation in a specific city. Most of all, we can further recommend travel routes satisfying the designated user profiles (e.g., gender, age, race) by leveraging people attributes in the user-contributed photos; for example, the best one-day trip in Manhattan for the Asian girls.

Another similar work is [14], which uses geo-tagged photos and textual blogs information on landmark generation, path discovering, and route planning. They merge incomplete paths inside a destination to suggest tourists with typical travel paths and stay times in a destination. For route planning, they model as a graph analysis problem and use dynamic programming as the solver. We also have the similar processes and extract travel patterns the from pictures but we want to emphasize that the major difference between our work and other related researches described above is that we bring in the concept of people attributes in the travel photos and consider these demographic information with the movements of photographer into a personalized travel recommendation framework. Besides, we have fundamentally different definitions on the travel patterns. That is, the travel patterns in this study are measured from the face detection results and further augmented by the face attributes (e.g., gender, age, race) extracted from the photos. By this novel aspect, we can mine more human attributes for effective travel personalization. For example, we will have the travel preferences about Caucasian males or Asian kids. Additionally, in the previous researches (e.g., [14, 2]), the travel patterns are defined over travel objects such as landmarks, events only. We will demonstrate in the next section that such automatically detected people attributes are informative for mobile travel recommendation and route planning.

3. OBSERVATIONS

3.1 Rich People Attributes in User-Contributed Photos

Using geo-tagged and time-stamped photos from social media as a resource for travel information mining have attracted a lot of researchers in recent years (e.g., [7, 2, 14, 5]). These large amounts of photo trajectories not only reveal the users' travel movements but are also promising for mining the demographic information about the locations by detecting people attributes on the photos. Authors in [1] have shown that users are willing to share photos for organization and (social) communication purposes – especially for travel photos. Meanwhile, such photos can be treated as the *social pixels* by travelers' cameras among travel locations (cf. Figure 1) [16]. It is promising to leverage such freely available user-contributed photos and further detect important people attributes. However, the previous works only focus on the statistics of the travel logs such as the popularity of locations but neglected the important and rich dimension of people attributes.

Meanwhile, in [11] Kumar et al. exploited the community-contributed photos for learning facial attributes (e.g., gender, age and race) which contribute to mining people attributes in large-scale media. Such rich attributes are shown having reasonable accuracy (>80%) for further applications. Therefore, we propose an approach to enable personalized travel recommendation by mining the parameterizing factors directly and automatically from the community-contributed photos – especially emphasizing on the (automatically) detected people attributes from the photos.

3.2 Correlation between Travel Patterns and People Attributes

By intuition, we know that some landmarks are female-favored, and some are male-favored. So are by other attributes such as race, age. Here we want to use entropy and mutual information [6] to measure the correlation between predicting next travel location and people attributes. The mutual information $I(X;Y)$ between two random variables X and Y is defined as follows:

$$I(X;Y) = H(X) - H(X|Y), \qquad (1)$$

where entropy $H(X)$ measures the uncertainty with a random variable X. The entropy reduction as introducing another random variable (i.e., Y) is the mutual information $I(X;Y)$ between the two random variables. Intuitively, the reduction means the help that random variable Y brings for predicting X.

Measured by entropy and mutual information and illustrated in Table 1, we demonstrate the relationship of people attributes and travel patterns in 5 locations sampled from 5 major worldwide cities. Taking the nearest five locations (indexed by j) into considerations as starting from location i, the entropy for the uniform choice is $H(L_{i\to j}) = 2.3219$. We will show how the entropy (uncertainties in choosing next visiting location) will be reduced as introducing mined (from community-contributed photos) knowledges. Here F denotes the calculated visiting frequencies between location i and j from the photo trips (cf. Figure 4(d)); A denotes the (detected) people attributes along with the photo trips; we use gender (i.e., male and female) only in this measurement. Thus, $H(L_{i\to j}|F)$[2] denotes the entropy of predicting the next location as given the mined travel frequencies (F). It is apparent that, from $H(L_{i\to j}|F)$, the mined travel frequency (F) helps choosing (recommending) the next travel location from the current one. Further introducing the people attributes (A), the recommendation will be more accurate; that is, salient entropy reduction is shown in $H(L_{i\to j}|A, F)$. Note that $I(L_{i\to j}; A|F) = H(L_{i\to j}|F) - H(L_{i\to j}|A, F)$, as depicted in the last column.

Taking Madison Square in Manhattan as an example (cf. the first row in Table 1), the mutual information $I(L_{i\to j}; A|F)$ is 0.5329 (bits), the reduction is about 25% of the entropy when given the people attributes (A). To interpret that intuitively, we can illustrate like this, if there are 4 random choices for the next destination, after knowing the people attribute (e.g., for the male only), the number of choice is down to 3. Therefore, we can see that the people attributes (A) have quite correlations with predicting travel locations $L_{i\to j}$. In this paper, we will show how to leverage such automatically mined people attributes for personalized travel recommendation.

4. SYSTEM OVERVIEW

Figure 2 shows the architecture of our system, which is divided into four main parts. At first, in order to mine the travel information within each city, we crawl the photos from the on-line photo-sharing websites (i.e., Flickr). We then use a mean-shift based method on geo-locations of these photos to generate the important locations on each city (Section 6.2) for the following user trip mining process. For the trip attribute pattern mining, the faces in the photos are firstly detected. The attributes are generated by applying people attribute detectors (Section 5).

Travel paths and locations mined from the community-contributed photos also contain rich people attributes from the detected people. For instance, if many faces in this location are detected as male, this destination is probably favored by male. This phenomenon can also be found in travel paths. We can further identify the demographic information (via people attributes) within travel paths by analyzing the associated photos. By mining the travel patterns users' day trips (Section 6.3), we propose two personalized travel recommendation applications – mobile travel recommendation (Section 7) and route planning (Section 8), which are further entailed by a probability Bayesian model and dynamic programming techniques.

Concept Definition

We first define some concepts used in the following sections:
Photo collections All the geo-tagged photos in the database. (i.e., all the points in Figure 4(a)).
Destination *Destinations* are the popular or important locations in a city, e.g., Brooklyn bridge in Manhattan, Colosseum in Rome, and Brandenburg Gate in Berlin. (i.e., the red point in Figure 4(c)).

[2]The detailed deviations can be referred to Section 7.

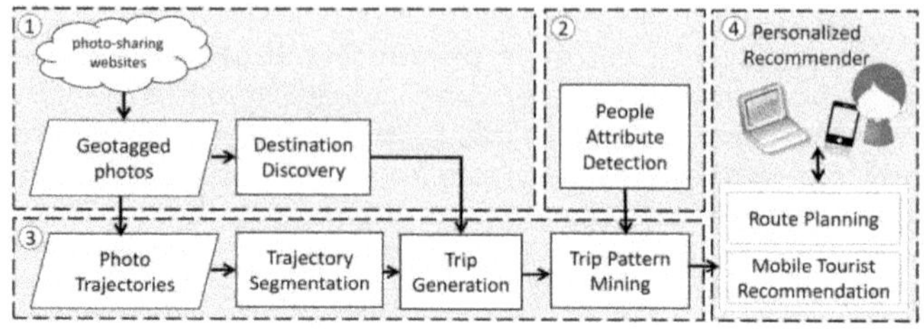

Figure 2: System Diagram: There are four main components. The first part contains data crawling process and destination generation (Section 6.2). After that, people attribute (i.e., gender, age, race) detection is applied on each photo (Section 5). The next step is the trip generation process and the attribute information of each trip is inferred by the detected faces in the trip (Section 6.3). Combined with the people attributes and the travel logs, we can build an personalized tourist recommender, such as mobile travel recommendation (Section 7) and route planning (Section 8).

Trajectory A collection of time series geo-tagged photos for a specific photographer.
Path & Route *Path* refers to a sequence of time series geo-tagged photos traversed by a user in one specific day (i.e., Figure 4(b)). After quantizing the geo-tagged photos to *destinations*, the results are defined as *route* (i.e., Figure 4(c)).
Trip An individual user's *trip* is the *route* with attribute information (i.e., Figure 4(d)).
Trip Segment A *trip segment* is a tuple with (start location, end location, attributes) and is a part of the *trip*. We will take the trip segments as major knowledge sources (or observed data) for mobile travel recommendation and route planning.

5. PEOPLE ATTRIBUTE DETECTION

In this work, we utilize nine people attributes including two gender attributes (female, male), four age attributes (kid, teen, middle-aged, elder) and three race attributes (Caucasian, African, Asian) to profile the travel preference of users. Currently, we only focus on the facial attributes since they represent rich information of people and can be learned through an adaptive framework [11]. Considering the scalability to deal with the increasing number of facial attributes, [11] proposes a generic framework for learning varying facial attributes adaptively. To begin with, we crawl the user-contributed photos from Flickr and extract the facial region by face detector. Further, the face images are decomposed into face components for learning and constructing a mid-level feature bank (by SVM) to describe varying facial attributes. Finally, Adaboost is conducted to select the most important mid-level feature set for the designated facial attribute.

5.1 Preprocessing

To construct a training dataset naturally with rich and diverse images close to real life, we crawl training images from social media (Flickr) containing abundant user-contributed photos. Moreover, the facial region is extracted from the

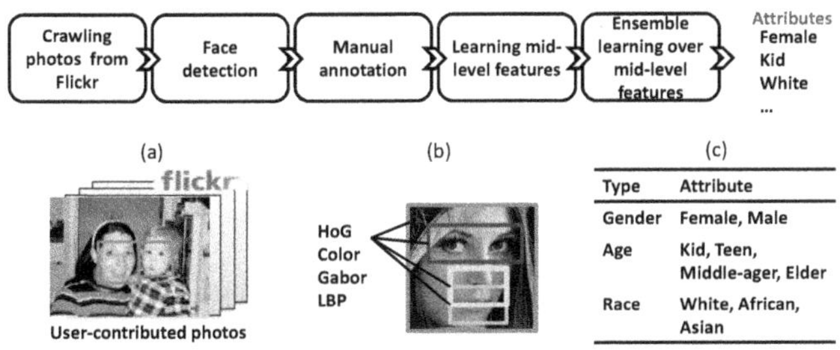

Figure 3: The framework of facial attribute detection: (a) crawling the user-contributed photos from social media and extracting the facial region by face detection to prepare the training images; (b) manually annotating the facial images for learning mid-level features by SVM; (c) utilizing Adaboost to learn the best combination of mid-level features for describing different facial attributes respectively.

whole image by face detection (cf. Figure 3(a)) and further applied facial feature detection [17] to locate important parts of a face such as eyes, philtrum and mouth. Features (e.g., edge, color, texture) extracted from different facial components pose different discriminating abilities across facial attributes. Therefore, we construct a mid-level feature bank based on those facial components for providing better generalization capability to deal with various facial attributes.

5.2 Mid-level Features

The preprocessed facial images are annotated manually as the training data to learn the mid-level features. A mid-level feature (Figure 3(b)) is a SVM classifier [3] with varying low-level features (e.g., Gabor filter, HoG, Color, Local Binary Patterns) extracted from different face components (e.g., whole face, eyes, philtrum, mouth). Those combinations constitute a feature bank to provide possible mid-level features required by facial attributes. Rather than using low-level features, mid-level features have better semantic meanings for describing facial attributes through multiple modalities. Note that, unlike image object classification, randomly selecting the images from other categories (attributes) as negative training data is impractical since attributes are often partially correlated such as female and Asian. Hence we simply group the attributes into several attribute type, for example, the attribute type "age" includes kid, teen, middle-ager and elder. Since the attributes with the same attribute type are mutually exclusive, thus providing negative training images with better discriminating capability. For example, we acquire the negative training images of kid attribute from the rest of the attributes belonging to the same attribute type (e.g., teen, middle-ager and elder).

5.3 Ensemble Learning for Different Attributes

For a facial attribute, the best combination of mid-level features is learned by Adaboost (Figure 3(c)). Here, we treat each mid-level feature as a weak classifier. The combined strong classifier represents the most important parts of that attribute, for example, <whole face, Gabor> is most effective for female attribute while <whole face, color> is most effective for African attribute. The important mid-level feature set for the designed facial attribute is adaptively selected and weighted through the boosting scheme. Experimenting in the benchmark data [11], the approach can effectively detect facial attributes and achieve more than 80% accuracy on the average. Meanwhile, the framework is generic for various facial attributes thus providing better scalability to precisely profile users for more attributes.

6. PHOTO TRIP GENERATION

The trip generation is a challenging problem because of the various trip types (e.g., itinerary durations) and different travel behaviors across demographic groups. We adopt the common frameworks, e.g., [14, 2], to mine the trips from the (noisy) user-contributed geo-tagged photos and further consider the people attributes in the photos. We conduct three main procedures: path extraction, destination discovery, and trip attribute pattern mining, to extract the observations (in trip segments between destinations) to be further incorporated in the next recommendation model.

We first use the time information in the photos to segment the *trajectories* from each user. These segments are with the limitation in one-day that can be seen as the one-day *paths* in the given city. The next processing is about the destination discovering because we try to map these uninformative *paths* into a higher level, i.e., *routes* which are based on the detected *destinations*. The next challenge is to give the attribute knowledge into the *routes*, resulting in the informative *trips*. These *trips* can be separated into *trips segments* and then will become the inputs in our proposed travel recommendation.

We emphasize here that, although people may visit places as a couple or group and usually not alone, in this beginning stage for proving the novel concept by leveraging people attributes in the photos for personalized recommendation, we focus on the individual travelers in this study first and we believe it can be extended to group travelers by further investigations; for example, conducting face clustering in the original travel patterns.

6.1 Path Extraction

We sort photos by the captured time for each user. The one-day paths are then detected by separating the sorted photos according to their date information. Also, we adopt the soft assignment to the photos which are at the boundary between two days, that is, we make each boundary photo belong to two paths, one is its original date path, another is the previous date path in order to handle the case that if a user's trip is across the midnight. The result paths are shown in Figure 4 (b).

6.2 Destination Discovering and Route Mapping

Because the generated paths are too noisy and complicated to mine the information, the next task is to refine these paths to a more informative level, *routes*, by quantizing the photos into the destinations. In the beginning, we apply mean-shift clustering procedure on the geo-tagged photos for each city, where each photo is represented by latitude and longitude coordinates, to discover the locations with high photo densities. Empirically, for mean-shift method, we use a flat kernel function and set the bandwidth parameter as 0.001, which is roughly the radius of a landmark, as mentioned in [12, 5, 7]. We use clusters containing at least 0.1% photos in the city and no less than 100 photos as destina-

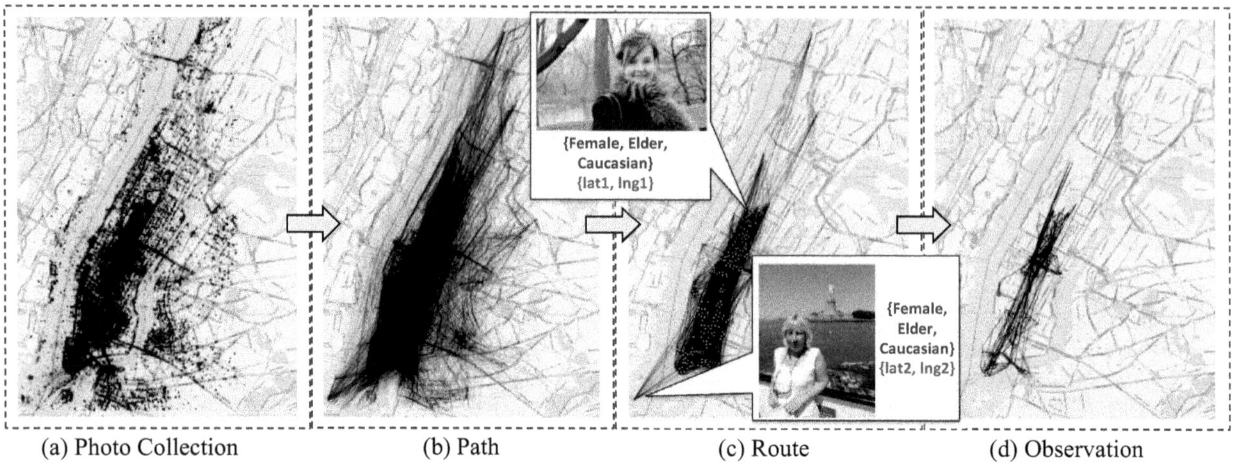

Figure 4: The photo trip generation process illustrated in Manhattan collection. (a) The collection of geo-tagged photos; each dot is the place where the photo is taken. After separating by date information on the photos for each user, the resulted travel *path*, which connects its photo sequences of the same user, is shown in (b). However, these noisy path trajectories are not informative. In (c), we first cluster these geo-tagged photos as *destinations*, representing locations of interests in the city and also marked as red points; we then quantize the paths into these discovered destinations as *routes*. The two photos are the examples for geo-tagged photos along with the trips, which contain the people attributes (i.e., gender, age, race) and the geo-location information (i.e., Lat for latitude, Lng for longitude) and can be further utilized to mine the relationship between attributes and travel behaviors. The *trips* with people attributes are shown in (d) which will finally become the learning data in our recommendation model. (Best seen in color)

tions. The red points in Figure 4 (c) illustrate the detected destinations on Manhattan via this procedure.

The path sequences of all users now can be translated into destination sequences, i.e., *routes*, by assigning the photo to the nearest destination if the distance between them is under a given threshold.

6.3 Trip Attribute Pattern Mining

A photographer can be seen as a human-sensor [16]; hence each detected face in the photos reveals not only the trip but also an observed people attributes. Besides, the detected face can be regarded as an individual sharing the same movements with this photographer. That is, we propagate the same movements from photographer to all the faces in the taken photos. For instance, given that there is a route sequence $(A \rightarrow B \rightarrow C)$ which is generated by an user. A, B, and C are the traversed destinations sequentially. All the detected faces in this route will all own the same route sequences and then result in many trips according to the face number. Although these trips have the same movement sequence, they might have different attributes based on the detection on the faces. Besides, all the trips generated from this route sequence will contain trip segments (e.g., $(A \rightarrow B)$ and $(B \rightarrow C)$ in this example). These trip segments are treated as the atomic references as the observation data for learning and recommendation later.

Formally, we define the trip T containing n destinations for a specific person (i.e., detected face) $u \in \mathbf{U}$ (i.e., $\mathbf{U}$ is the set of users) as $T_u = (L_{1_u} \rightarrow L_{2_u} \rightarrow ... \rightarrow L_{n_u}, \mathbf{A_u})$ where $L_{i_u} \in \mathbf{L}$ (i.e., $\mathbf{L}$ is the set of destinations) is the sequentially traversed destinations of user u and $\mathbf{A_u}$ is a tuple containing the detected attributes such as gender and age. For example, in Figure 4 (c), the two photos have the same (detected) attributes (female, elder, Caucasian), where each dimension represents the gender, age, and race accordingly.

7. TOURIST RECOMMENDATION MODEL

For personalized recommendation, we tackle the following scenario: "I am a male, and I am at Central Park now. What is the next suggested destination for me?" Obviously, the inputs of this framework include the target user u's profile A_u, composed of known people attributes, u's present location L_i, and the output is the recommended next destination L_j.

To recommend the optimal next destination L^*, this problem can be formulated as follows:

$$L^* = argmax_{L_j} P(L_j | A_u, L_i, \mathbf{\Theta}) \;\; \mathbf{\Theta} = \{\mathbf{F}, \mathbf{A}\}, \quad (2)$$

where $\mathbf{\Theta}$ is our learned tourist model composed of the travel frequencies between the destinations ($\mathbf{F}$) and detected attributes in photos ($\mathbf{A}$). Intuitively, we will recommend the proper destination that most tourists visit and matches the target user's profile A_u. That is why we need to mine both $\mathbf{F}$ and $\mathbf{A}$, the existing travel preferences among the destinations, from the large-scale community-contributed photos.

Until now, we have the trips with attribute patterns $T_{u \in \mathbf{U}} = (L_{1_u} \rightarrow L_{2_u} \rightarrow ... \rightarrow L_{n_u}, \mathbf{A_u})$. And each trip $T_{u \in \mathbf{U}}$ can be regarded as a sequence of trip segments as described above and which then become the observation dataset of our recommendation model.

This section describes a way of constructing the learning tourist knowledge that takes two factors into account: (1) the sequence correlation between destinations ($P(L_{i \rightarrow j})$ or denoted as $P(L_{ij})$), and (2) the people attribute patterns on the movements ($P(A|L_{ij})$).

7.1 Bayesian Learning Model

We adopt Bayesian learning model as our recommendation model because Bayesian has shown effective in recommendation systems and, most importantly, it can be applied for real-time mobile recommendation and immediate route planning service. It is the first attempt for us and can be replaced by any other recommendation models. By Bayes' theorem, the probability that the location L_j is the suggested destination given a start location L_i and the attribute value $\mathbf{A_u}$ of a specific user u is:

$$P(L_{i\to j}|\mathbf{A_u}) = \frac{P(L_{i\to j},\mathbf{A_u})}{P(\mathbf{A_u})} = \frac{P(L_{i\to j})P(\mathbf{A_u}|L_{i\to j})}{P(\mathbf{A_u})}, \quad (3)$$

where $P(L_{i\to j})$ is the probability that moving from location L_i to location L_j. Intuitively, it is equivalent to that we choose L_i as a start location (with the probability $P(L_i)$) (i.e., given L_i) and then transit to L_j (with the probability $P(L_j|L_i)$) and can be jointly formulated as $P(L_i)P(L_j|L_i)$. Therefore, the Equation 3 will become

$$P(L_{i\to j}|\mathbf{A_u}) = \frac{P(L_i)P(L_j|L_i)P(\mathbf{A_u}|L_{i\to j})}{P(\mathbf{A_u})} \quad (4)$$

In other words, based on the target user profile and his current location and given the observation data $\mathbf{\Theta} = \{\mathbf{F},\mathbf{A}\}$, the optimal prediction of next location is the destination L^* such that Equation 4 is maxmized,

$$L^* = argmax_L\{P(L_j|L_i)P(\mathbf{A_u}|L_{i\to j})\} \quad (5)$$

We assume the independence between different types of attributes (i,e,. gender and race are independent), such that the joint probability $P(\mathbf{A_u}|L_{i\to j})$ can be further expressed as the product of the marginals,

$$L^* = argmax_L\{P(L_j|L_i)\prod_{a_u\in\mathbf{A_u}} P(a_u|L_{i\to j})\} \quad (6)$$

The a_u is one of the tuple of $\mathbf{A_u}$ (i.e., gender). $P(a_u|L_{i\to j})$ and $P(L_j|L_i)$ in the product above are easy to be estimated from the frequencies of the training corpus (i.e., observation data):

$$P(a_u|L_{i\to j}) = \frac{count(L_{i\to j} \wedge \mathbf{A_u} = a_u)}{count(L_{i\to j})} \quad (7)$$

$$P(L_j|L_i) = \frac{count(L_{i\to j})}{\sum_{j\in\mathbf{L}} count(L_{i\to j})} \quad (8)$$

The $count(L_{i\to j})$ is the total number of observations that start at L_i and end at L_j. Similarly, The $count(L_{i\to j} \wedge \mathbf{A_u} = a_u)$ is the total number of observations that start at L_i and end at L_j with the attribute a_u.

7.2 Background Smoothing

We cannot ignore the possibility that the user will be in the location or want to go to the location that beyond our observed travel logs. For example, if a male is now in L_i, and there is no male which starts from L_i to any other locations in the historical data, we cannot predict the next location for this user due to the zero probability. Therefore, in order to deal with the unobserved events, we need to add a smoothing factor in the probabilistic model. Intuitively, we take destination popularity into consideration for the location correlation. This information is obtained from the destination generation process for each location L_j. The background probability is defined by,

$$P_{C.L}(L_j) = \frac{number\ of\ photos\ in\ the\ destination\ L_j}{number\ of\ photos\ in\ the\ city\ C} \quad (9)$$

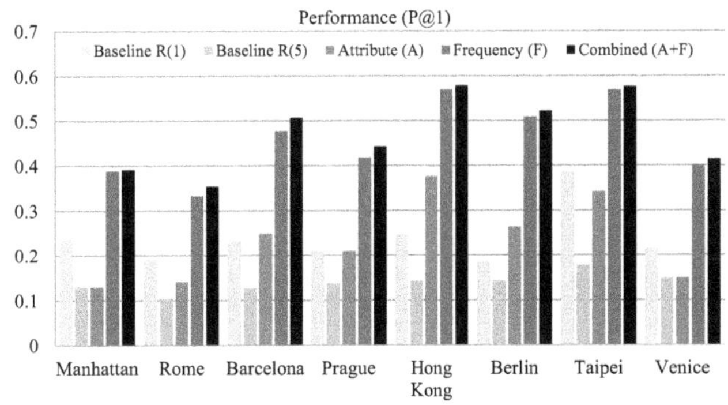

Figure 5: Mobile recommendation performance of different methods on eight worldwide cities. The knowledge-based methods, i.e., frequency (F), attribute (A), and combined (F+A), perform better than naively choose the first near location (R(1)) or the top 5 nearest (R(5)). Best seen in color.

For attribute probability, we use the city C's background attribute information to smooth the attribute effect.

$$P_{C.A}(a_k) = \frac{number\ of\ people\ with\ the\ attribute\ a_k}{number\ of\ people\ in\ this\ city\ C} \quad (10)$$

It must be noted that the background information of attributes is based on the detected faces, which may include the trips staying in the same location (i.e., it generates no trip segment) or the faces in the photos which does not quantizing into destinations.

We adopt a linear interpolation of the maximum likelihood model with the collection background information, using the coefficient α and β to control the influence of background model.

When we substitute Equation (9), (10) into Equation (6), we get the following final estimate for the joint probability:

$$L^* = argmax_L\{((1-\alpha)P(L_j|L_i) + \alpha P_{C.L}(L_j)) \prod_{a_k\in\mathbf{A_u}} ((1-\beta)P(\mathbf{a_k}|L_{ij}) + \beta P_{C.A}(\mathbf{a_k}))\}. \quad (11)$$

To avoid floating-point underflow when computing products of probabilities, all of the computations are in log-space.

Because the term $((1-\alpha)P(L_j|L_i)+\alpha P_{C.L}(L_j))$ considers the "frequency" of movements between locations, the recommendation using this probability is regarded as *frequency-based method* (F). Similarly, using the term $\prod_{a_k\in\mathbf{A_u}}((1-\beta)P(\mathbf{a_k}|L_{ij})+\beta P_{C.A}(\mathbf{a_k}))$ in recommendation is the *attribute-based method* (A). The combination of the F and A (i.e., Equation 11) is denoted as "F+A".

8. ROUTE PLANNING

The *route planning* problem can be treated like this: starting from location L_s and ending at location L_e, we want to go through N interesting destinations, and we have designated profile (or attributes) A_u (e.g., male).

We can take the graph-based method to solve the problem. A graph is generally composed of nodes, edges, and the weights on the edges. **Nodes**: each destination in the city is a node in the graph. **Edges**: The edge connects two nodes. From our learning model, we can calculate score of edges from the paths connecting the two destinations, however, parameterized by the user profile A_u. Because we want

Table 2: The 4 million geo-referenced photos collected from eight major cities in the world.

City	Images	Trips with face	Face in trips	Trip Segments
Manhattan	718,194	1,621	5,871	26,734
Rome	494,483	523	1,684	12,289
Barcelona	538,027	467	1,523	6,108
Prague	289,304	304	857	6,326
Hong Kong	446,813	379	1,393	4,316
Berlin	530,298	294	778	3,639
Taipei	579,033	585	3,242	3,658
Venice	334,513	199	606	3,140
Total	3,930,665	4,372	15,954	66,210

to go through popular landmarks rather than obscure ones, $P(L_i)$ should be placed into consideration. The other factor is the distance between candidate destinations; users do not prefer a devious journey, so we need a penalty function to diminish the overall route distance. Besides, we do not want to visit a destination twice, so we add the constraint that if the destination has been visited, the weight connecting the destination (from the current destination) is 0. Thus the weights for the edges can be formulated as:

$$s_{ij} = \begin{cases} 0 & , \textit{if } j \textit{ was visited} \\ P(L_i)P(L_{ij}|A_u) + \frac{\omega}{1+dist(L_i,L_j)}, & \textit{otherwise} \end{cases} \tag{12}$$

where $dist(L_i, L_j)$ is the geo-distance between destination L_i and L_j. The former term can be derived from Section 7. The latter term, $\frac{\omega}{1+dist(L_i,L_j)}$, is a penalty function of distance, and ω is the weight for this penalty function.

Because of the smoothing technique mentioned in Section 7.2, it is a fully connected and directed graph. The route planning problem is to recommend best travel route from L_s to L_e via N other destinations. We define the route R as:

$$R = \{r_0, r_1, ..., r_N, r_{N+1}, \} \tag{13}$$

where r_i is the i-th destination of the route R. By definition, $r_0 = L_s$, and $r_{N+1} = L_e$. In addition, s_{ij} is the score from destination i to j. We will locate a route that connecting the starting and ending destinations that maximize the scores among the traversed edges. Thus, the route we want to find is:

$$R^* = argmax_R\{\sum_{k=0}^{N} s_{r_k r_{k+1}}\} \tag{14}$$

Therefore, the route problem can be treated as the shortest path problem. In our constructed graph, the path with the highest score is the route we expect for recommendation. As mentioned in Section 7.2, we can get L^*, which is the maximum score between current and the next destination given A_u (designated user profile). Hence we can solve this problem by dynamic programming to derive the best route.

9. EXPERIMENTS

Our dataset was collected by downloading images and photo metadata using Flickr API for the major cities such as Manhattan, Rome and Barcelona. Each city's boundary can be determined by the Wikimapia[3], which is an on-line collaboratively map service containing the user-contributed geographic coordinates. We first issue a roughly rectangle boundary query and then use the precise boundary information to remove the photos outside the city. Table 2 summarizes the dataset statistics. These real travel logs are practical for interpreting the performance (by accuracy) of our recommendation algorithm. Although there are total about 4 millions images, we only experiment on the trips which contain detected attributes, i.e., those trips with face detected. In total, there are about 16K faces in the 4,372 trips as shown in the third and fourth columns in Table 2. The observations $(L_i, L_j, \mathbf{A})$ are generated by separating each trip into segments and duplicating these segments according to the detected face number in the trip. That is, faces belonging to the same trip share the same observations but have different attribute information (Section 6). Without loss of generality, we discard the trip segments not including in at least 2 different people.

For the processing time of our framework, the backend processes, including people attribute detection, trip generation, and learning prediction model are all in the off-line procedures which can be separated into different data splits and tasks to be processed in the distributed computation framework (e.g., Hadoop/MapReduce). The efficiency of the on-line recommendation scenarios can be easily achieved by the proposed Bayesian probability model. For on-line time cost, we measured on four randomly selected cities using the non-optimized MATLAB codes. On the average, it takes 0.0032 (sec) for personalized mobile recommendation. For route planning, we issued 5 queries per city, with randomly selected start/end locations and fixed 3 destinations in the midway; the averaged computation time is 3.5076 (sec).

9.1 Mobile Travel Recommendation

The first experiment is designed to verify the performance of our probability model on travel recommendation. We adopt a 5-fold cross-validation approach for the experiment. That is, the observations (i.e., the combination of $(L_i, L_j, \mathbf{A})$) are first split into 5 folds; 5 iterations of training and testing are performed; the training set contain 4 folds iteratively. Instances in the testing fold are excluded if their initial locations are not seen in the training set because they can not benefit from the recommendation model. For the background smoothing factors, α and β, we conduct a sensitivity test which varies the parameters by increments of 0.1 between 0 and 1. The best performance is measured by the average cross-validation accuracy, which is defined by *precision at one (P@1)* for the recommended destination. We set the parameters as those performed the best in this experiment.

In our experiment, we consider three kinds of people attributes, i.e., gender, age, and race, where gender $\in$ {male, female}, age $\in$ {elder, middle-aged, teenager, kid}, and race $\in$ {Caucasian, African, Asian}. For each kind of attribute, we apply the detectors for an input face and assign this face to the class with the highest score. Take gender as an example; if the score from male detector is higher than female's, this face will be classified as a male.

For measuring the frequency of attributes in Equation 7, it just needs to count on how many peoples in the same movement sequence having the same attribute value a_u (e.g., $a_u = male$).

9.1.1 Impact of Background Smoothing

The trade-off parameters α and β in the proposed algorithm influence the relative contribution from the background destination popularity and the people's attribute dis-

[3]www.wikimapia.org

Table 3: Improvements in P@1 for mobile travel recommendation across eight worldwide cities by exploiting the mined travel patterns and people attributes. R(5) is the baseline that recommends randomly choosing the top 5 nearest destinations. F represents the method which considers the visiting frequency between locations only. F+A combines the people attributes mined from photos and the F-based method. The mined knowledges, either travel frequencies and people attributes, both are helpful for mobile travel recommendation. We further categorize the city locations into different classes determined by prediction entropy $H(L_{ij}) = H(P(L_{i \to j}))$, measured in the collection and predicting by the travel frequencies only. The entropy $H(L_{ij})$ is higher as more diverse and hard choices for recommending the next travel destination. As observed, the relative gain between F and F+A (cf. the sixth and the last columns) increase for the difficult predictions.

City	Entropy	R(5)	F	F+A	F vs. F+A (%)	City	Entropy	R(5)	F	F+A	F vs. F+A (%)
Manhattan	$H(L_{ij}) \geq 0$	0.13	0.39	0.39	0.5	Hong Kong	$H(L_{ij}) \geq 0$	0.14	0.57	0.58	1.6
	$H(L_{ij}) \geq 1$	0.13	0.35	0.35	0.6		$H(L_{ij}) \geq 1$	0.14	0.41	0.43	4.6
	$H(L_{ij}) \geq 2$	0.11	0.28	0.28	0.03		$H(L_{ij}) \geq 2$	-	-	-	-
Rome	$H(L_{ij}) \geq 0$	0.10	0.33	0.35	6.5	Berlin	$H(L_{ij}) \geq 0$	0.14	0.51	0.52	2.6
	$H(L_{ij}) \geq 1$	0.10	0.28	0.30	8.5		$H(L_{ij}) \geq 1$	0.12	0.39	0.41	6.0
	$H(L_{ij}) \geq 2$	0.09	0.23	0.25	8.5		$H(L_{ij}) \geq 2$	0.08	0.28	0.32	13.5
Barcelona	$H(L_{ij}) \geq 0$	0.13	0.48	0.51	6.4	Taipei	$H(L_{ij}) \geq 0$	0.18	0.57	0.58	1.3
	$H(L_{ij}) \geq 1$	0.12	0.38	0.41	9.6		$H(L_{ij}) \geq 1$	0.16	0.43	0.44	1.7
	$H(L_{ij}) \geq 2$	0.12	0.26	0.30	14.7		$H(L_{ij}) \geq 2$	-	-	-	-
Prague	$H(L_{ij}) \geq 0$	0.14	0.42	0.44	6.1	Venice	$H(L_{ij}) \geq 0$	0.15	0.40	0.41	3.5
	$H(L_{ij}) \geq 1$	0.14	0.38	0.41	6.4		$H(L_{ij}) \geq 1$	0.14	0.37	0.38	4.5
	$H(L_{ij}) \geq 2$	0.10	0.30	0.30	-0.2		$H(L_{ij}) \geq 2$	0.11	0.29	0.30	3.5

tributions in each city. We find that for most of the cities, i.e., Manhattan, Rome, Barcelona, the optimal α is below 0.4, except for Hong Kong that has a higher α value (0.8). This phenomenon probably is caused by the sparse distribution of the observation data of Hong Kong such that most of the destinations have few faces detected. For other cities, the trips spread out well over the destinations, and can accurately predict using the training corpus.

9.1.2 The Recommendation Performance

Figure 5 shows the performance of the destination recommendation. We compare our knowledge-based methods with two baselines which randomly recommend the next destination by the top 1 (i.e., R(1)) or top 5 (i.e., R(5)) nearest destinations. The baselines are intuitive and proper because usually people will choose the nearby location as their next destination. As observed, the knowledge-based methods (i.e., frequency, combined) outperform the two baselines over 20% with respect to P@1. The method with attribute only sometimes performs worse than top 1 random due to the dense location distribution in these cities, incorporating the attribute into frequency factors generally increases the performance, which indicates that the attributes indeed bring up additional benefits besides those travel frequencies between destinations.

9.2 The Impact of People Attributes

In Figure 5, we can see that with the help of the location frequency mined from the historical travel logs, the performance is much better than the two baseline methods. The method with attribute only also improves but not so much as the method with frequency only. The phenomenon is reasonable since for major landmarks the visiting sequences between them are stable and people of different attributes might all likely travel between them. Therefore, we look at a more difficult testing location subset where the uncertainty of the number of choices for the next destination is large, i.e., where the conditional entropy $H(L_{ij})$ is above a certain threshold. A location with a higher movement (or prediction) entropy $H(L_{ij})$ means that the choices of the next stop are more diverse for the people who leave from this location. For these cases, the attribute information is more useful to aid the performance of recommendation.

Table 3 presents the performance gain between different methods. We compare the random choice among the five nearest R(5) baseline with the two knowledge-based methods. As shown in Table 3, the improvement comparing with baseline degrades as the entropy increases. The gain between the frequency (F) and the combined method (F+A) usually increases when the testing subset becomes more harder to predict ($H(L_{ij}) \geq 0$ to $H(L_{ij}) \geq 1$). There are some missing entries in Table 3 due to the lack of testing sets.

9.3 Route Planning

In the route planning framework, we take the graph-based method to solve this problem and the scores (over edges) are all based on the above destination recommendation steps which have been shown effective through the experiment (Section 9.1).

Initially we recruit eight testers to use the designed route planning system for travel planning on the cities they are familiar with. The ratings are satisfactory and consistent with their expectations. Here we list 3 cases from 3 major cities and try to analyze the results[4].

In the case of the routes from Central Park to Battery Park in Manhattan (see Figure 6(a)), we can see that Metropolitan Museum of Art is famous that it becomes a must-see landmark for people no matter what gender they have; Intrepid Sea, Air & Space Museum, a military and maritime history museum, is apparently male-tended. Note that the route planning is suggested according to the user profiles (i.e., male and female) and the learned travel preferences between destinations, automatically mined from the community-contributed photos.

In the case of the routes from Pincio to Piramide di Caio Cestio in Rome (see Figure 6(b)), it shows that females prefer going to Fontana Dei Quattro Flumi, while males like visiting Vatican Museum. In this case, we hypothesize that

[4]Note that our system assumes the higher score between two destinations reflects the fact that the traffic between them is accessible. We do not directly concern whether there are some barriers (e.g. river) or traffic barriers via the route.

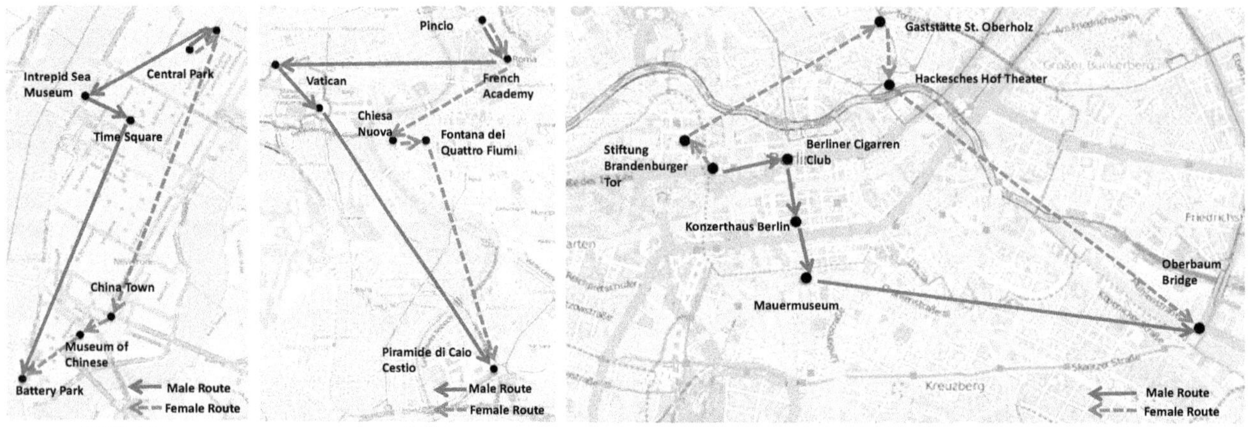

(a) Manhattan (b) Rome (c) Berlin

Figure 6: The route planning samples, with designated profiles – male vs. female, in 3 cities: (a) Manhattan, (b) Rome, and (c) Berlin. The blue route is for male, while the red one for female. Both routes in the same city are fixed at the same starting and end locations (or destinations). In addition, they must go through 3 other destinations in midway. Our route planning system could recommend different routes considering the given user profiles such as gender, age. From these results, Intrepid Sea, Air & Space Museum (i.e., Intrepid Sea Museum in (a)) and Berliner Cigarren Club tend to be suggested to males. (Best seen in color.)

the total distance might matter; that is the route through Vatican is longer.

In the case of the path from Stiftung Brandenburger Tor to Oberbaum Bridge in Berlin (see Figure 6(c)), Berliner Cigarren Club seems male-favored, while Hackesches Hof Theater is suggested for the female route. A leisurely route with theater visiting is more attractive than the cigarette museum to females. Besides, Mauermuseum in the route of male is the famous crossing point on the Berlin Wall.

Generally speaking, there are some landmarks very popular with both males and females, but it is without doubt that there are still some landmarks favored by only males or females according to the recommended routes of the same starting and ending destinations. By such attribute knowledge, our system is able to provide personalized route planning given the users profiles (i.e., gender, race, age)

10. CONCLUSIONS

In this work, we propose a probabilistic personalized travel recommendation model which adopts the automatically mined knowledges from the travel photo logs and the automatically detected people attributes in the photo contents. By information-theoretic measures and experiments in eight major cities, we confirm that people attributes are effective for mining demographics for travel landmarks and paths and very helpful for personalized travel recommendation and route planning. Meanwhile, people attributes are orthogonal to the travel logs alone and can further yield more satisfactory results especially in more challenging recommendations. For the future work, we are conducting experiments on more people attributes and adjust the probabilistic model for such diverse attributes to address more capabilities in personalization. Besides, the more competitive recommender models need to be investigated as well. We also want to expand our model with more contexts such as travel durations, traveling seasons. We believe such location- and individual-aware models are promising for further applications such as advertisement.

11. REFERENCES

[1] M. Ames et al. Why we tag: motivations for annotation in mobile and online media. In *ACM CHI*, 2007.

[2] Y. Arase et al. Mining people's trips from large scale geo-tagged photos. In *ACM MM*, 2010.

[3] C.-C. Chang et al. *LIBSVM: a library for support vector machines*, 2001. Software available at http://www.csie.ntu.edu.tw/ cjlin/libsvm.

[4] A.-J. Cheng et al. Gps, compass, or camera?: investigating effective mobile sensors for automatic search-based image annotation. In *ACM MM*, 2010.

[5] M. Clements et al. Using flickr geotags to predict user travel behaviour. In *ACM SIGIR*, 2010.

[6] T. M. Cover et al. *Elements of Information Theory*. Wiley, 1991.

[7] D. J. Crandall et al. Mapping the world's photos. In *WWW*, 2009.

[8] Y. Gao et al. W2go: a travel guidance system by automatic landmark ranking. In *ACM MM*, 2010.

[9] Q. Hao et al. Equip tourists with knowledge mined from travelogues. In *WWW*, 2010.

[10] R. Ji et al. Mining city landmarks from blogs by graph modeling. In *ACM MM*, 2009.

[11] N. Kumar et al. Facetracer: A search engine for large collections of images with faces. In *ECCV*, 2008.

[12] Y. Li et al. Landmark Classification in Large-scale Image Collections. In *IEEE ICCV*, 2009.

[13] D. Liu et al. Location sensitive indexing for image-based advertising. In *ACM MM*, 2009.

[14] X. Lu et al. Photo2trip: generating travel routes from geo-tagged photos for trip planning. In *ACM MM*, 2010.

[15] T. Mei et al. Knowledge discovery from community-contributed multimedia. *IEEE MultiMedia*, 17, October 2010.

[16] V. K. Singh et al. Social pixels: genesis and evaluation. In *ACM MM*, 2010.

[17] P. Viola et al. Rapid object detection using a boosted cascade of simple features. In *IEEE CVPR*, 2001.

[18] Y. Zheng et al. Mining interesting locations and travel sequences from gps trajectories. In *WWW*, 2009.

[19] Y. Zheng et al. Learning travel recommendations from user-generated gps traces. *ACM Trans. Intell. Syst. Technol.*, 2, January 2011.

[20] Y. Zheng et al. Recommending friends and locations based on individual location history. *ACM Trans. Web*, 2011.

Automatic Tag Generation and Ranking for Sensor-rich Outdoor Videos

Zhijie Shen†, Sakire Arslan Ay†, Seon Ho Kim‡, Roger Zimmermann†
†School of Computing, National University of Singapore, Singapore 117417
‡Integrated Media Systems Center, University of Southern California, Los Angeles, CA 90089
{z-shen, sakirear, rogerz}@comp.nus.edu.sg, seonkim@usc.edu

ABSTRACT

Video tag annotations have become a useful and powerful feature to facilitate video search in many social media and web applications. The majority of tags assigned to videos are supplied by users – a task which is time consuming and may result in annotations that are subjective and lack precision. A number of studies have utilized content-based extraction techniques to automate tag generation. However, these methods are compute-intensive and challenging to apply across domains. Here, we describe a complementary approach for generating tags based on the geographic properties of videos. With today's sensor-equipped smartphones, the location and orientation of a camera can be continuously acquired in conjunction with the captured video stream. Our novel technique utilizes these sensor meta-data to automatically tag outdoor videos in a two step process. First, we model the viewable scenes of the video as geometric shapes by means of its accompanied sensor data and determine the geographic objects that are visible in the video by querying geo-information databases through the viewable scene descriptions. Subsequently we extract textual information about the visible objects to serve as tags. Second, we define six criteria to score the tag relevance and rank the obtained tags based on these scores. Then we associate the tags with the video and the accurately delimited segments of the video. To evaluate the proposed technique we implemented a prototype tag generator and conducted a user study. The results demonstrate significant benefits of our method in terms of automation and tag utility.

Categories and Subject Descriptors

H.3.3 [**Information Storage and Retrieval**]: Information Search and Retrieval

General Terms

Algorithms, Design, Human Factors

*Area Chair: Daniel Gatica-Perez

Keywords

Video tags, location sensors, mobile video, geospatial

1. INTRODUCTION

Searching large repositories of videos for meaningful results is still a challenging problem. Furthermore, there is a pressing need for solutions since the amount of collected video is growing rapidly, in part due to technical advances in video capture devices. For example, smartphones which are carried by users all the time have lowered the barrier for recording video and the quality of these devices has reached a level that makes their video usable for many applications.

The most popular method for allowing users to search video corpuses is through textual annotations, commonly known as *tags* [1]. The meaning of tags (or keywords) can be anything that is related to the content of the video, for example location, people or animal names, event or action descriptions, *etc.* The generation of meaningful tags remains a major challenge. Traditional methods fall into two categories: (1) manual annotations by users and (2) automatic generation by means of content-based extraction methods. Both approaches suffer from some limitations. Manual annotations are laborious, often ambiguous and their uneven quality has been well documented [27, 24]. Tag generation based on content-based methods are very challenging for open domains and usually very compute-intensive.

Here we present an unconventional and complementary approach that shows significant promise and applies potentially to a large number of videos given that they satisfy two pre-conditions. First, we assume that videos are annotated with a rich set of meta-data that is obtained from GPS and compass sensors. Second, we require that videos are shot in an environment where the sensors are fully functional (especially the GPS), which currently means outdoors. While the first requirement may seem onerous at first glance, it is easily achievable today. The required hardware is cost-effectively available in the form of smartphones. Only a small recording app is necessary to enable millions of devices to be instantly compatible with our approach. As part of our project we have created two such recording apps for Android and iOS. The second pre-requisite is the availability of location information. While this will exclude some types of videos, it is applicable for a significant fraction of all videos. Location-based keywords were shown to be a major source of information and to provide high utility. For example among the 143 all-time most popular tags on Flickr (http://www.flickr.com/photos/tags/), 49 are the names of locations or geographic objects. Another study has reported

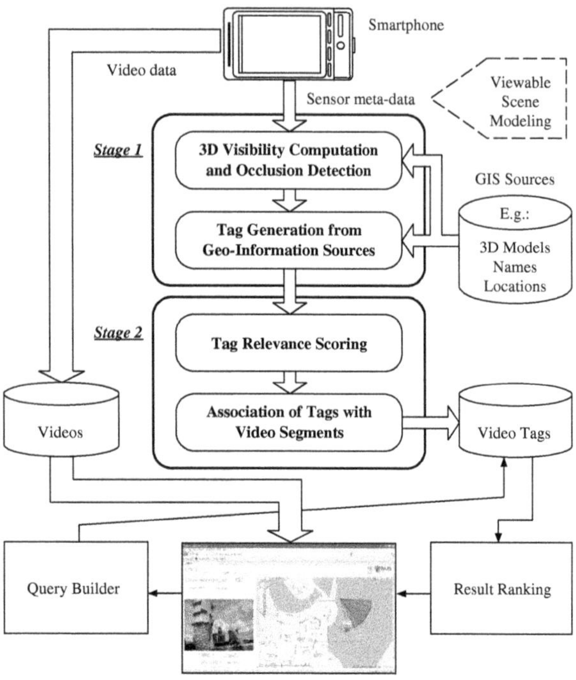

Figure 1: The process flow of the main processing steps for automatic tag generation.

that 28% of the Flickr tags are location related [23] and a third example is the LSCOM [17] set of concepts, which is well established for video annotations and widely acknowledged, and 20% of which are in the domain of location.

Figure 1 illustrates the overall architecture of our proposed tag generation approach and highlights its components. The system has two major processing stages which are outlined below. Users collect sensor-annotated videos with special recording apps and upload them to a server. The collected meta-data are utilized to describe the geographical coverage of the video scenes based on a *viewable scene model* [2]. In the first stage, the object information for the covered geographical region are retrieved from various geo-information services and visible objects are identified through 3D visibility computations. Occlusion detection is performed to remove hidden objects. The system then generates descriptive textual tags based on the object information retrieved from the geo-information services, such as names, types, locations, dimensions, *etc.* Currently we generate tags obtained from a limited number of sources, but one of the benefits of our approach is that tag generation can be extended in many ways, for example by employing geo-ontologies, event databases and Wikipedia parsing techniques. In the second stage, six relevance criteria are introduced to score the tag relevance to the scenes, *i.e.*, closeness to the *FOVScene* center, distance to the camera position, horizontally/vertically visible angle ranges/percentages of the object. Some attributes of the object information retrieved from the geo-information services are analyzed to identify the important landmarks. After scoring tag relevance, the video segments for which the tags are relevant to are determined. Unlike many other video tagging techniques, our system can associate tags precisely with the video sections in which they appear, rather than the whole video clip. Therefore, when a user searches videos for a certain tag, only those relevant video sections are returned. The ranked tags can be utilized by a video repository to allow search through textual keywords. Here are the specific contributions of this paper:

- The proposed technique is fully automatic. It also does not require any training set.
- The method is highly scalable since its processing is performed on the meta-data, which is small in size relative to the video data.
- Tags of high quality and objectivity are generated based on geospatial sensor properties which are mapped into a number of relevant (geo-)information databases.
- Tags are associated with clearly delimited segments of videos and are hence highly selective and ranked according to their relevance.

In the remaining sections of the paper we describe the detailed methods underlying our approach and the tools we have built for experimental verification. The results we have obtained illustrate that the proposed method works exceedingly well and we conjecture that it may open many future uses under a wide variety of application scenarios. Specifically, the rest of this paper is organized as follows. Section 2 contains a survey of the related work and Section 3 provides the background information on sensor data acquisition. Section 4 details the two major stages of our auto-tagging technique. Section 5 introduces the prototype implementation of the proposed technique and provides some examples of the tag generation and ranking. Section 5 also reports results of a user study. Finally, Section 6 concludes the paper.

2. RELATED WORK

Previously, researchers have leveraged content-based techniques to automatically tag videos. Naphade *et al.* [18] surveyed a number of studies for detecting video semantic concepts [17] and summarized some existing concept detection approaches and evaluation frameworks that are based on low-level content features. Recently, there have been further developments in this direction [20, 26, 7]. Siersdorfer *et al.* [22] pointed out the significant redundancy among the video content on social media sites and they exploited this characteristic to construct connections among videos and then propagate tags among similar videos. However, bridging the semantic gap through the sole use of content-based techniques is very difficult, as recently emphasized by Jain *et al.* [6]. Context (such as user and device information, and the video location), can serve as a supplement for understanding media semantics. Furthermore, a significant challenge is how the user should enter video search criteria into a site. The currently preferred method is textual keywords (employed by such commercial systems as Google, Bing and Yahoo). Our technique recognizes this preference and utilizes the contextual meta-data acquired from the sensors on smartphones to generate tags. As a benefit our technique does not require any training datasets and it reduces the skew in the long-tail distribution of tags often found in current systems where a small fraction of videos have many tags, but a significant portion have none. Of course our technique is amenable to content-based methods, and in fact may benefit such approaches in that it can reduce the set of videos which need to be processed with specific concept detectors. Though our system does not currently integrate such techniques, we plan to explore this in the future.

One technique similar to ours is *SEVA*, a sensor enhanced video annotation system which enables searching videos for the appearances of particular objects [14]. The authors make the strong assumption that every object has an attached sensor. Therefore, their technique can be applied only to videos that are collected within a controlled environment. In our work we investigate a broader problem and determine the representative tags for the geographic objects of user-generated outdoor videos. Furthermore, we consider the full geometry and visibility of objects, whereas *SEVA* assumes a single location for each object.

There are a number of studies that exploit the camera context. Toyama *et al.* [25] introduced a meta-data powered image database which indexes photographs using location and time. This work specifically explores methods for acquiring location tags, optimizing an image database for efficient geo-tagged image search and exploiting meta-data in a graphical user interface for browsing. Additional techniques in this direction have been proposed [16, 19]. Recently, Cao *et al.* [3] proposed a method to identify high-confidence tags and to propagate them based on time, location, and visual similarity among images. Some other studies demonstrated the usage of the geo-referenced photos to create tourism planning [15, 4]. These aforementioned context-aware techniques share two common characteristics: they deal only with images and use only GPS data as their sensory input. However, our technique uniquely defines a more precise video scene description (based on multi-sensor meta-data) and queries which objects a video shows by utilizing data from geo-information services. In addition, unlike the image-based techniques, our method also explores the temporal characteristics of videos. Moreover, we tag the videos according to the captured visible content rather than the camera position.

3. PRELIMINARIES

The basis for our tag generation approach is a description of the video content based on the geospatial properties of the scenes it captures. Here we provide a brief summary of our prior work on geospatial video annotation for completeness of the discussion [2], and a short description of our geospatial video recording apps developed for Android and iOS.

3.1 Description of Viewable Scene in Videos

A fundamental step in our work is the annotation of video content based on the geographical coverage of the video scenes in the geo-space. The meta data from camera-attached sensors are used to model the coverage areas of the video scenes as spatial objects. We put forward a *viewable scene model* which describes the scenes visible in the video based on the camera's *field of view* (FOV). Figure 2 illustrates a camera's viewable scene volume in 3D space. Accordingly, the 3D viewable scene can be described using the following parameters: (1) the camera position p read from a positioning device (*e.g.*, GPS), (2) the camera direction vector in 3D $\vec{d}$ which is obtained from a digital compass, (3) the horizontal and vertical camera viewable angles θ and ϕ which describe the angular extent of the scene filmed by the camera [5], and (4) the visibility range R which is the maximum distance from the camera location at which all the objects within the camera's field of view can be clearly recognized. R defines an upper bound on the distance searched in retrieving the visible objects. In this study, for simplicity, we assume that the camera is always level, then the $\vec{d}$ points towards the camera heading on the horizontal plane only. The horizontal visible angle range when the camera is pointing towards direction $\vec{d}$ will be given by $[\alpha, \beta]$ where $\alpha = d - \theta/2$ and $\beta = d + \theta/2$ (d is the direction angle of vector $\vec{d}$ with respect to North). Overall the camera viewable scene at time t is denoted by the tuple $FOVScene(t, p, \vec{d}, \theta, R)$ or $FOVScene(t, p, [\alpha, \beta], R)$.

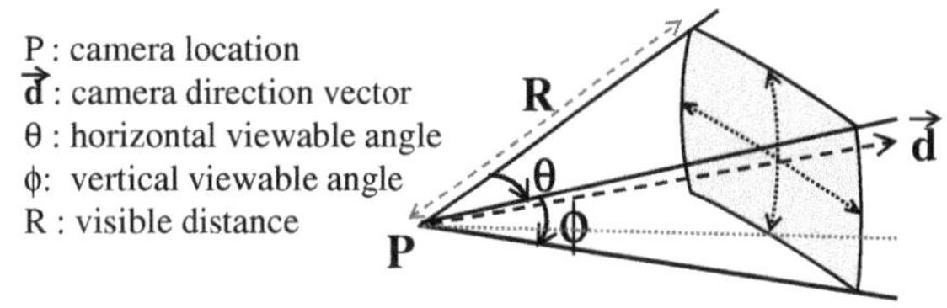

Figure 2: Illustration of *FOVScene* model in 3D.

3.2 Geospatial Video Recording Application

We created geospatial video recording applications for both Android- and iOS-based mobile phones. Our apps acquire, process and record the location and orientation meta-data along with the video streams. They can record H.264 encoded videos at DVD-quality resolution. To obtain the camera orientation, the apps employ the sensor data acquired from the orientation and accelerometer sensors. Camera location coordinates are acquired from the embedded GPS sensor. The collected meta-data is formatted with the JSON data-storage and -interchange format. Each meta-data item in the JSON data corresponds to the viewable scene information of a particular video frame. For the synchronization of meta-data with video content, each meta-data item is assigned an accurate timestamp and video time-code offset referring to a particular frame in the video. The sensor meta-data are sampled every second. The recorded geospatial videos can be immediately uploaded to our search portal, where users can submit queries to retrieve the videos and watch them via a web interface. Figure 3 shows screenshots of the Android app.

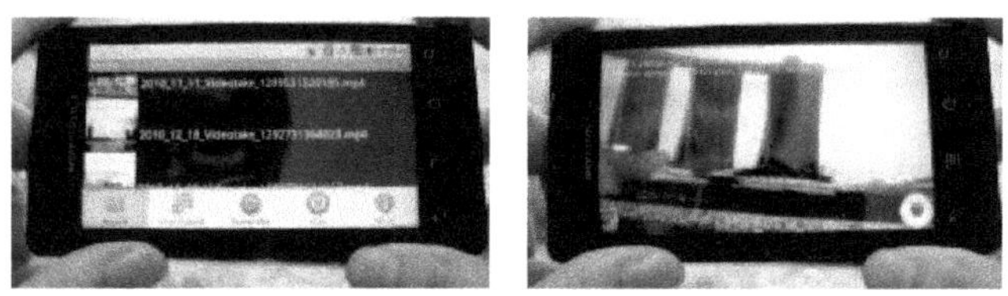

Figure 3: Screenshots of the Android app.

4. AUTOMATIC TAG GENERATION

After videos and sensor meta-data have been recorded, automatic video tagging can be applied. We first provide a formal definition of the problem and introduce some notations used in the rest of the section. Next, we describe our algorithm for finding visible objects in the video, which is based on the viewable scene model described in Section 3.1. This is followed by a detailed discussion on the automatic tag generation and ranking. We introduce six visual criteria for assessing the relevance of the generated tags. Lastly, we explain our method for associating tags with the video segments in which they appear.

(a) (b)

Figure 4: (a) A snapshot from one video that shows the skyscrapers around Singapore Marina Bay; (b) the corresponding view of Google Earth 3D buildings from the same location and camera direction.

4.1 Problem Formulation

Let $V=\{V_1, V2, ..., V_n\}$ be the set of video files with associated sensor meta-data denoted by $M=\{M_1, M_2, ..., M_n\}$, such that M_i contains the meta-data for video V_i sampled at every second. The scene information for V_i at time t is given by $M_i(t)= FOVScene(t,\ p,\ [\alpha,\beta],\ R)$, where p is the camera location and $[\alpha,\beta]$ is the horizontal visible angle.

To identify the objects visible in the video, our system retrieves information about the geographical objects for the covered region from two geo-information systems: OpenStreetMap (http://www.openstreetmap.org/) which is a free service providing editable maps of the world and GeoDec [21] which is an interdisciplinary and collaborative project developed at the University of Southern California (USC). Let $\{o_1, o_2, ...o_k\}$ be the set of geographic object descriptions (in 2D or 3D) retrieved from these systems. Then the set of all geographic object information is given by $O=\bigcup_{i=1}^{k} o_i$.

Given a set of geographic objects O for a region in geo-space and a set of video files V with associated sensor meta-data M, we have designed effective algorithms for the following steps: (1) determining the visible objects in video V_i by querying O through the meta-data M_i and extracting textual information about the visible objects to serve as tags, (2) scoring and ranking the tags based on the geospatial and temporal properties of their appearances in the video, and associating tags with the video segments where they appear.

4.2 Determination of Visible Objects in Videos

Our first step is to determine which objects have been captured in the video. The viewable scene information calculated based on the sensor meta-data identifies the geographic region covered in the video. However in order to describe the video semantics, further information about the geographic objects in the captured scene needs to be acquired. These objects may include buildings, landmarks, roads, parks, mountains or any other geo-object that is associated with a location. In our system, we retrieve information about these objects from two geo-information services, namely OpenStreetMap and GeoDec. These systems provide sophisticated information, such as name, type, location, polygon outline and even a 3D model of the geographic objects in geo-space. These 3D models reproduce the visual scene of the real world. For example, Figure 4(a) shows a snapshot extracted from one of our captured videos while Figure 4(b) illustrates the corresponding 3D models with the Google Earth interface. In order to determine the objects that appear in the right-hand figure, we query the geo-information services and retrieve all the objects within a certain distance R around the camera location points. A custom R value can be applied to affect the level of detail required in the tagging process. Next, the objects that are within the videos' viewable scenes are extracted through geometrical computations. A considerable challenge is that determining the actually visible objects is not straightforward due to occlusions.

4.2.1 *Visibility Determination based on FOV Scene*

DEFINING 3D VISIBILITY QUERIES. Figure 5(a) visualizes the viewable scene of the aforementioned video snapshot on Google Earth (the visible area is highlighted in blue while the occluded area is highlighted in yellow). Not all the objects are equally visible in the highlighted areas. We classify them into three categories according to their visibility level:

1. *Front Object*: An object to which there exists a line-of-sight horizontal tracing ray from the camera location which does not intersect with any other objects (see Figure 5(b)). The buildings labeled with alphabets belong to this category. In Figure 5(a), the front objects enclose the front area highlighted in blue.
2. *Vertically Visible Object*: An object which is not in the front but is vertically visible because its height exceeds what the front object is blocking. When the vertical viewable angle range of the object is wider than the angle of the object right in front of it, the object will be marked as vertically visible. The buildings labeled with numbers in Figure 5(a) belong to this category. Note that an object can be vertically visible even behind several objects.
3. *Occluded Object*: An object which is neither front nor vertically visible, therefore it is completely occluded.

When the query algorithm retrieves objects within the viewable scene, the object set will also include occluded objects. Thus, we need to devise a more sophisticated method to retrieve the visible objects only. Here we propose a 3D visibility query, inspired by the study of Lee *et al.* [10]. In this study, the authors introduce a technique to determine the visible objects and their visible angle ranges when observing from a specific viewpoint. One limitation of this technique is that the visibility computation is restricted within 2D space and is based only on the outline of the footprint of the objects. Therefore, the vertically visible objects will be considered as occluded by the front objects and will be eliminated. For example, when their method is applied, the Fullerton Hotel completely blocks the camera's sight to the skyscrapers in the back, which is not the case in reality as seen in Figure 5(a). Hence it is necessary to extend the method to 3D space to satisfy the demands of our system.

A 3D visibility query takes an object set O and the sensor

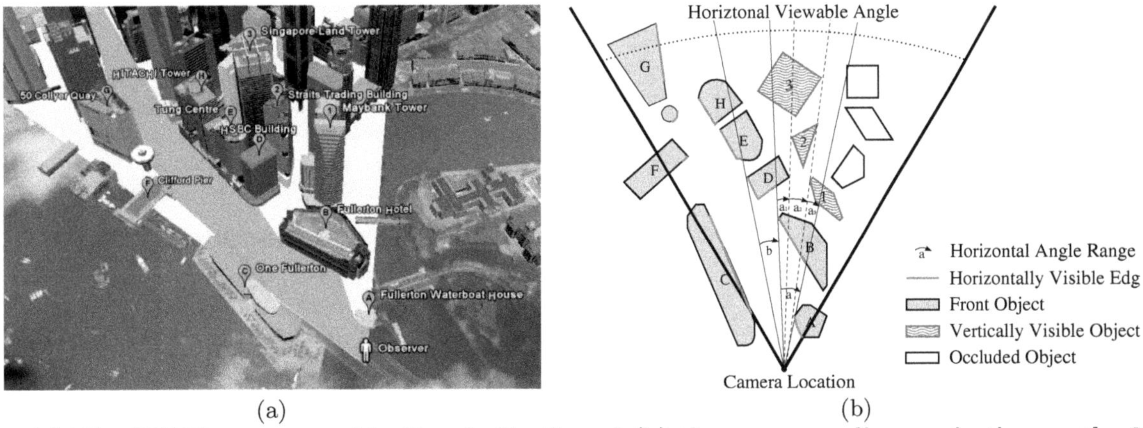

Figure 5: (a) The *FOVScene* mapped in Google Earth and (b) the corresponding projection on the 2D plane.

meta-data $M_i(t)$ (*i.e.*, the camera location p and the camera viewable angle range $[\alpha, \beta]$ at time t) as inputs, and returns a set of the visible objects and their horizontally and vertically visible angle ranges $\{(o : [\mu_h, \nu_h], [\mu_v, \nu_v])\}$. Notably, we not only obtain the visible objects, but also quantify their degree of visibility with angle ranges, which will later be used for tag ranking.

PROCESSING 3D VISIBILITY QUERIES. As illustrated in Figure 5(b), each visible object has a horizontal angle range (such as a for B and b for D), which indicates the visual width of it. However, a horizontal angle range may not only be associated with one visible object. For example, the non-front object 2 is also located in the range a. In a general case, since we consider vertical visibility as well, at an arbitrary horizontal angle value within $[\alpha, \beta]$ there may exist multiple visible objects, which are sorted according to their horizontal occlusion, forming a visible object queue. Hence, we define an *atomic horizontal angle range*, within which the visible object queue is the same at every angle value. In Figure 5(b), the range a is not atomic because there exist some angles whose visible object queues are different. On the other hand, the three sub-ranges of a are all atomic and respectively associated with unique object queues, *i.e.*, $(a_1 : \{B, D, 3\})$, $(a_2 : \{B, 2, 3\})$ and $(a_3 : \{B, 1\})$.

We next propose an incremental algorithm to determine the queue of visible objects associated with an atomic range as follows. Initially the queue is empty. When a new object arrives, the algorithm will check the horizontal occlusion between the newcomer and the objects in the queue one-by-one, stopping at the first object that is horizontally occluded by the newcomer or at the queue tail. If the newcomer is not entirely vertically occluded, it will be inserted right before the last checked object or into the queue tail. Afterwards, the vertical visibility of the objects behind the newcomer will be checked, and the ones that are wholly occluded by the newcomer will be removed from the queue (*e.g.*, the NTUC Center in Figure 6(a)). The process will stop when no more objects can be added to the queue. The final result will consists of the objects that are sorted according to their horizontal occlusion and are visible to some extent. Figure 6(b) shows an example of the result queue.

Algorithm 1 sketches the overall procedure of processing the 3D visibility query. To initialize the algorithm a mock object $\emptyset$ is introduced, which is assumed to be infinitely far away from the camera and have zero height, so that it is always occluded by any object. First, for each object,

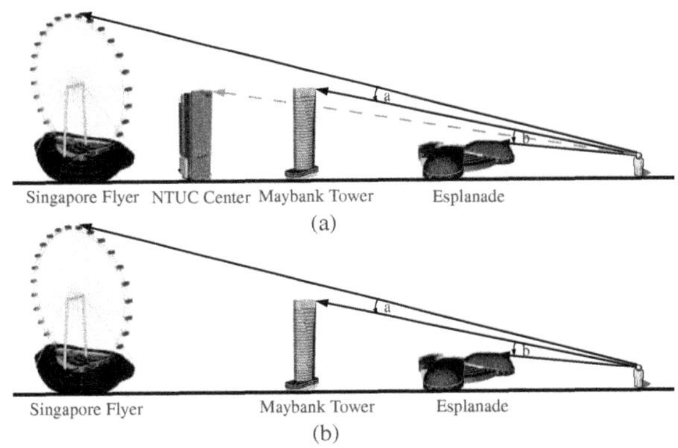

Figure 6: Demonstration of vertical occlusion.

the part of the horizontal angle range that is outside the camera viewable range is filtered from further computation to improve the performance. The camera viewable angle range $[\alpha, \beta]$ is split into a number of atomic horizontal angle ranges, in each of which the candidate objects will be added to the corresponding queue according to both horizontal and vertical occlusion, as is described above. The procedure *HorizontalOcclusion*() implements the 2D horizontal occlusion proposed by Lee *et al.* [10], while *VerticalOcclusion*() checks whether the object is entirely vertically occluded or not. At the end, the algorithm post processes the internal data structure and outputs the set of visible objects and their visible angle ranges, *i.e.*, $R = \{(o : [\mu_h, \nu_h], [\mu_v, \nu_v])\}$.

Note that the visibility query outlined in Algorithm 1 returns the set of visible objects only for a single *FOVScene*. Hence, this query needs to be repeated for every *FOVScene* in the video. We will discuss the visible object determination and ranking for an entire video file in Section 4.3.2.

EFFECTS OF SENSOR ERRORS ON VISIBILITY. The accuracy of the viewable scene calculation is somewhat dependent on the precision of the camera location and heading measurements obtained from the GPS and compass sensors. Zandbergen et al. [29] evaluates the accuracy of locations obtained using different positioning modes on the 3G iPhone. The A-GPS locations, which is the measurement mode used in our iPhone recording software, achieves an average median error of 8m, which is small compared to the size of the viewable scene we consider (*e.g.*, at full zoom-out about 13,000m^2 when R=300m). Additionally, there are techniques (*e.g.*, Kalman filter) to manage uncertainty and accuracy issues from insufficient and inaccurate

Algorithm 1: 3D Visibility Query Processor

```
Input  : the camera location p and viewable range [α, β]
         the set of objects O = {o}
Output: the set of visible objects and their visible angle
         ranges R = {(o : [μ_h, ν_h], [μ_v, ν_v])}
R_tmp = {([α, β] : {∅})}
foreach o ∈ O do
    [α_i, β_i] = [α, β] ∩ HorizontalRange(o)
    if [α_i, β_i] is empty then go to next loop
    foreach ([α_j, β_j] : O_j) ∈ R_tmp do
        [α_k, β_k] = [α_i, β_i] ∩ [α_j, β_j]
        if [α_k, β_k] is empty then go to next loop
        R_tmp = R_tmp − ([α_j, β_j] : O_j)
        O'_j ← O_j, O''_j ← O_j
        [α_l, β_l] = [α_j, β_j] − [α_k, β_k]
        R_tmp = R_tmp + ([α_l, β_l] : O'_j)
        for t = 1, 2, ..., Size(O''_j) do
            if HorizontalOcclusion(o, O''_j[t], p, [α_k, β_k]) ∧
            VerticalOcclusion(o, O''_j[t − 1], p) then
                Insert o into O''_j at t
                foreach o'' ∈ O''_j ∧ o'' after o do
                    if VerticalOcclusion(o'', o, p) then
                        Remove o'' from O''_j
                leave loop
        R_tmp = R_tmp + ([α_k, β_k] : O''_j)
R = PostProcess(R_tmp)
```

data. An error in the compass heading may be more significant. However, since the sensor meta-data used in this study have a fine sampling granularity (1 sample/sec), the amount of overlap between two consecutive FOVs is usually large. The missing visible objects in some video frames due to errors in the compass readings will probably still appear in the adjacent frames. However, such errors might have a minor effect on the tag scores (see Section 4.3). But any false positives would have very low scores and be ignored in the final video tagging. We plan to further elaborate on the robustness of our method and investigate possible error recovery techniques as part of our future work.

4.2.2 Assigning Tags to Visible Objects

To generate textual tags for visible objects we utilize the object set O retrieved from our geo-information sources, which contain detailed information about the objects, such as name, type, location, address, *etc.* A sample schema for object information looks as follows:

```
"id":<Object ID>,
"name":<Object name>,
"type:<Type of the object>,
"coordinates":<Outline of the object>,
"center":<Center point of the object>
"address":<Address of the object>,
"description":<Detailed description of the object>,
"websites":<List of supplementary websites>
```

In our prototype we use the names of visible objects to serve as tags. As described in the introduction, location and geographic names play an important role within all types of tags associated with videos and images of media sharing and search sites. Note that our method could be used to further add versatile information to the visible objects, and expand the tag type beyond the geographic domain. For example, we could easily incorporate event databases (*e.g.*, Upcoming, http://upcoming.yahoo.com/), and use geo-information and time to extract event-information tags. Moreover, natural language processing methods can be introduced to generate better and more descriptive tags. In our prototype implementation, if there exists a Wikipedia page for a visible object, we use this fact to upgrade its rank. The content of such pages can be processed in depth to further expand the tags, which is certainly an option in the future.

4.3 Scoring and Ranking of Tags

The visual appearance of objects within video scenes can be quite diverse. As an example, an object that is close to the camera would usually be seen clearly, whereas another object which is far away from the camera may be barely recognizable. Consequently, object tags should have different importance or relevance based on how the corresponding object appears in the video scene. Tag ranking [13] is an indispensable process to increase the effectiveness of tags, especially when the tag cardinality is large (*e.g.*, dozens of tags are generated for most of our test videos). Hence we need to prioritize the tags, which in other words means to prioritize the visible objects.

4.3.1 Scoring Tag Relevance for each FOV Scene

We propose to assess and quantify the relevance of visible objects in an individual *FOVScene* according to the six relevance criteria below.

- *Closeness to the FOVScene Center*: Research indicates that people tend to focus on the center of an image [9]. Based on this observation, we favor objects whose horizontal visible angle range is closer to the camera direction, which is the center of the scene, and score it with the formula $S_1 = 1 - \frac{|middle([\mu_h,\nu_h]) - d| \times 2}{|\alpha - \beta|}$ where $middle()$ returns the middle angle of the horizontal visible range $[\mu_h, \nu_h]$.
- *Distance*: A closer object is likely to be more prominent in the video. We formulate the score for the distance criterion as $S_2 = \min\{\frac{1}{distance(p, center(o))}, 1\}$ where *center*() returns the coordinate of the object center, and *distance*() computes the distance from the camera to the object center.
- *Horizontally and Vertically Visible Angle Ranges*: An object that occupies a wider range of the scene (either along the width or height) is more prominent. The normalized scores for these two criteria can be computed with the formulas $S_3 = \frac{|\mu_h - \nu_h|}{\theta}$ and $S_4 = \frac{|\mu_v - \nu_v|}{\phi}$, where θ and ϕ are the horizontal and vertical viewable angles, respectively.
- *Horizontally and Vertically Visible Percentages*: These two criteria focus on the completeness of the object's appearance in the video. The video scenes that show a larger percentage of an object are preferable over scenes that show only a small part of it. The scoring formulas are $S_5 = \frac{|\mu_h - \nu_h|}{width(o)}$ and $S_6 = \frac{|\mu_v - \nu_v|}{height(o)}$ where *width*() and *height*() return the maximal horizontally and vertically visible angle ranges without occlusion.

After obtaining the scores for each criterion, we linearly combine them to compute the overall score of an object in an individual *FOVScene*, *i.e.*, $S_{fov} = \sum_{i=1}^{6} w_i S_i$, where w_i represents the weight to adjust the contribution of each criterion to the overall score.

Additionally, we promote the scores of well-known objects (or landmarks), which are more likely to be searched for.

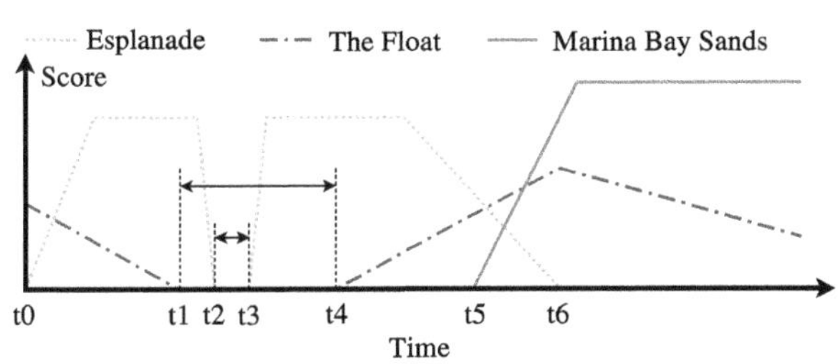

Figure 7: Demonstration of the temporal continuity of object occurrences.

The object information retrieved from the geo-information services include several clues to identify important landmarks. For example, in OpenStreetMap data, some landmarks (*e.g.*, the Singapore Flyer) are given an "attraction" label. Others are augmented with links to the Wikipedia pages, which might be an indirect hint for object importance, since something described in Wikipedia is believed to be important. In the future, we also plan to further adjust the scores according to visual information. To summarize, we can score the visible objects and subsequently their tags based on both relevance and supplemental information from the geo-information systems and thus determine their rank in each *FOVScene*.

4.3.2 Association of Tags with Video Segments

So far we have focused on tag ranking within a single video frame (*i.e.*, for an *FOVScene*). However due to the nature of videos, the temporal trends of the scores during a period should be explored. Figure 7 shows an example of score variations over time: the Esplanade receives the top score in the first half while the Marina Bay Sands takes the first place in the second half. These score variations (increase, decrease, reaching a peak or dropping to zero) are caused by the movement and the rotation of the camera. An important observation from this example is that we can in fact determine the segment where an object stays visible by detecting the two boundaries where the score starts from and returns to zero. For example, in Figure 7 the Esplanade is considered visible from t_3 to t_6. As an important contribution of our technique it can detect what objects appear in the video as well as when they appear. In other words, we can specifically associate a tag with a certain segment (or segments) of the video. To the best of our knowledge, none of the prior studies on video tagging does this. Another observation in Figure 7 is that the segments $[t_0, t_2]$ and $[t_3, t_6]$ are very close to each other. This short time gap between two segments may be caused by camera-shake or some other unexpected actions of the videographer. It may not really disturb human visual perception of continuity. As a further improvement, we set a threshold to merge close segments (*e.g.*, the segments $[-, t_1]$ and $[t_4, +]$ are too far to be merged), preventing videos from becoming too fragmented. Notably, the segmentation discussed above is logical and dynamic in that we do not physically split the videos.

Finally, for each segment associated with an object, we calculate its overall scores. Formally, let $S_{fov}(t)$ denote the score that the object obtains for the *FOVScene* at time t, and $\underline{t^i}$ and $\overline{t^i}$ respectively denote the start and the end time of the ith segment among the ones where the object appear. Then the score of the object for this segment can be computed through the formula $S^i_{seg} = \int_{\underline{t^i}}^{\overline{t^i}} S_{fov}(t)dt$. All the video segments associated with the object are ranked based on this score. Furthermore, we can compute the score of the object for the whole video via formula $S_{clip} = \sum_{i=1}^{n} S^i_{seg}$, where n is the number of the segments associated with the object. Similarly, the objects, or the tags in consequence, can be sorted according to this score. In summary, by applying the entire process including visibility checking and scoring, we can obtain (1) the sorted segments related to each tag, and (2) all the sorted tags of a video.

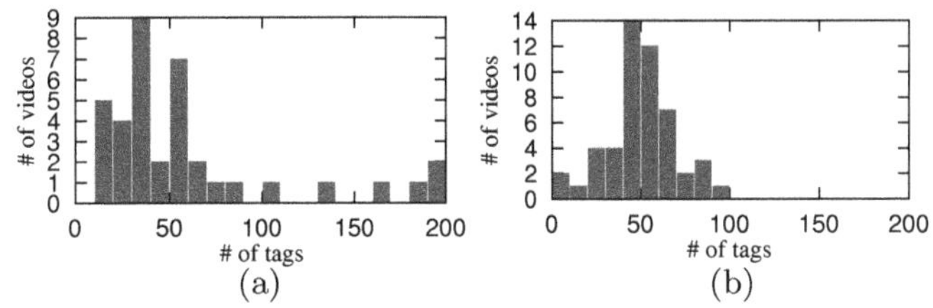

Figure 8: Distribution of the number of the generated tags for (a) Singapore and (b) USC videos.

5. EXPERIMENTAL EVALUATION

We built a prototype of our auto-tagging system and generated tags for a set of videos captured with our Android app. To evaluate the effectiveness of these tags, we conducted a user study. We will first describe our prototype and then illustrate some examples of tag generation and ranking. Lastly, we will report the results of the user study.

5.1 Prototype and Dataset Setup

Our prototype implements all stages described in Figure 1. That is, it processes the video sensor meta-data, queries several geo-information systems (*i.e.*, OpenStreetMap and GeoDec), computes the visible objects, extracts the tags, associates them with the video clips and segments, scores them, and finally stores them for video indexing. To demonstrate the usage and utility of our auto-tagging system, we also implemented a simple keyword-based search engine that outputs the related video segments or video clips, ordered according to their ranking scores.

We evaluated our prototype with two geographic sites where we captured videos: the downtown of Singapore and the University of Southern California (USC) campus. For the former site our prototype retrieves the geo-information from OpenStreetMap which is an open and free service built with voluntary contributions of users, and therefore some attributes for some objects might be missing. For example, although some geographic landmark objects have Wikipedia articles on the web, the links to most of these articles are missing in the dataset. Hence we additionally implemented a Wikipedia crawler to retrieve the missing links. Moreover, for the object dimensions OpenStreetMap only provides the footprint outline so that the object height is not available for vertical visibility check. To overcome this, we either automatically parsed the associated Wikipedia entries to look for clues of the object height, or estimated its object height according to its name and type (*e.g.*, 200m is given to a "tower" while 0m is given to a "river"). Another possible solution as well as future work can be to recover the missing information from visual clues. For the USC site, our prototype works with detailed 3D models retrieved from the GeoDec system, therefore the visibility check results are quite accurate for the videos captured at this site.

We have collected 87 outdoor video clips (37 in Singapore

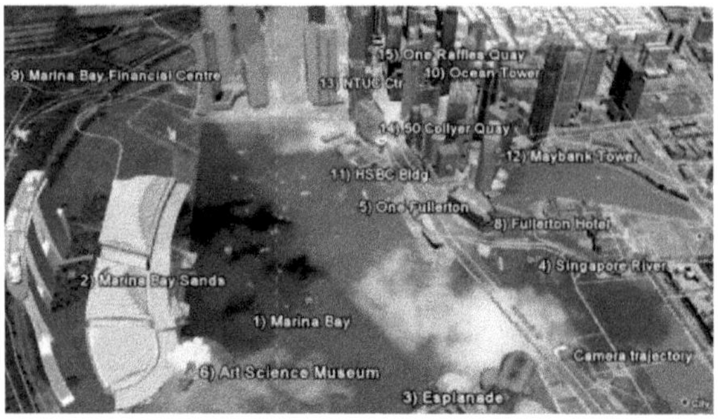

(a)

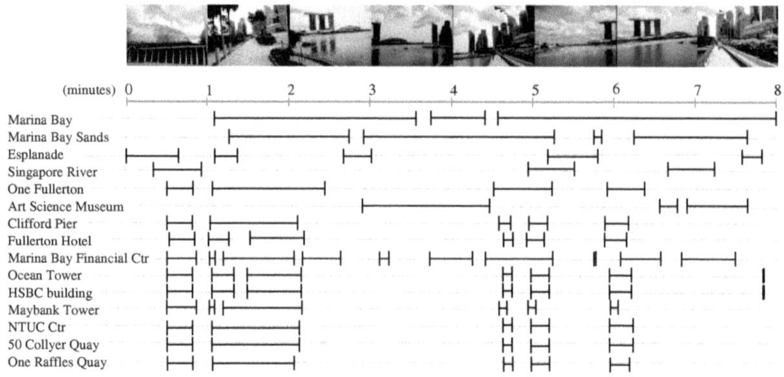

(b)

Figure 9: Illustration of automatically generated tags for an example video from Singapore Marina Bay. (a) Visualization of camera trajectory and top 15 tags on Google Earth interface; (b) list of the video segments where the top 15 tags appear.

and 50 at USC) and the accompanied sensor data for evaluation. The lengths of the videos vary from 1 minute to 16 minutes. We used our prototype to generate the tags for this video collection. It took 22.73 minutes for our prototype to process all these videos one-by-one on a desktop computer with a 2.83 GHz quad-core CPU and 3 GB of memory. The results show that our technique is effective: for the videos in Singapore our prototype generated 60 tags on average while for the USC videos it generated 49. Figures 8(a) and 8(b) show that the majority of videos receive dozens of tags. This is very positively different from a recent study [8] which reports that more than half of the videos on MySpace have just 1 to 5 tags. Additionally, manual tag cardinality is extremely uneven among web objects [11, 12]. Therefore, the promising productivity of our technique can secure assignment of adequate textual information for all videos, ensuring a high probability that no videos remain un-tagged.

5.2 Examples of Tag Generation and Ranking

Next we provide some specific example results of tag generation and ranking facilitated by the prototype implementation introduced in Section 5.1. Figure 9 illustrates the tags generated for a video taken at Singapore Marina Bay and the video segments related to each tag. Figure 9(a) visualizes the trajectory that the camera follows (along Esplanade Drive) on Google Earth and marks the top 15 tags generated for this video. Our auto-tagging system returned more than 100 tags, however we only list the top 15 in this example. Note that the tags are ordered from the most relevant to the least. Figure 9(b) lists the video segments where the tags appear in the video and shows some example frames (extracted every minute). As can be seen in the images, the Marina Bay and Marina Bay Sands, which are listed at the top of tag list, appear clearly in the video for several minutes. The tags listed lower in the list belong to objects that either appear for a short amount of time in the video or are far from the camera.

In Figure 10 we illustrate an example search for the USC campus videos. We search for the keyword "Bovard Auditorium," which refers to a well-known landmark within the campus. Some representative frames from the top six video segments are shown in Figure 10. As seen in the images, the top results clearly show the landmark from different viewpoints. One important aspect to note is that the tagging system successfully eliminates the occluded views of the landmark. As an example, in Figure 11(a), Bovard Auditorium is blocked by another building, therefore even though the camera is close and pointing in its direction, it does not appear in the video. The viewable scene for this video frame is illustrated in Figure 11(b). Figures 11(c) and (d) show another video frame and viewable scene illustration where the building is occluded only partially. Our auto-tagging system successfully eliminates the video scenes with occlusions similar to Figure 11(a). When a building is partially occluded, as illustrated in Figure 11(c), it will include those scenes in the resulting segments, however it will assign a lower rank score since the building appears within a small range in the viewable scene (see Section 4.3.1).

Figure 10: Top six results for "Bovard Auditorium."

(a) (b)

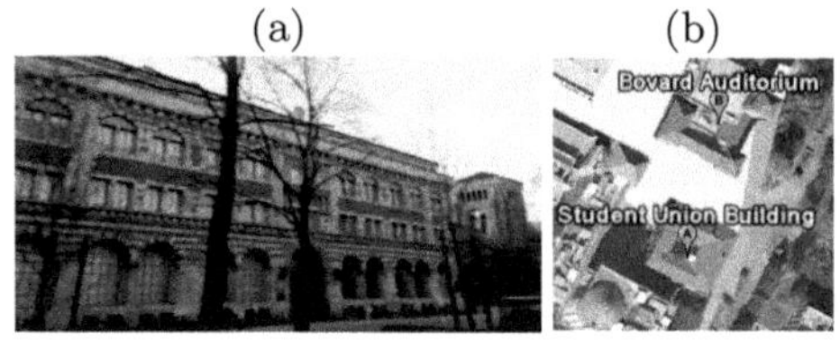

(c) (d)

Figure 11: Occluded and partially occluded view of "Bovard Auditorium."

5.3 User Study

There are few comparable techniques to ours that utilize geographic properties to automatically generating tags for videos, especially exploiting sensor data. Moreover, it

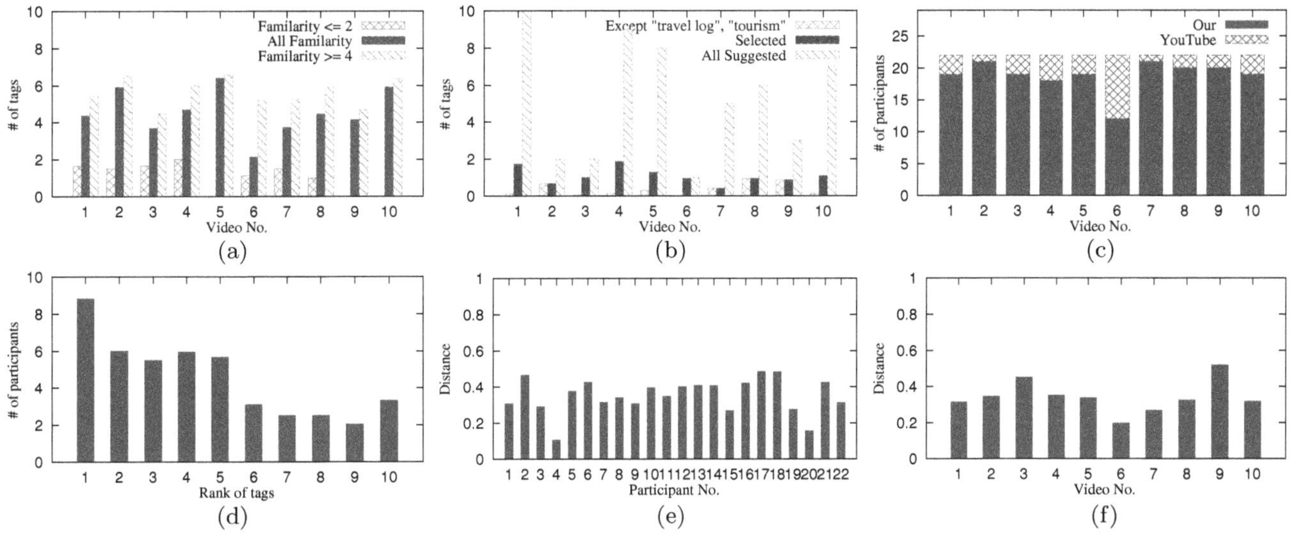

Figure 12: (a) The average number of selected tags in our tag set; (b) the number of tags Youtube suggested and the average number of selected tags from them; (c) the preference of participants regarding the two group of tags; (d) the average selectivity of the tags on each rank; (e) the average distance between our ranks and each participant's expectations on all videos, and (f) all participants' expectations on each video.

is difficult to use acknowledged datasets (*e.g.*, TRECVID, http://trecvid.nist.gov/) for our experiments due to the lack of enough sensor data in those sets. Thus, we believe that a user study is an appropriate methodology to evaluate the usefulness of the tags generated by our system and the similarity between our ranking and human expectations. In the user study, twenty-two people participated: 10 males and 12 females including students, professionals, research staff and faculty. The participants were chosen among people who are living or used to live in Singapore since we used our own video clips captured there showing some recognizable places and landmarks. The participants were requested to carefully watch the chosen videos, which had a total length of about 32 minutes and covered various recognizable landmarks within an approximately $4 \times 4\text{km}^2$ area of central Singapore. They answered a comprehensive set of predefined questions after finishing watching each video clip.

In the study, ten video clips were selected and uploaded to YouTube. While uploading, the tags suggested by YouTube (a feature of YouTube) were recorded to be used in the questionnaire. Questions were prepared to check the following: (1) the familiarity of the participants with the place where the video clip was captured (1 – least, 5 – most), (2) the relevance of the tag set generated by our system and the tag set suggested by YouTube, (3) the preference of the participants between the two tag sets, (4) the similarity of the relevance ranking in our tag set with the ranking by humans. Note that, without loss of generality, we used only the top ten relevant tags generated from our prototype, so that testers' focus is not distracted with too many tags. Additionally, in the actual questionnaire, we hid the sources of the two tag sets to ensure an unbiased comparison. Figures 12(a)–(e) summarize the results of the user study.

5.3.1 Selectivity of Relevant Tags

First, we analyze how the tags generated by our system were selected by participants. Figure 12(a) shows the average number of tags selected. Each selected tag was recognized and considered relevant to the video by participants. For most videos, around 4–6 tags out of 10 were considered relevant. An observation is that the familiarity of the filming locations to the participants has a significant impact on their choice of relevant tags. The participants who are more familiar with the locations selected more tags, and vice versa – a result which corresponds to our expectations. Another observation is that Video No. 6 received a noticeably low tag selectivity comparing to other videos. This video was captured along the street behind Orchard Road where there exist several landmarks so that a higher number of relevant tags could be expected. However, since these landmarks all face towards Orchard Road, the participants were troubled in recognizing them from the back (demonstrated by the average familiarity score of a mere 1.82). This case also demonstrates that the orientation of certain objects can be another criteria for tag ranking, which will be another extension in our future work.

In comparison, Figure 12(b) shows that the number of suggested tags from YouTube differs a lot across the videos, and the number of selected tags was no more than two for all the videos – significantly lower than ours. A critical problem of the suggested tags from YouTube is that they are too general without the recognition of location names and most suggested tags try to describe the activities in the videos. For example, "travel log" and "tourism" are associated with many of these 10 videos. Such tags are not desirable for search because they are less differential and user queries are usually quite specific [28]. If these tags are excluded, the selectivity of the remained tags is even lower. Overall, the participants showed a very strong preference to our tag set as illustrated in Figure 12(c).

5.3.2 Similarity of Tag Ranks to User Expectations

Next, we analyze how the relevance ranking of tags generated by our system was perceived by the study participants. Without loss of generality, a higher ranked tag can be recognized as a relevant one by an increased number of participants. Figure 12(e) demonstrates that the higher ranked tags were actually selected by more participants. It is an indirect confirmation that the participants agreed with our rankings to some extent. For a precise comparison, we introduce a metric, *ranking distance*, to quantify the similarity of two ranked tag sequences: T_α generated by our system and T_β listed by human participants on the same tag set $\{t_1, t_2, \ldots, t_n\}$. Ranking follows a total ordering, such that the sequence $T = t_{k_1} \prec t_{k_2} \prec \cdots \prec t_{k_n}$ can be transformed into an equivalent collection of binary relations $\{t_{k_i} \prec t_{k_j} | \forall i, \forall j, 1 \leq i < j \leq n\}$. Let $binary()$ denote the transformation and $||\bullet||$ denote the size of the collection. We can formally define the normalized distance between T_α and T_β with the formula $dist_{\alpha\beta} = \frac{||binary(T_\alpha) - binary(T_\beta)||}{||binary(T_\alpha)||}$ where the numerator indicates the number of conflict binary relations of the two tag sequences.

Figure 12(e) demonstrates the average distance between our and each participant's ranked tag sequence for all the videos. The average distance is approximately 0.35, implying that the system's and the participants' rankings are more similar than different. Importantly, even though each participant ranked the tags based on personal perception, the distances among different participants were quite close. This indicates that the criteria chosen for our ranking algorithm reflect common human perceptions well. Figure 12(f), which plots the average distance of the system's ranking to all participants' for each video, encouragingly illustrates consistent results. The distance on each video does not fluctuate widely, implying that our ranking algorithm is generally applicable to various videos.

6. CONCLUSIONS

We propose an unconventional and novel technique that leverages sensor-equipped smartphones and geo-information databases to automatically generate high quality tags for outdoor videos. We use the viewable scenes of videos obtained from sensor meta-data to query visible objects from geo-information databases and generate descriptive tags about these visible objects. The obtained tags are ranked according to how they appear in the videos' viewable scenes. We have built a prototype based on our technique and conducted a user study. The results demonstrate that our technique is very effective in retrieving tags and ranking their relevance to the video scenes. Furthermore, our technique is extensible as we can incorporate other types of databases (*e.g.*, event information) to generate tags in other domains. Our method is also complementary to existing content-based methods.

Acknowledgment

We would like to acknowledge that this research was carried out at the Centre of Social Media Innovations for Communities (COSMIC), sponsored and supported by the Singapore National Research Foundation and Interactive & Digital Media Program Office, MDA.

7. REFERENCES

[1] M. Ames and M. Naaman. Why We Tag: Motivations for Annotation in Mobile and Online Media. In *CHI*, 2007.

[2] S. Arslan Ay, R. Zimmermann, and S. H. Kim. Viewable Scene Modeling for Geospatial Video Search. In *ACM Multimedia*, 2008.

[3] L. Cao, J. Luo, and T. S. Huang. Annotating Photo Collections by Label Propagation According to Multiple Similarity Cues. In *ACM Multimedia*, 2008.

[4] Y. Gao, J. Tang, R. Hong, Q. Dai, T. S. Chua, and R. Jain. W2Go: A Travel Guidance System by Automatic Landmark Ranking. In *ACM Multimedia*, 2010.

[5] C. H. Graham, N. R. Bartlett, J. L. Brown, Y. Hsia, C. C. Mueller, and L. A. Riggs. *Vision and Visual Perception*. John Wiley & Sons, Inc., 1965.

[6] R. Jain and P. Sinha. Content Without Context is Meaningless. In *ACM Multimedia*, 2010.

[7] Y. G. Jiang, C. W. Ngo, and S. F. Chang. Semantic Context Transfer across Heterogeneous Sources for Domain Adaptive Video Search. In *ACM Multimedia*, 2009.

[8] Y. Jin, M. Hu, H. Singh, D. Rule, M. Berlyant, and Z. Xie. MySpace Video Recommendation with Map-Reduce on Qizmt. In *IEEE ICSC*, 2010.

[9] T. Judd, K. Ehinger, F. Durand, and A. Torralba. Learning to Predict Where Humans Look. In *ICCV*, 2009.

[10] K. C. K. Lee, W.-C. Lee, and H. V. Leong. Nearest Surrounder Queries. *IEEE TKDE*, 2010.

[11] K. Lerman and L. Jones. Social Browsing on Flickr. *Arxiv preprint cs0612047*, 2006.

[12] X. Li, L. Guo, and Y. E. Zhao. Tag-based Social Interest Discovery. In *WWW*, 2008.

[13] D. Liu, X. S. Hua, L. Yang, M. Wang, and H. J. Zhang. Tag Ranking. In *WWW*, 2009.

[14] X. Liu, M. Corner, and P. Shenoy. SEVA: Sensor-Enhanced Video Annotation. In *ACM Multimedia*, 2005.

[15] X. Lu, C. Wang, J. M. Yang, Y. Pang, and L. Zhang. Photo2Trip: Generating Travel Routes from Geo-Tagged Photos for Trip Planning. In *ACM Multimedia*, 2010.

[16] M. Naaman, S. Harada, Q. Wang, H. G. Molina, and A. Paepcke. Context Data in GeoReferenced Digital Photo Collections. In *ACM Multimedia*, 2004.

[17] M. Naphade, J. R. Smith, J. Tesic, S.-F. Chang, W. Hsu, L. Kennedy, A. Hauptmann, and J. Curtis. Large-Scale concept ontology for multimedia. *IEEE Multimedia*, 2006.

[18] M. R. Naphade and J. R. Smith. On the Detection of Semantic Concepts at TRECVID. In *ACM Multimedia*, 2004.

[19] A. Pigeau and M. Gelgon. Building and Tracking Hierarchical Geographical & Temporal Partitions for Image Collection Management on Mobile Devices. In *ACM Multimedia*, 2005.

[20] G. J. Qi, X. S. Hua, Y. Rui, J. Tang, T. Mei, and H. J. Zhang. Correlative Multi-Label Video Annotation. In *ACM Multimedia*, 2007.

[21] C. Shahabi, F. Banaei-Kashani, A. Khoshgozaran, L. Nocera, and S. Xing. GeoDec: A Framework to Effectively Visualize and Query Geospatial Data for Decision-Making. *IEEE Multimedia*, 2010.

[22] S. Siersdorfer, J. San Pedro, and M. Sanderson. Automatic Video Tagging using Content Redundancy. In *SIGIR*, 2009.

[23] B. Sigurbjörnsson and R. van Zwol. Flickr Tag Recommendation based on Collective Knowledge. In *WWW*, 2008.

[24] F. M. Suchanek, M. Vojnovic, and D. Gunawardena. Social Tags: Meaning and Suggestions. In *ACM CIKM*, 2008.

[25] K. Toyama, R. Logan, and A. Roseway. Geographic Location Tags on Digital Images. In *ACM Multimedia*, 2003.

[26] M. Wang, X. S. Hua, X. Yuan, Y. Song, and L. R. Dai. Optimizing Multi-Graph Learning: Towards A Unified Video Annotation Scheme. In *ACM Multimedia*, 2007.

[27] R. Yan, A. Natsev, and M. Campbell. A Learning-based Hybrid Tagging and Browsing Approach for Efficient Manual Image Annotation. In *CVPR*, 2008.

[28] K. Yang, X. S. Hua, M. Wang, and H. J. Zhang. Tagging Tags. In *ACM Multimedia*, 2010.

[29] P. A. Zandbergen. Accuracy of iPhone Locations: A Comparison of Assisted-GPS, WiFi and Cellular Positioning. *Transactions in GIS*, 2009.

Using Graphics Rendering Contexts to Enhance the Real-Time Video Coding for Mobile Cloud Gaming*

Shu Shi[†], Cheng-Hsin Hsu[‡], Klara Nahrstedt[†], and Roy H. Campbell[†]
[†]Department of Computer Science
University of Illinois at Urbana-Champaign
201 N Goodwin Ave., Urbana, IL 61801, USA
[‡]Deutsche Telekom Inc., R&D Lab
5050 El Camino Real, Ste. 221, Los Altos, CA 94022, USA
[†]{shushi2, klara, rhc}@illinois.edu, [‡]cheng-hsin.hsu@telekom.com

ABSTRACT

The emerging cloud gaming service has been growing rapidly, but not yet able to reach mobile customers due to many limitations, such as bandwidth and latency. We introduce a 3D image warping assisted real-time video coding method that can potentially meet all the requirements of mobile cloud gaming. The proposed video encoder selects a set of key frames in the video sequence, uses the 3D image warping algorithm to interpolate other non-key frames, and encodes the key frames and the residues frames with an H.264/AVC encoder. Our approach is novel in taking advantage of the run-time graphics rendering contexts (rendering viewpoint, pixel depth, camera motion, etc.) from the 3D game engine to enhance the performance of video encoding for the cloud gaming service. The experiments indicate that our proposed video encoder has the potential to beat the state-of-art x264 encoder in the scenario of real-time cloud gaming. For example, by implementing the proposed method in a 3D tank battle game, we experimentally show that more than 2 dB quality improvement is possible.

Categories and Subject Descriptors

H.5.1 [**Multimedia Information System**]: Video

General Terms

Design, Measurement

Keywords

Cloud Gaming, Mobile Devices, Real-Time Video Coding, 3D Image Warping

*Area chair: Pal Halvorsen. The co-author Cheng-Hsin Hsu (chsu@cs.nthu.edu.tw) is now with the Department of Computer Science at National Tsing Hua University, Taiwan.

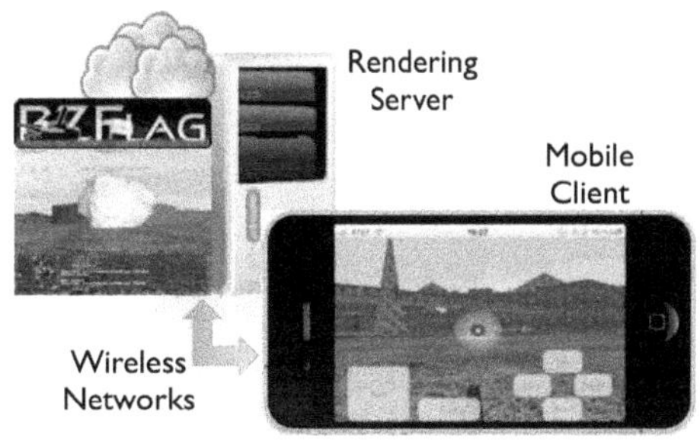

Figure 1: Mobile cloud gaming system prototype

1. INTRODUCTION

The emerging cloud gaming service, represented by OnLive [1], has rapidly expanded its market among gamers and attracted a lot of attention from researchers. The concept of cloud gaming is to render 3D video game on cloud server and send game scenes as 2D video to game players through broad-band networks. The control signals (mouse, keyboard, or game controller events) are sent back to cloud server to interact with the game application. Therefore, this cloud-based gaming service allows gamers to play the most advanced 3D video games without buying any high-end graphical hardware. However, cloud gaming also has some limitations. First, it depends on high bandwidth networks to deliver game video. Second, it is critical to the network latency since long latency seriously impairs the interactive performance of video games [4]. These restrictions make cloud gaming unavailable to the users having no high-quality network connections, and in particular, the mobile users who have problems with both the bandwidth and latency of wireless networks. For example, OnLive [1] requires a wired network connection with no less than 5Mbps constant bandwidth to provide 720p 30fps interactive gaming services. Limited services are provided to Wi-Fi users and no service at all is available to mobile network users.

We have built an experiment platform to better study the cloud gaming experience for mobile users. An open source 3D tank battle game, BZFlag[1], is rendered on a

[1]http://www.bzflag.org. We render and play this game in the first person perspective shooting mode.

powerful workstation. The game scenes are captured from the OpenGL frame buffer and scaled to the resolution of 640×480, which is sufficient to present enough details on the small screen of mobile phones. The captured frames are then encoded in real-time to a video stream and sent to mobile client through wireless networks. We set the target video frame rate to 30 fps to provide smooth gaming experience even for motion intensive games. The user control signals received by mobile client are sent back to rendering server for game interaction. Figure 1 shows an illustration of the system. Our research aims to improve the mobile gaming experience, and we focus on the following issues:

- *Bandwidth*: Since we are considering the mobile devices using wireless mobile networks as the client in our cloud gaming system, the available network bandwidth is very limited for streaming game video. Our system should minimize the network bandwidth usage and we set the target to only 1Mbps, which requires a compression ratio more than 100:1[2] to encode the game video in our system configuration.

- *Quality*: The reduction of network bandwidth should not compromise the video quality. For example, it is not favorable to use large quantization parameters in video encoding because the blurred video impairs the gaming experience.

- *Interaction Latency*: We define *interaction latency* as the time from the generation of user interaction request till the appearance of the first updated game frame on the mobile client. The largest portion of the *interaction latency* in a cloud gaming system is the network round trip latency between the rendering server and the mobile client. The previous work [4] showed that 100 ms is the largest tolerable latency for the first person shooting game. However, the latency of most wireless networks can easily go beyond this limit. For example, measurement studies [11, 17] reported 700+, 300+, and 200+ ms latencies in GPRS, EDGE, and UMTS cellular networks. To a great extent, the mobile cloud gaming experience depends on how to reduce *interaction latency*.

- *Real-Time*: The 30 fps frame rate requires that the rendering and encoding of every frame should be completed in 33ms. The real-time processing requirement is strict in our system because any delay will be added to the *interaction latency*.

An intuitive and conventional approach is to compress the game frames with a real-time H.264/AVC video encoder [22]. However, compared to the general-purpose offline H.264/AVC encoder, the real-time H.264/AVC encoder cannot leverage on various optimizations that require a few seconds of lookahead buffer [5]. As a result, the real-time H.264/AVC encoder has a much lower encoding efficiency and may fail to meet both *bandwidth* and *quality* requirements in some situations. In addition, this approach provides no help to reduce *interaction latency*. Therefore, rather than focusing only on the video coding component, we look at the problem from a system's perspective and find a different approach. Since the video encoder runs together with the 3D game engine, we are able to obtain the graphics rendering contexts (such as rendering viewpoint, pixel depth, camera motion, etc.) while capturing images from the frame buffer. In this paper, we present how to take advantage of graphics rendering contexts to address the four issues mentioned above.

We propose a 3D image warping assisted real-time video coding method that can not only improve the video encoding performance, but also be extended to reduce the *interaction latency* of our mobile cloud gaming system. The basic idea of our method is to select the key frames in the game video at first, and then use the 3D image warping algorithm [12] to interpolate other intermediate frames. Finally, H.264/AVC is used to encode all key frames and warping residues (the difference between the interpolation result and the original image frame) for each intermediate frame. The interpolation allows us to encode warping residues with much lower bit rate, and assign more bit rate to encode key frames. In the ideal situation, if all intermediate frames are perfectly interpolated and no residues need to be encoded, we can assign all bit rate to encode key frames for better video quality. Thus, the encoding performance of our method depends on the quality of the interpolation method we use.

3D image warping is a well-known image-based rendering (IBR) technique and fits in our coding method very well. Given the pixel depth and rendering viewpoint, the algorithm can efficiently warp an image to any new viewpoint. The shortcoming of 3D image warping is the warping artifact. Holes are generated when there is no pixel in the input image to reference when drawing the new image. In order to overcome the warping artifacts and maximize the warping quality, we introduce several optimization techniques that select the most appropriate key frames based on camera motion. The proposed coding method achieves high video coding efficiency. We evaluate the method in our mobile cloud gaming system and find that our method has the potential to beat the state-of-the-art x264 coder [5] in real-time.

Our work is novel in applying the rendering contexts and 3D image warping to assist real-time video coding. Many concepts used in our paper have been proposed by earlier researchers in different scenarios. For example, Levoy [8] proposed to use polygons to assist JPEG/MPEG compression. 3D image warping has been similarly applied for different purposes in various remote rendering systems [10, 2, 6] and other applications [16, 13]. However, we believe we are the first to study using the rendering contexts to assist real-time video coding in the area of cloud gaming, and we present the best solution so far to integrate the graphics rendering contexts and IBR techniques into video coding.

For the rest of the paper, we first summarize the related work in Section 2. Section 3 introduces in details how the proposed coding method works and how to optimize the key frame selection. Implementation issues are covered in Section 4. We evaluate our coding method as well as several optimization strategies in Section 5. Section 6 discusses the limitation of our coding method and how it can be extended for *interaction latency* reduction. Section 7 concludes the whole paper and presents our future work.

2. RELATED WORK

We summarize the related work from two aspects: 3D image warping in remote rendering systems, and real-time video coding technologies.

[2]The bandwidth of an uncompressed 30 fps, 640×480, YUV420 video is approximately 105Mbps

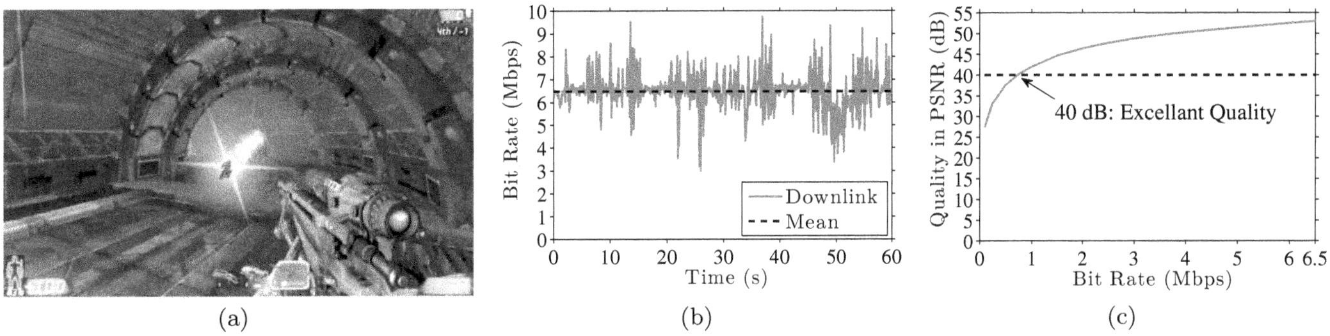

Figure 2: (a) Screenshot of *Unreal Tournament III*, (b) OnLive streaming rate, and (c) coding efficiency of a general purpose video coder.

2.1 Remote Rendering & 3D Image Warping

Cloud gaming is a type of remote rendering system, which renders the graphics content on a different machine from where it is displayed. Levoy [8] proposed to used the simplified polygons to assist the image compression in such remote rendering systems. However, this compression scheme requires the client to have a graphics rendering pipeline as well and real-time polygon simplification is difficult for complex dynamic graphics.

Giesen et al. [6] took a similar approach to ours. They tried to improve the performance of x264 encoding by building in 3D image warping to assist motion estimation. Their approach takes advantage of x264 to efficiently compress all warping residues, but also suffers from processing 3D image warping in blocks. As a comparison, our method warps the image at pixel level and our major concern is to select appropriate reference frames based on camera motion.

Bao and Gourlay [2] built a remote walkthrough environment based on 3D image warping. They proposed the idea of superview warping and view compensation to overcome warping artifacts. View compensation is to transmit only reference frames and warping residues to the client for display. We improve their solution in using better coding tools (H.264/AVC) and selecting multiple reference frames to reduce warping residues.

Mark [10] added a 3D image warping module to the conventional graphics pipeline to increase the rendering frame rate. Only key frames are rendered and other intermediate frames are interpolated by 3D image warping. Although it is an opposite problem to ours, which is to "remove" the actually rendered frames, many of our approaches, such as using multiple reference frames and how to generate reference frames, are inspired by Mark's work. The core idea behind both works is to exploit the frame-to-frame coherence in graphics rendering with image based rendering techniques.

2.2 Real-Time Video Coding

Nearly all video coding standards are based on hybrid video coders, which exploit spatial correlation using transform coding and temporal redundancy using motion prediction [21, Section 9.3]. These video coders are composed of a series of operations, such as transform coding, motion estimation, and entropy coding, where each operation incurs additional coding delay [18]. Unlike *general purpose* video coders that employ long look-ahead coding windows and complex coding tools for high coding efficiency, *real-time* video coders, such as [20, 3, 9], work under several constraints [15, 18]: (i) no bidirectional prediction, (ii) one-pass rate control, (iii) low buffer occupancy, (iv) intra refresh coding, and (v) strict encoding deadline, as low as 16.67 ms per frame. No bidirectional prediction eliminates the delay imposed by the frame reordering buffer, and two-pass rate control is inherently infeasible for real-time video coding. Moreover, low buffer occupancy and intra refresh coding ensure that individual coded frames do not exceed a maximum size, and thus coded frames can be directly streamed to the network without being buffered. Furthermore, when extremely low coding delay, in the order of nanoseconds, is required, intra-frame video coders [7, 14] can be used at an expense of significantly lower coding efficiency.

Because of the aforementioned constraints, compared to general purpose video coders, real-time video coders suffer from a much lower coding efficiency [5]. To illustrate the coding *inefficiency* of real-time video coders, we conducted the following experiment. We installed the OnLive thin client [1] on a dual-core laptop, which was connected to 10Mbps Ethernet. We played *Unreal Tournament III: Titan Pack*, a first-person shooter game illustrated in Figure 2(a), for 60 seconds, and we captured all downlink network packets. We also captured the rendered 720p video from the laptop's frame buffer, and saved it as a raw video file. From the network trace, we plot the OnLive streaming rate in Figure 2(b), which indicates that real-time OnLive encoder produces a stream at a fairly high bit rate: 6.49Mbps on average. Next, we encoded the raw video at several bit rates using x264 [5], which is a general purpose H.264/AVC encoder. We plot the resulting rate-distortion curve in Figure 2(c). This figure shows that x264 can encode the OnLive stream very well at rather low bit rates: x264 achieves 40+ dB at 1Mbps. In summary, Figure 2 reveals that real-time video coding is very challenging; even the state-of-art OnLive video coder suffers from coding inefficiency.

3. 3D IMAGE WARPING ASSISTED VIDEO CODING

In this section, we present how the proposed 3D image warping assisted video coding method works. Table 1 summarizes the notations and variables used.

3.1 Overview

To give one sentence overview of the proposed coding method: we select a set of key frames (named R frame)

Table 1: Notations and Variables

Name	Description
I_x	Image map of frame x. I'_x denotes the distorted image after passing I_x through image encoder and decoder.
D_x	Depth map of frame x. D'_x denotes the distorted depth after passing D_x through depth encoder and decoder.
v_x	Rendering viewpoint of frame x.
$\tilde{I}_x^y$	$\tilde{I}_y^x = warping(<I_x, D_x>, v_x \rightarrow v_y)$, the result image of warping $<I_y, D_y>$ from viewpoint v_y to v_x.
Δ_x^y	$\Delta_x^y = I_x - \tilde{I}_x^y$. The warping residue of frame x. Δ_x is used when the reference is not clearly specified.
$ref(x)$	The reference R frame for I_x.
$\mathcal{S}$	A set of all source video frames.
$\mathcal{R}$	A set of all R frames. $\|\mathcal{R}\|$ denotes the number of R frames in the set.
$\mathcal{W}$	A set of all W frames. $\|\mathcal{W}\|$ denotes the number of W frames in the set.
r	The actual bit rate of the encoded video. r_S denotes the bit rate of the whole video, r_{R_I}, r_{R_D}, and r_W denote the bit rate of R frame image, R frame depth, and W frame, respectively.
req	The target bit rate set for video encoding. req_S denotes the target bit rate of the whole video, req_{R_I}, req_{R_D}, and req_W are used to configure x264 to encode image, depth, and residue.
b	b_x denotes the size of the encoded frame x.
t	t_X denotes the time of playing the frame set. t_S denotes the video time. t_{R_I}, t_{R_D}, and t_W denote the time to play the component frames. Since the frame rate is the same, $t_X \propto \|X\|$.

in the video sequence based on the graphics rendering contexts extracted from the 3D video game engine, use the 3D image warping algorithm to interpolate other intermediate frames (named W frame) with the selected R frames, and encode the R frames and warping residues of W frames with x264. Our method can improve the coding performance by assigning more bit rate to encode the more important R frames and less bits for W frame residues. Figure 3 shows the framework in block diagrams and how data flows.

The core idea of our method is to exploit the frame-to-frame coherence. It is similar to motion estimation in many ways. For example, the concept of R/W frame is close to I/P frame in motion estimation. However, with the support of graphics rendering contexts, our method runs much faster than the search based motion estimation algorithms, and thus is more efficient in the real-time cloud gaming scenario.

Although the tools we use in this paper should look familiar to the researchers in the area of 3D/multi-view video coding, there are some major differences between our work and 3D/multi-view video coding [13]. First, 3D/multi-view video coding approaches only use IBR techniques to deal with different views at the same time spot while we apply 3D image warping to synthesize frames of different time. Second, in order to obtain accurate camera parameters for IBR, the cameras used in 3D/multi-view coding are usually statically deployed. Thus, only the object movements are studied and no camera motion needs to be considered. Besides, the depth capturing is usually not accurate enough for high quality IBR. On the contrary, we are able to extract accurate camera and depth information directly from 3D video game engine, which set us free to focus on other issues. Last, in 3D/multi-view video coding, only the actually captured frames can be selected as reference frames. But as we will introduce later in this section, we can also select the frames that do not exist in the video sequence as the reference frame. Our work is also different from the projects that apply 3D image warping techniques to generate stereo views from 2D sources [16]. It is because the 2D-3D conversion systems usually focus on high quality warping while our system concentrates on coding performance improvement. This core difference leads to very different frame selection strategies and system framework.

In the following subsections, we introduce different components in our proposed coding method, starting with 3D image warping.

3.2 3D Image Warping

3D Image warping is a well-known image-based rendering technique firstly proposed by McMillan [12]. The algorithm takes three inputs: (1) a depth image ($<I_x, D_x>$) that contains both color and depth maps; (2) the image's rendering viewpoint (v_x) that includes the camera position coordinate, the view direction vector, and the up vector; (3) a new viewpoint (v_y). The output of the algorithm is the color image at the new viewpoint ($\tilde{I}_y^x$). Figure 4 shows an illustration.

The key advantage of image warping algorithm is its complexity. The algorithm scans the image only once and it takes only a few arithmetic operations to process each pixel. Therefore, the algorithm is very computationally efficient and requires no graphical hardware support. The shortcoming of image warping is that it brings warping artifacts. Holes are generated when the occluded objects become visible in the new viewpoint because there is no pixel in the input image to reference when drawing the new image. It is also called the *exposure* problem.

Now we explain how to apply the 3D image warping algorithm to assist video coding. Given a source video frame set $\{I_x | x \in \mathcal{S}\}$, if we also know the depth map $\{D_x | x \in \mathcal{S}\}$ and viewpoint $\{v_x | x \in \mathcal{S}\}$ of each frame, we can select a group of R frames as $\mathcal{R}$ and the rest frames are all W frames as $\mathcal{W}$. The warping version $\{\tilde{I}_x^{ref(x)'} | x \in \mathcal{W}\}$ can be generated by running 3D image warping algorithm for every W frame. We have

$$\tilde{I}_x^{ref(x)'} = warping(<I'_{ref(x)}, D'_{ref(x)}>, v_{ref(x)} \rightarrow v_x)$$

where $I'_{ref(x)}$ and $D'_{ref(x)}$ are the distorted version of passing the original $I_{ref(x)}$ and $D_{ref(x)}$ through both encoder and decoder ($v_{ref(x)}$ is not distorted because we always apply lossless encoding for viewpoints). $ref(x)$ denotes the reference R frame for I_x. Since the application scenario is real-time video coding, any frame can only reference from previous frames. Thus $ref(x) < x$. Then we calculate the difference between the warping results and the original video frames as the warping residue $\{\Delta_x^{ref(x)'} | x \in \mathcal{W}\}$, where

$$\Delta_x^{ref(x)} = I_x - \tilde{I}_x^{ref(x)}$$

Finally, we encode the video sequence using the depth image of all R frames $\{<I_x, D_x> | x \in \mathcal{R}\}$, residues of all W

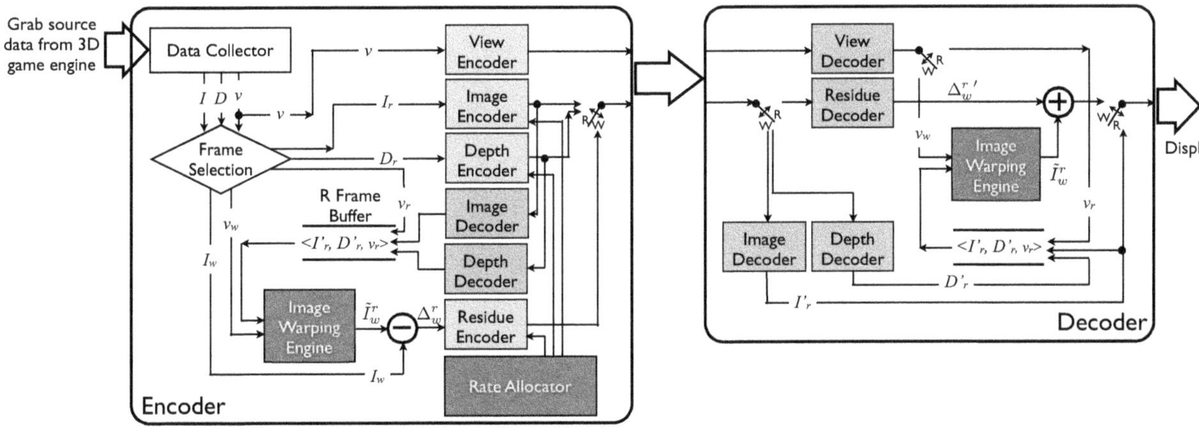

Figure 3: Framework of the 3D image warping assisted video encoder and decoder

frames $\{\Delta_x | x \in \mathcal{W}\}$ (Δ_x is used as the short for $\Delta_x^{ref(x)'}$), and all viewpoint information $\{v_x | x \in \mathcal{S}\}$.

On the decoder side, if the received video frame is R frame, we are able to decode I'_r, D'_r and v_r. I'_r should be directly displayed on the mobile screen and at the same time saved in the buffer together with D'_r and v_r. If the video frame is W frame, we get the distorted residue Δ'_w and the viewpoint v_w. We run 3D image warping algorithm for the saved R frame to calculate the warping frame $\tilde{I}_w^{r'}$, and then retrieve the target image frame I'_w by adding Δ'_w to $\tilde{I}_w^{r'}$.

3.3 Rate Allocation

The motivation of using 3D image warping in video coding is to reduce the signals of W frames so that they can be more efficiently encoded. The saved bit rate is applied to encode the more important R frames. Here we introduce the rate allocation strategy used in our coding method.

We first analyze the relationships between the different video bit rate components. We can represent the overall rate r_S as follows:

$$r_S = r_{R_I} + r_{R_D} + r_W \tag{1}$$

where

$$r_{R_I} = \frac{\sum_{x \in \mathcal{R}} b_{I_x}}{t_S}, \quad r_{R_D} = \frac{\sum_{x \in \mathcal{R}} b_{D_x}}{t_S}, \quad r_W = \frac{\sum_{x \in \mathcal{W}} b_{\Delta_x}}{t_S}$$

We did not consider the rate for encoding viewpoints in Eq. (1) because the rate used for encoding viewpoint vectors (36 bytes per frame before compression) is neglectable compared with the rate used for image frame compression. Fortunately, x264 allows us to set a target bit rate *req_r* when encoding a video sequence, and it automatically adjusts the encoding parameters to meet the requirement.

$$req_{R_I} \approx \frac{\sum_{x \in \mathcal{R}} b_{I_x}}{t_{\mathcal{R}}} \tag{2}$$

$$req_{R_D} \approx \frac{\sum_{x \in \mathcal{R}} b_{D_x}}{t_{\mathcal{R}}} \tag{3}$$

$$req_W \approx \frac{\sum_{x \in \mathcal{W}} b_{\Delta_x}}{t_{\mathcal{W}}} \tag{4}$$

Therefore, we do not need to manage the encoding size of every single frame but just find the appropriate bit rate req_{R_I}, req_{R_D}, and req_W to configure x264. We can apply Eq. (2), (3), (4) to Eq. (1):

$$r_S \approx \frac{\|R\| \cdot (req_{R_I} + req_{R_D}) + \|W\| \cdot req_W}{\|R\| + \|W\|} \tag{5}$$

Currently, we are using a static strategy in the rate allocation. We allocate a fixed portion of the overall available bit rate $f_R \cdot r_S$ to R frames, where $0 < f_R < 1$. We run experiments for each f_R value and find that 0.5 is a favorable value. The bit rate allocated for R frame depth map encoding is the half of the bit rate allocated for color map encoding because the depth map is not affected by image textures. In practice, we also find that depth encoding can achieve very high quality (50+ dB) with a relatively low bit rate (600Kbps). Therefore, we set a threshold T_{depth} for depth encoding to allocate no more bit rate than T_{depth}. Considering that we run x264 separately for three different components and the difference between the request bit rate and the actual encoded bit rate may be accumulated, we dynamically change req_W based on the actual bit rate of R frame encoding. As a result, given a target bit rate req_S, the bit rates of different components are calculated as follows:

$$req_{R_D} = \min(T_{depth}, \frac{\|R\| + \|W\|}{3 \cdot \|R\|} \cdot f_R \cdot req_S) \tag{6}$$

$$req_{R_I} = \frac{\|R\| + \|W\|}{\|R\|} \cdot f_R \cdot req_S - req_{R_D} \tag{7}$$

$$req_W = req_S + \frac{\|R\|}{\|W\|} \cdot (req_S - r_{R_D} - r_{R_I}) \tag{8}$$

3.4 Frame Selection

The rate allocation strategy is based on one assumption that the warping residues of W frames contain much less signals and can be encoded more efficiently than original image frames. However, this assumption may not be true if R frames are not carefully selected. In this subsection, we introduce three different frame selection strategies.

Fixed Interval

The *fixed interval* frame selection is the most intuitive solution. Starting from the first frame of the video sequence, we select the frames sequentially to form groups. All frame

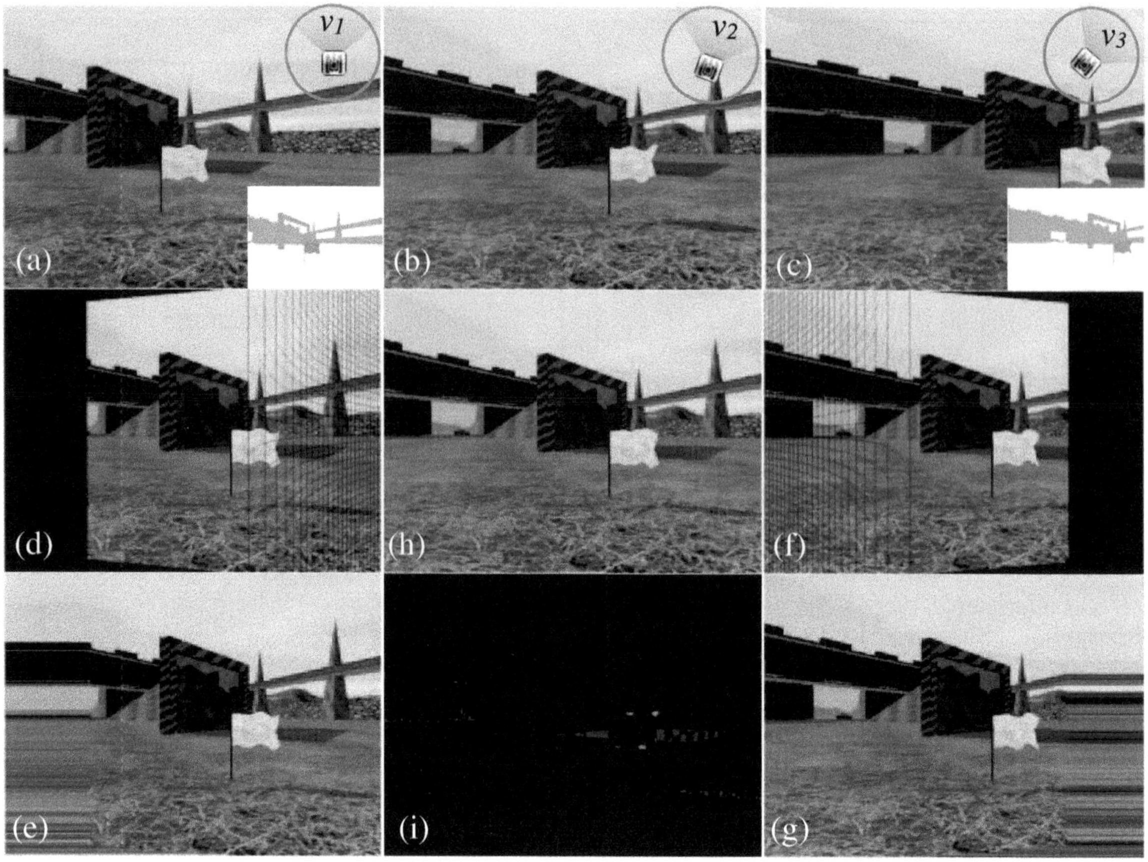

Figure 4: An illustration of how 3D image warping, double warping, and hole filling work: (a) the depth image frame $< I_1, D_1 >$ at viewpoint v_1; (b) the image frame I_2 at viewpoint v_2; (c) the depth image frame $< I_3, D_3 >$ at viewpoint v_3; (d) $\tilde{I}_2^1$ without hole filling; (e) $\tilde{I}_2^1$ with hole filling; (f) $\tilde{I}_3^1$ without hole filling; (g) $\tilde{I}_3^1$ with hole filling; (h) the warping result of double warping from v_1 and v_3 to v_2, with hole filling; (i) the difference between (h) and (b)

groups have the same fixed size, which is defined as *warping interval*. The first frame of each group is selected as R frame and the rest are W frames. The R frame in the group is referenced by all W frames of the same group. As long as the *warping interval* remains small, the viewpoints of the frames in the same group are likely to be close to each other so that 3D image warping can help remove most pixels.

The *fixed interval* solution is easy to implement. It does not require any other graphics rendering contexts except the rendering viewpoint and pixel depth required by 3D image warping. The rate allocation for *fixed interval* is also simplified. We do not need to dynamically change the bit rate request because the ratio of R and W is fixed all the time.

Dynamic Interval

One big disadvantage of the *fixed interval* solution is that it is too conservative in selecting W frames. For example, if the virtual camera remains static, all the frames will have the same background scene. Using only one R frame is enough for the whole static sequence. However, the *fixed interval* solution keeps generate R frames every *warping interval*. Toward this issue, we propose a *dynamic interval* strategy. The *dynamic interval* approach processes the encoding in the same way as *fixed interval*, with only one difference. The encoder needs to compare the viewpoint of the currently processing frame with the viewpoint of the previously encoded R frame. If two viewpoints are identical, which means the virtual camera remains static, then the current frame is selected as W frame.

The major benefit of this optimization is that the R frame number can be significantly reduced if the video sequence has a lot of static scenes. The reduction of R frame number allows the rate allocation module in our encoder to allocate more bit rate for R frame encoding (Eq. (6), (7)).

Double Warping

This approach uses the same strategy with *dynamic interval* for static sequences, and adds new optimization techniques for motion sequences. The warping artifacts caused by camera moving are difficult to fix. For example, Figure 4 shows an illustration of using 3D image warping for the images in a camera panning sequence. Pixels of a large area are missing in the warping result because those pixels do not exist in the source image. According to the previous work [19, 10], such artifacts can be effectively fixed by warping from another reference frames which have the missing pixels, or so called *double warping*. According to the example in Figure 4, if the target viewpoint v_2 is on the right side of the source

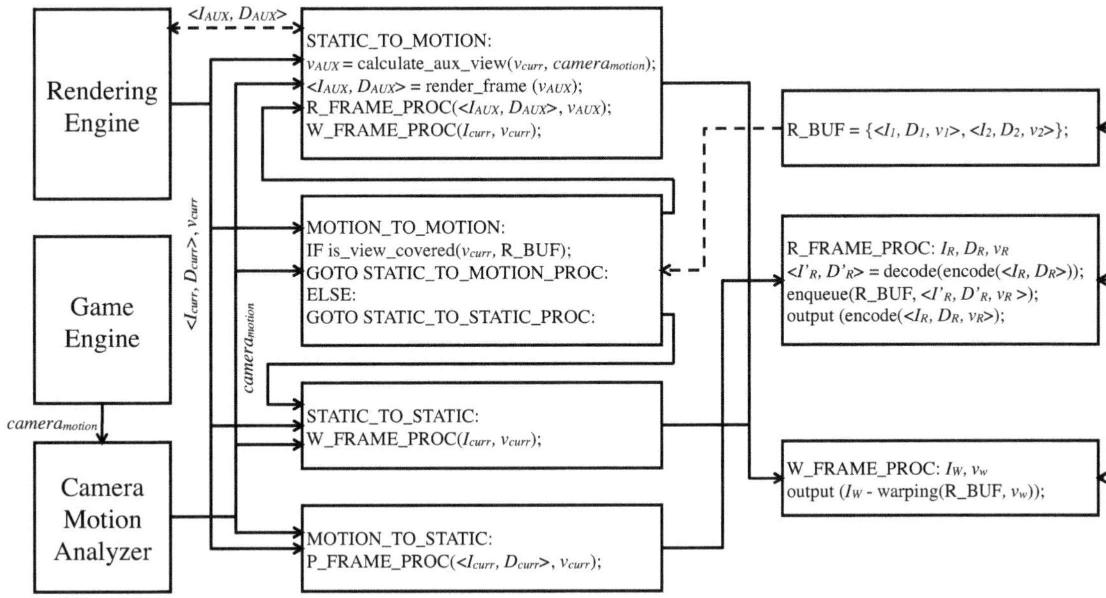

Figure 5: *Double warping* frame selection

viewpoint v_1, the viewpoint v_3 of the second reference frame should be selected on the right side of v_2 to provide the best coverage. However, in the scenario of cloud gaming, when the virtual camera is panning right, the frame I_3 is actually rendered later than I_2, which means when I_2 is encoded, there is no I_3 available for *double warping* reference.

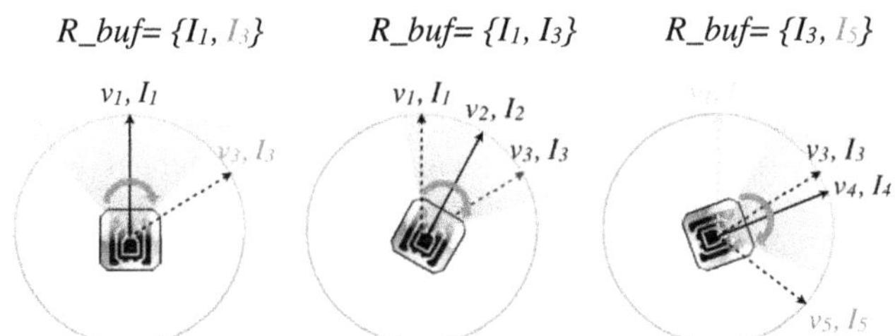

Figure 6: An illustration of the generation of auxiliary frames

In order to solve this problem, we modify in the 3D video game engine to render auxiliary frames for *double warping*. Figure 5 shows the work flow of *double warping* in details. We elaborate the whole flow in an example shown in Figure 6. Initially, the viewpoint is at v_1 and the image frame I_1 is captured. If a panning right motion is detected, the encoder will not only encode the current frame I_1, but also request the game engine to render the frame I_3 at the viewpoint v_3. I_3 does not exist in the game video sequence, but is generated only to support *double warping* for all intermediate viewpoint between v_1 and v_3. Both I_1 and I_3 are selected as R frames and saved in the buffer. As time goes by, the viewpoint pans right to v_2. It is well covered by two R frames I_1 and I_3. Thus I_2 is selected as W frames and *double warping* is applied to calculate the residue. If the viewpoint keeps moving to v_4, which is out of the coverage area of I_1 and I_3, the encoder will ask the game engine to render a new auxiliary frame I_5 at the viewpoint v_5. I_5 will be selected as R frame, added to the buffer to replace I_1. Both I_3 and I_5 are used to support the double warping of I_4.

Compared with the previous two frame selection strategies, *double warping* is able to improve the encoding performance further by reducing the warping residues created in motion sequences and using fewer R frames. *Double warping* not only takes the rendering viewpoint and pixel depth for 3D image warping, but also detects the camera motion events in the 3D video game engine and reuses the rendering engine to generate auxiliary frames.

4. IMPLEMENTATION

We have implemented an off-line version of the proposed video coder in our cloud gaming prototype system. In this section, we introduce some implementation issues and share some lessons we have learned.

The latest version of x264 is used in our system to encode the image map, depth map, and warping residues. We configure x264 as a real-time encoder to meet the requirement of our cloud gaming system. Table 2 lists the parameters for a real-time configuration.

Table 2: Real-Time x264 Encoding Settings

Setting	Description
`--bframes 0`	No bidirectional prediction
`--rc-lookahead 0`	No frame type and rate control lookahead
`--sync-lookahead 0`	No threaded frame lookahead
`--force-cfr`	Constant frame rate timestamp
`--sliced-threads`	Sliced-based threading model
`--tune zerolatency`	Implies all above real-time settings
`--preset fast`	A good balance between speed and quality
`--keyint 4`	Use small GOP size

The encoding of depth and residue is quite tricky in our current implementation. Our encoder produces the depth map as a 16-bit grey scale image. Because the current x264 does not natively support 16-bit color, it automatically converts the depth map to 8-bit image before encoding it, which leads to huge quality degradation. Therefore, we decompose the 16-bit depth map into two 8-bit sub-images: D^H and D^L. D^H contains the 8 more significant bits of every pixel and D^L has the 8 less significant bits. Then we encode D^H with the lossless mode of x264 by setting `--qp = 0`. D^L is encoded in a similar method to the image map. The residue frame can not be directly encoded by x264 either because it is a 9-bit color image (the difference of two 8-bit color image). Although x264 has the 9-bit support, we have found that in practice, the 9-bit x264 encoding does not generate good quality results and expensive operations are needed to prepare the 9-bit residue frame for the x264 input. Hence, we are taking an alternative approach by creating a new 8-bit image Δ^{+-} with the same width but twice height. The upper part of Δ^{+-} stores the pixels with positive value in Δ and the lower part has the negative pixels (reversed values). We use x264 to encode Δ^{+-} with the same parameters for image map and depth map.

We apply a hole filling technique in 3D image warping to fill all the holes with the color of their nearest neighbors (Figure 4 shows two examples). In the implementation, we found out that the hole filling is actually very important to our video coding method because the H.264/AVC encoder cannot effectively deal with the warping residues caused by hole pixels. It usually results in using even more bits to encode the residue of one hole pixel than the whole original image block. We plan to try other hole filling techniques proposed in [10, 2].

We set the GOP size for R frame encoding to 1 to force that every R frame is encoded using intra-prediction. This is because in the situation of mobile cloud gaming, the mobile networks are less likely to provide reliable end-to-end transmission. We should set the GOP to a small number so that the system does not take too long to read the next I frame if an I frame is lost. In our work, all W frames are dependent on their reference R frame. Thus, a larger than 1 GOP size for R frame encoding can possibly be scaled up to a huge loss when the network drops an intra-predicted R packets. Even though all R frames are encoded with intra-prediction, our encoder can still suffer when the R frame of a long static sequence is lost. We consider solving this problem in the future work by integrating different reliable transmission approaches.

5. EVALUATION

In this section, we use the cloud gaming prototype system to evaluate the performance of our proposed 3D image warping assisted video coding. Since we currently only have implemented an off-line version encoder, we need to record the game video first and then pass the raw frames to our encoder. We captured two BZFlag game video sequences: *pattern* and *free-style*. *Pattern* contains 315 frames, which is a 10 second play with four different motions (pan left, pan right, move forward, and move backward) currently supported by the mobile client implemented by us. Four motions are all played in the same pattern: pause for about one second and then move for about one second. *Free-style* contains 4072 frames, which is a 2 minute 15 second video

Table 3: Default Encoding Settings

Setting	Description
$reqs$ = 1Mbps	The target video bit rate
$f_R = 0.5$	Half bit rate is allocated for R frames
$T_{depth} = 700$	The threshold for depth encoding
`R_GOP` = 1	GOP for R frame encoding
`W_GOP` = 4	GOP for W frame residue encoding
`warp_int` = 4	*Warping interval* used only by the *fixed interval* and *dynamic interval* approaches

captured during the actual BZFlag game play. We encode the 2 video sequences with three different scripts: *fix_single*, *dyn_single*, and *dyn_double*, which stand for three different frame selection strategies: *fixed interval*, *dynamic interval*, and *double warping*, respectively. Table 3 lists the default setting for all scripts. We compare the results with the performance of using x264 directly for real-time encoding. The x264 encoding is configured using the real-time setting in Table 2. The default target bit rate is also set to 1Mbps. We present all experimental results in Figure 7.

The rate-distortion curves are presented in Figures 7(a) and 7(b). Both figures indicate that *dyn_double*, which stands for *double warping* optimization, has the best performance of all three approaches. It also outperforms x264 for about 2-3 dB at any given rate. In Figure 7(c), we plot the PSNR value of every frame in sequence *pattern* and we can see how each encoding approach actually works. The line of *dyn_double* shows periodic and prominent rises in PSNR because *double warping* uses the least number of R frames, and allocates the highest rate to encode R frames. Therefore all frames in the static scene can benefit a lot. However, since less bit rates are allocated for W frames, the PSNR of motion frames drop fast. For the first two motions (pan left and pan right), the frame quality can still maintain in a high level because *double warping* can generate high quality warping results. For the last two motions (move forward and move backward), the quality drops significantly because *double warping* can not correctly handle some special graphical effects, such as shadows. Figure 8 is the frame number 300 (PSNR=24.35dB) in *pattern* sequence using *dyn_double*. It shows that that the major problem comes from the shadow in front ground.

Figure 8: Shadow problem for *double warping*

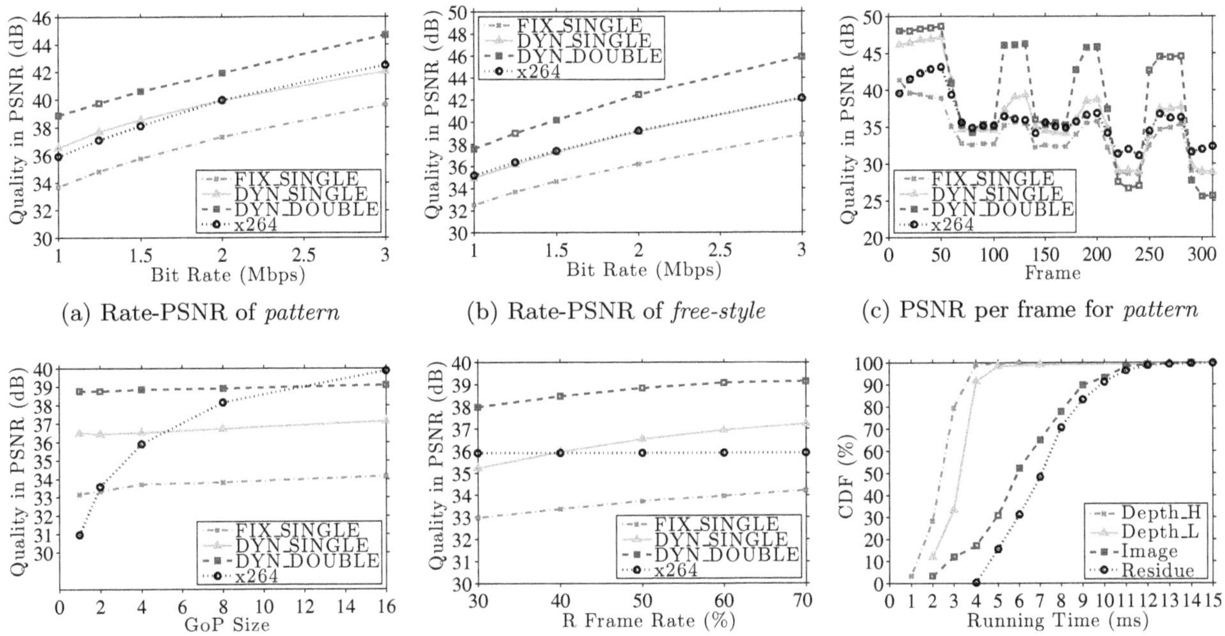

(a) Rate-PSNR of *pattern* (b) Rate-PSNR of *free-style* (c) PSNR per frame for *pattern*

(d) Rate-GOP of *pattern* (e) Rate-f_R of *pattern* (f) Encoding Runtime

Figure 7: Experiment Results

We also compare the performance under different setting parameters. For example, Figure 7(d) studies the relationship between PSNR and the GOP size. The figure shows no obvious difference in encoding quality of the proposed approaches with different GOP settings. However, the performance of x264 encoding increases significantly as the GOP size increases, and can beat our best performance (*dyn_double*) when GOP size is 16. We also test different f_R in Figure 7(e). Considering the line (*dyn_double*) having the best performance, the increase is less obvious for $f_R > 0.5$. Thus, we keep selecting $f_R = 0.5$ for all our experiments because assigning less bit rate for W frame can deteriorate the frames with bad quality although the average PSNR may increase.

Finally, the encoding and decoding complexity of the proposed coding method is evaluated. For video encoding, each W frame runs 3D image warping (either single warping or double warping) and the encoding of Δ. Each R frame needs to encode and decode I, D^H, and D^L. We plot the runtime of all components in Figure 7(f) and find that 90% of D^H and D^L frames are encoded within 4 ms, and 90% of I, and Δ frames are encoded within 10 ms (experiments were run on a Linux server with an Intel i7 2.8Ghz CPU and 4GB memory). Therefore, we believe there is enough room to optimize for 30 fps real-time encoding. For video decoding, we compare the overheads of our coding method with x264 decoding. Each R frame decodes I, D^H, and D^L and each W frame runs 3D image warping and decodes Δ. Assuming the decoding time of Δ and I is comparable to the decoding time of the original image frame, the added complexity of our method over x264 is the decoding of I for auxiliary frames (a subset of R frames), the decoding of D^H, D^L for all R frames, and the 3D image warping for every frame. Our experiments indicate that usually less than 10% of all frames are selected as R frames and the 3D image warping operation can be optimized to as low as 1.7 ms per frame (640×480) [23]. Therefore, we consider the overheads are acceptable. In addition, since our scheme is on top of H.264, the decoder can take advantage of the hardware acceleration module. The extra memory operations should not be a bottleneck as mobile devices become more and more powerful.

6. DISCUSSION

Another important feature of our coding method is to reduce *interaction latency*. When the mobile client receives the user commands to change the rendering viewpoint, rather than waiting for the server updates transmitted through the high latency network, the mobile client can immediately synthesize the image frame at the new rendering viewpoint by warping the R frames saved in the buffer. A similar *double warping* approach can be used to render auxiliary frames in advance to reduce warping artifacts since there is no warping residue available to the synthesized frame. Although the same name (auxiliary frame) and the same technique (*double warping*) are used, there are core differences between this latency reduction approach and the *double warping* coding approach. The auxiliary frames we have discussed in this paper are selected based on the already known camera motion and will surely be reference by other W frames. However, the auxiliary frames in the latency reduction approach will only be useful when unexpected user interaction happens. We will study this tradeoff between network bandwidth and interaction latency in the future work.

There are limitations of our proposed video coding method. First, it only works with cloud gaming systems or other remote rendering systems where the video encoder can extract graphics rendering contexts from the rendering engine in real-time. It may not achieve the best performance in the motion intensive games rendered in the third person perspective (e.g., real-time strategy and sports games) because the motion in the video is not mainly caused by the movement of virtual cameras. Second, the coding performance of the proposed video coding methods drops fast if the majority of pixels in the image frames are animations, foreground object actions, or special rendering effects (e.g., shadows). This is because the proposed video coding methods rely on the warping residues to encode those pixels, which are allocated relatively less bit rate. Even though, we believe our coding method can still be attractive to cloud gaming service providers. This is mainly because the first person perspective games usually require more intensive graphics rendering and are more suitable for cloud gaming. For example, according to the current game catalog of OnLive, more than half are the first person shooting, action, or racing games that can potentially benefit from our coding scheme. In order to extend the proposed coding method for all games, we are actively pursuing to integrate the proposed warping assisted coding scheme as a coding mode into x264 (similar to intra/inter mode), so that certain graphic effects, regions, and games can be encoded using traditional H.264 standard.

7. CONCLUSION

We have introduced the concept of using graphics rendering contexts in real-time video coding. Different from the conventional video coding approach, we are taking advantage of the pixel depth, rendering viewpoints, camera motion pattern, and even the auxiliary frames that do not actually exist in the video sequence to assist video coding, and we prove that the approach of integrating more components in the system has the potential to outperform the state-of-art H.264/AVC coding tools in the real-time cloud gaming scenario. The proposed approach is even more useful to serve mobile game clients because it can also help compensate the high latency introduced by wireless networks.

8. REFERENCES

[1] Onlive support documents. http://www.onlive.com/.

[2] P. Bao and D. Gourlay. Remote walkthrough over mobile networks using 3-D image warping and streaming. *IEE Proceedings on Vision, Image and Signal Processing*, 151(4):329–336, August 2004.

[3] U. Bayazit. Macroblock data classification and nonlinear bit count estimation for low delay H.263 rate control. In *Proc. of IEEE International Conference on Image Processing (ICIP'99)*, pages 263–267, Kobe, Japan, October 1999.

[4] T. Beigbeder, R. Coughlan, C. Lusher, J. Plunkett, E. Agu, and M. Claypool. The effects of loss and latency on user performance in unreal tournament 2003. In *Proc. of NetGames'04*, pages 144–151, Portland, OR, August 2004.

[5] J. Garrett-Glaser. x264: The best low-latency video streaming platform in the world, January 2010. `http://x264dev.multimedia.cx/archives/249`.

[6] F. Giesen, R. Schnabel, and R. Klein. Augmented compression for server-side rendering. In *Proc. of VMV'08*, pages 207–216, Konstanz, Germany, October 2008.

[7] Y. Lee and B. Song. An intra-frame rate control algorithm for ultra low delay H.264/AVC coding. In *Proc. of ICASSP'08*, pages 1041–1044, Las Vegas, NV, March 2008.

[8] M. Levoy. Polygon-assisted jpeg and mpeg compression of synthetic images. In *Proceedings of SIGGRAPH '95*, pages 21–28. ACM, 1995.

[9] Y. Liu, Z. Li, and Y. Soh. A novel rate control scheme for low delay video communication of H.264/AVC standard. *IEEE Transactions on Circuits and Systems for Video Technology*, 1(17):68–78, January 2007.

[10] W. Mark. *Post-Rendering 3D Image Warping: Visibility, Reconstruction, and Performance for Depth-Image Warping*. PhD thesis, University of North Carolina at Chapel Hill, Department of Computer Science, 1999.

[11] J. Marquez, J. Domenech, J. Gil, and A. Pont. Exploring the benefits of caching and prefetching in the mobile web. In *Proc. of WCITD'08*, Pretoria, South Africa, October 2008.

[12] L. McMillan. *An Image-Based Approach to Three Dimensional Computer Graphics*. PhD thesis, 1997.

[13] S. Milani and G. Calvagno. A cognitive approach for effective coding and transmission of 3D video. In *Proc. of the ACM International Conference on Multimedia (MM'10)*, pages 581–590, Firenze, Italy, October 2010.

[14] M. Nadeem, S. Wong, and G. Kuzmanov. An efficient realization of forward integer transform in H.264/AVC intra-frame encoder. In *Proc. of SAMOS'10*, pages 71–78, Samos, Greece, July 2010.

[15] H. Reddy and R. Chunduri. MPEG-4 low delay design for HDTV with multi-stream approach. Master's thesis, Swiss Federal Institute of Technology, Lausanne (EPFL), 2006.

[16] A. Redert, M. de Beeck, C. Fehn, W. Ijsselsteijn, M. Pollefeys, L. Van Gool, E. Ofek, I. Sexton, and P. Surman. Advanced three-dimensional television system technologies. In *Proceedings of 3DPVT'02*, pages 313 – 319, 2002.

[17] O. Riva and J. Kangasharju. Challenges and lessons in developing middleware on smart phones. *IEEE Computer*, 41(10):77–85, October 2008.

[18] R. Schreier, A. Rahman, G. Krishnamurthy, and A. Rothermel. Architecture analysis for low-delay video coding. In *Proc. of ICME'06*, pages 2053–2056, Toronto, Canada, July 2006.

[19] S. Shi, M. Kamali, K. Nahrstedt, J. C. Hart, and R. H. Campbell. A high-quality low-delay remote rendering system for 3D video. In *Proc. of the ACM International Conference on Multimedia (MM'10)*, pages 601–610, Firenze, Italy, October 2010.

[20] T. Tran, L. Liu, and P. Westerink. Low-delay MPEG-2 video coding. In *Proc. of VCIP'98*, pages 510–516, San Jose, CA, January 1998.

[21] Y. Wang, J. Ostermann, and Y. Zhang. *Video Processing and Communications*. Prentice Hall, 1st edition, 2001.

[22] T. Wiegand, G. Sullivan, G. Bjntegaard, and A. Luthra. Overview of the H.264/AVC video coding standard. *IEEE Transactions on Circuits and Systems for Video Technology*, 13(7):560–576, July 2003.

[23] W. Yoo, S. Shi, W. Jeon, K. Nahrstedt, and R. Campbell. Real-time parallel remote rendering for mobile devices using graphics processing units. In *Proc. of ICME'10*, pages 902 –907, july 2010.

Modeling Social Strength in Social Media Community via Kernel-based Learning*

Jinfeng Zhuang †, Tao Mei ‡, Steven C. H. Hoi †, Xian-Sheng Hua ‡, Shipeng Li ‡
† Nanyang Technological University, 50 Nanyang Avenue, Singapore 639798
‡ Microsoft Research Asia, Beijing 100080, China
{zhua0016, chhoi}@ntu.edu.sg, {tmei, xshua, spli}@microsoft.com

ABSTRACT

Modeling continuous social strength rather than conventional binary social ties in the social network can lead to a more precise and informative description of social relationship among people. In this paper, we study the problem of social strength modeling (SSM) for the users in a social media community, who are typically associated with diverse form of data. In particular, we take Flickr—the most popular online photo sharing community—as an example, in which users are sharing their experiences through substantial amounts of multimodal contents (e.g., photos, tags, geo-locations, friend lists) and social behaviors (e.g., commenting and joining interest groups). Such heterogeneous data in Flickr bring opportunities yet challenges to the research community for SSM. One of the key issues in SSM is how to effectively explore the heterogeneous data and how to optimally combine them to measure the social strength. In this paper, we present a kernel-based learning to rank framework for inferring the social strength of Flickr users, which involves two learning stages. The first stage employs a kernel target alignment algorithm to integrate the heterogeneous data into a holistic similarity space. With the learned kernel, the second stage rectifies the pair-wise learning to rank approach to estimating the social strength. By learning the social strength graph, we are able to conduct collaborative recommendation and collective classification. The promising results show that the learning-based approach is effective for SSM. Despite being focused on Flickr, our technique can be applied to model social strength of users in any other social media community.

Categories and Subject Descriptors

H.4.m [**Information Systems**]: Information Systems Applications—*Miscellaneous*

General Terms

Algorithms, Experimentation, Performance

Keywords

Social networks, kernel-based learning, learning to rank

* This work was performed at Microsoft Research Asia.
Area chair: Cees Snoek.

MM'11, November 28–December 1, 2011, Scottsdale, Arizona, USA.

1. INTRODUCTION

Social network mining, from communication networks, to friendship networks, to professional and organizational networks, has attracted a surge of interests in both industrial and academic communities. Most traditional studies focus on detecting *binary* relation ties between people (e.g., friends or not). Such a coarse indicator is not precise enough to give insight about the strength of social relationship among people. Some recent work, e.g., the study in [28], has attempted to address the problem of modeling the strength of social connections instead of simple binary linkage. Inferring precise social strength can facilitate a variety of applications, including friendship linkage prediction, item recommendation, social search, and so on.

In this paper, we investigate the challenging problem of Social Strength Modeling (SSM) of users in the social media communities. In particular, we take Flickr, one of the most popular online photo-sharing sites, as the social media platform in our study. Flickr contains rich user-generated contents, including shared photos, user-annotated tags, comments, and so on. Analogous to other social networking sites, e.g., Facebook and LinkedIn, each Flickr user can add other users into his contact list to indicate their friendship. Users can also create and join interest groups where users share photos of common interests and comments with each other. Besides the explicit mutual linkage between users, the uploaded photos and their associated metadata (e.g., tags, comments, etc.) can also be leveraged to infer the implicit relationship between users. The multimodal information available on Flickr poses opportunities yet challenges for the research on SSM.

One key challenge of SSM is to effectively explore and combine heterogeneous data from multiple modalities to measure the social strength in a principled way. Previous work on Flickr data mining has predominately focused on image-only or tag-only analysis. Other rich metadata has not been well exploited. To overcome this limitation, we present a novel framework for social strength modeling by unifying multi-modal heterogeneous data through a kernel-based machine learning approach. In particular, we suggest to use *kernel machine* [5] to model user similarity in each modal-

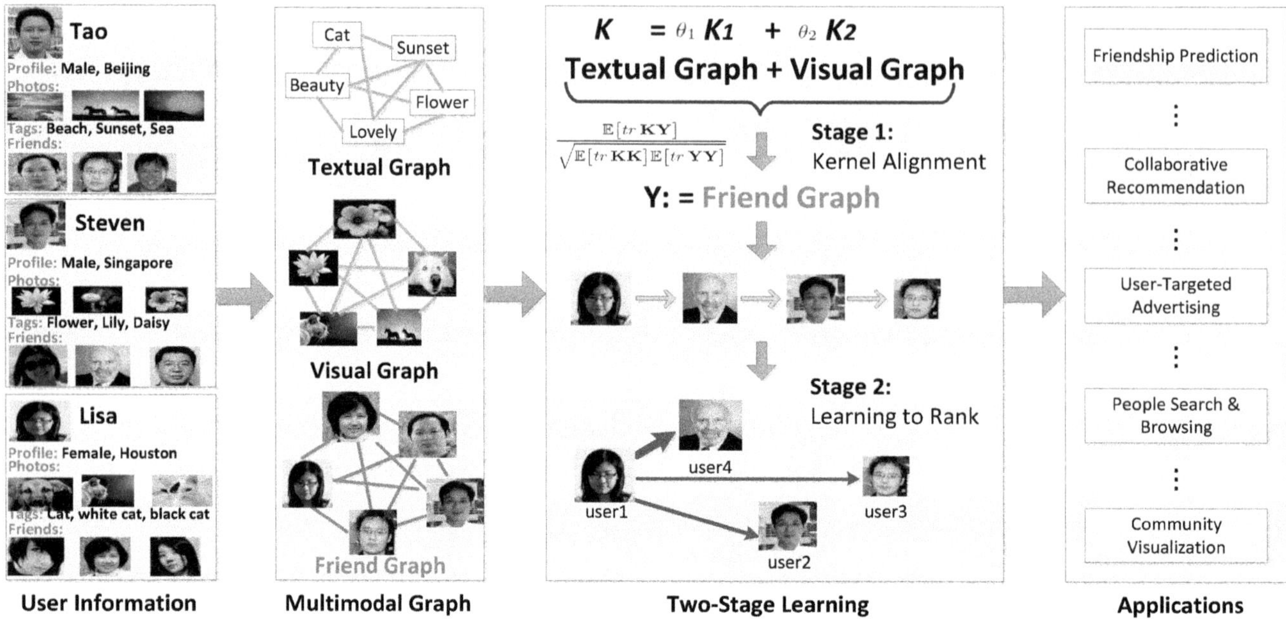

Figure 1: The proposed kernel-based learning to rank framework. The first panel shows the data associated with users, based on which we build three graphs in the second panel (only three kinds of graphs presented for illustration). In the third panel, we first learn the weight θ by maximally aligning the combination of textual and visual graphs to the friend graph, and then we adopt learning to rank framework with logistic loss to estimate the social strength. The learned social strength can lead to a wide variety of applications in the fourth panel.

ity, and then propose a two-stage learning scheme to measure the social strength by kernel-based techniques.

Specifically, we assume the final proximity graph of users is a linear combination of multiple proximity graphs, which are derived from the multiple modalities in Flickr. Each proximity graph is built by defining a kernel function on one modality. Figure 1 shows the proposed framework. At the first learning stage, we propose to combine the multiple proximity graphs by learning the optimal combination weights by following the kernel target alignment (KTA) principle [4, 7]. At the second stage, we propose a kernel-based learning to rank approach to model the social strength with the optimal kernel learned from the first stage. The proposed two-stage learning approach is able to model the social strength of users by exploring multimodal heterogeneous data in a systematic and comprehensive way. It is worth noticing that although we take Flickr as an example of social media community (as Flickr opens a public way to access its rich metadata), the proposed learning-based approach can be applied to any kind of community, such as Facebook and LinkedIn, in which users are also associated with rich multimodal metadata. The learned continuous social strength between users can facilitate a number of social media applications. In particular, we apply our technique to the social tasks of item recommendation and collective classification.

In summary, this paper makes the following contributions:

- We study the problem of modeling continuous social strength among users in a social media community. To the best of our knowledge, there are few works towards this target in the multimedia research community.
- We propose a novel two-stage kernel-based learning framework for social strength modeling, which effectively integrates heterogeneous data by optimally combining multiple kernels, and learns to rank social strength by a kernel-based learning to rank approach.
- We conduct experiments to evaluate the performance on a real-world dataset, and propose a wide variety of applications based on the learned social strength.

The rest of the paper is organized as follows. Section 2 formulates the problem of social strength modeling on Flickr data. Section 3 introduces the framework. Section 4 shows the experiments. Section 5 reviews related work, followed by the conclusion in Section 6.

2. PROBLEM FORMULATION

This section gives the problem definition of social strength modeling. Table 1 lists the key notations. First, we formally define the problem of social strength modeling with Flickr data as follows.

DEFINITION 1 (SOCIAL STRENGTH MODELING). *Given a collection of Flickr users $\mathcal{U}$, the goal of a* social strength modeling *problem is to learn a function $f : \mathcal{U} \times \mathcal{U} \rightarrow \mathbb{R}_+$ such that $f(u_i, u_j)$ measures the strength of social relationship between user u_i and user u_j.*

In the above definition, a basic element is a Flickr user $u_i \in \mathcal{U}$, which can be defined below.

DEFINITION 2 (FLICKR USER). *Each* Flickr user *$u_i \in \mathcal{U}$ is modeled as a three-dimensional tuple $u_i := [\mathcal{P}, \mathcal{N}, \mathcal{G}]$, where $\mathcal{P} = \{p_i : i \in \mathbb{N}_z\}$ is a collection of Flickr photos uploaded by user u_i, $\mathcal{N} \subset \mathcal{U}$ is the collection of users who appear in the contact list of user u_i, $\mathcal{G}$ is the collection of interest groups joined by user u_i.*

Figure 2: Example of the multimodal information associated with a typical Flickr user (left), a Flickr image (middle), and a Flickr interest group (right). The definition in Section 2 is a formalization of these data.

Table 1: List of key notations.

Notation	Description
$\mathbb{N}_u$	$\{1, \ldots, u\}$, a set of integers up to u †
N_u	$\lvert\mathbb{N}_u\rvert$, the cardinality of $\mathbb{N}_u$
u_i	the i-th Flickr user
$\mathcal{U}$	$\{u_i : i \in \mathbb{N}_u\}$, a collection of N_u users
$X, T, D, L, \mathcal{C}$	attributes of a Flickr image: content, tags, date, location, and comments
$\mathcal{P}, \mathcal{G}, \mathcal{N}$	a collection of Flickr photos, groups, and friends, respectively
#	the number of some object
$K, \mathbf{K}$	a similarity (kernel) function and matrix
tr $\mathbf{K}$	the trace of $\mathbf{K}$
$\lVert\mathbf{K}\rVert_F$	$:= \sqrt{\text{tr}\ \mathbf{KK}}$, the Frobenius norm of $\mathbf{K}$
$\mathbf{K}^\top$	the transpose of $\mathbf{K}$

†: We generalize the notation $\mathbb{N}_u$ and N_u to other objects, i.e., the sub-script u can be k, g, and c for indexing the *kernel*, *group*, and *comment*, respectively.

In the above definition, $\mathcal{N}$ and $\mathcal{G}$ indicate the explicit social relationship and organizations of Flickr users, and $\mathcal{P}$ may be beneficial to discovering some implicit relationship between users. Figure 2 shows the example of a typical Flickr user. "Your Photostream," "Your Contacts," and "Your Groups" correspond to $\mathcal{P}$, $\mathcal{N}$, and $\mathcal{G}$, respectively.

The contact list $\mathcal{N}$ indicates the binary social ties between users. Note that the friend relationship given by $\mathcal{N}$ is always asymmetric, which can be naturally handled by our proposed learning to rank framework in the next section. We employ $\mathcal{N}$ as the training data of known social strength for building our model.

The set $\mathcal{G}$ is the interest groups that user u_i has joined. For each $g \in \mathcal{G}$, it is created and self-organized by registered Flickr users. Users belonging to the same group tend to share photos of common interests. The right picture in Figure 2 shows a popular interest group.

The images $\mathcal{P}$ are useful to find implicit social relationship since they contain rich context information that expresses interests and social behaviors between users. We formally define a Flickr image as follows.

Definition 3 (Flickr image). *A Flickr image is defined as a 5-dimensional tuple* $P := [X, T, D, L, \mathcal{C}]$, *where*

- $X \in \mathcal{X} \subset \mathbb{R}^{d_x}$ *is the visual content with some fixed-length feature representation,* d_x *is the dimension of the visual descriptors;*
- $T \in \mathcal{T} \subset \mathbb{R}^{d_t}$ *is a vector representing the tags associated with* X*,* d_t *is the size of tag vocabulary;*
- D *is the date that* X *is created;*
- $L := [latitude, longitude] \in \mathbb{R}_+ \times \mathbb{R}_+$ *is the location where* P *is created;*
- $\mathcal{C} := \{[U, C]_i \in \mathcal{U} \times \mathbb{R}^{d_t} : i \in \mathbb{N}_c\}$ *is a collection of comments of* P*, where the first component* U *is the user who posts the comment and the second component* C *is the content of the comment.*

The rich context information $(T, D, L, \mathcal{C})$ besides the uploaded photo X encodes the social behaviors among different users. The middle panel of Figure 2 shows the typical behaviors of a Flickr user. In this paper, we incorporate this context information into a unified discriminative framework to model the social strength.

3. SOCIAL STRENGTH MODELING

In this section, we propose a kernel-based learning framework for social strength modeling.

3.1 Motivations

As shown in Figure 2, the first challenge is how to effectively combine the heterogeneous data associated with a user. Note that we can compute the similarity K under different modality, which is akin to a kernel function in the kernel machines, such as support vector machine and kernelized logistic regression. This inspires us to adopt the multiple kernel learning (MKL) scheme to integrate the multiple modalities, which has been actively studied in recent years [12]. Although not always yielding better results than single kernel chosen by cross-validation [3], it is regarded as one of the principle way to combine heterogeneous data sources. Therefore, we adopt the state-of-the-art MKL algorithm to weight each modality [4].

Second, we notice the social strength essentially ranks the degree of affinity between a pair of people. Therefore, we adopt the pair-wise learning to rank framework to further rectify the social strength based on the learned K in the first stage. Compared with generative models, such a discriminative model often enjoys better generalization ability [23]. Moreover, it avoids both the latent variable assumption and the parametric-form assumption of generative model functions, which make the learning more compact and precise.

We first discuss how to measure the similarity of Flickr users by defining a variety of kernel functions $\{K\}$ on different modalities of Flickr data. We then present a kernel learning technique to determine the optimal combination weights of multiple kernels, by following the kernel target alignment principle [4, 7]. Finally, based on the learned kernel, we formulate the social strength modeling problem in a pair-wise kernel-based learning to rank task, which can be efficiently solved in an iterative manner as the import vector machine (IVM) [31].

3.2 Kernels for Measuring User Similarity

For machine learning algorithms, the kernel trick is an important technique for mapping observations from a general set into a much higher- and possibly infinite dimensional inner product space without explicitly computing the mapping. Typically, each kernel $k : \mathcal{S} \times \mathcal{S} \to \mathbb{R}$ on a set $\mathcal{S}$ essentially defines the way of measuring similarity between data instances in $\mathcal{S}$. In this section, we present a series of candidate kernel functions in different modalities for measuring the similarity of Flickr users, which will be further explored with other kernel methods for inferring social strength.

3.2.1 User Similarity in Visual Space

For visual feature representation, we adopt the bag-of-(visual) word (BoW) model [18]. Specifically, we first extract the local descriptors of Scale-Invariant Feature Transform (SIFT) for each image [14]. All these descriptors are quantized into d_x groups by a K-means clustering process. Given an image, we assign each of its SIFT descriptors to a nearest cluster. Then, each image is converted into a fixed length of feature vector $\mathbf{x} \in \mathbb{R}^{d_x}$, where d_x is the size of visual vocabulary. The i-th component of this vector counts the frequency of SIFT descriptor assigned to cluster i. We measure the visual similarity between image $\mathbf{x}_i$ and $\mathbf{x}_j$ by a Gaussian kernel:

$$s(\mathbf{x}_i, \mathbf{x}_j) = \exp\Big\{-\frac{\|\mathbf{x}_i - \mathbf{x}_j\|^2}{\sigma^2}\Big\},$$

where σ is a kernel parameter. For a specific user u, we use the centroid of the images belonging to u to represent this user in the visual space, i.e.,

$$\bar{\mathbf{u}} = \sum_i \frac{\mathbf{x}_i}{|u|},$$

where $|u|$ is the number of images belonging to user u, $\mathbf{x}_i$ is one image uploaded by u. Thus, the similarity $K^1(u_i, u_j)$ between user u_i and u_j in the visual space can be given by

$$K^1(u_i, u_j) := \exp\Big\{-\frac{\|\bar{\mathbf{u}}_i - \bar{\mathbf{u}}_j\|^2}{\sigma^2}\Big\}.$$

As it is difficult to obtain an optimal bandwidth parameter σ, we set it as the average Euclidean distance empirically.

3.2.2 User Similarity in Text Space

Note that each uploaded photo can be associated with a set of tags provided by the user. We adopt the bag-of-word model to represent the textual information of a user [2]. Specifically, we collect all the tags and build a tag dictionary with size d_t. The tags of a user are converted into a feature vector in $\mathbb{R}^{d_t}$ by the traditional *tf-idf* weighing method. Here, the inverse document frequency is the number of users containing that tag. In this way, a user u_i can be represented by a vector $\mathbf{z}_i \in \mathbb{R}^{d_t}$. We employ the normalized linear kernel for measuring the user similarity in the text space which is widely used for text classification:

$$K^2(u_i, u_j) := \frac{\mathbf{z}_i^\top \mathbf{z}_j}{\sqrt{\mathbf{z}_i^\top \mathbf{z}_i}\sqrt{\mathbf{z}_j^\top \mathbf{z}_j}}.$$

Compared with the visual kernel K^1, the tag-based kernel K^2 carries more semantic information.

3.2.3 User Similarity by Mutual Comments

The interaction between users reflects the social connection between each other. For example, if two users post comments on each other's photos frequently, probably strong social ties exist between them. In general, people who are friends in real life would communicate more frequently. We can collect the mutual comment information between users to construct a symmetric link graph, in which each vertex represents a user and the edge weight is the number of comments between two users. Thus, we have

$$K^3(u_i, u_j) := \#comment \text{ between } u_i \text{ and } u_j.$$

When $i = j$, the kernel value is the frequency that u_i has ever posted to himself.

3.2.4 User Similarity by Common Interest Groups

The Flickr users can create or join in *Flickr interest groups*, which consists of a collection of users who share common interest or taste on photos of particular styles. Such interest groups can help users to find people or photos of their interest. Researchers have proposed techniques (e.g., [17, 15]) to analyze the structure and themes of the groups due to their importance in organizing Flickr users. Intuitively, people among which strong social connections exist are more likely to join the same interest groups, as they may affect each other and share similar interests. Therefore, we can use the number of common interest groups to measure the similarity between people:

$$K_u^4(u_i, u_j) := \#group \text{ both } u_i \text{ and } u_j \text{ joined}.$$

When $i = j$, the kernel value is the number of groups that u_i has joined.

3.2.5 User Similarity by Mutual Friends

Each Flickr user has a contact list, which can be deemed as "friends." When two users share many common friends, it is reasonable to infer that they have strong social connection to each other. Naturally, we can count this number as the kernel value to quantify this modality:

$$K^5(u_i, u_j) := \#friend \text{ belong to both } u_i \text{ and } u_j.$$

3.2.6 User Similarity via Geo-tags

The images in a social media site are usually associated with geo-tags, which indicates the latitude and longitude parameters where the photos are taken. If two users have traveled to the same place frequently, it is reasonable to conclude they are similar to each other (since they would like to travel to the same places). Similar to the representation in the text space, we use the bag-of-geotag to compute the similarity between users:

$$K^6(u_i, u_j) \; := \; \#\textit{location} \text{ where both } u_i \text{ and } u_j \text{ took photos.}$$

At the diagonal position of K^6, the value is the number of places the user has been to. The raw geo-tags are in form of longitude and latitude pairs. We discretize it by dividing the whole globe into tiles. Each location is represented by its corresponding tile.

3.2.7 User Similarity via Favorite Photos

One important function provided by Flickr is that users can mark their favorite photos (fave). Assuming the number of faves correlates to the social strength, we define

$$K^7(u_i, u_j) := \#\textit{photo} \text{ both } u_i \text{ and } u_j \text{ favor.}$$

The rationale underlying this assumption is that users who like the same photos tend to be friends. This may not be true in real case. However, through the KTA algorithm we learn the weights of these kernels, which provides us insight about which modalities are indeed informative for detecting social strength in the multimedia research community.

The similarity measures $K_u^{1\sim7}$ are not necessarily positive semi-definite (p.s.d.). We can force these measures to be p.s.d. to construct kernels by adding a properly scaled identity matrix to the corresponding similarity matrix.

3.3 Optimal Combination of Multiple Kernels

In the above, we define various kernel functions for similarity measures in different modalities. The next challenge is to find the best way of combining these modalities, which plays a key role in social strength modeling. Specially, our goal is to determine a linear combination of multiple kernels to fuse all modalities for measuring the similarity, parameterized by a weight vector $\boldsymbol{\theta} \in \mathbb{R}^{N_k}$:

$$K(u_i, u_j; \boldsymbol{\theta}) = \sum_{t=1}^{N_k} \theta_t K^t(u_i, u_j), \qquad (1)$$

where K^t is the kernel defined under the t-th view of the users, and N_k is the number of modalities (or views).

One naive way is to manually set the weights of different modalities, which however highly relies on domain knowledge and cannot find the optimal combination. In this section, we present a kernel-based learning technique to find the optimal combination of multiple kernels by following the principle of KTA [4, 7].

Specially, given the target matrix $\mathbf{Y}$ ($\mathbf{Y} \in \mathbb{R}^{N_u \times N_u}$), which encodes the existing known relationship among users (through explicit friend lists), we adopt the *kernel alignment* [7] to measure the quality of kernel $\mathbf{K}$ with respect to the target matrix $\mathbf{Y}$ as follows.

DEFINITION 4 (KERNEL ALIGNMENT). *Let $\mathbf{K}, \mathbf{Y} \in \mathbb{R}^{N_u \times N_u}$ be two kernel matrices such that $\|\mathbf{K}\|_F \neq 0$ and $\|\mathbf{Y}\|_F \neq 0$. Then, the* alignment *between $\mathbf{K}$ and $\mathbf{Y}$ is defined by*

$$\rho(\mathbf{K}, \mathbf{Y}) = \frac{\mathbb{E}\big[tr\, \mathbf{KY}\big]}{\sqrt{\mathbb{E}\big[tr\, \mathbf{KK}\big]\mathbb{E}\big[tr\, \mathbf{YY}\big]}}.$$

Note that the kernel matrices usually have to be centered ($\mathbb{E}[K_{ij}] = 0$) [4]. This centering step can be computed by

$$[\mathbf{K}]_{ij} := K_{ij} - \frac{1}{N_u}\sum_{i=1}^{N_u} K_{ij} - \frac{1}{N_u}\sum_{j=1}^{N_u} K_{ij} + \frac{1}{N_u^2}\sum_{i,j=1}^{N_u} K_{ij}.$$

Given the target graph represented by matrix $\mathbf{Y}$, we maximize the alignment ρ over $\mathbf{K}$ to solve the kernel. The matrix $\mathbf{Y}$ is observed from the Flickr platform. For example, in a friend prediction task, $\mathbf{Y}$ is the mutual contact graph constructed from the profile of each Flickr users. We assume the target kernel matrix is in form of $\mathbf{K} = \sum_{t=1}^{N_k} \theta_t \mathbf{K}^t$ consistent with equation (1), where $0 \leqslant \theta_t \leqslant 1, \sum_t \|\theta_t\|_2 = 1$. Thus the target variable is reduced from $\mathbb{R}^{N_u \times N_u}$ to $\mathcal{M} := \{\|\boldsymbol{\theta}\|_2 = 1 \text{ and } \boldsymbol{\theta} \geqslant 0\}$. The following theorem guarantees the optimal solution can be computed efficiently [4].

THEOREM 1. *The solution $\boldsymbol{\theta}^*$ of the optimization problem*

$$\max_{\boldsymbol{\theta} \in \mathcal{M}} \rho(\mathbf{K}, \mathbf{Y}) \;:\; \mathbf{K} = \sum_{t=1}^{N_k} \theta_t \mathbf{K}^t$$

is given by $\boldsymbol{\theta}^* = \boldsymbol{\theta}^*/\|\boldsymbol{\theta}^*\|$, where $\boldsymbol{\theta}^*$ is the solution of the following quadratic program:

$$\boldsymbol{\theta}^* = \arg\min_{\boldsymbol{\theta} \geqslant \mathbf{0}} \boldsymbol{\theta}^\top \mathbf{M} \boldsymbol{\theta} - 2\boldsymbol{\theta}^\top \mathbf{a},$$

where $\mathbf{a}$ is the vector $[tr\, \mathbf{K}^1\mathbf{Y}, \ldots, tr\, \mathbf{K}^{N_k}\mathbf{Y}]^\top$ and $\mathbf{M}$ is the matrix $[\mathbf{M}]_{kl} := tr\, \mathbf{K}^k\mathbf{K}^l$, for $k, l \in \mathbb{N}_k$.

3.4 Kernel-based Learning to Rank

After obtaining a similarity measure $K_u : \mathcal{U} \times \mathcal{U} \mapsto \mathbb{R}$ in the form of equation (1), we consider a discriminative model to estimate the social strength between two users. Let z be a $\{0,1\}$-valued latent variable to indicate whether there is a connection between two users. The social connection strength inference is about to estimate the probability $P(z_{ij} = 1|u_i, u_j)$. To this purpose, we build a logistic normal model based on training pairs. The connection between Flickr users come from the mutual contact $\mathcal{N}$ in Flickr user profile, i.e., $z_{ij} = 1$ if u_j is in the contact list of u_i.

We use a linear model $f(u_i, u_j) = \mathbf{w}^\top(\Phi(u_i) - \Phi(u_j))$ parameterized by $\mathbf{w}$ to predict the social strength between u_i and u_j, where the function $\Phi(\cdot) : \mathcal{U} \to \mathbb{R}^d$ maps a user U to a feature representation under some specific modality, i.e., $K_u(u_i, u_j) = \Phi(u_i)^\top \Phi(u_j)$. The intuition is if two users u_i and u_j are similar to each other, the difference of their prediction scores $\mathbf{w}^\top(\Phi(u_i) - \Phi(u_j))$ should be driven to 0. Thus, we solve $\mathbf{w}$ by minimizing the regularized loss:

$$\min_{\mathbf{w}} \frac{\lambda}{2}\|\mathbf{w}\|_2^2 + \sum_{u_i, u_j \in \mathcal{U}} l\Big(y_{ij}, \mathbf{w}^\top(\Phi(u_i) - \Phi(u_j))\Big), \qquad (2)$$

where λ is a hyper-parameter controlling the trade-off between regularization and loss of prediction. The label y_{ij} ($y_{ij} = 1 - z_{ij}$) takes value in $\{0,1\}$ indicating the connection between u_i and u_j. When u_i has u_j as a friend, we set $y_{ij} = 0$. The function $l(\cdot,\cdot) : \mathbb{R} \times \mathbb{R} \to \mathbb{R}_+$ measures the loss of prediction. We adopt the logistic loss $l(y_1, y_2) = \ln(1+e^{-y_1 y_2})$ instead of hinge loss in traditional SVM-based ranking model, as it can predict the probability of classification result. Then, we can estimate the social strength by

$$P(y_{ij} = 1|u_i, u_j) = \frac{e^{f(u_i,u_j)}}{1 + e^{f(u_i,u_j)}}.$$

According to the representor theorem [20], the solution of the above problem can be expressed in form of $f(\hat{u}) = \sum_j \alpha_j K(\hat{u}, \hat{u}_j)$, where $\boldsymbol{\alpha}$ is the weight of training pairs, $\hat{u}_j := [u_{j1}, u_{j2}]$ is an ordered "support" pair of users. Thus the dual objective can be written as

$$\min_{\boldsymbol{\alpha} \in \mathbb{R}^{N_p}} \frac{1}{N_p} \mathbf{1}^\top \ln\left(\mathbf{1} + e^{-\mathbf{y} \circ (\widehat{\mathbf{K}} \boldsymbol{\alpha})}\right) + \frac{C}{2} \boldsymbol{\alpha}^\top \widehat{\mathbf{K}} \boldsymbol{\alpha}, \tag{3}$$

where N_p is the number of training pairs, $\widehat{\mathbf{K}} \in \mathbb{S}^{N_u^2 \times N_u^2}$ is the kernel matrix evaluated from a kernel function $\widehat{K} : (\mathcal{U} \times \mathcal{U}) \times (\mathcal{U} \times \mathcal{U}) \rightarrow \mathbb{R}$, i.e., defined on the user pairs. The kernel $\widehat{K}$ of two pairs $\hat{u}_i$ and $\hat{u}_j$ is computed by

$$\begin{aligned} \widehat{K}(\hat{u}_i, \hat{u}_j) &= (\Phi(u_{i1}) - \Phi(u_{i2}))^\top (\Phi(u_{j1}) - \Phi(u_{j2})) \\ &= K_u(u_{i1}, u_{j1}) + K_u(u_{i2}, u_{j2}) \\ &\quad - K_u(u_{i1}, u_{j2}) - K_u(u_{i2}, u_{j1}), \end{aligned}$$

where $K_u : \mathcal{U} \times \mathcal{U} \mapsto \mathbb{R}$ is in the form of (1). The dual objective (3) can be solved efficiently by IVM [31].

3.4.1 Training Pair Selection

Constructing the training pair is not trivial for both effectiveness and efficiency purposes. When a user u_j appears in the contact list of u_i, it is likely that u_j is a friend of u_i in real life or that the content uploaded by u_j is of interest to u_i. Therefore, we can treat (u_i, u_j) as a positive pair directly when training the model. However, it is not so trivial for the case of negative pairs. It is a common case that u_i has not noticed his friend u_j has registered. Thus, u_i does not add u_j into his contact list. If we simply treat (u_i, u_j) as negative training pairs, the learned model would fail to predict such latent friends. One of our important applications is to reveal such potential friends. It calls for elaborate strategies for sampling negative pairs.

Moreover, there exists computational necessity for training pair sampling. Suppose each user has N_p friends on average, we would have $\mathcal{O}(N_p \times (N_u - N_p) \times N_u)$ training pairs in total. Such a large set of pairs makes it difficult to directly apply the pair-wise learning to rank algorithm. Moreover, some training pairs are not helpful for learning the models. The study in active learning shows a small fraction of discriminative training data can often yield satisfying performance. We then propose the following two-stage scheme for sampling pairs.

First, we choose the pairs of users that are least likely to be friends to construct negative training pairs. To this end, for each user u_i, we sort the values $K^t(u_i, u_j), j \in \mathbb{N}_u$ with $t \in \mathbb{N}_k$ in ascending order. The users with small similarity to u_i are excluded from the potential friend list of u_i. Since we have multiple N_k kernels defined on users, it is unclear to adopt which one for the sampling purpose. Here we employ a very conservative scheme, that is, we choose the top N_e users that appear in the top N ($N > N_e$) users of u_i under all the similarity measures K^t. For constructing positive pairs, we use K^3 after filtering out the friends according to the contact list, i.e., the kernel counting the mutual comments, to determine the ones most frequently communicating with u_i as positive pairs.

Second, we adopt the active sample selection scheme in IVM during the training phase [31]. Due to the logistic loss function of (2), the solution is non-sparse. However, many of the samples are not necessary to yield a useful solution. We can actively select a pair to expand the set of support vectors at each iteration. In this way, the learning can be significantly sped up while the efficacy of the learned model is preserved.

In summary, the proposed framework relies on a series of similarity measures from various modalities without any assumption how these measures are obtained. Therefore, any extension of this work only needs to design new features or add new factors to instantiate these measures.

3.5 Applications

The proposed social strength modeling can lead to a variety of applications, including but not limited to:

- **Friendship Prediction.** In Flickr, each user can add other users into his/her contact list. However, when users are known to each other in real life, or they share quite similar interest in photo styles, the friendship link may not exist explicitly due to the limited searching and browsing functionality. Our framework can predict the implicit links between Flickr users by leveraging the various content and context information.
- **Collaborative Recommendation.** It is very useful to improve user experience by recommending proper objects to users, e.g., interest groups and favorite photos. Such item recommendation tasks can be benefited from the modeled strength as the popularity of these terms are correlated with the social strength among people. Affinity propagation algorithms can be designed based on the learned social strength graph.
- **User-Targeted Advertising.** Similar to recommendation, we can provide user-targeted advertising to a connected component consisting of similar users, so that the advertisements are relevant to user interest through a propagation among similar users.
- **User Search & Browse.** We can rank the user search results according to their social strengths with the one who conducted the query. The user is more likely to find out the targets of his interest. This technique can compensate the lack of informative words matching with the query. Therefore, we expect the results based on traditional simple keyword matching can be greatly improved.
- **Community Visualization.** The applications of visualizing people's social network could be improved by scaling/shading links according to the estimated relationship strengths.

4. EXPERIMENT

Table 2: The statistics of the collected Flick data.

#user	#group	#image	#tag	#contact
5,000	109,205	5,001,601	116,372	81,447

We evaluated the proposed social strength modeling techniques on a real-world data set collected from Flickr. We start from a random user as seed and expand the crawling according to its friend list in a breadth-first search manner. We stopped at 5,000 users as we consider such a scale is enough to work with to conduct reliable conclusions. All

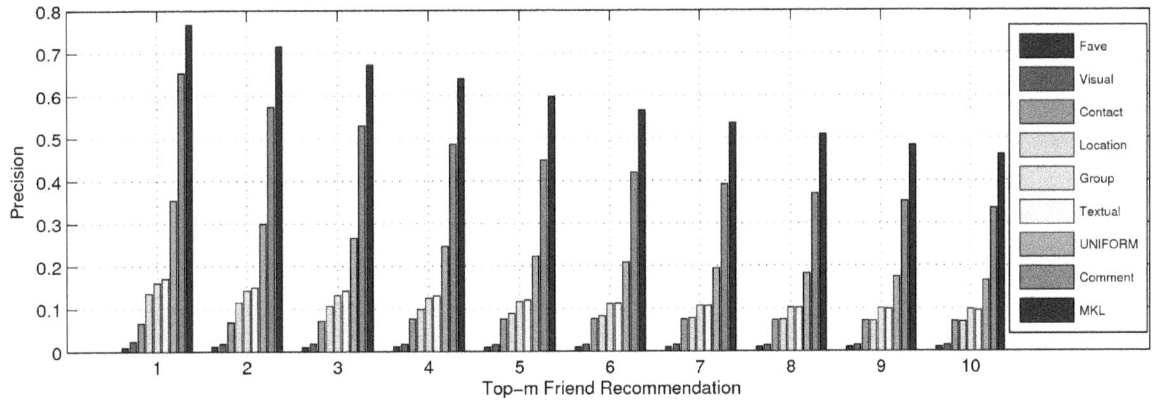

Figure 3: The average accuracy of top-10 friend recommendation by single and combined multiple kernels.

Table 3: The base kernels and the weights by KTA in the friend and group recommendation task.

Kernel	1	2	3	4	5	6	7
Name	Visual	Textual	Comment	Group	Contact	Location	Fave
Friend	.0042	.1007	.6488	.0637	.1042	.0499	.0285
Group	.0183	.1687	.5065	N/A	.2030	.0397	.0299

the associated metadata (as defined in Section 2) are downloaded in the XML format. We evaluate the effectiveness of social strength modeling on recommendation tasks.

4.1 Friend Recommendation

The essence of SSM is to infer the acquaintance between two people. Therefore, the most direct criterion of SSL is to measure the friend recommendation accuracy. It is also an important application for social network sites (including Flickr, though it is not initially designed for social purpose).

We randomly choose 4,000 users for training purpose. The target kernel matrix $\mathbf{Y}$ in Section 3.3 is the friend indicating matrix. The i-th row of $\mathbf{Y}$ is a binary vector indicating whether a user is in the contact list of user u_i. We adopt the learning to rank to infer the social strength based on kernels maximally aligned to $\mathbf{Y}$. For each kernel matrix $\mathbf{K}$, we normalize it by dividing each row with the maximal value at that row. Then we use $\mathbf{K} = (\mathbf{K} + \mathbf{K}^{\top})/2$ to make it symmetric. For the ones not satisfying the positive semi-definite (p.s.d.) property (this can be examined by eigen-decomposition), we add $\delta\mathbf{I}$ to make them p.s.d. The valuated kernels include:

- *Single*: A single kernel defined in Section 3.2. By examining the kernel one-by-one, one can observe the effect of each modality clearly;
- *Uniform*: Each kernel is assigned the same kernel weight. This is the baseline showing the result of simple combination, which serves as baseline method;
- *MKL*: The the proposed multiple kernel learning method introduced in Section 3.3 for combining the modalities.

Given a test user, we sort the values in a descending order and extract the top users as recommended friends. The learned weights of the kernels are presented in Table 3. The self-explanatory name of kernel implies its definition in Section 3.2. The top-10 friend recommendation results are plotted in Figure 3, from which we can have the following observations.

First, MKL yields the best performance among all the evaluated kernels. Its top-1 accuracy approaches 80%, and top-10 accuracy approaches 50%. Such relatively high accuracy confirms that inferring social strength on multimedia site is possible. It could open a new perspective for social network mining. For m from 1 to 10, MKL significantly outperforms other kernels. Specially, the naive unform combination only reports half of the accuracy of MKL. This fact verifies the efficacy of the proposed method. Moreover, it implies that the underlying single kernels are complementary. It coincides with the previous conclusion that MKL is effective at concatenating heterogeneous data.

Second, the *Comment* kernel (K^3) reports the second best result. Recall the definition of K^3, it's the number of mutual comments among Flickr users. Its good results show that the *mutual communication* is still the most informative modality when inferring social strength. This fact is consistent with the large volume of works on social network analysis, most of which are mutual communication based. Moreover, note that K^3 is also better than uniform combination. It means some of the modality is actually noisy. Therefore, learning the modality weight in a principle manner is crucial.

Third, we can analyze the contribution of each modality from the results of every single kernel. Specifically:

- The *Textual* kernel (K^2) reports the second best accuracy among all the single kernels, though it is worse than K^3. We can conclude that the photos of friends exhibit stronger semantically similarity.
- The *Visual* kernel (K^1) reports very poor performance. This could be possibly explained by the semantic gap. Besides, we use the mean of photos to measure visual similarity due to the difficulty of dealing with a large scale of photos. This also could lose much information.
- The *Fave* kernel (K^7) produces the worst performance among the 7 base kernels. With m varying from 1 to 10, its accuracy is most zero consistently. This fact means it is not useful when inferring social strength.

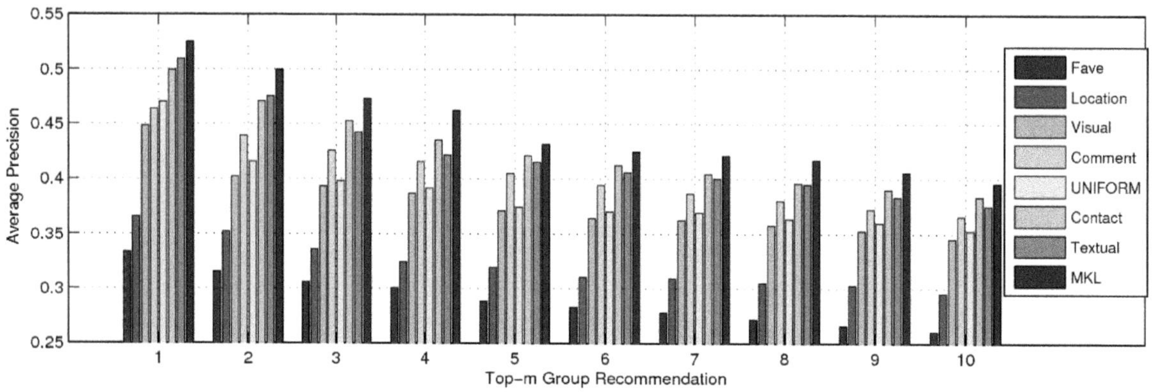

Figure 4: The average accuracy of top-10 group recommendation by single and combined multiple kernels.

- The *Group* kernel (K^4) is quite similar to *Textual* kernel. Their performance can be explained in the same manner as the group membership indicates the semantics of users' photos.
- The *Location* kernel (K^6) is helpful as friends have higher probability residing or taking pictures at the same place.

4.2 Group Recommendation

In this section, we evaluate the interest group recommendation task based on social strength modeling. For the user u_i and group g_k, the recommendation score p is

$$p(u_i, g_k) = \sum\nolimits_j f(u_i, u_j)\delta(u_j, g_k),$$

where $\delta(u_j, g_k) \in \{0, 1\}$ indicates whether u_j belongs to g_k, f is the social strength predicted by MKL method. We use the *Group* kernel as the target kernel matrix $\mathbf{Y}$ for alignment. We filter out the 1,000 most popular groups for prediction (actually the number of groups is larger than the number of users). We use the average recommendation accuracy to measure performance, as shown in Figure 4. The weights of the six base kernels are listed in Table 3.

We have the following observations from the results. First, MKL outperforms the other candidate kernels as in the case of friend recommendation. The top-10 accuracy is about 40%. It is practical to recommend interest groups to users. This fact confirms the efficacy of MKL again. The *uniform* combination only ranks the 4-th position among the eight methods. It is worse than two base single kernels. Therefor, careless kernel combination can hurt the performance as some kernels are noisy.

For the single kernels, the *Textual* kernel performs the best among the six kernels. We conclude that semantic information is the most important for predicting group membership. This is in contrast to friend recommendation, where mutual friendship is more informative. Each interest group has focused themes. The user annotated tags express the semantics of the photos and thus are more useful.

Difference from friend recommendation, the *Contact* kernel is almost as good as the Textual kernel. We conjecture that user-user relationship is correlated with user-group membership. Both content and social behavior contribute to social strength modeling. The accuracy of *Fave* and *Location* kernels is far from satisfactory. It is a bit surprising that the *Fave* kernel is even worse than the *Location* kernel. Intuitively, the location info is not for group recommendation as it is too coarse, while the *Fave* kernel carries the taste of photos of users, which is related to group membership. The kernel weight learned in Table 4 is quite different from the results in Table 3. Our framework omits the latent variable modeling process such that it can be task dependent.

4.3 Semi-supervised Classification

A prior similarity matrix defined over the input samples is crucial for the semi-supervised learning (SSL) (e.g., [30, 32]) as it characterizes the clustering or the manifold structure of the data. Such unsupervised information is helpful for classification purposes as similar data usually share similar labels. The social strength graph learned in this paper can play an important role for the SSL. We can plug it into [32], which is one of the most influential SSL algorithms, to predict the *gender* and the *location* of a Flickr user. For the first task, we predict the *gender* of a user (i.e., male or female). For the second, we first detect the most frequent location from all the locations associated with a user, and then predict whether s/he has been there. The target matrix $\mathbf{Y}$ is set as the contact graph for both tasks. We set the ratio of the supervised samples to the overall samples as 0.7. The parameters in the SSL algorithm are tuned by the cross-validation.

Figure 5 shows the results. We see that MKL performs the best in both tasks. This verifies that the modalities are complementary for the classification tasks. Regrading the single kernel, the *Textual* kernel performs the best, even comparable with MKL for the location prediction task. Recall that this also holds for the friend and group recommendation tasks. We see that the tag-based kernel is the most effective for SSM. The reason is that the semantic information carried by tags is the most meaningful for characterizing a user. On the other hand, among the four tasks, the *Fave* kernel performs the worst. Recall that it is defined by the count of photos users like. However, it is usually dominated by the quality of photos, instead of social relationship.

5. DISCUSSION AND RELATED WORK

Our work in this paper is closely related to the following research topics: 1) Flickr data mining, 2) social strength modeling, and 3) learning to rank.

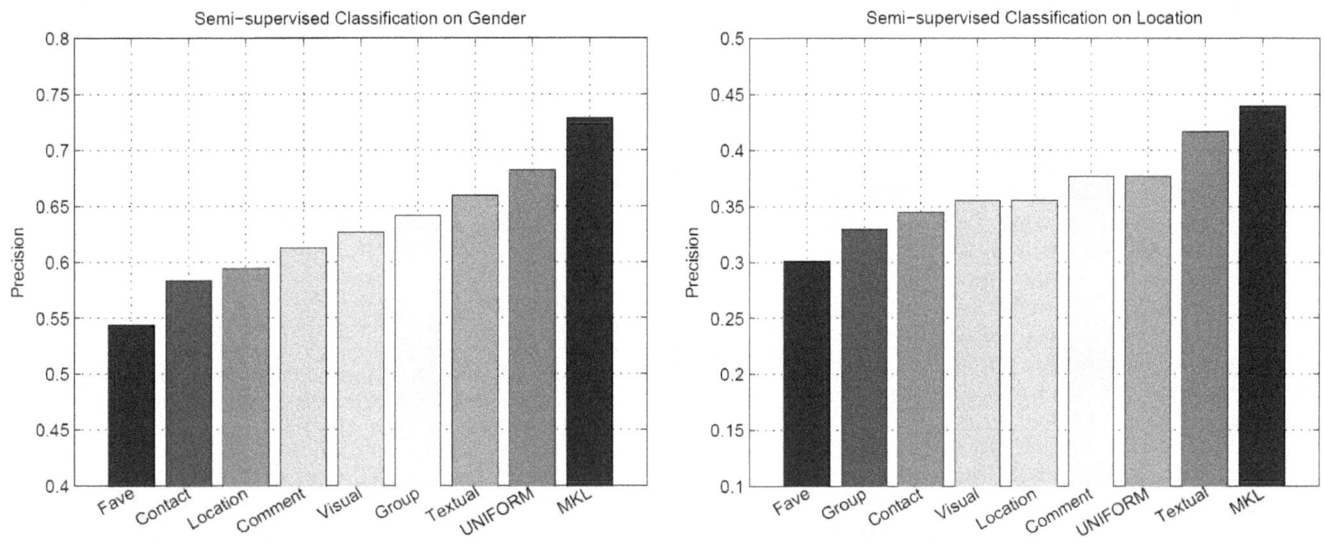

Figure 5: The evaluation of inferred social strength graph for semi-supervised classification. The left figure is the accuracy of *gender* prediction, the right figure is the accuracy of *location*.

5.1 Data Mining with Flickr Data

There exists rich research on mining Flickr data. In [16], the author conducted probabilistic latent semantic analysis on the Flickr interest groups, where each group is abstracted to be a collection of tags annotated to the images belonging to this group. This work is group-oriented and it is unclear how strong the relationship between users is. Due to the subjective and noisy process in group generating and expanding, Negoescu *et al.* proposed methods to hierarchically organize groups and model users and groups equally [15] [17]. These works are also *group-oriented.*

There are works focused on how to make use of the metadata of Flickr images to facilitate other applications. For example, geo-tag analysis [10] [21], automatic tag annotation [25], tag modeling [26]. These techniques are related to our work as they analyze both Flickr images and their annotated tags. However, all these studies are *image-orientated*, which cannot solve our *user-orientated* problem which involves heterogenous forms of data. Our proposed framework by predicting the social strength incorporates the rich content and context information on Flickr effectively, whereas previous works cannot make use of multiple modalities effectively.

5.2 Social Strength Modeling

Our task in this work is to infer the social strength among Flickr users. This connects to social strength modeling or link predictions, where quite a few representative works exists [1, 8, 9, 22, 24, 28]. However, few existing works make use of the rich content and context data of Flickr images to infer the social relationship between Flickr users. Moreover, our motivation here is to help users find out who exhibits similar interest in photo sharing. Thus our technique should be content-driven, instead of mutual communication-based on traditional works.

The unique characteristics of Flickr data provides more flexibility in social network mining. The idea of using Flickr data to infer social relationships has been recently proposed [19, 27, 29]. Wu *et al.* tried to reveal the closeness of people by face detection techniques [27]. However, this work is severely limited by the range of useable images. Singla *et al.* identified the social relationships between individuals in consumer photos with the principled Markov logic networks [19]. Due to the diversity of the images in Flickr, this rule-based method is not applicable for our task. Yu *et al.* intended to recommend a user's images to a known interest group based on supervised classification, where the initial group membership is deemed as label information [29]. As aforementioned, the initial group membership is subjective, incomplete, and noisy, which may not be reliable enough to serve as supervised information.

Recently, visual similarity, especially face similarity, has been leveraged to discover the relationship between roles in a movie [8] [24]. Our work is different from those in that we are investigating the heterogeneous forms of data in a more complex context, i.e., social communities. Xiang *et al.* proposed a hybrid generative-discriminative model which assumes a latent variable measuring the social strength computed from the user profile similarities [28]. The interactive activities are results of such latent variables. However, the profile data of Flickr is not so complete since it is not initially designed to be a social network site. It is not sufficient to infer the social strength solely based on the profile similarities. In addition, separating the interaction graph from profile similarity graph increases modeling complexity.

5.3 Multiple Kernel Learning to Rank

Our main technique is built on two topics, *kernel learning* and *learning to rank*. The most crucial element of a kernel method is *kernel*, which is in general a function that defines an inner product between any two examples in some induced Hilbert space [6]. Recent years have witnessed the active research of learning effective kernels automatically from data [12]. The most popular example technique for kernel learning is *Multiple Kernel Learning* [12], which aims at learning a linear (or convex) combination of a set of predefined kernels in order to identify a good target kernel for the applications. Besides the work of improving the efficiency of MKL, a number of extended MKL techniques have been proposed to improve the regular linear MKL method (e.g., [4, 11]). Here we adopt the two-stage method proposed by Cortes *et al.* [4] as it is computationally simple and works well both theoretically and practically. We learn the weight of each modality by maximizing the inner product between the combined kernel and the target kernel, which can be task dependent to make our solution more flexible.

Learning to rank is an active research topic in machine learning and information retrieval community [13]. It provides a principled and effective paradigm for IR applications. Here we are aware that the social strength essentially ranks the degree of affinity among people. If we can rank such relationship properly, then we can solve the SSM problem. Thus, we borrow the key idea of learning to rank to use and rectify the kernels learned in the first stage.

6. CONCLUSION

Instead of detecting binary social ties in traditional social networking, this paper studies how to infer the continuous social strength in the social media communities. The learned graph is more delicate and informative and can be applied in a lot of important applications, including friend prediction, item recommendation, visualization, and so on. Our key ideas are threefold: 1) leveraging the multiple data sources to compute multiple similarity functions, which can be enforced to satisfy positive semi-definite property to construct valid kernels, 2) employing the kernel target alignment algorithm to learn the weight of each modality and using the weighted summation of base kernels as the ideal kernel, and 3) devising the learning to rank framework based on the learned kernel to infer the social strength. Our techniques are discriminative and do not require any assumption of the underlying parametric statistical models that governs the social strength. Empirical results verified its effectiveness. We hope this work could call for more attention to the social strength modeling in this community.

7. REFERENCES

[1] L. A. Adamic and E. Adar. Friends and neighbors on the web. *Social Networks*, 25: 211–230, 2001.

[2] R. A. Baeza-Yates and B. A. Ribeiro-Neto. *Modern Information Retrieval.* ACM Press / Addison-Wesley, 1999.

[3] C. Cortes. Invited talk: Can learning kernels help performance? In *Proc. of ICML*, page 161, 2009.

[4] C. Cortes, M. Mohri, and A. Rostamizadeh. Two-stage learning kernel algorithms. In *ICML*, pages 239–246, 2010.

[5] C. Cortes and V. Vapnik. Support-vector networks. *Machine Learning*, 20(3):273–297, 1995.

[6] N. Cristianini and J. Shawe-Taylor. *An introduction to support Vector Machines: and other kernel-based learning methods.* Cambridge University Press, New York, NY, USA, 2000.

[7] N. Cristianini, J. Shawe-Taylor, A. Elisseeff, and J. S. Kandola. On kernel-target alignment. In *Proc. of Advances in Neural Information Processing Systems*, pages 367–373, 2001.

[8] L. Ding and A. Yilmaz. Learning relations among movie characters: A social network perspective. In *Proc. of ECCV*, pages 410–423, 2010.

[9] E. Gilbert and K. Karahalios. Predicting tie strength with social media. In *Proc. of CHI*, pages 211–220, 2009.

[10] L. S. Kennedy, M. Naaman, S. Ahern, R. Nair, and T. Rattenbury. How flickr helps us make sense of the world: context and content in community-contributed media collections. In *ACM Multimedia*, pages 631–640, 2007.

[11] M. Kloft, U. Brefeld, S. Sonnenburg, P. Laskov, K.-R. Muller, and A. Zien. Efficient and accurate l_p-norm multiple kernel learning. In *Proc. of Advances in Neural Information Processing Systems*, 2009.

[12] G. R. G. Lanckriet, N. Cristianini, P. L. Bartlett, L. E. Ghaoui, and M. I. Jordan. Learning the kernel matrix with semidefinite programming. *Journal of Machine Learning Research*, 5:27–72, 2004.

[13] T.-Y. Liu. Learning to rank for information retrieval. In *Proc. of SIGIR*, page 904, 2010.

[14] D. G. Lowe. Distinctive image features from scale-invariant keypoints. *Int. J. Comput. Vision*, 60(2):91–110, 2004.

[15] R. A. Negoescu, B. Adams, D. Q. Phung, S. Venkatesh, and D. Gatica-Perez. Flickr hypergroups. In *Proc. of ACM Multimedia*, pages 813–816, 2009.

[16] R. A. Negoescu and D. Gatica-Perez. Analyzing flickr groups. In *Proc. of CIVR*, pages 417–426, 2008.

[17] R. A. Negoescu and D. Gatica-Perez. Topickr: flickr groups and users reloaded. In *Proc. of ACM Multimedia*, pages 857–860, 2008.

[18] D. Nister and H. Stewenius. Scalable recognition with a vocabulary tree. In *Proc. of IEEE Conference on Computer Vision and Pattern Recognition*, pages 2161–2168, June 2006.

[19] J. L. P Singla, H Kautz and A. Gallagher. Discovery of social relationships in consumer photo collections using markov logic. In *Proc. of CVPR workshop*, 2008.

[20] B. Schölkopf, R. Herbrich, and A. J. Smola. A generalized representer theorem. In *Proc. of COLT/EuroCOLT*, pages 416–426, 2001.

[21] P. Serdyukov, V. Murdock, and R. van Zwol. Placing flickr photos on a map. In *Proc. of SIGIR*, pages 484–491, 2009.

[22] P. Singla and M. Richardson. Yes, there is a correlation: - from social networks to personal behavior on the web. In *Proc. of WWW*, pages 655–664, 2008.

[23] V. N. Vapnik. *Statistical Learning Theory.* Wiley, 1998.

[24] Y. Wang, T. Mei, and X.-S. Hua. Community discovery from movie and its application to poster generation. In *Proc. of International MultiMedia Modeling Conference*, pages 107–117, 2011.

[25] L. Wu, S. C. H. Hoi, R. Jin, J. Zhu, and N. Yu. Distance metric learning from uncertain side information with application to automated photo tagging. In *Proc. of ACM Multimedia*, pages 135–144, 2009.

[26] L. Wu, X.-S. Hua, N. Yu, W.-Y. Ma, and S. Li. Flickr distance. In *Proc. of ACM Multimedia*, pages 31–40, 2008.

[27] P. Wu and D. Tretter. Close & closer: social cluster and closeness from photo collections. In *Proc. of ACM Multimedia*, pages 709–712, 2009.

[28] R. Xiang, J. Neville, and M. Rogati. Modeling relationship strength in online social networks. In *Proc. of WWW*, pages 981–990, 2010.

[29] J. Yu, D. Joshi, and J. Luo. Connecting people in photo-sharing sites by photo content and user annotations. In *Proc. of ICME*, pages 1464–1467, 2009.

[30] D. Zhou, O. Bousquet, T. Lal, J. Weston, and B. Schlkopf. Learning with local and global consistency. In *Advances in Neural Information Processing Systems*, 2005.

[31] J. Zhu and T. Hastie. Kernel logistic regression and the import vector machine. In *Proc. of Advances in Neural Information Processing Systems*, pages 1081–1088, 2001.

[32] X. Zhu, Z. Ghahramani, and J. D. Lafferty. Semi-supervised learning using gaussian fields and harmonic functions. In *Proc. of International Conference on Machine Learning*, pages 912–919, 2003.

Audio-Visual Grouplet: Temporal Audio-Visual Interactions for General Video Concept Classification

Wei Jiang Alexander C. Loui
Corporate Research and Engineering, Eastman Kodak Company, Rochester, NY
{wei.jiang, alexander.loui}@kodak.com

ABSTRACT

We investigate general concept classification in unconstrained videos by joint audio-visual analysis. A novel representation, the Audio-Visual Grouplet (AVG), is extracted by studying the statistical temporal audio-visual interactions. An AVG is defined as a set of audio and visual codewords that are grouped together according to their strong temporal correlations in videos. The AVGs carry unique audio-visual cues to represent the video content, based on which an audio-visual dictionary can be constructed for concept classification. By using the entire AVGs as building elements, the audio-visual dictionary is much more robust than traditional vocabularies that use discrete audio or visual codewords. Specifically, we conduct coarse-level foreground/background separation in both audio and visual channels, and discover four types of AVGs by exploring mixed-and-matched temporal audio-visual correlations among the following factors: visual foreground, visual background, audio foreground, and audio background. All of these types of AVGs provide discriminative audio-visual patterns for classifying various semantic concepts. We extensively evaluate our method over the large-scale Columbia Consumer Video set. Experiments demonstrate that the AVG-based dictionaries can achieve consistent and significant performance improvements compared with other state-of-the-art approaches.

Categories and Subject Descriptors

H.3.1 [**Information Storage and Retrieval**]: Content Analysis and Indexing; H.4.m [**Information Systems Applications**]: Miscellaneous; H.3.m [**Information Storage and Retrieval**]: Miscellaneous

General Terms

Algorithms, Experimentation

Keywords

Audio-visual grouplet, video concept classification, temporal audio-visual interaction, foreground/background separation

*Area chair: Cees G.M. Snoek

MM'11, November 28–December 1, 2011, Scottsdale, Arizona, USA.

1. INTRODUCTION

This paper investigates the problem of automatic classification of semantic concepts in generic, unconstrained videos, by joint analysis of audio and visual content. These concepts include general categories, such as scene (*e.g.*, beach), event (*e.g.*, birthday, graduation), location (*e.g.*, playground) and object (*e.g.*, dog, bird). Generic videos are captured in an unrestricted manner, like those videos taken by consumers on YouTube. This is a difficult problem due to the diverse video content as well as the challenging conditions such as uneven lighting, clutter, occlusions, and complicated motions of both objects and camera.

Large efforts have been devoted to classify general concepts in generic videos, such as TRECVID high-level feature extraction [32] and Columbia Consumer Video (*CCV*) concept classification [18]. Most previous works classify videos in the same way they classify images, using mainly visual information. Specifically, visual features are extracted from either 2D keyframes or 3D local volumes, and these features are treated as individual static descriptors to train concept classifiers. Among these methods, the ones using the Bag-of-Words (*BoW*) representation over 2D or 3D local descriptors (*e.g.*, SIFT [23] or HOG [8]) are considered state-of-the-art, due to the effectiveness of BoW features in classifying objects [13], events [32], and human actions [21].

The importance of incorporating audio information to facilitate semantic concept classification has been discovered by several previous works [5, 18, 37]. They generally use a multi-modal fusion strategy, *i.e.*, early fusion [5, 18, 37] to train classifiers with concatenated audio and visual features, or late fusion [5, 37] to combine judgments from classifiers built over individual modalities. Different from such fusion approaches that avoid studying temporal audio-visual synchrony, the work in [16] pursues a coarse-level audio-visual synchronization through learning a joint audio-visual codebook based on atomic representations in both audio and visual channels. However, the temporal audio-visual interaction is not explored in previous video concept classification methods. The temporal audio-visual dependencies can reveal unique audio-visual patterns to assist concept classification. For example, as illustrated in Figure 1, by studying the correlations between temporal patterns of visual and audio codewords, we can discover discriminative audio-visual cues, such as the unique encapsulation of visual basketball patches and audio basketball bouncing sounds for classifying the "basketball" concept, and the encapsulation of visual stadium patches and audio music sounds for classifying

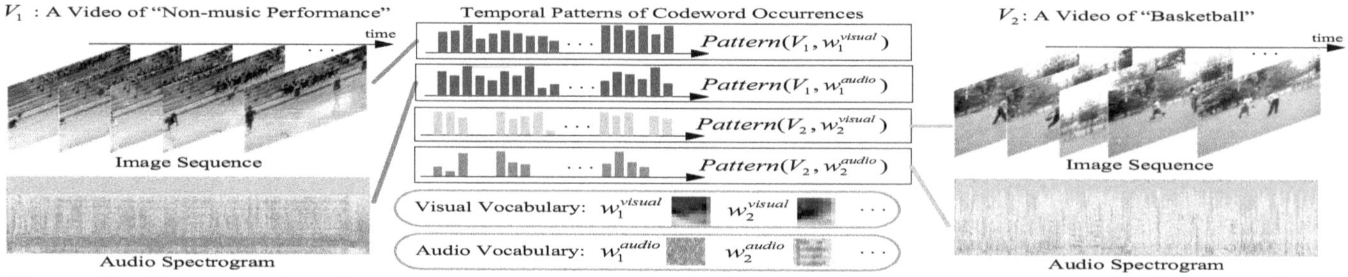

Figure 1: Discovery of audio-visual patterns through temporal audio-visual interactions. w_i^{visual} and w_j^{audio} are discrete codewords in visual and audio vocabularies, respectively. By analyzing the correlations between the temporal histograms of audio and visual codewords, we can discover salient audio-visual cues to represent videos from different concepts. For example, the highly correlated visual basketball patches and audio basketball bouncing sounds provide a unique pattern to classify "basketball" videos. The highly correlated visual stadium patches and audio background music are helpful to classify "non-music performance" videos. In comparison, discrete audio and visual codewords are less discriminative than such audio-visual cues.

the "non-music performance" concept [1]. To the best of our knowledge, such audio-visual cues have not been studied before in previous literatures.

From another perspective, beyond the traditional BoW representation, structured visual features have been recently found to be effective in many computer vision tasks. In addition to the local feature appearance, spatial relations among the local patches are incorporated to increase the robustness of the visual representation. The rationale behind this is that individual local visual patterns tend to be sensitive to variations such as changes of illumination, views, scales, and occlusions. In comparison, a set of co-occurrent local patterns can be less ambiguous. Along this direction, pairwise spatial constraints among local interest points have been used to enhance image registration [12]; various types of spatial contextual information have been used for object detection [10] and action classification [24]; and a grouplet representation has been developed to capture discriminative visual features and their spatial configurations for detecting the human-object-interaction scenes in images [39].

Motivated by the importance of incorporating audio information to help video concept classification, as well as the success of using structured visual features for image classification, in this paper, we propose an Audio-Visual Grouplet (*AVG*) representation. Each AVG contains a set of audio and visual codewords that have strong temporal correlations in videos. An audio-visual dictionary can be constructed to classify concepts using AVGs as building blocks. The AVGs capture not only the individual audio and visual features carried by the discrete audio and visual codewords, but also the temporal relations between audio and visual channels. By using the entire AVGs as building elements to represent videos, various concepts can be more robustly classified than using discrete audio and visual codewords. For example, as illustrated in Figure 2, The AVG that captures the visual bride and audio speech gives a strong audio-visual cue to classify the "wedding ceremony" concept, and the AVG that captures the visual bride and audio dancing music is quite discriminative to classify the "wedding dance" concept.

2. OVERVIEW OF OUR APPROACH

Figure 3 summarizes the framework of our system. We discover four types of AVGs by exploring four types of temporal audio-visual correlations: correlations between visual foreground and audio foreground; correlations between visual background and audio background; correlations between visual foreground and audio background; and correlations between visual background and audio foreground. All of these types of AVGs are useful for video concept classification. For example, as illustrated in Figure 3, to effectively classify the "birthday" concept, all of the following factors are important: the visual foreground people (*e.g.*, baby and child), the visual background setting (*e.g.*, cake and table), the audio foreground sound (*e.g.*, cheering, birthday song, and hand clapping), and the audio background sound (*e.g.*, music). By studying the temporal audio-visual correlations among these factors, we can identify unique audio-visual patterns that are discriminative for "birthday" classification.

To enable the exploration of the foreground and background audio-visual correlations, coarse-level separation of the foreground and background is needed in both visual and audio channels. It is worth mentioning that due to the diverse video content and the challenging conditions (*e.g.*, un-

[1]Detailed definition of "non-music performance" can be found in [18].

Figure 2: An example of AVG-based audio-visual dictionary. Each AVG is composed of a set of audio and visual codewords that have strong temporal correlations in videos. The AVG that captures the visual bride and audio speech (AVG: w_1^{visual}, w_2^{visual}, w_1^{audio}) gives a unique audio-visual cue to classify "wedding ceremony," and the AVG that captures the visual bride and audio dancing music (AVG: w_1^{visual}, w_2^{visual}, w_2^{audio}) is discriminative to classify "wedding dance." In comparison, discrete visual or audio codewords can be ambiguous for classification.

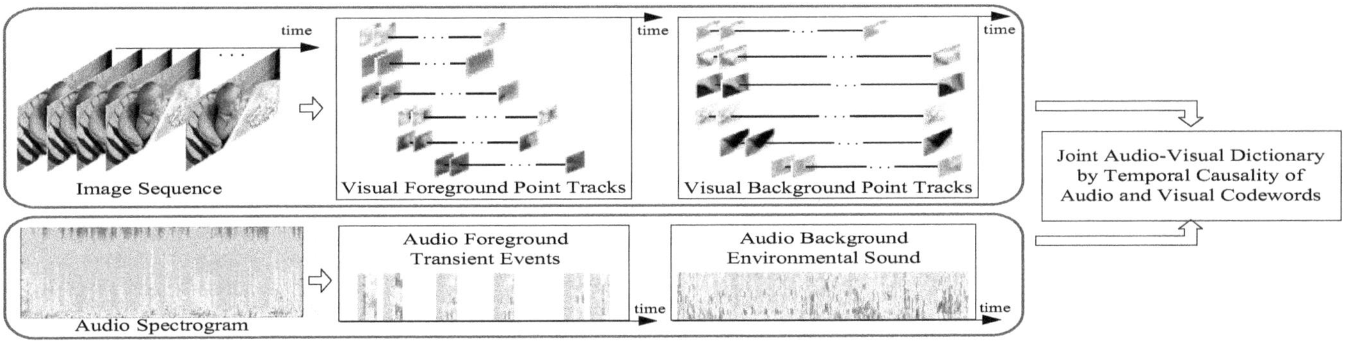

Figure 3: The overall framework of the proposed joint audio-visual analysis system. The example shows a "birthday" video, where four types of audio-visual patterns are useful for classifying the "birthday" concept: (1) the visual foreground baby with the audio foreground events such as singing the birthday song or people cheering, since a major portion of birthday videos have babies or children involved; (2) the visual foreground baby with the audio background music; (3) the visual background setting such as the cake, with the audio foreground singing/cheering; and (4) the visual background cake with the audio background music.

even lighting, clutter, occlusions, complicated objects and camera motions, and the unstructured audio sounds with overlapping acoustic sources), precise visual or audio foreground/background separation is infeasible in generic videos. In addition, exact audio-visual synchronization can be unreliable most of the time. Multiple moving objects usually make sounds together, and often the object making sounds does not synchronically appear in video. To accommodate these issues, different from most previous audio-visual analysis methods [3, 7, 15, 31] that rely on precisely separated visual foreground objects and/or audio foreground sounds, our proposed approach has the following characteristics.

- We explore statistical temporal audio-visual correlations over a set of videos instead of exact audio-visual synchronization in individual videos. By representing the temporal sequences of visual and audio codewords as multivariate point processes, the statistical pairwise nonparametric Granger causality [14] between audio and visual codewords is analyzed. Based on the audio-visual causal matrix, salient AVGs are identified, which encapsulate strongly correlated visual and audio codewords as building blocks to classify videos.
- We do not pursue precise visual foreground/background separation. We aim to build foreground-oriented and background-oriented visual vocabularies. Specifically, consistent local points are tracked throughout each video. Based on both local motion vectors and spatiotemporal analysis of whole images, the point tracks are separated into foreground tracks and background tracks. Due to the challenging conditions of generic videos, such a separation is not precise. The target is to maintain a majority of foreground (background) tracks so that the constructed visual foreground (background) vocabulary can capture mainly visual foreground (background) information.
- Similar to the visual aspect, we aim to build foreground-oriented and background-oriented audio vocabularies, instead of pursuing precisely separated audio foreground or background acoustic sources. In generic videos, the foreground sound events are usually distributed unevenly and sparsely. Therefore, the local representation that focuses on short-term transient sound events [6] can be used to capture the foreground audio information. Also, the Mel-Frequency Cepstral Coefficients (*MFCCs*) extracted from uniformly spaced audio windows roughly capture the overall information of the environmental sound. Based on the local representation and MFCCs, audio foreground and background vocabularies can be constructed, respectively.

We extensively evaluate our approach over the large-scale CCV set [18], containing 9317 consumer videos from YouTube. The consumer videos are captured by ordinary users under uncontrolled challenging conditions, without post-editing. The original audio soundtracks are preserved, which allows us to study legitimate audio-visual interactions. Experiments show that compared with the state-of-the-art multimodal fusion methods using BoW representations, our AVG-based dictionaries can capture useful audio-visual cues and significantly improve the classification performance.

3. BRIEF REVIEW OF RELATED WORK

3.1 Audio-Visual Concept Classification

Audio-visual analysis has been largely studied for speech recognition [15], speaker identification [31], and object localization [4]. For example, with multiple cameras and audio sensors, by using audio spatialization and multi-camera tracking, moving sound sources (*e.g.*, people) can be located. In videos captured by a single sensor, objects are usually located by studying the audio-visual synchronization along the temporal dimension. A common approach, for instance, is to project each of the audio and visual modalities into a 1D subspace and then correlate the 1D representations [3, 7]. These methods have shown interesting results in analyzing videos in a controlled or simple environment, where good sound source separation and visual foreground/background separation can be obtained. However, they cannot be easily applied to generic videos due to the difficulties in both acoustic source separation and visual object detection.

Most existing approaches for general video concept classification exploit the multi-modal fusion strategy instead of using direct correlation or synchronization across audio and visual modalities. For example, early fusion is used [5, 37] to concatenate features from different modalities into long vectors. This approach usually suffers from the "curse of dimensionality," as the concatenated multi-modal feature can be very long. Also, it remains an open issue how to construct suitable joint feature vectors comprising features from different modalities with different time scales and different distance metrics. In late fusion, individual classifiers are built for each modality separately, and their judgments are combined to make the final decision. Several combination strategies have been used, such as majority voting, linear combination, super-kernel nonlinear fusion [37], or SVM-based meta-classification combination [22]. However, classifier combination remains a basic machine learning problem. The best strategies depend on particular tasks.

Recently, an Audio-Visual Atom (*AVA*) representation has been developed in [16]. Visual regions are tracked within short-term video slices to generate visual atoms, and audio energy onsets are located to generate audio atoms. Regional visual features extracted from visual atoms and spectrogram features extracted from audio atoms are concatenated to form the AVA representation. An audio-visual codebook is constructed based on the AVAs for concept classification. The audio-visual synchrony is found through learning the audio-visual codebook. However, the temporal audio-visual interaction remains unstudied. As illustrated in Figure 1, the temporal audio-visual dependencies can reveal unique audio-visual patterns to assist concept classification.

3.2 Visual Foreground/Background Separation

One of the most commonly used techniques for separating foreground moving objects and the static background is background subtraction, where foreground objects are detected as the difference between the current frame and a reference image of the static background [11]. Various threshold adaptation methods [1] and adaptive background models [33] have been developed. However, these approaches require a relatively static camera, small illumination change, simple and stable background scene, and relatively slow object motion. When applied to generic videos for general concept classification, the performance is not satisfactory.

Motion-based segmentation methods have also been used to separate moving foreground and static background in videos [20]. The dense optical flow is usually computed to capture pixel-level motions. Due to the sensitivity to large camera/object motion and the computation intensity, such methods cannot be easily applied to generic videos either.

3.3 Audio Source Separation

Real-world audio signals are combinations of a number of independent sound sources, such as various instrumental sounds, human voices, natural sounds, *etc.* Ideally, one would like to recover each source signal. However, this task is very challenging in generic videos, because only a single audio channel is available, and realistic soundtracks have unrestricted content from an unknown number of unstructured, overlapping acoustic sources.

Early Blind Audio Source Separation (*BASS*) methods separate audio sources that are recorded with multiple microphones [28]. Later on, several approaches have been developed to separate single-channel audio, such as the factorial HMM methods [30] and the spectral decomposition methods [35]. Recently, the visual information has been incorporated to assist BASS [36], where the audio-video synchrony is used as side information. However, soundtracks studied by these methods are mostly mixtures of human voices or instrumental sounds with very limited background noise. When applied to generic videos, existing BASS methods cannot perform satisfactorily.

4. VISUAL PROCESS

We conduct SIFT point tracking within each video, based on which foreground-oriented and background-oriented temporal visual patterns are generated. The following details the processing stages.

4.1 Excluding Bad Video Segments

Video shot boundary detection and bad video segment elimination are general preprocessing steps for video analysis. Each raw video is segmented into several parts according to the detected shot boundaries with a single shot in each part. Next, segments with very large camera motion are excluded from analysis. It is worth mentioning that in our case, these steps can actually be skipped, because we process consumer videos that have a single long shot per video, and the SIFT point tracking can automatically exclude bad segments by generating few tracks over such segments. However, we still recommend these preprocessing steps to accommodate a large variety of generic videos.

4.2 SIFT-based Point Tracking

We use Lowe's 128-dim SIFT descriptor with the DoG interest point detector [23]. SIFT features are first extracted from a set of uniformly sampled image frames with a sampling rate of 6 fps (frames per second) [2]. Then for adjacent image frames, pairs of matching SIFT features are found based on the Euclidean distance of their feature vectors, by also using Lowe's method to discard ambiguous matches [23]. After that, along the temporal dimension, the matching pairs are connected into a set of SIFT point tracks, where different point tracks can start from different image frames and last variable lengths. This 6 fps sampling rate is empirically determined by considering both the computation cost and the ability of SIFT matching. In general, increasing the sampling rate will decrease the chance of missing point tracks, with the price of increased computation.

Each SIFT point track is represented by a 136-dim feature vector. This feature vector is composed by a 128-dim SIFT vector concatenated with an 8-dim motion vector. The SIFT vector is the averaged SIFT features of all SIFT points in the track. The motion vector is the averaged Histogram of Oriented Motion (*HOM*) along the track. That is, for each adjacent matching pair in the track, we compute the speed and direction of the local motion vector. By quantizing the 2D motion space into 8 bins (corresponding to 8 directions), an 8-dim HOM feature is computed where the value over each bin is the averaged speed of the motion vectors from the track moving along this direction.

4.3 Foreground/Background Separation

Once the set of SIFT point tracks are obtained, we separate them as foreground or background with the following two steps, as illustrated in Figure 4. First, for two adjacent frames I_i and I_{i+1}, we roughly separate their matching SIFT pairs into candidate foreground and background pairs based on the motion vectors. Specifically, we group these matching pairs by hierarchical clustering, where the grouping criterion is that pairs within a cluster have roughly the same moving direction and speed. Those SIFT pairs in the biggest cluster are treated as candidate background pairs, and all other

[2]In our experiment, the typical frame rate of videos is 30 fps. Typically we sample 1 frame from every 5 frames.

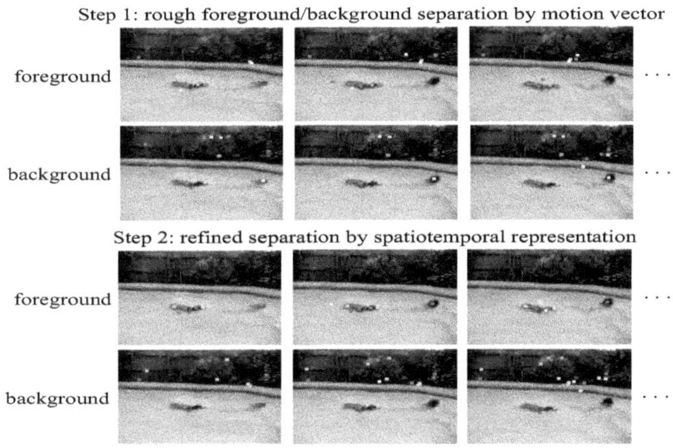

Figure 4: Example of foreground/background separation of SIFT point tracks. A rough separation is obtained by analyzing local motion vectors. The result is further refined by spatiotemporal analysis over entire images.

pairs are treated as candidate foreground pairs. The rationale is that foreground moving objects usually occupy less than half of the entire screen, and points on the foreground objects do not have a very consistent moving pattern. In comparison, points on the static background generally have consistent motion and this motion is caused by camera motion. This first step can distinguish background tracks fairly well for videos with moderate planar camera motions that occur most commonly in generic videos.

In the second step, we further refine the candidate foreground and background SIFT tracks by using the spatiotemporal representation of videos. A spatiotemporal X-ray image representation has been proposed by Akutsu and Tonomura for camera work identification [2], where the average of each line and each column in successive images are computed. The distribution of the angles of edges in the X-ray images can be matched to camera work models, from which camera motion classification and temporal video segmentation can be obtained directly [19]. When used alone, such methods cannot generate satisfactory segmentation results in many generic videos where large motions from multiple objects cannot be easily discriminated from the noisy background motion. The performance drops even more for small resolutions, *e.g.*, 320×240 for most videos in our experiments. Therefore, instead of pursuing precise spatiotemporal object segmentation, we use such a spatiotemporal analysis to refine the candidate foreground and background SIFT tracks. The spatiotemporal image representation is able to capture camera zoom and tilt, which can be used to rectify those candidate tracks that are mistakenly labeled as foreground due to camera zoom and tilt. Figure 4 shows an example of visual foreground/background separation by using the above two steps.

4.4 Vocabularies and Feature Representations

Based on the foreground and background SIFT point tracks, we build a visual foreground vocabulary and a visual background vocabulary, respectively. The BoW features can be computed using the vocabularies, which can be used directly for concept classification. Also, the temporal patterns of codeword occurrences can be computed to study the correlations between audio and visual signals in Section 6.

From Section 4.2, each SIFT point track is represented by a 136-dim feature vector. All foreground tracks from the training videos are collected together, based on which the hierarchical K-means technique [27] is used to construct a D-word foreground visual vocabulary $\mathcal{V}^{f-v}$. Similarly, a D-word background visual vocabulary $\mathcal{V}^{b-v}$ is constructed with all of the training background tracks. In our experiments, we use relatively large vocabularies, $D=4000$, based on findings from previous literatures [38] that when the vocabulary size exceeds 2000, the classification performance tends to saturate. That is, we can alleviate the influence of the vocabulary size on the final classification performance.

For each video V_j, all of its foreground SIFT point tracks are matched to the foreground codewords. A soft weighting scheme is used to alleviate the quantization effects [17], and a D-dim foreground BoW feature $\mathbf{F}_j^{f-v}$ is generated. Similarly, all of the background SIFT point tracks are matched to the background codewords to generate a D-dim background BoW feature $\mathbf{F}_j^{b-v}$. In general, both $\mathbf{F}_j^{f-v}$ and $\mathbf{F}_j^{b-v}$ have their impacts in classifying concepts, *e.g.*, both the foreground people with caps and gowns and the background stadium setting are useful to classify "graduation" videos.

To study the temporal audio-visual interactions, the following histogram feature is computed over time for each of the foreground and background visual vocabularies. Given a video V_j, we have a set of foreground SIFT point tracks. Each track is labeled to one codeword in vocabulary $\mathcal{V}^{f-v}$ that is closest to the track in the visual feature space. Next, for each frame I_{ji} in the video, we count the occurring frequency of each foreground codeword labeled to the foreground SIFT point tracks that have a SIFT point falling in this frame, and a D-dim histogram H_{ji}^{f-v} can be generated. Similarly, we can generate a D-dim histogram H_{ji}^{b-v} for each image frame I_{ji} based on vocabulary $\mathcal{V}^{b-v}$. After this computation, for the foreground $\mathcal{V}^{f-v}$ (or background $\mathcal{V}^{b-v}$), we have a temporal sequence $\{H_{j1}^{f-v}, H_{j2}^{f-v}, \ldots\}$ (or $\{H_{j1}^{b-v}, H_{j2}^{b-v}, \ldots\}$) over each video V_j.

5. AUDIO PROCESS

Instead of pursuing precisely separated audio sound sources, we extract background-oriented and foreground-oriented audio features. The temporal interactions of these features with their visual counterparts can be studied to generate useful audio-visual patterns for concept classification.

5.1 Audio Background

Various descriptors have been developed to represent audio signals in both temporal and spectral domains. Among these features, the MFCCs feature is one of the most popular choices for many different audio recognition systems [5, 31]. MFCCs represent the shape of the overall spectrum with a few coefficients, and have been shown to work well for both structured sounds (*e.g.*, speech) and unstructured environmental sounds. In soundtracks of generic videos, the foreground sound events (*e.g.*, an occasional dog barking or hand clapping) are distributed unevenly and sparsely. In such a case, the MFCCs extracted from uniformly spaced audio windows capture the overall characteristics of the background environmental sound, since the statistical impact of the sparse foreground sound events is quite small. Therefore, we use the MFCCs as the background audio feature.

For each given video V_j, we extract the 13-dim MFCCs from the corresponding soundtrack using 25 ms windows with a hop size of 10 ms. Next, we put all of the MFCCs from all training videos together, on top of which the hierarchical K-means technique [27] is used to construct a D-word background audio vocabulary $\mathcal{V}^{b-a}$. Similar to visual-based processing, we compute two different histogram-like features based on $\mathcal{V}^{b-a}$. First, we generate a BoW feature $\mathbf{F}_j^{b-a}$ for each video V_j by matching the MFCCs in the video to codewords in the vocabulary and conducting soft weighting. This BoW feature can be used directly for classifying concepts. Second, to study the audio-visual correlation, a temporal audio histogram sequence $\{H_{j1}^{b-a}, H_{j2}^{b-a}, \ldots\}$ is generated for each video V_j as follows. Each MFCC vector is labeled to one codeword in the audio background vocabulary $\mathcal{V}^{b-a}$ that is closest to the MFCC vector. Next, for each sampled image frame I_{ji} in the video, we take a 200 ms window centered on this frame. Then we count the occurring frequency of the codewords labeled to the MFCCs that fall into this window, and a D-dim histogram H_{ji}^{b-a} can be generated. This H_{ji}^{b-a} can be considered as temporally synchronized with the visual-based histograms H_{ji}^{f-v} or H_{ji}^{b-v}.

5.2 Audio Foreground

As mentioned above, the soundtrack of a generic video usually has unevenly and sparsely distributed foreground sound events. To capture such foreground information, local representations that focus on short-term local sound events should be used. In [6], Cotton *et al.* have developed a local event-based representation, where a set of salient points in the soundtrack are located based on time-frequency energy analysis and multi-scale spectrum analysis. These salient points contain distinct event onsets, *i.e.*, transient events. By modeling the local temporal structure around each transient event, an audio feature reflecting the foreground of the soundtrack can be computed. In this work, we follow the recipe of [6] to generate the foreground audio feature.

Specifically, the Automatic Gain Control (*AGC*) is first applied to equalize the audio energy in both time and frequency domains. Next, the spectrogram of the AGC-equalized signal is taken for a number of different time-frequency tradeoffs, corresponding to window length between 2 to 80 ms. Multiple scales enable the localization of events of different durations. High-magnitude bins in any spectrogram indicate a candidate transient event at the corresponding time. A limit is empirically set on the minimum distance between successive events to produce 4 events per second on average.

A 250 ms window of the audio signal is extracted centered on each transient event time, which captures the temporal structure of the transient event. Within each 250 ms window, a 40-dim spectrogram-based feature is computed for short-term signals over 25 ms windows with 10 ms hops, which results in 23 successive features for each event. These features are concatenated together to form a 920-dim representation for each transient event. After that, PCA is performed over all transient events from all training videos, and the top 20 bases are used to project the original 920-dim event representation to 20 dimensions.

By putting all the projected transient features from all training videos together, the hierarchical K-means technique [27] is used again to construct a D-word foreground audio vocabulary $\mathcal{V}^{f-a}$. We also compute two different histogram-like features based on $\mathcal{V}^{f-a}$. First, we generate a BoW feature $\mathbf{F}_j^{f-a}$ for each video V_j by matching the transient features in the video to codewords in the vocabulary and conducting soft weighting. Second, a temporal audio histogram sequence $\{H_{j1}^{f-a}, H_{j2}^{f-a}, \ldots\}$ is generated for each video V_j as follows. Each transient event is labeled to one codeword in the audio foreground vocabulary $\mathcal{V}^{f-a}$ that is closest to the transient event feature. Next, for each sampled image frame I_{ji} in the video, we take a 200 ms window centered on this frame. Then we count the occurring frequency of the codewords labeled to the transient events whose centers fall into this window, and a D-dim histogram H_{ji}^{f-a} can be generated. Similar to H_{ji}^{b-a}, H_{ji}^{f-a} can be considered as synchronized with H_{ji}^{f-v} or H_{ji}^{b-v}.

6. AVGS FROM TEMPORAL CAUSALITY

Recently, Prabhakar *et al.* have shown in [29] that the sequence of visual codewords produced by a space-time vocabulary representation of a video sequence can be interpreted as a multivariate point process. The pairwise temporal causal relations between visual codewords are computed within a video sequence, and visual codewords are grouped into causal sets. Evaluations over social game videos show promising results that the manually selected causal sets can capture the dyadic interactions. However, the work in [29] relies on nicely separated foreground objects, and causal sets are manually selected for each individual video. The method cannot be used for general concept classification.

We propose to investigate the temporal causal relations between audio and visual codewords. Our target is to capture the co-occurrences of audio and visual patterns over time. The rough foreground/background separation of both temporal SIFT point tracks and audio sounds enables a meaningful study of such temporal relations. For the purpose of classifying general concepts in generic videos, all of the following factors have their contributions: foreground visual objects, foreground audio transient events, background visual scenes, and background environmental sounds. Therefore, we explore their mixed-and-matched temporal relations to find salient AVGs that can assist the final classification.

6.1 Point-process Representation of Codewords

From the previous sections, for each video V_j, we have 4 temporal sequences: $\{H_{j1}^{f-v}, H_{j2}^{f-v}, \ldots\}$, $\{H_{j1}^{f-a}, H_{j2}^{f-a}, \ldots\}$, $\{H_{j1}^{b-v}, H_{j2}^{b-v}, \ldots\}$, and $\{H_{j1}^{b-a}, H_{j2}^{b-a}, \ldots\}$, with vocabularies $\mathcal{V}^{f-v}$, $\mathcal{V}^{f-a}$, $\mathcal{V}^{b-v}$, and $\mathcal{V}^{b-a}$, respectively. For each vocabulary, *e.g.*, the foreground visual vocabulary $\mathcal{V}^{f-v}$, each codeword w_k in the vocabulary can be treated as a point process, $N_k^{f-v}(t)$, which counts the number of occurrences of w_k in the interval $(0,t]$. The number of occurrences of w_k in a small interval dt is $dN_k^{f-v}(t) = N_k^{f-v}(t+dt) - N_k^{f-v}(t)$, and $E\{dN_k^{f-v}(t)/dt\} = \lambda_k^{f-v}$ is the mean intensity. For theoretical and practical convenience, the zero-mean process is considered, and $N_k^{f-v}(t)$ is assumed as wide-sense stationary, mixing, and orderly[3] [25]. Point processes generated by all D codewords of vocabulary $\mathcal{V}^{f-v}$ form a D-dim multivariate point process $\mathbf{N}^{f-v}(t) = (N_1^{f-v}(t), \ldots, N_D^{f-v}(t))^T$. Each video V_j gives one realization (trial) of $\mathbf{N}^{f-v}(t)$ with counting vector $(h_{j1}^{f-v}(t), h_{j2}^{f-v}(t), \ldots, h_{jD}^{f-v}(t))^T$, where $h_{jk}^{f-v}(t)$ is the value over the k-th bin of the histogram H_{jt}^{f-v}. Similarly, D-dim multivariate point processes $\mathbf{N}^{f-a}(t)$, $\mathbf{N}^{b-v}(t)$,

[3]The statistical properties of the process are time-invariant; the numbers of codewords in intervals separated widely in time are independent; given a sufficiently small interval, the number of codewords in the interval is at most one.

and $\mathbf{N}^{b-a}(t)$ can be generated for vocabularies $\mathcal{V}^{f-a}$, $\mathcal{V}^{b-v}$, and $\mathcal{V}^{b-a}$, respectively.

6.2 Temporal Causality among Codewords

Granger causality [14] is a statistical measure based on the concept of time series forecasting, where a time series Y_1 is considered to causally influence a time series Y_2 if predictions of future values of Y_2 based on the joint history of Y_1 and Y_2 are more accurate than predictions based on Y_2 alone. The estimation of Granger causality usually relies on autoregressive models, and for continuous-valued data like electroencephalogram, such model fitting is straightforward.

In [25], a nonparametric method that bypasses the autoregressive model fitting has been developed to estimate Granger causality for point processes. The theoretical basis lies in the spectral representation of point processes, the factorization of spectral matrices, and the formulation of Granger causality in the spectral domain. In the following, we describe the details of using the method of [25] to compute the temporal causality between audio and visual codewords. For simplicity, we temporarily omit indexes $f-v$, $b-v$, $f-a$, and $b-a$, w.l.o.g., since Granger causality can be computed for any two codewords from any vocabularies.

6.2.1 *Spectral representation of point processes*

The pairwise statistical relation between two point processes $N_k(t)$ and $N_l(t)$ can be captured by the cross-covariance density function $R_{kl}(u)$ at lag u:

$$R_{kl}(u) = \frac{E\{dN_k(t+u)dN_l(t)\}}{dudt} - I\left[N_k(t)=N_l(t)\right]\lambda_k\delta(u),$$

where $\delta(u)$ is the classical Kronecker delta function, and $I[\cdot]$ is the indicator function. By taking the Fourier transform of $R_{kl}(u)$, we obtain the cross-spectrum $S_{kl}(f)$. Specifically, the multitaper method [34] can be used to compute the spectrum, where M data tapers $\{q_m\}_{m=1}^{M}$ are applied successively to point process $N_k(t)$ (with length T):

$$S_{kl}(f) = \frac{1}{2\pi MT}\sum\nolimits_{m=1}^{M}\tilde{N}_k(f,m)\tilde{N}_l(f,m)^*, \qquad (1)$$

$$\tilde{N}_k(f,m) = \sum\nolimits_{t_p=1}^{T} q_m(t_p)N_k(t_p)\exp(-2\pi i f t_p).$$

The symbol * is the complex conjugate transpose. Equation (1) gives an estimation of the cross-spectrum using one realization, and such estimations of multiple realizations are averaged to give the final estimation of the cross-spectrum.

6.2.2 *Granger causality in spectral domain*

For multivariate continuous-valued time series Y_1 and Y_2 with joint autoregressive representations:

$$Y_1(t) = \sum\nolimits_{p=1}^{\infty} a_pY_1(t-p) + \sum\nolimits_{p=1}^{\infty} b_pY_2(t-p) + \epsilon(t),$$

$$Y_2(t) = \sum\nolimits_{p=1}^{\infty} c_pY_2(t-p) + \sum\nolimits_{p=1}^{\infty} d_pY_1(t-p) + \eta(t),$$

their noise terms are uncorrelated over time and their contemporaneous covariance matrix is:

$$\Sigma=\begin{bmatrix}\Sigma_2 \Upsilon_2\\ \Upsilon_2 \Gamma_2\end{bmatrix}, \Sigma_2=\mathrm{var}(\epsilon(t)), \Gamma_2=\mathrm{var}(\eta(t)), \Upsilon_2=\mathrm{cov}(\epsilon(t),\eta(t)).$$

We can compute the spectral matrix as [9]:

$$\mathbf{S}(f) = \begin{bmatrix} S_{11}(f)\ S_{12}(f)\\ S_{21}(f)\ S_{22}(f)\end{bmatrix} = \mathbf{H}(f)\Sigma\mathbf{H}(f)^*, \qquad (2)$$

where $\mathbf{H}(f)=\begin{bmatrix} H_{11}(f)H_{12}(f)\\ H_{21}(f)H_{22}(f)\end{bmatrix}$ is the transfer function depending on coefficients of the autoregressive model. The spectral matrix $\mathbf{S}(f)$ of two point processes $N_k(t)$ and $N_l(t)$ can be estimated using Eqn. (1). By spectral matrix factorization we can decompose $\mathbf{S}(f)$ into a unique corresponding transfer function $\tilde{\mathbf{H}}(f)$ and noise processes $\tilde{\Sigma}_2$ and $\tilde{\Gamma}_2$. Next, the Granger causality at frequency f can be estimated according to the algorithm developed in [9]:

$$G_{N_l\to N_k}(f) = \ln\left(\frac{S_{kk}(f)}{\tilde{H}_{kk}(f)\tilde{\Sigma}_2\tilde{H}_{kk}(f)^*}\right), \qquad (3)$$

$$G_{N_k\to N_l}(f) = \ln\left(\frac{S_{ll}(f)}{\tilde{H}_{ll}(f)\tilde{\Gamma}_2\tilde{H}_{ll}(f)^*}\right). \qquad (4)$$

The Granger causality scores over all frequencies are then summed together to obtain a single time-domain causal influence, *i.e.*, $C_{N_k\to N_l} = \sum_f G_{N_k\to N_l}(f)$, and $C_{N_l\to N_k} = \sum_f G_{N_l\to N_k}(f)$. In general, $C_{N_k\to N_l} \neq C_{N_l\to N_k}$, due to the directionality of the causal relations.

6.3 AVGs from the Causal Matrix

Our target of studying temporal causality between audio and visual codewords is to identify strongly correlated AVGs, where the direction of the relations is usually not important. For example, a dog can start barking at any time during the video, and we would like to find the AVG that contains correlated codewords describing the foreground dog barking sound and the visual dog point tracks. The direction of whether the barking sound is captured before or after the visual tracks is irrelevant. Therefore, for a pair of codewords represented by point processes $N_k^{s_k}(t)$ and $N_l^{s_l}(t)$ (where s_k or s_l is one of the following $f-v$, $f-a$, $b-v$, and $b-a$, indicating the vocabularies the codeword comes from), the nonparametric Granger causality scores from both directions $C_{N_k^{s_k}\to N_l^{s_l}}$ and $C_{N_l^{s_l}\to N_k^{s_k}}$ are summed together to generate the final similarity between these two codewords:

$$C(N_k^{s_k}, N_l^{s_l}) = C_{N_k^{s_k}\to N_l^{s_l}} + C_{N_l^{s_l}\to N_k^{s_k}}. \qquad (5)$$

Then, for a pair of audio and visual vocabularies, *e.g.*, $\mathcal{V}^{f-v}$ and $\mathcal{V}^{f-a}$, we have a $2D\times 2D$ symmetric causal matrix:

$$\begin{bmatrix} \mathbf{C}^{f-v,f-v} & \mathbf{C}^{f-v,f-a}\\ \mathbf{C}^{f-a,f-v} & \mathbf{C}^{f-a,f-a}\end{bmatrix}, \qquad (6)$$

where $\mathbf{C}^{f-v,f-v}$, $\mathbf{C}^{f-a,f-a}$, and $\mathbf{C}^{f-v,f-a}$ are $D\times D$ matrices with entries $C(N_k^{f-v}, N_l^{f-v})$, $C(N_k^{f-a}, N_l^{f-a})$, and $C(N_k^{f-v}, N_l^{f-a})$, respectively.

Spectral clustering can be applied directly based on this causal matrix to identify groups of codewords that have high correlations. Here we use the algorithm developed in [26] where the number of clusters can be determined automatically by analyzing the eigenvalues of the causal matrix. Each cluster is called an AVG, and codewords in an AVG can come from both audio and visual vocabularies. The AVGs capture temporally correlated audio and visual codewords that statistically interact over time. Each AVG can be treated as an audio-visual pattern, and all AVGs form an audio-visual dictionary. For a given video V_j, the original SIFT point tracks and audio features can be mapped to AVGs and generate an audio-visual dictionary-based feature. The simplest way to compute this dictionary-based feature is to aggregate the original BoW features over individual visual and audio vocabularies. For instance, for an AVG containing codewords $w_1^{f-a},\dots,w_n^{f-a}$ from $\mathcal{V}^{f-a}$, and $w_1^{f-v},\dots,w_m^{f-v}$ from $\mathcal{V}^{f-v}$, the value over the corresponding bin in the dictionary-based feature of video V_j is: $\sum_{p=1}^{n}F_{jp}^{f-a}+\sum_{p=1}^{m}F_{jp}^{f-v}$. F_{jp}^{f-a} (F_{jp}^{f-v}) is the value over the p-th bin in the BoW feature

$\mathbf{F}_j^{f-a}$ ($\mathbf{F}_j^{f-v}$) over $\mathcal{V}^{f-a}$ ($\mathcal{V}^{f-v}$). Classifiers such as SVMs can be trained using this feature for concept classification.

A total of four audio-visual dictionaries are generated in this work, by studying the temporal causal relations between different types of audio and visual codewords. They are: dictionary $\mathcal{D}^{f-v,f-a}$ by correlating $\mathcal{V}^{f-v}$ and $\mathcal{V}^{f-a}$, $\mathcal{D}^{b-v,b-a}$ by correlating $\mathcal{V}^{b-v}$ and $\mathcal{V}^{b-a}$, $\mathcal{D}^{f-v,b-a}$ by correlating $\mathcal{V}^{f-v}$ and $\mathcal{V}^{b-a}$, and $\mathcal{D}^{b-v,f-a}$ by correlating $\mathcal{V}^{b-v}$ and $\mathcal{V}^{f-a}$. As illustrated in Figure 3, all of these correlations reveal useful audio-visual patterns for classifying concepts.

7. EXPERIMENTS

We evaluate our algorithm over the large-scale CCV set [18], containing 9317 consumer videos from YouTube. These videos are captured by ordinary users under unrestricted challenging conditions, without post-editing. The original audio soundtracks are preserved, in contrast to other large-scale news or movie video sets [21, 32]. This allows us to study legitimate audio-visual interactions. Each video is manually labeled to 20 semantic concepts by using Amazon Mechanical Turk. More details about the data set and category definitions can be found in [18]. Our experiments take similar settings as [18], *i.e.*, we use the same training (4659 videos) and test (4658 videos) sets, and one-versus-all χ^2-kernel SVM classifiers. The performance is measured by Average Precision (*AP*, the area under uninterpolated PR curve) and Mean AP (*MAP*, averaged AP across concepts).

7.1 Performance of Concept Classification

To demonstrate the effectiveness of our method, we first evaluate the performance of the state-of-the-art BoW representations using different types of individual audio and visual features exploited in this paper, as well as the performance of their various early-fusion combinations. The AP and MAP results are shown in Figure 5. These BoW representations are generated using the same method as [18]. The results show that the individual visual SIFT, audio MFCCs, and audio transient event feature perform comparably overall, each having different advantages over different concepts. The combinations of audio and visual BoW representations through multi-modal fusion can consistently and significantly improve classification. For example, by combining the three individual features ("SIFT+MFCCs+Trans"), compared with individual features, all concepts get AP improvements, and the MAP is improved by over 33% on a relative basis. Readers may notice that our "SIFT" performs differently than that in [18]. This is because we have only a single type of SIFT feature (*i.e.*, SIFT over DoG keypoints) and generate the BoW representation using only the 1×1 spatial layout, while several types of keypoints and spatial layouts are used in [18]. Actually, our "MFCCs" performs similarly to that in [18], due to the similar settings for feature extraction and vocabulary construction.

Next, we compare the classification performance of using individual foreground and background audio and visual vocabularies (*i.e.*, $\mathcal{V}^{f-v}$, $\mathcal{V}^{f-a}$, $\mathcal{V}^{b-v}$, and $\mathcal{V}^{b-a}$), as well as using various types of audio-visual dictionaries (*i.e.*, $\mathcal{D}^{f-v,f-a}$, $\mathcal{D}^{f-v,b-a}$, $\mathcal{D}^{b-v,f-a}$, and $\mathcal{D}^{b-v,b-a}$). Each audio-visual dictionary contains about 300 AVGs on average. The results are shown in Figure 6. Also, the four types of audio-visual-dictionary-based features are concatenated together to train concept classifiers so that the advantages of all dictionaries in classifying different concepts can be exploited. This is the

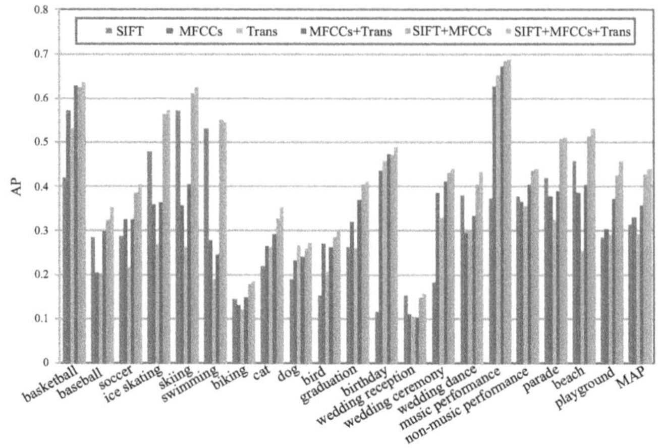

Figure 5: Comparison of various BoW representations as well as their early-fusion combinations.

"All A-V Dictionaries" approach shown in Figure 6. From the figure, we can see that for individual vocabularies, visual foreground performs better than visual background in general, while audio background performs better than audio foreground. Such results are within our expectation, because of the importance of the visual foreground in classifying objects and activities, as well as the effectiveness of audio background environmental sounds in classifying general concepts as shown by previous work [5, 18]. Compared with the visual foreground, visual background wins over "wedding ceremony" and "non-music performance," because of the importance of the background settings for these concepts, *e.g.*, the arch, flower boutique, and seated crowd for "wedding ceremony," and the stadium or stage setting for "non-music performance." In the audio aspect, audio foreground outperforms audio background over three concepts, "dog," "birthday," and "music performance," because of the usefulness of capturing consistent foreground sounds in these concepts.

Through exploring the temporal audio-visual interaction, the audio-visual dictionaries generally outperform the corresponding individual audio or visual vocabularies. For example, the MAP of $\mathcal{D}^{f-v,f-a}$ outperforms those of $\mathcal{V}^{f-v}$ and $\mathcal{V}^{f-a}$ by more than 10%, the MAP of $\mathcal{D}^{b-v,b-a}$ outperforms those of $\mathcal{V}^{b-v}$ and $\mathcal{V}^{b-a}$ by more than 20%, *etc.* By combining all types of dictionaries together, compared with individual audio or visual vocabularies, all concepts get consistent, significant AP improvements, and the overall MAP is improved by more than 50%. In addition, compared with direct multi-modal fusion without temporal audio-visual interaction (*i.e.*, "SIFT+MFCCs+Trans"), our "All A-V Dictionaries" approach has consistent AP gains over all concepts, with a 12% MAP gain overall. For 12 concepts (*e.g.*, "baseball," "ice skating," *etc.*) the APs are improved by more than 10%. The results demonstrate the effectiveness of extracting useful AVGs to classify general video concepts.

7.2 Visualization of AVGs

In Figure 7, we show some examples of the AVGs that are identified as carrying unique audio-visual patterns to classify different concepts. Such visualization helps us to subjectively and intuitively evaluate the effectiveness of our approach. Each example shows some visual and audio codewords grouped together in an AVG. Each visual codeword is shown as some local points in a video that are very similar to the codeword. For each audio codeword, we show the

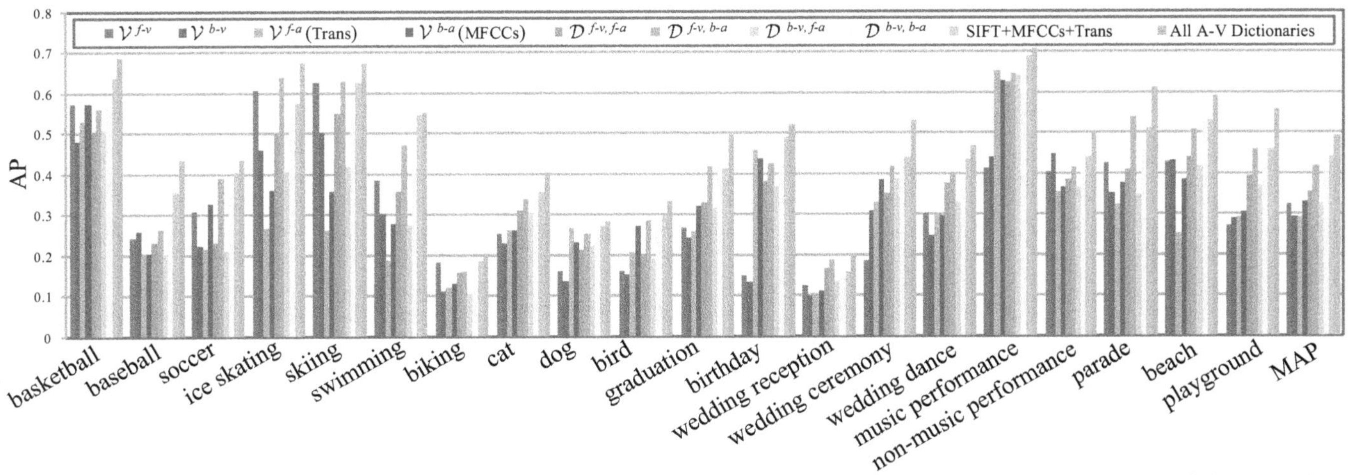

Figure 6: Comparison of individual foreground/background audio/visual vocabularies and audio-visual dictionaries.

spectrogram of the soundtrack over a 200 ms window, where the audio feature in this short window is very similar to the codeword. For the clarity of visualization, for each AVG, we show only a few codewords that co-occur in the same video. An actual AVG typically has about 20~30 codewords.

From the visualization we can see that by studying the temporal interactions of foreground and background audio and visual codewords, we can group inter-related audio and visual codewords into meaningful AVGs. Such AVGs provide discriminative audio-visual cues for classifying various concepts. The examples also confirm our assumption that all of the four types of audio-visual foreground/background interactions are important. For example, the visual foreground basketball player with audio foreground whistling and cheering sounds give a unique cue to classify "basketball" videos; the visual foreground bride and audio background music form a useful pattern to classify "wedding dance" videos; the visual background playground equipments and audio foreground children's cheering and laughing sounds are useful to classify "playground" videos; and the visual background sand and water together with audio background wind blowing sound are discriminative to classify "beach" videos.

8. CONCLUSION

We proposed an AVG representation by studying the statistical temporal causality between audio and visual codewords. Each AVG encapsulates inter-related audio and visual codewords as a whole package, which carries unique audio-visual patterns to represent the video content. By conducting coarse-level foreground/background separation in both visual and audio channels, four types of AVGs were extracted from four types of temporal audio-visual correlations, correlations between visual foreground and audio foreground codewords, between visual foreground and audio background codewords, between visual background and audio foreground codewords, and between visual background and audio background codewords. Experiments over large-scale consumer videos demonstrate that all four types of AVGs provide discriminative audio-visual cues to classify various concepts, and significant performance improvements can be obtained compared with state-of-the-art multi-modal fusion methods using BoW representations. It is worth mentioning that our method has some limitations. For videos that we cannot get meaningful SIFT tracks or extract meaningful audio transient events, our method will not work well.

9. ACKNOWLEDGEMENT

We would like to thank the authors of [6] and [25] for sharing their code with us, and for Shih-Fu Chang for many useful discussions.

10. REFERENCES

[1] T. Aach and A. Kaup. Bayesian algorithms for adaptive change detection in image sequences using Markov random fields. *Signal Processing: Image Communication*, vol. 7, pages 147-160, 1995.

[2] A. Akutsu and Y. Tonomura. Video tomography: An efficient method for camerawork extraction and motion analysis. *ACM Multimedia*, 1994.

[3] Z. Barzelay and Y. Schechner. Harmony in motion. In *Proc. IEEE CVPR*, pages 1-8, 2007.

[4] M.J. Beal, N. Jojic, and H. Attias. A graphical model for audiovisual object tracking. *IEEE Trans. PAMI*, 25(7):828-836, 2003.

[5] S. Chang, D. Ellis, W. Jiang, K. Lee, A. Yanagawa, A. Loui, and J. Luo. Large-scale multimodal semantic concept detection for consumer video. In *Proc. ACM MIR*, pages 255-264, 2007.

[6] C. Cotton, D. Ellis, and A. Loui. Soundtrack classification by transient events. In *IEEE ICASSP*, Prague, Czech Republic, 2011.

[7] M. Cristani, B. Manuele, and M. Vittorio. Audio-visual event recognition in surveillance video sequences. *IEEE Trans. Multimedia*, 9(2):257-267, 2007.

[8] N. Dalal and B. Triggs. Histograms of oriented gradients for human detection. In *Proc. IEEE CVPR*, pages 886-893, 2005.

[9] M. Ding, Y. Chen, and S.L. Bressler. Granger causality: Basic theory and applications to neuroscience. In *S. Schelter, N. Winterhalder, J. Timmer, Handbook of Time Series Analysis, Wiley, Wienheim*, 2006.

[10] S. Divvala, D. Hoiem, J. Hays, A. Efros, and M. Hebert. An empirical study of context in object detection. In *IEEE CVPR*, Miami, Florida, 2009.

[11] S.Y. Elhabian, K.M. El-Sayed. Moving object detection in spatial domain using background removal techniques - State-of-art. *Recent Patents on Computer Science*, 1(1):32-54, 2008.

[12] O. Enqvist, K. Josephson, and F. Kahl. Optimal

Figure 7: Examples of AVGs carrying useful audio-visual cues to classify concepts. For each AVG, we only show a few codewords that co-occur in an example video. For each video, visual codewords are marked by colored circles in a sampled image frame, each color indicating one visual codeword. Audio codewords are shown as the spectrograms of soundtracks over 200 ms windows. Only 2 audio codewords are given for each AVG. For instance, in the first example "basketball" video, we show 3 visual codewords and 2 audio codewords in an AVG.

correspondences from pairwise constraints. In *IEEE ICCV*, Kyoto, Japan, 2009.

[13] M. Everingham, L. Van Cool, C.K.I. Williams, J. Winn, and A. Zisserman. The Pascal visual object classes (VOC) challenge. *IJCV*, 88(2):303-338, 2010.

[14] C. Granger. Investigating causal relations by econometric models and cross-spectral methods. *Econometrica*, 37(3):424–438, 1969.

[15] K. Iwano, T. Yoshinaga, S. Tamura, and S. Furui. Audio-visual speech recognition using lip information extracted from side-face images. *EURASIP Journal on ASMP*, 2007(1):4-12, 2007.

[16] W. Jiang, C. Cotton, S. Chang, D. Ellis, and A. Loui. Audio-visual atoms for generic video concept classification. *ACM TOMCCAP*, 6:1-19, 2010.

[17] Y. Jiang, C.W. Ngo, and J. Yang. Towards optimal bag-of-features for object categorization and semantic video retrieval. In *ACM CIVR*, pages 494-501, 2007.

[18] Y. Jiang, G. Ye, S. Chang, D. Ellis, and A. Loui. Consumer video understanding: A benchmark database and an evaluation of human and machine performance. In *ACM ICMR*, Trento, Italy, 2011.

[19] P. Joly and H.K. Kim. Efficient automatic analysis of camera work and microsegmentation of video using spatiotemporal images. *Signal Processing: Image Communication*, 8(4):295-307, 1996.

[20] Y. Ke, R. Sukthankar, and M. Hebert. Event detection in crowded videos. In *IEEE ICCV*, Brazil, 2007.

[21] I. Laptev, M. Marszalek, C. Schmid, and B. Rozenfeld. Learning realistic human actions from movies. In *IEEE CVPR*, Alaska, 2008.

[22] W.H. Lin and A. Hauptmann. News video classification using svm-based multimodal classifiers and combination strategies. In *Proc. ACM Multimedia*, pages 323-326, 2002.

[23] D.G. Lowe. Distinctive image features from scale-invariant keypoints. *IJCV*, 60(2):91-110, 2004.

[24] M. Marszalek, I. Laptev, and C. Schmid. Actions in context. In *IEEE CVPR*, Miami, Florida, 2009.

[25] A. Nedungadi, G. Rangarajan, N. Jain, and M. Ding. Analyzing multiple spike trains with nonparametric granger causality. *Journal of Computational Neuroscience*, 27(1):55-64, 2009.

[26] A. Ng, M. Jordan, and Y. Weiss. On spectral clustering: Analysis and an algorithm. In *NIPS*, 2001.

[27] D. Nistér and H. Stewénius. Scalable recognition with a vocabulary tree. In *Proc. IEEE CVPR*, pages 2161-2168, 2006.

[28] D.T. Pham and J.F. Cardoso. Blind separation of instantaneous mixtures of non stationary sources. *IEEE Trans. Signal Processing*, 49(9):1837-1848, 2001.

[29] K. Prabhakar, S. Oh, P. Wang, G. Abowd, and J.M. Rehg. Temporal causality for the analysis of visual events. In *IEEE CVPR*, San Francisco, 2010.

[30] S.T. Roweis. One microphone source separation. In *NIPS*, pages 793–799, 2001.

[31] M. Sargin, H. Aradhye, P.J. Moreno, and M. Zhao. Audiovisual celebrity recognition in unconstrained web videos. In *IEEE ICASSP*, Taipei, 2009.

[32] A.F. Smeaton, P. Over, and W. Kraaij. Evaluation campaigns and TRECVid. In *Proc. ACM MIR*, pages 321-330, 2006.

[33] C. Stauffer and E. Grimson. Learning patterns of activity using realtime tracking. *IEEE Trans. PAMI*, 22(8):747-757, 2000.

[34] A. Walden. A unified view of multitaper multivariate spectral estimation. *Biometrika*, 87(4):767–788, 2000.

[35] B. Wang and M.D. Plumbley. Investigating single-channel audio source separation methods based on non-negative matrix factorization. In *Proc. ICArn*, pages 17-20, 2006.

[36] W. Wang, D. Cosker, Y. Hicks, S. Saneit, and J. Chambers. Video assisted speech source separation. In *Proc. IEEE ICASSP*, pages 425–428, 2005.

[37] Y. Wu, C.Y. Lin, E.Y. Chang, and J.R. Smith. Multimodal information fusion for video concept detection. In *Proc. IEEE ICIP*, pages 2391–2394, 2004.

[38] J. Yang, Y. Jiang, A. Hauptmann, and C. Ngo. Evaluating bag-of-visual-words representations in scene classification. *ACM MIR*, pages 197–206, 2007.

[39] B. Yao and L. Fei-Fei. Grouplet: A structured image representation for recognizing human and object interactions. In *IEEE CVPR*, San Francisco, 2010.

News Contextualization with Geographic and Visual Information*

Zechao Li[1,2], Meng Wang[3], Jing Liu[1], Changsheng Xu[1,2] and Hanqing Lu[1,2]
[1]Institute of Automation, Chinese Academy of Sciences, Beijing China 100190
[2]China-Singapore Institute of Digital Media, 21 Heng Mui Keng Terrace, Singapore 119613
[3]School of Computing, National University of Singapore, Singapore
{zcli, jliu, csxu, luhq}@nlpr.ia.ac.cn, eric.mengwang@gmail.com

ABSTRACT

In this paper, we investigate the contextualization of news documents with geographic and visual information. We propose a matrix factorization approach to analyze the location relevance for each news document. We also propose a method to enrich the document with a set of web images. For location relevance analysis, we first perform toponym extraction and expansion to obtain a toponym list from news documents. We then propose a matrix factorization method to estimate the location-document relevance scores while simultaneously capturing the correlation of locations and documents. For image enrichment, we propose a method to generate multiple queries from each news document for image search and then employ an intelligent fusion approach to collect a set of images from the search results. Based on the location relevance analysis and image enrichment, we introduce a news browsing system named NewsMap which can support users in reading news via browsing a map and retrieving news with location queries. The news documents with the corresponding enriched images are presented to help users quickly get information. Extensive experiments demonstrate the effectiveness of our approaches.

Categories and Subject Descriptors

H.3.3 [**Information Storage and Retrieval**]: Information Search and Retrieval; H.5.1 [**Information Interfaces and Presentation**]: Multimedia Information System

General Terms

Algorithms, Experimentation

Keywords

News location relevance, Image enrichment, NewsMap

*Area chair: Cees Snoek

1. INTRODUCTION

With the proliferation of news documents on the Internet, online news reading becomes an important approach for information acquisition in people's daily lives. People can access and browse news on either some main web portals, such as MSN and Yahoo!, or large news websites, such as CNN, AOL and MSNBC. It is reported by Newspapers Association of America (NAA) that, in US, there are more than 100 millions of unique visitors on several major news websites monthly and the number is nearly 2/3 of all adult Internet users[1]. However, existing news presentation usually has the following two limitations:

(1) Lack of location-based organization. Existing studies demonstrate that users usually have high priority in getting news information about some specific places, such as his/her country, working city and hometown [29]. Most large news websites can organize news documents according to the involved countries, such that a rough personalization can be accomplished by identifying the user's location based on IP address. Of course we can search for news documents by giving a location name as query on many news websites, but the location names contained in news documents are usually noisy and this will degrade the search performance.

(2) Incomprehensive visual information. A picture is worth a thousand words. The associated pictures, as the complement of news text, are able to provide readers additional information or help them get information quickly. However, the pictures contained in news documents are usually very few. In fact, a statistical analysis on a randomly collected dataset (see the description about the dataset in Section 6) shows that more than half of the news documents do not contain any picture and only less than 5% of the news documents contain more than one picture.

To address these problems, we propose approaches to contextualize news documents with geographic and visual information respectively. We employ a matrix factorization approach to analyze the location relevance for each news document, and enrich the document with a set of web images. It is well known that the key part of a news document is "4W" elements: "Who", "When", "Where" and "What" [22]. Our approaches are actually able to enhance the three of them, namely, "Who", "Where" and "What". The enhancement

[1]http://www.naa.org/TrendsandNumbers.aspx

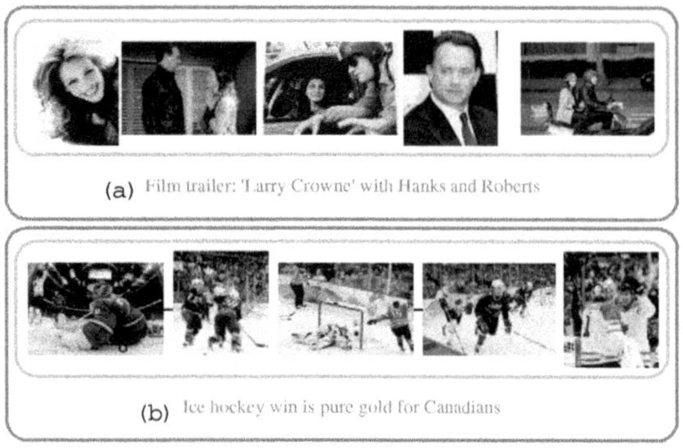

Figure 1: Examples for demonstrating how images can complement the text information of news documents. By providing illustrative images, we can let users get more information, such as the "Who" and "What" elements in news documents (see (a) and (b), respectively).

of "Where" is obvious as we can estimate the location relevance for the document. The other elements are enhanced by the image enrichment. For example, as shown in Fig. 1, when reading a news document about a new movie of Julia Roberts, the user may be interested in who this actor is. When reading a news document about an ice hockey competition, the user may be interested in what the sport is like. By providing several illustrative images, our approach is able to provide the user with more vivid and comprehensive information that complements the text document.

Our approaches work as follows. We employ a toponym extraction and expansion process to extract the location names from news documents. However, they are usually noisy and incomplete. For example, there are many documents that contain multiple locations or do not contain any location. The relevance of locations can be inferred by mining the content of news documents and their correlations. For example, a news document discussing about "Olympic 2008" may not contain a location name, but we can infer its relevance to "Beijing" by exploring other topic-related but location-indicated news documents. To address this problem, we propose a probabilistic matrix factorization algorithm, called Correlation Consistent Probabilistic Matrix Factorization (CCPMF), to analyze the location relevance of documents. For image enrichment, a set of web images is collected with the help of Google image search. The title and main body of each document are analyzed to generate queries with different lengths for image search, and we then employ an intelligent fusion method to merge the search results. The pictures contained in news documents will also be explored in the image enrichment process.

Based on the news location analysis and image enrichment approaches, we introduce a news browsing system named NewsMap. Users can browse the map and click a place, and the system will show the news documents that are relevant to the place. It also supports news search with a textual location query. The enriched images are presented together with the title and summary for each news document such that users can quickly get necessary information. We employ a PageRank approach that incorporates both the location relevance and the time information to rank news documents.

Our contribution can be summarized as follows:

1) We propose a matrix factorization based algorithm to analyze the location relevance for news documents. In comparison with the conventional matrix factorization approach, our method investigates the news content correlation and location co-occurrence and thus achieves much better performance.

2) We propose an approach to enrich news documents with a set of web images. A set of techniques, such as query generation, rank aggregation and duplicate detection are integrated to find appropriate images. Although it involves several existing techniques, such as rank aggregation and duplicate detection, our approach that generates queries with different lengths and then fuses their search results is novel, and it can also be applied in other applications.

3) Based on the location relevance analysis and image enrichment, we introduce a news browsing system named NewsMap, which supports users in browsing news documents via a map.

The rest of this paper is organized as follows. Section 2 reviews related work. In Section 3 and Section 4, we introduce the location relevance estimation and image enrichment approaches for news documents, respectively. We introduce the NewsMap system in Section 5. Experimental results are reported in Section 6. We conclude the paper with future work in Section 7.

2. RELATED WORK

Since our work involves news location analysis and enriching text documents with images, we mainly review previous work along these two directions.

2.1 Media Geolocation

Media geolocation has attracted great research interest in recent years for its many potential applications, such as media search, recommendation and travel assistance.

Hays and Efros [13] proposed an image geolocation approach which locates an image by finding its nearest neighbors in a GPS-tagged dataset. Serdyukov et al. [28] proposed a text-driven method to analyze the geographic information of Flickr images. A language model based on tags is learned for each grid of map and the location of an image is determined by these models. Existing work has shown that the performance of web image geolocation can be improved by combining textual and visual features [3, 7]. The literature regarding video geolocation is relatively sparse. Kelm et al. [19] proposed an approach that combines textual and visual models to find the grid of a video. Christel et al. [4] proposed a method to tag video sequences with latitude and longitude information. It supports users in browsing videos via a map with all of the places discussed in the videos. However, it cannot handle noisy and incomplete place names. While both providing map interface for browsing, our NewsMap system provides a snap view that illustrates the news titles and the related images in order to help readers get information quickly (details will be introduced in Section 5). More details about image and video geolocation can be found in [23, 39]. Different from the geolocation of image and video that needs to explore visual content and tag information, our task is to analyze the relevance levels of the location names contained in news documents. Therefore, in this work we employ a matrix factorization approach with exploring the correlation of news documents and locations.

The task of finding a geographic focus of a web page was first proposed in [10]. Two methods are investigated, one is by analyzing the geographic location of the hosts linking into the site and the other is based on the detection and disambiguation of location name. The methods in [1, 41] rely on propagating the confidence weights of locations up to the root of the gazetteer taxonomy to determine the place each name refers to. But these methods cannot be applied to our task as we do not have links among news documents. Co-occurrence models are used to disambiguate place names in [25]. In this method, Wikipedia is used to generate a co-occurrence model, which can be used to improve average precision in the geographic information retrieval system. However, the task of [25] is place name disambiguation, while our target is to analyze the location relevance of documents and it is able to handle the noisy and incomplete locations for documents. Geographical Information Retrieval (GIR), which is the augmentation of Information Retrieval with geographic metadata, is also related to our work. To provide the necessary framework for evaluating GIR systems, a track named GeoCLEF [12] started from 2005. GIR tries to exploit geographical references in text for targeted and improved retrieval. Different from the tasks of GeoCLEF and GIR, the target of our work is to analyze the location relevance of documents and support users to search news by place names as queries.

Currently, there are several systems that support news browsing with geographic information, such as World News Map[2] and Yahoo News Map[3]. However, the geolocation is only performed at country level based on several simple heuristics. The NewsMap system introduced in our work can support news browsing with locations at different scales and can provide much better user experience.

2.2 Text Visualization

There exists work that aims to find images to describe or enrich text documents. WordsEye [6] employed semantic representation to synthesize 3D scenes from text. Joshi et al. [18, 40] proposed a story picturing system that is able to find a set of pictures to describe a fragment of a text. In their approach, key phrases are extracted from the text to retrieve images, which are then ranked using lexical annotations and visual content. In [40], the picturability is measured in terms of the ratio of the frequencies under regular web versus image search. Graphics is used to spatially arrange the images to represent the story. Several methods are also proposed to find or synthesize an image to describe a web page [16, 30]. However, there is little work on enriching news documents with media information. The most related work is [8] and [9]. Delgado et al. [8, 9] proposed methods to assist users in reading news by providing images. However, the methods select images from a fixed database based on their text information, such as tags, whereas our approach applies image search tools to find images from the web. In addition, the methods by Delgado et al. add images for each sentence, whereas our work finds several images to enrich the whole news document together with the original pictures. In fact, the scheme by Delgado et al. is more likely designed for tools that assist children and elderly, whereas our approach can enhance context information for general users.

[2]http://www.tsmaps.com/

[3]http://isithackday.com/hacks/placemaker/map.php

3. LOCATION RELEVANCE ANALYSIS

In this section, we elaborate our news location analysis approach, which consists of two steps: (1) toponym extraction and expansion and (2) matrix factorization based relevance analysis.

3.1 Toponym Extraction and Expansion

We obtain a toponym list from the news data set with toponym extraction and expansion approach based on external knowledge resources. The process is described as follows.

First, we employ OpenNLP[4], a homogeneous package based on a machine learning approach using maximum entropy, to extract toponym candidates from news documents. Second, we remove several candidates that do not have geo-coordinates in Wikipedia[5]. The next step is to expand the toponym list and eliminate geographical ambiguity. For example, there are two places named "Paris", one in France and the other in US. We take each toponym candidate as a query and submit it to GeoNames[6], which will return a list of related place names. We collect the corresponding "Name", "Country", "Latitude" and "Longitude" information for each returned item. We parse the returned items and deduplicate the toponym list by exploring the information of "Country" and geo-coordinates. Meanwhile, we employ the information of "Country" and geo-coordinates to eliminate ambiguity among the toponym candidates (note that the information of "Country" contains hierarchical administrative division, such as country and state).

3.2 Matrix Factorization Relevance Analysis

Up to now, we have obtained a toponym list including a set of locations, and we can find the locations contained in each news document. However, a problem is that the locations found in such way are usually noisy. It comes from two facts. First, several location names contained in a news document are not very relevant. For example, considering a news document that describes the wedding of a celebrity, the document may contain some place names about the bride, such as where she was born and the hometown name of the bride, but these locations are not relevant enough in comparison with the location where the wedding is hold. The second fact is that several relevant locations may not appear in the documents. Clearly, to accurately analyze the most relevant location for a news document needs understanding of the news content and it is a challenging NLP problem. Existing studies demonstrate that the semantic space spanned by text keywords can be approximated by a smaller subset of salient words of the original space [38]. News content has the low rank property as well. Therefore, considering a relevance score matrix $\mathbf{R}$ of which the (i, j)-th element indicates the relevance of the i-th toponym and j-th document, $\mathbf{R}$ could be approximated by the product of two low-rank matrices $\mathbf{P}$ and $\mathbf{E}$. These two low rank matrices are the latent feature representations of locations and news contents. Thus the relevance analysis problem becomes the task of estimating the location-document relevance matrix with information loss minimization, and we employ matrix factorization to estimate the location-document relevance matrix. We further explore the correlation of locations and news

[4]http://incubator.apache.org/opennlp/

[5]http://www.wikipedia.org/

[6]http://www.geonames.org/

documents, i.e., the relevance scores of highly correlated locations or similar documents should be close. Therefore, we propose a Correlation Consistent Probabilistic Matrix Factorization (CCPMF) algorithm to simultaneously integrate the multiple assumptions.

We first introduce some notations. Assume there are M locations and N news documents. Let $\mathbf{R} \in \mathcal{R}^{M\times N}$, $\mathbf{P} \in \mathcal{R}^{H\times N}$, $\mathbf{E} \in \mathcal{R}^{H\times N}$, $\mathbf{C} \in \mathcal{R}^{M\times M}$ and $\mathbf{S} \in \mathcal{R}^{N\times N}$ denote the location-document relevance matrix, location latent feature matrix, document latent feature matrix, location correlation matrix, and document correlation matrix, respectively. Denote by $\mathbf{R}^0$ the location-document appearance matrix, i.e., R^0_{ij} if the i-th location is contained in the j-th document, and otherwise $R^0_{ij} = 0$. The matrices $\mathbf{P}$ and $\mathbf{E}$ indicate latent feature representations that we need to estimate in the matrix factorization approach. We usually set $H < \min(M, N)$ and it is the rank of $\mathbf{R}$.

To mine the latent relations among the sparse data set, Probabilistic Matrix Factorization (PMF) [27] can be employed which approximates $\mathbf{R}$ as a product of two lower-rank matrices. However, it does not take the correlations of locations and documents into account, i.e., the facts that the relevance scores of highly correlated locations or similar documents should be close. Therefore, we extend the PMF approach to CCPMF to further consider the correlations of locations and documents.

PMF is a probabilistic linear model with Gaussian observation noise, which is defined as

$$p(\mathbf{R}^0|\mathbf{P}, \mathbf{E}, \sigma_R^2) = \prod_{i=1}^{M}\prod_{j=1}^{N}[\mathcal{N}(R^0_{ij}|\mathbf{p}_i^T\mathbf{e}_j, \sigma_R^2)]^{\delta_{ij}}, \quad (1)$$

where $\mathcal{N}(x|\mu, \sigma^2)$ is the Gaussian probability density function with mean μ and variance σ^2, and δ_{ij} is the indicator function that satisfies $\delta_{ij} = 1$ if $R^0_{ij} > 0$, and otherwise $\delta_{ij} = 0$.

Zero-mean spherical Gaussian priors are placed on the two lower-rank matrices:

$$p(\mathbf{P}|\sigma_P^2) = \prod_{i=1}^{M}\mathcal{N}(\mathbf{p}_i|0, \sigma_P^2\mathbf{I}), \quad (2)$$

$$p(\mathbf{E}|\sigma_E^2) = \prod_{j=1}^{N}\mathcal{N}(\mathbf{e}_j|0, \sigma_E^2\mathbf{I}), \quad (3)$$

where $\mathbf{I}$ is the identify matrix.

Through a Bayesian inference, the poster distribution over $p(\mathbf{P}, \mathbf{E}|\mathbf{R}^0, \sigma_R^2, \sigma_P^2, \sigma_E^2)$ can be obtained. Maximizing the log-posterior is equal to minimizing the following equation:

$$\mathcal{L} = \frac{1}{2}\sum_{i=1}^{M}\sum_{j=1}^{N}\delta^R_{ij}(R^0_{ij} - R_{ij})^2 + \frac{\lambda_P}{2}\mathrm{Tr}[\mathbf{P}^T\mathbf{P}] + \frac{\lambda_E}{2}\mathrm{Tr}[\mathbf{E}^T\mathbf{E}], \quad (4)$$

where $\mathbf{R} = \mathbf{P}^T\mathbf{E}$, $\lambda_P = \sigma_R^2/\sigma_P^2$, $\lambda_E = \sigma_R^2/\sigma_E^2$ and $\mathrm{Tr}[\cdot]$ denotes the trace operation on a matrix.

To consider the inter-correlations, CCPMF embeds the correlations of locations and documents as two consistency constraints on PMF, which can be described by the graphical model in Fig. 2. CCPMF is formulated to minimize the

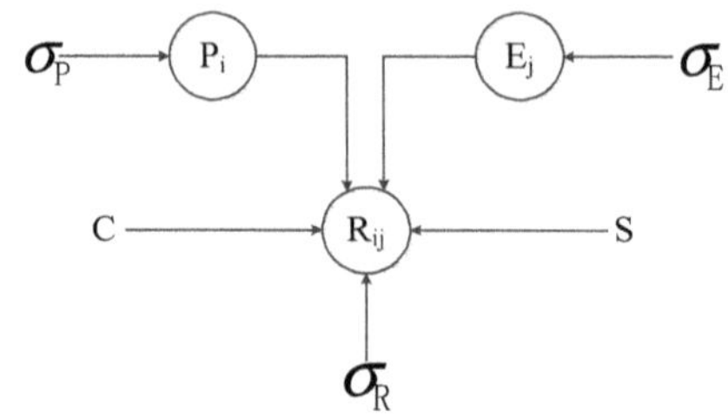

Figure 2: The graphic model for Correlation Consistent Probabilistic Matrix Factorization (CCPMF).

following equation.

$$\mathcal{L} = \frac{1}{2}\sum_{i=1}^{M}\sum_{j=1}^{N}\delta_{ij}(R^0_{ij} - R_{ij})^2 + \frac{\lambda_P}{2}\mathrm{Tr}[\mathbf{P}^T\mathbf{P}] + \frac{\lambda_E}{2}\mathrm{Tr}[\mathbf{E}^T\mathbf{E}] + \frac{\lambda_C}{2}F_C(\mathbf{R}) + \frac{\lambda_S}{2}F_S(\mathbf{R}) \quad (5)$$

In comparison with the conventional PMF approach, the C-CPMF method further incorporates two terms $F_C(\mathbf{R})$ and $F_S(\mathbf{R})$, which consider the location correlation and document correlation, respectively, and λ_C and λ_S are two positive weighting parameters. The term $F_C(\mathbf{R})$ enforces the relevance scores of highly correlated locations to be close while $F_S(\mathbf{R})$ enforces the relevance scores of highly similar documents are close. Although several parameters are involved in our formulation, we will observe its effectiveness in the experiments in Section 6.

The term $F_C(\mathbf{R})$ is defined as

$$F_C(\mathbf{R}) = \frac{1}{2}\sum_{k=1}^{N}\sum_{i,j=1}^{M}(R_{ik} - R_{jk})^2 C_{ij} = \mathrm{Tr}[\mathbf{R}^T\mathbf{L}^C\mathbf{R}], \quad (6)$$

where $\mathbf{L}^C = \mathbf{D}^C - \mathbf{C}$ is the Laplacian matrix and $\mathbf{D}^C$ is a diagonal matrix defined as $D^C_{ii} = \sum_{m=1}^{M} C_{im}$.

Similar to $F_C(\mathbf{R})$, $F_S(\mathbf{R})$ can be represented as

$$F_S(\mathbf{R}) = \frac{1}{2}\sum_{k=1}^{M}\sum_{i,j=1}^{N}(R_{ki} - R_{kj})^2 S_{ij} = \mathrm{Tr}[\mathbf{R}\mathbf{L}^S\mathbf{R}^T], \quad (7)$$

where $\mathbf{L}^S$ and $\mathbf{D}^S$ are defined similar to $\mathbf{L}^C$ and $\mathbf{D}^C$.

Based on Eq. 6 and Eq. 7, Eq. 5 can be rewritten as

$$\mathcal{L} = \frac{1}{2}\sum_{i=1}^{M}\sum_{j=1}^{N}\delta_{ij}(R^0_{ij} - R_{ij})^2 + \frac{\lambda_P}{2}\mathrm{Tr}[\mathbf{P}^T\mathbf{P}] + \frac{\lambda_E}{2}\mathrm{Tr}[\mathbf{E}^T\mathbf{E}] + \frac{\lambda_C}{2}\mathrm{Tr}[\mathbf{R}^T\mathbf{L}^C\mathbf{R}] + \frac{\lambda_S}{2}\mathrm{Tr}[\mathbf{R}\mathbf{L}^S\mathbf{R}^T]. \quad (8)$$

We adopt gradient descent to solve the above optimization problem over $\mathbf{P}$ and $\mathbf{E}$.

To implement CCPMF, we need to define $\mathbf{C}$ and $\mathbf{S}$, i.e., the correlation matrices for locations and documents.

For the correlation of locations, we adopt Google distance [5]. Let d_{ij} denote the Google distance between the i-th and j-th locations and then C_{ij} is defined as

$$C_{ij} = e^{-\frac{d_{ij}^2}{\sigma_C^2}}, \quad (9)$$

where σ_C is set to the median value of the pairwise distances.

For the correlation of documents, we represent the title, summary and main body of each news document with TF-IDF histograms. Therefore, we can estimate the cosine similarity of the titles, summaries and main bodies of each two news documents. Denote by $\mathbf{S}^t$, $\mathbf{S}^s$ and $\mathbf{S}^b$ the similarity matrices got in this way. We simply fuse them to get $\mathbf{S}$, i.e.,

$$\mathbf{S} = \alpha\mathbf{S}^t + \beta\mathbf{S}^s + (1 - \alpha - \beta)\mathbf{S}^b. \quad (10)$$

We simply set the parameters α and β to 1/3.

It is worth mentioning that different from the location-document appearance matrix $\mathbf{R}^0$ which is usually highly sparse, the relevance matrix $\mathbf{R}$ may not be sparse. However, we can easily sparsify $\mathbf{R}$ by setting the elements that are below a threshold to 0. This can facilitate the inverted indexing structure in large-scale search.

4. IMAGE ENRICHMENT

Our image enrichment approach consists of two steps. The first step is query generation, which forms a set of queries by analyzing both the titles and main bodies of news documents, and the second step is image mining and selection.

4.1 Query Generation

To retrieve images from the external sources, it is necessary to extract queries from news documents. A simple method is to adopt the title as query to search. However, current search engines cannot handle long queries well, and usually very limited results or even no result are returned for complex queries [14, 21]. Here we propose an approach to extract a set of queries.

The first step is performing stemming and removal of punctuation and stop-words for the whole news documents. We then need to identify several query terms from each news document. However, a news document is usually too long, which makes the query term selection difficult. Given the fact that the title of a news document is usually a good summarization of the whole document that is manually constructed by a specialist, and it is reasonable to select the query terms from the title. Considering there are several news documents with fairly long titles, we rank the title terms according to their correlation with the content of main body and only select top terms. Denote by $\mathcal{T} = \{term_1, term_2, ..., term_u\}$ and $\mathcal{B} = \{term_1^{'}, term_2^{'}, ..., term_v^{'}\}$ the set of terms in the title and main body, respectively. The importance score of $term_i$ can thus be estimated as

$$score(term_i) = \frac{1}{v}\sum_{j=1}^{v} exp(-\frac{d^2(term_i, term_j^{'})}{\sigma^2}). \quad (11)$$

Here $d(term_i, term_j^{'})$ is the Google distance between $term_i$ and $term_j^{'}$ and σ is the median value of all $d(term_i, term_j^{'})$. We select the top c terms in $\mathcal{T}$ with the highest importance scores. In the cases that $u < c$, we simply select $c - u$ terms from $\mathcal{B}$ with the highest TF-IDF values to complement $\mathcal{T}$.

The images are collected based on the c query terms with the help of online image search tools. However, there is a dilemma here: usually using more query terms for search can obtain more accurate and descriptive images, but it will also get less search results or even no result returned. For example, we consider a query term set {"Yao Ming", "Olympic", "torch", "representative", "nervous"}. If we use each single term to search, such as "Yao Ming" or "torch", the resulting images are not descriptive for the news document. If we use the combination of multiple terms such as "Yao Ming Olympic torch" to search, better results can be collected. But if we use all the terms, i.e., "Yao Ming Olympic torch

(a) Ming Yao

(b) torch

(c) Ming Yao torch

(d) Ming Yao torch Olympic representative nervous

Figure 3: Top image search results of (a) "Ming Yao", (b) "torch", (c) "Ming Yao torch" and (d) "Ming Yao torch Olympic representative nervous". From the results we can see the dilemma: the descriptiveness of the results from too few query terms is not good due to the lack of context information, and long queries cannot return reasonable results due to the limitation of search engines in handling complex queries.

representative nervous", the returned results are limited and are also irrelevant to the whole story. Figure 3 demonstrates the comparison of the top results of different queries.

To address this problem, we propose an approach that first generates all the combinations of the terms as queries for search and then fuse the search results by assigning appropriate weights to the queries that are of different lengths. Clearly, from the c terms, we can generate $L = \sum_{k=1}^{c}\binom{c}{k} = 2^c - 1$ queries with their lengths varying from 1 to c.

4.2 Image Mining and Selection

We issue each query on Google image search engine and collect the top h ranked results. Thus our next task is to fuse the L ranking lists, which is a rank aggregation problem. Generally there are two approaches for rank aggregation, namely, score-based fusion and rank-based fusion [35, 37, 24]. Here we adopt the score-based fusion approach. For each image in a ranking list, we can define its relevance score based on its position. But note that there are several news documents that originally contain pictures and we also take their information into the relevance score estimation. That means, the search results that are closer to the original pictures will be assigned higher scores. Therefore, considering x_i is the image at the k-th ($k \geq 1$) position of the j-th ranking list, its relevance score is defined as

$$s_j(x_i) = \mu(1 - \frac{k-1}{h}) + (1 - \mu)\max_{x \in \mathcal{O}} sim(x, x_i), \quad (12)$$

where $\mathcal{O}$ is the set of original pictures contained in the news document. Here we simply set the parameter μ to 0.5.

In score-based fusion, all the L search results are merged and we also find the duplicates based on their URL informa-

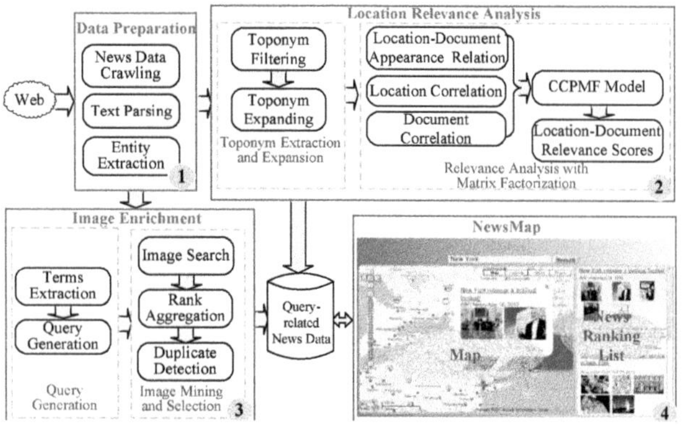

Figure 4: The schematic illustration of NewsMap.

tion. Note that in traditional rank aggregation, each ranking list is usually assigned a tunable weight [31]. But in our approach, we assign a distinct weight to all ranking lists of a specific query length as our target is to modulate the affect of different query lengths. That means, the queries with the same number of terms have the same weight, i.e.,

$$\theta = \theta_{1:L} = (\underbrace{\eta_1, \ldots, \eta_1}_{\binom{c}{1}}, \ldots, \underbrace{\eta_k, \ldots, \eta_k}_{\binom{c}{k}}, \ldots, \underbrace{\eta_c}_{\binom{c}{c}}) \tag{13}$$

where η_k is the weight for the $\binom{c}{k}$ queries with length k.

The fused score of x_i can be written as

$$s(x_i) = \sum_{j=1}^{L} \theta_j s_j(x_i). \tag{14}$$

The weights $\eta_1, \eta_2, \ldots, \eta_c$ are established based on a training set. The process is as follows. Given a collection of documents, for each image collected in the ranking lists, we manually label their ground truths. Then in the rank aggregation, we tune the weights to the values that optimize the average NDCG@10 [15] with grid search.

We generate a ranking list based on the fused scores $s(x_i)$, and then adopt the approach in [32] to perform duplicate detection for all these images and for each duplicate pair we remove the one with lower rank. After that, we select the top $r - |\mathcal{O}|$ images to complement the original pictures in $\mathcal{O}$, where $|\mathcal{O}|$ is the size of $\mathcal{O}$. Therefore, for each document we have r images, either from the original pictures or the web.

5. APPLICATION: NEWSMAP

We introduce a news browsing system, NewsMap, based on the news location analysis and image enrichment approaches. It assists users in getting news about a specific place with browsing a map. By clicking an interested place on the map, we will list ranked news documents with those enriched images as well as the titles. News search by a place name as a query is also supported. The framework of NewsMap is presented in Fig. 4, from which we can see that the whole system mainly contains four components.

First, we collect and process large-scale news data. These documents are parsed into titles, summaries, texts, URLs and images. Necessary text preprocessing steps, including word separation and stop-words filtering, are performed. We then extract entities including location and time.

The second and third components are the location analysis and image enrichment introduced in Section 3 and Section 4, respectively.

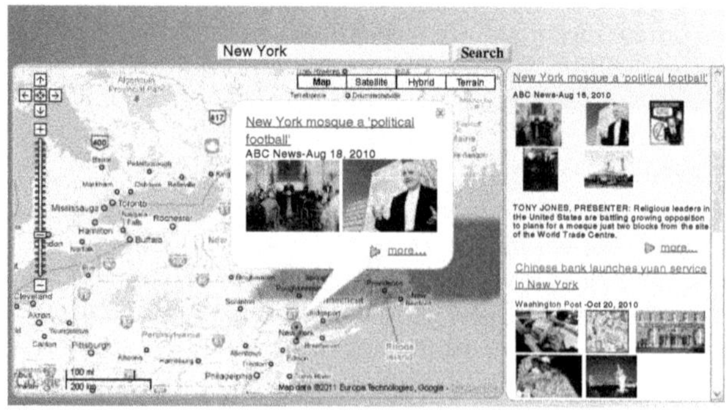

Figure 5: The user interface of NewsMap.

The fourth component is result ranking and visualization. There are many ranking algorithms [26, 34, 33, 36, 11]. Here we adopt a PageRank [26] approach with considering both location relevance and news timeliness. It will prioritize the following three kinds of news: (1) the news documents that are highly relevant to query location; (2) latest news; and (3) the news documents that have many closely related news reports (they usually indicate important news information that has been intensively reported). They actually indicate three properties for news presentation and search: relevance, timeliness and importance.

The time information is an important aspect for news. We quantize the time stamp of each news document as a number of "YYYYMMDD". For example, the time "Sep. 12 2010" will be quantized to be 20100912. Denote by $date_k$ the quantized date of the k-th document and we then normalize the numbers with two steps:

$$date_k = \frac{date_k - \min_j(date_j)}{\max_j(date_j) - \min_j(date_j)}; \tag{15}$$

$$date_k = \frac{date_k}{\sum_j date_j}. \tag{16}$$

Through CCPMF, we have obtained a relevance score between the query location and each news document. Denote by $score_k$ the relevance score between the location and the k-th document. We normalize them as follows.

$$score_k = \frac{score_k}{\sum_j score_j} \tag{17}$$

In the PageRank algorithm [26], we set the static ranking score of the k-th document to

$$r_k^0 = \frac{date_k + score_k}{2}. \tag{18}$$

An iterative process is then implemented by performing

$$r_k^{iter} = (1-y) r_k^0 + y \sum_j \frac{S_{kj}}{\sum_m S_{mj}} r_j^{iter-1}, \tag{19}$$

until $iter \geq 1$ achieves the pre-determined number. Here, S_{ij} is the similarity between the i-th and j-th document, and y is the damping factor (we simply set it to 0.85 [2]).

A preliminary UI of the NewsMap system is presented in Fig. 5, which is developed based on Google Map API. By submitting a location query (in the top textbox) or clicking a place on the map, the highest ranked news document with its title and the top 2 illustrative images is presented as a pop-up window positioning on the queried location of the map. The detailed ranking results about this location are shown in the right part with title, summary and

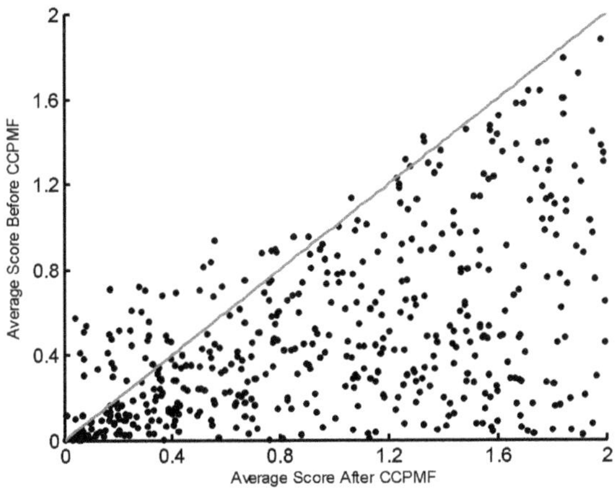

Figure 6: The comparison of the distribution of the average scores between before and after location refinement. We can see that for most news documents the locations after refinement are more relevant.

illustrative images (including the original pictures and the images enriched by our approach). In this way, the users can quickly get information about the news without reading its main body. Although UI is a very important part for such a system, a more detailed investigation is beyond our current scope and we leave it to our future work.

6. EXPERIMENTS

We elaborate our experiments on a dataset that contains news documents from multiple websites. We first introduce our experimental settings and then provide empirical justification of our approaches.

6.1 Experimental Settings

We collect a large data set from four websites, including ABCNews.com, BBC.co.uk, CNN.com and Google News. There are 135,308 news documents and 69,144 news images. By removing duplicates, there are 48,429 news documents and 20,862 news pictures in total.

From the news documents, there are 6,293 distinct location names extracted. By performing the filtering and expansion process, there are 4,742 locations remained.

To get the image similarity in Eq. 12, we extract 1000-dimensional bag-of-visual-words features from each image and adopt cosine similarity. In location relevance analysis, the rank H of latent matrices is set to 100 and the parameters λ_P, λ_E, λ_C and λ_S are set to 0.001, 0.001, 2^{-3} and 2^{-4}, respectively. Notation that these values are small because the corresponding regularizes are not normalized. In image enrichment, we set $h = 20$, i.e., we collect the top 20 ranked results for each query. The parameters c and v are set to 5 (this number is set with considering multiple factors, such as the typical length of a news document and the space that the images occupy).

In empirical evaluation, we need to manually label several ground truths, including the relevance between a location and a news document and the relevance of an image with respect to a document. We establish three relevance levels: very relevant, relevant and irrelevant. For the relevance between location and news document, the manual labeling is mainly according to the following principles. "Very relevant" means that the location is an important information clue for the news, such as the news exactly happens at that place, "relevant" means that the news document is related to the news but its relationship with the major event of the news is not strong, and "irrelevant" means that, whether or not the location appears in the news document, it is not related to the major event of the news. For the relevance of image, the labeling principles are mainly as follows. "Very relevant" means that the image well describes the story of the event of the news. "Relevant" means that, although it may not match the event of the news, the image is able to provide information about several important elements of the news, such as the people and activity, and "irrelevant" means that the images do not provide information about understanding the news and its important elements.

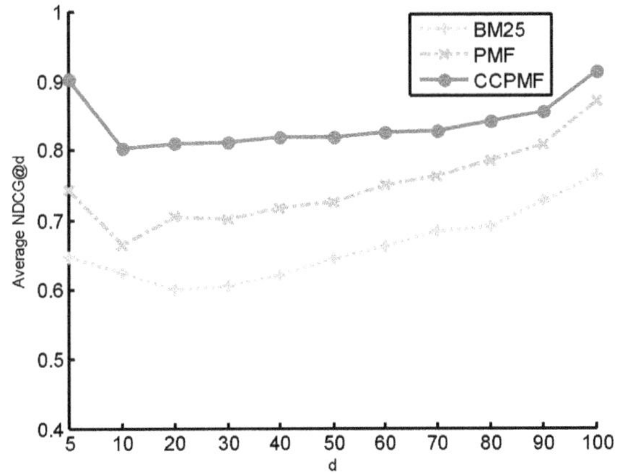

Figure 7: The search performance comparison of these three methods.

We also involve several user studies. All the user studies are conducted with 30 users frequently reading news online. They come from two countries with age from 20 to 35.

6.2 Experimental Results

6.2.1 On Location Relevance Analysis

We conduct two groups of experiments to evaluate our location relevance analysis.

Firstly, we randomly select 500 documents from the whole data set and then perform a location refinement process. For each document, we compare the relevance of locations before and after performing refinement. For the locations before performing refinement, we directly collect the distinct location names in the document. Supposing there are l locations in the document, we also collect the l locations with the highest relevance scores after performing CCPMF. Then each location of the news document is manually checked to decide whether it is really relevant. We assign score 2, 1, and 0 to indicate very relevant, relevant and irrelevant, respectively. In this way, we can obtain two average relevance scores for the locations in each document, one before and one after location refinement. Figure 6 illustrates the distribution comparison of the average scores, from which we can see that, for most news documents, the scores have been boosted after performing location refinement. The mean results of the scores before and after performing location refinement are 0.492 and 0.954, respectively. This indicates the effectiveness of our relevance analysis approach.

The second group of experiments validates the location relevance analysis by news search. We randomly select 100 location names from our toponym list. We then perform search in our news data set and rank the search results with

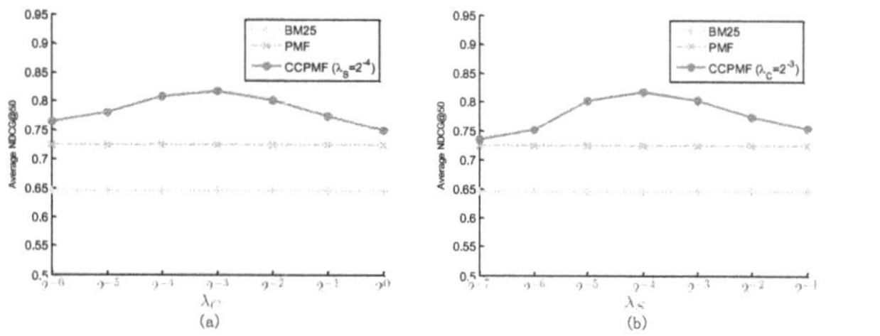

Figure 8: The performance of tuning the two parameters λ_C and λ_S. (a): varying λ_C while fixing $\lambda_S = 2^{-4}$; (b): varying λ_S while fixing $\lambda_C = 2^{-3}$.

the relevance scores obtained by CCPMF. We compare our approach with the following two methods:

(1) BM25 ranking model ($b = 0.75$ and $k_1 = 2.0$) [17].

(2) Probabilistic Matrix Factorization (PMF) model [27]. The comparison of our approach with the PMF algorithm is able to validate the effectiveness of the two correlation terms in Eq. 5.

The average NDCG comparison of the three methods is illustrated in Fig. 7. From the results we can see that the search performance with the proposed relevance analysis approach significantly outperforms the other two methods.

We also test the sensitiveness of the two parameters λ_C and λ_S. Here we fix the performance evaluation metric to average NDCG@50. We first fix λ_S to 2^{-4} and tune λ_C. The performance curve is illustrated in Fig. 8 (a). We then fix λ_C to 2^{-3} and tune λ_S, and the performance curve is illustrated in Fig. 8 (b). From the results we can see that CCPMF outperforms the BM25 and PMF approaches when the two parameters vary in a wide range.

6.2.2 *On Image Enrichment*

As previously introduced, in image enrichment we need a training set to learn the weights of η_1, η_2, η_3, η_4 and η_5. Therefore, we randomly select 300 news documents to be the training set. We assign scores 2, 1 and 0 to the relevance levels of "very relevant", "relevant" and "irrelevant", respectively, and then tune the weights to their optimal values by maximizing the average NDCG of the final ranking lists.

We perform image enrichment on all the other news documents. Figure 9 provides several examples. We first evaluate our rank aggregation approach. We compare our approach with the following two methods:

(1) **Naive Search**: Performing image search by regarding the whole document title as a query on Google image.

(2) **Naive Fusion**: Performing image search with each term in the news title (instead of multi-term combinations) and then fusing the results as in 4.2.

To save manual labeling effort, we randomly select 1,000 news documents from the whole data set for evaluation. If for a query there is no result returned, we set its NDCG value to 0. Figure 10 illustrates the average NDCG comparison of these three methods. We can see that our approach remarkably outperforms the other two methods. This demonstrates the effectiveness of our query generation and image collection approach.

We also conduct a user study to compare the news documents with and without image enrichment. Each user is

Figure 9: Several examples of the web images collected by our approach. Here we only show the news titles and the five collected images.

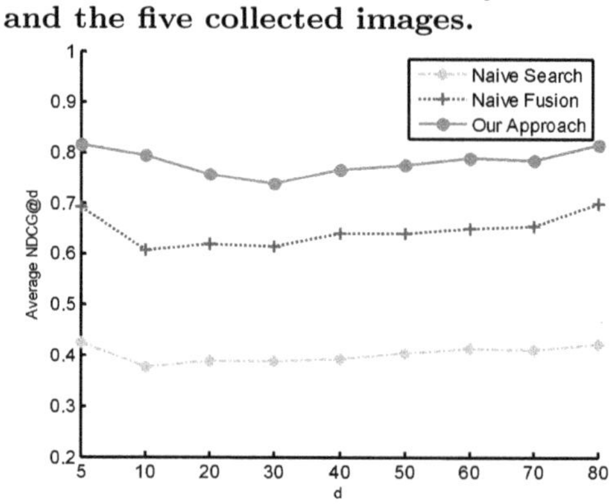

Figure 10: The average NDCG comparison results of image enrichment using these three methods.

asked to freely browse news documents and compare these two versions. They can choose "better", "much better" and "comparable" options for the comparison of these two versions. If the enriched images provide useful information, the users will regard the version after image enrichment better. Otherwise, if the enriched images are fairly irrelevant, users will judge that the original version is better as the images provide no information and they will be distractive. We quantize the results as follows. We assign score 1 to the worse version and the other version is assigned a score 2, 3 and 1 if it is better, much better and comparable than this one, respectively. The average rating scores and the standard deviation values are illustrated in Table 1. From the results we can clearly see the preference of users towards the version after image enrichment. We also perform a two-way ANOVA test [20] and the results are illustrated in the table as well. The p-values demonstrate that the superiority of our version is statistically significant.

6.2.3 *On the News Ranking in NewsMap*

In the above experiments, we have evaluated the location relevance analysis and image enrichment components. Now we evaluate our ranking approach in the NewsMap system.

Table 1: The left part illustrates the average rating scores and standard deviation values from the user study on the comparison of news documents before and after image enrichment. The right part illustrates the ANOVA test results.

After image enrichment vs. Before image enrichment		The factor of ranking schemes		The factor of users	
After image enrichment	Before image enrichment	F-statistic	p-value	F-statistic	p-value
2.367 ± 0.669	1.100 ± 0.305	58.486	1.970×10^{-8}	0.313	0.999

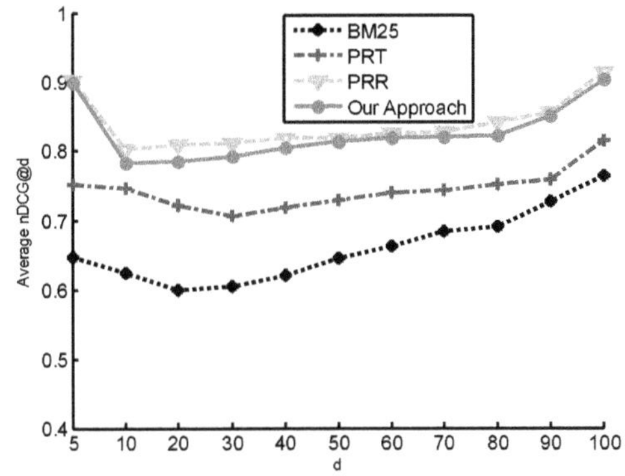

Figure 11: The search relevance comparison of different ranking methods.

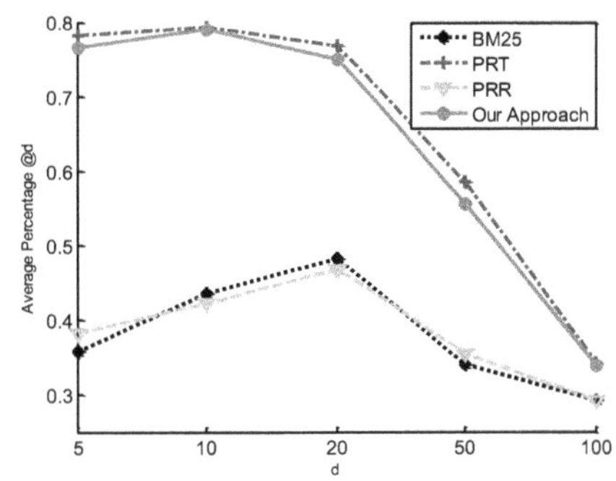

Figure 12: The timeliness comparison of different ranking methods. The vertical axis is the average percentage of the latest news (in the latest week before our data collection process) of the top d results.

We compare our approach with the following methods:

(1) **PRT**: PageRank with content timeliness as the static ranking, i.e., the right part of Eq. 18 is set to $date_k$.

(2) **PRR**: PageRank with location relevance as the static ranking, i.e., the right part of Eq. 18 is set to $score_k$.

(3) **BM25**: ranking with the BM25 model [17].

We evaluate the relevance of searching results with the 100 queries as in Section 6.2.1. The comparison among PRT, PRR, BM25 and ours is shown in Fig. 11. It is observed that BM25 achieves the worst performance, and PRR achieves the best performance. Actually, our approach is very close to PRR, but our method and PRT are better in terms of timeliness, which is demonstrated in Fig 12. We make a simple statistic analysis about the number of documents happening in the latest week before the time we finished our data collection, and the average ratio over 100 queries for top $d(d = 5, 10, 20, 50, 100)$ results is used to evaluate the news timeliness. From the both respects, i.e., relevance and timeliness, our method has more satisfied performance.

We then conduct user study to compare our approach with each of the three methods in terms of the interestingness of returned results, which is actually integrated the news relevance, timeliness and importance. In each pairwise comparison, the users are allowed to perform search with any location name and compare the two ranking lists. They can choose "better", "much better" and "comparable" options for the comparison of each two ranking schemes based on the interestingness. We then quantize the results as follows. We assign score 1 to the worse ranking scheme and the other scheme is assigned a score 2, 3 and 1 if it is better, much better and comparable than this one, respectively. The average rating scores and the standard deviation values of the three comparisons are illustrated in Table 2 - 4, respectively. From the results we can see the preference of users towards our proposed ranking approach. We also perform a two-way ANOVA test [20], and the results are shown in the tables as well. It is observed that the performance of our method statistically significantly outperforms others.

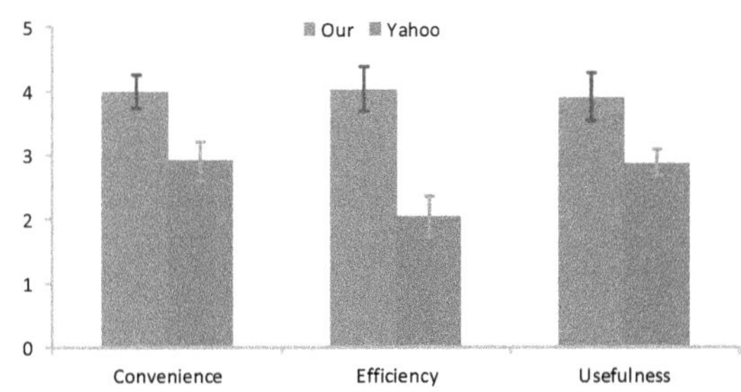

Figure 13: The comparison of NewsMap and Yahoo News Map in different aspects.

6.2.4 *On the Comparison of NewsMap and Yahoo News Map*

Now we conduct user study to evaluate the performance of the overall system and compare it with the Yahoo News Map system. Participants were required to give scores from 1 to 5 (greater score indicates better result) in terms of the following aspects while they freely searched and browsed the results: **Convenience** (the system should be convenient for users to search and browse news), **Efficiency** (it should cost users little time to learn the news content and comprehensive information.) and **Usefulness** (it is necessary for news retrieval system to provide useful information.). The results are illustrated in Fig. 13, which shows the mean scores and standard deviations. It can be observed that the proposed NewsMap system outperforms Yahoo News Map in different aspects.

7. CONCLUSIONS AND FUTURE WORK

This paper proposes methods that can estimate the relevance of locations for a given document and enrich it with web images. For location relevance analysis, we employ a novel matrix factorization method, and for image enrichment we propose methods to generate queries for search

Table 2: The left part illustrates the average rating scores and standard deviation values from the user study on the comparison of our ranking method and PRT. The right part illustrates the ANOVA test results.

Our method vs. PRT		The factor of ranking schemes		The factor of users	
Our method	PRT	F-statistic	p-value	F-statistic	p-value
$\mathbf{1.967 \pm 0.615}$	1.233 ± 0.504	14.682	6.306×10^{-4}	0.151	1.000

Table 3: The left part illustrates the average rating scores and standard deviation values from the user study on the comparison of our ranking method and PRR. The right part illustrates the ANOVA test results.

Our method vs. PRR		The factor of ranking schemes		The factor of users	
Our method	PRR	F-statistic	p-value	F-statistic	p-value
$\mathbf{1.933 \pm 0.640}$	1.261 ± 0.521	11.154	2.300×10^{-3}	0.139	1.000

Table 4: The left part shows the average rating scores and standard deviation values from the user study on the comparison of our ranking method and BM25. The right part illustrates the ANOVA test results.

Our method vs. BM25		The factor of ranking schemes		The factor of users	
Our method	BM25	F-statistic	p-value	F-statistic	p-value
$\mathbf{2.033 \pm 0.490}$	1.100 ± 0.305	47.765	1.355×10^{-7}	0.219	1.000

and then intelligently fuse the results. A news browsing system named NewsMap is introduced based on the relevance analysis and image enrichment approaches, which can support users in browsing and retrieving news with a map. We conduct experiments on a large dataset and the results demonstrate the effectiveness of our approaches.

Our work can be further extended along several directions. First, we can further organize the news with a topic discovery component. Second, our system can be useful in news recommendation as long as we can identify the profiles of users or their interests in local news. Finally, we will consider the critical analysis of the effectiveness and extend CCPMF to other potential applications such as shopping and several local services.

8. ACKNOWLEDGMENTS

This work was supported by the National Natural Science Foundation of China (Grant No. 60903146, 60833006 and 90920303), and 973 Program (Project No. 2010CB327905).

9. REFERENCES

[1] E. Amitay, R. Sivan, and A. Soffer. Web-a-where: Geotagging web content. In *Proceedings of ACM SIGIR*, pages 273–280. Sheffield, UK, July 2004.

[2] S. Brin and L. Page. The anatomy of a large-scale hypertextual web search engine. In *Proceedings of ACM WWW*, pages 107–117, April 1998.

[3] L. Cao, J. Yu, J. Luo, and T. S. Huang. Enhancing semantic and geographic annotation of web images via logistic canonical correlation regression. In *Proceedings of ACM Multimedia*, pages 125–134. China, 2009.

[4] M. G. Christel, A. M. Olligschlaeege, and C. Huang. Interative maps for a digital video library. *IEEE Multimedia*, 7(1):60–67, March 2000.

[5] R. L. Cilibrasi and P. M. B. Vitanyi. The google similarity distance. *IEEE Trans. on Knowledge and Data Engineering*, 19(3):370–383, March 2007.

[6] B. Coyne and R. Sproat. Wordseye: An automatic text-to-scene conversion system. In *Proceedings of Annual Conference on Computer Graphics and Interactive Techniques*, pages 487–496. Los Angeles, USA, August 2001.

[7] D. J. Crandall, L. Backstrom, D. Huttenlocher, and J. Kleinberg. Mapping the world's photos. In *Proceedings of ACM WWW*, pages 761–770. Madrid, Spain, April 2009.

[8] D. Delgado, J. Magalhães, and N. Correia. Assisted news reading with automated illustrations. In *Proceedings of ACM Multimedia*, pages 1647–1650. Firenze, Italy, October 2010.

[9] D. Delgado, J. Magalhães, and N. Correia. Automated illustration of news stories - improving the readers experience. In *Proceedings of IEEE International Conference on Semantic Computing*, pages 73–78, September 2010.

[10] J. Ding, L. Gravano, and N. Shivakumar. Computing geographical scopes of web sources. In *Proceedings of International Conference on Very Large Data Bases*, pages 545–556. San Francisco, USA, September 2000.

[11] B. Geng, L. Yang, C. Xu, and X.-S. Hua. Content-aware ranking for visual search. In *CVPR*, pages 3400–3407, 2010.

[12] F. Gey, R. Larson, M. Sanderson, H. Joho, P. Clough, and V. Petras. Geoclef: The clef 2005 cross-language geographic information retrieval track overview. In *CLEF'05*, pages 908–919, 2005.

[13] J. Hays and A. A. Efros. Im2gps: estimating geographic information from a single image. In *Proceedings of IEEE CVPR*, pages 1–8, 2008.

[14] S. Huston and W. B. Croft. Evaluating verbose query processing techniques. In *Proceedings of ACM SIGIR*, pages 291–298, July 2010.

[15] K. Järvelin and J. Kekäläinen. Cumulated gain-based evaluation of ir techniques. *ACM Trans. on Information Systems*, 20(4):422–446, October 2002.

[16] B. Jiao, L. Yang, J. Xu, and F. Wu. Visual summarization of web pages. In *Proceedings of ACM SIGIR*, pages 499–506. Geneva, Switzerland, July 2010.

[17] K. S. Jones, S. Walker, and S. E. Robertson. A probabilistic model of information retrieval: development and comparative experiments. *Information Processing and Management*, 36(6):779–808, November 2000.

[18] D. Joshi, J. Z. Wang, and J. Li. The story picturing engine: Finding elite images to illustrate a story using mutual reinforcement. In *Proceedings of ACM Workshop on Multimedia Information Retrieval*, pages 119–126, 2004.

[19] P. Kelm, S. Schmiedeke, and T. Sikora. Video2gps: Geotagging using collaborative systems, textual and visual features. In *Proceedings of MediaEval*. Pisa, Italy, 2010.

[20] B. M. King and E. M. Minium. *Statistical Reasoning in Psychology and Education*. Wiley, New York, 1999.

[21] G. Kumaran and V. R. Carvalho. Reducing long queries using query quality predictors. In *Proceedings of ACM SIGIR*, pages 564–571. Boston, USA, July 2009.

[22] Z. Li, J. Liu, X. Zhu, and H. Lu. Multi-modal multi-correlation person-centric news retrieval. In *Proceedings of ACM CIKM*, 2010.

[23] J. Luo, D. Joshi, J. Yu, and A. Gallagher. Geotagging in multimedia and computer vision—a survey. *Multimedia Tools and Applications*, 51(1):187–211, October 2010.

[24] X. Olivares, M. Ciaramita, and R. van Zwol. Boosting image retrieval through aggregating search results based on visual annotations. In *Proceedings of ACM Multimedia*, pages 189–198. Canada, October 2008.

[25] S. Overell and S. Rüger. Using co-occurrence models for placename disambiguation. *International Journal of Geographical Information Science*, 22(3):265–287, March 2008.

[26] L. Page, S. Brin, R. Motwani, and T. Winograd. *The PageRank Citation Ranking: Bringing Order to the Web*. Technical Report, Stanford Digital Library Technologies Project, 1999.

[27] R. Salakhutdinov and A. Mnih. Probabilistic matrix factorization. In *Advances in Neural Information Processing Systems*, pages 1257–1264, 2007.

[28] P. Serdyukov, V. Murdock, and R. van Zwol. Placing flickr photos on a map. In *Proceedings of ACM SIGIR*, pages 484–491. Boston, USA, July 2009.

[29] J. F. Sturm. Site matters: The value of local newspaper web sites. Technical report, NAA, 2009. http://www.naa.org/TrendsandNumbers/Research.aspx.

[30] J. Teevan, E. Cutrell, D. Fisher, S. M. Drucker, G. Ramos, P. Andre, and C. Hu. Visual snippets: Summarizing web pages for search and revisitation. In *Proceedings of International Conference on Human factors in computing systems*, pages 2023–2032. Boston, USA, April 2009.

[31] C. C. Vogt and G. W. Cottrell. Fusion via a linear combination of scores. *Information Retrieval*, 1(3):151–173, October 1999.

[32] B. Wang, Z. Li, M. Li, and W.-Y. Ma. Large-scale duplicate detection for web image search. In *Proceedings of IEEE International Conference on Multimedia Expo*, pages 353–356. Toronto, Canada, July 2006.

[33] M. Wang, X.-S. Hua, R. Hong, J. Tang, G.-J. Qi, and Y. Song. Unified video annotation via multi-graph learning. *IEEE Trans. on Circuits and Systems for Video Technology*, 19(5):733–766, March 2009.

[34] M. Wang, X.-S. Hua, J. Tang, and R. Hong. Beyond distance measurement: Constructing neighborhood similarity for video annotation. *IEEE Trans. on Multimedia*, 11(3):465–473, February 2009.

[35] R. Yan and A. G. Hauptmann. The combination limit in multimedia retrieval. In *Proceedings of ACM Multimedia*, pages 339–342, November 2003.

[36] Y. Yang, D. Xu, F. Nie, J. Luo, and Y. Zhuang. Ranking with local regression and global alignment for cross media retrieval. In *Proceedings of ACM Multimedia*, pages 175–184, October 2009.

[37] L. Zhang, L. Chen, F. Jing, K. Deng, and W.-Y. Ma. Enjoyphoto—a verticcal image search engine for enjoying high-quality photos. In *Proceedings of ACM Multimedia*, pages 367–376. USA, October 2006.

[38] R. Zhao and W. I. Grosky. Narrowing the semantic gap—improved text-based web document retrieval using visual features. *ACM Trans. on Multimedia*, 4(2):189–200, June 2002.

[39] Y. Zheng, Z. Zha, and T.-S. Chua. Research and applications on georeferenced multimedia: a survey. *Multimedia Tools and Applications*, 51(1):77–98, October 2010.

[40] X. Zhu, A. B. Goldberg, M. Eldawy, C. R. Dyer, and B. Strock. A text-to-picture synthesis system for augmenting communication. In *Proceedings of National Conference on Artificial Intelligence*, pages 1590–1595. Vancouver, Canada, July 2007.

[41] W. Zong, D. Wu, A. Sun, E.-P. Lim, and D. H.-L. Goh. On assigning place names to geography related web pages. In *Proceedings of ACM/IEEE-CS joint conference on Digital libraries*, pages 354–362. New York, USA, June 2005.

Multi-Modal Constraint Propagation for Heterogeneous Image Clustering*

Zhenyong Fu
Department of Computer Science and Engineering
Shanghai Jiao Tong University, Shanghai, China
zhyfu@sjtu.edu.cn

Horace H.S. Ip
Department of Computer Science
City University of Hong Kong, Hong Kong
cship@cityu.edu.hk

Hongtao Lu†
Department of Computer Science and Engineering
Shanghai Jiao Tong University, Shanghai, China
htlu@sjtu.edu.cn

Zhiwu Lu
Institute of Computer Science and Technology
Peking University
Beijing, China
luzhiwu@icst.pku.edu.cn

ABSTRACT

This paper presents a multi-modal constraint propagation approach to exploiting pairwise constraints for constrained clustering tasks on multi-modal datasets. Pairwise constraint propagation methods have previously been designed primarily for single modality data and cannot be directly applied to multi-modal data or a dataset with multiple representations. In this paper, we provide an effective solution to the multi-modal constraint propagation problem by decomposing it into a set of independent multi-graph based two-class label propagation subproblems which are then merged into a unified problem and solved by quadratic optimization. We also show that such a formulation yields a closed-form solution. Our approach allows the initial pairwise constraints to be propagated throughout the entire multi-modal dataset. The propagated constraints are further used to refine the similarities between the objects for subsequent clustering tasks. The proposed method has been tested in constrained clustering tasks on two real-life multi-modal image datasets and shown to achieve significant improvements with respect to the single modality methods.

Categories and Subject Descriptors

H.3.1 [**Information Storage and Retrieval**]: Content Analysis and Indexing

*Area chair: Cees Snoek
†The corresponding author.

MM'11, November 28–December 1, 2011, Scottsdale, Arizona, USA.

General Terms

Algorithms, Experimentation, Performance.

Keywords

Pairwise Constraint Propagation, Multi-Modal Analysis

1. INTRODUCTION

In constrained clustering tasks, we exploit the available prior knowledge to guide the clustering process. Examples of prior information for constrained clustering include relative comparisons [5], pairwise constraints [20], and cluster sizes [25]. Prior knowledge on whether two objects belong to the same cluster or not are expressed respectively in terms of must-link constraints and cannot-link constraints. Generally, such pairwise constraints, unlike the class labels of data, do not provide explicit class information and are therefore considered a weaker form of supervisory information. In many situations, pairwise constraint relationships between data points are more readily available than the actual class label of the data. In this paper, we focus our attention on constrained clustering problems based on pairwise constraints. In general, while it is possible to infer pairwise constraints from domain knowledge or user feedback, in practice, the availability of such constraints is scarce. Hence, one line of research in constrained clustering aims to fully utilize the information inherent in the available pairwise constraints through constraint propagation.

It should be noted that the problem of pairwise constraint propagation differs from that of label propagation and is more challenging in the following aspects: (a) unlike class labels for data, pairwise constraints in general do not provide explicit class information; (b) it is in general not possible to infer class label directly from the pairwise constraints which simply state whether a pair of data belong to the same class or not; (c) for a dataset of size n, there are potentially $O(n^2)$ pairwise constraints that can be inferred through constraint propagation, while there are only $O(n)$ class labels that need to be inferred for the data in label propagation.

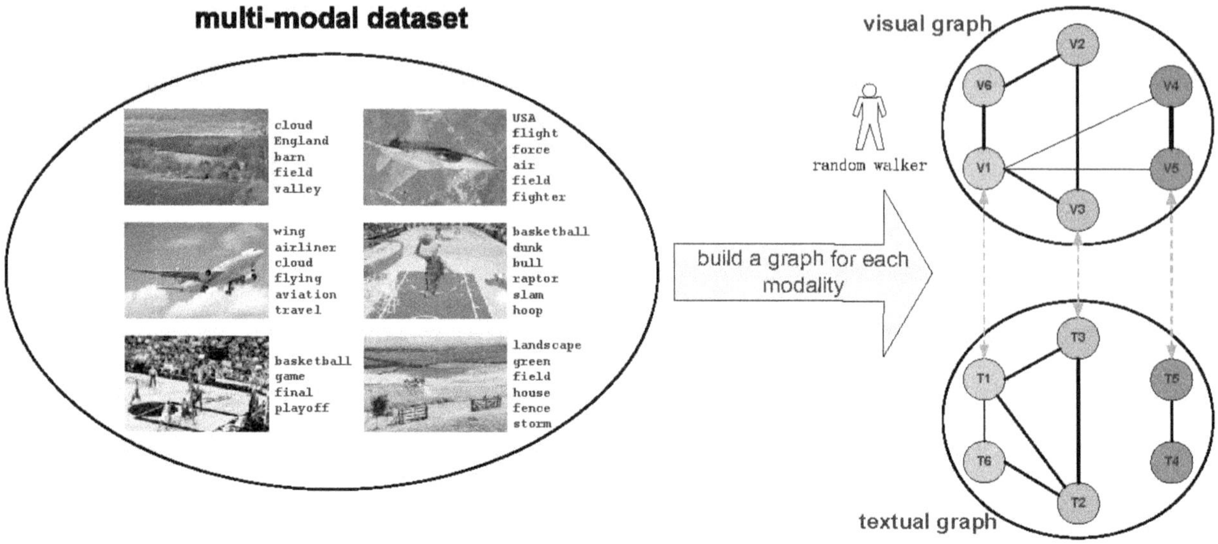

Figure 1: Illustration of our proposed scheme for multi-modal pairwise constraint propagation. For the images from multi-modal dataset (here from the Flickr website), we build a graph for each modality and then define a random walk process on these graphs. Besides the inner-graph walking, the random walker can also jump among different graphs.

Several approaches have been proposed in the past to deal with the challenging problem of pairwise constraint propagation, such as Kamvar et al.'s spectral learning (SL) [8], Lu and Carreira-Perpinan's affinity propagation (AP) [11], Wang and Davidson's flexible constrained spectral clustering [22], Li et al.'s pairwise constraint propagation by semidefinite programming (SDP) [10], and Lu and Ip's exhaustive and efficient pairwise constraint propagation (E^2CP) [13]. However, these methods can only be applied to data within a single modality or presented in a single representation. In reality, there are many datasets with multiple modalities or multiple representations. For example, images found on the Web can either be described by their visual characteristics or by the surrounding texts. Another example is the images from photo sharing websites, such as Flickr[1]. These images can typically be represented using two separate modalities, based respectively on the visual features and the user-provided textual tags. Figure 1 shows image samples from the Flickr website. From Figure 1, it can be observed that in a multi-modal dataset, different modality features typically reflect different aspects of the data and provide information that complements each other.

In this paper, we consider the problem of pairwise constraint propagation on the multi-modal dataset. Our approach is motivated by Lu and Ip's work [13] that provides a tractable framework and a closed-form solution for exhaustive constraint propagation on a dataset. It should be noted however that their method was developed for single modality data only. In this work, we generalize the constraint propagation framework for the multi-modal situations. More specifically, we first construct multiple graphs for the multi-modal data, with one graph for each of the modalities. We then define a random walk process on these graphs. As shown in Figure 1, on each node of every graph, a walker has the probabilities of jumping to the same node on other graphs during the random walk process. The probability of choosing a particular graph at a special node is determined by the graph's prior probability and the stationary probabilities of the corresponding nodes in different graphs. Hence, the transition probabilities among the nodes on multiple graphs can be further computed. According to such transition probabilities, we consider any pair of instances with higher transition probability should also have similar constraint settings with respect to other instances. This insight can be formulated as a series of independent multi-graph based constraint propagation subproblems. A graph regularization framework is applied to solve these subproblems through a series of quadratic optimizations. Furthermore, we also show that the set of constraint propagation subproblems can be unified and solved as a single quadratic optimization problem. At the same time, we show that the formulation has a closed-form solution. It should be stressed that while our solution is based on semi-supervised learning (label propagation) techniques, it does not require any initial class labels.

For constrained clustering, the propagated constraints obtained by our multi-modal constraint propagation are used to refine the similarities among data points for the subsequent clustering process. To evaluate the effectiveness of the proposed method, we select two real-life image datasets with multiple representations for constrained clustering tasks. Our approach has several attractive and novel features: 1) our method is directly applicable to multi-class problems; 2) it can simultaneously deal with both must-link and cannot-link constraints; 3) as a solution for multi-modal problems, it can propagate pairwise constraints across multi-modal instances and can handle any number of data modalities; 4) it allows soft constraints, i.e., the pairwise constraints can be associated with confidence scores; and 5) it has a closed-form solution. To the best of our knowledge, our algo-

[1]http://www.flickr.com/

rithm represents the first solution for the problem of pairwise constraint propagation on multi-modal datasets. Our experimental results have shown that the proposed method can achieve significant improvements with respect to the state-of-the-art methods which have been primarily designed for single modality data.

The remainder of this paper is organized as follows. Section 2 analyzes related works. In section 3, we first overview the graph regularization framework of Lu and Ip's E^2CP algorithm for single modality data, and then present our multi-modal constraint propagation algorithm. Experimental results are shown in section 4. Section 5 draws the conclusion on this paper.

2. RELATED WORK

Pairwise constraints have been widely used in the context of clustering with side information [24, 8, 1, 9], where it has been shown that the presence of appropriate pairwise constraints can often improve the performance. One way to deal with pairwise constraints is to trivially set the similarities between the constrained data to 1 and 0 for must-link and cannot-link constraints, respectively [8]. This approach only adjusts the similarities between constrained data without propagating the constraint information to other data. In contrast, in [11], the pairwise constraints are propagated to unconstrained data using Gaussian process. However, as noted in [11], this method makes certain assumptions for constraint propagation especially with respect to two-class problems. An heuristic approach for multi-class problems is also discussed. In [10], pairwise constraint propagation is formulated as a semidefinite programming (SDP) problem. Although this optimization-based method is not limited to two-class problems, it incurs extremely large computational cost for solving SDP and is not particularly scalable to large datasets. Moreover, the authors only report the results on small-scale datasets. In [22], Wang and Davidson proposed a flexible constrained spectral clustering algorithm, which can be solved in polynomial time and also allows soft constraints. However, their method is only valid for two-class problems, and invalid for multi-class problems. Another work of Wang and Davidson in [21] suffers from the same limitation. Lu and Ip proposed an exhaustive and efficient pairwise constraint propagation method, which makes use of semi-supervised learning for pairwise constraint propagation [13]. Their work provides a tractable framework that shows how pairwise constraints are propagated independently and then accumulated into a conciliatory closed-form solution. Their method achieves superior performance compared to previous methods. Recently, Fu et al. provide a solution to the problem of pairwise constraint propagation within single modality data based on a symmetric graph regularization framework [6]. Under this framework, they show that pairwise constraint propagation with symmetric manner is equivalent to solving a Lyapunov matrix equation which is commonly found in control systems problems. Another related research area to our work is the multiview learning, which aims to learn from instances that have multiple representations [27, 15, 7, 23]. Our approach is inspired by multiview learning and semi-supervised learning. Particularly, we generalize the idea of multiview learning to the area of pairwise constraint propagation and formulate the multi-modal constraint propagation as a problem of multiple independent label propagations on multiple graphs.

3. MULTI-MODAL CONSTRAINT PROPAGATION

In this section, we first overview the E^2CP algorithm under a graph regularization framework, followed by the details of our proposed multi-modal pairwise constraint propagation algorithm.

3.1 Constraint Propagation for Single Modality Data

Given a dataset of n objects $\mathcal{X} = \{x_1, \dots, x_n\}$ and two sets of pairwise constraints, denoted respectively by $\mathcal{M} = \{(x_i, x_j)\}$ where x_i and x_j should be in the same class and $\mathcal{C} = \{(x_i, x_j)\}$ where x_i and x_j should be in different classes, the goal of pairwise constraint propagation is to propagate these pairwise constraints across the entire dataset and then classify $\mathcal{X}$ into k classes.

Let $G = (V, W)$ be an undirected, weighted graph defined on the dataset, i.e., $V = \mathcal{X}$. The elements in the similarity matrix $W = [w(i,j)]_{n\times n}$, denotes the similarity between two data points, x_i and x_j. For modeling the local neighborhood relationships between the data points, we adopt the k-nearest neighbor graph construction manner, in which $w(i,j) = 0$ if x_j is not among the k-nearest neighbors (k-NN) of x_i. We set $w(i,i) = 0$ for $1 \le i \le n$ to avoid self-reinforcement, and set $W = (W + W^T)/2$ to ensure that W is symmetric. The graph Laplacian L of G is defined as $L = D - W$, where $D = [d(i,i)]_{n\times n}$ is a diagonal matrix with $d(i,i) = \sum_j w(i,j)$. The normalized graph Laplacian $\bar{L}$ of G is defined as

$$\bar{L} = D^{-1/2} L D^{-1/2} = I - D^{-1/2} W D^{-1/2},$$

where I is the identity matrix. It should be noted that $\bar{L}$ is symmetric and positive semidefinite, with its eigenvalues being in the interval [0,2] [2].

The smoothness of a vectorial function $\boldsymbol{f} : \mathcal{X} \to \mathcal{R}$ on the graph can be measured by

$$\Omega(\boldsymbol{f}) = \frac{1}{2} \sum_{i,j} w_{ij} \left(\frac{f(x_i)}{\sqrt{d_{ii}}} - \frac{f(x_j)}{\sqrt{d_{jj}}}\right)^2 = \boldsymbol{f}^T \bar{L} \boldsymbol{f},$$

where $\boldsymbol{f} = (f(x_1), \dots, f(x_n))^T$. The smaller is $\Omega(\boldsymbol{f})$, the smoother is $\boldsymbol{f}$. This measurement penalizes large changes between data points that are strongly connected.

To propagate the constraints on single modal data, we first represent the two types of pairwise constraints with a single matrix $Y = \{Y_{ij}\}_{n\times n}$:

$$Y_{ij} = \begin{cases} +1, & (x_i, x_j) \in \mathcal{M}; \\ -1, & (x_i, x_j) \in \mathcal{C}; \\ 0, & \text{otherwise.} \end{cases} \tag{1}$$

It is trivial to note that Y is a symmetric matrix.

We further define $F = \{F_{ij}\}_{n\times n}$ as the matrix that represents the final results of the propagated pairwise constraints. As shown in Figure 2, when we focus on a single data point x_i in $\mathcal{X}$, we use $Y_{i\cdot}$ and $Y_{\cdot i}$ to respectively denote the i-th row and i-th column with respect to x_i in Y. Similarly, we use $F_{i\cdot}$ and $F_{\cdot i}$ to respectively denote the i-th row and i-th column with respect to x_i in F. It can be observed that $Y_{i\cdot}$ and $Y_{\cdot i}$ is the initial pairwise constraints between x_i and all the other data points in $\mathcal{X}$ prior to constraint propagation.

Propagating the constraint relationships related to x_i can be viewed as a two-class semi-supervised learning problem,

	x_1	x_2	x_3	x_4	x_5	x_6	x_7
x_1	0	-1	1	0	0	0	1
x_2	-1	0	0	-1	0	0	0
x_3	1	0	0	0	0	-1	0
x_4	0	-1	0	0	0	0	0
x_5	0	0	0	0	0	0	0
x_6	0	0	-1	0	0	0	-1
x_7	1	0	0	0	0	-1	0

Figure 2: One example of pairwise constraints indicator matrix as defined in (1). When we focus on a single node, such as x_3 here, pairwise constraint propagation can be viewed as a two-class semi-supervised learning problem in the row and column direction, respectively.

where the "positive class" is the must-link relationship and the "negative class" is the cannot-link relationship. If we only use $Y_{\cdot i}$, i.e. to propagate the constraints along the vertical direction of Y, according to the graph regularized label propagation [26], pairwise constraint propagation with respect to x_i can be formulated as

$$\min_{F_{\cdot i}} \frac{1}{2}\eta\|F_{\cdot i} - Y_{\cdot i}\|_2^2 + \frac{1}{2}F_{\cdot i}^T \bar{L} F_{\cdot i},$$

where $\eta > 0$ is the regularization parameter. We note that since for each data point in $\mathcal{X}$ we can similarly formulate a label propagation subproblem and the objective functions of these subproblems are all nonnegative, we can therefore merge all of the subproblems into a single optimization problem. That is

$$\min_{F_v} \frac{1}{2}\eta\|F_v - Y\|_F^2 + \frac{1}{2}\mathrm{tr}(F_v^T \bar{L} F_v),$$

where $\mathrm{tr}(Z)$ stands for the trace of a matrix Z and $\|\cdot\|_F$ is the Frobenius norm. So, the results of the vertical pairwise constraint propagation F_v is:

$$F_v = \eta(\eta I + \bar{L})^{-1}Y.$$

Similarly, if we only work with $Y_{i\cdot}$, i.e. to propagate the constraints along the horizontal direction of Y, the pairwise constraint propagation problem has the solution:

$$\min_{F_{i\cdot}} \frac{1}{2}\eta\|F_{i\cdot} - Y_{i\cdot}\|_2^2 + \frac{1}{2}F_{i\cdot}\bar{L}F_{i\cdot}^T$$

Using the same argument as given above, after merging all the subproblems for horizontal pairwise constraint propagation, we have

$$\min_{F_h} \frac{1}{2}\eta\|F_h - Y\|_F^2 + \frac{1}{2}\mathrm{tr}(F_h \bar{L} F_h^T),$$

and the results of horizontal pairwise constraint propagation F_h is:

$$F_h = \eta Y(\eta I + \bar{L})^{-1}.$$

If we consider constraint propagation along one direction only, i.e. either vertically or horizontally, it is possible that a column (or a row) contains no pairwise constraints (for example, see the fifth column in Figure 2. That is, the entries of this column (or row) may all be zeros, and for such cases, no constraint propagation will occur along this column (or row). This problem can be dealt with by performing the pairwise constraint propagation process twice, first along the vertical direction, and then along the horizontal direction. If we use the vertical results F_v as the initial constraints in the horizontal propagation, for the pairwise constraint propagation on single modality data, we obtain the following closed-form solution:

$$F = \eta^2(\eta I + \bar{L})^{-1}Y(\eta I + \bar{L})^{-1}. \quad (2)$$

3.2 Constraint Propagation for Multi-Modal Data

We now focus our attention on the problem of multi-modal pairwise constraint propagation. We first define the problem of pairwise constraint propagation on multiple graphs. For multi-modal data or data with multiple representations, assume we have defined S undirected and symmetric graphs, $G_s = (V, W_s), s = 1, \dots, S$, on the dataset, where S denotes the number of modalities or representations. Each element of the similarity matrix $W_s = [w_s(u,v)]_{n\times n}$, $w_s(u,v)$, measures the similarity between x_u and x_v on the s-th modality. It should be noted that these graphs share the same set of vertices while having different similarity matrices. As in the situation of pairwise constraint propagation on a single graph, for multiple graphs, we still have only a single constraint matrix as defined by equation (1) that defines the available initial constraints among the data. In other words, for multi-modal data, we define the pairwise constraints on the instances but not on the modalities.

With respect to each graph G_s, as in [2], for the vertex $u \in V$, we denote its degree on G_s as $d_s(u) = \sum_v w_s(u,v)$. The volume of graph G_s is defined as $\mathrm{vol}_s V = \sum_{u\in V} d_s(u) = \sum_{u\in V, v\in V} w_s(u,v)$. The natural random walk on G_s can be defined as follows. That is, for any pair vertexes u and v on G_s, their transition probability on G_s is

$$p(u \to v|G_s) = w_s(u,v)/d_s(u), \quad (3)$$

and the stationary probability of u on G_s is

$$p(u|G_s) = d_s(u)/\mathrm{vol}_s V. \quad (4)$$

Let $p(G_s)$ $(1 \le s \le S)$ denote the prior probabilities of the random walker choosing the graph G_s, and we have $p(G_s) \succeq 0$ and $\sum_s p(G_s) = 1$. Then the posterior probability to choose the graph G_s at vertex u is

$$\begin{aligned} p(G_s|u) &= \frac{p(G_s,u)}{\sum_{G_s} p(G_s,u)} \\ &= \frac{p(u|G_s)p(G_s)}{\sum_{G_s} p(u|G_s)p(G_s)}. \end{aligned} \quad (5)$$

For any pair vertexes u and v, their transition probability on multiple graphs can be computed as

$$p(u \to v) = \sum_{G_s} p(u \to v|G_s)p(G_s|u). \quad (6)$$

In addition, the stationary probability of vertex u on multiple graphs is computed as

$$p(u) = \sum_{G_s} p(u|G_s)p(G_s). \quad (7)$$

Given the above random walk process among multiple graphs, we can decompose the multi-modal pairwise constraint propagation into a series of two-class semi-supervised learning subproblems on multiple graphs, in which each subproblem can be solved by the multiview label propagation technique [27].

Let F denote the results of pairwise constraint propagation on multiple graphs. For a single data point x_i, its vertical pairwise constraint propagation on multiple graphs can be formulated as

$$\min_{F_{\cdot i}} \frac{1}{4} \sum_{u,v \in V} p(u)p(u \to v)(F_{ui} - F_{vi})^2 + \frac{1}{2}\eta \sum_{u \in V} p(u)(F_{ui} - Y_{ui})^2.$$

Intuitively, the first term in the objective function forces the settings of pairwise constraint with respect to x_i to change as slowly as possible between strongly connected vertexes (reflected by their transition probability). At the same time, the second term forces the constraint propagation results to fit the initial constraints as much as possible. The tradeoff between these two requirements is measured by the regularization parameter η.

Let P denote the transition probability matrix with its elements being $p(u \to v)$, and Π the diagonal stationary probability matrix with its diagonal elements being $p(u)$. Define the matrix $\hat{L}$ as

$$\hat{L} = \Pi - \frac{\Pi P + P^T \Pi}{2}. \quad (8)$$

It can be shown that $\sum_{u,v \in V} p(u)p(u \to v)(F_{ui} - F_{vi})^2 = 2F_{\cdot i}^T \hat{L} F_{\cdot i}$ (the verification is given in Appendix I). Thus, the above vertical constraint propagation problem can be transformed to

$$\min_{F_{\cdot i}} \frac{1}{2}\eta(F_{\cdot i} - Y_{\cdot i})^T \Pi (F_{\cdot i} - Y_{\cdot i}) + \frac{1}{2} F_{\cdot i}^T \hat{L} F_{\cdot i}$$

Given that the objective functions of the constraint propagation for all x_i's subproblems are all nonnegative, we can merge all of them into a single quadratic optimization problem. That is

$$\min_{F_v} \frac{1}{2}\eta \mathrm{tr}((F_v - Y)^T \Pi (F_v - Y)) + \frac{1}{2}\mathrm{tr}(F_v^T \hat{L} F_v). \quad (9)$$

Differentiating the objective function in equation (9) with respect to F_v and setting it to zero, we can find that the results of the vertical propagation F_v on multiple graphs become:

$$F_v = \eta(\eta\Pi + \hat{L})^{-1}\Pi Y. \quad (10)$$

Similarly, for a data point x_i, its horizontal pairwise constraint propagation on multiple graphs can be formulated as

$$\min_{F_{i \cdot}} \frac{1}{4} \sum_{u,v \in V} p(u)p(u \to v)(F_{iu} - F_{iv})^2 + \frac{1}{2}\eta \sum_{u \in V} p(u)(F_{iu} - Y_{iu})^2.$$

Using the same argument as given above, we merge all of horizontal constraint propagation subproblems into a single quadratic optimization problem as follow:

$$\min_{F_h} \frac{1}{2}\eta \mathrm{tr}((F_h - Y)\Pi(F_h - Y)^T) + \frac{1}{2}\mathrm{tr}(F_h \hat{L} F_h^T), \quad (11)$$

and hence the results of horizontal constraint propagation F_h on multiple graphs become

$$F_h = \eta Y \Pi (\eta \Pi + \hat{L})^{-1}. \quad (12)$$

Moreover, by combining the results of vertical and horizontal propagation together, the final result of pairwise constraint propagation on multiple graphs F is

$$F = \eta^2 (\eta\Pi + \hat{L})^{-1} \Pi Y \Pi (\eta\Pi + \hat{L})^{-1}. \quad (13)$$

It should be noted that if we define W as

$$w(u,v) = \sum_s p(G_s) \frac{w_s(u,v)}{\mathrm{vol}_s V},$$

then we have $W = \Pi P$. It is noteworthy that if all of the similarity matrices are symmetric, then W will also be symmetric and we have $\Pi P = P^T \Pi$ and $W = (\Pi P + P^T \Pi)/2$. We can then view W as the similarity measurement for the data points on multiple graphs. Moreover, note that $p(u) = \sum_v w(u,v)$, so we can also view the matrix $\hat{L} = \Pi - W$ as the multi-graph Laplacian. Hence, (9) and (11) can be viewed as a formulation for multi-modal constraint propagation problem under the framework of multi-graph regularization.

3.3 The MMCP Algorithm

Once we have the constraint propagation result F, we can incorporate F into a constrained clustering algorithm. As in [13], we refine the similarities between the data points on multiple graphs according to F using the following refinement method,

$$w^\star(u,v) = \begin{cases} 1 - (1 - F_{uv})(1 - w(u,v)), & F_{uv} \geq 0; \\ (1 + F_{uv})w(u,v), & F_{uv} < 0. \end{cases} \quad (14)$$

It can be seen that the above refinement will increase the similarity when $F_{uv} > 0$ and decrease it when $F_{uv} < 0$.

Let $W^\star = [w^\star(u,v)]_{n \times n}$ be the refined similarity matrix according to equation (14). We adopt the spectral clustering algorithm [19] with $W^\star$ to form clusters. Finally, the constrained clustering algorithm that makes use of our approach is shown in Algorithm 1. The proposed multi-modal constraint propagation method will be denoted as MMCP in the following.

3.4 Complexity Analysis

For a dataset of size n, our MMCP algorithm includes an inverse matrix computation of an $n \times n$ matrix and performs matrix multiplication of two $n \times n$ matrices twice. The time complexity of MMCP is therefore $O(n^{2+\alpha})$ ($\alpha \approx 0.376$) [3, 4]. Since this time complexity is nearly proportional to the total number of all possible pairwise constraints (i.e. $n(n-1)/2$), our MMCP can be considered computationally efficient. Moreover, our MMCP incurs significantly less computational cost than [10], given that constraint propagation based on semidefinite programming has a time complexity of $O(n^4)$.

Algorithm 1 Multi-Modal Constraint Propagation

Input: A dataset of n objects $\mathcal{X} = \{x_1, x_2, \ldots, x_n\}$, which has multiple representations. And the set of must-link constraints $\mathcal{M} = \{(x_u, x_v)\}$, the set of cannot-link constraints $\mathcal{C} = \{(x_u, x_v)\}$, and the number of classes k.
Output: Cluster labels for the objects in $\mathcal{X}$.

1. Form multiple symmetric similarity matrices $W_s = [w_s(u,v)]_{n \times n}, s = 1, \ldots, S$.
2. Generate the initial constraint matrix Y with $\mathcal{M}$ and $\mathcal{C}$ using (1).
3. For each graph G_s, define a random walk on it with the transition probabilities as (3) and the stationary probabilities as (4).
4. Given the graphs prior probabilities $p(G_s)$ $(1 \leq s \leq S)$, compute the transition probabilities of the random walk on multiple graphs as (6) and the stationary distribution as (7).
5. Denote by P the matrix with the elements $p(u \to v)$, and Π the diagonal matrix with the diagonal elements $p(u)$. Let $W = (\Pi P + P^T \Pi)/2$ represent the similarity matrix on multiple graphs. Form the matrix $\hat{L}$ as (8).
6. Compute the constraint propagation result F by (13).
7. Adjust the similarity matrix W using F through (14).
8. Form k classes by applying the spectral clustering on the refined similarity matrix $W^{\star}$.

4. EXPERIMENTAL RESULTS

In this section, we evaluate the performances of our MMCP on two multi-modal image datasets. The first dataset, in which there are 11 categories and totally 8564 instances, contains images crawled from the photo sharing website Flickr and we call it Flickr-11[2]. The second is the Corel dataset, which consists of 5,000 images from 50 Corel Stock Photo CDs. Each CD includes 100 images on the same topic (class), giving a total of 50 classes. We call it Corel-5000.

For comparison, the results of four notable and most related constrained clustering algorithms for single source data, Kamvar et al.'s spectral learning (SL) [8], Kulis et al.'s semi-supervised kernel k-means (SSKK) [9], Lu and Carreira-Perpinan's affinity propagation (AP) [11] and Lu and Ip's exhaustive and efficient constraint propagation (E^2CP) [13], are also reported. In addition, we use the normalized cuts (NCuts) [17], which is effectively a spectral clustering algorithm but without considering pairwise constraints, as the baseline method. The single modality algorithms will yield multiple results, one for each of the modalities. It should be noted however that the MMCP, which works simultaneously on multiple modalities, will give only one set of results for the multi-modal dataset which we used to compare with the respective results obtained from each of the modalities using the single modality methods.

[2]http://ci.sjtu.edu.cn/dataset/flickr11/

Figure 3: Sample images from 11 categories of the Flickr-11 dataset.

In the following, We first describe the experimental setup, including the performance measure and the parameter selection. Then we compare our MMCP with the other five methods on Flickr-11 and Corel-5000.

4.1 Experimental Setup

In order to evaluate these algorithms, we compare the clustering results with the available ground-truth data labels, and employ the *Normalized Mutual Information* (NMI) as the performance measure [18]. For two random variables X and Y, the NMI is defined as:

$$NMI(X,Y) = \frac{I(X,Y)}{\sqrt{H(X)H(Y)}},$$

where $I(X,Y)$ is the mutual information between X and Y, and $H(X)$ and $H(Y)$ are the entropies of X and Y, respectively. Note that $0 \leq \text{NMI} \leq 1$, and the larger is the NMI, the better is the result. To evaluate the algorithms under different settings of pairwise constraints, we exploit the ground-truth data labels and generate a varying number of pairwise constraints randomly for each dataset. That is, we randomly choose a pair of data points from each dataset. If they have the same class labels, we generate a must-link constraint, otherwise a cannot-link constraint. Each experiment is randomly run 20 times and the averaged NMI is reported.

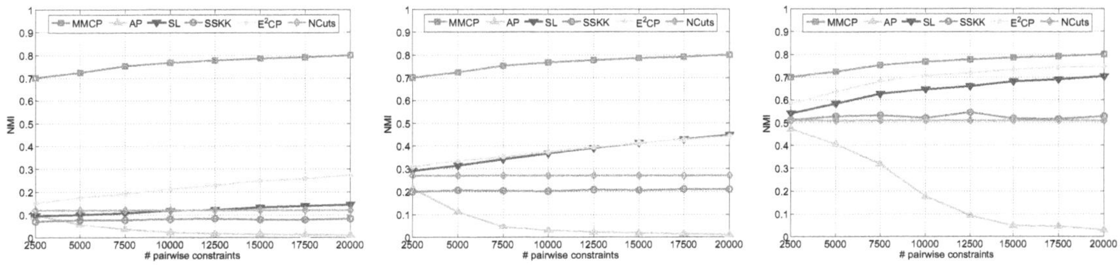

(a) global (b) local (c) text

Figure 4: Clustering results on the three modalities of Flickr-11 dataset with different number of pairwise constraints: NMI vs. Number of constraints. (a) Results on the visual global modality. (b) Results on the visual local modality. (c) Results on the textual modality.

For each multi-modal image dataset, we construct three types of representations (three modalities), i.e. visual global feature, visual local feature and textual description. The first two features are derived from visual appearance and the third is from textual annotation. For the visual global feature, we extract and combine a 64-dimensional color histogram (LAB) [16] and a 128-dimensional wavelet texture [14] to form the global feature vector. We adopt the Chi-Square kernel as the similarity measure between global feature vectors. For our visual local feature, we extract the SIFT descriptors of 16×16 pixel blocks computed over a regular grid with spacing of 8 pixels. Then we perform k-means clustering on the extracted feature vectors to form a vocabulary of 600 visual keywords. Based on this visual vocabulary, we then define a spatial Markov kernel [12] for the construction of the similarity graph. As the textual feature, for two textual vectors, we first compute their *cosine* distance and then compute the Gaussian similarity. For the three modalities, we set the prior graph probabilities to 0.05, 0.2, and 0.75 for the visual global, visual local, and textual features, respectively. In addition, we set $\eta = 0.25$ and $k = 5$ in our experiments. All the algorithms are implemented in Matlab, running on 2.67GHz and 32GB RAM server.

4.2 On Flickr-11

The first dataset used in our experiments were crawled from the Flickr website. We choose eleven categories and, for each category, we download 2000 images and their user-provided textual tags. We manually filtered out the unrelated images to the corresponding category. The eleven categories and the corresponding number of images (within brackets) in the remaining images are airplane (813), auto (924), dog (943), turtle(833), elephant(652), NBA (921), laptop (683), piano (678), farm (716), cityscape (1007) and library (394). We randomly select 5 examples from each category which are shown in Figure 3. For the user-provided textual tags, we remove the stop words and then check the remaining tags against the WordNet to remove those tags that do not exist in WordNet. Moreover, we choose the most frequent 1000 words as the text vocabulary of Flickr-11. With this text vocabulary, we generate the textual representation for the Flickr-11 images.

In the experiments, we compare the clustering performance of the six algorithms using different number of pairwise constraints. The clustering results on Flickr-11 are shown in Figure 4, from which we can see that our MMCP consistently and significantly outperforms the other five algorithms on all of the data modalities under different settings of pairwise constraints. On each of the modalities, as the number of constraints grows, the performance of our MMCP improves more significantly than those of AP and SSKK. In contrast, AP and SSKK perform unsatisfactorily, and in some cases, their performances have been degraded to that of NCuts. As to SL and E^{2}CP, although their performances also benefit from the increasing number of constraints, but due to the fact that they only make use of one data modality at a time, our MMCP consistently outperforms them on each data modality. In addition, in Table 1, we compare our MMCP with the linearly combining E^{2}CP, which linearly combine multiple similarity matrices together and then perform the E^{2}CP algorithm. From Table 1, we

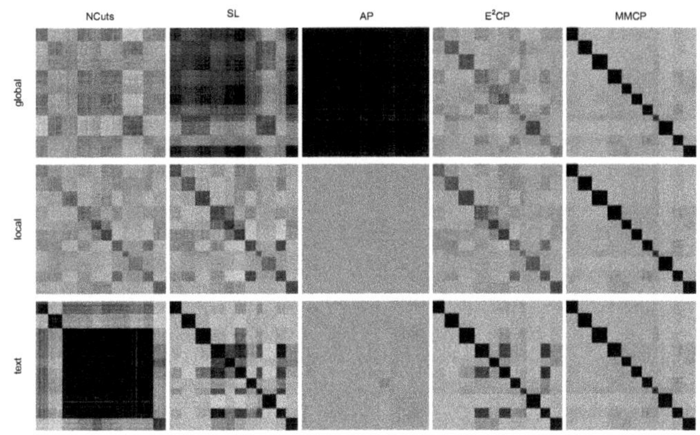

Figure 5: Distance matrices of the low-dimensional representations for the three modalities of Flickr-11 dataset (first row: visual global modality; second row: visual local modality; third row: textual modality) obtained by NCuts, SL, AP, E^{2}CP and MMCP, respectively. The darker is a pixel, the smaller is the distance.

#constraints	**5,000**	**10,000**	**15,000**	**20,000**
LC-E^{2}CP	0.690	0.726	0.753	0.770
MMCP	0.724	0.768	0.785	0.801

Table 1: Clustering results (NMI) of MMCP and linearly combining E^{2}CP on Flickr-11

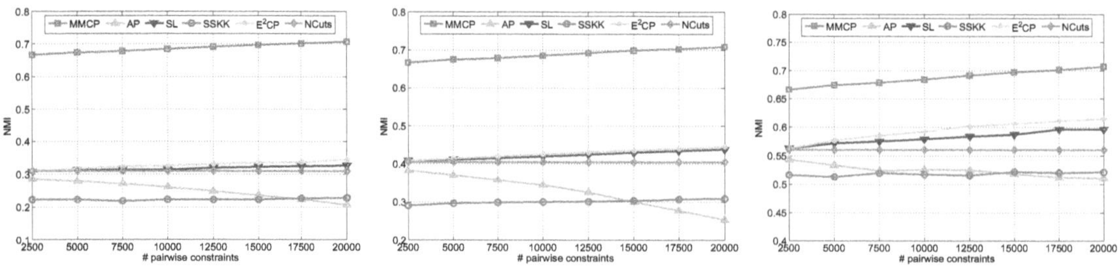

(a) global (b) local (c) text

Figure 6: Clustering results on the three modalities of Corel-5000 dataset with different number of pairwise constraints: NMI vs. Number of constraints. (a) Results on the visual global modality. (b) Results on the visual local modality. (c) Results on the textual modality.

can find that although E^{2}CP benefits from the simple combination of the modalities, the performances of our MMCP are still better than linearly combining E^{2}CP.

To help visualize the effect of our MMCP which exploits the pairwise constraints for clustering, we show the distance matrices of the low-dimensional data representations obtained by NCuts, SL, AP, E^{2}CP and our MMCP in Figure 5. We can find that the block structure of the distance matrices of the data representations obtained by our MMCP on each data modality is significantly more obvious, as compared to those of the data representations obtained by NCuts, SL, AP and E^{2}CP. This means that after refining the similarities among the data by our MMCP, each cluster associated with the new data representation becomes more compact and the different clusters become more separated.

It should be noted that the pairwise constraints used here are actually very sparse. The total number of pairwise constraints that can potentially be defined for the Flickr-11 dataset with $n = 8564$ is 36,666,766, i.e. $(n^2 - n)/2$. In our experiments, for example, the 2,500 pairwise constraints used for constrained clustering represent only about 0.006% of the total number of pairwise constraints that our MMCP eventually generated through constraint propagation for the entire dataset.

4.3 On Corel-5000

The clustering results on Corel-5000 are shown in Figure 6, from which two observations can be drawn. Firstly, our MMCP can achieve the best performance on all of the data modalities. After incorporating the pairwise constraints into clustering, the improvement achieved by our MMCP is very significant compared with NCuts, the baseline unconstrained method. The two methods of AP and SSKK that also consider the constraint information give unsatisfactory performance. Significantly, these two methods do not perform better than NCuts. Secondly, when the number of pairwise constraints grows, we find a consistent and obvious improvement in the performance of our MMCP, but the other three constrained clustering methods, i.e. AP, SL and SSKK, do not present this trend in constrained clustering. The performance of AP even degrades when the number of pairwise constraints increases. Similar to the situation on the Flickr-11 dataset, although the performances of E^{2}CP also benefits from the increasing number of constraints, due to the fact that it only makes use of one data modality at a time, our MMCP consistently outperforms it on each data modality. The comparison of our MMCP and linearly combining E^{2}CP

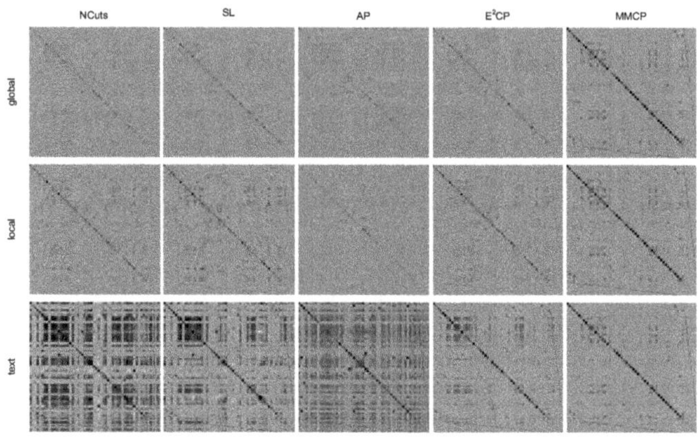

Figure 7: Distance matrices of the low-dimensional representations for the three modalities of Corel-5000 dataset (first row: visual global modality; second row: visual local modality; third row: textual modality) obtained by NCuts, SL, AP, E^{2}CP and MMCP, respectively. The darker is a pixel, the smaller is the distance.

#constraints	5,000	10,000	15,000	20,000
E^{2}CP	0.635	0.649	0.663	0.674
MMCP	0.675	0.685	0.698	0.708

Table 2: Clustering results (NMI) of MMCP and linearly combining E^{2}CP on Corel-5000

on Corel-5000 is listed in Table 2, from which we can see that our MMCP outperforms linearly combining E^{2}CP.

The distance matrices of the low-dimensional data representations obtained by NCuts, SL, AP, E^{2}CP and our MMCP on Corel-5000 dataset are shown in Figure 7. Once again, we find that compared to other methods, our MMCP has the most obvious diagonal block structure on each data modality. This is because the propagated pairwise constraints obtained by our MMCP can correctly reflect the underlying class relationships among data points, thus the following process of refining the similarities between instances can be effective, i.e. make the objects from the same class more compact and the objects from different classes more separated.

(a) glocal

	k=5	k=10	k=15	k=20	k=25
NCuts	0.117	0.146	0.149	0.147	0.149
SL	0.145	0.145	0.141	0.134	0.126
AP	0.009	0.006	0.006	0.005	0.005
E^2CP	0.274	0.261	0.243	0.225	0.206
MMCP	0.801	0.803	0.797	0.791	0.774

(b) local

	k=5	k=10	k=15	k=20	k=25
NCuts	0.275	0.267	0.267	0.270	0.273
SL	0.448	0.427	0.388	0.378	0.355
AP	0.010	0.006	0.006	0.006	0.006
E^2CP	0.442	0.429	0.402	0.392	0.375
MMCP	0.801	0.803	0.797	0.791	0.774

(c) text

	k=5	k=10	k=15	k=20	k=25
NCuts	0.512	0.551	0.620	0.622	0.623
SL	0.703	0.674	0.663	0.660	0.655
AP	0.030	0.027	0.024	0.023	0.021
E^2CP	0.747	0.760	0.753	0.744	0.739
MMCP	0.801	0.803	0.797	0.791	0.774

Table 3: The performances (NMI) of five methods with respect to different k values.

4.4 The Influence of Parameters

We analyze the influence of parameters in our MMCP and other related methods in this section. In particular, we conduct experiments with different settings of k (the number of the nearest neighbors) and η (the regularization parameter) respectively on the Flickr-11 dataset. Firstly, we perform experiments with different k values and show the results of NCuts, SL, AP, E^2CP and our MMCP in Table 3, where we apply 20,000 initial pairwise constraints and fix $\eta = 0.25$. It can be seen that among the four methods that consider the constraint information, the results of AP are consistently bad and the other three methods all perform worse for greater k. Contrarily, NCuts that does not take the prior constraint information into consideration performs more stable than the constrained clustering algorithms. However, the performances of our MMCP are still much better than those of Ncuts. Finally, we report the performance of E^2CP and MMCP with respect to different values of the regularization parameter η in Figure 8, where we use 20,000 initial pairwise constraints and fix $k = 5$. From Figure 8, we can find that the performances of E^2CP and MMCP are both stable when $\eta > 0.2$. Moreover, MMCP consistently outperforms E^2CP on each data modality under different settings of the regularization parameter η.

5. CONCLUSIONS

In this paper, we have proposed a novel multi-modal pairwise constraint propagation approach to propagate the pairwise relationships, including must-link and cannot-link constraints, across the entire multi-modal dataset. Previous works have been developed primarily for single modality data and cannot be directly applied to multi-modal data. Our method solved the problem of pairwise constraint propagation on the multi-modal dataset by decomposing it into a set of independent multi-graph based two-class label propagation subproblems which are then unified and solved as a single quadratic optimization problem. At the same time, we show that the formulation has a closed-form solution. It should be noted that while our solution is based on semi-supervised learning (label propagation) techniques, it does not require any explicit class labels. Our approach has the following novel characteristics: 1) it is applicable to multi-class problems; 2) it can simultaneously handle both must-link and cannot-link constraints; 3) as a solution for multi-modal problems, it can propagate pairwise constraints across multi-modal instances and can handle any number of data modalities; 4) it allows soft constraints, i.e., the pairwise constraints can be associated with confidence scores; and 5) it has a closed-form solution. The proposed method has been tested in constrained clustering tasks on two real-life multi-modal image datasets and shown to achieve significant improvements with respect to the single modality methods.

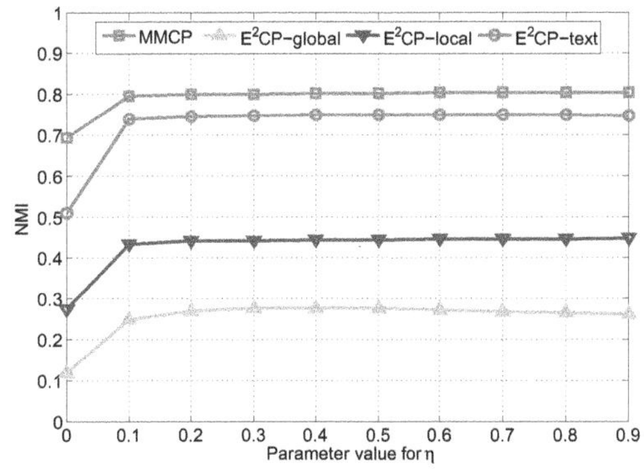

Figure 8: The performance (NMI) of E^2CP and our MMCP with respect to different settings of the regularization parameter η.

6. ACKNOWLEDGMENTS

We would like to thank the anonymous reviewers for their insightful suggestions. The work described in this paper is supported by NSFC (No. 60873133), the National High Technology Research and Development Program of China (No. 2008AA02Z310), 973 (No. 2009CB320901), a City University of Hong Kong matching grant (No. 9678017) to an Australian ARC Linkage project (LP100100466), and the National Natural Science Foundation of China under Grant Nos. 60873154 and 61073084.

7. REFERENCES

[1] S. Basu, M. Bilenko, and R. Mooney. A probabilistic framework for semi-supervised clustering. In *SIGKDD*, 2004.

[2] F. Chung. *Spectral graph theory*. American Mathematical Society, 1997.

[3] H. Cohn, R. Kleinberg, B. Szegedy, and C. Umans. Group-theoretic algorithms for matrix multiplication. In *FOCS*, 2004.

[4] D. Coppersmith and S. Winograd. Matrix multiplication via arithmetic progressions. *Journal of symbolic computation*, 9(3):251–280, 1990.

[5] A. Frome, Y. Singer, F. Sha, and J. Malik. Learning globally-consistent local distance functions for shape-based image retrieval and classification. In *ICCV*, 2007.
[6] Z. Fu, Z. Lu, H. Ip, Y. Peng, and H. Lu. Symmetric graph regularized constraint propagation. In *AAAI*, 2011.
[7] B. Gao, T. Liu, T. Qin, X. Zheng, Q. Cheng, and W. Ma. Web image clustering by consistent utilization of visual features and surrounding texts. In *ACM Multimedia*, 2005.
[8] S. Kamvar, D. Klein, and C. Manning. Spectral learning. In *IJCAI*, 2003.
[9] B. Kulis, S. Basu, I. Dhillon, and R. Mooney. Semi-supervised graph clustering: a kernel approach. In *ICML*, 2005.
[10] Z. Li, J. Liu, and X. Tang. Pairwise constraint propagation by semidefinite programming for semi-supervised classification. In *ICML*, 2008.
[11] Z. Lu and M. Carreira-Perpinán. Constrained spectral clustering through affinity propagation. In *CVPR*, 2008.
[12] Z. Lu and H. Ip. Image categorization by learning with context and consistency. In *CVPR*, 2009.
[13] Z. Lu and H. Ip. Constrained spectral clustering via exhaustive and efficient constraint propagation. In *ECCV*, 2010.
[14] B. Manjunath and W. Ma. Texture features for browsing and retrieval of image data. *IEEE Transactions on Pattern Analysis and Machine Intelligence*, 18(8):837–842, 1996.
[15] S. Rüping and T. Scheffer. Learning with multiple views. In *Proc. ICML Workshop on Learning with Multiple Views*, 2005.
[16] L. Shapiro and G. Stockman. *Computer Vision.* Prentice Hall, 2003.
[17] J. Shi and J. Malik. Normalized cuts and image segmentation. *IEEE Transactions on Pattern Analysis and Machine Intelligence*, 22(8):888–905, 2000.
[18] A. Strehl and J. Ghosh. Cluster ensembles—a knowledge reuse framework for combining multiple partitions. *The Journal of Machine Learning Research*, 3:583–617, 2003.
[19] U. von Luxburg. A tutorial on spectral clustering. *Statistics and Computing*, 17(4):395–416, 2007.
[20] K. Wagstaff and C. Cardie. Clustering with instance-level constraints. In *ICML*, 2000.
[21] X. Wang and I. Davidson. Active spectral clustering. In *ICDM*, 2010.
[22] X. Wang and I. Davidson. Flexible constrained spectral clustering. In *SIGKDD*, 2010.
[23] X. Wang, W. Ma, G. Xue, and X. Li. Multi-model similarity propagation and its application for web image retrieval. In *ACM Multimedia*, 2004.
[24] E. Xing, A. Ng, M. Jordan, and S. Russell. Distance metric learning with application to clustering with side-information. In *NIPS*, 2003.
[25] L. Xu, W. Li, and D. Schuurmans. Fast normalized cut with linear constraints. In *CVPR*, 2009.
[26] D. Zhou, O. Bousquet, T. Lal, J. Weston, and B. Schölkopf. Learning with local and global consistency. In *NIPS*, 2004.
[27] D. Zhou and C. Burges. Spectral clustering and transductive learning with multiple views. In *ICML*, 2007.

APPENDIX

In this appendix, we will give a short illustration about how to verify the equation

$$\sum_{u,v\in V} p(u)p(u\to v)(F_{ui}-F_{vi})^2 = 2F_{\cdot i}^T\hat{L}F_{\cdot i} \tag{15}$$

The left part in equation (15) can be decomposed as follows

$$\begin{aligned}
&\sum_{u,v} p(u)p(u\to v)(F_{ui}-F_{vi})^2 \\
= &\sum_{u,v} p(u)p(u\to v)F_{ui}^2 && \text{(16a)}\\
+ &\sum_{u,v} p(u)p(u\to v)F_{vi}^2 && \text{(16b)}\\
- &\sum_{u,v} 2p(u)p(u\to v)F_{ui}F_{vi} && \text{(16c)}
\end{aligned}$$

(16a) is equal to

$$\sum_{u,v} p(u)p(u\to v)F_{ui}^2 = \sum_u p(u)F_{ui}^2 \sum_v p(u\to v) = \sum_u p(u)F_{ui}^2$$

(16b) is equal to

$$\sum_{u,v} p(u)p(u\to v)F_{vi}^2 = \sum_v F_{vi}^2 \sum_u p(u)p(u\to v).$$

Since $\sum_u p(u)p(u\to v) = p(v)$, we have

$$(16b) = \sum_v p(v)F_{vi}^2 = \sum_u p(u)F_{ui}^2 = (16a).$$

Especially, (16a) and (16b) are all equal to $F_{\cdot i}^T\Pi F_{\cdot i}$, where Π is the diagonal stationary probability matrix with its diagonal elements being $p(u)$.

Moreover, it can be seen that

$$\sum_{u,v} p(u)p(u\to v)F_{ui}F_{vi} = F_{\cdot i}^T(\Pi P)F_{\cdot i},$$

and

$$\sum_{v,u} p(v)p(v\to u)F_{vi}F_{ui} = F_{\cdot i}^T(P^T\Pi)F_{\cdot i},$$

where P denote the transition probability matrix with its elements being $p(u\to v)$. Thus,

$$(16c) = F_{\cdot i}^T(\Pi P + P^T\Pi)F_{\cdot i}.$$

In summary, the left part in equation (15) equals to

$$2F_{\cdot i}^T\Pi F_{\cdot i} - F_{\cdot i}^T(\Pi P + P^T\Pi)F_{\cdot i} = 2F_{\cdot i}^T(\Pi - \frac{\Pi P + P^T\Pi}{2})F_{\cdot i}$$

If we define

$$\hat{L} = \Pi - \frac{\Pi P + P^T\Pi}{2},$$

we will get the final conclusion, i.e. the formula (15):

$$\sum_{u,v\in V} p(u)p(u\to v)(F_{ui}-F_{vi})^2 = 2F_{\cdot i}^T\hat{L}F_{\cdot i}.$$

Implicit Experiences as a Determinant of Perceptual Quality and Aesthetic Appreciation

Wendy Ann Mansilla[1], Andrew Perkis[1], Touradj Ebrahimi[1, 2]
1. Centre for Quantifiable Quality of Service in Communication Systems (Q2S)
Norwegian University of Science and Technology, Trondheim, Norway
2. Multimedia Signal Processing Group
École Polytechnique Fédérale de Lausanne, Lausanne, Switzerland
{wendy.mansilla, andrew, touradj.ebrahimi}@q2s.ntnu.no

ABSTRACT
Since the Dadaist refusal of the conventional standards in art, followed by Fluxus` rejection of art as a commodity, and recently, the popularity of Internet and technology in art, artworks have become difficult to recognize as artworks in themselves. Modern works of art are no longer readily only seen today, more often fully experienced. The processing of an aesthetic experience needs a new understanding in terms of the changing context of art and the experiential perspective of art recipients. In the multimedia arena, the valid assumption is that, evaluations of aesthetic experiences are mostly based on the accessible information on the surface of the medium. Several research groups in psychology question the singularity of exterior-level assumptions demonstrating that there are modulating factors that affect aesthetic experiences and one of these is implicit experience. In this paper, we review the significance of empirical aesthetics in psychology and from the artistic point of view combined with a technical and experiential perspective. We also discuss our approach of considering the implications of implicit experiences to the modelling of Quality of Experience (QoE) where this is used as a measurement of perception and aesthetic judgment of contemporary and modern works of art.

Categories and Subject Descriptors
H.1.2 [**Information Systems**]: Models and Principles—Human Factors; H.5.1 [**Information Systems**]: Information Interfaces and Presentation—Evaluation/Methodology

General Terms
Design, Experimentation, Human Factors

Keywords Art, Empirical Aesthetic, Implicit Experiences, QoE, Aesthetic Experience, Aesthetics of Digital Error

*Area Chair: Aisling Kelliher.

1. INTRODUCTION
For nearly a century, the mode of art reception and definition has dramatically changed, and with the new electronic art, video art, Internet-art and non-art among others, the line between art and commodity is blurring. The conventional ideal of beauty as a criterion for valued artistic work is replaced by the idea of pleasure, sensation or of interest, a story, and a political statement, all of which boil down to the viewers' experience.

Nowadays, many properties investigated by early psychological studies are difficult to apply in contemporary and modern artworks. Art has evolved into a sophisticated form whose value is highly contested - from Dadaism followed by Fluxus, and the rise of art manifestoes and activisms (e.g. Situationist International), the usual accepted visual structure no longer serves as a prevailing standard in art schools or in art movements. With the increasing importance of the Internet in everyday life, new forms of representation are brought forward. Along with the advances in video technology is the growing demand for photographic and cinematographic art content that requires electronic transmission and feedback. The imperfect world of the Internet and technology in general has inspired artists to see beauty in the erroneous digital world. These new paradigms of representation and its transforming social functions require examination from a psychological as well as a technological point of view in order to explicitly understand aesthetic experience.

Today, artistic work is valued for its distinctive artistic style or technique. The need to develop these individually distinctive styles has encouraged artists to rely on new technology to push innovation. These innovations and technologies have a significant impact on the viewers of art or other forms of aesthetic experience. The technical progress has also produced a dramatic effect on the viewers` quality expectations when encountering aesthetic stimulus that use technology. Ensuring quality in a technology-driven visual presentation no longer relies solely on Quality of Service (QoS) conventions (i.e. guaranteed service-related features from the content provider's perspective based on an objective measure). Perception of quality in aesthetic content needs to be addressed from the user's experiential perspective. As expectations of technological consumption change, there is increasing need for new mechanisms to understand the evolving user experience, and so research on multimedia quality has shifted its focus to QoE [13, 38, 56].

In this paper, we review prior literature related to empirical aesthetics and experience moderating variables such as perceptual fluency and expertise on art and its implications for aesthetic judgment and assessment of user perception. We also describe our empirical approach in investigating the importance of implicit experiences. In the final section, we draw some conclusions and describe the future directions of the current work.

2. VIEW OF EMPIRICAL AESTHETICS

The processing of aesthetic experience is complex and highly subjective, and is therefore challenging to empirically quantify and understand. Judging an aesthetic stimulus involves intricate interactions between various mechanisms such as emotion, cognition, and interactions with the environment. In psychology, a long history of research has been founded on the influence of visual features on aesthetic judgment (since [14]). Today, empirical aesthetics in psychology is recognized as not only visually oriented but also strongly connected to hedonic experience [26]. Determining and validating all possible factors that influence aesthetic appreciation has rich research potential within the field of empirical aesthetics [52].

Within the field of Human-Computer Interaction (HCI), several studies have demonstrated that aesthetics in visual design enhance perceived usability [50, 51] and improve cognitive task performance [34, 47]. There is also an increasing recognition that "what is beautiful may not always be usable" which results in a shift in focus towards a more experiential orientation in HCI. The traditional notion of beauty which implies usability or utility [50] is challenged by the findings that such correlation does always exist [20, 53]. In addition, beyond HCI`s focus on user needs, aesthetics in product design is found to be influential on learning [40], user preference [8], enjoyment and fun [6, 9], and impulsive buying [36].

Compared to psychology and HCI, there are only a few empirical studies on aesthetic quality in the field of multimedia signal processing [7, 28]. Most of these studies are centred on determining the visual attributes of an image, which is sometimes followed by a proposal for an algorithm that can potentially automate the prediction of aesthetic quality. These studies typically categorize visual features based on intuition or common technical criteria. Based on these features, non-expert users are asked to rate the subjective quality of an image. In some cases, the statistical results are fed to a computer to discriminate between aesthetically pleasing and displeasing materials.

Aesthetic judgment is influenced not only by the psychophysical variables (such as intensity, brightness, saturation, size, contrast, colour, and clarity) used in quality related or other empirical aesthetics studies but also by several other known factors. All these influencing variables can be used as a foundation in multimedia and information technology research. These include conditions such as exposure effect [5, 57], familiarity [58], prototypicality [33], and compositional organization [1, 55]. There are also other features such as preference for symmetrical over asymmetrical counterparts [44], curved over sharp objects [2] [46], and complex over simple stimuli [23]. It was also observed that implicit experiences affect processing of art [45]. In addition, art reception can also be modulated by social variables that are for instance affected by situational demands [52]. It seems that in order to understand or even predict aesthetic judgment towards a stimulus, it is important to recognize that aesthetic processing experience happens in several stages. Leder et al. [26], proposed a model that involves five stages in an aesthetic processing experience (perceptual analyses, implicit memory integration, explicit classification, cognitive mastering and evaluation).

The technical and visual attributes of the stimulus that the majority of the multimedia processing studies are concerned with happens mostly at the perceptual analysis layer. At this stage, features that can be extracted automatically or easily are examined. In addition, the psychophysical variables can already be detected spontaneously at this level. This is followed by the implicit processing stage where the role of influencing variables such as prior implicit experience or initial affective state takes place. Memory associations such as familiarity and prototypicality contribute to processing at this level, which can be influenced by aesthetic fluency (i.e. viewer's level of art experience and expertise).

The processing stage called explicit classification is concerned with the analysis of content and style. The type of artwork and the expertise of the viewer can have a considerable impact on the result at this stage. An art expert commonly processes information through the analysis of style-related features, while an art novice is commonly influenced by the content-related processing [11]. Leder et al. [26] noted that processing of styles requires some expertise and that without explicit learning about artistic styles it could be hard to classify artworks [10, 37]. Furthermore, analysis and development of an art style is usually learned through formal education or acquired with expertise in discourse on subjects related to art. Consistent with this assumption, research on expertise in various domains shows that experts indeed generally perceive things that novices cannot [39]. More specifically, experts and novices evaluate, create and experience art differently [25]. However, there are also evidences that non-expert art observers can also decode and understand works of art beyond just the external level [19] and that stylistic processing skill can also be acquired through implicit experiences [13].

Despite quantitative demonstrations that perception of aesthetic judgments in a product or technological design is remarkably stable overtime [20] or that anything beautiful has a pragmatic quality [50]; study results sometimes vary and can be explained by methodological inconsistencies, or lack of judgmental process [21]. Perhaps, aesthetic judgment simply needs further examination at a deeper level of interaction or construction [35], 17] and thus, one of the aims of the current study is to verify how other modulating variables can contribute to further this understanding.

3. AESTHETIC QUALITY AND PERCEPTUAL FLUENCY

What determines whether we see beauty or trash in a medium depends on various psychological mechanisms. The visual quality of a stimulus affects the viewer's aesthetic judgment through perceptual fluency [43, 52]. This effect happens when higher quality material is judged more positively than the lower quality material because of the experience of processing "ease". A visual object is considered to be high in perceptual fluency when it is easier to see and evaluate.

When processing ease is due to the "surface" qualities of a material, the experience of fluency is perceptual and is influenced by variables such as simple repetition, contrast, presentation duration, etc. [42]. Although these external features are more popular in academic studies when associating fluency with aesthetic evaluations, there are other levels in the experience of processing ease. Another type is conceptual fluency, and is influenced by variables like semantic priming, predictability, context congruity, etc. [42]. Although conceptual priming is more content-oriented, Reber et al. [42] pointed out that perceptual and conceptual manipulations of fluency tend to result in similar effects on judgment.

Repeated exposure to a medium leads to familiarity. Familiarity enhances liking and in psychology this phenomenon is associated with fluency. Familiar stimuli are processed faster and elicit less attention orienting than novel stimuli [24, 12]. Familiar stimuli are also viewed as more attractive than novel ones [57]. In one of our own studies, using a multimedia processing approach, we presented a stereoscopic 3D scenario augmented with familiar and novel actors and applied equal amounts of degradation on both stimuli. We have confirmed that when the viewer is presented with a double stimuli test condition of a familiar and novel signal, the stimuli with higher fluency (more familiar) signals result in more positive perceived quality evaluations [31]. One of the conclusions that confirm that perceived quality influences aesthetic judgment is the information processing bias towards natural scenes [42]. Natural scenes elicit pleasure and are seen as beneficial to physical and mental well being [4], and are also seen as highly tolerant to quality degradations compared to man-made scenes [52].

Several studies propose that high perceptual fluency is associated with positive affect and results in more favourable evaluations [26, 42]. It is also known that increased fluency results in a higher judgment of liking, but does not enhance judgment of disliking [30]. The result of our prior study on the link between familiarity, affect, and perception of quality further supports this conclusion, suggesting that when a viewer is presented with a double stimuli test condition having an equal degradation of a familiar and a novel signal, the stimulus that is more personally relevant (which increases fluency) is evaluated to be more enjoyable than the less relevant or novel one [31].

Various facets within psychology research question the singularity of the surface-level assumption demonstrating there are modulating factors that affect aesthetic judgment [45]. One modulating factor is implicit experience such as previous exposure to mental concepts or prior bodily sensations that influence a viewer's mood at the time of judgment.

In the case of modern or contemporary works of art or even for most of the technologically-driven content such as augmented reality or mixed electronic media, the classical approach to present attractiveness or beauty has often been reduced or completely modified. According to Popper [41], with increasing technological usage and influences, art has become "virtualized" where the impression of reality felt by perceivers of art is not only provided by vision and hearing but also by other bodily sensations. He points out that the difference between virtualized and traditional art is that the artistic intentions of today involve humanization of technology - driven by basic human needs or utility and hedonism.

Our prevalent exposure to Internet malfunctions, technical errors, and computer crashes is changing the way we create, appreciate and consume aesthetic forms today. Thus, quality distortions or degradations typically produced as a result of technological imperfections are often applied to an artwork for the purpose of making it look aesthetically attractive. In some cases, there is no longer a separation between degradation and visual work, which renders the material too complex to perceive by some naïve art viewers.

It seems that in appreciating modern and contemporary artworks or digital media, experience prevails more than biological intuition. To explain the complex world of art, it seems timely to look beyond the accessible information bearing on the material. Examining the potentials of the unconscious exposure to those media that some may find technically or artistically contesting, might provide answers as to why one can appreciate works of art that are not typically visually beautiful or low in technical quality. This paper aims to challenge the traditional way of viewing perceived quality in the domain of multimedia signal processing, thus broadening the concept of QoE by including aspects of art.

4. IMPLICIT EXPERIENCE

People tend to encode the world based on what immediately occupies their mind [22, 49]. Aside from the properties of the stimulus, research on the impact of priming on aesthetic judgment and behaviour suggests that prior implicit experiences also regulate aesthetic judgments. This effect (also known as cognitive accessibility) is most commonly demonstrated by priming studies. Such studies show that the encoding of behaviour is guided by which mental concepts are accessible at the moment of impression encoding. Priming increases the perceptual fluency of mental concepts in the presence of primes related to those concepts [3].

We shall use the term implicit experience in our QoE studies to refer to prior stimulus mental concept exposures. Implicit experience because it is not necessary to have conscious awareness of the priming stimuli for such an experience to affect aesthetic processing. In social psychology, priming is administered by presenting contextual cues (primes) to the perceiver who is unaware of the relationship of the stimulus to the measured dependent variable [3, 48].

In one of the studies by Reber, et al., ([43], Study 1), pictures of everyday objects (e.g. birds, plane, desk) were primed with matched or mismatched contours (i.e. highly degraded contour of either the target image or a different image). The participants who were unaware of fluency manipulations, recognized matched contours faster and resulted in more positive evaluations when compared to the unmatched contours. The result of visual priming is also consistent with the manipulations of presentation duration and figure-ground contrast where increase in perceptual fluency leads to a more positive evaluation of the perceived stimuli [42, 54].

Implicit experiences interfere with human visual judgment and information processing and therefore, we believe that it is important to investigate the conditions necessary to incorporate this variable to our QoE and multimedia aesthetics studies. In the next section we describe our experimental approach designed to support and discuss the potential impact of implicit experiences on the quality and aesthetic judgment of modern and contemporary visual contents.

5. MEASURING QUALITY OF EXPERIENCE

We present three studies that compare the effects of implicit experiences on the QoE. Study 1 involves measurement of the immediate response (i.e. QoE) of viewers with no previous test conditions or manipulations; Study 2 investigates the introduction of implicit experience by manipulation of primes in the form of a performance task followed by measurement of QoE; and Study 3 further explores the target mental concepts by employing three conditions: exploration of images found on the Internet, performance task, and assessment of QoE.

5.1 General Methodology

All studies in the current research were conducted in a dimly lit room. Subjects were tested one at a time and upon arrival, were constructively asked if they were in a positive state of health and mood. This verification was followed by instructions and distribution of a score sheet. Data were collected from the participants by marking on a given sheet of paper. The stimuli used in all studies were displayed on a 17-inch display screen, with participants located at a distance of approximately 80-90 cm from the display.

Participants in each study were told that they would take part in several unrelated studies that involved viewing, exploration and evaluation of modern and contemporary art. It is somehow important to assure a representative mode of art reception especially in the context of a laboratory experiment and prior to each study, the viewers were told that they would be involved in an experiment concerning reception of aesthetics to invite a positive mental state [26, 27].

Prior to data collection, participants were also informed that initial impressions provide more valuable answers. They were also instructed not to let production-related bias such as resolution quality influence their ratings. Furthermore, they were also informed that the experimental films were produced in the 1960s and the images of paintings that they would be seeing were not at their highest resolutions (approximately within the range of 500 x 480 to 640 x 480 pixels).

Participants in all studies had normal or corrected to normal vision. They were regular Internet users (i.e. used the Internet at least 5 times per week), had extremely low to average art knowledge and interest and had visited no more than two museums and art exhibitions in the prior three years. None of the study participants had previously participated in prior experiments conducted as part of this research.

5.2 Stimuli

Three types of stimuli were selected, representing popular contemporary forms of art highly accessible through the Internet and contemporary art museums. These stimuli were selected not only because of their challenging artistic style and composition, but also because of their known persistence, influence and constantly evolving forms.

5.2.1 Stimuli 1: Digital Reproductions of Modern and Contemporary Paintings

30 digital reproductions of modern and contemporary paintings were used in the current research (see Table 1). These paintings incorporated properties of a medium that are inspired by technical imperfections that disrupt their reality or by digital errors that may disrupt how these artworks are communicated (see Figure 1). Images used were all desaturated to approximately 70 percent because huge differences in saturation levels can have an effect on the viewer's evaluation [32].

Table 1. List of modern and contemporary paintings used in the current study

Artist	Title	Style
Alexa Meade	Spectacle, Jaimie Power Exchange, Natura Morts, BluePrint, Synthesized, Self Contained, Blue Print Installation, & Alexa Painting	Takes the imperfections of the traditional two dimensional painting into the physical world which can be categorized as Hyperrealism
Andy Denzler	Bedroom Portrait series, The Human Nature Project, In to the Black Woods, Transition II, Waterfall Crossing, Body & Faces Study 4, Equinox, & Falcon Street	Resemble snapshots of events that have quality or encoding issues. Style is between Photorealism and Abstract Expressionism.
Joseph Beuys	Konigstochter Sieht Island, Painting Version 1-90, & Schwangere und Schwan	Torn hole on paper or abstractly emphasized body parts (fat) with minimalistic representation (Neo-expressionism).
Gregory Thielker	Under the Unminding Sky series	Photorealistic paintings from the water on the windshield perspective that can effectively obscure viewing (Hyperrealism).
Gerhard Richter	Family series	Uses blurring edges technique to create an illusion of a photorealist early portrait photograph (Hyperrealism).
Picasso	Guernica, & Bust of a Woman with a Hat	Abstract and distorted representations of three-dimensional subjects on canvas (Cubism).
Andy Warhol	Self Portrait, 1986	Image appears to have a technical screen print misalignment (Pop-art).
Richard Hamilton	Swingeing London 67 series	Photorealistic and blurring technique (Pop-art).
Sigma Polke	Ziegenwagon	Collage-like and technically pixelated painting technique (Pop-art).

a.) Paintings by Andy Denzler

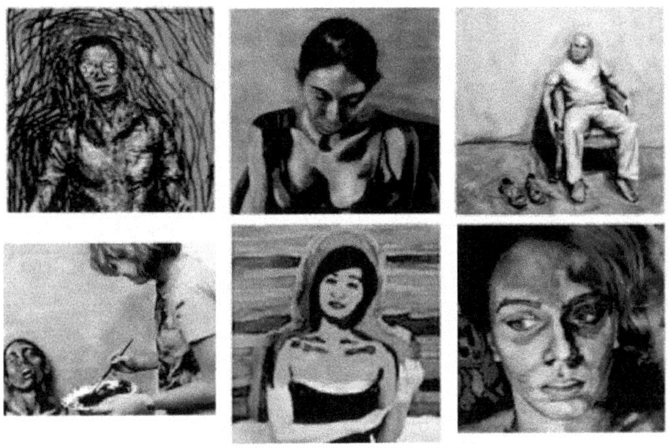

b.) Paintings by Alexa Meada

Figure 1. Snapshots of selected digital reproductions of contemporary paintings (posted with written permissions from the artists).

5.2.2 Stimuli 2: Experimental Art Films

Four experimental art films produced by Wolf Vostell, John Cavanaugh, Eric Andersen, and Peter Kennedy, whose works exploit the narrative potentials of distortions found on analogue transmissions from the 1960s. These films were downloaded from YouTube and edited to last approximately 40-50 seconds each.

5.2.3 Stimuli 3: Internet Images of the Aesthetics of Digital Error

The Internet is a rich resource for capturing digital images with an artistic style that takes computational errors as the chosen subject, Typing “glitch + art” into the Google search engine, (for details see Figure 2) results in 228 images within a single webpage. Each image has a mouse over functionality that allows the viewer to see images at higher dimensions including image title, metadata or sometimes a short text.

Figure 2. Snapshot of images of the aesthetics of digital error found on the Internet

5.3 Study 1: Aesthetic Fluency Test

In this study, immediate fluency was measured using the QoE impairment assessment scale. This study is intended to verify the potential perceived quality tolerance level of naïve participants when presented with experimental art films.

5.3.1 Method

Study 1 involved 22 participants consisting of 9 female and 13 male subjects, with a mean age of 31 years old (SD = 4.46). Participants were PhD students, Masters students, and government and research institution employees. They were residents of Norway, Denmark and the Netherlands. The stimulus set for this study is described earlier in section 5.2.2. After the participants were examined for their visual acuity, given instructions, and constructively verified for their emotional state, they viewed one experimental art film for training and three actual test data (randomly presented). Each movie lasted from 40 to 50 seconds followed by a black screen for 20s to give participants time to record their quality impairment assessment. Using a 5-point quality impairment scale (1 as being very annoying and 5 meaning imperceptible), the participants marked their ratings on a sheet of paper.

5.3.2 Results and Discussion

Using a quality impairment scale, naïve participants rated the aesthetic quality of films characterized by aesthetic distortions as annoying (mean = 1.70, std. deviation = 0.69) and reported them to be questionable and hard to understand. The result is obvious and to be expected, but valuable in verifying the relationship between aesthetic fluency and aesthetic judgment on such stimuli. Although the intention of the artists was to use distortions on analogue transmissions to complement the narrative of the films used in the current study, a non-expert viewer was unable to understand such a purpose. The result also provided the basis to further our investigations on the effects of fluency manipulations in increasing the appreciation of such kind of art material. Art appreciation in modern and contemporary art films requires more than a reported positive mental and physical state, therefore it seems important to investigate how other variables can contribute in modulating it.

5.4 Study 2: Style Comparison Test as an Implicit Experience

Study 2 aimed at verifying the potential perceived quality tolerance scale of naïve participants when presented with experimental art films after an exposure to a primed concept.

5.4.1 Method

Study 2 involved 20 subjects consisting of 8 female and 12 male subjects with a mean age of 30 years old (SD = 3.0). Participants were Masters and PhD students, and government employees based in Norway. The stimulus set is described earlier in section 5.2.1 for digital reproductions of paintings and in section 5.2.2 for experimental art films.

After the participants were verified for their physical and mental states and given instructions, they proceeded with the style comparison task. In this task, participants were asked to judge whether two succeeding stimuli were similar or different in artistic style. They performed four practice trials and 30 experimental trials. Each trial started with the presentation of a lightly coloured fixation cross in the centre of the screen for 500ms. Next, two digital copies of paintings at 800ms each with 300ms white screen intervals were shown. After showing these two images a gray screen was shown at 2500ms to allow the participants to identify the style similarity of the paired images (i.e. by marking yes or no on a score sheet). At the end of the first test, subjects were asked if the experience was positive or negative (or if it is boring, stressful, neutral or fun) to confirm their positive state. The majority of the participants found the experiment as a positive or otherwise neutral experience.

The second scale followed immediately after an instruction was given. One film was shown for training followed by three actual test data of experimental art films (randomly presented). Each movie lasted from 40 to 50 seconds followed by a black screen at 20s to allow some time for recording quality impairment assessment (by marking 1 as being very annoying and 5 meaning imperceptible or no quality issues on a score sheet).

Before ending the entire session, participants were asked if it ever crossed their minds during the experiments that the first scale was related to the second. None of the participants reported awareness of any connection between the two scales. Participants were also asked to identify images or names of artists that they can immediately remember from the previous experiment (data was recorded but not analysed).

5.4.2 Results and Discussion

The percentage performance and mean QoE scores were sampled across participants in Study 2. Based on the binary response (yes/no) gathered from the style comparison task, the percentage performance score of each participant was calculated by adding the total number of correctly identified styles divided by the total number of actual test data (N = 30) and then multiplied by one hundred. The percentage performance of each participant was then used as an independent variable to perform a linear regression analysis with the calculated mean quality impairment rating (in a 5-point scale) across participants as a dependent variable.

The translated data was analyzed with the Statistical Package for the Social Sciences (SPSS), a simple linear regression and correlation was extracted to analyze the relationship between aesthetic style comparison score and measured quality ratings (QoE). Based on the linear regression (see Figure 4) and correlation analysis computed for Study 2, there was a positive (R-squared value = 0.729) significant relationship between aesthetic comparison style score and QoE. Furthermore, the results show that 85% of the variability in QoE could be explained by the participant's success in the aesthetic comparison scale (see Figure 4 & 5).

Using a quality impairment scale, naïve participants rated the aesthetic quality of the films as less annoying than Study 1 (mean = 2.86, std. deviation = 0.8). The Independent Samples Mann-Whitney U Test was calculated and the results suggest that there is a statistically significant difference between the underlying distributions of the QoE scores in Study 1 and the QoE scores in Study 2 ($z = -4.05$, $p < 0.05$, mean rank for Study 1 = 14.25, & mean rank for Study 2 = 29.48).

It seems that adding a primed concept leads to a higher quality assessment. The result of the mean QoE scores in Study 2 is higher than in Study 1 but is not sufficient to conclude that an increase in implicit experience correlates to an increase of tolerance to aesthetic distortions on films. In the next section we describe our final study conducted to verify the relationship between QoE and primed mental concepts.

Model Summary

Model	R	R Square	Adjusted R Square	Std. Error of the Estimate
1	.854[a]	.729	.714	.42749

a. Predictors: (Constant), Comparison_Score

Figure 4. Linear regression diagram with mean QoE rating as dependent variable and aesthetic comparison score as independent variable on Study 2

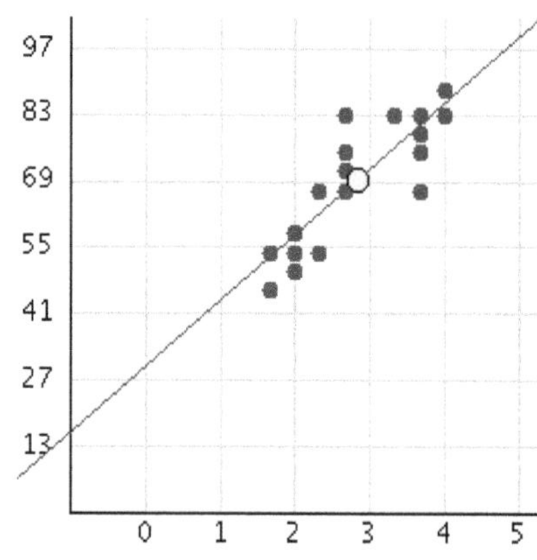

Figure 5. Scattered plot showing relationship between QoE rating (horizontal) and comparison test score (vertical) on Study 2, with center of mass represented by a yellow dot.

5.5 Study 3: Art Exploration and Style Comparison Test as Implicit Experiences

This study further examines the effect of increasing visual access to target mental concepts to the QoE.

5.5.1 Method

This study was conducted with 18 participants consisting of 10 female and 8 male subjects, with a mean age of 29 years old (SD = 5.5). Participants from this experiment were mostly undergraduate and Masters students, freelance and research institution employees, residing in Norway and Denmark. The stimulus set is described earlier in section 5.2.1 for digital reproductions of paintings, section 5.2.2 for experimental art films, and section 5.2.3 for Internet images.

After verifying the participant's physical and mental states an instruction was given followed by a brief training session. They were told that a question would be asked after the exploration session referring to the images viewed. In the actual session, participants were instructed to freely explore the prepared image search results of "glitch + art" at the google.com website for about 60 seconds (see section 5.2.3). The viewers were told not to explore deeper into the website links of each image but rather they were advised to place the cursor on each images to see textual cues. At the end of the session, they were asked to shortly describe on paper some images that they can immediately recall (data were recorded but not analysed).

Subjects performed another task after an instruction was given. In this task, participants were asked to identify whether two succeeding stimuli were similar or different in artistic style (the same scale as in Study 2 was used). They were given 4 practice trials and 30 experimental trials. Each trial started with the presentation of a lightly coloured fixation cross in the centre of the screen for 500ms. Next, two digital copies of paintings at 800ms each with 300ms white screen interval were shown. After showing these two images a gray screen was shown at 2500ms to allow the participants to identify the style similarity of the paired images (i.e. by marking yes or no on a score sheet). The majority of the participants found the experiment as positive or otherwise neutral.
The final scale followed immediately after an instruction was given. One film was shown for a practice trial followed by 3 actual test data of experimental art films (randomly presented). Each movie lasted from 40 to 50 seconds followed by a black screen shown for 20s to facilitate QoE assessment. Finally, participants were asked if they were aware of any experimental connections among three scales conducted during the experiments. No one expressed any awareness of any connections.

5.5.2 Results and Discussion

The percentage performance and mean QoE scores were sampled across participants in Study 3 and translations were the same as in Study 2. Using SPSS, a linear regression and the correlation analysis for Study 3 was calculated. Results suggest that there is a positive (R-squared value = 0.708) significant relationship between aesthetic comparison score and QoE (see Figure 6). Furthermore, results show that 84% of the variability in QoE could be explained by the participant's success in the aesthetic style comparison scale (see Figure 7).

The Independent Samples Mann-Whitney U Test was calculated in SSPS and the results suggest that there is a statistically significant difference between the underlying distributions of the QoE scores in Study 3 and QoE scores in Study 2 (z = -2.09, p = 0.037, mean rank for Study 2 = 15.98, & mean rank for Study 3 = 23.42). The results suggest that an increase in primed concept can lead to a more positive quality impairment assessment.

The Independent Samples Kruskas-Wallis Test was also calculated across all three studies and results show that there is a statistically significant difference among QoE scales (p <0.05, test statistic, H = 29.80). The computed mean rank across test conditions show that Study 3 ranks the highest QoE score amongst studies (mean rank value of Study 1 = 15, Study 2 = 35, and Study 3 = 44). These results further suggest that implicit experiences can influence QoE ratings.

Model Summary

Model	R	R Square	Adjusted R Square	Std. Error of the Estimate
1	.842^a	.708	.690	.34575

a. Predictors: (Constant), Comparison_Score

Figure 6. Linear regression diagram with QoE rating as dependent variable and aesthetic comparison score as independent variable on Study 3.

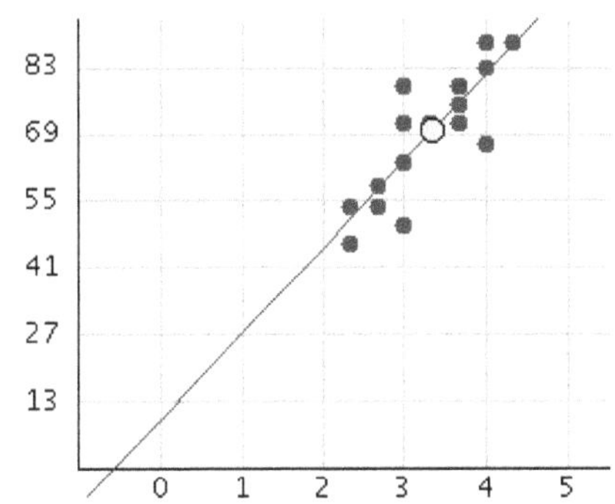

Figure 7. Scattered plot showing relationship between QoE rating (horizontal) and comparison test score (vertical) on Study 3, with center of mass represented by a yellow dot.

6. GENERAL DISCUSSION

In the current research, data was analyzed with SPSS, a simple linear regression and correlation was extracted to analyze the relationship between aesthetic style comparison score and measured quality ratings (QoE). Results suggest that there is a positive significant relationship between aesthetic processing score and QoE. Results show that that 85 % of the variability in QoE on Study 2 and 84 % on Study 3 could be explained by the participant's success in the aesthetic style comparison measure.

The effects of manipulations of fluency through primes (in the form of aesthetic style comparison task) in Study 2 and Study 3 as compared to Study 1 is demonstrated through a box and whiskers plot (see Figure 8). An increase access to mental concepts seems to lead to higher tolerance level in viewing films appearing to have quality issues (median of QoE score on Study 2 = 2.67 and Study 3 = 3.5 as compared to the lower value of median on Study 1 = 1.67). Study 3, which involves highest access to target mental concepts, results to higher positive ratings amongst test conditions. The results across three studies demonstrate that an increase in implicit experience correlates to an increase in QoE ratings.

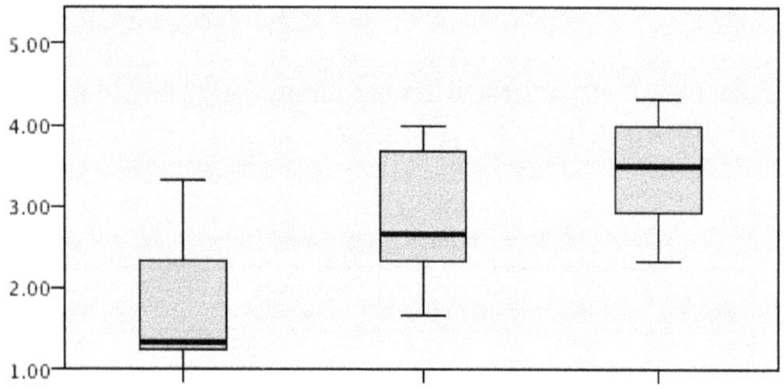

Labels	Study 1	Study 2	Study 3
Min	1	1.67	2.33
Q_1	1.33	2.33	3
Median	1.33	2.67	3.5
Q_3	2.2475	3.67	3.9175
Max	3.33	4	4.33

Figure 8. Box & whiskers plot of the QoE ratings of the 3 studies considered in the current research. The line in the middle of the box shows the median. The lower and upper limits of the box correspond to the first (Q1) and third (Q3) quartiles.

7. LIMITATIONS & FUTURE RESEARCH

Several limitations have to be considered when interpreting the results of the current research. First, the studies performed are limited to the assessment of visual aesthetics and may not generalize to other modalities such as sound, music or virtual and interactive environments. It would be interesting to investigate if audiovisual data or the presence of interactivity can produce similar results. Second, although the studies employed approximately 20 naïve participants for each formal scale, validity of the measures remains to be examined on other groups of participants and on other media. Third, it should be noted that the majority of the samples of participants used in the current research share a common cultural exposure or background. Considerable differences in culture might also be a source of bias given that art development varies across cultures. It is therefore recommended to replicate the current experimental structure to participants with significant differences in cultural exposure, background and language. Fourth, although the participants were told that the experiments involve reception of art to evoke a positive state (as suggested by psychologists) and were constructively asked if they were in a positive state prior to each experiments, there is also a possibility that other internal or unconscious concerns may affect the evaluations of the participants, however, validating the presence of such an element is beyond the scope of the current work. It would also be interesting to see how negative affect can influence the results of the current study. For instance, there are observations that viewers tend to analyze artwork more holistically if the perceiver is in a positive state and more analytically if in a negative mood [16]. Fifth, although evidence suggests that aesthetic response to a stimulus with various presentation duration only marginally differ [20, 29], it may also be possible that immediate aesthetic responses are inaccurate or that automatic and conscious processes do not always lead to the same aesthetic judgment [26]. Finally, further psychometric properties (e.g. test and retest stability) were not included in the current study.

8. CONCLUSION AND FUTURE WORK

In this paper we have investigated that aside from exterior-level properties of a visual stimulus, implicit experiences modulate aesthetic judgment and quality perception. Such implicit experiences interfere with human visual judgment and information processing and therefore, we believe that it is essential to examine the conditions necessary to incorporate this variable in assessing QoE of visual multimedia contents involving aesthetics.

Using three studies, we were able to show that access to prior mental concepts (i.e. implicit experiences), could potentially influence the perceptual quality judgment of an art novice viewer. The absence of prior mental concepts seems to lead to a more critical evaluation of quality than those test conditions that provide prior implicit experiences that could potentially lead to perceptual fluency.

We have also observed a potential relationship between aesthetic performance tasks and QoE evaluations. Our data suggests that higher performance on aesthetic style comparison test leads to a more positive evaluations of perceptual quality.

We have investigated the potential power of implicit experiences as an influential catalyst of perceptual change. The positive result of increasing access to mental concept implies that we should consider re-examining our approaches in traditional empirical evaluations of aesthetic judgment of multimedia to include the potential impacts of implicit experiences. We have also demonstrated that by considering the implications of implicit experiences using the traditional quality measurement, we can come up with a potential approach to predict QoE.

Our next step is to further investigate implicit experience and other modulating factors (e.g. complexity of the stimulus) using various controlled conditions (e.g. effects of the duration of the subjects exposure to the stimuli, the use of verbal, audio and/or other visual mental concepts). We believe that these could lead to a better understanding of empirical aesthetics of multimedia and provide more understanding on how we can recreate or predict real-world conditions involving aesthetic appreciation in a laboratory experiment.

2. ACKNOWLEDGMENTS

This work has been funded by "Centre for Quantifiable Quality in Communication Systems, Centre of Excellence" appointed by Research Council of Norway.

10. REFERENCES

[1] Arnheim, R. (1988). The power of the center. Berkeley, CA: University of California Press.

[2] Bar, M., & Neta, M. (2006). Humans prefer curved visual objects. Psychological Science, 17, 645-648.

[3] Bargh, J.A. & Chartrand, T.L. (2000). The mind in the middle: A practical guide to priming and automaticity research. In H.T. Reis & C.M. Judd (Eds.), Handbook of research methods in social and personality psychology, New York: Cambridge University Press.

[4] Berman, M. G., Jonides, J., & Kaplan, S. (2008). The cognitive benefits of interacting with nature. Psychological Science, 19, 1207-1212.

[5] Bornstein, R. F. (1989). Exposure and affect: Overview and meta-analysis of research, 1968–1987. Psychological Bulletin, 106 (2), 265-289.

[6] Caroll, J.M., & Thomas, J.C.(1988). Fun. SIGCHI Bulletin, 19, 21-24.

[7] Cerosaletti C. D. & Loui A. (2009). Measuring Perceived Aesthetic Quality of Photographic Images. In Proceedings of the First International Workshop on Quality of Multimedia Experience (QoMEX), 47-52.

[8] Cober, R.T., Brown, D.J., Levy, P.E., Cober, A.B., & Keeping, L.M. (2003). Organizational web sites: web site content and style as determinants of organizational attraction. International Journal of Selection and Assessment, 11, 158-169.

[9] Creusen, M., & Snelders, D. (2002). Product appearance and consumer pleasure. In: Green, W.S. &, Jordan, P.W. (Eds.), Pleasure with Products: Beyond Usability. Taylor & Francis, London, 69-75.

[10] Cupchik, G. C. (1992). From perception to production: A multilevel analysis of the aesthetic process. In G. C. Cupchik & J. Laszlo (Eds), Emerging visions of the aesthetic process: Psychology, semiology, and philosophy. New York: Cambridge University Press, 61-81.

[11] Cupchik, G. & Laszlo, J. (1992). Emerging visions of the aesthetic process: Psychology, semiology, and philosophy. New York: Cambridge University Press.

[12] Desimone, R., & Duncan, J. (1995). Neural mechanisms of selective visual attention. Annual Review of Neuroscience, 18, 193-222.

[13] Ebrahimi, T. (2009). Quality of multimedia experience: past, present and future. In Proceedings of the 17th ACM International Conference on Multimedia, 3-4.

[14] Fechner, G.T. (1876). Vorschule der aesthetik. Leipzig, Germany: Breitkoff & Hartel.

[15] Field, D. J., & Brady, N. (1997). Visual sensitivity, blur and the sources of variability in the amplitude spectra of natural scenes. Vision Research, 37, 3367-3383.

[16] Forgas, J.P. (1995). Mood and judgment: The Affect Infusion Model (AIM). Psychological Bulletin, 117, 39-66.

[17] Frohlich, D.M. (2004) 'Beauty as a design prize' Human-Computer Interaction, 19 (4), 359-366.

[18] Gordon, P. C., & Holyoak, K. J. (1983). Implicit learning and generalisation of the 'mere exposure' effect. Journal of Personality and Social Psychology, 45, 492-500.

[19] Hasenfus, C. Martindale, C. & Birnbaum, D. (1983). Psychological reality and cross-media artistic styles. Journal of Experimental Psychology: Human Perception and Performance, 9 (6), 841-863.

[20] Hassenzahl, M. (2004). The interplay of beauty, goodness, and usability in interactive products. Human–Computer Interaction, 19, 319-349.

[21] Hassenzahl, M. & Monk, A. (2010). The Inference of Perceived Usability From Beauty. In Human Computer Interaction, 25 (3), 235-260.

[22] Higgins, E. T. (1996). Knowledge activation: Accessibility, applicability, and salience. In E. T. Higgins & A. Kruglanski (Eds.), Social psychology: Handbook of basic principles New York: Guilford, 133-168.

[23] Jacobsen, T. (2004). Individual and group modelling of aesthetic judgment strategies. British Journal of Psychology, 95, 41-56.

[24] Jacoby, L.L. & Dallas, M. (1981). On the relationship between autobiographical and perceptual learning. Journal of Experimental Psychology: General, 110, 306-340.

[25] Kozbelt, A., & Seeley, W. P. (2007). Integrating art historical, psychological, and neuroscientific explanations of artists' advantages in drawing and perception. Psychology of Aesthetics, Creativity, and the Arts, 1, 80-90.

[26] Leder, H., Belke, B., Oeberst, A., & Augustin, D. (2004). A model of aesthetic appreciation and aesthetic judgments. British Journal of Psychology, 95, 489-508.

[27] Leder, H., Tinio, P. P. L., Fuchs, I. M., & Bohrn, I. (2010). When attractiveness demands longer looks: the effects of situation and gender. Quarterly Journal of Experimental Psychology, 63 (9), 1858-1871.

[28] Li, C. & Chen. T. (2009). Aesthetic visual quality assessment of paintings. IEEE Journal of Selected Topic in Signal Processing, 3 (2), 236-252.

[29] Lindgaard, G., Fernandes, G., Dudek, C., & Brown, J. (2006). Attention web designers: You have 50 milliseconds to make a good first impression! Behaviour & Information Technology, 25, 115-126.

[30] Mandler, G., Nakamura, Y., & Van Zandt, B. J. S. (1987). Nonspecific effects of exposure on stimuli that cannot be recognized. Journal of Experimental Psychology: Learning, Memory, and Cognition, 15, 646-648.

[31] Mansilla, W. A., Perkis A., & Ebrahimi T. (2009). Exposure effect on experience and visual perception in stereoscopic visual presentations. In Proceedings of the 6th International Conference on Advances in Computer Entertainment Technology, 332-335.

[32] Mansilla, W. A., Puig, J., Perkis A., & Ebrahimi T. (2010). Chroma Space: Affective Colours in Interactive 3D World. In Proceedings of the 18th ACM International Conference on Multimedia, 1441-1444.

[33] Martindale, C., Moore, K., & Borkum, J. (1990). Aesthetic preference: Anomalous findings of Berlyne's psychobiological theory. American Journal of Psychology, 103, 53-80.

[34] Moshagen, M., Musch, J., & Goritz, A.S. (2009). A blessing, not a curse: experimental evidence for beneficial effects of visual aesthetics on performance. Ergonomics, 52, 1311-1320.

[35] Norman, D. (2004). Introduction to this special section on beauty, goodness, and usability. Human Computer Interaction, 19 (4), 311-18.

[36] Parboteeah, D.V., Valacich, J.S., & Wells, J.D. (2009). The influence of website characteristics on a consumer's urge to buy impulsively. Information Systems Research, 20, 60–78.

[37] Parsons, M. J. (1987). How we understand art: A cognitive developmental account of aesthetic experience. Cambridge: Cambridge University Press.

[38] Perkis, A., Rahayu, F., Reiter, U., You, J., & Ebrahimi, T. (2010). Quality of experience for high definition presentations Case: Digital Cinema. In High-Quality Visual Experience: Creation, Processing and Interactivity of High-resolution and High-dimensional Video Signals. Springer-Verlag.

[39] Phelps, R. H., & Shanteau, J. (1978). Livestock judges: How much information can an expert use? Organizational Behavior and Human Performance, 21, 209-219.

[40] Pomales-Garcia, C., Liu, Y., & Mendez, D. (2005). Web-based distance learning technology: does appearance matter. In: Human Factors and Ergonomics Society Annual Meeting Proceedings, 755-758.

[41] Popper, Frank (2007). From Technological to Virtual Art. MIT Press, Cambridge, MA, U.S.A.

[42] Reber, R., Schwarz, N., & Winkielman, P. (2004). Processing Fluency and Aesthetic Pleasure: Is Beauty in the Perceiver's Processing Experience? Personality & Social Psychology Review, 8 (4), 364-382.

[43] Reber, R., Winkielman, P., & Schwarz, N. (1998). Effects of perceptual fluency on affective judgments. Psychological Science, 9, 45-48.

[44] Rhodes, G., & Tremewan, T. (1996). Averageness, exaggeration and facial attractiveness. Psychological Science, 7, 105-110.

[45] Schwarz, N., & Clore, G. L. (1996). Feelings and phenomenal experiences. In E. T. Higgins & A. Kruglanski (Eds.), Social psychology: Handbook of basic principles. New York: Guilford, 433- 465.

[46] Silvia, P. J., & Barona, C. M. (2009). Do people prefer curved objects? Angularity, expertise, and aesthetic preference. Empirical Studies in the Arts, 27, 25-42.

[47] Sonderegger, A., & Sauer, J. (2010). The influence of design aesthetics in usability testing: effects on user performance and perceived usability. Applied Ergonomics 41, 403-410.

[48] Srull, T. K., & Wyer, R. S. (1979). The role of category accessibility in the interpretation of information about persons: Some determinants and implications. Journal of Personality and Social Psychology, 37, 1660-1672.

[49] Stapel, D. A. (2003). Making sense of hot cognition: Why and when description influences our feelings and judgments. In J. P Forgas, K. D. Williams, & W. von Hippel (Eds.), Social judgments: Implicit and explicit processes New York: Cambridge University Press, 227-250.

[50] Tractinsky, N., Katz, A.S., & Ikar, D. (2000). What is beautiful is usable. Interacting with Computers ,13, 127–145.

[51] Tractinsky, N., & Lowengart, O. (2007). Web-store aesthetics in e-retailing: a conceptual framework and some theoretical implications. Academy of Marketing Science Review, 11, 1-18.

[52] Tinio, P. P. L., Leder, H., & Strasser, M. (2010). Image quality and the aesthetic judgment of photographs: Contrast, sharpness, and grain teased apart and put together. Psychology of Aesthetics, Creativity, and the Art.

[53] van Schaik, P., & Ling, J. (2009). The role of context in perceptions of the aesthetics of web pages over time. International Journal of Human– Computer Studies, 67, 79-89.

[54] Willems S. & Van der Linden M. (2006). Mere exposure effect: A consequence of direct and indirect fluency-preference links, Consciousness and Cognition, 15, 323–341.

[55] Wilson, A., & Chatterjee, A. (2005). The assessment of preference for balance: Introducing a new test. Empirical Studies of the Arts, 23, 165-180.

[56] You, J., Reiter, U., Hannuksela, M., Gabbouj, & M., Perkis, A. (2010) Perceptual-based Quality Assessment for Audio-visual Services - A Survey. Signal Processing: Image Communication, 25(7), 482-501.

[57] Zajonc, R. B. (1968). Attitudinal effects of mere exposure. Journal of Personality and Social Psychology Monograph Supplements, 9(2), 1-27.

[58] Zajonc, R.B. (1998). Emotions. In: Filbert, D.T., Fiske, S.T. and Lindzey, G. (Eds.). The Handbook of Social Psychology (4th ed.). The Handbook of Social Psychology, 1, 591-632.

Searching the Past: An Improved Shape Descriptor to Retrieve Maya Hieroglyphs *

Edgar Roman-Rangel [1, 2]
eroman@idiap.ch

Carlos Pallan Gayol [3]
pallan.carlos@gmail.com

Jean-Marc Odobez [1, 2]
odobez@idiap.ch

Daniel Gatica-Perez [1, 2]
gatica@idiap.ch

[1] Idiap Research Institute, Martigny, Switzerland
[2] École Polytechnique Fédérale de Lausanne (EPFL), Lausanne, Switzerland
[3] National Institute of Anthropology and History (INAH), Mexico City, Mexico

ABSTRACT

Archaeologists often spend significant time looking at traditional printed catalogs to identify and classify historical images. Our collaborative efforts between archaeologists and multimedia researchers seek to develop a tool to retrieve two specific types of ancient Maya visual information: hieroglyphs and iconographic elements. Towards that goal we present two contributions in this paper. The first one is the introduction and analysis of a new dataset of 3400+ Maya hieroglyphs, whose compilation involved manual search, annotation and segmentation by experts. This dataset presents several challenges for visual description and automatic retrieval as it is rich in complex visual details. The second and main contribution is the in-depth analysis of the Histogram Of Orientation Shape Context (HOOSC), and more precisely, the development of 4 improvements that were designed to handle the visual complexity of Maya hieroglyphs: open contours, mixture of thick and thin lines, hatches, large instance variability, and a variety of internal details. Experiments demonstrate that the adequate combination of our improvements to retrieve Maya hieroglyphs, provides results with roughly 20% more precision compared to the original HOOSC descriptor. Complementary results with the MPEG-7 shape dataset validate (or not) the proposed improvements, showing that the design of appropriate descriptors depends on the nature of the shapes one deals with.

Categories and Subject Descriptors

H.3 [**Information Storage and Retrieval**]: Information Search and Retrieval—*Retrieval models*; I.4 [**Image Processing and Computer Vision**]: Feature Measurement—*Feature representation, size and shape*

*Area chair: David Shamma

MM'11, November 28–December 1, 2011, Scottsdale, Arizona, USA.

General Terms

Algorithms, Experimentation

Keywords

Archaeology, Maya, Image retrieval, Hieroglyphs, Shape

1. INTRODUCTION

One of the many ways in which computer vision and multimedia retrieval can help improve the work of archaeologists and curators is by developing a machine that can rank automatically digital versions of historical materials according to visual similarity. Such a tool will have many positive implications within the realm of Cultural Heritage, starting with a significant decrease in the usual time spent looking manually at traditional printed catalogs (e.g., [16, 28]). This is in particular the case for the understanding of pre-Columbian cultures like the Maya, who developed highly sophisticated writing and counting systems based on hieroglyphs. Our collaborative efforts between archaeologists and multimedia researchers seek to develop tools capable of efficiently retrieving two specific types of highly encoded visual information: namely, Maya hieroglyphs (syllabic and word glyphs) and Maya iconographic elements (Maya art). Specifically on this paper, we deal with a subclass of the Maya hieroglyphic system: that of syllables or syllabographs.

1.1 Our contributions

The first contribution of this paper is the introduction of a new dataset of Maya syllabic hieroglyphs for automatic visual analysis. This dataset has been collected by expert manual identification, annotation, and segmentation of hieroglyphs that appear in Maya inscriptions of the Mexican territory, it has been generated by the National Anthropology and History Institute of Mexico (INAH) through the AJIMAYA project, and it has been complemented with a few glyphs taken from other sources [16, 20, 28]. In total, it comprises 24 positive syllabic classes containing 1200+ glyphs, and other 2100+ examples in a negative class. To the best of our knowledge, this is the largest Maya syllabic dataset ever analyzed with computer vision techniques.

The second and main contribution of this work is the improvement of the Histogram of Orientation Shape Context (HOOSC) [23], a shape descriptor recently proposed to retrieve complex shapes such as Maya hieroglyphs. Similar to traditional shape descriptors like the Shape Context [3] (SC), the HOOSC takes as input a set of points. This robust descriptor combines the log-polar regional segmentation of the Shape Context with a distribution of orientations (HOG-like) description [7], and it has proven to work well in retrieval tasks with small databases in the order of a few hundred glyphs. Our improvements include: 1) a reformulation of the input to be described, going from a set of points sampled from the raw and typically thick contours of the shape, to a set of points taken from thinned versions of them. This addresses the problem of inaccurate description that arises as a consequence of the rough lines often found in Maya hieroglyphs that generate duplicate contours; 2) traditionally, only a subset of points from the input is used in the description to avoid expensive computations, in contrast we propose an efficient way to integrate the complete set of points, leading to more robust descriptors while still avoiding redundancy and high computing cost; 3) we increased the discriminative power of the descriptor by using only the most informative portion of the spatial context; 4) as complement to the implicit position that the HOOSC already features, we included the explicit relative self-position within the global shape of each described point.

We conducted several experiments to validate our improvements on the Maya syllabic dataset. Our results show that their adequate combination results in better retrieval performance, with an increment of approximately 20% of average precision, in comparison with the original HOOSC [23]. Complementary experiments with the MPEG-7 Core Experiment CE-Shape-1 test set [12] allowed us to validate which of the proposed improvements are suitable to describe other shape data sources in function of the nature of the shapes at hand.

1.2 The Maya hieroglyphic source

The pictorial collection we analyze is not a modern construct, it was devised several hundred years ago by a now extinct civilization: the ancient Maya culture. The Maya is generally regarded as the epitome of ancient (pre-industrial) civilizations in the Americas, with many of its achievements comparable to those of the Old-World cultures that developed in Egypt, Greece, Rome, Sumer, and Babylon, to name but a few. Of concern here are the Maya hieroglyphic writing and Maya visual narrative or iconography (a substrate of Maya Art), which are often more sophisticated than its Old-World counterparts.

Roughly outlined, the ancient Maya was one of the several civilizations belonging to a cultural super-area called Mesoamerica, which encompassed the major parts of what are now the countries of Mexico, Guatemala, Honduras, Belize, and El Salvador (see Fig. 1). The Maya culture began to flourish during a chronological period called the Preclassic (c.a., BC 2000 - 250 AD), in a region labeled as the Maya lowlands, which encompassed an area roughly the same size of modern Germany. Although their development was differential according to region and speed, generally speaking, their heyday is regarded to have occurred during the subsequent Classic period (c.a., AD 250 - 900), and it was then when their hieroglyphic writing and the highly encoded iconographic imagery attained the levels of sophistication and consistency that we can rightly regard as a coherent, self-contained visual system, capable of conveying speech and ideas with admirable precision, even when compared

Figure 1: Maya region.

Figure 2: Examples of syllabographs: (a) 'a, and (b) b'a; and logographs: (c) KAB', (d) SUUTZ', and (e) K'AHK'. Images from [16, 28].

with our "new-era" devices for information exchange: e.g., alphabets, syllabaries, graphic conventions, and so forth.

In a nutshell, any ancient script could be defined as a system for the visual recording of information through signs (graphemes) related in some way to the meanings (lexemes) and sounds (phonemes) that conform any given speech [5]. Only briefly, we note here that linguists generally ascribe the Maya writing system to the class of the so-called logosyllabic writing systems, to which a large number of other ancient-world scripts belong, such as the Anatolian from Syria, or the Hiragana from Japan. These writing systems are primarily composed of two distinct categories of signs: syllabographs and logographs. The former are visual signs which encode only specific phonetic value (i.e., phonemes) and almost always comprise a consonant-vowel or single aspirated vowel structure. On the other hand, logographs encode both sound and meaning (roughly equivalent to the notion of "word-signs"), and the vast majority of them have a consonant-vowel-consonant structure, noting that the embedded vowel could be either simple or complex, thus making possible forms like KAB' (earth); SUUTZ' (bat) and K'AHK' (fire). Fig. 2 shows as visual examples 2 syllables and 3 logographs.

Currently, almost 1000 different glyphs (semantic classes) have been identified, including both syllabographs and logographs. However, only 80% have been deciphered and are readable today. Note that these semantic classes might be represented with instances containing high level visual variability, which increments as the temporal and spatial gaps increase. For the purpose of creating an image dataset with the highest applicability for retrieval, and under the logic of a progressing scheme, we decided to focus exclusively on syllabic signs reserving logographs for later stages, going from relative simplicity towards increased complexity, which in future work would ultimately lead to the retrieval of queries performed over Maya iconographic elements. Thus, for the set of glyphs herein presented, we reach 24 classes, relying on their higher frequency of occurrence over other syllabic signs, thus facilitating the labor of manual localization, segmentation, extraction, and annotation by archaeologists; and allowing to have enough material for experimentation.

1.3 Outline

The remaining of this paper is organized as follows. Section 2 highlights some of the most recent related work. Section 3 introduces the novel dataset used in this work. Section 4 describes the HOOSC and presents the improvements we propose. Section 5 describes the protocol we followed to test our method. In section 6 we present and discuss the results. Finally, in section 7 we present our conclusions.

2. RELATED WORK

Retrieval from image and shape representations have been approached in several ways. In [17] local viewpoint-invariant features are computed for specific areas automatically detected, providing robustness to image clutter, partial visibility, occlusion, and changes in viewpoint or lighting conditions. A review of shape representation and retrieval is found in [31], where the authors compare descriptors which mainly differ according to whether they describe contours or regions, and according to the locality scope of the description.

Some works rely on the robust Shape Context descriptor [3] and tackle the resulting set-to-set matching problem using linear programming optimization methods [32]. With similar approach, shapes can be represented by sets of local contour segments organized as trees, and used to perform search of shapes based on a particle filtering framework [15]. Descriptive object shape models can be learned combining long salient bottom-up contours [26], where a latent SVM learning formulation tunes the scores of a many-to-one contour matching approach used to deal with the random fragmentation that might occur in the contours. However, these techniques might not be computationally efficient enough when the set size increases as a consequence of dealing with complex shapes. The generalized version of the Shape Context explored in [18] uses quantized descriptors and local orientation information, which results in faster retrieval implementations and obtains better results than the original SC. In general, modeling objects by bags-of-visterms has proven very efficient [21, 25, 29], even though some issues related to the loss of spatial information arise with this representation. A bag-of-features approach able to retains spatial information has been proposed recently in [6].

Skeletal shape representations have been also studied. In [27], both the geometric and topological information of 3-D objects is combined in the form of a skeletal graph, using graph matching techniques to match and compare skeletons. The shape recognition problem is also approached with a graph matching algorithm in [1], based on object silhouettes where geodesic paths between skeleton endpoints are compared without considering the topological graph structure. Appearance-based object representations of local descriptors are explored in [8, 19, 24] to describe shape images as visual vocabularies of boundary fragments. For instance, in [8] a local segment network representation is used. More recently, shape retrieval has been boosted with graph techniques like local diffusion process [30] and graph transduction [2], achieving very good retrieval results. However, rather than dealing with shapes, these methods focus on retrieval of silhouettes with no internal details, and very often with closed and well defined boundaries.

In the specific field of automatic visual analysis of historical and cultural datasets, the work in [4] investigates how to formulate region-of-interest queries, and perform retrieval with relevance feedback. In [13], a system to retrieve paintings and photos of art objects using content and metadata is presented. Description and retrieval of Chinese characters has been broadly studied. For instance, the work in [14], detects visual patterns and trends in image collections of ancient Chinese paintings, lending to a correct identification of the artist style. In [33], Chinese calligraphy characters are retrieved using contour shapes and interactive partial-distance-map-based high-dimensional indexing that speeds up the performance. Another interesting work in cultural heritage is presented in [10], where artist identification is achieved using wavelets that characterize brushstrokes of several van Gogh paintings.

Finally, with an archaeological approach, a set of rules such as single symmetry axis and morphology is used in [9] to recognize a single polymorphic Mesoamerican symbol by describing its variations as sets of discrete curves. Previous works on description and retrieval of Mayan hieroglyphs achieved competitive results in small datasets up to a few hundreds of glyphs [22, 23]. In particular, in [23] the HOOSC descriptor is proposed and shown to be promising.

3. DATA

The complex manual process commonly followed by archaeologists to obtain digital versions of the hieroglyphs, and the laborious manual search needed to rank them according to visual similarity, are two of the main motivations to conduct this research. We found it relevant to present a brief outline of how the data has been compiled and organized. Namely, the overall process is as follows:

1. At archaeological sites, digital photographs of inscriptions are taken during the night. Instances with variations in the illumination are gathered to achieve high levels of detail (e.g., to study eroded inscriptions).
2. Line drawing are obtained by tracing the inner features of the inscriptions on top of multi-layers photographs.
3. Manual segmentation, search, and identification of hieroglyphs is done consulting existing glyphic catalogs.
4. Experts transcript manually the identified glyphs. i.e., map the phonetic value of each Maya sign into alphabetical conventions.
5. When needed, transliteration is performed to represent ancient Maya speech into modern alphabetic forms.
6. Morphemes and lexemes are obtained through morphological segmentation.
7. Grammatical analysis is done to indicate the function of each of these elements.
8. Finally, the translation of ancient Maya text into a modern target language is achieved, e.g., English.

Figure 3 shows the first and second steps of this process.

Figure 3: First two steps in the collection process.

Table 1: Thompson numbers, visual examples, and sounds for the classes of the Maya syllabic dataset.

T1	T17	T23	T24	T25	T59

/u/	/yi/	/na/	/li/	/ka/	/ti/
T61	T82	T92	T102	T103	T106

/yu/	/li/	/tu/	/ki/	/ta/	/nu/
T110	T116	T117	T126	T136	T173
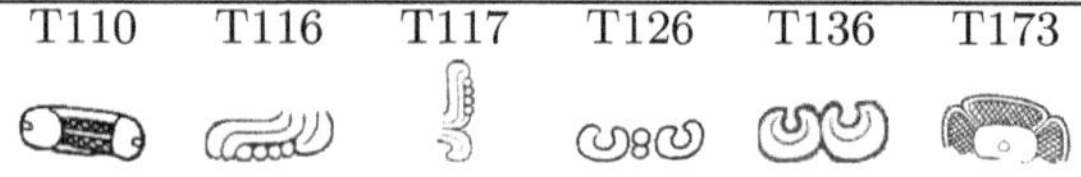					
/ko/	/ni/	/wi/	/ya/	/ji/	/mi/
T178	T181	T229	T501	T534	T671
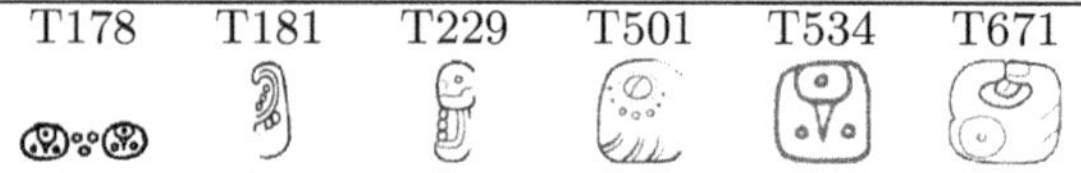					
/la/	/ja/	/'a/	/b'a/	/la/	/chi/

The goal of this work is to improve the third step of this process. To that purpose, we collected a dataset which comprises 1270 Maya glyphs belonging to 24 syllabic classes, plus 2128 extra glyphs that do not correspond to any of the 24 classes and that are grouped in a negative class. The glyphs have been gathered from different archaeological sources, including the AJIMAYA project of INAH, the Macri and Looper syllabic catalog [16]; the Thompson catalog [28]; and the website of the Foundation for the Advancement of Mesoamerican Studies, FAMSI [20]), generating what to our knowledge is the largest dataset of Maya glyphs that has been analyzed with automatic techniques.

As simple as it might sound, this task required non-trivial work of archaeologists expert in Mayan iconography, who spent several months looking manually for the images in complex inscriptions. A dataset like this cannot be produced by non-trained annotators. Table 1 shows one visual example of each positive class, along with their Thompson number which traditionally is used as identifier, and their syllabic value, i.e., their sound. Note that this dataset posits many challenges in terms of visual complexity due to the richness in internal details of its elements, their variability, the fact that some of the classes might be visually similarity, and that conversely some glyphs inside each class might not be as similar as expected in visual terms.

The instances in this dataset correspond to glyphs that often appear in inscriptions from 4 main subregions of the Maya area (Petén, Usumacinta, Motagua, and Yucatán), and the participation of archaeologists in our team helped validating the localization and segmentation of each instance within the inscriptions. Finally, each glyph was manually aligned to the orientation most commonly seen for its class.

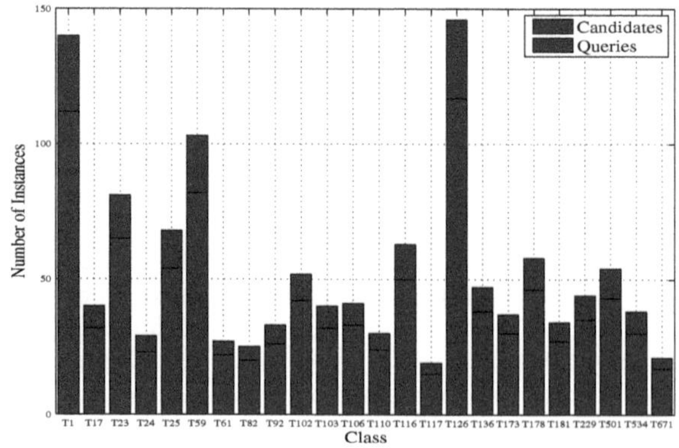

Figure 4: 1270 glyphs distributed over 24 classes.

We divided the dataset into two subsets. Approximately 80% of the glyphs from each class are in the first subset (candidates, denoted by G_C), comprising 1004 instances and leaving the remaining 266 glyphs ($\approx$20%) in the seconds subset (queries, denoted by G_Q). Fig. 4 shows the number of glyphs in each class.

The dataset features many of the complex phenomena presented in Maya glyphs. For instances, the class T534 shown in Table 1 is a "pars pro toto" version of T178 (i.e., a fraction of the original sign containing diagnostic features that account for the whole), both referring to syllable *la*. Since we address the retrieval problem from a visual perspective rather than semantic, and taking advantage of the availability of data, we decided to treat them as two different classes.

The negative class was gathered from the same sources, taking at random as many glyphs as possible. Note that some of the glyphs in this class might be logographs.

4. OUR APPROACH

This section explains the HOOSC descriptor introduced in [23], which is motivated to cope with several drawbacks from the Shape Context (SC) [3] and Generalized Shape Context (GSC) [18] descriptors. This section also explains the approach used to perform retrieval using the HOOSC as shape descriptor. Finally, we present the improvements we propose to the HOOSC.

4.1 HOOSC descriptor

The HOOSC is a robust shape descriptor that combines the log-polar regional formulation of the Shape Context (SC) [3], with a distribution of orientations (HOG-like) description [7]. According to [23], for a given shape whose contours are represented by a set P of N points, a HOOSC descriptor $hoosc_i$ is a vector that describes the point p_i as a function of the distribution of the local orientations of the $N-1$ remaining points.

This descriptor is computed on a log-polar space whose origin ($\theta = 0, \rho = 0$) corresponds to the position of p_i. The remaining points are distributed over 12 angular intervals accounting for a complete perimeter, and 5 distance intervals (that we refer to as *rings*) covering in total as twice as the average pairwise distance between every pair of points in the

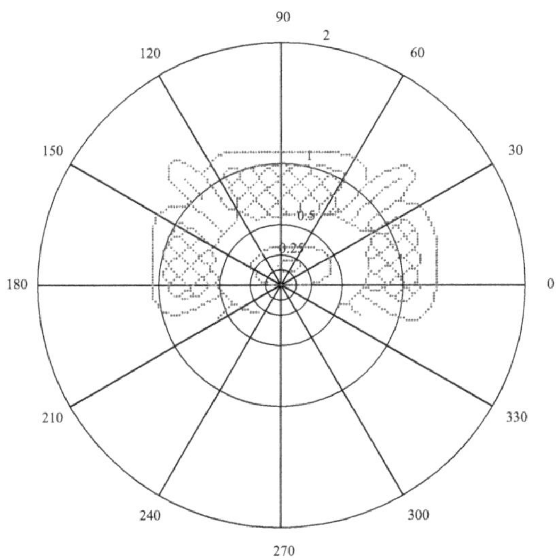

Figure 5: Pivots (red) and points (blue) on the 60 log-polar regions (12 orientations and 5 rings).

shape P, thus resulting in a space of 60 log-polar regions as shown in Fig. 5.

More precisely, let us denote by P_i^r the subset of points falling within the r-th region with respect to the point p_i:

$$P_i^r = \{p_j \in P \colon p_j \neq p_i, (p_j - p_i) \in R_r\}, \quad (1)$$

where $p_j - p_i$ means vector difference, and R_r denotes one of the 60 regions in the log-polar grid indexed by r.

The region R_r is further characterized by a histogram of the local orientations in P_i^r. Since the histogram is encoded with 8 bins, the final $hoosc_i$ descriptor has 480 dimensions [1]. To take into account uncertainty in orientation estimation and to avoid hard binning effects, the distribution of local orientation is calculated through a kernel-based approach for orientation density estimation. More precisely, the density for angle θ in the log-polar region R_r of point p_i, is denoted by $h_i^r(\theta)$,

$$h_i^r(\theta) = \sum_{p_j \in P_i^r} \mathcal{N}\left(\theta; \theta_j, \sigma^2\right), \quad (2)$$

where $\mathcal{N}\left(\theta; \mu, \sigma^2\right)$ is the value at angle θ of a Gaussian of mean μ and variance σ^2 ($\sigma = 10°$ works well in practice). The actual value of the 8-bins orientation histogram in bin $[a, b]$ is obtained by integrating the density $h_i^r(\theta)$ within this interval. Independent normalization of each of the 5 rings is suggested in [23]. The final HOOSC descriptor $hoosc_i$ for point p_i is the concatenation of all the 60 histograms h_i^r after the normalization:

$$hoosc_i = \left[h_i^1, h_i^2, \ldots, h_i^{60}\right]. \quad (3)$$

Note that SC and GSC [3, 18] compute either the number of points in each region or its dominant local orientation, resulting in 60 and 120 dimensional descriptors respectively. However, previous attempts demonstrated that those methods are not as suitable to describe Maya hieroglyphs effectively [22, 23].

[1]Though both log-polar bins and orientation bins are components of histograms, we use the terms region and bins to refer to them respectively.

4.2 Shape retrieval with the HOOSC

Computing the HOOSC descriptor for every point of a given shape can be thought of as describing the shape from different perspectives, which allows for a robust representation of the shape. However, direct comparisons of shapes is difficult because the number of points might differ from one shape to other, and solving the point-to-point correspondence problem is computationally expensive in some cases.

Often, the k-means algorithm is used to quantize the descriptors and build a bag of visual words or visterms (*bov*), such that shapes are more efficiently described. Two shapes can be further compared by simply computing the distance between their respective *bov* [18, 23]. To perform shape retrieval, we rank the *bov* of candidate-shapes according to their L1 similarity with respect to the *bov* of a given query-shape, as proposed in [23].

4.3 Improving the HOOSC descriptor

Several limitations arise as consequences of the HOOSC construction (large dimensionality, redundancy in the description, the need to find a trade off between the number of points for the description and computational efficiency), and the nature of the considered shapes (thick and thin lines, noisy shapes, hatched drawings, instance variability, complex internal details). In the following, we explain four improvements we propose to the HOOSC descriptor that address these limitations and that are key to achieve good retrieval results when dealing with Maya syllabic instances, as shown in section 6.

Thinned contours as input. Computing HOOSC descriptors for a set of points sampled along the raw contours of a shape works well with silhouettes and shapes whose internal details are not of crucial importance. This also performs well when accurate contours can be easily extracted. However, the Maya glyphs often present lines of different degrees of thickness, both along the contours as well as in their internal details. Thus, the use of contour extractors sometimes generates "double" contours as shown in Fig. 6(a), which can result in noisy descriptors and in an increase of intra-class variability.

We propose the use of thinning algorithms [11] to preprocess the binary shapes and estimate thinned versions of their contours, as the one shown in Fig. 6(c). This often provides more input to the HOOSC descriptor.

Pivot points. Instead of computing descriptors for each of the points in the whole input set P, usually only a uniformly sampled subset of points P' is considered in order to make the description computationally efficient [3, 23]. This means that each point p_i' is described using all the other points in P' to compute the HOOSC histograms explained in section 4.1. Fig. 6(b) illustrates in red a subset of points sampled from original set in 6(a). Attention is needed to ensure that P' is large enough to describe the shape in a reliable way.

We propose to compute HOOSC descriptors at each point in the subset P' as a function of *all* the points in the original set P, rather than only on those belonging to P'. The resulting descriptors will be more accurate, yet will remain computationally efficient. We call the points in P' "pivots" to differentiate them from the points in P, which are simply referred to as "points". Fig. 6(d) shows in red the selected pivots from the set of points in 6(c).

Spatial span of the descriptor. As shown in Fig. 5, the most internal regions of the log-polar space usually include

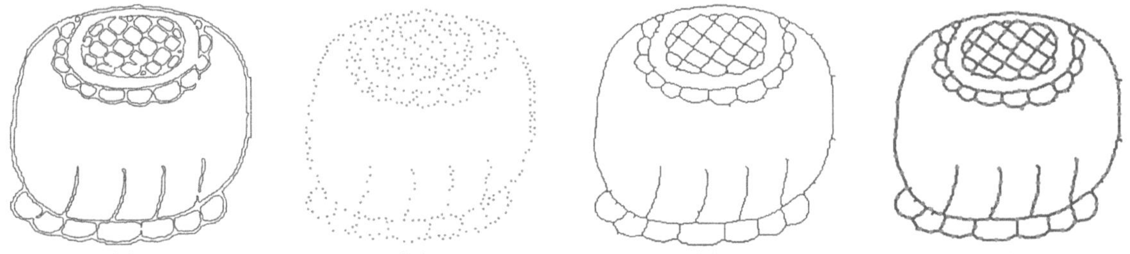
(a) (b) (c) (d)

Figure 6: Different contour extractions and subsampling. (a) from raw contour. (b) subsampling of points from the contours in (a). (c) from thinned contours. (d) the pivots of (c) in red. (Best viewed as pdf).

very few points (sometimes only the point to be described is in those regions). Also very often, many of the external regions are empty or only contain points that are close to the inner boundary of the ring. These two facts might result in several empty or noisy sections of the 480-D HOOSC vector that can affect the representation accuracy.

Since the most discriminative information is found in the intermediate spatial scope of the log-polar space, we use only the 288 dimensions of the descriptor that correspond to rings 2, 3, and 4. This reduces the dimensionality of the vector while improving its discriminative power.

Explicit spatial position. The HOOSC implicitly encodes continuous information about the position of each pivot within the shape, e.g., few observations in the lower regions of the log-polar grid means that the pivot point is located towards the bottom of the image.

The descriptive ability of the HOOSC can be improved further if the position is explicitly incorporated within the descriptor. We concatenate the coordinates (x_i, y_i) of each pivot p'_i, as two additional dimensions in the descriptor, thus representing the relative position within the bounding box encapsulating the glyph, i.e., within the interval [0,1]. With this normalization, the distance between the information explained by the position of two descriptors weights approximately twice the distance between the information contained in each of their rings.

5. EXPERIMENTS

In this section we describe the experimental protocol followed to evaluate the improvements proposed in section 4.

5.1 Evaluated methods

On the syllabic Maya dataset, we evaluated the Generalized Shape Context (GSC) [18] and five different variants of the HOOSC descriptor: HOOSC0 is the original method explained in section 4.1. The HOOSC1 takes as input thinned versions of the shape contours. The HOOSC2 describes the subsampled pivot points with respect to the whole set of points. HOOSC3 trims the log-polar space and only uses intermediate spatial scope (i.e., only rings 2, 3, and 4). Finally in HOOSC4, the relative self-position is explicitly incorporated within the description. As a consequence of the modifications proposed in section 4.3, the vectors named as HOOSC3 and HOOSC4 only have 288 and 290 dimensions respectively, instead of 480 as is the case of the HOOSC0, HOOSC1, and HOOSC2. Table 2 summarizes the differences between the 5 evaluated methods, note that these improvements are key to achieve good retrieval performance.

Table 2: The 5 HOOSC variants evaluated in this paper in the Maya syllabic dataset. Improvements are highlighted in blue.

HOOSC	0	1	2	3	4
Contours	Raw	Thin	Thin	Thin	Thin
Pivots from	Pivots	Pivots	Points	Points	Points
Rings	1:5	1:5	1:5	2:4	2:4
self-position	NO	NO	NO	NO	YES

5.2 Evaluation protocol

We followed [23] to decide the number of pivot points to be described. With GSC and HOOSC0 we use one tenth of the number of points in the original raw contours, constraining it when possible to be at least 100 points, i.e., $max(10\%, 100)$. Sampling from thinned contours usually results in less points than sampling from the double lines generated by the raw contour. To avoid very sparse pivot-sets when sampling from thinned contours, we increased the sampling rate to $max(20\%, 150)$, obtaining on average the same number of pivots per glyph than in the raw contour cases: 161.7 and 169.5 respectively.

From the subset of candidate-glyphs (denoted G_C, see end of section 3), we randomly selected 1500 descriptors (i.e., GSC or HOOSC#) in each of the 24 positive classes, and using k-means clustered them into 2500 visual words. Then, we estimated the *bov* of each glyph in G_C and G_Q, and performed retrieval experiments to evaluate the retrieval precision. Our results are reported as Mean Average Precision (mAP). More precisely, for each method mentioned in Table 2 we implemented the following protocol:

1. Compute the descriptors, (i.e., GSC or HOOSC#).
2. Learn a visual vocabulary, using only descriptors in G_C of the 24 classes. This ensures that the vocabulary does not contain information about the queries in G_Q.
3. Describe every glyph in G_C and G_Q as a *bov* distribution over the resulting vocabulary.
4. Query from G_C using each glyph of G_Q, rank the retrieved vector, and compute the retrieval precision.

Additionally, we repeated the retrieval experiment adding to G_C all the glyphs of the negative class, and representing them by their *bov* computed over the visual vocabulary. This experiment is referred to as "24+1".

5.3 Applicability to other datasets

As already stated, our research is mainly motivated by the current needs of the archaeological community and the

Table 3: HOOSC variants evaluated in the A-MPEG-7 dataset. Improvements are highlighted in blue.

HOOSC	0	5	6	7	4
Contours	Raw	Raw	Raw	Raw	Thin
Pivots from	Pivots	Points	Points	Points	Points
Rings	1:5	1:5	2:4	1:5	2:4
self-position	NO	NO	NO	YES	YES

complexity of the glyphs they need to deal with. That said, to further asses which of our improvements are suitable and beneficial to describe and retrieve shape data of different nature, we conducted experiments on the MPEG-7 Core Experiment CE-Shape-1 test set [12]. This dataset comprises 70 classes of silhouettes with 20 instances each. We divided it randomly at the same rate as the Maya dataset: 80% G_C and 20% G_Q, and repeated the experimental protocol described in section 5.2.

The original HOOSC descriptor was not designed to handle neither rotation nor reflexion since hieroglyphs under this transformation may have different meanings. Thus, we started by manually aliging 283 instances (≈20%) that were either rotated or reflected, and tested the HOOSC variants summarized in Table 3. In our experiments we refer to this version of the data as A-MPEG-7. Later, we tested the best HOOSC variant on the original unaligned MPEG-7 dataset. To handle the rotation issue, we followed the same approach used in [3], where the tangent vector at each pivot is treated as the positive x-axis of the reference log-polar, thus resulting in a theoretical rotation invariant descriptor.

6. RESULTS

We present the results obtained with our improvements on retrieval experiments with the Maya syllabic dataset. We also show results of the generalization of these improvements to retrieve common shapes, i.e., the MPEG-7 dataset.

6.1 Maya syllabic glyphs

The first row of results in Table 4 shows the mean Average Precision (mAP) of each method evaluated using the 24 positive classes. The original method (HOOSC0) obtains a precision 12% higher than the GSC in absolute terms. Changing the input to be thinned contours makes the description more robust and leads to better retrieval results (HOOSC1). The mAP of HOOSC2 shows that taking into account all the points for the description improves the results. We also notice that computing the descriptors at the complete set of points P, does not provide substantial improvements (results not shown). When we trim the HOOSC to only its intermediate distance scope (rings 2, 3, and 4) as in the case of the HOOSC3, the resulting descriptors are shorten while leading to a slightly higher precision. Finally, the explicit addition of the self-position (HOOSC4) allows for a mAP result of 0.532, for a total improvement of almost 20% in absolute terms with respect to the original HOOSC.

The classes might vary in terms of size and visual complexity. We present in Fig. 7 the per-class average precision AP versus the standard recall. These curves correspond to the 5 classes with the highest AP and the 3 with the lowest AP. Although class T117 has very few instances (see Fig. 4), it is the one with highest average precision. This is because it contains unique features that are not shared with any other class, such as its vertical orientation and the circles in the right hand side. Similar trends occur with classes T534 (inverted face), T229 (one circle in a superior section, and some circles in a vertical arrangement on the left hand side), T59 (concentric circles and quasi parallel lines), and T501 (circles and lines in specific internal regions).

Table 4: mAP for the 6 methods evaluated in the Maya dataset: GSC, and HOOSC0 to HOOSC4.

Classes	GSC	HOOSC				
		0	1	2	3	4
24	0.236	0.350	0.422	0.492	0.502	**0.538**
24 + 1	0.195	0.201	0.281	0.341	0.341	**0.374**

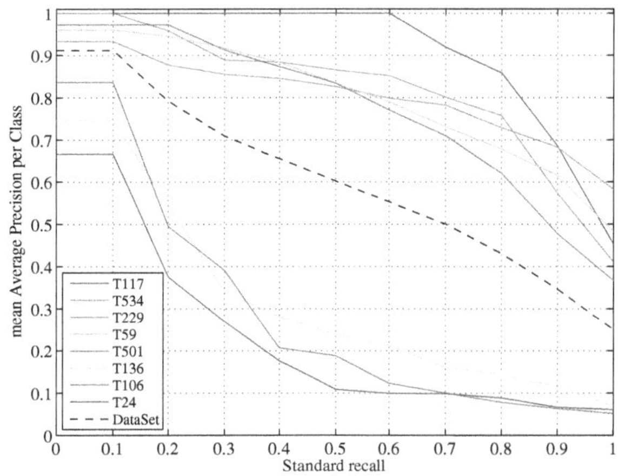

Figure 7: mAP precision vs standard recall for the whole collection (dashed line), plus the corresponding results for the 5 classes with highest average precision and the three with lowest average precision.

The curve of class T136 degrades relatively fast because its instances are often confused with class T126 (Table 5). We observed a similar behavior with class T24 which is confused with classes T1, T17, and T23. In the case of class T106, the high variability among their instances, which could be split into two visual subclasses, results in a relative low precision. Despite the relative low precision for few classes, note that on average the precision is acceptable as shown in the dashed line in Fig. 7, and in the examples of Table 5.

Finally, the second row of results in Table 4 presents the mAP when the 2128 elements in the negative class are incorporated within the pool G_C. Note that the degradation roughly follows the same trend as before, keeping the method with our improvements as the best one in both cases.

6.2 Visual retrieval machine

One of the long term objectives of our research is the implementation of an accurate visual retrieval system for Maya hieroglyphs. This tool will allow archaeologists to quickly search in large corpus for instances of visual queries. Fig. 8 shows an example of the preliminary version of this system. Such a tool, once improved, will ameliorate the amount of time invested by archaeologists in manual searches, and might also help in the training of scholars learning about the Maya writing system. A video illustrating this initial tool is available at http://www.idiap.ch/project/codices/demos.

Table 5: Retrieval results. The first and second columns show the name of each class and one random query, followed by its Top 15 retrieved candidate-glyphs in ascending order from left to right. Relevant glyphs are enclosed in a gray square.

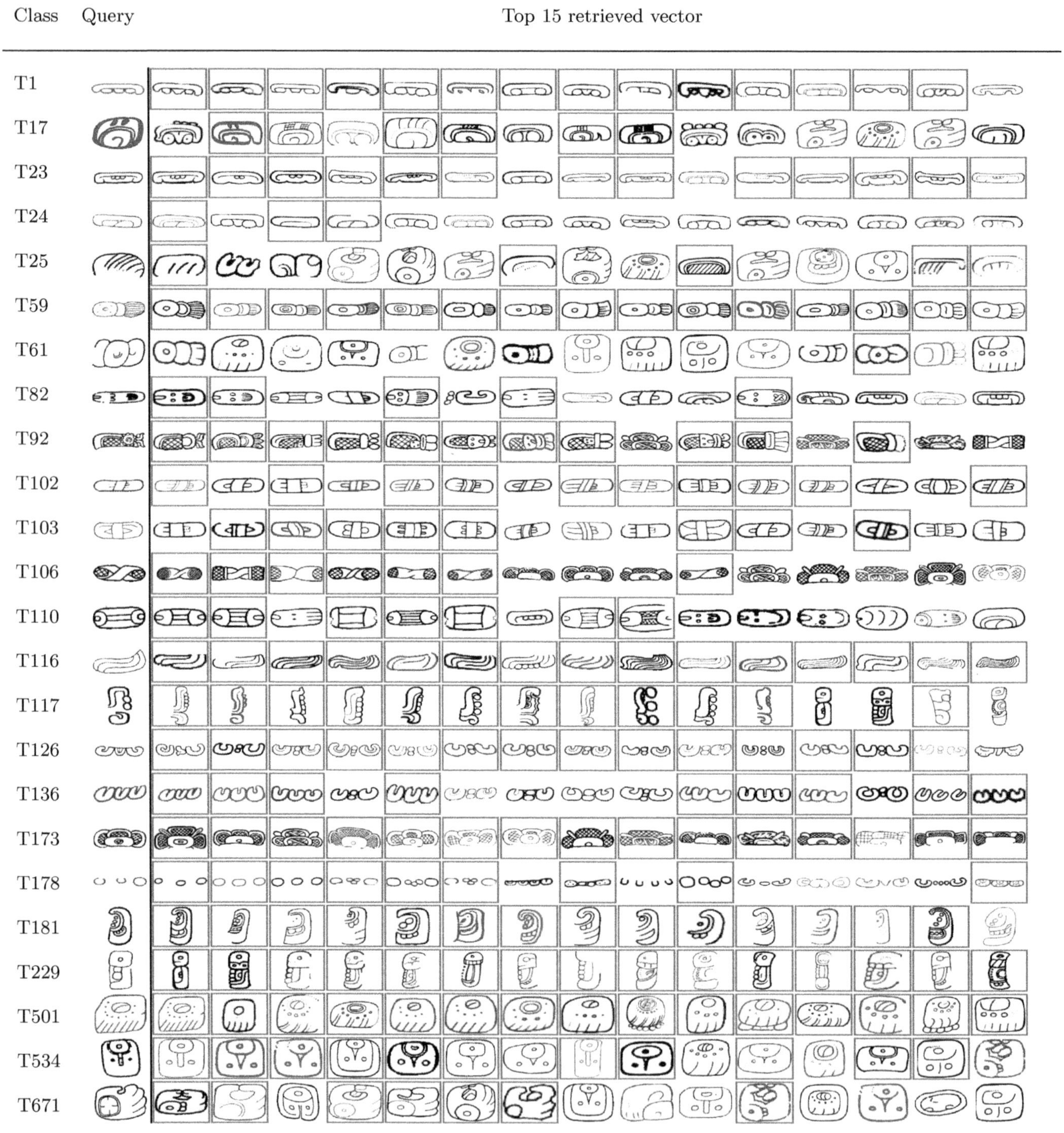

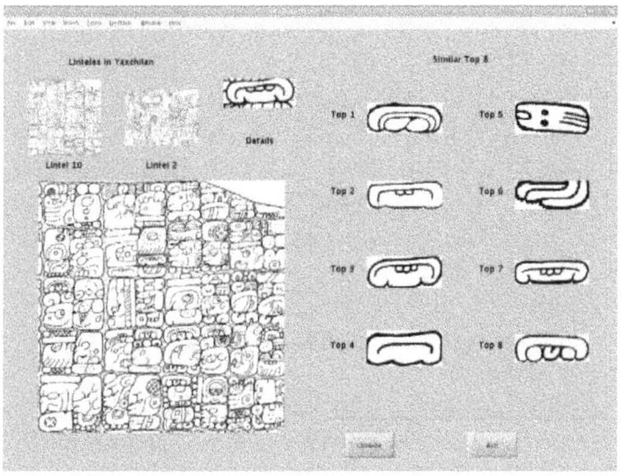

Figure 8: The segmented instances that are most similar to a selected glyph are retrieved from a database (Best viewed as pdf).

Table 6: *mAP* and *bes* for the methods evaluated in the A-MPEG-7 dataset.

Classes	GSC	HOOSC				
		0	4	5	6	7
mAP	0.813	0.848	0.790	0.852	0.849	**0.867**
bes	0.882	0.905	0.848	0.908	0.906	**0.918**

6.3 Results on the MPEG-7 dataset

Previous methods tested on this dataset for retrieval tasks are compared via the *Bull's eye* score (*bes*) [2], we present our results in terms of both *mAP* and *bes*. Table 6 shows the results for the GSC and the evaluated variants of the HOOSC on the A-MPEG-7 dataset.

The HOOSC4 which uses our 4 improvements and that works the best with the Maya hieroglyphs does not perform as well with the MPEG-7 dataset. The reason is due to two factors: a) as these shapes are dominantly filled and clean convex silhouettes with very well defined boundaries, the morphological thinning transformation results in a loss of information and in descriptors with lower discriminative power. For these shapes, directly sampling the descriptors from the raw contours produces better results as shown with the HOOSC5 to HOOSC7 in table 6; b) unlike to the Maya hieroglyphs, where using the 5 *rings* (the whole spatial scope) adds noise to the description, using the 5 *rings* with the MPEG-7 silhouettes does not harm the description and the retrieval performance remains competitive as shown by HOOSC5 and HOOSC6. We can see that computing descriptors at pivots with respect to the whole set of points, and incorporating the relative self-position in the descriptor provide good results (HOOSC7).

Finally as explained in section 5.3, we incorporated robustness to rotation and experimented with the original unaligned shape instances achieving results of 0.733 of *mAP* and 0.811 of *bes* with the HOOSC7. Examples of this experiment are shown in Table 7, we can see that while rotated instances are well retrieved, the HOOSC is not robust to reflected shapes yet. It is important to mention that the quality of the hieroglyphs varies drastically due to the nature of the documents from which they are extracted. Thus, some improvements of the HOOSC descriptor (thinning and using only rings 2, 3, 4) are specifically designed to deal with noise (e.g., due compression). In contrast, the MPEG-7 shape dataset is cleaner.

Table 7: 15 queries randomly chosen from the MPEG-7 dataset and their corresponding Top 7 retrieved candidates via the HOOSC7 method.

Query	Top						
	1	2	3	4	5	6	7

7. CONCLUSIONS

We compiled a large set of Maya glyphs that comprises 3400+ instances distributed over 24 positive and 1 negative classes. This dataset presents several challenges for automatic visual description, and to the best of our knowledge is the largest one that has been analyzed with automatic tools.

We analyzed the Histogram Of Orientation Shape Context (HOOSC) descriptor with a set of retrieval experiments of Maya hieroglyphs. We proposed four improvements to the descriptor that achieve roughly 20% absolute improvement in terms of retrieval precision compared to the original HOOSC. Overall, our results demonstrate that relevant elements are retrieved first for most of the cases, and that only a few of them fail, either because of their intra-class variability or because of the high visual similarity across some classes. To validate the generalization of our improvements, we evaluated them on a general shape dataset, the MPEG-7 dataset. We found that two out of these four improvements proposed to describe complex shapes are also suitable to describe convex and clean silhouettes. Although the HOOSC was not designed to handle rotations, we found that this feature is easy to incorporate. Future work is still required to provide the HOOSC with robustness against reflection.

Overall, we believe that the proposed descriptor is suitable for general shapes and that it will be able to handle other shape datasets, to the condition that the right combinations of the options presented here is used, depending on the target shapes. We expect that our methodology will eventually be implemented into real systems to support queries of scholars in Maya archaeology and that, in the long term, it will be suitable for interaction with general audiences like museum visitors.

8. ACKNOWLEDGMENTS

We thank the support of the Swiss National Science Foundation through the CODICES project, of INAH through the AJIMAYA project, and of the European Network of Excellence PASCAL2 through student travel funds.

9. REFERENCES

[1] X. Bai and L. J. Latecki. Path Similarity Skeleton Graph Matching. *IEEE Trans. PAMI*, 30(7):1282–1292. 2008.

[2] X. Bai, X. Yang, L. J. Latecki, W. Liu, and Z. Tu. Learning Context-Sensitive Shape Similarity by Graph Transduction. *IEEE Trans. PAMI*, 32(5):861–874. 2010.

[3] S. Belongie, J. Malik, and J. Puzicha. Shape Matching and Object Recognition Using Shape Contexts. *IEEE Trans. PAMI*, 24(4):509–522. 2002.

[4] N. Boujemaa, V. Gouet, and M. Ferecatua. Approximate Search vs. Precise Search by Visual Content in Cultural Heritage Image Databases. *Proc. MIR Workshop ACM-MM*. 2002.

[5] J. K. Browder. Place of the High Painted Walls: The Tepantitla murals and the Teotihuacan writing system. PhD thesis. University of California. 2005.

[6] Y. Cao, C. Wang, Z. Li, L. Zhang, and L. Z. Spatial-bag-of-features. *Proc. IEEE CVPR*. 2010.

[7] N. Dalal and B. Triggs. Histograms of Oriented Gradients for Human Detection. *Proc. IEEE CVPR*. 2005.

[8] V. Ferrari, L. Fevrier, F. Jurie, and C. Schmid. Groups of Adjacent Contours for Object Detection. *IEEE Trans. PAMI*, 30(1):36–51. 2008.

[9] Y. Frauel, O. Quesada, and E. Bribiesca. Detection of a Polymorphic Mesoamerican Symbol Using a Rule-based Approach. *Pattern Recognition*, 39(7):1380–1390. 2006.

[10] C. R. Johnson, E. Hendriks, I. Berezhnoy, E. Brevdo, S. Hughes, I. Daubechies, J. Li, E. Postma, and J. Z. Wang. Image Processing for Artist Identification - Computerized Analysis of Vincent van Gogh's Painting Brushstrokes. *IEEE Signal Processing Magazine, Special Issue on Visual Cultural Heritage*, 25(4):37–48. 2008.

[11] L. Lam, S.-W. Lee, and C. Y. Suen. Thinning Methodologies a Comprehensive Survey. *IEEE Trans. PAMI*, 14(9):869–885. 1992.

[12] L. J. Latecki, R. Lakamper, and T. Eckhardt. Shape Descriptors for Non-rigid Shapes with a Single Closed Contour. *Proc. IEEE CVPR*. 2000.

[13] P. H. Lewis, K. Martinez, F. S. Abas, M. F. A. Fauzi, S. C. Y. Chan, M. Addis, M. J. Boniface, P. Grimwood, A. Stevenson, C. Lahanier, and J. Stevenson. An Integrated Content and Metadata Based Retrieval System for Art. *IEEE Trans. Image Processing*, 13(3):302–313. 2004.

[14] J. Li and J. Z. Wang. Studying Digital Imagery of Ancient Paintings by Mixtures of Stochastic Models. *IEEE Trans. Image Processing*, 13(3):340–353. 2003.

[15] C. Lu, L. J. Latecki, N. Adluru, X. Yang, and H. Ling. Shape Guided Contour Grouping with Particle Filters. *Proc. IEEE ICCV*. 2009.

[16] M. Macri and M. Looper. The New Catalog of Maya Hieroglyphs. Vol. 1 The Classic Period Inscriptions. University of Oklahoma Press : Norman. 2003.

[17] K. Mikolajczyk and C. Schmid. Scale and Affine Interest Point Detectors. *IJCV*, 60(1):63–86. 2004.

[18] G. Mori, S. Belongie, and J. Malik. Efficient Shape Matching Using Shape Contexts. *IEEE Trans. PAMI*, 27(11):1832–1837. 2005.

[19] A. Opelt, A. Pinz, and A. Zisserman. A Boundary-fragment Model for Object Detection. *Proc. ECCV*. 2006.

[20] M. Pitts and L. Matson. Writing in Maya Glyphs. Foundation for the Advancement of Mesoamerican Studies, Inc. 2008.

[21] P. Quelhas, F. Monay, J. M. Odobez, D. Gatica-Perez, T. Tuytelaars, and L. V. Gool. Modeling Scenes with Local Descriptors and Latent Aspects. *Proc. IEEE ICCV*. 2005.

[22] E. Roman-Rangel, C. Pallan, J.-M. Odobez, and D. Gatica-Perez. Retrieving ancient maya glyphs with shape context. *Proc. IEEE ICCV, Workshop on eHeritage and Digital Art Preservation*. 2009.

[23] E. Roman-Rangel, C. Pallan, J.-M. Odobez, and D. Gatica-Perez. Analyzing Ancient Maya Glyph Collections with Contextual Shape Descriptors. *IJCV, Special Issue in Cultural Heritage and Art Preservation*, 94(1):101âĂŞ117. 2011.

[24] J. Shotton, A. Blake, and R. Cippola. Contour-based Learning for Object Detection. *Proc. IEEE ICCV*. 2005.

[25] J. Sivic and A. Zisserman. Video Google: A Text Retrieval Approach to Object Matching in Videos. *Proc. IEEE ICCV*. 2003.

[26] P. Srinivasan, Q. Zhu, and J. Shi. Many-to-one Contour Matching for Describing and Discriminating Object Shape. *Proc. IEEE CVPR*. 2010.

[27] H. Sundar, D. Silver, N. Gagvani, and S. Dickinson. Skeleton Based Shape Matching and Retrieval. *Proc. IEEE International Conference on Shape Modeling and Applications*. 2003.

[28] J. E. S. Thompson. A Catalog of Maya Hieroglyphs. University of Oklahoma Press : Norman. 1962.

[29] J. Willamowski, D. Arregui, G. Csurka, C. R. Dance, and L. Fan. Categorizing Nine Visual Classes Using Local Appearance Descriptors. *Proc. ICPR, Workshop on Learning for Adaptable Visual Systems*. 2004.

[30] X. Yang, S. Koknar-Tezel, and L. J. Latecki. Locally Constrained Diffusion Process on Locally Densified Distance Spaces with Applications to Shape Retrieval. *Proc. IEEE CVPR*. 2009.

[31] D. Zhang and G. Lu. Review of Shape Representation and Description Techniques. *Pattern Recognition*, 37(1):1–19. 2004.

[32] Q. Zhu, L. Wang, Y. Wu, and J. Shi. Contour Context Selection for Object Detection: A set-to-set Contour Matching Approach. *Proc. ECCV*. 2008.

[33] Y. Zhuang, Y. Zhuang, Q. Li, and L. Chen. Interactive High-dimensional Index for Large Chinese Calligraphic Character Databases. *ACM TALIP*, 6(2). 2007.

Shedding Light on Shadow: Real-time Interactive Artworks based on Cast Shadows or Silhouettes*

Christian Jacquemin
LIMSI-CNRS
& Univ. Paris-Sud
91400 Orsay, France
christian.jacquemin@limsi.fr

Georges Gagneré
Didascalie.net
1 rue Duvergier
75019 Paris, France
gg@didascalie.net

Benoit Lahoz
L'ange Carasuelo
9 chemin du Trou Samson
95150 Taverny, France
benoit.lahoz@carasuelo.org

ABSTRACT

Digital shadowing is a source of interest in immersive and interactive artworks because it enhances the feeling of presence, and because it is a very intuitive and engaging interaction "device". After a presentation of some major pieces in shadow-based artwork along two categories (silhouette-based digital shadows and cast shadow-based digital shadows), we propose a real-time software platform that can produce these two types of shadows from video capture and image processing. The processing is divided into image analysis for shadow extraction, calibration, and special effects. It is made highly flexible and parameterized, so that it can fit various configurations. Two specific configurations are illustrated because of their genericity: one for infrared light silhouette-based shadow and live performance, and one for both digital shadowing categories and interactive art installations with visible light. We then present some of the applications of such a platform through various live performances made by two theater companies involved in a collaborative project with scientists. The examples confirm the wide variety of scenographic setups in which shadow can be involved as a key component.

Categories and Subject Descriptors

H.5.1 [Information Systems]: Information Interfaces and Presentation—Multimedia Information Systems; Artificial, Augmented, and Virtual Realities; J.5 [Arts and Humanities]: Performing Arts (e.g. dance, music)

General Terms

Algorithms, Design, Experimentation, Human Factors

Keywords

Augmented Reality, Real-time Image Processing, Digital Art, Digital Shadow, Video-scenography, Interactive art

*Area chair: Aisling Kelliher

MM'11, November 28–December 1, 2011, Scottsdale, Arizona, USA.

1. INTRODUCTION

Shadow is a recurring theme in arts, literature, and philosophy since the Antiquity and Plato's "Cave" where cast shadows symbolize the limited perception of the world by its prisoners. Shadows in the visual arts have mainly appeared since the Renaissance through early perspective artworks. They were used to enhance the 3D perception of the scenes, and made light sources explicit. For this reason, perspective and shadows can be considered as early attempts to render artworks immersive by giving the user a feeling of "being there". In addition to immersion and perspective perception, shadows were also used to give a sense of volume through shading. When combined with the real world, as in the case of Masaccio's fresco "Tribute Money" in Santa Maria del Carmine (Florence), the light source of the artwork could be purposely chosen to coincide with a physical light source in the church, thus making this type of artwork an example of early Augmented Reality. Last, shadows have also be used for their symbolic meaning, representing evilness and hidden dark sides of humanity.

For similar purposes of immersion and augmentation of the real world, shadows can also be found in contemporary visual artworks, and we are mostly interested in interactive digital arts in which video-projection reveals and highlights shadows through "digital shadows". Since this domain is made up of a wide variety of works, and since the technological setups are quite diverse and rarely documented, our purpose in this article is to offer a synthetic and cohesive artistic analysis of recent digital works that refer to shadows, together with an accurate description of our technological platform for developing shadow-based artworks. To our knowledge, this is the first attempt to unify a body of works that have played a significant role in the recent developments of digital arts. This article intends to cover both the descriptive and analytical artistic sides, and to address both the technological and scientific issues raised by that type of work.

In Section 2, we present interactive digital works that use virtual shadow as a major component of the installation. These works are subdivided into two categories depending on the input used to produce the virtual shadow, whether cast shadow or silhouette. Section 3 describes two combinations for the relative positioning of a video-projector, a camera, and a light source together with a platform developed for the implementation of virtual shadow-based real-time interactive artworks. Last, in Section 4, several virtual shadowing installations and performances based on the platform are described and analyzed together with their applications in social and educative activities.

2. DIGITAL SHADOW ARTWORKS

Interactive artworks based on shadow offer an augmented visualization of the physical world through the addition of a digital shadow. Because of this configuration, all these works can be classified as Augmented Reality installations in which the physical world is overlaid with digital information, here the video-projected augmented shadow. We define two categories of shadow-based artworks depending on the source of the digital shadow: Cast Shadow-Based Shadow (CSBS) artworks for a physical shadow generally combined with video-projection, or Silhouette-Based Shadow (SBS) artworks for digital shadow built from a silhouette capture (see Figure 1).

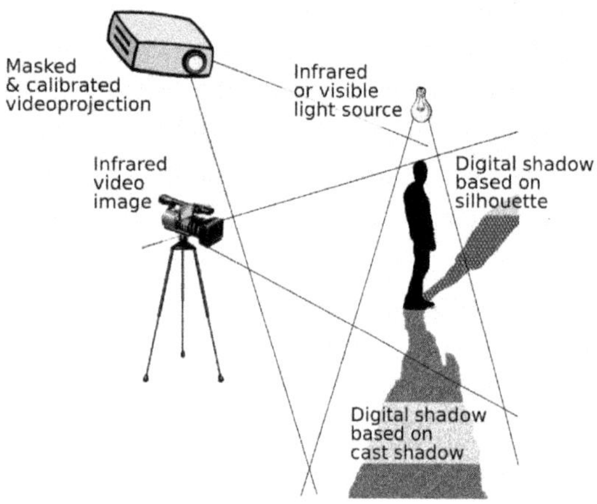

Figure 1: Cast Shadow-Based Shadow (CSBS) through physical light occlusion, and Silhouette-Based Shadow (SBS) through silhouette projection.

The first category, CSBS artworks use a physical light shadow as a basis of the visualization, and therefore rely on the extraction of the visible or non-visible shadow cast by an occluder (the onlooker) with respect to a visible or an infrared (IR) light source. In these works the digital shadow is produced from the capture of a cast shadow, and the digital shadow must be accurately registered with the cast shadow it originates from. If the light source is in the visible range, the overlaid digital shadow must fill accurately the dark area of the cast shadow with video-projected light. In the case of IR lighting, the digital shadow reveals the invisible shadow through video-projection.

The second category, SBS artworks, is based on the extraction of the onlookers' silhouette and its digital conversion into a virtual cast shadow with no corresponding physical light source. Since the virtual shadow is video-projected, it is generally brighter than the background contrary to a digital shadow based on cast shadow that is projected into a dark area. For SBS artworks, registration is less critical than for CSBS works since there is no physical shadow it has to be aligned with. The criteria for alignment in SBS are mainly perceptual: the onlooker has to be convinced that the shadow is really hers. The belief in the virtual shadow by actors does not depend solely on visual clues, but mainly results from the correspondence between their own movements and the perceived shadow motions. At the visual level, two main constraints exist however: the feet of the shadow should be located at the user's feet, and the orientation of the shadow should correspond to the shadow that would be cast if the camera was replaced by a light source. At the behavior level, the time delay between the shadow capture and the virtual shadow display should be short enough to make the actor perceive that her own gestures are synchronized with the shadow movements. We will return to these issues in Section 4 when examining digital shadow-based artworks. SBS and IR lit CSBS artworks can be confused because of the invisibility of the physical IR-light cast shadow in CSBS.

2.1 Cast Shadow-Based Shadow (CSBS) Artworks

Our interest in shadow-based artwork started when working on video-scenography rehearsals for a theater play in which one of the spotlights was partially masked by a grid-shaped gobo[1]. Instead of considering video-projection and spot-lighting as two conflicting entities, we were exploring various mixes of these two types of light such as blending the video-projection with a dimmed colored spotlight. When using the gobo, we came to the idea of video-projecting inside the shadows of the gobo. For this purpose, we took a picture of the partially shadowed stage from the video-projector location. Through a quick thresholding and calibration procedure, this picture was then converted into a black and white bitmap and used to mask the video-projection in the lit parts of the stage so that it would only be visible in the shadows of the gobo. Masking and calibration were approximate, but the inaccuracies of these processes instead of harming the visual rendering, provided the spectators with a nice feeling of depth and volume. Later we decided to rework this setup in an interactive manner by analyzing a live video image, extracting automatically the dark zones, and using them as masks for the video-projection. This is one of the purposes of the platform presented in Section 3.

Cast shadow has been used in several artworks to reveal a "hidden" image that can only be perceived under specific conditions of lighting (a unique and accurately located point source) and shadowing (on a plane projection surface). For example, Tim Noble and Sue Webster[2] build sculptures out of garbage or familiar objects to reveal images that transcend the reality of these objects by showing unexpected shadow shapes such as a portrait or a sitting couple. These works reverse the traditional meaning of shadow that represents dark impulses or irrationality.

CSBS works draw their effects from the additive properties of emitted light. In the case of a single light source, the light intensity in a shadowed zone is weaker than in the neighboring lit zone. For very powerful light sources, the darkness of shadowed zones can be used to reveal video-projection that is too dimmed to be perceived in the lit zone (e.g. "Body movies" by Lozano-Hemmer mentioned below). For the case of two or more light sources, CSBS works can reveal video-images that are only visible if only one of the light sources is received. In "Movie-in-Shadow" [9], two video-projected images with complementary colors are accurately superimposed so that the resulting image is a uniform

[1] A "gobo" is a piece of metal with shaped holes that is placed in front of the spotlight and produces a pattern of light.
[2] http://www.timnobleandsuewebster.com/

white color. By occluding one of the two light sources, the passers-by reveal the complementary image inside their cast shadows. A similar revelation process is offered by Rafael Lozano-Hemmer in "Body Movies"[3] by showing video images inside the cast shadows of the passers-by. These shadows are projected at various scales depending on the distance of the onlookers that are blocking the light of the spotlights. The variety in shape and scale of the silhouettes is combined with the video stream into a single fantastic scene.

Cast shadows can also be used in a playful way as a complementary graphical element to sculpture, whether static or in motion. Kumiya Mashita[4] and Fred Eerdekens[5] both use a light spot that projects a single and clear cast shadow of a sculpture on a wall. The shadow reveals shapes of the sculpture that cannot be seen from the normal onlookers position, and combines them with the visible shapes of the sculpture into a coherent and puzzling artwork. Closer to the topic of our research, even though it has no digital process, the "Night Shadow Project" by Michael Neff[6] consists in outlining the shadows cast by public lighting at night. It has in common with our work to augment the cast shadow (graphically in his work and digitally in our approach), and to leave a trace of a light effect even when the conditions have changed (through painting in his work, and through graphical feedback in ours).

All the CSBS artworks we have presented so far do not make use of digital shadowing techniques, but rely instead on a visible light shadow. On the contrary, the artworks presented in the next sub-section (2.2) are based on digital shadows obtained through the video capture and extraction of the silhouette. To our knowledge, these works represent the mainstream approach to digital shadowing even though it can also be based on cast shadow capture. The interesting feature of CSBS artworks is that they can result in the complementary association of video-projection light with spotlights or natural lights. Our hybrid platform described in Section 3 can process both CSBS and SBS setups.

2.2 Silhouette-Based Shadow (SBS) Artworks

"Shadow Play" is an Asian traditional form of theater that spread through Europe at the 18th Century and known in France as "Ombres Chinoises" (Chinese Shadows). Whereas originally designed for articulated flat puppets, Shadow Play has since been extended to whole or partial human body animations. The basic setup consists in using a strong and horizontal light beam to project the silhouette of the puppets or performers on a semi-opaque surface. This traditional form of theater has been retargeted to digital art by capturing the video image of a silhouette and using it as a mask for synthesizing a virtual shadow through video-projection.

The SBS digital artworks can be roughly divided into two categories depending on whether the virtual shadow is used as an interactor or as a visual and aesthetic component in the installation. The reason for using a silhouette-based shadow as an interactor, is to "simplify" the onlooker's presence in the installation by turning her into a legible and simple black shape. The silhouette keeps enough similarity with the body to make interaction transparent and intuitive, while it avoids clutterring up the visual rendering of the work with a realistic view of the user. In such installations, it is generally the border of the silhouette that serves as an interactor.

A pioneering use of the SBS setup is "Videoplace" created by Myron Krueger in 1977. Originally designed as a responsive environment, this artwork developed "the basis for a new aesthetic medium based on real-time interaction between men and machines" [6]. The performer invited to play in "Videoplace" was interacting with the computer-generated images through her SBS shadow. The innovation in "Videoplace" was to consider interacting through the user's shadow as the main artistic issue in this environment, upstaging the visual rendering accordingly. Despite such early shadow-based approaches to interaction, there remains numerous possibilities and future exciting artworks that can certainly further this line of artistic research, such as David Rokeby's "Silicon Remembers Carbon"[7].

Some of the most representative examples of SBS installations are Zachary Booth Simpson's "Mine-Control"[8] works. In his works, the silhouette contour is used as an obstacle to control a flow, the bouncing of a ball, the motion of an animal and the waves on a surface. In his article [8], Golan Levin quotes several digital artworks controlled by hand and arm shadows, including his own work "Messa di Vocce"[9] (in collaboration with Zach Lieberman, Jaap Blonk, and Joan La Barbara), in which silhouette is used to generate visual elements combined with voice analysis.

The SBS artworks that exploit shadow as an aesthetic component generally do not assign a specific interactive function to the user's shadow projection. The shadow can be taken as it is, as a schematic and yet recognizable trace of a presence. Such SBS digital artworks are the ones closest to the ancestral form of shadow play. Scott Snibbe's "Outward Mosaic"[10] collects onlookers' animated shadows into a live and refined gallery of multi-scale loop videos of shadows. The control relationship between the user and her shadow is reversed when the shadow appearance is modified by the user's behavior. In Philip Worthington's "Shadow Monsters"[11] hand shadows are turned into monster's head profiles through the addition of frightening graphical elements.

Live performance has also a strong interest in introducing shadows on stage for various scenographic purposes. For example in Philippe Decouflé's "Sombrero"[12] ballet, shadow is used for scale effects or mirror behaviors. A wide range of shadow-based scenery effects are also presented in Chunky Move's "Mortal Engine" dance performance. These effects combine music- and gesture-controlled generative graphics with silhouette capture to immerse the dancer's shadow into a flow of hypnotic visual effects.

By altering the behavior of the shadow and introducing discrepancies between the shadow appearance and the human body that produces it, the pseudo-shadow is likely to question our presence to the world. Zachary Booth Simpson's "Shadow"[13] with Adam Frank presents a virtual shadow

[3]http://www.lozano-hemmer.com/body_movies.php
[4]http://kumiyamashita.com
[5]http://www.fred-eerdekens.be/
[6]http://michaelneff.com/
[7]http://homepage.mac.com/davidrokeby/src.html
[8]http://www.mine-control.com/
[9]http://www.flong.com/projects/messa/
[10]http://www.snibbe.com/projects/interactive/
[11]http://www.worthersoriginal.com/viki/
[12]http://www.culturekiosque.com/dance/-reviews/decoufle_sombrero.html
[13]http://www.mine-control.com/shadow.html

that has no physical cause, and that reacts to and combines with the onlooker's own cast shadows. Similarly, "Digital Shadow"[14] by Alessandro Corsini and colleagues introduces so-called rebellious shadows that quit their mirror behavior to switch to unexpected motions corresponding to previous recordings of the same silhouette. We will present similar investigations in Section 4 for live performance with children, teen-agers, and young disabled adults.

Last, shadow can also be used in artworks as a medium between the real world and a virtual one. In the "Abstract"[15] installation by Joëlle Bitton, visitors are invited to a meditation Japanese garden world by discovering it through their transparent shadows. In the Augmented Virtuality installation "Gate 3.5"[16] by Bertrand Planes, the onlookers have their shadow projected inside a 3D virtual world. In addition to enhancing their feeling of presence in the virtual world, the shadow also serves the purpose of a kind of "non-tactile" contact with the virtual world, and a discovery of its geometry through virtual shadow-based exploration.

3. PLATFORM FOR SHADOW-BASED INSTALLATIONS

This section describes a generic platform for shadow and silhouette extraction, and its use for various output effects through image synthesis. The input to this software is an IR monochromatic image that possibly contains both a silhouette and its cast shadow. The output is one or two virtual shadows rendered from one or both of them.

The setup for experimenting with shadows is presented in Figure 2. It shows the most complex case with two types of cast shadows: the blocking of the video-projector light and the blocking of the spotlight (visible or IR light). The video-projector light shadowing is considered as an uninteresting parasite shadow. We therefore focus only on the cast shadow that results from blocking the light emitted by the light-spot. In the case of visible light, the digital shadow must be calibrated to the physical shadow. The setup for digital shadowing offers a wide variety of combinations that have been studied exhaustively by Chan and Gagneré [4]. They mostly depend on the relative positions of the user, the camera, the video-projector, the spotlight, and the "screen". We only focus on two emblematic and illustrative ones; they are illustrated by Figures 3 and 4.

First, Figure 3 shows a top view of a configuration dedicated to SBS that has been investigated by the theater companies involved in the project and in this article. In this configuration, a translucent screen is located behind the performer and receives both the video-projection and a powerful IR light so that the performer's silhouette can be easily extracted from the lit background. Rear video-projection avoids the performer's occlusion of the video-projector light that otherwise can occur in front projection. This configuration is well-suited for live performance because the shadow is clearly visible for the audience, and does not require complex calibration procedures. It has been used in several performances and educational activities with children by the theater companies. They are presented in Section 4.

Second, the configuration shown in Figure 4 has only been exploited in the laboratory work for tuning up the platform. This second configuration relies on image analysis for the extraction of physical cast shadow.

[14]http://www.digitale-medien-bremen.de/

[15]http://www.superficiel.org/joelle/art/pages/abstract.htm

[16]http://www.bertrandplanes.com/-pages/Gate35%20Panorama.php

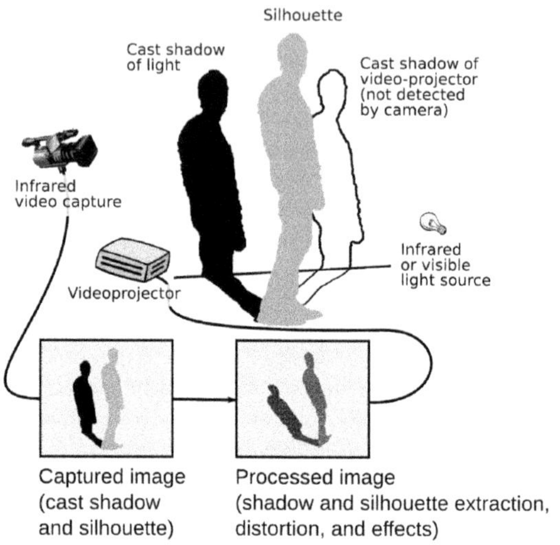

Figure 2: Image input/output in the platform for shadow-based works.

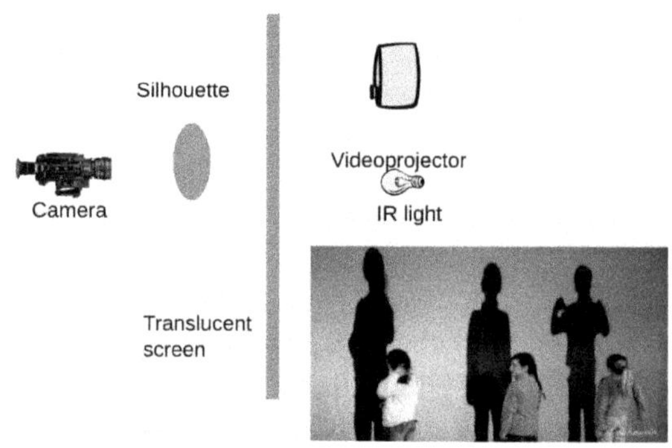

Figure 3: Top view of SBS IR light configuration, and sample performance.

The two main steps in computational processing for digital shadow-based installations are "image analysis" for real-time shadow or silhouette detection, and visual effects through "image synthesis" (see Figure 5). Both are implemented with GPU-programming (shaders) for optimization and portability purposes.

The image analysis modules extract two masks from an input B&W video image, corresponding respectively to cast shadow and silhouette by distinguishing the pixels according to their homogeneity: shadows tend to be more homogeneous than silhouettes. The image analysis modules are followed by an image synthesis component that uses the shadow and silhouette masks to render a virtual shadow from one of these elements or both, and adds optional artistic effects such as fire, water, particles, virtual 3D components, etc. In the case of cast shadow input (CSBS works), the output shadow is calibrated so as to be embedded into the cast shadow. In the case of silhouette input (SBS works), the virtual shadow is generally displayed as a fake cast shadow, anchored at the feet of the onlooker, and projected opposite to the camera considered as a virtual light source.

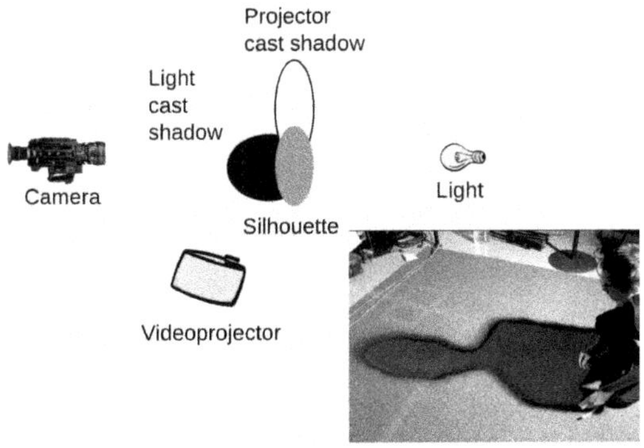

Figure 4: Top view of IR or visible light CSBS and SBS, and sample laboratory capture.

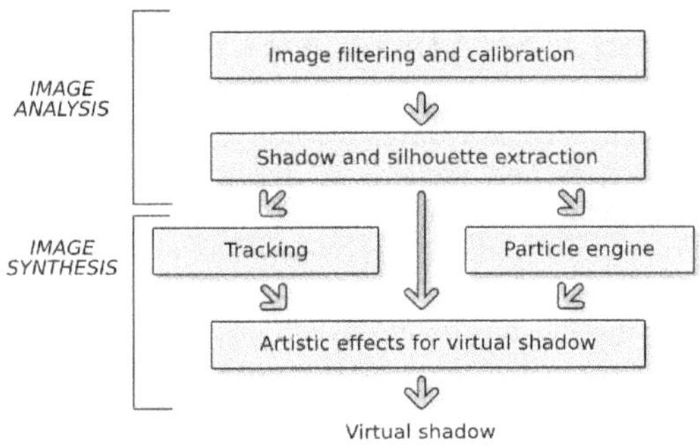

Figure 5: Full pipe-line.

We examine these two components (image analysis and image synthesis) in turn.

3.1 Real-time Image Analysis

Computer Vision plays a central role in Augmented Reality applications because it is used for registering the virtual elements with the physical world through 3D reconstruction and calibration procedures. Since the augmentation of shadow in CSBS and SBS artworks is based on the video-projection of a digital shadow, these works belong to Spatial Augmented Reality (SAR) described by Bimber et al. [2]. In SAR, video-projection is used to overlay digital information on the physical world by carefully registering the digital information with its corresponding location inside the physical world.

In CSBS works, the cast shadow of the user blocking a light beam (whether visible or IR) must be extracted. In SBS works, the user's silhouette has to be obtained and projected from a virtual point light into the digital scene. In both cases, cast shadow and silhouette detection are made in the IR spectrum to avoid visual feedback by capturing the video-projected image by the video camera (video-projector light contains very little IR and is almost invisible to an IR video capture). The IR lighting is obtained either by using an IR spotlight if the installation is in the dark, or by using a visible light spotlight that contains IR in the case of CSBS works. In both cases, video capture for image processing is made solely in the monochromatic IR spectrum.

Whereas IR image analysis has been extensively studied to track objects that emit IR light, the issue in our work is to track parts of the image that do not receive IR light: either cast shadows due to the user's occlusion (Figure 4), or silhouette of the user(s) standing in front of a bright surface or a translucent surface on which IR light is projected (Figure 3). The image processing part of SBS works is a simplified form of chroma keying in which a silhouette is separated from its background. Instead of color separation, silhouette extraction relies here on light intensity separation and background subtraction because it is made on a monochromatic IR image. Similarly, cast shadow extraction is also based on the detection of darker areas in the image. The modules for image processing are given in Figure 6.

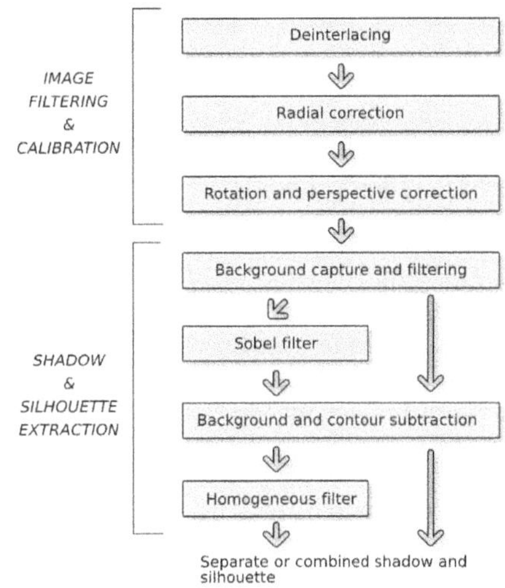

Figure 6: Image analysis pipe-line.

After video deinterlacing, the first part of image processing concerns image calibration. First, the deinterlaced IR image is transformed into a plane image through lens radial correction. Then two transformations are applied (rotation and perspective) in order to register the image to the user's position in the scene. After calibration the video-projection of the cast shadow matches the physical cast shadow in case of a CSBS installation.

The second step in image processing consists in cast shadow and silhouette extraction. First a background image is computed through a median and Gaussian filter on 5 images captured over 70 frames [7]. The background contours are filtered and combined with the background image for shadow and silhouette extraction through background subtraction. Contours are highlighted in the extraction process because some of the renderings use them either for aesthetic purposes (outlining the shadow edge) or for functional purposes (using the contour of the shadow for interaction). Background subtraction is based on logarithmic intensities because it results in better quality, and is less sensitive to threshold selection [11]. A final filter separates the cast shadow from the silhouette by using the property of background subtraction resulting in more homogeneous regions in the shadowed part of the scene than in its mobile parts [7].

3.2 Real-time Image Synthesis

The masks associated with shadow and silhouette are used by the image synthesis modules to generate virtual shadows. Three main components build up the image synthesis part of the platform: a module for computing and highlighting the bounding boxes around the two masks, a particle engine, and the rendering modules for visual effects.

The tracking module relies mainly on a geometry shader that computes the minimal and maximal coordinates of the shadow and silhouette areas to obtain and display their bounding boxes. These data can be used, for example, by the particle engine to attract particles towards the center of the bounding boxes, and make them converge towards the shadow or the silhouette whatever their positions in the field of view of the camera. The bounding box is calculated on a sub-sampled image to reduce the computational cost.

The particle engine belongs to the category of physics engines. They are very popular in the game and digital art communities where they are used to add realism to animation. Particles are point masses that are controlled by a force and interactions with other particles or with obstacles. We have developed an open GPU framework for animating and rendering particles. Fragment shaders compute the particle dynamics and vertex shaders update the positions through vertex texture fetch. The engine allows for the computation of particles bouncing on the contour of an object (here the shadow or the silhouette) according to the surface norm.

Two artistic particle renderings have been studied. First, an ambient visual display shows falling particles as white drops, and lets them bounce on the surface of the shadows. Second an interactive rendering shows particles as words that are attracted by the center of the shadow, and bounce on its surface. If the shadow remains still for a while, the words will eventually stabilize on its surface.

The last processing pass of virtual shadow rendering consists of a wide variety of fragment shaders that take as input the calibrated and distinguished areas of shadow and silhouette, and use them to generate various visual renderings of a digital shadow that are projected in the physical shadow in the case of CSBS artworks, or anchored to the user's feet and projected on a plane surface (wall, vertical screen, or floor) for SBS works. We only focus on a few rendering modules that were of particular interest for the technical development of artistic installations.

The purpose of the colorimetric compensation [1] module is to "erase" the shadow by video-projecting a bright virtual shadow that compensates the decrease of illumination due to cast shadow. This module is targeted for CSBS installations with a visible light. Since no full visible light range video capture is available in our setup, the compensation cannot rely on a captured image and on the comparison of the lit and non-lit areas. It is based on the manual tuning of a uniform lighting of the floor surface. Better results could be obtained through live color video capture.

The feedback module is mainly intended for installations with non-visible light. Its purpose is to reveal a shadow (whether CSBS or SBS) and to display it with a feedback rendering loop in order to make the trace of the user's motion explicit. This module can be applied to various video fillings of the digital shadow: uniform color, texture, or video. This effect also gives the onlookers a clue to the user's motion speed according to the length of the shadow feedback trail.

In the same vein as the particle engine, two modules for fire and a water effects modify the shadow masks at the pixel level, based on a simple physics of fire or water, and a noise texture to add randomness to the motion and the coloring. In the fire module, the shadow is colored with a moving and distorted fire texture, and the border pixels are displaced towards the top of the image in combination with the noise texture. The geometric distortion and color changes of the water effects are controlled by particle displacements generated by the particle module described above.

Last, an Augmented Reality module is the combination of a texture or a fixed video and a mask that highlights a foreground element of the image on which the shadow can be cast. This kind of simple augmentation can only work for an image of a plane shadowed surface such as a fence or a wall. For more complex geometrical scenes, it is necessary to reconstruct the geometry of the photo or video as described by Jacquemin, et al. [5]. Another solution is to use the shadow for Augmented Virtuality by projecting the flat shadow inside a 3D virtual scene, in which the geometry can be used to compute the shadowed areas.

4. SAMPLE SHADOW ARTWORKS

As an application of the platform described in the preceding section, this section focuses on examples of SBS artworks, and offers new insights to digital shadowing. There are natural motivations for using SBS in the performing arts: The tradition of Shadow Play makes the audience conventionally understand the SBS as a shadow projection of the actor and dancer due to a virtual horizontal light placed in the audience. The lack of continuity between the performer and her shadow does not break this rule. On the contrary, it reinforces the magical effect of projection that can be found in many traditional narratives such as Plato's "Cave" or Pliny's "Clay modeler Butades". Last, using a shadow cast on a floor is not easily perceived by an audience because the perspective dramatically diminishes the visual effect of horizontal images, and because a single spotlight makes it difficult to light up the whole stage.

4.1 Sample SBS Dance Scenography

SBS has played a major role in the theater play "Les Révélations d'une ombre"[17] by co-author Georges Gagneré. In this play the seemingly autonomous shadow of a dancer played in time and space with the performer. Four real-time effects were used

- In Figure 7.a, the SBS setup allows us to produce in real-time chronophotographic views of the dancer's movements, inspired by the famous 19th century Muybridge's studies on human locomotion. The various shadows are triggered by notes of music played on stage by a saxophonist.

- Again through the SBS setup, the live shadow of the dancer is shrunk and put in a virtual maze as if she were located inside a video-game (see Figure 7.b). The dancer moves her body and finds the appropriate interactions that will make her progress.

- Figure 7.c shows the cast shadow of the dancer in the white video-projected light behind a screen. The silhouette is shot by a camera in front of the stage and is symmetrically projected as a digital shadow on the second half of the screen. This setup allows us to create several doubles with delays and buffered images that multiply the possibilities of additional characters.

[17]http://www.didascalie.net/lrdo

- Last, with the SBS setup and a symmetry of the projection, the dancer plays with her shadow to discover strange topologies musically created in real-time by a saxophonist (see Figure 7.d).

Figure 7: "Les Révélations d'une ombre", 2009.

The use of the setup presented in Figure 3 offers appropriate conditions to allow the SBS be out of the performer's control. It opens the possibilities to experiment a dialogue in real-time with the living shadow projection of the dancer (among others, inspiring autonomous shadow examples are the "Peter Schlemihl's Remarkable Story" by Adelbert von Chamisso, or "The Shadow" by Hans Christian Andersen). The theme of the monstrous metamorphosis was developed for expressing the secrete ambitions of control from the musician character towards his dancing creature. The setup offered possibilities to develop an initiatic quest by having the shadow counterpart making an extraordinary journey to free the obsessed spirit of her creator.

4.2 Sample SBS Theater Scenography

The purpose of "L'ange Carasuelo company" SBS work is to make possible a shared experience between scientists, artists, technicians, and audience. One of its goals is to propose a shared and simple "shadow tool" for artistic and educative purposes, considering that many performance artists, technicians, and citizens find digital technologies challenging as creative tools whereas they are commonly used for entertainment (e.g. video-games).

This work in strongly related with the deep meaning of the shadow, as a connection between us, our "invisible world", and the real world. Based on this assumption, the research started from a corpus of texts and representations from Carl Jung's work, recent digital shadow works mentioned in Section 2, and Haruki Murakami's novels. This ternary relationship had important consequences on the use of the platform, both for artistic and mediation approaches.

Firstly, writing with (and somehow, for) the tool implied a shift in the roles of each member in the artistic team. Artists had to be able to deal with technical constraints for performance design, and technicians had to understand the artistic needs, and propose "on the fly" some simple, fast, and efficient digital environments. Secondly, shadow was used to inform the audience and the performer of the space and time structure of the virtual world, by shifting our point of view on the world, offering an open gate to our own imagination. As detailed in the next section, the digital shadow played the role of an avatar that could enlarge the consequences of our motions in an immersive context. This point was particularly meaningful during the workshops we organized at the "ESSEC Business" School, hosting physically and sensorially handicapped students.

4.2.1 Technical constraints and believability

The first appropriation of the platform was to organize workshops, brain-storming, and discussions with the partners. Thanks to the artistic collaborative company "didascalie.net" and to the efforts made jointly by the artistic and technical participants, we designed "Tolalusulo"[18], a workable version of the tool that could be used to experiment various scenographic setups based on different configurations of the tracking and projection surfaces. We finally chose a frontal installation such as the one described in Figure 3 integrating: an IR translucent screen for vertical projection, a shiny floor to reflect the IR light behind the feet so that the IR camera in front the screen could catch the whole silhouette of the performers, a video-projector, and a set of theatre spotlights equipped with visible light filters installed behind the screen.

The main trouble we had to face was that our setup was shrinking the space in which the participants could perform. Restricted to one meter away from the screen, this narrow stage band was constraining the actor to a kind of 2.5-dimensional space. As a consequence we decided to write the show with this constraint: our characters would be enclosed in his space, and their shadows would deploy in a 3D space behind the screen. A kind of unconscious personal space was suddenly revealed by their independent shadows. In this way, the 2.5D performing space was expanded to a much larger world (3D space plus time, with the possibility of going back in time) through 2D shadows. Since we could not use traditional spotlights on the performers, we decided to keep the performers in the dark and to swap the roles: darken the actor, while lighting up her (digital) shadow.

These constraints, combined with a time delay through software recording capabilities, became the main ingredients of a story we wrote on stage. A text was written by Benoît Lahoz based on Haruki Murakami's novels, and the opening nights took place in L'apostrophe, Cergy and Le Cube, Issy-les-Moulineaux during Winter 2011 (Figure 8.e). Working with the platform impacted significantly our writing practices, and oriented us toward a layer-based compositing style. The story turned into a journey into layers of memories and social data received by the characters, in which the shadow was a kind of guide and a support for letting them reveal their deep personal values.

SBS was also used as an interactor with virtual objects like a 3D moving wall, a 2D fluid wallpaper, etc. Both the shadow as a self-representation and as an interactor were tightly coupled to make it understandable by the audience. In some scenes, the shadow was projected onto a 3D virtual world used as a stage background. Opening a 3D world to the shadow had to be believable for both the performer and the audience so that it could be perceived as a projection into a fragile Augmented Virtuality environment.

Believability was also a major issue in the experimentation workshops with pupils, students, and individuals (January 2010-June 2011). Early 2010, the major negative comment

[18] http://www.didascalie.net/tolalusulo

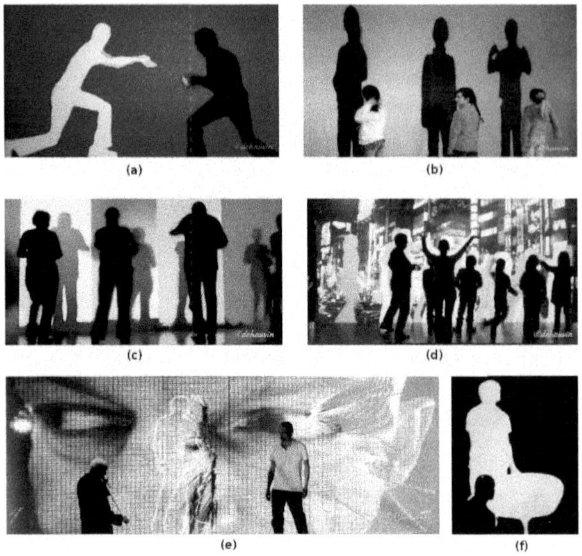

Figure 8: Taverny workshops, 2010, and "Un petit à côté du monde" play, 2011.

on SBS setup was about latency. The 6-year old pupils were the most concerned by this issue. In 2011 we reached approximately 30 frames per second and reduced so much the latency that it became almost imperceptible, although still noticed by the performers. This persistent observation unlocked another interpretation of the participants: What is actually important is not a merge between our cast shadow and the projected shadow, but the possibility for a performer to identify herself with her own shadow. As soon as we can identify ourselves with the projected black shape, all possible distortions can be applied without cancelling this personal identification. This consideration opened a very large way for dramatic experimentations: What is happening, in what kind of world, between the moment I move and the moment my shadow moves?

4.2.2 Shadow deconstruction

The first intention for the performance was to open a visual space-time to be experimented with on stage, both by the characters and the audience. It was based on shadow spatial deconstruction by casting it on diversely oriented volumes, and on temporal deconstruction through latency rendering that would result in time-inconsistent shadow. Our hypothesis was: as the character (then the audience) focuses on her shadow, she provisionally breaks her so-called unity to enter a deeper space-time of dreams, memories, and information structures. This assumption is related to the concept of theater that opens a space-time window inside the audience's own chronology, in which the spectator explores her own personality through identification and catharsis. Our research focused on Carl Jung's work on shadow, "collective unconscious" and "metaphysical reality".

By dealing with technology we played with four dimensions (3D space + time) to enter this particular world. The two main tools were: mapping the SBS on a 3D based virtual space, and increasing or decreasing the latency while performing. Thus the performer was informed of her presence in this world through her shadow, by travelling a space larger than the stage (corresponding to a specific mental space) in a deconstructed time: delaying the past while allowing the audience to catch a glimpse of the future.

The complex relationship between light source, projection surface, and obstacle made the shadow take a difficult to grasp piecewise pass (like when our shadow is cast on perpendicular surfaces and broken into scattered pieces). Consequently, the shadow cast on the "walls" of this virtual space had to be made in a realistic manner to look believable. As the scenery had to be portable, we used a procedural process to map the shadow image on a virtual space (as described by Jacquemin et al. [5]). These constraints revealed a parallel between the technological problems we had to resolve and the inner questions of the performance similar to the issues raised by Sheppard et al. in [10] on the way a dance performance can be staged in a very technological telepresence environment.

Our deconstructed character, receiving information from too many sources, was about to travel in a virtual world deconstructed in space and time. Layers of information were represented by vertically and horizontally controllable perpendicular surfaces on which the cast shadow revealed prerecorded pictures, videos, and structures (especially Rutt/-Etra-like heightfields), and then zoomed to other spaces.

By opening virtual spaces, we took the risk to make the performer disappear by not being strong enough to inhabit and "dominate" the virtual environment. To do so the performer had to enter in a genuine relationship with the shadow: she had to keep in mind what she made one second ago and then react by inventing another continuity while performing inside the moving space. Through this process the technology became a tool for improvisation: the performer, with the help and creativity of the technicians playing live, was able to inform herself of what she was doing and of the consequences of these acts in an oscillating time. Ultimately immobility suddenly closed the spaces and stopped the time, in a kind of rhythmic ritual experience, not so far of the origins of theater.

4.2.3 Shadow plays

Based on these issues, we built a few games for workshops with children and teen-agers:

- The "Shadow Phone" in which 4 participants were playing the "mirror game" with their own shadow before we shuffled the shadow videos so they could play live with someone else's shadow (Figures 8.b & c).
- The "Shadow Ballet" in which 6 video-captures of dancing children were buffered and projected as shadow silhouettes with various delays in different colors on a picture or video background. It ended up into a "dance floor of the past moment" in which each child tried to recognize the shadows' owners (Figure 8.d).
- In "What is inside my shadow", children were prompted to use their shadow to reveal a chosen picture or video, and comment on it aloud while making it visible.
- "My image that belongs to us" proposed to the participants to create a collective image with their own shadow in a sequential manner, each of them leaving a trace of their presence on the screen.
- "Shadow Pong" was an adaptation of the well-known Pong game that could be played by 2 participants using their shadow as interactor.

Other games were implemented with motion freezing, horizontal shadow flipping, buffering, inverting colors, etc., always associated with a debriefing and observation time.

The imagination and creative skills of the participants were practiced with their whole body, so that the interface with the virtual world was not reduced to a limited device such as a joystick or a Wiimote. The whole body was used to make the members of the audience understand the continuity between us, our shadow, and the virtual world, and make them feel projected into their own "shadow world" (imagination, unconsciousness, etc.).

Working with people who have physical, linguistic, or perceptive disabilities, far from limiting the possibilities multiplied them. For example, a partially-blind student passed long hours drawing the background of a platform game, and then used the shadow as an avatar. In this way his whole body (and not only his eyes or fingers) was involved into the game. Time latency was staged with students suffering from dyspraxia who were actually experiencing a latency between stimuli reception and processing. This correspondence between the real human and the virtual shadow resulted in interesting discussions with the participants and offered us some drama material for the theater play we were building together: What is happening during this transitional time? Is the time of imagination, fiction, and poetry?

Perceptive amplification was the main issue in this collective experience. In sharing this tool, we acquired knowledge and competences that led our artistic research to unexplored paths that we could never have found on our own. This was made possible thanks to the partnership between scientists, artists, education and civil society staff, and individuals.

4.3 Art/science collaboration process

The realization of the software platform and its use for performances and pedagogical workshops shows how scientific and technological works intertwine with artistic creation and offer new perspectives for both disciplines.

The first intuition shared by scientists, engineers and artists in their collaborative project was to use the shadow to build a bridge between real and virtual worlds. We already said that by covering a space the shadow gives a proof of presence. This is not easy to fully understand (children do it only around five years old), but it is playful to experiment. Playing with the shadow of a performer or an onlooker results in new interactions setup between the real and virtual worlds. Starting from a digital shadow, we imagined concrete artistic situations to physically interact with digital augmentation of the physical world.

The first point was that building a digital shadow was a very difficult step either for scientists and engineers or for artists and stage directors. The use of visible and invisible lights, video-projector, camera, computer, and projection surfaces, the spatial relationship between the performer/onlooker and her shadow resulted in a complex experimental environment. Finally, the scientific methodology was of a great help to decompose the complexity and to choose the appropriate setups. An amazing result was that the computer program does not grasp the concept of shadow. What a child's brain can do in one second is unachievable by the most powerful computer. Consequently the whole staff (scientific, technical or artistic) had to make common choice to build the digital shadow and to accept limitations in its use: we shared a common object, built it from scratch, and learned together, step by step, how to use it in an augmented environment.

The art/science collaboration process refutes the notion of progress and implements well a post-modernist approach to life in which errors and bugs, practices and habits, meaning and concepts count more than technological achievements and scientific advances. As a consequence, such a collaboration can only mature if both parts collaborate in an empathic and listening manner, and accept to dismiss their preconceived views on technological art. Such a need is well illustrated by Sheppard et al. in [10] in the TED tele-immersive dance environment experience, in which bugs, delays, and discrepancies are used as artistic tools, shifting from an approach where they should be avoided to a set-up in which they are integrated and controlled by the dancers.

At the beginning of our collaboration, performers played with the digital shadow as an additional character, and explored its autonomy. They imagined scenes that induced specific scientific or technological explorations to make possible interactions. Conversely, the scientists and engineers explored "by themselves" interesting properties of the digital shadows that had aesthetic qualities, and brought original set-ups to artists. For instance, tracking and particle effects were suggested by artists, but water and fire effects came from a scientific exploration of the particle engine applied to distort the digital shadow. To have built together a common object allowed independent creativity from each participant and genuine investigation producing relevant results in each field (scientific publication or shows), and finally helped to reach new territories of collaboration.

This process took several months before being mature. It was not planned when the collaboration started. We regularly used to express the need of a common vocabulary to understand the multiple and seemingly divergent emerging points of view. But the success in collaboration came from fully sharing a common object and its setups, a digital shadow interacting with a virtual world in an augmented environment. As we wrote in part 2, there are two main setups for dealing with shadows: CSBS and SBS. We just explained why we first explored the SBS. Nevertheless, current developments are actually led by the scientific partner who convinced his artistic partners to explore the CSBS and develop its potentialities. The initial exploration of the autonomous shadow, and the consequent common experience, can apply now to other contexts in which a cast-shadow can be transformed from inside. New artistic ideas will come from forthcoming workshops involving light designers, stage directors, and scientists. We hope to produce some works that will develop the digital part of the CSBS framework.

In our project, the shadow theme took a shape that allowed to produce in the same time scientific knowledge and artistic experiments. We were certainly helped by the original double nature of the shadow: it played a important part in the discovery of our world (principally in astronomy and in cognition as shown by Casati [3]), and it was for all time a favored mean to tell stories. Using it to explore Augmented Reality gave us the opportunity to find out new topics of research and practice.

4.4 Artistic dissemination and sustainability

Working with technologies inside a collective project made us question the economic aspects of project: How could we share the results and the tool when the project is finished?

We had to find affordable solutions to install a basic software suite and consider the best low-cost "tool quality-sharing opportunities". Incidentally or not, these three aspects of our approach (technical, psychological, and social) were always tightly linked to our artistic experiments with SBS digital shadow on-stage. The necessity to share a common object brings the scientific and technical partners to organize the software platform introduced in Section 3 through shader modules that can be easily used to build by-product softwares suiting artistic needs. When compared with previous ad-hoc in-house approaches, it offers major improvements in the quality of shadow extraction for artistic design, and makes new configurations accessible for pedagogical workshops with pupils. The GPU-based approach to digital shadowing of the research team made this porting possible and opened the door to many additional special effects. We used SBS as a representation of a semi-dependent shadow of the performers, enhanced with time delay, frame buffering, and distortion effects. Blending modes between distinct effects were, in this case, very useful to deconstruct the shadow and make it enter in the digital world of the video.

Each involved artist proposed numerous, various and specific experiments to allow pupils and audience to play with their own shadows and discover a wide variety of creative worlds. This creativity was also shared by librarians who brought their own proposals to feed workshops with references and activities about shadows. We also shared our new skills with other dance and theater companies. Taking apart the financial aspects, the cost of working with technologies introduces a new parameter of power in the arts world depending on how knowledgeable the people are with the technology. A way for helping to overcome these power issues is to make clearer the technological dependencies between partners. It makes networking possible and results in stronger collaborations. We tried to find the most affordable hardware and software solutions for the platform in connection with a wide art-activist community including free software developers. And two companies used "Tolalusulo" to work with digital shadows: Anne Morel and Sans Titre Production deal with gender themes in two recent shows. Christophe Greilsammer and L'Astrolabe Cie created a performance from the famous Andersen's tale "The Shadow". This collaboration process produces a state of mind in the use of shadows that arguably results in a new type of exchange with the audience and with "external" artists.

5. CONCLUSION AND PERSPECTIVES

The success of the workshops leads the artists to think about simplified derived setups on common hardware and software to broadly disseminate the creative and pedagogical tools. A designer will make improvements in this direction. Moreover, numerous interactions already developed in the platform by engineers and scientists offer exciting perspectives to create new stories and performances.

Playing with the shadows implied a close relationship between the performer and a screen. Attempts have been made to break the flatness of the screen by using a 3D world in which shadows were walking around. This can surely be developed with 3D stereoscopic projections. But an alternative has been suggested by the scientific team to deeper explore the possibilities offered by CSBS in interactive environments using traditional lighting. This exploration will be a future development of the current project, involving in addition both a space designer and a light designer.

By demystifying the digital aspect of the work and focusing on the meaning in the art piece (even if working with technologies) our new practice entails necessary changes in our beliefs to be successful.

6. ACKNOWLEDGEMENT

This project has been funded by Région Île-de-France as a PICRI Project. We are grateful to Médiathèque Taverny, Le Cube Issy-les-Moulineaux, La Filature Mulhouse, Plateforme Virage, and CNRS for their support. Most of all we are very grateful to all the participants in this project: Valérie Bajcsa, Wai Kit Chan, Loïs Drouglazet, Catherine Lazaro, Olivier Pfeiffer, Renaud Rubiano and Jean-Marc Vézien, .

7. REFERENCES

[1] O. Bimber, A. Emmerling, and T. Klemmer. Embedded entertainment with smart projectors. In ACM SIGGRAPH 2005 Courses, SIGGRAPH '05, New York, NY, USA, 2005. ACM.

[2] O. Bimber and R. Raskar. Spatial Augmented Reality: Merging Real and Virtual Worlds. A. K. Peters, Ltd, Montreal, 2005.

[3] R. Casati. La découverte de l'ombre. Albin Michel, Paris, 2002.

[4] W. K. Chan and G. Gagneré. Tllslo (toute la lumière sur l'ombre) - les configurations du dispositif. Technical report, LIMSI-CNRS, July 2010.

[5] C. Jacquemin, B. Planes, and R. Ajaj. Shadow casting for soft and engaging immersion in augmented virtuality artworks. In Proceedings of the 15th international conference on Multimedia, MULTIMEDIA '07, pages 477–480, New York, NY, USA, 2007. ACM.

[6] M. W. Krueger. Responsive environments. In AFIPS National Computer Conference, volume 46 of AFIPS Conference Proceedings, pages 423–433. AFIPS Press, 1977.

[7] A. Leone and C. Distante. Shadow detection for moving objects based on texture analysis. Pattern Recogn., 40:1222–1233, April 2007.

[8] G. Levin. Hands up! A visual essay on the 'Media Art Pose', September 2006. http://www.flong.com/texts/essays/essay_pose/.

[9] Y. Minomo, Y. Kakehi, M. Iida, and T. Naemura. Transforming your shadow into colorful visual media: multiprojection of complementary colors. Comput. Entertain., 4, July 2006.

[10] R. M. Sheppard, M. Kamali, R. Rivas, M. Tamai, Z. Yang, W. Wu, and K. Nahrstedt. Advancing interactive collaborative mediums through tele-immersive dance (ted): a symbiotic creativity and design environment for art and computer science. In Proceeding of the 16th ACM international conference on Multimedia, MM '08, pages 579–588, New York, NY, USA, 2008. ACM.

[11] Q.-Z. Wu and B.-S. Jeng. Background subtraction based on logarithmic intensities. Pattern Recogn. Lett., 23:1529–1536, November 2002.

Towards Peer-Assisted Rendering in Networked Virtual Environments*

Minhui Zhu
National University of Singapore

Sebastien Mondet
University of Oslo

Géraldine Morin
University of Toulouse

Wei Tsang Ooi
National University of Singapore

Wei Cheng
Manovega Pte. Ltd.

ABSTRACT

This paper introduces a new technique, called peer-assisted rendering, that aims to enable interactive navigation in a 3D networked virtual environment using a resource-constrained device, by speeding up the rendering. A resource-constrained client requests part of the rendered scenes from other peers with similar viewpoints within the virtual environment, and merges the rendered parts into its own view. This approach is more scalable than previous solutions based on server-based pre-rendering. The goal of this paper is to make a strong case for the feasibility of peer-assisted rendering through the following two messages. First, by analyzing a large number of user traces from a popular virtual world called *Second Life*, we show that there are surprisingly many users with similar viewpoints and encompass large number of common objects in their viewing areas, indicating that a client can potentially find multiple other peers that can assist in rendering. Second, by combining three different rendering methods, each contributing to rendering of different classes of objects in the scene, we show that it is possible for a client to render the scene efficiently with little visual artifacts.

Categories and Subject Descriptors

I.3.2 [**Graphics Systems**]: Distributed/network graphics

General Terms

Performance, Measurement, Design

Keywords

Peer-Assisted Rendering, Image-based Rendering, Networked Virtual Environments, Resource-constrained Devices

1. INTRODUCTION

Networked virtual environments (NVEs) are becoming an important class of distributed multimedia applications and are getting increasing attention commercially, with applications such as online education, teleconferencing, and entertainment. For example, *Second Life*, a user-generated NVE built by Linden Lab, reports more than 21 million accounts registered and about 55,000 concurrent users as of April 2011.

On the other hand, as Internet access via hand-held devices becomes prevalent, there is an increasing demand from users to access NVE interactively with these devices. Hardware manufacturers have been enhancing mobile device's performance and capabilities, with 3G and IEEE 802.11 chips, better computational capabilities, and higher screen resolutions, enabling rich multimedia applications. Some devices are even equipped with GPUs (Graphical Processing Units), improving the audio-visual experience. These GPUs, however, are still limited in their processing capability. For instance, NVidia's GoForce 5300 does not contain any 3D engine[1], but instead is designed to decode a large amount of multimedia formats. Powerful GPUs, such as PowerVR SGX graphics processor, which can support between 7–28 MPoly/s, are only available on high end devices, such as iPhone 4 and Palm Pre. These GPUs, however, increase the power consumption of the devices dramatically [20]. Hence, despite an increase in the networking capability, rendering high quality and realistic 3D scenes on mobile devices remains a bottleneck for mobile access to NVE.

A common approach to enable mobile access to NVE is to reduce the rendering workload at the mobile client, by migrating the rendering tasks elsewhere. We say that the mobile client is assisted by an *assistant* that renders on behalf of the mobile client, and we call the mobile client the *assistee*.

A large class of previous work on mobile access to NVE can be classified under the *server-assisted rendering* approach. A server acts as the assistant and continuously renders the 3D scene according to the assistee's viewpoint (defined by a set of synthetic camera parameters). The resulting rendered images are encoded as a video stream and transmitted to the assistee for decoding and display.

There are two main issues with server-assisted rendering. First, the approach is not scalable. 3D rendering and video encoding are computationally expensive operations. Sterkin [26] reported that a high-end server can support only 14 simultaneous assistees using this approach. One can expand the server capacity to support more assistees. For instance, Shi et al. proposed moving 3D rendering and video encoding into a cloud [25]. While such cloud-based solution provides the convenience and flexibility of instantiating a rendering server as needed, the rendering cost still increases linearly with the number of clients.

Second, server-assisted rendering introduces additional latency. NVE is a highly interactive application. With server-assisted ren-

*Area chair: Xian-Sheng Hua

[1] http://en.wikipedia.org/wiki/GoForce

MM'11, November 28–December 1, 2011, Scottsdale, Arizona, USA.

dering, however, its takes at least one round-trip time for the new viewpoint to be rendered at the assistee. Bao and Gourlay have proposed a method to reduce the interaction latency, by warping the rendered images received from the server immediately at the assistee when viewpoint changes [1]. Despite introducing some visual artifacts due to warping, this approach works well generally. It is limited, however, to a static, single user, virtual world (such as building walk-through). In a dynamic scene (e.g., with multiple moving avatars), the warp image would not have included the updated avatars, causing these avatars to appear frozen as the viewpoint changes.

1.1 Peer-Assisted Rendering

These drawbacks of the existing proposals motivate the need for a scalable method to support rendering of dynamic scenes from a complex multi-user virtual environments on a mobile device.

This paper introduces a new technique to reduce the rendering workload of an assistee, by distributing the rendering tasks to other clients, or peers, in the same virtual world. We call this approach *peer-assisted rendering*. Clients accessing the virtual world are heterogeneous in nature. Some clients are running on hosts with good rendering capabilities (most desktops are equipped with GPU). These clients can act as assistants, render parts of the scene separately, and send them to the assistee. We call the partial scene rendered at the assistants *rendering elements*. The assistee then merges the rendering elements to create its view of the scene.

A fundamental question that peer-assisted rendering approach needs to address is how to split the rendering tasks and what is a rendering element. In our design, we choose to have three types of rendering elements, to balance between the rendering load on the assistee and the assistants, to maintain interactivity, and to minimize visual artifacts.

The first type of rendering elements consists in the furthest objects, the sky, and the ground. These objects are rendered as one single depth-enabled image by the assistants according to their own viewpoint. We call this image the *background impostor*. Since the assistants are rendering them for their own use in any case, rendering the background impostor does not incur much additional overhead.

The second type of rendering elements consists in the static near objects. These objects are rendered as individual images by the assistants. We call these rendering elements the *object impostors*. The objects are also rendered according to the viewpoint of the assistants, so it incurs very little additional overhead for them. Moreover, the assistants may already use some of these rendering elements for themselves (e.g. for rendering shadows, and reflections). The impostors and the corresponding depth maps are sent to the assistee, which warps them to its view point.

The final type of rendering elements consists of dynamic objects, such as other avatars. These objects are rendered locally by the assistee as "normal" 3D objects.

We now explain how to generate a new rendered image when the assistee changes its viewpoint. When the viewpoint of the avatar changes, the background impostors are warped using McMillan and Bishop's Image Warping Algorithm [19] and are composed into the assistee's background. Since the background impostors consists of far objects, it changes very little as the viewpoint changes. Warping the background impostors therefore does not incur much visual artifacts. If background and near objects are warped from the same image, however, exposure gaps often appear (holes in background). These near objects are therefore rendered separately to reduce the exposure gaps when the viewpoint changes (the occluded parts would be rendered by the assistants anyway, c.f. Section 3.1). Finally, in order to maintain interactivity with other avatars, the assistee renders all other close/dynamic objects itself. This way, their updates or movements are reflected with minimal delay and maximal quality at the assistee.

The strengths of peer-assisted rendering are the following. First, it is more scalable than a server-assisted approach. It uses the rendering capability of other clients of the environment to partially render the scene on behalf of the assistee. Second, it reuses rendered elements from the assistants. The rendering elements from the assistants are rendered according to their own viewpoint – and it is something that they already do anyway. Third, it can adapt to the rendering capability of the assistee. By tuning the classification of objects into rendering elements, we can trade off visual artifacts with the rendering workload at the assistee. Finally, by rendering the moving avatars locally at the assistee, peer-assisted rendering maintains the interactivity between the user and the virtual environment.

1.2 Contributions

There are many hurdles and research challenges in realizing peer-assisted rendering practically. In fact, too many to be addressed in a single paper. This paper, as the first paper introducing this concept, aims to establish a solid case for the efficacy of peer-assisted rendering. We choose to address two fundamental questions in this paper: (i) are there enough assistants with similar viewpoints and common objects to help an assistee? (ii) what is the quality of the scene rendered at the assistee as user navigates around the scene?

To answer the first question, we analyze mobility and object traces from a popular NVE named Second Life. We show that there are surprisingly many avatars with significant overlaps in viewing frustum, and most assistees can find enough assistants to cover a large number of objects in their viewing frustum.

To answer the second question, we build a renderer that simulates the peer-assisted rendering process, and show that the resulting rendered quality is close to that if rendered fully by the assistee.

1.3 Organization

The rest of this paper is organized as follows. Section 2 presents relevant past research efforts. Section 3 describes how the rendering is done. Section 4 defines two similarity metrics and describes how assistants are chosen. Section 5 shows the setup and the results of our experiments. Section 6 presents the results of the Second Life trace analysis. Finally, Section 7 discusses the challenges for future work. we conclude in Section 8.

2. RELATED WORK

Navigating through, and interacting with, a large NVE on a mobile phone with limited computational capacity is challenging. The computational demand to render the 3D scene in NVE leads to low rendering frame rate. A common technique to improve the frame rate is to reduce the details of 3D content within the NVE. Previous work has proposed to simplify the geometry of 3D models [10] or filter out objects (by making them invisible) on the mobile client [17]. Despite improving the frame rate, these techniques reduce the quality of the rendered scene.

To maintain high level-of-details in the scene and high frame rate at the same time, *server-based rendering* schemes, was proposed [7, 21]. With this approach, the client continuously sends its viewpoint to the server. The server renders the 3D scene according to the client's viewpoints as a sequence of images, and transmits the resulting sequence to the client for display as a video stream.

To reduce the bandwidth consumed by transmissions of the rendered scene to the clients, warping-based techniques have been proposed. The idea is that the server transmits only selected rendered scenes, along with the depth maps of each scene. These rendered scenes are accurately rendered by the server. The clients interpolates between the rendered scene, by warping the given images to target viewpoint [5, 2]. Chang and Ger [5] proposed that the server creates a layered depth image of the scene corresponding to the mobile client's viewpoint. The layered image is then transmitted to the client for warping; layered image gives good result even with exposure gaps. Bao and Gourlay [2] propose that the clients generate subsequent frames locally using 3D warping upon receiving the rendered scene. Differences between the rendered images and the warped images for the next viewpoint are requested from the server.

Shi et al. [23] use warping for mobile clients in a slightly different context: in their setting, the input data is a 3D video stream. A dedicated proxy transforms the 3D video into well-chosen 2D frames and depth maps to be sent to the mobile client. These proxies may distribute the computational problem among various independent machines, and move the rendering process closer to the client, which improves interactivity. The availability of such powerful proxies, however, is not realistic for Internet-based NVE applications. The latency of the latter setup has been then improved by warping from multiple images. To get reference images well suited for warping, a *viewpoint prediction* algorithm is used [24]. Prediction/prefetching algorithms for server-side image-based pre-rendering are also studied by Lazem et al. [12].

Another approach is based on pre-rendered panoramic images. In Boukerche and Pazzi's system [3], the server receives the mobile user's viewpoint and warps from a panoramic view in cylindrical coordinates for the client. Lei et al. [13] suggested that the client warps the scene himself from a portion of the panorama. In both works, a buffering method is proposed for anticipating the pre-rendering.

Chen et al. [6] propose an on demand image-based networked visualization method. The client can pull pre-rendered multi-resolution images from a web-server.

The proposed approaches above are not scalable. The server (or proxy) either has to render 3D scenes along with real-time video encoding for each client according to its successive viewpoints, or has to pre-render a large database of possible scenes (like panoramic or movie) to cover the 3D environment. These server operations are computationally expensive. Hence, an increasing number of clients may quickly exhaust the server's capabilities. To allow more mobile users to connect simultaneously, Lamberti et al. [11] use a cluster-based rendering farm based on *Chromium*[2] OpenGL implementation.

To reduce the computing load of the server, some of the work mentioned [6, 3, 13] propose to buffer some pre-rendered scenes. Caching may lead to synchronization issues in large scale NVEs, such as Second Life, where the rendered scenes are dynamic. Even for the static part of the scenes, it would require the pre-rendering, and the storage, of huge amounts of images, consuming computing resources.

Boukerche et al. [4] improve their previous system [3] from a scalability point of view. The authors use peer-to-peer distribution to share the images rendered by the server. A peer can find other peers that visit the same "region of interest" and ask them for images. The spirit of their work is similar to ours, but using only a single image, the technique works best for static scenes. Most other pieces of work related to P2P techniques in NVEs have stressed on performing load-balancing for the network and/or server resources. One example of P2P optimization for NVEs is Ke and Zimmermann's [15] spatialised audio streaming system. They aim at improving the delivery of audio streams while minimizing the latency using a P2P bandwidth balancing model. Regarding the actual 3D objects, Cheng et al. [8] investigate the streaming of progressive meshes within a P2P NVE. They partition the meshes into chunks and show how a node can lookup for the provider of a given chunk. Within the ASCEND project[3], Hu et al. [9] considers improvements on P2P techniques for sharing 3D content. Their focus, however, is to share geometric data of the scene and does not concern rendering.

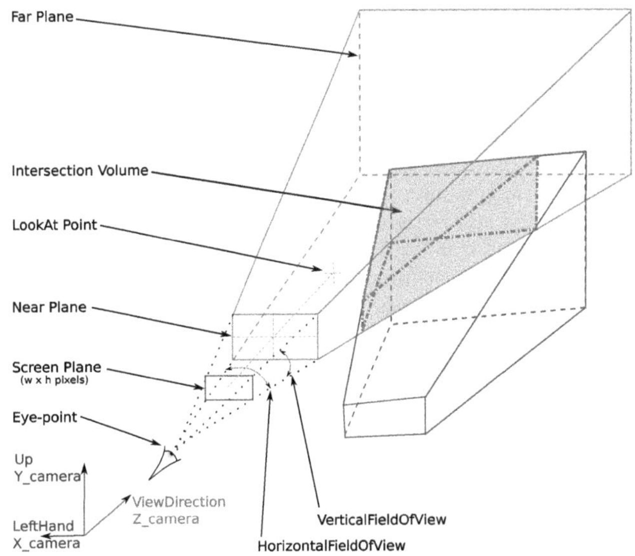

Figure 1: The frustum-related vocabulary.

3. ASSISTEE RENDERING

We now elaborate on how the assistee utilizes different rendering elements from the assistants to produce the rendered scene. We first briefly review the classical rendering pipeline and introduce some notations. Then, we detail the concept of warping from a single image introduced by McMillan and Bishop [19]. The next subsection explains the partitioning of the scene and defines the notion of an impostor, as we use it here. Finally, we show the composition of the different rendering elements and evaluate the quality and efficiency of the assisted rendering.

3.1 3D Rendering

To establish a common vocabulary for the rest of the paper, we now briefly explain how 3D rendering is typically done. Rendering is the process of automatically generating a 2D image from a set of virtual 3D objects. The set of objects potentially visible from a given viewpoint is delimited by a volume called the *frustum*; Figure 1 provides details about the vocabulary related to the viewpoint. As most users in an NVE have horizontal view directions, our study in Section 4 uses simplified parameters for the viewpoint definitions: we consider the position of the user ("eye-point"), his view direction, and his viewing angle ("horizontal field of view"). In most NVE applications, the process is implemented in three steps. The first step, *perspective transformation*, uses a geometric function to transform all 3D objects contained in the frustum. Its complexity

[2]http://chromium.sourceforge.net/

[3]http://ascend.sourceforge.net/

is linear in the numbers of 3D geometric primitives within the frustum. The next step, *projection* to the 2D screen plane, removes the depth coordinate. Finally, the *rasterisation* step converts the continuous image on the screen plane into a pixel array in the rendered image. The depth value is kept for each pixel, and used to manage per-pixel occlusions (with the *Z-Buffer* algorithm). This per-pixel depth information can be stored as the *depth map* of the image and may be used for 3D image warping (c.f. 3.2). Note that all objects within the frustum are processed through the rendering pipeline, since occlusions are treated by the last step *–Z-Buffer–* of the pipeline. Any object within the frustum of an assistant, even if occluded, is rendered and may be re-used by the assistee for warping. Moreover, note that the overall complexity of the rendering is a linear function of the number of triangles, or polygons, in the scene for the first two parts (*perspective transformation* and *projection*), and linear in the number of pixels for the *rasterization*. Of course, GPUs do implement these operations in parallel on geometric elements for the first two parts, and on pixels for the rasterization.

3.2 Single Image Warping

We now briefly explain 3D image warping. In the context of peer-assisted rendering, image warping is used to generate a view from the camera of the assistee when viewpoint changes, taking advantage of the depth information kept by standard rendering engines (e.g. OpenGL-based). Exact warping can be done for certain camera moves: homographies are exact for rotations around the "eye-point", or also, for arbitrary motion of a planar object.

The image rendered from a given viewpoint A, associated with its depth map, contains enough information to re-render (or *warp*) adequately all the pixels visible by A from a different viewpoint B. The correctness of the rendering is up to the quantization of the image information due to the rasterization step and of the depth due to its storage in the depth map. Pixels visible from B but not from A, however, will not be present in the warped image; this creates well known artifacts called *exposure gaps*. Exposure gaps may be thwarted by merging multiple reference images [23]. Mark et al. [18] present a concise review on these methods and provide a more elaborated transformation, which depends on more information from the rendering process.

Pixels visible from B that are occluded in A may be hidden by a different object, or by self occlusion. Self occlusion occurs when the angle between the two view points is more than the change of normal in the silhouette edge of the object. Although it is hard to quantify, the number of occlusion due to a different object seem to be higher than the number of self occlusion in NVE that have a complex scene with many objects. Therefore, we propose to warp objects of the scene independently, to reduce the number of exposure gaps caused by object occlusions.

In terms of complexity, 3D image warping is fast since it is linear in the number of pixels of the image being warped.

3.3 Decomposition of the scene

With the background on 3D rendering and 3D image warping, we can now elaborate on how the assistee renders its scene. The assistee partitions the scene into three classes of rendering elements: background objects, near static objects, and dynamic objects. These rendering elements can be rendered by different assistants, warped independently, before being combined by the assistee (Figure 2).

Such partitioning has two main advantages. First, warping static nearby objects independently from the background significantly reduces the number and size of exposure gaps. To understand this, consider the alternative where the assistant renders the near objects

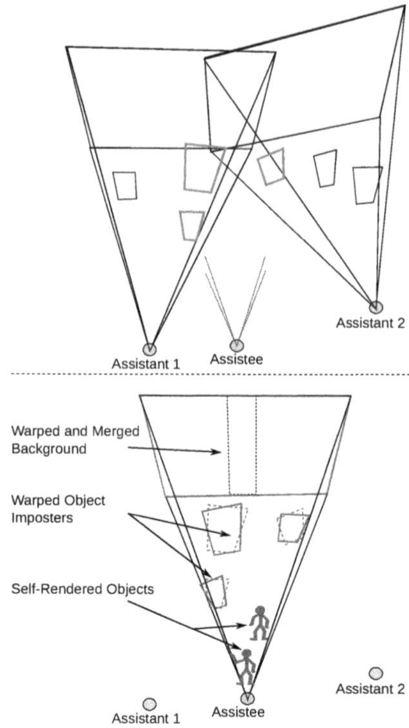

Figure 2: In the upper figure, an assistee may recover the three (green) objects in his frustum –not drawn entirely for clarity– from two neighboring peers. Both assistant provide the background. In the lower figure, the assistee has warped the three impostors, warped and combined the two backgrounds, and rendered locally only the dynamic objects –here the two red little guys– and merged these rendering objects together.

together with the background objects as one impostor. The pixels corresponding to the background region occluded by the near objects would not be available when the image is warped, creating an exposure gap. Rendering the background objects and near objects as separate images eliminates such exposure gaps. In a way, we are rendering images with multiple layers, similar to the idea behind layered depth images [22]. Second, by partitioning the scene into different rendering elements, the rendering workload can be distributed to more than one assistants, leading to a more flexible and scalable solution. Different assistants may be chosen. The choice of the assistant is discussed in Section 4.

Here is how the partitioning is done. First, objects that are of distance d and above from the eye-point of the assistee are grouped together to form the background objects (we use half of the far plane distance as d in our work). We also force the ground to be in the background so that it does not suffer from exposure gaps. Second, static objects that are within distance d from the eye-point of the assistee are grouped into impostors. Grouping is done using scene graph – a tree that organizes objects in the scene into a hierarchy based on spatial position of the objects. An impostor is a rendered image of a group of objects that corresponds to a subtree in the scene graph. We can adjust how fine we want to partition the scene by moving up and down the scene graph. In our examples, we have between 20 and 120 impostors.

Finally, dynamic objects such as avatars that are within distance d from the eye-point of the assistee form the third partition. These objects are rendered as 3D objects locally.

3.4 Hybrid Rendering

To generate the rendered scene, the assistee combines the three classes of rendering elements, two of which are warped, and one is rendered regularly. The assistee, upon encountering a new object in its frustum or upon experiencing large visual artifacts in rendering of an object, sends a request to an assistant based on the assistant selection algorithm (see Section 4) for the corresponding impostor. The assistant renders the requested objects as an impostor and sends them, together with the corresponding depth map, to the assistee. The same is done for the background impostor. This hybrid rendering is illustrated by Figure 2.

Instead of making the assistants generate the impostors according to the assistee's viewpoint, we choose to use warping at the assistee. The assistee knows the viewpoint of the assistant from which the impostors come from, and uses this information to warp them to its own viewpoint. This approach improves the overall latency for two reasons. First, the assistant does not need to get updates of the assistee's viewpoint, which would increase the network round-trips. Second, by reusing the assistants' depth-enabled images, the assistee can move in the scene and continue warping without requiring any additional information.

The scene at the assistee now consists of a warped background, warped impostors and moving objects within distance *d* from the eye-point (including the avatars). The assistee now renders the scene using regular graphics pipeline. The composition of the three types of rendering objects is also performed by the last step (Z-buffer) of the graphics pipeline, using the depth information of the 3D objects of the background and of the impostors.

Figure 3 shows an example that illustrates the whole process and a ground truth rendered image for comparison.

3.5 Computational Complexity

The complexity of the classical rendering process depends on both the number of polygons in the scene and the number of pixels in the screen (Section 3.1). the complexity of a warping pass, however, depends only on the number of pixels of the warped image. Thus, the traditional 3D graphics pipeline does not benefit much from the smaller display size of a mobile device, whereas warping does [19]. The complexity of warping is comparable to the complexity of the rasterization step of 3D rendering. Hence, when warping an object, the time spent in the *perspective transformation* step and the *projection* step is saved, compared to 3D rendering. Moreover, grouping the objects simplifies warping further: in 3D rendering, objects are rasterized independently, whereas objects being warped together lead to a single pass on the pixel array. In particular, warping the background objects into a single image avoids considering the objects that are far away one-by-one. Note the resolution of the grouping (how many objects per impostors) may be chosen: more object per impostors leads to less impostors, which lowers the complexity of the rendering at the expense of more visual artifacts (exposure gaps).

4. ASSISTANCE

The goal of this study is to prove the concept for peer-assisted rendering. We consider the scheme where a mobile device profits from rendering work already done, and cached, by other peers. The assistee will have to build its view of the scene by using image warping from the rendering results (object images) from other viewpoints (c.f. Section 3). Therefore, the assistee needs to find other peers that can provide him with, at least, partial rendering results corresponding to his viewpoint, i.e., other peers that see a part of what he sees. In order to show that this peer-assisted scheme is viable in the current usage of *Second Life*, we need to define

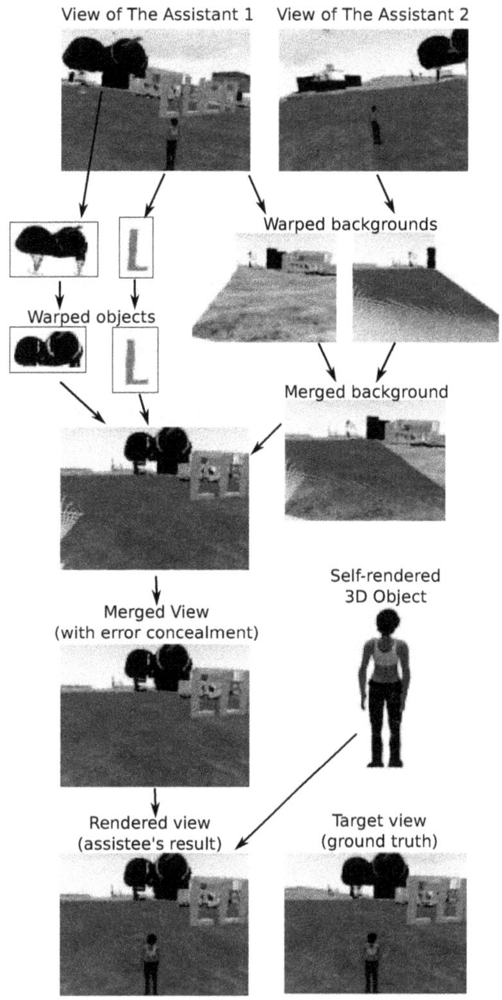

Figure 3: An example of hybrid rendering at the assistee: Assistant 1 provides the impostors and a part of the background, Assistant 2 provides a complementary part of the background, and the dynamic object (the avatar) is rendered locally.

notions of similarity for avatar views. In the remaining of this section, we build two similarity criteria which reflect how much the assistant may help with object images or for background warping.

4.1 Quantifying View Similarity

We define similarity metrics as a measure between the assistee and a set of candidate assistants. These metrics measure the capacity of a set of potential assistants in providing the objects impostors and background to the assistee. We define two similarity measures, object similarity and viewpoint similarity, below.

We first define the notion of *object similarity* between an assistant and an assistee. This similarity measure counts the ratio of the number of objects that falls into the viewing frustum of both the assistant and the assistee, to the number of objects in the viewing frustum of the assistee. The idea here is that, if an object falls into the frustum of the assistee, it is needed by the assistee, and if it also falls into the viewing frustum of the assistant, then it can be rendered as an impostors by the assistant.

There is an additional factor to consider, however. The impostor would not be helpful to the assistee if the difference in the viewing

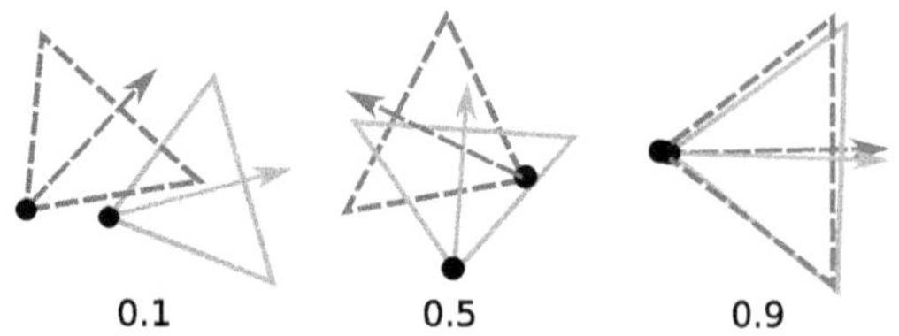

Figure 4: Pairs of 2D viewpoints and their overlapping area ratios. Viewpoint similariry is computed by filtering with the angle between viewing directions.

angle of the assistant and assistee to the object is large. Warping of the impostor in this case would generate large visual artifacts. In the worst case, the assistant and assistee could be facing each other with the object in between. In this case, the impostor from the assistant would be useless. As such, we filter out assistants whose differences in viewing angle with respect to the assistee's viewing angle is larger than a threshold, and set the similarity to zero.

This metric naturally generalizes to more than one candidate assistant, by considering the number of object shared between the assistee and any of the candidate assistants, thus taking into account the complementarity of the assistants.

The object similarity is indicative of the amount of data that can be shared between the assistant and the assistee, but it involves point in polygon query, which could be expensive, especially on the assistee that is already resource-constraint. We introduce another similarity measure that is easier to calculate and approximate the object similarity, called *viewpoint similarity*. Viewpoint similarity computes the *area* of the intersection between the view frustum of the assistant and the assistee.

To compute viewpoint similarity, we only consider 2D view frustum in the `xy-plane`. We ignore the z-angle, the angle between the vector `z_camera` and the horizontal plane (c.f. Figure 1), since most users have a horizontal viewing direction. We also ignore the near-plane. Hence, the 2D viewpoint of a peer is modeled by a triangle: the `position` is the vertex, facing the edge projection of the `far-plane`, and the two remaining edges are defined by the sides of the 3D frustum (see Figure 4).

Two viewpoints are then compared using the overlapping area between two 2D viewpoints, that is, the projection of the "intersection volume" on the horizontal plane (c.f. Figure 1). We compute the similarity as the ratio between the overlapping area and the area of the assistee. The similarity for a pair of avatars thus ranges between 0 and 1, with 1 representing the same viewpoint (c.f. Figure 4).

As in object similarity, we set the similarity between two avatars to zero when the angle between their view directions is larger than a threshold (we use the default horizontal FOV setting in Second Life, which is 91 degree). To extend this metric to multiple assistants, we compute the intersection between the assistee's 2D viewpoint and the union of all assistants' 2D viewpoints whose viewing angle lies within the threshold.

In Section 6, we show that the viewpoint similarity is very close to object similarity, thus, we use only viewpoint similarity to select the assistants, as explained in the next section.

4.2 Selecting Assistants

We now formally define how an assistee can determine which assistant(s) to use, using viewpoint similarity as the metric.

Let a be the assistee, and $\mathcal{A}$ be the set of candidate assistants in the system, whose difference in viewing angle with respect to the viewing angle of the assistee is below the given threshold. Define $VS(a,\mathcal{S})$, where $\mathcal{S} \subseteq \mathcal{A}$ is a subset of $\mathcal{A}$, as the viewpoint similarity between the assistee a and the assistants in $\mathcal{S}$. The assistant selection problem can be defined as follows: Given a and $\mathcal{A}$, find

$$\mathcal{S}_{max} = \arg\max_{\mathcal{S} \subseteq \mathcal{A}} VS(a,\mathcal{S})$$

A naive approach would involve enumerating all the possible subsets of $\mathcal{A}$, which takes exponential time. Instead, we choose to use a $O(kn)$ greedy algorithm to approximate $\mathcal{S}$, where k is the number of assistants chosen, and n is the size of $\mathcal{A}$. The algorithm works as follows. First, the assistee sets $\mathcal{S}$ to empty. It then picks the assistant such that the addition of this assistant to the set $\mathcal{S}$ would increase the value of $VS(a,\mathcal{S})$ the most. It repeats either until we have k assistants in $\mathcal{S}$, until the value of $VS(a,\mathcal{S})$ is larger than VS_{th}, or until $\mathcal{S}$ does not increase after increasing k by one.

The next section shows the efficiency of the proposed selection for finding good assistants.

Figure 5: Position and Viewing Direction of Assistants.

5. RESULTS

5.1 Experimental Setup

We now present the rendering results from a scene in Second Life using peer-assisted rendering, with assistants selected using our greedy algorithm. Our goal here is to establish the efficacy of peer-assisted rendering through a simple, illustrative experiment.

We modified the Second Life client to include a user interface to position assistants in a Second Life region. This modification allows our experiment to be reproducible. We changed the rendering pipeline of Second Life so that it is capable of partially render a scene as background and object impostors.

In our experiments, we placed 10 assistants into a region named Mauve in Second Life. The impostors rendered by these assistants are stored and used in our assistee simulator. The location and viewing direction of the assistants are shown in the map in Figure 5.

The assistee simulator is a rendering client that we developed. This simulator simulates peer-assisted rendering by receiving, as input, the positions, the viewing parameters, and the impostors rendered by the assistants. The simulator then renders the scene in real-time. User can navigate in the virtual environment by interacting through the keyboard. For each frame, the simulator runs the assistant selection algorithm, and picks the best assistants out of the 10 candidates. Once the best assistants are chosen, the simulator renders the scene by warping the impostors, composting the warped impostors, concealing the errors in the resulting frame, mixing in the 3D objects, and finally displaying the result.

Figure 6: Rendering results with different number of assistants and the ground truth. From Left to Right: one assistant, three assistants, five assistants, ground truth.

Figure 7: Rendering results with different viewpoint similarities and the ground truth. From Left to Right: 0.6, 0.8, 1.0, ground truth.

5.2 Rendering Results

We present here the rendering results at the assistee. To understand the effect of the number of assistants and to validate the viewpoint similarity criteria between the assistants and assistee, we show the rendering results when different number of assistants are chosen and when a different similarity threshold is used.

Figure 6 shows the rendering results of the first frame if the assistant selection algorithm chooses 1, 3, and 5 assistants respectively. The ground truth is also shown for comparison. As expected, as the number of assistants chosen increases, the amount of visual artifacts reduces. Interestingly, with one assistant only, the majority of the impostors and a large part of the background are rendered properly already. This observation supports the usefulness of viewpoint similarity and our assistant selection algorithm.

Figure 7 shows the rendering results if the assistant selection algorithm stops running when the viewpoint similarity threshold exceeds a given value (VS_{th} = 0.6, 0.8 and 1.0). A threshold of 1.0 means that the assistant selection algorithm stops only after it fails to find any assistant that can improve the similarity. Here, we can visually quantify the impact of viewpoint similarity, even for impostors. As viewpoint similarity increases, the amount of visual artifacts reduces. Even with a viewpoint similarity of 1.0, however, we still have visual artifacts due to warping. Three kind of visual artifacts are visible: sampling issues (e.g., on the ground), exposure gaps (corresponding to white pixels on the image), and synchronisation issues (e.g., on the TV wall). Whereas exposure gaps issues are inherent to warping (as discussed in Section 3.1), we see here that using multiple assistants reduce significantly these issues. For sampling, many papers have addressed this resolution problem in the context using splatting, meshing [18] or more sophisticated modeling like LDI trees (e.g., [22]). The error concealment using splatting is illustrated on Figure 3. In the future, we want to take advantage of our object-based implementation for solving the sampling issue. The last issue causing the mixed images on the TV screens could be solved by changing the similarity metric to favor updated assistants.

We now show the result of our peer-assisted rendering on this set of 10 assistants, with $k = 10$ and $VS_{th} = 1$. Our assistee navigates through the scene as a user controls its trajectory. In this sequence, we are able to get an average similarity of 0.9. The number of assistants used varies between 3 and 6 (average is 4.1) depending on the position of the assistee.

Figure 8 shows the rendered results for every 20 frames. The exposure gaps appearing in the sequence are due to the quantization of the rasterization, and could be solved by a more careful (and a little more complex) warping. Note however that no exposure gap due to occlusion between objects occurs, as in the classical warp from a single image.

5.3 Communication Overhead

We now discuss the communication overhead incurred by peer-assisted rendering. Using our proposed approach, the data traffic from the assistants to the assistee consists of rendering elements, which are sent only when the set of chosen assistants changes. Further, the rendering elements of background objects and static near objects can be cached and reused. Thus, when the assistee moves slowly in the NVE (e.g., walking), new rendering elements are sent infrequently and the communication overhead is kept small.

Using video-based server-assisted rendering approaches [7, 21], the server continuously sends the rendered scene as a video to the assistee. Thus, the communication cost increases with time.

In our experiment above, we navigate the assistee in the vicinity of the assistants for about 1.5 minutes, generating a total of 2328 frames. Compressing these frames as a high quality MPEG-4 video[4] yields a 14 MB video. On the other hand, the navigation of the assistee causes all 10 assistants to eventually send their impostors and associated depth maps to the assistee. We compressed the impostors using JPEG and the depth maps using lossless fpzip [16], resulting in total data size of only 2 MB. Figure 9 shows the cumulative communication overhead over time in our experiment for the first 1000 frames. For peer-assisted rendering, the overhead is bursty – a large burst of data is sent when a new assistant is chosen. The rendering elements, however, can be cached and reused to

[4]We use mencoder with variable bit rate option, average bit rate of 500 kbps, 10 frames per GOP, and no B-frames.

Figure 8: Every 40 frames of an image sequence generated by hybrid rendering: background, and nearby objects are warped, both avatars are rendered locally. The second row shows the corresponding ground truth images.

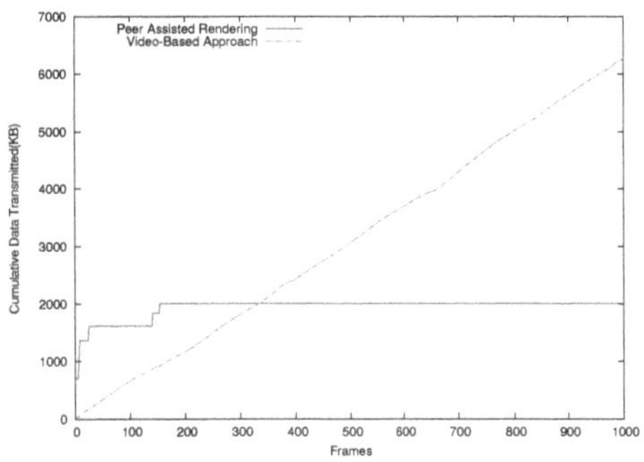

Figure 9: Cumulative communication overhead.

render a new frame if no new assistant is chosen. Thus, the communication overhead remains flat most of the time.

6. ANALYSIS OF SECOND LIFE TRACES

Having established the efficacy of distributed rendering, we now focus on answering another fundamental question. Will there be enough supply of assistants with common viewpoints or objects? To answer this question, we analyze a large collection avatar traces from Second Life to study the viewpoint similarity and object similarity between the avatars from a real, popular virtual world.

The traces are collected following similar procedure as those described by Liang [14]. There are two separate groups of experiments, one to collect avatar mobility traces, and the other to collect object traces. The collection of avatar mobility traces is conducted with a customized, command-line based, Second Life client that acts as a bot. We placed this bot in the region in which we want to collect the avatar mobility traces. The bot receives state updates from the server. These updates contain the position and viewing direction of each avatar. These information are logged by the bot every 10 seconds. The collection of object traces are done by moving the bot systematically in a region. As the bot receives new objects information from the server, it logs the position the objects.

We use traces from three regions in Second Life: Sunland, Japan Resort, and Freebies. We choose a one-hour period to analyze in this paper. Previous analysis of traces in Second Life have shown little hour-to-hour variability in the characteristics of the avatar mobility. Basic trace information is summarized in Table 1, showing the number of records (each record contains information about one avatar at one time instance) and the number of unique avatars (how many unique avatars visited the region within the trace period) for the time period.

We calculate the distribution of similarity between the avatars as follows. We explain the steps for viewpoint similarity, but the steps for object similarity is the same.

For each region, for each time t in the trace, and for each avatar a that appears in time t in the trace, we do the following. We compute the viewpoint similarity between this avatar a and all the other avatars in the region at time t, and find the avatar with the highest viewpoint similarity with a. In other words, we find the highest viewpoint similarity over all possible pairs (a,i) where $i \neq a$. Let's denote this maximum value of viewpoint similarity as $VS_{max}(a,t)$. We then average $VS_{max}(a,t)$ over all time t where a exists in the region during the period of analysis to obtain the average maximum viewpoint similarity $\bar{VS}_{max}(a)$ for each avatar a. We plot the CDF for $\bar{VS}_{max}(a)$ for the three regions in Figure 10.

In the same figure, we also plotted the CDF for average maximum viewpoint similarity for each avatar a and two other avatars, and similarly, for three other avatars. The sets of two or three avatars are considered exhaustively since we want here to prove the existence of good potential assistants –unlike in Section 5 where a greedy strategy is preferred to limit the computation time.

The results can be interpreted as follows. Take Japan Resort for example. Consider an assistee that uses k assistants. If k is 1, then on average, more than 20% of the avatars have an assistant that has viewpoint similarity of about 0.7. If two assistants are used ($k = 2$), then every avatar can find two assistants with combined viewpoint similarity of 0.85 or above. Following this interpretation, for all three regions that we analyzed, we can see that there is a significant amount of avatars with high viewpoint similarity, especially if we use two assistants. In all cases, more than half of the avatars can find two assistants with viewpoint similarity above 0.6.

Figure 10 also indicates that, as the number of assistants chosen increases to three, the improvement in the viewpoint similarity is limited, and in some cases, even reduces. The decrease is because for some assistees only two candidate assistants are passing the filtering on viewing angle difference: the number of samples for best-2 and best-3 is thus different.

The second row of Figure 10 plots the object similarity (defined in Section 4.1), calculated for a set of two or three assistants the same way as for the viewpoint similarity. We can see that half of

Region Name	Date/Time Collected	Number of Records	Number of Unique Avatars
Freebies	12:00, 23 January 2011	5786	71
Japan Resort	12:00, 23 January 2011	5912	61
SUNLAND	12:00, 23 January 2011	2516	53

Table 1: Information on Second Life Traces Used

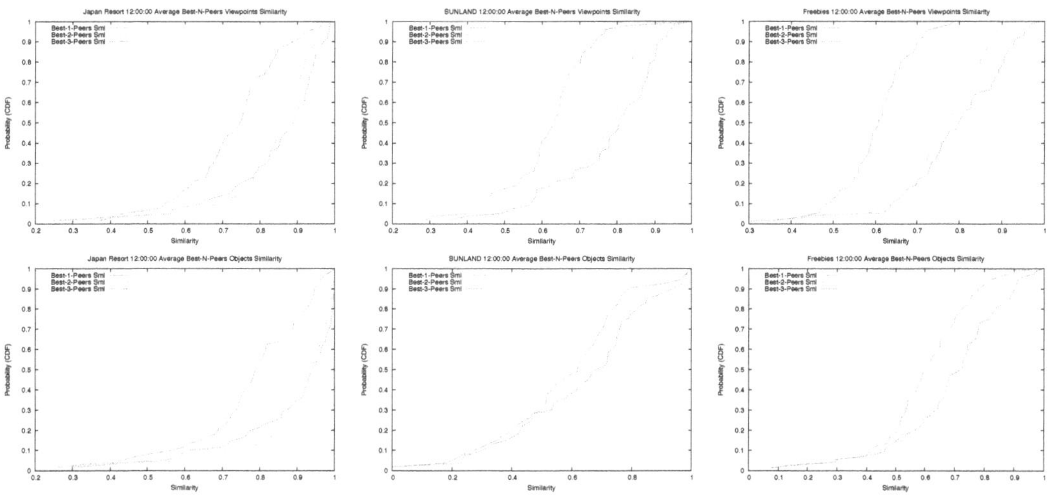

Figure 10: CDF for Viewpoint (top) and Object Similarity (bottom) for three regions: Japan Resort (left), SUNLAND (center), Freebies (right).

the assistee have an average of at least 0.5 object similarity with the best assistant, and this value improves to at least 0.7 if the assistee uses two assistants. In other words, two assistants can provide impostors for 70% of the objects half of the time. Just like viewpoint similarity, as we increase the number of assistants, the object similarity does not improve dramatically.

These trace analysis shows that in a practical NVE, even when there are only tens of avatars in a region, it is feasible to find enough peers that share similar viewpoint and a common set of objects in the viewing frustum, which is one of the fundamental conditions for peer-assisted rendering to be practical. This result further supports the efficacy of the peer-assisted rendering.

7. RESEARCH CHALLENGES

We have presented a first case for using peer assistance in rendering complex dynamic 3D scenes on mobile devices, showing clearly that there are supply of peers with similar viewpoint in a popular NVE, and a simplified rendering can yield good quality. In this section, we want to point out the coming challenges for pushing the idea of peer-assisted rendering further.

Our work did not consider yet the transmission issues. Bandwidth, loss rate, and latency between the assistee to a chosen assistant can effect the interactivity and rendering quality at the assistee, and need to be considered. Thus, the overall system needs to trade off among: (C1) computational cost on the assistee, (C2) quality of the rendered scene on assistee, (C3) the quality of the assistant, (C4) the resources at the assistant, and (C5) bandwidth requirements. In this paper, we have started addressing the constraints (C1) and (C2) on the assistee. For (C1), the proposed rendering scheme based on rendering elements is already flexible since the grouping strategy can be adapted. Different rendering elements could easily be added (e.g., billboards) for objects that are flat enough. For (C2), we have shown that the quality of the rendered images is satisfying. The frame rate, and its dependence to the rendering solution needs to be studied. In particular, we could imagine adapting the rendering to meet a minimum frame rate requirement, considering other characteristics of the assistant(s) and the network. For choosing the assistant (C3), we have proposed a metric based on geometric properties (position, frustum) of the assistant(s) relative to the assistee. These metrics extend to a set of assistants, which is important since covering the background is necessary for a complete representation of the scene. We have also shown that this geometric similarity approximates well enough the object metric proposed, and thus is usable for choosing assistant for impostors. Other characteristics of the assistant, such as availability in terms of resources (C4), could be taken into account. If the assistant has spare CPU or GPU cycles, we could then let the assistant warp for the assistee (or perform 3D rendering for the assistee). In that case, the assistee will have to send in its geometric parameters (position, frustum) and the assistant may have to download some part of the scene he is not seeing himself. Finally, the network conditions have to come into play. Synchronization issues, due to network latency, will occur and have to be measured. The network proximity (RTT) could also contribute to the metric measuring the quality of an assistant. More generally, network conditions could drive the strategy of the assistee: keep warping the background from an image received at a previous cycle if the network bandwidth is low.

These criteria (C1 – C5) are often incompatible with each other. Trading off these different criteria is non-trivial and is the next step that our research will undertake.

Other open issues in peer-assisted rendering include incentives and security. We have assumed that assistants are honest and altruistic. In practice, users need incentives to contribute bandwidth and rendering capacity to help other users. One approach could be to reward the assistants with virtual money (e.g., Linden Dollars in Second Life), either from the server or from the assistee. Another interesting issue is security. Such peer-assisted scheme needs to be robust against malicious users. A malicious rendering assistant may provide the wrong scene to the assistee, making the NVE unusable to the assistee. A malicious assistee might seek assistance from other users even though it might not need it, wasting the resources of the other users (a denial of service attack). Preventing malicious assistant and assistee are interesting open issues that we plan to look into in the future.

8. CONCLUSION

We have proposed a method for easing the access to NVE with a device with limited rendering capacities. Our approach is scalable: rendering assistance comes from other peers. It is also *tunable:* we can adjust the classification of the rendering elements to allow a trade-off between rendering quality and computational cost. We first show through an experimental setup that our approach provides satisfying rendering quality and a lower complexity for the assistee while keeping low overhead for the assistants. Then, by analyzing traces from Second life, we show that the density of avatars is sufficient to insure a high probability of finding an appropriate rendering assistant.

9. REFERENCES

[1] P. Bao and D. Gourlay. A framework for remote rendering of 3-D scenes on limited mobile devices. *IEEE Trans. on Multimedia*, 8(2):382 – 388, April 2006.

[2] P. Bao and D. Gourlay. Collaborative walkthrough using 3D warping. In *Proceedings of ICCCE '08*, pages 1110–1115, Kuala Lumpur, Malaysia, 2008.

[3] A. Boukerche and R. W. N. Pazzi. Remote rendering and streaming of progressive panoramas for mobile devices. In *Proceedings of ACM MULTIMEDIA '06*, pages 691–694, Santa Barbara, CA, USA, 2006.

[4] A. Boukerche, R. Werner, and N. Pazzi. A peer-to-peer approach for remote rendering and image streaming in walkthrough applications. In *Proceedings of IEEE ICC '07*, pages 1692 –1697, june 2007.

[5] C.-F. Chang and S.-H. Ger. Enhancing 3D graphics on mobile devices by image-based rendering. In *Proceedings of IEEE PCM '02*, pages 1105–1111, London, UK, 2002.

[6] J. Chen, I. Yoon, and W. Bethel. Interactive, internet delivery of visualization via structured prerendered multiresolution imagery. *IEEE Trans. on Visualization and Computer Graphics*, 14(2):302–312, 2008.

[7] L. Cheng, A. Bhushan, R. Pajarola, and M. E. Zarki. Real-time 3D graphics streaming using MPEG-4. In *Proc. of the IEEE/ACM Workshop on Broadband Wireless Services and Applications*, 2004.

[8] W. Cheng, D. Liu, and W. T. Ooi. Peer-assisted view-dependent progressive mesh streaming. In *Proceedings of ACM MULTIMEDIA '09*, pages 441–450, Beijing, China, 2009.

[9] S.-Y. Hu. A case for 3D streaming on peer-to-peer networks. In *Proceedings of Web3D '06*, pages 57–63, Columbia, Maryland, 2006.

[10] H. Z. Jie Feng. Efficient view-dependent LOD control for large 3D unclosed mesh models of environments. In *Proceedings of IEEE ICRA '04*, pages 2723–2728, 2004.

[11] F. Lamberti, C. Zunino, A. Sanna, A. Fiume, and M. Maniezzo. An accelerated remote graphics architecture for PDAs. In *Proceedings of Web3D '03*, pages 55–ff, Saint Malo, France, 2003.

[12] S. Lazem, M. Elteir, A. Abdel-Hamid, and D. Gracanm. Prediction-based prefetching for remote rendering streaming in mobile virtual environments. In *IEEE Intl. Symp. on Signal Processing and Information Technology*, pages 760 –765, December 2007.

[13] Y. Lei, Z. Jiang, D. Chen, and H. Bao. Image-based walkthrough over Internet on mobile devices. In *Proc. of Grid and Cooperative Computing*, pages 728–735, 2004.

[14] H. Liang, R. N. Silva, W. T. Ooi, and M. Motani. Avatar mobility in user-created networked virtual worlds: measurements, analysis, and implications. *Multimedia Tools and Applications*, 45(1-3):163–190, 2009.

[15] K. Liang and R. Zimmermann. Cross-tree adjustment for spatialized audio streaming over networked virtual environments. In *Proceedings of NOSSDAV '09*, pages 73–78, Williamsburg, VA, USA, 2009.

[16] P. Lindstrom and M. Isenburg. Fast and efficient compression of floating-point data. *IEEE Trans. on Visualization and Computer Graphics*, 12:1245–1250, September 2006.

[17] J. Lluch, R. Gaitan, E. Camahort, and R. Vivo. Interactive three-dimensional rendering on mobile computer devices. In *Proceedings of ACM SIGCHI '05*, pages 254–257, 2005.

[18] W. R. Mark, L. McMillan, and G. Bishop. Post-rendering 3D warping. In *Proceedings of I3D '97*, pages 7–ff., Providence, RI, 1997.

[19] L. McMillan and G. Bishop. Plenoptic modeling: an image-based rendering system. In *Proceedings of SIGGRAPH '95*, pages 39–46, 1995.

[20] B. Mochocki, K. Lahiri, and S. Cadambi. Power analysis of mobile 3D graphics. In *Proc. of the Conf. on Design, Automation and Test in Europe*, pages 502–507, Munich, Germany, 2006.

[21] Y. Noimark and D. Cohen-Or. Streaming scenes to MPEG-4 video-enabled devices. *IEEE Computer Graphics and Applications*, 23(1):58–64, 2003.

[22] J. Shade, S. Gortler, L.-w. He, and R. Szeliski. Layered depth images. In *Proceedings of SIGGRAPH '98*, pages 231–242, 1998.

[23] S. Shi, W. J. Jeon, K. Nahrstedt, and R. H. Campbell. Real-time remote rendering of 3D video for mobile devices. In *Proceedings of ACM MULTIMEDIA'09*, pages 391–400, Beijing, China, 2009.

[24] S. Shi, M. Kamali, K. Nahrstedt, J. C. Hart, and R. H. Campbell. A high-quality low-delay remote rendering system for 3D video. In *Proceedings of ACM MULTIMEDIA '10*, pages 601–610, Firenze, Italy, 2010.

[25] W. Shi, Y. Lu, Z. Li, and J. Engelsma. Scalable support for 3D graphics applications in cloud. In *Proceedings of IEEE CLOUD '10*, pages 346–353, 2010.

[26] A. Sterkin. Interactive 3D streaming. Research@Intel Blog, June 2008. Retrieved 1 April 2010.

BlueStreaming: Towards Power-Efficient Internet P2P Streaming to Mobile Devices*

Yao Liu[1] Fei Li[1] Lei Guo[2] Yang Guo[3] Songqing Chen[1]

[1]Department of Computer Science, George Mason University, {yliud, lifei, sqchen}@cs.gmu.edu

[2]Microsoft Corporation, Mountain View, CA, USA, leguo@microsoft.com

[3]Bell Labs, Alcatel-Lucent, yang.guo@alcatel-lucent.com

ABSTRACT

P2P streaming applications are very popular on the Internet today. However, a mobile device in P2P streaming not only needs to continuously receive streaming data from other peers for its playback, but also needs to continuously exchange control information (e.g., buffermaps and file chunk requests) with neighboring peers and upload the downloaded streaming data to them. These lead to excessive battery power consumption on the mobile device.

In this paper, we first conduct Internet experiments to study in-depth the impact of control traffic and uploading traffic on battery power consumption with several popular Internet P2P streaming applications. Motivated by measurement results, we design and implement a system called BlueStreaming that effectively utilizes the commonly existing Bluetooth interface on mobile devices. Instead of activating WiFi and Bluetooth interfaces alternatively, BlueStreaming keeps Bluetooth active all the time to transmit delay-sensitive control traffic while using WiFi for streaming data traffic. BlueStreaming trades Bluetooth's power consumption for much more significant energy saving from shaped WiFi traffic. To evaluate the performance of BlueStreaming, we have implemented prototypes on both Windows and Mac to access existing popular Internet P2P streaming services. The experimental results show that BlueStreaming can save up to 46% battery power compared to the commodity PSM scheme.

Categories and Subject Descriptors

C.2.4 [**Distributed Systems**]: Distributed applications

General Terms

Measurement, Design, Experimentation

Keywords

P2P, Internet Mobile Streaming, Bluetooth, Power Saving

1. INTRODUCTION

Internet Peer-to-Peer (P2P) streaming applications are very popular today. For example, PPTV [1], PPStream [2], SopCast [3], and QQLive [4] are all Internet-scale P2P streaming systems that provide hundreds of TV channels and serve millions of Internet users every day. As a result, CNN has started to use P2P technology provided by Octoshape to deliver high quality live video to its users [5]. According to Cisco's report [6], today, global P2P TV systems have generated over 280 petabytes (and 6% of) Internet video traffic per month, and is growing at a rate of 47% annually.

In tandem with the fast-growing Internet streaming services, mobile devices are pervasively used today. For example, it has been reported that iPad users generated 2.5 times more Internet traffic than iPhone users for accessing popular services such as USAToday, Google Maps, Bloomberg, eBay after its release [7]. To support mobile Internet accesses, 802.11 and the third generation (3G) wireless networks are also quickly developing. For example, WiFi operates in more than 595,000 public hotspots [8]. Jupiter Research also estimated that 65% households in the United States have home-deployed WiFi access points (APs) [9].

However, using mobile devices to receive Internet streaming services can quickly exhaust the limited battery supply because receiving Internet streaming services often involve continuous and bulk data transmissions, decoding, rendering, and displaying. Among them, wireless data transmissions consume a significant amount of energy. For example, it was reported that the WiFi radio on HTC Tilt 8900 series consumes up to 5x more power than the base energy consumption of the phone [10]. A lot of efforts have been made to save battery power consumed by the wireless network interface cards (WNICs) by exploiting sleep opportunities via proxying [11], batching [12], PSM-throttling [13], etc. However, existing power saving strategies mainly focus on client/server (C/S) based streaming applications. Compared to C/S based streaming, Internet P2P streaming can further aggravate the battery power consumption on mobile devices due to the following unique characteristics.

First, different from C/S based streaming, a client participating in P2P streaming needs to continuously exchange extra control traffic, such as buffermaps and fine-grained data chunk requests, with neighbors. Such control traffic, on the one hand, greatly facilitates the streaming content distribution in a scalable manner. On the other hand, it also remarkably increases the total number of IP packets transmitted and reduces the inter-packet delays, which further reduces the sleep opportunities of the WNIC.

Second, critical to the scalability of a P2P system, a client participating in P2P streaming has to upload the downloaded content to other neighboring peers. Such uploading requirement does not exist in C/S based streaming. The uploading traffic increases the total traffic volume for a P2P client, resulting in more battery power consumption.

Third, a client participating in P2P streaming receives streaming content from multiple sources instead of a single server. Further-

*Area Chair: Surender Chandra

MM'11, November 28–December 1, 2011, Scottsdale, Arizona, USA.

more, these streaming sources are changing dynamically along time since a P2P client often needs to frequently connect to new neighbors to download missing file chunks. In addition, the dynamics of the streaming sources result in different round-trip times to the client, making data receiving at the client side totally random, and making it difficult for the WNIC to switch into the power saving mode (PSM).

In this paper, we first conduct Internet measurements to study in-depth the impact of Internet P2P streaming on battery consumption on mobile devices with several popular Internet P2P streaming applications. Our measurement results show that: (1) a client in P2P streaming needs to transmit an extremely large number of small packets for control traffic (e.g., twice as many as streaming data packets). Such a large number of frequent and delay-sensitive control packets not only increase the traffic volume, but also significantly reduce the inter-packet delay and the potential sleep time of the WNIC on the mobile device; (2) the amount of uploading traffic a mobile client needs to transmit to its neighbors changes from time to time and from application to application, ranging from 10 Kbps to over 1.5 Mbps. In addition to increasing the transmission load on the WNIC, such highly un-predictable uploading further reduces the inter-packet delay and the sleep opportunities of the WNIC for power saving; and (3) a client in P2P streaming receives packets from dynamically changing sources (e.g., 3 to 20 peers), making it difficult to employ server or client-centric traffic shaping techniques to save power consumption on mobile devices.

Motivated by the measurement results, we seek to address these challenges for power-efficient Internet mobile P2P streaming services. Accordingly, we propose and design the BlueStreaming system by leveraging the commonly existing Bluetooth interface on mobile devices. In BlueStreaming, instead of having WiFi and Bluetooth interfaces to work alternatively, we always keep Bluetooth active to transmit delay-sensitive control traffic. With intelligent traffic shaping techniques applied on the WiFi interface for data traffic, the extra battery power consumed by the Bluetooth interface can be over-compensated by the greater power saving on the WiFi interface. Furthermore, the uploading traffic from the client is opportunistically scheduled on both interfaces to minimize battery power consumption incurred.

To evaluate the performance of BlueStreaming, we have implemented prototypes on both Windows and Mac OS to participate in several popular Internet P2P streaming services. Our experimental results show that BlueStreaming can effectively reduce battery power consumption by up to 46% without affecting streaming quality. In summary, this paper makes the following contributions:

- Through Internet measurement and analysis, we show that when a mobile device participates in Internet P2P streaming services, its battery power consumption is highly affected by its control traffic, uploading traffic, and the dynamics of neighboring peers.
- We design and implement BlueStreaming, a power-efficient Internet P2P streaming system that takes into account the unique characteristics of Internet P2P streaming and trades Bluetooth's power consumption for greater power saving on the WiFi interface via intelligent traffic shaping.
- We evaluate our BlueStreaming prototype with popular Internet P2P streaming applications in both infrastructure and hybrid modes, and show that BlueStreaming can improve energy saving by up to 46% compared to the commodity PSM scheme.

The remainder of the paper is organized as follows. Section 2 describes some related work. We present our measurement results in Section 3 and the design of BlueStreaming in Section 4. The implementation is described in Section 5 and the evaluation is discussed in Section 6. We make concluding remarks in Section 7.

2. BACKGROUND AND RELATED WORK

With pervasive wireless Internet accesses, power saving has been considered on the commodity WNIC. Today most WNIC can operate in two power modes: Constantly Awake Mode (CAM) and PSM. It has been reported in [10] that a mobile smartphone in CAM uses as much as 1120 mW power, while it consumes much less power of 72 mW in PSM. In practice, commodity WiFi devices often use adaptive PSM (PSM-A) instead of static PSM. PSM-A switches between CAM and PSM modes. If there is no network activity (idle) for a pre-determined time period, called *idle timeout interval*, the WiFi interface would switch to PSM by sending a NULL data frame with the `Pwr Mgt` field set to 1. It only wakes up to check the Traffic Indication Map (TIM) per beacon interval (e.g., 100 ms). The WiFi interface can notify AP that it is ready to receive buffered data by sending another NULL data frame with the `Pwr Mgt` field set to 0. To further improve the energy efficiency, a lot of prior work has sought to exploit idle opportunities for the WNIC. For example, μPM [14] allows the WiFi interface to exploit short intervals in terms of microseconds between MAC frames to enter the low power mode. Catnap [12], on the other hand, exploits large sleep intervals by scheduling TCP transfers at the granularity of application data units with the help of workload hints.

Meanwhile, since mobile devices commonly have equipped with multiple network interfaces that have different power consumption rates, research has been conducted on alternatively activating different interfaces for battery power saving, focusing on substituting a high-power consumption interface with a low-power consumption interface whenever possible. For example, Agarwal et al. proposed to wake up the WiFi interface for incoming calls using GSM radio [15]. In CoolSpots [16], policies were proposed to intelligently switch between the Bluetooth and WiFi interfaces. However, CoolSpots is not appropriate for today's Internet streaming delivery to mobile devices because Bluetooth alone cannot afford the constant bandwidth demanded by modern streaming applications (see Section 4.1). In contrast to CoolSpots that uses the two interfaces alternatively, BlueStreaming uses both WiFi and Bluetooth interfaces simultaneously, and relies on the greater power saving on the WiFi interface to overcompensate the extra power consumption incurred by the Bluetooth interface.

Focusing on Internet streaming to mobile devices, Bertozzi et al. proposed to switch off the WiFi interface during playback and turn it on when running out of streaming buffer [17]. Linear prediction was proposed to select sleep time intervals for the WNIC [18]. PSM-throttling [13] utilizes client-side reshaping of TCP traffic to improve energy saving. Compared to existing work, this study shows that a client in P2P streaming not only generates extra uploading traffic, but also transmits highly frequent and delay-sensitive control traffic, making direct adoption of existing solutions ineffective.

3. MEASUREMENT AND ANALYSIS

To investigate the battery power consumption on mobile devices in popular Internet P2P streaming applications, in this section, we conduct measurements with several existing Internet P2P streaming applications. We then analyze the traffic in-depth in order to study underlying factors that impact the battery power consumption.

3.1 Methodology and Result Overview

To study the battery power consumption on mobile devices in receiving P2P streaming services, we first use a 2nd generation iPod Touch (iTouch) running iOS 3.1.2 to receive streaming services. We conduct experiments with TVUPlayer [19], and Justin.tv [20]. To the best of our knowledge, TVUPlayer is the only P2P based

Table 1: Summary of Statistics on Laptop

Name	Architecture	Encoding Rate (Kbps)	Total # of IP Packets	Total # of Contro Packets	Total # of Streaming Packets	Sleep Time (%)	Average# of Neighbors
PPTV	P2P	400	191716	116819	70873	4.42	12
PPS	P2P	396	433935	322779	85180	0.09	20
SopCast	P2P	530	305826	202240	92457	0.99	3
QQLive	P2P	500	293474	183814	108827	7.12	4
J.tv	C/S	433	123655	56689	66966	21.44	N/A

streaming application available on iTouch at the time of this measurement, while Justin.tv is a C/S based Internet streaming service.

In these experiments, we set up Wireshark to listen on the same channel to capture all incoming/outgoing packets. Since we log packets at the data-link layer, we are able to get frame control information from IEEE 802.11 headers. We use `Pwr Mgt` flag in the frame control field to determine the Power Management mode that the WiFi interface will switch to after the transmission of the current frame. All experiments are run for 30 minutes and are conducted with a dedicated AP running 802.11g in order to minimize traffic contention.

We set both TVUPlayer and Justin.tv to watch channels with the same streaming rate (281 Kbps), and examine the potential power consumed by the WiFi interface. Our results show that during 30 minutes test, C/S based Justin.tv allows the WNIC to sleep for 83% time, while in P2P based TVUPlayer, the WNIC can only sleep for 26% time, meaning 3 times more power consumption in receiving P2P streaming services. Given that iOS uses an extremely aggressive PSM-A policy (idle timeout interval is only about 20-25 ms [10]), the energy performance of TVUPlayer on other mobile devices could be even worse.

Although the above results provide an overview of the power inefficiency P2P streaming services for mobile devices, TVUPlayer is not as widely used as other P2P based Internet streaming services such as PPTV (PPLive is renamed as PPTV), PPStream (PPS), SopCast and QQLive, each of which serves millions of Internet users daily. To study in-depth the battery power consumption of mobile devices in these applications, we further conduct experiments with a laptop computer since these applications do not have a version for mobile devices. We again compare their results against C/S based Justin.tv (J.tv) [21]. In these experiments, the laptop computer connects to a dedicated AP running 802.11n and watches different channels of these popular applications. The laptop runs Windows 7 with `Maximum WiFi Power Saving` enabled. Again, Wireshark is used to capture all incoming and outgoing packets to/from the laptop at the data-link layer. Because each peer in P2P streaming is required to upload to its neighbors and such uploading throughput can be highly un-predictable (we will show later in Section 3.3), we thus conduct experiments at various times of a day and first present the results of tests that involve the least amount of uploading traffic. This makes the comparison against C/S based J.tv more meaningful because otherwise the additional high uploading from a mobile device undoubtedly increases the battery power consumption. Note that these tests are not necessarily accessing unpopular channels, since uploading of a peer is also affected by a number of other factors.

Table 1 summarizes some raw data based on the traces we have collected in the experiments. Note that *Total # of Streaming Packets* refers to the downloaded streaming data packets only. Although the video encoding rates are different across four P2P applications, it is not necessarily correlated to the amount of time that the WiFi interface has spent in the PSM: both PPTV and PPS stream at similar rates, but they have different power efficiency; SopCast allows the WiFi interface to sleep for less than 1% of the session time with a streaming rate of 530 Kbps, but at a similar rate of 500 Kbps in QQLive, the WiFi interface operates in the PSM for 7% of the session time, and is the most power efficient.

Nevertheless, compared to C/S based J.tv in which the WiFi operates in the PSM for 21% of the session time, none of these four popular P2P streaming applications is power efficient. Note that all above experiments involve a small amount of uploading traffic. If the laptop has to upload more to neighboring peers, the power efficiency of P2P streaming applications would be even worse (we will show soon in Section 3.3).

While the sleep time varies in different P2P streaming applications, above results on both the mobile device and the laptop show that compared to C/S based streaming, a mobile client in existing P2P streaming applications is much less power efficient. As aforementioned, this is likely due to the uploading and control traffic. To quantify their impact, next we further analyze the incoming and outgoing traffic to/from our testing client.

3.2 Impact of Control Traffic

Figures 1, 2, 3, and 4 show more detailed traffic analysis in the above experiments for PPTV, PPS, SopCast, and QQLive, respectively. Figure 1(a) shows the packet size distribution of PPTV. As indicated by this figure, the packet size distribution is highly bimodal. Via reverse-engineering, we find that only about 37% packets are streaming packets with the size around 1408 bytes while about 60% packets have a size less than 300 bytes. Similarly, Figures 2(a), 3(a), and 4(a) show that there are more than 74%, 66%, and 62% small packets in the streaming sessions of PPS, SopCast, and QQLive, respectively.

Recall that existing P2P streaming systems mainly use a pull based mesh structure, in which neighboring peers need to frequently exchange control information. For example, peers exchange `buffermaps` to determine data chunk availability among neighbors. Peers also need to send out `file chunk requests` to retrieve missing streaming data chunks. In addition, PPTV, PPS, Sopcast, and QQLive all use UDP to transmit packets. Thus, these small packets can only be control traffic of the P2P protocol. Via reverse-engineering, it is confirmed that these packets include both buffermaps exchanged with neighbors and file chunk requests sent to neighbors.

Table 1 shows that in all these P2P streaming applications, there are more control packets (the 5th column) than streaming data packets (the 6th column). PPS even generated about 3 times more control packets than data packets. Regardless of the total traffic amount of these control packets, such a large number of control packets can significantly reduce the the inter-packet delay and thus idle time of the WiFi interface. This would result in more battery power consumption. Figures 1(b), 2(b), 3(b), and 4(b) show the inter packet delay distribution in these experiments. In these figures, `Inter Streaming Packet` delay considers only ingress streaming data packets. `Inter Control Packet` delay considers both incoming and outgoing control packets, and `Inter`

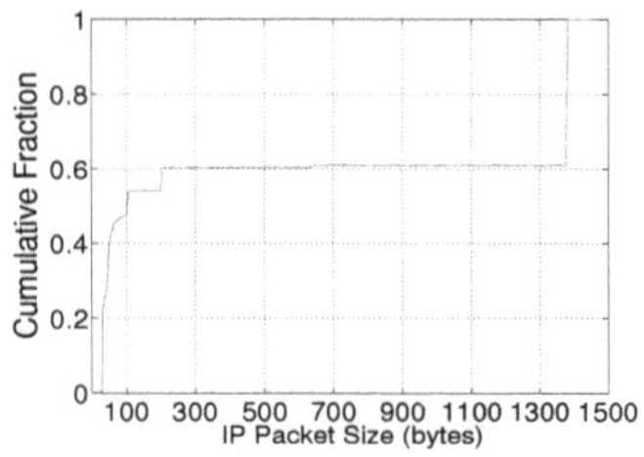

(a) Packet Size (CDF)

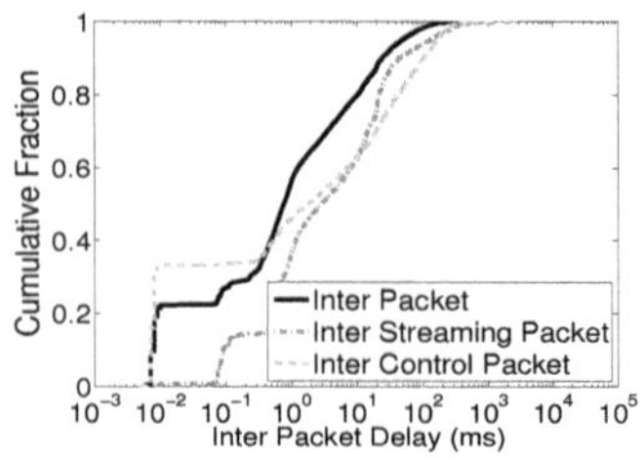

(b) Inter Packet Delay (CDF)

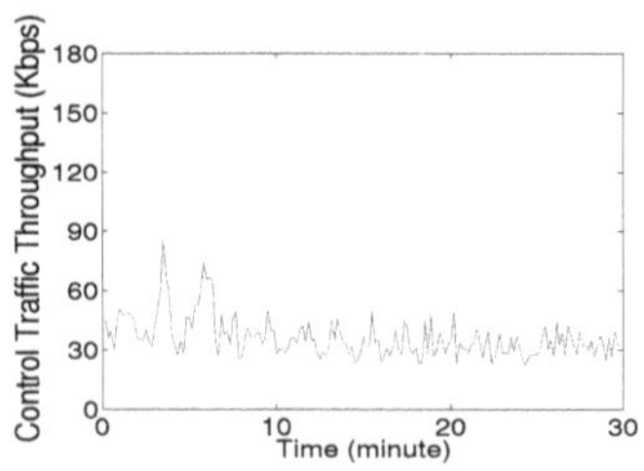

(c) Control Traffic Throughput

Figure 1: PPTV (400Kbps)

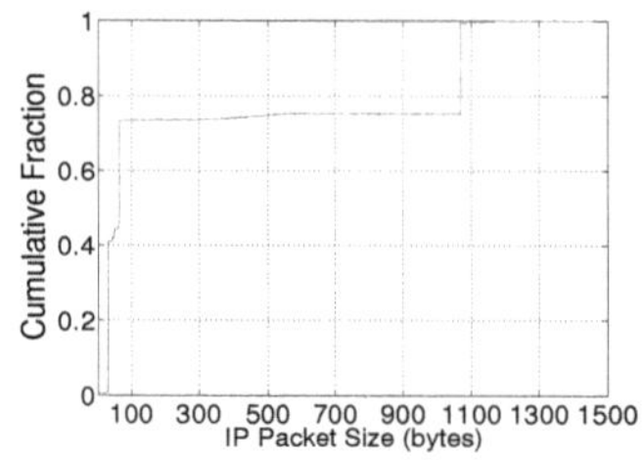

(a) Packet Size (CDF)

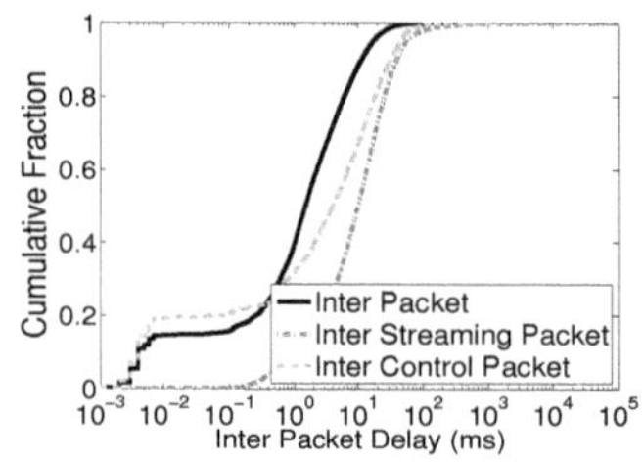

(b) Inter Packet Delay (CDF)

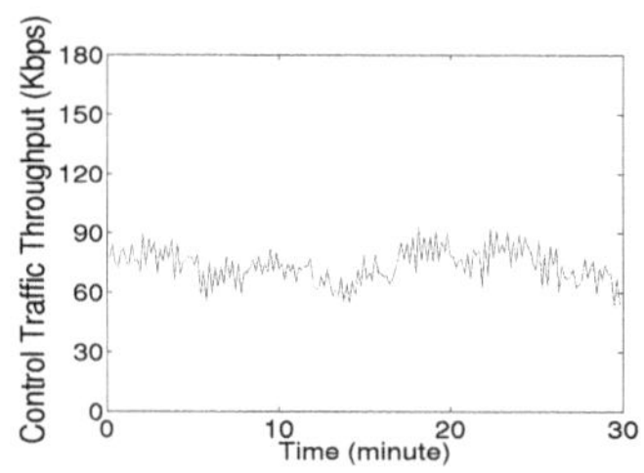

(c) Control Traffic Throughput

Figure 2: PPS (396Kbps)

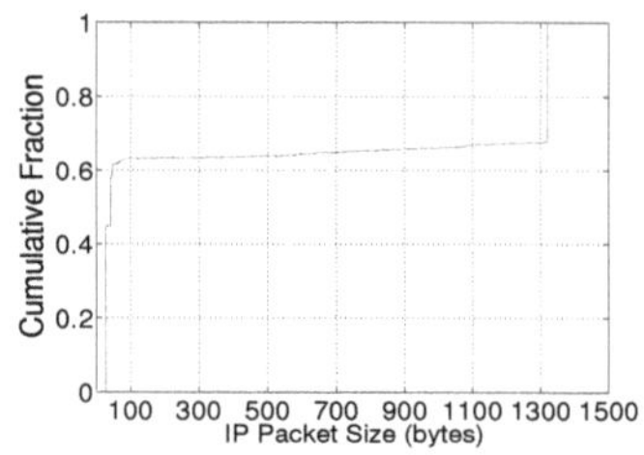

(a) Packet Size (CDF)

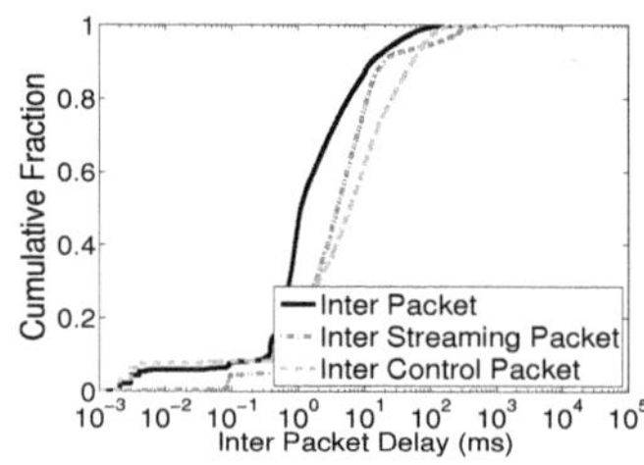

(b) Inter Packet Delay (CDF)

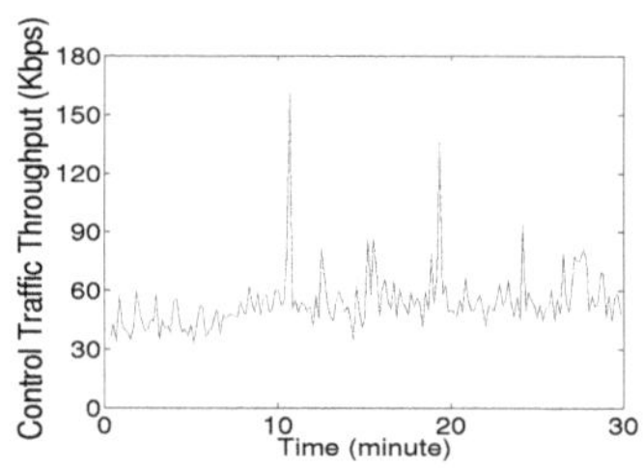

(c) Control Traffic Throughput

Figure 3: SopCast (530Kbps)

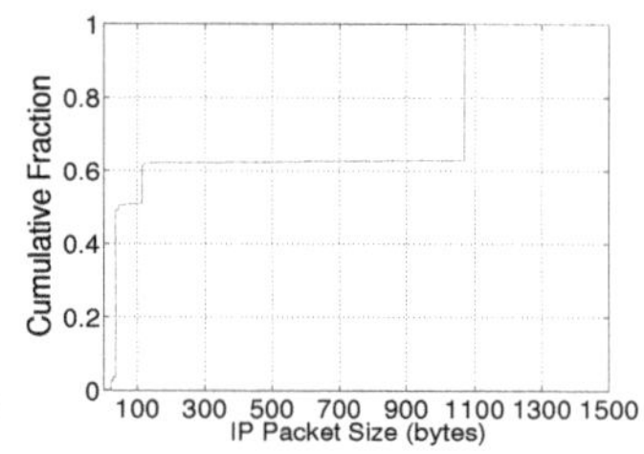

(a) Packet Size (CDF)

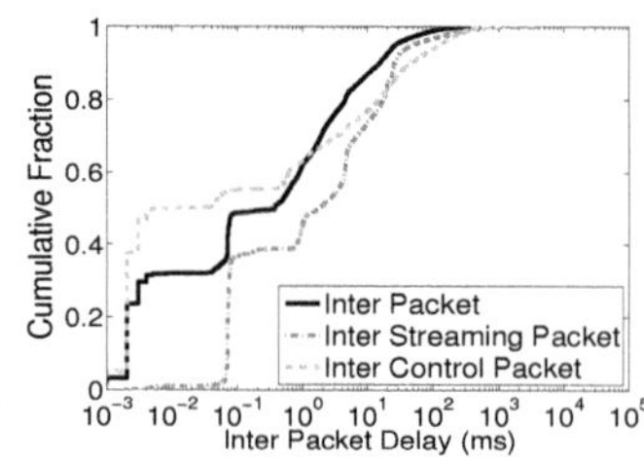

(b) Inter Packet Delay (CDF)

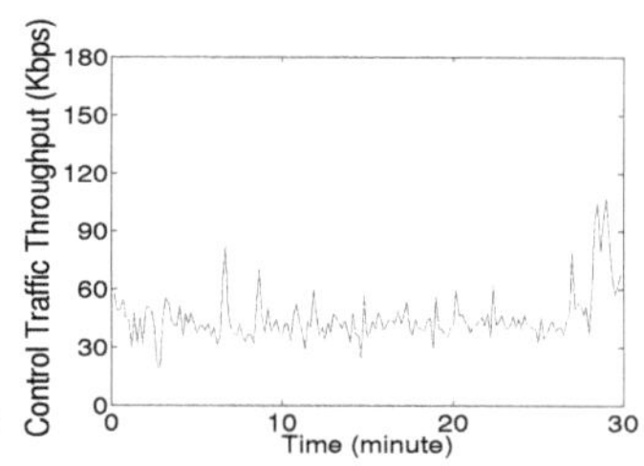

(c) Control Traffic Throughput

Figure 4: QQLive (500Kbps)

`Packet` delay takes all packets transmitted into account. As shown in these figures, while 10% and 3% successive streaming packets of PPTV and PPS arrive with a delay larger than 100 ms (meaning opportunities for power saving), about 60% control packets in PPTV and 42% in PPS are sent/received within 1 ms from the preceding one. This causes the overall Inter Packet delay to significantly deviate from Inter Streaming Packet delay patterns.

Although control packets are much more frequent than streaming data packets, the throughput of control traffic is relatively small. As shown in Figures 1(c), 2(c), 3(c), and 4(c), the throughput of control traffic of the four P2P streaming applications is less than 100 Kbps for most of the time. In these figures, the throughput is averaged over 10 seconds. The relatively small control traffic throughput is mainly due to the small size of control packets. This is a very important feature that we could explore to save power consumption in BlueStreaming in Section 4. Although control traffic may increase with the increase of uploading, typically the control traffic throughput is still much smaller than the streaming data rate.

3.3 Impact of Uploading Traffic

The measurement results we have presented above involve a minimum amount of uploading traffic. In practice, a P2P client may upload more and the uploading throughput may also change from time to time. Figure 5 shows the uploading variations of our client with a minimum uploading average and a maximum uploading average in our over fifty 30-minute tests at various time. As shown in this figure, the throughput of uploading traffic could reach as high as over 1 Mbps in PPTV, PPS, and SopCast. Such a high uploading throughput clearly consumes more battery power. As shown in Table 3, with a larger amount of uploading traffic transmitted, the sleep time (%) of the WiFi interface in all four applications de-

Table 3: Comparison of Sleep Time (%)

	PPTV	PPS	SopCast	QQLive
MAX	4.42	0.09	0.99	7.12
MIN	0.08	0.00	0.22	4.33

creases significantly, and in PPS it even could not switch into the PSM at all.

3.4 Impact of the Number of Neighbors

Both control traffic and uploading traffic are affected by the number of neighbors a peer communicates with at a time. A larger number of neighbors not only increase the control information exchanged with different peers and the uploading traffic amount, but also divide large idle time intervals into smaller ones because the response time of different peers to our client varies significantly. During the experiments, we have kept track of the number of peers that our streaming client downloaded data from. As shown in the last column of Table 1, during the 30-minute test, our client in QQLive exchanges streaming data with 4 neighboring peers on average every 10 seconds, while it involves 12 neighbors on average in PPTV.

Summary of Measurement Results: Our study shows that in Internet P2P streaming (1) although of small throughput, the control traffic is highly frequent, which remarkably reduces the potential sleep time of the WiFi interface; (2) the uploading required from a peer changes dynamically and could reach a very high throughput, which directly affects the battery power consumption and worsens the client side traffic pattern; (3) the dynamics of peers' neighbors directly affect both control and uploading traffic, and the variance

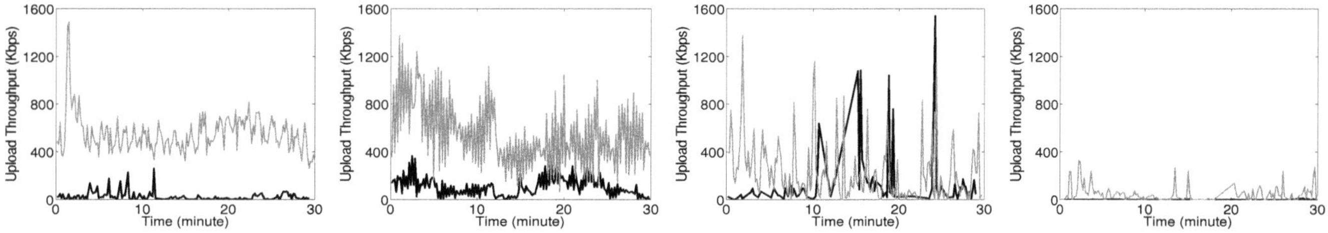

(a) PPTV (b) PPS (c) SopCast (d) QQLive

Figure 5: Variation of Upload Throughput (averaged over 10 seconds)

Table 2: Simple Strategies Do Not Work Well

Name	Total # of Streaming	Sleep Time (%)	Distortion/Freeze Time (%)
PSM-A	109800	5.24	0
Bluetooth only	37228	N/A	96
WiFi with traffic shaping	121598	26.89	38

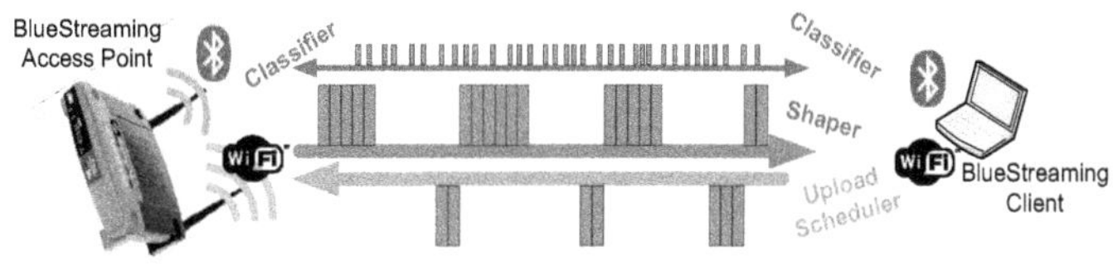

Figure 6: Overview of BlueStreaming Architecture

of response time among neighbors further shortens inter-packet delay.

4. DESIGN OF BLUESTREAMING

As discussed in the last section, P2P streaming differs from traditional client-server based streaming on the additional control traffic, uploading traffic, and data receiving from multiple peers. These can lead to excessive battery power consumption on mobile devices.

4.1 Motivation

To save power consumed for data transmission, an intuitive solution is to always switch to a low power interface, e.g., Bluetooth connection when available. Another solution is to use WiFi interface only, but aggressively shapes the traffic by brutally buffering all packets for long enough and transmit them in a very large MAC frame periodically.

We implement both of these schemes. Table 2 shows the results when accessing a QQLive channel of 500 Kbps for 30 minutes. `Bluetooth only` saves energy consumption by only using Bluetooth for all transmissions. However, Bluetooth alone cannot afford the constant bandwidth demanded by the application. As a result, Table 2 shows that the client with `Bluetooth only` receives about only 34% streaming data packets compared to PSM-A. This causes the playback to be frozen all the time during the entire streaming session.

On the other hand, in WiFi with traffic shaping, the control packets are also buffered and sent in burst periodically via WiFi. Table 2 shows that such an approach can make the WiFi interface to sleep for 26% of the session time. However, the delayed control packets have caused the client to receive 10% more streaming packets, indicating the delay-sensitivity of control traffic. Moreover, by analyzing the captured frames of the playback and comparing with those captured in PSM-A (since we do not have access to the original video), we find that quality degradation (playback freezing or distortion) happens for a total of 684 seconds, which is 38% of the entire streaming session.

The above results demonstrate that these intuitive strategies using either interface may cause problems in both user perceived quality and the efficiency of transmission. We next present our design of BlueStreaming to intelligently utilize both WiFi and commonly existing Bluetooth interfaces on mobile devices for Internet P2P streaming accesses.

4.2 BlueStreaming Overview

To efficiently deal with control traffic in P2P streaming, BlueStreaming leverages the Bluetooth interface on a mobile device to transmit control traffic. For this purpose, BlueStreaming always classifies the incoming and outgoing traffic to/from a client into two classes: ingress/egress control traffic and ingress/egress data traffic. BlueStreaming uses Bluetooth to transmit both ingress and egress control traffic. In addition, since uploading is inevitable and Bluetooth is always active in BlueStreaming, Bluetooth also uploads to neighbors whenever there is available bandwidth. The WiFi interface is mainly used for streaming data downloading, as well as uploading opportunistically upon excessive uploading.

Figure 6 depicts the architecture of BlueStreaming. Logically, BlueStreaming consists of three main components: the traffic classifier at both the AP and the client sides to decouple control traffic from streaming data traffic, the traffic shaper at the client side for shaping data traffic to save battery power, and the uploading scheduler at the client side to handle uploading traffic. The successful design of these three components, however, needs to address the following challenges:

- *traffic classifier*: given that in most P2P streaming, control traffic and data traffic use the same channel (port number), how can control traffic be decoupled from data traffic transparently (transparent to the application)?
- *traffic shaper*: since most existing P2P streaming traffic is delivered over UDP and a client often dynamically communicates with a set of different peers at a time, how shall BlueStreaming shape the downstream traffic to a client?
- *uploading scheduler*: because uploading from a peer is necessary and critical to the scalability of a P2P system, how does a client perform uploading while minimizing the corresponding battery power consumption?

4.3 Traffic Classifier: Diverting Control Traffic to Bluetooth

Since Bluetooth operates with about 20% power compared to WiFi in an active state, with BlueStreaming, a mobile device seeks to use Bluetooth to transmit the large number of small delay-sensitive control packets in order to put the WiFi interface into sleep mode for a longer time. This requires Bluetooth to provide sufficient bandwidth to transmit control traffic. Commodity Bluetooth interfaces today typically offer a low data rate of 1 Mbps or so. Although we have shown in Section 3 that control traffic may fluctuate from time to time depending on a number of factors such as the number of neighbors, the control traffic rate is often very low. Using Bluetooth to transmit control traffic also needs to consider the time sensitivity of control packets. A previous study shows that the delay of the control traffic would cause repetitive requests of the same data chunks [22]. Thus, to ensure timely delivery of control packets, in BlueStreaming, the Bluetooth interface stays active all the time so that control packets are transmitted without any delay.

To transmit control packets via Bluetooth, control traffic must be separated from data traffic at runtime. In BlueStreaming, the traffic classifier is responsible for decoupling control packets from data packets. Since there are both incoming and outgoing control packets, the traffic classifier works at both the AP and the client sides. Because (1) the current design of BlueStreaming aims to be application transparent, (2) both control traffic and data traffic in typical P2P streaming services use a same port, and (3) the classification must be real time, BlueStreaming has to avoid deep packet inspection for any application specific information.

Thus, in BlueStreaming, we leverage a feature that we have found via our measurement for runtime packet decoupling. In Section 3, Figures 1(a), 2(a), 3(a), and 4(a) show the packet size distribution. As shown in these figures, the control packets are of a much smaller size compared to that of streaming data packets. Thus, in BlueStreaming, we leverage the packet size to differentiate different types of packets. Although the classification is based on our observation in the measurements, we have further conducted measurements with these P2P streaming services for prolonged time in order to validate its accuracy.

Once the control traffic is decoupled, it is easy to divert to the Bluetooth interface. Upon packet arrival, merging received packets from different interfaces is straightforward since these P2P streaming applications use UDP.

4.4 Traffic Shaper: Shaping Ingress Streaming Traffic

After all control packets are diverted to the Bluetooth channel, only data traffic is transmitted through WiFi. Thus, more energy could be saved by exploiting the idle time of the WiFi interface.

Figures 1(b), 2(b), 3(b), and 4(b) show the inter-packet delays. As shown in these figures, although the Inter Packet delay distribution of WiFi (without control traffic) is similar to the distribution of Inter Streaming Packet delay, the increase of sleep opportunity due to control traffic elimination is still small. This is likely due to the multiple uploading peers instead of only a single server. Multiple uploading peers have different response time to this client, resulting in different ingress streaming packet arrival time as observed in our measurement.

Thus, after diverting control traffic, BlueStreaming still needs to handle incoming traffic from different neighboring peers. A natural scheme is to do traffic shaping at the AP. Since BlueStreaming mainly deals with UDP based streaming, the traditional TCP based traffic shaping in the client-server based architecture, such as PSM-throttling, does not work. In addition, due to the QoS requirements of Internet streaming services, such streaming packets cannot be buffered for too long.

To this end, in the traffic shaper, BlueStreaming utilizes the buffer maintained by the WiFi AP: the streaming packets arrived over time are combined into a single MAC frame burst. As a result, the interval between bursts is significantly enlarged and the WiFi interface can exploit these opportunities to switch into the PSM.

To minimize the change to AP, the traffic shaper in BlueStreaming works by not sending the NULL or PS-Poll frame even when the TIM indicates that there are buffered frames for the client. This forces the AP to continue to buffer frames destinated to this client. A subtle issue here is to determine when to wake up and retrieve buffered data. In BlueStreaming, we set it based on: (1) streaming bitrate, (2) effective WiFi bandwidth, and (3) QoS requirements. The first two are easy to determine. The third one, however, is highly application dependent. On the one hand, it impacts the client perceived streaming quality directly, although the playout buffer can absorb most of such delay. On the other hand, P2P applications usually use a timer to determine if any data chunk needs to be re-requested. For certain chunks that are not received in time, they will either be forfeited if their deadline has already passed or they will be requested again [22]. Hence, if streaming packets are buffered at the AP for too long, the application would believe such packets are lost, and request them again.

On the other hand, if the WiFi interface keeps staying in the sleep mode without responding to AP's beacon messages, the AP would believe that the client is no longer associated. After a pre-determined timeout interval, the AP would start dropping its buffered frames. Thus, how long the data packets should be buffered is critical, which directly determines the sleep duration of the WiFi interface.

Taking all the above considerations into account, we set the packet buffering duration as follows:

$$T_{buf} = min\Big(T_{re-req} \times (1 - \frac{Rate}{BW_{WiFi}}), T_{AP-timeout}\Big) \quad (1)$$

where T_{re-req} is the re-request timer of P2P applications, $Rate$ is the bitrate of the streaming channel, BW_{WiFi} is the estimated bandwidth of the WiFi link, and $T_{AP-timeout}$ is the timeout duration after that the AP starts to drop buffered data for the client.

4.5 Uploading Scheduler: Scheduling Upload Wisely

In P2P streaming, peers should upload data to neighbors. This is the key to the scalability of any P2P application. But such uploading brings new complexities. First, uploading to other peers of the downloaded data directly incurs the consumption of the uploading bandwidth and battery power. Second, uploading incurs a comparable number of control packets. Third, uploading is very dynamic and hard to predict in P2P streaming since it depends on how many peers the client is serving at a time. As a result, uploading may seriously offset our energy saving efforts.

Aiming to solve these issues efficiently so that the minimum battery power is consumed for such uploading, we design an uploading scheduler working at two levels: *Priority-based Bluetooth Uploading* and *Opportunistic WiFi Uploading*. In short, BlueStreaming tends to fully utilize the always-on Bluetooth first, and then opportunistically utilize WiFi for uploading if needed.

4.5.1 *Priority-based Bluetooth Uploading*

In the previous measurement, we have shown that control traffic, although resulting in a large number of packets, occupies a small portion in the traffic volume. Utilizing Bluetooth for control traffic transmission typically consumes less than 20% of the available Bluetooth bandwidth. This leaves a lot of Bluetooth bandwidth unused because the Bluetooth interface in BlueStreaming is always active. Thus, when there are uploading packets pending, un-used Bluetooth bandwidth is firstly exploited to transmit the uploading traffic. Since Bluetooth is kept active to transmit frequent control traffic, diverting uploading packets to it does not incur much more power consumption.

While the above idea works intuitively, a design pitfall is the delay of control packets due to the streaming data uploading to neighbors. In order to ensure timely delivery of control packets, upstream data packets should not be diverted to Bluetooth when the bandwidth utilization of Bluetooth reaches a threshold. For this purpose, different priorities should be assigned to control traffic and data traffic. A higher priority should always be given to the control packets when data packets also present.

4.5.2 Opportunistic WiFi Uploading

Since WiFi provides a much higher data rate compared to Bluetooth, when high uploading is demanded and it cannot be completed by Bluetooth, BlueStreaming considers to opportunistically use WiFi to deliver uploading traffic in burst. For this purpose, similar to downstream/incoming packets, intermittent upstream/outgoing packets are combined and sent at a higher data rate by buffering outgoing streaming packets for a certain amount of time at the network layer at the client side.

The timing in the above process is critical. Although it is appealing to buffer the packets for long enough and then transmit them in a very large MAC frame, it would impact the performance of the requesting peer and may cause our BlueStreaming client to receive excessive repetitive requests. This can further increase the number of control packets and negatively impact the throughput of the Bluetooth channel. In order for WiFi to upload with a minimum consumption of extra battery power, the scheduler should work seamlessly with the PSM mechanism on the client.

Thus, to opportunistically utilize WiFi for uploading when needed, the uploading scheduler schedules to transmit burst uploading traffic before or right after "shaped" downstream traffic based on the PSM configuration.

- If the idle timeout interval used in PSM is only based on outgoing traffic activities, BlueStreaming starts to upload while the WiFi interface is in PSM. It will switch from PSM to CAM and the transmission is scheduled to finish right before the start of downstream packet transmissions. Note that the end-timing of uploading is not stringent, because the AP will not start to send buffered downstream packets until it receives a NULL wake-up or PS-Poll frame from the client. Under such a scheduling policy, the time spent for downloading streaming packets would be counted toward the idle timeout interval.
- If the idle timeout interval for PSM is based on both incoming and outgoing traffic activities, the scheduler can schedule the uploading via WiFi after being notified by the AP that it has no more buffered data packets.

In either case, the client can sleep for:

$$T_{sleep} = min\Big(T_{re-req} \times (1 - \frac{Rate}{BW_{WiFi}}), T_{APtimeout}\Big) - \frac{SIZE_{Up-Buf}}{BW_{WiFi}} \quad (2)$$

where $SIZE_{Up-Buf}$ denotes the volume of uploading packets buffered in the outgoing buffer at the client side.

5. IMPLEMENTATION

To evaluate the performance of BlueStreaming, we have implemented prototype systems on both Mac OS and Windows. In this section, we discuss some implementation and deployment issues.

5.1 Prototype Implementation

Our current prototypes run on laptops since laptops have implemented more complete Bluetooth profiles including Personal Area Network (PAN) as desired by BlueStreaming. BlueStreaming could be totally AP-transparent if control traffic can be separated at the transport layer. However, as we mentioned before, existing P2P streaming applications do not differentiate control traffic from data traffic at the transport layer. Therefore, we need a traffic classifier at both the AP and the client sides. We prototyped BlueStreaming AP using a MacBook as AP for both WiFi and Bluetooth. It shares its wired Ethernet connection via WiFi and Bluetooth interfaces. In a nutshell, the traffic classifier works at the IP layer. It intercepts packets at the IP layer, modifies destination addresses, and re-injects the packets to the corresponding interfaces.

The traffic shaper utilizes the buffer maintained at the WiFi AP by allowing the client not to wake up even if it has buffered packets. For this purpose, we implement a buffer at the network layer of our AP, which buffers downstream data packets and then forwards to the link layer in burst periodically. The buffering time is set according to Equation (1).

The upload scheduler is implemented at the client side. In our experiments, the idle timeout interval of PSM set by the driver is solely based on outgoing network activities. Therefore, we schedule outgoing uploading traffic before the bursty downloading of incoming traffic. To implement this, we set up a client side buffer at the network layer to buffer its outgoing packets. It also logs the timestamp of the first arrived packet of the latest incoming burst via WiFi, and determines when to start transmitting bursty uploading traffic based on Equation (2).

5.2 Infrastructure vs. Hybrid Mode

BlueStreaming can be deployed in two modes in practice: (1) an Infrastructure mode where a dedicated AP provides both WiFi and Bluetooth connections, and (2) a Hybrid mode where an intermediate device is used.

A BlueStreaming client needs both WiFi and Bluetooth interfaces, so that both interfaces can be used in parallel. In an infrastructure mode, the AP also needs to have both interfaces so that a BlueStreaming client and the AP can direct different types of traffic to different subnets (e.g. wireless LAN and bluetooth PAN).

In practice, however, a Bluetooth-enabled AP is not so common compared to a WiFi AP. If WiFi AP does not support Bluetooth, we allow a BlueStreaming client to operate in a hybrid mode by utilizing other Bluetooth-enabled network devices nearby. The intermediate devices should have a Bluetooth interface as well as a connection to the AP (wired or wireless). In practice, the hybrid mode can be easily deployed by using a plug-and-play Bluetooth dongle. In this mode, a BlueStreaming client can form an ad-hoc network with the intermediate device, and ask it to relay its traffic.

Another natural concern is the range mismatch problem of WiFi and Bluetooth. The expected communication range of WiFi is about 100 meters, while Bluetooth often covers only about 10 meters. In BlueStreaming, the hybrid mode can help deal with this issue. That is, with a relay in the middle, the communication distance of Bluetooth can double. Multi-hop relay could also be leveraged if necessary. We will study the impact of relay in the hybrid mode in the next section. If there is no relay possible at all, the user has to use WiFi as before.

On the other hand, the new Bluetooth standard may shed light on this range mismatch issue. For example, with the development of Bluetooth 4 [23], Bluetooth can improve its coverage to 50 meters or more. Better yet, with new low energy techniques, such an improved communication range may not necessarily increase the energy consumption.

5.3 Channel Selection and Competition Avoidance

Co-existence of Bluetooth and WiFi has attracted a lot attention during the past years, because Bluetooth and WiFi may operate in the same spectrum. When a Bluetooth transmission and a WiFi transmission happen at the same frequency, interferences could happen and packets may be lost.

Recent advances of wireless technology have made significant progress to address this problem. For example, hardware vendors today commonly use specific co-existence algorithms to handle Bluetooth and WiFi traffic intelligently when both interfaces are in operation. Operating systems such as Windows 7 also implement Adaptive Frequency Hopping (AFH) to minimize interferences. In our experiments, our laptop is equipped with the latest Bluetooth/WiFi combo chipset from Broadcom and runs Windows 7. We will study retransmissions rates in Section 6.4.

6. PERFORMANCE EVALUATION

6.1 Experimental Setup

To evaluate BlueStreaming, we run our Windows prototype to access PPTV, PPS, SopCast, and QQLive. A laptop (MacBook) is set as the BlueStreaming Access Point for both WiFi and Bluetooth, and WiFi runs 802.11n at 2.4GHz. A second laptop runs Windows 7 and acts as the BlueStreaming client to run the four applications. The third laptop associates with the AP and captures WiFi traffic in a promiscuous mode. In a hybrid mode, a fourth laptop is used to relay the control traffic between our testing client and the AP by associating with the AP via WiFi, while the AP turns off its Bluetooth interface and only serves as AP for WiFi. In all experiments, laptops are placed 3 meters from each other except that the traffic sniffer (the third laptop) and our testing client (the second laptop) are placed close to each other.

6.2 Energy Saving in the Infrastructure Mode

We first examine the effectiveness of BlueStreaming in infrastructure mode. For each of the four applications, three tests are conducted: (1) `PSM-A` (without BlueStreaming), (2) BlueStreaming with only the traffic classifier enabled, and (3) BlueStreaming with all three components enabled. Because there is always uploading traffic from our testing client, the traffic shaper has to work with the uploading scheduler in order to maximize power saving. So we did not test BlueStreaming with only the traffic classifier and the shaper enabled. Each of these tests is conducted for 30 minutes. For each application, three tests are carried out consecutively in the hope that the Internet conditions and dynamics of these P2P services have not remarkably changed.

Table 4: PPTV at 400 Kbps

Name	Total # of Streaming	Total # of Control	Sleep Time (%)	Consumed Energy(J)
PSM-A	66465	147554	0.56	2005
Classifier only	66121	121512	25.82	1745
BlueStreaming	70622	132466	60.50	1090

Table 4 gives an overview of the power saving on our testing client when accessing a channel of 400 Kbps in PPTV. During all three tests, our testing client receives smooth playback and captured frames show no quality degradation when compared to that in PSM-A. However, the amount of the battery power consumed by the WiFi interface for receiving streaming data is vastly different. With `PSM-A`, the WiFi interface spent only 10 seconds in the PSM and more than 99% of the session time in the active mode. When the traffic classifier is enabled, the amount of power saving is greatly improved: the WiFi interface spent more than 25% of session time in the PSM. When BlueStreaming is fully enabled, the WiFi interface spent over 60% time in the PSM, a 134% improvement over the case with only the traffic classifier enabled.

The additional sleep time of WiFi does not necessarily mean additional energy saving since BlueStreaming keeps Bluetooth active all the time and thus constantly consumes some battery power. We need to take that into account to evaluate the total power consumption of BlueStreaming. Since we do not use an instrument to measure the absolute battery consumption, we rely on the specification given in [16] and [10] to estimate the total power consumed. That is, the WiFi interface consumes 1120 mW in the CAM and 72 mW in the PSM; the Bluetooth interface consumes 120 mW in the active mode, and 25 mW in the idle mode. Note that we consider Bluetooth to be always active, which is conservative for the total power saving. The last column of Table 4 shows that considering the total power consumption of both the WiFi and Bluetooth interfaces, the classifier only and BlueStreaming can save over 13% and 46% energy, respectively, when compared to `PSM-A`.

Figure 7 further shows the Inter Packet Delay distribution of WiFi traffic in these three tests. Compared to Figure 7(a), Figures 7(b) and 7(c) show that the Inter Packet delay distribution and Inter Streaming Packet delay are similar to each other, indicating the effectiveness of `Traffic Classifier` in diverting control traffic and exploiting sleep opportunities for the WiFi interface. In particular, Figure 7(c) shows a very pronounced bimodal pattern when all BlueStreaming components are enabled: about 95% packets arrive within 1 ms of the preceding one, while the rest arrive over 600 ms of the preceding packet, demonstrating the effectiveness of downstream traffic shaping.

Figure 8 further plots a snapshot (10 seconds) of the traffic pattern on the WiFi interface of our testing client in these three tests. Both incoming and outgoing packets are included. Figure 8(a) shows the traffic pattern when `PSM-A` is used. The traffic pattern shows a stair-case shape, and the small intervals between successive packets imply few opportunities for the WiFi interface to switch into PSM. Streaming with the classifier only can divert the frequent control packets to Bluetooth, resulting in more sleep opportunities as shown in Figure 8(b). However, due to the variation of response time from different neighbors, the traffic pattern is still not bursty enough. With the help of `Traffic Shaper` in BlueStreaming, Figure 8(c) shows that bursty traffic is sent more regularly and periodically, given that the interval between bursts is determined by Equation (1).

Table 5: QQLive at 500 Kbps

Name	Total # of Streaming	Total # of Control	Sleep Time (%)	Consumed Energy(J)
PSM-A	109800	206259	5.24	1917
Classifier only	105702	190428	34.37	1584
BlueStreaming	103600	187311	52.89	1234

Table 5 shows the results of our testing client accessing a 500 Kbps channel in QQLive. The table shows that although QQLive transmits 50% more packets than PPTV, it has more power saving in `PSM-A` and `Classifier-only` than in PPTV. This is likely due to the smaller variation of response time from a different number of neighboring peers. However, the request time-out T_{re-req} of QQLive is smaller than that of PPTV (based on our reverse en-

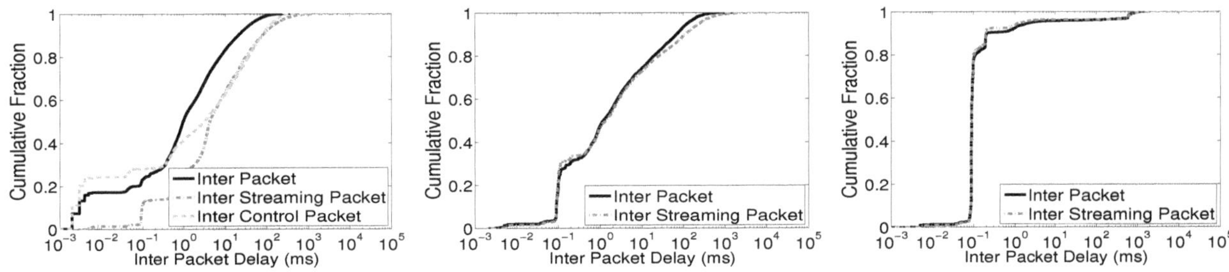

(a) PSM-A (b) Classifier only (c) BlueStreaming

Figure 7: PPTV 30-min Tests: Inter Packet Delay of WiFi (CDF)

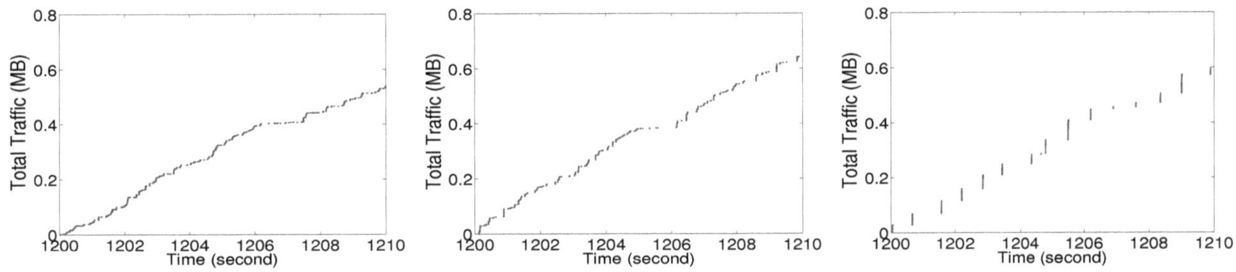

(a) PSM-A (b) Classifier only (c) BlueStreaming

Figure 8: Traffic Pattern of PPTV

gineering), and thus traffic shaping is less effective for QQLive. Even so, the extra amount of battery power saved by applying traffic shaping and upload scheduling is still prominent: the WiFi interface spent more than 52% of the session time in the PSM.

While omitting detailed results of PPS and SopCast due to page limit, we also show the overall energy saving for them in Figure 9, where *Blue-I* means BlueStreaming under the infrastructure mode and *Blue-H* means BlueStreaming under the hybrid mode. Because PPS has a very small request time-out value, our client saves about 10% energy in BlueStreaming compared to PSM-A. SopCast, on the other hand, has a larger T_{re-req} smiliar to that of PPTV, and thus our client can save about 45% energy with BlueStreaming.

6.3 Hybrid Mode

We have shown that BlueStreaming is effective in saving power in the infrastructure mode where the AP supports both Bluetooth and WiFi. In practice, if Bluetooth is out of range or the AP does not support Bluetooth, we propose to use the hybrid mode. In this section, we evaluate BlueStreaming in hybrid mode with a relay node in the middle. The intermediate node forms a Bluetooth Adhoc network with our BlueStreaming client, and joins the subnet of BlueStreaming AP via the WiFi connection.

Since control traffic in P2P streaming is delay-sensitive, a particular concern on the hybrid mode is the delay of relaying, which could increase the response time at the application layer and deteriorate streaming quality. Because of the highly dynamic nature of P2P streaming overlay, we could not directly use application layer response time to compare the delay in different scenarios. Instead, we use `Ping` to measure the approximate round trip time from our BlueStreaming client to the AP via different paths, and estimate the increased control traffic delay. In short, the control traffic could be delivered under three scenarios: (1) `PSM-A` via a direct WiFi connection when BlueStreaming is not enabled; (2) `BlueStreaming-Infrastructure` via a direct Bluetooth connection; and (3) `BlueStreaming-Hybrid` via a relayed Bluetooth device. For `PSM-A` and `BlueStreaming-Infrastructure`, we use standard `Ping` to measure the RTT. For `BlueStreaming-Hybrid`, we run a customized `Ping` at our BlueStreaming client that measures the RTT of the *relayed* connection to AP.

We send out one `Ping` request every 1 second with 32 bytes payload, which is the payload of a typical control packet. For each scenario, we take the average of 400 RTT results. Table 6 shows that with a direct 802.11n WiFi connection, the RTT is about 3 ms; with a direct Bluetooth connection in the infrastructure mode, the RTT increases to about 22 ms on average, which is likely due to the smaller throughput of Bluetooth; with a relayed Bluetooth connection in the hybrid mode, the RTT slightly increases to 25 ms, which is due to the additional WiFi transfer occurred between the relay node and the WiFi AP. Apart from the potentially increased control traffic response time, the streaming quality during the tests has no degradation in either the infrastructure or hybrid mode.

Figure 9 further summarizes the average energy consumption across four applications in these tests. The figure shows that the estimated energy consumption is comparable in both modes.

Due to high dynamics of P2P streaming overlay, it is not appropriate to say if one mode is better/worse than the other in terms of power saving even if they have demonstrated slightly different performance on energy consumption. Nevertheless, it is reasonable to conclude that BlueStreaming running in both modes can achieve good power saving.

6.4 Retransmission Rate

Throughout our experiments, we have been using 802.11n at 2.4 GHz band (instead of 5 GHz), which is the same band that Bluetooth operates on. In addition to that, using `airport scan` on the MacBook to scan all available WiFi APs nearby, we find that all non-overlapping channels (channel 1, 6, and 11) of 2.4 GHz are occupied by more than 6 APs each during our experiments because our experiments are done in a lab covered by the AP hotspots. Because we run our experiments during 1pm to 5pm local time, there are a lot of wireless users around, meaning lots of background traf-

Table 6: RTT based on customized Ping

Name	RTT (ms)
PSM-A	3
BlueStreaming-Infrastructure	22
BlueStreaming-Hybrid	25

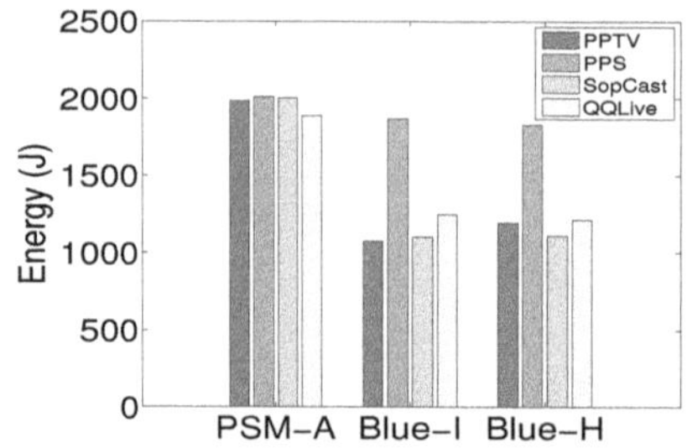

Figure 9: Energy Consumption Comparisons

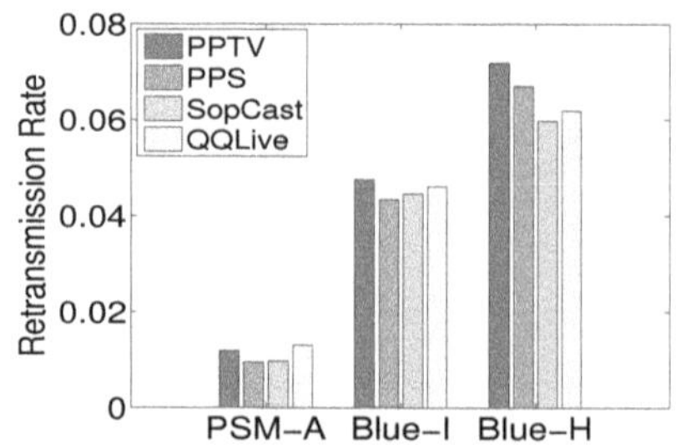

Figure 10: Retransmission Rates

fic. Both sharing 2.4 GHz band and significant background traffic may cause collisions and interferences.

To examine the situation of such intereferences, we study the re-transmission rate during our experiments. Figure 10 depicts the average retransmission rate of WiFi traffic throughout our experiments. The result shown in the figure is the mean of five runs. When the Bluetooth interface is not used, the retransmission rate under `PSM-A` across four applications is about 0.01. When we turn on BlueStreaming and use the infrastructure mode to transmit P2P streaming traffic, the retransmission rate increases to above 0.04. This shows in our environment, actively using Bluetooth does mildly increase retransmissions. When BlueStreaming uses an intermediate node to relay control traffic in the hybrid mode, the retransmission rate increases to about 0.06, possibly because the relay node uses WiFi to communicate with our BlueStreaming AP and deliver control traffic. Even so, the streaming quality in the experiments is not degraded, demonstrating the practicability of BlueStreaming. In an environment with less background traffic, the retransmission rate could further decrease.

7. CONCLUSION

Recently the Internet has witnessed the rapid increase of P2P streaming traffic and the quick shift of using mobile devices for Internet accesses. Unfortunately, accessing delay-sensitive streaming services on a mobile device is hindered by the limited battery power supply, because a mobile client in P2P streaming needs to transmit more traffic, including uploading to neighbors as well as exchanging a large number of control packets with neighbors. In order to enable power-efficient P2P streaming to mobile devices, in this work, we have designed and implemented BlueStreaming, a system that simultaneously utilizes WiFi and commonly existing Bluetooth interfaces. The energy consumed by the Bluetooth interface is effectively over-compensated by the greater power saving on the WiFi interface. Extensive experiments with our implemented prototypes demonstrate the effectiveness and practicability of BlueStreaming.

8. ACKNOWLEDGEMENT

We appreciate constructive comments from our shepherd Surender Chandra and anonymous referees. The work is partially supported by NSF under grants CNS-0746649, CNS-1117300, CCF-0915681, CCF-1146578, and AFOSR under grant FA9550-09-1-0071.

9. REFERENCES

[1] "PPTV (previously PPLive)," http://www.pptv.com/.

[2] "PPStream," http://www.ppstream.com/.

[3] "SopCast," http://www.sopcast.com/.

[4] "QQLive," http://live.qq.com/.

[5] "CNN Live Video," http://www.cnn.com/help/liveflash.html.

[6] "Cisco VNI," `http://www.cisco.com/en/US/solutions/collateral/ns341/ns525/ns537/ns705/ns827/white_paper_c11-481360.pdf`.

[7] "Apple's iPad Generates 2.5x the Wireless Data Traffic Generated by the iPhone," `http://bytemobile.com/news-events/2010/archive_260410.html`.

[8] "WiFi," http://v4.jiwire.com/search-hotspot-locations.htm.

[9] V. Bychkovsky, B. Hull, A.K. Miu, H. Balakrishnan, and S. Madden, "A Measurement Study of Vehicular Internet Access Using In Situ Wi-Fi Networks," in *Proc. of ACM MOBICOM*, 2006.

[10] E. Rozner, V. Navda, R. Ramjee, and S. Rayanchu, "NAPman: Network-Assisted Power management for WiFi Devices," in *Proc. of ACM MobiSys*, 2010.

[11] S. Chandra and A. Vahdat, "Application-specific Network Management for Energy-Aware Streaming of Popular Multimedia Formats," in *Proc. of USENIX Annual Technical Conference*, 2002.

[12] F. Dogar, P. Steenkiste, and K. Papagiannaki, "Catnap: Exploiting High Bandwidth Wireless Interfaces to Save Energy for Mobile Devices," in *Proc. of ACM MobiSys*, 2010.

[13] E. Tan, L. Guo, S. Chen, and X. Zhang, "PSM-throttling: Minimizing Energy Consumption for Bulk Data Communications in WLANs," in *Proc. of IEEE ICNP*, 2007.

[14] J. Liu and L. Zhong, "Micro Power Management of Active 802.11 Interfaces," in *Proc. of ACM MobiSys*, 2008.

[15] Y. Agarwal, R. Chandra, A Wolman, P. Bahl, K. Chin, and R. Gupta, "Wireless Wakeups Revisited: Energy Management for Voip over Wi-Fi Smartphones," in *Proc. of ACM MobiSys*, 2007.

[16] T. Pering, Y. Agarwal, R. Gupta, and R. Want, "CoolSpots: Reducing the Power Consumption of Wireless Mobile Devices with Multiple Radio interfaces," in *Proc. of ACM MobiSys*, 2006.

[17] D. Bertozzi, L. Benini, and B. Ricco, "Power Aware Network Interface Management for Streaming Multimedia," in *Proc. of IEEE WCNC*, 2002.

[18] Y. Wei, S. M. Bhandarkar, and S. Chandra, "A Client-side Statistical Prediction Scheme for Energy Aware Multimedia Data Streaming," *IEEE Transactions on Multimedia*, vol. 8, no. 4, 2006.

[19] "TVUPlayer," http://itunes.apple.com/us/app/id323640984.

[20] "Justin.tv," http://itunes.apple.com/us/app/id358612216.

[21] "Justin.tv," http://www.justin.tv.

[22] Y. Liu, F. Li, L. Guo, and S. Chen, "Reducing Data Request Contentions for Improved Streaming Quality," in *Proc. of ACM NOSSDAV*, 2010.

[23] "Bluetooth 4," http://www.gizmodo.com.au/2010/04/bluetooth-4-0-uses-less-power-while-extending-range/.

Peer-Assisted Texture Streaming in Metaverses

Ke Liang, Roger Zimmermann, Wei Tsang Ooi
School of Computing
National University of Singapore
Singapore, 117417
{liangke, rogerz, ooiwt}@comp.nus.edu.sg

ABSTRACT

User-extensible metaverses need an effective way to disseminate massive and dynamic 3D contents (*i.e.*, meshes, textures, animations, etc.) to end users, and at the same time maintain a low consumption of server bandwidth. Peer-to-peer (or peer-assisted) technologies have been widely considered as a desirable complementary solution to efficaciously offload servers in large-scale media streaming applications. However, due to both the bandwidth constraints of heterogeneous users and unpredictable access patterns of latency-sensitive 3D contents, it is very challenging to cut the server bandwidth cost in metaverses. In this paper, we propose a peer-assisted texture streaming architecture to minimize the server bandwidth consumption without degrading the end-user satisfaction. We propose a game-theoretic peer selection strategy which achieves a good trade-off between performance and complexity. Our algorithm is light-weight, and can efficiently utilize the bandwidth of users in a fully decentralized manner by enabling each peer (*i.e.*, user) to quickly select its content providers who can satisfy the requests of the peer within the latency constraint of the content. We evaluate our algorithm through an extensive comparison study based on simulations using realistic data (*i.e.*, avatar mobility traces and textures) collected from Second Life. The simulation results show that the proposed algorithm can effectively reduce the server bandwidth consumption without degrading the user experience.

Categories and Subject Descriptors

C.2.4 [**Computer-Communication Networks**]: Distributed Systems—*Distributed applications*; C.4 [**Performance of Systems**]: Performance attributes

General Terms

Algorithms, Design, Theory

Keywords

Peer-assisted streaming, game-theoretic algorithm

*Area Chairs: Surender Chandra.

1. INTRODUCTION

Recent years have witnessed a significant growth in *metaverses*, defined as online 3D immersive networked virtual worlds, where each user, represented by an *avatar*, can socialize with other users and interact with user-generated 3D contents. Unlike massively multiplayer online games (MMOGs), where users install the whole static 3D contents in advance via DVDs or patches downloaded offline from the Internet, the metaverses need to stream interactive 3D contents to users live over the Internet, according to their visibility or interests. Specifically, when avatars move around in a metaverse, their immediate environment will be downloaded dynamically from the metaverse server to the corresponding users. Considering the fact that a significant portion (over 50%) of the server bandwidth is consumed by transmission of the *textures*[1] of 3D contents in metaverses [22], we focus on texture streaming in this study and refer to 3D contents as textures throughout the paper.

Most commercial metaverses (*e.g.*, Second Life [27] and ActiveWorlds [2]) are currently deployed using a client/server (C/S) scheme, where centralized servers are used to maintain the states of metaverses and online users, and to distribute 3D contents to users. Throughout the paper, we use the term content, texture, and 3D content interchangeably. Since users do not store the entire virtual world, but download the contents from dedicated servers when needed, the server bandwidth costs can be huge when the amount of contents and the number of online users increases. For example, according to the economic report from Second Life [28] in the third quarter of 2010, the user hours (*i.e.*, the sum of the combined length of all user sessions) per month is roughly 35 million hours. From Tables 2 and 3 in Section 5, we can observe that the average amount of texture data sent from the servers per user hour is 263 MB. Therefore, roughly 9 petabytes (PB) of texture data will be delivered from the servers to users monthly. As a consequence, one of the most important and formidable challenges facing the metaverse providers is to reduce the server bandwidth consumption.

A natural way to offload servers is to utilize bandwidth and caches of online users using peer-to-peer (P2P) technologies, *i.e.*, enable online users to serve one another. We use the term peer, avatar and user interchangeably thereafter. With the assistance of *peers*, the server bandwidth cost can be reduced, and the scalability and affordability of the system can be improved. More specifically, a peer can download the required contents from other peers via sending

[1]A texture is simply a bitmap image that is used to provide surface coloring for a 3D model.

requests to them, which may send back the corresponding contents if they have available bandwidth. In order not to degrade the user satisfaction of metaverses, all the required contents need to be downloaded within a certain *latency constraint* measured in seconds. If a peer fails to download the required textures from other peers within the latency constraint, it will send the requests directly to dedicated servers, thus consume bandwidth on the server side. Since the server is not replaced but complemented by the peers, we refer to such systems as peer-assisted systems. To minimize the server bandwidth cost, peers need to select appropriate peers as their content *providers*, respecting the available bandwidth of peers and latency constraints of the contents.

Peer selection strategies, which aim to reduce the server bandwidth consumption, have been extensively studied in peer-assisted media streaming systems, including live [17,19] and video-on-demand (VoD) [16,30] P2P streaming. Unfortunately, current peer selection strategies for live or VoD P2P streaming systems cannot be easily applied to 3D content delivery, due to the unpredictable and non-linear request patterns of 3D content.

More specifically, in live P2P streaming systems, every peer has the same request pattern and it does not usually request the contents that precede the playback timestamp (assuming it has been stored in its cache if seeking is allowed). In VoD P2P streaming systems, every peer can (mostly) predict the contents it needs in the near future. Therefore, the media contents in both live and VoD streaming systems are viewed as one-dimensional (*i.e.*, time) data files. In texture streaming systems, however, the contents are viewed as data files that are stored in a multi-dimensional space (*i.e.*, locations). Peers with different download and upload capacities download the contents on demand according to their unpredictable behaviors *per se*, such as walking, running and flying in metaverses. Moreover, the number of potential content providers for each peer in live or VoD P2P streaming systems is large, and thus the sets of content providers of peers are less overlapping. However, in texture streaming systems, the potential content providers of a peer (*e.g.*, an avatar) are mostly its neighbors in the virtual world. Hence the number of potential content providers is small and the sets of content providers of peers are highly overlapping. This makes the design of peer-assisted texture streaming much more challenging compared with live or VoD P2P streaming systems. Prior research on peer selection strategies in peer-assisted texture streaming systems has paid little attention to the issue of optimally utilizing the bandwidth of heterogeneous peers while respecting the latency constraints of textures.

In this paper, we design a decentralized peer selection strategy for peer-assisted texture streaming with heterogeneous peers. The proposed peer selection strategy has a rapid convergence rate, and it can minimize the server bandwidth consumption while respecting the latency constraints of textures. It is important to point out that we seek to reduce the server bandwidth consumption via optimally utilizing the available network capacities of peers, hence the focus of this paper is not on incentive mechanisms [18] that aim to increase the available network resources.

Note that a practical peer selection strategy should be performed in a decentralized manner. We believe the peer selection strategy in such peer-assisted texture streaming systems can be characterized in a game-theoretic setting, and thus inherit its decentralized and practical nature. Specifically, requests sent by peers can be viewed as players in a game, where each is associated with a weight which is the size of the requested texture. Each player in the game is selfish and will try to minimize her own cost. In other words, peers will send their requests to underloaded providers. We formulate the server bandwidth minimization problem as an asymmetric congestion game, and we show that its equivalent problem is to minimize the *potential* of the game.

The rest of the paper is organized as follows. We model the peer-assisted texture streaming system and formulate the server bandwidth minimization problem in Section 2. We describe our game-theoretic peer selection algorithm in Section 3. The convergence time of the proposed algorithm is analyzed in Section 4. Section 5 details the evaluation of the proposed peer selection algorithm. The simulation results show that the proposed peer-assisted system can achieve a much lower server bandwidth consumption in comparison with existing algorithms. Finally, we discuss related work and conclude the paper in Sections 6 and 7, respectively.

2. SYSTEM MODEL

The most popular metaverse today is Second Life [27], where the virtual world consists of non-overlapping and independent regions. Each region is managed by a server that maintains the states of all objects and avatars within the region. To simply the discussion, we restrict our focus to a single region in Second Life. Once a peer logs in, it contacts the server which ensures the persistency of the region by continually sending relevant updates of objects and avatars to the peer through the network. In addition, the server determines the relevant subset of data that is required by each peer according to its location and visibility.

Each peer can freely roam around within the region and interact with other peers and objects within its *area-of-interest* (AoI), which is defined as a circular space around the peer with a given radius. The peers in the AoI of a peer are called AoI neighbors. Each peer needs to download the textures within its AoI that are not stored in its *cache* as it is moving in the region. After receiving the demanded textures, it will store them in its cache, from where a view is rendered according to the spatial information (*e.g.*, location and orientation) of the objects that the textures apply to. The size of the cache is determined by the metaverse provider or peers themselves. We assume that the default cache size of each peer is 128 MB (default cache size of users in Second Life). A simple but effective cache replacement algorithm is used in our setting: the cached textures that are far way from the avatar will be replaced with the newly downloaded textures when the cache is full.

To cut the server bandwidth cost, every peer is allowed to download the required textures from other peers by sending requests to others. If a peer receives requests from other peers, it is regarded as a content *provider* of those peers, and we assume every peer can be a provider to others. These requests are processed by content providers in a FIFO (First In First Out) manner. To maintain a good user satisfaction, all the requested textures must be delivered within a certain time limit, defined as the *latency constraint* of textures. If a peer fails to obtain the requested textures from its content providers within the latency constraint (due to the upload constraints of its content providers), it will send the requests to the server, thus consuming server bandwidth.

2.1 Notations and Definitions

Let P and T denote the set of online peers and the set of textures in a region, respectively. The size of texture $i \in T$, denoted by w_i, is measured in units of kilobytes (*i.e.*, KB). Let r_i^j denote the request sent by peer j for texture i, and the *weight* of the request r_i^j be the size of the requested texture (*i.e.*, w_i). The latency constraint for each texture is denoted by d, measured in seconds. Without loss of generality, we assume online peers are heterogeneous and have different upload capacities. Let u_i denote the upload capacity of peer i, measured in kilobytes per second, *i.e.*, KB/s. It is critical to note that the upload capacity is assumed to be the only bottleneck in the system, since the bottleneck caused by the constrained download capacities of peers can be eliminated by reducing the number of requests accordingly.

Let $R_i = \cup_{j \in P}\{r_i^j\}$ be the set of requests sent by all peers for texture i. Since every texture is unique, we have $R_i \cap R_j = \emptyset$ for any two textures i and j. In order to avoid receiving duplicate textures which would significantly increase bandwidth overhead and server bandwidth cost, every request is sent to only one of the peers. In other words, every request has only one provider. Similarly, let $S_i \subseteq P$ be the set of peers that have texture i in their caches. The information of S_i can be piggybacked into the updates sent by the server through the network. The *load* of peer i, denoted by l_i, is defined as the total weights of requests sent to peer i. The *height* of request r_k^i (sent by peer i) at peer j, denoted by $h_k^{i,j}$ (since every request is unique and has only one provider), is defined as the load of peer j directly after request r_k^i arrives at peer j. The notations that will be used throughout this paper are summarized in Table 1.

2.2 Problem Formulation

Since the amount of data that can be delivered by peer i within the latency constraint is $d \cdot u_i$, the server will disseminate the rest of the amount of data, if any, to the corresponding peers that sent their requests to peer i. Therefore, the server will send $\max\{l_i - d \cdot u_i, 0\}$ of data due to the inadequate upload capacity of peer i. Our goal is to minimize the bandwidth consumption at the server while respecting the upload capacities of heterogeneous peers, which can be formally stated as follows:

$$(\mathbf{F1}) \min \sum_{i \in P} \max\{\sum_{R_k \neq \emptyset} \sum_{i \in S_k} x_k^{j,i} w_k - d \cdot u_i, 0\} \quad (1)$$

$$\text{s.t.} \sum_{i \in S_k} x_k^{j,i} = 1, \ \forall r_k^j \in R_k \quad (2)$$

$$x_k^{j,i} \in \{0, 1\}, \ \forall r_k^j \in R_k. \quad (3)$$

Term	Definition
P	Set of online peers.
T	Set of textures.
u_i	Upload capacity of peer $i \in P$.
w_i	Size of texture $i \in T$.
r_k^i	Request sent by peer i for texture k.
R_k	Set of requests for texture k. $R_k = \cup_{i \in P}\{r_k^i\}$
S_k	Set of peers that have texture k in their caches.
l_i	Load of peer $i \in P$.
$h_k^{i,j}$	Height of request r_k^i at its provider, peer j.
d	Latency constraint of textures.

Table 1: List of notations and their definitions.

As shown in Eq. 3, $x_k^{j,i}$ is an indicator variable indicating whether the request r_k^j is sent to peer i. Specifically, if r_k^j is sent to peer i, $x_k^{j,i} = 1$; otherwise $x_k^{j,i} = 0$. Eq. 2 shows that every request has only one provider. The load of peer i is

$$l_i = \sum_{R_k \neq \emptyset} \sum_{i \in S_k} x_k^{j,i} w_k. \quad (4)$$

Note that the equivalent problem of minimizing the bandwidth consumption at the server is to maximize the total amount of data that is transmitted by peers within the latency constraint of textures (*i.e.*, d seconds), which can be formulated as follows:

$$(\mathbf{F2}) \max \sum_{j \in P} \sum_{k \in T} w_k x_k^{j,i} \quad (5)$$

$$\text{s.t.} \sum_{i \in S_k} \sum_{k \in T} w_k x_k^{j,i} \leq d \cdot u_i, \ \forall r_k^j \in R_k, \quad (6)$$

$$x_k^{j,i} \in \{0, 1\}, \ \forall r_k^j \in R_k. \quad (7)$$

It can be observed that the alternative formulation (*i.e.*, **F2**) is a multidimensional knapsack problem [24], which is NP-complete [13] in general. Many approaches have been proposed to solve it, such as LP-relaxation [25], the primal-dual method [6] and dynamic programming [26].

We would like to point out that centralized approaches are not desirable for the design of peer selection strategies in peer-assisted texture streaming systems since a global connectivity information and the request information is required to obtain a feasible solution. Therefore, the computation to solve **F1** (Eq. 1) or **F2** (Eq. 5) will be invoked upon churn (*i.e.*, peer's leaving or joining) and avatar mobility that significantly changes the set of requests. As the number of peers increases, the overhead of communication and processing is not tolerable in practice.

Although there exist decentralized [23] and online [6] [9] algorithms that compute approximate solutions within polylogarithmic communication rounds, they are based on the assumption that each peer has the same capacity and is aware of global information, *i.e.*, it knows about loads and upload capacities of peers, and the connectivity information between any two peers. However, we consider the scenario where peers have different upload capacities and each requested texture needs to be downloaded within the latency constraint. As a result, existing centralized or decentralized algorithms which aiming to solve Eq. 5 in the formulation **F2** are not suitable for peer-assisted texture streaming. By combining Eq. 1 and Eq. 4, **F1** can be simplified to

$$\min \sum_{i \in P} \max\{l_i - d \cdot u_i, 0\}, \quad (8)$$

where $\max\{l_i - d \cdot u_i, 0\}$ is the amount of bandwidth consumed by the server due to the inadequate upload capacity of peer i. Therefore, we transform **F1** into an asymmetric load balancing problem: how to distribute the loads on *overloaded* peers ($l_i > d \cdot u_i$) to *underloaded* peers ($l_i < d \cdot u_i$).

The objective of this paper is to design a light-weight peer selection strategy that can be implemented in a decentralized and online fashion. To this end, we model the peer selection strategy as a *congestion game* and thus inherit its practical and decentralized nature, which has been successfully used to model load balancing problems in P2P networks as well as many other real world applications due to its conceptual simplicity.

3. SERVER BANDWIDTH MINIMIZATION

We first describe the concept of congestion games and Nash equilibrium. Then we present a peer selection strategy based on an asymmetric weighted congestion game to minimize server bandwidth cost in a decentralized fashion.

3.1 Congestion Games

The classical congestion games have been investigated for many years. A congestion game, denoted by G, can be defined as a tuple $(N, M, (A_i)_{i\in N}, (f_e)_{e\in M})$, where $N = \{1, ..., n\}$ denotes the set of *players* and $M = \{1, ..., m\}$ denotes a set of *facilities*. Each player $i \in N$ is assigned a finite set of strategies A_i and a cost function f_e is associated with facility $e \in M$.

To play the game, each player i selects a strategy $a_i \subseteq A_i$, where $A_i \subseteq M$ is the strategy set of player i. The strategy profile, denoted by $\mathbf{a} = (a_i)_{i\in N}$, is defined as a vector of strategies selected by all the players. Similarly we use the notation $\mathcal{A} = \times_{i\in N} A_i$ to denote the set of all possible strategy profiles. A congestion game is *symmetric* if all the players have the same strategy set, *i.e.*, $\forall i, j \in N, A_i = A_j$; otherwise it is *asymmetric*. A congestion game is *weighted* if each player i is specified a weight w_i. The cost of player i for the strategy profile $\mathbf{a}$ is given by $c_i(\mathbf{a}) = f_{a_i}(\mathbf{a}, w_i)$.

The goal of each player in congestion games is to minimize her own cost without trying to optimize the global situation. That is, all players will try to lower their own cost by changing their strategies individually. A *pure Nash equilibrium* is defined as a steady state in which no players have an incentive to change their strategies.

DEFINITION 1 (PURE NASH EQUILIBRIUM [21]). *A strategy profile $\mathbf{a} \in \mathcal{A}$ is said to be a pure Nash equilibrium of G if for all players $i \in N$ and each alternate strategy $a_i' \in A_i$,*

$$c_i(a_i, \mathbf{a}_{-i}) \le c_i(a_i', \mathbf{a}_{-i}), \tag{9}$$

where $\mathbf{a}_{-i} = (a_j)_{j\in N\setminus\{i\}}$ denotes the list of strategies of the strategy profile $\mathbf{a}$ for all players except i.

Congestion games have a fundamental property that a pure Nash equilibrium always exists [11]. To analyze convergence properties of congestion games (*i.e.*, the time from any state to a pure Nash equilibrium), we introduce the definition of potential function for congestion games.

DEFINITION 2 (POTENTIAL FUNCTION [10]). *A function $\Phi : \mathcal{A} \to R$ is a potential for game G if $\forall \mathbf{a} \in \mathcal{A}$, $\forall a_i, a_j \in A_i$,*

$$c_i(a_i, \mathbf{a}_{-i}) \le c_i(a_j, \mathbf{a}_{-i}) \Rightarrow \Phi(a_i, \mathbf{a}_{-i}) \le \Phi(a_j, \mathbf{a}_{-i}). \tag{10}$$

Therefore, $\mathbf{a}^*$ is a Nash equilibrium if and only if

$$\mathbf{a}^* = \arg\min_{\mathbf{a}\in\mathcal{A}} \Phi(\mathbf{a}). \tag{11}$$

An ϵ-Nash equilibrium is an approximate Nash equilibrium, which is defined as a state in which no player can reduce her cost by a multiplicative factor of less than $1 - \epsilon$ by changing her strategy.

3.2 Minimizing Server Bandwidth Cost

We show that the server bandwidth minimization problem can be formulated as an asymmetric weighted congestion game, denoted by G, which is defined as

$$G = (N, M, (A_i)_{i\in N}, (f_e)_{e\in M}), \tag{12}$$

where $N = \cup_{k\in W} R_k$ and $M = \cup_{k\in W} S_k$ correspond to the set of requests and peers (*i.e.*, providers) in our scenario, respectively. Each request $i \in N$ has a weight w_i (*i.e.*, the size of the requested texture), and each peer $i \in M$ has an upload capacity u_i. The strategy set of request i, denoted by A_i, is the set of peers M_i that have stored the requested texture in their caches. Since every request is sent to only one of the peers at a time, G is a *singleton* congestion game, *i.e.*, $\forall i \in N$, $a_i \in A_i$.

The strategy profile of G, denoted by $\mathbf{a} = (a_i)_{i\in N}$ corresponds to the peer selection profile, and $\mathcal{A} = \times_{i\in N} A_i$ corresponds to the set of all possible peer selection profiles. The cost of request i given a peer selection profile $\mathbf{a}$ is defined as

$$c_i(\mathbf{a}) = \min\{\max\{h_i - d \cdot u_j, 0\}, w_i\}, \tag{13}$$

where $j = a_i$ is the peer selected by request i and h_i is the *height* of request i at peer j. Clearly, for each peer $j \in M$, the sum of the cost of requests that select peer j is

$$\sum_{a_i=j} c_i(\mathbf{a}) = \sum_{a_i=j} \min\{\max\{h_i - d \cdot u_j, 0\}, w_i\} \tag{14}$$

$$= \max\{l_j - d \cdot u_j, 0\}, \quad \forall a_i \in \mathbf{a}. \tag{15}$$

Recall that $\max\{l_j - d \cdot u_j, 0\}$ is the amount of data that the server will disseminate to the corresponding peers due to the upload capacity limitation of peer j. We define the potential function of G is as the sum of the cost of all requests:

$$\Phi(\mathbf{a}) = \sum_{j\in M} \sum_{a_i=j} c_i(\mathbf{a}) = \sum_{j\in M} \max\{l_j - d \cdot u_j, 0\}. \tag{16}$$

Therefore, the problem of minimizing the server bandwidth cost can be solved by minimizing the potential function of the corresponding congestion game. The peer selection profile, *i.e.*, $\mathbf{a}$, has a significant impact on the server bandwidth cost, which is minimized if $\mathbf{a}$ is a pure Nash equilibrium (*i.e.*, $\mathbf{a} = \mathbf{a}^*$ as shown in Eq. 11).

3.3 Peer Selection Strategy

Based on the established connection between the congestion game G (see Eq. 12) and the server bandwidth cost minimization problem, an optimal peer selection strategy can be thought of as an optimal strategy profile, *i.e.*, a pure Nash equilibrium of G. It has been shown that finding a pure Nash equilibrium in a congestion game is PLS-complete [11], hence the number of changes of the strategy profile required from one state to any pure Nash equilibrium is exponentially large. Therefore, our goal is to quickly reach an *approximate* Nash equilibrium from any state by enabling each peer to change its strategies for its requests according to a *bounded jump rule* (see lines 11 and 14 in Algorithm 1), which will be discussed later in this section.

It is worth to point out that the offline peer selection strategies are undesirable in practice due to both the additional delay they incur to find appropriate content providers for all peers, and the inefficient utilization of peer bandwidth (since the peer bandwidth cannot be used to delivery texture data during the process of finding a good peer selection strategy). Furthermore, metaverses are highly dynamic environments such that churn, avatar mobility, and time-varying peer capacities will significantly degrade the feasibility and efficiency of offline peer selection strategies.

We introduce a light-weight peer selection strategy, shown in Algorithm 1, which reduces the server bandwidth cost by enabling each peer to repeatedly *update* its strategy for each texture that it requests. More specifically, all requests are sent by peers in a repeated fashion, *i.e.*, the strategy of each request can be changed if (1) the current content provider of the request is overloaded, and (2) the corresponding peer finds an underloaded provider within the latency constraint.

Algorithm 1: Peer selection for each peer $i \in P$.

1 Let t be the local time of peer i;
2 Let t_k be the time when r_k^i is generated;
3 Let a_i^k be the provider of the request r_k^i;
4 **foreach** $r_k^i \in R_k$ **do**
5   Contact a peer j from $S_k(d)$ u.a.r. ;
6     $a_i^k \leftarrow j$;
7   Send r_k^i to peer a_i^k;
8   Let h_k^i be height of r_k^i at peer j;
9   **if** $h_k^i \leq d \cdot u_j$ **then**
10   Stop contacting other peers;
11   **while** $t \leq t_k + d$ *and* $h_k^i - (d - t + t_k)u_{a_i^k} \geq w_k$ **do**
12   Contact a peer j' from $S_k(d - t + t_k)$ u.a.r. ;
13   Let $l_{j'}$ be the load of peer j';
14   **if** $l_{j'} \leq (d - t + t_k)u_{j'}$ **then**
15             $a_i^k \leftarrow j'$;
16   Send r_k^i to peer a_i^k;
17   **else**
18   Go to line 11;
19   Let h_k^i be height of r_k^i at peer j';
20   **if** $h_k^i < w_k + (d - t + t_k) \cdot u'_j$ **then**
21   Stop contacting other peers;
22   Send the request for texture k directly to the server;

Our approach is an online algorithm such that each peer performs the peer selection process and the texture transmission process in parallel. Each request is sent to a peer once it is generated (line 7 in Algorithm 1). Each peer i can change its strategy for each request in a repeated fashion if the bounded jump rule is satisfied. Also, our algorithm is light-weight such that each peer i needs to contact u.a.r. (*i.e.*, uniformly at random) only one other peer in $S_k(d')$ for each request r_k^i with latency constraint d' at one time, where $S_k(d') = \{i \in S_k : l_i < d'u_i\}$. The information of S_k (the set of peers that have texture k in their caches) is maintained at the server and can be piggybacked onto the update packets in practical implementations. The current latency constraint (*i.e.*, $d' = d - t + t_k$) of the request is calculated at the requesting peer, where t and t_k are the current time and the time when the request is generated, respectively. It is worth noting that every peer in S_k has the same probability being selected, although some peers have failed to satisfy the bounded jump rule in previous rounds. Because both requests and caches of peers are highly dynamic due to the avatar mobility.

The key idea of the bounded jump rule is to restrict the change of strategies such that the potential of the system decreases monotonically. Since all requests are processed by their content providers in a FIFO fashion, the peers that have the requests which can be processed within their latency constraints will not consider changing their current strategies (see lines 9 and 20 in Algorithm 1). From the perspective of congestion games, those requests (*i.e.*, players in games) have no incentives to change their strategies since their costs cannot be reduced (for pure Nash equilibrium) or not significantly reduced (for ϵ-Nash equilibrium).

More formally, for a given request r_k^i (sent by peer i for texture k) at peer a_i^k with a weight w_k and a height $h_k^i(t)$, by Eq. 13, the cost of r_k^i at time t is

$$c_{r_k^i}(\mathbf{a}(t)) = \min\{\max\{h_k^i(t) - (d - t + t_k)u_{a_i^k}, 0\}, w_k\},$$

where $\mathbf{a}(t)$ is the strategy profile of all peers at t, and $(d - t + t_k)$ is the latency constraint of texture k at t. This implies

$$c_{r_k^i}(\mathbf{a}(t)) = w_k \iff h_k^i(t) - (d - t + t_k)u_{a_i^k} \geq w_k. \quad (17)$$

Therefore, a peer will consider to change its strategy for its requests only when the costs of requests equal their weights, otherwise it will stop contacting other peers (line 21 in Algorithm 1). If the requesting peer of request r_k^i (*i.e.*, peer i) finds another peer j' at t (line 12 in Algorithm 1) during the repeated update process (the loop from line 11 to line 21 in Algorithm 1) such that $l_{j'}(t) \leq (d - t + t_k)u_{j'}$, it will send the request r_k^i to peer j'. It is worth noting that multiple peers may find peer j' and send requests to peer j' at the same time. In the worst case, only the first request can be processed by peer j' since peers process requests in a FIFO manner. Finally, the request will be sent to the server if $c_{r_k^i}(\mathbf{a}(t)) = w_k$ for any $t \in [t_k, t_k + d]$. It should be noted that no requesting peer will change its selection mid-way during a download, since it will stop contacting other content providers if it can download the request texture from the current content provider (lines 9 and 20 in Algorithm 1).

With the bounded jump rule, it is easy to observe that the potential function of game G is monotonically decreasing such that for a given set of requests and $\forall t_1, t_2$, we have

$$t_1 \leq t_2 \implies \Phi(\mathbf{a}(t_1)) \geq \Phi(\mathbf{a}(t_2)). \quad (18)$$

Furthermore, our algorithm applies to a fully distributed and concurrent setting such that all peers can change their strategies for their requests at the same time without a centralized coordination.

4. ANALYSIS

Recall that the proposed peer selection strategy follows principles and mechanisms of congestion games, and thus it is carried out in a repeated fashion (see Algorithm 1). More specifically, every peer i will repeatedly contact a provider j in S_k for each texture k that it requests (*i.e.*, r_k^i), and it will change its strategy for the request (*i.e.*, a_i^k) if the bounded jump rule (see lines 11 and 14 in Algorithm 1) is satisfied. In addition, peers perform this process individually without centralized coordination.

We formulate the problem of minimizing the server bandwidth cost as a congestion game, and we define the potential of the congestion game as the server bandwidth cost (see Eq. 16), which is minimized when a Nash equilibrium (a steady state) is reached. With the proposed bounded jump rule, a steady state is a ϵ-Nash equilibrium of the congestion game. Therefore, a critical question to investigate is *how fast does the system reach a ϵ-Nash equilibrium from any state?* In what follows, we seek to investigate the upper bound of the convergence time of our peer selection strategy.

Recall that the potential function of the game G with the bounded jump rule is monotonically decreasing in the presence of concurrent changes of peers' strategies (peers update their content providers (*i.e.*, peers in M) individually), because peers only consider to change the strategies of the requests that are sent to overloaded peers. More specifically, peer i will change the content provider of request r_k^i, if and only if $h_k^{i,j} - (d - t + t_k)u_j \geq w_k$ (ee Eq. 17 and Line 11 in Algorithm 1), where t and t_k are the local time and the time when the request is generated, respectively. The equivalent condition is $h_k^{i,j} + (t - t_k)u_j - w_k \geq d \cdot u_j$. Therefore, we can analyze the convergence rate of the proposed peer selection strategy via analyzing the convergence rate of the corresponding congestion game.

THEOREM 1. *Given a game $G = (N, M, (A_i)_{i\in N}, (f_e)_{e\in M})$ that satisfies the bounded jump rule, where $N = \cup_{k\in W} R_k$ and $M = \cup_{k\in W} S_k$ is the set of requests and content providers, respectively. Then a ϵ-Nash equilibrium can be reached within $O(\log n)$ rounds, where n is the number of online peers.*

PROOF. Let $\Phi(t)$ be the potential of the game at time t. According to Eq. 16, we have $\Phi(t) = \sum_{k\in R(t)} w_k$. Similarly, let $S(t) = \cup_{k\in R(t)} S_k(d)$ be the set of underloaded peers at time t, where $S_k(d) = \{i \in S_k : l_i < d \cdot u_i\}$ denotes the set of underloaded peers that have texture k in their caches. Let $n = |P|$ and $m_t = |S(t)|$ be the number of online peers and underloaded content providers at time t, respectively.

Note that a pure equilibrium can be reached at time t if (1) $\Phi(t) = 0$ (all requests can be delivered by peers within the latency constraint), or (2) $m_t = 0$ (no more underloaded content providers). Therefore, we introduce a non-increasing function $\Psi(t) = m_t\Phi(t)$ to analyze the convergence rate of proposed peer selection strategy.

At time $t+1$, let $\mathbf{x} = \{x_1, x_2, ..., x_{m_t}\}$ be a vector, where x_i denote the total size of requests that migrate to peer $i \in S(t)$. Obviously, $\Phi(t) = \sum_{i=1}^{m_t} x_i$. By applying Cauchy-Schwarz inequality to $\mathrm{E}[\Psi(t+1)]$, which is the expected value of $\Psi(t+1)$, we have the following:

$$\begin{aligned}\mathrm{E}[\Psi(t+1)] &= \mathrm{E}[m_{t+1}\Phi(t+1)] \\ &\leq \left(\mathrm{E}[m_{t+1}^2]\mathrm{E}[\Phi^2(t+1)]\right)^{\frac{1}{2}}. \quad (19)\end{aligned}$$

Noting that the square root function $f : x \to \sqrt{x}$ and the function $g : x \to x^2$ are convex functions, we apply Jensen's inequality to Eq. 19 and get

$$\begin{aligned}\mathrm{E}[\Psi(t+1)] &\leq \mathrm{E}[m_{t+1}]\mathrm{E}[\Phi(t+1)] \\ &= \sum_{m=1}^{m_t} m \Pr(m_{t+1} = m)\mathrm{E}[\Phi(t+1)|m_{t+1} = m], \quad (20)\end{aligned}$$

where m is the number of underloaded content providers in $S(t+1)$ at time $t+1$. The expected value of the potential function given m is

$$\begin{aligned}\mathrm{E}[\Phi(t+1)|m_{t+1} = m] &= \Phi(t) - \frac{\binom{m-1}{m_t-1}}{\binom{m}{m_t}} \sum_{i=1}^{m_t} x_i \\ &= \left(1 - \frac{m}{m_t}\right)\Phi(t). \quad (21)\end{aligned}$$

Combining Eq. 21 and Eq. 20, we have the following:

$$\begin{aligned}\mathrm{E}[\Psi(t+1)] &\leq \sum_{m=1}^{m_t} m\left(1 - \frac{m}{m_t}\right)\Phi(t)\Pr(m_{t+1} = m) \quad (22) \\ &\leq \frac{m_t}{4}\Phi(t)\sum_{m=1}^{m_t}\Pr(m_{t+1} = m) = \frac{1}{4}\Psi(t). \quad (23)\end{aligned}$$

Let τ be the number of rounds that a ϵ-Nash equilibrium (*i.e.*, $\Psi(t+\tau) = O(1)$) is reached from time t. By Lemma 2 (see right column), we have

$$\mathrm{E}[\tau|\Psi(t)] \leq \log\left(\frac{\Psi(t)}{\Psi(t+\tau)}\right) = \log(\Psi(t)). \quad (24)$$

Note that the maximum value of of $\Psi(t)$ is $|T|n^2$ ($|T|$ is the total number of textures), which occurs in the case when every peer requests all the textures in the region. Therefore, $\mathrm{E}[\tau] \leq 2\log(|T|n)$. By Markov's inequality, we have that

$$\Pr(\tau \geq 40\log(|T|n)) \leq \frac{\mathrm{E}[\tau]}{40\log(|T|n)} = 0.05. \quad (25)$$

This implies that $\Pr(\tau \leq 40\log(|T|n)) \geq 0.95$. As a result, with a high probability, a ϵ-Nash equilibrium can be reached from any state within $O(\log n)$ rounds. □

LEMMA 2. *Let $X_1, X_2, ...$ denote a sequence of non-negative random variables and assume that for all $i \geq 0$*

$$\mathrm{E}[X_i|X_{i-1} = x_{i-1}] \leq \alpha \cdot x_{i-1}$$

for some constant $\alpha \in (0, 1)$. Furthermore, fix some constant $x^* \in (0, x_0]$ and let τ be the random variable that describes the smallest t such that $X_t \leq x^*$. Then,

$$\mathrm{E}[\tau|X_0 = x_0] \leq \frac{2}{\log(1/\alpha)} \cdot \log\left(\frac{x_0}{x^*}\right). \quad (26)$$

PROOF. The complete proof is shown in [12]. □

Theorem 1 indicates that the proposed peer selection strategy can rapidly reach a ϵ-Nash equilibrium within $O(\log n)$ communication rounds from any state, where n is the total number of online peers in the region.

5. EVALUATION

We now evaluate our peer-assisted texture streaming system using a comprehensive simulation program with input from realistic traces collected from the most popular metaverse application - Second Life. We choose Second Life to conduct our evaluation, as the Second Life Viewer[2] and OpenMetaverse[3] are open source and provide functionalities to collect the texture information and location information of avatars from Second Life servers.

For comparisons, we have also simulated the following three peer selection algorithms using the same implementation settings with the proposed algorithm: (1) C/S scheme, where all the requests are solely served by the centralized server; (2) FLoD [15], where each peer can send its requests to AoI neighbors; if AoI neighbors fail to respond, it will send the requests to the server; (3) BAPS [7], which allocates the upload capacities of peers into channels and each peer will select the provider that in the currently connected channels;

[2]`http://wiki.secondlife.com/wiki/Source_downloads`
[3]`http://openmetaverse.org/`

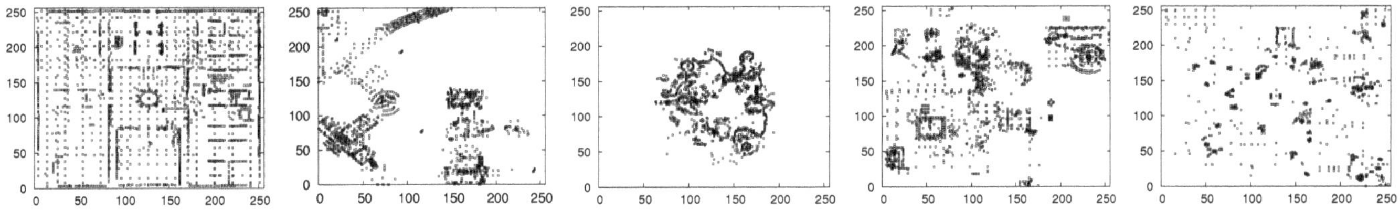

(a) Freebies (b) Waterhead (c) Orientation Island (d) Mauve (e) Japan Resort

Figure 1: 2D positions of textures in different regions, each of which is 256×256 meters.

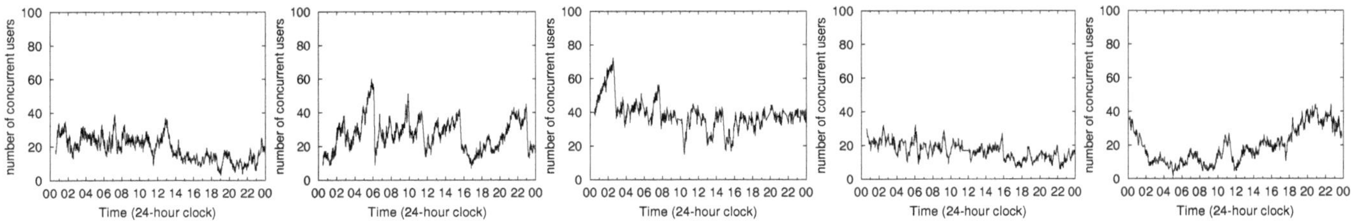

(a) Freebies (b) Waterhead (c) Orientation Island (d) Mauve (e) Japan Resort

Figure 2: Number of concurrent users in different regions during a day.

Region	Number/Size of Textures	User Hours
Freebies	2940 / 0.71 GB	201.1
Waterhead	407 / 0.21 GB	580.1
Orientation Island	87 / 0.56 GB	604.7
Mauve	621 / 0.57 GB	270.7
Japan Resort	551 / 0.41 GB	364.5

Table 2: Total number and size of textures and user hours of different regions during a day.

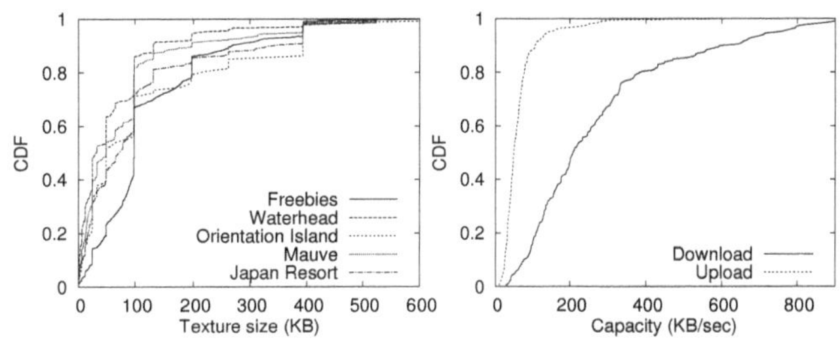

(a) Texture size (b) Peer bandwidth

Figure 3: Distribution of (a) textures sizes, and (b) peer bandwidth.

if the provider is overloaded, it will pick a peer from AoI neighbors as the provider; if that fails, it will randomly select a peer beyond of the AoI; eventually the request will go to the server if no appropriate provider is found.

5.1 Data Collection and Simulation Setup

We collect the realistic texture information of 5 regions (*i.e.*, Freebies, Waterhead, Orientation Island, Mauve, and Japan Resort) from Second Life. The 2D positions of textures, and the distributions of texture sizes of different regions are shown in Figures 1 and 3(a), respectively. The total size of textures and user hours (*i.e.*, the sum of the combined length of all user sessions) during a day in these regions are summarized in Table 2. Before logging into each region, we clear the cache of our client to store all the textures after we log in. After logging into each region, we move our avatar within the region step by step. Specifically, we stop the avatar at each step and wait for all textures within the AoI to be downloaded and rendered before moving to the next step until the whole region is covered, and all textures within the region have been downloaded. When logged into the regions with cleared cache, a regular client requires 10 to 20 seconds to download all the textures within the avatar's AoI. We choose 5 and 10 seconds as two latency constraints of textures attempting to improve the user experience.

It is worth noting that we only collect the textures of objects instead of avatars, since the positions of textures on avatars may change over time due to the mobility and behavior of avatars. Since a texture can be applied to multiple objects that exist in different locations, textures can have multiple positions in our simulations.

We set up a discrete-event simulation using the one-day avatar mobility traces of the 5 regions from Second Life. Each collected mobility trace is a time series with a sampling rate of 10 seconds. The unique ID of each avatar and its trajectory are used to reproduce the movement of avatars. As shown in Figure 2, the number of concurrent users changes over time. We assume that every peer joins the system with a cleared cache, hence peers will request all the textures in their AoIs immediately after they join the system. As avatars move around in the virtual world, they will request the textures within their AoI that are not stored in their caches. The default cache size is set to 128 MB for each peer. We use a simple but efficient cache replacement algorithm which evicts textures that are farther away from the avatar with newly downloaded textures.

To evaluate the proposed algorithm in a heterogeneous environment, every peer is assigned an upload capacity and a download capacity randomly selected from a realistic data set collected from dslreports.com [5], as shown in Figure 3(b). Note that peers (especially peers with wireless access) may have bandwidth (both upload and download) fluctuations, we assume that each peer can utilize 80% of their assigned capacities most of the time for downloading or sending textures. It is worth to point out that the bandwidth distribution of peers has no impact on the convergence rate of the proposed peer selection strategy, as shown in Theorem 1. The AoI radius of each peer is set to be 64 m, which is the default value in Second Life.

5.2 Server Bandwidth Consumption

Recall that our main objective is to reduce the server bandwidth consumption via utilizing the network capacities of participating peers, hence the main performance metric in our simulation is the average server bandwidth consumption in one day. Three different algorithms are evaluated using collected avatar mobility traces during a day. We sum up the total amount of textures required and total amount of texture data that is delivered by the server.

Table 3 shows the efficiency of different schemes in terms of server bandwidth consumption when the latency constraint of all textures is set to 5 seconds, *i.e.*, all the required textures should be delivered (from peers or the server) to the destinations within 5 seconds. We see that all the algorithms except the C/S scheme can reduce the server bandwidth consumption in all the regions via utilizing the bandwidth of participating peers. It can be observed that the proposed peer selection strategy outperforms the other alternatives by a substantial margin in any region.

Table 4 shows the server bandwidth consumption when the latency constraint of all textures is set to 10 seconds. Since relaxing the latency constraint of textures increases the number of requests that peers can satisfy, the server bandwidth consumption is reduced significantly. It is worth noting that relaxing the latency constraint of textures inevitably degrades the user satisfaction.

In the case when the number of textures is large (*e.g.*, the Freebies region with 2940 textures), the number of requests is large. Therefore the server bandwidth consumption is high due to the inadequate capacities of peers which cannot satisfy all the demand. Nevertheless, the proposed algorithm can save 23% and 39% of server bandwidth consumed by the C/S scheme in the Freebies region when the latency constraints of textures are 5 seconds and 10 seconds, respectively. In the case when the number of textures is relatively small (*i.e.*, less than 1000), peer-assisted schemes can save a large amount of server bandwidth. Moreover, we see in Tables 3 and 4 that the proposed peer selection strategy significantly outperforms existing algorithms since it can utilize the peer capacities more efficiently than FLoD and BAPS.

5.3 Server Request Ratio

Another performance metric we use is the server request ratio, which is defined as the percentage of requests in the region that are successfully served by the server. Intuitively, a higher server request ratio results in both a higher server bandwidth consumption and a higher server load. Figures 4 and 5 show the distribution of server request ratio of different algorithms when the latency constraints of textures are 5 seconds and 10 seconds, respectively.

We observe in Tables 5 and 6 that our peer selection strategy achieves a lower expected server request ratio than other existing algorithms in all regions and under all implementation settings. This is because the requests with the proposed peer selection strategy can be sent to underloaded peers rapidly within the latency constraint of textures, so that the peers' bandwidth is efficiently utilized. Therefore, the server load and bandwidth consumption can be reduced (since fewer requests will be processed). Benefitting from this, the system scalability can be improved.

Region	FloD	BAPS	Proposed
Freebies	76.3 %	66.3 %	**50.5** %
Waterhead	25.1 %	20.1 %	**10.2** %
Orientation Island	20.1 %	15.9 %	**7.5** %
Mauve	47.4 %	42.1 %	**31.8** %
Japan Resort	45.4 %	42.7 %	**30.2** %

Table 5: Expected server request ratio (smaller is better) in different regions, when the latency constraint of textures is 5 seconds.

Region	FloD	BAPS	Proposed
Freebies	66.3 %	49.6 %	**35.8** %
Waterhead	13.4 %	10.2 %	**6.6** %
Orientation Island	12.6 %	8.3 %	**5.7** %
Mauve	37.4 %	30.1 %	**20.1** %
Japan Resort	35.6 %	32.8 %	**19.4** %

Table 6: Expected server request ratio (smaller is better) in different regions, when the latency constraint of textures is 10 seconds.

Region	Communication Overhead	
	$d = 5$ Seconds	$d = 10$ Seconds
Freebies	2.36 KB/s	2.16 KB/s
Waterhead	0.26 KB/s	0.12 KB/s
Orientation Island	0.08 KB/s	0.06 KB/s
Mauve	1.02 KB/s	0.86 KB/s
Japan Resort	1.04 KB/s	0.88 KB/s

Table 7: Averaged communication overhead per peer under different latency constraints (*i.e.*, d) of textures in different regions.

5.4 Overhead

Since the protocol overhead incurred is naturally an important metric for every distributed algorithm, we investigate the communication overhead incurred by the proposed peer selection strategy in the last group of simulations. We compute the average overhead per peer as shown in Table 7. It is easy to observe that the communication overhead of our algorithm is very low, with a consumption of less than 3 KB/s per peer in all regions. This is because each peer contacts only one peer for each request at each round, and the sizes of request packets and their corresponding acknowledge packets are usually small (less than 100 bytes per packet). Considering that the requests are processed in a FIFO fashion at each peer, we believe that the processing overhead is reasonable in practice.

6. RELATED WORK

Peer-to-peer or peer-assisted 3D streaming systems for networked virtual environments have been studied extensively. They allow peers to store the 3D contents they receives in caches, and share their network resources and caches to serve others. Varvello *et al.* [29] proposed a structured P2P architecture (implemented on the top of Kad [20]) where all the 3D objects are stored in the participating peers instead of centralized servers. Peers need to query their required objects in Kad, and wait for the data before rendering

Region	Server Bandwidth Consumption (GB)				Fraction of Saved Bandwidth		
	C/S	FLoD	BAPS	Proposed	FLoD	BAPS	Proposed
Freebies	215.6	201.1	183.5	166.1	6.7 %	14.8 %	**23.0 %**
Waterhead	17.5	8.4	6.6	2.8	52.2 %	62.2 %	**84.1 %**
Orientation Island	20.3	11.1	10.5	5.4	45.2 %	48.1 %	**73.4 %**
Mauve	21.6	17.6	16.4	13.7	18.3 %	23.8 %	**36.4 %**
Japan Resort	32.6	25.4	24.7	19.4	22.1 %	24.2 %	**40.5 %**

Table 3: Server bandwidth consumption (smaller is better) and the fraction of saved bandwidth (larger is better) of different algorithms during a day, when the latency constraint of textures is set to 5 seconds.

Region	Server Bandwidth Consumption (GB)				Fraction of Saved Bandwidth		
	C/S	FLoD	BAPS	Proposed	FLoD	BAPS	Proposed
Freebies	215.6	189.9	161.0	131.4	11.9 %	25.3 %	**39.0 %**
Waterhead	17.5	5.1	3.0	1.3	70.9 %	82.8 %	**92.2 %**
Orientation Island	20.3	7.7	6.5	3.2	61.9 %	68.2 %	**84.0 %**
Mauve	21.6	14.9	12.5	9.3	30.5 %	41.8 %	**56.5 %**
Japan Resort	32.6	21.3	20.3	12.6	34.6 %	37.9 %	**61.3 %**

Table 4: Server bandwidth consumption (smaller is better) and the fraction of saved bandwidth (larger is better) of different algorithms during a day, when the latency constraint of textures is set to 10 seconds.

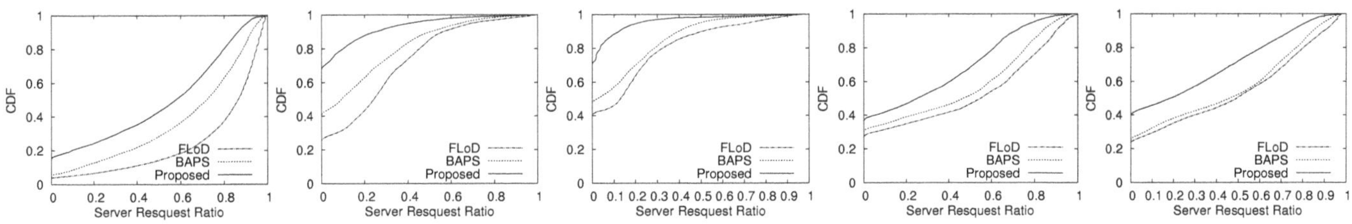

(a) Freebies (b) Waterhead (c) Orientation Island (d) Mauve (e) Japan Resort

Figure 4: Distribution of server request ratio (smaller is better) in different regions during a day, when the latency constraint of textures is set to 5 seconds.

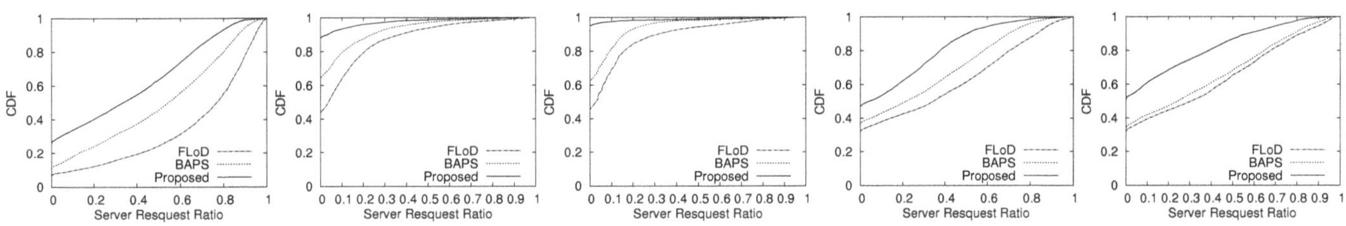

(a) Freebies (b) Waterhead (c) Orientation Island (d) Mauve (e) Japan Resort

Figure 5: Distribution of server request ratio (smaller is better) in different regions during a day, when the latency constraint of textures is set to 10 seconds.

those objects in their virtual environments. This pure P2P architecture suffers from low consistency (due to the query delay) and persistency (due to the avatars' mobility).

Hu *et al.* [15] proposed FLoD, which is the first framework for peer-assisted 3D streaming in metaverses. FLoD enables each peer to send its requests to a randomly chosen AoI neighbor, thus reduce the server bandwidth cost. If the AoI neighbors fail to respond, the peer will send the requests to the server. To minimize the server bandwidth cost in FLoD respecting the bandwidth constraints of peers, Chien *et al.* [7] proposed a bandwidth aware peer selection algorithm, named BAPS, that improves the utilization of peer bandwidth via bandwidth reservation.

Our objective is to minimize the server bandwidth cost by enabling peers to rapidly select underloaded content providers in a decentralized manner. The key idea is to balance the loads of peers. A number of algorithms have been proposed for dynamic load balancing, which is modeled as a weighted congestion game with selfish and non-cooperative users. A steady state in this context is a pure Nash equilibrium, in which no user is willing to change her/his strategy. Since the idea of using a potential function to measure the closeness to a Nash equilibrium was introduced by Even-Dar *et al.* [10], a number of protocols (*e.g.*, [8] [14]) have been proposed to balance the loads sequentially, *i.e.*, the migration events take place one at a time, and costs on users are updated immediately. More recently, concurrent protocols (*e.g.*, [4] [3] [1]) for load balancing have been proposed to improve the convergence time by allowing users to change their strategies concurrently. We adopt the concept of these load balancing techniques by applying it to peer selection strategy in peer-assisted 3D streaming systems.

Our system distinguishes itself from all existing systems in the following two important aspects. First, we consider the latency requirements of 3D contents, and design a light-weight peer selection strategy to minimize the server bandwidth respecting the latency constraints of contents and the bandwidth constraints of peers. Second, the peer' bandwidth is optimally utilized in a decentralized manner.

7. CONCLUSION

In this paper we have introduced a peer-assisted texture streaming system for metaverses that minimizes the server bandwidth cost without degrading the end-user satisfaction. We formulate the problem of server bandwidth minimization as a congestion game, and use the concept of congestion games to design a peer selection strategy. Our algorithm is light-weight, online, and can efficiently utilize the bandwidth of heterogeneous peers in a decentralized manner by enabling each peer to repeatedly update its content providers independently and concurrently. We evaluate our algorithm through an extensive comparison study based on simulations using realistic texture information and avatar mobility traces collected from Second Life. As shown by our simulation results, the proposed algorithm can effectively reduce the server bandwidth cost and increase the scalability of metaverses. Encouraged by our results from this paper, we are currently working on a real-world deployment of our proposal as an extension to Second Life.

Acknowledgment

This research has been funded in part by A*Star SERC PSF grant 082 101 0028.

8. REFERENCES

[1] H. Ackermann, S. Fischer, M. Hoefer, and M. Schöngens. Distributed Algorithms for QoS Load Balancing. In *SPAA '09: 21st Annual Symposium on Parallelism in Algorithms and Architectures*, pages 197–203, 2009.

[2] ActiveWorlds. Online: http://www.activeworlds.com.

[3] B. Awerbuch, Y. Azar, and R. Khandekar. Fast Load Balancing via Bounded Best Response. In *SODA '08: 19th Annual ACM-SIAM Symposium on Discrete Algorithms*, pages 314–322, 2008.

[4] P. Berenbrink, T. Friedetzky, L. A. Goldberg, P. Goldberg, Z. Hu, and R. Martin. Distributed Selfish Load Balancing. In *SODA '06: 17th Annual ACM-SIAM Symposium on Discrete Algorithm*, pages 354–363, 2006.

[5] Broadband Reports and Speed Test Statistics. Online: http://www.dslreports.com/archive.

[6] N. Buchbinder and J. Naor. The Design of Competitive Online Algorithms via a Primal-Dual Approach. *Foundations and Trends in Theoretical Computer Science*, 3:93–263, 2009.

[7] C.-H. Chien, S.-Y. Hu, and J.-R. Jiang. Bandwidth-Aware Peer-to-Peer 3D Streaming. In *NETGAMES '09: 8th Annual Workshop on Network and Systems Support for Games*, 2009.

[8] S. Chien and A. Sinclair. Convergence to Approximate Nash Equilibria in Congestion Games. In *SODA '07: 18th Annual ACM-SIAM Symposium on Discrete algorithms*, pages 169–178, 2007.

[9] Y. Emek, M. M. Halldórsson, Y. Mansour, B. Patt-Shamir, J. Radhakrishnan, and D. Rawitz. Online Set Packing and Competitive Scheduling of Multi-Part Tasks. In *PODC '10: 29th ACM Symposium on Principles of Distributed Computing*, pages 440–449, 2010.

[10] E. Even-Dar and Y. Mansour. Fast Convergence of Selfish Rerouting. In *SODA '05: 16th Annual ACM-SIAM Symposium on Discrete Algorithms*, pages 772–781, 2005.

[11] A. Fabrikant, C. Papadimitriou, and K. Talwar. The Complexity of Pure Nash Equilibria. In *STOC '04: 36th Annual ACM Symposium on Theory of Computing*, pages 604–612, 2004.

[12] Fischer, Simon and Olbrich, Lars and Vöcking, Berthold. Approximating Wardrop Equilibria with Finitely Many Agents. *Distributed Computing*, 21:129–139, 2008.

[13] M. R. Garey and D. S. Johnson. *Computers and Intractability: A Guide to the Theory of NP-Completeness.* W. H. Freeman & Co., 1990.

[14] P. W. Goldberg. Bounds for the Convergence Rate of Randomized Local Search in a Multiplayer Load-balancing Game. In *PODC '04: 23rd Annual ACM Symposium on Principles of Distributed Computing*, pages 131–140, 2004.

[15] S.-Y. Hu, T.-H. Huang, S.-C. Chang, W.-L. Sung, J.-R. Jiang, and B.-Y. Chen. FLoD: A Framework for Peer-to-Peer 3D Streaming. In *INFOCOM '08*, pages 1373 –1381, 2008.

[16] Y. Huang, T. Z. Fu, D.-M. Chiu, J. C. Lui, and C. Huang. Challenges, Design and Analysis of a Large-scale P2P-VOD System. In *SIGCOMM '08: ACM SIGCOMM Conference on Data Communication*, 2008.

[17] S. Liu, R. Zhang-Shen, W. Jiang, J. Rexford, and M. Chiang. Performance Bounds for Peer-Assisted Live Streaming. In *SIGMETRICS '08: International Conference on Measurement and Modeling of Computer Systems*, pages 313–324, 2008.

[18] R. T. B. Ma, S. C. M. Lee, J. C. S. Lui, and D. K. Y. Yau. A Game Theoretic Approach to Provide Incentive and Service Differentiation in P2P Networks. In *SIGMETRICS '04: International Conference on Measurement and Modeling of Computer Systems*, pages 189–198, 2004.

[19] N. Magharei and R. Rejaie. PRIME: Peer-to-Peer Receiver-drIven MEsh-Based Streaming. In *INFOCOM '07: 26th IEEE International Conference on Computer Communications*, pages 1415 –1423, 2007.

[20] P. Maymounkov and D. Mazières. Kademlia: A Peer-to-Peer Information System Based on the XOR Metric. In *IPTPS '01: 1st International Workshop on Peer-to-Peer Systems*, pages 53–65, 2002.

[21] N. Nisan, T. Roughgarden, E. Tardos, and V. V. Vazirani. *Algorithmic Game Theory.* Cambridge University Press, 2007.

[22] I. A. Oliver, A. H. Miller, and C. Allison. Virtual Worlds, Real Traffic: Interaction and Adaptation. In *MMSys '10: 1st Annual ACM SIGMM Conference on Multimedia Systems*, 2010.

[23] A. Panconesi and M. Sozio. Fast Distributed Scheduling via Primal-Dual. In *SPAA '08: 20th Annual Symposium on Parallelism in Algorithms and Architectures*, pages 229–235, 2008.

[24] J. Puchinger, G. R. Raidl, and U. Pferschy. The Multidimensional Knapsack Problem: Structure and Algorithms. *INFORMS Journal on Computing*, 2010.

[25] A. Schrijver. *Theory of Linear and Integer Programming.* John Wiley & Sons, Inc., 1986.

[26] A. Schrijver. *Combinatorial Optimization: Polyhedra and Efficiency.* Springer, 2003.

[27] Second Life. Online: http://secondlife.com.

[28] The Second Life Economy. Online: http://blogs.secondlife.com/tags/quarterly_economic_report.

[29] M. Varvello, C. Diot, and E. Biersack. P2P Second Life: Experimental Validation Using Kad. In *INFOCOM '09*, pages 1161–1169, 2009.

[30] J. Wang, C. Huang, and J. Li. On ISP-friendly Rate Allocation for Peer-assisted VoD. In *MM '08: 16th ACM International Conference on Multimedia*, pages 279–288, 2008.

Cloud Download: Using Cloud Utilities to Achieve High-quality Content Distribution for Unpopular Videos *

Yan Huang [1], Zhenhua Li [2*], Gang Liu [1], and Yafei Dai [2]
[1] Tencent Research, Shanghai, China
[2] EECS, Peking University, Beijing, China
{galehuang, lizhenhua1983 *, ganghust, daiyafei} @gmail.com

ABSTRACT

Video content distribution dominates the Internet traffic. The state-of-the-art techniques generally work well in distributing popular videos, but do not provide satisfactory content distribution service for *unpopular videos* due to low data health or low data transfer rate. In recent years, the worldwide deployment of cloud utilities provides us with a novel perspective to consider the above problem. We propose and implement the *cloud download* scheme, which achieves high-quality video content distribution by using cloud utilities to *guarantee the data health* and *enhance the data transfer rate*. Specifically, a user sends his video request to the cloud which subsequently downloads the video from the Internet and stores it in the cloud cache. Then the user can usually retrieve his requested video (whether popular or unpopular) from the cloud with high data rate in any place at any time, via the intra-cloud data transfer acceleration. Running logs of our real deployed commercial system (named VideoCloud) confirm the effectiveness and efficiency of cloud download. The users' average data transfer rate of unpopular videos exceeds 1.6 Mbps, and over 80% of the data transfer rates are more than 300 Kbps which is the basic playback rate of online videos. Our study provides practical experiences and valuable heuristics for making use of cloud utilities to achieve efficient Internet services.

Categories and Subject Descriptors

C.2.4 [**Distributed Systems**]: Distributed applications

General Terms

Design, Measurement, Performance

*Area chair: Surender Chandra.
This paper is a joint work of Tencent Research and Peking University. The first two organizations/authors have made their unique and equally important contributions.

MM'11, November 28–December 1, 2011, Scottsdale, Arizona, USA.

1. INTRODUCTION

Video content distribution dominates the Internet traffic. A recent Cisco report [1] says that nearly 90% of all the consumer IP traffic is expected to consist of video content distribution, including web video like YouTube [2], P2P (peer-to-peer) video like BitTorrent [3] and PPLive [4], and so on in 2012. Therefore, achieving *high-quality* video content distribution over the Internet is of great significance for both academia and industry. Here the meaning of *high-quality* is two-fold: *high data health* and *high data transfer rate*. The metric *data health* is initially used in the BitTorrent protocol [3]. It denotes the number of available full copies of the shared file in a BitTorrent swarm. For example, the data health 1.0 means one full copy is available, and a swarm with data health less than 1.0 is called an *unhealthy* swarm because no peer in the swarm can get a full copy. In this paper, we keep using *data health* to represent the data redundancy level of a video file. High data health implies that the user is able to obtain a full copy of the video, and high data transfer rate enables the advanced function of online video streaming (including live streaming [5] and on-demand streaming [6]).

The state-of-the-art techniques of video content distribution mainly include CDN (content distribution network like Akamai [7]) and P2P. CDN is the traditional technique that optimizes the performance of Internet content distribution by strategically deploying edge servers at multiple locations (often over multiple ISP networks). These edge servers cooperate with each other by replicating or moving data according to data popularity and server load. An end user usually obtains a copy of data from a nearby edge server, so that the data transfer rate is greatly enhanced and the load on the original data source is reduced. However, for the sake of limited storage and bandwidth capacity, it is not cost-effective for CDN to replicate unpopular videos to edge servers [8], considering that there are many more unpopular videos than popular videos over the Internet. Moreover, CDN is a charged facility that only serves the content providers who have paid, rather than a public utility of the Internet. Consequently, it is impractical to count on CDN for efficient distribution of unpopular videos.

Different from CDN, P2P content distribution mainly relies on the unstable but numerous end users to form peer-to-peer data swarms [3, 9], where data is directly exchanged between neighboring peers. The real strength of P2P shows when a popular video is distributed, because a popular video is shared by a number of peers and more peers usually imply higher data health and higher degree of download parallelism, which further lead to higher data transfer rate. As to an unpopular video, it is often difficult to find a corresponding peer swarm. Even if the peer swarm exists, the few peers are unlikely to have high data health or high data transfer rate, and thus each peer has to stay online for long hours to wait for the download completion — a tedious process of low energy efficiency. In a word, although CDN and P2P generally work well in distributing popular videos, neither of them is able to provide satisfactory content distribution service for unpopular videos, due to low data health or low data transfer rate.

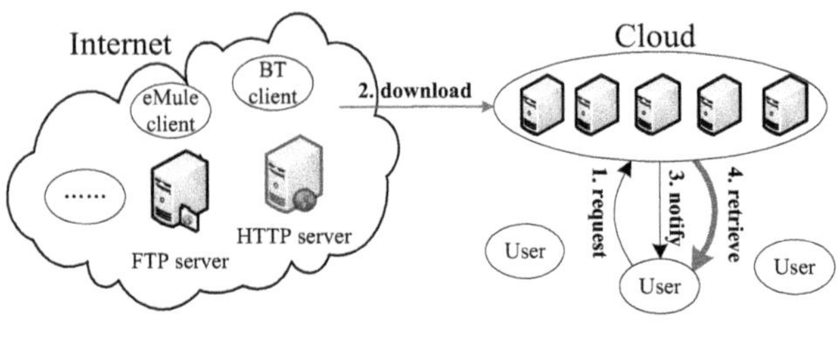

Figure 1: Principle of cloud download.

In recent years, the worldwide deployment of cloud utilities [10, 11] provides us with a novel perspective to consider the above problem. In this paper, we propose and implement the *cloud download* scheme, which achieves high-quality video content distribution by using cloud utilities to *guarantee the data health* and *enhance the data transfer rate.* The principle of cloud download is depicted in Figure 1. Firstly, a user sends his video request to the cloud (see Arrow 1 in Figure 1). The video request contains a file link which can be an HTTP/FTP link, a BitTorrent [3]/eMule [9] link, and so on [1]. Subsequently, the cloud *downloads* the requested video from the file link and stores it in the cloud cache (see Arrow 2 in Figure 1) to guarantee the data health of the video ≥ 1.0 (each video also has a duplicate in the cloud cache for redundancy). Then the cloud notifies the user (see Arrow 3 in Figure 1) and the user can usually *retrieve* [2] his requested video (whether popular or unpopular) from the cloud with high data rate (see Arrow 4 in Figure 1) in any place at any time, via the intra-cloud data transfer acceleration (which will be addressed in detail in Section 3.2). In practice, the cloud does not need to notify the user when his requested video is available. Instead, the user actively checks the download progress by himself and takes corresponding actions. That is to say, Arrow 3 in Figure 1 can also be replaced by "3. check".

Besides, an important derivative advantage brought by cloud download is the *user-side energy efficiency.* An Internet user often has to keep his computer (and network interface card) powered-on for long hours (says t_1) only to download an unpopular video [12]. During this process, a lot of energy is wasted because the major components (including CPU, memory, disk, etc.) keep working but are not efficiently used. Cloud download uses the cloud servers to download the requested videos, so its users do not need to be online; in fact, they do not need to open their computers at all — this is the reason why we also call "cloud download" as "offline download". When the requested video is available in the cloud, the user can usually retrieve it in short time (says t_2). Thus, cloud download significantly reduces the user-side energy cost (by the ratio $\frac{t_1-t_2}{t_1}$). The detailed energy efficiency analysis will be presented in Section 4.5.

The only drawback of cloud download lies in that for some videos, the user must wait for the cloud to download it and thus he cannot view the video at once. The abovementioned waiting time is denoted as the *view startup delay.* Note that CDN and P2P also have their view startup delay to buffer a certain amount of data for a smooth view startup of the video (e.g., buffer the first several minutes' data for a 100-minute video). This drawback is effectively alleviated by the *implicit and secure data reuse among the users* of cloud download. For each video, the cloud only downloads it from the Internet when it is requested for the first time, and the subsequent requests are directly satisfied by using the cached copy with very low view startup delay (except when the cached copy is replaced). Such data reuse is more secure than the explicit data reuse among P2P users (which is susceptible to the Sybil attack [13], Eclipse attack [14], DHT attack [15], and so on), because it is completely handled by the cloud and is oblivious to users. According to the real-system performance, the data reuse rate among the users reaches 87%, indicating that most video requests are satisfied instantly with very low view startup delay.

Since June 2010, we have deployed a large-scale commercial cloud download system (named VideoCloud [16]) on top of the QQCyclone platform [17], using a "micro" data center composed of 426 commodity servers. VideoCloud has attracted over 6 million registered users and supports most of the mainstream content distribution protocols like HTTP, FTP, BitTorrent, eMule, and so on. Currently, VideoCloud receives over 0.2 million video requests sent from around 50000 users per day, and most of the requests are issued for unpopular videos. The data center of VideoCloud has been deployed across four major ISPs in China and is planned to cover more domains. The user's monetary cost for cloud download service differs from Amazon S3 [18] and Microsoft Azure [19], but is more similar to Dropbox [20]. Specifically, the user of VideoCloud is charged according to his cloud storage capacity and regardless of the bandwidth consumed. Any registered user is allocated with 5-GB free storage, and extra storage is charged in unit of 5 GB.

The system running logs confirm the effectiveness and efficiency of cloud download. For example, the users' average data transfer rate of unpopular videos exceeds 1.6 Mbps, and over 80% of the data transfer rates are more than 300 Kbps which is the basic playback rate of online videos [2, 21]. In comparison, when the *common download method* is used, the average data transfer rate is merely 0.57 Mbps, and 70% of the data transfer rates are less than 300 Kbps. The common download method denotes the common way in which a user downloads video content from the Internet, e.g., using a web browser or a P2P client software to download a video. Besides, compared with the common download method, cloud download reduces the user-side energy cost by around 92%.

To sum up, our contributions in this paper are as follows:

[1]The cloud does not accept keywords as the video request, because one keyword or a combination of several keywords may correspond to multiple videos with different contents in the Internet.

[2]Here we use *retrieve* to distinguish with *download.* In this paper, *download* means the cloud obtains data from the Internet while *retrieve* means the user obtains data from the cloud.

1. We analyze the state-of-the-art techniques of video content distribution (i.e., CDN and P2P) and discover that neither of them is able to provide satisfactory content distribution service for unpopular videos. Driven by this problem, we propose and implement the novel cloud download scheme, which achieves high-quality video content distribution by using cloud utilities to guarantee the data health and enhance the data transfer rate. The only drawback of cloud download, i.e., the view startup delay, is effectively alleviated by the implicit and secure data reuse among the users.

2. We have deployed VideoCloud, a large-scale commercial cloud download system. And we present its system architecture and design techniques, as well as our observations, analysis, and insights. Our study provides practical experiences and valuable heuristics for making use of cloud utilities to achieve efficient Internet services.

3. We evaluate the performance of VideoCloud via its running logs using three major metrics: data transfer rate, view startup delay, and energy efficiency. The evaluation results confirm the effectiveness and efficiency of cloud download.

2. RELATED WORK

As the backbone bandwidth and end user access bandwidth of the Internet continuously increase, people have been putting forward higher and higher demand on video content distribution. The pixel resolution evolves from CIF (common intermediate format, 352*288), VGA (video graphics array, 640*480), to HD (high-definition, 1280*720), and the playback mode evolves from view-after-download to view-as-download. In the past 15 years, high-quality video content distribution has been a very hot research topic in both industry and academia [22], in particular the state-of-the-art techniques: CDN and P2P. The advantages and disadvantages of CDN, P2P, and cloud download have been addressed in the previous section. In recent years, some researchers recognize that both CDN and P2P have their limitations and thus propose novel schemes by combining or optimizing CDN and P2P.

On top of ChinaCache [23], the biggest commercial CDN service provider in China, Yin et al. developed a *hybrid CDN-P2P* live streaming system (named LiveSky [24]) to incorporate the strengths on both sides: the scalability of P2P, and the quality control capability and reliability of CDN. Although the hybrid CDN-P2P architecture inevitably brings extra deployment complication and maintenance cost, LiveSky achieves lower burden on the CDN network and higher working efficiency of peer streaming for popular videos. However, for unpopular files, it is difficult and inefficient for the few users to form a peer swarm, and then the performance of LiveSky will be like that of a common CDN.

Wu et al. [25] refocused on the importance of servers in P2P streaming systems and thus proposed the *server-assisted P2P* streaming scheme. Via a 7-month running trace of a commercial P2P live streaming system, named UUSee [26], they found that the total available bandwidth of the 150 streaming servers could not meet the increasing demand of download bandwidth from hundreds of channels (a channel can be seen as a peer swarm), although the total upload bandwidth of peers also increased with download demand. So they proposed an allocation algorithm of server bandwidth, named Ration, which could proactively predict the minimum server bandwidth demand of each channel, based on historical information. Therefore, each channel can be guaranteed with desirable streaming quality. Ration has the similar shortcoming as LiveSky because every channel of UUSee can be seen as a very popular video. For unpopular videos, Ration would work like the traditional client-server video streaming scheme.

Recent years have seen a strong trend in *extremely high-quality* video content distribution like online HDTV (high-definition TV) [27] and cinematic-quality VoD (video-on-demand) [28]. Undoubtedly, extremely high-quality videos can provide Internet users with wonderful viewing experiences; however, the content distribution of extremely high-quality videos (in particular those unpopular videos without powerful CDN support) over the highly dynamic Internet environments has still been a very challenging problem. The latest practical solution may be Novasky [28], an operational "P2P storage cloud" for on-demand streaming of cinematic-quality videos over a high-bandwidth network (i.e., the campus network of Tsinghua University). The limitation of Novasky is obvious: it works on a high-bandwidth campus network which is much more stable and homogeneous than the real Internet. Cloud download uses cloud utilities to guarantee the data health of videos and meanwhile enhance the data transfer rate to quite high and stable. Thus, cloud download can be taken as a promising solution to the future extremely high-quality video content distribution over the Internet.

3. SYSTEM DESIGN

In this section, we present the system architecture and design techniques of VideoCloud, as well as our observations, analysis, and insights.

3.1 System Overview

As depicted in Figure 2, the architecture of VideoCloud is mainly composed of five building blocks: 1) *ISP Proxies*, 2) *Task Manager*, 3) *Task Dispatcher*, 4) *Downloaders*, and 5) *Cloud Cache*. The detailed hardware composition of each building block is listed in Table 1. Note that all the information of Memory, Storage, and Bandwidth refers to one server. We do not list the CPU information since the performance of CPU is not important for our system which is data (bandwidth and storage) intensive rather than computation intensive. In total, the system utilizes 426 commodity servers, including 300 chunk servers making up a 600-TB cloud cache, 80 download servers with 26 Gbps of Internet bandwidth, and 33 upload servers with 20 Gbps of Internet bandwidth. Every server runs the Suse Linux v10.1 operating system. Now we describe the organization and working process of the system by following the message and data flows of a typical cloud download task.

The user of VideoCloud should have installed its client software [16]. The client software is able to recognize which ISP the user locates at from the user's IP address (with the help of an embedded and periodically updated IP-ISP mapping file), so the video request is firstly sent to the corresponding ISP Proxy by the client software (see Arrow 1 in Figure 2). Each ISP Proxy maintains a *request queue* to control the number of requests sent to the Task Manager (see Arrow 2 in Figure 2), so that the Task Manager is resilient

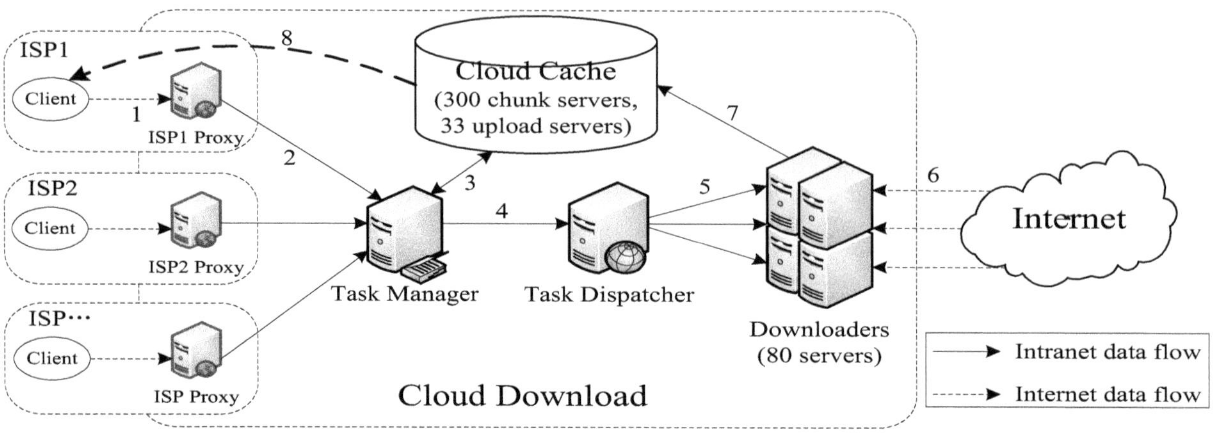

Figure 2: System architecture of cloud download.

Table 1: Hardware composition of VideoCloud.

Building Block	Number of servers	Memory	Storage	Bandwidth
ISP Proxy	4	8 GB	250 GB	1 Gbps (Intranet), 0.3 Gbps (Internet)
Task Manager	4	8 GB	250 GB	1 Gbps (Intranet)
Task Dispatcher	3	8 GB	460 GB	1 Gbps (Intranet)
Downloaders	80	8 GB	460 GB	1 Gbps (Intranet), ~0.325 Gbps (Internet)
Cloud Cache	300 chunk servers, 33 upload servers, and 2 index servers	8 GB	4 TB (chunk server), 250 GB (upload server)	1 Gbps (Intranet), ~0.6 Gbps (Internet)

to request upsurge in any ISP. Presently, VideoCloud has set four ISP Proxies in the four major ISPs in China: China Telecom [29], China Unicom [30], China Mobile [31], and CERNET (China Education and Research Network) [32]. If the user does not locate at any of the four major ISPs (such users take a small portion), his video request is sent to a random one of the four ISP Proxies. We plan to set more ISP Proxies in more ISPs in the future.

On receiving a video request, the Task Manager firstly checks whether the requested video has a copy in the Cloud Cache (see Arrow 3 in Figure 2). If the video request is a BitTorrent/eMule link, the Task Manager examines whether the Cloud Cache contains a video which has the same hash code with that contained in the BitTorrent/eMule link [3]. Otherwise, the Task Manager directly examines whether the file link is repeated in the Cloud Cache. If the requested video actually has a copy, the user can directly and instantly retrieve the video from the Cloud Cache (see Arrow 8 in Figure 2). Otherwise, the Task Manager forwards the video request to the Task Dispatcher (see Arrow 4 in Figure 2).

The Task Dispatcher assigns the video request to one server (called a "downloader") in the Downloaders for data downloading (see Arrow 5 in Figure 2). For example, if the video request is a P2P request, the assigned downloader will act like a common peer to join the corresponding peer swarm. The Task Dispatcher is mainly responsible for balancing the bandwidth loads of the 80 downloaders. The number of downloaders (80) is empirically determined to guarantee that the total download bandwidth (26 Gbps) exceeds the peak load of download tasks (nearly 20 Gbps till now). Each downloader executes multiple download tasks in parallel in order to fully utilize its download bandwidth (around 0.325 Gbps) (see Arrow 6 in Figure 2), and the Task Dispatcher always assigns a newly incoming video request to the downloader which has the lowest download data rate.

As long as the downloader accomplishes a download task, it computes the hash code of the downloaded video and attempts to store the video in the Cloud Cache (see Arrow 7 in Figure 2). The downloader firstly checks whether the video has a copy in the Cloud Cache (using the hash code). If the video is repeated, the downloader simply discards it. Otherwise, the downloader checks whether the Cloud Cache has enough unused space to store the new video. If the Cloud Cache does not have enough unused space, it deletes some cached videos to get enough unused space to store the new video. The concrete cache architecture, cache capacity planning, and cache replacement strategy will be investigated in Section 3.2, Section 3.4, and Section 3.5, respectively.

When the abovementioned video store process is finished, the user can usually retrieve the requested video from the Cloud Cache (see Arrow 8 in Figure 2) in any place at any time. Since the user's ISP information can be acquired from his video retrieve message (see Arrow 4 in Figure 1), the Cloud Cache takes advantage of the intra-cloud ISP-aware data upload technique to restrict the retrieve data flow within the same ISP as the user's, so as to enhance the data transfer rate and avoid the inter-ISP traffic cost.

3.2 Data Transfer Acceleration

A critical problem of cloud download is how to accelerate the data transfer (i.e., retrieve) process so that the user can

[3] A BitTorrent/eMule link contains the hash code of its affiliated file in itself, while an HTTP/FTP link does not.

obtain his requested video (whether popular or unpopular) from the cloud with high data rate in any place at any time. Considering that the cross-ISP data transfer performance degrades seriously and the inter-ISP traffic cost is often expensive [33, 34], we solve this problem via the intra-cloud ISP-aware data upload technique. Since the user's real-time ISP information can be acquired from his video retrieve message, the Cloud Cache takes advantage of its ISP-aware upload servers to restrict the retrieve data flow within the same ISP as the user's, so as to enhance the retrieve data rate and avoid inter-ISP traffic cost. Specifically, as shown in Figure 3, the Cloud Cache consists of 300 chunk servers, 33 upload servers, and 2 index servers which are connected by a DCN (data center network). A specific number of upload servers are placed in each ISP, proportional to the data traffic volume in each ISP. The video requests come from tens of ISPs, but most of them come from the four major ISPs in China: China Telecom [29], China Unicom [30], China Mobile [31], and CERNET [32]. Figure 4 demonstrates the number of users, the number of video requests, and the data traffic volume in each ISP in one day. Thereby, the Cloud Cache places 21, 10, 1, and 1 upload servers in the four major ISPs respectively at the moment. If the user locates at other ISPs, we randomly choose an upload server to transfer the corresponding data.

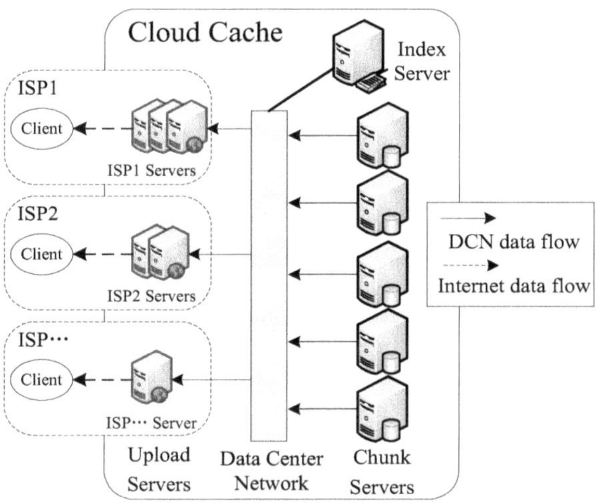

Figure 3: Architecture of the Cloud Cache.

Every video is segmented into chunks of equal size to be stored in the chunk servers, and every chunk has a duplicate for redundancy, so the 300 chunk servers can accommodate a total of $\frac{300 \times 4 \text{ TB}}{2} = 600$ TB unique data. In order to achieve load balance and exploit the chunk-correlation in the same file, all the chunks of a video are stored together into the chunk server with the biggest available storage capacity. The duplicate chunks of a video must be stored in another chunk server. There exists an index server (as well as a backup index server) which maintains the metadata of chunks for chunk search and validation. The metadata is a list of n-tuples like < *file hash code, file link, number of chunks, physical location of the first chunk, physical location of the first duplicate chunk* >.

The DCN in the Cloud Cache adopts the traditional three-tier tree structure to organize the switches, composed of a core tier in the root of the tree, an aggregation tier in the middle, and an edge tier at the leaves of the tree. The index servers, chunk servers, upload servers, and downloaders are connected to the switches at the edge tier. Suppose a user A locating at ISP1 wants to retrieve a video f stored in a chunk server S, and the Cloud Cache has placed 10 upload servers ($U_1, U_2, \cdots, U_{10}$) in ISP1. The chunks of f are firstly transferred from S to a random upload server (says U_4) in ISP1, and then transferred from U_4 to the user A. The transfer process is not store-and-forward but pass-through: as soon as U_4 gets a complete chunk of f, U_4 transfers the chunk to A. f would not be cached in U_4 because the intra-cloud end-to-end bandwidth is quite high (1 Gbps) and we do not need to make things more complicated than necessary.

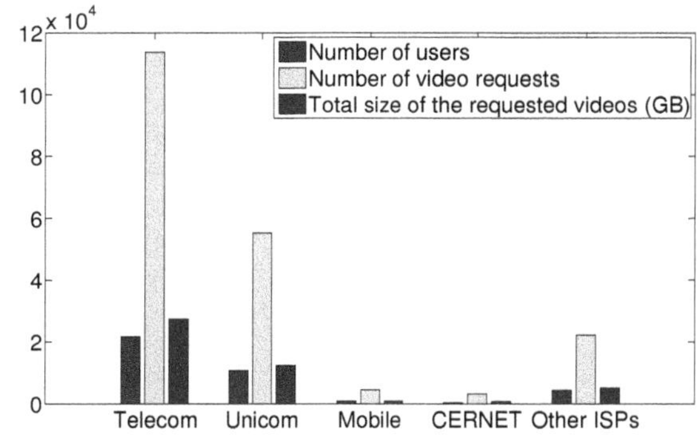

Figure 4: Number of users, number of video requests, and data traffic volume in each ISP in one day.

3.3 Download Success Rate Improvement

Although cloud download guarantees the data health of the requested video (≥1.0) after the video is downloaded by the cloud, it cannot guarantee to download every requested video successfully. In this subsection, we construct a simple model to analyze the download success rates of cloud download and *common download* (the data reuse among users is not considered). *Common download* is the common way in which a user downloads video content from the Internet. Considering the highly dynamic and complicated Internet environments, the target of our model is to illustrate the long-term expected trend, rather than the accurate prediction in a short period.

Whether we use common download or cloud download, the download success rate of a requested HTTP/FTP file only depends on the accessibility of the file link (1-accessible or 0-inaccessible). According to our measurements of the accessibility of numerous HTTP/FTP file links submitted to VideoCloud, the average download success rate of HTTP/FTP files is:

$$R_1 = R_1' = 0.414.$$

The download success rate of a requested P2P file is much more complicated because the accessibility of a peer is a stochastic variable. Consider a P2P swarm consisting of n peers sharing a file f. The time limit is T hours, that is to say, each peer must draw his conclusion in T hours: 1-download success or 0-download failure. In average, each peer stays online for t hours in the time limit (T hours) and the data health of a single peer is h ($h<1.0$). For a common peer P, during the t hours when P is online, P is expected to encounter $\frac{n \cdot t}{T}$ online peers (n is the average number of peers in a peer swarm), assuming the online time of each peer is independent. Since the data health of a single peer is h, the download success rate of P is expected to be:

$$R_2 = 1 - (1-h)^{\frac{n \cdot t}{T}}.$$

Cloud download uses a stable peer P' (in fact, P' is a cloud server) to join in the P2P swarm, so the online duration t for P' is $t = T$. Then the download success rate of P' is expected to be:

$$R_2' = 1 - (1-h)^n.$$

Among all the video requests, let α denote the fraction of HTTP/FTP file requests, and β denote the fraction of P2P file requests. Thus, the overall download success rates of common download and cloud download are expected to be:

$$R = \alpha \cdot R_1 + \beta \cdot R_2, \text{ and } R' = \alpha \cdot R_1' + \beta \cdot R_2'.$$

Our 17-day measurements of VideoCloud show that $h = 0.4$, $n = 5.4$, $\frac{t}{T} = 0.12$, $\alpha = 27.4\%$, and $\beta = 72.6\%$. As a result,

$$R = 31.8\%, \text{ and } R' = 79.3\%.$$

The expected download success rates (R and R') are depicted in Figure 5 to compare with the real performance of VideoCloud. The real-system average download success rate is 81.4%.

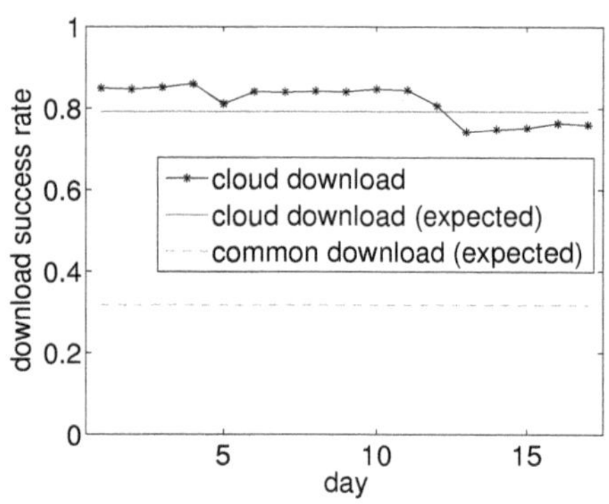

Figure 5: Download success rate in each day.

3.4 Cache Capacity Planning

The biggest hardware and energy cost of the VideoCloud system comes from the Cloud Cache, in particular the 300 chunk servers making up a 600-TB cloud cache. In this subsection, we address the reason why the cache capacity is planned as 600 TB.

VideoCloud has over 6 million registered users. It is impossible to allocate each user with unlimited cloud cache capacity. Instead, each registered user is allocated with a 5-GB free cloud cache at the moment, because 5 GB is around the size of a common TV play series [4]. Given that the average size of requested videos is 379 MB, we regard a cloud cache which accommodates more than 13 videos (5 GB / 379 MB = 13.5) as basically enough to satisfy a common user's requirement. Extra storage is charged in unit of 5 GB. According to our statistics, almost all the users of VideoCloud are 5-GB free users, which is quite similar to the situation of Dropbox [20]. Consequently, over 6 million registered users need more than 29000 TB of cache capacity *in the worst case*. The *worst case* happens under the following three conditions: 1) Every user fully utilizes its 5-GB cloud cache [5]; 2) There is no data reuse among the users; and 3) The data in a user's cloud cache is stored *forever* unless it is retrieved by the user (this condition will be replaced by a more practical and economical condition later on). It is difficult to predict the extent of the first and second conditions because they depend on users' behaviors and may vary enormously as time goes by. Therefore, to change the third condition is our only choice. The third condition is replaced by a practical and economical condition: 3) The data in a user's cloud cache is stored *for one week* unless it is retrieved by the user. The store period (one week) is an empirical parameter according to our operating experiences of VideoCloud, i.e., almost all the users (over 95%) retrieve their requested videos within one week after the requested video is available. Currently, VideoCloud receives around 0.22 million video requests per day and the average size of requested videos is 379 MB, so the total cloud cache capacity *in the worst case* should be:

$$C = 379 \text{ MB} \times 0.22M \times 7 = 584 \text{ TB}.$$

To cope with the fluctuations in the daily number of video requests, the total cloud cache capacity is planned as $C' = 600$ TB, slightly larger than $C = 584$ TB. Via the 600-TB cloud cache, the data reuse rate among the users reaches 87%, indicating that most video requests are satisfied instantly (i.e., with very low view startup delay).

3.5 Cache Replacement Strategy

Although the current cloud cache capacity (600 TB) can well handle the current daily number of video requests (around 0.22 million), it is quite likely that the number of video requests will be much higher than 0.22 million in some day. For example, if the daily number of video requests increases to 2.2 million, what shall we do? Obviously, it is impossible for us to construct a 6000-TB cloud cache made up of 3000 chunk servers — the hardware and energy cost are far beyond our affordability. As a result, some data must be replaced to make efficient utilization of the limited cloud cache capacity, where the cache replacement strategy plays a critical role. In this subsection, we investigate the performance of the most commonly used cache replacement strategies, i.e., FIFO (first in first out), LRU (least recently used), and LFU (least frequently used) via real-trace driven simulations. The trace is a 17-day system log (refer to Section 4.1 for detailed information) of VideoCloud. The metrics are two-fold: 1) *cache hit rate*; and 2) *size of replaced data*, which illustrates the I/O cost of chunk servers. We hope the cache hit rate to be as high as possible, while the size of replaced data to be as small as possible.

As shown in Figure 6 and Figure 7, among the three cache replacement strategies, FIFO performs the worst, and LFU performs the best to achieve the highest cache hit rate and the smallest size of replaced data. The cache capacity is set to 70 TB, and using other cache capacities rather than

[4]Amazon Cloud Drive [35] also sets 5 GB as the basic cloud storage capacity provided to its users.

[5]Since almost all the users of VideoCloud are 5-GB free users at the moment, we regard every user as a 5-GB free user for computation convenience.

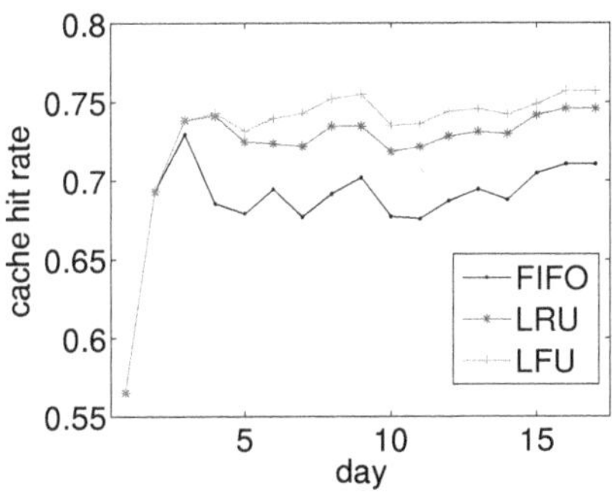

Figure 6: Cache hit rate.

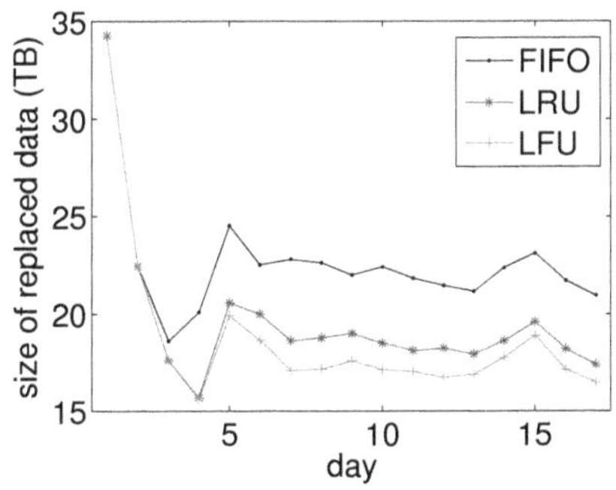

Figure 7: Size of replaced data.

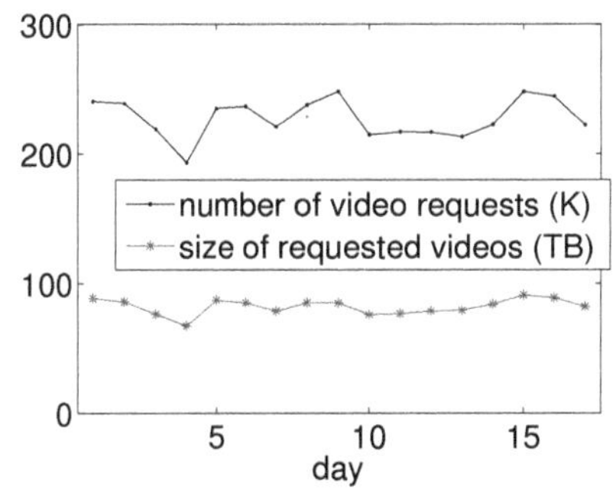

Figure 8: Daily statistics.

70 TB generates the similar results. Therefore, the Cloud Cache of VideoCloud adopts the LFU cache replacement strategy for future scalability. Delving more deeply, LFU has been recognized to be especially suitable for a system where the popularity of data objects does not change very much over a specific time period (one day or one week) [36]. VideoCloud has the abovementioned property because most of the data objects are unpopular videos whose popularity hardly changes much.

4. PERFORMANCE EVALUATION

4.1 Dataset

We use the complete running log of the VideoCloud system in 17 days, from January 1, 2011 to January 17, 2011 to evaluate the performance of cloud download. The log includes the performance information of around 3.87 million video requests, involving around one million unique videos. Most of the videos are .rmvb (around 40%) and .avi files (around 20%). 27.4% of the requested videos are HTTP/FTP files, and the remaining are BitTorrent/eMule files. The total size of the requested videos is 1400 TB, and the total size of the unique videos is 280 TB. The daily statistics are plotted in Figure 8. For each video request, we record its *user id*, *file link*, *file hash code*, *file type*, *file size*, *video request time*, *download duration time* (of the cloud downloader), *retrieve duration time* (of the users), *cache hit status* (1-hit, 0-miss), *download success status* (1-success, 0-failure), and so on.

Figure 9 indicates that the popularity distribution of the requested videos in 17 days is highly skewed, approximately following the Zipf model [37]. Let x denote the popularity ranking of a video file, and let y denote the popularity of the file. Then we have the following fitting equation:

$$log(y) = -a \cdot log(x) + b,$$

which is equal to

$$y = 10^b \cdot x^{-a},$$

where $a = 0.8464$ and $b = 11.3966$. More in detail, 97.1% of the videos receive less than one request per day while merely 0.09% of the videos receive more than ten requests per day (we empirically use the indicator "ten requests per day" as the boundary between popular and unpopular videos), demonstrating that almost all the requested videos in VideoCloud are unpopular. Besides, around 83% of the requests are issued for unpopular videos. As mentioned in Section 1, our cloud download scheme aims to provide efficient content distribution service for unpopular videos, so we only evaluate the performance corresponding to unpopular videos in the following subsections.

4.2 Metrics

We use three major metrics as follows to evaluate the performance of a cloud download system.

1. *Data transfer rate* denotes the data rate when a user retrieves his requested video from the cloud. Specifically, data transfer rate $= \frac{\text{file size}}{\text{retrieve duration time}}$.

2. *View startup delay* denotes how long a user must wait for the cloud to download his requested video. For a video request, if the cache hit status is 1-hit, the view startup delay is taken as 0; otherwise, the view startup delay is regarded as the download duration time of the cloud downloader.

3. *Energy efficiency* denotes how much energy is saved by using cloud download, compared with the common download method. In particular, we consider the *user-side* energy efficiency and the *overall* energy efficiency, respectively.

4.3 Data Transfer Rate

Since the data transfer rate is computed by dividing the file size by the retrieve duration time, in this subsection we firstly present the CDF of file size (in Figure 10), the CDF of retrieve duration time (in Figure 11) and the CDF of data transfer rate (in Figure 12), and then try to discover their relations.

The average file size is 379 MB, which is close to the common size of a 100-minute video, given the fact that around 60% of the requested videos are .rmvb and .avi files. From Figure 10, we find that 16% of the files are smaller than 8MB, most of which are demo videos, pictures, and documents. The reason lies in that many video content providers like to attach the introductions, snapshots, or advertisements to the videos.

The average retrieve duration time is 32 minutes. From Figure 11, we see that 73% of the files are retrieved in less than 32 minutes, and 93% of the files are retrieved in less than 100 minutes so that if the file is a 100-minute video, it can be viewed with high playback continuity (the user can choose either mode: view-as-download or view-after-download).

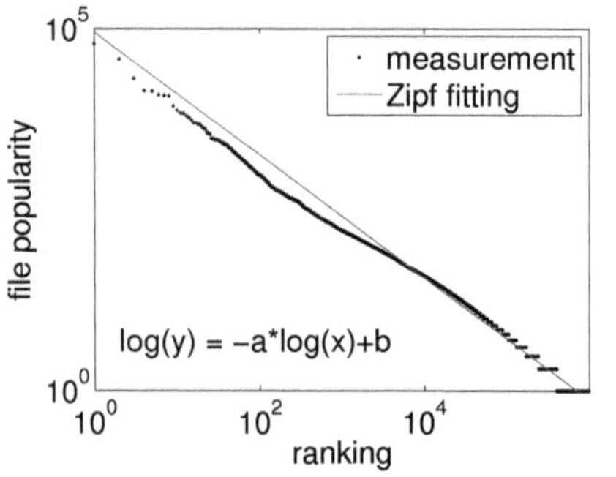

Figure 9: Popularity distribution of requested videos.

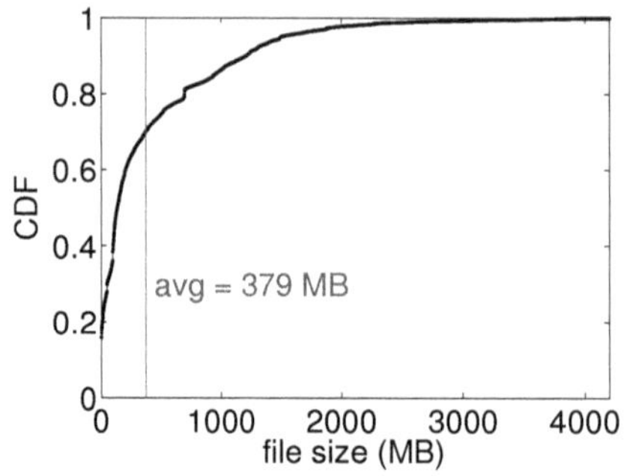

Figure 10: CDF of file size.

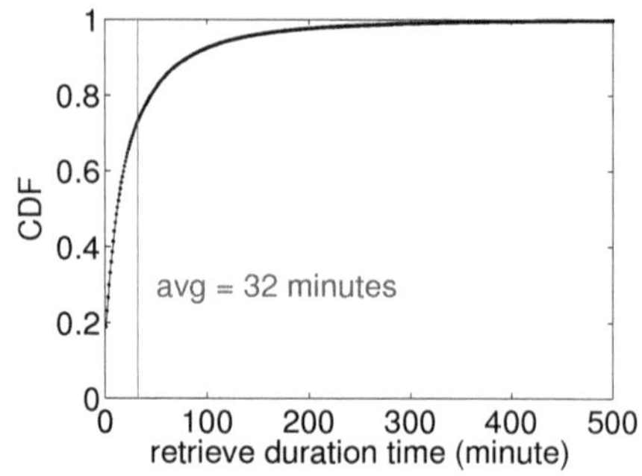

Figure 11: CDF of retrieve duration time.

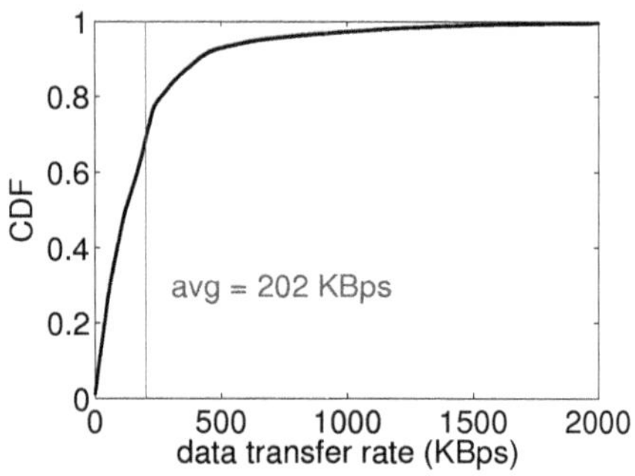

Figure 12: CDF of data transfer rate.

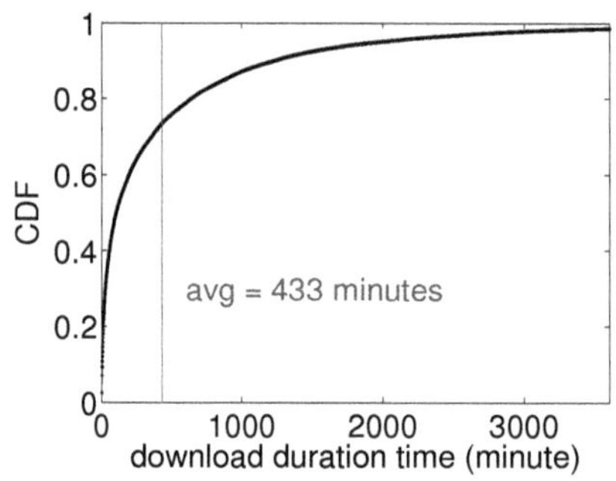

Figure 13: CDF of download duration time.

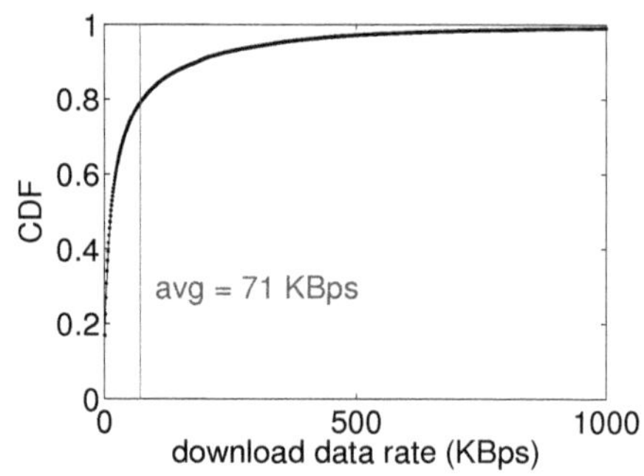

Figure 14: CDF of download data rate.

The average data transfer rate is 202 KBps (> 1.6 Mbps). As shown in Figure 12, over 80% of the data transfer rates are more than 37.5 KBps (= 300 Kbps) which is the basic playback rate of online videos [2, 21]. The main reason why around 20% of the data transfer rates are less than 300 Kbps is that the user does not locate at the four major ISPs in China (as mentioned in Section 3.2) and thus his video retrieve data flow crosses multiple ISPs. More in detail, the data transfer rate in each ISP is plotted in Figure 15.

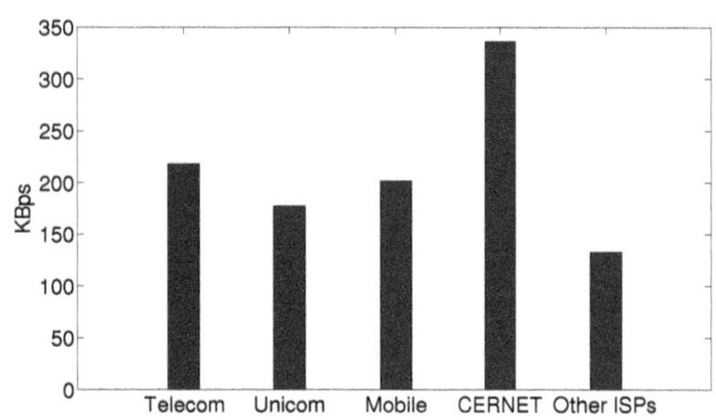

Figure 15: Data transfer rate in each ISP.

We discover a simple but accurate relation among the average file size, the average data transfer rate, and the average retrieve duration time, that is

$$\frac{\text{the avg file size (379 MB)}}{\text{the avg data transfer rate (202 KBps)}} = \text{the avg retrieve duration time (32 minutes).} \quad (1)$$

This is a very useful equation which illustrates that if we take some measures (e.g., to invest more upload servers with higher upload bandwidth, or deploy more upload servers in more ISPs) to further enhance the data transfer rate, the retrieve duration time is expected to decrease inverse-proportionally. Thereby, we can find a proper tradeoff point between the data transfer rate and the retrieve duration time for future design.

4.4 View Startup Delay

View startup delay is effectively alleviated by the implicit and secure data reuse among the users in VideoCloud. For a video request, if the cache hit status is 1-hit (i.e., the requested video has been stored in the cloud cache), the view startup delay is taken as 0; otherwise, the view startup delay is the download duration time. Thus, we firstly present the CDF of download duration time (in Figure 13) and the CDF of download data rate (in Figure 14), and then get the amortized view startup delay.

The average download duration time is 433 minutes and the average download data rate is 71 KBps (= 0.57 Mbps). In the previous subsection, we discover the relationship (see Equation (1)) among the average file size, the average data transfer rate, and the average retrieve duration time. However, this relationship does not exist as to the download duration time and the download data rate:

$$\frac{\text{the avg file size (379 MB)}}{\text{the avg download data rate (71 KBps)}} = 91 \text{ minutes} \ll \text{the avg download duration time (433 minutes).} \quad (2)$$

The reason is that most download events have too low

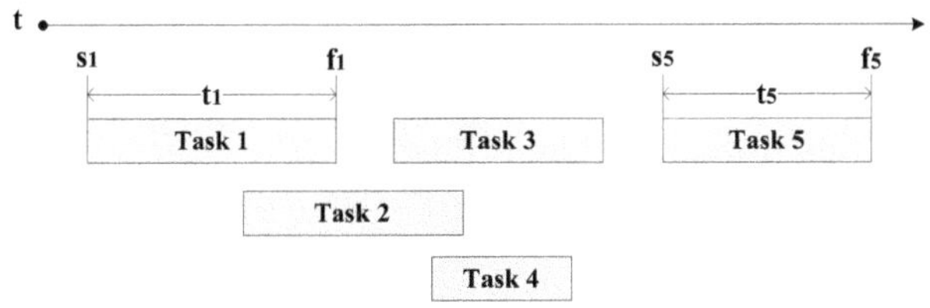

Figure 16: Download parallelism of a user i.

download data rate, e.g., 22% of the download rates are less than 2 KBps, 45% less than 10 KBps, and 70% less than 37.5 KBps (= 300 Kbps). In particular, 79% of the download data rates are less than the average download data rate (71 KBps).

As mentioned in Section 3.3, the data reuse rate among the users in VideoCloud reaches 87%, so the amortized view startup delay = $87\% \cdot 0 + 13\% \cdot$ 433 minutes = 56 minutes. We will make efforts to further reduce the amortized view startup delay, although this may be a challenging work.

4.5 Energy Efficiency

It is difficult for VideoCloud to record the accurate energy cost of each user, so we leverage the approximate power consumption of a PC (personal computer) to estimate the average energy cost of the users. According to a recent IDC report [38], laptop sales have occupied about 70% of the PC sales. And using the average statistics of the Dell PCs [39], the power consumption of a laptop is about 50 W and that of a desktop is about 250 W. Thereby, the average power consumption of a PC is estimated as

$$P_1 = 50W \cdot 70\% + 250W \cdot 30\% = 110W.$$

Our 17-day system log includes the performance information of $N = 3.87M$ video requests. Without cloud download, the energy cost for the users to accomplish all the video requests is denoted as E_1. To properly estimate E_1, the *download parallelism* of each user must be taken into account. As shown in Figure 16, in the common download way, suppose the user i starts Task 1 at the time s_1 and finishes Task 1 at the time f_1, and then the download duration time of Task 1 is $t_1 = f_1 - s_1$. The meanings of the symbols for Task 2/3/4/5 are similar. Then the *download parallelism* of the user i is computed as

$$p_i = (\sum_{j=1}^{5} t_j)/(f_3 - s_1 + f_5 - s_5),$$

and the energy cost of the user i is computed as

$$e_i = P_1 \cdot (f_3 - s_1 + f_5 - s_5) = P_1 \cdot (\sum_{j=1}^{5} t_j)/p_i.$$

As a result, E_1 is estimated as

$$E_1 = \sum_{i=1}^{m} e_i = 2.21M \text{ KWH},$$

where m denotes the total number of users and KWH = Kilowatt Hour.

By using cloud download, the energy cost of the whole system is:

$$E_2 = E_c + E_u,$$

where E_c denotes the energy cost of the cloud utilities and E_u denotes the energy cost of the users. Since each server in the cloud works in all the time and the average power consumption of a server is $P_2 = 700W$, E_c is estimated as:

$$E_c = P_2 \cdot S \cdot 17 \text{ days} = 700W \cdot 426 \cdot 17 \text{ days} = 0.12M \text{ KWH},$$

where S is the total number of servers in VideoCloud. And E_u is estimated in the same way we estimate E_1:

$$E_u = \sum_{i=1}^{m} e'_i = 0.18M \text{ KWH},$$

where e'_i is the energy cost of the user i in retrieving his requested videos from the cloud. Therefore,

$$E_2 = E_c + E_u = 0.12M \text{ KWH} + 0.18M \text{ KWH} = 0.3M \text{ KWH}.$$

In conclusion, the *user-side* energy efficiency is

$$\frac{E_1 - E_u}{E_1} = \frac{2.21M - 0.18M}{2.21M} = 92\%, \qquad (3)$$

and the *overall* energy efficiency of the total cloud download system (cloud + users) is

$$\frac{E_1 - E_2}{E_1} = \frac{2.21M - 0.3M}{2.21M} = 86\%. \qquad (4)$$

5. CONCLUSION AND FUTURE WORK

Video content distribution is becoming a kill application of the Internet owing to the users' inflating requirements on both video quantity and quality, so it is of great importance to investigate how to achieve high-quality content distribution for both popular and unpopular videos. In this paper, we firstly analyze the state-of-the-art techniques. We find they generally work well in distributing popular videos, but do not provide satisfactory content distribution service for unpopular videos. In fact, there are many more unpopular videos than popular videos over the Internet. Therefore, we propose and implement the novel cloud download scheme, which utilizes cloud utilities to achieve high-quality content distribution for unpopular videos. Running logs of our real deployed commercial system confirm the effectiveness and efficiency of cloud download. Our study provides practical experiences and valuable heuristics for making use of cloud utilities to achieve efficient Internet services.

Still some future work remains. Firstly, it is possible to extend the application of cloud download to smaller or private organizations. In our opinion, even a company or a university can build a cloud download system like VideoCloud as its private cloud system to facilitate its users. For example, we discover that in many companies some employees may keep their computers all night on to continue an unfinished download task after they leave the company, which is rather energy-*inefficient*. Since the design of cloud download (described in Section 3) is quite simple and practical, a company can invest in building a private (small-scale) cloud download system and then encourage its employees to send every download request to the cloud.

Secondly, as mentioned in Section 3.3, although cloud download has improved the download success rate of requested videos to 81.4%, download failure still exists. In fact, it is very difficult to judge the download failure of a video request. Given that the most powerful web search engine has just discovered less than 1% of all the things existing in the Internet [40], it is impossible to tell a user whether his requested video can be obtained at last if we keep on trying. Consequently, we have to tell the user his video request is *judged to have failed* at the "right" time. Then the key point is: what is the "right" time? In another words, what is the rule to judge the failure of a video request? Presently, we choose a simple judging rule which takes into account both the download duration time and the download progress (i.e., the download completion fraction of the requested video). The rule is: check the download progress periodically; if the download progress does not change in the latest period, the video request is judged to have failed. The current period is empirically set to be 24 hours. Next step we plan to further analyze the system log to discover more factors that influence the failure of video requests and consider a more accurate failure judging algorithm.

Finally, as a large-scale commercial system in its first version, VideoCloud tends to adopt traditional/straightforward design in constructing each component so that the deployment and debugging are easy to handle. We realize there is still considerable optimization space for novel/original design to take effect. This paper is the first step of our efforts, and we are dedicated to obtaining more lessons and insights on our way.

6. ACKNOWLEDGEMENTS

This work is supported by the National Basic Research Program of China under Grant 2011CB302305 and the National Natural Science Foundation of China under Grants 61073015 and 60873051. We would like to thank Fuchen Wang and Yue Cao for their valuable help.

7. REFERENCES

[1] The Cisco Visual Networking Index report. http://newsroom.cisco.com/dlls/2008/ekits/Cisco_Visual_Networking_Index_061608.pdf.

[2] YouTube we site. http://www.youtube.com.

[3] The BitTorrent protocol specification. http://www.BitTorrent.org/beps/bep_0003.html.

[4] PPLive web site. http://www.pptv.com.

[5] X. Zhang, J. Liu, B. Li, and T. Yum. "CoolStreaming/DONet: A Data-driven Overlay Network for Peer-to-Peer Live Media Streaming," In IEEE INFOCOM, 2005.

[6] C. Huang, J. Li, and K. Ross. "Can Internet Video-on-Demand be Profitable?" In ACM SIGCOMM, 2007.

[7] Akamai web site. http://www.akamai.com.

[8] J. Kangasharju, J. Roberts, and K.W. Ross. "Object replication strategies in content distribution networks," Computer Communications, vol. 25, no. 4, 2002, pp. 376 - 383.

[9] eMule web site. http://www.eMule.org.

[10] M. Armbrust, A. Fox, R. Griffith, A.D. Joseph, R. Katz, A. Konwinski, G. Lee, D. Patterson, A. Rabkin, I. Stoica, and others. "Above the Clouds: A Berkeley View of Cloud Computing," Berkeley Tech. Rep., 2009.

[11] A. Greenberg, J. Hamilton, D.A. Maltz, and P. Patel. "The cost of a cloud: research problems in data center networks," SIGCOMM Computer Communication Review, vol. 39, no. 1, 2008, pp. 68 - 73.

[12] K. Roth and K. McKenney. "Energy Consumption by Consumer Electronics in U.S. Residences," Final Report to the Consumer Electronics Association (CEA), Jan. 2007.

[13] J. R. Douceur. "The sybil attack," In IPTPS 2002, Cambridge, MA, March 2002, pp. 251 - 260.

[14] A. Singh, T. Ngan, P. Druschel, D. Wallach. " Eclipse attacks on overlay networks: Threats and defenses," In IEEE INFOCOM, 2006.

[15] E. Sil and R. Morris. " Security considerations for peer-to-peer distributed hash tables," In IPTPS, 2002.

[16] The VideoCloud web page (March 2011). http://xf.qq.com/help_video.html.

[17] The QQCyclone platform. http://xf.qq.com.

[18] Amazon S3 web site. http://aws.amazon.com/s3.

[19] MS Azure. http://www.microsoft.com/windowsazure.

[20] Dropbox web site. http://www.dropbox.com.

[21] Youku web site. http://www.youku.com.

[22] D. Wu, Y. Hou, W. Zhu, Y. Zhang, and J. Peha. "Streaming video over the Internet: approaches and directions," IEEE Transactions on Circuits and Systems for Video Technology, vol. 11, no. 3, 2001.

[23] The ChinaCache CDN web site. http://www.chinacache.com.

[24] H. Yin, X. Liu, T. Zhan, V. Sekar, F. Qiu, C. Lin, H. Zhang, and B. Li. "Design and deployment of a hybrid CDN-P2P system for live video streaming: experiences with LiveSky," In ACM Multimedia, 2009, pp. 25 - 34.

[25] C. Wu, B. Li, and S. Zhao. "On Dynamic Server Provisioning in Multichannel P2P Live Streaming," to appear in IEEE/ACM Transactions on Networking.

[26] UUSee web site. http://www.uusee.com.

[27] http://www.webtvwire.com/category/internet-hdtv.

[28] F. Liu, S. Shen, B. Li, B. Li, H. Yin, and S. Li. "Novasky: Cinematic-Quality VoD in a P2P Storage Cloud," In IEEE INFOCOM, 2011.

[29] China Telecom. http://www.chinatelecom.com.cn.

[30] China Unicom. http://www.chinaunicom.com.cn.

[31] China Mobile. http://www.10086.cn.

[32] CERNET (China Education and Research Network) web site. http://www.cernet.edu.cn.

[33] H. Xie, Y.R. Yang, A. Krishnamurthy, Y.G. Liu, and A. Silberschatz. "P4P: Provider portal for applications," In ACM SIGCOMM, 2008.

[34] D.R. Choffnes, and F.E. Bustamante. "Taming the torrent," In ACM SIGCOMM, 2008.

[35] Amazon Cloud Drive web site. https://www.amazon.com/clouddrive/learnmore.

[36] S. Podlipnig and L. Boszormenyi. " A survey of web cache replacement strategies," ACM Computing Surveys, vol. 35, no. 4, 2003, pp. 374 - 398.

[37] L. Breslau, P. Cao, L. Fan, G. Phillips, and S. Shenker. "Web caching and Zipf-like distributions: Evidence and implications," In IEEE INFOCOM, 1999, pp. 126 - 134.

[38] The IDC Desktop and Laptop Sales report. http://news.techworld.com/sme/3227696/desktop-and-laptop-sales-to-grow-this-year.

[39] Dell web site (March 2011). http://www.dell.com.

[40] B. Croft, D. Metzler, and T. Strohman. "Search engines: Information retrieval in practice," Addison-Wesley, USA, 2009.

Generating Story Variants with Constrained Video Recombination*

Alberto Piacenza, Fabrizio Guerrini, Nicola Adami, Riccardo Leonardi
Department of Information Engineering, University of Brescia, Italy
{firstname.lastname}@ing.unibs.it

Jonathan Teutenberg, Julie Porteous, Marc Cavazza
School Of Computing, Teesside University, Middlesbrough, UK
{J.Teutenberg,J.Porteous, M.O.Cavazza}@tees.ac.uk

ABSTRACT

We present a novel approach to the automatic generation of filmic variants within an implemented Video-Based Storytelling (VBS) system that successfully integrates video segmentation with stochastically controlled re-ordering techniques and narrative generation via AI planning. We have introduced flexibility into the video recombination process by sequencing video shots in a way that maintains local video consistency and this is combined with exploitation of shot polysemy to enable shot reuse in a range of valid semantic contexts. Results of evaluations on output narratives using a shared set of video data show consistency in terms of local video sequences and global causality with no loss of generative power.

Categories and Subject Descriptors

I.2.10 [**Artificial Intelligence**]: Vision and Scene Understanding—*Video Analysis*

General Terms

Algorithms

Keywords

Interactive Storytelling, Logical Story Unit, Markov Chains, Narrative Modeling

1. INTRODUCTION

The original idea behind interactive cinema, since Činčera's *Kinoautomat*, was to allow user preferences to modify the unfolding of the narrative, whilst preserving the overall story world. However, the "branching narrative" approach to interactive films has eventually been abandoned due to the exponential cost attached to the shooting of filmic material for all alternative scenes, and the adverse effects on spectators' filmic experience of mandatory interaction at branching points [13]. Another limitation of branching video applied to cinema is that it depends largely on local decision points and is unable to make use of global filmic properties, falling short of core narrative principles which, since Aristotle, have emphasised the overall shape of dramatic action.

This double limitation of video content generation explains why most recent research in Interactive Storytelling (IS) has taken place using computer graphics [21] and more recently computer games engines [24], which provide a visual medium facilitating the dynamic generation of visual content, e.g. through built-in mechanisms for keyframed animation generating motion sequences that can still be split and recombined through scripting and other mechanisms. These systems have increasingly adopted the visual codes of film itself, through real-time camera control and simplified forms of real-time editing. Yet, despite recent progress in graphics rendering and wide-scale acceptance of 3D animation in film, the visual quality of video is still far superior to that of real-time generated graphics.

Current interest in storytelling applied to video is dominated by the storyfication or emergent storytelling paradigm [27]. Storyfication, which stems from a different perspective on narrative than the one traditionally associated to film, is about using temporal and semantic relationships to attribute meaning to a sequence of events, e.g. forming a life narrative from personal videos. Conversely, the challenge of Video-Based Storytelling (VBS) for films that we are addressing consists in generating alternative stories from the same baseline content whilst preserving its dramatic nature and global narrative properties, by transposing recent advances of automatic narrative generation back to the field of video. These correspond to different variants of a given film, each exhibiting different narrative properties, but each constituting a proper drama, albeit with a different course of action. This achievement would constitute an important step towards interactive films, but it makes it necessary to leverage the combinatorial properties of individual video segments beyond the simple reordering of short sequences.

Narrative generation techniques developed in IS support generation using global dramatic properties and contextual phenomena. This would make it possible to capitalise on the "Kuleshov effect" which explains how identical shots[1] featuring characters receive a different interpretation by the viewers depending on their context. However, this requires a semantics of individual video units compatible with the

*Area chair: Susanne Boll

[1]Shots are sequences of continuous still images (frames) as filmed through a single, uninterrupted camera take [12].

MM'11, November 28–December 1, 2011, Scottsdale, Arizona, USA.

global logic of AI-based narrative generation. Another important aspect for content recombination is to be able to derive flexible units of content from the baseline video material. This also overcomes the need to manually tag fixed individual units of content, which requires significant effort and may not be compatible with dynamic changes in context that are at the heart of the narrative variant philosophy.

Interactive Narratives rely on the ability to dynamically generate the sequence of narrative actions rather than following pre-defined branching points. Narrative generation thus plays a central role, since it supports the propagation of changes introduced by the user: either initial preferences that will trigger a wholly different story variant, or real-time interventions, which will alter the course of an unfolding story, leading to a "recomputation" of future story actions. Techniques underlying narrative generation, such as planning, operate by maintaining causal consistency (narrative actions being formalised through pre- and post-conditions) over the entire narrative, from the point in time where new information is provided until the state defined as the story end. Narrative generation can thus be applied at any point in time, and the frequency at which new information can be taken into account defines the sampling rate of interaction [24]. However, in the case of our first VBS prototype, there is still an additional overhead in the amount of processing required to automatically refine individual video units to be used in the subsequent generation of the remainder of the narrative. For that reason, we have focussed our examples on narrative generation, with user interaction limited to an initial parameterisation of story properties that will determine the overall nature of the story variant. Our underlying planner has previously demonstrated its potential for anytime interactivity when used with 3D graphics content [24].

Our technical solution, which we present in this paper, features in a small-scale (by filmic standards), yet fully-implemented and functional VBS system which we use as an illustration throughout the paper. The system uses Michael Radford's screen adaptation of Shakespeare's play *The Merchant of Venice* [25] as its baseline video. The paper is organised as follows: in Section 2 we provide the motivation for this work while relating to previously proposed IS systems. Section 3 introduces the key elements of our system's architecture. In Sections 4 and 5 the video processing technology needed to achieve VBS is described while narrative generation is discussed in Section 6. Finally, Section 7 presents early evaluation results, and we conclude by discussing future work and current limitations.

2. RELATED WORK AND MOTIVATION

The development of video-based storytelling is an active area of Multimedia systems research, and several prototypes based on the storyfication paradigm [27] have been introduced by Brooks [6], Aguierre Smith et al [28, 29], Cesar et al [8], Bocconi et al [4], Zsombori [32] and Shen et al [27]. These systems organise user-contributed content [8] into a narrative [27] or support the generation of personalised documentaries [6, 4, 32]; most of them aim at organising video content into a narrative format, rather than modifying a pre-existing narrative structure. One common feature of these systems is their commitment to semantic categorisation of basic video units, which is consistent with a bottom-up approach, aiming at producing semantic consistency from local principles. These semantic categories are often generated through manual tagging, which assumes, but is also consistent with, a static unit of content.

These early works adopt a discourse oriented perspective (see the importance of shots as units in [14], or rhetorical relations in [3]), without considering the global properties of the plot. Zsombori et al [32] developed authoring and delivery tools for interactive television as part of the NM2 project. Their approach relied on improvements to branching narrative techniques and didn't exploit AI techniques such as planning, hence their system is unable to reason about global narrative properties and maintain global causal consistency (a fact acknowledged by the authors [32]). Other approaches such as IDC [26] and AUTEUR [22] reason at the level of individual actions to output a restricted set of short videos and have made reference to some planning concepts, although mostly restricted to action description. Jung et al [18] considered the narrative properties of video content and emphasised the locality of dramatic actions but also recognised the need for editorial relations to support the narrative structure. It could be said that these systems included the elementary components of planning actions, but without connecting them to modern planning algorithms which operate on global rather than local constraints.

The challenge we are addressing is to reconcile this narrative approach with the visual quality that only video can provide. Our VBS system has different narrative objectives than the systems discussed above and hence is closer in its philosophy to those IS systems that use (top-down) plan-based narrative generation with 3D graphics. In IS, state-of-the-art plan-based narrative generators such as [24] are capable of generating complex narratives containing 40+ narrative actions and working consistently on the global aspects of an output narrative, which we see as a key factor in the induction of a narrative experience for authored media.

Our earlier approach [23] attempted to directly combine state-of-the-art plan-based narrative generation with video content. It used somewhat naive mappings between planning actions and video segments with the consequence that the output was restricted to variants that were simple rearrangements of the original input story, without fundamentally changing the original semantics of the actions. In other words, there was a mismatch between our semantic/action level and our narrative level: the two limitations we faced were i) the static nature of our basic video units and ii) the lack of sophistication of our semantic representation.

In this paper we shall describe how these limitations have been addressed as part of our new prototype. Our solution involved the development of a shared semantic representation that facilitated the conceptual integration of video processing and narrative generation based on AI planning techniques for story consistency. For instance, the automatic categorisation of emotional aspects of video can provide some form of baseline semantic analysis which is both relevant to narrative aspects and also to how users tend to consume filmic media [19]. This approach enables the generation of planning compatible actions as units of recombination in a way that was previously not possible, thus enabling the construction of completely new filmic variants.

3. SYSTEM OVERVIEW

An overview of the architecture of our system is shown in Fig. 1. The output is a system generated filmic variant of the baseline input movie or potentially a completely new

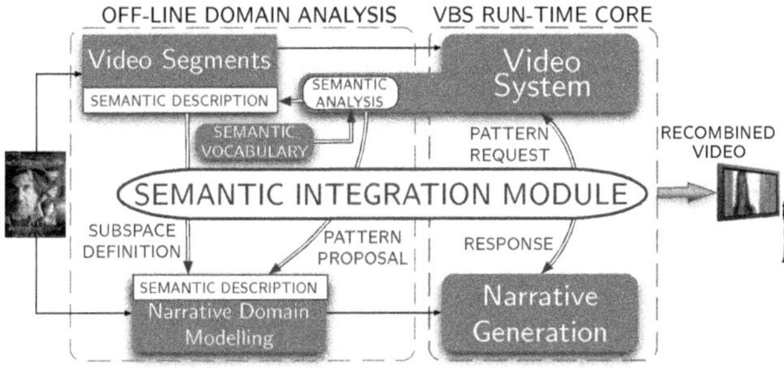

Figure 1: Architecture of the VBS system: a baseline video is analysed and a semantic subspace is created within the semantic integration module and then shared with the domain model; the integration module handles communication between the video system and the narrative generation modules to automatically produce novel filmic variants through video recombination.

story except for the locations and the actors involved (their role and interaction may be completely different from those of the original). The heart of the system is a video integration module which acts as the nexus between the analysis of the input video and the generation of narrative variants for output. The integration of video analysis and narrative generation is achieved via the use of a shared semantic representation which enables communication between the content automatically identified by the video system and the model of the narrative domain used for narrative generation.

During an initial phase of domain analysis, low-level features of the input baseline video are processed to determine basic contextual information (such as characters and locations) and subdivided into shots which form the building blocks for recombined video generation. Also during the domain analysis phase, a representation of the narrative domain is created which includes specification of key narrative actions to be defined for subsequent narrative generation. Then, at the end of the domain analysis phase, the identified shots and narrative actions are mapped to points in the shared semantic representation. These points are defined in terms of semantic features such as the presence of different characters and their mood and provide a common vocabulary for communication between the system components.

In the VBS core, the narrative generation module outputs story variants in response to user input. These variants (sequences of narrative actions) must be constructed in a way that ensures the generation of a consisent plot or preserves the consistency of a modified one. This can't be done without video analysis level reasoning about local causality and consistency and hence our approach integrates it with a joint though separate high level reasoning about global narrative properties. Each action in an output narrative can map to multiple points in the shared semantic subspace (see Section 4), so the video presentation of individual narrative actions isn't limited to any single segment of the baseline video (as it is with the naive mapping used in [23]); instead, appropriate video subparts for a narrative action can be selected from any video segments which map to relevant points for that action in the semantic subspace, while preserving fundamental consistency in the content. This is a powerful result since it provides a complete decoupling of the narrative model and the baseline video content which is only described by its semantics. Importantly, this enables the presentation of completely novel filmic variants.

Another innovative feature of the system is that the output of video processing is able to place constraints on the narrative generation. In particular, the list of semantic descriptors identified in the baseline video are used to create a fully shared semantic subspace, so the planner can avoid the actions mapping to semantics not present in the video.

The VBS system supports two different modalities for the creation of the recombined video, each reflecting the direction of the flow of semantic information in the core. The narrative-driven setup is done online and consists of the video system answering specific requests for desired content from the narrative side expressed using the semantic vocabulary. In the video system-driven setup, the latter tries to identify possible narrative actions by mixing video segments according to internal models that can be derived from the integration of consistent pieces of content (in terms of locations, involved characters, and similar models of interactions). The video clips and the associated semantic information are then proposed to the narrative generator, which will add them to its domain model if they are deemed adequate.

4. VIDEO MODELING

The baseline video is initially described in terms of the semantic vocabulary and modeled to allow effective content recombination. Subsection 4.1 details the automatic algorithms for preliminary temporal segmentation of the original movie into logical basic segments – the building blocks for recombined video. Subsection 4.2 introduces the intermediate level semantic vocabulary that is used to communicate between the narrative domain and the video system. Semantic modeling of video content, necessary for the video recombination process, is detailed in Subsection 4.3.

4.1 Video Segmentation

From a high level point of view, the movie can be separated into a succession of semantically consistent segments, also called *Logical Story Units* (or LSUs) [30], each one conveying a concept of the story being narrated. Alternatively, at the most basic level, a video can be divided into *shots*. Each LSU is therefore a sequence of temporally adjacent shots conveying a common concept in the context of the story. Both shots and LSUs represent fundamental entities with which the video system constructs new video sequences.

The video system first extracts the shots from the film by applying a shot boundaries detector [5] [20]. The algorithm used in this system is based on the classical twin comparison method, employed on statistical color intensity distributions of adjacent frames: an abrupt variation in the color distribution is interpreted as a shot boundary. Particular types of shot boundaries, e.g. dissolves, are also taken into account through a suitable dissolve model [1].

LSUs are then formed starting from the shot segmentation. In [30], a video is represented by a Scene Transition Graph (STG). The nodes of the graph are clusters of visually similar and temporally close shots and the edges represent the shot transitions. It is also shown that the STG can be decomposed into separated cyclic subgraphs through the removal of so-called cut-edges and that each subgraph identifies a LSU. This process is shown in Fig. 2.

In the current implementation, visual clustering is per-

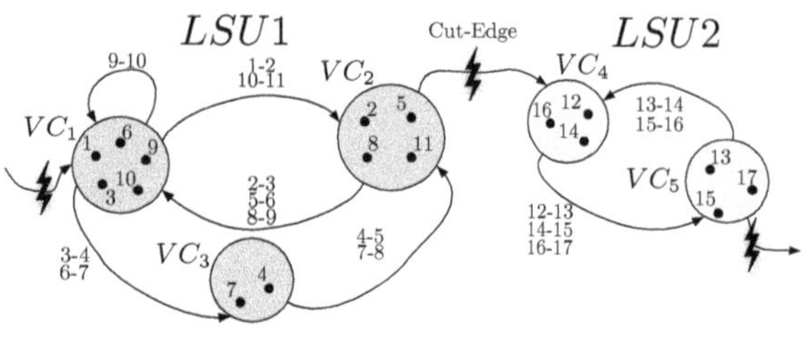

Figure 2: LSU segmentation using visual clusters of shots and temporal transitions. The clusters, VC_1–VC_5, are obtained through hierarchical clustering; points inside clusters represent individual shots. The numbers on the links refer to shot transitions.

formed by extracting a codebook of visual words by dividing shot keyframes in square blocks and then running a Tree-Structured Vector Quantization algorithm [16] to LUV color space values of the blocks. The codebook size is determined by controlling the distortion on the reconstructed keyframe. Then, a shot similarity measure is defined by averaging the distortion increase caused by representing each shot using the codebook of the other. Last, the final shot visual clusters are obtained through hierarchical clustering as in [2].

4.2 Intermediate Semantic Representation

The video system annotates the extracted shots using several semantic *tags* that describe intermediate level concepts specified in an agreed vocabulary. The tags allow the definition of a *semantic subspace* in which video content is described. In particular, each shot is described by a *semantic point* of the subspace, that is an instance of the tags describing the semantic point abstraction. We used the following tags:

- **Characters:** A list of characters present in the shot, specified by an anonymous *name* tag, e.g. A, B, ∅ or {A,B}, and the prevalent *mood* of the individual characters, taking one of three possible values: positive, negative or neutral.
- **Field:** A ternary value indicating the *field* of vision of the camera: close-up, medium or wide.
- **Environment:** Three binary values for the general shot environment (when applicable): *time* (day or night), *location* (indoor or outdoor), and *crowd* presence (present or not).

The selection of the tags is important both for the video synthesis and for the narrative generation. The former must have sufficient information on the shots to recombine them without losing consistency. In turn, narrative generation must be able to describe the actions from a more abstract level, but, at the same time, the tags can't delve into too much detail to avoid complicating the mapping between narrative actions and semantic description. In the light of these considerations, it is clear that, aside from the characters present in the shot, their prevalent mood is also necessary to accurately convey the high level meaning of the narrative action, e.g. positive mood for merry actions. All other tags are necessary for the coherence of the recombined content, by allowing mixing of shots that are set in the same context.

4.3 Semantic Modeling of Scenes

As illustrated in Fig. 2, each LSU can be modeled as a completely connected STG, where the nodes represent clusters of visually similar shots. In order to describe the LSU using the semantic vocabulary, the shots belonging to the LSU must be re-clustered, using their semantic description. The initial nodes in the STG may be split in subgraphs. The resulting new graph transforms the initial LSU to a Markov chain, that is referred to as a *Semantic Story Unit* (SSU). In an SSU, instead of using the visual clusters described in Subsection 4.1, we introduce the concept of *semantic clusters*, that are built grouping the shot of the given LSU according to their semantic tag values. The SSU entity introduced in this work joins the temporal LSU concept with the semantic description of the shots to obtain a model that captures the structural semantic behavior of the scenes.

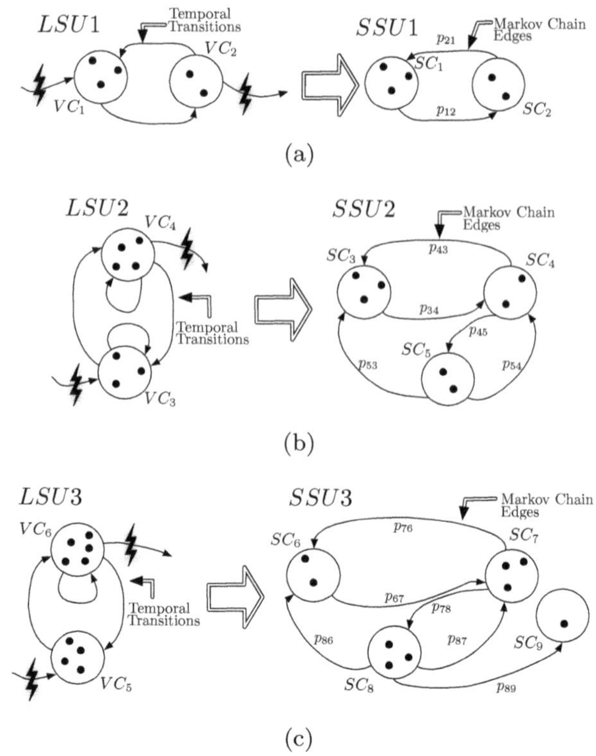

Figure 3: SSU generation in various *VC*-*SC* correspondence cases: (a) the visual clusters and the semantic clusters are perfectly matched, (b) one of the visual cluster has spawned two different semantic clusters, (c) additional cut-edge added.

The construction of an SSU is depicted in Fig. 3. In case (a), the visual clusters (VC) and the semantic clusters (SC) are perfectly matched. In case (b), instead, one visual cluster contains shots with different semantics and hence has spawned two different *SC*s. As a consequence of the spawning, the cyclic properties of the original LSU may be lost; in particular the chain could contain sink nodes, hence introducing additional cut-edges. An example of this situation is illustrated in case (c).

The Markov chain that constitutes the SSU possesses a transition probability P. The transition probabilities between the nodes are evaluated using the number of actual temporal shot transitions. In general, p_{ij} is computed by dividing the number of temporal transitions that go from shots of the cluster SC_i to shots of the clusters SC_j, divided by the number of shots in the cluster SC_i. In Fig. 3 the auto-transitions associated with the probabilities p_{ii} have been omitted for clarity. For example, assuming that the visual clusters of $LSU1$ in Fig. 2 are perfectly matched to the semantic clusters of the corresponding SSU, as in case (a) of Fig. 3, the transition probability matrix would be:

$$P = \begin{bmatrix} p_{11} & p_{12} & p_{13} \\ p_{21} & p_{22} & p_{23} \\ p_{31} & p_{32} & p_{33} \end{bmatrix} = \begin{bmatrix} 0.2 & 0.4 & 0.4 \\ 0.75 & 0 & 0.25 \\ 0 & 1 & 0 \end{bmatrix}$$

For sink nodes, such as SC_9 in case (c) of Fig. 3, a unitary probability is assigned to their auto-transition.

5. VIDEO RECOMBINATION

This section details the cooperation workflow between the narrative construction and video system modules: the information exchange taking place between the two subsystems and the technologies for video recombination.

5.1 Semantic Information Exchange

After semantic analysis of the baseline video the *semantic subspace* is defined by organizing the available resources for use by the system, namely, the semantic points.

Part of the domain model is a manually constructed mapping between high-level actions and so-called *semantic patterns*. The patterns are a list of semantic points that need to be present in the considered action for correctly conveying the high level meaning, e.g., a semantic pattern of a dialogue could be constituted by two points with character A and two points with the same environmental tags and character B. With the available semantic points known, the model can be updated to avoid those not present in the original content.

Examples of the semantic information exchanged in the modalities described in Section 3 are depicted in Fig. 4. Part (a) shows the video-driven set up where, aside from the semantic subspace definition, the video system also provides a list of semantic patterns generated via the *semantic patterns proposal* of Subsection 5.2. This video-driven setup is motivated by its detailed knowledge of the movie structure, i.e. it can put together novel semantic patterns using the conceptual information. Moreover, the visual content for these narrative actions is of high quality by construction.

In the narrative-driven setup (part (b) of the figure), a *semantic pattern request* is sent to the video system as it chooses the next narrative action. The pattern requested is obtained through the mapping between the narrative actions and the semantic vocabulary, with suitable parameters for characters and location pertinent to the action.

When the video system is able to satisfy the request, the narrative generator is notified to provide the subtitles to add to the shots. Since the narrative generator is constrained by the semantic subspace definition, the request can in principle be satisfied. However, in certain cases the video system can fail (see Subsection 5.2), which forces the story generator to rewind its engine and to find an alternative narrative action.

5.2 Semantic Clusters Recombination

This subsection formalizes the SSU-based innovative techniques for the manipulation of Markov chains (SSU transition graphs) for the generation of the recombined video, namely the substitution and deletion of semantic clusters belonging to a given SSU and pairwise Semantic Story Units fusion respectively.

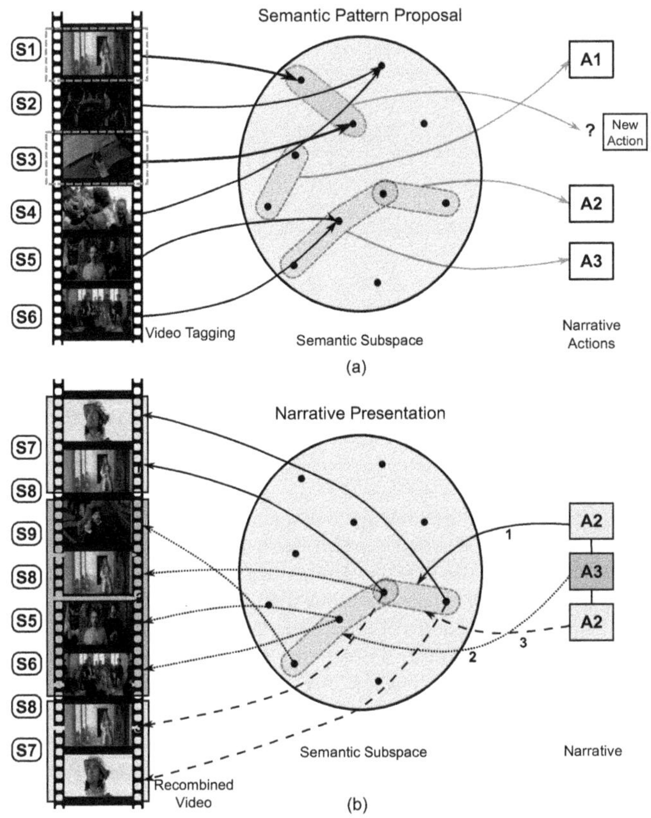

Figure 4: Mapping between video and narrative using the shared semantic subspace: each action is mapped to a semantic pattern and the patterns are depicted as a shaded region in the subspace. In (a) the video system proposes semantic patterns as possible actions and the resulting recombined video is assessed and in (b) the narrative generator requests recombined video with given semantic patterns associated with a narrative composed by three actions. The dashed arrows (label 3) denote a successive request of the same pattern as that of label 1.

5.2.1 Semantic Cluster Substitution and Deletion

When the video system receives a semantic pattern request, it generates a shot sequence after having constructed a suitable SSU. To properly answer to a pattern request, the ideal situation is to have an SSU composed by semantic clusters which have a one-to-one correspondence with the needed semantic points. In that case, the system would perform a random walk across the Markov chain model of the SSU. From any given node, a shot is chosen with the only constraint being to preserve causality of visual information.

Auto-transitions in the SSU are not desirable since shots described by the same semantic points played back to back introduce visual flicker. Hence, an operator $D[\cdot]$ puts the diagonal values of P to 0 and uniformly redistributes the probability among the other columns. Obviously, the redistribution of some probability perturbs the transition matrix.

If no perfectly matching SSU is found, the video system tries to generate a new target SSU that satisfies the pattern, starting from so-called candidate SSUs. A given SSU is a potential candidate to be modified into the target SSU if

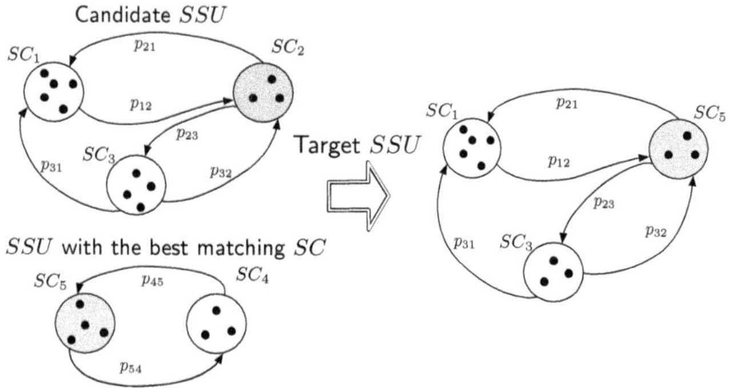

Figure 5: Semantic cluster substitution: some shots in SC_5 (green) are substituted into SC_2 (red).

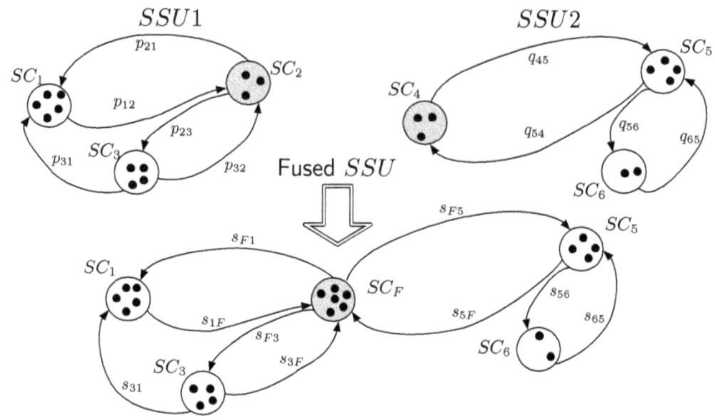

Figure 6: SSU fusion process: the fused SSU has aggregated SC_2 from $SSU1$ and SC_4 from $SS2$, that represent the same semantic point, into the fused cluster SC_F. Auto-transitions are omitted.

both these conditions are satisfied: the candidate SSU has at least a matching semantic point with the target SSU and it has no less semantic clusters than the target SSU so as not to generate artificial cluster transitions. To avoid the complete loss of the existing logical structure, only two operations are allowed: substitution and deletion of semantic clusters. The rationale under this process is to minimize the changes to the underlying structure of the candidate SSU inherited by the original video content. When semantic criteria are not applicable, low level visual distortion (the shot similarity measure introduced in Section 4.1) is used instead.

The algorithm for choosing the best candidate SSU is based on satisfying as many semantic points as possible, starting from the most numerous one in terms of requested points. The tie-breaking criteria among candidates is the fewest number of shots that are unrelated to the desired semantic clusters. At the end of this process, the semantic clusters of the best candidate SSU with unrelated semantic points must be substituted and those in excess must be deleted to adhere to the semantic pattern.

First, let us concentrate on cluster substitution. Fig. 5 depicts such a situation. The candidate SSU has SC_1 and SC_3 satisfying the semantic pattern, but SC_2 does not and need to be substituted. Our objective is to preserve the number of shots in SC_2 so that the transition matrix is not perturbed. Then, we try to find a matching semantic cluster in some other SSU that satisfies the requested semantic point and that has sufficient shots: in the example, SC_5 is subsampled and put in place of SC_2. If more than one cluster fits, then the closer one in terms of average shot similarity is selected. Alternatively, if no matching semantic cluster has enough shots, the visually closer clusters are exhausted in sequence until the number of needed shots is satisfied. In the case that more semantic clusters need to be substituted, the process is repeated sequentially.

Last, excess semantic clusters may need to be deleted. This operation is more penalizing because it is bound to perturb the transition matrix, since some cluster transitions disappear and hence this is equivalent to reducing the number of dimensions of P. Moreover, some diagonal value may acquire non-zero values, that is some auto-transition may also appear in the target SSU. Again, $D[\cdot]$ needs to be applied before performing the random walk for shot selection.

The video system should compute a cost to highlight how much of the original SSU structure has been lost to answer the request; if this exceeds a threshold the video system responds with failure, indicating that the request can't be satisfied. In this work, the cost associated with the construction of the target SSU is $C = w_c \cdot n_c + w_d \cdot n_d + w_a \cdot n_a$, where n_c is the number of substituted shots, n_d is the number of deleted shots, n_a is the number of shots auto-transitions before the application of $D[\cdot]$ and w_c, w_d and w_a are the associated weights ($w_d > w_a > w_c$ for the reasons above).

5.2.2 Semantic Story Units Fusion

In the video system driven setup, the video system tries to generate new possible narrative actions by fusing SSUs and obtain new semantic patterns. Such a new semantic pattern is proposed for evaluation thanks to the generation of an example video clip. If it is possible to attach a high level meaning to the clip then the semantic pattern and the narrative actions describing it are added to the set of narrative actions. Obviously, single, non-trivial SSUs are first proposed because they are obtained directly from the corresponding LSUs, which likely reflect narrative actions of the original plot. In addition, the video system tries to combine different SSUs to obtain a sequence of shots that may convey some complex meaning. For example, if two SSUs associated to dialogues are mixed, the fused SSU could possibly represent a new dialogue between multiple characters.

Obviously, it is necessary to fuse only SSUs that have a minimum degree of coherence. In this work, we exhaustively try fusing only pairs of SSUs that have at least a matching semantic cluster. Fig. 6 illustrates the case where two semantic clusters, SC_2 and SC_4, share the same semantic point and as such it is decided to merge them into the fused SSU SC_F, while trying to inherit as much structure as possible from the individual participating SSUs.

Formally, starting from the $SSU1$ with transition matrix P and $SSU2$ with transition matrix Q, we construct a fused SSU with transition matrix S. We will use Fig. 6 as a working example. The concerned transition matrices are:

$$P=\begin{bmatrix} p_{11} & p_{12} & p_{13} \\ p_{21} & p_{22} & p_{23} \\ p_{31} & p_{32} & p_{33} \end{bmatrix}, Q=\begin{bmatrix} q_{44} & q_{45} & q_{46} \\ q_{54} & q_{55} & q_{56} \\ q_{64} & q_{65} & q_{66} \end{bmatrix}, S=\begin{bmatrix} s_{FF} & s_{F1} & s_{F3} & s_{F5} & s_{F6} \\ s_{1F} & s_{11} & s_{13} & s_{15} & s_{16} \\ s_{3F} & s_{31} & s_{33} & s_{35} & s_{36} \\ s_{5F} & s_{51} & s_{53} & s_{55} & s_{56} \\ s_{6F} & s_{61} & s_{63} & s_{65} & s_{66} \end{bmatrix}$$

To preserve the original structures, all the transitions between the clusters inherited by the originals should be preserved (in our case, between SC_1 and SC_3 and between SC_5 and SC_6). The transitions to and from the fused cluster should be weighted by the numbers of shots in the original clusters (defined as n_2 and n_4, respectively), as this reflects the relative importance of the individual component clusters. The most practical solution is therefore to extend the transition matrices P and Q, rearranging them in the same row order as S and identifying the individual semantic clusters that will be fused with the final fused clusters, as in:

$$P^* = \begin{bmatrix} p_{FF} & p_{F1} & p_{F3} & 0 & 0 \\ p_{1F} & p_{11} & p_{13} & 0 & 0 \\ p_{3F} & p_{31} & p_{33} & 0 & 0 \\ 0 & 0 & 0 & 0 & 0 \\ 0 & 0 & 0 & 0 & 0 \end{bmatrix}, \quad Q^* = \begin{bmatrix} q_{FF} & 0 & 0 & q_{F5} & q_{F6} \\ 0 & 0 & 0 & 0 & 0 \\ 0 & 0 & 0 & 0 & 0 \\ q_{5F} & 0 & 0 & q_{55} & q_{56} \\ q_{6F} & 0 & 0 & q_{65} & q_{66} \end{bmatrix}$$

where F in P^* identifies with SC_2 in P and F in Q^* identifies with SC_4 in Q. Then, the fused SSU transition matrix S is constructed by concatenating the rows of S_F, S_P and S_Q, where S_P and S_Q are the rows of P^* and Q^* respectively corresponding to the non-fused SCs and S_F are the rows corresponding to the fused clusters (in this case a single row), obtained by computing:

$$S_F = \frac{n_2}{n_2 + n_4} P_F^* + \frac{n_4}{n_2 + n_4} Q_F^*$$

where again n_2 and n_4 are the shots number in the original SC_2 and SC_4 clusters being fused. With this formulation, no new transitions between semantic clusters are introduced. The resulting matrix is therefore:

$$S = \begin{bmatrix} & & S_F & & \\ p_{1F} & p_{11} & p_{13} & 0 & 0 \\ p_{3F} & p_{31} & p_{33} & 0 & 0 \\ q_{5F} & 0 & 0 & q_{55} & q_{56} \\ q_{6F} & 0 & 0 & q_{65} & q_{66} \end{bmatrix}$$

6. NARRATIVE INTEGRATION

Each story variant proposes a different sequence of narrative actions. We have described in previous sections how action variants could be generated from common video footage using semantic representations. To assemble a consistent story, it is necessary to preserve the global consistency of actions: this is achieved using AI Planning techniques, which can handle the combinatorics of individual actions whilst preserving the overall story logic as previously described [31]. For the narrative generation, we use a forward-chaining state-based planner (bottom half of Fig. 1).

In this section we consider the key enablers of narrative integration in the system: the narrative domain actions and mappings from them to semantic patterns; and the use of the shared semantic space in constraining narrative generation (further details of the planner can be found in [23]).

6.1 Mapping Narrative Actions to Semantics

The domain model used by our planner corresponds to narrative states and is formalised using the PDDL language [15]. The states refer to categories of actions and character attributes, both generic and specific to the baseline plot. Narrative actions contain variables that are instantiated at run time with the names of specific characters, objects, locations corresponding to video semantics.

Also specified during the domain analysis are mappings between the narrative actions and points in the shared semantic subspace. As with the narrative actions these mappings from actions to semantics contain variables which are ground at run time by assigning values to character, object, and location variables. Action and semantics share the same variable assignments. The mapping used for action translation in our implementation results in semantic sequences of between 2 and 4 semantic points. As we show in the evaluation, this is sufficient for representing what are for the most part binary character interactions, though systems with larger-scale actions may require longer sequences with a greater authorial overhead in encoding the mapping.

6.2 Constrained Narrative Generation

In storytelling systems that feature computer generated presentation, every potential narrative action is guaranteed to have a valid presentation. With a shift to presentation based on recombination of pre-recorded video data, this guarantee no longer holds. Our narrative planning procedure therefore must be capable of adapting the generation process to avoid areas of the narrative space for which video data is not available. These adaptations are two-fold: static modifications that can be applied to any narrative generated for the given domain and video data; and dynamic modifications to recover from unexpected presentation failure.

In Subsection 4.2 we described the process of automatically extracting the parameters for our semantic abstraction from a set of video data. As VBS systems do not permit on-line dynamic content generation the semantic subspace available for presentation is determined prior to narrative generation. Static analysis can then ensure the planner constructs narratives using only those actions that map to sequences of semantics that are a subset of those available. This is achieved by performing a filtering procedure as the variables in each narrative action are ground (by substitution with specific character names and so on), which applies the action-semantics mapping and accepts only those actions that map to semantics appearing in the video, avoiding those for which no representative shot exists in the video data.

This static filtering process guarantees the exclusion of single actions which cannot be presented given the available video data, however it may not exclude all necessary actions. For example, when the requested semantics map to a logical structure that is radically different from SSUs in the original video, this request may be declined. Thus the planner must be able to recover from failure during plan construction.

Failure occurs at one of two points depending on the execution process. If all semantic requests are processed prior to presentation, then the unpresentable action can be removed from the domain and a new plan constructed. However, to enable reactive narrative generation, planning and execution must be interleaved [7] so when failure is detected presentation of earlier actions may already have begun. This is the situation assumed in our approach which achieves online failure recovery by removing the failed action from the domain and re-planning from the previous accepted action. This results in slightly longer narratives as there are fewer decision points at which the narrative can 'work around' a failure. The effect of this in practice is explored in Section 7.

7. EXPERIMENTAL RESULTS

Experiments were conducted to evaluate the filmic variants generated by our VBS system in terms of: narrative variant

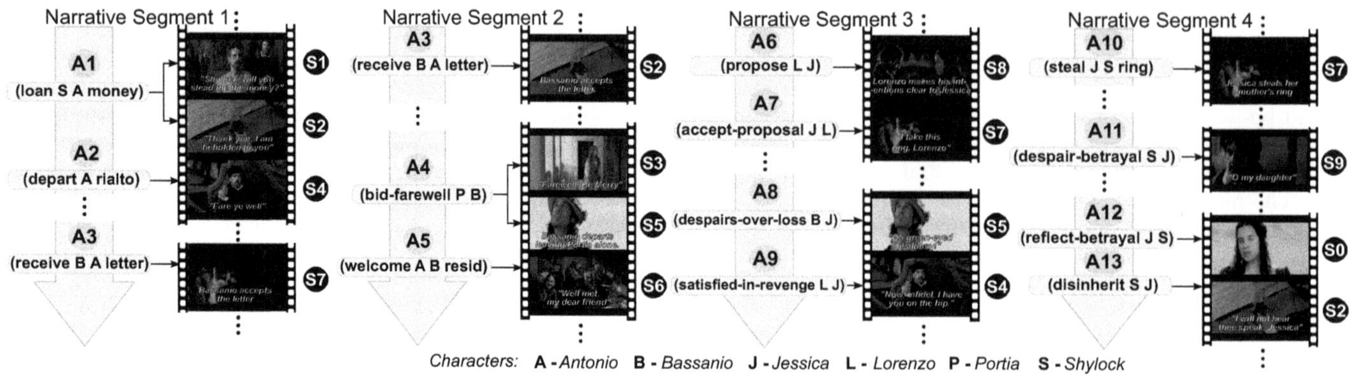

Figure 7: Sample VBS system output: shown running downwards are excerpts of four narratives generated using our *Merchant of Venice* domain model; each narrative shows a number of actions alongside a selection of video shots chosen by the system for the visual presentation of that action (see text for further detail).

generation; consistency and comprehensibility; and visual quality. The results of this evaluation are discussed below.

7.1 Generated Filmic Variants

Fig. 7 shows excerpts from filmic variants generated by our VBS system. Each narrative includes selected actions along with system chosen video shots for visual presentation. The narratives highlight a number of important points:

- The generative possibilities afforded by our plan-based approach result in a large space of potential narratives and the figure shows four very different narratives from this space: narrative 1 contains elements of the original play, a loan is established (A1) and a letter received telling of the perilous circumstances of the benefactor (A3); narrative 2 tells of a profligate character deserting his wife (A2) and later receiving the indulgent welcome of a good friend (A5); narrative 3 tells of romance (A6, A7), lost love (A8) and revenge (A9); and narrative 4 tells a very different tale of familial betrayal (A11), despair (A12) and disinheritance (A13).
- Individual narrative actions can appear in different narratives with different visual presentations (shots) used in each. For example, action A3 is in narratives 1 and 2 but its presentation differs: shot S7 in narrative 1 and S2 in narrative 2. This is possible because different shots are described by the same semantic point. Importantly, this flexibility allows the VBS system to exploit large video corpora enabling multiple presentations on subsequent runs or similar narratives.
- A single shot can be used in multiple semantic contexts because the same semantic pattern can be part of the mapping to diverse narrative actions, e.g., shot S2 appears in both narrative 1 and 2 in totally different contexts.

7.2 Generative Power

The power of a narrative generator can be expressed in terms of expected narrative path length n, and the number of choices at each narrative step (i.e. branching factor) b. The size of the space of narratives that can be generated from a given initial state is: b^n. Here the branching factor is described in terms of the number of characters in the narrative c, and the average number of actions each character has available to them a, giving $b = c \cdot a$.

As outlined in Section 6.2, a pattern request can fail and so the average number of actions a can be reduced. In this case, if p is the fraction of actions removed, then the size of the narrative space becomes $((1-p)(c \cdot a))^n$. However, since removing actions forces the narrative to circumnavigate affected regions of the previous path, n is expected to increase when actions are removed and hence narrative possibility is not compromised.

To evaluate how these changes affect the generative power in practice, we have calculated the branching factor for our *Merchant of Venice* domain and narrative lengths from our three example initial states. Fig. 8 shows the effect on branching factor and length that randomly removing increasing number of actions from the domain has. The error bars show one standard deviation based on 9 repeats over 3 narrative initial states. The high variance is to be expected, as narrative spaces are well known to be non-uniform [9].

The three narratives averaged a branching factor of 8 when all actions were available. In most cases this was around 4 actions for each of two on-stage characters. As actions are removed the branching factor follows the expected downward trend decreasing linearly with number of actions. Interestingly, the increase in length as convoluted narratives are required to work around unpresentable actions more than compensates for the decrease in branching factor. The rapid rise in average narrative length n seen in Fig. 8 means that the overall space of narratives the planner draws from actually increases in size.

When using the entire footage of the original *Merchant of Venice* film to source video data there are still 6% of the actions in our example domain with no corresponding semantics. This appears near the left of Fig. 8 where the branching factor has not yet reduced, but produces narratives that are around 3 actions longer. The greater possibilities enabled by these additional actions in the narratives more than makes up for the slight decrease in options for character actions. In fact, the narrative space is on average 11 times larger than that being explored when all actions are available.

It should also be noted that when more than 15% of actions were removed prior to narrative generation, runs occurred in which no valid narrative could be found. This is due to the planner encountering dead-ends or low branching factor regions in the narrative space. The rate of failure began at 18% (when 85% of actions remain), and rose as high as 90% (only 60% of all actions remain). So as a rule of thumb it appears that sufficient video is required to cover at least 85% of a domain for successful narrative generation.

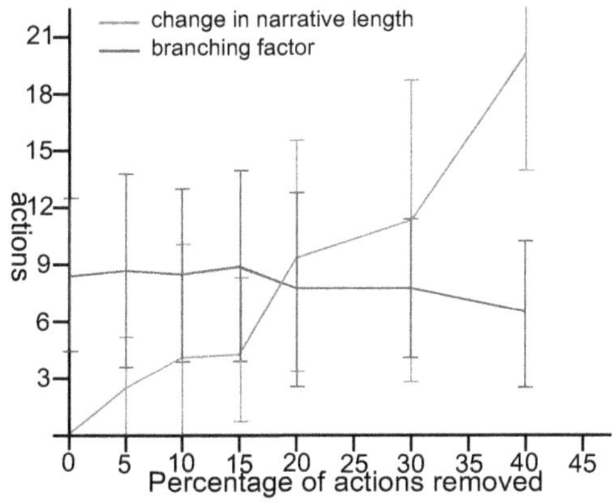

Figure 8: The change in generative power after constraining available video, measured in branching factor size and increase in narrative length.

7.3 Narrative Comprehensibility

We also explored how comprehensible the narratives output by our VBS system were to users. The QUEST model [17] represents narratives as a conceptual graph that provides measures that are able to rate the relative quality of comprehension questions. Asking users to assign goodness of answer (GOA) values to question-answer pairs and assessing their correlation with QUEST-predicted quality has proven a useful technique for measuring presentation's effect on comprehension in IS [10]. An additional benefit of this approach over free-form questionnaires is that it eliminates the need for qualitative assessment of user responses.

Correlation between the QUEST model's expected quality of question-answer pairs and user ratings would provide strong evidence that our VBS system produces easily comprehended narratives. To determine if this is so, we created a narrative and video sequence for each of our three example initial states. Four questions and four answers were randomly selected from the QUEST model of each of our three narratives. This gave 16 question-answer pairs for each narrative, which were presented to 10 participants for a total of 480 evaluations. Participants were asked to watch the video for a narrative and rate the goodness of each answer for each question with a value from 1 (very bad) to 5 (very good).

User responses were compared against measures of reachability and arc distance in the QUEST graph for each narrative. We set expected values for the GOA with 5 (very good) for those with arc distance 1, 4 for those with arc distance 2, and so on, with 1 (very bad) expected for question-answer pairs that are unreachable in the QUEST graph. The mean difference between these expected values and those of the participants was 1.07 – significantly lower than the 1.6 mean that would result from random selection. This was significant with $p < 0.01$ by a two-tailed single sample T-test. Furthermore, the correlation between user GOA and the arc distance measure was 0.49 by Pearson product-moment coefficient, which can be interpreted as somewhere between a medium and large correlation [11] (see page 116). Given that no normalisation between participants' results was performed and that the relationship between our arc distance measure and GOA is not necessarily linear, this level of correlation is strong evidence that the video-based presentation of stories has not compromised comprehensibility.

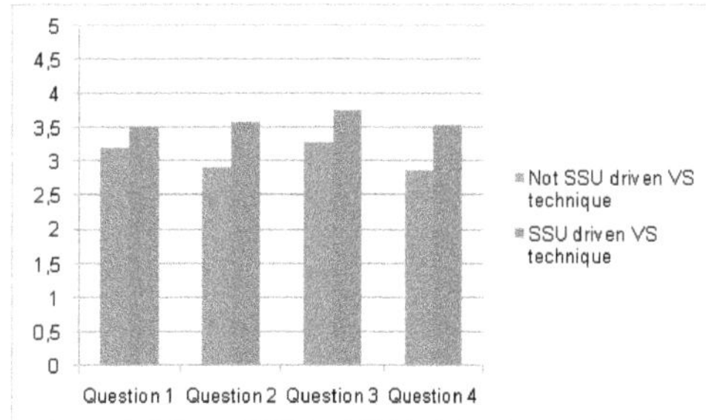

	SSU driven		*Not SSU driven*	
	Mean	Conf. Int.	Mean	Conf. Int.
Question 1	3.19	0.34	2.88	0.31
Question 2	3.23	0.35	2.50	0.41
Question 3	3.50	0.27	3.00	0.29
Question 4	3.23	0.31	2.57	0.31

Figure 9: Visual Quality Test Results: users were questioned about shot adequacy, coherency, transitions and enjoyability of videos generated with and without our SSU techniques (see text for detail).

7.4 Visual Quality

We also ran subjective tests on the quality of video content by generating recombined video clips, of about 4 minutes, relating to two alternative plots. For comparison, the same plots were used to generate video that didn't exploit the SSU techniques from Section 5.2; instead, output video was formed by taking shots satisfying the semantic patterns guaranteeing only causality of the shots in the same narrative action. These 4 videos were shown in random order to users, who were asked the following questions for each video:

- *Shot duration adequacy*: if the pace of the shots seems right to the user, not too frenetic nor too slow.
- *Shot content coherency*: if the shots visual content is consistent with the subtitles meaning, conveying the narration.
- *Actions Transition*: if the transition between consecutive narrative actions is smooth or it appears artificial.
- *Overall enjoyability*: if the recombined video is pleasant, with emphasis on perception rather than understanding.

Again, the answers were integer grades ranging from 1 (low quality) to 5 (high quality). Fig. 9 reports the Mean Opinion Score (MOS) of the answers, along with the 95% confidence interval. From the grades given to the content quality provided by the VBS system, it can be concluded that the users were generally satisfied with the experience, although there is still room for improvement. Also, Fig. 9 highlights that the shot recombination technology benefits from the SSUs underlying structure inherited by the LSUs.

8. CONCLUSIONS

The paper overviews a complete implementation of an innovative VBS system that fully integrates AI planning with a sophisticated video analysis and recombination process. The integration has been enabled through the definition of a common semantic vocabulary that permits cooperation between planning and video processing. This also extends the flexibility of the planning by removing the limits imposed by using only actions originally scripted in the baseline video. Moreover, the intermediate level semantics also guarantee that the actual video content played back is more closely tailored to the intended high level meaning of the narrative actions. The system showcases novel techniques for manipulating the Markov models representing semantic story units.

Our experimental results show that the alternative narratives generated through scripted video recombination achieve promising grades from user tests and highlight the importance of the SSU-based technology presented here in exploiting the underlying logical structure of the original content.

9. ACKNOWLEDGMENTS

This work has been funded (in part) by the European Commission under grant agreement IRIS (FP7-ICT-231824).

10. REFERENCES

[1] N. Adami and R. Leonardi. Identification of editing effect in image sequences by statistical modeling. In *Proc. Picture Coding Symposium (PCS)*, pages 157–160, Portland, OR, USA, 1999.

[2] S. Benini, P. Migliorati, and R. Leonardi. Hierarchical structuring of video previews by leading cluster analysis. *Signal, Image and Video Processing*, 4(4):435–450, 2010.

[3] S. Bocconi, F. Nack, and L. Hardman. Using Rhetorical Annotations for Generating Video Documentaries. In *IEEE Int. Conf. on Multimedia and Expo (ICME)*, pages 1070–1073, Netherlands, 2005.

[4] S. Bocconi, F. Nack, and L. Hardman. Automatic generation of matter-of-opinion video documentaries. *Journal of Web Semantics*, 6(2):139–150, 2008.

[5] J. Boreczky and L. Rowe. Comparison of video shot boundary detection techniques. *Electronic Imaging*, 5(2):122–128, 1996.

[6] K. M. Brooks. Do Story Agents Use Rocking Chairs? The Theory and Implementation of One Model for Computational Narrative. In *Proc. ACM Multimedia Conf.*, pages 317–328, New York, NY, USA, 1996.

[7] M. Cavazza, F. Charles, and S. J. Mead. Character-based interactive storytelling. *IEEE Intelligent Systems*, 17(4):17–24, 2002.

[8] P. Cesar, D. Bulterman, and L. Soares. Human-centered television: directions in interactive television research. *ACM Trans. on Multimedia Computing, Communication and Applications*, 4(4), 2008.

[9] Y.-G. Cheong and R. M. Young. Narrative generation for suspense: Modelling and evaluation. In *Proc. 1st Joint Int. Conf. on Interactive Digital Storytelling (ICIDS)*, pages 144–155, 2008.

[10] D. Christian and M. Young. Comparing cognitive and computational models of narrative structure. In *Proc. of the National Conf. of the American Association for AI (AAAI)*, pages 385–390, San Jose, CA, USA, 2004.

[11] J. Cohen. *Statistical power analysis for the behavioral sciences*. Academic Press, New York, 1988.

[12] C. Cotsaces, N. Nikolaidis, and I. Pitas. Video shot detection and condensed representation. *IEEE Signal Processing Magazine*, 23(2):28–37, 2006.

[13] C. Crawford. *Chris Crawford on Game Design*. New Riders Publishing, 2003.

[14] G. Davenport, T. Smith, and N. Pincever. Cinematic Primitives for Multimedia. *IEEE Computer Graphics and Applications*, 11(4):67–74, 1991.

[15] A. Gerevini and D. Long. Technical report, 2005. http://www.cs.yale.edu/homes/dvm/papers/pddl-bnf.pdf.

[16] A. Gersho and R. M. Gray. *Vector Quantization and Signal Compression*. Kluwer Academic, 1992.

[17] A. C. Graesser and D. Hemphill. Question answering in the context of scientific mechanisms. *Journal of Memory and Language*, 30(2):186–209, 1991.

[18] B. Jung, J. Song, and Y. Lee. A narrative-based abstraction framework for story-oriented video. *ACM Trans. on Multimedia Computing, Communication and Applications*, 3(2), 2007.

[19] C. Lanz, S. Nowak, and U. Kühhirt. Determination of categories for tagging and automated classification of film scenes. In *Proc. 8th European Conf. on Interactive TV (EUROITV)*, pages 297–300, Finland, 2010.

[20] G. Lupatini, C. Saraceno, and R. Leonardi. Scene break detection: A comparison. In *Proc. Workshop on Research Issues In Data Engineering (RIDE)*, pages 34–41, Orlando, FL, USA, 1998.

[21] M. Mateas and A. Stern. Structuring Content in the Façade Interactive Drama Architecture. In *Proc. 1st Conf on AI and Interactive Digital Entertainment (AIIDE)*, Marina Del Rey, USA, 2005.

[22] F. Nack. *AUTEUR: The Application of Video Semantics and Theme Representation for Automated Film Editing*. PhD thesis, 1996.

[23] J. Porteous, S. Benini, L. Canini, F. Charles, M. Cavazza, and R. Leonardi. Interactive Storytelling via Video Content Recombination. In *Proc. ACM Multimedia Conf.*, pages 1715–1718, Italy, 2010.

[24] J. Porteous, M. Cavazza, and F. Charles. Applying Planning to Interactive Storytelling: Narrative Control using State Constraints. *ACM TIST*, 1(2):1–21, 2010.

[25] M. Radford. MGM Home Ent. (Europe) Ltd., 2004. The Merchant of Venice (film adaptation).

[26] W. Sack and M. Davis. IDIC: Assembling Video Sequences from Story Plans and Content Annotations. In *Proc. ICMCS*, pages 14–19, Boston, USA, 1994.

[27] E. Shen, H. Lieberman, and G. Davenport. What's Next?: Emergent Storytelling from Video Collection. In *Proc. 27th Int. Conf. on Human Factors in Computing Systems (CHI)*, pages 809–818, USA, 2009.

[28] T. Smith and G. Davenport. The Stratification System. A Design Environment for Random Access Video. In *3rd Int. Workshop on Network and Operating System Support for Digital Audio and Video, (NOSSDAV)*, pages 250–261, California, USA, 1992.

[29] T. Smith and N. Pincever. Parsing Movies In Context. In *Proc. Summer Usenix Conf.*, Nashville, USA, 1991.

[30] M. M. Yeung and B.-L. Yeo. Time-constrained clustering for segmentation of video into story units. In *Proc. Int. Conf. on Pattern Recognition (ICPR)*, volume 3, pages 375–380, Wien, Austria, 1996.

[31] R. Young. Creating Interactive Narrative Structures: The Potential for AI Approaches. In *Notes of the AAAI Spring Symposia on AI and Interactive Entertainment*, pages 81–82, Stanford, CA, 2000.

[32] V. Zsombori, M. Ursu, J. Wyver, D. Williams, and I. Kegel. ShapeShifting Documentary: A Golden Age. In *Proc. 6th European Conf. on Interactive TV (EUROITV)*, pages 40–50, 2008.

Personalizing Automated Image Annotation using Cross-Entropy

Xirong Li　Efstratios Gavves　Cees G.M. Snoek
Marcel Worring　Arnold W.M. Smeulders

Intelligent Systems Lab Amsterdam, Informatics Institute, University of Amsterdam
Science Park 904, 1098XH Amsterdam, The Netherlands
{x.li,e.gavves,c.g.m.snoek,m.worring,a.w.m.smeulders}@uva.nl

ABSTRACT

Annotating the increasing amounts of user-contributed images in a personalized manner is in great demand. However, this demand is largely ignored by the mainstream of automated image annotation research. In this paper we aim for personalizing automated image annotation by jointly exploiting personalized tag statistics and content-based image annotation. We propose a cross-entropy based learning algorithm which personalizes a generic annotation model by learning from a user's multimedia tagging history. Using cross-entropy-minimization based Monte Carlo sampling, the proposed algorithm optimizes the personalization process in terms of a performance measurement which can be flexibly chosen. Automatic image annotation experiments with 5,315 realistic users in the social web show that the proposed method compares favorably to a generic image annotation method and a method using personalized tag statistics only. For 4,442 users the performance improves, where for 1,088 users the absolute performance gain is at least 0.05 in terms of average precision. The results show the value of the proposed method.

Categories and Subject Descriptors

H.3.1 [**Information Storage and Retrieval**]: Content Analysis and Indexing—*Indexing methods*; I.2.6 [**Artificial Intelligence**]: Learning—*Concept learning*

General Terms

Algorithms, Experimentation, Human Factors

Keywords

Automated image annotation, Personalization, Personal multimedia tagging history, Cross-entropy optimization

Area chair: Wu-chi Feng

1. INTRODUCTION

Annotating large personal collections of pictures on smart phones, personal computers, and the web is of great social importance. With the size of such collections growing so rapidly, full manual annotation is unfeasible. Thus, automatic image annotation is crucial, but this is challenging due to the well-known semantic gap: "the lack of coincidence between the information that one can extract from the visual data and the interpretation that the same data have for *a user in a given situation*" [24]. Much work has been conducted to (partially) bridge the gap by learning a mapping between visual features and objective semantics [6,9,20,22,26,27]. However, in the above efforts the *user* factor in the semantic gap is completely ignored. Clearly, users have personal preferences for image subjects. For instance, some users collect pictures of flowers, while others may favor images of cars. This real-world phenomenon suggests that an off-the-shelf image annotation system is unlikely to be universally applicable to the large variations in personal albums. The absence of personal information in devising image annotation models results in unsatisfactory annotations.

Some research has been conducted towards personalizing automated image annotation [4,5,14,21]. Sawant et al. were among the first to leverage user tagging preferences, with their novel observation that "a user's previously used tags can be the best determinants of her future uploads" [21]. Interestingly, their study revealed that simply annotating a user's new images with tags most frequently used by the same user in the past yields a much higher accuracy than several automated methods. This result leads the authors to conclude that prediction by personal tag statistics is a reasonable upper bound on personalized image annotation performance.

In this paper we study the problem of *personalizing automated* image annotation in a social web context. We tackle the problem by proposing a generic framework which jointly exploits generic content-based image annotation and personal multimedia tagging history. We present a learning algorithm which optimizes the personalization process in terms of a performance measurement which can be arbitrarily chosen. Due to this technical advantage, we go beyond the performance upper bound of personalized image annotation established in [21].

2. RELATED WORK

Instead of proposing a new generic image annotation model, this paper studies the personalization of automated image annotation. We first review recent progress in generic image annotation, and then we discuss related work on image annotation personalization.

2.1 Generic Image Annotation

A considerable amount of papers have been published for generic image annotation [6, 9, 13, 15, 22, 23, 25, 26]. We divide existing work into content-based methods and content-context-based methods.

The content-based methods predict tags purely based on image content analysis [6, 9, 13, 22, 25, 26]. Li and Wang [9] train a multivariate Gaussian mixture model for each tag, while Support Vector Machines are used in [22]. Liu et al. [13] annotate images by maximizing the joint probability of images and tags. The authors in [26] perform image annotation by learning a mapping into a common feature space where both images and tags are represented. They rank tags in terms of their distance to a test image in the common space. In contrast to per-tag modeling, k-nearest-neighbors based methods make predictions by propagating tags to the unlabeled image from its visual neighbors [16]. Weighted nearest neighbors are considered in [6]. Sparse reconstructions are employed in [25] to reduce the chance of incorrectly including neighbors which are semantically irrelevant to the unlabeled image. To enhance content-based image annotation, contextual information on the creation of an unlabeled image has been investigated [15, 23]. In [15], GPS data, indicating where the image was captured, is employed, whereas in [23], camera metadata such as shutter speed and focal length describing how the image was captured is studied. In both content-based and content-context-based methods, all users are treated equally, without taking personal preferences into account.

Work such as [3, 12, 29] studies learning image annotation models from social-tagged images. Datta et al. [3] treat user tags as positive feedback to incrementally update an existing model. Liu et al. [12] and Zhu et al. [29] measure both image-wise visual similarity and tag-wise semantic similarity to refine existing annotations. These methods learn from the social community but do not consider personalized image annotation.

2.2 Personalized Image Annotation

Recently some papers have appeared towards automated approaches to personalized image annotation [4, 5, 14, 21]. According to whether user interaction is needed, we divide existing work into two types of methods, automatic methods and semi-automatic methods.

The automatic methods achieve personalization by inferring from personal digital calendars [5] or multimedia tagging history [21], or training a generic model on personal collections [4]. In [5], Gallagher et al. explore the possibility of using personal calendar event annotations to label images. The rationale for the idea is based on the coincidence between the calendar event and image capture time. Calendar annotations are not always available. More importantly, tagging a calendar event is different from tagging an image. Therefore, personalizing image annotation based on the calendar tagging history seems questionable. Assuming that context-constrained images such as those captured at the same location have a similar visual style, Duan et al. [4] propose a probabilistic model where styles are viewed as latent variables. While learning from visual features of high dimensionality requires many labeled examples, the number of personal images for a specific user is relatively small and many of them are unlabeled. Hence, learning models using personal collections alone seems problematic. To overcome the problem, Liu et al. [14] propose a semi-automatic method, by first learning a generic model for each tag using images from a professional photo forum. They then solicit user feedback to adapt the learned model to personal collections. The difficulty in obtaining user feedback for thousands of tags puts the scalability of the semi-automatic method into question. Moreover, in [4,5,14], personal tagging history, a strong clue for building personalized annotation models, is untouched.

In [21], Sawant et al. propose to combine personal tagging history, in the form of tag frequency, and predictions made by a content-based image annotation system [9] in a Naïve Bayes formulation. They conclude that combining tagging history and content analysis is inferior to using the history alone. We argue that their conclusion is true but for their Naïve Bayes model only. In that model the performance of the individual pieces of evidence is not considered. In contrast, we propose a personalization model which is directly optimized in terms of the prior annotation performance. As a consequence, we reach the novel conclusion that combining the personal tagging history and content analysis yields better personalized image annotation.

The rest of the paper is organized as follows. We formulate the personalization problem and elaborate the proposed personalization model in Section 3. We setup experiments in Section 4, with results analyzed in Section 5. We conclude the paper in Section 6.

3. PERSONALIZED IMAGE ANNOTATION

3.1 Problem Formalization

Let u be a user for whom we want to provide personalized image annotation. Let $X_{u,past}$ be a set of images the user has already labeled, and $X_{u,future}$ a set of unlabeled images the user wants to have tags for. We use w to denote a tag and $V = \{w_1, \ldots, w_m\}$ for a large vocabulary. For each image $x \in X_{u,future}$, we aim to annotate it with tags from the vocabulary such that the annotations are relevant with respect to the image from the user's standpoint. To do so, we use both information from the user as well as the social web community. So let X_{comm} indicate images in the community, and $X_{u,past}$ is a subset of X_{comm}. We define $G_u(x, w)$ as a *personalized* image annotation function whose output is a confidence score of the tag w being relevant to the image x. This allows us to rank tags by $G_u(x, w)$ in descending order and preserve the top ranked tags as annotations of unlabeled images for this particular user.

Personalized image annotation is a complex task. It is unlikely that an image annotation function based on a single modality can capture all relevant characteristics. We therefore need to look at the problem from multiple perspectives. Ideally, we exploit varying evidence such as content-based image annotation driven by diverse features [6, 11], tag statistics in personal collections and networks [21], personal daily activities [5], geographic context [15], or camera metadata [23]. In this study, we focus on combining content-based annotation and personal tag statistics, as they are

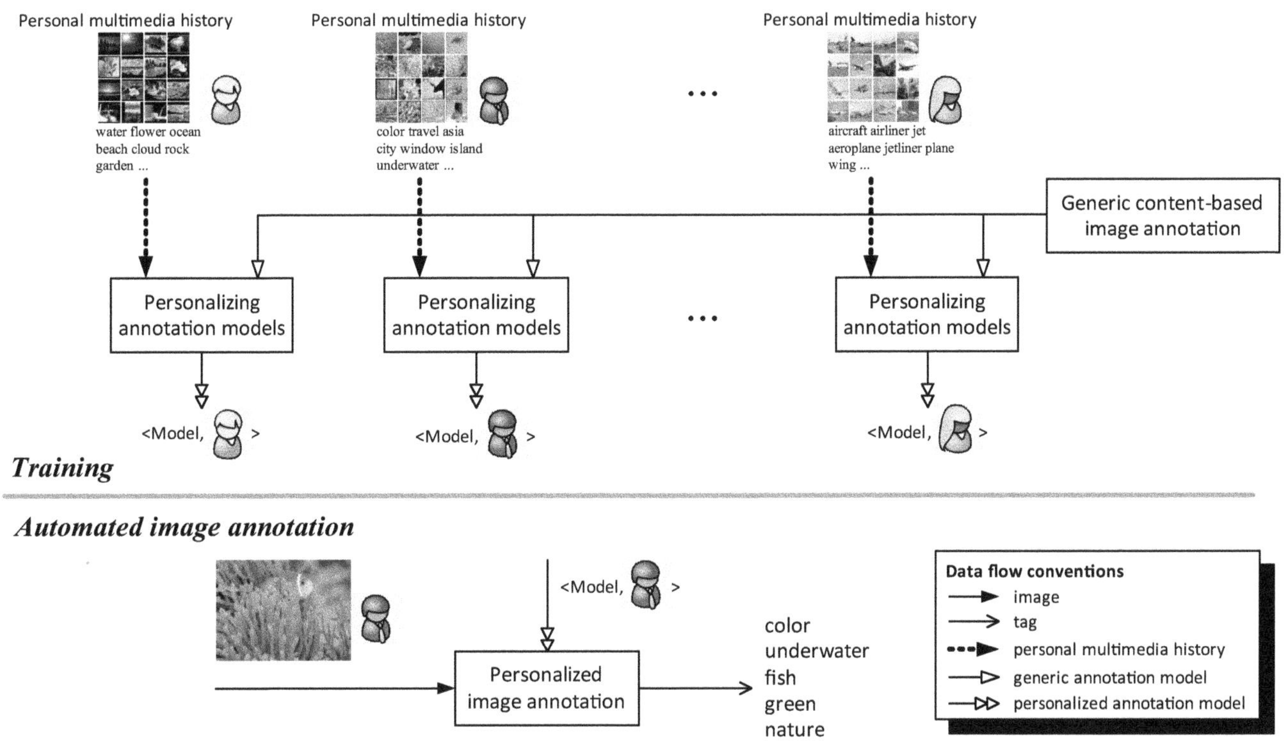

Figure 1: The proposed framework for *personalizing* automated image annotation. For a given user, we deliver a personalized image annotation model, by jointly exploiting content-based image annotation and the user's multimedia tagging history.

two fundamental elements related to the problem and are often more accessible than other elements. Nevertheless, to make our discussion general, we consider combining annotation functions driven by multiple sources of evidence. To that end, let $\{g_1(x,w),\ldots,g_t(x,w)\}$, with $g_j(x,w) \in [0,1]$, $j=1,\ldots,t$, be a set of such image annotation functions. As combining these functions can be viewed as a multi-modal fusion problem, we choose to use a linear weighted sum, an effective strategy for multi-modal fusion according to [1]. The importance of individual tags varies per user, so tag-dependent weights are necessary. To formalize the above notion, for each tag w_i, $i=1,\ldots,m$, we express a parameterized version of $G_u(x,w)$ as

$$G_{u,\Lambda}(x,w_i) = \sum_{j=1}^{t} \lambda_{i,j} g_j(x,w_i), \tag{1}$$

where $\{\lambda_{i,j}\}$ are non-negative weighting parameters, and $\Lambda = [\lambda_{i,j}]_{m\times t}$ is the parameter matrix. While $\lambda_{i,j}$ indicates the importance of $g_j(x,w_i)$ for predicting w_i, their summation, namely $\sum_{j=1}^{t}\lambda_{i,j}$, reflects the importance of w_i for annotating the personal collection. By optimizing the weights per user, we obtain personalized image annotation models.

To find the optimal weights for a given user, we need information about what tags the user is likely to use for tagging her/his personal collections. We assume that a user's tagging preference is relatively consistent within a certain period. Therefore, the images the user has already labeled $X_{u,past}$ are the prime candidates. To make the above notion operational, we need to formulate an optimization goal per user. Let $rank(V|x,G_{u,\Lambda})$ be a ranking of the vocabulary V for an image $x \in X_{u,past}$, obtained by sorting tags in descending order by $G_{u,\Lambda}(x,w)$. Let $\mathbf{w}_x$ be the set of tags assigned to x by its user, serving as ground truth to assess $rank(V|x,G_{u,\Lambda})$. We define

$$E(rank(V|x,G_{u,\Lambda}),\mathbf{w}_x)$$

as a performance measure function which produces a real-valued score indicating ranking quality. As we learn from a set of images, rather than from a single image, we define a set-level performance measure as

$$S(X,\Lambda) = \frac{1}{|X|}\sum_{x\in X} E(rank(V|x,G_{u,\Lambda}),\mathbf{w}_x), \tag{2}$$

where $|\cdot|$ is the cardinality of a set. Putting everything together, we formulate the problem of personalizing automated image annotation for a given user as solving the following optimization problem:

$$\Lambda^* = \operatorname*{argmax}_{\Lambda} S(X_{u,past},\Lambda), \tag{3}$$

subject to

$$0 \le \lambda_{i,j} \le 1. \tag{4}$$

Solving Eq. 3 yields the optimal parameters for the personalized model defined in Eq. 1, which are then used to annotate new, yet unlabeled, images of the user. We illustrate the proposed framework in Fig. 1.

3.2 Personalization using Cross-Entropy

Finding a solution for the optimization problem in Eq. 3 is nontrivial. As the performance measure function E is often not differentiable, a standard gradient-ascent based algorithm is inapplicable. A common approach to such a problem is Monte Carlo simulation. But, when the parameter space is large, as in our case, finding Λ^* or its good approximation by random sampling is a rare event. A crude Monte Carlo approach would imply an unfeasibly large simulation effort. A solution for rare event search is offered by the cross-entropy method [19], which iteratively optimizes an arbitrary function by importance sampling. We first describe the cross-entropy method in general, and then present a cross-entropy based learning algorithm for solving Eq. 3.

3.2.1 The Cross-Entropy Method

Imagine that our goal is to maximize an objective function $S(\Lambda)$, and its maximum is found at Λ^*. The cross-entropy method [19] assumes that Λ is a random variable following a parametric distribution $p(\Lambda;\Theta)$ which is specified by an (unknown) hyper parameter Θ. In a nutshell, the method consists of the following two steps executed iteratively:

Step 1. Randomly generate n samples using $p(\Lambda;\Theta)$; We use $\{\Lambda^{(1)},\ldots,\Lambda^{(n)}\}$ to denote the n samples.

Step 2. Select the top s samples $\{\widehat{\Lambda}^{(1)},\ldots,\widehat{\Lambda}^{(s)}\}$ by sorting the n samples in descending order by $S(\Lambda)$, where the selected samples are called *elite* samples. Re-estimate Θ by maximum likelihood estimation on the s elite samples.

From the second step we see that the hyper parameter Θ is updated in terms of the elite samples. As a consequence, the probability of generating good samples is progressively increased, making Λ converge towards its optimal value. The procedure repeats until it hits certain stop criteria. For instance, the performance does not improve or the number of iterations exceed a given threshold. We compute Λ^* as the expectation of $p(\Lambda;\Theta)$.

The theoretical foundation of the two-step procedure is that, the original optimization problem can be tackled by iteratively solving the following problem,

$$\Theta^* = \underset{\Theta}{\operatorname{argmax}} \int_{\Lambda} I(S(\Lambda) \geq \gamma) p(\Lambda;\Theta) d\Lambda, \quad (5)$$

where I is an indicator function, and γ is a given level. The rationale for Eq. 5 is that a good choice of Θ shall generate more elite Λ with $I(S(\Lambda \geq r)) = 1$. We use T to indicate the number of iterations in total and $q = 1,\ldots,T$ to index a specific iteration. For a given level $\gamma^{(q)}$, let $\Theta^{(q)}$ be the solution to Eq. 5. By constructing an increasing sequence of levels $\{\gamma^{(q)}\}$, and correspondingly finding a sequence of hyper parameters $\{\Theta^{(q)}\}$ by solving Eq. 5, the optimal solution is progressively approached. When $\gamma^{(T)}$ is close to $S(\Lambda^*)$, the expectation of $p(\Lambda;\Theta^{(T)})$ will be close to Λ^*.

So in each iteration, our goal is to find Θ such that the cross entropy between $p(\Lambda;\Theta^{(q)})$ and $p(\Lambda;\Theta)$ is minimized. According to [19], minimizing the cross entropy turns out to be maximum likelihood estimation on those elite samples with $S(\Lambda) \geq \gamma^{(q)}$. To see how this conclusion results in the second step of the cross-entropy method, let $\{\widehat{\Lambda}^{(1,q)},\ldots,\widehat{\Lambda}^{(s,q)}\}$ be the s elite samples found in the q-th iteration. By setting $\gamma^{(q)} = S(\widehat{\Lambda}^{(s,q)})$, $\Theta^{(q)}$ is the result of maximum likelihood estimation on $\{\widehat{\Lambda}^{(1,q)},\ldots,\widehat{\Lambda}^{(s,q)}\}$.

3.2.2 The Cross-Entropy based Learning Algorithm

We now present an algorithm for image annotation personalization, on the basis of the cross-entropy method. For reasons of simplicity, we assume that the weighting parameters $\{\lambda_{i,j}\}$ are independent of each other. Each parameter $\lambda_{i,j}$ follows a distribution $p(\lambda_{i,j};\theta_{i,j})$, and $\Theta = [\theta_{i,j}]_{m\times t}$ is the hyper parameter matrix. Moreover, we choose binomial distributions to be the distribution family, because the parameter of a binomial distribution, namely $\theta_{i,j}$, directly measures the impact of $\lambda_{i,j}$ on the personalization process. If a larger (smaller) value of $\lambda_{i,j}$ contributes more to the objective function $S(X_{u,past},\Lambda)$ in the current learning round, $\theta_{i,j}$ increases (decreases) such that a larger (smaller) value is more likely to be assigned to $\lambda_{i,j}$ in next rounds. Concretely, in the q-th iteration, we first randomly generate a sequence of n samples, $\{\Lambda^{(1,q)},\ldots,\Lambda^{(n,q)}\}$, where

$$\lambda_{i,j}^{(l,q)} \leftarrow \frac{1}{N} Binomial(N,\theta_{i,j}^{(q-1)}), \text{ for } l = 1,\ldots,n. \quad (6)$$

Note that to satisfy the constraints that $0 \leq \lambda_{i,j} \leq 1$, we divide the output of the Binomial function by the number of trials. Subsequently, we find s elite samples from the n samples by sorting them in descending order according to our objective function $S(X_{u,past},\Lambda)$. As we have mentioned in Section 3.2.1, the optimal $\Theta^{(q)}$ is found by maximum likelihood estimation on the s elite samples. For a Binomial distribution, this amounts to averaging over the elite samples, namely

$$\theta_{i,j}^{(q)} = \frac{1}{s}\sum_{l=1}^{s} \widehat{\lambda}_{i,j}^{(l,q)}. \quad (7)$$

Since the expectation of $\frac{1}{N}Binomial(N,\theta)$ is θ, the optimal set of weights Λ^* found by the proposed algorithm is $\Theta^{(T)}$.

We summarize our algorithm in Table 1. As there is no need to compute gradients for the objective function, the proposed algorithm can optimize the personalization process in terms of a performance measure which can be arbitrarily chosen. Moreover, its convergence is theoretically guaranteed by the underlying cross-entropy method [19].

Concerning the complexity of our algorithm, the main computational effort is spent on evaluating $S(X_{u,past},\Lambda)$. We assume that the generic annotation functions $\{g_j(x,w)\}$ are precomputed. For a given Λ, the complexity of constructing a tag rank for an image is $O(m\cdot t + m^2)$, and con-

Table 1: The proposed cross-entropy based learning algorithm for optimizing automated image annotation per user.

INPUT: A user's multimedia tagging history $X_{u,past}$, base image annotation functions $\{g_1,\ldots,g_t\}$,

OUTPUT: optimized weights Λ^* for the personalized image annotation function $G_{u,\Lambda}(x,w)$.

1. Initialize $\Theta^{(0)}$
2. for $q = 1,\ldots,T$
3. Randomly generate $\{\Lambda^{(1,q)},\ldots,\Lambda^{(n,q)}\}$ using Eq. 6
4. Evaluate the generated samples using Eq. 2, and select the s elite samples
5. Obtain $\Theta^{(q)}$ by maximum likelihood estimation on the s samples using Eq. 7
6. $\Lambda^* \leftarrow \Theta^{(T)}$

sequently $O(|X_{u,past}| \cdot (m \cdot t + m^2))$ for the entire training set. Notice that the evaluations of the n parameters $\{\Lambda^{(l,q)}\}$ are independent of each other. The computation associated with each image is also independent of other training images. Therefore, the algorithm can be easily parallelized.

4. EXPERIMENTAL SETUP

To verify our proposal of personalized image annotation, we conduct a series of experiments on realistic personal image sets collected from the social web.

4.1 Data Sets

Community Image Set X_{comm} for building a content-based image annotation system. We use a set of 3.5 million images randomly sampled from Flickr by our earlier work [10]. Because batch-tagged images are often (nearly) duplicate and of low tagging accuracy, such images are not helpful for content-based image annotation. Also, we want tags to be meaningful. With these two considerations, we remove batch-tagged images and tags not defined in WordNet [17]. We use the remaining 800K images as X_{comm}. Since tags with very low frequency are unlikely to be well predicted, we preserve tags assigned to at least 100 images, and thus obtain a vocabulary V with $m = 5,073$ tags.

Personal Image Sets X_u for testing personalized image annotation. As this work studies how to personalize automated image annotation, the personal image sets for evaluation should be independent of the 800K community image set. To that end, we choose NUS-WIDE [2], which consists of 20K Flickr images after the same preprocess as we used for the community set. We aim to learn from a user's multimedia tagging history. Therefore, for each user, instead of splitting her/his image set at random, we divide the set into two distinct subsets, namely *Past* and *Future*, such that images from *Past* were uploaded before images from *Future*. The *Past* and *Future* sets are instantiations of $X_{u,past}$ and $X_{u,future}$ defined in Section 3.1. To reveal how much personal tagging history is required for the history information to be useful, we conduct a study on 5,315 users with varying amounts of personal tagging history, as shown in Table 2. The number of images in the *Past* sets ranges from 1 to 205, with an average value of 7.9. The *Future* set has similar statistics. For each user, we use $X_{u,past}$ for training and $X_{u,future}$ for evaluation. Note that we treat each test image as unlabeled. Its user tags are merely used for ground-truth purposes.

4.2 Base Image Annotation Functions

We choose two state-of-the-art models, *PersonalPreference* [21] and *Visual* [11], which predict tags using tag statistics and visual content, respectively.

PersonalPreference. We choose this function for its good performance for personalized image annotation, as suggested in [21]. Given an unlabeled image x from a user u, the PersonalPreference model simply annotates x with the most frequent tags in $X_{u,past}$. Let $P(w|X)$ be the tag distribution in a social-tagged image set X, computed as

$$P(w|X) \approx \frac{\text{freq}(w|X) + \epsilon}{\sum_{j=1}^{m} \text{freq}(w_j|x) + \epsilon \cdot m}, \quad (8)$$

where freq$(w|X)$ is the number of images labeled with w in X, and ϵ is a small positive constant for smoothing. We express the PersonalPreference version of $g(x, w)$ as

$$g_{pp}(x, w) = P(w|X_{u,past}). \quad (9)$$

Table 2: We build personalized image annotation models for 5,315 users with varying amounts of personal tagging history. The amount of tagging history per user is measured by $|X_{u,past}|$.

$\lvert X_{u,past}\rvert$	Number of users
1	1,422
$2 \sim 9$	2,554
$10 \sim 49$	1,221
≥ 50	118

Visual. This model as introduced in our previous work [11] predicts tags purely based on image content. Our experiments show that it outperforms ALIPR [9], the content-based model used in [21]. Given an image x represented by a visual feature f, the Visual model first finds k neighbor images visually close to x from the community image set X_{comm}, and then selects the most frequent tags in the neighbor set as annotations of x. To overcome the limitation of single features in describing image content, predictions made based on individual features are uniformly combined. We express the Visual version of $g(x, w)$ as

$$g_v(x, w) = \frac{1}{|F|}\left(\sum_{f \in F} \frac{\text{freq}(w|X_{x,f,k})}{k} - \frac{\text{freq}(w|X_{comm})}{|X_{comm}|}\right), \quad (10)$$

where F is a set of features, and $X_{x,f,k}$ are the k visual neighbors of x with the visual similarity defined by f.

To implement Eq. 10, we choose three decent visual features as follows: COLOR, CSLBP, and GIST. The COLOR feature is a 64-d global feature, combining the 44-d color correlogram [8], the 14-d texture moments [28], and the 6-d RGB color comments. The CSLBP feature is a 80-d center-symmetric local binary pattern histogram [7], capturing local texture distributions. The GIST feature is a 960-d feature describing dominant spatial structures of a scene by a set of perceptual measures such as naturalness, openness, and roughness [18]. The parameter k is set to 500.

By incorporating the two complementary base functions, $g_{pp}(x, w)$ and $g_v(x, w)$, into our unified framework, we aim for good personalized image annotation.

4.3 Implementation

Parameters of the Proposed Model. There are $m = 5,073$ tags and $t = 2$ base image annotation functions. We empirically set the parameters of the algorithm described in Table 1 as follows: $n = 10$, $s = 2$, and $T = 200$. The computational time of the algorithm is linearly proportional to the size of the training data. For a user with 50 tagged images for training, each learning round costs approximately 42 seconds in our prototype system.

Evaluation Criteria. We use precision at top 1 (P@1) and precision at top 5 (P@5) to evaluate the accuracy of the top predicted tags. To evaluate entire tag rankings, we use average precision (AP), a good combination of precision and recall. The personalization process is optimized in terms of AP. The performance for a given user is averaged over all test images of this user.

4.4 Experiments

Experiment 1: User Tagging Consistency. We aim to verify to what extent our conjecture about user tagging consistency made in Section 3.1 is valid. Due to the lack of golden criteria for judging consistency, we compare the divergence between tag distribution of the same user and from different users. Given two users u_i and u_j, we compute the Jensen-Shannon divergence between $P(w|X_{u_i,past})$ and $P(w|X_{u_j,future})$, where the probability masses are computed using Eq. 8. So $i = j$ indicates intra-user divergences, while $i \neq j$ indicates inter-user divergences.

Experiment 2: Comparing Models. We compare the proposed model with the following three baselines: two generic models, namely CommunityPreference and Visual, and one personalized model, PersonalPreference. CommunityPreference annotates an image by simply predicting the most frequent tags within the community set. Visual and PersonalPreference, as mentioned in Section 4.2, are two ingredients in the proposed model.

5. RESULTS

5.1 Experiment 1: User Tagging Consistency

The intra-user and inter-user divergence matrix is shown in Fig. 2, where the diagonal line denotes the intra-user divergences. For a better view of the four user groups in Table 2, we randomly select 100 users from each group, and arrange the matrix in ascending order in terms of $|X_{u,past}|$. For users with a very short tagging history as shown in the top left corner of Fig. 2, the intra-user divergences are smaller than their inter-user counterparts within the same group. But the difference is relatively small, largely due to the fact that the lack of tagging history makes the estimated tag distributions less distinguishable. As the amount of the tagging history increases, we observe a more clear difference between intra-user divergences and inter-user divergences. See for instance $|X_{u,past}| \geq 50$ as shown in the bottom right corner of Fig. 2. Viewing the inter-user divergences as a baseline, we conclude that the tagging preferences of the same user is relatively consistent.

5.2 Experiment 2: Comparing Models

Personalized Models versus Generic Models. As shown in Table 3, when a user's personal tagging preference is unknown, content-based prediction, i.e, the *Visual* model, with an AP score of 0.091, is much better than *CommunityPreference* with an AP score of 0.044. Once a user's tagging history is available, the simple *PersonalPreference* model, with an AP score of 0.232, clearly outperforms content-based prediction. The statement is valid even for $|X_{u,past}| = 1$. The result is consistent with the observation made by [21] that a user's previously used tags are important for predicting her/his future uploads.

Comparing Two Personalized Models. As shown in Table 3, the proposed model compares favorably to *PersonalPreference* under all evaluation criteria. In contrast to [21] where *PersonalPreference* is considered as an upper bound on image annotation performance, our model surpasses the "upper bound".

We compare the two personalized models, given users with varying amounts of personal tagging history. In the extreme case, there are 1,422 users, each having only one tagged images available for training. For 67% of the 1,422 users, we observe improvements, with a relative gain of 8% in terms of AP. Richer tagging history results in better personalized models in general.

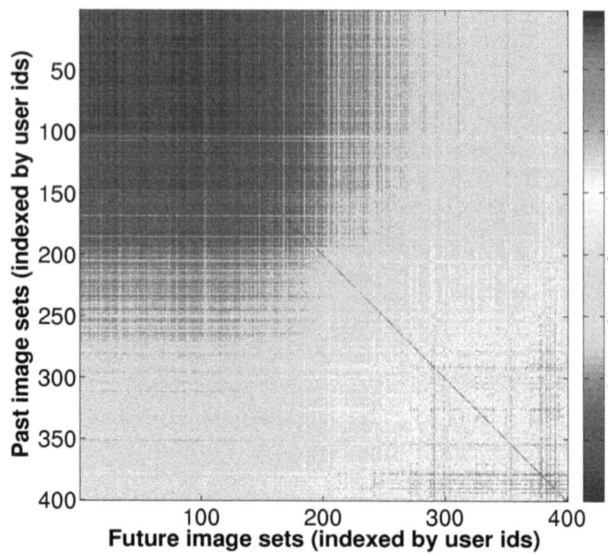

Figure 2: Experiment 1. User tagging consistency. The axes represent the *Past* and *Future* sets of 400 users with $|X_{u,past}|$ ranging from 1 to 168. Each entry in the matrix is the Jensen-Shannon divergence between the tag distribution in a *Past* set and in a *Future* set. The matrix is asymmetrical due to inter-user tagging divergences. The diagonal line indicates intra-user divergences. Best viewed in color.

For a comprehensive study, we make a per-user comparison between our model and *PersonalPreference*. The **absolute** improvement in terms of AP is shown in Fig. 3. For 4,442 out of the 5,315 users in our experiments, the proposed model is better than *PersonalPreference*. For 1,088 users, we obtain an absolute improvement of at least 0.05 in terms of AP. We provide in Table 4 a close-up view of the two extremes of the performance curve. In the worst case (Bottom 1), the two ground truth tags 'peninsula' and 'winchester' correspond to abstract notions with rare frequency in the community set. As a consequence, the *Visual* model fails to predict these two tags, resulting in a worse personalized model compared to *PersonalPreference*. In the best case (Top 1), our model, by ranking 'balloon' at the top, improves AP from 0.333 to 1. Overall the proposed algorithm strikes a proper balance when combining *PersonalPreference* and *Visual* in the process of model personalization.

We also look into the scenario when richer personal tagging history is available. For 94.9% of the 118 users with $X_{u,past}| \geq 50$, we observe improvements when compared to *PersonalPreference*. While in the worse case there is a relative loss of 4%, in a successful case we reach a relative improvement of 60%. For a better understanding of (un)successful cases, we illustrate two of them in Fig. 4. For both cases, due to the divergence between the tag distribution in *Past* and in *Future*, PersonalPreference yields relatively lower performance, with AP scores of 0.285 and 0.195, respectively. For the successful case, however, pictures of flowers can be well annotated by the *Visual* model, with an average precision of 0.343. By cross-entropy based

Table 3: **Experiment 2. Comparing the overall performance of generic and personalized image annotation models. The amount of personal tagging history is reflected by $|X_{u,past}|$. Scores are averaged over users. A gray cell indicates the top performer.**

	$\lvert X_{u,past}\rvert = 1$			$\lvert X_{u,past}\rvert = 2 \sim 9$			$\lvert X_{u,past}\rvert = 10 \sim 49$			$\lvert X_{u,past}\rvert \geq 50$			MEAN		
Annotation models	*P@1*	*P@5*	*AP*	*P@1*	*P@5*	*AP*	*P@1*	*P@5*	*AP*	*P@1*	*P@5*	*AP*	*P@1*	*P@5*	*AP*
CommunityPreference	0.033	0.046	0.036	0.044	0.058	0.043	0.058	0.088	0.053	0.077	0.106	0.061	0.045	0.063	0.044
Visual [11]	0.175	0.108	0.079	0.198	0.128	0.090	0.249	0.164	0.105	0.304	0.200	0.118	0.206	0.132	0.091
PersonalPreference [21]	0.271	0.233	0.194	0.403	0.273	0.219	0.571	0.398	0.302	0.610	0.437	0.328	0.411	0.295	0.232
This paper	**0.307**	**0.244**	**0.209**	**0.439**	**0.293**	**0.245**	**0.597**	**0.419**	**0.328**	**0.655**	**0.469**	**0.356**	**0.445**	**0.313**	**0.257**

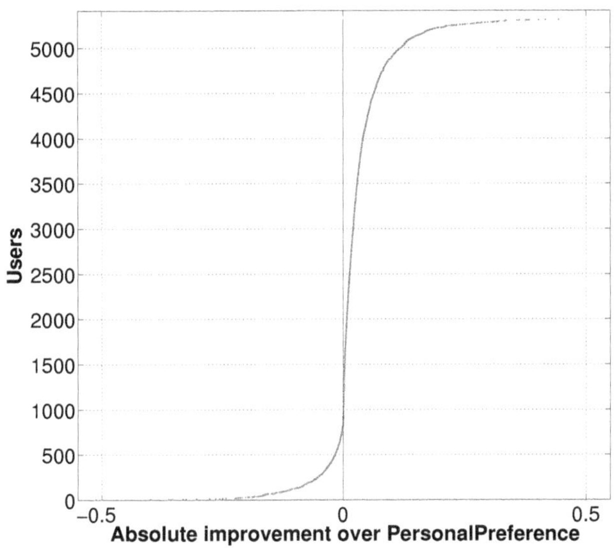

Figure 3: Experiment 2. Comparing two personalized models: The proposed model *versus* PersonalPreference. The performance measure is average precision. For the majority of users in consideration, we obtain personalized image annotation with a higher accuracy.

learning, our model reaches an AP of 0.455. Since images in the worst case are heavily edited, making image content analysis more difficult, *Visual* performs badly, with an average precision of 0.073. We conclude that unless both base image annotation functions fail, the combined model in general yields better or at least comparable performance, compared to the base functions.

Finally, we present some qualitative results in Table 5. The proposed algorithm emphasizes tags which are less frequent, yet more meaningful than the most frequent tags which tend to be general. To summarize, both quantitative and qualitative results verify the effectiveness of the proposed algorithm for personalizing automated image annotation.

6. DISCUSSION AND CONCLUSIONS

Automated image annotation is an important yet challenging research problem. In this paper, we study a novel aspect of the problem: *personalization* – personalizing generic image annotation models with respect to a given user.

We confirm the observation from previous work [21] that personal tagging preference is a strong source of evidence for predicting a user's future annotation. Similar to [21], our experiments also show that a model simply using personal tagging statistics clearly outperforms a content-based model [11] which exploits multi-feature visual content analysis. This nontrivial phenomenon implies that the landscape of personalized image annotation is much different from generic image annotation. Let us now look back at the fundamental challenge in image annotation, namely the semantic gap [24]. The objective aspect of the gap might be ultimately surmounted by machine vision, which aims for an understanding of the visual content independent of the user. Since the human interpretation of the content depends on the specific user in a given situation [24], personalization is essential for solving the subjective aspect of the gap. Thus, to fully bridge the semantic gap, personal information such as tagging history is a factor of major importance. Nevertheless, we challenge the conclusion of [21] that annotating images using personal tagging statistics is a performance upper bound for personalized image annotation.

To personalize generic image annotation models, we propose a linear fusion framework which jointly exploits a user's personal multimedia tagging history and content-based image annotation. The proposed cross-entropy based model enables the personalization process to be optimized in terms of an (arbitrarily) chosen performance measure. It is due to this technical innovation that we can go beyond the performance upper bound defined in [21].

We have conducted an extensive evaluation on 5,315 realistic users with varying amounts of personal tagging history. For the majority of users in consideration, the proposed personalization model surpasses the "upper bound". In an extreme scenario, where a user has only one tagged image available for training, we observe improvements for 67% of these one-training-image users, with a relative gain of 8% in terms of average precision. In general, richer personal tagging history leads to better personalized annotation models. These results clearly verify the effectiveness of the proposed framework for personalized image annotation.

Thus far, we have successfully exploited two heterogenous image annotation functions in the proposed framework. Since our framework is general, other annotation functions driven by varied evidence could be easily added in the future.

Acknowledgements

We thank the anonymous reviewers for their valuable feedback. This work was partially sponsored by the EC-FP6 VIDI-Video, the STW SEARCHER, and the FES COMMIT projects.

Table 4: A close-up of the two extremes in Fig. 3. Images ranging from Top 1 to Top 6 (Bottom 1 to Bottom 6) have the largest (least) absolute improvements, when comparing our model to the *PersonalPreference* model. In the context of personalization image annotation, we consider user tags as the ground truth. The function $g_v(x,w)$ indicates the *Visual* model [11], $g_{pp}(x,w)$ for the *PersonalPreference* model [21], and $G_u(x,w)$ for the proposed model. For each model, the top ranked tags are shown. Correct annotations are marked by an *italic* font.

		Annotation results					Annotation results		
	Truth	$g_v(x,w)$	$g_{pp}(x,w)$	$G_u(x,w)$		Truth	$g_v(x,w)$	$g_{pp}(x,w)$	$G_u(x,w)$
Top 1 	balloon	flower pink macro cat girl	mickey school *balloon* high gym	*balloon* gym high school mickey	**Top 2** 	market	beach water car street food	vendor indian *market*	*market* indian vendor bw two
Top 3 	rabbit sit sitting pose portrait	dog cat *pet* *animal* cute	cute coaster summer color sweet	*animal* *pet* *portrait* *bunny* young	**Top 4** 	toy anniversary	flower food nature garden dog	duke *toy* *anniversary* ho lady	*toy* *anniversary* ho lady duke
Top 5 	navy ship	boat bus harbour water river	usa *navy* *ship* alabama museum	*ship* *navy* usa museum alabama	**Top 6** 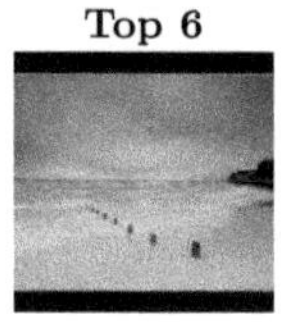	beach coast water storm weather	cloud sky sunset *beach* *water*	panorama canon rip ocean *weather*	*beach* *storm* *weather* rock rip
Bottom 1 	peninsula winchester	bridge building house city river	*peninsula* *winchester* water square fountain	fountain water square navy pier	**Bottom 2** 	nj squirrel explore	animal zoo night mountain building	*nj* *squirrel* halloween dog ny	manhattan ny dog parade *nj*
Bottom 3 	microphone	bw blackandwhite street people portrait	*microphone* music	music *microphone* smile vienna subway	**Bottom 4** 	elephant	tree animal nature green bird	*elephant* dog mutt collar	dog *elephant* mutt collar plant
Bottom 5 	toledo windmill	sky night cloud bridge blue	*windmill* holland sky landscape cloud	sky holland landscape cloud *windmill*	**Bottom 6** 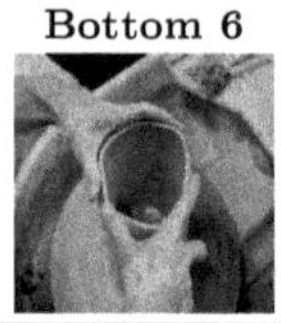	pottery ceramic wheel me	food flower dog macro cat	*pottery* *wheel* disaster big *ceramic*	disaster big bowl *wheel* *pottery*

7. REFERENCES

[1] P. Atrey, M. Hossain, A. El Saddik, and M. Kankanhalli. Multimodal fusion for multimedia analysis: a survey. *Multimedia Syst.*, 16(6):345–379, 2010.

[2] T.-S. Chua, J. Tang, R. Hong, H. Li, Z. Luo, and Y.-T. Zheng. NUS-WIDE: A real-world web image database from National University of Singapore. In *CIVR*, 2009.

[3] R. Datta, D. Joshi, J. Li, and J. Wang. Tagging over time: real-world image annotation by lightweight meta-learning. In *ACM Multimedia*, 2007.

[4] M. Duan, A. Ulges, T. Breuel, and X.-Q. Wu. Style modeling for tagging personal photo collections. In *CIVR*, 2009.

[5] A. Gallagher, C. Neustaedter, L. Cao, J. Luo, and T. Chen. Image annotation using personal calendars as context. In *ACM Multimedia*, 2008.

[6] M. Guillaumin, T. Mensink, J. Verbeek, and C. Schmid. TagProp: Discriminative metric learning in nearest neighbor models for image auto-annotation. In *ICCV*, 2009.

[7] M. Heikkilä, M. Pietikäinen, and C. Schmid. Description of interest regions with local binary patterns. *Pattern Recogn.*, 42:425–436, 2009.

[8] J. Huang, S. Kumar, M. Mitra, W. Zhu, and R. Zabih. Image indexing using color correlograms. In *CVPR*, 1997.

[9] J. Li and J. Wang. Real-time computerized annotation of pictures. *IEEE Trans. Pattern Anal. Mach. Intell.*, 30(6):985–1002, 2008.

[10] X. Li, C. Snoek, and M. Worring. Learning social tag

(a) A successful case

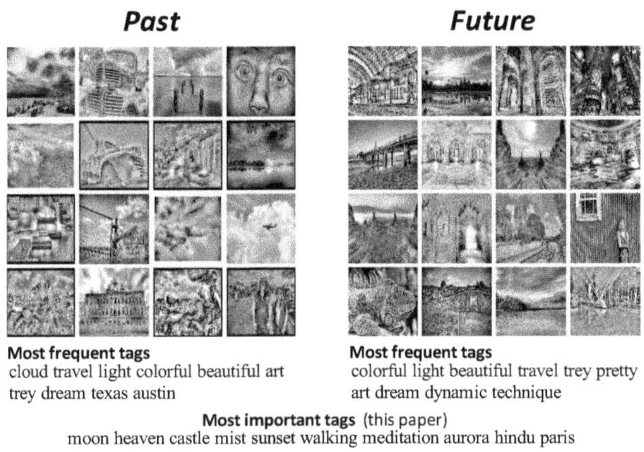

(b) An unsuccessful case

Figure 4: Illustrating successful and unsuccessful cases of image annotation personalization when rich personal tagging history ($|X_{u,past}| \geq 50$) are available for training. We personalize the *Visual* model $g_v(x, w)$ in terms of a user's *Past* and apply the personalized model $G_u(x, w)$ to annotate the user's *Future* images. In (a), $g_v(x, w)$ is stressed due to its good performance in *Past*, resulting in a relative improvement of 60% over PersonalPreference $g_{pp}(x, w)$. In (b), both $g_v(x, w)$ and $g_{pp}(x, w)$ perform poorly, resulting in a relative loss of 4% against $g_{pp}(x, w)$. Compared to $g_v(x, w)$ and $g_{pp}(x, w)$, unless both base functions fail, our algorithm generally yields better or at least comparable performance.

Table 5: Important tags *versus* frequent tags. The most important tags within a user's tagging vocabulary are found by sorting tags in descending order using $\sum_{j=1}^{t} \lambda_{i,j}$. Recall that $\lambda_{i,j}$ reflects the importance of an image annotation function $g_j(x, w)$ for predicting tag w_i. As the cross-entropy method was original invented for rare event search [19], our model recognizes tags which are less frequent yet more meaningful. For instance, 'sheep' and 'basket' for User 1, 'stage' and 'racing' for User 2, and 'house' and 'sunlight' for User 3.

	Top ranked tags	
$X_{u,past}$ of User 1	*Frequency*	*Importance*
	washington	sheep
	animal	dock
	wildlife	tent
	vancouver	peanut
	outdoor	basket
	nature	snake
	pet	feather
	female	holiday
	bird	black
	rescue	rooster
$X_{u,past}$ of User 2	*Frequency*	*Importance*
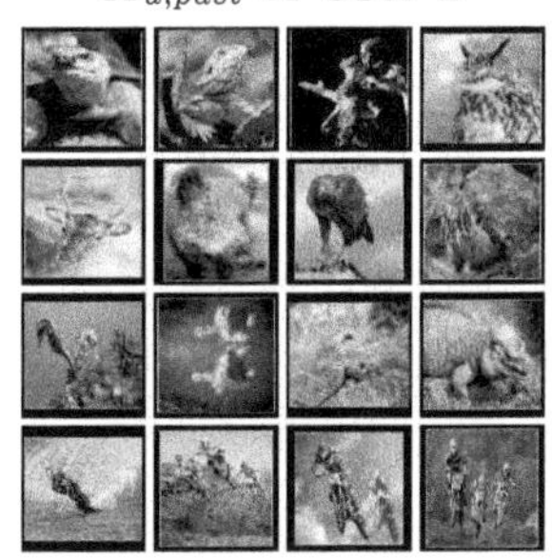	image	stage
	picture	music
	photo	racing
	animal	aquarium
	zoo	bird
	nature	swim
	austria	angry
	tier	mare
	google	flying
	art	floral
$X_{u,past}$ of User 3	*Frequency*	*Importance*
	cloud	land
	brasil	tunnel
	road	house
	sky	sol
	brazil	sunlight
	car	field
	blue	rural
	highway	ga
	landscape	muscle
	green	pb

relevance by neighbor voting. *IEEE Trans. Multimedia*, 11(7):1310–1322, 2009.

[11] X. Li, C. Snoek, and M. Worring. Unsupervised multi-feature tag relevance learning for social image retrieval. In *CIVR*, 2010.

[12] D. Liu, X.-S. Hua, M. Wang, and H.-J. Zhang. Image retagging. In *ACM Multimedia*, 2010.

[13] J. Liu, B. Wang, M. Li, Z. Li, W. Ma, H. Lu, and S. Ma. Dual cross-media relevance model for image annotation. In *ACM Multimedia*, 2007.

[14] Y. Liu, D. Xu, I. Tsang, and J. Luo. Textual query of personal photos facilitated by large-scale web data. *IEEE Trans. Pattern Anal. Mach. Intell.*, 33(5):1022–1036, 2011.

[15] J. Luo, J. Yu, D. Joshi, and W. Hao. Event recognition: viewing the world with a third eye. In *ACM Multimedia*, 2008.

[16] A. Makadia, V. Pavlovic, and S. Kumar. Baselines for image annotation. *Int. J. Comput. Vision*, 90(1):88–105, 2010.

[17] G. Miller. WordNet: a lexical database for english. *Commun. ACM*, 38(11):39–41, 1995.

[18] A. Oliva and A. Torralba. Modeling the shape of the scene: a holistic representation of the spatial envelope. *Int. J. Comput. Vision*, 42(3):145–175, 2001.
[19] R. Rubinstein and D. Kroese. *The Cross-Entropy Method: A Unified Approach to Combinatorial Optimization, Monte-Carlo Simulation, and Machine Learning*. Springer-Verlag, New York, 2004.
[20] P. Sandhaus and S. Boll. Semantic analysis and retrieval in personal and social photo collections. *Multimedia Tools Appl.*, 51(1):5–33, 2011.
[21] N. Sawant, R. Datta, J. Li, and J. Wang. Quest for relevant tags using local interaction networks and visual content. In *ACM MIR*, 2010.
[22] Y. Shen and J. Fan. Leveraging loosely-tagged images and inter-object correlations for tag recommendation. In *ACM Multimedia*, 2010.
[23] P. Sinha and R. Jain. Classification and annotation of digital photos using optical context data. In *CIVR*, 2008.
[24] A. Smeulders, M. Worring, S. Santini, A. Gupta, and R. Jain. Content-based image retrieval at the end of the early years. *IEEE Trans. Pattern Anal. Mach. Intell.*, 22(12):1349–1380, 2000.
[25] J. Tang, R. Hong, S. Yan, T.-S. Chua, G.-J. Qi, and R. Jain. Image annotation by knn-sparse graph-based label propagation over noisily tagged web images. *ACM Trans. Intell. Syst. Technol.*, 2:14:1–14:15, 2011.
[26] J. Weston, S. Bengio, and N. Usunier. Large scale image annotation: learning to rank with joint word-image embeddings. *Mach. Learn.*, 81:21–35, 2010.
[27] L. Wu, S. Hoi, R. Jin, J. Zhu, and N. Yu. Distance metric learning from uncertain side information with application to automated photo tagging. In *ACM Multimedia*, 2009.
[28] H. Yu, M. Li, H.-J. Zhang, and J. Feng. Color texture moment for content-based image retrieval. In *ICIP*, 2002.
[29] G. Zhu, S. Yan, and Y. Ma. Image tag refinement towards low-rank, content-tag prior and error sparsity. In *ACM Multimedia*, 2010.

Cross Media Hyperlinking for Search Topic Browsing *

Song Tan§ Chong-Wah Ngo§ Hung-Khoon Tan† Lei Pang§
songtan@student.cityu.edu.hk cwngo@cs.cityu.edu.hk
thkhoon@utar.edu.my leipang3@student.cityu.edu.hk

Department of Computer Science§
City University of Hong Kong
Kowloon, Hong Kong

Faculty of Information & Communication Technology†
University Tunku Abdul Rahman
Perak, Malaysia

ABSTRACT

With the rapid growth of social media, there are plenty of information sources freely available online for use. Nevertheless, how to synchronize and leverage these diverse forms of information for multimedia applications remains a problem yet to be seriously studied. This paper investigates the synchronization of multiple media content in the physical form of hyperlinking them. The ultimate goal is to develop browsing systems that author search results with rich media information mined from various knowledge sources. The authoring enables the vivid visualization and exploration of different information landscapes inherent in search results. Several key techniques are studied in this paper for developing these browsing features. These techniques include content mining and selection from web videos, space-time alignment of multiple media, and augmenting of search result with *when* and *what* information. We conduct both quantitative and user studies on a large video dataset for performance evaluation. Comparison with traditional techniques including storyboard summarization and video skimming are also presented.

Categories and Subject Descriptors

H.3.3 [**Information Search and Retrieval**]: Retrieval models

General Terms

Algorithms Performance Experimentation

Keywords

Video browsing, media content synchronization, event extraction, visual summarization

*Area chair: Dick Bulterman

MM'11, November 28–December 1, 2011, Scottsdale, Arizona, USA.

1. INTRODUCTION

Browsing search results while digesting the key information from massive pool of returned data is by no means an easy task. The existing web retrieval techniques mostly concentrate on targeted search and present the results by relevancy ranking. Visualizing different facets of information offered by search results is often not supported. In the domain of multimedia particularly, a mechanism that could facilitate the navigation of unexplored results and switch of new search focus is highly demanded. One example of text-based exploratory search is the Google "Wonder Wheel" [1]. In this system, a wheel shows search terms related to a given query. By rolling different wheels, the users are exposed to diverse sub-topics related to the original query.

Developing tools such as Google Wonder Wheel for multimedia search exploration, nevertheless, faces two practical obstacles. First, audio-visual content is difficult to be analyzed if compared to text-based articles due to the semantic gap problem. The meta-data provided by users could be subjective and incomplete. There is no solution for the semantic organization of search results, for examples, to support visualization of thousands of web videos returned for a query topic. Second, web videos of hot topics are massively uploaded to the Internet. It is not surprise to see that these videos are inter-related with partially overlapped visual content [13, 20]. In general, there is no consensus of how these somewhat related but diverse and continue evolving clips should be managed for search results presentation. The information offered by a clip itself is normally short and concise. Providing an overview to visualize different facets of a search topic from thousands of short clips intuitively is a task different from the traditional video condensation [22].

This paper addresses the problems of search topic browsing for web videos through the hyperliking of visual and textual snippets mined from multiple online resources. We consider two issues that enable search result authoring for information exploration: uncover the semantic themes (or events) of a topic; and organize content of short clips for matching potential events. We refer the former issue as *event extraction*, and the later as *visual summarization*. Given hundreds or thousands of returned web videos, video segments which are near-duplicate of each others are first extracted. These segments could be implicitly grouped as visual snippets for signifying different events or themes of a search topic. The problem of *visual summarization* is tackled by uncovering the essential information which is frequently found in video clips. On the other hand, various knowledge sources including wikipedia pages and news articles are collected to

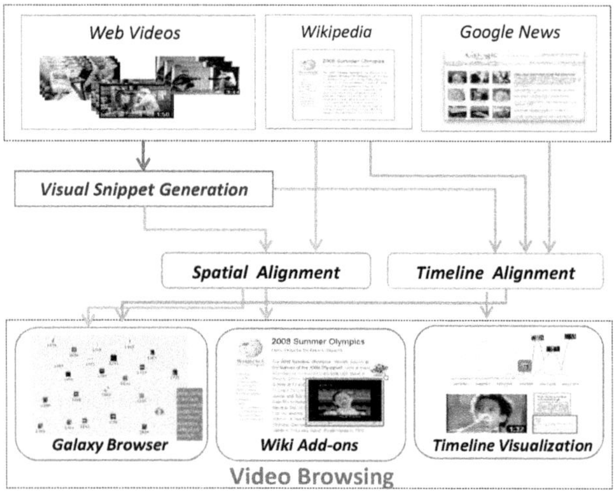

Figure 1: Overview of framework for cross media hyperlinking.

form the pool of textual cues potentially useful for describing visual snippets. Content alignment is then performed *temporally* and *spatially* to synchronize the visual and textual snippets from the video clips and knowledge sources respectively. The outcomes are "media hyperlinks" which link visual snippets with semantic description of events including the when and what information. Meanwhile, hyperlinks are also created for wikipedia pages whenever suitable videos describing the textual snippets are found. In brief, the problem of *event extraction* is tackled by exploiting external sources and aligning multiple information cues.

Figure 1 gives an overview of the proposed framework. First, web videos of a search topic are threaded to form islands of visual snippets based on partial near-duplicate processing (Section 3). Temporal alignment synchronizes the snippets with timeline extracted from wikipedia and news articles by network flow algorithm (Section 4). Meanwhile, spatial alignment matches the snippets with wikipedia page at the sentence level by tag cloud modeling (Section 5). Based on this space-time alignment, three browsing systems: timeline visualization (TL), wiki add-ons (WA) and galaxy browser (GA) are built (Section 6). TL allows timeline based visualization of search topics, and WA enables cross-reference interaction between different media. GA treats each visual snippet as a constellation and integrates TL and WA for exploratory search.

The main contributions of this paper are twofold. First, a computational framework is proposed for mining visual snippets, and more importantly, synchronizing the snippets with multiple online knowledge sources. Second, the framework seamlessly activates variants of browsing mechanisms for more efficient search result visualization and exploration.

2. RELATED WORK

Linear browsing, which clicks-and-plays clips sequentially, has been a traditional way of navigating search results. Nevertheless, different from text-based browsing, watching a long list of web videos of each lasts for a few minutes could be a tedious task. Grasping the overall picture of a search topic from watching hundreds of returned short clips also sounds infeasible. There have been numerous efforts indeed for improving the browsing efficiency from different viewpoints, including relationship mining, search re-ranking and multi-video summarization.

In commercial search engines such as YouTube, video cowatch statistics is a popular technique for video *relationship mining* [4]. The statistics, gathered from millions of web users, are derived by measuring the videos which are cowatched in the same viewing session. The suggested videos by cowatch are likely to be similar, and therefore, have a higher chance of falling into the same event of a topic. Nevertheless, while this feature (known as "related videos") is useful in general, the cowatch statistics does not explicitly tell the connection among videos. A more appealing mechanism is by depicting the video relationship through storyline. Early studies along this line include [7, 11, 18, 26, 28]. These works however are mostly constrained in the domain of news videos, where there are abundant professional-made text transcripts to be explored for constructing the story structure of a topic. For example, the mediaWalker developed by [10] provides a novel browsing interface for users to trace the development of news topics. The interface is built upon a directed graph structure that chronologically chains evolving events for browsing [11]. Similar work has also been demonstrated by [26] which represents evolving and peripheral events of news videos as a topic structure for browsing and summarization. Extending these works to web video domain, nevertheless, faces serious difficulties mainly due to the problem of "sparse text". Specifically the user-supplied text description is less reliable for building of topic structure to describe diverse video content. A recent effort by [15] is to densify the sparse text of web videos by a bipartite graph reinforcement model. The textual information are propagated and enriched by simply connecting videos which share common keywords. The propagated information, however, is limited and imprecise as text cue is considered as the only channel for spreading texts, while visual content similarity is ignored. As evidenced by [15] in the experiments, the amount of text after densification remains limited in describing topics. The work in [24] recently investigated the feasibility of constructing event structure for web videos by clustering user meta-data and visual feature trajectories. As shown in [24], constructing such structure is difficult as the features are rather noisy compared to news domain.

Another viewpoint for search results presentation is by *re-ranking* the retrieval list according to sub-topics [27, 29]. One typical approach is to optimize not only the relevancy but also the novelty of returned results. In other words, the search list is diversified by removing duplicate or highly similar documents. For multimedia search, in particular, this strategy is highly effective for preventing from the repeated watch of similar videos. A recent work which demonstrated the efficient elimination of duplicate web videos from search result is by [25], where both content and context features are integrated for real-time processing. Nevertheless, the approach in [25] can only effectively deal with full duplicates. For partial near-duplicates [20], which commonly exist in web videos, have not been seriously explored for re-ranking or sub-topic retrieval. Incorporating human interaction to refine search results is also a popular way of re-ranking. Well-known systems include InforMedia XVR [8], VisionGo [17] and RotorBrowser [5]. These systems, nevertheless, mainly focus on rapid localization of relevant items for targeted search, while lacking of mechanism for presenting different views of search results. In [6], thread-based video browsing was developed for visualizing the results from various search dimensions such as time, high-level concepts and visual proximity. However, as threads are defined as the linked sequences of shots and each thread is viewed separately, it is difficult to infer event-level information from threads for describing search topics.

Multi-video summarization has been studied recently to condense large amount of videos for providing a gist overview of search results [9, 14, 23, 21]. A straightforward approach is by extending the algorithms for single-video summarization [23], where the similarity notion is not restricted to within the shots of a video but the pool of shots from multiple videos. Techniques such as maximal marginal relevancy (MMR) and minimum description length (MDL) were employed to select the best set of shots from multiple videos for summarization [14, 23]. The recent work in [9] presented an approach for mining the "key shots" to summarize the search results. The key shots are identified by near-duplicate keyframe detection. With key shots, informative tags are further extracted to generate visual-textual storyboard. Meanwhile, key shots are also optimally assembled based on their time order in the original clips for sequential skimming. Another work by [21] shown the use of external knowledge such as Google Trends to chronologically order web videos for timeline based visualization.

3. VISUAL SNIPPETS GENERATION

Web videos of a topic, though visually diverse, are always somewhat correlated. Given a large set of videos associated with sparse text, the task is to mine the snippets that are capable of depicting the major patches of information in these videos. For instance, given the videos about "Beijing Olympics 2008", the candidate snippets are the videos describing major events such as "torch relay", "Fuwa Mascots" and "Michael Phelps swimming". A commonly observed phenomenon in social media is that the important events of a topic are often discussed by a large group of Internet users and in a short period of time. For video websites, this phenomenon turns into the fact that similar videos of an event, possibly captured from different viewpoints and in different snapshots of time, are massively uploaded. In addition, some video segments are cut from a video and then pasted into other videos with modifications such as supplement of captions and sound effects [13, 20]. This phenomenon gives clue that a practical way of mining visual snippets without the employment of semantics is by detecting the partial near-duplicate segments among videos. With this assumption, we define two terminologies here. *Thread* refers to as a near-duplicate segment that is commonly shared by videos. *Visual snippet* refers to as the set of videos which are interlinked, either directly or transitively, by at least one thread. In the remaining of this section, we present our framework for partial near-duplicate detection, which integrates and refines several existing works in the literature.

Figure 2 shows an overview of our framework which is composed of three stages. The first stage processes videos by uniformly sampling keyframes and extracting local interest points [16]. The keyframes are represented with bag-of-visual-words (BoW). For efficiency, BoW of $20K$ words is built on a vocabulary tree of two layers and indexed with inverted file structure [19]. To minimize the effect of quantization loss due to the use of BoW, hamming embedding [12] is

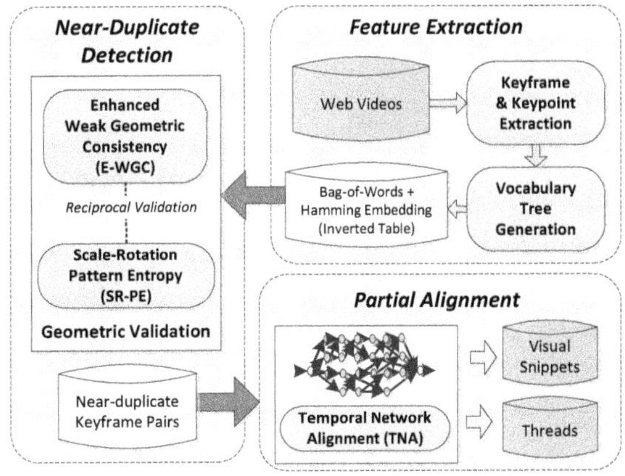

Figure 2: Framework of visual snippet generation.

employed to generate a short signature for each word. In the second stage, near-duplicate (ND) keyframes are retrieved based on BoW matching and signature verification. Basically each keyframe is treated as a query, and the set of candidate ND keyframes are retrieved. To verify the candidate NDs, reciprocal validation is performed by cross-checking the geometric parameters estimated by two algorithms: enhanced weak geometric consistency (E-WGC) [12, 31] and scale-rotation invariant pattern entropy (SR-PE) [30]. Both E-WGC and SR-PE estimate the scale and rotation parameters of two keyframes but with different approaches. E-WGC utilizes the by-product of local interest point detection to estimate parameters, and thus is sensitive to the robustness of point detection. SR-PE relies directly on the BoW matches for estimation, and thus is sensitive to the quality of BoW retrieval. We leverage this fact by performing candidate pruning whenever E-WGC and SR-PE give inconsistency estimation. In the third stage, the set of ND keyframes are consolidated to generate threads. We employ temporal network [20] which efficiently aligns the ND keyframes between videos by imposing temporal constraints. The set of aligned keyframes are then extracted from videos to form threads. Meanwhile, the videos which are linked through threads are also grouped to form visual snippets.

Figure 3 shows an example of visual snippets mined from the search topic "US presidential election 2008" which consists of 738 videos. Our framework extracted a total of 54 visual snippets. For illustration purpose, some of the snippets are aligned with the events in wiki timeline shown in Figure 3(c).

4. TEMPORAL ALIGNMENT

The temporal alignment aims to arrange the important web videos of a topic according to milestone events, and in addition, create hyperlinks for cross-referencing the videos and timeline information available online. One knowledge source which includes the event timeline is wikipedia [2], as shown in Figure 3(c). An intuitive approach for alignment is by directly matching the meta-data of web videos and the text description of event timeline. However, such matching may not be reliable since both ends contain only the snapshot description about events, of either a sparse set of texts from a video or a few short sentences from wiki page. In this section, we present a novel way of alignment by considering

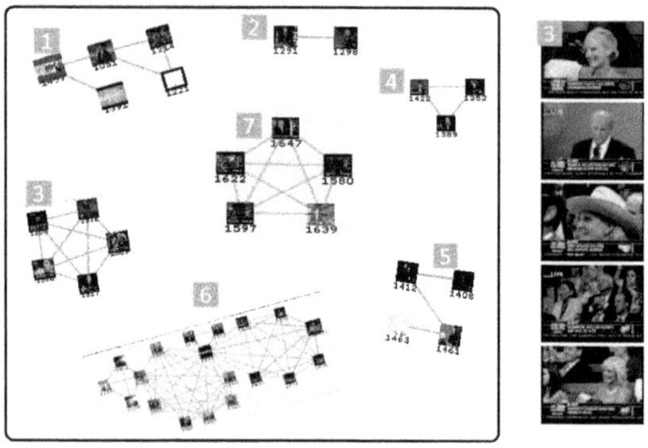

(a) Visual snippet (b) Keyframes

1. 2004 July 27 – *Barack Obama delivers the keynote address at the Democratic National Convention.*
2. 2008 August 25–28 – *The Democratic National Convention convenes in Denver, Colorado.*
3. 2008 September 1–4 – *2008 Republican National Convention convenes in Minneapolis-St. Paul, Minnesota.*
4. 2008 September 24 – *The first segment of Sarah Palin's interviews with Katie Couric airs on CBS News.*
5. 2008 October 2 – *Joe Biden and Sarah Palin appear at the vice presidential debate at Washington University in St. Louis.*
6. 2008 October 7 - *John McCain and Barack Obama appear at the second presidential debate at Belmont University, Tennessee.*
7. 2008 November 4 – *Election Day: Barack Obama and Joe Biden win 52.92 percent of the popular vote and 365 electoral votes to John McCain and Sarah Palin's 45.66 percent and 173 electoral votes.*

(c) Timeline

Figure 3: Examples of visual snippets for the search topic "US presidential election 2008". The correspondences between snippets (a) and events in wiki timeline (c) are labeled with numbers. The keyframes for snippet "3" are listed in (b).

four different sources: wiki page, news articles, videos and threads.

4.1 Problem Formulation

We employ a graph model, as illustrated in Figure 4, for temporal alignment. The model is composed of four layers of heterogeneous nodes. The nodes residing at the first layer represent the event entries extracted from a wikipedia page, while the second-level nodes are news ariticles related to a search topic. The third and forth layers are respectively the web videos and their threads. The edges between adjacent layers specify the similarity between nodes. Note that there are no edges between nodes of a layer. The problem of alignment is to find a path, which traverses from an event entry and reaches a thread, that optimizes the total similarity between any two adjacent nodes along the path. Denote the graph as $\mathbf{G}(\mathbf{N},\mathbf{E})$, where $\mathbf{N}$ is the set of nodes and $\mathbf{E}$ is the set of edges. We formulate the problem as *network flow optimization*, and the objective function is to maximize:

$$\text{maximize} \sum_{e_{ij} \in \mathbf{E}} f(e_{ij}) w(e_{ij}) \quad (1)$$

where the flow $f(e_{ij})$ is a binary indicator with value equals to 1 if nodes i and j are connected, and 0 otherwise. The term $w(e_{ij})$, which will be described in Section 4.1.1, signifies the importance (or weight) of an edge. Specifically, the optimization seeks for a path that has the largest capacity for carrying the flow through different layers (or information sources) of the graph. The capacity is characterized by the edge weights along the path. The result of optimization is a set of heterogeneous documents cross-referencing each other.

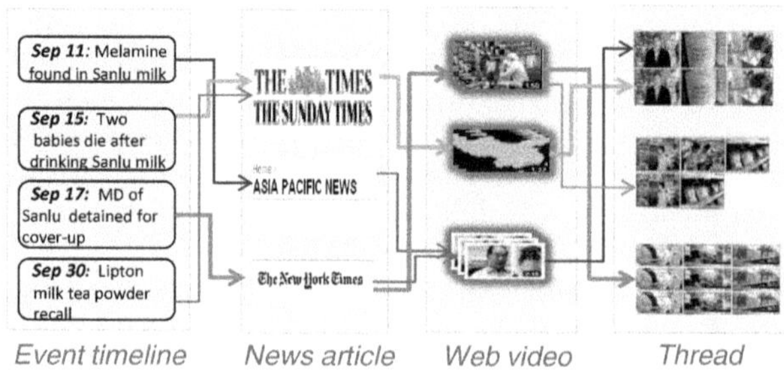

Figure 4: An illustration of graph model for aligning heterogeneous information sources.

There are three major significances with the introduction of the graph model in Figure 4. First, the second-layer news articles serve as "intermediate agents" before matching the meta-data of a web video and the short passage of an event entry in wikipedia. This layer densifies and enriches the amount of informative text for matching. In other words, both video and event entry can align with each other even in the extreme case where there are no common words between them, as long as there is a news article which bridges them. Second, only the videos belong to threads are considered for alignment. These videos are likely to be representative since they contain near-duplicate segments which are repeatedly reused for signifying major events and changes of perspective. Third, the result of aligning heterogeneous information sources can be directly utilized to develop the browsing interface which will be described in Section 6.

4.1.1 Edge Weighting

There are two kinds of edges in $\mathbf{G}$ for inter-relating different natures of nodes: binary and weighted edges. The former is for specifying visual similarity while the later is for text similarity. The binary edges basically group together the set of web videos according to the threads which are mined using the approach described in Section 3. Or equivalently, the edges link videos to their corresponding threads. The value of an edge is either 1 or 0 depending on the belonging of a video to a thread. The weighted edge, on the other hand, is used for characterizing node proximity, for example, between an event entry (or web video) $\mathcal{W}$ and a news articles $\mathcal{N}$. The edge weight is quantified using text cue as following:

$$Sim(\mathcal{W},\mathcal{N}) = \sum_{w \in \mathcal{W} \cap \mathcal{N}} \text{TF-IDF}(w) \quad (2)$$

Both nodes $\mathcal{W}$ and $\mathcal{N}$ are represented by a set of keywords. The similarity basically measures the number of common keywords in both nodes. Nevertheless, direct counting the number of common keywords may overlook the contribution of certain words to the similarity value. This is because the matching is usually conducted between a long article (news) and a short passage (wikipedia event entry) or a sparse set of texts (meta-data of a web video). In Equation (2), instead, the importance of a keyword w is weighted by TF-IDF computed based on the news article $\mathcal{N}$.

4.1.2 Network Flow Algorithm

The formulation in Equation (1) is typically a constrained binary programming problem that can be solved using network flow maximization [3]. By network flow, each edge e_{ij} is characterized by two terms, weight $w(e_{ij})$ and flow $f(e_{ij})$. Two artificial nodes, source n_{src} and sink n_{sink} nodes, are introduced. The source node is connected to all nodes of event entries such that all paths are originated from this node. Meanwhile, sink node is connected to all threads such that this is a node where all paths terminate. The solution of network flow should obey the equilibrium constraint so that the optimal path must not be broken at any point from the source to sink. This constraint can be characterized by network flow conservation where the net inflows and the outflows at a particular node must be equal to zero. In other words, Equation (1) can be effectively solved subject to the following conditions:

$$\sum_{e_{in} \in E_{in}(n)} f(e_{in}) - \sum_{e_{out} \in E_{out}(n)} f(e_{out}) = 0, \quad \forall n \in \mathbf{N} \quad (3)$$

$$\sum_{e_{out} \in E_{out}(n_{src})} f(e_{out}) = 1 \quad (4)$$

$$\sum_{e_{in} \in E_{in}(n_{sink})} f(e_{in}) = 1 \quad (5)$$

$$0 \leq f(e_{ij}) \leq 1, \quad \forall e_{ij} \in \mathbf{E} \quad (6)$$

where $E_{in}(n)$ and $E_{out}(n)$ denote the set of in-coming edges and out-going edges of node n respectively. Equations (3) to (6) impose the flow conservation constraints to control a well-behaved weight transfer from the source to sink node. The unimodality property [3] of network flow formulation ensures that the solution must be binary. Thus, the set of nodes traversed by the optimal path indicated by $f(.) = 1$ constitutes the solution. This path, which contributes the largest accumulated weights, corresponds to the various information sources that are best aligned. Since there always exists a valid path from the source to sink, by convexity property, Equation 1 will converge into a global solution [3].

In the implementation, we target to align each event entry in wikipedia page to a web video, as long as the accumulated weights of the path are significantly large. Thus, the network flow algorithm is iteratively run, in a way that the current optimal path is removed from the graph before the start of next iteration. The procedure stops when all the event entries are attempted for temporal alignment.

4.2 Efficient and Robust Alignment

The size of graph can become large when there are hundreds to thousands of web videos to be matched. On the other hand, the alignment also becomes difficult when the objective is to select one video out of this excessive number of noisy and diverse clips for matching against an event entry. An efficient solution is by detecting the potential hot times of a search topic, and then performing temporal alignment separately for each hot time. In other words, in each alignment, only the event entries, news articles and videos that fall within the hot time are considered for matching. This results in faster and more robust alignment, owing to a smaller pool of candidate videos which have higher likelihood to be matched is considered by the network flow algorithm.

We adopt the strategy in [21] to detect the hot times of a search topic. The detection is based on the statistics from Google Trends and Youtube video upload count. The former, especially, provides the search volume index to summarize the number of queries for a topic on Google search engine across time. The index reflects the temporal changes of user interest, and the peaks of index approximate the occurrence of milestone events under a topic. Similar observation is also found for Youtube video upload count, but there is normally a time lag between these two statistics. Similar to [21], we use month as the unit of hot time, and identify the hot months by first fusing the statistics from search volume index and video upload count. Thresholding technique is then employed to sample the hot months of a search topic. Temporal alignment is carried out sequentially for each detected hot month to align the event entries and video clips uploaded within the month.

To guarantee reliable matching, the recall of representative news articles is important. For example, using search query topic such as "US Presidential Election 2008" will easily result in miss of articles about critical events such as "Sarah Palin's teen daughter pregnant", which has impact for Palin's candidacy. To tackle this problem, the frequent keyword sets associated with each hot month are mined for retrieving online news articles. The keyword sets are obtained by the tri-gram frequent itemset mining algorithm. The examples of keyword sets include "democratic national convention", "barack obama debate" and "palin teen pregnant". These sets broaden the coverage of a search topic, and are more discriminative in recalling back the relevant and representative articles for temporal alignment.

5. SPATIAL LINKING

While timeline information provides valuable clue for event detection and alignment, not all the wiki pages have a well-structured time-event entries as shown in Figure 3(c). The wiki page of a topic is usually a free-style description of text composed of sections, paragraphs and sentences. The narration of an event could happen at a sentence, a paragraph, or even arbitrarily in different sections of a page. Furthermore, several events may be interchangeably reported, but altogether depicting the evolution of a topic. In most cases, the time information could be missing or is ambiguous to be resolved if without the analysis of contextual relationship among sentences. In short, temporal alignment between events and web videos could be difficult when the time cue is weakly described.

Instead of performing temporal alignment, this section describes the extraction of textual snippets directly from wiki pages by matching with web videos. We name this process as "spatial alignment" since time cue is not explicitly utilized, and more importantly, the matching is conducted directly at the sentence level. Intuitively, the matching could be difficult, since in contrast to temporal alignment, additional cues such as timeline and news articles are not available for exploitation. To guarantee robust alignment, we leverage the tag cloud pooled from the web videos of a visual snippet for matching. More specifically, rather than brute-force matching the sentences and videos for finding the best alignment, the matching is conducted between sentences and visual snippets.

The problem statement of spatial alignment is defined as follows. Denote $\mathcal{V}$ as the tag cloud of a visual snippet, and $\mathbf{S} = \{\mathcal{S}_1, \mathcal{S}_2, \ldots, \mathcal{S}_m\}$ as the set of m sentences from a wiki page. The task is to find the best sentence $\mathcal{S}^*$ that narrates

$\mathcal{V}$:

$$\mathcal{S}^* = \arg max_{\mathcal{S}_k \in \mathbf{S}}\{\mathcal{V} \cap \mathcal{S}_k\} \quad (7)$$

where the matching is based on counting the number of keywords in a sentence that also appear in the visual snippet. In our implementation, more than one sentence, specifically a passage of several sentences, might be extracted for a $\mathcal{V}$ if the retrieved sentences with high match are spatially close to each other. This also ensures that the contextual narration among sentences be well preserved for describing $\mathcal{V}$. The end result of alignment is a set of $(\mathcal{V}, \mathcal{S}^*)$ pairs. We further select one or several videos from a snippet which contribute the most number of words to tag cloud of $\mathcal{V}$ as the representatives. These videos are hyperlinked to the corresponding wiki page at the sentence-level for cross-reference browsing.

Using visual snippets as the unit for matching offers several advantages. First, a snippet, which is formed by videos inter-linked by threads, offers a denser and more comprehensive description of one or several events. Thus, the richer set of texts ideally will provide a better ground for more reliable sentence-level matching. Second, redundant matching, such as the repeated match of similar videos to different sentences, can be avoided. This is simply because the sets of partially near-duplicate videos have been clustered by snippets before matching. Third, the number of snippets is significantly less than videos, and thus the matching can be carried out more efficiently.

6. TOPICAL BROWSING

The techniques presented in sections 4 and 5 enable three types of browsing systems: (a) timeline based visualization, (b) wiki add-ons, and (c) galaxy browsing, as illustrated in Figure 5. Each system has its own features, and offers different experiences for exploring search topics. Timeline based visualization links together web videos and news articles of milestone events, while providing a gist overview of event evolution over time. Wiki add-ons, on the other hand, cross-references wikipedia pages and web videos, where a user can jump back and forth between two different media. Galaxy browsing supports the exploration and identification of information patches, by showing a galaxy view of visual snippets and how different videos are inter-linked with each other. A user can slide cursor to navigate different snippets and zoom in to view the detailed information.

Among these three systems, timeline based visualization explicitly links the major videos and news articles of events to time. The available key events offered by the pool of retrieved videos of a search topic are revealed to users by indicating the time of occurrence on the trend chart. In Figure 5(a), a user can click an event label on the trend chart, and the system will prompt an essential video together with textual snippets summarizing the event. The snippets are extracted from wiki timeline and the news articles which are most aligned with the web video based on the network flow algorithm as described in Section 4.1.2. By further clicking the link associated with news snippet, the corresponding online news article will be shown. The trend chart also gives clues to the relative importance of events, which provides another dimension for users to navigate the search result.

While timeline visualization is efficient in depicting the temporal evolution of a search topic, there are topics which are not well structured with time. Even there is, the time information may not be available online for use. Wiki add-ons gives another view of browsing search result when timeline is not available, and is especially suitable for users who have little or no knowledge about the events of a search topic. As shown in Figure 5(b), when reading a wiki page, users can click sentence for viewing one or multiple videos hyperlinked to the description.

Galaxy browsing bundles timeline visualization and wiki add-ons, in addition, visualizes the video relationship in the form of visual snippets. Each snippet is hyperlinked with text snippets which may include *when* and *what* information extracted from wikipedia pages based on temporal and spatial alignment. The snippets help users quickly understand the information they encounter, and make decision about which navigational path to follow. By clicking a snippet, the system will bring users to the set of available information. As shown in Figure 5(c), these include the timeline of event under investigation and the paragraphs extracted from wiki page with key sentences being highlighted.

7. EXPERIMENTS

We used the web video dataset in [24] consisting of 22 search topics and approximately 22,000 web videos for performance evaluation. The topics were selected based on the top 10 news happened during 2006 to 2009 as recommended by CNN, TIMES and Xinhua. The search topics, as listed in Table 1, were issued to YouTube and all the returned videos were crawled to construct the dataset. Table 1 shows the details of dataset for 22 search topics, along with the number of snippets and threads being generated by our approach in Section 3. We manually check the result. The accuracy of threading is approximately 80%. About 60% of snippets are semantically meaningful. Noisy snipppets are mostly formed due to anchor person shots and logos.

The collected dataset shown in Table 1 basically covers different characteristics of search topics for experimental evaluation. The topics differ in terms of duration persistence and content complexity. For example, the videos about topic-18 (Iran nuclear program) last for several years from 2006 to 2009, while the videos about topic-7 (Virginia tech massacre) only span for one month from April to May of year 2007. However, the persistence of a search topic does not necessarily imply the complexity of a topic. For example, topic-22 (Michael Jackson dead) lasts for few months but the videos comprise a series of sub-topics like "cardiac arrest", "moonwalk", "memorial tribute" and "last rehearsal". In contrast, the videos for topic-12 (California wildfire) happen periodically for several years, but the content is relatively homogeneous.

7.1 Objective Evaluation

We conduct evaluation separately for temporal alignment and spatial linking. The experiment for temporal alignment is carried out for 9 topics which have the timeline information as shown in Table 1. While for spatial linking, we filter few topics which have no English version of wiki pages from experiments. In both experiments, the video titles, descriptions and tags are extracted as the meta-data. Standard pre-processing such as stop word removal and Porter stemming is applied to the meta-data before matching.

Temporal Alignment. We compare our approach based on network flow algorithm with a baseline which matches the event entries extracted from wiki timeline and the meta-data of videos directly. The baseline is basically a greedy ap-

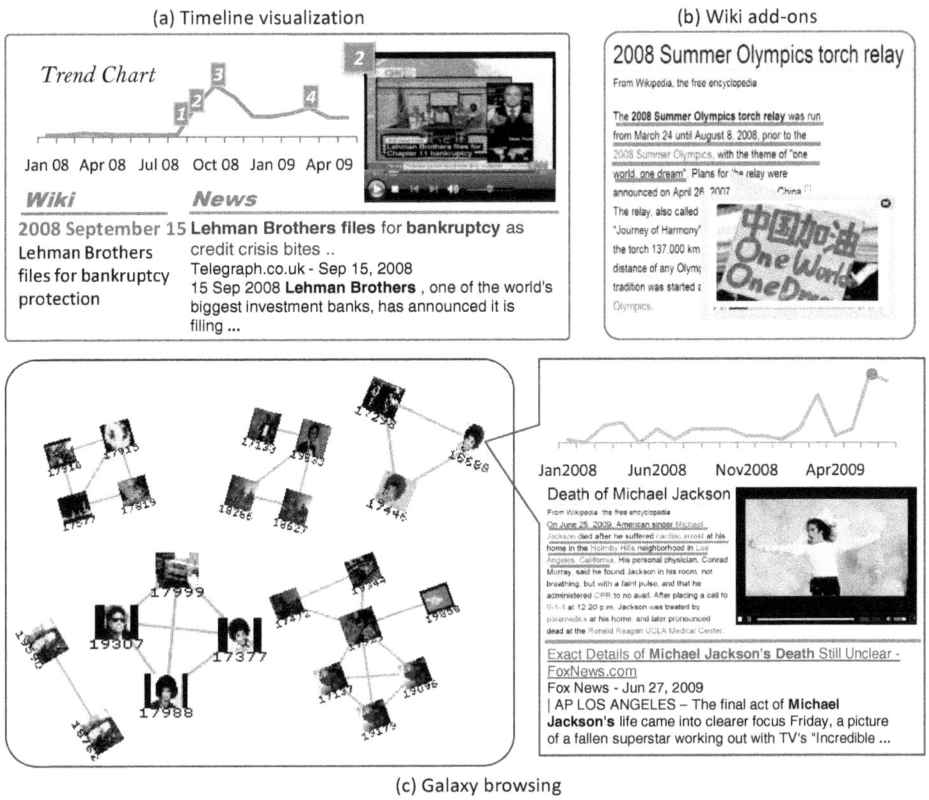

Figure 5: The three developed browsing systems based on media content synchronization.

proach similar to [21], where one-to-one matching between videos and events is performed within each hot month of a topic. Similar to our approach, the video-event similarity is measured based on the accumulated tf-idf score between them. The major difference between both methods are: our approach considers news articles as the bridge for matching event entries and videos, and in addition, threads mined from the set of returned videos are used to filter less important videos from matching. We evaluate the performance based on precision and recall. Recall measures the number of events being matched to relevant videos. Precision examines the ability of an approach in reducing the false alarm among the established matches. A match is regarded as relevant when the video is related or partially related to the target event. Since "relevancy" is subjective, as long as the event is the main focus of video, we regard the match as relevant. Since our approach also considers news articles, we impose an additional constraint that the matched news article should also be somewhat related in order to acknowledge an match as relevant.

Table 2 shows the result of temporal alignment. The result indicates that our approach outperforms baseline in terms of precision and recall. Especially, among the established alignments, approximately 75% of them are regarded as relevant, which is significantly better than the baseline. Few topics, however, are suffered from lower precision due to the fact that the underlying events are entangling and not discriminative. For instance, topic-1 (Economic collapse) contains the keywords "bank", "mortgage" and "federal" in several entries of events. Similarly for topic-10 (Melamine) where the common keywords in events are "Sanlu", "Milk" and "Melamine". The recalls for both approaches are not high. This is simply because wiki page tends to give a more detailed description of a topic than videos. For instance in topic-4 (Mumbai terror attack), there are event entries describing the preparation before the terror attack such as arming with weapon, leaving for Mumbai by ship and the route. We do not find any videos which could match to these events. Similar observation is also found for topic-1 (Economic collapse) and topic-21 (Swine flu). In general, compared to baseline, our approach benefits from the proposed graph model in the way that the news articles are able to densify the sparse text in video meta-data and lead to better alignment performance. The use of threads also enhances the chance of matching relevant videos to events.

Spatial Linking. To show the benefit of using visual snippets for matching sentences, we compare our approach to a baseline which matches the meta-data of popular videos to sentences. The popularity of a video is measured based on user view count. For each topic, we rank the videos by popularity and select a subset of them for matching. Table 3 shows the results in terms of precision. Because the result of baseline approach is noisy in general, the precision is calculated up to a depth of k, where k is the number of events detected by our approach. As indicated in Table 3, our approach using the tag cloud pooled from visual snippets offers a much better performance than the baseline. From our analysis, popular videos are mostly interesting videos but are not necessarily informative. In addition, without employing visual snippets to constraint the matching, some sentences are matched to videos of similar version. This in-

Table 1: Dataset

ID	Topic	Video #	Visual Snippet #	Thread #	Timeline (News #)
1	Economic collapse	1025	76	95	Yes (84)
2	US president election 2008	738	54	91	Yes (96)
3	Beijing olympics	1098	60	121	
4	Mumbai terror attack	423	42	52	Yes (65)
5	Russia Georgia war	749	63	112	Yes (42)
6	Somali pirates	410	47	60	
7	Virginia Tech massacre	682	59	72	Yes (32)
8	Israel attack gaza	802	72	113	
9	Beijing olympic torch relay	655	42	74	
10	Melamine	783	54	81	Yes (68)
11	Sichuan earthquake	1458	139	254	
12	California wildfires	426	10	14	
13	London terrorist attacks	784	58	122	
14	Oil price	759	49	65	
15	Myanmar cyclone	613	80	133	
16	Kosovo independence	524	24	38	
17	Russia presidential election	1335	96	120	
18	Iran nuclear program	1056	85	145	Yes (72)
19	Israeli-Palestine peace	586	31	54	
20	Korea nuclear test	1060	88	118	Yes (32)
21	Swine flu	1153	78	105	Yes (146)
22	Death of Michael Jackson	1865	139	252	

Table 2: Performance evaluation for temporal alignment. The parenthesis in the second column indicates the number of hot months.

ID	Event #	Detected events	*Our approach* Prec	*Our approach* Rec	*Baseline* Prec	*Baseline* Rec
1	30 (3)	6	0.33	0.07	0.17	0.03
2	26 (5)	8	0.62	0.19	0.25	0.08
4	4 (1)	2	1.00	0.50	1.00	0.50
5	17 (1)	3	1.00	0.18	0.33	0.06
7	6 (1)	2	1.00	0.33	0.50	0.17
10	31 (2)	10	0.40	0.13	0.50	0.16
18	3 (1)	2	1.00	0.67	0.50	0.33
20	3 (1)	3	0.67	0.67	0.67	0.67
21	22 (1)	4	0.50	0.10	0.25	0.05
Mean		5	0.73	0.31	0.46	0.23

deed indicates the significance of having visual snippets for minimizing redundant matches.

By investigating the hyperlinking results, among the correct alignments, basically a match between a visual snippet and sentence(s) indicates a different event. By comparing this result to temporal alignment, more events, of average 10 events per topic, are detected. This is because sentences are contextually more informative compared to the wiki timeline which summarizes events with short descriptions. Take the sentence from topic-10 (Melamine): "A number of countries have imposed blanket bans on Chinese milk products or its derivatives, among which are Bangladesh, ... and Malaysia which have imposed specific bans on mainland Chinese dairy products which have tested positive for Melamine" as an example. The context provides informative background for reliable matching of the sentence with video meta-data. For topics where timeline information is not available, for example topic-11 (Sichuan earthquake), the detected events include "when and where it happens", "the aftermath" and "the memorial". The extracted sentences corresponding to these events provide objective description for summarizing different facets of visual snippets mined from this topic.

Table 3: Precision for spatial alignment. The parenthesis indicates the number of near-duplicate videos being linked to a wiki page.

ID	Detected events	*Our approach*	*Baseline*
1	6	0.83	0.83 (2)
2	9	0.67	0.33 (2)
3	9	0.89	0.56 (4)
4	7	0.71	0.71
5	16	0.81	0.69 (2)
6	15	0.67 (2)	0.20
7	4	0.75	0.75 (3)
8	8	0.75	0.75
9	6	0.67	0.00 (4)
10	6	0.50	0.33 (3)
11	11	0.82	0.55 (2)
14	2	0.50	1.00 (2)
15	7	0.71	0.71 (2)
16	7	0.57	0.43
17	14	0.64	0.32
18	12	0.83	0.25 (3)
21	14	0.64	0.57
22	17	0.88	0.41 (4)
Mean	10	0.71	0.52

7.2 User Studies

We conduct subjective evaluation to compare five video browsing systems: timeline based visualization (TL), wiki add-ons (WA), galaxy browsing (GA), video skimming (VS) and static storyboard (SB). The aim of evaluation is to study the practicality of these systems for browsing and exploring the returned web videos of a search topic. VS and SB are two classical ways of browsing videos [22]. We adopt the implementation in [9] for developing VS and SB. VS concatenates the key shots of web videos chronologically to generate a synopsis video. In [9], key shots are defined as the set of near-duplicate shots. In our implementation, we treat the set of threads mined using our framework as the key shots. SB, on the other hand, is a textual-visual board that puts together the keyframes and tags extracted from key shots as a static summarization of videos.

We define the following four criteria for evaluating the browsing systems:

- *Coverage*: To what degree the presented multimedia content retains the coverage of a search topic?
- *Precision*: Is the presented content always precise and relevant to a search topic?
- *Conciseness*: Is the presented content always concise and contains no redundant information?
- *Presentation*: To what degree the organization, presentation and functionality of the browsing system help in exploring the events in a topic?

The first three criteria basically assess the ability of a system in mining the essential information from web videos. The information should cover as much key events as possible, while being capable of minimizing the irrelevant and redundant events. The last criterion examines whether the mined content are presented in a manner that allows the efficient exploration of different events in a topic. We further define two criteria for evaluating the overall user experience in using a browsing system:

- *Engagement*: How useful the browsing system is in providing guidance for exposing the different sub-topics of a search topic?
- *Acceptance*: Will the browsing system lead to better user experience, if it is being used by social media websites such as YouTube and Wikipedia?

We invite 16 evaluators from different education backgrounds including computer science (12), linguistics (1), law (1), industry (1) and business (1). All the evaluators are familiar with video social media websites such as YouTube. The average age of evaluators is 28 and the standard deviation is 3.5. In the evaluation, topics are randomly assigned such that each topic is evaluated by four human subjects. Each evaluator is requested to use different browsing systems to explore videos under a topic. To minimize the carryover effect, evaluators are instructed to leave "wash-out" time between evaluating different systems. Furthurmore, the effect is also counterbalanced by assigning different order of topics for different subjects. After finishing exploring a topic, an evaluator is asked to rate the five[1] systems based on the aforementioned criteria. The rating is in the scale of 1 to 7, with 7 being the highest score (highly confident), and 1 being the lowest (not acceptable).

We summarize the evaluation result by averaging the rating for each topic from all the 16 evaluators. Figures 6(a) to 6(d) show the statistics for the first four criteria. Overall, the evaluators give higher rating to our three proposed systems than video skimming (VS) and storyboard (SB). From

[1]For the case where a topic does not have timeline information, only four browsing systems will be evaluated.

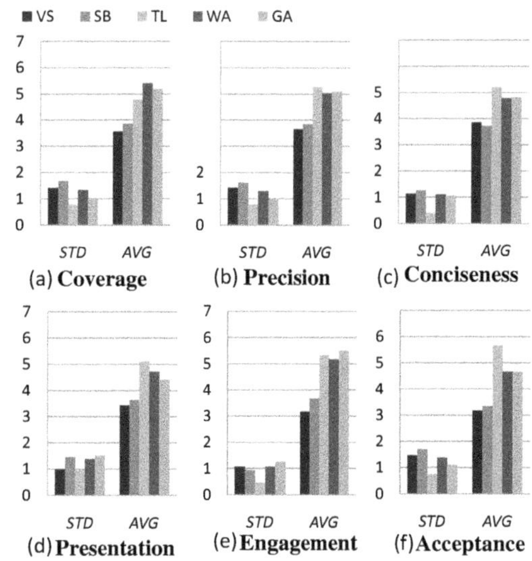

Figure 6: The average rating (AVG) and standard deviation (STD) of user studies for video skimming (VS), story board (SB), timeline visualization (TL), wiki add-ons (WA) and galaxy browsing (GA).

our analysis, evaluators indeed rely on the context description to understand the visual content. SB which provides a list of static images with sparse tag description is not informative in general. The concatenated keyshots in VS, on the other hand, do not preserve the event relationship and result in the poorest performance in terms of the criteria coverage and precision. Timeline visualization (TL), in contrast, encodes a wealth of descriptions extracted from wiki event timeline and news snippets, and achieves the highest score in the criteria presentation and conciseness. The trend chart, especially, offers a gist overview of key events for exploring search topics. Comparing all the systems, wiki add-ons (WA), which gives detailed description of a topic and is supplemented with aligned videos, obtains the highest score in coverage. However, the presented content is not as precise and concise as TL and galaxy browsing (GA). GA, interestingly, obtains high scores in all the four criteria. The feedbacks from evaluators indicate that the information presented by GA is comprehensive, but for ordinary users, GA is also relatively complicated to use than TL and WA.

Figures 6(e) and 6(f) show the rating for the overall user experience of using the five systems. The proposed TL, WA and GA show significantly better performance than VS and SB in terms of the two criteria engagement and acceptance[2]. GA achieves the highest score in search engagement. Most evaluators agree that GA is comprehensive and provides better guidance for exploring different details of a topic. The evaluators indicate that GA is especially suitable for browsing search topics of rich visual content such as topic-3 (Beijing Olympics), topic-4 (Mumbai terror attack), and topic-11 (Sichuan earthquake). For topics such as topic-1 (Economic collapse) and topic-18 (Iran nuclear program)

[2]The conclusion is based on AVONA (analysis of variance) test. First, the calculated F value exceeds the tabulated F value for p=0.001. Second, the 5% least significant difference between the means of any two systems also shows that the three proposed systems are significantly better.

which require understanding of background history, WA is still the best choice. TL, on the other hand, is benefited from the provision of timeline for browsing the event evolution of a search topic. Majority of evaluators give high rating that they would like to use TL for browsing videos in social media. In general, the feedbacks collected from evaluators indicate that the ability of synchronizing various online resources for content presentation is an interesting feature for multimedia information search.

8. CONCLUSIONS

We have presented our work for visualization and exploration of video search results by cross hyperlinking of different media. The visual content selection, based on automatic thread and snippet generation, provides a solid ground for elegant matching of various knowledge sources such as news articles and wikipedia pages. The proposed algorithms allow the effective extraction of events for augmenting search results with rich information. The user evaluation on the three developed browsing systems clearly indicates the advantages of search result authoring for information browsing and exploration.

Currently, we consider media content synchronization for three major knowledge sources: Youtube videos, Wikipedia and Google news. Future extension includes the generalization of alignment algorithms when more heterogeneous sources are incorporated. Potential issue to study is information extraction from contradictory content and diverse formats. In terms of computational complexity, our work does not support real-time synchronization of media in response to a user query. Processing one thousand videos could take about 1 to 2 days using a dual core CPU. Most of the computational time is consumed by the extraction of visual snippets. When distributed computing is considered, however, a search topic is expected to be available for browse within few hours. As "Google Wonder Wheel", it is suffice to show the search result augmenting and visualization for popular topics, which can be offline processed and mined from query log analysis.

ACKNOWLEDGEMENT

The work described in this paper was fully supported by a grant from the Research Grants Council of the Hong Kong Special Administrative Region, China (CityU 119610).

9. REFERENCES

[1] Google wonder wheel. http://www.googlewonderwheel.com/.

[2] Wikipedia. en.wikipedia.org/.

[3] R. K. Ahuja, T. L. Magnanti, and J. B. Orlin. *Network Flows: Theory, Algorithms, and Applications.* Prentice Hall, Reading, Massachusetts, 1993.

[4] S. Baluja, R. Seth, D. Sivakumar, Y. Jing, J. Yagnik, S. Kumar, D. Ravichandran, and M. Aly. Video suggestion and discovery for YouTube: Taking random walks through the view graph. In *WWW*, 2008.

[5] O. de Rooij, C. G. M. Snoek, and M. Worring. Query on demand video browsing. In *ACM Multimedia*, 2007.

[6] O. de Rooij and M. Worring. Browsing video along multiple threads. *IEEE Trans. on Multimedia*, 12(2):121–130, Feb 2010.

[7] P. Duygulu, J. Y. Pan, and D. A. Forsyth. Towards auto-documentary: Tracking the evolution of news stories. In *ACM Multimedia*, 2005.

[8] A. G. Hauptmann, W. H. Lin, R. Yan, J. Yang, and M. Y. Chen. Extreme video retrieval: Joint maximization of human and computer performance. In *ACM Multimedia*, 2006.

[9] R. Hong, J. Tang, H. K. Tan, C. W. Ngo, S. Yan, and T. S. Chua. Beyond search: Event driven summarization for web videos. *ACM TOMCCAP*, 2011.

[10] I. Ide, T. Kinoshita, T. Takahashi, S. Satoh, and H. Murase. mediawalker: A video archive explorer based on time-series semantic structure. In *ACM Multimedia*, 2007.

[11] I. Ide, H. Mo, N. Katayama, and S. Satoh. Topic threading for structuring a large-scale news video archive. In *CIVR*, 2004.

[12] H. Jegou, M. Douze, and C. Schmid. Hamming embedding and weak geometric consistency for large scale image search. In *ECCV*, 2008.

[13] J. R. Kender, M. L. Hill, A. Natsev, J. R. Smith, and L. Xie. Video genetics: A case study from YouTube. In *ACM Multimedia*, 2010.

[14] Y. Li and B. Merialdo. Multi-video summarization based on AV-MMR. In *CBMI*, 2010.

[15] L. Liu, L. Sun, Y. Rui, Y. Shi, and S. Yang. Web video topic discovery and tracking via bipartite graph reinforcement model. In *WWW*, 2008.

[16] D. Lowe. Distinctive image features from scale-invariant keypoints. *IJCV*, 60(2), Nov 2004.

[17] H. B. Luan, S. Y. Neo, H. K. Goh, Y. D. Zhang, S. X. Lin, and T. S. Chua. Segregated feedback with performance-based adaptive sampling for interactive news video retrieval. In *ACM Multimedia*, 2007.

[18] S. Y. Neo, T. Ran, and et. al. The use of topic evaluation to help users browse and find answer in news video corpus. In *ACM Multimedia*, 2007.

[19] D. Nistĺer and H. Stewĺenius. Scalable recognition with a vocabulary tree. In *CVPR*, 2006.

[20] H. K. Tan, C. W. Ngo, R. C. Hong, and T. S. Chua. Scalable detection of partial near-duplicate videos by visual-temporal consistency. In *ACM Multimedia*, 2009.

[21] S. Tan, H. K. Tan, and C. W. Ngo. Topical summarization of web videos by visual-text time-depedent alignment. In *ACM Multimedia*, 2010.

[22] B. T. Truong and S. Venkatesh. Video abstraction: A systematic review and classification. *ACM TOMCCAP*, 3(1), 2007.

[23] F. Wang and B. Merialdo. Multi-document video summarization. In *ICME*, 2009.

[24] X. Wu, Y. Lu, Q. Peng, and C. W. Ngo. Mining event structure from web videos. *IEEE Multimedia Maganize*, 18(1), Jan 2011.

[25] X. Wu, C. W. Ngo, A. G. Hauptmann, and H. K. Tan. Real-time near duplicate elimination for web video search with content and context. *IEEE Trans. on Multimedia*, 11(2):196–207, Feb 2009.

[26] X. Wu, C. W. Ngo, and Q. Li. Threading and autodocumenting in news videos. *IEEE Signal Processing Magazine*, 23(2):59–68, Mar 2006.

[27] C. Zhai, W. Cohen, and J. Lafferty. Beyond independent relevance: Methods and evaluation metrics for subtopic retrieval. In *ACM SIGIR*, 2003.

[28] Y. Zhai and M. Shah. Tracking news stories across different sources. In *ACM Multimedia*, 2005.

[29] B. Zhang, H. Li, Y. Liu, L. Ji, W. Xi, W. Fan, Z. Chen, and W.-Y. Ma. Improving web search results using affinity graph. In *ACM SIGIR*, 2005.

[30] W. L. Zhao and C. W. Ngo. Scale-rotation invariant pattern entropy for keypoint-based near-duplicate detection. *IEEE Trans. on Image Processing*, 19(2), Feb 2009.

[31] W. L. Zhao, X. Wu, and C. W. Ngo. On the annotation of web videos by efficient near-duplicate search. *IEEE Trans. on Multimedia*, 12(5), July 2010.

3D Cinematography Principles and Their Applications to Stereoscopic Media Processing*

Chun-Wei Liu
National Taiwan University
Taipei, Taiwan
dreamway@cmlab.csie.ntu.edu.tw

Tz-Huan Huang
National Taiwan University
Taipei, Taiwan
tzhuan@csie.ntu.edu.tw

Ming-Hsu Chang
National Taiwan University
Taipei, Taiwan
winble@cmlab.csie.ntu.edu.tw

Ken-Yi Lee
National Taiwan University
Taipei, Taiwan
kez@cmlab.csie.ntu.edu.tw

Chia-Kai Liang
Lytro, Inc.
Mountain View, California USA
liangck@gmail.com

Yung-Yu Chuang
National Taiwan University
Taipei, Taiwan
cyy@csie.ntu.edu.tw

ABSTRACT

This paper introduces 3D cinematography principles to the field of multimedia and illustrates their usage in stereoscopic media processing applications. These principles include (1) maintaining coordination among views, (2) having a continuous depth chart, (3) placing rest areas between strong 3D shots, (4) using a shallow depth of field for shots with excessive depth brackets, and (5) being careful about the stereoscopic window. Taking these principles into account, we propose designs for stereoscopic extensions of two popular 2D media applications—video stabilization and photo slideshow—to provide a better 3D viewing experience. User studies show that by incorporating 3D cinematography principles, the proposed methods yield more comfortable and enjoyable 3D viewing experiences than those delivered using naive extensions of conventional 2D methods.

Categories and Subject Descriptors

I.4.9 [**Computing Methodologies**]: Image Processing and Computer Vision—*Applications*

General Terms

Algorithms, Human Factors, Experimentation.

Keywords

Stereoscopic media, 3D cinematography principles, stereoscopy, video stabilization, photo slideshow.

1. INTRODUCTION

The success of 3D movies has ignited the so-called "3D revolution" and has paved the way to rapid deployment of 3D equipment. Stereoscopic and autostereoscopic displays have been deployed in theaters, billboards, televisions, computer screens, and even mobile devices. Binocular consumer cameras can be found now at very affordable prices. The wide deployment of stereoscopic displays and binocular cameras has made the capture and display of stereoscopic media easy, and has led to more such media. Thus we are seeing the advent of the stereoscopic multimedia era. Unfortunately, in spite of the rapid progress in stereoscopic hardware for both acquisition and display, little progress has been made on the software side, especially for consumer 3D media processing.

Professional 3D movie makers either use proprietary programs or even the current generation of 2D tools for 3D film editing. The fast deployment of stereoscopic equipment calls for more attention to be paid to research on stereoscopic media editing operations, especially those beyond professional 3D film editing. There are many operations that are not important to professionals but are essential for consumers. For example, in the film industry, visual quality and the comfort of 3D movie viewing often involve careful planning and controlling of several conditions, such as stable camera paths and depth of field. For a stable camera path, it is important that viewers keep their eyes on the objects or regions of interest without having to track shaky movements. For depth of field, it is critical for viewers to maintain convergence on the objects or regions without over-adjusting their ciliaris, which can lead to feelings of dizziness. Unfortunately, such planning and controls are unlikely for consumers when taking casual home or travel videos. Thus, additional processing is needed to ensure comfort when watching consumer stereoscopic videos. As another example, although stereoscopic photo slideshows have very little use in 3D filmmaking, consumers may find them very useful.

The main contribution of this paper is to introduce 3D cinematography principles and to incorporate these principles into 3D media processing algorithms for the rendering of 3D results that yield more comfortable viewing experiences. We use stereoscopic video stabilization and stereoscopic photo slideshows as two examples that demonstrate the use of these principle in stereoscopic media processing. For video stabilization, conventional monocular stabilization algorithms do not take into account binocular constraints and can destroy the important coordination between views. The resulting imagery could lead to eye strain or could end up not stereoscopic at all. During stabilization, we take into account such constraints to maintain binocular relationships between views and to deliver videos that can be viewed with com-

*Area chair: Dick Bulterman

MM'11, November 28–December 1, 2011, Scottsdale, Arizona, USA.

fort. As 3D media often have increased visual complexity and extended reading times, 3D photo browsing requires a smoother and gentler transition style than its 2D counterpart. 3D filmmakers often use depth placement, active depth cuts, and floating windows to adjust depth strength and smooth viewers' oculo-muscular activities [19]. In addition, for scenes with depth variation, viewers might fail to converge to layers with excessive depths, and could thus experience eye strain. To reduce this eye strain, one could blur the layers that viewers find it difficult to converge to. Such principles are useful in creating comfortable stereoscopic photo slideshows.

The rest of this paper is organized as follows. In Section 2, we discuss related work, and in Section 3 we introduce the 3D cinematography principles. In Sections 4 and 5 we demonstrate two applications which incorporate these principles: stereoscopic video stabilization and stereoscopic photo slideshows. In Section 6 we present our experiments, and in Section 7 we conclude and describe future work.

2. RELATED WORK

Stereoscopy and 3D cinematography. With the development of 3D cinema, tremendous effort has been expended to better understand the biological and physiological foundations of stereopsis. This includes studies on the stereo asymmetry effect [10] and on visual discomfort [12]. There are editing tools for 3D cinema [9, 26], but most of them directly manipulate the disparity map without high-level parameters such as eye positions. Recently, Lang et al. proposed a nonlinear disparity mapping method to allow users to adjust the perceived depth of a 3D film [13]. Koppal et al. proposed a viewer-centric editor for stereoscopic cinema [11] which allows manipulation using stereo parameters such as interocular distance, field of view, and location. All these tools are interactive tools specially designed for 3D filmmaking. They are designed mainly for adjusting effects along the new dimension created by 3D media, such as re-rendering after changing the interocular distance. These effects and operations often exist only in stereoscopic media and not in 2D media.

In this paper, we focus on generic stereoscopic media processing operations such as video stabilization and photo slideshows: operations that also exist for 2D media but that cannot be achieved using these 3D cinema editing tools. The only work we were able to find along this direction was Lo et al.'s work, which allows users to perform copy and paste for stereoscopic images [17] and Chang et al.'s work on content-aware stereoscopic image resizing [1].

Video stabilization. Most 2D video stabilization methods follow a three-step framework consisting of motion estimation, motion compensation, and image composition [20]. A common motion estimation approach for video stabilization is to estimate a dominant planar homography that stabilizes a large planar region in the video. In additional to 2D motion estimation, 3D motion estimation has also been explored [15] using structure-from-motion techniques. Note that although 3D motion estimation is used, the videos are still 2D. The goal of motion compensation is to remove high-frequency jitters from the estimated camera motion. This is the component that most video stabilization algorithms attempt to improve; many methods have been proposed for this, including particle filters, regularization and Kalman filters. Lee et al.'s method, a rare exception that does not follow this three-step framework [14], directly compensates for camera motion by smoothing feature trajectories. These methods all take as input a 2D video and output a stabilized 2D video. In contrast, Smith et al.'s video stabilization method takes a multi-view video as the input [24], but uses the surrounding views only to help stabilize the central view. Thus, as only the centric video is stabilized, the output is still a 2D video.

Photo slideshows. The plain display styles of popular tools for slideshows such as Picasa [22] tend to be dull. Music has been used to accompany the slideshows to create a more pleasant viewing experience. Chen et al. [2] have attempted to synchronize the emotions evoked by auditory stimulus of music and visual content of photos. By coordinating emotions in both auditory and visual contents, emotional expression is enhanced and user's photo browsing experience could be enriched. Photo2Video [8] (and Microsoft's Photo Story [21]) generates a set of 2D panning and zooming camera motions within a photo to create more vivid slideshows. Tiling Slideshow [3] provides users with a more pleasant browsing experience by displaying photos in a tiled fashion in tempo with background music. To better browse landmark photos, Photo Tourism [25] (and Microsoft's Photosynth) analyzes spatial relations among photos to allow users to interactively switch between spatially related photos. Photo Navigator [7] enhances the photo browsing experience for spatially related photos by attempting to make users feel that they are personally in the scenes and are revisiting the place. We are not aware of any system specifically designed to synthesize slideshows for stereoscopic photos.

3. 3D CINEMATOGRAPHY PRINCIPLES

Although 3D films have recently become popular, 3D cinematography actually has quite a long history, during which filmmakers have introduced several 3D cinematography principles to reduce viewing discomfort and to enhance the feeling of immersion when watching 3D films. For example, because of the increased visual complexity and extended reading time, 3D films usually require a smoother, gentler editing style than their 2D counterparts. Some of these principles are not only useful for professional filmmaking but also for stereoscopic image and video processing. In this section we discuss some of these principles [19] that could be relevant to stereoscopic media processing.

1. Maintain coordination among views. Stereoscopic displays simulate human stereoscopic vision by showing two images, one per eye. For stereoscopic vision to work, our two eyes must see images that are identical in all characteristics, except for a slight horizontal shift in object position, called *disparity*. Any other discrepancies in color, lighting, timing, focus, or image geometry can lead to an unconscious overload of the visual system. Depending on the intensity of the image defects, the audience may experience less-than impressive 3D effects, discomfort such as eye strain and headaches, or eventually a total loss of depth perception with double-vision effects.

From this most important guiding principle, we learn that left and right images should be processed in perfect coordination. Independent applications of 2D processing methods on the left and right views potentially introduce desynchronization and mismatch between views. For example, for 3D video stabilization, independent stabilization on the left and right videos can lead to vertical parallaxes due to zoom and rotation discrepancies. In addition, horizontal disparities can become inconsistent across frames, leading to inconsistent depth perception of objects. Similarly, for other popular editing operations such as color adjustment, tone mapping, depth-of-field blurring or inpainting, photographic mismatches in focus, lightness, contrast, blur, or textures can also result in unpleasant 3D effects.

2. ***Have a continuous depth chart.*** During preproduction, filmmakers often draw a *depth chart* to plan shots and gauge their feasibility. A depth chart illustrates the distribution of the depth budget through time. This can include the depth strength curves of the closest point, the farthest point, and the attention point. Figure 1 is an example. The portion of the depth range defined by the closest and the farthest depths used in a shot is called the *depth bracket.* A *depth jump* occurs if the depth brackets of two neighboring shots are too far apart. This forces the viewers to adjust their convergence from one shot to another. For example, if the previous shot (*out shot*) is a wide shot behind the screen and the next shot (*in shot*) is a close-up shot in front of the screen, the audience has to search for the correct convergence point in the next shot because it is too far away from the convergence point of the previous shot. In this case, stereopsis is interrupted and the suspension of disbelief is disturbed.

The respect of depth positions from shot to shot is called depth continuity. Depth continuity can be achieved by not cutting between shots for which the audience cannot immediately fuse in 3D the incoming left and right images. Another solution in 3D cinematography is to employ active depth cuts, in which the outgoing and incoming shots are reconverged toward each other over a few frames around the cut, thus leading the audience's convergence from the out-shot depth to the in-shot position. Reconvergence can be achieved by either converging the cameras in shooting or horizontally shifting the image planes in postproduction. By horizontally shifting the images, we effectively place the depth bracket at different depth positions. This approximates the effects of adjusting the vergence in the postprocessing. By placing the depth bracket at different depth positions, we can reduce the severity of the depth jumps while maintaining the 3D shapes of the shots. The standard 3D cinematography procedure for active depth cuts introduced by Steve Schklair is as follows (quoted from Mendiburu's book [19]):

1. *Bring the attention point of the out shot up to the screen plane.*

2. *Cut to the in shot, with its focus point placed in the very same depth.*

3. *Keep moving the convergence point, up to the in shot's correct depth.*

This procedure will direct viewers to follow the convergence directions without a blink. The movement should be just fast enough not to be detected, and slow enough to be easily followed. It is not necessary to place the depth transition point on the screen depth plane as long as it can bring shots to common ground and keep the dynamic convergence at a constant velocity.

One final note on depth jumps is that forward and backward jumps are not equal. Jumping from foreground to background is less stressful than the other way around. When jumping from background to foreground, the incoming convergence point is closer to the audience, and we must squint to restore stereopsis. This is more disturbing than moving from foreground to background, where we need only relax our visual muscles.

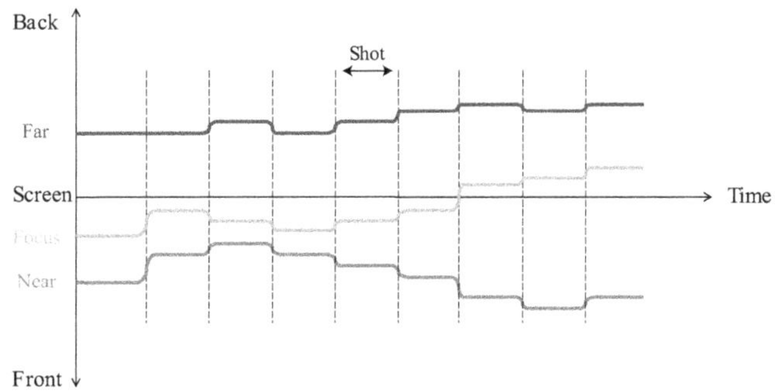

Figure 1: An example of a depth chart used in 3D cinematography. A depth chart shows the depth distribution of shots along time, and can include depth curves for the closest (red), farthest (blue), and attention (green) points. The depth range defined by the closest depth and the farthest depth of a shot is called the shot's depth bracket.

3. ***Place rest areas between strong 3D shots.*** Viewers can experience eye strain if they stare at strong 3D effects for too long. Thus, it is recommended that strong 3D shots should be interspersed with low 3D sequences, called *rest areas* because they give the audience a chance to rest their visual systems.

4. ***Use a shallow depth of field for shots with excessive depth brackets.*** 3D displays have range limitations. When objects are beyond the so-called comfort zone, i.e. too far away or too close, it is difficult for humans to perform depth fusion. In addition, for images of objects close to us as well as those far from us, although we can fuse them as long as they are within the comfort zone, we cannot simultaneously fuse, on the same picture, objects that are too far away from each other. In 3D cinematography, if the foreground and the background are too far away from each other, a shallow depth of field is often used to isolate the characters and to draw the audience's attention to the main character.

5. ***Be careful about the stereoscopic window.*** The stereoscopic window is a very important feature in 3D cinematography. When we look at a 3D photo, we are actually looking at a 3D world through a window defined by the edges of the display. Consider the case when a face is hiding behind the left edge of the display: your right eye sees about half of the face, including the nose. Your left eye does not see the nose, as it has been blocked by the left edge. A stereoscopic window violation occurs if the face is interpreted as being in front of the screen, because the face should not be occluded by the edge if it is in front of the screen. In 3D cinematography this problem is solved often by applying masks on the sides of the frame to hide what the eyes should not see: this is called "floating the stereoscopic window". The other related rule is to avoid the main character's hitting the top edge of the screen, as it would create the illusion that the screen is curved toward the audience.

Although these principles were developed for 3D film production, we advocate their use in the post-processing of stereoscopic media. When extending 2D media authoring methods to their 3D counterparts, in addition to the requirements for the original problems, these principles should be taken into account to ensure proper 3D content creation.

Different sets of principles may apply to different media and authoring operations. Among these principles, Principle 1 is fundamental; almost every stereoscopic media authoring method should obey it. Principles 2 and 3 are more relevant for temporal media editing. When the authoring operators cause changes in the depth bracket, Principle 4 should be taken into account. For example, the image stitching, or photomontage, operation combines multiple images together and takes union of their depth brackets. In this case, algorithm designers could choose to either select images with similar depth ranges or could instead apply shallow depth-of-field effects on the composites to avoid excessive depth ranges. Principle 5 plays a role when authoring operators re-frame media, such as when cropping, compositing, or resizing. These operators should ensure that objects of interest do not hit the frame border. In the next two sections, we use video stabilization and photo slideshows as examples that demonstrate how these principles can be incorporated in 3D media authoring.

4. STEREOSCOPIC VIDEO STABILIZATION

Amateur videos often exhibit annoying jitter due to the shaky motion of an unsteady hand-held camera. This jitter is aggravated with stereoscopic video because it requires more muscular and brain activity to follow shaky convergence points. To improve the experience of watching such videos, one important task is stereoscopic video stabilization, that is, the removing of unwanted perturbations in stereoscopic videos caused by unstable camera motions.

At first sight, a stereoscopic video is no more than two streams of videos. Thus, a naive solution would be to apply conventional 2D video stabilization on both video streams independently. However, this seldom works well because a stereoscopic video is a pair of videos that are not independent but are correlated. The naive method, as it completely ignores the coordination and synchronization between the two views as described in the principles of Section 3, can yield an unwanted vertical parallax as well as inconsistent horizontal disparities. The former destroys depth perception as the left and right views are not perfectly horizontally aligned any more, and the latter leads to shimmering artifacts. The inconsistent time-varying horizontal disparities are interpreted as time-varying depths by our brains. Thus, viewers perceive that objects move forward and backward arbitrarily.

Therefore, it is important during stabilization to add constraints to maintain horizontal alignment and consistent disparity. Our method achieves stereoscopic video stabilization by incorporating these constraints into the optimization process of Lee et al.'s 2D video stabilization method [14]. We first extract feature trajectories from the input video and build correspondences of features across the left and right views (Section 4.1), and then find an optimized set of transformations to smooth out these trajectories under these constraints (Section 4.2). Figure 2 visualizes the process. Figure 2(a) shows the per-stabilization feature trajectories over time for the left view of the *children* sequence. Note that these trajectories are jaggy due to camera shakes. The algorithm finds a set of transforms for each view to deform the video volumes for both views jointly, yielding smooth trajectories in the deformed video volumes, as shown in Figure 2(b) (left view). Once the features move smoothly after transformation, the transformed video sequence appears stabilized.

(a)

(b)

Figure 2: Visualization of feature trajectories (of the *children* sequence). (a) A frame from the left video, overlapped with its extracted feature trajectories before stabilization: these trajectories twist around in the video volume. After stabilization, feature trajectories become smoother in the transformed video volumes (b). Once trajectories become smooth, the transformed video sequence looks stabilized.

4.1 Feature Trajectory Retrieval

Robust feature trajectory extraction from video is crucial for trajectory-based video stabilization methods. Trajectories must be concatenated and pruned carefully to avoid the serious errors that arise from false matches. We basically follow the procedure in [14] to retrieve feature trajectories. However, since our input is a stereoscopic video, we take advantage of the two different views of the scene that we have at each time instance. Additional stereo constraints can be used to verify feature matches, greatly reducing the chance of false matches. Furthermore, in addition to matching features temporally to lengthen trajectories, we must also match features across views to obtain the correspondences between features in the left and right frames. These correspondences help us to maintain horizontal alignment and consistent disparity. That is, after stabilization, we require that any pair of features matched across the left and right frames has vertical coordinates and disparity similar to that before stabilization.

Feature detection. Our current implementation uses SIFT [18] for its accuracy and robustness in different lighting and blurring conditions. We detect SIFT features for each frame of both views.

Feature verification. Good feature matches between the left and right images reveal disparities, essentially leading to a sparse but accurate depth estimation of the scene. In addition, good matches in the temporal domain reveal information about camera shaking. Both are essential for our algorithm. However, noisy matches can ruin these estimates. Since we have images of two different views, for more robust matching, we apply RANSAC [4] to estimate a fundamental matrix [6] which encodes the two-view geometry for each time instance. Feature matches failing the fundamental matrix constraint are regarded as false matches and are omitted from further processing.

Trajectory tracking. After obtaining the features for each frame of both videos, our algorithm retrieves robust feature trajectories by making a forward sweep across each video. To extend trajectories from the current frame to the next frame, four steps—addition, linking, propagation by optimization, and pruning—are performed [14]. In addition to trajectories, we also have feature correspondences between the left and right images for each time instance from the previous step.

4.2 Stabilization by Optimization

We formulate the stabilization of stereoscopic video as a nonlinear optimization problem in the spatio-temporal domain. In the temporal domain, feature trajectories should behave smoothly so that the video is stabilized. In the spatial domain, we require that matched features are horizontally aligned and maintain consistent disparity. More precisely, for a stereoscopic video with n frames, we find a set of similarity transformations $\{T_l, T_r\} = \{T_l^i, T_r^i | 1 \le i \le n\}$ with respect to the left frames I_l^i and the right frames I_r^i to stabilize the video. The optimal set of transformations should minimize the following objective function:

$$E_t(T_l, T_r) + \lambda_s E_s(T_l, T_r), \qquad (1)$$

where E_t and E_s represent the temporal smoothness and the stereoscopic constraints of the transformed/stabilized stereoscopic video, respectively. λ_s is the weighting parameter balancing those two objective terms.

We define the smoothness function E_t as a weighted combination of the trajectory roughness function E_r, the zoom-factor function E_z, and uncovered function E_u. E_r represents the roughness of feature trajectories, which is related to the trajectory accelerations. For the j-th trajectory $\xi_j = \{p_j^i | 1 \le i \le n\}$, where p_j^i is the feature of ξ_j at the i-th frame, the acceleration $a_j^i(T)$ of ξ_j at the i-th transformed frame can be defined as

$$a_j^i(T) = T^{i+1} p_j^{i+1} - 2T^i p_j^i + T^{i-1} p_j^{i-1}. \qquad (2)$$

The roughness of a transformed trajectory is the sum of its accelerations along time. By summing up the weighted roughness values of all trajectories, we obtain the roughness cost term for a set of transforms

$$E_r(T_l, T_r) = \sum_{v=\{l,r\}} \sum_{\xi_j} \sum_{i=2}^{n-1} w(j,i,v) \| (T_v^i)^{-1} a_i^t(T_v) \|^2. \qquad (3)$$

We use the weighting function w to control the importance of each trajectory. The weighting function w is essentially a hat function which puts more weight on the middle of the trajectory and less to either end, as the ends of a trajectory are often less reliable. When the trajectory ξ_j does not have a corresponding feature at time i or view v, we set $w(j, i, v) = 0$.

When zooming in, a frame must be upsampled, which can lead to degraded quality. This is especially bad for stereoscopic videos, because excessive quality degradation often leads to a loss of depth perception. Therefore we attempt to prevent the zoom factors from being much larger than 1; we use the following zoom-factor function E_z^i to limit the zoom-factor s of each transform:

$$E_z(T_l, T_r) = \sum_{v=\{l,r\}} \sum_{i=1}^{n} [s_v^i > 1](s_v^i - 1)^4, \qquad (4)$$

where $[f]$ is an indicator function which returns 1 when the argument f is true and 0 otherwise. Note that although E_z is non-differentiable, it is so only at the point $s_v^i = 1$; therefore it does not complicate optimization in practice. Finally, we use E_u to penalize transforms which lead to large uncovered areas in the transformed videos [14].

Although minimizing E_t can generate two smooth videos for the left and right videos respectively, those two videos may not jointly make for a good stereoscopic viewing experience, as discussed above. For comfortable stereoscopic video viewing, any asymmetry between the left and right frames should be eliminated. Any discrepancy between the left and right transformations can lead to vertical offsets for matching pairs, resulting in eye strain when watching the stabilized video.

The term E_s in Equation (1) is designed to measure the stereoscopic quality of the stabilized video. The transformation set minimizing Equation (1) should strike a balance between video stabilization and stereoscopic quality, and thus provide the best visual experience.

Specifically, let $(p_{j,l}^i, p_{j,r}^i)$ denote a matched feature pair in frames I_l^i and I_r^i. Their horizontal disparity $(p_{j,l}^i - p_{j,r}^i)[x]$ yields an estimate for the depth. To provide consistent horizontal disparity for consistent depth perception, the transformed horizontal disparity should be close to the original disparity. At the same time, to maintain horizontal alignment, the vertical disparity should be close to zero. Therefore, we define the stereoscopic energy E_s as

$$E_s(T_l, T_r) = \sum_{i=1}^{n} E_s(T_l^i, T_r^i), \qquad (5)$$

$$E_s(T_l^i, T_r^i) = \sum_{j=1}^{N(i)} \| (T_l^i p_{j,l}^i - T_r^i p_{j,r}^i) - d_j^i \|^2, \qquad (6)$$

$$d_j^i = [(p_{j,l}^i - p_{j,r}^i)[x], 0]^{\mathrm{T}}, \qquad (7)$$

where $N(i)$ is the number of matched feature pairs at time i and d_j^i is a guiding disparity vector for matching pair $(p_{j,l}^i, p_{j,r}^i)$ which requires consistent horizontal disparity and zero vertical disparity. Here, the operator $[x]$ extracts the x-component of a 2D vector. (5) is optimized using the Levenberg-Marquardt algorithm. The initial solution is the set of uniform scale transformations with the scaling factor $s = 1.01$.

5. STEREOSCOPIC PHOTO SLIDESHOWS

Photo slideshows provide a more enjoyable photo browsing experience. Although interesting 2D slideshow effects have been studied extensively in previous work [8, 3, 7], they are not necessarily well-suited to stereoscopic photo viewing. The design of a good stereoscopic photo slideshow is not a trivial task. Without special care, viewers might experience discomfort when viewing stereoscopic slideshows. We focus on plain slideshows in which transitions are inserted between photos. Whereas common transitions for 2D media such as fade and wipe effects mainly serve cosmetic purposes only, for stereoscopic slideshows, transitions are an essential part of a comfortable viewing experience.

As explained in Section 3, depth jumps can lead to viewer discomfort. If two neighboring stereoscopic photos have very different depth brackets, it will require more effort from the viewer to switch between them, in terms of accommodation and convergence. If we are allowed to change the order in which the photos are displayed, we can reorder them to yield a better depth chart with fewer depth jumps (Section 5.1). Otherwise, if we are not allowed to change the order, for example, when the photos must be displayed in chronological order, we can use active depth cuts to introduce transitions between photos that will reduce the depth jump and resulting viewer discomfort (Section 5.2). Finally, for photos with excessive depth brackets, viewer discomfort may arise from an inability to focus on both ends of the images at the same

Figure 3: Depth charts of the slideshows. (a) The depth chart of original (blue curve) and reordered (red curve) image sequences with Δ_{ROI}. (b) The image sequence reordered using Δ_{ROI}. (c) The original sequence. (e) The sequence reordered using Δ_{JSD}. (d) The depth brackets of the original sequence. (f) The depth brackets of the reordered sequence (e).

time. According to the 3D cinematography principle, we can in this case apply shallow depth-of-field effects to blur part of the images to direct viewer attention to a narrower but more comfortable depth bracket (Section 5.3).

5.1 Photo Reordering

According to the principles of Section 3, we want to reorder the photos such that the depth jumps are as small as possible. We have explored two ways of estimating the depth jump. The first option takes into account regions of interest (ROIs). As humans tend to pay more attention to ROIs, disparity differences are weighted by their saliency values.

Given two stereoscopic photos I^i and I^j, we first calculate their disparity maps D^i and D^j as well as their saliency images Φ^i and Φ^j. As our method does not require very accurate maps, we employ a conventional binocular stereo algorithm [23] and a saliency estimation method [5]. The saliency-weighted depth jump Δ_{ROI} between these two stereoscopic images is defined as

$$\Delta_{ROI}(I^i, I^j) = \frac{1}{W}\sum_p(\Phi^i(p)+\Phi^j(p))\|D^i(p)-D^j(p)\|, \quad (8)$$

where $W = \sum_p(\Phi^i(p) + \Phi^j(p))$ is the sum of both saliency images for normalization. Δ_{ROI} is essentially the saliency-weighted average depth difference between two images.

Although it may seem to make sense to take ROIs into account, there is no guarantee that the viewer is focused on the ROIs when switches happen. Thus, the second option is to measure the depth jump, taking into account only the depth bracket but not ROIs. A depth bracket is simply the depth histogram Ψ^i of the disparity map D^i. We use Jensen-Shannon divergence to estimate the similarity between two histograms and define the divergence-based depth jump Δ_{JSD} as

$$\Delta_{JSD}(I^i, I^j) = H\left(\frac{\Psi^i + \Psi^j}{2}\right) - \frac{H(\Psi^i) + H(\Psi^j)}{2}, \quad (9)$$

where $H(\Psi)$ is the Shannon entropy for distribution Ψ.

Once we have evaluated the pairwise distance Δ between any pair of images, given a set of n images, the goal of reordering is to find a permutation π which minimizes the sum of depth jumps between neighboring images,

$$\sum_{i=1}^{n-1} \Delta(I^{\pi(i)}, I^{\pi(i+1)}). \quad (10)$$

This problem can be reduced to the classical traveling salesman problem, which is NP-hard. However, there are efficient approximation algorithms for it.

Figure 3 shows the results of the reordering. Figure 3(c) is the original sequence, and Figure 3(b) is the sequence reordered using Δ_{ROI}. Figure 3(a) shows the depth charts of both sequences. The blue curve shows the depth chart of the original sequence and the red one represents that of the reordered sequence. Reordering clearly reduces the number of depth jumps. Figure 3(d) shows the depth histogram of the original sequence. Reordered with Δ_{JSD}, we obtain the sequence shown in Figure 3(e), the depth histograms of which are shown in Figure 3(f). The depth jumps are similarly reduced here. Although these two measures lead to different reordering results, in practice, both effectively reduce the stress of accommodation and convergence between cuts; we did not observe significant differences between the two.

5.2 Active Depth Cuts

Two neighboring stereoscopic images that have very different depth brackets result in a depth jump in the depth chart and subsequent viewer discomfort. To remedy this problem, a simple solution is to apply active depth cuts. The procedure is as follows.

1. Gradually shift the depth bracket of the *out image* so it is centered at the screen.
2. Switch to the *in image* whose depth bracket is centered at the screen.
3. Gradually shift the depth bracket of the in image back to its original position.

The depth brackets can be safely shifted by translating two images horizontally to make them closer or further away. Note that as suggested in Section 3, shifting the depth brackets back to the screen also helps to relieve viewer tension if the previous photo had a strong 3D effect. For step 2, there are various ways to switch from the out images to the in image. We have explored clean cuts, blends, and fades. Experiments showed that active depth cuts with fades yield the best results. Details are provided in Section 6.

5.3 Shallow Depth-of-Field Effects

For photographs with excessive depth brackets, we apply shallow depth-of-field filtering to bring viewer attention to a narrower but more comfortable depth bracket. The effective bracket can be gradually shifted by gradually shifting the focus of the shallow depth-of-field effects. This way, viewers can still view the whole photo but without viewing discomfort as they only focus on part of the excessive depth bracket at one time.

We designed a modified Gaussian filter to blur the images based on the disparity maps. For normal Gaussian filters, a parameter σ is universally applied to all pixels of an image. In our design, each pixel p's σ is dynamically adjusted according to the difference of the in-focus disparity value and p's disparity value. Let $G(p;\sigma)$ denote the filter which applies a Gaussian function with standard deviation σ on p. Our disparity-based blur filter for p is defined as

$$B(p;t,\sigma) = G\left(p;\left(\frac{(D(p)-t)}{\max(D)-\min(D)}\right)^2\sigma\right), \quad (11)$$

where σ is the standard deviation, t is the in-focus disparity value (the regions with disparity t are in focus), D is the disparity map, $D(p)$ is the disparity value of p, and $\max(D)$ and $\min(D)$ represent the maximal and minimal disparity values in D. By varying σ in proportion to the distance from the pixel's disparity to the in-focus disparity, regions whose disparity values are further from t will be more blurred. This effectively simulates depth-of-field effects. Figure 4 shows the left and right images, their disparity maps, and images with different focus settings.

To summarize, the proposed stereoscopic slideshow system works as follows.

- If allowed, reorder the photo sequence to yield a more continuous depth chart.
- During image display, if the depth bracket of the image is excessive, apply shallow depth-of-field blur filtering to gradually direct the viewer's attention from the foreground to the background.

Figure 4: Depth-of-field blur. (a) and (b) are the left and right images, respectively, (c) and (d) their disparity maps, (e) resultant left image when focusing on the butterfly in the foreground, (f) that when focusing on the leaves in the background, and (g) and (h) another example with different focuses.

- During image transitions, if there is a large depth jump between the in image and the out image, use active depth cuts. In addition, when switching from the out image to the in image, use fade-in or fade-out effects to gradually switch from the out image to a blank image and then to the in image.

6. EXPERIMENTAL RESULTS AND USER STUDIES

Since there is no objective metric for measuring the stereoscopic quality of stabilization and of slideshows, subjective user studies were conducted to evaluate our methods. In these studies, stereoscopic media were displayed on a Samsung 3D monitor 2233RZ with a Nvidia 3D Vision Solution. We adopted the 5-point Likert-scale as the evaluation scoring form for all questions (score 1 for the worst and 5 the best).

(a) original (b) Deshaker (c) Lee et al. (d) the proposed method

Figure 5: First row: stereoscopic matching pairs of the *csiegirl* sequence at frame 163. Second row: the feature trajectories of the sequence. (a) The original input, the results of (b) Deshaker, (c) Lee et al. [14], and (d) the proposed method. Note that for better visualization, we plot only a portion of the matching pairs and trajectories used in our algorithm.

6.1 Stereoscopic Video Stabilization

For evaluating stereoscopic video stabilization, we used three stereoscopic videos with different characteristics: a camera moving around a static scene (*csiegirl*), a camera following a single main moving object (*redgirl*), and a static camera with multiple moving objects (*children*). As we are not aware of other methods specifically designed for stereoscopic videos, we can only make comparisons with conventional algorithms designed for monocular videos by applying them individually on the left and right videos. The compared methods include the shareware Deshaker and Lee et al.'s method [14].

Figure 5 shows the feature trajectories and the stereoscopic matching pairs of the *csiegirl* sequence before and after processing. Frames are shown in the form of red/blue anaglyph. The top row shows the positions of the feature pairs and the bottom row shows the trajectories after stabilization. For a better 3D viewing experience, the connecting lines of feature pairs should remain horizontal after stabilization in the top row. The bottom row shows the trajectories after stabilization. For a more stabilized video, the trajectories should become smoother. Only our method simultaneously smoothes the feature trajectories and keeps the feature points well-aligned on the same scanlines. In contrast, although the method of Lee et al. generates smooth trajectories, it introduces large vertical disparity drifts which cause viewing discomfort. This is evident from the top of Figure 5(c). After stabilization, the left and right feature pairs are no longer horizontally aligned. Deshaker uses smaller transformations for stabilization and thus generates a less stabilized result, as evident by the rougher trajectories shown in the bottom of Figure 5(b).

We further examine the horizontal and vertical disparity changes due to stabilization in Figures 6. These plots show the average differences between the original disparities of the feature pairs and the disparities after stabilization for each frame. The best 3D video should contain zero vertical offset. As views with larger vertical offsets are not vertically aligned, they correspond to greater difficulty for viewers in perceiving 3D. For horizontal disparity, larger and more inconsistent changes respectively mean more deviation from the original depth and more inconsistency of depth perception. Thus, for both vertical offsets and horizontal disparities, the smaller the average differences, the better the viewing experience. Compared to other methods that do not jointly stabilize the left and right views, our method yields the closest disparities to the original disparities for the feature pairs both horizontally (Figure 6 left) and vertically (Figure 6 right), and thus ensures better depth perception. Lee et al.'s approach yields the greatest average differences because their approach has more freedom to move the cameras. When the two views are not constrained properly, such freedom leads to more deviations between the two views. Deshaker does better in this respect, but still yields greater differences than the proposed method. While the results of Lee et al. appear very stable when viewed independently, the large horizontal disparity variation cause the results to be unstable along the depth axis. Moreover, the large vertical disparity deviation makes it difficult for users to fuse depth perception.

Thirty evaluators with normal stereoscopic vision were invited to participate in the user study. They were requested to indicate their satisfaction from the following perspectives:

1. *Stabilization.* What do you think about the 2D spatial stabilization of the video?
2. *Depth continuity.* What do you think about the depth stabilization of the video?
3. *Stereoscopic effect.* What do you think about the comfort and the stereoscopic effect in the video?
4. *Experience.* How does the stabilization effect help you experience the video?
5. *Acceptance.* How much are you willing to adopt the stabilization effect?

Figure 7 shows the results. Generally, our method outperforms others in all aspects because we jointly optimize the

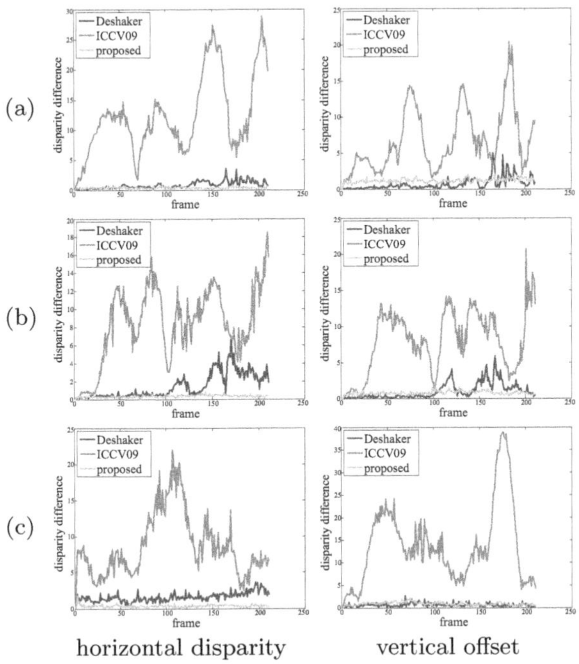

Figure 6: The averaged absolute changes of the horizontal disparities (left) and vertical offsets (right) of the matching pairs before and after stabilization in the (a) *children*, (b) *csiegirl*, and (c) *redgirl* sequences.

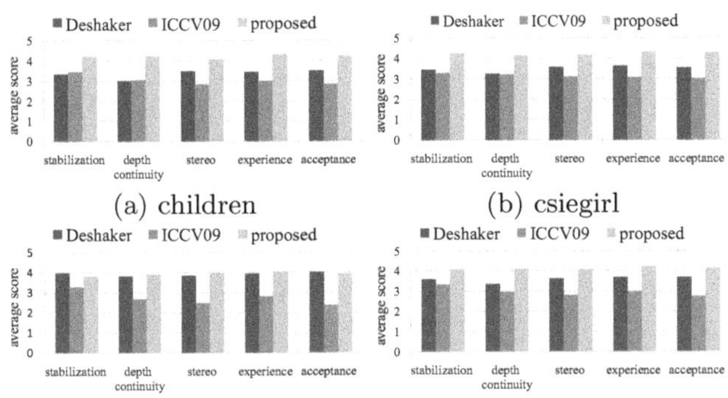

(a) children (b) csiegirl

(c) redgirl (d) average

Figure 7: Results of user studies for stabilization for the three test sequences (a) *children*, (b) *csiegirl*, (c) *redgirl*, and their average (d).

temporal smoothness and the stereoscopic quality. One interesting observation is that although the method of Lee et al. was very stable, it consistently received the lowest score. We conclude therefore that maintaining coordination among views and avoiding depth jumps, as described in Section 3, is more important than maintaining temporal smoothness for stereoscopic videos. Finally, because the test videos are not long, the users did not experience eye strain in our experiments. However, we believe that for longer videos, Deshaker and Lee et al.'s methods will lead to eye strain due to their inferior stereoscopic quality.

6.2 Stereoscopic Photo Slideshows

As mentioned above, instead of developing pleasing transition and presentation effects, we focus on the depth smoothness of photo transitions for comfortable stereoscopic perception. To find a good transition effect, we conducted a user study, experimenting with the depth shift method and combining it with three basic transition effects—clean cut (no effect), fade-in/fade-out, and blending— commonly used in slideshows to switch between photos. Hence there are a total of six possible options. Fifteen evaluators were invited to participate in the user study, six of whom were expert users familiar with stereo vision and slideshows. The eight 960x720 stereoscopic photos shown in Figure 3 were used for the evaluation. The evaluators were requested to indicate their satisfaction with respect from the following perspectives:

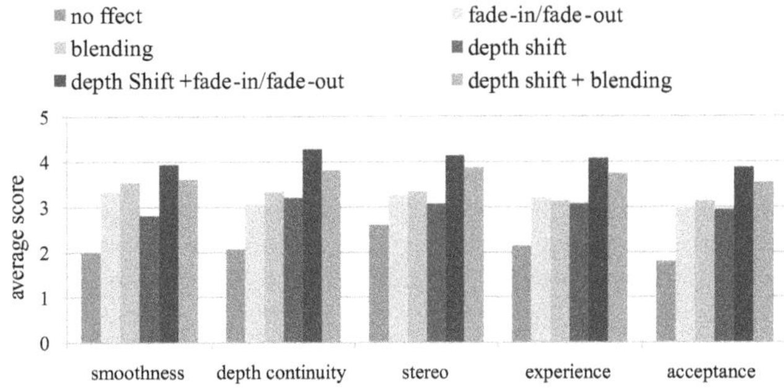

Figure 8: Results of the user study for stereoscopic photo slideshows. Six options were explored by switching on/off depth shift and combining with three basic transition effects—clean cut (no effect), fade-in/fade-out, and blending. Depth shift with fade-in/fade-out yielded the best performance.

1. *Smoothness.* What do you think about the smoothness of photo transitions?

2. *Depth continuity.* What do you think about the smoothness of the depth (disparity) variation on the display of each photo?

3. *Stereoscopic effect.* What do you think about the comfort and stereoscopic effect of the slideshow?

4. *Experience.* To what extent does the transition effect help you experience the trip?

5. *Acceptance.* How much are you willing to adopt the transition effect?

Figure 8 shows the results, which show that the depth shift method greatly enhances the viewing experience regardless of the transition effect used. We also found that clean cut is not a good transition, especially for stereoscopic images. Even with depth shift, it received even lower scores than fade or blending without depth shift in terms of depth continuity and stereoscopic effects. This is because viewers have to search for convergence points from scratch very quickly. The combination of depth shift and fade-in/fade-out achieved the best results since the inserted blank image allowed users to relax and also reduced the greatest differences of depths and colors between the in and out images. One point worth noting is that some subjects seemed to be able to adapt to large depth variations; for them, the effect of the depth shift method did not seem obvious.

6.3 Limitations

Although the proposed methods yield a better 3D viewing experience, they have their limitations. For example, the stereoscopic video stabilization algorithm relies on the robust extraction of feature trajectories. If not provided with a sufficient number of feature trajectories, the method could fail. In our experience, the method requires at least ten feature trajectories passing through a frame for reliable results. Stereoscopic slideshows require a reasonable estimation of disparity values to provide good shallow depth-of-field effects. Inaccurate disparities could cause artifacts.

7. CONCLUSIONS

We have introduced a set of stereoscopic cinematography principles and have adapted them to stereoscopic media processing. We have not only introduced the first methods for stereoscopic video stabilization and stereoscopic photo slideshows, but more importantly, we have shown that it is essential to consider these empirical principles when working on stereoscopic media processing. With the growing popularity and ubiquity of 3D media, we believe that there will soon be a strong demand for these methods; these principles are important to their success.

In the future, for stereoscopic video stabilization, we would like to explore 3D approaches; for stereoscopic slideshows, we would like to incorporate more interesting effects. We would also like to see how well these principles could help other stereoscopic media processing operations such as color adjustment, tone mapping, depth-of-field blurring, inpainting, and morphing. We would also like to explore additional stereoscopic cinematography principles for these operations. We have here investigated the utilization of only some 3D cinematography principles. Other principles could find their roles in other applications. For example, the rules about the stereoscopic window could be important when extending photographic recomposition [16] to stereoscopic images.

Acknowledgments

This work was supported by the National Science Council of Taiwan, under contracts NSC100-2628-E-002-009 and NSC100-2622-E-002-016-CC2.

8. REFERENCES

[1] C.-H. Chang, C.-K. Liang, and Y.-Y. Chuang. Content-aware display adaptation and interactive editing for stereoscopic images. *IEEE Trans. Multimedia*, 13(4):589–601, August 2011.

[2] C.-H. Chen, M.-F. Weng, S.-K. Jeng, and Y.-Y. Chuang. Emotion-based music visualization using photos. *Proc. 14th Intl. Multimedia Modeling Conf.*, 4903:358–368, Jan. 2008.

[3] J.-C. Chen, W.-T. Chu, J.-H. Kuo, C.-Y. Weng, and J.-L. Wu. Tiling slideshow. In *Proc. ACM Multimedia*, pages 25–34, 2006.

[4] M. A. Fischler and R. C. Bolles. Random sample consensus: A paradigm for model fitting with applications to image analysis and automated cartography. *Communications of the ACM*, 24(6):381–395, 1981.

[5] J. Harel, C. Koch, and P. Perona. Graph-based visual saliency. In *Advances in Neural Information Processing Systems (NIPS)*, 2006.

[6] R. Hartley and A. Zisserman. *Multiple View Geometry in Computer Vision*. Cambridge University Press, 2004.

[7] C.-C. Hsieh, W.-H. Cheng, C.-H. Chang, Y.-Y. Chuang, and J.-L. Wu. Photo navigator. In *Proc. ACM Multimedia*, pages 419–428, October 2008.

[8] X.-S. Hua, L. Lu, and H.-J. Zhang. Automatically converting photographic series into video. In *Proc. ACM Multimedia*, pages 708–715, 2004.

[9] T. Kawai, T. Shibata, T. Inoue, Y. Sakaguchi, K. Okabe, and Y. Kuno. Development of software for editing of stereoscopic 3D movies. In *Proc. Stereoscopic Displays and Virtual Reality Systems IX*, 2002.

[10] F. L. Kooi and A. Toet. Visual comfort of binocular and 3D displays. *Displays*, 25(2-3):99 – 108, 2004.

[11] S. Koppal, C. L. Zitnick, M. Cohen, S. B. Kang, B. Ressler, and A. Colburn. A viewer-centric editor for stereoscopic cinema. *IEEE Computer Graphics and Applications*, 31(1):20–35, 2011.

[12] M. Lambooij, W. A. IJsselsteijn, M. Fortuin, and I. Heynderickx. Visual discomfort and visual fatigue of stereoscopic displays: A review. *Journal of Imaging Science and Technology*, 53(3):1–14, 2009.

[13] M. Lang, A. Hornung, O. Wang, S. Poulakos, A. Smolic, and M. Gross. Nonlinear disparity mapping for stereoscopic 3D. *ACM Trans. Graph.*, 29(4):Article 75, 2010.

[14] K.-Y. Lee, Y.-Y. Chuang, B.-Y. Chen, and M. Ouhyoung. Video stabilization using robust feature trajectories. In *Proc. ICCV*, pages 1397–1404, 2009.

[15] F. Liu, M. Gleicher, H. Jin, and A. Agarwala. Content-preserving warps for 3D video stabilization. *ACM Trans. Graph. (Proc. SIGGRAPH)*, 28(3):Article 44, 2009.

[16] L. Liu, R. Chen, L. Wolf, and D. Cohen-Or. Optimizing photo composition. *Computer Graphic Forum*, 29(2):469–478, 2010.

[17] W.-Y. Lo, J. V. Baar, C. Knaus, M. Zwicker, and M. Gross. Stereoscopic 3D copy & paste. *ACM Trans. Graph.*, 29(6), 2010.

[18] D. Lowe. Distinctive image features from scale-invariant keypoints. *IJCV*, 60:91–110, 2004.

[19] B. Mendiburu. *3D movie making: Stereoscopic digital cinema from script to screen.* Focal Press, 2009.

[20] C. Morimoto and R. Chellappa. Evaluation of image stabilization algorithms. In *Proc. ICASSP*, volume V, pages 2789–2792, 1998.

[21] Photo Story. `http://www.microsoft.com/`.

[22] Picasa. `http://picasa.google.com/`.

[23] D. Scharstein and R. Szeliski. A taxonomy and evaluation of dense two-frame stereo correspondence algorithms. *IJCV*, 47(1-3):7–42, 2002.

[24] B. M. Smith, L. Zhang, H. Jin, and A. Agarwala. Light field video stabilization. In *Proc. ICCV*, pages 341–348, 2009.

[25] N. Snavely, S. M. Seitz, and R. Szeliski. Photo tourism: Exploring photo collections in 3D. *ACM Trans. Graph.*, 25(3):835–846, 2006.

[26] C. Wang and A. A. Sawchukg. Disparity manipulation for stereo images and video. In *Proc. Stereoscopic Displays and Applications XIX*, 2008.

Towards Multi-Semantic Image Annotation with Graph Regularized Exclusive Group Lasso *

Xiangyu Chen[†‡§] Xiao-Tong Yuan[§] Shuicheng Yan[§†] Jinhui Tang[♮]
Yong Rui[♯] and Tat-Seng Chua[†‡]

[†] NUS Graduate School for Integrative Sciences and Engineering,
[§] Department of Electrical and Computer Engineering, [‡] School of Computing, NUS
[♯]Microsoft Advanced Technology Center,
[♮]Nanjing University of Science and Technology

ABSTRACT

To bridge the *semantic gap* between low level feature and human perception, most of the existing algorithms aim mainly at annotating images with concepts coming from only one semantic space, e.g. cognitive or affective. The naive combination of the outputs from these spaces will implicitly force the conditional independence and ignore the correlations among the spaces. In this paper, to exploit the comprehensive semantic of images, we propose a general framework for harmoniously integrating the above multiple semantics, and investigating the problem of learning to annotate images with training images labeled in two or more correlated semantic spaces, such as *fascinating nighttime*, or *exciting cat*. This kind of semantic annotation is more oriented to real world search scenario. Our proposed approach outperforms the baseline algorithms by making the following contributions. 1) Unlike previous methods that annotate images within only one semantic space, our proposed multi-semantic annotation associates each image with labels from multiple semantic spaces. 2) We develop a multi-task linear discriminative model to learn a linear mapping from features to labels. The tasks are correlated by imposing the exclusive group lasso regularization for competitive feature selection, and the graph Laplacian regularization to deal with insufficient training sample issue. 3) A Nesterov-type smoothing approximation algorithm is presented for efficient optimization of our model. Extensive experiments on NUS-WIDE-Emotive dataset ($56k$ images) with 8×81 emotive cognitive concepts and Object&Scene datasets from NUS-WIDE well validate the effectiveness of the proposed approach.

Categories and Subject Descriptors

H.3.1 [**Information Storage and Retrieval**]: Content Analysis and Indexing-indexing methods

*Area chair: Nicu Sebe

MM'11, November 28–December 1, 2011, Scottsdale, Arizona, USA.

General Terms

Algorithms, Performance, Experimentation

Keywords

Multi-Semantic Image Annotation, Exclusive Group Lasso

1. INTRODUCTION

With the popularity of photo sharing websites, new web images on a wide variety of topics have been growing at an exponential rate. At the same time, the contents of images are also enriched and more diverse than ever before. In order to manege this huge amount and variety of images, there is a basic shift from content-based image retrieval to concept-based retrieval techniques. This shift has motivated research on image annotation which offers a series of challenges in media content processing techniques. The *semantic gap* [17] between high-level semantics and low-level image features is still one of the main challenging problems for image classification and retrieval. Moreover, image semantics can be viewed at two levels: Cognitive level and Affective level [10]. The two spaces of image semantics are interrelated and should be used together to reinforce each other in order to improve accuracy of concept detection and in particular, to detect complex concepts involving both types of basic concepts.

However, existing studies on image semantic annotation mainly aim at the assignment of either the cognitive concepts or affective concepts to a new item separately. Moreover, they fail to take into consideration the correlation between concepts from different spaces. For example, certain cognitive concepts (such as *snake* and *tiger*) are usually attached with negative emotion, while other concepts (such as *beach* and *sunset*) are associated with positive emotions. As a result, the complex concepts consisting of concepts from different spaces cannot be inferred easily. For detecting these complex concepts, the current learning process requires huge amount of efforts for extracting different types of cognitive and emotive features and is thus generally unaffordable for large-scale image dataset. Moreover, it is hard to generate concepts from different semantic spaces simultaneously because they require the use of different techniques to be applied to different semantic spaces, and the aggregation of results of individual concepts from different spaces is usually unable to model the meanings of complex query in the real-world search task. This motivates us to harmoniously embed these two or more semantic spaces into one general

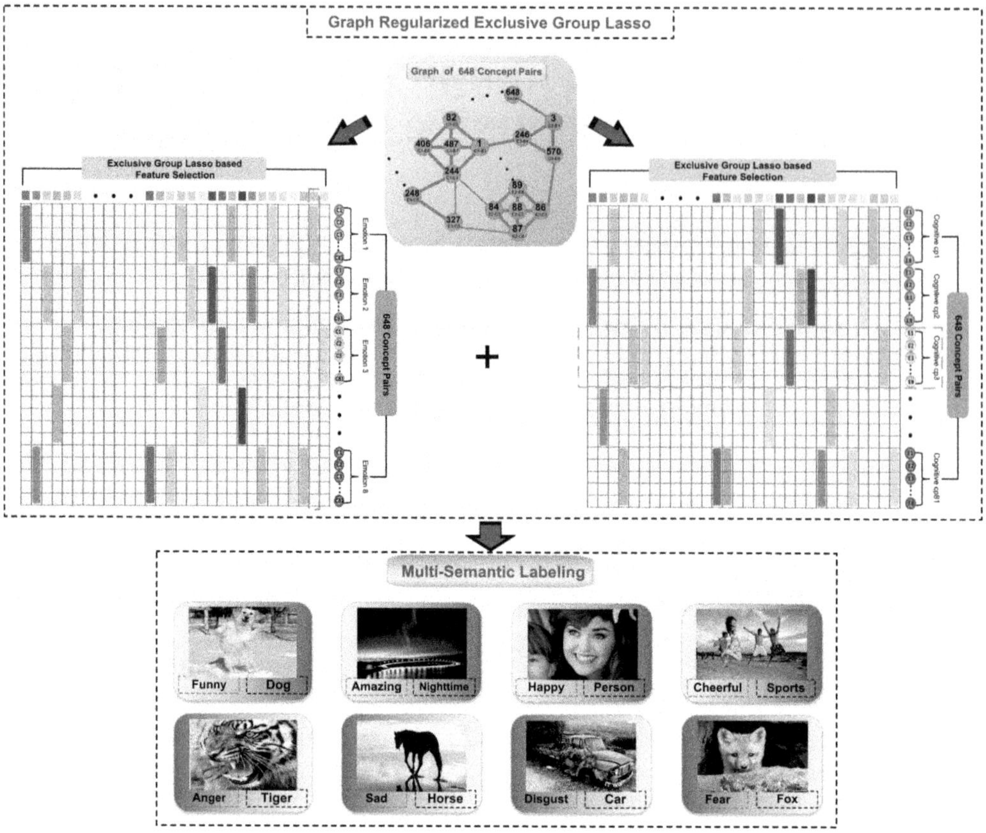

Figure 1: System overview of our proposed Multi-Task Learning scheme for Image Annotation with Multi-Semantic Labeling (IA-MSL). The training data are simultaneously labeled in both cognitive (81 concepts) and emotive semantic (8 concepts) spaces. The system is trained with a multi-task linear regression model regularized by a graph term, and an exclusive group lasso term. The graph term (middle of the top part) encourages correlation of the $648 = 8 \times 81$ emotive-cognitive concept pairs among tasks. While the exclusive group lasso term encourages sparse feature sharing across different cognitive concepts under the same emotive category (left of the top part) and different emotive concepts under the same cognitive category (right of the top part), which also captures the negative correlations among different emotive/cognitive categories.

framework for annotating the deeper and multi-semantic labels to images. In this paper, we are particularly interested in explicit multi-semantic [1] image annotation under the unified generic visual features. This framework not only works well on cognitive and affective spaces but can also be applied to other multi-space semantics such as object and scene.

In recent years, the semantic-based image annotation has become one of the most important research directions in multimedia community, which focuses on developing automatic annotation algorithms to extract the semantic meaning of images. For cognitive semantics, we usually assign appropriate cognitive concepts to the image for representing and identifying its visual contents. Affective semantics are represented in adjective form and describe the intensities of feelings, moods or sensibility evoked in users when viewing images, such as Amusement, Awe, Contentment, Excitement, Anger, Disgust, Fear and Sad [21, 22]. For popular cognitive or affective queries, the returned images can fill many result pages in popular search engines, but many will not satisfy the deeper requirement of complex and multi-semantic retrieval. For example, most commercial systems can handle the individual emotional/cognitive words well, like searching only for "cat" or searching only with the word "exciting". But for the case of searching for images with the query "exciting cat", the precision of result will be degraded because most images are only precisely labeled with either affective concepts or cognitive concepts and the desired multi-semantic labeled sample images are really rare due to the lack of mature and efficient comprehensive semantic image annotation technique.

Learning to annotate the comprehensive semantic to images in multi-semantic spaces is a challenging problem in the real world applications. In this paper, we propose a novel and promising approach, namely, Image Annotation with Multi-Semantic Labeling (IA-MSL), to annotate images simultaneously with labels in two or more correlated spaces. The key challenge with IA-MSL is the large number of classes involved in training due to the combination of multiple semantic spaces. Thus, some classes may suffer from the problem of insufficient training samples. One

[1]The *multi-semantic* (or *polysemy*) retrieval has been explored in [14] for multi-modality (visual and textual) based image retrieval, in which a visual object or text word may belong to several concepts. For example, a "horizontal bar" object can belong to high jump or pole vault event. Differently, the term multi-semantic used in this paper emphasizes that an image can be labeled in multiple semantic spaces.

naive solution to avoid this issue is to train the classifiers within each semantic space and then combine the outputs from these semantic spaces for the ultimate combinational semantic prediction in an *enrichment* manner, which imposes the conditional independency assumption. More formally, by saying enrichment of a classifier from two semantic spaces $\mathcal{L}^1$ and $\mathcal{L}^2$, we mean to train two such classifiers (with confidence label vector output) in $\mathcal{L}^1$ and $\mathcal{L}^2$ separately, and then obtain multi-semantic confidence vector y of test sample x using the following strategy

$$y = y^1 \otimes y^2,$$

where $y^1 \in \mathbb{R}^{|\mathcal{L}^1|}$ and $y^2 \in \mathbb{R}^{|\mathcal{L}^2|}$ are the label confidence vectors of x from semantic space $\mathcal{L}^1$ and $\mathcal{L}^2$, respectively, and $\otimes$ denotes the Kronecker product. In such a scheme, given an image observation x, we made the semantic space independent assumption, i.e., $P(l^1, l^2 \mid x) = P(l^1 \mid x)P(l^2 \mid x)$, $\forall l^1 \in \mathcal{L}^1, l^2 \in \mathcal{L}^2$. Although simple for implementation, the apparent limitation of enrichment scheme is that it ignores the correlations among the semantic spaces. To deal with such an issue and harness the correlations across the semantic spaces, we propose to formulate IA-MSL as a regularized multi-task discriminative analysis model, where individual tasks are defined as learning linear discriminative models for individual complex semantic concepts $\{(l_1, l_2) \mid l_1 \in \mathcal{L}_1, l_2 \in \mathcal{L}_2\}$. We propose to learn all the tasks in a joint manner by imposing two types of regularization, the graph Laplacian regularization and exclusive group lasso regularization. The graph Laplacian regularization captures the correlation clues to refine concept classifier, especially in cases with insufficient training samples. For each semantic space, since the image features are typically exclusively shared among different concepts in this space, we also exploit a so called exclusive-group-lasso regularizer to capture such negative correlations among category groups, which performs on the unified generic features, greatly reducing the cost of extracting different types of feature for different semantic spaces. Taking the NUS-WIDE-Emotive dataset as an example, in both emotive space $\mathcal{L}_1$ with 8 concepts and cognitive space $\mathcal{L}_2$ with 81 concepts, it is reasonable to assume that if an image feature is important for one of several concepts, it is less likely for this feature to be also important for the other concepts. Such an exclusive regularization mechanism is empirically shown to be effective to boost the multi-semantic labeling performance

1.1 Our Contributions

The major contributions of this paper are three-fold:

- We propose a novel framework for Image Annotation with Multi-Semantic Labeling (IA-MSL), which exploits the high-level semantic of images from two or more semi-orthogonal label spaces;
- As an implementation of IA-MSL, we develop a multi-task discriminative analysis model to learn a proper linear mapping from features to labels. The proposed model simultaneously considers co-occurrent relationship among tasks through the graph Laplacian regularization, and the negative relationship among tasks in feature sharing.
- A Nesterov-type smoothing approximation algorithm is developed for efficient optimization of the proposed model. Empirical results on real-world large scale datasets validate the efficiency and effectiveness of our approach.

1.2 Related Work

1.2.1 Image Annotation in Unitary Semantic Space

Many multi-label/unitary-label annotation algorithms were proposed and well studied to assign labels to each image for a fixed image collection crawled from websites such as Flickr. For this fixed data set, images are assigned with either cognitive concepts or emotive concepts, or other semantic concepts from a unitary semantic space.

For the image annotation in cognitive semantic space [18, 41], multi-label propagation is a hot and promising research direction. Many methods were proposed to exploit the interrelations among different labels [29, 33, 40, 34] since some class labels may correlate to each other. For example, Ueda and Saito [31] proposed a generative model for multi-label learning that explicitly incorporates the pairwise correlation between any two class labels. A Bayesian model is introduced in [9] to assign labels through underlying latent representations. Qi *et al.* [27] proposed a unified Correlative Multi-Label (CML) framework to simultaneously classify labels and model correlations between them. Liu *et al.* [20] utilized constrained nonnegative matrix factorization (CNMF) to optimize the consistency between image similarity and label similarity. Zhu *et al.* [45] suggested a maximum entropy model for exploring the label correlation for multi-label learning. In the setting of large-scale multi-label annotation, Chen *et al.* [4] proposed the Kullback-Leibler divergence based multi-label propagation, which encodes the label information of an image as a unit label confidence vector and imposes inter-label constraints and manipulates labels interactively.

For image annotation in emotive semantic space, most researchers mainly focus on emotive feature analysis and extraction. The popularly adopted methods include Support Vector Machines (SVMs), Random Forest, the C4.5 tree classifier and Naive Bayes classifier method. For example, Machajdik *et al.* [21] investigated methods to extract and combine low-level features that represent the emotional content of an image from psychology and art theory views. For classification, they adopted the Naive Bayes classifier to annotate images with emotive concepts. Wang *et al.* [35] developed and extracted special integrated histogram features and utilize support vector regression for automatically emotional image annotation. In [38], an SVM framework for supervised learning of emotion categories was also adopted with extracting the holistic image features. Besides the specific features, many other works also utilized the generic features. Hayashi *et al.* [12] adopted the RGB color feature and classified the images through neural network. Wu *et al.* [37] adopted SVM method for affective image classification based on general color and texture features.

Different from the above body of efforts on image annotation in unitary semantic space, we propose and investigate the problem of multi-semantic image annotation to meet the requirement of real-world search conditions.

1.2.2 Multi-task Learning

Recently, there have been a lot of interests around multi-task learning (MTL), both in theory and practice. The idea behind this paradigm is that, when the tasks to be learned are similar enough or are related in some sense, it may be advantageous to take into account these relations between tasks. Several works have experimentally highlighted the benefit of such a framework [3]. In general, MTL can be addressed through a regularization framework [7]. For example, the joint sparsity regularization favors to learn a common subset of features for all tasks [1, 26], while the exclusive sparsity regularization is used for exclusive feature selection across tasks in [44]. Our method follows the regularized MTL framework. In contrast to the existing regularization that only considers the model parameters dependent, our proposed regularization is characterized by data as well as model parameters, and thus is much more informative.

1.2.3 Group Sparse Inducing Regularization

Learning models regularized by group sparse inducing penalties have been widely studied in both machine learning [39, 43] and signal processing fields [15, 8]. Let $w \in \mathbb{R}^d$ be the n parameters to be regularized. Denote $\mathcal{I} = \{1, ..., d\}$ the variable index and $\mathcal{G} = \{g_i \subseteq \mathcal{I}\}_{i=1}^{l}$ a set of variable index groups. The group formation varies according to the given grouping or hierarchical structure. Denote $\|w_{\mathcal{G}}\|_{p,q} := \sum_{g \in \mathcal{G}} \|w_g\|_p^q$ the $\ell_{p,q}$-norm defined over groups $\mathcal{G}$, where $\|w_g\|_p^q := \left(\sum_{j \in g} |w_j|^p\right)^{q/p}$. The $\ell_{2,1}$-norm regularizer is used in group Lasso [39] which encourages the sparsity on group level. Jacob *et al.* [13] proposed the overlap group Lasso and graph Lasso as variants of group Lasso to handle overlapping groups. Another group sparsity inducing regularizer is the $\ell_{\infty,1}$-norm which is widely used in multi-task learning problems [19, 42]. When $p = 1, q = 2$, the $\ell_{1,2}$-norm has recently been studied in the exclusive-Lasso model [44] for the multi-task learning and elitist-Lasso model [16] for audio signal denoising. Unlike the group Lasso regularizer that assumes covariant variables in groups, the exclusive Lasso regularizer models the scenario when variables in the same group compete with each other to be selected in the output.

2. OUR PROPOSED SCHEME

2.1 Problem Statement

Given a labeled dataset $\{x_i, l_i\}_{i=1}^{N}$, where $x_i \in R^d$ is the feature vector of the i-th image and l_i is the associated image label. In this study, we assume that l_i is obtained from two or mote different spaces of labeling. Formally, $l_i = \{l_i^k\}_{k=1}^{K}$ where $l_i^k \subseteq \mathcal{L}^k$ is the label(s) of image i in the k-th labeling space equipped with label set $\mathcal{L}^k$. It is noteworthy the difference between our multi-semantic labeling classification and the so called multi-label classification. In the latter problem, the labels associated with an image is from a unitary semantic space, e.g., object category. Differently, in our setting, we are interested in the case that the labels associated with the same image are obtained from different semantic spaces, e.g., object category and emotion. Indeed, for each space k, the label l_i^k can be a multi-label vector in this space. In the following descriptions, for simplicity and clarity purpose, we consider without loss of generality that the labels are obtained from $K = 2$ semantic spaces. Denote $\mathcal{L} = \mathcal{L}_1 \times \mathcal{L}_2$ the Cartesian products of $\mathcal{L}^1$ and $\mathcal{L}^2$. Let $y_i \in R^{|\mathcal{L}|}$ be the zero-one label matrix indicating whether x_i is jointly labeled as $l^1 \in \mathcal{L}^1$ and $l^2 \in \mathcal{L}^2$. By concatenating the columns of label matrix y_i, we get an $|\mathcal{L}|$ dimensional label vector, which is also denoted by y_i in the rest of this paper. Given the training feature-label set $\{x_i, y_i\}_{i=1}^{N}$, we are interested in the problem of learning a linear mode $y = Wx$ such that the label of an unseen test sample can be predicted via this model. Naively, one could utilize the following multivariate least squares regression (LSR) model

$$\min_{W} \left\{ J(W) := \frac{1}{2}\|Y - WX\|^2 \right\}, \tag{1}$$

where $X = [x_1, ..., x_n] \in \mathbb{R}^{d \times n}$ is the feature matrix with each column a training image feature, $Y = [y_1, ..., y_n] \in \mathbb{R}^{|\mathcal{L}| \times n}$ is the label matrix with each column a training image label vector, $W \in \mathbb{R}^{|\mathcal{L}| \times d}$ is the parameter to be estimated. Obviously, the proceeding LSR forms an MTL since the objective J in (1) can be rewritten as:

$$J(W) = \sum_{j=1}^{|\mathcal{L}|} \frac{1}{2}\|Y_j - W_j X\|^2, \tag{2}$$

where $Y_j \in \mathbb{R}^n$ and $W_j \in \mathbb{R}^d$ are the j-th row of Y and W, respectively. In the preceding MTL formulation, we are to learn $|\mathcal{L}|$ different linear regression models (tasks) $Y_j = W_j X$, $j = 1, ..., |\mathcal{L}|$. In this naive formulation, the tasks are learned independently to each other.

For better performance, it is often beneficial to take into account the relationships across tasks by imposing certain regularization to the objective (2). Particular, in the setting of our multi-semantic labeling problem, there are two types of correlations among tasks should be considered.

- **Exclusive feature selection:** In each semantic space, our objective is to differentiate the related categories. Motivated by the exclusive feature sharing previously considered in [44], we may expect a negative correlation among categories, namely, if a visual feature is deemed to be important for one category, it becomes less likely for this feature to be an important feature for the other categories. In order to capture such an exclusive feature selection nature among categories in each semantic space, we propose to utilize an $\ell_{2,1}^2$-norm regularizer analog to the ℓ_1^2-norm regularizer used in the exclusive Lasso model [44].

- **Concepts correlation:** Another important regularization we should explore is the semantic relationship between the combinational concepts in $\mathcal{L}$. This is of particular interest in our work due to the insufficient sample issue severely occurs in multi-semantic annotation. That is, some of the combinational labels in $\mathcal{L}$ are supported by very few or even zero training samples. For example, in our emotion-category dataset, although the category "dog" and the emotion "happy" are supported by plenty of samples, the combinational label ("dog", "happy") is not supported by any sample in the training set. Obviously, for any label j without training samples, $Y_j = 0$, and thus the corresponding W_j will be a zero vector through naive model (2). To handle this issue, one natural way is to propagate the correlation among concepts to their corresponding model parameters. As we will see shortly, the Google similarity distance [6] is a simple and effective choice to describe the correlation among concepts.

Next, we describe in detail the two types of regularization we imposed to the naive MTL model (2). Figure 1 gives an illustration of the pipeline of the proposed framework.

2.2 An Exclusive Group Lasso Regularizer

In this subsection, we address the regularization of feature exclusive selection across tasks. Let $\mathcal{G}^1$ of size $|\mathcal{L}^1|$ be a group of label index set in $\mathcal{L}$ constructed as follows: each element $g \in \mathcal{G}^1$ is an index set of combinational labels $(l^1, l^2) \in \mathcal{L}$ which share a common $l^1 \in \mathcal{L}^1$. For example, for the category-emotion label spaces, each group in $\mathcal{G}^1$ is the combination of emotion labels of a certain category. Similarly, we can construct $\mathcal{G}^2$ of size $|\mathcal{L}^2|$ associated with label set $\mathcal{L}^2$. Let us consider the following regularizer:

$$\Omega(W) := \frac{1}{2}\sum_{i=1}^{d}\left(\|W^i_{\mathcal{G}^1}\|^2_{2,1} + \|W^i_{\mathcal{G}^2}\|^2_{2,1}\right), \quad (3)$$

where $\|W^i_{\mathcal{G}^k}\|^2_{2,1} = \left(\sum_{g\in\mathcal{G}^k}\|W^i_g\|_2\right)^2$, $k = 1, 2$, and $W^i \in \mathbb{R}^{|\mathcal{L}|}$ is the i-th column of W, $W^i_g \in \mathbb{R}^{|\mathcal{L}|}$ is the restriction of vector W^i on the subset g by setting $W^i_j = 0$ for $j \neq g$. For each feature i, the $\ell^2_{2,1}$-norm regularizer $\|W^i_{\mathcal{G}^k}\|^2_{2,1}$ can be viewed as a group Lasso extension of ℓ^2_1 regularizer used in exclusive Lasso [44]. Similar to the analysis in [44], one can confirm that $\|W^i_{\mathcal{G}^k}\|^2_{2,1}$ is sparse inducing and it encourages exclusive selection of features at the level of group $g \in \mathcal{G}^k$. In other words, for each feature i, it tends to assign larger weights to some important groups while assigning small or even zero weights to the other groups.

2.3 A Graph Laplacian Regularizer

We explore in this subsection the semantic relationships between concepts. Suppose that we are given a similarity matrix $P \in \mathbb{R}^{|\mathcal{L}|\times|\mathcal{L}|}$ that stores the pairwise similarity score between concepts. The larger P_{jk} is, the more similar two concepts j and k are, and vice verser. We propose to use the following graph regularizer

$$\Psi(W) := \frac{1}{2}\sum_{j,k=1}^{|\mathcal{L}|} P_{jk} \parallel W_j - W_k \parallel^2 . \quad (4)$$

The intuition behind the preceding regularizer is that closely related concepts should have similar regression weights. Different from the $\Omega(W)$ in previous subsection that describes the negative correlation among tasks, the graph regularizer $\Psi(W)$ models the positive correlation among tasks by transferring the weight information among neighboring concepts. Such a mechanism is particularly helpful for robust learning of weights for some combinational concepts only supported by very few or even zero instances in the training set. Denote $L = D - P$ the Laplacian matrix where D is a diagonal matrix whose diagonal entries are the row sums of P. $\mathrm{Tr}(\cdot)$ represents the matrix trace operation. We may equivalently reexpress (4) as the following compact form

$$\Psi(W) = \frac{1}{2}\mathrm{Tr}[W^T LW].$$

Generally speaking, the similarity matrix P can be defined based on any reasonable co-currency measurement such as Google distance [6] and Flickr distance [36]. In our implementation, P is obtained by applying the Normalized Google similarity Distance (NGD) proposed by Cilibrasi and Vitanyi [6]. NGD is simply estimated by exploring the textual information available on the Web. The distance between two concepts is measured by the Google page counts when querying both concept names to the Google search engine. It assumes that the words and phrases acquire meaning from the way they are used in society. Since Google has indexed a vast number of web pages, and the common search term occurs in millions of web pages, this database can somewhat reflect the term distribution in society. Formally, $NGD(x, y)$ between two concepts x and y is defined as

$$NGD(x,y) = \frac{\max\{\ln f(x), \ln f(y)\} - \ln f(x,y)}{\ln N - \min\{\ln f(x), \ln f(y)\}},$$

where $f(x)$, $f(y)$, and $f(x, y)$ in this paper denote the number of images from training data containing concept-pair $x \in \mathcal{L}^1 \times \mathcal{L}^2$ (e.g. emotive-cognitive pair), $y \in \mathcal{L}^1 \times \mathcal{L}^2$, both x and y, respectively. N is the total number of images in training data. We then define $P(x, y) = \exp\{-N(x, y)/\eta\}$ where η is a tunable parameter. The similarity matrix P can also be calculated by other co-occurrent technologies such as Flickr distance [36].

2.4 Graph Regularized Exclusive Group Lasso

Based on the discussion in the previous two subsections, we propose to extend the naive MTL model (1) to the following graph regularized exclusive Lasso MTL:

$$\min_W \left\{ F(W) := \underbrace{J(W) + \lambda\Omega(W)}_{\text{exclusive group Lasso}} + \underbrace{\gamma\Psi(W)}_{\text{graph regularizer}} \right\}. \quad (5)$$

As aforementioned, Equation (5) formulates a regularized MTL with $|\mathcal{L}|$ tasks, each of which learns a linear regression model for certain combinational concept in $\mathcal{L}$. The first two terms in (5) form an exclusive group Lasso objective. The regularizer $\Omega(W)$ encourages the exclusive relationships across tasks. The graph Laplacian regularizer $\Psi(W)$ enforces the semantic correlation among tasks. Through the regularized MTL formulation (5), the parameters W can be learned in a joint manner. It is straightforward to verify that the objective $F(W)$ in (5) is convex but non-smooth since all the three components are convex whereas $\Omega(W)$ is non-smooth. We will develop in the next section an efficient method to optimize problem (5). Once the optimal parameter W^* is obtained, the label vector of a test sample with feature x is given by $y = W^*x$. Such a vector can be used for performance evaluation over testing data.

3. OPTIMIZATION

The non-smooth structure of $\Omega(W)$ makes the optimization of problem (5) a non-trivial task. The general purpose subgradient method as used in [44] is applicable but it typically ignores the structure of problem and suffers from slow rate of convergence. Our idea for optimization is to approximate the original non-smooth objective by a smooth function and then solve the latter by utilizing some off-the-shelf fast algorithms. In this section, we derive a Nesterov's smoothing optimization method [24] to achieve this purpose.

3.1 Smoothing Approximation

It is standard to know that for any vector $p \in \mathbb{R}^n$, its ℓ_2-norm $\|p\|_2$ has a max-structure representation $\|p\|_2 = \max_{\|v\|_2\leq 1}\langle p, v\rangle$. Based on this simple property and the smoothing approximation techniques originally from [24], function $\Omega(W)$ can be approximated by the following smooth function

$$\Omega_\mu(W) = \frac{1}{2}\sum_{i=1}^{d}\left(q^2_{\mathcal{G}^1,\mu}(W^i) + q^2_{\mathcal{G}^2,\mu}(W^i)\right), \quad (6)$$

where

$$q_{\mathcal{G}^k,\mu}(W^i) := \max_{\|V^{i,k}_{\mathcal{G}^k}\|_{2,\infty}\leq 1} \langle W^i, V^{i,k}\rangle - \frac{\mu}{2}\|V^{i,k}\|_2^2. \quad (7)$$

Herein, μ is a parameter to control the approximation accuracy. Formally, we have the following result on approximation accuracy of Ω_μ towards Ω:

PROPOSITION 1. *Assume that $\|W^i\|_2 \leq R$. Then $\Omega_\mu(W)$ is a μ-accurate approximation to $\Omega(W)$, that is*

$$\Omega_\mu(W) \leq \Omega(W) \leq \Omega_\mu(W) + C\mu, \quad (8)$$

where $C \equiv \sqrt{2}dR\left(|\mathcal{L}^1|^2 + |\mathcal{L}^2|^2\right)/2$.

The proof follows the similar arguments as in [24]. Proposition 1 shows that for fixed $\mu > 0$, the function Ω_μ can be seen as a uniform smooth approximation of function Ω.

For a fixed W^i, denote $V^{i,k}(W^i)$ the unique minimizer of (7) for $k = 1, 2$, respectively. It is easy to check that for $k = 1, 2$, $\forall g \in \mathcal{G}^k$,

$$V_g^{i,k}(W^i) = \frac{W_g^i}{\max\{\mu, \|W_g^i\|_2\}}.$$

The following result states that Ω_μ is differentiable and its gradient can be analytically calculated:

THEOREM 1. *Function $\Omega_\mu(W)$ is well defined, convex and continuously differentiable with gradient*

$$\nabla\Omega_\mu(W) = \left[\nabla\Omega_\mu(W^1), ..., \nabla\Omega_\mu(W^d)\right], \quad (9)$$

where for $i = 1, ..., d$,

$$\nabla\Omega_\mu(W^i) = q_{\mathcal{G}^1,\mu}(W^i)V^{i,1}(W^i) + q_{\mathcal{G}^2,\mu}(W^i)V^{i,2}(W^i). \quad (10)$$

Moreover, $\nabla\Omega_\mu(W)$ is Lipschitz continuous with the constant

$$L_\mu = \left(\frac{2\sqrt{2}R}{\mu} + |\mathcal{L}^1|^2 + |\mathcal{L}^2|^2\right)d. \quad (11)$$

The proof is given in Appendix A.

3.2 Smooth Minimization via APG

Based on the results in the previous subsection, we now propose to solve the following smooth optimization problem as an approximation to the non-smooth problem (5):

$$\min_W \{F_\mu(W) := J(W) + \lambda\Omega_\mu(W) + \gamma\Psi(W)\}. \quad (12)$$

Given a fixed $\mu > 0$, by Theorem 1 it is easy to see that the objective F_μ is differentiable with gradient

$$\nabla F_\mu(w) = (WX - Y)X^T + \lambda\nabla\Omega_\mu(W) + \gamma LW.$$

Therefore, we can apply any first-order methods, e.g., proximal gradient descent [23] and BFGS [25], to optimize the smooth objective (12). In our implementation, for simplicity and efficiency, we employ the Accelerated Proximal Gradient method [30] to optimize the smoothed problem (12). The algorithm is formally described in Algorithm 1. For a fixed μ, it is shown that APG has $\mathcal{O}(1/t^2)$ asymptotical convergence rate bound, where t is the time instance. If we describe convergence in terms of the number of iterations needed to reach an ϵ solution, i.e., $|F_\mu(w) - \min F_\mu| \leq \epsilon$, then by choosing $\mu \approx \epsilon$ the rate of convergence is $O(1/\epsilon)$. It is noteworthy that the convergent complexity of Algorithm 1 depends on constant $1/L_\mu$ which is dominated by the factor μ when it is small. To further accelerate Algorithm 1 for extremely small μ, one may apply the continuation technique as suggested in [2].

Algorithm 1 Smooth minimization for Problem (12)

Input: $X \in \mathbb{R}^{d\times n}$, $Y \in \mathbb{R}^{|\mathcal{L}|\times d}$, $\mathcal{G}^1$, $\mathcal{G}^2$, λ, γ, μ.
Output: $W^t \in \mathbb{R}^{|\mathcal{L}|\times d}$
Initialization: Initialize W_0, V_0 and let $\alpha_0 \leftarrow 1$, $t \leftarrow 0$.
repeat
  $U_t = (1-\alpha_t)W_t + \alpha_t V_t$,
  Calculate $\nabla\Omega_\mu(U_t)$ according to (9), (10), and L_μ according to (11).
  $V_{t+1} = V_t - \frac{1}{\alpha_t L_\mu}\left(-(Y - WX)X^T + \lambda\nabla\Omega_\mu(U_t) + \gamma LW\right)$,
  $W_{t+1} = (1-\alpha_t)W_t + \alpha_t V_{t+1}$,
  $\alpha_{t+1} = \frac{2}{t+1}$, $t \leftarrow t+1$.
until Converges

4. EXPERIMENTS

To validate the effectiveness of IA-MSL, we conduct extensive experiments on two large scale image datasets: NUS-WIDE-Emotive; and NUS-WIDE-Object&Scene [5]. The NUS-WIDE-Emotive set contains two types of semantic labels: cognitive concept category with 81 tags and emotion category with 8 affective tags. The underlying image diversity and complexity make it a good test bed for multi-semantic image annotation experiments. The publicly available NUS-WIDE-Object&Scene is a subset of NUS-WIDE [5] obtained after noisy tag removal. It is also annotated in two sematic spaces: the scenes category with 33 tags and objects category with 31 tags, which is also suitable for our test. Moreover, since unitary semantic is a special case of multi-semantic, we also compare our proposed algorithm with existing methods on NUS-WIDE-Emotive with individual cognitive semantic and emotive semantic, separately. We report quantitative results on both datasets, with an emphasis on the comparison with the state-of-the-art related algorithms in terms of annotation accuracy.

4.1 Datasets

NUS-WIDE-Emotive dataset is an emotion version of the publicly available NUS-WIDE-LITE [5] database consisting of 55,615 images. Two kinds of semantic labels are associated to each image: an 81-D label vector indicating its relationship to 81 cognitive object categories and an 8-D label vector indicating its relationship to the 8 affective semantic concepts(tightly related to tags yet relatively high-level). For cognitive semantic, the 81-D object category label vector for each image is currently available from NUS-WIDE. For the emotive semantic concepts, we adopt the similar categories as studied in [21, 22]: Amusement, Awe, Contentment, Excitement, Anger, Disgust, Fear, Sad to represent the 8 different types of positive and negative emotions. To label the emotive ground truth on this dataset, the images were peer rated in a web-survey where the participants could select the best fitting emotional category from the eight categories. 10 human subjects with almost equal gender distribution and with ages ranging from 23 to 30 years old have helped to achieve the annotation task. For each image the category with the most votes was selected as the ground truth. Images with inconclusive human votes were removed from the set. For our experiment, We randomly select half of the images for training and the rest for testing. On image features, we use a 1134-D feature as a concatenation of 225-D blockwise color moments, 128-D wavelet texture, 75-D edge direction histogram, 64-D color histogram, 144-D color correlogram and 500-D bag of visual words [5].

NUS-WIDE-Object&Scene [5] are two subsets from NUS-WIDE. In this paper, we select 50,000 images from these two datasets. It consists of two kinds label categories: 31 concepts for object category and 33 concepts for scene category. Each image is assigned with a 31-D object label vector and a 33-D scene label vector. For evaluation, we construct a training set of size 25,000 whilst the rest are used for testing. The same 1134-D feature as used for the previous dataset is also applied here.

4.2 Baselines and Evaluation Criteria

We systematically compare our proposed IA-MSL with six baseline algorithms as listed in Table 1. Amongst them,

- The *support vector machines* (SVM) is a baseline for binary-class classification problem. Here we use its multi-class version by adopting the conventional one-vs-all strategy.
- The Naive Multi-task Learning (NMTL) refers to the independent MTL regression model (2).
- The SVM-E and NMTL-E are two enrichment (recall the definition of enrichment method in Section 1) methods of SVM and NMTL, respectively.
- The Multi-task Learning with Graph Laplacian (MTLG) and Multi-task Learning with Exclusive Lasso (MTLE) are two special cases of the regularized MTL framework (5), by setting $\lambda = 0$ and $\gamma = 0$, respectively.

In order to further study the performance in unitary semantic space, we also compare IA-MSL with several state-of-the-art annotation algorithms as listed in in Table 2, on each semantic space of NUS-WIDE-Emotive.

Many measurements are used to evaluate multi-label annotation performance for concepts propagated to the unlabeled images, e.g., ROC curve, precision recall curve, Average Precision (AP), and so on. In this work, we adopt one of the most widely used criteria, AUC (area under ROC curve) [11], for annotation accuracy evaluation on each category, and Mean AUC (MAUC) for average performance evaluation on the entire dataset. All experiments are conducted on a desktop PC equipped with Intel dual-core CPU (frequency: 3.0 GHz) and 32G bytes physical memory.

4.3 Experiment-I: NUS-WIDE-Emotive

On NUS-WIDE-Emotive, we category all labels into 648 (8 emotions × 81 objects) combination classes. The ground truth of 648 labels is derived by simple Cartesian product of 8 emotive labels and 81 cognitive labels. Some of these 648 multi-semantic labels suffer from the issue of insufficient training samples, which is not rare in real world retrieval scenario. In such a multi-semantic setting, we compare IA-MSL with six baselines listed in Table 1. Table 3 lists the quantitative results. Note that for each of the 8 emotive classes, its AUC is obtained by averaging over the 81 AUCs associated with this emotion but for different object categories. The AUCs for 81 object categories are calculated similarly but omitted from this conference submission due to space limit. From these results we are able to make the following observations:

Table 1: The baseline algorithms.

Name	Methods
SVM	Support Vector Machine
SVM-E	The enrichment of SVM from individual spaces.
NMTL	Naive MTL as in (2)
NMTL-E	The enrichment of N-SVM from individual spaces.
MTLG	Regularized MTL with only graph Laplacian
MTLE	Regularized MTL with only exclusive group Lasso

Table 2: The baseline algorithms for comparison in individual semantic spaces of NUS-WIDE-Emotive.

Name	Methods
SVM	Support Vector Machine
LNP	Linear Neighborhood Propagation [32]
EGSSC	Entropic Graph Semi-Supervised Classification [28]
LSMP	Large-scale Multi-label Propagation [4]

- IA-MSL simultaneously outperforms the competing methods in MAUC and AUCs on all of the 8 emotive classes.
- On comparison between IA-MSL and NMTL, since both utilize the same features, the improvement of the former over the latter is supposed to stem from the fact that IA-MSL explicitly encodes exclusive group lasso and graph Laplacian regularizer in discriminative analysis. As simplified versions of IA-MSL, MTLG and MTLE are both superior to NMTL but inferior to IA-MSL.
- It is interesting to note that the enrichment methods SVM-E and NMTL-E outperform SVM and NMTL, respectively. This is not surprising since both SVM and NMTL suffer from the insufficient training sample problem in multi-semantic spaces, while SVM-E and NMTL-E bypass this problem by training and testing in unitary space, and then fusing the results in individual spaces as final output.

To show the convergence performance of the proposed smoothing approximation optimization scheme developed in Section 3, we illustrate in Figure 2 the objective value ($F_\mu(W)$) in (12) convergence curve on NUS-WIDE-Emotive. It can be observed that the algorithm converges fast in less than 100 iterates. As a first-order information, the smoothing approximation method used in IA-MSL scales well w.r.t. the sample size N and feature dimensionality d. In our practice, a typical training time on this dataset is about 512 seconds. The per query time of IA-MSL is about 0.05 second.

By setting the semantic space number $K = 1$, IA-MSL is immediately applicable to unitary semantic image annotation. We have also compared IA-MSL with baselines in Table 1. Table 4 lists the results for 8 emotive classes. Table 5 lists the corresponding results for 81 cognitive object

Table 3: The MAUCs of different image annotation algorithms on the NUS-WIDE-Emotive for 648 Concepts.

Methods	SVM	SVM-E	NMTL	NMTL-E	MTLG	MTLE	IA-MSL
Amusement	55.7	57.9	60.0	61.2	65.7	66.1	**71.1**
Excitement	54.2	56.2	64.4	65.2	68.1	71.2	**75.4**
Awe	56.8	57.9	64.7	64.9	65.0	67.8	**69.7**
Contentment	67.0	68.9	75.1	76.4	76.4	80.9	**83.7**
Disgust	30.2	31.3	35.4	36.0	34.1	35.1	**37.0**
Anger	59.1	60.7	67.2	68.1	68.3	72.0	**77.2**
Fear	54.2	55.7	59.7	60.0	61.5	64.3	**68.9**
Sad	61.2	62.3	67.4	67.8	68.1	70.8	**73.6**
MAUC %	54.8	56.1	62.0	63.1	65.1	66.1	**69.6**

Table 4: The AUCs and MAUC of different image annotation algorithms on the NUS-WIDE-Emotive for 8 Emotive Categories.

AUC %	SVM	NMTL	MTLG	MTLE	IA-MSL
Amusement	73.0	76.0	77.9	77.9	**78.1**
Excitement	34.8	64.6	66.9	66.9	**67.2**
Awe	28.5	70.0	71.2	71.2	**72.2**
Contentment	33.2	65.2	67.1	67.0	**68.2**
Disgust	25.1	68.7	73.3	73.3	**75.8**
Anger	32.1	64.9	67.3	67.2	**69.8**
Fear	30.2	68.6	71.2	71.1	**72.7**
Sad	26.1	73.5	36.9	74.5	**75.6**
MAUC %	36.1	67.8	70.1	71.1	**73.7**

Table 5: The MAUCs of different image annotation algorithms on the NUS-WIDE-Emotive for 81 object concepts.

Methods	SVM	NMTL	MTLG	MTLE	IA-MSL
Group1	71.1	75.4	78.8	80.3	**86.4**
Group2	57.0	74.5	78.1	79.6	**85.7**
Group3	53.7	76.2	79.1	80.4	**86.4**
Group4	54.3	79.1	82.3	83.8	**89.9**
Group5	40.1	72.4	74.8	76.3	**84.3**
Group6	35.0	75.0	78.3	79.9	**86.3**
Group7	25.1	75.6	79.1	80.6	**86.8**
Group8	9.1	72.6	76.0	77.5	**83.4**
MAUC %	42.7	75.1	78.5	80.2	**86.1**

categories. To make the table compacter, we sort the 81 concepts according to the descending order of training sample number and evenly divide them into 8 groups. The AUCs in Table 5 are obtained by averaging over each of these 8 concept groups. From the results in both tables we can see that IA-MSL also outperforms the baselines for unitary semantic annotation. Moreover, we also compare IA-MSL with several representative unitary semantic image annotation algorithms on NUA-WIDE-LITE as listed in Table 6. It can be seen that our method outperforms the state-of-the-arts methods.

One direct application of IA-MSL is real world image retrieval with multi-semantic query words. On NUS-WIDE-Emotive, by inputting the emotive-cognitive query word "Amusement Dog", the returned top 6 ranked images by IA-MSL, NMTL and SVM are shown in Figure 3.

4.4 Experiment-II: NUS-WIDE-Object &Scene

On this dataset, we category all labels into three setting: 33 scene classes, 31 object classes and 1023 (33 scene × 31 concepts) combination classes. The ground truth of 1023 labels is also derived by Cartesian product of 33 scene labels and 31 object labels. Again, some of these 1023 multi-semantic labels suffer from the issue of insufficient training samples. We compare IA-MSL with six baseline algorithms as shown in Table 1. Table 7 lists the quantitative results. To make the results more compactly, we sort the 1033 concepts in the descent order of training sample number and evenly divide them into 5 groups. The AUCs in Table 7 are obtained by averaging over each of these 5 concept groups. As can be observed that IA-MSL outperforms the competing methods in MAUC and AUCs on all the 5 concept groups. It is noted that on Group 5, all the involved comparing algorithms return AUC value 0. This is unsurprising since Group 5 is composed of those concepts with very few or even zero training samples, and thus all the algorithms fail including. A typical running time for training on this dataset is about 470 seconds. The per query time of IA-MSL is about 0.08 second.

Table 6: The unitary semantic annotation results on NUS-WIDE-LITE.

Methods	SVM	LNP	EGSSC	LSMP	IA-MSL
MAUC	38.5	74.5	75.0	78.3	81.5

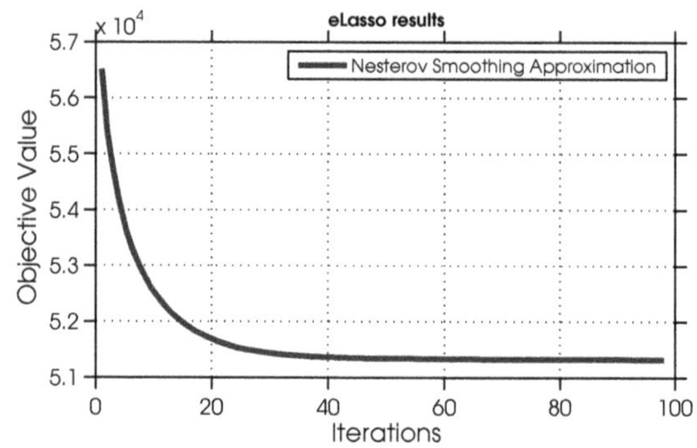

Figure 2: Convergence curve of IA-MSL on NUS-WIDE-EMOTIVE dataset.

Specially, in the setting of unitary semantic image annotation, we have also compared IA-MSL with the algorithms listed in Table 2. Table 8 and Table 9 list the corresponding results for 31 objects and 33 scenes, respectively. In order to present the concise and compact results, we sort both the 31 objects and 33 scenes based on the descent order of training sample number and evenly divide each of them into 5 groups. The AUCs are obtained by averaging over each of these 5 groups. From the results, we observe again that IA-MSL also outperforms the baselines for unitary semantic annotation.

5. CONCLUSION

In this paper, we proposed the IA-MSL method to explore multi-semantic meaning of images based on two or more semi-orthogonal label spaces from multi-semantic. We formulated this challenging problem as a multi-task discriminative analysis model, where individual tasks are defined by learning the linear discriminative model for individual complex semantic concepts. We considered all the tasks in a joint

Table 7: The MAUCs of different image annotation algorithms on the NUS-WIDE-Object&Scene for 1023 Concepts.

Methods	SVM	SVM-E	NMTL	NMTL-E	MTLG	MTLE	IA-MSL
Group1	61.3	62.5	79.8	81.2	82.5	84.6	**86.7**
Group2	50.0	51.9	65.8	67.2	71.3	72.4	**78.7**
Group3	41.2	42.1	50.5	52.1	55.0	56.5	**75.8**
Group4	5.3	5.5	5.6	6.1	6.2	7.3	**13.0**
Group5	0	0	0	0	0	0	**0**
MAUC %	38.0	40.2	47.2	48.6	51.0	52.5	**61.3**

Figure 3: Some exemplar results of query search and ranking by IA-MSL (top row), NMTL (middle row) and SVM (bottom row) on NUS-WIDE-Emotive with the query: "Amusement Dog". The red border indicates correct result while the green one incorrect.

Table 8: The MAUCs of different image annotation algorithms on the NUS-WIDE-Object&Scene for 31 object concepts.

Methods	SVM	NMTL	MTLG	MTLE	IA-MSL
Group1	71.2	72.6	77.8	79.9	**87.4**
Group2	58.9	71.6	76.5	78.6	**84.1**
Group3	40.4	75.1	80.1	82.2	**88.7**
Group4	21.3	75.3	80.3	82.4	**87.9**
Group5	10.1	74.8	79.8	81.3	**87.0**
MAUC %	44.5	73.8	78.9	81.0	**87.5**

Table 9: The MAUCs of different image annotation algorithms on the NUS-WIDE-Object&Scene for 33 scene concepts.

Methods	SVM	NMTL	MTLG	MTLE	IA-MSL
Group1	70.0	72.4	78.8	81.5	**87.0**
Group2	57.1	59.6	64.5	67.2	**83.7**
Group3	39.8	73.8	79.3	82.0	**88.1**
Group4	19.1	72.5	78.9	81.1	**87.6**
Group5	9.0	72.1	77.6	80.3	**86.8**
MAUC %	43.3	72.3	77.8	80.5	**87.1**

manner by imposing two types of regularization on parameters, the graph Laplacian regularization and exclusive group lasso regularization. A Nesterov-type smoothing approximation method is developed for model optimization. The proposed algorithm was tested on two image benchmarks built for multi-semantic annotation. We validated the superiority of IA-MSL in terms of both accuracy and efficacy. In future, we can attach a few sub-categories to each category of the aforementioned 8 Emotive Categories to expand our search range towards real world search scenario.

6. ACKNOWLEDGEMENTS

We would like to acknowledge to the support of "NExT Research Center" funded by MDA, Singapore, under the research grant: WBS:R-252-300-001-490, and the partially support of NUST Research Funding NO. 2011ZDJH09.

7. REFERENCES

[1] A. Argyriou, T. Evgeniou, and M. Pontil. Convex multi-task feature learning. *Machine Learning*, 73 (3):243–272, 2008.

[2] S. Becker, J. Bobin, and E. Candes. NESTA: A fast and accurate first-order method for sparse recovery. *SIAM J. on Imaging Sciences*, 4(1):1–39, 2011.

[3] R. Caruana. Multi-task learning. *Machine Learning*, 28(1):41–75, 1997.

[4] X. Chen, Y. Mu, S. Yan, and T.-S. Chua. Efficient large-scale image annotation by probabilistic collaborative multi-label propagation. In *ACM MM*, 2010.

[5] T.-S. Chua, J. Tang, R. Hong, H. Li, Z. Luo, and Y.-T. Zheng. NUS-WIDE: A real-world web image database from national university of singapore. In *ACM CIVR*, 2009.

[6] R. Cilibrasi and P. M. B. Vitanyi. The google similarity distance. *IEEE Transactions on Knowledge and Data Engineering*, 19(3):370–383, 2007.

[7] T. Evgeniou and M. Pontil. Regularized multi–task learning. In *SIGKDD*, 2004.

[8] M. Fornasier and H. Rauhut. Recovery algorithm for vector-valued data with joint sparsity constraints. *SIAM Journal on Numerical Analysis*, 46(2):577–613, 2008.

[9] T. Griffiths and Z. Ghahramani. Infinite latent feature models and the indian buffet process. In *NIPS*, 2005.

[10] A. Hanjalic. Extracting moods from pictures and sounds: Towards truly personalized TV. *Signal Processing Magazine*, 23(2):90–100, 2006.

[11] J. A. Hanley and B. J. McNeil. The meaning and use of the area under a receiver operating characteristic (ROC) curve. *Radiology*, 143(1):29–36, 1982.

[12] T. Hayashi and M. Hagiwara. Image query by impression words-the IQI system. *IEEE Transactions on Consumer Electronics*, 44(2):347–352, 1998.

[13] L. Jacob, G. Obozinski, and J.-P. Vert. Group lasso with overlap and graph lasso. In *ICML*, 2009.

[14] K. Kesorn. *Multi-Model Multi-Semantic Image Retrieval*. PhD Thesis, Queen Mary, University of London, 2010.

[15] M. Kowalski. Sparse regression using mixed norms. *Applied and Computational Harmonic Analysis*, 27(3):303–324, 2009.

[16] M. Kowalski and B. Torreesani. Sparsity and persistence: Mixed norms provide simple signals models with dependent coefficient. *Signal, Image and Video Processing*, 3(3):251–264, 2009.

[17] M. Lew, N. Sebe, C. Djeraba, and R. Jain. Content-based multimedia information retrieval: State-of-the-art and challenges. *ACM Trans. Multimedia Comput. Commun. Appl.*, 2(1):1–19, 2006.

[18] D. Liu, X.-S. Hua, L. Yang, M. Wang, and H.-J. Zhang. Tag ranking. In *WWW*, 2009.

[19] H. Liu, M. Palatucci, and J. Zhang. Blockwise coordinate descent procedures for the multi-task lasso, with applications to neural semantic basis discovery. In *ICML*, pages 649–656, 2009.

[20] Y. Liu, R. Jin, and L. Yang. Semi-supervised multi-label learning by constrained non-negative matrix factorization. In *AAAI*, 2006.

[21] J. Machajdik and A. Hanbury. Affective image classification using features inspired by psychology and art theory. In *ACM MM*, 2010.

[22] J. A. Mikels, B. L. Fredrickson, G. R. Larkin, C. M. Lindberg, S. J. Maglio, and P. A. Reuter-Lorenz. Emotional category data on images from the international affective picture system. *Behavior Research Methods*, 37(4):626–630, 2005.

[23] Y. Nesterov. *Introductory Lectures on Convex Optimization: A Basic Course*. Kluwer, 2004.

[24] Y. Nesterov. Smooth minimization of non-smooth functions. *Mathematical Programming*, 103(1):127–152, 2005.

[25] J. Nocedal and S. J. Wright. *Numerical Optimization*. Springer-Verlag, 2006.

[26] G. Obozinski, B. Taskar, and M. Jordan. Joint covariate selection and joint subspace selection for multiple classification problems. *Journal of Statistics and Computing*, 20(2):231–252, 2009.

[27] G.-J. Qi, X.-S. Hua, Y. Rui, J. Tang, T. Mei, and H.-J. Zhang. Correlative multi-label video annotation. In *ACM MM*, 2007.

[28] A. Subramanya and J. Bilmes. Entropic graph regularization in non-parametric semi-supervised classification. In *NIPS*, 2009.

[29] J. Tang, S. Yan, R. Hong, G.-J. Qi, and T.-S. Chua. Inferring semantic concepts from community-contributed images and noisy tags. In *ACM MM*, 2009.

[30] P. Tseng. On accelerated proximal gradient methods for convex-concave optimization. *submitted to SIAM Journal of Optimization*, 2008.

[31] N. Ueda and K. Saito. Parametric mixture models for multilabeled text. In *NIPS*, 2002.

[32] F. Wang and C. Zhang. Label propagation through linear neighborhoods. In *ICML*, 2006.

[33] M. Wang, X.-S. Hua, R. Hong, J. Tang, G.-J. Qi, and Y. Song. Unified video annotation via multi-graph learning. *IEEE Transactions on Circuits and Systems for Video Technology*, 19(5):733–746, 2009.

[34] M. Wang, X.-S. Hua, J. Tang, and R. Hong. Beyond distance measurement: Constructing neighborhood similarity for video annotation. *IEEE Transactions on Multimedia*, 11(3):465–476, 2009.

[35] W.-N. Wang, Y.-L. Yu, and S.-M. Jiang. Image retrieval by emotional semantics: A study of emotional space and feature extraction. In *IEEE SMC*, 2006.

[36] L. Wu, X.-S. Hua, N. Yu, W.-Y. Ma, and S. Li. Semi-supervised multi-label learning by constrained non-negative matrix factorization. In *ACM MM*, 2008.

[37] Q. Wu, C. Zhou, and C. Wang. Content-based affective image classification and retrieval using support vector machines. *Affective Computing and Intelligent Interaction*, 37(84):239–247, 2005.

[38] V. Yanulevskaya, J. C. van Gemert, K. Roth, A. K. Herbold, N. Sebe, and J. M. Geusebroek. Emotional valence categorization using holistic image features. In *ICIP*, 2008.

[39] M. Yuan and Y. Lin. Model selection and estimation in regression with grouped variables. *Journal of the Royal Statistical Society. Series B*, 68(1):49–67, 2006.

[40] Z.-J. Zha, X.-S. Hua, T. Mei, J. Wang, G.-J. Qi, and Z. Wang. Joint multi-label multi-instance learning for image classification. In *CVPR*, 2008.

[41] Z.-J. Zha, L. Yang, T. Mei, M. Wang, and Z. Wang. Visual query suggestion. In *ACM MM*, 2009.

[42] J. Zhang. A probabilistic framework for multi-task learning. Technical report, CMU-LTI-06-006, 2006.

[43] P. Zhao, G. Rocha, and B. Yu. The composite absolute penalties family for grouped and hierarchical variable selection. *The Annals of Statistics*, 37(6A):3468–3497, 2009.

[44] Y. Zhou, R. Jin, and S. C. Hoi. Exclusive lasso for multi-task feature selection. In *AISTATS*, 2010.

[45] S. Zhu, X. Ji, W. Xu, and Y. Gong. Multi-labelled classification using maximum entropy method. In *ACM SIGIR*, 2005.

APPENDIX

A. PROOF OF THEOREM 1

PROOF. Fixe an $i \in \{1, ..., d\}$. Analog to the standard analysis and results (see, e.g. [24, Theorem 1]) we can derive that $q_{\mathcal{G}^k,\mu}(W^i)$, $k = 1, 2$, is well defined and continuously differentiable with gradients given by

$$\nabla q_{\mathcal{G}^k,\mu}(W^i) = V^{i,k}(W^i),$$

which is Lipschitz continuous with constant

$$L^i_{k,\mu} = \frac{1}{\mu}. \tag{A.1}$$

By chain rule of derivative we get that for $k = 1, 2$,

$$\frac{1}{2}\nabla q^2_{\mathcal{G}^k,\mu}(W^i) = q_{\mathcal{G}^k,\mu}(W^i)V^{i,k}(W^i),$$

which proves the (10), and consequently (9).

To prove the Lipschitz continency of $\nabla\Omega_\mu(W)$, one may first confirm the Lipschitz continuousness of $\frac{1}{2}\nabla q^2_{\mathcal{G}^k,\mu}(W^i)$, $k = 1, 2$,

$$\begin{aligned}
& \|q_{\mathcal{G}^k,\mu}(W^i)\nabla q_{\mathcal{G}^k,\mu}(W^i) - q_{\mathcal{G}^k,\mu}(U^i)\nabla q_{\mathcal{G}^k,\mu}(U^i)\|_2 \\
= \; & \|q_{\mathcal{G}^k,\mu}(W^i)\nabla q_{\mathcal{G}^k,\mu}(W^i) - q_{\mathcal{G}^k,\mu}(W^i)\nabla q_{\mathcal{G}^k,\mu}(U^i) \\
& + q_{\mathcal{G}^k,\mu}(W^i)\nabla q_{\mathcal{G}^k,\mu}(U^i) - q_{\mathcal{G}^k,\mu}(U^i)\nabla q_{\mathcal{G}^k,\mu}(U^i)\|_2 \\
\le \; & |q_{\mathcal{G}^k,\mu}(W^i)| \cdot \|\nabla q_{\mathcal{G}^k,\mu}(W^i) - \nabla q_{\mathcal{G}^k,\mu}(U^i)\|_2 \\
& + \|\nabla q_{\mathcal{G}^k,\mu}(U^i)\|_2 \cdot |q_{\mathcal{G}^k,\mu}(W^i) - q_{\mathcal{G}^k,\mu}(U^i)| \\
\le \; & \left(\frac{\sqrt{2}R}{\mu} + |\mathcal{L}^k|^2\right)\|W^i - U^i\|_2
\end{aligned} \tag{A.2}$$

where the last equality follows the basic facts: (i) constant in (A.1), (ii) $|q_{\mathcal{G}^k,\mu}(W^i)| \le \|W^i_{\mathcal{G}^k}\|_{2,1} \le \sqrt{2}R$, (iii) $\|\nabla q_{\mathcal{G}^k,\mu}(U^i)\|_2$ $\|V^{i,k}(U^i)\|_2 \le |\mathcal{L}^k|$, and (iv) $|q_{\mathcal{G}^k,\mu}(W^i) - q_{\mathcal{G}^k,\mu}(U^i)| \le \|\mathcal{L}^k\|\|W^i - U^i\|_2$ (due to the boundness of $\nabla q_{g,\mu}$ in (iii)). By combining (6) and (A.2) we establish the validity of (11). □

Reading between the Tags to Predict Real-World Size-Class for Visually Depicted Objects in Images

Martha Larson, Christoph Kofler, Alan Hanjalic
Multimedia Information Retrieval Lab, Delft University of Technology
Delft, The Netherlands
{m.a.larson, c.kofler, a.hanjalic}@tudelft.nl

ABSTRACT

Multimedia information retrieval stands to benefit from the availability of additional information about tags and how they relate to the content visually depicted in images. We propose a generic approach that contributes to improving the informativeness of image tags by combining generalizations about the distributional tendencies of physical objects in the real world and statistics of natural language use patterns that have been mined from the Web. The approach, which we refer to as 'Reading between the Tags,' provides for each tag associated with an image, first, a prediction concerning *corporeality*, i.e., whether or not the tag denotes a physical entity, and, then, concerning the real-world size of that entity, i.e., large, medium or small. Mining takes place using a set of Language Use Frames (LUFs) that are composed of natural language neighborhoods characteristic of tag classes. We validate our approach with a series of experiments on a set of images from the MIRFLICKR data set using ground truth created with standard crowdsourcing techniques. The main experiments demonstrate the effectiveness of our approach for size-class prediction. A further experiment shows that size-class prediction can be improved and made image-specific using general and relatively small sets of visual concepts. A final experiment confirms that the set of LUFs can also be chosen automatically via statistical feature selection.

Categories and Subject Descriptors

H.3.1 [**Information Search and Retrieval**]: Content Analysis and Indexing

General Terms

Algorithms, Experimentation

Keywords

User-contributed tags, Image annotation, Size, Real-world scale, Selectional restrictions, Lexico-syntactic patterns, Crowdsourcing

1. INTRODUCTION

User-contributed tags are helpful for image browsing and retrieval and their utility can be further improved if the relationship between a tag and the visual content of an image can be made more specific. We propose a technique, 'Reading between the Tags', which applies a lightweight approach in order to generate generic information that can be used to improve tag informativeness. Our proposed technique combines the distributional tendencies of physical objects in the real world with general Web text statistics to make a best guess about tag sizes. In particular, we are interested in predicting if a tag corresponds to a physical entity depicted in the image and, if it does, whether that entity is small, medium or large. The best guess is based on the tag identity alone, i.e., without making use of image content, and predicts an image-independent tag size class. This initial prediction constitutes a prior concerning the content of the actual image. Visual information derived from the image can then be incorporated in order to generate a prediction of tag size-class that is image specific. In contrast to other approaches that rely exclusively on visual analysis and tag distributions to refine tags, our approach makes use of auxiliary information on objects' physical properties that is automatically derived from the neighborhoods of tags when they are used as words in natural language.

If we consider the two images in Figure 1 as images in a large image collection, it is easy to imagine cases in which a user image need is satisfied by one image, but not the other, e.g., by the left image of the boy racing his cars and not by the right image of the cars racing at the racetrack. The user stands to benefit if the tag *car* associated with each image were enriched with information concerning the real-world size of the car depicted. This example illustrates our underlying motivation for predicting the size-classes of visually depicted objects in images: additional information about the size of the objects in images denoted by tags is useful to support the user in searching and browsing image collections. Ultimately, such size information could also make a contribution to tag ranking or tag propagation.

Flickr: Mydaas! Flickr: Martin Pettitt

Figure 1. Two examples of car racing: small cars vs. large cars

Now consider the two images in Figure 1, not as images per se, but rather as depictions of two real world situations involving car racing. It would be rather odd or unnatural if one of the cars pictured in the situation on the left would engage in a race with one of the cars on the right. Our approach is based on the observation that situations in the real, physical world tend to be characterized by a single, specific scale. It exploits the generalization that natural events and interactions in the real world are somewhat less prone to take place between objects of radically different sizes. Instead, the co-occurrence distribution of physical objects in the real world displays a trend towards dependency on size. We refer to this tendency as *scale specificity*.

*Area Chair: Kiyoharu Aizawa

MM'11, November 28–December 1, 2011, Scottsdale, Arizona, USA.

Note that scale specificity is not merely a style or composition property of the images in Figure 1, but derives from the physical configuration of the real-world situation or event that is depicted in the image. Further, notice that we do not claim that scale specificity is an inviolable rule. In an extraordinary situation, the toy car *could* race against the professional racecar. Rather, scale specificity is a *tendency* that applies to naturally occurring real-world situations. Our basic insight, whose usefulness is supported by our experimental results, is that the tendency towards scale specificity in real-world situations is strong enough to be successfully exploited for helping to improve the informativeness of tags.

Our 'Reading between the Tags' approach leverages scale-specificity effects in two parallel domains: the natural language domain and the image domain. As an example from the natural language domain, two real-world situations are presented in Figure 2. In the case of the flower, it is perfectly natural that the girl is holding it in her hand. However, in the case of a car, it is more natural for the girl to be standing beside it since it is too large for her to hold in her hand.

Flickr: dæxus

Flickr: clappstar

Figure 2. Natural interaction of a girl's hand with a flower (left); in contrast a car is too big to fit in the girl's hand (right)

Natural language is produced by human beings, who frequently discuss or describe the real, physical world that exists around them. If scale-specific events and interactions are natural in the real world, then it is to be expected that language describing scale-specific situations occurs, in general, more frequently than language describing situations that are not scale specific. With respect to this example, we would anticipate that people would more frequently say or write a sentence describing a situation in which a girl holds a flower in her hand than one describing a situation where a girl holds a car in her hand. The girl's hand can be considered as existing on the same scale as the flower, but not on the same scale as the car. Instead, descriptions of a girl standing beside the car could be anticipated to be more frequent.

Scale-specific effects are particularly strong when humans are involved since humans have limited physical powers that constrain their interaction with the world around them. Within a relatively well-defined range, humans have certain limits to their size and their power of strength and sight. These constraints have the effect of limiting human actions and interactions to specific scales and these situations have clear manifestations in natural language. We elaborate on these constraints in Section 3.2, where we use them to select effective language use patterns.

The main contribution of this paper is a novel approach, 'Reading between the Tags', that combines the scale-specific tendencies of real-world situations with natural language use patterns reflecting scale specificity to automatically generate size-class predictions for tags. The basic approach functions independently of the visual content of images and instead uses statistics of natural language use patterns involving tag-words that occur frequently in general Web text. The basic approach generates a best guess, which, as will be shown by the experiments, provides a strong prior related to image content. The performance of the basic approach can be further enhanced by additional information from general visual concepts by exploiting scale-specificity in the image domain.

We turn now to an example from the image domain. In natural events and interactions, if we assume that physical entities tend to interact on the same scale, then images captured of physical, real-world situations can be expected to reflect scale-specificity. In the image on the left in Figure 3, a mongoose interacts with a flower. Both entities can be considered roughly small scale and the situation is quite natural and ordinary. The presence of the visual concept *flower* signals the small scale of the image and thereby the small size of entities in its visual context, here, the mongoose. Note that we do not claim that it is impossible for a mongoose to interact with a substantially larger entity such as a fire truck. Our observation is that scale-specific situations tend to be sufficiently more natural and commonplace and for this reason enjoy an elevated frequency with respect to their representations, which we exploit in our approach.

Frequently, the composition of images serves to enhance scale-specific effects. Photographers' inclination to move in or to zoom in on subjects may arise from a conscious effort to 'fill the frame with stuff' [18], or from a desire to ensure that image subject matter is clearly visible. Although photographers also vary composition, with respect to other considerations such as depth of field, in general we would expect images to exhibit a tendency to include salient depictions of objects on one scale, to the exclusion of objects on other scales, especially larger objects.

Flickr: Tambako the Jaguar

Flickr: khowaga1

Figure 3. Small-scale scale specificity: a mongoose interacts with a flower (left); Large-scale scale specificity: a windmill pictured against the sky (right)

How the photographer fills the frame impacts not only the physical entities depicted in the image, but also the presence of other visual concepts. In this case, we point out that especially the presence of general concepts (e.g., sky, water, night, flower), such as those that constitute the basis for much work in the area of visual concept detection [11][24], serve as clues to image scale. The connection is weak, but strong enough to be exploited for our purposes of making tags more informative. In the image on the right in Figure 3, the windmill is a relatively large physical object and the photographer must stand back to capture it in its entirety and naturally captures part of the sky. The same point applies to the image of the race at the racetrack on the right in Figure 1. Sky, in these cases, is a general visual concept that can be expected to occur with an elevated frequency in images that depict scale-specific situations when the scale is relatively large. The experiments we carry out using visual concepts are intended to demonstrate the usefulness of this distributional tendency and abstract away from the noise of visual concept detector output by making use of ground-truth visual concept labels.

The main research question addressed by this paper is Q1: Can the principle of 'Reading between the Tags' successfully combine the tendency toward scale-specificity with statistics on natural language use patterns to predict tag-class? We also address two auxiliary questions. Q2: Can visual concepts occurring in images be used to refine the prediction of the basic approach? Q3: Do statistically selected language use patterns demonstrate scale-specificity effects and can they support tag-class prediction?

The paper is organized as follows. We overview related work in the relevant sub-domains and explain the motivations and mechanics of the approach in detail. Then, we report on our main experiments that demonstrate the effectiveness of the basic principle of 'Reading between the Tags', which uses natural language use pattern statistics estimated using Web text. In two further experiments, we show the potential of visual concepts to further refine size-class prediction and also demonstrate the robustness of our approach to the choice of features. We conclude with a summary of our main findings and an outlook on future work.

2. BACKGROUND AND RELATED WORK

2.1 Making tags more informative

Much recent work has been devoted to both exploiting and improving the tags users apply to images, with the goal of providing better support for image browsing and retrieval. Tags are notoriously noisy and the user intent behind them might be vague, lazy, highly personal or even malicious—all factors which make tags in their 'raw' form less appropriate for general use. An overview of work on tags and image semantics can be found in [22]. Here, we highlight individual examples as necessary to illustrate key contributions most closely related to ours. Our work shares the same motivation as work on 'tagging tags', i.e., refining tags by assigning them properties [26]. For example, if an image is tagged *balloon*, the approach adds the information that the tag designates a *red* balloon. In [26], tag properties are extracted using visual features. In contrast, our work exploits linguistic patterns, making use of visual features in the form of visual concepts as a supplement. In [16], the usefulness of tags is improved by ranking them with respect to their relevance to the visually depicted content of an image. The work in [23] uses tag co-occurrence and aggregation to generate recommendations of tags for images on Flickr. Tags are de-noised by combining visual features with tag co-occurrence in [14]. In [15], votes from visually similar neighbors are used to improve the relevance score of a tag, which can then be integrated into a retrieval algorithm. Like these approaches, 'Reading between the Tags' strives to improve the usefulness of tags for users. Because it makes use of general Web text statistics that reveal information not directly available from tag co-occurrence or visual features, it has a potential to be used to further enhance any of the techniques mentioned here.

2.2 Language Use Statistics from the Web

Mining large text corpora using lexico-syntactic patterns is a well-established technique, with early roots in computational linguistics [9]. More recently, techniques have employed Web text data, including [13][12][21] and also the well-known Google Similarity Distance (GSD) [3], which estimates the similarity between words and phrases using counts of search results returned by Google. The massive quantities of data available on the Web make it a source of useful approximations of the frequency of word use, as shown by [13][3]. Most approaches use the number of hits returned by a search engine to approximate the frequency of a given language use pattern. We go one step further and also exploit the assumption that the frequency of a language use pattern reflects the relative ordinariness of a given event or interaction in the real world. Like many approaches, including [9], we use specific linguistic neighborhoods in order to mine meaning from text.

2.3 The Linguistics of Physical Properties

'Reading between the Tags' relies on the ability of linguistic contexts to signal physical properties such as corporeality and size. Word co-occurrences in text have been used in the literature to discover many aspects of semantics. For example, in [25] attributes of animals are mined from Wikipedia to form the basis for visual classifiers. This and related techniques directly exploit lexical co-occurrences. For example, on the basis of observing many occurrences of 'the pink flower' in natural language text, we can identify 'pink' as a possible attribute of a flower. This example is highly simplified, but it serves to illustrate the difference of existing techniques with our own. Notice the problem we encounter in the case of size. Finding occurrences of 'the elephant is small' and the 'the mouse is small' does not shed light on the absolute size of these entities in the real world: small for an elephant is enormous for a mouse. Instead, we propose an indirect technique of accessing information on the physical properties of objects that exploits scale specificity and is based on the principles of cognitive linguistics, which regards language as interdependent on human perception of the real, physical world.

Human perception is encoded into language at a relatively low lexico-syntactic level by *proto-semantic features*, which for the purposes of this paper can be taken to be physical properties that are related to objects' form, shape or structure. Computer vision has previously made limited but productive use of such linguistic features [4][6]. They are useful because they are more abstract than low-level visual features, but not as high-level as other linguistic features (such as words) [4] and for this reason have the potential to generalize well.

Proto-semantic features have been successfully exploited for natural language processing tasks, notably word sense disambiguation [20]. Examples of helpful selectional patterns involving proto-semantic features can be found in many languages: across languages the verb *drink* is used with liquids; the Chinese-language noun classifier 座 *zuò* is generally used with large entities like buildings and mountains; and the English preposition *along* is used with an object that is long and path-like. In our approach, we make use of the selectional restrictions of verbs requiring physical existence of their objects (*measure* and *weigh*) as well as relative restrictions on physical configurations imposed by prepositions (*in*, *on*, *at*) on their objects.

Proto-semantic features are manifested in language in a rather indirect manner and, as a result, many speakers are unaware of their existence. However, since they do contribute to determining the immediate neighborhoods of words, it is reasonable to expect physical properties to be reflected in short phrases extracted from textual descriptions or discussion. From the perspective of our approach, if the statistics of short phrases can capture the scale-specificity of events and interactions described in text, then their use is to be preferred over other more intensive, and potentially less robust, text analysis techniques.

The relationship between spatial language and human visual perception of space has been well researched, e.g., [8], but its systematic exploitation in practical multimedia applications has remained elusive. In [4], the difficulty of exploiting human-perceived proto-semantics in multimedia analysis is related to the great power of human language to generalize and also its ability to introduce unexpected distortions. The 'Reading between the Tags' approach, however, applies a lightweight technique that relies on large-scale statistics and is able to tease out information from human language that is related to scale specificity and exploit it to support the enrichment of tags.

3. TAG-CLASS PREDICTION APPROACH

3.1 Corporeality Prediction

Corporeality prediction involves predicting for each tag assigned to an image whether or not that tag denotes a *physical entity* (pe) visually depicted in the image. We sharpen the notion by defining a physical entity as '...a subject which has a mass and which casts a distinct shadow.' This formal definition of physical entity provides a reference for making decisions in any borderline cases that are encountered when annotating our test data with ground truth (cf. Section 4.1). Not all tags assigned to images by users (e.g., *cool* and *tomorrow*) can be interpreted as denoting concepts with an independent, self-contained existence. Such cases are not considered entities and we designate them *not a physical entity* (no-pe). Of the tags that do designate entities, many will designate entities that have no physical nature, but are rather abstract, non-corporeal concepts such as *friendship*, *love*, *violence*, *Facebook* and *bedtime*; these are also designated no-pe. Note that we define our task such that the success of corporeality prediction is always judged with respect to the combination of tag and image, and not with respect to the tag in isolation. The consequence is that a tag, e.g., *pizza*, is considered pe with respect to an image that actually depicts an identifiable pizza and no-pe with respect to an image that depicts a family at an Italian restaurant waiting for their pizza to arrive. Note that our basic tag-class prediction approach generates a best guess for the corporeality of a given tag that does not take the image itself into account. We judge it, however, with respect to image-dependent ground truth labels since these best reflect its ultimate usefulness to the user.

3.1.1 Language Use Frames (LUFs)

Under the 'Reading between the Tags' approach, we predict the corporeality of tags by making use of their language use patterns, in particular, the frequency with which they appear in natural language text in the neighborhood of specific words. We assume that the relative frequency of use patterns reflects the relative naturalness or commonness of a particular sort of real world event. For example, if *iPad* and *friendship* are two tags associated with a Flickr image, we can gather evidence on whether these tags potentially designate physical entities in the photo by looking at the frequency of their occurrence in certain linguistic neighborhoods. We expect that in general language use, the string of words 'The iPad measures...' will be relatively more frequent than 'The friendship measures...', simply because an iPad is a physical object and it is not at all odd to subject it to the act of weighing.

We refer to strings of the form 'The X measures' and 'The X weighs' as language use frames (LUFs). They are, simply put, lexico-syntactic patterns whose commonality in natural language use reveals something about the physical properties (in this case corporeality) of the tag substituted in for X. We make an estimate of use frequency by filling in the X in the LUF with a tag and using the resulting string to query the Yahoo! search engine. Any mainstream search engine would serve as well. We refer to this estimate as a LUF-score and prediction methods that make use of LUF-scores and LUF-based approaches. At the time of writing, the string 'the friendship measures' returns six hits using the Yahoo! search engine and the string 'the iPad measures' returns 1,300, this difference is used by our approach as evidence that an iPad is a physical entity and friendship is not.

3.1.2 Predicting Corporeality with LUF-Scores

Corporeality prediction is carried out under our approach by using statistics gathered from the LUFs as features that provide input to a classification decision. Specifically, each image is represented by a set of four LUF-scores, $\{LUF_1, LUF_2, LUF_3, LUF_4\}$ returned by four different queries, as illustrated in Figure 4.

1	2	3	4
the <tag> measure	the <tag> measures	the <tag> weigh	the <tag> weighs

Figure 4. LUFs used for corporeality prediction

Using two separate LUFs with two versions of the verb accommodates plural tags. Note that we are not interested in what occurs after the verb, since it can be anticipated to be highly specific, e.g., '2 cm' or '500 lbs', and, due to proto-semantics, the presence of the verb is already adequate evidence that the weighing or measuring has occurred. We choose to build LUF frames based on weighing and measuring since these are arguably the only interactions that can potentially be applied to *all* physical objects.

We apply two approaches for predicting corporeality with LUF-scores. The first is a simple rule that makes use of a threshold imposed on the sum of the four LUF-scores (*N=4*) to predict the corporeality class (*CC*) for a given tag as illustrated in Eq. (1).

$$\mathrm{CC(tag)} = \begin{cases} \text{no-pe}, & \sum_{i=1}^{N} \mathrm{LUF_i(tag)} < \theta \\ \text{pe}, & \sum_{i=1}^{N} \mathrm{LUF_i(tag)} \geq \theta \end{cases} \quad (1)$$

The threshold θ is estimated on our development set, which is mutually exclusive from the test set. We use this simple rule to investigate if our approach can yield basic, stable performance independently of the availability of large amounts of labeled training data. The second approach is a learning approach that uses standard classifiers; the input is the set of LUF-scores in Figure 4 and the output is the pe/no-pe decision.

The baseline for corporeality prediction is provided by WordNet [5], a large database containing words in the English language. WordNet includes information on whether a particular sense of a word designates a physical entity. This approach has been used for determining whether a tag is a physical entity in [26].

3.2 Size-class Prediction

Size prediction is applied to all tags that have been determined to designate physical entities by the corporeality prediction step just described. Note that previous work using image object size, e.g., [1], focuses on size in terms of how much of the frame that the object fills. Here, we are interested in the physical size of the object in the real-world situation depicted in the image. Each tag is assigned to one of three size categories (small, medium or large) depending on the real-world size of the physical entity visually depicted in the image. For completeness, we describe our definition of the size classes in detail. These definitions informed the labeling of ground truth (cf. Section 4.1). Small (s) is differentiated from non-small using the question 'Is it bigger than a breadbox?' used in the well-known game 'Twenty Questions' presumably for its ability to reduce entropy in an arbitrary real-world setting during the decision process of identifying objects [2]. Non-small objects are differentiated into medium (m) and large (l) objects using the question 'Does it fit into a delivery van?' These two questions correspond respectively to objects of the size that individual humans can manipulate and also transport with their bare hands and that objects that individual humans can manipulate or transport with non-specialized transport equipment. Our goals in assuming these size classes are threefold: (1) We wish to avoid arbitrary cutoffs. (2) We would like intuitive size classes matching users' natural conceptualization of the world with an eye to our ultimate goal of improved image browsing and search. (3) Natural size divisions pertinent for human perception and interaction can be anticipated to provide a good correspondence with language use patterns.

3.2.1 Language Use Frames (LUFs)

Similarly to the case of corporeality prediction, we predict the size class by using series of scores that represent the number of hits returned by Yahoo! when queried with specific Language Use Frames (LUFs) into which the tag has been substituted. However, for size prediction we exploit insight derived from scale-specificity effects. As mentioned in the introduction, such effects can be expected to be somewhat more stable in events and interactions involving humans because of the relatively limited and predictable range of human size, strength and vision. Humans can interact with their hands with small objects located at relatively short range. Human sight, however, is much wider ranging and does not involve physical interaction: for this reason, human perception and observation can involve large objects that are located at a distance.

These trends are reflected in language use. For example, we expect, 'He put the needle in his pocket' to be relatively more frequent than phrases in which large objects are manipulated, e.g., 'He put the windmill in his pocket.' Notice that both describe actions that do not take place on a daily basis. Both a needle and a windmill would be slightly strange objects to put in one's pocket. However, because the needle corresponds to a scale-specific event we expect it to occur relatively more frequently than the case of the windmill. The elevated frequency of the event is reflected in an elevated frequency of language use patterns. The statistics in the second row of Table 1 show that this expectation is borne out in practice when the relative commonness of language use is approximated by our standard procedure of counting the number of hits returned by the Yahoo! search engine. A further benefit of exploiting the presence of humans in events and interactions is the relative frequency of their mention. We speak and write regularly about ourselves, our friends and other people we know, and in this sense, using LUFs that exploit human experience with the world helps to ensure that we have enough data for solid estimation.

Table 1. Scores for size class frame examples. The score is the number of hits returned by Yahoo! when queried with an exact query consisting of the LUF with the tag substituted in.

	Language Use Frame (LUF)	Scores for example tags needle (S)	hobbit (M)	windmill (L)
S	the <tag> in her hand	541	0	1
	the <tag> in his pocket	42	0	0
M	the <tag> beside her	5	29	0
	the <tag> on his left	6	3	0
L	the <tag> in the distance	9	0	185
	the <tag> on the horizon	4	22	47

In order to form the LUF frame, we use only those parts of phrases that are directly related to physical configuration, i.e., 'the <tag> in his pocket'. This truncation allows the LUFs to pick up on manipulation events involving a wide range of verbs (cf. 'he carried the needle in his pocket' and 'he hid the needle in his pocket'). Notice that despite the truncation we keep the focus on situations involving humans by including the possessive pronouns 'his' and 'her'. Natural interaction with medium objects involves predominantly proximity rather than manipulation. For this reason, we expect 'She turned to the <tag> beside her' to be relatively commonplace when <tag> is a medium physical object and truncation leads to the LUF 'the <tag> beside her.' In Table 1, it can be seen that this expectation is borne out when the relative commonness of language use is approximated by our standard procedure of counting the number of hits returned by Yahoo! in response to specific queries. Together, the examples in Table 1 illustrate the interaction of the three types of LUFs used for size-predictions with examples of tags from the three size classes. It can be seen that LUF-scores can fluctuate a great deal and do not always give the correct decision individually. For example, *hobbit* produces a relatively high score with respect to the large LUF in the final line of the table. We surmise that it is important that multiple LUFs are used to contribute to size-class decisions.

3.2.2 Predicting Size-Class with LUF-Scores

In our main experiment, we use 18 frames like those in Table 1 that we selected according to the considerations discussed above: {LUF_1, LUF_2, LUF_3, LUF_4, LUF_5...LUF_{18}}, cf. Figure 5.

1	2	3	4	5	6	7	8	9	10	11	12	13	14	15	16	17	18
S								M								L	
the <tag> in her hand	the <tag> in his hand	the <tag> in her pocket	the <tag> in his pocket	the <tag> between her fingers	the <tag> between his fingers	the <tag> in her mouth	the <tag> in his mouth	the <tag> beside her	the <tag> beside him	the <tag> at her side	the <tag> at his side	the <tag> on her right	the <tag> on his right	the <tag> on her left	the <tag> on his left	the <tag> in the distance	the <tag> on the horizon

Figure 5. LUFs used for size-class prediction

Each frame is associated with a size classes small (LUF_1–LUF_8), medium (LUF_9–LUF_{16}), and large (LUF_{17}–LUF_{18}). In practice, the balance of frames over size classes was determined using the development set. Note that an auxiliary experiment using LUFs statistically selected from Web text in Section 5.4 will reveal our approach to be independent of the specific details of the design of the LUF inventory.

As above, we first introduce a simple rule approach to distinguish between `s`, `m`, and `l` for size-class prediction.

$$\mathrm{SC(tag)} = \arg\max_{c \in C} \sum_{i=1}^{N_c} \mathrm{LUF_i(tag)} \qquad (2)$$

As shown in Eq. (2), we predict tag size-classes by using the largest LUF size-class sum of the three defined size classes ($C=\{s, m, l\}$), where N_c is the number of LUF frames of a given size class. In case of equal LUF size-class sums, we break the tie by deciding for the smaller class. Our second approach is again a learning approach that makes use of standard classifiers. The input to the approach is the set of LUF-scores in Figure 5 and the output is the `s/m/l` decision.

We note that a possible alternative to using LUFs for size prediction is to develop a large knowledge resource listing tags and their corresponding sizes. The LUF-based approach is superior to that approach because it can handle a large range of words (i.e., it is not necessary to know what a hobbit is, or have previously hand-classified *hobbit* as a medium physical entity in order to determine its size class). Since the distribution of tags, including the image tags on Flickr, follows a power law distribution [23], approximately half of the tags occurring will only occur once, making them difficult to look up in the dictionary. The LUF approach on the other hand, can generate a prediction for any tag and relies only on a minimum number of tag mentions having already appeared on the Web.

3.3 Size-class Prediction with Visual Concepts

We experiment with incorporating LUF-scores and visual concepts in order to enhance the performance of size-class prediction and to generate an image-specific size-class prediction. As mentioned in the introduction, we conjecture that general visual concepts that are present in an image provide additional information about the scale of the image and thereby also about the size-class of tags denoting physical entities present in the image. The examples in Figure 6 serve to illustrate how challenging exploitation of visual concepts will be in practice. Both of these images are tagged *windmill* and the tag designates a depicted physical entity. Ideally, we would like to use visual concepts to discriminate between the small windmill on the left and the large one on the right.

Flickr: jchong

Flickr: Darwin Bell

Figure 6. Potential contribution of visual concepts in two specific cases. Both images are tagged *windmill.*

The lack of the visual concept *sky* in the photo on the left could be an important clue that it is not a large-scale image, which would in turn serve to indicate that the windmill is not large. However, it would not be unnatural to have shot these children outside with some sky visible in the frame, so the absence of sky is possibly a rather weak indicator. In the picture on the right, sky does correlate with a large-scale image, which would suggest a large-scale windmill. However, the flower in the front can, in other settings, suggest a small-scale image. Visual concepts can potentially send a contradictory message about a given image. From these examples we surmise that we should probably expect only modest improvement in the size-class predictions of tags by integrating general visual concepts and that we will need to use multiple visual concepts that have been identified as being particular helpful for this purpose. We form a simple set that combines the LUF-scores for a given tag of an image and the visual concepts depicted in that image: {LUF_1, LUF_2, LUF_3, LUF_4, LUF_5...LUF_n, VIS_1, VIS_2...VIS_m}. We select visual concepts for inclusion in the set using simple feature selection techniques and carry out size-class prediction using a classifier.

4. EXPERIMENTAL FRAMEWORK

4.1 Data Set

The data set used in our experiments is a subset of the MIRFLICKR25000 set [10]. From this set, we sampled a set of 5,000 images (500 images for development and 4,500 images for test) for use in our experiments. We restricted ourselves to images with between 5–10 tags resulting in a total number of 35,659 tags (3,627 tags in the development set and 32,032 tags in the test set). MIRFLICKR data are issued with human-generated ground truth for visual concepts appearing in the images.

The ground truth was created by a standard crowdsourcing procedure carried out on MTurk—Amazon's Mechanical Turk. MTurk is a platform that makes it possible to distribute tasks over human workers, who receive a small payment for successful task completion. Our crowdsourcing task involved a series of questions concerning each Flickr photo and its associated tags. Workers were asked to judge for each of the tags whether or not it was associated with a physical object depicted in the image and, if so, what the size was. A common understanding of these notions among workers was facilitated by a detailed set of definitions and examples. Each image and its tags were annotated by three workers and we adopted the majority opinion as our ground truth label. Inter-annotator agreement surpassed the generally accepted level of 0.7 (kappa 0.740 for corporeality and 0.713 for size) [19]. Before being allowed to annotate images, workers were required to pass a recruitment test, through which the quality of their annotation work was scrutinized. Once admitted, further checks and controls were imposed in order to ensure that quality was maintained. In total, 56 distinct workers annotated the published tasks. MIRFLICKR (http://press.liacs.nl/mirflickr/) is publically available and our ground truth will be available via the MediaEval multimedia benchmark (http://www.multimediaeval.org/).

4.2 Experimental Setup

We carry out prediction with both simple rules and with classifiers. We experiment with four standard classifiers: a decision tree (J48), a rule-based classifier (JRip), a support vector machine (SNO), and a Naïve Bayes classifier. The decision tree and the rule-based classifier are non-parametric algorithms which have the ability to select the most useful features to use. Naïve Bayes is a generative classifier and included because of its simplicity and familiarity, although we expect it to be suboptimal since it is prone to over-fitting. We use the classifier implementations from the Weka data mining framework [7]. Our simple rule results use a parameter set on the development set and our classification results are generated using 5-fold cross validation on our test set. We report results in terms of Weighted Precision (WP) and Weighted Recall (WR), defined as the precision and recall for each class weighted by class size.

5. EXPERIMENTAL RESULTS

We report on our experiments that validate the 'Reading between the Tags' approach and answer our research questions. Sections 5.1 and 5.2 present the results of the basic approach, which generates best-guess classes for image tags independently of image content. Section 5.3 presents results of image-specific size class prediction accomplished by incorporating visual concepts into the classifier. Finally, Section 5.4 presents results with automatic LUF selection.

5.1 Corporeality Prediction

5.1.1 Baseline performance

In order to provide a check that our predictions are non-trivial, we use a *dominant class baseline.* We calculate the larger class on our ground truth and predict all tags as belonging to this dominant class. For the total number of 32,032 tags, 11,482 are labeled in the ground truth as `pe` and 20,550 as `no-pe`, corresponding to a dominant class baseline performance of 0.412/0.642 (WP/WR).

As mentioned in Section 3.1.2, we also compare our corporeality prediction (i.e., pe vs. no-pe decision) with a baseline generated using lookup in WordNet. We generate a *WordNet baseline* by assigning a tag to the category (pe and no-pe) that characterizes the majority of its senses as listed in WordNet. If a tag does not appear in WordNet it is classified as no-pe. This approach correctly classified 4,780/11,482 pe's and 17,701/20,550 no-pe's, corresponding to a performance of 0.690/0.702 (WP/WR).

5.1.2 Prediction methods

The results of the methods used for predicting pe and no-pe, reported in terms of Weighted Precision (WP) and Weighted Recall (WR), are given in Table 2. The simple rule in Eq. (1) uses the optimum θ as determined on the development set ($\theta=300$).

Table 2. Results for corporeality prediction

Condition		WP/WR
Dominant class baseline		0.412/0.642
WordNet baseline		0.690/0.702
Simple rule	Eq (1)	0.653/0.670
Classifiers	Decision tree	**0.754/0.757**
	Rule-based class.	0.720/0.722
	SVM	0.718/0.646
	Naïve Bayes	0.554/0.595

The LUF-based approaches (i.e., the simple rule and the classifiers) outperform the dominant class baseline. The simple rule correctly classifies 2,904/11,482 pe's and 18,569/20,550 no-pe's. Its comparatively good performance demonstrates that LUF-based approaches are relatively independent of the availability of large amounts of training data. Notice that the simple rule is more conservative than WordNet in hypothesizing pe's. The decision tree yields the best classification result (correctly classified: 5,730/11,482 pe's and 18,513/20,550 no-pe's), outperforming the WordNet baseline by ca. 6%, absolute. This approach is slightly less conservative than WordNet in hypothesizing pe's.

5.2 Size-class Prediction

We evaluate size-class prediction from two different perspectives. The first is *three-way size-class prediction,* which reports performance only on the tags that we have already determined to denote physical entities. This perspective gives us information on how well we can predict size class in isolation. The second is *four-way size-class prediction,* which reports performance on all tags and reflects the ability of our approaches to predict no-pe, s, m vs. l. It is more challenging to achieve overall improvement under this second perspective. We include it since it provides us with an indication of the difference that tag prediction can potentially make in an application setting where both corporeality and size matter. Practically, we accomplish four-way prediction by first distinguishing pe vs. no-pe and then splitting pe into s, m or l. For our experiments, we use the pe/no-pe decision drawn from our best performing pe/no-pe prediction method, namely, the decision tree classifier in the previous section.

5.2.1 Baselines

As with corporeality prediction, in order to be certain that we are producing meaningful results, we compare our approach with the *dominant class baseline* under which all labels are assigned to the largest class attested in the ground truth. For the 11,482 ground-truth-labeled pe tags, 3,422 are ground-truth-labeled as s, 2,897 as m, and 5,163 as l, corresponding to a baseline performance of 0.202/0.450 (WP/WR) for three-way and 0.412/0.642 (WP/WR) for four-way prediction.

5.2.2 Prediction methods

The results of prediction of tag size class are presented in Table 3.

Table 3. Results for size-class prediction

Condition	3-way WP/WR (s | m | l)	4-way WP/WR (s | m | l | no-pe)
Baseline	0.202/0.450	0.412/0.642
Simple rule Eq. (2)	0.673/0.635	0.665/0.692
Decision tree	**0.831/0.834**	**0.709/0.727**
Rule-based	0.821/0.819	0.704/0.724
SVM	0.680/0.602	0.638/0.686
Naïve Bayes	0.663/0.598	0.640/0.685

The LUF-based approaches (i.e., the simple rule and the classifiers) outperform the dominant class baseline. The decision tree delivers the best performance.

In order to test size-class classification using exclusively simple rules, we ran an additional condition in which the pe/no-pe decision uses the simple rule in Eq. (1) and the subsequent s/m/l decision in Eq. (2). This approach achieves a three-way size class classification performance of 0.699/0.688 (WP/WR), which beats the baseline. Four-way size class performance does not improve over the baseline—it is held back by the relative conservativeness, mentioned above, of the simple rule in hypothesizing pe's. Although the performance achieved using exclusively simple rules is not particularly dramatic it is important since it means that in any setting in which size-class information on tags could be used, a weak, but potentially helpful prediction, can be supplied by a very lightweight method that makes use of a search engine and a threshold. Further, our experiments revealed that a better pe/no-pe decision would allow our approach for size-class prediction to really come into its own. We tested size-class prediction using oracle information on which tags correspond to physical entities. In this case, the four-way size-class prediction performance rises to 0.859/0.822 (WP/WR) for the simple rule and 0.901/0.894 (WP/WR) for the best classifier.

The results of these experiments allow us to answer our first research question Q1 positively: the principle of 'Reading between the Tags' can indeed successfully combine the tendency toward scale-specificity with statistics on natural language use patterns in order to predict tag-class.

5.3 Incorporating Visual Concepts

We now carry out size-class prediction experiments as above, except that we add information about the presence of visual concepts within the images. Adding visual concept information makes it possible to predict a size-class that is image specific.

We make use of two different sources of information on the visual concepts that are present in the images. First, we investigate the visual concepts used in the MIRFLICKR data set, choosing the 20 most frequent concepts for which ground truth annotations are available as our visual concept candidate set.[1] Second, we investigate visual concepts that occur in the widely-used visual concept ontology LSCOM (http://www.lscom.org/). To build our visual concept candidate set for LSCOM concepts, we exploit our ground truth concerning tag classes. In particular, there is a large intersection between physical entity tags and the visual concepts

[1] animals, car, clouds, female, flower, food, indoor, lake, male, night, people, plant_life, river, sea, sky, structures, sunset, transport, tree, and water. (We exclude portrait, which reflects composition.)

included in LSCOM. We assume if an image is tagged with a tag that we know denotes a physical entity, we can consider that tag to be evidence that a specific visual concept occurs in that image. We apply feature selection (CfsSubsetEval implementation in Weka, combined with Best First search) to generate a list of physical entity tags that are highly predictive of the size-class of their sister physical entity tags (i.e., other physical entity tags used to tag the same image). Then, we retain all physical entities that also correspond to concepts in LSCOM. Note that although we can assume the presence of a LSCOM visual concept whenever it corresponds to one of the ground-truth tags of an image, we cannot use our ground-truth tags as an exhaustive source of information concerning the presence of LSCOM concepts. Exhaustive LSCOM annotations would presumably have yielded a more dramatic illustration of the impact of the presence of visual concepts on tag size-class prediction, but our non-exhaustive set is well-suited for our present purpose of demonstrating the size-class disambiguating effects of adding information concerning visual concepts to LUF vectors.

We carry out classification using the decision tree, our best classifier from Section 3.2. Results are reported in Table 4. Visual concepts are selected $\{VIS_1, VIS_2...VIS_m\}$ for inclusion in the LUF vector by applying brute-force search to our candidate visual concept lists to discover a set of concepts that provide optimal classification performance. The first condition uses development data optimization: we select the visual concept set using the development data. The second condition involves test set optimization: we explore ideal performance by choosing the visual concept set using the test data. For both conditions we use the physical entities as determined by our best `pe/no-pe` decision (i.e., the decision tree with WP/WR of 0.754/0.757, cf. Table 2).

Table 4. Size-class prediction incorporating visual concepts

Visual Concept Set	Dev. set opt. 3-way WP/WR (s | m | l)	Test set opt. 3-way WP/WR (s | m | l)
MIRFLICKR	0.846/0.849	0.857/0.858
LSCOM	0.847/0.849	0.849/0.851

All conditions demonstrate improvement over the best 3-way classification with the decision tree (0.831/0.834).

Development set optimization yields three useful concepts from the MIRFLICKR candidate set: `night`, `transport`, and `water` and three useful concepts from the LSCOM candidate set: `birds`, `garden` and `flowers`. Test set optimization yields a similar set of concepts from the MIRFLICKR candidate set (`night`, `lake`, `water`, and `structures`) but a relatively less similar set of concepts from LSCOM (`tower`, `bride`, `garden`, and `clouds`), which we attribute to the specificity of the candidate set for the content of the test images. The inclusion of `bride` is quite interesting. Investigation of the data revealed that the presence of this concept helps to properly classify the tag *groom,* which provides evidence of the power of visual concepts to correct cases of systematic LUF score misclassification.

In sum, we see that the addition of information on the presence of visual concepts delivers a modest, but appreciable improvement over the use of LUF-scores alone. These results confirm the idea that visual information, which potentially also reflects scale as illustrated by Figure 3 and Figure 6, can complement the basic 'Reading between the Tags approach' to tag-class prediction, allowing us to give a positive answer to Q2. However, a caveat is in order. The improvement achieved in three-way prediction is currently not large enough to make a difference in four-way prediction, for which more sophisticated optimization will be needed. Note that these experiments are intended to confirm the *potential* of exploiting visual concepts. This step is only the first on the path towards ultimately deploying visual concepts to improve tag-class prediction in an applied setting. In such a case, noisy visual concept detector output would be used rather than the ideal used here.

5.4 Automatic feature discovery

In our final experiment, we make use of a set of frames that were statistically selected from Web text as being useful for the purpose of size-class classification. We queried Yahoo! with combinations of the tags in our development set and 16 prepositions[2] expressing notions of place gathered from [17]. For each `{tag, preposition}` pair, we executed the following pattern of queries: `the <tag> <preposition> {her, his, the}`. We choose this pattern because the definite article 'the' helps to filter out contexts not involving referential nouns and the possessive pronouns help keep the focus on situations involving humans. For each results list (we cut off at a maximum of 750 results) we collected word strings including the query and the following word, the 'context word' needed to complete the LUF. The result was ca. 2.5 million candidates from which we selected those combinations of query and context word occurring more than 10 times, resulting in 448 frames. For each tag in our development set we collected LUF-scores using the collected frames and we applied feature selection (CfsSubsetEval combined with Best First search) to select a final list of 18 representative size-class frames illustrated in Figure 7.

1	2	3	4	5	6	7	8	9	10	11	12	13	14	15	16	17	18
the <tag> in the window	the <tag> over his face	the <tag> in his district	the <tag> under her chin	the <tag> in her hand	the <tag> on the floor	the <tag> over the threshold	the <tag> on her plate	the <tag> near the airport	the <tag> on her hat	the <tag> in her mouth	the <tag> in the pan	the <tag> inside the ears	the <tag> under the pillow	the <tag> in his mouth	the <tag> in the van	the <tag> near the horizon	the <tag> on his breath

Figure 7. Automatically discovered size-class prediction LUFs

We repeated our size-class prediction experiments using the 18 automatically discovered LUFs using the best classification result from the corporeality prediction (decision tree with WP/WR of 0.754/0.757). The results—presented in Table 5—demonstrate that automatically discovered LUFs achieve performance comparable to that of the hand-designed LUFs reported in Table 3.

Table 5. Results for size-class prediction using automatically discovered LUFs (cf. original LUFs in Table 3)

Condition	3-way WP/WR (s | m | l)	4-way WP/WR (s | m | l | no-pe)
Decision tree	**0.824/0.827**	**0.708/0.726**
Rule-based class.	0.811/0.809	0.701/0.723
SVM	0.674/0.601	0.634/0.685
Naïve Bayes	0.681/0.603	0.640/0.686

These results indicate that the LUF-based approach to tag-class prediction works independently of a particular choice of LUFs. Surprisingly, the automatic selection process 'rediscovers' LUFs that were used in the initial experiment (e.g., `the <tag> in her`

[2] `in, inside, on, at, over, above, under, underneath, beneath, below, near, by, next to, between, among, opposite`

hand). Even more revealing is the fact that the discovered LUFs appear to reflect the sort of scale-specificity that the original LUFs were designed to exploit (i.e., the <tag> on her plate would pick up on small scales and the <tag> near the airport on larger scales). Another interesting observation is that the discovered LUF the <tag> in the van corresponds exactly to our definition of a medium object ('fits into a delivery van') chosen to reflect natural human conceptual notions of medium, providing supporting evidence in the pertinence of that choice to human conceptualization of size class. In sum, we are able to determine that if LUFs are selected statistically, they perform well and also demonstrate the same sort of scale-specific patterns that we assumed helpful at the onset, which constitutes a positive answer to our third research question Q3. This confirmation of the usefulness of scale-specific LUF supports our original conjecture that although scale-specific effects of real-world situations are a general tendency rather than a hard-and-fast rule, the tendency is still strong enough to be exploitable for tag size-class prediction.

6. DISCUSSION

To gain additional insight into 'Reading between the Tags', we dug deeper into the results generated by our LUF-based predictions in order to better understand their limitations and potential. Our manual review of results led to some interesting observations. First, we found that for the tags associated with the two images in Figure 8, the LUF-based approach is able to make a pe/no-pe decision while WordNet cannot.

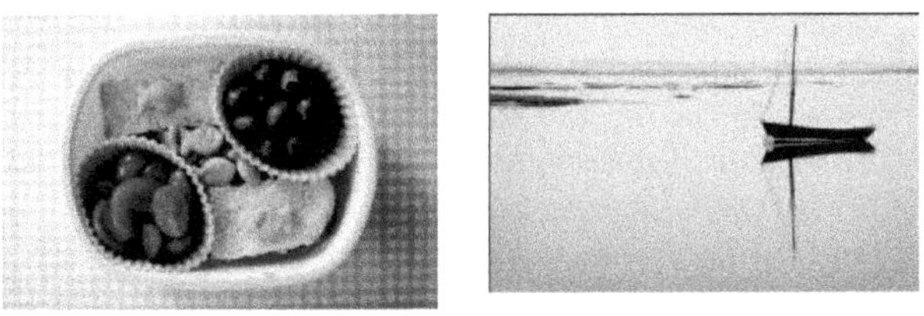

Figure 8. Images tagged *bento box* (left) and *dingy* (right): LUF-scores succeed, but WordNet fails to produce a corporeality prediction for these tags.

The left image is tagged *bento box*, which designates a physical entity not listed in WordNet at the time that the experiments were performed. The right image is tagged *dingy*, a misspelling of *dinghy*, which is the type of boat pictured. Misspellings are often based on pronunciations of words and, as a result, certain misspellings are widespread. We discovered that our approach is able to handle such misspellings, which would never be included in WordNet. We counted the total number of tags in our test set that WordNet could not return a result for: 14,617 of the 32,032 tags, or 46%. The size of this percent supports our conclusion that the LUF-based approach provides a superior solution.

Investigation of the results of the image-specific size-class prediction incorporating visual concepts reported in Section 5.3 turned up individual results strongly suggesting that additional information about visual concepts depicted in images does indeed make the contribution expected. Both images in Figure 9, for example, were tagged with the tag *animals*, once referring to small toy animals in the picture on the left, once to an actual animal, a tiger. The classifier correctly identified the *animals* tag as 'small' in the left-hand case and 'medium' in the right-hand case. This example suggests that the visual concept *water* helped to distinguish the two cases by signaling the relatively larger scale of the right image and thus contributing information concerning the size of the animal in question. Other examples of tags in our test data set for which the incorporation of visual concepts made it possible to correctly disambiguate size are: *bag, brush, cross, engine, fountain, flag, horse, poster* and *robot.*

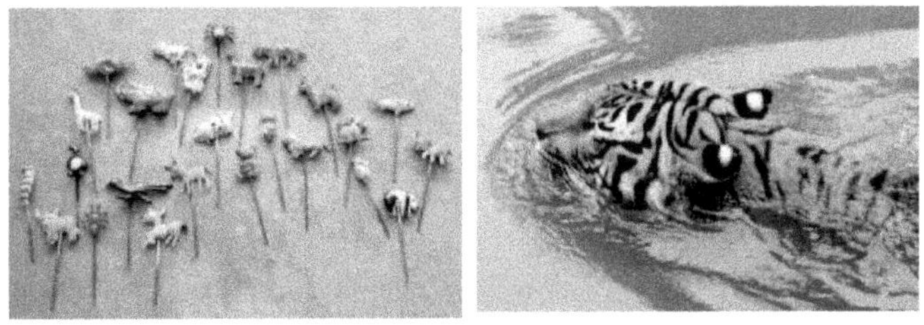

Figure 9. Example showing the positive influence of the presence of visual concepts on size-class prediction performance. Both are tagged *animals*; left is 'small', right is 'medium'.

Further, we carried out statistics on our ground truth tags to assess the feasibility of using the ground truth size-class labels to create a dictionary that would allow us to predict tag size class by looking up the most common size for a give tag. Of the 32,032 tags in our test set, 45% occurred only one time, meaning that they could not be covered by a look up strategy. As expected, the long-tail distribution of tags makes dictionary look up an unappealing alternative to LUF-based approaches. LUF-scores possess a further advantage over dictionary look-up for the application of image-specific tag-size prediction. If an entity is multi-size (i.e., has different size realizations when it appears in different images, like *car* in Figure 1) then it is likely to also occur in the real world in different sizes. Such multi-size entities could be expected to be described in different Web texts with different size realizations (e.g., we expect to find a mixture of passages about toy cars and passages on racecars). We anticipate that given enough LUF frames, tags will exhibit LUF-score patterns that are capable of reflecting whether or not they may designate multi-sized entities. This information could potentially be exploited by the classifier and thereby further aid image-specific tag size-class prediction.

7. CONCLUSION AND OUTLOOK

We have proposed a novel approach 'Reading between the Tags' that combines scale-specific tendencies of the real world with statistics derived from general Web text in order to enhance image tags with additional information about the corporeality and size of the entities that they denote. The approach is grounded in principles of proto-semantics from cognitive linguistics that serve to guarantee its universality and, practically speaking, its ability to handle an arbitrary user tag associated with an arbitrary image in a generic image collection. We have evaluated the approach on a set of Flickr images associated with a large number (more than 30K) of tags.

Our experimental findings bring to light two aspects that make the 'Reading between the Tags' approach a valuable tool in the arsenal of techniques that can be applied to improve the informativeness of tags and enhance their contribution to semantic multimedia indexing. First, our approach is able to generate a best guess prediction for tag corporeality and tag size class using only a small amount of development data and text statistics from the Web. As such, it constitutes an extremely cheap source of information about arbitrary tags that is waiting on the Web to be gathered for exploitation. If labeled training data is available, performance can be further improved by using classifiers. A key point is that our approach can handle a wide range of tags, including obscure and misspelled cases, for which a strategy involving look-up in a knowledge resource, such as WordNet or a dictionary specifying common sizes for tags, would fail to generate a prediction. Second, our approach has demonstrated potential to be able to exploit visual concepts occurring in images to differentiate image-specific size in the case of multi-size tags, i.e., tags designating entities of different sizes when used with different images. This point is quite important due to the prevalence of multi-sized tags. Using the ground truth of our test set we estimated that 25% of tags designating physical entities are multi-size tags, namely the real-world size of the visually depicted physical entity that they designate can vary from image to image.

Our future work will focus on exploiting the information inherence in the co-occurrence of tags and of tags and visual concepts. In particular, we will focus on multi-sized tags and investigate how the interaction of LUF-based information concerning all the tags of an image can be exploited. We will also explore the practical use of visual concepts, which will involve taking the noisy output of visual concept detectors into account. As mentioned at the onset, we anticipate that tags that are supplemented with size-class information will support users in search and browsing. However, we also see great potential for the 'Reading between the Tags' approach to supplement any approach that can make use of additional information about tags. We expect that it has a contribution to make to tag ranking and can also provide additional information that can be exploited for tag propagation. Specifically, in the future we will investigate the ability of information generated by the LUF-approach to aid image-level decisions such as zoom-level detection and iconicity classification.

User-contributed tags have recently proven themselves to be important sources of information for improving semantic annotation of multimedia. Our work suggests that the potential of community-contributed information is far from exhausted, and that the Web itself is replete with text that is relevant to the content of images. By leveraging general tendencies about the physical world, the 'Reading between the Tags' approach is able to unlock new dimensions of potential that are currently lying latent within the information reserves on the Web.

8. ACKNOWLEDGMENTS

The research leading to these results has received funding from the European Commission's 7th Framework Programme (FP7) under grant agreement № 216444 (PetaMedia).

9. REFERENCES

[1] Berg, T.L., and Berg, A.C. 2009. Finding iconic images, In *Proc. of the Internet Vision Workshop at the Conference on Computer Vision and Pattern Recognition (CVPR '09),* 1-8.

[2] Brodley, C., Lane, T., and Stough, T. 1999. Knowledge Discovery and Data Mining. *American Scientist.* 87(1), 5410.

[3] Cilibrasi, R.L. and Vitanyi, P.M.B. 2007. The Google Similarity Distance. *IEEE Trans. on Knowl. and Data Eng.* 19(3), 370-383.

[4] Doursat, R. and Petitot, J. 2005. Bridging the gap between vision and language: A mophodynamical model of spatial categories. In *Proceedings of the International Joint Conference on Neural Networks (IJCNN '05).*

[5] Fellbaum, C. 1998. *WordNet: An Electronic Lexical Database.* Bradford Books.

[6] Gupta, A. and Davis, L.S. 2008. Beyond Nouns: Exploiting Prepositions and Comparative Adjectives for Learning Visual Classifiers. In *Proceedings of the 10th European Conference on Computer Vision: Part I (ECCV '08),* 16-29.

[7] Hall, M., Frank, E., Holmes, G., Pfahringer, B., Reutemann, P., and Witten, I. H. 2009. The WEKA Data Mining Software: An Update. *SIGKDD Explorations*, 11(1).

[8] Hayward, W. and Tarr, M. 1995. Spatial language and spatial representation. *Cognition.* 55(1), 39-84.

[9] Hearst, M. 1992. Automatic acquisition of hyponyms from large text corpora. In *Proceedings of the 14th conference on Computational linguistics – Vol. 2 (COLING '92)*, 539-545.

[10] Huiskes, M.J. and Lew, M.S. 2008. The MIR Flickr retrieval evaluation. In *Proceedings of the ACM International Conference on Multimedia Information Retrieval (MIR '08)*, 39-43.

[11] Huiskes, M.J., Thomee, B., and Lew, M.S. 2010. New trends and ideas in visual concept detection: the MIR Flickr retrieval evaluation initiative. In *Proceedings of the ACM International Conference on Multimedia Information Retrieval (MIR '10)*, 527-536.

[12] Hung, S.-H., Lin, C.-H., and Hong, J.-S. 2010. Web mining for event-based commonsense knowledge using lexico-syntactic pattern matching and semantic role labeling, *Expert Systems with Applications*, 37(1), 341-347.

[13] Keller, F. and Lapata, M. 2003. Using the web to obtain frequencies for unseen bigrams. *Comput. Linguist.* 29(3), 459-484.

[14] Lee, S., Neve, W.D., and Ro, Y.M. 2010. Tag refinement in an image folksonomy using visual similarity and tag co-occurrence statistics. *Image Commun.* 25(10), 761-773.

[15] Li, X., Snoek, C.G.M., and Worring, M. 2008. Learning tag relevance by neighbor voting for social image retrieval. In *Proceedings of the ACM International Conference on Multimedia Information Retrieval (MIR '08)*, 180-187.

[16] Liu, D., Hua, X.-S., Yang, L., Wang, M., and Zhang, H.-J.. 2009. Tag ranking. In *Proceedings of the International World Wide Web Conference (WWW '09)*, 351-360.

[17] Purdue Online Writing Lab, Retrieved April 11, 2011, from http://owl.english.purdue.edu/owl/resource/594/01/

[18] Quick Shot Artist. *How to Compose a Picture,* Retrieved April 11, 2011, from http://quickshotartist.com/Compose/

[19] Randolph, J. J. 2008. *Online Kappa Calculator.* Retrieved April 10, 2011, from http://justus.randolph.name/kappa

[20] Resnik, P. 1997. Selectional preference and sense disambiguation. In *Proc. of the SIGLEX Workshop on Tagging Text with Lexical Semantics: Why, What, and How?*, 52-57.

[21] Sánchez, D. 2010. A methodology to learn ontological attributes from the web. *Data & Knowledge Engineering*, 69(6), 573-597.

[22] Sawant, N., Li, J., Wang, J. 2011. Automatic image semantic interpretation using social action and tagging data. *Multimedia Tools and Applications*, 51(1), 213-246.

[23] Sigurbjörnsson, B. and van Zwol, R. 2008. Flickr tag recommendation based on collective knowledge. In *Proceedings of the International World Wide Web Conference (WWW '08)*, 327-336.

[24] Snoek, C. G. M. and Worring, M. 2009. Concept-Based Video Retrieval, *Foundations and Trends in Information Retrieval*, 4(2), 215-322.

[25] Wan, K.-W., Roy, S. 2010. Identifying and learning visual attributes for object recognition. In *Proceedings of the International Conference on Image processing (ICIP'2010)*, 3893-3896.

[26] Yang, K., Hua, X.-S., Wang, M., and Zhang, H.-J. 2010. Tagging tags. In *Proceedings of ACM Multimedia (MM '10)*, 619-622.

Exploiting the Entire Feature Space with Sparsity for Automatic Image Annotation *

Zhigang Ma
DISI, University of Trento, Italy
ma@disi.unitn.it

Yi Yang
SCS, Carnegie Mellon University, USA
yiyang@cs.cmu.edu

Feiping Nie
CSE, University of Texas at Arlington, USA
feipingnie@gmail.com

Jasper Uijlings
DISI, University of Trento, Italy
uijlings@disi.unitn.it

Nicu Sebe
DISI, University of Trento, Italy
sebe@disi.unitn.it

ABSTRACT

The explosive growth of digital images requires effective methods to manage these images. Among various existing methods, automatic image annotation has proved to be an important technique for image management tasks, *e.g.*, image retrieval over large-scale image databases. Automatic image annotation has been widely studied during recent years and a considerable number of approaches have been proposed. However, the performance of these methods is yet to be satisfactory, thus demanding more effort on research of image annotation. In this paper, we propose a novel semi-supervised framework built upon feature selection for automatic image annotation. Our method aims to jointly select the most relevant features from all the data points by using a sparsity-based model and exploiting both labeled and unlabeled data to learn the manifold structure. Our framework is able to simultaneously learn a robust classifier for image annotation by selecting the discriminating features related to the semantic concepts. To solve the objective function of our framework, we propose an efficient iterative algorithm. Extensive experiments are performed on different real-world image datasets with the results demonstrating the promising performance of our framework for automatic image annotation.

Categories and Subject Descriptors

H.3.3 [**Information Search and Retrieval**]: Selection Process; I5.2 [**Design Methodology**]: Feature Evaluation and Selection; I4.10 [**Image Respresentation**]: Statistical

General Terms

Algorithms, Experimentation, Theory

*Area chair: Qi Tian

MM'11, November 28–December 1, 2011, Scottsdale, Arizona, USA.

Keywords

Image Annotation, Semi-supervised Learning, Sparse Feature Selection, Manifold Learning

1. INTRODUCTION

With the popularity of digital cameras, an overwhelming number of digital images are present in our world. The advancement of computer network and storage technology, on the other hand, has led to many websites such as Flickr for people to share these images. Confronted with these countless images, we have to think about how to organize and utilize them effectively. Image annotation is one technique that can facilitate the management of these image resources by associating keywords or detailed text descriptions with images. Rich and accurate annotation is critical for efficient image indexing, retrieval, organization and management.

However, the sheer amount of images makes it infeasible to annotate all the images manually. Hence, automatic image annotation has received a lot of research interest.

Tagging is one popular way for image annotation by leveraging a great number of image resources from the Web-scale datasets such as Flickr. These user-generated images are annotated with user-defined tags and therefore can be used in the research on image annotation. The tagging approach for annotation is typically realized through two processes, searching and mining. The searching process aims to find the similar images of the unannotated images from the Web-scale datasets while the mining process extracts annotation from the textual information of these retrieved similar images. Research on this topic has already shown progress in automatic image annotation [23][19]. For instance, in [23], Wang *et al.*, have proposed a new image tagging system by leveraging the Web-scale images. The system first searches for similar images on the Web and then mines the images found to obtain their annotations. However, user-tagged images are potentially noisy because the tags may not reflect the concepts but something outside images, thus leading to degraded performance of image annotation.

Another effective way, namely, the labeling approach, has also been studied widely for automatic image annotation. Among the various labeling methods, learning-based automatic annotation has gained the most popularity. Learning-based methods [13][4][29] require pre-labeled samples as the training data to learn the models for image annotation. Since images are usually represented by different features, much work [9][25][24] has focused on optimizing the feature selection process in their annotation frameworks. By finding the discriminative subset of original features and elim-

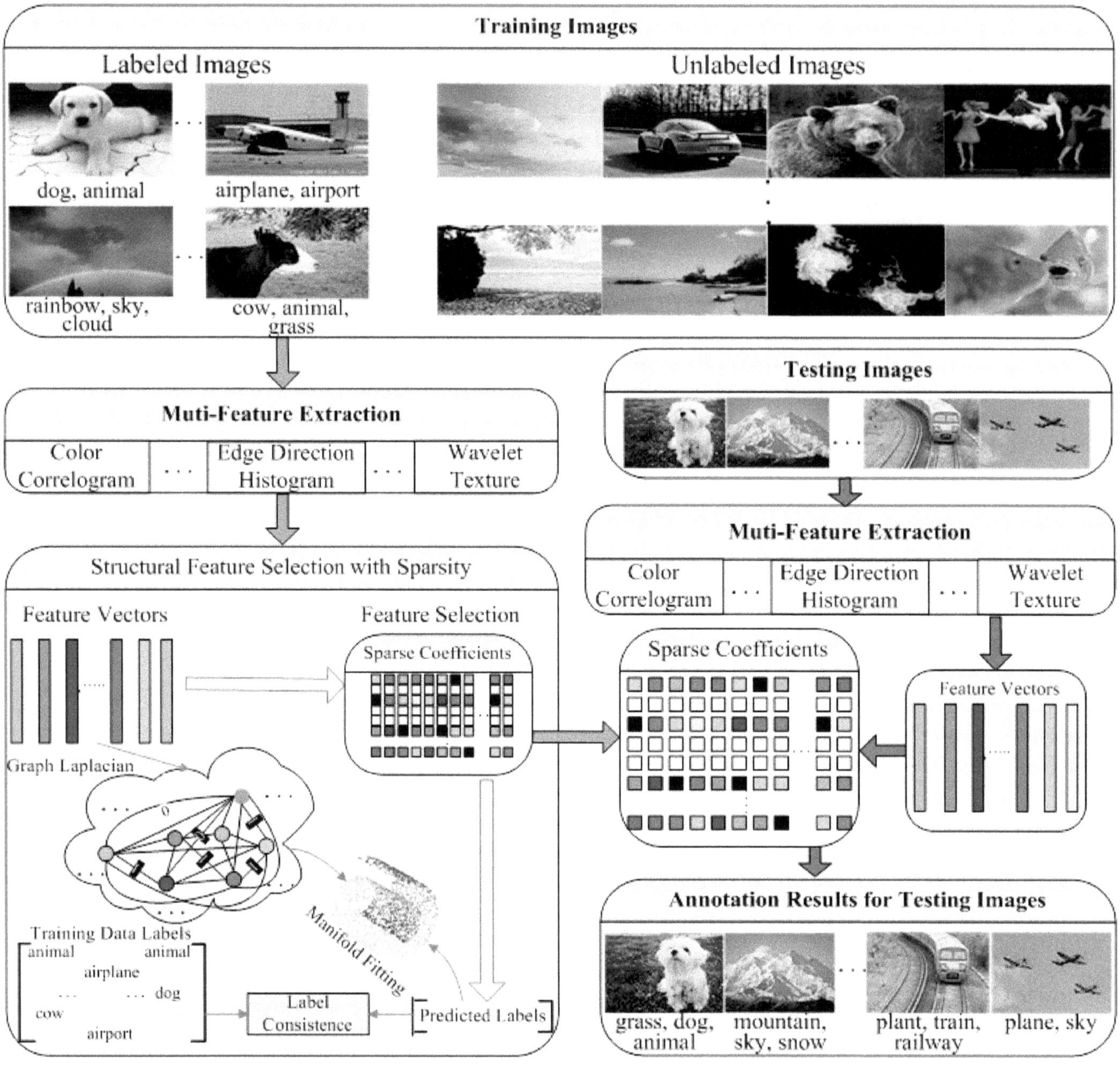

Figure 1: The illustration of our SFSS image annotation framework.

inating the noise, feature selection can help improve image annotation performance. On the other hand, a large body of feature selection algorithms are available to be utilized for image annotation. Yet these methods have certain drawbacks themselves. Classical feature selection algorithms such as Fisher Score [8] compute the weights of different features, rank them accordingly and then select features one by one. These classical algorithms generally evaluate the importance of each feature individually and neglect the useful information of the correlation between different features. Another problem is that they can only use labeled training samples for feature selection, which have excessive cost in human labor. In many practical applications, however, we only have limited labeled data and a large number of unlabeled data. Motivated by this fact, semi-supervised feature selection has been proposed. For example, in [31], Zhao *et al.* have presented an algorithm based on the spectral graph theory but similarly to Fisher Score [8], their method selects features one by one. To overcome the disadvantage of selecting features individually, a plethora of state of the art approaches such as [25][24][17] have proposed to extract features jointly across all data points. Nonetheless, [25][24][17] still implement their methods in a supervised way.

To progress beyond the current image annotation methods, we propose a novel semi-supervised annotation framework inspired by the recent work in feature selection [17][25][32] and semi-supervised learning [18][20]. As mentioned before, previous feature selection methods have not considered selecting feature jointly across all data points in the semi-supervised scenario. Therefore, our work aims to utilize both labeled and unlabeled data to select features while simultaneously consider the correlation between them. We call the new method in our framework Structural Feature Selection with Sparsity (SFSS). Figure 1 illustrates how our method works for image annotation. All the training and testing images are first represented by feature vectors. The graph Laplacian is constructed based on both labeled and unlabeled training data. Then sparse feature selection and label prediction are conducted simultaneously by satisfying both label consistence with the training data labels and the manifold fitting on data structure. By selecting the most relevant features, the sparse coefficients can be applied to the feature vectors of the testing images for annotation. The main contributions of our work are as follows:

- Our method is a semi-supervised joint feature selection algorithm with sparsity, which can select the discriminative features by exploiting the whole feature space. Furthermore, our method can simultaneously learn a classifier for image annotation during the feature selection.
- The advantages of both manifold learning and joint feature selection are leveraged together, which is verified by the image annotation results of extensive experiments.
- Our method yields good results even if few labeled samples are available, which makes it attractive for real-world image datasets.

The rest of this paper is organized as follows. In section II, we review related work on feature selection, semi-supervised learning and automatic image annotation. We then illustrate the formulation of our framework and propose the solution and an algorithm for solving the objective function in section III. Experiments are given in section IV and section V concludes this paper.

2. RELATED WORK

Our work is geared towards more satisfactory image annotation performance. As feature selection and semi-supervised learning are both effective ways in multimedia analysis, we combine them in our framework for image annotation. In this section, we briefly review three related research topics, *i.e.*, feature selection, semi-supervised learning and automatic image annotation.

2.1 Feature Selection

Feature selection aims to extract important features and reduce the noise to better represent the original data. As a result, it can help increase accuracy. Furthermore, feature selection can boost computational efficiency on the classification side but also on the feature extraction side by only extracting those that are relevant for classification.

Traditional feature selection algorithms use fully labeled data and leverage the labels for feature selection. For instance, Fisher Score [8] evaluates the relevance of a feature according to the label distribution of the data. Previous works have demonstrated their good performance. However, as they evaluate features one by one the computational cost is very high. In contrast, a recently popular approach, *i.e.*, sparsity-based feature selection extracts features jointly across all data points [32][17][26]. This approach originated from the idea that the underlying representations of many real-world processes are often sparse. Hence, feature selection can be achieved by searching the sparse representation of the data. The most well-known sparse model is the $l1$-norm regularization. In [3], Cai *et al.* use an $l1$-regularized regression model to select features jointly instead of evaluating each feature independently. A family of works have also been rendered to extend the $l1$-norm regularization to the $l1/lq$-norm regularization which can better exploit the pairwise correlation among groups of features. In [32], Zhao *et al.* use spectral regression with $l_{2,1}$-norm constraint to evaluate features jointly and their method can effectively remove redundant features. In [17], Nie *et al.* also leverage joint $l_{2,1}$-norm minimization on both loss function and regularization for feature selection. These methods have shown to be prominent in feature selection and thus can facilitate clustering, classification, annotation and many other applications. Taking into account the benefits of sparse feature selection, we apply it to our framework as well. But different from the state of the art, we extend it to a semi-supervised way.

2.2 Semi-Supervised Learning

Semi-supervised learning uses both labeled and unlabeled data for different tasks in machine learning. The motive lies in the fact that labeled data are expensive to obtain while abundant unlabeled data are easy to acquire and helpful to improve the performance of the learning tasks. In [33], Zhu reviews different approaches for semi-supervised learning in the past. A major paradigm for semi-supervised learning is to construct graph to utilize manifold structure for learning process.

A considerable number of methods based on the graph Laplacian have been proposed so far. In [10], He has proposed to incrementally learn an adaptive subspace by preserving the semantic structure of the image space for image retrieval. Yang *et al.* have proposed a semi-supervised approach for cross media retrieval in [27]. In [22], Wang *et al.* have integrated multiple graphs into a regularization and optimization framework for video annotation. In [18], Nie *et al.* have proposed a Flexible Manifold Embedding framework which utilizes label information from labeled data together with a manifold structure from both labeled and unlabeled data, and applied their framework to dimensionality reduction and showed better results than other state of the art semi-supervised algorithms. From these previous works we learn that semi-supervised learning can leverage the whole data distribution, thus resulting in promising performance for different applications. As a result, we also incorporate the graph Laplacian based semi-supervised learning into our framework to facilitate the feature selection. The improvement of feature selection can consequently lead to better image annotation performance, which is the focused application in our work.

2.3 Automatic Image Annotation

Image annotation correlates labels that describe semantic concepts to images. It is basically a classification problem as it has to decide which classes an image may belong to. Annotation is usually realized by exploiting the correspondence between visual features and semantic concepts of the images. Since manual annotation is time-consuming and has excessive cost in human labor, the existing research works are mainly focused on automatic image annotation.

Present approaches for automatic image annotation are based on different theories. One approach is to use different probabilistic models to predict the semantic concepts for unlabeled images, *e.g.*, in [30] a probabilistic model connecting the visual features and the textual words has been proposed for automatic image annotation. However, using probabilistic models inevitably brings in parameter estimation, which is a complex process. Another approach for automatic image annotation is based on graph construction by mining the data structure. For example, in [16], Liu *et al.* have proposed to construct an adaptive similarity graph to exploit the data distribution to facilitate image annotation and the experimental results demonstrate the advantage of their method. Another widely adopted approach for automatic image annotation is applying classifiers to obtain the semantic concepts of images. Many works have been presented using this methodology. For instance, Gao *et al.* scale up SVM classifier by incorporating the feature hierarchy and boosting and then apply the classifier to image annotation in [9].

Researchers have made great progress in feature selection, semi-supervised learning and automatic image annotation respectively. However, few works have been rendered to incorporate the latest advanced techniques of feature selection and semi-supervised learning into one framework for image annotation. Zooming into details, we notice that the current semi-supervised feature selection algorithms usually select features one by one while joint feature selection generally belongs to either supervised or unsupervised genre. Meanwhile, the potential of applying feature selection to improve image annotation remains largely unexplored. To bridge the gap, in this paper we propose a unified framework for image annotation by leveraging both the state of the art feature selection and semi-supervised learning methodology.

3. METHODOLOGY

In this section, we first illustrate the formulation of our Structural Feature Selection with Sparsity (SFSS) framework. Then a detailed approach is rendered to solve the objective function of SFSS.

3.1 Formulation of Proposed Framework

Most traditional feature selection algorithms suffer from the limitation of evaluating features one by one, *i.e.*, they select features independently without considering the correlations between different features [8]. Aiming to exploit relational information among the features and select them jointly, recent works have applied $l_{2,1}$-norm based models to their algorithms [32][17][26]. These algorithms can select the most discriminating features with joint sparsity, thus boosting the feature selection performance. The algorithms can be generalized as to solve the following problem:

$$\min_{W} loss(W) + \gamma \|W\|_{2,1}, \tag{1}$$

where W is a projection matrix used for feature selection and $loss(W)$ is the loss function. γ is a regularization parameter. Suppose $W \in \mathbb{R}^{d\times c}$, then its $l_{2,1}$-norm is defined as:

$$\|W\|_{2,1} = \sum_{i=1}^{d} \sqrt{\sum_{j=1}^{c} W_{ij}^2} \tag{2}$$

As shown in previous works [17][26], regularization using the $l_{2,1}$-norm of W makes the optimal W corresponding to (1) sparse, which means that some of its rows shrink to zero. Consequently, W can be viewed as the combination coefficients for the most discriminative features. Feature selection is then realized by W where only the features associated with the non-zero rows in W are selected.

Various algorithms have been developed by applying different loss functions [1][32][17]. Despite the efficacy, these $l_{2,1}$-norm based feature selection algorithms generally work in the supervised way, in other words, they utilize labeled data to evaluate features. If very few labeled data are leveraged, it may induce over-fitting. On the contrary, if these methods use a large number of labeled data, the cost will be quite high.

Semi-supervised learning can exploit both the labeled data and unlabeled data, which makes it appropriate in practical applications where only a few labels are available. Besides, previous works have shown that semi-supervised learning has great potential to boost the learning performance when properly designed [7]. Considering the benefits of semi-supervised learning, we therefore extend the objective function in (1) to semi-supervised scenario.

To begin with, we briefly introduce the fundamental principle of the graph Laplacian, which is widely used in semi-supervised learning and adopted in our method.

Denote $X = [x_1, x_2, ..., x_n]$ as the training data matrix where m data are labeled. $x_i \in \mathbb{R}^d (1 \le i \le n)$ is the i-th datum and n is the total number of the training data. Let $Y = [y_1, y_2, ..., y_m, y_{m+1}, ..., y_n]^T \in \{0,1\}^{n\times c}$ be the label matrix. c stands for the class number and $y_i \in \mathbb{R}^c (1 \le i \le n)$ is the label vector with c classes. Let Y_{ij} denote the j-th datum of y_i then $Y_{ij} = 1$ if x_i is in the j-th class, while $Y_{ij} = 0$ otherwise. If x_i is not labeled, y_i is set to a vector with all zeros, namely, $\forall i > m$, $y_i|_{i=(m+1)}^{n} = 0^{c\times 1}$. Define a weight matrix G, whose element G_{ij} reflects the similarity between x_i and x_j as

$$G_{ij} = \begin{cases} 1 & x_i \text{ and } x_j \text{ are } k \text{ nearest neighbors;} \\ 0 & \text{otherwise.} \end{cases}$$

The graph Laplacian is then constructed through $L = D - G$ where L is the graph Laplacian matrix and D is a diagonal matrix with $D_{ii} = \sum_{j=1}^{n} G_{ij}$.

Manifold Regularization [2] is the most well-known approach based on the graph Laplacian to extend many algorithms to semi-supervised way. Its popularity lies in the facts that multimedia data normally possess a manifold structure, which has been shown in many works [28][15] and that Manifold Regularization can explore such manifold structure. We therefore apply it to the loss function in (1) and get the following objective function:

$$\arg\min_{W,b} Tr\left(W^T X L X^T W\right) + \mu \left\|X_l^T W + 1_n b^T - Y_l\right\|_F^2 + \gamma \|W\|_{2,1}. \tag{3}$$

A brief explanation for the above objective function is as follows. X_l and Y_l denote the labeled training data and their ground truth labels respectively. $b \in \mathbb{R}^c$ is the bias term and $1_n \in \mathbb{R}^n$ denotes a column vector with all its n elements being 1. μ and γ are parameters to balance the regression and the $l_{2,1}$-norm of W. Though the objective in (3) is semi-supervised, the features selected through it are merely best related to the known ground truth labels Y_l through the regression $\mu \left\|X_l^T W + 1_n b^T - Y_l\right\|_F^2$. Following the recent transductive classification algorithm [34][33], we expect the selected features to accurately reflect all the labels of the training data where many of them are unlabeled. Therefore, we define a predicted label matrix as $F = [f_1, \dots f_n]^T \in \mathbb{R}^{n\times c}$ for all the training data in X. Note that $f_i \in \mathbb{R}^c (1 \le i \le n)$ is the predicted label vector of $x_i \in X$. F is supposed to be consistent with the ground truth labels of the training data and be smooth on the manifold structure so it can be optimized through the following objective function [34][33]:

$$\min_F \sum_{l=1}^{c} \left[\frac{1}{2} \sum_{i,j=1}^{n} (F_{il} - F_{jl})^2 G_{ij} + \sum_{i=1}^{n} U_{ii} (F_{il} - Y_{il})^2\right], \tag{4}$$

where F_{il} is the l-th element of f_i and U is a diagonal matrix whose diagonal element $U_{ii} = \infty$ if x_i is labeled and $U_{ii} = 1$ otherwise. For later usage, we name U as a decision rule matrix for convenience. (4) can be rewritten as:

$$\min_F Tr\left(F^T L F\right) + Tr\left((F-Y)^T U (F-Y)\right), \tag{5}$$

where $Tr(\cdot)$ denotes the trace operator. L in the above function can also be constructed by some other sophisticated methods, *e.g.*, the one in [27] to exploit the manifold structure. The framework shown in (5) has been widely applied to multimedia content analysis such as video annotation [21], cross media retrieval [27], *etc.*, where different methods were adopted to compute the matrix L.

Further inspired by the work in [18] which has proved the advantage of incorporating predicted labels F into Manifold Regularization, we propose our ultimate objective function as:

$$\arg\min_{F,W,b} Tr\left(F^T LF\right) + Tr\left((F-Y)^T U(F-Y)\right) + \mu\left\|X^T W + 1_n b^T - F\right\|_F^2 + \gamma\|W\|_{2,1}. \quad (6)$$

Our framework can solve for F, W and b at the same time. Since W selects the features most related to the class labels, it can be used directly for image annotation. For any unseen images denoted by X', their label matrix $F' = X'^T W + 1_n b^T$.

It is worth mentioning that although (6) looks similar to the objective function $\arg\min_{F,W,b} Tr(F^T LF) + Tr((F-Y)^T U(F-Y)) + \mu\|X^T W + 1_n b^T - F\|_F^2 + \gamma\|W\|_F^2$ in [18], the $l_{2,1}$-norm regularization $\|W\|_{2,1}$ in our framework makes it different from [18]. First of all, our framework is able to select the discriminative features across all the data points with joint sparsity. It can be applied to feature selection while the method in [18] is dedicated to classification and dimensionality reduction. Since our method is able to select a denoised and compact feature subset, it can enhance the accuracy as well as efficiency. On top of that, our framework further differs from [18] in the way to obtain W. In [18], W is calculated easily in a closed form. In contrast, the $l_{2,1}$-norm in our framework is non-smooth which makes it difficult to be solved. To deal with this problem, we propose an efficient algorithm to obtain W and elaborate it subsequently.

3.2 Solution

The objective problem of (6) can be solved as follows.

First, by setting the derivative of (6) *w.r.t* b to zero, we have:

$$\begin{aligned} & 2\mu(X^T W + 1_n b^T - F) = 0 \\ \Rightarrow\ & 1_n^T 1_n b^T = 1_n^T F - 1_n^T X^T W \\ \Rightarrow\ & b^T = \frac{1}{n}(1_n^T F - 1_n^T X^T W) \end{aligned} \quad (7)$$

Substituting b^T in (6) with (7), the problem becomes:

$$\begin{aligned} & \arg\min_{F,W} Tr\left(F^T LF\right) + Tr\left((F-Y)^T U(F-Y)\right) \\ & +\mu\left\|X^T W + \frac{1}{n}1_n 1_n^T F - \frac{1}{n}1_n 1_n^T X^T W - F\right\|_F^2 + \gamma\|W\|_{2,1} \\ \Rightarrow\ & \arg\min_{F,W} Tr\left(F^T LF\right) + Tr\left((F-Y)^T U(F-Y)\right) \\ & +\mu\left\|(I - \frac{1}{n}1_n 1_n^T)X^T W - (I - \frac{1}{n}1_n 1_n^T)F\right\|_F^2 + \gamma\|W\|_{2,1}, \end{aligned} \quad (8)$$

where I is an identity matrix. Using H to represent $I - \frac{1}{n}1_n 1_n^T$, we arrive at:

$$\arg\min_{F,W} Tr\left(F^T LF\right) + Tr\left((F-Y)^T U(F-Y)\right) + \mu\left\|HX^T W - HF\right\|_F^2 + \gamma\|W\|_{2,1}. \quad (9)$$

Note that $H = H^T = H^2$. By setting the derivative of (9) *w.r.t* F to zero, we have:

$$\begin{aligned} & 2LF + 2U(F-Y) - 2\mu H(HX^T W - HF) = 0 \\ \Rightarrow\ & (L + U + \mu H)F = UY + \mu HX^T W \\ \Rightarrow\ & F = PQ, \end{aligned} \quad (10)$$

where $P = (L + U + \mu H)^{-1}$ and $Q = UY + \mu HX^T W$. Substituting F in (9) with (10), the problem becomes:

$$\begin{aligned} & \arg\min_{W} Tr\Big(Q^T P^T LPQ + Q^T P^T UPQ - Q^T P^T UY \\ & - Y^T UPQ + \mu(W^T X - Q^T P^T)H^T H(X^T W - PQ)\Big) \\ & + \gamma\|W\|_{2,1} \\ \Rightarrow\ & \arg\min_{W} Tr\Big(Q^T P^T (L+U)PQ - Q^T P^T UY - Y^T UPQ \\ & + \mu W^T XHX^T W - \mu W^T XHPQ - \mu Q^T P^T HX^T W \\ & + \mu Q^T P^T HPQ\Big) + \gamma\|W\|_{2,1} \end{aligned} \quad (11)$$

Since $Tr(Q^T P^T UY) = Tr(Y^T UPQ)$ and $Tr(\mu W^T XHPQ) = Tr(\mu Q^T P^T HX^T W)$, (11) becomes:

$$\begin{aligned} & \arg\min_{F,W} Tr\Big(Q^T P^T (L + U + \mu H)PQ - 2Q^T P^T UY \\ & + \mu W^T XHX^T W - 2\mu Q^T P^T HX^T W\Big) + \gamma\|W\|_{2,1} \\ \Rightarrow\ & \arg\min_{W} Tr\Big(Q^T P^T P^{-1} PQ - 2Q^T P^T (UY + \mu HX^T W) \\ & + \mu W^T XHX^T W\Big) + \gamma\|W\|_{2,1} \\ \Rightarrow\ & \arg\min_{W} Tr\Big(Q^T P^T Q - 2Q^T P^T Q + \mu W^T XHX^T W\Big) \\ & + \gamma\|W\|_{2,1} \end{aligned} \quad (12)$$

As $Q = UY + \mu HX^T W$, we thus have:

$$\begin{aligned} & \arg\min_{W} Tr\Big(\mu W^T XHX^T W - (UY + \mu HX^T W)^T P^T \\ & (UY + \mu HX^T W)\Big) + \gamma\|W\|_{2,1} \\ \Rightarrow\ & \arg\min_{W} Tr\Big(\mu W^T XHX^T W - \mu Y^T UPHX^T W \\ & - \mu W^T XHP^T UY - \mu^2 W^T XHP^T HX^T W\Big) + \gamma\|W\|_{2,1} \\ \Rightarrow\ & \arg\min_{W} Tr\Big(W^T (XH(\mu I - \mu^2 P)HX^T)W \\ & - 2\mu Y^T UPHX^T W\Big) + \gamma\|W\|_{2,1}. \end{aligned} \quad (13)$$

Denoting $XH(\mu I - \mu^2 P)HX^T$ by A and $\mu XHPUY$ by B respectively, we obtain the following quadratic problem to solve:

$$\arg\min_{W} Tr\left(W^T AW\right) - 2Tr\left(B^T W\right) + \gamma\|W\|_{2,1}. \quad (14)$$

3.3 Algorithm

To solve the problem in (14), we use the Lagrangian function and rewrite it as:

$$Tr\left(W^T AW\right) - 2Tr\left(B^T W\right) + \gamma\|W\|_{2,1}. \quad (15)$$

Denote $W = [w^1, ..., w^d]^T$ with w^i as its i-th row. By setting the

Algorithm 1: The SFSS algorithm.

Input:
The training data $X \in \mathbb{R}^{d\times n}$;
The training data labels $Y \in \mathbb{R}^{n\times c}$;
Parameters μ and γ.

Output:
Converged $W \in \mathbb{R}^{d\times c}$.

1: Compute the graph Laplacian matrix $L \in \mathbb{R}^{n\times n}$;
2: Compute the decision rule matrix $U \in \mathbb{R}^{n\times n}$;
3: $H = I - \frac{1}{n}1_n 1_n^T$;
4: $P = (L+U+\mu H)^{-1}$;
5: $A = XH(\mu I - \mu^2 P)HX^T$;
6: $B = \mu XHPUY$;
7: Set $t=0$ and initialize $W_0 \in \mathbb{R}^{d\times c}$ randomly;
8: **repeat**
Compute the diagonal matrix D_t as:
$$D_t = \begin{bmatrix} 2\left\|w_t^1\right\|_2 & & \\ & \cdots & \\ & & 2\left\|w_t^d\right\|_2 \end{bmatrix};$$
Update W_{t+1} as: $W_{t+1} = (D_tA+\gamma I)^{-1}D_tB$;
$t = t+1$.
until *Convergence*;
9: Return W.

derivative of (15) *w.r.t* W to zero, we have:

$$\begin{aligned} &2AW - 2B + 2\gamma D^{-1}W = 0 \\ &\Rightarrow W = (A+\gamma D^{-1})^{-1}B = (DA+\gamma I)^{-1}DB, \end{aligned} \tag{16}$$

where D is a diagonal matrix with its diagonal element $D_{ii} = 2\left\|w^i\right\|_2$. Therefore, we propose the detailed iterative approach in Algorithm 1 to solve the objective problem in (14). Next, we show that Algorithm 1 converges, which mainly follows our previous work in [17][26].

THEOREM 1. *The objective shown in (14) monotonically decreases until converging to the global optimum using the iterative approach in Algorithm 1.*

PROOF. The step to compute W_{t+1} in Step 8 of Algorithm 1 performs the following operation:

$$\begin{aligned} &\arg\min_W Tr\left(W^TAW\right) - 2Tr\left(B^TW\right) + \gamma Tr\left(W^TD_t^{-1}W\right) \\ &\Rightarrow \arg\min_W Tr\left(W^TAW\right) - 2Tr\left(B^TW\right) + \gamma\sum_i \frac{\left\|w^i\right\|_2^2}{2\left\|w_t^i\right\|_2} \end{aligned} \tag{17}$$

It can be inferred from (17) that W_{t+1} is the minimum of $Tr\left(W^TAW\right) -2Tr\left(B^TW\right) + \gamma\sum_i \frac{\left\|w^i\right\|_2^2}{\left\|w_t^i\right\|_2}$. Therefore we have:

$$\begin{aligned} &Tr\left(W_{t+1}^TAW_{t+1}\right) - 2Tr\left(B^TW_{t+1}\right) + \gamma\sum_i \frac{\left\|w_{t+1}^i\right\|_2^2}{2\left\|w_t^i\right\|_2} \\ &\le Tr\left(W_t^TAW_t\right) - 2Tr\left(B^TW_t\right) + \gamma\sum_i \frac{\left\|w_t^i\right\|_2^2}{2\left\|w_t^i\right\|_2} \end{aligned} \tag{18}$$

If

$$\sum_i \left\|w_{t+1}^i\right\|_2 - \sum_i \frac{\left\|w_{t+1}^i\right\|_2^2}{2\left\|w_t^i\right\|_2} \le \sum_i \left\|w_t^i\right\|_2 - \sum_i \frac{\left\|w_t^i\right\|_2^2}{2\left\|w_t^i\right\|_2}, \tag{19}$$

by incorporating it to (18) we can get:

$$\begin{aligned} &Tr\left(W_{t+1}^TAW_{t+1}\right) - 2Tr\left(B^TW_{t+1}\right) + \gamma\sum_i \left\|w_{t+1}^i\right\|_2 \\ &\le Tr\left(W_t^TAW_t\right) - 2Tr\left(B^TW_t\right) + \gamma\sum_i \left\|w_t^i\right\|_2, \end{aligned} \tag{20}$$

which proves that the objective function value in (14) monotonically decreases until convergence. Note that it is easy to prove (19) as follows. It is known that $2ab \le a^2+b^2$. If $b \neq 0$, we have [17]:

$$\begin{aligned} &a \le \frac{a^2}{2b} + \frac{b^2}{2b} \\ &\Rightarrow a - \frac{a^2}{2b} \le b - \frac{b^2}{2b} \end{aligned} \tag{21}$$

By substituting a and b with $\sum_i \left\|w_{t+1}^i\right\|_2$ and $\sum_i \left\|w_t^i\right\|_2$ respectively in (21), we obtain (19). Consequently (20) also holds. It can be proved that the objective of our framework is convex, we therefore can conclude that the proposed approach converges to the global optimum. □

4. EXPERIMENTS

In this section, we conduct extensive experiments to study the performance of our framework for automatic image annotation. We also compare the annotation results of our method with four other algorithms.

4.1 Image Datasets

We choose three image datasets, *i.e.*, Corel-5K [12][11], MSRA-MM [14] and NUS-WIDE [6] in our experiments. The following is a brief description of the three datasets.

Corel-5K: This dataset is comprised of real-world images from COREL image CDs. In our experiment, we use the standard dataset used in [12][11]. Corel-5K consists of 5,000 images from 50 different categories, *i.e.*, there are 50 concepts in total.

MSRA-MM: The dataset used in our experiments is a subset of the original MSRA-MM 2.0 dataset, which includes 50,000 images related to 100 concepts. However, 7,734 images within it are not associated with any labels. We have removed these images and obtained a subset of 42,266 labeled images. Three feature types used in [25], namely Color Correlogram, Edge Direction Histogram and Wavelet Texture are combined in our experiments to represent the images considering the computational efficiency.

NUS-WIDE: It consists of 269,000 real-world images collected from Flickr. Since 59,653 images of this dataset are not labeled, we have removed them and used the remaining 209,347 labeled images associated with 81 concepts in our experiments. The images are also represented by the combination of Color Correlogram, Edge Direction Histogram and Wavelet Texture.

4.2 Compared Methods

In our experiments, we compare our SFSS framework with one classical and three state of the art methods for automatic image annotation. Detailed information of them is given as follows.

- Fisher Score (F-score) [8]: It depends on fully labeled training data to select features with the best discriminating ability.
- Group Lasso with Logistic Regression (GLLR) [25]: It selects both sparse and discriminative groups of homogeneous features by group lasso extended with logistic regression.
- Feature Selection via Joint $l_{2,1}$-Norms Minimization (FSNM) [17]: It employs joint $l_{2,1}$-norm minimization on both loss

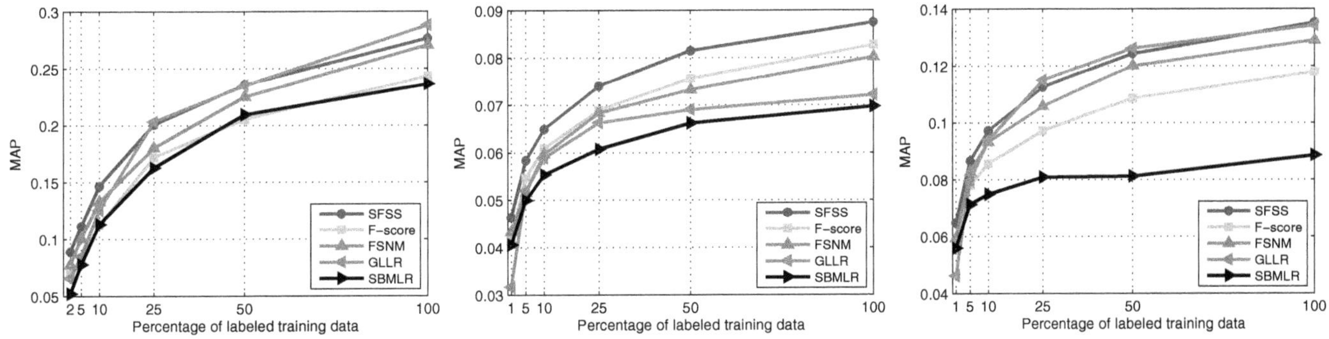

(a) Corel-5K (b) MSRA-MM (c) NUS-WIDE

Figure 2: Performance variance *w.r.t* the percentage of labeled training data. When 10% or less of the data are labeled our method outperforms all other algorithms. When 25% or more of the data are labeled, our method yields top performance or, in the MSRA-MM dataset significantly better performance.

Table 1: A brief comparison between the different methods.

Method	Supervision	Feature Selection with Sparsity	Classifier Generation
SFSS	Semi	Yes	Yes
F-score [8]	Full	No	No
GLLR [25]	Full	Yes	Yes
FSNM [17]	Full	Yes	No
SBMLR [5]	Full	Yes	No

Table 2: Performance comparison (MAP±Standard Deviation) when 2% (Corel-5K) or 1% (MSRA-MM&NUS-WIDE) training images are labeled.

	Corel-5K	MSRA-MM	NUS-WIDE
SFSS	**0.090±0.008**	**0.047±0.002**	**0.065±0.002**
F-score [8]	0.069±0.006	0.041±0.002	0.058±0.003
GLLR [25]	0.066±0.008	0.032±0.008	0.046±0.007
FSNM [17]	0.078±0.007	0.043±0.002	0.059±0.002
SBMLR [5]	0.052±0.004	0.040±0.002	0.056±0.003

function and regularization to realize feature selection across all data points.

- Sparse Multinomial Logistic Regression via Bayesian L1 Regularisation (SBMLR) [5]: It exploits sparsity by using a Laplace prior and is used for multi-class pattern recognition. It can also be utilized for feature selection.

Following [17], for FSNM we first select features and then conduct classification with the regularized least square regression. Similarly, F-score and SBMLR are used to perform feature selection and we use regularized least square regression subsequently to learn classifiers from the data represented by the selected features.

A brief comparison between the properties of our method and the other ones is given in Table 1.

4.3 Experiments Setup

To begin with, we randomly generate a training set for each of the three datasets. The training set comprises n samples, among which m samples are labeled. We set n as 2500 for the Corel-5K dataset and 10000 for both the MSRA-MM and NUS-WIDE datasets. The rest of the images of each dataset work as the corresponding testing set which is used to evaluate the annotation performance.

Table 3: Performance comparison (MAP±Standard Deviation) when 5% training images are labeled.

	Corel-5K	MSRA-MM	NUS-WIDE
SFSS	**0.112±0.009**	**0.059±0.002**	**0.087±0.003**
F-score [8]	0.083±0.007	0.055±0.002	0.078±0.002
GLLR [25]	0.085±0.010	0.052±0.001	0.079±0.001
FSNM [17]	0.101±0.007	0.051±0.002	0.082±0.002
SBMLR [5]	0.078±0.005	0.050±0.002	0.071±0.003

Table 4: Performance comparison (MAP±Standard Deviation) when 10% training images are labeled.

	Corel-5K	MSRA-MM	NUS-WIDE
SFSS	**0.147±0.009**	**0.065±0.001**	**0.097±0.002**
F-score[8]	0.113±0.003	0.061±0.002	0.086±0.003
GLLR [25]	0.126±0.015	0.059±0.001	0.094±0.002
FSNM [17]	0.133±0.009	0.060±0.001	0.093±0.003
SBMLR [5]	0.113±0.013	0.055±0.002	0.075±0.007

For MSRA-MM and NUS-WIDE, we set m as 1%, 5%, 10%, 25%, 50% and 100% of the total training images respectively. However, to cover all the semantic concepts in Corel-5K, at least 50 labeled training data are required. Thus, slightly different from the settings of the other two datasets, m is set as 2%, 5%, 10%, 25%, 50% and 100% of the total training images for Corel-5K. The results with different m are reported accordingly. The generation of training and testing sets is conducted 5 times for each dataset and the average results are reported.

There are two types of parameters to be tuned in our experiments. The first one is the parameter k that specifies the k nearest neighbors used to compute the graph Laplacian matrix L and it is set to 15 for all three datasets. The second one represents the regularization parameters, which are denoted as μ and γ in (6) in our framework. GLLR, FSNM and regularized least square regression also have such kind of parameters. We tune all these parameters from $\{0.001, 0.01, 0.1, 1, 10, 100, 1000\}$ and report the best results of corresponding methods.

To evaluate the annotation performance, we compare the labels obtained through different classification approaches with the ground truth labels for the testing sets. Among various evaluation metrics, Mean Average Precision (MAP) is stable and has good discrimin-

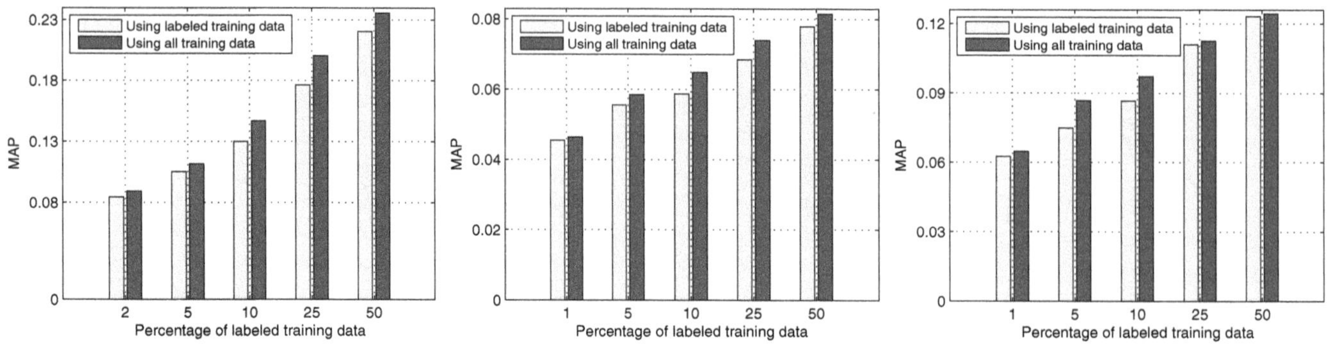

(a) Corel-5K (b) MSRA-MM (c) NUS-WIDE

Figure 3: The influence of unlabeled data on annotation. The blue bar corresponds to our semi-supervised algorithm, namely, SFSS as used in Figure 2. The yellow bar corresponds to the case when only labeled data are used (no unlabeled data). The largest relative improvement of 11%-13% is obtained when 10% training data are labeled. The large difference clearly shows that using unlabeled data improves annotation results.

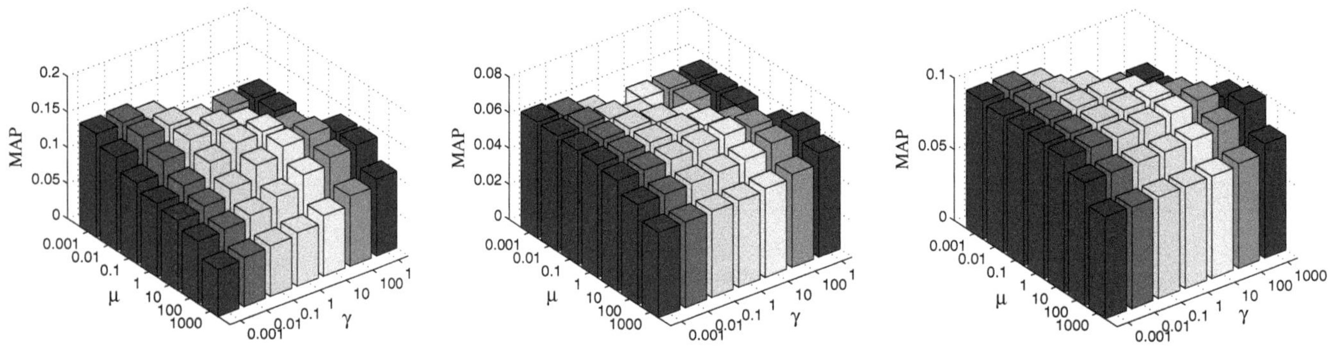

(a) Corel-5K (b) MSRA-MM (c) NUS-WIDE

Figure 4: Performance variance *w.r.t* μ and γ. The figure displays different annotation results when using different pairs of μ and γ. It can be seen that when μ and γ are close in value, the annotation performance is generally better than the case when they differ too much from each other.

ating capability. It is now widely used to evaluate accuracy so we use MAP in our experiments as well.

4.4 Image Annotation Results

Figure 2 shows the annotation results when different percentages of data are labeled. Table 2 to Table 4 show the results when 2% (Corel-5K) or 1% (MSRA-MM&NUS-WIDE), 5% and 10% of the training data are labeled. We have the following observations from the experimental results: 1) As the number of labeled training samples increases, performance obviously increases. 2) Our method is the only one which has consistently high scores on all three datasets. All other methods have varying degrees of success on each dataset. 3) When 25% or more of the training data are labeled, our method is competitive with the best algorithms compared or better. However, our advantage over other supervised algorithms decreases in general. On the Corel-5K dataset GLLR [25] slightly outperforms our method; on the NUS-WIDE dataset our method is competitive with GLLR [25]; on the MSRA-MM dataset our method outperforms all other methods. 4) Finally, when less than 25% of the data are labeled, our method consistently outperforms other methods on all three datasets. This is especially visible on the Corel-5K and MSRA-MM datasets.

The good performance of our SFSS framework can first be attributed to the appealing property that it can select features jointly across the whole feature space. The incorporation of the sparse model facilitates the feature selection by finding the discriminative features, which can assist in learning a robust classifier for image annotation in return. Exploiting the correlation between the predicted labels, the ground truth labels and the data structure also contributes to the good performance. Moreover, besides labeled data, our method can leverage the unlabeled data in the training stage so that it can learn the manifold structure.

4.5 Influence of the Unlabeled Data

As our method uses both labeled and unlabeled data for feature selection, we conduct an experiment to discover the influence of the unlabeled data on the annotation results.

In this experiment, we leave out the unlabeled data in the training sets and only use labeled training data as the input of our framework. Then we compare the results with the ones that are achieved by using the entire training set including both labeled and unlabeled data. The experiment is done on all the three datasets with 2% (Corel-5K) or 1% (MSRA-MM&NUS-WIDE), 5%, 10%, 25% and 50% training data labeled. The results are displayed in Figure 3.

We observe that on all datasets using unlabeled data in addition to the labeled data yields better results over using the labeled data alone: When 10% of the data are labeled, by also using unlabeled data we obtain relative improvements of 13% on the Corel-5K dataset, 11% on the MSRA-MM dataset and 12% on the NUS-WIDE dataset. We conclude that using unlabeled data clearly improves annotation results.

4.6 Parameter Sensitivity Study

To understand how the two parameters μ and γ in our framework can affect the annotation performance, we perform an experiment on the parameter sensitivity in which 10% training data are labeled. Figure 4 demonstrates the MAP variance *w.r.t* μ and γ. It is interesting to notice that the performance is generally better when μ and γ are comparable in value.

The phenomenon is supposed to be related to the trait of the dataset. However, to discover the root cause is not simple and it is out of the scope of our current focus.

5. CONCLUSION

In this paper we have proposed a new classification framework for automatic image annotation. Our work integrates several state of the art innovations from semi-supervised learning and feature selection, leading to a framework with the following desirable properties. First, our method jointly selects the discriminative features across the entire feature space. In addition, our method can learn the manifold structure from both labeled and unlabeled data. We performed experiments on three real-world image datasets. Results showed that if most of the training data are labeled, our method consistently yields competitive or better accuracy than other methods. When the majority of the data are unlabeled, our method clearly outperforms other methods on all three datasets. Using unlabeled data to boost classification performance is particularly important for image data as high quality manual labeling is expensive. We thus conclude that our method is suitable for large-scale image annotation.

6. ACKNOWLEDGMENTS

The work of Z. Ma, J. Uijlings, and N. Sebe was supported by the Glocal FP7 IP and the S-PATTERNS FIRB projects. The work of Y. Yang was partially supported by the National Science Foundation under Grants No. IIS-0917072, and CNS-0751185. Any opinions, findings, and conclusions or recommendations expressed in this material are those of the author(s) and do not necessarily reflect the views of the National Science Foundation.

7. REFERENCES

[1] A. Argyriou, T. Evgeniou, and M. Pontil. Multi-task feature learning. In *Advances in Neural Information Processing Systems (NIPS)*, 2007.

[2] M. Belkin, P. Niyogi, and V. Sindhwani. Manifold regularization: A geometric framework for learning from labeled and unlabeled examples. *Journal of Machine Learning Research*, 12:2399–2434, 2006.

[3] D. Cai, C. Zhang, and X. He. Unsupervised feature selection for multi-cluster data. In *Proceedings of the ACM international conference on Knowledge discovery and data mining (ACM SIGKDD)*, 2010.

[4] G. Carneiro, A. B. Chan, P. J. Moreno, and N. Vasconcelos. Supervised learning of semantic classes for image annotation and retrieval. *IEEE Transactions on Pattern Analysis and Machine Intelligence*, 29(3):394–410, March 2007.

[5] G. Cawley, N. Talbot, and M. Girolami. Sparse multinomial logistic regression via bayesian l1 regularisation. In *Advances in Neural Information Processing Systems (NIPS)*, 2006.

[6] T.-S. Chua, J. Tang, R. Hong, H. Li, Z. Luo, and Y.-T. Zheng. Nus-wide: A real-world web image database from national university of singapore. In *ACM International Conference on Image and Video Retrieval (CIVR)*, pages 8–10, July 2009.

[7] I. Cohen, F. G. Cozman, N. Sebe, M. C. Cirelo, and T. S. Huang. Semisupervised learning of classifiers: Theory, algorithms, and their application to human-computer interaction. *IEEE Transactions on Pattern Analysis and Machine Intelligence*, 26(12):1553–1567, December 2004.

[8] R. O. Duda, P. E. Hart, and D. G. Stork. *Pattern Classification (2nd ed.)*. Wiley-Interscience, New York, USA, 2001.

[9] Y. Gao, J. Fan, X. Xue, and R. Jain. Automatic image annotation by incorporating feature hierarchy and boosting to scale up svm classifiers. In *Proceeding of the ACM International Conference on Multimedia (ACM MM)*, 2006.

[10] X. He. Incremental semi-supervised subspace learning for image retrieval. In *Proceeding of the ACM International Conference on Multimedia (ACM MM)*, 2004.

[11] S. C. H. Hoi, W. Liu, and S.-F. Chang. Semi-supervised distance metric learning for collaborative image retrieval and clustering. *ACM Transactions on Multimedia Computing, Communications, and Applications*, 6(3):18:1–18:26, 2010.

[12] S. C. H. Hoi, M. R. Lyu, and R. Jin. A unified log-based relevance feedback scheme for image retrieval. *IEEE Transactions on Knowledge and Data Engineering*, 18(4):509–524, 2006.

[13] R. Jin, J. Y. Chai, and L. Si. Effective automatic image annotation via a coherent language model and active learning. In *Proceeding of the ACM International Conference on Multimedia (ACM MM)*, 2004.

[14] H. Li, M. Wang, and X.-S. Hua. MSRA-MM 2.0: A large-scale web multimedia dataset. In *Proceedings of the IEEE International Conference on Data Mining Workshops*, pages 164–169, December 2006.

[15] Y.-Y. Lin, T.-L. Liu, and H.-T. Chen. Semantic manifold learning for image retrieval. In *Proceeding of the ACM International Conference on Multimedia (ACM MM)*, 2005.

[16] J. Liu, M. Li, W.-Y. Ma, Q. Liu, and H. Lu. An adaptive graph model for automatic image annotation. In *Proceeding of the 8th ACM international workshop on Multimedia information retrieval*, 2006.

[17] F. Nie, H. Huang, X. Cai, and C. Ding. Efficient and robust feature selection via joint l21-norms minimization. In *Advances in Neural Information Processing Systems (NIPS)*, 2010.

[18] F. Nie, D. Xu, T. W. Hung, and C. Zhang. Flexible manifold embedding: A framework for semi-supervised and unsupervised dimension reduction. *IEEE Transactions on Image Processing*, 19:1921–1932, 2010.

[19] B. C. Russell, A. Torralba, K. P. Murphy, and W. T. Freeman. Labelme: A database and web-based tool for image annotation. *International Journal of Computer Vision*, 77(1-3):157–173, 2008.

[20] V. Sindhwani, P. Niyogi, and M. Belkin. Linear manifold regularization for large scale semi-supervised learning. In *Workshop on Learning with Partially Classified Training Data, International Conference on Machine Learning*, 2005.

[21] M. Wang, X.-S. Hua, R. Hong, J. Tang, G.-J. Qi, and

Y. Song. Unified video annotation via multi-graph learning. *IEEE Transactions on Circuits and Systems for Video Technology*, 19(5):733–746, 2009.

[22] M. Wang, X.-S. Hua, X. Yuan, Y. Song, and L.-R. Dai. Optimizing multi-graph learning: towards a unified video annotation scheme. In *Proceeding of the ACM International Conference on Multimedia (ACM MM)*, 2008.

[23] X.-J. Wang, L. Zhang, F. Jing, and W.-Y. Ma. Annosearch: Image auto-annotation by search. In *IEEE Computer Society Conference on Computer Vision and Pattern Recognition (CVPR)*, pages 1483–1490, June 2006.

[24] F. Wu, Y. Han, Q. Tian, and Y. Zhuang. Multi-label boosting for image annotation by structural grouping sparsity. In *Proceeding of the ACM International Conference on Multimedia (ACM MM)*, 2010.

[25] F. Wu, Y. Yuan, and Y. Zhuang. Heterogeneous feature selection by group lasso with logistic regression. In *Proceeding of the ACM International Conference on Multimedia (ACM MM)*, 2010.

[26] Y. Yang, H. T. Shen, Z. Ma, Z. Huang, and X. Zhou. L21-norm regularized discriminative feature selection for unsupervised learning. In *International Joint Conferences on Artificial Intelligence (IJCAI)*, 2011.

[27] Y. Yang, D. Xu, F. Nie, J. Luo, and Y. Zhuang. Ranking with local regression and global alignment for cross media retrieval. In *Proceeding of the ACM International Conference on Multimedia (ACM MM)*, 2009.

[28] Y. Yang, Y. Zhuang, F. Wu, and Y. Pan. Harmonizing hierarchical manifolds for multimedia document semantics understanding and cross-media retrieval. *IEEE Transactions on Multimedia*, 10(3):437–446, 2008.

[29] Z. Zha, X. Hua, T. Mei, J. Wang, G. Qi, and Z. Wang. Joint multi-label multi-instance learning for image classification. In *IEEE Computer Society Conference on Computer Vision and Pattern Recognition (CVPR)*, 2008.

[30] R. Zhang, Z. M. Zhang, M. Li, W.-Y. Ma, and H.-J. Zhang. A probabilistic semantic model for image annotation and multi-modal image retrieval. In *IEEE International Conference on Computer Vision (ICCV)*, 2005.

[31] Z. Zhao and H. Liu. Semi-supervised feature selection via spectral analysis. In *Proceedings of the SIAM International Conference on Data Mining*, 2007.

[32] Z. Zhao, L. Wang, and H. Liu. Efficient spectral feature selection with minimum redundancy. In *Proceedings of the AAAI Conference on Artificial Intelligence*, 2010.

[33] X. Zhu. Semi-supervised learning literature survey. In *Technical Report 1530, University of Wisconsin, Madison*, 2007.

[34] X. Zhu, Z. Ghahramani, and J. Lafferty. Semi-supervised learning using gaussian fields and harmonic functions. In *Proceedings of the Twentieth International Conference on Machine Learning (ICML)*, 2003.

Colorizing Tags in Tag Cloud: A Novel Query-by-Tag Music Search System

Ju-Chiang Wang[1,2], Yu-Chin Shih[1,2], Meng-Sung Wu[2], Hsin-Min Wang[2] and Shyh-Kang Jeng[1]

[1] Department of Electrical Engineering, National Taiwan University, Taipei 106, Taiwan

[2] Institute of Information Science, Academia Sinica, Taipei 115, Taiwan

{asriver, ycshih, wums, whm}@iis.sinica.edu.tw, skjeng@cc.ee.ntu.edu.tw

ABSTRACT

This paper presents a novel content-based query-by-tag music search system for an untagged music database. We design a new tag query interface that allows users to input multiple tags with multiple levels of preference (denoted as an MTML query) by colorizing desired tags in a web-based tag cloud interface. When a user clicks and holds the left mouse button (or presses and holds his/her finger on a touch screen) on a desired tag, the color of the tag will change cyclically according to a color map (from dark blue to bright red), which represents the level of preference (from 0 to 1). In this way, the user can easily organize and check the query of multiple tags with multiple levels of preference through the colored tags. To effect the MTML content-based music retrieval, we introduce a probabilistic fusion model (denoted as GMFM), which consists of two mixture models, namely a Gaussian mixture model and a multinomial mixture model. GMFM can jointly model the auditory features and tag labels of a song. Two indexing methods and their corresponding matching methods, namely pseudo song-based matching and tag affinity-based matching, are incorporated into the pre-learned GMFM. We evaluate the proposed system on the MajorMiner and CAL-500 datasets. The experimental results demonstrate the effectiveness of GMFM and the potential of using MTML queries to search music from an untagged music database.

Categories and Subject Descriptors

H.3.3 [**Information Storage and Retrieval**]: Information Search and Retrieval; H.5.3 [**Group and Organization Interfaces**]: Web-based interaction; H.5.5 [**Sound and Music Computing**]: System.

General Terms

Algorithms, Performance, Experimentation, Human Factors.

Keywords

Tag cloud-based music query interface, MTML query, content-based music information retrieval, probabilistic fusion model.

*Area Chair: Lexing Xie

1. INTRODUCTION

With the explosive growth of music collections, music information retrieval (MIR) has been extensively studied in recent years. There are many ways to retrieve pieces of desired music, e.g., query by humming/singing [1], query by example [2], query by meta-information, and query by tag [3]. In this paper, we study the query-by-tag MIR task. Specifically speaking, we propose a novel content-based MIR system, which allows users to input a query of multiple tags with multiple levels of preference by colorizing desired tags in a web-based tag cloud interface to search music from an untagged music database.

There are several tagged music resources for researchers to investigate users' tagging behavior among music tracks. For example, Last.fm is a collaborative social tagging network that collects information about users' music habits in terms of music tags. However, the tagging resources collected by Last.fm may encounter a problem called tagger bias [3], which is originated from the completely non-constrained tagging environment in Last.fm. Consequently, several web-based music tagging games have been created with the objective of collecting useful tags, e.g., MajorMiner.org [4], Tag A Tune [5], and the Listen Game developed by D. Turnbull [6]. In these tagging games, music clips are randomly assigned to taggers in order to reduce the tagger bias. However, the collected music tags have only been assigned to existing music tracks; in other words, there are no tags available for new tracks. The so-called "cold start" issue has motivated research into a number of interesting topics, such as automatic music tag annotation and tag-based music retrieval from an untagged music database.

Unlike the traditional meta-information (e.g., artist(s) name, track name, and album name) and well-defined categories (e.g., genre and emotion) annotated by domain experts, music tags are free text labels generated by common Internet users. Because these tags are annotated without constraint, they can be noisy (e.g., misspelled, redundant, irrelevant, and unlimited in term numbers). It is believed that a tag will enter the common musical vocabulary once it is adopted by a large number of users, and thereby extracting tags with high term frequencies can intuitively reduce the noisy factors. This leads gradually to the emergence of the so-called folksonomy, which is a full-scale taxonomy of music that reflects the current usage among Internet users [7]. The point of view about music tags motivates several current tag-based music search interfaces. For example, Last.fm[1] highlights or enlarges

[1] http://www.last.fm/charts/toptags

those commonly used tags for users to search music information in question, such as web pages, related artists, and music playlists. This kind of interface is also known as the tag cloud, which becomes one of the key visual elements in Web 2.0. The tags in a tag cloud are usually single words and are normally listed alphabetically, and the importance of each tag is shown with font size or color [8]. Tag cloud facilitates browsing and navigating all available tags alphabetically and by popularity. There are several developments of tag cloud interface in different visual layouts [9-11]. In sum, tag cloud provides an intuitive 2-dimensional layout that reflects aggregations of tag-usage statistics. However, a tag in the traditional layout of tag cloud is usually a hyperlink that directs to a collection of items that are associated with the tag, i.e., a user can only choose a single tag at once (e.g., Last.fm), which can not completely describe the information need. Although tag cloud reveals some tagging statistics derived from the data behind the interface, it does not provide users with any interaction. In light of the above discussions, as shown in Figure 1, we propose a novel tag-based music query interface that allows users to input a query comprised of multiple tags with multiple levels of preference (denoted as an MTML query hereafter) by colorizing desired tags in a tag cloud. As will be detailed in Section 3, the tag cloud in the interface not only provides the tagging statistics of the music content but also allows users to interact with it to organize the query by manipulating the colors of the desired tags.

We believe that the MTML query can help facilitate content-based music retrieval for two reasons.

1) Unlike images, which often contain only a few clearly identifiable objects, a piece of music can be described in nature by multiple music tags. The tags can include different types of musical information, such as genre, mood, instrumentation, personal preferences, original artist(s), and particular usages. A user can assign tags of the same type or different types to a specific song, and this may lead to specific tag co-occurrence (denoted as *co-tag* hereafter) patterns among auditorily similar songs. For example, instrumental or timbre tags, such as guitar, drum, rap, saxophone, and piano, are inspired by auditory cues directly. These instrumental tags usually result in a series of consequent tags, e.g., electric guitar, distortion, and drum commonly result in rock, loud, and metal tags; saxophone and piano are often assigned together with jazz or soft tags. Therefore, retrieving music with a certain co-tag pattern is more effective than retrieving music with a single tag. For example, if a person tags the song "Trouble" performed by "Coldplay" with "male, pop, piano, and slow" tags, he may use those tags to search for other songs that are similar to "Trouble" later. A single tag query like "pop" is very ambiguous, but combining a number of tags provides a clearer description of the desired song.
2) A song in a tagged music database has multiple tags with different counts. The tag count corresponds to the number of users who have annotated the song with the tag, i.e., it shows the tag popularity. Therefore, the MTML query can be directly matched with the *tag count distribution* of each song in a *tagged music database* to retrieve relevant music. The MTML query can also be matched with the *tag affinity distribution* of each song in an *untagged music database*. The tag affinity distribution of an untagged song consists of the confidence degree given by each tag predictor. The MTML query actually gives a more precise query than a single tag query and a simple binary multi-tag query.

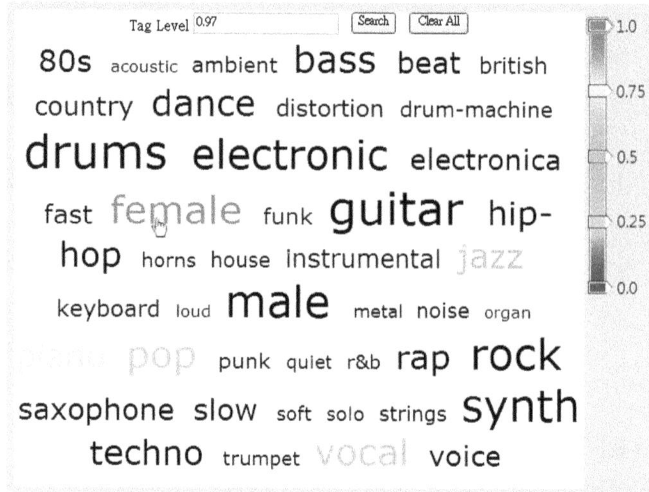

Figure 1. The screenshot of the tag cloud-based music search interface that allows a user to input a query consisting of multiple tags with multiple levels of preference by colorizing desired tags in the tag cloud. When moving the mouse pointer on a tag, the "Tag Level" (0.00~1.00) is shown in the value box in the top of the figure. The user can clicks and holds the left mouse button to change the color and level of the tag. After manipulating the colors of the desired tags, the user can click the search button to retrieve the desirable music. According to the color map in the rightmost of the figure, the user has inputted "female" with 0.97, "jazz" with 0.58, "piano" with 0.73, "pop" with 0.28 and "vocal" with 0.82.

To effect the MTML content-based music retrieval, we propose a Gaussian Multinomial Fusion Model (GMFM), which consists of two mixture models, namely a Gaussian mixture model (GMM) and a multinomial mixture model (MMM). The GMFM can jointly model the auditory features and tag labels of a tagged song. The tag cloud for the target untagged music database can be generated by automatic music tagging based on the GMFM learned from a limited tagged training music database. We also propose two indexing methods and their corresponding matching methods, namely, pseudo song-based matching and tag affinity-based matching, based on the GMFM.

The major contribution of this paper is threefold.

1) We address a new query scenario for music information retrieval, i.e., query by multiple tags with multiple levels of preference (denoted as an MTML query).
2) We design a new tag query interface that allows users to input an MTML query by colorizing desired tags in a tag cloud.
3) We propose a novel probabilistic fusion model, i.e., GMFM, which jointly model the auditory features and tag labels of a tagged song, and two indexing/matching methods based on the GMFM to effect the MTML content-based music retrieval.

The remainder of this paper is organized as follow. In Section 2, we discuss related work. In Section 3, we present our tag cloud-based MIR interface. Section 4 contains an overview of the proposed MTML-based MIR system. In Section 5, we describe the audio signal processing part. In Section 6, we introduce the GMFM and our MTML-based MIR methods. We discuss the evaluation of the proposed system in Section 7. In Section 8, we summarize our conclusion and discuss feature work.

2. RELATED WORK

A number of interfaces and approaches have been proposed for music retrieval using music tags. In [12], the authors propose a similarity measure in the space of social audio features and demonstrate an advanced music retrieval interface to retrieve songs by selecting a tag in a tag cloud on a mobile device. The tag cloud is user dependent; in other words, it only displays tags corresponding to a user's music collection. The tag cloud-based retrieval scenario is basically the same as that in Last.fm. Turnbull et al. [13] model the feature distribution of each tag with a GMM and estimate the model's parameters with a weighted mixture hierarchies expectation maximization algorithm. Hoffman et al. [14] propose a Codeword Bernoulli Average (CBA) method to model a tag's probability based on a song-level vector quantized feature representation. The training efficiency and tag prediction performance highly depend on the quality of the pre-trained codebook. Our recent work [15] applies a binary ensemble classifier comprised of SVM and AdaBoost to each tag to model its corresponding music features. The extended work in [16] shows that the tag prediction performance can be improved by considering the tag count information in auto-tagger training. All the above systems only consider retrieving music with a single tag.

In [7], Levy et al. apply text-based information retrieval (IR) techniques to music collections. They represent a music track with a joint vocabulary made up of social tags and muswords, where muswords are the quantized terms that represent the auditory characteristics of a segment-based signal in a track. The authors utilize two IR models to retrieve music in a query-by-example fashion. Each track in the music database is represented as a scaled concatenation of a bag-of-tags (BOW) vector and a bag-of-muswords (BOM) vector, denoted as BOW+M. Then, they apply the probabilistic latent semantic analysis (PLSA) model on the vector representations of songs to enhance the music retrieval effectiveness and efficiency. However, in their experiments, the music database is not completely untagged because a certain percentage of label information is used in the BOW+M representation. Recently, the latent aspect model of music tags has been extended to handle open vocabulary tags [17]. The open vocabulary tags, which contain many noisy labels, are reduced to a small set of topic labels using Latent Dirichlet Allocation (LDA), and then classifiers are trained on the transformed topic labels. Although they accept free text queries, which are equivalent to multi-tag queries, they do not consider the preference of each tag.

The Heard It system [18] creates an intelligent tag-based music retrieval system with three connected components: a social game, a learning machine, and a music understanding component. First, a social Internet game [19] is developed such that players can listen to music and share their opinions online. A player actually plays with a machine instead of other players but the player is not aware of this. The design increases the playability of the game. The objective is to have players verify whether a music clip should be associated with a pre-defined tag or not. Through the game, a large amount of reliable music tags with associated music clips have been collected and used to train automatic music tagging classifiers. These classifiers are then applied to predict new songs with pre-defined tags. Finally, a content-based music search system is established, and users can retrieve or generate a music playlist via multiple tags. The tags are categorized into 6 classes, namely, emotion, characteristics, genre, instrumentation, use of music, and vocal. Users can select desired tags from the 6 classes or type the tag words in the pre-defined tag set, as shown in Figure

(a) (b)

Figure 2. The tag query interface of Herd It. Users can (a) select tags from the pre-categorized menu or (b) enter the tag words in the search box.

2. The categorization of tags helps users organize their music needs. However, users can only enter multiple *binary* tags without preference levels, and the tags in the menu do not show the social information or data distribution behind the interface.

In a word, the abovementioned tag-based MIR approaches or systems accept either single or multiple tags typed in or selected from a tag list or a tag cloud. None of them consider the preference level of a tag. However, in the proposed tag-based MIR system, the tag cloud in the interface not only provides the tagging statistics of the music content but also allows users to interact with it to organize the query by manipulating the colors of the desired tags. As will be detailed in Section 6, in the proposed GMFM, the GMM and MMM are learned in a single stage, while the models in [7, 14, 17] are learned in two stages. In this paper, we do not deal with the open vocabulary tags since the current MTML interface does not allow users to enter tags not covered by the tag cloud.

3. TAG CLOUD-BASED MIR INTERFACE

As the screenshot of the proposed web-based MIR interface shown in Figure 1, there is a music tag cloud where the font size of a tag corresponds to the popularity according to the tag frequency in the music database. Since the music database is originally untagged, the tag cloud is generated via automatic tagging, i.e., the font size of a tag is determined by the accumulated confidence degree among music clips given by the corresponding tag predictor. All tags are allocated alphabetically and initialized to black color. In the rightmost, there is a color map (from dark blue to bright red), in which each color represents a tag level ranging from 0.00 to 1.00. When a user clicks and holds the left mouse button on a desired tag, the color of the tag will change cyclically according to the color map, and the corresponding tag preference level will be synchronized with the tag color and shown in the value box of "Tag Level" in the top of the interface. Once the user releases the left mouse button, the current color and level of the selected tag will be stored. The color changing period is set to 3 seconds, i.e., the tag color changes gradually from dark blue (0.00) to bright red (1.00) in 3 seconds, and then retrogresses from bright red (1.00) to dark blue (0.00) in another 3 seconds. The user can move the mouse pointer back to a previously colored tag to modify its color and level. In this way, the user can easily organize and check the query of multiple tags with multiple levels of preference through the colored tags. When the user clicks the "search" button, the interface will submit the selected tags with corresponding levels of preference to the music search system, and then a ranked music list with related materials will be returned to the user.

Since users can obtain tagging statistics behind the MIR system from the tag cloud display, we believe that the tag cloud-based query interface can help users organize their desired musical concepts. For example, users can readily know the popularity of a tag through the font size. They may compromise their information needs by selecting some popular tags in order to retrieve more music tracks. Besides, there are infinite kinds of possible MTML queries. Slight changes to the MTML query may lead to different music ranking results. In other words, users can interact with the music query interface to further discover music in the database.

Currently, the tag-colorizing interface is implemented as a desktop interface. However, it can be directly applied to a smart mobile device where users can simply press and hold on the desired tags through its touch screen. The tag cloud layout can fit the pinch-to-zoom mechanism and be clearly displayed on the small touch screen. With such an interface, users can easily search music by inputting an MTML query through a *mouse* or a *finger* without the need of typing any words or values. We can also implement the desktop interface by using a scrolling bar for each tag. Users can increase or decrease the preference for a particular tag more instantaneously by using a mouse to control the scrolling function. However, the scrolling function-based interface may not be able to show tagging statistics of the music database.

4. SYSTEM OVERVIEW

In Section 3, we have described how users can enter the MTML query through the tag cloud-based interface to retrieve music. In this section, we will give an overview on the proposed MTML content-based music search system.

As shown in Figure 3, the proposed MTML content-based music search system is implemented in two phases: *feature indexing phase* and *music retrieval phase*. In the feature indexing phase, each music clip in the untagged music database is indexed as a fixed-dimensional vector based on the clip's audio features. We use two indexing approaches: indexing with the *auditory posterior distribution* of a music clip by using an auditory feature reference, or indexing with the *tag affinity distribution* of a music clip given by automatic music tagging. In the retrieval phase, given an MTML query from the proposed tag-colorizing interface, the content-based music search system will return a ranked list of relevant music clips by vector matching. We apply two matching methods, namely *pseudo song-based matching* and *tag affinity-based matching*; each corresponding to one of the two indexing approaches. In pseudo song-based matching, an MTML query is first transformed into a pseudo song (i.e., the predicted auditory posterior distribution of the MTML query), and then matched with the music clips in the database in the space of auditory posterior distribution. In tag affinity-based matching, an MTML query is directly used to match with the music clips in the database in the space of tag affinity distribution. Table 1 summarizes the two implementations of the MTML music search system.

4.1 Tag Affinity Prediction

We assume that human memory stores a series of latent co-tag patterns that are difficult to describe. When tagging a song, people usually choose one or more of these patterns according to the auditory characteristics of the song. Although we cannot describe the latent co-tag patterns and auditory characteristics exactly, we believe that there is a strong link between them. Therefore, as shown in Figure 4, we introduce a hidden layer of latent classes of music features (denoted as the *latent feature class* hereafter) into the prediction flow of tag affinity distribution to link the latent co-tag patterns and auditory features.

Table 1. The two implementations of the MTML music search system.

Name	Indexing Vector	Matching Method
System 1	Auditory Posterior Distribution	Pseudo Song-based Matching
System 2	Tag Affinity Distribution	Tag Affinity-based Matching

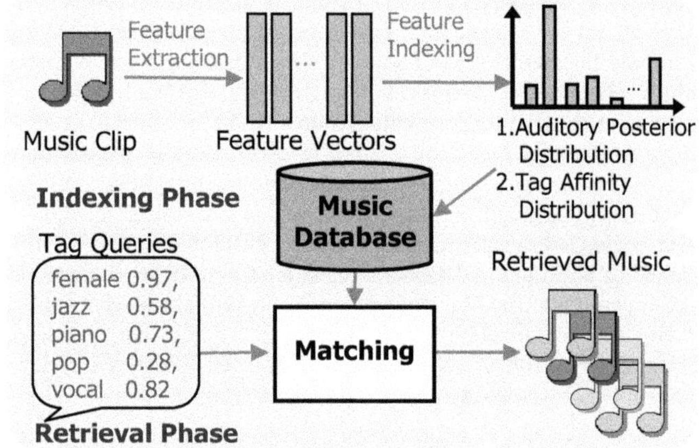

Figure 3. The flowchart of the proposed MTML content-based music search system.

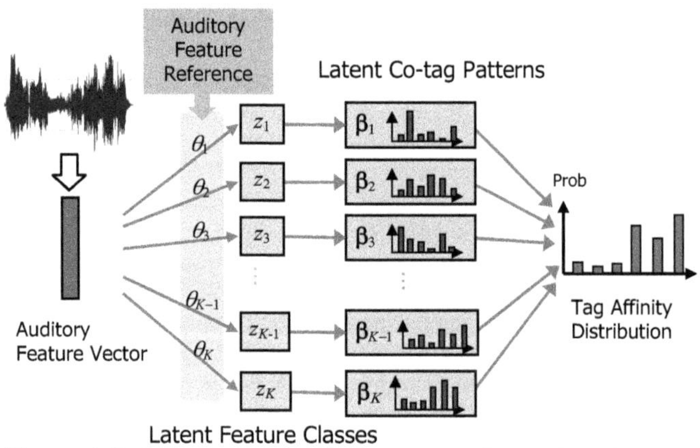

Figure 4. Indexing a music clip by automatic tagging: the prediction flow of tag affinity.

Assume there are K latent feature classes z_k, k=1,…,K. Each class z_k represents a group of auditory feature vectors, and its corresponding latent co-tag pattern is denoted as $\boldsymbol{\beta}_k$. A music clip is first extracted into an auditory feature vector. Then, the posterior probability (denoted as θ_k) of latent feature class z_k of the clip can be computed according to a pre-trained auditory feature reference. With $\boldsymbol{\beta}_k$, k=1,…,K, we can predict the tag affinity distribution for an untagged clip based on the value of θ_k, k=1,…,K. For example, if a clip's auditory features can be described completely by a certain latent feature class z_1, i.e., θ_1=1, and θ_i=0 for all i≠1, then its tag affinity distribution would exactly follow $\boldsymbol{\beta}_1$. To implement the idea, we assume that the tag labels with counts of a tagged song can be modeled by an MMM, where each latent co-tag pattern corresponds to a component multinomial distribution with parameter $\boldsymbol{\beta}_k$, k=1,…,K, and the auditory feature vector of the song can be modeled by a GMM, which corresponds to the aforementioned auditory feature reference. The two mixture models (MMM and GMM) condition on the same set of latent feature classes, i.e., a mixture component in MMM corresponds to a specific mixture component of GMM. The fusion of MMM and GMM leads to the GMFM.

4.2 Pseudo Song Estimation

In System 1 in Table 1, by using the GMFM, the MTML query is folded in into the latent co-tag patterns to estimate a pseudo song in the auditory posterior distribution representation. As shown in Figure 5, an MTML query is transformed into a posterior probability vector $\boldsymbol{\lambda}$ whose k-th component is the posterior probability λ_k of latent feature class z_k, k=1,…,K. We assume that λ_k, k=1,…,K, derived from the MTML query have a similar property with the auditory posterior distribution θ_k, k=1,…,K, that is used to index music clips in the untagged music database. For example, if an MTML query is extremely like $\boldsymbol{\beta}_1$, the folding-in process will yield a dominative posterior λ_1 on z_1, i.e., λ_1=1, and λ_i=0 for all $i\neq 1$, which means that the MTML query is extremely relevant to the song whose auditory posterior distribution is dominated by θ_1. Therefore, the pseudo song derived from the MTML query can be used to match with the clips in the untagged music database.

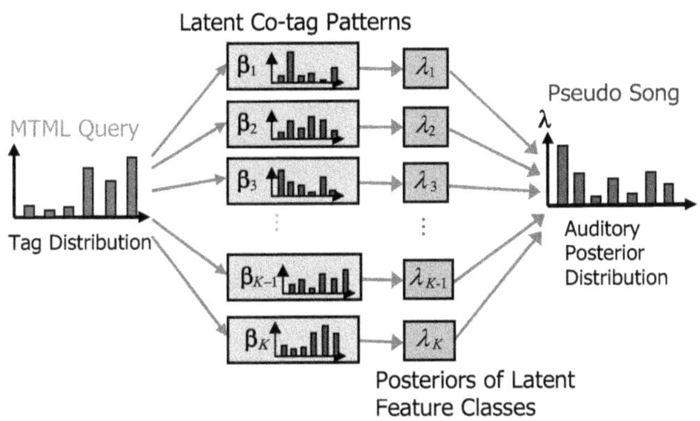

Figure 5. The estimation of the pseudo song (in the auditory posterior distribution representation) from an MTML query (in the tag distribution representation).

5. AUDIO SIGNAL PROCESSING

In this section, we describe the audio signal processing part in this work. To enhance the training efficiency and conform to the property of our music tagging modeling method, we adopt the segment-based audio feature representation instead of the frame-based one. A music clip in the database will be divided into segments and each segment is represented by a fixed-dimensional feature vector consisting of short-term temporal features and long-term perceptive features.

5.1 Audio Segmentation

Our audio segmentation is based on a measure of audio novelty proposed in [20]. An example segmentation result is shown in the bottom panel of Figure 6. We first compute the cosine measure of Mel-frequency cepstral coefficient (MFCC) vectors between any pairs of two frames (non-overlapping with size of 50ms) in a music clip, and build a self-similarity matrix, which can be visualized as a square image in the top panel of Figure 6. The color scale of a pixel in the image is proportional to the similarity. Then, we can

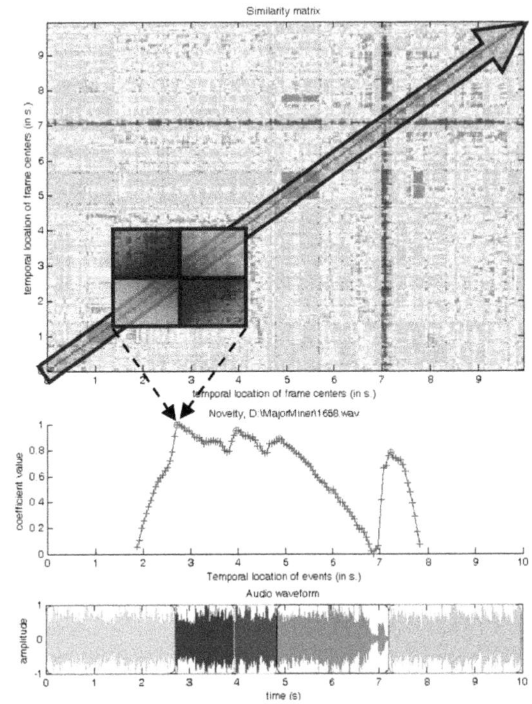

Figure 6. An illustration of audio segmentation.

obtain a time-aligned novelty curve, as shown in the middle panel of Figure 6, by convolving a checkerboard kernel with a radial Gaussian taper along the diagonal of the self-similarity matrix. The radial Gaussian taper of width H is defined as:

$$G(a,b)=\exp\left\{-4\times\left[\left(\frac{a-H/2}{H/2}\right)^2+\left(\frac{b-H/2}{H/2}\right)^2\right]\right\}, \qquad (1)$$

where a, b = 1,…,H, are the horizontal and vertical indexes of the Gaussian taper, respectively. Therefore, we only need to calculate a diagonal strip of width H when constructing the self-similarity matrix. In this work, H is set to 64 (3.2sec). Finally, the local peaks of the novelty curve, as marked by circles in the middle panel of Figure 6, are selected as segment boundaries. To prevent feature extraction failures caused by insufficient data, we require the length of each segment to be at least 1 second.

Audio segmentation will divide a music clip into a dynamic number of segments with dynamic lengths. For the convenience of implementation, all the segments of a music clip are extracted into a segment-based feature vector and treated equally in training and testing. We will describe in detail the processing of segments in a music clip in Section 6.

5.2 Music Feature Extraction

To extract music features, we utilize MIRToolbox 1.3 [21], a free software that comprises approximately 50 audio/music feature extractors and statistical descriptors. As shown in Table 2, we consider seven categories of features in this work, namely, dynamic, fluctuation, rhythm, spectral, timbre, pitch, and tonal features. We set default values for parameters in MIRToolbox, such as the length of frame and hop size. Short-term (frame-based) features are represented by their mean and standard deviation calculated over the segment. After feature extraction, each segment is represented by a 180-dimensional feature vector.

Table 2. The music features and the corresponding dimension used in the segment-based feature vector.

Type	Feature Description	Dim
dynamic	rms	2
fluctuation	peak, centroid	3
rhythm	event density, pulse clarity, tempo, attack time, attack slope	7
spectral	centroid, spread, skewness, kurtosis, entropy, flatness, rolloff at 85%, rolloff at 95%, brightness, roughness, irregularity	22
timbre	zero crossing rate, spectral flux, low energy, MFCC, delta MFCC, delta-delta MFCC, zero crossing rate	78
pitch	pitch value, inharmonicity	4
tonal	key strength, key clarity, key mode possibility, HCDF, chroma peak, chroma centroid, chroma	61

6. METHODOLOGY

This section presents the methodology of the MTML music search system, which is developed based on observations from the tagged music resources. We take several music clips from the MajorMiner dataset, as shown in Table 3, as examples. Each music clip in 10 seconds long has its tag labels with counts. These music clips can be grouped into two sets according to their tags, i.e., the clips in a set have a similar tag count distribution. However, the clips in a set in Table 3 may not be grouped together based on the auditory features since there exists a gap between the similarity of auditory features and the similarity of tag count distributions. The gap may come from insufficient auditory feature extraction or representation. It is believed that the tag count distribution of a music clip represents human perception about the clip. If we group music according to the auditory features only, the grouping results may be beyond human expectation. Therefore, certain supervisions based on tag labels with counts should be considered when estimating the distribution of auditory features. However, it is impossible to collect infinite music data with label information. In this work, our objective is to jointly learn a probabilistic model that considers both the auditory features and the tag labels with counts from a limited training dataset. We hope that the model can approximately cover the mostly realistic situations. In our model, we treat the tag labels with counts of a music clip as a text feature. Therefore, a music clip contains two types of features, i.e., the auditory features and the tag features. Both of them will contribute in model learning, but the contributions may not be equal.

6.1 The Gaussian Multinomial Fusion Model

As described in Sections 4.1 and 4.2, we would like to model the auditory feature vectors by a GMM and model the tag labels with counts by an MMM. We propose a fusion model called Gaussian Multinomial Fusion Model (GMFM) to combine the GMM and MMM. We assume that both GMM and MMM have the same number of mixtures, each mixture-component-pair of GMM and MMM conditions on the same latent feature class z_k, k=1,…,K, and the corresponding Gaussian and multinomial distributions have the same mixture prior π_k. All available tags are represented as a sequence of M tags, denoted as $\mathbf{w}=(w_1,w_2,\ldots,w_M)$. Suppose we have a tagged music dataset in which the music clips are divided into a total of N segments, and each segment, denoted by s_i, i=1,…,N, is extracted into a segment-based feature vector. A segment s_i is represented by an {auditory, tag-counts} feature pair denoted by $\{\mathbf{x}_i, \mathbf{c}_i\}$, where $\mathbf{x}_i$ is the auditory feature vector of s_i ; $\mathbf{c}_i$ is the vector of tag counts (i.e., a bag-of-tags vector) of the music clip from which s_i is originated (i.e., the tag labels with counts of a music clip are shared by all its component segments); and $c(i, j)$, j=1,…,M, denotes the count of the j-th tag w_j in $\mathbf{c}_i$. The likelihood functions of GMM and MMM for segment s_i are formulated in Eqs. (2) and (3), respectively,

$$p(\mathbf{x}_i \mid s_i, \Lambda) = \sum_k \pi_k N(\mathbf{x}_i \mid \boldsymbol{\mu}_k, \boldsymbol{\Sigma}_k), \quad (2)$$

$$p(\mathbf{w} \mid s_i, \Lambda) = \sum_k \pi_k MN(\mathbf{w} \mid \mathbf{c}_i, \boldsymbol{\beta}_k) = \sum_k \pi_k \prod_j \beta_{kj}^{\,c(i,j)}, \quad (3)$$

where $N(\cdot)$ is a Gaussian distribution with parameters $\boldsymbol{\mu}_k$ and $\boldsymbol{\Sigma}_k$; $MN(\cdot)$ is a multinomial distribution with the parameter $\boldsymbol{\beta}_k$, where its j-th component β_{kj}, j=1,…,M, represents the probability of the j-th tag in the k-th latent co-tag pattern; Λ represents the parameter set of the GMFM. Given the training music dataset, the joint log-likelihood L over all segments is defined as follows:

$$\begin{aligned} L &= \sum_i \log p(\mathbf{x},\mathbf{w} \mid s_i, \Lambda) = \sum_i \log\left[p(\mathbf{x} \mid s_i, \Lambda)^{\rho}\, p(\mathbf{w} \mid s_i, \Lambda)^{(1-\rho)}\right] \\ &= \sum_i \rho \log p(\mathbf{x} \mid s_i, \Lambda) + (1-\rho)\log p(\mathbf{w} \mid s_i, \Lambda) \quad (4) \\ &= \sum_i \left\{ \rho \log \sum_k \pi_k N(\mathbf{x}_i \mid \boldsymbol{\mu}_k, \boldsymbol{\Sigma}_k) + (1-\rho)\log \sum_k \pi_k \prod_j \beta_{kj}^{\,c(i,j)} \right\}. \end{aligned}$$

where the power weight ρ, which ranges between 0 and 1, is used because the log-likelihoods of GMM and MMM are not in a comparable scale. The role of ρ will be discussed later.

6.2 Model Inference with the EM Algorithm

The GMFM can be fitted by maximizing the joint log-likelihood L in Eq. (4) with respect to the mixture weight π_k, Gaussian parameters $\boldsymbol{\mu}_k$ and $\boldsymbol{\Sigma}_k$, and multinomial parameters $\boldsymbol{\beta}_k$, k=1,…,K. We apply the Expectation Maximization (EM) algorithm to estimate the model parameters. Both types of features, namely the auditory features and the tag features, of a segment should contribute to the posterior probability of a latent feature class z_k. Therefore, in the E-step, the posterior probability of z_k given s_i is the weighted combination of the corresponding posterior probability of the

Table 3. An example 2-group clustering result of music clips from the MajorMiner dataset based on their human labeled tags.

Group	Artist Name – Song Name – Clip Starting Time	Associated Music Tags (Tag Counts)
1	Cast - Two of a Kind - 2:20	bass(3),drum(5),electric guitar(2),guitar(5),male(5),pop(3),rock(5),vocal(2)
	The Kinks - Dedicated Follower of Fashion - 1:30	bass(2),drum(4),guitar(5),male(4),pop(2),rock(4),vocal(2)
	Suede - You Belong to Me - 1:30	bass(2),drum(3),guitar(4),male(4),pop(2),rock(5)
	New Order - Turn My Way - 2:40	bass(2),drum(3),guitar(3),male(3),pop(2),rock(4),vocal(2)
2	Intermix - Sonic Ritual - 4:20	beat(2),dance(2),electronic(3),electronica(5),house(2),synth(4),techno(4)
	Underworld - Air Towel - 1:00	beat(2),dance(3),electronic(4),electronica(4),house(2),synth(5),techno(3)

GMM, i.e., $p(z_k | \mathbf{x}_i, s_i)$, and that of the MMM, i.e., $p(z_k | \mathbf{w}, s_i)$, as expressed in the following:

$$p(z_k | s_i) \equiv \alpha \cdot p(z_k | \mathbf{x}_i, s_i) + (1-\alpha) \cdot p(z_k | \mathbf{w}, s_i)$$
$$= \alpha \cdot \frac{\pi_k N(\mathbf{x}_i | \boldsymbol{\mu}_k, \boldsymbol{\Sigma}_k)}{\sum_q \pi_q N(\mathbf{x}_i | \boldsymbol{\mu}_q, \boldsymbol{\Sigma}_q)} + (1-\alpha) \cdot \frac{\pi_k \prod_j \beta_{kj}^{\ c(i,j)}}{\sum_q \pi_q \prod_j \beta_{qj}^{\ c(i,j)}}, \tag{5}$$

where α is a *leverage factor* for adjusting the contributions of the auditory features and the co-tag distribution.

In the M-step, we maximize the expected log-likelihood over the posterior probability $p(z_k | s_i)$ with respect to the model parameters. The update rules for the model parameters are as follows:

$$\pi_k' \leftarrow \frac{1}{N} \sum_i p(z_k | s_i), \tag{6}$$

$$\boldsymbol{\mu}_k' \leftarrow \frac{\sum_i p(z_k | s_i) \mathbf{x}_i}{\sum_i p(z_k | s_i)}, \tag{7}$$

$$\boldsymbol{\Sigma}_k' \leftarrow \frac{\sum_i p(z_k | s_i)(\mathbf{x}_i - \boldsymbol{\mu}_k')(\mathbf{x}_i - \boldsymbol{\mu}_k')^T}{\sum_i p(z_k | s_i)}, \tag{8}$$

$$\beta_{kj}' \leftarrow \frac{\sum_i c(i,j) p(z_k | s_i)}{\sum_q \sum_i c(i,q) p(z_k | s_i)}. \tag{9}$$

The posterior probability of a latent feature class z_k in Eq. (5) plays a linkage between the GMM and the MMM, and determines the identical mixture weight π_k of the two models in Eq. (6).

The reason why we use the addition of the two mixture models' posterior probabilities rather than the product to estimate the posterior probability of z_k in Eq. (5) is that they have very different scales. From our experiences, the likelihood of the Gaussian PDF could be extremely small (could even become 0 due to the limited computing power) owing to the high dimension of the auditory feature vector. If product is used, the learning process could be overwhelmingly dominated by the auditory features, and the learning of MMM would highly depends on the feature aggregation of the GMM. Although the GMM learned in this way may be tight, the MMM could be very loose. This does not fit our goal of learning a GMFM with properly balanced feature aggregation that leads to good performance.

The leverage factor α is designed to be tuned and validated in the experiments. Note that in Eq. (4), ρ will not affect the estimation of model parameters in the joint log-likelihood maximization process because the log-likelihood terms of the two mixture models in Eq. (4) can be maximized independently. In practice, ρ plays a role in balancing and generating a reasonable L if we require a stopping criterion based on L during the iterative model fitting process. In this work, we readily set ρ to be equal to α. The learning process of GMFM is summarized in Algorithm 1.

Algorithm 1. The learning process of GMFM

Input: Initial model parameters $\{\boldsymbol{\mu}_k^{(0)}, \boldsymbol{\Sigma}_k^{(0)}, \boldsymbol{\beta}_k^{(0)}\}$, k=1,…,K;
Training segments $\{\mathbf{x}_i, \mathbf{c}_i\}$, i=1,…,N; Leverage factor α;
Stopping ratio r;

Output: Learned model parameters $\{\hat{\pi}_k, \hat{\boldsymbol{\mu}}_k, \hat{\boldsymbol{\Sigma}}_k, \hat{\boldsymbol{\beta}}_k\}$;

```
Initialize a set of equal π_k^(0) that sum to 1;
Iteration index t ← 0;
Compute L(t) with Eq. (4) using {π_k^(0), μ_k^(0), Σ_k^(0), β_k^(0)};
while (L(t)-L(t-1))/L(t) > r or t = 0 do
    Compute the posterior probability using Eq. (5);
    t ← t+1;
    Update {π_k^(t), μ_k^(t), Σ_k^(t), β_k^(t)} using Eqs. (6) ~ (9);
    Compute L(t) with Eq. (4) using {π_k^(t), μ_k^(t), Σ_k^(t), β_k^(t)};
end while
```

6.3 Music Retrieval with MTML Queries

As summarized in Table 1, there are two ways to apply the GMFM to the MTML content-based MIR system. Both Systems 1 and 2 need to first convert each music clip in the database into a set of auditory posterior distribution vectors. Given a music clip S, it is first extracted into a set of segment-based feature vectors denoted as $\mathbf{x}_t$, t=1,…,T. Then, the auditory posterior distribution of segment $\mathbf{x}_t$, denoted as vector $\boldsymbol{\theta}_t$, is computed with the GMM in the pre-learned GMFM:

$$\theta_{tk} \leftarrow p(\mathbf{x}_t | z_k, \Lambda) = \frac{\pi_k N(\mathbf{x}_t | \boldsymbol{\mu}_k, \boldsymbol{\Sigma}_k)}{\sum_q \pi_q N(\mathbf{x}_t | \boldsymbol{\mu}_q, \boldsymbol{\Sigma}_q)}. \tag{10}$$

where θ_{tk} is the k-th component in $\boldsymbol{\theta}_t$.

In System 1, each music segment in the database is indexed by its $\boldsymbol{\theta}$ computed by Eq. (10). Then, a given MTML query $\tilde{\mathbf{c}}$, whose component is denoted as $\tilde{c}(j)$, j=1,2…,M, is folded in into the MMM to estimate a pseudo song $\boldsymbol{\lambda}$ whose component λ_k, k=1,…,K, is estimated by

$$\lambda_k \leftarrow p(z_k | \mathbf{w}, \tilde{\mathbf{c}}, \boldsymbol{\beta}_k) = \frac{\pi_k \prod_j \beta_{kj}^{\ \tilde{c}(j)}}{\sum_q \pi_q \prod_j \beta_{qj}^{\ \tilde{c}(j)}}. \tag{11}$$

The pseudo song has a similar property with the auditory posterior distribution $\boldsymbol{\theta}$ as explained in Section 4.2. Therefore, we apply the well-known vector space model to compute the cosine similarity between the pseudo song and each music segment in the database. The music segments in the database are ranked by sorting the similarities from high to low. The ranking position of a music clip in the database is the *averaged* ranking positions of its component segments.

In System 2, the GMFM-based automatic tagger predicts the tag affinity distribution of each music clip in the untagged music database. Given a music clip S, we first predict the tag affinity of S's component segment $\mathbf{x}_t$, t=1,…,T. The affinity of tag w_j for segment $\mathbf{x}_t$ is computed by

$$p(w_j | \mathbf{x}_t) = \sum_k \theta_{tk} \beta_{kj}. \tag{12}$$

Assume each segment in a music clip is treated equally, the affinity of tag w_j for S is computed by

$$p(w_j | S) = \frac{1}{T} \sum_{t=1}^{T} p(w_j | \mathbf{x}_t). \tag{13}$$

Given an MTML query, we use the same standard matching function, i.e., the cosine similarity, to compare an MTML query $\tilde{\mathbf{c}}$, and the tag affinity distribution of each music clip in the database.

Since the two systems may complement each other, we can perform a ranking ensemble on their ranking results. The system is denoted as System 3 in the experiments.

7. EVALUATION AND RESULTS

In this section, we first examine the convergence of GMFM learning and the parameter α. Then, we evaluate the MTML content-based MIR system on the MajorMiner [4] and CAL-500 datasets.

The MajorMiner dataset is obtained from the MajorMiner website, which uses a game to gather informative free text labels for music. Each player labels randomly given music clips (each about 10 seconds long) by listening to them without any meta-information. If two players assign the same text label to a music clip, the label is adopted by the system. Hence, each music clip's tag count is at least 2. We crawled all the music clips associated with the most commonly used 76 tags from the MajorMiner website in March 2011. The resulting dataset contains 2,472 music clips. In the dataset, the count of a tag given to a music clip is at most 12.

The CAL-500 dataset consists of 500 clips of western popular songs [14]. The length of a clip ranges from 3 seconds to more than 22 minutes. Each clip has been manually labeled by at least three humans following 174 pre-defined text labels. We select a subset of 111 tags, which cover categories of genre, instrumentation, usages, and vocals. In this work, the "soft-assignment" scores of tags between 0 and 1 are transformed into positive integer counts ranging from 1 to 14 for model training.

7.1 Examination of GMFM Learning

We fit the GMFM on the MajorMiner dataset to examine the convergence of the training log-likelihood. The initial GMM is derived by applying the K-means algorithm on a small portion of available segment-based vectors. The initial MMM is randomly generated and the parameters of each mixture component are normalized to sum to unity. From Figure 7(a), we can see that the log-likelihood of the GMFM (K=32) increases monotonically till the stopping criterion that the log-likelihood is increased by less than 0.0001 is reached. Note that K represents the number of latent feature classes. We also perform an automatic tagging experiment with the GMFM to validate the parameter α. The experiment is executed in a three-fold cross-validation manner, i.e., two-thirds of music clips for training and the remaining for testing. We repeat 20 runs to get the average tag prediction performance in terms of AUC (area under the ROC curve) per clip at different K and α. In each run, the dataset is divided into three folds at random. As shown in Figure 7(b), the GMFM achieves better tagging performance when α is between 0.5 and 0.7. The results indicate that the auditory features should contribute more in GMFM learning. In the following MIR experiments, α is set to the value that gives the best performance in Figure 7(b). Although the performance curves in Figure 7(b) vary slightly with K, they have a similar concave tendency. The performance is improved as K increases since a larger K yields a higher resolution of the latent feature class. But the improvement is not linearly proportional to the increase in K, and it starts to saturate at around K=256 as will be described in detail later.

7.2 Evaluation of the MTML MIR System

To evaluate the proposed MIR system, we need a set of MTML queries; and for each query, we need the relevant/irrelevant labels of music clips in the dataset. Recall that each music clip in the dataset is associated with tags and their counts, i.e., $c(i, j)$, j=1,…,M; thus, the tag labels with counts of each clip can be used as a test MTML query. Then, given an MTML query, the proposed content-based MIR system searches the music clip itself as well as other music clips that are perceptually similar to it. How-

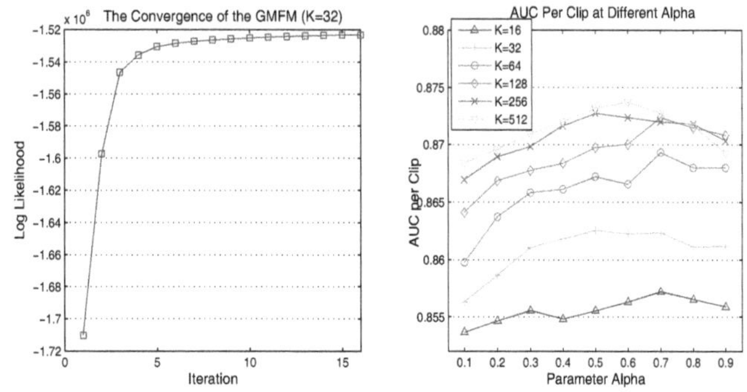

(a) (b)

Figure 7. (a) The log-likelihood computed in Eq. (4) at each iteration of GMFM learning; (b) the automatic tagging performance in terms of AUC per clip with different K and α.

ever, since relevance information is not available and manual labeling is not feasible, we generate the relevance information based on the tag labels with counts of music clips in the dataset. We assume that two music clips will be considered relevant by a user if they have a highly similar tag count distribution, i.e., the cosine similarity between their tag count distributions is close to 1. For example, the music clips in a group in Table 3 are considered mutually relevant. Therefore, the ground-truth relevance R between two clips can be defined as the cosine similarity (in the range 0 to 1) between their tag count distributions. If we take the tag count distribution of a clip S_1 as an MTML query, the ground-truth relevance for clip S_2 can be calculated as the cosine similarity between the tag count distributions of S_1 and S_2. In this way, we can generate the relevance information for each MTML query.

We repeat three-fold cross-validation 20 times on the MajorMiner dataset. In each run, the dataset is divided into three folds at random. We use 1,648 clips for training the GMFM and 824 clips for MIR testing. The tag label of each track in the test set is taken as an MTML query; hence, there are 824 MTML queries. Given a query in turn, the retrieval system will rank the 824 music clips based on their audio content. The same manner is applied on the CAL-500 dataset except that we perform five-fold cross-validation. The ranked results are compared with the ground-truth relevance. To evaluate the retrieval performance, we apply the discounted cumulative gain (DCG) and normalized DCG (NDCG) [22]. DCG is formulated as follows:

$$\mathrm{DCG}@P = R(1) + \sum_{i=2}^{P} \frac{R(i)}{\log_2 i}, \tag{14}$$

where $R(i)$ is the ground-truth relevance of the i-th music clip on the ranked list. The ground-truth relevance of a retrieved music clip will contribute to DCG a non-negative value discounted logarithmically proportional to its ranked position. The DCG at P is proportional to how relevant the top P retrieved music clips are to the query. If a system retrieves more relevant clips and highly relevant clips have higher positions, it will obtain a higher DCG. If we only consider the ranking of the retrieved clips and disregard the relevance degree with respect to the whole database, we can use the normalized DCG, which is formulated as follows:

$$\mathrm{NDCG}@P = \frac{\mathrm{DCG}@P}{\mathrm{IDCG}@P}, \tag{15}$$

where IDCG@P, which guarantees the ideal NDCG@P value will be 1, is the best DCG@P that can be obtained given a set of re-

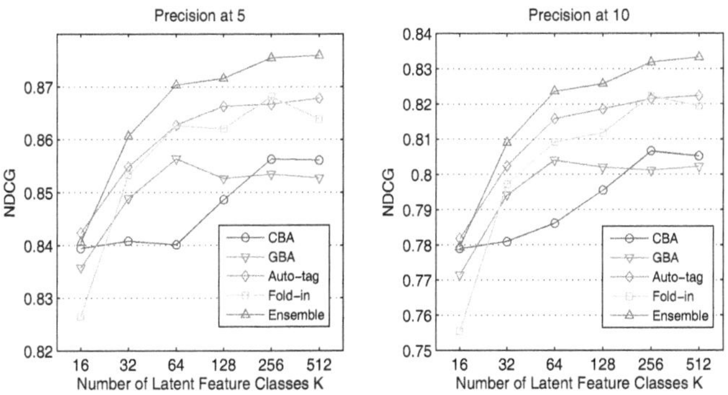

Figure 8. The NDCG results for the MajorMiner dataset.

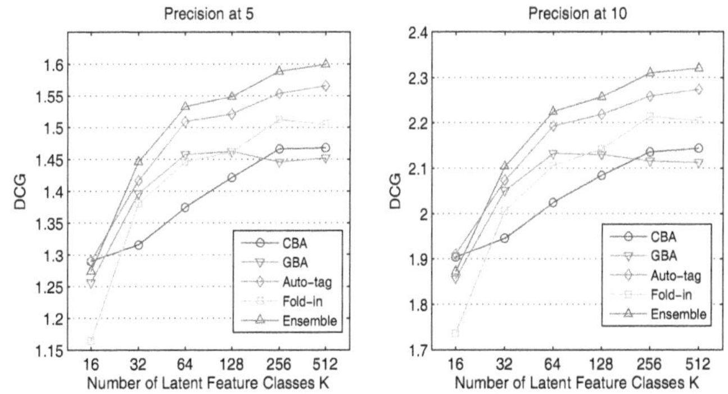

Figure 9. The DCG results for the MajorMiner dataset.

trieved clips. NDCG is practically meaningful because most users only care about the ranking of the top ranked results.

7.2.1 MIR Methods Compared

We evaluate the Fold-in method (i.e., System 1 in Table 1), the Auto-tag method (i.e., System 2 in Table 1), and the Ensemble method (i.e., System 3 mentioned in Section 6.3). The number of latent feature classes is set between 16 and 512. We also implement three methods as the baselines, namely, the codebook Bernoulli Average (CBA) method [14], the Gaussian Bernoulli Average (GBA) method, and the Random method. The CBA method starts with an unsupervised training of a codebook on available auditory feature vectors, and then each music clip is encoded as a bag-of-codewords vector. Next, a binary classifier for each tag is learned based on estimating a set of Bernoulli distributions, each corresponding to a codeword. There are several improvements with GMFM versus CBA. First, CBA is performed in a two-step learning manner in which the label information is not considered in codebook training and the learning of Bernoulli distributions fully depends on the vector grouping of the codebook. Second, CBA is not designed to model the co-tag phenomenon and tag counts since it employs an independent classifier for each tag and a Bernoulli distribution for each codeword. Third, the use of vector quantization for encoding a song limits the generalization of CBA so that it usually requires a large codebook to achieve good performance and model adaptation is not feasible when there are new songs or tag labels. In the GBA method, the codebook is replaced by a GMM. Note that K represents the size of codebook in CBA and the number of Gaussian components in GBA. The Random method is implemented in two ways: 1) randomly generating a pseudo song for an MTML query, and 2) indexing a clip with a randomly generated tag affinity. The performance of the Random method is the average performance of the two implementation ways. We also investigate the performance of the query-by-example (QBE) method. Compared with the Fold-in method, which uses the pseudo song estimated from an MTML query to search music, the QBE method uses the auditory posterior distribution of the associated music clip.

7.2.2 Results of MIR Experiments

The results of MIR experiments on the MajorMiner dataset in terms of mean NDCG@5, NDCG@10, DCG@5, and DCG@10 are shown in Figures 8 and 9, respectively. It can be found that the performance in general monotonically increases with K, but the improvements are gradually reduced. For the MajorMiner dataset, we suggest to use K=256 because of its performance and computational efficiency. From the figures, it is obvious that our methods, in particular System 2 (Auto-tag) and System 3 (Ensemble), out-

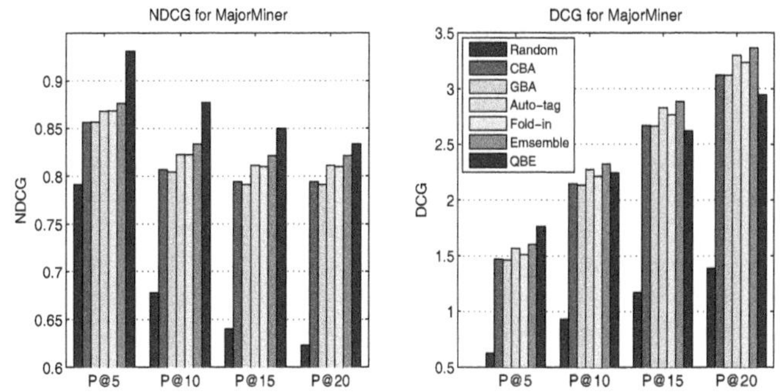

Figure 10. The comparison of the best performance of all methods on the MajorMiner dataset.

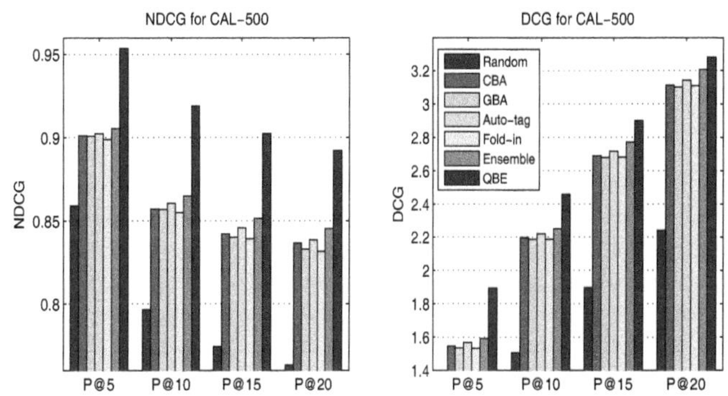

Figure 11. The comparison of the best performance of all methods on the CAL-500 dataset. The DCG@5 of the Random method is not shown because it is worse than 1.4.

perform the baselines in all cases. There could be two reasons for the superiority of System 2 (Auto-tag) over System 1 (Fold-in). First, System 2 matches the MTML query with the music clips in the database in the tag label space, based on which the ground-truth relevance R is estimated, while System 1 does matching in the auditory posterior space. Second, the GMM is fitted better than the MMM in GMFM learning because the GMFM favors the GMM and auditory features more according to α. However, the two systems can be combined as System 3 (Ensemble) to further improve the performance. The results verify that System 1 and System 2 complement each other. Although the ensemble method performs well, for the online computational efficiency, we suggest using System 2 since the folding-in procedure in System 1 may suffer from an additional step of estimating the pseudo song from the input MTML query online.

The comparison of the best performance of all methods evaluated on the MajorMiner and CAL-500 datasets are shown in Figures 10 and 11, respectively. From the figures, it is obvious that all methods outperform the Random method significantly. The QBE method is originally designed to evaluate the upper bound performance of the Fold-in method. However, it is interesting to find that QBE does not always outperform Fold-in. The reason could be as follows. The pseudo song transformed from a music clip *S*'s tag labels should have a near identical auditory posterior distribution with *S* ideally. However, the MMM learned from the latent feature classes and tag labels with counts of the training music clips may transform *S*'s tag labels with counts (i.e., the MTML query) into a pseudo song that may benefit from the ground-truth relevance estimated from the tag labels with counts in the music database, although it does not share a similar auditory posterior distribution with *S*,. This is reasonable if tag bias or noisy tags exist in the training dataset. Compared with MajorMiner, CAL-500 is a more well-labeled dataset, in which all the pre-defined tags are verified to the music clips (the tags in MajorMiner are not, due to the nature property of social tagging resources). As can be seen in Figure 11, the performance of CBA and GBA gets closer to that of Auto-tag, and CBA and GBA even outperform Fold-in in some cases, in contrast to the results for MajorMiner in Figure 10. Since the noisy factors in realistic tagged music resources can be dealt by topic modeling as discussed in [7, 17], the GMFM, which employs the concepts of topic modeling, has the advantage as well. The observation that the QBE method performs an outstanding result in terms of the NDCG metric also indicates that the similarity from auditory posterior distribution $\boldsymbol{\theta}$ encoded by the GMM does properly match human's perceptual similarity.

8. CONCLUSION AND FUTURE WORK

In this paper, we have addressed a new tag-based query scenario for music information retrieval, i.e., query by multiple tags with multiple levels of preference. The MTML query scenario is accomplished by a query-by-tag MIR system with a novel tag query interface that allows users to search music by colorizing desired tags in a tag cloud. In addition to music, the tag-colorizing interface can also be applied to other multimedia documents, e.g., images and videos. To effect the content-based music retrieval, we have introduced a novel probabilistic fusion model GMFM, which consists of a GMM and an MMM, to jointly model the auditory features and tag labels of a song. Two indexing methods and their corresponding matching methods, namely pseudo song-based matching and tag affinity-based matching, are incorporated into the pre-learned GMFM. The experimental results have demonstrated the effectiveness of GMFM and the potential of using MTML queries to search music from an untagged music database.

Our future work is fivefold. First, with the tag-colorizing interface, users have the opportunity to interact with the interface and discover music in the database. We can also apply a user feedback scenario. In this way, we can collect the tags associated with a set of originally untagged music. The newly collected tagged music can be used to adapt the GMFM by using the Maximum a Posteriori (MAP) algorithm. Second, the GMFM can be extended to fit out a self-organizing map (SOM) of music tags. In this way, the tag cloud will have a more intelligent layout, which shows more information about tags to attract people to play and discover music with the system. Third, the usability of the proposed tag cloud-based interface should be further evaluated on a large untagged music database. In this paper, we only evaluate the technical method that realizes the interface on two small tagged music databases. Hopefully, we can cooperate with a music website or Internet radio station such that the user experience of the system could be practically evaluated. Fourth, we will further consider the usability of the tag cloud-based interface and the scrolling function-based interface. The integration of these two interfaces is also worthy of study. Fifth, we want to extend our method to deal with the open vocabulary tags. We do not consider the open vocabulary tags currently since the MTML interface does not allow users to enter tags not covered by the tag cloud. However, the interface will be more flexible if it also allows users to key in tags.

9. ACKOWLEDGEMENTS

This work was supported in part by Taiwan e-Learning and Digital Archives Program (TELDAP) sponsored by the National Science Council of Taiwan under Grant: NSC 100-2631-H-001-013. We thank the anonymous reviewers and our shepherd Dr. Lexing Xie for their help comments.

10. REFERENCES

[1] N. Kosugi, et al. A practical query-by-humming system for a large music database. In *Proc. of ACM MM*, 2000.

[2] W.-H. Tsai, H.-M. Yu, and H.-M. Wang. A query-by-example technique for retrieving cover versions of popular songs with similar melodies. In *Proc. of ISMIR*, 2005.

[3] P. Lamere. Social tagging and music information retrieval. *J. New Music Res.*. 37(2), pp. 101-114, 2008.

[4] M. I. Mandel and D. P. W. Ellis. A web-based game for collecting music metadata. *J. New Music Res.*. 37(2), pp. 151–165, 2008.

[5] E. Law and L. von Ahn. Input-agreement: A new mechanism for data collection using human computation games. In *Proc. of ACM CHI*. pp. 1197-1206, 2009

[6] D. Turnbull, et al. A game-based approach for collecting semantic annotations of music. In *Proc. of ISMIR*, 2007.

[7] M. Levy and M. Sandler. Music information retrieval using social tags and audio. *IEEE Trans. on Multimedia*. 11(3), 383-395, 2009.

[8] http://en.wikipedia.org/wiki/Tag_cloud

[9] Owen Kaser and Daniel Lemire. Tag-cloud drawing: Algorithms for cloud visualization. In *Proc. of WWW*, 2007.

[10] S. Lohmann, J. Ziegler, and L. Tetzlaff. Comparison of tag cloud layouts: Task-related performance and visual exploration. T. Gross et al. (Eds.). *INTERACT 2009*, Part I, pp. 392–404, 2009.

[11] K. Knautz, S. Soubusta, and W.G. Stock. Tag clusters as information retrieval interfaces. In *Proc. of the 43rd Annual Hawaii International Conference on System Sciences (HICSS-43)*, 2010.

[12] M. Kuhn, R. Wattenhofer and S. Welten. Social audio features for advanced music retrieval interfaces. In *Proc. of ACM MM*, 2010.

[13] D. Turnbull, L. Barrington, D. Torres, and G. Lanckriet. Semantic annotation and retrieval of music and sound effects," *IEEE Trans. on Audio, Speech and Lang. Process.*. 16(2), pp. 467–476, 2008.

[14] M. Hoffman, D. Blei, and P. Cook. Easy as CBA: A simple probabilistic model for tagging music. In *Proc. of ISMIR*, 2009.

[15] H.-Y. Lo, J.-C. Wang, and H.-M. Wang. Homogeneous segmentation and classifier ensemble for audio tag annotation and retrieval. In *Proc. of IEEE ICME*, 2010.

[16] H.-Y. Lo, S.-D. Lin, and H.-M. Wang. Audio tag annotation and retrieval using tag count information. In *Proc. of MMM*, 2011.

[17] E. Law, B. Settles, and T. Mitchell. Learning to tag from open vocabulary labels. In *Proc. of ECML*, 2010.

[18] http://herdit.org/music/

[19] http://apps.facebook.com/herd-it/

[20] J. Foote and M. Cooper. Media segmentation using self-similarity decomposition," In *Proc. of SPIE Storage and Retrieval for Multimedia Databases*, 2003.

[21] O. Lartillot and P. Toiviainen. A Matlab toolbox for musical feature extraction from audio. In *Proc. of DAFx*, 2007.

[22] K. Jarvelin and J. Kekalainen. Cumulated gain-based evaluation of IR techniques. *ACM Trans. on Info. Syst.*. 20(4), pp. 422–446, 2002.

Creating Personalized Memories from Social Events: Community-Based Support for Multi-Camera Recordings of School Concerts

Rodrigo Laiola Guimarães[1], Pablo Cesar[1], Dick C.A. Bulterman[1], Vilmos Zsombori[2], Ian Kegel[3]

[1] CWI: Centrum Wiskunde & Informatica
Science Park 123, 1098 XG
Amsterdam, The Netherlands
+31 20 592 9333

[2] Department of Computing
Goldsmiths, University of London
London, SE14 6NW, UK
+44 (0)20 7078 5152

[3] BT Research & Technology
Adastral Park, IP5 3RE
Ipswich, UK
+44 (0)1473 642916

rlaiola@cwi.nl, p.s.cesar@cwi.nl, dick.bulterman@cwi.nl, v.zsombori@gold.ac.uk, ian.c.kegel@bt.com

ABSTRACT

The wide availability of relatively high-quality cameras makes it easy for many users to capture video fragments of social events such as concerts, sports events or community gatherings. The wide availability of simple sharing tools makes it nearly as easy to upload individual fragments to on-line video sites. Current work on video mashups focuses on the creation of a video summary based on the characteristics of individual media fragments, but it fails to address the interpersonal relationships and time-variant social context within a community of diverse (but related) users. The aim of this paper is to reformulate the research problem of video authoring, by investigating the social relationships of the media 'authors' relative to the performers. Based on a 10-month evaluation process, we specify a set of guidelines for the design and implementation of socially-aware video editing and sharing tools. Our contributions have been realized and evaluated in a prototype software that enables community-based users to navigate through a large common content space and to generate highly personalized video compilations of targeted interest within a social circle. According to the results, a system like ours is a valid alternative for social interactions when apart. We hope that our insights can stimulate future research on socially-aware multimedia tools and applications.

Categories and Subject Descriptors

H.1.2 [**Models and Principles**]: User/Machine Systems – *Human factors*. H.5.1 [**Information Interfaces and Presentation**]: Multimedia Information Systems – *Audio, Video*.

General Terms

Design, Experimentation, Human Factors, Management.

Keywords

Web-Mediated Communication, Privacy, Video Authoring, Video Sharing and Information Management.

*Area Chair: Hari Sundaram.

1. INTRODUCTION

The place: the Exhibition Hall in Prague. The date: August 23, 2009. *Radiohead* is about to start their concert. The band invites fans to capture personal videos, distributing 50 Flip cameras. The cameras are then collected, and the videos are post-processed along with Radiohead's audio masters. The resulting DVD captures the concert from the viewpoint of the fans, making it more immersive and proximal than typical concert productions (see: radiohead-prague.nataly.fr).

The concert of Radiohead typifies a shift in the way music concerts – and other social events – are being captured, edited, and remembered. In the past, professionals created a full-featured video, often structured according to a generic and anonymous narrative. Today, advances in non-professional devices are making each attendee a potential cameraperson who can easily upload personalized material to the Web, mostly as collections of raw-cut or semi-edited fragments. From the multimedia research perspective, this shift makes us reflect and reconsider traditional models for content analysis, authoring, and sharing.

The existence of many content fragments of common social events has resulted in innovative work on individual fragment retrieval. These include tools for the automatic extraction of instrumental solos and applause sections [11], and crowd-sourcing techniques that use the direct or indirect behavior of participants for improving retrieval results [16]. Once a collection of candidate fragments has been identified, other researchers have explored community video remixing [14] and automatic algorithmic solutions for synchronizing and organizing user-generated content (UGC) from popular music events [8][15]. All these solutions have focused on various properties of the video/audio content. Nevertheless, none of them has considered the social relationships between performers, users, and recipients of the media. They thus missed an opportunity for creating videos exploiting the social relationships between people participating in the same event.

This paper considers the case in which performers and the audience belong to the same social circle (e.g., parents, siblings and classmates at a typical school concert). Each participating member of the audience records content for personal use, but they also capture content of potential group interest. This content may be interesting to the group for several reasons: it may break the monotony of a single camera viewpoint, it may provide alternative (and better) content for events of interest during the concert (solos, introductions, bloopers), or it may provide additional views of events that were not captured by a person's own camera. It is important to understand that the decision to use substitute or

Table 1. Handling Multi-Camera Recordings of Concerts.

	Preparation, capturing	*Relationship btw performers and people recording*	*Intelligent processes*	*Purpose*
"Professional" DVD	Scripted	Professional	Human director (planning)	Complete coverage
Anonymous UGC Mashup	Ad-Hoc	Similar likings, idols	Video search, video analysis	Complete coverage
Socially-aware community	Ad-Hoc	Family & friends	Video analysis, video authoring	Memories, bonds

additional content will be made in the particular context of each user separately: the father of the trombone player is not necessarily interested in the content made by the mother of the bass player *unless* that content is directly relevant for the father's needs. Put another way, by integrating knowledge of the structure of the social relationships within the group, content classification can be improved and content searching and selection by individual users can be made more effective.

In order to understand the role of the social network among group members in a multi-camera setting, consider the comparison presented in Table 1. This table compares the use of multi-camera content in three situations: by a (professional) video crew creating an archival production, by a collection of anonymous users contributing to a conventional user-generated content mashup, and within a defined social circle as input for differentiated personal videos. (Semi-)Professional DVD-style productions often follow a well-defined narrative model implemented by a human director, and are created to capture the essence of a total event. Anonymous UGC mashups are created from ad-hoc content collections, often based on the primary and secondary content classification methods discussed above. In socially-aware communities, friends and family members capture, edit and share videos of small-scale social events with the main purpose of creating personal (and not group) memories. Interested readers can view a video that illustrates the general concept of personalized community videos[1], and an example of a personal video generated by our system[2].

One of the major differentiators of our work is that its primary purpose is not the creation of an appealing video summary version of the event or the creation of a collective collaborative community work. Instead, our system is intended to be a resource that facilitates the reuse of collective contents for individual needs. Rather than using personal fragments to strengthen a common group video, our work takes groups fragments to increase the value of a personal video. Each of the videos created by our system will be tailored to the needs of particular members of the group – the video created for the father of the trombone player will be different from the one for the mother of the bass player, even though they may share some common content.

This paper considers the following three research questions in the context of a video editing system for school concerts:

1. Can a socially-aware group editing system be defined in terms of existing social science theories and human-centered processes, and if so, which?
2. Does the functionality provided by a socially-aware editing system provide an identifiable improvement over other approaches for creating personalized videos?
3. Can these improvements be validated in end-user studies?

Our work has concentrated on the modeling of parents of students participating in a high school concert. In this scenario, parents capture recordings of their children for later viewing and possible sharing with friends and relatives. Working with a test group at a local high school, we investigate how focused content can be extracted from a broad repository, how content can be enhanced and tailored to form the basis of a micro-personal multimedia message packet, that can be eventually transferred and shared with family and friends (each with different degrees of connectedness with the performer and his/her parents). Results from a ten months evaluation process provide useful insights into how a socially-aware authoring and sharing system should be designed and architected, for helping users in nurturing their close circle. The evaluation process with a core group of parents included preliminarily focus groups, recording of a high school concert, and evaluation of the prototype application, and reflection on the overall process and experience.

This paper is structured as follows. Section 2 discusses related work with the intention of contextualizing our contributions. Then, Section 3 identifies key requirements for socially-aware video authoring and sharing systems. These requirements are gathered from interviews and focus groups, while social theories motivate our work. Section 4 answers the first research question, providing guidelines to realize systems that meet those requirements. Then, Section 5 reports on results and findings regarding utility and usefulness, thus directly responding the second and third research questions. Lastly, Section 6 dedicates to the discussion of open-ended questions and concluding remarks.

2. RELATED WORK

A number of research efforts have addressed the use of media for content analysis, semantic annotations, and video mashup generation of video concerts. Naci and Hanjalic [11] report on a video interaction environment for browsing records in music concerts, in which the underlying automatic analyzer extracts the instrumental solos and applause sections in the concert videos, and also the level of excitement along the performances. Fans of a band can be useful for improving content retrieval mechanisms [16]; where a video search engine allows for user-provided feedback to improve, extend, and share, automatically detected results in concepts from video footage recorded during a rock n' roll festival. Kennedy and Naaman [8] describe a system for synchronization and organization of user-contributed content from live music events, creating an improved representation of the event that builds on the automatic content match. While the previous examples provide useful mechanisms for handing multi-camera video recordings, more recent papers focus on particular applications. Martin and Holzman [10] describe an application that can combine multiple streams for news coverage in a cross-device and context-aware manner. Shrestha et al., [15] report on an application for creating mashup videos from YouTube[3] recordings of concerts. They present a number of content management mechanisms (e.g., temporal alignment and content quality assessment) that then are used for creating a multi-camera

[1] http://www.youtube.com/user/TA2Project#p/u/6/re-uEyHszgM

[2] http://www.youtube.com/user/TA2Project#p/u/4/Ho1p_zcipyA

[3] The services and technologies mentioned in this paper, if unknown, could very easily be identified via a simple Internet search, therefore they will not be Web-referenced.

video. Results in that paper indicate that the final videos are perceived almost as if created from a professional video editor.

While a system designed following our guidelines applies many of the technologies and mechanisms presented in those papers – content alignment tools, automatic semantic annotation – we extend the problem space to small-scale social events, in which the social bonds between people plays a major role. Where performers and people capturing the event are socially related, and the recordings will act in the future as common memories. Our work complements past research by providing an experimental methodology to design tools that allows people to remember and share video experiences with the aim of fostering strong ties.

Our work builds on previous findings in event modeling [18] and video abstraction/summarization [17]. The main difference of our work lays on the fact that we do not aim at providing a complete description of the shared event, but a better understanding of how community media can serve individual needs. Closely related to our work are topics such as home video management and navigation [1], and photo albums creation [12]. However, we go one step further by allowing users to navigate, annotate, and utilize multi-camera recordings: other material contributed by other participants of a shared event.

3. MOTIVATION

Recognizing the importance of looking at common media assets as a cornerstone for the sharing of family experiences [19], the guidelines introduced in this paper provides the basis for systems aiming to help smaller groups of people (such as a family, a school class or a sporting club) viewing, creating, and sharing personalized videos. From the technical perspective, a system should combine the benefits of personal focus – knowing whom you are talking with – within the context of temporally asynchronous and spatially separated social meeting spaces. The motivation of our work is rooted in the inherent necessity of people for socializing and for nurturing relationships. One important aspect of our work is that we decided to follow an inter-disciplinary approach in which both technology and social issues were addressed. At the core of this approach was establishing a long-term relationship with a group of parents within the target school as a basis for requirements analysis, concept evaluation and system validation.

3.1 Social Science Fundamentals

The experimental methodology presented in this paper is based on two social science theories: the strength of the interpersonal ties and the social connectedness. Further argumentation about the social theories guiding our work can be consulted in [7].

Based on a number of interviews (see Section 3.2), we can conclude that current social media approaches are not adequate for a family or a small social group for storing and sharing collections of media that is personal and important to them. Our assumption is validated by other studies [5], which concluded that social media applications like Facebook do not take into account the interpersonal tie strength of the users. Granovetter [6] defines interpersonal ties as:

"...a combination of the amount of time, the emotional intensity, the intimacy (mutual confiding), and the reciprocal services which characterize the tie."

If we were to design a video sharing system intended for family and friends, we would exploit the social bonds between people by taking into account their personal relationships (*intimacy*). The system would provide mechanisms for personalizing the resulting videos (*adding personal intensity*) with some effort (*amount of time*), and would allow the recipient to acknowledge and reply to the creator (*reciprocity*).

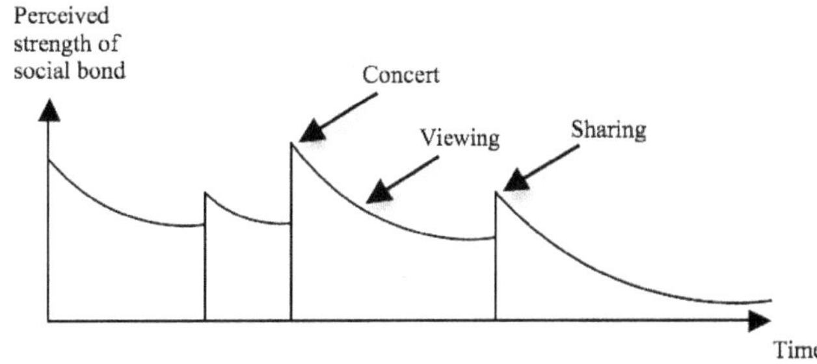

Figure 1. A schematic view of the perceived strength of social bond over time in relation to our scenario.

Social connectedness theory helps us to understand how social bonds are developed over time, and how existing relationships are maintained. Social connectedness happens when one person is aware of another person, and confirms his awareness [13]. Such awareness between people can be natural and intense or lightweight. As reported elsewhere, even photos [19] and sounds [3] can be good vehicles for creating the feeling of connectedness. Figure 1 illustrates a schematic view of the perceived strength of a social bond over time, showing reoccurring shared events ("interaction rituals" in the Durkheim sense [4]), with a fading strength of the social bond in between. The peaks in the figure correspond to intense and natural shared moments, when people participate in a joint activity (e.g., a music concert) re-affirming their relationships and extending their common pool of shared memories. The smaller peaks correspond to social connectedness actions, such as sending a text message or sharing a personalized video of the shared event, that build on such shared memories. If we were to follow the social connectedness theory, we would design a system that mediates the smaller peaks and thus helps in fostering relationships over time.

3.2 Family Interviews and Focus Groups

In order to better understand the problem space, we involved a representative group of users at the beginning of the evaluation process. The first evaluation, in 2008, consisted of interviews with sixteen families across four countries (UK, Sweden, Netherlands, and Germany). The second evaluation, in-depth focus groups – with three parents each – was run in the summer of 2009 in the UK and in December 2009 in the Netherlands. Further information about these two preliminarily user-centered evaluations can be found elsewhere [20]. Since our requirements for socially-aware video editing and sharing systems are partially derived from the results, we will summarize here key findings about current practices and challenges about media sharing.

As social connectedness theory suggests, many participants engaged in varied forms of media sharing as they felt that reliving memories and sharing experiences help bring them (and other households) together. Parents e-mailed pictures of the kids playing football to the grandparents, shared holiday pictures via Picasa, or on disk, or using Facebook, enabling friends and families to stay in touch with each other's lives. Nevertheless, the interviewed people said that if they shared media, they would do so via communication methods they perceived as private and then only to trusted contacts. There was a general reticence from the parents towards existing social networking sites. From the focus groups it became clear that current video sharing models do not fit the needs of family and friends. Much richer systems are needed and will become an essential part of life for family relationships.

A number of parents reported photography as a hobby and would routinely edit their shared images. Their children, on the other hand, even if interested in photography, seemed less keen to manually edit the pictures, and declared a strong preference for automatic edits or relied on their parents. The participants would then discuss the incidents relating to the pictures later on with friends and family, on the phone or at the next reunion. Home videos tended to be watched far less frequently, although the young pre-teen participants appreciated them and were described by their parents as having *"worn the tape[s] down"* from constant viewing when much younger.

In general the participants' responses converged to:

- A willingness to engage in varied forms of recollections through recorded videos;
- A clear requirement for systems that could be trusted as ensuring privacy;
- A positive reaction to the suggestion of automatic and intelligent mechanisms for managing home videos.

In each case, creating personalized presentations (tailored for family use) remained a core issue.

3.3 Requirements

The general user needs, social theories and initial interviews with focus groups have lead to a number of requirements for community-support for multi-camera recordings of shared events:

- *Connectedness*: it should provide tools and mechanisms for maintaining relationships over time. The goal is not so much on supporting high intensity moments – the event – but for the small peaks of awareness (recollection of the event);
- *Privacy and control*: current video sharing models do not fit the needs of family and friends. New systems should address their concerns, and target social community-based use cases;
- *Effortless*: people are reluctant to invest time in processes they consider that could be done automatically. Future systems should include automatic processes for analyzing, annotating, and creating videos of the shared event;
- *Effort, intimacy and reciprocity*: while such automatic processes lower the burden for the user, they do not conform with existing social theories. Since we do not want to limit the joy of handcrafting videos for others, systems should offer optional manual interfaces for personalization purposes.

We used these requirements as the basis for specifying the guidelines discussed in the next section.

4. SOCIALLY-AWARE VIDEO AUTHORING SYSTEMS

This section specifies the general guidelines for a socially-aware video authoring and sharing system. Such guidelines have been realized in a system called *MyVideos*. *MyVideos* was developed as a collection of configurable processes, each of which allowed us to study one or more aspects of the development of socially-aware video systems. Note that the purpose of this paper is not to describe any one component in detail, but to illustrate the interplay of facilities required to support social media sharing. The design and architecture are direct results from the evaluation process reported in this paper.

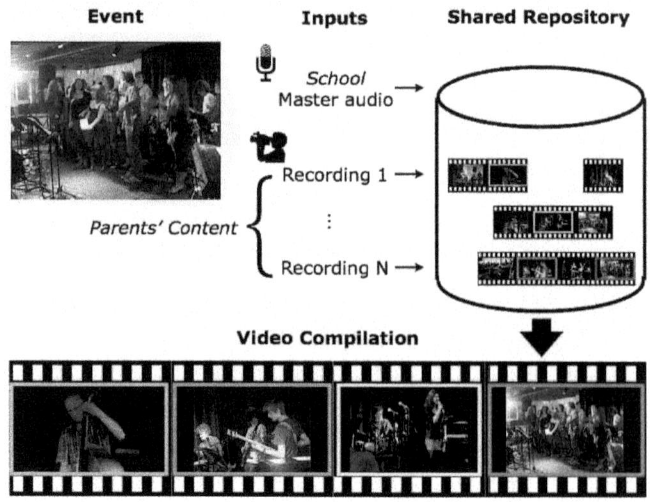

Figure 2. High-level workflow of *MyVideos*.

4.1 High-Level Workflow

The high-level workflow of socially-aware authoring systems is sketched in Figure 2. The input material includes the video clips that the parents agreed to upload, together with a master track recorded by the school. All the video clips are stored in a shared video repository that also serves as a media clip browser in which parents, students, and authorized family members can view (and selectively annotate) the videos. Privacy and a protected scope for sharing is a key component of the system. Each media item is automatically associated with the person who uploaded it, and there are mechanisms for participants to restrict sharing of certain clips. Participants can use their credentials for navigating the repository – those parts allowed to them – and for creating and sharing different stories intended for different people.

At capturing time, there are no specific filming requirements for users. They can record what they wish using their own camera equipment. The goal is to recreate a realistic situation, in which friends and families are recording at a school concert. This flexibility comes at a cost, however, since most existing solutions that work well in analyzing input datasets are not that useful for our use case. As indicated in the related work [15], handling user-generated content is challenging, since it is recorded using a variety of devices (e.g., mobile phones), the quality and lightning are not optimal, and the length of the clips is not standard. As described below, each clip is automatically analyzed and tagged with information on performer, instrument, song, and special events. In practice, this automatic annotation must be fine-tuned manually, either by parents/users or by a school curator.

4.2 Guidelines

In order to support the social theories described in Section 3.1 and requirements in Section 3.3, *MyVideos* incorporates a number of automatic, semi-automatic and manual processes that assist in the creation of personal memories of an event. These processes balance convenience and personal effort when making targeted, personalized videos. Emotional intensity is provided thanks to a recommendation algorithm that searches for people and moments that might bring memories to the user. For mediating intimacy, *MyVideos* provides users the means to enrich videos for others by including highly personalized content such as audio, video, and textual comments. With these approaches we intend to increase the feeling of connectedness, particularly among family members and friends who could not attend the social event.

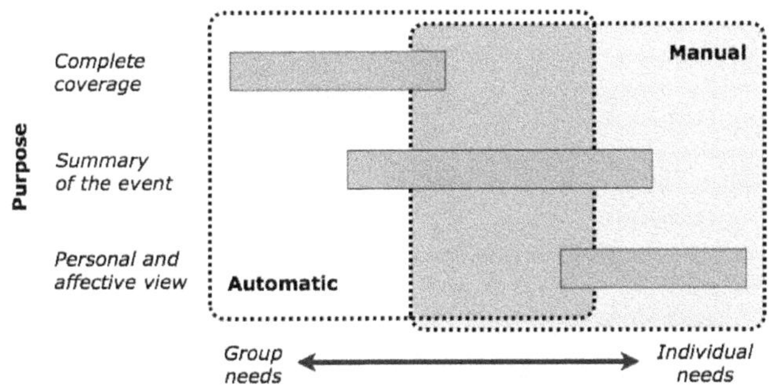

Figure 3. Comparison between automatic and manual generation of video compilations. Automatic methods are not sufficient for creating personal and intimate memories.

4.2.1 *Reflecting Personal Effort*

Users of *MyVideos* can automatically assemble a story based on a number of parameters such as people to be featured, songs to be included, and duration of the compilation. Such selection triggers a narrative engine that, in less than three minutes, creates an initial video using the multi-camera recordings. The narrative engine selects the most appropriate fragments of videos in the repository based on the user preferences and assembles them following basic narrative constructs.

Given an example query:

SelectedPersons=[Julia, Jan Hans];

SelectedSong=[Cry Me River];

SelectedDuration=[3minutes].

The algorithm extracts the chosen song from the master audio track, and uses its structure as backbone for the narration. It then selects all the video content aligned with the selected audio fragment; the master video track provides a good foundation and a possible fall back for the event fragments that are not well covered by individual recordings. The *audio* object is the leading layer and, in turn, it is made of *AudioClips*. This structure generates a sequence of all the songs that relate to the query. As soon as the length of the song sequence extends beyond the *SelectedDuration*, the compilation is terminated. The *video* object has the role of selecting appropriate video content in sync with the audio. An example of the selection criteria is the following:

1. Select video clip that is in sync with the audio;
2. Ensure time continuity of the video;
3. If there are more potential clips that ensure continuity, select those with *Person* annotations matching the user choices stored in *SelectedPersons*;
4. If the result consists of more clips, select those whose *Instruments* annotation match the instruments that are active in the audio layer;
5. If the result consists of more clips, select those whose *Person* annotation matches the persons currently playing a solo.

Once the automatic authoring process is complete, a new video compilation is created in which the selected song and people are featured. As reported elsewhere [21], such narrative constructs have been developed and tested together with professional video editors. Our assumption, based on the social theories, was that automatic methods – while useful – were not sufficient for creating personal memories of an event. Such assumption is validated by our results (Section 5). Figure 3 shows a comparison between automatic and manual generation of mashups. Automatic techniques are better suited for group needs such as a complete coverage or a summary of the event, but are not capable of capturing subtle personal and affective bonds. We argue instead for hybrid solutions, in which manual processes allow users to add their personal view to automatically assembled videos.

MyVideos provides such interfaces for manually fine-tuning video compilations. Users can improve and personalize existing productions by including other video clips from the shared repository. For example, a parent can add more clips in which his daughter is featured for sharing with grandma, or he can instead add a particularly funny moment from the event when creating a version for his brother. Results of the evaluation indicate that users liked such functionality, which automatic processes are not able to provide – it is quite complicated to design an algorithm that detects "funny" events based on personal stories!

4.2.2 *Supporting Emotional Intensity*

Another assumption leading the design of *MyVideos* was that users are particularly interested in finding video clips in which people close to them are featured. Results of the evaluation indicate that emotional searchers were the most popular. Our system incorporates a recommender algorithm that it is optimized based on the profile of the logged user. This optimization takes into account semantic annotations associated to the user's media and on the subjects that more frequently appear on his recordings.

The core of the navigation interface for visualizing the multi-camera recordings is such optimized recommender algorithm that returns relevant fragments of video clips based on given parameters. *MyVideos* implements four different filters for emotional searches: instruments, songs, people, and cameras. The first filter will return video clips in which a particular instrument appears. The second one will return those belonging to a specific song during the concert. The third filter will query about the close friends and family member of the logged users. And the last one will return video clips taken by one of the cameras (e.g., the camera of the user logged in or the camera of his wife). These filters can be combined in complex queries, thus simplifying the searching process. For example, a father can request for his son and daughter playing "Cry Me River", since he remembers this was a very emotive moment of the concert.

Given an example query:

SelectedPersons=[Julia, Jan Hans];

SelectedSong=[Cry Me River].

The result will be:

QueryPersons(Julia, Jan Hans) ∩ *QueryEvents(Cry Me a River)*

The query algorithm works as follows:

1. Select fragments of the video clips matching the query; in case of complex queries select intersecting the sets
2. If the result consists of one fragment, return it
3. If the result consists of more than one fragment, order the resulting list based on:
    - The requested person;
    - The annotations associated to the video clips uploaded by the logged user (affection parameter);
    - The subjects that appear more frequently in the video clips uploaded by the logged user (affection parameter).

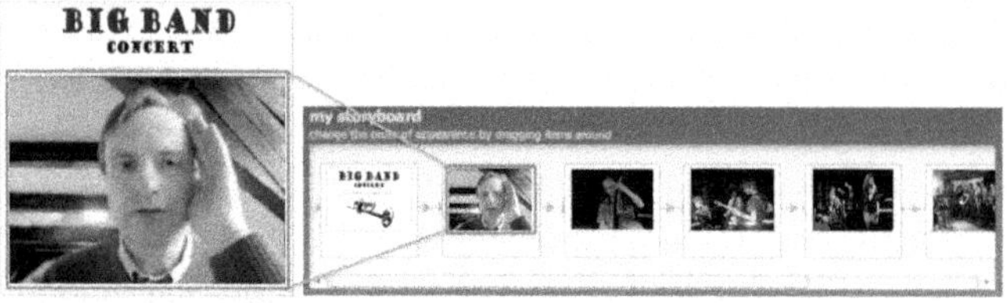

Figure 4. Elements of an authored video composition: the parent has included an introductory image and a video for making it more personal and intimate.

In addition to the query interface that allows users to find moments of the videos that they particularly remember, *MyVideos* offers optional manual interfaces for improving semantic annotations. When users are searching for specific memories, it might happen that results are not accurate due to mistakes in the annotations. Our system allows users to correct such annotations while previewing individual clips. For example, they can change / add / remove the name of the performer and the title of the song. Moreover, they can add extra annotations (e.g., solo). According to our results, such functionality was appreciated even though some participants were reluctant to make changes they consider the system should have done correctly in the first place.

4.2.3 Supporting Intimacy and Enabling Reciprocity

Apart from allowing fine-tuning of assembled videos, our system enables users to perform enrichments. *MyVideos* provides mechanisms for including personal audio, video, and textual commentaries. For example, these could be recordings of oneself (the author of the production) or subtitles aligned with the video clips commenting the event for others. Users can as well record an introductory audio or video, leading to more personalized stories. Figure 4 illustrates some elements of an authored video, where a parent has created his own version of a concert. Moreover, he has added some personal assets, such as an introductory image and a video recording of himself that acts as the message envelope. According to our results, this functionality (we call it "Capture Me") would be used by all but one of our participants.

Our application addresses reciprocity by enabling life-long editing and enriching of compiled videos. As indicated before, videos created with our tool can be manually improved and enriched using other assets from the repository, adding personal video and audio recordings, and including subtitles or textual comments. This is possible because of the underlying mechanism used for creating compilations. A high-level description language, in our case SMIL, allows us to temporally describe the contents of the compilation. The actual video clips are included by reference, and never modified or re-encoded. In other words, we do not burn a new compilation, but just describe it in a SMIL file that then is shared with other people. As shown in a previous publication [2], there are benefits of such approach. In the context of this paper, the main benefit is that it enables people to comment, enrich, and improve existing compilations. Thus, users receiving an assembled video can easily include further timed comments as a reciprocity action for the original sender. A grandmother might add a *"Isn't Julia cute?!"* reply in a reciprocal message to her son.

4.2.4 Guidelines relative to Requirements

In addition to reflecting *effort* and supporting *emotional intensity*, *intimacy*, and *reciprocity*, *MyVideos* also aims at other requirements identified in Section 3.3, as discussed below.

Using a trusted storage media server (provided by the school) fulfills the requirement of privacy. Parents can upload the material from the concerts to a common media repository. The repository is a controlled environment, since it is provided and maintained by the school, instead of being an external resource controlled by a third-party company. Moreover, all the media material is tagged and associated with the parent who uploaded it, and there are mechanisms so parents can decide not to share certain clips in which their children appear. Users can use their credentials for navigating the repository – those parts allowed to them – and for creating different stories for different people.

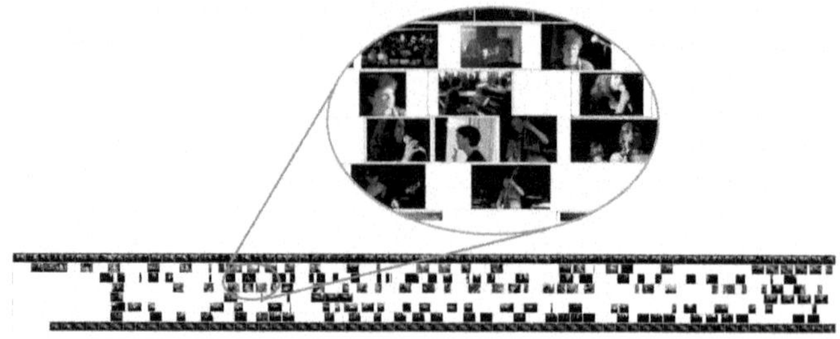

Figure 5. Temporal alignment of a real life data set from a concert, where a community of users recorded video clips.

The requirement on effortless is met by the provision of a number of automatic processes that analyze and annotate the videos, and that help users to navigate media assets and to create memories. First, our system uses two automatic tools for analyzing and annotating the ingested video clips: a temporal alignment and a semantic video annotation tools. The temporal alignment tool is used to align all of the individual video clips to a common time base. The core of the temporal alignment algorithm is based on perceptual time-frequency analysis with a precision of 10ms. Figure 5 shows the results of the temporal alignment of a recorded real life dataset (more information on the datasets will be provided in Section 5.1). The level of accuracy of our tool is of around 99%, improving other state-of-the-art solutions [8][15]. Since the focus of this paper is not on content analysis, we will not further detail this part of the system. The interested reader can find the algorithm and its evaluation elsewhere [9]. The Semantic Video Annotation Suite provides basic analysis functions, similar to the ones reported in [15]. The tool is capable of automatically detecting potential shot boundaries, of fragmenting the clips into coherent units, and of annotating the resulting video sub-clips. Second, our system uses other automatic processes for visualizing media assets and for effortless creation of videos. As introduced in the previous subsections, users can navigate the video clips using a recommender algorithm, and they can automatically generate a video compilation from the multi-camera recordings.

These automatic tools provide a baseline-personalized video. Our personalization extension tools allow further transformation to highly targeted presentations from a common media resource. In order to promote easy user sharing, the client aspects of *MyVideos* have been implemented a full-fledge Web application. The system is hosted on a dedicated research testbed with a high bandwidth symmetrical Internet connection and virtualized processor clusters dedicated to hosting Web applications and serving video. In our architecture, each school would rent space and functionality on the testbed, in order to make systems like ours available to their community. In our current implementation, the testbed space was provided to members of the community.

5. EVALUATIONS

The evaluation reported in this paper is part of an extended study to better understand the intersection of social multimedia and social interactions. The final intention is to provide technological

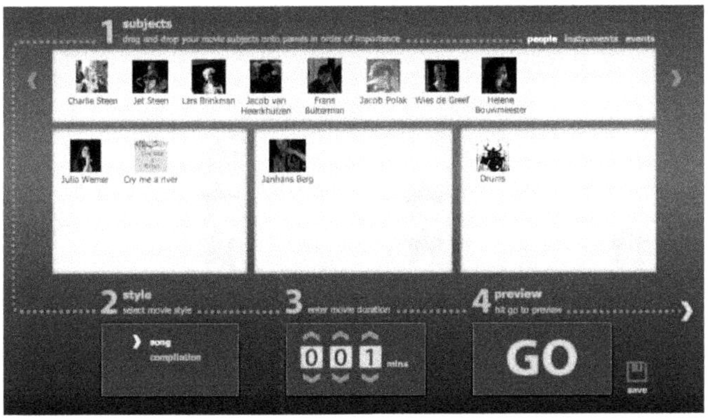

Figure 6. Interface for automatically assembling stories.

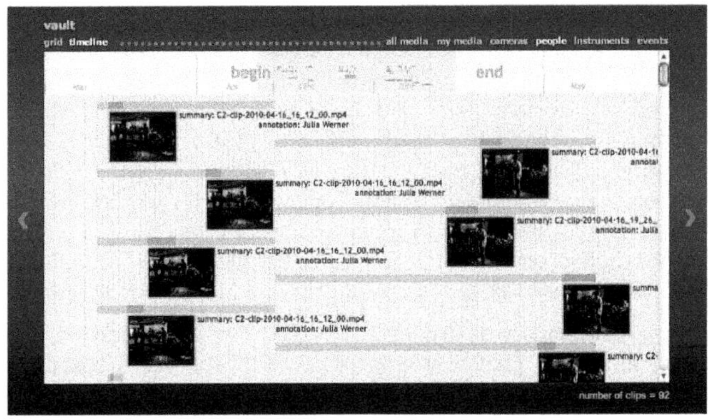

Figure 7. Interface for navigating video clips (timeline).

solutions for improving social communications between families living apart. Potential users have been involved in the process since the beginning, starting with interviews and focus groups, leading up to an evaluation of the prototype. A set of parents from a high school in Amsterdam has been actively collaborating with this research. Starting in December 2009, the parents were invited to a focus group that took place in Amsterdam; in April 2010 they recorded (together with some researchers) a concert of their children; in July 2010 they used our prototype application with the video material recorded in that concert. This section reports on the evaluations carried out during this journey.

In particular, we are interested in whether the functionality provided by a socially-aware editing system provides an identifiable improvement over other approaches for creating personalized videos. Ultimately, we are not that interested in physiological issues related to specific interfaces. Instead we want to better understand the social interactions around our system and how well social connectedness is supported. In order to validate our assumptions we ran a number of experiments: some testing the functionality and others involving users. The next subsections detail the experiments, report on the results and analyze them.

5.1 Experiments

5.1.1 Video Recordings

The first set of experiments consisted in the recording of three different concerts: a school rehearsal in Woodbridge in the UK, a jazz concert by an Amsterdam local band called the Jazz Warriors, and a school concert at the St. Ignatius Gymnasium in Amsterdam. The intention behind these concert recordings was twofold: to better understand the problem space and to gather real life datasets that could be used for testing the functionality.

In the first concert, Woodbridge, a total of five cameras were used to capture the rehearsals. The master camera was placed in a fixed location, front and centre to the rehearsal, set to capture the entire scene (a 'wide' shot) with no camera movement and an external stereo microphone in a static location near to the rehearsal performance. This experiment was very useful for testing the automatic processes provided by our system: the temporal alignment algorithm, the semantic video annotation suite, the automatic authoring tool, and the recommender system for visualizing multi-camera recordings.

Then, at the end of November 2009 a concert of the Jazz Warriors was captured as part of an asset collection process. The goal of the capture session was to gain experience with an end-user setup that would be similar to that expected for the Amsterdam school trial. The concert took place on 27 November 2009 at the Kompaszaal, a public restaurant and performance location in Amsterdam. The Jazz Warriors is a traditional big band with approximately 20 members. In total eight (8) cameras were used to capture the concert, where two cameras were considered as 'masters' and were placed at fixed locations at stage left and stage right. In total, we collected more than 200 video clips and approximately 80 images. The longest video clip was 50min, the shortest 5s.

The first two concerts were primarily experimental, providing us enough material for fine-tuning the automatic and manual processes. On 16 April 2010 the concert from the Big Band (St. Ignatius Gymnasium) was recorded. In this case parents took part in the recordings and provided the research team with all the material. In total around 210 media objects were collected for a concert lasting about 1h and 35 minutes. Twelve (12) cameras were used; two of them used as the master cameras. These recordings were used for evaluating the prototype.

5.1.2 Prototype Evaluation

In cooperation with a local high school, a core group of seven people were recruited, among relatives and friends of the kids that performed in the third concert, for evaluating the prototype. The rationale used for recruitment was to gather as many roles as possible for better understanding the social needs of our potential users. The participants were three high school students, a social scientist, a software engineer, an art designer and a visual artist, resulting in a variety of needs that may influence the video capturing, editing and sharing behaviors. All the participants were Dutch. The average age of the participants was 37.1 years (SD = 20.6 years); 3 participants (42.8%) were female. Among our participants, 3 had children (ranging in age from 14 to 17 years). All participants were currently living in the Netherlands, but an uncle of a performer that lives in the US was recruited to serve as an external participant (the only one that was not present in the concert recordings). The prototype evaluation was conducted over a two–month span in the summer of 2010 (Jul-Sep).

The review group was kept small so that we could establish directed and long-term relationships. The qualitative nature of our interactions provided us with a deep understanding of the ways in which people currently share experiences to foster strong ties. The participants represent a realistic sample for the intended use case: all the parents have kids going to the same high school, all of them tend to record their kids, and some of them have some experience with multimedia editor tools. Moreover, the parents were involved in previous focus groups dating from December 2009 and they recorded their kids playing in the Big Band concert (April 2010). The goals of the study make it impossible to do crowdsource testing, since users of the system should be people that care about the actual content of the videos.

We used multiple methods for data collection, including in person interviews, questionnaires, and interaction with the system. Figure 6 shows the interface our participants used for automatically assembling stories. Users only have to select the subject matter (people, songs, instruments) and two parameters (style, and duration). Then, by pressing the "GO" button, a story will be automatically assembled. Figure 7 shows how a user can browse temporally – there are other navigation interfaces – the multi-camera video material. In the figure, the video clips in which a performer connected to the user appears are highlighted in orange.

The experiment consisted of 2 sessions. The initial session was used to collect background information about video recording habits, their intentions behind these habits and their social relations around media. We also used this session as an opportunity to understand how the participants conceptualize the concert. The second (in-depth) session was dedicated to capture video editing practices and media sharing routines of the participants based on their interactions with the system.

5.1.3 London Student Study

Another smaller and more incidental evaluation was performed for validating and contrasting the results obtained when evaluating the prototype. In this case, we asked a broader group of British students about their social media habits. We then introduced the system to them, and let them play with it for a full day. A total of 20 kids completed the questionnaires. The students were from London high schools and were between 14 and 18 years old.

5.2 Results

Figure 8 shows the results of some of the questionnaires filled by the participants in Amsterdam. In all the cases, the participants interacted with the system visualizing media assets and creating stories. The top part (a) shows their responses to questions related to media capturing, editing, and sharing. The bottom part (b) shows their answers to the questions related to utility and usefulness, including comparisons to other existing solutions.

Regarding common practices, all participants reported they record videos in social events (e.g., family gatherings and vacation trips). However, most of them said that they barely looked at the recorded material afterwards (see Figure 8 (a)). For most of them, video editing is time consuming and way too complicated. Nevertheless, some are familiar with video editing tools. When prompted if and how they share their videos, our participants repeatedly said that in general they do not post personal videos on the Web. While the youngest participants argued their personal videos were not interesting enough to share on social networking services, for our older respondents privacy was the main reason not to share personal videos on the Web. On the other hand, all participants do appreciate watching videos on YouTube, and most of them have a Facebook account. However, only a few do collaborative tagging of videos and/or photos.

The responses from the London high school questionnaires are captured in Figure 9. In general, we can talk about a generation that has gowned up watching and sharing digital videos. Regarding *MyVideos*, the kids graded it similarly than the evaluators of the prototype, indicating that our results can be generalized further than initially expected.

5.3 Findings

Based on our observations, responses to the questionnaires, and analysis of the collected audio/video, we present here our findings regarding *effort*, *emotional intensity*, and *intimacy*. We end this

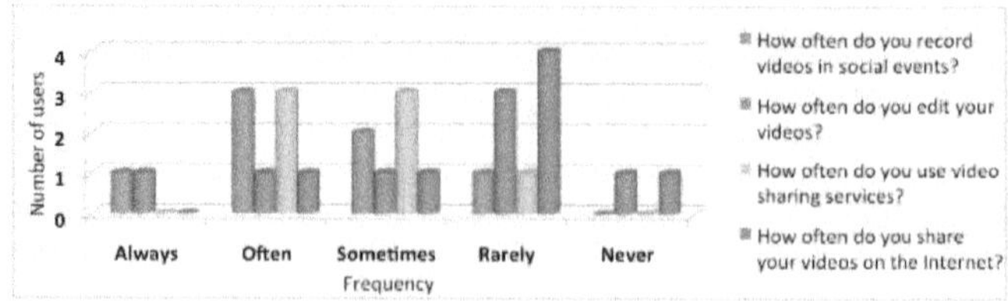

a) Social media habits

Questions		**Questionaire Results**
Q01. Did you like *MyVideos*?		👍👍👍👍👍👍👍
Q02. Does *MyVideos* help you recalling memories of social events?		👍👍👍👍👍👍👍
Q03. Would you like to see what other parents and friends have recorded in the same event?		👍👍👍👍👍👍👍
Q04. Is *MyVideos* better than traditional systems to browse videos recorded by other people?		👍👍👍👍👍👎👎
Q05. Is *MyVideos* better than traditional systems to find people you care about?		👍👍👍👍👎👎👎
Q06. Would you add/correct more metadata by using *MyVideos*?		👍👍👍👍👍👎👎
Q07. Is the material you capture enough to create video productions?		👍👍👎👎👎👎👎
Q08. Would you create more video stories with *MyVideos* (compared to existing tools)?		👍👍👍👍👍👍👎
Q09. Would you create videos stories faster using *MyVideos* (compared to existing tools)?		👍👍👍👍👍👍👍
Q10. Would you create video stories more easily using *MyVideos* (compared to existing tools)?		👍👍👍👍👍👍👎
Q11. Would you fine-tune automatic generated video stories by using manual tools?		👍👍👍👍👍👎👎
Q12. Would you personalize videos by adding yourself to the story? ("capture me")		👍👍👍👍👍👍👎
Q13. Which approach did you like the most?	Automatic	👍👍👍
	Manual	👍👍👍👍
Q14. Would you share more videos with *MyVideos*?		👍👍👍👍👍👍👎
Q15. Is *MyVideos* safer than other video sharing systems?		👍👍👍👍👎👎👎
Q16. Would you pay for *MyVideos*?		👍👍👍👍👎👎👎

Key: 👍 (Yes) 👎 (No)

b) Utility and Usefulness of *MyVideos*.

Figure 8. Results of the questionnaire in Amsterdam.

subsection with a discussion on how our experimental method relates to strong ties and social connectedness theories.

5.3.1 Effort

In general the participants liked *MyVideos* and considered its functionality useful, since it allowed them to use recordings done by others (see Q01-05 in Figure 8 (b)). A surprising outcome during the prototype evaluation was that participants were not really into editing before sharing videos. Participants rarely edited the video clips they have captured. We believe this behavior is motivated by the immediacy paradigm offered by successful commercial video sharing systems such as YouTube. However, the automatic authoring process was generally appreciated,

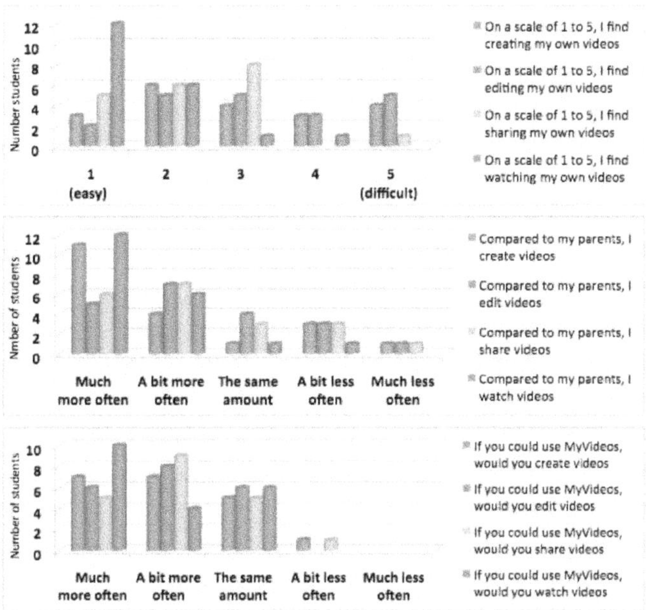

Figure 9. Results of the questionnaire to high school students in London (14-18 years old).

making the users feel as they could create stories faster and easier (Q08-10 and Q13 in Figure 8 (b)). Overall, the assembled videos were considered visually compelling. As an example, Figure 10 presents the comments of a user while interacting with the system.

Although participants found the assembled videos appealing, they wanted (manual) tools to further personalize the stories (see Q11-13 in Figure 8 (b)). Nevertheless, the participants considered that creating memories require using the optional manual processes included in the system. Optional manual processes for personalizing and fine-tuning were welcomed and requested.

"I want more portraits of my daughter (in this automatic generated compilation)... is it possible to edit an existing movie (in the Editor)?" (Father of a performer)

5.3.2 Emotional Intensity

The participants appreciated the filter (recommendation) functions offered by *MyVideos* because such features skip all the rest and focus on the topics of interest (Q04). Interestingly, with the users we spoke to, a person was considered featured in a video (and suitable for search) only if it was a prominent shot (e.g., close-up or solo). Most of the participants reported they would not be interested in a shot in which the subject of their interest barely appears. We believe the relative low score on "Is *MyVideos* better than traditional systems to find people you care about?" (Q05) is because this version of the system did not have quality filters.

"If he is in the background but he is on the shadow it is OK but I would like to see a video in which he really shows up... My mother (performer's grandma) would not enjoy seeing this video of him because there is not much to see" (Uncle of a performer)

When we prompted our participants about how much time they were willing to spend in adding/correcting annotations, they were quite resistant, arguing that this process demands too much effort. Nevertheless, the questionnaires show an improvement over existing solutions (see Q06 in Figure 8 (b)).

5.3.3 Intimacy

Regarding the optional manual processes, for most of our participants the 'capture me' function – functionality for including

Figure 10. A participant using the automatic authoring tool.

personal assets (as shown in Figure 4) in a video compilation – was seen as a way to personalize videos for a target audience. As shown in the results (see Q12), such functionality was generally appreciated. Some of the participants told us they would use this functionality when creating a birthday present video, for instance.

5.3.4 Social Connectedness

Based on the participants' comments, reactions, and answers to the questionnaires, we can conclude that participants appreciated the benefits of such a system and considered it as a valuable vehicle for remembering events, thus improving social connectedness. In particular, participants largely agreed that *MyVideos* would help them in recalling memories from social events (see Q02). Moreover, they agreed that *MyVideos* would allow them to create more videos and to share them with others (see Q08, Q12 and Q14 in Figure 8 (b) and Figure 9). As shown in Figure 1, social connectedness theory, all these actions represent the small peaks of awareness we intended to mediate with socially-aware video authoring and sharing tools.

In general, participants were proud about their own productions, but in most cases they were actively looking for video clips of their close friends and relatives. They complained – and desperate - when the quality of the video was not good enough or when the metadata of the videos was wrong. And most importantly, they wanted to share video clips featuring members of their close circle. *"Can I send it now?"* was the reaction of one of the participants after seeing a video clip he especially liked.

While these results are highly valuable and relevant, we are aware that they are not complete. It is our intention to develop technological solutions for togetherness, but there is no simple solution for such a complex problem. Doing this requires a number of steps, where each one needs to be developed and tested in turn. Our next step in this direction is to run long field trials, for obtaining stronger evidences on how productions and relationships evolve over time.

6. DISCUSSIONS AND CONCLUSIONS

This paper reports on a 10-month evaluation process that investigates mechanisms and principles for togetherness and social connectivity around media. The contribution is a set of guidelines for a new paradigm of multimedia authoring tools: socially-aware video editing and sharing. Our experimental methodology has lead to the specification of a set of guidelines for nurturing strong ties and improving social connectedness. These guidelines have been realized and evaluated through a prototype tool that allows users to navigate, create and share videos from a social event – a concert – they took part in. Our user studies contemplated a short-term evaluation in the UK and a long-term process in the Netherlands, in which people actively participated and recorded a concert of their relatives. As shown in this paper, our experimental methodology aims at meeting the requirements needed for social communities that are not addressed by existing social media Web applications. It aims at improving *connectedness* by *effortless* interaction, providing support for *emotional intensity*, *intimacy* and *reciprocity*.

Our results and findings lead to some open questions, we expect to answer in future studies. For example, it looks surprising that users liked *MyVideos* (e.g. Q01-04 in Figure 8 (b)), but they did not find it much "safer". Based on previous interviews and other studies, we believe this is because more senior users are by default concerned about uploading material outside their reach (even though it is a controlled environment). More specific studies and trials are needed for gaining better insight about this issue. Another interesting question is whether people actually need authoring tools. One might believe that often, people are satisfied with capturing an event in some primitive form perhaps more so than producing something more sophisticated. We argue that this belief is rooted in the models offered by current authoring and sharing tools, such as YouTube. Our findings illustrate that, if offered the right paradigm, users will create and share more sophisticated productions. Apart from results of our preliminarily interviews, we can observe that users want others' content to create their own productions (Q03 and Q07 in Figure 8 (b)) and that users feel that they would create more videos using our prototype (Q08). After all, storytelling has been (and will be) a primarily way of communicating between people.

During this process we did not intend to focus on a specific piece of software, but to take a broader look at the process and its implications. Our final intention is to reformulate the research problem of multimedia authoring by emphasizing the importance of the social relationships between the media 'authors' relative to the performers. We believe our findings are relevant for future research in this new direction: socially-aware authoring and sharing tools. Essentially, we hope these insights can stimulate others, even as we use the insights to further our own work.

7. ACKNOWLEDGEMENTS

The research leading to these results has received funding from the European Community's Seventh Framework Programme (FP7/2007-2013) under grant agreement no. ICT-2007-214793. Special thanks to partners involved in the *MyVideos* demonstrator.

REFERENCES

[1] Abowd, G.D., Gauger, M., and Lachenmann, A. 2003. The Family Video Archive: an annotation and browsing environment for home movies. In *Proceedings of the ACM SIGMM International Workshop on Multimedia Information Retrieval*, pp. 1-8.

[2] Cesar, P., Bulterman, D.C.A., Jansen, J., Geerts, D., Knoche, H., and Seager, W. 2009, Fragment, Tag, Enrich, and Send: Enhancing the Social Sharing of Videos. *ACM TOMCCAP*, 5(3): article number 19.

[3] Dib, L., Petrelli, D., and Whittaker, S. 2010. Sonic souvenirs: exploring the paradoxes of recorded sound for family remembering. In *Proceedings of the ACM Conference on Computer Supported Cooperative Work*, pp. 391-400.

[4] Durkheim, E. 1971. The elementary forms of the religious life. Allen and Unwin.

[5] Gilbert, E. and Karahalios, K. 2009. Predicting tie strength with social media. In *Proceedings of the SIGCHI Conference on Human Factors in Computing Systems*, pp. 211-220.

[6] Granovetter, M.S. 1973. The Strength of Weak Ties. *American Journal of Sociology*, 78(6): 1360-1380.

[7] Guimarães, R.L., Cesar, P., Bulterman, D.C.A., Kegel, I., and Ljungstrand, P. 2011. Social Practices around Personal Videos using the Web. In *Proceedings of the ACM International Conference on Web Science*.

[8] Kennedy, L.S. and Naaman, M. 2009. Less talk, more rock: automated organization of community-contributed collections of concert videos. In *Proceedings of the International Conference on World Wide Web*, pp. 311-320.

[9] Korchagin, D., Garner, P.N. and Dines, J. 2010. Automatic Temporal Alignment of AV Data with Confidence Estimation. In *Proceedings IEEE International Conference on Acoustics, Speech and Signal Processing*.

[10] Martin, R. and Holtzman, H. 2010. Newstream: a multi-device, cross-medium, and socially aware approach to news content. In *Proceedings of EuroITV*, pp. 83-90.

[11] Naci, S.U. and Hanjalic, A. 2007. Intelligent browsing of concert videos. In *Proceedings of the ACM International Conference on Multimedia*, pp. 150-151.

[12] Obrador, P., Oliveira, R., and Oliver, N. 2010. Supporting personal photo storytelling for social albums. In *Proceedings of the ACM International Conference on Multimedia*, pp. 561-570.

[13] Rettie, R. 2003. Connectedness, awareness and social presence. In *Proceedings of the Annual International Workshop on Presence*.

[14] Shaw, R. and Schmitz, P. 2006. Community annotation and remix: a research platform and pilot deployment. In *Proceedings of the ACM international Workshop on Human-Centered Multimedia*, pp. 89-98.

[15] Shrestha, P., de With, P.H.N., Weda, H., Barbieri, M., and Aarts, E.H.L. 2010. Automatic mashup generation from multiple-camera concert recordings. In *Proceedings of the ACM International Conference on Multimedia*, pp. 541-550.

[16] Snoek, C., Freiburg, B., Oomen, J., and Ordelman, R. 2010. Crowdsourcing Rock N' Roll Multimedia Retrieval. In *Proceedings of the ACM International Conference on Multimedia*, pp. 1535-1538.

[17] Truong, B.T. and Venkatesh, S. 2007. Video abstraction: A systematic review and classification. *ACM TOMCCAP*, 3(1).

[18] Westermann, U. and Jain, R. 2007. Toward a Common Event Model for Multimedia Applications. *IEEE Multimedia*, 14(1): pp. 19-29.

[19] Whittaker, S., Bergman, O., and Clough, P. 2010. Easy on that trigger dad: a study of long term family photo retrieval. *Personal Ubiquitous Computing*, 14(1): pp. 31-43.

[20] Williams, D., Ursu, M.F., Cesar, P., Bergstrom, K., Kegel, I. and Meenowa, J. 2009. An emergent role for TV in social communication. In *Proceedings EuroITV*, pp. 19-28.

[21] Zsombori, V., Frantzis, M., Guimarães, R.L., Ursu, M.F., Cesar, P., Kegel, I., Craigie, R. and Bulterman, D. 2011.Automatic Generation of Video Narratives from Shared UGC. In *Proceedings of the ACM Conference on Hypertext and Hypermedia*, pp. 325-334.

Why Did the Prime Minister Resign?

Generation of Event Explanations from Large News Repositories

Frank Nack
ISLA, Informatics Institute
University of Amsterdam
Postbus 94323,
1098 XH Amsterdam, The Netherlands
nack@uva.nl

Ichiro Ide*
Graduate School of Information Science
Nagoya University
Furo-cho, Chikusa-ku,
Nagoya 464-8601, Japan
ide@is.nagoya-u.ac.jp

ABSTRACT

One of the common parts of news is to provide the background for a current event, such as the resignation of a Prime Minister. This paper addresses a framework that facilitates semi-automated authoring of explanatory audio-visual news topics in a retrospective style for the domain of politics based on already edited new stories available in the repository of the news corporation. The aim is to facilitate a journalist with an audio-visual body based on which he/she can finalize the explanatory piece. The proposed framework enhances current state of the art video summarization by allowing the combination of different news stories into one coherent explanation about a topic of the current news. The framework introduces techniques that exploit demoscopic data in form of polls for the development of the general story outline; the automatic retrieval of relevant material by using a combination of event templates and automatic news summarization over topic threads; and the generation of the final video by applying a set of trimming rules. Example generations are presented and discussed and an outline of future work is presented.

Categories and Subject Descriptors

H.5.1 [**Multimedia Information Systems**]: Video; I.7.2 [**Document Preparation**]: Multi/mixed media

General Terms

Human Factors, Design

Keywords

Multimedia authoring, template, topic, topic thread, event, automated video editing, story generation, video archive

*This work was done during his stay at Informatics Institute, University of Amsterdam.

*Area chair: Susanne Boll

MM'11 November 28–December 1, 2011, Scottsdale, Arizona, USA.

1. INTRODUCTION

A news program on TV is regularly scheduled and reports current events. They follow typically a particular format, i.e. they start with the head story, followed by international news, national news, sports, and the weather, where each part forms a series of individual stories that are presented by an anchor person. A news program can include live material, e.g. recorded interviews by field reporters, expert opinions, and opinion polls, or editorial content, i.e. short background information that explains a current event.

In particular, the editorial content for short background information in form of audio-visual material requires a complex and resource demanding production process, structured for very rapid assembly of material from very diverse sources [13]. The aim is to facilitate background information to a headline of the news program in form of an explanatory news story, for example about the resignation of a national government. This type of story needs to explain within a given time span that fits the overall news structure, what the government has achieved or not, and what was the final reason that lead to its fall. The making of this clip requires that the most significant events during the government are selected, where two aspects are important. First, the events need to speak to the society's memory so that the audience can reflect about the presentation. Second, the story represents the information bias of the news corporation as any news is presented with some bias. From the point of view of a responsible editorial journalist, the most complex aspects of this authoring process is to identify the significant events for a given topic and present it according to the broadcaster's ideological presentation style. Usually the journalist will make use of his/her own memory shaped by his/her work focus, to establish the story line and develop the explanatory voice over. During the process, he/she will frequently access the news corporation's repository, to ensure that the relevant content is available in the appropriate format. The whole process needs to be performed on a very short notice.

In this paper we present work that is directed towards the application of IT support for the outlined production process, including the automation of the message construction, query, asset creation, and packaging processes [8]. The aim is to facilitate the journalist with an audio-visual start-up video that chronologically presents crucial events where the order explains the topic under investigation. The goal of the research is to establish a framework of techniques that facilitates semi-automated authoring of explanatory audio-visual news topics in a retrospective style for the domain of politics based on already edited news stories available in the repository of the news corporation. The relevance of the events chosen to explain the causal chain results from a connection of the story events to positive or negative developments of tracking polls that cover the period in which the topic under consideration occurred. In that way, the proposed authoring framework makes use of the collective memory of the viewers, as the used clips function as "triggers" to well-known events that have been popularized already on TV. The choice and order of events represent the general practice of the broadcasting corporation to take advantage of a topic by selecting some story events and sacrificing others to better present the particular point of view of the news organization. Thus, the presented framework includes techniques that establish the often expected aim for objectivity but also facilitates a biased analysis of the topic under investigation. On both aspects, namely, content selection and its final presentation, we aim to demonstrate and assess the applicability and acceptability of this framework in a news production environment.

In the following, we first define a number of key attributes of our framework, and then describe the basic elements of the framework. These are the exploitation of poll data for the development of the general story outline; the automatic retrieval of related material by using a combination of event templates and automatic news summarization over topic threads; and the final generation of the media material through automated editing. Finally, we assess our achievements thus far, and provide an overview of further work.

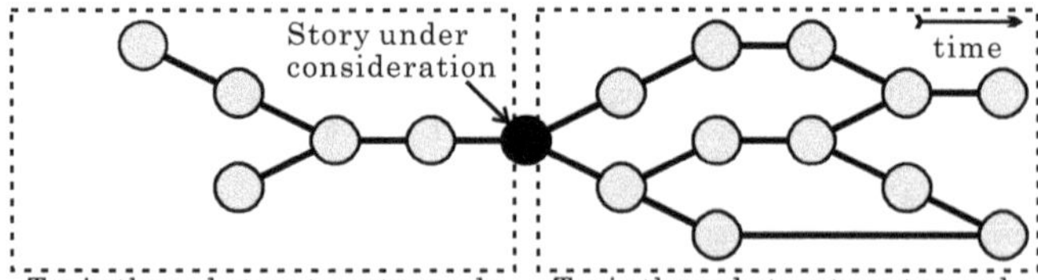

Figure 1: Example of a topic thread structure originating from a story under consideration.

2. RELATED WORK

There are in particular three fields in multimedia research that are relevant for the approach described in this paper: news video semantics, semi-automated multimedia authoring, and event representation.

There is a large body of work within multimedia related to news videos. The predominant amount of work focuses on helping with semantic video retrieval [9, 19], which is relevant for the detection of topics in non-annotated material. Other works cover the aspect of video summarization [4, 5, 18], which address the problem of distilling appropriate videos from large corpora. Work on topic clustering points into the same direction [14], only that here the interest is not so much to support the retrieval of video but rather to extract the connection between news stories over time. The problem with these approaches is that they mainly focus either on the structural extraction of a single news show or try to concatenate the different threads of one news story over time. The combination of different story threads is so far not addressed, though the work of Ide et al. on "mediaWalker" [10] is the closest reaching into this direction. Its aim is to establish and exploit the chronological semantic structure in a large-scale broadcast news video archive. The results of the mentioned work, especially work on the message construction and asset querying processes, provide us with the basis for the part in our framework that aims at connecting different news stories into an explanatory video for a particular topic currently discussed in the news.

Multimedia authoring, seen as the idea of allowing an endless montage of audio-visual assets into new items, inspired a great deal of research in computer environments that embody mechanisms to interpret, manipulate or generate audio-visual media [3, 8, 12, 13, 15]. All these works address the various steps within multimedia production [8], always assuming that there is an author involved in the process. We also assume an author in the production loop, in particular for the making of the voice over, but we aim for an automated production process that addresses the parts message construction (establish the story line) and packaging (trim the retrieved material for the final output) [8].

In recent years, substantial work has been provided for the modeling of multimedia events [1, 17, 21]. The proposed models are relevant as they model time and space, objects and persons, as well as causal and correlative relationships between events for particular domains. In that way, they represent the basic questions about any particular event from the point of view of news, namely —who, what, when, where, why, and how (see in particular [16]). We follow a similar path but represent contextualised political events, in form of collections of particular useful document sources and the particular way how they should be interpreted so that the system can establish the potential main events. We also make use of a combination of topic-based and template-based content identification techniques so that the material for the established events can be retrieved.

3. PROPOSED FRAMEWORK

In this section we explain the key steps of the framework we propose for the semi-automatic generation of videos that explain a current news event in a retrospective view. As we use particular terms throughout the paper, we first define those. We base the definition of these terms on two sources, namely the Topic Detection and Tracking (TDT) workshop series organized by NIST [6] and the work by Ide et al. [10]. The definitions of the first three adopt TDT's view, while the latter two follow those introduced by Ide et al.

- Event: Some incident that occurred at some specific time and place along with all necessary preconditions and unavoidable consequences.
- Story: A topically cohesive segment of news that includes two or more declarative independent clauses about a single event.
- Topic: A seminal event or activity, along with all directly related events and activities.
- Topic thread: A sequence of related stories chained chronologically. It may contain several topics.
- Topic thread structure: A directed graph composed of topic threads terminating/originating from a specified story.

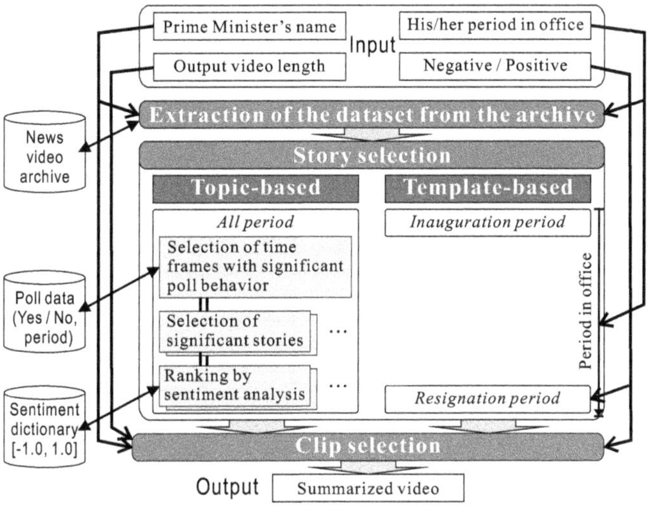

Figure 2: Outline of the generation process.

As shown in Fig. 1, a topic thread structure represents the development of news topics along the time-line concerning a story under consideration.

3.1 Outline

The overall structure of our framework covers three essential phases: First, it needs to determine the topics that the retrospective video should cover. Next, it identifies the essential events that need to be covered. Finally, it establishes the final presentational form of the video. Figure 2 shows the flow of the process.

Note here that our framework mainly covers the generation of the video itself. Amendments certainly need to be performed once the responsible journalist has finalized the voice over based on the event order established in the video.

For the ease of readability, we will use the resignation of a Prime Minister as the example of a current news event to be retrospectively analyzed. The assumed bias for the explanations and the example generations (see section 4) is negative. However, a positive video could be generated by reverting the bias to positive and then apply the related structures. Detailed explanations on each phase follows.

3.2 Dataset

The video data used in our work comes from the NII-TVRECS archive [11], which consists of a Japanese news show recorded daily for more than ten years (1,800– hours). The video data is accompanied with closed-caption, and is segmented into stories by the method described in [10].

From this archive, the proposed framework extracts all stories during the period that contains the Prime Minister's name mentioned as a subject in the closed-caption. For this, morphological analysis[1] and syntactic analysis[2] were applied to all closed-caption texts during the period.

[1]A Japanese morphological analyzer JUMAN developed at Kyoto University was used. It is available for download from `http://nlp.kuee.kyotou.ac.jp/nl-resource/juman-e.html`.

[2]A Japanese syntactic analyzer KNP developed at Kyoto University was used. It is available for download from `http://nlp.kuee.kyoto-u.ac.jp/nl-resource/knp-e.html`.

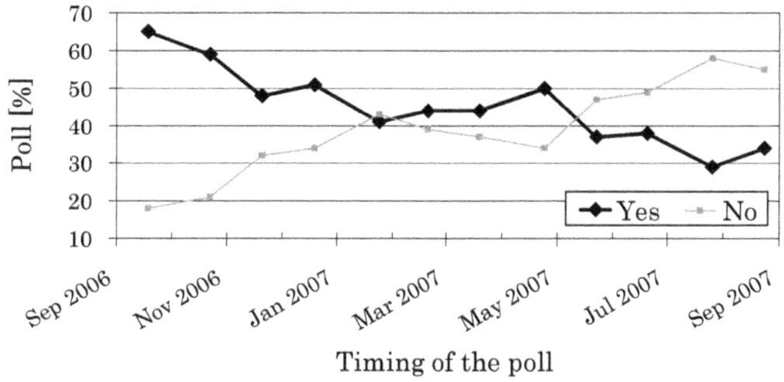

Figure 3: Example of the transition of polls (N_{PM} = "Shinzo Abe")[3].

3.3 Input

In order to generate an explanatory video, information is required that provides the essential content and presentation constraints. In our framework, we request the following input parameters for a Prime Minister's resignation:

- Topic: The Prime Minister's name N_{PM}
- Topic duration: His/her period in office $(D_{\mathrm{inaug}}, D_{\mathrm{resig}})$
- Bias: Positive/Negative
- Output video length: $D_{\mathrm{vid\_length}}$

The generated output is a video that covers essential events, which facilitates a retrospective view on the topic. For our example, this means that a video needs to be generated so that it presents a description of a Prime Minister's key actions in an attempt to explain his/her resignation.

3.4 Story selection

Since our system is designed to be applied in the political domain and should produce an explanatory video to be understood by the audience, we make use of demoscopic polls (see an example in Fig. 3) as an external reference that should establish the key moments to be considered. As the presented opinions relate to real events, we try to identify those and in that way we make use of the collective memory of the viewers, as the used clips function as "triggers" to well-know events during the time period of the topic that needs to be explained. The duration of the polls follows the time-frame p_i $(i = 1, 2, ..., P)$ with a period of approximately one month between two consecutive monthly poll measurements while the Prime Minister was in office, where the end of the last day of the poll is considered as the boundary.

Stories that become sources of the final output video are selected by a combination of two strategies: topic-based and template-based. The former is designed to automatically extract related stories that can be linked to the patterns of crucial poll descriptions, while the latter describes prototypical events that establish a plausible introduction to and finish of the output video. Details of each strategy follow.

3.4.1 Topic-based story selection

Significant stories are selected in a bottom-up approach, making use of poll patterns that presumably coincide with major events in political news, and utilizing the features extracted from the topic thread structure concerning each story. The selection is performed in the following steps:

1. Time-frames p_i $(i = 1, ..., P)$, where potentially significant events may exist, are determined according to crucial poll patterns.
2. The amount of events to be required for the video are calculated.
3. Stories that cover the major events within each time-frame p_i are estimated according to the clues obtained from topic thread structures.
4. The estimated stories are ranked according to sentiments (negative/positive), in order to be selected as a final story that represent the time period.

Details of the four steps follows.

Step 1: Selecting time-frames according to poll patterns.

In order to determine the time-frame where a significant event may have occurred, we refer to polls available from an external source[3]. The polls consist of ratios on the approval ("Yes") or the disapproval ("No") of the government led by the Prime Minister in focus. Figure 3 shows an example of the transition of polls for the government of the Japanese Prime Minister Shinzo Abe. The system determines either positive or negative poll pattern and selects poll positions according to the bias strategy selected by the journalist. Each pattern is defined as follows:

- Positive poll pattern
  - The "Yes" rate rises above θ_{v_p}.
  - The "Yes" rate increases more than θ_{c_p} per time-frame.
  - The "Yes" rate exceeds the "No" rate.
- Negative poll pattern
  - The "Yes" rate drops below θ_{v_n}.
  - The "Yes" rate decreases more than θ_{c_n} per time-frame.
  - The "No" rate exceeds the "Yes" rate.

The number of significant poll patterns detected is denoted as N_{poll}. Once this number is calculated, it needs to be determined how many events need to be detected to represent a crucial moment.

Step 2: Determining the overall video structure.

This step actually covers two aspects of the video generation, namely content identification as well as structure definition. Both parts cannot be separated from each other. The type of video we talk about here follows an already established pattern in broadcasting news, which is as follows: The anchor person introduces the topic explained in the video. The video then starts with some introductory video clips followed by a presentation of the poll graph, on which the crucial data point is highlighted. This is followed by clips of events that explain the data. This alteration between poll graph description and explanatory clips is then followed in alternating fashion until the end, where the video concludes with the topic that needs to be explained.

[3]The "Monthly survey on political attitude" by NHK Broadcasting Culture Research Institute was used as the source. It is updated monthly at `http://www.nhk.or.jp/bunken/research/yoron/seijiishiki/list_seijiishiki1.html`, and also published in "The NHK Monthly Report on Broadcast Research".

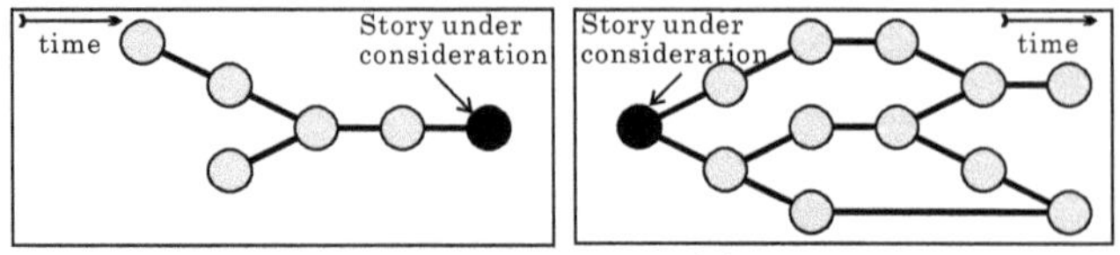

(a) Terminal story (b) Original story

Figure 4: Terminal/original story in a topic thread structure. Stories concerning general structures such as the one shown in Fig. 1 are neither a terminal nor an original story.

Applying this general pattern of retrospective explanation, where the retrospective part is formed through a chronological presentation of events, requires that the pattern can be applied within the given time constraints. For that a calculation is performed that establishes the number of events that can be presented within each part of the video (Intro, poll blocks, and Final). This depends on the time period needed to be covered and the cognitive complexity of the potential clips (e.g. the image of a poll graph can be comprehended within $T_{\text{poll}} = 3$ seconds, where an event clip is usually composed of shots with different frame ratios and varying content complexity resulting in a length of somewhere between 30 to 50 seconds [7]).

The calculation in our framework is as such: The start point is the overall time of the final video ($D_{\text{vid\_length}}$). From that we subtract $N_{\text{poll}}T_{\text{poll}}$, and the remaining time is divided into equal blocks covering the introduction, the explanatory events, and the conclusion, where we follow Gregory's setup of shot ratio comprehension [7]. Depending on the remaining time and the complexity of the middle structure, i.e. the number of critical poll parts needed to be explained, a decision is made on the amount of events to be shown for each explanatory part (see 3.4.2 for the calculation of the values for the Intro and the Final parts). At the end of this calculation, the basic structure of the video is established. It may look like this: {Intro (2), Poll 1, Expl 1(2), Poll 2, Expl 2 (2), Poll 3, Expl 3 (2), Poll 4, Final (2)}, where the numbers in brackets represent the amount of stories to be collected for each part. Note that this structure does not provide any editing on the material yet. The final editing of the by then, established clips will be described in 3.5.

We will now estimate which story may contain an event that may well explain a particular poll pattern.

Step 3: Selecting significant stories during the determined time-frame.

First, stories that are assumed to contain significant events are selected according to the "topic thread structure" proposed by Ide et al. [10]. This is done regardless to the established bias. Since a topic thread structure represents the flow of topics preceding and succeeding a story under consideration, we considered that analyzing its structure leads to the evaluation of the significance of the story.

From topic thread structures concerning each story in a time-frame, the story is selected as a candidate of significant stories, if either of the following two criteria is satisfied:

- Original/terminal story: The story in-focus terminates or originates a topic thread structure (Figure 4).
- Density: More than θ_{d_d} stories appear along the topic thread structure within θ_{d_p} days before/after the story.

The established set of potential stories now needs to be organized so that the amount of events calculated in Step 2 can be extracted.

Step 4: Ranking the selected stories based on sentiment analysis.

Finally, sentiment analysis is applied to all the stories selected in the previous step. It is performed in the following manner, which yields a normalized value in the range of $[-1.0, 1.0]$:

1. For each term that appears in a story, look-up a sentiment dictionary and assign a p/n value that represents the positiveness/negativeness of the term if it exists.
2. Sum-up all the p/n values and normalize it with the number of terms that were assigned a value.

For the sentiment dictionary, Takamura et al.'s dictionary on semantic orientation of words[4] [20] was used, which is composed of pairs of a word and a value between -1.0 (negative) and 1.0 (positive).

The stories are ranked according to their p/n values, and selected according to the following rules:

- Select the top θ_s stories for a positive poll pattern.
- Select the least θ_s stories for a negative poll pattern.

The number θ_s reflects the value established for the various blocks calculated for the overall video structure. For our example in Step 2, θ_s is 2.

The outcome of the presented four steps is an editing list that contains the IDs of the stories to be included in the final output video. Still missing are the videos for the Intro and the Final parts of the video. Those are established through a template-based story selection process.

3.4.2 Template-based story selection

We make use of templates for the design of the Intro and Final parts of the explanatory video, as they usually portray, according to their rhetoric function, stereotypical events. These events are usually not very much commented on while being shown and only marginally influence the polls and would be hence difficult to detect with the outlined topic-based techniques.

The function of the Intro part is to establish the retrospect setting. Depending on the topic, there are stereotypic events that the potential viewer of the clip will immediately identify. We gather such types of events in the template that is associated with the topic. For the current example, this means that a typical Intro event for a retrospect on a Prime Minister's reign is the "inauguration speech". Showing this is in fact a convention among broadcasters for news related explanatory videos, so much so that a particular term is available to make this sequence easily retrievable.

[4]Available for download from `http://www.lr.pi.titech.ac.jp/~takamura/pndic_en.html`.

The Final part of the video usually provides the resolution to the initial query, meaning that the topic under consideration is actually presented. For our example, this could mean to portray a conflict between a government and opposition in a sequence where the Prime Minister at the end resigns due to the heavy criticism. Our framework reflects on these issues by providing template structures that are related to a topic. We based our design on explanatory videos generated by human editors for the NHK evening news.

Below we describe both the positive and negative events we search for in the presented order. Search here means to look for word sets associated with the event (e.g. the "inauguration speech") to retrieve stories for the Intro and the Final parts. For the Intro part, we make use of the positive part of the template, while for the Final part, we make use of the part that represents best the aimed for bias. The list of positive events for the topic "resignation" looks like this (the terms in [] describe some of the concepts we search for):

- Inauguration speech (this is always shown) or if not available use the Prime Minister talking in Parliament [Prime Minister, N_{PM}, Inauguration], alternative [Prime Minister, N_{PM}, Parliament]
- If additional material is needed for the Intro part:
  - The Prime Minister visits a foreign country (for each nation there might be preferences here for particular countries) [Prime Minister, N_{PM}, China, US, Germany, ...]
  - The Prime Minister announces a positive budget [Prime Minister, N_{PM}, budget, positive]
  - The Prime Minister presents a positive economical view [Prime Minister, N_{PM}, good economy, improving economy, industry, presentation]
  - The Prime Minister wins a prize [Prime Minister, N_{PM}, prize, receive, ceremony]
  - Government party wins a by-election [Prime Minister, N_{PM}, election, win]

The list of negative events for the topic looks like this:

- Conflict with the opposition and Prime Minister resigns [Prime Minister, N_{PM}, may resign, opposition party names, leader, party, criticize] and [Prime Minister, N_{PM}, resignation, leaving office]
- If additional material is needed for the Final part (if none of those is already part of the above conflict):
  - The Prime Minister has personal or health problems [Prime Minister, N_{PM}, health, hospital, way to hospital]
  - Government Party loses a by-election [Prime Minister, N_{PM}, election, loss]
  - The Prime Minister or a minister has juridical problems [Prime Minister, N_{PM}, fraud, party members, ministers]
  - The Prime Minister announces a negative budget [Prime Minister, N_{PM}, budget, negative]
  - The Prime Minister presents a negative economical view [Prime Minister, N_{PM}, weak economy, high inflation, deflation, industry, presentation]

The amount of elements to be presented depends, in accordance to Step 2 in 3.4.1, on the temporal duration of non-covered poll material. In the proposed framework, stories at the beginning and the end of the entire time-line are selected according to this strategy:

- Inauguration speech
  Select from the period $\{p_1, ..., p_{P_{\text{inaug}}}\}$, the first story that contains the term "inauguration speech" (Number of stories $N_{\text{inaug}} = 1$).
- Opening stories
  Depending to the period $\{p_1, ..., p_{P_{\text{opening}}}\}$ before the occurrence of the first positive/negative poll pattern, N_{opening} stories are selected according to the following criteria:
  - $N_{\text{opening}} = 1$ (if $P_{\text{opening}} \leq 2$ [TF])
  - $N_{\text{opening}} = 2$ (if 2 [TF] $< P_{\text{opening}} \leq 4$ [TF])
  - $N_{\text{opening}} = 3$ (if $P_{\text{opening}} > 4$ [TF])
- Closing stories
  Depending on the period $\{p_{P-P_{\text{closing}}+1}, ..., p_P\}$ after the poll has dropped below θ_{v_c}, N_{closing} stories are selected according to the following criteria:
  - $N_{\text{closing}} = 1$ (if $P_{\text{closing}} \leq 2$ [TF])
  - $N_{\text{closing}} = 2$ (if 2 [TF] $< P_{\text{closing}} \leq 4$ [TF])
  - $N_{\text{closing}} = 3$ (if $P_{\text{closing}} > 4$ [TF])

At the end of the complete story selection process, an editing list is established with the selected stories in a chronological order. The identified material still needs to be trimmed so that it fits the overall time constraint set by the journalist.

3.5 Editing for the final output

This part of the framework establishes in a semi-automatic fashion the final output video. There are basically two steps that need to be performed, namely the generation of the poll inserts and the final trimming of the stories.

Step 1: Generation of the graphical inserts.

The graphical inserts serve as the introduction of significant turning points and facilitate the corner stones of the retrospective structure. Figure 5 contains four different examples of such inserts. Generating such inserts automatically can be achieved by using formal descriptions of the various components (e.g. axis, title, highlight circles, etc.) and layout rules for achieving presentational coherence as described in [2]. However, they are currently generated manually.

Step 2: Editing of the story clips and finalization of the video.

The final generation step requires that the selected story videos are trimmed so that the given time constraint for the overall length is kept. Based on the allocated material, the length for each clip is calculated as such: When the length of the summarized video is set to T, the length for video clips that should be cropped from each story is decided as

$$T_{\text{clip}} = \frac{T - N_{\text{poll}} T_{\text{poll}}}{\theta_s N_{\text{poll}} + N_{\text{inaug}} + N_{\text{opening}} + N_{\text{closing}}}. \quad (1)$$

The automatic cropping in our framework follows the approach described in [13], which provides a planner for news composition based on 22 rules for the automated clipping of a shot and juxtaposition of shots. In [13], the material to be edited was raw material produced for a particular purpose. Trimming could be achieved in that system by adjusting the video at the beginning or the end. We are, however, confronted with the problem that the selected video stories are already edited and hence the required section is not necessarily found at the beginning or the end of a story clip. We addressed this issue as follows, where the strategies for explanatory parts are slightly different to those used for Intro and Final parts.

For the explanatory videos, we search in every clip for the topic (here the Prime Minister's name N_{PM}) in the closed-caption. The related time code is taken and then a duration of T_{clip} seconds is clipped from this point into the clip. In case a cut is detected in this part, which means that a new section in the video story has been reached, the sequence is shifted forward. In case the shot only portrays the Prime Minister, i.e. in form of a statement, we make use of the knowledge that our material is already edited, and assume that the real event is covered before. The selected part then starts with the images of the event and resolves with the statement of the Prime Minister. In cases where the Prime Minister's name could not be found, we pick the head news, that is the first video clip after the intro section of the anchorperson and take the first T_{clip} into that part of the story video. The assumption is that this is the main event to which the poll refers to.

For the clipping of the Intro and the Final parts, we take a slightly different strategy. For the detection of relevant sections of the video story, we make use of the terms associated to the positive or negative events for a topic, as outlined in 3.4.2. The rule is that for the Intro part, the positive template setting is chosen, while for the Final part, the template setting is chosen according to the aimed for bias. In both cases, the first event in the template set of events associated with a topic will always be the default. For the Intro part, the transcript of the selected source video is analyzed for the combination of the terms available in the concept list, for our example "Prime Minister", N_{PM}, and "inauguration". The sequence with the highest number of these three terms in the closed-caption is chosen. If it is longer than T_{clip} seconds, it will be clipped from its end on, as it is always easier to cut into an action than terminating on the end of an action. In case the number of events to be covered by the Intro part is larger than one, the list of additional events is sequentially worked through. Identifying suitable points is again based on the distribution of the concepts over the clip where the highest concentration to a particular point in the video determines the entrance point for trimming. The time code of this point is taken, over which T_{clip} is evenly placed. In case the terms are separated and distributed over the source video, one fraction of the Intro part is created for the topic (here the Prime Minister), which covers half of T_{clip}. Then the remaining half is applied on the first identified term that follows the topic in the positive or negative term list of the event. For example, if the event is "The Prime Minister visits a foreign country" and the first matching term is "China", this is the part on which the remaining shot time is applied to. If there are more than one section that can be chosen, the rule will apply that faces are more important than non-face videos (based on the fact that people recognize faces easier than landscapes).

The clipping of the Final part basically follows the above rules. However, the Final part will always be the last to be edited as its duration is usually longer than the other clips. The reason is that the first part of the negative event set, which asks for a controversy between Prime Minister and opposition, asks for the presentation of all opposition parties. Depending on the amount of parties in parliament, this might exceed the given temporal constraint, as clips need to be long enough to identify the different representatives of the parties (note that it is not necessary to cut on what they say, as the final soundtrack will be done manually).

The generation of the Final part therefore begins with a recalculation of the actually used time, as some of the already trimmed parts could be shorter than the assigned time constraint. In that case, this remaining time is used for the Final part. The first part to be generated for the Final part is the actual topic, in our example, the Prime Minister's resignation. For that the terms "resignation", "Prime Minister", and "leaving office" are searched from the closed-captions. As all three terms are associated to a joint fraction in the story source, the "leaving office" part is trimmed backwards into the "Prime Minister's speech". If the "leaving office" part is too long, the window is shifted so long into the "Prime Minister's speech" that the latter covers half of T_{clip}. If both parts are temporarily separated, they are individually located and half of the duration T_{clip} is assigned to each. They are then joined into one sequence, with the part of the Prime Minister resigning first.

Once the topic is covered, the remaining time is provided for trimming the controversy section. The story video is first searched for a sequence where the terms "Prime Minister" and "may resign" are detected. In case both appear around the same temporal proximity, the first appearance of each is taken as a start point. Then the occurrence of the term "opposition" or the different party names are searched for. Occurrences are marked, and the number of identified spots is summed up. One occurrence of a shot with the the Prime Minister is added and the remaining time is devised by that figure, to allow for equal presentation. The trimming of each identified part starts at the end of each shot and extends in reverse direction for the calculated time. Only the part of the Prime Minister follows the identification and overlay pattern, as the identified point may be part of a longer section. All the parts are then concatenated.

The final outcome is an editing list of video IDs and associated start and end times, as well as the IDs of inserts and their duration. The video generated with this framework at least needs an Intro part, one event in the middle and the Final part, all connected by two poll images. Thus, the shortest video possible is 132 seconds long. The generated video is the basis the journalist then starts working with, meaning that other events can be added, or the order or the material itself can be altered.

4. EXAMPLE

We applied the framework to four cases of resignation of Japanese Prime Ministers within the period from September 2006 to June 2010. Figure 5 is an example of a negative summary on Japanese Prime Minister Shinzo Abe.

The patterns searched for in the poll data are established based on an evaluation of the available poll data in combination with existing story fragments, resulting in the values in Table 1. The portrayed events represent explanations of pointed out patterns in the poll diagrams.

Table 1: Values of parameters for generating the example(s).

Parameter	Value	Parameter	Value
N_{PM}	"Shinzo ABE"	N_{inaug}	1 story
D_{inaug}	Sept. 26, 2006	P	13 time frames
D_{resig}	Sept. 26, 2007	θ_{d_d}	7 days
$D_{\text{vid}_\text{length}}$	5 minutes	θ_{d_p}	80 %
θ_{v_p}	60 %	T_{poll}	3 seconds
θ_{c_p}	10 %	P_{opening}	2 time frames
θ_{v_n}	30 %	N_{opening}	1 story
θ_{c_n}	10 %	P_{closing}	3 time frames
N_{poll}	4	N_{closing}	2 stories
θ_s	2 stories	T_{clip}	24 seconds

Table 2: Events composing the summary. "To" events represent clips generated by the topic-based approach and "Te" events represent clips generated by the template-based approach.

Event	Description
Te1-1	Inauguration
Te1-2	Trip to China
To1-1	Return of party members after they had been expelled
To1-2	Meeting between party members to discuss the procedure of that return
To2-1	Prime Minister handles a crisis about a North Korean nuclear test
To2-2	Minister has to step down because he referred to women as "child-bearing machines"
To3-1	Government confirmed that pension records are mismanaged
To3-2	Crisis about North Korean refugees
To4-1	Opposition wins the election to the Upper House
Te2-1	US Airbase extension under discussion (this is the edited conflict sequence)
Te3-1	Prime Minister's resignation (this is the resignation and leave office section)

The actual processing time excluding the manual editing part for one Prime Minister was approximately 1 minute on a SUN Blade 100 work station. However, since most of this process could be done offline on the archive side at the time of capturing the video as a daily batch process, the proposed framework does not require much online processing.

The actual events are described in Table 2. Clips Te1-1 and Te1-2 are examples of the Intro part trimming, where clip Te1-1 represents the inauguration speech and clip Te1-2 additional material, here the example of a trip to China. Clips T1-1 to To3-1 follow the general editing pattern explained in 3.4.1. Clip To3-2 contains a reverse ordering also described in 3.4.1. Clip To4-1 is again normally trimmed following the explanatory pattern. The keyframe for clip Te2-1 only shows the first part of an controversial topic sequence described in 3.5. The actual sequence of the opposition contains five clips, one for each opposition leader. Clip Te3-1 is another example of this part, as it contains the announcement of the Prime Minister about his resignation and a shot that shows him leaving the parliament building.

(Te1-1) Sept. 26, 2006 #5 → (Te-2) Oct. 8, 2006 #1 → (P1) Poll: Dec., 2006 →

(To1-1) Nov. 21, 2006 #4 → (To1-2) Nov. 22, 2006 #5 → (P2) Poll: Feb., 2007 →

(To2-1) Jan. 15, 2007 #3 → (To2-2) Jan. 30, 2007 #3 → (P3) Poll: June, 2007 →

(To3-1) May 23, 2007 #6 → (To3-2) June 2, 2007 #1 → (P4) Poll: Aug., 2007 →

(To4-1) Aug. 6, 2007 #2 → (Te2-1) Sept. 9, 2007 #1, Sept. 10, 2007 #1 →

(Te3-1) Sept. 11, 2007 #1, Sept. 12, 2007 #1

Figure 5: Example of a negative summary created by the proposed framework (N_{PM} = "Shinzo ABE", $(D_{\mathrm{inaug}}, D_{\mathrm{resig}})$ = (Sept. 26, 2006, Sept. 26, 2007), $D_{\mathrm{vid\_length}}$ = 5 minutes). Each clip is represented by a thumbnail image. Below are shown the clip ID, date of broadcast, and the story ID.

We evaluated this clip and one other of the four generated explanatory videos by comparing their content with the content and style of explanation videos actually created by NHK, the broadcaster (we call those further on "NHK video"). In the comparison with the NHK video about Prime Minister Abe's resignation, where only two thirds of this version was accessible, we found that clips Te1-1 to To1-2 covered the same events, though with different video material. Clip To2-1 was not at all used in the NHK video but instead a story about the resignation of a minister due to fraud. Clips To2-2 and To3-1 are then again covering the same events but with different video material. The event of clip To3-2 in our video is again not used in the NHK video, which addresses instead the suicide of a cabinet Minister. For the period of our clips To4-1 to Te3-1, unfortunately, there was no comparison available. It is also apparent that the NHK uses less strict pattern of insertion of demoscopic material. The pattern in the NHK video was three events, and then a succession of two events separated by poll inserts. An additional difference was that the inserts in the NHK video were animated, though the presented information was the same. Both ours and the second NHK video were much shorter than the video of Fig. 5, as Prime Minister Kunio Hatoyama only showed dropping poll rates. The two videos showed hence the same pattern, the same events but again with different video material. We also asked Japanese colleagues to state how reasonable the created videos were (we showed the video and provided them with a comment about the event portrayed in the video). All stated that the presented events could explain the pattern indicated in the preceding poll but if the events were always the most important they did not dare to say. It all depended on the voice over.

5. DISCUSSION

The approach described in this article is but a small step towards the intelligent editing of explanatory news video. Nevertheless, we believe that the work undertaken informs research into the automated generation of video beyond the summarization of a single news show. The proposed framework in the current state describes the general pipeline of steps to generate event explanations for the domain of news in a chronological and retrospective manner. As the approach works in real time the system takes the first established story. We demonstrated that the coupling of topic-based and template-based automatic authoring works well for a video repository that contains already edited material for a consistent domain, as in our case, news. The chronological approach of representing events in combination with story threads can also be applied to similar description structures, such as the review of a year (What were the highlights of 1999?) or the collection of major events in a person's life (Why was Elisabeth Taylor famous?). In particular the latter example is what we aim for next, namely larger story structures in form of obituaries.

The achieved results with respect to event identification and automatic retrieval of related material propose that the framework can be utilized to ease the work of journalists, i.e. leave it to the system to find the essential events for a particular case of explanation and provide this as a start point for the journalist to then finalize the video. The two examples of generated material are, with respect to structure and content, comparable to those versions generated by professionals at a broadcasting company. Besides providing a larger set of templates and technology to establish those, it would be interesting to see if professionals (editors or journalists) would save time with the proposed framework, assuming that some re-editing and the occasional search for better material might occur. This question, however, can only be answered with a long-time user test, which is beyond the current state of the environment.

With the current state of the framework, we could demonstrate that the template-approach allows a directed access to relevant data sources that then facilitates the development of the explanatory video. In the presented case, the demoscopic poll data allowed the identification of significant points in time that potentially can indicate pointers to relevant events. It needs to be seen if other topics in politics in particular or other domains like entertainment provide similar semantic correlations between the topic and a presentation form that facilitates a temporal as well as semantic structure to establish an explanation for the topic. It needs to be stated that the system will not work in case the demoscopic data is not available. However, different sources can provide similar data, e.g. demoscopic analysis of twitter tweets. It then needs to be investigated how these sources can take the role of triggers for the related events.

As also demonstrated in this paper, our approach might not necessarily generate the appropriate events and might also establish a different presentation form (i.e. using different video material) as those chosen by professional editors or journalists. Though the response on our generated examples showed that the events made sense, we are also aware of the fact that the news domain is a thankful medium, where the visual content merely provides a carpet for the dominant voice over. The relation between image and audio, therefore, needs further investigation. At the moment, all we can state is that the framework introduces a biased angle, though that is again referring to the closed-caption and hence to the soundtrack. Additional descriptors need to be introduced into the template that can support a similar sentiment analysis as is used for the transcript evaluation.

We need to admit that the formalization of the current template schema is rather ad-hoc. The design is mainly based on the analysis of the particular event type we were interested in. Even though the overall approach of using contextualised keywords works, it needs to be investigated how far this can be correlated to the ontologies already in use within broadcasting organizations. In the same context, it is not yet clear if the strict planning of a fixed presentation pattern does not result in neglecting significant material. The overall format, though, is appropriate as it reflects the common broadcasting style for presenting such types of explanations. It is worthwhile to investigate how different presentation forms would influence the structure of the templates associated to a topic. In this context, it would also be interesting to investigate how the already existing audio track can be used for the selection of video clips or for the final presentation generation. In particular, the latter can contribute to an approach towards complete automation of the production process.

Though the described approach works, we still need to verify with journalists in how much it fits their needs. In particular, the ways how they could alter the structures easily if they wish to work with different events needs to be investigated. We currently consider to either automatically provide, or facilitate the user to edit, alternative storylines.

6. CONCLUSION

We presented a framework for the semi-automated authoring of explanatory audio-visual news topics in a retrospective style for the domain of politics, which follows a hybrid approach that couples an automatic topic-based approach of story generation with template-based generation of the introduction and the final parts of the video. We demonstrated that the approach works for in an environment that can depend on already edited material, such as the news repository of a broadcaster. The next further developments will focus on the integration of the developed technologies into a complete system and further research on additional template types.

7. ACKNOWLEDGMENTS

Parts of this work were supported by the Grants-in-Aid for Scientific Research (21013022, 21700103, 2300036), the Excellent Young Researchers Overseas Visit Program (21-5324) from JSPS, and a joint research project between Nagoya University, University of Amsterdam, NetCompass, Ltd. and National Institute of Informatics.

8. REFERENCES

[1] P. Appan and H. Sundaram. Networked multimedia event exploration. In *Proceedings of the 12th ACM International Conference on Multimedia*, pages 40–47, October 2004.

[2] J. Bateman, J. Kleinz, T. Kamps, and K. Reichenberger. Towards constructive text, diagram, and layout generation for information presentation. *Comput. Linguist.*, 27:409–449, September 2001.

[3] D. C. A. Bulterman and L. Hardman. Structured multimedia authoring. *ACM Trans. Multimedia Comput. Commun. Appl.*, 1:89–109, February 2005.

[4] M. G. Christel, A. G. Hauptmann, H. D. Wactler, and T. D. Ng. Collages as dynamic summaries for news video. In *Proceedings of the 10th ACM International Conference on Multimedia*, pages 561–569, December 2002.

[5] E. Dumont, B. Mérialdo, S. Essid, W. Bailer, H. Rehatschek, D. Byrne, H. Bredin, N. E. O'Connor, G. J. F. Jones, A. F. Smeaton, M. Haller, A. Krutz, T. Sikora, and T. Piatrik. Rushes video summarization using a collaborative approach. In *Proceedings of the 2nd ACM TRECVid Video Summarization Workshop*, pages 90–94, October 2008.

[6] J. G. Fiscus and G. R. Doddington. Topic detection and tracking evaluation overview. In J. Allan, editor, *Topic detection and tracking*, pages 17–31. Kluwer Academic Publishers, Norwell, MA, USA, 2002.

[7] J. R. Gregory. *Some Psychological Aspects of Motion Picture Montage.* Ph.D. Thesis, University of Illinois., 1961.

[8] L. Hardman, Z. Obrenoviĉ, F. Nack, B. Kerhervé, and K. Piersol. Canonical processes of semantically annotated media production. *Multimedia Systems*, 14:327–340, 2008.

[9] A. G. Hauptmann, R. Yan, and W.-H. Lin. How many high-level concepts will fill the semantic gap in news video retrieval? In *Proceedings of the 6th ACM International Conference on Image and Video Retrieval*, pages 627–634, July 2007.

[10] I. Ide, T. Kinoshita, T. Takahashi, H. Mo, N. Katayama, S. Satoh, and H. Murase. Exploiting the chronological semantic structure in a large-scale broadcast news video archive for its efficient exploration. In *Proceedings of APSIPA Annual Summit and Conference 2010*, pages 996–1005, December 2010.

[11] N. Katayama, H. Mo, I. Ide, and S. Satoh. Mining large-scale broadcast video archives towards inter-video structuring. In *Advances in Multimedia Information Processing —PCM2004 5th Pacific Rim Conference on Multimedia Proceedings, Part II*, volume 3332 of *Lecture Notes in Computer Science*, pages 489–496, December 2004.

[12] R. Laiola Guimarães. Automatic and manual processes in end-user multimedia authoring tools: where is the balance? In *Proceedings of the 18th ACM International Conference on Multimedia*, pages 1699–1700, October 2010.

[13] F. Nack and W. Putz. Designing annotation before it's needed. In *Proceedings of the 9th ACM International Conference on Multimedia*, pages 251–260, October 2001.

[14] S.-Y. Neo, Y. Ran, H.-K. Goh, Y. Zheng, T.-S. Chua, and J. Li. The use of topic evolution to help users browse and find answers in news video corpus. In *Proceedings of the 15th ACM International Conference on Multimedia*, pages 198–207, September 2007.

[15] A. Scherp and S. Boll. Context-driven smart authoring of multimedia content with xSMART. In *Proceedings of the 13th ACM International Conference on Multimedia*, pages 802–803, November 2005.

[16] A. Scherp, T. Franz, C. Saathoff, and S. Staab. F–a model of events based on the foundational ontology dolce+DnS ultralight. In *Proceedings of the 5th International Conference on Knowledge Capture*, pages 137–144, September 2009.

[17] A. Scherp, R. Jain, M. Kankanhalli, and V. Mezaris. Modeling, detecting, and processing events in multimedia. In *Proceedings of the 18th ACM International Conference on Multimedia*, pages 1739–1740, October 2010.

[18] F. Shipman, A. Girgensohn, and L. Wilcox. Generation of interactive multi-level video summaries. In *Proceedings of the 11th ACM International Conference on Multimedia*, pages 392–401, November 2003.

[19] C. G. M. Snoek, M. Worring, and A. G. Hauptmann. Learning rich semantics from news video archives by style analysis. *ACM Trans. Multimedia Comput. Commun. Appl.*, 2:91–108, May 2006.

[20] H. Takamura, T. Inui, and M. Okumura. Extracting semantic orientations of words using spin model. In *Proceedings of the 43rd Annual Meeting of the Association for Computational Linguistics*, pages 133–140, June 2005.

[21] U. Westermann, S. Agaram, B. Gong, and R. Jain. Event-centric multimedia data management for reconnaissance mission analysis and reporting. In *Proceedings of the 14th ACM International Conference on Multimedia*, pages 499–500, October 2006.

The Director's Lens: An Intelligent Assistant for Virtual Cinematography *

Christophe Lino
IRISA/INRIA Rennes
Campus de Beaulieu
35042, Rennes Cedex, France
christophe.lino@inria.fr

Marc Christie
IRISA/INRIA Rennes
Campus de Beaulieu
35042, Rennes Cedex, France
marc.christie@irisa.fr

Roberto Ranon
HCI Lab, University of Udine
via delle Scienze 206
33100, Udine, Italy
roberto.ranon@uniud.it

William Bares
Millsaps College
1701 North State St Jackson
MS 39210
bareswh@millsaps.edu

ABSTRACT

We present the *Director's Lens*, an intelligent interactive assistant for crafting virtual cinematography using a motion-tracked hand-held device that can be aimed like a real camera. The system employs an intelligent cinematography engine that can compute, at the request of the filmmaker, a set of suitable camera placements for starting a shot. These suggestions represent semantically and cinematically distinct choices for visualizing the current narrative. In computing suggestions, the system considers established cinema conventions of continuity and composition along with the filmmaker's previous selected suggestions, and also his or her manually crafted camera compositions, by a machine learning component that adapts shot editing preferences from user-created camera edits. The result is a novel workflow based on interactive collaboration of human creativity with automated intelligence that enables efficient exploration of a wide range of cinematographic possibilities, and rapid production of computer-generated animated movies.

Categories and Subject Descriptors

H.5.1 [**Multimedia Information Systems**]: Animations, Video

General Terms

Algorithms, Human Factors

Keywords

Virtual Cinematography, Motion-Tracked Virtual Cameras, Virtual Camera Planning

*Area chair: Dick Bulterman

1. INTRODUCTION

Despite the numerous advances in the tools proposed to assist the creation of computer-generated animations, the task of crafting virtual camera work and edits for a sequence of 3D animation remains a time-consuming endeavor requiring skills in cinematography and 3D animation packages. Issues faced by animators encompass: (i) creative placement and movement of the virtual camera in terms of its position, orientation, and lens angle to fulfill desired communicative goals, (ii) compliance (when appropriate) with established conventions in screen composition and viewpoint selection and (iii) compliance with continuity editing rules which guide the way successive camera placements need to be arranged in time to effectively convey a sequence of events.

Motivated in part to reduce this human workload, research in automated virtual camera control has proposed increasingly sophisticated artificial intelligence algorithms (e.g. [10, 5, 9, 17, 2, 20]) that can in real-time generate virtual camera work that mimics common textbook-style cinematic sequences. However, this combination of increased automation and decreased human input too often produces cinematography of little creative appeal or utility since it minimizes the participation of filmmakers skilled in "taking ideas, words, actions, emotional subtext, tone and all other forms of non-verbal communication and rendering them in visual terms" [6]. Additionally, existing systems rely on precoded knowledge of cinematography and provide no facility to adapt machine-computed cinematography to examples of human-created cinematography.

This paper introduces the *Director's Lens*, whose novel workflow is the first to combine the creative intelligence and skill of filmmakers with the computational power of an automated cinematography engine.

1.1 Overview

Our Director's Lens system follows a recent trend in previsualization and computer-generated movies, by including a motion-tracked hand-held device equipped with a small LCD screen that can be aimed like a real camera (see Figure 4) to move a corresponding virtual camera and create shots depicting events in a virtual environment.

In the typical production workflow, the filmmaker would film the same action from different points of view, and then

Figure 1: Screenshot of *Director's Lens* user interface in *Explore Suggestions* mode.

later select, trim and combine shots into sequences and ultimately create a finished movie. Our system instead proposes a workflow in which shooting and editing are combined into the same process. More specifically, after having filmed a shot with the motion-tracked device, the filmmaker decides where a cut should be introduced (i.e. trim the shot) and the system will compute a set of suitable camera placements for starting the subsequent shot. These suggestions represent semantically and cinematically distinct choices for visualizing the current narrative, and can keep into account consistency in cinematic continuity and style to prior shots. The filmmaker can visually browse the set of suggestions (using the interface shown in Figure 1), possibly filter them with respect to cinematographic conventions, and select the one he or she likes best.

Once a suggestion is selected, it can be refined by manually moving the virtual camera into a better position, angle, or adjusting lens zoom, and shooting can start again. In addition, movies with shots composed of still cameras can be quickly generated with just keyboard and mouse.

The system exploits an annotated screenplay which provides the narrative context in the form of text descriptions of locations, subjects, and time-stamped actions, with links to the 3D models employed in the scene. The system uses the screenplay to provides on-screen information about timing of actions and dialog while shooting and provides our cinematography engine requisite knowledge about the 3D geometry and animation being shot. To generate the suggestions, the cinematography engine leverages both its knowledge of classical cinematography rules [3], and the knowledge it gets by analyzing the compositions created by the filmmaker.

1.2 Contributions and Outline

In the emergent *Virtual Moviemaking* approach [4], realtime 3D graphics and motion-tracked virtual cameras are used in all production phases to provide creative team members with the ability of both reduce the time needed for previsualization, and to enable them to enjoy immediate and direct control of the process, from pre-production to production. For example, designed virtual sets can be interactively explored to accurately plan shots and refine creative ideas or virtual props before actual shooting takes place.

Our system aims at improving Virtual Moviemaking processes by introducing, for the first time, the combination of manual control of the virtual camera with an intelligent assistant. This provides a filmmaker with a way to interactively and visually explore, while shooting, a wide variety of possible solutions for transitioning from a shot to another, including some perhaps not considered otherwise, and instantly see how each alternate would look like without having to walk and turn around with the motion-tracked device (or move a virtual camera around with keyboard and mouse). In addition, in the innovative production workflow we propose, shooting and editing are combined in a seamless way, thus enabling very rapid production of animated storyboards or rough movies for previsualization purposes.

Furthermore, a novice filmmaker could use the system as a hands-on learning tool to quickly create camera sequences that conform to the textbook guidelines of composition and continuity in cutting from one shot to the next.

Finally, our work constitutes the first effort towards automatically learning cinematography idioms from live human camera work, and therefore building systems that are able to learn from examples of human experts, instead of trying to pre-encode a limited number of situations.

This paper is structured as follows. In Section 2 we review related work. Section 3 describes how the system computes the suggestions, while Section 4 illustrates the Director's Lens interface layout and functionality. Section 5 discusses implementation details, limitations and results from preliminary users' feedback. Finally, Section 6 concludes the paper and outlines future work.

2. RELATED WORK

Cinematographers over time developed a rich canon of conventions for filming commonly recurring types of shots (a continuous take of camera recording) and sequences (an ordered series of shots). For example, cinematic convention suggests that in filming two characters facing one another in conversation, alternating shots of the two characters should depict one gazing left-to-right and the other right-to-left. In filming the first shot of such a sequence, the camera is placed on one side of an imaginary line-of-interest passing through the characters, and successively placing the camera on the same side of this line preserves continuity by repeating the established facing directions of the characters. [3].

In composing the visual properties of a shot, a cinematographer may vary the size of a subject in the frame or the relative angle or height between camera and subject. Shot sizes include extreme close-up, close-up, medium, long, and extreme long in which a subject's size in the frame appears progressively smaller or more distant. A filmmaker can also use editing decisions such as shot duration and the frequency of cuts to artful effect. [3].

2.1 Automated Virtual Camera Planning

The research field of automated camera planning, which combines expertise in Computer Graphics and Artificial Intelligence has sought to reduce the burden of manually placing and moving virtual cameras by bringing to bear increasingly sophisticated intelligence to emulate the composition and editing decisions found in traditional film.

Early efforts in automated camera control computed virtual camera locations from pre-programmed displacement vectors relative to the subject(s) being viewed, e.g. [12]. Attempts to model the editing transitions between shots have relied on idiom-based approaches which encode established conventions for filming common scenarios (e.g. groups of actors in conversation) using hierarchical state machines to model and transition between commonly used shot types [15]. These approaches fall short when a user needs to film scenarios not anticipated by the pre-coded state machines.

Seeking to better handle unanticipated scenarios and arbitrary user-specified viewing goals, constrained-optimization camera planners compute virtual camera placements from user-specified declarative constraints on how subjects should appear by view angle, size and location in the frame, and avoidance of occlusion. Typically, heuristic search-based or optimization techniques repeatedly generate and evaluate the quality of candidate camera shots until a satisfactory camera placement is found [10, 5]. To reduce the computational complexity, the 3D scene space can be partitioned into regions that yield semantically distinct shots by distance, view angle, and relative position of subjects [8]. Extensions to tackle camera path-planning problems have been proposed in offline [7] or online contexts [14]. The quality of the output often depends on carefully formulating the constraint parameters and importances making it difficult for users to obtain a specific desired shot.

Automatically producing virtual camera behavior coupled with narrative planning entails encoding and reasoning about coherent narrative discourse and cinematography to visualize a story. Along this line, a few systems have been proposed, e.g. CamBot [11] and Darshak [17] which can compute a full movie from a script while maintaining consistent rhetorical structure. These approaches however operate in offline contexts.

A recent proposal [20] combines all these lines of research and is able to, starting from a script of the movie, compute camera motion and edits in real-time by partitioning the 3D scene space into *Director Volumes* that combine semantic and visibility information about subjects, and then searching optimal cameras (also enforcing composition rules) inside the best volume.

In summary, existing automated virtual camera planners can in realtime generate camera placements, movements, and edits to visualize sequences of live or pre-recorded events in virtual 3D worlds. The resulting computer-generated camera work is generally adequate for mechanically reproducing cinematic sequences that conform to anticipated textbook scenarios such as groups of virtual actors in conversation. However, crafting truly artful cinematography often requires human judgement of when and how to creatively depart from textbook rules (see [22]). Unfortunately, existing automated virtual camera planners provide little or no facility for a human filmmaker to interject his or her creativity into the planner's operation.

Passos et. al. [21] also recognize the need to look beyond relying on programmers to encode cinematography knowledge in their system, which uses a neural network, to enable users to train an editing agent by selecting between a small set of virtual cameras each filming a moving car from different vantage points. Our system instead uses a much deeper model of cinematography accounting for continuity, cinematic style, and composition constraints and utilizes an intuitive motion-tracking and touch-screen interface that allows a user to craft his own compositions.

2.2 Computer-based Assistants for Movie Production

Commercial systems like FrameForge 3D [16] enable a user to create a virtual set and place cameras for producing storyboards and previsualization, but do include intelligent automated assistance to find suitable camera angles and framings or to plan camera paths.

Intelligent storyboarding research systems provide assistance in creating storyboards. For example, Longboard [18] integrates a sketch-based tablet interface to a discourse and camera planner. The user defines a script and then sketches a storyboard, from which the system produces animatics and renders scenes, possibly adding shots and actions if the user or the script did not specify them. In a form of interplay similar to that of our system, the user has the possibility of either accepting or rejecting the suggested shots by specifically adding constraints on certain frames or by adding new frames to the storyboard. However, Longboard is meant to be used as an offline generator, not as a shooting assistant.

Adams and Venkatesh [1] have proposed a mobile assistant for amateur movie makers where the user selects a narrative template and a style, and the system displays shot directives (i.e. how to film a specific part of the event) by generating 3D simplified first-person renderings that illustrate what the camera should frame and how. The renderings are meant to assist the user while shooting in the field.

2.3 Motion-tracked Cameras for Movies

Early virtual reality researchers studied different user interaction metaphors for users to control the position and orientation of a virtual camera by moving a six-degree of freedom motion sensor [24]. This technique of animating a virtual camera using a hand-held motion sensor has found high-profile application in the previsualization (planning) and filming of feature films including *Polar Express* (2004), *Beowulf* (2007), and *Avatar* (2009). Computer game productions such as *Command and Conquer: Red Alert 3, and Resident Evil 5* have also used these devices to create in-game cinematics. Commercially-available systems (e.g., Intersense VCAM, NaturalPoint Insight VCS) couple camera-like bodies or camera mounts with 3DOF (orientation) or 6DOF (orientation and position) sensors, whose readings are mapped onto the virtual camera parameters (position, orientation) and provide buttons or levers to adjust lens zoom angle. These devices have replaced typical mouse, keyboard, and joystick camera controls with intuitive motion-sensing control, but they operate with the same complex software interfaces of 3D modeling tools, which are not designed around cinematic organizational concepts of scene, sequence, and shot. Nor can they easily manage and browse a variety of alternate cinematic visualizations side-by-side.

3. COMPUTING SUGGESTIONS

The core of our system relies on the automated generation of a large range of suggested cameras and on the ranking of these suggestions according to the last frame of the current shot.

In order to generate appropriate shots with relation to the story, our system requires the provision of an annotated screenplay. This screenplay specifies a set of actions (possibly overlapping in time) as they occur in a sequence of scenes by specifying, for each one, the starting and ending times, the involved subjects/objects (if any), a relevance value, and a textual description of the action. Actions may be attached to a character or an object (e.g. "Parsons walks to the table"), or describe any general event (e.g. "Characters are entering the canteen"). In addition, the screenplay includes the names of particular 3D model parts for the subjects, which are required to perform appropriate screen composition in computing suggestions (e.g. for a character, body part, head part and eyes parts). An excerpt of the annotated screenplay for a scene from Michael Radford's *1984* is provided below:

```
Screenplay "1984"
  Scene "Canteen"
  Location "Canteen"
   Actor Smith
     body "SmithBody"
     head "SmithHead"
     leftEye "SmithLeftEye"
     rightEye "SmithRightEye"
   Actor Syme
    ...
   Action "A pours gin"
     Relevance 5
  begin 0 end 4
     Character "Smith"
   Action "A drinks gin"
     Relevance 5
     begin 4 end 12
  Character "Smith"
   Action "A turns"
     Relevance 3
     begin 10 end 18
     Character "Smith"
   Action "A speaks to B"
     Relevance 9
     begin 18 end 21
     Character "Smith"
     Character "Syme"
 ...
end screenplay
```

As the user requests a list of suggestions (at time in the movie we denote t_s) our system performs a three-step computation:

- from the screenplay the system selects the list of all actions overlapping time t_s or occurring within a second after time t_s (this enables to suggest a shot which anticipates an action);
- for each selected action, the set of key subjects (characters, objects, buildings) is extracted and a dynamic spatial partitioning process generates a wide collection of viewpoints ensuring both a complete coverage of the key subjects and actions as well as significant enough difference between viewpoints (see detailed description in next Section). Each viewpoint represents a suggested starting point for a shot;
- each suggestion is then ranked by considering the enforcement of cinematic continuity rules between the current viewpoint and the suggested viewpoint, the quality of the composition in the shot (how elements are spatially organized on the screen), the relevance of the suggestion with relation to the action and the quality of the transition between the current shot and the suggestion.

3.1 Dynamic Spatial Partitions

We employ *Director Volumes*, a technique proposed by [20] to compute dynamic spatial partitions in the space of viewpoints around key subjects (a key subject may be a character or any object of the environment). As displayed in Figure 3, the area around some subjects configurations (a typical two-character configuration in the Figure, but one, three or more character configurations are also considered) is partitioned with relation to shot distance (Close-Up, Medium Shot, Long shot, Extreme Long Shot) and with relation to relative angle of the camera against the key subjects (Internal, External, Apex, Parallel and Subjective see [3]). For a one-subject shot this would be Front, Left, Right, Profile, 3/4 Left, 3/4 Right. These dynamic spatial partitions are based on Binary Space Partitions (BSPs) which are recomputed every time a change occurs in the 3D environment

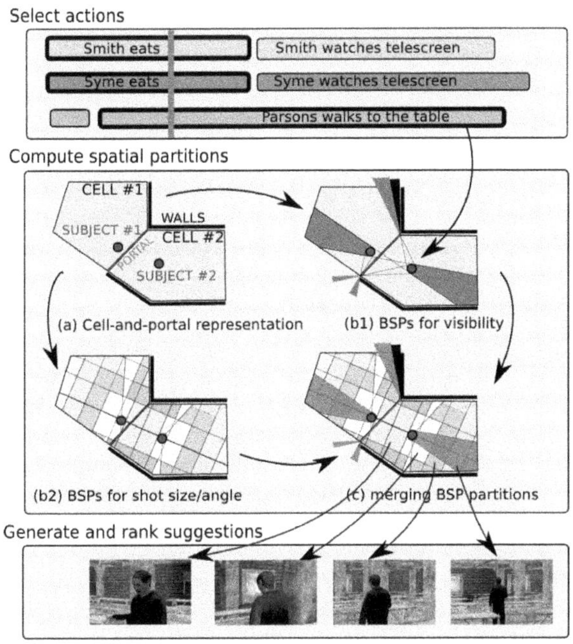

Figure 2: The automated computation of suggestions. Each selected action in the screenplay leads to the computation of a set of spatial partitions (each partitionned area represents a typical shot of the action). Suggestions are computed and ranked for each area.

(due to character or object motion). Each partition is qualified with a semantic tag representing its shot distance and relative angle to subjects.

In a parallel step, we compute a second level of dynamic spatial partitions to identify visibility of key-subjects. We analyze the 3D environment to build a visibility graph [23] (a graph which connects convex cells extracted from the environment which share a common portal, the portal representing a potential occluder). We use the graph to propagate full visibiltiy, partial visibility and no visibility for each key-subject and tag spatial partitions accordingly.

Finally, we rely on BSP-tree merging techniques to compose the information from the Director Volumes and the visibility graph into a single representation. Using this technique, all regions generated by the partitions represent viewpoints with different tags, meaning that whatever viewpoint is selected in a region, it will yield a similar result in terms of shot distance, relative angle to framed subjects and visibility.

For each region, our process generates three suggestions: a high-angle shot, a low-angle shot, and a medium angle shot, and for each of these suggestions, a default screen composition is computed by enforcing the rule of the thirds (key-subjects are spatially arranged on the screen to appear at the intersection of the line of the thirds [3]).

The overall process is described in Figure 2.

3.2 Ranking Suggestions

Once a set of suggestions is computed (for a two-subject configuration, over 240 shots are generated and for a one-subject configuration, 120 shots are generated), our system performs a quality ranking process, whose result is used when displaying the suggestions to the user (see Section 4).

The quality $q_s > 0$ of a suggestion s is defined as the product of qualities assessing specific features of s:

$$q_s = Q_{cont}(s) \cdot Q_{comp}(s) \cdot Q_r(s) \cdot Q_t(s)$$

with

$$Q_{cont}(s) = Q_{loi}(s) \cdot Q_{change}(s)$$

where Q_{cont} measures the enforcement of *continuity* rules, Q_{loi} measures compliance with *line-of-interest* rule and last, Q_{change} measures compliance with the change-in-angle-or-size rule. Q_{comp} represents the satisfaction of composition rules, Q_r represents the relevance of the suggestion with relation to the current action's relevance, and Q_t represents the quality of the transition between the current shot and the suggestion. All the $Q_i(s)$ functions return positive real values.

In the following subsection, we detail how $Q_i(s)$ functions are computed.

3.2.1 Respecting Continuity in the Cut

Cinematographic conventions related to continuity in cuts are well established. Such conventions typically maintain the spatial coherency in cuts (do not invert key subjects on the screen), the motion coherency (key subjects moving in the same direction on successive shots) and the composition continuity (successive shots of the same subjects will maintain similar composition). We rely on the following continuity rules to establish the ranking $Q_{cont}(s)$:

- **Line-of-interest continuity**: in actions which involve two or more key subjects, once the camera is located on one side of the line-of-interest (imaginary line linking two key subjects), the camera should not cross this line in successive shots, unless using an extreme long shot (that re-establishes the key subjects in relation to the environment). The system ranks all suggestions on the opposite side of the Line-of-interest with a low value.
- **Change in angle or size**: When considering two shots portraying the same subject, there should be at

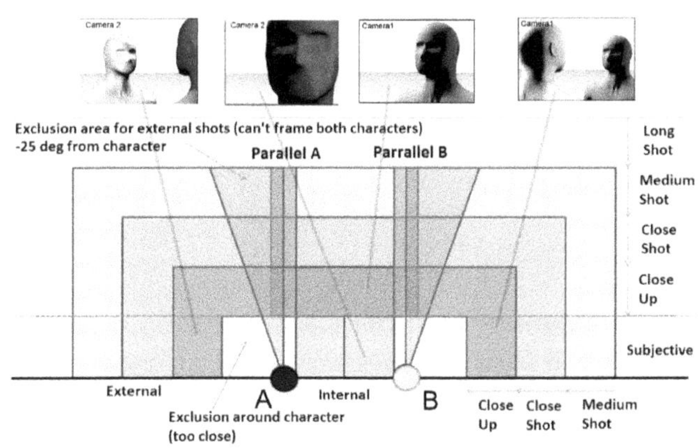

Figure 3: Spatial partitions around two subjects define areas of characteristic viewpoints referred to as Director Volumes (see [20]).

least a thirty-degree difference in orientation with relation to the key subject, or a notable difference in the size of the subject in the shot. For this purpose we compute the difference in angle and size between the current shot and the suggested shot. Only suggestions with noticeable difference in size are ranked positively (here we consider a change of at least two units in size, a unit being a step between two shots in the range of Extreme Close Shot, Close Shot, Medium Close Shot, Long Shot and Extreme Long Shot). Suggestions that subtend an angle lower than 30 degrees to the subject are ranked with a low value.

3.2.2 *Respecting Classical Composition Rules*

Suggestions computed by the system try to enforce the classical rule of the thirds. When considering characters, the composition is set so that their eyes (an element to which spectators look at in priority when gathering elements in a picture) are located at the intersection of two equally spaced horizontal lines and two equally spaced vertical lines on the screen. We thus measure as an Euclidean distance the difference between the ideal composition and the composition computed by the system to asses the quality of a viewpoint. Bad compositions are ranked with low values.

3.2.3 *Relevance of the Shot w.r.t. Current Action*

Relevance is measured by exploring the capacity of the shot to enhance a viewer's comprehension of the action. Each action has a relevance value that encodes its importance for the story (*e.g.* representing whether the action is a foreground action, an establishing action, or a background action). Shots that depict more relevant actions, from relevant viewpoint enforce the comprehension of the story and will have a higher quality.

3.2.4 *Quality in Transitions Between Shots*

Quality in transitions (a transition is a cut between shots) is measured by using transition matrices. A transition matrix is a stochastic matrix used to describe the transitions of a Markov chain. We encode our transitions with a right stochastic matrix, i.e a square matrix where each row consists of nonnegative real numbers summing to 1. Each value t_{ij} of the matrix T (i being the row index, and j the column index) corresponds to the probability of performing a cut from Director Volume i to Director volume j. We use three different matrices depending on whether the transition is performed inside the same action, between related actions, or between unrelated actions. The quality of the transition is given by an affine function $y = ax + b$, where $a > 0, b > 0$ and x is equal to the value t_{ij}^k related to the transition in the corresponding matrix T_k. The values in the matrices therefore represent user preferences in performing cuts, and in our approach, the values are updated by a learning process described in Section 3.3.

3.3 Learning from the User Inputs

We rely on a simple reinforcement learning technique to update the probabilities in the transition matrices, using the cuts already performed by the user. Three distinct transition matrices are encoded depending on whether the transition is performed:

1. **during the same action (matrix T_A)**: the two consecutive shots are conveying the same action;
2. **between related actions (matrix T_R)**: the two consecutive shots are conveying two different actions, but the actions have a causal link (e.g. in case of dialog, the first action being "Syme speaks Smith" and the second one "Smith answers to Syme" for instance). A causal link is established when the two actions share the same key subjects;
3. **between unrelated actions (matrix T_U)**: the two consecutive shots are conveying two different actions, and there is no causal link between them;

These transition matrices actually define preferences in using some transitions between shots over others. A shot is identified by its type (orientation to subject) and its size (extreme long to extreme close-up). Our system learns the transition matrices from the user inputs, by analyzing the successive choices in shot types performed by the user. The learning process operates as follows. Each time the user selects a suggestion as the new shot, we first determine the transition matrix T_k to consider by analysing whether (1) the successive conveyed actions are the same, (2) the actions are different but are causally linked, or (3) the actions are different and they have no causal link. Then all the values t_{ij}^k of the row i of the corresponding matrix T_k (where i is the shot type of the current shot), are updated in the following way: let the newly selected shot be of type n, the value t_{in}^k will be increased, and the values $t_{ij}^k, j \neq n$ of row i will be accordingly updated such that $\sum_i t_{ij} = 1$.

The probabilities in the matrices influence the quality of a shot by ranking preferred cuts higher (the quality of transition $Q_t(s)$ is expressed as a function of t_{ij}^k).

4. THE DIRECTOR'S LENS SYSTEM

In this Section, we describe the interface and user interactions with the Director's Lens system. To demonstrate the system, we will use as example a reconstruction from a sequence of Michael Radford's *1984* movie, together with a set of 70 actions which describe in details the events occurring over the scene. The scene is composed of 5 key subjects (Syme, Parsons, Julia, Smith and an anonymous member of the party).

4.1 User Input Devices

The Director's Lens system features a 7-inch HD LCD touch-screen mounted to a custom-built dual handgrip rig (see Figure 4) that can be paired with either a 3DOF or 6DOF motion sensor. When used with a 3DOF sensor (rotation controls camera aim direction), the two thumb sticks control camera position, and buttons adjust lens zoom, movement/zoom speed, and record/playback functions. When paired with an optical 6DOF tracking system, a rigid cluster of reflective markers is fixed to the device and one of the thumb sticks is configured to increase or decrease lens zoom angle. The spatial configuration (position/orientation) read by the tracking sensor is synchronized with the spatial configuration of the virtual camera in the system, so that (besides a distance scaling factor that can be adjusted) movements of the motion-tracked device will correspond to analogous movements of the virtual camera in the 3D scene.

The system can also be used with just a desktop or notebook computer and a mouse. In this mode, the preferred workflow is primarily one of clicking to select a suggested

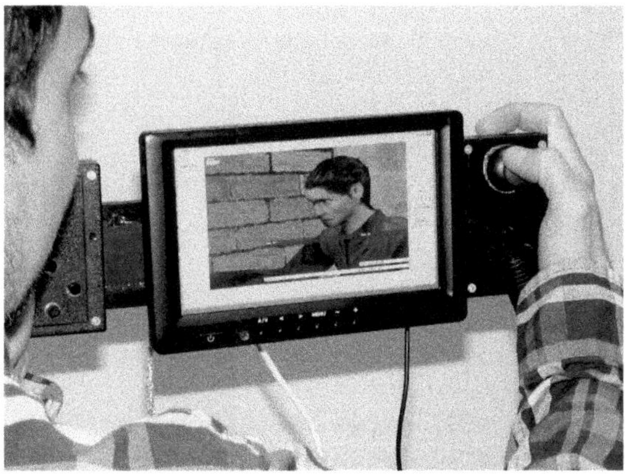

Figure 4: Our hand-held virtual camera device with custom-built dual handgrip rig and button controls, a 7-inch LCD touch-screen.

camera placement for each shot to very rapidly compose a virtual 3d movie made with shots featuring static cameras.

4.2 User Interface and Interaction

The user's interaction with Director's Lens is divided into two interface modes: (i) *explore suggestions* (Figure 1) and (ii) *camera control/movie playing* (Figure 5).

4.2.1 Explore Suggestions Interface

The *explore suggestions* interface (Figure 1) displays the suggestions for beginning a new shot from any instant in the recorded movie. The suggestions are presented as small movie frames, arranged in a grid whose rows and columns correspond to visual composition properties of the suggested cameras. More specifically, the horizontal axis from left-to-right varies by decreasing shot length (or distance) in order of extreme long, long, medium, close-up, and extreme close-up. The vertical axis from top-to-bottom presents suggestions from a variety of camera heights in order of high, medium, and low. For example, Figure 1 shows the suggestions that are proposed to transition from a shot depicting the actions "Syme eats" to a new shot where two parallel actions occur: "Syme eats" (which continues from the previous shot) and "Smith speaks to Syme" (the last frame of the previous shot is shown in the reel at the bottom left). Notice, for example, that all suggestions in the top row are viewed by cameras positioned above the virtual actors.

When more than one suggestion is generated for each shot length and camera angle, the system displays a stack of frames in that grid position, where the top one is the most highly ranked (of all the suggestions in the stack). If the user wishes to explore a stack (s)he can expand the actually displayed suggestions for a grid column, row, or cell, by clicking on the corresponding column/row heading. For example, Figure 5 shows the suggestions grid expanded to display all suggestions for medium length / medium angle shots.

When the suggestions do not refer to the first instant in the movie (i.e., there are previous shots), the system allows the user to visually filter the presented suggestions on the basis of respect of cinematography rules, namely the line of interest, and minimum change in angle or size with respect to the previous shot's last frame. For example, in Figure 1 we have selected to display only suggestions that respect the line of interest rule (i.e., the camera is on the same side of the line of interest as in the previous shot last frame), while Figure 5 shows just suggestions where the camera is at least 30 ° difference in orientation with relation to the key subject (with respect to the previous shot of the last frame).

The user selects a suggested shot by touching its icon in the grid. The larger image framed in the reel at the bottom left represents the previous shot to assist the user in choosing or modifying a suggestion to best follow its predecessor, and shows the currently selected suggestion to its right. The user finally confirms his or her choice and goes to the *camera control/movie playing* interface.

4.2.2 Camera Control / Movie Playing Interface

The *camera control/movie playing* screen (see Figure 6) allows the filmmaker to view the recorded movie or manually take control of the camera to record a shot. The interface features a single large viewport to display the 3D scene as viewed from a virtual camera corresponding to the filmmaker's choice for the current instant in the movie or corresponding to the position/orientation of the motion-tracked device (when the tracking of the device is enabled).

When camera tracking is not enabled, the *Play* button allows one to play-pause the animation, and visualize it from the currently recorded shots, while *Previous Shot* and *Next Shot* buttons enables to move in the recorded movie by shot. With these functionalities, the user can review the recorded movie, and decide where to introduce a cut - this is implicitly introduced when one asks the system to explore suggestions.

When camera tracking is enabled, the virtual camera is driven by the motion tracking and lens zoom controls of the hand-held device. The tracking starts from the currently used camera, so that, if the user is coming from the *explore suggestions* interface after having selected a suggestion, tracking starts from the virtual camera in the configuration associated with that suggestion. By using the *Turn on Recording* button, the user starts/Stops recording of the stream of virtual camera position, orientation, and lens angle input data. Starting recording also starts playback of the pre-produced animated character action and digitized audio dialog.

A graphic overlay can appear over the camera image to display an animated timeline of the unfolding character actions and dialog. Horizontal bars along each row represent one character's actions or dialog. The length of each bar represents the duration of that event. Bars scroll by as the animation plays to indicate the passage of time. This allows the filmmaker to move the camera at the precise time in anticipation of an upcoming screenplay action or spoken dialog event. The overlay also displays the framing properties (e.g. medium, low, etc.) of the current camera view.

Figure 7 demonstrates an example in which the system suggests shots which match the composition of the user's previous shot. In this scene, Smith pours a bottle while seated facing Syme. The user has composed a shot (shown in the right image in the Figure) in which Smith fills the rightmost third of the frame and gazes to the left and the camera is to his lefthand side. Consequently, when we click to enable the line of interest filter, the system generates suggestions in which no viewpoints violate the line of interest by placing the camera on Smith's righthand side. Furthermore, all shots display Smith on the rightmost third of the

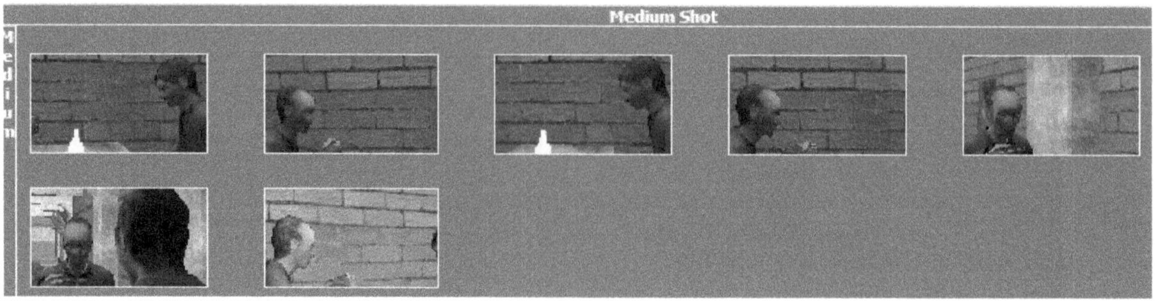

Figure 5: Screenshot of the interface in Explore Suggestions mode with expansion of medium shots and medium camera angles that were visualized in Figure 1, with additional enabling of the *Change in Angle* visual filter. Compare the resulting suggestions with the last frame of the previous shot that is shown in the bottom left part of Figure 1.

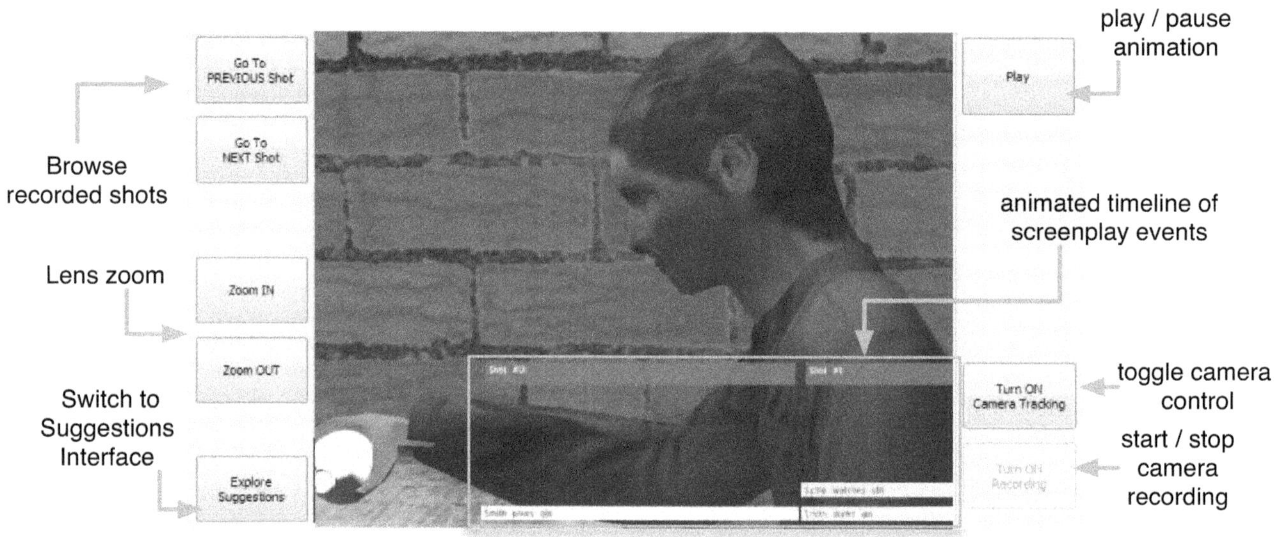

Figure 6: Screenshot of the interface in Camera Control / Movie Playing mode. The overlay horizontal bars show an animated timeline of screenplay events and their duration, together with an indication of the camera angle and framing that is currently being used in the movie.

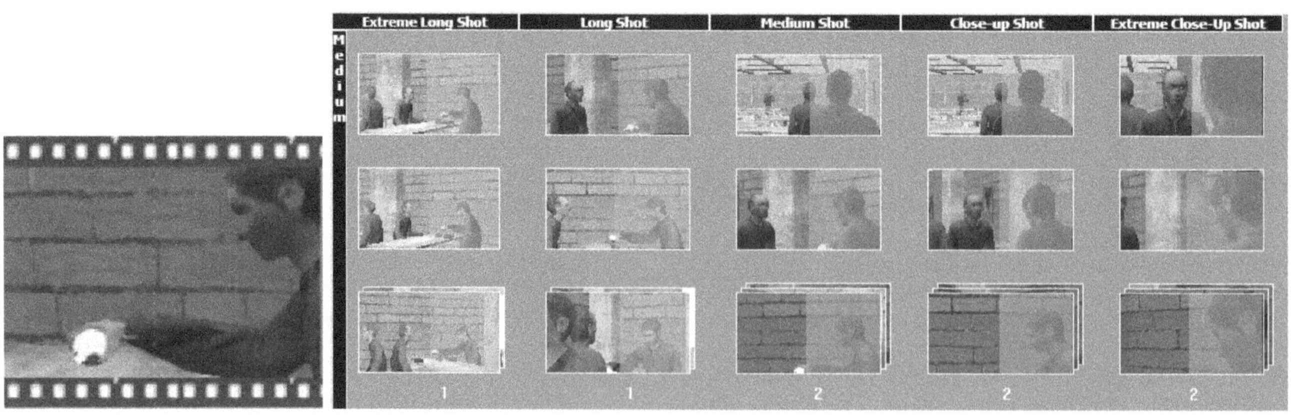

Figure 7: Given user's composition for the current shot (shown in the left image), the system suggests shots (right image) which satisfy continuity rules of editing.

frame. Also note suggested compositions leave more room ahead of Smith's face, as did the user's composition.

5. RESULTS

Our system is coded in C++ and uses the OGRE real-time rendering engine, and a custom-written abstraction layer to interface to a variety of button and joystick input devices and motion trackers. In our tests we used 6DOF rigid body reflective markers with an A.R.T. optical tracker with 16 cameras covering a workspace of 4×8 meters. The application runs on a computer whose video output is routed over an HDMI cable to the small LCD touch screen. The largest computational cost of the cinematography engine is in finding visibility and director's volumes, which depend on the geometric complexity of the scene and the variations in position of the key subjects. In the pictured example, the computation of suggestions takes around a second on a Intel Core i7 2.13 GHz notebook, which is acceptable since this computation is not required to happen in real-time.

5.1 Applicability to Other Scenarios

The examples shown in the paper features mostly dialog actions involving two or three characters, and also generic actions (e.g. "Parsons walks to the table") for which proper suggestions are computed. In general, the system can model any event where one character or object, or group of objects (*e.g.*, cars driving, architectural elements) is involved, and propose suggestions to properly frame it using different angles and shot lengths. Note that for many situations (e.g. shooting of architecture, or crowds) there are not many cinematographic conventions other than using establishing shots first, and then closer shots. However, in general, the cinematography knowledge the system uses can be expanded by designing additional Director Volumes for specific cases or using the automatically learned tables of transitions. For situations that involve, in the same instant, more than three characters, the system could be extended by employing the method of hierarchical lines of action [19].

Scenes involving very fast action can be a bit problematic as the system might generate suggestions that are good for the considered instant, and decrease in quality after a short delay, for example because the framed character moves aways or is covered by some moving objects. This kind of situation would require the system either to consider animations occurring in an interval of time, instead of an instant, or to suggest camera movements, instead of just starting frames. However, this would be of much greater computational cost than deriving suggestions for single instants. In these cases, however, the filmmaker can at worst ignore the suggestions and deal with the situation by taking manual control.

Finally, the system computes all suggestions using a single fixed lens field of view. However, the user can quickly adjust the field of view by manual control. The system's search algorithm can be extended by taking into account variations on lens angle. In practice, the set of lens angles to consider would be limited to model the cinematography practice of using a small number of user-selected "prime" or standard lenses.

5.2 User Feedback

While we do not currently have results from formal and extensive user evaluations, a few videographers have tried the system, reporting great satisfaction in using it.

In general, users found the system workflow refreshing compared to mouse-based solutions, were very willing to try it, and could rapidly use it to produce results. In our tests, after a very brief introduction to the system, users familiar with camerawork could shoot a 3 minutes video of the 1984 scene in around 10-15 minutes, including taking decisions on camera angles and cuts. For comparison, producing a video for same animation sequence took an expert user a few hours of work using 3DS Max. The reason for the huge difference in time comes from the fact that with typical animation software tools one is forced to a workflow where cameras have to be manually positioned and animated, and then the shot can be watched, and often one has to go back and forth between cameras modifications and testing the result. Furthermore, there's the complexity of manually keeping track of timings and motion curves, making sure that edits occur in the correct place and time.

While the use of a motion-tracked virtual camera is surely pivotal in reducing the amount of time needed, we can hypothesize that suggestions also played a role, as in general users needed to make very small movements to refine the suggestions and find their ideal starting camera positions. Moreover, from our feedback with professionals in the development of motion-tracked virtual cameras, we know that having to walk around in the tracked space to explore angles and distances is perceived as a real issue. Finally, users more experienced in real cameras work appreciated on-screen information overlays of character actions and their timing while shooting.

The interface for browsing suggestions by shot distance and height was considered easy to learn and effective for a videographer, and the possibility of quickly visualizing many alternatives was very appreciated, though not all users agreed with each suggestion. This is expected since the perceived quality of a suggestion is a subjective factor, which changes from one videographer to another. However, users' attitude towards the cinematography engine work was positive, mainly because the the system does not force one to any shooting or editing style, and suggestions can be ignored: however, many times they caused the videographer to consider solutions he had not thought about, thus enhancing creative thinking and exploration.

6. CLOSING REMARKS

While a few experiments have been done in combining human expertise with automatic camera planners, we believe that this work is the first attempt at innovating the shooting process of CG animations by providing intelligent and adaptive automatic support in creating shots. In the shooting of CG movies, videogame cinematic scenes and machinima, the system has the potential of making the process much easier and quicker than current methods. From our early tests, unlike existing automated systems which rely on pre-coded cinematic knowledge to cover all anticipated scenarios, our interactive approach proves effective even if no suggested viewpoint is "perfect" in the user's creative judgement.

Future work includes conducting extensive user evaluations to precisely assess the user satisfaction of the various system features, and measure task completion time with and without the automated assistance capability.

We plan also to focus on methods to improve the recorded

camera tracks. For example, one could think of a "steady-cam" filter to avoid using a tripod for non-handheld camera style, or apply post-processing algorithms to recorded video to improve apparent camera movement as proposed by Gleicher and Liu [13].

Motion-sensing virtual cameras offer an opportunity to easily capture shots in the context of screenplay actions providing a rich corpus for machine learning. Further work in this novel direction could eliminate the re-programming needed to encode knowledge for new numbers and arrangements of actors, shots, and transitions, and also provide an effective way to incorporate more sophisticated stylistic capabilities into automatic camera planners.

6.1 Acknowledgements

Thanks to Dean Wormell of InterSense for discussions on the use of motion-sensing virtual cameras in movie productions. Thanks to Nick Buckner, Tyler Smith, Alex Olinger, and Lihuang Zhu for constructing our virtual camera device. William Bares acknowledges support of a Millsaps College sabbatical award. Roberto Ranon acknowledges the financial support of the PRIN project *Descriptive Geometry and Digital Representation: intelligent user interfaces to support modeling and navigation in 3D graphics application for architecture and design*. This work has been funded in part by the European Commission under grant agreement IRIS (FP7-ICT-231824).

7. REFERENCES

[1] B. Adams and S. Venkatesh. Director in your pocket: holistic help for the hapless home videographer. In *Proceedings of the 12th ACM International Conference on Multimedia*, pages 460–463. ACM Press, 2004.

[2] D. Amerson, S. Kime, and R. M. Young. Real-time cinematic camera control for interactive narratives. In *Proceedings of the 2005 ACM SIGCHI International Conference on Advances in computer entertainment technology*, pages 369–369. ACM Press, 2005.

[3] D. Arijon. *Grammar of the Film Language*. Hastings House Publishers, 1976.

[4] Autodesk. The new art of virtual moviemaking. Autodesk whitepaper, 2009.

[5] W. Bares, S. McDermott, C. Boudreaux, and S. Thainimit. Virtual 3D camera composition from frame constraints. In *Proceedings of the 8th ACM international conference on Multimedia*, pages 177–186. ACM Press, 2000.

[6] B. Brown. *Cinematography: Theory and Practice: Image Making for Cinematographers, Directors, and Videographers*. Focal Press, 1st edition, 2002.

[7] M. Christie, E. Languénou, and L. Granvilliers. Modeling camera control with constrained hypertubes. In *Proceedings of the Constraint Programming Conference (CP 2002)*, pages 618–632. Springer-Verlag, 2002.

[8] M. Christie and J.-M. Normand. A semantic space partitioning approach to virtual camera control. In *Proceedings of the 2005 Eurographics Conference*, pages 247–256. Blackwell Publishing, 2005.

[9] N. Courty, F. Lamarche, S. Donikian, and E. Marchand. A cinematography system for virtual storytelling. In *Proceedings of the 2003 International Conference on Virtual Storytelling*, volume 2897, pages 30–34, November 2003.

[10] S. M. Drucker and D. Zeltzer. Camdroid: a system for implementing intelligent camera control. In *Proceedings of the 1995 Symposium on Interactive 3D Graphics*, pages 139–144. ACM Press, 1995.

[11] D. Elson and M. Riedl. A lightweight intelligent virtual cinematography system for machinima generation. In *Proceedings of the 3rd Conference on AI for Interactive Entertainment (AIIDE)*, 2007.

[12] S. Feiner. Apex: An experiment in the automated creation of pictorial explanations. *IEEE Computer Graphics & Applications*, pages 29–37, 1985.

[13] M. L. Gleicher and F. Liu. Re-cinematography: improving the camera dynamics of casual video. In *Proceedings of the 15th international conference on Multimedia*, pages 27–36. ACM Press, 2007.

[14] N. Halper, R. Helbing, and T. Strothotte. A camera engine for computer games: managing the trade-off between constraint satisfaction and frame coherence. In *Proceedings of the 2001 Eurographics Conference*, pages 174–183. Blackwell Publishing, 2001.

[15] L. He, M. F. Cohen, and D. H. Salesin. The virtual cinematographer: a paradigm for automatic real-time camera control and directing. In *Proceedings of the 23rd ACM conference on Computer graphics and interactive techniques (SIGGRAPH '96)*, pages 217–224. ACM Press, 1996.

[16] Innoventive-Software. Frameforge3d, 2007.

[17] A. Jhala. *Cinematic discourse generation*. PhD thesis, 2009.

[18] A. Jhala, C. Rawls, S. Munilla, and R. M. Young. Longboard: A sketch based intelligent storyboarding tool for creating machinima. In *Proceedings of the 2008 FLAIRS Conference*, pages 386–390, 2008.

[19] K. Kardan and H. Casanova. Virtual cinematography of group scenes using hierarchical lines of actions. In *Proceedings of the 2008 ACM SIGGRAPH symposium on Video games*, pages 171–178. ACM Press, 2008.

[20] C. Lino, M. Christie, F. Lamarche, G. Schofield, and P. Olivier. A real-time cinematography system for interactive 3D environments. In *Proceedings of the 2010 ACM SIGGRAPH/Eurographics Symposium on Computer Animation*, pages 139–148. ACM Press, 2010.

[21] E. B. Passos, A. Montenegro, E. W. G. Clua, C. Pozzer, and V. Azevedo. Neuronal editor agent for scene cutting in game cinematography. *Comput. Entertain.*, 7:57:1–57:17, 2010.

[22] B. Peterson. *Learning to See Creatively*. Watson-Guptill, 1988.

[23] S. J. Teller and C. H. Sequin. Visibility preprocessing for interactive walkthroughs. In ACM, editor, *Proceedings of the 18th ACM annual conference on Computer graphics and interactive techniques (SIGGRAPH)*, pages 61–69, 1991.

[24] C. Ware and S. Osborne. Exploration and virtual camera control in virtual three dimensional environments. *Proceedings of the 1990 symposium on Interactive 3D graphics (SI3D 90)*, pages 175–183, 1990.

Reliving On Demand: A Total Viewer Experience

Vivek K. Singh[1*], Jiebo Luo[2], Dhiraj Joshi[2], Phoury Lei[2], Madirakshi Das[2], Peter Stubler[2]
[1] University of California, Irvine, [2] Kodak Research Laboratories, Rochester, NY, USA
singhv@uci.edu, {jiebo.luo, dhiraj.joshi, phoury.lei, madirakshi.das, peter.stubler}@kodak.com

ABSTRACT
Billions of people worldwide use images and videos to capture various events in their lives. The primary purpose of the proposed media sharing application is digital *re-living* of those events by the photographers and their families and friends. The most popular tools for achieving this today are still static slide-shows (SSS) which primarily focus on visual effects rather than understanding the semantics of the media assets being used, or allowing different viewers (e.g. friends, family, who have different relationships, interests, time availabilities, and familiarities) any control over the flow of the show. We present a novel system that generates an aesthetically appealing and semantically drivable audio-visual media show based on several reliving dimensions of events, people, locations, and time. We allow each viewer to interact with the default presentation to 'on-the-fly' redirect the flow of reliving as desired from their individual perspectives. Moreover, each reliving session is logged and can be shared with other people over a wide array of platforms and devices, allowing sharing experience to go beyond the sharing of the media assets themselves. From a detailed analysis of the logged sessions across different user categories, we have obtained many interesting findings on the reliving needs, behaviors and patterns, which in turn validate our design motivations and principles.

Categories and Subject Descriptors
H.5.2 [INFORMATION INTERFACES AND PRESENTATION]: User Interfaces - Interaction styles. H.5.4 [INFORMATION INTERFACES AND PRESENTATION]: Hypertext/Hypermedia-Navigation

General Terms
Design, Human Factors.

Keywords
Reliving, sharing, semantic, interaction, slide-show, spatio-temporal navigation

1. INTRODUCTION
Human beings have always felt the need to chronicle parts of their daily lives. From the paintings of cave men, to oral ballads and story-telling, to commissioned portraits in the medieval era, we notice a clear human desire to record and preserve aspects of their lives to relive at later points in time. The 20th century saw the emergence of personal cameras to undertake this chronicling process, and today nearly every family chronicles parts of their lives using photos and videos. This chronicling and data capturing was done for two important reasons. First, for the participants themselves to *relive* the events of their lives at later points of time; second, for them to *share* these events in their lives with other friends and family, who were not present at the events but would still be interested in knowing how the event (e.g. the vacation, or the wedding, or the trip) went by. The importance of sharing is underscored by the *billions* of image uploads per month on social media sites such as Facebook, Flickr, and Picasa. As shown in Fig. 1, digital reliving has become ubiquitous on many platforms and devices.

Figure 1. People don't merely share images, they want to re-live and share their experiences with others. It is important to enable digital reliving on ubiquitous platforms (web, home, hardcopy) and devices (TV, PC, smart phones, tablets, digital picture frames, kiosks, photobooks).

The massive growth in data *creation* aspect has highlighted two major issues with the techniques available for *consumption* of such data. First, the sheer volume of images implies that it becomes difficult for participants to relive specific memories (e.g. in terms of events, locations, people), without searching through a huge collection of media. Second, sharing one's images with multiple family members and friends in one's diverse social network implies that each person has a different interest level and perspective when looking at the images. Sharing across different users requires catering to users with different time availability, different motivations, different interests, and different perspectives. These different perspectives have traditionally been ignored by both research and commercial applications. In fact, while sophisticated tools are being created to bridge the *semantic gap* on the organizer or the producer side of media collections, very little effort is being put into bridging the *intent gap* on the *recipient* side of the media sharing equation.

*Area Chair: Dick Bulterman

* Work was done when the author was interning at Kodak Research Laboratories, Eastman Kodak Company, Rochester, NY, USA.

Considering these factors, we present a novel system for digital *reliving* and *sharing*. We describe an approach for generating *dynamic* media-shows (which are inspired by, but significantly richer than *static* slide-shows which are currently the most popular mode of photo playback). These media reliving experiences are aesthetically pleasing yet semantically drivable based on people, locations, events, and time - attributes that have been successfully employed by multimedia community to characterize stories in social media settings such as Facebook [16]. Very importantly, we no longer consider the recipient to be a passive consumer, but rather someone who can interact with and redirect the flow of this media-stream based on different semantic facets. This redirection occurs in an aesthetically pleasing manner and on-the-fly (i.e. without the need to re-start the show or re-compiling the data collection). Further, the users can directly interact with the show (e.g. by clicking directly on 'Hotspots' i.e. any of the faces being shown) rather than having to use a search box with "advanced" settings which appear inelegant and may disrupt the media flow. Thus, the proposed system provides users an elegant tool for reliving their personal, or their friend's media collection while interacting directly with it as and when they desire, to reroute the media flow along any desired semantic axis. As will become clearer, media reliving is different from both media search and media browsing. Media search involves clear user intent. The intent is significantly weaker in media browsing [6]. Media reliving provides a valuable middle ground for user interaction and intent clarity, and does so in an aesthetically pleasing manner.

The design of the system and its evaluation by users with different roles and demographic backgrounds (e.g. age, gender, family roles) also provided some unique insights into the process of digital re-living. While most viewers appreciated the ability to semantically re-route the media stream, their methods of interacting with it varied significantly across different demographic factors. Hence we also present our findings about the semantic axis (time, location, person, and events) that is most frequently used for rerouting the media stream, and how this distribution changes across different demographic groups. The findings are interesting, and may affect the design of ours as well as other reliving efforts in near future.

The outline for the rest of this paper is as follows. Section 2 describes the related work. Section 3 describes our design principles. We discuss the proposed reliving approach in section 4. Section 5 discusses implementation details, while section 6 describes our in-depth analysis and findings on the user feedback, as well as user interaction patterns. We present out conclusions in Section 7.

2. RELATED WORK

A number of commercial products provide similar features. For example, iPhoto, Picasa, Flickr, and Facebook all provide ways to upload and share pictures. However, the slide-shows supported are basic, with little to no user interaction present at *run time*. Hence they do not allow a user to bridge the intent gap. The FaceMovie feature in Picasa is an interesting innovation that tries to assemble images of the same person at different ages in a dynamic slide-show. Therefore, in a way it tries to understand the face/person semantics but again does not provide any user interaction tools at run time.

The multimedia community has seen multiple efforts in understanding the content of the images and bridging the semantic gap. For example, very good surveys of work in this direction are provided in [19][6]. Earliest attempts to understand the user intentions at run time were documented by "relevance feedback" work [18] that allows users to click on a desired image to see similar images. Recently multiple approaches like 'exploratory search' [15], 'faceted browsing' [24] have also started guiding the user towards their desired content. We draw inspiration from these works, but focus on supporting direct user interaction with an already running aesthetically pleasing reliving experience.

The most common way of reliving image collections till date has been static slide-shows. Notable research efforts have been made to change this paradigm [3][5][23]. Tiling slide-shows [4] create dynamic (multiple tiles of images at the same time) slide-shows with (matching beat) music to improve user experience. iSlideshow [5] aims at understanding the 'content' of the images and creates collages of images based on concepts and supports transitions that dissolve at face ROI (region of interest). Again while these works show a clear research trend in understanding the semantics of media for better slide-shows, they do not provide any user-interaction or handle the intent gap. In [23], songs are identified to accompany image collections in media shows.

Hardcopies are also useful for reliving. HP's photo collage effort [22] allows for creation of aesthetically pleasing collages of pictures. However it focuses on static collages rather than dynamic audio-visual media experiences. In another recent work that focuses on photobook creation from social media [16], media in one's social network is matched with text queries (where, when, what, who) and then arranged into a printed photo book. Works like [1] provide a rich media authoring tool set to define media shows. However, the show needs to be defined *before* (i.e at 'compile-time') the user can view it. Similarly, the system in [3] allows viewers to edit videos for shared (or personal) consumption later. In contrast, we focus on providing an effective tool that allows users to redirect the flow *while* they are viewing it (i.e. at run-time).

User interaction is a key aspect of human centered multimedia in general and is particularly important to media sharing and reliving. The recent emphasis on interactive search and browsing (closely related to our work) bears testimony to the importance of human in the loop. Along these lines, the interactive search engine in MediaMill [20] allows users to rapidly review video content and revise their search strategies on the fly. For mobile video browsing, in [8] a three-level design space consisting of video segments, entire video, and collection of related videos is proposed to characterize the complexity of navigation.

The multimedia community has recognized that human centered computing systems should be "multimodal, proactive, and easily accessible to a wide range of users" [9]. We take to heart this philosophy in defining the design principles of our work.

3. DESIGN PRINCIPLES

We postulate that reliving systems should be *user controllable*, *semantically drivable*, and *aesthetically pleasing*. These principles have had multiple design implications for the system developed.

1) User controllable: To bridge the user intent gap we allow viewers to interact with, and redirect the media flow as and when desired (users can of course also just choose to sit back and enjoy the ongoing media flow).We support *interaction on the fly*, allowing users to interact with the system and redirect the flow without causing it to stop and re-boot. This is significant as we believe that systems that stop and reconfigure each time a new input setting is desired cannot provide satisfying reliving experience.

Figure 3: A blow-up of the media reliving interface showing all the features.

2) Semantically drivable: The user control cannot be just linear (e.g. pause, play) but rather needs to be semantically drivable. We consider *media (image, video) as portals to memory and experience space.* Users are interested in reliving significant events in their lives rather than viewing "IMG_0667.jpg" per se. Hence we want to provide users the tools to navigate their experience space (and not merely the media space). Specifically, we leverage on *events as organizing units* (as the human memory is believed to be largely episodic i.e. event driven) [10]. To support the experiential navigation, we follow the adage of *"less is more"* and focus only on well understood semantic axes of *time, location,* and *people* which can also be detected quite robustly. We make a design choice to keep a minimalistic number of axes to keep browsing easy yet robust.

3) Aesthetically pleasing: Aesthetics of the presentation are just as important as the media assets selected in the reliving experience. Hence features such as reflective music, background and transition effects are integral parts of the system designed. We support *dynamic presentation* i.e. present fast-paced multi-photo composites which enhance holistic event level reliving, and produce a more lively experience. Lastly, rather than focusing on mono-media (e.g. just images) we *support multimedia.* We think that the users employ more than one media (images, videos, music) to capture their lives, and enjoy a better reliving experience when multiple media are presented to them synergistically.

4. OUR APPROACH

4.1 System overview

Fig. 2 provides an overview of our media reliving system. The system pre-processes the media collection for each user to extract different event and geographical clusters, and obtains their corresponding metadata (location, time, and people). The combination of media collection and the metadata is next used to create an aesthetically pleasing media show. At run-time however, the viewer can choose to interact with the system, and the presentation is dynamically adapted to match user intent. Specifically the presentation order of events and the relative screen presence given to each photo within the event are re-computed based on user input. We also maintain a log of user-interactions, which allows us to identify different patterns as discussed in section 6.2.

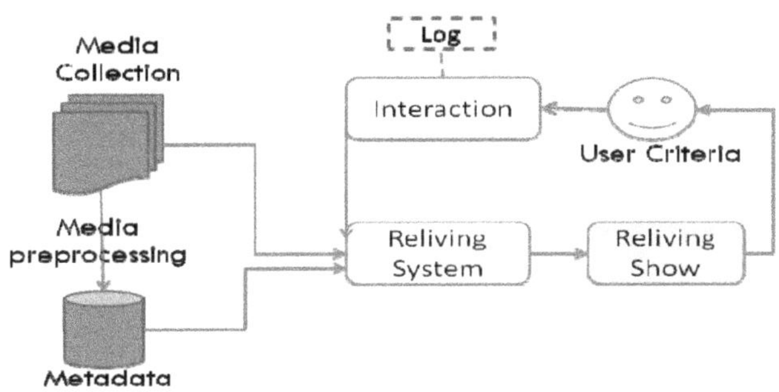

Figure 2. The high-level design of our reliving system.

A screenshot of the developed system is shown in Fig 3. As can be seen, the user has the option to passively view the default media show, or actively control the flow through the semantic axes of places, people, and time. At any given event the user is also provided the option to preview the next few events and jump forward or backwards. The user can also control the pace of the slide-show and pause to look at important images if desired. Lastly, the system can automatically go into 'full-screen' mode and back to show and hide the controlling toolbars depending on whether the user is interacting with the system.

4.2 Media reliving flow

The steps required for dynamic re-ordering and presentation reconfiguration are shown in Fig. 4. The system performs the pre-processing to cluster the media collection into events and extracts the corresponding metadata. The system chooses 'time' as the default criterion to generate the media show. However, each time a user selects a new criterion, the system reorders the event collection based on the criterion. Next, it determines the suitability of each image inside the event media sub-collection, based on the criterion. Depending on the number of relevant images found suitable, a presentation layout is selected. Similarly, based on the criterion, the transition method across images and background music are selected. The image set is shown in order and the show continues until a new criterion is selected by the user (in our current version, the show loops back to the beginning when all the pictures corresponding to a user-criterion have been displayed). In the following sections, we describe each component in more detail.

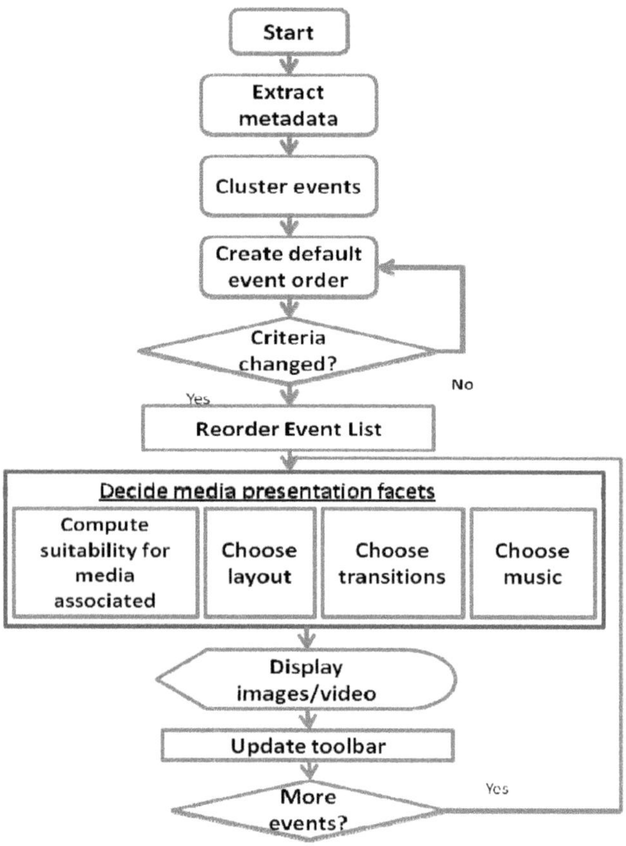

Figure 4. A flow diagram of the reliving system.

4.3 Extracting metadata (Pre-processing)

As shown in Fig. 5, the system computes three types of metadata for each image/video in the media collection.

1) Media descriptors: i.e. Type (photo/video), URL, and resolution.

2) Aesthetic value descriptor: This was obtained using an image value descriptor based on some of the attributes described in [12][11][7] including colorfulness, contrast, sharpness, spatial distributions of edges and colors, and faces.

3) Semantic metadata: (Timestamp, location, and people): The location was obtained from the combination of directly encoded GPS values, and folder directory names at coarse level. The folder names were geo-coded using Google API. The people pictured in a collection were detected using the Omron face detection algorithm similar to [21]. We developed an algorithm that uses facial similarity to automatically group faces into clusters. Face clusters were labeled once for each data set.

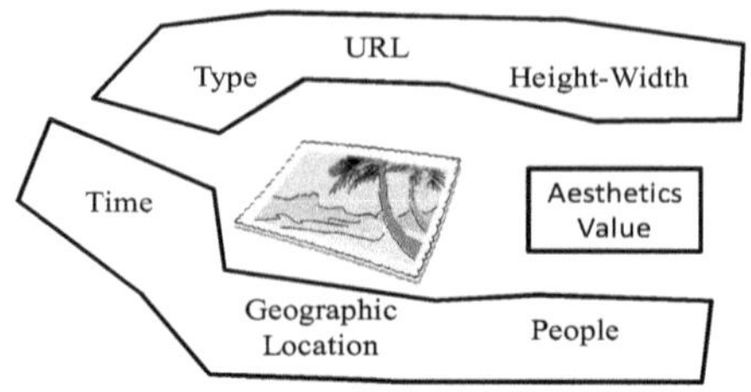

Figure 5. Metadata computed for each media element.

4.4 Clustering events

Once the system has the time-stamps for each media element, it performs event clustering using the algorithm in [13]. This algorithm is based on temporal information and visual similarity, attempting to match user's perceptions of real-life events. The histogram of time differences between adjacent images or videos is clustered into two classes: time differences that correspond to event boundaries, and those that do not. Color block-based visual similarity is used to refine the event boundaries. Once the media elements are clustered into events, the system computes the aggregated time-span, location-span and people list for the event.

The overall process of meta-data extraction for identifying the current toolbar options to be provided is shown in Fig. 6. From the geographical location axis perspective, the system clusters the data into geographical locations from which events are captured. The geographic locations computed are used as options on the 'places' browsing axis. The geographical clustering was performed using a mean-shift algorithm similar to [2].

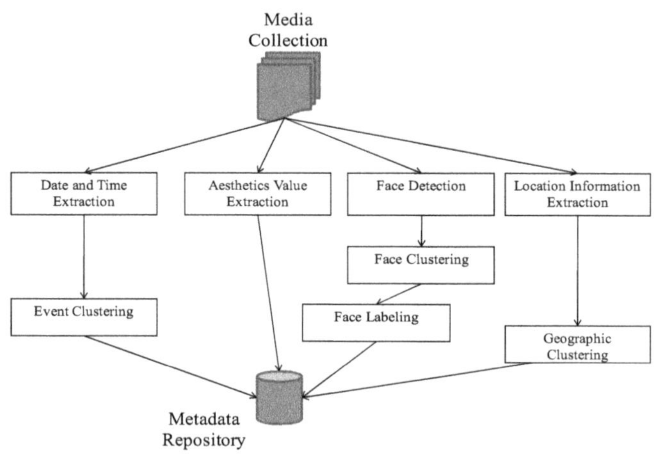

Figure 6. The metadata extraction process.

4.5 Reordering of the event list

The system uses time as the default ordering criterion for an event collection. Hence the show moves in a chronological order until the user chooses to interact with it.

The event list can be reordered according to different criteria. Each event is granted a matching score (α_1) based on the criterion selected. This matching score is combined with the previous matching score (α_2) using a weighted averaging scheme.

$$\alpha_{1(t+1)} = w_1 \cdot \alpha_{1(t)} + w_2 \cdot \alpha_{2(t)}$$

While the associated weights (w_1, w_2) ratio was heavily biased towards the new match, the presence of a dampening factor helps to create a smoother transition across criteria, and also adds some randomness (i.e. the users do not see *exactly* the same show each time a particular value is chosen) to the created show. The precise computation is as follows:

1) Time: If the criterion selected is a particular time value (v_1), the matching criterion w_1 is defined as the normalized time difference between v_1 and the considered event's start time. We decided to go only in one direction (i.e. chronologically increasing) as an initial feedback from users suggested that they become confused by jumping back and forth in time. Hence for an event **e**, the matching score is computed as:

$$w_1 = 1 - \frac{e.startTime - v_1}{\mathrm{e_{last}.\,startTime} - v_1}$$

where $\mathbf{e}_{\text{last}}$ is the event with the latest start time. All events with start times before the selected value are assigned a w_1 value of zero.

2) People: If the criterion selected is a person (or a group of people), w_1 is computed based on the number of that person(s) images (both in ratio and absolute numbers) in the event media collection. Therefore, if a user clicks on "Jenny's" face, the event collection that contains a large number of images, and most of which have Jenny's face is likely to attain a high matching score. Thus for selection of users p_1 *through* p_n, the matching score is computed as:

$$w_1 = 0.5 * \frac{e.numPics(p_1 \square \ldots \square p_n)}{|\mathrm{e.\,numPics}|} + 0.5 * \frac{|e.numPics|}{|\mathrm{e_{max}.\,numPics}|}$$

where $\mathrm{e_{max}}$ refers to the event with the largest photo collection.

3) Location: If the user selects a particular location (v) as their criterion, the matching score w_1 is computed as the normalized distance between the chosen location and the event's geo-location. We have used [latitude, longitude] pairs to represent the centroid location of events.

$$w_1 = \frac{\|v - e.loc\|}{\sqrt{180^2 - 90^2}}$$

where the normalization has been undertaken based on the maximum possible distance in the lat-long representation space.

4.6 Deciding media presentation facets

Once the system has an ordered list of events whose images and video need to be presented in the reliving session, it proceeds to compute a score for each individual image/video. This score dictates which images are shown and determines their screen presence (time and screen real-estate).

4.6.1 Computing score for each image

The relevance of each image in reliving is computed as a weighted average of its aesthetic properties as well as semantic aspects (where relevant). We next describe score computation with respect to different reliving dimensions.

1) Time & Location: Images receive a score purely based on their aesthetic value metadata computed during the pre-processing step.

2) People: The images are given a score based on the combination of multiple semantic factors based on the people selected (i.e. p_1 through p_n) in the criterion

a). r1=$(p_1 \square \ldots \square p_n)$ present in the image? (A binary 1, 0 score)

b). r2= size of the face(s) in pixels

c). r3= position of the face centroid

d). r4= $\frac{|(p_1 \square \ldots \square p_n)|}{|total\ NumFaces|}$

e). r5= aesthetic value factor

(a) two images (b) three images

(a) four images (b) five images

Figure 7. Examples of different layout templates.

Figure 8. 'Default' layout template (left) and a template with mixed landscape and portrait frames (right).

4.6.2 Choosing the layout

Ideally the layout should be aesthetically pleasing but relevant to show the media (images or videos) in a given event. For a given event, the layout is selected such that the number of images or video shown is an integer factor of the total number of images or videos in the event. The page layouts with two, three, four or five images are pre-designed, as shown in Fig. 7. If the number of images is not a direct factor, a default layout as shown in Fig. 8 is selected. A light weight automatic cropping algorithm (see Section 4.7) is used if necessary to fit the images into a template. A set of rules is also used to determine whether to use a template with more landscape frames or portrait frames.

4.6.3 Choosing the transition

We wanted to create a dynamic experience for users viewing the images. Hence instead of changing single images (or even collections) one by one, we decided to allow each image/ frame inside the 'image collage' to transit dynamically. The actual transition method depends on the reliving criterion. It was selected to be slide-in/slide-out for the 'time' and 'location' criteria. For the people based interaction, we chose to implement a novel face-to-face transition effect. Our approach gives an effect of the person's face being used as a 'wormhole' to progress from one image or video to another. Note that our transition effect is different from Picasa FaceMovie wherein a subsequent picture bearing a face of the same person is superimposed on top of the current picture to perfectly align the face in size and position.

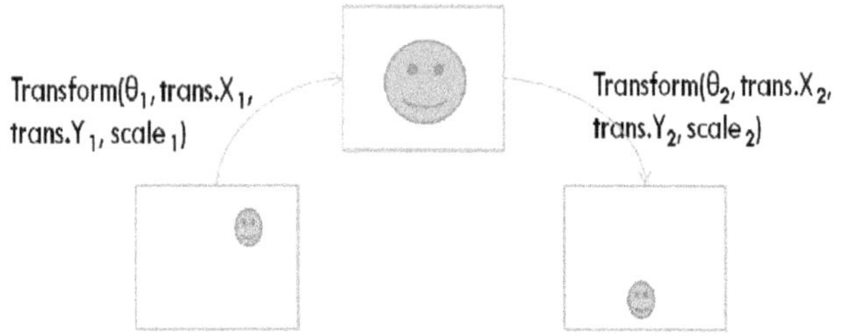

Figure 9. Creating face-to-face transitions.

As shown in Fig. 9, an affine transformation (rotation, translation, and scale) is computed to move the current face in the current image or video into a predefined size-orientation intermediate frame. At the same time a transformation to move from the intermediate frame according to the face into the next image is also computed. When both these transformations are applied in tandem as a smooth transition, the above mentioned face-to-face transition effect is produced.

We consider this an interesting feature as most currently available presentation mechanisms do not create any transitions based on the semantics of the images being shown.

4.6.4 Choosing the music

This step selects semantically relevant music to accompany the media to be displayed. The music is selected based on the current user criterion chosen. For the 'time' criterion, music is selected based on the season (e.g. music for seasons spring, summer, autumn, and winter) of the event; for criterion 'people', music is selected based on the generation of the person(s) selected (e.g. music for the generation of Baby-boomers and generations X, Y, and Z); for criterion 'location' the system searches into a database of geolocation-characterized music and chooses the one that is closest to the location of the event. A database of geo-characterized music has been constructed by manually searching for music using location specific text queries in an annotated music database (here YouTube). Locations for which characteristic music was obtained were identified based on popular tourist destination locations. A library of close to 100 songs exists in the current system. The library is extensible but that is beyond the scope of this paper.

Note though that during reliving, an event can be arrived at using one (or a combination of multiple) user criteria. In other words, an event has multiple facets (e.g. people, time) associated with it. The accompanying music is based on the current facet chosen to guide the media show. Hence the media for the same event may be accompanied by different types of music depending on how the event is arrived at in different or even the same reliving sessions.

4.7 Presenting the media

Once computing the suitability, layout, transition, and choosing the accompanying music for media is accomplished, this step displays the images or video, one event at a time. The images or video are granted screen time based on their suitability score (as described in Section 4.5). Within an event, images and video are displayed in a purely temporal order so as to present a clear temporal flow to the reliving user. The images that did not meet the minimum threshold (i.e. were semantically or aesthetically not satisfactory), are not included in the reliving session.

At times, the orientation of the images or video (landscape or portrait) may not match with the screen space allotted to them based on the selected layout. In order to resolve this issue, the system performs a light weight auto-zoom-crop to maintain as much semantic content as possible. For the criterion 'people', the auto-zoom-crop attempts to preserve the chosen person's face in the center of the frame. If the criterion is not 'people' and images or video contains faces, the auto-zoom-crop attempts to preserve as many faces as possible. If no faces are found in images or video, auto-zoom-crop attempts to conserve the center portion of images while sacrificing the outer parts.

In order to avoid the problem of having multiple images or video transitioning out of the screen at the same time (and leaving large blank screen spaces), we have implemented a token passing scheme between different holes, which allows only one image or video frame/hole to be blank on the screen at a given time.

The system also creates or selects a background image based on user selection (for time criterion, a representative image is selected from the current event, for people criterion, a mosaic of faces in the collection is created as background, and for location criterion, a location snapshot from Google maps is used as background). The background shows-up at the start of the event and compensates for empty holes during transitions. Background images also provide the users a sense of transition between events as they change during reliving.

4.7.1 Miscellaneous navigation and playback controls

As shown in Fig. 3, we also provide a number of navigation controls. The arrow at the end of the place or people navigation bar can be used to bring in new icons.

In particular, for the events, a "preview" function is provided for a user to scroll through ranked events without interrupting the current media flow. This is done by showing a sample image or video of the event as a representative thumbnail and giving (mouse-over) details of the event type and number of images or videos in them. This is akin to "channel surfing using the picture-in-picture feature in TV.

In addition, a set of intuitive playback controls (play/pause, ffwd, fbwd, next event, previous event, playback speed) are provided. Occasionally, the users want to merely control the temporal flow of their reliving experience. Hence we allow them to increase/decrease the speed of playback and pause at important events as they desire. Similarly, sometimes the users may want to 'skip' or 'rewind' events in the show.

4.7.2 Video integration

Videos are played along with the associated photos. Note that we manage the audio playback such that the ambient music is on mute when the video has its own sound track.

4.8 Updating the toolbars

The user navigation toolbars are updated based on the content of the event being displayed. The 'time' browsing toolbar is simply highlighted with the month or year of the current event, to establish a timeframe. Other aspects of this toolbar remain constant and allow users to switch to any time instance at will. The 'people' toolbar shows people relevant to the event being displayed. The 'location' toolbar shows locations of nearby events. The 'people' and 'location' toolbars also contain certain slots that, if requested, could be populated by "people" or "locations" randomly chosen from the user collection. The rationale behind this randomization is to allow the user to take a random leap in the reliving experience space if they get bored with the current selection.

4.9 Logging viewer sessions

We record various details of user reliving sessions. This serves two purposes. Firstly, it helps us in our analysis of user behavior across different demographics. Secondly, we expect users to consider sharing their reliving sessions with others as a form of experiential media. The idea is akin to sharing a book with others which already has underlines, highlights, or a Facebook/Youtube media element which shares the 'likes' or comments on it, or sharing one's play-list in addition to the actual song collection.

The recording for this purpose is done in an XML formatted log file, which captures the details of the event, the associated media elements being shown, the layout, as well as the contents of the axes being displayed. In addition, the type of click (hot-spot or axis) and the time-stamp are recorded. Thus such a record contains enough details to re-play or re-enact an entire reliving session if required. Fig. 10 shows a segment of a sample log file.


```
<Interaction>
        <Click>
                <GlobalEventID>urn:guid:f1337996-3c28-4345-b4fb-c4f1b788fc05</GlobalEventID>
                <SortedEventID>0</SortedEventID
                <TimeStamp>10:17:47 AM</TimeStamp>
                <Criteria_type>gps</Criteria_type>
                <Criteria_value>61.2175937710438 , -149.898739309764</Criteria_value>
                <HotSpotClick>False</HotSpotClick>
        </Click>
        <Snapshot>
                <Locations>
                        <loc>-149.898739309764,61.2175937710438</loc>
                        <loc>-73.508556462585,40.5956603174603</loc>
                        <loc>102.757525301205,25.1018832329317</loc>
                        <loc>104.195397,35.86166</loc>
                        <loc>6.09306585111111,52.7236709366667</loc>
                </Locations>
                <People>
                        <peo>Jiebo</peo>
                        <peo>Joyce</peo>
                        <peo>Xinping</peo>
                        <peo></peo>
                        <peo></peo>
                </People>
                <SortedEvents>
                        <eve>urn:guid:f1337996-3c28-4345-b4fb-c4f1b788fc05</eve>
                        <eve>urn:guid:f1337996-3c28-4345-b4fb-c4f1b788fc05</eve>
                        <eve>urn:guid:f1337996-3c28-4345-b4fb-c4f1b788fc05</eve>
                        <eve>urn:guid:f1337996-3c28-4345-b4fb-c4f1b788fc05</eve>
                        <eve>urn:guid:f1337996-3c28-4345-b4fb-c4f1b788fc05</eve>
                        <eve></eve>
                </SortedEvents>
                <PicsShown>
                        <pic>c:\data\jiebo\cvpr2008\103_5972.jpg</pic>
                        <pic>c:\data\jiebo\cvpr2008\103_5973.jpg</pic>
                        <pic>c:\data\jiebo\lijiang-shangrila-day2\108_0043.jpg</pic>
                        <pic>c:\data\jiebo\lijiang-shangrila-day2\108_0044.jpg</pic>
                </PicsShown>
        </Snapshot>
</Interaction>
```


Figure 10. A partial snapshot of a sample XML to record different interactions.

5. IMPLEMENTATION DETAILS

The system for reliving media collections has been implemented in C# language using Visual Studio 2010. Multiple features from the Windows Presentation Foundations were employed to make implementation easier when dealing with multiple media (image/video) types and undertaking animation effects on them.

The implemented system employs multiple multimedia processing techniques (viz. face detection, face recognition, event clustering, image geo-clustering, aesthetics value detection) under the hood. We have tried to adopt and customize many existing algorithms by computer vision and multimedia communities wherever appropriate rather than 're-inventing the wheel' ourselves.

The images used for the experiments were downloaded from web albums (Picasa, Flickr) of our volunteer participants. The pre-processing (face clustering, event detection, location clustering) was automatically undertaken by the system. The participant input was required at two time instances: once in labeling the clustered people faces, and second (if necessary for non-geotagged data) to label the media folders with a geo-encodable name.

6. EXPERIMENTS

We conducted two sets of experiments to study the performance of our created system. In the first experiment we compared the user satisfaction with our system to their favorite reliving software (e.g. iPhoto, Picasa, Facebook, ACDSee). We also studied the effect of demographic factors on the choice of features by the users. We tried to study which axes and methods of interaction were adopted by the users and how they varied over different gender and family roles.

Both the experiments were conducted using 11 family media collections. Some statistics are shown in the table below. Each collection was pre-processed and made available for users including 1st (owner of collection) 2nd (immediate family member of the collection owner, e.g. spouse, parents, or children) and 3rd parties (friends, other relatives, and acquaintances of the collection owner) to undertake their reliving sessions.

Age of contributing photographers	23 to 56
No. of images/ videos in the collection	2,091 to 10,522
No. of calendar years in time span	3 to 10
No. of tagged people in the collection	26 to 137
No. of places in the collection	19 to 45

We recorded a total of 35 reliving sessions undertaken by 26 different (14 male, 12 female) participants who interacted with the system in first (11 times), second (13), and third party (11) roles. Some participants undertook multiple roles (e.g. once as 1st party and once as a 3rd party for some other collection). However there was no overlap between 1st and 2nd party roles, as the participants belonged to 11 different families and their friends. Each of the participants was provided with a laptop containing their pre-processed media as well as the reliving system. Each participant was requested to spend at least 15 minutes in a reliving session in their home or office settings. The average time recorded for each session however was 30.14 minutes.

6.1 Experiment 1: Comparison with commercially available options

In this experiment we interviewed 20 of the aforementioned participants and asked them for feedback on the system used. The aim of this experiment was to study the usefulness of our new system (called 'Relive!') as compared to their current favorite system. The current favorites of users included Picasa, iPhoto, and many others (e.g. Facebook, ACDSee). The users were asked to rate the systems based on 7 criteria listed in the following table. The first three criteria jointly correspond to the design principles '*user controllable*' and '*semantically drivable*' described in section 3. Next two questions correspond to the '*aesthetically pleasing*' design principle. Lastly we asked the users to rate their overall quality of experience and mention their feature wish-list.

EVALUATION CRITERIA
1. Experience Control: Did you feel that you could redirect the flow of the experience as / when desired (on the fly)?
2. Personalization: Did you feel that you could obtain a personalized reliving experience from this system?
3. Reminiscence: Did you feel like you were reminded of the relevant events in your life?
4. Liveliness: How exciting and lively did you find the experience?
5. Aesthetics and Ambience: Was it a pleasant and rich experience?
6. Overall Quality of Experience: How happy were you with the experience?
7. Feature wish-list: What new features do you most wish to add?

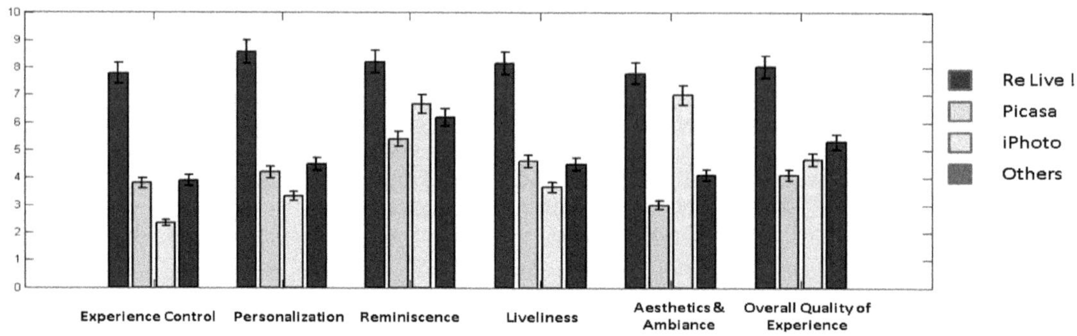

Figure 11. Comparing user-ratings for Relive! with existing multimedia organizer and viewer systems. The colored bars represent the average values and the error bars at the top indicate the 90% confidence intervals.

A summary of average user ratings (between 1 and 10) for the 6 quantitative questions is shown in Fig. 11. It is clear that the users rated the proposed media reliving system significantly higher in all six criteria . The Relive! system outperformed others most significantly in terms of '*experience control*' and '*personalization*' which resonate strongly with our design principles of creating a *semantically drivable* and *user-controlled* reliving system. Amongst other systems used, the users rated the aesthetics and ambiance of reliving sessions in iPhoto the highest.

6.2 Experiment 2: Use of different features across different user demographics

We conducted experiments to study the relative importance of different interaction axes, and how this varied across different demographics. Gender and Participation Role were chosen to be the two fundamental axes for analysis. Participation Roles were defined as aforementioned 1st party, 2nd party, and 3rd party.

As previously mentioned we recorded a total of 35 reliving sessions undertaken by 26 different participants. A total of 1,365 interactions were recorded in this (1,055 minute) process, which translated to slightly more than 1 click per minute. Hence the users liked to interact reasonably *actively* with the system. This is still much longer than typical browsing/strong interaction based reliving (e.g. Facebook), where we expect the mean time between clicks to be in order of seconds (e.g. ~7 seconds reported in [24] for a related task). Slide-shows, conversely provide no interaction mechanism, hence we would expect mean time between interactions to be in the order of minutes (e.g. 5 minutes).

We undertook detailed analysis across demographics based on the following questions:

1) Which demographic set interacts most actively with the reliving application, and which prefers to watch it passively?

The table shows clicks/minute recorded for different demographic groups.

Females	1.14	1.49	1.13	1.01
Males	1.41	1.25	2.08	1.43
Both	1.30	1.27	1.28	1.35
	All	1st party	2nd party	3rd party

As the above table indicates, we found that in general males tend to be more active than females. We also found that 3rd party users tend to interact most actively. The male and female behaviors however are quite different across their roles as first, second, or third parties.

Figure 12: Number of clicks (normalized to percentage) across different semantic axes.

Figure 13. 'Stickiness': Time spent viewing the show after click on different semantic axes

2) Which semantic axis is used most frequently by the users?

We also noticed that the most commonly used type of interaction was the skipping a few (one or more) events based on preview. This could imply that users have a 'surfing the channels' kind of mindset and perhaps get bored by seeing all the details (sometimes the event could contain up to 100 images) of an event. In fact in our user interviews, many suggested a more enhanced previewing and summarization support. This is a subject we will address in the near future. Our current attention is focused on the three semantic axes of people, places, and time (i.e. *'who, where, and when')* and how people interact with them in reliving settings.

Based on 747 clicks on different semantic axes, we found that the most frequently used axis for semantic interaction in the reliving sessions is 'People' (data shown as percentages in Fig. 12). 'People' was the most frequently used axis across (almost) all demographics. The only exception was 3rd party interaction in which 'Places' was the most frequently used criterion.

We also studied the stickiness i.e. 'the time spent viewing the show after a click' on the different semantic axes and found that the average time spent before changing semantic axis was 80.13 seconds. The relative time spent viewing the show after clicks (normalized as percentages) is shown in Fig. 13. Based on time spent, we found that 'Places' is most popular reliving criteria. It was the leader across all demographic groups except 1st person, where people tend to use 'Time' predominantly. Interestingly, we found no significant differences in male and female interaction patterns across different axes.

On the whole, we found that the use of different semantic axes peaked with different types of participants. *'Time' was the most frequently used by 1st party participants*, and *'People' are most frequently used in 2nd party interactions*. This makes intuitive sense as the primary participant is most likely to remember the time of occurrence of something they want to see. 2nd party users were basically family members hence their interest in 'People' also makes sense. Lastly, *'Places' are most commonly employed by 3rd party users*. They are typically least close to the people in the pictures and hence tend to be attracted to different 'Places' in the collection.

3) What are the common interaction patterns, and do they vary by demographics?

Lastly, we analyzed the interaction patterns i.e. 2nd order behavior such as which axis led to another in the user interaction-experience space. Transition graphs across the different semantic axes are shown Fig. 14. We noticed that more than half (51%) of interactions are loopback types (i.e. the same axis is used again). This indicates that users have a tendency to stay on one axis until something in another axis catches their attention.

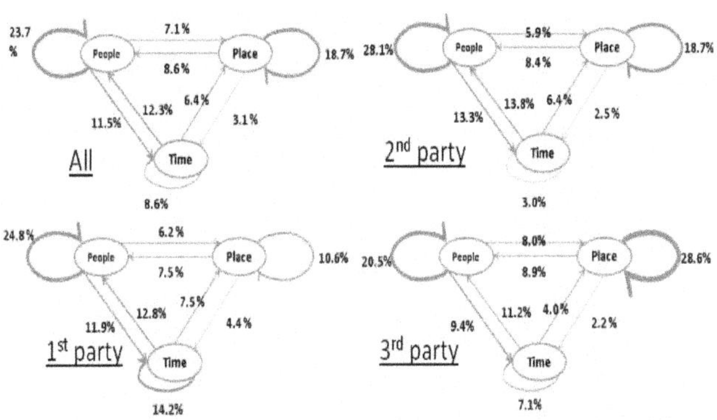

Figure 14. Transition graphs across the semantic axes.

We can again see the 'People' axis dominating and the 'Places' axis showing up prominently in the 3rd party case. We also notice that very few interaction patterns involve going from 'Places' to 'Time'. It is very small and in fact noticeably lesser than even its converse, i.e. 'Time" to 'Places' flow. This indicates that thinking of time first and then choosing across locations seems more common than thinking of place first and then choosing the time involved. On the other hand, the figure shows more pronounced movements between "People" and "Time" axes across all demographics somewhat indicating that users might be interested in viewing people across time.

6.3 Discussions

6.3.1 Reliving vs. retrieval vs. browsing

We would like to clearly differentiate between the problem focused "reliving on demand" with that of "media management". We consider media (image, video) as simply the portal into the user experience space. Media by itself is uninteresting unless it performs a function (e.g. reliving, sharing) for the human user.

Hence, while information retrieval is a valid problem in different contexts, it is clearly different from our focus. That said, a user can indeed search for certain media content along individual axis of time, location, people and event, or a combination thereof.

Similarly, while browsing has the potential for supporting 'reliving'; it typically occurs piece-meal, in an ad hoc manner. It does not create a holistic media show by combining multiple media elements in an aesthetically pleasing and multimedia enriched manner.

In a sense, reliving is well positioned between retrieval and browsing, and can be tailored towards either need to a large extent. We draw inspiration and support from the classification of users by clarity of their intent as "browsers", "surfers", and "searchers" in [6].

Our user study also indicates that there are different flavors of reliving with different viewers. We are pleased that such behavioral differences validate our design motivations and principles, at the core of which is to put the viewer in the driver's seat so that each individual can achieve a satisfying reliving experience.

6.3.2 Platforms

As we alluded in the introduction, digital reliving takes on all kinds of ubiquitous platforms (web, home, hardcopy) and devices (TV, PC, smart phones, tablets, digital picture frames, kiosks, photobooks). We believe the proposed media reliving system is suitable and adaptable for all of them. In fact, the selection and relative importance of different axes might become an important design consideration in devising both static (e.g. photo-book) and constrained real-estate (e.g. mobile) reliving scenarios.

6.3.3 Accuracy of media processing algorithms

The developed reliving system employs multiple multimedia processing techniques (viz. face detection, face recognition, event clustering, image geo-clustering, aesthetics value prediction) under the hood. These algorithms are not all 100% accurate. However the inaccuracies did not cause any observable disruption to the user experience (none of the 26 participants mentioned any issues with it). This can partially be attributed to the design choice made to focus on relatively robust semantic axes. The three axes of navigation are built on fairly reliable sources– 1) location from reliable clustering of geotags or (user given) folder names; 2) time from reliable camera metadata, 3) face information from reliable face clustering with user verification and labeling.

The underlying event clustering is based on reliable timestamps; and visual aesthetics is a soft factor that adds variety to the presentation. In summary, none of the potential errors would disrupt the user experience because the errors are benign (e.g. a missed face is often unnoticed). More importantly, the user attention is tightly geared to the far more engrossing reliving task rather than any single specific attribute or characteristic.

6.3.4 Relations to social media and cloud computing

We are currently witnessing an explosive growth in number of pictures and media elements being shared online across different media sites. Facebook (which has the strongest social aspect) has more picture uploads than any other site (around 2.4 billion new photo uploads each month). This clearly highlights the importance of social sharing as pivotal to how media will be managed and used in the near future. Similarly, all this data is being made available in the cloud for anybody (with permission), anywhere to access it, thus empowering people to share their multimedia experiences with ease and enjoyment [14].

With all this proliferation and data explosion, the tools which allow users to engage with such media assets would become ever more relevant. We have adopted the approach of doing this based on the fundamental human purpose of media capture; that of reliving it. Our effort is focused on the postulate that the process of reliving would be different for each user with whom this data is shared. People will have different time availability, interest level and primary semantic axes across which they would like to relive these events. Realizing this, to the best of our knowledge, ours is the first attempt at providing the recipients with the flexibility and control to choose their axes, interests, and speed of engagement with the social media shared by others. We see this as providing the very valuable middle ground of user engagement between every-click-browsing and passive slide-show viewing. Our system transforms gracefully into those two extreme cases but also allows the interaction and reliving to occur on demand.

7. CONCLUSIONS AND FUTURE WORK

We have developed and evaluated a novel media reliving system that produces aesthetically appealing and semantically drivable multimedia slide-show based on reliving dimensions of events, people, locations, and time. We allow each viewer to interact with the default presentation to dynamically redirect on the fly the flow of reliving as desired from their individual perspectives. Furthermore, using the logged reliving sessions we have discovered many interesting findings on the reliving needs, behaviors and patterns of different users, validating our design motivations and principles. The patterns learned (e.g. varying importance of people, place, and time based on 1st, 2nd or 3rd party interactions) would provide guidelines for our future versions, as well as potentially for others designing reliving applications. Our studies have confirmed that liberty to navigate along the dimensions of "time, location, and people" and the freedom to change paths as and when desired are essential to *true reliving*, which cannot be currently realized even in state-of-the-art image viewing systems. We strongly believe that the proposed "Reliving on Demand" paradigm will redefine the way people view and experience multimedia in personal and networked environments.

There are a few major improvement opportunities. Users are interested in having the option of using multiple axes to perform search-like functions. The event thumbnails can be made more informative (e.g., mouse-over expansion to multiple samples of an event). Duplicates and duds can be excluded (at least with an option given that detection algorithms can make errors). It may be desirable to tag favorites while reliving (so one can playback all favorites at the end or they can given favorite treatment later on for the same or different viewers). Finally, more data mining and recommendation can be done to further enrich and empower media sharing.

Acknowledgments: We thank the numerous participants who contributed their pictures and time, and provided valuable input.

8. REFERENCES

[1] D. C. A. Bulterman. Using SMIL to encode interactive, peer-level multimedia annotations. *ACM Symposium on Document engineering, 2003.*

[2] L. Cao, J. Luo, A. Gallagher, X. Jin, J. Han, T. S. Huang. A Worldwide Tourism Recommendation System Based on Geotagged Web Photos. *IEEE Int. Conf. on Acoustics, Speech, and Signal Processing*, 2010.

[3] R. G. Cattelan, C. Teixeira, R. Goularte, and M. D. G. C. Pimentel. Watch-and-comment as a paradigm toward ubiquitous interactive video editing. *ACM Trans. Multimedia Comput. Commun. Appl.* 4(4), Article 28, 2008.

[4] J.-C. Chen, W.-T. Chu, J.-H. Kuo, C.-Y. Weng, and J.-L. Wu. Tiling Slideshow. *ACM Int. Conf. on Multimedia*, 2006.

[5] J. Chen, J. Xiao, and Y. Gao. iSlideShow: A Content-aware Slideshow System. *Int. Conf. on Intelligent User Interfaces*, 2010.

[6] R. Datta D. Joshi, J. Li and J.Z. Wang, Image Retrieval: Ideas, Influences, and Trends of the New Age. *ACM Computing Surveys*, 40(2), 2008.

[7] R. Datta and J. Z. Wang. ACQUINE: Aesthetic Quality Inference Engine - Real-time Automatic Rating of Photo Aesthetics. ACM Int. Conf. on Multimedia Information Retrieval, 2010.

[8] J. Huber, J. Steimle, M. Mühlhäuser. Toward More Efficient User Interfaces for Mobile Video Browsing: An In-Depth Exploration of the Design Space. *ACM Int. Conf. on Multimedia*, 2010.

[9] A. Jaimes, D. Gatica-Perez, N. Sebe, and T. Huang. Human-Centered Computing: Toward a Human Revolution. *IEEE Computer*, 40(5), 30-34, 2007.

[10] R. Jain. EventWeb: Events and Experiences in Human Centered Computing. *IEEE Computer*, 2008.

[11] W. Jiang, A.C. Loui, C.D. Cerosaletti. Automatic Aesthetic Value Assessment in Photographic Images. *IEEE Int. Conf. on Multimedia and Expo,* 2010.

[12] Y. Ke, X. Tang, and F. Jing. The Design of High-Level Features for Photo Quality Assessment. *IEEE Int. Conf. on CVPR*, 2006.

[13] A. C. Loui, A. Savakis. Automated Event Clustering and Quality Screening of Consumer Pictures for Digital Albuming. *IEEE Trans. on Multimedia*, 5(3), 2003.

[14] W.-Y. Ma. Rethinking Multimedia Search in the "Clients + Cloud" Era. *ACM Int. Workshop on Large-scale Multimedia Retrieval and Mining*, 2009.

[15] G. Marchionini. Exploratory Search: From Finding to Understanding. ACM Communications, 49(4), 41-46, 2006.

[16] M. Rabbath, P. Sandhus P, S. Boll. Automatic Creation of Photo Books from Stories in Social Media, *ACM Int. Workshop on Social Media*, 2010.

[17] K. Ren, R. Sarvas, and J. Ćalić. Interactive Search and Browsing Interface for Large-scale Visual Repositories, *Multimedia Tools and Applications*, 2010.

[18] Y. Rui, T.S. Huang, and S. Mehrotra. Content-Based Image Retrieval with Relevance Feedback in MARS. *IEEE Int. Conf. Image Processing*, 1997.

[19] A. W. M. Smeulders, M. Worring, S. Santini, A. Gupta, and R. Jain. Content-Based Image Retrieval at the End of the Early Years. *IEEE Trans. Pattern Anal. Mach. Intell.* 22(12), 1349-1380, 2000

[20] C.G.M. Snoek, K.E.A. van de Sande, O. de Rooij, B. Huurnink, E. Gavves, D. Odijk, M. de Rijke, Th. Gevers, M. Worring, D.C. Koelma, A.W.M. Smeulders. The MediaMill TRECVID 2010 Semantic Video Search Engine. *NIST TRECVID Workshop*, 2010.

[21] P. Viola and M. Jones. Rapid Object Detection using a Boosted Cascade of Simple Features. *IEEE Int. Conf. on Computer Vision and Pattern Recognition*, 2001.

[22] J. Xiao, X. Zhang, P. Cheatle, Y. Gao, and C. B. Atkins. Mixed-Initiative Photo Collage Authoring. *ACM Int. Conf. on Multimedia*, 2008.

[23] S. Xu, T. Jin, F. C. M. Lau. Automatic Generation of Music Slide Show Using Personal Photos. *IEEE Int. Symposium on Multimedia*, 2008.

[24] K.-P. Yee, K. Swearingen, K. Li, and M. Hearst. Faceted Metadata for Image Search and Browsing. *ACM SIGCHI Conf. on Human factors in Computing Systems*, 2003.

Bilinear Deep Learning for Image Classification

Sheng-hua Zhong
Department of Computing
The Hong Kong Polytechnic University
Hung Hom, Kowloon
999077 Hong Kong, P. R. China
csshzhong@comp.polyu.edu.hk

Yan Liu
Department of Computing
The Hong Kong Polytechnic University
Hung Hom, Kowloon
999077 Hong Kong, P. R. China
csyliu@comp.polyu.edu.hk

Yang Liu
Department of Computing
The Hong Kong Polytechnic University
Hung Hom, Kowloon
999077 Hong Kong, P. R. China
csygliu@comp.polyu.edu.hk

ABSTRACT
Image classification is a well-known classical problem in multimedia content analysis. This paper proposes a novel deep learning model called bilinear deep belief network (BDBN) for image classification. Unlike previous image classification models, BDBN aims to provide human-like judgment by referencing the architecture of the human visual system and the procedure of intelligent perception. Therefore, the multi-layer structure of the cortex and the propagation of information in the visual areas of the brain are realized faithfully. Unlike most existing deep models, BDBN utilizes a bilinear discriminant strategy to simulate the "initial guess" in human object recognition, and at the same time to avoid falling into a bad local optimum. To preserve the natural tensor structure of the image data, a novel deep architecture with greedy layer-wise reconstruction and global fine-tuning is proposed. To adapt real-world image classification tasks, we develop BDBN under a semi-supervised learning framework, which makes the deep model work well when labeled images are insufficient. Comparative experiments on three standard datasets show that the proposed algorithm outperforms both representative classification models and existing deep learning techniques. More interestingly, our demonstrations show that the proposed BDBN works consistently with the visual perception of humans.

Categories and Subject Descriptors
I.2.0 [**Artificial Intelligence**]: General *–cognitive simulation*;
I.2.6 [**Artificial Intelligence**]: Learning *–connection and neural nets*

General Terms: Algorithm

Keywords: Deep learning, bilinear discriminant projection, image classification.

1. INTRODUCTION
Image classification, a classical problem in multimedia content analysis, aims to understand the semantic meaning of visual information and determine the category of the images according to some predefined criteria [1]. Existing image classification methods can be roughly divided into two broad families of approaches: parametric and nonparametric classifiers. Parametric classifiers, also known as learning-based classifiers, require an intensive training phase of the classifier parameters (e.g., the parameters of SVM [2], Boosting [3], fragments and object parts [4], decision trees [5], web graphs [6], hierarchical classification models [7], etc.). To date, the leading image classifiers are parametric classifiers, particularly SVM-based methods. Nonparametric classifiers make their classification decisions directly on the data, and require no training of parameters [8]. Recently, in the literature on multimedia, many papers focused on the specific applications; for instance, landmark image classification [9], sports genre & view type classification [10], age images classification [11] and affective images classification [12] [13]. In addition, camera metadata are utilized for classification [14].

Despite more than fifteen years of extensive research, image classification for real-world applications remains a well-known challenge in the field of multimedia. But humans, even children, do not have difficulty with classifying images. Before the age of 25 months, children have already developed the ability to recognize novel three-dimensional objects [15]. Motivated by this fact, researchers in the fields of cognitive science and neuroscience have conducted pioneering work on modeling the human brain using computational architectures. Among these computational architectures, deep architecture composed of multiple layers of parameterized nonlinear modules is a representative paradigm that has achieved notable success in modeling the human visual system.

In this paper, we focus on designing a proper deep architecture and corresponding learning algorithms for the tasks of image classification. The latest research results and findings from neuroscience have indicated that the deep model is consistent with the physical structure, evolution of intelligence, and propagation of information in the human visual cortex. Thus, it shows great potential to provide human-like judgment using a human-like system in tasks of multimedia content analysis. The following sections contain a detailed discussion from three aspects:

1) Deep architecture is identical to the multi-layer physical structure of the human visual cortex. The neocortex, which is associated with many cognitive abilities, has a complex multi-layer hierarchy [16]. The laminar structure and a multi-layer illustration of the neocortex are shown in Figure 1. The neocortex can be roughly divided into six functionally distinct layers from Molecular layer I to Multiform layer VI. Layer IV in the primary visual cortex (V1) is further divided into four layers, labeled 4A, 4B, 4Cα, and 4Cβ. Therefore, dozens of cortical layers are involved in generating even the simplest vision [17].

*Area Chair: Nicu Sebe.

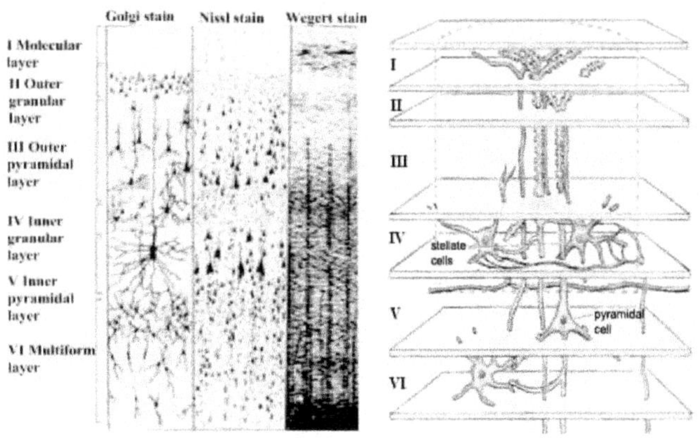

(a)Laminar structure of the neocortex (b) Multi-layer illustration of the neocortex

Figure 1. Multi-layer structure of the cerebral cortex.

2) The development of intelligence follows with the multi-layer structure. From an evolutionary viewpoint, the phylogenetically most recent part of the brain is the neocortex. In humans and other primates, starting from catarhinians, the multi-layers structure began to appear in the neocortex [18]. Therefore, a deep architecture actually represents the result of human intelligence evolution. It thus provides a possible way to achieve the ultimate target of multimedia content analysis, which is to enable the computer to understand images semantically as humans do.

3) The manner in which data is delivered in a deep architecture is a good simulation of the information propagation in the visual cortex. There are several reasons for believing that our visual systems contain multi-layer generative models in which top-down connections can be used to generate low-level features of images from high-level representations, and bottom-up connections can be used to infer the high-level representations that would have generated an observed set of low-level features [19]. Single cell recordings and the reciprocal connectivity between cortical areas [20] both suggest a hierarchy of progressively more complex features in which each layer can influence the layers below it.

From considerations in the field of neuroscience, deep model is chosen in this paper for the task of image classification. To better adapt the image data and the image classification application, we propose a novel deep model called bilinear deep belief network (BDBN) with a new deep architecture and a new deep learning algorithm.

The deep architecture of BDBN is designed by referencing the human visual system and the human procedure of perception. In the primary visual cortex, all the way through the optic tract to a nerve position is a direct correspondence from an angular position in the field of view of the eye, just like a matrix. Therefore, the input layer and all hidden layers in BDBN are constructed by a set of second-order planes, which are also consistent with the natural tensor structure of images. All of these planes are fully connected with the adjacent ones until the output layer, which is a vector to indicate the label of the images.

Based on this new deep architecture, we propose a novel deep learning algorithm with three stages: bilinear discriminant initialization, greedy layer-wise reconstruction, and global fine-turning. The rationale for three-stage learning comes from the phenomenon of two peaks of activation in the visual cortex areas. With regard to object recognition, the early peak is related to the activation of an "initial guess" based on the discriminative knowledge that has been acquired, while the late peak reflects the post-recognition activation of conceptual knowledge related to the recognized object [21]. In most existing deep models, "post activation" is modeled by the fine-tuning stage, but the "initial guess" process is neglected. In our model, two peaks of activation and the propagation of information in the visual cortex are faithfully realized.

We model the peak activation of the "initial guess" by preserving the discriminant information of the labeled data to the greatest extent. Most existing deep models initialize the parameter space in a random manner and gradually approximate a locally optimal solution by learning. Unfortunately, a bad initial parameter space may lead to a poor local optimum and thus seriously affect the following learning procedure. To address this problem, we utilize a bilinear discriminant strategy to construct a second-order plane from the lower layer. The symmetrically weighted connections between these two adjacent layers are used as the initial parameter space for further learning. Moreover, the discriminant-based "initial guess" brings an additional advantage to the meaningful architecture. Currently, the number of neurons in each layer is fixed and pre-defined intuitively. In our model, the size of the deep architecture is determined based on the optimum dimension for retaining the discriminant information.

Last but not least, we develop our deep model under a semi-supervised learning framework because of the insufficiency of the labeled images in real-world applications. However, when relying on the efforts of experienced human annotators, labeled instances are often difficult, expensive, or time consuming to obtain [22]. By contrast, with the growing availability of a large number of images from photo-sharing sites such as Flickr, abundant unlabeled data are available [23].

The remainder of this paper is organized as follows. Related work on deep learning is reviewed in Section 2. A novel deep architecture and a new deep learning algorithm are introduced in Section 3. Section 4 shows the performance of the proposed techniques in real image classification tasks and Section 5 concludes this paper.

2. RELATED WORK ON DEEP LEARNING

Different from shallow learning models, deep learning is about learning multiple levels of representation and abstraction that helps to make sense of data. Besides evidence from neuroscience, some theoretical analyses from machine learning also provide support for the argument that deep models are more compact and expressive than shallow models in representing most learning functions, especially highly variable ones. For example, to model the d-dimensional parity function, Gaussian SVM uses $O(d2^d)$ parameters while deep learning only needs $O(d^2)$ parameters with $O(log_2 d)$ hidden layers [24]. The effectiveness of a deep model makes it promising for use in solving hard learning problems, for example, in semantically identifying the class of images from low-level visual features.

The performance of deep learning has been notable, especially after the introduction of the deep belief networks (DBN) model. The learning procedure of DBN can be divided into two stages: abstracting information layer by layer and fine-tuning the whole deep network to the ultimate learning target [25]. Figure 2 shows a DBN with one input layer H^1, three hidden layers H^2, H^3, H^4, while x is the unfolding vector of input data, and y is the learning target. In the first stage, DBN pairs each feed-forward layer with a feed-back layer that attempts to reconstruct the input of the layer from the output. In Figure 2, the layer-wise reconstruction happens between H^1 and H^2, H^2 and H^3, H^3 and H^4, which is implemented by a family of Restricted Boltzmann Machines (RBMs) [26]. After a greedy unsupervised learning of each pair of layers, the lower-level features are progressively combined into more compact high-level representations. The whole deep network is then refined using a contrastive version of the "wake-sleep" algorithm via a global gradient-based optimization strategy.

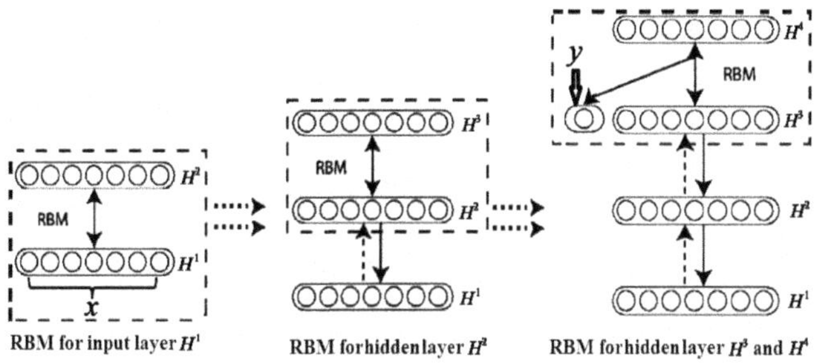

Figure 2. Structure of the deep belief network (DBN).

Owing to this two-stage fast greedy learning, deep learning has also exhibited a notable performance under a situation of insufficient training data [27]. Weston et al. simply leveraged shallow algorithms to deep architecture and already achieved a competitive performance in semi-supervised learning tasks [28]. DBN-rNCA is a semi-supervised learning algorithm that combines DBN architecture and neighborhood component analysis (NCA) techniques for dimensionality reduction [27]. Experimental validations have demonstrated that DBN-rNCA obviously improves the performance of handwritten digit recognition by using abundant unlabeled data. Zhou et al. proposed a new semi-supervised classifier called discriminative deep belief network (DDBN) [29], which integrated the abstraction ability of DBN for unlabeled data and the discriminative ability of the backpropagation strategy for labeled data. Moreover, empirical validations in various real-world applications have shown that DBN performs impressively in analyses of visual data, such as in image classification [27], image annotation [30], and image retrieval [31].

In recent years, deep convolutional architectures have been attracting an increasing amount of attention because of their ability to preserve the space structure and resistance to small variations in the images [32][33]. As early as in 1989, LeCun et al. proposed a convolutional network that used a feature detection layer followed by a feature pooling layer as the basic module, and that was trained to minimize the overall loss for classification [34]. While the convolutional nets are deep, i.e., including a series of multiple detection/pooling modules, they do not seem to suffer from the convergence problems that plague deep fully-connected neural nets [35]. Similar with DBN, deep convolutional network (DCNN) has no distinct feature extractor and classifier. All of the layers in DCNN are trained from data in an integrated fashion. Currently, DCNN has been successfully used to extract spatial features [36] and spatial-temporal features [33] in different applications, such as image classification [6] [37] and human action recognition [38].

3. BILINEAR DEEP LEARNING MODEL

In this section, we propose a novel learning framework based on bilinear deep belief network (BDBN). Our bilinear deep belief network, which is aimed at the task of image classification, is demonstrated in Section 3.1. The bilinear discriminant initialization stage is discussed in Section 3.2. Section 3.3 contains details of the greedy layer-wise reconstruction. The global fine-tuning process of the whole deep network is described in Section 3.4. We provide the procedure of BDBN in Section 3.5.

3.1 Bilinear Deep Belief Network

Let X be a set of data samples as shown below:

$$X = [\mathbf{X}_1, \mathbf{X}_2, ..., \mathbf{X}_k, ..., \mathbf{X}_K] \quad (1)$$

where $\mathbf{X}_k$ is a sample datum in the image space $\mathbb{R}^{I \times J}$ and K is the number of sample data. Let Y be a set of labels corresponding to X, which can be seen as:

$$Y = [\mathbf{y}_1, \mathbf{y}_2, ..., \mathbf{y}_k, ..., \mathbf{y}_K] \quad (2)$$

And $\mathbf{y}_k$ is the label vector of $\mathbf{X}_k$ in $\mathbb{R}^C$, where C is the number of classes.

$$y_k^c = \begin{cases} 1 & \text{if } \mathbf{X}_k \in c\text{th class} \\ 0 & \text{if } \mathbf{X}_k \notin c\text{th class} \end{cases} \quad (3)$$

Based on the given training set, the aim in image classification is to learn a mapping function from the image set X to the label set Y, and then classify the new coming data points according to the learned mapping function.

To address the problem of image classification, we propose a novel bilinear deep learning technique BDBN. Figure 3 shows the architecture of BDBN. A fully interconnected directed belief network includes input layer H^1, hidden layer $H^2, ..., H^N$, and one label layer La at the top. The input layer H^1 has $I \times J$ units, and this size is equal to the dimension of the input features. In our model, we use the pixel values of sample datum $\mathbf{X}_k$ as the original input features. In the top, the label layer has C units, which is equal to the number of classes. The search of the mapping function from X to Y is transformed to the problem of finding the optimum parameter space θ^* for the deep architecture.

The learning procedure of our proposed BDBN is listed below:

1. The strategy of bilinear discriminant projection is utilized to construct a projection to map the original data into a discriminant bilinear subspace.
2. The initial symmetrically weighted connections are constructed between adjacent layers according to the "initial guess" based on the discriminant information. The size of the deep architecture is determined automatically based on the optimum dimension to retain the discriminant information.
3. After the architecture of the next layer is determined, the parameter space is refined by the greedy layer-wise information reconstruction using RBMs as building blocks.
4. Repeat the first to third stages until the parameter space θ in all N layers is constructed.
5. In the "post activation" stage, the whole deep model is fine-tuned to minimize the classification error based on backpropagation.

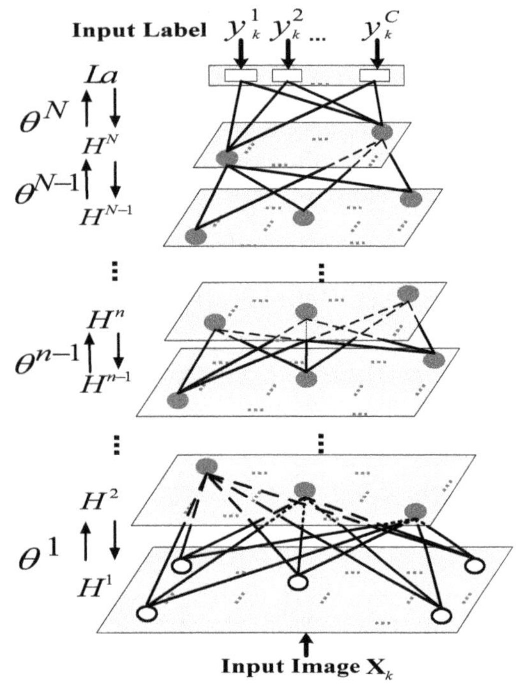

Figure 3. Architecture of the bilinear deep belief network.

3.2 Bilinear Discriminant Initialization

In this subsection, we introduce the bilinear discriminant projection (BDP), which is used to extract the discriminant information from the original image datasets.

Given the labeled training data points $\mathbf{X}_1,\mathbf{X}_2,\ldots,\mathbf{X}_L \in \mathbb{R}^{I\times J}$, without unfolding the input data to vectors, BDP aims to find two projection matrices $\mathbf{U}\in\mathbb{R}^{I\times P}$ and $\mathbf{V}\in\mathbb{R}^{J\times Q}$ such that by $\mathbf{TX}_s=\mathbf{U}^T\mathbf{X}_s\mathbf{V}$ (s = 1, ..., L), just as depicted in Figure 4, the latent representation $\mathbf{TX}_1,\mathbf{TX}_2,\ldots,\mathbf{TX}_L\in\mathbb{R}^{I\times J}$ can be obtained.

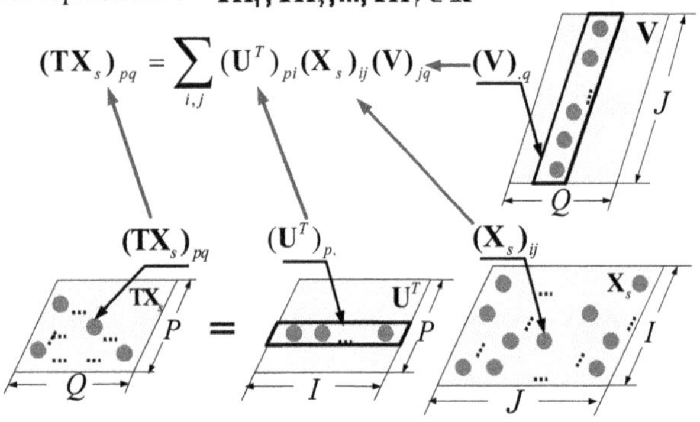

Figure 4. Latent representation with projection matrices U and V.

In order to preserve the discriminant information in the learning procedure, the objective function of BDP could be represented as follows:

$$\arg\max_{\mathbf{U},\mathbf{V}} J(\mathbf{U},\mathbf{V})=\sum_{s,t=1}^{K}\|\mathbf{U}^T(\mathbf{X}_s-\mathbf{X}_t)\mathbf{V}\|^2(\alpha\mathbf{B}_{st}-(1-\alpha)\mathbf{W}_{st})$$
$$s.t.\ \mathbf{U}^T\mathbf{U}=\mathbf{I}_P,\ \ \mathbf{V}^T\mathbf{V}=\mathbf{I}_Q \tag{4}$$

where $\alpha\in[0,1]$ is the parameter used to balance the between-class weights $\mathbf{B}_{st}$ and the within class weights $\mathbf{W}_{st}$, which are defined as follows [39][40]:

$$\mathbf{B}_{st}=\begin{cases}\frac{1}{n_d}-\frac{1}{n_c}, & \text{if } \mathbf{y}_s^c=\mathbf{y}_t^c=1,\\ \frac{1}{n_d}, & \text{else,}\end{cases}\quad,\ \mathbf{W}_{st}=\begin{cases}\frac{1}{n_c}, & \text{if } \mathbf{y}_s^c=\mathbf{y}_t^c=1,\\ 0, & \text{else,}\end{cases} \tag{5}$$

where $\mathbf{y}_s^c$ denotes the class label of datum point $\mathbf{X}_s$, n_d is the number of data points in all classes and n_c is the number of data points in class c, where $c\in\{1,\ldots,C\}$.

By simultaneously maximizing the distances between data points from different classes and minimizing the distances between data points from the same class, the discriminant information is preserved to the greatest extent in the projected feature space. Optimizing $J(\mathbf{U},\mathbf{V})$ is a non-convex optimization problem with respect to the projection matrices $\mathbf{U}$ and $\mathbf{V}$. However, solving $\mathbf{U}$ (or $\mathbf{V}$) with fixed $\mathbf{V}$ (or $\mathbf{U}$) is a convex optimization problem. Let $\mathbf{E}_{st}=\alpha\mathbf{B}_{st}-(1-\alpha)\mathbf{W}_{st}$, with the fixed $\mathbf{V}$. The optimal $\mathbf{U}$ is composed of the first P eigenvectors of the following eigendecomposition problem:

$$\mathbf{D}_\mathbf{V}\mathbf{u}=\lambda\mathbf{u} \tag{6}$$

where $\mathbf{D}_\mathbf{V}=\sum_{st}\mathbf{E}_{st}(\mathbf{X}_s-\mathbf{X}_t)\mathbf{V}\mathbf{V}^T(\mathbf{X}_s-\mathbf{X}_t)^T$. Similarly, with the fixed $\mathbf{U}$, the optimal $\mathbf{V}$ is composed of the first Q eigenvectors of the following eigendecomposition problem:

$$\mathbf{D}_\mathbf{U}\mathbf{v}=\lambda\mathbf{v} \tag{7}$$

where $\mathbf{D}_\mathbf{U}=\sum_{st}\mathbf{E}_{st}(\mathbf{X}_s-\mathbf{X}_t)^T\mathbf{U}\mathbf{U}^T(\mathbf{X}_s-\mathbf{X}_t)$.

Therefore, we can alternately optimize $\mathbf{U}$ (with a fixed $\mathbf{V}$) and $\mathbf{V}$ (with a fixed $\mathbf{U}$). The above steps monotonically increase $J(\mathbf{U},\mathbf{V})$ and since the function is upper bounded, it will converge to a critical point with transformation matrices $\mathbf{U}$, $\mathbf{V}$.

The sizes of P and Q are determined by the number of positive eigenvalues in $\mathbf{D}_\mathbf{V}$ and $\mathbf{D}_\mathbf{U}$, respectively, since adding the eigenvectors corresponding to the nonpositive eigenvalues will not increase $J(\mathbf{U},\mathbf{V})$ in Equation (4). As a result, the original dimension $I\times J$ is automatically reduced into $P\times Q$.

3.3 Greedy Layer-Wise Reconstruction

The sample data set $\mathbf{X}$ is inputted to the deep architecture as the input layer H^1 to construct an RBM with the first hidden layer H^2.

The energy of the state ($\mathbf{h}^1,\mathbf{h}^2$) in the first RBM is:

$$\begin{aligned}&E\left(\mathbf{h}^1,\mathbf{h}^2;\theta^1\right)\\&=-(\mathbf{h}^1\mathbf{A}^1\mathbf{h}^2+\mathbf{b}^1\mathbf{h}^1+\mathbf{c}^1\mathbf{h}^2)\\&=-\sum_{i=1,j=1}^{i\le I,j\le J}\sum_{p=1,q=1}^{p\le P^2,q\le Q^2}h^1_{ij}A^1_{ij,pq}h^2_{pq}-\sum_{i=1,j=1}^{i\le I,j\le J}b^1_{ij}h^1_{ij}-\sum_{p=1,q=1}^{p\le P^2,q\le Q^2}c^1_{pq}h^2_{pq}\end{aligned} \tag{8}$$

where $\theta^1=\left(\mathbf{A}^1,\mathbf{b}^1,\mathbf{c}^1\right)$ are the model parameters between the input layer H^1 and first hidden layer H^2. $A^1_{ij,pq}$ is the symmetric interaction term between the input unit (i,j) in H^1 and the hidden unit (p,q) in H^2. b^1_{ij} is the $(i,j)^{th}$ bias of layer H^1 and c^1_{pq} is the $(p,q)^{th}$ bias of layer H^2. $I \times J$ is the number of units in H^1, while $P^2 \times Q^2$ is the number of units in H^2. Therefore, the first RBM has the following joint distribution:

$$P\left(\mathbf{h}^1,\mathbf{h}^2;\theta^1\right)=\frac{1}{Z}e^{-E\left(\mathbf{h}^1,\mathbf{h}^2;\theta^1\right)}=\frac{e^{-E\left(\mathbf{h}^1,\mathbf{h}^2;\theta^1\right)}}{\sum_{\mathbf{h}^1}\sum_{\mathbf{h}^2}e^{-E\left(\mathbf{h}^1,\mathbf{h}^2;\theta^1\right)}} \quad (9)$$

where Z is the normalization constant. The probability of the model assigned to $\mathbf{h}^1$ in H^1 is:

$$P\left(\mathbf{h}^1\right)=\frac{1}{Z}\sum_{\mathbf{h}^2}e^{-E\left(\mathbf{h}^1,\mathbf{h}^2;\theta^1\right)}=\frac{\sum_{\mathbf{h}^2}e^{-E\left(\mathbf{h}^1,\mathbf{h}^2;\theta^1\right)}}{\sum_{\mathbf{h}^1}\sum_{\mathbf{h}^2}e^{-E\left(\mathbf{h}^1,\mathbf{h}^2;\theta^1\right)}} \quad (10)$$

And the log-likelihood of $P\left(\mathbf{h}^1\right)$ is:

$$\log P\left(\mathbf{h}^1\right)=\log\sum_{\mathbf{h}^2}e^{-E\left(\mathbf{h}^1,\mathbf{h}^2;\theta^1\right)}-\log\sum_{\mathbf{h}^1}\sum_{\mathbf{h}^2}e^{-E\left(\mathbf{h}^1,\mathbf{h}^2;\theta^1\right)} \quad (11)$$

Gibbs sampling from an RBM proceeds by sampling $\mathbf{h}^2$ given $\mathbf{h}^1$, then sampling $\mathbf{h}^1$ given $\mathbf{h}^2$, and so on. The conditional distributions over input state $\mathbf{h}^1$ in layer H^1 and hidden state $\mathbf{h}^2$ in layer H^2 are given by the logistic functions Equation (12) and Equation (13), where $\sigma(x)=\frac{1}{1+\exp(-x)}$.

$$p\left(\mathbf{h}^2\mid\mathbf{h}^1\right)=\prod_{p,q}p\left(h^2_{pq}\mid\mathbf{h}^1\right), p\left(h^2_{pq}=1\mid\mathbf{h}^1\right)=\sigma\left(\sum_{i=1,j=1}^{i\le I,j\le J}h^1_{ij}A^1_{ij,pq}+c_{pq}\right) \quad (12)$$

$$p\left(\mathbf{h}^1\mid\mathbf{h}^2\right)=\prod_{i,j}p\left(h^1_{ij}\mid\mathbf{h}^2\right), p\left(h^1_{ij}=1\mid\mathbf{h}^2\right)=\sigma\left(\sum_{p=1,q=1}^{p\le P^2,q\le Q^2}A^1_{ij,pq}h^2_{pq}+b_{ij}\right) \quad (13)$$

Denote $\mathbf{h}^2(t)$ for the tth of $\mathbf{h}^2$ sample from the chain, starting at $t=0$ with $\mathbf{h}^1(0)$, which is the input observation for the RBM, and $(\mathbf{h}^2(t),\mathbf{h}^1(t))$ for $t\longrightarrow\infty$ is a sample from the Markov chain. Therefore, we can calculate the derivative of Equation (11) with respect to the parameter $\theta^1=\left(\mathbf{A}^1,\mathbf{b}^1,\mathbf{c}^1\right)$ below:

$$\begin{aligned}\frac{\partial\log p(\mathbf{h}^1(0))}{\partial\theta^1}&=-\sum_{\mathbf{h}^2(0)}p(\mathbf{h}^2(0)\mid\mathbf{h}^1(0))\frac{\partial E(\mathbf{h}^2(0),\mathbf{h}^1(0))}{\partial\theta^1}+\\&\sum_{\mathbf{h}^2(t)}\sum_{\mathbf{h}^1(t)}p(\mathbf{h}^2(t),\mathbf{h}^1(t))\frac{\partial E(\mathbf{h}^2(t),\mathbf{h}^1(t))}{\partial\theta^1}\end{aligned} \quad (14)$$

The idea of the Contrastive Divergence [41] algorithm using the difference between two Kullback-Liebler divergences is to take t small (typically $t=1$) to run the chain for only one step. When $t=1$, the derivative to the model parameter $\mathbf{A}^1$ can be obtained by Equation (15),

$$\begin{aligned}&\frac{\partial\log P(\mathbf{h}^1(0))}{\partial\mathbf{A}^1}\\&=-\sum_{\mathbf{h}^2(0)}P(\mathbf{h}^2(0)\mid\mathbf{h}^1(0))\frac{\partial E(\mathbf{h}^2(0),\mathbf{h}^1(0))}{\partial\mathbf{A}^1}+\sum_{\mathbf{h}^2(1)}\sum_{\mathbf{h}^1(1)}P(\mathbf{h}^2(1),\mathbf{h}^1(1))\frac{\partial E(\mathbf{h}^2(1),\mathbf{h}^1(1))}{\partial\mathbf{A}^1}\\&=<\mathbf{h}^1(0)\mathbf{h}^2(0)>_{data}-<\mathbf{h}^1(1)\mathbf{h}^2(1)>_{recon}\end{aligned} \quad (15)$$

where $\langle\cdot\rangle_{data}$ denotes an expectation with respect to the data distribution and $\langle\cdot\rangle_{recon}$ denotes the "reconstruction" distribution of data after one step. This leads to a simple learning rule for performing the stochastic steepest ascent in the log probability of the training data in Equation (16) and Equation (17).

$$A^1_{ij,pq}=\vartheta A^1_{ij,pq}+\Delta A^1_{ij,pq} \quad (16)$$

$$\Delta A^1_{ij,pq}=\varepsilon_{\mathbf{A}}(<h^1_{ij}(0)h^2_{pq}(0)>_{data}-<h^1_{ij}(1)h^2_{pq}(1)>_{recon}) \quad (17)$$

Other parameters in the θ^1 update function can be calculated in a similar manner.

$$b^1_{ij}=\vartheta b^1_{ij}+\Delta b^1_{ij}=\vartheta b^1_{ij}+\varepsilon_{\mathbf{b}}(h^1_{ij}(0)-h^1_{ij}(1)) \quad (18)$$

$$c^1_{pq}=\vartheta c^1_{pq}+\Delta c^1_{pq}=\vartheta c^1_{pq}+\varepsilon_{\mathbf{c}}(h^2_{pq}(0)-h^2_{pq}(1)) \quad (19)$$

where ϑ is the momentum and $\varepsilon_{\mathbf{A}}$, $\varepsilon_{\mathbf{b}}$, $\varepsilon_{\mathbf{c}}$ are the learning rate of model parameters $\mathbf{A}$, $\mathbf{b}$, and $\mathbf{c}$.

As far as we know, all existing deep learning models determine the structure, such as the sizes of the hidden layers, based on intuition. In our proposed model, we intend to provide a more meaningful architecture by integrating the determinative information from labeled data. To integrate discriminative information obtained from bilinear discriminant projection for classification, we have two procedures: determining the sizes of hidden layers and calculating the discriminative initial symmetrically weighted connections.

As described before, we find a bilinear projection that can automatically reduce the original dimension $I\times J$ to $P\times Q$ through the transformation matrices $\mathbf{U}^1$ and $\mathbf{V}^1$. As a result, the number of neurons in layer H^2 is determined by the row and column size of the transformation matrices $\mathbf{U}^1$ and $\mathbf{V}^1$.

$$P^2=row(\mathbf{U}^1),\ Q^2=column(\mathbf{V}^1) \quad (20)$$

Furthermore, in existing deep learning models, the weights of the symmetrical connections $\mathbf{A}$ are initialized to small random values chosen from a zero-mean Gaussian with a standard deviation of about 0.01. Differently from them, we set the discriminative transformation parameters obtained from the bilinear discriminant projection as the initial weights of the symmetrical connections by Equation (21).

$$A^1_{ij,pq}(0)=(\mathbf{U}^1_{ip})^T\mathbf{V}^1_{jq} \quad (21)$$

The above discussion is the greedy layer-wise abstraction for the first layer H^1 with its next adjacent layer H^2. Similar operations can be performed on the higher layer pairs.

3.4 Global Fine-Tuning

Above, we use the greedy layer-by-layer algorithm to learn a deep model with the help of discriminant information obtained from bilinear discriminant projection. In this section, we use backpropagation through the whole deep model to fine-tune the parameters $\theta = [\mathbf{A}, \mathbf{b}, \mathbf{c}]$ for optimal reconstruction.

In the greedy layer-by-layer information abstraction stage, a global search has been performed for a sensible and good region in the whole parameter space. Therefore, before proceeding to the process of fine-tuning, we have already constructed a good data concept extraction model. In our model, backpropagation is utilized to adjust the entire deep network to find good local optimum parameters $\theta^* = [\mathbf{A}^*, \mathbf{b}^*, \mathbf{c}^*]$ to effectively classify the data. In this stage, the learning algorithm is used to minimize the classification error $[-\sum_l \mathbf{y}_l \log \hat{\mathbf{y}}_l]$, where $\mathbf{y}_l$ and $\hat{\mathbf{y}}_l$ are the correct label and the output label value of labeled sample datum $\mathbf{X}_l$ in X^L.

3.5 Bilinear Deep Learning Algorithm

In this section, the detailed procedure of the BDBN is described in Algorithm 1.

Algorithm 1: Bilinear Deep Belief Network

Input: Training data set X, Labeled samples X^L in X
Corresponding labels set Y
Number of layers N, Number of epochs E
Number of labeled data L, Parameter α
Between-class weights $\mathbf{B}_{st}$, Within class weights $\mathbf{W}_{st}$
Initial bias parameters $\mathbf{b}$ and $\mathbf{c}$
Momentum ϑ and learning rate $\varepsilon_{\mathbf{A}}$, $\varepsilon_{\mathbf{b}}$, $\varepsilon_{\mathbf{c}}$

Output: Optimal parameter space $\theta^* = [\mathbf{A}^*, \mathbf{b}^*, \mathbf{c}^*]$

for $n = 1, \ldots, N$ **do**
  for $e = 1, \ldots, E$ **do**
    if $n = 1$
      $T^n = X^L$
    else
      for $l = 1, \ldots, L$ **do**
        $\mathbf{T}_l^n = \sigma(\mathbf{T}_l^{n-1} A^{n-1} + c^{n-1})$
      end for
    end if
    while not convergent **do**
      $\mathbf{D}_V = \sum_{st} \mathbf{E}_{st} (\mathbf{T}_s^n - \mathbf{T}_t^n) \mathbf{V}\mathbf{V}^T (\mathbf{T}_s^n - \mathbf{T}_t^n)^T$
      $\mathbf{D}_U = \sum_{st} \mathbf{E}_{st} (\mathbf{T}_s^n - \mathbf{T}_t^n)^T \mathbf{U}\mathbf{U}^T (\mathbf{T}_s^n - \mathbf{T}_t^n)$
      Fix **V**, compute **U** by solving $\mathbf{D}_V \mathbf{u} = \lambda \mathbf{u}$
      Fix **U**, compute **V** by solving $\mathbf{D}_U \mathbf{v} = \lambda \mathbf{v}$
    end while
    Determine the size of the next layer
    $P^{n+1} = row(\mathbf{U}^n)$, $Q^{n+1} = column(\mathbf{V}^n)$
    Compute initial weights of the connections
    $A^n_{ij,pq}(0) = (\mathbf{U}^n_{ip})^T \mathbf{V}^n_{jq}$
    Calculate the state of the next layer

$$p\left(h^{n+1}_{pq} = 1 \mid \mathbf{h}^n\right) = \sigma\Big(\sum_{i=1,j=1}^{i \le P^n, j \le Q^n} h^n_{ij} A^n_{ij,pq} + c^n_{pq}\Big)$$

$$p\left(\mathrm{h}^n_{ij} = 1 \mid \mathbf{h}^{n+1}\right) = \sigma\Big(\sum_{p=1,q=1}^{p \le P^{n+1}, q \le Q^{n+1}} A^n_{ij,pq} h^{n+1}_{pq} + b^n_{ij}\Big)$$

    Update the weights and biases

$$A^n_{ij,pq} = \vartheta A^n_{ij,pq} + \varepsilon_{\mathbf{A}} (< h^n_{ij}(0) h^{n+1}_{pq}(0) >_{data} - < h^n_{ij}(1) h^{n+1}_{pq}(1) >_{recon})$$

$$b^1_{ij} = \vartheta b^1_{ij} + \varepsilon_{\mathbf{b}} (h^1_{ij}(0) - h^1_{ij}(1))$$

$$c^1_{pq} = \vartheta c^1_{pq} + \varepsilon_{\mathbf{c}} (h^2_{pq}(0) - h^2_{pq}(1))$$

  end for
end for
Calculate optimal parameter space $\theta^* = \arg\min_\theta [-\sum_l \mathbf{y}_l \log \hat{\mathbf{y}}_l]$

4. EXPERIMENTS AND RESULTS

In this section, three standard datasets with different kinds of visual data are used to demonstrate the performance of the proposed BDBN. The first dataset is the Caltech101, a standard dataset for image classification, which includes images of 100 different objects plus a background category [42]. In this paper, we use images from the first five categories. The second dataset is the Urban and Natural Scene. This dataset is composed of 2,688 color images with eight categories [43]. The third dataset is the CMU pose, illumination, and expression (PIE) dataset [44].

For simplicity, we set the balance weight α as 0.5 in our experiments. For parameters such as the learning rate and the momentum in the deep learning model, we simply follow the general setting of previous work on deep learning [45], although a more careful choice may lead to better performance. For example, in greedy layer wise learning, the number of epochs is fixed at 30 and the learning rate η is equal to 0.1.The initial momentum ϑ is 0.5. After five epochs, the momentum is set to 0.9. In the fine-tuning stage, the method of conjugate gradients is utilized and three line searches are performed in each epoch until convergence.

We compare the performance of BDBN with other representative classifiers, including k-nearest neighbor (KNN), support vector machines (SVM) [46], transductive SVM (TSVM) [47], neural network (NN) [48], EmbedNN [28], Semi-DBN [45], DBN-rNCA [27], DDBN [29], and DCNN [37]. KNN, a typical nonlinear classifier, is always used as the baseline for comparisons of performance. In this paper, we set k equal to 3. SVM and NN are two powerful methods of classification. EmbedNN is the semi-supervised version of NN with deep architecture. Semi-DBN, DBN-rNCA, and DDBN are the semi-supervised versions of DBN. As a new deep learning model, DCNN demonstrated great classification ability due to its ability to preserve visual locality and space structure.

4.1 Experiments on Caltech101

In this experiment, we work on the frequently used subset of the Caltech101 [29], which includes 2,935 images from the first five categories: 435 images of ''Faces,'' 435 images of ''Faces_easy,'' 798 images of ''Motorbikes,'' 467 images of ''Back_google,'' and 800 images of ''Airplanes.'' As shown in Figure 5, the images in the same category vary greatly.

Figure 5. Sample images from the dataset Caltech101.

First, we compare the classification accuracy of different methods with a various number of labeled data. Because the number of images in each category in Caltech101 is different, 50 images are randomly selected for each category to form the test set and the rest to form the training set. As the previous setting in [29], the number of labeled data is equal to 5, 25, 50, and 75 per category, respectively. We perform 10 random splits and report the average results over the 10 trials. As shown in Table 1, the performance of BDBN on this dataset is stable and impressive.

Table 1. Classification accuracy rate (%) on the test data with different number of labeled data per category on Caltech101.

Num./Cat.	5	25	50	75
KNN	44.60	58.20	63.20	64.60
SVM	49.80	66.20	67.40	68.20
TSVM	50.00	70.20	70.50	72.80
NN	53.20	64.00	66.80	70.60
EmbedNN	51.20	55.50	58.60	64.00
Semi-DBN	55.40	65.80	67.60	69.60
DBN-rNCA	55.80	64.20	65.40	69.80
DDBN	58.30	71.40	72.00	74.20
DCNN	58.20	70.80	73.40	75.20
BDBN	**61.80**	**71.60**	**75.60**	**78.80**

Then, we compare the convergence of the proposed BDBN with two other deep learning models: Semi-DBN and DDBN, all of which have a fine-tuning stage. Figure 6 shows that BDBN converges much more quickly than Semi-DBN and DDBN. Although they are all deep learning models, BDBN requires an average of 106 iterations in comparison to 290 iterations for Semi-DBN and 161 iterations for DDBN. The improvement comes from the strategy of bilinear discriminant projection. This strategy helps BDBN to achieve a better "initial guess" when constructing the symmetrically weighted connections between layers.

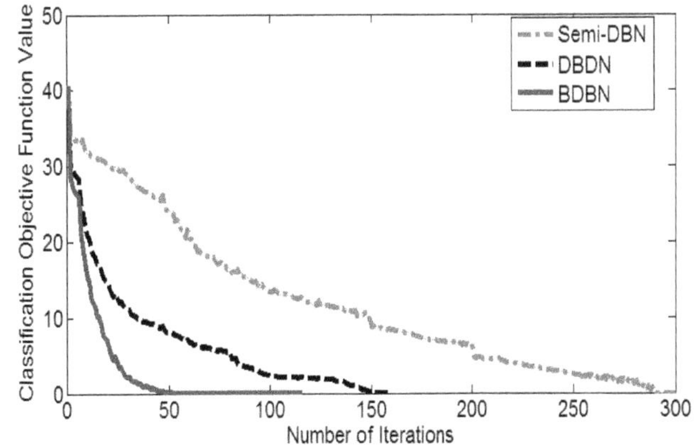

Figure 6. Convergence curve of Semi-DBN, DDBN and BDBN on Caltech 101.

In the third experiment, we visualize the parameter space between the input layer and the first hidden layer of BDBN. Some samples are shown in Figure 7. Obviously, BDBN abstracts the shape information from the training data and delivers it to the deeper layer for the determination of image classes.

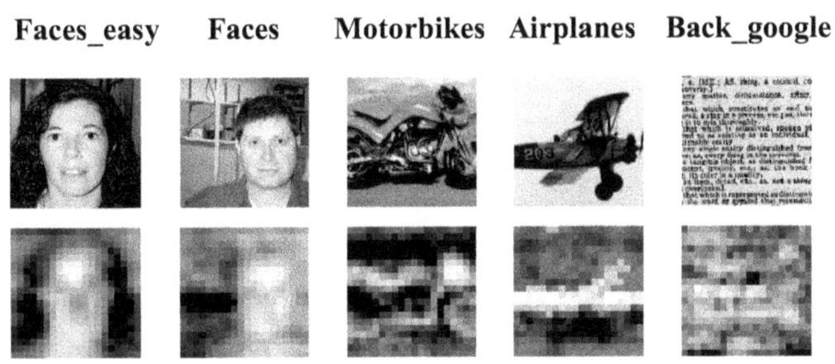

Figure 7. Some samples of parameter space visualization between the input layer and the first hidden layer of BDBN.

4.2 Experiments on Urban and Natural Scene

In this section, we demonstrate the performance of BDBN on the Urban and Natural Scene dataset [43]. This dataset is composed of 2,688 color images with eight categories, namely "coast & beach," "highway," "open country," "tall building," "forest," "street," "mountain," and "city center." In the preprocessing stage, images are downsampled to 32×32 as the input of BDBN. In our experiment, 50 images are randomly selected from each category to form the test set and the rest of the images are used for training. Sample images of each category are shown in Figure 8.

All existing deep learning models determine the structure, such as the sizes of the hidden layers, based on researchers' intuition. In our model, the number of the neurons in each layer can be determined automatically based on bilinear discriminant strategy. Table 2 demonstrates this advantage by comparing the real running time and classification accuracy of BDBN with other five neural networks. The number of labeled data is equal to 5, 25, 50 and 75 per category, respectively. We perform 10 random splits and report the average results over the 10 trials. For BDBN, the number of neurons in layer H^1 is the size of the input image, i.e. 32×32.

Figure 8. Sample images from the Urban & Natural Scene.

The number of neurons in H^2, H^3, H^4 is 24×24, 21×21, and 19×20, respectively. The classical setting of neurons numbers in H^2, H^3, H^4 are 500, 500, and 2000, according to previous publications. The results with different sizes of the deep architecture are provided for the models under comparison. In the table, "_d" is used to represent the compared models with the same size of BDBN, and "_c" is utilized to represent the compared models with the classical sizes. Clearly, BDBN has lower time complexity and better classification accuracy.

In Figure 9, we discuss the limitation of image classification based on visual similarity. Figure 9 (a) is a representative image of "Street", and Figure 9 (b) is a representative image of "Highway". Figure 9 (c) is classified to be "Highway" by BDBN and all other classifiers in this experiment, although the ground-truth of this image is "Street". Only according to visual similarity, Figure 9 (b) and Figure 9 (c) should be grouped together. However, human can give the correct judgment of Figure 9 (c) by referencing the buildings and cars along the street, which is a kind of contextual cueing acquired from past experiences of regularities. We list it as the future work of integrating contextual cueing in the deep modeling.

(a) (b) (c)

Figure 9. Limitation of image classification via visual similarity. (a) A representative image of "Street". (b) A representative image of "Highway". (c) The misclassified image. The ground-truth category of it is "Street" and the misclassified category is "Highway".

4.3 Experiments on CMU PIE

In this part, we demonstrate the performance of BDBN on image dataset of the CMU PIE dataset [44]. The CMU PIE face dataset contains 68 subjects with a total of 41,368 face images. The face images were captured by 13 synchronized cameras and 21 flashes, under varying pose, illumination and expression. As with the general setting of experiments to build the sub dataset [50], we use all the images under different illuminations and expressions with five near frontal poses (C05, C07, C09, C27, C29). In this way, about 170 images with the resolution of 32×32 are obtained for each individual. The preprocessing is applied following the general setting of experiment [50].

In the above experiments, the convolutional deep learning model demonstrates a better performance than other existing deep models. Therefore, in the experiment for dataset PIE, we compare the robustness of our deep model BDBN with that of the convolutional deep model DCNN. For the dataset, 120 images are randomly selected for each person to form the training set and the rest to form the test set. We perform 10 random splits and report the average results over the 10 trials.

First, we compare the influence from different number of labeled data with the same extent of noise. Of the 120 images for each person, different numbers of images are randomly selected and labeled while the others remain unlabeled. The number of labeled

Table 2. Comparisons of run-time (s) and classification accuracy (%) with different labeled numbers and different deep architectures.

Num. / Cat.	5		25		50		75	
	Run-time(s)	Acc.(%)	Run-time(s)	Acc.(%)	Run-time(s)	Acc.(%)	Run-time(s)	Acc.(%)
NN_d	**378**	22.25	1340	30.50	2693	31.50	5796	32.75
NN_c	438	22.50	3602	27.25	6791	30.25	9948	32.50
EmbedNN_d	435	26.75	1373	32.50	2722	35.00	5913	37.50
EmbedNN_c	523	27.50	3702	32.75	6831	36.50	10219	38.25
Semi-DBN_d	769	29.50	1275	33.50	2402	37.25	5945	40.25
Semi-DBN_c	1394	30.50	3467	34.25	7792	37.70	22887	39.50
DBN-rNCA_d	712	29.25	1156	35.25	2209	36.50	5197	41.25
DBN-rNCA_c	1134	30.75	3223	35.25	6565	37.00	18452	42.50
DDBN_d	658	31.25	1051	37.00	2126	41.25	5142	49.20
DDBN_c	1045	32.00	2987	38.25	5292	42.50	16737	51.00
BDBN	392	**35.25**	**963**	**42.50**	**2056**	**50.75**	**5101**	**55.25**

data per subject is equal to 5, 10, 20 and 40. The Gaussian white noise with a mean of 0 and a variance 0.003 is added to the intensity image. According to the average classification results shown in Figure 10 (a), it is obvious that the classification accuracy increases with the number of labeled data. In addition, BDBN exhibits better performance than DCNN under all conditions.

Second, we compare the influence from different extents of noise with same number of labeled data. Here, we fix the number of labeled data per subject to be 10. The variance of Gaussian white noise changes from 0.005 to 0.02. From Figure 10 (b), although the classification accuracy decreases along with the increase of noise in both BDBN and DCNN, our technique performs better. Thus, we are able to conclude that, although DCNN is famously invariant to variations or noises [32][33], our proposed BDBN is more robust than DCNN.

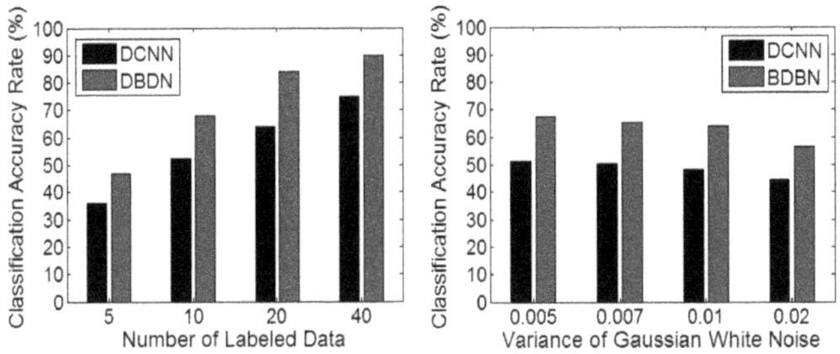

(a) (b)

Figure 10. (a) Classification Accuracy rate (%) with different number of labeled data (b) Classification Accuracy rate (%) with different extents of noise.

Why does BDBN always performs better than DCNN for noisy images? Figure 11 is intended to provide some interpretation from the data reconstruction. The images with Gaussian white noise with a mean of 0 and variance of 0.005 are inputted to BDBN, as shown in the first row. The results of the reconstruction in every layer are shown from the second to the fourth row. It is apparent that, after three layer-wise information reconstructions, the noises have been removed. In addition, the reconstructed images are more similar to the original images shown in the fifth row.

Figure 11. The reconstruction of BDBN in every layer. The first row shows the noisy images. The reconstruction results of every layer are shown from the second to the fourth row. The original images are shown in the fifth row.

5. CONCLUSION AND FUTURE WORK

In this paper, we propose a novel learning model, BDBN for a classical multimedia content analysis task, image classification. BDBN has several attractive characters. First, the novel deep architecture of BDBN simulates the multi-layer physical structure of the visual cortex and enables the preservation of the natural tensor structure of the input image in the information propagation. Second, the three-stage learning of BDBN faithfully realizes the procedure of object recognition by human beings, especially for the "initial guess" part, which has never been modeled in deep learning. Third, the bilinear discriminant initialization of BDBN not only prevents the propagation of information from falling into a bad local optimum but also provides a more meaningful setting for deep architecture. Fourth, the semi-supervised learning ability of BDBN causes the proposed deep techniques to work well with an insufficient number of labeled data. Experiments on three real-world image classification tasks not only show the distinguishing classification ability of BDBN but also clearly demonstrate our intention of providing a human-like image analysis by referencing the human visual system and perception procedure. Future work will be explored from two aspects. The first possible extension is providing more semantic understanding of the images by integrating contextual cueing in deep modeling. The second direction is utilizing deep learning for multimedia content analysis in a large scale dataset with noisy tags.

6. ACKNOWLEDGMENTS

This research was supported by HK PolyU 5245/09E.

7. REFERENCES

[1] F. Moosmann, E. Nowak and F. Jurie, "Randomized Clustering Forests for Image Classification", In *PAMI*, 2008.

[2] A. Kumar , C. Sminchisescu, "Support kernel machines for object recognition", In *ICCV*, 2007.

[3] A. Opelt, M. Fussenegger, A. Pinz, and P. Auer, "Weak hypotheses and boosting for generic object detection and recognition", In *ECCV*, 2004.

[4] J. Yang, K.Yu, Y. Gong, T. Huang, "Linear spatial pyramid matching using sparse coding for image classification", In *CVPR*, 2009.

[5] A. Bosch, A. Zisserman, X. Munoz, "Image classification using random forests and ferns", In *ICCV*, 2007.

[6] D. Mahajan, and M. Slaney, "Image classification using the web graph", In *ACMMM*, 2010.

[7] M.H. Tsai, S.F. Tsai, T.S. Huang, "Hierarchical image feature extraction and classification", In *ACMMM*, 2010.

[8] O. Boiman, E. Shechtman, M. Irani, "In defense of nearest-neighbor based image classification", In *CVPR*, 2008.

[9] X. Xian, C.S. Xu, J.Q. Wang, "Landmark image classification using 3D point clouds", In *ACMMM*, 2010.

[10] L.F. Li, N Zhang, L.Y. Duan, Q.M. Huang, J. Du, L. Guan, "Automatic sports genre categorization and view-type classification over large-scale dataset", In *ACMMM*, 2009.

[11] W.T. Chu, W.L. Liu, J. Y. Yu, "Age classification for pose variant and occluded faces", In *ACMMM*, 2010.

[12] J. Machajdik and A. Hanbury, "Affective image classification using features inspired by psychology and art theory," In *ACMMM*, 2010.

[13] R. Valenti, A. Jaimes, N. Sebe, "Sonify your face: facial expressions for sound generation", In *ACMMM*, 2010.

[14] Z. Li, H.Z. Luo, J.P. Fan, “Incorporating camera metadata for attended region detection and consumer photo classification”, In *ACMMM*, 2009.

[15] G. Wallis, H. Bülthoff, “Learning to recognize objects”, In *Trends. Cogn. Sci,* 1999.

[16] T. Lee, D. Mumford, “Hierarchical Bayesian inference in the visual cortex”, In *JOSAA*, 2003.

[17] G. Leuba, R. Kraftsik, “Changes in volume, surface estimate, 3-dimensional shape and total number of neurons of the human primary visual-cortex from midgestation until old-age”, In *Inat. Embryol.*, 1994.

[18] R. A. Barton, “Neocortex size and behavioural ecology in primates”, In *Royal Society of London*, 1996.

[19] G. E. Hinton, “Learning Multiple Layers of Representation”, In *Trends. Cogn. Sci*, 2007.

[20] D. J. Felleman, D. C. Van Essen, “Distributed hierarchical processing in the primate cerebral cortex”, In *Cereb. Cortex.*, 1991.

[21] R. VanRullen, S. J. Thorpe, "The time course of visual processing: from early perception to decision-making," In *JOCN,* 2001.

[22] X. Zhu, “Semi-supervised learning literature survey,” Technical report 1530, Univ. of Wisconsin-Madison, 2006.

[23] R. Gross, L. Sweeney, F. D. la Torre, S. Baker, “Semi-supervised learning of multi-factor models for face de-identification,” In *CVPR*, 2008.

[24] H. Larochelle, D. Erhan, A. Courville, J. Bergstra, and Y. Bengio, “An empirical evaluation of deep architectures on problems with many factors of variation”, In *ICML*, 2007.

[25] G. E. Hinton, S. Osindero, Y. Teh, “A fast learning algorithm for deep belief nets”, In *Neural Comput.*, 2006.

[26] P. Smolensky, “Information processing in dynamical systems: foundations of harmony theory”, In *Parallel Distributed Processing: Explorations in The Microstructure of Cognition*, vol. 1: Foundations, MIT Press, pp. 194-281, 1986.

[27] R.R. Salakhutdinov, G.E. Hinton, “Learning a nonlinear embedding by preserving class neighbourhood structure”, In *AISTATS*, 2007.

[28] J. Weston, F. Ratle, R. Collobert, “Deep learning via semi-supervised embedding”, In *ICML*, 2008.

[29] S.S. Zhou, Q.C. Chen, and X.L. Wang. "Discriminate Deep Belief Networks for Image Classification", In *ICIP*, 2010.

[30] Z. Wang, D. Xia, E.Y. Chang, “A deep-learning model-based and data-driven hybrid architecture for image annotation”, In *VLS-MCMR, ACM*, 2010.

[31] E. Hörster, and R. Lienhart, “Deep networks for image retrieval on large-scale databases”, In *ACMMM*, 2008.

[32] H. Lee, R. Grosse, R. Ranganath, A.Y. Ng, “Convolutional deep belief networks for scalable unsupervised learning of hierarchical representations”, In *ICML*, 2009.

[33] G. Taylor, R. Fergus, Y.L. Cun and C. Bregler, “Convolutional learning of spatio-temporal features,” In *ECCV*, 2010.

[34] Y.L. Cun, B. Boser, J.S. Denker, D. Henderson, R.E. Howard, W. Hubbard, L.D. Jackel, “Backpropagation applied to handwritten zip code recognition,” In *Neural Comput.*, 1989.

[35] Y. Bengio, and Y.L. Cun, “Scaling Learning Algorithms towards AI,” In *Large-Scale Kernel Machines*, 2007.

[36] R. Memisevic, G.E. Hinton, “Learning to represent spatial transformations with factored higher-order Boltzmann machines,” In *Neural Comput.*, 2010.

[37] K. Jarrett, K. Kavukcuoglu, M. Ranzato, and Y.L. Cun, “What is the best multi-stage architecture for object recognition?”, In *ICCV*, 2009.

[38] S. Ji, W. Xu, M. Yang, K. Yu, “3D convolutional neural networks for human action recognition,” In *ICML*, 2010.

[39] S. Yan, D. Xu, B. Zhang, H.J. Zhang, Q. Yang and S. Lin, “Graph embedding and extension: a general framework for dimensionality reduction”, In *PAMI*, 2007.

[40] M. Sugiyama, “Dimensionality reduction of multimodal labeled data by local fisher discriminant analysis”, In *JMLR*, 2007.

[41] G.E. Hinton, “Training products of experts by minimizing contrastive divergence”, In *Neural Comput.*, 2002.

[42] F.F. Li, R. Fergus, P. Pernoa, “Learning generative visual models from few training examples: an incremental Bayesian approach tested on 101 object categories”, In *CVPR* , 2004.

[43] A. Oliva and A. Torralba, “Modeling the shape of the scene: A holistic representation of the spatial envelope, ” In *IJCV*, 2001.

[44] T. Sim, S. Baker, “The CMU pose, illumination, and expression database”, In *PAMI*, 2003.

[45] Y. Bengio, P. Lamblin, D. Popovici, H. Larochelle, “Greedy layer-wise training of deep networks”, In *NIPS*, 2006.

[46] B. E. Boser, I. M. Guyon, and V. N. Vapnik, “A training algorithm for optimal margin classifiers”, In *COLT*, 1992.

[47] R. Collobert, F. Sinz, J. Weston, L. Bottou, “Large scale transductive SVMs, In *JMLR*”, 2006.

[48] T.M. Mitchell, “Machine Learning”, 1997.

[49] Y. Lecun, L. Bottou, Y. Bengio and P. Haffner. “Gradient-based learning applied to document recognition,” In *Proceedings of the IEEE,* pp. 2278-2324, 1998.

[50] X.F. He, D. Cai, and P. Niyogi, “Tensor subspace analysis”, In *NIPS*, 2005.

Retrieval-based Face Annotation by Weak Label Regularized Local Coordinate Coding *

Dayong Wang†, Steven C.H. Hoi†, Ying He†, Jianke Zhu‡
†School of Computer Engineering, Nanyang Technological University, Singapore.
‡College of Computer Science, Zhejiang University, Hangzhou, 310027, China.
{s090023, chhoi, yhe}@ntu.edu.sg, jkzhu@zju.edu.cn

ABSTRACT

Retrieval-based face annotation is a promising paradigm in mining massive web facial images for automated face annotation. Such an annotation paradigm usually encounters two key challenges. The first challenge is how to efficiently retrieve a short list of most similar facial images from facial image databases, and the second challenge is how to effectively perform annotation by exploiting these similar facial images and their weak labels which are often noisy and incomplete. In this paper, we mainly focus on tackling the second challenge of the retrieval-based face annotation paradigm. In particular, we propose an effective Weak Label Regularized Local Coordinate Coding (WLRLCC) technique, which exploits the local coordinate coding principle in learning sparse features, and meanwhile employs the graph-based weak label regularization principle to enhance the weak labels of the short list of similar facial images. We present an efficient optimization algorithm to solve the WLRLCC task, and develop an effective sparse reconstruction scheme to perform the final face name annotation. We conduct a set of extensive empirical studies on a large-scale facial image database with a total of $6,000$ persons and over $600,000$ web facial images, in which encouraging results show that the proposed WLRLCC algorithm significantly boosts the performance of the regular retrieval-based face annotation approaches.

Categories and Subject Descriptors

H.3.3 [**Information Storage and Retrieval**]: Information Search and Retrieval; I.2.6 [**Artificial Intelligence**]: Learning

General Terms

Algorithms, Experimentation

Keywords

web facial images, auto face annotation, unsupervised learning

1. INTRODUCTION

In the digital era today, people can easily capture a photo by all kinds of digital devices, and share it through the internet by various online tools, such as web photo sharing portals (e.g., Flickr) or social networks (e.g., Facebook). Among vast digital images and photos shared on the internet, a considerable amount of them are related to human facial images because they are closely related to social activities of human beings. The rapid growth of facial images has created many research problems and opportunities for a variety of real-world applications. An important technique in this area is *automated face annotation*, which aims to tag human names to a novel unlabeled facial image automatically.

Auto face annotation is beneficial to a number of real-world applications. For example, using auto face annotation techniques, online photo sharing sites or social networks can automatically annotate users' uploaded photos to facilitate online photo search and management tasks. Auto face annotation can also be applied in news video domain to detect important persons appeared in the videos to facilitate news video retrieval and summarization tasks.

Typically, face annotation is formulated as an extended face recognition problem, in which face classification models are trained from a collection of well-controlled labeled facial images using supervised machine learning techniques [3, 25, 38, 41, 44]. Such approaches are referred to as "model-based face annotation" techniques. Despite being studied extensively, they suffer from several common drawbacks. First, it is usually time-consuming and expensive to collect a large amount of human-labeled training facial images. Second, it is difficult to generalize the models when new training data or novel persons are added, in which an intensive re-training process is usually required. Last but not least, the annotation or recognition performance often scales poorly when the number of persons/classes is very large.

Recent studies [33] have attempted to explore a promising retrieval-based annotation paradigm for facial image annotation by mining the world wide web (WWW), where a mass number of weakly labeled facial images are freely available. Instead of training explicit classification models by the regular model-based face annotation approaches, the retrieval-based face annotation (RBFA) paradigm aims to tackle the automated face annotation task by exploiting content-based image retrieval (CBIR) techniques [27, 37] in mining massive weakly labeled facial images on the web. Such a paradigm was somewhat inspired by the search-based image annotation techniques [34] for generic image annotation since face annotation can be generally viewed as a sub-problem of generic image annotation [10, 11, 29, 32, 36], which has been extensively studied but remains a very challenging open problem.

In general, there are two main challenges faced by the emerging retrieval-based face annotation (RBFA) technique. The first challenge is how to efficiently retrieve a short list of most similar facial images from a large facial image database, which typically relies on an effective content-based facial image retrieval solution. The

*Area chair: Lexing Xie

MM'11, November 28–December 1, 2011, Scottsdale, Arizona, USA.

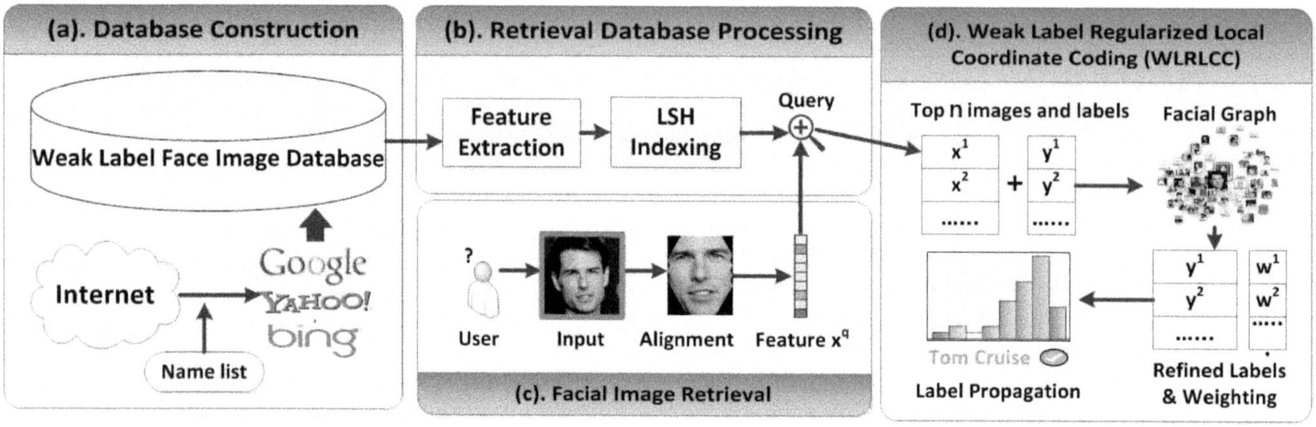

Figure 1: The system flow of the Retrieval-based Face Annotation (RBFA) scheme. (a) We collect weakly-labeled facial images from WWW using a web search engine; (b) We perform face detection and alignment, then extract GIST features from the detected faces, and finally apply LSH [9] to index the high-dimensional facial features; (c) A query facial image uploaded by the user is transformed into a feature vector with the same preprocessing step; using our content-based facial image retrieval engine, a short list of top-n most similar facial images and their associated names are retrieved and passed to the next learning and annotation stage; (d) The proposed WLRLCC scheme is applied to return the final list of (ranked) annotated face names.

second challenge is how to effectively exploit the short list of candidate facial images and their weak label information for the face name annotation task, which is critical because the associated labels of web facial images are often noisy and incomplete due to the nature of web images.

In this paper, we investigate the retrieval-based face annotation scheme by mainly addressing the second challenge. In particular, we propose a novel Weak Label Regularized Local Coordinate Coding (WLRLCC) technique to tackle the retrieval-based face annotation problem, which attempts to boost the annotation performance by a unified learning scheme, which exploits the local coordinate coding in achieving more effective features and makes use of the graph-based regularization to enhance the weak label simultaneously. In particular, given a query facial image for annotation, we firstly search for a short list of top-n most similar facial images from a weakly labeled web facial image database. After that, we apply the proposed WLRLCC algorithm to obtain a more discriminative local coordinate coding representation and an enhanced label matrix as well. Finally, we apply an effective sparse reconstruction scheme for the final facial name annotation. As a summary, the main contributions of this paper include:

- We propose a novel Weak Label Regularized Local Coordinate Coding (WLRLCC) technique, which constructs an effective sparse coding and enhances the weak label by exploiting both the local coordinate coding and graph-based weak label regularization principles.
- We propose an efficient algorithm to solve the proposed WLRLCC problem, and conduct extensive experiments to evaluate the proposed algorithm for automated face annotation on a large-scale web facial image database.

The rest of this paper is organized as follows. Section 2 reviews related work. Section 3 briefly introduces the proposed retrieval-based face annotation (RBFA) framework. Section 4 presents the proposed Weak Label Regularized Local Coordinate Coding (WLRLCC) scheme together with an effective face name annotation solution based on sparse reconstruction. Section 5 shows the experimental results of our empirical studies. Finally, Section 6 discusses the limitations, and Section 7 concludes this paper.

2. RELATED WORK

Our work is closely related to several groups of research work.

The first group is the studies of face detection, verification, and recognition. Comprehensive surveys on such topics can be found in [42, 14]. Although traditional face recognition methods can be extended for auto face annotation, they usually suffer from some common drawbacks. For example, they often require high-quality facial image databases collected in well-controlled environments. This drawback has been partially improved by some recent work on benchmark studies of unconstrained face detection and verification techniques on facial images collected from the web, such as the LFW benchmark [16, 21, 4]. However, traditional face recognition techniques have to train explicit classification models, which usually scale poorly when the number of persons/classess is large and are nontrivial to re-train the models when adding new training data or additional persons.

The second group is the studies of face annotation on collections of personal/family photos. Several studies [30, 7, 8] have mainly focused on the annotation task on collections of personal/family photos, which often contain rich context clues, such as personal/family names, social context, GPS tags, timestamps, etc. In addition, the number of persons/classess is usually quite small, making such annotation tasks less challenging. These techniques usually achieve fairly impressive annotation results, and some techniques have been successfully deployed in commercial applications, e.g., Apple iPhoto and Microsoft easyAlbum [8].

The third group is the studies of face annotation in mining weakly labeled facial images on the web. Some studies consider a human name as the input query, and mainly aim to refine the text-based search results by exploiting visual consistency of facial images, which is closely related to automatic image re-ranking problems. For example, [22] proposed a graph-based model for finding the densest sub-graph as the most related result. Le and Satoh [17] proposed a new local density score to represent the importance of each returned images. Unlike these studies of filtering the text-based retrieval results, some studies have attempted to directly annotate each facial image with the names extracted from its caption information. For example, [2] proposed a possibility model combined with a clustering algorithm to estimate the relationship between the facial images and the names in their captions. Finally, our work is closely related to some recent studies on the retrieval-based face annotation paradigm [33], which have attempted to attack the automated face annotation problem by exploiting content-based facial image retrieval techniques in mining web facial images. Some recent work [37] mainly addressed the first challenge of the RBFA paradigm, in which an effective image representation has been proposed by employing both the local and global features. Another recent work is the unsupervised label refinement (ULR) technique in [33] to address the second challenging problem where the initial weak label is enhanced by mining the facial graph information over the whole retrieval database. The work in the paper differs from the ULR scheme in several aspects. First, the ULR scheme is difficult to handle huge databases due to its high computational cost, while the proposed WLRLCC algorithm is applied only to a short list of most similar images. Second, the simple majority voting scheme of the ULR scheme might not be effective enough in exploiting the short list of most similar images; in contrast, the proposed WLRLCC algorithm comprehensively resolves this problem by fully exploiting the short list of top similar images via a unified optimization scheme of learning both sparse features and enhanced labels.

The fourth group is the studies of generic image annotation. The commonly studied techniques usually apply existing object recognition techniques to train classification models from human-labeled training images or attempt to infer the correlations probabilities between query images and annotation keywords [10, 11, 5, 13]. In recent years, the search-based image annotation paradigm in mining web images has attracted more and more research attention [34, 24, 31, 23]. Some studies in this area have attempted to develop efficient content-based indexing and searching techniques to facilitate the annotation/recognition tasks. For example, Russell et al. [24] developed a large collection of web images with ground truth labels to facilitate object recognition research. Wang et al. [34] proposed an efficient search-based annotation scheme for auto image annotation by combining both textural and visual information. There are also some studies that aim to address the final annotation process with effective label propagation. For example, Wright et al. [35] proposed a classification algorithm based sparse representation, which predicts the label information based on the class-based feature reconstruction. Tang et al. [29] presented a sparse graph-based semi-supervised learning (SGSSL) approach to annotate web images. Wang et al. [32] proposed another sparse coding based annotation framework (MSR), where the label-based graph is used to learn a linear transformation matrix for feature dimension reduction, and sparse reconstruction is employed for the subsequent label propagation step. Wu et al. [36] proposed to select heterogeneous features with structural Grouping Sparsity and suggested a Multi-label Boosting scheme (MtBGS) for feature regression, in which a group sparse coefficient vector is achieved for each class (category) and further used for predicting new instances. Wu et al. [37] proposed a multi-reference re-ranking (MRR) scheme for improving the retrieval process.

Finally, we note that the proposed learning methodology for WLRLCC is partially inspired by some existing works in machine learning, including local coordinate coding [40, 15], graph-based semi-supervised learning [45, 6] and multi-label learning [28].

3. RETRIEVAL-BASED FACE ANNOTATION FRAMEWORK

In this section, we briefly introduce the proposed Retrieval-based Face Annotation (RBFA) paradigm. Figure 1 illustrates the proposed framework, which consists of the following four major stages: (i) data collection of facial images from WWW, (ii) facial image preprocessing and high-dimensional facial feature indexing, (iii) content-based facial image retrieval for a query facial image, (iv) face annotation by the proposed Weak Label Regularized Local Coordinate Coding (WLRLCC) algorithm. The details of each stage are described as follows.

The first stage, as shown in Figure 1(a), is to collect a database of weakly labeled facial images, which can be crawled from WWW. In particular, we can choose a list of desired human names and submit them to existing web search engines (e.g., Google) for crawling their related web facial images. As the output of this crawling process, we obtain a collection of web facial images, each of them is associated with some human names. Given the nature of web images, these facial images are usually noisy, which may be incorrect or incomplete. We thus refer to such web facial images with noisy names as weakly labeled facial images.

The second stage, as shown in Figure 1(b), is to pre-process the weakly label facial image database, including face detection, face alignment, facial feature representation, and high dimension feature indexing. For facial region detection and alignment, we adopt OpenCV and the unsupervised face alignment technique proposed in [43]. For facial feature representation, we extract the GIST features [26] to represent the extracted facial regions. Finally, we apply the Locality-Sensitive Hashing (LSH) [9] to index the GIST features in our solution.

The previous two stages must be done before annotating a query facial image. The next two stages are related to online processes of annotating a query facial image. As shown in Figure 1(c), given a query facial image, we conduct a similar face retrieval process to find a short list of most similar faces (e.g., top-n similar faces) from the indexed face databases using the LSH technique.

After obtaining the top-n most similar faces, the last stage is to apply the proposed Weak Label Regularized Local Coordinate Coding (WLRLCC) algorithm for name annotation, as shown in Figure 1(d). Specifically, the proposed WLRLCC algorithm learns local coordinate coding for each of the similar facial images and enhances the weak label matrix via an iterative optimization process. Based on the learning results, a sparse reconstruction algorithm is applied to perform the final face name annotation. Next we present the details of the proposed WLRLCC technique.

4. WEAK LABEL REGULARIZED LOCAL COORDINATE CODING (WLRLCC)

In this section, we present the proposed Weak Label Regularized Local Coordinate Coding algorithm for the face annotation task based on a list of top-n most similar facial images. We first introduce some preliminaries and notations, followed by the problem formulation and the proposed algorithms, respectively. Finally, we discuss the sparse reconstruction method for the final name annotation.

4.1 Preliminaries

Consider a query facial image $x^q \in \mathbb{R}^d$, a d-dimension feature vector with some unknown class label denoted as y^q. The goal of a retrieval-based face annotation task is to estimate y^q based on the retrieval result from a large facial image database. Assume the short list of top-n most similar facial images to x^q are $\{(x^i, y^i)_{i=1}^n\}$, where $y^i \in \{1, 2, \ldots, m\}$ is the name label of its corresponding facial image x^i, and m is the total number of classes (names) among all the top-n facial images.

Let us denote by the feature matrix of the retrieval results $X =$

$[x^1, x^2, \ldots, x^n]$. We represent the initial name information with a class-membership-indicator matrix $\tilde{Y} \in \mathbb{R}^{n\times m}$, where $\tilde{Y}_{i\star}$, the i-th row of matrix, denotes the class label vector for x^i, $\tilde{Y}_{ij} = 1$ if $j = y^i$, and $\tilde{Y}_{ij} = 0$ otherwise. Due to the nature of web images, the initial "weak" label information $\tilde{Y}$ is often noisy and incomplete. Thus, it is critical to find some effective solution to enhance the initial weak label information. Finally, it is common to know that facial images usually follow some manifold structure, which motivates us to apply the local coordinate coding [40] to find a more effective sparse representation.

4.2 Problem Formulation

4.2.1 *Sparse Features via Local Coordinate Coding*

Sparse representation has been successfully applied in many applications, e.g., face recognition [35], graph construction [29], and feature selection [36], etc. Let us denote by $x \in \mathbb{R}^d$ some observed feature vector for reconstruction, and consider an under-determined system of linear equation as follows:

$$x = [D, I]\begin{bmatrix} s \\ \xi \end{bmatrix} = D \cdot s + I \cdot \xi,$$

where D is the overcomplete dictionary, I is an identity matrix, and ξ is a noise term. If the solution s is sparse enough, it should be recovered by solving the following convex optimization problem:

$$\min_{[s;\xi]} \sigma_{\text{SC}}([s;\xi]), \quad \text{s.t.} \quad x = D\cdot s + I \cdot \xi \tag{1}$$

where the sparsity penalty function is defined as $\sigma_{\text{SC}}(\cdot) = \|\cdot\|_1$. We can apply the same idea to reconstruct the sparse representation s^i of the i-th facial image x^i in the top-n retrieval results based on the dictionary $B = [X, I] \in \mathbb{R}^{d\times(n+d)}$ as follows:

$$\hat{s}^i = \arg\min_{\hat{s}} \frac{1}{2}\|x^i - B\hat{s}\|^2 + \lambda \cdot \sigma_{\text{SC}}(\hat{s}), \text{ s.t. } \hat{s}_i = 0 \tag{2}$$

where $\hat{s}^i = [s^i; \xi^i]$, s^i is the sparse coding of x^i, and ξ^i is the coefficient related to the noise of the facial image. The constraint $\hat{s}_i = 0$ is to avoid using x^i itself for reconstruction.

Following the Local Coordinate Coding (LCC) [40], it is important to exploit the locality information for the linear embedding of high dimensional data on the manifold. In contrast to traditional sparse coding, the intuition of LCC is to assign a larger coefficient to the dictionary item that is closer to the encoding item. Specifically, instead of adopting the sparsity term $\sigma_{\text{SC}}(\hat{s})$ directly, a locality weight is assigned to each element in $\hat{s}$. Thus, the regularizer of LCC is formulated as follows:

$$\sigma_{\text{LCC}}(\hat{s}) = \sum_{k=1}^{n+d} |\hat{s}_k| \cdot \|B_{\star k} - x^i\|^2 \tag{3}$$

where $B_{\star k}$ is the k-th column of dictionary B, and $\hat{s}_k$ is the k-th element of $\hat{s}$.

The regularizer $\sigma_{\text{LCC}}(\hat{s})$ in LCC has a close relationship with the non-negative sparse coding (NNSC) [15], in which all the elements in $\hat{s}$ are forced to be non-negative:

$$\sigma_{\text{NNSC}}(\hat{s}) = \sum_k \hat{s}_k, \text{ s.t. } \hat{s} \geq 0 \tag{4}$$

In the above regularizer, because of the non-negative constraint, a dictionary item that is close to the input item x^i (i.e., small $\|B_{\star k} - x^i\|^2$) is more likely to be active (nonzero) in NNSC, which in some sense is similar to LCC. By this motivation, we propose to combine the two regularizers to strengthen the locality constraint, which will also simplify our optimization problem. As a result, we can reformulate the optimization of learning the sparse representation for x^i as follows:

$$\begin{aligned} e(\hat{s}; x^i) = \min_{\hat{s}} \frac{1}{2}\|x^i - B\hat{s}\|^2 + \lambda \sum_{k=1}^{n+d} \hat{s}_k \cdot \|B_{\star k} - x^i\|^2 \\ \text{s.t. } \hat{s}_k \geq 0, k = 1, 2, \ldots, n+d \text{ and } \hat{s}_i = 0. \end{aligned} \tag{5}$$

Finally, we can give the formulation of the non-negative local coordinate coding problem for all the facial images in the top-n retrieval results:

$$E_1(\hat{S}; X) = \sum_{i=1}^{n} e(\hat{s}; x^i). \tag{6}$$

where $\hat{S} \in \mathbb{R}^{(n+d)\times n} = [S; \Xi]$, $S \in \mathbb{R}^{n\times n}$ is the local coordinate coding of X, and $\Xi \in \mathbb{R}^{d\times n}$ is the noise matrix.

4.2.2 *Weak Label Enhancement*

The previous formulation shows that the j-th local sparse coefficient s_j^i of facial image x^i essentially encodes the locality information between x^i and $x^j, j \neq i$. Specifically, a larger value of s_j^i indicates that x^j is more representative of x^i, i.e., having a larger contribution to the reconstruction of x^i. In addition, from a view of graph-based semi-supervised learning, for any two facial images, the smaller their local distance, the more likely they should belong to the same person. As a result, a larger value of s_j^i implies that the name labels of x^i and x^j are more likely to be the same.

Based on the above motivation, we can give the following formulation to enhance the initial weak label matrix $\tilde{Y}$ as follows:

$$E_2(Y, S) = \min_{Y\geq 0} \frac{1}{2}\sum_{i,j} s_j^i \|Y_{i\star} - Y_{j\star}\|^2 + \lambda\|(Y - \tilde{Y})\circ M\|_{\text{F}}^2 \tag{7}$$

M is a "sign" matrix $M = [sign(\tilde{Y}_{ij})]$ where $sign(x) = 1$ if $x > 0$ and 0 otherwise, and $\circ$ denotes the Hadamard product of two matrices. In the above objective function, the first term enforces that the class labels of two facial images x^i and x^j to be similar if the local sparse coefficient s_j^i is large, and the second term is a regularization term that prevents the refined label matrix being deviated too much from the initial weak matrix. Since the initial label matrix is noisy and incomplete, we apply the regularization of the second term on only these nonzero elements in $\tilde{Y}$.

In general, the optimal solution to the problem in Eq. (7) is dense; however, the ideal true label matrix is often very sparse. Following the suggestion in [33], we introduce some convex sparsity constraints to take into the consideration of sparsity, i.e., $\|Y_{i\star}\|_1 \leq \varepsilon, \varepsilon \geq 1$, where $i = 1, 2, \ldots, n$ (we choose $\varepsilon = 1$ in this work). These constraints are included to limit the number of name labels assigned to each facial image.

4.2.3 *Weak Label Regularized Local Coordinate Codin*

The above two optimization tasks of "sparse feature learning" and "label enhancement" are performed separately. In particular, the sparse features S are first learned from the optimization in Eq. (5), and then used by the optimization in Eq. (7) to refine the label matrix Y. To better exploit the potential of the two learning approaches, we propose the Weak Label Regularized Local Coordinate Coding (WLRLCC) scheme, which aims to reinforce the two learning tasks via a unified optimization framework. Specifically, the optimization of WLRLCC can be formulated as follows:

$$Q(\hat{S},Y) = E_1(\hat{S};X) + E_2(Y,S) = \min_{\hat{S},Y} \frac{1}{2}\|B\hat{S} - X\|_F^2 + \lambda_1 tr(\mathbf{1}\cdot(\hat{S}\circ V)) + \lambda_2 tr(Y^\top LY) + \lambda_3\|(Y-\tilde{Y})\circ M\|_F^2 \quad \text{s.t. } \hat{S}_{ii}=0, \|Y_{i\star}\|_1 \le 1, i=1,2,\ldots,n,\ \hat{S}\ge 0, Y\ge 0 \tag{8}$$

where $V \in \mathbb{R}^{(n+d)\times n}$, $V_{ij} = \|B_{\star i} - X_{\star j}\|^2$, $L = D - S$, D is a diagonal matrix, with $D_{ii} = \frac{\sum S_{i\star}+\sum S_{\star i}}{2}$, $Y \in \mathbb{R}^{n\times m}$, $\mathbf{1}$ is all-one-element matrix with dimension $n \times (n+d)$, $\circ$ denotes the Hadamard product of two matrices, and $tr(\cdot)$ denotes a trace function. In the above, $\lambda_2 tr(Y^\top LY)$ is a label smoothness regularizer which connects between the label matrix and the sparse features.

Remark. Although WLRLCC is similar to some existing sparse representation schemes, it differs from the existing approaches in two major aspects. First, instead of using the traditional sparse representation for semantic graph construction, a non-negative local coordinate coding algorithm is adopted, which exploits the advantages of both NNSC [15] and LCC [40]. Second, WLRLCC employs a unified optimization scheme to solve both sparse feature learning and label enhancement in an iterative approach; as a result, the enhanced label information is also exploited by the sparse coding step, which in some sense becomes a weakly supervised sparse learning approach while traditional sparse coding is often unsupervised.

4.3 Optimization

The optimization problem in Eq. (8) is generally non-convex. To solve this challenging optimization, we propose to solve $\hat{S}$ and Y alternatively by iteratively solving two optimization steps: (1) *Code Learning*, and (2) *Label Learning*. The step of updating $\hat{S}$ can be transformed into a weighted non-negative sparse coding problem, and the step of updating Y is a quadratic programming problem.

4.3.1 Code Learning

By first fixing the label matrix Y and ignoring the constant terms, the optimization problem in Eq. (8) can be reformulated as follows:

$$Q_Y(\hat{S}) = \min_{\hat{S}} \frac{1}{2}\|B\hat{S} - X\|_F^2 + tr(\mathbf{1}\cdot(\hat{S}\circ Z)) \quad \text{s.t. } \hat{S}_{ii}=0, i=1,2,\ldots,n, \text{and } \hat{S}\ge 0 \tag{9}$$

where $Z = \lambda_1 V + \lambda_2 U$, $U \in \mathbb{R}^{(n+d)\times n}$, for all $j=1,2,\ldots,n$, if $i \le n$, $U_{ij} = \frac{1}{2}\|Y_{i\star} - Y_{j\star}\|^2$; otherwise $U_{ij} = 0$. The other variables follow the same definitions in Eq.(8).

The optimization problem in Eq. (9) can be further separated into a series of sub-problems for each coding coefficient $\hat{S}_{\star i}$ of facial image $X_{\star i}$. Each sub-problem is a weighted non-negative sparse coding problem, which can be written into the following optimization:

$$\min_{\hat{s}\ge 0} \frac{1}{2}\|B\hat{s} - X_{\star i}\|^2 + \lambda_1 \sum_{k=1}^{n+d} \hat{s}_k \cdot Z_{ki} \quad \text{s.t. } \hat{s}_i = 0. \tag{10}$$

In our approach, we adopt the Fast Iterative Shrinkage and Thresholding Algorithm (FISTA) [1], a popular and efficient algorithm for the linear inverse problem that has been already implemented for sparse learning in [19]. Since we aim to solve the problem related to only the top-n images in the retrieval results, where n is usually small, FISTA is efficient enough for our application.

4.3.2 Label Learning

Similarly, by fixing $\hat{S}$ and ignoring the constant terms, the optimization problem in Eq.(8) can be reformulated as follows:

$$Q_{\hat{S}}(Y) = \min_{Y} tr(Y^\top LY) + \lambda\|(Y-\hat{Y})\circ M\|_F^2 \quad \text{s.t. } Y\ge 0, \|Y_{i\star}\|_1 \le 1, i=1,2,\ldots,n. \tag{11}$$

where $\lambda = \frac{\lambda_3}{\lambda_2}$, and the other variables follow the same definitions in Eq.(8). The optimization problem is a quadratic program with a series of closed and convex constraints (ℓ_1 ball). In order to efficiently solve this problem, we first vectorize the label matrix $Y \in \mathbb{R}^{n\times m}$ into a column vector $\bar{y} = vec(Y) \in \mathbb{R}^{(n\cdot m)\times 1}$, and then rewrite the previous optimization problem as follows:

$$Q(\bar{y}) = \min_{\bar{y}\ge 0} \bar{y}^\top \Psi \bar{y} + \mathbf{c}^\top \bar{y}, \text{ s.t. } \forall i, \sum_{k=0}^{m-1} \bar{y}_{k\cdot n+i} \le 1. \tag{12}$$

where $\Psi = I_m \otimes L^\top + \lambda R$, I_m is an identity matrix with dimension $m\times m$, $R = diag(vec(M))$, $\mathbf{c} = -2\lambda R^\top \cdot vec(\tilde{Y})$, and $\bar{y}_j$ is the j-th element in $\bar{y}$. In order to solve this problem, we employ the multi-step gradient scheme [1] and the efficient Euclidean projection algorithm [20].

Specifically, in the multi-step gradient scheme, in order to achieve the optimal solution $\bar{y}^\star$, we recursively update two sequences $\{\bar{y}^{(k)}\}$ and $\{z^{(k)}\}$, where k is the iteration step. Commonly at each iteration k, the variance $z^{(k)}$ is named as the search point and used to construct the combination of the two previous approximate solutions $\bar{y}^{(k-1)}$ and $\bar{y}^{(k-2)}$. In our problem, the sub-block problem is defined as:

$$\bar{y}^{(k+1)} = \arg\min_{\bar{y}\ge 0} \frac{t}{2}\|\bar{y} - \mathbf{v}\|^2, \text{ s.t. } \forall i, \sum_{k=0}^{m-1} \bar{y}_{k\cdot n+i} \le 1. \tag{13}$$

where $\mathbf{v} = z^{(k)} - \frac{1}{t}\mathbf{g}$ and $\mathbf{g} = 2\Psi z^{(k)} + \mathbf{c}$, t could be a fixed positive constant or searched in a backtracking step [1]. The key problem is to solve Eq. (13) efficiently. In our work, we employ the Euclidian projection algorithm [20], which has been shown as an efficient solution to such kind of ℓ_1 ball constrained problem with linear time complexity of $O(n)$ as compared with other algorithms of $O(n\log(n))$.

Further, in order to apply the Euclidian projection algorithm, we split $\bar{y}$ into a series of m-dimension sub-vectors with $\bar{y}^i = [\bar{y}_{k\cdot n+i}]_{k=0}^{m-1}$, where $i = 1,2,\ldots,n$, and similarly we can split the vector $\mathbf{v}$. Specifically, each optimal solution $\bar{y}^{i\star}$ for sub-vector $\bar{y}^i$ can be achieved by solving the following problem:

$$\bar{y}^{i\star} = \arg\min_{\bar{y}^i\ge 0} \frac{t}{2}\|\bar{y}^i - v^i\|^2, \quad \text{s.t. } \|\bar{y}^i\|_1 \le 1. \tag{14}$$

The problem in Eq. (14) has a non-negative constraint, which is different from the one in [20]. The optimal solution to this problem is given as:

$$\bar{y}_j^{i\star} = sign(v_j^i)\cdot \max(|v_j^i| - \lambda^\star, 0), j = 1,2,\ldots,m. \tag{15}$$

where $sign(\cdot)$ is the sign function in Eq. (7), $\bar{y}_j^i$ and v_j^i are the j-th elements in $\bar{y}^i$ and v^i, and $\lambda^\star$ is the optimal solution for the dual form of Eq. (14). Suppose $S = \{j|v_j^i \ge 0\}$, the value of $\lambda^\star$ can be computed as follows:

$$\lambda^\star = \begin{cases} 0 & \sum_{k\in S} v_k^i \le 1, \\ \bar{\lambda} & \sum_{k\in S} v_k^i > 1. \end{cases} \tag{16}$$

where $\bar{\lambda}$ is the unique root of function $f(\lambda) = \sum_{k\in S}\max(|v_k^i| - \lambda, 0) - 1$, which is continuous and monotonically decreasing in $(-\infty,\infty)$. The root $\bar{\lambda}$ can be achieved by a bisection search in linear time complexity of $O(dim(\bar{y}^i))$. It is well-known that the multi-step gradient scheme converges at $O(\frac{1}{k^2})$, where k is the iteration step, indicating our optimization can be solved efficiently.

4.4 Face Name Annotation

After obtaining the sparse coding matrix S and the enhanced label matrix Y, the last key step of our framework is to perform the face name annotation. First, the query facial image x^q is also projected into the local coordinate coding space. In particular, the new coding s^q w.r.t. x^q can be achieved by solving the following optimization problem:

$$[s^q;\xi^q] = \arg\min_{\hat{s}\geq 0} \frac{1}{2}\|B\hat{s} - x^q\|^2 + \lambda \sum_k \hat{s}_k \cdot \|B_{\star k} - x^q\|^2 \quad (17)$$

where the parameter setting is the same as the previous WLRLCC algorithm.

Although the manifold structure is supposed to be well fitted in the new local coordinate space, it is still unsuitable to directly use a one-vs-one similarity measure for face name annotation. For the second step, we employ a sparse reconstruction scheme in the local coordinate coding space to recover the potential weighting vector w^q for name annotation in the label space. The optimization problem is given as follows:

$$\min \|w^q\|_1 \quad \text{s.t. } s^q = S_{I_n} \cdot w^q \quad (18)$$

where $S_{I_n} = S + I_n$, S is the local coordinate codes obtained from the previous step and I_n is an $n \times n$ identity matrix.

Finally, the label vector y^q can be directly computed by:

$$y^q = Y^\top \cdot w^q$$

The value $y^q_k, k \in \{1, 2, \ldots, m\}$ measures the confidence of the k-th name being assigned to the query facial image x^q; as a result, a name with a large confidence value will be ranked on the top position for the final annotation result.

5. EXPERIMENTAL RESULTS

To evaluate the performance of the proposed Weak Label Regularized Local Coordinate Coding (WLRLCC) algorithm, we conduct an extensive set of experiments to compare WLRLCC with other annotation algorithms on a large real-world weakly labeled facial images database. In the following subsections, we first briefly introduce the construction of our weak labeled facial image database. We then discuss the compared algorithms and their parameter settings. Finally, we present and discuss the experimental results.

5.1 Experimental Testbed

To build our experimental testbed, we first collected a name list consisting of 6000 popular actor and actress names downloaded from the **IMDb** website http://www.imdb.com. We collected those names with the billboard: "Most Popular People Born In **yyyy**" of **IMDb**, where **yyyy** is the born year. e.g., the webpage [1] presents all the actors and actresses who were born in 1975 in the popularity order. Our name list covers the actors and actresses who were born between 1950 and 1990. We submitted each name from the list as a query to search for related web images by Google image search engine. The top 200 retrieved web images were crawled automatically. After that we adopt the OpenCV toolbox to detect the faces and adopt the Deformable Lucas-Kanade (DLK) algorithm [43] to align facial images into the same well-defined position. The non-face-detected web images were ignored directly. As a result, we collected over 600,000 facial images in our database. We refer to this database as the "retrieval database", which will be used for facial image retrieval during the auto face annotation process.

In order to evaluate the effect of different database sizes, we also built three subsets of the whole database by including the images belonging to a subset of P most popular persons. For example, when choosing $P = 400$, we will choose the top $\frac{P}{40} = 10$ names from the name list of each year. We denote such a new database as "GDB-040K", which means that there are about over 40,000 images in this sub-database. Following the same method, we totally construct four databases in different sizes, i.e., GDB-040K, GDB-100K, GDB-200K, GDB-600K.

We also built a "test dataset" by randomly choosing 120 names from our name list. We submitted each of these names as a text query to Google image search and crawled about 200 images from the top 200-th to 400-th search results. Note that we did not consider the top 200 retrieved images since they had already been collected in the retrieval database. This aims to examine the generalization performance of the proposed technique for unseen facial images. Since these facial images are often noisy, in order to form the ground truth labels for the test dataset, we requested our staff to manually examine the retrieved facial images and remove those irrelevant facial images for each name. As a result, the test database consists of about 1,600 facial images with on average about 10 to 15 facial images for each person.

5.2 Compared Algorithms and Metric

To evaluate the performance of the proposed WLRLCC algorithm, we compare it against a number of different algorithms, including a common baseline based on weighted majority voting and five state-of-the-art algorithms for face/image annotation. Most of these algorithms were proposed in recent years, which have been briefly introduced in Section 2. As a fair comparison, we adopted the same GIST features [26] to represent all the facial images. To evaluate the annotation performances, we adopted the *hit rate* at the top-t annotated results as the performance metric, which measures the likelihood of having the true label among the top-t annotated names for a query facial image. The list of compared algorithms and their parameter settings are discussed as follows:

- "SMW": a baseline algorithm that simply adopts the softmax weighted majority voting, which assigns a weighting coefficient w_i to the label vector $\tilde{Y}_{i\star}$ by $w_i = \frac{s(x^q,x^i)}{\sum_{j=1}^n s(x^q,x^j)}$, where $s(\cdot,\cdot)$ is defined as $s(x^q,x^i) = \frac{1}{1+\exp(-\|x^q-x^i\|^2)}$.
- "S-Recon": the sparse label reconstruction algorithm [35]. The label of x^q is predicted as $y^q = Y^\top \cdot s^q$, where s^q is the sparse representation of x^q achieved with Eq.(1).
- "SGSSL": the kNN Sparse Graph-based Semi-Supervised Learning algorithm [29], where parameters are set according the ones given by the authors.
- "MRR": the Multi-Reference Re-ranking algorithm [37]. The parameters setting follows the authors' suggestions of $N_p = 320$ and $\alpha = 8$. After the re-ranking step, the SMW algorithm is employed for the final name annotation.
- "MtBGS": the Multi-label Boosting by selecting heterogeneous features with structural Grouping Sparsity [36]. The parameters λ_1 and λ_2 are tuned via cross validation. As only one kind of feature is used, the number of groups in MtBGS is set to 1 in our experiment.
- "MSC" : the multi-label sparse coding framework, in which label information is used to build the semantic graph for feature embedding [32]. The parameter λ in the graph construc-

[1] http://www.imdb.com/search/name?birth_year=1975

tion and label propagation steps are determined via cross validation. The parameter β is set to 0.1 according to the paper.

- "WLRLCC": the proposed Weak Label Regularized Local Coordinate Coding algorithm. The parameter λ_2 in Eq. (8) is related to the *Code learning* step and *Label learning* step, where its contribution also depends on the setting of λ_1 and λ_3, respectively. In our experiments, we set λ_2 to 0.1, and tune λ_1 and λ_3 via cross validation. For the parameter in Eq. (17), we set it to the same value as λ_1.

Furthermore, we discuss the cross validation issue. For all the compared algorithms, we only conducted it in the experiments on the GDB-040K; as a result, the parameters with the best average hit rate results are directly used in the following experiments based on GDB-100K, GDB-200K, and GDB-600K, which is also helpful to evaluate the parameter sensitivity. In particular, for the experiments on GDB-040K, we randomly divide the test dataset into two parts of equal size, in which one part is used as the validation set to find the optimal parameters by a grid search, and the other part is used for performance evaluation. Such a procedure is repeated 10 times and the average performance is computed over the 10 trials, in which the parameters with the best average hit rate performance are recorded. For the experiments on GDB-100K, GDB-200K and GDB-600K, we also split the test database into two parts, and randomly selected one for performance evaluation with the previous recorded parameters. For all the algorithms, we report both the average performances and their standard deviations.

5.3 Impact of Top-n and Top-t Settings

Top-n	t=1	t=3	t=5	t=7	t=9	t=10
10	**0.570**	0.731	0.773	0.793	0.804	0.808
20	0.529	0.703	0.779	0.798	0.810	0.817
30	0.511	0.683	0.760	0.800	0.818	0.822
40	0.497	0.669	0.740	0.784	0.822	**0.832**
50	0.470	0.659	0.737	0.769	0.804	0.818
100	0.413	0.605	0.693	0.748	0.777	0.792
200	0.362	0.552	0.638	0.692	0.738	0.756

Table 1: The hit rate performance of baseline algorithm SMW with different settings of Top-n faces and Top-t names.

This experiment aims to evaluate the impact on the final annotation performance by varied settings of n and t values for Top-n retrieved facial images and Top-t annotated names. Table 1 shows the annotation performance of the baseline SMW algorithm with different settings of n and t values on the GDB-040K database. In this experiment, the initial weak label $\tilde{Y}$ is used as we aim to examine the relationship between n and t in the original database.

Several observations can be drawn from the experimental results. First of all, when n is fixed, increasing the value of t generally leads to better annotation performance. However, the improvement becomes marginal when t is larger than some threshold. Second, when increasing the value of n, the annotation performance decreases for a small t value (e.g., Top-t=1), but increases for a large t value (e.g., Top-$t = 10$). However, when n is large enough (i.e., Top-$n > 40$), increasing n definitely leads to degrade the annotation performance for all the t values. Finally, we found that a small n value often results in a high precision and a low recall of any top-t retrieval results, while a large n value often produces a high recall and a low precision.

The previous observations are beneficial to determining appropriate parameters in our experiments. Since SMW is a simple weighted majority voting algorithm without any re-ranking, it prefers the retrieval result with a high precision; thus its parameter n for Top-n retrieved images is set to 10. On the other hand, the other algorithms usually carrying a re-ranking or sample selection step typically prefer a high recall of the retrieved results such that a potentially larger pool of facial images can be exploited for re-ranking. Thus, the parameter n for all the other algorithms is set to 40.

5.4 Evaluation of Label Enhancement

This experiment aims to evaluate the performance of the refined label matrix Y. To ease our discussion, we only present the results of the proposed WLRLCC algorithm on the most noisy GDB-600K database. Similar observations can also been observed on the other databases by employing different algorithms. The WLRLCC algorithm is firstly applied to learn the local coordinate coding and enhance the label matrix. After that, both the refined label matrix Y and the initial weak label matrix $\tilde{Y}$ are used in the face name annotation step. The comparison results are presented in Figure 2.

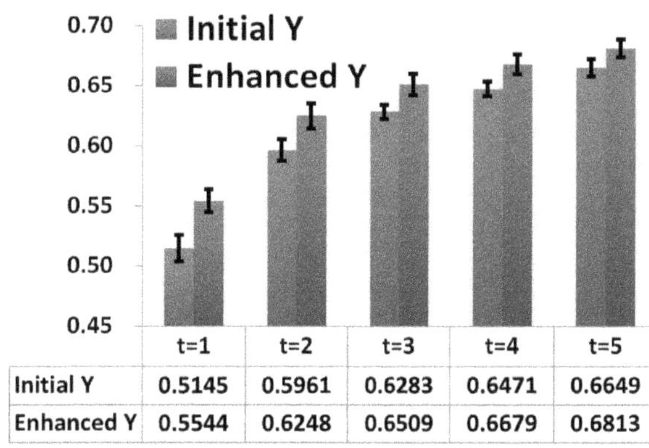

Figure 2: Evaluation of the enhanced label matrix Y on the GDB-600K database.

From the experimental results, it is obvious to observe that the enhanced label matrix Y significantly boosts the annotation performance, especially for small t values. This means that the proposed WLRLCC algorithm can efficiently exploit the graph-based locality information to refine the initial weak label matrix. In the following experiments, in order to evaluate the encoding results of the proposed WLRLCC algorithm, we will directly adopt the refined label matrix Y for all the compared algorithms to enable a fair comparison.

5.5 Evaluation of Auto Face Annotation

In this experiment, we compare the proposed WLRLCC algorithm with other algorithms on the GDB-040K database. Figure 3 and Table 2 show the average annotation performance at different t values, in which both mean and the standard deviation are reported. We can draw some observations for the results.

First of all, it is clear that the proposed WLRLCC algorithm consistently performs better than the other algorithms, especially for small t values. Considering Top-$t = 1$, the performance of the baseline SMW algorithm is about 60.8%. Using other more sophisticated annotation algorithms, much better results are achieved, e.g., MtBGS achieves 74.2% which is the best among all the other compared algorithm, except the proposed algorithm WLRLCC, which can further boost the performance to 77.5%. The promising result validates the effectiveness of the proposed WLRLCC algorithm for

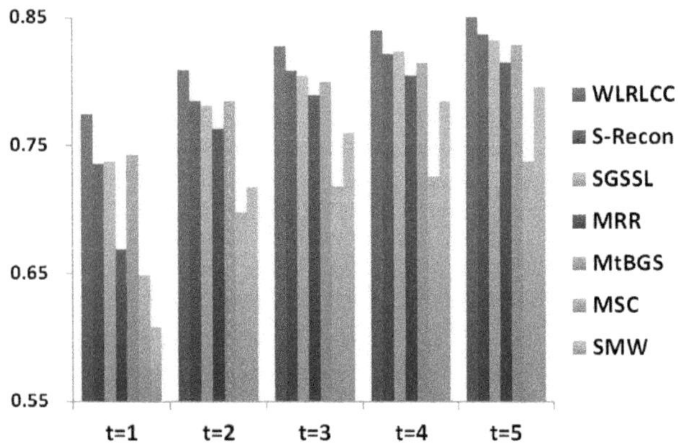

Figure 3: The comparison among WLRLCC and other algorithms on database GDB-040K.

improving the retrieval-based face annotation task. Secondly, similar to the observation obtained from Figure 2, more performance improvement is achieved by the WLRLCC algorithm for a small Top-t value, which is more critical for real applications. In practice, we mainly focus on a small t value since users usually would not be interested in a long list of annotated names. Thirdly, the annotation performance of MSC becomes worse when the t value for Top-t is too large. The MSC algorithm relies on a well-defined label matrix, which is used for graph construction and feature embedding. Although the label matrix Y is refined, it would still be noisy comparing to the manual labels.

	t=1	t=2	t=3	t=4	t=5
WLRLCC	0.7745 ± 0.012	0.8089 ± 0.010	0.8273 ± 0.010	0.8396 ± 0.009	0.8501 ± 0.009
S-Recon	0.7351 ± 0.010	0.7845 ± 0.010	0.8080 ± 0.010	0.8213 ± 0.008	0.8366 ± 0.007
SGSSL	0.7375 ± 0.013	0.7806 ± 0.009	0.8043 ± 0.009	0.8233 ± 0.009	0.8320 ± 0.009
MRR	0.6688 ± 0.014	0.7626 ± 0.009	0.7888 ± 0.009	0.8045 ± 0.009	0.8148 ± 0.011
MtBGS	0.7424 ± 0.013	0.7846 ± 0.013	0.7996 ± 0.011	0.8140 ± 0.011	0.8283 ± 0.010
MSC	0.6483 ± 0.013	0.6980 ± 0.013	0.7179 ± 0.013	0.7258 ± 0.011	0.7374 ± 0.010
SMW	0.6076 ± 0.015	0.7173 ± 0.009	0.7596 ± 0.008	0.7846 ± 0.007	0.7958 ± 0.007

Table 2: The comparison among WLRLCC and other algorithms on database GDB-040K.

5.6 Evaluation of Varied Database Sizes

In this experiment, we aim to examine the relationship between the annotation performance and the size of the retrieval database: GDB-040K, GDB-100K, GDB-200K, and GDB-600K. The experiment results are presented in Figure 1 and Table 3, where both the average performance and the standard deviation are presented. To be clear, we only show the annotation result with Top-$t = 1$, which is the most important case for the annotation task.

We can draw some observations from the results. First of all, similar to the previous observations, the WLRLCC algorithm consistently achieves the best annotation performance among all the compared algorithms for different database sizes. Second, it is clear that the annotation performance will decrease when increasing the size of the retrieval database, which is similar to the observation of the facial image retrieval in [37]. Note that there are two different ways for increasing the database sizes. One is to increase the number of facial images for each person, which is beneficial to the annotation task as more potential images are included, as shown in [33]; the other is to increase the number of unique persons, which could increase the difficulty of facial image retrieval and thus would degrade the annotation performance. The increase of database size in this experiment belongs to the second case. Third, the result also illustrates that the facial annotation problem remains a challenging problem, especially for large scale retrieval databases where accurate facial image retrieval could be a bottleneck for the annotation task, which is out of the scope of discussions in this paper.

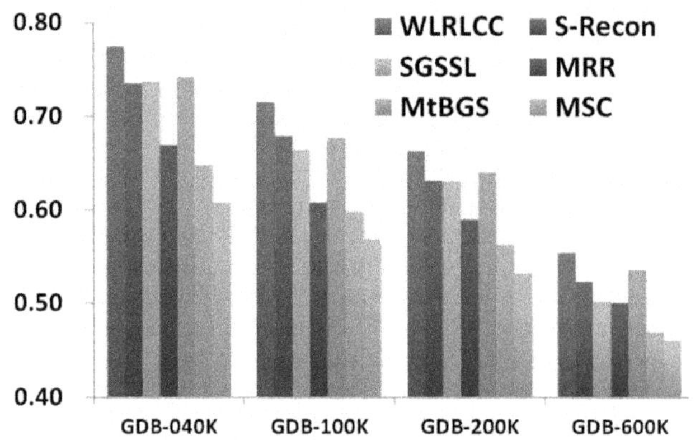

Figure 4: The comparison between WLRLCC and other algorithms on GDB-040K, GDB-100K,GDB-200K, and GDB-600K, with Top-t=1

5.7 Evaluation of Running Time Cost

In this section, we aim to evaluate the running time cost of the proposed WLRLCC algorithms, which consists of two major steps: (i) code learning and (ii) label learning. We adopt the FISTA [1] algorithm for solving the first problem, and implement the algorithm presented in Section 4.3.2 for the special QP problem in the second problem. To further reduce the running time, we also evaluate the performance of adopting PCA for dimension reduction over the original 512-dim GIST feature. We randomly select 1000 images from the retrieval database for PCA training. All the experiment results are presented in Table 4, where W-k denotes the new feature dimension is k after doing PCA projection.

Several observations can be drawn from these experiment results. First of all, the WLRLCC algorithm takes a bit longer time than the other algorithms, about 1.2 second for each query, as it has to code the feature and enhance the label together. Secondly, by using the PCA dimension reduction technique, the running time could be considerably reduced without introduce much performance degradation. For example, for the new 200-dim feature, the WLRLCC algorithm needs only about 0.63 second, but still achieves the best annotation performance, about 76.2%. Thirdly, when the dimension of the new feature space is small enough, the annotation performance of WLRLCC will decrease fast without more shrinkage in running time, which means there is a trade-off between the running time and the annotation performance. In this experiment, the suggested range of new feature dimension is about $[200, 300]$.

Besides the dimension reduction techniques, some other techniques could also been used for acceleration. In [39], Yang and Zhang propose a Gabor kernel based scheme to reduce the number

	WLRLCC	S-Recon	SGSSL	MRR	MtBGS	MSC	SMW
GDB-040K	0.7745±0.012	0.7351±0.010	0.7375±0.013	0.6688±0.014	0.7424±0.013	0.6483±0.013	0.6076±0.015
GDB-100K	0.7156±0.011	0.6789±0.009	0.6644±0.012	0.6080±0.010	0.6766±0.011	0.5981±0.012	0.5689±0.011
GDB-200K	0.6625±0.012	0.6314±0.008	0.6301±0.011	0.5898±0.008	0.6405±0.010	0.5628±0.012	0.5323±0.013
GDB-600K	0.5544±0.010	0.5228±0.007	0.5015±0.011	0.5005±0.008	0.5359±0.009	0.4694±0.010	0.4600±0.013

Table 3: Comparison between WLRLCC and other algorithms on GDB-040K, GDB-100K, GDB-200K, and GDB-600K (top-t=1).

	S-Recon	SGSSL	MRR	MtBGS	MSC
Time (s)	0.023 ± 0.007	0.971 ± 0.023	0.175 ± 0.016	0.414 ± 0.103	0.104 ± 0.191
Hit Rate	0.7351 ± 0.010	0.7375 ± 0.013	0.6688 ± 0.014	0.7424 ± 0.013	0.6483 ± 0.013
	WLRLCC	W-400	W-300	W-200	W-100
Time (s)	1.205 ± 0.041	0.959 ± 0.017	0.773 ± 0.028	0.63 ± 0.020	0.524 ± 0.030
Hit Rate	0.7745 ± 0.012	0.7639 ± 0.013	0.7619 ± 0.134	0.7615 ± 0.011	0.7403 ± 0.116

Table 4: The running time comparison of different algorithms and the annotation performance of different dimension reduction from the original 512-dim GIST feature(Top-t=1). W-k means the new feature dimension is k.

of atoms in dictionary, which could greatly reduces the computational cost for coding. In order to solve the large scale problem efficiently, some approximated algorithms are also proposed for sparse coding problem (e.g., LISTA [12], CoD [18], and so on.). These algorithms could also be adopted into our problem for running time reduction, which will be included in our further works.

5.8 Evaluation of Parameter Sensitivity

For the proposed WLRLCC algorithm, the best parameters λ_1 and λ_3 are found by a grid search on the GDB-040K database, which are also adopted in the experiments on other databases. Figure 5 shows the grid search results, where the ranges for λ_1, λ_3 are $\{0.005, 0.01, 0.1, 1, 3, 5\}$. From the figure, we observe that the performance of WLRLCC tends to be stable in some region $\lambda_1 \in [0.005, 0.1]$ and $\lambda_3 \in [0.1, 3]$. We thus choose $\lambda_1 = 0.01$ and $\lambda_3 = 1$ in our experiments, which are also adopted in the other three experiments on varied-scale databases. As shown in Figure 4, the encouraging performance of WLRLCC indicates that it is generally robust in the parameter setting for similar experiments.

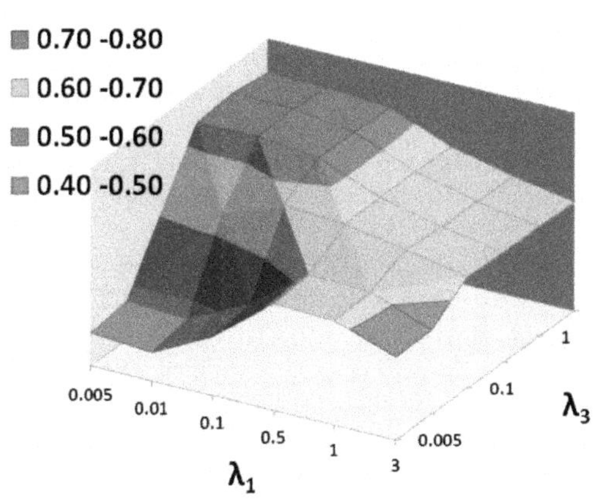

Figure 5: The grid search result of WLRLCC on GDB-040K.

6. DISCUSSIONS

There are two main assumptions for the proposed WLRLCC algorithm: (i) Although the initial weak label matrix is noisy and incomplete, the majority of its information remains beneficial; (ii) Two similar faces in the feature space share the same (close) name label. Typically, a generic image annotation problem also satisfies these assumptions. Our algorithm thus can be directly applied to a generic image annotation problem with a larger ε value for the multi-label task. On the other hand, the WLRLCC algorithm is usually limited by the discriminative ability of features, it would achieve a better performance on a special type of image annotation than generic image annotation problem.

The proposed retrieval-based face annotation scheme can be applied to many real-world applications. For example, it can be used to examine if a user uploads a celebrity's photo as his/her own avatar in a real-name social network. It can also be used for personal photo management in photo sharing web sites, where millions of unlabeled images are uploaded everyday.

For future work, we will address the issues of developing more efficient algorithms for the WLRLCC algorithm, including approximate sparse coding algorithms. In addition, instead of handling both the feature coding and label refinement steps in online manners, another way is to solve these problems over the whole retrieval database in an off-line manner. Future work will examine how to combine these two schemes effectively.

7. CONCLUSION

This paper investigated the retrieval-based face annotation problem and presented a promising framework to attack this challenge by mining massive weakly labeled facial images freely available on WWW. To improve the annotation performance, a novel Weak Label Regularized Local Coordinate Coding (WLRLCC) algorithm was proposed, which effectively exploits the principles of both local coordinate coding and graph-based weak label regularization. Using the achieved representative local coordinate coding and enhanced label matrix, a sparse reconstruction scheme is proposed for face name annotation. We conducted extensive experiments and found that the proposed WLRLCC algorithm achieved encouraging results on a large-scale web facial image testbed.

Acknowledgements

This work was supported by the Singapore National Research Foundation Interactive Digital Media R&D Program, under research grant NRF2008IDM-IDM004-006. Jianke Zhu was supported by Fundamental Research Funds for the Central Universities.

8. REFERENCES

[1] A. Beck and M. Teboulle. A fast iterative shrinkage-thresholding algorithm for linear inverse problems. *SIAM J. Img. Sci.*, 2:183–202, March 2009.

[2] T. L. Berg, A. C. Berg, J. Edwards, and D. Forsyth. Who's in the picture. In L. K. Saul, Y. Weiss, and L. Bottou, editors, *NIPS*, Cambridge, MA, 2005. MIT Press.

[3] T. L. Berg, A. C. Berg, J. Edwards, M. Maire, R. White, Y. W. Teh, E. G. Learned-Miller, and D. A. Forsyth. Names and faces in the news. In *CVPR*, pages 848–854, 2004.
[4] Z. Cao, Q. Yin, X. Tang, and J. Sun. Face recognition with learning-based descriptor. In *CVPR*, 2010.
[5] G. Carneiro, A. B. Chan, P. Moreno, and N. Vasconcelos. Supervised learning of semantic classes for image annotation and retrieval. *IEEE Tran. PAMI*, pages 394–410, 2006.
[6] O. Chapelle, B. Schölkopf, and A. Zien, editors. *Semi-Supervised Learning*. MIT Press, MA, 2006.
[7] J. Y. Choi, W. D. Neve, K. N. Plataniotis, and Y. M. Ro. Collaborative face recognition for improved face annotation in personal photo collections shared on online social networks. *IEEE Transactions on Multimedia*, 13, 2011.
[8] J. Cui, F. Wen, R. Xiao, Y. Tian, and X. Tang. Easyalbum: an interactive photo annotation system based on face clustering and re-ranking. In *CHI*, pages 367–376, 2007.
[9] W. Dong, Z. Wang, W. Josephson, M. Charikar, and K. Li. Modeling lsh for performance tuning. In *CIKM*, 2008.
[10] P. Duygulu, K. Barnard, J. de Freitas, and D. Forsyth. Object recognition as machine translation: Learning a lexicon for a fixed image vocabulary. In *ECCV*, 2002.
[11] J. Fan, Y. Gao, and H. Luo. Multi-level annotation of natural scenes using dominant image components and semantic concepts. In *ACM Multimedia*, pages 540–547, 2004.
[12] K. Gregor and Y. LeCun. Learning fast approximations of sparse coding. In J. Fürnkranz and T. Joachims, editors, *ICML*, pages 399–406. Omnipress, 2010.
[13] A. Hanbury. A survey of methods for image annotation. *J. Vis. Lang. Comput.*, 19:617–627, October 2008.
[14] E. Hjelmås and B. K. Low. Face detection: A survey. *In CVIU*, 83:236–274, 2001.
[15] P. O. Hoyer. Non-negative sparse coding. *CoRR*, cs.NE/0202009, 2002.
[16] G. B. Huang, M. Ramesh, T. Berg, and E. Learned-Miller. Labeled faces in the wild: A database for studying face recognition in unconstrained environments. Technical Report 07-49, University of Massachusetts, Amherst, October 2007.
[17] D.-D. Le and S. Satoh. Unsupervised face annotation by mining the web. In *ICDM*, pages 383–392, 2008.
[18] Y. Li and S. Osher. Coordinate descent optimization for l1 minimization with application to compressed sensing; a greedy algorithm. *Inverse Problems and Imaging*, 2009.
[19] J. Liu, S. Ji, and J. Ye. *SLEP: Sparse Learning with Efficient Projections*. Arizona State University, 2009.
[20] J. Liu and J. Ye. Efficient euclidean projections in linear time. In *ICML*, pages 657–664, Montreal, Quebec, Canada, 2009.
[21] H. V. Nguyen and L. Bai. Cosine similarity metric learning for face verification. In *ACCV, 2010.*, June 2008.
[22] D. Ozkan and P. Duygulu. A graph based approach for naming faces in news photos. In *CVPR*, 2006.
[23] X. Rui, M. Li, Z. Li, W.-Y. Ma, and N. Yu. Bipartite graph reinforcement model for web image annotation. In *ACM Multimedia*, pages 585–594, Augsburg, Germany, 2007.
[24] B. C. Russell, A. Torralba, K. P. Murphy, and W. T. Freeman. Labelme: A database and web-based tool for image annotation. *Int. J. Comput. Vision*, 77(1-3):157–173, 2008.
[25] S. Satoh, Y. Nakamura, and T. Kanade. Name-it: Naming and detecting faces in news videos. *IEEE MultiMedia*, 6(1):22–35, 1999.
[26] C. Siagian and L. Itti. Rapid biologically-inspired scene classification using features shared with visual attention. *IEEE Trans. Pattern Anal. Mach. Intell.*, 29:300–312, 2007.
[27] A. W. M. Smeulders, M. Worring, S. Santini, A. Gupta, and R. Jain. Content-based image retrieval at the end of the early years. *IEEE Tran. Pattern Anal. Mach. Intell.*, 22(12): 1349–1380, 2000.
[28] Y.-Y. Sun, Y. Zhang, and Z.-H. Zhou. Multi-label learning with weak label. In *AAAI*. 2010.
[29] J. Tang, R. Hong, S. Yan, T.-S. Chua, G.-J. Qi, and R. Jain. Image annotation by knn-sparse graph-based label propagation over noisily tagged web images. *ACM Trans. Intell. Syst. Technol.*, 2:14:1–14:15, February 2011.
[30] Y. Tian, W. Liu, R. Xiao, F. Wen, and X. Tang. A face annotation framework with partial clustering and interactive labeling. In *CVPR*, 2007.
[31] C. Wang, F. Jing, L. Zhang, and H.-J. Zhang. Image annotation refinement using random walk with restarts. In *ACM Multimedia*, pages 647–650, 2006.
[32] C. Wang, S. Yan, L. Zhang, and H.-J. Zhang. Multi-label sparse coding for automatic image annotation. In *CVPR*, 0:1643–1650, 2009.
[33] D. Wang, S.C.H. Hoi, and Y. He. Mining weakly labeled web facial images for search-based face annotation. In *SIGIR*, 2011.
[34] X.-J. Wang, L. Zhang, F. Jing, and W.-Y. Ma. Annosearch: Image auto-annotation by search. In *CVPR*, 2006.
[35] J. Wright, A. Y. Yang, A. Ganesh, S. S. Sastry, and Y. Ma. Robust face recognition via sparse representation. *IEEE Trans. Pattern Anal. Mach. Intell.*, 31(2), 2009.
[36] F. Wu, Y. Han, Q. Tian, and Y. Zhuang. Multi-label boosting for image annotation by structural grouping sparsity. In A. D. Bimbo, S.-F. Chang, and A. W. M. Smeulders, editors, *ACM Multimedia*, pages 15–24. ACM, 2010.
[37] Z. Wu, Q. Ke, J. Sun, and H.-Y. Shum. Scalable face image retrieval with identity-based quantization and multi-reference re-ranking. In *CVPR*, pages 3469–3476, 2010.
[38] J. Yang and A. G. Hauptmann. Naming every individual in news video monologues. In *ACM Multimedia Conference*, pages 580–587, New York, NY, USA, 2004.
[39] M. Yang and L. Zhang. Gabor feature based sparse representation for face recognition with gabor occlusion dictionary. In *ECCV*, pages 448–461, 2010.
[40] K. Yu, T. Zhang, and Y. Gong. Nonlinear learning using local coordinate coding. In Y. Bengio, D. Schuurmans, J. Lafferty, C. K. I. Williams, and A. Culotta, editors, *NIPS*, pages 2259–2267, 2009.
[41] L. Zhang, L. Chen, M. Li, and H. Zhang. Automated annotation of human faces in family albums. In *ACM Multimedia*, 2003.
[42] W. Zhao, R. Chellappa, P. J. Phillips, and A. Rosenfeld. Face recognition: A literature survey. *ACM Comput. Surv.*, 35(4):399–458, 2003.
[43] J. Zhu, S.C.H. Hoi, and L.V. Gool. Unsupervised face alignment by robust nonrigid mapping. In *ICCV*, 2009.
[44] J. Zhu, S.C.H. Hoi, and M.R. Lyu. Face Annotation Using Transductive Kernel Fisher Discriminant. *IEEE Transactions on Multimedia.*, 10(1):86–96, 2008.
[45] X. Zhu, Z. Ghahramani, and J.D. Lafferty. Semi-supervised learning using gaussian fields and harmonic functions. In *The Twentieth International Conference on Machine Learning (ICML-2003)*, pages 912–919, 2003.

Learning to Judge Image Search Results [*]

Xinmei Tian [†]
University of Science and Technology of China
Hefei, Anhui, China 230027
xinmeitian@gmail.com

Yijuan Lu
Texas State University
San Marcos, TX 78666
yl12@txstate.edu

Linjun Yang
Microsoft Research Asia
Beijing, China 100190
linjuny@microsoft.com

Qi Tian
University of Texas at San Antonio
San Antonio, TX 78249
qitian@cs.utsa.edu

ABSTRACT

Given the explosive growth of the Web and the popularity of image sharing Web sites, image retrieval plays an increasingly important role in our daily lives. Search engines aim to provide beneficial image search results to users in response to queries. The quality of image search results depends on many factors: chosen search algorithms, ranking functions, indexing features, the base image database, *etc.* Applying different settings for these factors generates search result lists with varying levels of quality. Previous research has shown that no setting can always perform optimally for all queries. Therefore, given a set of search result lists generated by different settings, it is crucial to automatically determine which result list is the best in order to present it to users. This paper proposes a novel method to automatically identify the best search result list from a number of candidates. There are three main innovations in this paper. First, we propose a preference learning model to quantitatively study the best image search result identification problem. Second, we propose a set of valuable preference learning related features by exploring the visual characters of returned images. Third, our method shows promising potential in applications such as reranking ability assessment and optimal search engine selection. Experiments on two image search datasets show that our method achieves about 80% prediction accuracy for reranking ability assessment, and selects optimal search engine for about 70% queries correctly.

Categories and Subject Descriptors

H.3.3 [**Information Search and Retrieval**]: Retrieval models

General Terms

Algorithm, Experimentation, Performance

Keywords

Image retrieval, search results performance comparison, reranking ability assessment

[†]This work was performed while the first author was a post-doctoral researcher at Texas State University.

[*]Area chair: Hari Sundaram

MM'11, November 28–December 1, 2011, Scottsdale, Arizona, USA.

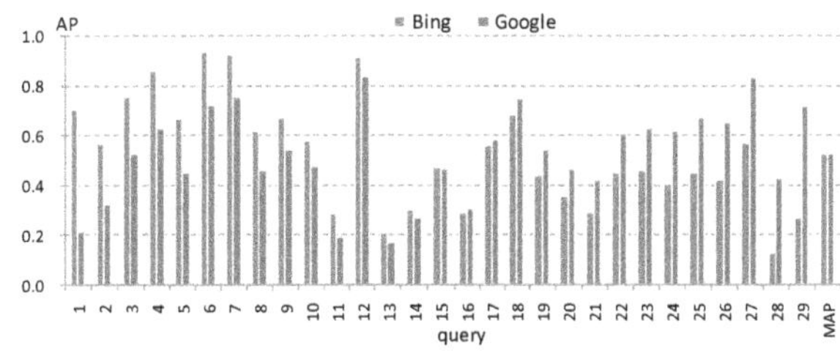

(a) AP@40 on each query and MAP over all queries for Bing and Google (queries are sorted according to their AP difference for better view).

(b) The top-10 images returned on query "White House".

Figure 1: Image search result comparison between Bing and Google.

1. INTRODUCTION

Given the explosive growth of the Web and the popularity of image sharing Web sites, image retrieval plays an increasingly important role in our daily lives. Extensive research has been conducted to retrieve images relevant to a given query. Many factors can influence image search results. Existing work aims to get better search results by focussing their efforts on various aspects of the search process, such as designing effective visual features [15, 16], building efficient image indexes [17], developing new ranking algorithms [6, 22] and designing user-friendly interface [24]. The algorithms used in these aspects generate result lists of varying quality when used with different settings. Following are two examples for illustration.

In our first example we compare image search results generated by two popular search engines, Bing and Google. We submitted 29 text queries to them, and collected the images they returned[1]. Fig. 1(a) gives the AP@40 (average precision, ref Section 5.1 for details) for each query of the two search engines and the overall performance MAP (mean AP over all queries). We find that although Bing and Google have comparable MAP values (52.24 and 52.36 respectively), their performance on individual queries is quite different. Google achieves better performance on about half the queries. For example, on the query "White House", the top images returned by Google are more related to the "White House" than those returned by Bing (Fig. 1(b)). If

[1]The data was collected in 2008.

Table 1: MAP@40 (×100) of Bing, Google, and after optimal search engine selection for each query.

	Bing	Google	$\text{Select}_{\text{Opt}}$
MAP@40	52.24	52.36	*60.71*

Table 2: MAP@20 (×100) of the text-based search (Text) and the two reranking methods, PRF and BR.

	Text	PRF	BR
MAP@20	50.28	60.65	63.64
Gain	-	20.62%	26.57%

an algorithm could automatically determine which search engine would generate a better result list for each query, one could achieve better performance by selecting the optimal search engine for each query. Table 1 shows the MAP value after this selection, which is 60.71, about 16% relative improvement over Bing and Google.

In our second example we compare the performance of text-based image search and visual reranking. Most existing image search engines are implemented by indexing and searching textual information associated with images, *e.g.*, surrounding text, URLs. The text-based image search approach is efficient for large scale image databases. However, it suffers when the associated text is incapable of adequately describing the image. To address this difficulty, visual reranking has been developed to refine the text search results by incorporating visual information from images. Recent research has shown that visual reranking can generally improve the performance of text-based image search to some extent [19, 22]. However, it is not guaranteed to benefit every query. It is widely observed that visual reranking can greatly improve retrieval performance for some queries, while for others reranking can even degrade the performance of the initial text-based search.

As an illustration, we apply two popular reranking methods, BR [19] and PRF [21], on a public image search dataset (Web353). This dataset was collected by Krapac *et al.* [13]. It contains 71478 images returned by a Web search engine for 353 general textual queries. Table 2 presents the average performance of the text-based search engine (Text) and the performance of the two reranking methods, in terms of MAP@20 over 353 queries. Table 3 lists the number of queries with improved, degraded, or equivalent performance after reranking. We find that, although overall performance of all 353 queries is improved, there are still around 100 queries (25 - 30 percent) that suffer performance decrease after reranking. By further investigating the reranking performance on each query, we find that the performance of many queries has decreased significantly. For some queries, the decrease in AP value is as great as 0.7. Thus, given a query, it becomes crucial for the search engine to predict its visual reranking performance and decide whether the visual reranking process should be performed or not. Doing so would allow us to avoid presenting reranking results which are even worse than text-based search results to users.

The above two examples raise the same problem: for a query, given a set of result lists, which one is the best (has the highest retrieval performance)? In other words, which result list should be presented to users? This paper aims to solve this problem: *given a set of search result lists returned by multiple search executions of a query, how can we design an algorithm to automatically compare the quality of those result lists in order to identify the result list with the highest performance.* To solve this problem, we build a model to investigate the quality of search results using machine learning. It consists of two stages: training and testing. In the training stage we explore the visual distribution characteristics of good and bad search result lists and derive a set of light-weight features to capture their differences. Then, by forming the search result lists of training queries into preference pairs, we derive a preference learning model (PLM) by training on these pairs with RankSVM [12]. Finally, in the testing stage, the developed PLM is applied to predict the preference score for search result lists of any testing query.

Table 3: The number of queries with improved, degraded, or equivalent performance after reranking.

♯queries	Improved	Unchanged	Degraded
PRF vs. Text	237	6	110
BR vs. Text	256	10	87

To the best of our knowledge this is the first attempt that automatically evaluates the quality of Web image search result lists. The proposed approach has a wide range of applications. For example, it is capable of selecting the best search engine to solve the problem in example 1 and automatically determining whether reranking can benefit the query to solve the problem in example 2. There are also many other promising potential applications. For example, given different search algorithm settings (various visual features, visual reranking methods, *etc.*), our approach can automatically select the optimum settings for each query.

The main contributions introduced in this paper are summarized as follows:

- We quantitatively study and formulate the image search result preference learning problem. We propose a novel framework and a set of valuable features to automatically compare the quality of image search result lists.
- Our proposed approach shows promising application potential for optimal search engine selection, merging of search result lists, and selecting the best visual feature and reranking approach for each individual query.
- Our work will explicitly guide the research in visual reranking ability estimation and provide a path for query difficulty modeling.

2. RELATED WORK

Image search plays an important role in our daily lives. Considerable research has been proposed to improve image search from various aspects, such as image annotation [2] and visual reranking [19, 21, 22]. All these research efforts have the same objective of returning good image search results to users. Different search result lists are generated by different image search methods and their performance on each query varies greatly. These works show their strength on certain aspects. There is no single method which can always work the best for all queries. Therefore, in addition to developing (overall) effective search approaches, it is also very important to select the most suitable search method for each query. Through this selection, better image search results can be derived. This paper conducts this best method selection for each query by investigating the quality of the image search result lists generated by different search methods. The search result list with the highest performance is picked out and presented to users.

The most related work to this paper is the query difficulty prediction. Query difficulty prediction in document retrieval has been explored for many years [3, 7, 8, 9, 11, 14, 23]. It aims to predict whether a query will have a high retrieval performance in a document collection. It includes two categories, pre-retrieval prediction and post-retrieval prediction. In pre-retrieval, query difficulty prediction attempts to evaluate search performance before the retrieval step [8, 9, 14]. It mainly relies on statistics of query terms over document collections. He and Ounis [8] proposed several pre-retrieval predictors by considering the intrinsic statistical features of queries, including query length, standard deviation of the inverse document frequency (idf) of terms in the query, query scope, and a simplified clarity score (SCS). Kwok *et al.* [14] employed support vector regression to train a query difficulty prediction model with simple features such as log document frequency and query term frequency. Imran and Sharan [9] proposed two pre-retrieval query difficulty predictors based on the co-occurrence information among query terms. They assumed that higher co-occurrence of query terms means more information is conveyed, which leads to an easier query or a lower query difficulty level.

In post-retrieval prediction, the retrieval step is conducted first and query difficulty prediction evaluates the performance of the returned results. Our work is most related to it. In [3], a clarity score was proposed that measures the ambiguity of a query through the Kullback-Leibler divergence between the language models created from top-retrieved documents and all documents in the collection. Hauff *et al.* [7] proposed an improved clarity score to solve the parameter sensitivity problem of the previous one. Elad Yom-Tov *et al.* [23] estimated the quality of search result lists by measuring the agreement between the top results returned by the full query and its sub-queries. Jensen *et al.* [11] predicted query difficulty by using features extracted from surrogate documents represented in the search result list to train a regression model. In image retrieval, little research has been conducted on query difficulty estimation. Xing *et al.* [20] used textual features to predict whether a query is difficult to be represented by images or not. This work does not investigate the image search performance, but only classifies the queries into two categories "easy" or "hard".

Query difficulty prediction estimates the performance of a search result list for a given query. Unlike query difficulty prediction, our work targets comparing several search result lists generated for a particular query. Instead of predicting their exact performance, we only need to know which search result list is better than the others. Furthermore, in query difficulty prediction, the search result lists are independent of each other since they are generated for different queries. In our problem, the compared search result lists are generated for the same query and are thus correlated. We can utilize the correlation between them. Additionally, both the query and documents in the query difficulty prediction problem are in the textual domain. In our problem queries are textual and images are visual, creating a more complex problem. Our image search result performance comparison problem faces many challenges. As a first attempt, this paper only focuses on exploiting visual information, which is the essential description of images. In the case where textual information of images (URL, surrounding texts *et al.*) is also available, we will further exploit the joint usage of textual and visual information for this problem in the future.

3. PROBLEM FORMULATION

For query q and an image collection $\{\mathbf{x}_1, \cdots, \mathbf{x}_N\}$, multiple search result lists can be derived using different search algorithms. Each search result list is a permutation/ranking of the N images sorted in descending order by their ranking scores, which are generated by the search algorithm . We use ranking list variable l to denote a search result list. Assuming there are n_q ranking lists generated for query q, they constitute a set of search result lists $\mathcal{L}^{(q)} = \{l_1, \cdots, l_{n_q}\}$. Our objective is to automatically determine which l in $\mathcal{L}^{(q)}$ has the highest performance,

$$l^* = \text{argmax}_{l \in \mathcal{L}^{(q)}} \ y(l), \tag{1}$$

where $y(l)$ denotes the performance of l. $y(l)$ can be measured by commonly used information retrieval measures, such as precision, recall, Average Precision (AP) [1] and Normalized Discounted Cumulated Gain (NDCG) [10].

For two ranking lists, the one with more relevant images ranked at the top gives a better performance than the one with fewer relevant images ranked at the top. If we have the ground truth label of each image (its relevance to query q), then $y(l)$ can be derived by using AP or NDCG and the best search result selection in problem (1) is straight forward. However, in real applications, the ground truth relevance labels for images are unavailable. In this situation, how can we know which ranking list performs better? In this paper, we propose to solve this problem via machine learning. Specifically, we want to learn a preference model $f(l) = \mathbf{w}^{\mathrm{T}}\psi(l)$ from a training set, where $\mathbf{w}$ is the weighting coefficient vector and $\psi(l)$ is a vector which reflects the characteristics of l. This model should satisfy the following constraints on the training set

$$\forall (l_i, l_j), \text{if } y(l_i) > y(l_j), \text{ then } f(l_i) > f(l_j). \tag{2}$$

For two ranking lists l_i and l_j in training set, if the ground truth performance $y(l_i)$ is better than $y(l_j)$ (l_i is preferred to l_j), $f(l_i)$ should be larger than $f(l_j)$. In other words, the ordinal relationship of pair $(f(l_i), f(l_j))$ must be consistent with that of $(y(l_i), y(l_j))$, to reflect the ground truth preference of two ranking lists.

In this paper we formulate the learning problem of $f(\cdot)$ by using the powerful RankSVM [12] algorithm. It minimizes the prediction errors on a set of training queries $\mathcal{Q} = \{q^{(1)}, \cdots, q^{(m)}\}$,

$$\min \ \frac{1}{2}\mathbf{w}^{\mathrm{T}}\mathbf{w} + C\sum \xi_{ijk} \tag{3}$$
$$s.t. \ \forall k, k = 1, \cdots, m. \ \forall (l_i, l_j) \in \mathcal{S}^{(q^{(k)})},$$
$$\mathbf{w}^{\mathrm{T}}\psi(l_i) \geq \mathbf{w}^{\mathrm{T}}\psi(l_j) + 1 - \xi_{ijk}, \ \xi_{ijk} \geq 0$$

where ξ is the slack variable and $C > 0$ controls the trade-off between model complexity and training errors. $\mathcal{S}^{(q)}$ is the set of preference ranking list pairs for query q generated from the ranking list set $\mathcal{L}^{(q)} = \{l_1, \cdots, l_{n_q}\}$

$$\mathcal{S}^{(q)} = \{(l_i, l_j) | y(l_i) > y(l_j); i, j = 1, \cdots, n_q\}. \tag{4}$$

The preference learning model $f(\cdot)$ can be derived by solving problem (3). Then, this model can be applied to any testing query q' for which ground truth relevance labels are unavailable. Suppose there are $n_{q'}$ ranking lists generated for this query, $\mathcal{L}^{(q')} = \{l_1, \cdots, l_{n_{q'}}\}$. $f(\cdot)$ can predict a value for each list. For any two ranking lists l_i and l_j, if $f(l_i) > f(l_j)$, we know that l_i performs better than l_j, and *vice versa.* The ranking list with the highest prediction value is the one which has the best performance.

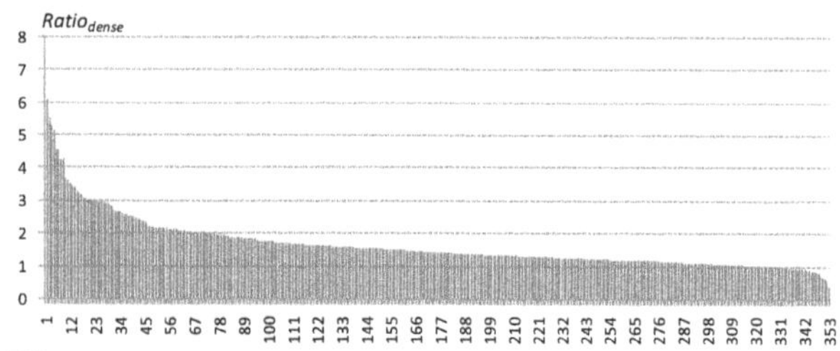

Figure 2: Sorted $Ratio_{dense}$ values in 353 queries.

4. FEATURE CONSTRUCTION

A crucial factor in $f(l) = \mathbf{w}^{\mathrm{T}}\psi(l)$ is the vector $\psi(l)$. It is not trivial to design a feature vector to capture visual characteristics of an arbitrary ranking list l. By analyzing the visual distribution of images in the collection, we propose a set of lightweight features.

4.1 Two Basic Assumptions

Given two ranking lists returned for query q over image collection $\{\mathbf{x}_1, \cdots, \mathbf{x}_N\}$, the key is to investigate the visual difference between relevant and irrelevant images. The relative feature vector $\psi(l)$ discussed in this paper is designed based on the following two basic assumptions:

- *Density Assumption*: Relevant images have higher density than irrelevant images;
- *Visual Similarity Assumption*: Relevant-relevant image pairs share higher visual similarity than relevant-irrelevant and irrelevant-irrelevant image pairs.

4.1.1 Density Assumption

Our density assumption is that relevant images have higher density than irrelevant images. To verify whether this assumption is true or not, we calculate the density of each of the N images in query q and then analyze their statistic characteristics. The density $p_{\mathbf{x}_i}$ for image $\mathbf{x}_i$ is calculated via Kernel Density Estimation (KDE)[18],

$$p_{\mathbf{x}_i} = \frac{1}{|\mathcal{N}(\mathbf{x}_i)|} \sum\nolimits_{\mathbf{x}_j \in \mathcal{N}(\mathbf{x}_i)} k(\mathbf{x}_i - \mathbf{x}_j), \tag{5}$$

where $\mathcal{N}(\mathbf{x}_i)$ is the set of neighbors of image $\mathbf{x}_i$ among the N images and $k(\mathbf{x})$ is a kernel function that satisfies both $k(x) > 0$ and $\int k(\mathbf{x})d(\mathbf{x}) = 1$. The Gaussian kernel is adopted in this paper and σ is empirically set as the average of pair-wise distances of all images.

Without ambiguity, we use $\mathbf{x}_i$ to denote both the image and its visual feature vector in this paper. Various visual features can be used in (5). In this paper we adopt the popular visual bag-of-word image representation. More details will be introduced in Section 5.1.

To show the density difference between relevant and irrelevant images, we calculate the average density of all relevant images $AvgDense_+$ and the average density of all irrelevant images $AvgDense_-$ in each query. They are calculated as,

$$AvgDense_+ = \frac{1}{|\mathcal{X}^+|} \sum\nolimits_{\mathbf{x}_i \in \mathcal{X}^+} p_{\mathbf{x}_i}, \tag{6}$$

$$AvgDense_- = \frac{1}{|\mathcal{X}^-|} \sum\nolimits_{\mathbf{x}_i \in \mathcal{X}^-} p_{\mathbf{x}_i}, \tag{7}$$

where $\mathcal{X}^+$ is the set of all relevant images and $\mathcal{X}^-$ is the set of all irrelevant images. $Ratio_{dense}$ is defined as, $Ratio_{dense} = AvgDense_+/AvgDense_-$.

We compute $Ratio_{dense}$ for all 353 queries in Web353 and plot them in Fig. 2 by sorting them in descending order.

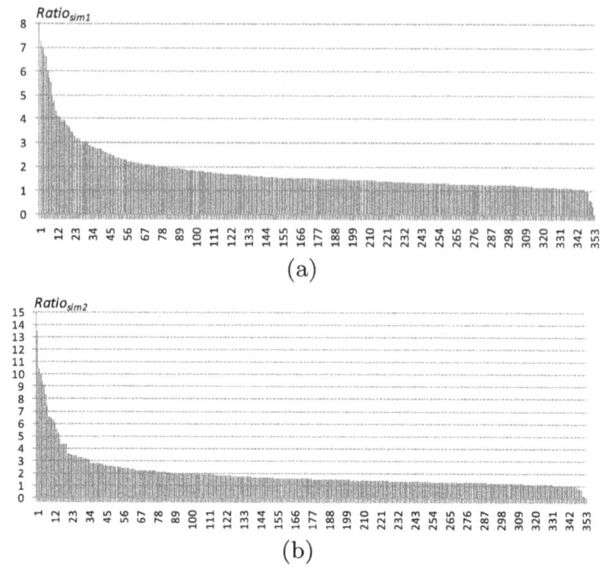

Figure 3: Sorted $Ratio_{sim1}$ (a) and $Ratio_{sim2}$ (b) on 353 queries.

From Fig. 2, we see that, among 353 queries, there are 329 queries whose average density of relevant images is larger than the average density of irrelevant images ($Ratio_{dense} > 1$). To verify whether $AvgDense_+$ is significantly larger than $AvgDense_-$, we further perform a statistical significance test. We used the T-test with a 5% level of significance. The T-test result shows that in 286 queries the average density of relevant images is significantly larger than the average density of irrelevant images. This phenomenon demonstrates that the density assumption holds for most queries.

4.1.2 Visual Similarity Assumption

Our visual similarity assumption is that relevant-relevant image pairs share higher visual similarity than relevant-irrelevant and irrelevant-irrelevant image pairs. For query q, we calculate the visual similarity $sim(\mathbf{x}_i, \mathbf{x}_j)$ for any image pair $(\mathbf{x}_i, \mathbf{x}_j)$. There are various ways to calculate $sim(\mathbf{x}_i, \mathbf{x}_j)$. We use the popular bag-of-visual words representation with intersection kernel [5].

To verify the visual similarity assumption we calculate the average similarity of relevant-relevant, relevant-irrelevant, and irrelevant-irrelevant image pairs for each query in the Web353 dataset. They are denoted as $AvgSim_{++}$, $AvgSim_{+-}$, and $AvgSim_{--}$ respectively. We plot the sorted $Ratio_{sim1} = \frac{AvgSim_{++}}{AvgSim_{+-}}$ and $Ratio_{sim2} = \frac{AvgSim_{++}}{AvgSim_{--}}$ in Fig. 3. It shows that, among 353 queries, there are more than 340 queries whose average similarity of relevant-relevant pairs is larger than the average similarity of relevant-irrelevant and irrelevant-irrelevant pairs. The statistical significance test (T-test with a 5% level of significance) reveals that $AvgSim_{++}$ is significantly larger than $AvgSim_{+-}$ in 347 queries, and $AvgSim_{++}$ is significantly larger than $AvgSim_{--}$ in 339 queries. This proves the validity of our visual similarity assumption.

Due to the well-known semantic gap problem, some queries (especially the queries with large intra-class appearance variance) are hard to be well represented by descriptive visual features. That is the reason why our two assumptions fail for some queries, as shown in Figs. 2 and 3. By further investigating the two assumptions on each query, we find that the assumptions are valid for the queries with small appearance variance, such as "pantheon rome", "flag Italy", "mona lisa",

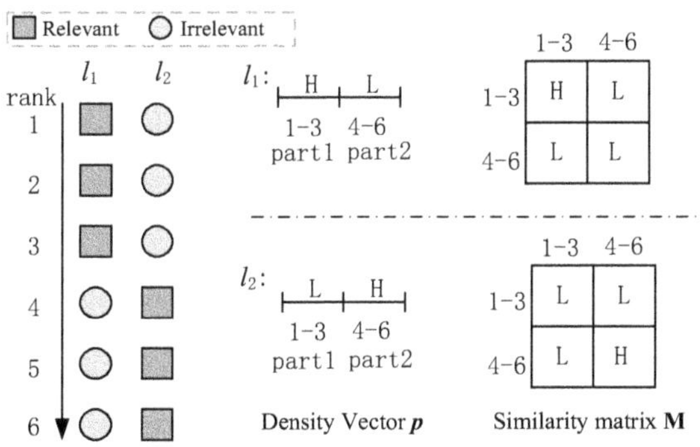

Figure 4: Illustration of density and similarity distribution difference between two ranking lists.

"log NBA", *etc.* They are likely to fail for the queries with large appearance variance, such as "flower", "dog", *etc.* Although the assumptions fail for some queries, they are valid for a majority of queries (Figs. 2 and 3). Therefore, it is reasonable to apply them in our method. Our experimental results reported in Section 5 also validate this.

4.2 Preference Learning Feature Extraction

Inspired by the above two assumptions, we propose a set of related features by mining the distribution of density and visual similarity in l. We demonstrate it by using a toy example for illustration, as shown in Fig. 4. Suppose there are 6 images returned for query q, 3 relevant (denoted by square) and 3 irrelevant (denoted by circle). Given the two ranking lists l_1 and l_2, obviously the performance of l_1 is better than l_2, *i.e.* $y(l_1) > y(l_2)$. According to the two assumptions, for the better ranking list l_1, its top ranked images should have high (H) density and share high visual similarity while bottom ranked images should have low (L) density and low visual similarity. This density and similarity distribution difference between the two ranking lists can be utilized for extracting preference learning related features.

4.2.1 Similarity Distribution Feature

For query q, given a ranking result l, a visual similarity matrix $\mathbf{M} \in \mathbb{R}^{N \times N}$ can be obtained by calculating pairwise image similarity. The (i, j) element m_{ij} in $\mathbf{M}$ denotes the visual similarity between the i-th ranked image and j-th ranked image. We split the N images into k groups along their ranks equally. As a consequence, the $N \times N$ similarity matrix $\mathbf{M}$ is split into $k \times k$ grids, as shown in Fig. 5. Then, we analyze the sub similarity matrix in diagonal blocks. Specifically, we calculate the mean and variance of similarities in each block to derive the similarity distribution feature vector F_{SD}:

$$F_{SD}(i) = [mean(\mathbf{M}^{(i,i)}), var(\mathbf{M}^{(i,i)})], i = 1, \cdots, k. \quad (8)$$

where $\mathbf{M}^{(i,i)}$ is the sub similarity matrix in block B_{ii}. Then, a $2k$-dimensional similarity distribution feature vector F_{SD} is derived. The intuition behind this feature is that, for a good ranking result list, more relevant images have higher ranks. In other words, images belonging to the top part may share higher similarity than those in other parts.

4.2.2 Density Distribution Feature

Similar to the visual similarity distribution feature, we also propose a density distribution feature based on the density assumption. For the N images $\{\mathbf{x}_1, \cdots, \mathbf{x}_N\}$, we can derive a density vector $\mathbf{p} = [p_1, \cdots, p_N]^{\mathrm{T}}$, where p_i is the

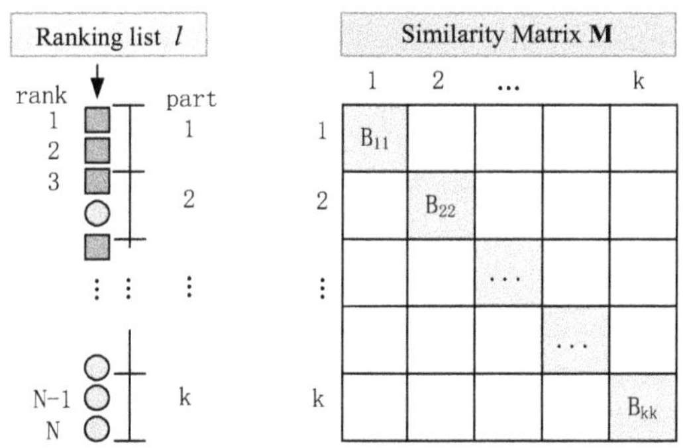

Figure 5: The N images are split into k parts along their ranks equally. Therefore, the $N \times N$ similarity matrix M is split into $k \times k$ blocks.

density of the i-th ranked image in l as defined in (5). We also split the N images into k groups and calculate the mean and variance of the density of the images in each part,

$$F_{DD}(i) = [mean(\mathbf{p}^{(i)}), var(\mathbf{p}^{(i)})], i = 1, \cdots, k. \quad (9)$$

where $\mathbf{p}^{(i)}$ is the sub density vector for images in part i. By concatenating $F_{DD}(i)$, $i = 1, \cdots, k$, we can get a $2k$-dimensional density distribution feature vector F_{DD}.

4.2.3 Feature from Top-T Ranked Images

Both F_{SD} and F_{DD} roughly capture the overall density and visual similarity distribution of all N images in l (mean and variance). The following features are designed to exploit them in fine granularity as a complementation. Especially in the case when users only focus on the performance of images ranked in the first several pages. Therefore, we propose a histogram of density and visual similarity to elaborately analyze the top-T ranked images in l.

Specifically, the density value is in range [0, 1] and we equally divide it into C-bins. Then, the densities of top-T ranked images $\{p_1, p_2, \cdots, p_T\}$ can be quantified into a C-bin histogram by mapping them into the corresponding bins. We denote this density histogram feature as F_{HD},

$$F_{HD}(c) = \frac{1}{T}|\{i|i = 1, \cdots, T, p_i \in c\text{-th bin}\}|, \quad (10)$$

where $c = 1, \cdots, C$.

Similarly, we can get a C-bin visual similarity histogram F_{HS} by mapping the $T \times T$ similarity matrix of the top-T ranked images into C-bins,

$$F_{HS}(c) = \frac{1}{T^2}|\{(i, j)|i, j = 1, \cdots, T, m_{ij} \in c\text{-th bin}\}|, \quad (11)$$

where $c = 1, \cdots, C$.

Given F_{SD}, F_{DD}, F_{HD}, and F_{HS}, the final preference learning feature vector $\psi(l)$ can be derived by concatenating these four individual features.

4.3 Training Sample Enlargement

We have shown how to extract the preference learning feature vector $\psi(l)$ for a ranking list l. We then build the preference learning model by training RankSVM on a set of queries $\{q^{(1)}, \cdots, q^{(m)}\}$, as presented in problem (3). In the training set, for each query, there are usually only a few ranking lists in $\mathcal{L}^{(q)}$, which may cause the small (insufficient) sample problem. For example, in our example 1 in Section 1, there are only two ranking lists (one from Bing and the other from Google). To solve this problem, we can construct additional ranking lists to enlarge the training set.

We can manually create ranking list l^{manual} for each query by permutating the N images in query q according to certain rules. Then, l^{manual} is added into the ranking list set $\mathcal{L}^{(q)}$:

$$\mathcal{L}^{(q)} \leftarrow \mathcal{L}^{(q)} \cup \{l^{manual}\} \quad (12)$$

In this paper, we create three manual ranking lists for each query, including:

1) Perfect ranking list: order all relevant images at the top and all irrelevant images at the bottom;

2) Worst ranking list: order all irrelevant images at the top and all relevant images at the bottom;

3) Random ranking list: permutate the images randomly.

Our experiments show that this training set enlargement works well for solving the small training sample problem.

5. EXPERIMENTS

5.1 Reranking Ability Assessment

In this section, we investigate the effectiveness of the proposed preference learning model (PLM) by applying it to reranking ability assessment. In reranking, each query q has two ranking lists: l_{Text} generated by text-based search engine and l_{rerank} generated by the reranking process. The *reranking ability* t_q^* is defined as the performance improvement of reranking over text-based search, $t_q^* = y(l_{rerank}) - y(l_{Text})$. The reranking ability measures to what degree reranking can improve text-based search results. For a query, if its reranking ability is positive (suitable to be reranked), the reranking result list will be presented to users; otherwise the text-based search result list will be presented. In other words, the search engine can achieve guaranteed performance enhancement by only reranking queries which are suitable for reranking while leaving the remaining unsuitable ones unchanged. With this motivation, we apply PLM to assess reranking ability. Specifically, with the model $f(\cdot)$, PLM can predict a value for l_{Text} and l_{rerank} respectively. The prediction difference $f(l_{rerank}) - f(l_{Text})$ is used to approximate the ground truth reranking ability t_q^*.

Dataset: In order to demonstrate the capacity of PLM for reranking ability assessment, we conduct experiments on a large public web image search dataset "Web353", collected by Krapac *et al.* [13]. This dataset consists of 71478 images returned by the French search engine Exalead [2] for 353 search queries, which were sampled from the most frequent terms searched by Exalead users. These 353 queries are very diverse and cover a broad range of topics, including landmark, design (painting, map, logo, flag), people (movie, sports, singer star), object (vehicle, instrument, building, sports tool), and others (animal, plant, product, place, event, abstract word). Queries are somewhat evenly distributed across these topics. For each query, there are about 200 images returned by Exalead. The ground-truth relevance label for each image is given a binary value: "relevant" or "irrelevant". In this dataset, there are 43.86% images labeled as relevant. For each query, we conduct BR (Bayesian Reranking) [19] to generate its reranking result l_{rerank}.

Ranking List Performance $y(l)$: For query q, given a ranking result list l, its ground truth performance $y(l)$ is measured via non-interpolated average precision (AP) [1], which is widely used in information retrieval. AP is the mean of the precision values obtained when each relevant image occurs. The AP of top-T ranked images is defined as

[2]http://www.exalead.com/search/image

$$\text{AP@}T = \frac{1}{Z_T}\sum_{i=1}^{T}[precison(i) \times rel(i)] \quad (13)$$

where $precison(i)$ is the precision of top-i ranked images and $rel(i)$ is a binary function denoting the relevance of the ranked image with "1" for relevant and "0" for irrelevant. Z_T is a normalization constant which is chosen to guarantee AP@$T = 1$ for a perfect ranking result list.

Model training: We use the leave-one-out method for PLM training. At each step we train the model on 352 queries and test this model on the leftover query. We repeat the process 353 times to ensure that each query has been used as test query at least once.

Image visual representation: The density and visual similarity features described in Section 4 are calculated based on visual representation of images. In this paper we use a bag-of-visual word histogram to visually represent an image. Scale-invariant feature transform (SIFT) [16] local descriptors are extracted from each image on a dense grid. Then, a codebook is generated by clustering all local descriptors into 1000 groups [5]. By quantizing local descriptors into visual words, each image is represented as a 1000-dimensional histogram. Spatial pyramid matching [15] is used to encode spatial information. Calculating the similarity between two histograms is done using an intersection kernel.

Evaluation: For each query q, there are two ranking lists: l_{Text} and l_{rerank}. The query's ground truth reranking ability is $t_q^* = y(l_{rerank}) - y(l_{Text})$, and the reranking ability estimated by the learned PLM is $t_q = f(l_{rerank}) - f(l_{Text})$. We evaluate PLM from the following two aspects.

1. *Prediction Accuracy* (AC):

$$\text{AC} = \frac{\sharp\text{Correctly predicted queries}}{\sharp\text{Total queries}} \quad (14)$$

Correctly predicted queries are those which satisfy $t_q^* t_q > 0$. AC examines whether PLM can correctly predict the binary relationship (improved or not) between the result lists of reranking and text-based search. In addition to this overall accuracy, we also examine the prediction accuracy P+, P− of positive and negative queries. A positive (negative) query is one in which reranking performs better (worse) than the text-based search, *i.e.*, $t_q^* > 0$ ($t_q^* < 0$). P+ and P− are defined as:

$$\text{P}+ = \frac{\sharp\text{Correctly predicted positive queries}(t_q^* > 0 \text{and} t_q > 0)}{\sharp\text{Total positive queries}}$$

$$\text{P}- = \frac{\sharp\text{Correctly predicted negative queries}(t_q^* < 0 \text{and} t_q < 0)}{\sharp\text{Total negative queries}}$$

We examine P+ and P− because we want to investigate the model's capacity for negative query detection as well as the percentage of sacrificed positive queries.

2. *Correlation Coefficient*: Accuracy only measures the binary prediction of reranking ability, *i.e.*, improved or not after reranking. To further verify the effectiveness of PLM in terms of reranking ability degree prediction, we check the consistency between the ground truth reranking ability vector $\mathbf{t}^* = [t^*_{q^{(1)}}, \cdots, t^*_{q^{(353)}}]^{\text{T}}$ and the one predicted by PLM $\mathbf{t} = [t_{q^{(1)}}, \cdots, t_{q^{(353)}}]^{\text{T}}$. As widely used in query difficulty prediction [11, 23], we calculate the Kendall's τ rank correlation coefficient between $\mathbf{t}^*$ and $\mathbf{t}$. Kendall's τ is defined as $\tau = \frac{n_c - n_d}{n_c + n_d}$, where n_c and n_d are the numbers of concordant and discordant pairs respectively. A pair of two queries $(q^{(i)}, q^{(j)})$ is concordant if the orders of $(t^*_{q^{(i)}}, t^*_{q^{(j)}})$ and $(t_{q^{(i)}}, t_{q^{(j)}})$ agree. Kendall's τ value falls within the range [-1, 1], where -1 means perfect negative correlation, 1

Table 4: Correlation coefficients and accuracy in *reranking ability assessment.*

		Kendall's τ	AC(%)	P+(%)	P-(%)
T=20	QD	0.0543	57.51	67.97	33.33
	PLM	0.3654	75.64	92.19	35.63
T=40	QD	0.1485	65.44	77.44	30.49
	PLM	0.4414	78.75	91.35	42.68
T=60	QD	0.0826	65.44	77.09	26.03
	PLM	0.4782	82.44	92.73	49.32
T=80	QD	0.1244	68.84	81.09	27.40
	PLM	0.4820	80.45	89.82	50.68
T=100	QD	0.1400	70.82	82.44	28.99
	PLM	0.4659	80.74	89.25	52.17

Table 5: MAP ($\times$100) comparison in *reranking ability assessment.* MAP is the mean of AP over all queries.

	Text	BR	Select$_{\text{QD}}$	Select$_{\text{PLM}}$	Select$_{\text{Opt}}$
MAP@20	50.28	63.64	59.65	**64.32**	*66.80*
MAP@40	45.24	57.37	55.29	**57.97**	*59.40*
MAP@60	43.06	54.35	51.89	**55.02**	*55.96*
MAP@80	42.60	52.90	51.24	**53.45**	*54.32*
MAP@100	43.08	52.99	51.65	**53.38**	*54.24*

means perfect positive correlation, and 0 means $\mathbf{t}^*$ and $\mathbf{t}$ are independent to each other.

Reranking Ability Assessment: We evaluate PLM at 5 truncation levels, *i.e.*, $y(l) = \text{AP@}T, T = \{20, 40, 60, 80, 100\}$. We implement the document query difficulty method proposed in [11] as a baseline, since this method conducts query difficulty prediction through supervised model training. Based on [11], we extract textual features for each image from its associated textual information (URL, surrounding text, *etc.*) and train a regression model. The reranking ability is denoted as the query difficulty difference between the two ranking lists (l_{Text} and l_{rerank}). We note the method in [11] as QD. Table 4 shows the Kendall's τ correlation coefficients and accuracy of our approach and the baseline QD. It reveals that our method outperforms QD in both correlation coefficients and accuracy. By further investigating P+ and P-, we conclude that PLM removes about half of the negative queries while keeping most positive queries. For example, in T=80, PLM detects 50.68% of the negative queries, preventing performance decrease, while sacrificing performance gain on only 10.18% of the positive queries.

With the predicted reranking ability, we can choose to execute reranking only on those queries whose reranking ability is positive. This operation can prevent large performance decreases on some queries, possibly improving the user experience. The reranking process selection for each query can also lead to a better overall performance (mean AP over all queries, MAP). We select a better one from l_{Text} and l_{Rerank} for each query via QD (Select$_{\text{QD}}$) and PLM (Select$_{\text{PLM}}$.) Table 5 lists the MAP values for text-based search (Text), reranking (BR), Select$_{\text{QD}}$, and Select$_{\text{PLM}}$. Column Select$_{\text{Opt}}$ shows the maximal MAP by selecting the best search result list between Text and BR for each query according to their ground truth performance, which gives the upper bound of the MAP value we can achieve. Table 5 shows that Select$_{\text{PLM}}$ performs better than both Text and BR, while Select$_{\text{QD}}$ only achieves a moderate performance between Text and BR. The reason why the QD method in [11] does not work well here is that textual features in image retrieval are not the essential descriptions for the images, therefore more noise (*e.g.*, mismatching between surrounding text and image content) may be introduced.

Table 6: MAP ($\times$100) comparison in reranking ability assessment for the queries which do not satisfy the assumptions.

	Text	BR	Select$_{\text{PLM}}$	Select$_{\text{Opt}}$
MAP@20	41.00	**41.29**	40.78	*47.51*
MAP@40	36.57	36.91	**37.20**	*41.09*
MAP@60	34.58	35.38	**35.46**	*38.37*
MAP@80	35.32	36.15	**36.16**	*38.92*
MAP@100	36.38	**37.90**	37.50	*40.19*

Table 7: MAP ($\times$100) comparison in reranking ability assessment for each of the 5 query categories (T=60).

	Text	BR	Select$_{\text{PLM}}$	Select$_{\text{Opt}}$
landmark	50.92	62.44	**63.75**	*64.88*
design	41.94	57.83	**58.59**	*59.00*
people	47.08	**61.61**	61.59	*62.08*
object	33.66	35.33	**36.64**	*39.00*
others	40.38	50.70	**51.31**	*52.10*

As we discussed in Section 4.1, the assumptions are not always valid for all queries. For those queries which do not satisfy the assumptions, the extracted preference learning features may be noisy. Consequently the preference prediction may be unreliable. To investigate the implication of the failures of the assumptions on the prediction results, we examined the performance of the proposed PLM on the 67 queries which do not satisfy either the density assumption or the visual similarity assumption. The experimental results show that our approach still achieves (50$\pm$4.9)% prediction accuracy (AC over $T = 20, 40, 60, 80, 100$) in reranking ability assessment, which is close to random prediction. And the Select$_{\text{PLM}}$ is comparable to Text and BR, as shown in Table 6. It reveals that our method does not worsen the search engine's performance even on the queries which do not satisfy the assumptions.

To further investigate the effectiveness of PLM for different categories of queries, the 353 queries are grouped into 5 categories: landmark (53), design (60), people (98), object (54) and others (88). We conducted experiments on each of the 5 categories. The experimental results show that our method works well on all query categories. The prediction accuracy (ACs) are 86.79%, 95.00%, 87.76%, 61.11%, 78.41% respectively. Even in the category "object", of which queries usually have images with a large visual appearance variance, moderate AC (61.11%) is obtained and the MAP value of Select$_{\text{PLM}}$ is better than both Text and BR, as shown in Table 7. Better performance is achieved in "landmark" and "design" since the images of those categories are more visually consistent. For "people", high AC is obtained, but the Select$_{\text{PLM}}$ is very close to BR. The reason is that BR already improves most of queries in this category a lot, hence the improvement space of PLM over BR is limited.

Reranking Feature Selection: PLM can also be applied to select optimal reranking features. The reranking

Table 8: **MAP (×100) comparison in *reranking feature selection* from {Text, BR_{SIFT} and BR_{CF}}**

	Text	BR_{SIFT}	BR_{CF}	$Select_{Random}$	$Select_{PLM}$	$Select_{Opt}$
MAP@20	50.28	63.64	60.21	58.04	**64.74**	*69.13*
MAP@40	45.24	57.37	53.99	52.20	**58.44**	*61.35*
MAP@60	43.06	54.35	50.65	49.35	**55.17**	*57.34*
MAP@80	42.60	52.90	49.20	48.23	**53.85**	*55.58*
MAP@100	43.08	52.99	49.08	48.38	**53.67**	*55.36*

Table 9: **MAP (×100) comparison in *reranking algorithm selection* from {Text, BR_{SIFT} and PRF_{SIFT}}.**

	Text	BR_{SIFT}	PRF_{SIFT}	$Select_{Random}$	$Select_{PLM}$	$Select_{Opt}$
MAP@20	50.28	63.64	60.65	58.19	**63.76**	*69.44*
MAP@40	45.24	57.37	54.75	52.45	**57.79**	*60.99*
MAP@60	43.06	54.35	51.97	49.79	**55.07**	*57.26*
MAP@80	42.60	52.90	50.68	48.73	**53.39**	*55.56*
MAP@100	43.08	52.99	50.57	48.88	**53.62**	*55.43*

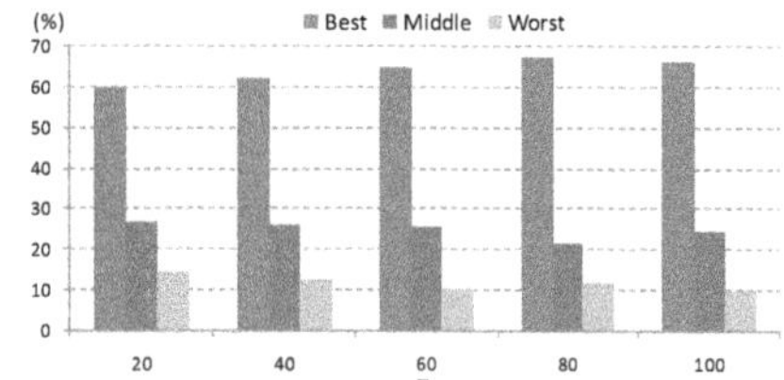

Figure 6: *Reranking feature selection.* Percentages of queries for which PLM selects the Best/Middle/Worst ranking list.

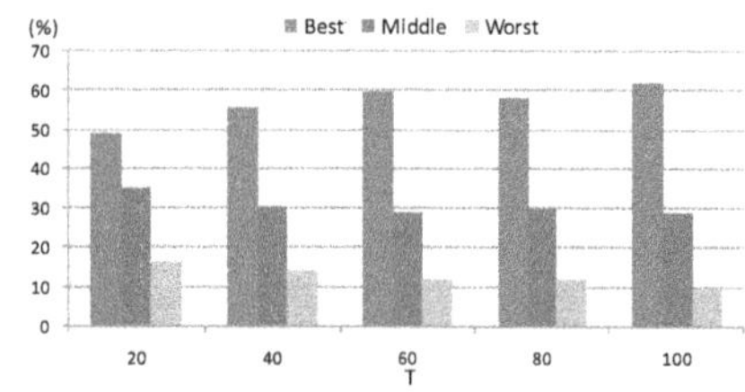

Figure 7: *Reranking algorithm selection.* Percentages of queries for which PLM selects the Best/Middle/Worst ranking list.

feature is the visual feature used in the reranking process which has a great influence on reranking performance. We use two different visual features for BR reranking and obtain their corresponding ranking lists. One feature is the aforementioned SIFT based bag-of-visual word histogram, denoted as SIFT. The other one is a combination of several low-level features adopted in [4], denoted as CF.

With two ranking lists generated by BR_{SIFT} and BR_{CF}, as well as the text-based search result list (Text), we apply PLM to select the best result list for each individual query. Table 8 gives the MAP comparison between their individual performances, as well as the performance after selection. We compare PLM with random selection. Without prior knowledge, random selection just selects from the three ranking lists randomly. It shows that our model $Select_{PLM}$ not only outperforms random selection $Select_{Random}$, but also outperforms all three individual ranking methods. In Fig. 6, we further give the % of the Best/Middle/Worst selection queries, which shows the percent of all queries for which our method chose each one of the three ranking lists. Fig. 6 clearly demonstrates that, for most queries (60%-70%), PLM selects the Best ranking list from {Text, BR_{SIFT}, BR_{CF}}. This is a substantial improvement over the random

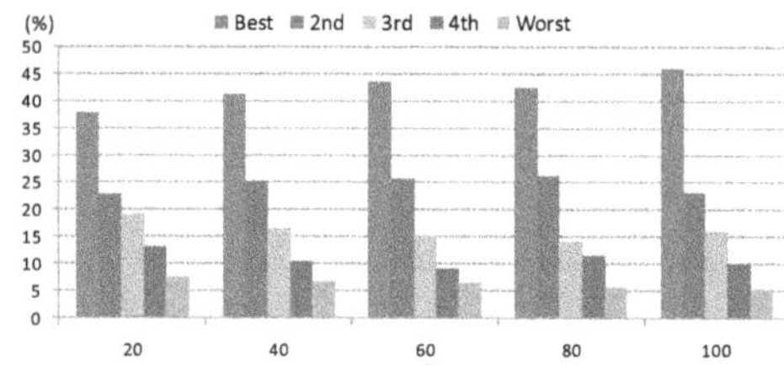

Figure 8: *Reranking feature and algorithm mixture selection.* Percentages of queries for which PLM selects the Best/2nd/3rd/4th/Worst ranking list.

selection method, which chooses the Best ranking list for 33.33% of queries, and verifies the effectiveness of our model.

Reranking Method Selection: Similar with reranking feature selection, PLM can also be applied to select the optimal reranking method for each query. This selection is conducted on reranking results generated by BR [19] and PRF [21]. The SIFT feature is used in both reranking methods. Table 9 and Fig. 7 give the MAP value comparison and % of the Best/Middel/Worst selection queries, respectively. It also demonstrates the effectiveness of our method in selecting better ranking method for each query.

Reranking Feature and Algorithm Mixture Selection: With two reranking features (SIFT and CF) and two reranking algorithms (BR and PRF), four reranking result lists are generated by their combination, *i.e.*, BR_{SIFT}, PRF_{SIFT}, BR_{CF} and PRF_{CF}. We further test PLM on this mixture selection. For each query, four reranking lists as well as the Text result list are ranked according to the value predicted by PLM. Table 10 gives the MAP value comparison We note an increase in performance after PLM selection, producing better results than all five basic methods and random selection. We also analyzed the number of queries for which PLM selects the i-th best ranking list ($i = 1, \cdots, 5$; $i = 1$ means the best and $i = 5$ means the worst), as shown in Fig. 8. It shows that PLM selects the Best/second best ranking list for about 40%/20% of the queries. It obviously outperforms random selection, which would select each of the five ranking lists for about 20% of the queries.

5.2 Search Engine Selection

In this section we investigate the effectiveness of the proposed method by applying it to optimal image search engine

Table 10: MAP (×100) comparison in *reranking feature and algorithm mixture selection* from {Text, BR_{SIFT}, BR_{CF}, PRF_{SIFT} and PRF_{CF}}.

	Text	BR_{SIFT}	BR_{CF}	PRF_{SIFT}	PRF_{CF}	$Select_{Random}$	$Select_{PLM}$	$Select_{Opt}$
MAP@20	50.28	63.64	60.21	60.65	54.00	57.76	**64.86**	*72.26*
MAP@40	45.24	57.37	53.99	54.75	49.67	52.20	**58.57**	*63.68*
MAP@60	43.06	54.35	50.65	51.97	47.52	49.51	**55.45**	*59.45*
MAP@80	42.60	52.90	49.20	50.68	50.68	49.21	**53.83**	*57.57*
MAP@100	43.08	52.99	49.08	50.57	47.58	48.66	**54.00**	*57.29*

selection and search result merging. Specifically, each query q has two ranking lists generated by two search engines: Bing and Google. Our objective is to determine which search engine returns better performance for any query q.

Dataset: A dataset was collected from two popular image search engines, Bing (Live) and Google. We selected 29 queries [3] from the top-1000 queries of Live Image Search and popular tags on Flickr. The 29 queries satisfy all the following three criteria: 1) *Popularity*: they are either top queries of Live Image Search or popular tags of Flickr; 2) *Broad topic coverage*: the 29 queries cover wide topics, *e.g.*, animals, plants, scene, objects, *etc.*; 3) *Including both simple and compound queries*: the 29 queries contain both simple queries which normally consist of one term (*e.g.*, "Cat", "Flower", *etc.*) and compound queries which are refined terms based on some certain attribute, *e.g.*, color ("White Cat"), time ("White House Night"), emotion ("Funny Dog"), *etc.* We submitted each query to Bing and Google respectively, and collected the top 1000 images returned, resulting in 50566 total images. For each query, the returned images are labeled as either "relevant" or "irrelevant". In this dataset, there are 42.23% images labeled as relevant.

To the best of our knowledge, there is no publicly available dataset which collects the search results of the same queries from several search engines and the queries are sampled from real query logs. To collect such a large query set is difficult since it may need the collaboration between academia and industry and it will involve a large amount of efforts in getting query logs from popular search engines , collecting the huge amount of data and employing human for labeling. As the first try, we collected a moderate-size dataset with 50K images [22] with the collaboration with Bing search. In the future, with the continuing collaboration with industry, we plan to collect a larger dataset from several search engines.

Experimental setting is the same as that in Section 5.1. We used the bag-of-visual words histogram for image representation and the leave-one-out method for model training.

Evaluation: For each query q, there are two ranking lists: l_{Bing} and l_{Google}. Each query's ground truth performance difference is denoted as $\delta_q^* = y(l_{Bing}) - y(l_{Google})$, and the performance difference estimated by PLM is $\delta_q = f(l_{Bing}) - f(l_{Google})$. We also evaluate PLM's preference prediction ability from the following two aspects:

1. *Prediction Accuracy* defined in (14). In this application, the correctly predicted queries are those which satisfy $\delta_q^* \delta_q > 0$, *i.e.*, the preference relationship between the two ranking lists is correctly predicted.

[3]Animal, Beach, Beijing Olympic 2008, Building, Car, Cat, Clouds, Earth, Flower, Fox, Funny Dog, George W. Bush, Grape, Hearts, Hello Kitty, Hiking, Mercedes Logo, Panda, Sky, Statue of Liberty, Sun, Trees, Wedding, White Cat, White House Night, White House, Winter, Yellow Rose, Zebra.

Table 11: Correlation coefficients and Accuracy in search engine selection from {Bing, Google}

	T=20	T=40	T=60	T=80	T=100
Kendall's τ	0.1724	0.1970	0.1232	0.1626	0.2315
AC(%)	62.07	68.97	65.52	79.31	75.86

2. Correlation coefficient: Kendall's τ correlation coefficients between the ground truth performance difference vector $\mathbf{\Delta}^* = [\delta^*_{q(1)}, \cdots, \delta^*_{q(29)}]^{\mathbf{T}}$ and the one predicted by our PLM $\mathbf{\Delta} = [\delta_{q(1)}, \cdots, \delta_{q(29)}]^{\mathbf{T}}$.

Search Engine Selection: We also evaluate 5 different Ts as in Section 5.1. Table 11 shows the correlation coefficients and accuracy. It shows that moderate correlation coefficients are achieved and the AC is more than 70% when T=80 and 100. It demonstrates that PLM can choose the better search engine between Bing and Google for the majority of queries. Therefore, better performance will be achieved after this suitable search engine selection. The MAP values of Bing ($Text_{Bing}$), Google ($Text_{Google}$) and the one generated after our PLM Selection ($Select_{PLM}$) are given in Table 12. Column $Select_{Opt}$ is the maximal MAP value arrived at by selecting the optimal search engine according to their ground truth. Table 12 shows that $Select_{PLM}$ achieves consistent performance improvements over both $Text_{Bing}$ and $Text_{Google}$ for all Ts. From Tables 11 and 12, we conclude that the proposed PLM method can be successfully applied to optimal search engine selection.

Search Results Merging: In search engine selection, for each query, we choose a better one between l_{Bing} and l_{Google}. In addition to this binary selection, we can also merge the two result lists to get a new one. For query q, when we have no idea of the performance of the two search results, they may contribute equally to the final merged result list. If we have the prior knowledge of which one is better than the other, then higher merging weight can be assigned to this better one. Our PLM can serve this role by using the predicted δ_q to set appropriate merging weights. To complete this goal, the $\mathbf{\Delta}$ is first normalized into [-1, 1]. We denote the normalized performance difference as $\tilde{\delta}_q$. Then, for query q, the merging weights for l_{Bing} and l_{Google} are defined as $w_{Bing} = \frac{1}{2}(1 + \tilde{\delta}_q)$ and $w_{Google} = \frac{1}{2}(1 - \tilde{\delta}_q)$ respectively ($w_{Bing} \geq 0$, $w_{Google} \geq 0$, $w_{Bing} + w_{Google} = 1$). To form the merged result list, we assign a merging score to each image in l_{Bing} and l_{Google}. The merging score for the i-th ranked images in l_{Bing} is $i \times (1 - w_{Bing})$. The merging score for the i-th ranked image in l_{Google} is $i \times (1 - w_{Google})$. The final merged ranking list is derived by sorting all images in l_{Bing} and l_{Google} in ascending order of their merging scores. The performance of this weighted merging result is given in Table 12, comparing with the equal merging in which $w_{Bing} = w_{Google} = 0.5$. The search engine selection

Table 12: MAP (×100) comparison in search engine selection and search results merging from {Bing, Google}

	$Text_{Bing}$	$Text_{Google}$	$Select_{Random}$	$Select_{PLM}$	$Select_{Opt}$	$Merge_{Equal}$	$Merge_{Weight}$
MAP@20	57.91	64.26	61.09	**65.80**	*71.51*	65.36	**67.21**
MAP@40	52.24	52.36	52.30	**56.12**	*60.71*	59.57	**59.80**
MAP@60	49.18	44.35	46.77	**50.78**	*54.63*	54.78	**55.85**
MAP@80	46.52	39.41	42.97	**47.77**	*50.64*	51.31	**52.76**
MAP@100	44.52	36.20	40.36	**45.16**	*48.18*	48.61	**49.83**

discussed above is actually a hard merge of the two search results with weight either 1 or 0. Table 12 clearly demonstrates that merging by leveraging our preference prediction outperforms equal merging.

6. CONCLUSION AND FUTURE WORK

In this paper, we proposed a method to automatically compare a set of ranking result lists for a given query by mining their visual information. The method is formulated within the RankSVM framework and a set of lightweight features are designed to reflect the visual difference between two ranking lists. The proposed method is successfully applied to reranking ability estimation and automatic search engine selection. Experimental results have demonstrated the effectiveness of our approach and its promising applications on reranking feature and model selection, as well as merging of image search results.

Currently, our preference learning model is built based on visual features of images only, and their textual information is not considered. In the future, we plan to further exploit this ranking list performance comparison problem by investigating both visual and textual features, to achieve better performance. Another direction of our future work is to apply this model to more potential applications, *e.g.*, query suggestion, query language selection and so on.

Acknowledgments This work was supported by Research Enhancement Program (REP) and start-up funding from the Texas State University, and was supported in part to Dr. Qi Tian by NSF IIS 1052851, Faculty Research Awards by Google, FXPAL and NEC Laboratories of America, respectively.

7. REFERENCES

[1] Trecvid video retrieval evaluation. hppt://www-nlpir.nist.gov/projects/trecvid/.

[2] G. Carneiro, A. Chan, P. Moreno, and N. Vasconcelos. Supervised learning of semantic classes for image annotation and retrieval. *PAMI*, 29(3):394–410, 2007.

[3] S. Cronen-Townsend, Y. Zhou, and W. B. Croft. Predicting query performance. *ACM SIGIR*, pages 299–306, 2002.

[4] J. Cui, F. Wen, and X. Tang. Real time google and live image search re-ranking. *ACM Multimedia*, pages 729–732, 2008.

[5] J. Deng, A. C. Berg, K. Li, and F.-F. Li. What does classifying more than 10,000 image categories tell us? *ECCV*, pages 71–84, 2010.

[6] B. Geng, L. Yang, C. Xu, and X.-S. Hua. Content-aware ranking for visual search. *CVPR*, pages 3400–3407, 2010.

[7] C. Hauff, V. Murdock, and R. Baeza-Yates. Improved query difficulty prediction for the web. *ACM CIKM*, pages 439–448, 2008.

[8] B. He and I. Ounis. Inferring query performance using pre-retrieval predictors. *SPIRE*, pages 43–54, 2004.

[9] H. Imran and A. Sharan. Co-occurrence based predictors for estimating query difficulty. *IEEE ICDM Workshops*, pages 867–874, 2010.

[10] K. Järvelin and J. Kekäläinen. Cumulated gain-based evaluation of ir techniques. *ACM Trans. Inf. Syst.*, 20(4):422–446, 2002.

[11] E. Jensen, S. Beitzel, D. Grossman, O. Frieder, and A. Chowdhury. Predicting query difficulty on the web by learning visual clues. *SIGIR*, pages 615–616, 2005.

[12] T. Joachims. Optimizing search engines using clickthrough data. *SIGKDD*, pages 133–142, 2002.

[13] J. Krapac, M. Allan, J. Verbeek, and F. Juried. Improving web image search results using query-relative classifiers. *CVPR*, pages 1094–1101, 2010.

[14] K.-L. Kwok, L. Grunfeld, H. L. Sun, and P. Deng. Trec 2004 robust track experiments using pircs. *TREC*, 2004.

[15] S. Lazebnik, C. Schmid, and J. Ponce. Beyond bags of features: Spatial pyramid matching for recognizing natural scene categories. *CVPR*, pages 2169–2178, 2006.

[16] D. G. Lowe. Distinctive image features from scale-invariant keypoints. *IJCV*, 60(2):91–110, 2004.

[17] K. Min, L. Yang, J. Wright, L. Wu, X.-S. Hua, and Y. Ma. Compact projection: Simple and efficient near neighbor search with practical memory requirements. *CVPR*, pages 3477–3484, 2010.

[18] E. Parzen. On estimation of a probability density function and mode. *The annals of mathematical statistics*, 33(3):1065–1076, 1962.

[19] X. Tian, L. Yang, J. Wang, Y. Yang, X. Wu, and X.-S. Hua. Bayesian video search reranking. *ACM Multimedia*, pages 131–140, 2008.

[20] X. Xing, Y. Zhang, and M. Han. Query difficulty prediction for contextual image retrieval. *ECIR*, pages 581–585, 2010.

[21] R. Yan, A. G. Hauptmann, and R. Jin. Multimedia search with pseudo-relevance feedback. *CIVR*, pages 238–247, 2003.

[22] L. Yang and A. Hanjalic. Supervised reranking for web image search. *ACM Multimedia*, pages 183–192, 2010.

[23] E. Yom-Tov, S. Fine, D. Carmel, and A. Darlow. Learning to estimate query difficulty: including applications to missing content detection and distributed information retrieval. *ACM SIGIR*, pages 512–519, 2005.

[24] Z.-J. Zha, L. Yang, T. Mei, M. Wang, and Z. Wang. Visual query suggestion. *ACM Multimedia*, pages 15–24, 2009.

Prediction of the Inter-Observer Visual Congruency (IOVC) and Application to Image Ranking*

Olivier Le Meur
University of Rennes 1
Campus de Beaulieu
35042 Rennes, France
olemeur@irisa.fr

Thierry Baccino
University of Paris VIII / LUTIN
30, avenue Corentin Cariou
75930 Paris, France
thierry.baccino@univ-paris8.fr

Aline Roumy
INRIA
Campus de Beaulieu
35042 Rennes, France
aline.roumy@inria.fr

ABSTRACT

This paper proposes an automatic method for predicting the inter-observer visual congruency (IOVC). The IOVC reflects the congruence or the variability among different subjects looking at the same image. Predicting this congruence is of interest for image processing applications where the visual perception of a picture matters such as website design, advertisement, etc. This paper makes several new contributions. First, a computational model of the IOVC is proposed. This new model is a mixture of low-level visual features extracted from the input picture where model's parameters are learned by using a large eye-tracking database. Once the parameters have been learned, it can be used for any new picture. Second, regarding low-level visual feature extraction, we propose a new scheme to compute the depth of field of a picture. Finally, once the training and the feature extraction have been carried out, a score ranging from 0 (minimal congruency) to 1 (maximal congruency) is computed. A value of 1 indicates that observers would focus on the same locations and suggests that the picture presents strong locations of interest. A second database of eye movements is used to assess the performance of the proposed model. Results show that our IOVC criterion outperforms the Feature Congestion measure [33]. To illustrate the interest of the proposed model, we have used it to automatically rank personalized photograph.

Categories and Subject Descriptors

H.4 [**Information Systems Applications**]: Miscellaneous; D.2.8 [**Software Engineering**]: Metrics—*complexity measures, performance measures*

General Terms

Experimentation, Human Factors

*Area chair: Kiyoharu Aizawa

MM'11, November 28–December 1, 2011, Scottsdale, Arizona, USA.

Keywords

visual dispersion, congruency, images ranking, eye tracking

1. INTRODUCTION

Idiosyncrasy is defined as an individualizing quality or characteristic of a person or group, and is often used to express peculiarity (from Wikipedia). Therefore idiosyncratic eye movements refer to as the difference between the visual scanpaths of observers viewing the same stimulus. More precisely, these differences concern the intrinsic features of visual fixations. For instance, there is a strong variability of fixation durations between and within observers as shown by [31]. In this paper, we define inter-observer visual congruency (IOVC) and we propose a new method to automatically compute it.

The causes explaining the visual dispersion are usually classified into either stimulus-dependent (or bottom-up) or observer-dependent features (or top down).

A first observer-dependent cause is the cultural difference as suggested by [27, 5]. These authors compared the visual scan pattern of two different populations, an American and an Asian one. The conclusion was Asian people tend to look more at the background and spend relatively less time on focal objects than American people. However, a recent study casts doubt on the influence of cultural differences on oculomotor behavior [32].

A second observer-dependent factor of variability is due to our prior knowledge or our prior experience as illustrated by [1]. They showed that the variability differs when observers looked at famous versus non-famous faces. Famous faces tend to decrease the dispersion of visual fixations just after the stimulus onset. The visual scanning is then affected by higher level information such as the eye-movement-based memory effect.

On the opposite, stimulus-dependent features influencing the dispersion between observers is related to the properties of the stimuli itself. For instance, Rousselet et al. [36] shows that human faces as well as animals attract our attention leading to a decrease of inter-observer variability. Contrary to the two previous factors that are observer-dependent, the properties of the stimuli and their characteristics can be easily extracted and analyzed automatically from the picture.

It is also important to note that the difference between observers' scanpath is time-dependent [29, 38]. They indeed showed that the consistency in fixation locations between observers decreases with prolonged viewing. To explain that, two hypotheses have been formulated: [29] shows that the influence of bottom-up mechanisms decreases with the viewing time and is progressively overridden after several seconds of viewing by top-down mechanisms. On the contrary [38] conjectures that bottom-up mechanisms are not time-dependent and that low-level visual features might keep their ability to attract our visual attention throughout the viewing. They therefore explained that the increase of inter-observer variability would be due to the growing influence of top-down mechanisms over time. Even if both papers propose different explanations, they all agree on the time dependency of IOVC and on the fact that bottom-up (or stimulus-dependent) mechanisms occur first.

In this study, we predict the inter-observer visual congruency that occurs in the first seconds of a picture observation. For a given picture, a score indicating the degree of visual congruence is computed. The computational model we propose, combines stimulus-dependent features which are solely inferred from the low-level visual features of the incoming picture. We train the model by using a large eye-tracking database. In this database, we consider the eye movements tracked in the first seconds of a picture observation. Observer-dependent features such as prior knowledge are not taken into account since they may vary from one observer to another. In order to get a general model that can apply to any picture, we propose a stimulus-dependent model. Therefore, our method predicts the dispersion based on the influence of stimulus characteristics, rather than individual observer characteristics.

There are very few studies dealing with the computational modeling of the inter-observer visual congruency. The closest work concerns a method to measure visual clutter. Note that IOVC and visual clutter defers since the former is the dispersion that exists between locations focused by observers whereas the latter is related to the amount of visual information in a scene. However both might be strongly correlated. The most popular method to measure the visual clutter has been proposed by Rosenholtz et al. [33]. The idea is to measure the visual clutter of a scene in order to avoid confusion and to speed up the visual processing of information. For instance, a possible application is to help people to find important information on a web site or simply on a screen. Rosenholtz et al.'s solution is based on a set of low-level visual features. Some of them will be reused in this study. Rosenholtz et al. assessed the performance of their algorithm by comparing the amount of clutter for a scene to the reaction time required to find a target in the same scene. In this paper as in [33], we use low-level visual features. However, our approach differs from [33] since the goal is different and since we not only use low-level visual features but also eye tracking measurements. More precisely, we use the visual scanpaths of observers in order to train a model. Our approach is supported by a number of studies suggesting that the degree of clutter present in the scene affects the deployment of our visual attention [17]. For instance, Ehinger et al. [9] measured the dispersion between observers to define an upper bound of model-predicted saliency [46]. Eye movements were collected when 14 observers performed a task of pedestrian detection in 912 outdoor scenes. The dispersion between observers was computed by a one-against-all method as proposed by [42]. Here we use the same measurement method for the inter-observer dispersion (as in [9]) and this provides a ground truth used in the learning phase of our algorithm. However the comparison between Ehinger et al. [9] stops there because Ehinger et al. propose a computational model to predict where observers look at, while searching for pedestrians. To infer the salient locations in this visual search context, they combined different guidance sources such as low-level saliency (by using Torralba's model [42]), target features (by using a person detector) and scene context. In our method, we do not predict where people look at. We predict the dispersion between observers indicating whether observers look at similar locations or not, while Ehinger et al. used the dispersion between observers as an upper bound for comparing performance of computational models with human fixations.

Eye movements are also often used to examine the usability of an interface. Golberg and Kotval [13] defined a number of metrics based on the analysis of fixation durations and saccade amplitudes. Cowen et al. [8] featured the efficiency of a visual search by examining the fixation distributions. Fixations concentrated in a small area indicate focused and efficient searching whereas sparse fixations would indicate lower search efficiency.

In this paper, we present a computational model of inter-observer visual congruency (IOVC). From a training set composed of eye tracking data, we build a prediction model by using a supervised approach. Our goal aims to give a score to a given picture that indicates whether the visual strategy of human observers is similar or not. From the eye tracking data, we set up a ground truth by computing for each picture the inter-observer congruency. By using a limited number of low-level visual features, a model is trained and is able to predict efficiently and automatically the dispersion between observers. This predicted score can be used in applications where the visual perception of a picture matters such as website design, advertisement. Indeed, it can help to rank images based on their capacity to attract our attention or help to measure the relevance of web design.

The paper is composed as follows. Section II gives an overview of the proposed approach. Section III describes how the IOVC is measured. A large database of eye tracking data is used for this purpose. Section IV is related to the extraction of visual features that are supposed to influence the attentional allocation. Section V concerns the learning and its performance. Section VI presents an application for ranking personalized pictures based on their interestingness. Finally, we conclude the paper.

In summary, our contributions include:

- a solution for predicting the inter-observer congruency. We use an eye tracking database to train a computational model;
- a novel scheme to estimate the depth of field for a scene is proposed which is simpler than existing methods;
- a new method to rank automatically personalized photographs. The ranking is based on pictures' interestingness.

2. SYSTEM OVERVIEW

Figure 1 illustrates the proposed approach. First, an image database with its corresponding eye tracking data is set up. The feature extraction step extracts different visual attributes for each picture of the training dataset. After the feature extraction, the training set along with eye tracking data is used to train a cluster-weighted model. The trained model is then used to predict the inter-observer congruency of a picture taken from a new data set.

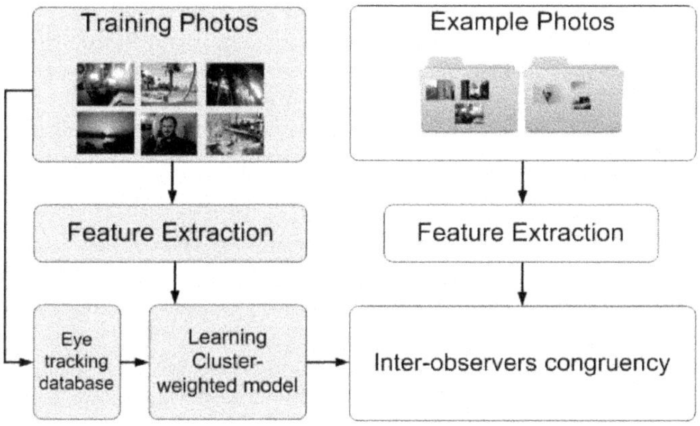

Figure 1: System overview.

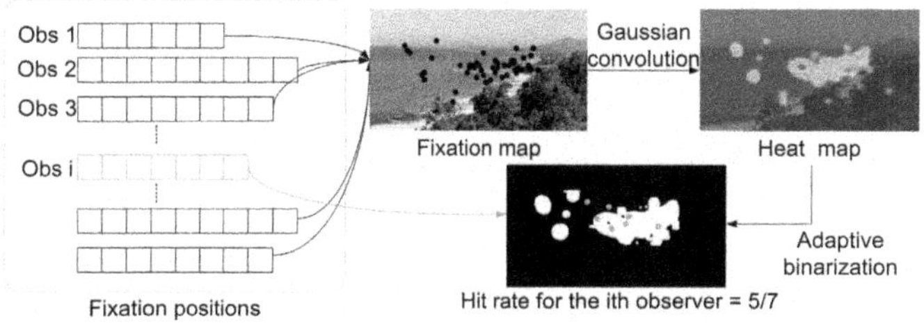

Figure 2: Measure of the inter-observer congruency. On the left, the spatial coordinates of visual fixations for each observer are given. By considering all fixations except those stemming from the ith observer, a heat map is computed (on the right). After an adaptive binarization, we count the number of fixations of the ith observer that fall into salient regions (white region on the bottom).

Once the estimation of model's parameters has been performed, personalized photograph can be ranked according to their interestingness. The interestingness of an image is related to its ability to attract and to hold our attention. The interestingness of a picture is thus similar to the inter-observer congruency.

3. MEASURING THE INTER-OBSERVER CONGRUENCY

3.1 Eye-tracking database

Judd et al.'s database [20] is used in this study. Let us first review the experimental protocol and the characteristics of this dataset. The database is composed of 1003 images of various contents. Images had different resolutions and were in a landscape or portrait orientation. Fifteen viewers were involved in the eye tracking tests. The users were males and females between the ages of 18 and 35. Two of the viewers were researchers and the others were naive viewers. They viewed each image for 3 seconds in a free-viewing task. Participants sat at a distance of approximately two feet from a 19 inch computer screen of resolution 1280×1024. The images subtended approximately 45 horizontally and 37 vertically of the observer's field of view. The number of pixel per degree is then about 23. This database can be downloaded from `http://people.csail.mit.edu/tjudd/index.html`.

3.2 Inter-observer congruency

To assess the inter-observer congruency, a one-against-all approach (also called leave one out) is used as in [42]. The first step consists in computing a 2D fixation distribution from the fixation data of all observers except one for a given picture. The fixation distributions were then convolved with a two-dimensional Gaussian. Each pixel of this map represents the probability to be fixated. The standard deviation of the Gaussian kernel is set at one degree to reflect estimates of foveal size. This map is then thresholded to select an image area having the highest probability of being fixated. The threshold is adaptively set in order to keep 25% of the image. The goal is now to compute the percentage of the visual fixations of the remaining observer that fall within salient parts of the threshold saliency map. This process was iterated for all observers. For a given picture, the variability between observers is the average of the aforementioned percentage over all subjects. As most of the dispersion values are in the range of 0.5 to 1, the scale has been stretch from 0 to 1. A value of 1 indicates that observers fixate the same areas. Conversely, a low value would suggest that the scan patterns are uncorrelated meaning a strong variability between subjects. Figure 2 illustrates the method for the ith observer.

Over the whole dataset, the average dispersion is of 72%, the median dispersion is of 76%. Figure 3 shows the distribution of the inter-observer congruency over the whole dataset. It is interesting to notice that, for a number of pictures, the congruency is maximal. This is due to the fact that a fixation point is defined by its spatial coordinates and by its neighborhood, representing one degree of visual angle (representing fovea's size). Figure 4 shows for different pictures the experimental congruency between observers. Results suggest that the congruency is small when there is nothing in the scene that catches our attention. In this context, areas that stand out the background are rare and the scene consistency is strong. As expected, the presence of human faces tends to increase the inter-observer congruency. It is indeed known that human faces attract in an effortlessly manner our attention.

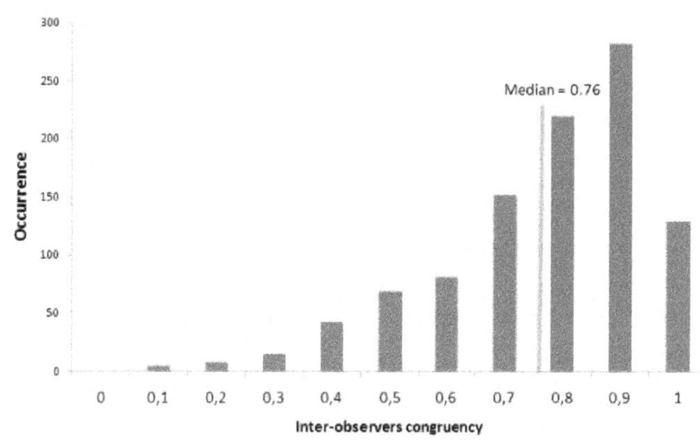

Figure 3: Distribution of the inter-observer congruency over Judd et al.'s dataset [20].

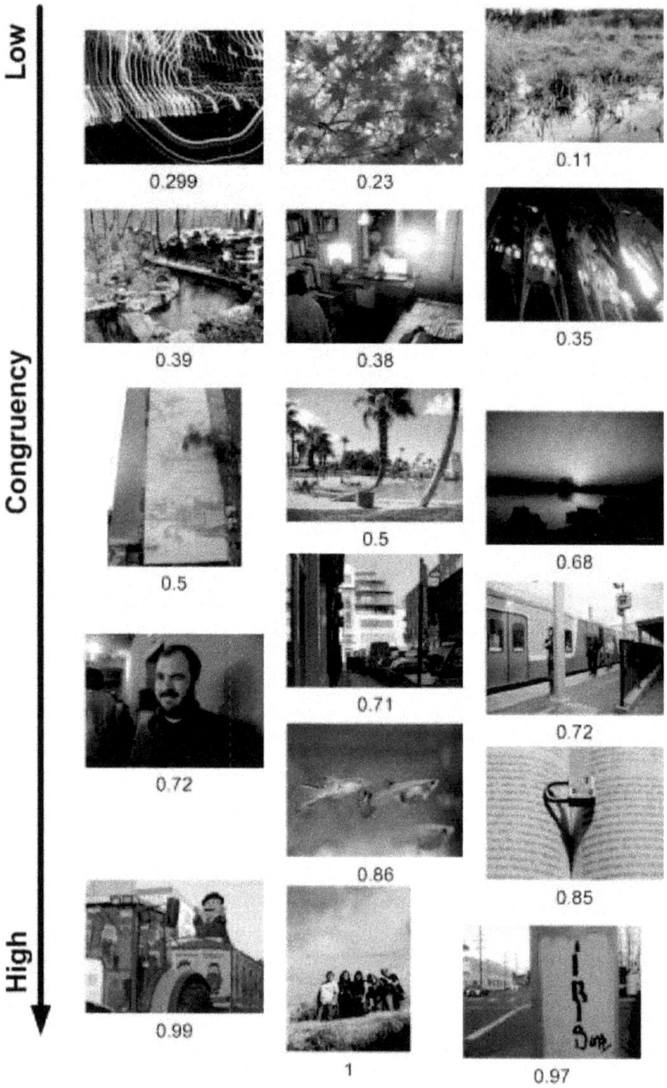

Figure 4: Examples of pictures associated with their corresponding inter-observer congruency. IOVC is in the range of 0 (strongest) to 1 (lowest).

4. EXTRACTION OF VISUAL ATTRIBUTES IMPACTING THE INTER-OBSERVER VARIABILITY

In this section, the visual features used to predict the inter-observer congruency are presented.

4.1 Face detection

As the human faces significantly impact our visual deployment, it is of importance to detect human faces. The face detector we use is the one proposed by OpenCV library. The face detector is based on Haar feature-based cascade classifier for object detection. This kind of detection has been initially proposed by [44] and improved by [23].

4.2 Color Harmony

Several studies showed that scene incongruency or inconsistency are factors influencing the inspection of an image [24, 14, 43]. Among the scene inconsistency factors (objects, size, etc), the color might be an important factor. For instance, Frey et al. [11] showed that overt attention is significantly influenced by the presence of color. The basic assumption was that the color presence might systematically increase the congruency. The conclusion of [11] is not so straightforward. Indeed, the influence of the color might depend on the picture's category.

In this study, the color inconsistency refers to the color harmony of the scene. We speculate that a scene with a strong consistent color harmony would be less visually disruptive than a scene with a poor color harmony. To measure the color harmony, we propose to follow the process of [6].

In [6], the notion of color harmony is based on the work of Matsuda [26, 39]. Figure 5 illustrates the height harmonic templates on the hue wheel. These templates, that may be rotated by an arbitrary angle, can be used to measure how aesthetically pleasing an image is.

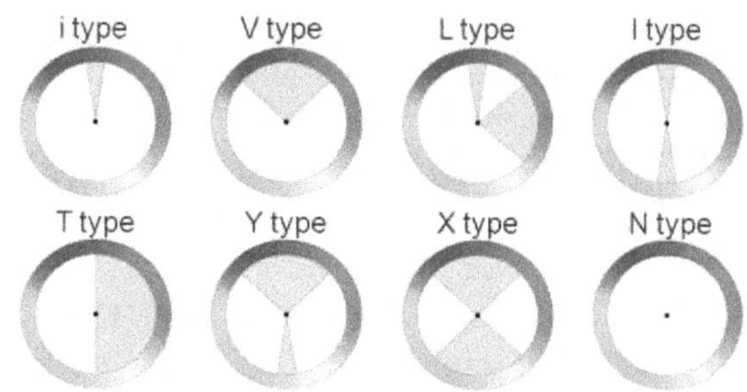

Figure 5: The seven color templates defined by [26] on the hue wheel. The templates may be rotated by an arbitrary angle (extracted from [6]). The template N is used for gray-scale images.

The color harmony of an input color picture I, called $CH(I)$ is computed by equation 1. We use similar notations as [6]. They are briefly reminded below:

$$CH(I) = \min_{m} F(I, (m, \alpha^*)) \quad (1)$$

where, $m \in \{i, I, L, T, V, X, Y\}$. The function F is defined as follows:

$$F(I, (m, \alpha^*)) = \sum_{i \in I} \left\| H(i) - E_{T_m(\alpha^*)}(i) \right\| \times S(i) \quad (2)$$

where H and S denote the hue and the saturation channels, respectively. The hue distance $\|.\|$ refers to the arc-length distance on the hue wheel (measured in radians). Hues that are enclosed in the sector of T_m are considered to have zero distance from the template. α^* defines the orientation of the template T_m that minimizes the distance F. As in [6], we use Brent's algorithm [30] to find the best orientation α^*. This kind of algorithm seeks a local minimum of a function in a given interval. $E_{T_m(\alpha^*)}(i)$ is the sector border hue of template T_m with orientation α^* that is the closest to the hue of pixel i. Figure 6 gives an example of two pictures extracted from [6]: one is the original whereas the second presents an optimized color harmony. The value F is given for each template.

4.3 Depth of Field

The Depth of Field (DoF) is defined as the distance between the nearest and farthest objects in a scene that appear

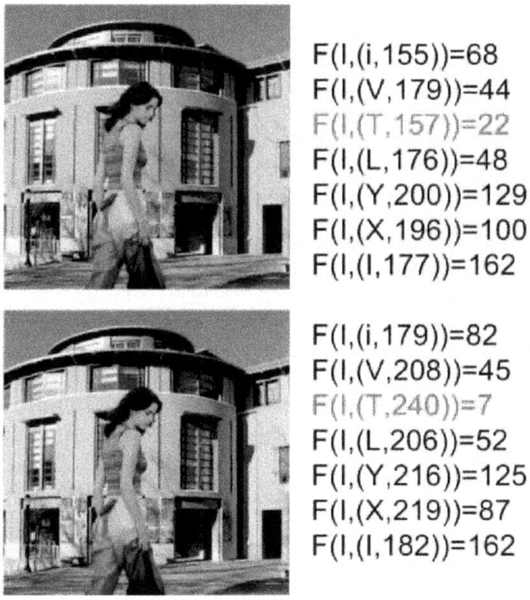

Figure 6: Original (top) and harmonized (bottom) picture extracted from [6]. On the right-hand side, the value $F(I,(m,\alpha^*))$ for each template m is given. The red value is the lowest one, called here $CH(I)$. The harmonized picture presents a lower CH value than the original one.

acceptably sharp in an image. A shallow DoF is often used to emphasize the region of interest in a picture. It is for instance used for portraiture photography. All background details are blurred whereas the nearest person (or object) is sharp, attracting our attention. An example is given figure 7 (a). When a large DoF is used, the opposite effect is achieved. The entire picture is sharp so that all the details of the scene are preserved. Picture of figure 7 (c) was taken with a large DoF.

Estimating the DoF is then of importance. As photographers can steer our visual attention towards a particular areas by controlling the DoF, the inter-observer variability might be contingent upon this artistic effect.

To determine the depth of field, the proposed algorithm relies on the fact that the shape of the horizontal/vertical derivatives histogram is modified after a blurring operation [22, 25]. The proposed scheme to compute the DoF of a picture is described below.

Let I the input picture and f_k the blurring kernel of size $k \times k$ ($k = \{3, 5, 7\}$). The blurring kernels are first applied on the luminance L of I and the vertical and horizontal derivatives are then computed. The vertical and horizontal derivatives are given by:

$$p_{xk} \quad \alpha \quad hist(I * f_k * d_x) \tag{3}$$

$$p_{yk} \quad \alpha \quad hist(I * f_k * d_y) \tag{4}$$

where $d_x = [1 \ -1]$ and $d_y = [1 \ -1]^T$.
For a pixel (i,j) and for a kernel k, we compute the KL-divergence between the distributions p_{xk} and p_{yk} and the original distributions p_{x1} and p_{y1}:

$$D_k(i,j) = \sum_{(n,m)\in W_{ij}} KL(p_{xk}|p_{x1})(n,m) + KL(p_{yk}|p_{y1})(n,m) \tag{5}$$

where, W_{ij} is a window centered on the pixel (i,j). In this study, all the experiments were performed using uniform kernels.

The KL-divergence for a given pixel located at (i,j) is given by the following formula:

$$KL(p|q)(i,j) = p_{ij} log(\frac{p_{ij}}{q_{ij}}) \tag{6}$$

The KL-divergence involves two probability density functions p and q. They both sum to 1. The KL-divergence is only defined when p_{ij} and q_{ij} are greater than zero. The quantity $0log0$ is considered as zero.

The use of the KL-divergence is especially interesting in the equation 7 because of its similarity with the DoF values. Indeed, D_k tends to zero when the distributions p_{xk} and p_{yk} are close to p_{x1} and p_{y1}, respectively. In this case, it means that the incoming picture is not sensitive to blur indicating that the picture is already blurred. The DoF is then low. When the value D_k increases, it suggests that the areas under analysis is rather sharp (DoF is probably high).

The DoF value is finally computed as follows:

$$DoF = \sum_{(i,j)\in I} \sum_k D_k(i,j) \tag{7}$$

Figure 7 (b) and (d) give the value of DoF for two examples. For the first one, the DoF is of 0.12 suggesting that the picture is composed of large blurred areas. As the DoF is greater than zero the picture probably presents a sharp areas, sensitive to a blurring operation. For the second picture, the DoF is of 0.75. Unlike the previous one, this picture is more sensitive to blurring operations, suggesting that most of the pictures are sharp. Figure 7 (b) and (d) illustrate in bright areas regions that are sensitive to blur. For the sake of visibility, the two pictures have been normalized in the range of 0 to 255 by using their own global maximum (3.56 and 4.68, respectively). This kind of map might be used to extract the region of interest when the DoF value is rather low, as proposed by [25].

4.4 Scene complexity

The amount of visual information as well as the visual clutter in a picture might contribute to explain the observers' variability [33]. Oliva et al. in [28] determined a list of factors that correlates with our representation of the visual complexity of a scene. Among them, the most important would be the quantity and the variety of objects, detail and color. To assess the visual complexity, three computational measures are used: the entropy, the number of regions and the amount of contours.

4.4.1 Entropy-based scene complexity

To compute the entropy of the incoming picture I, we follow a similar approach of the one described in [33]. The complexity of the scene is the sum of the entropies of wavelet subbands. The procedure is described below:

1. The input picture is first converted into the Lab color space;

(a) Original (b) DoF=0.12 (c) Original (d) DoF=0.75

Figure 7: (a) and (c) two original pictures. (b) and (d) indicates areas sensitive to blur in dark. The bright areas correspond to unfocus areas. DoF, standing for Depth of Field, indicates whether the picture is sensitive to blur (deep DoF) or not (shallow DoF).

2. Each component is transformed by using a 2D dyadic wavelet transform. The level number is set to 2;

3. A non parametric method is used to compute the probability distribution of wavelet coefficients. The entropy for each subband is computed as $E = -\sum_i p_i log(p_i)$, where, p_i is the probability distribution of wavelet coefficients for a given subband.

4. We sum the subband entropies for each component $\{L, a, b\}$;

5. The final complexity C is obtained by using the pooling of [33]: $C = 0.84 \times E_L + 0.08 \times E_a + 0.08 \times E_b$, where E_L, E_a and E_b represent the entropy of the component L, a and b, respectively.

   Figure 8 gives two complexity values C for two pictures.

4.4.2 *Color mean shift segmentation*

The color mean-shift segmentation has been proposed by [7]. Based on a bilateral filtering, the color mean-shift segmentation associates each pixel of the incoming picture with a significant mode of the joint domain density located in the neighborhood of the considered pixel. The software designed by [4] and available at `http://coewww.rutgers.edu/riul/research/code/EDISON/index.html` is used to perform the segmentation.

The sizes of the filtering kernel (h_s, h_r) (by using the notations of [7]) are both set to 5. M is the minimum number of pixels enclosed by a region (equal to 1 percent of the input resolution).

Figure 8 shows two segmented pictures ((b) and (d)). The number of regions of the segmented picture is also given. This value is used to feature the visual complexity of the scene.

4.4.3 *Amount of contours*

Edges play an important role in our perception. For instance, Baddeley and Tatler [2] showed that edges correlate with fixation location in real-world scenes better than luminance contrast.

To measure the amount of contours in an image, Sobel edge detectors are used to detect horizontal, vertical and diagonal edges. The kernel has a size of 3×3. These kernels are applied on each level of a Gaussian pyramid. The number of levels is equal to 3. For each level, we compute the average energy of the Sobel detectors (by averaging over the level the squared output of Sobel filter). This process is performed for each level of the pyramid and for the three components $\{L, a, b\}$. For a given component, we combine the energy across scale by taking the average. Finally, to get a single measure, the average energy value is computed across the three components.

5. LEARNING: DESCRIPTION AND PERFORMANCE

5.1 Learning

Each image is then represented by a features vector, having a dimension of 6. The dimensionality of the features vector is not reduced as the number of dimension is low.

The estimation of the inter-observer congruency is equivalent to the estimation of the joint probability density function $p(IOVC, \mathbf{v})$. The random variable $IOVC$ represents the inter-observer visual congruency whereas $\mathbf{v}$ is the feature vector containing the six indicators. To infer the relationship between these two random variables, a learning algorithm is used. We follow the same procedure described in [40, 34] and use software kindly provided by [34]. We just remind the main aspects of this learning procedure.

The learning consists in estimating the relationship between a measure of congruency and the extracted visual features described in the previous section. A cluster-weighted model (CWM) initially proposed by [12] is used. This is a generalization of Gaussian mixture, in which each Gaussian function expressed a part of the relationship between the input and the output distributions. The joint PDF $p(IOVC, \mathbf{v})$ is given by:

$$p_\theta(IOVC, \mathbf{v}) = \sum_{i=1}^{N} p(c_i)p(\mathbf{v}|c_i)p(IOVC|\mathbf{v}, c_i) \quad (8)$$

where $IOVC$ is the inter-observer congruency and $\mathbf{v}$ refers to the image features. N is the number of clusters. Each cluster is decomposed in three factors:

- $p(c_i)$ is the weight of the cluster c_i;

(a) Original (b) Segmented (C=14.67dit/pel;Reg=103) (c) Original (d) Segmented (C=14.72dit/pel;Reg=72)

Figure 8: (a) and (c) two original pictures. (b) and (d) are the segmented pictures. C and Reg stand for the complexity measure and the number of regions, respectively.

- $p(\mathbf{v}|c_i)$ is a multivariate Gaussian with mean μ_i and covariance matrix $\sum_i$:

$$p(\mathbf{v}|c_i) = \frac{exp\left[-\frac{1}{2}(\mathbf{v}-\mu_i)^T(\sum_i)^{-1}(\mathbf{v}-\mu_i)\right]}{(2\pi)^{L/2}\left|\sum_i\right|^{1/2}} \quad (9)$$

- $p(IOVC|\mathbf{v}, c_i)$ is the probability of the inter-observer congruency $IOVC$ given the input data in the cluster i:

$$p(IOVC|\mathbf{v}, c_i) = \frac{exp\left[-\frac{1}{2}(IOVC - w_i^T\mathbf{v}^*)^2\right]}{\sqrt{2\pi}\sigma_i} \quad (10)$$

  This is a Gaussian function with a variance equal to σ_i^2 and a mean dependent on the input feature $\mathbf{v}^*$ (same as $\mathbf{v}$ with a value 1 concatenated to its end) and a weight vector w_i. This vector indicates the weight of each input data.

Parameters of the model θ, ($p(c_i)$, μ_i, $\sum_i$, σ_i^2, w_i, with $i = 1...N$) are estimated using the Expectation-Maximization algorithm [18].

As explained in [15], in data-rich situation, it would be possible to split the data into three parts (a training set, a validation set and a test set). As this is not the case here (1000 pictures), we use the Bayesian Information Criterion (BIC) to define the model complexity. The BIC is given by:

$$BIC = -2 \times loglik + d \times \log S \quad (11)$$

where d is the number of free parameters depending on the number of clusters, S is the size of the dataset and $loglik$ is the maximized log-likelihood:

$$loglik = \sum_{n=1}^{S} \log p_{\widehat{\theta}}(IOVC, \mathbf{v}) \quad (12)$$

where $p_{\widehat{\theta}}(IOVC, \mathbf{v})$ is defined in equation 8. $\widehat{\theta}$ are the estimated parameters of the model.

Figure 9 presents the BIC values in function of N (the number of clusters). $N = 9$ is a good trade-off between complexity and quality of prediction. This value allows to predict quite efficiently the inter-observer congruency without over fitting the training data. Indeed, over fitting the data would lead to an almost perfect prediction but the risk is to loss the generalization property. As mentioned by [10], it is important to accept error to make less error. By using $N = 9$, we respect this first point. Concerning the quality of prediction, the ground truth and the predicted values of $IOVC$ are correlated $r(2004) = .34$, $p < .001$ (Pearson coefficient) and $r(2004) = .28$, $p < .001$ (Spearman coefficient).

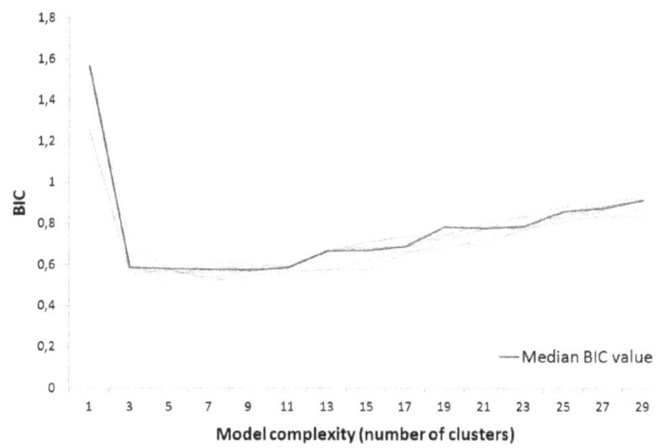

Figure 9: BIC in function of the model complexity. Several trials have been performed (light red curves). The dark red curve gives the median BIC values.

Remark: during the learning phase, we didn't use the face detector in order to limit the impact of false alarms on the estimated parameters. Instead, hand-label data are used indicating for each picture of the dataset the number of faces present.

5.2 Performance

A qualitative and quantitative evaluation of the proposed approach has been performed. Figure 11 presents some qualitative results. Figure 11 gives 10 pictures (top): the first five pictures have a high IOVC whereas the last five pictures present a small IOVC. These results are consistent with our own subjective evaluation. The first five pictures of figure 11 are much more interestingness than the last five pictures. In other words, it would be difficult to predict where an observer would focus on this kind of pictures. To illustrate this point, saliency maps of these pictures are computed using [21] (bright areas correspond to salient areas). These maps are more or less relevant and they do not differentiate pictures of Figure 11 whereas IOVC scores can do. IOVC scores could be used to estimate saliency maps relevance. A high IOVC score would suggest that the saliency map has to be very focussed as for the fourth picture on the top row (Figure 11).

A quantitative evaluation is also performed by using another eye tracking database. This database is composed of 27 pictures and can be downloaded from `http://www.irisa.fr/temics/staff/lemeur/visualAttention/`. We compute the Pearson correlation coefficient between IOVC stemming from this new ground truth and our prediction. Both are correlated $r(54) = .27$, $p < .17$. The correlation is not significant due to the small number of pictures in this database. In addition, the face detector fails to detect the human faces on 5 pictures due to the varying face poses. This lack of accuracy in the detection lowers the correlation coefficient.

The proposed method is compared to the Feature Congestion measure of Rosenholtz et al. [33]. This measure aims to evaluate the visual clutter of a scene. The software available on Rosenholtz's web page is used. We run the Feature Congestion measure on the aforementioned dataset. The correlation coefficient between the Feature Congestion measure and IOVC of this dataset is $r(54) = -0.15$, $p < .43$. The correlation is negative since a high visual clutter might be interpreted as a weak congruency.

5.3 Limitations

The proposed model is relevant in order to predict the dispersion of observers only in free-viewing task. In the introduction, we have dressed a list of factors influencing the dispersion between observers. One factor that was not mention is the task to perform. For instance, if we measure the inter-observer congruency when the task is to detect pedestrians, the inter-observer congruency is very high, indicating that observers share the same strategy to perform the task. To illustrate this point, we compute the inter-observer congruency over the whole eye tracking database of Ehinger [9] (some details are given in the introduction). The average dispersion is of 82%, the median dispersion is of 88%. Compared to the dispersion measured on Judd's database, there is a significant difference (unpaired t-test, $F(1, 1356) = 8.28$, $p < .001$).

Another limitation concerns the influence of the viewing time on the dispersion. It has been shown that the dispersion is time-dependent and increases with the time viewing. This feature is here not taken into account. For the targeted application, this feature was not judged as fundamental.

The last limitation concerns the limited accuracy of the detector we use. More specifically, as the presence of face plays an important role, the face detector has to be as efficient as possible.

6. IMAGE RANKING BASED ON INTERESTINGNESS

The interestingness of an image is related to its ability to attract and to hold our attention. For instance, to give a score of interestingness, Flickr (`http://www.flickr.com`) uses a combination of several parameters such as comments, annotations, favorites, etc. This is an excellent indicator but it requires a feedback or an effort of the users. An indicator based on the content analysis, such as the proposed method, might help evaluating the immediate interest of an image.

The proposed method can then be used in a context of photos browsing and automatic photograph organization. As in [35, 25, 37, 45], we propose to organize a large set of photograph. However the proposed ranking is based on the picture interestingness. This is different from state-of-the-art methods. For instance, Luo and Tang [25] proposed to rank images according to their quality. This score is based on composition, lighting, focus controlling and color. Although there are some similarities among the extracted features (such as the DoF), better photo quality does not mean more relevant or interestingness, as mentioned in [25]. For instance, Judd et al. [19] show that the dispersion between observers depends on image complexity and that fixations from lower-resolution images (low quality) can predict fixations on higher-resolution images (high quality).

To illustrate the proposed method, we propose to sort forty nine images. We run the proposed model on these pictures in order to estimate their interestingness. Figure 10 illustrates the results by showing the pictures ranked according to their interestingness. The first picture (top-left) has the most important IOVC whereas the picture having the lowest IOVC appears at bottom-right. On the last pictures, we can notice that there is nothing that stands out the background. In other words, it would be very difficult to predict for this kind of picture where an observer would focus on.

7. CONCLUSION

In this paper we proposed a new criterion to automatically estimate the visual congruence between observers. We have evaluated our method qualitatively and quantitatively. We showed that our IOVC criteria outperforms the Feature Congestion measure of [33] since the absolute value of the correlation between the ground truth IOVC and our criterion is larger than with the Feature Congestion measure of [33]. The predicted IOVC can be used in image processing applications where the visual perception of a picture matters such as website design, advertisement. For instance, we considered ranking personalized photograph: pictures are sorted out in function of their predicted IOVC.

However, the proposed method is still an approximation of the 'true' IOVC. It can best estimate short-term IOVC, that is the IOVC experienced in the first instant of a picture observation. In order to improve this method, it would be necessary to consider both higher level factors such as those proposed by [41] and higher level cognitive factors like the scene coherence [16]. Taking into account these factors is difficult because of their complexity.

In future work it is planned to build a new eye tracking database in order to improve the training and the performance assessment. The influence of higher level information such as the type of the scene (indoor, outdoor...) will also be examined. Last but not the least, we will consider more IOVC-based applications. One of them is related to photo-quality assessment as presented in [3, 25]. The use of the predicted IOVC might be combined with other image ranking work.

8. REFERENCES

[1] R. Althoff and N. Cohen. Eye-movement-based memory effect: a reprocessing effect in face perception.

Figure 10: 49 pictures of various contents sorted out in function of their interestingness (from top-left (highest congruency) to bottom-right (lowest congruency)).

Jounral Of Experimental Psychology-Learning Memory and Cognition, 25(4):997–1010, 1999.

[2] R. Baddeley and B. Tatler. High frequency edges (but not contrast predict where we fixate: A bayesian system identification analysis. *Vision Research*, 46:2824–2833, 2006.

[3] S. Bhattacharya, R. Sukthankar, and M. Shah. A coherent framework for photo-quality assessment and enhancement based on visual aesthetics. In *in ACM Multimedia International conference*, 2010.

[4] C. Christoudias, B. Georgescu, and P. Meer. Synergism in low-level vision. In *16th International Conference on Pattern Recognition*, volume IV, pages 105–155, 2002.

[5] H. Chua, J. Boland, and R. Nisbett. Cultural variation in eye movements during scene perception. In *Proceedings of the National Academy of Sciences*, volume 102, pages 12629–12633, 2005.

[6] D. Cohen-Or, O. Sorkine, R. Gal, T. Leyvand, and Y. Xu. Color harmonization. In *ACM Transactions on Graphics (Proceedings of ACM SIGGRAPH)*, volume 56, pages 624–630, 2006.

[7] D. Comaniciu and P. Meer. Mean shift: A robust approach toward feature space analysis. *IEEE Trans. Pattern Analysis and Machine Intelligence*, 24:603–619, 2002.

[8] L. Cowen, L. Ball, and J. Delin. An eye-movement analysis of web-page usability. In L. S. V. Ltd, editor, *People and Computers XVI-Memorable yet invisible: Proceedings of HCI 2002*, pages 317–335, 2002.

[9] K. Ehinger, B. Hidalgo-Sotelo, A. Torralba, and A. Oliva. Modeling search for people in 900 scenes. *Visual Cognition*, 17:945–978, 2009.

[10] H. Einhorn. Accepting erro to make less error. *Journal of Personality Assessment*, 50(3):387–395, 1986.

[11] H. Frey, C. Honey, and P. Konig. What's color got to do with it? the influence of color on visual attention in different categories. *Journal of Vision*, 8(14), October 2008.

[12] Gershnfel. *The nature of mathematical modelling.* Cambridge, Univ. Press, 1999.

[13] H. Golberg and X. Kotval. Computer interface evaluation using eye movements: methods and constructs. *International Journal of Industrial Ergonomics*, 24:631–645, 1999.

[14] R. Gordon. Attentional allocation during the perception of scenes. *Journal of Experimental Psychology: Human Perception and Performance*, 30:760–777, 2004.

[15] T. Hastie, R. Tibshirani, and J. Friedman. *The elements of statistical learning.* Springer Series in Statistics, 2001.

[16] J. Henderson. Regarding scenes. *Current Directions in Psychological Science*, 16:219–222, 2007.

[17] J. Henderson, M. Chanceaux, and T. Smith. The influence of clutter on real-world scene search:

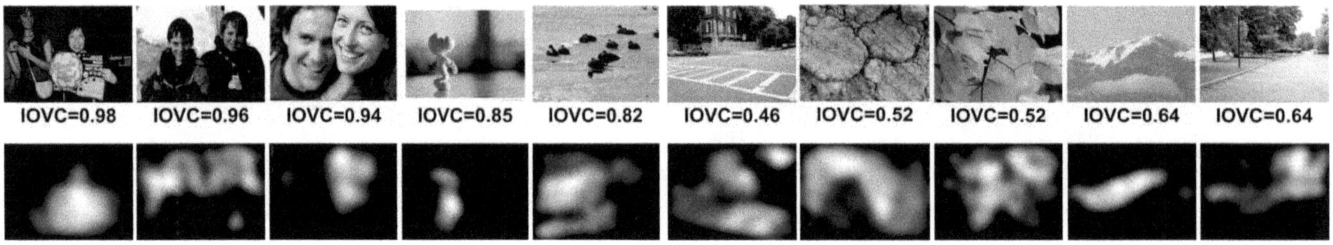

Figure 11: Top: pictures having high IOVC (first five) and pictures having low IOVC (last five). Bottom: saliency maps of pictures. Bright areas correspond to the most salient parts.

Evidence from search efficiency and eye movements. *Journal of Vision*, 9(1), January 2009.

[18] M. Jordan and R. Jacobs. Hierarchical mixtures of experts and the em algorihtm. *Neural Computation*, 6:181–214, 1994.

[19] T. Judd, F. Durand, and A. Torralba. Fixations on low-resolution images. *Journal of Vision*, 11(4), 2011.

[20] T. Judd, K. Ehinger, F. Durand, and A. Torralba. Learning to predict where people look. In *ICCV*, 2009.

[21] O. Le Meur, P. Le Callet, D. Barba, and D. Thoreau. A coherent computational approach to model the bottom-up visual attention. *IEEE Trans. On PAMI*, 28(5):802–817, May 2006.

[22] A. Levin. Blind motion deblurring using image statistics. In *NIPS*, 2006.

[23] R. Lienhart and J. Maydt. An extended set of haar-like features for rapid object detection. In *ICIP*, volume 1, pages 900–903, 2002.

[24] G. Loftus and N. Mackworth. Cognitive determinants of fixation location during picture viewing. *Journal of Experimental Psychology: Human Perception and Performances*, 4:565–572, 1978.

[25] Y. Luo and X. Tang. Photo and video quality evaluation: focussing on the subject. In *ECCV*, pages 386–399, 2008.

[26] Y. Matsuda. Coor design. In *Asakura Shoten*, 1995.

[27] R. Nisbett. *The geography of thought: how Asians and Westerners think differently... and why.* New York: Free Press, 2003.

[28] A. Oliva, M. Mack, M. Shrestha, and A. Peeper. Identifying the perceptual dimensions of visual complexity of scenes. In *26th annual meeting of the Cognitive Science Society Meeting*, 2004.

[29] D. Parkhurst, K. Law, and E. Niebur. Modelling the role of salience in the allocation of overt visual attention. *Vision Research*, 42:107–123, 2002.

[30] W. Press, S. Teukolsky, W. Vetterling, and B. Flannery. *Numerical Recipes in C: the art of Scientific Computing.* Cambridge University Press, New York, NY, USA, 1992.

[31] K. Rayner. Eye movements in reading and information processing: 20 years of research. *Psychological Bulletin*, 124(3):372–422, 1998.

[32] K. Rayner, M. Catelhano, and J. Yang. Eye movements when looking at unusual-weird scenes: are there cultural differences? *Journal of Experimental psychology: learning, Memory and cognition*, 35(1):154–259, 2009.

[33] R. Rosenholtz, Y. Li, and L. Nakano. Measuring visual clutter. *Journal of Vision*, 7(2), March 2007.

[34] M. Ross and A. Oliva. Estimating perception of scene layout properties from global image features. *Journal Of Vision*, 10(1), Januray 2010.

[35] C. Rother, L. Bordeaux, Y. Hamadi, and A. Black. Autocollage. In *in ACM Transactions on Graphics (SIGGRAPH)*, 2006.

[36] G. A. Rousselet, M. J.-M. Macé, and M. Fabre-Thorpe. Is it an animal? is it a human face? fast processing in upright and inverted natural scenes. *Journal of Vision*, 3:440–455, 2003.

[37] X. Sun, H. Yao, R. Ji, and S. Liu. Photo assessment based on computatinal visual attention model. In *ACM Multimedia*, pages 541–544, 2009.

[38] B. W. Tatler, R. J. Baddeley, and I. D. Gilchrist. Visual correlates of fixation selection: effects of scale and time. *Vision Research*, 45:643–659, 2005.

[39] M. Tokumaru, N. Muranaka, and S. Imanishi. Color design support system considering coor harmony. In *IEEE International Conference on Fuzzy Systems*, pages 378–383, 2002.

[40] A. Torralba and A. Oliva. Depth estimation from image structure. *IEEE Pattern Analysis and Machine Intelligence*, 24(9):1226–1238, 2002.

[41] A. Torralba and A. Oliva. Statistics of natural image catagories. *network*, 14:391–421, 2003.

[42] A. Torralba, A. Oliva, M. Castelhano, and J. Henderson. Contextual guidance of eye movements and attention in real-world scenes: the role of global features in object search. *Psychological review*, 113(4):766–786, 2006.

[43] G. Underwood and T. Foulsham. Visual saliency and semantic incongruency influence eye movements when inspecting pictures. *The Quarterly journal of experimental psychology*, 59(11):1931–1949, 2006.

[44] P. Viola and M. Jones. Rapid object detection using a boosted cascade of simple features. In *CVPR*, 2001.

[45] C.-G. Yeh, Y. Ho, B. Barsky, and M. Ouhyoung. Personalized photograph ranking and selection system. In *ACM Multimedia*, 2010.

[46] Q. Zhao and C. Koch. Learning a saliency map using fixated locations in natural scenes. *Journal of Vision*, 11(3):1–15, 2011.

Modeling 3D Articulated Motions with Conformal Geometry Videos (CGVs) *

Dao T. P. Quynh Ying He Xiaoming Chen Jiazhi Xia Qian Sun Steven C. H. Hoi
School of Computer Engineering
Nanyang Technological University
Singapore
daot0006|yhe|xmchen|xiaj0002|sunq0004|chhoi@ntu.edu.sg

ABSTRACT

3D articulated motions are widely used in entertainment, sports, military, and medical applications. Among various techniques for modeling 3D motions, geometry videos (GVs) are a compact representation in that each frame is parameterized to a 2D domain, which captures the 3D geometry (x, y, z) to a pixel (r, g, b) in the image domain. As a result, the widely studied image/video processing techniques can be directly borrowed for 3D motion. This paper presents conformal geometry videos (CGVs), a novel extension of the traditional geometry videos by taking into the consideration of the isometric nature of 3D articulated motions. We prove that the 3D articulated motion can be uniquely (up to rigid motion) represented by (λ, H), where λ is the conformal factor characterizing the intrinsic property of the 3D motion, and H the mean curvature characterizing the extrinsic feature (i.e., embedding or appearance). Furthermore, the conformal factor λ is pose-invariant. Thus, in sharp contrast to the GVs which capture 3D motion by three channels, CGVs take only one channel of mean curvature H and the first frame of the conformal factor λ, i.e., approximately $1/3$ the storage of the GVs. In addition, CGVs have strong spatial and temporal coherence, which favors various well studied video compression techniques. Thus, CGVs can be highly compressed by using the state-of-the-art video compression techniques, such as H.264/AVC. Our experimental results on real-world 3D motions show that CGVs are a highly compact representation for 3D articulated motions, i.e., given CGVs and GVs of the same file size, CGVs show much better visual quality than GVs.

Categories and Subject Descriptors

H.5.1 [**Multimedia Information Systems**]: Video

General Terms

Algorithms, Design

*Area chair: Wei Tsang Ooi

Keywords

Geometry videos, conformal geometry videos, 3D articulated motion, deformable objects, video compression, H.264/AVC, conformal parameterization, isometric transformation.

1. INTRODUCTION

The media and entertainment industry has experienced explosive growth in the last decade. Computer animated characters are now necessary components of many applications, including video games, movies, social virtual world, human computer interface designs, mass communication and psychological studies. In order to make these animated characters convincing, they require sophisticated facial expressions and body motions. Thus, 3D motion/video is an emerging research topic. Recent advances in 3D scanning technology, such as multi-view photometric stereo [25], template based space-time registration [15], fringe projection [38], etc, allow the acquisition of 3D motions in real-time. However, the captured 3D motions are usually represented by bulky, irregular polygonal meshes, which poses substantial challenges for modeling and compression.

Geometry image [3] is an emerging technique that intelligently encodes the 3D geometry into an image format, in which each pixel r, g, b represents a 3D vertex x, y, z. Geometry images naturally bridge two research fields, image processing and geometric processing, thus, one can borrow the widely studied image processing techniques (e.g., compression [9] [19]) to 3D geometry. Geometry videos (GVs) extend geometry images to capture 3D motion in a video format. It has been shown that geometry video is effective in modeling 3D facial expressions [34] and 3D animation [2].

With a widespread belief within the media community that a 3D surface has three functional freedoms (i.e., x, y, and z of each vertex), the existing research of geometry compression relies on the ambient space $\mathbb{R}^3$ in which the surface is embedded and focuses on the extrinsic properties. However, the classical result in differential geometry shows that a surface can be uniquely determined up to rigid motion by its first fundamental form and mean curvature H. With conformal parameterization, the first fundamental form is completely encoded into conformal factor λ, which is the scaling factor of infinitesimal patches of surface. In other words, a 3D surface has only two degrees of freedom, one characterizing its intrinsic feature (i.e., metric) and the other for the extrinsic feature (i.e., embedding), see Fig 1. Inspired by this, this paper presents *conformal geometry videos (CGVs)*, a novel extension of the traditional GVs for modeling general 3D motions of articulated models, which are approximate isometric transformation. By parameterizing 3D motions using conformal parameterizations, we partition the 3D motion into two video sequences λ and H, where the conformal factor λ encodes the intrinsic feature, the mean curvature H encodes the extrinsic feature. Observing that 3D articulated motions are approximate isometric transformations, conformal factor λ, the intrinsic feature, remains unchanged, i.e., it is invariant to 3D poses. Thus, different frames distinguish only by their extrinsic feature H. As a result, we only need to handle the pose-dependent mean curvature. This leads to a highly compact representation that takes only approximately 1/3 the space of conventional geometry videos. In addition, CGVs have strong spatial and temporal coherence, and can be heavily compressed further by using the state-of-the-art video compression techniques, such as H.264/AVC. Our experimental results on real-world 3D motions demonstrate that CGVs outperforms the conventional GVs by providing a more compact and effective modeling framework for 3D articulated motions.

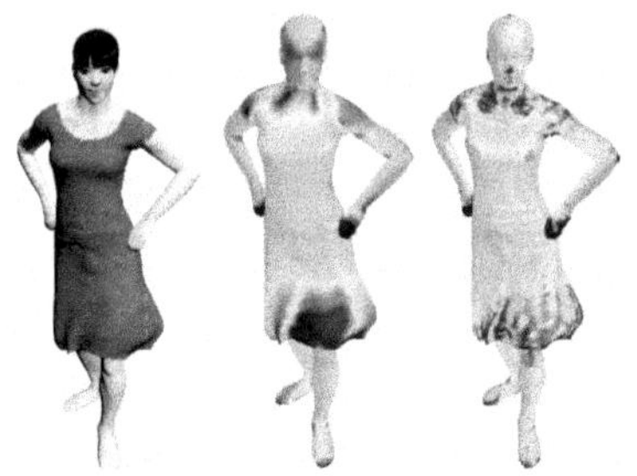

(a) 3D model (b) λ (c) H

Figure 1: With conformal parameterization, the 3D geometry can be determined (uniquely up to rigid motion) by its conformal factor λ and mean curvature H. λ and H are rendered in color for illustration purpose.

So as presented above, CGV naturally bridges 3D motion modeling and 2D video processing,allowing us to borrow the well-studied video processing technique (e.g., H.264) to model and compress 3D motion data. The specific contributions of this paper include:

- We present CGV, which naturally extend the conventional GV framework by taking into the consideration of the approximate isometric nature of articulated 3D motion.
- We present a set of algorithms to construct CGVs, including geometric feature detection and tracking, constrained polycube conformal parameterization, polycube flattening, and optimization-based 3D motion reconstruction.
- We show that CGVs have stronger spatial and temporal coherence than that of GVs and natural videos, and such redundancy can be significantly removed by the powerful compression tools available in H.264/AVC.

2. PREVIOUS WORK

This section reviews the related work in three different research fields, 3D motion processing, video compression, and global conformal parameterization, which are naturally integrated by the proposed conformal geometry video framework.

2.1 3D motion processing

Recent advances in 3D scanning technology [25] [13] [15] [38] allow us to capture the 3D human motion in real time, which also pose significant challenges in data processing. Each frame of the scanned motion is given in its own scanner space other than in the object space. Therefore, from the analysis and processing point of view, it's highly desirable to align or register the captured data in the object space. Feature tracking is the key technique to find the correspondence among different frames of 3D motion. Wang *et al.* presented a data-driven approach for video speed precise facial tracking and expression retargeting [31]. To handle surface matching with noise, occlusion and clutter, Wang *et al.* adopted least square conformal parameterization simplifying the 3D human face registration problem to a 2D image matching problem [29]. Mitra *et al.* proposed an algorithm to register large sets of unstructured point clouds of moving and deforming objects without computing correspondences [17]. Wang *et al.* developed an efficient non-rigid 3D motion tracking algorithm to establish inter-frame correspondences that facilitate the temporal study of subtle motions in facial expressions [30].

Since the scanned 3D motion is usually bulky, compression becomes an emerging problem in 3D motion data transmission and storage. Han *et al.* proposed time-varying meshes (TVM) by extending the block matching algorithm from 2D video to 3D meshes [6]. By considering both spatial and temporal redundancies, the compression ratio of TVM is between $6:1$ and $50:1$ [7]. Yamasaki *et al.* proposed algorithms of intra-frame and inter-frame coding for both geometry and color texture of TVM [36].

Another approach to compress 3D motions is GVs. Briceño *et al.* parameterized the synthetic animated mesh sequence onto a rectangle domain and then formed GVs [2]. They classified the frames as I-Frames and P-Frames and then used 2D wavelet-based techniques to compress the geometry video. Taking the advantage of approximate isometric feature of facial expressions, Xia *et al.* [34] developed an expression-invariant 3D face parameterization algorithm that can guarantee the exact feature correspondence, which favors the geometry video compression by using the state-of-the-art H.264/AVC.

2.2 Video compression

Video compression has been extensively studied in the past several decades. The traditional 2D video compression techniques can be categorized as prediction, transformation, quantization and entropy coding, see [21] for a comprehensive survey. H.264/AVC is the state-of-the-art video coding standard [10], which is able to achieve very low bitrates by employing many advanced compression techniques such as block-size adaptive intra-frame prediction, quarter-pixel-precision multi-frame motion estimation, block-size adaptive transformation and quantization, high-performance CABAC entropy coding [32]. CGVs are fundamentally different than natural videos and traditional GVs in that CGVs show strong coherence in both temporal and spatial domains, which is particularly suitable for H.264/AVC compression (see Section 5.2 for more details).

2.3 Global conformal parameterization

The research area of global surface parameterization has a long and fruitful tradition in computer graphics community [20]. Conformal parameterization has drawn particular attention due to its many promising properties, such as angle preserving, intrinsic to the geometry, insensitive to resolution/tessellation, etc.

Gu and Yau [5] pioneered a global conformal parameterization algorithm for surfaces with arbitrary genus. They analyzed the structure of the space of all global conformal parameterizations of a given surface and found all possible solutions by constructing a basis of the underlying linear solution space. The resulting parameter lines minimize angle distortion but may have a rather large metric distortion. Furthermore, the space of global conformal parameterizations is too rigid to allow a local alignment of the parameter lines at given surface features. Many follow-up works have been proposed to improve the conformal parameterization quality by reducing the area distortion and allowing user control on the singularities and/or parameter lines, such as [11] [14] [37], just name a few.

Polycube map is a variant of the global parameterization in that the parametric domain (i.e., a polycube) can be embedded in $\mathbb{R}^3$ rather than the abstract charts in $\mathbb{R}^2$. Polycube parameterization has several unique advantages over the chart based parameterization, which are particularly useful for conformal geometry video constructions: 1) The parametric domain mimics the geometry of the 3D shape, thus, the area distortion can be significantly reduced. 2) The user can easily control the location of singularities and direction of parameter lines. 3) Polycube can be flattened to a 2D rectangular domain, such that the boundary is axis aligned. Thus, one can sample the input 3D model into a completely regular geometry image.

There are several approaches to parameterize 3D models to polycube domain. Tarini *et al.* [23] pioneered the concept of polycube mapping. However, as direct projection from 3D model to polycube is used, their method is not bijective, since two vertices may share the same projected image on the polycube. Wang *et al.* [27] introduced an intrinsic approach that is guaranteed to be a diffeomorphism. However, in this scheme it is difficult to control the polycube map, i.e., a feature on the 3D model may not be mapped to a desired location on the polycube. In their follow-up work, Wang *et al.* [28] proposed the user-controllable polycube map where the users can explicitly specify the pre-images of the polycube corners. Lin *et al.* [16] proposed an automatic approach to construct the polycube map of non-trivial topology. He *et al.* [8] proposed a divide-and-conquer approach to compute polycube map of large-scale models. Xia *et al.* [33] presented an editable polycube map framework that allows the users to easily specify the mapping constraints and post-edit the parameterization. Wan *et al.* [26] presented an optimization framework to find the optimal polycube mapping by trading off the area distortion and the complexity of the polycube.

Although there are extensive research in surface parameterization, little progress has been reported on motion data parameterization, in which the key challenge is to keep the temporal and spatial coherence. Xia *et al.* proposed an algorithm to expression-invariant parameterization algorithm for 3D human faces [34]. Their method computes the harmonic field on a topological annulus and then builds the bijective parameterization by tracing the integral curves of the harmonic field. This method works well for 3D faces which have simple topology and geometry. However, it is difficult to extend their method for parameterization of general 3D articulated motions, which may have much more complicated geometry and topology than human faces.

3. CONFORMAL GEOMETRY VIDEOS

3.1 Conformal representation of 3D surfaces

We use the following notations throughout this paper:

λ	Conformal factor
H	Mean curvature
K	Gaussian curvature
$\mathbf{r}$	an oriented 2-manifold surface
$\triangle$	Laplace-Beltrami operator
M	Motion sequence, M_i is the ith frame
$k_t^{M_i}(x,x)$	Heat Kernel Signature of point $x \in M_i$

A classical question in differential theory is which data are sufficient to describe a surface in space up to rigid motions.

Let $\mathbf{r}(u,v)$ be the surface embedded in $\mathbb{R}^3$ and $(\cdot,\cdot)$ be the dot product. Let $E=(\mathbf{r}_u,\mathbf{r}_u)$, $F=(\mathbf{r}_u,\mathbf{r}_v)$,and $G=(\mathbf{r}_v,\mathbf{r}_v)$ be the coefficients of the first fundamental form, where $\mathbf{r}_u$ and $\mathbf{r}_v$ are the tangent vectors.

$$I=(d\mathbf{r},d\mathbf{r})=Edu^2+2Fdudv+Gdv^2$$

Let $L=(\mathbf{r}_{uu},\mathbf{n})$, $M=(\mathbf{r}_{uv},\mathbf{n})$, and $N=(\mathbf{r}_{vv},\mathbf{n})$ be the coefficients of second fundamental form, where $\mathbf{n}$ is the normal.

$$II=(d\mathbf{r},d\mathbf{n})=Ldu^2+2Mdudv+Ndv^2$$

According to the fundamental theorem of surfaces, if E, F, G, L, M, N are given functions of u and v, sufficiently differentiable, which satisfy the Gauss-Codazzi equations and the added conditions that $EG-F^2>0$, $E>0$, $G>0$, there exists a surface, uniquely determined except for its position in space, which has respectively as its first and second fundamental forms the quadratic forms $Edu^2+2Fdudv+Gdv^2$ and $Ldu^2+2Mdudv+Ndv^2$. This theorem guarantees not only the existence of a surface, provided the conditions are met, but also that if two surfaces have the same fundamental forms, they are congruent.

Figure 3: 3D human motions are approximate isometric (i.e., metric preserving). Given various poses of a subject, we compute the geodesic distance with the source point at his head and render the isolines of the resultant geodesic distance fields. Clearly, the geodesic distances (or the metrics) are intrinsic features, that are highly consistent and invariant to the poses.

Note that under conformal parameterization, the u- and v- parameter lines are orthogonal, so $F=(\mathbf{r}_u,\mathbf{r}_v)=0$. Considering Gauss-Codazzi equations contain three equations, there are only two degrees of freedoms among the six coefficients, E, F, G, L, M and N. In general, a 3D surface can be uniquely (up to rigid motion) determined by the first fundamental form and mean curvature, which is stated in the following theorem [4].

Theorem 1. A closed surface $\mathbf{r}\in\mathbb{R}^3$ with conformal parametrization is determined by its conformal factor λ and mean curvature H uniquely up to rigid motion, where

$$\begin{aligned}\triangle\ln\lambda &= \lambda^2K\\ H\mathbf{n} &= \triangle\mathbf{r},\end{aligned}$$

$\triangle$ is the Laplace-Beltrami operator and K the Gaussian curvature.

Intuitively speaking, conformal factor can be thought of as scaling infinitesimal patches of the surface, while mean curvature characterizes how the shape is embedded in $\mathbb{R}^3$. Theorem 1 states that

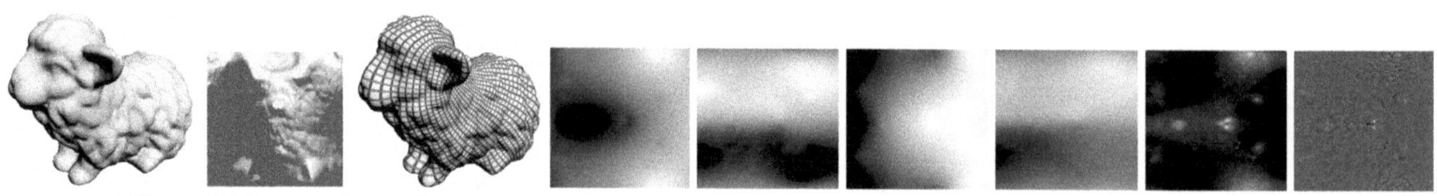

(a) 3D model (b) Parametric domain (c) Conformal parameterization (d) GI x channel (e) GI y channel (f) GI z channel (g) GI all channels (h) CGI λ channel (i) CGI H channel

Figure 2: Encoding 3D geometry into conformal factor λ and mean curvature H. The 3D model (a) is conformally parameterized to a rectangular domain (b). The texture mapping in (c) illustrates the angle preserving property of conformal parameterization, i.e., the u- and v-parameter lines are orthogonal everywhere. The traditional geometry image (GI) captures 3D geometry into three grayscale images (d)-(f) or a color image (g), in which each vertex coordinate (x, y, z) is represented by the color of a pixel (r, g, b) . In contrast, conformal geometry image (CGI) encodes the 3D shape (uniquely up to rigid motion) by its conformal factor (h) and mean curvature (i), which is more storage efficient than the traditional geometry image.

a surface can be uniquely represented (up to rigid motion) by its conformal factor λ and mean curvature H rather than the absolute coordinate (x, y, z). The traditional geometry images have to save $3n$ data, i.e., each pixel has three channels, where n is the number of pixels in the geometry image. In sharp contrast, using conformal parameterization, we can encode 3D shape into a conformal geometry image which only takes $2n$ space without loss of any information. Figure 2 shows an example of representing the 3D model using the conformal (λ, H) representation.

3.2 Conformal representation of 3D motions

With conformal parameterization, the traditional geometry image can be converted into conformal geometry image, in which $1/3$ space can be saved immediately. Thus, it is very natural to ask how can we extend geometry video to conformal geometry video. Observe that 3D motions of articulated objects (e.g., human, animals) are approximate isometric, i.e., the geodesic distances are preserved as show in Figure 3. Since the conformal factor λ is an intrinsic feature that depends on the metric only, it is invariant to the poses as well. As a result, we only need to capture the mean curvature H in the conformal geometry video. This is characterized in the following theorem:

Theorem 2. Consider a conformally parameterized *deformable* model $\mathbf{s}(u, v, t)$, where t is the time and (u, v) are the isothermal parameters. If the deformation $\mathbf{s}(u, v, \cdot)$ is isometric, then the conformal factor $\lambda(u, v, \cdot)$ is independent of time t. Furthermore, the 3D motion $s(\cdot, \cdot, t)$ can be completely reconstructed by using $\lambda(\cdot, \cdot, 0)$ and $H(\cdot, \cdot, t)$ for $\forall t$.

We omit the proof as it is straightforward. The general framework for constructing conformal geometry videos is shown in Algorithm 1.

Remark 1. The above framework is very general in that various conformal parameterization algorithm can be applied depending on the geometry and/or topology of the input 3D motion,. Furthermore, algorithms may also differ in the strategies of encoding, compression and decoding. For example, different strategies of discretization of λ and H will lead to different encoding/decoding algorithms; one has many choices on the video compression techniques, such as H.264/AVC, MPEG, etc. This paper focuses on the 3D articulated motions, which can be parameterized to polycube domain. We compress CGVs using H.264/AVC and reconstruct 3D motions by an optimization approach. The details of our algorithm are presented in Section 4 and 5.

Remark 2. As the 3D shape is uniquely determined up to rigid motion (i.e., rotation and translation) by conformal factor λ and mean curvature H, we need to eliminate the rigid motion ambiguity. Note that a 3D rigid motion can be uniquely determined by given the coordinates of four non-coplanar points (a.k.a. anchor points). Comparing to the number of vertices in each frame, the storage of these four anchor points can be ignored.

Remark 3. A conformal geometry video with k frames takes $nk + n + 4k$ space, where n is the number of pixels/vertices in each frame. In contrast, the traditional geometry video takes $3nk$ space. Thus, CGVs take approximately $1/3$ space of GVs, thus, CGVs are more compact and space efficient than GVs.

Remark 4. The proposed conformal geometry videos are fundamentally different than the natural videos (NVs) and traditional geometry videos. First, CGVs contain only one channel, i.e., mean curvature H, while both GVs and NVs have three channels, i.e., (x, y, z) or (r, g, b). Second, the conformal factor λ and mean curvature H are independent, while the three channels of GVs are not independent. Third, CGVs show stronger spatial and temporal coherence than GVs and NVs (see Section 5.2 for discussion).

Figure 4 demonstrated the CGV and GV of the deformed cloth.

Algorithm 1: Constructing Conformal Geometry Videos

Parameterization (Sec 4):
Given a 3D isometric motion M with k frames, conformally parameterize M such that all the salient features are consistently mapped to the parametric domain, which guarantees the intrinsic features (e.g., metric, conformal factor, Gaussian curvature, etc) are pose invariant.

Encoding (Sec 5.1):
Compute the conformal factor λ_1 for the first frame M_1.
Compute the mean curvature $H_i, i = 1, \cdots, k$ for every frame M_i.
For each frame M_i, choose four non-coplanar anchor points, and record their locations, denoted by l_i, which is used to eliminate the reconstruction ambiguity.
Output the conformal geometry video $\lambda_1, H_1, \cdots, H_k$ and $l_1, \cdots, l_k$.

Compression (Sec 5.2):
Apply the video compression technique to the mean curvature sequence $H_i, i = 1, \cdots, k$.

Decoding (Sec 5.3):
To recovery the i-th frame M_i, compute the 3D shape from λ_1 and H_i.
Eliminate the rigid motion ambiguity by using the locations of four anchor points l_i.

Since the cloth deformation is perfectly isometric, the λ channel characterizing the intrinsic property is pose-invariant (see Row 2). Thus, CGVs only need to keep one frame of λ and all frames of H. GVs, however, differ significantly for all channels for every frame.

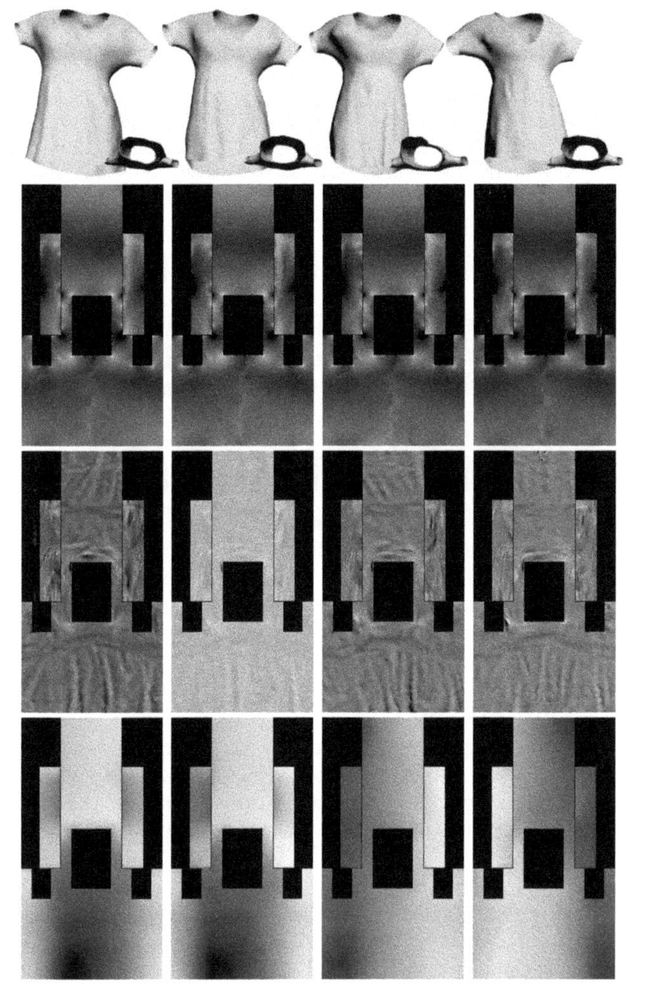

(a) (b) (c) (d)

Figure 4: Geometry videos vs conformal geometry videos. The given cloth deformation (row 1) is perfectly isometric, so the conformal factor λ (row 2) is pose-invariant. As a result, CGVs only need to capture the mean curvature H (row 3), which characterizes the extrinsic feature. The traditional geometry video (row 4), in sharp contrast, differs significantly in all channels.

4. CONFORMAL PARAMETERIZATION OF 3D ARTICULATED MOTIONS

As mentioned in Section 2.2, there are many conformal parameterization algorithms available. However, most of them parameterize the 3D models into charts with irregular boundaries, which may cause numerical issues when reconstructing the curved boundary. In this paper, we use conformal polycube parameterization for two reasons: First, the parametric domain is a 3D shape that mimics the geometry of the input model, thus, the area distortion can be controlled in an easy and intuitive manner. Second, polycube has regular atlas in that each polycube face is the union of squares. Thus, each chart has axis-aligned boundaries, which facilitates the encoding and decoding.

The input of our algorithm is a sequence of captured 3D motion, each frame is represented by a triangle mesh. Note that the scanned 3D motion data are usually given in the reference system of the scanner without registration in object space, thus, they do not have correspondence between two frames. To construct conformal geometry videos, all the salient features must be *consistently* parameterized to the desired locations on the parametric domain, otherwise, the conformal factor may not be pose-invariant.

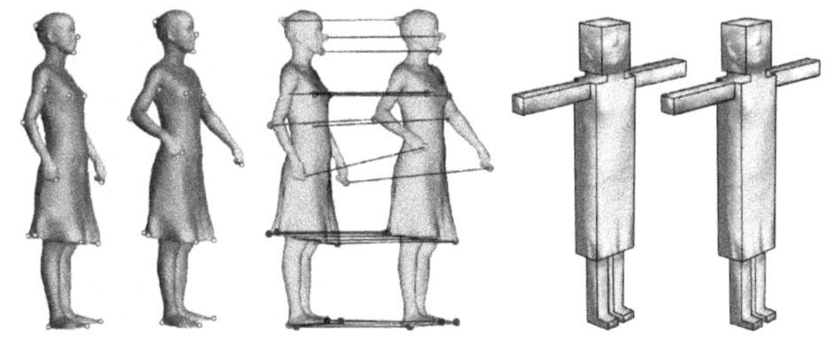

(a) (b) (c)

Figure 5: Feature detection and tracking. (a) The heat kernel signature (HKS), where blue (resp. red) represents low (resp. high) HKS value, and the detected feature points. (b) Feature points tracking between two adjacent frames. (c) By our constrained polycube mapping algorithm, different poses can be parameterized to the polycube in a consistent manner.

Feature detection For each frame M_i, we compute the Heat Kernel Signature (HKS) [22] $k_t^{M_i}(x,x)$ for each point $x \in M$, with a short diffusion time ($t = 0.007$ in our experiments). Then we use the local maxima of the HKS to identify the feature points [18]. In practice, we consider a point p to be a feature point on M_i if $k_t^{M_i}(p,p) > k_t^{M_i}(x,x)$ for all x in the two-ring neighborhood of point p. Figure 5(a) shows the computed HKS with relative large time and the detected geometric feature points.

Feature tracking Give two adjacent frames M_i and M_{i+1}, we detect the set of feature points $P \subseteq M_i$ and $Q \subseteq M_{i+1}$ by geometric feature detection. For each point $p \in P$, we find the correspondence $q \in Q$ using the method [18] and record the distance of the candidate pair (p,q). We then choose the pair with the shortest distance as the ground truth matching, and find the correspondence of feature points between M_i and M_{i+1} by isometric matching [18]. Note that not every feature point in P is mapped to Q and vice versa. In practice, we discard the pairs with distance 4 times lager than that of the pair with the shortest distance. Figure 5(b) shows the correspondence among the feature points between M_i and M_{i+1}.

Constrained conformal polycube parameterization Once we find the correspondence of the salient features in the 3D motion, we can parameterize it to the polycube domain by using the editable polycube map approach [33]. This method is able to parameterize a complex 3D model to the polycube such that the user-specified constraints on the 3D model can be accurately mapped to the desired location on the polycube. Given the first frame M_i with the detected features (e.g., head, hands, feet, etc), we sketch their desired locations on the polycube, and compute the polycube map using [33]. Then we parameterize M_i, $i > 1$, to the same polycube domain with the feature constraints tracked by the heat kernel signature. Next, we apply a Laplacian smoothing to the computed polycube maps, which leads to high quality conformal parameterization (see Figure 6(d)). Finally, we cut the 3D polycube open and flatten it to a rectangle domain in $\mathbb{R}^2$ (see Figure 6(c)).

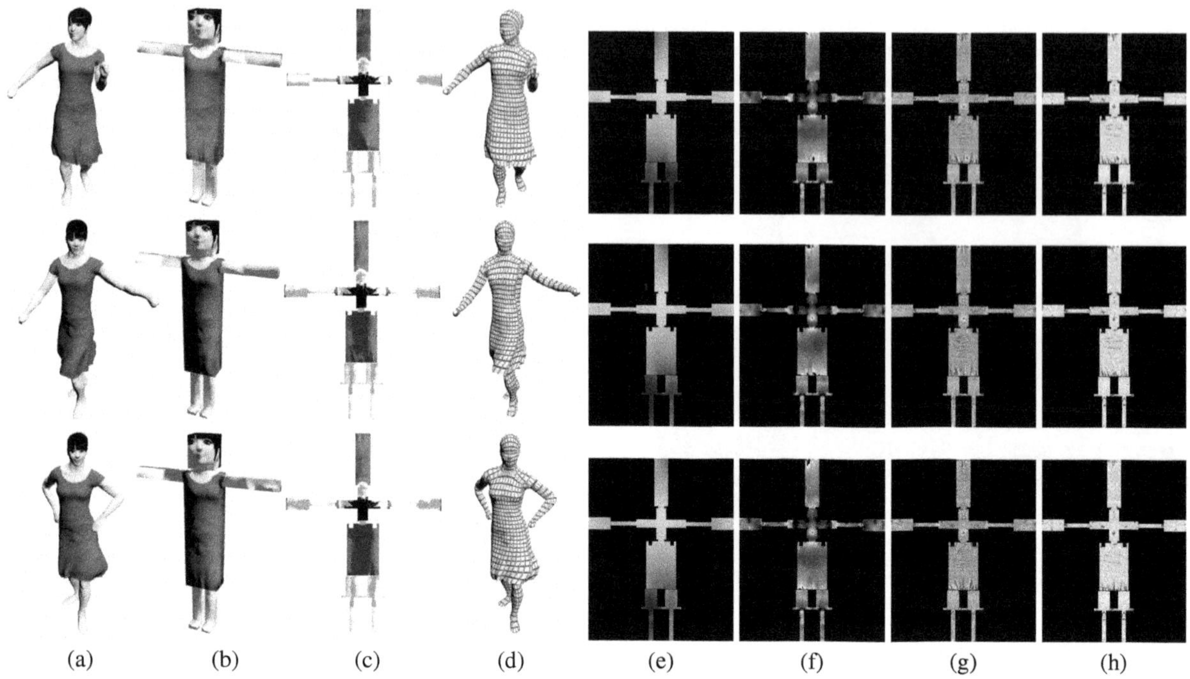

Figure 6: **The samba sequence. (a) 3D motion. (b) Conformal polycube parameterization. (c) Flattened polycube to $\mathbb{R}^2$. (d) Checkerboard texture mapping induced by the polycube parameterization. (e) Geometry videos (x, y and z channels). (f) and (g) show the λ and H channels of conformal geometry videos. To better visualize the pose-dependent feature of mean curvature, we render H with color in (h).**

5. COMPRESSION WITH CGVS

5.1 Encoding

In the continuous setting, the conformal factor measures the scaling of the infinitesimal patches of the surface. In discrete setting, each 3D pose M_i is represented by a quadrilateral mesh. Let $Nb(v)$ denote the four neighbors of vertex v (if v is a polycube corner, $Nb(v)$ contains 3 or 5 elements). We approximate conformal factor of a vertex v as the average lengths of the edges adjacent to v, i.e.,

$$\lambda(v) = \frac{1}{|Nb(v)|} \sum_{p \in Nb(v)} l(v, p),$$

where $l(v, p)$ is the length of edge $\{v, p\}$. The discrete mean curvature of vertex v is approximated as

$$H(v) = (\triangle v, \mathbf{n}),$$

where the discrete Laplace-Beltrami operator is

$$\triangle v = v - \frac{1}{|Nb(v)|} \sum_{p \in Nb(v)} p.$$

As mentioned before, the conformal factor λ is pose-invariant if the 3D motion is perfectly isometric. However, such isometric motion is quite rare in real-world applications. In fact, most of the 3D articulated motions are approximate isometric, thus, the conformal factor λ is not a constant. To accurately reconstruct M_i ($i > 1$), we choose a set of key frames in the 3D motion, and then define the conformal factor image for each key frame. In practice, $k/10$ key frames (i.e., one key frame in every 10 frames) of conformal factor lead to satisfactory results in our experiments (see Section 6 for the details).

5.2 Compression

The conformal geometry video contains k frames of mean curvature H and m key frames of conformal factor λ, where $m(\ll k)$ is specified by the user. We partition conformal geometry video into two independent grayscale video sequences, each of them is compressed by H.264/AVC in 4:0:0 YUV format at various bitrates. For comparison, the compression of traditional geometry videos with three channels is compressed similarly except in 4:4:4 YUV format.

We have conducted a statistical analysis on the samba sequence in the format of CGVs, GVs and NVs, respectively. As shown in Figure 7(a)-(c), the conformal factor λ and mean curvature H of CGVs are more concentrated into a smaller number of buckets. We also compared CGV to GV and NV in Figure 7(d) by using the Prewitt based histograms [35]. It has been observed that CGVs also provide more concentrated results in the histogram distributions. Furthermore, Figure 7(e) compares the mean square errors (MSEs) for the conformal factor (only applied to the key frames) and mean curvature (all frames) of CGVs, GVs, and the corresponding NVs after a 32x32 full search motion estimation at a given QP(=8). Clearly, the MSEs of CGVs are smaller than that of the NVs and GVs. This proves that the redundancy in CGVs can be significantly removed by motion estimation, which is the most powerful and effective tool in H.264/AVC. The above statistical results show that CGV pixels are highly correlated in both spatial and temporal domain. The results are also consistent with our subjective observations - we found that the neighboring frames of CGV are very similar in appearance, and the neighboring pixels share similar pixel values. On the other hand, the H.264/AVC standard mainly takes advantage of removing the spatial and temporal redundancies of video sequences to achieve compression. Consequently, our CGV is very suitable to be compressed with H.264/AVC.

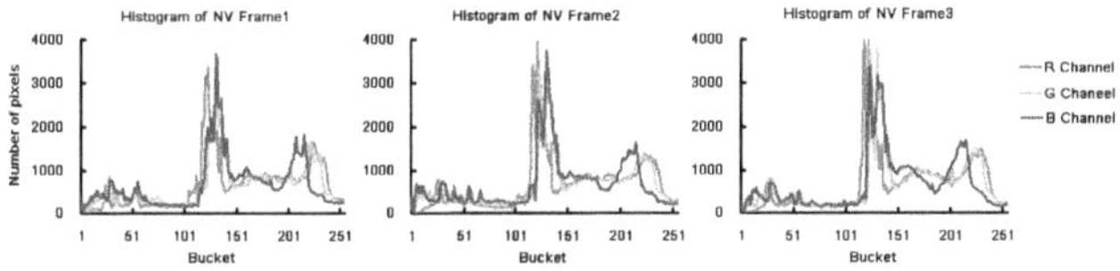

(a) Pixel value distribution of natural videos (NVs)

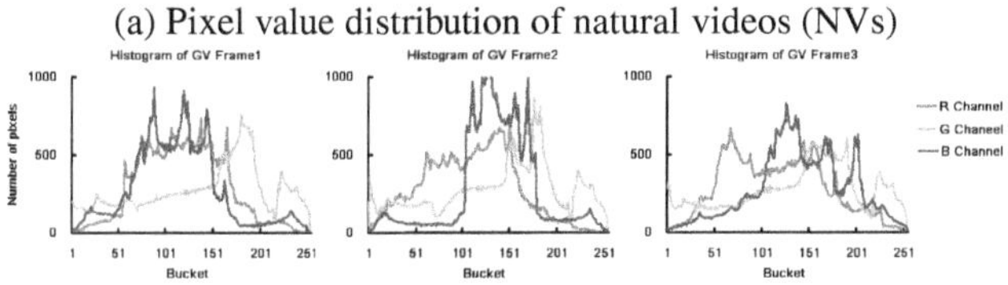

(b) Pixel value distribution of geometry videos (GVs)

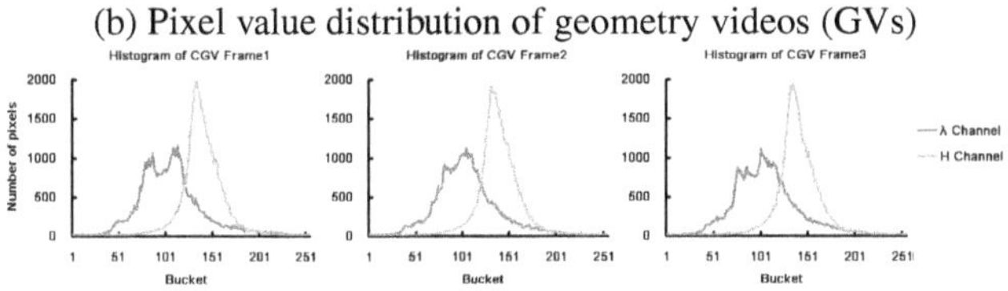

(c) Pixel value distribution of conformal geometry videos (CGVs)

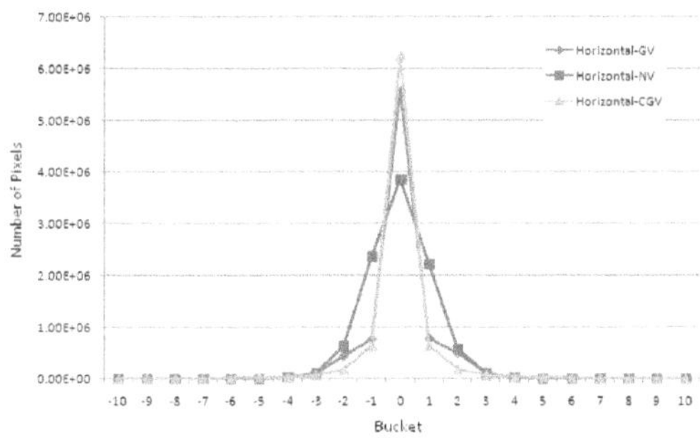

(d) Prewitt-based histogram comparison

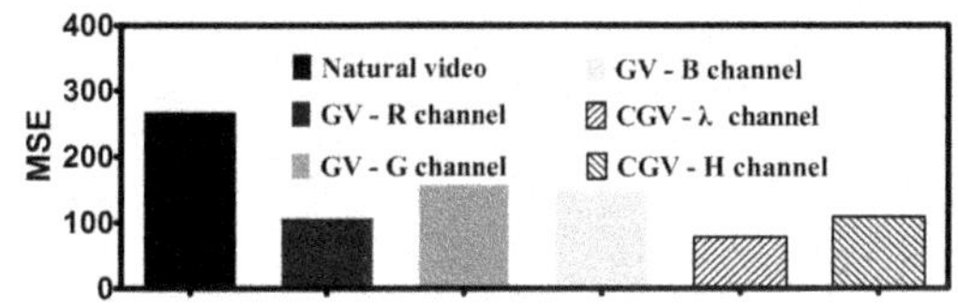

(e) Mean square error (MSE) after a 32x32 full search motion estimation

Figure 7: CGVs are fundamentally different than GVs and NVs in that CGVs have stronger spatial and temporal coherence as shown by the smaller MSE. Also, the pixel values of CGVs are concentrated on a small number of buckets.

5.3 Decoding

To reconstruct the 3D geometry from the conformal geometry video, we solve the following optimization problem:

$$\min \sum_{v_i} (\| \Delta v_i \|^2 - H_i^2)^2 + \sum_{v_i} |\lambda(v_i)^2 - \lambda_i^2|^2, \quad (1)$$

where λ_i is the decoded conformal factor of v_i, and Δv_i gives the mean curvature vector of vertex v_i. Note that one can reconstruct the geometry uniquely up to rigid motion (i.e., rotation and translation) from (λ, H). We eliminate the ambiguity of rigid motion by using the locations of four non-degenerate anchor points.

Note that Eqn. 1 is a non-linear programming, thus, it is difficult to obtain the global optimal in general. In our implementation, we take advantage of the spatial and temporal coherence of conformal geometry videos. As the location of four anchor points are already known, we compute the rigid motion between the anchor points of the frame M_{i-1} and frame M_i. Next we apply this rigid motion to the reconstructed geometry M_{i-1} and then use it as the initial guess for the current frame. This strategy works very well in practice.

6. EXPERIMENTAL RESULTS

This section presents the experimental results of modeling 3D motions using our conformal geometry video framework. We also compare our CGVs with the traditional GVs.

Test sequences: We conducted experiments on 5 real-world human motion datasets (samba, march, squat, handstand and bouncing) and 1 synthetic dataset (cloth deformation). The human motion is approximately isometric transformation where the motion is composed of a few non-rigidly moving parts. The samba sequence consists of 200 frames, the march and squat 250 frames, the handstand and bouncing 174 frames. Each of frame in human motion datasets has 250k vertices. The synthetic cloth deformation is isometric, and consists of 450 frames with 160k vertices in each frame.

H.264/AVC configuration: We have used the H.264/AVC reference software (JM14.2 version) to encode the test sequences. The compression procedure is as we described in Section 5.2. To have different video qualities, we encoded each sequence at different bitrates by changing the quantization parameters (QPs) in the range of -24 to -4 (please note that we have adopted the negative QPs in order to encode high-quality videos). Each test sequence is encoded at 30 frames per second with IPBPB GOP structure, 32x32 full search motion estimation and CABAC entropy coding. The intra-frame period was set to 30 and the Rate Distortion Optimization (RDO) was turned on.

3D motion compression results: To make a fair comparison between GVs and CGVs, we chose the compressed GVs and the compressed CGVs with similar file sizes (i.e., similar bitrates). Table 1 shows the low, medium and high bitrates of GVs and CGVs that we chose for the comparison on 5 human motion sequences and the cloth sequence. Then we reconstructed the 3D motion from the compressed GVs and CGVs. For the synthetic cloth deformation which is isometric, we only need one frame of the conformal factor. For the 3D human motions which are approximate isometric, we set $k/10$ key frames (i.e., one key frame every 10 frames) for the conformal factor.

Table 1: The bitrates of GVs and CGVs of 6 tested sequences

	Low Bitrate	Medium Bitrate	High Bitrate
GV samba	1526.86	2616.42	5594.50
CGV samba	1463.30	2433.94	5013.71
GV march	1104.69	1886.72	3060.75
CGV march	965.73	1852.06	2975.82
GV squat	1148.10	1960.72	3308.69
CGV squat	1097.78	1870.92	3290.72
GV handstand	1087.69	1939.89	3241.26
CGV handstand	940.54	1606.60	2820.94
GV bouncing	1270.20	2247.14	3745.29
CGV bouncing	1184.47	2223.89	3826.06
GV cloth	1249.14	2173.03	3763.88
CGV cloth	1212.08	2137.01	3004.56

Figures 8 and 9 show the experimental results on two real datasets and one synthetic dataset. We observed that both CGVs and GVs perform well in high bitrates. However, GVs perform poorly in low bitrates, see the artifacts (non-smoothness, self-intersection, fold-over, etc) in the reconstructed 3D motion. In contrast, CGVs generate 3D motions with much better quality even in low bitrates. For quantitative comparison between GVs and CGVs, we measured the

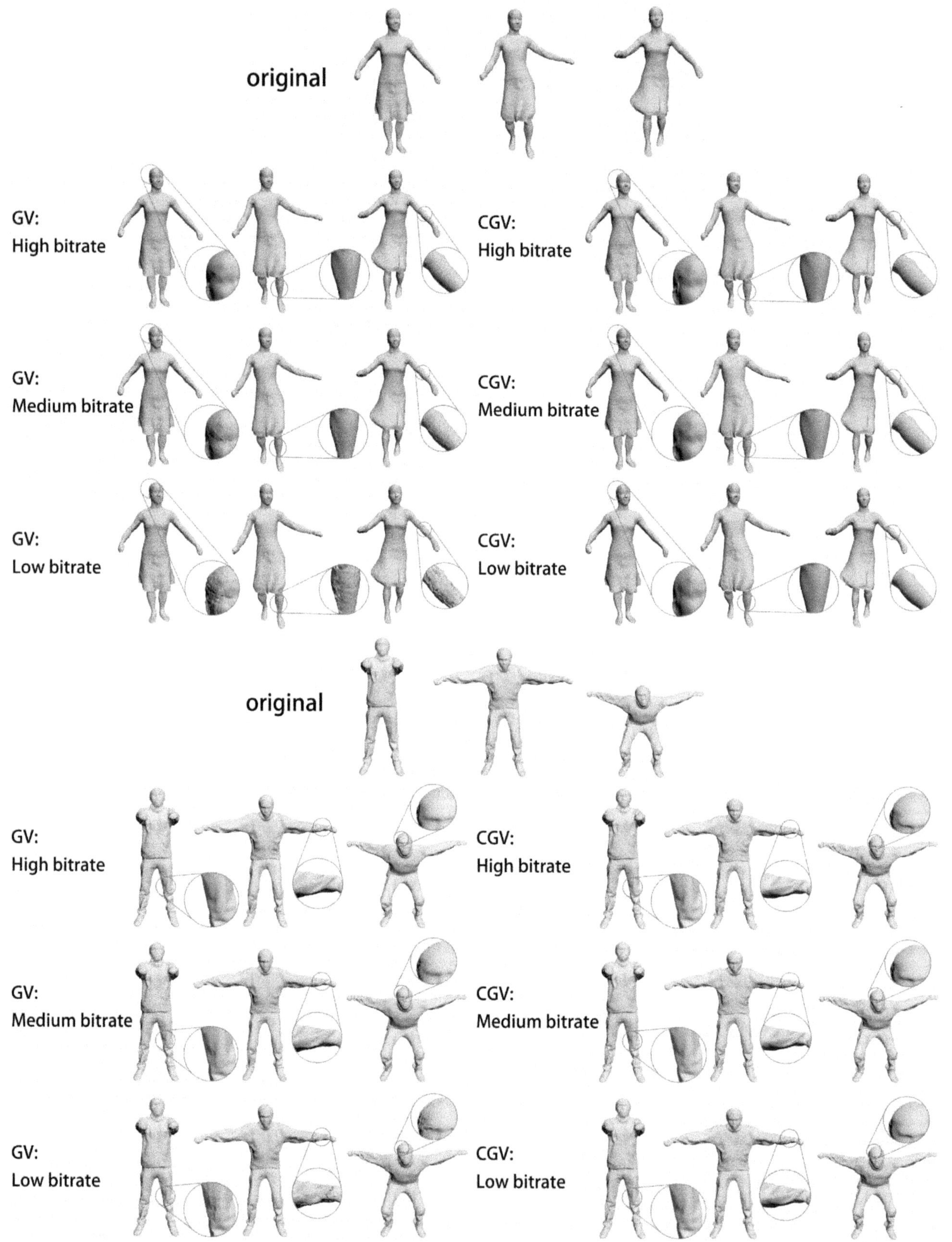

Figure 8: Experimental results on the samba (top) and squat (bottom) sequences with high, medium and low bitrates for GVs and CGVs. Note that the quality of CGVs generated 3D motion does not drop too much when bitrate is reduced. In contrast, GVs perform poorly on low bitrates. Images are rendered in high resolution that allows close-up evaluation.

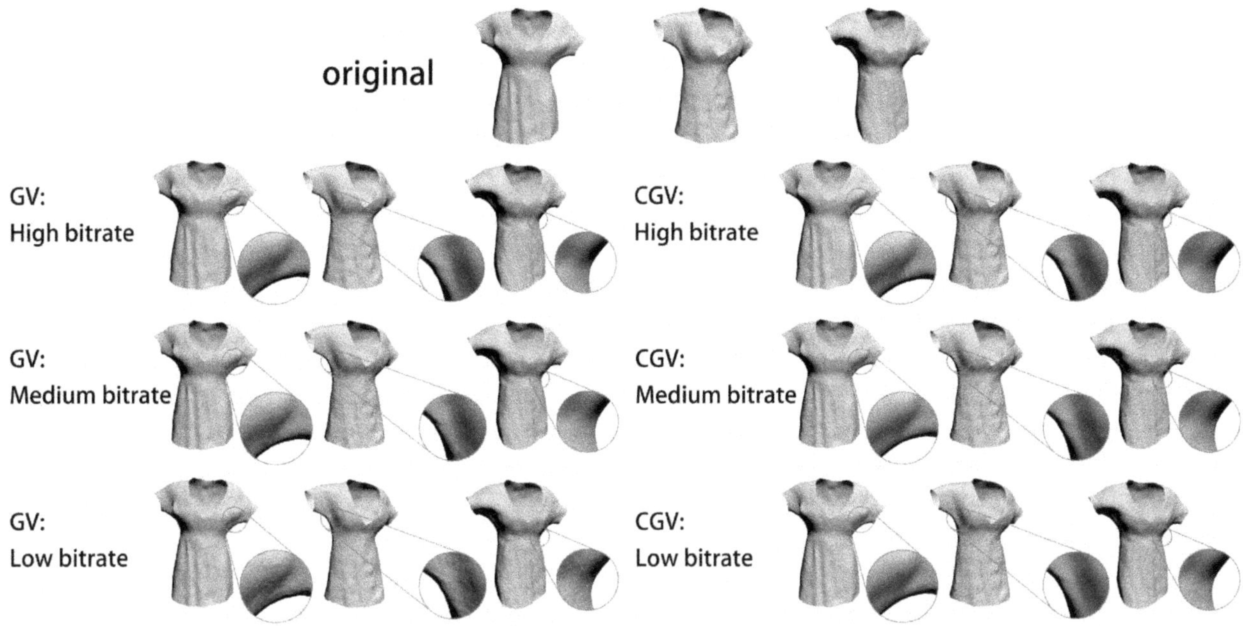

Figure 9: The cloth sequence with high, medium and low bitrates for GVs and CGVs. Note the artifacts (such as non-smoothness, self-intersection, fold-over, etc) on the GVs with low bitrates, while CGVs with similar bitrates lead to visually pleasing results without obvious artifacts.

compression quality by computing the smoothness metric [12],

$$\sqrt{\frac{1}{|V|}\sum_{i=1}^{|V|}\| \triangle v_i - \triangle v_i'\|^2},$$

where v_i and $v_i^{'}$ are the vertices in the original and reconstructed meshes respectively. This smoothness metric characterizes the local change of differential coordinates and is used for measurement of shape quality. The smaller the value of the smoothness metric, the closer the reconstructed model to the original model and visually more pleasing. Conversely, the larger the value of the smoothness metric, the less smooth the reconstructed data(e.g. blocking artifacts) and visually less pleasing. As we show in the Table 2 the normalized smoothness metric of all the datasets, CGVs consistently outperform GVs since GVs encode x/y/z directly which is very sensitive to the block artifacts in low and medium bitrates. In sharp contrast, CGVs encode the 3D geometry into conformal factor and mean curvature, and reconstruct x/y/z by solving an optimization problem that naturally preserves the smoothness of the 3D motion (based on the assumption that 3D articulated motions are spatially smooth, which is true for 3D human and animals). Thus, CGVs are visually more pleasing than GVs.

The time statistics were measured in seconds on a PC with 2.66 GHz CPU and 4GB RAM: Feature detection takes 9s on the first frame and tracking in subsequent frames is done in real time, parameterization 1s/frame, compression 12s/frame, decompression real time, 3D reconstruction 23s/frame. In reconstruction part, our current solver is conjugate gradient with linear convergence rate. Other advanced solvers (e.g. BFGS) can significantly improve the performance.

7. CONCLUSIONS

This paper presented conformal geometry videos (CGVs), a novel extension of the traditional geometry videos by taking into the consideration of the isometric nature of 3D articulated motions. We showed that the 3D articulated motion can be uniquely determined

Table 2: The normalized smoothness metric of GVs and CGVs of 6 tested sequences, with unit 10^{-4}

	Low Bitrate	Medium Bitrate	High Bitrate
GV samba	6.51	2.69	1.79
CGV samba	2.97	1.96	1.72
GV march	8.68	4.91	3.20
CGV march	3.46	2.01	1.85
GV squat	6.86	4.01	2.75
CGV squat	2.21	1.17	1.16
GV handstand	9.82	5.55	3.53
CGV handstand	3.71	2.89	2.68
GV bouncing	9.54	5.36	3.40
CGV bouncing	5.63	4.49	4.24
GV cloth	2.20	1.19	0.73
CGV cloth	0.76	0.56	0.46

(up to rigid motion) by (λ, H), where λ is the conformal factor characterizing the intrinsic property of the 3D motion, and H the mean curvature characterizing the extrinsic feature (i.e., embedding or appearance). The rigid motion ambiguity can be easily eliminated by the locations of four non-degenerate anchor points. Since the conformal factor λ is pose-invariant, CGVs take only 1/3 the storage requirement of the traditional GVs. Our statistical tests showed that CGVs have strong spatial and temporal coherence, which is highly desirable for H.264/AVC compression. We applied conformal geometry videos to model real-world 3D human motions and synthetic cloth deformation and demonstrated that that CGVs outperform GVs with better quality and less space complexity.

There are several research directions that are worth to investigate in the future. First, as the real-world 3D motions are only approximate isometric, we need to define the conformal factor for a certain number of key frames. In our current implementation, we set one key frame among every 10 frames. Although simple, this strategy is obviously far from optimal, as the locations of key frames are data dependent. We will develop an optimization approach to determine the locations of the key frames. Second, decoding 3D motion from λ and H is to solve a degree 4 nonlinear programming. We use the conjugate gradient approach in our current implementation. Adopting advanced solvers or GPU based solvers can improve the performance. Third, we assume that the input 3D motion data are closed and error-free. However, the captured 3D motions always have various defects, such as holes, noise, etc. It would be interesting to investigate techniques for parameterizing and modeling such incomplete data.

Acknowledgement

This work was supported by National Research Foundation (NRF) under grant NRF2008IDM-IDM004-006. The 3D human motion and cloth datasets are courtesy of [24] and [1] respectively. We would like to thank the anonymous reviewers for their constructive comments.

8. REFERENCES

[1] D. Bradley, T. Popa, A. Sheffer, W. Heidrich, and T. Boubekeur. Markerless garment capture. *ACM Trans. Graph.*, 27(3), 2008.

[2] H. M. Briceño, P. V. Sander, L. McMillan, S. Gortler, and H. Hoppe. Geometry videos: a new representation for 3d animations. In *SCA*, pages 136–146, 2003.

[3] X. Gu, S. J. Gortler, and H. Hoppe. Geometry images. *ACM Trans. Graph.*, 21:355–361, July 2002.

[4] X. Gu, Y. Wang, and S.-T. Yau. Geometric compression using Riemann surface structure. *Communications in Information and Systems*, 3(3):171–182, 2003.

[5] X. Gu and S.-T. Yau. Global conformal surface parameterization. In *SGP*, pages 127–137, 2003.

[6] S.-R. Han, T. Yamasaki, and K. Aizawa. Time-varying mesh compression using an extended block matching algorithm. *TCSVT*, 17(11):1506–1518, 2007.

[7] S.-R. Han, T. Yamasaki, and K. Aizawa. Geometry compression for time-varying meshes using coarse and fine levels of quantization and run-length encoding. In *ICIP*, pages 1045–1048, 2008.

[8] Y. He, H. Wang, C.-W. Fu, and H. Qin. A divide-and-conquer approach for automatic polycube map construction. *Comput. Graph.*, 33:369–380, 2009.

[9] H. Hoppe and E. Praun. *Advances in Multiresolution for Geometric Modelling*, chapter Shape compression using spherical geometry images., pages 27–46. Springer-Verlag, 2003.

[10] ITU-T. The h.264/avc standard. *ITU-T Rec. H.264*, 2008.

[11] F. Kälberer, M. Nieser, and K. Polthier. Quadcover - surface parameterization using branched coverings. *Comput. Graph. Forum*, 26(3):375–384, 2007.

[12] Z. Karni and C. Gotsman. Spectral compression of mesh geometry. In *SIGGRAPH*, pages 279–286, 2000.

[13] T. P. Koninckx and L. Van Gool. Real-time range acquisition by adaptive structured light. *TPAMI*, 28:432–445, 2006.

[14] Y.-K. Lai, M. Jin, X. Xie, Y. He, J. Palacios, E. Zhang, S.-M. Hu, and X. Gu. Metric-driven rosy field design and remeshing. *TVCG*, 16:95–108, 2010.

[15] H. Li, B. Adams, L. J. Guibas, and M. Pauly. Robust single-view geometry and motion reconstruction. *ACM Trans. Graph.*, 28(5), 2009.

[16] J. Lin, X. Jin, Z. Fan, and C. C. L. Wang. Automatic polycube-maps. In *GMP*, pages 3–16, 2008.

[17] N. J. Mitra, S. Flöry, M. Ovsjanikov, N. Gelfand, L. Guibas, and H. Pottmann. Dynamic geometry registration. In *SGP*, pages 173–182, 2007.

[18] M. Ovsjanikov, Q. Mérigot, F. Mèmoli, and L. Guibas. One point isometric matching with the heat kernel. *Comput. Graph. Forum*, 29:1555–1564, 2010.

[19] G. Peyré and S. Mallat. Surface compression with geometric bandelets. *ACM Trans. Graph.*, 24:601–608, 2005.

[20] A. Sheffer, E. Praun, and K. Rose. Mesh parameterization methods and their applications. *Found. Trends. Comput. Graph. Vis.*, 2:105–171, 2006.

[21] G. Sullivan and T. Wiegand. Video compression - from concepts to the H.264/AVC standard. In *Proceedings of the IEEE*, pages 18–31, 2005.

[22] J. Sun, M. Ovsjanikov, and L. Guibas. A concise and provably informative multi-scale signature based on heat diffusion. In *SGP*, pages 1383–1392, 2009.

[23] M. Tarini, K. Hormann, P. Cignoni, and C. Montani. Polycube-maps. *ACM Trans. Graph.*, 23(3):853–860, 2004.

[24] D. Vlasic, I. Baran, W. Matusik, and J. Popovic. Articulated mesh animation from multi-view silhouettes. *ACM Trans. Graph.*, 27(3), 2008.

[25] D. Vlasic, P. Peers, I. Baran, P. Debevec, J. Popović, S. Rusinkiewicz, and W. Matusik. Dynamic shape capture using multi-view photometric stereo. *ACM Trans. Graphics (Proc. SIGGRAPH Asia)*, 28(5), Dec. 2009.

[26] S. Wan, Z. Yin, K. Zhang, H. Zhang, and X. Li. A topology-preserved optimization algorithm for polycube mapping. *Computers & Graphics*, 2011.

[27] H. Wang, Y. He, X. Li, X. Gu, and H. Qin. Polycube splines. *Computer-Aided Design*, 40(6):721–733, 2008.

[28] H. Wang, M. Jin, Y. He, X. Gu, and H. Qin. User-controllable polycube map for manifold spline construction. In *SPM*, pages 397–404, 2008.

[29] S. Wang, Y. Wang, M. Jin, X. Gu, and D. Samaras. 3d surface matching and recognition using conformal geometry. In *CVPR (2)*, pages 2453–2460, 2006.

[30] Y. Wang, M. Gupta, S. Zhang, S. Wang, X. Gu, D. Samaras, and P. Huang. High resolution tracking of non-rigid motion of densely sampled 3d data using harmonic maps. *IJCV*, 76(3):283–300, 2008.

[31] Y. Wang, X. Huang, C. Lee, S. Zhang, Z. Li, D. Samaras, D. Metaxas, A. Elgammal, and P. Huang. High resolution acquisition, learning and transfer of dynamic 3D facial expressions. In *CGF*, pages 677–686, 2004.

[32] T. Wiegand, G. Sullivan, G. Bjontegaard, and A. Luthra. Overview of the H.264/AVC video coding standard. *TCSVT*, 13:560–576, 2003.

[33] J. Xia, I. Garcia, Y. He, S.-Q. Xin, and G. Patow. Editable polycube map for gpu-based subdivision surfaces. In *I3D*, I3D '11, pages 151–158, 2011.

[34] J. Xia, Y. He, D. T. P. Quynh, X. Chen, and S. C. H. Hoi. Modeling 3d facial expressions using geometry videos. In *ACM Multimedia*, pages 591–600, 2010.

[35] J. Xia, D. T. P. Quynh, Y. He, X. Chen, and S. C. H. Hoi. Modeling and compressing 3d facial expressions using geometry videos. *TCSVT*, accepted, 2011.

[36] T. Yamasaki and K. Aizawa. Patch-based compression for time-varying meshes. In *ICIP*, pages 3433–3436, 2010.

[37] Y.-L. Yang, J. Kim, F. Luo, S.-M. Hu, and X. Gu. Optimal surface parameterization using inverse curvature map. *TVCG*, 14:1054–1066, 2008.

[38] S. Zhang and P. Huang. High-resolution, real-time 3d shape acquisition. In *CVPRW'04 Vol. 3*, page 28, 2004.

Random Partial Paired Comparison for Subjective Video Quality Assessment via HodgeRank *

Qianqian Xu
Graduate University, Chinese Academy of Sciences, Beijing 100049, China
qqxu@jdl.ac.cn

Tingting Jiang⋆
National Engineering Lab. for Video Technology, Key Lab of Machine Perception (MOE), School of EECS, Peking University, Beijing 100871, China
ttjiang@pku.edu.cn

Yuan Yao⋆
School of Mathematical Sciences, Key Lab. of Machine Perception (MoE), Peking University, Beijing 100871, China
yuany@math.pku.edu.cn

Qingming Huang⋆
Graduate University, Chinese Academy of Sciences, Beijing 100049, China
qmhuang@jdl.ac.cn

Bowei Yan
School of Mathematical Sciences, Peking University, Beijing 100871, China
yanbowei@gmail.com

Weisi Lin
School of Computer Engineering, Nanyang Technological University, Nanyang 639798, Singapore
wslin@ntu.edu.sg

ABSTRACT

Subjective visual quality evaluation provides the ground-truth and source of inspiration in building objective visual quality metrics. Paired comparison is expected to yield more reliable results; however, this is an expensive and time-consuming process. In this paper, we propose a novel framework of ***HodgeRank on Random Graphs*** (HRRG) to achieve efficient and reliable subjective Video Quality Assessment (VQA). To address the challenge of a potentially large number of combinations of videos to be assessed, the proposed methodology does not require the participants to perform the complete comparison of all the paired videos. Instead, participants only need to perform a random sample of all possible paired comparisons, which saves a great amount of time and labor. In contrast to the traditional deterministic incomplete block designs, our random design is not only suitable for traditional laboratory and focus-group studies, but also fit for crowdsourcing experiments on Internet where the raters are distributive over Internet and it is hard to control with precise experimental designs.

Our contribution in this work is three-fold: 1) a HRRG framework is proposed to quantify the quality of video; 2) a new random design principle is investigated to conduct paired comparison based on Erdös-Rényi random graph theory; 3) Hodge decomposition is introduced to derive, from incomplete and imbalanced data, quality scores of videos and inconsistency of participants' judgments. We demonstrate the effectiveness of the proposed framework on LIVE Database. Equipped with random graph theory and HodgeRank, our scheme has the following advantages over the traditional ones: 1) data collection is simple and easy to handle, and thus is more suitable for crowdsourcing on Internet; 2) workload on participants is lower and more flexible; 3) the rating procedure is efficient, labor-saving, and more importantly, without jeopardizing the accuracy of the results.

*Area chair: Wei-tsang Ooi.
⋆Corresponding author.

Categories and Subject Descriptors

H.5.1 [**Information Interfaces and Presentation**]: Multimedia Information Systems—*Evaluation/methodology*; C.4 [**Performance of Systems**]: Design studies; H.1.2 [**Models and Principles**]: User/Machine Systems—*Human factors*

General Terms

Performance, Experimentation, Human Factors

Keywords

Subjective Video Quality Assessment, HodgeRank, Random Graphs, Persistence Homology

1. INTRODUCTION

With the rapid development and wide applications of digital media devices, the number of videos available is growing at an explosive rate. The Video Quality Assessment (VQA) issue, has drawn increasing attention from researchers during recent years, and now plays an important role in a broad range of applications, e.g. video enhancement, reconstruction, compression, communication, displaying, registration, printing, watermarking, etc.

The existing methods of VQA can be divided into two categories: subjective assessment and objective assessment. In subjective viewing tests, video sequences are shown to a group of viewers and then their opinions are recorded and averaged to evaluate the quality of each video sequence. This testing process is labor-intensive and time-consuming. Therefore, there has been an increasing demand to build intelligent, objective quality measurement models [33, 24, 27, 34, 15] to predict perceived video quality automatically. Subjective experiments are often used to provide the ground-truth and verification for objective models. In typical Mean Opinion Score (MOS) test [1], individuals are asked to give a rating from Bad to Excellent (Bad-1, Poor-2, Fair-3, Good-4, and Excellent-5) to grade the quality of a video. However, such a test may suffer the following problems [8]:

1. Unable to concretely define the concept of scale;
2. Dissimilar interpretations of the scale among users;
3. Difficult to verify whether a participant gives false ratings either intentionally or carelessly.

Therefore, to address the problems above, recent investigations turn to an alternative approach with paired comparison [8]. In a paired comparison test, a participant is simply asked to compare two videos simultaneously, and vote which one has the better quality based on his/her perception. Therefore individual decision process in paired comparison is simpler than in the typical MOS test, as the five-scale rating is reduced to a dichotomous choice.

However, paired comparison approach leaves a heavier burden on participants with a larger number of comparisons. For example, we are given 15 distorted versions of 1 reference video, i.e. 16 videos in total to be compared; by adopting the MOS, it only needs to perform 15 judgments. However, it requires $\binom{16}{2}$ =120 comparisons if adopting the complete design in existing paired comparison method [8]. When the number of videos to be judged is large, it may be practically impossible, or at least unacceptable from the viewpiont of the participants. If the testing time for a single participant lasts too long [2], participants may become lack of patience and thus may input random decisions carelessly or intentionally. Therefore, how to make paired comparison method efficient and applicable in reality has become an urgent issue in the VQA community.

To address this issue, we propose in this paper a novel methodology which is not only suitable for traditional laboratory and focus-group studies, but also fit for crowdsourcing experiments, i.e. ***HodgeRank on Random Graphs***.

Our rationale is that, since the number of videos to be judged can be large, we do not ask a single participant to perform the complete comparison of all the video pairs. Instead, every participant only needs to commit to a fraction of all possible comparisons. Hence it raises a question: how to choose the pairs that will be viewed by participants? There has been a large literature in statistics on deterministic incomplete block design [9]. However, these designs are not suitable for crowdsourcing on Internet where the raters are distributive over Internet with varied backgrounds and it is hard to control with traditional experimental designs. To meet this challenge, we propose a random design based on Erdös-Rényi random graph theory [12], the simplest scheme among other choices, where video pairs are independently presented to a participant for rating. Equipped with a recent new development of Hodge theoretical approach to statistical ranking [18], we can infer a reliable global ranking from such data.

In HodgeRank, it shows that every edge flow representing paired ranking can be resolved into two orthogonal components, a gradient flow that represents the l_2-optimal global ranking and a divergence-free flow (cyclic) that measures the validity of the global ranking obtained—if this is large, it indicates that the data does not have a good global ranking. This divergence-free flow can be further decomposed orthogonally into a curl flow (locally cyclic) and a harmonic flow (locally acyclic but globally cyclic); these provide information on whether inconsistency in the ranking data arises locally or globally. In applications, one should avoid large global inconsistency which indicates some serious conflicts of interests in ranking data. Through Erdös-Rényi random graphs, we can efficiently control this kind of inconsistency.

We demonstrate the effectiveness and generality of the proposed framework on LIVE Database [3]. Experimental results show that the proposed framework is promising and has potentially wide applications in subjective VQA.

Our contribution in this work is three-fold:

1. We propose a novel framework of HodgeRank with random graphs to quantify the quality of video. The advantages of our framework over the traditional ones are: 1) data collection is simple, easy to handle, and thus is more suitable for crowdsourcing on Internet; 2) workload on participants is lower and more flexible; 3) the rating procedure is efficient, labor-saving, and more importantly, without jeopardizing the accuracy of the results. As we shall see later, under such models the $O(n^2)$ complete paired comparisons can be reduced to $O(n^{3/2})$, with a lower bound of $O(n \log n)$.
2. A new random design principle is investigated to conduct paired comparison based on Erdös-Rényi random graph theory;
3. Hodge decomposition on graphs is introduced to derive, from incomplete (where every participant may only give partial comparisons) and imbalanced (where different video pairs may receive different number of comparisons) data, quality scores of videos and the inconsistency of participants' judgments.

The remainder of this paper is organized as follows. Section 2 contains a review of related works. Then Section 3 establishes the statistical ranking models based on the Hodge decomposition theory, as well as the principles for random sampling grounded in random graph theory. The detailed experiments are demonstrated in Section 4. Section 5 presents the conclusive remarks along with discussion for future work.

2. RELATED WORK

2.1 Paired Comparison

Paired comparison generally refers to any process of comparing entities in pairs by raters to judge which entity in each pair is preferred. The method of paired comparison has been widely studied in social choice, psychology, statistics, and computer science [32, 21, 9, 28, 5]. It has also drawn increasing attention from the machine learning community as it may be adapted to classification problems [14, 13, 16].

Among various approaches to analyzing paired comparison results, a recent framework based on combinatorial Hodge Theory [18] will be adopted in this paper, which is particularly suitable for the analysis of incomplete and imbalanced data distributed on a graph. Our work exploits such a HodgeRank approach with random graph models in the setting of subjective video quality assessment.

2.2 Crowdsourcing

With the advent of ubiquitous Internet access, it becomes more and more popular to ask an Internet crowd to conduct experiments on their personal computers [17, 6]. This new distributed model advocates mass collaboration and the wisdom of the commons. The main difference between crowdsourcing and ordinary outsourcing is that a task is carried out by an unspecific Internet crowd rather than a specific group of people. For example, researchers can seek help from the Internet crowd to conduct user studies on image annotation [30, 26], document relevance [4], and document evaluation [22].

Most recently, a crowdsourceable framework [8] has been proposed for VQA which adopts a paired comparison approach. However, one major shortcoming of [8] lies in that it makes a strong assumption that all paired data collected are complete which is impossible for large number of videos. In this paper, we present a new principle to deal with possibly incomplete and imbalanced data distributed on random graphs, which reduces the sampling complexity and is easy to implement in crowsourcing VQA on internet.

2.3 Inconsistency Checking

After collecting the paired data from the participants, there is a need to assess the consistency of judgment as not every participant is trustworthy. They may input random decisions carelessly or intentionally. Like traditional social choice theory with complete and balanced data, the method in [8] proposes Transitivity Satisfaction Rate (TSR) to measure the consistency of a participant's judgments, which checks all the transitive triangles such that A> B >C >A. The TSR is defined as the number of judgment triplets (e.g., the three preference relations among A, B, and C) satisfying transitivity divided by the total number of triplets where transitivity may apply; thus, the value of the TSR is always between 0 and 1. If a participant's judgments are consistent throughout all the rounds of an experiment, the TSR will be 1; otherwise it will be less than 1.

However, TSR is only based on complete and balanced paired comparison data. When the paired data is incomplete with missing edges, HodgeRank will give us a general treatment of inconsistency where both triangular and global cycles are considered.

3. HODGERANK ON RANDOM GRAPHS

In this section, we propose a new random design principle to conduct paired comparison and analyze data for a reliable global ranking and inconsistency. Our sampling mechanism exploits the Erdös-Rényi random graphs, a simple but efficient approach in our study. Other random graphs can be applied into the framework, which are left for future studies. HodgeRank is a particularly suitable tool to analyze paired comparison data in such graphs by adapting to their topological structures. We first explain how to develop a statistical ranking model based on Hodge theory on general graphs, and then describe the principles that the random selection must adhere to.

3.1 HodgeRank on Graphs

Let $\wedge = \{1, ..., m\}$ be a set of participants and $V = \{1, ..., n\}$ be the set of videos to be ranked. Paired comparison data is collected as a function on $\wedge \times V \times V$, which is *skew-symmetric* for each α, i.e. $Y^{\alpha}_{ij} = -Y^{\alpha}_{ji}$ representing the degree that α prefers i to j. The simplest setting is the binary choice, where[1]

$$Y^{\alpha}_{ij} = \begin{cases} 1 & if\ \alpha\ prefers\ i\ to\ j, \\ -1 & otherwise. \end{cases} \quad (1)$$

General Y^{α}_{ij} can be used to represent paired comparison grades, *e.g.* $Y^{\alpha}_{ij} > 0$ refers to the degree that α prefers i to j and the vice versa $Y^{\alpha}_{ji} = -Y^{\alpha}_{ij} < 0$ measures the dispreference degree [18]. In this paper we shall focus on binary choice, to avoid the scale ambiguity issue discussed early. However the theory can be applied to the general case.

Such paired comparison data can be represented by a directed graph, or hypergraph, with n nodes, where each directed edge between i and j refers the preference indicated by Y^{α}_{ij}. Figure 1 shows an illustration of such hypergraph.

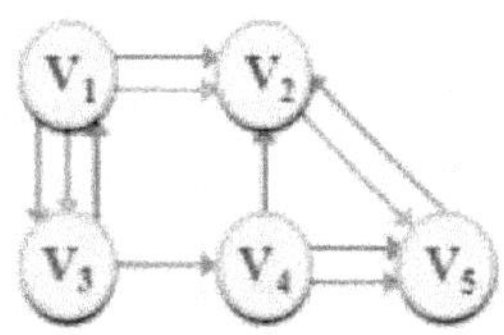

Figure 1: An example of paired comparison hypergraph for 5 videos.

A nonnegative weight function $\omega : \wedge \times V \times V \longrightarrow [0, \infty)$ is defined as,

$$\omega^{\alpha}_{ij} = \begin{cases} 1 & if\ \alpha\ makes\ a\ comparison\ for\ \{i,j\}, \\ 0 & otherwise. \end{cases} \quad (2)$$

It may reflect the confidence level that a participant compares $\{i, j\}$ by taking different values, which is however not pursued in this paper.

Following [18], the statistical rank aggregation problem is looking for some global ranking score $s : V \to R$ such that

$$\min_{s \in \mathbb{R}^{|V|}} \sum_{i,j,\alpha} \omega^{\alpha}_{ij}(s_i - s_j - Y^{\alpha}_{ij})^2, \quad (3)$$

which is equivalent to the following weighted least square problem

$$\min_{s \in \mathbb{R}^{|V|}} \sum_{i,j} \omega_{ij}(s_i - s_j - \hat{Y}_{ij})^2, \quad (4)$$

where $\hat{Y}_{ij} = (\sum_{\alpha} \omega^{\alpha}_{ij} Y^{\alpha}_{ij})/(\sum_{\alpha} \omega^{\alpha}_{ij})$ and $\omega_{ij} = \sum_{\alpha} \omega^{\alpha}_{ij}$.

A graph structure arises naturally from ranking data as follows. Let $G = (V, E)$ be a paired ranking graph whose vertex set is V, the set of videos to be ranked, and whose edge set is E, the set of video pairs which receive some comparisons, i.e.

$$E = \left\{ \{i,j\} \epsilon \binom{V}{2} \mid \sum_{\alpha} \omega^{\alpha}_{i,j} > 0 \right\}. \quad (5)$$

In classical statistical paired ranking theory, a paired ranking is called *complete* if each participant α in $\wedge$ gives a total judgment of all videos in V; otherwise it is called *incomplete*. It is *balanced* if the paired comparison graph is k-regular with equal weights $\omega_{ij} = \sum_{\alpha} \omega^{\alpha}_{ij} \equiv c$ for all $\{i, j\} \in E$; otherwise it is called *imbalanced*. A complete and balanced ranking induces a complete graph with equal weights on all

[1]If ties occur, we randomly split them into either preference.

edges. The existing paired comparison methods in VQA often assume complete and balanced data [8]. However, this is an unrealistic assumption for real world data. For example, in crowdsourcing, different video pairs might receive different number of comparisons, which leads to different edge weights ω_{ij}. Nevertheless, as to be shown below, it is efficient to utilize a simple random design based on Erdös-Rényi random graph theory where for each participant some video pairs are chosen randomly. The HodgeRank approach adopted in this paper enables us a unified scheme which can deal with incomplete and imbalanced data.

The minimization problem (4) can be generalized to a family of *linear models* in paired comparison methods [9]. To see this, we first rewrite (4) in another simpler form. Assume that for each edge as video pair $\{i,j\}$, the number of comparisons is n_{ij}, among which a_{ij} participants have a preference on i over j and a_{ji} vice versa. So $a_{ij}+a_{ji}=n_{ij}$ if no tie occurs. Therefore, for each edge $\{i,j\}\in E$, we have a preference probability estimated from data $\hat{\pi}_{ij}=a_{ij}/n_{ij}$. With this definition, the problem (4) can be rewritten as

$$\min_{s\in \mathbb{R}^{|V|}} \sum_{\{i,j\}\in E} n_{ij}(s_i - s_j - (2\hat{\pi}_{ij}-1))^2, \tag{6}$$

since $\hat{Y}_{ij}=(a_{ij}-a_{ji})/n_{ij}=2\hat{\pi}_{ij}-1$ due to equation (2).

General *linear models*, which are firstly formulated by G. Noether [25], assume that the true preference probability can be fully decided by a linear scaling function on V, i.e.

$$\pi_{ij} = \text{Prob}\{i \text{ is preferred over } j\} = F(s_i^* - s_j^*), \tag{7}$$

for some $s^* \in \mathbb{R}^{|V|}$. F can be chosen as any symmetric cumulated distributed function. When only an empirical preference probability $\hat{\pi}_{ij}$ is observed, we can map it to a skew-symmetric function by inverse of F,

$$\hat{Y}_{ij} = F^{-1}(\hat{\pi}_{ij}), \tag{8}$$

where $\hat{Y}_{ij}=-\hat{Y}_{ji}$. However, in this case, one can only expect that

$$\hat{Y}_{ij} = s_i^* - s_j^* + \varepsilon_{ij}, \tag{9}$$

where ε_{ij} accounts for the noise. The case in (6) takes a linear F and is often called a *uniform model*. Below we summarize some well known models which have been studied extensively in literature [9].

1. *Uniform* model:

$$\hat{Y}_{ij} = 2\hat{\pi}_{ij} - 1. \tag{10}$$

2. *Bradley-Terry* model:

$$\hat{Y}_{ij} = \log\frac{\hat{\pi}_{ij}}{1-\hat{\pi}_{ij}}. \tag{11}$$

3. *Thurstone-Mosteller* model:

$$\hat{Y}_{ij} = F^{-1}(\hat{\pi}_{ij}). \tag{12}$$

where F is essentially the Gauss error function

$$F(x) = \frac{1}{\sqrt{2\pi}}\int_{-x/[2\sigma^2(1-\rho)]^{1/2}}^{\infty} e^{-\frac{1}{2}t^2}dt. \tag{13}$$

Note that unknown constants σ and ρ will only contribute to a rescaling of the solution of (4).

4. *Angular transform* model:

$$\hat{Y}_{ij} = \arcsin(2\hat{\pi}_{ij} - 1). \tag{14}$$

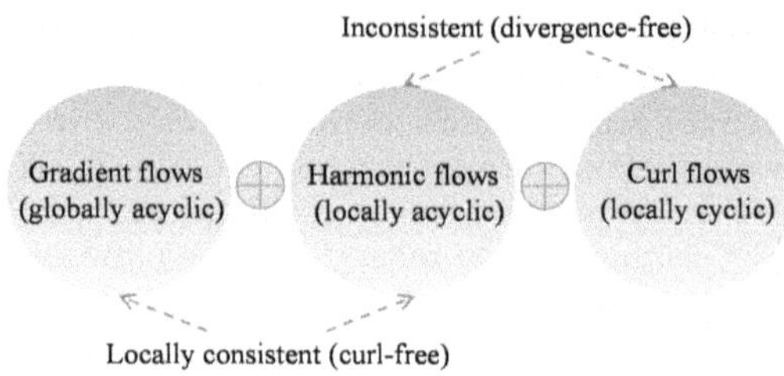

Figure 2: Hodge decomposition of paired rankings.

Different models will give different $\hat{Y}_{ij}$ from the same observation $\hat{\pi}_{ij}$, followed by the same weighted least square problem (4) for the solution. Therefore, a deeper analysis of problem (4) will disclose more properties about the ranking problem.

HodgeRank on graph $G=(V,E)$ provides us such a tool, which characterizes the solution and residue of (4), adaptive to topological structures of G. The following theorem adapted from [18] describes a decomposition of $\hat{Y}$, which can be visualized as edge flows on graph G with direction $i\to j$ if $\hat{Y}_{ij}>0$ and vice versa. Before the statement of the theorem, we first define the triangle set of G as all the 3-cliques in G.

$$T = \left\{\{i,j,k\}\epsilon\binom{V}{3} \,|\{i,j\},\{j,k\},\{k,i\}\epsilon E\right\}. \tag{15}$$

Equipped with T, graph G becomes an abstract simplicial complex, the clique complex $\chi(G)=(V,E,T)$.

Theorem 1 [Hodge Decomposition of Paired Ranking] Let $\hat{Y}_{ij}$ be a paired comparison flow on graph $G=(V,E)$, i.e. $\hat{Y}_{ij}=-\hat{Y}_{ji}$ for $\{i,j\}\in E$ and 0 otherwise. There is a unique decomposition of $\hat{Y}$ satisfying

$$\hat{Y} = \hat{Y}^{(1)} + \hat{Y}^{(2)} + \hat{Y}^{(3)}, \tag{16}$$

where

$$\hat{Y}_{ij}^{(1)} = \hat{s}_i - \hat{s}_j, \quad \text{for some } \hat{s}\in\mathbb{R}^V, \tag{17}$$

$$\hat{Y}_{ij}^{(2)} + \hat{Y}_{jk}^{(2)} + \hat{Y}_{ki}^{(2)} = 0, \text{ for each } \{i,j,k\}\in T, \tag{18}$$

$$\sum_{j\sim i}\omega_{ij}\hat{Y}_{ij}^{(2)} = 0, \text{ for each } i\in V. \tag{19}$$

The decomposition above is *orthogonal* under the following inner product on $\mathbb{R}^{|E|}$, $\langle u,v\rangle_\omega = \sum_{\{i,j\}\in E}\omega_{ij}u_{ij}v_{ij}$.

The following provides some remarks on the decomposition.

1. $\hat{Y}_{ij}^{(1)}$ is a rank two skew-symmetric matrix and gives a linear score function $\hat{s}\in\mathbb{R}^V$ up to a translation constant. We thus call $\hat{Y}^{(1)}$ a *gradient flow* since it is given by the difference (discrete gradient) of the score function $\hat{s}$ on graph nodes,

$$\hat{Y}_{ij}^{(1)} = (\delta_0\hat{s})(i,j) := \hat{s}_i - \hat{s}_j, \tag{20}$$

where $\delta_0:\mathbb{R}^V\to\mathbb{R}^E$ is a finite difference operator (matrix) on G. $\hat{s}$ can be chosen as any least square solution of (4), where we often choose the minimal norm solution,

$$\hat{s} = \Delta_0^\dagger\delta_0^*\hat{Y}, \tag{21}$$

where $\delta_0^* = \delta_0^T W$ ($W = \text{diag}(\omega_{ij})$), $\Delta_0 = \delta_0^* \cdot \delta_0$ is the unnormalized graph Laplacian defined by $(\Delta_0)_{ii} = \sum_{j\sim i} \omega_{ij}$ and $(\Delta_0)_{ij} = -\omega_{ij}$, and $(\cdot)^\dagger$ is the Moore-Penrose (pseudo) inverse. On a complete and balanced graph, (21) is reduced to the $\hat{s}_i = \frac{1}{n-1}\sum_{j\neq i} \hat{Y}_{ij}$, often called *Borda Count* as the earliest preference aggregation rule in social choice [18].

2. $\hat{Y}^{(2)}$ satisfies two conditions (18) and (19), which are called *curl-free* and *divergence-free* conditions respectively. The former requires the triangular trace of $\hat{Y}$ to be zero, on every 3-clique in graph G; while the later requires the total sum (inflow minus outflow) to be zero on each node of G. These two conditions characterize a linear subspace which is called *harmonic flows.*

3. The residue $\hat{Y}^{(3)}$ actually satisfies (19) but not (18). In fact, it measures the amount of intrinsic (local) inconsistancy in $\hat{Y}$ characterized by the triangular trace. We often call this component *curl flow.* In particular, the following relative curl,

$$\text{curl}^r_{ijk} = \frac{|\hat{Y}_{ij} + \hat{Y}_{jk} + \hat{Y}_{ki}|}{|\hat{Y}_{ij}| + |\hat{Y}_{jk}| + |\hat{Y}_{ki}|} \in [0, 1], \tag{22}$$

can be used to characterize triangular intransitivity; $\text{curl}^r_{ijk} = 1$ iff $\{i, j, k\}$ contains an intransitive triangle of $\hat{Y}$. Note that computing the percentage of $\text{curl}^r_{ijk} = 1$ is equivalent to calculating the Transitivity Satisfaction Rate (TSR).

Figure 2 illustrates the Hodge decomposition for paired comparison flows. The readers may refer to [18] for the detail of theoretical development. Below we just make a few comments on the application of HodgeRank in our setting.

1. To find a global rankng $\hat{s}$ in (21), recent developments of Spielman-Teng [31] and Koutis-Miller-Peng [23] give fast (almost linear in $|E|\text{Poly}(\log|V|)$) algorithms for this purpose.

2. Inconsistency of $\hat{Y}$ has two parts: global inconsistency measured by harmonic flow $\hat{Y}^{(2)}$ and local inconsistency measured by curls in $\hat{Y}^{(3)}$. Due to the orthogonal decomposition, $\|\hat{Y}^{(2)}\|^2_\omega/\|\hat{Y}\|^2_\omega$ and $\|\hat{Y}^{(3)}\|^2_\omega/\|\hat{Y}\|^2_\omega$ provide percentages of global and local inconsistencies, respectively.

3. A nontrivial harmonic component $\hat{Y}^{(2)} \neq 0$ implies the fixed tournament issue, i.e. for any candidate $i \in V$, there is a paired comparison design by removing some of the edges in $G = (V, E)$ such that i is the overall winner.

4. One can control the harmonic component by controlling the topology of clique complex $\chi(G)$. In a loop-free clique complex $\chi(G)$ where $\beta_1 = 0$, harmonic component vanishes. In this case, there are no cycles which traverse all the nodes, e.g. 1>2>3>4> ...>n>1. All the inconsistency will be summarized in those triangular cycles, e.g. i>j>k>i.

Theorem 2. The linear space of harmonic flows has dimension equal to β_1, i.e. the number of independent loops in clique complex $\chi(G)$, which is called the first order Betti number.

Fortunately, for Erdös-Rényi random graphs, it is not hard to obtain graphs whose β_1 are zero.

3.2 Erdös-Rényi Random Graphs

Erdös-Rényi random graphs $G(n, p)$ start from n vertices and draw their edges independently according to a fixed probability p. Such random graph model is chosen to meet the scenario that in crowdsourcing ranking raters and videos come in an unspecified way. Among various models, Erdös-Rényi random graph is the simplest one equivalent to I.I.D. sampling. Therefore, such a model is systematically studied in the paper. Other random graph models (e.g. k-regular, preference attachment) can also be developed with HodgeRank on general graphs, which is however left to our future pursuit.

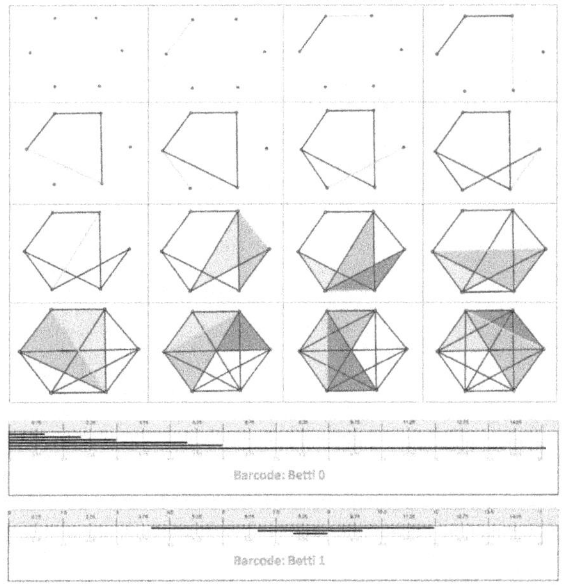

Figure 3: Persistence barcodes of Betti numbers.

However, to exploit Erdös-Rényi random graphs in crowdsourcing experimental designs, one has to meet some conditions depending on our purpose:

1) *The resulting graph should be connected, if we hope to derive global scores for all videos in comparison*;

2) *The resulting graph should be loop-free in its clique complex, if we hope to get rid of the global inconsistency in harmonic component.*

The two conditions can be easily satisfied for large Erdös-Rényi random graphs.

Theorem 3. Let $G(n, p)$ be the set of Erdös-Rényi random graphs with n nodes and edge appearance probability p. Then the following holds as $n \to \infty$,

1. [Erdös-Rényi 1959] [12] if $p \succ \log n/n$, then $G(n, p)$ is almost always connected; and if $p \prec \log n/n$ then $G(n, p)$ is almost always disconnected;

2. [Kahle 2009] [19] if $p = O(n^\alpha)$, with $\alpha < -1$ or $\alpha > -1/2$, then the expected β_1 of the clique complex $\chi(G(n, p))$ is almost always equal to zero, i.e. loop-free.

These theories imply that when p is large enough, Erdös-Rényi random graphs will meet the two conditions above with high probability. In particular, almost linear $O(n \log n)$ edges suffice to derive a global ranking, and with $O(n^{3/2})$ edges harmonic-free condition is met.

However, it remains a question how to ensure that a given graph instance satisfies the two conditions? This issue is important since in the future we might even develop further experimental designs beyond merely Erdös-Rényi random graphs, e.g., considering confidence levels on edges. Fortunately, recent development in computational topology provides us such a tool, persistent homology.

3.3 Persistence Homology Barcodes

Persistence homology is firstly introduced by [11] in computational topology, and later developed by [35] into an algebraic theory. Roughly speaking, it provides us an online algorithm to compute the Betti numbers when simplexes enter in a sequential way. For more details of persistent homology, readers may refer to the surveys in [7, 10]. Here we just discuss in brief the application of persistent homology to monitor the number of connected components (β_0) and loops (β_1) .

To use persistent homology, we will put the nodes, edges and triangles in $\chi(G) = (V, E, T)$ in a linear order, such that a node appears no later than its associated edge and an edge no later than its associated triangle. For example, in random graph designs for video comparisons, we can assume the videos (nodes) come in a certain order (e.g. production time, or all created in the same time), after that pairs of videos (edges) are presented to us independently one by one. A triangle $\{i, j, k\}$ is created whenever all the three associated edges appeared. Persistent homology may return the evolution of the number of connected components (β_0) and the number of independent loops (β_1) at each time when a new node/edge/triangle is born. Figure 3 illustrates a birth process of clique complex and its associated Betti numbers (β_0 and β_1) that are computed and plotted by JPlex [29].

With the aid of persistent homology, one can compute the mean Betti numbers for random graphs. For example, with 16 videos ($n = 16$), the expected β_0 and β_1 (with 100 random graphs) are plotted in Figure 4(a). Note that with $p > 0.7$ with high probability the expected β_1 for $G(16, p)$ equals to 0. This phase transition probability will drop as the number of nodes increases, and this can be seen from the cases of $n = 32$ ($p > 0.5$) and $n = 64$ ($p > 0.4$), as plotted in Figure 4(b) and (c). As [19] shows, this probability asymptotically drops at the rate $p \sim n^{-1/2}$.

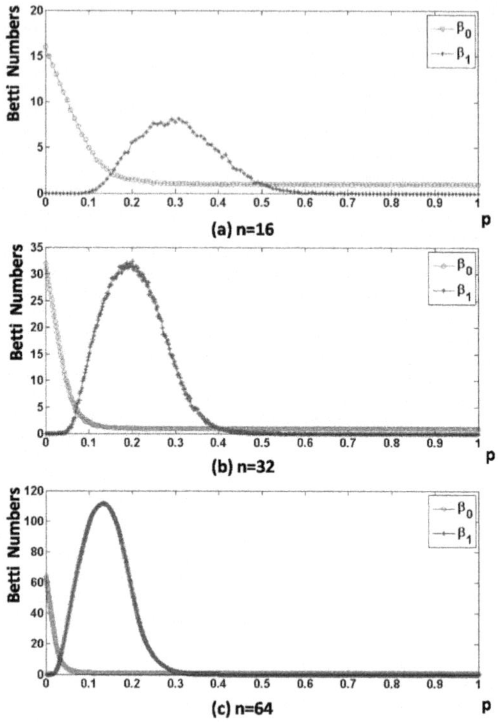

Figure 4: Average Betti numbers of random graphs.

4. EXPERIMENTS

In this section, we systematically evaluate the effectiveness of our proposed HRRG method for subjective VQA. First, the dataset used for the experiments is briefly explained, followed by the experimental design of obtaining paired comparison data. Next, a procedure is presented to obtain the ground-truth as a set of complete data. Finally, the results with incomplete data are demonstrated with three random sampling schemes.

4.1 Dataset

We adopt the publicly-accessible database for VQA, LIVE Database [3], which includes 10 different reference videos and 15 distorted versions of each reference, for a total of 160 videos. The distorted videos are obtained using four different distortion processes—MPEG-2 compression (4 distorted videos per reference), H.264 compression (4 distorted videos per reference), lossy transmission of H.264 compressed bitstreams through simulated IP networks (3 distorted videos per reference) and lossy transmission of H.264 compressed bitstreams through simulated wireless networks (4 distorted videos per reference). Nine out of ten videos are 10 seconds long, while the 10th video is 8.68 seconds long. Seven sequences have a frame rate of 25 frames per second, while the remaining three have a frame rate of 50 frames per second. The videos are diverse in content and include a wide range of objects, textures, motions and camera movements. In subjective testing, the observers are asked to provide their opinion of video quality on a continuous scale. In other words, the MOS is adopted to analyze the perceived quality of each video. Note that we do not use the subjective scores in LIVE [3], we only borrow the video sources it provides. Different from LIVE [3], we propose to assess video quality with paired comparison.

4.2 Paired Data Collection

We now present our experiment design for collecting the set of paired data. The complete comparisons of this video database will require $10 \times \binom{16}{2} = 1200$ decisions. Considering that the order of presentation may bias final results, we need to balance them out at the design stage. A complete balancing-out would be achieved by repeating the whole experiment with the order that each pair reversed. However, this is too expensive and time-consuming. Therefore, our playlists will be based on a random permutation of 1200 test pairs with a random within-pair order. Moreover, we hope to avoid the situation with successive pairs of test videos from the same reference, to avoid contextual and memory effects in their judgments of quality. For this purpose, after the playlist is constructed, our program would go over the entire playlist to determine if adjacent pairs correspond to the same reference. If such a case is detected, one of the pairs would be swapped with another randomly chosen pair in the playlist which does not suffer from the same problem.

A benefit of such a random presentation scheme is to make it impossible for participants to cheat our system by inputting "smart" answers. This is because the order of each pair and the order within each pair are totally random in

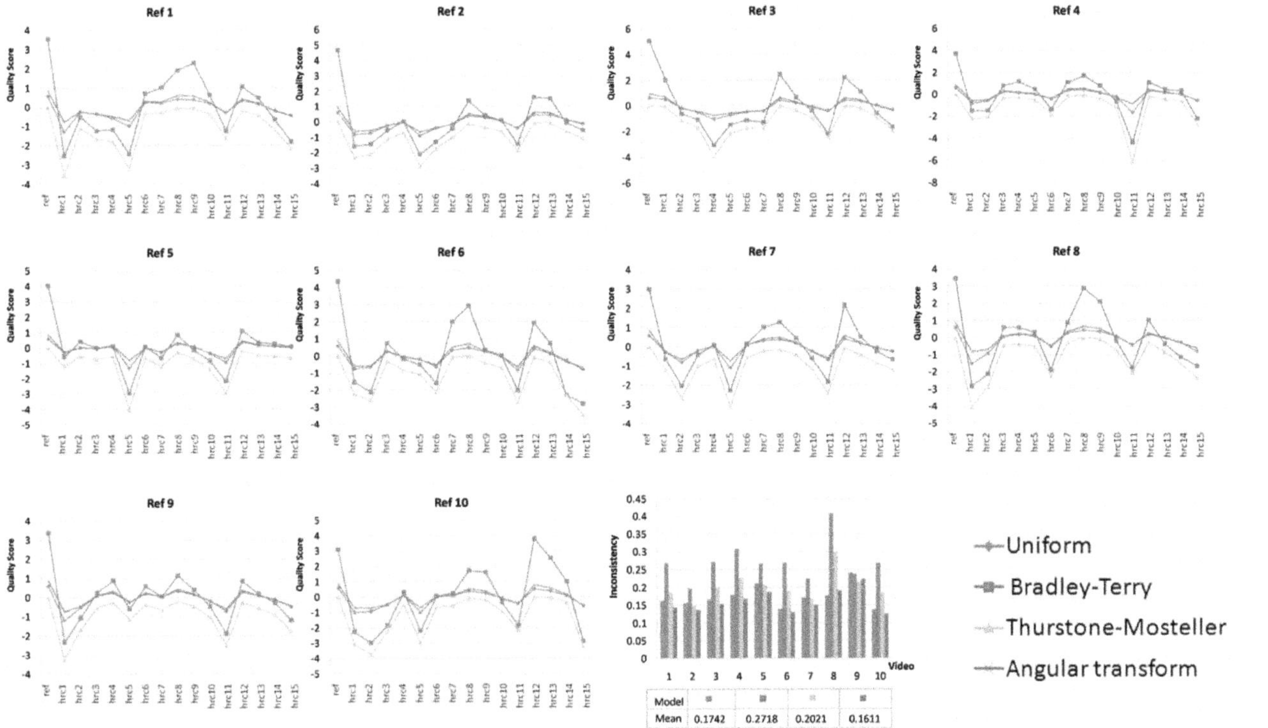

Figure 5: Global ranking scores and inconsistency distribution of 32 complete rounds on Live Database [3]. The *Angular transform* model has the smallest mean inconsistency at 0.1611 shown by the purple line.

each experiment, and the order is not disclosed to the participants before the test.

Before starting the experiment, each participant is briefed about the goal of the experiment and given a short training session to familiarize themselves with the testing procedure. In the testing process, videos are displayed at their native resolutions to prevent any distortions due to scaling operations performed by software or hardware. As each comparison takes approximately 30-40 seconds, the total time for each subjective experiment will vary from 10 up to 14 hours. According to [2], the execution time of one experiment by each observer should not exceed 30 minutes. Thus, we split the playlist into 30 sessions where each session consists of 40 video pairs and thus will not exceed a half hour. Finally 209 random observers, each of whom perform varied number of comparisons, provide 41800 paired comparisons in total. These paired comparisons can compose 32 rounds of complete comparisons. Because each round needs 1200 paired comparisons, the total number of comparisons for 32 rounds is $38400 = 32 \times 1200$.

The results of paired comparisons can be collectively summarized by $Y_{ij}^{\alpha,r}$, where for each reference video $r = 1, \dots, 10$, $Y_{ij}^{\alpha,r}$ follows the same definition in Section 3.1 with $\alpha = 1, \dots, 32$ for round (group) index. Note that the experiments below will run in the same way for each reference video, whence the index r will be omitted when we don't need to specify it. For each reference video, such paired comparison data can be represented by a directed graph (or hypergraph) with 16 nodes, and between every pair of nodes there are 32 directed edges indicating the preferences.

4.3 Experimental Results

4.3.1 Ground-truth

The purpose of this paper is to show that with some random samplings, incomplete data could provide good approximation of the results from the complete data. In other words, HodgeRank with incomplete data could well approximate the global ranking derived from complete data. Therefore, results obtained from 32 rounds of complete comparisons are treated as the ground-truth in our experiment. HodgeRank with such a complete and balanced data will be reduced to the Borda Count following (21). The *total inconsistency* is measured by

$$\text{Inc.Total}(\hat{Y}) = \frac{\|\hat{Y} - \hat{Y}^{(1)}\|_\omega^2}{\|\hat{Y}\|_\omega^2} = \frac{\sum_{ij} \omega_{ij}(\hat{s}_i - \hat{s}_j - \hat{Y}_{ij})^2}{\sum_{ij} \omega_{ij} \hat{Y}_{ij}^2}, \tag{23}$$

which equals to the sum of $\|\hat{Y}^{(2)}\|_\omega^2 / \|\hat{Y}\|_\omega^2$ (*global/harmonic inconsistency*) and $\|\hat{Y}^{(3)}\|_\omega^2 / \|\hat{Y}\|_\omega^2\|$ (*local/curl inconsistency*). We also define the *harmonic percentage* as the ratio

$$\text{Percentage.Harm}(\hat{Y}) = \frac{\|\hat{Y}^{(2)}\|_\omega^2}{\text{Inc.Total}(\hat{Y})}. \tag{24}$$

With complete and balanced data, global/harmonic inconsistency vanishes according to Section 3.1.

Global ranking scores $\hat{s}$ for each reference and inconsistency distribution are given in Figure 5, where "ref" represents 10 different reference videos in Live Database [3] and "hrc1-15" are 15 distorted versions of each reference. It can be seen that Hodge decomposition with *Angular transform* model has the smallest mean inconsistency. Therefore, we will adopt this model in the following experiments for incomplete data.

4.3.2 Results of Incomplete Data

In the following experiments, we adopt the Kendall rank correlation (τ) coefficient [20] to measure the rank correlation between global rankings from complete and incomplete data. Given two global scores x_i and y_i on V, define $X_{ij} = \text{sign}(x_i - x_j)$ and $Y_{ij} = \text{sign}(y_i - y_j)$. Then Kendall's τ coefficient is defined as

$$\tau(x, y) = \frac{\sum_{\{i,j\}\in E} X_{ij} Y_{ij}}{\sqrt{\sum X_{ij}^2 \cdot \sum {Y_{ij}}^2}}, \tag{25}$$

which measures the percentage of concordance ($X_{ij}Y_{ij} > 0$) minus the percentage of mismatch ($X_{ij}Y_{ij} < 0$) between two rankings. The coefficient is normalized such that two identical rankings produce a correlation of $+1$, while a ranking and its perfect inverse gives a -1, and the expected correlation of two random rankings is 0.

As illustrated in Section 3.3 Figure 4, for $n = 16$, if more than 25% random edges are added, the resulting graph is connected with high probability, and with more than 70% edges, the resulting clique complex is loop-free with high probability. Connectivity is necessary if we would like to derive a global score on all videos. The existence of harmonic ranking may jeopardize the global score by incurring the fixed tournament issue. To illustrate this point, Figure 6 shows the Kendall's τ, total inconsistency, harmonic inconsistency, and percentage of harmonic over total inconsistency, against the edge sampling percentage ranging from 20% to 80%. In this example, harmonic inconsistency accounts for more than 50% total inconsistency before 25% edges, and rapidly drops to zero after 70% edges (where Kendall's τ coefficient goes beyond 0.9 and total inconsistency stabilizes below 0.2).

Therefore in the following experiments, to avoid the possible issue of harmonic ranking, we choose an upper bound for the thresholding probability above, *i.e.* 75% ($120 \times 0.75 = 90$) for $n = 16$ node graphs. In this case, with high probability the total inconsistency will be fully characterized by the local inconsistency. For general large Erdös-Rényi graphs, we can choose any upper bound for $p = O(n^{-1/2})$ with $O(n^{3/2})$ edges. Note that such a choice is only a sufficient condition to avoid harmonic ranking. In the cases where harmonic inconsistency is small enough, one can choose much smaller thresholding probability, up to $p = O(n^{-1} \log n)$ with almost linear $O(n \log n)$ edges which is the lower bound to guarantee connectivity.

In the following, we study three random sampling schemes, guided by this principle from Erdös-Rényi random graphs. These sampling schemes exhibit an increasing order of freedom, which is thus increasingly adaptive to crowdsourcing applications.

The following sampling schemes are the same for each r of the reference video. The first sampling scheme, called here *group balanced random sampling*, draws 75% random pairs from each round $\alpha \in \{1, \ldots, 32\}$ of complete comparisons. Note that each group thus has the same number of pairs. The second scheme, called here *group imbalanced random sampling*, draws 75% random paired comparisons from the whole collection over $\alpha = 1, \ldots, 32$, with some groups covering possibly more than 75% of edges while others less. The third one, called here *sufficient-coverage random sampling*, simply draws arbitrary number of paired comparisons from the whole collection, with the only requirement that at least 75% distinct pairs are covered. We will examine the average performance of each sampling. Other complicated sampling schemes are possible. However, we focus on the three schemes here due to their simplicity and thus can be regarded as a foundation for further developments.

All the three sampling schemes above could guarantee that 75% distinct pairs of 16 videos are compared, whence with high probability the harmonic ranking induced from such data vanishes.

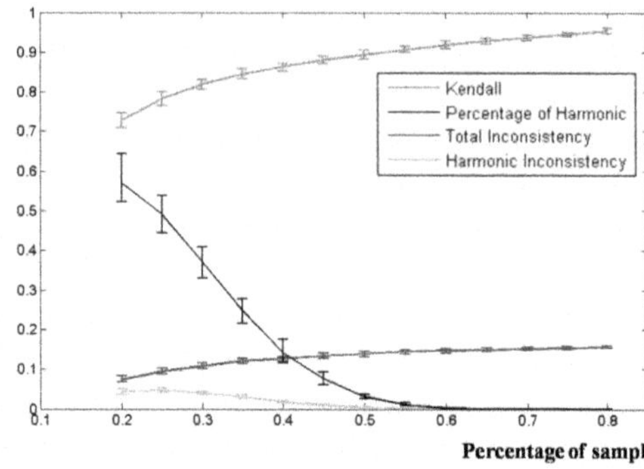

Figure 6: Inconsistency decomposition and Kendall's τ to ground truth, versus percentage of edge samples. Results are averaged over 10 reference videos with 100 bootstrapped samples.

Table 1: Kendall's τ and inconsistency of Exp-I.

	min	mean	max	std
Kendall's τ	0.9567	0.9716	0.9917	0.0058
Inconsistency	0.1643	0.1740	0.1817	0.0032

Exp-I: group balanced random sampling

The first sampling scheme is studied here. For each of the 10 reference videos, and for each of the 32 groups of complete paired comparisons, 75% (i.e. 90) video pairs are drawn independently without replacement from 120 edges. The name, *group balanced random sampling*, refers to the fact that each group contains the same number of pairs. Then, HodgeRank (4) is applied to obtain quality scores of each video from this incomplete dataset. To ensure the statistical stability, we run the random sampling process 100 times.

Table 1 shows the mean Kendall's τ and inconsistency results of 100 times achieved by this scheme. From these experimental results, we make the following comments.

First, it is shown that this sampling approach could provide good approximate results of the complete data, with an average Kendall's τ of 0.9716.

Second, we observe that the mean inconsistency of this

Table 2: Kendall's τ and inconsistency of Exp-II.

	min	mean	max	std
Kendall's τ	0.9550	0.9699	0.9867	0.0066
Inconsistency	0.1661	0.1734	0.1812	0.0031

sampling scheme (0.1740) is only slightly higher than the complete data (0.1611), which is within our acceptable level.

In a summary, these results show that the random sampling mechanism based on random graph theory is good in providing approximations of complete data via HodgeRank.

Exp-II: group imbalanced random sampling

Different from Exp-I, for each of the 10 reference videos, in this experiment we randomly select 75% of all paired comparisons, i.e. $32 \times 120 \times 0.75 = 2880$ comparisons. The number of pairs selected from each of the 32 rounds in this case might be different, where the name, *group imbalanced random sampling*, comes from. However, the total number of the selected samples for each reference video is the same to Exp-I.

Table 2 shows the mean Kendall's τ-coefficients and inconsistencies which indicates that this method could produce comparable results of Exp-I. The Kendall's τ between the ground-truth and the 100 random experiments has an average of 0.9699 ± 0.0066 (in contrast to 0.9716 ± 0.0058 in Exp-I), while the average inconsistency is 0.1734 ± 0.0031 (in contrast to 0.1740 ± 0.0032 in Exp-I).

Exp-III: sufficient-coverage random sampling

Our last experiment is to examine the performance under *sufficient-coverage random sampling* settings. That is, we randomly sample arbitrary number of pairs from each of 32 rounds, with the only requirement that at least 75% (90) edges of the graph are covered, i.e. at least a paired comparison occurs on 75% (90) distinct video pairs. Due to the multiple comparisons between a pair of videos, a natural question is raised that how many percentage of samples are needed to reach this 75% coverage. Similar to Erdös-Rényi random graph theory on simple graphs, Figure 7 draws percentage of samples versus median number of edges (or distinct pairs) covered. As we can see, after 4% of samples on this hypergraph, with high probability 75% distinct pairs will be covered.

Moreover, Table 3 shows the mean Kendall's τ-coefficient and inconsistency of 100 random experiments. The high average performance (0.9337 ± 0.0415 for Kendall's τ and 0.2256 ± 0.0606 for inconsistency) shows the promising application of this simple sampling scheme.

More complicated sampling schemes can be developed based on various combinations of the prototype methods above. Considering a more practical situation, the available time that can be used for testing of each participant may be distinctly different. From this point of view, the number of pairs (k) shown to participants can be adjusted according to their time limit. That is, when a participant's time is comparatively adequate, k can be set up as a larger value and thus could provide opportunity for him/her to view more pairs. But if he/she is under the pressure of limited time, k should be smaller. In the extreme case for online crowdsourcing experiments, a complete random sampling scheme can be used to select both participants and video pairs randomly. As shown above, HodgeRank and random graph theory can guide us to find the global ranking efficiently.

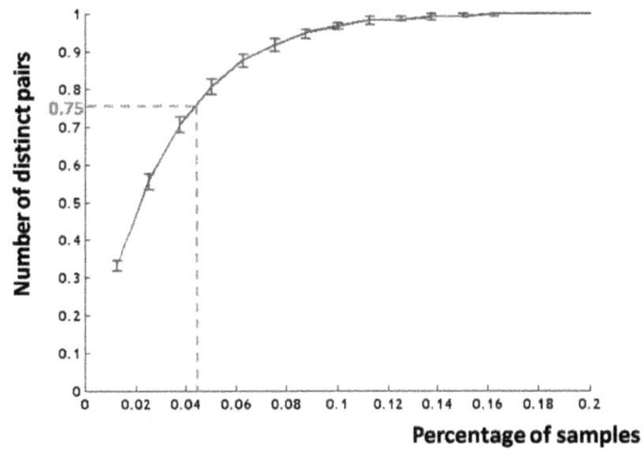

Figure 7: Percentage of samples versus number of distinct pairs. For each percentage level, the experiments are repeated 100 times and the median number of distinct pairs with [0.25, 0.75] confidence interval are plotted in the figure.

Table 3: Kendall's τ and inconsistency of of Exp-III.

	min	mean	max	std
Kendall's τ	0.8067	0.9337	0.9857	0.0415
Inconsistency	0.1623	0.2256	0.3777	0.0606

5. CONCLUSIONS

In this paper, we have proposed an efficient approach called ***HodgeRank on Random Graphs*** towards subjective VQA. Our approach is based on random graph theory and HodgeRank on graphs. In particular, we study three random sampling schemes inspired by Erdös-Rényi random graph theory, followed by HodgeRank to analyze the incomplete and imbalanced data collected in these ways. In these sampling schemes, participants only need to perform a random fraction of all possible paired comparisons. But with a sufficiency of coverage satisfied, HodgeRank may give reliable results without jeopardizing the accuracy of the result. In contrast to the traditional deterministic incomplete block designs, our random design is not only suitable for traditional laboratory and focus-group studies, but also fit for crowdsourcing experiments on Internet.

Additionally, we would like to point out here that inconsistencies are not necessarily due to untrustworthy inputs of the participants but may very well be an inherent characteristic of the data. In future, we plan to focus on this problem to investigate into more sophisticated techniques to detect the part of the inconsistencies only resulting from the careless inputs of participants. Moreover, with the rapid advent of technologies on rich user interface, the proposed framework can be extended to assess users' experience in interactive applications with an online learning setting where random graph models may take into account of sampling order (e.g. preference attachment graphs), which will also be part of our future work.

6. ACKNOWLEDGMENTS

This work was supported in part by National Basic Research Program of China (973 Program): 2009CB320906, in part by National Natural Science Foundation of China: 61025011, 60833006 and 61071157, in part by Beijing Natural Science Foundation: 4092042, and in part by the SINGAPORE MINISTRY OF EDUCATION Academic Research Fund (AcRF) Tier 2: T208B1218. Yuan Yao also thanks Microsoft Research-Asia for its support.

7. REFERENCES

[1] *ITU-R Recommendation P.800. Methods for subjective determination of transmission quality*, 1996.

[2] *ITU-R Methodology for the Subjective Assessment of the Quality of Television Pictures*. 2002.

[3] LIVE video quality assessment database. `http://live.ece.utexas.edu/research/quality/`, 2008.

[4] O. Alonso, D. Rose, and B. Stewart. Crowdsourcing for relevance evaluation. *SIGIR Forum*, 42(2):9–15, 2008.

[5] K. Arrow. A difficulty in the concept of social welfare. *Journal of Political Economy*, 58(4):328–346, 1950.

[6] D. Brabham. Crowdsourcing as a model for problem solving: an introduction and cases. *Convergence*, 14(1):75, 2008.

[7] G. Carlsson. Topology and data. *Bulletin of the American Mathematical Society*, 46(2):255–308, 2009.

[8] K.-T. Chen, C.-C. Wu, Y.-C. Chang, and C.-L. Lei. A crowdsourceable QoE evaluation framework for multimedia content. pages 491–500. ACM Multimedia, 2009.

[9] H. David. *The method of paired comparisons.* 2nd Ed., Griffin's Statistical Monographs and Courses, 41. Oxford University Press, New York, NY, 1988.

[10] H. Edelsbrunner and J. Harer. Computational topology : an introduction. 2010.

[11] H. Edelsbrunner, D. Letscher, and A. Zomorodian. Topological persistence and simplification. *Discrete and Computational Geometry*, 28(4):511–533, 2002.

[12] P. Erdos and A. Renyi. On random graphs i. *Publ. Math. Debrecen*, 6:290–297, 1959.

[13] Y. Freund, R. Iyer, R. Shapire, and Y. Singer. An efficient boosting algorithm for combining preferences. *Journal of Machine Learning Research*, 4(6):933–969, 2004.

[14] T. Hastie and R. Tibshirani. Classification by pairwise coupling. *Annals of Statistics*, 26(2):451–471, 1998.

[15] A. Hekstra, J. Beerends, D. Ledermann, F. de Caluwe, S. Kohler, R. Koenen, S. Rihs, M. Ehrsam, and D. Schlauss. PVQM-A perceptual video quality measure. *Signal Processing: Image Communication*, 17:781–798, 2002.

[16] R. Herbrich, T. Graepel, and K. Obermayer. *Large margin rank boundaries for ordinal regression.* MIT Press, 2000.

[17] J. Howe. The rise of crowdsourcing. *Wired Magazine*, 14(6):176–183, 2006.

[18] X. Jiang, L.-H. Lim, Y. Yao, and Y. Ye. Statistical ranking and combinatorial Hodge theory. *Mathematical Programming*, 2010.

[19] M. Kahle. Topology of random clique complexes. *Discrete Mathematics*, 309:1658–1671, 2009.

[20] Kendall, Maurice, and J. Gibbons. *Rank Correlation Methods.* Oxford University Press, 1990.

[21] M. Kendall and B. Smith. On the method of paired comparisons. *Biometrika*, 31(3-4):324–345, 1940.

[22] A. Kittur, E. Chi, and B. Suh. Crowdsourcing user studies with Mechanical Turk. pages 453–456. SIGCHI conference on Human factors in computing systems, 2008.

[23] I. Koutis, G. Miller, and R. Peng. Approaching optimality for solving sdd systems. FOCS '10 51st Annual IEEE Symposium on Foundations of Computer Science, 2010.

[24] J. Lubin. The use of psychophysical data and models in the analysis of display system performance. pages 163–178. Digital Images and Human Vision, 1993.

[25] G. Noether. Remarks about a paired comparison model. *Psychometrika*, 25:357–367, 1960.

[26] S. Nowak and S. Ruger. How reliable are annotations via crowdsourcing: a study about inter-annotator agreement for multi-label image annotation. International conference on Multimedia information retrieval, 2010.

[27] M. Pinson and S.Wolf. A new standardized method for objectively measuring video quality. *IEEE Transactions on Broadcasting*, 50(3):312–322, September 2004.

[28] T. Saaty. A scaling method for priorities in hierarchical structures. *Journal of Mathematical Psychology*, 15(3):234–281, 1977.

[29] H. Sexton and M. Johansson. JPlex: a java software package for computing the persistent homology of filtered simplicial complexes. `http://comptop.stanford.edu/programs/jplex/`, 2009.

[30] A. Sorokin and D. Forsyth. Utility data annotation with Amazon Mechanical Turk. pages 1–8. Computer Vision and Pattern Recognition Workshops, June 2008.

[31] D. Spielman and S.-H. Teng. Nearly-linear time algorithms for graph partitioning, graph sparsification, and solving linear systems. STOC '04 Proceedings of the thirty-sixth annual ACM symposium on Theory of computing, 2004.

[32] L. Thurstone. The method of paired comparisons for social values. *Journal of Abnormal and Social Psychology*, 27:384–400, 1927.

[33] C. van den Branden Lambrecht and O. Verscheure. Perceptual quality measure using a spatiotemporal model of the human visual system. *SPIE Conference on Human Vision and Electronic Imaging*, 2668(1):450–461, March 1996.

[34] Z. Wang, L. Lu, and A. Bovik. Video quality assessment based on structural distortion measurement. *Signal Processing: Image Communication*, 19(2):121–132, February 2004.

[35] A. Zomorodian and G. Carlsson. Computing persistent homology. *Discrete and Computational Geometry*, 33(2):249–274, 2005.

Saving Bitrate vs. Pleasing Users: Where is the Break-Even Point in Mobile Video Quality?

Wei Song, Dian W. Tjondronegoro, Michael Docherty
Faculty of Science and Technology, Queensland University of Technology
2 George Street, Brisbane, 4000, Australia
{w1.song, dian, m.docherty} @qut.edu.au

ABSTRACT

This paper presents a comprehensive study to find the most efficient bitrate requirement to deliver mobile video that optimizes bandwidth, while at the same time maintains good user viewing experience. In the study, forty participants were asked to choose the lowest quality video that would still provide for a comfortable and long-term viewing experience, knowing that higher video quality is more expensive and bandwidth intensive. This paper proposes the lowest pleasing bitrates and corresponding encoding parameters for five different content types: cartoon, movie, music, news and sports. It also explores how the lowest pleasing quality is influenced by content type, image resolution, bitrate, and user gender, prior viewing experience, and preference. In addition, it analyzes the trajectory of users' progression while selecting the lowest pleasing quality. The findings reveal that the lowest bitrate requirement for a pleasing viewing experience is much higher than that of the lowest acceptable quality. Users' criteria for the lowest pleasing video quality are related to the video's content features, as well as its usage purpose and the user's personal preferences. These findings can provide video providers guidance on what quality they should offer to please mobile users.

Categories and Subject Descriptors

H.5.1 [**Multimedia Information Services**]: Evaluation/methodology. H.5.2 [**User Interfaces**]: User-centred design

General Terms

Design, Experimentation, Human Factors.

Keywords

Acceptability, mobile video, quality, bitrate, encoding parameters, user profile, content type.

1. INTRODUCTION

Mobile video refers to the various forms of videos viewable on mobile devices, which can be downloaded and streamed in real time. Minimizing video bitrate is an important issue in mobile delivery for three main reasons. First, wireless networks prefer low bitrate to adapt to different bandwidth conditions. Second, users prefer low bitrate as most network providers normally charge for data usage. Third, video providers need to save costs associated with serving the content, especially if the users and amount of videos are rapidly growing. However, low video bitrate could lead to poor video quality, which would not be pleasing to watch. In general, lower bitrate corresponds to lower video quality under a particular video format. Fortunately, there is a nonlinear relationship between a user's perceived quality and the video's bitrate [1]. This offers an opportunity to find the lowest possible bitrate that will still provide an acceptable video quality.

There are existing studies that have proposed the lowest acceptable bandwidth requirement for mobile TV quality [2-4]. However, these studies were subject to restrictions from older generation mobile devices with lower display resolution and relatively low bitrate choices (which would suit older network bandwidths). Thus, the results derived from the previous studies are not always suitable for current scenarios. Moreover, a recent study has identified that the lowest acceptable video quality is not equal to the lowest quality for long term viewing, and users' requirements may change with more experience of watching mobile video [5].

This paper presents a user study on mobile video quality requirements, aiming to find the lowest requirement for a pleasing viewing experience, thereby maintaining a balance between users' satisfaction and bandwidth (cost) saving. The study was designed so that users would choose a desired video quality that would be comfortable for long term viewing, while considering that the bandwidth increases if they want higher quality. Based on the results and analysis, this paper presents important discoveries in mobile video user experience, namely:

- the mapping of video bitrates to the subjective judgment of quality pleasantness,
- impact of content type, video encoding parameters and user profile on mobile video viewing experience, and
- users' selection processes and their criteria for the lowest pleasing quality for different content types.

The rest of this paper is organized as follows. Section 2 provides a review of previous studies on mobile video quality assessment. Section 3 describes the details of our user study, while Section 4 presents the results from both quantitative and qualitative analysis. Section 5 further discusses some related issues, and then the paper is concluded in Section 6.

2. RELATED WORK

Many studies have demonstrated qualitatively that users' requirements for mobile video depend on both social and psychological factors, including consumption model, service, user

*Area Chair: Mor Naaman

MM'11, November 28–December 1, 2011, Scottsdale, Arizona, USA.

profile, contexts and the video quality [6]. Video quality is influenced by the technical elements of the video processing, such as spatial and temporal resolution and quantization; as well the features in the specific video content such as motion and texture complexity.

For mobile video delivery, saving a user's data download costs can be achieved by video bitrate reduction. There are three main factors influence bitrate: resolution, frame rate, and quantization parameters. Resolution reduction scales the size of the frames by transmitting fewer pixels, thereby reducing the level of detail in the frame. Frame rate reduction drops frames, which leads to frame jump. Scaling quantization levels drops chrominance or DCT coefficients, resulting in a loss of colors and detail. Moreover, in block-based video codec (e.g. H.264/AVC, MPEG, and WMV), blockiness and blurriness can be aggravated by coarser quantization [7]. Fortunately, the degradation in perceived video quality is not proportionate to the decrease in bitrate [1]. Thus, many researchers continue to explore methods to achieve a good user experience using perceptual quality oriented strategies.

The commonly used method for evaluating perceptual quality is the scale-based subjective quality assessment using 5/9/11-scales, recommended by ITU [9]. However, the scale-based assessment overburdens participants, especially when they struggle to determine a proper score for the quality of a video. Binary choice method is therefore suggested to use in assessing acceptability of mobile TV (one kind of mobile videos) by McCarthy and Knoche et al. [3, 10]. The idea of acceptability is to identify the lowest acceptable quality level [10, 11]. In Knoche et al.'s user study [3], the impacts of image resolution, bitrate and content type on acceptability rating were addressed under the conditions of the maximum resolution of 320x240 pixels and the maximum encoding bitrate of 448kbps, which were restricted by the technology and devices at that time. In their further study [4], although a mobile device with higher screen resolution was used, the examined image resolution was still only up to 480x360 pixels. As image size (resolution) has a significant impact on perceived video quality [3, 12], the previous studies using small screens, or testing for lower resolutions do not adequately address current issues. Since then, mobile devices have improved rapidly, supporting higher resolutions and having increased memory and processing capability. Moreover, people are generally more experienced with viewing high definition (HD) quality than they were previously. It is probable that the users' requirements regarding mobile video quality have changed due to the improvements in mobile devices and the increased experience of viewing mobile videos.

A recent user study used a more current model of a mobile device and tried to address more issues related to the user experience of mobile videos [5]. The qualitative study on users' criteria on acceptability assessment revealed that a user's opinion of whether or not a video's quality is acceptable is different from whether the user is willing to watch it in the long-term. Therefore, we should differentiate them by stating that the *lowest quality for pleasing use* refers to the minimum quality that users would accept for regular viewing; and the *lowest acceptable quality* refers to the minimum quality that users would be willing to watch.

Previous qualitative studies have addressed how users assess mobile video quality. In [3], the reasons for unacceptable quality for different content types, including animation, music, sports and news, depend on issues such as text detail, object detail, shot type, facial detail, jerky pictures, audio fidelity, color and contrast. In [13], visual quality factors were defined for different content, including details, erroneousness, blurriness, motion, clarity, text readability, and so on. Both studies confirmed that the criteria for visual quality are different for different content types, which is commonly explained by the features of content types. However, the question remains: are there other reasons related to the criteria?

The cost versus performance issue in the multimedia domain has been discussed in [14], and it was found that there is a trade-off between quality of service (QoS) and price. When the price is perceived as too high, users would rather select the lowest acceptable QoS. Otherwise, they would tend to select the highest available level of QoS. Price is a commercial factor and the affordable price depends on each individual. In most real cases, users do not know how much they are spending on the video that they are watching. As most networks charge by data-flow, users generally hope to achieve the best quality at the lowest cost possible. When the networks do not have a data quota, network traffic control mechanisms may not always provide users with the highest possible quality, even though the network providers generally hope to obtain high user satisfaction. Hence, it is important to identify the threshold of quality in mobile videos, which maintains an acceptable balance between network and bandwidth.

3. USER STUDY

This study was designed to find the optimal video quality that users would be pleased to regularly watch on their mobile devices. To mimic real world scenarios, a popular representative of currently available mobile phones (i.e. the iPhone) was chosen as the test tool. The test videos were selected to represent the various characteristics of encoded video.

3.1 Equipment

This study was carried out on an iPhone 3GS with 16GB storage, 3.5-inch (75mmx50mm) widescreen Multi-Touch display, and 480x320-pixel resolution at 163 ppi. It supports H.264/AVC video format's baseline profile, up to 1.5 Mbps, 640x480 pixels, and 30 frames per second. It supports AAC-LC audio format, up to 160 Kbps, 48kHz.

3.2 Test Materials

To represent the typical video content of mobile TV [15-17], we used five video content types in the user study, namely, news, music, animation, sports and movie, as described in Table 1.

It is important to use real material for a user-oriented study [18], therefore all videos were selected from recorded news and sports videos, trailers of movies and animations, and a clip of music TV. The test video content was selected to be representative of the content types, and comparable with previous studies [2, 3]. Each test video was encoded using various combinations of parameters: quantization parameter (QP), spatial resolution (SR) and frame rate (FR). From these combinations, we obtained 30 test clips, which have different qualities in terms of bitrates. The 30 test clips were then divided into three groups L, M and H, corresponding to three SR: 320x240 pixels, 480x320 pixels, and 640x480 pixels respectively. The purpose of this SR-based group separation is to compare the impact of various image resolutions as different mobile devices support different display resolutions.

Table 2 shows the encoding parameters of the 10 test clips in each of the SR groups, which are presented in bitrate ascending order.

To remove any additional (and unwanted) quality impairments, the test clips were all encoded at high resolutions (>=1280x720) and high bitrates (>2048kbps). To meet the requirements of the testing device (iPhone), the video format was defined as H.264/AVC baseline 3.0. As this paper does not evaluate the effect of audio, the videos were encoded using a uniformly high quality of audio AAC, 64kbps and 48kHz to ensure participants would understand the content and enjoy the viewing experience.

Table 1. Description of test video content types

 Animation (An) Planet 51 trailer (2:16)	 Movie (Mo) The Back-up Plan trailer (2:20)	 Music (Mu) Miley Cyrus – 7 Things MV (3:30)
 News (Nw) A clip from Channel TEN news in 2009 (3:50)	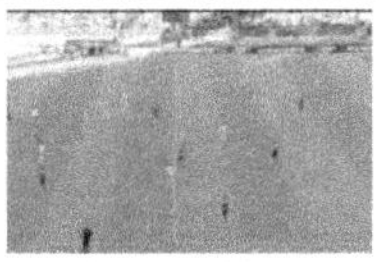 Sports (Sp) A clip from Spain vs. South Africa in FIFA 2009 (5:20)	

Table 2. Encoding parameters for one SR group (e.g. 320x240, 480x320, and 640x480)

No.	QP	FR (fps)	No.	QP	FR (fps)
Clip1	40	12.5	Clip 6	32	25
Clip 2	40	25	Clip 7	28	12.5
Clip 3	36	12.5	Clip 8	28	25
Clip 4	36	25	Clip 9	24	12.5
Clip 5	32	12.5	Clip 10	24	25

3.3 Participants

Participants were recruited in the lounge area outside of a university library, where, based on our observations, the activity of viewing mobile videos often occurs. We offered coffee vouchers for their time and emphasized that they should participate in the study as naturally as possible, and that there would be no assessment made on their viewing performance. 40 participants took part in the quality assessment test for all the five content types. The participants comprised an equal number of males and females, in the age range of 17-35 (average age = 23.2). All participants reported normal color vision and confirmed that they had not previously watched the test videos, which was important to determine if the impact of content recognition needed to be considered [19]. We also collected other participants' profiles related to their experience using mobile video, as listed in Table 3. A participant could have multiple preferences for video content type, and his/her prior experience in watching mobile video was classified based on whether he/she had used mobile video for over six months and whether he/she watched mobile videos at least once a week. The information was used to perform statistical analysis on the effect of user profile on the quality acceptability. In addition, it should be pointed out that there were two participants who worked in the area of image or video processing. However, as we did not find any significant difference in their assessments compared to other participants, we included these two participants in the subsequent data analysis for greater external validity.

Table 3. Participants' profiles (Out of 40)

Experience in watching mobile video	
• Frequency: at least once a week	21 (52.5%)
• Duration: less than six months	20 (50%)
Preference for content types	
• Animation	11 (27.5%)
• Movie	24 (60%)
• Music	16 (40%)
• News	10 (25%)
• Sports	12 (30%)

3.4 Procedure

To guide the participation, we told participants that the purpose of this study and the test scenario was as follows: "*This study aims to find out what quality of mobile video is the lowest acceptable for common use, based on the user's viewing experience.*" [,,,] "*In this study, the quality of your viewing video is adjustable. BUT the scenario is that the higher the quality you watch, the more the bandwidth (cost) you would have to spend. Your task is to adjust the quality of video to reach an optimal trade-off between viewing experience and cost. The optimal trade-off means that you should pick up the lowest quality possible, but you would still feel comfortable (i.e. pleased) to watch and are willing to use this kind of quality of videos regularly.*"

Further explanation was as follows: *"The scenario is that you want to have a nice viewing experience but sometimes the network bandwidth does not support very high quality video or you may worry that it would cost too much on your data plan. We are experimenting to find the quality borderline where you can still enjoy the watching experience, but the bandwidth (cost) is the lowest possible. So we are asking you to select the lowest quality that you feel would be comfortable and enjoyable to watch regularly."*

After ensuring the participants understood the task, the data collection procedure started and was completed in 20-25 minutes with three steps. Step1: participant's profile collection. Step 2: the participant randomly chose the video contents. While watching, they could adjust the video quality to decide the preferred quality under the scenario of cost saving. Step 3: a short interview (about five minutes) was performed to further understand the user's experience.

To ensure that the first two steps could be achieved smoothly, we custom designed an iPhone application, of which screenshots are shown in Figure 1. First of all, the participant's profile was required, including name (or nickname), age, gender, content type preference, and experience in viewing mobile video. All the information was collected by choosing an answer for each question as shown in Figure 1(a). Then, the participant chose one type of content and played the test videos by touching the corresponding cells in the content list (Figure 1(b)). For example, if the news video was chosen, the cells with name "News L", "News M" and "News H" had to be watched one after another in any order. Each cell corresponded to a spatial resolution group, containing 10 test clips encoded with different combinations of QP and FR parameters (see Table 2). Check marks were used to remind the participants which videos had been viewed.

To consider the possible effect of a change in direction of quality (i.e. low to high or high to low), we asked half of the participants to view the test clips in a bitrate ascending order and the other half to view the videos in a descending order. During the ascending order viewing, the first displayed video quality was the clip with the lowest bitrate. He/she could switch to a higher quality by swiping up or right on the middle of the screen (illustrated in Figure 1(d)). When the current video was at a higher quality level, the participant could also shift to a lower quality by swiping down or left. After swiping, the next quality video continued to play from the current playback time (with up to one-second's overlap) rather than from the beginning. This was to minimize the effect of quality switch on people's viewing. After quality adjustments participants could choose to keep watching until the end of the video content or stop watching once they determined the lowest pleasing quality. All data of user's information and interactions while viewing videos were stored into a database file and exported to our machine for data analysis, as well as viewed from a results page (Figure 1(c)) by participants for their interest.

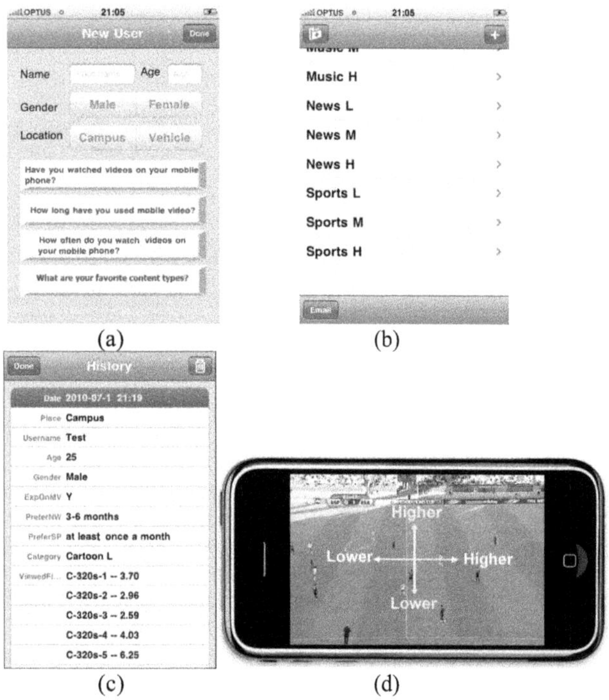

Figure 1. Screenshots of the test iPhone application

The main advantage of using the custom designed iPhone application during the user study is that data collection could be automatically and implicitly performed without interrupting participants' viewing. The streamlined test process was faster and participants were less likely to become tired and bored.

Generally, the follow-up interview was very short and took less than five minutes. Two main questions were asked.

- What criteria did you use to select the desired video quality?
- Is there any difference between your criteria for different content types? Why?

4. RESULTS

We used both quantitative and qualitative data for our analysis. The quantitative data were obtained from tracking users' interactions with the test tool while they were choosing the acceptable video quality. The qualitative data were obtained from interviews to provide further discussion on related issues.

In order to perform statistical analysis, we firstly transformed each subject's evaluation into binary data to denote whether a certain video quality is acceptable for pleasurable viewing or not, with 1 and 0 respectively. At a given resolution, the video clips that had lower quality (based on their bitrate) than the selected lowest acceptable clip were regarded as "unacceptable"; whilst those clips with higher quality will be regarded as "acceptable". In total, 6000 quality assessments (0/1) were obtained from the 150 test clips used by 40 participants.

Using this data, we calculated the *acceptability* for each clip. In this paper, "acceptability" refers to the percentage of participants accepting a video quality as the lowest pleasing quality. The acceptability was then used to indicate the required quality to meet the user's requirements.

Using the binary data from the 6000 quality assessments, we also conducted *Binary Logistic Regression* analysis to examine whether the user viewing experience is influenced by various factors, such as video encoding parameters, content type, viewing order and user profiles. Post-hoc within-subject tests were followed using a non-parametric *McNemar's* test to compare the difference between two related conditions for dichotomous data [20].

From the recorded quality-selection tracks, user's behavior when selecting their required video qualities can also be probed. In this part, two non-parametric methods, the *Kruskal-Wallis* test and the *Mann-Whitney* test [20], were used to compare the medians of multiple and two groups of continuous data of spent time.

4.1 Acceptability and Encoding Parameters

Figure 2 shows the mean acceptability lines of pleasing quality for all kinds of content types and resolution groups (i.e. the percentage of each test clip was rated as acceptable). From this graph, it can be observed that the acceptability is different from content to content, and from resolution to resolution. In general, a movie video gains much lower acceptability than others, whereas a news video gains higher acceptability. Moreover, the difference between content types reduces with the increase of resolution from 320x240 pixels to 640x480 pixels. The next subsection will further verify this phenomenon with statistical analysis.

For the purpose of differentiating the degree (or extent) of users' satisfaction, we define four stages of the acceptability, 0-40%, 41-60%, 61-80%, 81-100% respectively. The acceptability of less than 40% should be avoided as it will disappoint users; 41-60% is the critical state, indicating a risk of annoying users; 61%-80% means that the quality can please most users; and over 80% can achieve high user satisfaction. Based on Figure 2, at the highest resolution of 640x480 pixels, QP<=32 can meet 80% of user requirements for all content types; while at 320x240 and 480x320 pixels resolutions, a higher quantization level (QP<=28) is needed for movies and sports than for other content types (QP=24). Due to the close relationship between perceptual video quality and bitrate [1], we draw the bitrate-acceptability curves for each content type (shown in Figure 3), and list the range of bitrates for acceptability distributions (shown in Table 4).

Using the same video encoder, different content types were encoded into different bitrates under the same encoding setting of QP, SR and FR. Figure 3 also shows an obvious effect of content type on the bitrate acceptability. In general, a video at a high resolution of 640x480 pixels needs a higher bitrate to reach the same acceptable quality as videos that were obtained at lower resolutions of 320x240 or 480x320 pixels (see Figure 3 (a, c-f)). This can be explained by the fact that a higher image resolution needs a higher encoding bitrate to reach the same objective quality. However, this tendency is not obvious for the movie video (see Figure 3 (b)), which may be due to participants' attitudes towards a movie, as highlighted in the next subsection of user criteria. For the sports video, the acceptability rises with the bitrate much more slowly than for other content types, as generally more encoding bits are required for fast motion content.

Based on the mapping between the encoding bitrate and the quality acceptability (as listed in Table 4), we suggest that at 320x240 pixels and 12.5fps, the encoding bitrate of mobile viewing should not be lower than 200kbps for animation, movie and music videos, 120kbps for news videos, and 250kbps for sports videos. To reach a high level of user satisfaction, the bitrate requirements should be: 200kbps for news, 300kbps for animation and music, 350kbps for movies, and 500kbps for sports with small and many objects (e.g. soccer).

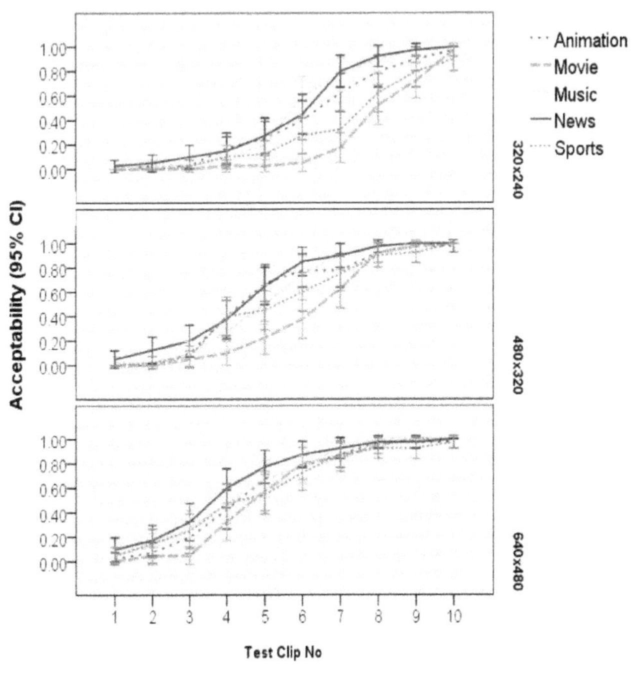

Figure 2. Mean acceptability of test clips for five content types

4.2 Influencing Factors on Quality Acceptability

To examine the impacts of various factors on quality acceptability, such as video encoding parameters, user profiles, content type and viewing order, we conducted a Binary Logistic Regression analysis. In this analysis, binary values indicating whether a quality is acceptable were used as dependent variables. Whereas nine predictors, namely: quantization parameter (QP), spatial resolution (SR), frame rate (FR), content type (CT), gender, age, frequency (of viewing mobile videos), duration (of viewing the video), and viewing order, were used as independent variables.

According to *Wald statistics* and the associated probabilities, which provide an index for the significance of each predictor, all the variables: QP, SR, FR, content type, gender, frequency, duration, and viewing order were found to provide significant contributions to the acceptability prediction ($p < .05$), except age ($z = 2.94, p > .05$).

To explore how these factors influence mobile user's acceptance of video quality, we performed a follow-up analysis for each of the influencing factors.

4.2.1 Effect of content type

A significant impact of content type was found as a result of the *regression analysis* ([$\chi^2(4)$=199.544, p<.001]). Since the same participants made the binary evaluations for each content type, we employed the McNemar test to compare the acceptability difference between any pairs of content types. The results showed that a significant impact of content type on quality acceptability is mainly reflected between movie and music, movie and news, and movie and animation (p<.05). This is consistent with the observation from Figure 2 that at the same encoding setting, the quality of movie video is less (likely to be) accepted than the other content types.

The statistical results also indicated that as the spatial resolution is decreased, more encoding setting points showed a significant effect on content type. For example, the apparent acceptability gap between movie and music exists at 5 points (in clip 5-9) for 320x240 pixels, but only 2 points (in clip 3-4) for 640x480 pixels (see also Figure 2). However, with respect to their bitrates, the difference in quality acceptance between various content types mainly concentrates on a relative low bitrate range, around 200 to 400 kbps regardless of the spatial resolution.

4.2.2 Effect of Encoding Parameters

Binary logistic regression analysis showed that the acceptability of video quality significantly increases with the:

- decrease of QP ([χ^2 (4)= 1337.234, p<.001]),
- increase of SR ([χ^2 (2)= 396.268, p<.001]), and
- increase of FR ([χ^2 (1)= 171.899, p<.001]).

The McNemar test revealed that when other encoding parameters are fixed, there were great differences among adjacent QP values, and between the lowest image resolution of 320x240 pixels and other resolutions (p<.001). However, the significant difference between 480x320 pixels and 640x480 pixels only occurred when content types were animation (p<.05) and movie (p<.001).

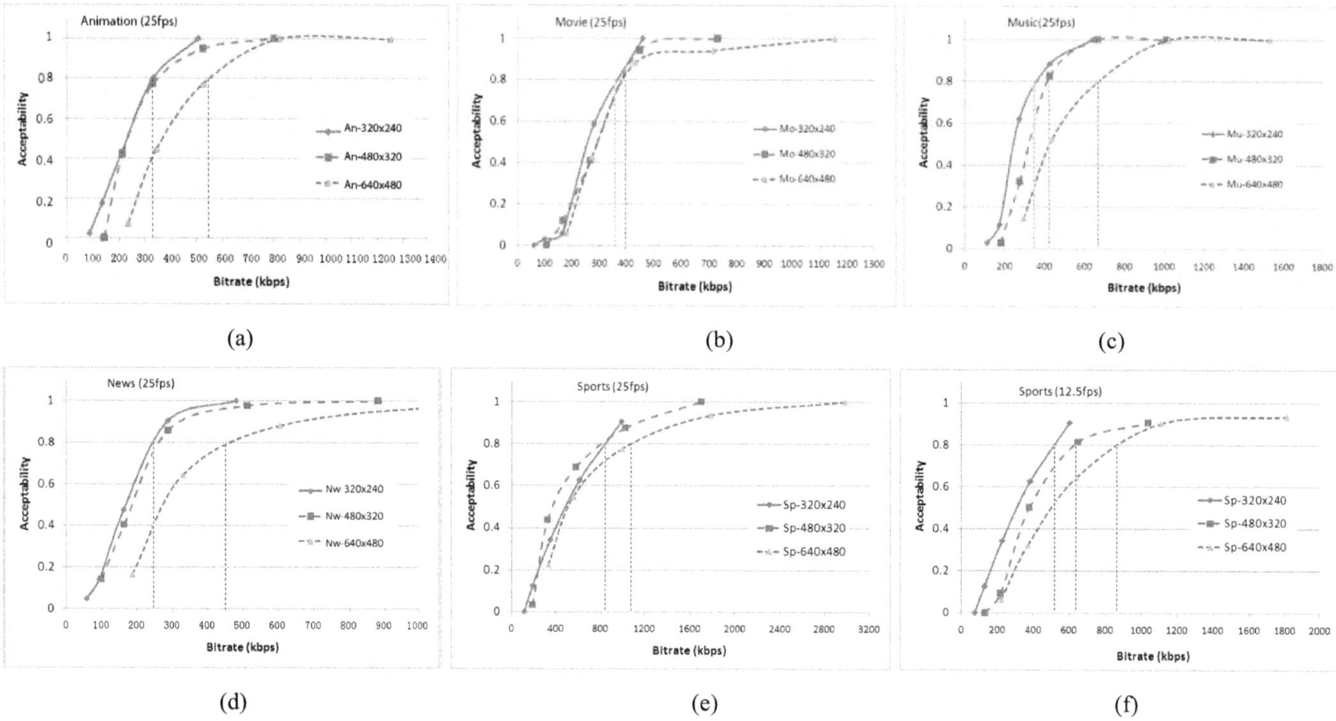

Figure 3. Relationships between bitrate and quality acceptability

Table 4. Mapping relationship between average bitrate and quality acceptability

Accept-ability (%)	SR (pixels)	FR (fps)	Animation	Movie	Music	News	Sports
41-60	320x240	12.5	180-230	230-290	210-250	120-150	250-380
		25	200-270	230-290	220-270	150-200	400-580
	480x320	12.5	200-230	230-290	260-300	140-180	320-450
		25	200-270	270-320	300-350	160-210	320-460
	640x480	12.5	300-350	270-310	350-430	210-280	420-600
		25	350-410	270-320	380-480	250-300	450-620
61-80	320x240	12.5	230-320	290-360	250-300	150-200	380-520
		25	270-350	290-380	270-350	200-250	580-850
	480x320	12.5	230-350	290-360	300-380	180-230	450-630
		25	270-350	320-390	350-400	210-260	460-850
	640x480	12.5	350-450	310-400	430-550	280-360	600-850
		25	410-550	320-400	480-670	300-450	620-1000

4.2.3 Effect of viewing order

A significant impact of viewing order ([χ^2 (1) = 7.242, p = .001]) showed that the quality acceptability obtained in the descending order (from high bitrate to low) was lower than that obtained in the ascending order. This conclusion is in accordance with the effect of image resolution order given in [3], where participants who viewed clips decreasing in image resolution were less likely to accept the video quality. However, the significant difference is related to content types. Separate Mann-Whitney U tests for each content type showed that the order influence was not significant for movie ([z = -.355, p = .723]) but was significant for animation, music, news and sports (p < .025). Due to the significant impact of viewing order, when analyzing the impacts of user profile, the dependency between order and user profile was considered.

4.2.3 Effect of User Profile

Logistic regression was used to test four characteristics of the user profile: gender, age, experience with mobile video: frequency (of at least once per week) and duration (whether having watched mobile video in the last six months). It was found that gender [$\chi^2(1)$=23.988, p<.001], frequency [$\chi^2(1)$=8.12, p=.004], and duration [$\chi^2(1)$=9.915, p=.002] significantly influenced users' experience. Figure 4 illustrates these effects. It was observed that frequent watchers (at least once per week) had a lower acceptability than those who do not often watch mobile video; while long-term experienced users (>6 months) had slightly more tolerance for a low video quality than the short-term or non-experienced users. Also, the acceptability score for women was much higher than that for men. However, this tendency was only distinct when viewing test clips in ascending order because gender had a significant interaction with viewing order in the quality evaluation ([$\chi^2(1)=104.731$, $p<.001$]).

There was no significant interaction between duration and order, and between duration and gender ($p>.05$). However, there were significant relationships between frequency and gender, and frequency and duration ($p<.001$) (shown in Figure 5). The effect of frequency on quality acceptability was mainly found in male and long-term users. In other words, among male and long-term users of mobile video, frequent viewers require higher pleasing quality than non-frequent viewers.

In our experiment, user's preference for a content type was not count-balanced. For example, less than 30% of participants liked news and sports and about 70% of them disliked news and sports. Due to the large gap, we could not state that the impact of user's preference is significant. However, an obvious difference of average acceptability between people who like and dislike the content types was observed. Figure 6 illustrates the average acceptability for animation and sports. In accordance with the conclusion in [19], we found that content types that match a user's preference generally collected a higher rating. For instance, people who like animation were more likely to accept a lower video quality. However, sports video took an opposite direction, whereby sports fan were less likely to accept lower video quality. We will conduct further discussions regarding this phenomenon through analyzing the interview data.

4.3 Quality Selection Patterns

In this experiment, we also recorded users' trajectories while selecting the final (pleasing) quality, including the video clip names and the quality-switching time in milliseconds. Since the data on the switching time was not in normality distribution (based on the *Kolmogorov-Smirnov* test $p<.05$), non-parametric tests were used instead. In general, the mean time for switching quality is about 3.342 seconds. The Kruskal-Wallis Test indicated that there was a significant difference among the mean time for the five video content types ([$\chi^2(4)=55.586$, $p<.001$]). The post-test using Mann-Whitney tests revealed that the average time spent on news video was much lower than that of other content types ($p<.001$); and the average time spent on sports video was significantly lower than animation but higher than news ($p<.001$) (see also Figure 7 (a)). Moreover, people spent much more time at the chosen quality level (mean = 4.487s) than other quality levels (mean = 2.792) ([$z=-16.384$, $p<.001$]).

When people opted for the quality close to the lowest pleasing threshold, two patterns of selection behaviors were observed. In Pattern 1, participants directly chose their target qualities without hesitation, while in Pattern 2, participants bounced to and from the lower or higher qualities to do a comparison before making their final decision. Pattern 1 mostly happened when viewing in the quality ascending order; while Pattern 2 was predominant in the quality descending order. This finding is most likely to be related to the test purpose of selecting the lowest pleasing quality. When users viewed videos from low quality to high quality, once they found the current quality was good enough and much better than the previous one, they could directly choose the current one as the lowest pleasing quality. However, when viewing from high to low, they often had to check at a low quality stage to see how poor the next quality would be, and they then returned to a desired quality stage, and compared several adjoining qualities to make the decision.

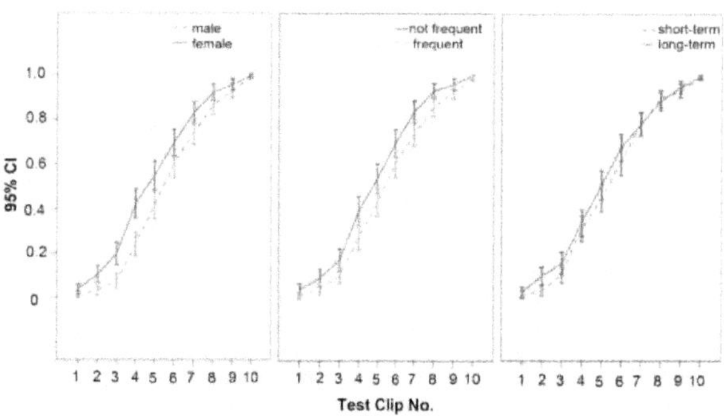

Figure 4. Effects of user profile (gender, frequency, duration) on quality acceptability

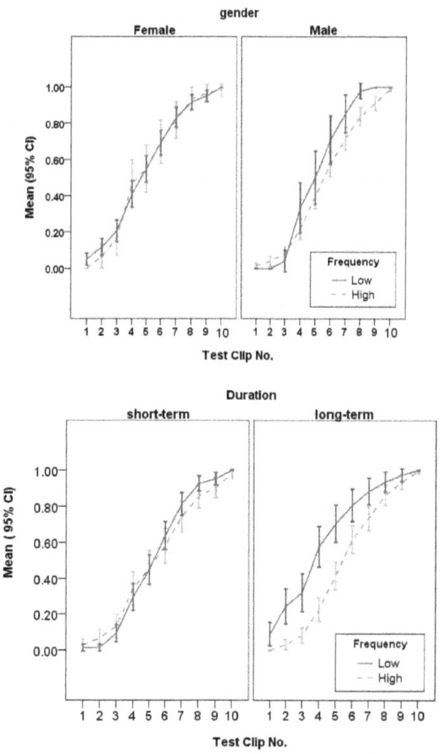

Figure 5. Relationships between frequency and gender, frequency and duration

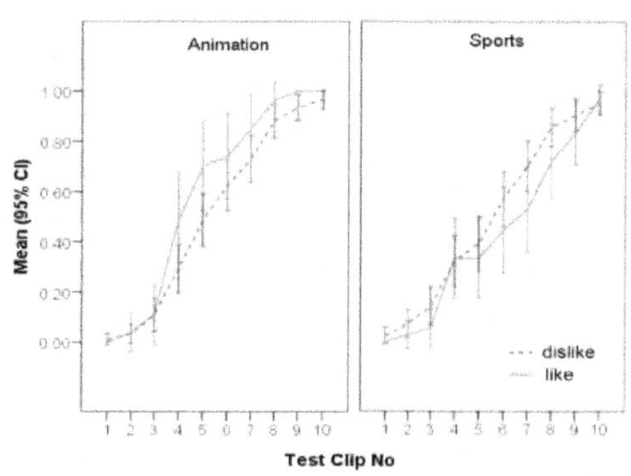

Figure 6. Effect of user's preference for content types on quality acceptability

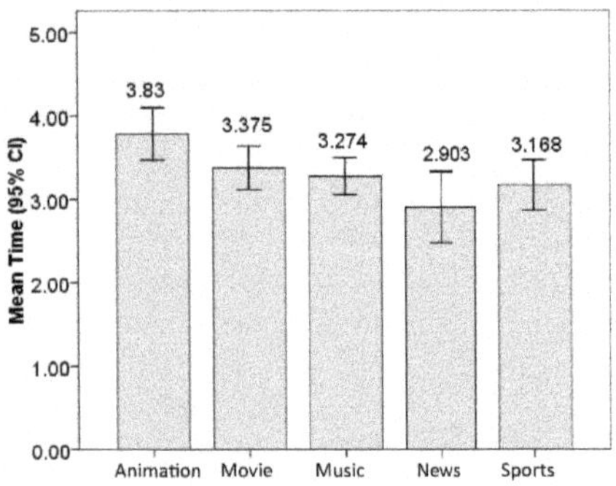

(a)

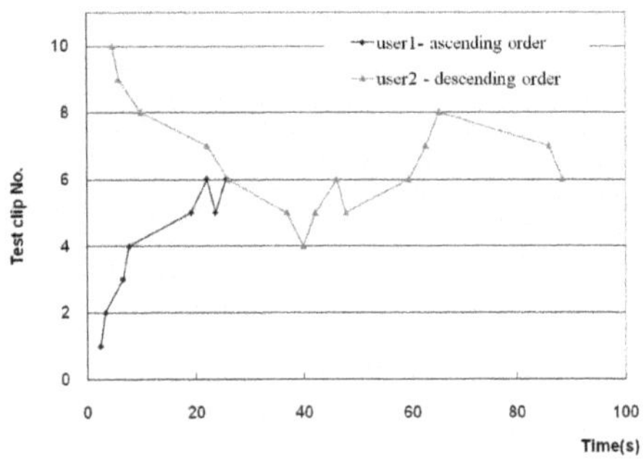

(b)

Figure 7. (a) Mean quality selection time for five content types (b) Examples of quality selection patterns

Although not dominant, pattern 2 still existed in the ascending order. The bouncing-back behavior usually occurred at the beginning of selecting a quality and within only one quality level from the key quality. Once the quality ruler was built, the following selections were direct and quick. Figure 7 (b) demonstrates two examples of pattern 2. Similarly, pattern 1 also appeared in the descending order. Furthermore, though belonging to the same pattern 2 in the descending order, some participants adjusted video qualities recognizably less frequently than others.

4.4 Criteria of Acceptable Quality

This section focuses on how users typically assess the acceptable quality of different content types for meeting their requirements of natural daily viewing. Our study confirmed that people have different assessment criteria for different content types [3,13,19], evidenced by the qualitative data from 28 interviewees' opinions. However, it is more interesting to know why users make different judgments and how their criteria explain the results from the quantitative analysis.

For movie video, one participant's words can represent the majority of other opinions: "*I have a higher quality requirement for movie than other video types. I need the actors or actresses' faces clear enough to recognize their expressions. Since movie is commonly watched in a HD quality on a cinema screen or a TV/PC screen, it should be also vivid on a mobile device screen; and HD is good if possible.*"

Obviously, affected by the experience of watching high definition (HD) films, users want a HD movie even on a small screen device. This is consistent with the assessment results about required bitrate and encoding parameters for the movie: at the highest resolution (640x480 pixels), a medium quantization quality (QP=32) can meet their needs; however, when the resolution drops (480x320, or 320x240 pixels), a higher quantization quality (QP = 28, 24 respectively) is needed to compensate for the loss of resolution.

For news video, audio quality and the synchronization of audio and video seem more important than video quality.

"... I don't like it if the speaker's lips movement doesn't match the speech."

"... I never thought of the news quality. Well, I mean I just watch what the websites show to me...."

"... It should be clear, but needn't be as clear as movie."

The difference in criteria for news and movie can be used to explain why news is accepted the easiest whereas it is most difficult to satisfy users with a movie.

For music video, participants mentioned the audio quality. Their focus is not mainly on the video quality, thus if the image is not too blurry or pixelated, they will accept it. Some participants also mentioned facial details, because the music video test clip contained a lot of close-up shots of singers. Despite the fact that the music video used was a fast-rhythm song, there was no statement about a "jerky picture", which was heavily commented about in the music content type in Knoche et al.'s study [3]. We think this arises from the selection of music video itself, as Knoche et al.'s explanation of "*the problem seemed to lie with a disruption of rhythm associated with the music being played*".

Participants had fewer requirements for animation. They mainly do not like blockiness, as smoothness is the key for achieving a pleasing quality. This is consistent with the fact that animation videos generally contain vivid colors, high contrast and frame changes.

"*It doesn't matter what the animation's quality is. I mean almost all given qualities were not bad, but if no blocks in the picture it will be nice. Also, I found that in some qualities, frame changed too fast, it made me feel a little bit uncomfortable.*"

For sports video, most participants agreed that when small objects exist, they need a higher quality compared to the big objects. The objects should also move smoothly.

To explore the opposite impact of user's preference for sports video on the acceptable video quality, we compared the interview data from both people who like and dislike a certain video content type. For news video, news fans do not necessarily require a high quality because their main purpose in watching news video was for information, which can be obtained by listening more than watching. However, for users who do not like news, they wanted the people's faces in the video to be clear (i.e. not too blurry). This finding is in accordance with the finding in [5], but inconsistent with [19]. In contrast, sports fans always wanted the video quality to be as high as possible so that they could clearly see the players and the ball on the small screen. As for other users who are not keen on sports, their attitudes are quite interesting. They thought that the players were too small to recognize on the small screen even in a high quality video. As such, for those users, high quality was not necessary for sports video. And they accepted a quality in which they could see enough of the game to understand what was going on and the movement was not jittery. The derived effects of preference for sports video contradicts the conclusion from [5], in which people who were fond of sports were more accepting of a lower quality. The conflict is associated with our study's evaluation scenario - cost saving but happy to use. Although the sports fans may accept a poor quality, they are more willing to pay more for a high quality.

5. DISCUSSION

To maximize user experience of mobile video, it is essential to understand users' requirements for video quality. This requirement is related not only to the video quality itself, but also to a user's profile. Studying the effect of user profile on quality acceptability can benefit personalized mobile video delivery. For example, a high quality of sports video is generally required in order to satisfy sports fans, whereas, a high quality of news video is needed to avoid disappointing occasional news watchers.

As for the acceptable bitrate, Knoche et al. [2, 3] previously stated that at 320x240 pixels resolution and 12.5 fps, movie and music requires about 200 kbps bitrate to be acceptable by 80% of participants; news only needed 100 kbps while football needed over 300 kbps. However, using the same conditions, our results indicate that the bitrate requirements are about one-and-a half times higher than Knoche et al.'s findings. For example, over 300kbps for animation, movie, music, 200kbps for news, and 520kbps for sports. However, the bitrate requirements for 40% of acceptability are similar to Knoche et al.'s results (see Table 4). We argue that the remarkable increase in expectation is due to two main reasons. Firstly, user's requirements for mobile video quality have increased, along with the development of video and mobile technologies. Current users have much more exposure to high-resolution videos than previously, and the enhanced experience in turn promotes the increase in a user's requirements (and expectations). This impact is demonstrated in our study by the user's criteria for movie videos (i.e. they want much higher quality as they are used to HD videos), and the requests for higher quality from frequent watchers of mobile video. Secondly, the lowest quality requirement for regular and pleasing viewing experience is generally higher than that of the lowest acceptable quality. Another possible reason is the change in social expectations of mobile video quality. The social expectations refer to the norms that give regularity to the behavior of watching mobile videos and make predictable interaction between members of the social group [21]. It is assumed that in 2005 [2, 3] people generally expected a relatively low video quality on a mobile device because the common devices did not have high display resolutions, nor were many high quality videos introduced to users. However, this paper does not have explicit evidence to show that effect. It will be an interesting study to obtain a deeper insight into this issue.

Considering the impact of content features (spatial and temporal complexity) on the encoding bitrate, we should point out that the lowest acceptable bitrates for various content types given in this paper are only the estimated range of bitrates as the exact bitrate depends on the individual video content itself. In spite of the bitrate differences among content types, a commonality can be observed in terms of the encoding parameters. That is, to achieve a good user experience (based on 80% of acceptability), the quantization parameter (QP) should be less than 28 under the resolution of 320x240 pixels and 32 under the resolution of 480x320 and 640x480 for animation, music and news; but for movie and sports, it should be less than 24, 28 and 32 under the three resolutions respectively. Moreover, it should be noted that the lowest acceptable bitrate for the five content types is dependent on the encoding standard of the H.264/AVC Baseline 3.0 profile, which is required by iPhone 3GS. In fact, the encoding bitrate varies across encoding standards (such as H.264 and WMV) and encoding levels (such as baseline and high profile). Since the usable encoding settings depend on the supported platform, the lowest acceptable bitrate might be different for different platforms.

With regards to the quality selection behavior, some users make a decision quickly but some are very careful. A question arose from this phenomenon: do people prefer an adjustable quality-providing mode or a direct quality-providing mode? The former allows users to change the quality level; while the latter refers to providing users with a fixed quality that is accepted by most people.

In this study, our aim is not to investigate how cost influences a user's requirements in the selection of mobile video quality, but using cost as an assumption condition to instruct users to select the lowest pleasing quality. The scenario-based user study aims to gain a closer user experience. The results can give video providers guidance on what quality they should offer to mobile users and in what range the quality should be adjusted.

6. CONCLUSION

Mobile video users prefer to watch high quality videos at the lowest possible bandwidth (which often directly means cost). Video providers want to provide optimal quality to please users, while maintaining storage savings and speeding up video delivery. To serve both requirements, the paper attempted to answer: "where is the break-even point in mobile video quality?" To answer this question, we performed a thorough user study on quality acceptability of mobile video for five typical content types: animation, movie, music, news and sports.

Through the statistical analysis, we address the significant impacts of content type, encoding parameter, and user profile on the acceptability of mobile video quality. It was found that: (i) the acceptability of video quality increases significantly with the decrease of the quantization parameter (QP) and the increase of spatial resolution (SR) and frame rate (FR); (ii) there is a stronger relationship between acceptability and content type at a relatively low bitrate range of 200 - 400kbps; (iii) female users and people who seldom watch mobile video are more likely to accept a lower quality than their counterparts.

We also provide general bitrate requirements and the corresponding encoding parameters for the five content types. It is suggested that: (i) with 80% of acceptability as the threshold, the encoding bitrate for a 320x240 pixel image resolution should be over 200kbps for news, 300kbps for animation and music, 350kbps for movie, and 500kbps for sports; (ii) at higher resolutions, such as 480x320 pixels and 640x480 pixels, a higher than 60% of acceptability can be achieved if the bitrate is greater than 300kbps for news, 400kbps for animation, movie, and music, and 800kbps for sports; and (iii) for videos with resolutions of higher than 480x320 pixels, a quantization parameter (QP) of less than 28 is required to meet the requirements for quality acceptability, regardless of the video content types.

Compared to previous work, we find that the lowest quality requirement for regular viewing is much higher than the lowest acceptable quality. This may be caused by not only the scenario difference between the pleasing and long-term use and the short time viewing, but also the increasing user demand for quality due to the advance of video technology and the growth of experience in watching mobile video. From the follow-up interviews, participants' criteria for selecting the lowest pleasing quality explain their different requirements for different content types. In general, users expect a high quality movie, even on a mobile device with a small screen. However, they do not expect high video quality for music and news, but rather, good sound and synchronization of audio and video. Those who like a particular video content type can usually accept a relatively low quality, but the opposite is found in sports' fans who expect higher quality sport videos to see their favorite players' details clearly. The criteria show that a pleasing quality significantly depends on a user's purposes and preferences for content types.

The findings from this study make connections between users' requirements and the underlying technical parameters, and add to our understanding about the influence of user profiles on their requirements. This study suggests that it is important for mobile video providers to take into consideration the increase in users' requirements, in order to deliver a pleasing video quality to users. For future work, it will be interesting to study in-depth how users' requirements have changed and how user profile, usage cost and environment, and social expectations affect the user experience in mobile video. Our ongoing research focuses on an extensive user study and user experience modeling of mobile video to establish optimal video delivery strategies and prediction models to meet mobile video user's satisfaction. We will also study the question raised in this paper on the effect of the quality-providing mode to seek a better interaction between users and video delivery systems. Other aspects of influencing user experiences of mobile video, such as cost and social expectation, may also be further explored.

7. REFERENCES

[1] VQEG. *Final report from the video quality experts group on the validation of objective models of video quality assessment, phase II*. VQEG, 2003.

[2] Knoche, H. and McCarthy, J. D. Design requirements for mobile TV. In *Proceedings of the Mobile HCI'05* (Salzburg, Austria, 2005). ACM, NY, 183-192.

[3] Knoche, H., McCarthy, J. D. and Sasse, M. A. Can small be beautiful?: assessing image resolution requirements for mobile TV. In *Proceedings of the 13th ACM Multimedia* (Hilton, Singapore, 2005). ACM, NY, 829-838.

[4] Knoche, H. and Sasse, M. A. The big picture on small screens: Delivering acceptable video quality in Mobile TV. *ACM Transactions on Multimedia Computing, Communications and Applications*, 5, 3 (2009), 1-27.

[5] Song, W., Tjondronegoro, D. and Docherty, M. Exploration and optimization of user experience in viewing videos on a mobile phone. *Int. J. Softw. Eng. Know.*, 8, 20 (2010).

[6] Buchinger, S., Kriglstein, S. and Hlavacs, H. A comprehensive view on user studies: survey and open issues for mobile TV. In *Proceedings of the 7th European Conference on Interactive Television* (Leuven, Belgium, 2009). ACM, NY,179-188.

[7] Leontaris, A. and Reibman, A. Comparison of blocking and blurring metrics for video compression. In *Proceedings of the IEEE International Conference on Acoustics, Speech and Signal Processing* (Philadelphia, USA, 2005), 585-589.

[8] Jumisko-Pyykkö, S. and Hannuksela, M. M. Does context matter in quality evaluation of mobile television? In *Proceedings of the 10th international conference on Human computer interaction with mobile devices and services* (Amsterdam, Netherlands, 2008). ACM, NY, 63-72.

[9] ITU-R Recommendation BT. 500-11:. *Methodology for the Subjective Assessment of Quality for Television Pictures*. 2004.

[10] McCarthy, J. D., Sasse, M. A. and Miras, D. Sharp or smooth?: comparing the effects of quantization vs. frame rate for streamed video. In *Proceedings of the SIGCHI Conference on Human Factors in Computing Systems* (San Francisco, USA, 2004). ACM, NY, 535-542.

[11] Jumisko-Pyykkö, S., Vadakital, V. K. M. and Hannuksela, M. M. Acceptance threshold: A bidimensional research method for user-oriented quality evaluation studies. *Int. J. Digital Multimedia Broadcasting* (2008), 1-20.

[12] Song, W., Tjondronegoro, D. and Azad, S. User-centered video quality assessment for scalable video coding of H.264/AVC standard. In *Proceedings of the 16th International Multimedia Modeling Conference* (Chongqing, China, 2010) Springer, 55-65.

[13] Jumisko-Pyykkö, S., Häkkinen, J. and Nyman, G. Experienced quality factors - qualitative Evaluation approach to audiovisual quality. In *Proceedings of the SPIE Multimedia on Mobile Devices* (2007) SPIE,1-12.

[14] Hands, D. S., Partridge, C., Cheng, K. and Jacobs, R. J. Price-dependent quality: Examining the effects of price on multimedia quality requirements. In *Proceedings of the SPIE the International Society for Optical Engineering on Human Vision and Electronic Imaing XII* (San Jose, California, USA, 2007). SPIE.

[15] Södergård, C. *Mobile television-technology and user experiences*. 506, VTT Information Technology, 2003.

[16] Carlsson, C. and Walden, P. Mobile TV-to live or die by content. In *Proceedings of the 40th Annual Hawaii International Conference on System Sciences (HICSS)* (2007). IEEE Computer Society, 51-57.

[17] O'Hara, K., Mitchell, A. S. and Vorbau, A. Consuming video on mobile devices. In *Proceedings of the SIGCHI on Human Factors in Computing Systems* (San Jose, CA, USA, 2007). ACM, NY, 857-866.

[18] Sasse, M. A. and Knoche, H. Quality in context-an ecological approach to assessing QoS for mobile TV. In *Proceedings of the 2nd ISCA/DEGA Tutorial & Workshop on Perceptual Quality of System* (Berlin, Germany, 2006).

[19] Jumisko-Pyykkö, S., Ilvonen, V. P. and Väänänen-Vainio-Mattila, K. A. Effect of TV content in subjective assessment of video quality on mobile devices. In *Proceedings of the Multimedia on Mobile Devices* (San Jose CA, 17-18 Jan 2005). SPIE, 243-254.

[20] Aron, A., Aron, E. and Coups, E. J. *Statistics for psychology*. Harlow: Pearson Education, 2009.

[21] Hines, R.H. Social expectations and cultural deprivation. *J. Negro Ed.* (1964), 136-142.

Implementation of the Discrete Wavelet Transform and Multiresolution Analysis in the Encrypted Domain *

Peijia Zheng, Jiwu Huang
School of Information Science and Technology
Sun Yat-Sen University
Guangzhou, 510006, China
zhengpj@student.sysu.edu.cn, isshjw@mail.sysu.edu.cn

ABSTRACT

Signal processing in the encrypted domain is a new technology for protecting valuable signals from insecure signal processing. Although there has been some research in the area, this field of research is still in its infancy.

In this paper, we propose a scheme for implementing discrete wavelet transform (DWT) and multi-resolution analysis (MRA) in a homomorphic encrypted domain. We first suggest a framework for performing DWT and inverse discrete wavelet transform (IDWT) in the encrypted domain and then conduct an analysis of data expansion and quantization errors on the framework. In order to solve the problem of data expansion, which is very important in practical applications, we then present a novel method for reducing data expansion in the case that both DWT and IDWT are performed. With the proposed method, multilevel DWT/IDWT can be performed with less data expansion in a homomorphic encrypted domain. We address the case of a two-dimensional Haar wavelet transform and give some experiments to demonstrate the advantages of our improved method. To the best of our knowledge, this is the first paper on the implementation of DWT and MRA in the encrypted domain.

Categories and Subject Descriptors

K.6.5 [**Computing Milieux**]: Management of Computing and Information Systems—*Security and Protection*

General Terms

Algorithms, Security.

Keywords

Discrete wavelet transform(DWT), multiresolution analysis (MRA), homomorphic encryption, signal processing the encrypted domain, data expansion, secure signal processing.

*Area chair: Tian-Tsong Ng

MM'11, November 28–December 1, 2011, Scottsdale, Arizona, USA.

1. INTRODUCTION

Signal processing in the encrypted domain, also referred to as secure signal processing (SSP), has received considerable attention in recent years [1]. This new technology may promise two kinds of application in the very near future. The first is when the owners and manipulators of data are two different parties. For example, in the scenario of network media distribution, the customer may be asked to embed a watermark in the media to trace illegal copies. Since the plain media are easily attacked by the customer during watermarking, a solution is to embed a watermark in the encrypted media, whose content is protected by the cryptosystems. Signal processing in the encrypted domain provides powerful tools to make such secure implementation possible. The second application is the one requires a query on the encrypted data. For example, in the situation of a remote access system based on biometric data, the user will send his/her sensitive information to obtain access to the server. If the server is untrustworthy, the user will face a serious privacy and security problem. Signal processing in the encrypted domain, combined with the cryptographic protocols, can provide an effective solution to this problem. The user may simply send out his/her encrypted information, and the server is able to discover from those encrypted data whether the person is enrolled in the database. Secure multi-party computation [2][3] plays a key role in the interactive activity. In this paper, we focus on the research on signal processing in the encrypted domain without considering the function of the cryptographic protocols.

Not all the cryptosystems are suitable for the tasks of data encryption in order to perform signal processing in the encrypted domain. The reason is that most cryptosystems, such as Data Encryption Standard (DES) and Advanced Encryption Standard (AES), do not retain the algebraic relations among the plaintexts after encryption. A special kind of cryptosystem, the homomorphic cryptosystem, is able to keep one or two algebraic structures of the plaintext, and so is particularly suitable for handling the task of data encryption. The existing homomorphic cryptosystems can be divided into two classes. The first one is the partially homomorphic cryptosystem which keeps only one algebraic structure of the plaintexts, such as the ElGamal cryptosystem [4], the Paillier cryptosystem [5] and the Damgård-Jurik cryptosystem [6]. The second one is the fully homomorphic encryption scheme proposed in [7], which allows to evaluate any circuits homomorphically.

There have been some related works on signal processing in the encrypted domain over the past few years. An interactive buyer-seller watermarking protocol for invisible watermarking was proposed in [8], in which the seller does not get to know the exact watermarked copy that the buyer receives. Bianchi *et al.* [9] conducted an investigation on the implementation of the discrete Fourier transform (DFT) as well as the fast Fourier transform (FFT) on encrypted signals. The authors have done a pioneering work in this field, despite the problem of quantization error and data expansion having not been tackled. In [10], the authors proposed a composite signal representation for fast and storage-efficient processing of encrypted signals. Though the composite signal representation restricts the freedom of the packed samples, the authors offered a new approach for reducing the size of encrypted signals. In [11] [12], the authors proposed schemes for privacy-preserving face recognition by using the Paillier cryptosystem. A finger code-based identity-matching algorithm in the encrypted domain is presented in [13].

The discrete wavelet transform (DWT) is a common tool used in the field of signal processing. With the different wavelet bases and decomposition levels, DWT can extract different kinds of information from the media. DWT is therefore very likely to be carried out in the encrypted domain. It is expected to be used as a building block for secure media watermarking, secure feature extracting and secure information retrieval. According to our best knowledge, there has been no reports yet on the implantation of DWT and multi-resolution analysis (MRA) in the encrypted domain.

This paper addresses the issue of implementing DWT and MRA in the encrypted domain. Firstly, we describe a framework for performing DWT and inverse discrete wavelet transform (IDWT) in a homomorphic-encrypted domain, and conduct the analysis of data expansion. We then derive an upper bound on the accumulated error for decomposition and reconstruction. The framework is a general one and can be used to perform linear operation on encrypted data. For instance, A pyramid algorithm in the encrypted domain can be built by using our strategy. Secondly, we propose an improved method, called the multiplicative inverse method, to remove the quantization factor without decryption. The proposed method can be seen as a solution of the data expansion in the encrypted domain. By using the improved method, MRA can be implemented homomorphically in the encrypted domain with much less data expansion. Finally, we study the case of 2D discrete Haar wavelet transform to substantiate our proposed technique and the multiplicative inverse method. By using our technique, one is well able to design a privacy-preserving face detection/recognition system based on wavelet transform, for example, the face detection scheme proposed by Viola *et al.* [14]. We also provide performance comparisons and explore parameters of the multiplicative inverse method.

The remainder of this paper is organized as follows. Section 2 gives an introduction to probabilistic homomorphic encryption and the Paillier cryptosystem. In Section 3, we describe a technique to implement DWT in the encrypted domain and provide the upper bound estimation. In Section 4, we discuss the implementation of IDWT in the encrypted domain. An improved method to remove the data expansion is presented in Section 5. Section 6 gives some simulation experiments of 2D DWT on an encrypted image. We conclude our paper and provide suggestions for future work in Section 7.

2. PAILLIER CRYPTOSYSTEM: PROBABILISTIC HOMOMORPHIC CRYPTOSYSTEM

Rivest *et al.* [2] first introduced the homomorphic cryptosystem as a privacy homomorphism, which is defined as an encryption function which allows operation of the ciphertexts without decrypting them into plaintexts. Specifically, an algebraic operation is performed in the plaintext space corresponding to another algebraic operation which is performed in the ciphertext space. If m_1 and m_2 are any two plaintexts, we have

$$D[E[m_1] \circ E[m_2]] = m_1 \diamond m_2 \tag{1}$$

where $D[\cdot]$ and $E[\cdot]$ are the decrypting operator and encrypting operator, respectively. Operator '$\circ$' denotes the algebraic operation performed in the ciphertext space and '$\diamond$ denotes the corresponding algebraic operation performed in the plaintext space.

A probabilistic cryptosystem is a kind of cryptosystem which introduces randomness to the encryption process. Goldwasser *et al.* [15] first proposed the concept of the probabilistic cryptosystem. Even in the case of the same plaintext encryption, it yields different ciphertexts. The probabilistic property is particularly useful in public key cryptosystems. Anyone can carry out the encryption with the public key, but the probabilistic public key cryptosystem can resist chosen plaintext attacks. The probabilistic property can therfore help the public key cryptosystem to achieve semantic security [3].

There are some cryptosystems which have both the probabilistic property and the homomorphic property, such as the cryptosystem proposed by Paillier [5]. The Paillier cryptosystem is a semantic secure public key cryptosystem. It has an additive homomorphic property. That is, for any two ciphertexts, one can compute the sum of their plaintexts as long as he/she knows the public key. Very recently, Gentry [7] proposed the first fully homomorphic encryption scheme by using lattice-based cryptography. This scheme supports to evaluate arbitrary depth circuits homomorphically. It is not so efficient in practice, however, owing to its high computation complexity. A brief introduction to the Paillier cryptosystem is presented as below.

Key generation. Select two large prime numbers p and q randomly, and compute their product N and the least common multiple λ of $p-1$ and $q-1$, respectively. That is

$$N = pq, \tag{2}$$

$$\lambda = \mathrm{lcm}(p-1, q-1). \tag{3}$$

Choose a random integer $g \in \mathbb{Z}^*_{N^2}$. $\mathbb{Z}^*_{N^2}$ denotes the subset of $\mathbb{Z}_{N^2}$ in which each element is relatively prime with N^2, $\mathbb{Z}_{N^2}$ is the set of the integer numbers modulo N^2. λ is the private key and (N, g) is the public key.

Encryption. Let $m \in \mathbb{Z}_N$ be the plaintext, so the corresponding ciphertext is computed as

$$c = E[m, r] = g^m r^N \bmod N^2 \tag{4}$$

where $r \in \mathbb{Z}^*_N$ is an integer chosen at random. According to the Paillier cryptosystem the ciphertext c is in $\mathbb{Z}^*_{N^2}$.

Decryption. Let $c \in \mathbb{Z}^*_{N^2}$ be the ciphertext. The plaintext corresponding to c can be computed as

$$D[c] = \frac{L(c^\lambda \bmod N^2)}{L(g^\lambda \bmod N^2)} \bmod N \tag{5}$$

where $L(\cdot)$ denotes the function

$$L(u) = \frac{u-1}{N}. \quad (6)$$

The following equalities show some useful homomorphic properties of the Paillier cryptosystem

$$D\left[E\left[m_1, r_1\right] E\left[m_2, r_2\right] \bmod N^2\right] = m_1 + m_2 \bmod N, \quad (7)$$

$$D\left[E\left[m, r\right]^k \bmod N^2\right] = km \bmod N, \ \forall k \in \mathbb{Z}_N. \quad (8)$$

These properties will be applied in the following sections to address the performance of DWT and MRA in the encrypted domain.

3. DISCRETE WAVELET TRANSFORM IN THE ENCRYPTED DOMAIN

In this section, we discuss how to model DWT in the encrypted domain and how to compute the upper bound on the encrypted wavelet coefficients.

3.1 Integer Approximation and Evaluation

DWT is a tool used widely in the field of signal processing. Compared with DFT, DWT has several advantages. One advantage is that DWT can capture both the frequency and location of the input signal. Another advantage is that, for a finite-length signal with the length n, the computational complexity of DWT is $O(n)$ while that of FFT, the fastest algorithm for computing DFT, is $O(n \log n)$.

According to Mallat's algorithm [16], DWT can be defined recursively as

$$a_j(k) = \frac{1}{\sqrt{2}} \sum_{l \in \mathbb{Z}} h_d(2k-l) a_{j-1}(l) \quad (9)$$

$$d_j(k) = \frac{1}{\sqrt{2}} \sum_{l \in \mathbb{Z}} g_d(2k-l) a_{j-1}(l) \quad (10)$$

where $h_d(k)$ and $g_d(k)$ are the low-pass decomposition filter coefficients and high-pass decomposition filter coefficients, respectively, and $j = 1, 2, 3, \ldots$ is the decomposition level of the input signal. $a_j(k)$ and $d_j(k)$, termed the approximation coefficients and detail coefficients respectively, can be computed from $a_{j-1}(k)$. $a_0(l)$ is defined as the input signal which is denoted by $x(l)$. For convenience, we sometimes use $X_j(k)$ to represent both $a_j(k)$ and $d_j(k)$.

Since both the plaintext and the ciphertext are represented by integers in the cryptosystem, all the signal data and the algorithm parameters must also be represented by integers. For the sake of simplicity, we will assume all the elements of the input signal are integers. That is $x(l) \in \mathbb{Z}$. Because $x(l)$ may not always be positive, the problem of how to represent negative integers in the cryptosystem should be carefully considered. Assuming N is the modulus used by the cryptosystem, we let $N \geq 2\sup\{|x(l)|\}+1$, where $\sup\{\cdot\}$ denotes the least upper bound operator performed on a sequence. For convenience, $\sup\{|x(l)|\}$ will be denoted by U_x in the following. We obtain $z(l) = x(l) \bmod N$ from $x(l)$ as

$$z(l) = \begin{cases} x(l), & \text{for } x(l) \geq 0 \\ x(l) + N. & \text{for } x(l) < 0 \end{cases} \quad (11)$$

Therefore there is a bijective function from $\{x(l)\}$ to $\{z(l)\}$, and we can obtain the exact value of $x(l)$ from $z(l)$. When $z(l)$ and N are known, $x(l)$ can be obtained from $z(l)$ by using (11), without confusion.

Generally speaking, the decomposition filter coefficients $h_d(k)$ and $g_d(k)$ are real numbers. In order to carry out the implementation of DWT in the encrypted domain, some suitable integer coefficients should be used instead of the real ones. Those integer coefficients can be obtained by quantizing $h_d(k)$ and $g_d(k)$. The quantization process can be described as

$$H_d(k) = \lfloor Q h_d(k) \rceil \quad (12)$$

$$G_d(k) = \lfloor Q g_d(k) \rceil \quad (13)$$

where $\lfloor \cdot \rceil$ is the rounding function and Q is the scaling factor determined by practical applications. We will assume Q is an integer in the following.

According to the above discussion, we give the recursive definition of the integer approximation of the DWT as

$$A_j(k) = \sum_{l \in \mathbb{Z}} H_d(2k-l) A_{j-1}(l) \quad (14)$$

$$D_j(k) = \sum_{l \in \mathbb{Z}} G_d(2k-l) A_{j-1}(l) \quad (15)$$

where $j = 1, 2, 3, \ldots$ and $A_0(l)$ is defined as equal to $x(l)$. Similarly, we sometimes use $S_j(k)$ to represent both $A_j(k)$ and $D_j(k)$.

Since all the computations are either integer multiplications or integer additions, (14) and (15) can be computed in the encrypted domain by using the homomorphic properties. In the case that the input signal is encrypted with the Paillier cryptosystem, by means of the equations (7) and (8), the implementation of the DWT in the encrypted domain is given as

$$E\left[A_j(k)\right] = \prod_{l \in \mathbb{Z}} E\left[A_{j-1}(k)\right]^{H_d(2k-l)} \quad (16)$$

$$E\left[D_j(k)\right] = \prod_{l \in \mathbb{Z}} E\left[A_{j-1}(k)\right]^{G_d(2k-l)} \quad (17)$$

where all the multiplications and exponentiations are carried out under the square of the modulus. The procedure for implementing multi-level DWT in the encrypted domain is shown in Fig. 1.

Although we mainly discuss in the encrypted domain based on the Paillier cryptosystem, our technique can easily be extend to the fully homomorphic cryptosystem. Assuming **Add**() and **Mult**() are the two algorithms in fully-homomorphic encryption corresponding to the plain addition and multiplication, respectively. Then (14) is implemented in the fully-homomorphic encrypted domain as

$$E\left[A_j(k)\right] = \underset{l \in \mathbb{Z}}{\mathbf{Add}}\left(\mathbf{Mult}\left(E\left[A_{j-1}(k)\right], E\left[H_d(2k-l)\right]\right)\right) \quad (18)$$

The framework developed in this paper can be extended to fully-homomorphic encryption in the similar way.

3.2 Expanding Factor and Upper Bound

In order to implement DWT in the encrypted domain by using (16) and (17), we need to consider certain issues. One is whether we are able to recover $S_j(k)$ from the decryption of $E[S_j(k)]$ without error. Another one is how to obtain the

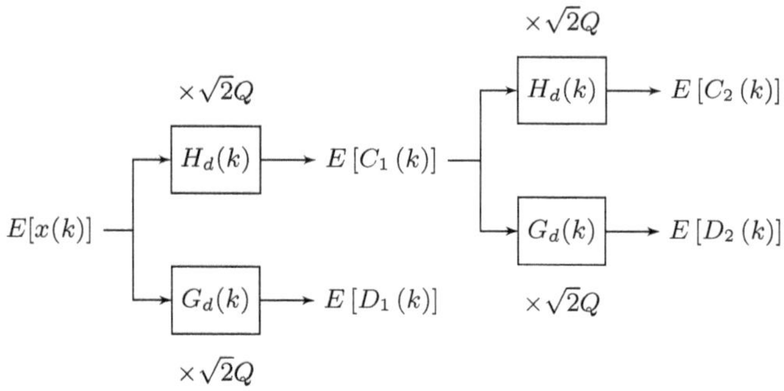

Figure 1: Block diagram of two-level DWT in the encrypted domain.

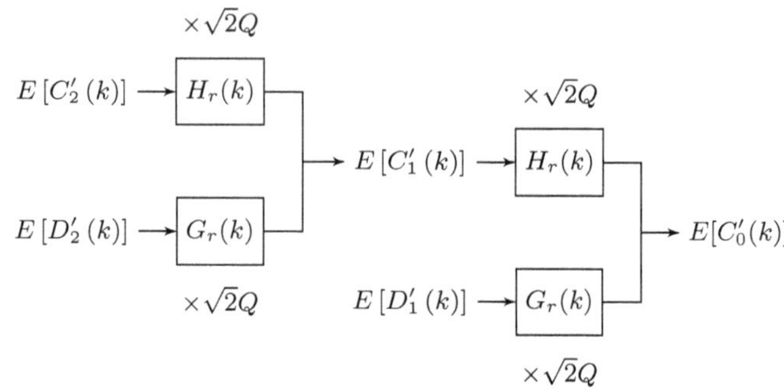

Figure 2: Block diagram of two-level IDWT in encrypted domain.

plain wavelet coefficient $X_j(k)$ when the recovery requirement is satisfied. Assuming the modulus of the cryptosystem is N, then $D[E[S_j(k)]]$ is equal to $Z_j(k) = S_j(k) \bmod N$. If all $S_j(k)$ are positive, we only need $\sup\{S_j(k)\} + 1 \leq N$ to recover $S_j(k)$ from $Z_j(k)$. This assumption may not be correct, however, since $S_j(k)$ can sometimes be negative. For the purpose of recovering the negative value of $S_j(k)$, the modulus N should satisfy the condition that $N > 2\sup_k\{|S_j(k)|\} + 1 = 2U_{S_j} + 1$. Then $S_j(k)$ can be obtained as

$$S_j(k) = \begin{cases} D[E[S_j(k)]], & \text{for } Z_j(k) < N/2 \\ D[E[S_j(k)]] - N. & \text{for } Z_j(k) > N/2 \end{cases} \quad (19)$$

Owing to the quantization process of wavelet filter coefficients, there will be an expanding factor K_j between $S_j(k)$ and $X_j(k)$. Therefore the plain wavelet coefficient $X_j(k)$ can be approximated as $\tilde{X}_j(k) = S_j(k)/K_j$. Hence, investigation of the expanding factor K_j and the upper bound U_{S_j} will make significant sense in terms of the practical implementation of DWT in the encrypted domain.

In the light of the above discussion, we express $S_j(k)$ by using $X_j(k)$ and K_j, that is,

$$S_j(k) = K_j X_j(k) + \epsilon_{S_j}(k) \quad (20)$$

where $\epsilon_{S_j}(k)$ denotes the accumulated error of the j-level implementation. From the above equation, we have $|S_j(k)| \leq K_j|X_j(k)| + |\epsilon_{S_j}(k)|$. Therefore a formal upper bound on $|S_j(k)|$ is expressed as

$$|S_j(k)| \leq \left\lfloor K_j \sup_k\{|X_j(k)|\} + \sup_k\left\{|\epsilon_{S_j}(k)|\right\} \right\rfloor \triangleq U_{S_j} \quad (21)$$

where $\lfloor\cdot\rfloor$ is the floor function. The value of $\sup\left\{|\epsilon_{S_j}(k)|\right\}$ and K_j depends on the quantization factor Q and the decomposition/reconstruction level of the DWT/IDWT. In the following, we discuss those issues in detail.

3.2.1 One-Level Decomposition

If we introduce a quantization error $\epsilon_{H_d}(k)$ in the process of (14), then the quantized low-pass decomposition filter coefficients in (12) can be expressed as $H_d(k) = Qh_d(k) + \epsilon_{H_d}(k)$. Assuming that the one-level approximation coefficients is computed by using (14), we obtain

$$A_1(k) = \sqrt{2}Qa_1(k) + \sum_{l\in\mathbb{Z}} x(l)\epsilon_{H_d}(2k-l) \quad (22)$$

from which we find that the expanding factor is $K_1 = \sqrt{2}Q$.

The upper bound on $A_1(k)$ is considered as below. It is obvious that $|\epsilon_{H_d}(k)| \leq 1/2$. According to the theory of wavelet analysis [17], $a_1(k)$ is the projection of $x(l)$ on a vector in the function space. By applying the *Bessel inequality* [18], we have $|a_1(k)|^2 \leq \|\mathbf{x}\|_2^2$, where $\|\cdot\|_2$ denotes the Euclidean norm operator performed on a vector. If $x(l)$ is a finite sequence of length n, then $\|\mathbf{x}\|_2^2 \leq nU_x^2$ and $\sum x(l) \leq nU_x$. By using substitution, we get an inequality

$$|A_1(k)| \leq \sqrt{2n}U_xQ + \frac{nU_x}{2}. \quad (23)$$

Similarly, an inequality on $D_1(k)$ can be obtained as

$$|D_1(k)| \leq \sqrt{2n}U_xQ + \frac{nU_x}{2}. \quad (24)$$

From the inequalities (23) and (24), we derive the upper bound on S_1 as $U_{S_1} = \lfloor\sqrt{2n}U_xQ + nU_x/2\rfloor$.

3.2.2 Generalization to Multi-Level Decomposition

Since the low-pass decomposition in (14) and the high-pass decomposition in (15) are equivalent for our analysis, without loss of generality, we first consider the low-pass decomposition. Assuming the $(j-1)$-level approximation coefficients have been obtained as $A_{j-1}(k) = K_{j-1}a_{j-1}(k) + \epsilon_{A_{j-1}}(k)$ with respect to the quantization error $\epsilon_{A_{j-1}}(k)$, and by using the substitution method, we have

$$A_j(k) = \sqrt{2}QK_{j-1}a_j(k) + \sum_{l\in\mathbb{Z}}\Big[Qh_d(2k-l)\epsilon_{A_{j-1}}(l) + K_{j-1}a_{j-1}(l)\epsilon_{H_d}(2k-l) + \epsilon_{H_d}(2k-l)\epsilon_{A_{j-1}}(l)\Big] \quad (25)$$

from which the recursive relations on the expanding factor and the accumulated error can be derived as

$$K_j = \sqrt{2}QK_{j-1} \quad (26)$$

$$\epsilon_{A_j}(k) = \sum_{l\in\mathbb{Z}}\Big[Qh_d(2k-l)\epsilon_{A_{j-1}}(l) + K_{j-1}a_{j-1}(l) \times \epsilon_{H_d}(2k-l) + \epsilon_{H_d}(2k-l)\epsilon_{A_{j-1}}(l)\Big]. \quad (27)$$

Since $A_0(l) = x(l)$, the recursion (26) starts with $K_0 = 1$. By applying $K_0 = 1$ in (26), we derive the j-level expanding

Table 1: The expanding factors and the upper bounds for different decomposition/reconstruction of DWT/IDWT in the encrypted domain

	The Expanding Factor	The Upper Bound on the Processed Data
1-level DWT	$\sqrt{2}Q$	$\lfloor \sqrt{2n}U_xQ + nU_x/2 \rfloor$
j-level DWT	$(\sqrt{2}Q)^j$	$\lfloor \sqrt{n}U_x(\sqrt{2}Q)^j + (\frac{n}{2}U_x)\sum_{r=0}^{j}(nQ+\frac{n}{2})^{j-r-1}(\sqrt{2}Q)^r \rfloor$
j-level IDWT	$(\sqrt{2}Q)^{2\tau-j}$	$\lfloor \sqrt{n}U_x(\sqrt{2}Q)^{2\tau-j} + (2nQ+n)^3\epsilon_{S_\tau,\text{sup}} + (nU_x)\sum_{r=0}^{\tau-j}(2nQ+n)^r(\sqrt{2}Q)^{2\tau-r} \rfloor$

factor as $K_j = (\sqrt{2}Q)^j$, which depends on the value of j and Q.

The upper bound on $\epsilon_{A_j}(k)$ can be evaluated as below. If $x(l)$ is a sequence with the length n, thanks to the *Bessel inequality*, $\left|\sum h_d(2k-l)\epsilon_{A_{j-1}}(l)\right|^2 \le \left\|\epsilon_{A_{j-1}}\right\|_2^2 \le n\left|\epsilon_{A_{j-1}}\right|$ and $\sum |a_j(l)|^2 \le \|\mathbf{x}\|_2^2$. Hence, an equivalent recursive relation on the upper bound of the accumulated error in (27) is given as

$$\left|\epsilon_{A_j}\right| \le \left(nQ + \frac{n}{2}\right)\left|\epsilon_{A_{j-1}}\right| + \frac{n}{2}U_xK_{j-1}. \quad (28)$$

Obviously, by using the initial condition $|\epsilon_{A_0}| = 0$ in (28), we can estimate the upper bound on $|\epsilon_{A_j}|$ as

$$\left|\epsilon_{A_j}\right| \le \left(\frac{n}{2}U_x\right)\sum_{r=0}^{j}\left(nQ+\frac{n}{2}\right)^{j-r-1}\left(\sqrt{2}Q\right)^r = \epsilon_{S_j,\text{sup}}. \quad (29)$$

Because $\left|\epsilon_{D_j}\right|$ is bounded by the same $\epsilon_{S_j,\text{sup}}$, we finally derive the upper bound on $S_j(k)$ as $U_{S_j} = \lfloor \sqrt{n}U_x\left(\sqrt{2}Q\right)^j + \epsilon_{S_j,sup}\rfloor$.

4. INVERSE DISCRETE WAVELET TRANSFORM IN THE ENCRYPTED DOMAIN

In this section, we build a new reconstruction mechanism of DWT in the encrypted domain and provide an upper bound on the accumulated quantization error.

4.1 Evaluation

According to the fast algorithm proposed by Mallat [16], IDWT can be defined recursively as

$$a_j(k) = \frac{1}{\sqrt{2}}\sum_{l\in\mathbb{Z}} h_r(k-2l)a_{j+1}(l) + g_r(k-2l)d_{j+1}(l) \quad (30)$$

where $h_r(k)$ and $g_r(k)$ are the low-pass reconstruction filter coefficients and high-pass reconstruction filter coefficients, respectively.

In order to carry out the implementation of IDWT in the encrypted domain, the reconstruction filter coefficients $h_r(k)$ and $g_r(k)$ must be first converted to suitable integers. Without loss of generality, we assume the integer reconstruction filter coefficients have the same quantization factor as the integer decomposition filter coefficients. Then the quantization process of the reconstruction filter coefficients is described as

$$H_r(k) = \lfloor Qh_r(k) \rceil \quad (31)$$

$$G_r(k) = \lfloor Qg_r(k) \rceil \quad (32)$$

where Q is the quantization factor which is identical to the one in (12) and (13).

A similar approach leads to the definition of the integer IDWT. Assuming we have already performed the τ-level integer DWT with a quantization factor Q, the integer IDWT is defined recursively as

$$A'_j(k) = \sum_{l\in\mathbb{Z}} H_r(k-2l)A'_{j+1}(l) + G_r(k-2l)D'_{j+1}(l) \quad (33)$$

where $j = \tau-1,\ldots,1,0$ is the reconstruction level and $D'_{j+1}(l)$ is defined as $D_{j+1}(l)Q^{2(\tau-j-1)}$. The superscript $'$ is added to denote the integer approximation of j-level reconstructed coefficients. Since the reconstruction starts from the τ-level decomposed coefficients, we define $A'_\tau(k) = A_\tau(k)$ and $D'_\tau(k) = D_\tau(k)$. Note that replacing $D_{j+1}(l)$ with $D'_{j+1}(l)$ in (33) is necessary, in order to add the integer detail coefficients $D_{j+1}(l)$ by the same scaling factor of the corresponding integer approximation coefficients $A'_{j+1}(l)$.

Since all the input arguments are integers, (33) can be computed in the encrypted domain as

$$E\left[A'_j(k)\right] = \prod_{l\in\mathbb{Z}} E\left[A'_{j+1}(l)\right]^{H_r(k-2l)} E\left[D'_{j+1}(l)\right]^{G_r(k-2l)} \quad (34)$$

For the value of $E\left[D'_{j+1}(l)\right]$, based on the homomorphic properties, it is easy to obtain $E\left[D'_{j+1}(l)\right]$ from $E\left[D_{j+1}(l)\right]$ as

$$E\left[D'_{j+1}(l)\right] = E\left[D_{j+1}(l)\right]^{Q^{2(\tau-j-1)}} \quad (35)$$

In Fig. 2, we show the procedure for implementing multi-level IDWT in the encrypted domain.

4.2 Upper Bound and Reconstruction Error

In order to evaluate the reconstruction performance, we must find an upper bound on the reconstruction errors. If some quantization errors are introduced in the process of (31) and (32), then we have $H_r(k) = Qh_r(k) + \epsilon_{H_r}(k)$ and $G_r(k) = Qg_r(k) + \epsilon_{G_r}(k)$. Assuming the $(j+1)$-level reconstruction coefficients have been obtained as $A'_{j+1}(k) = K'_{j+1}a_{j+1}(k) + \epsilon_{A'_{j+1}}(k)$ and $D'_{j+1}(k) = K'_{j+1}d_{j+1}(k) + \epsilon_{D'_{j+1}}(k)$. By using simple substitution in (33), we have

$$\begin{aligned} A'_j(k) = \sqrt{2}QK'_{j+1}A_j(k) + \sum_{l\in\mathbb{Z}} \Big[& Qh_r(k-2l)\epsilon_{A'_{j+1}}(l) \\ & + Qg_r(k-2l)\epsilon_{D'_{j+1}}(l) + K'_j a_{j+1}(l)\epsilon_{H_r}(k-2l) \\ & + K'_j d_{j+1}(l)\epsilon_{G_r}(k-2l) + \epsilon_{H_r}(k-2l)\epsilon_{A'_{j+1}}(l) \\ & + \epsilon_{G_r}(k-2l)\epsilon_{D'_{j+1}}(l) \Big]. \end{aligned} \quad (36)$$

If $x(l)$ is a sequence of finite length n, by using the similar deduction presented in Section 3.2.2, we obtain recursive relations for the expanding factor and the accumulated error as

$$K'_j = \sqrt{2}QK'_{j+1}, \quad (37)$$

$$\left|\epsilon_{A'_j}\right| \le (2nQ+n)\left|\epsilon_{A'_{j+1}}\right| + nU_x K'_{j+1}. \quad (38)$$

Moreover, since we reconstruct the signal from the τ-level decomposed coefficients, the initial condition of the recursion is $K'_\tau = (\sqrt{2}Q)^\tau$ and $\left|\epsilon_{A'_\tau}\right| = \left|\epsilon_{A_\tau}\right| = \epsilon_{S_\tau,\text{sup}}$. Hence, it is easy to obtain the expanding factor as $K'_j = (\sqrt{2}Q)^{2\tau-j}$. For the upper bound on the accumulated error, we have

$$\begin{aligned}\left|\epsilon_{A'_j}\right| &\le (2nQ+n)^3 \epsilon_{S_\tau,\text{sup}} \\ &+ (nU_x)\sum_{r=0}^{\tau-j}(2nQ+n)^r\left(\sqrt{2}Q\right)^{2\tau-r} \\ &= \epsilon_{S'_j,\text{sup}}.\end{aligned} \quad (39)$$

Thus, the upper bound on $A'_j(k)$ is given as $\lfloor\sqrt{n}U_x\left(\sqrt{2}Q\right)^{2\tau-j} + \epsilon_{S'_j,\text{sup}}\rfloor$. In particular, by applying $j=\tau$ in (39), we obtain an upper bound on the reconstruction error of the reconstruction mechanism in the encrypted domain.

The expanding factors and the upper bounds on the transform coefficients for different decomposition/reconstruction are summarized in Table 1.

5. IMPROVEMENT TO REDUCE DATA EXPANSION

In this section, we discuss the data expansion in the encrypted domain and propose an improved method to remove the expanding factor in the case of performing both DWT and IDWT.

5.1 Data Expansion in the Encrypted Domain

The data expansion is caused by the quantization of the filter coefficients. Each implementation of one-level DWT (or IDWT) in the encrypted domain will almost expand the plain value by a fixed factor, $\sqrt{2}Q$. The data expansion will become important in three situations. The first is the implementation of MRA in the encrypted domain. As discussed in Section 3.2 and Section 4.2, the expanding factor K will enlarge exponentially as the decomposition/reconstruction level increases. The second is the processing of multi-dimensional signals. If i is the dimension of the input signal, then K will also increase exponentially as i increases. The third is the case where both DWT and IDWT are performed, such as watermarking, compression, filtering and feature extraction. The procedures are shown in Fig. 3. In these applications, the data expansion is twice that of the one where single DWT/IDWT is performed.

Moreover, the scale factor Q decides the quantization precision of filter coefficients. Therefore Q implies the precision of the approximation of integer DWT/IDWT. In general, Q must be large enough to satisfy the precision requirement determined by practical applications. Let us consider a simple example below. Assume the input is a 2D signal encrypted with the Paillier cryptosystem whose modulus N is 1024 bits. The application requires Q to be 64 bits. Five level DWT and IDWT are performed on the encrypted

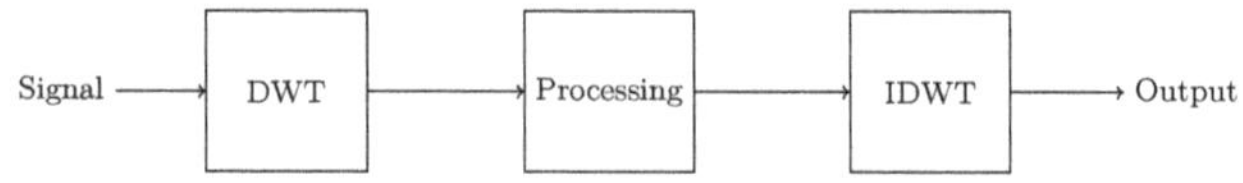

Figure 3: Block diagram of ordinary signal processing based on DWT. The processing includes watermarking, compressing, filtering and feature extraction, etc.

signal. Based on the analysis above, the final processed data is at least 1920(=(64×2+1)×5×2) bits. This means the plain value of the processed data is much larger than $\lceil (N-1)/2 \rceil$. And we cannot correctly recover the desired value from $D[E[S_j(k)]]$ by using (19). The data expansion greatly limits the application of the encrypted DWT/IDWT in practice.

5.2 Rational Filter Coefficients Wavelets

Let us consider rational filter coefficients wavelets, such as the Haar wavelet, the CDF 5/3 wavelet [19] and the biorthogonal spline wavelet family [20]. In mathematics, any rational number can be expressed as a quotient of two relatively prime numbers. If we assume the wavelet filters are of finite length, then there is a least common multiple among all the denominators. We denote the least common multiple by L. When the quantization factor Q is the multiple of L, that is,

$$Q \bmod L = 0 \quad (40)$$

the quantization processes (12), (13), (31) and (32) will product no quantization error. Without loss of generality, we assume Q is equal to L for rational filter coefficients wavelets in the following. This is easily achieved for most rational filter coefficient wavelets, such as the Haar wavelet, the CDF 5/3 wavelet and the biorthogonal spline wavelet family.

Since there is no quantization error in the quantization process, the deduction of the relationship between $S_j(k)$ and $X_j(k)$ becomes very elegant. Specifically, $\epsilon_{H_d}=0$, $\epsilon_{G_d}=0$ and $S_1(k)=\sqrt{2}QX_1(k)$. By using these initial conditions in (14) and (15), we obtain

$$S_j(k) = \left(\sqrt{2}Q\right)^j X_j(k). \quad (41)$$

Similarly, for the case of performing IDWT in the encrypted domain, $S'_j(k)$ is expressed as

$$S'_j(k) = \left(\sqrt{2}Q\right)^{2\tau-j} X'_j(k). \quad (42)$$

If τ-level IDWT is performed, then the plain value of the processed data is given as

$$S'_0(k) = \left(2Q^2\right)^\tau x(k). \quad (43)$$

5.3 Multiplicative Inverse Method

According to the definition of the homomorphic cryptosystem, all the plain-domain computation takes place in the finite ring $\mathbb{Z}_N$. When $S'_0(k)$ is greater than $\lceil (N-1)/2 \rceil$, we cannot obtain the correct value from $D[E[S'_0(k)]]$ by using (19). Since the data expansion is very common in the encrypted domain, the issue of recovering correct value from $D[E[S'_0(k)]]$ faces serious challenge. Therefore a method to remove the data expansion in the encrypted domain will be necessary for practical applications. We propose our improved method in the following.

We first give a assumption, i.e., Q is relatively prime with N. This assumption is proved reasonable in Section 5.4. To make the cryptosystem hard to break, p and q are always two large prime numbers greater than 2. Therefore $N = pq$ is relatively prime with 2. Since Q and 2 are both relatively prime with N, the expanding factor $K = 2^{\tau} Q^{2\tau}$ is relatively prime with N. Owing to the properties of the finite ring $\mathbb{Z}_N$, there is an element $\Theta \in \mathbb{Z}$, such that,

$$\Theta \cdot K \bmod N = 1 \tag{44}$$

where Θ is the modular multiplicative inverse of K in $\mathbb{Z}_N$. Θ is most efficiently computed by using the Euclidean algorithm [21].

In order to remove the data expansion, we multiply Θ on both sides of (43) to take away the factor K. According to the properties of the module multiplication and the equation (44), we have

$$\begin{aligned}\left(\Theta \cdot S_0'(k)\right) \bmod N &= (\Theta \cdot K \bmod N) \cdot (x(k) \bmod N) \\ &= x(k) \bmod N. \end{aligned} \tag{45}$$

The upper bound on $x(k)$ is naturally less than $\lfloor (N-1)/2 \rfloor$. Therefore we can recover the correct value of $x(k)$ from $(\Theta S_0'(k)) \bmod N$. The above process can be carried out in the encrypted domain by using the homomorphic properties,

$$E\left[S_0'(k)\right]^{\Theta} = E\left[\Theta \cdot S_0'(k) \bmod N\right] = E\left[x(k) \bmod N\right]. \tag{46}$$

The multiplicative inverse method requires no additional information about $x(k)$, so it does not need any interactive protocols to transfer information. It is carried out by the person who performs DWT/IDWT in the encrypted domain. Note that we cannot multiply some module multiplicative inverse on (41) to remove the scaling factor. The reason is that the wavelet coefficient $X_j(k)$ is not always an integer. Whereas $x(k)$ in (43) is always an integer, so the expanding factor K can be removed with the multiplicative inverse method.

Although there is a scale factor between the plain value of $E\left[S_0'(k)\right]$ and the desired value $x(k)$, we can remove the scaling factor without decryption. In the case $D\left[E\left[S_0'(k)\right]\right]$ exceeds $\lceil (N-1)/2 \rceil$, the decryption cannot output the expected result, but we still obtain the desired value $x(k)$ with the multiplicative inverse method.

5.4 Proof of the Assumption

We consider the probability that Q is relatively prime with N. Sine N is a product of two prime numbers p and q, the assumption that Q is relatively prime with N is equivalent to that Q is relatively prime with both p and q. The element in $\mathbb{Z}_N$, which is not relatively prime with N, is either the multiple of p or the multiple of q. The multiples of p in the ring $\mathbb{Z}_N$ are listed as

$$0,\ p,\ 2p,\ 3p,\ \cdots,\ (q-1)p,$$

and the multiples of q in the ring $\mathbb{Z}_N$ are listed as

$$0,\ q,\ 2q,\ 3q,\ \cdots,\ (p-1)q.$$

Therefore the number of the elements which are not relatively prime with N in $\mathbb{Z}_N$ is $(N+1-p-q)$. We compute

Figure 4: Encrypted image using the secure cryptosystem with a key longer than 1024 bits.

the probability that Q is not relatively prime with N, i.e.,

$$P = \frac{N+1-p-q}{N} = 1 + \frac{1}{N} - \frac{1}{p} - \frac{1}{q}. \tag{47}$$

The security of the cryptosystem increases as the value of N increases. It is reasonable to consider the situation where both p and q tend to infinity. $\frac{1}{N}$, $\frac{1}{p}$ and $\frac{1}{q}$ tend to zero as both of p and q tend to infinity. Therefore the probability that Q is relatively prime with N tends to one in the same manner. That is

$$\lim_{p,q\to\infty} P = 1 + \lim_{N\to\infty} \frac{1}{N} - \lim_{p\to\infty} \frac{1}{p} - \lim_{q\to\infty} \frac{1}{q} = 1 \tag{48}$$

from which we obtain that Q is relatively prime with N when p and q are sufficiently large.

In fact, N should be 1024 bits long according to [5]. Choosing two primes of equal length will make the cryptosystem more difficult to break. Without loss of generality, we consider the case that p and q are of equal length. We compute the probability P under the condition that N is 1024 bits long. Since both p and q are 512 bits long, we have

$$\frac{1}{p} = \frac{1}{q} = 2^{-512} \approx 7.4583 \times 10^{-155}, \tag{49}$$

$$\frac{1}{N} = 2^{-1024} \approx 5.5627 \times 10^{-309}. \tag{50}$$

The probability P is evaluated as

$$P \approx 1 + 5.5627 \times 10^{-309} - 2 \times 7.4583 \times 10^{-155} \approx 1. \tag{51}$$

This means the probability P is almost equal to one. Therefore the assumption that Q is relatively prime with N is reasonable in practical applications.

6. EXPERIMENTS AND PERFORMANCE ANALYSIS

In this section, we investigate the use of our proposed technique and the multiplicative inverse method for media processing.

6.1 Simulation Experiments

We choose the grayscale image 'Lena' of $512 \times 512 \times 8$ bits as the plain signal. We exploit 2D Haar wavelet in the experiments and choose two primes for our cryptosystem, i.e.,

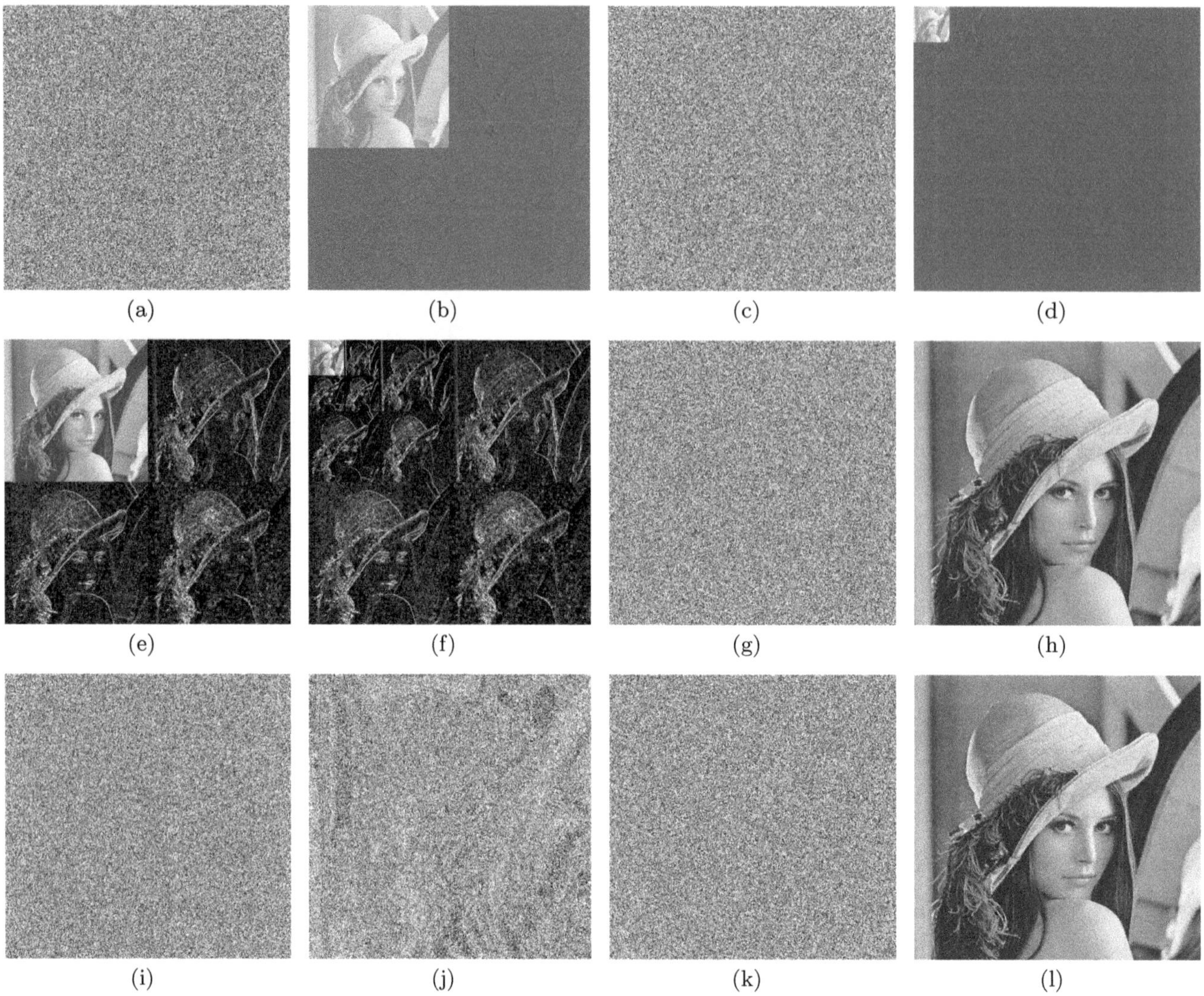

Figure 5: 2D Haar wavelet transform on an encrypted image: (a) One-level decomposition; (b) Decryption of one-level decomposition; (c) Three-level decomposition; (d) Decryption of three-level decomposition; (e) Contrast enhancement of one-level decomposition; (f) Contrast enhancement of three-level decomposition; (g) Three-level reconstruction; (h) Decryption of three-level reconstruction; (i) Five-level reconstruction; (j) Decryption of the new reconstruction; (k) The reconstruction with the multiplicative inverse method; (l) Result with the multiplicative inverse method.

$p = $ 9124096438171898962507570330221592470936908683613826010222874120352771834353040209664805046240893943174592905232588226985963062204933329673339949274073133 and $q = $ 2624504701366621622376486977663882833260732271643397089032621456092547481202656356838326913432117528590720429153417667854310169901529304328379156928626395 1. The product of p and q is longer than 1024 bits. The upper bound U_x on the image is 255. Obviously, U_x is much smaller than the value of $\lfloor (N-1)/2 \rfloor$, so the encryption can be carried out without confusion. We show the encrypted image in Fig. 4, which is secure enough to protect the image. We take this encrypted image as the input signal and begin the experiment as below.

Firstly, we perform one-level DWT on the encrypted image. Since all the denominators of the filter coefficients are 1, the least common multiple L is equal to 1. Let the quantization factor Q be 1. According the upper bounds we have derived, the integer coefficients Q_{S_1} is bounded by 261120, which is less than $\lfloor (N-1)/2 \rfloor$. We can recover the plain wavelet coefficients. The experiment result is shown in Fig. 6(a)-6(b).

Secondly, we perform three-level DWT on the encrypted image. After simple computation, we have the upper bound $Q_{S_3} = 1044480$, which is also less than $\lfloor (N-1)/2 \rfloor$. In Fig. 6(c)-6(d), we show the experimental result of this step. In order to make the wavelet transforms look clear, we modify the contrast and show them in Fig. 6(e)-6(f).

Thirdly, we perform three-level IDWT on the encrypted wavelet coefficients. We show the result and its decryption in Fig. 6(g)-6(h). Since the upper bound $Q_{S'_3} = 8355840 < \lfloor (N-1)/2 \rfloor$, the decryption looks the same as the plain image.

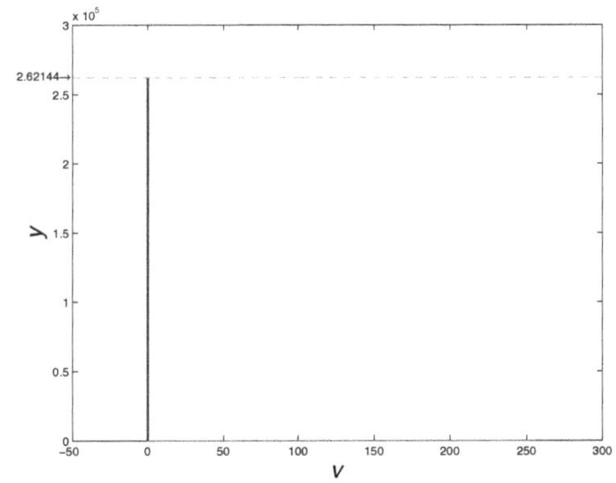

Figure 6: Error histogram. v is the bin location and y denotes the frequency count. There are 262144 samples in the test image.

In the simulation experiments above, we show the validity of the proposed framework, which helps to implement DWT/IDWT in the encrypted domain.

6.2 Multiplicative Inverse Method

For the sake of simplicity, we let $Q = 2^{64}$ be the quantization factor of the Haar wavelet filter coefficients. We first perform five-level DWT on the input encrypted image and then perform five-level IDWT on the encrypted transform coefficients. We show the encrypted reconstruction and its decryption in Fig. 6(i)-6(j). Obviously, the decryption image looks like a noisy image. It is quite different from the plain image that we expect to get. By using the multiplicative inverse method, we compute the power of the reconstruction data with an exponent Θ. Θ is the inverse element of the expanding factor. The processed result and its decryption is shown in Fig. 6(k)-6(l). The decryption seems the same as the original image 'Lena'. In order to detail the differences of those two images, we count the number of the error. The error histogram is given in Fig. 6, where all the samples are in zero valued bin. Therefore we obtain that there is no distortion between the two images.

6.3 Performance Comparison

The multiplicative inverse method is still useful when the recovery requirement is satisfied. We can use it to reduce the value range of the processed data. Let us consider the third step of the experiments in Section 6.1. We perform the multiplicative inverse method on the encrypted reconstruction data. The decryption of the processed result is identical to Fig. 5(l). In order to compare Fig. 5(h) and Fig. 5(l), we perform a logarithm function on both matrices and plot the first rows in Fig. 7. The shapes of both curves are the same, while the curve with the improved method lies far below the other one. This means the multiplicative inverse method greatly reduces the value range of the processed data in the encrypted domain.

6.4 Investigating the Θ value

We can compute Θ efficiently by using the Euclid algorithm. The value of Θ mainly depends on four parameters: the quantization factor Q, the wavelet reconstruction level τ, the cryptosystem's modular N and the dimension i of the input signal. We investigate the value of Θ for some popular rational filter wavelet bases, including the Haar wavelet, the CDF 5/3 wavelet and the biorthogonal spline 1.3 wavelet. The input signal is assumed to be one dimension. Since a 1024 bits Θ is a lengthy string, we compute the value of Θ with a small key cryptosystem, i.e. $N = 106060113287377$. In Table 2, we summarize the value of the expansion factor K and its multiplicative inverse Θ for some frequently-used reconstruction levels.

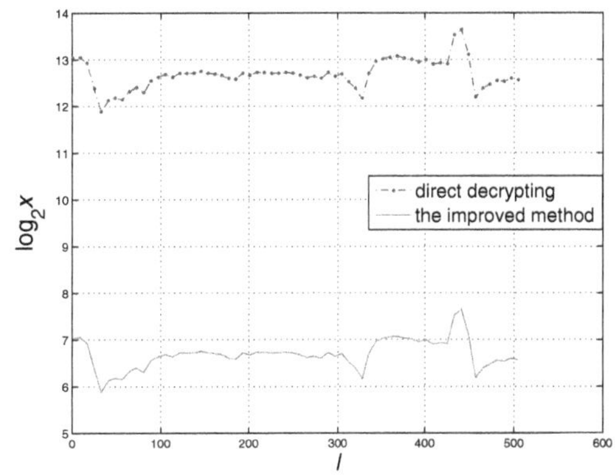

Figure 7: Value range comparison. l denotes the position of the sample and x is the value of the sample.

7. CONCLUSIONS AND FUTURE WORKS

This paper has investigated the implementation of DWT and MRA in a homomorphic encrypted domain, and tackled the problem of data expansion in practical applications. The main contributions are listed as follows:

1. We have described a technique to implement DWT and MRA in the encrypted domain by using homomorphic properties. Compared with plaintext DWT, DWT in the encrypted domain will greatly expand the plain value of signals. Thus we have derived an upper bound on the expanded data, irrespective of what kind of wavelet is involved.

2. For a class of wavelet transform, we have presented a method to perform DWT/IDWT in the encrypted domain without any quantization error. Based on that transform, an improved method is proposed to remove the expanding factor without decryption. The proposed method broadens the capacity of signal processing with the same cryptosystem parameters.

3. We have investigated the case of 2D Haar wavelet transform in our experiments. The experiments confirm the validity of our framework and demonstrate the advantages of the improved method.

Though an unscrupulous user can perform DWT on the encrypted data, it is impossible for him/her to extract any information from the transform coefficients. The reason is that the wavelet transforms on encrypted data is in encrypted form and he/she does not have the private key for decryption. Therefore, the technique described in this paper and the proposed algorithm are well suitable for secure and privacy-preserving multimedia applications, such as secure media filtering, secure feature extraction, secure face detection and secure watermarking.

The limitations of the proposed method are as follows. 1) The implementation of DWT in the homomorphic encrypted

Table 2: The expanding factor K and its multiplicative inverse Θ for three types of wavelet: the Haar wavelet, the CDF 5/3 wavelet and the biorthogonal spline 1.3 wavelet. The modulus is $N = 10606011328737$7.

Reconstruction level	The Haar Wavelet		The CDF 5/3 Wavelet		The Biorthogonal Spline 1.3 Wavelet	
	K	Θ	K	Θ	K	Θ
1	2	53030056643689	128	65458976169553	512	95909829007921
2	4	79545084965533	16384	105742916903644	262144	33123960628322
3	8	92802599126455	2097152	83685580044073	134217728	65937968722684
4	16	99431356206916	268435456	32968984361342	68719476736	93759978856674
5	32	49715678103458	34359738368	81459844425971	35184372088832	39541370123942

domain results in the store and computation overhead. With the existing homomorphic encryptions, the store overhead is very large since the input samples need to be encrypted separately. The homomorphic encryption turns the plain-domain operations (e.g. multiplications) to the cipher-domain operations (e.g. exponentiation), so the computation overhead is much larger than the plain one. 2) The proposed multiplicative inverse method which removes the expanding factor in the encrypted domain takes effect under the constraint that both DWT and IDWT are performed.

The future works will be in two aspects. One is to address the issues regarding the above limitations. It is necessary but very challenging to propose a method to reduce the store overhead. A fast algorithm to speed up the computation in the encrypted domain is also very meaningful. The other one is the extension of the multiplicative method. It can be extended to a general one for other cryptosystems and other signal transforms, for example, the DFT in the encrypted domain.

Acknowledgements

This work was supported by 973 Program (2011CB302204) and NSFC (61070167).

8. REFERENCES

[1] Z. Erkin, A. Piva, S. Katzenbeisser, RL Lagendijk, J. Shokrollahi, G. Neven, and M. Barni. Protection and retrieval of encrypted multimedia content: when cryptography meets signal processing. *EURASIP Journal on Information Security*, 2007:1–20, 2007.

[2] R.L. Rivest, L. Adleman, and M.L. Dertouzos. On data banks and privacy homomorphisms. *Foundations of secure computation*, pages 169–178, 1978.

[3] O. Goldreich, S. Micali, and A. Wigderson. How to play ANY mental game. In *Proceedings of the nineteenth annual ACM symposium on Theory of computing*, pages 218–229, 1987.

[4] T. ElGamal. A public key cryptosystem and a signature scheme based on discrete logarithms. pages 10–18, 1985.

[5] P. Paillier. Public-key cryptosystems based on composite degree residuosity classes. In *Advances in Cryptology–EUROCRYPT' 99*, pages 223–238. Springer, 1999.

[6] I. Damgård and M. Jurik. A generalisation, a simpli. cation and some applications of paillier's probabilistic public-key system. In *Public Key Cryptography*, pages 119–136. Springer, 2001.

[7] C. Gentry. Fully homomorphic encryption using ideal lattices. In *Proceedings of the 41st annual ACM symposium on Theory of computing*, pages 169–178, 2009.

[8] N. Memon and P.W. Wong. A buyer-seller watermarking protocol. *Image Processing, IEEE Transactions on*, 10(4):643–649, 2001.

[9] T. Bianchi, A. Piva, and M. Barni. On the implementation of the discrete fourier transform in the encrypted domain. *Information Forensics and Security, IEEE Transactions on*, 4(1):86–97, 2009.

[10] T. Bianchi, A. Piva, and M. Barni. Composite signal representation for fast and storage-efficient processing of encrypted signals. *Information Forensics and Security, IEEE Transactions on*, 5(1):180–187, 2010.

[11] Z. Erkin, M. Franz, J. Guajardo, S. Katzenbeisser, I. Lagendijk, and T. Toft. Privacy-preserving face recognition. In *Privacy Enhancing Technologies*, pages 235–253. Springer, 2009.

[12] A.R. Sadeghi, T. Schneider, and I. Wehrenberg. Efficient privacy-preserving face recognition. *Information, Security and Cryptology–ICISC 2009*, pages 229–244, 2010.

[13] T. Bianchi, S. Turchi, A. Piva, R.D. Labati, V. Piuri, and F. Scotti. Implementing fingercode-based identity matching in the encrypted domain. In *Biometric Measurements and Systems for Security and Medical Applications (BIOMS), 2010 IEEE Workshop on*, pages 15–21.

[14] P. Viola and M.J. Jones. Robust real-time face detection. *International journal of computer vision*, 57(2):137–154, 2004.

[15] S. Goldwasser and S. Micali. Probabilistic encryption. *Journal of computer and system sciences*, 28(2):270–299, 1984.

[16] S.G. Mallat. A theory for multiresolution signal decomposition: The wavelet representation. *Pattern Analysis and Machine Intelligence, IEEE Transactions on*, 11(7):674–693, 1989.

[17] I. Daubechies. *Ten lectures on wavelets.* Society for industrial and applied mathematics, 2004.

[18] W. Rudin. *Functional Analysis. 1991.* McGraw-Hill, New York.

[19] A. Cohen, I. Daubechies, and J.C. Feauveau. Biorthogonal bases of compactly supported wavelets. *Communications on pure and applied mathematics*, 45(5):485–560, 1992.

[20] S. Godavarthy. Generating spline wavelets. In *Proceedings of the 36th annual Southeast regional conference*, pages 8–14. ACM, 1998.

[21] A.J. Menezes, P.C. Van Oorschot, and S.A. Vanstone. *Handbook of applied cryptography.* CRC, 1997.

Multiple Feature Hashing for Real-time Large Scale Near-duplicate Video Retrieval *

Jingkuan Song
School of ITEE
The University of Queensland
QLD 4072, Australia
uqjsong1@uq.edu.au

Yi Yang
School of Computer Science
Carnegie Mellon University
Pittsburgh, PA 15213
yiyang@cs.cmu.edu

Zi Huang
School of ITEE
The University of Queensland
QLD 4072, Australia
huang@itee.uq.edu.au

Heng Tao Shen
School of ITEE
The University of Queensland
QLD 4072, Australia
shenht@itee.uq.edu.au

Richang Hong
School of Computer and Information
Hefei University of Technology
hongrc.hfut@gmail.com

ABSTRACT

Near-duplicate video retrieval (NDVR) has recently attracted lots of research attention due to the exponential growth of online videos. It helps in many areas, such as copyright protection, video tagging, online video usage monitoring, etc. Most of existing approaches use only a single feature to represent a video for NDVR. However, a single feature is often insufficient to characterize the video content. Besides, while the accuracy is the main concern in previous literatures, the scalability of NDVR algorithms for large scale video datasets has been rarely addressed. In this paper, we present a novel approach - Multiple Feature Hashing (MFH) to tackle both the accuracy and the scalability issues of NDVR. MFH preserves the local structure information of each individual feature and also globally consider the local structures for all the features to learn a group of hash functions which map the video keyframes into the Hamming space and generate a series of binary codes to represent the video dataset. We evaluate our approach on a public video dataset and a large scale video dataset consisting of 132,647 videos, which was collected from YouTube by ourselves. The experiment results show that the proposed method outperforms the state-of-the-art techniques in both accuracy and efficiency.

Categories and Subject Descriptors

H.3.3 [**Information Search and Retrieval**]: Search Process; H.3.1 [**Content Analysis and Indexing**]: Indexing

General Terms

Algorithms, Measurement, Experimentation

---

*Area chair: Lei Chen

Keywords

Near-duplicate, video retrieval, hashing, large scale

1. INTRODUCTION

With the rapid development of the Internet techniques, video capturing devices, and video editing softwares, the number of online videos continues to grow at an astonishing speed. Meanwhile, the video-related services, such as video sharing, monitoring, advertising and recommendation, inspire online users' interests and participation to video-related activities, including uploading, downloading, commenting, and searching. A substantial number of videos are uploaded and shared on social websites in each single day. It has been shown that there are a large number of near-duplicate videos (NDVs) on the Web, which are generated in different ways, ranging from simple reformatting, to different acquisitions, transformations, editions, and mixtures of different effects [18, 19, 30]. The presence of massive NDVs imposes strong demand for effective near-duplicate video retrieval (NDVR) in many novel applications, such as copyright enforcement, video tagging, online video usage monitoring, video database cleansing, cross-modal divergence detection, video result re-ranking, and so on. To list a few, a typical scenario could be that a Web user wants to get some novel videos but ends up with lots of NDVs in the top-ranked search results returned by the search engine. Another situation could be that a video producer expects to avoid their copyright protected videos being shared on the Internet. Both occasions require NDVR techniques to achieve their goals.

During recent years, much research effort have been made to NDVR [18, 7, 21, 32, 36]. Most of the existing algorithms usually adopt the following framework for NDVR. First, a video is divided into a sequence of keyframes extracted by time sampling or shot-boundary detection algorithms. These keyframes are represented by their visual features, such as color histogram, local points, Local Binary Pattern(LBP), etc. The sequence of the keyframes' features is then regarded as the signature of the video. For the sake of NDVR, the system needs to compare the similarity between the signatures of the query video and each dataset video and return the dataset videos which are most similar to the query example. Generally, there are three typical approaches to measure the similarity between two videos represented by a sequence of keyframes. The first one takes spatial and temporal constraints into consideration by employing sliding window for NDVR [8, 29]. The second approach computes pair-wise correlation/distances of each pair of keyframes from the two video clips, where the temporal information is not considered [13, 11]. The third kind is to combine all the keyframes into a single compact signature at video level [9, 29]. In this way, the similarity between video clips can be directly computed according to the global signature of the videos. The performance of the three approaches is data dependent. Different NDVR performance can be achieved while different video datasets are used.

Intuitively, the multiple features of video clips, each of which reflects the specific information of video data, are complementary to each other. Simultaneously utilizing the multiple features is helpful for disambiguation. For example, local signature is less robust to the changes in frame rate, video length, captions and global signature is sensitive to changes in contrast, brightness, scale, rotation, camera viewpoint, and so on. It is difficult, if not impossible, to find a single visual feature which is robust to all types of variations. It is therefore particularly important to exploit multiple features for the sake of NDVR, where various variations and distortions could take place between NDVs. For instance, it is easy to figure out that Fig.1(a) and Fig.1(b) are NDVs by the local features. Yet, their global features, such as HSV feature, are apparently different from each other. On the other hand, however, although Fig.1(c) and Fig.1(d) are NDVs, their local features are different from each other because of many captions in Fig.1(d). Only little work adopts multi-feature [31]. In that paper, the authors utilize contextual information including view counts, time duration and thumbnail image for fast identification of NDVs. However, using multiple visual features has not been well addressed.

Figure 1: Two groups of NDVs. Please refer to color images for better illustration.

The scalability of NDVR algorithm is becoming a more and more critical research issue as the number of videos is growing rapidly and most of the video content features are highly complex. How to construct efficient indexing structures to facilitate fast search over large scale video datasets is important for online NDVR, which demands real-time response. Many indexing methods in database literature have been proposed to support multimedia search, such as tree-structures [3], dimensionality reduction [28], hashing [6], and others [5]. However, these indexing methods mainly aim to improve the efficiency while the accuracy is not the concern. How to better preserve the near-duplicate relationships among videos in the indexing structure needs to be further studied.

In this work, we propose a new hashing algorithm, namely Multiple Feature Hashing (MFH), for accurate and efficient NDVR based on multiple visual features. To this end, multiple features (i.e., global and local visual features) of videos are analyzed to obtain the hash codes, which are more accurate to represent video content. Here we regard a video as a sequence of keyframes. Inspired by the recent study which shows that it is beneficial for multimedia semantics understanding to exploit the non-linear manifold structure of multimedia data [12, 33, 34], we propose to make use of the manifold information of keyframes when learning the hash codes for keyframes. Different from [27, 35] which can only make use of single feature to learn the hash code of keyframes, the individual structural information of each feature type is preserved in MFH proposed in this paper. Therefore MFH is more capable to make best use of the available information contained in different feature types for a more accurate NDVR. To cope with large scale data, MFH simultaneously learns the hash codes of the training data as well as a series of hash functions to infer the hash code of the videos which are outside the training set, making it apparently different from existing related work such as self-taught hashing [35] and spectral hashing [27]. NDVs are expected to have the same or similar hash codes. Once the hash codes are obtained, only Hamming distance calculation is performed to compute the similarity between videos. Such an operation is very fast, making it possible to perform NDVR over large scale video datasets in real time. It is worth highlighting the follow aspects of this paper.

1. We propose a new framework to exploit multiple local and global features of video data for NDVR. While most of the traditional NDVR algorithms use a single local or global feature, we use multiple features to improve the NDVR performance. We show that the combination of multiple local and global features is more capable to characterize the video content and thus yields better performance.

2. We propose a new hashing algorithm MFH which learns hash codes of the training videos and a group of hash functions to generate hash codes for the videos outside the training set. As far as we know, it is the first hashing algorithm on multiple features which is able to preserve the local structural information of each individual feature and also globally consider all the local structures in the optimization.

3. We have constructed a large scale video dataset consisting of 132,647 videos which have 2,570,554 keyframes. This dataset will be released to public so that other researchers will be able to use it as a test bed. Experiment results validate the proposed algorithm in both efficiency and accuracy.

The remainder of this paper is organized as follows. In section 2, we briefly discuss the related work. The details of MFH is presented in section 3. Extensive experiment results are given in section 4. Lastly, we draw a conclusion in section 5.

2. RELATED WORK

Our work is closely related to NDVR, multiple feature fusion, and hashing.

2.1 NDVR

NDVR and its related applications such as video copy and similarity detection have been actively studied in all kinds of real world applications [30]. During recent years, various approaches using different features and matching algorithms have been proposed for NDVR [18, 19, 29, 36]. The existing literatures on NDVR can be roughly divided into two groups, i.e., global feature based approaches and local feature based approaches respectively.

Many of the existing global feature based NDVR approaches emphasize the rapid identification of NDVs [4, 18, 19, 29]. In these works, videos are represented by compact global features. These approaches perform quite well in handling almost identical videos. For example, in [29], the authors adopt HSV to represent their keyframes and further generate a video signature by cumulating all the keyframes in the video. This representation achieves fast retrieval speed as well as high accuracy in their dataset. However, a limitation is that global feature based approaches usually become less effective in handling video copies with layers of editing cosmetics [30]. Meanwhile, global feature based approaches rely heavily on the selected feature types since different feature only performs well in certain specific aspects.

As an alternative to global feature based approaches, local feature based approaches have also attracted much research attention. Features such as color, texture and shape extracted at the keyframe level are further segmented into multiple region units, and are particularly suitable for retrieving NDVs with complex variations. The well-known local feature based approaches include keypoint based local feature detection approach (e.g., SIFT [14]) and some others [2]. However, the local based approaches are computationally expensive and not applicable to large scale NDVR. In [30], Wu et al. propose to construct a hierarchy structure to take advantage of both local feature and global feature. They first filter our part of the videos according to color histogram, and then employ pairwise comparison among keyframes by interest points matching. This hierarchy method improves the performance of NDVR. However, pairwise comparison among keyframes by local feature matching is impractical for large scale video datasets due to the heavy computation cost. Besides, using the global feature HSV only to filter out a large portion of videos might be inaccurate, because some NDVs may have quite different HSV feature, as shown in Fig.1(a) and Fig.1(b). Some recent proposals (e.g., [18, 16]) have also considered designing new features(spatial-temporal feature) or new similarity measuring methods to be adapted to videos characters. Nonetheless, they are single feature methods. Some (e.g., [17])has also considered scalability issue. They use keyframes to query within large-scale video archive. However, their main contribution is to investigate different keyframe samplings of the reference video database in order to evaluate the possible trade-off between accuracy and scalability. No new indexing methods are proposed and it is also a single feature method.

2.2 Multiple feature fusion

Given that multimedia data can be represented by multiple features, it becomes an important research topic to properly combine the evidences derived from different features. The key problem lying here is how to identify the similarity or correlation between two observations represented by multiple features. Late fusion strategies and early fusion strategies are the traditional methods for multiple-source fusion.

The late fusion algorithms [22, 24, 25] first generate separate results from different features, and then combine these results together by different strategies. The methods do not consider the correlation among features. Besides, as indicated in [20], late fusion is computationally more expensive for training. The early fusion strategies try to combine multiple features at the input stage [20]. For example, the algorithms proposed in [5] project different features into a unified space in which their applications can be performed. However, the individual structural information of each individual feature can not be well preserved and the computation cost is heavy. Some others (e.g., [32]) utilize tensor to incorporate multiple features, but it focuses on transductive learning.

2.3 Hashing

Hashing is an important approach to achieve fast similarity search. Many hashing methods have been proposed, such as locality sensitive hashing (LSH) [6], spectral hashing [27], self-taught hashing [35], and so on. Hashing methods implement fast nearest neighbor search in sub-linear time by mapping highly similar data points together. LSH [6, 10] uses a family of locality sensitive hash functions composed of linear projection over random directions in the feature space. The intuition behind is that for at lease one of the hash functions, nearby data points have high probability of being hashed into the same state. Recent compact binary code approaches [23] (e.g., spectral hashing, self-taught hashing) are possible to perform real-time search due to the quick similarity computation by using bit XOR operation in the Hamming space. The primary challenge on binary code methods is how to generate the compact binary codes for the data points. A good code requires that similar data in the original space should be mapped into similar binary codes. Spectral hashing utilizes spectral graph partitioning in the learning phase to get the hash codes of training data, which is similar to self-taught hashing. But to calculate the binary codes for a new data point, spectral hashing assumes that the data are uniformly distributed in a hype-rectangle, which is very restrictive, and self-taught hashing has to learn new classification models based on the result of learning phase. None of them takes consideration of multiple features. In this paper, we propose the first Multiple Feature Hashing (MFH) algorithm to learn a group of hash functions which can be utilized to map the keyframes into the Hamming space.

3. MULTIPLE FEATURE HASHING

The proposed framework based on multiple feature hashing (MFH) for NDVR is shown in Fig.2, which comprises two phases. In the first phase which is offline, we use the proposed MFH algorithm to learn a series of s hash functions $\{h_1(\cdot), ..., h_s(\cdot)\}$, each of which generates one bit hash code for a keyframe according to the given multiple features. Each keyframe has s bits. Using the derived hash functions $\{h_1(\cdot), ..., h_s(\cdot)\}$, each keyframe for a dataset video can be represented by the generated s-sized hash codes in linear time. In the second phase which is online, the query video's keyframes are also represented by s-sized hash codes mapped from the s hash functions. NDVR can be efficiently achieved where only efficient XOR operation on the hash codes is performed to compute the similarity between two videos.

The key research issue is how to train the hash functions which affect both accuracy and efficiency. In this section, we detail the proposed MFH algorithm. It is worthy noting that MFH is a general one which can be potentially applied to other large scale search applications where the data is represented by multiple features.

3.1 Terms and Notations

Let v be the number of features[1]. Given an integer $g \leq v$, $(x^g)_t \in \mathbb{R}^{d_g * 1}$ denotes the g-th feature of t-th training data, where d_g is the dimensionality of the g-th feature. Suppose there are n training keyframes in total. $X^g = [(x^g)_1, (x^g)_2, ..., (x^g)_n] \in \mathbb{R}^{d_g * n}$ is the feature matrix corresponding to the g-th feature of all the training data. $x_t = [(x^1)_t^T, (x^2)_t^T, ..., (x^v)_t^T]^T \in \mathbb{R}^{d \times 1}$,

[1]In our system, each keyframe is represented by the local feature LBP and the global feature HSV color histogram. Therefore, $v = 2$ here. Yet, MFH is able to deal with more feature types when $v > 2$.

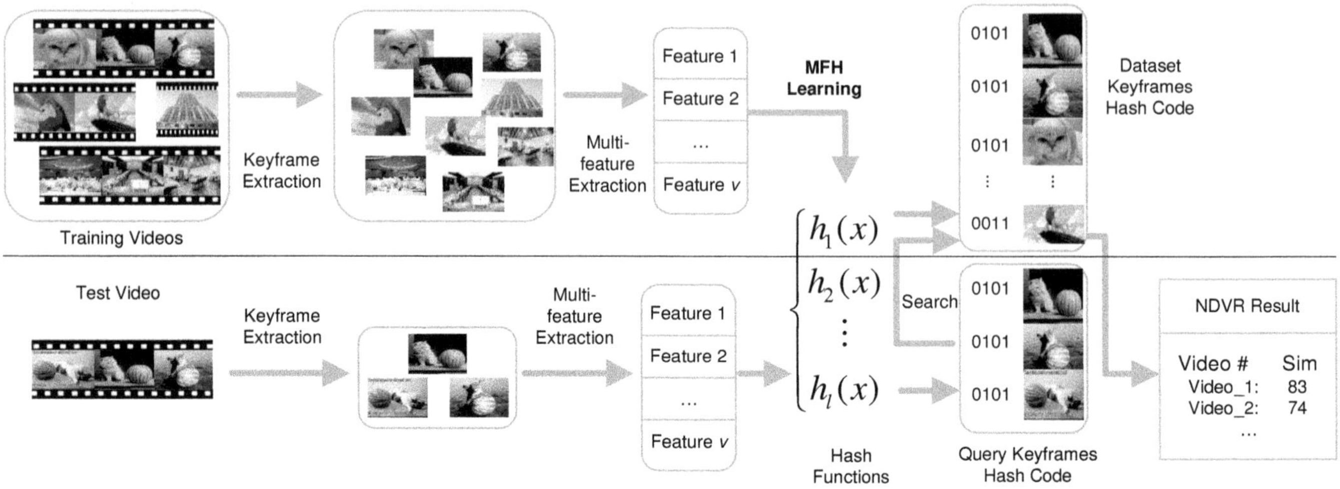

Figure 2: The Proposed Framework for NDVR

where $d = \sum_{g=1}^{v} d_g$, is the vector representation of the t-th training keyframe using all of the features and $X = [x_1, x_2, ..., x_n] \in \mathbb{R}^{d*n}$. MFH aims to learn a series of hash functions $\{h_1(\cdot), ..., h_s(\cdot)\}$, where s is the number of hash functions, i.e., the length of the hash code. Each of the s hash functions generates one bit hash code of the input keyframe. We further denote $Y = [(y_1)^T, ..., (y_n)^T]^T \in^{n \times s}$ as the hash codes of the training keyframes corresponding to all features and $Y^g = [(y_1^g)^T, ..., (y_n^g)^T]^T \in^{n \times s}$ as the hash codes of the training keyframes derived from the g-th feature.

3.2 The objective function of MFH

As demonstrated in [12, 15, 26, 27, 34, 35], it is beneficial to exploit the local structure of the training data to infer an accurate and compact representation, especially for multimedia data. While in [27, 35], the local structural information has been utilized to learn the hash codes, there are still two major limitations. First, both the algorithms proposed in [27, 35] are two-step training approaches. During the training phase, the hash codes of the training data are first generated according to which the hash functions are then defined. This may incur overfitting when generating the hash codes of training data because only local structure information is considered. Second, the algorithms proposed in [27, 35] can not deal with multiple features. Although a straightforward way is to concatenate the multiple features to produce a high dimensional vector, the structural information of each feature type will be lost.

To exploit the individual structural information of each individual feature, we define v affinity matrices $A^g \in \mathbb{R}^{n \times n}$ $(1 \le g \le v)$, one for each feature as follows:

$$(A^g)_{pq} = \begin{cases} 1, \text{ if } (x^g)_p \in \mathcal{N}_k((x^g)_q) \text{ or } (x^g)_q \in \mathcal{N}_k((x^g)_p) \\ 0, \text{ else} \end{cases} \quad (1)$$

where $\mathcal{N}_k(\cdot)$ is the k-nearest-neighbor set and $1 \le (p, q) \le n$.

To learn the hash codes $(y^g)_t$ from the g-th feature, a reasonable criterion is that similar items in the original space should have similar binary codes, which can be formulated as the following minimization problem:

$$\min_{Y^g} \sum_{p,q=1}^{n} (A^g)_{pq} \left\| (y^g)_p - (y^g)_q \right\|_F^2 . \quad (2)$$

Given a training keyframe x_t, we hope the overall hash codes y_t should be consistent with the hash codes $y_t^g|_{g=1}^v$ derived from each feature. In this way, the local structure information on each single feature is also globally considered and optimized. Therefore, we have the following minimization problem:

$$\min_{Y^g, Y} \sum_{g=1}^{v} \sum_{p,q=1}^{n} (A^g)_{pq} \left\| (y^g)_p - (y^g)_q \right\|_F^2 + \gamma \sum_{g=1}^{v} \sum_{t=1}^{n} \left\| y_t - (y^g)_t \right\|_F^2 \quad (3)$$

where γ is the parameter to balance the two parts. It is easy to see from Eq.3 that the individual manifold structure of each feature type is preserved (the first term) and all the manifold structures are also globally considered in the optimization (the second term).

Recall that we intend to learn the hash codes of the training keyframes and a series of hash functions $\{h_1(\cdot), ..., h_s(\cdot)\}$ in a joint framework. We propose to simultaneously learn the hash codes of the training keyframes and the hash functions by minimizing the empirical error of the hash functions *w.r.t.* the learnt hash codes Y. The proposed final objective function of MFH is given by:

$$\begin{aligned} \min_{Y, Y^g, W, b} \quad & \sum_{g=1}^{v} \sum_{p,q=1}^{n} (A^g)_{pq} \left\| (y^g)_p - (y^g)_q \right\|_F^2 \\ & + \gamma \sum_{g=1}^{v} \sum_{t=1}^{n} \left\| y_t - (y^g)_t \right\|_F^2 \\ & + \alpha \sum_{l=1}^{s} \left(\sum_{t=1}^{n} \| h_l(x_t) - y_{tl} \|_F^2 + \beta \Omega(h_l) \right) \\ \text{s.t.} \quad & \begin{cases} y_t \in \{-1, 1\}^s, (y^g)_t \in \{-1, 1\}^s \\ YY^T = I \end{cases} \end{aligned} \quad (4)$$

where $\Omega(h_l)$ is a regularization function over h_l, α and β are the parameters, $\mathbf{1} \in \mathbb{R}^{n \times 1}$ is a column vector with all ones, and y_{tl} is l-th bit hash code for x_t. In Eq.4, $y_t \in \{-1, 1\}^s$ and $(y^g)_t \in \{-1, 1\}^s$ enforce the hash codes of y_t and $(y^g)_t$ to be binary codes. As we will show later on, the constraint $YY^T = I$ is imposed to avoid the trivial solution. For the simplicity of implementation for large scale datasets, we adopt the linear transformation as the hash function. More specifically, given a keyframe represented by its

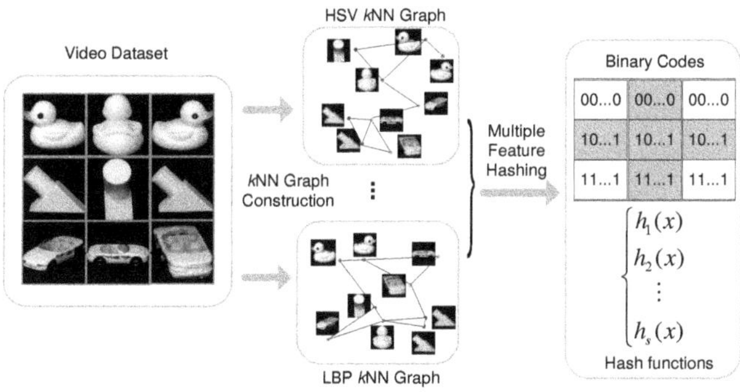

Figure 3: Multi-Feature Hashing

feature x_t, the l-th ($1 \le l \le s$) hash function h_l is defined as

$$h_l(x_t) = w_l^T x_t + b_l \tag{5}$$

where $w_l \in \mathbb{R}^{d\times 1}$ is the transformation matrix and $b_l \in \mathbb{R}$ is the bias term.

Let us define $W = [w_1, w_2, ..., w_s] \in \mathbb{R}^{d\times s}$, $b = [b_1, b_2, ..., b_s] \in \mathbb{R}^{1\times s}$ and $\mathbf{1}$ is a vector of all ones. Then we rewrite our objective function as follows:

$$\begin{aligned}
\min_{Y,Y^g,W,b} \quad & \sum_{g=1}^{v}\sum_{p,q=1}^{n} (A^g)_{pq} \left\| (y^g)_p - (y^g)_q \right\|_F^2 \\
& +\gamma \sum_{g=1}^{v}\sum_{t=1}^{n} \left\| y_t - (y^g)_t \right\|_F^2 \\
& +\alpha \left(\left\| X^T W + \mathbf{1}b - Y \right\|_F^2 + \beta \left\| W \right\|_F^2 \right) \\
\textbf{s.t.} \quad & \begin{cases} y_t \in \{-1,1\}^s, (y^g)_t \in \{-1,1\}^s \\ YY^T = I \end{cases}
\end{aligned} \tag{6}$$

In Eq.6, the term $\left\| X^T W + \mathbf{1}b - Y \right\|_F^2$ learns the hash functions to generate hash codes for the data. Meanwhile, it can be also interpreted as a regularizer in which global information is enclosed. Compared with the hashing algorithms proposed in [27, 35] where only local information is considered, it may eliminate the problem of overfitting, making the learning more robust. The objective function shown in Eq.6 is equivalent to the balanced graph partitioning and it is an NP-hard problem. Following [27], we relax the constraints $y_t \in \{-1,1\}^s, y_t^g \in \{-1,1\}^s$ to make the problem computationally trackable. The relaxed objective function is given by

$$\begin{aligned}
\min_{Y,Y^g,W,b} \quad & \sum_{g=1}^{v}\sum_{p,q=1}^{n} (A^g)_{pq} \left\| (y^g)_p - (y^g)_q \right\|_F^2 \\
& +\gamma \sum_{g=1}^{v}\sum_{t=1}^{n} \left\| y_t - (y^g)_t \right\|_F^2 \\
& +\alpha \left(\left\| X^T W + \mathbf{1}b - Y \right\|_F^2 + \beta \left\| W \right\|_F^2 \right) \\
& \textbf{s.t.} YY^T = I
\end{aligned} \tag{7}$$

3.3 Solution of MFH

In this subsection, we detail the approach to optimize the objective function of MFH. By setting the derivative of Eq.7 *w.r.t.* b to zero, we get:

$$\begin{aligned}
& \mathbf{1}^T \left(X^T W + \mathbf{1}b - Y \right) = 0 \\
& \Rightarrow b = \frac{1}{n} \left(\mathbf{1}^T Y - \mathbf{1}^T X^T W \right)
\end{aligned} \tag{8}$$

By setting the derivative of Eq.7 *w.r.t.* W to zero, we get:

$$X \left(X^T W + \mathbf{1}b - Y \right) + \beta W = 0. \tag{9}$$

Substituting b in Eq.9 by Eq.8, we have

$$\begin{aligned}
& XX^T W + X\mathbf{1} \left(\frac{1}{n} \left(\mathbf{1}^T Y - \mathbf{1}^T X^T W \right) \right) - XY + \beta W = 0 \\
& \Rightarrow W = \left(X L_c X^T + \beta I \right)^{-1} X L_c Y,
\end{aligned} \tag{10}$$

where $L_c = I - \frac{1}{n}\mathbf{1}\mathbf{1}^T$ is the centering matrix. Note that $L_c = (L_c)^T = L_c (L_c)^T$. Replacing W and b by Eq.8 and Eq.10 respectively, we have

$$\begin{aligned}
& X^T W + \mathbf{1}b - Y \\
= \; & X^T W + \mathbf{1}\frac{1}{n} \left(\mathbf{1}^T Y - \mathbf{1}^T X^T W \right) - Y \\
= \; & L_c X^T W - L_c Y \\
= \; & L_c X^T \left(X L_c X^T + \beta I \right)^{-1} X L_c Y - L_c Y
\end{aligned} \tag{11}$$

Let $M = \left(X L_c X^T + \beta I \right)^{-1}$. $\left\| X^T W + \mathbf{1}b - Y \right\|_F^2 + \beta \left\| W \right\|_F^2$ can be rewritten as:

$$\begin{aligned}
& \left\| X^T W + \mathbf{1}b - Y \right\|_F^2 + \beta \left\| W \right\|_F^2 \\
& = tr Y^T \left(L_c X^T M X L_c - L_c \right)^T \left(L_c X^T M X L_c - L_c \right) Y \\
& + \beta tr \left(W^T W \right) \\
& = tr Y^T \left(L_c X^T M X L_c L_c X^T M X L_c - 2 L_c X^T M X L_c + L_c \right) Y \\
& + \beta tr \left(Y^T L_c X^T M M X L_c Y \right) \\
& = tr \left(Y^T \left(L_c X^T M M^{-1} M X L_c - 2 L_c X^T M X L_c + L_c \right) Y \right) \\
& = tr Y^T \left(L_c - L_c X^T M X L_c \right) Y \\
& = tr Y^T B Y
\end{aligned}$$

where B is defined as:

$$B = \left(L_c - L_c X^T \left(X L_c X^T + \beta I \right)^{-1} X L_c \right) \tag{12}$$

Meanwhile, we have

$$\sum_{p,q=1}^{n} (A^g)_{pq} \left\| (y^g)_p - (y^g)_q \right\|_F^2 = tr \left((Y^g)^T L^g Y^g \right) \tag{13}$$

where $L^g = N^g - A^g$ is the Laplacian matrix of the g-th feature and N^g is the diagonal matrix with its diagonal element $N_{ii}^g = \sum_j A_{ij}^g$. Note that $\sum_{g=1}^{v}\sum_{t=1}^{n} \left\| y_t - (y^g)_t \right\|_F^2$ can also be written as $\sum_{g=1}^{v} \left\| Y - Y^g \right\|_F^2$. Then the objective function shown in Eq.7

becomes

$$\begin{aligned}\min_{Y,Y^g} \quad & \sum_{g=1}^{v}\left(tr\left((Y^g)^T L^g Y^g\right)+\gamma\left\|Y-Y^g\right\|_F^2\right)\\ & +\alpha tr\left(Y^T B Y\right)\\ \textbf{s.t.} \quad & Y^T Y = I. \end{aligned} \tag{14}$$

Setting the derivative of Eq.14 *w.r.t.* Y^g to be zero, we have

$$\begin{aligned} & 2L^g Y^g - 2\gamma(Y - Y^g) = 0 \\ & \Rightarrow Y^g = \gamma(L^g + \gamma I)^{-1} Y \end{aligned} \tag{15}$$

Let $C^g = \gamma(L^g + \gamma I)^{-1}$. Note that $C^g = (C^g)^T$. Then we arrive at

$$Y^g = C^g Y \tag{16}$$

Replace Y^g with Eq.16, the objective function in Eq.14 becomes:

$$\min_{YY^T=I} tr(Y^T D Y). \tag{17}$$

where D is defined as

$$\begin{aligned} D &= \sum_{g=1}^{v}\left(C^g L^g C^g + \gamma(I - C^g)^2\right) + \alpha B \\ &= \gamma\sum_{g=1}^{v}(I - C^g) + \alpha B \end{aligned} \tag{18}$$

The optimization problem shown in Eq.17 can be solved by performing the eigen-value decomposition of D. Y can be obtained by the s eigenvectors of D corresponding to the s smallest eigenvalues[2]. In summary, the training processing of the proposed MFH algorithm is listed as follows.

Algorithm 1 The MFH algorithm.

> **for** $g = 1$ to v **do**
>   **for** $p = 1$ to n **do**
>   **for** $q = 1$ to n **do**
>   Compute $L^g_{p,q}$ according to 13;
>   **end for**
>   **end for**
> **end for**
> Compute B according to Eq.(12);
> Compute D according to Eq.(18);
> Compute Y by performing eigenvalue decomposition on D.
> Output W and b according to Eq.10 and Eq.8.

Once W and b are obtained, they can be readily used to generate the hash codes of database keyframes as well as query keyframes. For example, given a keyframe x_t, we first compute its relaxed hash code y_t in continuous domain by $y_t = W^T x_t + b$. Then, we binarize it by comparing each dimension of y_t with its median of all dimensions. If it is greater than the median, we set it as 1. Otherwise, we set it as -1. To represent a video clip, Wu et al. proposed to averaging the visual feature of all its keyframes as the representation the whole video clip [29]. Following Wu's way, we can also generate the hash codes for a video clip by averaging the relaxed codes of all its keyframes and then binarize them. As a result, each video clip is represented by a single s-bit hash code. In this work, we use the above video representation to avoid pairwise keyframe comparisons. The number of common bits along all dimensions shared by two videos is approximated as the video similarity.

For better understanding of MFH, we give an illustration in Fig.3. Given a set of videos, to explore the individual manifold structure, we first construct kNN graph on each individual feature space. Then we learn the hash codes of each video under the criterion that similar items in the original space should have similar hash codes by solving the objective function Eq. 14 which preserves the local structure information of each individual feature and also globally considers the local structures among all the features. Meanwhile, a series of hash functions are simultaneously learned.

4. EXPERIMENTS

We experimentally evaluate the performance of MFH and compare it with existing state-of-the-art methods.

4.1 Experiment Setting

4.1.1 Video datasets

We used two datasets in the experiments.

CC_WEB_VIDEO Dataset [1] is provided by CityU of Hong Kong and CMU. It consists of 24 sets of video clips (totally 13,129 video clips) downloaded from video sharing websites including Google Video, Yahoo! Video, and YouTube using specific keywords. For each set of videos, the most popular video is selected as the query video, and all the other videos within the set are manually labeled to get the ground truth.

Combined Dataset is a larger video dataset created by ourselves by adding CC_WEB_VIDEO to our video dataset downloaded from YouTube. We choose the most popular 400 queries to query the videos from YouTube. Those queries are selected from Google Zeitgeist. Each year, Google examines billions of queries that people around the world have typed into Google search to discover the Zeitgeist saved in Google Zeitgeist Archives. We collect Google Zeitgeist Archives from 2004 to 2009, and choose the most popular 400 queries to search YouTube. The downloaded number of videos for each query is up to 1000. We crawled more than 150K YouTube videos from July 2010 to September 2010. After filtering out the videos who sizes are greater than 10M, the Combined Dataset contains 132,647 videos in total, which is more than twice as big as the one used in [18]. To our best knowledge, this is the biggest Web video dataset for experimental purpose. We further extract 2,570,554 keyframes from these videos. This dataset will be released to public so that other researchers will be able to use it as a test bed.

4.1.2 Visual features

On the CC_WEB_VIDEO dataset, shot-based sampling method is used to extract key-frames and there are 398,078 keyframes extracted in total. These keyframes are provided in the dataset. We further extract LBP feature on the keyframes as a local feature, which will be used together with the existing global feature HSV provided by dataset.

On the Combined Dataset, we firstly detect the shots from which the keyframes are extracted. Then we extracted two features for each keyframe, which are HSV and LBP, to be used as a global feature and a local feature respectively. HSV is a global color histogram with 162 dimensions and LBP is a local content feature with 256 dimensions.

[2]The trivial solution corresponding to the eigenvalue of zero is removed

4.1.3 Algorithms for comparison

To evaluate NDVR accuracy and efficiency, we present an extensive comparison of the proposed method with a set of existing NDVR methods, which are briefly described as follows.

Global feature based method: We use the global color histogram method as a baseline method. Each keyframe is represented as a color histogram feature vector. Each video is finally defined as a feature vector of a normalized color histogram over all the keyframes in the video.

Local feature based method: Wu et al. [29] proposed a hierarchical method to first use global color histograms to detect near-duplicate videos with high confidence and filter out very dissimilar videos. Then local feature is applied to identify the remaining uncertain videos with high accuracy.

Spatiotemporal feature based method: Shang et al. [18] introduced a compact spatiotemporal feature to represent the videos. This feature leverages relative gray-level intensity distribution within a frame and temporal structure of videos along frame sequence. Two feature selection methods, namely CE-based spatiotemporal feature and LBP-based spatiotemporal feature are proposed to generate the compact video signature. A new index structure is also proposed to index the signatures based on inverted file in order to achieve real-time retrieving performance.

Self-taught hashing: Zhang et al. [35] designed compact binary codes for a large number of documents so that semantically similar documents are mapped to similar codes. Then the search can be quickly done in the Hamming space. Also, to obtain the codes for previously unseen documents,it trains classifiers via supervised learning based on the binary codes learned from the training data. Here we extend it for video representation.

Spectral hashing: Weiss et al. [27] utilizes the results of graph Laplacian eigenvectors to the Laplace-Beltrami eigenfunctions of manifolds to generate compact binary codes of data points by assuming that the data are uniformly distributed in a hype-rectangle.

We also implemented single feature MFH, which is a special case of our MFH, to prove the significance of using multiple features. For simplicity, we let MFH_hsv and MFH_lbp represent the single feature case of our MFH. Similarly, let ST_lbp and ST_ce represent the two spatiotemporal feature based methods used in [18], and GF, LF, STH and SPH represent global feature based method, local feature based method, self-taught hashing and spectral hashing respectively.

4.1.4 System environment and evaluation metrics

All of the experiments are implemented on a computer which has Intel(R) Core(TM) i7 2.93GHz 8 processors, 16 GB RAM and 64-bit Windows 7 Enterprise N operating system. Following the work in [18], we also adopt the metric MAP (Mean Average Precision) to evaluate the performance. Among evaluation measures, MAP has been shown to have especially good discrimination and stability. We further use precision-recall curve to evaluate the performance on both datasets. Time efficiency is calculated on Matlab R2010a for all the comparison methods.

4.2 Results on CC_WEB_VIDEO

We first test different methods on the CC_WEB_VIDEO dataset. The same 24 queries as in [29, 18] are used. The MAP results and precision-recall curves of different methods can be seen in Table 1 and Fig.4 respectively.

From Table1, we can see that the proposed MFH achieves best results on MAP, although the margins are minor. Fig.4 shows that GF performs poorly compared with other four methods which have quite similar performance. This is probably because the dataset

Table 1: Comparison of MAP on CC_WEB_VIDEO

Methods	GF	LF	ST_lbp	ST_ce	MFH
MAP	0.892	0.952	0.953	0.950	0.954

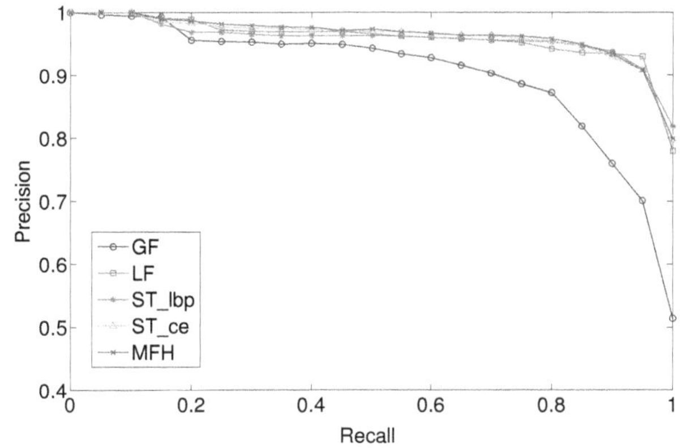

Figure 4: Comparison of precision and recall on CC_WEB_VIDEO.

is not big enough and thus less noises can be introduced for most methods. The performance of different methods cannot be fully explored. Next, we focus on the large dataset.

4.3 Results on Combined Dataset

To further test the accuracy and scalability of MFH, we test MFH on the Combined Dataset and compare it with existing methods. More specifically, we use the same 24 queries and groundtruth as in [29, 18] to search the whole Combined Dataset. There are several parameters need to be tuned for some of the algorithms. For each parameter we have a set of candidate values, and then we iteratively combine the parameters to form various parameter settings. For each parameter combination we run the same experiment to evaluate its impact on the performance. Finally, the parameter setting which results in the best performance is selected for each method. For the parameters in MFH, SPH and STH, including γ,α,β, we tune them from $10^{-6}, 10^{-3}, 10^{0}, 10^{3}, 10^{6}$ and tune the length of the binary code from 200 to 400. On this large Combined Dataset, we cannot compare with local feature based method LF proposed in [29] because this method utilizes interest points matching to measure the similarity of two keyframes. It is impractical in such a large dataset with 2,570,554 keyframes. We are also unable to extract the spatiotemporal features ST_lbp and ST_ce, because it takes extremely long time for our computer to extract the features from 132,647 videos. As a result, only methods including GF, STH, SPH, MFH_hsv, MFH_lbp, and MFH are compared. The results on MAP, search time are shown in Table 2. To have a clear visualization, averaged precision-recall curves are depicted in Fig.5. We also report the Average Precision (AP) of each query in Fig.6. From Table 2 and Fig.5, we have the following observations.

- MFH achieves the highest MAP and outperforms existing methods by large margins. Especially, MFH can have more than 86% MAP, while SPH has less than 60% MAP.
- SPH, STH and MFH all construct binary codes for the videos and perform the search using in the Hamming space. Even in the Matlab environment, they can search the large dataset

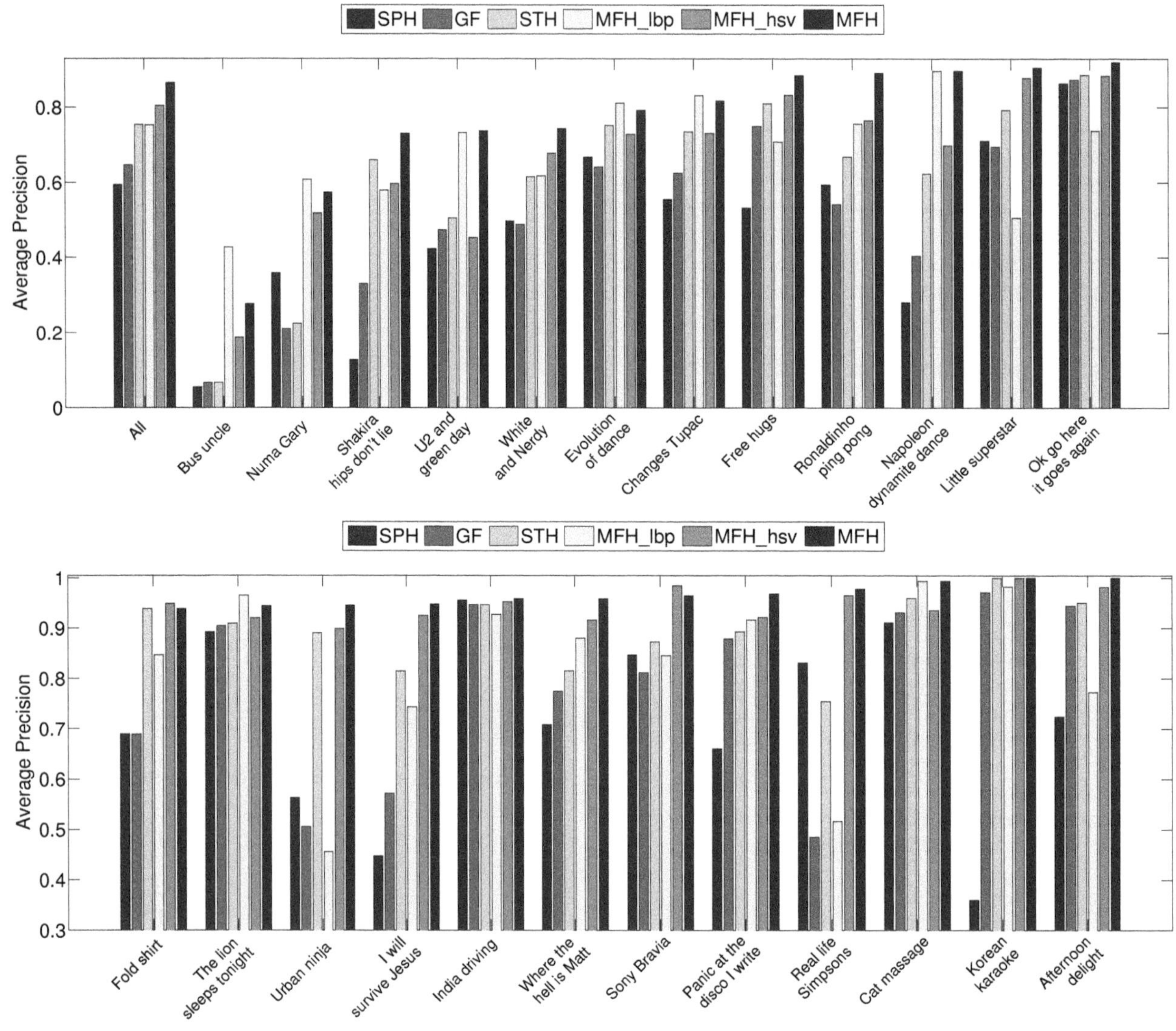

Figure 6: Comparison of AP corresponding to each query on the Combined Dataset. 'All' indicates the MAP of all the 24 queries.

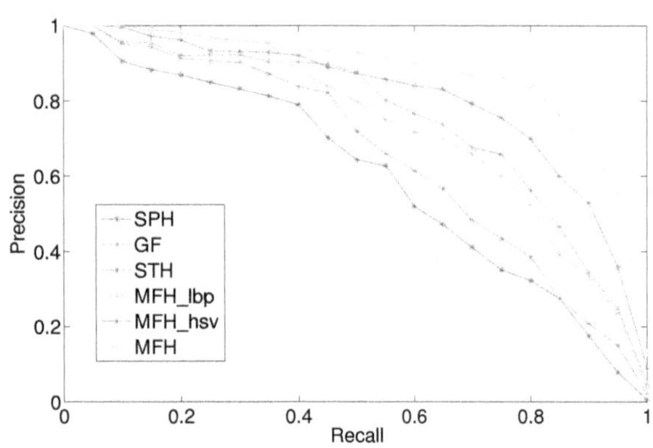

Figure 5: Comparison of precision and recall on the Combined Dataset.

within 1 second. However, SPH's performance is really unsatisfactory probably because the video dataset is not in accordance with the assumption that all the data points are uniformly distributed in a hyper-rectangle in the high-dimensional space. This also shows that MFH is more capable of preserving local data distribution information.

Table 2: Comparison of MAP and time on Combined Dataset

Methods	MAP	Time(s)
SPH	0.5941	0.4907
GF	0.6466	1.3917
STH	0.7536	0.6439
MFH_lbp	0.7526	0.6445
MFH_hsv	0.8042	0.4508
MFH	0.8656	0.5533

- GF performs search using the Euclidean distance and its performance is not good either. Its accuracy is much worse than that of MFH. Furthermore, its search time is about 2-3 times longer than hashing methods.

- MFH outperforms MFH_lbp and MFH_hsv in general, which demonstrates the effectiveness of combining multiple features in NDVR.

From Fig.6, we also observe that MFH_lbp is worse than MFH_hsv for the overall MAP. However, for some queries, such as 'Bus uncle' and 'U2 and green day', MFH_lbp achieves much better accuracy than MFH_hsv. This shows that different types of features can character some part of the visual content, and they can only perform well in some certain situations.

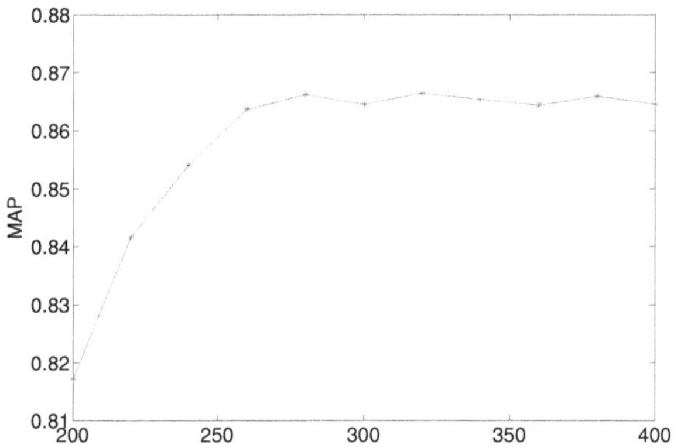

(a) The MAP of different code length

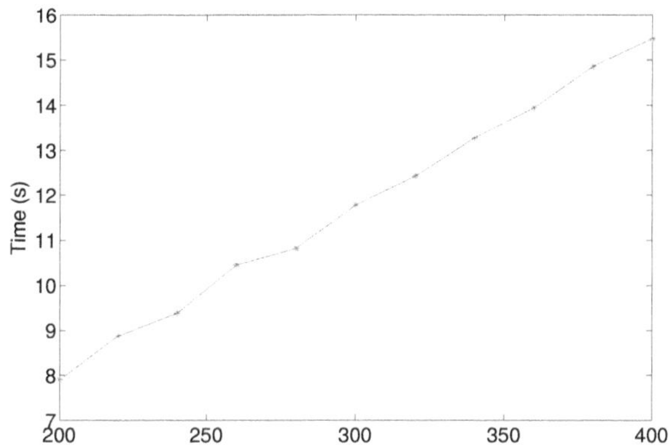

(b) The time cost of different code length

Figure 7: The performance variations of different code lengths

4.4 Parameter sensitivity study for MFH

In this subsection we test different parameter settings for our MFH to see the performance variation. There are four parameters in our proposed models: 1) γ, α and β shown in Eqn.7, and 2) s, the length of the binary code. We firstly find the best performance of s by fixing γ, α and β. Then we fix s and one of the parameters in γ, α and β, to report the MAP while the other two parameters are changing. In our paper, we tested $s = 200, 220, ..., 400$ and $\gamma, \alpha, \beta = 10^{-6}, 10^{-3}, 10^{0}, 10^{3}, 10^{6}$.

Among different combinations, MFH gains the best performance when $s = 320, \gamma = 10^{-3}, \alpha = 1$ and $\beta = 10^{-6}$. By fixing $s = 320$, we show the MAP variations on γ, α and β in Fig.8. Generally speaking, in order to obtain better performance, β should not be larger than 10^3, as shown in Fig.8(a) and Fig.8(b). We observe from Fig.8(a), Fig.8(b) and Fig.8(c) that the MAP is not very sensitive to the parameter γ and α when β is smaller than 10^3.

By fixing $\gamma = 10^{-3}, \alpha = 1$ and $\beta = 10^{-6}$, we show the performance variations on different code lengths in Fig.7. When the binary code length is less than 280, the MAP improves dramatically with the increase of binary code length. After that, the MAP keeps steady until reaching peak when $s = 320$. Then, the MAP fluctuates with slight drop until $K = 400$. This indicates that the longest binary code length can not guarantee the best MAP. When $s > 320$, the MAP declines slightly probably because a longer code may contain more noises. An approximately linear increasing trend for query time is illustrated in Fig.7(b). This is reasonable since it has a linear relationship with the code length.

5. CONCLUSION AND FUTURE WORK

In this paper, we have proposed a new multiple feature hashing (MFH) method for large scale NDVR. Compared with the existing algorithms, MFH has two major advantages. First, instead of using single feature, MFH employs a machine learning approach to exploit the local structure of each individual feature and fuse multiple features in a joint framework. Such a method is more stable to well characterize the video content. Second, the MFH method is proposed here to also accelerate the query speed. The extensive experiments verify the superior performance of our method on efficiency and accuracy over existing methods. In the future we intend to incorporate the temporal correlation of the keyframes within the same video to further improve the performance.

6. ACKNOWLEDGEMENTS

We are grateful to Dr Wu Xiao for providing us the CC_WEB_VIDEO dataset and to Dr Lifeng Shang for sharing the experiment results of his algorithm [18] with us. This work was supported by Australia Research Council under research Grant ARC DP1094678 and partially supported by National Science Foundation under Grants No. IIS-0917072 and CNS-0751185. Any opinions, findings, and conclusions or recommendations expressed in this material are those of the author(s) and do not necessarily reflect the views of the National Science Foundation.

7. REFERENCES

[1] Cc_web_video: Near-duplicate web video dataset. In *http://vireo.cs.cityu.edu.hk/webvideo*.

[2] H. Bay, T. Tuytelaars, and L. V. Gool. Surf: Speeded up robust features. In *ECCV*, pages 404–417, 2006.

[3] C. Böhm, S. Berchtold, and D. A. Keim. Searching in high-dimensional spaces: Index structures for improving the performance of multimedia databases. *ACM Computing Surveys*, 33(3):322–373, 2001.

[4] S. Cheung and A. Zakhor. Fast similarity search and clustering of video sequences on the world-wide-web. *IEEE Trans. on Multimedia*, 7(3):524–537, 2005.

[5] B. Cui, A. K. H. Tung, C. Zhang, and Z. Zhao. Multiple feature fusion for social media applications. In *SIGMOD*, pages 435–446, 2010.

[6] M. Datar, N. Immorlica, P. Indyk, and V. S. Mirrokni. Locality-sensitive hashing scheme based on p-stable distributions. In *Symposium on Computational Geometry*, pages 253–262, 2004.

[7] Z. Huang, L. W. 0002, H. T. Shen, J. Shao, and X. Zhou. Online near-duplicate video clip detection and retrieval: An accurate and fast system. In *ICDE*, pages 1511–1514, 2009.

[8] Z. Huang, H. T. Shen, J. Shao, B. Cui, and X. Zhou. Practical online near-duplicate subsequence detection for continuous

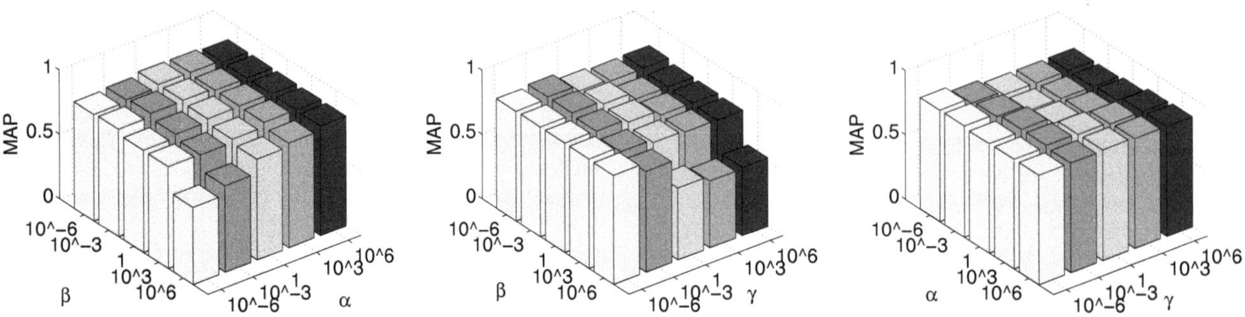

(a) γ is fixed as 10^{-3}. (b) α is fixed as 10^{0}. (c) β is fixed as 10^{-6}.

Figure 8: The MAP variations of different parameter settings

video streams. *IEEE Trans. on Multimedia*, 12(5):386–398, 2010.

[9] Z. Huang, H. T. Shen, J. Shao, X. Zhou, and B. Cui. Bounded coordinate system indexing for real-time video clip search. *ACM Trans. Inf. Syst.*, 27(3), 2009.

[10] A. Joly and O. Buisson. A posteriori multi-probe locality sensitive hashing. In *ACM Multimedia*, pages 209–218, 2008.

[11] A. Karpenko and P. Aarabi. Tiny videos: A large data set for nonparametric video retrieval and frame classification. *IEEE Trans. Pattern Anal. Mach. Intell.*, 33(3):618–630, 2011.

[12] Y.-Y. Lin, T.-L. Liu, and H.-T. Chen. Semantic manifold learning for image retrieval. In *ACM Multimedia*, pages 249–258, 2005.

[13] J. Liu, Z. Huang, H. T. Shen, and B. Cui. Correlation-based retrieval for heavily changed near-duplicate videos. *ACM Trans. Inf. Syst.*, 2011.

[14] K. Mikolajczyk and C. Schmid. A performance evaluation of local descriptors. *IEEE Trans. Pattern Anal. Mach. Intell.*, 27(10):1615–1630, 2005.

[15] F. Nie, D. Xu, I. W.-H. Tsang, and C. Zhang. Flexible manifold embedding: a framework for semi-supervised and unsupervised dimension reduction. *IEEE Trans. Img. Proc.*, 19(7):1921–1932, 2010.

[16] S. Poullot, O. Buisson, and M. Crucianu. Scaling content-based video copy detection to very large databases. *Multimedia Tools Appl.*, 47(2):279–306, 2010.

[17] S. Poullot and S. Satoh. Detecting screen shot images within large-scale video archive. In *ICPR*, pages 3203–3207, 2010.

[18] L. Shang, L. Yang, F. Wang, K.-P. Chan, and X.-S. Hua. Real-time large scale near-duplicate web video retrieval. In *ACM Multimedia*, pages 531–540, 2010.

[19] H. T. Shen, X. Zhou, Z. Huang, J. Shao, and X. Zhou. Uqlips: a real-time near-duplicate video clip detection system. In *VLDB*, pages 1374–1377, 2007.

[20] C. Snoek, M. Worring, and A. W. M. Smeulders. Early versus late fusion in semantic video analysis. In *ACM Multimedia*, pages 399–402, 2005.

[21] H.-K. Tan, X. Wu, C.-W. Ngo, and W.-L. Zhao. Accelerating near-duplicate video matching by combining visual similarity and alignment distortion. In *ACM Multimedia*, pages 861–864, 2008.

[22] S. Tollari and H. Glotin. Web image retrieval on imageval: evidences on visualness and textualness concept dependency in fusion model. In *CIVR*, pages 65–72, 2007.

[23] A. Torralba, R. Fergus, and Y. Weiss. Small codes and large image databases for recognition. In *CVPR*, 2008.

[24] D. R. Turnbull, L. Barrington, G. Lanckriet, and M. Yazdani. Combining audio content and social context for semantic music discovery. In *SIGIR*, pages 387–394, 2009.

[25] M. Wang, X.-S. Hua, R. Hong, J. Tang, G.-J. Qi, and Y. Song. Unified video annotation via multigraph learning. *IEEE Trans. Circuits Syst. Video Techn.*, 19(5):733–746, 2009.

[26] M. Wang, X.-S. Hua, J. Tang, and R. Hong. Beyond distance measurement: constructing neighborhood similarity for video annotation. *IEEE Trans. on Multimedia*, 11(3):465–476, 2009.

[27] Y. Weiss, A. Torralba, and R. Fergus. Spectral hashing. In *NIPS*, pages 1753–1760, 2008.

[28] M. Wichterich, I. Assent, P. Kranen, and T. Seidl. Efficient EMD-based similarity search in multimedia databases via flexible dimensionality reduction. In *SIGMOD*, pages 199–212, 2008.

[29] X. Wu, A. G. Hauptmann, and C.-W. Ngo. Practical elimination of near-duplicates from web video search. In *ACM Multimedia*, pages 218–227, 2007.

[30] X. Wu, C.-W. Ngo, A. G. Hauptmann, and H.-K. Tan. Real-time near-duplicate elimination for web video search with content and context. *IEEE Trans. on Multimedia*, 11(2):196–207, 2009.

[31] X. Wu, W.-L. Zhao, and C.-W. Ngo. Near-duplicate keyframe retrieval with visual keywords and semantic context. In *CIVR*, pages 162–169, 2007.

[32] Z. Wu, S. Jiang, and Q. Huang. Near-duplicate video matching with transformation recognition. In *ACM Multimedia*, pages 549–552, 2009.

[33] Y. Yang, D. Xu, F. Nie, J. Luo, and Y. Zhuang. Ranking with local regression and global alignment for cross media retrieval. In *ACM Multimedia*, pages 175–184, 2009.

[34] Y. Yang, Y. Zhuang, F. Wu, and Y. Pan. Harmonizing hierarchical manifolds for multimedia document semantics understanding and cross-media retrieval. *IEEE Trans. on Multimedia*, 10(3):437–446, 2008.

[35] D. Zhang, J. Wang, D. Cai, and J. Lu. Self-taught hashing for fast similarity search. In *SIGIR*, pages 18–25, 2010.

[36] X. Zhou, X. Zhou, L. Chen, A. Bouguettaya, N. Xiao, and J. A. Taylor. An efficient near-duplicate video shot detection method using shot-based interest points. *IEEE Trans. on Multimedia*, 11(5):879–891, 2009.

Learning Heterogeneous Data for Hierarchical Web Video Classification *

Xian-Ming Liu
Harbin Institute of Technology
No. 92, West Dazhi Street
Harbin, P.R. China
xmliu@hit.edu.cn

Hongxun Yao
Harbin Institute of Technology
No. 92, West Dazhi Street
Harbin, P.R. China
h.yao@hit.edu.cn

Rongrong Ji
Harbin Institute of Technology
No. 92, West Dazhi Street
Harbin, P.R. China
rrji@hit.edu.cn

Pengfei Xu
Harbin Institute of Technology
No. 92, West Dazhi Street
Harbin, P.R. China
pfxu@hit.edu.cn

Xiaoshuai Sun
Harbin Institute of Technology
No. 92, West Dazhi Street
Harbin, P.R. China
xiaoshuaisun@hit.edu.cn

Qi Tian
University of Texas at San Antonio
One UTSA Circle
San Antonio, TX, USA
qitian@cs.utsa.edu

ABSTRACT

Web videos such as YouTube are hard to obtain sufficient precisely labeled training data and analyze due to the complex ontology. To deal with these problems, we present a hierarchical web video classification framework by learning heterogeneous web data, and construct a bottom-up semantic forest of video concepts by learning from meta-data. The main contributions are two-folds: firstly, analysis about middle-level concepts' distribution is taken based on data collected from web communities, and a concepts redistribution assumption is made to build effective transfer learning algorithm. Furthermore, an AdaBoost-Like transfer learning algorithm is proposed to transfer the knowledge learned from Flickr images to YouTube video domain and thus it facilitates video classification. Secondly, a group of hierarchical taxonomies named *Semantic orest* are mined from YouTube and Flickr tags which reflect better user intention on the semantic level. A bottom-up semantic integration is also constructed with the help of semantic forest, in order to analyze video content hierarchically in a novel perspective. A group of experiments are performed on the dataset collected from Flickr and YouTube. Compared with state-of-the-arts, the proposed framework is more robust and tolerant to web noise.

Categories and Subject Descriptors

H.3.1 [**Information Storage and Retrieval**]: Content Analysis and Indexing

*Area chair: Nicu Sebe

MM'11, November 28–December 1, 2011, Scottsdale, Arizona, USA.

General Terms

Algorithms, Experimentation

Keywords

Transfer Learning, Web Video Classification, Hierarchical Taxonomy, Semantic Forest, Heterogeneous Data, Video Annotation, Video Search

1. INTRODUCTION

Coming with the explosive growth of Internet, video content analysis is a critical but challenging research topic, especially based on the difficulties to organize and search a huge scale of online videos. Different from an image, a video is difficult to understand because of its temporal relationship among each frame and the complex semantics. Especially, the video taggings are very expensive to fully acquired, resulting in the huge difficulty to train robust and effective video classifiers. In this work, we aim at investigating a more effective video classification / annotation strategy by learning video classifiers from the image domain.

Compared with the situations in classical video classifications, we have several new challenges when data is coming from the Internet. Regardless the low-level visual features and the semantic gap, the current video analysis methods usually suffer from several problems: Firstly, most video content analysis schemes require a certain amount of labeled data to train the models, and the labels are typically propagated in a top-down manner. For instance, each video shot is given a set of labels and the frames within this shot are inherent from these labels. This is usually unacceptable when dealing with huge scale of Web videos in terms of the labeling efficiency as well as the organization complexity. Secondly, instead of typically classifying the given tens or hundreds of categories, the Web videos are tagged with thousands or even more labels in total which are complicatedly correlative among each other. Therefore, traditional methods would not be capable to deal with this situation.

These drawbacks of the current approaches will cause inaccurate video contents understanding. In this paper, we are motivated at leveraging the cross-community knowledge across heterogeneous data towards automatic Web-based video classification. The cross-community data are used in two ways: firstly, a novel transfer learning algorithm is developed to make use heterogeneous auxiliary data; secondly, a hierarchical ontology, the *Semantic orest* is proposed, which represents the semantics of the Web data and fits for transferred heterogeneously, from metadata of multiple communities in a data-driven manner. In more details, we collected large-scale video data from YouTube and Web images rom Flickr. Then by applying the proposed transfer learning algorithm, YouTube videos are classified using the knowledge learned from Flickr images. To integrate the classification results from frame-level into a higher semantic level, a bottom-up integration is performed based on a so-called *Semantic orest*. Compared with the traditional approaches, our framework has the following novelties and contributions:

1. **Framework**: a novel Web video analysis framework is proposed in this paper by utilizing the cross-community heterogeneous data. By exploring the huge amount of user-labeled data from the Web, we are trying to figure out an efficient way of using these data, which is important for building video content analysis platform on a Web scale.
2. **Transfer Learning Strategy**: Though many transfer learning algorithms are proposed in recent years, there is still not an ultimate solution that works well in all scenarios. Therefore, it is still important to investigate the underlying principles for the task of classifying YouTube videos using Flickr images, and develop a specific strategy for this task, despite a lot of theoretical efforts have been made on this topic.
3. **Semantic Forest - Web Ontology**: Ontology plays an important role in video / image classification tasks when the category number gets large. We construct a hierarchical ontology named *Semantic orest* in a data-driven approach and it organizes the semantic items within the Web data efficiently.
4. **Bottom-Up perspective**: To avoid the drawback in labeling video data, we view the video content analysis in a Bottom-Up perspective instead of the traditional Top-Down manner. The semantic of video clips is bottom-up integrated based on Semantic Forest, which has been quantitatively validated to be very effective later in this paper.

Above researches have covered several challenging research topics, including transfer learning, semantic representation, and ontology construction.

1.1 Related Work

Video classification and annotation is a hot research topic in this decade and a lot of methods are proposed in recent years [25][24][30]. TRECVID [1] provided an opportunity to the research on visual event detection and recognition on a standard dataset, and lots of approaches were built [2][6][7], most of which focused on finding better features or combinations and fused multiple classifiers together. Laptev [15] utilized the bag-of-word framework proposed by Sivic and Zisserman [22] and introduced a spatial-temporal local descriptor resulting good performance on a Hollywood Movie database, which is labeled using the movie scripts. However, all of these methods require large amount of labeled data, which is unrealistic in real application.

Some other work also aimed at dealing with the taxonomy and ontology problem, which is critical for classification and annotation tasks according to the observation that semantic items are correlated with each other. In the image domain, the ImageNet [9] provided an effective dataset and also the ontology for image classification and object recognition. While in video domain, few work focused on this topic. Yanagawa *et al.* [28] developed a set of baseline concepts detectors called Columbia374-baseline for 374 visual concepts chosen from LSCOM ontology and Yuen *et al.* also extended LabelMe to videos and constructed LabelMe Video [32]. A more recent work showed an alternative solution for automatic discovery and organization of descriptive concepts (labels) within large real-world corpora of user-uploaded multimedia in [3]. It used YouTube meta-data to build the classification taxonomy dynamically. Xie *et al.* also organized the concept forest in a probabilistic way, distinguished with traditional ways of treating semantic concepts as isolated nodes [27]. Besides, the concepts are correlated with each other, considering these correlations, Qi *et al.* proposed a CML method for video annotation, which obtained better performance than treating them independently as traditional approaches did [19].

As web communities such as Flickr and YouTube becoming popular, more researches concentrate on making use of these web sources to provide additional information to multimedia analysis. TRECVID has already included web videos in its current training and testing data since 2010. In [14], the author made use of Flickr images and tags calculating a new semantic metric for video classification. While in [23] and [26] YouTube metadata including user descriptions, comments and search logs were introduced to video classification and annotation procedure and provided more flexible and robust solutions for web videos. For TRECVID and consumer videos, web information was also incorporated to provide either additional training data or auxiliary information [10] [11]. Duan *et al.* [11] used transfer learning and pyramid matching to learn from YouTube video and then applied the classifiers to consumer videos.

To make better use the auxiliary web data, transfer learning [18] is naturally introduced. For both image and video analysis, lots of transfer learning approaches were built to adapt heterogeneous auxiliary data to the target domain, aimed at transferring knowledge learned from either documents or metadata to visual information. These approaches usually assume a bias in classification hyper-plane or assign a prior assumption from the source domain to the target domain. Yang *et al.* [29] proposed an Adaptive-SVM to transfer discriminative information from the source video domain to the target TRECVID domain. An Adaptive Multiple Kernel Learning (A-MKL) was also proposed in [11] to minimize both the structural risk functional and the mismatch between data distributions from the source and target domains, by extending Multiple Kernel Learning and Pyramid Matching methods. As discussed in previous part of this paper, the semantic concepts are correlated, the similar principle was introduced to transfer learning by Qi in [20] by transferring relational information across heterogeneous

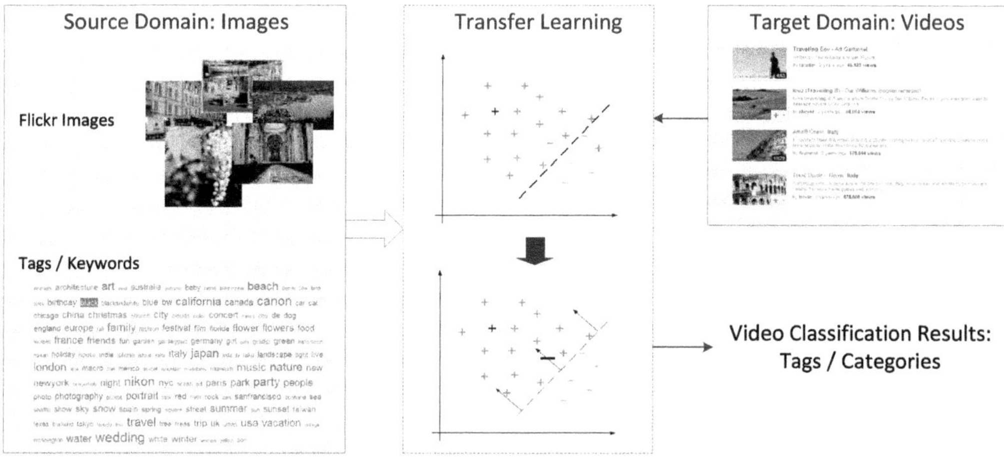

Figure 1: A candidate solution of web video classification and annotation by introducing additional sources, compared with traditional video classification framework.

data and applied in image classification. Similar issue was also discussed in [21]. More details about transfer learning please refer a survey by Yang *et. al* [18].

However, considering the following situation for video classification, the metadata or auxiliary data of web videos are utilized as additional information to help the classification tasks, labeled data is still hard to obtain. Using the auxiliary information such as tags and keywords as the labels of video clips will not only introduce extra noise, but also impossible to explicitly decide which shot or scene of the given video clip should have positive response to a specific tag.

A candidate solution is to use Flickr images as the source training data and transfer learning methods such as A-SVM [29] or A-MKL [11] are further adopted to transfer the discriminant information to the target YouTube video domain, as shown in Figure 1. A better result would be appreciated because the images are further incorporated as additional resource and hence provide more labeled training data.

Though positive, some problems still exist in this idea: Currently, the transfer learning strategies still fail to deal well with the heterogeneous situation, which is the exact one for transfer learning of taggings from from Flickr images to YouTube videos. Another crucial problem is that the existing works in heterogeneous transfer learning omits the concepts organization - the ontology or taxonomy.

1.2 Organization

Considering those problems mentioned above, a general framework of our solution is introduced in Section 2. By analyzing some statistical results from both Flickr and YouTube data, we discover the topic drifting phenomenon between heterogeneous data resources and introduce a novel transfer learning algorithm to annotate video frames by utilizing Flickr images' information in Section 3. Further, to cope with the complex semantic relation-ships, a hierarchical taxonomy named as Semantic Forest is mined from both video and image domains, based on which a bottom-up semantic integration is performed to build hierarchical semantic representation for Web videos in Section 4. In section 5, a group of experiments are designed on a large scale dataset to validate our framework and Section 6 concludes the whole paper.

2. GENERAL FRAMEWORK

A general framework of the proposed method is shown in Figure 2. It can be divided into two parts: 1) Transferring from Flickr images to YouTube videos; 2) Semantic Forest construction and bottom-up semantic integration for video clips. Compared with the prototype of candidate solution in Figure 1, two main modifications are shown in Figure 2. One is the novel transfer learning algorithm from the view of semantic concepts redistribution based on AdaBoost [12]. The other is the semantic integration procedure after the classification of video shots, which are the major contributions of this paper.

The system starts with extracting SIFT descriptors [16] within both the source Flickr images and YouTube videos. Then it constructs Bag-of-Words using K-Means clustering [22]. By analyzing the statistical distributions of semantic concepts over Bag-of-Words across from Flickr images to YouTube video key frames, a redistribution assumption is made and further we propose an AdaBoost-style transfer learning algorithm to transfer the discriminative information from Flickr images to YouTube videos, hence classify each video shot's key frames.

By adopting an unsupervised method over metadata from both Flickr and YouTube, a hierarchical ontology, the *Semantic orest*, is built up according to tags' correlations. Finally, the semantic integration is performed to integrate the semantic concepts in low levels in a bottom-up manner, and thus describe the video clip content as a hierarchical semantic representation. To demonstrate our framework, an YouTube video classification application is set up between large-scale Flickr images and YouTube video clips. Some other potential applications also include hierarchical video browsing, web video tag suggestion, and keyword based video retrieval.

3. LEARNING FROM HETEROGENEOUS DATA

In this section, we want to answer the questions in the following three aspects:

1. Phenomenon: What's the difference of semantic concept-

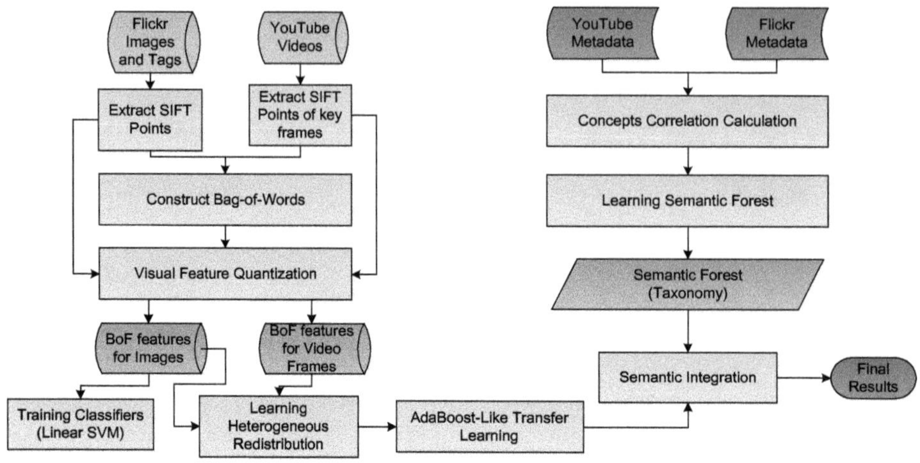

Figure 2: The Framework of the proposed method: Learning heterogeneous data for Web video classification

s distributions across different communities and media, explicitly from Flickr to YouTube?

2. Principles: Why the difference of distributions occurs and what's underlying this phenomenon? This could be principles for analyzing information transferring process between different communities.

3. Solutions: How to build efficient and effective algorithms to transfer discriminative information between heterogeneous data? Furthermore, how to connect different media sources and communities?

3.1 Heterogeneous Nature from Flickr to YouTube

In order to discover the underlying distribution principles of semantic concepts over different data resources, a group of statistical efforts have been done between collections of Flickr images and YouTube video clips. In this paper, we use the NUS-WIDE dataset [8], which contains 260,000 Flickr images and their corresponding tags as well as 2,000 YouTube videos collected from youtube by ourselves.

SIFT descriptors [16] on interesting points are extracted on both the entire Flickr image collection and the key frames of YouTube videos. Then K-means clustering is performed to construct Bag-of-Word following the classical work "Video Google" in [22]. Without loss of generality, we set the cluster number to be 500 as most approaches do, then adopt hard assign to assign each SIFT point to the nearest cluster center, which therefore achieves the vector quantification. Figure 3 shows this process. A major consideration in the BoW construction is whether or not to use the YouTube video data. YouTube videos are usually of lower quality than Flickr images and thus will add certain amount of noise. However, by incorporating them into the BoW construction will reduce the influence of domain shift. In this paper, we compare both strategies and the conclusion is to use both of them.

Each visual word in the dictionary is a compact representation of middle-level semantic concept according to [4][5] and also can reflect the semantic meaning [13]. We treat the visual words as the basic elements that semantic concepts are consisted of, and then analyze the distributions of semantic concepts on the visual words over both Flickr images and YouTube video key frames. Let's denote Flickr image and YouTube video collections contain sets of semantic concepts as $T_{image} = \{t_{i,k}\}$, $T_{video} = \{t_{v,k}\}$ respectively. And further assume they share the same dictionary $\mathcal{D}$ (this is reasonable since they are spanned in the identical d-dimensional feature space $\mathcal{F}^d$). For each semantic concept t in both T_{image} and T_{video}, its distribution on the middle-level concepts $\mathcal{D}$ is defined as:

$$P(t|\mathcal{D}) = \sum_{s \in S_t} p(t, s|\mathcal{D}) \tag{1}$$

where S_t is the samples correspond to concept t. From an intuitive point of view, similar visual content should appear similarly even though within different data sources. However, our observation is totally different. To measure this similarity of two probability distributions of the same concept from Flickr and YouTube data collections respectively,

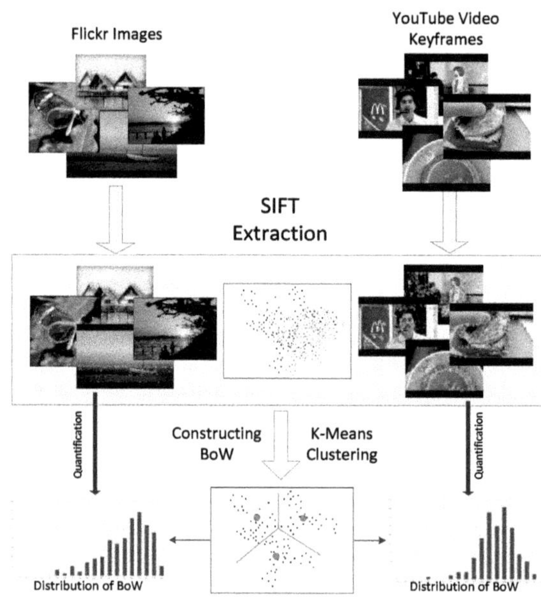

Figure 3: SIFT extraction and Bag-of-Word construction for Flickr images and YouTube video key frames.

a balanced KL-Divergence is introduced as follow:

$$D_{KL}(t_{v,k}, t_{i,k}) = D_{KL}(t_{v,k} \| t_{i,k}) + D_{KL}(t_{i,k} \| t_{v,k}) \quad (2)$$

which means to what extent two probabilistic distributions are different. The detailed results are shown in Table 1. It is obvious that most concepts vary greatly in different domains, but they are still related with each other to some degree by distributed similarly.

So what are the reasons of this phenomenon? We consider following potential factors:

1. Descriptor: We use SIFT points in the feature detection and description phase, which is invariant to *scale*, *translation*, and *rotation*. Similar SIFT points from Flickr images and YouTube video frames are still able to be matched as shown in Figure 4. Thus, this factor is not one of the reasons.

2. BoW Construction: As illustrated in previous part, we use SIFT points from both Flickr and YouTube to construct the dictionary. And considering the data scale we utilized, the obtained Bag-of-Words representations are robust and stable. Thus, the BoW construction is not the reason either.

3. Heterogeneous Distribution: We compare some tags' distributions over the 500 visual words between Flickr images and YouTube videos, and some of the results are shown in Figure 5. It can be observed that there are significant probabilistic distribution shifts between different Flickr and YouTube for each concept. Therefore, we attribute the *Heterogeneous henomenon* to the re-distribution of concepts.

Figure 4: SIFT points matching between Flickr image and YouTube video frame. The left part is from Flickr, and the right one is from YouTube.

However, previous researches on transfer learning and multimedia retrieval usually omitted this fact and focused on transfer learning on feature space or decision hyper-plane. In this work, we focus on the re-distribution of mid-level concepts and make the following assumption:

LEMMA 1. (Redistribution of Semantic Concepts across communities)
Semantic concepts t_i and t_v from different communities sharing the identical feature space but different distribution over middle-level concepts ($p(t_v|\mathcal{D}) \neq p(t_i|\mathcal{D})$), is able to transfer to each other by redistributing middle level concepts as

$$p(t_v|\mathcal{D}) = \prod_{d_k \in \mathcal{D}} \eta_k^{v,i} p(t_i|d_k) = \eta \times P(t_i|\mathcal{D}) \quad (3)$$

where $\vec{\eta} = \{\eta_1, \eta_2, ..., \eta_{|\mathcal{D}|}\}$ is the redistribution parameter vector.

The lemma indicates that *the transfer learning can be viewed in a middle-level concepts' redistribution perspective*, which answers question 1 and 2 at the beginning of this section.

Table 1: Balanced KL-Divergence on the same tag between different media sources.

	Airport	Animal	Bear	Boats	Bridge	Buildings	Cars	Cityscape
Airport	0.1205							
Animal		0.0471						
Bear			0.0666					
Boats				0.1351				
Bridge					0.2068			
Buildings						0.0657		
Cars							0.1560	
Cityscape								0.2762

3.2 AdaBoost-Like Transfer Learning

According to the above analysis, a straightforward algorithm which transfers Flickr images' discriminative information to YouTube videos is shown in Algorithm 1 based on the *edistribution Lemma*:

Algorithm 1:

Input: Linear classifier $f(x_i) = \mathbf{w}_i x_i$ for concept t
Output: Linear classifier $g(x_v) = \mathbf{w}_v x_v$ for concept t

```
foreach visual word d_k ∈ D do
    Estimate p(t_i|d_k) and p(t_v|d_k);
    Compute η_k = p(t_v|d_k) / p(t_i|d_k);
end
η⃗ = {η_k};
g(x_v) = η⃗ · f(x_i);
return g(x_v)
```

The basic idea of Algorithm 1 is to estimate the redistribution coefficients vector $\vec{\eta}$ from image domain to video domain, and hence re-organize the classifier $f(x_i) = \mathbf{w}_i x_i$ for concept t in image domain to adapt for the videos and obtain the target classifier $g(x_v)$. This is the direct conclusion from *edistribution Lemma*. However, we want to impose some further considerations as follows:

1. Since the labeled video data is hard to obtain, it is impossible to fully and accurately estimate both $p(t_v|d_k)$ and the redistribution coefficient vector $\vec{\eta} = \{\eta_k\}$;

2. This algorithm assumes that all visual words are equally contributed to semantic concept t, which not holds all the time in the real case (where different concepts usually bias different visual words).

To solve these problems, we propose an AdaBoost-Like transfer learning algorithm as an extension of Algorithm 1. Equation (3) can be approximated by choosing the most representative visual words with the most discriminative information as follows:

$$p(t_v|\mathcal{D}) = \prod_{d_k \in \mathcal{D}} \eta_k^{v,i} p(t_i|d_k) \simeq \prod_{d_k \in \widetilde{\mathcal{D}}} \eta_k^{v,i} p(t_i|d_k) \quad (4)$$

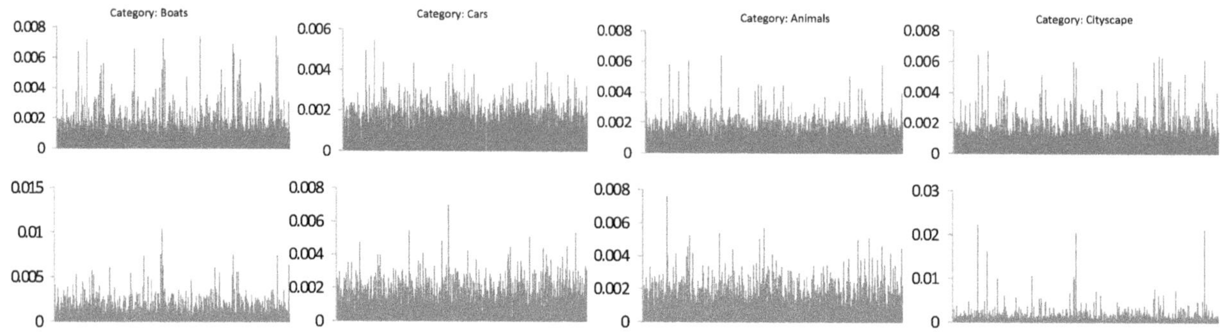

Figure 5: Semantic Concepts' distribution on visual words between Flickr images and YouTube video clips. The red ones are distribution of Flickr images on visual words, and the blue ones are the distribution of YouTube videos.

where $\widetilde{\mathcal{D}}$ is a subset of $\mathcal{D}$ with the most discriminative information. Then the transfer learning problems becomes a visual word selection and redistribution process, which can be easily solved by adopting the boosting idea. Thus, we naturally resort to the AdaBoost algorithm as shown in Algorithm 2.

Algorithm 2: AdaBoost-Like Transfer Learning Algorithm

Input: Linear Distribution $H_i = \mathbf{w}_i x_i$ for concept t, Loop L

Output: Linear Distribution H_v for concept t

Learn classifier $f(x_i)$ for images ;

Initialization: $H_v^{(0)} = H_i$, $\mathbf{w}_k = p(t_i|d_k)$, $W = \{w_k\}$;

for $l = 1, ..., L$ **do**

  Calculate training error on target domain according to $W^{(l)}$, $\epsilon^{(l)}$ on H_v^l ;

  Set $\beta_l = \epsilon^{(l)}/(1-\epsilon^{(l)})$;

  Update weight vector $w_k^{(l+1)} = w_k^{(l)} \beta_l^{1-\frac{1}{N}\sum|h^{(l)}(x)-y|}$;

  Update $w_k^{(l+1)} = \frac{w_k^{(l+1)}}{\sum w_k^{(l+1)}}$;

end

Output hypothesis $H_v = \sum w_K^{(l+1)} x_k$;

Apply hypothesis H_v on $f(x) \rightarrow f(H_v(x_v))$;

In Algorithm 2, the distribution $p(t_v)$ is initialized by the distribution on images collection $p(t_i)$, and the hypothesis for target domain $H_v^{(0)}$ is initialized with H_i from image domain. In each round of iteration, the middle level semantic concepts with lower response to target domain are weakened and the ones with higher response strengthened according to classifying error on the target domain samples. This is intuitive that the algorithm modifies the middle-level concepts' distribution to adapt the new domain.

In our application, we use linear-SVM trained on the Flickr image domain as the initial classifier, and this algorithm can be easily extended to any other type of classifiers. Besides, kernel methods are also available on this framework, by changing the hypothesis into kernel formulation. We use all the Flickr images to train the initial SVMs and in order to learn the hypothesis, a small part of YouTube videos are manually labeled and incorporated.

The AdaBoost-Like algorithm requires less labeled data in the target domain than Algorithm 1 because no probabilistic distribution on the target domain is needed to be estimated, and the training data is just used to evaluate the error of the current hypothesis. On the other hand, the AdaBoost-Like algorithm selects middle-level concepts by modifying the redistribution.

3.2.1 *Deep Insight of AdaBoost-Transfer*

There are mainly two concerns about the proposed AdaBoost-Transfer: the effect of emphasizing certain features and the robustness of AdaBoost methods. For the first concern, SIFT descriptors deal well with the scale change and are invariant to various situations. Thus, the detected SIFT points in both Flickr image domain and the YouTube video domain lie in the same feature space but distributed differently. The AdaBoost-Transfer aims at selecting the most stable feature under the unified hypothesis, and thus improves classification accuracy.

As to the second concern, the user tags on the Internet are noisy and not reliable enough, which may potentially lead to un-robustness of AdaBoost method. As addressed in the previous researches [31] and [20], this problem could be get rid of by using redundant data. In this paper, we introduce redundant data by using large-scale images and videos and thus eliminate the sensitiveness of AdaBoost algorithm.

3.2.2 *Relationship with Other Work*

The essence of this algorithm is to change the concepts' distribution over middle-level concepts followed by *edistribution Lemma*, instead of assuming the distribution over raw feature space, which is the basic idea of A-SVM. Another related work is CCCL [20] which also use AdaBoost for transfer learning. However, CCCL chooses categories to involve relationships between different categories in each round. Our work is motivated by resolving the nature of domain transfer from Flickr to YouTube.

4. CONSTRUCTION SEMANTIC FOREST

4.1 Semantic Forest

Semantic Forest is a hierarchical cross-community taxonomy consists with a group of trees representing the ontology for each category, which aims at building an efficient organization of semantic concepts covering various communities. To mine useful information from huge-scale metadata on the web, the construction of Semantic Forest follows a data-driven approach. This could benefit especially from the fact that the web is dynamic and changing all the time.

The principles in *Semantic orest* construction are: The links between nodes are determined by their co-occurrences: More co-occurred tags tend to be connected more strongly in the taxonomy. The level of each node is determined by its importance, which is indicated by the frequency. We denote the tag collection and their correlations as $\mathbf{N} = \{n_i\}$ and $\mathbf{E} = \{e_{i,j} | n_i, n_j \in \mathbf{N}\}$, where

$$e_{i,j} = \frac{e_{i,j}^{Flickr} \cdot e_{i,j}^{YouTube}}{e_{i,j}^{Flickr} + e_{i,j}^{YouTube}} \quad (5)$$

is the harmonic-mean of the correlations between concept i and j in both Flickr and YouTube, and satisfying

$$\mathbf{e}_i^{Flickr} = \sum_{n_j \in \mathbf{N}} e_{i,j}^{Flickr} = 1, \mathbf{e}_i^{YouTube} = \sum_{n_j \in \mathbf{N}} e_{i,j}^{YouTube} = 1 \quad (6)$$

after normalization. This formulation considers both communities and response only when in both of the two communities the concepts are correlated with each other.

For each category of semantic concepts, we build a semantic tree representing the ontology within this category. After TF-IDF processing, useless tags are removed. Considering computation cost and data redundancy in the large scale web data, a direct but effective method is applied to extract semantic concepts approximately: Its basic idea is to first select the most important nodes in graph $G = (\mathbf{N}, \mathbf{E})$, then partition all nodes into sub-groups as their sub-trees, and finally select representative tags in each sub-tree. We iteratively perform this operation in each round until convergent. In each round, the nodes with top averaged degree is treated as more important and defined as:

$$\arg\max_i \frac{ei}{|e_i|_1}, e_i = \sum_j e_{i,j} \quad (7)$$

where the L1 norm is defined as the count of non-zero elements in each row vector $e_i = \{e_{i,j}\}$.

Considering a real situation that even single concept could make sense for multiple categories, for instance, "Apple" could be either a kind of fruit belonging to "Food" or a kind of computer (tag could be added to the semantic forest in multiple times). Algorithm 3 shows the detailed process of constructing Semantic Forest.

Following this process, the obtained Semantic Forest is a group of K-Trees. Other operations such as punch and trim can be easily integrated into the K-Trees.

Compared with former work mainly using linguistic models such as WordNet [17], the proposed *Semantic orest* emphasizes on using a data-driven approach to automatically learn the representation and organization structure fitting for Web multimedia semantics, therefore is more appropriate for classifying Web videos and images than the traditional approaches. Another advantage is by using the large-scale data, the noisy tags are eliminated because of their small occurrences.

Algorithm 3: Constructing Semantic Forest

Output: Semantic Forest $\mathcal{F} = \{Tree_i\}$

Calculate $\mathbf{E}^{Flickr} = \{e_i^{Flickr}\}$ and $\mathbf{E}^{YouTube} = \{e_i^{YouTube}\}$;

Construct $\mathbf{E} = \frac{\mathbf{E}^{Flickr}\mathbf{E}^{YouTube}}{\mathbf{E}^{Flickr}+\mathbf{E}^{YouTube}}$ and $\mathcal{N}$;

$\forall Tree_i \in \mathcal{F}, Tree_i = Null$;

Select top K tags as roots for each tree following Eq. (8)

$r_i, r_2, ..., r_K$ And $\forall Tree_i \in \mathcal{F}, Tree_i = r_i$;

for $l = 1, ...L$ **do**

  foreach $Tree_i$ **do**

    foreach *node* t_i^l *on the l-th level of* $Tree_i$ **do**

      Find K best nodes related with t_i^l according to Eq. (5);

      Add these nodes as children of t_i^l;

    end

  end

end

4.1.1 *Why Flickr and YouTube?*

In this part, the reason why use Flickr + YouTube tags to construct the Semantic Forest is explained. Since the most popular tags on YouTube is related with music, movie, and pop singers, it is hard to extract effective information for video classification. Figure 6 shows an example of taxonomy tree extracted by only using YouTube information. Basically speaking, this is totally useless for efficient video annotation. However, the Flickr community does not focus on these aspects, and thus can remove useless information by using the harmonic average

$$e_{i,j} = \frac{e_{i,j}^{Flickr} \cdot e_{i,j}^{YouTube}}{e_{i,j}^{Flickr} + e_{i,j}^{YouTube}}. \quad (8)$$

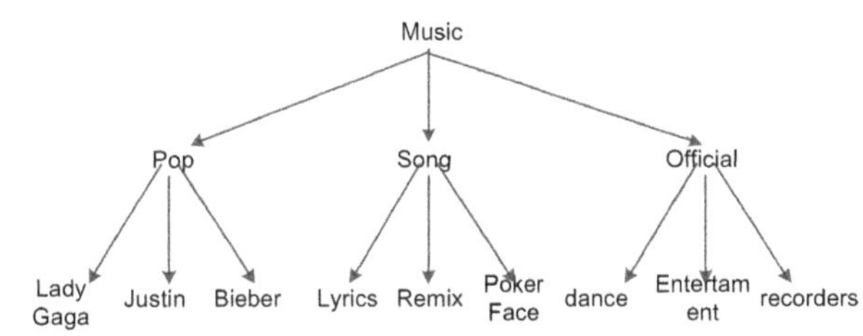

Figure 6: Taxonomy tree extracted only using YouTube information.

The most popular root concepts after filtering by Flickr become "Football", "Island" and "Africa" *et. al.* Due to the limitation of space, full semantic forest cannot be shown here.

4.2 Bottom-Up Semantic Integration

A bottom-up semantic integration is performed on the semantic forest, in order to integrate low-level semantic concepts into high-level ones. In our application of web video classification, this process is used to integrate the specific classification results of video key frames to more general concepts representation by using higher level semantics, including shots, scenes and video clips levels. All the operations are based on the assumptions that: classification on each higher level concept is determined by not only itself, but also the children concept collection C. This can be formulated as:

$$\tilde{p}(A) = (1-\lambda)p(A) + \lambda \sum_{c_i \in C} p(c_i)p(A|c_i) \qquad (9)$$

where $p(c_i)$ is the classification probability of child concept c_i, λ is a normalization factor to ensure that $\lambda \sum p(A|c_i) = 1$, $p(A)$ is the classification probability of concept A itself, and $\tilde{p}(A)$ is the final output result.

This integration is performed iteratively until reaching the top of each semantic tree. For each input video clip, the final classification result is the vector with every element representing classification score on corresponding semantic tree. This process is intuitively shown in Figure 7.

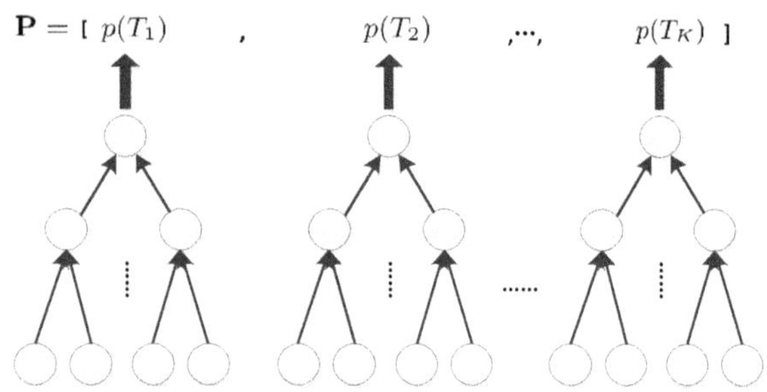

Figure 7: Classification result on semantic forest for the input video clip.

5. EXPERIMENTS

5.1 Preliminary

The data in our experiments include mainly two parts. For the image domain, NUS-WIDE dataset collected from Flickr is used, which contains 260,000 images, including corresponding tags. For the video domain, we collected 2,000 video clips from YouTube together with their keywords, descriptions and categories. 100 key frames are uniformly selected from each video clips without video shot detection, thus totally 200,000 video key frames are obtained. For the feature extraction, all Flickr images and 10,000 video key frames all over the dataset are chosen as input for K-Means clustering and construct the dictionary, by applying a Difference of Gaussian detector. Figure 8 shows examples of both images and videos.

To construct the Semantic Forest, we crawled 20,000 keywords using API provided by Flickr and Google YouTube respectively, and select most frequent 1,000 from these to construct the Semantic Forest. We set $K = 6$ in the construction which means each parent node has at most 6 children in the semantic tree. Thus the max depth of each semantic tree is 4.

5.2 Experimental Results

We compare various video classification scenarios on different setting and different algorithms in this section. 260,000 Flickr images and only 200 manually labeled YouTube video clips are used as training samples, by assigning each video with only one label. For the testing video examples, the keywords used to query on YouTube are stored as the ground truth. This leads to potential performance drop because not all the keywords are reasonable labeled by users.

Table 2: Performance Comparison with various methods

	Visual Word Construction	
	Flickr Only	Flickr & YouTube
VideoOnly	–	0.347
NoAdaBoost	0.283	0.314
AdaBoostTrans	0.304	0.326

Table 3: Experiments of the proposed method compared with other algorithms.

Category	VideoOnly	NoAdaBoost	AdaBoostTrans
Airport	0.212	0.054	0.072
Animal	0.048	0.138	0.136
Bear	0.417	0.417	0.306
Boats	0.072	0.344	0.469
Bridge	0.490	0.074	0.296
Buildings	0.911	0.465	0.854
Cars	0.373	0.630	0.451
cityscape	0.214	0.407	0.407

5.2.1 *Video Classification Performance*

Table 2 show the performance of the framework proposed in this paper compared with other methods, which are explained in details as follows:

VideoOnly - train a linear-SVM classier for each class using those 200 manually labeled videos as training samples and no Flickr images are incorporated in the training procedure.

NoAdaBoost - train a linear-SVM classier for each class using only Flickr images and no transfer learning strategy is used.

AdaBoostTrans - train a linear-SVM classier for each class using only Flickr images and labeled video data is used in the AdaBoost-Like transfer learning process.

The **VideoOnly** method uses only precisely labeled video clips as training data, which performs best but needs most human label. The performance of this method is the upper bound of video classification algorithms in our assumption.

Another observation is that the performance will improve by constructing dictionary using both Flickr images and YouTube video frames instead of using Flickr images only. This increases visual features' diversity and thus makes visual words more robust in representing visual content.

Table 4 shows detailed performance comparison on eight different categories. Since we don't incorporate motion feature into the training stage, all methods perform poorly on concepts such as "Animal" and "Airport". "Animal" videos are usually about moving animals beyond the ability of SIFT features, and "Airport" is really hard since airport is a very dynamic scene.

On the other hand, for some complex concepts such as "cityscape", we achieve better and more stable performance. This is because solely video data cannot provide sufficient information for these complex concepts, and large-scale Flickr images will make it much easier to solve this problem.

Figure 8: Examples of Flickr images and YouTube videos used in the experiments.

Table 4: Performance of semantic integration on Semantic Forest.

VideoOnly	0.347
AdaBoostTrans	0.326
AdaBoost-SemanticForest	**0.354**

An overall conclusion is that, the AdaBoost-Like transfer learning algorithm utilizes Flickr images to extend the representation ability of visual words, and also improves the stability of classifiers learned from image domain.

5.2.2 *Semantic Forest and Semantic Trees*

In this section, we emphasize on analyzing the effects of Semantic Forest and Semantic Trees.

The usefulness of taxonomy in classification, detection and recognition has been proved in many researches [17][23][19]. We apply semantic integration process on the extracted Semantic Forest, for which the classification results are shown in Table 4.

AdaBoost-SemanticForest - refers to adding learned semantic forest to AdaBoostTrans scenario to integrate semantic concepts in a bottom-up manner.

It is shown that the integration results are better than other approaches, even exceed the method directly using precisely labeled videos in training. This improvement can be attributed to the correlation and hierarchical structure of Semantic Forest, which integrates the classification results of related concepts to the target concept. Another question: Does the level of semantic trees affect the performance of video classification? In this subsection, we show some results on semantic integration using semantic trees with different levels. Figure 9 shows the average video classification precision of se-mantic integration using different semantic trees with different levels.

We change the size of children for each node (K) and the level of semantic forests L. The results are shown in Figure 9. More levels will incorporate more semantic concepts and thus improve performance, but will increase time cost as well. For the reason of balance, we set the level $L = 4$. The other issue we want to discuss is the number of children K. A larger K will integrate more concepts in fewer levels, thus when $K = 8$, the performance curve increase more sharply. But this will introduce non-relevant concepts into classification, based on which the performance cure slows down as the level of semantic forest grows.

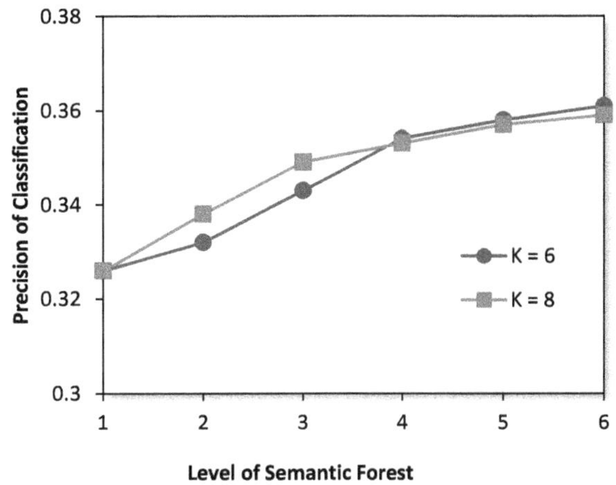

Figure 9: Performance of Semantic Forest integration under different depths and different children numbers.

6. CONCLUSION

This paper analyzes the heterogeneous phenomenon between different media. We assume the domain transfer from Flickr to YouTube is not caused by feature representation but the redistribution of middle-level semantic concepts. Subsequently, a simple but effective transfer learning algorithm is proposed using an AdaBoost-Like algorithm. Another contribution of this paper is the construction of the so-called semantic forest. To make use of keyword correlation into video classification, we build the semantic forest by mining concepts relationships within both Flickr and YouTube website. Based on this hierarchical taxonomy, a semantic integration operation is performed to integrate lower-level concepts to higher level ones. Several groups of experiments are performed on NUS-WIDE image database and 2,000 videos collected from YouTube.com. The experiment results show that our algorithm is both effective and efficient.

7. ACKNOWLEDGEMENT

This work was supported by National Natural Science Foundation of China (Grant No. 61071180 and Key Program Grant No.čž61133003), and in part to Dr. Qi Tian by NSF IIS 1052851, Faculty Research Awards by Google, FXPAL and NEC Laboratories of America, respectively.

8. REFERENCES

[1] Trecvid 2010 website. `http://www-nlpir.nist.gov/projects/tv2010`, 2010.

[2] A. Amir, J. Argillander, M. Campbell, A. Haubold, G. Iyengar, S. Ebadollahi, F. Kang, M. R. Naphade, A. P. Natsev, J. R. Smith, J. Tesic, and T. Volkmer. Ibm research trecvid-2005 video retrieval system. 2005.

[3] H. Aradhye, G. Toderici, and J. Yagnik. Video2text: Learning to annotate video content. In *I International Conference on Data Mining*, pages 144–151, 2009.

[4] Y.-L. Boureau, F. Bach, Y. LeCun, and J. Ponce. Learning mid-level features for recognition. In *I Computer Vision and attern ecognition*, pages 2559–2566, 2010.

[5] Y.-L. Boureau, J. Ponce, and Y. LeCun. A theoretical analysis of feature pooling in visual recognition. In *International Conference on Machine Learning*, pages 111–118, 2010.

[6] M. Campbell. Ibm research trecvid - 2006 video retrieval system. In *C Video etrieval valuation*, 2006.

[7] S.-F. Chang, W. Hsu, L. Kennedy, L. Xie, A. Yanagawa, E. Zavesky, and D.-Q. Zhang. Columbia university trecvid-2005 video search and high-level feature extraction. In *C Video etrieval valuation*, 2005.

[8] T.-S. Chua, J. Tang, R. Hong, H. Li, Z. Luo, and Y. Zheng. Nus-wide: a real-world web image database from national university of singapore. In *Conference on Image and Video etrieval*, pages 1–9, 2009.

[9] J. Deng, W. Dong, R. Socher, L.-J. Li, K. Li, and F.-F. Li. Imagenet: A large-scale hierarchical image database. In *I Computer Vision and attern ecognition*, pages 248–255, 2009.

[10] L. Duan, I. W.-H. Tsang, D. Xu, and S. J. Maybank. Domain transfer svm for video concept detection. In *I Computer Vision and attern ecognition*, pages 1375–1381, 2009.

[11] L. Duan, D. Xu, I. W.-H. Tsang, and J. Luo. Visual event recognition in videos by learning from web data. In *I Computer Vision and attern ecognition*, pages 1959–1966, 2010.

[12] Y. Freund and R. E. Schapire. A decision-theoretic generalization of on-line learning and an application to boosting. In *uropean Conference on Computational Learning heory*, pages 23–37, 1995.

[13] R. Ji, H. Yao, X. Sun, B. Zhong, and W. Gao. Towards semantic embedding in visual vocabulary. In *Computer Vision and attern ecognition*, pages 918–925, 2010.

[14] Y.-G. Jiang, C.-W. Ngo, and S.-F. Chang. Semantic context transfer across heterogeneous sources for domain adaptive video search. In *ACM International Conference on Multimedia*, pages 155–164, 2009.

[15] I. Laptev, M. Marszalek, C. Schmid, and B. Rozenfeld. Learning realistic human actions from movies. In *I Computer Vision and attern ecognition*, 2008.

[16] D. G. Lowe. Distinctive image features from scale-invariant keypoints. *International ournal of Computer Vision*, 60:91–110, 2004.

[17] M. Marszalek and C. Schmid. Semantic hierarchies for visual object recognition. In *I Computer Vision and attern ecognition*, 2007.

[18] S. J. Pan and Q. Yang. A survey on transfer learning. *I ransactions on nowledge and Data ngineering*, 22:1345–1359, 2010.

[19] G.-J. Qi, X.-S. Hua, Y. Rui, J. Tang, T. Mei, and H.-J. Zhang. Correlative multi-label video annotation. In *ACM International Conference on Multimedia*, pages 17–26, 2007.

[20] G.-J. Qi, Y. Rui, Q. Tian, and T. Huang. Towards cross-cateogory knowledge propagation for learning visual concepts. In *I Computer Vision and attern ecognition*, pages 897–904, 2011.

[21] M. Rohrbach, M. Stark, G. Szarvas, I. Gurevych, and B. Schiele. What helps where - and why? semantic relatedness for knowledge transfer. In *I Computer Vision and attern ecognition*, pages 910–917, 2010.

[22] J. Sivic and A. Zisserman. Video google: A text retrieval approach to object matching in videos. In *International Conference on Computer Vision*, pages 1470–1477, 2003.

[23] Y. Song, M. Zhao, J. Yagnik, and X. Wu. Taxonomic classification for web-based videos. In *I Computer Vision and attern ecognition*, pages 871–878, 2010.

[24] M. Wang and X.-S. Hua. Active learning in multimedia annotation and retrieval: A survey. *ACM ranscation on Intelligent System and echnolgy*, 2, 2011.

[25] M. Wang, X.-S. Hua, R. Hong, J. Tang, G.-J. Qi, and Y. Song. Unified video annotation via multi-graph learning. *I ranscation on Circuits and System for Video echnology*, 19, 2009.

[26] Z. Wang, M. Zhao, Y. Song, S. Kumar, and B. Li. Youtubecat: Learning to categorize wild web videos. In *I Computer Vision and attern ecognition*, pages 879–886, 2010.

[27] L. Xie, R. Yan, J. Tesic, A. Natsev, and J. R. Smith. Probabilistic visual concept trees. In *ACM International Conference on Multimedia*, pages 867–870, 2010.

[28] A. Yanagawa, S.-F. Chang, L. Kennedy, and W. Hsu. Columbia university's baseline detectors for 374 lscom semantic visual concepts. Technical report, Columbia University ADVENT, 2007.

[29] J. Yang, R. Yan, and A. G. Hauptmann. Cross-domain video concept detection using adaptive svms. In *ACM International Conference on Multimedia*, pages 188–197, 2007.

[30] Y. Yang, D. Xu, F. Nie, J. Luo, and Y. Zhuang. Ranking with local regression and global alignment for cross media retrieval. In *ACM Multimedia Conference*, pages 175–184, 2009.

[31] Y. Yao and G. Doretto. Boosting for transfer learning with multiple sources. In *I Computer Vision and attern ecognition*, pages 1855–1862, 2010.

[32] J. Yuen, B. C. Russell, C. Liu, and A. Torralba. Labelme video: Building a video database with human annotations. In *International Conference on Computer Vision*, pages 1451–1458, 2009.

Coached Active Learning for Interactive Video Search*

Xiao-Yong Wei
Machine Intelligence Laboratory
College of Computer Science
Sichuan University
610065, Chengdu, China
cswei@scu.edu.cn

Zhen-Qun Yang
Machine Intelligence Laboratory
College of Computer Science
Sichuan University
610065, Chengdu, China
jessicayang@scu.edu.cn

ABSTRACT

Active learning with uncertainty sampling has been popularly employed in implementing interactive video search, due to its promise to reduce labeling efforts. However, since the ultimate goal of interactive search is to find as many relevant shots as possible, the purely explorative learning strategy always places conventional active learning in a dilemma whether to explore uncertain areas for a better understanding of query distribution or to harvest in certain areas for more relevant instances. In this paper, we propose a novel paradigm of active learning, where a coaching process is introduced to guide the leaner by jointly consulting an estimated prior query distribution and a posterior query distribution indicated by current classifier outcomes. To bypass the difficulty of estimating the prior query distribution from a limited number of labeled relevant instances, we propose to estimate the distribution using a set of semantic distributions which are statistically from the same distributions as the labeled relevant instances. With the coaching of both prior and posterior query distributions, the learning can be conducted and scheduled with a global perspective, and thus can explicitly balance the trade-off between exploitation and exploration. The results of the experiments on TRECVID 2005–2009 datasets validate the efficiency and effectiveness of our approach, which outperforms the conventional active learning methods with uncertainty sampling and also shows superiority to several state-of-the art interactive video search systems.

Categories and Subject Descriptors

H.3.3 [**Information Storage and Retrieval**]: Information Search and Retrieval

General Terms

Design, Algorithms, Performance, Experimentation

Keywords

Coached Active Learning, Interactive Search, Querying Function

1. INTRODUCTION

Interactive video search is an efficient supplement to automatic search. In automatic search, a user provides an initial query (usually a text sentence) as the only input and sits beside in the rest of the searching process, in the hope that the system is able to figure out her/his query intention *automatically* and returns the relevant shots on demand. However, due to the limited ability of machine to reason *semantically* (due to the semantic gap), the performance of automatic search is still unsatisfactory in contrast to that of interactive search. The trick of interactive search lies in further involving the user in the searching process to help the machine understand her/his intention by providing *relevance feedback*. More specifically, every time the system returns a list of shots, a user can selectively label some shots as "relevant" or "irrelevant". The labels will be used as evidence for the system to refine its guess about the user's query intention and thus start a new round of search. The process repeats recursively until a satisfactory resulting list is reached or the user gives up. As most users cannot keep constant patience with the iterative labeling, learning their query intention *effectively* is critical in designing an interactive search system.

A commonly adopted scheme for this purpose is active learning [1], which speeds up the process by reducing the number of shots needed to be labeled. In active learning, the search is considered a recursive process to train a classifier which distinguishes relevant shots from irrelevant ones. The training is generally conducted on the labeled instances (with relevant shots as positive examples and irrelevant ones as negative) and repeats every time when freshly labeled instances are obtained through the users' labeling. To reduce the efforts of labeling, existing approaches try to select the most informative shots to query users. In terms of a support vector machine (SVM) learner, this can be done conveniently by sampling the shots closest to the separating hyperplane (i.e., the decision boundary), because those are the shots the machine is most uncertain of. Once being labeled, this will potentially cause a significant change of the hyperplane in the next round so as to improve the classifier. This greedy strategy is termed as *uncertainty sampling* [2–9].

Even being popularly employed, however, uncertainty sampling has been found not of a "kindred soul" with video search. The spirit of uncertainty sampling is to reduce the efforts of labeling by avoiding querying users with shots that the machine is most confident with, e.g., those farthest from the hyperplane on the positive side. Nevertheless, in video search, those shots are exactly what the users are looking for and delay of labeling them may frustrate the users at early stages, resulting in abortion of the learning. In other words, uncertainty sampling aims to achieve a high quality classifier at the final stage and thus is not eager to "harvest" relevant shots returned by the precursor classifiers. In interactive video search (especially at early stages), we concentrate more on the harvest and put less emphasis on the quality of the final classifier, a conflict also observed by A. G. Hauptmann *et al.* [10]. The problem can be related to an open question known as trade-off between

*Area chair: Marcel Worring

MM'11, November 28–December 1, 2011, Scottsdale, Arizona, USA.

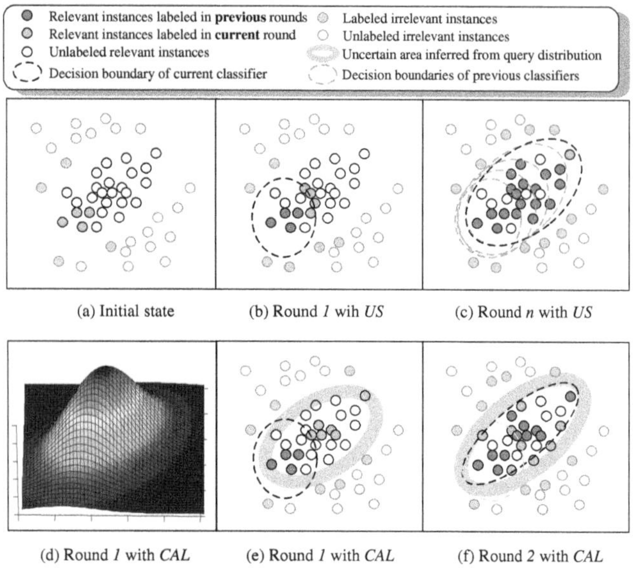

Figure 1: Learning with uncertainty sampling (US) and coached active learning (CAL): (a) initial state (of both US and CAL), several instances are labeled by users from the ranked list by initial search; (b) round 1 with US, the first classifier is trained, US samples those along the decision boundary to query next; (c) round n with US, after gradual expansion with numerous rounds, the decision boundary finally approaches to optimal; (d) round 1 with CAL, a query distribution is estimated; (e) round 1 with CAL, the first classifier is trained, CAL samples instances at two places to query next, namely in the dense area of the estimated query distribution and in uncertain area (estimated based on query distribution and classifier outputs); and (f) round 2 with CAL, query distribution and the uncertain area are re-estimated, the decision boundary is roughly close to optimal with only *two* rounds.

exploitation and exploration [11, 12], where a learner always hesitates whether to utilize knowledge at hand for obtaining immediate rewards or to explore the unknown area for improving future gains. It is a dilemma encountered by any learning process conducted on an unknown distribution, but has not been addressed sufficiently by prior studies of active learning.

In this paper, we propose a novel paradigm of active learning, which is able to estimate the probability density function (*pdf*) of the underlying query distribution to avoid the risk of learning on a completely unknown distribution. The estimated *pdf*, together with the distribution of the current classifier outcomes, will be used to guide the sampling, in the way that we give priority to two types of instances to query next, namely instances in the dense area (for boosting the harvest) and instances in the uncertain area (for figuring out the real decision boundary). The proportion of the two types can be controlled with a balancing factor determined on the harvest history, so that we encourage exploitation if the number of freshly labeled relevant shots maintains a growth momentum statistically, and otherwise we encourage exploration. This can balance the exploitation and exploration in a more principled way. In the sense that the learning is jointly guided with the estimated query distribution and distribution of the classifier outcomes, we name it as coached active learning (CAL) to distinguish it from conventional approaches without the coaching process. Compared with existing methods in active learning, CAL offers the following advantages:

- *Predictable Query Distribution*: Conventional approaches of active learning usually assume the query distribution is unknown, because it is difficult to estimate with only a limited number of labeled instances available. We argue that the query distribution is predictable in the scenario of video search. To bypass the difficulty of estimating it on labeled instances directly, we use a statistical test to find training examples which are from the same distribution(s) as the labeled instances, and use the distribution(s) of those examples to predict that of the query. More specifically, by taking the advantage of the widely available labels of semantic concepts[1] (e.g., Large-Scale Concept Ontology for Multimedia (LSCOM) [14]), we can group training examples into non-exclusive groups with each group representing a certain semantic element. For example, a group representing "airplane" can be collected from training examples being labeled as *airplane*. Furthermore, intersection and union operations can be used on existing groups for generating new groups representing more specific or general semantic elements, e.g., a group representing "military personnel" can be generated using the intersection of groups *military* and *people* (i.e., *military*∩*people*). During query time when labeled instances are available, we can compare them to each group and finally locate groups which are statistically from the same distribution(s) as the labeled instances. The groups can presumably represent different semantic aspects of the query, and their distributions thus can be used as predictors to estimate that of the query. For example, the query distribution of "find an airplane in sky" can be predicted with the distributions of groups *airplane*, *sky* and *airplane*∩*sky*. The details will be given in Section 3.
- *Rapid Convergence*: Without known query distribution, conventional active learning is often conducted in a purely exploratory manner and converges slowly. As shown in Figures 1(a) to (c), with uncertainty sampling, the expansion of the decision boundary is dependent on the freshly labeled instances, i.e., those closest to the decision boundary of the last round. A new boundary is thus stickily attached to that of the last round. It may take numerous rounds for the learner to figure out the optimal boundary. In contrast, supposing the query distribution has been well estimated, the proposed method can explore the target space in a more greedy manner, in the way that, to approximate the shape of the optimal boundary, we preferentially select two types of instances to query next: those in the dense area of the estimated query distribution (to search the center of the optimal boundary), and those in the uncertain areas where the learner still gets confused after consulting the estimated query distribution and the distribution of current classifier outputs (to search the real boundary, the way of estimating the uncertain areas will be given in Section 4). As shown in Figures 1(d) to (f), this helps the learner discover the optimal boundary rapidly.
- *Exploitation versus Exploration*: As aforementioned, the proposed method can balance the trade-off between exploitation and exploration through a balancing factor determined on harvest history. When the algorithm is encouraging exploitation, users can continuously find relevant shots and keep their patience with labeling, while the algorithm is encouraging exploration, the decision boundary is expanded towards uncertain area so as to increase the chance of locating more relevant shots in a long run. As we will show in Section 4, the

[1]These annotation collections are previously developed for training concept classifiers to fulfill the task of high-level concept indexing in TRECVID [13].

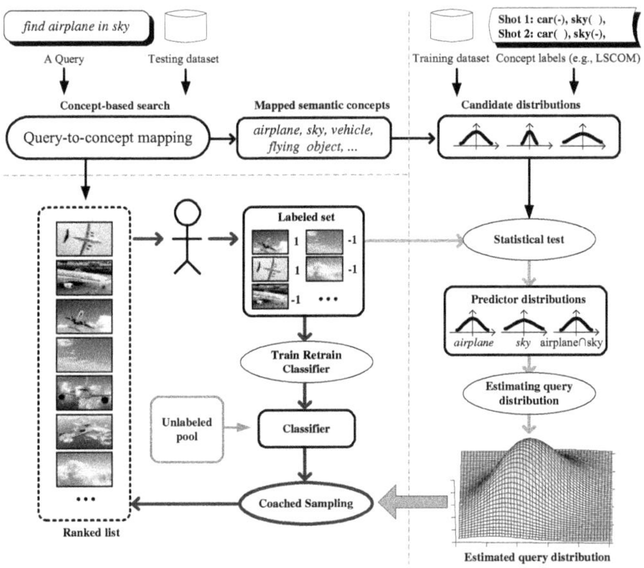

Figure 2: Interactive search framework consisting of three modules (divided by the red dashed lines): initial search (upper-left), query modeling (right), and coached active learning (bottom-left).

proposed method is not only able to choose the appropriate timing of exploitation or exploration through the balancing factor, but also able to control the step size of exploiting or exploring. To sum up, the balance scheme aims to maximize the harvest as well as minimize the users' efforts on labeling.

- *User Patience Maintenance*: It is of great importance to satisfy users with as many relevant shots as possible at the first few rounds of learning, not only for maintaining their enthusiasm on labeling, but also for collecting enough examples for training classifier. To this end, some of the existing methods even force users to annotate a fix number of instances at the first round [9]. However, it is impractical in video search because a coarse classifier at an early stage is often incapable of identifying enough relevant shots, a common issue observed by many authors [8,15]. In this paper, with the help of the estimated *pdf*, the proposed method can help the leaner locate the densest area of the query distribution where the relevant shots are abundant, and prevents the learning from unexpected abortion.

With the coached active learning, the framework of our interactive video search is shown in Figure 2. It consists of three modules: initial search, query distribution modeling, and coached active learning. We employ a concept-based search method [16] to perform the initial search, which returns not only an initial ranked list for labeling, but also a set of concepts semantically related to the query. In query modeling, every time when the labeled set is updated by freshly labeled shots, we find semantic groups which are statistically from the same distribution(s) as the labeled relevant shots through a statistical test (the semantic concepts obtained in the initial search will be used here to reduce the number of candidate distributions to compare), and use their distributions as predictors to estimate a query distribution. During the coached active learning, the estimated query distribution together with the distribution of the current classifier outputs will be used to coach the sampling process, which selects unlabeled shots to organize a new ranked list to query the user in the next round. The remainder of this paper is organized as follows. In Section 2, we review the existing work in active learning. Section 3 introduces our method for modeling query distribution and Section 4 describes the details of the proposed coached active learning. The experimental results and performance comparison are given in Section 5. Finally, Section 6 concludes this paper.

2. RELATED WORK

Active learning has been intensively studied over the last two decades due to its effectiveness in reducing the cost of data labeling, and has been applied to solve a diverse range of problems such as text classification [2, 17, 18], natural language processing [3] and speech recognition [19]. In this section, we mainly review active learning within the scenario of multimedia computing. For a more comprehensive survey, the reader is referred to [20].

The term *active learning* in literature is popularly referred to as pool-based active learning [17], where a classifier is trained iteratively on a small set of labeled instances and a large pool of unlabeled instances. In every iteration of learning, the major task is to selectively sample instances from the unlabeled pool to query users, so as to retrain the classifier with the updated labeled set in the next round. The sampling strategy, which is designed to minimize the number of instances needed to be labeled, is thus the core of active learning and a fundamental mark that distinguishes one existing method from others. Two strategies are popularly used: uncertainty sampling [2–9], and query-by-committee [17, 18, 21].

Uncertainty sampling is probably the most commonly employed framework, where the idea is to select the instances that the learner is most uncertain of their labels. A variety of methods have been proposed. For a binary classification problem using a probabilistic model, it can be done by simply querying the instances whose posterior probability of being positive is nearest 0.5 [2], or more generally (and possibly most popularly), by using *entropy* to measure the uncertainty of an instance based on its posteriors probability predicted by the current classifier(s) [3, 4]. In multimedia computing with active learning, the SVM classifier is widely adopted [5–9, 11], with which uncertainty sampling can be straightforwardly implemented to select the instances closest to the separating hyperplane where the classifier is usually confused and works awkwardly.

Different from uncertainty sampling in which inference is normally obtained through a single hypothesis (boundary), query-by-committee (QBC) organizes a committee with several classifiers for making a decision with the "wisdom of the crowds" [17, 18, 21]. Instances whose predicted labels are most inconsistent among committee classifiers are usually candidates to query next. Although being claimed to reduce the classification error and variance more efficiently than a single expert (classifier), QBC introduces computational burden in training more classifiers. Therefore, it is seldom used in large-scale video indexing and retrieval.

Additional to uncertainty sampling and QBC, there are other sampling strategies proposed with different premises, for example, of maximizing the expected model change (e.g., [22]), and of reducing the expected generalization error (e.g., [23]). The reader is referred to [20] for more details.

In the scenario of multimedia computing, uncertainty sampling with a SVM classifier is still considered the most prevalent scheme. However, the scheme is mainly investigated on image classification and retrieval (e.g., [6, 8, 9]), and there are comparably few discussions in the video domain ([5, 7]). It may be partially due to the expensiveness of conducting experiments on large-scale video datasets involving human users. Another important (probably more essential) reason is that the current way of using active learning for reducing labeling efforts may delay of the harvest of relevant instances, which is inconsistent with the ultimate goal of video retrieval [10, 24]. The algorithm proposed by Mitra *et al.* [11] is one of the few works we found to address this open question of exploitation-exploration dilemma within the context of active learning (even not for multimedia computing). The algorithm adaptively estimates a confidence factor based on the population proportion of relevant instances to irrelevant ones along the current separating hyperplane, so as to encourage exploitation when the two groups of instances are well balanced (an indication that the current decision boundary is approaching the optimal position) and to encourage exploration otherwise. However, on one hand, the searching along the boundary is expensive on a larger-scale dataset. On the other hand, without knowing the prior query distribution, the step size of exploitation or exploration is still difficult to decide, which may either causes an unstable learning (if the step size is too larger) or slows down convergence (if the size is too small).

In this paper, we address the exploitation-exploration dilemma in a more principled way by taking into consideration both the prior query distribution and posterior distribution (indicated by current classifier outputs). In other words, the prior query distribution can roughly indicate where the optimal boundary should be, while the posterior distribution indicates where the current local boundary resides. The schedule can be more reasonable by taking a more global perspective. As we will show in Section 4, our proposed method is able to schedule not only the timing (as in [11]) but also the step sizes for exploitation or exploration.

Considering the way of incorporating prior data distribution into active learning, our work is also related to [6], in which, prior to the learning, the authors divide the target dataset by clustering and learn the prior distributions of the clusters in advance. The knowledge about those prior distributions is then used to weight the uncertainty of an unlabeled instance with reference to which cluster it belongs to. However, the parameters for clustering (e.g., number of clusters) are difficult to be determined adaptively with this method. More importantly, it is well known that instances in the same cluster of a feature space may carry diverse semantic information, because instances that are similar in low-level feature space do not necessarily have the semantic meanings. The method is thus difficult to be utilized to estimate the query distribution.

3. MODELING QUERY DISTRIBUTION

After each round of labeling, we will obtain a labeled set $\mathcal{L}$ consisting of two subsets: $\mathcal{L}^+$ and $\mathcal{L}^-$ including instances having been labeled as "relevant" and "irrelevant", respectively. Since $\mathcal{L}^+$ is just an incomplete sampling of the query distribution with limited number of instances, it is different from inferring the query distribution from $\mathcal{L}^+$ directly. We propose an indirect way to infer the query distribution: first we find training examples which are statistically from the same distribution of those in $\mathcal{L}^+$; then we use the distribution(s) of those training examples (much more abundant than $\mathcal{L}^+$) to approximate that of the query. A practical way is to organize examples in the training set into nonexclusive groups according to the semantics they carry, so that groups which are from the same distribution as $\mathcal{L}^+$ can reflect different semantic aspects of the query. In this case, our query modeling can also be explained as a method that uses the pre-learned semantic groups to guess the query intension.

3.1 Organizing Semantic Groups

In organizing training examples into semantic groups, we propose to maximize the semantic generalizablity of the resulting groups with the hope that they can semantically cover as many queries as possible. We use *concept combination* to achieve this goal. The idea is first organizing examples into elementary groups of concepts, and then combining those groups to create new groups covering more complicated semantics. Given one of the abundantly available concept definition and annotation collections (e.g., LSCOM), we let G_i denote the set of shots labeled with concept i. Intersection or union operators are then used to combine those sets into new groups (such as $G_{i\cap j}$ and $G_{i\cup j}$). The combination can be done recursively among existing groups (G_i's, $G_{i\cap j}$'s and $G_{i\cup j}$'s) to achieve more complicated ones, as long as the number of training examples in every combined group is larger than a fixed threshold (say 30), so that the group is statistically meaningful.

The concept combination is powerful and practical. A similar idea has been discussed in [25] and also been utilized to generate pseudo-queries in [26]. In [25], the authors find that by the pair-wise combination of any two among 1000+ known concepts in LSCOM is possible to cover half million queries. For example, using intersection of two elementary groups of concepts *airplane* and *sky*, the query "find shots of aircraft in sky" can be fairly well interpreted. Similarly, with the union of concepts like *car*, *bus*, and *truck* it is possible to explain "find shots of ground vehicle". Note that the resulting groups are nonexclusive. To facilitate the discussion, unless otherwise specified, we will simply use G in the following description to refer to any one of the resulting groups.

3.2 Mapping between $\mathcal{L}^+$ and Semantic Groups

With $\mathcal{L}^+$, the set including instances labeled as "relevant", we need to find groups that are from the same distribution as those in $\mathcal{L}^+$. This is a two-sample test problem which has a solid foundation in statistics. For this purpose, we employ the widely-used two-sample Hotelling T-Square test [27], a test that determines if two samples are from the same multivariate distribution. By denoting $\mathbf{X}^+$ the set of the feature vectors of instances in $\mathcal{L}^+$, and $\mathbf{X}^G$ the set of feature vectors of examples in any semantic group G, the Hotelling's two-sample T-Square statistic is

$$t^2 = \frac{|\mathcal{L}^+||G|}{|\mathcal{L}^+| + |G|}(\boldsymbol{\mu}^+ - \boldsymbol{\mu}^G)'\mathbf{W}^{-1}(\boldsymbol{\mu}^+ - \boldsymbol{\mu}^G) \qquad (1)$$

where $|\mathcal{L}^+|$ and $|G|$ are the number of instances/examples in $\mathcal{L}^+$ and G respectively, $\boldsymbol{\mu}^+$ and $\boldsymbol{\mu}^G$ are the mean vectors of $\mathbf{X}^+$ and $\mathbf{X}^G$, and $\mathbf{W}$ is called the unbiased pooled covariance matrix estimate which is calculated as

$$\mathbf{W} = \frac{(|\mathcal{L}^+| - 1)\Sigma^+ + (|G| - 1)\Sigma^G}{|\mathcal{L}^+| + |G| - 2} \qquad (2)$$

where Σ^+ and Σ^G are the covariance matrices of $\mathbf{X}^+$ and $\mathbf{X}^G$. Please refer to [27] for more details.

Conducting Hotelling test which uses $\mathcal{L}^+$ to compare with candidate semantic groups (G's) one by one is time-consuming, because the number of G's can be up to a scale of hundreds of thousands. We employ two techniques to address this problem. First, we represent each G with three parameters ($|G|, \boldsymbol{\mu}^G, \Sigma^G$) which we can learn offline. As $\mathcal{L}^+$ can also be represented in a similar way, the test is thus performed between parameters instead of the direct comparison between instances in $\mathcal{L}^+$ and examples in G, effectively avoiding the intensive computation. Second, we reduce the number of candidate groups to compare by pruning groups not semantically related to the query. To this end, we borrow the idea of query-to-concept mapping, a technique mapping a query to concepts that are semantically related, which is the foundation of successful concept-based search and has been experimentally validated by a number of researchers [16, 28–30]. More specifically, at query time, we use query-to-concept mapping to select a set of concepts (denoted as C) which are semantically related to the query. In Hotelling test, we only test $\mathcal{L}^+$ with groups that concern any concept in C. For example, if *car* is one of the concepts in C, we only investigate groups G_{car}, $G_{car \cap road}$, $G_{car \cup bus}$ and so on. In our experiment, this reduces the number of candidate groups to a scale of thousands, significantly accelerating the comparison.

3.3 Estimating Query Distribution

With $\mathcal{L}^+$ and semantic groups selected in the last section, we use a gaussian mixture model (GMM) to estimate the distribution of the current query Q. Instances in $\mathcal{L}^+$ are used as training examples in GMM. Denoting the set of selected groups as $\mathcal{P}$ (predictor set), the probability density function (*pdf*) of the Q in GMM is:

$$P(\boldsymbol{x}|Q) = \sum_{G \in \mathcal{P}} \omega_G P(\boldsymbol{x}|G) \tag{3}$$

where $\boldsymbol{x}$ is the feature vector of any instance/example, $P(\boldsymbol{x}|G)$ is the *pdf* of semantic group G, and ω_G is the weight for $P(\mathbf{x}|G)$ with the summation of all ω_G equal to one. Assuming each G is generated by a multivariate normal distribution, $P(\boldsymbol{x}|G)$ can be estimated by

$$P(\boldsymbol{x}|G) = \frac{1}{(2\pi)^{k/2}|\Sigma^G|^{1/2}} \exp\left(-\frac{(\boldsymbol{x}-\boldsymbol{\mu}^G)'(\Sigma^G)^{-1}(\boldsymbol{x}-\boldsymbol{\mu}^G)}{2}\right) \tag{4}$$

where k is the dimension of the feature space, and $|\Sigma^G|$ is the determinant of Σ^G. To estimate the weights ω_G, we employ the most popular and well-established algorithm expectation-maximization (EM). With the instances in $\mathcal{L}^+$ as training examples, EM seeks a best set of weights ω_G^* (i.e., $\{\omega_1^*, \omega_2^*, \cdots, \omega_{|\mathcal{P}|}^*\}$) which maximizes the GMM likelihood

$$\{\omega_1^*, \omega_2^*, \cdots, \omega_{|\mathcal{P}|}^*\} = \underset{\{\omega_1, \omega_2, \cdots, \omega_{|\mathcal{P}|}\}}{\text{argmax}} \prod_{i=1}^{|\mathcal{L}^+|} P(\boldsymbol{x}_i|Q). \tag{5}$$

To accelerate the convergence of EM, we assign each predictor distribution an initial weight

$$\omega_i^0 = \frac{sim(\mathcal{L}^+, G_i)}{\sum_{G \in \mathcal{P}} sim(\mathcal{L}^+, G)} \tag{6}$$

where *sim*(.) is a function to compute similarity of two distributions. We implement this function as

$$\begin{aligned} sim(\mathcal{L}^+, G) = \exp\bigg\{ -\frac{1}{2}\Big(&\sqrt{(\boldsymbol{\mu}^+ - \boldsymbol{\mu}^G)'(\Sigma^+)^{-1}(\boldsymbol{\mu}^+ - \boldsymbol{\mu}^G)} \\ &+ \sqrt{(\boldsymbol{\mu}^G - \boldsymbol{\mu}^+)'(\Sigma^G)^{-1}(\boldsymbol{\mu}^G - \boldsymbol{\mu}^+)}\Big)\bigg\}. \end{aligned} \tag{7}$$

The similarity is indeed determined by the averaged Mahalanobis distance between the mean vectors of the two distributions (i.e., the part calculated in the braces of Eq. (7)), with the intuition that the closer G's distribution to $\mathcal{L}^+$'s, the larger the contribution of $P(\boldsymbol{x}|G)$ to $P(\boldsymbol{x}|Q)$. The EM will start from the initial ω_i^0 and finally converges to ω_G^*. Since EM is a commonly known algorithm, we do not further describe its details due to space limitation.

4. COACHED ACTIVE LEARNING

As described in Section 2, the core of the active learning is the sampling strategy which always tries to select the most informative instances to query the user so as to reduce the number of instances needed to be labeled. In this section, we describe the use of the estimated query distribution together with the distribution of classifier outcomes to coach the sampling.

To balance exploitation and exploration when sampling, we implement a function $\rho(x)$ to compute the priority of selecting an instance to query next. That is

$$\rho(x) = \lambda\, Harvest(\boldsymbol{x}) + (1-\lambda)\, Explore(\boldsymbol{x}) \tag{8}$$

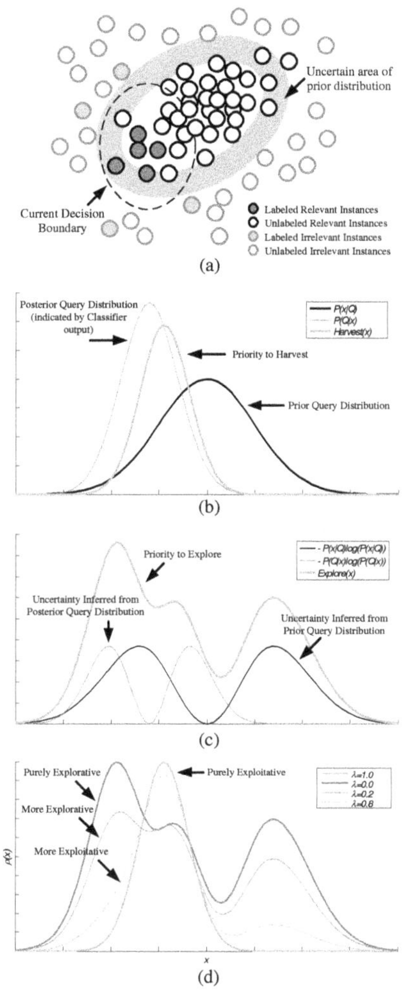

Figure 3: Illustration of Exploitative Priority and Explorative Priority: (a) an example of a query distribution in target space, (b) the prior and posterior distributions and the distribution of the corresponding exploitative priority *Harvest*($\boldsymbol{x}$), (c) the distributions of the uncertainties determined on the prior and posterior distributions and the distribution of the corresponding explorative priority *Explore*($\boldsymbol{x}$), and (d)the effect of using λ to balance exploitation and exploration.

where $Harvest(\boldsymbol{x})$ is a function to compute how likely the exploitation will be boosted if selecting $\boldsymbol{x}$ to query next, $Explore(\boldsymbol{x})$ computes how likely the exploration will be improved if selecting $\boldsymbol{x}$ to query next, and λ is a balancing factor to control the exploitation-exploration trade-off. In our proposed method, the use of λ is mainly for determining the timing of exploitation and exploration, and the step size is controlled in $Harvest(\boldsymbol{x})$ and $Explore(\boldsymbol{x})$ respectively. We will introduce the implementations of $Harvest(\boldsymbol{x})$ and $Explore(\boldsymbol{x})$ first, and then turn to λ.

4.1 Exploitative Priority

To boost the exploitation, one will intuitively select instances with high posterior probabilities $P(Q|\boldsymbol{x})$ to label. However, as the current classifier is trained with $\mathcal{L}^+$ (a biased sampling of relevant instances to Q), instances with high $P(Q|\boldsymbol{x})$ are not necessarily lying in the densest area of query distribution. To encourage the exploitation to shift towards the dense area where the instances have high prior probabilities $P(\boldsymbol{x}|Q)$, we implement the $Harvest(\boldsymbol{x})$ as

$$Harvest(\boldsymbol{x}) = P(\boldsymbol{x}|Q)P(Q|\boldsymbol{x}). \tag{9}$$

The function indeed adjusts the posterior probability of $\boldsymbol{x}$ by further considering its prior probability. As in Figure 3(b), the function will put higher priority to harvest the instances between the centers of prior and posterior distributions, instead of those around the center of the posterior distribution. Through the iterative harvesting, the center of posterior distribution will move to the center of the prior distribution step by step. The step size is indirectly controlled with respect to the distance between the two centers.

4.2 Explorative Priority

Uncertainty sampling is a commonly employed strategy to encourage exploration, where the uncertainty is usually estimated on the classifier outputs which indicate the posterior query distribution. Nevertheless, the estimated uncertainty can only reflect a local decision boundary of the current classifier which may be far from the optimal one. By considering both prior and posterior probabilities, we implement $Explore(\boldsymbol{x})$ as

$$Explore(\boldsymbol{x}) = \left\{-P(\boldsymbol{x}|Q)\log(P(\boldsymbol{x}|Q))\right\} \times \left\{-P(Q|\boldsymbol{x})\log(P(Q|\boldsymbol{x}))\right\}. \tag{10}$$

Noting that the parts in the first and second pairs of braces are the entropies of prior probability $P(\boldsymbol{x}|Q)$ and posterior probability $P(Q|\boldsymbol{x})$ respectively, which indicate the uncertainties inferred from prior and posterior "knowledge" about the query distribution. Eq. (10) is intuitively a summarization of these two uncertainties. As shown in Figure 3(c), $Explore(\boldsymbol{x})$ puts high priority on exploring the instances residing in the intersection of the uncertain areas of prior and posterior distributions. There are three peaks in the distribution of $Explore(\boldsymbol{x})$. The leftmost one is the highest peak which corresponds to the area both the prior and posterior distributions are most uncertain of, and the area where the left side of the optimal boundary is probably located. The peak in the middle corresponds to the area where prior and posterior distributions have a conflict in understanding. As shown in Figure 3(a), the area corresponds to the region where the current decision boundary passes through the central area of the prior distribution, and it is thus also worth exploring to clarify the misunderstanding (if the centers of prior and posterior distributions are aligned exactly, the middle peak will disappear.) The rightmost peak corresponds to the area far from the current decision boundary but the prior distribution "thinks" that the right side of the optimal boundary should be located there. Exploring this area helps to clarify the right side of the optimal boundary. If the query distribution is well estimated, exploring the areas under the three peaks will have the effect of pulling the current boundary towards the optimal one. The step size of the exploration is indirectly controlled by the distance between the current decision boundary and the "imagined" optimal one by prior distribution.

4.3 Balancing exploitation and exploration

To balance the exploitation-exploration trade-off *adaptively*, every time when $\mathcal{L}^+$ is updated by freshly labeled instances, we update λ based on the harvest history, i.e., number of relevant shots obtained in each round. We encourage exploitation when there are potentially more relevant shots to label, and encourage the exploration otherwise. To distinguish the data in different rounds, we add a subscript i (indicating the i-th round) for both $\mathcal{L}^+$ and λ. The λ_{i+1}, balancing factor at the $(i+1)$-th round, can then be updated as

$$\lambda_{i+1} = \lambda_i + \frac{|\mathcal{L}^+_{i+1}| - \bar{R}}{\bar{R}} \tag{11}$$

where $|\mathcal{L}^+_{i+1}|$ is the number of shots in $\mathcal{L}^+_{i+1}$, and $\bar{R}$, which we present later, is the expected number of relevant shots to be labeled in the $(i+1)$-th round. In Eq. (11), λ increases when the previous round harvested more relevant shots than expected, so that the learner will put more emphasis on exploitation, otherwise, λ decreases resulting in more emphasis on exploration. When the updating in Eq. (11) causes λ out of the interval [0,1], we cut its value to the corresponding boundary. The expected number of relevant shots $\bar{R}$ in the $(i+1)$-th round, is computed according to the harvest history as

$$\bar{R} = \sum_{k}^{i} \frac{1}{(i-k+1)^2} |\mathcal{L}^+_k| \tag{12}$$

which is a weighted summarization of the number of shots harvested so far. On the basis of fact that the weight $\frac{1}{(i-k+1)^2}$ decreases dramatically from the current round to those of the previous rounds, the result of Eq. (12) is mainly influenced by the harvest of several most recent iterations. The intuition is that we expect to harvest in the new round a little bit more than the number of relevant shots we have harvested recently. The effect of balancing with λ is illustrated in Figure 3(d), where the distribution of the priority function $\rho(x)$ appears more similar to that of exploitative priority $Harvest(\boldsymbol{x})$ if λ is larger, and more similar to that of the explorative priority $Explore(\boldsymbol{x})$ otherwise.

5. EXPERIMENT

We conduct experiments mainly using the TRECVID 2005 (TV05) test set, which is composed of news videos collected from multilingual sources including English, Chinese and Arabic, with a total length of 85 hours (45,765 shots). Twenty four search topics, together with their ground-truth provided by TRECVID'05, are used in the experiments. We only use the text queries, imagining that most users perform search with a short description of words.

We represent each video shot with a concept vector which is composed of the detection scores on the shot by a set of semantic concept detectors. In our case, we use VIREO-374 [31] which includes detectors for 374 LSCOM semantic concepts, the largest detector set available. The dimensionality of our concept vector is thus 374. The concept vector model has been popularly employed in TRECVID, and has been experimentally proven to be more reliable than low-level features (e.g., color, texture).

In the experiments, for each query, the video shots being labeled as "relevant" are put in a list ordered by the sequence in which they are labeled. Following the TRECVID evaluation, we use average precision (AP) to evaluate the list. To aggregate the performance over multiple queries, we use the mean of their APs (known as MAP).

5.1 Learning Candidate Semantic Distributions

With the method introduced in Section 3.1, we learn the candidate semantic distributions using LSCOM [14], the largest concept definition and annotation collection publicly available. LSCOM includes 2000+ concepts, of which 449 have been labeled on the development dataset of TRECVID 2005. To be practical, when learning semantic groups using the *concept combination*, we limit our interests to semantic groups being combined with no more than 2 concepts. After filtering out those with less than 30 training examples, we obtain 79514 non-exclusive sets of semantic groups including 334 groups with only one concepts (e.g., G_{fire}), 9501 groups by combining two concepts with the intersection operation (e.g., $G_{airplane \cap sky}$), and 69679 groups with the union operation (e.g., $G_{airplane \cup sky}$). We then learn from each group G three parameters, namely the group size $|G|$, the mean vector $\boldsymbol{\mu}^G$, and the covariance matrix Σ^G, to represent a candidate semantic distribution. To further fulfill the normality assumption in Section 3.3, we perform Mardia's test [27] on each distribution to check its similarity to the multivariate normal distribution and filter out those being rejected in the test. This finally results in 23046 candidate distributions which will be used at query time to estimate the query distribution. The results can be found at our demo webpage[2]. Note that the learning of these distributions has been done offline without increasing the online time cost.

5.2 Comparison with Uncertainty Sampling

To compare the performance of our method to conventional approaches of active learning, we conduct an experiment of interactive search involving 12 searchers (volunteers aging from 19 to 26, 3 females and 9 males, 8 undergraduates and 4 graduates) on 3 personal computers with exactly the same configuration (Intel(R) Core(TM) i3 CPU M3502.27GHz, 2GB Memory). Due to the expensiveness of the human experiment, we only compare our coached active learning (*CAL*) with the most popularly employed uncertainty sampling (*US*), which chooses the instances closest to the SVM separating hyperplane to query next. In this case, each searcher has to conduct a total of 48 searches (24 TV05 queries for each method). To avoid the situation that the users might be negatively involved in searching new queries when they were frustrated by some "difficult" queries previously, the users are recommended to separate the task into several times within twelve weeks with each time at most 6 queries being taken. Queries are assigned to a user in stochastic order and experimented at each time with a randomly selected active learning method (i.e., the order of using *CAL* or *US* is also stochastic). We restrict the interval between the searches with *CAL* and *US* on a same query to at least four weeks, for reducing the effect that a user's experience on searching the query with one method may facilitate the searching with another.

The two sampling strategies are experimented within the same user interface as shown at our demo webpage[2], and the interactive search is conducted with the framework we present in Figure 2 (to search with *US*, we replace the active learning module with uncertainty sampling). For initial search, we employ the work in [16], a concept-based search method which has been reported to have encouraging results. All searches are experimented using the TRECVID model of interactive search, where a search has to be finished within 15 minutes, but users can give up early if they feel that there is no hope to find new relevant shots.

5.2.1 Results of Interactive Search

Figure 4 shows the results of performance comparison of *CAL* and *US*, where the MAP at each number of examined shots is the average MAP of 12 users. As a reference, we also plot the change of balancing factor λ in *CAL*. It is easy to see that *CAL* outperforms *US* across the X-axis.

There are basically three stages of the searching process with *CAL*. The first stage is from point 0 to the point around 900, where *CAL* demonstrates a dramatical climbing, contributing 58.96% of the total MAP growth. At the top-200 shots, the initial climbing, which contributes 22.12% of the total MAP growth, may attribute to concept-based search, because it has been widely reported that the relevant shots are mainly distributed at the top-200 of the ranked list returned by a concept-based search. The climbing continues up to the point around 900, contributing 36.84% of the total MAP growth. It can be explained that the prior query distributions estimated in *CAL* successfully lead the classifiers to the dense areas. The abundant relevant shots there results in fruitful harvest and stimulates the MAP growth. There are two evidences to support this analysis. First, *US*, which has also benefited from concept-based search, exhibits an obvious slow-down

[2]http://www.cs.cityu.edu.hk/~xiaoyong/CAL/

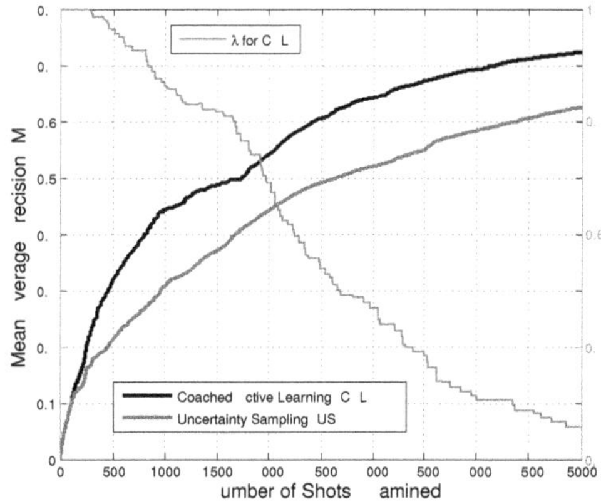

Figure 4: Performance comparison of Coached Active Learning and Uncertainty Sampling at increasing depths of results, using the TRECVID 2005 test set. The MAP at each point is the average of MAPs of 12 users. The balancing factor λ for *CAL* is also the average over 24 queries and across 12 users.

on MAP growth (from 0.1% growth per shot to 0.04%) after the initial harvest. Second, the corresponding λ is as high as 0.95, an indication that *CAL* is encouraging exploitation, i.e., pushing the classifier to the dense area according to our design in Section 4.1. The second stage is from point near 900 to 1500, where the climbing of *CAL* slows down with the MAP growing mildly, contributing 8.37% of the total MAP growth. In this stage, *CAL* may have reached its limit on harvesting in the dense area. This is inferred from the fact that the median number of relevant shots of TV05 queries is 214, and the majority of relevant should have been harvested after examining the top-1000 shots if an appropriate sampling function was used. Accordingly, the λ in this stage first drops down significantly to encourage the exploration of uncertain areas, and remains nearly horizontal in the rest of the stage to enable harvesting of newly discovered relevant shots. The third stage spans the rest of the X-axis, contributing 32.67% of the total MAP growth. In stage-3, the climbing of *CAL* speeds up again, but not as dramatically as in stage-1. From the change of λ, we can see that after the "adjustment" in stage-2, *CAL* totally shift its focus from exploitation to exploration in stage-3. This is reasonable because after examining the top-1500 shots, the majority of the relevant shots should have been located, and the learners have to detect new relevant shots substantially relying on exploration.

Compared with that of *CAL*, MAP of *US* increases more gently overall. The major disadvantage of *US* is that by always encouraging exploration and ignoring harvesting, *US* can easily frustrate the users and cause an early give-up of search. This is confirmed by the detailed performance comparison in Figure 5, where the final MAPs are obtained by evaluating the top-1000 shots in ranked lists that have been submitted after the 15-minute search and averaged over 24 TV05 queries. One can easily find that the performance superiority of *CAL* over *US* are more apparent among those "difficult" queries (in which both approaches exhibit moderate MAPs) than among the rest. For example, *CAL* obtains performance gains over *US* on queries "G. Bush entering or leaving a vehicle" and "Condoleeza Rice" by 1700% and 185.71% respectively. However, those of queries "tanks or other military vehicles" and "a ship or boat" are just by 18.84% and 17.83% respectively, even the MAPs on these two queries are comparably high. The former two queries include named entities. It is well known that this type of queries is too specific to enable an initial search without text-based search

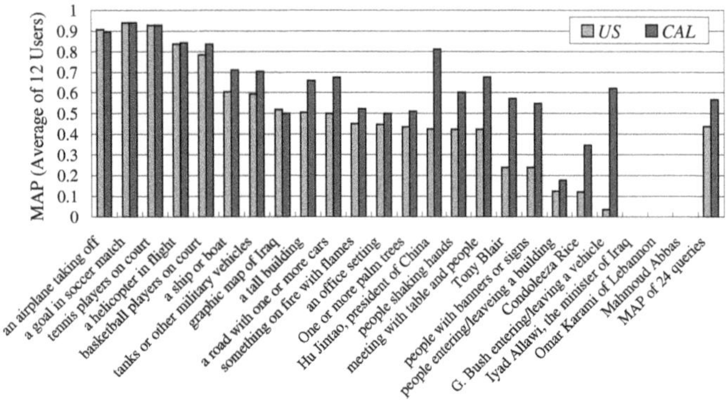

Figure 5: Performance comparison of *CAL* and *US* over 24 TRECVID 2005 queries. The MAP for each query is the average of APs of 12 users. The texts of queries have been manually modified to fit the figure.

modules to collect enough instances. This is exactly what happened in our concept-based search, which thus returns insufficient relevant shots to satisfy the users in the beginning. In the pure exploration-oriented *US*, it becomes even worse and finally causes the user to give up early. On the contrary, *CAL*, with the help of prior knowledge on query distribution, may have better chance to locate the dense areas and consequentially encourage the users on labeling in the succeeding iterations. It is worth mentioning that there are two queries "an airplane taking off" and "graphic map of Iraq", where *US* demonstrates slightly higher performance gain than *CAL* by 3.57% and 1.39% respectively. This type of queries are called person-thing queries according to the definition of TRECVID [13], where the query sentences can be directly matched to well-trained concept detectors (e.g., *airplane*, *map*). As reported by several authors [32,33], concept-based search performs very well in this type of queries, and the MAPs are thus determined mainly on the effectiveness of users in labeling. Therefore, it is fair to say that the exception for these two queries is probably a random phenomenon.

5.2.2 *Study of User Patience on Labeling*

To further study the effects of different sampling strategies on user patience, in Table 1, we present some statistics recorded during the experiment, including the users' records of maximum, average, and minimum numbers of shots examined per query, and maximum, average, and minimum numbers of irrelevant shots continuously encountered before submitting current labels in each round. The statistics show that users are evidently more patient with *CAL* than with *US*, indicated by their willingness to examined more shots overall and patience of waiting when irrelevant shots are continuously appeared. The maximum numbers of irrelevant shots continuously encountered before each submission are collected from the query "Mahmoud Abbas", where initial search fails to find any irrelevant shots. In this extreme case, the users are still able to examine 215 shots with *CAL* before giving up, 42 more than with *US*. Therefore, it is evident that *CAL* is better capable of keeping users' enthusiasm on labeling than *US*.

It is worth mentioning that compared with conventional active learning like *US*, even *CAL* has introduced two additional processes for estimating query distribution and adjusting step size of exploration, the online time cost per round for *CAL* estimation is only 0.531 seconds on average. According to our questionnaire, no searcher has noticed the difference between the online time costs of *CAL* and *US* (0.108 seconds per round).

Table 1: Statistics about users patience on labeling.

Mehtod	#Examined Shots			#Irrelevant Shots		
	Max	Avg.	Min	Max	Avg.	Min
CAL	5462	2445	166	215	64	15
US	4806	2037	107	173	32	13

5.3 Insights into Query Modeling

In this section, we are interested in which semantic distributions are selected for a certain query and whether they are able to simulate the query distribution. For each query, by sorting the selected semantic distributions according to their GMM weights (i.e., ω in Eq. (3)), Table 2 shows the 24 TV05 queries, corresponding concepts selected in the initial concept-based search (ordered by their semantic similarities to the query), and the semantic distributions (only top-3 are shown for space limitation) selected when searches have been finished (within the limitation of 15 minutes). Note that the results presented in the last column are randomly selected from one of the 12 users, because it is different from user to user.

In the second column, it is easy to observe that both the selected concepts and the order are seemingly reasonable. Basically, the top-3 concepts in this column have also been included by the selected semantic distributions that rank at the top-3 of the third column, a phenomenon consistent with our first intuition that concepts which are the most semantically related to a query should have the largest contributions (i.e., with the largest GMM weights). However, there are some distributions which have been obtained by combining concepts with the largest semantic similarities that are not necessarily being ranked at the top in the third column. For example, the concept *tank*, which ranks first in the second column for query "tanks or other military vehicles", does not even appear among the top-3 in the third column. The reason is that although some concepts seem the best ones for explaining a query *semantically*, their distributions may fail to explain the query distribution *statistically*, because their training examples might be insufficient and thus may provide biased statistical clues about the query distribution. In the example, concept *tank* might be too specific for a query relating to "military vehicles". Its distribution is less representative than those of concepts *military* and *vehicle* which cover more relevant instances and thus have been finally selected. Another interesting observation is that some concepts falsely selected by query-to-concept mapping have been successfully eliminated by the statistical test. For instance, the concept *boat* and *canoe*, which are selected for the query "An airplane take off" because they semantically share a common parent "vehicle" with "airplane", have been eliminated shortly after the statistical test. To sum up, the inconsistency between semantic and statistical concept selection reflects the limitation of purely semantics-based query-to-concept mapping. In CAL, the statistical test following the mapping can serve to compensate this limitation.

To further investigate whether the selected distributions can simulate the query distribution, we employ multi-dimensional scaling (MDS) to reduce the dimension of the feature space into 2D, so that every distribution related to the simulation process can be visualized. We also learn a distribution from relevant instances of each query to represent the real distribution. Figure 6(a) shows that the simulated distribution for query "a road with one or more cars" matches the real one very well, with a slight shift of distribution center, and a minor rotation. In addition, the shape of the simulated distribution appears "slimmer" than the real one, a common phenomenon observed among queries. This is due to the use of detection scores for composing feature vectors in our experiment. On the

Table 2: Selection of concepts and semantic distributions for TRECVID 2005 queries. Concepts are ordered by their similarities to corresponding queries. Semantic distributions are ordered by GMM weights.

Queries	Concept Selection			Selection of Semantic Distributions
Condoleeza Rice	face	food	sky	face, sky, food
Iyad Allawi, the minister of Iraq	face	leader	individual	N/A
Omar Karami, the minister of Lebannon	face	leader	individual	N/A
Hu Jintao, president of China	face	leader	individual	individual, face, individual∩single_person_male
Tony Blair	face	tony_blair	body_part	face, body_part∪crowd, face∩tie
Mahmoud Abbas	face	leader	individual	N/A
A graphic map of Iraq, Bagdhad marked	map	chart	road	map, map∪chart, map∪text_on_artificial_background
Tennis players on the court	tennis	court	sport	sport, tennis, tennis∩sport
People shaking hands	person	body_part	police	person∪body_part, person∩military_personnel, personnel∩military
A helicopter in flight	helicopter	running	walking	helicopter, helicopter∩sky, airplane∩sky
G. Bush entering/leaving a vehicle	face	vehicle	walking	face∩road, vehicle, vehicle∩walking
Something on fire with flames and smoke	smoke	sky	food	smoke, explosion_fire, smoke∩weapon
People with banners or signs	person	chart	group	group, protester∪group, business_people
One or more people or a building	building	person	tower	building, tower, building∩urban
A meeting with table and people	meeting	crowd	furniture	meeting, crowd, meeting∩tie
A ship or boat	boat	ship	canoe	boat, boat∩waterway, boat∩urban
Basketball players on the court	basketball	court	tennis	basketball, basketball∪face, basketball∩sport
One or more palm trees	tree	protester	caucasian	caucasian, caucasian∩male_person, tree
An airplane off	airplane	boat	canoe	airplane, airplane∩urban, airplane∩building
A road with one or more cars	road	car	sidewalk	road∩car, road, sidewalk
Tanks or other military vehicles	tank	military	vehicle	vehicle∩military, military, military∩smoke
building	building	tower	road	building, tower, building∩overlaid_text
A goal in a soccer match	soccer	football	furniture	soccer, football, sport
An office setting	office	sitting	store	office, store, office∩talking

Table 3: Performance comparison on TRECVID 2005-2009 between *CAL* and the best interactive search systems (*Best*). The results are evaluated with the average of InfAP over topics.

	2006	2007	2008	2009
Best	0.303	0.362	0.194	0.246
CAL	0.422	0.493	0.331	0.380

TRECVID 2005 development set, where the detectors are trained, the detectors perform more accurately than on the TRECVID 2005 test set, so that the distribution shape of detection scores on corresponding positive examples will be more centralized than that of the test set. To illustrate this effect, in Figures 6(b) and (c), we compare the real query distribution with that of its biggest contributor distribution *car∩road* which is learned on the intersection set of groups *car* and *road*. In Figures 6(b) and (c), we can see that the scatter plots of relevant instances of the query and the positive examples for *car∩road* resemble each other considerably, with the latter one more crowded around its center. Therefore, the distribution of Figure 6(c) is "slimmer" than that of Figure 6(b).

5.4 Comparison with State-of-the-art

First we compares our proposed method with two state-of-the-art systems: (1) MediaMill'05 [34], the best interactive search system reported in TRECVID 2005, (2) Extreme Video Retrieve (EVR) [10], the one reported with comparable performance to MediaMill'05. For EVR, we can only compare to the MAP of the method called manual paging with variable pagesize (*MPVP*) in [10], because even there are other methods proposed in the paper which can beat *MPVP*, but no exact MAPs are reported. The results show that our method (with MAP 0.565) outperforms MediaMill'05 (MAP 0.414) and EVR (MAP 0.406) by 36.53% and 39.22% respectively.

Give the fact that MediaMill'05 and EVR have evolved over the last five years, we further extend the comparison to the best interactive systems reported in TRECVID 2006–2009 [35–38] respectively. To bypass the difficulty of conducting the expensive human experiments, we use machine searchers with *CAL* instead. A machine search is an agent program who "knows" the groundtruth and behaves in the interactive process according to the patience parameters we have learned in Table 1. Following the standard of TRECVID, we use inferred average precision (InfAP) to evaluate each list. Table 3 shows the results. It is easy to see that *CAL* outperforms the best interactive systems by 35.25%, 38.82%, 36.94%, 70.62%, and 54.47% on TRECVID 2006–2009 respectively. It again confirms that *CAL* has a state-of-the-art performance.

6. CONCLUSION

We have presented our proposed approach called coached active learning, where a coaching process jointly considering both prior and posterior query distributions is introduced to guide the leaner, which makes the learning well-targeted, as well as effectively and efficiently avoids the conventional way of purely explorative searching in target space. We show that the prior distribution is predictable by using semantic distributions, which are statistically from the same distribution(s) as the labeled relevant instances, as predictors. Furthermore, with both prior and posterior query distributions available, we can explicitly schedule the timing of exploitation and exploration and control the step sizes of harvesting and exploring, which is a desirable feature in interactive video search. The experiments involving human users demonstrate encouraging results of the proposed approach in both keeping user patience and ensuring faster convergence. The experimental results also show that our interactive search with the proposed learning method outperforms two state-of-the-art systems in terms of MAP.

Although the comparison with existing active learning methods is limited due to the expensiveness of human experiments, we believe the proposed approach is more importantly a scheme which has addressed the open question of exploitation-exploration tradeoff in the video search domain. Once the comparisons with more sampling strategies have been conducted in the future, we can replace the *Harvest* or *Explore* function (or even the way of estimating the balancing factor) in Eq. (8) with the winner strategy accordingly. We will include these experiments in our future investigation.

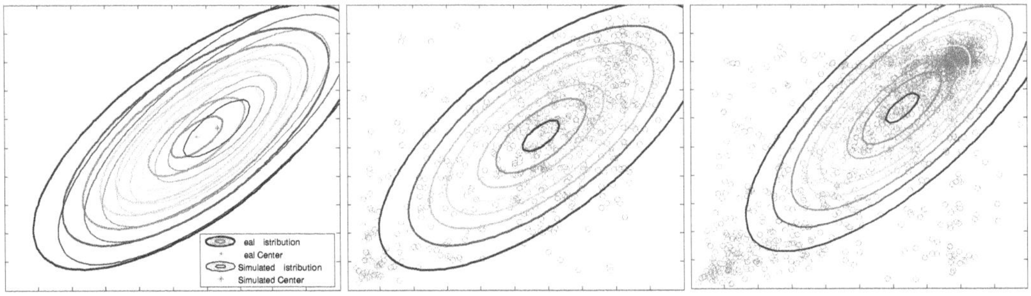

(a) Real vs. Simulated Distr. (b) Real Query Distribution (c) Semantic Distribution car∩road

Figure 6: Models related to distribution of query "a road with one or more cars": (a) contour plots of the real query distribution and the one simulated by GMM, (b) contour plot of the real query distribution and the scatter plot of relevant instances, (c) contour plot of the semantic distribution obtained by combining concepts *car* and *road* and corresponding scatter plot.

7. ACKNOWLEDGMENTS

The work described in this paper was fully supported by a grant from the National Natural Science Foundation of China (No. 61001148).

8. REFERENCES

[1] D. A. Cohn and et. al. Active learning with statistical models. *Journal of Artificial Intelligence Research*, 4:129–145, 1996.

[2] D. Lewis and W. Gale. A sequential algorithm for training text classifiers. In *ACM SIGIR Conference on Research and Development in Information Retrieval,*, pages 3–12, 1994.

[3] M. Tang, X. Luo, and S. Roukos. Active learning for statistical natural language parsing. In *Annual Meeting of the Association for Computational Linguistics*, pages 120–127, 2002.

[4] C. Zhang and T. Chen. An active learning framework for content-based information retrieval. *IEEE Transactions on Multimedia*, 4(2):260–268, 2002.

[5] M. Naphade and J. Smith. Active learning for simultaneous annotation of multiple binary semantic concepts. In *IEEE Int. Conf. on Multimedia and Expo*, pages 77–80, 2004.

[6] H. T. Nguyen and A. Smeulders. Active learning using pre-clustering. In *International Conference on Machine Learning*, 2004.

[7] R. Yan and et. al. Automatically labeling video data using multi-class active learning. In *IEEE Intl. Conf. on Computer Vision*, 2003.

[8] L. Wang and et. al. Bootstrapping svm active learning by incorporating unlabelled images for image retrieval. In *IEEE Comp. Soci. Conf. on Computer Vision and Pattern Recognition*, 2003.

[9] S. Tong and E. Chang. Support vector machine active learning for image retrieval. In *ACM Multimedia*, pages 107–118, 2001.

[10] A. G. Hauptmann, W.-H. Lin, R. Yan, J. Yang, and M.-Y. Chen. Extreme video retrieval: joint maximization of human and computer performance. In *ACM Multimedia*, pages 385–394, 2006.

[11] P. Mitra and et. al. A probabilistic active support vector learning algorithm. *IEEE Trans. Patt. Anal. Mach. Intell.*, 26:413–418, 2004.

[12] T. Osugi, D. Kun, and S. Scott. Balancing exploration and exploitation: A new algorithm for active machine learning. In *IEEE International Conference on Data Mining*, pages 330–337, 2005.

[13] A. F. Smeaton, P. Over, and W. Kraaij. Abstract evaluation campaigns and trecvid. In *ACM SIGMM Int. Workshop Multimedia Information Retrieval*, pages 321–330, 2006.

[14] M. Naphade, J. R. Smith, J. Tešić, S.-F. Chang, W. Hsu, L. Kennedy, A. Hauptmann, and J. Curtis. Large-scale concept ontology for multimedia. *IEEE Multimedia*, 13(3):86–91, 2006.

[15] P. G. Matthieu and M. Cord. Retin al: An active learning strategy for image category retrieval. In *IEEE Conf. on Image Processing*, pages 2219–2222, 2004.

[16] X.-Y. Wei, C.-W. Ngo, and Y.-G. Jiang. Selection of concept detectors for video search by ontology-enriched semantic spaces. IEEE Transactions on Multimedia, 10(6):1085–1096, 2008.

[17] A. McCallum and K. Nigam. Employing em and pool-based active learning for text classification. In *The Fifteenth International Conference on Machine Learning*, pages 350–358, 1998.

[18] S. Tong and D. Koller. Support vector machine active learning with applications to text classification. In *International Conference on Machine Learning*, pages 999–1006, 2000.

[19] G. Tur and et. al. Combining active and semi-supervised learning for spoken language understanding. *Speech Communication*, 45(2):171–186, 2005.

[20] B. Settles. Active learning literature survey. Computer Sciences Technical Report 1648, University of Wisconsin–Madison, 2009.

[21] V. S. Iyengar, C. Apte, and T. Zhang. Active learning using adaptive resampling. In *ACM SIGKDD International Conference on Knowledge Discovery and Data Mining*, pages 92–98, 2000.

[22] B. Settles, M. Craven, and S. Ray. Multiple-instance active learning. *Advances in Neural Information Processing Systems (NIPS)*, 20:1289–1296, 2008.

[23] X. Zhu and et. al. Combining active learning and semi-supervised learning using gaussian fields and harmonic functions. In *ICML 2003 workshop on The Continuum from Labeled to Unlabeled Data in Machine Learning and Data Mining*, pages 58–65, 2003.

[24] M.-Y. Chen, M. Christel,and et. al. Putting active learning into multimedia applications: dynamic definition and refinement of concept classifiers. In *ACM Multimedia*, pages 902–911, 2005.

[25] X.-Y. Wei, Y.-G. Jiang, and C.-W. Ngo. Concept-driven multi-modality fusion for video search. *IEEE Transactions on Circuits and Systems for Video Technology*, 21:62–73, 2011.

[26] B. Zhang, Q. Xiang, and et. al. Comprehensive query-dependent fusion using regression-on-folksonomies: a case study of multimodal music search. In *ACM Multimedia*, pages 213–222, 2009.

[27] K. V. Mardia, J. T. Kent, and J. M. Bibby. *Multivariate analysis*. Academic Press, 1979.

[28] C. G. M. Snoek, B. Huurnink, and et. al.. Adding semantics to detectors for video retrieval. *IEEE Transactions on Multimedia*, 9(5):975–986, 2007.

[29] S.-Y. Neo, J. Zhao, M.-Y. Kan, and T.-S. Chua. Video retrieval using high level features: Exploiting query matching and confidence-based weighting. In *Int. Conf. on Image and Video Retrieval*, 2006.

[30] J. Cao, H.-F. Jing, and et. al. Distribution-based Concept Selection for Concept-based Video Retrieval. In *ACM Multimedia*, 2009.

[31] Y.-G. Jiang, C.-W. Ngo, and J. Yang. Towards optimal bag-of-features for object categorization and semantic video retrieval. In *Int. Conf. on Image and Video Retrieval*, 2007.

[32] X.-Y. Wei and C.-W. Ngo. Fusing semantics, observability, reliability and diversity of concept detectors for video search. In *ACM Multimedia*, 2008.

[33] Y.-G. Jiang and et. al. Semantic context transfer across heterogeneous sources for domain adaptive video search. In *ACM Multimedia*, 2009.

[34] C. G. M. Snoek and et. al. The MediaMill TRECVID 2005 semantic video search engine. In *NIST TRECVID*, 2005.

[35] A. G. Hauptmann, M.-Y. Chen, and et. al. Multi-Lingual broadcast news retrieval. In *NIST TRECVID*, 2006.

[36] Murray Campbell, Alexander Haubold, and et. al. IBM Research TRECVID-2007 video retrieval system. In *NIST TRECVID*, 2007.

[37] C. G. M. Snoek and et. al. The MediaMill TRECVID 2008 semantic video search engine. In *NIST TRECVID*, 2008.

[38] C. G. M. Snoek and et. al. The MediaMill TRECVID 2009 semantic video search engine. In *NIST TRECVID*, 2009.

Learning Concept Bundles for Video Search with Complex Queries*

Jin Yuan
National University of Singapore
yuanjin@comp.nus.edu.sg

Zheng-Jun Zha
National University of Singapore
zhazj@comp.nus.edu.sg

Yan-Tao Zheng
Institute for Infocomm Research of Singapore
yantaozheng@gmail.com

Meng Wang
National University of Singapore
eric.mengwang@gmail.com

Xiangdong Zhou
Fudan University of China
xdzhou@fudan.edu.cn

Tat-Seng Chua
National University of Singapore
chuats@comp.nus.edu.sg

ABSTRACT

Classifiers for primitive visual concepts like "car", "sky" have been well developed and widely used to support video search on simple queries. However, it is usually ineffective for complex queries like "one or more people at a table or desk with a computer visible", as they carry semantics far more complex and different from simply aggregating the meanings of their constituent primitive concepts. To facilitate video search of complex queries, we propose a higher-level semantic descriptor named "concept bundle", which integrates multiple primitive concepts, such as "(soccer, fighting)", "(lion, hunting, zebra)" etc, to describe the visual representation of the complex semantics. The proposed approach first automatically selects informative concept bundles. It then builds a novel concept bundle classifier based on multi-task learning by exploiting the relatedness between concept bundle and its primitive concepts. To model a complex query, it proposes an optimal selection strategy to select related primitive concepts and concept bundles by considering both their classifier performance and semantic relatedness with respect to the query. The final results are generated by fusing the individual results from these selected primitive concepts and concept bundles. Extensive experiments are conducted on two video datasets: TRECVID 2008 and YouTube datasets. The experimental results indicate that: (a) our concept bundle learning approach outperforms the state-of-the-art methods by at least 19% and 29% on TRECVID 2008 and YouTube datasets, respectively; and (b) the use of concept bundles can improve the search performance for complex queries by at least 37.5% on TRECVID 2008 and 52% on YouTube datasets.

Categories and Subject Descriptors

H.3.3 [**Information Storage and Retrieval**]: Information Search and Retrieval

*Area chair: Hari Sundaram

General Terms

Algorithm, Performance

Keywords

Concept Bundle, Primitive Concept, Complex Query, Multi-task Learning, Video Search

1. INTRODUCTION

Witnessing the booming of social video sharing on the Internet, many commercial search engines, such as Google, Microsoft Bing and Yahoo!, are offering video search services by using textual metadata associated with videos. The performance of text-based video search is generally unsatisfactory, as the textual metadata associated with videos are usually noisy, incomplete and sometimes inconsistent with the video content.

To better describe video content, recent research efforts utilize a set of visual concepts as intermediate descriptors to facilitate video search [22, 24, 30, 38]. In concept-based video search, user query is usually mapped to related concepts, and a ranked list of video segments is generated by fusing the individual search results from related concepts. This fusion strategy transforms the query semantics into a set of primitive concepts and performs the retrieval by aggregating the search results from different concepts. This approach works well for queries that could be well matched with one or more primitive concepts, even though the concept detection performance is generally unsatisfactory [10].

However, simple aggregation of results from primitive concepts may fail for video search with complex queries, such as "police fighting protester", "persons fighting in the soccer match" etc., because they carry semantics that are more complex than and different from simply aggregating the meanings of their constituent primitive concepts. To interpret complex queries well, in this paper, we move one-step beyond primitive concepts and propose a higher-level semantic descriptor named "concept bundle". A concept bundle is defined as a composite semantic concept that integrates multiple primitive concepts, such as ("soccer", "fighting"), ("lion", "hunting", "zebra"), and ("lady", "laughing", "interview") etc. Carrying higher-level semantics, concept bundle is expected to deliver more precise descriptions of video contents, and thus better meet the video search requirement in a finer granularity. For example, in Figure 1, the complex query "persons dancing in the wedding" can be better answered by using the concept bundle ("dance", "wedding") than the typical concept-based video search approach which

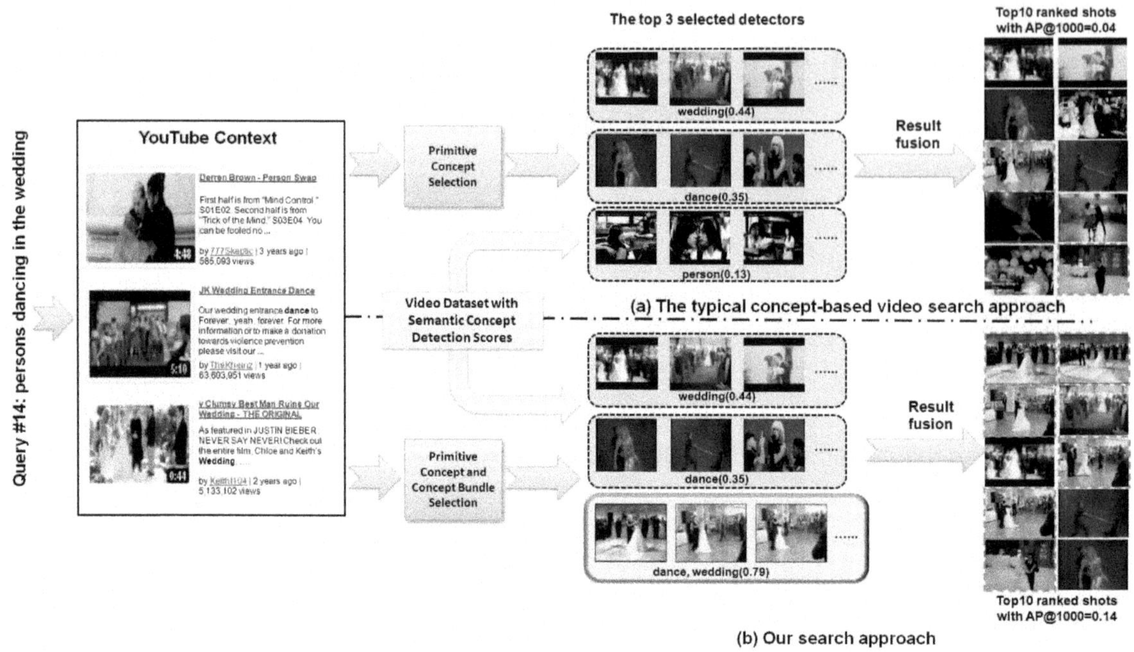

Figure 1: Illustration of the search procedure in the traditional concept-based video search (part (a)) and our search approach (part (b)) for the complex query "persons dancing in the wedding". In our search approach, the selected concept bundle ("dance", "wedding") is semantically closer to the query. We list the top 10 retrieved video shots by these two approaches, where the rank lists are ordered from left to right and top to bottom (positive samples are marked in red boxes).

uses only the primitive concepts. The reason is that the concept bundle ("dance", "wedding") is semantically closer to this query, and thus can better satisfy the complex query than that of the primitive concepts.

However, there are three challenges in learning concept bundles and performing complex query search. First, it is intractable to learn all the possible concept bundles for the practically unconstrained set of queries. Hence it is important to select informative concept bundles to learn. Second, compared to primitive concepts, the positive samples for concept bundles are usually scarce. This poses difficulty in deriving robust concept bundle classifiers. Third, to achieve a good search performance in complex query search, we need to select proper set of concept bundles to interpret the users' query in addition to primitive concepts.

To address these problems, our method first automatically selects informative concept bundles, with each bundle comprising two or more primitive concepts. We define the informative concept bundles as those frequently used in users' queries and whose constituent primitive concepts tend to co-occur in videos. Thus, the informativeness of a concept bundle can be measured based on its frequency on the suggested queries by Web video search engine and the concept co-occurrence in the tags of Web videos. Second, we learn a robust classifier for each selected concept bundle under the framework of SVM based multi-task learning. Our premise is that since the "concept bundle" is an intersection among its primitive concepts both in terms of semantics and data exemplars, the primitive concept classifiers share a common part in the decision space, which characterizes the firing region of the "concept bundle". We thus formulate each primitive concept classifier as a linear combination of two parts: a private classifier for this primitive concept and a communal classifier for the concept bundle. The concept bundle classifier (i.e., the communal classifier) can be obtained by jointly learning the primitive concept classifiers.

To search a complex query, we propose an optimal selection strategy to map the query to related primitive concepts and concept bundles by considering their classifier performance and semantic relatedness with respect to the query. The final search results are generated by fusing the individual results from these selected primitive concepts and concept bundles. We evaluate the proposed approaches on two video datasets: TRECVID 2008 and YouTube datasets. Compared to the state-of-the-art methods, our concept bundle learning approach achieves at least 19% and 29% performance improvements on TRECVID 2008 and YouTube datasets respectively. For video search, the use of concept bundles can characterize the complex queries well and improve the search performance by at least 37.5% and 52% on TRECVID 2008 and YouTube datasets respectively.

To summarize, we propose a higher-level semantic descriptor named "concept bundle" for video search of complex queries. The main contributions of this paper are:

- We develop a method to select informative concept bundles, based on its frequency on the suggested queries by Web video search engine and concept co-occurrences in Web videos.
- We develop a concept bundle learning algorithm based on the multi-task learning framework to overcome the sparse positive sample problem.
- We propose an optimal strategy to select primitive concepts and concept bundles to model complex query and perform the search.

The rest of this paper is organized as follows. We review related work in Section 2. In Section 3, we elaborate the concept bundle learning approaches including informative concept bundle selection, concept utility estimation, as well as concept bundle classifier learning. Section 4 describes the process of complex query search.

Experimental results on TRECVID 2008 and YouTube datasets are reported in Section 5, followed by the conclusion in Section 6.

2. RELATED WORK

Acting as semantic descriptors of video contents, visual concepts have been found to be effective for video search with simple queries [22]. The MediaMill-101 [23] utilizes a corpus of 101 concepts for concept-based video search, while Columbia374 [34] and VIREO-374 [14] leverage a larger set of 374 concept classifiers for video search. To learn a robust classifier for primitive concept, researchers focus on concept classifier learning algorithm, ranging from supervised learning [14] [23] [37] [38], semi-supervised learning[12] [29], cross domain learning[6] [17] [35], to multi-label learning [20], etc. In particular, Snoek el at. [23] utilized region-based features and temporal image features to achieve generic concept detection, and Jiang el at. [14] explored the part-based low level visual features, namely bag-of-visual-words (BoW) local features, for concept detection. Zha et al. proposed a statistical active learning algorithm for concept detection[38]. Wang el at. [29] proposed to learn a concept classifier from multiple graphs with optimal fusion weights. Naphade el at. [17] proposed to exploit cross domain classifiers and boost classifier performance based on concept inter-relation and fusion. Qi el at. [20] developed a multi-label learning approach by modeling individual classifiers and their correlation in a single graphical model formulation.

With individual concept classifiers, Aly et al. [1] utilized logical AND operator to combine two individual concepts into a combination, and computed its detection results by simply fusing the results from the individual classifiers. However, aforementioned, simply aggregating primitive concepts usually fails in learning concept bundle. Despite the effectiveness of existing works in modeling primitive concepts, they can not be directly adopted for learning concept bundle classifiers. In particular, the supervised learning methods [14] suffer from the sparse positive sample problem, since the positive samples of concept bundles are usually scare. The semi-supervised learning approaches [29] explore unlabeled samples to overcome the insufficient training sample problem, but neglect the relations between the primitive concepts in a bundle. These relations are usually useful in learning concept bundles. Multi-label learning methods [20] jointly learn primitive concepts by exploiting inter-concept relations. However, they focus on boosting the performance for primitive concepts instead of concept bundles. In this paper, we develop an effective approach for learning concept bundles. Our approach is based on the framework of multi-task learning [2, 7], which has been applied in wide areas such as object categorization [36], multi-device indoor localization [40] etc. By exploiting the relatedness between concept bundle and its primitive concepts, our approach is able to overcome the sparse positive sample problem and generates robust concept bundle classifiers.

In concept-based video search, it needs to select appropriate set of concepts to interpret users' queries. Existing concept selection methods can be divided into three categories: text-based, ontology-based, and visual-based [22]. The basic text-based selection methods rely on exact text matching between query and concept description [4]. The drawback of exact text matching is its ignorance of potentially relevant classifiers not covered directly by the query. To discover potential classifiers, some works directly estimate word relatedness between query and concept by using information from the Web including normalized Google distance [5] and Flickr distance [33], while other works expand query words or concept descriptions by Web source [11]. For example, Neo et al [19] expanded the query words using internet news articles for better interpretation of query semantics. The expanded query words are then used for classifier selection, either by direct text matching or the ontology-based selection. Jiang et al [13] argued that the Flickr context is more suited to reflect the co-occurrence statistics of words in image context rather than textual corpus; they proposed to estimate query-concept similarity by exploiting the context information associated with Flickr images. As an alternative to the text-based query expansion method, the ontology-based selection approach utilizes vocabularies such as WordNet [8] to select concepts. A number of ontology reasoning techniques have been developed for estimating the linguistic relatedness of words, which are widely used in concept selection such as RES [19], Lesk [18] etc. The results of the text-based or ontology-based selection approaches are independent from the visual dataset. These approaches may fail for some queries on which the visual feature plays an important role. In such case, the visual-based selection approach might be a valuable additional strategy [22]. The visual-based selection approaches [18] [21] [27] select appropriate concepts based on the detection scores of the classifiers to the query image/video examples. For example, Natsev et al. [18] formulated concept classifier selection as a discriminative learning problem. Their algorithm maps the query images into the space spanned by concept classifier probabilities. Subsequently, they used support vector machines to learn which concept classifiers are the most relevant. Because of the good performance by the text-based selection approach [13], in this paper, we select related concepts for a query by using YouTube text information. Furthermore, we consider concept classifier performance when performing selection.

With the selected classifiers, concept-based video search retrieves video segments by fusing the individual search results from these classifiers [1]. The crucial task in fusion strategy is the estimation of the weights of individual results. Chang et al. [4] determined the weights based on a text matching score between each concept and query, while Wei et al. [32] determined the weights according to the cosine distance between concepts and query. Not only using the text-matching score, Wang et al. [27] measured the weights by a linear combination of two scores: text matching score and visual matching score. In this paper, we estimate the concept weights by using the text matching score.

In summary, we propose a new semantic descriptor called "concept bundle" to interpret complex queries in concept-based video search. A novel multi-task SVM algorithm is developed to learn the concept bundle classifier. To search a complex query, we select related primitive concepts and concept bundles by considering both the semantic relatedness and classifier performance.

3. LEARNING CONCEPT BUNDLE

In this Section, we first propose an approach to select informative concept bundles in Section 3.1, then we elaborate our concept bundle learning algorithm in Section 3.2.

3.1 Informative Concept Bundle Selection

Given a concept corpus $\{C_k\}_{k=1}^{K}$ containing K primitive concepts, it is intractable to learn all the $2^K - K - 1$ possible concept bundles. In this research, we propose to learn the informative concept bundles, which are selected according to two criteria: users' interest and co-occurrence of the involved primitive concepts in video data. The users' interest of a concept bundle can be measured based on the occurrence frequency of this bundle in users' queries, while the co-occurrence of the involved primitive concepts can be inferred from the tags of Web videos. We use external sources from YouTube to help calculate the informativeness of concept bundle. For each individual concept C_k, we submit it to YouTube video search engine as a query and collect the queries suggested by the search engine. These suggested queries are normally related to the concept [39]. We also download the tags of the top ranked videos in the search results. As a result, we obtain a set of suggested queries and a set of tag files, where each tag file records the tags contained in a specific video. Based on these metadata, the informativeness of the concept bundle $(C_1, C_2, \cdots, C_M)$ is defined as

$$I(C_1, \cdots, C_M) = \alpha \frac{N_q(C_1, ... C_M)}{\sum_{m=1}^{M} N_q(C_m)} + (1-\alpha) \frac{N_t(C_1, ... C_M)}{\sum_{m=1}^{M} N_t(C_m)} \quad (1)$$

where $N_q(C_1, ... C_M)$ is the number of queries containing the bundle $(C_1, C_2, \cdots, C_M)$, $N_t(C_1, ... C_M)$ is the number of tag files that include $(C_1, C_2, \cdots, C_M)$, and α is a balance weight. The first term represents users' interest on the concept bundle $(C_1, C_2, \cdots, C_M)$ which is measured by its normalized frequency in the suggested queries. The second term measures the co-occurrence of these M concepts in video tags. We combines these two terms with a weight α to measure the informativeness.

Based on the above measurement, we select the informative bundles whose informativeness exceeds a certain threshold. However, it is computationally heavy to compute the informativeness for all the possible concept bundles. Here we adopt a dynamic programming approach to compute the informativeness in a bottom-up approach. We sequentially compute the informativeness of concept pairs, triples, quadruples, and so on. For any concept m-tuple $(C_1, C_2, \cdots, C_m)$, if its informativeness is less than a threshold, then we can discard any $(m+1)$-tuple that covers $(C_1, C_2, \cdots, C_m)$ since its informativeness will certainly be less than the threshold.

3.2 Learning Concept Bundle Classifier

3.2.1 *Concept Utility Estimation*

Intuitively, the M concepts in the concept bundle $(C_1, C_2, \cdots, C_M)$ may have different utilities for learning the concept bundle classifier. Take the concept bundle ("children","sitting","classroom") as an example. While most of the positive samples in the primitive concept "classroom" may be relevant to the concept bundle, and it may not be true for concepts "children" and "sitting". Thus, the classifier of the concept "classroom" should have a larger contribution to the concept bundle as compared to the other concepts. Here, we estimate the concept utilities in advance of learning the concept bundle.

For each concept C_m in the concept bundle $(C_1, C_2, \cdots, C_M)$, we collect the tags of the videos retrieved by C_m in Section 3.1 to form a tag document. As a result, we obtain M tag documents for the M concepts. We then regard $(C_1, C_2, \cdots, C_M)$ as a term and compute its term frequency and inverse document frequency (*tf-idf*) [16] scores with respect to all the M documents. These M *tf-idf* scores are then normalized as $\{\beta_m\}_{m=1}^M$ which reflect the importance of the M primitive concepts with respect to the concept bundle.

3.2.2 *Classification Algorithm*

Given a concept bundle $(C_1, C_2, ... C_M)$, we denote $\mathcal{D}_m = \{\mathbf{x}_i^m, y_i^m\}_{i=1}^{N_m}$, $\mathcal{D}_O = \{\mathbf{x}_i^O, y_i^O\}_{i=1}^{N_O}$ as the training samples of the primitive concept C_m $(1 \leq m \leq M)$ and the concept bundle respectively. N_m, N_O are the numbers of samples in $\mathcal{D}_m$ and $\mathcal{D}_O$ respectively; $\mathbf{x}_i^m, \mathbf{x}_i^O \in \mathbb{R}^d$ are the d-dimensional feature vectors of the i-th samples; and $y_i^m, y_i^O \in \{1, -1\}$ are binary labels indicating $\mathbf{x}_i^m$, $\mathbf{x}_i^O$ to be a positive or negative sample. Our goal is to learn a classifier $f(\mathbf{x})$ for the concept bundle $(C_1, C_2, ... C_M)$ based on the training samples $\{\mathcal{D}_m\}_{m=1}^M \bigcup \mathcal{D}_O$.

Since the concept bundle $(C_1, C_2, ... C_M)$ is an intersection among its M primitive concepts in terms of both semantic and data exemplars, we assume that the concept classifiers $\{f_m(\mathbf{x})\}_{m=1}^M$ of the M primitive concepts usually share a common area in the decision space, which characterizes the firing regions of the concept bundle. We thus formulate each $f_m(\mathbf{x})$ as a combination of two parts: a private classifier and a communal classifier. The communal classifier is actually the concept bundle classifier $f(\mathbf{x})$, which is shared among all its constituent primitive concepts. Here, we formulate each classifier as:

$$\begin{aligned} f(\mathbf{x}) &= \mathbf{w}\phi(\mathbf{x}) \\ f_m(\mathbf{x}) &= \mathbf{w}_m\phi(\mathbf{x}) + \beta_m \mathbf{w}\phi(\mathbf{x}) \end{aligned} \quad (2)$$

where $\mathbf{w}$ and $\{\mathbf{w}_m\}_{m=1}^M$ are model parameters; $\phi(\cdot)$ is the feature map function projecting the original feature $\mathbf{x}$ into the transformed space; and β_m is the weight parameter described in Section 3.2.1 that indicates the utility of the m-th primitive concept in learning the concept bundle classifier $f(\mathbf{x})$.

Aforementioned, learning concept bundles suffers from the sparse positive sample problem. Here, we consider two cases: (a) there is no positive sample for a given concept bundle (the training data for the concept bundle is unavailable); and (b) the training data for the concept bundle is available. For the sake of simplicity, we only introduce the formulation for case (b), and the corresponding algorithm for case (a) is actually the corresponding unsupervised counterpart, which can be inferred by deleting the terms related to the samples in $\mathcal{D}_O$. We derive $f(\mathbf{x})$ by jointly learning the concept classifiers $\{f_m(x)\}_{m=1}^M$ as:

$$\begin{aligned} \min_{\{\mathbf{w}_m\}_{m=1}^M, \mathbf{w}} \quad & \tfrac{\lambda M}{2}||\mathbf{w}||^2 + \tfrac{1}{2}\sum_{m=1}^{M}||\mathbf{w}_m||^2 + C(\sum_{m=1}^{M}\sum_{i=1}^{N_m}\xi_i^m + \sum_{i=1}^{N_O}\xi_i) \\ s.t. \quad & y_i^m(\mathbf{w}_m\phi(\mathbf{x}_i^m) + \beta_m\mathbf{w}\phi(\mathbf{x}_i^m)) \geq 1 - \xi_i^m \\ & y_j^O\mathbf{w}\phi(\mathbf{x}_j^O) \geq 1 - \xi_j, \quad \xi_i^m, \xi_i \geq 0 \\ & m = 1, 2, ...M \quad i = 1, 2, ...N_m \quad j = 1, 2, ...N_O \end{aligned} \quad (3)$$

where the first and second terms are the two regularization terms to prevent "overfitting", and the third term is the penalty on the training errors. λ and C are the tradeoff parameters, and ξ_i^m is the slack variable. The objective function in Eq. (3) can be rewritten as the following (primal) Lagrangian function:

$$\begin{aligned} L_P = & \tfrac{\lambda M}{2}||\mathbf{w}||^2 + \tfrac{1}{2}\sum_{m=1}^{M}||\mathbf{w}_m||^2 + C(\sum_{m=1}^{M}\sum_{i=1}^{N_m}\xi_i^m + \sum_{i=1}^{N_O}\xi_i) \\ & - \sum_{m=1}^{M}\sum_{i=1}^{N_m}\alpha_i^m(y_i^m(\mathbf{w}_m\phi(\mathbf{x}_i^m) + \beta_m\mathbf{w}\phi(\mathbf{x}_i^m)) - (1 - \xi_i^m)) \\ & - \sum_{i=1}^{N_O}\alpha_i(y_i^O\mathbf{w}\phi(\mathbf{x}_i^O) - (1 - \xi_i)) - \sum_{i=1}^{N_O}\mu_i\xi_i - \sum_{m=1}^{M}\sum_{i=1}^{N_m}\mu_i^m\xi_i^m \end{aligned} \quad (4)$$

where $\mu_i^m, \mu_i > 0$, $\alpha_i^m, \alpha_i \geq 0$ are the Lagrange multipliers. We minimize the Lagrangian function by setting its derivative with respect to $\mathbf{w}$, $\mathbf{w}_m$, ξ_i^m and ξ_i to zero respectively. This results in:

$$\begin{aligned} \mathbf{w}_m &= \sum_{i=1}^{N_m}\alpha_i^m y_i^m \phi(\mathbf{x}_i^m) \\ \mathbf{w} &= \begin{cases} \dfrac{\sum_{m=1}^{M}\beta_m\mathbf{w}_m}{\lambda M} & for\ case\ (a) \\ \dfrac{\sum_{m=1}^{M}\beta_m\mathbf{w}_m + \sum_{i=1}^{N_O}\alpha_i y_i \phi(\mathbf{x}_i^O)}{\lambda M} & for\ case\ (b) \end{cases} \\ \alpha_i^m &= C - \mu_i^m, \quad \alpha_i = C - \mu_i \end{aligned} \quad (5)$$

In Eq. (5), $\mathbf{w}_m$ is a linear combination of the training samples $(\mathbf{x}_i^m, y_i^m)_{i=1}^{N_m}$ which is the same as the expression in the typical SVM approach. In the unsupervised learning algorithm for case (a), $\mathbf{w}$ is a linear combination of the training samples of the M primitive concepts. This expression of $\mathbf{w}$ is similar with the expression of the Combine Weighted fusion [1]. However, the primitive concept classifiers here are jointly learned rather than independently learned as in [1]. Additionally, the primitive concepts with large β_m will contribute significantly to the concept bundle classifier $\mathbf{w}$. In the supervise learning for case (b), the expression of $\mathbf{w}$ consists of the classifiers of the primitive concepts as well as the training samples from the concept bundle. Substituting Eq. (5) into its Lagrangian function, we get the Lagrange dual objective function expressed in a matrix form as:

$$L(\mathbf{A}) = \arg\max_{\mathbf{A}}[-\mathbf{A}^T\mathbf{P}\mathbf{A} + \mathbf{1}\mathbf{A}] \tag{6}$$

where

$$\mathbf{A} = \begin{bmatrix}\alpha_1^1 & \dots & \alpha_{N_1}^1 & \dots & \alpha_1^M & \dots & \alpha_{N_M}^M & \alpha_1 & \dots & \alpha_N\end{bmatrix}^T$$

$$\mathbf{1} = \begin{bmatrix}1 & 1 & 1 & \dots & 1 & 1 & 1 & \end{bmatrix}$$

$$\mathbf{P} = \begin{bmatrix} \frac{1}{2}(\frac{\beta_1^2}{\lambda M}+1)\kappa_{11} & \dots & \frac{1}{2\lambda M}\beta_1\beta_M\kappa_{1M} & \frac{1}{2\lambda M}\beta_1\kappa_{1O} \\ \dots & \dots & \dots & \dots \\ \frac{1}{2\lambda M}\beta_M\beta_1\kappa_{M1} & \dots & \frac{1}{2}(\frac{\beta_M^2}{\lambda M}+1)\kappa_{MM} & \frac{1}{2\lambda M}\beta_M\kappa_{MO} \\ \frac{1}{2\lambda M}\beta_1\kappa_{O1} & \dots & \frac{1}{2\lambda M}\beta_M\kappa_{OM} & \frac{1}{2\lambda M}\kappa_{OO} \end{bmatrix}$$

$$\kappa_{ij} = \begin{bmatrix} y_1^i\mathcal{K}(\mathbf{x}_1^i, \mathbf{x}_1^j)y_1^j & \dots & y_1^i\mathcal{K}(\mathbf{x}_1^i, \mathbf{x}_{N_j}^j)y_{N_j}^j \\ y_2^i\mathcal{K}(\mathbf{x}_2^i, \mathbf{x}_1^j)y_1^j & \dots & y_2^i\mathcal{K}(\mathbf{x}_2^i, \mathbf{x}_{N_j}^j)y_{N_j}^j \\ \dots & \dots & \dots \\ y_{N_i}^i\mathcal{K}(\mathbf{x}_{N_i}^i, \mathbf{x}_1^j)y_1^j & \dots & y_{N_i}^i\mathcal{K}(\mathbf{x}_{N_i}^i, \mathbf{x}_{N_j}^j)y_{N_j}^j \end{bmatrix}$$

where $\mathcal{K}(,)$ is a kernel function and κ_{ij} represents the kernel matrix of the training samples from the concept i and j. The optimization problem expressed in Eq. (6) can be solved using SMO algorithm [3].

4. BUNDLE-BASED VIDEO SEARCH

Given a query Q, the typical concept-based video search approach first maps this query into related primitive concepts before computing the relevance of each video entry with respect to the query. In our search model, we map the query into related primitive concepts and concept bundles. For the sake of simplicity, we use the word "bundle" to imply both a primitive concept and a combined semantic concept (concept bundle) in this section.

4.1 Mapping Query to Bundles

4.1.1 *formulation*

Based on the pre-built bundle corpus $\mathcal{S} = \{\mathcal{C}_1, ..., \mathcal{C}_K\}$, we need to select related bundles $\{\mathcal{C}_1, ..., \mathcal{C}_L\}$ $(L < K)$ for each query Q. Our selection approach selects related bundles (denoted as a set $sub(\mathcal{S})$) from $\mathcal{S}$ according to two criterions: (1) $sub(\mathcal{S})$ should preferably contain the bundles with high semantic relatedness with respect to query Q; and (2) $sub(\mathcal{S})$ should introduce as little errors as possible. We make a tradeoff between these two criterions by a weight parameter C, and the formulation is expressed as:

$$\arg\min_{sub(\mathcal{S})} C * (1 - Sem(sub(\mathcal{S}))) + (1 - C) * Er(sub(\mathcal{S})) \tag{7}$$

where $Sem(sub(\mathcal{S}))$ measures the semantic relatedness of the bundles in $sub(\mathcal{S})$ with respect to the query Q, and $Er(sub(\mathcal{S}))$ is the errors produced by the classifiers of the bundles in $sub(\mathcal{S})$.

4.1.2 *Semantic Relatedness Estimation*

Different concepts have different semantic relatedness to query Q, and this semantic relatedness can be estimated by the text matching score [4]. In our approach, we use the *tf-idf* score between the query and concept to represent this text matching score. For each query Q, we first generate a parse tree [15] by using OpenNLP [1]. We then select the nouns and verbs from the parse tree as the salient words since they are found to be more important than articles, adjectives or adverbs [28]. Finally we take these selected salient words as a term and compute its *tf-idf* scores with respect to the K video tag documents of the bundles in $\mathcal{S}$, where each tag document is a collection of the video tag files downloaded from YouTube website (see Section 3.2.1). We normalize all the *tf-idf* scores in $\mathcal{S}$ as the bundle utilities $\{\beta_i\}_{i=1}^{|\mathcal{S}|}$. The semantic relatedness of $sub(\mathcal{S})$ is defined as the sum of the bundle utilities in $sub(\mathcal{S})$:

$$Sem(sub(\mathcal{S})) = \sum_{s_i \in sub(\mathcal{S})} \beta_i \tag{8}$$

4.1.3 *Error Estimation*

The performance of the pre-built bundle classifiers are quite different, and we want to select relevant classifiers that introduce as little errors as possible. Let $Er(sub(\mathcal{S}))$ be the misclassification probability of a sample $\mathbf{x}$ by the classifiers in $sub(\mathcal{S})$, which we express as:

$$Er(sub(\mathcal{S})) = \sum_y P(\hat{y} \neq y|\mathbf{x})P(y) \tag{9}$$

where $P(y)$ is the prior probability of sample $\mathbf{x}$ with label y, and $P(\hat{y} \neq y|\mathbf{x})$ is the misclassification probability of sample $\mathbf{x}$ ($\hat{y}$ is the predicted label). In our problem, we define two labels: $y \in \{1, -1\}$, where $y = 1$ means that $\mathbf{x}$ is a positive sample for query Q, and $y = -1$ otherwise. Based on these two labels, we transform Eq. (9) into Eq. (10) as:

$$\begin{aligned} Er(sub(\mathcal{S})) = & P(\hat{y} = -1|\mathbf{x}, y = 1)P(y = 1) \\ & + P(\hat{y} = 1|\mathbf{x}, y = -1)P(y = -1) \end{aligned} \tag{10}$$

Let $\mathbf{y^b} \in \mathcal{Y} = \{1, -1\}^L$ denote the L dimensional label vector of a sample $\mathbf{x}$ with respect to the bundles of $sub(\mathcal{S})$, where L is the number of bundles in $sub(\mathcal{S})$. A sample is positive if it satisfies all the bundles in $sub(\mathcal{S})$, and negative even if it is just irrelevant to one bundle in $sub(\mathcal{S})$. Thus, the label of a positive sample is $\mathbf{y^b} = \{1\}^L$, and that of a negative sample is $\mathbf{y^b} \in \mathcal{Y}/\{1\}^L$. As a result, we express the probabilities $P(\hat{y} = -1|\mathbf{x}, y = 1)$ and $P(\hat{y} = 1|\mathbf{x}, y = -1)$ as:

$$\begin{aligned} P(\hat{y} = -1|\mathbf{x}, y = 1) &= 1 - \prod_i^L P(\hat{y}_i^b = 1|\mathbf{x}, y_i^b = 1) \\ P(\hat{y} = 1|\mathbf{x}, y = -1) &= \max_{\mathbf{y^b} = \mathcal{Y}/\{1\}^L} \prod_i^L P(\hat{y}_i^b = 1|\mathbf{x}, y_i^b) \end{aligned} \tag{11}$$

where y_i^b is the i-th label of $\mathbf{y^b}$, and $\hat{y}_i^b$ is the predicted label by the i-th bundle classifier in $sub(\mathcal{S})$. In Eq.(11), for a positive sample, its every individual label y_i^b is 1, thus $P(\hat{y} = -1|\mathbf{x}, y = 1)$ can be directly calculated; For a negative sample, since its individual label y_i^b is uncertain, we set $P(\hat{y} = 1|\mathbf{x}, y = -1)$ to be the maximum misclassification probability among all the possible label assignments($\mathbf{y^b} \in \mathcal{Y}/\{1\}^L$).

To estimate the unknown probabilities in Eqs. (10) and (11), we resort to a validation dataset. We estimate the conditional probabilities $P(\hat{y}_i^b = 1|\mathbf{x}, y_i^b = 1)$ and $P(\hat{y}_i^b = 1|\mathbf{x}, y_i^b = -1)$ to be

[1] http://incubator.apache.org/opennlp/

the proportion of positive (negative) samples of the i-th bundle being classified as positive on the validation set. While for the prior probabilities $P(y=1)$ or $P(y=-1)$, we estimate them to be the proportion of positive(negative) samples over the total number of all samples on the validation set.

4.1.4 *Implementation*

In our approach, we employ an optimal function to select a set of related bundles to interpret a query. However, the computation cost will be high if we try all the possible sets (the time complexity is $O(2^K)$). Here, we develop a greedy algorithm to speed up the selection procedure. We first select a bundle from $\mathcal{S}$ with the minimal value of Eq. (7), and then incrementally add a bundle that maximally reduces the value of Eq. (7). This incremental process is stopped when the value of Eq. (7) cannot be further reduced by the remaining bundles. In our implementation, the sub-bundles of an selected bundle will no longer be evaluated and selected by the algorithm. The rationale is that a bundle is semantically closer to the query than its sub-bundles. We summarize the process of mapping-query-to-bundles in Algorithm 1.

Algorithm 1 Mapping-query-to-bundles

1: **Input:** The query Q, the pre-built bundle corpus $\mathcal{S}=\{\mathcal{C}_k\}_{k=1}^{K}$, the weight parameter C
2: **Output:** the related bundle set $sub(\mathcal{S})$
3: **Process:**
4: $\{\beta_k\}_{k=1}^{K} \longleftarrow$ Semantic_Relatedness_Estimation(Q, $\mathcal{S}$)
5: $sub(\mathcal{S})=\varnothing$
6: **while** there exists an unselected bundle s_i in $\mathcal{S}$ such that the value of Eq. (7) can be reduced **do**
7: $\quad \arg\min_{s_i} C*(1-Sem(sub(\mathcal{S})\cup s_i))+(1-C)*Er(sub(\mathcal{S})\cup s_i)$
8: $\quad sub(\mathcal{S})=sub(\mathcal{S})\cup s_i$
9: **end while**
10: return $sub(\mathcal{S})$.

4.2 Fusion

Different from the typical video search approach that fuses the results from related primitive concepts, our approach generates the final results by fusing the individual results from the related bundles. Given a selected bundle set $sub(\mathcal{S})$, with each bundle has a classifier f^l, we compute the relevance score of each keyframe with respect to the complex query as

$$Score(x)=\sum_{l=1}^{|sub(\mathcal{S})|}\beta_l\frac{1}{1+e^{-f^l(\mathbf{x})}} \tag{12}$$

where β_l is the utility value of the l-th bundle. The calculation of β_l is described in Section 4.1.2. Finally, we use the relevance scores of all the keyframes to rank the final search results.

5. EXPERIMENTS

5.1 Experimental Setup

We conducted experiments on two video datasets. The first one is the benchmark TRECVID 2008 dataset [26] (called "*TV08*" for short). The training set of "*TV08*" contains 110 videos with 18,120 keyframes from the TRECVID 2007 development dataset. We used it to train the classifiers of the concept bundles where the corresponding primitive concepts are the Columbia374 [34]. The validation set contains 109 videos with 18,142 keyframes from the TRECVID 2007 testing dataset. We used it to estimate the classifier performance used in concept bundle selection. The testing set contains 219 videos with 35,766 keyframes from the TRECVID 2008 testing dataset. It is used to test the performance of concept bundle classifiers and query search. The ground truth of the concept bundles is obtained through a manually labeling process, and that of the queries is provided by the TRECVID 2008 official release.

The other real-world video data is collected from YouTube Web site. We selected 41 representative primitive concepts from the popular tags in YouTube (see Table 1). These concepts cover a wide variety of semantics, including entertainment, arts, communication, sports, and animal etc. We submitted each concept to YouTube and collected the related queries suggested by the search engine. From the suggested queries, we selected 20 complex queries as listed in Table 2. Furthermore, we submitted each concept as a query to YouTube video search engine and downloaded the top 80 returned videos. To ensure that each query has some relevant videos, we submitted each query to YouTube and downloaded about 10 relevant videos. This gives rise to a total of 3,420 videos. After removing the duplicates, we obtained a total of 3,349 videos. We then extracted keyframes from these videos and obtain around 158,000 keyframes. This dataset is randomly separated into a training subset containing 2,002 videos with about 90,000 keyframes, a validation subset containing 990 videos with about 50,000 keyframes, and a

Table 1: The 41 Primitive Concepts Selected from Popular Video Tags in YouTube

astronaut	baby	basketball	beach
car	cat	children	cooking
crash	dance	fighting	fire
flood	horse	house	hunting
interview	kitchen	lady	laughing
lion	moon land	motorcycle	mouse
office	person	police	protester
race	riding	river	sea
singing	soccer	street	telephone
television	tree	vehicle	wedding
zebra			

Table 2: The 20 Queries on YouTube Dataset

ID	Query
1	Astronauts carrying out moon landing
2	A person is cooking in kitchen
3	A person is riding a horse
4	Baby is laughing
5	Cars crashing in a race
6	Cat and mouse
7	Children are singing
8	House in flood
9	Lady laughing in an interview
10	Lady make a telephone call in office
11	Lady on the beach with sea visible
12	Lions hunting zebras
13	Motorcycles racing at night
14	Persons dancing in the wedding
15	Persons fighting in street
16	Persons interviewing in street
17	Persons playing basketball in street
18	Police fighting protester
19	Soccer fighting
20	Vehicle fires

Table 3: The 40 Informative Concept Bundles on "*TV08*" dataset (The concept bundles in bold are evaluated in our experiment)

1	classroom,room	21	meeting,room
2	glasses,sunglasses	22	building,cityscape
3	basketball,stadium	23	**office,person**
4	**airplane,sky**	24	airplane,military
5	hand,handshaking	25	dance,street
6	bathroom,room	26	bird,sky
7	**building,sky**	27	house,room
8	athlete,sports	28	bus,driver
9	police,protester	29	car,police
10	**bridge,waterway**	30	**nighttime,street**
11	**street,vehicle**	31	face,hand
12	**crowd,outdoor**	32	mountain,snow
13	outdoor,sport	33	**animal,person**
14	swimmer,swimming	34	**computer,office**
15	animal,dog	35	landscape,sky
16	**flower,vegetation**	36	**dining_room,food**
17	clouds,sky	37	**computer_or_television _screens,person**
18	car,vehicle	38	desert,landscape
19	airplane,airport	39	mountain,sky
20	**ship,waterway**	40	car,desert

testing subset including 357 videos with about 18,000 keyframes. To obtain the ground truth, we conducted a manual labeling procedure. Specifically, each keyframe is labeled as a positive or negative sample with respect to the primitive concepts, the to-be-evaluated concept bundles, and the queries. We invited five subjects to manually label the keyframes. Each keyframe is labeled by at least three subjects, and the ground truth is established through majority voting. Since the downloaded top ranked videos are very noisy, the positive samples of the primitive concepts, the concept bundles and the queries are very sparse.

To represent the content of keyframes, we extracted three visual features: 166-dimensional color histogram, 100-dimensional edge distribution histogram and 96-dimensional texture cooccurrence. They are concatenated into a 362-dimensional feature vector.

5.2 Evaluation on Concept Bundle Learning

Based on the primitive concepts, we selected informative concept bundles according to their informativeness measured in Eq. (1). We conducted this selection on the 374 primitive concepts of "*TV08*" dataset and 41 primitive concepts of "*YouTube*" dataset. In calculating the informativeness of a concept bundle, we set the weight α in Eq. (1) to 0.5 to equally emphasize the co-occurrence of primitive concepts and users' interest on this concept bundle. For informative concept bundle selection, we set the threshold as the average informativeness of all the bundle candidates. In particular, the threshold is set to 0.25 for "*TV08*" dataset and 0.2 for "*YouTube*" dataset. As a result, we obtained 40 concept bundles on "*TV08*" dataset (see Table 3), and 38 concepts bundles on "*YouTube*" dataset (see Table 4).

From Tables 3 and 4, it is evident that some concept bundles are quite useful to model complex query, such as ("street","nighttime") for query "a street scene at night" and ("computer","office") for query "one or more people at a table or desk with a computer visible" on "*TV08*" dataset. However, some concept bundles are useless. For example, ("animal", "dog"), ("car", "vehicle") etc, are actually equivalent to primitive concepts since they are synonym or hyponym conveying similar semantics. Such concept bundles can be easily identified by Wordnet [8]. Thus, we employed Wordnet to filter out such concept bundles. After that, we selected a subset of concept bundles in Tables 3 and 4 to evaluate since the labeling of ground truth is labor-intensive. These selected concept bundles are those that will be used in our search task. For example, in Table 3, the third concept bundle ("basketball", "stadium") is not selected since it is not related to any "*TV08*"'s queries. As a result, we selected 13 concept bundles (bold font) in Table 3 and 22 concept bundles (bold font) in Table 4.

Table 4: The 38 Informative Concept Bundles on "*YouTube*" dataset (The concept bundles in bold are evaluated in our experiment)

1	**lady,telephone**	20	horse,race
2	**baby,laughing**	21	motorcycle,ride
3	car,race	22	**person,television**
4	**fighting,street**	23	**lady,office**
5	**dance,wedding**	24	baby,dance
6	race,river	25	cat,fighting
7	crash,motorcycle	26	car,race,river
8	**police,protester**	27	**fire,vehicle**
9	dance,street	28	**children,singing**
10	**horse,riding**	29	**interview,lady**
11	**motorcycle,race**	30	crash,vehicle
12	race,street	31	motorcycle,street
13	**car,race,crash**	32	**astronaut,moon land**
14	kitchen,sea	33	interview,protest
15	**lion,hunting,zebra**	34	**cooking,kitchen**
16	**cat,mouse**	35	**fighting,soccer**
17	dance,lady	36	**basketball,street**
18	**house,tree**	37	**beach,sea**
19	car,police	38	**flood,river**

On "*TV08*" dataset, we directly used Columbia374 primitive concept classifiers, while on "*YouTube*" dataset we trained the primitive concept classifiers using the Support Vector Machine (SVM). In the SVM algorithm, we used the empirically successful Gaussian kernel $exp(-\gamma||\mathbf{x}_i - \mathbf{x}_j||^2)$ as the kernel function where γ is the scaling parameter. A fivefold cross-validation process was conducted on the training set to determine the parameters.

As described in Section 3.2.2, we have considered two cases in our classification algorithm: Unsupervised Learning case (UL) without using the training samples for the concept bundles and Supervised Learning case (SL) using the training samples. Although all the concept bundles have training samples in our datasets, we still trained two kinds of the classifiers by the UL and SL approaches for each selected concept bundle in order to make a complete comparison with the following four existing methods:

- Support Vector Machine (SVM): This approach directly builds a SVM classifier for each concept bundle based on its training samples without using the primitive concepts. The Gaussian kernel is adopted and the parameters are estimated through a fivefold cross-validation process.

- Concept Fusion (CF) [1]: This approach generates the detection result list of a concept bundle by fusing the individual results from its primitive concept classifiers. Here we adopt the Combine Weighted fusion operation, and the fusion weight of each primitive concept is equal to its utility value with respect to the concept bundle.

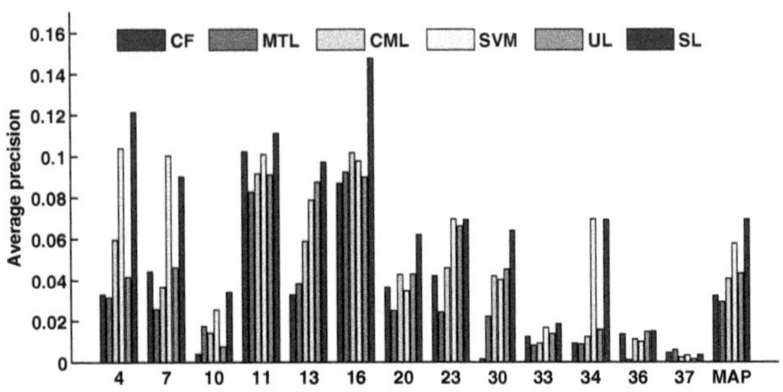

Figure 2: The performance on 13 concept bundles of *"TV08"* dataset as measured by AP@1000

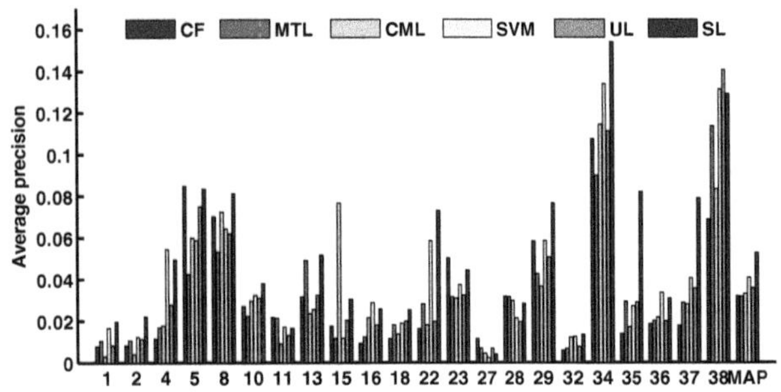

Figure 3: The performance on 22 concept bundles of *"YouTube"* dataset as measured by AP@1000

- Multi-label Learning Approach (CML) [20]: For each concept bundle, this approach jointly learns its involved primitive concepts on their training data, and outputs the predicted probabilities on all the primitive concepts for each testing sample. We then generates the detection result of the concept bundle using the CF approach.

- Multi-Task Learning Approach (MTL) [2]: This approach takes each involved primitive concept of a concept bundle as a learning task, and jointly learns these tasks with a shared parameter part. In the implementation, we adopt the modified Huber loss function as suggested in [2], and solve the optimization problem by the stochastic gradient descent method. After obtaining the results of the involved primitive concepts of a concept bundle, it generates the detection result of the concept bundle using the CF approach.

The performance is measured by the widely used non-interpolated Average Precision (AP) [26]. We averaged the APs over all the concept bundles to obtain the Mean Average Precision (MAP) as a measure of the overall performance.

Figures 2 and 3 illustrate the performance of our UL and SL methods as compared to that of CF, SVM, CML and MTL approaches. The following observations are obtained:

- The best performance is achieved by the SL approach with a MAP of 0.069 on *"TV08"* dataset and 0.053 on *"YouTube"* dataset. As compared to the results of many concept detection techniques which could achieve the MAP above 0.1 for primitive concepts, the performance of concept bundle learning is much lower. This is because the positive samples of concept bundle are much fewer than that of the primitive concepts.

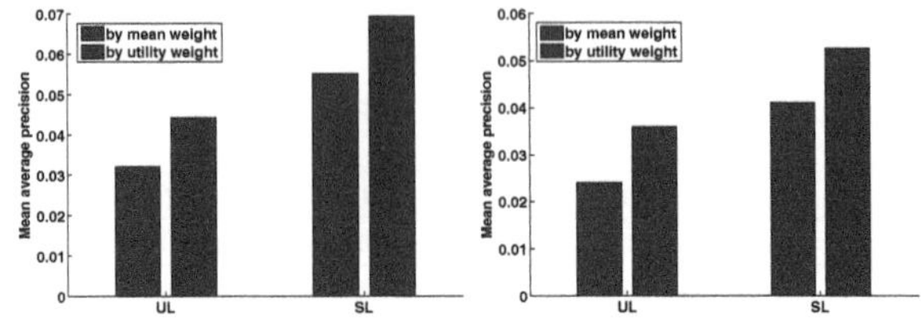

(a) TV08 Dataset (b) YouTube Dataset

Figure 4: The effectiveness of concept utility in UL and SL

- The SVM approach achieves a MAP of 0.058 on *"TV08"* dataset and 0.041 on *"YouTube"* dataset. Compared to the SVM approach, the improvement by the SL approach is about 19.0% and 29.3% on *"TV08"* and *"YouTube"* datasets respectively. This improvement re-affirms our view that jointly learning the concept bundles and their primitive concepts can overcome the sparse positive sample problem, and thus be able to achieve good performance.

- The UL approach only has a MAP of 0.043 on *"TV08"* and 0.036 on *"YouTube"* dataset, with a corresponding 25.0% and 11.8% performance degradation as compared to the SVM approach. This is because our UL approach is unsupervised and does not require the training samples of concept bundles.

- The other approaches CF, MTL, CML all have a poorer performance as compared to UL, SVM and SL approaches. This is because CF, MTL, CML approaches focus on learning the individual primitive concepts instead of concept bundle, and the results of the concept bundle are actually generated by the fusion operation. As discussed before, simply aggregating primitive concepts cannot interpret concept bundle well.

To evaluate the effectiveness of concept utility in our UL and SL approach, Figure 4 shows the performance comparison of the UL and SL approaches by using our utility weights or simply adopting mean weights ($\beta = \frac{1}{m}$ in Eq.(2)). We can see that using utility weights leads to better performance. This demonstrates that the concept utility could correctly estimate the degree of relatedness of primitive concepts with respect to the concept bundle. Taking the concept bundle ("person","office") on *"TV08"* dataset as example, the utilities for the primitive concepts "person" and "office" are 0.13 and 0.87 respectively. This enables the concept bundle ("person","office") to achieve an AP of 0.069 by the SL approach, instead of an AP of 0.035 by the SL approach using the mean weights.

5.3 Evaluation on Search Performance

Although the overall concept detection performance is not satisfactory, however, as pointed in [10], we are able to achieve standard text-based search performance for video when several thousand of detectors with modest performance are available. In this section, we evaluate the performance of our search approach. We conducted experiments on all the 48 queries in *"TV08"* search task and 20 queries on *"YouTube"* dataset. In our experiments, we employed the SL algorithm to train the classifiers for concept bundles. The weight parameter C in Eq.(7) was set to 0.8 due to its leading to the best performance (see Table 6). The probabilities in Section 4.1.3 were obtained through evaluating the classification results of the classifiers on the validation dataset.

In the first experiment, we evaluated the effectiveness of concept bundles in the overall search performance. We compared the

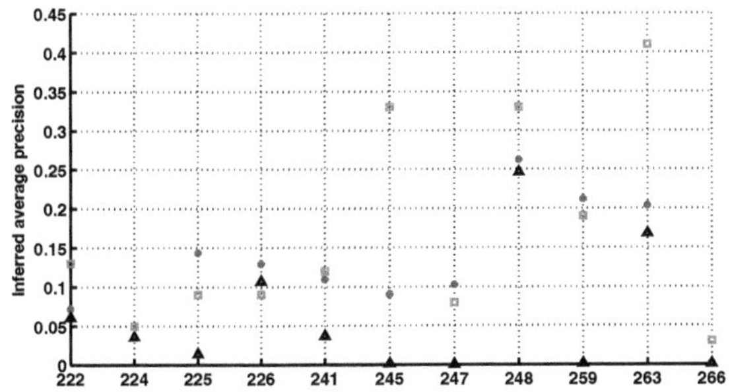

Figure 5: The detailed performance of the selected 11 queries on "*TV08*" dataset as measured by inferred AP@1000, where the rectangle is the best performance achieved by the official submissions on "*TV08*" search task, star and triangle are the performance achieved by our search approach using and not using concept bundles respectively

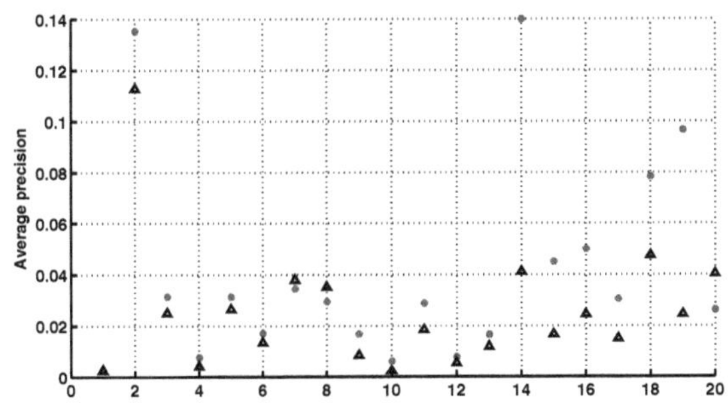

Figure 6: The detailed performance of the 20 queries on "*YouTube*" dataset as measured by AP@1000, where the star and triangle are the performance achieved by our search approach using and not using concept bundles respectively

search performance on two cases by: (1) mapping the query to related primitive concepts and concept bundles (using the concept bundles); and (2) mapping the query to only related primitive concepts (without using the concept bundles). Here, the search without concept bundles is performed using the same approach as in Section 4, but the concept bundles are not involved. Table 5 shows the comparison of search performance. On "*TV08*" dataset, we adopted the Inferred Average Precision (Inferred AP) as provided by TRECVID [26] to evaluate the performance of each query and the overall performance is measured by the Inferred Mean Average Precision (Inferred MAP). The overall results demonstrate that, by using concept bundles, our search algorithm can improve the Inferred MAP on "*TV08*" dataset from 0.04 to 0.055 and the MAP on "*YouTube*" dataset from 0.025 to 0.038. The relative improvements are 37.5% and 54.7%, respectively. These improvements are not marginal but considerable in the context of video search, which is an extremely difficult task due to the high diversity of video content [22]. Here, statistical significance test is not applied to examine the results. The reason is that significance test is normally ineffective in evaluating video search systems due to the high variance among the query topics [9].

Figures 5 and 6 show the detailed performance of our search algorithm on each query by using and not using the concept bundles. Actually, not all the queries could be mapped to concept bundles. On "*TV08*" dataset, only 11 queries could be mapped to concept bundles in our experiments, while the remaining queries are modeled using only primitive concepts and could achieve the same performance as the approach without using the concept bundles. Here, we only list the comparison results on these 11 queries. In Figure 5, on "*TV08*" dataset, our search approach using concept bundles outperforms that without using concept bundles on all the 11 queries. Among these queries, the performance of 5 queries (224, 225, 226, 247, 259) have significantly better performance as compared to the TRECVID official results. On "*YouTube*" dataset, our search approach using the concept bundles performs better on 17 queries, worse on 3 queries as compared to that without using the concept bundles. After analyzing these 3 queries (7,8,20), we find the search performance degradation is caused by the poor performance of the concept bundle classifiers (28,38,27 in Figure 3).

Table 5: The comparison of video search performance by using or not using concept bundles as measured by inferred MAP@1000 ("*TV08*") or MAP@1000 ("*YouTube*")

	using concept bundles	not using concept bundles
TV08	0.055	0.040
YouTube	0.038	0.025

Table 6: The video search performance by using different weights C in Eq. (7)

	C=0	C=0.2	C=0.4	C=0.6	C=0.8	C=1
TV08	0.031	0.031	0.031	0.038	**0.055**	0.052
YouTube	0.026	0.026	0.026	0.030	**0.038**	0.035

Furthermore, we evaluated the performance variation with different weights C (see Eq. (7)). Table 6 shows the search results under different weights C. The best performance is achieved when $C = 0.8$. The smaller value of C will lead to a rapid performance degradation, and the larger value of C will slightly reduce the search performance. This result demonstrates that the semantic relatedness is more important than the classifier performance in concept selection. When $C < 0.4$, the concept selection results are dominated by selecting the high performance concepts, and thus the search performance is stable.

Finally, Table 7 lists the performance comparison between our search approach and the two state-of-the-art approaches [31, 13] on "*TV08*" dataset. In [31], a multi-level fusion framework is developed by considering the semantics, observability, reliability and diversity for classifier selection, while in [13] the Flickr context is analyzed and used for classifier selection. In our approach, we utilize concept bundles to help learn the complex queries, and as a result we could achieve a significant improvement. Figure 7 further compares our results with the official submissions on "*TV08*" dataset. Among all the 82 submissions, our approach, using only concept based query process, ranks third, while the top two TRECVID official submissions adopted a combination of concept and image/video examples matching. For example, the best performing system [25] contains three modalities: text matching, concept-based search, and image/video example matching.

6. CONCLUSIONS

Table 7: The search performance comparison between our search approach and the state-of-the-art approaches on "*TV08*" dataset

	Wei et al [31]	Jiang et al [13]	Our approach
TV08	0.042	0.050	0.055

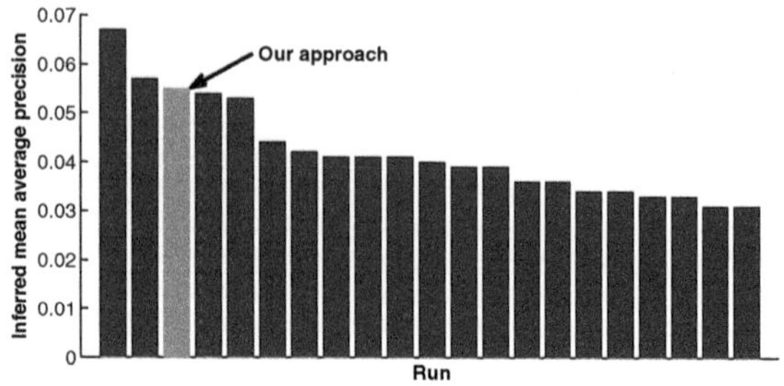

Figure 7: Inferred MAP comparison with the top-20 (out of 82) official submissions of the automatic video search task in TRECVID 2008

In this paper, we proposed to learn a higher-level semantic descriptor named "concept bundle" to facilitate video search for complex queries. To ensure the informativeness of concept bundles, we devised a selection process based on concept bundle frequency in the suggested queries by Web video search engine and the concept co-occurrence in the tags of Web videos. We then proposed a multi-task SVM algorithm to build the concept bundle classifier by jointly learning its involved primitive concept classifiers. We further proposed an algorithm to map complex queries to the concept bundles and primitive concepts by considering their semantic relatedness and classifier performance. The experiments were conducted on "*TV08*" and "*YouTube*" datasets and demonstrated that the concept bundles could characterize complex queries well and achieve promising performance as compared to the state-of-the-art approaches.

This paper begins a new research direction to model complex queries by using concept bundles. The current approach utilizes the training samples of primitive concepts to help learn the concept bundle classifier. However, given a positive sample of a certain primitive concept, only one or more regions of the sample are actually related to the target concept bundle. Thus, one of our future works is to identify the related regions when learning concept bundles. In addition, we will study the performance of our approach on a larger set of concepts and queries.

7. ACKNOWLEDGEMENT

This work was supported by A*Star Research Grant R-252-000-437-305 and NSFC Grant 61073002.

8. REFERENCES

[1] R. Aly, D. Hiemstra, and R. Ordelman. Building detectors to support searches on combined semantic concepts. Proc. of the SIGIR workshop on Multimedia Information Retrieval, 2007.

[2] R. K. Ando and T. Zhang. A framework for learning predictive structures from multiple tasks and unlabeled data. The Journal of Machine Learning, 2005.

[3] F. R. Bach, G. R. G. Lanckriet, and M. I. Jordan. Multiple kernel learning, conic duality, and the smo algorithm. Proc. of Int. Conf. on Machine Learning, 2004.

[4] S. F. Chang, W. Hsu, and et.al. Columbia university trecvid-2006 video search and high-level feature extraction. TRECVID Workshop, 2006.

[5] R. L. Cilibrasi and P. M. B. Vitanyi. The google similarity distance. IEEE Transactions on Knowledge and Data Engineering, 2007.

[6] L. X. Duan, I. W. Tsang, D. Xu, and S. J. Maybank. Domain transfer svm for video concept detection. Proc. of IEEE Int. Conf. on Computer Vision and Pattern Recognition, 2009.

[7] T. Evgeniou and M. Pontil. Regularized multi-task learning. Proc. of the ACM SIGKDD Int. Conf. on Knowledge discovery and data mining, 2004.

[8] C. Fellbaum. Wordnet: an electronic lexical database. The MIT Press, 1998.

[9] A. Hauptmann and W.-H. Lin. Assessing effectiveness in video retrieval. Proc. of the ACM Int. Conf. on Image and Video Retrieval, 2005.

[10] A. Hauptmann, Y. R. Yan, and W.-H. L. etc. Can high-level concepts fill the semantic gap in video retrieval? a case study with broadcast news. *IEEE Transactions on Multimedia*, 2007.

[11] X. Hu, L. Tang, and H. Liu. Enhancing accessibility of microblogging messages using semantic knowledge. In *Pro. of the ACM Int. Conf. on Information and knowledge management*, 2011.

[12] W. Jiang, S.-F. Chang, T. Jebara, and A. C. Loui. Semantic concept classification by joint semi-supervised learning of feature subspaces and support vector machines. Proc. of IEEE European Conf. on Computer Vision, 2008.

[13] Y. G. Jiang, C. W. Ngo, and S. F. Chang. Semantic context transfer across heterogeneous sources for domain adaptive video search. Proc. of ACM Int. Conf. on Multimedia, 2009.

[14] Y. G. Jiang, J. Yang, C. W. Ngo, and A. G. Hauptmann. Representations of keypoint-based semantic concept detection: A comprehensive study. *IEEE Transactions on Multimedia*, 2009.

[15] C. Manning and H. Schutze. Foundations of statistical natural language processing. MIT Press, 1999.

[16] C. D. Manning, P. Raghavan, and H. Schĺźtze. *An Introduction to Information Retrieval*. Cambridge University Press, Cambridge, England, online edition (c) edition, April 2009.

[17] M. R. Naphade and J. R. Smith. On the detection of semantic concepts at trecvid. Proc. of ACM Int. Conf. on Multimedia, 2004.

[18] A. P. Natsev, A. Haubold, J. Tešić, L. Xie, and R. Yan. Semantic concept-based query expansion and re-ranking for multimedia retrieval. Proc. of the ACM Int. Conf. on Multimedia, 2007.

[19] S. Y. Neo, J. Zhao, M. Y. Kan, and T. S. Chua. Video retrieval using high level features: Exploiting query matching and confidence-based weighting. Proc. of ACM Int. Conf. on Image and Video Retrieval, 2006.

[20] G. J. Qi, X. S. Hua, Y. Rui, J. H. Tang, T. Mei, and H. J. Zhang. Correlative multi-label video annotation. Proc. of ACM Int. Conf. on Multimedia, 2007.

[21] C. G. M. Snoek, B. Huurnink, L. Hollink, and et.al. Adding semantics to detectors for video retrieval. *IEEE Transactions on Multimedia*, 2007.

[22] C. G. M. Snoek and M. Worring. Concept-based video retrieval. *Foundations and Trends ®in Information Retrieval*, 2009.

[23] C. G. M. Snoek, M. Worring, J. C. V. Gemert, J. M. Geusebroek, and A. W. M. Smeulders. The challenge problem for automated detection of 101 semantic concepts in multimedia. Proc. of ACM Int. Conf. on Multimedia, 2006.

[24] S. Tang, J. T. Li, and et al. Trecvid 2008 high-level feature extraction by mcg-ict-cas. In TRECVID Workshop, 2008.

[25] S. Tang, J. T. Li, and et al. Trecvid 2008 participation by mcg-ict-cas. In TRECVID Workshop, 2008.

[26] TRECVID. http://trecvid.nist.gov/.

[27] D. Wang, X. Liu, L. Luo, J. Li, and B. Zhang. The importance of query-concept-mapping for automatic video retrieval. Proc. of ACM Int. Conf. on Multimedia, 2007.

[28] K. Wang, Z. Y. Ming, and T. Chua. A syntactic tree matching approach to finding similar questions in community-based qa services. Proc. of the 32nd ACM SIGIR, 2009.

[29] M. Wang, X. S. Hua, R. C. Hong, and et.al. Unified video annotation via multi-graph learning. IEEE Transactions on Circuits and Systems for Video Technology, 2009.

[30] M. Wang, X. S. Hua, J. H. Tang, and R. C. Hong. Beyond distance measurement: Constructing neighborhood similarity for video annotation. *IEEE Transactions on Multimedia*, 2009.

[31] X.-Y. Wei and C.-W. Ngo. Fusing semantics, observability, reliability and diversity of concept detectors for video search. Proc. of the ACM Int. Conf. on Multimedia, 2008.

[32] X. Y. Wei, C. W. Ngo, and Y. G. Jiang. Selection of concept detectors for video search by ontology-enriched semantic spaces. *IEEE Transactions on Multimedia*, 2008.

[33] L. Wu, X. S. Hua, N. Yu, W. Y. Ma, and S. Li. Flickr distance. Proc. of the ACM Int. Conf. on Multimedia, 2008.

[34] A. Yanagawa, S. F. Chang, L. Kennedy, and W. Hsu. Columbia university's baseline detectors for 374 lscom semantic visual concepts. ADVENT Technical Report 222-2006-8, 2007.

[35] J. Yang, R. Yan, and A. G. Hauptmann. Cross-domain video concept detection using adaptive svms. Proc. of ACM Int. Conf. on Multimedia, 2007.

[36] X. T. Yuan and S. C. Yan. Visual classification with multi-task joint sparse representation. Proc. of IEEE Int. Conf. on Computer Vision and Pattern Recognition, 2010.

[37] Z. J. Zha, X. S. Hua, T. Mei, and et al. Joint multi-label multi-instance learning for image classification. Pro. of the ACM Int. Conf. on Computer Vision and Pattern Recognition, 2008.

[38] Z. J. Zha, M. Wang, Y. T. Zheng, and et al. Interactive video indexing with statistical active learning. *IEEE Transactions on Multimedia*, 2011.

[39] Z. J. Zha, L. J. Yang, T. Mei, M. Wang, and Z. F. Wang. Visual query suggestion. Pro. of the ACM Int. Conf. on Multimedia, 2009.

[40] V. W. Zheng, S. J. Pan, Q. Yang, and J. J. Pan. Transferring multi-device localization models using latent multi-task learning. Proc. of the Int. Conf. on Artificial intelligence, 2008.

Flicker Effects in Adaptive Video Streaming to Handheld Devices

Pengpeng Ni[1,2], Ragnhild Eg[1,3], Alexander Eichhorn[1], Carsten Griwodz[1,2], Pål Halvorsen[1,2]
[1]Simula Research Laboratory, Norway
[2]Department of Informatics, University of Oslo, Norway
[3]Department of Psychology, University of Oslo, Norway

ABSTRACT

Streaming video over the Internet requires mechanisms that limit the streams' bandwidth consumption within its fair share. TCP streaming guarantees this and provides lossless streaming as a side-effect. Adaptation by packet drop does not occur in the network, and excessive startup latency and stalling must be prevented by adapting the bandwidth consumption of the video itself. However, when the adaptation is performed during an ongoing session, it may influence the perceived quality of the entire video and result in improved or reduced visual quality of experience. We have investigated visual artifacts that are caused by adaptive layer switching – we call them *flicker effects* – and present our results for handheld devices in this paper.

We considered three types of flicker, namely noise, blur and motion flicker. The perceptual impact of flicker is explored through subjective assessments. We vary both the intensity of quality changes (*amplitude*) and the number of quality changes per second (*frequency*). Users' ability to detect and their acceptance of variations in the amplitudes and frequencies of the quality changes are explored across four content types. Our results indicate that multiple factors influence the acceptance of different quality variations. Amplitude plays the dominant role in delivering satisfactory video quality, while frequency can also be adjusted to relieve the annoyance of flicker artifacts.

Categories and Subject Descriptors

H.1.2 [**Models and Principles**]: User/Machine Systems – *Human factors*; H.5.1 [**Information Interfaces and Presentation**]: Multimedia Information Systems – *Video*

General Terms

Experimentation, Human Factors

Keywords

Subjective video quality, Video adaptation, Layer switching

*Area Chair: Wu-chi Feng

1. INTRODUCTION

To cope with the Internet's varying bandwidth, many video streaming systems use adaptive and scalable video coding techniques to facilitate transmission. Furthermore, transfer over TCP is currently the favored commercial approach for on-demand streaming [1, 11, 14, 19] where video is progressively downloaded over HTTP. This approach is not hampered by firewalls, and it provides TCP fairness in the network as well as ordered, lossless delivery. Adaptation to the available bandwidth is controlled entirely by the application.

Several feasible technical approaches for performing adaptation exist. One frequently used video adaptation approach is to structure the compressed video bit stream into layers. The based layer is a low-quality representation of the original video stream, while additional layers contribute additional quality. Here, several scalable video codec alternatives exist, including scalable MPEG (SPEG) [6], Multiple Description Coding (MDC) [4] and the Scalable Video Coding (SVC) extension to H.264 [17]. The other alternative is to use multiple independent versions encoded using, for example, the advanced video coding (AVC) [8], which supports adaptation by switching between streams [1, 11, 14, 19]. Thus, video streaming systems can adaptively change the size or rate of the streamed video (and thus the quality) to maintain continuous playback and avoid large start-up latency and stalling caused by network congestion.

Making adaptation decisions that achieve the best possible user perception is, on the other hand, an open research field. Current video scaling techniques allow adaptation in either the spatial or temporal domain [17]. All of the techniques may lead to visual artifacts every time an adaptation is performed. An algorithm must take this into account and, in addition, it must choose the time, the number of times, and the intensity of such adaptations.

This paper reports on our investigation of the types of visual artifacts that are specific for frequent bandwidth adaptation scenarios:

- **Noise flicker** is a result of varying the signal-to-noise-ratio (SNR) in the pictures. It is evident as a recurring transient change in noise, ringing, blockiness or other still-image artifacts in a video sequence.
- **Blur flicker** is caused by repeated changes of spatial resolution. It appears as a recurring transient blur that sharpens and unsharpens the overall details of some frames in a video sequence.
- **Motion flicker** comes from repeated changes in the

video frame rate. The effect is a recurring transient judder or jerkiness of naturally moving objects in a video sequence.

When the frequent quality fluctuations in the streamed video are perceived as flicker, it usually degrades the experienced subjective quality. However, noise, blur and motion flicker as such can not be considered deficient. Active adaptation to changes in available bandwidth is generally preferable to random packet loss or stalling streams, and not every quality change is perceived as a flicker effect. Essentially, the perceptual effect of flicker is closely related to the *amplitude* and *frequency* of the quality changes. This paper explores the acceptability of flicker for a handheld scenario.

In figure 1, we show sketches of simple streaming patterns for both spatial and temporal scaling. Figure 1(a) depicts a video stream encoded in two layers; it consists of several subsequent segments, where each segment has a duration of t frames. The full-scale stream contains two layers (L0 and L1), and the low quality stream (sub-stream 3) contains only the lower layer (L0), it is missing the complete L1 layer. For these, the number of layers remains the same for the entire depicted duration, meaning that neither of the two streams flickers. The other two examples show video streams with flicker. The *amplitude* is a change in the spatial dimension, in this example the size of the L1 layer (in other scenarios, this may be the number of layers). The *frequency* determines the quality change period, i.e., how often the flicker effect repeats itself. In this example, sub-stream 1 changes its picture quality every t frames (2 blocks in the figure), whereas sub-stream 2 changes every $3t$ frames (6 blocks in the figure). Figure 1(b) shows a similar example of how the amplitude and frequency affect the streaming patterns in the temporal dimension. Here, the *amplitude* is a change in the temporal dimension. In this example, we index video segments by their temporal resolutions since only temporal scalability is in our concern. The full-scale stream can be displayed at a normal frame rate. Sub-stream 3 drops frames regularly and can be displayed at a constant low frame rate. Neither of the two streams flickers in the temporal dimension. Hence, we say that the full-scale stream contains layer L1, whereas sub-stream 3 contains only layer L0. Sub-stream 1 and 2 halve the normal frame rate at a regular interval of $2t$ and $4t$ time units, respectively. Therefore, the layer variations in sub-streams 1 and 2 have the same amplitude, but the changes appear at different frequencies.

To provide the best possible video quality for a given available bandwidth, the applications need to select the most suitable options from several streaming patterns. Considering the alternatives in figures 1(a) and 1(b), three sub-stream alternatives can be used if the full quality stream cannot be provided. Therefore, to get a better understanding of human quality perception of *flicker*, we have performed a subjective field study with a special focus on handheld devices. We have considered state-of-the-market encoding techniques represented by the H.264 series of standards. Our goals are (1) to evaluate the influence of the main influential factors on acceptability, and (2) to find the range of these factors' levels. With these answers we hope to minimize the flicker effect in layer variation. We evaluate the effect of noise, blur and motion flicker on four different types of video content. For each video type, we tested several levels of frequency and amplitude. In total, we performed 5088 individual assessments.

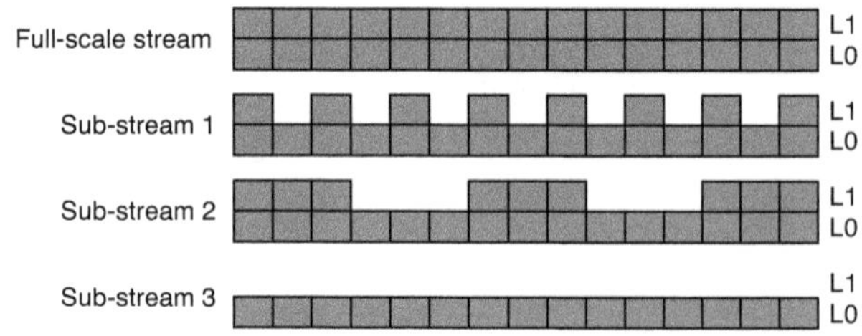

(a) Scaling in spatial dimension

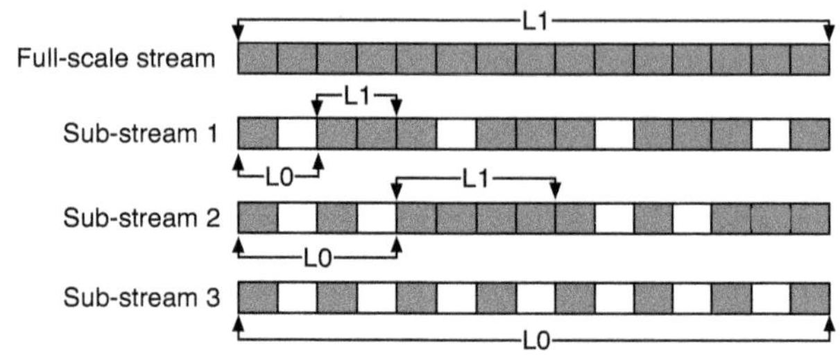

(b) Scaling in temporal dimension

Figure 1: Illustration of streaming patterns for scalable video.

From our results, we observe that the perception of quality variation is jointly influenced by multiple factors. Amplitude and frequency have significant impact on subjective impression. Most notably, when decreasing the quality switching frequency for flicker in the spatial domain, including noise and blur flickers, users' acceptance scores of the video quality tend to be higher. Moreover, the different flicker and content types are found to influence perceived quality in their own ways.

The paper is structured as follows. The experiment design is presented in section 3. Section 4 analyzes user responses and reports the analytical results. In section 5, we discuss our findings. Finally, section 6 concludes the paper.

2. RELATED WORK

To the best of our knowledge, very little work considers the flicker effect in the video quality domain. In [16], the National Telecommunications and Information Administration General Model (NTIA GM) introduced combined measures for the perceptual effects relating to different types of impairments, such as, blurriness, blockiness, jerkiness, etc. Kim et al. [9] proposed a scalability-aware video quality metric, which incorporated spatial resolution with frame rate and SNR distortion into a single quality metric. However, none of these objective metrics have considered the temporal variation of different impairments. Some subjective tests evaluate the visual quality of scalable video; for instance, the effect of quality degradation in the temporal and spatial dimensions is explored in [10, 12, 13]. The closest related work [20], points out that the frequency and amplitude of layer changes influence the perceived quality and should therefore be kept as small as possible. However, that user study limits itself to SNR scalability and does not take the influence of video content characteristics into account.

3. EXPERIMENT DESIGN

3.1 Randomized Block Design

We conduct subjective experiments to explore the impact of noise, blur and motion flicker on the perception of video quality. In addition to the three different adaptation domains (SNR for noise flicker, spatial resolution for blur flicker and temporal resolution for motion flicker), the overall video quality is influenced by other factors including amplitude, frequency and content characteristics (see section 3.2). All of these are design factors studies in our experiment. We do not limit ourselves to a single genre of video content, but we do not aspire to cover all semantic categories. We explore four content types, which are selected as representatives for extreme values of low and high spatial and temporal information content. In our experiments, the subjects are asked to rate their acceptance of the overall video quality. Due to the fluctuating state of videos that flicker, we predict flicker to be perceived differently than other artifacts. We add a Boolean score on perceived stability, which we expect to provide us with more insight into the nature of the flicker effects (see section 3.4). Finally, we measure participants' response time, which is the time between the end of a video presentation and the time when they provide their response.

The repeated measures design [2] of these experiments ensures that each subject is presented with all stimuli. The repeated measures design offers two major advantages: First, it provides more data from fewer people than, e.g., pairwise comparison studies. Second, it makes it possible to identify the variation in scores due to individual differences as error terms. Thus, it provides more reliable data for further analysis. This study employs an alternative to the traditional full factorial repeated-measures design that is called Randomized Block Design. It blocks stimuli according to flicker type and amplitude level. A stimuli block consists of a subset of test stimuli that share some common factor levels and can be examined and analyzed alone. Stimuli are randomized within each block and blocks are randomized to an extent that relies solely on the participant, as they are free to choose which block to proceed with.

The randomization of stimuli levels ensures that potential learning effects are distributed across the entire selection of video contents and frequency levels, and, to a degree, also amplitudes and flicker type. Moreover, we hope to minimize the effect of fatigue and loss of focus by dividing stimuli into smaller blocks and allowing participants to complete as many blocks as they wish, with optional pauses between blocks.

3.2 Content Selection and Preparation

As the rate distortion performance of compressed video depends largely on the spatial and temporal complexity of the content, the flicker effect is explored across four content types at different extremes. Video content is classified as being high or low in spatial and temporal complexity, as recommended in [7] and measured by spatial information (SI) and temporal information (TI) metrics, respectively. Four content types with different levels of motion and detail are selected based on the metrics (figure 2). To keep the region of interest more global and less focused on specific objects, we avoid videos with dictated points of interest, such as a person speaking. It is beyond the scope of the current investigation to generalize the results to all video content.

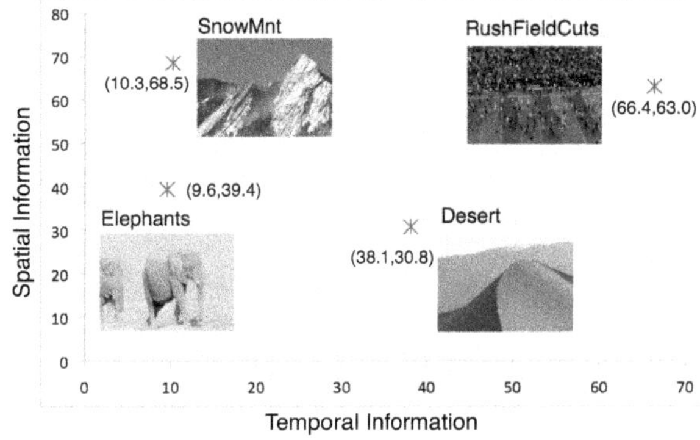

Figure 2: Test sequences.

Raw video material is encoded using the H.264/SVC reference software, JSVM 9.19, with two-layer streams generated for each type of flicker, as portrayed in figure 1. The amplitude levels of the layer variations are thus decided by the amount of impairment that separates the two layers. Table 1 summarizes the factor levels of amplitude, frequency, and content, according to the different flicker stimuli, noise, blur, and motion. For noise flicker stimuli, constant quantization parameters (QP) are used to encode a base layer L0 and an enhancement layer L1. Since the latter is encoded with QP24 for all test sequences, the amplitude levels and variations in video quality are represented by the QPs applied to L0 for noise flicker stimuli. Similarly, with blur flicker stimuli, amplitude is represented by spatial downscaling in L0, and temporal downscaling in L0 defines the amplitude for motion flicker stimuli.

To simulate the different flicker effects that can arise in streamed video, video segments from the two layers are alternately concatenated. Different frequencies of layer variation are obtained by adjusting the duration of the segments. For simplicity, we use only periodic duration. Corresponding to six frequency levels, six periods in terms of the L1 frame rate are selected, which include 6, 10, 30, 60, 90 and 180 frames for both noise and blur flicker stimuli. Since short durations for changes in frame rate are known to lead to low acceptance scores [13], the periods for motion flicker stimuli are limited to 30, 60, 90 and 180 frames.

a) Noise flicker

Amplitude	L1	QP24
	L0	QP28, QP32, QP36, QP40
Period	6f, 10f, 30f, 60f, 90f, 180f	
Content	RushFieldCuts, SnowMnt, Desert, Elephants	

b) Blur flicker

Amplitude	L1	480x320
	L0	240x160, 120x80
Period	6f, 10f, 30f, 60f, 90f, 180f	
Content	RushFieldCuts, SnowMnt, Desert, Elephants	

c) Motion flicker

Amplitude	L1	30fps
	L0	15fps, 10fps, 5fps, 3fps
Period	30f, 60f, 90f, 180f	
Content	RushFieldCuts, SnowMnt, Desert, Elephants	

Table 1: Selection of factor levels

3.3 Participants

In total, 28 participants (9 female, 19 male) were recruited at the University of Oslo, with ages ranging from 19 to 41 years (mean 24). They volunteered by responding to posters on campus with monetary compensation rewarded to all. Every participant reported normal or corrected to normal vision.

3.4 Procedure

This field study was conducted in one of the University of Oslo's library with videos presented on 3.5-inch iPhone of 480x320 resolution and brightness levels at 50%. Participants were free to choose a seat among the available lounge chairs but were asked to avoid any sunlight. They were told to hold the device at a comfortable viewing distance and to select one of the video blocks to commence the experiment. The 12-second long video segments were presented as single-stimulus events, in accordance with the ITU-T Absolute Category Rating method [7]. Each video stimulus was displayed only once. Video segments were followed by two response tasks, with responses made by tapping the appropriate option on-screen. For the first, participants had to evaluate the perceived stability of the video quality by answering "yes" or "no" to the statement "I think the video quality was at a stable level". The second involved an evaluation of their acceptance of the video quality, where they had to indicate their agreement to the statement "I accept the overall quality of the video" on a balanced 5-point Likert scale. The Likert scale includes a neutral element in the center and two opposite extreme values at both ends. A positive value can be interpreted as an acceptable quality level, a neutral score means undecidedness, while a negative score indicates an unacceptable quality level. Upon completion of a block, participants could end their participation, have a short break, or proceed immediately to the next block. Participants spent between 1.5 and 2 hours to complete the experiment.

4. DATA ANALYSIS

4.1 Method of Analysis

The current study explores the influence of amplitude and frequency of video quality shifts for three types of flicker stimuli, noise, blur and motion, as well as video content characteristics, on the perception of stability, the acceptance of video quality and response time. Control stimuli with constant high or low quality are included as references to establish baselines for the scores provided by participants. Stability scores and rating scores are processed separately, grouped according to flicker type. Thus responses are analyzed in six different groups, with control stimuli included in all of them. Since the perception of stability relies on detection, scores are binary and are assigned the value "1" for perceived stability of quality, and the value "0" for the opposite. Rating scores are assigned values ranging from -2 to 2, where "2" represents the highest acceptance, "0" the neutral element, and "-2" the lowest acceptance.

Consistency of acceptance scores is evaluated by comparing scores for control stimuli of constant high or low quality. Whenever a low quality stimulus scores better than the corresponding high quality stimulus, this is counted as a conflict. Conflicts are added up for each participant. If the acceptable number of conflicting responses is exceeded, the participant is excluded as an outlier. An acceptable number of conflicts stays within 1.5 times the interquartile range around the mean as suggested by [2, 3]. For the blur stimuli group this excluded two participants (12.5%), two for the motion stimuli group (10.5%), and none for the noise stimuli group.

Consistency of response times is also evaluated in order to eliminate results that reflect instances in which participants may have been distracted or taken a short break. Thus, any response time above three standard deviations of a participant's mean is not included in the following analyses.

Stability scores are analyzed as ratios and binomial tests are applied to establish statistical significance. As for acceptance scores, these are ordinal in nature and are not assumed to be continuous and normally distributed. They are therefore analyzed with the non-parametric Friedman's chi-square test [18]. The Friedman test is the best alternative to the parametric repeated-measures ANOVA [5], which relies on the assumption of normal distribution; it uses ranks to assess the differences between means for multiple factors across individuals. Main effects are explored with multiple Friedman's chi-square tests, applied to data sets that are collapsed across factors. Confidence intervals are calculated in order to further investigate the revealed main effects, assessing the relations between factor levels. Multiple comparisons typically require adjustments to significance levels, such as the Bonferroni correction. Yet, such adjustments can increase the occurrence of Type II errors, thus increasing the chances of rejecting a valid difference [15]. In light of this, we avoid the use of adjustments and instead report significant results without corrections. This procedure requires caution; we avoid drawing definite conclusions and leave our results open to interpretation. Repeated-measures ANOVA tests are finally introduced when analyzing response times.

4.2 Response Times

None of the repeated-measures ANOVA tests reveals any effect of amplitude, frequency or content on response time, for any type of flicker. In fact, response times seem to vary randomly across most stimuli levels. Possibly, this may be related to individual effort in detecting stability. If so, the video quality variation did not increase the decision-making effort. We may even surmise that participants evaluated the stability of video quality with a fair degree of confidence.

4.3 Noise Flicker Effects

The perceived stability of noise flicker stimuli is generally low and varies little over the different periods, as seen in table 2(a). However, the response percentage reflecting stable video quality is slightly higher for video segments of 180 frames. A significantly larger share of responses for the control stimuli reports video quality to be stable, as opposed to unstable, refer to the top and bottom lines in table 2(a). Due to the small difference between layers for QP28, it is plausible that the vast majority of participants do not perceive the flicker effect, which would explain why two thirds report stable quality, see the top line in table 2(b). Meanwhile, the higher rate of reported stability for non-flicker stimuli fits well with predictions. It indicates that participants detect and identify flicker as instability, whereas constant quality is experienced as stable, even when it is poor.

a) Period

Options	Stable	Unstable	P-value	Signif.
HQ	95.3%	04.7%	2.04e-71	+
6f	30.6%	69.4%	3.32e-12	-
10f	30.0%	70.0%	6.18e-13	-
30f	30.3%	69.7%	1.44e-12	-
60f	31.6%	68.4%	3.71e-11	-
90f	32.5%	67.5%	3.65e-10	-
180f	41.2%	58.8%	0.002	-
LQ	71.3%	28.7%	1.80e-14	+

b) Amplitude

Options	Stable	Unstable	P-value	Signif.
QP28	65.8%	34.2%	3.66e-12	+
QP32	27.7%	72.3%	4.49e-23	-
QP36	21.7%	78.3%	3.51e-37	-
QP40	15.6%	84.4%	8.74e-56	-

Table 2: Perceived quality stability for Noise flicker (+ Stable, - Unstable, (*) not significant), HQ = constant high quality, LQ = constant low quality.

Main effects are found with Friedman's chi-square tests for period ($\chi^2(5) = 69.25, p < .001$), amplitude ($\chi^2(3) = 47.98, p < .001$) and content ($\chi^2(3) = 27.75, p < .001$). The means and confidence intervals presented in figure 3(a) show that acceptance scores become increasingly higher than the constant low quality controls for periods of 60 frames and above. Figure 3(b) displays the decrease in acceptance with larger amplitudes, while figure 3(c) shows only small variations in acceptance scores depending on content type. As for potential interactions, figure 4 illustrates how mean acceptance scores vary across content types, with a tendency to increase as amplitude decreases or period increases. Moreover, the scores point to possible interactions, particularly between period and amplitude.

4.4 Blur Flicker Effects

For blur flicker stimuli, perceived video quality stability is again low across the different periods, accompanied by high perceived stability ratios for control stimuli, summarized in table 3(a). Furthermore, participants tend to judge the video quality as unstable at both amplitude 240x160 and amplitude 120x80, see table 3(b). This is also consistent with expectations, suggesting again that flicker is detectable and perceived to be unstable.

Friedman's chi-square tests reveal main effects for period ($\chi^2(6) = 41.79, p < .001$), amplitude ($\chi^2(1) = 14.00, p < .001$) and content ($\chi^2(3) = 33.80, p < .001$). As seen in figure 5(a), the mean acceptance scores are generally low across periods, only at 60 frames and above do they approach the acceptance of constant low quality. Moreover, there are little variations in acceptance according to amplitude and content, see figures 5(b) and 5(c). However, figure 6 illustrates how the differences in acceptance scores become greater when considering interactions. Similar to noise flicker, acceptance tends be higher for longer periods, but more markedly for the amplitude 240x160. Also acceptance scores for the Desert and Elephants clips appear to be higher than the RushFieldCuts and SnowMnt clips.

a) Period

Options	Stable	Unstable	P-value	Signif.
HQ	100%	00.0%	3.85e-34	+
6f	11.6%	88.4%	1.50e-17	-
10f	11.6%	88.4%	1.50e-17	-
30f	11.6%	88.4%	1.50e-17	-
60f	13.4%	86.6%	7.12e-16	-
90f	12.5%	87.5%	1.08e-16	-
180f	17.0%	83.0%	6.75e-13	-
LQ	81.2%	18.8%	1.42e-11	+

b) Amplitude

Options	Stable	Unstable	P-value	Signif.
240x160	19.3%	80.7%	4.89e-31	-
120x80	06.6%	93.5%	2.57e-67	-

Table 3: Perceived quality stability for Blur flicker (+ Stable, - Unstable, (*) not significant).

4.5 Motion Flicker Effects

Low perceived stability ratios are evident across all periods for motion flicker stimuli, presented in table 4(a). As expected, the vast majority of participants think that the video quality is stable for constant high quality control stimuli but not for constant low quality; there are more responses that correspond to perceived instability for low quality control stimuli. This is potentially explained by the lack of fluency of movement that occurs at lower frame rates. The stability scores for amplitude may also reflect a bias towards reporting jerkiness as instability, as listed in table 4. However, stability is reported more frequently for larger periods and better frame rates; this indicates influences from both period and amplitude on perceived quality stability.

Friedman's chi-square tests uncover main effects for all factors, including period ($\chi^2(3) = 7.82, p < .05$), amplitude ($\chi^2(3) = 41.62, p < .001$), and content ($\chi^2(3) = 27.51, p < .001$). However, the main effect for period is very close to the significance threshold (p=0.0499), which is likely the reason for the relatively flat distribution of acceptance scores observed in figure 7(a). Amplitude and content type, on the other hand, have larger effects on quality acceptance, as seen in figures 7(b), 7(c) and 8.

a) Period

Options	Stable	Unstable	P-value	Signif.
HQ	90.8%	09.2%	4.43e-47	+
30f	14.3%	85.7%	7.85e-35	-
60f	16.2%	83.8%	4.08e-31	-
90f	18.0%	82.0%	1.08e-27	-
180f	20.6%	79.4%	2.44e-23	-
LQ	40.8%	59.2%	0.0029	-

b) Amplitude

Options	Stable	Unstable	P-value	Signif.
15fps	43.8%	56.2%	0.045	(*)
10fps	15.1%	84.9%	2.62e-33	-
5fps	07.4%	92.6%	2.82e-52	-
3fps	02.9%	97.1%	1.82e-67	-

Table 4: Perceived quality stability for Motion flicker (+ Stable, - Unstable, (*) not significant).

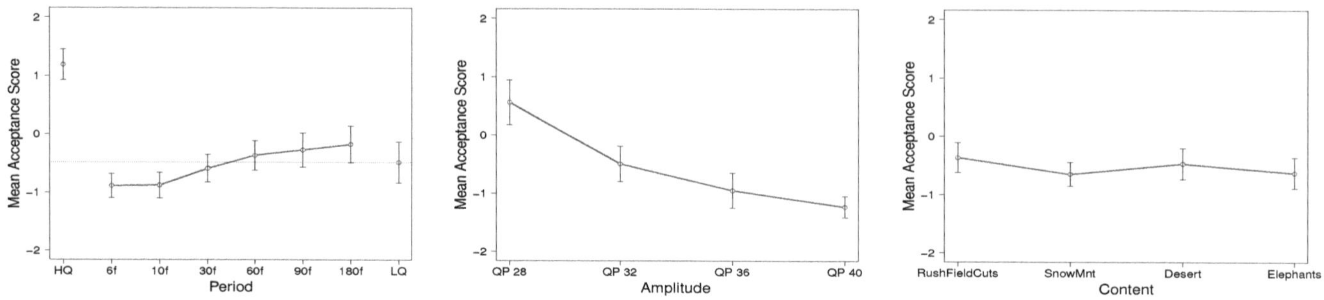

(a) (b) (c)

Figure 3: Effects of period, amplitude and content on Noise flicker stimuli. Error bars represent 95% confidence intervals.

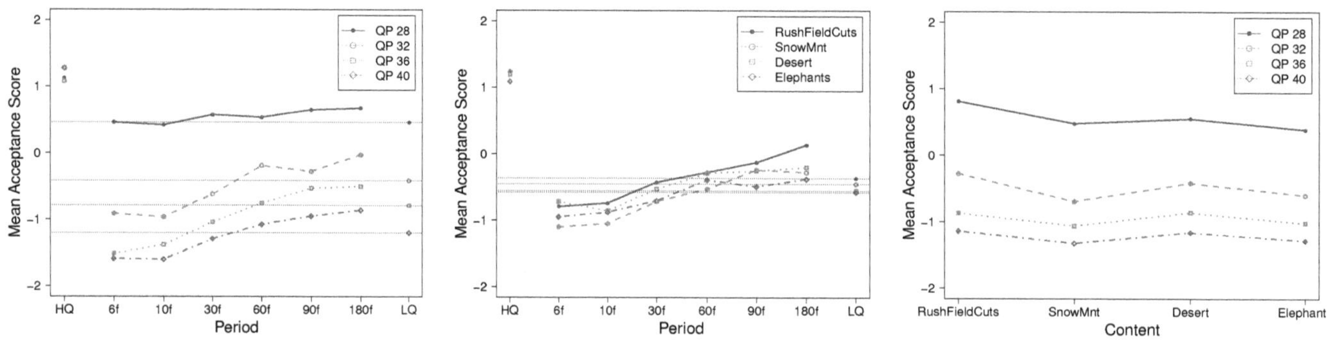

(a) Period effects according to amplitude (b) Period effects according to content (c) Content effects according to amplitude

Figure 4: Explored interactions for Noise flicker. (HQ = constant high quality, LQ = constant low quality)

5. DISCUSSION

5.1 Period Effect

The period of flicker is a major influential factor for flicker in the spatial dimension. Significant differences between acceptance scores given to different periods in noise flicker can be found in figure 3(a), and for blur flicker in figure 5(a). In figures 6(a) and 6(b), we can highlight three period ranges that influence the overall quality acceptance: low acceptance for short periods, acceptance higher than the low-quality control stimuli for moderate periods, and stagnating for long periods. Stagnation is less pronounced in figures 4(a) and 4(b).

In figure 4(b), the average across all amplitudes is shown for individual contents, reinforcing that the effect is independent of the content. At high frequencies ($< 30f$ or $< 1sec$ respectively), the flicker is perceived as more annoying than constant low quality for all different content types. Starting at moderate frequencies ($30 \sim 60f$ or $1 \sim 2s$), the quality is considered as better than a constant low quality for some content types. At low frequencies ($> 60f$ or $> 2s$), the quality is in most cases regarded as better than a constant low quality. For both flicker types in the spatial dimension, this is significant across amplitudes (figures 4(a) and 6(a)), content (figures 4(b) and 6(b)), but counter-examples exist (see the top line in figure 6(a)).

In the temporal dimension, the period does not seem to have a significant influence on the motion flicker. There are only small differences between acceptance scores for different periods, ranging from $30f$ to $180f$ (see figures 7(a), 8(a) and 8(b)). When the amplitude of temporal downscaling is small, scores are higher than for the low-quality control stimuli (figures 8(a), 10(a)). No period ranges can be highlighted.

A general observation for all three flicker types is that adaptive video streaming can outperform constant low quality streams, but the switching period must be considered in relation to the flicker amplitudes.

5.2 Amplitude Effect

The amplitude is the most dominant factor for the perception of flicker. This seems reasonable since the visual artifacts become more apparent with increasing amplitude when alternating between two quality versions. Our statistical results, presented in section 4, show this and evaluate the strength of the influence. The noise flicker effect is not detectable for the majority of our participants (see Q28 in table 2(b)) at low flicker amplitudes, where visual artifacts are less obvious. In the case of motion flicker, close to 50% of the responses show that changes between frame rates of 15fps and 30fps are not detectable. When the amplitude grows, meaning that the lower frame rate is reduced further, the detectability of quality fluctuation grows as well (see table 4(b)). The detectability shows the same changing trend for noise and blur flicker. The effect of flicker at different period lengths becomes significant only if the flicker artifacts are clearly detectable from the increase of flicker amplitude.

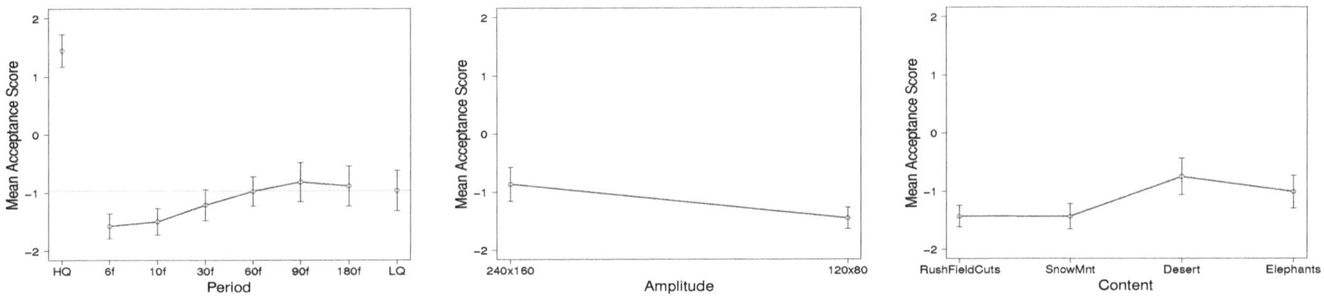

(a) (b) (c)

Figure 5: Effects of period, amplitude and content on Blur flicker. Error bars represent 95% confidence intervals.

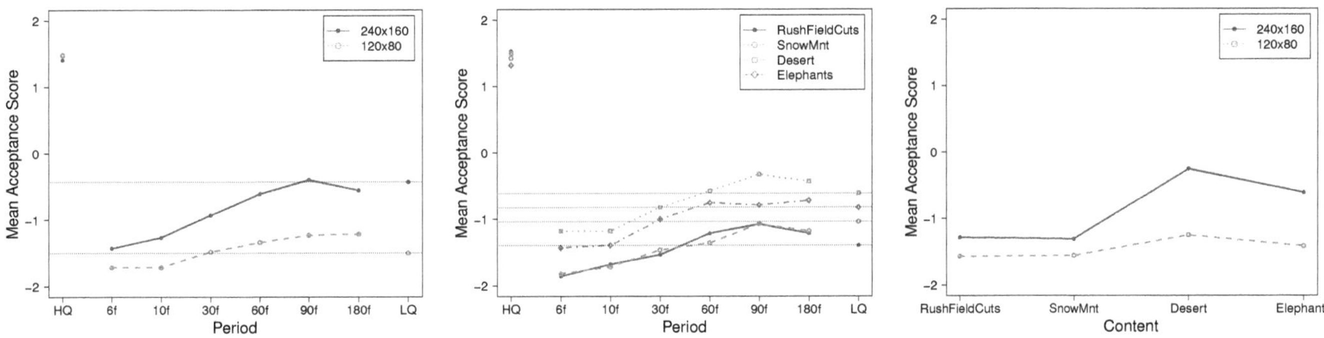

(a) Period effects according to amplitude (b) Period effects according to content (c) Content effects according to amplitude

Figure 6: Explored interactions for Blur flicker. (HQ = constant high quality, LQ = constant low quality)

In noise and motion flicker, we find an amplitude threshold below which the flicker is considered better than the low-quality control stimuli for all content types. Figures 9 and 10 show amplitudes above and below the threshold. In our experiments, an increase of the amplitude above 8 QPs for noise flicker or 10 fps (one third of the original frame rate) for motion flicker brings significant flicker effect that may make frequent adaptation worthless to perform (see figures 9(b) and 10(b)). While it is possible to obtain a benefit by choosing a suitable period for SNR variation, only the amplitude is critical for frame rate variation.

For blur flicker, we have tested only two amplitude levels (see figure 6(a)). Although the difference between them significant, the range we have selected does not cover enough amplitudes to draw further conclusions. The user experience of watching up-scaled video that was originally half or a quarter of the native display resolution of a handheld device turned out to yield low acceptance. Given the fact that our content is chosen from a wide range of spatial and temporal complexities (figure 2), this indicates that the change of spatial resolution should not exceed half the original size in order to deliver a generally acceptable quality. Further investigations are necessary to find acceptability thresholds for amplitude levels of blur.

5.3 Content Effect

Content seems to play a minor role for flicker, but its effect varies across different flicker types. For noise flicker, the effect of content is not significant (figure 3(c)). We observe weak interaction effects between period and content (figure 4(b)), but no interaction between amplitude and content. In figure 4(c), we see that the acceptance scores vary only slightly between content for the noise flicker although the chosen amplitudes cover a large part of the scale. However, a significant effect of content can be found in both blur and motion flicker (figures 5(c) and 7(c)). Content interacts slightly with amplitude as well. For blur flicker, the Desert and Elephant sequences get significantly different scores than RushFieldCuts and SnowMnt, see figure 6(c). For motion flicker, the SnowMnt sequence is least influenced by the loss of frame rate and always has significantly higher scores, see figures 8(b), 8(c) and 10. The observation means different content characteristics can influence the perception of flicker.

The SnowMnt and RushFieldCuts sequences have more complex texture details then the other two content types and are therefore more strongly affected by the loss of spatial resolution. Additionally, SnowMnt contains significantly less motion; half of the sequence moves slowly around the snow mountain at fairly constant distance. The lack of relative movement between objects in the scene may limit the visible effect of frame dropping. However, video classification based only on two simple metrics of spatial and temporal information does not cover enough content features that are related to human perception. Region of interest, the scope and direction of motion etc. may also have influences on visual experience. In our experiments, 15fps has the effect that the scores for two test sequences are on the

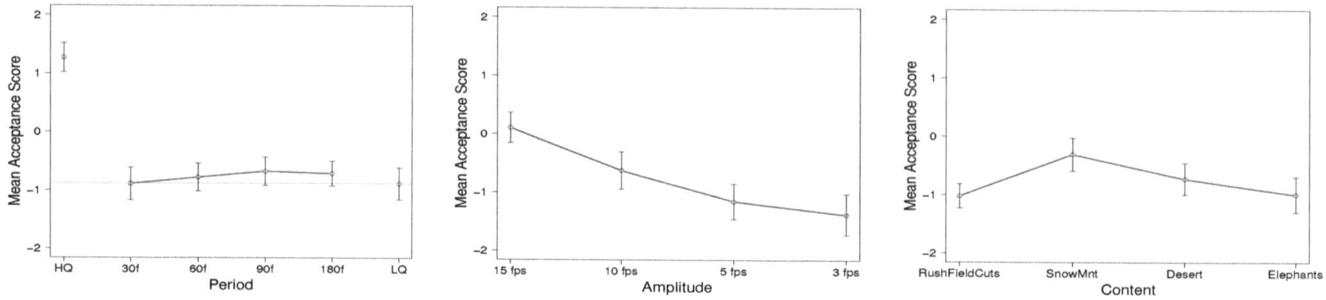

(a) (b) (c)

Figure 7: Effects of period, amplitude and content on Motion flicker stimuli. Error bars represent 95% confidence intervals.

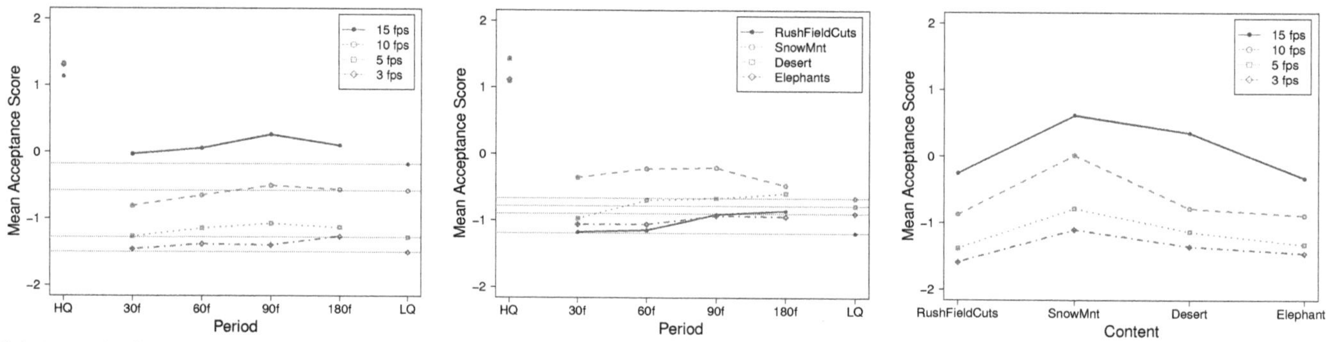

(a) Period effects according to amplitude (b) Period effects according to content (c) Content effects according to amplitude

Figure 8: Explored interactions for Motion flicker. (HQ = constant high quality, LQ = constant low quality)

negative part of the scale (see figure 10(a)), while the two sequences have quite different temporal complexity according to the TI metric, introduced in section 3. More advanced feature analysis is needed for further explanation of these phenomena.

5.4 Applicability of the Results

The results of our study can help improve the adaptation strategy in streaming systems or bit-rate controller for processing scalable video. Among three dimensions, SNR scalability is the most recommended adaptation option. When switching SNR layer, quality differences should be limited to less than 4 QPs to avoid additional visual artifacts. However, if larger quality shift is necessary, a quality level should be kept stable for at least 2 seconds.

The knowledge is applicable for both SVC-type and AVC-type systems – We have used SVC, but the results should be equally important/relevant for AVC-type systems like those used in modern HTTP streaming systems. For SVC, this knowledge helps to schedule the different enhancement layers and decide which to drop in case of congestion. For AVC, it helps determining how to code the different layers in order to increase quality if congestion forces the application to choose another quality layer.

6. CONCLUSION

To understand the human perception of video quality adaptation in fluctuating bandwidth scenarios, like streaming to handheld devices over wireless networks, we have performed a series of subjective assessment experiments using iPhones and iPods. We have identified three types of visual artifacts caused by adaptive bit-rate variations, the noise, blur and motion flicker effects. Furthermore, for these flicker effects we investigated how users experience quality changes at different amplitudes and frequencies, using several content types. Our results show that multiple factors influence the quality with respect to flicker effects in different scenarios. Among the influential factors, low frequency can relieve the annoyance of flicker effect in spatial dimension, but below a threshold (on the scale of a few seconds), decreasing frequency further does not have any significant effect. On the other hand, the amplitude has a dominant effect across spatial and temporal dimensions and should be kept as low as possible for satisfactory visual quality. Finally, blur and motion flicker effect on different content types varies even for the same amplitude. Videos with complex spatial details are particularly affected by blur flicker, while videos with complex and global motion require higher frame rate for smooth playback effect.

There are still numerous questions to answer and experiments to perform which is ongoing work. We are currently expanding our experiments to HD displays to see if there are differences in the findings as compared to the performed iPhone experiments. We are also interested in other content features and their influences on user perceived quality. We will consider in particular whether content with a unique focus point (e.g. speaking person) in a scene leads to different

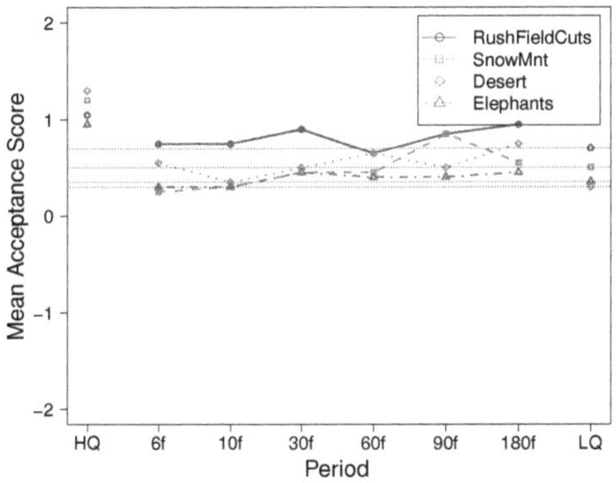

(a) Amplitude = QP28

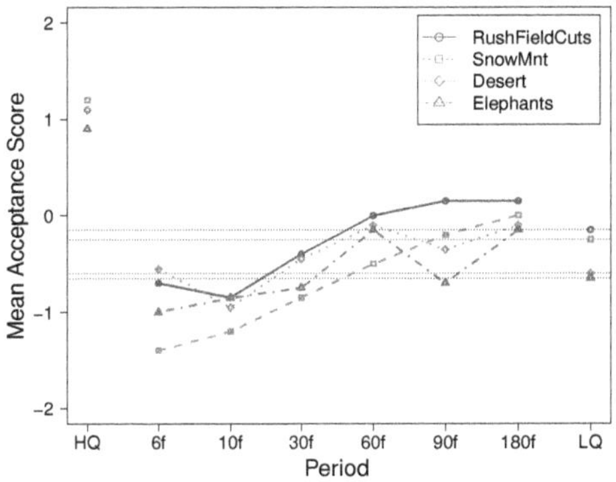

(b) Amplitude = QP32

Figure 9: Mean acceptance scores for two top amplitude levels in Noise flicker. (HQ = constant high quality, LQ = constant low quality)

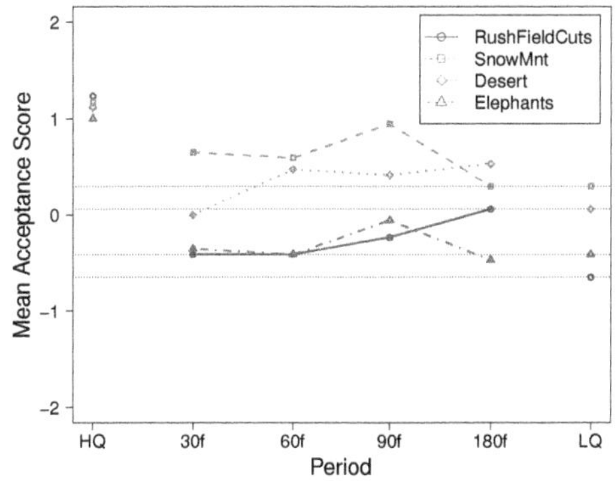

(a) Amplitude = 15fps

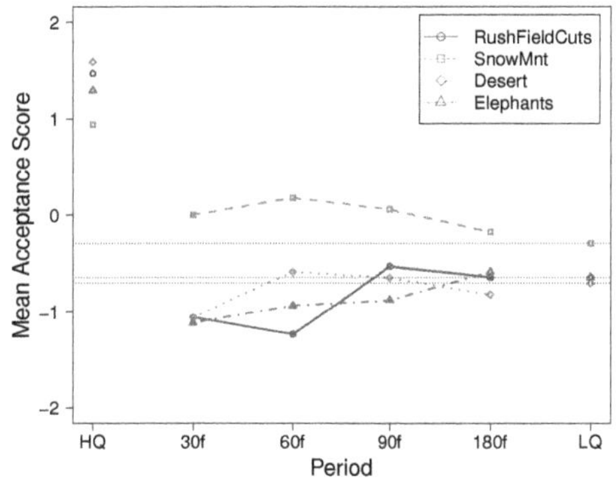

(b) Amplitude = 10fps

Figure 10: Mean acceptance scores for two top amplitude levels in Motion flicker. (HQ = constant high quality, LQ = constant low quality)

results, whether connecting temporal and spatial complexity to regions of interest makes a difference, and how camera motion vs. content motion affects results.

7. ACKNOWLEDGMENTS

The authors would like to thank the volunteer participants. This work is sponsored by the Norwegian Research Council under the Perceval project (project number 439838), the Verdione project (project number 187828) and the iAD centre for Research-based Innovation (project number 174867).

8. REFERENCES

[1] ADOBE. HTTP dynamic streaming on the Adobe Flash platform. http://www.adobe.com/products/-httpdynamicstreaming/-pdfs/httpdynamicstreaming_wp_ue.pdf, 2010.

[2] COOLICAN, H. *Research Methods and Statistics in Psychology*, 4 ed. Hodder Arnold, 2004.

[3] FRIGGE, M., HOAGLIN, D. C., AND IGLEWICZ, B. Some implementations of the boxplot. *The American Statistician 43*, 1 (Feb. 1989), 50–54.

[4] GOYAL, V. K. Multiple description coding: Compression meets the network. *IEEE Signal Processing Magazine 18*, 5 (September 2001), 74–93.

[5] HOWELL, D. C. *Statistical Methods for Psychology*, 5 ed. Duxberry, 2002.

[6] HUANG, J., KRASIC, C., WALPOLE, J., AND FENG, W. Adaptive live video streaming by priority drop. In *in Proceedings of the IEEE International Conference on Advanced Video and Signal Based Surveillance* (2003), pp. 342–347.

[7] INTERNATIONAL TELECOMMUNICATIONS UNION. *ITU-T P.910. Subjective video quality assessment methods for multimedia applications*, 1999.

[8] ITU-T AND ISO/IEC JTC 1. *Advanced Video Coding for Generic Audiovisual services, ITU-T Recommendation H.264*, Apr. 2003. ISO/IEC 14496-10(AVC).

[9] KIM, C. S., JIN, S. H., SEO, D. J., AND RO, Y. M. Measuring video quality on full scalability of H.264/AVC scalable video coding. *IEICE Trans. on Communications E91-B*, 5 (2008), 1269–1278.

[10] MCCARTHY, J. D., SASSE, M. A., AND MIRAS, D. Sharp or smooth?: Comparing the effects of quantization vs. frame rate for streamed video. In *Proceedings of the SIGCHI conference on Human factors in computing systems* (2004), pp. 535–542.

[11] MOVE NETWORKS. Internet television: Challenges and opportunities. Tech. rep., Move Networks, Inc., November 2008.

[12] NI, P., EICHHORN, A., GRIWODZ, C., AND HALVORSEN, P. Fine-grained scalable streaming from coarse-grained videos. In *Proceedings of the 18th International Workshop on Network and Operating*

Systems Support for Digital Audio and Video (NOSSDAV) (2009), pp. 103–108.

[13] Ni, P., Eichhorn, A., Griwodz, C., and Halvorsen, P. Frequent layer switching for perceived quality improvements of coarse-grained scalable video. *Springer Multimedia Systems Journal 16*, 3 (2010), 171–182.

[14] Pantos, R., Batson, J., Biderman, D., May, B., and Tseng, A. HTTP live streaming. http://tools.ietf.org/html/draft-pantos-http-live-streaming-04, 2010.

[15] Perneger, T. V. What's wrong with Bonferroni adjustments. *British Medical Journal 316*, 7139 (1998), 1236–1238.

[16] Pinson, M., and Wolf, S. A new standardized method for objectively measuring video quality. *IEEE Trans. on Broadcasting 50*, 3 (Sept. 2004), 312–322.

[17] Schwarz, H., Marpe, D., and Wiegand, T. Overview of the scalable video coding extension of the h.264/avc standard. *Circuits and Systems for Video Technology, IEEE Transactions on 17*, 9 (sept. 2007), 1103–1120.

[18] Sheldon, M. R., Fillyaw, M. J., and Thompson, W. D. The use and interpretation of the Friedman test in the analysis of ordinal-scale data in repeated measures designs. *Physiotherapy Research International 1*, 4 (1996), 221–228.

[19] Zambelli, A. Smooth streaming technical overview. http://learn.iis.net/page.aspx/626/smooth-streaming-technical-overview, 2009.

[20] Zink, M., Künzel, O., Schmitt, J., and Steinmetz, R. Subjective impression of variations in layer encoded videos. In *Proceedings of International Workshop on Quality of Service* (2003), pp. 137–154.

An Empirical Evaluation of Battery Power Consumption for Streaming Data Transmission to Mobile Devices*

Yao Liu[1] Lei Guo[2] Fei Li[1] Songqing Chen[1]
[1]Department of Computer Science
George Mason University
{yliud, lifei, sqchen}@cs.gmu.edu
[2]Microsoft Corporation
Mountain View, CA, USA
leguo@microsoft.com

ABSTRACT

Internet streaming applications are becoming increasingly popular on mobile devices. However, receiving streaming services on mobile devices is often constrained by their limited battery power supply. Various techniques have been proposed to save battery power consumption on mobile devices, mainly focusing on how much data to transmit and how to transmit.

In this paper, we conduct an experiment-based study with 11 Internet streaming applications using different streaming protocols. Our goal is to empirically investigate the battery power consumption on the wireless network interface for receiving streaming data via different approaches. Through measurement and analysis, we find that (1) the Chunk-based streaming is widely used in practice and it is most power-efficient because the traffic shaping technique is adopted to utilize PSM on mobile devices to save battery power consumption; however, it may cause quality degradation from time to time; (2) reducing streaming data transmission (by switching to a lower streaming quality) can marginally help save battery power consumption in RTSP, Pseudo streaming, and Chunk-based streaming applications; but it is effective for P2P streaming applications; (3) P2P streaming to mobile devices is not power-efficient because of the additional transmission of control traffic and uploading traffic; and reducing upload alone does not help for battery power saving. Our investigation provides new insights and some guidelines for the current Internet mobile streaming services and calls for further research on more power-efficient and scalable Internet mobile streaming protocols.

Categories and Subject Descriptors

C.2.4 [**Distributed Systems**]: Distributed applications

General Terms

Measurement, Experimentation

Keywords

Internet Mobile Streaming, Battery Power Consumption, Power Saving, Data Transmission

*Area chair: Wei-Tsang Ooi

MM'11, November 28–December 1, 2011, Scottsdale, Arizona, USA.

1. INTRODUCTION

Internet streaming to mobile devices is gaining increasingly popularity in practice. For example, CTV [1], CCTV [2], WTV [3], ImgoTV [4], and NHKworld [5] all allow iOS users to access their live TV programming content via 3G or WiFi network. SPBtv [6] supports more diverse platforms including iOS, Android, Windows Mobile, and Blackberry. It also provides a great variety of live TV channels from different countries. Orb [7] and AirVideo [8] allow users to access media content stored on their home computers. Justin.tv [9] even enables users to watch live streaming content broadcasted by other users. Many cellular network providers in the US today also provide streaming services to their subscribers, including Verizon's VCast [10] and AT&T's Mobile TV [11].

Different from their counterpart of streaming to desktop computers, Internet streaming to mobile devices is even more challenging because of the variety of the mobile platforms and operating systems, less reliable wireless connections, slower CPU, limited battery supply, etc. Among these factors, the limited battery supply is a critical constraint because most of the time mobile devices are battery-powered. Since the network transmission could consume a significant portion of the battery power, power saving on the wireless network interface card (WNIC) has been a major direction of many research efforts. The battery consumption of the WNIC mainly depends on the following two aspects: (1) how much data is transmitted during the streaming session? (2) how is such data transmitted?

The first aspect is very intuitive. Under the same circumstances of all other factors, transmitting more data would make the WNIC work longer and thus consume more battery power. In practice, a user can choose a low quality version of the same video clip and expects less battery power consumption. This is easy to do because the current practice from the industry often provides multiple versions of the same video clip with different quality (encoding rate) for users to choose from.

While choosing a low quality version is simple for end-users and only requires server support in advance, how to transmit data in order to reduce battery power consumption is much more complicated. Since today most of the commodity network interface card is supported with the IEEE 802.11 power saving mode (PSM) by default, it is straightforward that the PSM should be utilized to minimize the battery power consumption during streaming services. However, the standard PSM has limited effectiveness for streaming applications since streaming applications often involve bulk data transmission in a continuous fashion, which would not provide many opportunities for the WNIC to switch into PSM. Thus, plenty of research has been conducted in order to make the WNIC to sleep as much as possible for streaming to mobile devices and a variety of power saving schemes have been proposed. For example, PSM-throttling [12] proposes a client-centric scheme to enable buffering at the server so that streaming data could be sent in burst in order to maximize the sleep time of the WNIC. Proxy buffering [13] suggests to buffer packets at a local intermediate proxy and send them in client-specific intervals. The key idea of these schemes is to shape the traffic so that they can be sent in burst without degrading the streaming quality. They mainly target client/server based streaming services. With the popularity of P2P based Internet streaming, SCAP [14] has also been designed to leverage the temporal locality of uploading and downloading data at the access point so that less data would be required to upload from a mobile client.

In this study, we aim to evaluate the battery power consumption for Internet streaming data transmission to mobile devices in the current practice. For this purpose, we conduct Internet experiments with 11 existing Internet streaming services. These experiments examine the impact of how streaming data is transmitted and how much data is transmitted during these streaming sessions. Our results indicate that (1) the Chunk-based streaming is widely used in practice and it is most power-efficient because the traffic shaping technique is adopted to utilize the PSM on mobile devices to save battery power consumption; however, it may cause quality degradation from time to time; (2) reducing streaming data transmission (by switching to a lower streaming quality) can marginally help save battery power consumption in RTSP, Pseudo streaming, and Chunk-based streaming applications; but it is effective for P2P streaming applications; (3) P2P streaming to mobile devices is not power-efficient because of the additional transmission of control traffic and uploading traffic; and reducing upload alone does not help for battery power saving.

Our measurement results indicate that there is no panacea for power saving in receiving Internet streaming on mobile devices and further research is desired to improve the power efficiency in receiving Internet streaming applications. A particular challenge comes from P2P based Internet streaming, in which neither traffic shaping helps, nor P2P specific schemes can provide sufficient battery power saving benefit.

In summary, we have made the following contributions:

- Through measurement and analysis, we have provided an update of the battery power efficiency on mobile devices in receiving Internet streaming services.
- We have qualitatively and quantitatively investigated the four approaches for streaming to mobile devices, compared their power consumption characteristics, and analyzed the underlying reasons.
- Our results provide new insights for future research on power saving schemes for Internet mobile streaming and call for a power-efficient, high quality, and scalable protocol for streaming to mobile devices.

The reminder of the paper is organized as follows. We briefly describe the background and our measurement methodology in Section 2 and Section 3. We study the impact of how data is transmitted on battery power efficiency in Section 4, and we investigate the impact of reduced transmission in Section 5. Some related work is described in Section 6 and we make concluding remarks in Section 7.

2. BACKGROUND

In this section, we briefly illustrate the streaming protocols that are currently being used by existing Internet mobile streaming applications.

2.1 RTSP Streaming

Real-time streaming protocol (RTSP) [15] is a standard Internet streaming protocol for the communication between a media player and a media server. RTSP is a stateful protocol that establishes a media session between the client and the server, and allows the client to execute VCR-like commands, such as play and pause. The client maintains a small buffer to absorb network jitter and ensure smooth playback. With RTSP, the streaming server delivers streaming data at the rate equivalent to the object encoding rate.

In practice, today YouTube [16] and Vuclip [17] use RTSP to deliver streaming content to mobile devices such as Blackberry, Nokia, and SonyEricssion mobile phones.

2.2 Pseudo Streaming

While RTSP is a standard streaming protocol, Internet streaming services today also widely use HTTP for streaming content delivery, which we call Pseudo streaming or progressive downloading. With Pseudo streaming, a client downloads the media file from a HTTP server. The playback can start before the entire file is downloaded. Pseudo streaming is used in many popular Internet streaming services today, including YouTube and Vuclip. For example, a mobile version of YouTube allows iOS and Android users to use Pseudo streaming to watch videos in their native browsers [16].

Fast Start [18] is often used in pseudo streaming. Fast Start allows the server to deliver the data at a higher speed than the encoding rate at the beginning of the session and then uses a low speed to deliver the rest of the file. This is to reduce the startup delay perceived by the users as well as smoothing some network jitter during the playback.

2.3 Chunk-Based Streaming

Chunk-based streaming also uses HTTP to deliver streaming content. However, unlike Pseudo streaming that downloads a single streaming file, the media content is segmented into many chunks in Chunk-based streaming, and a client periodically queries the streaming server for new file chunks.

Many streaming services today are Chunk-based, including Apple HTTP Live Streaming [19], Flash HTTP Streaming [20], and Microsoft Smooth Streaming [21]. In this study, we focus on Chunk-based streaming implemented by Apple Inc, which was made available on iOS 3.0 in July 2009. CTV [1], CCTV [2], W.TV [3], ImgoTV [4], Justin.tv [9], NHKworld [5], SPBtv [6], and AirVideo [8] all use Chunk-based streaming. Among them, AirVideo is different from other seven applications in that it allows a user to set up streaming server at a desktop computer, which transcodes the video content and delivers to the mobile device.

Typically, in Chunk-based streaming, the media content is encoded as MPEG-4 audio and video, and transported via TCP using MPEG-2 Transport Stream (MPEG2-TS). They are assembled into `.ts` files using File Segmenter at the server side. A `.ts` file typically contains 10 second media content. For streaming access, a client queries the server for index files (`.m3u8`), which provides information about availability and location of `.ts` files. Then the client requests the listed media (`.ts`) files in order. The client usually queries the server for streaming content about every 10 seconds and the server replies with links to several `.ts` files, each of which contains media content for the next a few (typically 10) seconds. These files are reassembled after being downloaded and fed into the Media Player for playback.

2.4 Peer-to-Peer (P2P) Streaming

Peer-to-Peer (P2P) has demonstrated in practice to be scalable for file sharing and Internet streaming. Lots of Internet streaming

Table 1: Measured Applications

Service	Protocol	Transport	Format
YouTube	RTSP	UDP	3GP/MP4
Vuclip	RTSP	UDP	3GP
YouTube	Pseudo Streaming	TCP	MP4
Vuclip	Pseudo Streaming	TCP	MP4
AirVideo	Chunk-Based	TCP	MPEG-TS
CTV	Chunk-Based	TCP	MPEG-TS
CCTV	Chunk-Based	TCP	MPEG-TS
W.TV	Chunk-Based	TCP	MPEG-TS
ImgoTV	Chunk-Based	TCP	MPEG-TS
Justin.tv	Chunk-Based	TCP	MPEG-TS
SPBtv	Chunk-Based	TCP	MPEG-TS
NHKworld	Chunk-Based	TCP	MPEG-TS
TVUPlayer	P2P Streaming	UDP	ASF

systems have adopted P2P techniques. For example, both PPLive and PPStream are large scale P2P assisted multi-channel Internet streaming systems. Within a P2P system, a peer downloads the streaming content for the playback from other users and uploads the downloaded content to other peers simultaneously. While different protocols have been extensively studied, in practice, most of deployed Internet P2P streaming systems today are mesh-based and they often use a pull approach for data acquisition. That is, peers in these systems need to request data chunks from a dynamically changing set of neighbors. To pull/request data from neighbors, a peer first needs to exchange data chunk availability information (e.g., buffermap) with neighbors. After knowing which data chunks available at which neighbors, the peer then sends *Streaming Data Chunk Requests* to request missing chunks from different neighbors. Typically, the unit of a data chunk is small (e.g., 1280 bytes) compared to the video file size. Thus such data chunk requests are fine-grained, and are highly frequent. Such buffermap messages and fine-grained data chunk requests are referred to as control messages [22].

TVUPlayer [23] uses a Peer-to-Peer protocol to distribute live streaming content. It is available on different platforms, targeting both desktop/laptop users (Windows, Mac OS) and mobile device users (iOS). Instead of TCP, it uses UDP for streaming delivery.

3. METHODOLOGY

To investigate the energy performance of WNIC under the four streaming protocols as we have discussed in Section 2, we conduct experiments with the streaming services shown in Table 1. In our experiments, we use a 2nd generation iPod Touch (iTouch) running iOS 3.1.2 to receive streaming services. Among these services, YouTube and Vuclip provide streaming services using both RTSP and Pseudo streaming. TVUPlayer is the only P2P streaming application available on iTouch at the time of this measurement. The rest 8 applications use Chunk-based streaming through HTTP on iTouch.

For streaming services from YouTube, Vuclip, and AirVideo, we first access video clips from both YouTube and Vuclip via the mobile browser on iTouch. Then we download the video clips to a desktop running a local AirVideo server, and access it using the AirVideo App on iTouch. For CTV, CCTV, W.TV, ImgoTV, Justin.tv, SPBtv, NHKWorld, and TVUPlayer, we watch a streaming channel from each service.

In the experiments, for streaming services delivered via Pseudo-streaming, Chunk-based streaming, and P2P streaming protocols, we use iTouch to receive these streaming services. Since RTSP is not implemented on iOS, we were not able to access YouTube or Vuclip via RTSP directly on our iTouch. Instead, we use a netbook running Windows 7 with `Maximum WiFi Power Saving` enabled. The netbook declares itself as a mobile device, and receives streaming data via RTSP from YouTube and Vuclip servers.

In order to record all the incoming and outgoing packets, we set up Wireshark to listen on the same channel as the iTouch/netbook in a promiscuous mode and capture all packets received/delivered by our testing device.

In this study, we focus on the battery power consumed by the streaming data transmission. In receiving streaming services on a mobile device, there are three major power drainage sources: the WNIC for streaming data transmission, the CPU for data decoding, and the display for data rendering. Among them, the battery power consumed by the WNIC is significant. For example, it has been reported that the WNIC accounts for about 40% total energy consumed in video streaming [24]. We also have confirmed this on iTouch. Basically, we have compared the battery lifetime when playing the locally stored video clip on the iTouch (the WNIC is turned off) and when playing the same video clip streamed from a local server. In a typical test, the battery can last for 8 hours and 20 minutes without network transmission, but it can only last for 5 hours 40 minutes with streaming from AirVideo. This means that the WNIC consumes about 32% battery power in the streaming session. Note that in the above experiment, the WNIC spends 73.5% of the session time in the PSM when receiving streaming data from the local server. If the WNIC spends less time in the PSM, it would consume more battery power.

To estimate the power consumed by the WNIC for streaming data transmission, we rely on the `Pwr Mgt` flag in the frame control information from IEEE 802.11 headers to determine the Power Management mode that the WiFi interface will switch to after the transmission of the current frame. Basically, we count the total time the WNIC spends in the sleep mode. So instead of giving the absolute value of energy consumed, we report and compare the percentage of time that the WNIC spends in the sleep mode. Please note that the sleep time of the WNIC is not necessarily proportional to the power consumption of WNIC. For example, as shown in [25], 30%, 50%, and 70% WNIC sleep time would translate to 0.67 (1/1.5), 0.57 (1/1.75), and 0.5 (1/2) WNIC battery power consumption (compared to when the WNIC is always on). Nevertheless, the sleep time is still a good indicator of the WNIC power consumption without using any external instrument.

As we focus on the battery power consumption at the WNIC for data transmission in the streaming sessions under the four different delivery protocols, we will investigate battery power efficiency under these four different approaches, centering around the two fundamental aspects, namely (1) how data is transmitted and (2) how much data is transmitted, in the following two sections.

4. IMPACT OF HOW TO TRANSMIT

As we discussed before, how the streaming data is transmitted directly affects how long the WNIC can stay in PSM. In this section, we thus first examine how data is transmitted under these different protocols, and the consequence of such transmission on the battery power consumption on mobile devices.

4.1 Chunk-based Streaming is Most Power-Efficient with Traffic Shaping

Figure 1 shows the throughput of traffic delivered to/from our testing device when YouTube is accessed via RTSP and Pseudo streaming protocols, and AirVideo is used with Chunk-based

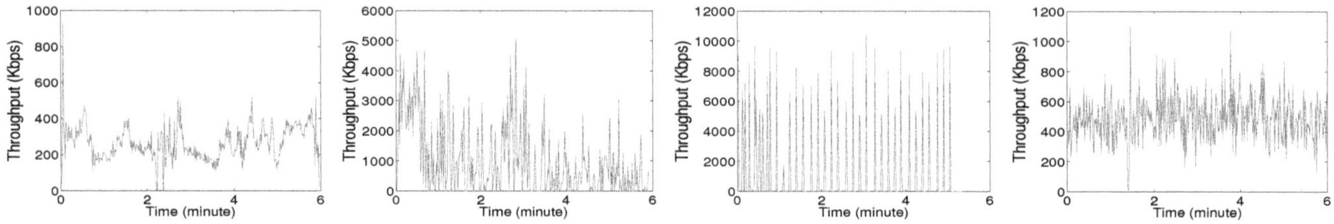

(a) RTSP (b) Pseudo Streaming (c) Chunk-based Streaming (d) P2P Streaming

Figure 1: Throughput (Kbps) in Delivering High Quality Video

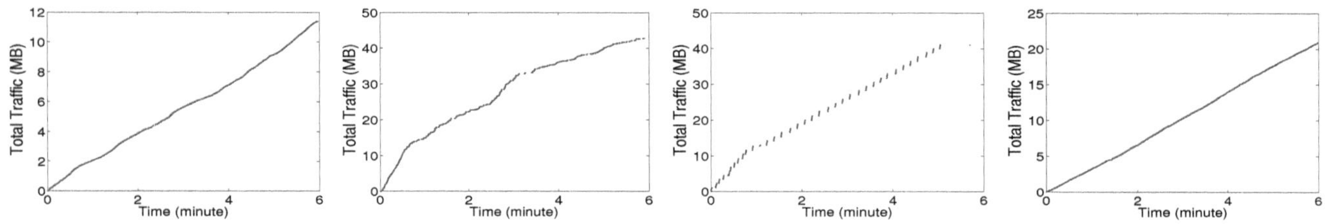

(a) RTSP (b) Pseudo Streaming (c) Chunk-based Streaming (d) P2P Streaming

Figure 2: Traffic Pattern in Delivering High Quality Video

streaming, as well as TVUPlayer is used with P2P streaming in one of their experiments. All these sessions last for 6 minutes. Figure 2 shows the corresponding traffic pattern during the 6-minute playback.

For RTSP as shown in Figure 1(a), the throughput varies between 200 Kbps and 400 Kbps, which is close to the delivered video's encoding rate of 246 Kbps. As a result, the accumulated traffic pattern shown in Figure 2(a) is close to a straight line.

Compared to RTSP that delivers YouTube video according to the video encoding rate, Figure 1(b) shows that when Pseudo streaming is used, the data is delivered at a much higher speed on average although the throughput decreases to the level close to the object encoding rate (654 Kbps) later. As shown in the figure, the average throughput at the beginning 30 seconds reaches 3 Mbps, which is 5 times of the object encoding rate. This would lead more data to be delivered ahead of the playback need. Correspondingly, Figure 2(b) confirms this result. Such a delivery method is called Fast Start as we have discussed in Section 2. The benefit of such delivering is to provide sufficient data to the player at the client slide to reduce the startup delay as well as smoothing out some network jitter.

For Chunk-based streaming, Figure 1(c) and Figure 2(c) show very different patterns from RTSP and Pseudo streaming when the same video clip (886 Kbps) is delivered via AirVideo. As we can observe from Figure 1(c), in AirVideo, the throughput has peaks peridocially, and the peak throughput could reach 11 Mbps (about 12 times of the object encoding rate). As a result, the traffic pattern is very bursty with a regular pattern as shown in Figure 2(c).

Figure 1(d) shows the throughput of P2P based TVUPlayer is about 450 Kbps on average while the object encoding rate is 281 Kbps. The throughput also varies from time to time, but there is no clear pattern as shown in Figures 1(b) or 1(c). Such a traffic pattern is due to additional traffic involved in P2P streaming applications since in P2P streaming, a peer needs to dynamically communicate with multiple neighbors to exchange buffermap information, request streaming data, and upload to neighbors as we have discussed in Section 2.4. Such control traffic and uploading traffic are highly dynamic, depending on the number of neighbors the client is communicating with at each moment.

To verify the impact of control traffic and uploading traffic in P2P streaming, we further plot packet size distribution (CDF) and upload throughput during this 6-minute session. Figure 3(a) shows that the packet sizes have a bi-modal pattern. Further packet inspection shows that all small packets are control packets with a size of 300 bytes or less, while all the larger packets are data packets containing file chunks. As shown in the figure, control packets account for more than 75% of total packets transferred. Such a large number of control packets significantly reduce the inter-packet delay and thus the idle time of the WNIC, resulting in more battery power consumption. Figure 3(b) shows the inter packet delay distribution. `Inter Streaming Packet` delay considers only ingress streaming data packets. `Inter Control Packet` delay considers both incoming and outgoing control packets, and `Inter Packet` delay takes all packets transmitted into account. While over 5% successive streaming packets of TVUPlayer arrive with a delay larger than 100 ms (meaning opportunities to sleep), about 65% control packets are sent/received within 10 ms from the preceding one. This causes the overall Inter Packet delay to significantly deviate from Inter Streaming Packet delay patterns. Apart from the extremely frequent control packets, Figure 3(c) shows that the uploading throughput also reaches as high as 300 Kbps. As a result, while the encoding rate of the video is 281 Kbps, the total throughput varies between 300 Kbps and 800 Kbps as shown in Figure 1(d). On the other hand, even with the control traffic and uploading traffic, Figure 2(d) shows that its traffic pattern is close to a straight line, similar to that of RTSP.

These results show that the streaming data are delivered differently under these four protocols. This results in significantly different battery power consumption on our mobile device: the WNIC sleeps the most in Chunk-based streaming (86.7%) and sleeps the least in RTSP streaming (23.1%) and P2P streaming (30.6%). In Pseudo streaming, the WNIC also sleeps for more than half of the session time (71.4%). Note that the video bit rates in RTSP and P2P streaming are 246 Kbps and 281 Kbps, much lower than these for Chunk-based and Pseudo streaming with the bit rates of 886 Kbps and 654 Kbps.

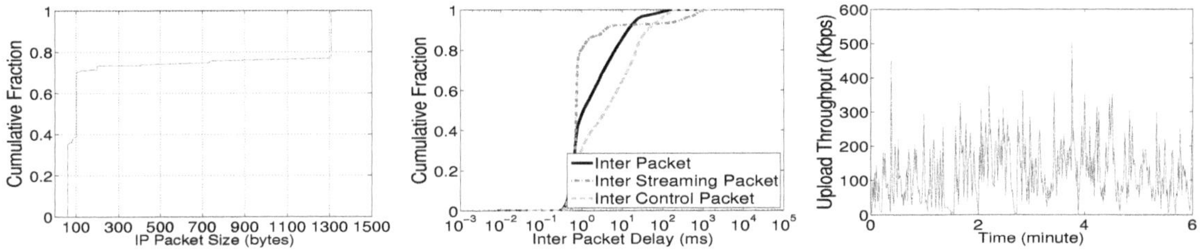

(a) Packet Size (CDF) (b) Inter Packet Delay (CDF) (c) Upload Throughput (Kbps)

Figure 3: Detailed Results of TVUPlayer (P2P streaming)

Table 2: Average WNIC Sleep Time (%) from Multiple Runs

RTSP	Pseudo	Chunk-based	P2P
23.2	72.2	86.4	29.7

While we only show detailed traffic patterns from one typical run (median of multiple runs), Table 2 shows the average WNIC sleep time over multiple experiments (5 runs) for different protocols. These results are consistent with the findings on the single runs we have presented.

Considering these results with the traffic throughput and traffic patterns we have observed in Figure 1 and Figure 2, we find that

- In Chunk-based streaming such as AirVideo, traffic shaping techniques are being used to deliver the data to mobile devices in burst, which leaves the WNIC on the mobile device into sleep mode for most of the time.
- In Pseudo streaming, the Fast Start technique can help transmit a large amount of data to the user at the beginning, which provides more opportunities for the WNIC to sleep when receiving the rest of data.
- In RTSP streaming, since the server delivers data according to the object encoding rate, it results in the least amount of sleep time of the WNIC.
- In P2P streaming, because a user has to frequently exchange control information and upload data to other peers, the WNIC cannot sleep for long time as in the Pseudo streaming or Chunk-based streaming.

4.2 Traffic Shaping is Widely Used, but it may Cause Quality Degradation

To investigate whether traffic shaping has been used in other services, we have conducted experiments with all other services. The results show that traffic shaping is being used in all these Chunk-based streaming applications: CTV, CCTV, W.TV, ImgoTV, Justin.tv, NHKworld, and SPBtv. Figure 4 shows the traffic pattern of 1 minute snapshot during a 6-minute streaming session. As indicated by these figures, traffic shaping is used in all of these applications for bursty data delivery. However, the burst length varies from application to application.

Correspondingly, Table 3 shows the sleep time of the WNIC in these sessions. As shown in this figure, the sleep time of the WNIC varies between 77% and 87% in all of these sessions, confirming the effectiveness of the traffic shaping on the battery power saving.

Although traffic shaping is very effective in Chunk-based streaming for saving battery power consumption on mobile devices, it has to be used carefully. Otherwise, it could affect the streaming quality perceived by end users. Figure 5 shows such a case in our experiments. The data receiving speed shown in Figure 5(a) fluctuates from time to time, and sometimes cannot catch up with the playback (for example, between 100 seconds to 200 seconds), resulting in playback freezing. This is not due to the bandwidth shortage because the thoughput shown in Figure 5(b) can reach higher than the video encoding rate (340 Kbps) even when the playback freezing happens. Therefore, how to choose the right burst length to use in the traffic shaping is important and deserves careful study. We leave it for our future study.

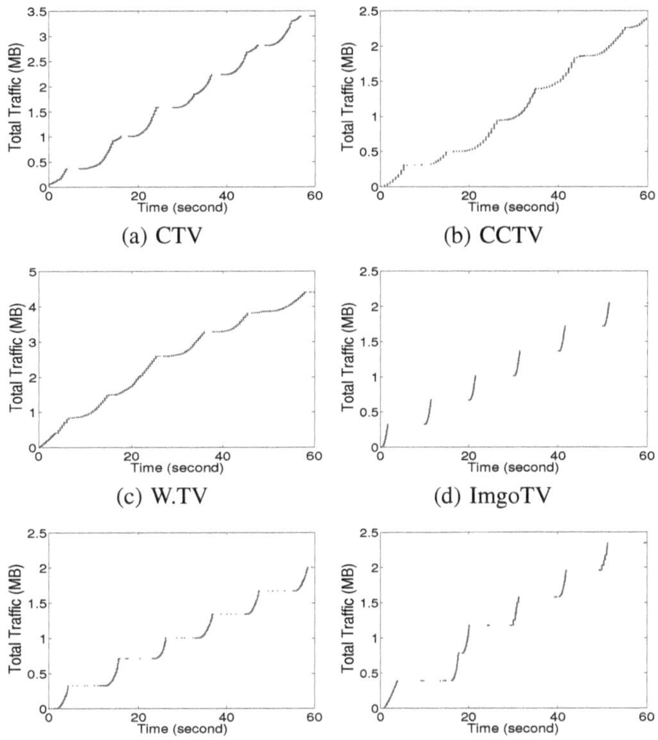

(a) CTV (b) CCTV (c) W.TV (d) ImgoTV (e) Justin.tv (f) NHKworld

Figure 4: Traffic Shaping is Used in All Chunk-based Streaming Applications

Table 3: WNIC Sleep Time (%)

AirVideo	CTV	CCTV	WTV
86.7	78.1	85.8	86.0
ImgoTV	Justin.tv	SPBtv	NHKworld
77.5	82.9	86.9	84.8

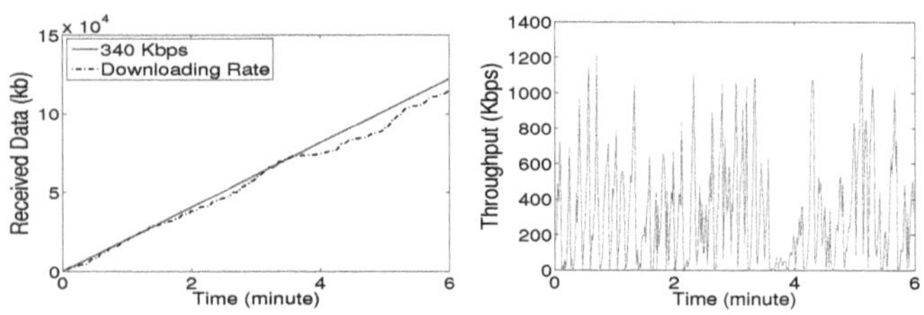

(a) Data Receiving vs. Playback (b) Throughput

Figure 5: CCTV at 340 Kbps

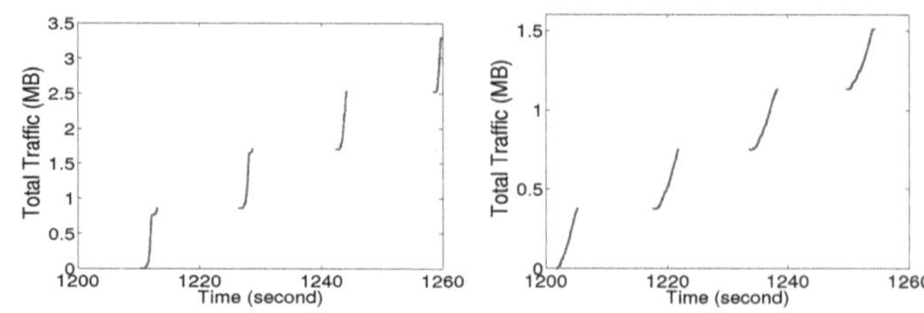

(a) SPBtv - 464 Kbps (b) SPBtv - 174 Kbps

Figure 8: SPBtv: Traffic Pattern

Table 4: WNIC Sleep Time (%) Comparison in High and Low Quality Streaming

	HighQ (Kbps)	Sleep Time (%)	LowQ (Kbps)	Sleep Time (%)
RTSP	246	23.1	81	33.0
Pesudo	654	71.4	247	80.3
Chunk	886	86.7	200	95.6
P2P	281	30.6	156	74.4

4.3 Summary

Through experiments and analysis on how data is transmitted under different protocols, our study shows traffic shaping is very helpful in Chunk-based streaming. However, due to protocol nature of constant bit rate sending, RTSP streaming can hardly apply traffic shaping to reduce battery power consumption on mobile devices.

Pseudo streaming could improve its power efficiency in two ways. One is to use Fast Start to deliver the entire file. The risk, however, is that a user may terminate the playback after viewing the clip for a few seconds. Another concern is the server capacity as the server may wish to reserve some bandwidth to serve other incoming requests. Besides fast streaming, the other option is to adopt traffic shaping technique, which practically turns into Chunk-based streaming.

On the other hand, P2P streaming is affected by both control traffic and uploading traffic. Whether such traffic can be reduced for power saving remains unclear and we will investigate in the next section.

5. IMPACT OF HOW MUCH TO TRANSMIT

As we have studied, how streaming is transmitted could significantly affect the power efficiency on mobile devices when receiving streaming with different approaches. Next we investigate whether reduced traffic amount would significantly reduce battery power consumption on mobile devices. Intuitively, a user may opt to a lower streaming quality with the expectation of less battery power consumption.

5.1 Reducing Streaming Quality Helps Little for All But P2P

To study the impact of reduced traffic amount, we instruct our device to access these streaming services again, but to video clips with lower quality in terms of the object encoding rate. Figure 6 and Figure 7 show the corresponding throughput and traffic patterns in these tests. Table 4 shows the corresponding power saving effectiveness.

Table 5: SPBtv – Impact of Reduced Streaming Data Transmission in Chunk-based Streaming

Quality	Encoding Rate (Kbps)	Total # of Packets	Sleep Time (%)
High	464	184689	86.9
Low	174	106756	90.2

For RTSP based streaming, as the streaming rate is reduced from 246 Kbps to 81 Kbps, Figure 6(a) shows the throughput of data transmission is also reduced from 200-400 Kbps to 50-150 Kbps, without taking full advantage of available bandwidth. The sleep time increases to 33%, and it is mostly because the downloading finishes 1 minute earlier than the viewing session as shown in Figure 2(a).

For Pseudo streaming, the YouTube server still sends streaming data at a very high rate at the beginning (about first 12 MB) as shown in Figures 1(b) and 2(b). However, because of reduced file size due to reduced video encoding rate (from 654 Kbps to 247 Kbps), only about 2 MB more content for the rest of playback is remaining to be downloaded. Thus, in this test, instead of switching to sleep mode opportunistically between successive transmissions as that in the High Quality streaming test, the WNIC can exploit larger intervals between bursts to sleep. As a result, the WNIC spends 9% more time in sleep mode.

For Chunk-based streaming using AirVideo, similar to its previous experiment with the High Quality video clip, a video chunk is delivered every 10 seconds, and packets are delivered in burst. Because of the reduced chunk size, the time spent on downloading each chunk is also reduced, and the WNIC can sleep longer after downloading each chunk. This is reflected with about 9% increase of the WNIC sleep time in Table 4.

However, surprisingly, in P2P streaming, although Figure 6(d) and Figure 7(d) do not show much difference from Figure 1(d) and Figure 2(d) except the decrease of the average throughput and the accumulated traffic amount, the increase of the power saving is significant: the sleep time of WNIC increases from 30% to 74%.

Overall, the sleep time increase of the WNIC due to the reduced streaming data amount is marginal or moderate (between 5% and 10%) for RTSP, Pseudo streaming, and Chunk-based streaming. But it is very effective for P2P based streaming.

While it is relatively intuitive for such a result in RTSP and Pseudo streaming due to their protocol nature of constant streaming (data sending) rate or Fast Start at the beginning, we further investigate why the impact of the reduced traffic amount is trivial in Chunk-based streaming and is significant in P2P streaming.

To verify the trivial power saving benefit in Chunk-based streaming by reducing streaming data transmission, we further conduct experiments with all other Chunk-based streaming services. Figure 8 shows the typical results with SPBtv. SPBtv allows users to ex-

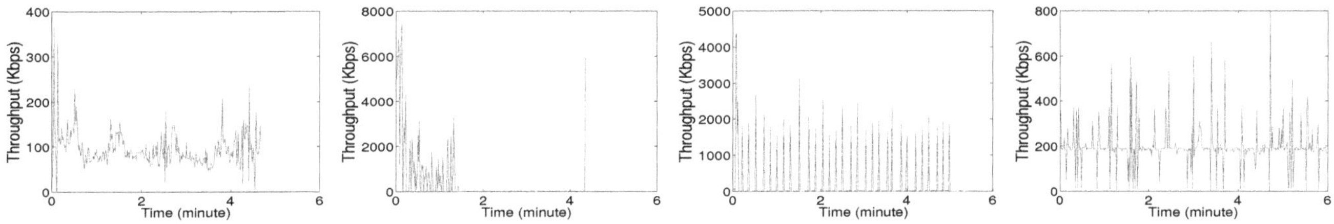

(a) RTSP (b) Pseudo Streaming (c) Chunk-based Streaming (d) P2P Streaming

Figure 6: Throughput (Kbps) in Delivering Lower Quality Video

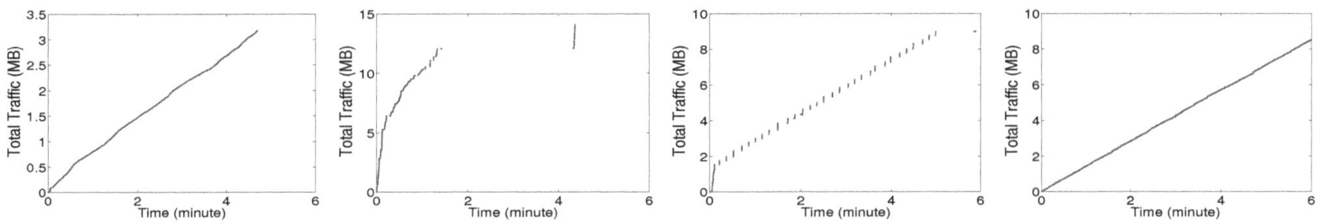

(a) RTSP (b) Progressive Download (c) Chunk-based Streaming (d) P2P Streaming

Figure 7: Traffic Pattern in Delivering Lower Quality Video

plicitly choose between High Quality and Low Quality. Through reverse-engineering, we find that: (1) for High Quality, the video bitrate is 400 Kbps and audio bitrate is 64 Kbps; (2) for Low Quality, the video bitrate is 110 Kbps and audio bitrate is also 64 Kbps. As we have described in Section 2, in HTTP streaming, a client would first query the server for index files (playlists). To support multiple quality levels of the same content, such index files can select appropriate files to request based on bandwidth conditions or the quality the client desires. Figure 8 compares the two streaming tests viewing High Quality (464 Kbps) and Low Quality (174 Kbps) live streaming content, respectively. Figure 8(b) indicates that when Low Quality video is accessed, the server also reduces its delivery rate. Given the access is done in non-peak hours and two tests were conducted consecutively, it is less likely due to the network congestion or the client side bandwidth limit. Our conjecture is that the server tends to reserve/allocate more resources to serve other/incoming High Quality streaming requests. Nevertheless, the server still uses traffic shaping when delivering the lower quality content. On the other hand, receiving lower quality streaming only makes the WNIC sleep about 3% more as shown in Table 5, thus confirming very limited effectiveness of reducing the streaming quality on battery power saving.

While the trivial power saving impact in Chunk-based streaming is mainly because of a reduced delivering rate from the server after the user switches to a lower quality video, P2P streaming is more complicated since it involves both control traffic and uploading traffic.

To study how this power saving happens in the lower quality P2P streaming, we further conduct experiments with TVUPlayer. Figure 9 shows more detailed results of TVUPlayer when it is used to access the Low Quality channel of 156 Kbps for one hour, while Figure 10 shows the results of watching a High Quality channel of 281 Kbps for one hour. Both of these two channels are unpopular. Figures 9(d) and 10(d) show the bandwidth spent on uploading to neighboring peers. For most of the time, there is little uploading to other peers in both sessions. Both sessions have similar traffic patterns and inter packet delays as shown in Figures 9(b) (c) and 10(b) (c).

Table 6: TVUPlayer – Impact of Reduced Streaming Data Transmission in P2P Streaming

Quality	Encoding Rate (Kbps)	Total # of Packets	Sleep Time (%)
High	281	502987	40.6
Low	156	220524	71.6

However, Figure 10(a) shows a different result from that in Figure 9(a). With a lower streaming quality, the percentage of control packets (these with small sizes of 300 bytes or less) is reduced by more than 15%. This is because control traffic also depends on the number of neighbors the client is communicating with during the streaming session even if both experiments are done with unpopular channels.

Table 6 lists the total number of data packets transmitted in these two sessions. With a reduced streaming quality session, the total number of packets is reduced by more than 50%, among which control packets are reduced even more as shown in Figure 10(a). Thus, when playing the video of 156 Kbps, the WNIC was able to sleep as much as 71.6% of the session time, while it can only sleep about 40.6% when watching the video of 281 Kbps. Clearly, the reduced total number of packets, including the control packets, in the lower quality streaming, leads to a longer sleep time of the WNIC.

5.2 Reducing Uploading Traffic in P2P Streaming Sometimes Helps

We have shown in the previous experiments that by switching into a lower quality video version, the mobile device in P2P streaming could save more battery power because of reduced data packets and control packets. For P2P streaming, data transmission also includes uploading to other peers. A peer in P2P systems has to upload to other peers for system scalability. But uploading to other peers is a heavy burden to mobile devices. We are wondering if we can reduce the uploading traffic amount to gain some power sav-

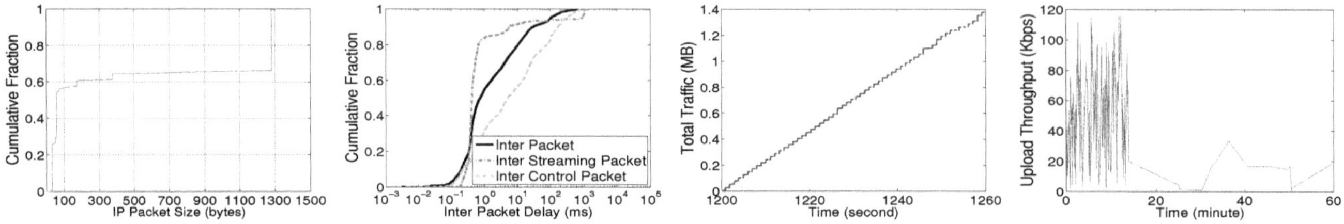

(a) Packet Size (CDF) (b) Inter Packet Delay (CDF) (c) Traffic Pattern (d) Upload Throughput

Figure 9: TVUPlayer - P2P Streaming for One Hour (156 Kbps) - Unpopular Channel

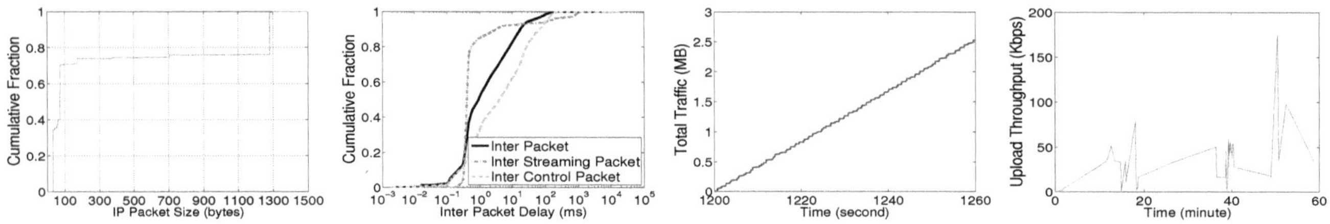

(a) Packet Size (CDF) (b) Inter Packet Delay (CDF) (c) Traffic Pattern (d) Upload Throughput

Figure 10: TVUPlayer - P2P Streaming for One Hour (281 Kbps) - Unpopular Channel

ing without switching to a lower quality video, as it is often not desirable by end-users.

5.2.1 *Upload Throttling Can Help*

Due to the concern of free-riders, P2P streaming systems today do not implement *tit-for-tat* as BitTorrent does [26]. As a result, most P2P applications would saturate the available uploading bandwidth when the channel has a large population. This is also true in TVUPlayer. Therefore, we want to study whether throttling uploading traffic in the P2P mobile streaming would reduce the power consumption.

Upload throttling is to throttle the uploading traffic to other peers. Since uploading to others is essential in P2P streaming systems and is the key to its scalability, throttling upload may help preserve battery power, but may be harmful to the entire P2P system. Because TVUPlayer does not allow us to set an uploading cap, we conduct the following experiments to test its effectiveness.

We instruct iTouch to watch a popular channel and an unpopular channel with a same streaming rate. The two experiments are conducted with the same network settings. The popular channel is accessed from 8 PM to 9 PM, and the unpopular one is accessed from midnight to 1 AM in the morning. Figure 10 shows the results of watching the unpopular channel of 281 Kbps, while Figure 11 shows the results of watching the popular channel of 281 Kbps. Since both channels are encoded with the same streaming rate, the CDF of packet size, as shown in Figure 10(a) and Figure 11(a), are largely similar. However, Figure 10(d) and Figure 11(d) show that when watching the popular channel, the device uploads much more traffic than when watching the unpopular one. Such uploading traffic results in a smaller percentage of large inter packet delay as shown in Figure 11(b).

As a result, Table 7 shows that while the WNIC can sleep about 40% of time when watching the unpopular channel, it can only sleep about 25% of time when watching the popular channel. The uploading overhead can result in 15% less sleep time. Note that in this popular channel session, the uploading is not excessive, as on average the uploading bandwidth is around 175 Kbps. If the uploading is higher, more battery power would have been consumed.

Table 7: Uploading Throttling (P2P)

Channel	Encoding Rate (Kbps)	Total # of Packets	Sleep Time (%)
Unpopular	281	502987	40.6
Popular	281	634527	25.9

These experiments show upload throttling can be effective, particular because these P2P streaming systems do not enforce *tit-for-tat*. Otherwise, the received streaming quality might be affected. In practice, these results imply that a user in P2P streaming can choose to watch the unpopular channels in order to preserve more battery power.

5.2.2 *Smart Caching at Access Point Does Not Help*

While upload throttling may not be fair to other peers in a P2P system, and potentially can affect the user's perceived streaming quality if *tit-for-tat*-like mechanisms are enforced, smart caching can alleviate this concern. Smart caching at access points (SCAP) [14] has been proposed to reduce/eliminate uploading in P2P applications by caching the downloaded data in the AP in case they need to be uploaded to other peers soon. For P2P streaming applications, a peer needs to quickly upload the downloaded content to others, and thus the AP only needs to maintain a small buffer to temporarily cache downstream data. When uploading is needed, the mobile device does not need to send the packet by itself. Instead, it sends a compressed packet telling the AP to do that for it. The AP will detect which cached packet to send and send the packet on behalf of the mobile device. Compared with upload throttling, SCAP could be transparent to the application. However, the mobile device still needs to receive requests from neighbors, and thus the control traffic generated by uploading is not eliminated.

We did not implement SCAP on our iTouch. Instead, to evaluate the potential benefit of using SCAP, we assume the best case in which all uploading traffic from the iTouch is eliminated to estimate the maximum power saving. We re-evaluate the trace shown in Figure 11 for watching a popular channel and we calculate the

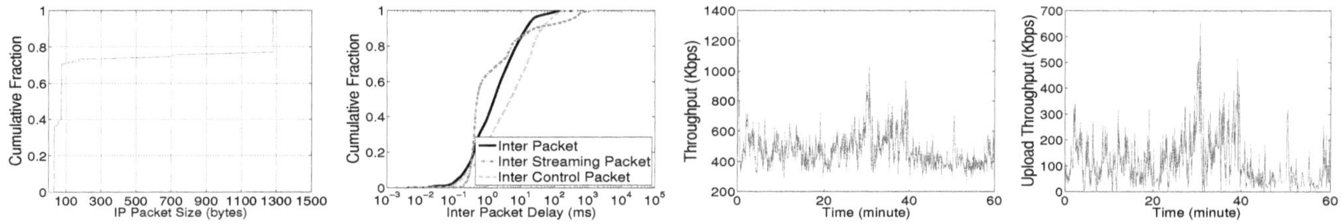

(a) Packet Size (CDF) (b) Inter Packet Delay (CDF) (c) Throughput (d) Upload Throughput

Figure 11: TVUPlayer - P2P Streaming for One Hour (281 Kbps) - Popular Channel

Table 8: Estimated Effectiveness of SCAP

	Encoding Rate (Kbps)	Total # of Packets	Sleep Time (%)
w/o SCAP	281	634527	25.9
SCAP	281	597746	26.4

potential power saving by counting all inter packet delays that are larger than the idle timeout interval as the sleep time of the WNIC. We have validated our method on our iTouch based on the data link layer control information for streaming sessions shown in previous sections. The error is less than 1%.

As shown in Table 8, compared to the case without using SCAP, SCAP only allows the WNIC to sleep 18 seconds more (less than 1 % of the session time). This surprising result, however, has some underlying reasons. Table 8 shows that the number of uploading packets saved by SCAP is relatively small (less than 40000), about 6% of the total number of packets. However, as shown in Table 7, twice more packets can be saved by watching an unpopular channel. This indicates that there is a significant portion of control traffic packets involved in uploading. Without removing these control packets, SCAP cannot increase many more opportunities for the WNIC to switch into the power saving mode.

These results on smart caching indicate that reducing uploading alone is not necessarily very helpful. The control traffic plays a very important role in P2P streaming and must be taken into consideration. This is why reducing the streaming quality or upload throttling are more effective, in which control packets are reduced proportionally.

5.3 Summary

The experiments in this section show that reducing transmission has trivial impact on power saving for mobile devices in RTSP, Pseudo streaming, and Chunk-based streaming, mainly because the server also reduces the sending rate when a lower quality streaming session is accessed although there is additional bandwidth available.

On the other hand, while reducing streaming quality is helpful for power saving in P2P streaming, it may not be desirable for end-users. Without sacrificing the streaming quality, simply reducing upload alone such as smart caching does not help, because the control traffic is not reduced. However, upload throttling can reduce both the uploading and control traffic, and thus can reduce the battery power consumption on the mobile device.

Considering both aspects, i.e., how to transmit and how much to transmit, during the streaming data transmission, in the current practice, we find Chunk-based streaming is more power-efficient than others. That is, a mobile user who wants to save battery power may always want to choose Chunk-based streaming delivery first if it is available. Pseudo streaming could be the next choice. On the other hand, different delivery approaches are not always available for the same video clip. Thus, Internet streaming service providers utilizing other approaches should adopt more power-saving techniques in order to better serve mobile users.

6. RELATED WORK

Along the popularity of wireless Internet accesses, a lot of research has been conducted on battery power saving on mobile devices. For example, Chandra studied typical Internet streaming services over wireless connections and concluded that 802.11 PSM does not save energy if the streaming rate is over 56 Kbps [27]. Anand et al. considered a self-tuning approach to adapt the WNIC's behavior to the access pattern and the intent of applications [28]. A power saving technique to reduce `energy × delay` product was proposed in [29]. Qiao et al. [30] proposed a smart power saving mode. Guo et al. designed a cooperative relay service in order to exploit the idle communication power of the WNIC for network throughput improvement [31]. Targeting streaming services delivered over the Internet to wireless devices, PSM-throttling leverages traffic shaping from the client side in order to allow the WNIC to sleep for a longer time [12]. This client-centric scheme eliminates the demand of infrasfrasture support as required by many previous schemes. For P2P applications such as P2P streaming running on wireless devices, Tan et al. designed SCAP [14] in order to reduce the power consumption on wireless devices by caching the uploading traffic at the AP. In SCAP, the upload from the wireless device can be performed directly from the AP instead of the wireless device, which could save both uploading bandwidth and battery power consumption on the wireless device. More recently, Xiao et al. studied the power consumption of mobile YouTube [32] and we have also examined resource utilization in different Internet mobile streaming architectures [33].

On the other hand, since mobile devices these days commonly have multiple network interfaces, plenty of work has considered to leverage the different power consumption rate of these interfaces [34, 35, 36, 37]. For example, CoolSpots [34] was proposed to intelligently switch between the Bluetooth and the WiFi interfaces. Agarwal et al. proposed to wake up the WiFi interface for incoming calls using the GSM radio [37]. Most recently, authors in [38] proposed Wiffler to reduce power consumption of mobile devices by augmenting 3G using WiFi.

While a lot of aforementioned efforts had aimed to reduce the battery power consumption by the wireless network interfaces on mobile devices, little is known about their feasibility and effectiveness for streaming to mobile devices. Furthermore, in the current practice, how streaming data is transmitted to mobile devices and how much data is transmitted under different protocols have not been thoroughly investigated. Our work in this study measures, analyzes, and compares the battery power efficiencies on data transmission under different delivery approaches. We have also explored potentials of various power saving techniques. Our results provide new insights for further improving the battery utilization on mobile devices when receiving Internet streaming services.

7. CONCLUSION

Along the pervasive usage of all kinds of mobile devices for Internet accesses, more and more streaming services are provided over the Internet to mobile users. However, receiving streaming services on mobile devices can consume a significant portion of the limited battery power supply. In this paper, we set to examine the battery power consumption on mobile devices in receiving such streaming services, focusing on streaming data transmission. Our measurement and analysis provide some new insights for providing power-efficient Internet mobile streaming services in the current practice. In particular, we show that Chunk-based streaming delivery is currently the most power-efficient approach with appropriate traffic shaping techniques. On the other hand, while P2P streaming is scalable and very promising, it is challenging to reduce the battery power consumption without sacrificing the streaming quality. Besides adding to the state-of-the-art, our results also provide some basis for next step research for more battery power-efficient and scalable Internet mobile streaming services.

8. ACKNOWLEDGEMENT

We appreciate constructive comments from our shepherd Wei-Tsang Ooi and anonymous referees. The work is partially supported by NSF under grants CNS-0746649, CNS-1117300, CCF-0915681, CCF-1146578, and AFOSR under grant FA9550-09-1-0071.

9. REFERENCES

[1] "CTV," http://itunes.apple.com/app/id340381556.
[2] "CCTV," http://itunes.apple.com/app/id331259725.
[3] "W.TV," http://itunes.apple.com/app/id318676629.
[4] "ImgoTV," http://itunes.apple.com/app/id349448995.
[5] "NHKworld," http://itunes.apple.com/app/id350732480.
[6] "SPBtv," http://itunes.apple.com/app/id356830174.
[7] "OrbLive," http://itunes.apple.com/app/id290195003.
[8] "Air Video," http://itunes.apple.com/app/id306550020.
[9] "Justin.tv," http://itunes.apple.com/app/id358612216.
[10] "Verizon Wireless: V CAST," http://products.vzw.com/index.aspx?id=video.
[11] "AT&T Mobile TV," http://www.att-mobiletv.com.
[12] E. Tan, L. Guo, S. Chen, and X. Zhang, "PSM-throttling: Minimizing Energy Consumption for Bulk Data Communications in WLANs," in *Proc. of IEEE ICNP*, Beijing, China, October 2007.
[13] S.Chandra and A.Vahdat, "Application-specific network management for energy-aware streaming of popular multimedia formats," in *Proc. of USENIX ATC*, 2002.
[14] E. Tan, L. Guo, S. Chen, and X. Zhang, "SCAP: Smart Caching in Wireless Access Points to Improve P2P Streaming," in *Proc. of IEEE ICDCS*, June 2007.
[15] "Real Time Streaming Protocol (RTSP)," http://www.ietf.org/rfc/rfc2326.txt.
[16] "Mobile YouTube," http://m.youtube.com.
[17] "Vuclip," http://m.vuclip.com.
[18] "Fast Start," `http://www.microsoft.com/windows/windowsmedia/technologies/bettertogether.aspx#faststart`.
[19] "Apple HTTP Live Streaming," http://tools.ietf.org/html/draft-pantos-http-live-streaming.
[20] "Flash HTTP Streaming," http://www.adobe.com/products/httpdynamicstreaming/.
[21] "Microsoft Smooth Streaming," http://www.iis.net/download/SmoothStreaming.
[22] X. Hei, C. Liang, J. Liang, Y. Liu, and K. Ross, "Insights into PPLive: A Measurement Study of a Large-Scale P2P IPTV System," in *Proc. of IPTV Workshop*, Edinburgh, Scotland, UK, May 2006.
[23] "TVUPlayer," http://itunes.apple.com/app/id323640984.
[24] J. Adams and G. Muntean, "Adaptive-Buffer Power Save Mechanism for Mobile Multimedia Streaming," in *Proc. of IEEE ICC*, 2007.
[25] F. Dogar, P. Steenkiste, and K. Papagiannaki, "Catnap: Exploiting High Bandwidth Wireless Interfaces to Save Energy for Mobile Devices," in *Proc. of ACM MobiSys*, 2010.
[26] Y. Huang, T. Fu, D. Chiu, J. Lui, and C.Huang, "Challenges, Design and Analysis of a Large-scale P2P-VoD System," in *Proc. of ACM SIGCOMM*, 2008.
[27] S. Chandra, "Wireless network interface energy consumption implications of popular streaming formats," in *Proc. of MMCN*, 2002.
[28] M. Anand, E. Nightingale, and J. Flinn, "Self-Tuning Wireless Network Power Management," in *Proc. of ACM MOBICOM*, Sept. 2003.
[29] H. Yan, R. Krishnan, S. A. Watterson, D. K. Lowenthal, and K. Li, "Client-Centered Energy and Delay Analysis for TCP Downloads," in *Proc. of IWQoS*, June 2004.
[30] D. Qiao and Kang G. Shin, "Smart Power-Saving Mode for IEEE 802.11 Wireless LANs," in *Proc. of IEEE INFOCOM*, 2005.
[31] L. Guo, X. Ding, H. Wang, Q. Li, S. Chen, and X. Zhang, "Exploiting Idle Communication Power to Improve Wireless Network Performance and Energy Efficiency," in *Proc. of IEEE INFOCOM*, April 2006.
[32] Y. Xiao, R. Kalyanaraman, and A. Yla-Jaaski, "Energy Consumption of Mobile YouTube: Quantitative Measurement and Analysis," in *Proc. of NGMAST*, Washington, DC, September 2008.
[33] Y. Liu, F. Li, L. Guo, and S. Chen, "A Measurement Study of Resource Utilization in Internet Mobile Streaming," in *Proc. of ACM NOSSDAV*, 2011.
[34] T. Pering, Y. Agarwal, R. Gupta, and R. Want, "CoolSpots: Reducing the Power Consumption of Wireless Mobile Devices with Multiple Radio interfaces," in *Proc. of ACM MobiSys*, Uppsala, Sweden, 2006.
[35] T. Armstrong, O. Trescases, C. Amza, and E. de Lara, "Efficient and Transparent Dynamic Content Updates for Mobile Clients," in *Proc. of ACM MobiSys*, Uppsala, Sweden, 2006.
[36] A. Rahmati and L. Zhong, "Context-for-wireless: Context-sensistive energy-efficient wireless data transfer," in *Proc. of ACM MobiSys*, 2007.
[37] Y. Agarwal, R. Chandra, A Wolman, P. Bahl, K. Chin, and R. Gupta, "Wireless Wakeups Revisited: Energy Management for Voip over Wi-Fi Smartphones," in *Proc. of MobiSys*, San Juan, Puerto Rico, 2007.
[38] A. Balasubramanian, R. Mahajan, and A. Venkataramani, "Augmenting Mobile 3G Using WiFi: Measurement, Design, and Implementation," in *Proc. of ACM MobiSys*, 2010.

Tennis Real Play: an Interactive Tennis Game with Models from Real Videos

Jui-Hsin Lai, Chieh-Li Chen, Po-Chen Wu, Chieh-Chi Kao, and Shao-Yi Chien

Graduate Institute of Electronics Engineering and Department of Electrical Engineering
National Taiwan University, Taipei, Taiwan
{juihsin.lai, chiehli.chen, pochen.wu.tw, chiehchi.kao}@gmail.com, sychien@cc.ee.ntu.edu.tw

ABSTRACT

Tennis Real Play (TRP) is an interactive tennis game system constructed with models extracted from videos of real matches. The key techniques proposed for TRP include player modeling and video-based player/court rendering. For player model creation, we propose a database normalization process and a behavioral transition model of tennis players, which might be a good alternative for motion capture in the conventional video games. For player/court rendering, we propose a framework for rendering vivid game characters and providing the real-time ability. We can say that image-based rendering leads to a more interactive and realistic rendering. Experiments show that video games with vivid viewing effects and characteristic players can be generated from match videos without much user intervention. Because the player model can adequately record the ability and condition of a player in the real world, it can then be used to roughly predict the results of real tennis matches in the next days. The results of a user study reveal that subjects like the increased interaction, immersive experience, and enjoyment from playing TRP.

Categories and Subject Descriptors

H.2.8 [**Information Systems**]: Database Applications—*Statistical database*; I.4.9 [**Image Processing and Computer Vision**]: Applications

General Terms

Algorithm, Design, Experimentation

1. INTRODUCTION

In recent years, a number of interactive videos have been proposed on the Internet. For example, there are now several such videos of magic shows on YouTube. These videos are unique in that users not only watch the videos but also participate in the show to guess the answers to magic tricks. It is our opinion that such interactive videos can engage user interest, and that the concept of interactive videos can be further extended.

In this paper, we propose Tennis Real Play (TRP), an interactive tennis game constructed from videos of real matches. TRP is inspired by advances in video analysis/annotation, video-based rendering, and interactive sports games. Previous relevant work is reviewed below.

Video Analysis/Annotation, like event annotation and content segmentation, is a popular and important topic because of the dramatic increase in the number of videos. Many previous studies on this issue have been published. For extraction of sport videos, Wang et al. [25] proposed a method to analyze video structure and automatically replay highlights of soccer videos. Wang and Parameswaran [26] analyzed the ball trajectories in tennis matches to detect player tactics for video annotation, and Zhu et al. [28] proposed recognition of player actions in tennis videos for event annotation. For content segmentation of tennis videos, Lai et al. [13] proposed methods for separating and reintegrating content to enrich videos of tennis matches. By applying these previously studied methods, a large number of videos can be organized so that users can immediately find highlights in a long video.

Video-based Rendering, which can be described as an extension of image-based rendering, is a method to rearrange video frames to create a new video. In studies of video-based rendering, Schodl et al. [23] proposed Video Textures to automatically cut videos into clips and re-loop them to create continuous animations. Efros et al. [2] proposed methods to recognize and classify player actions in football videos. Using such clips of player actions, new actions can be synthesized. Inamoto and Saito [9] rendered a free-view football game from videos from multiple cameras, with the free-view synthesis yielding a fresh viewing experience. Lai et al. [12] proposed Tennis Video 2.0, which rendered multiple players in continuous motion at the same time to create a more interesting viewing experience.

Interactive Sports Games are a popular form of entertainment. In particular, the interactive tennis game in Wii Sports [1] is one of the most well-known among such games. Innovative user interfaces such as those of Wiimote and Wii Fit provide a more realistic gaming experience and changes the way people play games. Not surprisingly, Wii has successfully engaged users throughout the world. In contrast to the interactivity in Wii, Play Station 3(PS3) places more

*Area chair: Pal Halvorsene

[1]Wii Sports. http://wiisports.nintendo.com/

MM'11, November 28–December 1, 2011, Scottsdale, Arizona, USA.

Figure 1: The user interface consists of four components: (a) the main screen of the rendering result, (b) the coordinates of the players and ball on XY-axis, (c) the coordinates of the players and ball on YZ-axis, and (d) motion paths in the player database.

emphasis on visual quality. Top Spin 3 [2] is one of the tennis games on PS3, and the realistic player postures and lighting effects offer the user a more vivid viewing experience. Inspired by both games, one of the aims of this study is to build a tennis game that offers an interactive experience similar to that of Wii along with vivid video texture.

TRP is an interactive tennis game system constructed with models extracted from videos of real tennis matches. As shown in the game frame in Figure 1(a), the textures of the players and the background court are extracted from real videos of matches, and player postures are immediately rendered according to the user's control. To implement TRP, we propose a system framework consisting of player model creation and player rendering, and a video with system overview is available on the website[3]. When creating a player model, projection to fiducial coordinates is proposed to normalize object sizes and the motion trajectories of segmented players. Next, a 4-state-transition model is proposed to model tennis players' behaviors. For player rendering, we propose methods to select suitable clips (moving/hit/standby) from the database. The most interesting and unique feature of our player rendering is that the movement abilities and hitting strength of a rendered player will depend on these clips and statistics in the videos of real matches. Subsequently, we construct a 3D model of the tennis court from the background image and build the game system on this model. As shown in Figures 1(b) and (c), the player's state is recorded in 3D coordinates and the game frame is rendered with a virtual camera. By combining the 3D model with techniques in video-based rendering, the proposed system can render game frames in different viewing angles. The contributions of this paper are listed below.

- To the best of our knowledge, this is the first work to integrate video-based rendering and interactive sports game, and all the rendering characters perform with the characteristics of the players in the real world. We can say that image-based rendering leads to a more interactive and realistic rendering.
- Conventional video games utilize expensive motion capture systems to build the player database which results in rather fixed action sets. Moreover, the player model cannot be updated often. The presented approach might be a good alternative for these methods. The users can even play with new players recorded in the sport video or their friends as the player in the home-made video.
- The game results of TRP can reflect the match results in real world because the game characters can adequately record the abilities and conditions of players in the match video. This property can then be used to roughly predict the results of real tennis matches in the next days.
- We provide viewers a new way to enjoy sports videos; viewers not only enjoy the match by watching videos but also have more immersive experience from playing match videos. In other words, a new match content can be integrated to the game as soon as a new match video is available without much user intervention.

The remainder of this paper is structured as follows. Section 2 describes in detail the generation of the player database, extraction of statistics, and player modeling. Clip selection, smoothing transitions, and system integration for player rendering are described in Section 3. Section 4 presents experimental results along with discussions. Finally, the major findings of the paper are summarized in Section 5.

2. PLAYER MODEL

Player model creation is a key component in TRP because player behaviors in the game including hitting preference and movement characteristics are controlled by the model. Each player has a unique player model in different tennis games. Consequently, the essence of this study is the creation of player models from videos of real matches.

2.1 Player Database

The first step in building the player database is to segment the player from the videos. The possible camera motions in tennis videos—panning, titling, and zooming—make the segmentation process quite difficult. Several previous studies have examined this problem. Lai et al. [14] projected video frames onto a sprite plane for background image generation, which was used for the segmentation of foreground objects. Han et al. [5] proposed a camera calibration module that employed the geometric layout in the form of a court model, which could then be used for player segmentation. The player database not only includes segmentation masks but also records where a player stands in each video frame. Nevertheless, the scale of each mask and position in the player database changes as a result of camera zooming or panning. Therefore, a procedure is required to normalize the database. For this purpose, we propose a fiducial coordinate system upon which all database information is projected. The fiducial plane is the tennis court in a fiducial coordinate system from bird's eye view, as shown in Figure 2.

Next, we assume that the bottom coordinates of the player mask (P_x, P_y) specify the position of the feet on the court. The normalized coordinates are presented as $(P_x^{'}, P_y^{'})$ by pro-

[2]Top Spin3. http://www.topspin3thegame.com/

[3]Demo videos. https://sites.google.com/site/juihsinlai/trp

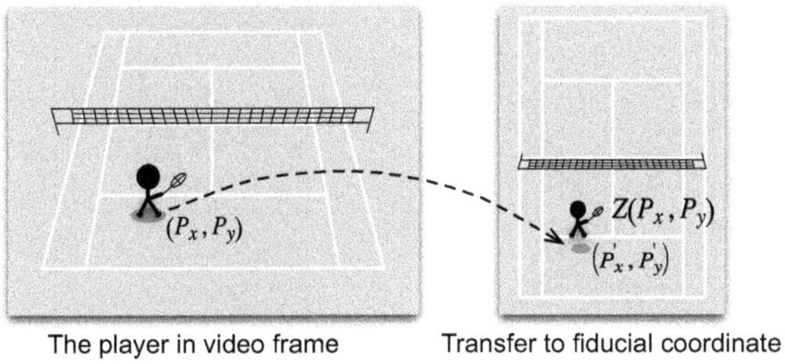

Figure 2: Illustration of player position and size normalization.

jecting (P_x, P_y) onto the fiducial coordinate system according to the following equations.

$$P_x' = G_x(P_x, P_y) = \frac{m_0 P_x + m_1 P_y + m_2}{m_6 P_x + m_7 P_y + 1}, \quad (1)$$

$$P_y' = G_y(P_x, P_y) = \frac{m_3 P_x + m_4 P_y + m_5}{m_6 P_x + m_7 P_y + 1}, \quad (2)$$

where m_0 to m_7 are the parameters of homography projection. As players are extracted from video frames, the sizes of the segmented players will be influenced by camera parameters and a player's position on the court. Therefore, two factors are considered to normalize player size: the projection parameters of the camera and the player's court position. The zooming rate parameters of the players can be estimated by calculating the deviation of $G_x(x, y)$ and $G_y(x, y)$ with respect to the horizontal and vertical zooming factors on the coordinates (P_x, P_y), respectively. Therefore, the normalized player size $Z(P_x, P_y)$ is obtained by multiplying the horizontal and vertical zooming factors, as expressed in the following equation.

$$Z(P_x, P_y) = \frac{\partial G_x(P_x, P_y)}{\partial P_x} \frac{\partial G_y(P_x, P_y)}{\partial P_y}. \quad (3)$$

As shown in Figure 2, the normalized player position and size can be calculated with perspective parameters and the player's position.

2.2 Hit Statistics

After building the database, it is necessary to extract the statistics of a player's characteristics in videos of their tennis matches. Determining a player's positions at the time of hitting is the key step in extracting this information because each hit strength and direction can be detected by the connection of positions at the time of hitting. To detect the time at which the player hits the ball, audio detection and ball trajectory analysis are applied. On the one hand, the hit sound is detected efficiently by the peak amplitude in an audio signal when the background noise is low. However, the hit sound is occasionally masked by an audience's cheer or a broadcaster's voice. To detect the hit time under loud background noise, information on ball trajectories is used instead of audio signals. According to the method of detecting the tennis ball trajectory in [13], the state of the ball can be modeled and used for hit time detection.

After their strengths and directions are detected, the hits must be further categorized. The hit categories include forehand volley, backhand volley, forehand stroke, backhand stroke, and drop shot. However, it is difficult to identify each hit category from videos with a single camera view. To simplify the identification process, two hit categories, forehand and backhand, are first labeled by the program. Several previous studies have investigated this problem. For example, Roh et al. [21] proposed a curvature scale space (CSS) to describe the characteristic shape features of the extracted players and used it to detect hit categories. However, we find that features in CSS cannot accurately identify hit categories in our experiments because players' shapes are dissimilar, and it is difficult to find common features in the same hit category. Using the methods in [28], we calculate and sum the values of optical flow on the right and left sides of the player. If the optical flow on the right side of the player is larger than that on the left side, the hit posture is regarded as a forehand. Otherwise, the hit posture is regarded as a backhand. The strength of forehand and backhand hits in various directions will be considered in Section 3.1.2.

Once forehand and backhand hits are categorized, we use the player position as a clue to identify volleys and strokes. The posture is identified as a volley if the player's position is close to the net and a stroke if player's position is far from the net. Although these assumptions are not always correct, most of the time they are true. In addition, the classification rates between stroke and volley can be improved by more information from different viewing angles of cameras. In sum, after detecting the hit time and identifying the hit category, each hit posture is classified as a forehand stroke, backhand stroke, forehand volley, or backhand volley.

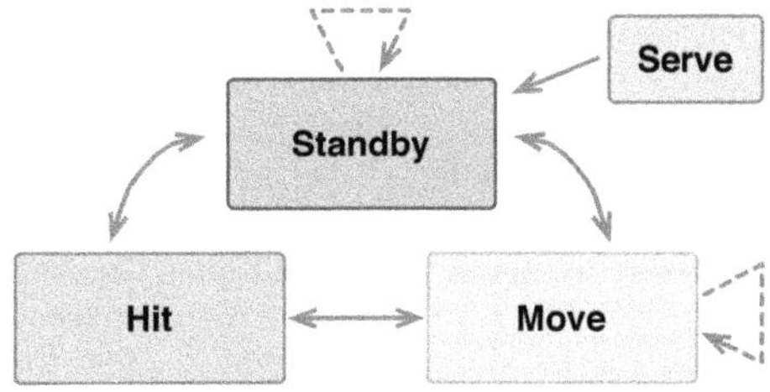

Figure 3: Proposed four-state-transition model for tennis player behaviors.

2.3 Behavior Model

Even after the player database has been constructed and the hit statistics generated, it remains difficult to vividly render a player's behavior without a behavior model. In previous studies of video-based rendering, Schodl and Essa [22] and Colqui et al. [1] synthesized new video clips by rearranging frames in the original video sequences. Both studies presented ingenious schemes to create new motions by displaying the original video clips in a different order. However, most of the objects in their test videos have simpler structures such as those of hamsters, flies, or fish. No human videos were used because human behaviors are more complex. For video-based rendering with human motions, Phillips and Watson [20] introduced template sequences and performed two forms of data-based action synthesis: "*Do as I Do*" and "*Do as I Say*". Although the results were impressive, the system could only synthesize actions based on templates of existing motion sequences. Furthermore, Flagg et al. [3] presented photo-realistic animations of human actions. By pasting numerous sensors on a human subject's body to detect motion, this study overcame many challenges encountered in synthesizing human actions and achieved vivid rendering effects. Nevertheless, this approach is not suitable for the present application.

In our opinion, a model that simulates the behavior of tennis players is needed. Therefore, we propose the four-state-transition model shown in Figure 3. The four states are *Serve*, *Standby*, *Move*, and *Hit*. The arrows in the figure represent the allowable state transitions. All the behaviors of tennis players during a match can be expressed by these state transitions. For example, a player may move right, wait to hit, and then perform a forehand stroke—a sequence which can be modeled by state transitions from *Move*, to *Standby*, to *Hit*. In the case of serving, a player may serve, run to a standby position, wait for the opponent's return, run to a hitting position, and then hit—a sequence which can be modeled as *Serve*, *Move*, *Standby*, *Move*, and *Hit*. As in the intra-state transitions for *Standby* and *Move* shown by the dotted lines in Figure 3, the same state may recur several times in rendering, the associated details of which are described in Section 3.1. Under this behavior model, the player database in Section 2.1 is further classified into four categories. As noted in Section 2.2, four different hitting postures—forehand stroke, forehand volley, backhand stroke, and backhand volley—are collected in the *Hit* category. Subsequently, actions between two hits are classified in the *Move* category. Action clips without movement in the *Move* category are then collected to form the *Standby* category.

3. PLAYER RENDERING

In this section, methods of player selection are proposed in which suitable clips are selected from the database to render the various motions and postures of players. For seamless connection between clips, the proposed approaches can smooth transitions in the player's shape, color, and motion. Subsequently, the game system is integrated with the rendered background court and foreground objects.

3.1 Database Selection

In previous studies focusing on video-based rendering, Schodl et al. [23] and Schodl and Essa [22] extracted textures of a video and synthesized new video clips by rearranging frames in the original video sequences. In both studies, the measure of similarity for video synthesis is the pixel difference between two frames. However, the methods in these studies were not suited for human rendering because the complexity of human images is higher than that of natural scenes used in previous studies. In previous studies of video-based rendering in humans, Kitamura et al. [11] used greater numbers of similarity measures such as motion vectors and contours, and both studies achieved more vivid visual effects. These studies should encourage the consideration of more similarity measures for better visual effects in human rendering. Nevertheless, the challenges are greater in player rendering because unlike the dedicated human videos from users captured in [3] and [11], the player database is constructed from videos of matches. In other words, the database may be incomplete for some postures, and thus lead to more difficult rendering. Therefore, in the proposed method for player rendering, the first step is to select appropriate player clips.

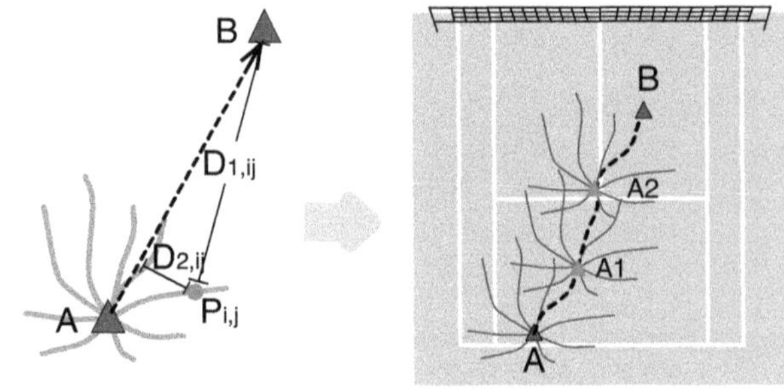

(a)Factors of similarity computation. (b)Selection result from A to B.

Figure 4: (a) Selecting a suitable motion clip to form a movement path from position A to position B by computing similarity. (b)Three motion clips forming a movement path.

3.1.1 *Clip Selection for Player Moving*

Suppose a motion path is to be rendered from position A to position B as illustrated in Figure 4(a), and that the best path is the shortest one (dotted line). Occasionally, it is difficult to find a clip from the player database that fits the dotted line, and multiple moving clips must be connected to form the moving posture. A critical problem is how to choose suitable moving clips to achieve seamless connections. Suppose there are n moving clips, and moving clip i, $i \in [1, n]$, is composed of l_i frames. $P_{i,j}$ is the player position in frame j of moving clip i in fiducial coordinates, $j \in [1, l_i]$. All player positions can form the possible movement trajectories such as those shown by the grey lines in Figure 4(a). The process of moving clip selection is to choose a motion path $[P_{i,1}, ..., P_{i,j}]$ which connects positions A and B. Three primary factors should be considered in moving clip selection: distance $\mathbf{D_{1,ij}}$, distance $\mathbf{D_{2,ij}}$, and index j.

- $\mathbf{D_{1,ij}}$ is the distance from position $P_{i,j}$ to position B. The selected moving clip should shorten the distance to the destination position B. As shown in Figure 4(a), the shorter the distance $\mathbf{D_{1,ij}}$, the better the motion path $[P_{i,1}, ..., P_{i,j}]$.
- $\mathbf{D_{2,ij}}$ is the distance from position $P_{i,j}$ to the shortest path. The selected moving clip should not be far from the shortest path. A shorter $\mathbf{D_{2,ij}}$ indicates that the rendered motion path from the selected clip is more efficient for player movement.
- A larger j is preferred because longer clips would make the rendering result smoother. In other words, a smaller j indicates that many shorter clips may be needed to render the motion path. This makes the path less smooth.

Taking these factors into consideration, the decision function at each position $P_{i,j}$ in moving clip selection is formulated as the sum of $\mathbf{D_{1,ij}}$, $\mathbf{D_{2,ij}}$, and j.

$$MD_{ij} = D_{1,ij} + D_{2,ij} - c_m j, \tag{4}$$

where c_m is a weighting coefficient to balance the effectiveness of clip length. The moving clip with the minimum value of MD_{ij} is recognized as the most suitable. Occasionally, the selection procedure is repeated several times and multiple clips are selected to form the motion path. As the illustration in Figure 4(b) shows, three clips, $\overline{AA_1}$, $\overline{A_1A_2}$, and $\overline{A_2B}$, form the motion path. It should be noted that the time to move from position A to position B depends on the player database. In other words, a shorter running time is needed if the player moves fast in various directions in the real video, which is recorded in the database as shown in Figure 1(d). The rendering of player motion based on extracted clips containing the movement characteristics of the player in videos of real match is one of the distinguishing features of TRP.

3.1.2 Clip Selection for Hitting

Unlike moving clip selection, the major factor considered in clip selection for hitting is the similarity of texture and shape between the final selected moving clip and the hitting clip. As the transition example in Figure 5 illustrates, the primary challenge is how to choose the hitting clip Hit to connect to the current frame CF_t in a seamless cascade. A reasonable assumption for a suitable connection is that the initial frames in a successive clip should be visually similar to the current clip. This requires computing the similarity between frames of the current clip and the initial frames of clips in the Hit category. HD_i, the distance between the initial frame of clip i and the current frame, is defined on the basis of textural and shape features. It is written as

$$HD_i = D_{tex,i} + c_h D_{shape,i}, \tag{5}$$

$$D_{tex,i} = \sum_x \sum_y |Hit_{i,1}(x,y) - CF_t(x,y)|^2, \tag{6}$$

where $D_{tex,i}$ is the textural similarity between the current frame $CF_t(x,y)$ and the initial frame of the successive clip $Hit_{i,1}(x,y)$. Note that the positions of the player masks in these clips are normalized (Section 2.1), and no alignment process is required in measuring textural similarity. $D_{shape,i}$ stands for the shape similarity derived with the Hausdorff-distance [7]. c_h is a weighting coefficient to balance the effectiveness of shape similarity. The clip Hit_i with the minimum HD_i is chosen as the successor clip.

For hitting properties, the hitting strengths are based on statistics from the player's performance in real videos. As an example in Figure 5, the blue and red charts show statistics for forehand and backhand strengths, respectively, in each direction (extracted in Section 2.2). To simulate the game, a Gaussian variable is added to the direction and strength of each hit. Note that different players in different videos have different statistics—a property which makes the proposed interactive game system more realistic. The rendering of hitting based on player characters is another distinguishing feature of TRP.

3.2 Smoothing Transitions

Occasionally, the next selected clip may not be sufficiently similar to the current clip, in which case the rendering result will appear awkward when the two are directly connected. For the example in Figure 5, the rendering result is not smooth if we cascade CF_t and $Hit_{1,1}$. In our observations, the dissimilarity between two clips comes from shape, color, and motion. To smooth the transition, we propose to insert transition frames between two cascading clips. The transition frames are calculated from the current clip and the next selected clip by considering the smoothness of shape, color, and motion. The number of transition frames can be dynamically determined by the value of the similarity measure in (5).

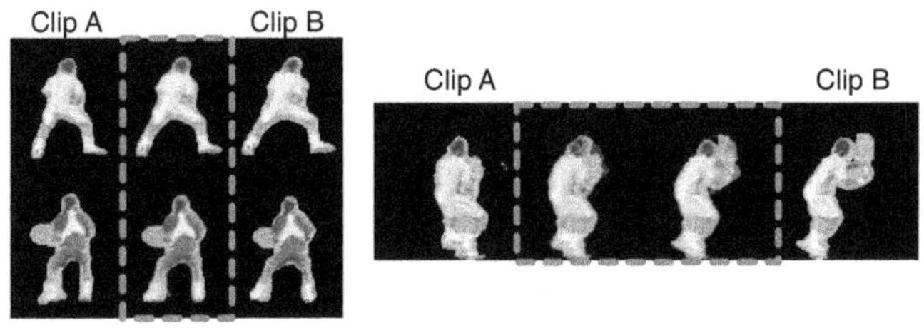

(a) Insert 1 transition frame (b) Insert 2 transition frames

Figure 6: Shape smoothing. (a) Insert one transition frame. (b) Insert two transition frames.

For shape smoothing, we attempt to interpolate the transition postures between two cascading clips. A well-known approach for shape transition is the image morphing method proposed by Seiz and Dyer [24]. With transition points labeled by users, image morphing can generate smooth transitions between two different images. Furthermore, a hierarchical and tile-based image warping scheme proposed by Gao and Sederberg [4] can improve the results. However, neither method can be directly applied to our application because it is impossible to manually label the transition points between any two clips in a massive database. Therefore, another challenge is how to automatically label the transition points. With the help of the feature detection method proposed in [18] and the feature descriptor in [16], feature points on the images can be automatically detected and matched. Suppose we wish to find the transition frames between two images: $I_1(i,j)$ and $I_2(i,j)$. $P_1(k)$ and $P_2(k)$ are the positions of feature points on $I_1(i,j)$ and $I_2(i,j)$, respectively. We propose to modify the cost function for view morphing by adding the distance between feature points as shown in the following equation.

$$W = \sum_i \sum_j |I_1(i,j) - \tilde{I}_2(i,j)|^2 + \lambda \sum_{k=1}^{n} |P_1(k) - \tilde{P}_2(k)|^2, \tag{7}$$

where $\tilde{I}_2(i,j)$ is the warping result of $I_2(i,j)$, $\tilde{P}_2(k)$ are the positions of the feature points in $\tilde{I}_2(i,j)$, n is the number of matched feature points, and λ is the weighting coefficient. The morphing process employs hierarchical and tile-based warping with the cost function (7). The process iteratively finds the minimum value of W and stops when W converges. As an example of shape smoothing in Figure 6(a), we insert one transition frame between clips A and B in which the player in the transition frame has an intermediate posture. Figure 6(b) is another example of shape smoothing with two transition frames. It can be observed that transition frames can effectively smooth the clip connection.

For color smoothing, the clips in the database are segmented from different time periods in a video. Therefore, each clip may have a different background because of changes in the weather. Occasionally, changes in background lighting conditions lead to luminance variation in the clips, making the transition unpleasing. To solve this problem, all clips in the database are normalized to the color of the court with Poisson Editing [19].

For motion smoothing, clips may have different movement speeds and directions. A discontinuity in the motion will

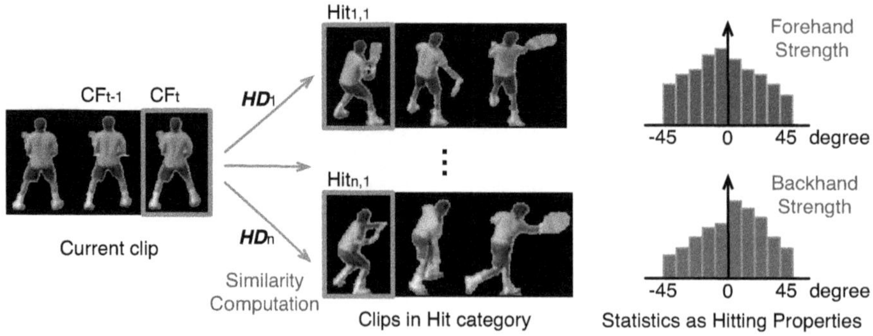

Figure 5: A suitable clip is chosen when the hitting clip has higher similarity to the current clip. The hitting properties of a player depend on statistics from real videos. The blue and red charts show hitting statistics for forehand and backhand strengths, respectively, in each direction.

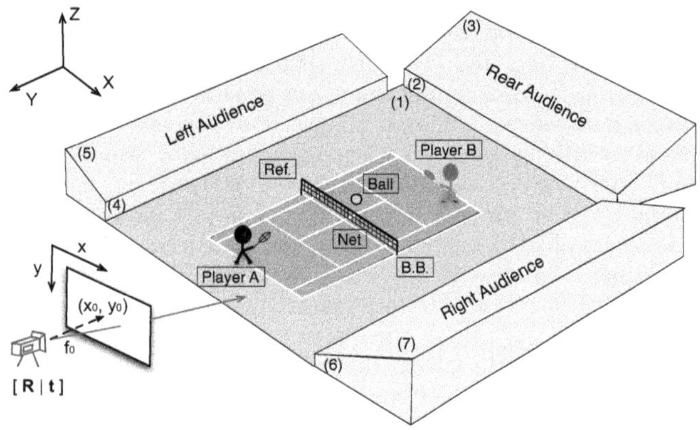

Figure 7: The structure of game system.

then make the rendering result discrete. To reduce discontinuities in motion, we provide an intermediate motion state to the transition frames. The intermediate motion state can be a linear interpolation of speed and direction between the two clips.

3.3 Game System

The entire game system includes rendering of not only the player rendering but also the background. The background is also an important component of a game system because a better rendering of it will increase the game's realism and user enjoyment. Inspired by the method proposed by Horry et al. [6] in "Tour Into the Picture" and the improved methods in [10], in TRP, 3D scenes are rendered from a 2D image once the user manually labels the 3D structure of the image. As the illustration in Figure 7 shows, the 3D structure of a tennis court can be roughly modeled by seven boards: (1) the floor, (2) the base of the rear audience, (3) the top of the rear audience, (4) the base of the left audience, (5) the top of the left audience, (6) the base of the right audience, and (7) the top of the right audience. The 2D scene rendered from the 3D structure is controlled by intrinsic and extrinsic parameters of the camera as follows:

$$\begin{bmatrix} x \\ y \\ 1 \end{bmatrix} \sim \begin{bmatrix} f_0 & 0 & x_0 \\ 0 & f_0 & y_0 \\ 0 & 0 & 1 \end{bmatrix} \begin{bmatrix} \mathbf{R} \mid \mathbf{t} \end{bmatrix} \begin{bmatrix} X \\ Y \\ Z \\ 1 \end{bmatrix}, \qquad (8)$$

Table 2: The computations per frame.

Items	Computation Units
Clip Selection	45
Smooth Transition	160 $\sim$ 270
Background Rendering	100
Foreground Rendering	20 $\sim$ 90

where f_0 is focal length and $[x_0, y_0]$ are the offset coordinates of the intrinsic parameters. The rotation matrix **R** and translation matrix **t** are extrinsic parameters. By modifying these camera parameters, we can render virtual 2D scenes from the 3D structure in any viewing angle. Incorporating foreground rendering into the 3D structure, the foreground objects in Figure 7 are rendered in the following order: Player B, net, referee, ball boy, ball[4], and Player A. In order to achieve more vivid player effects, we also model the light source and draw player shadows by warping player shapes according to the position of light sources. To model the motion blur effect of a fast-moving ball, alpha blending and multiple-ball rendering are used. More vivid rendering results can be generated by attending to these details.

4. EXPERIMENTS AND DISCUSSION

4.1 Rendering Results

We designed a graphic user interface to show rendering results at a resolution of 720 × 480 (Figure 1(a)), XY positions of players and ball on fiducial coordinates (Figure 1(b)), YZ positions of players and ball on fiducial coordinates (Figure 1(c)), and motion paths of players A and B (Figure 1(d)). In particular, Figures 1(b) and (c) clearly illustrate that the game system is built upon a 3D model. Figure 1(d) shows the potential motion paths of players, all of which are based on a database extracted from real videos of matches to record movement properties. Table 1 shows the information of tennis players in the game and also includes the match videos where the players extracted from. Because many *Motion* and *Hit* clips in the player database are similar, we only select some clips with various moving

[4]If the depth of the ball is deeper than that of the net, the rendering priority of the ball is higher than that of the net.

Table 1: **Information of player database and the match videos where the players extracted from.**

Tennis Video	Player Name	# of Clips in Motion	# of Clips in Hit
2009 French Open Semi Final	Roger Federer	27	12
2009 Wimbledon Open Semi Final	Serena Williams	22	12
2007 Australia Open Final	Roger Federer	29	26
2009 French Open Semi Final	Juan Martin del Potro	28	12
2009 Wimbledon Open Semi Final	Elena Dementieva	22	12

paths and hitting postures in the real-time game rendering. As shown in Table 1, 5 real tennis players are available in the game, and the number of clips in *Motion* and *Hit* states are also listed.

To control the player in the game, we analyzed the XYZ-axis acceleration signals of Wiimote through the Blue-tooth protocol for user's gesture recognition. The hitting strength of a player in the game is proportional to the statistics in the match video and user's force feedback. We suppose the hitting strength from statistics is $\mathbf{F_s}$, the user's force feedback is $\mathbf{F_u}$, and the hitting strength of the player in the game is $\mathbf{F_s} \cdot \alpha\mathbf{F_u}$, where α is the parameter for the normalization.

4.1.1 Viewing Effect

Further rendering results are shown in Figure 8. Figures 8(a) and (b) show players competing on a court at the French Open. To give more vivid visual effects, shadows of foreground objects are added to the court surface. Furthermore, the score is seamlessly painted on the court with alpha blending. To increase excitement, the player's hitting energy is shown accumulating during the game with the bars in the upper-right and lower-left corners. The player produces a powerful stroke accompanied by a fire ball when the hitting energy is full, as shown in Figure 8(b). Figure 8(d) shows players competing on a court at Wimbledon. Figure 8(e) shows a player and an animated character on a court at the Australia Open, and Figure 8(f) shows two animated characters on a court at the US Open. These images demonstrate that the rendering effects are quite realistic and resemble real videos.

The position of the camera is far from the tennis court in Figures 8(b), (d), (e), and (f), whereas it is behind player A in Figures 8(c), (g), (h), and (i). With changes in the viewing angle, the visual effects of TRP are more vivid and offer more novel experiences to users. Furthermore, the proposed methods of database selection can determine suitable clips and connect them to form various player movements and postures. The smoothing transitions effectively reduce the awkward effects caused by directly connecting two clips. A demo video showing the player and background renderings is available from the link of system overview in Section 1.

We find that the some rendering clips were still not smooth enough. Because the morphing process needs to iteratively refine the transformation, the much dissimilar clips will need more computation time to get better results. However, the requirement of real-time performance is always the critical factor in the game rendering; thus some clip connections cannot be refined to be perfect during the game. The number of discontinuous motion will decrease if the computer as the game server has higher computation capability.

4.1.2 Computational Analysis

TRP is an interactive tennis game and requires real-time rendering performance during user interaction. As mentioned in Section 3, the computations for rendering include clip selection, smoothing transitions, background rendering, and foreground rendering. Note that, the computation time of player rendering in proportion to the number of player clips, and the numbers of clips are listed in Table 1.

We set the computation of background rendering as 100 computation units (CUs) per frame and normalized the CUs for the other steps as shown in Table 2. Foreground rendering requires 20 to 90 CUs per frame depending on the position of camera. For example, the computational load is heavy when the camera position is close to the player as in Figure 8(c), because a larger foreground area must be rendered. Note that the computations for background rendering do not decrease when foreground computations increase, because the former is independent of the latter. Clip selection would process and depend on the current pose of the user. Due to the partial selection of player database, clip selection only costs 45 CUs, and it would be linearly increased when clip number increases. Smoothing transitions require extensive computations to detect feature points, execute the morphing process, and perform Poisson Editing. In the experiments, smoothing transition requires 160 to 270 CUs per frame depending on the size of foreground players, which costs the most computation in the game rendering. We made a multi-thread program and employed a PC with Intel i7 2.6GHz CPU to achieve a rendering performance of 720 × 480 and 30 fps, providing users with a more comfortable gaming experience.

4.2 Game Prediction with Player Statistics

Player rendering with hitting statistics and movement properties extracted from real videos is a key feature of TRP. A player's performance in TRP may reflect that player's performance in a real video. Therefore, we designed an experiment to observe whether the performances of players in TRP correlate with those in a real video. The experimental results are shown in Table 3. Two real videos were used: the men's semi-final of the French Open and the women's semi-final of Wimbledon, both in 2009. From the match records, the percentage of games won by Roger Federer in the former is 51%. The percentage of games won by Serena Williams in the latter is 54%.

To simulate a match with TRP, both players were controlled by the computer. A Gaussian variable was added in the direction and strength of hits to model the player in the real video. The simulations were run for 5 and 3 sets for the French Open and Wimbledon, respectively. The per-

Figure 8: Rendering results. Rendering results. (a)-(c) Two players competing on a French Open court. (d),(g) Two players competing on a Wimbledon court. (e),(h) A player and an animated character competing on an Australia Open court. (f),(i) Two animated characters competing on a US Open court.

centage of games won by Roger Federer was 55%, and that by Serena Williams was 61%. Therefore, the performance of a player in TRP can reflect that player's performance in real videos, although the former slightly overestimates the latter. We realize that match results are difficult to predict because player performance depends not only on hitting and moving but also on emotions, the weather, and chance. Nevertheless, we might still test how well the simulated results of TRP hold in general. For example, it would be interesting to use TRP to predict the results of Federer's performance in the 2009 French Open final and in the 2007 French Open. This could potentially show whether Federer's technique has advanced or regressed.

4.3 Subjective Evaluations

For the user study, we designed subjective evaluations for twenty undergraduates who played TRP for the first time, and the game environment was captured in our demo video. Of the twenty evaluators, eleven had a habit of watching videos of tennis matches whereas the rest did not. Sixteen evaluators had a habit of playing games on PS3 or Wii, whereas the others did not. Five questions were designed to evaluate the experience of playing TRP, and four were designed to compare the experiences of playing TRP, Wii Sports, and Top Spin 3 on PS3.

Before the subjective evaluations, evaluators were required to watch videos of tennis matches. Subsequently, they were required to play TRP and score their satisfaction on a five-point scale, i.e., 1, very unsatisfied; 2, somewhat unsatisfied; 3, no difference; 4, somewhat satisfied; and 5, very satisfied. The five questions were as follows:

Q.1 Did you have interactions with the video content from playing TRP?

Q.2 Did you have an immersive experience with the game of tennis from playing TRP?

Q.3 Was it entertaining and interesting to play TRP?

Q.4 Do you think that TRP is an innovative multimedia application?

Q.5 Are you more willing to play TRP after watching videos of tennis matches?

The average scores and standard deviations of the evaluations are listed in Figure 9. The results show that evaluators identify with increased interaction, immersive experience, and enjoyment from playing TRP. Furthermore, they highly

Table 3: The percentage of games won in real videos and in results simulated by Tennis Real Play.

Game Video	Name of Player A	Name of Player B	Game Points A-B	Game(%)	Simulation(%)
2009 French Open S.-F.	Roger Federer	Juan Martin del Potro	3-6, 7-6, 2-6, 6-1, 6-4	51 : 49	55 : 45
2009 Wimbledon Open S.-F.	Serena Williams	Elena Dementieva	6-7, 7-5, 8-6	54 : 46	61 : 39

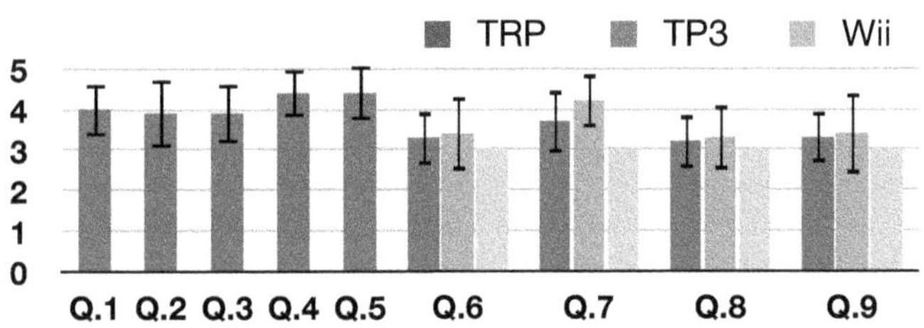

Figure 9: Results of subjective evaluation. The bars' heights are the average scores, and the black lines show the standard deviations.

agree that TRP is an innovative multimedia application and are more willing to play it after watching videos of tennis matches.

In the next phase, evaluators were required to play the tennis games in Wii Sports(Wii), Top Spin 3(TP3) on PS3, and TRP. They were told to use Wii as the standard of comparison and give a score of 1 to 5 for their experience with TP3 and TRP, i.e., 1, much worse; 2, somewhat worse; 3, no difference; 4, somewhat better; 5, much better. The four questions were as follows:

Q.6 Comparing the entertainment levels of each game, what do you think of the performance of TP3 and TRP?
Q.7 Comparing the realism of the visual effects, what do you think of the performance of TP3 and TRP?
Q.8 Comparing the interactiveness of each game, what do you think of the performance of TP3 and TRP?
Q.9 Comparing your preferences for each game, what do you think of the performance of TP3 and TRP?

The average scores and standard deviations of the evaluations are listed in Figure 9. The primary advantages of Wii are the innovations in user-interactive dialogue (e.g., Wiimote). TRP also employs Wiimote for interactive dialogue. From the results in Figure 9, the performances of TRP in regard to visual effects, interactiveness, and preference are all higher than for Wii. Some subjects noted that TRP has vivid rendering effects and realistic player properties which provided them with a more interesting and enhanced experience. Compared to TRP, the primary advantages of TP3 are its vivid rendering effects of the court and the players. The performances of TRP are slightly lower than those of TP3 in terms of entertainment, visual effects, and preference. However, we feel that the performances of TRP are still outstanding because TP3 requires dozens of individuals to build the game model and draw textures. In contrast, all of the materials in TRP are simply extracted from real videos. Furthermore, this feature may also lead to a new framework in game production; the latest game of TRP will be available after a real tennis match is played.

5. CONCLUSION AND EXTENSION

Inspired by video analysis/annotation, video-based rendering, and interactive sports games, an interactive tennis game—TRP—constructed using models extracted from videos of real tennis matches is proposed. As techniques for player model creation, we propose a database normalization process and a 4-state-transition behavioral model of tennis players. For player rendering, we propose clip selection, smoothing transitions, and a framework combining a 3D model with video-based rendering. Experiments show that vivid rendering results can be generated with low computational requirements. Moreover, the player model can adequately record the ability and condition of a player, which can then be used to roughly predict the results of real tennis matches. User studies reveal that subjects like the increased interaction, immersive experience, and enjoyment from playing TRP. They also show that evaluators rate the visual effects, interactiveness, and preference for TRP higher than those for Wii Sports but slightly lower than those for Top Spin 3. However, unlike building complex scene models or drawing player textures in Top Spin 3, all of the materials in TRP are extracted from videos of real matches. This property can also provide a new framework for game production; the latest game of TRP will be available after a tennis match is played.

Basically, some steps of the application can be improved by utilizing a powerful computation server, which can increase the rendering smoothness discussed in Section 4.1.1, or the existing techniques. For example, a few recent methods for shape [8] [17] and color interpolation [15] which might be useful to render more vivid viewing effects. However, the real-time constraint is one of reasons why we do not prefer these techniques. Furthermore, there are some papers addressing on pose estimation of tennis player [28] and retrieval of hitting statistics [27], but we only put emphasis on player rendering and system integration.

Limitations of the current system include the restrictions in the viewing angles and resolutions of the rendered game frame. For example, the system cannot render arbitrary views of the player, and the rendered game frame is blurry if the resolution of the tennis video is insufficiently high. Nevertheless, the limitation in viewing angles can be overcome if multiple videos from different cameras are made available. By constructing a database of multiple court models and players, the system can render game frames from any viewing angle. To overcome the limitation of low resolution, super-resolution techniques may be employed to preserve more details from the real video.

For future studies, our top priority is to extend the application of the proposed methods to other sports videos. The proposed methods in player model creation and player rendering will be modified. For example, the techniques of database normalization, clip selection, and smoothing transitions can be applied to videos of football games. Specifically, the proposed four-state-transition model of tennis players can be replaced by a transition model for football players (i.e., shot-pass-stop-motion). In this way, the framework in TRP can be extended to other sports videos to create games such as Football Real Play and Baseball Real Play.

6. REFERENCES

[1] G. Colqui, M. Tomita, T. Hattori, and Y. Chigusa. New video synthesis based on flocking behavior simulation. In *International Symposium on Communications, Control and Signal Processing*, pages 936–941, 2008.

[2] A. A. Efros, A. C. Berg, G. Mori, and J. Malik. Recognizing action at a distance. In *Proceedings of the Ninth IEEE International Conference on Computer Vision*, pages 726–733, 2003.

[3] M. Flagg, A. Nakazaway, Q. Zhangz, S. B. Kang, Y. K. Ryu, I. Essa, and J. M. Rehg. Human video textures. In *Proceedings of the 2009 symposium on Interactive 3D graphics and games*, pages 199–206, 2009.

[4] P. Gao and T. W. Sederberg. A work minimization approach to image morphing. *The Visual Computer*, pages 390–400, 1998.

[5] J. Han, D. Farin, and P. H. N. de With. Broadcast court-net sports video analysis using fast 3-d camera modeling. *IEEE Transactions on Circuits and Systems for Video Technology*, pages 1628–1638, 2008.

[6] Y. Horry, K.-I. Anjyo, and K. Arai. Tour into the picture: Using a spidery mesh interface to make animation from a single image. In *Proceedings of the 24th annual conference on Computer graphics and interactive techniques*, pages 225–232, 1997.

[7] D. Huttenlocher, G. Klanderman, and W. Rucklidge. Comparing images using the hausdorff-distance. *IEEE Transactions on Pattern Analysis and Machine Intelligence*, 15:850–863, 1993.

[8] T. Igarashi, T. Moscovich, and J. F. Hughes. As-rigid-as-possible shape manipulation. In *Proceedings of ACM SIGGRAPH 05*, pages 1134–1141, 2005.

[9] N. Inamoto and H. Saito. Free viewpoint video synthesis and presentation of sporting events for mixed reality entertainment. In *Proceedings of the 2004 ACM SIGCHI International Conference on Advances in Computer Entertainment Technology*, pages 42–50, 2004.

[10] H. W. Kang, S. H. Pyo, K.-I. Anjyo, and S. Y. Shin. Tour into the picture using a vanishing line and its extension to panoramic images. *Computer Graphics Forum*, 20(3):132–141, 2001.

[11] Y. Kitamura, R. Rong, Y. Hirano, K. Asai, and F. Kishino. Video agent: interactive autonomous agents generated from real-world creatures. In *Proceedings of the 2008 ACM symposium on Virtual reality software and technology*, pages 30–38, 2008.

[12] J.-H. Lai, C.-L. Chen, C.-C. Kao, and S.-Y. Chien. Tennis video 2.0: A new presentation of sports videos with content separation and rendering. *Journal of Visual Communication and Image Representation*, 22(3):271–283, 2011.

[13] J.-H. Lai and S.-Y. Chien. Tennis video enrichment with content layer separation and real-time rendering in sprite plane. In *Proceedings of IEEE International Workshop on Multimedia Signal Processing, MMSP 2008*, pages 672–675, 2008.

[14] J.-H. Lai, C.-C. Kao, and S.-Y. Chien. Super-resolution sprite with foreground removal. In *IEEE International Conference on Multimedia and Expo*, pages 1306–1309, 2009.

[15] A. Levin, D. Lischinski, and Y. Weiss. Colorization using optimization. *ACM Transactions on Graphics*, 23(3):689–694, 2004.

[16] D. Lowe. Distinctive image features from scale-invariant keypoint. *International Journal of Computer Vision*, 60(2):91–110, 2004.

[17] D. Mahajan, F.-C. Huang, W. Matusik, R. Ramamoorthi, and P. Belhumeur. Moving gradients: A path-based method for plausible image interpolation. *ACM Transactions on Graphics*, 28(3):42:1–42:11, 2009.

[18] K. Mikolajczyk and C. Schmid. Scale and affine invariant interest point detectors. *International Journal of Computer Vision*, pages 63–86, 2004.

[19] P. Pérez, M. Gangnet, and A. Blake. Poisson image editing. In *Proceedings of ACM SIGGRAPH 03*, pages 313–318, 2003.

[20] P. M. Phillips and G. Watson. Generalising video textures. In *Proceedings of the Theory and Practice of Computer Graphics*, pages 726–733, 2003.

[21] M.-C. Roh, B. Christmas, J. Kittler, and S.-W. Lee. Gesture spotting for low-resolution sports video annotation. *Pattern Recognition*, 41(3):1124–1137.

[22] A. Schodl and I. A. Essa. Controlled animation of video sprites. In *Proceedings of the 2002 ACM SIGGRAPH/Eurographics symposium on Computer animation*, pages 121–127, 2002.

[23] A. Schodl, R. Szeliski, D. H. Salesin, and I. Essa. Video textures. In *Proceedings of the 27th annual conference on Computer graphics and interactive techniques*, pages 489–498, 2000.

[24] S. M. Seitz and C. R. Dyer. View morphing. In *Proceedings of the 23rd annual conference on Computer graphics and interactive*, pages 21–30, 1996.

[25] J. Wang, C. Xu, E. Chng, K. Wah, and Q. Tian. Automatic replay generation for soccer video broadcasting. In *Proceedings of the 12th Annual ACM International Conference on Multimedia MULTIMEDIA '04*, pages 32–39, 2004.

[26] J. R. Wang and N. Parameswaran. Analyzing tennis tactics from broadcasting tennis video clips. In *Proceedings of the 11th International Multimedia Modelling Conference*, pages 102–106, 2005.

[27] X. Yu, C. H. Sim, J. R. Wang, and L. F. Cheong. A trajectory-based ball detection and tracking algorithm in broadcast tennis video. In *Proceedings of IEEE International Conference on Image Processing*, pages 1049–1052, 2004.

[28] G. Zhu, C. Xu, Q. Huang, W. Gao, and L. Xing. Player action recognition in broadcast tennis video with applications to semantic analysis of sports game. In *Proceedings of the 14th annual ACM international conference on Multimedia*, pages 431–440, 2006.

Celerity: A Low-Delay Multi-Party Conferencing Solution *

Xiangwen Chen
Dept. of Information Engineering
The Chinese University of Hong Kong

Minghua Chen
Dept. of Information Engineering
The Chinese University of Hong Kong

Baochun Li
Dept. of Electrical and Computer Engineering
The University of Toronto

Yao Zhao
Alcatel-Lucent

Yunnan Wu
Facebook Inc.

Jin Li
Microsoft Research

ABSTRACT

In this paper, we attempt to revisit the problem of multi-party conferencing from a practical perspective, and to rethink the design space involved in this problem. We believe that an emphasis on low end-to-end delays between any two parties in the conference is a must, and the source sending rate in a session should adapt to bandwidth availability and congestion. We present *Celerity*, a multi-party conferencing solution specifically designed to achieve our objectives. It is entirely Peer-to-Peer (P2P), and as such eliminating the cost of maintaining centrally administered servers. It is designed to deliver video with low end-to-end delays, at quality levels commensurate with available network resources over arbitrary network topologies where *bottlenecks can be anywhere in the network*. This is in contrast to commonly assumed P2P scenarios where bandwidth bottlenecks reside only at the edge of the network. The highlight in our design is a distributed and adaptive rate control protocol, that can discover and adapt to arbitrary topologies and network conditions quickly, converging to efficient link rate allocations allowed by the underlying network. In accordance with adaptive link rate control, source video encoding rates are also dynamically controlled to optimize video quality. We have implemented *Celerity* in a prototype system, and demonstrate its superior performance over existing solutions in a local experimental testbed and over the Internet.

Categories and Subject Descriptors

C.2.4 [**COMPUTER-COMMUNICATION NETWORKS**]: Distributed System—*Distributed applications*; H.4.3 [**INFORMATION SYSTEMS APPLICATIONS**]: Communications Applications—*video conferencing*

General Terms: Algorithms, Design, Experimentation, Performance

Keywords: Peer-to-peer, Multi-party video conferencing, Low delay, Utility maximization, Arbitrary network topology

1. INTRODUCTION

With the availability of front-facing cameras in high-end smartphone devices (such as the Samsung Galaxy S and the iPhone 4), notebook computers, and HDTVs, *multi-party* video conferencing, which involves more than two participants in a live conferencing session, has attracted a significant amount of interest from the industry. Skype, for example, has recently launched a monthly-paid service supporting multi-party video conferencing in its latest version (Skype 5) [1]. Skype video conferencing has also been recently supported in a range of new Skype-enabled televisions, such as the Panasonic VIERA series, so that full-screen high-definition video conferencing can be enjoyed in one's living room. We argue that these new conferencing solutions have the potential to provide an immersive human-to-human communication experience among remote participants. Such an argument has been corroborated by many industry leaders: Cisco predicts that video conferencing and tele-presence traffic will increase ten-fold between 2008-2013 [2].

While traffic flows in a live multi-party conferencing session are fundamentally represented by a multi-way communication process, today's design of multi-party video conferencing systems are engineered in practice by composing communication primitives (*e.g.*, transport protocols) over uni-directional feed-forward links, with primitive feedback mechanisms such as various forms of acknowledgments in TCP variants or custom UDP-based protocols. We believe that a high-quality protocol design must harness the full potential of the multi-way communication paradigm, and must guarantee the stringent requirements of low end-to-end delays, with the highest possible source coding rates that can be supported by dynamic network conditions over the Internet.

From the industry perspective, known designs of commercially available multi-party conferencing solutions are either largely server-based, e.g., Microsoft Office Communicator, or are separated into multiple point-to-point sessions (this approach is called Simulcast), e.g., Apple iChat. Server-based solutions are susceptible to central resource bottlenecks, and as such scalability becomes a main concern when multiple conferences are to be supported concurrently. In the Simulcast approach, each user splits its uplink bandwidth equally among all receivers and streams to each receiver separately.

*The area chair coordinating the review of this manuscript and approving it for publication was Prof. Wei Tsang Ooi.
This work was partially supported by the General Research Fund grants (Project No. 411008, 411209, 411010, and 411011) and an Area of Excellence Grant (Project No. AoE/E-02/08), all established under the University Grant Committee of the Hong Kong SAR, China, as well as two gift grants from Microsoft and Cisco.

Though simple to implement, Simulcast suffers from poor quality of service. Specifically, peers with low upload capacity are forced to use a low video rate that degrades the overall experience of the other peers.

In the academic literature, there are recently several studies on peer-to-peer (P2P) video conferencing from a utility maximization perspective [3–8]. Among them, Li *et al.* [3] and Chen *et al.* [4] may be the most related ones to this work (we call their unified approach Mutualcast). They have tried to support content distribution and multi-party video conferencing in multicast sessions, by maximizing aggregate application-specific utility and the utilization of node uplink bandwidth in P2P networks. Specific depth-1 and depth-2 tree topologies have been constructed using tree packing, and rate control was performed in each of the tree-based one-to-many sessions. However, they only considered the limited scenario where bandwidth bottlenecks reside at the edge of the network, while in practice bandwidth bottlenecks can easily reside in the core of the network [9, 10]. Further, all existing industrial and academic solutions, including Mutualcast, did not explicitly consider bounded delay in designs, and can lead to unsatisfied interactive conferencing experience.

1.1 Contribution

In this paper, we reconsider the design space in multi-party video conferencing solutions, and present *Celerity*, a new multi-party conferencing solution specifically designed to maintain low end-to-end delays while maximizing source coding rates in a session. *Celerity* has the following salient features:

- It operates in a pure P2P manner, and as such eliminating the cost of maintaining centrally administered servers.
- It can deliver video at quality levels commensurate with available network resources over *arbitrary network topologies*, while maintaining *bounded end-to-end delays*.
- It can automatically adapt to unpredictable network dynamics, such as cross traffic and abrupt link failures, allowing smooth conferencing experience.

Enabling the above features for multi-party conferencing is challenging. First, it requires a new formulation that allows systematic solution design over arbitrary network capacity constraints. In contrast, existing P2P system design works with performance guarantee commonly assume bandwidth bottlenecks reside at the edge of the network. Second, maximizing session rates subject to bounded delay is known to be NP-Complete and hard to solve approximately [11]. We take a practical approach in this paper that explores all 2-hop delay-bounded overlay trees with polynomial complexity. Third, detecting and reacting to network dynamics without *a priori* knowledge of the network conditions are non-trivial. We use both delay and loss as congestion measures and adapt the session rates with respect to both of them, allowing early detection and fast response to unpredictable network dynamics.

The highlight in our design is a distributed rate control protocol, that can discover and adapt to arbitrary topologies and network conditions quickly, converging to efficient link rate allocations allowed by the underlying network. In accordance with the adaptive link rate control, source video encoding rates are also dynamically controlled to optimize video quality in arbitrary and unpredictable underlay network conditions.

The design of *Celerity* is largely inspired by our new formulation that specifically takes into account arbitrary network capacity constraints and allows us to explore design space beyond those in existing solutions. Our formulation is overlay-link based and has a number of variables linear in the number of overlay links. This is a significant reduction as compared to the number of variables exponential in the number of overlay links in an otherwise tree-based formulation. We believe our approach is applicable to other P2P system problems, to allow solution design beyond the common assumption in P2P scenarios that the bandwidth bottlenecks reside only at the edge of the network.

Notation	Definition
$\mathcal{L}$	Set of all physical links
V	Set of conference participating nodes
E	Set of directed overlay links
C_l	Capacity of the physical link l
$a_{l,e}$	Whether overlay link e passes physical link l
$\boldsymbol{c}_m$	Overlay link rates of stream m, $\boldsymbol{c}_m = [c_{m,e}, e \in E]$
$\boldsymbol{y}$	Total overlay link traffics, $\boldsymbol{y} = \sum_{m=1}^{M} \boldsymbol{c}_m$
D	Delay bound
$R_m(\boldsymbol{c}_m, D)$	Session m's rate within the delay bound D
$q_l(z)$	Price function of violating link l's capacity constraint
p_l	Lagrange multiplier of link l's capacity constraint
$\mathcal{G}(\boldsymbol{c}, \boldsymbol{p})$	Lagrange function of variables $\boldsymbol{c}$ and $\boldsymbol{p}$

Note: we use bold symbols to denote vectors, e.g., $\boldsymbol{c} = [\boldsymbol{c}_1, \ldots, \boldsymbol{c}_M]$.

Table 1: Key notations.

We have implemented a prototype *Celerity* system using C++. By extensive experiments in a local experimental testbed and on the Internet, we demonstrate the superior performance of *Celerity* over state-of-the-art solutions Simulcast and Mutualcast.

Due to space limitation, all proofs and pseudo-codes are in our technical report [12].

2. PROBLEM FORMULATION AND CELERITY OVERVIEW

One way to design a multi-party conferencing system is to formulate its fundamental design problem, explore powerful theoretical techniques to solve the problem, and use the obtained insights to guide practical system designs. In this way, we can also be clear about potential and limitation of the designs, allowing easy system tuning and further systematic improvements. Table 1 lists the key notations used in this paper.

2.1 Settings

Consider a network modeled as a directed graph $G = (\mathcal{N}, \mathcal{L})$, where $\mathcal{N}$ is the set of all physical nodes, including conference participating nodes and other intermediate nodes such as routers, and $\mathcal{L}$ is the set of all physical links. Each link $l \in \mathcal{L}$ has a nonnegative capacity C_l and a nonnegative propagation delay d_l.

Consider a multi-party conferencing system over G. We use $V \subseteq \mathcal{N}$ to denote the set of all conference participating nodes. Every node in V is a source and at the same time a receiver for every other nodes. Thus there are totally $M \triangleq |V|$ sessions of (audio/video) streams. Each stream is generated at a source node, say v, and needs to be delivered to all the rest nodes in $V - \{v\}$, by using overlay links between any two nodes in V.

An overlay link (u, v) means u can send data to v by setting up a TCP/UDP connection, along an underlay path from u to v pre-assigned by routing protocols. Let E be the set of all directed overlay links. For all $e \in E$ and $l \in \mathcal{L}$, we define

$$a_{l,e} = \begin{cases} 1, & \text{if overlay link } e \text{ passes physical link } l; \\ 0, & \text{otherwise.} \end{cases} \quad (1)$$

The physical link capacity constraints are then expressed as

$$a_l^T y = \sum_{e \in E} a_{l,e} \sum_{m=1}^{M} c_{m,e} \le C_l, \quad \forall l \in \mathcal{L},$$

where $c_{m,e}$ denotes the rate allocated to session m on overlay link e and $a_l^T y$ describes the total overlay traffic passing through physical link l.

Remark: In our model, the capacity bottleneck can be anywhere in the network, not necessarily at the edges. This is in contrast to a common assumption made in existing P2P works that the access links of participating nodes are the only capacity bottlenecks.

2.2 Problem Formulation

In a multi-party conferencing system, each session source broadcasts its stream to all receivers over a complete overlay graph on which every link e has a rate $c_{m,e}$ and a delay $\sum_{l \in \mathcal{L}} a_{l,e} d_l$. For smooth conferencing experience, the total delay of delivering a packet from the source to any receiver, traversing one or multiple overlay links, cannot exceed a delay bound D.

A fundamental design problem is to maximize the overall conferencing experience, by properly allocating the overlay link rates to the streams subject to physical link capacity constraints. We formulate the problem as a network utility maximization problem:

$$\textbf{MP}: \quad \max_{c \ge 0} \quad \sum_{m=1}^{M} U_m\left(R_m(\boldsymbol{c}_m, D)\right) \qquad (2)$$

$$\text{s.t.} \quad a_l^T y \le C_l, \quad \forall l \in \mathcal{L}. \qquad (3)$$

The optimization variables are $\boldsymbol{c}$ and the constraints in (3) are the physical link capacity constraints.

$R_m(\boldsymbol{c}_m, D)$ denotes session m's rate that we obtain by using resource $\boldsymbol{c}_m$ *within the delay bound* D, and is a concave function of $\boldsymbol{c}_m$ as we will show in Corollary 1 in the next section.

The objective is to maximize the aggregate system utility. $U_m(R_m)$ is an increasing and strictly concave function that maps the stream rate to an application-specific utility. For example, a commonly used video quality measure Peak Signal-to-Noise Ratio (PSNR) can be modeled by using a logarithmic function as the utility [4] [1]. With these settings and observations, $U_m(R_m)$ is concave in $\boldsymbol{c}$ and the problem **MP** is a concave optimization problem.

Remarks: (i) The formulation of **MP** is an overlay link based formulation in which the number of variables per session is $|E|$ and thus at most $|V|^2$. One can write an equivalent tree-based formulation for **MP** but the number of variables per session will be *exponential* in $|E|$ and $|V|$. (ii) Existing solutions, such as Simulcast and Mutualcast, can be thought as algorithms solving special cases of the problem **MP**. For example, Simulcast can be thought as solving the problem **MP** by using only the 1-hop tree to broadcast content within a session. Mutualcast can be thought as solving a special case of the problem **MP** (with the uplinks of participating nodes being the only capacity bottleneck) by packing certain depth-1 and depth-2 trees within a session.

2.3 Celerity Overview

Celerity builds upon two main modules to maximize the system utility: (1) a *delay-bounded video delivery* module to distribute video at high rate given overlay link rates (i.e., how to compute and achieve $R_m(\boldsymbol{c}_m, D)$); (2) a *link rate control* module to determine $\boldsymbol{c}_m$.

[1]Using logarithmic functions also guarantees (weighted) proportional fairness among sessions and thus no session will starve at the optimal solution [13].

Video delivery under known link constraints: This problem is similar to the classic multicast problem, and packing spanning (or Steiner) trees at the multicast source is a popular solution. However, the unique "delay-bounded" requirement in multi-party conferencing makes the problem more challenging. We introduce a delay-bounded tree packing algorithm to tackle this problem (detailed in Section 3).

Link rate control: In principle, one can first infer the network constraints and then solve the problem **MP** centrally. However, directly inferring the constraints potentially requires knowing the entire network topology and is highly challenging. In *Celerity*, we resort to design adaptive and iterative algorithms for solving the problem **MP** in a distributed manner, without *a priori* knowledge of the network conditions (detailed in Section 4).

We high-levelly explain how *Celerity* works in a 4-party conferencing example in Fig. 1. We focus on session A, in which source A distributes its stream to receivers B, C, and D, by packing delay-bounded trees over a complete overlay graph shown in the figure. We focus on source A and one overlay link (B, C), which represents a UDP connection over an underlay path B to E to F to C. Other overlay links and other sessions are similar.

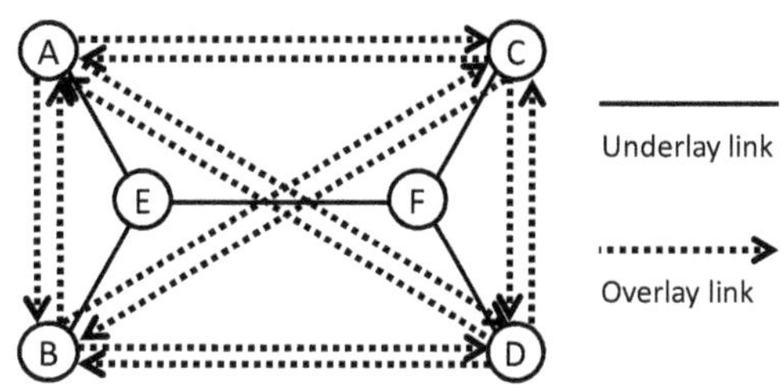

Figure 1: An illustrating example of 4-party (A, B, C, and D) conferencing over a dumbbell underlay topology. E and F are two routers. Solid lines represent underlay physical links. To make the graph easy to read, we use one solid line to represent a pair of directed physical links. Dash lines represent overlay links.

We first describe the control plane operations. For the overlay link (B, C), the head node B works with the tail node C to *periodically* adjust the session rate $c_{A,(B,C)}$ according to *Celerity*'s link rate control algorithm. Such adjustment utilizes control-plane information that source A piggybacks with data packets, and loss and delay statistics experienced by packets traveling from B to C. We show such local adjustments at every overlay link result in globally optimal session rates.

The head node B also *periodically* reports to source A the session rate $c_{A,(B,C)}$ and the end-to-end delay from B to C. Based on these reports from all overlay links, source A *periodically* packs delay-bounded trees using *Celerity*'s tree-packing algorithm, calculates necessary control-plane information, and delivers data and the control-plane information along the trees.

The data plane operations are simple. *Celerity* uses delay-bounded trees to distribute data in a session. Nodes on every tree forward packets from its upstream parent to its downstream children, following the "next-children" tree-routing information embedded in the packet header. *Celerity*'s tree-packing algorithm guarantees that (i) packets arrive at all receivers within the delay bound, and (ii) the total rate of a session m passing through an overlay link e does not exceed the allocated rate $c_{m,e}$.

In the following two sections, we first present the designs of the two main modules in *Celerity*. We then describe how they are implemented in physical peers in Section 5.

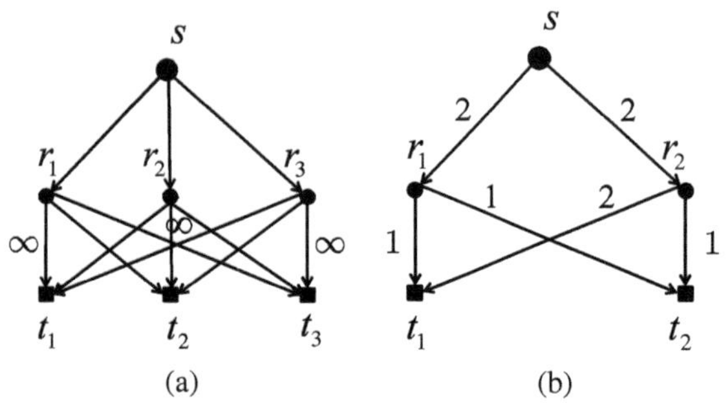

Figure 2: (a) Illustration of the directed acyclic sub-graph over which we pack delay-bounded 2-hop trees. (b) Critical cut example. Source s and its two receivers t_1, t_2 are connected over a directed graph. The number associated with a link represents its capacity.

3. PACKING DELAY-BOUNDED TREES

Given overlay link rate vector $\boldsymbol{c}_m$ and delay for every overlay link e (i.e., $\sum_{l \in \mathcal{L}} a_{l,e} d_l$), achieving the maximum broadcast/multicast stream rate under a delay bound D is a challenging problem. A general way to explore the broadcast/multicast rate under delay bounds is to pack delay-bounded Steiner trees. However, such problem is *NP*-hard [14]. Moreover, the number of delay-bounded Steiner trees to consider is in general exponential in the network size.

In this paper, we pack 2-hop delay-bounded trees in an overlay graph of session m, denoted by $\mathcal{D}_m$, to achieve a good stream rate under a delay bound. Note by graph theory notations, a 2-hop tree has a depth at most 2. Packing 2-hop trees is easy to implement. It also explores all overlay links between source and receiver and between receivers, thus trying to utilize resource efficiently. In fact, it is shown in [3, 4] that packing 2-hop multicast trees suffices to achieve the maximum multicast rate for certain P2P topologies. We elaborate our tree-packing scheme in the following.

We first define the overlay graph $\mathcal{D}_m$. Graph $\mathcal{D}_m$ is a directed acyclic graph with two layers; one example of such graph is illustrated in Fig. 2a. In this example, consider a session with a source s, three receivers $1, 2, 3$. For each receiver i, we draw two nodes, r_i and t_i, in the graph $\mathcal{D}_m$; t_i models the receiving functionality of node i and r_i models the relaying functionality of node i.

Suppose that the prescribed link bit rates are given by the vector $\boldsymbol{c}_m$, with the capacity for link (i, j) being $c_{m,(i,j)}$. Then in $\mathcal{D}_m$, the link from s to r_i has capacity $c_{m,(s,i)}$, the link from r_i to t_j (with $i \neq j$) has capacity $c_{m,(i,j)}$, and the link from r_i to t_i has infinite capacity. If the propagation delay of an edge (i, j) exceeds the delay bound, we do not include it in the graph. If the propagation delay of a two-hop path $s \to i \to j$ exceeds the delay bound, we omit the edge from r_i to t_j from the graph. As a result, every path from s to any receiver t_i in the graph has a path propagation delay within the delay bound.

Over such 2-layer sub-graph $\mathcal{D}_m$, we pack 2-hop trees connecting the source and every receiver using the greedy algorithm proposed in [15]. Below we simply describe the algorithm and more details can be found in [15].

Assuming all edges have unit-capacity and allowing multiple edges for each ordered node pair. The algorithm packs unit-capacity trees one by one. Each unit-capacity tree is constructed by greedily constructing a tree edge by edge starting from the source and augmenting towards all receivers. It is similar to the greedy tree-packing algorithm based on Prim's algorithm. The distinction lies in the rule of selecting the edge among all potential edges. The edge whose removal leads to least reduction in the multicast capacity of the residual graph is chosen in the greedy algorithm. We show an example to illustrate how the tree packing algorithm works in details in our technical report [12, Sec. 3].

The above greedy algorithm is very simple to implement and its practical implementation details are further discussed in Section 5. Utilizing the special structure of the graph $\mathcal{D}_m$, we obtain performance guarantee of the algorithm as follows.

Theorem 1. *The tree-packing algorithm in [15] achieves the minimum of the min-cuts separating the source and receivers in $\mathcal{D}_m$ and is expressed as*

$$R_m(\boldsymbol{c}_m, D) = \min_j \sum_i \min\{c_{m,(s,i)}, c_{m,(i,j)}\}. \tag{4}$$

Furthermore, the algorithm has a running time of $O(|V||E|^2)$.

Hence, our tree-packing algorithm achieves the maximum delay-bounded multicast rate over the 2-layer subgraph $\mathcal{D}_m$. The achieved rate $R_m(\boldsymbol{c}_m, D)$ is a concave function of $\boldsymbol{c}_m$ as summarized below.

Corollary 1. *The delay-bounded multicast rate $R_m(\boldsymbol{c}_m, D)$ obtained by our tree-packing algorithm is a concave function of the overlay link rates $\boldsymbol{c}_m$.*

4. OVERLAY LINK RATE CONTROL

4.1 Considering Both Delay and Loss

We revise original formulation to design our link rate control algorithm with both queuing delay and loss rate taken into account. Adapting link rates to both delay and loss allows early detection and fast response to network dynamics.

Consider the following formulation with a penalty term added into the objective function of the problem **MP**:

$$\textbf{MP}-\textbf{EQ}: \max_{c \geq 0} \quad \mathcal{U}(\boldsymbol{c}) \triangleq \sum_{m=1}^{M} U_m\left(R_m(\boldsymbol{c}_m, D)\right) - \sum_{l \in \mathcal{L}} \int_0^{\boldsymbol{a}_l^T \boldsymbol{y}} q_l(z)\, dz \tag{5}$$

$$\text{s.t.} \quad \boldsymbol{a}_l^T \boldsymbol{y} \leq C_l, \quad \forall l \in \mathcal{L}, \tag{6}$$

where $\int_0^{\boldsymbol{a}_l^T \boldsymbol{y}} q_l(z)\, dz$ is the penalty associated with violating the capacity constraint of physical link $l \in \mathcal{L}$, and we choose

$$q_l(z) \triangleq \frac{(z - C_l)^+}{z}, \tag{7}$$

where $(a)^+ = \max\{a, 0\}$. If all the constraints are satisfied, then the second term in (5) vanishes; if instead some constraints are violated, then we charge some penalty for doing so.

Remark: (i) The problem **MP-EQ** is equivalent to the original problem **MP**. Because any feasible solution $\boldsymbol{c}$ of these two problems must satisfy $\boldsymbol{a}_l^T \boldsymbol{y} \leq C_l$, and consequently the penalty term in the problem **MP-EQ** vanishes. Therefore, any optimal solution of the original problem **MP** must be an optimal solution of the problem **MP-EQ** and vice versa. (ii) It can be verified that $-\sum_{l \in \mathcal{L}} \int_0^{\boldsymbol{a}_l^T \boldsymbol{y}} q_l(z)\, dz$ is a concave function in $\boldsymbol{c}$; hence, $\mathcal{U}(\boldsymbol{c})$ is a linear combination of concave functions and is concave. However, because $R_m(\boldsymbol{c}_m, D)$ is the minimum min-cut of the overlay graph $\mathcal{D}_m$ with link rates being $\boldsymbol{c}_m$, $\mathcal{U}(\boldsymbol{c})$ is not a differentiable function [16].

We apply Lagrange dual approach to design distributed algorithms for the problem **MP-EQ**. The advantage of adopting distributed rate control algorithms in our system is that it allows robust adaption upon unpredictable network dynamics.

The Lagrange function of the problem is given by:

$$\mathcal{G}(\boldsymbol{c},\boldsymbol{p}) \triangleq \sum_{m=1}^{M} U_m\left(R_m(\boldsymbol{c}_m, D)\right) - \sum_{l\in\mathcal{L}} \int_0^{\boldsymbol{a}_l^T \boldsymbol{y}} q_l(z)\,dz - \sum_{l\in\mathcal{L}} p_l\left(\boldsymbol{a}_l^T \boldsymbol{y} - C_l\right), \quad (8)$$

where $p_l \geq 0$ is the Lagrange multiplier associated with the capacity constraint in (6) of physical link l. p_l can be interpreted as the price of using link l. Since the problem **MP-EQ** is a concave optimization problem with linear constraints, strong duality holds and there is no duality gap. Any optimal solution of the problem and one of its corresponding Lagrangian multiplier is a saddle point of $\mathcal{G}(\boldsymbol{c},\boldsymbol{p})$ and vice versa. Thus to solve the problem **MP-EQ**, it suffices to design algorithms to pursue saddle points of $\mathcal{G}(\boldsymbol{c},\boldsymbol{p})$.

4.2 A Loss-Delay Based Primal-Subgradient-Dual Algorithm

There are two issues to address in designing algorithms for pursuing saddle points of $\mathcal{G}(\boldsymbol{c},\boldsymbol{p})$. First, the utility function $\mathcal{U}(\boldsymbol{c})$ (and consequently $\mathcal{G}(\boldsymbol{c},\boldsymbol{p})$) is not everywhere differentiable. Second, $\mathcal{U}(\boldsymbol{c})$ (and consequently $\mathcal{G}(\boldsymbol{c},\boldsymbol{p})$) is not strictly concave in $\boldsymbol{c}$, thus distributed algorithms may not converge to the desired saddle points under multi-party conferencing settings [4].

To address the first concern, we use subgradient in algorithm design. To address the second concern, we provide a convergence result for our designed algorithm.

To proceed, we first compute subgradients of $\mathcal{U}(\boldsymbol{c})$. The proposition below presents a useful observation.

Proposition 1. *A subgradient of $\mathcal{U}(\boldsymbol{c})$ with respect to $c_{m,e}$ for any $e \in E$ and $m = 1, \ldots M$ is given by*

$$U_m'(R_m)\frac{\partial R_m}{\partial c_{m,e}} - \sum_{l\in\mathcal{L}} a_{l,e}\frac{(\boldsymbol{a}_l^T\boldsymbol{y} - C_l)^+}{\boldsymbol{a}_l^T\boldsymbol{y}}$$

where $\frac{\partial R_m}{\partial c_{m,e}}$ is a subgradient of $R_m(\boldsymbol{c}_m, D)$ with respect to $c_{m,e}$.

Motivated by the pioneering work of Arrow, Hurwicz, and Uzawa [17] and the followup works [18] [19], we propose to use the following *primal-subgradient-dual* algorithm to pursue the saddle point of $\mathcal{G}(\boldsymbol{c},\boldsymbol{p})$: $\forall e \epsilon M$, $m = 1, ...M$, $\forall l \epsilon \mathcal{L}$,

Primal-Subgradient-Dual Link Rate Control Algorithm:

$$c_{m,e}^{(k+1)} = c_{m,e}^{(k)} + \alpha\left[U_m'\left(R_m^{(k)}\right)\frac{\partial R_m^{(k)}}{\partial c_{m,e}} - \sum_{l\in\mathcal{L}} a_{l,e}\frac{(\boldsymbol{a}_l^T\boldsymbol{y}^{(k)} - C_l)^+}{\boldsymbol{a}_l^T\boldsymbol{y}^{(k)}} - \sum_{l\in\mathcal{L}} a_{l,e}p_l^{(k)}\right]_{c_{m,e}^{(k)}}^+ \quad (9)$$

$$p_l^{(k+1)} = p_l^{(k)} + \frac{1}{C_l}\left[\boldsymbol{a}_l^T\boldsymbol{y}^{(k)} - C_l\right]_{p_l^{(k)}}^+ \quad (10)$$

where $\alpha > 0$ represents a constant step size for all iterations, and

$$[b]_a^+ = \begin{cases} \max(0, b), & a \leq 0; \\ b, & a > 0. \end{cases}$$

We have the following observations for the algorithm in (9)-(10):

- It is known that $\sum_{l\in\mathcal{L}} a_{l,e}\frac{(\boldsymbol{a}_l^T\boldsymbol{y}-C_l)^+}{\boldsymbol{a}_l^T z}$ can be interpreted as the packet loss rate observed at overlay link e [20]. The intuitive explanation is as follows. The term $(\boldsymbol{a}_l^T\boldsymbol{y} - C_l)^+$ is the excess traffic rate offered to physical link l; thus $\frac{(\boldsymbol{a}_l^T\boldsymbol{y}-C_l)^+}{\boldsymbol{a}_l^T\boldsymbol{y}}$ models the fraction of traffic that is dropped at l. Assuming the packet loss rates are additive (which is a reasonable assumption for low packet loss rates), the total packet loss rates seen by the overlay link e is given by $\sum_{l\in\mathcal{L}} a_{l,e}\frac{(\boldsymbol{a}_l^T\boldsymbol{y}-C_l)^+}{\boldsymbol{a}_l^T\boldsymbol{y}}$.
- It is also known that p_l updating according to (10) can be interpreted as queuing delay at physical link l [21]. Intuitively, if the incoming rate $\boldsymbol{a}_l^T\boldsymbol{y} > C_l$, then it introduces an additional queuing delay of $\frac{\boldsymbol{a}_l^T\boldsymbol{y}-C_l}{C_l}$ at link l. If otherwise $\boldsymbol{a}_l^T\boldsymbol{y} \leq C_l$, then the queueing delay is reduced by an amount of $\frac{C_l-\boldsymbol{a}_l^T\boldsymbol{y}}{C_l}$ unless hitting zero. The total queuing delay observed by the overlay link e is simply the sum $\sum_{l\in\mathcal{L}} a_{l,e}p_l$.
- It turns out that the utility function, the subgradients, packet loss rate and queuing delay are sufficient statistics to update $c_{m,e}$ independently of the updates of other link rates. This way, we can solve the problem **MP-EQ** without knowing the physical network topology and physical link capacities.

The algorithm in (9)-(10) is similar to the standard primal-dual algorithm, but since $\mathcal{U}(\boldsymbol{c})$ is not differentiable everywhere, we use subgradient instead of gradient in updating the overlay link rates $\boldsymbol{c}$. If we fix the dual variables $\boldsymbol{p}$, then the algorithm in (9) corresponds to the standard subgradient method [22]. It maximizes a non-differentiable function in a way similar to gradient methods for differentiable functions — in each step, the variables are updated in the direction of a subgradient. However, such a direction may not be an ascent direction; instead, the subgradient method relies on a different property. If the variable takes a sufficiently small step along the direction of a subgradient, then the new point is closer to the set of optimal solutions.

Establishing convergence of subgradient algorithms for saddle-point optimization is in general challenging [18]. We explore convergence properties for our primal-subgradient-dual algorithm in the following theorem.

Theorem 2. *Let $(\boldsymbol{c}^*, \boldsymbol{p}^*)$ be a saddle point of $\mathcal{G}(\boldsymbol{c},\boldsymbol{p})$, and $\bar{\mathcal{G}}^{(k)}$ be the average function value obtained by the algorithm in (9)-(10) after k iterations:*

$$\bar{\mathcal{G}}^{(k)} \triangleq \frac{1}{k}\sum_{i=0}^{k-1}\mathcal{G}\left(\boldsymbol{c}^{(k)}, \boldsymbol{p}^{(k)}\right).$$

Suppose $\left|U_m'(R_m(\boldsymbol{c}_m))\right| \leq \bar{U}$, $\forall m = 1, \ldots, M$, where $\bar{U}$ is a constant, then we have

$$-\frac{B_1}{2\alpha k} - \frac{\Delta^2}{2}\alpha \leq \bar{\mathcal{G}}^{(k)} - \mathcal{G}(\boldsymbol{c}^*, \boldsymbol{p}^*) \leq \frac{B_2}{2k} + \frac{\Delta^2}{2}\max_{l\in\mathcal{L}} C_l^{-1},$$

where $B_1 = \left\|\boldsymbol{c}^{(0)} - \boldsymbol{c}^*\right\|^2$ and $B_2 = \left[\boldsymbol{p}^{(0)} - \boldsymbol{p}^*\right]^T diag\left(C_l, l \in \mathcal{L}\right)\left[\boldsymbol{p}^{(0)} - \boldsymbol{p}^*\right]$ are two positive distances depending on $(\boldsymbol{c}^{(0)}, \boldsymbol{p}^{(0)})$, and Δ is a positive constant depending on $\bar{U}$ and $(\boldsymbol{c}^{(0)}, \boldsymbol{p}^{(0)})$.

Remarks: (i) The results bound the time-average Lagrange function value obtained by the algorithm to the optimal in terms of distances of the initial iterates $(\boldsymbol{c}^{(0)}, \boldsymbol{p}^{(0)})$ to a saddle point. In particular, the averaged function values $\bar{\mathcal{G}}^{(k)}$ converge to the saddle point value $\mathcal{G}(\boldsymbol{c}^*, \boldsymbol{p}^*)$ within a gap of $\max\left(\alpha, \max_{l\in\mathcal{L}} C_l^{-1}\right)\frac{\Delta^2}{2}$, at a rate of $1/k$. (ii) The requirement of the utility function is easy to satisfied; one example is $U_m(z) = \log(z + \epsilon)$ with $\epsilon > 0$. (iii) Our results generalize the one in [18] in the sense that the result in [18] only applies to the case of uniform step size, while we allow different p_l to update with different step size $\frac{1}{C_l}$, which is critical for p_l to be interpreted as queuing delay and thus practically measurable. Our results also have less stringent requirement on the utility function than the one in [18]. (iv) Although the results may not warranty convergence in the strict sense, our experiments over LAN testbed and on the Internet in Section 6 show the algorithm quickly stabilizes around optimal operating points. Obtaining stronger convergence results that confirm our practical observations are of great interests and is left for future work.

4.3 Computing Subgradients of $R_m(\boldsymbol{c}_m, D)$

A key to implementing the Primal-Subgradient-Dual algorithm is to obtain subgradients of $R_m(\boldsymbol{c}_m, D)$. We first present some preliminaries on subgradients, as well as concepts for computing subgradients for $R_m(\boldsymbol{c}_m, D)$.

Definition 1. *Given a convex function f, a vector ξ is said to be a subgradient of f at $x \in$ **dom**f if*

$$f(x') \geq f(x) + \xi^T(x' - x), \forall x' \in \mathbf{dom} f,$$

where **dom**$f = \{x \in \mathbf{R}^n \| |f(x)| < \infty\}$ *is the domain of f.*

For a concave function f, $-f$ is a convex function. A vector ξ is said to be a subgradient of f at x if $-\xi$ is a subgradient of $-f$.

Next, we define the notion of a *critical cut*. For session m, let its source be s_m and receiver set be $V_m \subset V - \{s_m\}$. A partition of the vertex set, $V = Z \cup \bar{Z}$ with $s_m \in Z$ and $t \in \bar{Z}$ for some $t \in V_m$, determines an s_m-t-cut. Define

$$\delta(Z) \triangleq \left\{(i, j) \in E | i \in Z, j \in \bar{Z}\right\}$$

be the set of overlay links originating from nodes in set Z and going into nodes in set $\bar{Z}$. Define the capacity of cut $(Z, \bar{Z})$ as the sum capacity of the links in $\delta(Z)$:

$$\rho(Z) \triangleq \sum_{e \in \delta(Z)} c_{m,e}.$$

Definition 2. *For session m, a cut $(Z, \bar{Z})$ is an s_m-V_m critical cut if it separates s_m and any of its receivers and $\rho(Z) = R_m(\boldsymbol{c}_m, D)$.*

We show an example to illustrate the concept of critical cut. In Fig. 2b, s is a source, and t_1, t_2 are its two receivers. The minimum of the min-cuts among the receivers is 2. For the cut $(\{s, r_1, r_2, t_1\}, \{t_2\})$, its $\delta(\{s, r_1, r_2, t_1\})$ contains links (r_1, t_2) and (r_2, t_2), each having capacity one. Thus the cut $(\{s, r_1, r_2, t_1\}, \{t_2\})$ has a capacity of 2 and it is an $s - (t_1, t_2)$ critical cut.

With necessary preliminaries, we turn to compute subgradients of $R_m(\boldsymbol{c}_m, D)$. Since $R_m(\boldsymbol{c}_m, D)$ is the minimum min-cut of s_m and its receivers over the overlay graph $\mathcal{D}_m$, it is known that one of its subgradients can be computed in the following way [16].

- Find an s_m-V_m critical cut for session m, denote it as $(Z, \bar{Z})$. Note there can be multiple s_m-V_m critical cuts in graph $\mathcal{D}_m$, and it is sufficient to find any one of them.

- A subgradient of $R_m(\boldsymbol{c}_m, D)$ with respect to $c_{m,e}$ is given by

$$\frac{\partial R_m(\boldsymbol{c}_m, D)}{\partial c_{m,e}} = \begin{cases} 1, & \text{if } e \in \delta(Z); \\ 0, & \text{otherwise.} \end{cases} \tag{11}$$

5. PRACTICAL IMPLEMENTATION

Using the asynchronous networking paradigm supported by the asynchronous I/O library (called `asio`) in the `Boost` C++ library, we have implemented a prototype of *Celerity* with about 17,000 lines of code in C++.

Celerity consists of three main functional components: link rate control module, tree-packing and critical cut calculation module, and data multicast engine. Fig. 3 describes the relationship between these components and where they physically reside.

In the following, we describe the functionality implemented by peers, some critical implementations, and operation overhead.

5.1 Peer Functionality

In our implementation, all peers perform the following functions:

- Peers in every broadcast tree forward packets from its upstream parent to its downstream children. Sufficient information about the children is embedded in the packet header, for a packet to become "self-routing" from the source to all leaf nodes in a tree.

- Every 200 ms, each peer calculates the loss rate and queuing delay of its incoming links and updates the rates of these links based on the link rate control algorithm. The peer then sends the updated rates to the corresponding senders to take effect.

- Every 300 ms, each peer sends the link state (including allocated rate and Round Trip Time) of all its outgoing links for each session to the session source.

Upon receiving link states from all the links, the source of each session uses the received link rates and the delay information to pack a new set of delay-bounded trees, and starts transmitting session packets along these trees. We set the delay bound to be 200 ms when packing delay-bounded trees in our implementation. When a source packs delay-bounded trees, it also calculates one critical cut and the derivative of the utility for its session based on the allocated link rates. The source embeds the information about the critical cut and the derivative of the utility in the header of outgoing packets. When these packets are received, a peer learns the derivative of the utility and whether a link belongs to the critical cut or not; it then adjusts the link rate accordingly.

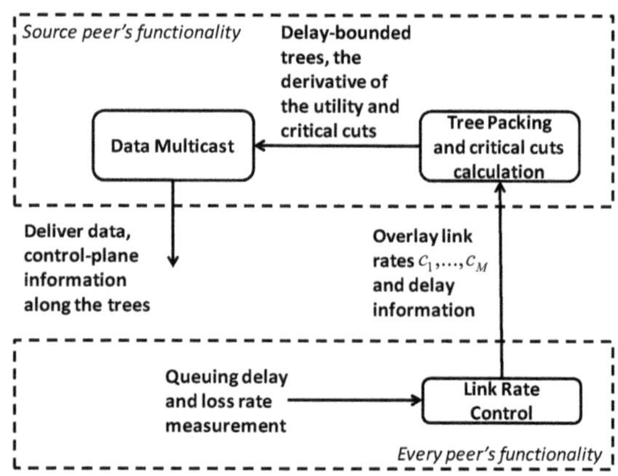

Figure 3: System architecture of *Celerity*.

5.2 Critical Cut Calculation

The calculation of critical cuts, i.e., the subgradient of $R_m(\boldsymbol{c}_m, D)$, is by the source of each session. It is the key to our implementation of the primal-subgradient-dual algorithm. There can be multiple critical cuts in one session, but it is sufficient to find any one of them. After the source collects the allocated session rates from all overlay links, it calculates the min-cut from itself to every receiver, and records the min-cut. Then the source compares the capacities of these min-cuts; the cut with the smallest capacity is a critical cut.

5.3 Utility Function

With respect to the utility function in our implementation, the PSNR (peak signal-to-noise ratio) metric is the de facto standard criterion to provide objective quality evaluation in video processing. The PSNR of a video stream coded at a rate z can be approximated by a logarithmic function $\beta \log(z + \delta)$ [4], in which a higher β represents videos with a larger amount of motion. δ is a small positive constant to ensure the function has a bounded derivative for $z \geq 0$. Due to this observation, we use a logarithmic utility function in our implementation.

5.4 Opportunistic Local Loss Recovery

Providing effective loss recovery in a delay-bounded reliable broadcast scenario, such as multi-party conferencing, is known to be challenging [23]. It is hard for error control coding to work efficiently, since different receivers in a session may experience different loss rates and thus choosing proper coding parameters to avoid unnecessary waste of throughput is non-trivial. If re-broadcasting the lost-packets is in use, it introduces additional delay and may cause packets missing deadlines and become useless.

In our implementation, we use network coding [23] [24] to allow opportunistic local loss recovery. For each overlay link e, if the trees of a session m do not exhaust $c_{m,e}$, the overlay-link rate dedicated for the session, then we send coded packets (i.e., linear combination of received packets of corresponding session) over such link e. As such, receiver of the overlay link e can recover the packets that are lost on link e locally by using the network coded packets. This way, Celerity provides certain flexible local loss recovery capability without incurring delay due to retransmission.

5.5 Fast Bootstrapping

Similar to TCP's Slow Start strategy, we implement a method in *Celerity* called "quick start" to quickly ramp up the session rates during conference initialization stage. The purpose is to bootstrap the system to close-to-optimal operating points when the conference just starts, during which period peers are joining the conference and nothing significant is going on. We achieve this by using large β in the utility functions and large step sizes in link rate adaptation during the first 30 seconds. After the initialization stage, we reset β and the step sizes to proper values and allow our system converge gradually, avoiding unnecessary performance fluctuation.

5.6 Operation Overhead

There are two types of overhead in *Celerity*: (i) *packet overhead*: each application-layer packet has a 46-byte header, containing critical cut information, derivative of the utility, packet sequence number, coding vector, and timestamp. (ii) *link-rate control and link-state report overhead*: every 200 ms, each peer adjusts the rates of its incoming links and sends them to their corresponding upstream senders. In our implementation, such rate-control overhead is 0.2 kbps per link per session. For the link state report overhead, each peer sends the link state of all its outgoing links for each session to the source of the session every 300 ms. In our implementation, for each peer, such link-state report overhead is 0.158 kbps per link per session. In Section 6.2, we report an overall operational overhead of 3.9% in our 4-party Internet experiment.

6. EXPERIMENTS

We evaluate our prototype *Celerity* system over a LAN testbed as well as over the Internet. The LAN experiments allow us to (i) stress-test *Celerity* under various network conditions; (ii) see whether *Celerity* meets the design goal – delivering high delay-bounded throughput and automatically adapting to dynamics in the network; (iii) demonstrate the fundamental performance gains over existing solutions, thus justifying our theory-inspired design.

The Internet experiments allow us to further access *Celerity*'s superior performance over existing solutions in the real world.

6.1 LAN Testbed Experiments

We evaluate *Celerity* over a LAN testbed illustrated in Fig. 4, where four PC nodes (A, B, C, D) communicate over a LAN dumbbell topology. The dumbbell topology represents a popular scenario of multi-party conferencing between branch offices. It is also a "tough" topology – existing approaches, such as Simulcast and Mutualcast, fail to efficiently utilize the bottleneck bandwidth and optimize system performance.

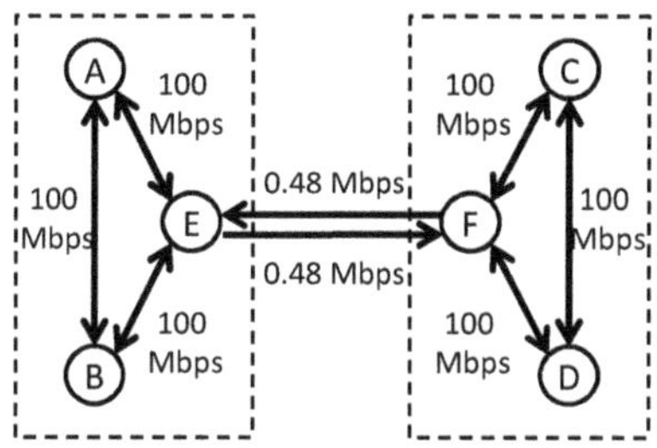

Figure 4: The "tough" dumbbell topology of the experimental testbed. Two conference participating nodes A and B are in one "office" and another twos nodes C and D are in a different "office". The two "offices" are connected by directed links between gateway nodes E and F, each link has a capacity of 0.48 Mbps. Link propagation delays are negligible.

In our experiments, all four nodes run *Celerity*. We run a four-party conference for 1000 seconds and evaluate the system performance. In order to evaluate *Celerity*'s performance in the presence of network dynamics, we reduce cross traffic and introduce link failures during the experiment. In particular, we introduce an 80kpbs cross-traffic from node E to node F between the 300th second and the 500th second, reducing the available bandwidth between E and F from 480 kbps to 400 kbps. Further, starting from the 700th second, we disconnect the physical link between A and E; this corresponds to a practical situation where node A suddenly cannot directly communicate with nodes outside the "office" due to middleware or configuration errors at the gateway E.

Figs. 6a-6d show the sending rate of each session (one session originates from one node to all other three nodes). For comparison, we also show the maximum achievable rates by Simulcast and Mutualcast, as well as the optimal sending rate of each session calculated by solving the problem in (2)-(3) using a central solver. Fig. 6e shows the utility obtained by *Celerity* and its comparison to the optimal. Fig. 6f shows the average end-to-end delay and packet loss rate of session A. Delay and loss performance of other sessions are similar to those of session A.

In the following, we explain the results according to three different experiment stages.

6.1.1 Absence of Network Dynamics

We first look at the first 300 seconds when there is no cross traffic or link failure. In this time period, the experimental settings are symmetric for all participating peers; thus the optimal sending rate for each session is 240 kbps.

As seen in Figs. 6a-6d, *Celerity* demonstrates fast convergence: the sending rate of each session quickly ramps up to 95% to the optimal within 50 seconds. Fig. 6e shows that *Celerity* quickly

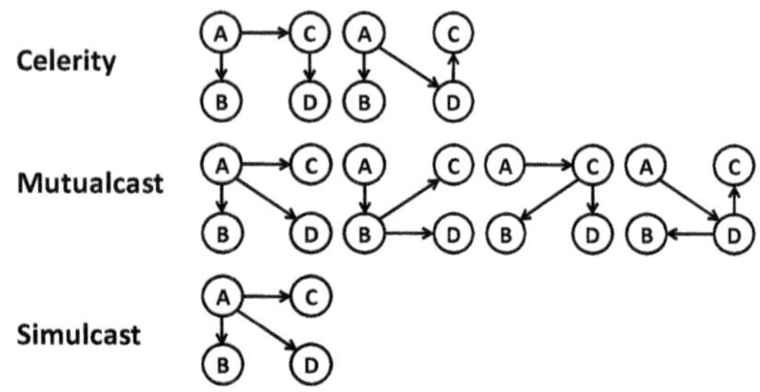

Figure 5: Session *A*'s trees used by *Celerity* (upon convergence), Mutualcast and Simulcast in the dumbbell topology, in the absence of network dynamics.

achieves a close-to-optimal utility. These observations indicate any other solution can at most outperform *Celerity* by a small margin.

As a comparison, we also plot the theoretical maximum rates achievable by Simulcast and Mutualcast in Figs. 6a-6d. We observe that within 20 seconds, our system already outperforms the maximum rates of Simulcast and Mutualcast.

Upon convergence, *Celerity* achieves sending rates that nearly double the maximum rate achievable by Simulcast and Mutualcast. This significant gain is due to that *Celerity* can utilize the bottleneck resource more efficiently, as explained below.

In Fig. 5, we show the trees for session *A* that are used by *Celerity*, Mutualcast and Simulcast in the dumbbell topology. As seen, Simulcast and Mutualcast only explore 2-hop trees satisfying certain structure, limiting their capability of utilizing network capacity efficiently. In particular, their trees consumes the bottleneck link resource twice, thus to deliver one-bit of information it consumes two-bit of bottleneck link capacity. For instance, the tree used by Simulcast has two branches $A \rightarrow C$ and $A \rightarrow D$ passing through the bottleneck links between *E* and *F*, consuming twice the critical resource. Consequently, the maximum achievable rates of Simulcast and Mutualcast are all 120 kbps. In contrast, *Celerity* explores all 2-hop delay-bounded trees, and upon convergence utilizes the trees that only consume bottleneck link bandwidth once, achieving rates that are close to the optimal of 240 kbps.

Fig. 6f shows the average end-to-end delay and packet loss rate of session *A*. As seen, the loss rate and delay are high initially, but decrease and stabilize to small values afterwards. The high loss rate and delay are due to *Celerity* increasing the rates aggressively during the initialization stage, in order to bootstrap the conference and explore network resource limits. *Celerity* quickly learns and adapts to the network topology, ending up with using cost-effective trees to deliver data. After the initialization stage, *Celerity* adapts and converges gradually, avoiding unnecessary performance fluctuation that deteriorates user experience. By adapting to both delay and loss, we achieve low loss rate upon convergence as compared to the case when only loss is taken into account [25].

6.1.2 Cross Traffic

Between the 300th second and the 500th second, we introduce an 80kpbs cross-traffic from node *E* to node *F*. Consequently, the available bottleneck bandwidth between *E* and *F* decreases from 480 kbps to 400 kbps. We calculate the optimal sending rates during this time period to be 200 kbps for sessions *A* and *B*, and remain 240 kbps for sessions *C* and *D*.

Seen in Figs. 6a-6d, *Celerity* quickly adapts to the bottleneck bandwidth reduction. *Celerity*'s adaptation is expected from its design, which infers from loss and delay the available resource and adapt accordingly. From Fig. 6f, we can see a spike in session *A*'s packet loss rate around 300th second, at which time the available bottleneck bandwidth reduces. The link rate control modules in *Celerity* senses this increased loss rate, adjusts, and reports the reduced (overlay) link rates to node *A*. Upon receiving the reports, the tree-packing module in *Celerity* adjusts the source sending rate accordingly, adapting the system to a new close-to-optimal operating point. At 500th second, the cross traffic is removed and the available bottleneck bandwidth between *E* and *F* restores to 480kbps. *Celerity* also quickly learns this change and adapts to operate at the original point, evident in Figs. 6a-6b.

6.1.3 Link Failure

Between the 700th second and the 1000th second, we disconnect the physical link between *A* and *E*. Consequently, node *A* cannot use the 2-hop threes with node *C* (*D*) being intermediate nodes; similarly node *C* (*D*) cannot use the 2-hop threes with node *A* being intermediate nodes. They can, however, still use the trees with node *B* as intermediate nodes. We compute the theoretical optimal sending rates during this time period to be 240 kbps for all sessions.

We observe from Fig. 6a that node *A*'s sending rate first drops immediately upon link failure, then quickly adapts to the new operating point of around 120 kbps, only half of the theoretical optimal. This is because *Celerity* only explores 2-hop trees for content delivery, while in this case 3-hop trees (e.g., $A \rightarrow B \rightarrow C \rightarrow D$) are needed to achieve the optimal. It is of great interest to explore beyond this 2-hop tree-packing limitation to further improve the performance without incurring excessive overhead.

In Figs. 6d, we observe session *D*'s rate first drops and then climbs back. This is because session *D happens* to use trees with node *A* being an intermediate node right before the link failure. The failure breaks these trees, and causes session *D*'s rate to drop dramatically. *Celerity* adapts and switches to use trees with node *B* as the intermediate node. Consequently, session *D*'s rate gradually restores to around the optimal. This observation shows the excellent adaptability of *Celerity* to abrupt network condition changes.

As a comparison, we observe that Simulcast's maximum achievable rates of session *A*, *C*, and *D* all drop to zero upon the link failure. This is because there is no direct overlay link between *A* and *C* (*D*) after the link failure. Consequently, Simulcast is not able to broadcast the source's content to all the receivers in these sessions, resulting in zero session rates.

6.2 Internet Experiments

Beside the prototype *Celerity* system, we also implement two prototype systems of Simulcast and Mutualcast, respectively. Both *Celerity* and Mutualcast use the same log utility functions in their rate control modules. We evaluate the performance of these systems in a four-party conferencing scenario over the Internet.

We use four PC nodes that spread two continents and tree countries to form the conferencing scenario. Two of the PC nodes are in Hong Kong, one is in Redmond, Washington, US, and the last one is in Toronto, Canada. This setting represents a common global multi-party conferencing scenario.

We run multiple 15-minute four-party conferences using the prototype systems, in a one-by-one and interleaving manner. We select one representative run for each system, and summarize their performance in Fig. 7.

Figs. 7a-7d show the rate performance of each session. As seen, all the session rates in *Celerity* quickly ramp up to near-stable values within 50 seconds, and outperforms Simulcast within 10 seconds. Upon stabilization, *Celerity* achieves the best throughput performance among the three systems and Simulcast is the worst. For instance, all the session rates in *Celerity* is 2x of those in Simulcast

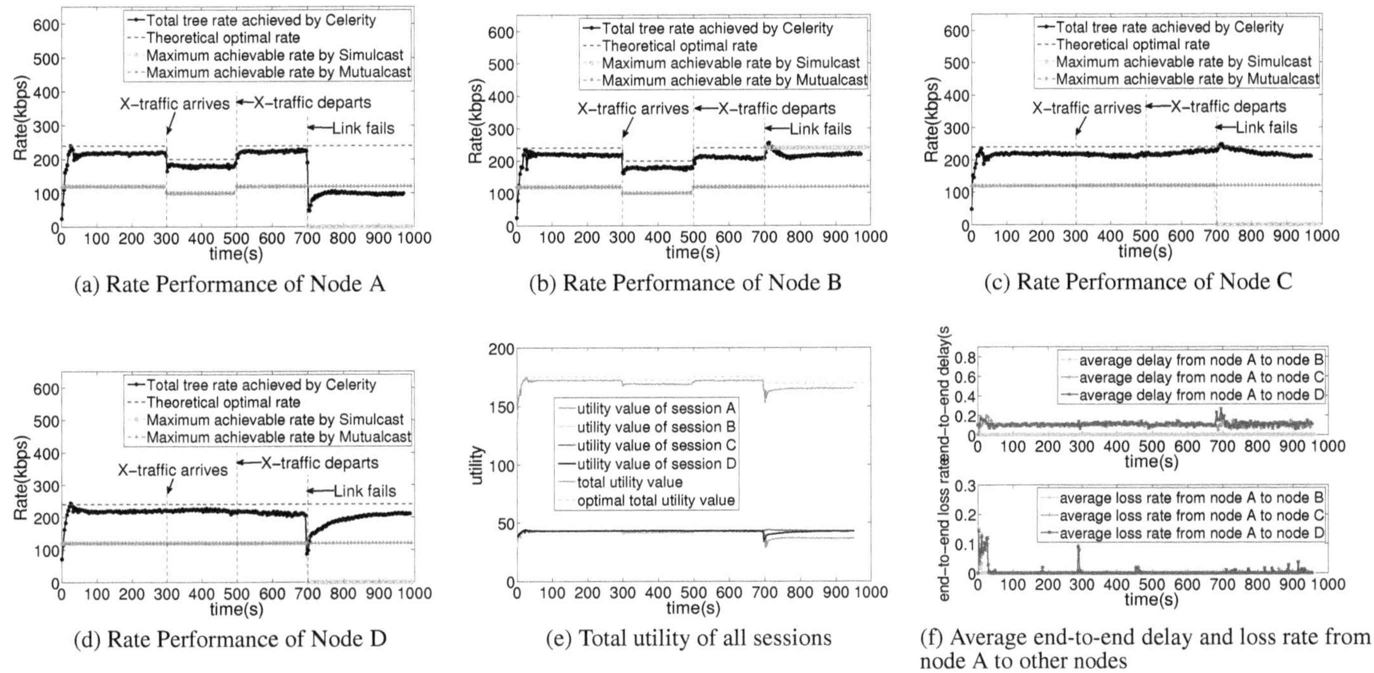

(a) Rate Performance of Node A

(b) Rate Performance of Node B

(c) Rate Performance of Node C

(d) Rate Performance of Node D

(e) Total utility of all sessions

(f) Average end-to-end delay and loss rate from node A to other nodes

Figure 6: Performance of *Celerity* over a dumbbell LAN testbed. (a)-(d): Sending rates and receiving rates of individual sessions. (e): Utility value achieved compared to the optimum. (f): End-to-end delay and loss rate of session *A*.

and Mutualcast, except in session C where Mutualcast is able to achieve a higher rate than *Celerity*.

We further observe *Celerity*'s superior performance in Fig. 7e, which shows the aggregate session rates, and in Fig. 7f, which shows the total achieved utilities. In both statistics, *Celerity* outperforms the other two systems by a significant margin. Specifically, the aggregate session rate achieved by *Celerity* is 2.5x of that achieved by Simulcast, and is 1.8x of that achieved by Mutualcast.

These results show that our theory-inspired solution *Celerity* can allocate the available network resource to best optimize the system performance. Mutualcast aims at similar objective but only works the best in scenarios where bandwidth bottlenecks reside only at the edge of the network [4].

Figs. 7g-7i show the average end-to-end loss rate and delay from source to receivers for session *A*, session *C* and session *D*. The results for session *B* is very similar to session *A* and is not included here. As seen, the average end-to-end delays of all sessions are within 200 ms, which is our preset delay bound for effective interactive conferencing experience. The average end-to-end loss rate for all sessions are at most 1%-2% upon system stabilization.

The overall operation overhead of *Celerity* in the 4-party Internet experiment is around 3.9%. In particular, the packet overhead accounts for 3.4%, and the link-rate control and link-state report overhead is around 0.5%.

7. CONCLUDING REMARKS

With the proliferation of front-facing cameras on mobile devices, multi-party video conferencing will soon become an utility that both businesses and consumers would find useful. With *Celerity*, we attempt to bridge the long-standing gap between the bit rate of a video source and the highest possible delay-bounded broadcasting rate that can be accommodated by the Internet where *the bandwidth bottlenecks can be anywhere in the network*. This paper reports *Celerity* solution as a first step in making this vision a reality: by combining a polynomial-time tree packing algorithm on the source and an adaptive rate control along each overlay link, we are able to maximize the source rates without any *a priori* knowledge of the underlying physical topology in the Internet. *Celerity* has been implemented in a prototype system, and extensive experimental results in a "tough" dumbbell LAN testbed and on the Internet demonstrate *Celerity*'s superior performance over the state-of-the-art solution Simulcast and Mutualcast.

As future work, we plan to explore source rate control mechanisms beyond the 2-hop tree-packing limitation in *Celerity* to further improve its performance without incurring excessive overhead.

8. REFERENCES

[1] Skype, "http://www.skype.com/intl/en-us/home."

[2] Cisco, "http://newsroom.cisco.com/dlls/2010/prod_111510c.html."

[3] J. Li, P. A. Chou, and C. Zhang, "Mutualcast: an efficient mechanism for content distribution in a P2P network," in *Proc. ACM SIGCOMM Asia Workshop*, Beijing, 2005.

[4] M. Chen, M. Ponec, S. Sengupta, J. Li, and P. A. Chou, "Utility maximization in peer-to-peer systems," in *Proc. ACM SIGMETRICS*, Annapolis, MD, 2008.

[5] İ. E. Akkuş, Ö. Özkasap, and M. Civanlar, "Peer-to-peer multipoint video conferencing with layered video," *Journal of Network and Computer Applications*, vol. 34, no. 1, pp. 137–150, 2011.

[6] M. Ponec, S. Sengupta, M. Chen, J. Li, and P. Chou, "Multi-rate peer-to-peer video conferencing: A distributed approach using scalable coding," in *IEEE International Conference on Multimedia and Expo*, New York, 2009.

[7] ——, "Optimizing Multi-rate Peer-to-Peer Video Conferencing Applications," *IEEE Trans. on Multimedia*, 2011.

[8] C. Liang, M. Zhao, and Y. Liu, "Optimal Resource Allocation in Multi-Source Multi-Swarm P2P Video Conferencing Swarms," *accepted for publication in IEEE/ACM Trans. on Networking*, 2011.

[9] A. Akella, S. Seshan, and A. Shaikh, "An empirical evaluation of

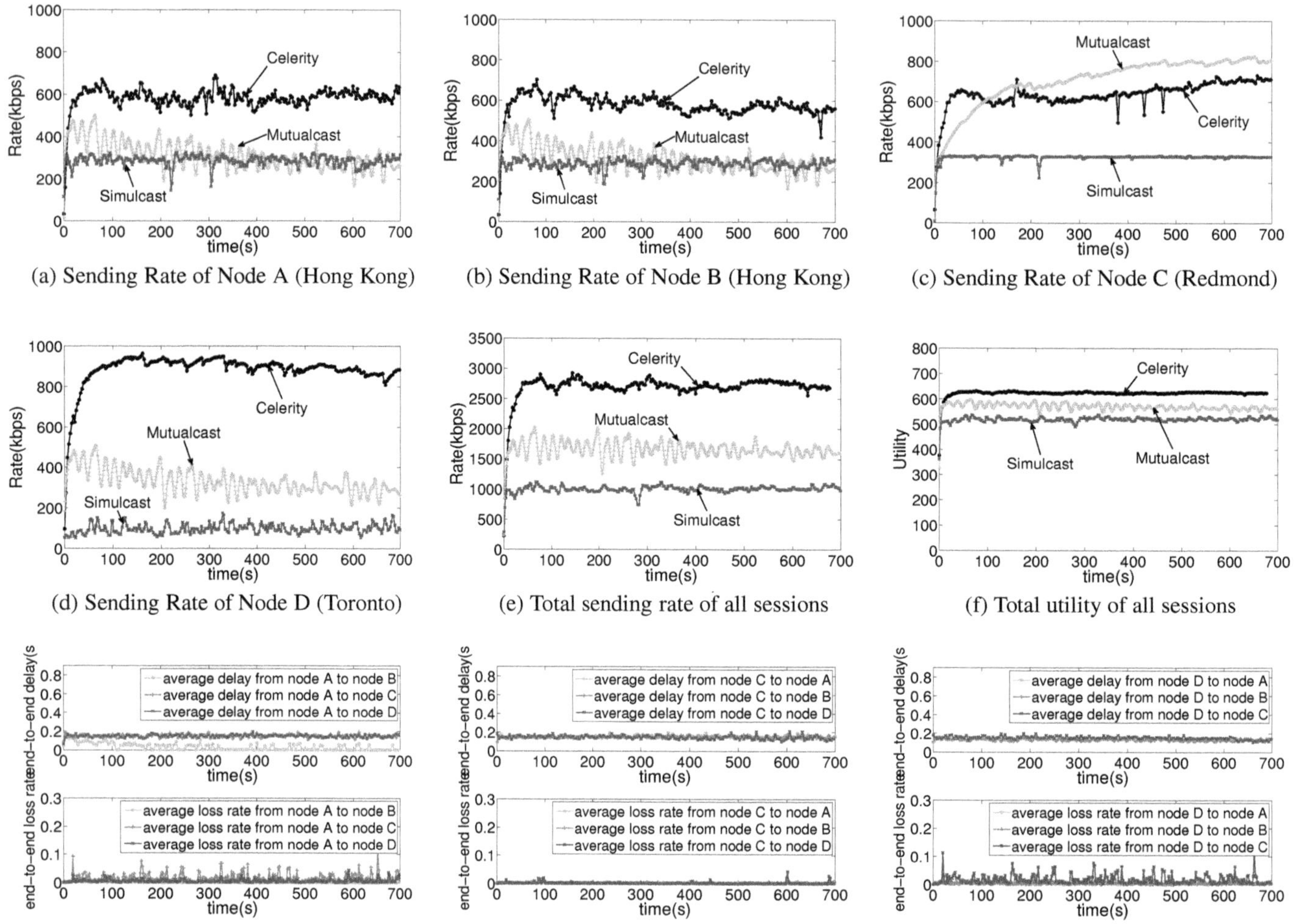

(a) Sending Rate of Node A (Hong Kong) (b) Sending Rate of Node B (Hong Kong) (c) Sending Rate of Node C (Redmond)

(d) Sending Rate of Node D (Toronto) (e) Total sending rate of all sessions (f) Total utility of all sessions

(g) Average end-to-end delay and loss rate from node A to other nodes (h) Average end-to-end delay and loss rate from node C to other nodes (i) Average end-to-end delay and loss rate from node D to other nodes

Figure 7: Performance of four-party conferences over the Internet, running prototype systems of *Celerity*, Simulcast, and the scheme in [4]. (a)-(d): Throughput of individual sessions. (e): Total throughput of all sessions. (f): Utility achieved by different systems. (g)-(h): End-to-end delay and loss rate of session A, C, and D for the *Celerity* system.

wide-area internet bottlenecks," in *Proc. of the 3rd Internet Measurement Conference*, 2003.

[10] N. Hu, L. E. Li, Z. M. Mao, P. Steenkiste, and J. Wang, "Locating internet bottlenecks: Algorithms, measurements, and implications," in *Proc. of ACM SIGCOMM*, 2004.

[11] V. Vazirani, *Approximation algorithms*. Springer Verlag, 2001.

[12] X. Chen, M. Chen, B. Li, Y. Zhao, Y. Wu, and J. Li, "Celerity: A low-delay multi-party conferencing solution," The Chinese University of Hong Kong, Hong Kong, Tech. Rep., 2011. [Online]. Available: http://arxiv.org/abs/1107.1138

[13] J. Mo and J. Walrand, "Fair end-to-end window-based congestion control," *IEEE/ACM Trans. Netw.*, no. 5, pp. 556 – 567, Oct. 2001.

[14] L. Guo and I. Matta, "QDMR: An efficient QoS dependent multicast routing algorithm," in *Proc. IEEE Real-Time Technology and Applications Symposium*, Canada, 1999.

[15] L. Lovasz, "On two minimax theorems in graph theory," *Journal of Combinatorial Theory, Series B*, vol. 21, no. 2, pp. 96–103, 1976.

[16] Y. Wu, M. Chiang, and S. Kung, "Distributed utility maximization for network coding based multicasting: A critical cut approach," in *Proc. IEEE NetCod 2006*, 2006.

[17] K. Arrow, L. Hurwicz, H. Uzawa, and H. Chenery, *Studies in linear and non-linear programming*. Stanford university press, 1958.

[18] A. Nedić and A. Ozdaglar, "Subgradient methods for saddle-point problems," *Journal of optimization theory and applications*, vol. 142, no. 1, pp. 205–228, 2009.

[19] R. Bruck, "On the weak convergence of an ergodic iteration for the solution of variational inequalities for monotone operators in Hilbert space," *Journal of Mathematical Analysis and Applications*, vol. 61, no. 1, pp. 159–164, 1977.

[20] F. Kelly, "Fairness and stability of end-to-end congestion control," *European Journal of Control*, vol. 9, no. 2-3, pp. 159–176, 2003.

[21] S. H. Low, L. Peterson, and L. Wang, "Understanding vegas: A duality model," *Journal of ACM*, vol. 49, no. 2, pp. 207–235, 2002.

[22] D. P. Bertsekas, *Nonlinear programming*. Athena Scientific Belmont, MA, 1999.

[23] J. Park, M. Gerla, D. Lun, Y. Yi, and M. Medard, "Codecast: a network-coding-based ad hoc multicast protocol," *Wireless Communications, IEEE*, vol. 13, no. 5, pp. 76–81, 2006.

[24] R. Ahlswede, N. Cai, S. Li, and R. Yeung, "Network information flow," *IEEE Trans. on Information Theory*, vol. 46, no. 4, pp. 1204–1216, 2000.

[25] X. Chen, M. Chen, B. Li, Y. Zhao, Y. Wu, and J. Li, "Celerity: Towards low-delay multi-party conferencing over arbitrary network topologies," in *ACM NOSSDAV*, 2011.

Contextual Synonym Dictionary for Visual Object Retrieval*

Wenbin Tang[†‡§†], Rui Cai[†], Zhiwei Li[†], and Lei Zhang[†]
[†]Microsoft Research Asia
[‡]Dept. of Computer Science and Technology, Tsinghua University
[§]Tsinghua National Laboratory for Information Science and Technology
tangwb06@gmail.com {ruicai, zli, leizhang}@microsoft.com

ABSTRACT

In this paper, we study the problem of visual object retrieval by introducing a dictionary of contextual synonyms to narrow down the semantic gap in visual word quantization. The basic idea is to expand a visual word in the query image with its synonyms to boost the retrieval recall. Unlike the existing work such as soft-quantization, which only focuses on the Euclidean (l_2) distance in descriptor space, we utilize the visual words which are more likely to describe visual objects with the same semantic meaning by identifying the words with similar contextual distributions (*i.e.* contextual synonyms). We describe the contextual distribution of a visual word using the statistics of both co-occurrence and spatial information averaged over all the image patches having this visual word, and propose an efficient system implementation to construct the contextual synonym dictionary for a large visual vocabulary. The whole construction process is unsupervised and the synonym dictionary can be naturally integrated into a standard bag-of-feature image retrieval system. Experimental results on several benchmark datasets are quite promising. The contextual synonym dictionary-based expansion consistently outperforms the l_2 distance-based soft-quantization, and advances the state-of-the-art performance remarkably.

Categories and Subject Descriptors

I.2.10 [**Vision and Scene Understanding**]: Vision

General Terms

Algorithms, Experimentation, Performance

Keywords

Bag-of-word, object retrieval, visual synonym dictionary, query expansion

*Area chair: Tat-Seng Chua

[†]This work was performed at Microsoft Research Asia.

MM'11, November 28–December 1, 2011, Scotsdale, Arizona, USA.

1. INTRODUCTION

To retrieve visual objects from a large-scale image database, most of the sophisticated methods in this area are based on the well-known bag-of-feature framework [14, 18], which typically works as follows. First, for each database image, local region descriptors such as the Scale Invariant Feature Transform (SIFT) [10, 20] are extracted. And then the high-dimensional local descriptors are quantized into discrete visual words by utilizing a visual vocabulary. The most common method to construct a visual vocabulary is to perform clustering (*e.g.* K-means) on the descriptors extracted from a set of training images; and each cluster is treated as a visual word described by its center. The quantization step is essentially to assign a local descriptor to its nearest visual word in the vocabulary in terms of Euclidean (l_2) distance using various approximate search algorithms like KD-tree [10, 15], Locality Sensitive Hashing [3] and Compact Projection [13]. After the quantization, each image is represented by the frequency histogram of a bag of visual words. Taking visual words as keys, images in the database are indexed by inverted files for quick access and search.

Visual descriptor quantization is a key step to develop a scalable and fast solution for image retrieval on a large scale database. However, it also brings two serious and unavoidable problems: *mismatch* and *semantic gap*.

Mismatch is due to the polysemy phenomenon, which means one visual word is too coarse to distinguish descriptors extracted from semantically different objects. This phenomenon is particularly prominent when the visual vocabulary is small. Fig. 1 shows some visual words from a vocabulary with 500K visual words constructed based on the Oxford Buildings Dataset [15]. The visual words in the first row are the top-5 nearest neighbors to the query word Q. Obviously these words describe objects with different semantic meanings (*e.g.* pillar, fence, wall), but have very close l_2 distances to Q. In a smaller visual vocabulary, they are very likely to be grouped into one word and lead to poor *precision* in retrieval. To address this problem, the simplest way to increase the discriminative capability of visual words is enlarging the vocabulary [15]. Other remarkable approaches working on this problem include bundling features [25], spatial-bag-of-features [1], hamming embedding and weak geometry consistency [5, 6], utilizing contextual dissimilarity measure [7], high-order spatial features [32], and compositional features [26], etc. In summary, by introducing additional spatial and contextual constraints into visual word matching, these approaches have made significant improvements on retrieval precision.

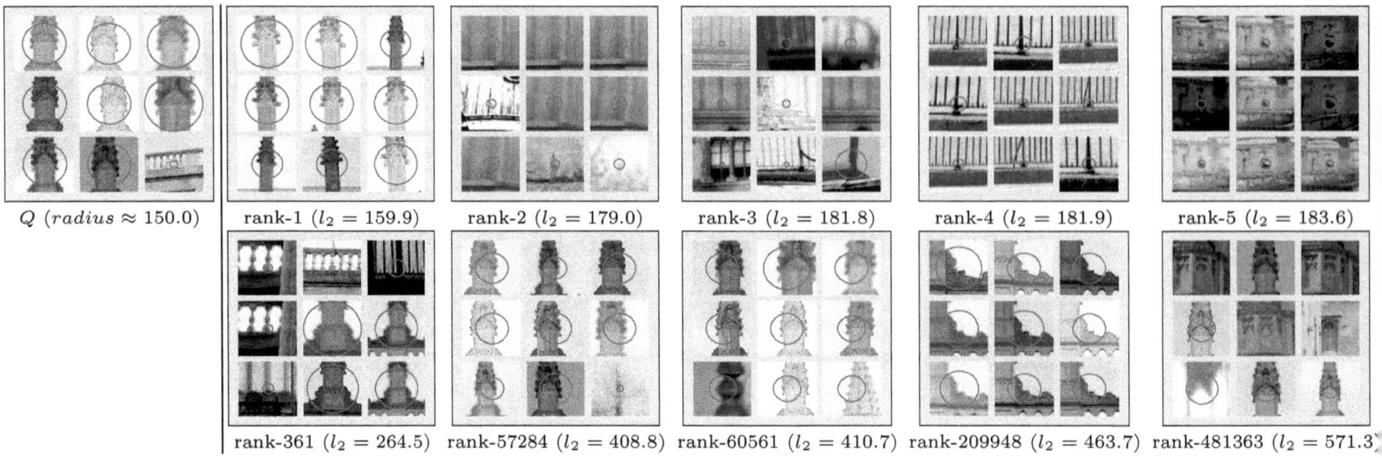

Figure 1: An example to illustrate the "semantic gap" between descriptors and semantic objects. Each visual word is represented by a panel containing 9 patches which are the closest samples to the corresponding cluster center. The Harris scale of each patch is marked with a red circle. Given the query word Q, its top-5 nearest neighbor words under l_2 distance are shown in the first row. The second row lists another 5 visual words (actually were identified by the algorithm in Section 2) which are more semantically related to the query word but are far away in the descriptor space. This example was extracted from a 500K vocabulary constructed based on the Oxford Building Dataset [15].

By contrast, semantic gap leads to the synonymy phenomenon, which means several different visual words actually describe semantically same visual objects. This phenomenon is especially obvious when adopting a large visual vocabulary, and usually results in poor *recall* performance in visual object retrieval [15]. In Fig. 1, there are another 5 visual words in the second row which are more semantically related to the query word Q but are far away from Q in the descriptor space. One of the reasons behind this phenomenon is the poor robustness of local descriptor algorithms. In fact, even those state-of-the-art local descriptors like SIFT are still sensitive to small disturbances (*e.g.* changes in viewpoint, scale, blur, and capturing condition) and output unstable and noisy feature values [19]. To increase the recall rate, a few research efforts have been devoted to reducing the troubles caused by synonymous words. One of the most influential techniques is the query expansion strategy proposed in [2], which completes the query set using visual words taken from matching objects in the first-round search results. Another method worthy of notice is soft-quantization (or soft-assignment), which assigns a descriptor to a weighted combination of nearest visual words [16, 21]. Statistical learning methods were also adopted to bridge semantic gap, *e.g.*, learning a transformation from original descriptor space (*e.g.* SIFT) to a new Euclidean space in which l_2 distance is more correlated to semantic divergence [17, 23]. A more direct approach was proposed in [12] to estimate the semantic coherence of two visual words via counting the frequency that the two words match with each other in a training set. A similar technique is also applied in [4], where spatial verifications are employed between the query and top-ranked images in the first-round result to detect matching points with different visual words, then the detected word pairs are viewed as synonyms and used to update the initial query histogram. Recently, there is another trend to bridge semantic gap in visual retrieval. The basic idea is to incorporate textual information to promote more meaningful visual features [8] or provide more accurate combinational similarity measure [24, 11]. For example, in [8], auxiliary visual words are identified by propagating the similarity across both visual and textual graphs. Incorporating textual information in visual retrieval is a promising research area as surrounding text is indeed available in many application scenarios (*e.g.* near-dup key-frame retrieval in video search [24]). However, this is beyond the scope of this paper, in which we still focus on leveraging pure visual information.

In this paper, we target at providing a simple yet effective solution to narrow down the semantic gap in visual object retrieval. In contrast, most aforementioned approaches are practically expensive. For example, query expansion needs to do multiple search processes; and its performance highly depends on the quality of the initial recall [2]. Learning-based methods [12, 17, 23] need to collect a set of matching point pairs as training data. To construct a comprehensive training set, it usually needs a large image database and has to run complex geometric verification algorithms like RANSAC on candidate image pairs to identify possible matching points. Even so, the obtained training samples (pairs of synonymous words) are still very sparse when the vocabulary size is large. Soft-quantization is cheap and effective, but in essence it can only handle the over-splitting cases in quantization. We argue that the existing l_2 distance-based soft-quantization is incapable of dealing with semantic gap. This is because visual words that are close in l_2 distance do not always have similar semantic meanings, as shown in Fig. 1.

However, the "expansion" idea behind soft-quantization and query expansion is very praiseworthy. It reminds us of the effective synonym expansion strategy in text retrieval [22]. For visual object retrieval, the main challenge here is how to identify synonyms from a visual vocabulary. In this paper, we once again borrow the experience from the text domain. In text analysis, synonyms can be identified by finding words

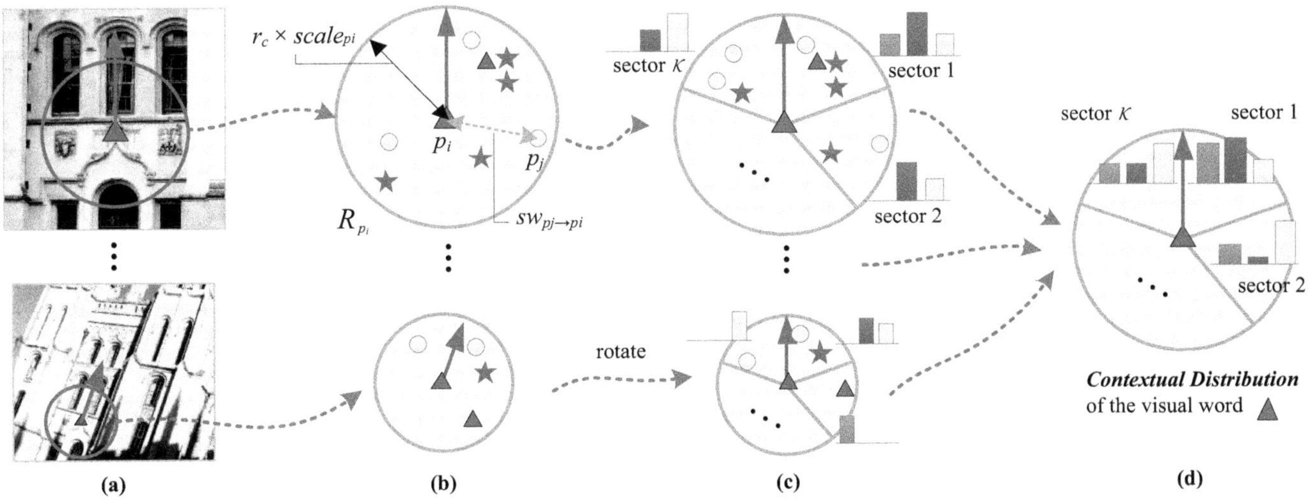

Figure 2: An illustration of the process to estimate the contextual distribution of a visual word ω_m. (a) For each instance p_i of the visual word, its visual context is defined as a spatial circular region R_{p_i} with the radius $r_c \times scale_{p_i}$; (b) A point in the visual context is weighted according to its spatial distance to p_i; (c) The dominant orientation of p_i is rotated to be vertical; R_{p_i} is partitioned into K sectors, and for each sector a *sub-histograms* is constructed; (d) The *sub-histograms* of all the instances of the visual word ω_m are aggregated to describe the contextual distribution of ω_m.

with similar contextual distributions [28], where the textual context refers to the surrounding text of a word. Analogically, we can define the visual context as a set of local points which are in a certain spatial region of a visual word. Intuitively, visual words representing the same semantic meaning tend to have similar visual contextual distributions. An evidence to support this assumption is the "visual phrase" reported in the recent literature of object recognition [27, 34, 26, 30, 29, 33, 32]. A visual phrase is a set of frequently co-occurring visual words, and has been observed to exist in visual objects from the same semantic category (*e.g.* cars). Besides co-occurrence, we also incorporate local spatial information to the visual contextual distribution as well as the corresponding contextual similarity measure[1]. Next, we define the "contextual synonyms" of a visual word as its nearest neighbors in terms of the contextual similarity measure. The ensemble of contextual synonyms of all the visual words is a *contextual synonym dictionary*, which can be computed offline and stored in memory for fast access. For retrieval, each visual word extracted on the query image is expanded to a weighted combination of its visual synonyms, then the expanded histogram is taken as the new query.

As a side-note, here we would like to make a distinction between the proposed *contextual synonym dictionary* and *visual phrase* in existing work. Actually, their perspectives are different. To identify visual phrases, the typical process is to first discover combinations of visual words and then group these combinations according to some distance measures. Each group is taken as a visual phrase. The related work usually works on a small vocabulary as the number of possible combinations increases in exponential order of the vocabulary size [27, 34]. Moreover, they can leverage supervised information (*e.g.* image categories) to learn distance measures between visual phrase (*e.g.* the Mahalanobis distance in [29], boosting in [26], and the kernel-based learning in [32]). In retrieval, visual phrase is considered as an additional kind of feature to provide better image representations. By contrast, the contextual synonym dictionary in this paper is defined on single visual word. There is no explicit "phrases" but embeds some implicit contextual relationships among visual words. Our approach can work on large vocabulary as the cost is just linear with the vocabulary size. For retrieval, the synonym dictionary is utilized to expand query terms and the image representation is still a histogram of visual words. Therefore, the contextual synonym dictionary can be naturally integrated into a standard bag-of-feature image retrieval system.

The rest of the paper is organized as follows. We introduce the visual context and contextual similarity measure in Section 2. Section 3 describes the system implementation to construct a contextual synonym dictionary, and presents how to apply the synonym dictionary to expand visual words in visual object retrieval. Experimental results are discussed in Section 4; and conclusion is drawn in Section 5.

2. VISUAL CONTEXTUAL SYNONYMS

In this section, we introduce the concepts of *visual context* and *contextual distribution*, as well as how to measure the *contextual similarity* of two visual words according to their contextual distributions.

To make a clear presentation and facilitate the following discussions, we first define some notations used in this paper. In the bag-of-feature framework, there is a visual vocabulary $\Omega = \{\omega_1, \ldots, \omega_m, \ldots, \omega_{\mathcal{M}}\}$ in which ω_m is the mth visual word and $\mathcal{M} = |\Omega|$ is the vocabulary size. Each extracted

[1]Although spatial information has been widely utilized to increase the distinguishability of visual words, the goal here is to identify synonymous words. Moreover, most spatial information in previous work just takes into account the context of an individual image patch; while in this paper, the spatial information of a visual word is the contextual statistics averaged over all the image patches assigned to that word.

local descriptor (SIFT) is assigned to its nearest visual word (*i.e.*quantization). As a result an image $\mathcal{I}$ is represented as a bag of visual words $\{\omega_{p_i}\}$ where ω_{p_i} is the visual word of the ith interest point p_i on $\mathcal{I}$. Correspondingly, we adopt (x_{p_i}, y_{p_i}) to represent the coordinate of p_i, and $scale_{p_i}$ to denote its Harris scale output by the SIFT detector. Moreover, for a visual word ω_m, we define its *instance set* $\mathbb{I}_m$ as all the interest points quantized to ω_m in the database.

2.1 Visual Contextual Distribution

In a text document, the context of a word is its surrounding text, e.g, a sentence or a paragraph containing that word. For an interest point p_i, there is no such syntax boundaries and we just simply define its visual context as a spatial circular region R_{p_i} centered at p_i. As illustrated in Fig. 2 (a) and (b), the radius of R_{p_i} is $r_c \times scale_{p_i}$, where r_c is a multiplier to control the contextual region size. Since the radius is in proportion to the Harris scale $scale_{p_i}$, R_{p_i} is robust to object scaling. The simplest way to characterize textual context is the histogram of *term-frequency*; similarly, the most straightforward definition of the visual contextual distribution of p_i is the histogram of visual words:

$$\mathcal{C}_{tf}(p_i) = [tf_1(p_i), \ldots, tf_m(p_i), \ldots, tf_{\mathcal{M}}(p_i)] \quad (1)$$

where tf_m is the term frequency of the visual word ω_m in the contextual region R_{p_i}.

Although $\mathcal{C}_{tf}$ can embed the co-occurrences among visual words, it is incapable of describing the spatial information, which has been proven to be important in many computer vision applications. To provide a more comprehensive description, in the following we introduce two strategies to add spatial characteristics to the visual context, namely *supporting weight* and *sector-based context.*

Supporting weight is designed to distinguish the contributions of two different local points to the contextual distribution of p_i, as shown in Fig. 2 (b). Intuitively, the one which is closer to the region center should be more important. Specifically, for an interest point $p_j \in R_{p_i}$, its *relative distance* to p_i is the Euclidean distance on the image plane normalized by the contextual region radius:

$$dist_{p_j \to p_i} = \frac{\|(x_{p_j}, y_{p_j}) - (x_{p_i}, y_{p_i})\|_2}{r_c \times scale(p_i)} \quad (2)$$

And the contribution (*supporting weight*) of p_j to p_i's contextual distribution is defined as:

$$sw_{p_j \to p_i} = e^{-dist^2_{p_j \to p_i}/2} \quad (3)$$

while in $\mathcal{C}_{tf}$, each p_j is considered to contribute equally to the histogram. Then, the contextual distribution definition incorporating supporting weight is:

$$\mathcal{C}_{sw}(p_i) = [c_1(p_i), \ldots, c_m(p_i), \ldots, c_{\mathcal{M}}(p_i)] \quad (4)$$

where

$$c_m(p_i) = \sum_{p_j} sw_{p_j \to p_i}, \quad p_j \in R_{p_i} \,\&\, \omega_{p_j} = \omega_m. \quad (5)$$

Sector-based context is inspired by the definitions of *preceding* and *following* words in text domain. In textual context modeling, the part before a word is treated differently with the part after that word. Analogously, we can divide the circular region R_{p_i} into several equal *sectors*, as shown in Fig. 2 (c). Actually, this thought is quite natural and

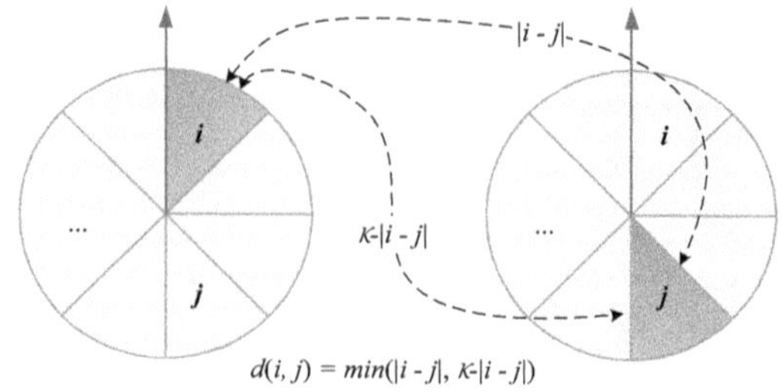

Figure 3: Definition of the *circle distance* between two sectors.

similar ideas have been successfully applied for both object recognition[9] and retrieval[1]. To yield rotation invariance, we also rotate R_{p_i} to align its dominant orientation to be vertical. Then, as illustrated in Fig. 2 (c), the sectors are numbered with $1, 2, \ldots, \mathcal{K}$ in clockwise starting from the one on the right side of the dominant orientation. After that, we compute the contextual distribution for each sector, denoted as $\mathcal{C}^k_{sw}$, and concatenate all these *sub-histograms* to construct a new *hyper-histogram* $\mathcal{C}_{sect}$ to describe the contextual distribution of R_{p_i}:

$$\mathcal{C}_{sect}(p_i) = [\mathcal{C}^1_{sw}(p_i), \ldots, \mathcal{C}^k_{sw}(p_i), \ldots, \mathcal{C}^{\mathcal{K}}_{sw}(p_i)] \quad (6)$$

It should be noticed that the length of $\mathcal{C}_{sect}$ is $\mathcal{K} \times \mathcal{M}$.

Contextual distribution of a visual word is the statistical aggregation of the contextual distributions of all its instances in the database, as shown in Fig. 2 (d). For a visual word ω_m, we average $\mathcal{C}_{sect}(p_i), \forall p_i \in \mathbb{I}_m$ to represent its statistical contextual distribution:

$$\mathcal{C}_m = [\mathcal{C}^1_m, \ldots, \mathcal{C}^k_m, \ldots, \mathcal{C}^{\mathcal{K}}_m], \; \mathcal{C}^k_m = \frac{1}{|\mathbb{I}_m|} \sum_{p_i \in \mathbb{I}_m} \mathcal{C}^k_{sw}(p_i). \quad (7)$$

$\mathcal{C}^k_m$ is a $\mathcal{M}$-dimensional vector whose n^{th} element $\mathcal{C}^k_m(n)$ is the weight of the visual word ω_n in the kth sector of ω_m. In this way, $\mathcal{C}_m$ incorporates abundant semantic information from instances in various images, and is more stable than the context of an individual image patch.

2.2 Contextual Similarity Measure

To identify visual synonyms, the remaining problem is how to measure the contextual similarity between two visual words. First of all, the contextual distributions $\{\mathcal{C}_m, 1 \leq m \leq \mathcal{M}\}$ should be normalized to provide a comparable measure between different visual words. Considering that $\mathcal{C}_m$ is essentially a hyper-histogram consisting of $\mathcal{K}$ sub-histograms, the most straightforward way is to normalize each sub-histogram $\mathcal{C}^k_m$ respectively. However, in practice we found the normalization of sub-histograms usually results in the lost of spatial density information. In other words, a "rich" sector containing a large amount of visual word instances is treated equally to a "poor" sector in the following similarity measure. To keep the density information, we perform a l_2-normalization on the whole histogram $\mathcal{C}_m$ as if it has not been partitioned into sectors.

Based on the l_2-normalized $\mathcal{C}_m$, the most natural similarity measure is the *cosine* similarity. However, the cosine similarity on $\mathcal{C}_m$ implies a constraint that different sectors (*i.e.*sub-histograms) are totally unrelated and will not be compared. This constraint is too restrict as sectors are only

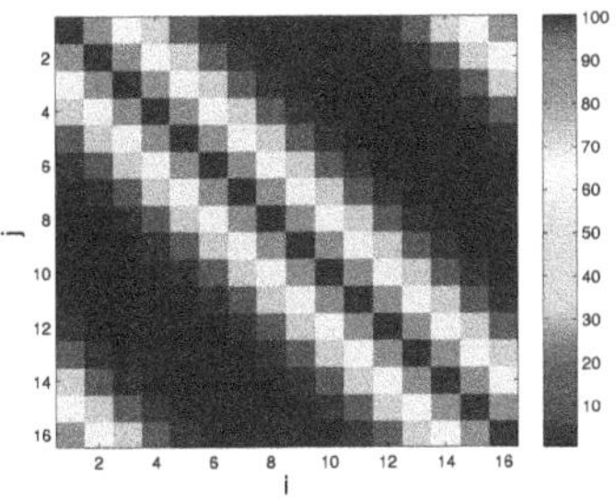

Figure 4: Visualization of the dislocation probability (%) when $\mathcal{K} = 16$.

a very coarse partition of a contextual region. Moreover, the dominant direction estimated by the SIFT detector is not that accurate. Therefore, the cosine similarity is easy to underestimate the similarity of two visual words really having close contextual distributions. To tolerate the dislocation error, in this paper the contextual similarity of two visual words ω_m and ω_n is defined as:

$$Sim(\omega_m, \omega_n) = \sum_{i=1}^{\mathcal{K}} \sum_{j=1}^{\mathcal{K}} \left(Sim^{sec}(\mathcal{C}_m^i, \mathcal{C}_n^j) \cdot \Phi(i,j) \right). \quad (8)$$

Here, Sim^{sec} is the weighted inner product of the two sub-histograms $\mathcal{C}_m^i$ and $\mathcal{C}_n^j$:

$$Sim^{sec}(\mathcal{C}_m^i, \mathcal{C}_n^j) = \sum_{v=1}^{\mathcal{M}} idf_v^2 \cdot \mathcal{C}_m^i(v) \cdot \mathcal{C}_n^j(v). \quad (9)$$

where the weight idf_v is the *inverse-document-frequency* of the visual word ω_v in all the contextual distributions $\{\mathcal{C}_m, 1 \leq m \leq \mathcal{M}\}$, to punish those popular visual words. Φ is a predefined $\mathcal{K} \times \mathcal{K}$ matrix whose (i,j)-element approximates the dislocation probability between the ith and j^{th} sectors. As shown in Fig. 3 and Fig. 4, $\Phi(i,j)$ is computed based on the exponential weighting of the *circle distance* between the corresponding sectors:

$$\Phi(i,j) = e^{-\frac{d(i,j)^2}{\mathcal{K}/2}}, \; d(i,j) = \min(|i-j|, \mathcal{K} - |i-j|). \quad (10)$$

According to the similarity measure, the "contextual synonyms" of a visual word ω_m are defined as those visual words with the largest contextual similarities to ω_m.

3. SYSTEM IMPLEMENTATIONS

In this section, we introduce the system implementation to construct the *contextual synonym dictionary* through identifying synonyms for every visual words in the vocabulary. Furthermore, we describe how to leverage the synonym dictionary in visual object retrieval.

3.1 Contextual Synonym Dictionary Construction

To construct the contextual synonym dictionary, the contextual distributions of all interest points in training images are first extracted. Next, the contextual distributions of visual words are obtained by aggregating of the distribution of all its instances. For a visual word ω_q, the contextual synonyms are then identified by searching for the visual words with largest contextual similarities.

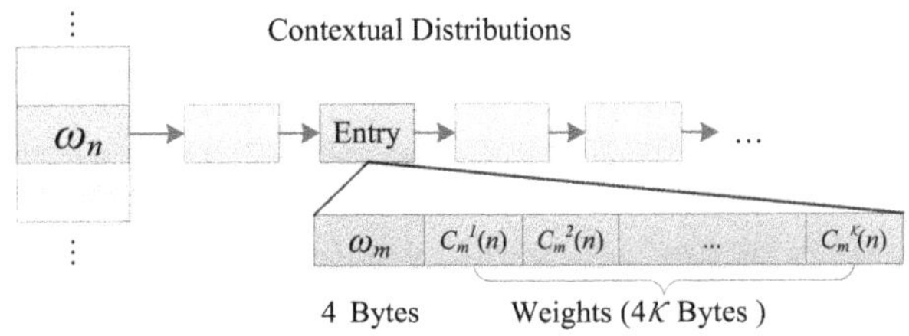

Figure 5: Inverted files to index contextual distributions.

Input: Training image set: $\{\mathcal{I}_1, \mathcal{I}_2, \ldots, \mathcal{I}_s\}$;
Output: Synonym Dictionary;
foreach *interest point* $p_i \in \{\mathcal{I}_1, \mathcal{I}_2, \ldots, \mathcal{I}_s\}$ **do**
  extract contextual distribution $\mathcal{C}_{sect}(p_i)$;
end
foreach *visual word* $\omega_m \in \Omega$ **do**
  $\mathcal{C}_m = [\mathcal{C}_m^1, \ldots, \mathcal{C}_m^k, \ldots, \mathcal{C}_m^{\mathcal{K}}]$, $\mathcal{C}_m^k = \frac{1}{|\mathbb{I}_m|} \sum_{p_i \in \mathbb{I}_m} \mathcal{C}_{sw}^k(p_i)$;
  Sparsify $\mathcal{C}_m$ to satisfy $\|\mathcal{C}_m\| \leq \|\mathcal{C}_{max}\|$;
end
Build inverted files as illustrated in Fig. 5;
foreach *visual word* $\omega_q \in \Omega$ **do**
  Initialize all *score*[] = 0;
  foreach *visual word* $(\omega_n, \mathcal{C}_q^1(n), \ldots, \mathcal{C}_q^{\mathcal{K}}(n)) \in \mathcal{C}_q$ **do**
    foreach *entry* $(\omega_m, \mathcal{C}_m^1(n), \ldots, \mathcal{C}_m^{\mathcal{K}}(n))$ *in the inverted list of* ω_n **do**
      $score[m] += \sum_{i,j=1}^{\mathcal{K}} idf_n^2 \cdot \mathcal{C}_q^i(n) \cdot \mathcal{C}_m^j(n) \cdot \Phi(i,j)$;
    end
  end
  The visual words with largest *score* are the synonyms of ω_q;
end

Algorithm 1: Synonym Dictionary Construction.

The brute-force way to find the most similar visual words is to linear scan all the visual words and compare the contextual similarities one-by-one. However, the computational cost is extremely heavy when dealing with a large visual vocabulary. For example, to construct the synonym dictionary for a vocabulary with 10^5 visual words, it needs to compute 10^{10} similarities. Therefore the linear scan solution is infeasible in practice. To accelerate the construction process, we utilize inverted files to index contextual distributions of visual words, as shown in Fig. 5. The inverted files are built as follows. Every visual word ω_n has an entry list in which each entry represents another visual word ω_m whose contextual distribution containing ω_n. An entry records the id of ω_m, as well as the weights $\{\mathcal{C}_m^k(n), 1 \leq k \leq \mathcal{K}\}$ of ω_n in ω_m's contextual distribution. Supposing there are $\|\mathcal{C}_q\|$ unique non-zero elements in ω_q's contextual distribution, it just needs to measure visual words in the corresponding $\|\mathcal{C}_q\|$ entry lists to identify synonyms. $\|\mathcal{C}_q\|$ is called the *contextual distribution size* of ω_q; and $\|\mathcal{C}\|_{avg}$ is the average of the contextual distribution sizes for all the visual words.

Sparsification Optimization : With the assistance of inverted files, the time cost to identity synonyms of specific visual word ω_q is $O(\|\mathcal{C}_q\| \times \|\mathcal{C}_{avg}\| \times \mathcal{K}^2)$, which is considerably less expensive than linear scanning. However, when large training set applied, the contextual distributions of visual words may contain thousands of visual words and make the construction process costly. To save the costs, in prac-

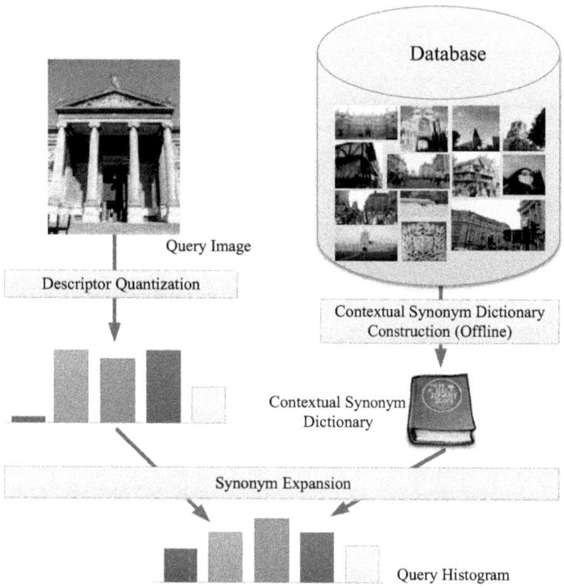

Figure 6: The framework of leveraging contextual synonym dictionary in visual object retrieval. The visual words in query image are expended to corresponding weighted combination of visual synonyms, and the augmented histogram is token as query.

tice we can make the contextual distribution more sparse by removing visual words with small weights in the histogram, to satisfy $\|\mathcal{C}_m\| \leq \|\mathcal{C}\|_{max}, \forall m \in [1, \mathcal{M}]$. Finally, the construction process is summarized in Algorithm 1.

Complexity Analysis : Each entry in the inverted files requests $4 \times (\mathcal{K}+1)$ bytes; and the total memory cost is around $4 \times (\mathcal{K}+1) \times \mathcal{M} \times \|\mathcal{C}\|_{avg}$ bytes without sparsification. The time cost to identify synonyms of one visual word is $O(\|\mathcal{C}\|_{avg}^2 \times \mathcal{K}^2)$; and the overall time complexity to construct the contextual synonym dictionary is $O(\|\mathcal{C}\|_{avg}^2 \times \mathcal{K} \times \mathcal{M})$. For example, given the vocabulary size $\mathcal{M} = 500K$, the sector number $\mathcal{K} = 16$ and the contextual region scale $r_c = 4$, the average contextual distribution size $\|\mathcal{C}\|_{avg} \approx 219$. The construction process requires about 7G memory and runs around 35 minutes on a 16-core 2.67 GHz Intel Xeon® machine. By employ sparsification, the contextual distribution size of a visual word do not exceed $\|\mathcal{C}\|_{max}$. Therefore, the space complexity is $O(\mathcal{K} \times \mathcal{M} \times \|\mathcal{C}\|_{max})$ and time complexity is $O(\|\mathcal{C}\|_{max}^2 \times \mathcal{K}^2 \times \mathcal{M})$. It should be noted that, since $\|\mathcal{C}\|_{max}$ is a constant, the computation cost is independent with the number of images in training set. A comprehensive study of different settings of $\|\mathcal{C}\|_{max}$ and the corresponding costs are given in Section 4.2.

3.2 Contextual Synonym-based Expansion

Now we explain how to leverage contextual synonym dictionary in visual object retrieval. The framework is similar to that proposed for soft-quantization. The basis flow is that each visual word extracted on the query image is expanded to a list of k_{nn} words (either l_2 nearest neighbors in soft-quantization or contextual synonyms in this paper). The query image is then described with a weighted combination of the expansion words. However, there are some differences that should be mentioned: (1) We only perform expansion on query images. Although expanding images in database is doable, it will greatly increase the index size and retrieval time. (2) Each local descriptor is only assigned to one visual word in quantization. The expanded synonym words are obtained via looking up the contextual synonym dictionary. (3) The weight of each synonym is in proportion to its contextual similarity to the related query word. The work flow is illustrated in Fig. 6.

Table 1: Information of the datasets.

Dataset	#Images	#Descriptors (SIFT)
Oxford5K	5,063	24,910,180
Paris6K	6,392	28,572,648
Flickr100K	100,000	152,052,164

Table 2: The approaches in comparison.

Approach	Parameters
Hard-Quantization	$\mathcal{M}$
l_2-based Soft-Quantization (Query-side)	$\mathcal{M}$, k_{nn}
Contextual Synonym-based Expansion	$\mathcal{M}$, k_{nn}, r_c, $\mathcal{K}$, $\|\mathcal{C}\|_{max}$

4. EXPERIMENTAL RESULTS

A series of experiments were conducted to evaluate the proposed contextual synonym-based expansion for visual object retrieval. First, we investigated the influences of various parameters in the proposed approach, and then compared the overall retrieval performance with some state-of-the-art methods on several benchmark datasets.

4.1 Experiment Setup

The experiments were based on three datasets, as shown in Table 1. The **Oxford5K** dataset was introduced in [15] and has become a standard benchmark for object retrieval. It has 55 query images with manually labeled ground truth. The **Paris6K** dataset was first introduced in [16]. It has more than 6000 images collected from Flickr by searching for particular Paris landmarks, and also has 55 query images with ground truth. The **Flickr100K** dataset in this paper has 100K images crawled from Flickr, and we had ensured there is no overlap with the Oxford5K and Paris6K datasets. We adopted SIFT as the local descriptor in the experiments, and applied the software developed in [20] to extract SIFT descriptors for all the images in these datasets.

Two state-of-the-art methods were implemented as baselines for performance comparison, i.e., hard-quantization and l_2-based soft-quantization, as shown in Table 2. For evaluation, the standard *mean average precision* (mAP) was utilized to characterize the retrieval performance. For each query image, the average precision (AP) was computed as the area under the precision-recall curve. The mAP is defined as the mean value of average precision over all queries. Table 2 also lists the parameters in these methods, which will be discussed in the following subsection.

To avoid over-fitting in the experiment, the query images were excluded in the contextual synonym dictionary construction process.

4.2 Contextual Synonym-based Expansion

In this subsection, we investigate the influences of the parameters in the proposed approach. We also gave a try to

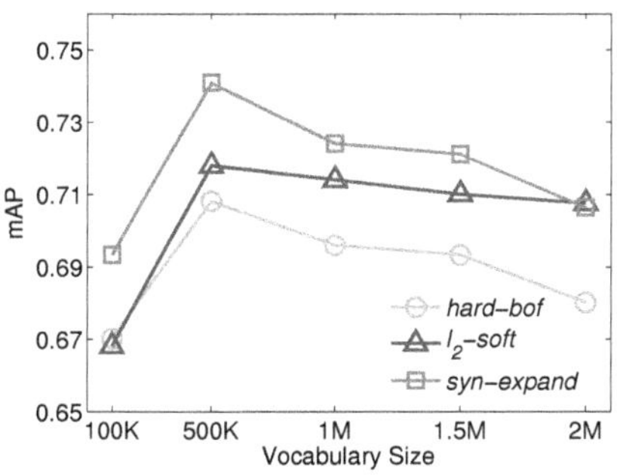

Figure 7: Performance comparisons of different approaches under different vocabulary sizes.

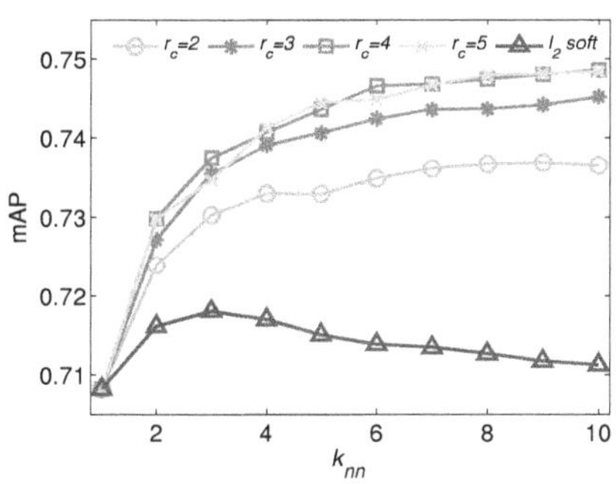

Figure 8: Performance comparisons of different approaches under different contextual region scales and different numbers of expansion words (vocabulary size $\mathcal{M}$=500K).

combine the l_2-based soft-quantization with our synonym-based expansion. All the evaluations in this part were based on the Oxford5K dataset.

Vocabulary Size $\mathcal{M}$. The three approaches in comparison were evaluated on five vocabulary sizes – 100K, 500K, 1M, 1.5M and 2M. For l_2-based soft-quantization and synonym-based expansion, the number of expansion words was set to 3, under which the best performance was achieved in [16]. The mAP values of different approaches under different vocabulary sizes are shown in Fig. 7. All the three approaches got the best performance on the 500K vocabulary. This is slightly different with the observation in [15] in which the best performance was on a vocabulary with 1M visual words. This may because the adopted SIFT detectors were different. An evidence to support this explanation is that in this paper even the baseline performance (with hard-quantization) is much higher than that reported in [15]. From Fig. 7, it is also noticeable that the performances of all the approaches drop when the vocabulary size becomes larger. This suggests that over-splitting becomes the major problem with a large vocabulary. This also explains why soft-quantization is with the slowest decreasing speed as it is designed to deal with the over-splitting problem in quantization. All the following experiments (unless explicitly specified) were based on the 500K vocabulary.

Number of Expansion Words k_{nn}. Both soft-quantization and the proposed synonym-based expansion need to determine the number of soft-assignment/expansion words. As shown in Fig. 8, k_{nn} was enumerated from 1 to 10 in the experiment. It is clear that the performance of soft-quantization drops when more expansion words are included. This makes sense as neighbors in l_2 distance could be noises in terms of semantic meaning, as the example shown in Fig. 1. This observation is also consistent with the results reported in [16], and proves that soft-quantization cannot help reduce semantic gaps in object retrieval. By contrast, the proposed synonym expansion works well when the expansion number increases. Although the performance is relatively stable when k_{nn} becomes large, the additional expansion words don't hurt the search results. This also suggests that the included contextual synonyms are semantically related to the query words.

Table 3: Performance comparison of the proposed approach under different sector numbers in contextual region partition.

$\mathcal{K}$	1	2	4	8	16	32
mAP	0.748	0.751	0.752	0.753	**0.755**	0.754

Table 4: Complexity and performance analysis of different contextual distribution sizes.

$\|\mathcal{C}\|_{max}$	∞	100	20
$\|\mathcal{C}\|_{avg}$	219.1	94.8	19.8
mAP	0.755	0.755	0.750
Memory	7.4GB	3.2GB	673MB
Syn. Dict. Const. Time	35min	19min	14min

Contextual Region Scale r_c. Fig. 8 also shows the performances of the proposed approach with different contextual region scales. We enumerated the multiplier r_c from 2 to 5, and found the performance becomes stable after $r_c = 4$. Actually, the Harris scales for most SIFT descriptors are quite small. We need a relatively large r_c to include enough surrounding points for getting a sufficient statistic to visual context. Therefore, r_c was set as 4 in the following experiments.

Number of Contextual Region Sectors $\mathcal{K}$. As introduced in Section 2.1, a contextual region is divided into several sectors to embed more spatial information. Different numbers of sectors were evaluated, as shown in Table. 3. The performance was improved with more sectors in the partition. However, the improvement is not significant when $\mathcal{K}$ is large. We selected $\mathcal{K} = 16$ in the experiments.

Contextual Distribution Size $\|\mathcal{C}\|_{max}$. We have analyzed the complexity to construct a contextual synonym dictionary in Section 3.1, and proposed to make the contextual distribution sparse with an upper bound threshold $\|\mathcal{C}\|_{max}$. Different $\|\mathcal{C}\|_{max}$ values were tested and the corresponding mAP, memory cost, and running time are reported in Table 4. Of course this restriction will sacrifice the characterization capability of contextual distribution. However, the retrieval performance only slightly drops with the compensation of significantly reduced memory and running time. One explanation of the small performance decrease is that the sparse operation also make the contextual distribution noise-free. In other words, words with small weights in context are very possible to be random noises.

Table 5: **Retrieval performances via integrating l_2-based soft-quantization and synonym expansion, respectively on two vocabularies of 500K and 2M.**

l_2 Soft-Quant.	Vocabulary		Synonym Expansion 1_{nn}	2_{nn}	3_{nn}	5_{nn}	10_{nn}
	500K	1_{nn}	0.708	0.734	0.741	0.748	0.755
		2_{nn}	0.716	0.742	0.747	0.752	**0.756**
		3_{nn}	0.718	0.744	0.749	0.753	0.755
	2M	1_{nn}	0.680	0.698	0.706	0.717	0.730
		2_{nn}	0.700	0.715	0.725	0.734	0.745
		3_{nn}	0.708	0.725	0.734	0.741	**0.751**

Integrate Soft-Quantization and Synonym Expansion. It is an intuitive thought to integrate soft-quantization and the proposed synonym expansion, as they target to deal with over-splitting and semantic gap respectively. We proposed a simple integration strategy, *i.e.*, doing soft-assignment first and then expanding each obtained soft word with its contextual synonyms. The motivation here is that over-splitting is in low-level feature space and should be handled before touching the high-level semantic problem. In the experiment we evaluated different combinations of expansion numbers for soft-quantization and contextual synonyms. The results are shown in Table 5, in which each column is with the same number of synonyms but different numbers of words ($1 \sim 3$) in soft quantization. We did the evaluations on two vocabularies. On the 500K vocabulary, the improvement of integration is not significant in comparison with only using contextual synonym expansion; however, the improvement on the 2M vocabulary is noticeable. This is because the over-splitting phenomenon is not that serious on the 500K vocabulary, and semantic gap is the main issue. While for the 2M vocabulary, both over-splitting and semantic gap become serious; and the two approaches complement each other. Of course we just shallowly touch the integration problem and leave the exploring of more sophisticated solutions to the future work.

4.3 Comparison of Overall Performance

The comparison of overall performance of different approaches on various datasets are shown in Table 6. To provide a comprehensive comparison, for each approach we adopted the RANSAC algorithm to do spatial verification for reranking the search results. Moreover,the query expansion strategy (denoted as QE in Table 6) proposed in [2] was also applied based on the RANSAC results to further improve the retrieval performance. The "query" in [2] represents an image but not a visual word, and the corresponding "query expansion" is different with the expansion in this paper. From Table 6, it is clear that the proposed contextual synonym-based expansion always achieved the best performance.

There are several interesting observations from Table 6. First, in the Oxford5K dataset, the performance gains of the RANSAC re-ranking are 3.0%, 3.3% and 3.9% for hard-quantization, l_2-soft quantization, and synonym-based expand, respectively. The spatial verification and re-ranking was only performed on the top-ranked images, thus the performances highly depend on the initial recall. With the assistance of synonym expansion, the recall is improved which makes the RANSAC more powerful. The additional improvements brought by the image-level query expansion (QE) are 4.9%, 3.9% and 1.7% respectively. The performance gains in syn-expand results are not as significant as those in two baselines. One possible explanation is that visual synonyms already narrow down the semantic gaps and leave little room for QE. It's noticeable that the mAP of syn-expand is even larger than l_2-soft + RANSAC on all the four experiments, this proves that the proposed approach is cheap and effective. Another observation is that, the improvements brought by RANSAC in Paris6K dataset is not as significant as those in Oxford5K. This may because that the queries in Paris6K dataset contain more positive cases(on average, each query in Paris6K has 163 positive cases, but only 52 for queries in Oxford5K), meanwhile the RANSAC is only performed on a small part of the first-round retrieval results.

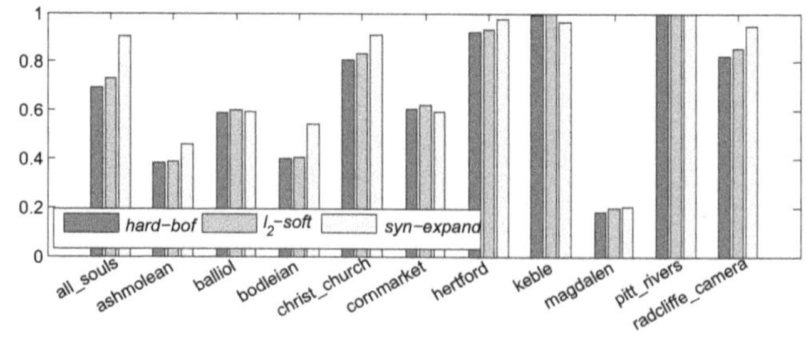

Figure 9: mAP of all the queries on the "Oxford5K+Flickr100K" dataset.

For the "Oxford5K+Flickr100K" dataset, we also present the mAP for all the 11 query buildings (five queries for each), as shown in Fig. 9. Our approach outperforms the baseline methods in most query buildings. However, it perform slightly worse than l_2-soft in balliol, cornmarket and keble. This may because of the noises in the synonym vocabulary. We leave the noise removing task as our future work.

The price has to be paid by the proposed approach is relatively slow speed in search, as expansion words increase the query length. Soft-quantization also suffers from the "long query" problem. With our implementation ($k_{nn} = 10$ and on the "Oxford5K+Flickr100K" dataset), the average respond time of hard-quantization is about 0.14 seconds while that of our approach was around 0.93 seconds. Fortunately, the response time is still acceptable for most visual search scenarios. Moreover, we noticed that there has been some recent research efforts [31] addressed on accelerating search speed for long queries.

To provide a vivid impression of the performance, we show four illustrative examples in Fig. 10. The search was performed on the "Oxford5K+Flickr100K" dataset. For each example, the precision-recall curves of the three approaches in Table 2 were drawn. From the precision-recall curves, it is clear that the gain of the proposed approach is mainly from the improvement of recall, which is exactly our purpose.

5. CONCLUSION

In this paper we introduced a contextual synonym dictionary to the bag-of-feature framework for large scale visual search. The goal is to provide an unsupervised method to reduce the semantic gap in visual word quantization. Synonym words are considered to describe visual objects with the same semantic meanings, and are identified via measur-

Table 6: Comparison of the overall performances of different approaches on various datasets.

	BOF			BOF + RANSAC			BOF + RANSAC + QE		
	hard-bof	l_2-soft	syn-expand	hard-bof	l_2-soft	syn-expand	hard-bof	l_2-soft	syn-expand
Oxford5K	0.708	0.718	**0.755**	0.738	0.751	**0.794**	0.787	0.790	**0.811**
Paris6K	0.696	0.705	**0.733**	0.702	0.710	**0.737**	0.776	0.776	**0.791**
Oxford5K+Flickr100K	0.672	0.688	**0.736**	0.707	0.722	**0.773**	0.758	0.767	**0.797**
Paris5K+Flickr100K	0.673	0.688	**0.722**	0.681	0.696	**0.730**	0.766	0.770	**0.785**

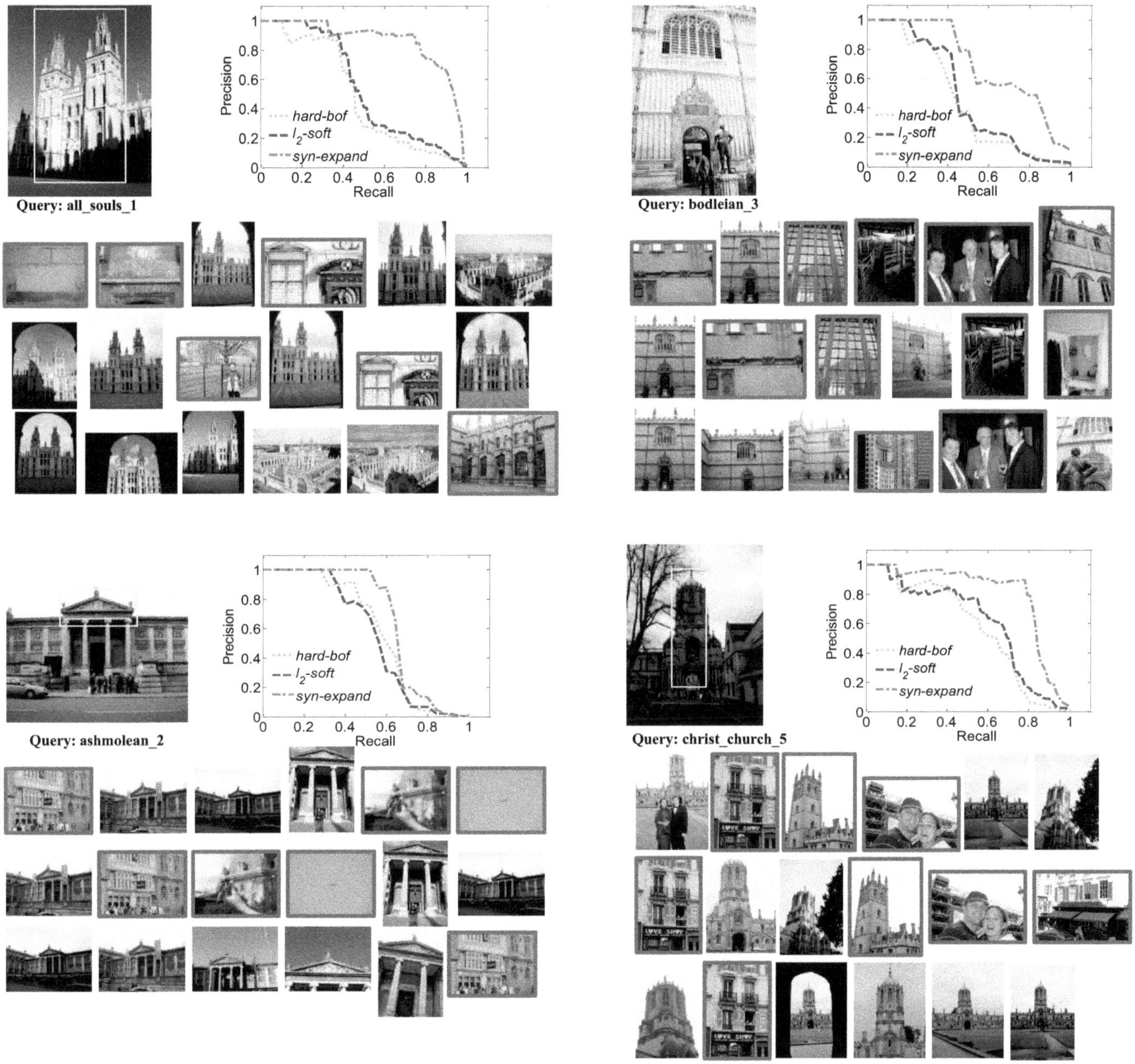

Figure 10: An illustration of search results and precision-recall curves for 4 example query images, all_souls_1 (upper-left), bodleian_3 (upper-right), ashmolean_2 (bottom-left) and christ_church_5 (bottom-right), on the "Oxford5K+Flickr100K" dataset. The three rows of search results correspond respectively to *hard-quantization*, *soft-quantization*, and *contextual synonym-based expansion*. False alarms are marked with red boxes.

ing the similarities of their contextual distributions. The contextual distribution of a visual word is based on the statistics averaged over all the image patches having this word, and contains both co-occurrence and spatial information. The contextual synonym dictionary can be efficiently constructed, and can be stored in memory for visual word expansion in online visual search. In brief, the proposed method is simple and cheap, and has been proven effective by exhaustive experiments.

This paper describes our preliminary study to leverage contextual synonyms to deal with semantic gaps, there is still much room for future improvement, *e.g.*, exploring a better strategy to deal with over-splitting and semantic gap simultaneously. Moreover, in future work we will investigate whether the contextual synonym dictionary can help compress a visual vocabulary. Another direction is to apply the synonym dictionary to applications other than visual search, *e.g.*, discover better visual phrases for visual object recognition.

6. REFERENCES

[1] Y. Cao, C. Wang, Z. Li, L. Zhang, and L. Zhang. Spatial-bag-of-features. In *CVPR*, pages 3352–3359, 2010.

[2] O. Chum, J. Philbin, J. Sivic, M. Isard, and A. Zisserman. Total recall: Automatic query expansion with a generative feature model for object retrieval. In *ICCV*, 2007.

[3] M. Datar, N. Immorlica, P. Indyk, and V. S. Mirrokni. Locality-sensitive hashing scheme based on p-stable distributions. In *SCG*, pages 253–262, 2004.

[4] E. Gavves and C. G. M. Snoek. Landmark image retrieval using visual synonyms. In *ACM Multimedia*, pages 1123–1126, 2010.

[5] H. Jegou, M. Douze, and C. Schmid. Hamming embedding and weak geometric consistency for large scale image search. In *ECCV*, pages I: 304–317, 2008.

[6] H. Jegou, M. Douze, and C. Schmid. Improving bag-of-features for large scale image search. *IJCV*, 87(3):316–336, 2010.

[7] H. Jegou, H. Harzallah, and C. Schmid. A contextual dissimilarity measure for accurate and efficient image search. In *CVPR*, 2007.

[8] Y. Kuo, H. Lin, W. Cheng, Y. Yang, and W. Hsu. Unsupervised auxiliary visual words discovery for large-scale image object retrieval. In *CVPR*, 2011.

[9] S. Lazebnik, C. Schmid, and J. Ponce. Beyond bags of features: Spatial pyramid matching for recognizing natural scene categories. In *CVPR*, pages 2169–2178, 2006.

[10] D. G. Lowe. Distinctive image features from scale-invariant keypoints. *IJCV*, 60(2):91–110, 2004.

[11] H. Ma, J. Zhu, M. R. Lyu, and I. King. Bridging the semantic gap between image contents and tags. *IEEE Transactions on Multimedia*, 12(5):462–473, 2010.

[12] A. Mikulík, M. Perdoch, O. Chum, and J. Matas. Learning a fine vocabulary. In *ECCV*, pages 1–14, 2010.

[13] K. Min, L. Yang, J. Wright, L. Wu, X.-S. Hua, and Y. Ma. Compact projection: Simple and efficient near neighbor search with practical memory requirements. In *CVPR*, pages 3477–3484, 2010.

[14] D. Nister and H. Stewenius. Scalable recognition with a vocabulary tree. In *CVPR*, pages 2161–2168, 2006.

[15] J. Philbin, O. Chum, M. Isard, J. Sivic, and A. Zisserman. Object retrieval with large vocabularies and fast spatial matching. In *CVPR*, 2007.

[16] J. Philbin, O. Chum, M. Isard, J. Sivic, and A. Zisserman. Lost in quantization: Improving particular object retrieval in large scale image databases. In *CVPR*, 2008.

[17] J. Philbin, M. Isard, J. Sivic, and A. Zisserman. Descriptor learning for efficient retrieval. In *ECCV*, pages 677–691, 2010.

[18] J. Sivic and A. Zisserman. Video Google: A text retrieval approach to object matching in videos. In *ICCV*, pages 1470–1477, 2003.

[19] T. Tuytelaars and K. Mikolajczyk. Local invariant feature detectors: A survey. *Foundations and Trends in Computer Graphics and Vision*, 3(3):177–280, 2007.

[20] K. E. A. van de Sande, T. Gevers, and C. G. M. Snoek. Evaluating color descriptors for object and scene recognition. *PAMI*, 32(9):1582–1596, 2010.

[21] J. van Gemert, C. J. Veenman, A. W. M. Smeulders, and J.-M. Geusebroek. Visual word ambiguity. *PAMI*, 32(7):1271–1283, 2010.

[22] E. M. Voorhees. Query expansion using lexical-semantic relations. In *SIGIR*, pages 61–69, 1994.

[23] S. A. J. Winder and M. Brown. Learning local image descriptors. In *CVPR*, 2007.

[24] X. Wu, W. Zhao, and C.-W. Ngo. Near-duplicate keyframe retrieval with visual keywords and semantic context. In *CIVR*, pages 162–169, 2007.

[25] Z. Wu, Q. Ke, M. Isard, and J. Sun. Bundling features for large scale partial-duplicate web image search. In *CVPR*, pages 25–32, 2009.

[26] J. S. Yuan, J. B. Luo, and Y. Wu. Mining compositional features for boosting. In *CVPR*, 2008.

[27] J. S. Yuan, Y. Wu, and M. Yang. Discovery of collocation patterns: from visual words to visual phrases. In *CVPR*, 2007.

[28] H. S. Zellig. *Mathematical structures of language.* Interscience Publishers New York, 1968.

[29] S. Zhang, Q. Huang, G. Hua, S. Jiang, W. Gao, and Q. Tian. Building contextual visual vocabulary for large-scale image applications. In *ACM Multimedia*, pages 501–510, 2010.

[30] S. Zhang, Q. Tian, G. Hua, Q. Huang, and S. Li. Descriptive visual words and visual phrases for image applications. In *ACM Multimedia*, pages 75–84, 2009.

[31] X. Zhang, Z. Li, L. Zhang, W.-Y. Ma, and H.-Y. Shum. Efficient indexing for large scale visual search. In *ICCV*, pages 1103–1110, 2009.

[32] Y. M. Zhang and T. H. Chen. Efficient kernels for identifying unbounded-order spatial features. In *CVPR*, pages 1762–1769, 2009.

[33] Y. M. Zhang, Z. Y. Jia, and T. H. Chen. Image retrieval with geometry preserving visual phrases. In *CVPR*, 2011.

[34] Y.-T. Zheng, M. Zhao, S.-Y. Neo, T.-S. Chua, and Q. Tian. Visual synset: Towards a higher-level visual representation. In *CVPR*, 2008.

Contextual Image Search* †

Wenhao Lu† Jingdong Wang‡ Xian-Sheng Hua‡ Shengjin Wang† Shipeng Li‡
†Tsinghua University, Beijing, P. R. China, {luwenhao, wsj}@ocrserv.ee.tsinghua.edu.cn
‡Microsoft Research Asia, Beijing, P. R. China, {jingdw, xshua, spli}@microsoft.com

ABSTRACT

In this paper, we propose a novel image search scheme, *contextual image search*. Different from conventional image search schemes that present a separate interface (e.g., text input box) to allow users to submit a query, the new search scheme enables users to search images by only masking a few words when they are reading through Web pages or other documents. Rather than merely making use of the explicit query input that is often not sufficient to express user's search intent, our approach explores the context information to better understand the search intent with two key steps: query augmenting and search results reranking using context, and expects to obtain better search results. Beyond contextual Web search, the context in our case is much richer and includes images besides texts. In addition to this type of search scheme, called *contextual image search with text input*, we also present another type of scheme, called *contextual image search with image input*, to allow users to select an image as the search query from Web pages or other documents they are reading. The key idea is to use the search-to-annotation technique and the contextual textual query mining scheme to determine the corresponding textual query, to finally get semantically similar search results. Experiments show that the proposed schemes make image search more convenient and the search results are more relevant to user intention.

Categories and Subject Descriptors

H.3.1 [**Information Storage and Retrieval**]: Content Analysis and Indexing; I.2.10 [**Artificial Intelligence**]: Vision and Scene Understanding

General Terms

Algorithms, Experimentation

Keywords

Image search, textual and visual context, contextual query augmentation, contextual reranking

†Area Chair: Nicu Sebe.
*This work was performed at Microsoft Research Asia.

Figure 1: Illustration of contextual image search with text input to remove the ambiguity of the query "apple". (a) corresponds to the results from the raw query "apple", (b) corresponds to the contextual search results in the context of introducing fruits, and the textual context includes *fruit*, *stem*, *knobby*, and so on, and (c) corresponds to the contextual search results in the context of introducing the Apple Inc., and the textual context include *company*, *logo*, *iphone*, and so on.

1. INTRODUCTION

Image search engines have been playing important roles for consumers to find desired images. Our investigation shows that search queries are often issued when people are browsing Web pages and working on emails, or other documents. In such cases, the context of the query from the associated document is useful to describe user's interest more clearly, e.g., disambiguate the query and hence help to capture the search intent. Better image search results are naturally expected with the help of the context. In this paper, we propose a novel image search scheme, *contextual image search*, which enables users to issue a query by masking textual words or selecting an image in a document and then combines its context information to find more relevant images in the case of *text input* and semantically similar images in the case of *image input*. Beyond contextual Web search, the context in our case is richer and contains visual components, and hence contextual image search is more challenging.

Let's look at several examples to illustrate how the context information facilitates image search. On the one hand, the context is capable of removing the possible ambiguity of a textual query. Given a query "apple" masked by a user, e.g., from `http://www.mahalo.com/apple-fruit`, merely from the word, it is not clear whether it refers to a fruit or a product logo. With its context including *fruit*, *stem*, *knobby* and so on, it is natural that the essential intent of the user is a fruit. The contextual image search results using the proposed technique are shown in Fig. 1(b). In the context of the Web page, `http://en.wikipedia.org/wiki/Apple_Inc.`, including *company*, *logo*, *iphone* and so on, the query "apple" refers to the product logo, and the contextual image search results correspond to Fig. 1(c).

Figure 2: Illustration of reranking image search results using textual context to help find images that better match the user intent implied from the textual context. (a) corresponds to search results of "George Bush", (b) shows the reranking results using the context from the document describing jokes of George Bush, and the textual context includes *joke*, *fool*, *prank*, and so on, and (c) shows the results from one commercial image search engine with the query "Funny George Bush". The results in (b) show that reranking using textual context can indeed take effect and even make the results better than the results in (c) obtained from the explicit query "Funny George Bush".

Figure 3: Illustration of reranking image search results using visual context. (a) shows the visual context of "Queen Victoria", (b) shows the image search results of "Queen Victoria" without contextual reranking, and (c) shows the image search results of "Queen Victoria" with visual contextual reranking, which are more consistent with the visual context in (a).

On the other hand, a user-masked query, even without ambiguities, may be insufficient to express the search intent. For example, the words "George Bush", masked by the user when he is reading the Web page whose content is relevant to jokes of George Bush, `http://www.gwjokes.com/`, has large probability to (of course may not always) mean to search for funny images as the *textual context* includes words such as *joke*, *fool*, *prank*, and so on. Then using the context to rerank search results, called *contextual reranking*, the corresponding reranking results will be more relevant to user intent, as shown Fig. 2(b). Compared the results with the manually-created query "Funny George Bush" in Fig. 2(c), the textually contextual reranking results look more satisfactory.

As another illustration that context can help express the search intent more clearly, Figs. 3(a), 3(b) and 3(c) show an example in which *visual context* for reranking takes effect when masking a textual query, "Queen Victoria" from `http://en.wikipedia.org/wiki/Queen_Victoria`. The visual context from this page is shown in Fig. 3(a), which reflects the user interest on classic images. Image search results without the help of the visual context and with its help are shown in Figs. 3(b) and 3(c), respectively. It can be observed that the results in Fig. 3(c) are more consistent with the content of the document and the style of the visual contexts.

Last, we present an example in Fig. 4 to show that the context helps to return semantically similar image search results when an image is selected as the input from a Web page. Fig. 4(a) shows the selected image from `http://www.istanbulvisions.com/religion.htm`. Our scheme first mines a few candidate queries from the surrounding texts of the duplicate search results

Figure 4: Illustration of contextual image search with image input. (a) corresponds to the selected image, (b) corresponds to the search results of the contextually determined textual query "Blue mosque", (c) corresponds to the reranked search results using the selected image as the seed of similar images.

(e.g., *More sizes* in Microsoft Bing image search and Google image search), and in this example, the candidate queries are "Blue mosque", "Istanbul", "Turkey travel", "Istanbul turkey", and then uses the textual context of the selected image, which includes the sentence, *The mosque is one of several mosques known as the Blue Mosque for the blue tiles adorning the walls of its interior*, to determine the textual query, which is "Blue mosque" in this example. Finally, the search results are shown in Fig. 4(b) and the reranked results with the selected image as the seed of similar images are shown in Fig. 4(c). In contrast, the *More sizes* feature in Microsoft Bing image search and Google image search can only return duplicated images. The *similar* features are not adoptable for only using image as the query input and it is not clear whether the performance is good when conducting similar image search on Microsoft Bing image search without text queries and on Google image search without the help of the surrounding texts.

To utilize context to make image search results more relevant to user intent, we propose two contextual image search schemes, with text input (masking textual words) mentioned in [19] and with image input (selecting an image). For the case of text input, it consists of the following steps. We first extract the context associated with the user input from the document. The context consists of two types: textual context and visual context. Second, we explore the textual context to remove the possible ambiguity for query augmentation. Third, the augmented query is used to perform first-round image search using the text-based image search technique to get a bunch of images. Finally, the textual and visual context information is used to rerank the images to make the results more relevant to user intent. For the case of image input, we use the search-to-annotation technique to mine a few candidate textual queries and then determine the final textual queries using the textual context of the selected image. Of course, the powerful learning-to-(re)ranking algorithms can be easily combined into our system. But the purpose of this paper is to design a system that can be easily deployed based on existing image search engines (e.g., Google's more size and similar search).

To summarize, this paper offers the following key contributions:

- We propose a contextual image search system that performs image search with the help of textual and visual contexts.
- For *contextual image search with text input*, we propose a contextual query augmentation manner to remove the query ambiguity by using the textual context. Particularly, we use the context to help select the most probable augmented query from the candidate augmented queries. Moreover we present a contextual reranking way, which uses the context to rerank search results, to make search results more relevant to user intent. Beyond contextual Web search, the visual context is additionally explored for reranking.

- We propose another search scheme *contextual image search with image input*, i.e., selecting an image from the Web page as the query, to get semantically similar search results.

2. RELATED WORK

A lot of efforts have been conducted to improve image search by helping user more clearly indicate the search intent and making use of the search intent effectively [3, 9, 17]. Most of them focus on presenting interfaces to enable users to express the search intent more conveniently and more clearly, but they do not explore any context information for image search. This type of image schemes can be referred as *image search without context*. In the following, we review *image search without context* and *image search in context* (but without using context), and then pose the promising scheme, *image search with context*.

Image search without context

The widely used commercial image search engines, including Google image search, Yahoo! image search and Microsoft Bing image search, provide an explicit interface, a *text input box*, to enable users to issue textual queries, and then rely only on the input to search the image database. However, a single textual query is frequently not sufficient to clearly indicate the search intent.

Some other image search engines provide features to allow users to upload or draw an image, i.e., issue a *visual query*, to illustrate the search intention visually. Tineye[1] enables users to update an image to trigger a content based image retrieval. Because of the gap between the image feature and the semantic content, such techniques succeed only in finding duplicate or near-duplicate images. An online similar image search engine[2] provides the feature of image search by sketch. However, merely using a visual example as the query for image search does not suffice because it is not guaranteed that visually similar images have similar semantic content.

To exploit the above two schemes for image search together, Microsoft Bing image search provides the *Similar images* feature. First, a user may issue a textual query to get the text-based image search results. Then, to help indicate the search intention more clearly, the user may select an image from the search results that is closer to what the user is interested in and use it to reorder the images according to the visual similarities. But it still suffers from the semantic gap as it is not clear what in an example image is indeed the search intention. The *similar* feature in Google image search seems to explore the surrounding text information to search similar images for the images in the database. However, it does not support the scenario of issuing a query in context that is not in the database, and it is not clear whether the performance is good, even supporting such a scenario.

Besides, commercial image search engines provide *explicit filters* to help users to clarify the search intent into some scopes. For example, Google image search presents options to allow users to find images of different sizes, different types (e.g., face, photo, clip art, and line drawing), or different dominant colors. Microsoft Bing image search additionally provides options to find images with faces or head & shoulders.

There are many other efforts on *interactive query indication* to improve image search. Relevance feedback [2, 11, 15, 26] is one of the most traditional techniques, which allows users to clarify the search intent by selecting a few positive and/or negative images. A so-called CuZero system [27] is proposed to embrace the frontier of interactive visual search for informed users, and specifically an interactive interface is presented to enable users to navigate seamlessly in the concept space at-will and simultaneously while displaying the results corresponding to arbitrary permutations of multiple concepts in real time. The CueFlik system [6] allows end-users to provide examples of images to quickly create their own rules for reranking the images. An interactive image search scheme [18, 24, 25] is proposed to help users find desired images with the requirement on how the concepts or colors are spatially distributed.

Image search in context

One of the most common scenarios where users want to perform image search is reading or writing a document which make users be interested in some matters related to the document. Therefore, to facilitate image search for this scenario, image search engines, including Google image search, Microsoft Bing image search, and Tineye, provide browser (such as IE and Firefox) plugins to enable users to mask keywords or select animage in Web pages so that an image search action can be performed without the necessity of issuing the query at the home page of an image search engine. Such schemes definitely accelerate image search. However, the very useful information besides the user input, called context, available from the document, is not explored for image search.

Image search with context

The concept "context" have different meanings in different application scenarios. For the scenario of object detection [4] in computer vision, the context is usually used to describe the interaction of different objects/concepts, for example, the co-occurrence of different objects in the similar scene. In the scenario of mobile search, the situation of performing image search, including location, time, action history, and search history, can be regarded as the context. In the scenario of personalized search, the personal information, including the personal interest, the search history and so on, are regarded as the search context. In this paper, we regard the surrounding textual and visual information of a query from the document as the context and focus on exploiting such context for image search, but it should be noted that the methodology in this paper can be applied to image search with other types of contexts.

Context information has other usages, e.g., user interests prediction [21] , media processing to bridge the sematic gap [7], in-image advertising [14], and image annotation using duplicate images [20]. Context has also been explored for Web search [5, 8]. But the context is only limited in textual components, and the rich visual context is not exploited. Perhaps, the most related problem is contextual image retrieval [22, 23], but it directly adopts the technique of textual context based Web search, without exploring the visual context. Moreover, we also support the image input for contextual image search.

3. SYSTEM OVERVIEW

The whole contextual image search system consists of two subsystems: database construction system and ranking system. In the database construction system, an image database, which may be a local database, or a global database that is crawled from the Internet, is built and organized as the search database. We extract the visual feature for each image, a bag-of-visual-words (BoW) representation in our implementation, and its text description from the document holding this image, which is obtained using the context capturing scheme that is described later. Then, we build an indexing system that depends on the text description, which makes it efficient to search images with a textual query given. Besides, each image is associated with a static rank, which is computed, for instance, from the static rank of the Web page holding this image.

The ranking system for *contextual image search with text input*

[1] http://www.tineye.com
[2] http://www.gazopa.com

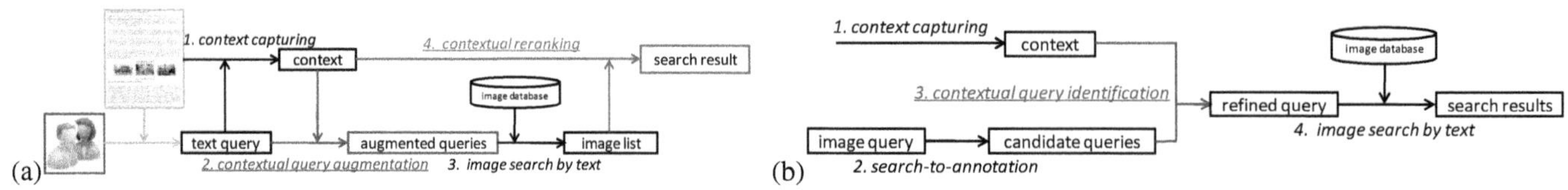

Figure 5: System overview of contextual image search with (a) text input and (b) image input.

is illustrated in Fig. 5(a). The typical input of this system is a few textual keywords masked by the user from a document. The output is a list of ranked images that are from the image database. The remaining system consists of four modules: context capturing, contextual query augmentation, image search by text, and contextual reranking.

1. *Context capturing* is to find a set of textual keywords, called textual context, and a set of images, called visual context, from the document, according to the spatial position of the query in the document.
2. *Contextual query augmentation* is to use the context to refine the query. The textual context is used to augment the query by removing the ambiguity.
3. *Image search by text* is to search images using the augmented query based on the text-based image search technique.
4. *Contextual reranking* aims to make use of both the textual and visual contexts to promote images that have similar contexts with the query.

The key novelty among the system lies in the second and fourth modules, which make use of context to improve the relevance of image search results.

Contextual image search with image input in Fig. 5(b), different from text input, performs two different steps: search to annotation and contextual query identification. *Search to annotation* aims to mine the candidate textual queries for the input image using the surrounding texts of the duplicate images of the input image obtained from the Web [20]. *Contextual query identification*, the key novelty of this scheme, exploits the surrounding texts of the input image and refine the candidate textual queries to finally get the textual queries.

In addition, our system supports the hybrid query, e.g., a pair of masked words and selected image, from a document. In this case, the search is completed by performing the first three step in our system with text input, and then doing visually similar image search, using the technique similar to "Similar images" in Microsoft Bing image search or "Similar" in Google image search. This is a natural extension and we will not present detail discussion on it.

3.1 Notations

The document that the user is reading is denoted as D, and it may contain texts, images, and even videos. The raw textual query, masked by the user from D, is denoted as q, and the raw image query is denoted as q_i. An image in the document is denoted as I^c. The context is denoted as C. It should be noted that the context may contain different types of components and will be described in detail later.

An image in the database is denoted by I_k, and it is associated with a pair of features, a visual feature $\mathbf{h}_k^v$ and a textual feature $\mathbf{h}_k^t$. We represent the image using the popular BoW representation. To obtain a BoW representation, we extract a set of maximally stable extremal regions (MSERs) [13] for each image, represent each region by a scale-invariant feature transform (SIFT) descriptor [10], and then quantize each SIFT descriptor with the k-means algorithm [16]. The BoW representation for an image description will lead to the benefit that the fast indexing and retrieval algorithms used in text search can be directly adopted for image retrieval, which is shown in the video google technique [16]. The textual feature of an image is obtained by using a vector space model to describe its associated textual contexts, and such a textual feature is widely used in existing commercial image search engines.

4. CONTEXTUAL IMAGE SEARCH WITH TEXT INPUT

The contextual image search problem can be formally formulated as follows. Given a query q and the associated document D, the goal is to order the images $\mathcal{I} = \{I_k\}_{k=1}^N$ by computing relevance scores $\mathcal{R} = \{r_k\}_{k=1}^N$ of their visual and contextual information and with the query q and the document D. Mathematically, we define the relevance score as the probability of I_k conditioned on the query and its associated document,

$$r_k = P(I_k|q, D). \qquad (1)$$

To formulate this conditional probability, we introduce the intermediate variables, an augmented query, $\bar{q}^*$, and a context, C^*, which are obtained from the user input and the document. Then Eqn. (1) can be written as follows,

$$P(I_k|q, D) \approx P(I_k|\bar{q}^*, C^*). \qquad (2)$$

This transformation is essentially based on the Bayesian estimation. The following equation will hold

$$P(I_k|q, D) = \sum\nolimits_{\bar{q},C} P(I_k|\bar{q}, C)P(\bar{q}, C|q, D) \qquad (3)$$

$$\approx P(I_k|\bar{q}^*, C^*), \qquad (4)$$

if $P(\bar{q}^*, C^*|q, D)$ is large enough. Here,

$$(\bar{q}^*, C^*) = \arg\max\nolimits_{\bar{q},C} P(\bar{q}, C|q, D). \qquad (5)$$

For convenience, we may drop * in the following description. With this decomposition, our problem can be solved in two steps: (1) processing the document to discover the context and the augmented query, and (2) ranking the images with the discovered context and augmented query.

To obtain the context and the augmented query, we transform the probability $P(\bar{q}, C|q, D)$ as follows,

$$P(\bar{q}, C|q, D) = P(\bar{q}|C, q)P(C|q, D). \qquad (6)$$

This factorization is reasonable because (1) the context is only dependent on the input query and the document and (2) the augmented query can be approximately determined by the query and its context. Therefore, the process can be finished in two steps, context extraction, i.e., discovering the context C^* according to q and D, and contextual query augmentation, i.e., finding $\bar{q}^*$, so that $P(\bar{q}^*|C^*, q)$ is maximized.

To evaluate $P(I_k|\bar{q}, C)$, we propose a two-step scheme. The first step is to perform text-based image search using the augmented query $\bar{q}$. The second step is to perform a reranking step by exploiting the context information. Essentially, the two-step scheme is equivalent to the following decomposition,

$$P(I_k|\bar{q}, C) \propto P(\bar{q}, C|I_k)P(I_k) = P(C|I_k)P(\bar{q}|I_k)P(I_k). \quad (7)$$

Here, $\propto$ holds with $\bar{q}$, C given. The terms, $P(\bar{q}|I_k)P(I_k)$, corresponds to the first step, and the rank model of existing text-based image search engines is essentially equivalent to this model, with $P(I_k)$ being the static rank. The term, $P(C|I_k)$, corresponds to the second step, contextual reranking.

In summary, the implementation of our system consists of the following modules: context capturing ($P(C|D, q)$), contextual query augmentation ($P(\bar{q}|C, q)$), image search by text ($P(\bar{q}|I_k)P(I_k)$), and contextual reranking ($P(C|I_k)$). In the following, we describe the four modules in detail.

4.1 Context Capturing

Context capturing aims to discover the visual and textual context for a query to rank images, as well as the context of an image for database construction. The textual and visual contexts, are denoted by C_t and C_v. The visual context of a query consists of a set of images from the same document and their local textual contexts $C_v = \{C_v^v, C_v^t\}$.

To extract the textual context of an image, we propose to use the vision-based page segmentation (VIPS) algorithm [1]. VIPS can extract the sematic structure of a Web page based on its visual representation. The VIPS algorithm first extracts all the suitable blocks from the Document Object Model tree in html, and then finds the separators between these blocks, where the separators denote the horizontal or vertical lines in a page visually crossing without blocks. Based on these separators, a Web page can be represented by a semantic tree in which each leaf node corresponds to a block. In this way, contents with different topics are distinguished as separate blocks in a Web page.

The VIPS algorithm can be naturally used for surrounding text extraction. For an image, we find the surrounding text from its corresponding block as a part of its textual context. Specifically, the textual context of an image includes $C_t = \{C_t^1, C_t^2, C_t^3\}$, with C_t^1, C_t^2, C_t^3 corresponding to image name and its description with a high weight, page title and document title with a middle weight, and other surrounding text with a low weight, respectively. The images in the database are actually processed using the above scheme to extract their associated textual contexts.

The extraction of textual context for masked keywords is relatively easy. Besides the page title and the document title, the neighboring words of the masked keywords are viewed as surrounding texts, and used as a part of the textual context, called local context. In this case, the textual context includes $C_t = \{C_t^2, C_t^3\}$.

4.2 Contextual Query Augmentation

We propose to make use of the textual context to augment the textual query to remove possible ambiguities. The augmented queries for a textual query q can be formed by combining q and the keywords from the textual context C_t. It might be a solution to use them as queries to search the images. However, obviously, augmented queries obtained in this way may not always be meaningful, and then the returned images may not be satisfactory. Therefore, rather than exploiting the textual context to directly augment queries, we use them as a support to disambiguate the query. To this goal, we first build a set of candidate augmented queries, $Q = \{\bar{q}_1, \bar{q}_2, \cdots, \bar{q}_n\}$, which can remove the ambiguities of the query q. Then, we vote each augmented query in Q using the context C_t.

The following presents a mathematical derivation and its implementation algorithm. We find an optimal augmented query, by checking the posterior of each candidate augmented query, given the context obtained from the document. Mathematically, the posterior can be computed as

$$P(\bar{q}|C_t, q) = \frac{P(C_t|\bar{q}, q)P(\bar{q}|q)}{P(C_t|q)} \propto P(C_t|\bar{q}, q)P(\bar{q}|q), \quad (8)$$

where $P(C_t|\bar{q}, q)$ is the likelihood of the augmented query with respect to the context C_t, and $P(\bar{q}|q)$ is the prior of the augmented query $\bar{q}$. The denominator $P(C_t|q)$ can be ignored because it is independent on $\bar{q}$ and hence is viewed as a constant.

In our implementation, the prior is computed as

$$P(\bar{q}|q) = 1/|Q|, \quad (9)$$

if $\bar{q} \in Q$, and $P(\bar{q}|q) = 0$ if $\bar{q} \notin Q$. This is reasonable because we have no any bias on the candidate augmented queries $\bar{q}$ if no context support.

The likelihood $P(C_t|\bar{q}, q)$ is used to evaluate the relevance between the context C_t and $\bar{q}$. To this end, we borrow the idea of evaluating the relevance between queries and documents. First, we extend the context to get $\bar{C}_t$, which is obtained by expanding the words in C, e.g., using synonyms, stemming, and so on [12]. Then, we adopt the Okapi BM25 algorithm that is used by search engines to rank documents with a search query. Given a candidate augmented query $\bar{q}$ containing n terms $\{q, q_1, q_2, \cdots, q_n\}$, with q being the raw query and q_i being the augmented words, the BM25 score between the extended context and this query is computed as

$$\text{score}(\bar{q}, C_t) = \sum_{i=1}^{n} \frac{idf(q_i) \times tf(q_i, \bar{C}_t) \times (k+1)}{tf(q_i, \bar{C}_t) + k(1 - b + b \times ndl(C_t))}, \quad (10)$$

where $tf(q_i, \bar{C}_t)$ is the term frequency of q_i in $\bar{C}_t$, $idf(q_i)$ is the inverse document frequency, $ndl(C_t) = |C_t|/|\tilde{C}_t|$ is normalized textual context length, $|C_t|$ and $|\tilde{C}_t|$ indicate the context length of C_t and the average context length in the database, and k and b are two parameters and chosen as $k = 2.0$ and $b = 0.75$ in our implementation. The likelihood is calculated as $P(C_t|\bar{q}, q) \propto \text{score}(\bar{q}, C_t)$. Then, the optimal augmented query is selected as

$$\bar{q}* = \arg\max_{\bar{q}} P(C_t|\bar{q}, q)P(\bar{q}|q) = \arg\max_{\bar{q}} \text{score}(\bar{q}, C_t). \quad (11)$$

In the cases that $P(C_t|\bar{q}, q)$ for all $\bar{q}$ has the similar values or that $P(C_t|\bar{q}*, q)$ is very small, i.e., the context is not enough to disambiguate the query, we keep the original raw query, $\bar{q} = q$.

4.3 Image Search by Text

Given the augmented query, we perform text-based image search (Microsoft Bing image search in our implementation), by matching the augmented query with the textual context of each image in the database. The text-based image search returns a list of images, ranked by the static score $P(I_k)$ and the relevances $P(\bar{q}_t|I_k)$ between the textual contexts of images and the query. Specifically, $P(\bar{q}_t|I_k) = \exp[\text{score}(\bar{q}_t, Q_k)]$, where the score is evaluated using Eqn. (10).

4.4 Contextual Reranking

Contextual query augmentation explores only the texts in the textual context that are related to the candidate augmented queries and useful to disambiguate the query. The remaining texts, e.g., describing the situation, and visual contextual, are also very important and useful for image ranking. In the example of Fig. 2, the words, *joke* in the textual context, can help promote funny images.

Therefore, this step, contextual reranking, aims to exploit the context information that presents hints on the search intent to reorder the results from text-based search so that top images are more consistent with the search intent.

Contextual reranking is different from the previous work on visual reranking. Visual reranking explores the visual similarities, reorders the visually similar images together, and at the same time the original order is kept as far as possible. Instead, contextual reranking aims to promote images that match the context better, and also wants to keep the original order as much as possible. Of course, we may also explore the visual similarities for the contextual reranking. But we find that the visual reranking does not make the search results improved in our case, especially when the visual context takes effect. Therefore, in our implementation, we investigate only context for reranking.

Textually contextual reranking

Contextual reranking aims to evaluate the probability, $P(C|I)$. We decompose it into two terms, $P(C|I) = P(C_t|I)P(C_v|I)$, to compute the reranking scores from the textual and visual contexts, respectively. Textually contextual reranking, to evaluate $P(C_t|I)$, is conducted as follows. The textual context except the query related context is helpful to describe the situation that may be of interest and is related to the search intent (as illustrated in Fig. 2). In our implementation, the score from the textual context is computed as the document similarity between the textual context and the text description of images in the search results, and specifically evaluated by the BM25 algorithm. The computation formula is similar to Eqn. (10). But differently, the score is computed between two reduced contexts, which are obtained by discarding the augmented query related words in the original textual contexts, because the augmented query related textual words have been explored in contextual query augmentation for text-based search and the remaining words are useful for reranking. Suppose the similarity from textual context is denoted by $\text{sim}_t(C_t, I_k)$, The probability $P(C_t|I_k)$ is computed as $P(C_t|I_k) \propto \exp(\text{sim}_t(C_t, I_k))$.

Visually contextual reranking

Visually contextual reranking, corresponding to evaluate $P(C_v|I)$, aims to promote the images that are similar to the images from the document that are relevant to the textual query. The similarity from the visual context can be evaluated from the bag-of-visual-words representation. Furthermore, to obtain better visual-words presentation, we perform an augmentation step, which is based on the following observations. 1) The images in a document usually have similar semantic content if their local textual contexts are very relevant to the query, and 2) if each local feature in the bag-of-visual-word representation is homogeneously regarded and not differentiated, some local features that may be irrelevant to the semantic content, e.g., coming from the background, will influence the performance.

In our implementation, we view each image as a document, and borrow the inverse document frequency (idf) technique to weight different visual words, which is often used in information retrieval and text mining to learn the weight for each word. First, we adopt a textual context based filter scheme to filter out images whose semantic contents may not be relevant to the visual query. To this end, we compute the similarity of local textual context of each image in the document with the textual query. The similarity is also evaluated based on the BM 25 algorithm, similar to Eqn. (10). Then, if the similarity is larger than a threshold, the corresponding image will be counted for the idf computing. Specifically, the weight of a visual word is set as $w_i = 1/idf(f_i)$ with f_i corresponding to a visual word, which is different from the conventional tf-idf weighting that aims to remove the meaningless words, while we aim to find the common pattern in the images, which is important for visual similarity computation in our case.

After the augmentation step, we turn to compute the similarity score between visual contexts and each image I_k in the search results from text-based image search. Suppose I_i^c is an image in the filtered visual context and its bag-of-words representation is written as a histogram vector $\mathbf{h}_i^c$, then the similarity between I_i^c and I_k is computed as the weighted histogram intersection,

$$\text{sim}_v(I_i^c, I_k) = \sum\nolimits_j \min(h_{ij}^c, h_{kj})w_j. \quad (12)$$

Then, we compute the similarity between the visual context and an image in the search results by finding the largest one among the similarities between images in the filtered visual context and the image,

$$\text{sim}_v(C_v, I_k) = \max\nolimits_{I_i \in C_v} \text{sim}_v(I_i^c, I_k)\delta_{[I_i]}. \quad (13)$$

Here $\delta_{[I_i]}$ is an indicator to show if I_i lies in the filtered visual context. The probability $P(C_v|I_k)$ is set as $P(C_v|I_k) \propto \exp(\text{sim}_v(C_v, I_k))$.

4.5 Overall Ranking

For one image I_k, its probability conditioned on the context and the augmented query can be computed by

$$\begin{aligned} P(I_k|C, \bar{q}) &\propto P(C|I_k)P(\bar{q}|I_k)P(I_k) & (14)\\ &= P(C_t|I_k)P(C_v|I_k)P(\bar{q}|I_k)P(I_k) & (15)\\ &\propto \exp\left[\lambda_1 \text{sim}_t + \lambda_2 \text{sim}_v + \lambda_3 \text{score}_i\right]. & (16) \end{aligned}$$

Here, $P(I_k) = 1$ as we actually get the top 1000 images that have larger static ranks and do not regard their static ranks homogeneously. sim_t, sim_v and score_i correspond to the similarities from the textual context, the visual context, and text-based image search, respectively, and λ_1, λ_2, and λ_3 are their associated weights, to adjust the degrees that we trust the three factors. $\lambda_1 = 0.2$, $\lambda_2 = 0.2$, and $\lambda_3 = 1$ in our implementation.

5. CONTEXTUAL IMAGE SEARCH WITH IMAGE INPUT

The following investigates the search scenario in which an image is selected as the query. In this case, our experiment shows that the search results are good to find duplicated images by performing CBIR if the bag-of-visual-words representation is used to describe an image, which is also demonstrated in the "More sizes" feature in Microsoft Bing image search and Google image search. Instead, we propose to search semantically similar images rather than duplicate images. The key idea of our approach is to mine the textual query from the selected image. Our approach consists of four steps as shown in Fig. 5(b), where the two key steps are search to annotation and contextual query identification. Search to annotation discovers the candidate textual queries using the technique [20], and contextual query refinement identifies the final textual queries using the context to refine the textual queries. Denote the selected image in this case as q_i, and the formulation is as follows,

$$\begin{aligned} q_t^* &= \arg\max p(q_t|q_i, D) & (17)\\ &= \arg\max \sum\nolimits_{C_t, \tilde{q}_t} p(q_t|\tilde{Q}_t, C_t)p(\tilde{Q}_t|q_i)p(C_t|q_i, D) & (18)\\ &\approx \arg\max p(q_t|\tilde{Q}_t^*, C_t^*). & (19) \end{aligned}$$

Here $C_t^* = \arg\max p(C|q_i, D)$ which corresponds to the context capturing step in Subsec. 4.1. $\tilde{Q}_t^* = \arg\max p(\tilde{Q}_t|q_i)$, which is corresponding to search to annotation for candidate textual query discovering. $p(q_t|\tilde{q}_t^*, C_t^*)$ corresponds to contextual query identification.

The search to annotation step for candidate textual query discovering is as follows. First, the duplicate images of the selected image is found from the Web images, e.g., using the technique similar to the "More sizes" feature in Microsoft Bing image search. Second, the surrounding texts of the obtained duplicated images are mined to get a list of candidate textual queries $\tilde{Q}_t^*$ using the technique [20]. More details could be found from [20]. The final textual queries could be obtained, from the candidate textual queries, $\tilde{Q}_t^*$, i.e., $q_t^* \in \tilde{Q}_t^*$. We evaluate $p(q_t|\tilde{Q}_t^*, C_t^*)$ using the Okapi BM25 algorithm, to get the score score$(\tilde{q}_t, C_t)$. using Eqn. (10).

In our system, we use the query that maximizes score$(\tilde{q}_t, C_t)$ as the final textual query q_t^*. Then, we use q_t^* as the textual query to search images in text-based image search. As an optional step, we rerank the search results using the "Similar image" feature in Microsoft Bing image search, by regarding the selected image from the user as the seed. It is not guaranteed that our approach can always get the exact textual query. Hence, besides presenting the search results from q_t^* to users, our system also presents a few images with other candidate textual queries, to give the chance to users to find possible desired images if the textual query from our approach is not as expected from the users.

6. EXPERIMENT

This section presents quantitative and visual evaluation results for *contextual image search with text input*. We only present visual results for *contextual image search with image input* and do not present the quantitative evaluation because the comparison is naturally clear and our scheme generates semantically similar images while traditional CBIR only gets visually similar images or duplicated images.

6.1 Setup

In our experiment, we implement one instance of contextual image search, specifically for the Web page. To make our system useable, we crawled image search results with textual queries from one existing commercial image search engine. There are 5000 top search queries and their candidate augmented queries (about 10000). For each query, we crawl about 1000 images, and totally we got about 15,000,000 images. For each image, we analyze its Web page and get its context using the aforementioned context capturing scheme.

Data set

We collect the data set to evaluate contextual image search from the search logs that were recorded when users tried the proposed search system. Specifically, we present the system to the users, and show how to use it to perform image search using the three examples shown in Figs. 1, 2 and 3. Then we allow the users to play with the system for about two hours. During the search process, we record each search session, including the Web page URL, and the selected query, into search logs. After all trials, we process the search logs and arrange search sessions together by merging the search sessions with the same raw query as a group of search queries. Totally, we got about 100 groups of search queries. On average, there are about 4 individual search sessions for each group. We randomly sampled 50 groups among them to build the ground truth for quantitative evaluation. These 50 groups of queries include different types, e.g., famous person, site, and products.

Ground truth

The ground truth of the search results are built as follows. For each search session, we ask annotators to label the results: contextual image search result and image search result only with the raw query. Besides the raw query, we also show the document to the annotators to allow annotators to get familiar with the context. To differentiate different relevance degrees, we adopted a graded relevance scale, and use four levels from level 0 (the least relevant) to level 3 (the most relevant). We asked 5 users to judge each search session, and then selected the most frequent level as the final level for each image. To avoid any bias on the labeling, those users were selected such that they have no special knowledge on image search and are initially unknown about the proposed technique.

Evaluation criteria

To evaluate the performance, we use the normalized discounted cumulative gain (nDCG) measure. DCG measures the usefulness, or gain, of a document based on its position in the result list. The gain is accumulated cumulatively from the top of the result list to the bottom with the gain of each result discounted at lower ranks. Two assumptions of DCG measure are that highly relevant documents are more useful when appearing earlier in a search engine result list (have higher ranks) and that highly relevant documents are more useful than marginally relevant documents, which are in turn more useful than irrelevant documents. Comparing a search engine performance from one query to the next cannot be consistently achieved using DCG alone, so the cumulative gain at each position (e.g., p) should be normalized across queries. This is done by sorting documents of a result list by the ground truth, producing an ideal DCG at position p. Mathematically, nDCG at a rank position p is calculated as

$$\text{nDCG}(p) = \text{DCG}(p)/\,\text{iDCG}(p), \tag{20}$$

$$\text{DCG}(p) = \sum\nolimits_{i=1}^{p} r_i/\log_2(i+1), \tag{21}$$

where r_i is the graded relevance of the result at position i, and calculated as $r_i = 2^{c_i} - 1$, with c_i the groundtruth level of the image at position i, iDCG(p) is an ideal DCG at position p. The nDCG values for all queries can be averaged to obtain a measure of the average performance for many queries.

6.2 Quantitative Evaluation

Given the raw query, the context information can be used to disambiguate the raw query to make search intention clearer or present more hints to make search intention more specific, by contextual query augmentation and contextual reranking, respectively. In the following, we compare the schemes, only using contextual query augmentation, only using contextual reranking, and using both the two schemes, with the baseline scheme that directly performs image search with the raw query.

We report nDCG scores at different positions of the schemes, only contextual query augmentation, only contextual reranking, and the whole scheme, for image search. Here we present the scores for the first 40 images because the investigation shows that users often only check the first 40 images (i.e., the first two pages of results). In addition, we also report the result of the baseline algorithm, using the raw query for image search. The comparison results are shown in Fig. 6. From this figure, it can be observed that both contextual query augmentation and contextual reranking can individually make search results improved. To have a deeper view of contextual reranking, we also present the nDCG curves of reranking only with textual context or visual context, respectively. Wherein, the textual context only based approach is essentially equivalent to the mixture models in [22]. We can see that both visual and textual contexts can help improve the relevance.

We also report the relative improvements of these schemes over the baseline algorithm at positions, {1, 5, 10, 20, 40}, which is

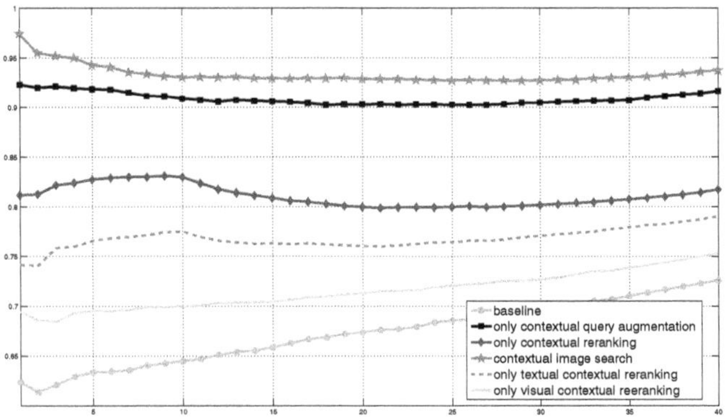

Figure 6: The quantitative evaluation of contextual image search. The average nDCG curves at different positions of the schemes, only using contextual query augmentation, only using contextual reranking, using both the two schemes, and the baseline algorithm without using the context, are presented. We can observe that context can help improve the performance. Particularly, the nDCG curves of reranking, with textual context and visual context, respectively, are also reported to illustrate the effects of the two contexts.

	A	B	C	D	E
1	56.16	47.94	30.13	18.83	11.30
5	48.82	44.97	30.62	20.87	9.746
10	44.28	40.93	28.70	20.20	8.497
20	37.88	34.04	18.76	12.94	5.823
40	29.11	26.22	12.62	8.873	3.752

Table 1: Relative improvements at positions {1, 5, 10, 20, 40} over the baseline scheme for five schemes: A - contextual image search, B - only contextual query augmentation, C - only contextual reranking D - only textual contextual reranking, and E - only visual contextual reranking. The unit is %.

shown in Tab. 1. It can be observed that the proposed contextual image search scheme even gets about 50% improvement over the baseline scheme.

6.3 Visual Results for Text Input

This subsection presents visual results to illustrate the contextual image search performance. To show the effects of contextual query augmentation, textual contextual reranking, and visual contextual reranking, we report the results in three categories.

Contextual query augmentation

We present two visual comparison results shown in Fig. 7. The first example is about famous soccer stars, "Ronaldo". The documents introducing these stars usually only use the name for convenience. We present two contextual search results, when masking the query *Ronaldo* from two Web pages, `http://news.bbc.co.uk/sport2/hi/football/8529228.stm` and `http://www.telegraph.co.uk/sport/football/cristianoronaldo/7234785/Cristiano-Ronaldo-Manchester-United-return-possible.html`, respectively. In the textual context from the former Web page includes *Brazil*, which suggests the search intent be "Ronaldo Brazil" [3] and the words, *Cristiano* and *Manchester*, in the textual context from the latter Web page,

[3]Actually, his full name is Ronaldo Luś Nazário de Lima, but less used due to the complexity. Therefore, we use "Ronaldo Brazil" as the augmented query.

(a) Results with the raw query "Ronaldo".

(b) Results with the augmented query "Ronaldo Brazil". The textual context includes *Brazil* and so on.

(c) Results with the augmented query "Cristiano Ronaldo". The textual context includes *Cristiano*, *Manchester* and so on.

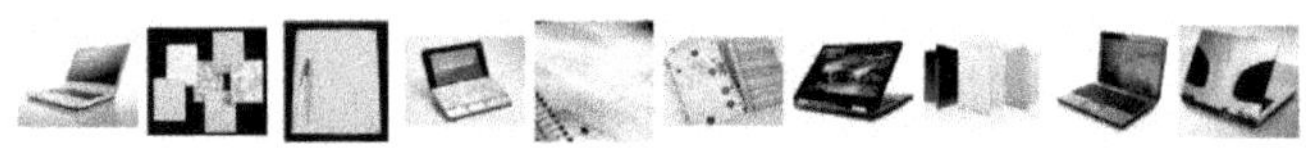

(d) Results with the raw query "notebook".

(e) Results with the augmented query "notebook paper". The textual context includes *paper*, *notepad*, *writing* and so on.

(f) Results with the augmented query "laptop". The textual context includes *laptop*, *computer*, *battery* and so on.

Figure 7: Visual illustration of contextual query augmentation.

suggests the search intent be "Cristiano Ronaldo". In another example, users masked the word "notebook" when reading the Web pages, `http://en.wikipedia.org/wiki/Notebook`, `http://www.consumeraffairs.com/news04/2006/08/dell_fire.html`, and the queries are augmented as "notebook paper" and "laptop", respectively, according to the context. The corresponding results are shown in Fig. 7.

Textually contextual reranking

The visual illustration of textually contextual reranking is presented in Fig. 8. Figs. 8(a) and 8(b) show the image search results without contextual reranking and with contextual reranking, when masking a raw query "Cambridge England" from `http://www.travelpod.com/travel-photo/flyin_bayman/castles_beer-06/1147366740/s-cambridge-punting.jpg/tpod.html`. The textual context of this query from the document contains the keywords *river*, *boat* and *floating*. Therefore, with textually contextual reranking, the images with rivers are promoted as shown in Fig. 8(b). As another example shown in Figs. 8(c) and 8(d), a user may issue a raw text query "Michael Jordan" when reading the Web page, `http://www.nba.com/jordan/mjslamdunk.html`. The textual context of this query contains keywords like *dunk* and *slam*. As a result, images with these keywords (or expanded words) in its textual contexts, which have large probability to illustrate slam dunks of Michael Jordan, are promoted. The two examples show that the textual context can help find images that are more consistent with user search intention.

Visually contextual reranking

We also show visual examples to illustrate visual context can also help clarify user search intention from the visually contextual reranking. The example in Fig. 3 has shown that

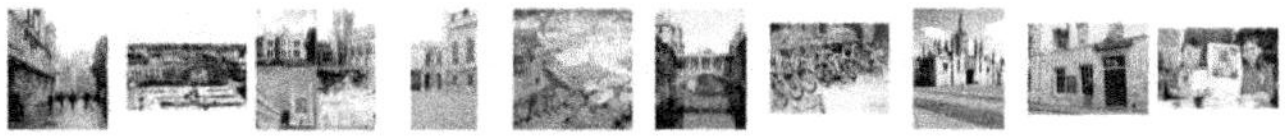

(a) Results of "Cambridge England" without contextual reranking.

(b) Results of "Cambridge England" with textual contextual reranking. The textual context contains *river*, *boat* and *floating*.

(c) Results of "Michael Jordan" without contextual reranking.

(d) Results of "Michael Jordan" with textual contextual reranking. The textual context contains *dunk* and *slam*.

Figure 8: Visual illustration of textually contextual reranking.

(a) Irrelevant

(b) Irrelevant

(c) Relevant

Figure 9: Image context for "Tower bridge". With the filtering scheme based on the relevance of the local textual context with the query, images in (a) and (b) are filtered out, and the image in (c) is left for visually contextual reranking.

visual context is helpful to find images that are more relevant to users. Here, we present another example with the query "Tower bridge" from `http://www.the-pass.co.uk/ArticleDetails.asp?ArticleID=123`. Its visual context is shown in Fig. 9, and with the filtering scheme based on the relevance of the local text context with the query, only the image in Fig. 9(c) is used for visual contextual reranking. The image search results without contextual reranking and with visually contextual reranking are shown in Figs. 10(a) and 10(b). From the two figures, we can see that the images with tower bridge under the night are ranked on the top after visual contextual reranking, which is more reasonable as the user, reading the document about tower bridge describing the scene under the night, may be more interested in such images.

6.4 Visual Results for Image Input

In the following, we show the visual results of our contextual image search scheme with image input. Fig. 12 shows the search results when a user selects the image shown in Fig. 11(a) as the search input from `http://arthistory.about.com/b/2009/05/05/the-artists-the-argument-the-epee-and-the-ear.htm`. The candidate textual queries from the surrounding texts of the duplicated images of the selected image are *Van gogh* and *Bandaged ear*. However, the surrounding text of the selected image and its name only contain *Van gogh*, not *Bandaged ear*. Hence, our scheme determines the final query as "Van gogh", and the corresponding search results are shown in Fig. 12(a). As an option, the user may select to see the reranking results with the selected

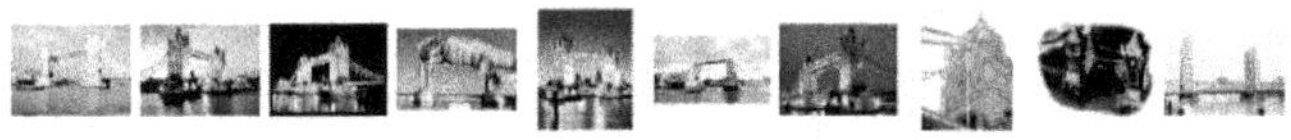

(a) Results of "Tower bridge" without contextual reranking.

(b) Results of "Tower bridge" with visually contextual reranking, which are more consistent with the visual context in Fig. 9.

Figure 10: Visual illustration of visually contextual reranking.

image as the seed, which are shown in Fig. 12(b). From the results, the user can see different versions of the selected image.

Fig. 13 shows another case when a user reads the Web page about Olympic `http://www.kentsport.org/london2012/groups_arts_nov08.asp` and becomes interested in the image in it shown in Fig. 11(b). By analyzing the surrounding texts of the duplicated images, we extract three candidate textual queries, *barcelona*, *barcelona olympics*, and *olympic mascot*. As the textual context of this selected image contains many occurrences of *olympic mascot*, the best textual query determined from the context would be "olympic mascot". The corresponding search results are shown in Fig. 13(a). Here, the name of the selected image, "barca_mascot.jpg", suggests *barcelona olympics* would be another textual query. Hence, our scheme in this case also suggests this to the user as an option and the corresponding results are shown in Fig. 13(b).

6.5 User Study

We conducted user studies to show that the proposed contextual image search is very convenient and helpful for users to perform image search. We recruit 30 volunteers, students from university campus and our research lab, to take part in the user study. Their grades vary from freshman to graduate grade 3. Their ages range from 19 to 24. All participants are Web image search engine users.

We first present a question to them. The question is about the situations where an image search action is triggered from their experiences. The answers show that there are three major situations to trigger users to perform image search: famous sites and people when reading documents, interesting objects heard or seen from other way, and meaningful things demanded in their work. The answers show that the proposed contextual image search scheme will make image search very convenient for users as image search actions often take place when reading documents.

Then, we allow them to use three image search engines: existing commercial image search engine with a text query input box, reduced contextual image search without using contexts, and our contextual image search. After using them about three hours, they give us the feedbacks on using them. The feedbacks show that 1) the latter two schemes for image search make them search image more efficient and convenient, and 2) search results of contextual image search are more satisfactory and most of them match their search intention very well although the intention is not indicated in the issued raw query.

7. CONCLUSION

In this paper, we present a contextual image search scheme that uses the context to better understand the search intent and expect better image search results. The context information, including the surrounding text, other main text information and the images, is first extracted from the document where the query is generated. We present two contextual image search cases, text input and image

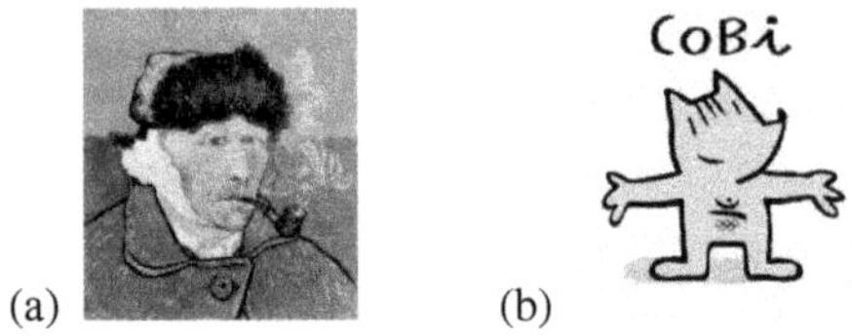

Figure 11: Image inputs for contextual image search.

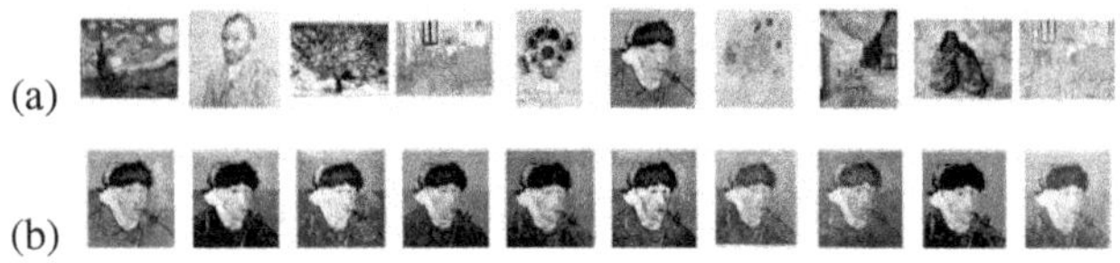

Figure 12: Visual results of contextual image search with the image input shown in Fig. 11(a). (a) corresponds to the search results of the contextually determined textual query "Van gogh", (b) corresponds to the reranked search results using the selected image as the seed of similar images.

input. The former case makes use of contexts to help augment the queries and rerank the search results. The later case exploits the textual contexts to determine a textual query to finally get semantically similar images rather than duplicate images. The experimental results and user studies justify that the proposed contextual image search scheme is very helpful and effective.

In the future, we will develop more general contextual image search, including mobile image search with wider contexts (e.g., position, time, and history). Moreover, we will extend contextual image search to contextual video search by applying the proposed methodology and investigating extra video contexts.

8. REFERENCES

[1] D. Cai, S. Yu, J.-R. Wen, and W.-Y. Ma. Vips: a vision-based page segmentation algorithm. Technical Report MSR-TR-2003-79, Microsoft, 2003.

[2] J. Cui, F. Wen, and X. Tang. Intentsearch: interactive on-line image search re-ranking. In *ACM Multimedia*, pages 997–998, 2008.

[3] R. Datta, D. Joshi, J. Li, and J. Z. Wang. Image retrieval: Ideas, influences, and trends of the new age. *ACM Comput. Surv.*, 40(2), 2008.

[4] S. K. Divvala, D. Hoiem, J. Hays, A. A. Efros, and M. Hebert. An empirical study of context in object detection. In *CVPR*, pages 1271–1278, 2009.

[5] L. Finkelstein, E. Gabrilovich, Y. Matias, E. Rivlin, Z. Solan, G. Wolfman, and E. Ruppin. Placing search in context: the concept revisited. *ACM Trans. Inf. Syst.*, 20(1):116–131, 2002.

[6] J. Fogarty, D. S. Tan, A. Kapoor, and S. A. J. Winder. Cueflik: interactive concept learning in image search. In *CHI*, pages 29–38, 2008.

[7] R. Jain. Multimedia information retrieval: watershed events. In *Multimedia Information Retrieval*, pages 229–236, 2008.

[8] R. Kraft, C.-C. Chang, F. Maghoul, and R. Kumar. Searching with context. In *WWW*, pages 477–486, 2006.

[9] M. S. Lew, N. Sebe, C. Djeraba, and R. Jain. Content-based multimedia information retrieval: State of the art and challenges. *TOMCCAP*, 2(1):1–19, 2006.

Figure 13: Visual results of contextual image search with the image input shown in Fig. 11(b). (a) corresponds to the search results of the contextually determined textual query "Olympic Mascot", (b) corresponds to the search results of the second possible textual query "Barcelona olympics".

[10] D. G. Lowe. Distinctive image features from scale-invariant keypoints. *International Journal of Computer Vision*, 60(2):91–110, 2004.

[11] Y. Luo, W. Liu, J. Liu, and X. Tang. Mqsearch: image search by multi-class query. In *CHI*, pages 49–52, 2008.

[12] C. D. Manning, P. Raghavan, and H. Schütze. *Introduction to Information Retrieval*. Cambridge University Press, 2008.

[13] J. Matas, O. Chum, M. Urban, and T. Pajdla. Robust wide baseline stereo from maximally stable extremal regions. In *BMVC*, 2002.

[14] T. Mei, X.-S. Hua, and S. Li. Contextual in-image advertising. In *ACM Multimedia*, pages 439–448, 2008.

[15] Y. Rui and T. S. Huang. A novel relevance feedback technique in image retrieval. In *ACM Multimedia (2)*, pages 67–70, 1999.

[16] J. Sivic and A. Zisserman. Efficient visual search of videos cast as text retrieval. *IEEE Trans. Pattern Anal. Mach. Intell.*, 31(4):591–606, 2009.

[17] A. W. M. Smeulders, M. Worring, S. Santini, A. Gupta, and R. Jain. Content-based image retrieval at the end of the early years. *IEEE Trans. Pattern Anal. Mach. Intell.*, 22(12):1349–1380, 2000.

[18] J. Wang and X.-S. Hua. Interactive image search by color map. *ACM TIST*, 3(1):26, 2012.

[19] J. Wang, W. Lu, X.-S. Hua, S. Wang, and S. Li. Contextual image search. Technical report, MSR-TR-2010-84, 2010.

[20] X.-J. Wang, L. Zhang, X. Li, and W.-Y. Ma. Annotating images by mining image search results. *IEEE Trans. Pattern Anal. Mach. Intell.*, 30(11):1919–1932, 2008.

[21] R. W. White, P. Bailey, and L. Chen. Predicting user interests from contextual information. In *SIGIR*, pages 363–370, 2009.

[22] X. Xing, Y. Zhang, and B. Gong. Mixture model based contextual image retrieval. In *CIVR*, pages 251–258, 2010.

[23] X. Xing, Y. Zhang, and M. Han. Query difficulty prediction for contextual image retrieval. In *ECIR*, pages 581–585, 2010.

[24] H. Xu, J. Wang, X.-S. Hua, and S. Li. Image search by concept map. In *SIGIR*, pages 275–282, 2010.

[25] H. Xu, J. Wang, X.-S. Hua, and S. Li. Interactive image search by 2d semantic map. In *WWW*, pages 1321–1324, 2010.

[26] R. Yan, A. Natsev, and M. Campbell. Multi-query interactive image and video retrieval: theory and practice. In *CIVR*, pages 475–484, 2008.

[27] E. Zavesky and S.-F. Chang. Cuzero: embracing the frontier of interactive visual search for informed users. In *Multimedia Information Retrieval*, pages 237–244, 2008.

MUSIZ: A Generic Framework for Music Resizing with Stretching and Cropping

Zhang Liu[†,‡], Chaokun Wang[‡,§,♮,♯], Yiyuan Bai[†,‡], Hao Wang[†,‡], Jianmin Wang[‡,§,♮]
[†]Department of Computer Science and Technology, Tsinghua University
[‡]School of Software, Tsinghua University, Beijing 100084, China
[§]Tsinghua National Laboratory for Information Science and Technology
[♮]Key Laboratory for Information System Security, Ministry of Education
[♯]Key Laboratory of Intelligent Information Processing, Institute of Computing Technology, CAS
{liuzhang08,byy06,wanghao07}@mails.thu.edu.cn, {chaokun,jimwang}@tsinghua.edu.cn

ABSTRACT

Content-aware music adaption, i.e. *music resizing*, in temporal constraints starts drawing attention from multimedia communities because of the need of real-world scenarios, e.g. animation production and radio advertisement production. The goal of music resizing is to change the length of a music track to a user preferred length using a series of basic operations, e.g. compression, prolonging, cropping and repeating. The only existing music resizing approach so far, called LyDAR, suffers from some limitations. For example, it cannot support prolonging a music track and cannot compress music pieces with very small stretch rates. In this paper, we propose MUSIZ, a generic framework for **MU**sic re**SIZ**ing. Observing the diversity of quality degradation for different segments, we propose the concept of *stretch-resistance* to measure the degree of quality degradation after a segment is stretched. MUSIZ stretches high stretch-resistance segments intensively and relieves low stretch-resistance segments to reduce the negative impact on the stretched music piece. For short length resizing requests, we develop a contiguity-preservative cropping algorithm to remove segments before stretching, while smoothing the abrupt change at the joint between two segments. Comprehensive experimental results show that MUSIZ is superior to the existing approaches.

Categories and Subject Descriptors

H.5.5 [**Information Interfaces and Presentation**]: Sound and Music Computing

General Terms

Algorithms

Keywords

Music resizing, music retargeting, stretch-resistance

*Area Chair: Tat-Seng Chua

MM'11, November 28–December 1, Scottsdale, Arizona, USA.

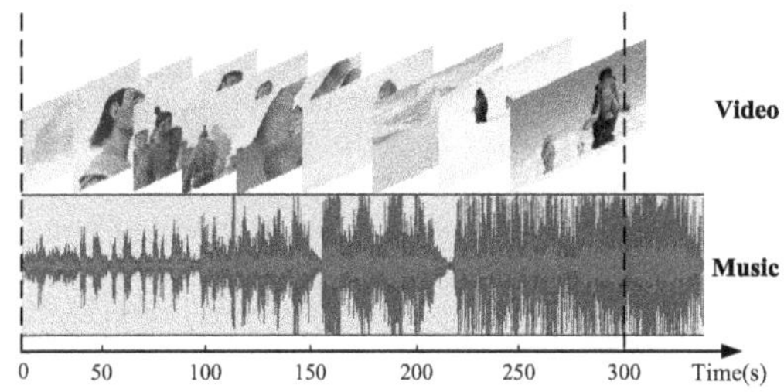

Figure 1: A use scenario of music resizing. The music track (335s) is selected as the background music of a video clip (300s).

1. INTRODUCTION

The task of content-aware media adaptation (CAMA) is content-based adjustment of a medium entity to satisfy given spatial or temporal constraints. For instance, an editor wants to adjust a 400×300 pixel resolution portrait to a 200 × 400 pixel resolution version so that it can be arranged in the layout of a magazine page. There exist many works on CAMA in spatial constraints (image [4, 24] and video [15, 25]), whereas few attention has been paid to CAMA in temporal constraints (music [19, 18]). However, a number of requirements on the latter are emerging. For example, in film post-production stage, a film editor wants to accompany a 300s animation with a 335s song as illustrated in Fig. 1.

We address content-aware music adaptation, i.e. *music resizing*, in this paper. The intuitive idea of music resizing is based on the discovery that stretch-resistance of different music segments may be different. The stretch-resistance measures the degree of quality degradation for a music segment after stretching (compression or prolonging). For high stretch-resistance segments, the quality degradation is slower than segments with low stretch-resistance, i.e. high stretch-resistance indicates the strong robustness against stretching. For example, the perceptual artifacts [16] can easily appear in the resized segments with human voices, especially in high tempo segments. In other words, the quality of a resized music segment with singing voice degrades more intensively than that of a voiceless segment with the same stretch rate [1]. This is because human hearing is more sensitive to human voice, compared with pure instrumental sound [7]. Inspired by this fact, music resizing technology stretches different parts in a music piece non-homogeneously. In order to decrease the quality degradation caused by stretching, music segments with high stretch-resistance

[1]The stretch rate, denoted as α, is defined as the ratio of the user preferred length T_u to the length of the original music piece $T_{\mathcal{M}}$, i.e. $\alpha = T_u/T_{\mathcal{M}}$

are stretched more significantly and the stretching amounts of low stretch-resistance segments are relieved.

The only existing music resizing approach proposed so far is LyDAR [19, 18] in which the structure of a music track is analyzed by parsing the corresponding lyrics file. Lyrics density, measured by number of words per second, is utilized to measure the stretch-resistance of a segment. Assuming that a segment with high lyrics density is more fragile than the one with lower lyrics density, segments are compressed with different stretch rates according to their lyrics densities. However, LyDAR suffers from the following limitations. Firstly, LyDAR cannot handle music tracks without lyrics, e.g. electronic music and light music. Secondly, LyDAR does not cope with the prolonging situation, i.e., the user preferred length is larger than the original length of the music piece, which is a common requirement for audio editing. Thirdly, the distribution of stretch-resistance within a lyrics sentence cannot be captured, because the structure analysis phase only utilizes lyrics files. A lyrics file in LRC format provides lyrics words and the start timestamps of each sentence. Thus, all parts within a music segment corresponding to a lyrics sentence share the same stretch-resistance. And we cannot capture details within a sentence, e.g. slow and silent parts at the end of a sentence, the absence and appearance of human voice within a sentence. Finally, LyDAR cannot support low stretch rate. Only stretching operation is used for resizing in LyDAR and the stretching operation will degrade the quality of music significantly when the stretch rate is smaller than a threshold, say $\alpha \leq 50\%$.

We propose **MUSIZ**, a generic framework for **MU**sic re**SIZ**ing, in this paper. First of all, both lyrics density (i.e. phoneme rate) and acoustic features (e.g. onset, pitch) are used to estimate the stretch-resistance. The stretch-resistance reveals how much degradation a stretching operation will cause on a music clip, i.e. the robustness against the time-scale stretch. After the distribution of stretch-resistance in a music track is obtained, the scheduling algorithm distributes the stretch amount to different parts in a music piece, aiming to minimize the quality degradation of the resized music piece. Specifically, segments, which are robust to stretch, are intended to be compressed or prolonged intensively, but segments, which are sensitive to stretch, are going to be prevented from over-stretching. To improve the quality of the resized music piece, some music clips will be removed from the original music piece if the user preferred stretch rate is much smaller than 100% (e.g. 50%). The removed music clips are well selected so that the cropped music track which consists of the remaining segments will sound smooth and fluent.

To the best of our knowledge, MUSIZ is the first work addressing the generic content-aware music resizing framework which is able to resize tracks in both compression and prolonging cases. The main contributions of our proposal are summarized as follows:

- We propose a content-aware music resizing framework which supports both compression and prolonging.
- We present a new stretch-resistance measurement by mixing lyrics density and content-based audio features for accurate quality degradation estimation.
- We develop an adaptive resizing algorithm which utilizes both stretching and cropping operations to alleviate the quality degradation of the resized music track.
- We design a music clip cropping algorithm, which eliminates the abrupt change at the joint between two segments after removing segments between them.
- We conduct both subjective and objective experiments on a music collection with 1230 music tracks and the results show that MUSIZ can resize music tracks effectively and efficiently.

The rest of this paper is structured as follows. Previous work are reviewed in Section 2. The overview of the proposed music resizing framework is presented in Section 3. Technologies involved in the structure analysis phase, e.g. segmentation and labeling, are detailed in Section 4. Section 5 discusses the music synthesis technologies, including the stretching and cropping algorithms. The experimental results are reported and analyzed in Section 6. Finally, we conclude this paper in Section 7.

2. RELATED WORK

Music resizing is related to various areas in music analysis and audio processing. In the section, we briefly survey the previous works, and point out the primary differences between them and the technology proposed in this paper.

2.1 Music Structure Analysis

Music structure analysis is a traditional task for music research communities, which aims to extract the high-level structure information from low level audio features. Foote *et al.* [13] presented methods of estimating the instantaneous audio novelty by analyzing self-similarity, instead of relying on particular acoustic cues or requiring training. Zhang *et al.* [29] developed a heuristic rule-based procedure to segment and classify audio signals into basic audio types, such as silence, speech and music, by using low level audio features. Dannenberg *et al.* [10] took repetition as a universal characteristic in musical structure modeling and developed the algorithms to find the approximate repeated patterns in a music object. Chai *et al.* [8] presented an algorithm to automatically analyze the repetitive structure of musical signals. Dynamic programming is used to detect the repetitions of each segment with fixed length in a music piece and the music structure is inferred by summarizing the repetition information. Abdallah *et al.* [3] used the optimized Markov chain Monte Carlo methods and the modified Wolff's algorithm to generate music segments. Barrington *et al.* [5] adopted a dynamic texture to represent a music fragment and segment a music piece by clustering audio fragment with a dynamic texture mixture model. Most currently, Weiss *et al.* [28] utilized the sparse shift-invariant probabilistic latent component analysis to detect repeated patterns in a music piece. For more comprehensive historical overview about the music structure analysis, we refer the reader to a recent survey [23].

2.2 Music Retargeting

Music retargeting is the most related topic to our work. The existing music retargeting technologies can be categorized into two classes, i.e. *time stretching* and *music thumbnailing*.

Time stretching is designed to change the speed of audio signal, preserving original frequency components. The overlap-add (OLA) based algorithms are a family of time stretching algorithms (e.g. the waveform similarity based overlap-add (WSOLA) algorithm [27] proposed by Verhelst). Recently Grofit *et al.* [14] proposed an enhanced WSOLA algorithm which avoided the perceptually significant transient (PST) sections during the procedure of stretching. The time stretching approaches focus on the signal-level scaling with small length variance. But our resizing framework processes a music piece in the music structure level.

Music thumbnailing (a.k.a. music summarization) is another way of music retargeting, which aims at generating a representative audio excerpt of a piece of music. The music thumbnail is composed of one or several clips from a song. Usually, the most repeated segments are extracted as the music thumbnails. For example, Logan *et al.* [25] proposed a clustering based and a hidden Markov model (HMM) based segmentation approaches, and then identified the most repeated segment from a piece of music. Cooper *et al.* [20] proposed the similarity matrix approach using the Mel-frequency

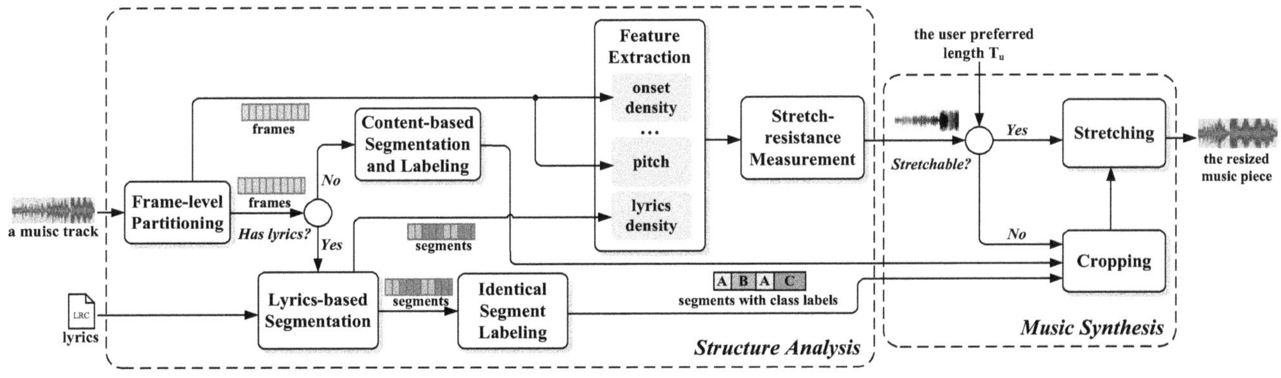

Figure 2: The proposed music resizing framework

cepstral coefficients (MFCC) to measure the similarity between different segments, so that the thumbnail of a music piece is the segment with the most number of similar segments. Bartsch [6] and Goto [21] took advantage of chroma based features, which project the entire spectrum onto 12 distinct semitones of the musical octave, to detect the repeated pattern in a piece of music. A heuristic method based on high-level features was used to find the most salient segment as the music thumbnail. Xu *et al.* [9] combined spectral power, amplitude envelope and MFCC as the features of segmentation and adopted a clustering approach to find the most frequent segment as the music summary. Levy *et al.* [17] proposed a timbre feature based clustering approach to music segmentation and the most repeated segment was selected as the thumbnail.

Goals of the music summarization and the music resizing are different. Music summarization focuses on finding the most representative clip in a music track, but it does not concentrate on the temporal requirement. So the length of the selected clip is often different from the user preferred length. Besides, music summarization does not care about the appreciation of the modified music track, e.g., the abrupt start and end of the selected clip may spoil the aesthetics of music. As a result, the music summarization is more suitable for music browsing or music retrieval tasks. E.g., Amazon.com provides a 30s sample for each music track. The goal of music resizing is to change the length of a music track to the user preferred length accurately, while relieving the quality degradation of the resized music track (in terms of fluency, integrity, continuity etc.). Thus, music resizing is designed as a music editing technique for automatic high quality temporal modification of music tracks, e.g. the background music production.

3. FRAMEWORK OVERVIEW

In this section, we propose our music resizing framework, i.e. MUSIZ. The input of MUSIZ are the audio file of a music track $\mathcal{M}$, the corresponding lyrics file (optional) as well as the user preferred length T_u. T_u is given by users and indicates whether the music track $\mathcal{M}$ needs to be compressed ($T_u < T_\mathcal{M}$) or prolonged ($T_u > T_\mathcal{M}$), where $T_\mathcal{M}$ represents the length of $\mathcal{M}$. After taking the inputs, MUSIZ then analyzes the music piece $\mathcal{M}$, and carefully modifies the audio content of the music piece so that the length of the modified music piece is exactly T_u.

The workflow diagram of the framework is shown in Fig.2. First of all, a music track is split into *frames* with fixed length, which is the basic unit of acoustic feature extraction and stretching in our framework. After that, the sequence of frames are divided into several sub-sequences and each sub-sequence is called a *segment*. We then calculate the similarity between segments, and similar or identical segments are labeled with the same tag. The labeled segments are useful when we want to remove some parts from the music piece. Methods of the music segmentation and labeling are different, depending on the existence of the corresponding lyrics (in LRC format). For music tracks with lyrics, the segmentation can be easily achieved by splitting the music track according to the lyrics sentences. Each segment corresponds to a sentence in lyrics. We then calculate the similarity between all pairs of segments based on the cross-correlation method. Two segments are considered to be identical segments if they are similar enough. Finally, identical segments are classified into a group and labeled with the same tag (e.g. 'A' or 'B'). For music tracks without lyrics, we extract the chroma features [6] for each frame. And then the repetition based structure analysis approach proposed by Chai *et al.* [8] is employed to segment the music track and label repeated segments. The structure of a music track is represented as a sequence of labeled segments (e.g. 'ABAC') as shown in Fig. 2.

The stretching operation degrades the quality of a frame and the quality degradation of different frames may vary [19, 18]. Before modifying the music track, we must determine how much quality degradation a frame will suffer from if it is stretched. Thus, we extract lyrics and acoustic features from frames, e.g. lyrics density, onset density and pitch. The *stretch-resistance* of a frame is estimated based on the features, revealing how much changes in these features are caused due to the stretching operation. Once the stretch-resistance information of all frames is obtained, MUSIZ schedules the stretch rate of each frame.

It is common sense that a music track cannot be compressed or prolonged with an arbitrary stretch rate. For example, the quality of a resized 15s music clip which is compressed from a 300s one is obviously intolerant ($\alpha = 5\%$). Similarly, we cannot accept a music clip which is stretched from a length 15s to 300s ($\alpha = 2000\%$) either. Therefore, we introduce the minimal stretch rate $\alpha_{\min}$ and the maximal stretch rate $\alpha_{\max}$ to prevent music tracks from being over-stretched. We call the music piece is *stretchable* with the stretch length T_u if the stretch rate $\alpha = T_u/T_\mathcal{M}$ is between $\alpha_{\min}$ and $\alpha_{\max}$. In other words, we use the stretching operation to resize a music piece only if $\alpha \in [\alpha_{\min}, \alpha_{\max}]$. In practice, we set $\alpha_{\min} = 80\%$ and $\alpha_{\max} = 200\%$.

If a music piece is *stretchable* with the user preferred length T_u, the stretching operation is executed to stretch the length of the music piece to the user preferred length. Note that, given the same stretch rate, the quality of low stretch-resistance frames degrades more severely than that of high stretch-resistance frames. To achieve a better quality of the resized music track, it is reasonable to schedule stretch rates over different frames according to their stretch-resistance. In detail, the stretching algorithm of MUSIZ stretches high stretch-resistance frames intensively, whereas decreases the stretching amount on low stretch-resistance frames.

During the stretching process, WSOLA [27] is used to scale all audio frames in the music piece.

If a music piece is not *stretchable* with the user preferred length T_u, MUSIZ has to tackle two difficult conditions, i.e. too long user preferred length in prolonging cases or too short user preferred length in compression cases. 1) *In the prolonging cases* (i.e. $\alpha > 100\%$), MUSIZ only needs to handle stretch rates ranging from 100% to 200%, i.e. $100\% < \alpha < 200\%$. Because, compared with prolonging some or all parts in the music track, it is more acceptable to repeat the entire music track several times when $\alpha \geq 200\%$. A real-world situation is the background music in a parade or ceremony (e.g. nation parade in Olympic games or a wedding), where the march is played repeatedly. We resize the music track in a repeating manner when $\alpha \geq 200\%$. In detail, we first get the *average stretch rate* $\tilde{\alpha} = \frac{\alpha}{\lfloor\alpha\rfloor}$. It is obvious that $100\% \leq \tilde{\alpha} < 200\%$ holds. After that, the music piece is resized with the average stretch rate $\tilde{\alpha}$. Finally, we repeat and concatenate the resized music piece $\lfloor\alpha\rfloor$ times. And the length of the concatenated clip is exactly α times of the length of the original music piece. Therefore, we only need consider $0 < \alpha < 200\%$ in the rest of this paper. 2) *In the compression cases* when the user preferred length is too short (i.e. $\alpha < \alpha_{\min}$), the cropping operation is executed to remove some parts from the music piece until the remaining music piece is *stretchable* with the user stretch length. Cropping is based on sequences of segments, because segments are relative independent elements in a music piece. In order to implement high quality cropping, we add a restriction to the cropping algorithm. The restriction is based on the labels which we get in the structure analysis phase. It demands that the sequence of segments between two segments s_i and s_j can be removed only if they can connect naturally.

Algorithm 1 illustrates steps of the music resizing algorithm. Key steps in MUSIZ are classified into two phases as shown in Fig. 2, i.e. *structure analysis* and *music synthesis*. In the following two sections, we detail the technologies of structure analysis and music synthesis, respectively.

Algorithm 1: MUSIC-RESIZING-ALGORITHM($\mathcal{M}$, T_u)

Input : $\mathcal{M}$ — the music piece to be resized;
T_u — the user preferred length;
Output : $\mathcal{M}_r$ — the resized music piece;
Calculate the stretch rate $\alpha = T_u/T_{\mathcal{M}}$;
Divide $\mathcal{M}$ into n ℓ-length frames $q_1 q_2 \cdots q_n$;
Split the frame sequence into segments and label identical segments;
Extract features and calculate the stretch-resistance of each frame;
if $\alpha \geq 200\%$ **then** $\tilde{\alpha} \leftarrow \frac{\alpha}{\lfloor\alpha\rfloor}$;
else $\tilde{\alpha} \leftarrow \alpha$;
if $\mathcal{M}$ *is* stretchable *with* T_u *(*$80\% < \tilde{\alpha} < 200\%$*)* **then**
  $\mathcal{M}_r \leftarrow$ Stretch $\mathcal{M}$ with stretch rate $\tilde{\alpha}$;
else
  $(\mathcal{M}', \alpha') \leftarrow$ Crop $\mathcal{M}$ with stretch rate $\tilde{\alpha}$;
  $\mathcal{M}_r \leftarrow$ Stretch $\mathcal{M}'$ with stretch rate α';
end if
if $\alpha \geq 200\%$ **then** $\mathcal{M}_r \leftarrow$ Repeat and concatenate $\mathcal{M}_r$ $\lfloor\alpha\rfloor$ times;
return $\mathcal{M}_r$;

4. STRUCTURE ANALYSIS

To perform high quality music resizing, it is necessary to obtain the structural information of a music track. The structure analysis phase includes *segmentation*, *segment labeling*, *feature extraction* and *stretch-resistance estimation*. Segmentation divides a music track into disjoint segments. And then we exploit the similarity between segments in order to extract the repetitive structures in a music track. Besides, the lyrics feature and acoustic features are extracted from segments and frames respectively. Finally, the stretch-resistance of frames is derived based on the lyrics and acoustic features extracted from segments and frames respectively.

4.1 Segmentation and Labeling

First of all, the music track $\mathcal{M}$ is divided into *frames*, i.e. $q_1 q_2 q_3 \ldots q_n$, where q_i is the ith frame and n is the number of frames in $\mathcal{M}$. The length of each frame t_ℓ is 2048 samples. We then split the entire music track, in form of a sequence of frames $q_1 q_2 \ldots q_n$, into non-overlapping sub-sequences of frames. Each sub-sequence of frames is called a *segment*, denoted as s_i. Furthermore, we calculate the similarity among segments. Similar segments are classified into a group and labeled with the same tag. Technologies used for segmentation and labeling are different, depending on whether the corresponding lyrics is available or not. Now we discuss the two kinds of segmentation and labeling methods, respectively.

For Music Tracks without Lyrics: The *content-based segmentation* is utilized to divide the music track into segments. We use the chroma based segmentation and labeling approach described in [8], because it is efficient and reliable most of time. Here we just summarize the primary steps of the method and refer the reader to [8] for detailed description. Firstly, the 12-dimensional chroma feature [6] is extracted for each frame. The 12 elements of the chroma feature represent the pitch classes C, C♯, D, D♯, E, F, F♯, G, G♯, A, A♯, B, separately. After the feature extraction, the music track is represented as a sequence of vectors $V = \mathbf{v_1 v_2} \ldots \mathbf{v_n}$, where $\mathbf{v_i}$ is the chroma vector of q_i and n is the number of frames in the music track. Secondly, we calculate the cosine distance $d_{i,j}$ between feature vectors $\mathbf{v_i}$ and $\mathbf{v_j}$ as

$$d_{i,j} = 0.5 \cdot \left(1 - \frac{\langle \mathbf{v_i}, \mathbf{v_j} \rangle}{\|\mathbf{v_i}\| \cdot \|\mathbf{v_j}\|}\right), \quad (1)$$

where $\langle \cdot, \cdot \rangle$ represents the dot product of two vectors and $\| \cdot \|$ is the L^2-norm of a vector. Distances of all frames with each other are calculated in a pairwise fashion and the results are organized as an $n \times n$ distance matrix $DM = [\, d_{i,j}]$. Thirdly, the sequence of all feature vectors V are divided into sub-sequences e_i of 200 vectors with 150 vectors overlapped, $e_i = \mathbf{v_{k_i}} \ldots \mathbf{v_{k_i+199}}$. For each sub-sequences e_i, the dynamic time wrapping (DTW) is used to match e_i against the vector sequence V_i, where $V_i = \mathbf{v_{k_i}} \ldots \mathbf{v_n}$. The matching result $r_i(j)$ represents the DTW distance between e_i and $\mathbf{v_j v_{j+1}} \ldots \mathbf{v_n}$, $k_i \leq j \leq n$. For each e_i, there may be multiple local minimum in $r_i(j)$ and each local minimum $r_i^*(\delta)$ indicates a repetition of e_i beginning at $\mathbf{v_{k_i+\delta}}$. Finally, consecutive sub-sequences, say $e_i \ldots e_{i+m}$, with similar repetitions are merged into one segment s. The segment and all its repeated duplications are labeled with the same tag.

For Music Tracks with Lyrics: If the lyrics file is available, the *lyrics-based segmentation* is used to split the music track into segments according to the lyrics sentences in the lyrics file. As shown in Fig. 3, the lyrics file in LRC format is organized as a series of lyrics sentences with the starting time of each sentence. The LRC lyrics files have been used for automatic lyrics display for a long time[2]. It is easy to find the LRC file corresponding to a music track on the Internet. Through the lyrics-based segmentation, the sequence of frames will be divided into segments according to the lyrics sentences. And each sub-sequence of frames corresponds to a lyrics sentence in the lyrics file. Note that empty sentences may exist in a lyrics file, indicating that the corresponding segments are pure instrumental music segments or silent segments. For example,

[2]http://en.wikipedia.org/wiki/LRC_file_format

[00:00.00]
[00:17.09]You only see what your eyes want to see
[00:22.00]How can life be what you want it to be
[00:25.43]You're frozen when your heart's not open
[00:27.43]
[00:34.88]You're so consumed with how much you get

Figure 3: A lyric fragment clipped from the LRC file of the song *Frozen* sung by Madonna.

there is an empty segment beginning at 27.43s and ending at 34.88s in the lyrics fragment illustrated in Fig. 3.

After the segmentation, we then find *identical* segments within a music piece by calculating the similarity between segments. We select the cross-correlation based similarity measurement method described in [13], which is widely adopted in many previous works, e.g. [20, 6]. To begin with, the segment s_i is denoted as a sequence of chroma feature vectors $\mathbf{v_i^1 v_i^2} \dots \mathbf{v_i^{l_i}}$, where $\mathbf{v_i^j}$ represents the chroma feature vector of the jth frame in s_i and l_i is the number of frames in s_i. Without loss of generality, we assume s_i is not longer than s_j, i.e., $l_i \leq l_j$. Then a cross-correlation function $C_{i,j}(k)$ between s_i and s_j is calculated as

$$C_{i,j}(k) = \frac{1}{l_i} \sum_{m=1}^{l_i} \langle \mathbf{v_i^m}, \mathbf{v_j^{m+k}} \rangle \,. \qquad (2)$$

After that, the similarity between segments s_i and s_j, denoted as $\Phi(s_i, s_j)$, is defined as

$$\Phi(s_i, s_j) = \max_{0 \leq k < l_j - l_i} C_{i,j}(k) \,. \qquad (3)$$

Two segments s_i and s_j are considered to be *identical* if $\Phi(s_i, s_j) \geq \lambda$, where λ is the *identical threshold* predefined in our framework, e.g. $\lambda = 0.4$. Finally, identical segments are classified into groups, and segments in the same group are labeled with the same tag.

4.2 Stretch Resistance Estimation

The stretching operation will change the content of frames. The human perpetual change degrades the quality of the music track. To determine how much quality degradation a frame will suffer from, we propose the concept of *semantic density* to describe the human perpetual status of a music frame. Furthermore, the stretch-resistance is modeled as the rate of change in semantic density. Given the same stretch amount, a music segment is considered to have high stretch-resistance if the change rate of the semantic density is small, and vice versa.

For a music frame, the semantic density is modeled as a linear combination of acoustic (e.g. onset density, pitch level) and lyrics features. Formally, given a frame q_i, the *semantic density* of q_i, denoted as d_i, is defined as

$$d_i = \langle \mathbf{w}, \mathbf{f}_i \rangle = \sum_{j=1}^{k} w^j f_i^j \,, \qquad (4)$$

where k is the number of features utilized to describe the semantic density, $\mathbf{w} = (w^1, w^2, \dots, w^k)^T$ is the weight vector used to balance the influences of different features on the semantic density and $\mathbf{f}_i = (f_i^1, f_i^2, \dots, f_i^k)^T$ is the feature vector of the frame q_i, whose elements indicate the perceptible status of a frame in different aspects such as singing rate, pitch, etc.

So, based on the semantic density, we define the stretch-resistance of a frame q_i, denoted as r_i, in form of a sigmoid function as

$$r_i = \frac{a}{b + e^{|\frac{\partial d_i}{\partial t_i}|}} \,, \qquad (5)$$

where d_i is the semantic density of q_i, t_i is the time length of q_i, and a, b are two real numbers used to normalize the range of r_i. On the right-hand side of Eq. 5, $|\frac{\partial d_i}{\partial t_i}|$ measures the change rate of semantic density after q_i is stretched. Large value of $|\frac{\partial d_i}{\partial t_i}|$ indicates the quality of q_i after stretching degrades intensively and, therefore, the stretch-resistance of q_i is low. For simplicity, we set $a = 2, b = 1$ to normalize the range of stretch-resistance to $(0, 1]$. Especially, $r_i = 1$ states the quality of frame q_i cannot be influenced by stretching, e.g. silent parts. We can use the differencing method to approximate the value of derivative $\frac{\partial d_i}{\partial t_i}$. In detail, given a frame with density d, we decrease (in compression cases) or increase (in prolonging cases) the length of the frame by a tiny value τ and get the new value of semantic density d'. The value of $|\frac{\partial d_i}{\partial t_i}|$ is estimated as $|\frac{d'-d}{\tau}|$.

In the implementation of MUSIZ, we adopt four music features to estimate the stretch-resistance of each frame. They are *onset density*, *zero-crossing rate*, *pitch* and *lyrics density*.

Onset refers to the beginning of an acoustic event, e.g. a perceptible change in intense or pitch of an acoustic signal. The *onset density* is defined as the number of onsets per second in a frame. Audio clips with high onset density are speedy. We employ the onset detection algorithm described in [12] to discover all onsets in the music piece. And then, we count the number of onsets $\mathcal{N}_i^{onset}$ in each frame q_i and calculate the onset density f_i^{onset} of q_i, i.e. $f_i^{onset} = \mathcal{N}_j^{onset}/t_\ell$, where t_ℓ is the length of a frame.

Zero-crossing rate is the rate of sign-changes along the waveform of a music track. It is often used to distinguish vocal segments from non-vocal segments in a music track [22]. To obtain the zero-crossing rate, we simply scan samples in a frame from the beginning to the ending, and count the number of sign-changes $\mathcal{N}_{zcr}$ between two adjacent samples during the scanning. The zero-crossing rate f_i^{zcr} of q_i is then calculated as $f_i^{zcr} = \mathcal{N}_{zcr}/t_\ell$.

Pitch represents the perceived fundamental frequency of audio signals. We adopt the YIN algorithm [11] to extract the pitch of a frame. Instead of maximizing the auto-correlation, YIN algorithm aims to find the period τ such that a cumulative mean normalized different function is minimized and, as a result, the fundamental frequency of frame q_i is $f_i^{pitch} = 1/\tau$.

Lyrics density [18] measures the singing rate in a sentence by parsing the lyrics words in the corresponding lyrics file. High lyrics density indicates the singer sings speedily, and vice versa. The lyrics density is useful for stretch-resistance calculation. Because, according to the observation of the human hearing perspective [7], the sense of human hearing is more sensitive to the manipulation of the human voice than that of the pure instrumental sound. In practice, there are many ways to define the lyrics density, e.g. word rate, letter rate. In this paper, we choose the phoneme rate as the lyrics density, since phonemes reveal the sound property of lyrics words, i.e. the pronunciation of words, more accurately. Formally, given a segment s_i with length t_i and the corresponding lyrics sentence lrc_i, the lyrics density f_i^{lrc} is defined as $f_i^{lrc} = \mathcal{N}_{ph}(lrc_i)/t_i$, where $\mathcal{N}_{ph}(lrc_i)$ is the number of phonemes in lyrics sentence lrc_i. All frames within a segment s_i share the same lyrics density f_i^{lrc}. To implement the word-phoneme translation, we use the CMU pronouncing dictionary 0.7a [3], which adopts the ARPAbet[4] symbol set for phoneme representation. Fig. 4 illustrates the translation from one lyrics sentence to phonemes with the CMU pronouncing dictionary.

Please note that acoustic features which are appropriate for stretch-resistance measurement are not limited. Other features can also be

[3]http://www.speech.cs.cmu.edu/cgi-bin/cmudict

[4]The ARPAbet symbol set consists of 39 phonemes, which is developed to represent the international phonetic alphabet (IPA) with ASCII characters.

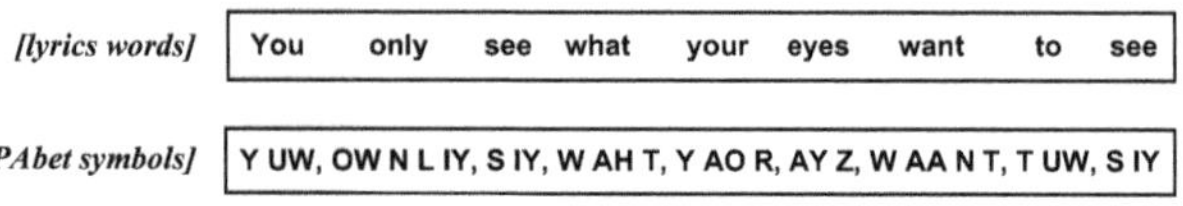

Figure 4: Translation from lyrics words to ARPAbet symbols with CMU pronouncing dictionary.

integrated in our resizing framework flexibly. Fig. 5 displays the distribution of stretch-resistance in a music track.

5. MUSIC SYNTHESIS

Based on the music structure information, we can modify the audio content of the music track so that the length of the synthesized music track is able to fit the temporal limitation of the application. Two basic operations are used in the synthesis phase of MUSIZ, i.e. *stretching* and *cropping*. In order to minimize the quality degradation of the entire music track, the stretching algorithm must determine whether and how much a frame should be stretched. Meanwhile, the cropping operation is probably used before stretching, if the user preferred length is much smaller than the length of the original music track.

5.1 Stretching Operation

In this subsection, we propose the stretching algorithm which distributes the stretching amounts over all frames in a music track according to their stretch-resistance. As shown in Algorithm 2, given the stretch rate $\alpha \in (0, 200\%)$ [5] , we first calculate the total time variation ΔT as

$$\Delta T = T_{\mathcal{M}} \cdot (\alpha - 1) \,, \tag{6}$$

where $T_{\mathcal{M}}$ is the time length of the original music piece. The user wants to prolong the music piece if $\Delta T > 0$. Otherwise, the music piece needs to be compressed when $\Delta T < 0$.

To schedule ΔT over frames, the stretching algorithm first divides ΔT into fixed-length time slices. The length of each time slice, denoted as δt, is predefined in our framework, e.g. $\delta t = 5ms$. Therefore, the stretching algorithm iterates $\lceil \frac{|\Delta T|}{\delta t} \rceil$ times for assigning all time slices. And the length of the last time slice may be smaller than δt. Meanwhile, for efficiently fetching the highest stretch-resistance frame, all frames are maintained in a priority queue in a descending order w.r.t. stretch-resistance.

The stretching process goes iteratively. At each iteration, the scheduling algorithm selects one frame, denoted as q_ϵ, from all frames in the music piece and distributes one time slice to q_ϵ. The q_ϵ is selected as

$$q_\epsilon = arg \max_{q_i \in \mathcal{M}} r_i \,. \tag{7}$$

After the time slice assignment, the length of q_ϵ increases (in prolonging cases) or decreases (in compression cases) by δt. As a result, the semantic density and stretch-resistance of q_ϵ are updated after the length of q_ϵ changes. Accordingly, the priority queue is also updated to maintain the descending order of frames w.r.t. stretch-resistance. The iteration does not stop until all $\lceil \frac{|\Delta T|}{\delta t} \rceil$ time slices are distributed. And the resized music track is generated by concatenating the stretched frames. During the stretching processing, we use the WSOLA algorithm [27] to stretch the audio content of all frame without altering the perceived frequency attributes of audio frames.

5.2 Cropping Operation

The stretching operation cannot guarantee that the quality of the stretched music piece is acceptable for audiences when the stretch

[5]In cases when $\alpha \geq 200\%$, the prolonging and repeating approach can convert α to the range $(0, 200\%)$ as discussed in Section 3.

Figure 5: The distribution of stretch-resistance of the song *Don't cry for me, Argentina* sung by Madonna. Lyrics density, onset density, zero-crossing rate and pitch are used. The color illustrates the stretch-resistance in the song. *Black* parts indicate the high stretch-resistance parts and *red* parts mean low stretch-resistance parts.

Algorithm 2: STRETCHING($\mathcal{M}$, α)

```
Input  : M — the music track to be resized;
         α — the stretch rate, α ∈ (0, 200%);
Output : M_r — the resized music piece;
if α = 1 then return M;
Get the total time variation ΔT;
Calculate the stretch-resistance for all frames, r_1, r_2, ..., r_n;
Q ← Create the priority queue of frames w.r.t. the stretch-resistance in
  a descending order;
for i ← 1 to ⌈|ΔT|/δt⌉ do
    q_i ← Select the frame with highest stretch-resistance from Q;
    Decrease (Increase) the length of q_i by δt;
    Update the stretch-resistance r_i of q_i;
end for
M_r ← Concatenate all resized frames q_1, q_2, ..., q_n;
```

rate is too small. For example, the average speed will be accelerated by 10 times when $\alpha = 10\%$. Even though high stretch-resistance segments can absorb more stretching amounts, the resized music piece still sounds noisy and uncomfortable. Notice that music is characterized by repetition [10], i.e., there are some repeated segments in a music track. Removing some segments from a music piece may be less harmful than over-stretching the music piece. Inspired by this, we propose a cropping-enable resizing approach, which mixes cropping operation and stretching operation adaptively. In particular, we want to remove some segments from the original music piece such that the length of the remaining music piece is near the user preferred length. The removed music segments are carefully selected so that the remaining segments can connect together naturally and fluently. After that, the remaining music piece is then stretched to the user preferred length by the stretching algorithm discussed in Section 5.1.

Cuttable Clip. In a music track, two segments may not connect naturally after the sequence of segments between them is removed. In other words, an abrupt change at the joint between the two segments may be generated. Because the melody and singing voices in a music track are continuous. To eliminate the abrupt change at the joint, we introduce the concept of *cuttable clip*.

A music track is able to be represented as a sequence of labeled segments through the structure analysis, e.g. $s_1 s_2 \ldots s_{10}$ with labels 'ABCDEBAECE' in Fig. 6. If we remove a sequence of consecutive segments from the original music piece, two segments which are not adjacent with each other will connect. For example, s_5 and s_9 will connect together if the sequence $s_6 s_7 s_8$ is removed from the original music piece. Now, we have to decide whether the segments $s_5 s_9$ ('EC') sound good. Notice that the tag sequence 'EC' exists in the original music track ($s_8 s_9$), which indicates that connection between s_5 and s_9 sounds natural and fluent. And the sequence $s_6 s_7 s_8$ is a *cuttable clip* in the music piece. Removing cuttable clips preserve the contiguity at the joint in the remaining segments. The definition of *cuttable clip* is shown as follows.

DEFINITION 1 (CUTTABLE CLIP). *Given a music track* $\mathcal{M} = (s_1, s_2, \ldots, s_n)$ *with the class tags* $\mathcal{C} = \{c_1, c_2, \ldots, c_m\}$, *a* cuttable clip *is a sequence of consecutive segments* $s_j s_{j+1} \ldots s_k$,

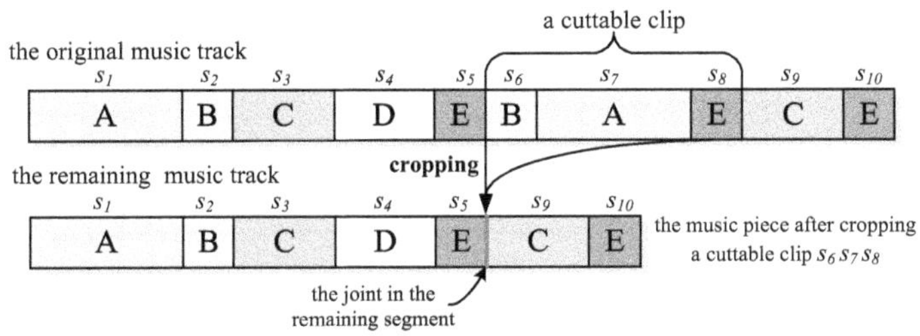

Figure 6: An example of cropping a cuttable clip. The original music track (*top*) contains $s_1s_2\ldots s_9s_{10}$ and one cuttable clip is $s_6s_7s_8$. The music piece after cropping the cuttable clip consists of $s_1s_2\ldots s_5s_9s_{10}$ (*bottom*) and the joint (*red line*) locates between s_5 and s_9.

Table 1: Segment Groups and Position List

Tag	Segment[length (s)]	Avg. length (s)	Position
A	$s_1[3.2]$, $s_7[3.2]$	3.2	1, 7
B	$s_2[1.0]$, $s_6[1.2]$	1.1	2, 6
C	$s_3[2.2]$, $s_9[2.1]$	2.15	3, 9
D	$s_4[2.0]$	2.0	4
E	$s_5[1]$, $s_8[0.9]$, $s_{10}[1]$	1.0	5, 8, 10

where $\exists\, s_i \in \mathcal{M}$ *such that* $tag(s_i) = tag(s_{j-1})$ *and* $tag(s_{i+1}) = tag(s_{k+1})$, $1 < j \leq k < n$.

The cuttable clip is not unique in a given segment sequence. To find out all cuttable clips in a sequence of segments, we create the position list of each segment class. The position list records all positions of segments belonging to the same segment class (ref. to Column 4 in Table 1). And we enumerate all the 2-combinations of position numbers in the position list of c_i. Each 2-combination (x, y) refers to a cuttable clip $s_{x+1}\ldots s_y$. For example, tag 'E' appears at position 5, 8 and 10 in Fig. 6. All 2-combinations of $\{5, 8, 10\}$ are $(5, 8)$, $(5, 10)$ and $(8, 10)$. The corresponding cuttable clips generated from the three 2-combinations are $s_6s_7s_8$ ('BAE'), $s_6s_7s_8s_9s_{10}$ ('BAECE') and s_9s_{10} ('CE').

Cropping Algorithm. Based on the concept of cuttable clips, we develop a cropping algorithm which removes cuttable clips in a greedy manner. Initially, a music piece is considered as a sequence of labeled segments. Then the cropping algorithm finds out all cuttable clips in the sequence of segments and selects one cuttable clip to remove. We repeat the above step until the length of the cropped music piece $T_{\mathcal{M}'}$ satisfies $T_u \in [\alpha_{\min} \cdot T_{\mathcal{M}'}, \alpha_{\max} \cdot T_{\mathcal{M}'}]$, i.e., the remaining music piece is *stretchable* with T_u.

As shown in Algorithm 3, the cropping algorithm begins with making a copy $\mathcal{M}_r$ of the original music track $\mathcal{M}$. Before the iteration begins, the current music piece $\mathcal{M}_r$ is checked whether its length falls in the stretchable range, i.e. $[T_{\mathcal{M}_r} \cdot \alpha_{\min},\ T_{\mathcal{M}_r} \cdot \alpha_{\max}]$. If the current version of the music piece $\mathcal{M}_r$ is $stretchable$, $\mathcal{M}_r$ is outputted directly for stretching. Otherwise, the cropping iteration starts. At each iteration, the position lists of segment groups are updated according to $\mathcal{M}_r$. After that, we find all cuttable clips in $\mathcal{M}_r$ and the set of cuttable clips is denoted as Λ. The algorithm then selects the best cuttable clip, denoted as e_{rm}, in Λ and removes e_{rm} from the current music piece. The criterion of the best cuttable clip selection is heuristic in this paper. The best cuttable clip e_{rm} is selected as the cuttable clip e which minimizes the difference between the user preferred length and the length of the music piece after removing the cuttable clip e from $\mathcal{M}_r$. Formally,

$$e_{rm} = arg \min_{e \in \Lambda} |T_{\mathcal{M}_r} - t_e - T_u|\ , \qquad (8)$$

where $T_{\mathcal{M}_r}$ is the length of the current music track, t_e is the length of the cuttable clip e and T_u is the user preferred length. The cropping algorithm keeps removing cuttable clips until the current music piece $\mathcal{M}_r$ is *stretchable*.

Algorithm 3: CROPPING($\mathcal{M}$, α)

Input : $\mathcal{M}$ — the music piece to be resized;
α — the stretch rate
Output : $\mathcal{M}_r$ — the remaining music piece;

$\mathcal{M}_r \leftarrow \mathcal{M}$;
while $\mathcal{M}_r$ *is not stretchable* **do**
  $\Lambda \leftarrow$ Find all cuttable clips in $\mathcal{M}_r$;
  if Λ *is* $\emptyset$ *or* ($\forall\, e \in \Lambda$, $T_{\mathcal{M}_r} - t_e \leq T_u$) **then**
    return error;
  $e_{rm} \leftarrow$ Evaluate lengths of all cuttable clips in Λ and select the best cuttable clip according to Eq. 8;
  $\mathcal{M}_r \leftarrow$ Remove e_{rm} from $\mathcal{M}_r$;
end while
return $\mathcal{M}_r$;

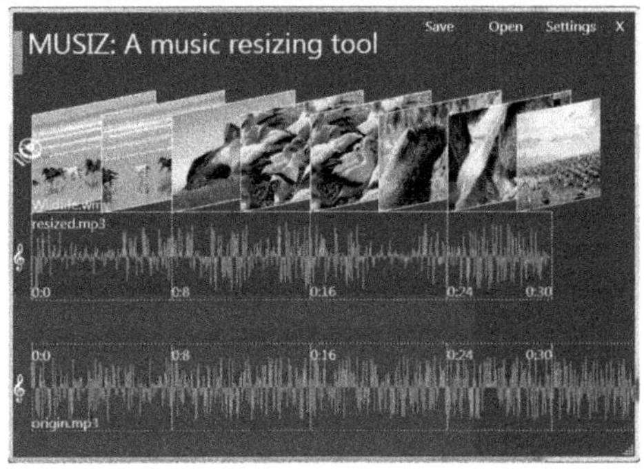

Figure 7: A screenshot of the GUI demo of MUSIZ. A music track (*bottom*) is reszied to a short version (*middle*) for accompanying a video clip (*top*). Some video frames are sampled to illustrate the video content along the time axis.

6. EXPERIMENTAL EVALUATION

In this section, we evaluate MUSIZ with subjective user studies and objective efficiency measurements.

We implemented the command-line version of MUSIZ in C++ and it was compiled with GCC 4.4.3 compiler. Acoustic features, e.g. onset, zero-crossing rate, were extracted with Marsyas [26], an open source audio processing software [6]. For efficient audio stretching, we used the SoundStretch [7] audio processing utility which was implemented based on the SoundTouch [8] library. Experiments related to the efficiency evaluation were conducted on a PC with Intel Q8200 2.3 GHz processors, 4 GB RAM, 1.5 TB hard disk, running Ubuntu 9.04 server edition. To confirm the utility of MUSIZ, we also developed a GUI demo as shown in Fig. 7. The demo was implemented based on the library of MUSIZ and the Microsoft Windows Presentation Foundation (WPF) technique for the GUI development. It permits the resizing of a music track by assigning a preferred length or the automatic generation of background music by giving a video/audio clip.

We collected 1230 music tracks (in MP3 format) and the corresponding lyrics files (in LRC format) from the Internet. The music collection contains different music genres, e.g. classical, popular. The distribution of music genres in the music collection is displayed in Table 2. For normalization, all music tracks were converted to the WAVE format with the same parameters (44, 100 Hz 16-bit mono). The size of all WAVE files is 25.2 GB in total and the average piece duration of the music collection is 260.88s.

[6] http://marsyas.info/
[7] http://www.surina.net/soundtouch/soundstretch.html
[8] http://www.surina.net/soundtouch/index.html

Table 2: Music Collection

Genre	# of tracks
Classical	30
Popular	726
Electronic	22
Hip-hop	83
Others	369

Table 3: Grade Points

Grade	Description
5.0	Imperceptible
4.0	Perceptible, but not annoying
3.0	Slightly annoying
2.0	Annoying
1.0	Very annoying

Table 4: Medians of Feature Distributions

Feature name (unit)	Abbr.	d^{med}
Lyrics density (# of phonemes per sec.)	lyric	4.849
Onset density (# of onsets per sec.)	onset	0.416
Zero-cross rate	zcr	2493.41
Pitch (Hz)	pitch	134

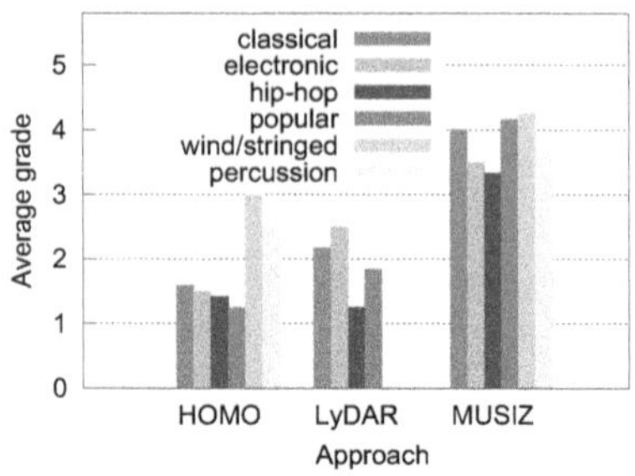

Figure 8: Comparison results of resizing algorithms (HOMO, LyDAR, MUSIZ) on different music types ($\alpha = 50\%$).

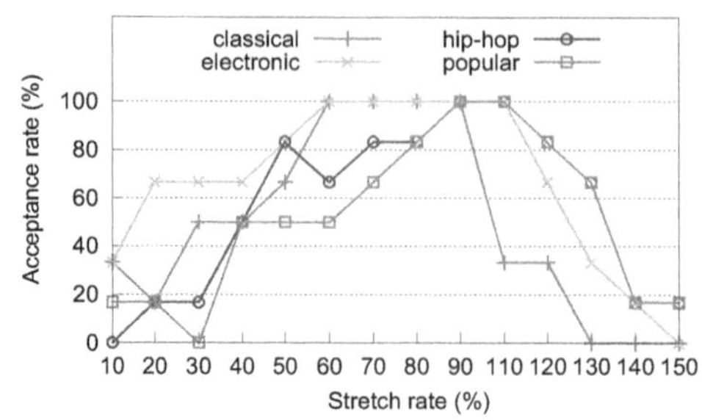

Figure 9: Effect of the stretch rate on the average user acceptance rate for different music genres.

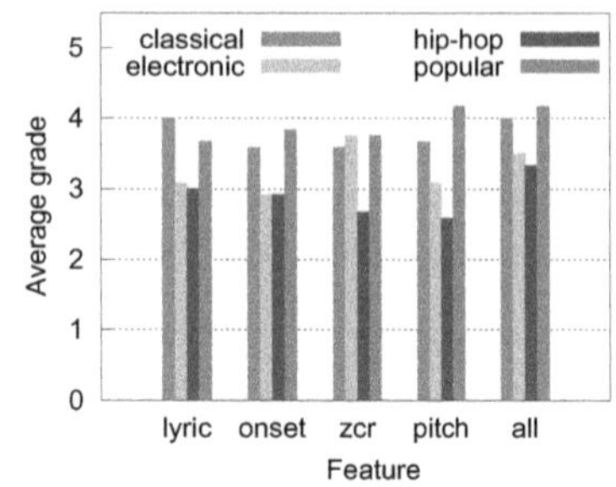

Figure 10: Effect of the feature on the average user acceptance rate for different music genres ($\alpha = 50\%$).

6.1 Weight Selection

The semantic density (ref. to Eq. 4) is a weighted sum of all features. It is really difficult to give a specific set of weights which are suitable for all music tracks. Thus, we assume that all features make the same contribution to the semantic density. However, the range of different features varies greatly. To normalize the range of features, we define the weight vector as

$$\mathbf{w} = (w_{lrc}, w_{onset}, w_{zcr}, w_{pitch}) = (\frac{1}{d^{med}_{lrc}}, \frac{1}{d^{med}_{onset}}, \frac{1}{d^{med}_{zcr}}, \frac{1}{d^{med}_{pitch}}), \quad (9)$$

where $w_{lrc}, w_{onset}, w_{zcr}, w_{pitch}$ represent the weights of lyrics density, onset density, zero-crossing rate and pitch, respectively. And d^{med}_x denotes the median of the distribution of feature x. To obtain the median, we calculate the distribution of the four features and the median of each feature distribution is shown in Table 4. Therefore, the weight vector we used in the evaluation is $\mathbf{w} = (w_{lrc}, w_{onset}, w_{zcr}, w_{pitch}) = (\frac{1}{4.849}, \frac{1}{0.416}, \frac{1}{2493.41}, \frac{1}{134}) = (0.206, 2.4038, 0.0004, 0.0075)$.

6.2 User Study

We conducted comprehensive user studies to evaluate the performance of MUSIZ. 12 experimented volunteers (2 participants were female and 10 participants were male) took part in the user studies. All of them were Master's or Ph.D. candidates from the School of Software and the Department of Computer Science and Technology at Tsinghua University. They were invited to listen to different versions of the resized music tracks and rate each resized version. During the audition process, each volunteer wore earphones to hear the original music tracks and their resized versions played on a PC. To alleviate the difference among audience perspectives, the experimental results were the average values derived from all audiences. It is necessary to clarify that all volunteers had experience of audio evaluations before joined our experiments and all of them understood English, because this background knowledge may affect the subjective judgments.

6.2.1 Comparative Study

This set of experiments compares the performance of MUSIZ with LyDAR [19, 18] and the traditional time stretching approach (HOMO) [27]. We used the SoundTouch library to implement the time stretching and we also implemented the LyDAR approach for comparison. We randomly selected 6 music tracks from 6 music types in our music collection, i.e. classical, popular, hip-hop, electronic, wind/stringed and percussion. In these types, classical, popular, hip-hop, electronic are music genres. Whereas, *percussion* denotes instrumental music pieces played by percussion instruments (e.g. drum). *Wind/stringed* represents instrumental music piece played by wind instruments (e.g. clarinet) or string instruments (e.g. violin).

Each music track was resized with HOMO, LyDAR as well as MUSIZ, respectively. The stretch rate was $\alpha = 50\%$ and all four features were used for stretch-resistance estimation in MUSIZ. Volunteers first listened to the original version of the music track, and then they listened to the resized versions of the music track with HOMO, LyDAR and MUSIZ, respectively. During evaluating the resized versions, volunteers were allowed to listen the original version for reference whenever they wanted. After listened one resized version (e.g., produced by HOMO), they assessed the quality on the resized version compared to the original version according to the ITU-R BS.1116-1 [1]. We adopted the ITU-R five-grade impairment scale [2], which was continuous with anchors as shown in Table 3. Volunteers were assigned another music track for evaluation if all resized versions of the music track were assessed.

As shown in Fig. 8, LyDAR performs better than HOMO in most of music genres, except for the hip-hop. The tempo of hip-hop music is flexible and noticeable, because it has strong rhythm segments (e.g. rapping, beatboxing). The lyrics density estimation in LyDAR cannot capture the rhythm changes within a sentence. As a result, speedy parts in a segment may be mistakenly estimated as slow parts because of other long speechless parts within the segment. MUSIZ adopts acoustic features (e.g. onset density and zero-crossing rate) and the length of feature extraction windows is very small. Thus, it can capture the speedy changes accurately. In all music genres, MUSIZ outperforms both HOMO and LyDAR. Note that the result of LyDAR representing *wind/stringed* and *percussion* are missing. Because LyDAR cannot process music tracks without lyrics and, therefore, experiments about *wind/stringed* and *percussion* are not conducted with LyDAR.

6.2.2 Effects of Genre

In this set of experiments, we examine the effects of music genres on the performance of our approach. We randomly selected 10

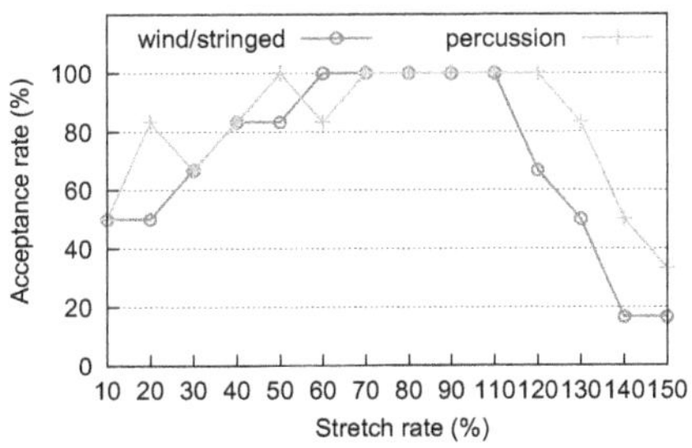

Figure 11: Effect of the stretch rate on the average user acceptance rate for different instruments (wind/stringed, percussion)

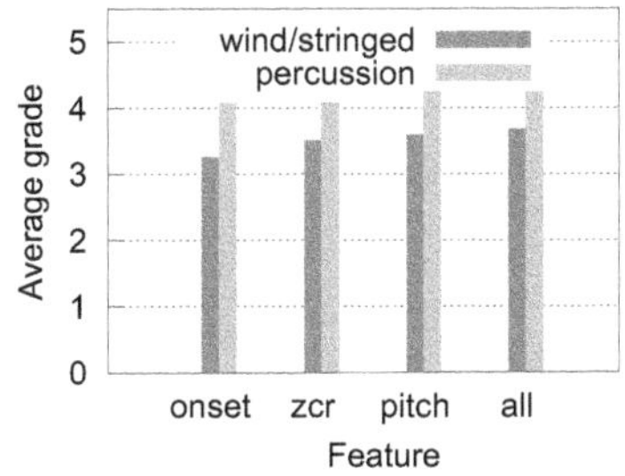

Figure 12: Effect of the features used on the average score for different instruments ($\alpha = 50\%$).

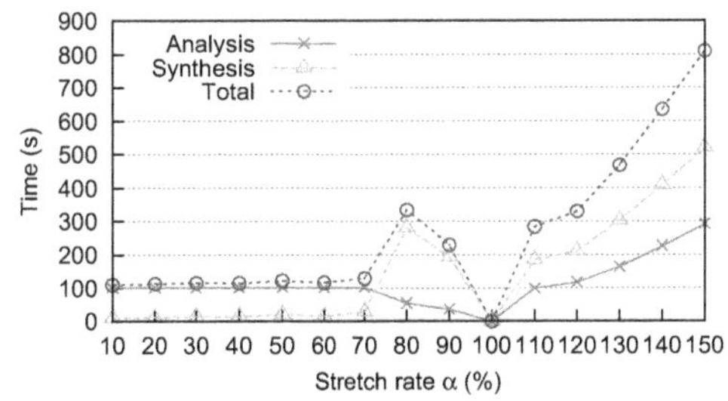

Figure 13: Effect of the stretch rate on execution time.

music tracks from each music genre. All four features were used for stretch-resistance in MUSIZ. Music track was resized by MUSIZ with a series of stretch rates, ranging from 10% to 150% at an interval of 10%. For each music track, the original version was firstly listened by volunteers for reference. They could choose to first evaluate the compressed versions or the prolonged ones. In compression cases ($10\% \leq \alpha \leq 90\%$), volunteers listened to different resized versions of a single music track in a descending order w.r.t. stretch rates. Note that the original version of the music track was available for volunteers during evaluating the resized version. Once listened to a resized version, volunteers were asked whether they accepted the resized version and they recorded the answers with *YES* or *NO*. We then calculated the average acceptance rate as $\frac{n_{acc}}{n_{total}}$, where n_{acc} is the number of acceptance records and n_{total} is the number of all records. The experiments process in the prolonging cases ($110\% \leq \alpha \leq 150\%$) is the same as that in the compression cases, except that volunteers listened to resized versions of a music track in an ascending order w.r.t. stretch rates.

As shown in Fig. 9, the quality of each music genre degrades when the stretch rate decreases or increases from 100%. Classical and electronic music tracks are robust against compression. Quality of popular music and hip-hop music degrades rapidly when the stretch rate decreases in the compression case. The tempo of classical music is low and there are few singing voices in electronic music. Meanwhile, human hearing is very sensitive to acceleration of human voices. Therefore, our resizing approach achieves high performance when the speed of singing voice is low or the music pieces are pure instrumental music. However, the quality of prolonged classical music tracks degrades rapidly, because the prolonging operation decelerates the speed of classical music whose tempo is very low originally.

Another set of experiments is going to explore the relation between genres and features used for stretch-resistance estimation in MUSIZ. For each music genre, we randomly select 8 music tracks. The stretch rate is $\alpha = 50\%$. For each music track, we generated five resized versions with MUSIZ, i.e. the music track using each feature (e.g. onset) individually and the one using all four features together. Similar to the comparative study in Section 6.2.1, volunteers were asked to listen to the original version and the five resized versions. For each resized version, volunteers assessed on the quality of this version with the five-grade impairment scale [2]. Finally, we got the average score of all grades in a music genre. As illustrated in Fig. 10, different types of music do benefits from different features. And the overview performance of music resizing enhances when we combine all features effectively.

6.2.3 *Effects of Instrument*

Now we intend to evaluate how instruments affect the performance of resizing. To eliminate the effects of singing voice, music tracks used in this set of experiments are pure instrumental music without human voice. As a result, the lyrics density cannot be used for stretch-resistance estimation. We classified the instrumental music tracks into two groups, i.e. *wind/stringed* and *percussion*. Music tracks in *percussion* are played with percussion instruments, e.g. drums and tambourines. Whereas, music tracks in *wind/stringed* are performed with wind and string instruments.

In the first set of experiments, 4 music tracks were randomly selected from each group. Each music track was resized with different stretch rates from 10% to 150% at an interval of 10%. Similar to the first set of experiments in Section 6.2.2, volunteers listened to different resized versions of a music track following a decreasing order w.r.t. the stretch rate (from 90% to 10%) in the compression cases, and an ascending order w.r.t. the stretch rate (from 110% to 150%) in the prolonging cases. After listening a revised version, volunteers were asked whether this version is acceptable. Finally, we calculated the acceptance rate of each music group. As shown in Fig. 11, *percussion* music is more suitable for resizing, compared with *wind/stringed* music. Because semantics of the *percussion* music is obscure and the sound is discrete. Therefore, the percussion music is robust to the cropping operation of MUSIZ.

In the second set of experiments, we fixed the stretch rate $\alpha = 50\%$ and varied the features used in MUSIZ. The assessment process is the same as the second set of experiments in Section 6.2.2. Volunteers were asked to grade the resized versions of a music track according to the ITU-R five-grade impairment scale [2]. Fig. 12 indicates that percussion music achieves better resizing quality than wind/stringed music. Moreover, the combination of all features leads to better quality of the resized music tracks than the versions resized with only one feature.

6.3 Efficiency Evaluation

To evaluate the efficiency of MUSIZ, we varied the stretch rate from 10% to 150% at an interval of 10%. All music tracks in our music collection were resized. We recorded *the average analysis time* and the *average synthesis time* . The analysis time represents the time of music structure analysis. Whereas, the synthesis time denotes the time cost on stretching and cropping for audio content. The sum of the average analysis time and the average synthesis time is the *average total execution time*.

As shown in Fig. 13, the analysis time is almost constant when $10\% \leq \alpha < 80\%$. The segmentation and labeling method is required before the cropping operation. The time cost of segmentation and labeling is not affected by the stretch rate. Besides, the synthesis time is relatively small and roughly increases with the stretch rate when $\alpha \leq 120\%$. This is leaded by the fact that the absolute time variation $|\Delta T|$ (ref. to Eq. 6)increases with the stretch rate. Both the analysis time and synthesis time decrease when α increases from 80% to 100%. In this range, the music piece is stretchable and only the stretching operation is used. The computational complexity of the resizing algorithm is determined by the absolute time variation $|\Delta T|$. $|\Delta T|$ decreases to 0 when α changes to 100%. Therefore, the analysis time and synthesis time decrease correspondingly.

The analysis time and synthesis time increase with α when $\alpha >$ 100%, which is also caused by the increment of $|\Delta T|$. In this situation, the larger $|\Delta T|$ is, the more times the stretching algorithm must iterate. Therefore, the total execution time increases linearly with the stretch rate.

6.4 Limitations

As the first generic music resizing framework, MUSIZ enables high quality temporal modification for music tracks. However, there still exist some limitations which should be improved. Firstly, the features used for stretch-resistance estimation are not limited to the four features we adopted in this paper. Exploring and verifying other features is a very meaningful work for music resizing. Secondly, the parameters (e.g. $\alpha_{\min}$, $\alpha_{\max}$, $\mathbf{w}$) used in MUSIZ are fixed for different music types. One interesting work is to investigate the relations between parameters and performance of MUSIZ for difference music types and, furthermore, obtain the optimal parameters for each music type. We believe the knowledge of music types will help to improve the performance of music resizing. Thirdly, we recruited 12 volunteers for the user studies in the research work because of the limitation on human resources. We will develop online music resizing applications which may attract more people to evaluate our system in the realistic settings.

7. CONCLUSIONS

Extensive applications demand to resize music pieces in time-constrained context. However, existing music resizing methods cannot meet the need of real world applications. In this paper, we proposed a generic music resizing framework, i.e. MUSIZ, which is conscious of the content structure of a music track and enables compression, prolonging and cropping operations. As the first attempt to exploit the general content-based music resizing framework, MUSIZ consists music structure analysis and music synthesis. Both lyrics density and content-based audio features are used to estimate the stretch-resistance of a music segment. Moreover, stretching and cropping operations are utilized to eliminate the quality degradation of the resized music track. Extensive experimental results demonstrate the effectiveness of MUSIZ.

In the future work, we plan to extend the proposed approach in two directions. Firstly, we are interested in exploiting other acoustic features for effective stretch-resistance estimation. Secondly, we will investigate the relationship between music types and the quality of resized music tracks, and therefore we can improve the effectiveness of MUSIZ based on the knowledge of music types.

8. ACKNOWLEDGMENTS

The work is supported by the National Natural Science Foundation of China (No. 60803016, No. 61073005, No. 61170064), the National HeGaoJi Key Project (No. 2010ZX01042-002-002-01), the ICT Key Laboratory of Intelligent Information Processing, CAS (No. IIP2010-2) and the Tsinghua National Laboratory for Information Science and Technology (TNLIST) Cross-discipline Foundation. We would like to thank the volunteers for participating the user study. We would also like to thank the anonymous reviewers and the shepherd for their insightful comments.

9. REFERENCES

[1] Methods for the subjective assessment of small impairments in audio systems including multichannel sound systems. *Recommendation ITU-R BS.1116-1*, 1994.

[2] General methods for the subjective assessment of sound quality. *Recommendation ITU-R BS.1284-1*, 1997.

[3] A. Abdallah, B. Sandler, C. Rhodes, and M. Casey. Using duration models to reduce fragmentation in audio segmentation. *Machine Learning*, 65(2-3):485–515, 2006.

[4] N. T. N. Anh, W. Yang, and J. Cai. Seam carving extension: a compression perspective. In *ACM Multimedia*, pages 825–828, 2009.

[5] L. Barrington, A. Chan, and G. Lanckriet. Modeling music as a dynamic texture. *IEEE TASLP*, 18(3):602–612, Mar 2010.

[6] M. A. Bartsch and G. H. Wakefield. Audio thumbnailing of popular music using chroma-based representations. *IEEE Transactions on Multimedia*, 7(1):96–104, 2005.

[7] P. Belin, R. J. Zatorre, P. Lafaille, P. Ahad, and B. Pike. Voice-selective areas in human auditory cortex. *Nature*, 403:309–312, Jan 2000.

[8] W. Chai and B. Vercoe. Music thumbnailing via structural analysis. In *ACM Multimedia*, pages 223–226, 2003.

[9] C.Xu, Y.Zhu, and Q.Tian. Automatic music summarization based on temporal, spectral and cepstral features. In *IEEE ICME*, pages 117–120, Nov 2002.

[10] R. B. Dannenberg and N. Hu. Pattern discovery techniques for music audio. In *ISMIR*, pages 63–70, 2002.

[11] A. de Cheveigné and H. Kawahara. YIN, a fundamental frequency estimator for speech and music. *The Journal of the Acoustical Society of America*, 111(4):1917–1930, 2002.

[12] S. Dixon. Onset detection revisited. In *Proc. of the Int. Conf. on Digital Audio Effects*, pages 133–137, Sept 2006.

[13] J. Foote. Visualizing music and audio using self-similarity. In *ACM Multimedia*, pages 77–80, 1999.

[14] S. Grofit and Y. Lavner. Time-scale modification of audio signals using enhanced wsola with management of transients. *IEEE TASLP*, 16(1):106–115, 2008.

[15] S. Kopf, J. Kiess, H. Lemelson, and W. Effelsberg. FSCAV: fast seam carving for size adaptation of videos. In *ACM Multimedia*, pages 321–330, 2009.

[16] J. Laroche and M. Dolson. Improved phase vocoder time-scale modification of audio. *IEEE TSAP*, 7(3):323–332, May 1999.

[17] M. Levy. A comparison of timbral and harmonic music segmentation algorithms. In *IEEE ICASSP*, pages 1433–1436, Apr 2007.

[18] Z. Liu, C. Wang, L. Guo, Y. Bai, and J. Wang. Lydar: A lyrics density based approach to non-homogeneous music resizing. In *IEEE ICME*, pages 310–315, 2010.

[19] Z. Liu, C. Wang, J. Wang, W. Zheng, and S. Shi. Structure-aware music resizing using lyrics. In *WWW*, pages 1155–1156, 2010.

[20] M.Cooper and J.Foote. Automatic music summarization via similarity analysis. In *ISMIR*, pages 81–85, Jul 2002.

[21] M.Goto. A chorus-section detecting method for musical audio signals. In *IEEE ICASSP*, pages 437–440, 2003.

[22] T. L. Nwe, A. Shenoy, and Y. Wang. Singing voice detection in popular music. In *ACM Multimedia*, pages 324–327, 2004.

[23] J. Paulus, M. Müller, and A. Klapuri. Audio-based music structure analysis. In *ISMIR*, pages 625–636, Aug 2010.

[24] A. Shamir and S. Avidan. Seam carving for media retargeting. *Communications of the ACM*, 52(1):77–85, 2009.

[25] L. Shi, J. Wang, L. Duan, and H. Lu. Consumer video retargeting: context assisted spatial-temporal grid optimization. In *ACM Multimedia*, pages 301–310, 2009.

[26] G. Tzanetakis. Music analysis, retrieval and synthesis of audio signals marsyas. In *ACM Multimedia*, pages 931–932, 2009.

[27] W. Verhelst. Overlap-add methods for time-scaling of speech. *Speech Communication*, 30(4):207–221, 2000.

[28] R. J. Weiss and J. P. Bello. Identifying Repeated Patterns in Music Using Sparse Convolutive Non-Negative Matrix Factorization. In *ISMIR*, pages 123–128, Aug 2010.

[29] T. Zhang and C. Kuo. Heuristic approach for generic audio data segmentation and annotation. In *ACM Multimedia*, pages 67–76, 1999.

Robust Visual Reranking via Sparsity and Ranking Constraints*

Nobuyuki Morioka†
The University of New South Wales & NICTA
Sydney, Australia
nmorioka@cse.unsw.edu.au

Jingdong Wang
Microsoft Research Asia
Beijing, China
jingdw@microsoft.com

ABSTRACT

Visual reranking has become a widely-accepted method to improve traditional text-based image search engines. Its basic principle is that visually similar images should have similar ranking scores. While existing methods are different in specifics, almost all of them are based on explicit or implicit pseudo-relevance feedback (PRF). Explicit PRF-based approaches, including classification-based and clustering-based reranking, suffer from the difficulty of selecting reliable positive and negative samples. Implicit PRF-based approaches, such as graph-based and Bayesian visual reranking, deal with such unreliability by making use of the initial ranking in a soft manner, but have limited capability of promoting relevant images and lowering down irrelevant images.

In this paper, we propose ℓ_1 square loss optimization based on sparsity and ranking constraints to detect confident samples which are most likely to be relevant to a query. Based on the discovered confident samples, we present an adaptive kernel-based scheme to rerank the images. The success of our proposed method comes from another important observation that irrelevant images, whether initially positioned at the top or bottom, are usually less-popular and more diverse than relevant images. Therefore, it is robust against outlier images and suitable when relevant images are multimodally distributed. The experimental results demonstrate significant improvement of our method over several existing reranking approaches on both MSRA-MM V1.0 and Web Queries datasets.

Categories and Subject Descriptors

H.3.3 [**Information Search and Retrieval**]: Retrieval models

*Area chair: Lexing Xie

†This work was performed when Nobuyuki Morioka was visiting Microsoft Research Asia as a research intern.

MM'11, November 28–December 1, 2011, Scotsdale, Arizona, USA.

Figure 1: Given a query "panda", (a) pseudo-relevance feedback selects the top images as positive relevant samples indicated in red, and (b) our proposed approach in this paper finds confident image samples indicated in cyan that are thought to be highly relevant to "panda" from the initial rank list via our sparsity and ranking constrained optimization framework.

General Terms

Algorithms, Experimentation, Performance

Keywords

Image Search Reranking, Non-negativity, Sparsity, ℓ_1 Loss

1. INTRODUCTION

Due to ever growing number of online images, image search and retrieval is one of active and challenging areas of multimedia research. Many image search engines such as Bing, Google and Yahoo! have relied on matching textual information of the images, including surrounding texts, titles, captions and URLs, against textual queries given by users. However, because the textual information fails to capture rich image content, their returned results are often inconsistent with the queries [7]. While visual features like color moments [21] and Scale Invariant Feature Transform (SIFT) [16] can be a substitute for the textual information, there is a huge semantic gap between such low-level statistical visual features and the high-level semantic concepts (or queries) [19].

Visual reranking which integrates both the textual and visual information is proposed to return visually satisfying search results. Based on the textual information, it first quickly scans through a whole database to generate a list of images that are potentially relevant to a given query. The images in the list are initially ranked according to their relevance scores calculated from their corresponding textual

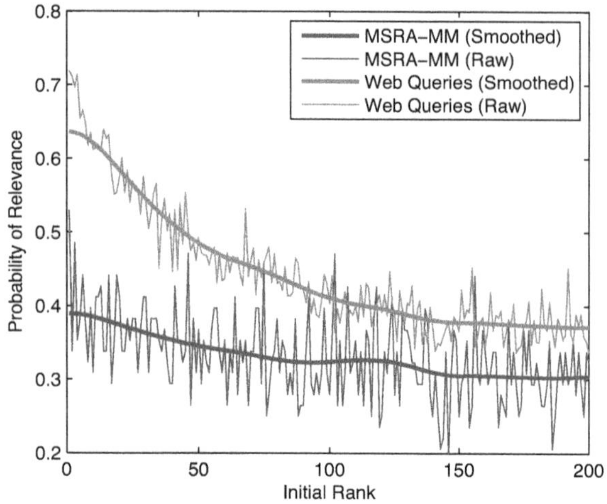

Figure 2: Probability of relevance vs. initial rank position for the MSRA-MM V1.0 and Web Queries datasets. Web Queries have initial ranks highly correlated with relevance. In contrast, MSRA-MM V1.0 contains more noise when the raw data is compared. When smoothed for further analysis, it has low, yet similar relevance probability across all rank positions. Thus, depending on the search engine or dataset used, the pseudo-relevance feedback assumption might not hold.

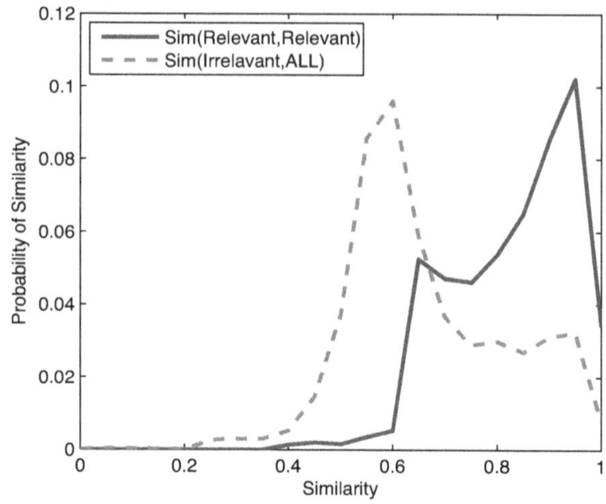

Figure 3: Distributions of visual similarity between images from MSRA-MM V1.0 plotted. The blue curve is the distribution of the similarity between relevant images. The red is the distribution of the similarity from irrelevant images to all images. The relevant images tend to share visual patterns with each other more often than irrelevant images.

information. Based on their visual similarities, the images are reordered such that visually similar images are reranked together.

The common idea in many existing reranking algorithms is that they implicitly or explicitly utilize pseudo-relevance feedback (PRF) [1]. Explicit PRF-based approaches, including classification-based [30] and clustering-based [4] approaches, take top images as pseudo-positive examples and/or bottom images as pseudo-negative examples to either train a classifier or cluster images to perform reranking. However, the selected pseudo-positive and pseudo-negative examples are not reliable and may potentially be false positives and false negatives respectively which will affect the reranking performance. Figure 1 (a) shows an example of such a scenario where the first two images from the initial ranking will be selected as pseudo-positive, but are in fact false positives. Figure 2 also illustrates that the PRF assumption may not always hold for every dataset used. In contrast, implicit PRF-based approaches, including graph-based [5, 7] and Bayesian visual reranking [23], overcome such unreliability by making use of the initial ranking in a soft manner. It encourages relevant images that are positioned at the bottom to move up by receiving reinforcement from other relevant images positioned at the top. However, its major shortcoming is that it cannot push down irrelevant images that are initially ranked high, as the irrelevant images tend to be more visually diverse than the relevant ones. The diversity of irrelevant images is depicted in Figure 3. Therefore, whether they are explicit or implicit, the PRF-based approaches suffer from an unreliable initial rank list where false positives may be selected as pseudo-positive examples.

The explicit PRF-based approaches can theoretically be improved by selecting different numbers (N) of top images for each query. According to our simple experiments performed on the publicly available MSRA-MM V1.0 dataset [28], manually selecting the best performing result from different N for each query improves the performance significantly as shown in Figure 4. Although it would be an interesting problem to automatically select N for each query, this is rather difficult to solve and only partially overcomes the unreliability issue. It can exclude irrelevant images that appear around the bottom part of the top images, but it cannot handle the cases similar to the one in Figure 1 where irrelevant images are occupying the first two positions. These irrelevant images will always get selected no matter what N is.

Therefore, we instead redefine the problem as finding a set of confident image samples that are relevant to the query from the top-ranked images. This can be seen as a relaxation, because the set of images considered are no longer need to be consecutive (starting from the very top), but are selectively chosen from the top-ranked images. To verify our intuition, another simple experiment is performed where a small number of relevant images from the ground truth are randomly sampled as reference points for reranking. The results are reported in Figure 4. With a small set of relevant samples, the performance improves - even better than when different N is chosen for each query.

Given the new problem of finding confident samples, this paper proposes two optimization methods based on sparsity and ranking constraints to solve the problem. The methods described in this paper utilize the fact that relevant images share visual patterns more often than irrelevant images do. After the confident samples are detected, we use them as reference points to rerank images with an adaptive kernel-based scheme. Our approach may be similar to the exemplar-based classification, but ours is fully unsupervised.

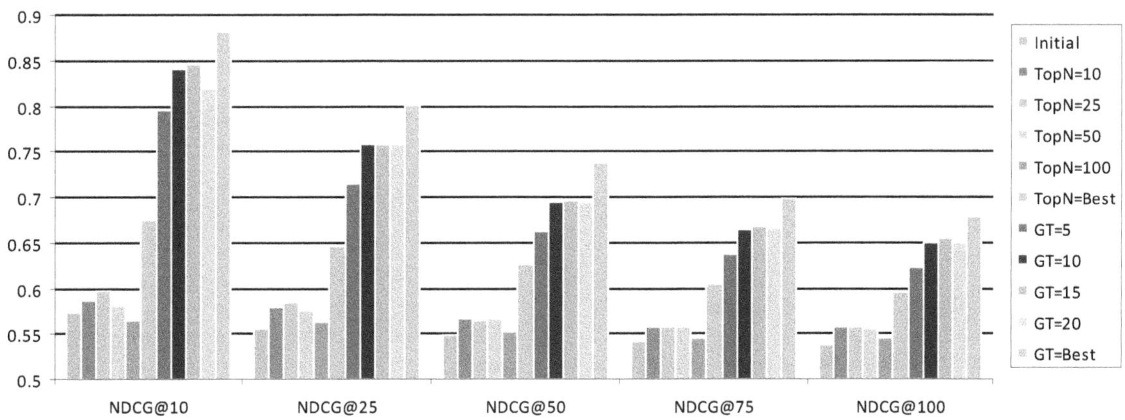

Figure 4: Simple experiments are performed on MSRA-MM V1.0 [28]. TopN=N selects top $N \in \{25, 50, 75, 100\}$ images as reference points for reranking. In contrast, for TopN=Best, we manually inspect different N and choose the best performing one for each query. Hence, its performance improvement can only be achieved theoretically. For GT=N, we manually pick a small number (N) of relevant images from top 100 images using the ground truth labels. While this is ideal, it achieves significantly better performance than PRF-based TopN - motivating our work on automatically detecting confident samples. NDCG is used for performance evaluation (c.f. Section 4.1)

In summary, the main contributions of this paper are as follows:

- We reformulate the new problem of finding confident images from the initial search results, which relaxes the assumption of the psuedo-relevance feedback and does not assume that all images in the top-N have to be relevant to a query.
- We propose and solve two ℓ_1 loss minimization problems with sparsity and ranking constraints, which result in discovering highly-confident samples and are robust against outlier images that are initially ranked highly.
- We rerank images based on the detected confident samples with a kernel-based approach, which successfully promotes relevant images and lowers down irrelevant images. This greatly improves the reranking performance.

The rest of this paper is organized as follows. Section 2 reviews existing work on visual reranking. Section 3 describes our robust visual reranking approach based on sparsity and ranking constrained optimization framework. Section 4 demonstrates the effectiveness of our approach empirically. Section 5 concludes this paper with the future work.

2. RELATED WORK

This section reviews existing visual reranking methods for both image and video retrieval, as the underlying mechanisms of reranking images and videos are generally similar. Broadly speaking, many existing reranking techniques are either supervised or unsupervised.

The supervised methods generally learn a model from human-labeled data offline and use it during the online reranking process [10, 31]. They tend to focus more on designing good reranking features. Other notable ones include using semantic concepts [18], exploiting the click-through data [6], and analyzing the contextual information [32]. On the other hand, the unsupervised methods are more practical than the supervised ones, as they do not assume any human-labeled data to perform reranking. They are either classification-based [14, 29, 30], graph-based [5, 7, 23] or clustering-based [4].

The classification-based method usually consists of three steps. First, under the pseudo-relevance feedback assumption originally introduced in text retrieval [1], both pseudo-positive and pseudo-negative images are sampled. Then, a classifier is trained using either SVM [30], boosting [29] or ranking SVM [14]. Finally, the trained classifier is used to score each image. The key limitation of this method is that the selected pseudo-positive and pseudo-negative images may not be truly-positive and truly-negative. Hence, it is not always guaranteed to learn a robust classifier.

In contrast to the classification-based method, the graph-based method [5, 7, 23] integrates both the initial ranking and visual consistency between images. It constructs a graph where every pair of visually similar images are connected by an edge and the initial rank information is propagated through the graph until convergence. Unfortunately, the graph-based method has no formal mechanism to explicitly penalize outlier images that are dissimilar from other images since it only reranks visually similar images together. Thus, in theory, if one irrelevant image is placed at the top of the initial search result, it will happily stay there because irrelevant images have often small similarities with other irrelevant images and be pushed down at a lower position only in the rare case of its few similar images having low initial ranks.

The clustering-based method groups images based on their visual similarity as well as the initial ranking information [4, 15]. In [4], the information bottleneck principle is used to derive the best groups that maximize mutual information between clusters and labels. It is shown to perform well on videos where near duplicate shots are often found. Typicality-based reranking [15] is concerned with finding samples that are typical among all relevant and irrelevant images by exploring the initial ranking too. The two approaches are based on the assumption that both relevant and irrelevant images are visually compact, which may hold in the benchmark TREC video retrieval evaluation [17]. But it does not hold in web image search as shown in Figure 3. Moreover, as concluded in [15], it relies heavily on the initial ranking and suffers from the drawback of graph-based methods where it is limited in lowering down irrelevant images that are initially ranked high. Typicality is also explored among visual words by [13].

To overcome this outlier problem, the noise resistant ranking method in [12] computes spectral decomposition of a Laplacian matrix and filters noisy images with sparse eigenbasis fitting. Our reconstruction-based approach with sparsity and ranking constraints also tackles the same problem, but directly seeks a sparse set of confident samples that are relevant to a query. These detected samples are used as reference points to perform reranking such that dissimilar and irrelevant images are ranked low. The sparsity constraint is also adopted in [22] to avoid overfitting of a linear ranking model in the context of directly optimizing ranking measures. In our case, the sparsity constraint is applied on the confident sample detection, not on the ranking model, to only select samples that are relevant with high confidence.

3. ROBUST VISUAL RERANKING

Before describing our approach in detail, we formerly define what visual reranking is. We let an initial ranking list and its corresponding set of visual features of one query be $\bar{\mathbf{r}} = [\bar{r}_1, \bar{r}_2, \cdots, \bar{r}_M]^T \in \mathbb{R}^M$ and $\mathbf{X} = [\mathbf{x}_1, \mathbf{x}_2, \cdots, \mathbf{x}_M]$ respectively where M is the total number of the returned results. We define reranking as:

$$\mathbf{r} = f(\mathbf{X}, \bar{\mathbf{r}}),$$

where f is a function of both $\mathbf{X}$ and $\bar{\mathbf{r}}$ returning another ranking list $\mathbf{r} = [r_1, r_2, \cdots, r_M]^T \in \mathbb{R}^M$ which is considered to be a refined version of $\bar{\mathbf{r}}$.

Our approach consists of two main steps as illustrated in Figure 5. The first step finds confident image samples from the initial search results. We define a function of detecting confident samples as:

$$\mathbf{c} = g(\mathbf{X}, \bar{\mathbf{r}}),$$

where $\mathbf{c}$ is a binary vector. If c_i is 1, then its corresponding image I_i is a confident sample that will be used later for reranking. The second step uses the detected confident samples as reference points to rerank the images and such a reranking step is defined as:

$$\mathbf{r} = h(\mathbf{X}, \mathbf{c}).$$

In the next two sections, we describe these two steps in detail.

3.1 Confident Sample Detection

Our confident sample detection is based on an intuition that relevant images share visual patterns with each other more often than irrelevant images, as the relevant ones tend to be less diverse compared to their counterparts. This is illustrated in Figure 3. Therefore, for each image, we first compute its total similarity degree to all other images in the initial ranking list. For a relevant image, it should be similar to other relevant images making its total similarity degree high. Whereas for an irrelevant image, it should be dissimilar to most images regardless of whether they are relevant or irrelevant. Hence, its total similarity degree should be low.

To measure the total similarity degree, we compute a kernel matrix $\mathbf{K} \in \mathbb{R}^{M \times M}$. Each entry k_{ij} of the matrix stores the similarity between two visual features $\mathbf{x}_i$ and $\mathbf{x}_j$, except that we set all self-similarities to 0. We sum the elements in each row of $\mathbf{K}$ to obtain a column vector $\mathbf{s} = \mathbf{Ke}$ where $\mathbf{e}$ is a vector of all ones. We let each entry s_i of $\mathbf{s}$ be the total similarity degree of an image indexed at i to all other images.

In order to analyze which images *mainly* contribute to the composition of $\mathbf{s}$, we propose a reconstruction-based approach which aims to minimize the error between $\mathbf{s}$ and $\mathbf{Kc}$. If a particular image contributes a lot, then it should be significantly similar to other images and it is most likely to be relevant to a query. As motivated from Figure 4, we only need a few confident samples that are truly relevant to the query to obtain good performance. To achieve this, we add a sparsity constraint on $\mathbf{c}$ to the reconstruction error yielding the following formulation:

$$\min_{\mathbf{c}} \|\mathbf{s} - \mathbf{Kc}\|_q^p + \alpha\phi(\bar{\mathbf{r}}, \mathbf{c}) \quad (1)$$
$$\text{s.t. } \mathbf{c} \in \{0,1\}^M,$$

where α is a trade-off parameter that balances the two terms and $\phi(.)$ takes $\bar{\mathbf{r}}$ as one of the input to include a preference of selecting confident samples based on the initial ranking list.

While the above formulation should result in finding a less complex and more robust solution that has as few non-zero entries as possible in $\mathbf{c}$ and achieving a low reconstruction error, it is a binary integer programming problem which is generally NP-hard. Since exhaustive search is computationally expensive, it is not feasible in practice to solve in that way. Hence, we introduce two relaxation schemes, namely non-negative least squares and bounded-variable least squares, such that it can be solved efficiently and effectively.

3.1.1 *Non-Negative Least Squares*

In this section, we describe how the formulation given in Eqn. (1) is relaxed into the non-negative least square problem which can theoretically be solved in a polynomial time. We introduce an auxiliary non-negative real vector $\mathbf{z} \in \mathbb{R}^M_{+,0}$ which infers $\mathbf{c}$ as follows:

$$\mathbf{c} = \mathbf{1}_{(\mathbf{z}>0)}, \quad (2)$$

where $\mathbf{1}_{(.)}$ is an element-wise indicator function returning 1 if z_i is positive and 0 otherwise. We replace $\mathbf{c}$ with $\mathbf{z}$ in Eqn. (1) to obtain the following minimization problem:

$$\min_{\mathbf{z}} \|\mathbf{s} - \mathbf{Kz}\|_1^2 + \alpha\|\mathbf{Dz}\|_1^2 \quad (3)$$
$$\text{s.t. } \mathbf{z} \geq \mathbf{0}.$$

The ℓ_1 square loss is adopted to measure the reconstruction error between $\mathbf{s}$ and $\mathbf{Kz}$, as the ℓ_1 loss has been shown to tolerate more against outlier images which do not really share visual patterns with other images [3]. This is not the case for the ℓ_2 loss which is known to be sensitive when outliers are present in data. As for the constraints on $\mathbf{z}$, we

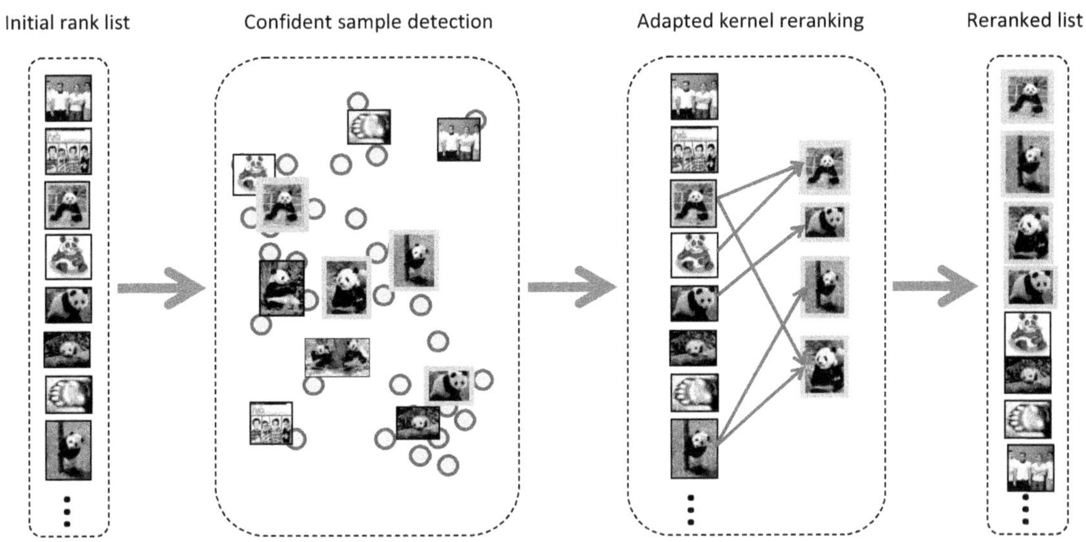

Figure 5: An illustration of robust visual reranking. In the second block, images with cyan bounding boxes correspond to the detected highly-confident samples. Blue circles indicate other images

have the ℓ_1 norm as the sparsity constraint and introduce a diagonal matrix $\mathbf{D}$ to include the initial ranking as prior information. The ℓ_1 norm is preferred over the ℓ_2 norm, as the latter does not encourage to suppress the entries in $\mathbf{z}$ to zero. Each diagonal entry of $\mathbf{D}$ acts as a weight for the corresponding entry in $\mathbf{z}$. The lower the weight, the higher the chance of the corresponding entry of $\mathbf{z}$ being non-zero and considered as a confident sample. Therefore, $\mathbf{D}$ biases the preference of choosing confident samples more towards the initially-highly-ranked images. We will discuss different solutions in instantiating the matrix $\mathbf{D}$ in Section 3.1.3.

The formulation given in Eqn. (3) may lead to an over-reconstruction of $\mathbf{s}$ by $\mathbf{Kz}$ where some entries of $\mathbf{s} - \mathbf{Kz}$ are negative. As a consequence, among the computed confident samples, some samples may not be truly relevant. The sparsity constraint on $\mathbf{z}$ can handle the problem as the over-reconstruction often results in high ℓ_1 norm of $\mathbf{z}$, but with no gaurantee. To handle this issue properly, we explicitly introduce another constraint of $\mathbf{s}-\mathbf{Kz} \geq \mathbf{0}$ to directly avoid it. This additional constraint in fact helps us to rewrite Eqn. (4) into the form similar to the well-studied non-negative least squares problem [8, 26] given as:

$$\min_{\mathbf{z}} \left\| \begin{bmatrix} \mathbf{e}^T\mathbf{s} \\ \mathbf{0} \end{bmatrix} - \begin{bmatrix} \mathbf{e}^T\mathbf{K} \\ \sqrt{\alpha}\mathbf{e}^T\mathbf{D} \end{bmatrix} \mathbf{z} \right\|_2^2 \quad \text{s.t. } \mathbf{z} \geq \mathbf{0}, \ \mathbf{s} - \mathbf{Kz} \geq \mathbf{0}. \tag{4}$$

This is essentially a quadratic programming problem which can be solved in a polynomial time with any standard quadratic programming solver. The images corresponding to the non-zero entries of the optimal $\mathbf{z}$ are treated as the confident samples of a query.

3.1.2 Bounded-Variable Least Squares

With the formulation given in Eqn. (4), $\mathbf{z}$ can be efficiently solved, but it potentially has one undesired consequence where $\mathbf{z}$ can take values larger than 1. This still results in selecting fewer truly-relevant images and more false-positive images to well fit the reconstruction of the irrelevant images. To resolve this issue, we introduce lower and upper bounds for $\mathbf{z}$ such that its entries will be between 0 and 1. This naturally guarantees the constraint of $\mathbf{s} - \mathbf{Kz} \geq \mathbf{0}$ and turns Eqn. (4) into bounded-variable least squares [2, 20] given as:

$$\min_{\mathbf{z}} \left\| \begin{bmatrix} \mathbf{e}^T\mathbf{s} \\ \mathbf{0} \end{bmatrix} - \begin{bmatrix} \mathbf{e}^T\mathbf{K} \\ \sqrt{\alpha}\mathbf{e}^T\mathbf{D} \end{bmatrix} \mathbf{z} \right\|_2^2 \quad \text{s.t. } \mathbf{0} \leq \mathbf{z} \leq \mathbf{1}. \tag{5}$$

The above formulation improves the ability of fitting the reconstruction of the relevant images well and excluding the irrelevant images with the help of the ℓ_1 loss. This allows us to further reduce false positives of the confident samples.

3.1.3 Sparsity and Ranking Constraints

The two proposed formulations are both driven by the sparsity and ranking constraints on $\mathbf{z}$. The sparsity constraint aims to discover a few images that are indeed relevant to the query such that they become reference points to perform the kernel-based reranking described later. The ranking constraint utilizes the initial ranking $\bar{\mathbf{r}}$ as an additional constraint on $\mathbf{z}$ such that initially high-ranked images have a higher chance of being selected as the confident samples. This is motivated by Figure 2 indicating top-ranked images often have a higher probability to be relevant. The ranking constraint is achieved by introducing a diagonal matrix $\mathbf{D}$ and linearly combining it with $\mathbf{z}$ in the ℓ_1 norm. The important question is how to set each diagonal entry d_{ii} of $\mathbf{D}$ in order to achieve the preference of the confident samples according to the initial ranking. We give three possible solutions, namely linear, step-wise and shrinkage, which are defined as follows:

$$d_{ii} = \eta(i + \nu), \tag{6}$$

$$d_{ii} = \eta\lceil(i + \nu)/\epsilon\rceil, \tag{7}$$

$$d_{ii} = \eta(\max(i - \epsilon, 1) + \nu)), \tag{8}$$

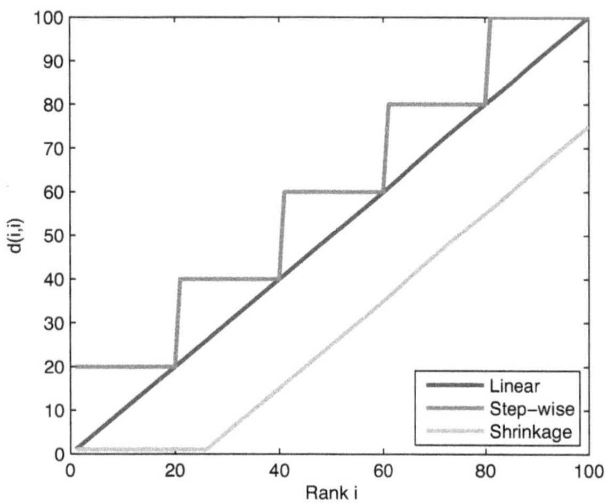

Figure 6: Three possible penalty matrices for the ranking constraint, namely linear in blue, step-wise in red and shrinkage in green.

where η acts like a normalization constant to make the entries of $\mathbf{D}$ sum up to 1. The diagonal entries of the three different matrices are plotted in Figure 6. In the case of $\mathbf{D}$ being set to an identity matrix, we have no confident sample preference towards the initial ranking, i.e. all images are equally likely to be a confident sample.

Our sparsity and ranking constraints differ from the adaptive Lasso [33], as we have either non-negativity or bounds to further constrain $\mathbf{z}$ and the weights defined in $\mathbf{D}$ are more natural to combine the additional useful initial ranking information. To make our problem computationally more feasible, we use $\|.\|_1^2$ instead of $\|.\|_1$ norm. Other penalty matrices, such as fused Lasso [24], ℓ_1 trend filtering [9] and generalized Lasso [25] where off-diagonal entries of the matrices are also non-zero, have been explored by the statistical community before. It is not yet clear and still open how we can utilize them in the reranking problem.

3.2 Adaptive Kernel-Based Reranking

After discovering the confident samples using one of the two optimization methods described, we use the kernel-based approach to rerank the images in the initial ranking list. We choose the kernel-based reranking over the graph-based reranking, due to its simplicity and computational efficiency. The justification of the kernel-based approach is also supported by Figure 3 presented earlier in this paper. The similarities between relevant images are generally higher than those between relevant and irrelevant images and between irrelevant images. Therefore, the relevant images receive higher support from the discovered confident samples while the irrelevant images receive lower support. Even when false-positive images are selected as confident samples, they will not promote the ranks of other irrelevant images to go up because the similarities to those irrelevant images are low.

To formalize, for each image, we compute its rank by summing the responses of the Gaussian kernels with the discovered confident samples which is given as:

$$r_i = \sum_{m=1}^{M} \mathbf{1}_{(z_m>0)} \exp\left(\frac{\|\mathbf{x}_i - \mathbf{x}_m\|^2}{2h^2}\right). \quad (9)$$

Instead of the Gaussian kernels used above, we may generalize the formula as:

$$r_i = \sum_{m=1}^{M} \mathbf{1}_{(z_m>0)} K(\mathbf{x}_i, \mathbf{x}_m). \quad (10)$$

Such a generalization is useful when the only available information is a kernel matrix (not raw visual features). This implies that the whole reranking algorithm can work directly from the kernel matrix, as the confident sample detection is also based on the kernel matrix.

In summary, we outline the whole reranking procedure as follows:

1. Retrieve visual features $\mathbf{X}$ of images in the initial rank list of a query.
2. Obtain a kernel matrix by computing cosine similarity between visual features (i.e. $\mathbf{K} = \mathbf{X}^T\mathbf{X} - \mathbf{I}$). We suppress self-similarity.
3. Compute the total similarity vector $\mathbf{s}$ by summing the columns of $\mathbf{K}$, i.e. $\mathbf{s} = \mathbf{K}\mathbf{e}$.
4. Find the optimal $\mathbf{z}$ according to Eqn. (4) or Eqn. (5) to find confident samples.
5. Infer the final rank $\mathbf{r}$ with Eqn. (9).

3.3 Time Complexity

We analyze the time complexity of our reranking algorithm. Given the initial ranking list of a query, we first compute a kernel matrix $\mathbf{K}$ which takes $O(M^2)$ where M is the length of the ranking list. To run the optimization to detect confident samples from the top N images, it runs ordinary least squares on an active set of variables over N iterations where each iteration takes $O(N^3)$. In practice, it often converges in significantly less than N iterations and the number of active variables at each iteration is also smaller than N. Therefore, it can be solved very efficiently. After the confident samples are found, the adaptive kernel-based reranking takes $O(MN)$ to compute reranked scores. Since the purpose of our algorithm is to rerank the initial search results, its speed is independent to the number of images in a database. On a desktop with 2.4GHz Intel Core Duo and 2GB memory, our MATLAB implementation takes about 0.3 seconds only to rerank each query for M and N being 850 and 100 respectively. We believe this is reasonable for a real-time application.

4. EXPERIMENTS

4.1 Experimental Setup

Experiments are conducted on the MSRA-MM V1.0 [28] and Web Queries [10] datasets both of which are publicly available for download. The MSRA-MM dataset consists of 68 diverse yet representative queries collected from the query log of Bing. In total, it contains 60,257 images and there are roughly 900 images for each query. As for the ground truth labels, it has three relevant levels from 0 to 2: (0) irrelevant, (1) fair, and (2) relevant. The Web Queries dataset, on the other hand, consists of 354 representative queries collected

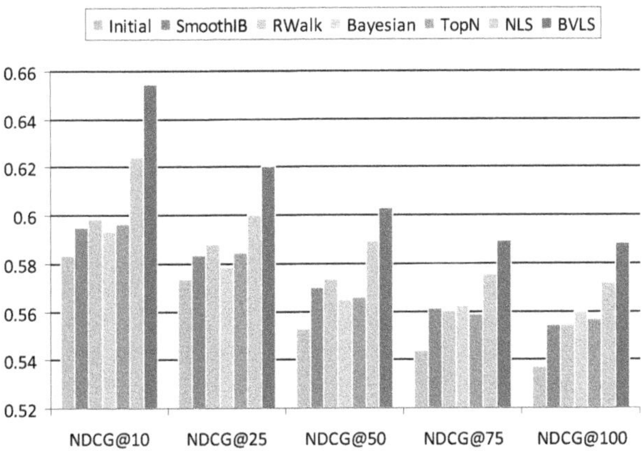

Figure 7: Experimental results on MSRA-MM V1.0.

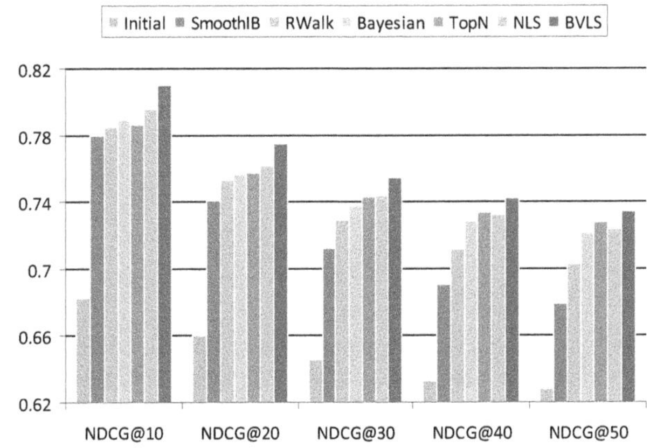

Figure 8: Experimental results on Web Queries.

from Google. In total, it contains 71,478 images and there are about 200 images for each query. In contrast to MSRA-MM, while the number of queries is much larger for Web Queries, the images returned per query are much low (some queries have less than 20 images). The ground truth labels are in binary: (0) irrelevant and (1) relevant.

As for the visual features, we use the thumbnail images instead of the original images to densely sample 128 dimensional SIFT descriptors from 16×16, 24×24 and 32×32 sized patches at every 8 pixels step from each image in both datasets with VLFeat [27]. Then, a random collection of 200,000 descriptors is used to learn 1024 visual words with k-means clustering and the bag-of-words descriptor is computed for each image. We include the spatial location information of each local feature as well [11]. To detect the confident samples, the top 100 images are considered as candidates for each query. Accordingly the dimension of the kernel matrix $\mathbf{K}$ becomes $M \times 100$ and the total similarity vector $\mathbf{s}$ is calculated from this matrix. The linear weight is adopted for $\mathbf{D}$ to induce the ranking constraint. For each experiment, the bandwidth for the adaptive kernel-based reranking is fixed as 0.8 and 1.5 for MSRA-MM and Web Queries respectively. To perform the actual optimization of non-negative least squares and bounded-variable least squares, we use MATLAB's lsqlin(.) which solves least squares with linear constraints.

In order to measure the reranking performance for each query, we adopt the Normalized Discounted Cumulated Gain (NDCG) which is a standard evaluation method in information retrieval when relevance levels are more than two. For a given query, the NDCG at position p can be calculated as

$$\text{NDCG@}p = \frac{1}{Z}\sum_{j=1}^{p} \frac{(2^{t_j}-1)}{\log(1+j)},$$

where t_j is the relevance level of the jth image in the refined ranking list. Z is a normalization constant which makes NDCG@p be 1 for a perfect ranking. For both MSRA-MM V1.0 and Web Queries datasets, Z is calculated based on the ground truth labels provided. To compute the overall performance, NDCGs are averaged over all queries for each dataset.

4.2 Performance Comparison

We compare the following reranking methods to demonstrate the effectiveness of our approach.

- SmoothIB [4] - A clustering based approach based on pseudo-relevance feedback and information bottleneck clustering over visual features with the help of the smoothed initial ranking.
- Random walk reranking (RWalk) [5, 7] - A popular graph-based method that integrates initial ranking and visual similarity between images.
- Bayesian reranking (Bayesian) [23] - Another graph-based method that exploits initial ranking by considering their pairwise difference.
- TopN - The top N images for each query are assumed to be confident samples and the adaptive kernel-based reranking (Eqn. (10)) is performed. N is tuned (as 25) in a brute-force manner to get the best performance.
- NLS - Confident samples are detected based on non-negative least squares (Eqn. (4)) and then the adaptive kernel-based reranking is performed.
- BVLS - Confident samples are detected based on bounded-variable least square (Eqn. (5)) and then the adaptive kernel-based reranking is performed.

Choice of the parameters for each existing method is critical for optimal performance. We have carefully evaluated different parameters and the best performing result is reported in the performance comparison for each method.

4.2.1 *MSRA-MM V1.0*

The results for the MSRA-MM dataset are shown in Figure 7. It is clear from the results that our reranking methods based on the confident sample detection outperform other existing reranking methods across all evaluated NDCGs. When compared against the improvement of both NLS and BVLS from the initial ranking, other reranking methods do not improve much especially for NDCGs at earlier positions. The main reason for this is that the PRF assumption, which is used explicitly in SmoothIB and TopN and implicitly in

Method	MAP
Initial	0.570
Smooth [4]	0.616
RWalk [5, 7]	0.634
Bayesian [23]	0.658
TopN	0.666
NLS	0.664
BVLS	**0.670**
Query-Rel. [10]	0.649

Table 1: Mean average precision evaluated for different reranking methods on the Web Queries dataset.

Graph and Bayesian, does not hold well for this dataset. As previously shown in Figure 2, the probability of relevance given a rank position stays relatively low and similar across all ranks. Hence, the results on this dataset demonstrate the robustness of our confident sampled-based rereanking methods against the unreliability of PRF.

4.2.2 Web Queries

Figure 8 shows that for the Web Queries dataset, the performance of all methods are generally better against the initial rank. This is because unlike the previous dataset, the pseudo-positive examples are more reliable for this dataset as shown in Figure 2. While the existing methods perform well on this dataset, BVLS achieves better performance. NLS achieves better results than TopN and Bayesian at earlier positions and comparable results at later positions. As consistently observed from these two datasets, for earlier NDCGs, BVLS achieves high performance - implying it is effective in pulling more relevant images to appear in the first 10 to 20 positions of the reranked list. This is useful in practice, as users tend to see the first 10 to 20 images more often than the images at later positions.

Since the relevance labels provided by this dataset are in binary, we also report mean average precision (MAP). BVLS and NLS obtain MAP of 0.670 and 0.664 respectively. The results for other reranking methods are shown in Table 1. For a fair comparison, we report the result for the query-relative feature reranking [10] based only on the visual features instead of the one utilizing both the visual and textual features, as both BVLS and NLS exploit the visual features only. It is worth noting that TopN achieve marginally better than NLS. This may be due to the fact that the PRF assumption holds well for Web Queries and the number of top images to consider is tuned extensively. Since MAP takes into account of the whole image list unlike NDCG, it suggests that while BVLS is effective in pulling the relevant images to high positions, it tends to not care too much about the ordering of the bottom images.

4.3 Empirical Analysis

This section analyzes our reranking algorithm in detail. In particular, we check the correctness of the detected confident samples and evaluate the parameters associated to the sparsity and ranking constraints as well as the kernel-based reranking.

4.3.1 The Correctness of Confident Samples

We evaluate how many of the confident samples detected with our approach are indeed correct according to the ground truth. We use precision to measure the performance of the confident sample detection. The results are reported in Table 2. When compared against the method that simply picks the top N number of images based on the PRF assumption, both of our optimization methods, in particular BVLS, achieve better precision. Not only our approach picks the confident samples more accurately, it also determines the number of confident samples for each query automatically.

Method	MSRA-MM	Web Queries
TopN=25	0.384/0.890	0.621
TopN=50	0.370/0.882	0.569
TopN=100	0.349/0.862	0.509
NLS	0.393/0.892	0.638
BVLS	**0.423/0.916**	**0.682**

Table 2: Precision of confident sample detection based on non-negative least squares (NLS) and bounded-variable least squares (BVLS). For MSRA-MM V1.0, since there are three different relevance levels, we evaluate the precision in two ways. The first is to only consider relevance scale of 2 being positive and the rest being negative. The second is to treat relevance scales of 2 and 1 as positive.

For qualitative analysis, Figure 9 shows the confident samples detected from images associated with the query of "panda" from the MSRA-MM dataset. While there are several irrelevant images in the initial ranking list (especially, the first two images are irrelevant), our confident sample detection has successfully discovered the confident samples that are relevant. The kernel-based reranking based on these confident samples achieves visually much better results.

4.3.2 The Sparsity and Ranking Constraints

In this section, we study the effect of changing both the sparsity parameter α and the ranking constraint for BVLS on MSRA-MM. We evaluate α in a range between 20 and 160 with a 20 step increment and use the three ranking constraints described in Section 3.1.3, i.e. linear, step-wise and shrinkage. We also compare against when no initial ranking preference is used, i.e. the ranking constraint matrix set to an identity. For all three ranking constraints, ν is set to 50, such that the weight assigned at each rank position does not decrease sharply. This is based on the observation of Figure 2 for MSRA-MM that the relevance probability is relatively uniform compared against Web Queries. For both step-wise and shrinkage constraints, ϵ is set to 10. η for all three constraints normalizes the sum of the diagonal entries of $\mathbf{D}$ to be 1.

The results are shown in Figure 10. For both NDCG@10 and NDCG@50, the peaks of the four different constraints (including no ranking constraint) are observed when the sparsity is 120. While the performance of no ranking constraint is still better than other existing reranking methods on this dataset (c.f. Figure 7), we can see the clear advantage of including the initial ranking as the confident sample selection preference. All three ranking constraints are better than the one with no ranking preference. For NDCG@10, the linear constraint clearly performs the best amongst the three ranking constraints, and for NDCG@50, all constraints achieve about the same performance. This suggests that un-

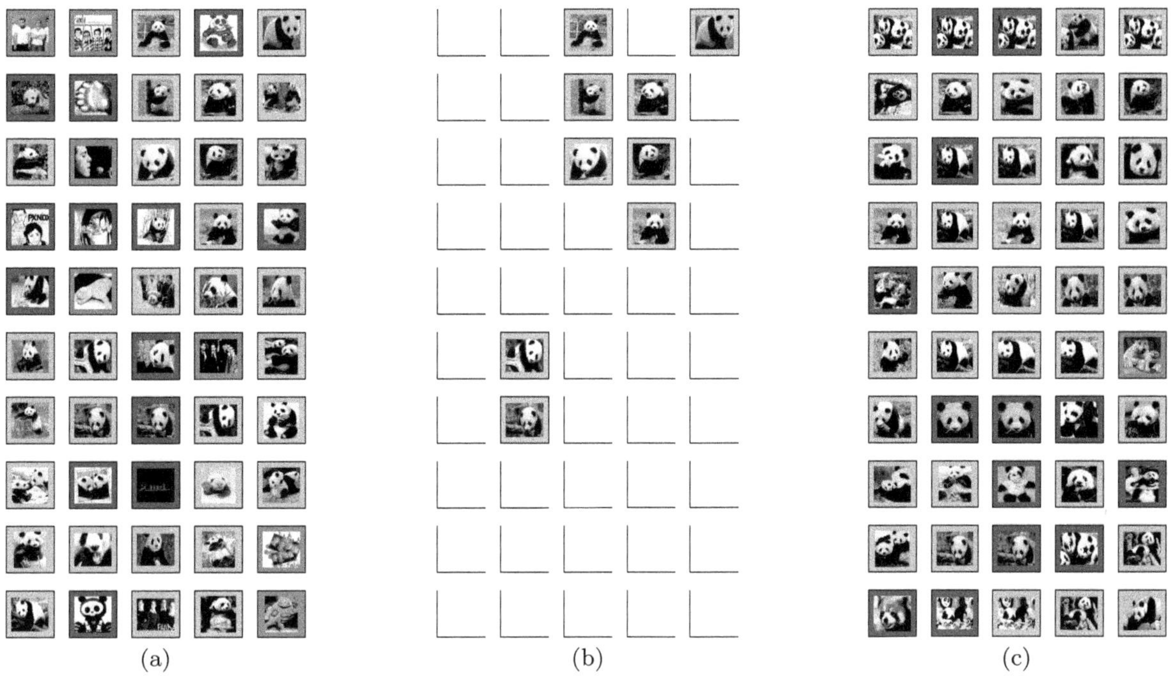

Figure 9: A qualitative analysis of our reranking approach for the query of "panda" from the MSRA-MM V1.0 dataset. (a) The first 50 images from the initial rank list shown. Each image has a color-coded border. Green, blue and red indicate relevance scales 2, 1 and 0 respectively. (b) Confident samples selected from the initial rank list are shown and unselected ones are suppressed for clarity. (c) The first 50 images of the reranked list shown.

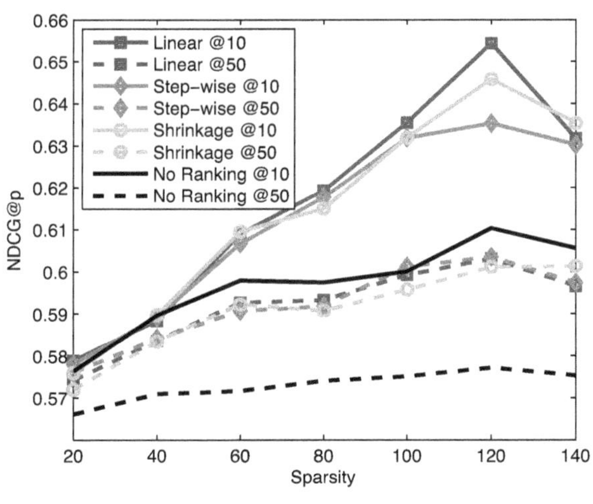

Figure 10: Different sparsity parameters and ranking constraints are evaluated. The ranking constraint improves from just having the sparsity constraint of z.

less we confidently know what kind of ranking constraint is suited for the dataset we use, it is better to use the simple linear constraint, as both step-wise and shrinkage require an additional parameter to be tuned.

4.3.3 The Bandwidth of Gaussian Kernel

The adaptive kernel-based reranking use a Gaussian kernel which requires the bandwidth parameter h to be tuned. It may be desirable to select a different bandwidth for each query. However, this is beyond the scope of this paper. Also, Figure 11 indicates that our approach is not very sensitive to the selection of the bandwidth parameter. We evaluate different bandwidths selected between 0.5 and 1.0 with a 0.1 step increment. While the appropriate bandwidth selection seems slightly critical to obtain the optimal performance for NDCG@10, other NDCGs is not so sensitive to the bandwidth selection.

5. CONCLUSION AND FUTURE WORK

In this paper, we have formulated a problem of finding confident image samples that are relevant to a given query. Two optimization solutions that exploit sparsity and ranking constraints are proposed, namely non-negative least squares and bounded-variable least squares. The detected confident samples are used as reference points for the kernel-based approach to rerank images. The experimental results have shown that the performance of our approach is significantly better than other existing reranking approaches. It can also be computed efficiently. For our future work, we would like to explore other optimization techniques to further reduce false-positive confident samples.

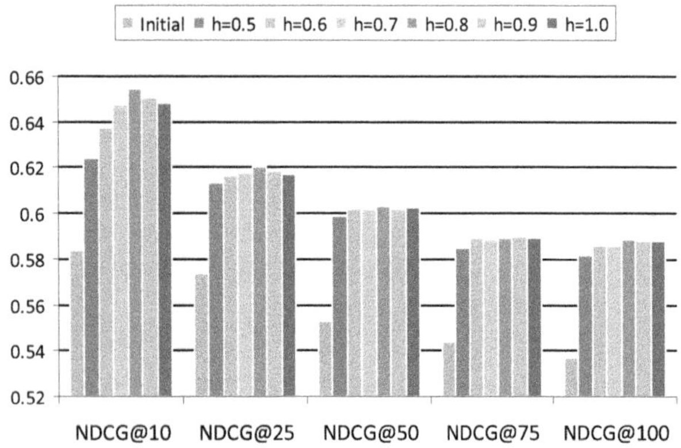

Figure 11: Different bandwidths of the Gaussian kernel used for reranking are evaluated on the MSRA-MM V1.0 dataset.

6. REFERENCES

[1] J. Carbonell, Y. Yang, R. Frederking, R. Brown, Y. Geng, and D. Lee. Translingual information retrieval. In *IJCAI*, 1997.

[2] T. Coleman and Y. Li. A Reflective Newton Method for Minimizing a Quadratic Function Subject to Bounds on Some of the Variables. *SIAM Journal on Optimization*, 1996.

[3] A. Eriksson and A. van Den Hengel. Efficient computation of robust low-rank matrix approximations in the presence of missing data using the L1 norm. In *CVPR*, 2010.

[4] W. Hsu, L. Kennedy, and S.-F. Chang. Video search reranking via information bottleneck principle. In *ACM Multimedia*, 2006.

[5] W. Hsu, L. Kennedy, and S.-F. Chang. Video search reranking through random walk over document-level context graph. In *ACM Multimedia*, 2007.

[6] V. Jain and M. Varma. Learning to re-rank: query-dependent image re-ranking using click data. In *WWW*, 2011.

[7] Y. Jing and S. Baluja. VisualRank: Applying PageRank to Large-Scale Image Search. *PAMI*, 2008.

[8] H. Kim and H. Park. Sparse non-negative matrix factorization via alternating non-negativity-constrained least squares for microarray analysis. *Bioinformatics*, 2007.

[9] S.-J. Kim, K. Koh, S. Boyd, and D. Gorinevsky. L1 trend filtering. *SIAM Review*, 2009.

[10] J. Krapac, M. Allan, J. Verbeek, and F. Jurie. Improving web-image search results using query-relative classifiers. In *CVPR*, 2010.

[11] S. Lazebnik, C. Schmid, and J. Ponce. Beyond Bags of Features: Spatial Pyramid Matching for Recognizing Natural Scene Categories. In *CVPR*, 2006.

[12] W. Liu, Y.-G. Jiang, J. Luo, and S.-F. Chang. Noise Resistant Graph Ranking for Improved Web Image Search. In *CVPR*, 2011.

[13] Y. Liu, T. Mei, and X.-S. Hua. CrowdReranking: exploring multiple search engines for visual search reranking. In *SIGIR*, 2009.

[14] Y. Liu, T. Mei, J. Tang, X. Wu, and X.-S. Hua. Learning to video search rerank via pseudo preference feedback. In *ICME*, 2008.

[15] Y. Liu, T. Mei, M. Wang, X. Wu, and X.-S. Hua. Typicality-Based Visual Search Reranking. *IEEE Transactions on Circuits and Systems for Video Technology*, 2010.

[16] D. Lowe. Distinctive Image Features from Scale-Invariant Keypoints. *IJCV*, 2004.

[17] M. Naphade, L. Kennedy, J. Kender, S.-F. Chang, J. Smith, P. Over, and A. Hauptmann. A Light Scale Concept Ontology for Multimedia Understanding for TRECVID 2005, 2005.

[18] A. Natsev, A. Haubold, J. Tesic, L. Xie, and R. Yan. Semantic concept-based query expansion and re-reranking for multimedia retrieval. In *ACM Multimedia*, 2007.

[19] A. Smeulders, M. Worring, S. Santini, A. Gupta, and R. Jain. Content-Based Image Retrieval at the End of the Early Years. *PAMI*, 2000.

[20] P. Stark and R. Parker. Bounded-variable least-squares: an algorithm and applications. *Computational Statistics*, 1995.

[21] M. Stricker and M. Orengo. Similarity of color images. In *SPIE Storage and Retrieval for Image and Video Datasets III*, 1995.

[22] Z. Sun, T. Qin, Q. Tao, and J. Wang. Robust Sparse Rank Learning for Non-Smooth Ranking Measures. In *SIGIR*, 2009.

[23] X. Tian, L. Yang, J. Wang, X. Wu, and X.-S. Hua. Bayesian Visual Reranking. *IEEE Transactions on Multimedia*, 2010.

[24] R. Tibshirani, M. Saunders, S. Rosset, J. Zhu, and K. Knight. Sparsity and smoothness via the fused lasso. *Journal of the Royal Statistics Society Series*, 2005.

[25] R. Tibshirani and J. Taylor. The Solution Path of the Generalized Lasso. *The Annals of Statistics*, 2010.

[26] M. van Benthem and M. Keenan. Fast algorithm for the solution of large-scale non-negativity constrained least squares problem. *Journal of Chemometrics*, 2004.

[27] A. Vedaldi and B. Fulkerson. VLFeat: An Open and Portable Library of Computer Vision Algorithms, 2008.

[28] M. Wang, L. Yang, and X.-S. Hua. MSRA-MM: Bridging Research and Industrial Societies for Multimedia Information Retrieval, 2009.

[29] R. Yan and A. Hauptmann. Co-retrieval: A boosted reranking approach for video retrieval. In *CIVR*, 2004.

[30] R. Yan, A. Hauptmann, and R. Jin. Multimedia Search with Pseudo-Relevance Feedback. In *CIVR*, 2003.

[31] L. Yang and A. Hanjalic. Supervised reranking for web image search. In *ACM Multimedia*, 2010.

[32] W. Zhou, Q. Tian, L. Yang, and H. Li. Latent visual context analysis for image re-ranking. In *CIVR*, 2010.

[33] H. Zou. The Adaptive Lasso and Its Oracle Properties. *Journal of the Americal Statistical Association*, 2006.

Motor Learning using a Kinematic-Vibrotactile Mapping targeting Fundamental Movements

Troy McDaniel, Morris Goldberg, Daniel Villanueva, Lakshmie Narayan Viswanathan, Sethuraman Panchanathan
Center for Cognitive Ubiquitous Computing
School of Computing, Informatics and Decision Systems Engineering
Arizona State University
Tempe, Arizona, USA 85281
{troy.mcdaniel, daniel.villanueva, lakshmie, panch}@asu.edu, mgoldberg@ieee.org

ABSTRACT
In this paper, we present a novel approach for teaching motor skills through the use of vibrotactile stimulation. We propose a kinematic-vibrotactile mapping that targets fundamental movements (basic building blocks of human motion) using saltatory vibration patterns where vibrations are delivered and interpreted as movement through a conceptual mapping. Two conceptual mappings are explored: the "follow me" concept and the push/pull metaphor. A user study, approved by a local ethics committee, was conducted to explore how these conceptual mappings affect learnability, recognition accuracy, response time and naturalness. Results show the approach to work effectively with a combination of vibration patterns under each conceptual mapping providing the most useful design.

Categories and Subject Descriptors
H.5.2 [User Interfaces]: Haptic I/O.

General Terms
Design, Experimentation, Human Factors.

Keywords
Vibrotactile, saltation, kinematic, fundamental movements.

1. INTRODUCTION
Movement is the bridge between us and our interaction with the world around us. To interact with our environment, we manipulate objects with our hands and body; verbally communicate through tongue and lip movements; and express ourselves or convey ideas through a combination of hand and body gestures, facial expressions and eye movements in addition to verbal cues and social touch. It goes without saying, then, the importance of movement in daily life for accomplishing tasks and goals, socializing with others, and maintaining one's health through exercise. To enrich our lives, we strive to expand our set of motor skills for enhancing our health through sports and exercise; for recreational purposes, such as sports, or as an artistic outlet, such as learning a new musical instrument; or for attaining career goals. The method in which a novel motor skill is taught, and how well the pedagogy aligns with the learning style of the student, will influence how effectively and efficiently the skill is mastered.

As most people are visual learners, individual or group instruction of movement and posture is typically delivered through a combination of verbal explanation and visual demonstration [1]. Verbal cues are often used to convey a high level description of the movement, but are often difficult to parse and translate into movement [2]; even so, they are useful as a complement to visual demonstration. Upon watching a visual demonstration of a movement, students will attempt to mimic the movement by mapping it onto their frame of reference. Feedback from a trainer takes the form of verbal explanation and/or visual demonstration, focusing on improving the movement or posture in question. During this stage, trainers will often make physical contact to complement their feedback; touch cues may be used to guide movement, or shift attention to limbs or areas of the body that are moving incorrectly or are of incorrect posture.

There are several shortcomings with the aforementioned pedagogical techniques for teaching motor skills. First, consider the challenges of group instruction. When trainers are nearby, students tend to learn more effectively [1], most likely due to improved motivation and feedback, and a clear view of the movement to be learned; but with a large group of students, this isn't always possible. Physical contact is a useful complement to verbal and visual cues, but it is sparse in a group setting, and in fact difficult to provide as only a portion of limbs and joints can be engaged at any moment [2]. Moreover, learning preferences are often overlooked, creating missed opportunities. In martial arts instruction [3], it is recommended to accommodate each student's learning preference: some students learn visually through demonstration, some auditorily through discussion and some kinesthetically through practice. However, individualized instruction is often difficult to achieve in large classes. In general, one-on-one instruction offers the benefits of working closely with a trainer. However, such instruction is expensive especially over a long period of time, and is therefore not affordable for many students.

Common are situations where our visual, auditory and/or haptic modalities are overloaded or unavailable for receiving motor instructions. For example, in a group scenario, our vision and hearing can quickly become overloaded with information due to

*Area Chair: Massimo Zancanaro

MM'11, November 28–December 1, 2011, Scottsdale, Arizona, USA.

distractions of other students. There are numerous examples where our modalities may be unavailable for use: in many sports, such as snowboarding [4] and swimming [5], students are unable to receive real-time feedback from trainers during the activity due to the physical separation or nature of the activity; while playing a musical instrument, real-time visual and auditory feedback is difficult to provide as vision and hearing are already overloaded with information from reading music, focusing on playing and listening to the sound [6]; and lastly, visual or auditory modalities may not be useful options when instructing students with sensory or perceptual impairments affecting vision or hearing.

To address one or more of the aforementioned issues associated with traditional pedagogy of motor skills, researchers have proposed augmented and virtual reality solutions utilizing multimedia content of images, video, audio, graphics and/or haptics. Although the majority of approaches are multimodal in that they either augment traditional methods or provide a complete multimedia experience, it is useful to categorize the approaches based on the specific modality that is augmented to improve motor learning: approaches may therefore be classified under the visual, auditory, kinesthetic or vibratory modality.

1.1 Visual Modality

Motor instruction and feedback VR and AR approaches targeting our visual modality engage our sight with multimedia content including images, video, animation and/or graphics. Within this category, the most common approaches are those of virtual reality in which one-on-one instruction and feedback is simulated. Often a head mounted display is used to enable users to compare their virtual representation's movement to a virtual expert's movement to correct movement errors in real-time [7][8]. However, the bulkiness and cost of most wearable VR systems may limit practicality. Moreover, this solution is limited in situations where our visual modality is overloaded or unavailable.

1.2 Auditory Modality

The benefits of sound and music are well known for motor learning and performance. Auditory feedback while playing a musical instrument is critical for self-evaluation; and musical rhythm helps with timing in dancing and exercise. Additionally, auditory-based motor instruction and feedback AR approaches have been proposed to more directly assist with motor learning. These approaches transform kinematic and/or kinetic data into sound, where sensors, such as accelerometers [9] or force sensors [10][11], extract motion cues. Unfortunately, as with the visual modality, there are many application scenarios where hearing may be overloaded or unavailable.

1.3 Kinesthetic Modality

Kinesthetic-based motor instruction and feedback AR approaches utilize robotics, exoskeletons or haptic devices to promote motor learning or rehabilitation through haptic guidance and/or resistance. A variety of systems have been proposed, both in the context of robot-assisted motor learning [12] and haptic guidance [13][14], with much focus on motor rehabilitation. Although studies have shown the benefits of haptic guidance for acquiring new motor skills or rehabilitation, these approaches are limited by cost and portability of equipment.

1.4 Vibratory Modality

Based on previous work, described in Section 2, vibrotactile stimulation for teaching motor movements seems to offer a promising alternative to the aforementioned approaches: vibration motors are small, lightweight, and inexpensive, and engage our tactile sense, avoiding overloaded or unavailable visual or auditory modalities; in addition to bridging the gap between distally located students and teachers as found in many sports. Proposed AR approaches cover a variety of applications for sports [4][5], music playing [6][18] and rehabilitation [2][15]. Support-based approaches (in this work, referred to as instruction-based) cue students to perform movements regardless of their performance, whereas feedback-based approaches provide stimulation linked to performance with the intent to correct errors [10]. Feedback-based vibrotactile stimulation has been shown to be useful for motor learning [2][6], which should come as no surprise given the importance of feedback while mastering new motor skills (see [2]); but feedback alone is not enough during motor training as we need to know the movement to be performed (be it a novel movement, or a movement that is part of a regimen provided by the trainer). Therefore, feedback-based approaches are often combined with visual and/or auditory instruction. However, as situations may arise where our visual or auditory modalities are overloaded or unavailable, vibrotactile instruction-based approaches cannot be dismissed.

Instruction-based approaches have been largely application-specific, making proposed vibrotactile cues difficult to generalize to other domains. Further, how vibrations map to movements (i.e., the kinematic-vibrotactile mapping), and how these mappings affect perception and motor performance, has received little attention. We propose an instruction-based approach to address these two limitations. Rather than target high-level, complex movements or movements related to a specific application, we target the basic building blocks of human motion: the fundamental movements [16]. As these basic movements may be combined to create almost any human motion, our approach is general enough to be applicable to a wide variety of application domains. The details of our proposed approach and system implementation are given in Section 3 and 4, respectively, but first we provide an overview of related work in Section 2. Next, in Section 5, we present a user study, approved by a local ethics committee, in which we systematically explored the design space to discover which vibrotactile instructions are the most natural for cueing fundamental movements. Lastly, Section 6 gives possible directions for future work.

2. RELATED WORK

2.1 Feedback-Based Approaches

In general, feedback-based approaches utilize vibrotactile stimulation to communicate errors in joint angles, positions or accelerations compared to some predefined movement or posture, typically of an expert or the user's own calibration profile in the case of physical therapy. Lindeman et al. [17] proposed the TactaPack: a wearable assistive device for physical therapy that utilizes wireless, attachable modules, each with an accelerometer and vibration motor, and its own processing and power capabilities. Vibrations (which take the place of a nudge) warn of limbs exceeding (or not reaching) acceleration ranges found during the calibration stage wherein a physical therapist leads the regimen. MusicJacket [6] is a wearable system that provides vibrotactile feedback to students learning to play the violin. Specifically, vibration motors on the arms and wrists as well as the torso, provide guidance for proper bowing movement and playing posture. The Tactile Interaction for Kinesthetic Learning

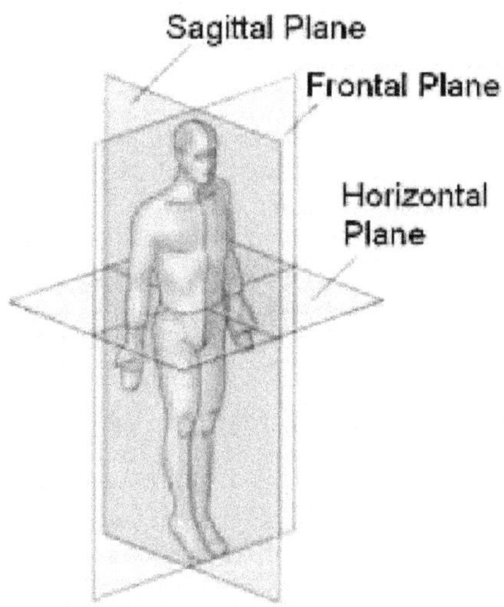

Figure 1. Sagittal, frontal and horizontal planes of the human body. Body posture shown is the anatomical position. Adapted from the Wikimedia Commons file "File:BodyPlanes.jpg".

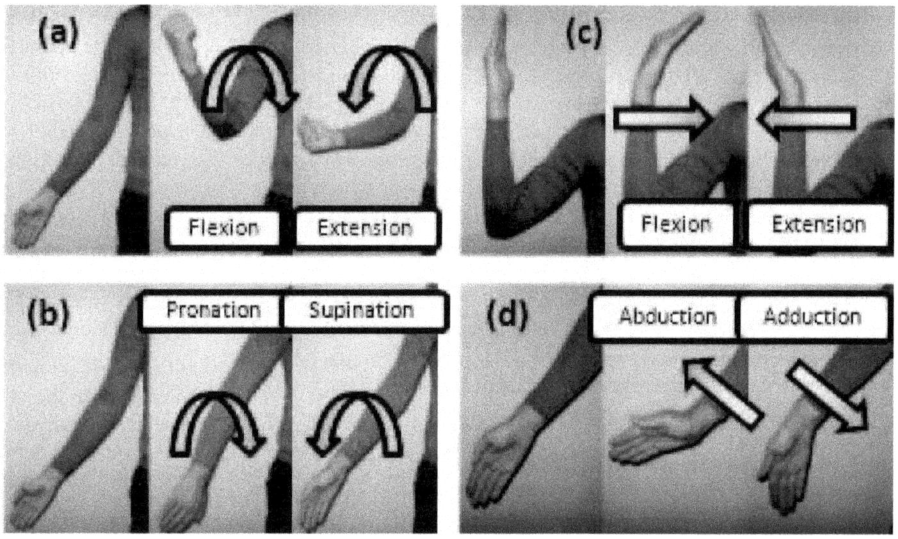

Figure 2. Visual demonstration of fundamental movements of the right arm (referred to in later sections) while in the anatomical position. (a) flexion and extension of the elbow joint; (b) rotations of the forearm; (c) flexion and extension of the wrist joint (shown in different position for visibility); and (d) abduction (radial deviation) and adduction (ulnar deviation) of the wrist joint.

(TIKL) wearable system, designed and implemented by Lieberman et al. [2], conveys which joints are in error through the location and intensity of vibrations, found based on comparisons with an expert's movement and the magnitude of error, respectively. A similar methodology is used by StrokeSleeve [15]; but unlike TIKL, which uses infrared motion tracking, StrokeSleeve uses magnetic tracking. Both TIKL and StrokeSleeve target the fundamental movements of the arm.

2.2 Instruction-Based Approaches

Instruction-based approaches communicate which movement to perform using spatio-temporal vibration patterns of varying levels of abstraction. The level of abstraction of instructions ranges from high-level ("step left foot forward", "lean forward", etc.) to low-level movements such as fundamental movements. In [5], vibrotactile pulses delivered to the left wrist of a swimmer conveyed the speed at which to swim (fast or slow when stimulation is on or off, respectively); and which arm to perform a stroke with depending upon the duration of the vibration (short or long). Mobile Music Touch (MMT) [18], developed by Huang et al., is a wearable glove that uses vibration pulses (one vibration motor for each finger) to help teach piano music subconsciously while away from the piano. Spelmezan et al. [4] proposed tactile motion instructions to enable snowboarding coaches to deliver real-time instruction and feedback to students as they are riding. Although the authors intended the instructions to be used for feedback (delivered automatically or by a coach), the cues could also be instruction-based to provide a supportive function regardless of user performance. An open response paradigm explored movements elicited from a set of vibration patterns that were gauged as useful. Subjects found single pulses to be vague, and preferred saltatory vibration patterns given their directionality. Although responses varied across participants in terms of the movement elicited by each pattern, a useful set of patterns was derived and tested under realistic snowboarding conditions. Spelmezan et al. also discovered that subjects interpreted vibrations as either pushing or pulling a limb. Lastly, in [19], we presented high-level spatio-temporal design guidelines for mapping vibrations to fundamental movements for the purpose of instruction-based motor learning. However, no formal user study was conducted to learn how design parameters affect the usefulness and naturalness of vibrotactile cues for motor learning. In the following section, we present our proposed conceptual methodology and system implementation.

3. KINEMATIC-VIBROTACTILE MAPPING

The aforementioned instruction or feedback-based approaches all facilitate motor learning through a kinematic-vibrotactile mapping. There are three stages within this mapping: (1) the design of the vibration signal to be applied to the skin; (2) the conceptual mapping of the perceived vibration signal to the movement it is intended to elicit or cue; and (3) the type of movement to be performed based on the cue. As discussed, kinematic-vibrotactile mappings have been application specific; we propose a novel, generic mapping, and shed light on several research questions through pilot testing and a formal user study.

3.1 Fundamental Movements

The human body is capable of five fundamental movements [16]: flexion, extension, abduction, adduction and rotation. Consider our posture being that of the anatomical position (see Figure 1); each fundamental movement occurs in one of three cross-sectional planes that divide the body into different halves. Flexion and extension occur within the sagittal plane about the frontal-horizontal axis. At a given joint, flexion or extension causes a decrease or increase in the joint angle, respectively. Abduction and adduction occur within the frontal plane about the sagittal-horizontal axis. Abduction is movement away from the sagittal plane, whereas adduction is movement toward the sagittal plane. Rotation occurs within the horizontal plane about the frontal-sagittal axis. Rotation of a limb toward the sagittal plane is pronation, whereas rotation of a limb away from the sagittal plane is supination. In this work, we limit movements to the right arm (see Figure 2) so that a thorough, exploratory study is feasible.

Given that we are targeting the basic building blocks of movement, this approach is intended for use by those just beginning to learn a complex movement. Typically, beginners are first taught which movements to perform, and after the student has become familiar with the movement or sequence of movements, the next goal is to perfect these movements [10]; and so, we hypothesize that imparting knowledge about which joints and structures are involved in the movement will be useful during the early stages of learning. With the addition of feedback-based instruction (see future work in Section 6), the proposed approach has the potential to scale well to users with a wide range of skill including experts. By linking real-time vibrotactile feedback with user performance, users will have the capability to master movements, and practice and self-evaluate their skill over time to retain a high degree of movement control and coordination.

3.2 Vibrotactile Stimulation

Saltation [20] is a perceptual illusion, often demonstrated by three vibration motors, spaced along a cross-section of the skin, actuated in sequence with three brief vibration pulses each. Rather than perceiving localized pulses at each motor, pulses feel as if they are spaced across the whole length of the array of motors. Saltation provides the illusion of apparent motion, which has an associated directionality, useful for motor learning applications [4][19]. For this reason, we've chosen to use saltatory vibration patterns as our form of vibrotactile stimulation. Of course, saltation isn't limited to only three motors or three pulses; spatio-temporal vibrations have many dimensions that affect perception of saltation: number of motors; motor spacing/placing; and the length, number and spacing between pulses (see [20]).

3.3 Conceptual Mapping

When mapping vibration patterns to movements, pedagogical concepts may be employed to better facilitate user understanding and learning. If certain vibration patterns naturally elicit movement without any training, teaching these concepts may not be necessary; however, it is difficult to find such vibrations given user variability and preferences. In this work, we explore two pedagogical concepts: the mimic or "follow me" concept, and the push/pull metaphor, both in the context of saltatory vibrations to cue fundamental movements—that is, our proposed kinematic-vibrotactile mapping. Our interest here is exploring how intuitive or natural these concepts are to users. A key design choice affecting the naturalness of a conceptual mapping is how the vibration motors are spaced and placed on the skin, or the configuration of motors. Given an infinitely large design space, pilot testing was done for each conceptual mapping in an effort to narrow down configurations for each fundamental movement.

3.3.1 Mimic or "Follow Me" Concept

The idea behind the "follow me" conceptual mapping is to simply follow the direction of vibration pulses as they move along a cross-section of the skin. Through pilot testing, we found that vibration directionality tangential to its assigned movement trajectory seems to be the most intuitive. For example, if we bend our arm at the elbow joint (flexion), the movement follows an arc; a vibration pattern with directionality orthogonal to our forearm would be tangential to this arc. Figure 3 (a)-(d) provides a visual depiction of configurations for each fundamental movement of the right arm, where, through pilot tests, configurations were narrowed down to those shown. These patterns were deemed the most natural, and were selected for evaluation. Below, we present observations made during pilot testing; but first, the following measurements were recorded when the system was not worn, and motors are identified using anatomical locations with respect to the arm held out in front of the user with the palm facing down: (a) elbow flexion/extension: inter-motor spacing of 2 in. (dorsal aspect to medial side) and 2.125 in. (medial side to volar aspect); (b) forearm rotations: inter-motor spacing of 2 in. (dorsal to medial side), 2 in. (medial side to volar aspect), 2.5 in. (volar aspect to lateral side) and 2 in. (lateral side to dorsal aspect); (c) wrist flexion/extension: inter-motor spacing of 1.25 in. (dorsal aspect to medial side) and 1.125 in. (medial side to volar aspect); and (d) wrist abduction/adduction: inter-motor spacing of 1.25 in. (medial side to center) and 1.375 in. (center to lateral side).

For elbow flexion/extension, saltation felt most natural when delivered to the volar aspect of the middle of the forearm or more proximal, near the elbow joint. The middle of the forearm should be avoided, however, to prevent confusion with vibrations for forearm rotations; as should more distal regions to avoid confusion with vibrations for wrist movements. For forearm rotations, saltation (conveyed by at least four motors) felt most natural anywhere on the forearm; but the middle portion is recommended to avoid vibrations for wrist and elbow movements. For wrist flexion/extension, saltation felt most natural when delivered to either side of the wrist joint (we used the medial side when the back of the hand is anterior to the palm of the hand). For any wrist movement, it is recommend to avoid placing motors across the wrist joint and onto the forearm as rotational movements will cause the forearm to move within the worn fabric, misaligning a configuration with its respective movement; in other words, if vibration patterns are to work well for any arm (or, limb, body, etc.) posture, then careful attention must be paid to spatial variations of motors as movements are performed. Also, avoid placing motors on the palm as it may be obtrusive. Lastly, for wrist abduction/adduction, saltation felt most natural when delivered to the back of the hand on or below the knuckles, where the generous surface area provides sufficient spacing between individual motors, as well as with vibrations targeting wrist flexion/extension. In general, to improve distinctness, vibration patterns targeting different fundamental movements, e.g., rotations versus elbow flexion/extension, should not share motors, and be as far apart as possible. Lastly, within a configuration, motors must be spaced such that directionality is easily perceived.

3.3.2 Push and Pull Metaphor

The push metaphor teaches us to perceive vibrotactile stimulation as "pushing" a limb; or "pulling a limb" in the case of the pull metaphor. Through pilot testing, vibrotactile stimulation that runs parallel to the limb, either across the joint that is to be articulated, or near the joint, seems to be the most intuitive. Whereas Spelmezan et al. [4] used either the push metaphor or the pull metaphor, we combine these into the push/pull metaphor, halving the needed number of motors, thereby making the system more cost effective and simplifying design and hardware. As an example, consider elbow flexion/extension: upon feeling a vibration running up the volar aspect of the forearm across the elbow joint, this vibration pattern would be perceived as pulling (or flexing) the forearm; if the vibration runs in the opposite direction, the pattern would be perceived as pushing (or extending) the forearm. A visual depiction of the configurations are shown in Figure 3 (e)-(h), and the following measurements were recorded, under the same conditions described in Section 3.3.1, and similarly presented: (e) elbow flexion/extension: inter-motor spacing of 4.25 in. (distal to center) and 2.75 in. (center to

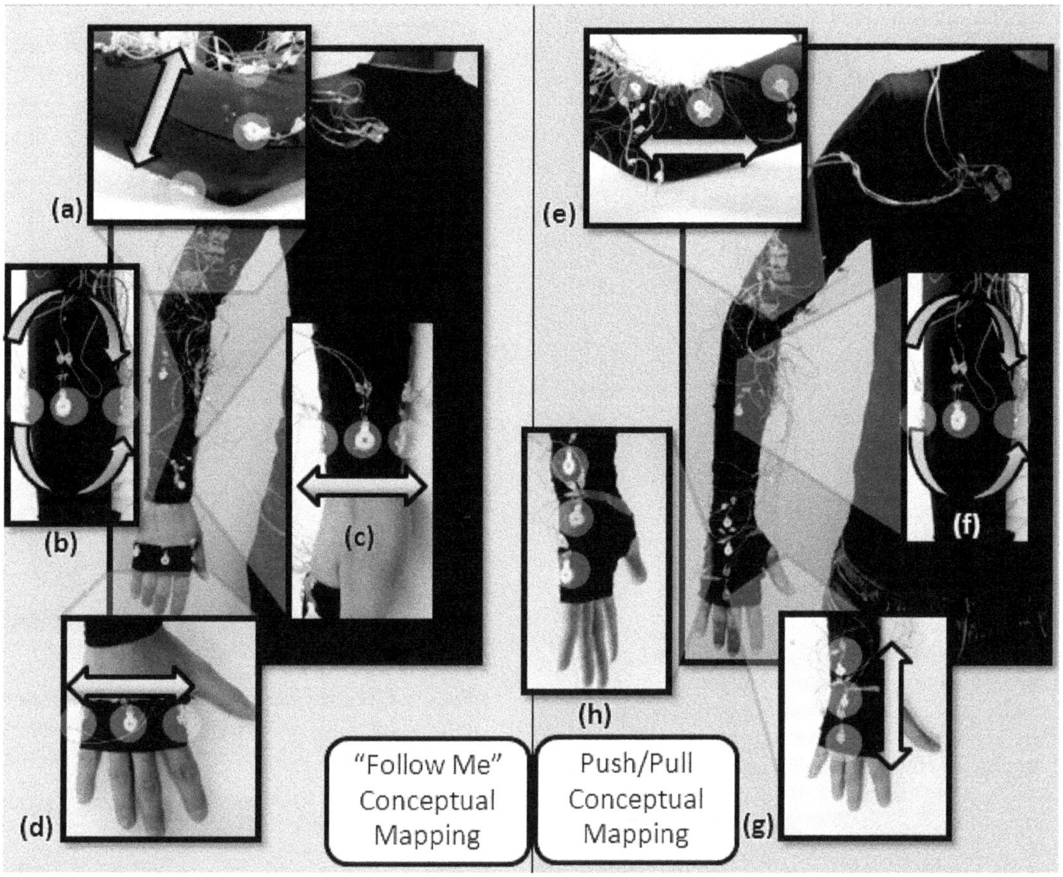

Figure 3. Vibration motor configurations (highlighted) and directionality (arrows) for "Follow Me" (left) and Push/Pull (right) conceptual mappings. Rotation pattern (f) is identical to (b), and so it uses the "follow me" rather than push/pull mapping. All movements use three motors except rotations (b) and (f) which use four motors equidistantly spaced around the forearm (the motor on the volar side of the forearm is not shown as it is occluded by the arm). For saltation, each motor vibrates for four brief pulses (with the exception of rotations, where motors vibrate for three pulses so that the total duration is reasonable) of a burst duration of 100 ms with an interstimulus interval of 60 ms. Moreover, before each pattern begins, a longer pulse (burst duration: 500 ms; interstimulus interval: 200 ms) is given at the starting motor to help capture the user's attention. This gives a total duration of 2.56 seconds for each pattern except rotations, which are of length 3.04 seconds. Rotations have a longer duration given that five motors in total are actuated (the vibration pattern comes full circle, ending on the starting motor).

proximal); (f) forearm rotations: same as (b); and for both (g) wrist flexion/extension and (h) wrist abduction/adduction, motor spacing measurements cannot be made, except for when the system is worn, as motors are each attached to separate garments; in any case, however, we can make measurements between motors of these two groups based on which motors share sections of garments: distal motors have a spacing of 1.625 in., center motors have a spacing of 1.75 in., and proximal motors have a spacing of 1.375 in.

For elbow flexion/extension, saltation felt most natural when delivered to the volar aspect of the arm across the elbow joint, with the center motor on the elbow joint. Motors should be generously spaced apart so that when the arm is fully flexed, the vibration pattern for extension may still be easily perceived. Vibration patterns for rotations were most intuitive when explained and delivered under the "follow me" concept (see previous subsection), so no push/pull version is proposed. For wrist flexion/extension, saltation felt most natural when delivered to either the palm or back of the hand, but it is recommended to avoid the palm; and as described before, for wrist movements, motors should not be placed posterior to the wrist joint (and hence onto the forearm) to avoid complications arising from forearm rotations. For wrist abduction/adduction, saltation felt most natural when delivered to the lateral side of the hand when the back of the hand is anterior to the palm.

4. SYSTEM IMPLEMENTATION

Figure 4 depicts the hardware of the system. The sleeve is part of a compression shirt (Men's medium; 84% polyester, 16% spandex). A LilyPad Arduino (ATmega328) microcontroller is powered using a LilyPad LiPower and a 2000 mAh Polymer Lithium Ion battery. To deliver power, stranded wires are used to reduce resistance. Thin, flexible, solid core wires are used to trigger motors. Wires are slack to provide flexibility when altering configurations, and to enable subjects to easily move while wearing the system. The microcontroller controls vibration motors (pancake motors; 150 Hz), attached with a small dab of hot glue that is easily removed when spatially altering motors. Motors are not directly connected to the microcontroller, but instead, are connected through nested 8-bit address latches (model#: 74HC259N). Within our implementation, latches are nested for two levels, enabling one microcontroller to support over 200 motors. Between a latch and a motor (each latch supports 7 motors) is a driver (Hi V & A Darlington Transistor Array; model#: ULN2004ANE4).

The firmware stored on the microcontroller was developed using the Arduino development environment. The firmware stores vibration patterns (a sequence of motor actuations of specific timings), triggered when received over Bluetooth. These commands are sent wirelessly from a GUI-based application that was developed using Visual C#. The GUI enables users to connect to the microcontroller, actuate motors individually or from pre-defined patterns, and start/stop a timer for recording response times.

5. EXPERIMENT

Aim: The purpose of this study is to explore the naturalness of the proposed kinematic-vibrotactile mapping; in particular, we wish to explore how the "follow me" concept and push/pull metaphor affect naturalness. Naturalness is primarily investigated through subjective feedback, but learning rate, recognition accuracy, and response time may also shed light on the usefulness of the conceptual mappings. It is important to note that the intuitiveness of a conceptual mapping is closely linked to motor spacing and placement (configuration); we've accounted for this through extensive pilot testing to find the most useful and natural configurations for each fundamental movement of the two conceptual mappings. Moreover, we cannot assume that vibration patterns, after being learned in one posture, will generalize to different postures. Ideally, however, we'd prefer *posture-free* vibration patterns that generalize well to other postures after being mastered in one training posture. To this end, we explore how well the proposed vibration patterns generalize to novel postures (various arm postures).

Subjects: The experiment involved 20 subjects, all Arizona State University students, divided between two conditions. The "follow me" condition involved 8 males and 2 females (age range: 19 to 27; mean: 24); and the push/pull condition also involved 8 males and 2 female (age range: 20 to 34; mean: 25). No subjects had motor or tactile impairments.

Procedure: Subject information including age, sex, height and weight was collected. The experiment was briefly explained to participants, after which they donned the wearable system, depicted in Figure 4 with configurations depending on their assigned condition (see Figure 3). The experiment consisted of three phases: a familiarization, training, and two-part testing phase. The experimenter explained the randomly assigned condition, which was either the "follow me" or push/pull conceptual mapping. During the entire study, with the exception of the second part of testing, subjects were asked to remain standing with their arms by their sides (training posture). During the familiarization phase, each vibration pattern of the assigned conceptual mapping was sequentially presented; before each presentation, the experimenter demonstrated the movement and explained the stimulation, relating it to its conceptual mapping. To avoid confusion, layman terminology (see Table 2) was used to specify fundamental movements: for example, 'wrist up' rather than 'wrist extension'. For simplicity, since wrist abduction/adduction is depended upon the posture of the hand with respect to the sagittal plane, they are taught in posture B (see Figure 5), and assumed to remain the same across different postures, 'Wrist Left' and 'Wrist Right', respectively. This assumption is made throughout the remainder of the paper including results and discussion. Once completing the first pass through the patterns, the vibration patterns were delivered once more. During the training phase, training trials were repeated unless the subject scored a recognition accuracy of at least 80% (7 out of 8 patterns) during a trial. A single training trial involved the random presentation of all eight vibration patterns, once each. Participants were told to respond with the movement the vibration cued, as quickly, but also as accurately, as possible. The experimenter informed the subject about the correctness of each response; if the movement was incorrect, the experimenter demonstrated the correct movement, and presented the pattern once more. During each phase, the experimenter recorded learning rate (training phase only), response correctness and response time. Learning rate is the number of training trials required before the subject passes on to testing. The correctness of

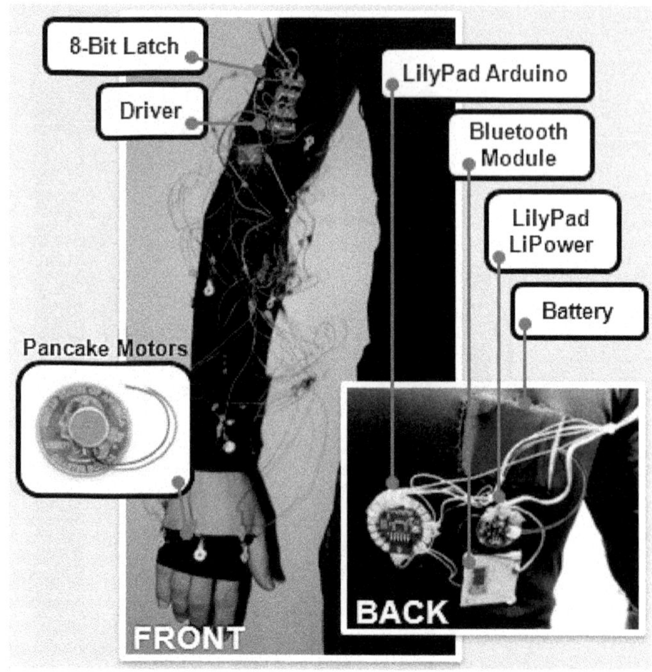

Figure 4. Hardware of system implementation depicting microcontroller, power supply, wireless communication module, actuators and other components.

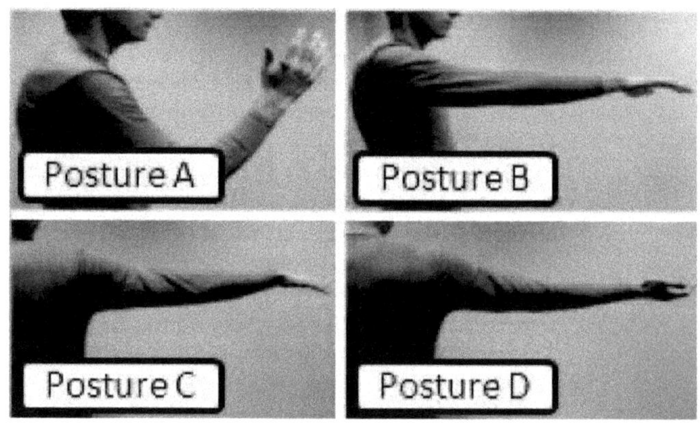

Figure 5. The four novel postures, A, B, C and D, used during the second part of the testing phase.

each response is used to derive recognition accuracy, or the percentage of correct responses. Response time is the duration between the start time of the presentation of the pattern, and the time at which the subject began performing the correct movement; if incorrect movements were performed first, but then corrected by performing the correct movement, within a time limit of 15 seconds, the response was marked as correct.

The first part of the testing phase was similar to the training phase with the exception that four trials (32 presentations total with four random presentations per pattern) were performed for each subject, and no feedback was given. During the second part of the testing phase, four new postures, depicted in Figure 5, were introduced. The experimenter demonstrated each posture, and explained how the arm should be slightly bent at the elbow while in each posture (not shown in figure) to allow extensions to be performed. Each vibration pattern was presented once for each posture, for a total of 32 presentations. Presentation pairs (*posture*, *vibration pattern*) were randomized. Before each presentation, the participant was informed which posture to change to, after which, the pattern was presented. No feedback was given. Finally, subjects were asked to fill out a questionnaire.

Results: The mean average number of learning trials was 1.9 (SD: 0.99) and 1.4 (SD: 0.7) for "follow me" and push/pull conditions, respectively. Recognition accuracies and classifications for each vibration pattern are summarized in Figure 6. For the "follow me" and push/pull conditions, the overall recognition accuracy for the first part of testing was 97% (SD: 8.8%) and 98% (SD: 6.1%), respectively; and 98% (SD: 8.1%) and 94% (SD: 14.5%) for the second part. Mean response times for each vibration pattern are summarized in Figure 7. For the "follow me" and push/pull conditions, the overall response time for the training phase was 3.6 s (SD: 1.59 s) and 2.8 s (SD: 0.72 s), respectively; for the first part of testing, 2.9 s (SD: 0.96 s) and 2.5 s (SD: 5.9 s); and for the second part of testing, 2.9 s (SD: 0.86 s) and 2.5 s (SD: 0.59 s). Table 1 summarizes results from the post-experiment questionnaire where subjects rated a series of questions using a Likert scale from 1 (low/difficult) to 5 (high/easy). Tables 2 summarizes results pertaining to the subjective naturalness of each vibration pattern, where subjects rated each pattern's naturalness as 'excellent' (perfect or near perfect), 'acceptable' (satisfactory) or 'unacceptable' (needs improvement).

Discussion:

- *Learning Rate:* The average number of learning trials did not differ significantly between conditions, $t(18)=1.30$, $p>0.2$, two-tailed, showing that both conceptual mappings were easy to learn.
- *Recognition Accuracy:* For the first part of testing, the overall recognition accuracy (across subjects) of each vibration pattern (and for either condition) is impressive at 90% or better, with most accuracies being in the high 90's (see Figure 6a). Moreover, a one-way repeated measure ANOVA revealed that recognition accuracies between vibration patterns did not differ significantly, $F(7,63)=1.52$, $p>0.05$, and $F(7,63)=0.93$, $p>0.05$, for the "follow me" and push/pull conditions, respectively. This shows that within each condition, patterns were distinct and easy to recognize. For the second part of testing in which novel postures were introduced, the overall recognition accuracy (across subjects and postures) of each vibration pattern (for either condition) is impressive given no prior training on the novel postures; as depicted in Figure 5b, most accuracies are 90% or better, showing that most patterns, for either condition, were still distinct and easy to recognize even for new postures. However, for the push/pull condition, wrist abduction and adduction were both below 90% at 88% (SD: 13.1%) and 75% (SD: 28.9%), respectively. A two-way repeated measure ANOVA revealed that the main effects for vibration pattern and posture were both significant, $F(7,63)=5.14$, $p<0.0002$, and $F(3,27)=4.33$, $p<0.05$, as well as their interaction, $F(21,189)=3.1$, $p<2\times10^{-5}$. Regarding the main effect of pattern type, Figure 6b suggests lower recognition accuracy for wrist adduction compared to other patterns, regardless of posture. Although we observed slight difficulties with recognizing this pattern while in posture A, B and C, it was posture D that presented the biggest challenge. Regarding the main effect of posture, we observed posture D to have lower overall recognition accuracy, regardless of pattern type, when compared to other postures. However, we observed that the patterns of wrist abduction and adduction created the most problems for participants while in posture D (interaction effect). Overall wrist abduction and adduction accuracy, while in posture D, were both very low at 50% (SD: 52.7%) each. As shown in the confusion matrix of Figure 5b, all five misclassifications of wrist abduction occurred in posture D, whereas half (five out of ten) misclassifications of wrist adduction occurred in posture D; most of the confusion happened between wrist movements. Subjective feedback confirmed the difficultly of recognizing wrist abduction and adduction patterns in posture D for the push/pull condition: many subjects commented that wrist abduction and adduction for push/pull were very difficult to recognize while in posture D due to the (rotated) hand posture. Indeed, in (8) of Table 1, which addresses subjective distinctness and ease of recognition, we see that wrist abduction/adduction were the lowest rated among other patterns in the push/pull condition.
- *Response Time:* After training, overall response times for either condition and for any pattern were impressive, at roughly three seconds or less. Figure 7 shows a general decrease in overall response time (across subjects) for vibration patterns as subjects progressed from training to the first part of testing; then seemingly stabilizing between the first and second part of testing with some small increases or decreases depending on the pattern and condition. A two-way repeated measure ANOVA revealed the main effect of phase type to be significant, $F(2,18)=15.87$, $p<1.1\times10^{-4}$ and $F(2,18)=15.53$, $p<1.21\times10^{-4}$, for "follow me" and push/pull conditions, respectively. Based on Figure 7, this suggests that with continued exposure to the patterns, reaction times improved, with perhaps the exception of the transition between the two parts of testing. This may be due to the introduction of the novel postures, or perhaps more time was needed before we saw further improvements in terms of response time. We hypothesize that over long term use, users will continue to become more proficient at recognizing and responding to the patterns. Only for the "follow me" condition was the main effect of pattern type significant, $F(7,63)=4.13$, $p<8.61\times10^{-4}$. Indeed, from Figure 7, we see that patterns for wrist abduction and adduction were recognized faster on average compared to other patterns. This coincides with subjective feedback: see (8) of Table 1. As expected, this indicates that more natural patterns (see Table 2) will lead to

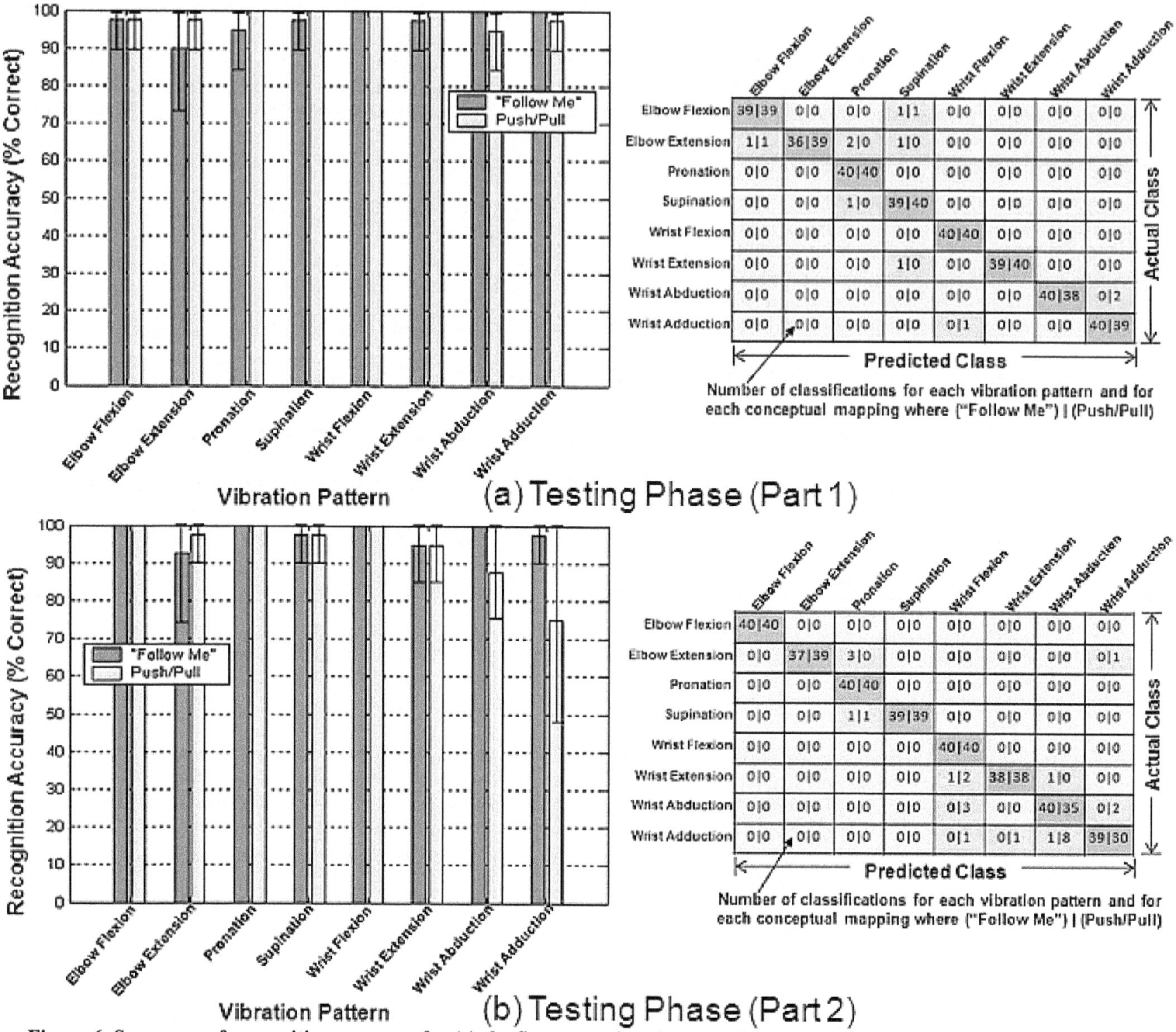

Figure 6. Summary of recognition accuracy for (a) the first part of testing, and (b) the second part of testing. Bar plots (left) show mean recognition accuracies (with standard deviation error bars) for each vibration pattern, averaged across subjects in (a) and averaged across subjects and novel postures in (b). Confusion matrices (right) show the number of times the actual vibration pattern (y-axis) has been classified as the predicted vibration pattern (x-axis), summed across subjects in (a) and summed across subjects and novel postures in (b), where summations are shown using the convention: "follow me" | push/pull. Although rotations appear under the push/pull condition, only the "follow me" concept was used to explain rotations.

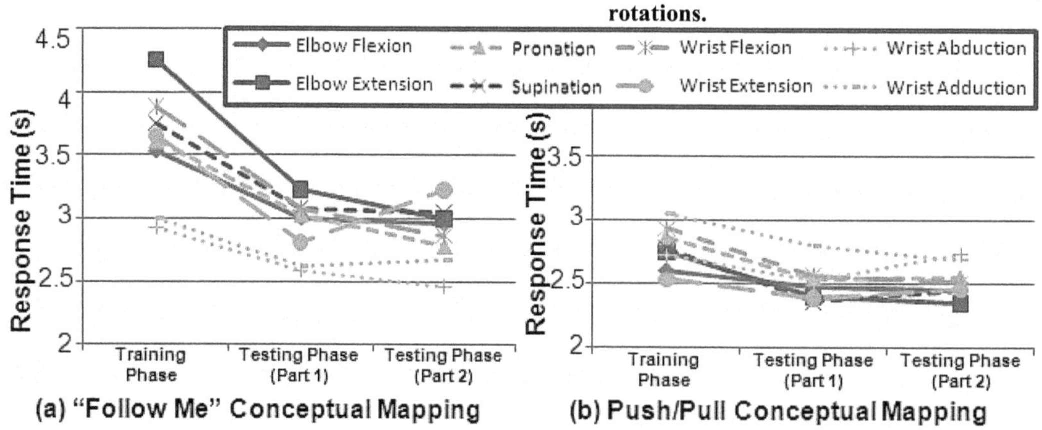

Figure 7. Summary of mean response time for each vibration pattern, averaged across subjects for training and first part of testing, and averaged across subjects and novel postures for second part of testing. Although rotations appear under the push/pull condition, they were always explained using the "follow me" concept.

Table 1. Results of post-experiment questionnaire. Subjects were trained using layman terminology such as 'wrist up' rather than 'wrist extension'. Rotations use the "follow me" concept, even though they also appear in push/pull condition.

Questions	Follow Me		Push/Pull	
	Mean	SD	Mean	SD
1) How easy was it to put on the suit?	3.6	0.42	4	0.67
2) How easy was it to take off the suit?	3.6	0.96	3.7	0.95
3) How easy was it to perform the movements with the suit on?	4.7	0.67	4.9	0.32
4) How comfortable was the suit?	4	0.82	3.9	0.88
5) How lightweight was the suit?	4.9	0.32	5	0
6) How silent were the suit's vibration	4.1	0.57	4.1	0.57
7a) How easy was it to learn the vibration pattern for 'wrist left' (Wrist Adduction)?	4.9	0.32	4	1.25
7b) ... for 'wrist right' (Wrist Abduction)?	4.9	0.32	4	1.05
7c) ... for 'wrist up' (Wrist Extension)?	4.3	0.67	4.9	0.32
7d) ... for 'wrist down' (Wrist Flexion)?	4.4	0.70	4.7	0.48
7e) ... for 'rotate right' (Supination)?	4.6	0.69	4.4	1.07
7f) ... for 'rotate left' (Pronation)?	4.6	0.69	4.4	1.07
7g) ... for 'elbow flex' (Elbow Flexion)?	4.1	0.88	4.9	0.32
7h) ... for 'elbow extend' (Elbow Extension)?	4	0.82	4.9	0.32
8a) How easy was it to recognize & respond to vibration for 'wrist left' (Wrist Adduction)?	5	0	3.8	1.03
8b) ... for 'wrist right' (Wrist Abduction)?	5	0	4	0.82
8c) ... for 'wrist up' (Wrist Extension)?	4.4	0.94	4.7	0.67
8d) ... for 'wrist down' (Wrist Flexion)?	4.5	0.96	4.7	0.67
8e) ... for 'rotate right' (Supination)?	4.3	0.63	4.3	1.06
8f) ... for 'rotate left' (Pronation)?	4.2	0.75	4.3	1.06
8g) ... for 'elbow flex' (Elbow Flexion)?	4	0.94	4.8	0.42
8h) ... for 'elbow extend' (Elbow Extension)?	3.9	0.99	4.8	0.42

Table 2. Number of votes (out of 10) for each vibration pattern where subjects were asked to vote patterns as 'excellent', 'acceptable' or 'unacceptable' in terms of naturalness. Summations of votes are shown using the convention: "follow me" \| push/pull. Rotations use the "follow me" concept, even though they also appear in push/pull condition.

Vibration Patterns	Excellent	Acceptable	Unacceptable
'Wrist Left' (Wrist Adduction)	9|0	1|6	0|4
'Wrist Right' (Wrist Abduction)	9|0	1|8	0|2
'Wrist Up' (Wrist Extension)	2|5	7|5	1|0
'Wrist Down' (Wrist Flexion)	2|4	7|6	1|0
'Rotate Right' (Supination)	6|7	4|2	0|1
'Rotate Left' (Pronation)	6|7	4|2	0|1
'Elbow Flex' (Elbow Flexion)	1|9	8|1	1|0
'Elbow Extend' (Elbow Extension)	1|8	8|1	1|1

- *Posture-Free Vibrations:* With the exception of wrist abduction/adduction for the push/pull condition, based on the impressive recognition accuracies when novel postures were introduced, along with consistent response times, we see that the proposed conceptual mappings and configurations generalize well to new postures that are different from the training posture. This is important as we cannot expect users to re-learn vibration patterns for every new posture they might encounter, which would be unrealistic for many applications. However, we cannot ignore that the vibration pattern for wrist abduction/adduction did not perform well for every posture. We hypothesize that the ideal solution will involve both conceptual mappings, utilizing the most natural patterns.

- *Subjective Feedback:* For the "follow me" condition, vibration patterns for wrist abduction/adduction were rated higher in terms of learnability and distinctness (see Table 1) as well as naturalness (see Table 2) where all but one subject rated the patterns as 'excellent' in terms of naturalness; whereas wrist abduction/adduction for the push/pull condition received no 'excellent' ratings—mostly 'acceptable' or 'unacceptable'. As previously mentioned, subjects felt the latter vibration patterns to be too similar and close to those of wrist flexion/extension. It seems obvious, then, that wrist abductions and adductions should be cued using the "follow me" conceptual mapping with the respective configuration. This will allow for sufficient spacing between wrist flexion and extension vibrations. Wrist flexion/extension under the push/pull condition received higher ratings for learnability and distinctness (Table 1) as well as naturalness (Table 2) compared to the "follow me" condition. Most ratings for the naturalness of wrist flexion/extension, for the "follow me" condition, fell under 'acceptable'; many subjects felt the vibration patterns were more appropriate for rotations, although these patterns were rarely misclassified as such—see Figure 6. The ideal configuration would have motors in a straight line such that the directionality is tangential to the arc of the motion; however, due to the curvature of the skin around the arm, especially around the wrist joint, there is a tradeoff between motor spacing and the curvature of the directionality. Enough spacing is required to provide the illusion of apparent motion, but with larger spacing, motors will cover a greater circumference around the arm. This is an inherent problem when using the "follow me" conceptual mapping to design configurations for flexion and extension, at least where there is limited flatness. Therefore, the conceptual mapping of push/pull seems to be a better option for movements of flexions and extensions. For elbow flexion/extension, there is a clear preference for the push/pull version—see Table 1 and 2. As shown in Table 2, most ratings were 'excellent' whereas most ratings for the "follow me" condition were 'acceptable'. As mentioned, for the "follow me" conceptual mapping, these patterns share the same problem as those for wrist flexion/extension. Indeed, we see that most misclassifications were with rotations—see Figure 6. Lastly, most subjects felt vibration patterns for rotations to be intuitive, easy to learn, and easy to recognize. It is therefore clear that a combination of patterns from the two conceptual mappings explored here is needed rather than using one concept to explain all kinematic-vibrotactile mappings. The most effective patterns from each conceptual mapping should be used: "follow me" wrist abduction/adduction, push/pull wrist flexion/extension, push/pull elbow flexion/extension, and "follow me" rotations.

6. Conclusion and Future Work

This work has proposed a novel kinematic-vibrotactile mapping for instruction-based motor learning, general enough to be used for a variety of applications involving the teaching of motor skills. Two conceptual mappings were explored, and findings indicate that vibration patterns from both mappings should be utilized to ensure learnability and usability. We hypothesize that the nature of the movement (joint/limb articulated, and its type of movement) largely influences how natural a conceptual mapping will be. For example, a vibration running up our arm across our elbow joint seems to be more indicative of flexion compared to a vibration running along the side of our arm near the elbow joint. Indeed, we saw that participants found the former to be more natural (Table 2) and recognized it faster (Figure 7). No experimental comparison with existing approaches has been performed given the difficultly of a direct comparison: our instruction-based approach is unique in that we target low-level, fundamental movements. However, as part of future work, we will perform a study to compare the performance of the proposed approach, for teaching beginners complex movements, with different instruction sets of higher levels of abstraction; the latter of which are commonly used among existing approaches for vibrotactile-based motor instruction. We hypothesize that our approach will be more effective by enabling beginners to gain a foundational understanding of the intricate articulations of complex movements. We are currently extending this approach to accommodate feedback-based motor learning; 6DOF Inertial Measurement Units (IMUs) will be used to measure joint angles and rates of change, and these inputs will drive the spatio-temporal characteristics of vibration patterns proposed here. More specifically, tactile rhythm will convey how to adjust movement speed, and vibrotactile spatial variations will convey how to adjust limb position. By integrating feedback into our instruction set, we will bridge the divide between instruction-based and feedback-based approaches, improving the scalability of the proposed approach by accommodating a greater range of skill level, from beginner to expert. Although simple, low-level movements, i.e., fundamental movements, were assessed here, this was a necessary step to discover distinct and natural vibration patterns that can be used to intuitively build and instruct more complex movements. We plan to conduct several application-oriented user studies to evaluate the aforementioned instruction/feedback based approach for learning complex movements. Specifically, we are targeting motor learning and/or rehabilitation for individuals with sensory, perceptual or physical disabilities. Lastly, we plan to explore how well these conceptual mappings and configurations generalize across the body.

7. Acknowledgements

This research was supported by a GPSA Research Grant awarded by ASU Graduate and Professional Students Association, the Graduate College, and Office of the Vice Provost for Research.

8. REFERENCES

[1] C. A. Kennedy and M. M. Yoke. 2009. *Methods of group exercise instruction*. Human Kinetics, Champaign, IL.

[2] J. Lieberman and C. Breazeal. 2007. Development of a wearable vibrotactile feedback suit for accelerated human motor learning. *Proc ICRA*, 4001-6.

[3] L. A. Kane. 2004. *Martial Arts Instruction*. YMAA Publication Center, Boston, MA.

[4] D. Spelmezan, M. Jacobs, A. Hilgers and J. Borchers. 2009. Tactile motion instructions for physical activities. *Proc CHI*, 2243-52.

[5] K. Förster, M. Bächlin and G. Tröster. 2009. Non-interrupting user interfaces for electronic body-worn swim devices. *Proc PETRA*, 38: 1-4.

[6] J. van der Linden, R. Johnson, J. Bird, Y. Rogers and E. Schoonderwaldt. 2011. Buzzing to play: lessons learned from an in the wild study of real-time vibrotactile feedback. *Proc. CHI*, 533-42.

[7] U. Yang and G. J. Kim. 2002. Implementation and evaluation of 'Just Follow Me': an immersive, VR-based motion-training system. *Presence: Teleoperators and Virtual Environments*, 11, 3 (June 2002), 304-23.

[8] P. T. Chua, R. Crivella, B. Daly, N. Hu, R. Schaaf, D. Ventura, T. Camill, J. Hodgins and R. Pausch. 2003. Training for physical tasks in virtual environments: tai chi. *Proc VR*, 87-94.

[9] M. Takahata, K. Shiraki, Y. Sakane and Y. Takebayashi. 2004. Sound feedback for powerful karate training. *Proc NIME*, 13–18.

[10] D. Drobny, M. Weiss and J. Borchers. 2009. Saltate!: a sensor-based system to support dance beginners. *Proc CHI*, 3943–48.

[11] A. O. Effenberg. 2005. Movement sonification: effects on perception and action. IEEE Multimedia, 12, 2 (April-June 2005), 53-59.

[12] K. Kosuge, T. Hayashi, Y. Hirata and R. Tobiyama. 2003. Dance partner robot - Ms DanceR. *Proc IROS*, 4, 3459-64.

[13] G. Grindlay. 2008. Haptic guidance benefits musical motor learning. *Proc Haptics Symposium*, 397-404.

[14] D. Feygin, M. Keehner and R. Tendick. 2002. Haptic guidance: experimental evaluation of a haptic training method for a perceptual motor skill," *Proc Haptics Symposium*, 40-47.

[15] P. Kapur, M. Jensen, L. J. Buxbaum, S. A. Jax and K. J. Kuchenbecker. 2010. Spatially distributed tactile feedback for kinesthetic motion guidance. *Proc Haptics Symposium*, 519-26.

[16] R. S. Behnke. 2006. *Kinetic anatomy*. Human Kinetics, Champaign, IL.

[17] R. W. Lindeman, Y. Yanagida, K. Hosaka, S. Abe. 2006. The TactaPack: a wireless sensor/actuator package for physical therapy applications. *Proc Haptics Symposium*, 337-41.

[18] K. Huang, T. Starner, E. Do, G. Weinberg, D. Kohlsdorf, C. Ahlrichs and R. Leibrandt. 2010. Mobile Music Touch: mobile tactile stimulation for passive learning. *Proc CHI*, 791-800.

[19] T. McDaniel, D. Villanueva, S. Krishna and S. Panchanathan. 2010. MOVeMENT: a framework for systematically mapping vibrotactile stimulations to fundamental body movements. *Proc HAVE*, 1-6.

[20] F. A. Geldard and C. E. Sherrick. 1972. The cutaneous 'rabbit': a perceptual illusion. *Science*, 178, 4057 (October 1972), 178 -79.

Affect-based Adaptive Presentation of Home Videos

Xiaohong Xiang
School Of Computing
National University Of Singapore
Singapore,117417
xiangxiaohong@comp.nus.edu.sg

Mohan S Kankanhalli
School Of Computing
National University Of Singapore
Singapore,117417
mohan@comp.nus.edu.sg

ABSTRACT

In recent times, the proliferation of multimedia devices and reduced costs of data storage have enabled people to easily record and collect a large number of home videos; furthermore, this collection is growing with time. With the popularity of participatory media such as YouTube and facebook, problems are encountered when people intend to share their home videos with others. The first problem is that different people might be interested in different video content. Given the numbers of home videos, it is a time-consuming and hard task to manually select proper content for people with different interests. Secondly, as short videos are becoming more and more popular in media sharing applications, people need to manually cut and edit home videos which is again a tedious task. In this paper, we propose a method that employs affective analysis to automatically create video presentations from home videos. Our novel method adaptively creates presentations based on three properties: emotional tone, local main character and global main character. A novel sparsity-based affective labeling method is proposed to identify the emotional content of the videos. The local and global main characters are determined by applying face recognition in each shot. To demonstrate the proposed method, three kinds of presentations are created for family, acquaintance and outsider. Experimental results show that our method is very effective in video sharing and the users are satisfied with the videos generated by our method.

Categories and Subject Descriptors

H.5.1 [**Information Interfaces And Presentation**]: Multimedia Information Systems

General Terms

Algorithms, Theory

Keywords

affect, adaptive presentation, home video

*Area Chair: Susanne Boll

1. INTRODUCTION

The advancement of technology has brought forth into daily life, a plethora of consumer devices such as digital cameras, digital video recorders and computers. Holidays, weddings, children's birthdays - those moments in life that we would like to hold on forever can now be preserved in the form of videos and images with the aid of such devices. On the other hand, sharing these rich media with family, friends and even outsiders via Internet has become a significant means of communication between people [1] due to the popularity of social community websites like Facebook and YouTube.

However, several issues are encountered when people want to share their home videos. First, significant redundancy within these video and image collections makes it boring and time-consuming to browse through. Second, we observe distinct individual preferences for such video and image content. This in turn makes it necessary to select and display different content to suit the diversity of preferences. Taking a birthday party video as an example, family members would probably be interested in media containing the host, rather than other unfamiliar guests. However, outsiders perhaps only care whether this media can interest them or not, if it is shared via Internet. Furthermore, it is impossible to keep all the media in online albums because of the restrictions on upload size and the limited capacity. As a result, it is probably a tedious job to choose and keep the desired videos or images. In the light of such prevailing problems, there is urgent need for an effective media synthesis method for creation of videos and images that are brief, rich and appropriate for individual preferences.

YouTube is one of the most well-known participatory platform providing a new generation of video sharing service in the contemporary online environment. Videos shared on it usually are relatively short [5], which means short video is more popular than longer video. Therefore, people might need to cut long videos into shorter and easily digestible versions. Nowadays, there have been a variety of video editing software available, like Boilsoft video cutter and VisiCrop. However, as far as we know, all of them require the user to manually choose the needed part by providing beginning and ending times for video segments. This is tedious and very time-consuming. Therefore, automatically analyzing the video and selecting the part needed for the user is preferred. We find that the automatic selection of desired segments of the videos is a preferable strategy.

Among the traditional multimedia analysis techniques, visual attention analysis [4] and semantic video analysis [23] are two well-known approaches. "Everyone knows what attention is. It is the taking possession of the mind, in clear and vivid form, of one out of what seem several simultaneously possible objects or trains of thought. Focalization, concentration of consciousness are of its essence. ...." [16]. Visual attention analysis is a multidisciplinary endeavor involving multiple fields such as cognitive psychology, computer vision and multimedia, etc. Semantic video analysis is to provide the semantic abstraction built on the original video data that is closer or even equal to the high-level understanding of human perceptual system. Both approaches aim to help understand the video content better. Recently, a new and important multimedia analysis technique, termed as affective video analysis [14], has been introduced to improve the understanding between media and human beings' feeling. Comparing with the former traditional techniques, affective video content analysis takes advantage of both psychological knowledge and computational methods to enable computers to recognize the emotion and affective states contained in the video. Consequently, applications based on this method are more consistent with human abstract thinking and cognitive process, which results in being more friendly, usable and natural. Combination of the affective video analysis and media synthesis not only realizes the automatic affect-based video analysis, classification and labeling, but also holds on all the attractive, strong-emotional and interesting moments. Affective video analysis has significant advantage in choosing and generating satisfactory, interesting and natural media. Exploiting the affective cues contained in home videos and presenting them adaptively are the interesting features of this paper.

In this paper, we propose a method to adaptively present home videos using affective video analysis. We achieve this with the following steps: First, we extract the affective states within home video content by affective video analysis. In order to get the corresponding affective label for each video clip, the shot-based audio and visual features are extracted separately, and input to the affective analysis model. Thereafter, the affective analysis model generates a corresponding affective label for the analyzed video shot. Simultaneously, the face recognition model also identifies the person contained in each shot according to the face database provided in advance, and labels the video as well. Consequently, two kinds of labels (affective label and face label) are present along with each video for the post processing. Second, three properties of video: emotional tone, local main character and global main character are found in each video and collection of videos by means of a modified tf.idf weight. Finally, we use these properties to connect different video clips and create presentations. Three example categories adopted from social groups identified in Social Science Research considered in this paper are: family, acquaintance and outsider respectively. Based on the experimental results, we show that our method can generate good presentations for each category. In this paper, our key contributions are:

- A novel sparsity-based affective labeling method is proposed to analyze the affective state in videos. Compared to existing approaches of affective analysis, our method is relatively simpler, and more intuitive.

- Three concepts: emotional tone, local main character and global main character are proposed. We demonstrate these to be important reference factors in generating adaptive presentations.

This paper is organized as follows. Section 2 reviews the related work to serve as a preamble, and Section 3 describe the proposed methodology. Section 4 presents the experimental results of the proposed methodology, and finally, conclusions are drawn in Section 5.

2. RELATED WORK

Within this section, we will review and discuss the related work on the adaptive presentation of home video and video content affective analysis.

2.1 Adaptive Presentation

CeWe Color [9] has provided CeWe Photobook software program to create photobooks as customer wishes with a variety of templates of backgrounds, layouts and designs. The concept of adaptive presentation has been innovatively exploited. Based on different objective, individual characteristics, and profiles, the presentation can be created adaptively to satisfy different demands. Since CeWe Photobook has got the support of the majority of customers and has become a popular gift among family and friends, we have reasons to believe that creating elegant, attractive and adaptive media presentations is promising.

Demerdash et al. [10] have proposed a framework for generating adaptive multimedia presentations by dynamic selection of files from a large data repository. They have made use of concepts from the fields of discourse analysis and rhetorical structure. They also exploited the technical(syntactic), semantic and relational textual annotation as well as context-sensitive rules and patterns of selection to create the presentation. Rabbath [22] et al. have realized that the representation of those photos in appealing physical photo books has been highly appreciated by many people, and sharing the photos via social networking sites is becoming a popular communication means in the world . Accordingly, it is reasonable to develop an approach to collect and bundle photos from the same events but uploaded by different persons into one story. They have taken advantage of content analysis of text and images to automatically and semi-automatically detect media elements and select photos of a specific story. Our method is the generalization of the Rabbath's work, using videos instead of photos.

Not too many papers have had efforts on adaptive media presentation, what's more, as far as we know, there is no study on the presentation of home videos. As we discussed earlier, with the increasing size of collection of home movies, adaptive presentation is needed.

2.2 The Emotion Model

Many psychological emotion models have been developed. They can be summarized into two categories: a) continuous emotion space [24, 3]; b) discrete emotion states [11, 15]. As a well-known and classical emotion model for the former, 3-D (Valence, Arousal, Control) emotion space can represent the entire scope of human emotions as a set of points in this coordinate space. Based on the fact Control dimension plays only a limited role in distinguishing various emotion states, the 2-D Valence-Arousal (V-A) emotion space allows a smooth passage from one state to another in an infinite set of values [14, 28]. Although the 3-D emotion model can represent rich affective states as pairs of (V,A), it is very difficult for people to present their emotional experiences using the values of valence and arousal. By comparison, people are used to making use of simpler words like happy, sad to depict their emotion. Consequently, the latter one naturally consists of a set of discrete words, like happy, sadness, fear, and angry, which are thought to be distinct to depict the affective experiences of human beings. Besides, taking advantage of discrete simple words to label, indexing and retrieving the videos are easier and in accord with the thinking of human beings.

In this paper, we choose the second emotion model to represent the affect within videos for the following consideration: first, because we collect affective ground truth from user study, a discrete emotion model can enable participants to express their emotional experience better. Second, it is easier to label videos with a single emotion compared to continuous dimensional emotion model. We identify the affect of each shot of video, and label them with happy, sad, fear, angry or neutral tags. If several adjacent shots are identified as the same affect, we label them with one affective tag.

2.3 Affective Video Analysis

As a newly developed multimedia analysis technique, affective video content analysis is still facing some challenges. One important issue encountered by the researchers is to fill the gap between the low level features and affective concepts. Kang [17] has performed an empirical study on the relationship between emotional events and low-level features of video data (color, motion and shot cut rate) and constructed Hidden Markov Models to detect emotional events: fear, sad, joy and normal. In addition, Xu and Hanjalic [14] have proposed a computational framework to map the low-level features extracted from video data on the 2-D emotion space which is characterized by the dimensions of arousal and valence. Arousal time curve and valence time curve along the video were constructed by the corresponding model of arousal and valence respectively to represent V-A content within video. Furthermore, they combined the obtained time curves into the so-called affect curve that can serve to determine the prevailing mood per segment of a video. Based on Xu's work, an improved 2D V-A emotion space has been proposed to represent and recognize the video's affective content [28]. The V-A emotion space has been divided into a set of typical fuzzy emotion subspaces through which discrete affective state can be represented in this continuous V-A space. Sun and Yu [27] have selected the video affective content units from the excitement intensity curves, and constructed Video Affective Tree (VAT). Based on the VAT, middle-level audio and visual affective features have been extracted. And then, HMMs-based video affective content recognizer has been utilized to classify the basic affective state of audience in terms of those features. A Bayesian framework has been proposed to detect the emotional states based on the shots arousal and content-based features [26].

As discussed above, all of these methods used to do affective analysis can be summarized into four categories: Gaussian Mixture Model [28], Hidden Markov Models [17, 27], Bayesian Model [26] and Support Vector Regression Model (SVR) [30]. They all differ from our proposed approach: sparsity-based affective analysis, which is one of our main contributions.

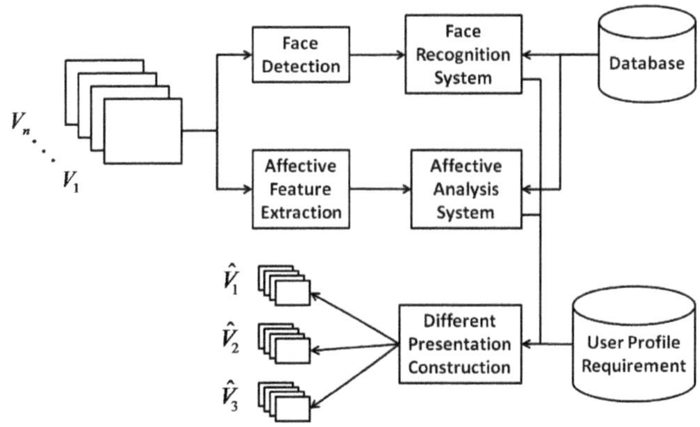

Figure 1: The overall framework of our proposed method

3. METHODOLOGY

In this section, we will discuss the details of the proposed method. Figure 1 shows the overall framework of our method. Shot is the basic unit of affective analysis and face recognition. So, a Singular Value Decomposition (SVD)−based approach [7] is first implemented to segment the video. After that, shot-based audio and visual feature vectors are extracted respectively as input to the affective analysis model. Simultaneously, faces are also detected as input to the face recognition model [29]. Then, affective and face labels are assigned to each shot, and treated as the terms in "document": shot and video. A modified t-f.idf weighed scheme is used to find the three "properties" of video: emotional tone, local main characters and global main characters. Based on them, adaptive presentations can be created for different target viewers. As our main contributions, the technique of affective analysis and the algorithms for the construction of presentation will be detailed in the following.

3.1 Affective Features Extraction

The relationship between emotional events and low level features has been studied by many researchers [2, 17]. For example, in the 'sad' event, the colors are usually "dark", and "low saturated", but "happy" event is along with 'bright' colors in general. So the color cue is taken into account to represent the emotional events. To compute the color feature, each frame of RGB color space is transformed into HSV color space, and then quantize the pixel values into 11 culture colors [13]. For key frames of each shot, we computed the histograms of 11 culture colors, as well as the mean and covariance of color histogram, saturation and value separately. A total of 17 features are extracted for each key frame, and composed into a visual feature vector. Totally, k number of visual feature vectors are extracted for shot with k key frames.

As we know, movies can express rich and strong emotions because of the meticulous editing of film editors. In contrast, natural home video without any editing not only has no strong emotional expression, but also it has much noise. However, audio can contain significant affective information. Thus, the audio features, such as pitch average, silence ratio, short time energy, zero-crossing rate, brightness and rolloff, were computed to construct the audio feature vector. So far, two kinds of feature vectors (k visual feature vectors and 1 audio feature vector) were constructed and normalized.

3.2 Affective Labeling

The approaches reported in the past papers can be classified into several categories: Gaussian Mixture Model, Hidden Markov Models, Bayesian Model and Support Vector Regression Model. Here, we propose a totally different model called *sparse representation of affect* to do the classification and labeling of affective video, which is one of the main contributions in our work.

How does the combination of low-level features contribute to affect has been a big open challenge in the area of affective computing, and most existing approaches have not yielded good results. Since we do not understand the phenomenon well, we thought of trying a radically different approach to tackle it. Therefore, we use many features resulting in a high-dimensional space from which we extract the right sparse representation. Compared to the above mentioned models, sparse representation of affect is an easier and more intuitive method for the affective analysis. Moreover, it is simpler, faster, and without restricted parameters which is useful with voluminous video data.

The problem of sparse representation has seen a recent surge of interest in the statistical signal processing areas [6]. The representation and compression of the signal is the original objective of studying the sparse representation. It has not been used to classify and recognize the affect within video before. Sparse representation essentially involves solving of a linear system of equations. Considering a linear equation $y = Ax$, where A is a real M-by-N matrix and $M < N$, the solution x is infinite. Sparse representation aims to solve it by choosing the optimization problem ℓ^0-norm solution, or ℓ^1-norm solution, or ℓ^2-norm solution.

$$\ell^i : \hat{x}_i = \arg\min_x \|x\|_i, \texttt{ subject to } y = Ax, i = 0, 1, 2 \quad (1)$$

where $\|\cdot\|_0$ denotes the ℓ^0-norm, which counts the number of nonzero entries in a vector. Many efficient methods are available when the solution is known to be sparse.

3.2.1 Sparse Representation

[27] have validated that motion, shot length and sound energy are robust and generic to measure the 'happy' content in a video. Specifically, high sound energy can present the 'happy' emotion or 'anger' emotion to some extent, but the 'sad' emotion is depicted by low sound energy. On the other hand, the difference of silence ratio can distinguish 'happy' and 'sad'. It is reasonable to assume that the feature vectors extracted from videos with different affect are distinctive. In other words, given two video clips with same affective state, the extracted feature vectors should be very similar. Although the division of affective features to distinguish emotional events is obscure, we can assume that a set of representative feature vectors for each affective event can be found as the basic feature vectors of that affective event subspace, and then each feature vector coming from that affective event can be represented as a linear combination of the corresponding basic feature vectors. We have to point out that the number of basic vectors is hoped to be as large as possible. We denote by $y \in \Re^D$ the feature vector of the test video clip with i-th affect, and $\{y_i^1, \cdots, y_i^k\}$ the k basic feature vectors of i-th affective event. Then the y can be represented by eq. (2).

$$\begin{aligned} y &= y_i^1\alpha_1 + y_i^2\alpha_2 + \cdots + y_i^k\alpha_k \\ &\doteq A_i\vec{\beta}_i, \vec{\beta}_i \in \Re^k \end{aligned} \quad (2)$$

$$\texttt{Where, } A_i = [y_i^1, y_i^2, ..., y_i^k] \quad (3)$$

$$\vec{\beta}_i = [\alpha_1, \alpha_2, ..., \alpha_k]^T \quad (4)$$

Unfortunately, it is difficult to learn if those feature vectors can represent that affect subspace in the affective space. For us, randomly choosing from thousands and hundreds of videos is the only way to get the basic feature vector. Obviously, it is impractical to achieve. Thanks to the property of linear combination, we can choose any feature vectors of the same affective event as the basic vectors [19]. If we assume that a given feature vector extracted from unknown affective video can only be represented by those basic vectors from the same affect-i, that is, only $\vec{\beta}_i$ is not zero vector. We can use the eq. (5) to summarize it.

$$y = A_1\vec{\beta}_1 + A_2\vec{\beta}_2 + \cdots + A_n\vec{\beta}_n = Ax \quad (5)$$

$$\texttt{where, } A = [A_1, \ldots, A_{i-1}, A_i, A_{i+1}, \ldots, A_n] \quad (6)$$

$$\begin{aligned} x &= [\vec{\beta}_1, \ldots, \vec{\beta}_{i-1}, \vec{\beta}_i, \vec{\beta}_{i+1}, \ldots, \vec{\beta}_n]^T \\ &= [\mathbf{0} \ldots \mathbf{0} * \mathbf{0} \ldots \mathbf{0}]^T \in \Re^{nk} \end{aligned} \quad (7)$$

A is called the 'sample matrix', each column is a sample, and the solution $x \in \Re^N, N = n \times k$, should be a sparse vector: $n-1$ of its entries should be zero, except for the ones associated with the correct emotional state. '$*$' represents the nonzero entries $\vec{\beta}_i$. We can obtain solution x by solving the linear equation $y = Ax$.

In our work, instead of fusion of visual feature vector and audio feature vector, we take advantage of the decision fusion theory. Visual sample matrix A_v and audio sample matrix A_a are constructed separately for two channels: visual and audio. Visual feature vector and audio feature vector are both extracted from shot to feed into the corresponding channel.

3.2.2 Sparse Solution

In sparse representation area, the basic idea of compressive sampling is: for certain types of signals, just a small number of nonadaptive samples carries sufficient information to approximate the signal well [6]. Research in this field can be categorized into two classes: sampling and reconstruction. The way to construct a signal approximation given a vector of noisy samples is the major algorithmic challenge in this research field.

In this paper, we exploit the discriminative nature of sparse representation to perform classification of affect content with-in videos. As discussed in the previous section, since the solution x is a sparse vector, we can treat it as a sparse and compressible signal, and then the test feature vector y corresponding to x is regarded as the compressive sample. In this way, the affective analysis problem is converted to the reconstruction of a sparse signal. The sparse representation is brought in the affective analysis for the first time. Our significant contribution is to convert the affective analysis problem into solving a linear equation, which makes the affective analysis easier, simpler, and more intuitive, compared to the traditional methods.

However, there is a serious problem encountered by affective analysis of home videos. The sample y inevitably contains noise, because the home video is generated by an amateur with low level device in any possible environment. In other words, the sample probably is incomplete and inaccurate. We hope the algorithm of construction of compressive signal is very robust to noise. Fortunately, COSAMP [19] has been proposed to be a practical and robust method for solving ℓ^1-minimization problem, that is. eq. (1):

$$\ell^1 : \hat{x}_1 = \arg\min_x \|x\|_1, \ \texttt{subject to} \ y = Ax$$

3.2.3 *Classification Based On Two Components*

Given a new test shot of home video, k visual feature vectors $y_v^1, ..., y_v^k$ are extracted from k key frames, and one audio feature vector y_a is extracted from the shot. We first compute their sparse representations $\hat{x}_v^1, ..., \hat{x}_v^k, \hat{x}_a$ via eq. (1). Ideally, the nonzero entries in $\hat{x}_v^1, ..., \hat{x}_v^k, \hat{x}_a$ will be related to the columns of corresponding sample matrix A_v and A_a, and we can easily do the classification. However, noise and modeling error will result in separating the sparse entries into multiple classes. So considering the global sparse representation, we classify test vectors based on how well the sparse entries associated with the samples of each classes.

In order to recognize the affect in a video shot, we define a new function δ_i that denotes the means to set the coefficients not for the i-th emotional state to zero. Specifically, for $x \in \Re^N$, $\delta_i(x) \in \Re^N$ is a new vector whose nonzero entries correspond to the coefficients belonging to i-th class in x. Given a test vector y and the corresponding approximation x, residual vector $R \in \Re^N$ is computed via eq. (8), where N is the number of classes.

$$R(i) = \|y - A\delta_i(\hat{x}_i)\| \ \texttt{for} \ i = 1, ..., N \tag{8}$$

Thus, given a shot's visual and audio feature vectors $y_v^1, ..., y_v^k, y_a$, corresponding residual vectors $R_v^1, ..., R_v^k, R_a$ are computed and normalized. We first calculate the global residual of the fusion of visual and audio by an average weighted scheme of eq. (9). And then eq. (10) is used to do classification.

$$R(i) = w_1 R_a(i) + w_2 \frac{\sum_{j=1}^{k} R_v^j(i)}{k} \tag{9}$$

$$\texttt{assign}(V_s) = \arg\min_i R(i) \tag{10}$$

Algorithm 1 summarizes the classification procedure.

Algorithm 1 The Algorithm For Classification of Emotion within Home Video

1. **Input:** sample matrix $A_v = [A_{v,1}, ..., A_{v,N}] \in \Re^{mxn}$ and $A_a = [A_{a,1}, ..., A_{a,N}] \in \Re^{pxq}$ for N emotional states.

   A test shot(V_s)'s visual feature vectors $y_v^1, ..., y_v^k \in \Re^m$ for k key frames, and audio feature vector $y_a \in \Re^p$.

2. Normalize the columns of A_v and A_a and feature vectors $y_v^1, ..., y_v^k, y_a$.

3. solve the ℓ^1-minimization problem:

   $\hat{x}_v^j = \arg\min_x \|x\|_1, \ \texttt{subject to} \ y_v^j = A_v x,$

   $\texttt{for} \ j = 1, ..., k$

   $\hat{x}_a = \arg\min_x \|x\|_1, \ \texttt{subject to} \ y_a = A_a x$

4. Compute the residual for each component:

   $R_v^j(i) = \|y_v^j - A_v\delta_i(\hat{x}_v^j)\| \ \texttt{for} \ j = 1, ..., k, i = 1, ..., N$

   $R_a(i) = \|y_a - A_a\delta_i(\hat{x}_a)\| \ \texttt{for} \ i = 1, ..., N$

5. Compute the global residual for shot:

   $R(i) = w_1 R_a(i) + w_2 \frac{\sum_{j=1}^{k} R_v^j(i)}{k}$ for $i = 1, ..., N$

6. **Output:** assign(V_s) = $\arg\min_i R(i)$

3.3 Presentation Construction

Before we create presentations of a collection of videos, we also have to recognize the faces in the videos to create the person labels of shot. In order to create the basic face database, the users in advance need to upload as many photos as possible, of individuals who they usually care, to train our face recognition model. Though it is tedious, fortunately, users just need to do it once. Once the basic face database is established, the PCA-based approach [29] can be applied to identify the human faces within shot and label each shot with the recognized face.

Through the affective model and face recognition model of our method, each shot has been assigned with several person labels and one emotional label. In order to obtain satisfying home video presentations by exploiting the labels of affect state and person, various rules need to be developed on the basis of the human perception of different purposes respectively. Next, we will introduce three significant concepts for constructing our presentation. These three proposed concepts are one of our contributions in this work.

3.3.1 *Properties Of Videos*

It is quite frequently possible that the original video is noisy, of low quality or has long boring segments. However we find some "inherent" properties contained in it. We listed them as follows:

- Emotional Tone
- Global Main Character
- Local Main Character

Specifically, in this paper, the main feeling of audience is considered as the emotional tone of that video, when he/she watches the video. Meanwhile, in one video, the persons the story is mainly related to are regarded as the main characters of this video. The main characters in one video are local, and yet, compared to the local main characters based on one video, main characters found from the whole collection of videos about the same theme are referred as global. Later, we will mainly explain why the three properties are chosen, describe how to define these three concepts in videos, and how to utilize them to select shots and construct the final presentation.

According to Murch [21], emotion is the most important factor when it comes to film editing: whether the cut reflects what the editor believes the audience should be feeling at that moment or not [2]. Therefore, emotional continuity is proposed as the most important goal of scene editing in film editing area to maintain the emotional flow of a movie or show. It is better to keep the overall tone continuity of the film, because that is what the audiences mostly experience. On the other hand, the audience attention span for our own home videos is often quite short, and the shots with strong emotion catch audience's attention mostly, since the interesting parts of a home video are intermixed with longer, less interesting regions. What's more, such video is often of poor quality resulting from abrupt camera movement or too short or too long views, making it uninteresting to watch while waiting for the next interesting segment [12]. Therefore, the final presentation must preserve the emotion of videos as much as possible and greatly attract audience's attention and interest.

People overwhelmingly attend to humans in images and videos with the faces dominating visual attention [8]. In other words, the faces within images/frames catch most attention of audiences. Based on this fact, the person labeling can be taken into account as an important cue for the construction of presentation. On the other hand, since we have made an assumption that the collection of videos is related to the same theme, the main persons existing in those videos are relatively constant. Thus, the idea of local main character and global main character make sense for videos.

The term frequency-inverse document frequency (tf.idf) weight [25] is a statistical measure used to evaluate how important a term is to a document in a collection or corpus. The weight of $tf - idf$ is calculated by eq. (11):

$$(tf - idf)_{i,j} = \frac{n_{i,j}}{\sum_k n_{k,j}} \times \log \frac{|D|}{|d : t_i \in d|} \qquad (11)$$

where $n_{i,j}$ is the number of occurrences of the considered term t_i in document d_j, $|D|$ is the total number of documents in the corpus, and $|d : t_i \in d|$ is the number of documents where the terms t_i appears.

It is a popular method often used in text mining and information retrieval. According to the definition of tf.idf, the importance of a term increases proportional to the number of times the term appears in that document but decreases with an increase in the frequency of the word in the collection. However, it conflicts with our definitions of emotional tone, and main characters. The emotion mostly felt by audience in video is the emotional tone of that video, which means that corresponding emotion term will appear with high frequency in all shots of that video. In this case, shot is regarded as 'document', one video is treated as the 'corpus'. Similarly, local main characters refer to the persons who appear with relatively high frequency in video, and global main characters are the set of person labels which are assigned in whole collection of videos more often. Therefore, the tf.idf weight of emotion term and person label can not really reflect the importance of the term, because it violates the intuition that the final weight should increase proportionally to the frequency of the label in the corresponding "corpus". So, anew tf.idf formulation which can really reflect the relationship between importance of label and its frequency in the corresponding "corpus" is introduced as the eq.(12).

$$w_i = \frac{n_{i,j}}{\sum_k n_{k,j}} \times (\log |D| - \log \frac{|D|}{|d : t_i \in d|}) \qquad (12)$$

A emotional term like "happy" or "neutral" has been assigned to each shot. In this case, we treat the shots as the documents, and video as corpus in modified tf.idf scheme, that is, $|D|$ is the total number of shots of video v_j, and

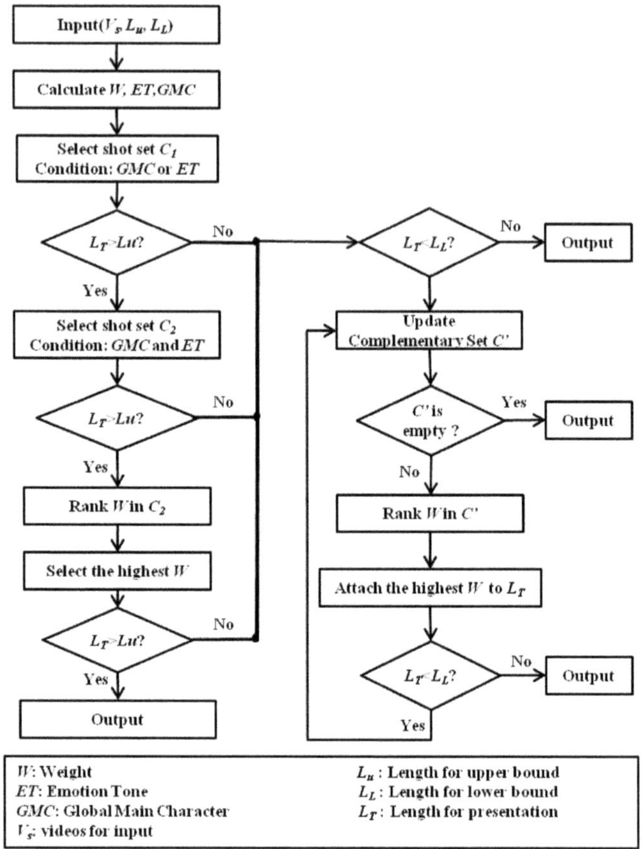

Figure 2: The algorithm details for family's presentation

$|d : t_i \in d|$ is the number of shots emotion state i is assigned to in video v_j. According to the formulation (12), each emotional term in video has a tf.idf weight. We treat emotional term with highest weight as the emotional tone of this video. We denote the tf.idf weight of emotion term i by w_i^e, so the emotional tone ET of the video is:

$$ET = \arg\max_i (w_i^e) \qquad (13)$$

Here, we point out that the emotional tone can tolerate or hide certain errors of affective labeling. Even if there are few errors in affective labeling, as long as the rate of errors is less than a threshold, the found emotional tone is also consistent with that of the video. We make use of the weights and emotional tone to select appropriate shots from each video for the construction of presentation.

Similar to the weight of emotional term, a weight $w_{i,j}^l$ called local character weight is computed for each person label in video v_j. Differing from local character weight computation, global character weight w_i^g is based on the whole collection of videos. Specifically, $|D|$ is sum of shots of whole collection of videos, and $|d : t_i \in d|$ is sum of shots person label i is assigned to in all videos.

In order to find local and global main characters of videos, we introduce two adaptive thresholds ε_l and ε_g as the judgement of local and global main characters respectively. When the local weight is larger than ε_l, the corresponding person label is one of main characters of that video. Similarly, comparing global character weight with global thresholds ε_g, the global main characters can be found. The formulations to find local main character and global main character are:

$$LMC_j = \{i | w_{i,j}^l \geqslant \varepsilon_l\} \quad (14)$$

$$GMC = \{i | w_i^g \geqslant \varepsilon_g\} \quad (15)$$

where LMC_j is the set of local main characters of video v_j, and GMC represents the set of global main character of collection of videos. The thresholds can vary for different videos, which is more reasonable. In our implementation, we choose the threshold as the half of maximum:

$$\varepsilon_l^j = 0.5 * \max_i(w_{i,j}^l) \quad (16)$$

$$\varepsilon_g = 0.5 * \max_{i,j}(w_{i,j}^g) \quad (17)$$

Here, ε_l^j is the threshold of v_j.

Algorithm 2 The Algorithm For Construction of Presentation For Acquaintance

1. **Input:** A set of video's shots $V_s = V_{s1}^1, ..., V_{sn}^1, ..., V_{s1}^N, ..., V_{sk}^N$ with emotional label and person labels; The required upper limit of length L_u and lower limit L_L.
2. Compute the weights of affective label and person labels via a modified tf.idf scheme separately: $w = \frac{n_{i,j}}{\sum_k n_{k,j}} \times (\log |D| - \log \frac{|D|}{|d:t_i \in d|})$
3. Find the emotional tone, local main characters and global main characters by corresponding threshold.
4. Select the shots with local main character labels or emotional tone labels, this shots set denotes by C_1, and update the complementary set C'.
5. If the total length L_τ is larger than L_u, go to (6); Otherwise go to (8).
6. Select the shots C_2 with LMC labels and ET labels out of C_1, update the complementary set C'. If the total length L_τ is larger than L_u, go to (7); Otherwise, go to (8).
7. Rank the weight w in C_2, select shots with high weight until the total length L_τ is shorter than L_u, and larger than L_L, the final set denotes by V_e, go to (10).
8. If the total length L_τ is shorter than L_L, go to (9); Otherwise, let $V_e = C_2$, go to (10).
9. Rank the weight w in complementary set C', select shots with high weight until the total length L_τ is shorter than L_u, and larger than L_L, the final set denotes by V_e, then go to (10).
10. **Output** A presentation constructed by shots in V_e in order of the shot's date.

3.3.2 Algorithms For Presentation

We now have already found the emotional tone, and local and global main characters of total collection of videos. Each video has three kinds of weight: emotional tone weight w_i^e, local main character weight w_i^l and global main character weight w_i^g. For different purposes of presentation, we focus on different weights to construct our characteristic presentations. Final presentation must satisfy that the order of the selected shots should be consistent with the original videos, and any other styles of film are not taken into account.

In the social sciences [18], a society can be viewed as a large group consisting of many smaller social groups. The members of a true social group should share some characteristics which is called "social interaction" in social sciences, such as representations, interests, values, ethnic or social background, and even kinship ties. There are two main types of social groups classified [18]. One is primary groups which are small groups with intimate, kinship-based relationships. The other one is secondary groups which are large groups including formal and institutional relationships. In contrast to the primary groups, they may last for years. Besides, the individuals which do not belong to the previous mentioned groups can be treated as the third group. In terms of this knowledge and 'social interaction', we identify 'family' as primary group, since it is more global and has a confident and firm tie, which make this group stable in any case. 'Acquaintance' is considered secondary group in humans' communication network, as it can be changed with events, environments, social identity, and even social status of individual. However, from the view of humans' communication network, it is relatively stable in one particular case. In addition, the individuals outside the previous two groups can be classified into one group named 'outsider' in this case. Therefore, we derive the three types of social groups for our presentation purposes.

- Presentation for family

  We focus on the global main characters (GMC) and emotional tone (ET) to generate a particular presentation for family members. Generally speaking, the main persons appearing in the videos relevant to the same theme are relatively constant, and the role of these videos relatively appears at most times. The persons who go through the whole videos perhaps are the main character of these videos, in other words, the main character of this theme perhaps is the owner of these videos. As the family members of the owner, they care more about the activities of their families rather than the others. According to the definition of global main character, global main characters play the lead in this video collection, that is, GMC represents the role of this theme. Therefore, the presentation focusing on the GMC is meaningful, on the other hand, we should keep the emotional tone of this collection in the terms of emotional continuity. The emotional tone is the primary emotion of that video the viewer should feel. Thus, the final presentation should preserve this property at least.

- Presentation for acquaintance

  We focus on the local main characters (LMC) and emotional tone (ET) to generate a presentation specially for acquaintance. Compared to the global main character, the local main characters only stand for a short focus or interest, that is, LMC represents the role of that specific video, which perhaps is just a scene in this theme. Relatively speaking, local main characters could be those persons who are related to the role of theme. In other words, in the home videos, the local main characters perhaps are the friends or acquaintance of owner based on the fact that the local main characters are recognized depending on the user's basic face database. Therefore, compared to the family members, acquaintances concern with the local main characters who perhaps are themselves more than global main characters. Meanwhile, the final presentation also should preserve the emotional tone as well because the emotional tone is the primary emotion of that video.

- Presentation for outsider

  Compared to family members and acquaintance, outsiders don't care what is the content of presentation but care about if this presentation can interest them. As we know, face and emotion within video both are the important aspects which can help video attract the viewers' attention. In our work, emotion of each shot has already been found by the affective labeling. Also, the face cue can be represented by the local and global main characters. A weighted scheme is used to combine the main character information and emotion information. Then the importance of shot increases proportionally to the value of weight w_t computed via eq. (18). Selecting shots with high weight w_t can not only preserve the emotional tone, but also keep the main characters of videos.

$$w_t = w_1 * w_i^e + w_2 \sum (w_j^l + w_j^g) \qquad (18)$$

Specifically, given the collection of videos V_s, the required upper and lower bound of length of presentation: L_u and L_L, the detailed algorithms for presentation will be shown. For family presentation focusing on the global main character and emotional tone, the process of constructing a family's presentation is shown in Figure 2. For presentation shown to acquaintance, it considers the factors of the local main characters and emotional tone. Therefore, the detailed algorithm is shown in algorithm 2. We select the shots with higher weight w_t computed by (18) to construct the needed presentation for outsiders. The presentation for outsiders is created by algorithm 3.

4. EXPERIMENTAL RESULTS

4.1 Affective Classification Results

We have observed that it is difficult to collect the home videos with emotion: 'fear' and 'angry'. So, in this paper, we just consider two kinds of emotions: happy and sad. We collect affective ground truth from user study. Six people (3 males and 3 females) are invited to accomplish this task. They are required to describe their affective states with "Happy", "Neutral", and "Sad" labels. To construct the visual and audio sample matrices respectively, 160 high quality natural images and 40 different audio are provided to those participants. All of these images and audio are downloaded from Google Image and YouTube. We assign an emotion label to audio or image, only if six participants all choose that label. Visual feature vector of high quality images selected from user study are used as the training sample in visual sample matrix. Similarly, the audio feature vector of audio

Algorithm 3 The Algorithm For Construction of Presentation For Outsider

1. **Input:** A set of video's shots $V_s = V_{s1}^1, ..., V_{sn}^1, ..., V_{s1}^N, ..., V_{sk}^N$ with emotional label weight w^e and person labels' local and global main character weight w^e and w^g, and the required upper limit of length L_u and lower limit L_L.
2. Compute the total weight (score) of shot: $w_t(s) = w_1 * (w^e(s) + w_2 \sum_j (w_j^l(s) + w_j^g(s))$ for labels of shot s in set V_s.
3. Rank all total weights w_t, consequently, shots in set V_s come into being a set $\hat{V}_s$ keeping the same order of ranked weights.
4. Select the first k shots in set $\hat{V}_s$ to satisfy that the total length L_τ of first k shots is larger than L_L, and shorter than L_u. Then let V_e is the set of selected shots.
5. **Output:** A presentation constructed by shots in V_e in order of the shot's date.

selected from user study are used as the training sample in audio sample matrix.

We constructed three different sample matrices. All sample matrices A_1, A_2 and A_3 randomly select their training samples from the ground truth as their columns. The columns of A_1, A_2 and A_3 can overlap but are not the same. We made a test data set from Google Image and YouTube. Then, shot segmentation is applied to segment those videos. The ground truth of shot was manually determined by three people. In order to evaluate our sparsity-based affective analysis method, two widely used metrics: precision and recall [20] are used.

We first designed an experiment: affective classification just considers the component of visual features of key frames and ignores the audio channel. Table 1 shows the results of this experiment.

		Precision	Recall
Sample Matrix A_1	Happy	62.5%	41.7%
	Sad	58.8%	76.9%
Sample Matrix A_2	Happy	71.9%	69.7%
	Sad	75.0%	76.9%
Sample Matrix A_3	Happy	76.7%	82.1%
	Sad	85.7%	81.1%

Table 1: The result of classifying affective states depending on visual features of key frames

From the table, we can see that on the whole, the classification based on the sample matrix A_3 has better performance than that based on A_1 and A_2. In addition, from the result, when A_3 is used as the sample matrix, most of the emotion contents: happy and sad are recognized exactly by the visual features.

Another experiment is designed to analyze the 'happy' and 'neutral' events depending on two channels: audio and visual. At the same time, we also list the results relying only on visual features. Table 2 shows the corresponding results of classification of 'happy' and 'neutral' based on fusion of audio and visual components, and just based on the visual component.

	Fusion of Two Components		Depending On Visual Feature	
	Happy	Neutral	Happy	Neutral
Precision	70.9%	64.1%	80.3%	52.0%
Recall	70.0%	66.1%	72.2%	65.7%

Table 2: The result of classifying affective states: 'Happy' and 'Neutral' depending on visual features and fusion of two component respectively

From the Table 2, we can see that, with the fusion of audio and visual component, the performance of classification of 'happy' decrease, but performance of 'neutral' is slightly up. This may be because in the home video, the noise in audio component is more than in the visual component because of the environment, which more influences the audio features of 'happy' shot compared to 'neutral' shot.

Emotion is a subjective feeling which relies on audiences perceptions. Talking about the emotion inevitably leads to a discussion about subjectivity. In addition, finding a good sample matrix is a very tough problem. Due to the limitation, home videos with emotion 'fear' and 'angry' are very less, only 'happy' and 'sad' have been tested. Therefore, it is difficult to compare our experimental results with the others' results in home video area. Further, we have obtained one significant insight that the sparse representation does appear to capture the relationship between low-level features and affect. We will do more experiments to substantiate this point in our next work.

4.2 Experimental Results For Presentation

It is very difficult to evaluate the quality of a video presentation as results are hard to quantify computationally and the related factors to consider are highly complex. Since there is no absolute measurement of presentation quality available, we evaluate the quality of our presentation with a user study. For the experiment, we invited 10 people as our test subjects. A total of 9 video presentations of three different theme videos were generated by our method, and used as the test videos. The information about three original videos and the generated presentations is summarized in Table 3.

Video	A	B	C
Theme	Holiday Trip	Birthday Party	Wedding Party
L_o	3m 47s	3m 34s	6m 10s
L_u	1m 10s	1m 10s	2m
L_L	40s	50s	1m 30s
L_f	42s	1m 6s	1m 37s
L_a	52s	1m 4s	1m 46s
L_s	1m 8s	1m 3s	1m 39s

Table 3: Details of original videos and the corresponding three presentations. Notes: Video A, B and C are the collections of several short videos; L_o refers to the total length of original video collection; L_u and L_L provided by user is the upper bound and lower bound of length of final presentation respectively; L_f, L_a and L_s are the length of created presentation for family, acquaintance and outsider respectively

Figure 3: Example of original videos. Note: The region in the yellow circle represents the detected face.

Before viewing the video presentations, the subjects were given the aim of these presentations and the relevant information: Video A is related to one specific holiday trip; Video B is related to a birthday party; Video C is related to a wedding party; We give an example of the original videos in Figure 3. L_o is the total length of original video collection; L_u and L_L provided by user is the upper bound and lower bound of length of final presentation respectively; L_f, L_a and L_s are the length of created presentation for family, acquaintance and outsider respectively. All relevant videos can be found in the URL: `http://mmas.comp.nus.edu.sg/NUSAAP/nusaap.html`. After viewing each presentation, each subject was asked to compare them with the original one, and rate the presentation on a scale of 1 to 5, with 1 represents worst, 5 represents excellent. Table 4 shows the results of the evaluation.

Presentation	A	B	C	Average
Family	3.8	3.5	4.5	3.9
Acquaintance	3.8	3.5	4.0	3.7
outsider	3.6	3.7	3.7	3.7

Table 4: Results of user study

From the table 4, we can see that on the whole, the presentations performed quite well with scores of over 3.5 in all. Looking at the scores of each individual summary, presentation for family members got the highest score in all videos except B. This can be explained: video B is a video of a birthday party in a small room. This result in that the GMC and LMC are almost the same. According to the rule for presentation construction, the presentation for family is very similar to the one for acquaintance. In addition, this video is created by a relatively low level camera, and in a narrow space with bad illuminance. All of these can affect the impression of this presentation, thus influencing the score of family presentation of video B.

Presentation for acquaintance scored high in video C but got the lowest score in video B among the three videos. As we discussed in previous paragraph, this is expected since the content of presentations for acquaintance and family are not apparently distinctive, and the quality of video B is low. The effect of this presentation decreases. Thus score is relatively low.

The scores of presentation for outsider are almost the same for all videos. Since an outsider presentation just cares if the content can mostly catch the viewer's attention, this presentation reflects the interesting parts in that collection. Therefore, subjects can easily judge this presentation.

5. CONCLUSIONS

In this paper, we propose a novel video affective analysis method and three properties of video for construction of home video representation. Sparse presentation of affective analysis is used to classify the affective state in home video for the first time. It appears to be a promising elegant and intuitive method. By decision fusion of visual component and audio component, the affective events 'happy' and 'sad' are detected with high accuracy based on a good sample matrix. Additionally, based on the proposed three properties of videos, home video presentations for family, acquaintance and outsider are automatically created. The test results are good and satisfactory.

In the future, we will aim to find a better sample matrix which may provide higher classification performance. We will extract more high level affective features to improve our model and classify more emotions. Furthermore, we will employ our sparsity-based affective analysis to detect the affective event in movies, which contains more affective events. We will also introduce aesthetics into our home video presentations, in order to create better presentations.

Acknowledgments

This research was done for CSIDM Project No. CSIDM-200801 partially funded by a grant from the National Research Foundation (NRF) administered by the Media Development Authority (MDA) of Singapore.

6. REFERENCES

[1] E. Babbie. *he practice of social research.* Wadsworth Pub Co, 2007.

[2] D. Bordwell, K. Thompson, and J. Ashton. *ilm art: An introduction.* McGraw-Hill, 1990.

[3] M. Bradley. Emotional memory: A dimensional analysis. *motions: ssays on emotion theory*, pages 97–134, 1994.

[4] C. Bundesen. A theory of visual attention. *sychological review*, 97(4):523, 1990.

[5] J. Burgess and J. Green. *You ube: nline video and participatory culture.* Polity Press, 2009.

[6] E. Candès. Compressive sampling. In *roceedings of the International Congress of Mathematicians*, volume 3, pages 1433–1452, 2006.

[7] Z. Cernekova, C. Kotropoulos, and I. Pitas. Video shot segmentation using singular value decomposition. In *roceedings of I International Conference on Multimedia and xpo*, volume 2, pages 301–304, 2003.

[8] L. Chen, X. Xie, X. Fan, W. Ma, H. Zhang, and H. Zhou. A visual attention model for adapting images on small displays. *Multimedia systems*, 9(4):353–364, 2003.

[9] C. Color. *Ce e hotoboo* . Photoworld, 2007.

[10] O. Demerdash, S. Bergler, L. Kosseim, and P. Langshaw. Generating Adaptive Multimedia Presentations Based on a Semiotic Framework. *Advances in Artificial Intelligence*, pages 417–421, 2005.

[11] P. Ekman. An argument for basic emotions. *Cognition & motion*, 6(3):169–200, 1992.

[12] A. Girgensohn, J. Boreczky, P. Chiu, J. Doherty, J. Foote, G. Golovchinsky, S. Uchihashi, and L. Wilcox. A semi-automatic approach to home video editing. In *roceedings of ACM symposium on User interface software and technology*, pages 81–89, 2000.

[13] E. Goldstein. *Sensation and perception.* Brooks/Cole Publishing, 1999.

[14] A. Hanjalic and L. Xu. Affective video content representation and modeling. *I ransactions on Multimedia*, 7(1):143–154, 2005.

[15] K. Hevner. Experimental studies of the elements of expression in music. *he American ournal of sychology*, 48(2):246–268, 1936.

[16] W. James. *he principles of psycholog(Vol. 2).* New York: Holt, 1890.

[17] H. Kang. Affective content detection using HMMs. In *roceedings of ACM international conference on Multimedia*, pages 259–262, 2003.

[18] A. Kuper and J. Kuper. *he social science encyclopedia.* Routledge/Thoemms Press, 1985.

[19] D. Needell and J. Tropp. CoSaMP: Iterative signal recovery from incomplete and inaccurate samples. *Applied and Computational Harmonic Analysis*, 26(3):301–321, 2009.

[20] D. Olson and D. Delen. *Advanced data mining techniques.* Springer Verlag, 2008.

[21] M. Ondaatje and W. Murch. *he conversations: alter Murch and the art of editing film.* Knopf, 2002.

[22] M. Rabbath, P. Sandhaus, and S. Boll. Automatic creation of photo books from stories in social media. In *roceedings of ACM SI MM wor shop on Social media*, pages 15–20, 2010.

[23] Y. Rui, T. Huang, and S. Chang. Image Retrieval: Current Techniques, Promising Directions, and Open Issues. *ournal of visual communication and image representation*, 10(1):39–62, 1999.

[24] J. Russell. A circumplex model of affect. *ournal of personality and social psychology*, 39(6):1161–1178, 1980.

[25] G. Salton and M. McGill. *Introduction to modern information retrieval*, volume 1. McGraw-Hill New York, 1983.

[26] M. Soleymani, J. Kierkels, G. Chanel, and T. Pun. A bayesian framework for video affective representation. In *Affective Computing and Intelligent Interaction and or shops*, pages 1–7, 2009.

[27] K. Sun and J. Yu. Video affective content representation and recognition using video affective tree and hidden Markov models. *Affective Computing and Intelligent Interaction*, pages 594–605, 2007.

[28] K. Sun, J. Yu, Y. Huang, and X. Hu. An improved valence-arousal emotion space for video affective content representation and recognition. In *roceedings of I International Conference on Multimedia and xpo*, pages 566–569, 2009.

[29] M. Turk and A. Pentland. Face recognition using eigenfaces. In *Computer Vision and attern ecognition*, pages 586–591, 1991.

[30] S. Zhang, Q. Tian, Q. Huang, W. Gao, and S. Li. Utilizing affective analysis for efficient movie browsing. In *roceedings of I International Conference on Image rocessing*, pages 1853–1856, 2010.

Example-based Video Remixing Support System*

Naoko Nitta
Department of Communication Engineering,
Osaka University,
2-1 Yamada-Oka, Suita, Osaka 565-0871, Japan
naoko@comm.eng.osaka-u.ac.jp

Noboru Babaguchi
Department of Communication Engineering,
Osaka University,
2-1 Yamada-Oka, Suita, Osaka 565-0871, Japan
babaguchi@comm.eng.osaka-u.ac.jp

ABSTRACT

Video remixes are generally created by sequentially arranging selected video clips and mixing them with other media streams such as audio clips and transition effects. Especially, mixing music clips often effectively improves the expressive quality of video clips. This paper proposes an example-based system for supporting average users in the 3 steps in video remixing: I)video shot sequence creation, II)music clip selection, and III)audio volume adjustment. The proposed system creates a template for a video remix and gives suggestions to users on an interface such as which video clips should be selected to create a video shot sequence and which music clips should be mixed to the created video shot sequence based on professionally created video remix examples. Then, the audio volume of each video shot is automatically adjusted based on its audio content so that the sounds in the video shots and the music clips would not interfere with each other. Experiments have verified that our system was able to create a video shot sequence whose quality was improved equally as the professionally created one by mixing the selected music clips, doubling the subjective scores from 1.7 to 3.7 on a scale of 1-5. Automatic audio volume adjustment improved the subjective scores by approximately 0.5 points on average. Further, the suggestions provided on the interface was evaluated useful by 5 subjects when creating a video remix by selecting 32 video clips and 4 music clips from 265 video clips and 180 music clips.

Categories and Subject Descriptors

H.5.1 [**INFORMATION INTERFACE AND PRESENTATION**]: Multimedia Information Systems—*Video*

General Terms

Design, Experimentation

Keywords

Video Remixing, Music Mixing, Examples, User Interface

*Area chair: Susanne Boll

1. INTRODUCTION

Video remixing, which is to create a new video by mixing a sequence of the selected original video clips with other media streams such as audio clips, graphics, texts, and video transition effects, is one of the ways to re-purpose the original video clips to make them more enjoyable to viewers. Especially, mixing a sequence of the selected video clips with music clips is a relatively easy but effective way to improve the expressive quality of the original video clips.

While the automation makes video remixing faster, it usually involves depriving users of control in video remixing, which is not always desirable [1]. Since the selection of video and music clips should largely depend on users' preferences, certain amount of control in selecting them should be given to users. Many video editing tools such as Adobe Premier [2] and Windows Movie Maker [3] have been developed to enable average users to create video remixes when given multiple video and music clips; however, the task is still time-consuming and the quality of the video remixes depends on the users' levels of technical or artistic skills. Therefore, the aim of this work is to develop a system which provides suggestions to users for selecting and arranging video and music clips.

As prior work for supporting video clip selection, Hitchcock visually presents the perceived quality of video clips using face icons [4], since they target on home videos which can often be of poor quality resulting from lack of professional capture skills. Further, a professionally authored template describing the temporal structure of a video shot sequence is used to give suggestions to users what kinds of video clips should be used as each shot [5]. In order to support users in the selection and arrangement of both video and music clips, Lazycut also presents a manually prepared template for the target video remix [6]. Such a template can be very helpful for average users to remix videos; however, how to prepare the template has not been discussed.

Let us note here that professionally created videos are usually composed of several scenes, each of which is a series of shots unified by their content, where each shot is recorded continuously by a camera. These shots are often arranged in sequence based on the film syntax [7] [8]. Music clips are usually mixed to a scene so as to maintain the feeling of continuity in the scene by establishing links across its constituent shots [9]. In professionally created videos, the music clips are generally chosen based on implicit aesthetic rules to establish links between video scenes and music clips. Thus, our proposed system firstly tries to learn the temporal structure of video shots and scenes [10] and the aesthetic compatibility between video scenes and music clips from professionally created video remix examples. Then, based on the learned video shot/scene structure, a template for a video remix is constructed and presented to users on an interface. Video clips can also be presented according to their suitability to the template so that users can easily select suitable video clips to the template [11]. Further, based on the learned aesthetic compatibility between video scenes and music clips, candidate music clips for a video scene can also be presented to users once all the video shots in the scene are selected and arranged.

Another issue to consider in music mixing is that, since the video clips can contain sound such as music and speech, mixing music clips can degrade the quality of video remixes due to the two different simultaneously playing sounds. Therefore, the audio volume of the video or music clips need to be adjusted appropriately to avoid the quality degradation of the generated video remixes. Our system learns how the audio volume is adjusted for each video clip in professionally created video remix examples, and based on the learned patterns, automatically adjusts the audio volume of the video clips selected by users based on their audio content.

In summary, the contributions of the work are:

1. A system which creates a template for a video remix and provides suggestions to users on an interface for selecting video clips based on their suitability to the template and for selecting music clips for the created video scenes based on their aesthetic compatibility is developed. The system also realizes the automatic audio volume adjustment in mixing video scenes and music clips, which has not been handled in existing systems.
2. Unlike the existing systems, the proposed system adopts an example-based approach which obtains the video remix template, the aesthetic compatibility, and the audio volume adjustment rules from professionally created video remix examples.
3. Experiments are conducted to verify the effectiveness of the example-based approach, which is based on standard machine learning techniques, in improving the video remixes even with a limited number of video remix examples. The usefulness of the suggestions provided on the interface is also subjectively evaluated.

The rest of the paper is organized as follows. After presenting the related work in Section 2, the system overview is given in Section 3. Sections 4–6 each describes the details of each process: video shot sequence creation, music clip selection, and audio volume adjustment, and Section 7 describes our proposed user interface and how users create a video remix by using the interface. Finally, experimental results are discussed in Section 8 and Section 9 concludes the paper.

2. RELATED WORK

As described in Section 1, there are some existing work to support average users in video remixing. Considering the average users' skills in capturing home videos, Hitchcock visually presents the perceived quality of video clips using face icons [4] so that users can easily select video clips of good perceived quality. Further, a manually prepared template is used in order to support users in the selection and arrangement of video and music clips [6]. While the template describes the temporal structure of the video and music clip sequences, how to create the template is not discussed and the template only describes the temporal duration and the hierarchical structure of shots and scenes. As the work considering more about the content of the video clips, Davis also proposed to use a professionally authored template which describes what kinds of video clips should be used as each video shot [5]. Canini et al. developed a user interface where users can select video clips based on the similarity of their emotional identity so that the emotional mood of the created video remix would be continuous [12].

On the other hand, there has been some work for automatically creating a video clip sequence by focusing on how certain types of video clips are arranged in sequence by considering the film syntax. Video clips are firstly characterized by their shot sizes, durations, camerawork, moving direction of objects, etc. and the syntax rules such as a scene has to have at least 3 video clips [7], 2 video clips of extremely different shot sizes, e.g. close-up and long shots, should not be connected, the duration of a video clip recorded with the camera fixed is up to 15 seconds, and a video clip recorded with the camera fixed precedes video clips recorded with the camera panning/zooming [8] are used to automatically select and arrange video clips.

Other work have tried to automatically synthesize video clips and music clips to improve their expressive quality. For example, Hua et al. proposed a method for automatically generating music-video-like videos by aligning visually similar video clips to repetitive segments in a music clip such as prelude, interlude, and coda [13]. Wang et al. also focused on the structure of a music clip and proposed to generate a music sports video by selecting the best video clip for each semantic music segment such as Intro, Verse, and Chorus considering their semantic content and tempo using certain user-defined rules [14]. Yoon et al. proposed to conserve the intent of the video-maker by segmenting video and music clips into segments of near-uniform flow and selecting the best video segment for each music segment based on their novelty, velocity and brightness and by using time-warping [15]. While these work all tried to synthesize video clips to a music clip, Mulhem et al. have proposed a method for synthesizing several music clips to a sequence of video clips by selecting the best music clip for a video clip based on heuristically determined rules about the aesthetic compatibility between video and music clips, more concretely, how the dynamic, motion, and pitch of video and music clips coincide with each other [16]. Inspired by Mulhem's work, Cristani et al. examined statistically which audio-visual features actually correlate with each other in the professional created documentary videos to determine a policy for selecting the most suitable music clip for a video clip taken by a camera mounted on a car [17].

Our work is similar to [17] in terms of observing professionally created video remixes to learn the patterns in the temporal structure of the video remixes related to the film syntax and in the aesthetic compatibility between video scenes and music clips. The novelty of our work is that, instead of observing how each audio or visual feature contributes to these patterns, machine learning techniques are used in our example-based approach. Based on the learned patterns, our system provides not only the video remix template but also helpful information for selecting video and music clips according to the template to users on an interface.

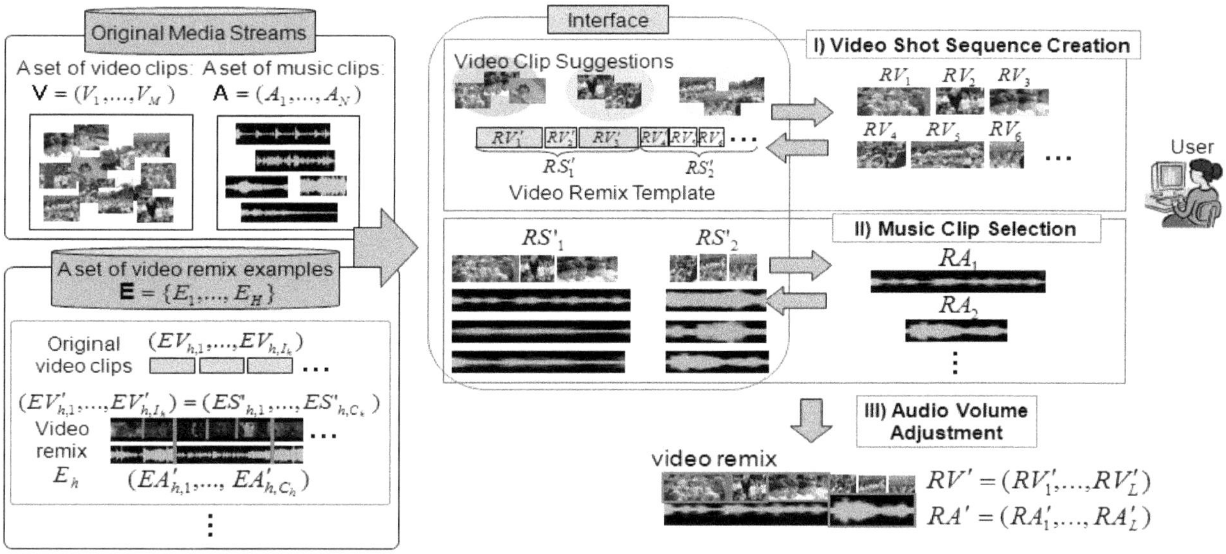

Figure 1: Overview of Example-based Video Remixing Support System

Finally, although playing the sound in a video clip sequence and music clips simultaneously can sometimes degrade the aesthetic quality of the video remixes, their audio volume adjustment has not been considered in previous work. In the same example-based framework, our system automatically adjusts the audio volume of the selected video clips.

3. EXAMPLE-BASED VIDEO REMIXING SUPPORT SYSTEM

The target of our work is to create a new video remix from multiple video and music clips. We adopt a video-driven approach, that is, a video shot sequence is firstly created, and then music clips are mixed to the created video shot sequence. More concretely, from a set of M video clips $\mathbf{V} = (V_1, \cdots, V_M)$ and a set of N music clips $\mathbf{A} = (A_1, \cdots, A_N)$, a video remix is created by the following 3 steps:

I) Video Shot Sequence Creation

L video clips $RV_l (l = 1, \cdots, L)$ are selected to create a sequence of L video shots $RV' = (RV'_1, \cdots, RV'_L) = (RS'_1, \cdots, RS'_D)$, where certain consecutive video shots $(RV'_{s_d}, \cdots, RV'_{e_d}) (1 \le s_d < e_d \le L; e_d + 1 = s_{d+1})$ construct the dth scene RS'_d. Note that L is specified by the user and the time duration of the video clip RV_l is adopted to obtain the video shot RV'_l.

II) Music Clip Selection

In professionally created video remixes, a music clip is often assigned to a video scene constructed by consecutive video shots. Therefore, for each scene RS'_d, a music clip RA_d is selected from $\mathbf{A}$ to create a sequence of D music excerpts $RA' = (RA'_1, \cdots, RA'_D)$, where the time duration of the music clip RA_d is adopted to obtain the music excerpt RA'_d so that the durations of RA'_d and of RS'_d are the same.

III) Audio Volume Adjustment

The audio volume of each video shot RV'_l is adjusted so that the sound in the video shots and the music excerpts would not interfere with each other.

Selecting and arranging appropriate video and music clips are often best performed by users [1]. Therefore, we develop an example-based video remixing support system for supporting average users in creating a new video remix based on the patterns learned from professionally created video remix examples. Figure 1 shows the overview of the system. The proposed system provides suggestions to users on the interface for the steps I) and II), so that users can efficiently and effectively select and arrange video and music clips, and automatically realizes the step III) by referring to a set of H video remix examples $\mathbf{E} = \{E_1, \cdots, E_H\}$. Each video remix E_h can be considered as aligned sequences of I_h video shots $EV'_h = (EV'_{h,1}, \cdots, EV'_{h,I_h}) = (ES'_{h,1}, \cdots, ES'_{h,C_h})$, where certain consecutive video shots $(EV'_{h,s_c}, \cdots, EV'_{h,e_c})$ $(1 \le s_c < e_c \le I_h; e_c + 1 = s_{c+1})$ construct the cth scene, and C_h music excerpts $EA'_h = (EA'_{h,1}, \cdots, EA'_{h,C_h})$. Additionally, a sequence of the original video clips $EV_h = (EV_{h,1}, \cdots, EV_{h,I_h})$ is given. Thus, a video remix example can be represented as $E_h = \{EV'_h, EA'_h, EV_h\}$. By referring to $\mathbf{E}$, the 3 steps are realized as follows:

I) Video Shot Sequence Creation

A set of video shot sequences of the video remix examples $\{EV'_h | h = 1, \cdots, H\}$ is used to learn which types of video shots/scenes should/should not be sequentially arranged to construct a video remix. Then, a video remix template for $RV' = (RV'_1, \cdots, RV'_L) = (RS'_1, \cdots, RS'_D)$, a sequence of L video shots constructing D video scenes which fits the learned patterns, can be generated and presented to the user on an interface. All video clips $V_m \in \mathbf{V}$ are also presented according to their suitability to the template and their perceived quality on the interface to support users in selecting and arranging the video clips according to the template. The time duration of each selected video clip is determined according to the template and can be automatically adjusted by using a technique such as [18] to obtain a video shot sequence.

II) Music Clip Selection

A set of pairs of a video scene and a music excerpt in

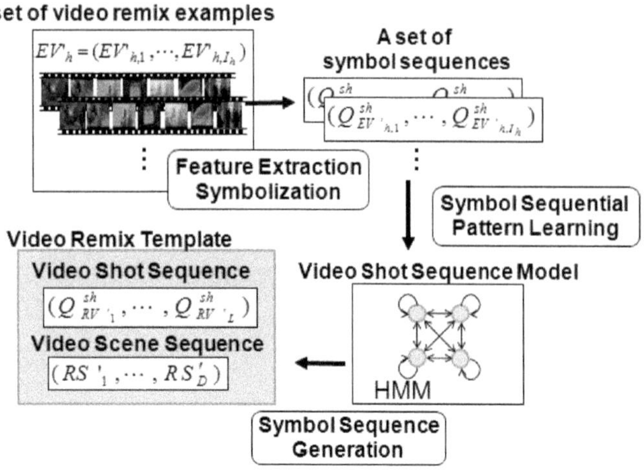

Figure 2: Video Remix Template Generation

video remix examples $\{(ES'_{h,c}, EA'_{h,c})|c = 1, \cdots, C_h; h = 1, \cdots, H\}$ is used to learn which types of video scenes and music excerpts are more likely to be mixed. Then, for each $RS'_d = (RV'_{s_d}, \cdots, RV'_{e_d})(1 \leq s_d < e_d \leq L; e_d + 1 = s_{d+1})$, the candidate music clips are selected from $\mathbf{A}$ based on the learned patterns and presented to users on the interface to support users in selecting the appropriate music clip RA_d.

III) Audio Volume Adjustment

A set of pairs of a video shot and its original video clip of video remix examples $\{(EV'_{h,i}, EV_{h,i})|i = 1, \cdots, I_h; h = 1, \cdots, H\}$ is used to learn how the audio volume of each original video shot has been adjusted. Then, the audio volume of each video shot RV'_l is automatically adjusted according to the learned patterns.

4. VIDEO SHOT SEQUENCE CREATION

This section describes how the video remix template is generated. How the users are supported in creating the video shot sequence on an interface is described in Section 7.

4.1 Feature Extraction

The video shot sequence creation step focuses on which types of video shots/scenes are arranged in sequence to create video remixes of good expressive quality. Therefore, we extract 5 types of aesthetic attributed features [19] [20], namely, the length, brightness, motion intensity, and presences and absences of camera motion and human objects from $EV'_{h,i}$ and V_m obtaining the feature vector $\mathbf{VF}^{sh}$. After the discretization of each feature dimension, all feature vectors in each discretized feature space are represented with a same symbol. Consequently, $EV'_{h,i}$ and V_m are represented by the symbols $Q^{sh}_{EV'_{h,i}}$ and $Q^{sh}_{V_m}$, respectively.

4.2 Video Remix Template Generation

This step generates the video remix template which describes a sequence of L video shots and D video scenes $RV' = (RV'_1, \cdots, RV'_L) = (RS'_1, \cdots, RS'_D)$ when L is specified by the user. Hidden Markov Model(HMM) is used to learn the temporal structure of every video remix example $EV'_h = (EV'_{h,1}, \cdots, EV'_{h,I_h})$, more concretely, which types of video shots/scenes should/should not be arranged in sequence. Since HMM is a generative model which can be used for randomly generating observable data given some hidden parameters, a sequence of video shots which is likely to be observed by the learned model can be generated as the template of a video shot sequence.

Figure 2 shows the overview of the video remix template generation. The video shot sequence of the hth video remix example $EV'_h = (EV'_{h,1}, ..., EV'_{h,I_h})$ is represented as a symbol sequence $(Q^{sh}_{EV'_{h,1}}, \cdots, Q^{sh}_{EV'_{h,I_h}})$. The maximum likelihood estimates of the HMM parameters are derived from the set of symbol sequences of H video remix examples by using the Baum-Welch algorithm [21]. Given the estimated HMM parameters, the probability of observing a symbol sequence can be computed with the forward algorithm [21], and a symbol sequence $(Q^{sh}_{RV'_1}, \cdots, Q^{sh}_{RV'_L})$, which is likely to be observed by the learned model, can be generated with genetic algorithm [22] as the template for the video shot sequence $RV' = (RV'_1, \cdots, RV'_L)$. The state sequence that is most likely to have generated the obtained symbol sequence can be derived by the Viterbi algorithm [21]. Then, when considering a repetitive state sequence corresponds to a scene, the sequence $(RV'_{s_d}, ..., RV'_{e_d})$ $(1 \leq s_d < e_d \leq L; e_d + 1 = s_{d+1})$ constructing RS'_d can be determined.

Table 1: Features for Music Clip Selection

	Characteristics	Features
Video Scenes	Color	Hue, Saturation, Brightness
	Amount of Activity	Visual Disturbance[20]
	Speed	Average Shot Length
Music Clips	Noisiness	Zero-Crossing Rate(ZCR)
	Brightness	Spectral Centroid
	Speed	Beat per Minute(BPM) [23]
	Loudness	Dynamic Range VSTD
	Emotion	MFCC Spectral Flatness Measure Spectral Crest Factor

5. MUSIC CLIP SELECTION

This section describes how the candidate music clips are selected for each video scene RS'_d. The candidate music clips are presented on the interface described in Section 7 to support users in selecting a music clip for each scene.

5.1 Feature Extraction

Assuming that the music clips which are compatible to video scenes of similar impression have similar impression and those compatible to video scenes of different impression have different impression, features representing the impression of video scenes and music clips are extracted. As discussed in [20], the color, the amount of activity, and the speed are related to the impression of video scenes. The impression of music is related to the noisiness, brightness, speed, and loudness [16] [24]. Further, features related to emotion-based classification [25] [26] are also considered to be related to the impression of music. Accordingly, features indicated in Table 1 are extracted from video scenes and music clips. Here, the visual disturbance [20] is defined as a measure of the motion variation within a video segment and can be obtained as the ratio of pixels with motions differ-

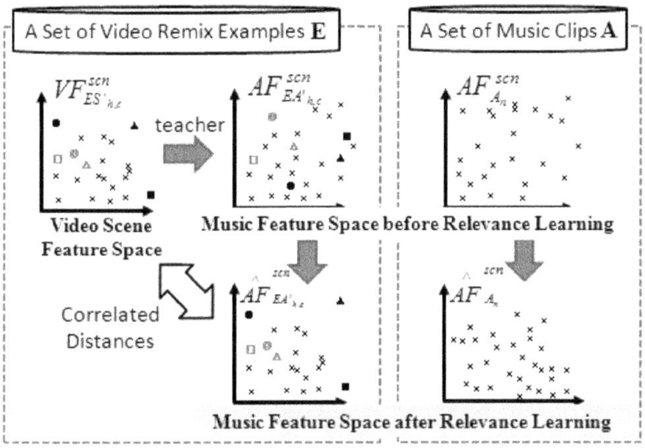

Figure 3: Music Feature Space Transformation

ent from the global motions which can be caused by camera motions. Dynamic range represents the difference between the quietest and loudest volumes, VSTD is the standard deviation of the short-time energy, and MFCC is the Mel-Frequency Cepstrum Coefficient.

18-dimensional feature vector and 19-dimensional feature vector, each of which is related to the visual and audio features described in Table 1, are extracted from the video scenes $ES'_{h,c}$ and RS'_d and from the music excerpts $EA'_{h,c}$ and the music clips A_n respectively. Then, they are transformed by Principal Component Analysis after normalization to obtain $\mathbf{VF}^{scn}$ and $\mathbf{AF}^{scn}$.

5.2 Music Feature Space Transformation

We aim at evaluating the similarity of impressions among video scenes and music clips by their distances in the video scene feature space and the music feature space, respectively. To this end, when the distances between video scenes are small in the video scene feature space, the distances between their mixed music excerpts, which are assumed to be compatible to both video scenes, should also be small in the music feature space, and when the distances between video scenes are large, the distance between the music excerpts mixed to each video scene, which are assumed to be incompatible to the other video scene, should also be large.

Thus, given a set of pairs of a video scene and a music excerpt in video remix examples $\{(ES'_{h,c}, EA'_{h,c})|c = 1, \cdots, C_h; h = 1, \cdots, H\}$, a non-linear mapping of the music feature space for $\mathbf{AF}^{scn}$ to another k-dimensional space for $\hat{\mathbf{AF}}^{scn}$ is learned by Relevance Learning based on the 3-layered perceptrons [27], so that the distances among the music excerpts $EA'_{h,c}$ in the transformed space would correlate to the distances among their mixed video scenes $ES'_{h,c}$ in the video scene feature space for $\mathbf{VF}^{scn}$.

To be more specific, the target mapping would transform an input feature vector $\mathbf{AF}^{scn}$ into $\hat{\mathbf{AF}}^{scn}$ with the weight coefficients of the 3-layered perceptrons. Given the distances between the video scenes $\mathbf{VF}^{scn}_{ES'_{h,c}}$ and $\mathbf{VF}^{scn}_{ES'_{h',c'}}$ $(h, h' = 1, \cdots, H, c, c' = 1, \cdots, C_h, h \neq h' \vee c \neq c')$ in the video scene feature space as the teacher distances, the weight coefficients are tuned so that the total error of the distances between $\hat{\mathbf{AF}}^{scn}_{EA'_{h,c}}$ and $\hat{\mathbf{AF}}^{scn}_{EA'_{h',c'}}$ from the teacher distances is minimized. A modified back propagation method is applied for the learning. The Euclidean distance is used as the distance. After the learning, the feature vector $\mathbf{AF}^{scn}_{A_n}$ for every $A_n \in \mathbf{A}$ is also transformed by the learned mapping. Figure 3 shows the overview of the music feature space transformation.

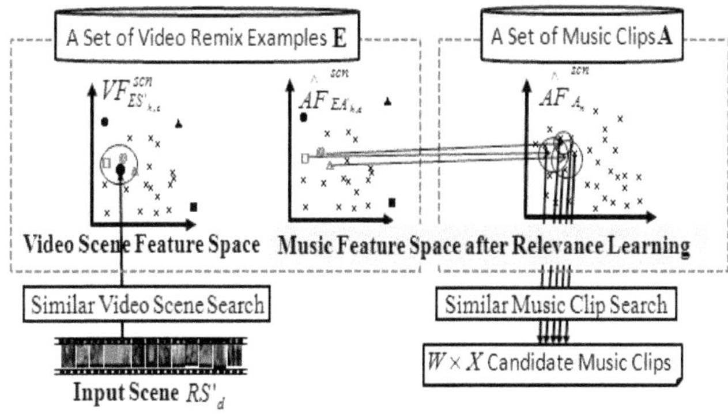

Figure 4: Similarity-based Music Clip Selection

5.3 Similarity-based Music Clip Selection

Assuming that music clips of similar impression are compatible to the video scenes of similar impression, a music clip compatible to the input video scene will be found around the music excerpts in the transformed music feature space, which are mixed with the video scenes close to the input scene in the video feature space. Figure 4 shows the overview of similarity-based music clip selection, which is composed of the following 2 steps:

Step 1: Similar Video Scene Search
For each video scene RS'_d, the W most similar example video scenes $ES'_{h,c}$ are retrieved from $\mathbf{E}$ based on the Euclidean distance of $\mathbf{VF}^{scn}_{RS'_d}$ to $\mathbf{VF}^{scn}_{ES'_{h,c}}$ for all $ES'_{h,c} \in \mathbf{E}$.

Step 2: Similar Music Clip Search
Each of the W retrieved similar video scenes, $ES'_{h,c}$, is mixed with the music excerpt $EA'_{h,c}$. For each of the W music excerpt $EA'_{h,c}$, the X most similar music clips are retrieved from $\mathbf{A}$ based on the Euclidean distance of $\hat{\mathbf{AF}}^{scn}_{EA'_{h,c}}$ to $\hat{\mathbf{AF}}^{scn}_{A_n}$ for all $A_n \in \mathbf{A}$.

6. AUDIO VOLUME ADJUSTMENT

This section describes how the audio volume of each video shot RV'_l is automatically adjusted.

6.1 Feature Extraction

In professionally created video remixes, the audio volume of the video shots or of the music excerpts is considered to be adjusted based on the audio content of the video shot such as speech, music, and environmental sound. Therefore, the audio features are extracted from each video shot. According to some work for audio scene classification and sound source discrimination [28] [29], in addition to the short-time energy, ZCR, spectral centroid, and MFCC described in Section 5.1, spectrum spread, spectral roll-off, high ZCR ratio, and low short-time energy ratio are effective for audio content classification. Further, the video shots whose audio volume are set louder than the volume of mixed music excerpts, such as the video shots with speech, often have a certain time duration. Therefore, the shot length is also extracted from

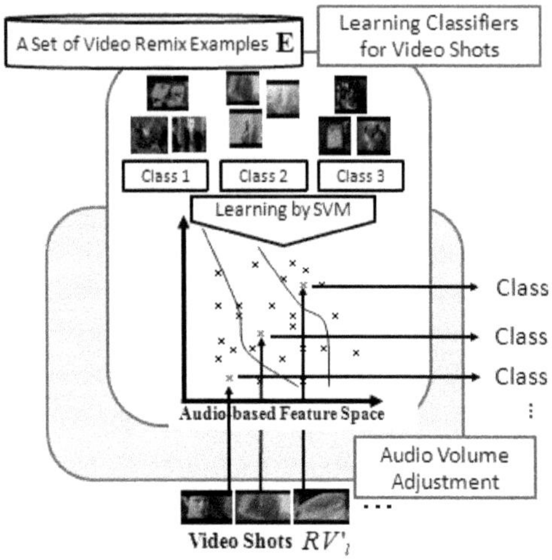

Figure 5: Audio Volume Adjustment

each video shot. In summary, 34-dimensional feature vector $\mathbf{AF}^{sh}$ related to the features discussed above is extracted from each video shot.

6.2 Audio Volume Adjustment by SVM

In professionally created video remixes, the audio volume of each video shot $EV'_{h,i}$ is set either louder or quieter than or equal to the mixed music excerpts. Therefore, given a set of pairs of a video shot and its original video clip of video remix examples $\{(EV'_{h,i}, EV_{h,i})|h = 1, \cdots, H, i = 1, \cdots, I_h\}$, the audio volume class $AC_{h,i}$ of $EV'_{h,i}$ can be manually determined. By using a set of pairs of the feature vector $\mathbf{AF}^{sh}_{EV'_{h,i}}$ of the video shot $EV'_{h,i}$ and its audio volume class $AC_{h,i}$ as the training data, discriminative classifiers for the 3 classes are learned by Support Vector Machine(SVM). Here, $AC_{h,i} = 1$, $AC_{h,i} = 2$, and $AC_{h,i} = 3$ indicate that the audio volume of the video shot $EV'_{h,i}$ is set louder than, quieter than, and equal to the mixed music excerpts, respectively. Then, the class for each video shot RV'_l is determined by the learned SVM classifiers to adjust its audio volume. Figure 5 shows the overview of the audio volume adjustment, which is composed of the following 2 steps:

Step 1: Learning Classifiers for Video Shots
SVM classifiers for the 3 classes are learned from a set of pairs of a video shot and its audio volume class $\{(EV'_{h,i}, AC_{h,i})|h = 1, \cdots, H, i = 1, \cdots, I_h\}$.

Step 2: Audio Volume Adjustment
The audio class AC_l for the video segment RV'_l is determined by the learned SVM classifiers. Then, according to AC_l, the audio volume of RV'_l is either turned up (Class 1), turned down (Class 2), or kept unchanged (Class 3).

Figure 6 shows a scatter plot of the first 2 principal component scores of the video shots $EV'_{h,i}$ which belong to each class for the video remix examples we have collected. Since this figure indicates that the video shots in Class 1 and those in other classes are relatively easily separable, a 2-class classifier for Class 1 and other classes and another 2-class classifier for Classes 2 and 3 are learned and used in a hierarchical manner as shown in Fig.7.

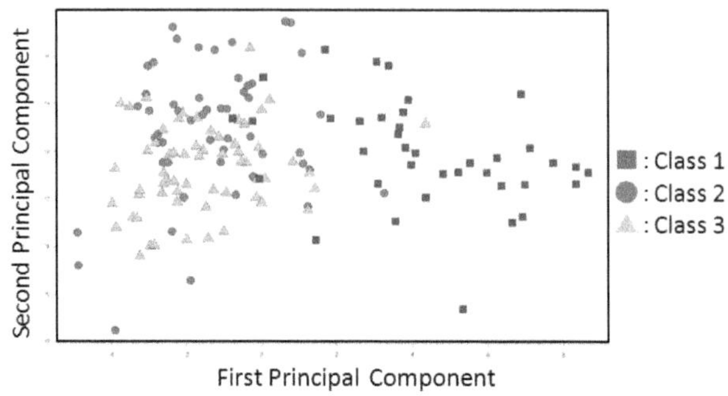

Figure 6: A Scatter Plot for Video Shots

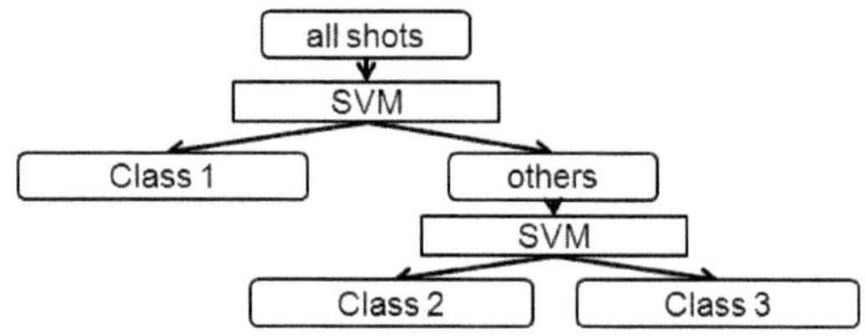

Figure 7: 2-layer Video Shot Classification by SVM

7. USER INTERFACE

In order to help users select a suitable video clip from $\mathbf{V}$ for every symbol $Q^{sh}_{RV'_l}$ in the template and a suitable music clip from $\mathbf{A}$ for every video scene RS'_d, a user interface composed of 4 panels: a)video remix template presentation panel, b)video clip browsing panel, c)video clip selection panel, and d)music clip selection panel as shown in Fig. 8 is developed. Focusing on 1)how to present many video clips in a limited display space so that their semantic cohesiveness is observable and 2)how to cut down the user's remixing time while improving the quality of the created video remixes, each panel is designed as follows.

a) Video Remix Template Presentation Panel
The symbol sequence generated in Section 4.2 is presented as the template for a video shot sequence. Each symbol is represented by a rectangle whose width represents the length feature value of the symbol. Additionally, the same symbol is represented by the same color. The user firstly selects a symbol to select a video clip for the corresponding symbol.

Further, the video scene sequence which is derived from the state sequence of the generated symbol sequence is presented as the template for a video scene sequence, indicating which consecutive video shots construct a scene. After selecting video clips for all the symbols in a scene, the user can select the scene to select a music clip for the corresponding scene.

b) Video Clip Browsing Panel
Video clips are presented considering their temporal order, which are related to their semantic cohesiveness. In order to realize it in a limited display space, a 3-dimensional book-style video clip browsing panel is developed, where each page presents a set of consecutive video clips recording the same event or scene. The pages are then assembled in their temporal order. For example, a video captured at a school field day can be presented by temporally assembling the pages display-

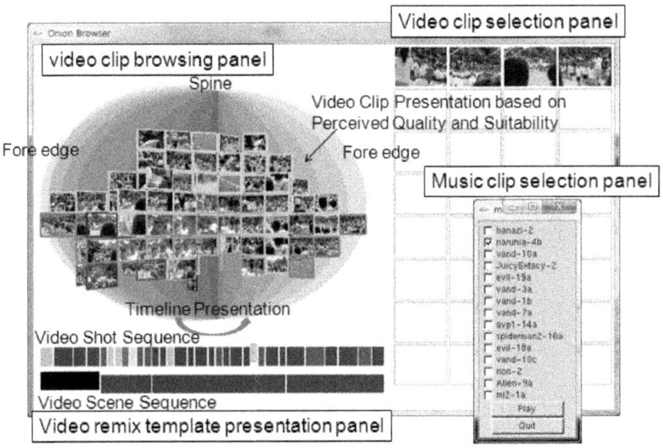

Figure 8: User Interface

ing video clips of each physical event such as the $4 \times 100m$ relay, the $100m$ sprinting, and the tug of war in their chronological order.

A video clip is represented by a key frame which is the first frame of the video clip. The key frame is arranged on a page according to its suitability $S(V_m, Q^{sh}_{RV'_l})$, which is determined based on the distance between the features of V_m and the center of the discretized feature space corresponding to the symbol $Q^{sh}_{RV'_l}$.

Moreover, the perceived quality of video clips can be bad due to abnormal camera motions or lighting conditions and these clips are less suitable to be selected for a video remix than those of good perceived quality. Thus, the perceived quality $P(V_m)$ of video clips V_m are evaluated based on the unstableness, jerkiness, brightness, and orientation similarly to [30]. Then, the key frame of V_m is arranged on a page by also considering its perceived quality $P(V_m)$.

Generally, a 3-dimensional interface can present more information than a 2-dimensional interface on a display of the same size. However, since the 3-dimensional points are projected to the 2-dimensional display, parts of the information can become unobservable due to the overlapping areas. Especially, in the 3-dimensional book-style browsing panel, the pages are more likely to be overlapped with each other in the areas around the spine of the book than in the areas around the fore edge of the book. Therefore, in order to arrange the video clips with the high perceived quality and suitability around the fore edge of the page while arranging those with the low perceived quality and suitability around the spine of the page, their positions in the PS coordinate system are projected to the XY coordinate system as shown in Fig. 9(b). Further, in order to avoid the overlaps of video clips in each page, grids are arranged in a page as shown in Fig. 9(c). Each video clip is assigned to the grid which is closest to its XY coordinate.

c) **Video Clip Selection Panel**
The video clip selection panel is composed of L rectangles, each of which corresponds to a symbol of the symbol sequence generated in Section 4.2. When a symbol

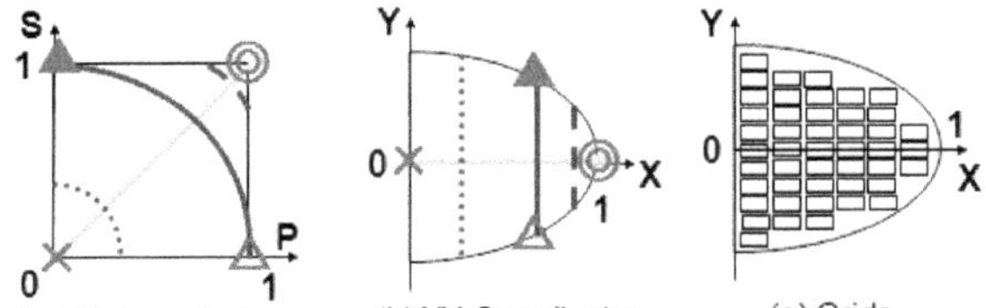

(a) PS Coordinates (b) XY Coordinates (c) Grids

Figure 9: Video Clip Presentation

is selected in the video remix template presentation panel, the corresponding rectangle is marked by a colored frame. The user can select a video clip for the symbol by dragging and dropping the corresponding key frame presented in the video clip browsing panel.

d) **Music Clip Selection Panel**
The music clip selection panel appears when a scene is selected in the video remix template presentation panel after all of its video shots are selected, presenting a list of candidate music clips suitable for the scene. The user can select a music clip and press "Play" button to play the video scene mixed with the selected music clip. When the user decides a music clip for the video scene, the user selects the music clip and presses "Quit" button.

By using the interface, a video remix can be created by repeating the following 5 steps.

1. When one of the symbol is selected in the video remix template presentation panel by a mouse click, the key frames of the video clips are arranged in the video clip browsing panel according to their suitability to the selected symbol and their perceived quality.
2. The user can browse the video clips by turning or rotating the pages. Selecting a key frame by a mouse click with the right button plays the corresponding video clip.
3. When a key frame is drag-and-dropped to the video clip selection panel, the video clip is inserted at the position of the symbol in the video remix.
4. After selecting all video clips composing a video scene, the user can select the video scene in the video remix template presentation panel to obtain a list of candidate music clips for the scene in the music clip selection panel.
5. In the music clip selection panel, the user can play the candidate music clips mixed with the video scene to decide the best music clip for the scene.

8. EXPERIMENTS

Our proposed method can work with any type of professionally created video remix examples as long as they are created by combining a set of video and music clips and can be represented as $E_h = \{EV'_h, EA'_h, EV_h\}$. As one of the representative professionally created video remixes whose original videos are easily available, trailers of 61 action movies were collected referring to The Internet Movie Database [31] for the experiments. The movie trailers were segmented into video scenes $ES'_{h,c}$ at music changes and into video shots $EV'_{h,i}$. For 45 video scenes, we were able to separately collect the mixed music clips $EA'_{h,c}$, which do not contain the audio signals contained in the mixed video scenes, by referring to soundtrack.net [32]. The original video clips $EV_{h,i}$ were collected from movies, and for 150 video shots $EV'_{h,i}$, their classes $AC_{h,i}$ were manually determined. As a result, 38, 52, and 60 video shots were obtained for Classes 1, 2, and 3. For a video shot sequence generation, the number of symbols resulting from the feature space discretization was 72 and the number of states in HMM was set to 4.

We also prepared a set of music clips $\mathbf{A}$ by collecting 123 pieces of music of various genres such as movie soundtracks, classical music, and popular music (Japanese-pop and Western-pop). They were manually segmented into music structure components such as Intro and Verse to obtain 180 music clips in total. When using home videos as a set of video clips $\mathbf{V}$, a 45-minute video recording a sports field day held by a kindergarten was used. The video was composed of 40 video segments. Since these segments are often recorded by moving the camera without switching it off, they were segmented based on their camera work so that the video segments with consistent features are used as video clips V_m. As a result, the video was segmented into 265 video clips in total. The lengths of the video clips ranged from 1 to 30 seconds with the average of 11 seconds. The frame rate of all video streams is 10fps and the sampling rate of all audio streams is 44100 Hz.

8.1 Evaluations of Music Clip Selection

In order to solely evaluate if the example-based approach is effective in selecting subjectively compatible music clips to an input video scene, we used scenes extracted from movie trailers, which are professionally created video shot sequences, as the test input scene. Since the aim of existing methods was to select a music clip for a video shot, their results can not be directly compared to our results of selecting a music clip for a video scene, which is composed of several video shots. Therefore, we compared our results with the professional decisions, which are the music excerpts actually mixed to the input scenes in movie trailers.

10 scenes were randomly extracted from movie trailers, and since more than one music clip can be compatible to the input scene, for each input scene,

Video 1: 3 music clips selected by our approach ($W = 3$ and $X = 1$)

Video 2: 3 music clips which are most similar to the music excerpts mixed with the 3 least similar video scenes $ES'_{h,i}$ to the input scene

Video 3: music excerpt which is actually mixed to the input scene in the movie trailer

Video 4: 3 music clips selected in the same way as for Video 1 without music feature space transformation

Video 5: 3 music clips selected in the same way as for Video 2 without music feature space transformation

were mixed. 10 subjects watched these 10 sets of the video scene mixed with the 13 different music clips and rated them with the score of 1-10 with 1 being very bad and 10 being very good. Figure 10 shows the average scores for the video scenes mixed with each type of music clips. For example, the score for Video 1 is the average of 10 subjects' average scores over the 3 video scenes mixed with the music clips selected by our system.

As a result of a paired t-test for the 100 subjective scores (for 10 sets of videos compared by 10 subjects), while the

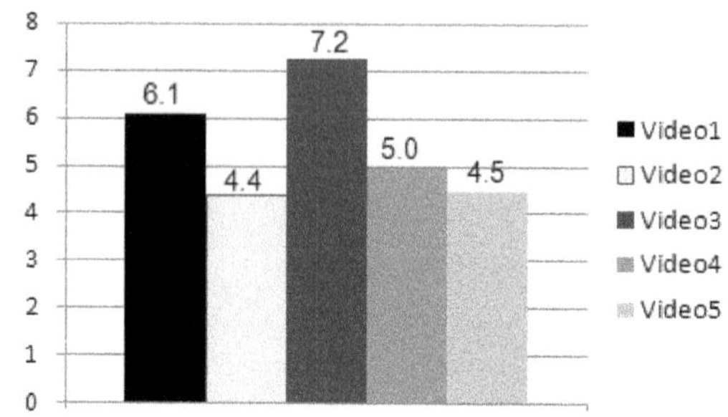

Figure 10: Average Subjective Scores for Video Scenes Mixed with Each Type of Music Clips

Table 2: Results of Audio Volume Adjustment

		True Class			
		Class 1	Class 2	Class 3	Total
Results	Class 1	33	0	1	34
	Class 2	3	34	11	48
	Class 3	2	18	48	68
Total		38	52	60	150

scores for Video 4 were only slightly better than those for Video 5 (0.47 ± 0.4 points higher (95% confidence interval), $t = 2.378$, $P < 0.02$), the scores for Video 1 were 1.72 ± 0.34 points higher than those for Video 2 ($t = 10.05$, $P < 1.0e-16$), indicating the effectiveness of the similarity-based music clip selection, and 1.11 ± 0.35 points higher than those for Video 4 ($t = 6.28$, $P < 1.0e-08$), indicating the effectiveness of the music feature space transformation in improving the similarity-based music clip selection. Although the scores for Video 3 were better than those for Video 1 (1.16 ± 0.38 points higher, $t = 6.02$, $P < 1.0e-07$), the scores for Video 1 were the closest to those for Video 3, indicating that the music clips selected by our approach were subjectively the closest to the professionally selected ones.

8.2 Evaluations of Audio Volume Adjustment

The effectiveness of the audio volume adjustment can be evaluated by using video shots in the movie trailers by examining how accurately their true classes can be determined. By using 10 shots randomly selected from the 150 video shots $EV'_{h,i}$ as the test data and the remaining 140 video shots as the training data, the accuracy, which is defined as the ratio of the video shots correctly classified as Class k to the actual number of shots in Class k, was evaluated by the cross-validation. Here, the accuracy was obtained by changing the number of the principal components separately for the 2 layers. As a result, the first 4 and 5 principal component scores, which obtained the best performance, are used for each layer in the following experiments. The overall classification results are shown in Table 2. The results indicate that the video shots whose sound should be turned up (Class 1) can be relatively easily determined, while more information is considered necessary for determining when to turn down the sound of the video shot (Class 2).

8.3 Evaluations of Created Video Remixes

Firstly, as the subjective evaluation of audio volume adjustment, 3 scenes were selected from movie trailers and all

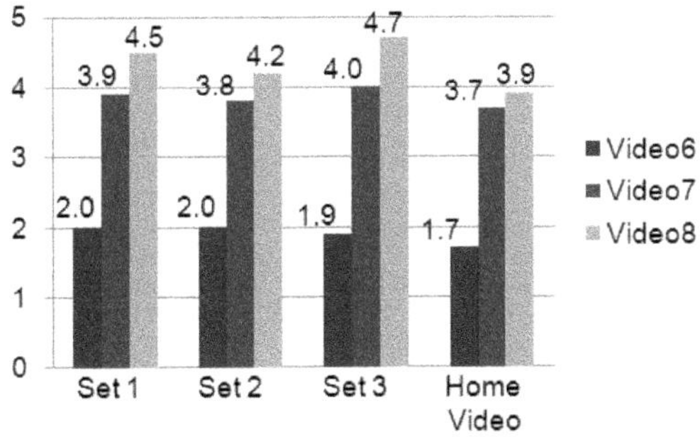

Figure 11: Subjective Scores for Video Remixes

video shots $EV'_{h,i}$ constructing the corresponding scene were obtained from the original movie. From the video shots,

Video 6: concatenation of the video shots
Video 7: Video 6 mixed with a music excerpt $EA'_{h,c}$
Video 8: Video 7 with the audio volume adjusted

were created. 10 subjects watched the 3 sets of these videos and rated them in the scale of 1-5 with 1 being very bad and 5 being very good. Figure 11 shows the scores for each video. As a result of a paired t-test for the 30 subjective scores for the 3 sets of videos compared by 10 subjects, the scores for Video 8 were 0.57 ± 0.28 points higher than those for Video 7 (95% confidence interval, $t = 5.13$, $P < 1.0e{-}04$), indicating the effectiveness of the audio volume adjustment.

Further, for subjective evaluations of the proposed 3 steps, by using 15 home video clips selected based on the suggestions provided by our system, Videos 6-8 were also created and rated by the same 10 subjects. The music clip selected by our system was mixed for Video 7. As shown in Fig. 11, the quality of the created video scene was improved after music clip selection, (the scores for Video 7 were 2 ± 0.96 points higher than those for Video 6 ($t = 6.63$, $P < 1.0e{-}4$)) in the same way as for professionally created video shot sequence (the scores for Video 7 were 1.93 ± 0.51 points higher than those for Video 6 ($t = 11.17$, $P < 1.0e - 11$)). Since video clips with good perceived quality are selected to create a video scene, visual features did not differ so much for home videos; and therefore, using movie trailers as examples was equally useful in the video clip sequence creation and music clip selection processes. However, after the audio volume adjustment, the quality did not improve for home videos (the scores for Video 8 were 0.2 ± 0.31 points higher than those for Video 7 ($t = 0.68$, $P < 0.52$)) as much as the professionally created video shot sequence. According to the subjects, Video 8 was rated lower for home videos due to the video shots with applause whose audio volume was turned down. Since the movie trailers used in the experiments did not contain shots with applause, how to handle such shots has not been correctly learned. Further, the difference in the audio characteristics between home videos and the examples can also have affected the results. For example, home videos tend to have more noise in the background. Thus, for remixing home videos, it would be better to use video remix examples which are professionally created also from home videos. As future work, more experiments with larger number of various types of examples are necessary.

8.4 Evaluations of Interface

Finally, we evaluated the usability of the interface. For comparison, we changed the user interface to have rectangle-

Table 3: Evaluations of Interface

		Subjects				
		A	B	C	D	E
Video Clip Selection	Proposed	4	5	4	4	4
	Comparative	3	4	3	3	3
Music Clip Selection	Proposed	5	4	3	5	5
	Comparative	2	5	3	3	1

shaped pages and arranged video clips in the order of the perceived quality in each page so that users can select them according to their perceived quality in a similar way to existing approaches. For our proposed system, 9 ($W = 3, X = 3$) candidate music clips are suggested, while the comparative system provides all music clips. 5 subjects used both interfaces to create a video remix composed of 4 scenes and 32 video clips from 265 home video clips and 180 music clips and evaluated the ease of video clip selection and the ease of music clip selection with the score of 1-5. Table 3 shows the results. The ease of video clip selection was evaluated slightly higher for the proposed system by all subjects since the template and the video clip arrangement were perceived as helpful suggestions. Since the perceived quality is also helpful information for selecting video clips, the scores for the comparative interface was also relatively good. For music clip selection, while some subjects liked the suggestions by the system, others complained about the limited number of candidates. Sometimes, the subjects did not like the music clips suggested by the system. One of the subjects also mentioned that since the system provides the candidate music clips based on the created video shot sequence, changing a video shot in the created video shot sequence deleted the music clip he had in mind from the candidate list. In order to give users more control in the music clip selection, providing all the music clips in the order of suitability to the created video shot sequence would be a better way for suggesting music clips. Further, some subjects suggested providing certain amount of semantic information or at least a page number in the pages of the book-style video clip browsing panel. The improvement of the interface by referring to these comments will be our future work.

9. CONCLUSION

This paper proposed a system for supporting average users in video remixing by using multiple video and music clips based on professionally created video remix examples. The proposed system firstly creates a template for a video remix and gives suggestions to users on an interface such as which video clips should be selected to create a video shot sequence and which music clips should be mixed to the created video shot sequence. Then, the audio volume of each video shot is automatically adjusted based on its audio content.

As the experimental results, the average subjective score for the music clips selected by our system was 6.1 on average, which was close to the score of professionally selected music clips 7.2. The objective evaluations revealed that the audio volume was adjusted correctly for 77% of video shots. Further, the quality of the video shot sequence created by using the proposed interface improved greatly after mixing music clips and audio volume adjustment from 1.7 to 3.9 in the scale of 1-5, which was similar improvement to professionally created video shot sequence. Although there is more space for improvement in the interface, the suggestions provided on the interface were subjectively evaluated useful in creating a video remix, especially the template and the suggestions of video clips. These experimental results all indicated the effectiveness of the example-based approach even with a limited number of video remix examples. As a future work, larger-scale experiments are necessary with larger number of various types of original video clips and video remix examples and by larger number of subjects.

Acknowledgment

This research was partially supported by a Grant-in-Aid for Young Scientists (B) 20700087 from JSPS and by Core Project from Microsoft Institute for Japanese Academic Research Collaboration. The authors would like to thank Jang-il Kim and Konomi Yoshida for their contributions to the development of the system.

10. REFERENCES

[1] A. Girgensohn, J. Boreczky, P. Chiu, J. Doherty, J. Foote, G. Golovchinsky, S. Uchihashi, and L. Wilcox. A semi-automatic approach to home video editing. In *Proc. ACM Symp. on User Interface Software and Technology*, pages 81–89, 2000.

[2] Adobe Premiere Pro CS5. `http://www.adobe.com/products/premiere/`.

[3] Windows Live Movie Maker. `http://windowslive.com/desktop/moviemaker/`.

[4] A. Girgensohn, S. Bly, F. Shipman, J. Boreczky, and L. Wilcox. Home video editing made easy - balancing automation and user control. In *Proc. Int'l Conf. on Human-Computer Interaction*, pages 464–471, 2001.

[5] M. Davis. Editing out video editing. *IEEE Multimedia*, 10(2):2–12, 2003.

[6] X.-S. Hua, Z. Wang, and S. Li. Lazycut - content-aware template-based video authoring. In *Proc. ACM Int'l Conf. on Multimedia*, pages 792–793, 2005.

[7] H. Sundaram and S.-F. Chang. Condensing computable scenes using visual complexity and film syntax analysis. In *Proc. IEEE Int'l Conf. on Multimedia and Expo*, pages 389–392, 2001.

[8] M. Kumano, Y. Ariki, K. Shunto, and K. Tsukada. Video editing support system based on video content analysis. In *Proc. Asian Conf. on Computer Vision*, pages 628–633, 2002.

[9] Y. Li and C.-C. J. Kuo. *Video Content Analysis Using Multimodal Information: For Movie Content Extraction, Indexing and Representation.* Kluwer Academic Publishers, 2003.

[10] N. Nitta and N. Babaguchi. Example-based video remixing. *Multimedia Tools and Applications*, 51(2):649–673, 2011.

[11] N. Nitta and N. Babaguchi. Example-based home video remixing. In *Proc. IEEE Int'l Conf. on Multimedia and Expo*, 2011.

[12] L. Canini, S. Benini, and R. Leonardi. Interactive video mashup based on emotional identity. In *Proc. European Signal Processing Conf.*, pages 1499–1503, 2010.

[13] X.-S. Hua, L. Lu, and H.-J. Zhang. Automatic music video generation based on temporal pattern analysis. In *Proc. ACM Int'l Conf. on Multimedia*, pages 472–475, 2004.

[14] J. Wang, C. Xu, E. Chung, L. Duan, K. Wan, and Q. Tian. Automatic generation of personalized music sports video. In *Proc. ACM Int'l Conf. on Multimedia*, pages 735–744, 2005.

[15] J.-C. Yoon, I.-K. Lee, and S. Byun. Automated music video generation using multi-level feature-based segmentation. *Multimedia Tools and Applications*, 41(2):197–214, 2009.

[16] P. Mulhem, M. S. Kankanhalli, J. Yi, and H. Hassan. Pivot vector space approach for audio-video mixing. *IEEE Multimedia*, 10(2):28–40, 2003.

[17] M. Cristani, A. Pesarin, C. Drioli, V. Murino, A. Roda, M. Grapulin, and N. Sebe. Toward an automatically generated soundtrack from low-level cross-modal correlations for automotive scenarios. In *Proc. ACM Int'l Conf. on Multimedia*, pages 551–559, 2010.

[18] Y. Kurihara, N. Nitta, and N. Babaguchi. Automatic appropriate segment extraction from shots based on learning from example videos. In *Proc. Pacific-Rim Symp. on Image and Video Technology*, pages 1082–1093, 2009.

[19] H. Zettl. *Sight Sound Motion: Applied Media Aesthetics.* Wadsworth Publishing, third edition, 1999.

[20] Z. Rasheed, Y. Sheikh, and M. Shah. On the use of computable features for film classification. *IEEE Trans. on Circuits and Systems for Video Technolgy*, 15(1):52–64, 2005.

[21] L. R. Rabiner. A tutorial on hidden markov models and selected applications in speech recognition. In *Proc. IEEE*, volume 77, pages 257–285, 1989.

[22] D. Whitley. A genetic algorithm tutorial. *Statistics and Computing*, 4:64–85, 1994.

[23] MixMeister BPM Analyzer. `http://www.mixmeister.com/bpmanalyzer/bpmanalyzer.asp`.

[24] T. Li, M. Ogihara, and Q. Li. A comparative study on content-based music genre classification. In *Proc. Int'l ACM SIGIR Conf. on Research and Development in Information Retrieval*, pages 282–289, 2003.

[25] P. Dunker, S. Nowak, A. Begau, and C. Lanz. Content-based mood classification for photos and music: A generic multi-modal classification framework and evaluation approach. In *Proc. Int'l Conf. on Multimedia Information Retrieval*, pages 97–104, 2008.

[26] P. Dunker, C. Dittmar, A. Begau, S. Nowak, and M. Gruhne. Semantic high-level features for automated cross-modal slideshow generation. In *Proc. Int'l Workshop on Content-Based Multimedia Indexing*, pages 144–149, 2009.

[27] K. Suzuki, H. Yamada, and S. Hashimoto. A similarity-based neural network for facial expression analysis. *Pattern Recognition Letters*, 28(9):1104–1111, 2007.

[28] H. Jiang, J. Bai, S. Zhang, and B. Xu. Svm-based audio scene classification. In *Proc. Int'l Conf. on Natural Language Processing and Knowledge Engineering*, pages 131–136, 2005.

[29] Y. Lavner and D. Ruinskiy. A decision-tree-based algorithm for speech/music classification and segmentation. *EURASIP J. on Audio, Speech, and Music Processing*, 2009, 2009.

[30] T. Mei, C.-Z. Zhu, H.-Q. Zhou, and X.-S. Hua. Spatio-temporal quality assessment for home videos. In *Proc. ACM Int'l Conf. on Multimedia*, pages 439–442, 2005.

[31] The International Movie Database. `http://www.imdb.com/`.

[32] Soundtracknet, The Art of Film and Television Music. `http://www.soundtrack.net/`.

Towards Low Bit Rate Mobile Visual Search with Multiple-Channel Coding

Rongrong Ji[⋆†♯]
[⋆]Peking University,
Beijing, 100871, China
rrji@pku.edu.cn

Ling-Yu Duan[⋆], Jie Chen[⋆]
[⋆]Peking University,
Beijing, 100871, China
{lingyu,cjie}@pku.edu.cn

Hongxun Yao[†]
[†]Harbin Institute of Technology,
Harbin, 150001, China
yhx@vilab.hit.edu.cn

Yong Rui[‡]
[‡]Microsoft China
Beijing, 100190, China
yongrui@microsoft.com

Shih-Fu Chang[♯]
[♯]Columbia University
New York, 10027, USA
sfchang@ee.columbia.edu

Wen Gao[⋆†]
[⋆]Peking University
Beijing, 100871, China
wgao@pku.edu.cn

ABSTRACT

In this paper, we propose a multiple-channel coding scheme to extract compact visual descriptors for low bit rate mobile visual search. Different from previous visual search scenarios that send the query image, we make use of the ever growing mobile computational capability to directly extract compact visual descriptors at the mobile end. Meanwhile, stepping forward from the state-of-the-art compact descriptor extractions, we exploit the rich contextual cues at the mobile end (such as GPS tags for mobile visual search and 2D barcodes or RFID tags for mobile product search), together with the visual statistics at the reference database, to learn multiple coding channels. Therefore, we describe the query with one of many forms of high-dimensional visual signature, which is subsequently mapped to one or more channels and compressed. The compression function within each channel is learnt based on a novel robust PCA scheme, with specific consideration to preserve the retrieval ranking capability of the original signature. We have deployed our scheme on both iPhone4 and HTC DESIRE 7 to search ten million landmark images in a low bit rate setting. Quantitative comparisons to the state-of-the-arts demonstrate our significant advantages in descriptor compactness (with orders of magnitudes improvement) and retrieval mAP in mobile landmark, product, and CD/book cover search.

Categories and Subject Descriptors

H.4 [**Information Systems Applications**]: Miscellaneous; I.4 [**Image Processing and Computer Vision**]: [Scene Analysis, Object recognition]

General Terms

Algorithms, System, Measurement

*Area chair: Marcel Worring

MM'11, November 28–December 1, 2011, Scotsdale, Arizona, USA.

Keywords

Mobile Visual Search, Compact Descriptor, Contextual Learning, Wireless Communication, Data Compression

1. INTRODUCTION

Handheld mobile devices, such as smart camera phones, have great potential for emerging mobile visual search and augmented reality applications, such as location recognition, scene retrieval, product search, or CD/book cover search. In real-world mobile visual search applications, the reference database typically has millions of images and can only be stored on the remote server(s). Therefore, online querying involves transferring the query image from the mobile device to the remote server. This query delivery is often over a relatively slow wireless link. As a result, the quality of the user experience heavily depends on how much information has to be transferred. This issue becomes even more crucial when we move towards streaming augmented reality applications.

Indeed, this time consuming query delivery is often unnecessary, since the server only performs similarity search rather than query image reconstruction. With the ever growing computational power on mobile devices, recent works have proposed to directly extract compact visual descriptor(s) from the query image on the mobile end [1][2][3][4][5], and then send this descriptor over the wireless link with a low bit rate. This descriptor is expected to be compact, discriminative, and meanwhile efficient in extraction to reduce overall query delivery latency. In particular, the research, development, and standardization of compact descriptors for visual search are involving big industry efforts from Nokia, Qualcomm, Aptina, NEC, *etc.* [6].

Aside from low latency wireless query delivery, the direct extraction of compact descriptors on the mobile end may also lighten the overcrowding network communication in the remote server infrastructure. Different from processing textual queries, the online visual search systems face a bandwidth challenge when simultaneously receiving tens of thousands of image queries. How to optimize the bandwidth consumption for scalable visual search remains yet to be explored. On the other hand, a mobile device is constrained by the energy of the battery, hence saving energy is critical. However, sending the entire image or high-dimensional signature throughout 3G network connections will result in serious energy consumption. On the contrary, as quanti-

Figure 1: The developed mobile visual search system with Multiple-channel Coding based compact Visual Descriptor (MCVD). Our system is deployed in both the HTC DESIRE G7 and the iPhone4 smart phones, working for applications such as mobile landmark search, mobile product search, and mobile CD/Book cover search.

tatively reported in this paper, it is more power saving to extract and send a very compact descriptor instead.

Towards low bit rate mobile visual search, previous local descriptors *e.g.* SIFT [7], SURF [8], and PCA-SIFT [9] are *over size*: Sending hundreds of such local descriptors typically costs over the size of the original image. On the other hand, aiming for zero latency wireless query delivery, the state-of-the-art compact local descriptors [2][3] are still not compact enough. For instance, to the best of our knowledge, the state-of-the-art CHoG descriptor [2] still involves $50 \times n$ bits, where n is the number of local features per image, typically over hundreds. Intuitively, a possible extremely "compact" solution seeks to compress these local descriptors into a Bag-of-Words (BoW) histogram [1]. But to maintain sufficient discriminability, the BoW histogram typically involves over thousands of codewords (as demonstrated in most existing works [1][2][10]), which degrades the compactness potential of the sent descriptor.

We argue that such a high-dimensional image signature (*e.g.* BoW histogram) can be further compressed, without any serious loss in its search performance. Given the state-of-the-art effective high-dimensional image signatures, we aim to learn a compression function to further convert these signatures into an extremely compact descriptor (say, hundreds of bits) at the mobile end. Our main idea is to exploit the rich contextual cues inherent to the mobile end (*e.g.* GPS, 2D barcode, or RFID tags) to supervise the design of descriptor compression, which can significantly reduce the descriptor size[1] by a supervised compression function learning to preserve the ranking capability of the raw high-dimensional signature.

We propose a **M**ultiple-channel **C**oding based compact **V**isual **D**escriptor (**MCVD**) to achieve the above goal. The MCVD consists of both offline learning and online extraction phases: Its offline learning involves learning an optimal channel division, as well as an optimal descriptor compression with respect to each channel:

- The channel division adaptively maps each reference database image into its best-matched "channel", either based on its contextual cues (*e.g.* GPS) or based solely on its visual statistics (*e.g.* BoW or GIST).
- Within each channel, we introduce a supervised robust PCA scheme for descriptor compression, with two contributions: (1) it captures the main visual statistics within reference images in this channel by a low rank matrix recovery, which filters out indiscriminative object appearances from the BoW histograms within this channel (*e.g.* intruding foreground objects and irrelevant background trees in landmark search, background clutters in product search); (2) it incorporates the ranking precision loss of these reference images to supervise the dimension reduction procedure, which preserves the retrieval capability of the original BoW.

The online extraction of MCVD converts an initial high-dimensional visual signature (*e.g.* BoW histogram) into a compact descriptor, typically hundreds of bits for zero-latency wireless transferring. It consists of two steps:

- map the query image into its corresponding channel based on either its visual statistics, or its related contextual cues, or both;
- compress the visual signature using a channel-specific function to transform the high dimensional signature into a low-dim, hit/non-hit binary code.

Finally, the MCVD outputs a compact, discriminative, and channel-specific binary code sequence with further entropy coding. It is decoded to regenerate the original BoW again at the server end. In essence, MCVD undergoes a sort of lossy compression but still preserves a high search precision with extremely small amount of bits, which can incorporate the contextual supervision into both the channel division and the compression learning stages.

Taking mobile landmark search for instance, we maintain a visual vocabulary of moderate size to search worldwide landmarks: Once a mobile user enters a given city, the server alerts the mobile to receive a downstream adaption (*e.g.* the channel division function with multiple intra-channel compression functions) to "teach" the mobile how to adaptively extract MCVD in this city. In online search, the mobile device firstly extracts an original high-dimensional descriptor, and compresses it into a compact MCVD descriptor for delivery. Figure 2 shows our scheme with contributions in the following three-fold:

(1) the extracted visual descriptor is extremely compact (*e.g.* typically 100 bits per query in landmark search). Comparing with the widely used BoW for mobile visual search, we achieve almost identical mAP at an 1:4000 compression rate. Comparing with the state-of-the-art CHoG descriptors [2], we achieve an 1:64 compression rate. Comparing with sending a small-size query image (typically 20KB), we even achieve an 1:1500 to 1:3125 compression rate.

(2) the channel division and intra-channel compression learning merit context aware scenarios, which well exploits the pervasive contextual cues in mobile computing (such as GPS, 2D barcodes, Base station, as well as RFID tags).

(3) in intra-channel compression learning, we pay specific attentions to the computational efficiency and storage feasibility on the mobile end, achieved by an offline supervised robust PCA which uses singular vector decomposition.

We introduce our low bit rate mobile visual search pipeline in Section 2. We then present our channel division and intra-channel compression in Section 3. Section 4 demonstrates our real-world implementations, including mobile landmark search and product/CD/book cover search. The former is validated in a ten million web landmark image database, as well as a landmark search benchmark; while the latter is validated on public available product/CD/book cover benchmarks. Finally, we review related work in Section 5 and

[1]We will show in Section 4 that in some cases it could even improve the search discriminability

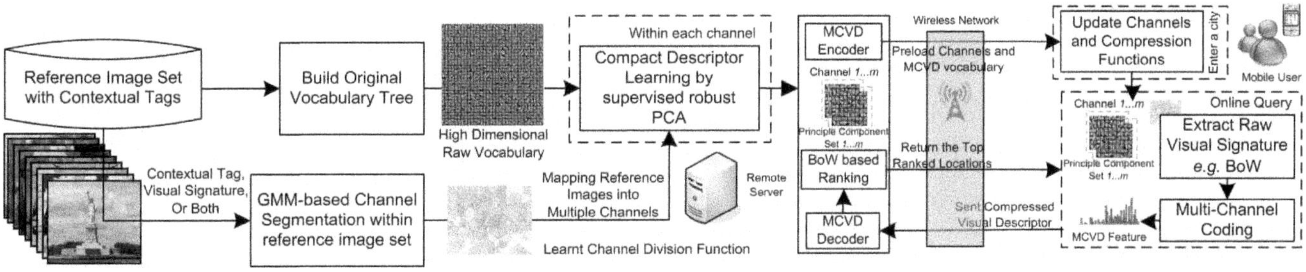

Figure 2: The proposed low bit rate mobile visual search framework using multiple-channel coding. Different from previous works in near-duplicated visual search, this framework emphasizes on extremely compact descriptor extraction directly on the mobile end. Towards zero-latency query delivery, approximate hundreds of bits visual descriptor is typically extracted from each query. To the best of our knowledge, it is the most compact descriptor with comparable discriminability to the state-of-the-arts [1][2][10][11].

discuss future research topics of the low bit rate mobile visual search in Section 6.

2. A LOW BIT RATE MOBILE VISUAL SEARCH FRAMEWORK

The proposed low bit rate mobile visual search framework follows the pipeline in Figure 2: At the mobile end, we extract the raw visual signature (such as local features or a Bag-of-Words histogram) from the query photo and compress (encode) this signature into a very compact descriptor. Instead of sending the query photo, we send this compact descriptor through a wireless link like a 3G network connection or WLAN at a low bit rate. At the remote server, this compact descriptor is decoded to form the raw visual signature, based on which we rank the image similarity using scalable indexing techniques such as vocabulary tree [10]. The key design of the above pipeline is our Multiple-channel Coding based compact Visual Descriptor (MCVD) in Section 3, which in a general sense integrates visual analysis, machine learning, and coding to provide an intelligent functionality in descriptor compression. In this section, we first introduce the pipeline of our low bit rate mobile visual search.

2.1 The Search Pipeline

Our MCVD consists of four phases as in Figure 2:

Step (1): The first phase is a "channel selection" in the mobile end. Its input can be any kind of initial high-dimensional visual descriptors, possibly with context cues. A typical instance is to use the Bag-of-visual-Words (BoW) histogram [10]. By comparing visual similarity, or contextual tag (such as GPS) based similarity, or both, the "channel selection" decides which channel(s) to use for mapping the raw BoW for the subsequent intra-channel compression.

Step (2): The second phase is to encode the raw BoW of an image with respect to the selected channel, which outputs a compact descriptor as our final MCVD result. This descriptor is further compressed into a codeword occurrence (hit/non-hit) histogram with Huffman coding.

Step (3): The encoded signature (with entropy coding), together with its channel identification, are transmitted over the wireless network.

Step (4): In the remote server, the decoding procedure is performed, following the pipeline of Huffman decoding, MCVD decoding, and BoW regeneration. The decompressed BoW is subsequently used for inverted indexing based search. In addition, BoW based spatial re-ranking can be applied, which however involves additional sending and matching the spatial layout coding of interest points [12].

2.2 Raw BoW Extraction with VT

Towards scalable visual search in a million scale database, vocabulary tree (VT) [10] based techniques were well exploited in previous works [1][13][14][15]. VT employs hierarchical K-means to partition local descriptors into quantized codewords. An h-depth VT with b-branch produces $m = b^h$ codewords, and the scalable search typically settles $h = 5$ and $b = 10$ [10]. Given a query photo I_q with J local descriptors $\mathbf{L}(q) = [L_1(q), ..., L_J(q)]$, VT quantizes $\mathbf{L}(q)$ by traversing the vocabulary hierarchy to find the nearest codeword, which converts $\mathbf{L}(q)$ to a BoW histogram $\mathbf{V}(q) = [V_1(q), ..., V_m(q)]$. In retrieval, an optimal ranking is supposed to minimize the following loss with respect to the ranking position $R(x)$ of each I_x (BoW feature $\mathbf{V}(x)$):

$$Loss_{Rank}(q) = \sum_{x=1}^{n} R(x)\ \mathbf{W}_x \cdot (\mathbf{V}(q) - \mathbf{V}(x)) \qquad (1)$$

where TF-IDF weighting is calculated in a way similar to its original form [16] in document retrieval:

$$\mathbf{W}_x = [\frac{n_1^x}{n^x} \times log(\frac{n}{n_{V_1}}), ..., \frac{n_m^x}{n^x} \times log(\frac{n}{n_{V_m}})] \qquad (2)$$

where n^x denotes the number of local descriptors in I_x; $n_{V_i}(x)$ denotes the number of local descriptors in I_x quantized into V_i; n denotes the total number of images in the database; n_{V_i} denotes the number of images containing V_i; $\frac{n_i^x}{n^x}$ serves as the term frequency of V_i in I_x; and $log(\frac{n}{n_{V_i}})$ serves as the inverted document frequency of V_i.

3. THE CHANNEL LEARNING PRINCIPLE

The state-of-the-art visual descriptors are typically high-dimensional and cost large amount of bits in wireless delivery. For instance, the well known SIFT local descriptor is 128×8 bits, which involves $128 \times 8 \times n$ bits per query (with n local features; n typical over hundreds). The state-of-the-art CHoG descriptor also involves $50 \times n$ bits. To further reduce the delivery size, the "bag" of local descriptors can be further quantized into a BoW, followed by a histogram compression such as [1]. However, to maintain sufficient discriminability, the histogram dimension of BoW is at least

10,000 (typically contains 0.1 to 1 million codewords in the state-of-the-art settings), which is against the compactness.

We divide and conquer this issue using *Channel Coding*, which maps each descriptor into a corresponding channel and then compress them correspondingly, making an optimal tradoff between compression rate and discriminability. The learnt channels and coding functions are of small size and can be online downloaded to the mobile or can be also easily pre-installed in the mobile end.

Learning Goal: Given database images $\mathbf{I} = \{I_i\}_{i=1}^n$, we offline extract n m-dim BoW [10][17] $\mathbf{V} = \{V_i\}_{i=1}^n$, typically is with dimensionality $m = 0.1 - 1$ million. All images may be bounded with contextual information such as GPS or base station tags. We aim to (1) learn a channel division function $\mathbf{C} = \{C_j\}_{j=1}^M$ to partition $\mathbf{I} = \{I_i\}_{i=1}^n$ into M channels, where $I_i \in C_j$ denotes I_i is assigned to channel C_j. The division function learning typically involves the contextual supervision *e.g.* GPS tags. (2) learn a codebook $\mathbf{U}_j \in \mathbb{R}_k$ for compact descriptor extraction in each C_j from $\mathbf{V} \in \mathbb{R}_m$, such that $k \ll m$, all of which are either pre-installed, or online updated to the mobile device once the mobile device is assigned to a given channel C_j, for example, the mobile user enters a geographical region.

3.1 Channel Definition

A channel refers to a way to subdivide (partition) the reference database, based on which a raw high-dimensional visual signature (such as BoW histogram) is mapped into one of these channels[2]. Within each channel, this signature is extremely compressed to form a channel dependent compact descriptor. For each database (such as a city scale landmark database or a product/CD/book cover database), there is a channel division function to partition the database images. Each channel has its own compression function. An example of channel constitution is shown in Figure 3.

The channel learning can be based on contextual tags (*e.g.* GPS or RFID) or can be based solely on the visual statistics of the high-dimensional signatures. Even when the original signature is delivered into a wrong channel, this signature is still compressed, but would result in less discriminative but compact descriptors.

3.2 Adaptive Channel Division Learning

Taking mobile landmark search as an example, we assume there are GPS tags $\mathbf{X} = \{x_i\}_{i=1}^n$ available. We then adopt a light but durable Gaussian Mixture Model (GMM) [18] to segment $\mathbf{I}$ into M channels. The geo-tagged database photos are assumed to be drawn from M landmark regions. We denote the ith component as w_i, with mean vector μ_i. We regard the GPS tags $\mathbf{X}$ of those photos belonging to the ith component as generated from the ith Gaussian with mean μ_i and covariance matrix $\sum$, following a normalized distribution $N(\mu, \sum)$.

Hence, we assign the jth photo into the ith channel based on its Bayesian posterior probability:

$$p(y = i|x_j) = \frac{p(x_j|y = i)P(y = i)}{p(x_j)} \tag{3}$$

where $p(x_j|y = i)$ is the probability that the channel (region)

[2]Here, the definition of channel differs from that in communication, which refers either to a physical transmission medium such as a wire, or to a logical connection over a multiplexed medium such as a radio channel.

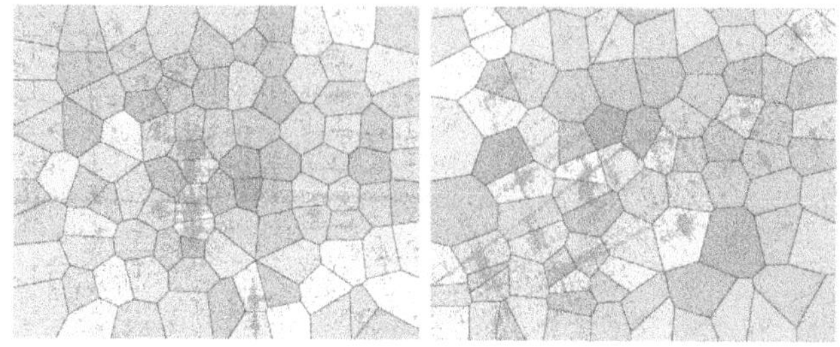

Figure 3: The channel division effects in mobile landmark search. GPS are employed in channel division and selection. In the above subfigures, the green nodes denote the spatial distribution of photos, and the black lines delineate the regions of different channels. The different saturation of red color reflects the length of MCVD. The left subfigure is the channel division in Beijing, the right subfigure is the channel division in New York City.

y of x_j is C_i, which follows the normalized distribution:

$$p(x_j|y = i) = \frac{exp\left[-\frac{1}{2}(x_j - \mu_i)^T \sum_i^{-1}(x_j - \mu_i)\right]}{(2\pi)^{\frac{M}{2}} ||\sum_i||^{\frac{1}{2}}} \tag{4}$$

where $(x_j - \mu_i)$ in such a case denotes the geographical distance between the jth photo and the ith region centroid.

Neither the component parameters nor the channel assignments for photos are known. We adopt an expectation maximization for segmentation: First, we estimate a Gaussian Mixture Model at the tth iteration denoted by (t) as:

$$\lambda_t = \left\{\mu_1(t), ...\mu_M(t), \sum_1(t), ... \sum_M(t), P_1(t), ...P_M(t)\right\} \tag{5}$$

Subsequently, we utilize an Expectation Maximization procedure to learn the optimal Gaussian component assignment $p(y = i|x_j, \lambda_t)$ for each x_j and the optimal Gaussian component parameters (P_i and μ_i) respectively.

In addition, we may lighten the influence of contextual supervision in channel division, since in some cases these tags are unavailable. In such case, the $p(x_j|y = i)$ in Equation 3 is refined based solely on the visual similarity between the jth photo and the ith Gaussian component as:

$$p(x_j|y = i) = \frac{exp\left[-\frac{1}{2}(F_j - F_{\mu_i})^T \sum_i^{-1}(F_j - F_{\mu_i})\right]}{(2\pi)^{\frac{M}{2}} ||\sum_i||^{\frac{1}{2}}} \tag{6}$$

F_j can refer to any easily computed set of visual features *e.g.* GIST or color histogram. In addition, features in Equation 6 can be (if needed) also a normalized combination of both contextual and visual features *e.g.* $< F_j, x_j >$.

3.3 Learning Intra-Channel Compression

To learn an optimal compression function within each channel, we have to address three practical issues: (1) the initial BoW histogram contains lots of irrelevant or noisy codewords, probably arising from intruding foreground objects and irrelevant background objects in mobile landmark search, or background clutters in mobile product search; (2) the storage of compression function should be minimal, for instance it is impossible to store an $1,000,000 \times 1000$ dimension reduction matrix, unless it is really sparse or has low rank (the former can be stored as a sparse matrix, and the latter can be efficiently approximated by using its singular

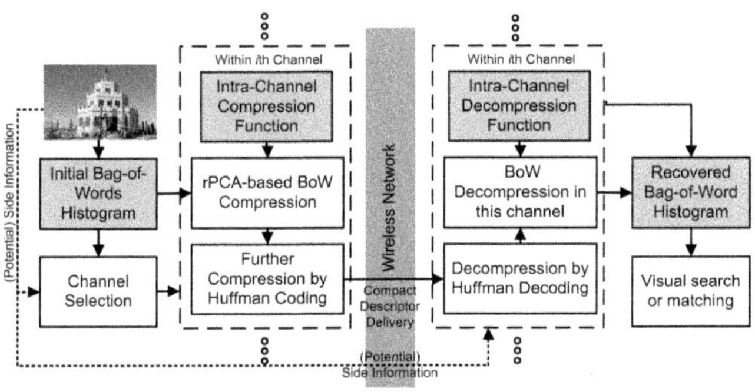

Figure 5: The channel learning principle consists of two phases: The first phase is to learn an optimal channel division based on either contextual information or visual statistics, or both. The second phase is to learn an optimal compression function with respect to each channel, based on the robust PCA learning with (possible) contextual supervision.

vectors); (3) the learnt dimension reduction function should be sufficiently discriminative in search, or in other words can preserve the ranking loss of the original high-dimensional BoW (without any compression) as much as possible.

We achieve the above goals based on a novel supervised robust PCA learning, with three basic considerations: (1) we learn a sparse error matrix to separate the noisy and unrepresentative visual elements from the raw BoW signatures in a given channel, based on which only the most representative and discriminative codewords are preserved; (2) we learn a low rank matrix for PCA extraction, based on which we only need to store the resulting singular vectors in the mobile storage card; (3) we allow to integrate the contextual supervision into the low rank matrix learning, which models the image ranking loss after compression to supervise the robust PCA extraction to preserve its ranking capability.

Ranking List for Learning: Given a channel C containing n' photos $[I_1, I_2, ..., I_{n'}]$, we randomly sample n_{sample} photos $[I'_1, I'_2, ..., I'_{n_{sample}}]$ as queries, which generates the following ranking list for this channel C:

$$\begin{aligned} Query(I'_1) &= [A^1_1, A^1_2, ..., A^1_R] \\ &\cdots \\ Query(I'_{n_{sample}}) &= [A^{n_{sample}}_1, A^{n_{sample}}_2, ..., A^{n_{sample}}_R] \end{aligned} \quad (7)$$

A^j_i is the ith element in the ranked result of the jth query; R is the number of result returned. By compressing the initial BoW, the resulting MCVD descriptor is expected to preserve the ranking order $[A^j_1, A^j_2, ..., A^j_R]$ for the jth query as much as possible. Hence, we inject the above ranking loss to supervise intra-channel learning[3].

Supervised Robust PCA learning: Given in total n_{sample} ranking lists with m-dimensional BoW in each channel, we formulate the original signature matrix as $\mathbf{D} \in \mathbb{R}^{m \times n}$. Typically, there are lots of noisy words in $\mathbf{D}$ from patches like foreground cars, people, and trees (for landmark search), or background clusters (for product/CD/book cover search). These words are meaningless in retrieval and can be modeled as additive errors $\mathbf{E} \in \mathbb{R}^{m \times n}$. Therefore, similar to [19], we consider $\mathbf{D}$ as being generated from a purified, low-rank matrix $\mathbf{P} \in \mathbb{R}^{m \times n}$[4] with an additive error matrix $\mathbf{E}$:

$$\mathbf{D} = \mathbf{P} + \mathbf{E} \quad (8)$$

The solution of the above question can be exactly learnt through optimizing the following loss with $\mathcal{L}_0$ form:

$$Min_{(\mathbf{P},\mathbf{E})} rank(\mathbf{P}) + \gamma||\mathbf{E}||_0 \quad subj\ to\ \mathbf{D} = \mathbf{P} + \mathbf{E} \quad (9)$$

Due to the nonconvex nature of Equation 9, following [19], we relax Equation 9 into the reformulation of the nuclear form of the low rank matrix $||\mathbf{P}||_* = \sum_i^k \sigma_i(\mathbf{P})$ with k singular vectors, together with the $\mathcal{L}_1$ form of the sparse error matrix $\mathbf{E}$. We then approximate the optimal $\mathbf{P}$ and $\mathbf{E}$ as:

$$Min_{(\mathbf{P},\mathbf{E})} ||\mathbf{P}||_* + \gamma||\mathbf{E}||_1 \quad subj\ \mathbf{D} = \mathbf{P} + \mathbf{E} \quad (10)$$

where $||\mathbf{P}||_* + \gamma||\mathbf{E}||_1$ is the convex envelope of $rank(\mathbf{P}) + \gamma||\mathbf{E}||_0$. As stated in [19], for almost all pairs $(\mathbf{P}_0; \mathbf{E}_0)$ consisting of a low-rank matrix $\mathbf{P_0}$ for compression matrix learning and a sparse matrix $\mathbf{E}_0$ for error removal, there is a uniquely definite minimizer:

$$\begin{aligned} (\mathbf{P}_0, \mathbf{E}_0) = \arg Min_{(\mathbf{P},\mathbf{E})} ||\mathbf{P}||_* + \gamma||\mathbf{E}||_1 \\ subj \quad \mathbf{D} = \mathbf{P} + \mathbf{E} \end{aligned} \quad (11)$$

Following the setting of [19], we also have $\gamma = m^{-\frac{1}{2}}$. Then the PCA is learnt from $\mathbf{P}$ by calculating a singular value decomposition matrix $\mathbf{M}_{m \times k}$ with k singular vectors to represent the original m dimensional signature. Such PCA decompositions subsequently produce the new $\mathbf{U}$ based on $\mathbf{U} = \mathbf{M}^T\mathbf{P}$, where $\mathbf{M}$ is built upon k singular vectors of $\mathbf{P}$. Subsequently, we only store the k singular vectors $\{\sigma'_i\}_{i=1}^k$ of $\mathbf{U}$ ($k \leq rank(\mathbf{U})$) on the mobile to compress BoW $\mathbf{V}$.

Beyond [19], we further incorporate the ranking loss into our objective function. Such loss comes from whether or not the learnt dimension reduction matrix ($M_{m \times k}$ from $\mathbf{P}$) can preserve the ranking list $[A^j_1, ..., A^j_R]$ for the jth query. To quantize this, we penalty the ranking loss for ith transformed BoW $\mathbf{U} \in \mathbb{R}_k$ from $\mathbf{V}_m\mathbf{M}_{m \times k}$:

$$\begin{aligned} &Loss(I'_i, \mathbf{P}) = \\ &\sum_{r=1}^{R} R(A^i_r)\mathbf{W}_{A^i_r}||\mathbf{M}\mathbf{U}_j(I'_i), \mathbf{V}(A^i_r)||_{L2} \end{aligned} \quad (12)$$

where $i \in [1, n_{sample}]$; $R(A^i_r)$ is the position of rth returning for ith query I'_i. The overall ranking loss $Loss_{Rank}\mathbf{P}$ is:

$$\sum_{i=1}^{n_{sample}} \sum_{r=1}^{R} R(A^i_r)\mathbf{W}_{A^i_r} \cdot (\mathbf{M}^{t-1}\mathbf{U}_j(I'_i) - \mathbf{V}(A^i_r)) \quad (13)$$

The ideal compression in a given channel C is then formulated as the low rank recovery of $\mathbf{P}$, with respect to the sparse error matrix $\mathbf{E}$ together with the ranking loss, where the compromising parameter θ controls both factors:

$$\begin{aligned} Min_{(\mathbf{P},\mathbf{E})} ||\mathbf{P}||_* + \gamma||\mathbf{E}||_1 + \theta Loss_{Rank}\mathbf{P} \\ subj \quad \mathbf{D} = \mathbf{P} + \mathbf{E} \end{aligned} \quad (14)$$

Optimization Procedure: Similar to [19], we adopt the proximal gradient approach in [20] to learn the optimal low-rank matrix $\mathbf{P_0}$ and a sparse matrix $\mathbf{E}_0$. In that sense,

[3]In the future, active sensing techniques can be also considered to sample queries for the subsequent learning.

[4]Our learning does not target at absolute low rank recovery of $\mathbf{P}$, instead our goal is to preserve the loss of ranking list distortions with the lowest number of singular vectors of $\mathbf{P}$.

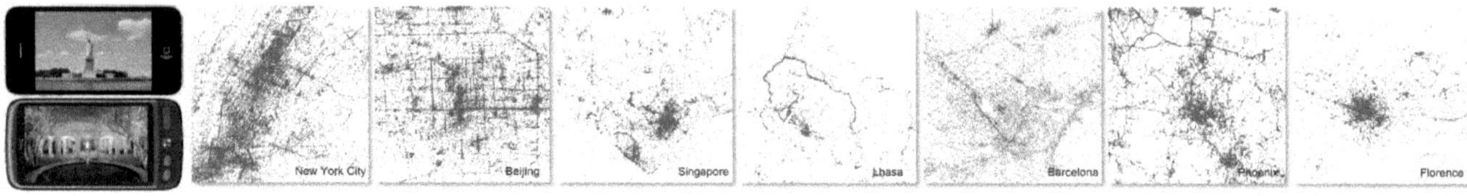

Figure 4: (a) Implementation platform of iPhone4 and HTC DESIRE G7; (b) Geographical photo distribution of *10MLandmarkWeb* in New York City, Beijing, Singapore, Lhasa, Barcelona, Phoenix, and Florence.

Table 1: Mobile memory (mb) and time (second) comparison (MCVD is with a vocabulary tree pruning to further reduce the storage space).

	Local Feature	BoW Generate	Mapping & Compression	Memory Cost
BoW	1.2s	0.14s	N/A	59MB(H=5, B=10)
MCVD	1.2s	0.038s	~ 0	0.69MB $\sim$ 3.44MB

the algorithm has a theoretical convergence rate of $O(t^{-2})$ where t is the iteration number. In each iteration, a Singular Value Decomposition is first calculated, then both $||\mathbf{P}||_*$ and loss in Equation 14 are evaluated. Learning is converged or stopped once the convergence rate is small enough, or the iteration reaches a given threshold (typically < 100)[5].

We summarize the input/output and pipeline of our rPCA based compression as three steps (for a higher-level search procedure please refer to Section 2.1): (1) Offline learn supervised rPCA and store the k principle components within each channel, which is online updated to the mobile; (2) Given an m-dim BoW histogram V extracted from the I_Q, the mobile device calculates the k principle components and binarizes them into k-bit hit/non-hit. (3) The k-bit MCVD descriptor is sent to the server, where the m-dim BoW is restored in a lossy manner.

Inter-Channel Coding: To address marginal queries or queries assigned to wrong channels, we may prefer to compress the raw signature by leveraging multiple channels, which is referred to *Inter-Channel Coding*, simulated to the Greedy N-Best Paths [15] in VT. Note that in such case, the resulting descriptor is in general N times larger than the single channel coding. In the remote server, the descriptor decoding follows a late fusion principle, which fuses the ranking list based on different decoded descriptors.

4. EXPERIMENTAL VALIDATIONS

Data Collection and Ground Truth Labeling: We have validated our proposed Multiple-channel Compact Visual Descriptor (MCVD) on both mobile landmark search and mobile product, CD/book cover search tasks. Our evaluations are conducted on the three following datasets:

(1) *he en Million Landmar images crawled from the eb (10MLandmar eb)*: We have collected over ten million geographical tagged photos from both Flickr and Paranomia using their APIs. Our photo collection covers the following seven cities: New York City, Beijing, Singapore, Lhasa, Barcelona, Phoenix, and Florence. In each city, to label the queries and their ground truths, we choose the 30 most dense regions and 30 random regions from its geographical map. For each region, we ask volunteers to manually identify one or more dominant views. Then, all near-duplicated photos to a given view are picked out in both the current region and its nearby regions. Finally, we randomly sample 5 labeled photos from each region as the query, which forms 300 queries in total with ground truths in each city.

(2) *he U landmar Benchmar (UBench)*: We also test our MCVD on the publicly available mobile landmark search benchmark dataset (the largest) from MPEG CDVS requirement subgroup [21], which contains 13,179 scene photos, organized into 198 landmark locations from the Peking University Campus. There are in total 6193 photos captured from professional cameras (SONY DSC-W290, Samsung Techwin <Digimax S830 / Kenox S830>, *etc.* with resolution 2592×1944) and 6986 from phone cameras (Nokia E72-1, HTC Desire, Nokia 5235, *etc.* with resolution 640×480, 1600×1200 and 2048×1536) respectively. Over 20 volunteers are involved in data acquisition, and each landmark is captured by a pair of volunteers: One using a professional camera and the other using a mobile phone, with a portable GPS. The average viewing angle variations are 10 degrees in nearby photos. Both blurring and shaking are more frequent occur in the mobile phone. There are 381 mobile queries from 198 landmarks (each contains 2 images), 33 reference images on average for each query. Each image in the reference list must be visually and truly matched against at least one of the queries of that object.

(3) *he roduct and CD/boo Cover Database (CBD)* contains Stanford mobile visual search database [22], UK-Bench near-duplicated benchmark [10], and a book cover dataset collected by the authors. Each product/CD/book has a category tag, which in practice could be acquired in the mobile device through 2D barcode, logo, or RFID, *etc.* However, to simplify more targeted evaluation, we leverage PCBD for unsupervised channel learning only.

Memory and Time Cost: We deploy our MCVD descriptor on HTC DESIRE G7 and iPhone4, as shown in Figure 4 (a). HTC DESIRE G7 is equipped with an embedded camera with maximal 2592×1944 resolution, a Qualcomm ARMV7 processor with 998.4MHz frequency, a 512M ROM + 576M RAM memory, 4G SD extended storage, and an embedded GPS. iPhone4 is equipped with similar memory setting. Table 1 further shows the memory and time cost of MCVD on the mobile phone. In extracting MCVD descriptor, the most time-consuming job is the local feature extraction, which could be further accelerated by random sampling, instead of detecting interest points [2][7]. Basically, zero latency is a subjective concept, involving time costs of MCVD, query delivery, search, and results returning. MCVD cost is listed in Table 1. Search costs about 30 ms per query. About query delivery, for quantitative and fair comparisons, we prefer the query bit rate, as the exact

[5] It is worth to mention that we target a lossy compression. That is, we aim to learn P with lower rank; meanwhile the negative effects of enforcing low rank learning on the retrieval ranking loss is minimized. Therefore, our learning phase is to find out the compromise between low rank and ranking discriminability. In addition, as BoW is by nature sparse we can assume matrix $\mathbf{E}$ is sparse. The above assumptions have been empirically proved with its amazing performance in real-world settings.

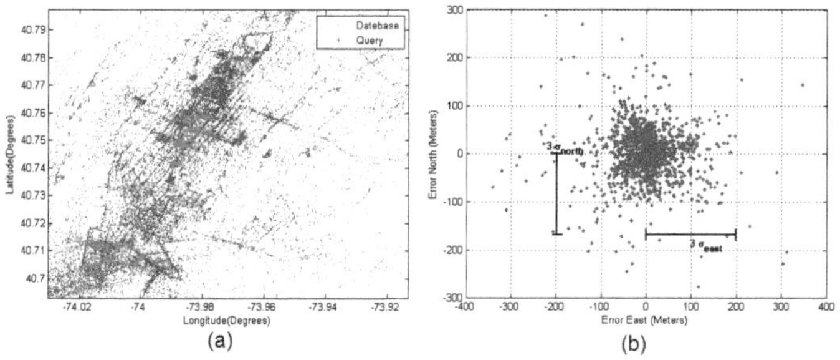

Figure 6: (a) the geographical distribution of the 600 queries in New York City; (b) the geographical error distribution of the search results to these queries (Queries are aligned in the red centroid point).

latency measurement in time heavily depends on the variable wireless connection.

Parameters: We extract SIFT [7] from each photo. A Vocabulary Tree [10] is built to generate the initial vocabulary **V**, which outputs a BoW $V(i)$ for each photo I_i. We denote the hierarchical level as H and branching factor as B. In a typical setting, we have $H = 5$ and $B = 10$, producing approximately 0.1 million words. We maintain an initial identical vocabulary in the mobile end. To reduce the memory cost of VT, tree pruning operation is applied.

For each city (or each application), we learn its channel division and channel coding scheme respectively, which is online downloaded to the mobile device once the user enters a given city (for mobile landmark search), or the user activates the product search functionality (for product search). This downstream adaption costs small bandwidth but brings about great benefits in zero-latency query delivery, involves typically 80KB downstream data and can be downstream in less than 2s in a typical 3G network. In addition, with the channel division, tree pruning may contribute to very small memory cost of the tree as well as efficient quantization as shown in Table 1. Regarding the effects of different channel numbers and marginal queries located near channel boarders, we provide evaluations in "Insights into Channel Learning" and Figure 10 and 11 subsequently.

Evaluation Criterion: We use mean Average Precision (mAP) to evaluate the system performance. Given in total Q queries, mAP is defined as follows:

$$mAP = \frac{1}{N_q}\sum_{i=1}^{N_q}\left(\frac{\sum_{r=1}^{N} P(r)}{\# - of - relevant - images}\right) \quad (15)$$

N_q is the number of queries; N the number of relevant images for the ith query; $P(r)$ is the precision at rank r.

Comparison Baselines: (1) *aw Bag-of- ords*: Transmitting the entire BoW has the lowest compression rate. However, it provides an upper bound in mAP with any BoW compression strategies. (2) *ID hresholding*: As a straightforward scheme, we only transmit the IDs of codewords with the highest IDF values as an alternative solution for vocabulary Compression. (3) *Aggregating Local Descriptors [11]*: The work in [11] adopted aggregate quantization to obtain compact signature. Its output is also a compressed codeword histogram originated from an initial vocabulary V. (4) *ree Histogram Coding [1]*: Chen *et al.* used residual coding to compress the BoW histogram, which is one of the most related works to our channel learning scheme. (5) *ithout Channel Division*: To quantize the advantages

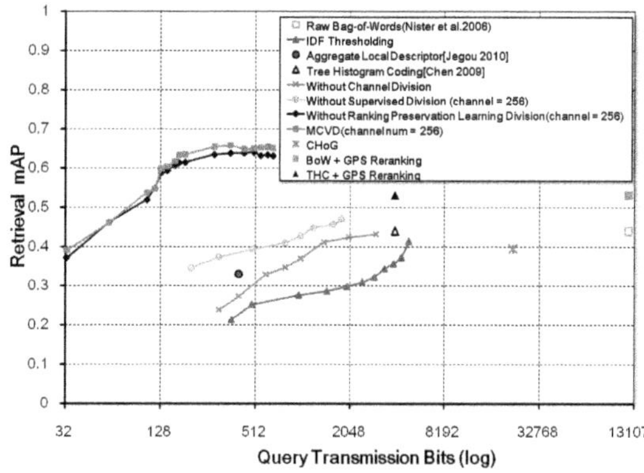

Figure 7: Rate distortion analysis of two typical cases of multiple-channel compact visual descriptor schemes with and without contextual information, with comparison to previous works in [1][2][10][11].

of our channel division, we also degenerate our approach by ignoring any channel division, *i.e.*, performing compression function learning over only one channel within each entire database. (6) *ithout Supervised Channel Division*: We further lighten the need of using contextual supervision in channel division to meet the scenarios of missing any contextual cues. We directly use visual clustering to subdivide each database into multiple channels, based on the L2 distance of the BoW signature of database images. To speed up the division process, only a small subset (sampling less than 10% of reference database images) is used to find out the cluster centroids. (7) *ithout an ing reservation Learning*: We validate our ranking sensitive learning in each channel by removing the ranking cost in compression learning (Equation 14). As a result, we learn the dimension reduction in its original form, capturing only the visual statistics rather than its ranking preservation capability. As shown latter, it would also degenerate the descriptor effectiveness. (9) *CHo [2]*: Finally, we compare our BoW compression based descriptor with the state-of-the-art compact local descriptor CHoG presented in [2].

Rate Distortion Analysis: Figure 7 compares the rate distortion with the state-of-the-arts in [1][2][10][11] in *10MLandmar eb*. We achieve the highest compression rate with equalized mAP distortions (horizontal view), or in other words maintain the highest search mAP with equalized compression rates (vertical view). We achieve less than 256 bits per image. Comparing with the raw high-dimensional BoW, we achieve identical mAP by 1:1,000 compression rate; comparing with the state-of-the-arts [1][2], we achieve 1:64; comparing with sending the JPEG query image (typically over 40 KB), we even achieve 1:2,500-1:3,125 compression rate. We also outperform Baseline (6) and (7) that are without supervised channel division or ranking preservation learning.

Insights into Channel Learning: *Impacts of Channel Number Variations*: One straightforward concern with MCVD might be the proper channel division by using contextual tags as well as the reliance on the context cues. So we provide two groups of quantitative evaluations.

First, we evaluate the impacts of different channel division numbers on MCVD in mobile landmark search. By setting the channel number identical to the database image number, we degenerate MCVD to GPS based location recognition. Figure 9 shows that directly using GPS cannot achieve the

Figure 8: Visualized Examples of the location recognition search results, as well as the product and book cover search results. Left image is the mobile photo query, the right images are the ranking list (the upper line: the ranking results using the initial Bag-of-Words; the lower line: the ranking results using our compact descriptor). The left subfigure shows the product, book search identities.

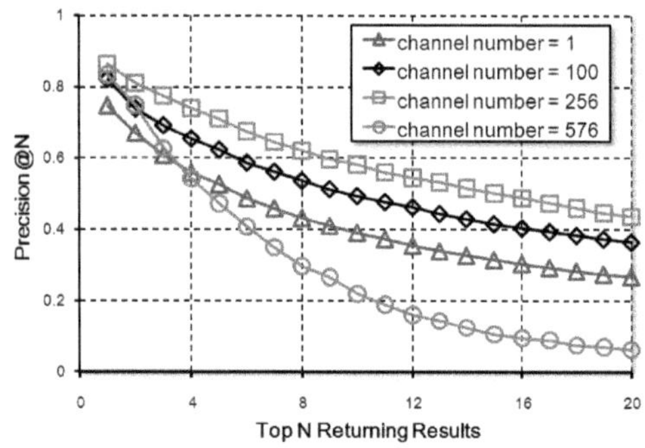

Figure 9: Precision@N with respect to the increasing of channel numbers in New York City. Note that neither too coarse nor too precise channel division is optimal, the later is partially due to some imprecise GPS tags that could result in assigning the test query into mistaken channels.

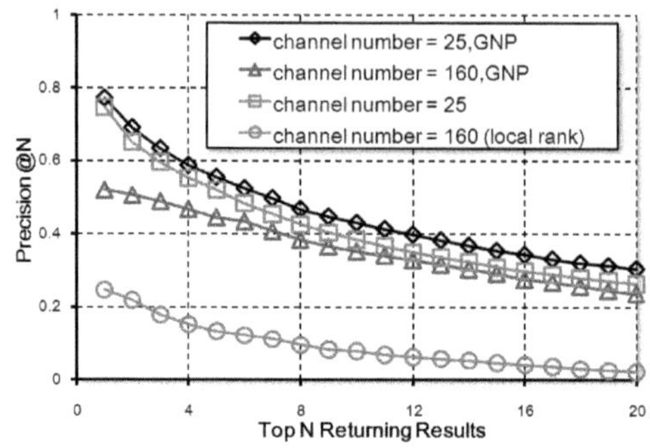

Figure 10: MCVD robustness in PKUBench by (a). adding contextual distractor. (b). for geographical marginal queries. "local ranking" denotes to search images in an individual channel only - seriously affected by marginal queries.

highest performance. One limitation comes from the noisy GPS acquisition, *e.g.* within dense buildings.

Second, without channel division (setting channel = 1), our scheme is degenerated into a solution without any contextual supervision. In such a case, our MCVD has a performance degeneration comparing with the well-tuned channel number (setting channel = 256), which reveals the advantages of contextual cues in helping visual descriptor extraction. In mobile landmark search experiments, given the best-tuned channel number, we have on average 3200 images within a radius range of on average 0.9km in each channel[6].

Channel Division obustness: Our channel division faces another challenge from the marginal queries: It is natural to imagine that the channel division would affect the queries happening at the margin of nearby channels (such as geographical nearby partitions in mobile landmark search). To demonstrate our robustness, we choose a landmark search scenario and sample a set of 100 queries located within 50 meters of channel margins (ten for each channel). Simulating the Greedy N-Best Paths (GNP) [15] in vocabulary search, we also incorporate multiple channels in coding, followed by a late fusion at the client end after getting N ranking lists of images from the N channels (in such case the coding length would be approximate N times larger). However, Figure 10 shows that, even without GNP, considerable robustness is still obtained with the marginal query sampling. Indeed, performance is moderately acceptable comparing with entering the correct channel. It is because we are doing global ranking at the entire image database, rather than doing the local ranking only within the image subset in each channel.

[6]Regarding to the top 1-4 returning, different channel numbers have less negative affects. In practice, we use cross validation to assign a best channel for each scenario

Robustness in Mobile Photographing Scenarios: Based on PKUBench, we evaluate MCVD robustness in five real-world mobile photographing cases. Figure 11 shows the visualized query results as well as the mAP degeneration for each photographing scenario:

(1) *cclusive Query* contains 20 mobile queries and 20 corresponding digital camera queries, occluded by foreground cars, people, and buildings.

(2) *Bac ground Clutters* contains 20 mobile queries and 20 corresponding digital camera queries taken far away from the landmark, probably containing nearby buildings.

(3) *Night and Cloudy Query Set* contains 9 mobile phone queries and 9 corresponding digital camera queries. The night query is seriously affected by the lightings.

(4) *Blurring and Shac ing Query Set* contains 20 mobile queries taken when the phone shacking and 20 corresponding digital camera queries with blurring or shacking.

(5) *Adding Distractors into Database* is to inject a set of distractor photos (6630 photos from Summer Palace provided in [21], visually similar to the landmark buildings in PKUBench) to PKUBench with random GPS tag within PKU compus.

Quantitative Validations in Product Search and CD/book Cover Search: We further validate our MCVD on the Product and CD/book Cover Database (PBDC), including three public available datasets including UKBench [10], Stanford MVS Benchmark [1], and a publicly available Book Cover database. For UKBench and Book Cover database, we sample the first image as the query and use the remaining images to build up the ground truth reference database. For Stanford MVS Benchmark, for each object category a query is matched to one top ground truth in reference dataset. Our method also reports promising mAP comparing with Baselines as shown in Figure 8 and Table 2.

Where the MCVD Codewords are Matched: Figure 12 further investigates where our MCVD descriptor is

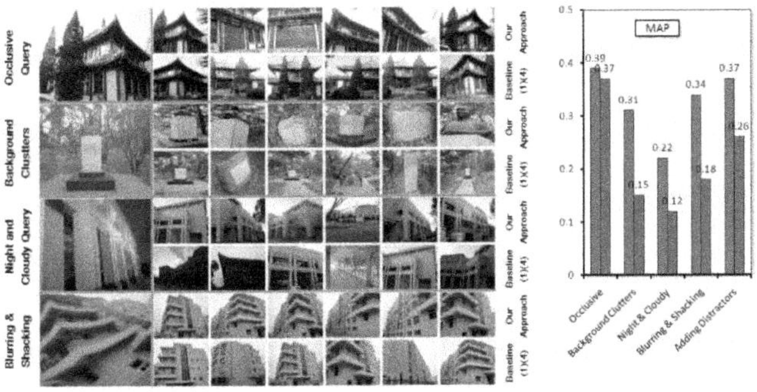

Figure 11: The robustness test of MCVD with respect to (1) Occlusive Query, (2) Background Clutters, (3) Night and Cloudy Query, (4) Blurring and Shacking Query, (5) Adding distractors. We compare our scheme with Baselines (1)(4) (blue bar: MCVD; red bar: BoW).

Table 2: mAP with respect to the compression rate for the product/CD/book cover databases.

	UKBench	Stanford MVS Benchmark	Book Cover
BoW	0.27/14.5KB	0.80/14.5KB	0.485/14.5KB
THS [1]	0.27/0.5KB	0.80/0.5KB	0.485/0.5KB
CHoG [2]	0.26/2.6KB	0.75/3.2KB	0.46/2.1KB
MCVD	0.35/0.4KB	0.88/0.2KB	0.62/200bits

matched from the query image to the database images, in which circles are associated with the matched local descriptors (recovered from MCVD) and different colors indicate different nonzero codewords (quantized from local descriptors). It is easy to see that, our MCVD only preserves a very small subset of local features detected in the query (originally approximate 300-400 features), which are dealt with as the most discriminative features.

Average Energy Consumption: On a mobile device, we are constrained by the battery life. Therefore, energy conserving is critical for mobile applications. One interesting investigation is the comparison of average mobile energy consumption in: (1) extracting and sending compact descriptors, (2) extracting and sending the BoW signature, and (3) sending the original query image. We empirically test the number of image queries the mobile can send before the battery runs out of power for 3G network connection. A typical phone battery has a voltage of 4.0V and a capacity of 1400mAH(or 20.2K Joules). Hence, for 3G connections, the maximum number of images that the mobile can send is 20.2k joules / 52.4 joules = 385 total queries. For the extraction and transmitting of our proposed multiple-channel compact visual descriptor, we would be able to perform 20.2k joules / 8.1 joules = 2494 total queries, which is 6× as many queries as transmitting the entire query image.

Our evaluations in Figure 13 reveals that sending both original query image and the high-dimensional descriptor would cost serious energy consumption, comparing with performing visual descriptor compression on the mobile and then sending the compact descriptor instead.

5. RELATED WORK

Combining with the ever growing wireless Internet services, mobile visual search has offered a wide range of applications, such as location recognition [14][23][24][25][26],

Figure 12: Case study of the spatial matching for our proposed low bit rate descriptors between query (left photo) and the top returning results. Different colors denote different nonzero codewords in the recovered BoW histogram from MCVD.

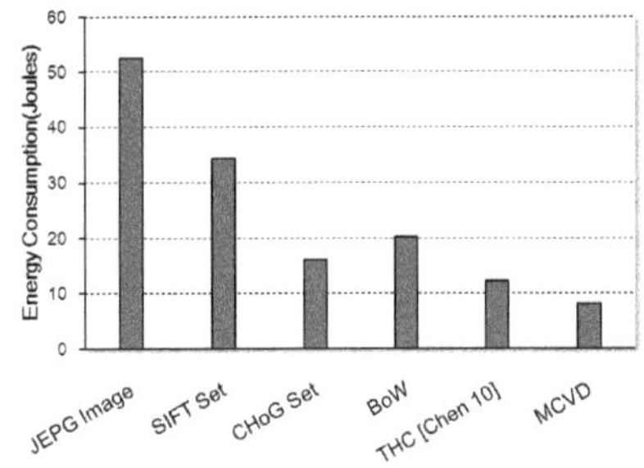

Figure 13: Average energy consumption comparison through the 3G wireless link, between transmitting the entire query image and the extraction and transmitting of MCVD and other compact descriptors.

landmark retrieval [27][28][29] product search, and CD/book cover search [5][10][12]. In general, most state-of-the-art mobile visual search systems are deployed based on approximate similarity matching techniques such as bag-of-words models [10][14][15] or hashing systems, typically with inverted indexing system to be scalable.

Coming with the ever growing computational power of mobile devices, recent works [1][2][3][4][5] have proposed to directly extract visual descriptors on the mobile devices for the subsequent low cost transmission. Although there are previous works in compact local descriptors such as SURF [8], GLOH [30], and PCA-SIFT [9], their compression rates and transmission efficiencies are not sufficient in the context of low bit rate wireless transmission. Consequently, recent works have focused on more compact visual content descriptions [1][2][3][4] that are specially designed for the mobile visual search scenarios.

A representative group of works come from compressing the local visual descriptors [2][3][5][31]. For instance, Chandrasekhar *et al.* proposed a Compressed Histogram of Gradients (CHoG) [2] for compressive local feature description in the mobile device, which adopts both Huffman Tree and Gagie Tree coding to compress each local feature into approximate 50 bits. The same authors in [3] proposed to compress the SIFT descriptor with Karhunen-Loeve Transform for mobile visual search, resulting into approximately 2 bits per SIFT dimension (128 in total). Tsai *et al.* [12] proposed to transmit the spatial layouts of descriptors. While local feature detectors typically extract $\sim 1,000$ points per image, the overall transmission is about 8KB, less than sending the query photo (typically over 20KB).

The recent work in [1] stepped forward by sending the bag-of-features histogram instead of the original local feature descriptors with position difference encoding of non-zero bins, which gained much higher compression rates with only slight loss in discriminability. The work in [1] reported an approximate 2 KB code per image for a vocabulary with 1M words, much less than directly sending the compact local descriptors (more than 5KB to the best of our knowledge). A recent review can be found at [5].

6. CONCLUSIONS AND FUTURE WORKS

In this paper, we present a low bit rate mobile visual search framework towards zero-latency query delivery even using a relatively slow wireless link. Our main idea is to directly extract a compact visual descriptor on the mobile end, with possible supervision from contextual cues such as GPS, barcode, or RFID. To this end, state-of-the-art visual descriptors such as BoW histograms have a relatively high dimensionality although effective. We propose to learn a multiple-channel coding scheme to further compress these high-dimensional signatures efficiently at the mobile end: First, we learn a channel division to subdivide the database images with possible contextual supervision; Second, in each channel, we learn its respective compression function based on a supervised robust PCA, which separates the noisy visual contents in compression, reduces the storage cost at mobile end, and preserves the ranking capability of the original high-dimensional BoW histogram. We evaluate MCVD on a million-scale mobile landmark search system and a mobile product and CD/book cover search system, with applications on Apple and Android cell phones. We report superior performances over the state-of-the-arts [1][2][10][11].

We envision the promising usage of compact visual descriptors in the ongoing industry standardizations and state-of-the-art research efforts, which possibly starts more practical scenarios in real world low bit rate applications. The proposed descriptor as well as the zero-latency search scheme would be at the very beginning of a significant and potentially huge activity, which is towards challenging but exciting research, development, and standardization of mobile search as well as mobile reality augmentation applications.

7. ACKNOWLEDGEMENT

This work was supported by National Basic Research Program of China (2009CB320902), in part by Chinese National Nature Science Foundation (60902057, 61071180) and CADAL Project Program. Correspondence should be addressed to lingyu@pku.edu.cn.

8. REFERENCES

[1] D. Chen, S. Tsai, V. Chandrasekhar, G. Takacs, J. Singh, and B. Girod. Tree histogram coding for mobile image matching. In *DCC*, 2009.

[2] V. Chandrasekhar, G. Takacs, D. Chen, S. Tsai, R. Grzeszczuk, and B. Girod. Chog: Compressed histogram of gradients a low bit-rate feature descriptor. In *CVPR*, 2009.

[3] V. Chandrasekhar, G. Takacs, D. Chen, S. Tsai, J. Singh, and B. Girod. Transform coding of image feature descriptors. In *VCIP*, 2009.

[4] M. Makar, C. Chang, D. Chen, S. Tsai, and B. Girod. Compression of image patches for local feature extraction. In *ICASSP*, 2009.

[5] B. Girod, V. Chandrasekhar, D. Chen, N.-M. Cheung, R. Grzeszczuk, Y. Reznik, G. Takacs, S. Tsai, and R. Vedantham. Mobile visual search. In *IEEE Signal Processing Magazine*, 2011.

[6] Y. Reznik. Compact descriptors for visual search. In *MPEG N11529*, 2010.

[7] D. Lowe. Distinctive image features from scale invariant keypoints. In *IJCV*, 2004.

[8] H. Bay, T. Tuytelaars, and L. Van Gool. Surf: Speeded up robust features. In *ECCV*, 2006.

[9] Y. Ke and R. Sukthankar. Pca-sift: A more distinctive representation for local image descriptors. In *CVPR*, 2004.

[10] D. Nister and H. Stewenius. Scalable recognition with a vocabulary tree. In *CVPR*, 2006.

[11] H. Jegou, M. Douze, C. Schmid, and P. Perez. Aggregating local descriptors into a compact image representation. In *CVPR*, 2010.

[12] S. Tsai, D. Chen, G. Takacs, V. Chandrasekhar, J. Singh, and B. Girod. Location coding for mobile image retrieval. In *MobileMedia*, 2010.

[13] D. Chen, S. Tsai, V. Chandrasekhar, *et al.* Inverted index compression for scalable image matching. In *DCC*, 2010.

[14] A. Irschara, C. Zach, J. Frahm, and H. Bischof. From structure-from-motion point clouds to fast location recognition. In *CVPR*, 2009.

[15] G. Schindler and M. Brown. City-scale location recognition. In *CVPR*, 2007.

[16] G. Salton and C. Buckley. Term-weighting approaches in text retrieval. In *Inform. Proc. and Manage.*, 1988.

[17] J. Sivic and A. Zisserman. Video google: a text retrieval approach to object matching in videos. In *ICCV*, 2003.

[18] C. Stauffer and W. Grimson. Learning patterns of activity using real-time tracking. In *PAMI*, 2000.

[19] J. Wright, A. Ganesh, S. Rao, Y. Peng, and Y. Ma.

[20] A. Beck and M. Teboulle. A fast iterative shrinkage-thresholding algorithm for linear inverse problems. In *SIAM Journal on Imaging Science*, 2009.

[21] R. Ji, L.-Y. Duan, T. Huang, H. Yao, and W. Gao. Pukbench: A contextual rich benchmark for mobile visual search. In *95th MPEG Meeting*. CDVS AD HOC Group Input Contribution, 2010.

[22] V. Chandrasekhar, D. Chen, S. Tsai, N.-M. Cheung, H. Chen, G. Takacs, Y. Reznik, R. Vedantham, R. Grzeszczuk, J. Bach, and B. Girod. The stanford mobile visual search dataset. In *ACM Multimedia Systems Conference*, 2011.

[23] W. Zhang and J. Kosecka. Image based localization in urban environments. In *3DVT*, 2006.

[24] J.-A. Lee, K.-C. Yow, and A. Sluzek. Image based information guide on mobile devices. In *Advances in Visual Computing*, 2008.

[25] J. Philipin, O. Chum, M. Isard, J. Sivic, and A. Zisserman. Object retrieval with large vocabulary and fast spatial matching. In *CVPR*, 2007.

[26] D. Crandall, L. Backstrom, and J. Kleinberg. Mapping the world's photos. In *WWW*, 2009.

[27] J. Hays and A. Efros. Img2gps: estimating geographic information from a single image. In *CVPR*, 2008.

[28] Y. Zheng, M. Zhao, Y. Song, and H. Adam. Tour the world: building a web-scale landmark recognition engine. In *CVPR*, 2009.

[29] X. Li, C. Wu, C. Zach, S. Lazebnik, and J.-M. Frahm. Modeling and recognition of landmark image collections using iconic scene graphs. In *ECCV*, 2008.

[30] K. Mikolajczyk and C. Schmid. Performance evaluation of local descriptors. In *PAMI*, 2005.

[31] V. Chandrasekhar, D. Chen, A. Lin, G. Takacs, S. Tsai, N. Cheung, Y. Reznik, R. Grzeszczuk, and B. Girod. Comparison of local feature descriptors for mobile visual search. In *ICIP*, 2010.

Honest Signals: How Social Networks Shape Human Behavior

Alex Pentland
MIT
Cambridge, MA USA
pntland@mit.edu

Abstract

How did humans coordinate before we had sophisticated language capabilities? Pre-linguistic social species coordinate by signaling, and in particular `honest signals' which actually cause changes in the listener. I will describe examples of human behaviors that are honest signals, and how they can be used to accurately predict and shape the outcomes of interactions (medical compliance, negotiation, trust assessment, depression screening, etc.). Understanding how human decision making is influenced by these pre-linguistic patterns of signaling also leads to very different ways to build incentives to change. In a recent trial we were able to change population behaviors using a social signaling strategy, and achieved twice the efficiency of standard behavior change schemes.

Categories & Subject Descriptors: H.5.1 Multimedia Information Systems

General Terms: Measurement, Performance, Design, Human Factors, Theory.

Bio

Alex `Sandy' Pentland directs MIT's Human Dynamics Laboratory and the MIT Media Lab Entrepreneurship Program, and advises the World Economic Forum, Nissan Motor Corporation, and a variety of start-up firms. He has previously helped create and direct MIT's Media Laboratory, the Media Lab Asia laboratories at the Indian Institutes of Technology, and Strong Hospital's Center for Future Health.

Sandy is one of the world's most-cited computer scientists, and a pioneer in computational social science, organizational engineering, mobile computing, image understanding, and modern biometrics. His research has recently been featured in Nature, Science, the World Economic Forum, Harvard Business Review, and the popular press.

MM'11, November 28–December 1, 2011, Scottsdale, Arizona, USA.
ACM 978-1-4503-0616-4/11/11.

Keynote Talk

"U are Happy Life": Telling the Future's Stories

Genevieve Bell
Intel Fellow and Director,
Interactions and Experience Research Intel Labs,
2111 NE 25th Avenue, JF2-78,
Hillsboro, OR 97124, USA
genevieve.bell@intel.com

Categories & Subject Descriptors: H.1.2 [User/Machine Systems]:Human factors; H.5.1 [Information Interfaces and Presentation]:Multimedia Information Systems

General Terms: Human Factors.

Bio

Genevieve Bell joined Intel in 1998 as a researcher in Corporate Technology Group's People and Practices Research team — Intel's first social science oriented research team. She helped drive the company's first non-U.S. field studies to inform business group strategy and products and conducted groundbreaking work in urban Asia in the early 2000s. Bell has been the driving force behind Intel's emerging user-experience focus: over the last decade, she has fundamentally changed how Intel envisions, plans, and develops its platforms.

Bell currently leads an R&D team of social scientists, interaction designers, human factors engineers, and a range of technology researchers to create the next generation of compelling user experiences across a range of internet-connected devices, platforms, and services. She will drive user-centered experience and design across the compute continuum.

Prior to joining Intel, Bell was a lecturer in the Department of Anthropology at Stanford University. She has written more than 25 journal articles and book chapters on a range of subjects focused on the intersection of technology and society. Her book, "Divining the Digital Future," co-authored with Prof. Paul Dourish, will be released by MIT Press in spring 2011.

Raised in Australia, Bell received her bachelor's degree in anthropology from Bryn Mawr College in 1990. She received her master's and doctorate degrees in anthropology from Stanford University in 1993 and 1998, respectively.

MM'11, November 28–December 1, 2011, Scottsdale, Arizona, USA.
ACM 978-1-4503-0616-4/11/11.

Digital Media Distribution – The Future

Arnaud Robert
Senior Vice President
Distribution Technology Group
Walt Disney Studios
Burbank, CA, USA
Arnaud.Robert@disney.com

ABSTRACT

Consumer devices and technologies are evolving faster than ever, allowing for rich, interactive user experiences. But more importantly, media consumption behavior and expectations are changing and the promise of digital media remains to be fulfilled. In this presentation, we will explore major technology trends, consumer trends, and how they intersect with the future digital media experiences and business models.

Categories and Subject Descriptors

A.m [**MISCELLANEOUS**]

General Terms

Human Factors.

Keywords

Digital Media, Technology and Consumer Trends.

Bio: Arnaud Robert is a renowned leader in digital media strategies, and in delivering innovative, cross-platforms consumer products for Disney, Technicolor, Microsoft, Nagravision-Kudelski and various start-ups.

As Senior Vice President of Technology at The Walt Disney Studios, Arnaud guides the Studio through the rapidly changing digital media ecosystem and manages the engineering, product development and user experience teams, as well as the piracy management efforts.

Arnaud received his PhD from the Swiss Institute of Technology and now also serves on the Media Council of the World Economic Forum and is a member of the National Academy of Engineering. Arnaud has 35 issued or pending patents, published over 30 broadly distributed scientific papers, and is a sought after speaker at corporate retreats and public events alike on wide range of topics from the future of digital entertainment to advances in signal processing.

MM'11, November 28–December 1, 2011, Scottsdale, Arizona, USA.
ACM 978-1-4503-0616-4/11/11.

Networking of Multimedia Women Event

Beyond Epsilon Science

"Where to Look and How to Realize New Opportunities"

Organizer and Moderator

Klara Nahrstedt
University of Illinois at Urbana-Champaign, USA
klara@illinois.edu

Speakers

Svetha Venkatesh
Curtin University of Technology, Australia
S.Venkatesh@curtin.edu.au

Nalini Venkatasubramanian
University of California, Irvine, USA
nalini@ics.uci.edu

Panelists

Dulce Ponceleon
IBM Almaden
USA
dulce@almaden.ibm.com

Maria Zemankova
National Science Foundation,
USA
mzemanko@nsf.gov

Susanne Boll
University of Oldenburg,
Germany
Susanne.Boll@informatik.uni-oldenburg.de

SUMMARY

"Networking of Multimedia Women" event is a continuation of an on-going conversation in the multimedia research community and efforts by the ACM SIGMM to engage and promote female researchers in multimedia community, enable networking of junior and senior female researchers, and give insights towards successful professional careers based on examples.

This year, the event will have a theme, called "Beyond Epsilon Science", where preeminent senior female researchers from academia, industry and government, Svetha Venkatesh, Nalini Venkatasubramanian, Dulce Ponceleon, Susanne Boll, and Maria Zemankova will present and discuss how to go beyond epsilon science, where to look for big ideas with high social impact, as well as how to obtain funding to realize these ideas, innovations and opportunities. Their current research projects and funding efforts, and their personal experiences will drive the event's discussions, awareness of major research and funding initiatives, answers to open questions and insights into successful professional careers.

MM'11, November 28–December 1, 2011, Scottsdale, Arizona, USA.
ACM 978-1-4503-0616-4/11/11.

Categories and Subject Descriptors

H.1.2[Multimedia Research]: Multimedia Applications; H.5.1 [Multimedia Interfaces and Presentation]:Multi-modal Situational Awareness, Autism Intervention Technologies

General Terms

.Multimedia Research

Keywords

Multimedia applications, Autism, Emergency Response, Multi-modal Situational Awareness Technologies, Intervention Technologies for Autism, Multimedia Interfaces, Multimedia Scalable Systems, Multimedia Information Gathering

1. Event Introduction

The event "Networking of Multimedia Women", held at the ACM Multimedia 2011, enables continuation of discussion and networking among junior and senior female researchers. The theme "Beyond Epsilon Science" drives the organization of the event. This year, the event starts with two talks that motivate and encourage researchers to look for big ideas and work on research problems that go beyond "epsilon science". The two talks are followed by a panel where panelists and audience engage in a discussion, presenting further major research ideas and initiatives, as well as methods on how to look for such big ideas and how to get them funded. Below we briefly present the talks, the panel and speakers/panelists biographies.

2. Talks and Speakers

The first talk, called "**When was the last time your project made you smile?: Doing Computer Science that builds Social Capital",** is presented by a leading researcher in multimedia processing and professor at the Curtin University, Australia**, Svetha Venkatesh.**

.

In this talk, Professor Ventakesh describes her close encounters in pursuit of early intervention technology for children with Autism Spectrum Disorder. ASD affects 1 in 150 children at an estimated cost of $3.2 million per sufferer, a figure that pales beside the cost to sufferers and parents in anxiety, anger, stress, and depression. Fast and reliable early intervention is critical, but current approaches are laborious and costly, and waiting lists are long. In response, she has partnered with Autism West and psychologists at the cutting edge of therapy to build early intervention software based on evidence-based learning theory that delivers stimulus of increasing complexity and adapts to learner performance. She shows why it changes the landscape of early intervention, and demonstrates the first iPad-based Waitlist program. She describes her journey, its challenges and when it made her smile.

Dr. Svetha Venkatesh holds the Inaugural John Curtin Distinguished Professorship. Venkatesh was elected a *Fellow of the International Association of Pattern Recognition* in 2004 for contributions to formulation and extraction of semantics in multimedia data. She is a *Fellow of the Australian Academy of Technological Sciences and Engineering*. She is on the editorial board of the both premier multimedia journals: *IEEE Transactions on Multimedia* and *ACM Transactions on Multimedia*, and a program member of several international conferences such as ACM Multimedia. Venkatesh has developed frontier technologies in large scale pattern recognition exemplified through 346 publications including 2 books, 12 book chapters, 78 journal and 254 conference publications. She has won over $12.1 million in competitive research funding since 1992. Venkatesh and her colleagues have filed 9 patents, of which 3 are full patents. One start-up company, spun out of these patents is Virtual Observer and based on the paradigm shifting methods that leverages mobile cameras to deliver wide area surveillance solutions. The technology won the Runner up in both the *WA Inventor of the year (Early stage) and Global Security Challenge* (Asia-Pacific) in 2007. A recent spin-out company is iCetana and is based on novel methods to find anomalies in video data. iCetana won the *Broadband Innovation Award* at the prestigious Tech23 in 2010.

The second talk, called "**Multimodal Situational Awareness for Societal-scale Emergency Response**", is presented by a leading researcher in multimedia systems, Professor **Nalini Venkatasubramanian**, from University of California, Irvine, USA.

In this talk, Professor Venkatasubramanian shows how technology and research can help save lives and property by responding effectively to natural and manmade disasters. Situational information is critical in disasters – effective response relies on extracting actionable awareness from multiple sources in crises. Multimedia information sources provide rich content (e.g. speech, audio, images, video, text, social media) regarding the evolving state of the disaster – this information is vital for creating awareness that leads to improved decision making and response. She will describe her research experiences in developing and deploying multimodal situational awareness technologies for emergency response. She will highlight key fundamental scientific research problems and solution strategies for the collection/dissemination of situational content and walk through the process of translating this to validation and deployment of real world system artifacts for the emergency response community. This work opens up new possibilities for the design of resilient, adaptive and scalable societal scale systems of the future.

Dr**. Nalini Venkatasubramanian** is currently a Professor in the School of Information and Computer Science at the University of California Irvine. She has had significant research and industry experience in the areas of distributed systems, adaptive middleware, pervasive and mobile computing, distributed multimedia and formal methods and has published extensively in these areas. As a key member of the Center for Emergency Response Technologies at UC Irvine, Nalini's recent research has focused on enabling resilient, scalable observation and analysis of situational information from multimodal input sources, techniques for dynamic adaptation of the underlying systems to enable information flow under massive failures and the dissemination of rich notifications to members of the public at large. Many of her research contributions have been incorporated into software artifacts which are now in use at various first responder partner sites. She is the recipient of the prestigious NSF Career Award, an Undergraduate Teaching Excellence Award from the University of California, Irvine in 2002 and multiple best paper awards. Prof. Venkatasubramanian has served in numerous program and organizing committees of conferences on middleware, distributed systems and multimedia and on the editorial boards of journals. She received her M.S and Ph.D in Computer Science from the University of Illinois in Urbana-Champaign. Prior to arriving at UC Irvine, Nalini was a Research Staff

Member at the Hewlett-Packard Laboratories in Palo Alto, California.

3. Panel and Panellists

The panel, called "**Beyond Epsilon Science – How to look and How to realize new opportunities**" includes panellists who are senior and preeminent multimedia researchers in the industry, academia and government, Dulce B. Ponceleon from IBM Research - Almaden, USA, Susanne Boll from University of Oldenburg, Germany, and Maria Zemankova from National Science Foundation, USA. The panel is moderated by Klara Nahrstedt from University of Illinois at Urbana-Champaign.

Dulce P. Ponceleon, *IBM Research – Almaden.*

Dr. Dulce Ponceleon is a Research Staff Member at IBM Research - Almaden since 1997, where she currently manages the Content Protection Group. Last year she was a recipient of the 26th Annual Tribute to Women (TWIN) Awards given by the YWCA of Silicon Valley in recognition of women who demonstrate excellence in industry. She is a technical contributor to the content protection standards for Blu-ray, i.e. Advanced Access Content System (www.aacsla.com) and the Technical Chair of 4C (www.4centity.com), a content protection standards for recordable and pre-recorded media. She is a key contributor to 4C's specifications for Secure Digital cards applications. She is IBM's Research Relationship Manager (RRM) for Media & Entertainment. In this role she brings the industry requirements to IBM' research labs world-wide and promotes partnership with other IBM organizations to strengthen and differentiate IBM's offerings. While at IBM she conducted research in multimedia, from multimedia analysis and retrieval to audio and video compression, video summarization, content protection and multimedia security. Previously, she worked at Apple Computer, Inc. where she was a key contributor to the first video & audio codec supported by Apple's QuickTime Conferencing, the first software-only videoconferencing system. Dr. Ponceleon has served in numerous program committees and held workshops, tutorials, and panels in the areas of multimedia and security. She is the author of numerous publications, 19 patents, and a chapter in the text book *Modern Information Retrieval: The Concepts and Technology behind Search (2nd Edition).* She received her M.S. and Ph.D. degrees in computer science from Stanford University. Last but not least she has a passion for mentoring and volunteering to encourage minorities to pursue technical careers.

Susanne Boll, *University of Oldenburg, Germany.*

Susanne Boll is Professor for Media Informatics and Multimedia Systems as Department of Computing Science at the University of Oldenburg, Germany. Also since 2002 she is a member of executive board of the OFFIS Institute for Information Technology (OFFIS) where she is scientific head of many international and national research projects in the field of semantic retrieval and intelligent user interfaces. She is leading the Human-Machine-Interaction Technology Cluster. In 2001, Susanne Boll received her doctorate with distinction at the Technical University of Vienna, Austria and her diploma degree with distinction in computer science at the Technical University of Darmstadt, Germany, in 1996.

Susanne Boll's research interests lie in the field of semantic retrieval of digital media, context-aware and location-based mobile systems, and intelligent user interfaces. She is member of the editorial board of the IEEE Multimedia Magazine and Associate Editor of the ACM Transactions on Multimedia Computing, Communications and Applications (ACM TOMCCAP) and Springer Multimedia Tools and Applications (MTAP). As an active member of the community, Susanne served on program committees for many international conferences and also co-organized several international events. Dr. Boll is an active member of SIGMM of the ACM and GI, and also a member of IEEE Computer Society.

Maria Zemankova, *National Science Foundation.*

Maria Zemankova joined the National Science Foundation (http://ww.nsf.gov) as a Program Director in the Information and Intelligent Systems (IIS) Division in 1988. She has been instrumental in developing initiatives on Scientific Databases, Digital Libraries, and Biodiversity and Ecosystem Informatics, and is currently involved in Information Integration & Informatics Program, Graphics & Visualization, Graduate STEM Fellows in K-12 Education (GK-12) Program and various cross-disciplinary initiatives. Maria likes to "re-new" herself from time-to-time. She spent a year (1993 - 1994) with The MITRE Corporation and a year (2000 - 2001) at the National Library of Medicine, NIH. She is Co-Editor-in-Chief of the Journal of Intelligent Information Systems (http://www.springerlink.com/content/1573-7675/), a member of ACM, AAAI, IEEE, Sigma Xi, and in 1992, she received the ACM SIGMOD Contributions Award.

Klara Nahrstedt, *University of Illinois at Urbana-Champaign*

Klara Nahrstedt is a professor at the University of Illinois at Urbana-Champaign, Computer Science Department. Her research interests are directed towards tele-immersive systems, Quality of Service (QoS) management in wired and wireless networks, and distributed, and pervasive mobile systems. She is the coauthor of the widely used multimedia books `Multimedia: Computing, Communications and Applications' published by Prentice

Hall, and 'Multimedia Systems' published by Springer Verlag. She is the recipient of the Early NSF Career Award, the Junior Xerox Award, the IEEE Communication Society Leonard Abraham Award for Research Achievements, the University Scholar Award, the Humboldt Research Award, and the Ralph and Catherine Fisher Professorship Chair. She was the editor-in-chief of ACM/Springer Multimedia Systems Journal, she was the general co-chair of ACM Multimedia 2006, the general chair of ACM NOSSDAV 2007, the general chair of IEEE Pervasive Computing and Communications (Percom) 2009. Currently, she is the associate editor of ACM Transactions on Multimedia Computing, Communications and Applications, and she is the elected chair of ACM Special Interest Group in Multimedia (2007-2013).

Klara Nahrstedt received her Diploma degree in mathematics and numerical analysis from Humboldt University, Berlin, in 1985. She was a research scientist in the Institute for Informatik in Berlin until 1989. In 1995 she received her PhD from the University of Pennsylvania in the Department of Computer and Information Science. She is the member of ACM and IEEE Fellow.

ACM Multimedia Interactive Art Program: Interaction Stations

David Tinapple and Todd Ingalls
School of Arts, Media and Engineering, Arizona State University, Tempe, AZ, USA

ABSTRACT
The Interaction Stations Exhibit features screen-based, interactive works that align with the new conference themes, and integrate into the physical setting of the conference center. In this paper we describe our motivation for this format, as well as the works selected and larger connections.

Categories and Subject Descriptors
J.5 [Computer Applications]: Arts and Humanities - fine arts

General Terms
Documentation, Arts Research and Practice, New Media Art, Interactive Art

Keywords
Culture, Multimedia Arts, Technology.

1. INTRODUCTION
Developing an art exhibit for a conference such as ACM Multimedia presents several challenges, one of the greatest being how to make the works presented seem integral to the conference experience. Rather than focus on a conceptual theme for the works, we choose to focus on a form that would allow us to place the work in the central space where the conference attendees will see the works throughout the span of the conference and be challenged to interact with them and with each other. The form we selected was screen based works that could be presented on large displays, placed on mobile stands.

Another challenge is attracting work from a wide array of international artists. One major hindrance for an artist working digitally is the transport and setup of equipment, screens, computers, projectors, etc.. In this exhibition, we decided to create a standardized "interaction station" consisting of a large LCD screen, speakers or headphones, and various optional input devices such as microphones, video cameras, or Kinect 3D cameras. With the basic hardware provided, it becomes much simpler and easier for a large number of artists to apply and participate.

2. OVERVIEW OF SELECTED WORKS
We selected 8 works for aesthetic and conceptual reasons as well as suitability for our proposed display platforms. We also selected works that would actively engage conference attendees in a physical interactive experience.

MM'11, November 28–December 1, 2011, Scottsdale, Arizona, USA.
ACM 978-1-4503-0616-4/11/11.

As might be expected, several of the works focus on media authoring, but also overlap with other conference themes.

The Infinite Adventure Machine by David Benqué[1] explores the new capabilities and limitations of storytelling given new technologies, input devices, and artificial intelligence. Using structure extracted from Russian folk-tales, the software allows users to generate narratives based on these fundamental narrative functions.

Irad Lee's *Spamology*[2] makes visible and audible the stories told by our email spam. *Spamology* is a audiovisual work creating a flowing 3D landscape based on 10 years and 2 million individual pieces of email spam. The data is visualized and sonified based on word frequency. The piece reveals what patterns exists in the spam and how these have changed over time.

*Matrice Active,*by Sophie Lavaud (conception-realisation) and Jean-François Jégo (interaction design)[3] is a work that allows the audience to explore an existing painting modeled in 3D. This exploration allows the viewer to manipulate and modify aspects of the painting's elements as well as define different states of the underlying system of composition.

André Sier's[4] piece, *uunnii-galáxias*, develops an interactive exploration of simulated cluster of galaxies spawned from an http database. Users may add new galaxies to the database.

Between Page and Screen, by Amaranth Borsuk[5] and completed in collaboration with Brad Bouse, is a software program and a printed book that contains no text but markers which allow for a type of augmented reality in which poetry is mapped to the surface of the book when viewed through the software.

The Digital Washboard, an installation by Derrick Giscloux[6] implementation by CreArtCom Studio[7], is a human movement driven musical and visual instrument. The interaction is based on the proprioceptive understanding of viewer's gestures.

Part game, part simulation, *.raindrops* by Deborah Schmidt , Martin Herrmann and Brian Eschrich[8] is an installation that uses viewer tracking as well as the ambient soundscape to explore a world of plants and flowers that need to be watered.

Finally, *AV Clash*, by André Carrilho and Nuno Correia, with Gokce Taskan [9] is a work that allows one to created audiovisual compositions that use sounds retrieved from freesound.org and uses the accompanying tags to decide what sounds to loop. The user can throw and knock visual representations of these sounds to create new clashes.

3. ACKNOWLEDGMENTS
We would like to thank the organizing committee for giving us this opportunity and working with us on its realization. We also wish to give special thanks to all who submitted works to the

ACM Multimedia Interactive Arts Exhibit. There were many fine works submitted that were not chosen for reasons of space or format.

4. REFERENCES

[1] www.davidbenque.com

[2] www.iradlee.com.

[3] http://www.sophielavaud.org.

[4] http://s373.net.

[5] http://www.amaranthborsuk.com.

[6] http://derrickgiscloux.free.fr.

[7] http://www.creartcom.eu.

[8] http://raindrops.at-random.de/en/1-10.

[9] http://avclash.com.

Panel

Serious Games

Organizer:

Abdulmotaleb El Saddik
University of Ottawa
elsaddik@mcrlab.uottawa.ca

PANEL OVERVIEW

Video games (digital computer games, short: games) are very popular and successful, both as leisure activity and contemporary information and communication medium in the digital age, and as relevant economic factor and prospering market, not only in the creative industries. Games tackle a diversity of research aspects, e.g. Computer Graphics, AI, Storytelling, interfaces and sensorics, authoring and production, usability and user experience or other ICT and multimedia technologies. Game technology and game techniques are broadly used by other application domains apart from pure entertainment as well. Prominent examples in the field of Serious Games (games 'more than fun') represent games for health, persuasive games, advergames or games for education and training, for instance in the form of multiplayer online games as tool to support collaborative learning settings.

Recently, numerous game-specific conferences – among others the Game Developers Conference (GDC), Future Play, Foundations of Digital Games (FDG), Games for Health or the GameDays – have been established to discuss underlying technology, methods and concepts of Games and Serious Games.

Categories & Subject Descriptors:

H.1.2 [User/Machine Systems]; H.5 [INFORMATION INTERFACES AND PRESENTATION]; K.8 [PERSONAL COMPUTING]: Games

General Terms: Design, Economics, Experimentation, Human Factors.

MM'11, November 28–December 1, 2011, Scottsdale, Arizona, USA.
ACM 978-1-4503-0616-4/11/11.

Further, dedicated game aspects are discussed at well-known, high ranked academic conferences such as the ACM conferences on Computer Graphics and interactive techniques (SIGGRAPH) or about human factors in computing system (CHI), the Artificial Intelligence for Interactive Digital Entertainment Conference (AIIDE), the international conference on computer supported learning (CSCL) or the European conferences on Technology-enhanced learning (EC-TEL) and Game-based learning (ECGBL).

The aim of this panel is to strengthen the tight link between serious games (the game industry and game research) and multimedia technologies (the multimedia community) and to encourage scientists and practitioners from both sides to communicate and profit from each other.

This Panel will open the discussion on serious games from multimedia perspectives and the panellists together with the audience will be discussing the following issues and questions:

Q1: Nowadays, the games industry represents one of the most prospering markets, not only in the creative industries. What do you think was the most significant change in the games industry during the last 20 years from a research/technology point of view?

Q2: Which big research steps regarding games and serious games do you expect within the next 5 years?

Q3: Which multimedia developments/innovations would you consider useful/helpful for the (serious) games industry in the future?

Q4: Which grand challenges do you see in the field of serious games – what are your main contributions?

Q5: How do you see the role of the (serious) games industry for the development and acceptance of new multimedia applications (games, simulations, social networks)?

Panel: Towards Synergy between the Open Source and the Research Multimedia Communities

Pablo Cesar
CWI, the Netherlands
p.s.cesar@cwi.nl

Wei Tsang Ooi
NUS, Singapore
ooiwt@comp.nus.edu.sg

Ben Moskowitz
OVC & Mozilla Foundation
ben@mozillafoundation.org

Zohar Babin
Kaltura
zohar.babin@kaltura.com

Dick Bulterman
CWI and Vrije Universiteit, the Netherlands
dick.bulterman@cwi.nl

Rainer Lienhart
University of Augsburg, Germany
lienhart@informatik.uni-augsburg.de

Robert Richter
Mozilla Foundation
bobby@mozillafoundation.org

ABSTRACT

This panel extends current efforts from the ACM Multimedia 2011 Organization Committee in taking an important step towards open source projects. The panelists include speakers who are among the leading figures from the open source community. The goal is to provide a shared space for discussion and interaction among consolidated and new open source projects and multimedia researchers.

Categories and Subject Descriptors

H.5.1 [**Information Interfaces and Representation**]: Multimedia Information Systems

General Terms

Algorithms, Design, Experimentation, Standardization

Keywords

Open Source Software, Multimedia

Statement

The open source software community has been instrumental in pushing multimedia state-of-the-art advances to millions of end users. The VLC[1] video player, for instance, has an average of 24 million downloads per month. Asterisk[2], an open source telephony software, has often been associated with the rise of VoIP in recent years; and OpenCV[3], a computer vision library, is widely used by government and companies (including Google, Yahoo! and Microsoft) to perform automatic recognition of faces and objects.

OpenCV is an example of fruitful synergy between the research and the open source communities. Rooted at Intel Research Lab, OpenCV receives various contributions from the research community, and it is widely used as an innovation instrument. Unfortunately, it is more an exception, than the norm. There are not many other large-scale open source projects that integrate results from different multimedia research areas (e.g., video search, peer-to-peer streaming). Research groups often develop disjoint, small projects as prototypes for showing specific results. While solid open source projects have emerged from academia and industrial research labs, they often do not reach other researchers as part of their development and user community.

The research community would benefit tremendously with open source projects that allows disparate research groups to contribute to a single software framework, reducing repetitive development effort, and allowing easier evaluation and comparisons among different algorithmic solutions. Managing a large-scale open source project, however, is a challenging task, and we believe the research community can learn many lessons from the successful open source community.

This panel aims to exploit synergy between these two isolated groups (researchers and open source projects), exploring the possible benefits and better understanding the existing challenges. The final goal is to provide a forum for investigating how innovation can be incorporated into existing open source projects or if new open source initiatives are needed in order to better serve the research community needs. We believe a closer exchange between the two groups would benefit both communities. On one hand, open source projects will get the visibility and attention their deserve, possibly attracting contributions from the research community and integrating latest research results into the projects. On the other hand, prominent researchers can learn more about current open source projects they can use as end-users and potentially contribute to; as well as the challenges associated to running successful large-scale open source projects.

This panel extends current efforts from the ACM Multimedia 2011 Organization Committee in taking an important step towards open source projects. The panelists include speakers who are among the leading figures from the open source community. The goal is to provide a shared space for discussion and interaction among consolidated and new open source projects and multimedia researchers.

[1]http://www.videolan.org/vlc/
[2]http://www.asterisk.org/
[3]http://www.opencv.org

MM'11, November 28–December 1, 2011, Scottsdale, Arizona, USA.
ACM 978-1-4503-0616-4/11/11.

Goals

Some of the goals of the panel, listed as questions, are the following:

- What are the current challenges for building open source software projects?
- What are the keys of a successful open source software project?
- How are research innovations being incorporated into open software projects?
- How can the research community get involved and benefit from existing open software projects?
- Would it be beneficial for the research community to work together to develop a large-scale open source software? If so, what are the challenges?

Open Source Projects and Participants

The panel will be hosted by the co-chairs of the ACM Multimedia 2011 Open Source Software Competition, who will act as representatives of the research community and lead the conversation. The intention is to invite leading figures from a number of representative projects that cover most of the areas of interest to the ACM Multimedia community. In particular, the following projects and initiatives will be represented:

OpenCV: OpenCV is a library of programming functions mainly aimed at real time computer vision, developed by Intel and now supported by Willow Garage. This cross-platform library focuses mainly on real-time image and video processing.

Ambulant[4]: The Ambulant Open SMIL Player is an open-source media player with support for SMIL 3.0. It is intended for researchers and developers who want an open-source player upon which they can build higher-level systems solutions for authoring and content integration, or within which they can add new or extended support for networking and media transport components.

[4]http://www.ambulantplayer.org/

Kaltura[5]: Kaltura is a software company based in New York that was founded in 2006. Kaltura's technology allows publishers and content owners to publish, manage, monetize, and analyze their video and other rich-media content. The main components of Kaltura's online video platform are based on open-source software, enabling any site to add advanced video and rich-media capabilities.

Mozilla's Popcorn.js[6]: Popcorn.js is an HTML5 javascript library that allows for integrating the web into video productions. It is an event framework for HTML5 media that utilizes the native HTMLMediaElement properties, methods, and events, normalizes them into an API, and provides a plugin system for community contributed interactions. For media makers, Popcorn.js allows video, audio, and other media to control elements of a web page.

Open Video Alliance[7]: The Open Video Alliance is a coalition of organizations and individuals committed to the idea that the power of moving image should belong to everyone.

Organizers

Dr. Wei Tsang Ooi (National University of Singapore, Singapore) is an Associate Professor at the Department of Computer Science, National University of Singapore. He received his Ph.D. from Cornell University in 2001. After spending a year as postdoctoral researcher at University of California, Berkeley, he returned to his alma mater, National University of Singapore, as a faculty member. He currently leads the NEMESYS research group, looking into various research issues in multimedia systems and networking.

Dr. Pablo Cesar (CWI: Centrum Wiskunde & Informatica, the Netherlands) is a tenure track researcher in the Distributed and Interactive Systems research group at CWI. He received his PhD from the Helsinki University of Technology in 2006. He has (co)authored over 40 articles about multimedia systems and infrastructures, social media sharing, interactive media, multimedia content modeling, and user interaction. He is involved in standardization activities (e.g., SMIL from W3C) and has been active in a number of European projects such as Passepartout, SPICE, iNEM4U, and TA2.

[5]http://corp.kaltura.org/

[6]http://popcornjs.org/

[7]http://openvideoalliance.org/

Job Opportunities and Career Perspective for Fresh Graduates of the Multimedia Community*

Yu-Ru Lin
College of Computer and Science
Northeastern University
Boston, MA 02115
yuruliny@gmail.com

Vincent Oria
Dept. of Computer Science
New Jersey Institute of Technology
Newark, NJ 07102
oria@njit.edu

K. Selcuk Candan
School of CIDSE
Arizona State University
Tempe, AZ 85281
candan@asu.edu

Lyndon Kennedy
Yahoo! Research
Santa Clara, CA 95054
lyndonk@yahoo-inc.com

Dulce Ponceleón
IBM Almaden
San Jose, CA 95120
dulce@almaden.ibm.com

Hari Sundaram
Arts Media and Engineering
Arizona State University
Tempe, AZ 85281
hari.sundaram@asu.edu

Rong Yan
Facebook
Palo Alto, CA 9304
rongyan@fb.com

Roger Zimmerman
Dept. of Computer Science
National University of Singapore
rogerz@comp.nus.edu.sg

ABSTRACT

The future of multimedia community depends on how the community effectively and efficiently recruits, nurtures and retains young talents. Students tends to decide on their majors based on job opportunities and the main question in every student mind while finishing a degree is "which jobs are out there for me?" In this panel, we have gathered people from both academia and industry to discuss job opportunities and career perceptive. The panel will try to basically answer two main questions: (1) Which are the jobs for the fresh graduates of our community? (2) What are the carrier paths in both academia and industry?

Categories and Subject Descriptors

A.1 [**INTRODUCTORY AND SURVEY**]:

General Terms

Human Factors

Keywords

career, academia industry, tenure

1. PANELISTS

K. Selcuk Candan: K. Selcuk Candan is a Professor of Computer Science and Engineering at the School of Computing, Informatics, and Decision Science Engineering at the Arizona State University and is leading the EmitLab research group. He joined the department in August 1997, after receiving his Ph.D. from the Computer Science Department at the University of Maryland at College Park. Prof. Candan's primary research interest is in the area of management of non-traditional, heterogeneous, and imprecise (in particular, multimedia, web, and scientific) data. His various research projects in this domain are funded by diverse sources, including the National Science Foundation, Department of Defense, Mellon Foundation, and various industrial research labs. He has published over 150 articles and many book chapters. He has also authored 9 patents. Recently, he co-authored a book titled "Data Management for Multimedia Retrieval" for the Cambridge University Press and co-edited "New Frontiers in Information and Software as Services: Service and Application Design Challenges in the Cloud" for Springer.

Recently, Prof. Candan served as an editorial board member of the Very Large Databases (VLDB) journal and the Journal of Multimedia. He has served in the organization and program committees of various conferences. In 2006, he served as an organization committee member for SIGMOD'06, the flagship database conference of the ACM and one of the best conferences in the area of management of data. In 2008, he served as a PC Chair for another leading, flagship conference of the ACM, this time focusing on multimedia research (MM'08). He also served in the review board of the Proceedings of the VLDB Endowment (PVLDB). In 2010, he was a program co-chair for ACM CIVR'10 conference and a program group leader for ACM SIGMOD'10. In 2011, he is serving as a general co-chair for the ACM MM'11 conference and is in the executive committee of ACM SIGMM. In 2012, he will serve as a general co-chair for ACM SIGMOD'12. In 2012, he will also serve in the organizing committees of ACM MM'12 and VLDB'12.

Dulce Ponceleón: Dr. Dulce Ponceleón is a Research

*Funding for the Doctoral Symposium was provided by NSF under award number 1138910

MM'11, November 28–December 1, 2011, Scottsdale, Arizona, USA.
ACM 978-1-4503-0616-4/11/11.

Staff Member at IBM Research - Almaden since 1997, where she currently manages the Content Protection Group. Last year she was a recipient of the 26th Annual Tribute to Women (TWIN) Awards given by the YWCA of Silicon Valley in recognition of women who demonstrate excellence in industry. She is a technical contributor and IBM representative to the content protection standards for Blu-ray, i.e. Advanced Access Content System (www.aacsla.com) and the Technical Chair of 4C (www.4centity.com), a content protection standards for recordable and pre-recorded media. She is a key contributor to 4C's specifications for Secure Digital cards applications. She is IBMŠs Research Relationship Manager (RRM) for Media & Entertainment. In this role she brings the industry requirements to IBM' research labs world-wide and promotes partnership with other IBM organizations to strengthen and differentiate IBM' s offerings. While at IBM she conducted research in multimedia, from multimedia analysis and retrieval to audio and video compression, video summarization, content protection and multimedia security. Previously, she worked at Apple Computer, Inc. where she was a key contributor to the first video & audio codec supported by Apple's QuickTime Conferencing, the first software-only videoconferencing system. She received her M.S. and Ph.D. degrees in computer science from Stanford University. She is the author of numerous publications, 19 patents, and a chapter in the text book Modern Information Retrieval: The Concepts and Technology behind Search (2nd Edition). Dr. Ponceleón has served in numerous program committees and held workshops, tutorials, and panels in the areas of multimedia and security.

Lyndon Kennedy: Lyndon Kennedy is a scientist at Yahoo! Labs in Santa Clara, CA, where he investigates techniques for automatically indexing, searching, and managing digital image and video collections. He received a Ph.D. degree in 2009 in Electrical Engineering from Columbia University, where he conducted research in the Digital Video and Multimedia Lab under the direction of Prof. Shih-Fu Chang. He also holds B.S. (2003) and M.S. (2005) degrees, both in EE from Columbia University.

His research has received several awards and honors. He was co-author of a paper awarded the IBM Student Paper Award at ICIP in 2004. In 2006 and 2009, he was co-author of papers nominated for the Best Paper awards at ACM Multimedia and the ACM Workshop on Social Media, respectively. In 2007, he was invited as part of a group of 8 top senior Ph.D. students in the multimedia field to participate in the IBM Watson Emerging Leaders in Multimedia Workshop.

Hari Sundaram: Hari Sundaram is currently an associate professor of media arts and computing, with the School of Arts Media and Engineering, and Computer Science at Arizona State University. He received his Ph.D. from the Department of Electrical Engineering at Columbia University in 2002. He is interested in understanding human activity in physical spaces, as well as in online social networks. In the former, he has investigated the design of immersive multimedia environments for stroke patient rehabilitation. Another way to think about this work: can we design machines to teach human beings specific physical skills that enable them to perform functional tasks? His work on social networks has focused on several broad themes: discovering communities, analyzing communication patterns, behavioral cascades, and design of social games for motivating work. We can use results from the work on community discovery, as an example, several scenarios: sparking innovation in conferences, creating cooperative behavioral cascades as well as in more meaningful information search. His research has won several awards (the best student paper award at JCDL 2007, the best ACM Multimedia demo award in 2006). He received the best student paper award at ACM Multimedia 2002, and the Eliahu I. Jury Award for best Ph.D. dissertation in 2002. He also received in 2000, a best paper award on video retrieval from IEEE Trans. On Circuits and Systems for Video Technology. He is an active participant in the Multimedia community; he is an associate editor at several major journals: ACM Transactions on Multimedia Computing, Communications and Applications (TOMCCAP), IEEE Multimedia and IEEE Transactions on Multimedia. He will co-organize the upcoming ACM SIG Multimedia 2011.

Rong Yan: Dr. Rong Yan is currently a Research Scientist in Facebook. He was a Research Staff Member in the IBM T. J. Watson Research Center from 2006 to 2009. Dr. Yan received his M.Sc. (2004) and Ph.D. (2006) degree from Carnegie Mellon University's School of Computer Science.

His research interests include digital and social media analysis, large-scale machine learning, data mining, information retrieval and computer vision. Dr. Yan received the BestPaper runner-up awards in ACM MM 2004 and ACM CIVR 2007. He led the technical efforts for building Facebook's face detection / recognition service, and designed the automatic video retrieval systems that achieve the best performance in the world-wide TRECVID evaluation in 2003 / 2005. He has received the IBM Research External Recognition Award in 2007. Dr. Yan has authored or co-authored 5 book chapters and more than 60 international conference and journal papers. He has served or is serving as co-chairs for 10 conferences / workshops and as a Program Committee member in more than 40 ACM / IEEE conferences. He gave tutorials and guest lectures at several major conferences and universities.

Roger Zimmerman: Roger Zimmermann is an Associate Professor with the Department of Computer Science at the National University of Singapore (NUS) where he is also an investigator with the Interactive and Digital Media Institute (IDMI). Prior to joining NUS he held the position of Research Area Director with the Integrated Media Systems Center (IMSC) at the University of Southern California (USC). He received his Ph.D. degree from USC in 1998. Among his research interests are distributed and peer-to-peer systems, collaborative environments, streaming media architectures, georeferenced video management, and mobile location-based services. He has co-authored a book, five patents and more than a hundred-twenty conference publications, journal articles and book chapters in the areas of multimedia and information management. He is an Associate Editor of the ACM Computers in Entertainment magazine and the ACM Transactions on Multimedia Computing, Communications and Applications journal. He is a Senior Member of the IEEE and a member of ACM

Industry Panel

Innovating the Multimedia Experience

Organizers and Moderators

Khaled El-Maleh
Qualcomm
kelmaleh@ qualcomm.com

Haohong Wang
TCL Research America
haohongwang@gmail.com

Panelists

Susie Wee
Cisco Systems

Heather Yu
Huawei Technologies USA

Zhengyou Zhang
Microsoft

James D. Johnson
IEEE Distinquished Lecturer

PANEL SUMMARY

In this panel, each panelist will present their view of the current state-of-the-art of research and product innovations in the three major areas of multimedia experience: visual, auditory and gaming. We will discuss examples of innovation that enhance the consumption and sharing of multimedia (video, audio, graphics etc.) and thus increase quality of user experience. Another major focus of this panel is to open the discussion on how to innovate new multimedia user experiences.

Categories and Subject Descriptors

H.1.2[User/Machine Systems]:Human factors; H.5.1 [Information Interfaces and Presentation]:Multimedia Information Systems

General Terms

Human Factors.

Keywords

Multimedia experience, Visual media, Auditory media, Gaming, Sharing, User experience

Khaled El-Maleh, *Qualcomm Inc.*

Khaled El-Maleh received his M. Eng. and Ph.D. from McGill University, Canada, and B. Sc. in EE and B. Sc. in Applied Math from King Fahd University (KFUPM), Saudi Arabia. He has been with Qualcomm, San Diego since 2000. Dr. El-Maleh's areas of expertise and interests include: design, implementation and quality evaluation of mobile multimedia systems with focus on speech and video compression/processing algorithms, innovation and technology transfer . He was a key member of the team who designed the first generation of mobile camcorder and video telephony solutions for both UMTS and CDMA networks. He was the video quality lead for Qualcomm chip unit and contributed to the design of media quality assessment tools with focus on automated on-chip quality testing. He is currently leading the multimedia engineering team in the Strategic IP Department of Qualcomm with focus on developing innovative technologies to enhance mobile multimedia user experience. In addition to his technical publications, he has filed more than 200 US and international patents covering video\image\speech processing and compression technologies, mobile learning and wireless power charging. He is a founding member of the International Workshop on Quality of Multimedia Experience (QoMEX) and served as the General Co-Chair for QoMEX 2009. He served/currently serving as the TPC Vice Chair (Tutorial Co-Chair) for Globecom 2010, TPC member for ACM Multimedia 2010, Steering Committee member for QoMEX 2010 and QoMEX 2011, Industry Co-Chair for ICME 2011, Industry Chair for SiPS 2011, Advisory Committee member of IEEE DSP/SPE 2011. He is currently serving as a member of the steering committee of ICME 2012-2014, Industry Panel Co-Chair of ACM Multimedia 2011, Industry Co-Chair for ICIP 2012, Special Sessions Co-chair for MMSP 2012, Tutorial Co-Chair for ICASSP 2013. He is a guest editor of two upcoming special journal issues on Quality of Multimedia User Experience (IEEE Signal Processing Magazine and European Journal of Signal and Image Processing)- to be published in 2011. Khaled is the recipient of Qualcomm first Career Thought Leader Award.

MM'11, November 28–December 1, 2011, Scottsdale, Arizona, USA.
ACM 978-1-4503-0616-4/11/11.

Haohong Wang, *TCL Research America*

Haohong Wang received the B.S. degree in computer science and the M.Eng. degree in computer applications both from Nanjing University, China, the M.S. degree in computer science from University of New Mexico, and the Ph.D. degree in Electrical and computer engineering from Northwestern University, Evanston, USA. He is currently the General Manager of TCL Research America, TCL Corporation, at Santa Clara, California, in charge of the overall corporate research activities in North America including 5 research labs at multiple locations. Prior to that he held various technical and management positions at AT&T, Catapult Communications, Qualcomm, Marvell, TTE and Cisco. Dr. Wang's research involves the areas of multimedia communications, 3D graphics, video analysis and processing, and 3DTV systems. He has published more than 50 articles in peer-reviewed journals and International conferences. He is the inventor of more than 40 U.S. patents and pending applications. He is the co-author of 4G Wireless Video Communications (John Wiley & Sons, 2009), and Computer Graphics (1997).

Dr. Wang is the Editor-in-Chief of the Journal of Communications (2008-), the Technical Program Chair of IEEE GLOBECOM 2010 (Miami) and the General Chair of IEEE ICME 2011 (Barcelona) and IEEE ICCCN 2011 (Maui). He chairs the IEEE Multimedia Communications Technical Committee (2010-2012), and is an elected member of the IEEE Visual Signal Processing and Communications Technical Committee (2005-), and IEEE Multimedia and Systems Applications Technical Committee (2006-). He is a member of the Steering Committee of IEEE Transactions on Multimedia. He has served as the Editor-in-Chief of the IEEE MMTC E-Letter (2009) and as an Editor (or Guest Editor) of IEEE Transactions on Multimedia, IEEE Communications Surveys & Tutorials, IEEE Communications Magazine, ACM Multimedia

Systems Journal and many others. He served as the General Chair of the 17th IEEE International Conference on Computer Communications and Networks (ICCCN 2008) (US Virgin Island).

Susie Wee, *Vice President and Chief Technology and Experience Officer of Collaboration and Communication at Cisco Systems*

Susie Wee is the Vice President and Chief Technology and Experience Officer of Collaboration and Communication at Cisco Systems where she is responsible for driving innovation and experience design in Cisco's collaboration products and software services. Prior to this, she was at Hewlett Packard in the roles of founding Vice President of the Experience Software Business and Chief Technology Officer of Client Cloud Services in HP's Personal Systems Group and Lab Director of the HP Labs Mobile and Media Systems Lab. Susie was the co-editor of the JPSEC standard for the security of JPEG-2000 images and the editor of the JPSEC amendment on File Format Security. She was formerly an associate editor for the IEEE Transactions on Circuits, Systems and Video Technology and for the IEEE Transactions on Image Processing. While at HP Labs, Susie was a consulting assistant professor at Stanford University where she co-taught a graduate-level course on digital video processing. Susie received Technology Review's Top 100 Young Innovators award, ComputerWorld's Top 40 Innovators under 40, the INCITs Technical Excellence award, and the Women In Technology International Hall of Fame award. She is an IEEE Fellow for her contributions in multimedia technology and has over 50 international publications and over 40 granted patents. Susie received her B.S., M.S., and Ph.D. degrees from the Massachusetts Institute of Technology.

Heather Yu, *Director, Media Technologies Research, Huawei Tech USA*

Heather Yu got her Ph.D. from Princeton University in 1998. Currently, she is the Director of the Huawei Media Networking Lab located at Bridgewater, NJ. With the mission of establishing a world class R&D team and leading the key multimedia technology innovations, she led the NJ team successfully accomplished the development of several new media technology research areas and a series of new technology innovations offering competitive edge capabilities and supporting various functionalities for Huawei's products. Before joining Huawei, she was with Panasonic Princeton Lab working on media communication, media processing, media security, and P2P technology research. Since graduated from Princeton, Heather served numerous positions in related associations, such as Chair of the IEEE Multimedia Communications Tech Committee, IEEE Communications Society Strategic Planning Committee member, IEEE Human Centric Communications emerging technology committee chair, Associate Editor in Chief for PPNA journal, AEs of several IEEE journals/magazines, and Conference chair and TPC chair for many conferences in the field. She holds 23 granted US patents and has many in pending. She published 70+ publications, including 4 books, P2P Networking and Applications, Semantic Computing, P2P Handbooks, and Multimedia Security Technologies for Digital Rights Management.

James D. Johnston, *IEEE Distinguished Lecturer, Audio Technology Pioneer*

James D. Johnston received his BSEE and MSEE from Carnegie-Mellon University. Mr. Johnston has been called the father of perceptual audio coding for his pioneering contributions that revolutionized digital audio. His accomplishments during a 26-year career at AT&T Bell Labs have, among other achievements, allowed for the distribution of digital music and digital radio over the Internet. He is presently an independent consultant having retired from the position of Chief Scientist at DTS, Inc. where he was working on a variety of acoustical modeling, preprocessing and postprocessing algorithms for audio capture, analysis, control, and presentation.

Dr. Johnston joined DTS Inc., from his position at Neural Audio. Prior to that, he worked for 5 years at Microsoft Corporation in the "Codecs", "Core Media Processing" and finally the video services groups as Audio Architect.

Dr. Johnston retired from AT&T Labs - Research, quartered at Florham Park, NJ, Speech Processing Software and Technology Research Department. Before that, he was employed by AT&T Bell Laboratories, in the Acoustics Research Department under Dr. J. L. Flanagan, and in the Signal Processing Research Department.

Dr. Johnston was the primary researcher and inventor of the MPEG-2 AAC audio coding algorithm, and a principle contributor to the "MP3" algorithm. He also represented AT&T in the ANSI accredited group X3L3.1, and X3L3.1 in the ISO-MPEG-AUDIO (MP3, AAC) arena.

Dr. Johnston was awarded the IEEE James L. Flanagan Signal Processing Field Award (2006); elected Fellow, Audio Engineering Society (1997); received AT&T Technology Medal and AT&T Standards Award (1998); received a New Jersey Inventor of the Year Award (2001); elected IEEE Fellow (2002).

Dr. Johnston's current research interests include acoustic scene modelling, loudspeaker design, loudspeaker pattern control, cochlear modelling, masking threshold models, stereo imaging models and stereo imaging sensitivity models, methods of reproducing soundfields either literally or perceptually, microphone and soundfield capture techniques, both actively steered and time-invariant, and speech and audio coding methods in general.

Zhengyou Zhang, *Principal Researcher at Microsoft, Affiliate Professor at University of Washington*

Zhengyou Zhang is a Fellow of the Institute of Electrical and Electronic Engineers (IEEE). He is the Founding Editor-in-Chief of the newly established IEEE Transactions on Autonomous Mental Development (IEEE T-AMD), and is on the Editorial Board of the International Journal of Computer Vision (IJCV), the Machine Vision and Applications, and the Journal of Computer Science and Technology (JCST). He was on the Editorial Board of the IEEE Transactions on Pattern Analysis and Machine Intelligence (IEEE T-PAMI) from 1999 to 2005, the IEEE Transactions on Multimedia (IEEE T-MM) from 2004 to 2009, the International Journal of Pattern Recognition and Artificial Intelligence (IJPRAI) from 1997 to 2008, among others. He is listed in Who's Who in the World, Who's Who in America and Who's Who in Science and Engineering.

Before joining Microsoft, Zhengyou worked at INRIA (French National Institute for Research in Computer Science and Control) for 11 years, and was a Senior Research Scientist since 1991, where he worked in the Computer Vision and Robotics group. In 1996-1997, he spent one-year sabbatical as an Invited Researcher at the Advanced Telecommunications Research Institute International (ATR), Kyoto, Japan.

He holds more than 80 US patents and has about 20 patents pending. He has published over 200 papers in refereed international journals and conferences, and is the author of several books.

1st International ACM Workshop on Music Information Retrieval with User-Centered and Multimodal Strategies (MIRUM)

Cynthia C.S. Liem
Delft University of Technology
Delft, The Netherlands
c.c.s.liem@tudelft.nl

Meinard Müller
Saarland University
and MPI Informatik
Saarbrücken, Germany
meinard@mpi-inf.mpg.de

Douglas Eck
Google Inc.
Mountain View, USA
deck@google.com

George Tzanetakis
University of Victoria
Victoria, Canada
gtzan@cs.uvic.ca

ABSTRACT

The 1st International ACM Workshop on Music Information Retrieval with User-Centered and Multimodal Strategies (MIRUM) at ACM Multimedia was proposed in order to gather experts from the Music and Multimedia Information Retrieval communities, as well as other neighboring fields. The workshop aims to provide a high-profile platform for presenting current work on Music Information Retrieval, with strong focus on user-centered and multimodal approaches. These focus areas are not only relevant to the Music Information Retrieval field, but equally recognized as emerging and relevant in the Multimedia domain. This way, a cross-disciplinary dialogue on open challenges can be initiated, facilitating new bridging opportunities and increased exchanges of expertise between communities. In this summary, we provide an overview of the 1st MIRUM workshop. After a description of the rationale and focus areas of the workshop, the accepted submissions and other program elements are summarized.

Categories and Subject Descriptors

H.5.5 [**Information Interfaces and Presentation**]: Sound and Music Computing

General Terms

Algorithms, Design, Experimentation, Human Factors

Keywords

Music Information Retrieval, Multimodal Music Processing, User-Centered Design, Cross-Domain Methodology Transfer

1. INTRODUCTION

Music is an outstanding example of a content type with many different representations, including audio recordings, symbolic scores, folksonomy descriptions and accompanying video material. Due to the existence of such complementary musical representations and information sources, music content is multimedia data by definition. However, at premier multimedia venues such as the ACM Multimedia Conference, research on music content has so far been much less represented than work focusing on visual content only.

With the 1st International ACM Workshop on Music Information Retrieval with User-Centered and Multimodal Strategies (MIRUM), the organizers would like to stimulate a change in this representation discrepancy, by attracting work on current emerging directions in Music Information Retrieval that also will be of relevance to Multimedia Information Retrieval researchers, as well as researchers from other neighboring fields that are already reaching out to the Multimedia domain. With the presented papers, keynote talk and panel discussion, a cross-disciplinary discussion is sought to identify shared open challenges, and create new bridging opportunities and increased exchanges of expertise between communities to address these challenges.

MM'11, November 28–December 1, 2011, Scottsdale, Arizona, USA.
ACM 978-1-4503-0616-4/11/11.

2. FOCUS AREAS

The MIRUM workshop identified user-centered and multimodal strategies in Music Information Retrieval research as its main focus areas, following current developments and initiatives in the field with potential relevance beyond the music research community [3]. More specifically, the following topics of interest were mentioned in the call for papers:

- Music multimedia content analysis;
- Visual and sensory information for music processing;
- Multimodal music search, retrieval and recommendation;
- Social networks and indexing for music applications;
- Music similarity measures at different specificity levels;
- Fusion of multimodal music information sources;
- Music knowledge representation and reasoning;
- Interactive music systems and retrieval;
- (Adaptive) user interaction and interfaces;
- User (context) models and personalization;
- Real-world issues;
- Evaluation methods and data understanding;
- Cross-domain methodology transfer.

3. PRESENTED PAPERS

22 technical papers were submitted for review to the MIRUM workshop. After a double-blind review process, 9 of these papers were selected for presentation at the workshop.

In [1], tf-idf techniques from textual document retrieval are transferred to the audio domain. A vector space model of MFCC coefficients is proposed and applied to music genre classification.

A well-represented task in Music Information Retrieval research is beat tracking. As an alternative to traditional approaches applying comb filters, autocorrelation or Short-Time Fourier Transforms, in [2] Nonstationary Gabor Transforms are proposed for this task, showing significant improvement over existing approaches.

While mood analysis of songs has typically been considered at the document level, it is recognized in [4] that mood is a time-varying concept. Techniques are proposed for estimating the musical mood trajectory in a song using both lyrics and audio features.

Motion is a modality naturally induced by music. The relation between gestures and the perception of pitched and non-pitched sounds is investigated and discussed in [5], revealing strong correlation between pitch and vertical gesture movement, and suggesting other more complex relationships between sound and motion parameters.

In [7], identification of geographically traditional-sounding music is investigated. With YouTube data as input, metric learning is applied to learn a perceptual space reflecting traditional-sounding proximity in a better way than would be the case for a conventional Euclidean space.

Using real-life listening data obtained from the last.fm service, in [8] artist clustering is performed through affinity propagation. Folksonomy analysis shows that this method is capable of identifying semantics-aware 'musical worlds'.

Inspired by object recognition in computer vision through a vocabulary tree approach, an analogous approach for music identification is proposed in [9], showing increased efficiency over other state-of-the-art methods.

In [10], content-based affective classification of music videos is studied. Affect classification results based on audio, visual and combined audiovisual features are investigated against ground truth obtained from a subjective user study.

Finally, in [11] a tempo-sensitive music search engine with multimodal inputs for wellness and therapeutic applications is presented, proposing different querying methods for facilitating tempo-based music search.

4. OTHER PROGRAM ELEMENTS

Dr. Roeland Ordelman, who is an R&D manager at the Netherlands Institute for Sound and Vision, will give the keynote talk [6] at the MIRUM workshop. The Netherlands Institute for Sound and Vision holds one of the largest audiovisual archives in Europe (including a considerable amount of music content). Referring to the practical end-user experiences in his institute, Dr. Ordelman will talk about exploitation possibilities of audiovisual data in the networked information society.

In addition, a panel discussion on bridging opportunities between the Music Information Retrieval community and its neighboring fields will be held featuring experts from multiple disciplines. This will be an interactive discussion that also will be open to input from the attending audience.

5. CONCLUSIONS

An overview of the 1st MIRUM workshop at ACM Multimedia was given. Despite being held for the first time, the workshop attracted a considerable amount of attention with a large paper submission volume, thus allowing for a full-day event. The organizers are confident that this resulted in an inspiring and multidisciplinary program, and hope that this will set up sustainable new cross-community bridges and expertise exchanges, increasing the presence and visibility of music content research work in the Multimedia community and stimulating joint future work.

6. REFERENCES

[1] K. Aryafar and A. Shokoufandeh. Music Genre Classification using Explicit Semantic Analysis. In *Proceedings ACM MIRUM 2011*, Scottsdale, Arizona, November 2011.

[2] A. Holzapfel, G. A. Velasco, N. Holighaus, M. Dörfler, and A. Flexer. Advantages of Nonstationary Gabor Transforms in Beat Tracking. In *Proceedings ACM MIRUM 2011*, Scottsdale, Arizona, November 2011.

[3] C. C. S. Liem, M. Müller, D. Eck, G. Tzanetakis, and A. Hanjalic. The Need for Music Information Retrieval with User-Centered and Multimodal Strategies (Workshop Theme Paper). In *Proceedings ACM MIRUM 2011*, Scottsdale, Arizona, November 2011.

[4] N. Nishikawa, K. Itoyama, H. Fujihara, M. Goto, T. Ogata, and H. Okuno. A Musical Mood Trajectory Estimation Method using Lyrics and Acoustic Features. In *Proceedings ACM MIRUM 2011*, Scottsdale, Arizona, November 2011.

[5] K. Nymoen, B. Caramiaux, M. Kozak, and J. Torresen. Analyzing Sound Tracings - A Multimodal Approach to Music Information Retrieval. In *Proceedings ACM MIRUM 2011*, Scottsdale, Arizona, November 2011.

[6] R. Ordelman. Audiovisual Archive Exploitation in the Networked Information Society. In *Proceedings ACM MIRUM 2011*, Scottsdale, Arizona, November 2011.

[7] C. Parker, D. Joshi, P. Lei, and J. Luo. Finding Geographically Representative Music via Social Media. In *Proceedings ACM MIRUM 2011*, Scottsdale, Arizona, November 2011.

[8] E. Tacchini and E. Damiani. What is a "Musical World"? An Affinity Propagation Approach. In *Proceedings ACM MIRUM 2011*, Scottsdale, Arizona, November 2011.

[9] T. Xu, A. W. Yu, X. Liu, and B. Lang. Music Identification via Vocabulary Tree with MFCC Peaks. In *Proceedings ACM MIRUM 2011*, Scottsdale, Arizona, November 2011.

[10] A. Yazdani, K. Kappeler, and T. Ebrahimi. Affective Content Analysis of Music Video Clips. In *Proceedings ACM MIRUM 2011*, Scottsdale, Arizona, November 2011.

[11] Y. Yi, Y. Zhou, and Y. Wang. A Tempo-Sensitive Music Search Engine with Multimodal Inputs. In *Proceedings ACM MIRUM 2011*, Scottsdale, Arizona, November 2011.

Third ACM International Workshop on Multimedia in Forensics and Intelligence (MiFor 2011)

Sebastiano Battiato
Image Processing Lab
University of Catania, Italy
battiato@dmi.unict.it

Sabu Emmanuel
School of Computer Engineering
Nanyang Technological University, Singapore
asemmanuel@ntu.edu.sg

Adrian Ulges
Multimedia Analysis and Data Mining Group
German Research Center for Arti£cial Intelligence (DFKI), Kaiserslautern, Germany
adrian.ulges@dfki.de

Marcel Worring
Intelligent Systems Lab Amsterdam
University of Amsterdam
The Netherlands
m.worring@uva.nl

ABSTRACT

This paper introduces the context of the workshop and the associated papers.

Categories and Subject Descriptors

H.4 [**Information Systems Applications**]: Miscellaneous

General Terms

Algorithms, Legal Aspects

Keywords

Forensic Mining, Computer Vision, Pattern Recognition, Multimedia Search, Privacy, Image Forgery

1. INTRODUCTION

The rapid growth of multimedia collections world-wide opens new challenges to multimedia technology with respect to crime prevention and investigation. The protection of images, video, and audio data from illegal use, as well as its exploitation in forensics and intelligence, have become serious challenges as the sheer data volume renders a full manual inspection by an expert impossible. Tools are needed to support the protection, management, processing, interpretation, and visualization of multimedia data in the different steps of the investigation process.

Many exciting solutions for related problems have been developed in the multimedia research community (including knowledge extraction, categorization, indexing, browsing and visualization), forming an excellent basis for forensics and intelligence. However, due to the complexity of the targeted material, the lack of structure and meta-data, and other application-specific constraints, approaches must be tailored, adapted, and extended.

MM'11, November 28–December 1, 2011, Scottsdale, Arizona, USA.
ACM 978-1-4503-0616-4/11/11.

2. WORKSHOP TOPICS AND PAPERS

The workshop is divided into two main topics. The first one deals with access to visual collections of data in a forensic setting. The second topics considers the improvement of privacy for users of social networking sites and how to control the authenticity of the data being transferred in the network.

2.1 Biometrics and retrieval in forensics

Content based image retrieval has a long tradition in the multimedia field. In [5] such techniques are adapted to support law enforcement in identifying criminal gangs and monikers based on graffiti analysis. They use a query by visual example paradigm and use the result to return an associated list of gang names.

Face recognition or matching can also be viewed as an image retrieval problem, but with very specific characteristics. Especially for forensic purposes it is a hard problem due to the uncontrollable circumstances. The work in [3] considers the quality of input samples used for face matching and how they affect performance in such a difficult context.

2.2 Privacy and Authenticity

Social networking sites have given an amazing impetus to sharing of multimedia data. The amount of data poses tremendous challenges in terms of privacy of users and authenticity of the data being transferred.

In [1] the problem is attacked at the social network operator level which are holding the data, aiming to provide enhanced privacy to the users of the sites. The proposed method is evaluated against a number of attacks.

Rather than considering the privacy of the user [2][4] consider the authenticity of the data being transferred. The paper [2] considers the problem of identifying whether the data has changed when transferred along the communication channel. Finally, [4] looks at the authenticity of an image itself when it is received. Are there any clues that can proof that the image has been tampered?

3. REFERENCES

[1] P. Atrey. A secret sharing based privacy enforcement mechanism for untrusted social networking operators. In *Proc. MiFor*, 2011.

[2] S. Battiato, G. Farinella, E. Messina, and G. Puglisi. A forensic signature based on spatial distributed bag of features for image alignment and tampering detection. In *Proc. MiFor*, 2011.

[3] M. de Marsico, M. Nappi, and D. Riccio. Measuring measures for face sample quality. In *Proc. MiFor*, 2011.

[4] Q. Liu. Detection of misaligned cropping and recompression with the same quantization matrix and relevant forgery. In *Proc. MiFor*, 2011.

[5] W. Tong, J.-E. Lee, R. Jin, and A. Jain. Gang and moniker identification by graffiti matching. In *Proc. MiFor*, 2011.

AIEMPro 2011: The 4th International Workshop on Automated Media Analysis and Production for Novel TV Services

Sid-Ahmed Berrani
Orange Labs - France Telecom
4 rue du Clos Courtel.
35510 Cesson-Sévigné - France
sidahmed.berrani@orange.com

Alberto Messina
RAI Radiotelevisione Italiana
Corso Giambone, 68
I-10135 Turin - Italy
a.messina@rai.it

ABSTRACT

The ACM AIEMPro 2011 workshop presents research on automated media content analysis and production for, amongst others, the development of novel TV services. The program of the workshop has two sessions. The first one is composed of three papers on video and TV content structuring and indexing. The second session is also composed of three papers on media production and retrieval systems and applications.

Categories and Subject Descriptors

H.4.0 [**Information Systems Applications**]: General

General Terms

Algorithm, Design, Experimentation, Performance, Theory

Keywords

Automatic media content analysis and indexing, media production, TV services.

1. INTRODUCTION

The workshop aims at exploring automated information extraction techniques and audiovisual content analysis tools to support future media production for novel TV services. This workshop follows in a series of previous events: the first one in conjunction with DEXA 2008 (AIEMPro08), the second one in conjunction with WIAMIS 2009 (AIEMPro09), and the third one in conjunction with ACM Multimedia 2010 (AIEMPro10). This year, the workshop is the result of a successful merge with the CBTV workshop (held in 2009 in conjunction with the IEEE International Symposium on Multimedia).

The significant increase in the amount of digital video content (TV channels in particular), and the diversification of broadcast possibilities and storage devices, have recently given rise to the emergence of many new services and novel TV programs consumption schemes and usage trends. These new services are aimed at making broadcast content available to consumers according to their needs, i.e. without any constraint on location and/or time and with the possibility to cherry pick and navigate according to the viewers desire. These services have been proven to be very effective in significantly increasing the content audience and open new niches for profitable use of broadcast content. Examples of such services are TV-on-demand, interactive TV, Catch-Up TV... This explosion of new media distribution and consumption paradigms and the corresponding new production workflows based on digital computer-based tools require an immediate revision of the traditional ways of making business in media industry. These evolutions are progressively substituting the traditional one-to-many broadcasting model. To cope with these trends, broadcasters are revolutionizing their point of view, trying to embrace these new models into their production and distribution facilities.

Leading experts all agree in recognizing automation of processes as one of the key for success in this scenario, because of the potential costs reduction introduced by it. This concept is grounded on several concurring factors in the media sector: a) switch over to Digital Television introduces more channels (meaning ore content items are produced/published); b) cross media production (web TV, Hybrid Broadcast/Broadband, multi-screen applications) means reuse of the same material in many different ways; c) improvements in infrastructure (IT) allows better content accessibility; d) recovery of Cultural Heritage implies archive digitization, annotation and multi-platform dissemination; e) budget limitations and shorter time-to-market mean number of media professionals cannot increase.

The cumulative effect of these factors can be summarized as follows: a lot more digital media items need to be produced by the same or reduced staff, and in a quicker and more cost-efficient way. As a consequence, the adoption of tools for intelligent analysis and synthesis of multimedia data are seen as substantial enabling factors in making interactive, multi-channel and multi-purpose productions value-returning.

The workshop aims thus at catalyzing the migration towards new ways of producing, broadcasting, and presenting media content, via the introduction of tools for automated multimedia analysis and understanding. At the same time, the workshop aims at helping academic researchers better understand the real-life key requirements that enable higher impact and wider adoption of these methods.

MM'11, November 28–December 1, 2011, Scottsdale, Arizona, USA.
ACM 978-1-4503-0616-4/11/11.

The program of AIEMPro 2011 includes 6 papers, accepted out of 11 submissions, grouped into two sessions: (1) Media Content Structuring and Indexing, and (2) Media Production and Retrieval Systems and Applications. Though the range of topics is quite diverse, including news story clustering, concept detection in live video stream, TV program structuring, video copy detection, speech recognition, media retrieval systems and architecture... The overall delivered picture is pointing very clearly to a future scenario in which automated analysis of content plays a crucial and indispensable role.

In fact, the careful analysis of this year's program as well as past editions' ones [6], makes foresee that future media production and distribution facilities will be integrated with a highly distributed and intelligent content analysis framework capable of supporting all the phases of the value chain. This will mainly allow broadcasters and media producers to make production processes and new services more efficient to be designed, deployed and maintained.

However, what is still missing is an overall and comprehensive view on how these technologies can collaborate with each other in the context of standard frameworks and architectures, and a robust analysis of performances that can be obtained in real use cases, i.e. where content differs from items used for developing algorithms and where new content and service paradigms arise on almost a daily basis.

These latter issues will be object of future efforts by the AIEMPro community at large.

2. WORKSHOP CONTENT SUMMARY

This Section gives some more detail about each of the accepted papers.

Session 1 presents research on Media Content Structuring and Indexing. Paper [2] proposes a sequence-based kernel approach for on-line high-level concept detection on live video streams. The technique efficiently computes the kernel function for an updated value for the current sliding window position based on information about matching elements from previous positions. The approach is tested on the TRECVID 2007 by analyzing, for distinct kernel functions, the required information needed to efficiently evaluate the kernel in the next sliding window, the memory and runtime complexity.

Paper [3] proposes a clustering approach for news stories to be used for news TV channels. It consists of several steps: shot boundary detection, commercial break detection/filtering, anchorperson detection, story aggregation and clustering. The bag of visual-words model and the bag of trajectory model are then used in order to describe objects present in news stories.

Paper [1] addresses the problem of unsupervised detection of recurrent audio segments in TV programs toward program structuring. Recurrent segments are the key elements in the process of program structuring. The paper focuses on a repeated sequence detection method and a set of basic audio descriptors. The objective of the study is to evaluate the effectiveness of considered method and descriptors and their ability to handle the wide range of existing audio recurrences. The idea is provide readers with a synthesis that allows them choosing the appropriate method for each kind of recurrences.

Session 2 deals with Media Production and Retrieval systems and applications. In Paper [5], a novel search environment is presented which collects as much metadata as possible in one single retrieval system. Authors explain how speech recognition can facilitate unlocking the archive by illustrating experiments and measuring the keyword recognition rate, rather than the pure word error rate. Conclusions are that keyword recognition rate is sufficient for efficient media retrieval in a search application.

Paper [7] deals with the picture-in-picture copy detection problem. It proposes a generalized spatial coding representation in which both the relative position and relative orientation is embedded in the spatial code of images key points. A novel formulation for spatial verification problem is also discussed and polynomial and non-polynomial algorithms to efficiently address the spatial verification problem are also introduced. Experiment results on TRECVID and MSRA datasets shows a 20% improvement over the classical hierarchical bag-of-words approach.

Paper [4] describes supporting most aspects of a media provider real workflows such as production, distribution, content description, archiving, and re-use of video items. Issues like lack of human resources, necessity of parallel media distribution, and retrieving previously archived content through editors or consumers are discussed.

3. REFERENCES

[1] A. Abduraman, S.-A. Berrani, J.-B. Rault, and O. Le Blouch. From audio recurrences to TV program structuring. In *Proc. of the ACM AIEMPro Workshop*, 2011.

[2] W. Bailer. Sequence-based kernels for online concept detection in video. In *Proc. of the ACM AIEMPro Workshop*, 2011.

[3] W.-T. Chu, C.-C. Huang, and W.-F. Cheng. News story clustering from both what and how aspects: using bag of word model and affinity propagation. In *Proc. of the ACM AIEMPro Workshop*, 2011.

[4] R. Knauf, J. Kürsten, A. Kurze, M. Ritter, A. Berger, S. Heinich, and M. Eibl. Produce. Annotate. Archive. Repurpose - accelerating the composition and metadata accumulation of TV content. In *Proc. of the ACM AIEMPro Workshop*, 2011.

[5] M. Matton and K. Braeckman. Speech recognition tools in a media retrieval system. In *Proc. of the ACM AIEMPro Workshop*, 2011.

[6] A. Messina, R. De Sutter, J.-P. Evain, M. Sano, and G. Friedland. 3rd International Workshop on Automated Information Extraction in Media Production (AIEMPro). In A. Del Bimbo, S.-F. Chang, and A. W. M. Smeulders, editors, *ACM Multimedia*, pages 1751–1752. ACM, 2010.

[7] S. Purushotham, Q. Tian, and C.-C. J. Kuo. Picture-in-picture copy detection using spatial coding techniques. In *Proc. of the ACM AIEMPro Workshop*, 2011.

WSM2011: Third ACM Workshop on Social Media

Steven C.H. Hoi
School of Computer Engineering, Nanyang Technological University
Singapore
chhoi@ntu.edu.sg

Michal Jacovi
IBM Haifa Research Lab
Israel
jacovi@il.ibm.com

Ioannis Kompatsiaris
CERTH - Informatics and Telematics Institute
Greece
ikom@iti.gr

Jiebo Luo
Kodak Research Labs
USA
jiebo.luo@kodak.com

Konstantinos Tserpes
Department of Informatics and Telematics, Harokopio University of Athens
Greece
tserpes@hua.gr

ABSTRACT

The Third Workshop on Social Media (WSM2011) continues the series of Workshops on Social Media in 2009 and 2010 and has been established as a platform for the presentation and discussion of the latest, key research issues in social media analysis, exploration, search, mining, and emerging new social media applications. It is held in conjunction with the ACM International Multimedia Conference (MM'11) at Scottsdale, Arizona, USA, 2011 and has attracted contributions on various aspects of social media including data mining from social media, content organization, geo-localization, personalization, recommendation systems, user experience, machine learning and social media approaches and architectures for large-scale data processing.

Categories and Subject Descriptors

H.4 [**Information Systems Applications**]: Miscellaneous; H3.1 [**Information Storage and Retrieval**]: Content Analysis and Indexing; I.4.9 [**Image Processing and Computer Vision**]: Applications; J.4 [**Computer Applications**]: Social And Behavioral Sciences

General Terms

Algorithms, Design, Management

Keywords

Social media, media analysis, social media search, social Web and networks

1. INTRODUCTION

Social networking sites, such as Flickr, Facebook and PicasaWeb, host billions of images and video, which have been annotated and shared among friends, or published in groups that cover a specific topic of interest. The availability of this mass amount of multimedia data along with the annotations and feedback by users creates a number of opportunities and research challenges as well as many exciting real-world applications. Unlike conventional multimedia data, social media contains much rich user-generated information, including social connections, multimodal content and descriptions, location and comments in various forms (ranking, votes, likes). Therefore, many approaches have been developed, which are able to handle and process such heterogeneous information towards resolving long-standing challenges in multimedia, e.g., multimedia understanding towards improving recommendation and personalization techniques.

WSM2011[1] continues the series of Workshops on Social Media in 2009[2] and 2010[3] and this year received 22 submissions from which the program committee accepted 10 as oral presentations. The workshop attracted contributions on various aspects of social media including data mining and information extraction from social media, content organization, geo-localization, personalization, recommendation systems, user experience, machine learning and social media approaches and architectures for large-scale data processing. The program also includes two keynote talks by recognized researchers on community detection and mining in social media and on large-scale social media analysis in facebook.

2. PAPER SUMMARY

Workshop papers elaborate on extracting useful information from social media, with methods to automatically detect and identify events or perform sentiment analysis in social media sharing web sites. More specifically, [9] tackles the problem of exploiting metadata attached to media and events (tags, description, geographic location) in order to create the missing link between an event description and its illustrating media documents. The presented approach not only detect events with high accuracy but also mines and identifies events that have not been published in popular event directories. In [8] a method for sentiment analysis (the mood of the author or her opinion with respect to a specific entity) by capturing textual patterns, inherently supporting multilingual or noisy content is presented.

MM'11, November 28–December 1, 2011, Scottsdale, Arizona, USA.
ACM 978-1-4503-0616-4/11/11.

[1] http://www.cais.ntu.edu.sg/~wsm2011/
[2] http://www.cais.ntu.edu.sg/~wsm2009/
[3] http://www.cais.ntu.edu.sg/~wsm2010/

Given the very large amount of media available, content organization is necessary and many papers address this challenge, including automatic tag suggestion, classification or more specific applications like alignment of different photo streams or sequences from different photographers for the same event [10]. In [5] the algorithm presented jointly uses four techniques to enhance classification: cross-domain learning that adapts previous classifiers learned from a source domain to classify new data in the target domain; semi-supervised learning that leverages information from unlabeled data to help training; multi-concept learning that uses concept relations to enhance individual concept detection; and active learning that improves the efficiency of manual annotation by actively querying users. In [3] visual characteristics in terms of the bag of word model and tagging behaviors are jointly considered for tag suggestion in Web videos.

Location information is important in shared media and papers either address the issue of missing geo-location information by automatically inferring the location from tags, visual cues and already geo-located media [4], or exploit this feature to map phenomena (e.g., the "scenicness" of a place) not easily observable through other means [7].

Personalized recommendations is a key application in social media-based environments since they are able to achieve high efficiency by incorporating multimedia content items, user-contributed annotations and the user's social network. The paper [6] presents a system implementing a travel recommender for places that are not necessarily touristic or famous, but rather are genuinely representative of the place and also match usersÕ personal interests. The recommendation system makes use of user photos from the image sharing community Flickr.

User aspects and user experience related issues are important topics and in [2] critical questions like what factors influence individual participation in social media conversations are addressed. The authors identify several key aspects of social media conversations, distinct from both online forum discussions and other social networks. These aspects include intrinsic and extrinsic network factors. There are three factors intrinsic to the network: social awareness, community characteristics and creator reputation. The factors extrinsic to the network include: media context and conversational interestingness.

Finally, the paper [1] is about an architecture for the sharing of social live streaming data (e.g. a stream of videos or a stream of documents produced by groups of people) including specific components such as the user interface and memory management.

In most of the papers, the important multimodal properties of social media are taken into account including joint distributions and similarities of tag, visual, temporal and location information during processing. Scalability is also an important challenge since all approaches include experiments in very large datasets and parallelizable architectures and techniques for multi-core CPUs are proposed.

3. CONCLUSIONS

The success of the Third Workshop on Social Media in terms of number and quality of papers shows that social media analysis, organization and information extraction remains a key, emerging topic. This year's contributions confirm that the utilization of aggregated collections of such media and the combination of their visual, textual, temporal, location and social context, provides the ingredients for a more thorough understanding of the various events, patterns and situations embedded or emerging in such data. Therefore, there is still a need for scalable and multi-modal approaches that are able to handle the massive amount of available data and provide useful information for a variety of applications.

To this end, the invited speakers will provide their insights on such future issues and specifically to the Issues and Challenges in Social Media Mining by Prof. Huan Liu from Arizona State University and to the Large-scale Social Media Analysis in Facebook, Dr. Rong Yan, Facebook Inc.

4. ACKNOWLEDGEMENTS

The WSM2011 workshop was supported by the European Commission under contracts FP7-215453 WeKnowIt - Emerging, Collective Intelligence for personal, organisational and social use and FP7-257774 SocIoS - Exploiting Social Networks for Building the Future Internet of Services for their support.

5. REFERENCES

[1] S. Barahmand and S. Ghandeharizadeh. Chase display of social live streams (soliss). In *International ACM Workshop on Social Media*, 2011.

[2] M. D. Choudhury and H. Sundaram. Why do we converse on social media? an analysis of intrinsic and extrinsic network factors. In *International ACM Workshop on Social Media*, 2011.

[3] W. T. Chu, C. J. Li, and J. Y. Yu. Tag suggestion and localization for web videos by bipartite graph matching. In *International ACM Workshop on Social Media*, 2011.

[4] G. Friedland, J. Choi, H. Lei, and A. Janin. Multimodal location estimation on flickr videos. In *International ACM Workshop on Social Media*, 2011.

[5] W. Jiang and A. Loui. Laplacian adaptive context-based svm for incremental video concept detection. In *International ACM Workshop on Social Media*, 2011.

[6] C. Kofler, M. L. Caballero, M. M. Blanco, V. Occhialini, and M. Larson. Near2me: An authentic and personalized social media-based recommender for travel destinations. In *International ACM Workshop on Social Media*, 2011.

[7] S. Newsam and L. Xie. Im2map: Deriving maps from georeferenced community contributed photo collections. In *International ACM Workshop on Social Media*, 2011.

[8] G. Papadakis, F. Aisopos, and T. Varvarigou. Sentiment analysis of social media content using n-gram graphs. In *International ACM Workshop on Social Media*, 2011.

[9] R. Troncy, B. Huet, and X. Liu. Using social media to identify events. In *International ACM Workshop on Social Media*, 2011.

[10] J. Yang and J. Luo. Photo stream alignment for collaborative photo collection and sharing in social media. In *International ACM Workshop on Social Media*, 2011.

ACM International Workshop on Social and Behavioral Networked Media Access (SBNMA'11)

Naeem Ramzan
Queen Mary University of London
London, United Kingdom
naeem.ramzan@eecs.qmul.ac.uk

Fei Wang
IBM T.J.Watson Research Center, USA
fwang@us.ibm.com

Charalampos Z. Patrikakis
Technological Education Institute of Piraeus, Greece
bpatr@telecom.ntua.gr

Peng Cui
Tsinghua University, China
cuip@tsinghua.edu.cn

Nikolaos Doulamis
National Technical Univ. of Athens, Greece
ndoulam@cs.ntua.gr

Shiqiang Yang
Tsingua University, China
yangshq@tsinghua.edu.cn

Gordon Sun
Tencent Technologies, China
gordonsun@tencent.com

ABSTRACT

In an endeavour to speak and prevail over some of the open problems that obstruct efficient networked media, this workshop will fetch together folks from a number of research communities, including but not limited to Multimedia Distribution and Access, Social Network Analysis, Multimedia Content Analysis, Behavioral Analysis, User Modelling Adaptation and Personalization. It is our credence that a synergetic approach involving the above mentioned research areas can surpass their individual potentials, leading to improved networked media access. The main objective of this workshop is to provide a forum to disseminate work that explicitly exploit the synergy between multimedia content analysis, behavioral modelling, personalisation, and next generation networking and community aspects of social networks. This synergetic methodology could produce high quality of experience for personalized multimedia access in networking environment.

Categories and Subject Descriptors

H.5.1 Multimedia Information Systems

General Terms

Experimentation, Design, Algorithms, Human Factors.

Keywords

Social, behavioral, adaptation, personalization, interaction, access.

1. INTRODUCTION

In recent years, there has been an unprecedented increase in the creation and consumption of digital information. In addition, people are increasingly well connected on the Internet through some social network sites, blogs, wikis and mashups. Some popular social and networked media platforms such as Facebook, Flicker, YouTube and Windows Live provide virtual platforms for all users to share their ideas, photos, videos and music, and all users are collaborating together to contribute to media production and sharing. In these networked media platforms, a large volume of users actively interact with each other, which not only influence each individual's behavior on information utilization, but also affect the system's performance. To improve user experience and level of service, it is of ample importance to analyze the impact of social and human behavioural factors on networked media platforms. This environment presents clear challenges to conventional information retrieval research, which is based mainly on individual activities.

2. CONTRIBUTION

This workshop aims at presenting work focusing on two major topics: The first is to address the question on how multimedia content analysis can be combined with information derived from behavioural modelling and social interactions in order to improve personalised content distribution. The second relates to the way in which personalised services can be offered to users, in a real time, ubiquitous seamless and comprehensive way, through a comprehensive context framework that targets Quality of Experience rather than the traditionally sought Quality of Service.

The main goal of this workshop is to provide a forum to disseminate work that explicitly exploit the synergy among multimedia content analysis, behavioural modelling, personalisation, next generation networking and community aspects of social networks by reviewing pressing needs, examining challenging research issues, and showing the state-of-the-art research and development in networked media information retrieval environment.

MM'11, November 28–December 1, 2011, Scottsdale, Arizona, USA.
ACM 978-1-4503-0616-4/11/11.

Hence, this workshop is distinct from and complementary to previous initiatives in that it involves the integration of user's behavioural modeling, multimedia content analysis, and seamless delivery techniques with information derived from networked communities and context awareness. The workshop will cover the following topics:

3. TOPICS OF INTEREST

This workshop is distinct from and complementary to previous initiatives in that it involves the integration multimedia content analysis techniques with information derived from users, networked communities, and context awareness. The aim of the workshop is to cover the following topics:

- Techniques for robust and scalable distribution of multimedia content.
- Social behaviour methods in the area of multimedia search, content delivery and scalable streaming
- Fundamental (theoretical and practical) challenges in behavioural modelling for networked media information retrieval
- Recent advances in behavioral modeling on networked media
- Robust distribution of multimedia services over heterogeneous networks and access technologies
- QoE of the multimedia communication over social/P2P networks
- Social networks analysis to multimedia content personalization and adaptation

4. WORKSHOP SUMMARY

The workshop is featured with 2 keynote talks, 7 full research and 4 invited papers. Due to the high amount of accepted and invited papers, it was decided to allocate time slot of 30 mins for invited paper and 20 mins for full research papers. The papers accepted for presentations are given below.

A number of approaches have investigated the multimedia content personalization and adaptation by social network analysis. In the paper entitled "A Hierarchical Multimodal Approach for Placing videos on the Maps using Millions of Flickr Photographs" Kelm et al. present a hierarchical, multi-modal approach for placing non-geotagged Flickr video on the map. Zhang et al. explore an approach that exploits YouTube video co-watch data to improve the performance of video taxonomic classification system in their paper "Improving Video Classification via YouTube Video Co-Watch Data". In "Using Media Related User Profiles to Personalize Multimedia Access over Social Networks" Argyriou et al. address the issue of personalized media access over the internet. Hu et al. in "Event Analytics via Social Media" analyze the response of users to public events through social media. Voulodimos et al. in "Employing Clustering Algorithms to Create User Groups for Personalized Context Aware Services Provision" present user preferences in the scope of social groups.

Accepted papers also focus on social behavior methods in the area of multimedia distribution. Brenner et al. in "Graph-Based Recognition in Photo Collections Using Social Semantics" show how to recognize people in consumer photo collections by employing a graphical model. Marian and Mathias in their paper "Pursuing the Holy Grail by interrelating user intentions and Bag of Visual Words to perform retrieval adaptation" present how the user's search behavior enhance the multimedia retrieval and adaptation. Alan Gomes presents how to represent and measure social interactions as behavioral contingencies in his paper "Measuring Media-based Social Interactions Provided by Smartphones Applications in Social Networks". Mirza et al. investigate in the use of eye tracking techniques in order to personalize image annotation and retrieval in "Gaze Movement Inference for User Adapted Image Annotation and Retrieval".

Savas et al. in "Adaptive Multi-view Video Streaming over P2P Networks Considering Quality of Experience" present a mesh-based P2P streaming architecture for Multi-view video that employs rate adaptation according to the findings to deliver the best QoE under diverse network conditions. Finally, in "Social and Behavioral Media Access: A Survey" Ramzan gives his position on the expected evolution of social and behavioral networked media access.

5. ACKNOWLEDGEMENTS

This workshop was partially supported by its affiliated projects: Saracen (FP7-248474), 3DLife (FP7-247688), PetaMedia (FP7-216444) and SA EMC^2 (FP7-287663).

Modeling and Representing Events in Multimedia

Vasileios Mezaris
Centre for Research and Technology Hellas
Informatics and Telematics Institute
Thermi 57001, Greece
bmezaris@iti.gr

Ansgar Scherp
University of Koblenz-Landau
Information Systems and Semantic Web
Universitätsstr. 1
Koblenz, Germany
scherp@uni-koblenz.de

Ramesh Jain
University of California
Donald Bren School of Information and Computer Sciences
Irvine, CA 92697, USA
jain@ics.uci.edu

Mohan Kankanhalli
National University of Singapore
School of Computing
Singapore 117590
mohan@comp.nus.edu.sg

Huiyu Zhou
Queen's University Belfast
ECIT Institute
Belfast, BT3 9DT, United Kingdom
h.zhou@ecit.qub.ac.uk

Jianguo Zhang
University of Dundee
School of Computing
United Kingdom
jgzhang@computing.dundee.ac.uk

Liang Wang
National Lab of Pattern Recognition
Beijing, China
wangliang@nlpr.ia.ac.cn

Zhengyou Zhang
Microsoft Research
One Microsoft Way, Redmond
WA, USA
zhang@microsoft.com

ABSTRACT

This paper presents an overview of the Joint Workshop on Modeling and Representing Events (JMRE), which is held as part of ACM Multimedia 2011. JMRE is concerned with the understanding of events from multimedia, and with using events in order to better organize and consume multimedia.

Categories and Subject Descriptors

H.1.0 [**Information Systems**]: Models and Principles

General Terms

Design, Human Factors, Management

Keywords

Multimedia, events, objects, event detection, event-based applications, event models, sparse representation

1. MOTIVATION

Events are ubiquitous in multimedia. We find them in the contents that we all have created, shared or simply encountered on the Internet: for example, images from a concert that we recently attended or an interesting location that we visited, amateur video footage from a friend's wedding ceremony, official footage from an important game of our favorite football team, or eye-witness descriptions and infrared satellite images of a devastating tornado that made it to the headlines. All these contents come in different media types (e.g. image, video, text) created by different devices under different conditions. What is common though for all these media items is that they all have captured and convey information about real-life events. Efficiently and effectively understanding these heterogeneous events from the available multimedia contents and using them in order to better organize, share, retrieve and consume the contents in any possible way raises a significant challenge in today's world.

The goals of the Joint Workshop on Modeling and Representing Events (JMRE), held as part of ACM Multimedia 2011, are documenting and advancing the state of the art in relation to the above challenge. JMRE comprises two parts, the International Workshop on Events in Multimedia (EiMM) and the International Workshop on Sparse Representation for Event Detection in Multimedia (SRED). JMRE'11 also features a keynote talk by Prof. Nack, titled "Event and story - an intricate relationship" [6].

2. EVENTS IN MULTIMEDIA (EIMM)

This year's *International Workshop on Events in Multimedia*[1] (EiMM'11) is the third edition of the series of EiMM workshops, following the very successful workshops of this series, EiMM'09[2], held in Beijing, China, as part of ACM Multimedia 2009 [7], and EiMM'10[3], held in Florence, Italy, as part of ACM Multimedia 2010 [8].

The focus of the EiMM series lies on how to detect, model, and process domain-level events, and on how to develop applications that make use of domain-level events in the context of multimedia data. The EiMM'11 workshop brings together researchers from the different areas of the multimedia research community, who are interested in understanding the concept of events. It presents research progress in the

[1] `http://www.uni-koblenz.de/confsec/eimm11/`
[2] `http://www.uni-koblenz.de/confsec/eimm09/`
[3] `http://www.uni-koblenz.de/confsec/eimm10/`

MM'11, November 28–December 1, 2011, Scottsdale, Arizona, USA.
ACM 978-1-4503-0616-4/11/11.

areas of event detection and processing in multimedia data, event representation and event models, events in the context of Web 2.0, architectures for event management, and interactive event-based applications and tools.

Specifically, the papers included in the EiMM'11 program address the following topics:

- Event-based organization of personal photo archives. Treating the images acquired by a single person during a period of several months as a photo archive, Tankoyeu et al. [9] use various contextual cues for organizing the photos into different events.

- Recognition of events and sub-events in photo albums. Assuming that an album contains photos of a single event, Mattivi et al. [4] exploit the multitude of photos in the album for detecting its event type (e.g. Baseball, Concert, Wedding), and then further organize the album's photos into pre-defined sub-events (e.g. for Wedding, into ceremony, party-eating, etc.).

- Recognition of dynamic events (e.g. running, walking) in video using visual cues. Ballas and Delezoide [1] build on recent work on local feature trajectories, to investigate the impact of a new trajectory filtering scheme and two new trajectory descriptors to the detection of such video events.

- Recognition of complex events (e.g. feeding an animal) in video using audio cues. Mertens et al. [5] exploit non-speech audio features for building "acoustic super-models" that detect complex events from low-level audio features, and show that even using audio alone they can achieve high recognition rates.

- Event-based analysis of the game flow in sports video. In [2], mid-level and possibly incomplete annotations of individual shots (expressing camera views, play types, etc.) are used for finding and representing the overall game flow as the series of major events (e.g. "scoring", "turn-over") of the game. This approach is tested in the domain of American football.

- Lifelog event analysis. In [3], several aspects of lifelog research and related technical challenges are discussed, and a complete web-based event management service for collaborative lifelog event analysis is presented.

3. SPARSE REPRESENTATION FOR EVENT DETECTION IN MULTIMEDIA (SRED)

The *International Workshop on Sparse Representation for Event Detection in Multimedia*[4] (SRED'11) is focused on modeling, detection and recognition of events using sparsity analysis and applications that make use of sparse learning for event analysis in the context of multimedia. It presents research highlights in the area of sparse representation for event analysis and crowd behaviour analysis.

Specifically, the papers included in the SRED'11 program address the following topics:

- Amateur video summarisation. In [10], Wang et al. present a kernel based sparse representation approach for directly summarising consumer videos, where a dictionary of subsequences is generated using the clustered frames with importance ranking.

- Unusual event detection in crowded scenes. Xu et al. introduce in [11] an approach for unusual event detection via sparse reconstruction of dynamic textures over an overcomplete basis set, with the dynamic texture described by local binary patterns from three orthogonal planes (LBPTOP).

[4]http://research.microsoft.com/en-us/um/people/zhang/SRED11/

4. ACKNOWLEDGMENTS

The EiMM'11 workshop was supported by the European Commission under contract FP7-248984 GLOCAL.

5. REFERENCES

[1] N. Ballas and B. Delezoide. Trajectories based descriptor for dynamic events annotation. In *Proc. JMRE'11 @ ACM Multimedia 2011*, Scottsdale, AZ, USA, Nov.-Dec. 2011.

[2] Y. Ding and G. Fan. Finding the Game Flow from Sports Video. In *Proc. JMRE'11 @ ACM Multimedia 2011*, Scottsdale, AZ, USA, Nov.-Dec. 2011.

[3] P. H. Kim and F. Giunchiglia. Lifelog Event Management: Crowd Research Case Study. In *Proc. JMRE'11 @ ACM Multimedia 2011*, Scottsdale, AZ, USA, Nov.-Dec. 2011.

[4] R. Mattivi, J. Uijlings, F. D. Natale, and N. Sebe. Exploitation of time constrains for (sub-)event recognition. In *Proc. JMRE'11 @ ACM Multimedia 2011*, Scottsdale, AZ, USA, Nov.-Dec. 2011.

[5] R. Mertens, H. Lei, L. Gottlieb, G. Friedland, and A. Divakarian. Acoustic Super Models for Large Scale Video Event Detection. In *Proc. JMRE'11 @ ACM Multimedia 2011*, Scottsdale, AZ, USA, Nov.-Dec. 2011.

[6] F. Nack. Event and story - an intricate relationship. Keynote talk. In *Proc. JMRE'11 @ ACM Multimedia 2011*, Scottsdale, AZ, USA, Nov.-Dec. 2011.

[7] A. Scherp, R. Jain, and M. Kankanhalli. Events in multimedia. In *Proc. ACM Multimedia 2009*, pages 1147–1148, Beijing, China, October 2009.

[8] A. Scherp, R. Jain, M. Kankanhalli, and V. Mezaris. Modeling, Detecting, and Processing Events in Multimedia. In *Proc. ACM Multimedia 2010*, pages 1739–1740, Firenze, Italy, October 2010.

[9] I. Tankoyeu, J. Paniagua, J. Stottinger, and F. Giunchiglia. Event Detection and Scene Attraction by Very Simple Contextual Cues. In *Proc. JMRE'11 @ ACM Multimedia 2011*, Scottsdale, AZ, USA, Nov.-Dec. 2011.

[10] Z. Wang, M. Kumar, J. Luo, and B. Li. Sequence-Kernel Based Sparse Representation for Amateur Video Summarization. In *Proc. JMRE'11 @ ACM Multimedia 2011*, Scottsdale, AZ, USA, Nov.-Dec. 2011.

[11] J. Xu, S. Denman, S. Sridaran, C. Fookes, and R. Rana. Dynamic Texture Reconstruction from Sparse Codes for Unusual Event Detection in Crowded Scenes. In *Proc. JMRE'11 @ ACM Multimedia 2011*, Scottsdale, AZ, USA, Nov.-Dec. 2011.

Joint ACM Workshop on Human Gesture and Behavior Understanding (J-HGBU'11)

Maja Pantic
Imperial College London, UK
m.pantic@imperial.ac.uk

Alex Pentland
MIT, Media Lab, MA, USA
pentland@mit.edu

Alessandro Vinciarelli
University of Glasgow
vincia@dcs.gla.ac.uk

Rita Cucchiara
Università di Modena e Reggio Emilia, Italy
cucchiara.rita@unimore.it

Mohamed Daoudi
TELECOM Lille1/LIFL, France
daoudi@telecom-lille1.eu

Alberto del Bimbo
Università di Firenze, Italy
delbimbo@dsi.unifi.it

ABSTRACT

The ability to understand social signals of a person we are communicating with is the core of social intelligence. Social Intelligence is a facet of human intelligence that has been argued to be indispensable and perhaps the most important for success in life. At the same time, human-centric multimedia applications for humans and about humans are becoming increasingly important. 3D modeled human-objects, like bodies, heads and faces are exploited for animation, security, and human computer interaction, while three dimensional motion of arms, legs and local body features is used for more complete human gesture, activity and behavior analysis. The Joint Human Gesture and Behavior Understanding (J-HGBU) workshop event consists of two parts focusing on these complementary challenges: the Workshop on Multimedia Access to 3D Human Objects (MA3HO'11) and the Workshop on Social Signal Processing (SSPW'11).

Categories and Subject Descriptors

H.1.2[User/Machine Systems]:Human factors; H.5.1 [Information Interfaces and Presentation]:Multimedia Information Systems

General Terms

Human Factors.

Keywords

Multimedia experience, Social signals, Human gestures, 3D human objects, Behavior understanding

1. WORKSHOP ON MULTIMEDIA ACCESS TO 3D HUMAN OBJECTS (MA3HO'11)

MA3HO'11 includes 6 long papers and 7 short papers, selected from 18 submissions. The subjects addressed include 3D human activity recognition, 3D human motion, 3D face expression recognition, 3D face recognition, 3D face and human body dataset, among others. Paper [1] presents a novel approach to identify and/or verify persons by using three-dimensional dynamic and structural features extracted from human motion depicted on image streams. Paper [2] models deformation of human as a combination of articulated and non-rigid surface deformation. A novel algorithm is proposed for motion segmentation to find articulated body components, together with hierarchical estimation of non-rigid structure from motion. Paper [3] presents a complete comparative review of recent multi-view 2D and 3D approaches for human action recognition. Paper [4] addresses the problem of automatic 3D facial expression recognition. Automatic feature point localization is followed by face segmentation into regions. Face regions are hence matched to reference models of the six prototypical expressions using Iterative Closest Points (ICP). Paper [5] presents 3DPeS: a new dataset for 3D/multi-view surveillance and forensic applications. This has been designed for the evaluation of research results in people re-identification, people detection, people segmentation and people tracking. The new assessed version of the dataset contains hundreds of video sequences of 200 individuals taken from a multi-camera distributed surveillance system over several days, with different light conditions. Paper [6] proposes a solution to 3D face recognition that supports accurate face matching also in cases where just some parts of probe scans are available. In the proposed approach, distinguishing traits of the face are captured by extracting keypoints of the 3D depth image and adopting local shape descriptors that measure how much the face depth changes in the keypoints neighborhood. Paper [7] presents an automatic approach to detect feature points on 3D human models. Instead of detecting all feature points simultaneously, this algorithm recursively detects feature points by using a multi-stage strategy. In paper [8] human motion understanding based on motion capture (mocap) data is investigated. Three approaches are considered: 1) the spatial domain approach, 2) the spatio-temporal domain approach and 3) the decision fusion approach. Paper [9] proposes a 3D perceptual shape feature-based approach for efficient body parts classification and pose estimation.. Paper [10] proposes a new and simple external camera calibration method based on several plane intersections observed with a low-cost depth camera. A second contribution consists in a body volume reconstruction method based on visual hull that is adapted and enhanced with the use of depth information. Paper [11] describes a pedestrian detection system that can be trained from the projected suggestive contours of the 3D models and an estimation of its 3D pose instead of using multiple 2D training view images. Paper [12] proposes 3D reconstruction from sparse 3D landmark models. A 3D recognizer is built for each landmark based on the 3D landmark model. Paper [13] describes a new dataset under construction at the Media Integration and Communication Center and the University of Florence. The dataset consists of high-resolution 3D scans of human faces from each subject, along with several video sequences of varying resolution and zoom level.

MM'11, November 28–December 1, 2011, Scottsdale, Arizona, USA.
ACM 978-1-4503-0616-4/11/11.

2. WORKSHOP ON SOCIAL SIGNAL PROCESSING (SSPW'11)

SSPW11 includes 4 long papers and 4 short papers, selected from 11 submissions. The subjects addressed include multimodal recognition, human activity recognition and human communication, among the others. Paper [14] discusses the EAR method and identifies three ways in which it can enrich research in psychology and related fields. Specifically, it is suggested that it can (1) provide ecological, behavioral criteria that are independent of self-report, (2) calibrate psychological effects against frequencies of real-world behavior, and (3) help with the assessment of subtle and habitual behaviors that evade self-report. Paper [15] describes the recent developments in behavioral signal processing aimed at understanding dyadic interactions in couple therapy. Paper [16] proposes a computational framework which has wide applicability, including the recognition of human social behaviors, the synthesis of natural animations for robots and virtual humans, improved multimedia content analysis, and the diagnosis of social and behavioral disorders like the autism spectrum disorder. Paper [17] investigates the various aspects involved in the perception and computation of the beauty trait. Paper [18] proposes to automatically predict the degree of coordination between dyadic partners performing an imitation task. A subjective evaluation of their coordination was obtained via a questionnaire addressed to human judges. Paper [19] addresses the automatically detection of the Big Five personality traits from short (30-120 seconds) self-presentations, by investigating the effectiveness of various simple non-verbal acoustic and visual social signals such as pitch, intensity, visual activity cues, head orientation and so on. Paper [20] proposes an approach for Automatic Personality Perception, the task of predicting the personality traits attributed by human listeners to speakers they listen to for the first time and they are not acquainted with. Paper [21] investigates a layered HMM architecture where the outputs from a lower layer are fed into the upper layer in order to train classifiers of complex classes of human activities. A conditioned HMM (CHMM) which inherits the structure from the latent-dynamic conditional random field based on directed graphs is proposed .

3. REFERENCES

[1] F. Gomez-Caballero, T. Shinozaki, S. Furui, K. Shinoda. Person authentication using 3D human motion. In Proc. ACM J-HGBU 2011Workshop, 2011.

[2] Rohith MV, C. Kambhamettu. Estimation and utilization of articulations in recovering non-rigid structure from motion using motion subspaces. In Proc. ACM J-HGBU 2011Workshop, 2011.

[3] M. Holte, A. University; C. Tran, M. Trivedi, T. Moeslund. Human Activity Recognition using Multiple Views: A Comparative Perspective on Recent Developments. In Proc. ACM J-HGBU 2011Workshop.

[4] P. Lemaire, M. Ardabilian, M. Daoudi, B. Ben Amor, L. Chen. Fully Automatic 3D Facial Expression Recognition using a Region-Based Approach. In Proc. ACM J-HGBU 2011Workshop.

[5] D. Baltieri, R. Cucchiara, R. Vezzani. 3DPeS: 3D People Dataset for Surveillance and Forensics. In Proc. ACM J-HGBU 2011Workshop.

[6] S. Berretti, A. Del Bimbo, P. Pala. 3D Partial Face Matching using Local Shape Descriptors. In Proc. ACM J-HGBU 2011Workshop.

[7] X. Pan, A. Agathos, Multi-stage Feature Point Detection for 3D Human Data. In Proc. ACM J-HGBU 2011Workshop.

[8] H. Kadu, C.-C. J. Kuo, M. Kuo. Human Motion Classification and Management Based on Mocap Data Analysis. In Proc. ACM J-HGBU 2011Workshop.

[9] G. Hu, Q. Gao, 3D Perceptual Shape Feature-based Body Parts Classification and Pose Estimation. In Proc. ACM J-HGBU 2011Workshop.

[10] E. Auvinet, F. Multon, J. Meunier, Body volume reconstruction using multiple depth cameras. In Proc. ACM J-HGBU 2011Workshop.

[11] S. Min Yoon, A. Kuijper, Simultaneous Detection of Pedestrians, their Pose, and the Camera Viewpoint using 3D Models. In Proc. ACM J-HGBU 2011Workshop.

[12] X. Xiao, C. Xu, J. Wang, M. Xu. Landmark Recognition and Retrieval: From 2D to 3D. In Proc. ACM J-HGBU 2011Workshop.

[13] Bagdanov, A. Del Bimbo, L. Masi. The Florence 2D/3D Hybrid Face Dataset. In Proc. ACM J-HGBU 2011Workshop.

[14] M. Mehl, F. Deters. The Sounds of Social Life: Naturalistic (Acoustic) Observation Sampling. In Proc. ACM J-HGBU 2011Workshop.

[15] P. Georgiou, M. Black S. Narayanan. Behavioral signal processing for understanding (distressed) dyadic interactions: Some recent developments. In Proc. ACM J-HGBU 2011Workshop.

[16] L-P. Morenc. Computational Study of Human Communication Dynamics. In Proc. ACM J-HGBU 2011Workshop.

[17] H. Gunes. A Survey of Perception and Computation of Human Beauty. In Proc. ACM J-HGBU 2011Workshop.

[18] E. Delaherche, M. Chetouani, Automatic recognition of coordination level in an imitation task. In Proc. ACM J-HGBU 2011Workshop.

[19] L. Batrinca, B. Lepri, F. Pianesi. Multimodal Recognition of Personality during Short Self-Presentations. In Proc. ACM J-HGBU 2011Workshop.

[20] A. Vinciarelli, G. Mohammadi. Automatic Attribution of Personality Traits Based on Prosodic Features. In Proc. ACM J-HGBU 2011Workshop.

[21] M. Glodek, L. Bigalke, M. Schels, F. Schwenker. Incorporating Uncertainty in a Layered HMM Architecture for Human Activity Recognition. In Proc. ACM J-HGBU 2011Workshop.

Medical Multimedia Analysis and Retrieval

Yu Cao
College of Engineering and Computer Science, The University of Tennessee at Chattanooga
Chattanooga, TN, 37403
Tel: +1-423-425-4351
yu-cao@utc.edu

Jayashree Kalpathy-Cramer
Department of Medical Informatics and Clinical Epidemiology,
Oregon Health & Science University
Portland, OR 97239
Tel: +1-503-494-3731
kalpathy@ohsu.edu

Devrim Ünay
Electrical and Electronics Engineering Dept. Bahçesehir University, Çıragan Caddesi 34353, Turkey
Tel: (+90) 212-3815700
devrim.unay@bahcesehir.edu.tr

ABSTRACT
Advances in sensor technology, processing speed, high-speed networking, and the massive digital storages are being incorporated into today's healthcare practice. Tremendous amounts of medical multimedia data are captured and recorded in digital format during the daily clinical practice, medical research, and education. Intelligent medical knowledge discovery and retrieval from medical multimedia data is very useful and highly desirable. Motivated by the huge potential benefits, we have organized the ACM International Workshop on Medical Multimedia Analysis and Retrieval (MMAR2011), held in conjunction with The Annual ACM International Conference on Multimedia (ACM Multimedia 2011). In this paper, we first introduce the background and overview of the workshop. Then we introduce the workshop review process, followed with a brief introduction of the accepted papers in this workshop, as well as the conclusion.

Categories and Subject Descriptors
H.2.4 [**Systems**]: Multimedia databases; H.5.1 [**Multimedia Information Systems**]; J.3 [**Computer Applications**] Medical information systems

General Terms
Algorithms, Performance, Design, Human Factors.

Keywords
Multimedia databases, Multimedia Information System, Medical Information System.

1. INTRODUCTION
Advances in sensor technology, processing speed, high-speed networking, and the massive digital storages are being incorporated into today's healthcare practice. Tremendous amounts of medical multimedia data such as CT images, cardiac ECHO videos, data from wearable sensors and textual patient records, are captured and recorded in digital format during the daily clinical practice and medical research. Medical multimedia analysis and retrieval research, with the goal of knowledge of knowledge discovery and intelligent searching from medical data, can be used to address many critical issues facing our health care system, biomedical research and education today. These issues include healthcare quality, cost, and safety, throughput of biomedical research, and the effective translation of research into patient care. Furthermore, advancing the appropriate use of Health Information Technology (Health IT), which includes the wide application of medical multimedia analysis and retrieval research, holds great promise for improving quality of health care, reducing medical errors, providing safer care at lower cost, and advancing biomedical research. At the same time, the unique characteristics and challenges of medical multimedia data (e.g., large volume, heterogeneous, and semantic-rich) provide a world-leading opportunity for bringing together research scientists and practitioners from diverse disciplines that seek the understanding of the fundamental principles and design strategies in multimedia systems and leverage those understandings to build real-world medical multimedia systems.

The goal of this workshop was to bring together researchers in the area of medical multimedia analysis and retrieval, and to provide a forum for multidisciplinary research opportunities, with a focus on the state of the art in successes, the assessment of the applicability of the obtained results in real-life applications, as well as the future directions in medical multimedia analysis and retrieval. Practical issues for the design, implementation, and integration of medical multimedia analysis and retrieval systems have been discussed. Further, to encourage a larger group of image analysis researchers to benefit from the databases and evaluations created in the context of ImageCLEF, we provided access to the medical databases and tasks of ImageCLEF on request. This could encourage a broader public and assure that results remain comparable.

Topics of interest include but are not limited to practical areas that span a variety of aspects of medical multimedia analysis and retrieval including: (1) Analysis and mining in medical multimedia data (e.g., MRI, CT, X-ray, Ultrasound, Impedance, Biomagnetic, Bioelectric Imaging, echo videos, time series data); (2) Content-based indexing and retrieval for medical multimedia data Medical ontologies in relationship to multimedia; (3) Visualization techniques for medical multimedia data Function, and structure from medical images; (4) Multiscale modeling for medical multimedia data, such as the development and the evolution of complex spatiotemporal patterns, at different scales; (5) Machine learning of disease correlations from mining medical multimedia data; (5) Clinical decision support systems based on medial multimedia analysis; (6) Practical applications of medical multimedia data analysis and retrieval; (7) Algorithms for medical image retrieval or classification using the ImageCLEF collection.

MM'11, November 28–December 1, 2011, Scottsdale, Arizona, USA.
ACM 978-1-4503-0616-4/11/11.

2. THE REVIEW PROCESS

We received ten submissions for this workshop. We reviewed the eight valid submissions as one of the ten was an incomplete submission and another was withdrawn. The authors have presented a wide range of approaches and sceneries in the area of medical multimedia analysis and retrieval. Each paper has been peer reviewed by at least three program committee members, who are experts in the various topics covered by the workshop. In addition, the workshop organizers examined the reviews for each paper and had extensive discussions with reviewers to reach a consensus for each paper. In the end, four papers were recommended for acceptance, the most important consideration is the quality: we want to ensure all the papers being accepted in this conference are consistent with the quality requirements of the main ACM MM conference. In addition to the four reviewed papers, we have one invited paper. The invited paper was also peer-reviewed by three experts to ensure the quality.

3. ACCEPTED PAPERS

All the five papers selected for publication are closely related to medical image analysis and retrieval. Among these five papers, one paper is related to pathological spatial context-enhanced medical image retrieval; two papers deal with medical image classification; one paper is focusing on feature extraction for medical images; and the last paper is concentrating on medical video analysis. In the following sub-sections, we will introduce each accepted paper in more detail.

Pathological Spatial Context-Enhanced Medical Image Retrieval: In the paper entitled "Hierarchical Spatial Matching for Medical Image Retrieval", Yang Song, Weidong Cai, and Dagan Feng propose a content-based medical image retrieval framework that utilize the pathological spatial context in the medical image. This paper aims to effectively extract and represent the spatial context of pathological tissues, and design a novel hierarchical spatial matching (HSM) method based on the spatial pyramid matching. The proposed method is able to (1) handle the translation variations of the main pathological object; (2) describe the spatial information surrounding the pathological object in an adaptive scale; and (3) compute image similarities with an optimally weighted distance function.

Medical Image Classification: The paper "Predicting modality from text queries for medical image retrieval" by Pierre Tirillym Kun Lu, and Xiangming Mu focuses on how to identify the medical image modality (e.g., CT image, MRI image, and etc). In this paper, taxonomy of queries and the specificities of the problem are described. Then, a Bayesian classifier is proposed to automatically predict the modality expressed in the queries, as well as two models to integrate these prediction to an image retrieval system. Experiments performed on data from the ImageCLEFMed 2009 and 2010 challenges show that the proposed approach can outperform current systems in precision, although the performance can differ significantly from one query to another. The paper "Towards the Improvement of Textual Anatomy Image Classification using Image Local Features" by Xiao-Bing Huang, Tian Zhao, Yu Cao, Xiangming Mu, and Pierre Tirilly introduces a new approach for anatomy classification using a hybrid approach. First, a mutual information (MI) based filter is applied to select a set of terms with top MI scores for each anatomical class and help reduce the noise existing in the raw text. Second, local features extracted from the images are transformed as visual descriptors. Last, a hybrid scheme on the results from the textual and visual methods is applied to achieve further improvement of the classification results. Experiments show that this hybrid scheme improves the results over the sole textual or visual method on different anatomical class settings.

Feature Extraction Method for Medical Images: The paper "Fast Fractal Stack: Fractal Analysis of Computed Tomography Scans of the Lung" by Alceu Costa, Joe Tekli, and Agma Traina introduces a new feature extraction method: the Fast Fractal Stack, or FFS. The extraction algorithm consists in decomposing the input grayscale image into a stack of binary images from which the fractal dimension values are computed, resulting in a compact and highly descriptive set of features. They evaluated FFS for the task of classification of interstitial lung diseases in computed tomography (CT) scans. The proposed approach performs well, improving the classification accuracy when compared to other feature extraction algorithms. Additionally, the FFS extraction algorithm is efficient.

Medical Video Analysis: In paper entitled "Video-based Motion Expertise Analysis in Simulation-based Surgical Training Using Hierarchical Dirichlet Process Hidden Markov Model", Qiang Zhang and Baoxin Li focus on the problem of building automated systems to achieve computational understanding of surgical skills, largely through analysis of motion data captured by video or other sensors. This paper extends the Hierarchical Dirichlet Process Hidden Markov Model (HDP-HMM) for this purpose. Spatial temporal interest points and visual words are employed. A histogram is constructed for each frame. For sequences of each motion expertise level, they infer an HDP-HMM model. Finally, the classification of the motion expertise level for a testing sequence is based on choosing a model that maximizes the likelihood of the given sequence.

4. CONCLUSIONS

Some of the grand challenges facing society include how to improve the health care quality, reduce the medical error, and lower the health care cost [1, 2]. Breakthrough research in biomedical informatics, which includes the cutting edge research in Medical Multimedia Analysis and Retrieval, holds great promise for contribute to address these challenging questions. Based on the high quality papers accepted by the conference, we are confident that the ACM MMAR 2011 event is an excellent reflection of the state of the art and it will contribute to the ultimate goal of transforming the health care system and biomedical research via innovative computing techniques.

We are very grateful for all of the contributing authors and the hard work of the program committee. We would also like to thank the organizers of ACM MM 2011 for sharing our vision.

5. REFERENCES

[1] (2011). *National Association for Healthcare Quality.* Available: http://www.nahq.org

[2] (2010). *World Health Organization: The World health report 2010.* Available: http://www.who.int/mediacentre/multimedia/podcasts/2010/whr_20101202/en/

Ubi-MUI 2011 ACM Workshop Summary

Ali Asghar Nazari Shirehjini, Sahin Albayrak
DAI-Labor
Technical University of Berlin
[Ali.Nazari, Sahin.Albayrak]@dai-labor.de

Abdulsalam Yassine
Alcatel-Lucent
Ottawa, Canada
Abdulsalam.Yassine@alcatel-lucent.com

ABSTRACT
Intelligent Environments have the vision of enhancing our everyday environment and interaction with its objects by sensing, computing, and communication capabilities. The major characteristics of such environments are the increasing number of embedded intelligent devices (*ubiquity*) into the background (*transparency*). These devices are expected to disappear or blend into the background and will be invisible to the user. However, because of this transparency, users fail to develop an adequate mental model for interaction with such environments. The Ubiquitous Meta User Interfaces (Ubi-MUI) ACM workshop provides a venue for the development of highly intuitive, multimedia supported meta user interfaces that bring transparency, predictability, and control into intelligent environments.

Categories & Subject Descriptors: H. Information system: H.1.2 User/machine systems- Human Factors

General Terms: Design, Experimentation, Human Factors

INTRODUCTION
The nature of intelligent environments has transformed the way humans interact with the surrounding objects. Such advancement is calling for new types of user interfaces that create an overall system image for intelligent environments in order to help users to better understand and engage in the environment [1]. In this sense, representative user interfaces are Ubiquitous Meta User Interfaces (Ubi-MUI) that could increase the transparency and predictability of the whole system by visualizing the environment's internal states, perception and decision making processes. Using Ubi-MUI, users could observe, analyze, understand, control, and customize the adaptive behavior and context-dependent interactions of their surrounding. In such environments, multimedia play two key roles: they support new ways of interaction that apply to multiple human senses, and they diffuse the content presentation in the user's environment. Addressing the challenges of such research venue is a community-spanning effort, necessitating the pooling of resources and experiences of different research groups. While workshops related to Multimedia, Ubiquitous Computing and Human Factors exists, the unique requirements of interaction with and within intelligent environments require an interdisciplinary approach. The aim of this workshop thus is to provide a link (1) between these different research groups and (2) between the academic communities and industry groups.

MM'11, November 28–December 1, 2011, Scottsdale, Arizona, USA.
ACM 978-1-4503-0616-4/11/11.

BACKGROUND
Nowadays, there is a growing research community in the field of interactive systems that can be deployed for intelligent environments. The major characteristics of such environments are the increasing number of embedded intelligent devices (*ubiquity*) into the background (*transparency*). These environments will have profound impact on the type, content and functionality of the emerging products and services [2]. The research in the area of multimedia support that applies to the human senses in user interfaces is still in its infancy stage for such environments. The majority of user interface design research is based on modeling relative user interface related knowledge (e.g. [3]). While somehow multimedia editors are included into the user interface model and task interpretations for example the work in [4] [5] and [6] to name few, these designs need to bring transparency, predictability, and control into intelligent environments. The open literature describes some studies which focus on human centric user interfaces for smart environments. A survey of such studies can be found in [7]. The methods of user-centered design have been extended to other interaction paradigms as well, as described in [8]. While the interaction between the human and the computer is relatively low in legacy user interfaces, this interaction is much higher with smart environments. The human user can interact using her/his senses. The interaction can actually occupy the same space of the surrounding environment where the user is living. This interaction makes the transfer of the user-centered awareness to become very rich and highly context-dependent [9].

IMPORTANT TOPICS FOR UBI-MUI RESEARCH

This workshop intends to cover research that addresses representation of intelligent environments, concept of meta user interfaces, and implementation and evaluation aspects. Below are the details of such topics in relevant to the Ubi-MUI workshop.

Representing Intelligent Environments. This topic focuses on the state-of-the-art in areas related to visualization and animation of sensing activities, decisions, and implicit interactions of intelligent systems, which allows users to understand and predict the behavior of the system. It touches on awareness creation for implicit interaction concepts using multimedia artifacts. Using avatars, storytelling, or gaming to introduce the functional capabilities and adaptive behavior of intelligent environments to novice users is also included in the scope of this topic.

Concepts for Meta User Interfaces. Currently there is a momentum for multimodal multimedia interfaces to control and modify implicit interactions and the environment's responsive activities. This workshop extends its coverage to include user interfaces to control and modify system behavior. In this context, the emphasis is given to supportive user interfaces that create a system face for intelligent environments, natural meta interaction concepts allowing users an easy access to multimedia environments (search, exploration, manipulation and control of media and devices), touch and gesture based interfaces, 3D displays and audio immersive systems for augmented-reality. Also, topics such as metaphors and coordination algorithms for distributed conflict management are considered.

Implementation, and Evaluation Aspects. Especially in user-centric interfaces, it is important to provide methods to evaluate the added-value of multimedia assisted meta user interfaces. That is, including user studies related to mental models for human-environment-interaction and meta user interfaces. The workshop seeks for novel approaches to effectively manage the complexity of development, real-time, de-centralized media-processing architectures, middleware architectures for sensor and multimedia integration. Implementation and evaluation that encompasses activity analysis and domain observations related to phenomena such as loss of control and over-automation Smart Multimedia sensors are particularly important.

CONCLUSION

This workshop extends the trend of using multimedia supported meta user interfaces in smart environments. The areas of the research topics described in the previous section are very relevant to Ubi-MUI and expected to increase the richness of the interaction with the smart environments. The main goal of the workshop is to foster collaboration among researchers in their areas of interest related to Ubiquitous Meta User Interfaces and allow a face-to-face exchange of ideas.

REFERENCES

[1] S. Komar. Challenges for Ubiquitous computing. Fifth International Conference on Networking and Services, 2009

[2] V. Coroama, J. Bohn, F. Mattern, Living in a smart environment—implications for the coming ubiquitous information society, in: Proceedings of the International Conference on Systems, Man and Cybernetics 2004 (IEEE SMC 2004), vol. 6, The Hague, 2004, pp. 5633–5638, The Netherlands, October 10-13

[3] D. Grammenos, S Kartakis, I Adami, C. Stephanidis, CAMILE: controlling AmI lights easily, in: Proceedings of the 1st ACM International Conference on Pervasive Technologies Related to Assistive Environments (PETRA 2008), 15–19 July 2008, Athens, Greece, [CD-ROM], New York, ACM Press, 2008.

[4] J.Y. Han. Low-cost multi-touch sensing through frustrated total internal reflection. In: UIST 2005: Proceedings of the 18th annual ACM symposium on User interface software and technology, ACM Press, New York, NY, USA, pp 115–118

[5] A. Wilson, S. Izadi, O. Hilliges, A. Garcia-Mendoza , D. Kirk. Bringing Physics to the Surface. In: In proceedings of the 21st ACM Symposium on User Interface Software and Technologies (ACM UIST), Monterey, CA, USA, 2008

[6] S. Boring, O. Hilliges, A. Butz. A wall-sized focus plus context display. In: Proceedings of the Fifth Annual IEEE Conference on Pervasive Computing and communications (PerCom) 2007

[7] Vredenburg K, Mao JY, Smith PW, Carey T (2002) A survey of user-centered design practice. In: CHI '02: Proceedings of the SIGCHI conference on Human factors in computing systems, ACM, New York, NY, USA, pp 471–478, 2002

[8] K. Luyten, C. Vandervelpen, J. Van Den Bergh, K. Coninx, Context-sensitive user interfaces for ambient environments: design, development and deployment, http://hdl.handle.net/1942/7935, in: Dagstuhl Seminar 05181: Mobile Computing and Ambient Intelligence: The Challenge of Multimedia (Dagstuhl Seminar 05181), 2005.

[9] A. Buts. User Interfaces and HCI for Ambient Intelligence and Smart Environments. Available at: http://cs.gmu.edu/~jpsousa/classes/895/readings/0533.pdf

The Third ACM International Workshop on Multimedia Technologies for Distance Learning (MTDL 2011)

Rynson W.H. Lau
Department of Computer Science
City University of Hong Kong
Hong Kong
+852-2788-7525
rynson@cs.cityu.edu.hk

Timothy K. Shih
Dept. of Computer Science and Info Engineering
National Central University
Taiwan
+886-(0)3-422-7151
timothykshih@gmail.com

Frederick Li
School of Engineering and Computing Sciences
University of Durham
United Kingdom
+44-(0)191-33-44299
frederick.li@durham.ac.uk

Neil Y. Yen
Dept. of Human Informatics and Cognitive Sciences
Waseda University
Japan
+81-(0)3-3203-4337
neil219@gmail.com

ABSTRACT
The MTDL 2011 workshop in its third edition aims to continue in the contribution and evaluation of the impact of multimedia technologies to e-Learning. This workshop is held in conjunction with the ACM Multimedia 2011 Conference in Scottsdale, Arizona, U.S.A.. As a cover paper of this workshop, we briefly summarize important issues to be addressed in e-learning in the first section, followed by a discussion of important issues proposed in the 5 papers accepted to the workshop (among the 9 submissions), plus 3 invited papers.

Categories and Subject Descriptors
D.2.10 [Design]: Methodologies, Representation.
H.1.2 [User/Machine Systems]: Human factors.
H.5.2 [User Interface]: User-Centered Design, Interaction styles.
I.4.9 [Image Processing and Computer Vision]: Applications.

General Terms:
Algorithms, Management, Performance, Design, Human Factors, Theory.

Keywords:
Multimedia Technologies, e-Learning, Distance Learning, Game-based Learning, Learning Methodologies

1. INTRODUCTION
Multimedia technologies are having a big impact in education at all levels, from schools to universities, and in all educational institutions and approaches ranging from face to face education to distance learning or open universities. With the blooming and generalization of Internet-based multimedia technologies, e-learning is moving toward another era with the development of new multimedia technologies and their integration with the pre-existing e-learning infrastructure. But to have a significant impact all this technology innovations should carefully address both pedagogical and technological perspectives to ensure their successful incorporation in e-learning.

MM'11, November 28–December 1, 2011, Scottsdale, Arizona, USA.
ACM 978-1-4503-0616-4/11/11.

This third ACM MTDL workshop aims to discuss problems, current studies, and solutions in how to use multimedia and communication technologies to improve e-learning. This workshop follows the success of the First ACM Workshop (MTDL 2009) held in Beijing, 2009 [1] and the Second ACM Workshop (MTDL 2010) held in Italy, 2010 [2]. The goal is to continue providing a public forum for researchers and practitioners to exchange new ideas and information regarding advancements in the state of the art of emerging multimedia and e-learning related issues from multidisciplinary perspectives. This workshop also facilitates to identify new research topics and envision the future.

Some of the open key issues for distance learning are how to integrate the new technology developments with the preexisting systems that are already in use in the educational institutions. For instance new mobile devices are continuously appearing and there are no widely accepted models about how to use effectively these devices in the educational domain. Besides, new approaches such as game-based learning or social learning are being proposed as a way to improve education but it is not clear how these approaches can be integrated in the learning flow. In addition, generalization of e-learning technologies has been based on the development of e-learning standards and specifications that simplify the reusability of contents and the interoperability across heterogeneous systems and platforms. Hence, new proposal should take into account these standardization initiatives.

In the next section, the main contributions of the five regular papers accepted and three invited papers in MTDL 2011 are outlined.

2. WORKSHOP PAPERS
In [3], Jailly et al. present an interactive multimedia interface allowing students to remotely control a spectrum analyzer. The focus of the paper is to build a mixed reality system to support collaborative training under a remote laboratory environment. The system also includes a VoIP tool and colored based widgets to support group awareness.

In [4], Ghosh et al. present a framework supporting distance education in rural areas of India and developing countries. It relies on a low-cost equipment, Home Infotainment Platform, to compliment Direct-To-Home (DTH) television network, allowing video lectures and asynchronous interaction to be delivery on a slow-speed Internet. The framework connects city-based expert teachers and students of rural areas.

In [5], Javahari et al. present a real-time collaborative multimedia education framework based on an N-tiers distributed architecture. The study emphasizes on sustaining support for a large number of live users to perform different learning activities, such as simulations, quizzes, and games. The case studies reveal the feasibility of the proposed framework.

In [6], Zhang et al. verify Association Link Network (ALN) having the Small-World characteristic. Given such a property and ALN can be constructed to semantically link up Web resources from the Internet, a new filtering algorithm is proposed to discover relevant Web resources for supporting Web-based learning.

In [7], Niu et al. present a user evaluation framework for Web-based learning systems. The evaluation and the guiding of users are throughout the whole process of learning. This paper analyzes users' learning behavior to provide personalized services. Preliminary experiments show the effectiveness for improving students' learning effects and the precision of user evaluation.

In [8], Li et al. consider to provide facilities supporting interactive tutoring activities. In the domain of learning cooking recipes, in particular, various retrieval functions are needed to provide learners with adequate references and access to various multimedia recipes in circumstances such as recipe adaptation and transferred learning. This paper provides an overview description of an intelligent tutoring system equipped with such advanced facilities.

In [9], Li and Watson present a game-based learning environment to support novice students learning programming. The proposed environment exploits game construction tasks to make the elementary programming more intuitive to learn. It also comprises concept visualization techniques, which allows students to visualize and learn key concepts in programming through game object manipulation.

In [10], Yen and Jin present a general model to identify the implicit correlations between shared learning resources and produce the reusable paths among resources. The context (i.e., geographical information) is considered to make real-time alternation to the generated paths to fulfill specific search scenario. The idea is implemented on iPads, serving as a preliminary instance of pervasive learning.

REFERENCES

[1] Shih, T.K., Lau, R.W.H., and Yen, N. 2009. "ACM International Workshop on Multimedia Technologies for Distance Learning (MTDL 2009)," *Proc. ACM MTDL 2009.*

[2] Shih, T.K., Lau, R.W.H., and Magnenat-Thalmann, N. 2010. "ACM International Workshop on Multimedia Technologies for Distance Learning (MTDL 2010)," *Proc. ACM MTDL 2010.*

[3] Jailly, B., Gravier, C., Preda, M., and Fayolle, J. 2011. "Interactive Mixed Reality for Collaborative Remote Laboratories," *Proc. ACM MTDL 2011.*

[4] Ghosh, H., Wattamwar, S., Oberoi, T., Shroff, G., Pal, A., Dasgupta, R., and Chakravarty, K. 2011. "A Novel Framework for Distance Education using Asynchronous Interaction," *Proc. ACM MTDL 2011.*

[5] Jayahari, K., Bijlani, K., and Mathew, A. 2011. "A-VIEW: Real Time Collaborative Multimedia e-Learning," *Proc. ACM MTDL 2011.*

[6] Zhang, S. and Luo, X. 2011. "Discovering Small-World in Association Link Networks For Web-based Learning," *Proc. ACM MTDL 2011.*

[7] Niu, K., Chen, W., Niu, Z., Li, Q., Gu, P., Li, Y., and Huang, Z. 2011. "A User Evaluation Framework for Web-Based Learning Systems," *Proc. ACM MTDL 2011.*

[8] Li, Q., Mao, X., and Xie, H. 2011. "Interactive Tutoring of Cooking Activities with Personalized Multimedia Recipe Search," *Proc. ACM MTDL 2011.*

[9] Li, F. and Watson, C. 2011. "Game-Based Concept Visualization for Learning Programming," *Proc. ACM MTDL 2011.*

[10] Yen, N.Y. and Jin, Q. 2011. "Discovery of Implicit Correlation between Shared Information in an Open Environment," *Proc. ACM MTDL 2011.*

ACM International Workshop on Interactive Multimedia on Mobile and Portable Devices (IMMPD'11)

Jiebo Luo
University of Rochester
Rochester, NY 14627, USA
jluo@cs.rochester.edu

Caifeng Shan
Philips Research
High Tech Campus 36
Eindhoven 5656 AE, The Netherlands
+31 40 2741601
caifeng.shan@philips.com

Ling Shao
The University of Sheffield
Mappin Street
Sheffield S1 3JD, United Kingdom
+44 114 222 5841
ling.shao@sheffield.ac.uk

Minoru Etoh
NTT DoCoMo
Yokosuka, Japan
etoh@nttdocomo.co.jp

ABSTRACT
With the mobile and portable devices become ubiquitous for people's daily life, how to design user interfaces of these products that enable natural, intuitive and fun interaction is one of the main challenges the multimedia community is facing. Following several successful events, the ACM International workshop on Interactive Multimedia on Mobile and Portable Devices (IMMPD'11) aims to bring together researchers from both academia and industry in domains including computer vision, audio and speech processing, machine learning, pattern recognition, communications, human-computer interaction, and media technology to share and discuss recent advances in interactive multimedia.

Categories and Subject Descriptors
F.1.2 [**Theory of Computation**]: Modes of Computation – *Interactive and reactive computation.* H.5.2 [**Information Systems**]: Information Interfaces and Presentation – *User Interfaces* I.1.2 [**Computing Technologies**]: Artificial Intelligence I.1.4 [**Computing Technologies**]: Image Processing and Computer Vision. I.1.5 [**Computing Technologies**]: Pattern Recognition

General Terms
Algorithms, Design, Experimentation, Measurement, Human Factors, Performance, Theory.

Keywords
Multimedia, Human-Computer Interaction, Consumer Electronics, Computer Vision, Pattern Recognition.

MM'11, November 28–December 1, 2011, Scottsdale, Arizona, USA.
ACM 978-1-4503-0616-4/11/11.

1. INTRODUCTION
With the development of silicon technologies, mobile and portable electronics devices, such as personal computers, mobile phones, digital cameras, and PDA, have become ubiquitous for people's daily life. These devices provide multimedia sources for entertainment, communication, and so on. How to design user interfaces of these products that enable natural, intuitive and fun interaction is one of the main challenges the multimedia community is facing.

Considering that mobile and portable devices are usually supplied with multiple sensors (e.g., camera and microphone), how to employ multimodal information for interaction has recently received much attention in both academia and industry. But interactive multimedia is still an under-explored field. Many challenges exist when moving to multimodal interaction: for example, how to annotate and search huge data acquired by using multiple sensors, especially in the unconstrained end-user environments? How to effectively extract and select representative multimedia features for human behavior recognition? How to select the fusion strategy of multimodal data for a given application? To address these challenges, we must adapt the existing approaches or find new solutions suitable for multimedia interaction on mobile and portable devices.

Multimedia interaction on mobile and portable devices is a hot topic, and records of recent ACM Multimedia conferences demonstrated this trend. Recent efforts have led to many exciting applications and products (prototypes). The major objectives of this workshop are: 1) collecting and seeking the recent advances in multimedia interaction; 2) exploiting potential challenges and possible advanced solutions in terms of theory and practice, and 3) illustrating the great value of multimedia interaction with successful real-world applications. The participants can also get in touch with a variety of recent techniques as well as the case studies of different tasks from multimedia interaction applications. This workshop can also serve to bridge laboratory research and industrial practice to a considerable degree.

This workshop builds upon the previous events organized by the workshop organizers: Special Session on Multimedia Understanding for Consumer Electronics, International Conference on Multimedia Modeling, 2011 and International Workshop on Interactive Multimedia for Consumer Electronics, ACM Multimedia, 2009. The targeted audiences are mainly researchers, engineers as well as graduate students working on relevant areas.

2. TOPICS OF INTEREST

Topics related to interactive multimedia on mobile and portable devices include:

- Multimedia description and markup
- Multimedia representation and annotation
- Multimedia search and retrieval
- Presence and environment sensing
- Face detection, tracking, and recognition
- Hand detection, tracking, and recognition
- Emotion/mood recognition
- Gesture/action/activity recognition
- Audio-visual recognition and interaction
- Novel interaction (accelerometer, touch screen, haptics, voice, etc.)
- Multimodal data modeling and fusion
- Multimedia content adaptation
- Context-aware services
- Interaction with depth-sensing

3. TECHNICAL PROGRAM

Based on review comments, eight papers are accepted for this half-day workshop, covering different related topics. The accepted papers are from industry and academia, representing diverse geographic locations including United States, Europe, Japan, Taiwan, and China.

The accepted papers are

- A Novel PRO-CAM based interactive display surface, Wenhong Yuan, et al. (University of Science and Technology of China, Nokia)
- Mobile Interactive Region-of-Interest Video Streaming with Crowd-Driven Prefetching, Derek Pang, et al. (Stanford University)
- Comp2Watch: Enhancing the Mobile Video Browsing Experience, Yu-Ming Hsu, et al. (National Taiwan University)
- Image Collection Summarization for Search Result Overviewing on Mobile Devices, Go Irie, et al. (NTT Corporation, Cornell University, The University of Tokyo)
- Interactive and Real-Time Generation of Home Video Summaries on Mobile Devices, Jianwei Niu, et al. (Beihang University, Nokia Research Center)
- Using Ephemeral Clustering and Query Logs to Organize Web Image Search Results on Mobile Devices, Gaël Dias and Jose Moreno (University of Beira Interior)
- System Level Power Allocation Algorithm for Mobile Devices for Full Playback Guarantee, Sachin Deshpande and Louis Kerofsky (Sharp Laboratories of America)

4. PROGRAM COMMITTEE

We would like to express our gratitude to the program committee, who worked very hard in reviewing papers and providing suggestions for their improvements. The Program Committee members and their affiliations are listed as follows.

- Xavier Binefa, University of Barcelona, Spain
- Andrea Cavallaro, Queen Mary University of London, UK
- Berna Erol, Ricoh Innovations, USA
- Yun (Raymond) Fu, SUNY at Buffalo, USA
- Ling Guan, Ryerson University, Canada
- Aki Harma, Philips Research, The Netherlands
- Winston Hsu, National Taiwan University, Taiwan
- Alejandro Jaimes, Telefonica I+D, Spain
- Tae-Kyun Kim, Cambridge University, UK
- Qian Lin, HP Labs, USA
- Alexander C. Loui, Kodak Research Labs, USA
- Xiaoming Liu, GE Global Research, USA
- Tao Mei, Microsoft Research Asia, China
- Anton Nijholt, University of Twente, The Netherlands
- Jean-Marc Odobez, IDIAP Research Institute, Switzerland
- Yoichi Sato, University of Tokyo, Japan
- Wolfgang Hurst, Utrecht University, The Netherlands
- Shihong Lao, Omron, Japan
- Kari Pulli, NVIDIA, USA
- Xiaoyi Jiang, University of Munster, Germany

Frontiers in Multimedia Search

Alan Hanjalic, Martha Larson
Multimedia Information Retrieval Lab
Department of Mediamatics
Delft University of Technology
Delft, The Netherlands
{a.hanjalic, m.a.larson}@tudelft.nl

ABSTRACT
This outline summarizes our tutorial "Frontiers in Multimedia Search", whose goal is to provide insights into the most recent developments in the field of multimedia retrieval and to identify the issues and bottlenecks that could determine the directions of research focus for the coming years. We present an overview of new algorithms and techniques, particularly concentrating on those innovative approaches that are informed by neighboring fields including information retrieval, speech and language processing and network analysis. We also discuss evaluation of new algorithms, in particular, making use of crowdsourcing for the development of the necessary data sets.

Categories and Subject Descriptors
H.3.1 [**Information Storage and Retrieval**]: Content Analysis and Indexing, H.3.3 [**Information Storage and Retrieval**]: Information Search and Retrieval

General Terms
Algorithms, Performance, Experimentation, Theory

Keywords
tutorial, multimedia, search, retrieval.

1. INTRODUCTION
Multimedia that cannot be found is, in a certain sense, useless. It is lost in a huge collection, or worse, in a back alley of the Internet, never viewed and impossible to reuse. Research in multimedia retrieval is directed at developing techniques that bring image and video content together with users—matching multimedia content and user needs. Over the past few years, the field of multimedia has directed substantial effort at developing efficient and scalable solutions for multimedia search and has reached an impressive level of achievement. Serious attention has been devoted to shaking off the comfortable habits that arose in the early years due to over-eager pursuit of hyped research topics and myopic focus on benchmark datasets and tasks.

The field generates a constant stream of new results, but they are scattered across different tracks and conferences. This fragmentation means that productive paths towards further improving the multimedia search results are challenging to identify. Moreover, enormous potential remains to be exploited by better integrating expertise from fields such as information retrieval (IR) and speech and language processing into the development of multimedia search paradigms.

MM'11, November 28–December 1, 2011, Scottsdale, Arizona, USA.
ACM 978-1-4503-0616-4/11/11.

The objective of this tutorial is to present an overview of research efforts at the frontiers of multimedia search. The tutorial represents an extension and improvement of the tutorial presented last year [1]. It is designed to guide participants in more effectively directing their own research effort and in abandoning assumptions about the nature of the field that have become outdated. In particular, we argue that it is necessary to keep the focus of our research efforts set on the ever-evolving needs of the user. The tutorial also aims at providing a solid introduction to techniques from the fields of IR and speech and language processing that are potentially valuable if deployed in a multimedia search context.

In the tutorial, we will first give an overview of "multimedia search in the wild," how and when we use multimedia access and retrieval technologies in our lives, both personal and professional. The overview makes clear the nature of multimedia search approaches that are needed to support us in our work and leisure activities. We go on by discussing the main bottlenecks, illustrated by specific examples that are currently preventing the adoption of multimedia search technology in practice. The core of the tutorial is constituted by the presentation of a set of cutting edge ideas, approaches and concrete techniques that show potential to effectively address these bottlenecks. Each case is illustrated by examples and experimental results.

This tutorial is aimed as researchers already working in multimedia retrieval, but looking for new challenges and new orientations. We also address new scientists and provide guidance in choosing how to best approach the multimedia search problem and which promising new research areas to explore. We have designed the tutorial to be relevant to researchers in both academia and industry, and we present for them a perspective on what we believe to be the future of multimedia search.

2. TUTORIAL OVERVIEW

2.1 Usefulness of Multimedia Search
We start the course program by addressing the same fundamental question as in the last year's installment of this tutorial, namely *how multimedia search can benefit people's personal and professional lives.* We do this by unraveling the multimedia search process and identifying the aspects that are critical when devising a multimedia search mechanism truly useful for people.

We often find ourselves pursuing specific *goals* in our personal lives or at work. These life-level goals are largely a function of our activities and often have a component with (potentially) a strong relationship to multimedia search, e.g., informing ourselves in order to make decisions, entertaining ourselves, building relationships with others and learning how to do specific activities. Goals are typically pursued by planning and carrying out a set of tasks. A multimedia search task is associated with a particular multimedia *content need.* The user's content need, also called an *information need*, is the user's conceptualization of what kind of results are necessary to complete the task. The content need encompasses the intellectual content of the item, aspects of the item related to style, aesthetics and provenance, (e.g., creator), as well as physical properties of the item (e.g., file type). The user expresses his/her information need as a *query*. The query can be implicit or explicit, and is typically *refined* by the user over the course of the search session to make it more effective. Refinement reflects attempts at making the query more effective or development in the underlying information need. The way a user formulates a query is dependent on personal knowledge and whether that person is a professional or a casual searcher. A large part of the challenge of multimedia search is to reconstruct the content needs of users based on their (typically imperfect) queries.

Once the query is specified, the next critical question to be addressed is *what a search system should offer a user.* The following main issues play a role here:

- **'Aboutness':** Will the system interpret the query of the user as an attempt to specify a distinguishing characteristic of the item or as an expression of what the item should be about, i.e., the subject matter treated by the item?
- **Diversity versus relevance:** Should the system offer a wide range of results and let the human help decide what is relevant or offer only a limited range of balanced results?
- **Transparency:** Should the system communicate to the user how the results are relevant to the query or attempt to represent some kind of confidence in the correctness or the completeness of the result?

2.2 Making the most of the user

In view of the above, exploiting the interaction of the user with the search system can be seen as the first step towards the development of multimedia search solutions that take the abovementioned usefulness aspects into account. Approaches that make the most of the user can employ several tactics. For example, they can enhance the query to better be able to reveal the user information need and search intent. Alternatively, they can enrich the collection by implicit or explicit metadata and in this way facilitate the calculation of the relevance of collection items to user queries. Approaches discussed include:

- Transaction Log Analysis: Information need inference through search/browsing history (e.g., click-throughs),
- Context modeling in multimedia search,
- (Visual) Query suggestion,
- User-supported query expansion,
- Helping users to choose where to start searching.

2.3 Making the most of the collection

In the next step, we discuss the relationships that exist in the collection and in the search environment, like, for example, similarities among documents, connections among users and interactions between users and documents. These relationships can provide rich information that can be exploited to improve multimedia search performance. Two categories of approaches and techniques working in this direction will be discussed:

- Maximizing the quality of the top-N search results using IR concepts and cross-modal analysis,
  - (Visual) Search reranking,
  - Query-class-dependent search,
  - Query performance prediction,
- Integrating social information from networked communities,
  - Tag propagation and de-noising using collaborative actions in a community of users,
  - Multimedia annotation and similarity computation using community-contributed metadata.

2.4 Making the most of multimedia items

Automatic indexing systems (e.g., speech recognition, audio event detection, semantic concept detection) are well known for their imperfections (indexing noise). Multimedia search paradigms are required that can robustly deal with these imperfections. Challenges, promising ideas and approaches working in this direction will be discussed, such as:

- Lessons learned from speech recognition (features engineering, confidence scores and lattices),
- Exploiting characteristics of multimedia items that are revealed using simple methods of structural analysis,
- Integrating information from external sources to reduce influence of indexing noise.

2.5 How to make impact?

As in last year's installment of our tutorial, we close by covering promising areas in which research topics can be formulated and opportunities to work within evolving new paradigms, including:

- **Cross-disciplinary work**: Understanding the multimedia production process, understanding human communication, cognition and physiology.
- **Crowdsourcing**: The creation of multimedia annotations can be divided into small tasks and carried out by workers on a crowdsourcing platform such as Amazon's Mechanical Turk in exchange for a small reward. If good task design and appropriate quality control can be imposed, crowdsourcing is viable for cost-effective generation of the groundtruth necessary for algorithm evaluation.
- **Benchmarking and Innovation challenges**: Drive forward the state of the art and allow for cross-site algorithmic comparison. We focus on two examples: the MediaEval benchmarking effort, which emphasizes human and social aspects of multimedia access and retrieval, and the ACM Multimedia Grand Challenge, which calls for solutions to challenges formulated by industry.

3. LITERATURE

The material for the tutorial consists of lecture slides and a list of conference and journal publications representative of the ideas and paradigms discussed in the tutorial. The literature list is made available online via a citeulike group with the name *mirfrontiers*, (http://www.citeulike.org/group/13276/library).

4. REFERENCES

[1] Alan Hanjalic and Martha Larson. Advances in multimedia retrieval, Part I: Frontiers in multimedia search. In *Proceedings of ACM MM '10*, 1773-1774.

Internet Multimedia Advertising: Techniques and Technologies

Tao Mei †, Ruofei Zhang ‡, Xian-Sheng Hua †
† Microsoft Research Asia
‡ Yahoo! Labs
{tmei, xshua}@microsoft.com; rzhang@yahoo-inc.com

ABSTRACT

The explosive growth of multimedia data on the Internet creates huge opportunities for multimedia advertising. In this tutorial, we present the techniques and technologies for Internet multimedia advertising. The tutorial aims at bringing together recent insights from the research on multimedia advertising that addresses the theoretical fundamentals, solution concepts, and the issues related to the development of modern multimedia advertising schemes.

Categories and Subject Descriptors

H.3.3 [**Information Storage and Retrieval**]: Information Search and Retrieval—*Selection process*; H.3.5 [**Information Storage and Retrieval**]: Online Information Services—*Web-based services*; H.5.2 [**Information Interfaces and Presentation**]: User interface—*User-centered design*

General Terms

Algorithms, Experiments, Human Factors

Keywords

Online advertising, multimedia advertising.

1. TUTORIAL DESCRIPTION

Advertising provides financial support for a large portion of today's Internet ecosystem. Compared to traditional means of advertising, such as a banner outside a store or textual advertisements in newspapers, multimedia advertising has some unique advantages: it is more attractive and more salient than plain text, it is able to instantly grab users' attention and it carries more information that can also be comprehended more quickly than when reading a text advertisement. Rapid convergence of multimedia, Internet and mobile devices has opened new opportunities for manufacturers and advertisers to more effectively and efficiently reach potential customers. While largely limiting itself to radio and TV channels currently, multimedia advertising is about to break through on the web using various concepts of internet multimedia advertising.

The explosive growth of multimedia data on the web also creates huge opportunities for further monetizing them with multimedia advertisements. Multimedia content becomes a natural information carrier for advertising in a way similar to radio wave to carry bits in digital communications. More and more business models are rolled out to freely distribute multimedia content and recoup the revenue from the multimedia advertisements it carries. With the increasing importance of online multimedia advertising, researchers from multimedia community have made significant progresses along this direction. This tutorial aims at: 1) reviewing and summarizing recent high-quality research works on internet multimedia advertising, including basic technologies and applicable systems, and 2) presenting insight into the challenges and future directions in this emerging and promising area.

This tutorial is based on our recently edited book on multimedia advertising [1], and survey papers on media and text advertising [2, 3]. It is appropriate to both graduate students and senior researchers working in the field of multimedia and/or online advertising, as well as industry practitioners who are working in the field of search engine development, video/image content providers, developers of video/image sharing portals and IPTV providers. Instead of in depth coverage of contemporary papers, this tutorial will introduce the important general concepts and themes of this timely topic. Moreover, we will also show extensive demos on contextual multimedia advertising.

The tutorial will address the following aspects in multimedia advertising: 1) introduction of traditional text advertising techniques, 2) understanding audience for user-targeted advertising, 3) image advertising which associates an image with a piece of advertisement, 4) video advertising which associate a video sequence with a set of advertisements, 5) mobile advertising which recommends context-aware and personalized entities to a give user, and 6) challenges and future directions.

2. REFERENCES

[1] X.-S. Hua, T. Mei, and A. Hanjalic. *Online Multimedia Advertising: Techniques and Technologies.* IGI Global, 2011.

[2] M. Karimzadehgan, W. Li, R. Zhang, and J. Mao. A stochastic learning-to-rank algorithm and its application to contextual advertising. In *Proceedings of International World Wide Web Conference*, pages 377–386, March 2011.

[3] T. Mei and X.-S. Hua. Contextual internet multimedia advertising. *Proceedings of the IEEE*, 98(8):1416–1433, August 2010.

MM'11, November 28–December 1, 2011, Scottsdale, Arizona, USA.
ACM 978-1-4503-0616-4/11/11.

Internet Video Search

Cees G. M. Snoek
ISLA, Informatics Institute
University of Amsterdam
Science Park 904, 1098 XH
Amsterdam, The Netherlands
cgmsnoek@uva.nl

Arnold W. M. Smeulders
ISLA, Informatics Institute
University of Amsterdam
Science Park 904, 1098 XH
Amsterdam, The Netherlands
arnoldsmeulders@uva.nl

ABSTRACT

In this tutorial, we focus on the challenges in internet video search, present methods how to achieve state-of-the-art performance while maintaining efficient execution, and indicate how to obtain improvements in the near future. Moreover, we give an overview of the latest developments and future trends in the field on the basis of the TRECVID competition - the leading competition for video search engines run by NIST - where we have achieved consistent top performance over the past years, including the 2008, 2009 and 2010 editions.

Categories and Subject Descriptors: H.3.3 Information Storage and Retrieval: Information Search and Retrieval
General Terms: Algorithms, Experimentation, Performance
Keywords: Visual categorization, video retrieval, information visualization

1. TUTORIAL DESCRIPTION

The scientific topic of video search is dominated by five major challenges:

a the *sensory gap* between an object and its many appearances due to the accidental sensing conditions;

b the *semantic gap* between a visual concept and its lingual representation;

c the *model gap* between the amount of notions in the world and the capacity to learn them;

d the *query-context gap* between the information need and the possible retrieval solutions;

e the *interface gap* between the tiny window the screen offers to the amount of data;

The semantic gap is bridged by forming a dictionary of visual detectors for concepts and events. The largest ones to date consist of hundreds of concepts excluding concept-tailored algorithms. It would simply take too long to achieve. Instead, we come closer to the ideal of one computer vision algorithm tailored automatically to the purpose at hand by employing example data to learn from. We discuss the advantages and limitations of a machine learning approach from examples. We show for what type of semantics the approach is likely to succeed or fail. In compensation for the absence of concept-specific (geometric or appearance) models, we emphasize the importance of good feature sets. They form the basis of the observational model by all possible color, shape, texture or structure invariant features help to characterize the concept and event at hand. Apart from good features, the other essential component is state-of- the-art machine learning in order to get the most out of the learning data.

We integrate the features and machine learning aspects into a complete internet video search engine, which has successfully competed in TRECVID. The multimedia system includes computer vision, machine learning, information retrieval, and human-computer interaction. We follow the video data as they flow through the efficient computational processes. Starting from fundamental visual features, covering local shape, texture, color, motion and the crucial need for invariance. Then, we explain how invariant features can be used in concert with kernel-based supervised learning methods to arrive at an event or concept detector. We discuss the important role of fusion on a feature, classifier, and semantic level to improve the robustness and general applicability of detectors. We end our component-wise decomposition of internet video search engines by explaining the complexities involved in delivering a limited set of uncertain concept detectors to an inpatient online user. For each of the components we review state-of-the-art solutions in literature, each having different characteristics and merits.

Comparative evaluation of methods and systems is imperative to appreciate progress. We discuss the data, tasks, and results of TRECVID, the leading benchmark. In addition, we discuss the many derived community initiatives in creating annotations, baselines, and software for repeatable experiments. We conclude the course with our perspective on the many challenges and opportunities ahead for the multimedia retrieval community.

Acknowledgments

This tutorial is supported by STW SEARCHER, FES COMMIT, and the IARPA ALADDIN via Department of Interior National Business Center contract number D11PC20067. Disclaimer: The views and conclusions contained herein are those of the authors and should not be interpreted as necessarily representing the official policies or endorsements, either expressed or implied, of IARPA, DoI/NBC, or the U.S. Government.

MM'11, November 28–December 1, 2011, Scottsdale, Arizona, USA.
ACM 978-1-4503-0616-4/11/11.

Semantic Computing in Multimedia

ACM Multimedia Tutorial

Simone Santini*
Universidad Autónoma de Madrid
Madrid, Spain
simone.santini@uam.es

ABSTRACT

This short overview describes teh contents of the tutorial *Semantic computing in multimedia*, which was offered to the participants of *ACM Multimedia 2011*.

Given the impossibility of summarizing properly the contents of the tutorial in just two pages, the purpose of this overview is mainly to introduce the reader to the relevant bibliography.

Categories and Subject Descriptors

H.5.1 [**Multimedia Information Systems**]: methodology; H.1.1 [**Systems and Information Theory**]: General systems theory

General Terms

Design,Human Factors,Standardization

Keywords

Semantics,multimedia semantics,context,logic

Semantics, as a cognitive computing topic (as opposed, for example, to the formal semantics of programming languages) began within artificial intelligence and then, beginning in the 1980s, faded from public attention following the then general decline of the interest in symbolic artificial intelligence [15]. Those were the heydays of connectionism, and connectionist machines, ex hypothesi, would not model semantics explicitly [5]. However, in the last ten years or so there has been a significant resurgence of the technical discourse on semantics, based on the diffused opinion that the large amount of data available today can be properly managed only through a qualitative leap in the processing capabilities of computing machines [2]. A semantic leap, as it is. This is true especially for multimedia data such as video and audio, whose temporal nature (and the consequent imposition of the temporality of the data to the user) makes browsing awkward [14]. Regardless of the correctness, or even the plausibility, of the preminence given to semantic for the solution of the data access problems (a relation on which the jury is still out [16, 18]), the relation between meaning and formal systems (for such are computers) has an obvious scientific significance *per se*, and it is a praiseworthy enterprise whose scientific and cultural value can stand on its own.

Semantics is a complex issue, with a history of many centuries and a variety of different points of view (see, for instance, [9, 6] for some bibliography). In order to do serious research on semantics, the computing scientist must be aware of important and complex theoretical questions, and of the solutions and models that the different schools of thought have proposed. The purpose of this tutorial is to provide such background. The idea is to equip researchers with enough technical and philosophical background to allow them to make original and significant contributions to the discipline of semantic computing.

The purpose of this tutorial is not primarily to give the attendance information on standards and programming techniques (which, by know, are fairly well known to the majority of the scientists in the area, and well accessible through a plethora of well written books), but to give them a better view of the larger topics in which semantics is embedded. It is my opinion that learning techniques and standards is the easy part of the job, something that, to quote a popular academic saying, *can be learnt for $5 worth of late fees at the local library.* The difficult part, the one that needs a face-to-face discussion is, as it is often the case, to know what to do with these standards and techniques, that is, to understand the general theory of semantics and how the different techniques fit in it.

The tutorial is divided in three parts: an introductory one, and two parts dedicated each one to one of two major classes of approaches: the logical and the hermeneutical. The introductory part contained a brief history of semantics and related disciplines, such as logics and semiotics, as well as a brief history of pictorial communication and of the discoursive practices that have surrounded the creation of pictures and videos. We shall not go into much depth (this part alone could easily provide material for a Ph.D. if developed fully), but I shall give the attendants enough background to understand the scope and the problems of multimedia communication, and those generated by the deceptively simple concept of multimedia semantics [1, 7].

The second part dealt mainly with logic and with the logical approach to of semantics. It covered, roughly, a terrain that goes from Tarski [17] and Carnap [3] to curent ontologies [11], with some emphasis on model theory and some foray into partially uncharted waters, such as the use of fuzzy

*This work was supported by the *Ministerio de Educación y Ciencia* under the grant N. MEC TIN2008-06566-C04-02, *Information Retrieval on different media based on multidimensional models: relevance, novelty, personalization and context.*

MM'11, November 28–December 1, 2011, Scottsdale, Arizona, USA.
ACM 978-1-4503-0616-4/11/11.

logic for multimedia modeling. This section, in turn, was divided in two part. The first, and longest, was a technical discussion on the different concepts of semantics that have been used in logic, with special emphasis on aspect of formal semantics and on traditional knowledge representation (including ontologies, the semantic web, and their relation to multimedia). The second part contained a brief excursus on the presuppositions that underlie this work. Traditional logic is a discipline of formal reasoning and never quite dealt with the content (viz. the semantics) of statements. Ever since Aristotle, the systematizatization of the syllogism operated by the Scolastics, all the way to the axiomatic programme of Russel and the Analytic Philosophy [8], logic has been a science of the *forms* of reasoning, without any reference to the contents of the reasoning activity. If one looks, for example, at the classification of syllogisms, one will find a classification into types of phrases (*Barbara Darii celarent,...*) and a division into figures based only on formal properties of the sentence. Nothing is said of the content of these sentences. The only notable exception is Hegel who, in his *objective* logic, considered that the forms of logic were the basis of metaphysics, that is, of ontology. Alas, every attempt at developing formally Hegel's logic has failed.

To say that the meaning of a document (multimedia or otherwise) can be characterized by a logic theory requires certain assumptions, at the basis of which is the idea that a document has a *content*, independent (more or less) of the linguistic means that are used to express it, and that exists (more or less) intact even if nobody is interpreting the document. We analyzed critically this view of meaning, its plausibility, and the limits of its validity. In particular, we shall consider the notion of *semantic games* as a possible formalization of the Wittgenstenian notion of meaning as use [19].

The incipit of the third part formed a continuum with the non-technical discussion of the second part. While analyzing the presuppositions of the logic approach to semantics, we began to look at alternative views, with a special emphasis on two areas: *hermeneutics* [12] and *structural semantics* [10]. We worked to understand the rôle of the reader in the creation of meaning, the rôle of the discoursive practices of media creation, and that of the cultural conventions that drive the way in which media should be interpreted. The study of signification carried out in this way unveiled several important characteristics for the design of semantic systems. Meaning is not an attribute of an image or a video, but something that arises when an artifact is used as part of an *activity*, and only takes meaning in the context of that activity. That is, meaning is created when an artifact is interpreted in a context, and as part of an activity. So, rather than modeling the content of documents, we should model the activities that require access to the images and the context in which these activities take place. We considered several possible solutions for context modeling, highliting that the variable nature of context makes it imperative to use mehtods less brittle that logic. Consequently, we studied *soft computing* solutions, starting from the solutions adopted in information retrieval and content based image retrieval [13]. We considered the techniques oriented to a semantic characterization of the data, from latent semantics and self-organizing maps in information retrieval, to semantic claassification and cooperative systems in content based image retrieval [4].

The participants to the workshop received a booklet of notes. An improved and continuously updated version of this material is available from the web page of the author: `www.ii.uam.es/~ssantini`

1. REFERENCES

[1] Gonzalo Abril. *Análisis crítico de textos visuales.* Madrid:Sintesis, 2007.

[2] T. Bench-Capon and G. Malcom. Semantics for interoperability: relating ontologies and schemata. Technical Report ULCS-02-029, Dept. of computer science, University of Liverpool, 2000.

[3] Rudolf Carnap. Empiricism, semantics, and ontology. *Review Internationale de Philosophie*, 4, 1950.

[4] Scott Deerwester, Susan T. Dumais, George W, Furnas, Thomas K, Landauer, and Richard Harshman. Indexing by latent semantic analysis. *Journal of the American Society for Information Science*, 41(6):391–407, 2000.

[5] Hubert Dreyfus. *What computers still can't do: a critique of artificial reason.* Cambridge, MA:The MIT Press, 1992.

[6] Umberto Eco. *A theory of semiotics.* Bloomington:Indiana University Press, 1979.

[7] Norman Fairclough. *Media Discourse.* Bloomsbury, paperback edition, 2009.

[8] Jerry Fodor. *Concepts.* Oxford:Oxford University Press, 1997.

[9] Horst Geckeler. *Semántica estructural y teoría del campo léxico.* Madrid:Gredos, 1976. Spanish translation of *Strukturelle Semantik und Wortfeldtheorie* by Marcos Martínez Hernández.

[10] A. J. Greimas. *Sémantique structurale.* Paris:Larousse, 1966.

[11] N. Guarino. Formal ontology and information systems. In *Proceedings of FOIS 98, Trento, Italy, 6–8 June*, pages 3–15. Amsterdam:IOS Press, 1998.

[12] Roy J. Howard. *Three faces of Hermeneutics.* Berkeley:University of California, 1982.

[13] S. Kaski. Computationally efficient approximation of a probabilistic model for document representation in the WEBSOM full-text analysis method. *Neural Processing letters*, 5(2), 1997.

[14] Yong Rui, Thomas S. Huang, and Sharad Mehrotra. Constructing table-of-content for videos. *Multimedia Systems*, 7(5):359–368, 1999.

[15] S. Russell and P. Norvig. *Artificial inteligence, a modern approach.* Upper Saddle River:Prentice Hall, 1995.

[16] Karen Sparck Jones. What's new about the semantic web? some questions. *ACM SIGIR Forum*, 38(2):18–23, 2004.

[17] Alfred Tarski. The semantic conception of truth and the foundations of semantics. *Philosophy and phenomenological research*, 4, 1944.

[18] Yorick Wilks. The semantic web as the apotheosis of annotation, but what are its semantics? In *Twentieth National Conference on Artificial Intelligence (AAAI'05)*, 2005.

[19] Ludwig Wittgenstein. *Philosophical Investigations.* Prentice Hall, 1973.

Tutorial on Multimedia Music Signal Processing

[Extended Abstract]

Gaël Richard
Institut Telecom, Telecom ParisTech, CNRS-LTCI
37 rue Dareau, 75014 Paris, France

Categories and Subject Descriptors

H.5.5 [**Sound and Music Computing**]: Methodologies and techniques, Modeling, Signal analysis, synthesis, and processing; I.5.4 [**Applications**]: Signal processing

General Terms

Algorithms, Theory

Keywords

Multimodal Music signal processing, Audio signal representations, Decomposition models, Music source separation

1. MOTIVATION

The enormous amount of unstructured audio data available nowadays and the spread of its use as a data source in many applications are introducing new challenges to researchers in information and multimedia signal processing. Automatic analysis of audio documents (music, radio broadcast audio streams,...) gathers several research directions including *audio indexing and transcription* (extraction of informative features leading to audio content recognition or to the estimation of high level concepts such as melody, rhythm, instrumentation or harmony,...), *audio classification* (grouping by similarity, by music genre or by audio events categories) and *content-based retrieval* (such as query by example or query by humming approaches).

In this context, the general field of *Music signal Processing* is receiving a growing interest and becomes more relevant and more visible in the audio community. Nevertheless, if much work is tackled in audio and music signal processing it is somewhat often presented only in specialized music or audio signal processing conferences. In the multimedia community, the focus of interest is often on the *image* or *video signal* with less emphasis on the audio signal and its potential for analyzing or interpreting a multimedia scene.

The aim of the proposed tutorial is then to provide a general introduction of audio signal processing which should be of broad interest for the multimedia community, to review the state of the art in music signal processing (this will be largely based on [1]) and to highlight with some examples the potential of music signal processing for multimedia streams.

MM'11, November 28–December 1, 2011, Scottsdale, Arizona, USA.
ACM 978-1-4503-0616-4/11/11.

2. INTENDED AUDIENCE AND BENEFICES

The tutorial will mostly target an intermediate audience which has some knowledge in multimedia but may not be familiar with audio and music signals. The tutorial will nevertheless include some more advanced concepts which should also be of broad interest to students, researchers and engineers who are more knowledgeable in audio but who are not familiar with decomposition models or audio source separation principles.

The expected benefices for the multimedia community include:

- *a better understanding of audio processing basics* and potential for multimedia streams indexing. The tutorial will also include a brief presentation of existing open source tools which allow to rapidly design an audio indexing module.

- *a better understanding of decomposition models for music signals* and how they can be efficiently used to represent the signal as a set of objects or sources (with application to audio source separation). This will be illustrated using a number of sound examples in the context of karaoke applications or other audio remixing applications.

- *a better understanding of the potential of multimodality* through multimedia music examples. The tutorial will highlight this aspect on using two specific examples (a multimedia drum transcription system and a cross modal music video search.

3. TUTORIAL CONTENT

As outlined above, the objective of the tutorial is first to introduce some basics of music signal processing, to provide some more insights on decomposition models which are at the heart of a number of audio signal processing methods and then to illustrate on some well chosen examples how audio processing tools are particularly interesting for music multimedia streams processing.

The tutorial is **scheduled on half a day** and is structured in four main parts:

- **Introduction**: this section will provide a general introduction on the domain of audio and music signal processing and will illustrate the interest of this domain through a number of recent applications [1]. A typical architecture of an audio classification system will also be given and further discussed on an illustrative music indexing task (e.g. music instrument automatic recognition [2]).

- **Signal representations and decomposition models**: this section will start with the traditional Fourier representation of audio signal and related transformations which are particularly well suited for music signal analysis (Constant Q transform, Mel-Frequency transform, chromagrams,...). Decomposition models will then be rapidly presented and will include in particular greedy decomposition models [3] and factorization models [4] which are becoming popular for a wide variety of problems.
- **Application:** the signal representations and decomposition models will then be applied to music sources separation with examples on singing voice extraction [5], drum track separation [6] and bass line separation [7].
- **Multimodality:** the potential of multimodality in music signal processing will then be highlighted through two specific examples: a multimodal drum track separation [8, 9] and audio-based video search for music videos [10]. This part will also be the occasion to discuss some very early results on experiments conducted on the fully multimodal, multiple sensors database released for the ACM Multimedia 2011 Grand challenge sponsored by Huawei/3Dlife[1].

4. BIOGRAPHY

Prof. Gaël Richard received the State Engineering degree from Telecom ParisTech, in 1990, the Ph.D. and *Habilitation à Diriger des Recherches* degrees from University of Paris-XI, respectively in 1994 and 2001. He then spent two years at the CAIP Center, Rutgers University (USA), in the speech processing group of Prof. J. Flanagan, where he explored innovative approaches for speech production. Between 1997 and 2001, he successively worked for Matra Nortel Communications and Philips Consumer Communications. In particular, he was the project manager of several large-scale European projects in the field of multimodal speaker verification and audio processing. He then joined Télécom ParisTech where he is now full Professor and Head of the Audio, Acoustics and Waves research group. Co-author of over 80 papers and inventor in a number of patents, he is also an expert for the European Commission in Audio and Multimedia signal processing. Pr. Richard is a member of the EURASIP, senior member of IEEE, Associate Editor of the IEEE Transactions on Audio, Speech and Language Processing and member of the Audio Acoustics Signal Processing Technical committee of the IEEE. `www.telecom-paristech.fr/~grichard/`

5. REFERENCES

[1] M. Mueller, D. Ellis, A. Klapuri, and G. Richard. Signal processing for music analysis. *IEEE Journal on Selected Topics in Signal Processing*, 2011, To appear.

[2] G. Richard. *Audio Indexing*. Information Science Reference - IGI Global, 2008.

[3] L. Daudet. Audio sparse decompositions in parallel : let the greed be shared ! *IEEE Signal Processing Magazine*, 27(2):90–96, Mar. 2010.

[4] P. Smaragdis and J. Brown. Non-negative matrix factorization for polyphonic music transcription. In *In IEEE Workshop on Applications of Signal Processing to Audio and Acoustics*, pages 177–180, 2003.

[5] B. David J.L Durrieu and G. Richard. A musically motivated mid-level representation for pitch estimation and musical audio source separation. *IEEE Journal on Selected Topics in Signal Processing*, 2011, under review.

[6] O Gillet and G Richard. Transcription and separation of drum signals from polyphonic music. *IEEE Transactions on Audio, Speech and Language Processing*, 16(3):529–540, March 2008.

[7] M. Ryynänen and A. Klapuri. Automatic transcription of melody, bass line, and chords in polyphonic music. *Computer Music Journal*, 32(3):72–86, 2008.

[8] O. Gillet and G. Richard. Enst-drums: an extensive audio-visual database for drum signals processing. In *7th International Conference on Music Information Retrieval, ISMIR 2006*, Victoria, Canada, October 2006.

[9] K. McGuinness, O. Gillet, N. O'Connor, and G. Richard. Visual analysis for drum sequence transcription. In *European Signal Processing Conference (Eusipco)*, Poznan, Pologne, sep 2007.

[10] S. Essid O. Gillet and G. Richard. On the correlation of automatic audio and visual segmentations of music videos. *IEEE Trans. on Circuit and Systems for Video Technology*, apr 2007.

[1] http://www.acmmm11.org/content-3Dlife-challenge.html

Acoustic and Multimodal Processing for Multimedia Content Analysis

Gerald Friedland
International Computer Science Institute
1947 Center Street, Suite 600
Berkeley, CA 94704-1198
fractor@icsi.berkeley.edu

ABSTRACT
This article summarizes the corresponding 3-hour tutorial at ACM Multimedia 2011.

Categories and Subject Descriptors
H3.1 [**Information Storage and Retrieval**]: Indexing methods; I4.8 [**Image Processing and Computer Vision**]: Scene Analysis—Sensor Fusion

General Terms
Experimentation

Keywords
Audio, Video, Multimodal, Multimedia Content Analysis

1. Motivation
Today's computers start to have enough computational power and enough memory to be able to process a large amount of data in different sensory modalities. This allows to improve the robustness of current content analysis approaches and attack problems that are impossible to solve using only a single modality. Just as a human analyst uses multiple sources of information to determine the content of a video, it seems obvious that for video content analysis, the investigation of clues across different sensor modalities and their combination can lead to better results than investigating only one stream of sensor input. This is especially true for the analysis of consumer-produced, "unconstrained" videos, such as YouTube uploads or Flickr content.

Many computer science curricula usually include basic image processing and computer vision classes but only rarely acoustic content analysis classes, and if so, acoustic analysis is often reduced to speech recognition. This results in multimedia content analysis in being mostly image and vision-centric. While visual information is a very important part of a video, acoustic information often complements it. Moreover, with multimodal integration and fusion being still a research topic, many multimedia researchers lack in-depth knowledge on how to combine and integrate modalities in an efficient and effective way.

2. Objectives
The objective of the tutorial is to introduce interested multimedia students and researchers who are not specialized in audio into the world of acoustic processing research with a focus on multimodal content analysis. For example, what is the accuracy of speech recognition after all and what open source options are there? Can I do indoor/outdoor detection with audio? How does an acoustic event detector work? What are the toolkits available for me to use? The goal is to enable the participants to include acoustic processing into their research as an addition to image, text, and visual video processing to enhance their multimedia content analysis results, especially on large scale video corpora. Because a 3-hour tutorial can neither replace a several semester lecture on the topic nor a degree in electrical engineering, the major purpose of this tutorial is to introduce basic concepts and technical terms, along with practical software toolkits and references to key literature. I hope to foster a high degree of cross-media fertilization that will benefit the multimedia community.

3. Outline
The following is a list of topics that the tutorial will cover:

- Useful and common filters
- Features for audio analysis
- Typical machine learning methods used for acoustic processing
- Evaluation methods of acoustic processing
- Example tasks of acoustic analysis
- Toolkits for acoustic analysis
- Multimodal integration
- Multimodal fusion
- Experimental setup for conducting multimodal experiments
- Acoustic and multimodal research challenges
- Discussion

4. Course Material
The course material will be based on a class taught on the same topic at UC Berkeley in the fall semester 2011. The participants will be handed the slides of the presentations. In addition, the attendees of the tutorial will have early access to the textbook materials "Introduction to Multimedia Computing" by G. Friedland and R. Jain which is going to appear at Cambridge University Press soon after the tutorial. The textbook complements the tutorial not only with additional explanation but also with pseudo code (for reference purposes) and exercises (for deepening the presented material).

5. About the Presenter
Dr. Gerald Friedland is a senior research scientist at the International Computer Science Institute (ICSI), a private lab affiliated with the University of California, Berkeley, where he leads multimedia content analysis research, mostly focusing on acoustic techniques. Projects he is involved include work on

MM'11, November 28–December 1, 2011, Scottsdale, Arizona, USA.
ACM 978-1-4503-0616-4/11/11.

acoustic methods for TRECVid MED 2011's video concept detection task, multimodal location estimation for consumer videos, and multimodal grounded perception for robots. Dr. Friedland has published more than 100 peer-reviewed articles in conferences, journals, and books. He is associate editor for ACM Transactions on Multimedia Computing, Communications, and Applications, is in the organization committee of ACM Multimedia 2011, and a TPC co-chair of IEEE ICME 2012. Dr. Friedland is the recipient of several research and industry recognitions, among them the European Academic Software Award and the Multimedia Entrepreneur Award by the German Federal Department of Economics. Most recently, he led the team that won the ACM Multimedia Grand Challenge in 2009.

Despite being mainly a researcher, Dr. Friedland is a passionate teacher. He teaches a class on the same topic on the fall semester at UC Berkeley and he is currently authoring a new textbook "Introduction to Multimedia Computing" together with Dr. Ramesh Jain, to appear at Cambridge University Press. He is also a proud founder, program director, and instructor of the IEEE International Summer School on Semantic Computing at UC Berkeley which fosters cross-disciplinary computer science research on content extraction.

Graphical Probabilistic Modeling and Applications in Multimedia Content Analysis

Xiao-Ping Zhang
Ryerson University
Toronto, Canada
xzhang@ee.ryerson.ca

Zhu Liu
AT&T Labs - Research
Middletown, NJ, USA
zliu@research.att.com

ABSTRACT
Graphical probabilistic models play an important role in modern machine learning and pattern recognition. In this half-day tutorial, we introduce the fundamentals of graphical probabilistic modeling, including Bayesian networks, Markov random fields, hidden conditional Random field, etc. We also discuss some applications of graphical probabilistic modeling in multimedia content analysis, for example, video segmentation, video event detection, video sequence matching, and image labeling. The audience will learn the basic of graphical models, and get familiar with the state of the art in multimedia content analysis systems.

Categories and Subject Descriptors
G.2.3 [**Discrete Mathematics**]: Graph Theory – *Applications.*

I.4.8 [**Image Processing and Computer Vision**]: Scene Analysis – *Time-varying imagery, Object recognition, Motion.*

General Terms
Theory, Algorithms, Performance, Management.

Keywords
Graphical Probabilistic Modeling, Multimedia Content Analysis, Hidden Conditional Random Field Model, Video Segmentation.

1. INTRODUCTION
With the rapidly growing popularity of multimedia content creation and sharing enabled by the high quality mobile video capture devices and the broadband wire or wireless connection, the volume of new content that is available to us is simply beyond our consumption capacity. For example, in the last year, video material uploaded to the YouTube video sharing service has increased from about 20 hours per minute to about 35 hours per minute. Tools that can automatically find the most relevant content according to our interests, specified manually or learned from our viewing history, are desired. Multimedia content analysis and understanding is an indispensable component in such tools and many other multimedia applications and services. It has been an active research area in the last two decades, and it has evolved to a combination and interconnection of many subjects such as audio and music processing, image and video processing, natural language processing, computer vision, and machine learning.

MM'11, November 28–December 1, 2011, Scottsdale, Arizona, USA.
ACM 978-1-4503-0616-4/11/11.

While multimedia content is associated with manually created tags and metadata, for example, pictures might have captions, videos might have summarizing text or category labels, these descriptors usually do not provide in-depth information and sometime inconsistent. As a complementary solution, multimedia content analysis provides a richer representation of the indexed content. For example, speech recognition can provide a text signal from the spoken content of videos and visual analysis might provide richer content tagging. The past few years have witnessed a considerable progress in this area, yet, as a field, multimedia content analysis is still in its infancy, facing many challenges and limitations. One of them is the well known semantic gap between the low level features and high level content meanings. Recently, encouraging results have been reported in many applications, for example, detecting events in video employing Hidden Markov Model (HMM), extracting high level visual concept from low level visual features by manifold learning, segmenting video content using the Hidden Conditional Random Field (HCRF) model, etc. Advanced techniques in machine learning have been found as a promising solution for filling the semantic gap.

Graphical models are the combination of probability theory and graph theory, and they provide a way to represent the joint distribution over all of the random variables by a product of factors each depending only on a subset of the variables. Such models are flexible and scalable to capture complex dependencies among large number of random variables. Many existing statistical models and methods find a unifying representation in graphical models. For example, Hidden Markov models, random Markov field, Kalman filter, etc. As an emerging framework in machine learning with enormous potential, graphical models have been introduced in the multimedia content analysis area, and are widely adopted in many applications. The intrinsic nature of multimedia content analysis tasks, including high dimension of the low level features, rich prior knowledge on the structure of multimedia content, as well as the complex temporal-spatial correlation among multiple modalities, find a perfect match for graphical models. There is no doubt that the application of graphical models in multimedia content analysis will keep thriving.

2. TUTORIAL OVERVIEW
The purpose of this tutorial is twofold: introducing the graphical models as a new framework of machine learning, and demonstrating the applications of graphical models in multimedia content processing domain. This tutorial is intended for researchers in the multimedia content analysis and understanding area as well as professionals working in related fields. Fundamentals in both graphical models and the multimedia content analysis will be covered in this tutorial, and there are no prerequisites for the

audience. The tutorial is designed to present a refreshing, broad perspective on graphic models, and in-depth examples on their application in multimedia content analysis. It will be valuable to experts in the constituent technologies such as multimedia indexing and search, content-based analysis who are looking to broaden their knowledge beyond their current areas of expertise. Specifically, the audience will: 1) Understand the basic of the graph theory and graphical models; 2) Learn special graphical models, including Hidden Markov models, Markov Random Field, and Conditional Random Field; 3) Get familiar with the general approaches in multimedia content analysis systems; and 4) Study a few examples on how to apply graphical models in multimedia content analysis tasks, for example, video event detection, video sequence matching, image labeling, etc; 5) Be able to determine which topics in multimedia content analysis are of interest to them for further study.

3. TUTORIAL TOPICS

This tutorial will include two parts: Part I – Introduction of Basic Theory, and Part II – Advances and Applications in Multimedia Content Analysis. Following are detailed outlines for each part.

Part I: Introduction of Basic Theory

- Bayesian Methods
- Graphical Models
- Hidden Markov Models (HMM)
- Markov Random Field (MRF)
- Conditional Random Field (CRF)

Part II: Advances and Applications in Multimedia Content Analysis

- Video Temporal Dynamics
- Identification of Digital Video based on Shot-level Sequence Matching
- Independent Component Analysis Mixture Hidden Markov Models (ICAMHMM)
- Video Event Detection using ICAMHMM
- ICA Mixture Hidden Conditional Random Field Model (ICAMHCRF) for Sports Event Classification
- Gaussian Mixture Conditional Random Field Modeling for Indoor Image Labeling
- Laplacian Mixture Conditional Random Field Model for Image Labeling
- Future Research Directions

The course material mainly consists of the lecture slides. We will demonstrate some video content analysis systems built on graphical models. Useful online links and resources will be listed for the interested audience for further research.

4. CONCLUSIONS

The graphical probabilistic models become an essential tool in many research areas. This tutorial is specifically designed for audiences in the multimedia field, introducing the recent progress of graphical models, and demonstrating how to apply them in multimedia content analysis systems. Understanding the advantage and limitation of graphical models, participants will be more comfortable at deploying this technique in problems at hand and determining research direction for future work.

Multimedia Tagging: Past, Present and Future

Jialie Shen
SMU
Singapore
jlshen@smu.edu.sg

Meng Wang
Hefei University of Technology
Hefei, China
eric.mengwang@gmail.com

Shuicheng Yan
NUS
Singapore
eleyans@nus.edu.sg

Xian-Sheng Hua
Microsoft
USA
xshua@microsoft.com

ABSTRACT

The tags have proved to be a very crucial mechanism to facilitate the effective sharing and organization of large scale of multimedia information. As a result, technical developments on intelligent multimedia tagging have attracted a substantial amount of efforts involving experts from information retrieval, multimedia computing and artificial intelligence (particularly computer vision). The truly interdisciplinary research has resulted in many algorithmic and methodological developments. Meanwhile, many commercial web systems (e.g., Youtube, Last.fm and Flickr) have successfully introduced a variety of toolkits to assist different users in discovering and exploring media content using tags. This tutorial aims to provide a comprehensive coverage on the evolution of research for developing multimedia tagging technologies and identify a range of major challenges for the further scholarly study in the coming years.

Categories and Subject Descriptors

H.3.3 [**Information Storage and Retrieval**]: Information Search and Retrieval

General Terms

Algorithms, Performance, Theory

1. INTRODUCTION

As size of online media collections grows rapidly, multimedia information retrieval (MIR) becomes an increasingly critical technique for effective multimedia document search and management. To facilitate the processes, it is necessary to annotate the multimedia objects with comprehensive textual information. Consequently, multimedia tagging has been actively studied by many different communities (e.g., multimedia, information retrieval, machine learning and computer version) [1, 2, 5]. It has been proven that the metadata can play a very important role in accurate, efficient and flexible multimedia organization and sharing process.

The studies on tagging process and the related intelligent tool development have a long history at the MM research. However, to the best of our knowledge, none of the previous tutorials focuses on multimedia tagging. The tutorial serves several purposes:

- It provides a detailed survey of state of the art for multimedia tagging systems, algorithms and their search applications.
- It gives a comprehensive review on fundamental challenges in design and validation of multimedia tagging systems.
- It aims to raise the awareness about importance of multimedia document tagging process and the related system development in the MM community, especially among researchers in the domain of multimedia content analysis, management and retrieval.

2. TUTORIAL OVERVIEW

Since the tags associated with multimedia documents affects performance of the search and data management system in many different ways, recent research demonstrates considerable diversity. Accordingly, the tutorial consists of five key parts, and is organized as follows.

2.1 Why Tagging Multimedia Documents?

The technological advancements in the newer-generation convergence products (e.g., smart phones, PDA and portal MP3 player) have offered people exceedingly convenient ways to acquire images, audio clips and videos. Access to the multimedia information is crucial to the users from different communities. It has been proven that certain amount of metadata can significantly enhance the efficiency of the multimedia data management and associated operations. Consequently, there has been increasing interest to study techniques for automatic generation of text annotation about the content. In particular, multimedia tagging is gaining in importance due to wide range of potential applications such as indexing, retrieval, and recommendation systems. The tutorial will start with a variety of real-world examples illustrating the popularity and importance of multimedia tagging. The examples will highlight the fundamental impacts of tags and tagging process, especially when being applied to large scale multimedia search and management under different contexts.

2.2 Image Tagging

In this part, we overview the previous research on image tagging from three independent but related aspects [2, 6]. They include automatic tagging, tag-to-region assignment and tag refinement (retagging). Accurate manual tagging is generally laborious and tedious when the image repository size becomes huge. Thus, an automatic process to assign

MM'11, November 28–December 1, 2011, Scottsdale, Arizona, USA.
ACM 978-1-4503-0616-4/11/11.

the tags to an image is highly desirable. Recently, many algorithms have been proposed for automatic image tagging, varying from classifier construction for individual semantic labels to learning statistical relevance models between images and keywords. In many cases, even after obtaining reliable tags decribing visual content at the image-level, we still need mechanisms to assign tags to particular regions within an image. It is very important to develop reliable content-based image retrieval and analysis systems. On the other hand, the image tags in real world could be imcompleted and imprecise. Consequently, tag refinement (or retagging) gaining a considerable momentum as a paradigm for tag quality enhancement. Based on how to model the refinement process, the existing approaches can be classified into three main categories: independent label propagation, correlative label analysis and graph-based optimization. The tutorial will compare and highlight different techniques. In addition, we will highlight the importance of acurrate tags on various real applications (e.g., online image search and personal image managment systems).

2.3 Beyond Image: Music and Video Tagging

In this unit, a variety of techniques proposed for effective tagging in information represented as music and video sequences are reviewed and analyzed. Comparing to image, music and video enjoy very different media characteristics. While the significant progress has been achieved in recent years, most of the existing approaches for tagging music and video documents still adopt a simple classification approach, and apply statistical machine learning classifiers directly on low level features [4, 3]. Thus, they suffer the shortcomings of (1) poor annotation accuracy, (2) deficiency of comprehensive evaluation and the associated result analysis based on large scale datasets, and (3) incomprehensive content representation, arising from inappropriate combination of multimodal and temporal information. At the core of these technical developments are intelligent algorithms for summarizing video content and detecting key concepts & their association accurately. For video and music sequences, there are various kinds of features. They could be motion for videos, timber for music and lyrics for music. The tutorial will highlight the importance and role of the cues about temporal dynamics in enhancing system performance. We also will explore the similarities and differences between the approches proposed for combining features extracted from various types of modalities.

2.4 Assistive Multimedia Tagging

In this part, we introduce assistive multimedia tagging, the efforts that accomplish multimedia tagging with human-computer joint exploration. Although great progress has been made in past a few years, automatic multimedia tagging can still hardly achieve satisfactory performance on real-world multimedia data that vary widely in genre, quality, context and content. Meanwhile, the power of human intelligence has been fully demonstrated in the Web 2.0 era. If well motivated, Internet users are able to provide high quaulity tag based annotation for large amount of multimedia data. Therefore, a set of new techniques have been developed by combining human and computer for more accurate and efficient multimedia tagging, such as batch tagging, active tagging, tag recommendation and tag refinement. These techniques are able to accomplish multimedia tagging by jointly exploring human and computer in different ways. This paper abbreviates them as 'assistive tagging' and conducts a comprehensive survey of existing research efforts on this theme. Here we categorize existing assistive tagging techniques into three paradigms: (1) tagging with data selection & organization; (2) tag recommendation; and (3) tag processing. We introduce the research efforts on each paradigm and summarize the methodologies. We also provide a discussion on several future trends in this research direction.

2.5 Open Problems

There is still a lot to be done in the research of the multimedia tagging. In the part, we will discuss a set of open problems for the research exploration in the future. Particularly, we are interested in the issuses related to mass scale multimedia tagging and its applications. For the most of existing technqiues, statistical machine learning algorithms play a key role in modeling multimedia content and their association with text keywords. One of the major limitation is that their performance largely depends on the limited size of the labelled training data set and how to obtain high quality learning examples. Moreover, it is a very challenging problem to perform large scale evaluation on multimedia tagging systems. In fact, how to quickly and cheaply construct test collections and corresponding ground truth information still remains open to the MM and IR research.

3. CONCLUSION

The main purpose of this tutorial is to explore recent efforts on developing multimedia tagging techniques and review differences between the approaches developed for various types of multimedia information, such as images, music and videos. Our tutorial also aims to provide a good coverage on the methodologies and systems developed by industry. We hope that two main learning outcomes can be achieved via this tutorial. In the short term, we expect that this tutorial will enable the participants to gain a fundamental understanding of multimedia tagging and key research challenges. From a long run perspective, we expect that the role of this tutorial is to foster more interactions between the scholars from different research areas to develop effective and scalable tagging techniques.

4. ACKNOWLEDGMENTS

Professor Jialie Shen is partially supported by the Mobile plus Cloud Computing Theme Research Program Award, Microsoft Research.

5. REFERENCES

[1] X. Li, C. G. M. Snoek, and M. Worring. Learning social tag relevance by neighbor voting. *IEEE Transactions on MM*, 2009.
[2] O. Nov and C. Ye. Why do people tag?: motivations for photo tagging. *Commun. ACM*, 2010.
[3] J. Shen, W. Meng, S. Yan, H. Pang, and X.-S. Hua. Effective music tagging through advanced statistical modeling. In *ACM SIGIR*, 2010.
[4] S. Siersdorfer, J. S. Pedro, and M. Sanderson. Automatic video tagging using content redundancy. In *ACM SIGIR*, 2009.
[5] M. Wang, B. Ni, X. S. Hua, and T.-S. Chua. Assistive multimedia tagging: A survey of multimedia tagging with human-computer joint exploration. *ACM Computing Surveys*, 2011.
[6] G. Zhu, S. Yan, and Y. Ma. Image tag refinement towards low-rank, content-tag prior and error sparsity. In *ACM MM*, 2010.

Eye Tracking Methodology and Applications to Images and Video

Harish Katti
School Of Computing
National University of Singapore
harishk@comp.nus.edu.sg

Mohan Kankanhalli
School Of Computing
National University of Singapore
mohan@comp.nus.edu.sg

ABSTRACT

Our tutorial introduces eye-tracking as an exciting, non-intrusive method of capturing user attention during human interaction with digital images and videos. We believe eye-gaze can play a valuable role in understanding and processing (a) huge volumes of image and video content generated as a result of human experiences and interaction with the environment (b) Personalization and in human-media interaction, having access to individual preferences and behavioral patterns would be a key component of such a system. Recent possibilities to seamlessly integrate eye-tracking into laptops and mobile devices opens up a plethora of possibilities for applications that can respond to human visual attention strategies. (c) Visual content design such as in advertising often employs techniques that guide user attention to produce visual impact and elements of surprise and emotion. Eye-gaze has been used as a tool to evaluate different choices of visual elements and their placement. (d) Affective analysis of images and videos is an ongoing and challenging area in multimedia research, show recent results on how eye-gaze and accompanying pupillary dilation information can aid affective analysis.

Categories and Subject Descriptors

H.4 [**Information Systems Applications**]: Multimedia application

General Terms

Experimentation, Human Factors

Keywords

Eye-tracking, visual attention

1. INTRODUCTION

This tutorial introduces eye-tracking as an exciting, non-intrusive method of capturing user attention during interaction with digital images and videos. The tutorial will focus on the following aspects,

- What is eye-tracking and what does it offer for multimedia researchers?
- Basic understanding of human anatomy, low and high level visual cognition, mathematical techniques underlying popular eye-tracking hardware and software.
- Introduction to experiment design, analysis and visualization and application scenarios.

The tutorial will consist of two parts of roughly equal duration. The first half will introduce eye-tracking methodology and potential use in experiments and applications involving human interaction with images and videos. Second half will focus on hands-on experiments and data-analysis using state-of-art eye tracking hardware and software.

2. MOTIVATION AND OVERVIEW OF TUTORIAL CONTENTS

We frequently encounter personal video and image collections having thousands of images, to millions of video clips on *YouTube* and billions of images on repositories such as *Flickr* or *Picasa*. Once such content is generated, it becomes useful and necessary to automate the process of understanding and storing it to enable subsequent use such as indexing and retrieval [3][7] and query processing, re-purposing for devices with different form factors [6]. Eye-tracking has good potential in bridging the *semantic gap* often encountered between sensory information such as images or video, and the semantic interpretations of the same [3]. The tutorial contents are aimed at researchers who want to understand the basics of eye-tracking and potential applications to image and video and is geared towards audience with diverse backgrounds ranging from psychology to engineering and computer science.A basic knowledge of programming and statistics will help, but is not a compulsory pre-requisite as the tutorial material will be self-contained and introductory in nature. Participants from different backgrounds will be exposed to methods that are complementary to their basic training.

Being non-invasive, spatio-temporal information tied to the human visual process, eye-gaze makes for an ideal candidate for Image and video understanding problems. In this tutorial, we describe important aspects of behavioural signals as shown in Fig. 1 and compare eye-tracking methodology against other forms of behavioural signal capture.

2.1 The phenomenon of Visual attention

Human Visual Attention (HVA) is the strategy employed by humans to to align a Region of Interest with the central region of the field of view. This process also involves ballistic movements of the eyes called *saccades*. This is followed by

MM'11, November 28–December 1, 2011, Scottsdale, Arizona, USA.
ACM 978-1-4503-0616-4/11/11.

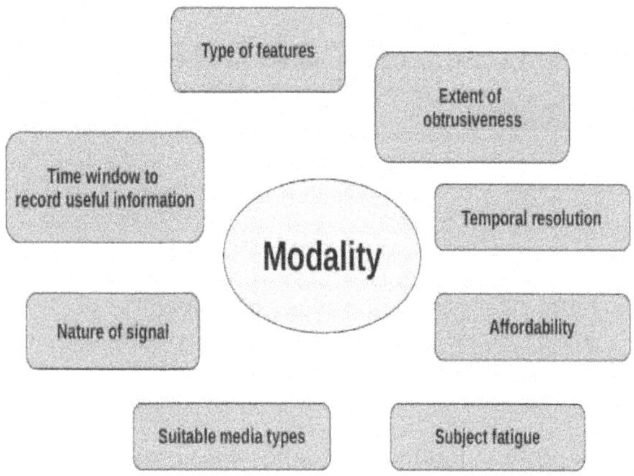

Figure 1: Important aspects to be considered while choosing a behavioural signal for human-media interaction.

a brief duration of *fixation* where the eye-gaze holds steady for a short while to inspect the Region of Interest. This is typically defined as a time-interval of $> 100ms$ where eye-gaze is limited within a visual angle of 1°. This strategy is critical to the limited capabilities of the Human visual system, as the total visual input from the environment is too overwhelming and oftentime redundant in large parts. beyond the visual properties of any semantic category, factors such as our real world model, short term memory and current task/intent, significantly influence Visual attention and subsequent understanding of an image [1]. This is illustrated in the following figure Fig. 2,

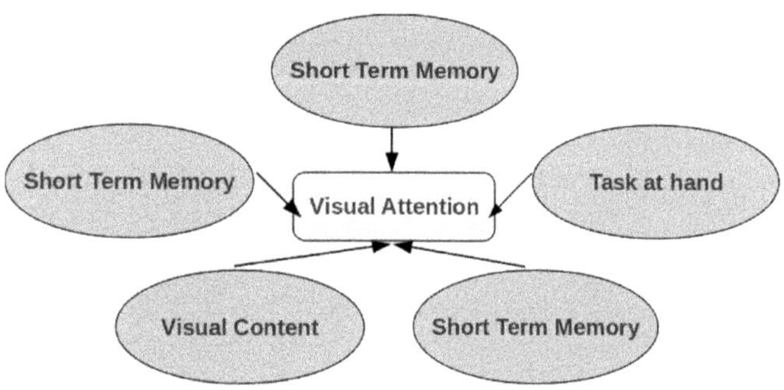

Figure 2: Different factors that affect human visual attention and subsequent understanding of images.

Each of these factors has been shown to influence visual attention. Visual attention is an important mechanism to isolate, selected regions of the visual field for more detailed observation. Hence it is important to acknowledge and if possible control the influence of these factors in human-image interaction. In this tutorial, we will explore the eye-tracking terminology, standard experimental paradigms and interesting applications relevant to image and video.

2.2 List of Topics

We explore typical experiment design for experiments involving images and video, the tutorial will also bring forth the difference between classical eye-tracking experiments in psychology and those likely to be done by media researchers based on our work with images [5][4][2], text [5] and ongoing work with video. Tutorial participants will be made familiar with eye-tracking experiment design.

The first half will cover the following topics,

- Defining the role of eye-gaze for an experimental study or application and preparation of stimulus set for image or video based experiment.
- Eye-tracking hardware choices ranging from low-cost open source, desktop based and mobile head-mounted options.
- Typical eye-gaze analysis and visualization methods for image and video based experiments.
- Interactive, eye-gaze contingent systems.

The second half will consist of a hands-on session covering the following topics,

- Aspects of analysis and visualization for image and video stimuli. This will be introduced with customized code accompanying the NUSEF dataset [4], as well as commercial software from SMI.
- Eye-tracking experiments with image and video stimuli using commercial trackers from SMI and also low-cost open source' based tracking.

2.3 Acknowledgements

This work is funded by the AStar, SERC grant, "Characterizing and Exploiting Human Visual Attention for Automated Image Understanding and Description".

3. REFERENCES

[1] G. L. Malcolm K. Rayner, T. J. Smith and J. M. Henderson. Eye movements and visual encoding during scene perception. *Psychological Science*, 20(1):6–10, 2009.

[2] H. Katti, S. Ramanathan, M. S. Kankanhalli, N. Sebe, T. S. Chua, and K. R. Ramakrishnan. Making computers look the way we look: exploiting visual attention for image understanding. In *Proceedings of the international conference on Multimedia*, MM '10, pages 667–670, New York, NY, USA, 2010. ACM.

[3] L. Jia J. Z. Wang R. Datta, D. Joshi. Image retrieval: Ideas, influences, and trends of the new age. *ACM Computing Survey*, 40(2), 2008.

[4] S. Ramanathan, H. Katti, M. S. Kankanhalli, T. S. Chua, and N. Sebe. An eye fixation database for saliency detection in images. *ECCV 2010*, 2010.

[5] Subramanian Ramanathan, Harish Katti, Raymond Huang, Tat-Seng Chua, and Mohan S. Kankanhalli. Automated localization of affective objects and actions in images via caption text-cum-eye gaze analysis. In *ACM International Conference on Multimedia 2009*, pages 729–732, 2009.

[6] A. Shamir and O. Sorkine. Visual media retargeting. In *SIGGRAPH ASIA '09: ACM SIGGRAPH ASIA 2009 Courses*, pages 1–13, New York, NY, USA, 2009. ACM.

[7] C. Snoek. Semantic image and video indexing in broad domains. *IEEE Transactions on Multimedia*, 9(5), 2007.

Alice's Worlds of Wonder: Exploiting Tags to Understand Images in terms of Size and Scale

Christoph Kofler
c.kofler@tudelft.nl

Martha Larson
m.a.larson@tudelft.nl

Alan Hanjalic
a.hanjalic@tudelft.nl

Delft Multimedia Information Retrieval Lab
Delft University of Technology, Mekelweg 4, 2628 CD Delft, The Netherlands

ABSTRACT

The 'Wonderlands of Size and Scale' system extends Flickr search functionality with a mechanism that exploits information implicit in image tag sets to filter images on the basis of characteristics related to size and scale. The innovative contribution of the 'Wonderlands' system is threefold: first, its use of an understanding of real-world physical entities depicted in images in terms of size and scale to filter images for display to the user; second, its application of our recently proposed 'Reading between the Tags' approach, which infers the real-world size of physical objects depicted in images by combining user-assigned image tags and natural language statistics mined from the Web; and, third, its trim realization of an engaging application that is implemented in a light-weight manner such that it can be executed as a live extension to the Flickr search engine. Results of a simple system-oriented evaluation support the conclusion that 'Wonderlands' reaches its aim of presenting users with images sorted with respect to the size- and scale-characteristics of their visually depicted content.

Categories and Subject Descriptors

H.3.1 [**Information Search and Retrieval**]: Content Analysis and Indexing; H.4 [**Information Systems Applications**]: Miscellaneous

General Terms

Algorithms, Design, Experimentation

Keywords

Image understanding, Tags, Real-world Size, Scale

1. INTRODUCTION

Community-based image collections have grown not only increasingly larger, but ever-more impressive in the diversity, quality, and novelty of images they contain. The collection of photos that has evolved on the preeminent online photo management and sharing application Flickr[1] is no exception. If users are to fully appreciate, explore and exploit the richness of these digital resources, new perspectives are needed that support them in accessing image collections along novel, less-obvious dimensions. The Yahoo! Image Challenge 'Novel Image Understanding' calls for efficient and meaningful technologies for organizing images and presenting them to users. 'Wonderlands of Size and Scale' addresses this challenge with a fully-operational extension to Flickr search that allows users to explore images with respect to dimensionality-related characteristics of their visually depicted content. The novelty of 'Wonderlands' lies in its ability to infer properties of size and scale of real-world physical entities depicted in images using information implicit in the tag sets added to images by users. Our system adopts the theme of 'Alice's Adventures in Wonderland', a 19th-century novel by Lewis Carroll. In the book, Alice, a little girl, falls down a rabbit hole into a fantasy world. In this world, she is alternately very small and very big, effectively taking on two different size- and scale-perspectives parallel to the dimensionality-related perspectives on Flickr images that we would like to present to users.

Our choice of 'size and scale' as an organizing principle for photos has two motivations. First, humans naturally make use of dimensionality in their understanding of the world around them. As part of the human conceptual system, size and scale constitute characteristics of depicted content that are relevant for the full-range of Flickr users, including both casual browsers and professional photographers. Further, size and scale hold a particular appeal for the human mind, providing not only an organizing principle, but apparently also a source of wonder and delight. The power of this appeal, and its particular relevance in the world of photography, is witnessed by the animated object catalogue Universcale [3] created by Nikon. Second, current image search technology and applications suffer restrictions on their size- and scale-aware search functionality, treated further in Section 2. In the remainder of this paper, we describe the system's functionality, underlying technology and the system implementation and then present evaluation results. We conclude with a brief discussion and outlook.

2. RELATED WORK AND SYSTEMS

This section overviews two areas of multimedia retrieval most closely related to 'Wonderlands': the notion of 'size' as applied to the task of indexing images and also the design considerations related to user experience of image search.

MM'11, November 28–December 1, 2011, Scottsdale, Arizona, USA.

[1] http://www.flickr.com/

2.1 'Size' in Image Indexing

The notion of size that we apply in 'Wonderlands' relates to the real-world size of the subject or subjects visible in an image together with the depicted surrounding environment. In contrast, in image indexing, 'size' is often taken to refer either to the outer dimensions of the image in pixels or to the proportion of the frame filled by the subject. Predictions of frame filling contribute to automatic selection among images portraying the same subject, as in the identification of canonical views for the selection of iconic images [5]. Note that frame-filling is not relevant to the notion of size we use.

In current applications, real-world size of the subjects of photos can be accessed via keywords such as 'small' and 'large' included in the metadata. Getty Image's Catalyst search engine [1] allows users to search a collection of stock photography. As a commercial collection, Getty's images are well-curated, making it possible to maintain a clean and complete set of annotations disambiguated into semantic categories, e.g., *Tiger* is a member of the category *Big Cat.* Via these categories, Catalyst is able to interpret 'small' and 'large' as physical properties and allows users to combine these properties with topical keywords. The combination is, however, restricted to images that have been explicitly annotated—the query *Tiger(Big Cat)* with *Large(Physical Description)* results in a selection of only four images. Our application directly addresses the challenge of working with Flickr images by exploiting not a single piece of metadata, but rather the entire set of user image tags.

We note that many photos on Flickr contain scale-specific terms in their descriptions and tag sets that are related to the dimensionality of the visually depicted content, e.g., *closeup, macro, landscape, panorama, portrait.* The use of these terms on Flickr suggests that size and scale are among the salient characteristics of photos, reinforcing our view that dimensionality-aspects of visual content is important to users for search. 'Wonderlands' pushes the functionality of Flickr a step further by generating size- and scale-aware image results for users without requiring them to explicitly make use of particular dimensionality terms while tagging images or formulating queries.

In particular, we conjecture that users searching for images might not be consciously aware that their information needs contain a specific dimensionality component. We contend that, like image style, the dimensional properties of the visually depicted content of an image is quite easy for users to recognize in images that satisfy their search needs, but quite difficult to articulate during the search process. As stated by [4], image search is often more exploratory than general Web search and search with respect to difficult-to-formulate image characteristics is presently not well supported. 'Wonderlands' seeks to redress the balance and provide users a way to explore images in terms of properties related to size and scale. In sum, currently existing technologies point to the usefulness of size- and scale-aware image search and browsing, but are restricted in that they fall short of supporting the user in fully exploiting this perspective on large, online photo-sharing collections such as Flickr.

2.2 Entertainment as a Goal of Image Search

Our system design is inspired by the insight that image search constitutes, in and of itself, a form of entertainment [4]. The importance and usefulness of this perspective is supported by the observation that Flickr offers users 'Interesting Photos' as a search option. The existence of search applications that provide exclusively fascination, pleasure and curiosity driven image search supports our view that entertainment is an important user goal for image search and should be taken into account in the design of image search systems. An example is a system offered by Multicolr Search Lab that allows users to explore interesting Flickr images by color alone [2]. We chose our 'Alice in Wonderland' theme to encourage users to interact playfully with our system and reinforce curiosity-driven search and browsing behavior.

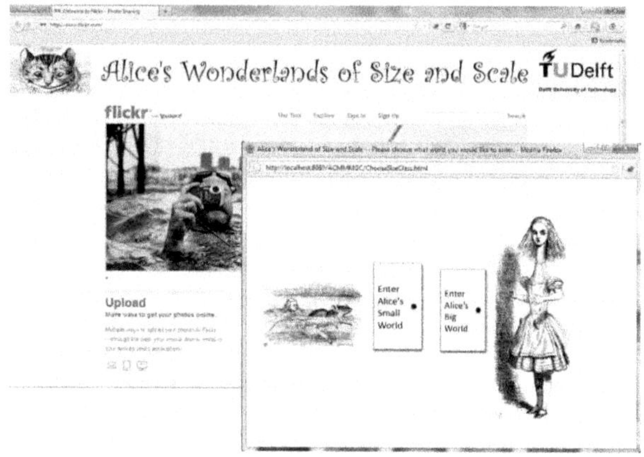

Figure 1: 'Wonderlands of Size and Scale'

3. THE 'WONDERLANDS' SYSTEM

The opening screen of 'Wonderlands', shown (behind) in Figure 1, carries a banner with the system name superimposed on the Flickr homepage. Using the Flickr homepage is intended to trigger the user to apply their usual Flickr search behavior in formulating queries for the system and signal that the system operates live on the entire Flickr image collection. The queries are entered into the Flickr search box. 'Wonderlands' pops up its entry screen, cf. Figure 1, which carries two illustrations of Alice drawn from the novel. Alice is pictured in her small state next to a door that invites, 'Enter Alice's Small World' and she is pictured in her large state next to a door that invites, 'Enter Alice's Big World'. When the user chooses a door, the results window opens and images start to appear. In 'Alice's Small World' the images put the user eye-to-eye with small sized objects pictured in small environments with limited range, giving the impression of seeing the world from the perspective of a small being viewing its environment from low to the ground. In 'Alice's Big World' the images give the user the big picture, the objects pictured are large and the perspective is a broad one. Examples of the two worlds for the user query 'car' are pictured in Figure 2. The appearance of the images in the world window tracks the random movement of the Cheshire Cat, one of the fantastical creatures from the novel with the power to appear and disappear at will. Within 'Wonderlands' his jumps serve to indicate that new images are in the process of loading.

3.1 The Theory of Wonderlands

The 'Wonderlands' concept leverages scale specificity manifested as a distributional trend on the sizes of physical objects tagged in Flickr images in order to identify images that belong to the 'Small World' vs. the 'Big World'. This section reviews the basic theory behind the implementation.

Figure 2: Alice's worlds for the query car.

3.1.1 Scale Specificity

The notion of scale specificity, which we first introduced in [6], describes the trend of physical objects to co-occur in real-world situations with other physical objects of roughly the same size. Scale specificity arises due to physical constraints in operation in the real world and can be observed in the domain of images (i.e., the situations that we capture when we take photos often involve objects of similar sizes) and also in the area of natural language (i.e., the situations that we frequently describe when we speak involve objects of similar sizes). Scale specificity is not a hard and fast rule, but rather has the status of a trend. The trend is, however, strong enough to be exploited for the purposes of image annotation, which we demonstrated in [6] by showing that scale specificity in the language domain could be leveraged by a 'Reading Between the Tags' system that processes user tags of an image, decides if they denote physical objects, and, if so, generates a prediction of the real world sizes of these objects. 'Wonderlands' extends the 'Reading Between the Tags' method by combining size-class decisions from the entire tag set of an image to generate a size- and scale-related prediction for that image, i.e., whether it belongs to the 'Small World' or the 'Big World'.

3.1.2 The Power of LUFs

The 'Reading Between the Tags' approach generates size-class predictions for image tags using Language Use Frames (LUFs). Each LUF consists of a sequence of words that characteristically occurs in natural language describing a situation of a particular scale. Example LUFs are: `the <tag> in her hand` and `the <tag> on the horizon`. To predict the size-class of a given tag, the tag is substituted into a LUF and the resulting string is used to query a search engine, in our case, Yahoo!. The number of hits returned is taken to reflect the association strength of a tag with a scale-specific natural language context, and by extension, the relative commonality of the object denoted by the tag in corresponding scale-specific real-world contexts. For example, the tag *teacup* is inferred to refer to a small object on the basis of the high scores returned by small-scale LUFs, e.g., `the teacup in her hand`, and the low scores of large-scale LUFs, e.g., `the teacup on the horizon`. The decision uses a LUF set balanced over different scales and applies either a simple rule, or if training data is available, a classifier, cf. [6].

3.1.3 Inferring Size and Scale from Tag Sets

Assignment of an image to one of Alice's worlds is based on the balance between class-sizes predicted for the tags in the tag set of the image. If a tag set contains more small than large tags, the image is assigned to the 'Small World' and if it contains more large than small tags it is assigned to the 'Big World'. In case of equal class-sizes, we break the tie by deciding for the 'Small World' class. Tags that cannot be determined to denote physical objects are ignored. If an image fails to have any classifiable tags, it is skipped, since no decision can be made.

3.2 System Architecture and Implementation

The 'Wonderlands' system is an extension to Flickr and is implemented as a client-server-based application consisting of a Java Servlet—which manages session and classification information—as a server component and a Firefox browser[2] plug-in—which uses Greasemonkey[3]—as a client component. Greasemonkey offers the possibility to execute JavaScript on websites and is triggered on specified URL patterns. We use Greasemonkey to route requests submitted through the actual Flickr website to the server component of our system in order to easily and seamlessly integrate our image classification algorithm into the Flickr website.

In order to allow the system to select pictures for Alice's worlds without surpassing the attention span of the user, we choose for an implementation that avoids the online calculation of LUF scores, a process that requires multiple search engine queries for multiple tags in order to classify one image. Instead, a fixed set of size-indicative tags is generated in advance using a development set of 500 images whose tags (3,627 in total) have been human annotated with size-class information (cf. [6] for more details of the annotation process). The tags most indicative of the size-classes of their sister tags (i.e., other tags in the same image tag sets) are chosen for inclusion. A standard feature selection procedure within the Weka data mining framework[4] (a decision tree classifier, J48, and CfsSubsetEval combined with Best First search) was applied to make the choice. The final set of size-indicative tags includes 219 tags;[5] this set is consulted via a look up while the system is running.

Our 'Wonderlands' system communicates with Flickr using the logic depicted in Algorithm 1, which shows the high-level functionality of the server component. The method `onStartSurfing()` (lines 1-3) is executed on the URL pattern `http://www.flickr.com/`, i.e., as soon as a user begins interacting with the Flickr website. The server component loads the 219 size-indicative tags and initializes the views that will subsequently be presented. As soon as the user enters a query in the Flickr search box, `onSearch()` (lines 4-6) is executed on the URL pattern `http://www.flickr.com/search/*` and starts a separate thread in order to classify images for size and scale in real-time. `runPictureClassifierThread(...)` (lines 12-25) first gathers real-time tag-based search results (i.e., images and corresponding tags) from the Flickr webservices[6] and classifies images as described in Section 3.1.3 by comparing the tag set of an image to the set of size-indicative tags. Both, 'Small World' and 'Big World' search results are collected until the user chooses which of Alice's worlds he wants to enter in the window depicted in Figure 1. As soon as the user has made a choice, `onSizeChoose()` (lines 7-8) is executed and sets

[2]http://www.mozilla.com/en-US/firefox/

[3]https://addons.mozilla.org/nl/firefox/addon/greasemonkey/

[4]http://www.cs.waikato.ac.nz/ml/weka/

[5]Examples: `lego`, `cake` (*small*) and `clouds`, `water` (*large*).

[6]http://www.flickr.com/services/api/flickr.photos.search.html

the required world size. From this point on, only search results corresponding to the user's choice are collected and the results view is presented to the user. The results view updates itself every 1500ms by calling `onPictureViewUpdate()` (lines 9-11) on the server component, which collects newly available search results from the classifier thread and displays them to the user, as shown in the examples of the two worlds presented in Figure 2. The source code of the 'Wonderlands' Flickr extension is available for download.[7]

Algorithm 1 High-level functionality of the server component of the system, which manages session and classification information.

```
    {onStartSurfing()}
 2: sizeIndicativeTags ← loadSizeIndicativeTags()
    initializeViews(sizeChooseView, pictureView)
 4: {onSearch()}
    searchThread ← runPictureClassifierThread(query, sizeIndicativeTags, flickrWebservice)
 6: sizeChooseView.display()
    {onSizeChoose()}
 8: searchThread.setSizeChoice(sizeChoice)
    {onPictureViewUpdate()}
10: newSearchResults ← searchThread.getResults()
    pictureView.display(newSearchResults)
12: {runPictureClassifierThread(...)}
    pictures ← FlickrWebservice.getPictures(query)
14: for all pictures p in pictures do
      tags ← FlickrWebservice.getTags(p)
16:   for all tags t in tags do
        if t ∈ (size ← sizeIndicativeTags[t]) then
18:       hist[size] ← hist[size] + 1
        end if
20:   end for
      p.sizeClass ← getMaxOccurrencesSizeClass(hist)
22:   if p.sizeClass = sizeChoice then
        newSearchResults.add(p)
24:   end if
    end for
```

4. EVALUATION

We carry out a system-oriented evaluation of the selection of images for Alice's worlds using human-generated ground truth pertaining to the scale of the image (closeup, medium range, or landscape shot). The human annotators were given examples of each of the categories to use as the basis for their decisions. Annotation was carried out within the framework of the same crowdsourcing task used to generate the size-class annotations for individual tags [6]. For the purposes of evaluation of 'Wonderlands', we consider an image to be correctly displayed in Alice's 'Small World' if it is a closeup shot and correctly displayed in Alice's 'Big World' if it is either a medium range or a landscape shot. As mentioned above, some images fail to have tags that denote physical entities and the 'Wonderlands' image classification algorithm does not generate a world-assignment for these images. We eliminated such images from the image set used for evaluation. The final evaluation set contained 1,633 images: 765 'Small World' images (closeup shots) and 868 'Big World' images (605 medium range shots + 263 landscape shots). In reality, we expect that the scale specificity reflected in Alice's worlds captures size- and scale-related characteristics of images other than the distinctions relating to range annotated in our ground truth. However, our chosen evaluation method is well suited as a straightforward check to reveal whether the system is sensitive to size- and scale-related characteristics over a relatively large number of cases.

'Small World' classification yielded 548 correctly classified and 217 incorrectly classified images; 'Big World' classification yielded 713 correctly classified and 155 incorrectly classified images, resulting in an overall classification performance of 0.773/0.772 (Weighted Precision/Weighted Recall). For comparison, the performance of the dominant class baseline (all images assigned to the 'Big World') is 0.283/0.532 (WP/WR). The large difference with this baseline supports the conclusion that the contrast between Alice's worlds will be consistently recognizable by the user and provides evidence that 'Wonderlands' is actually able to carry out decisions that reflect an understanding of images on the basis of size and scale.

5. DISCUSSION AND OUTLOOK

We have presented, 'Wonderlands', a system that provides users with perspectives on Flickr search results reflecting size- and scale-related characteristics of images. 'Wonderlands' represents the first real-world application of the approach proposed in [6]. Currently, 'Wonderlands' makes use of tags that denote physical objects depicted in images. Future work will involve integrating dimensionality terms from tag sets. We will also carry out user tests to determine which aspects of size and scale reflected by the images selected to populate Alice's worlds are most helpful and interesting for users who are searching or browsing Flickr. The larger challenge ahead is integrating information derived from multimedia content analysis into 'Wonderlands' in a manner that does not slow down the system, but still succeeds in enhancing user appreciation of the wonder of Alice's worlds.

6. ACKNOWLEDGMENTS

The research leading to these results has received funding from the European Commission's 7th Framework Programme under grant agreement Nr. 216444 (PetaMedia).

7. REFERENCES

[1] Getty Images - Catalyst. http://www.gettyimages.com/Catalyst/, last accessed: 01.08.2011.

[2] Multicolr Search Lab - Idée Inc. http://labs.ideeinc.com/multicolr/, last accessed: 01.08.2011.

[3] Nikon | Feel Nikon | Universcale. http://www.nikon.com/about/feelnikon/universcale/, last accessed: 01.08.2011.

[4] P. André, E. Cutrell, D. S. Tan, and G. Smith. Designing novel image search interfaces by understanding unique characteristics and usage. In *INTERACT '09*, pages 340–353, 2009.

[5] T. Berg and A. Berg. Finding iconic images. In *Computer Vision and Pattern Recognition Workshops 2009*, pages 1–8, 2009.

[6] M. Larson, C. Kofler, and A. Hanjalic. Reading between the tags to predict real-world size-class for visually depicted objects in images. In *ACM Multimedia 2011*, this proceedings.

[7] http://tinyurl.com/alicewow/

Scalable Mobile Video Question-Answering System with Locally Aggregated Descriptors and Random Projection

Guan-Long Wu[†], Yu-Chuan Su[⊙], Tzu-Hsuan Chiu[⋆], Liang-Chi Hsieh[⊕], Winston H. Hsu[‡]
{garywgl[†], r96098[⋆], winston[‡]}@csie.ntu.edu.tw, spooky@cmlab.csie.ntu.edu.tw[⊙],
viirya@gmail.com[⊕]
National Taiwan University, Taipei, Taiwan

ABSTRACT

We present a scalable mobile video Question-Answering system with locally aggregated descriptors and random projection using user-generated videos all around the world for ACM Multimedia 2011 Technicolor challenge: "precise event recognition and description from video excerpts." Our proposed system takes a video excerpt as a query and explores its canonical semantics of that. We collect a public events video dataset containing 7 topics with 1963 YouTube videos to evaluate our proposed system. The experiment results show that our proposed video feature representation outperforms a state-of-the-art near-duplicate retrieval based on color histogram. The signature generated by random projection not only ensures real-time efficiency but also achieves a competitive MAP performance with original feature.

Categories and Subject Descriptors: H.3.3 [Information Search And Retrieval]: Search process; H.3.1 [Content Analysis and Indexing]: Abstracting methods

General Terms: Experimentation, Performance

1. INTRODUCTION

Targeting on the topic of "precise event recognition and description from video excerpts" for ACM Multimedia 2011 Technicolor Challenge, we present a novel and promising mobile video Question-Answering (QA) system. Comparing to the traditional text search interface, our proposed video QA system based on video excerpts helps users to investigate the semantics in a video effectively. Users do not need to come up with the appropriate keywords as query, and the QA system returns the top 5 ranked semantics once they upload a query video. The snapshot of our proposed system is illustrated in Figure 1.

There are two main challenges for the proposed system. The first is how a system processes the explosive growing user-generated videos efficiently. Take YouTube as an example, according to Wikipedia, YouTube receives more than 3 billion views per day and users upload more than 24 hours of videos per minute. The second is how to explore the multilingual semantics in a video excerpt. YouTube reported that around three quarters of data are uploaded outside the US. However, people in different countries use different languages to annotate videos. To tackle these challenges, searching video content directly by video excerpts can retrieve multilingual information more intuitively than keywords, because public event videos are similar in visual appearances. Therefore, we can explore the video semantics in multiple languages based on near-duplicate video retrieval.

Figure 1: The snapshot of mobile video QA system.

In this paper, we present a scalable video QA system with locally aggregated descriptors and random projection. We review the related work briefly in Section 2. Description of our proposed work is presented in Section 3. We show the experiment results and discuss them in Section 4, and conclusion is given in Section 5.

2. RELATED WORK

2.1 Question-Answering System

A QA system requires meeting precise information need of user by natural language or media. A typical text-based QA system answers questions written in natural language by text automatically. Nowadays, it is an important issue to leverage the resources of the community websites which have a large amount of archives to answer user's question by finding the most related question. Wang *et al.* [7] propose a new retrieval framework for community-based QA to tackle the similar question matching problem based on syntactic tree structure. However, the knowledge base of the work

MM'11, November 28–December 1, 2011, Scottsdale, Arizona, USA.

is Yahoo! Answers and it cannot be applied on YouTube easily due to the lack of structural data for text semantics. Therefore, the effectiveness of typical text-based QA system is limited.

For multimedia QA, Multimedia contents are suitable for answers in several types of questions. For example, user can easily learn to tie shoelaces by watching a demo video clip instead of reading a paragraph describing the steps. Li *et al.* [5] propose a multimedia QA system named *Video Reference* where the input is a sentence of question and the output is the most relevant video on YouTube. Although it leverages the video contents on YouTube, it still uses text as queries only.

2.2 Near-duplicate Video Retrieval

Near-duplicate video retrieval has been receiving much attention in recent years due to the rapid growth of online video services. Most existing works on duplicate-video retrieval focus either on videos that are very similar in visual content or video copy detection.

For videos similar in visual content, it turns out that simple color histogram may provide reasonable result. Using 24 bins color histogram in HSV color space, Wu *et al.* achieve 0.891 MAP on CC_WEB_VIDEO dataset [8]. However, color histogram is insufficient for "semantic duplicate" video detection, and it is also insufficient for partial duplicate video detection, which is a common situation in video QA system. "Semantic duplicate" means the videos share a same semantic definition (e.g. public events) although they are not very similar in visual appearance. To detect partial duplicate videos, temporal network that utilizes the temporal relation in video segments are introduced [6]. Despite its success, the method requires more storage and computational cost than signature-based methods, which limits the scalability of the system.

Video copy detection aims to find videos that come from the same source video but undergo different distortions. To solve the problem, Douze *et al.* [3] proposed a complicated frame matching method. Although such method provides high precision for duplicate video detection even the video suffers from severe degradation, the complex computation hinders the scalability and is thus not suitable for the proposed video QA system.

3. DESCRIPTION OF PROPOSED WORK

3.1 System Overview

Our proposed system is composed by an online part and an offline part. The illustration is shown at Figure 2. In the offline part, videos from YouTube or other video sharing websites are processed, and video feature vectors are extracted by the video feature extraction component. The contextual data of video (e.g. title, tags, description) is used in video profile generation and every video has its own profile which is constructed by leveraging Google Search and Wikipedia.

In the online part, the system compares the query feature vector from a video except uploaded by a user to the ones in database, and finds the top ranking database videos as candidates. Then, the canonical semantics selection ranks the items in candidate profiles and returns the top ranked semantic items to the user. The technical detail of video representation extraction is described in Section 3.2 and Section 3.3, and the descriptions of video profile generation and canonical semantics selection are shown in Section 3.4.

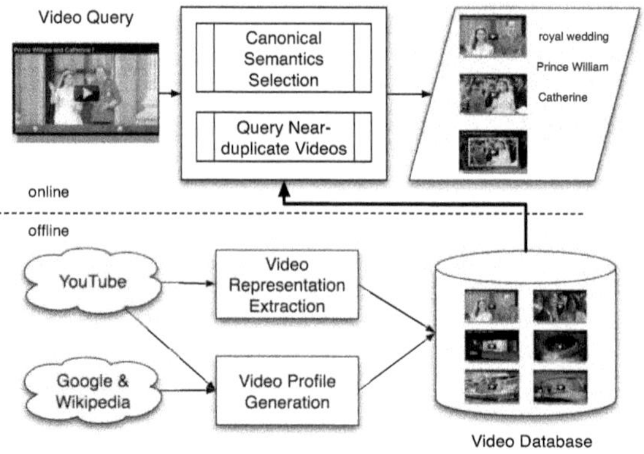

Figure 2: The architecture of our proposed system.

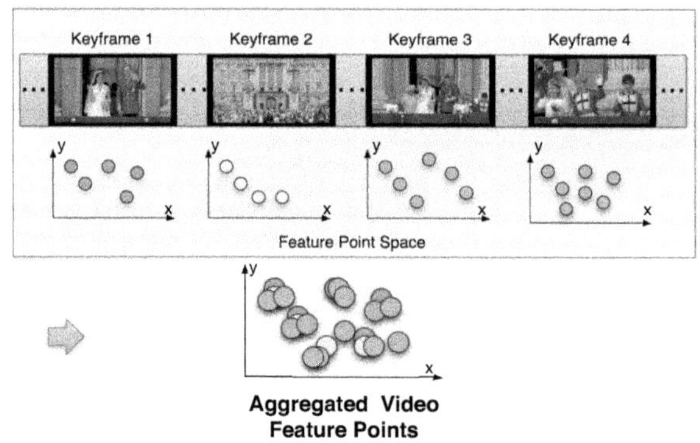

Figure 3: A sample video representation for a video of "Wedding of Prince William and Catherine Middleton."

3.2 Video Representation

Local features have been shown to be very discriminative visual features. Several methods have been proposed to transform local features to an image-wise vector representation. Among them, the vector of locally aggregated descriptors (VLAD) [4] was proposed to remedy the quantization errors suffered by the popular bag-of-word method. Based on VLAD, the system generates a vector which aggregates difference of the SIFT descriptors and the codebook centers in all keyframes. Note that keyframes are extracted by abrupt-shot detection to represent a video. The illustration is shown at Figure 3.

In our implementation, the number of center is set to 64 and the 128 dimensions of Hessian-Affine SIFT points are extracted from video keyframes so that the dimension of the feature vector is 8192. The distance metric is L_2 distance.

3.3 Dimension Reduction for Scalable Computation

In order to reduce the storage and computation time for comparing videos in database, we use a random projection in the dimension reduction process. Random projection (RP) is an effective dimension reduction method for wide range of domains. Bingham *et al.* [2] show the performance comparison between the random projection and other dimension reduction techniques (e.g. principle component analysis and discrete cosine transform) in image and text data. RP has a comparable performance with others but the computation cost is greatly reduced.

RP uses random matrix $R(i,j) = r_{ij}$ which follows the Gaussian distribution but it is usually not met in practice due to the higher computation cost. Achlioptas [1] presents a simpler random matrix following a probability distribution:

$$r_{ij} = \begin{cases} +1 & \text{with probability } \frac{1}{2}, \\ -1 & \text{with probability } \frac{1}{2} \end{cases} \quad (1)$$

In practice, the above equation has a lower computation cost because the integer mathematics operation is faster than floating point mathematics operation.

Assume the original dimension of feature vector is D and the reduced dimension is N, the dimension of random projection matrix is $[D \times N]$. Equation 1 is used to generate the projection matrix in our proposed work.

After applying the random projection to the feature vector, we get a reduced vector V and we quantize the vector V based on the equation:

$$V_i = \begin{cases} 1 & \text{if } V_i \geq 0, \\ 0 & \text{if } V_i < 0 \end{cases} \quad (2)$$

to generate the signature. We use hamming distance as the distance metric.

The effectiveness of using random projection can be discussed from two perspectives: computation cost and storage. For the computation cost issue, it is intuitive that the computation time for hamming distance is less than norm-2 distance because hamming distance can be calculated using XOR operation and counting the bits set after the XOR operation. For the storage issue, an original feature vector requires $D \times 8$ bytes (the storage of double floating point is 8 bytes) to store, and the signature uses $\frac{N}{8}$ bytes only. Thus, the signature-based representation reduces both the storage and the computation cost. We show the mean average precision performance of signature using different number of bits and the original feature representation in section 4.

3.4 Canonical Video Semantics Selection

In this part, the system completes the canonical video semantics selection in two phases. The first phase is the Wikipedia profile generation using Google Search and it is an offline process. For each video, the video title is used as the query keywords in Google Search and the titles of the top T_p returned wikipedia article form the profile of the video.

For instance, if a user uses "President Barack Obama 2009 Inauguration" as a query and Google Search returns the wikipedia articles such as "Inauguration of Barack Obama," "United States presidential inauguration" and "Presidency of Barack Obama," etc. The main reason of using Google Search instead of the default searching mechanism[1] in Wikipedia is that Google Search provides more accurate ranked results in general.

The second phase, it is an online query process, the canonical semantics selection. For a query video excerpt, the feature vector of the query is extracted. Then, the system returns the ranking list according to the similarity between the query video and the videos in the database. The canonical video semantics of the query is voted by the top T_v videos in the returned ranking list and the ranking items in their profiles. The equation 3 lists the scoring function:

$$score(i) = \sum_{r \in T_v} \sum_{\exists i \in profile_r} \frac{1}{\sqrt{rank_r}} \frac{1}{\sqrt{rank_i}} \quad (3)$$

i represents a semantic item in a video profile, $rank_r$ shows the ranking based on distance of video vectors, and $rank_i$ describes the ranking in a video profile.

In our proposed system, the interface shows the top 5 video semantics. We compare the performance of Prec@5 based on the method but using our proposed video representation and a color-based feature [8] in the Section of experiment result.

4. EXPERIMENT RESULTS

4.1 Video Dataset

To evaluate the performance of our proposed system, we collect a public event video dataset using YouTube API. The 7 public events listed below are selected and the topic is used as the query terms to collect video data:

1. "2011 Tohoku earthquake and tsunami"
2. "apple ipad 2 steve jobs"
3. "Beijing Olympics 2008 Opening ceremony"
4. "President Barack Obama 2009 Inauguration"
5. "September 11 attacks"
6. "Wedding of Prince William and Catherine Middleton"
7. "windows 98 crash bill gates"

For each topic, we utilize YouTube API to download the top 100 videos according to "relevance," "published," "viewCount," and "rating," respectively, and the results are then aggregated together. Hence, there should be no more than 400 videos in a query topic. At the end, the dataset contains 1963 videos with 89618 keyframes. The size of video files (flv format) is about 27 GB. We label the ground truth of these videos and 626 videos are verified belonging to one of the 7 event topics.

4.2 Experiment Setup

In the experiment of this work, the dimension of the proposed local-feature-based video representation is 8192, and the dimension of the color-based feature is 24 following the setting of [8]. The programs are implemented using Python and run at a machine contains an 8-core CPU and 48GB memory. In canonical semantics selection, the top 20 videos are considered in the voting step.

4.3 Performance Comparison

Figure 4 shows the mean average precision (MAP) comparison of our proposed feature and the color-based baseline for the ground truth videos in semantic duplicate retrieval. We use each ground truth videos as a query and calculate average precision using leave-one out method where the query depth is 50 (The query video must be removed from database for each query.) Finally, the mean average precision for each event topic is calculated.

The MAP of our proposed video feature outperforms the color-based baseline, except for the "September 11 attacks" event topic. We conjecture the reason is that the visual

[1]http://en.wikipedia.org/wiki/Special:Search

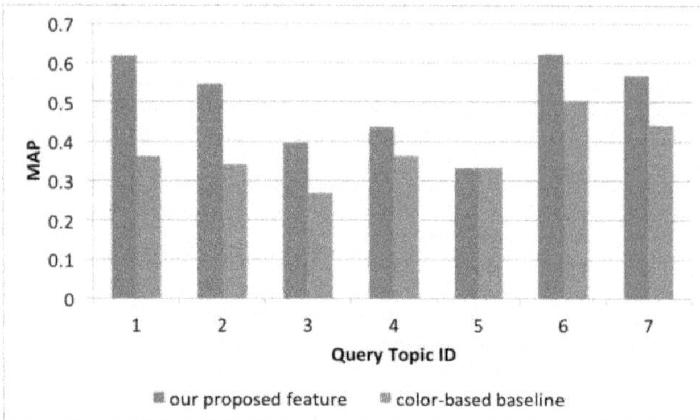

Figure 4: The MAP comparison of our proposed feature and the color-based baseline for the ground truth videos in semantic duplicate retrieval.

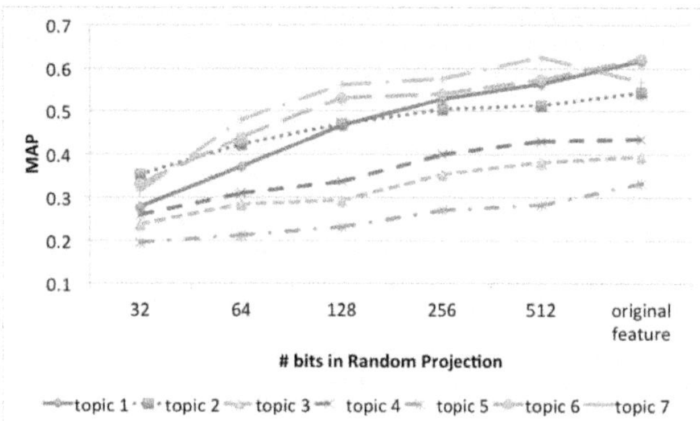

Figure 5: The MAP comparison of different number of bits in Random Projection for the ground truth videos in semantic duplicate retrieval.

pattern (e.g. explosion) in "September 11 attacks" is not captured well by local features.

Figure 5 shows the MAP comparison of different number of bits in RP for the ground truth videos in semantic duplicate retrieval. The MAP performance decreases when using less number of bits to represent a video in general cases. However, the 512 bits configuration achieves a satisfactory performance comparing to the original features and saves lots of storage and computation cost.

Figure 6 shows the precision at 5 of documents retrieved (P@5) comparison between our proposed feature and the color-based baseline for canonical video semantics. We randomly select 20 ground truth videos for each topic. If the number of ground truth videos for a topic is less than 20, we choose all of that. For each video, we let users label whether each of the 5 canonical video semantic is relevant. It's worth noting that the comparison between the performances is more important than the exact value, because the words or sentences well describing a video varies in number.

The P@5 of our proposed feature outperforms the color baseline in 5 topics, but it is worse in "September 11 attacks" and "Windows 98 crash bill gates." It probably contains more than one factor to affect the subjective QA performance. However, in the same video semantics selection mechanism,

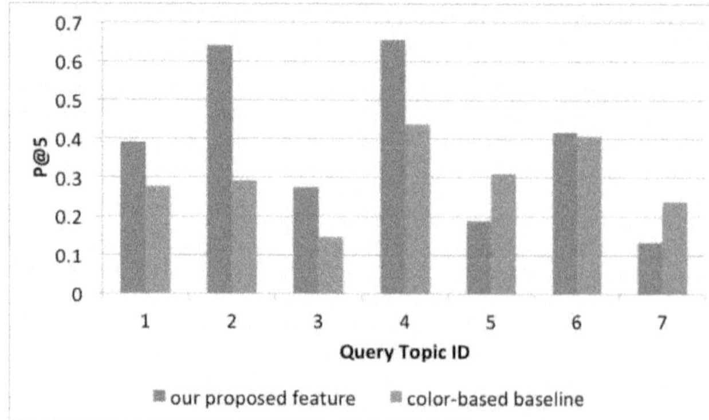

Figure 6: The P@5 comparison of our proposed feature and the color-based baseline for canonical video semantics.

our proposed feature provides higher P@5 than the color-based baseline.

5. CONCLUSION

We propose a scalable mobile video Question-Answering system with locally aggregated descriptors and random projection. User can simply record the interested video excerpt by mobile phone and upload it to our system to get the possible video semantics. Note that users do not need to provide any textual information in this scenario. The snapshot of our proposed system is shown in Figure 1. Thus we consider that it is a promising solution to target at ACM Multimedia Technicolor Challenge.

For scalable computation, our experiment results show the signature-based video representation using random projection to reduce the storage usage and computational cost effectively and reaches a corresponding performance comparing to the original feature representation.

6. REFERENCES

[1] D. Achlioptas. Database-friendly random projections: Johnson-lindenstrauss with binary coins. *J. Comput. Syst. Sci.*, 66, 2003.
[2] E. Bingham et al. Random projection in dimensionality reduction: applications to image and text data. In *ACM SIGKDD*, 2001.
[3] M. Douze et al. Inria-lear's video copy detection system. In *TRECVID*, 2008.
[4] H. Jégou et al. Aggregating local descriptors into a compact image representation. In *IEEE CVPR*, 2010.
[5] G. Li et al. Video reference: question answering on youtube. In *ACM MM*, 2009.
[6] H.-K. Tan et al. Scalable detection of partial near-duplicate videos by visual-temporal consistency. In *ACM MM*, 2009.
[7] K. Wang et al. A syntactic tree matching approach to finding similar questions in community-based qa services. In *ACM SIGIR*, 2009.
[8] X. Wu et al. Practical elimination of near-duplicates from web video search. In *ACM MM*, 2007.

Photo Search by Face Positions and Facial Attributes on Touch Devices

Yu-Heng Lei, Yan-Ying Chen, Lime Iida, Bor-Chun Chen, Hsiao-Hang Su, Winston H. Hsu
National Taiwan University, Taipei, Taiwan
{ryanlei, yanying}@cmlab.csie.ntu.edu.tw,
{limeiida, siriushpa}@gmail.com, b95901019@ntu.edu.tw, winston@csie.ntu.edu.tw

ABSTRACT

With the explosive growth of camera devices, people can freely take photos to capture moments of life, especially the ones accompanied with friends and family. Therefore, a better solution to organize the increasing number of personal or group photos is highly required. In this paper, we propose a novel way to search for face images according facial attributes and face similarity of the target persons. To better match the face layout in mind, our system allows the user to graphically specify the face positions and sizes on a query "canvas," where each attribute or identity is defined as an "icon" for easier representation. Moreover, we provide aesthetics filtering to enhance visual experience by removing candidates of poor photographic qualities. The scenario has been realized on a touch device with an intuitive user interface. With the proposed block-based indexing approach, we can achieve near real-time retrieval (0.1 second on average) in a large-scale dataset (more than 200k faces in Flickr images).

Categories and Subject Descriptors

H.3.1 [**Content Analysis and Indexing**]: Indexing methods; H.5.2 [**User Interfaces**]: Input devices and strategies

General Terms

Algorithms, Design, Experimentation, Performance

Keywords

Face attributes, Face retrieval, Touch-based user interface, Block-based indexing

1. INTRODUCTION

When browsing photos, what makes that image memorable? MIT Media Relations [6] pointed out that images with people in them are the most memorable, followed by images of human-scale space and close-ups of objects. The phenomenon becomes more obvious in consumer photos because most of them contain family members or close friends that users care about and usually keep in mind. Users may forget where or when they took the photos but they would not forget their friends and family. Therefore, they can make use of facial attributes and face identities to effectively formulate their search intentions. Furthermore, reviewing the retrieved images probably recalls more scenes in users' memory. For example, Alice seems standing next to me and an African kid sitting in the middle. The imagination of the photo in mind can be organized intuitively by graphically arranging people on a query "canvas" and refined by designating more face attributes and identities (Fig. 1). Although consumer photos naturally lack of annotations, automatic facial attribute and identity recognition techniques would make the scenario more economical and scalable.

Recently, some efforts attempt to capture users' intention by allowing them to visually describe the image content and layout on a query canvas. [1] revisits the problem

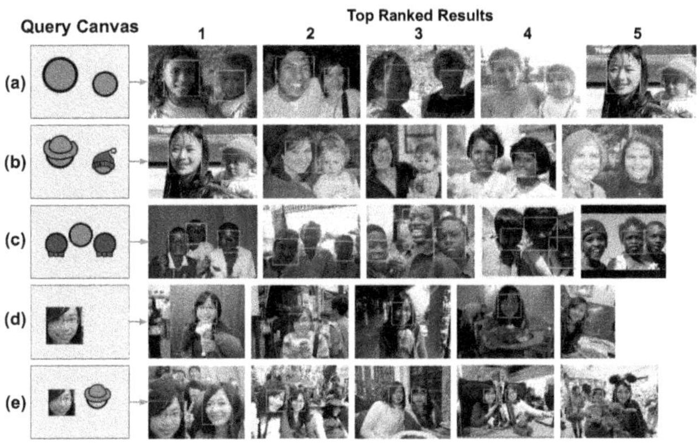

Figure 1: Example queries and top 5 retrieval results from our image search system. (a) specifies two arbitrary faces with the larger one on the left and the smaller one on the right. (b) further constrains that the left face has attributes "female" and "youth" and the right face has attribute "kid." (c) specifies two faces of "male" and "African" on the left and right, in addition to an arbitrary face on the center. (d) specifies a particular face in the database at the desired position and in the desired size. (e) specifies the previous database face on the left, and a face of "female" and "youth" on the right.

of sketch-based image search for scene photos. However, the gap between the user's mind and their specified query can still be large even in such a system. For instance, users with poor drawing skills may have a hard time describing their intention accurately. In addition, many object details are naturally difficult to sketch, such as the age of a face. To deal with this sketching difficulty, [7] allows the user to formulate a 2-D "semantic map" by placing text boxes of various search concepts at desired positions and in desired sizes. However, it does not address the problem for discovering specific persons in the intended scene and is therefore inapplicable to managing consumer photos. Meanwhile, typing text is not a simple operation on touch panels even though both sketch-based and concept-based queries target at better user experience.

Recent trends reveal that the popularity of touch devices brings new chances and challenges to image organization. In this paper, we propose a novel system for searching consumer photos by exploiting computer vision technologies in estimating facial attributes and face similarity. Rather than laboriously sketching detailed appearances [1] or typing text [7], our work allows users to formulate a query canvas by placing "icons" of desired facial attributes (Fig. 1 (b)(c)), a specific face instance (Fig. 1 (d)), or a specific face instance with a wildcard face (Fig. 1 (e)) at desired positions and in desired sizes. Moreover, we provide aesthetics filtering to retain images of better composition, colorfulness, and contrast, thus enhancing visual experience and saving time for reviewing poor photographic (usually unintended) image candidates. The scenario has been realized on a touch device with an intuitive user interface. To tackle the computation overheads for searching face positions in large-scale datasets, we propose a block-based indexing approach enabling rapid on-line retrieval response (0.1 second on average). The real system currently processes more than 200k faces in Flickr images and the number is scalable to larger photo collections.

2. OBSERVATIONS AND SYSTEM OVERVIEW

When looking for a photo in mind, it is difficult and inefficient for users to indicate the exact file location in the storage even though they are well categorized by time or geo-locations. Some prevailing photo sharing websites employ crowd-sourcing to obtain free tags semantically associated to images, but the mechanism can not be duplicated to personal photo organizer because users are not expected to actively annotate their photos. Although current commercial photo management software begin to exploit technologies in face recognition and face clustering, such solutions still lack the capability of searching for scenes with faces deployed in a specific layout. In light of this observation, our proposed system (Fig. 2) attempts to make consumer photo management faster and easier. As the contributions of this paper, we are (1) to analyze "wild photos" with no tag information at all by automatic facial attribute detection (Sec. 3) and face similarity estimation (Sec. 4), (2) to enhance visual experience by aesthetic filtering which removes image candidates of poor photographic qualities (Sec. 5), (3) to advance search pattern from query by single face instance to query by multiple attributed faces allocated on a canvas (Sec. 6.1, 6.2), and (4) to support rapid and accurate search

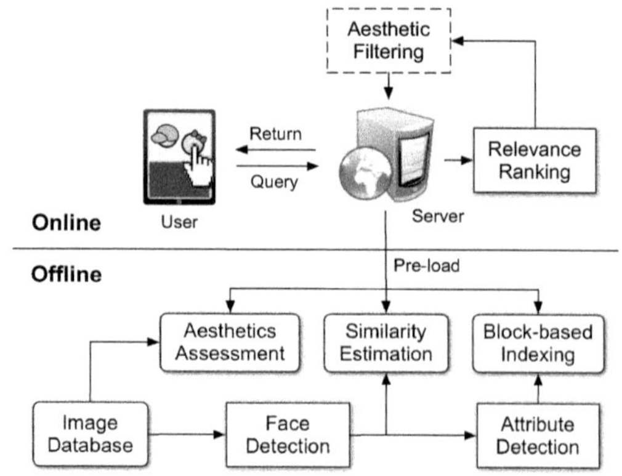

Figure 2: Framework of the proposed system. Photos are analyzed by facial attribute detection, face similarity estimation, aesthetics assessment, and block-based indexing in the off-line process.

for face positions by the proposed block-based indexing approach (Sec. 6.3).

3. DETECTING FACE ATTRIBUTES

Facial attributes possess rich information about people and have been shown promising for seeking specific persons in face retrieval and surveillance systems. In this work, we utilize eight people attributes including two of gender (female, male), three of age (kid, youth, elder) and three of race (Caucasian, Asian, African) to categorize faces in large-scale photos. We will extend to more facial attributes in the future. In the training phase, all the attributes are learned through a combination of Support Vector Machines (SVM) and Adaboost similar to [4]. Firstly, we crawl user-contributed photos from Flickr and extract facial regions by a face detector. Further, the face images are annotated manually and decomposed into different face components (e.g., whole face, eyes, nose, mouth), from each of which various low-level features (e.g., Gabor filter, HOG, Grid color moments, and local binary patterns) are extracted. A mid-level feature learned is an SVM classifier with a specific low-level feature extracted from a specific face component. Finally, the optimal mid-level features for the designated facial attribute are selected and weighted through Adaboost. The combined strong classifier represents the most important parts of that attribute, for example, <Gabor, whole face> is most effective for female attribute while <color, whole face> is most effective for African attribute.

Experimenting in the benchmark data [4], the approach can effectively detect facial attributes and achieve more than 80% accuracy on the average. Meanwhile, the framework is generic for various facial attributes thus providing better scalability to precisely profile users for more attributes. The real-valued attribute scores are normalized to the interval (0,1) by a sigmoid function before they are used.

4. ESTIMATING FACE SIMILARITIES

To enable search through face appearance, we adapt the face retrieval framework [2]. The advantage of this framework includes: (1) efficiency, which is achieved by using sparse representation of face image with inverted indexing,

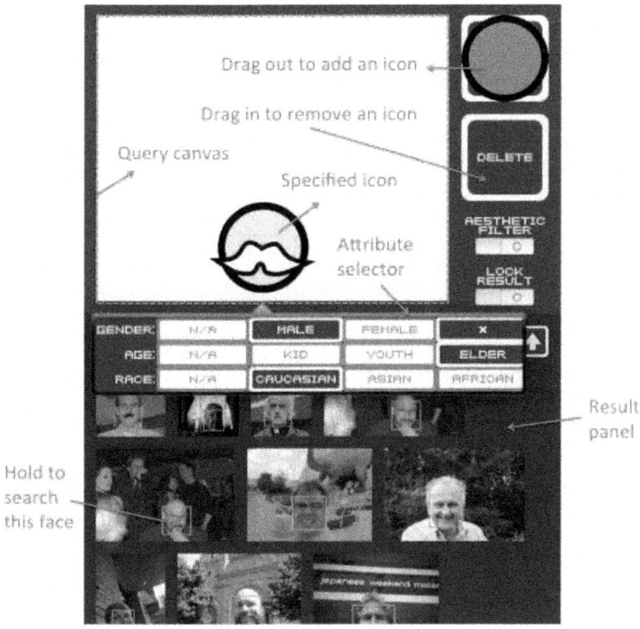

Figure 3: The touch-based interface of our system. Users can formulate a query by adding face icons from the top-right control panel and dragging the icons into canvas at desired positions. When clicking icons, a pop-up window will show up for attribute selection. Users can browse the query results on bottom and hold any faces back to query canvas to find out more images with the similar faces.

and (2) leveraging identity information, which is done by incorporating the identity information into the optimization process for codebook construction. Both of the above two points are suitable for our system. In details, detected faces are first aligned into canonical position, and then component-based local binary patterns are extracted from the images to form feature vectors. Sparse representations are further computed from these feature vectors based on a learned dictionary combined with extra identity information. By incorporating such framework into our system, the user can not only specify positions and attributes of the face but also use a face image itself with position as the query. The real-valued similarity scores are normalized to the interval (0,1) before they are used.

5. ASSESSING PHOTO AESTHETICS

The function of filtering based on photo aesthetics is also integrated in the proposed system. According to the work [5], the bag-of-aesthetics-preserving features are extracted to model the photo aesthetics at the global scope in our paper. These features have the following advantages: 1) photos can be modeled in multiple resolutions by its decomposition method; 2) photos can be described from different aesthetic aspects, including color, texture, saliency, and edge, by applying patchwise operations proposed in [5]; 3) contrast information, which humans are more sensitive to, is taken into consideration. Therefore, based on these features, the aesthetic properties of photo composition, colorfulness, contrast, etc., can be modeled jointly.

6. PHOTO SEARCH ON TOUCH DEVICES

6.1 User Interface

Since our system is extremely suitable for a touch-based interface, we have implemented the user interface on a tablet device, as shown in Figure 3. The user can drag faces from top-right onto the canvas, and the result will be displayed in the result panel in real time. Holding a face icon invokes an popup attribute selector. We have designed a total of 48 face icons (3 x 4 x 4) to describe the attribute combinations. To search by similarity, the user can hold a face in the result panel, and use the new icon on the top-right to find similar faces in other photos. There is also a simple aesthetic filter to help find photos with better looks.

6.2 Ranking Function

First note that in our system, coordinates are always represented as a fraction of the image width or height. This allows the computation to be adapted to the various aspect ratios in the query canvas or the database images. For a (query image, target image) pair, denoted as (q, t), the ranking problem is casted as a greedy version of maximum bipartite matching, with the two sets Q and T being the query image and the target image, respectively. Also note that bipartite matching ensures each face is matched at most once. By greedy, we mean the first query face is matched first by choosing the best matching face available. This significantly reduces the computational cost and coincides with the idea that the first face coming to the user's mind is the most important. The matching score between a face in the query q and a face in the target t is proposed as a linear combination of face similarity, face attributes, face center position, and face size:

$$\begin{aligned} match(q,t) = {} & w_{sim}\left(Sim(q,t)\right) + \\ & w_{attr}\left(\prod_{\alpha=1}^{|\alpha|} Attr(q,t)\right)^{1/|\alpha|} + \\ & w_{pos}\left(1 - \frac{d_c}{\sqrt{2}}\right) + w_{size}\left(1 - \frac{d_w + d_h}{2}\right) \end{aligned} \tag{1}$$

The first term is the similarity score between q and t. The second term is the geometric mean of all the three attribute scores ($|\alpha| = 3$). If an attribute is not specified, it is counted as 1. Notice in the UI, face similarity and face attributes are not specified at the same time. The third and the fourth terms are to normalize the errors in position and size to the interval (0,1), where d_c is the L2 distance between the face centers, and d_w and d_h are the L1 distances between the face widths and heights.

The overall matching score is then proposed as the arithmetic mean of the individual matching scores:

$$score(Q,T) = \frac{1}{max(|Q|,|T|)} \sum_{q,t \in M} match(q,t) \tag{2}$$

M denotes the set of matched faces. |Q| and |T| in the denominator are the number of faces in the query image and the target image, so if the numbers are different, there is a huge penalty in the overall score.

6.3 Block-based Indexing

We apply a block-based method to spatially index all the database faces. Since the face center coordinates, width and height, denoted as x, y, w, and h, are fractions, the infinitely many numbers in the interval (0,1) make indexing computationally infeasible and quantization too sensitive. Therefore, we first quantize each of the four variables into L levels, and pre-define overlapping blocks of various valid (x,y,w,h) combinations and use them throughout the system. Notice that not all the L^4 combinations are valid blocks. The mapping between an (x,y,w,h) pair and a block id can be easily achieved by representing a block id as an L-nary number of 4 digits. This mapping is both unique and storage-free. We can then build an inverted index to record, for each block id, the image id's that contain a face in this block and all of their attribute scores. Of course, examining only faces in the block of the query is still too sensitive. So in on-line search, the system runs a small "sliding window" to compute the scores of faces in neighboring blocks. The range of the sliding window indicates the level of tolerance.

For multiple-face queries, each face is processed separately. It is important that we enforce constraints that each target face can be matched at most once, and that each query face matches at most one face in the same target image.

7. EXPERIMENTS

In this section, we describe the dataset and implementation details, and evaluate the performance on the joint ranking of face attributes, face position, and face size. For the performance on face similarity and photo aesthetics, please refer to the corresponding references [2] and [5]. For a video demonstration of the system, please visit our project page: `http://www.csie.ntu.edu.tw/~winston/projects/face`

7.1 Dataset and Implementation details

The dataset is composed of two portions. As mentioned in section 3, we crawl a large number of user-contributed photos from Flickr as the main portion. For similar face retrieval, 732 daily photos containing 1,248 faces are added to the dataset as the second portion. After face detection by a commercial but free API [3], together there are 115,487 images containing 244,491 faces in the dataset (2.117 faces per image).

Similar face retrieval is intended only for the second portion, so only the pairwise similarity scores in the second portion are estimated, and faces in the first portion have zero similarity scores. For the weights in the ranking function, we empirically choose $w_{sim} = 2.00$, $w_{attr} = 0.70$, $w_{pos} = 0.20$, and $w_{size} = 0.10$. This reflects the user's intention that face similarity and attributes are much more important when they are specified. For block-based indexing, we choose the number of quantization levels as $L = 20$, and the sliding window for tolerance is 5 levels in position and 4 levels in size. Aesthetic filtering is optionally applied to the initial result, which keeps images of top 50% aesthetic ranks in the final result.

With the index and metadata preloaded, the proposed system reports a typical running time of 0.10 second on a 16-core, 2.40GHz Intel Xeon server with 48GB of RAM. The storage cost is 112MB.

7.2 Performance Evaluation

In order to evaluate our system, we manually create eight different queries containing different search intentions listed in the table 1. We then ask twenty people to do the evaluation by showing them the queries with top 10 results retrieved by our system, and ask them whether the retrieved result is relevant to the query. Table 1 shows the average results from twenty users. Query tasks 1 through 4 all have precision higher than 90%. The precision decreases as the query becomes more complicated. This is because the attribute detector itself has errors. When there are many attributes in a query, it becomes harder to find images with all correctly detected attributes, For instance, if the attribute detector has 80% detection rate, when there are three attributes specified in a query, only 51% of the images are correctly detected by the attribute detector. Query task 7 has the lowest P@10. This is probably because it is naturally hard for the attribute detector to find whether a kid is a male or female.

Table 1: Precision@10 of 8 selected queries.

#	Query Intention	P@10
1	Single face (top-left)	0.99
2	Single face (profile canvas)	0.93
3	Single face (close-up)	0.99
4	Two faces (left and right)	0.97
5	Single face (male, youth)	0.75
6	Male (left) and female (right)	0.53
7	Female kid (left) and male kid (right)	0.29
8	Three faces on top and two below	0.68

8. CONCLUSIONS

Our work proposes a novel way for effectively organizing and searching consumer photos by positioning attributed faces at desired positions and in desired sizes on a query canvas. Meanwhile, we can automatically detect facial attributes and measure face similarity in the off-line process to provide rapid on-line photo search. Integrated with aesthetics assessment, we can further save time for browsing photos with poor quality. The scenario has been realized on a touch device with an easy-to-use interface and has achieved fast retrieval response by the proposed block-based indexing approach.

9. REFERENCES

[1] Y. Cao et al. Edgel index for large-scale sketch-based image search. *CVPR*, 2011.

[2] B.-C. Chen, Y.-H. Kuo, Y.-Y. Chen, K.-Y. Chu, and W. Hsu. Semi-supervised face image retrieval using sparse coding with identity constraint. *ACM Multimedia*, 2011.

[3] face.com API. `http://developers.face.com`.

[4] N. Kumar et al. Facetracer: A search engine for large collections of images with faces. *ECCV*, 2008.

[5] H.-H. Su, T.-W. Chen, C.-C. Kao, S.-Y. Chien, and W. Hsu. Scenic photo quality assessment with bag of aesthetics-preserving features. *ACM Multimedia*, 2011.

[6] A. Trafton. What makes an image memorable? *MIT Media Relations*, 2011.

[7] H. Xu et al. Image search by concept map. *SIGIR*, 2010.

Towards Textually Describing Complex Video Contents with Audio-Visual Concept Classifiers

Chun Chet Tan[†], Yu-Gang Jiang[‡], Chong-Wah Ngo[†]

[†]Dept of Computer Science, City University of Hong Kong, Kowloon, Hong Kong

[‡]School of Computer Science, Fudan University, Shanghai, China

cctan2@student.cityu.edu.hk, ygj@fudan.edu.cn, cwngo@cs.cityu.edu.hk

ABSTRACT

Automatically generating compact textual descriptions of complex video contents has wide applications. With the recent advancements in automatic audio-visual content recognition, in this paper we explore the technical feasibility of the challenging issue of precisely recounting video contents. Based on cutting-edge automatic recognition techniques, we start from classifying a variety of visual and audio concepts in video contents. According to the classification results, we apply simple rule-based methods to generate textual descriptions of video contents. Results are evaluated by conducting carefully designed user studies. We find that the state-of-the-art visual and audio concept classification, although far from perfect, is able to provide very useful clues indicating what is happening in the videos. Most users involved in the evaluation confirmed the informativeness of our machine-generated descriptions.

Categories and Subject Descriptors

I.2.10 [**Artificial Intelligence**]: Vision and Scene Understanding—*Video analysis*

General Terms

Algorithms, Experimentation, Measurement

Keywords

Textual descriptions of video content, audio-visual concept classification.

1. INTRODUCTION

Precise video content description is useful for many applications such as video search. Commercial search engines have been using some content-relevant texts, such as those extracted from captions/contexts of online videos and scripts of movies and TV series. However, these textual annotations provided by humans are far from adequate for enormous online videos which often neither have scripts nor meaningful captions. This motivates the need of developing automatic solutions for generating video content descriptions.

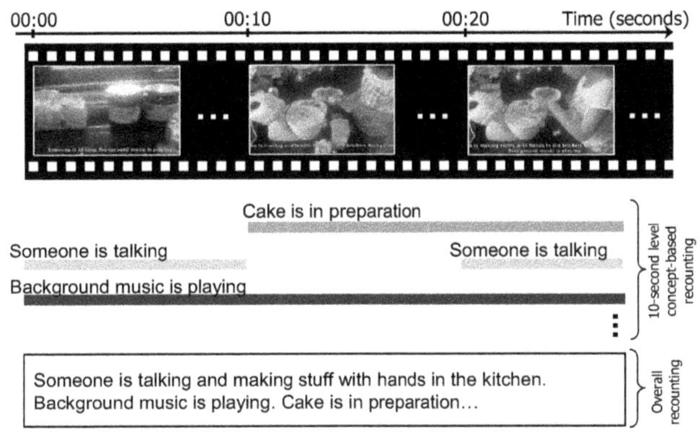

Figure 1: Video content recounting with audio-visual concept classifiers. Given a video (shown on the top), our proposed approach first classifies several audio-visual concepts, and then automatically produces textual descriptions based on the concept classification results.

In [3], an interesting method was proposed for textually describing videos. However, this approach was applied to simple data from constrained scenarios and is therefore infeasible to be implemented for real-world complex videos. Fortunately, in recent years there have been many research efforts devoted to visual and audio content recognition. For example, in [5], Laptev et al. proposed a very effective method based on spatial-temporal interest points for learning human actions in Hollywood movies. Jiang et al. [2] used a multimodal approach for complex video event recognition in Internet videos, and in [6], Lee et al. tried to identify semantic concepts in consumer videos by using audio feature alone. In each of the aforementioned works on content recognition, the authors have shown promising results on real-world video data. Although these content recognition techniques are still far below perfect, recent studies have found them helpful for many applications, such as video search [1, 9].

In this paper, we conduct a pilot study to explore the technical feasibility of automatically describing complex video contents. Our approach is grounded on the cutting-edge techniques for recognizing visual and audio semantics in videos. According to the recognition outputs, video contents are automatically described at both short clip level and entire video level. The mapping from content recognition results to textual descriptions is done by simple rule-based methods. Using a set of Internet videos containing three complex event topics, we study to what extent the imperfect automatic audio-visual concept classifiers can contribute to textual video content recounting. Carefully designed user studies verify the promise of our idea. Figure 1 shows an example of content description output by our approach. In the following, we first present our proposed approach, and then describe experiments and discuss results.

2. VIDEO CONTENT RECOUNTING

Our proposed video content recounting framework consists of two major components: audio-visual concept learning and rule-based textual description generation.

2.1 Audio-Visual Concept Learning

Central to automatic content recounting is the recognition of semantic contents in videos. To this end, we develop automatic classifiers for identifying a set of audio/visual semantic concepts. We follow the state-of-the-art approaches in [5, 2, 6]. Specifically, we extract three kinds of audio-visual features: 2D static SIFT [7], 3D spatial-temporal interest points (STIPs) [4], and MFCC audio descriptors. For SIFT, we use two standard detectors DoG [7] and Hessian Affine [8], and each detected local image patch is described by a 128-dimentional gradient histogram. STIPs are detected at multiple spatial and temporal scales. Laptev's method [4] is adopted to locate keypoints with significant local variation in both space and time. Histogram of Oriented Gradients (HOG; 72 dimensions) and Histogram of Optical Flow (HOF; 90 dimensions) descriptors are computed for the detected STIPs. Eventually HOG and HOF descriptors are concatenated into a 162-dimensional vector for each STIP. In contrast to the two visual descriptors that are computed based on sparse detectors, the MFCC features are densely extracted in the audio track of the videos — we compute a 60-dimensional MFCC feature in every 32ms temporal window, and nearby windows have 16ms overlap.

Now that we have multiple SIFT, STIP, and MFCC descriptors extracted from each video. The popular bag-of-word representation is then applied to convert the 3 sets of descriptors separately into 3 fixed-dimensional feature vectors. We use hierarchical k-means to generate a visual vocabulary of 4,000 words for both STIP and MFCC, and two smaller vocabularies of 500 words for DoG-SIFT and Hessian-SIFT respectively. The choices of visual or audio vocabulary size are based on empirical evidences from the prior studies in [5, 2].

In audio-visual concept learning, we use each 10-second video clip, instead of the entire video, as a data sample, so that we can obtain finer-grained audio-visual clues for content recounting. For SIFT feature, two spatial layers (1×1 and 2×2) are used in the vector quantization process, producing a 5,000-dimensional feature vector for each 10-second clip ($1 \times 1 \times (2 \times 500) + 2 \times 2 \times (2 \times 500)$). For STIP and MFCC, no spatial/temporal partitioning is used.

With the three types of audio-visual features, we use SVM classifier for concept learning. Following [2], given an audio/visual concept, depending on the type of the concept, we empirically pick the best suitable feature to train a SVM classifier. The concepts used in our experiments and their training data will be introduced in the experiment section.

2.2 Concept-based Content Recounting

The second stage of our approach is to utilize the concept classification results to generate content recounting. For this, we take a simple rule-based approach by predefining a set of templates according to the concepts under consideration.

Before generating the textual descriptions, we first try to predict high-level events happening in the target videos based on audio-visual concept classification. The high-level event prediction can be used for alleviating the effect of noisy concept classification. We manually define a $k \times l$ event-concept relevancy matrix $\mathbf{R}$ for this purpose, where k is the number of events and l is the number of concepts. Since practically k is very likely to be in the scale of a few hundreds, it is feasible to let humans fill in this relevancy matrix. The entries of the matrix are either $+1$ for concepts with strong positive correlations to the event, or -1 for those with negative correlations to the event. For example, concept "outdoor" is assigned with a value -1 while "kitchen" is given a value of $+1$ for event "making a cake". With the relevancy matrix, we use the following equation for predicting the presence of each event in a video:

$$p = \mathbf{R} \times c, \tag{1}$$

where c is a l-dimensional concept classification score vector for the video, and p is a k-dimensional event prediction score vector. In our experiments, we only consider the case where each video contains a single event, and thus the final selected event corresponds to the index in p with maximum prediction score.

This simple event prediction process helps the recounting by preventing conflicts in concept occurrence caused by noisy classification. For example, the automatic concept classification may predict that the background scene of a video changes from indoor "kitchen" to "outdoor", and then flips back to "kitchen" again. In this case, if the video is predicted with an event "making a cake", the noisy "outdoor" classification will not be used in recounting since it conflicts with "making a cake" according to the event-concept relevancy matrix $\mathbf{R}$.

Next we describe the rules for generating textual descriptions. In this pilot exploratory work, we consider three types of concepts: human action concepts (e.g., "walking"), scene concepts (e.g., "kitchen"), and audio sound concepts (e.g., "cheering"). The templates used for recounting are predefined based on these concepts. Our first template is based on the classification of concepts "crowd" – if it is detected, we use "Several people are..." as subject phrase. Otherwise we use "Someone is...". The subject phrase is then concatenated with the action and scene phrases accordingly based on the identified action/scene concepts. For example, if "crowd" and "walking" concepts are identified simultaneously, then we output "Several people are *walking*". If both action (e.g., "walking") and background scene (e.g., "kitchen") concepts are identified, we form sentences like "someone is *walking* in the *kitchen*". Sometimes scene concepts may be identified but no people related concept is found. In this case, we use phrases describing scene setting only, such as "The background is a *baseball field*". In addition, if there are multiple scene concepts identified, we only generate a sentence based on the one with the highest confidence. This way we can further reduce noisy classification and make the final recounting more concise and less wordy. The overall recounting mecha-

Table 1: **Audio-visual concepts used in our experiments.**

Human Action Concepts	Scene Concepts	Audio Concepts
walking	kitchen	outdoor rural
running	outdoor with grass/tree	outdoor urban
squatting	baseball field	indoor quiet
standing up	crowd	indoor noisy
making stuff with hands	cake close-up	speech comprehensible
batting baseball		music
		cheering
		clapping

nism is pretty generic — it is very easy to incorporate more concepts and/or templates into the framework for more detailed video recounting.

We use the same set of simple templates described above to generate descriptions at both 10-second clip level and entire video level. The entire video level recounting is generated by removing all the redundant (duplicate) phrases from the 10-second level descriptions.

3. EXPERIMENTS

3.1 Experimental Setup

Experiments are performed on Internet videos from NIST TRECVID 2010 multimedia event detection (MED) task[1]. The MED task was set up to foster automatic content recognition and recounting techniques for complex videos. Three events were defined in MED 2010: "assembling a shelter", "baseball batting a run in", and "making a cake". Our target in this work is to automatically produce textual descriptions for the MED test videos that contain at least one of the events (140 videos in total). For the audio-visual concepts, we use 19 concepts defined by Columbia University [2]. Labels of these concepts are also provided by [2] on 7,156 10-second clips from 565 training videos, i.e., each 10-second clip of the 565 training videos has been manually labeled w.r.t. the 19 concepts[2]. We use STIP feature for human action concept classification, SIFT feature for scene classification, and MFCC feature for classifying audio concepts. The classifiers are then applied to 10-second clips of the 140 test videos to generate audio-visual concept classification scores. During recounting, a concept is treated as true if it has a classification score larger than 0.4.

We conduct subjective user studies to evaluate the recounting performance. Figure 2 displays the user-interface design. Recounting score ranges from 1 to 5 (from very bad to very good), indicated by the number of color-highlighted hearts shown in the figure. Before the evaluation, the users were instructed and guided about the score assignment in detail using several example videos. During the evaluation, videos were randomly assigned to users and each video was scored by at least three independent users. As introduced earlier, evaluation is conducted on both 10-second clip level and entire video level. The evaluation interfaces for both are similar, except that for the 10-second level recounting, the textual descriptions below the video are online updated as the video is playing.

3.2 Results and Analysis

We first report event prediction performance based on the audio-visual concept classification outputs, as described in Section 2.2. Since concept classification is performed on 10-second clip level, there are two ways to consolidate the predictions for generating the overall concept vector, c, by using the "mean" and the "max" values of concept scores over all 10-second clips in a video. We report performance of both strategies. Overall, the event prediction accuracy of both "mean" and "max" strategies is equal to 89.3%. Table 2 summarizes the number of misses and false alarms for each event. "Max" has less misses for event "batting a run in". This is because some concepts only occur once throughout the baseball videos, e.g., "running" or "cheering". On the other hand, the "max" strategy gives negative impact for event "making a cake". This may be due to the fact that "making a cake" is a long-term event with many concepts happening continuously (e.g., "kitchen", "making stuff with hands", etc.), for which "mean" strategy is more reliable. Since there is no clear winner between the two, we only report recounting results using "max" in the following.

Now we summarize the recounting evaluation results from user studies. In total there are 43 human evaluators involved in this subjective scoring process. Figure 3 shows the user scores for both 10-second clip level and entire video level recounting. Overall, the results are very encouraging - about 1/3 of the videos received full score 5 hearts, and another 1/2 of them were given 3–4 hearts. Comparing videos of the three events separately, "batting a run in" videos have more positive feedbacks than the other two, which is probably due to the fact that this event has relatively more consistent (and easy-to-identify) background scene pattern. Videos with the "assembling a shelter" event, on the other hand, are more difficult to recount since the scene/object settings of this event have very large intra-class variations.

Figure 2: User evaluation interface. A video is displayed on the top and its textual description is given under it. Users were asked to score the recounting quality by assigning 1-5 hearts shown at the bottom.

Table 2: Concept-based event prediction results. We report the number of misses and false alarms (FA) for each event, using two consolidation strategies: "mean" and "max".

Event (true positive video #)	"Mean"		"Max"	
	#Miss	#FA	#Miss	#FA
Assembling a shelter (46)	2	13	2	13
Batting a run in (47)	6	1	2	2
Making a cake (47)	7	1	11	0

[1]http://www.nist.gov/itl/iad/mig/med10.cfm

[2]The audio-visual concept annotations were downloaded from http://www.ee.columbia.edu/ln/dvmm/researchProjects/MultimediaIndexing/TRECVID2010MED/TRECVID2010MED.htm

Figure 4: Recounting result examples. The left two are good, while the right one is a bad result example, where the outdoor street scene was mistakenly recognized as indoor kitchen. This is mainly due to the low coverage of our current audio-visual concept library which only contains a specific outdoor concept "outdoor with grass/tree".

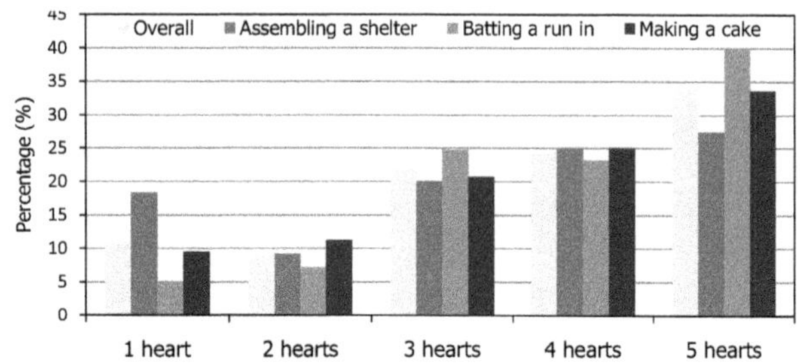

(a) 10-second clip level recounting

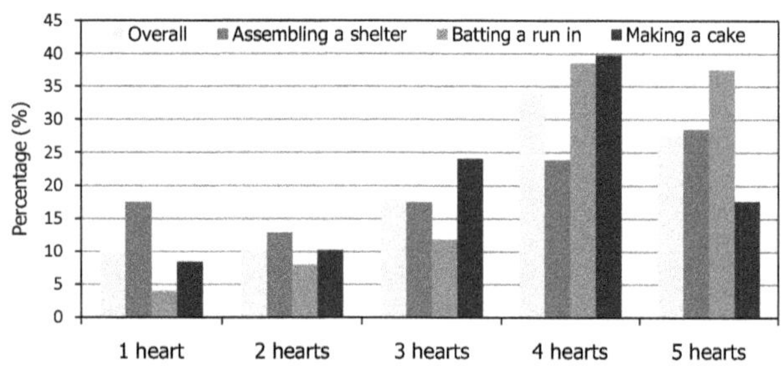

(b) entire video level recounting

Figure 3: User evaluation results of automatic content recounting on (a) 10-second clip level, and (b) entire video level. Scores were marked by 1-5 hearts indicating recounting quality varying from very bad to very good. Overall, users involved in the evaluation were quite satisfied with the results. Entire video level recounting is a bit worse than that on the 10-second level since it is more challenging to generate short and descriptive overall summaries.

User evaluation results of the two levels of recounting do not differ too much, except that the entire video level recounting received a smaller number of full scores (5 hearts). This indicates that there may be some missing clues or conflicts resulted from the generation of the overall recounting, which deserves deeper analysis that will be done in our future work. Figure 4 shows some examples with both good and bad recounting outputs.

4. CONCLUSIONS

We have conducted a pilot study towards the challenging goal of generating video content descriptions automatically. Our focus is particularly on the utilization of audio-visual concept classifiers obtained based on the state-of-the-art content recognition techniques. Using a set of Internet videos and 19 audio-visual concept classifiers as a showcase, we have observed that simple rule-based recounting method is already able to generate very encouraging results. Our main contribution of this work is to show that the imperfect classification of audio-visual concepts can be exploited for effectively describing complex video contents. There are still many ways to improve the current prototype system. Significant ones include the utilization of advanced natural language processing (NLP) techniques for generating more elegant textual descriptions, and the extension of our concept library to cover more real-world audio-visual settings.

Acknowledgement

The work described in this paper was fully supported by a grant from the Research Grants Council of the Hong Kong Special Administrative Region, China (CityU 119709). YGJ is supported by Fudan University New Faculty Start-up Grant.

5. REFERENCES

[1] A. Hauptmann, R. Yan, W.-H. Lin, M. Christel, and H. Wactlar. Can high-level concepts fill the semantic gap in video retrieval? a case study with broadcast news. *IEEE Transactions on Multimedia*, 9:958–966, 2007.

[2] Y.-G. Jiang, X. Zeng, G. Ye, S. Bhattacharya, D. Ellis, M. Shah, and S.-F. Chang. Columbia-UCF TRECVID2010 multimedia event detection: Combining multiple modalities, contextual concepts, and temporal matching. In *NIST TRECVID Workshop*, 2010.

[3] A. Kojima, T. Tamura, and K. Fukunaga. Natural language description of human activities from video images based on concept hierarchy of actions. *International Journal of Computer Vision*, 50:171–184, 2002.

[4] I. Laptev. On space-time interest points. *International Journal of Computer Vision*, 64:107–123, 2005.

[5] I. Laptev, M. Marszałek, C. Schmid, and B. Rozenfeld. Learning realistic human actions from movies. In *IEEE Conference on Computer Vision and Pattern Recognition*, 2008.

[6] K. Lee and D. P. W. Ellis. Audio-based semantic concept classification for consumer video. *IEEE Transactions on Audio, Speech and Language Processing*, 18:1406–1416, 2010.

[7] D. G. Lowe. Distinctive image features from scale-invariant keypoints. *International Journal Computer Vision*, 60:91–110, 2004.

[8] K. Mikolajczyk and C. Schmid. Scale and affine invariant interest point detectors. *International Journal of Computer Vision*, 60(1):63–86, 2004.

[9] C. G. M. Snoek and M. Worring. Concept-based video retrieval. *Foundations and Trends in Information Retrieval*, 4(2):215–322, 2009.

Evaluating a Dancer's Performance using Kinect-based Skeleton Tracking

Dimitrios Alexiadis, Petros Daras
Informatics and Telematics Institute, Thessaloniki, Greece
{dalexiad, daras}@iti.gr

Philip Kelly, Noel E. O'Connor
CLARITY: Centre for Sensor Web Technologies, Dublin City University, Ireland
{philip.kelly, noel.oconnor}@dcu.ie

Tamy Boubekeur
Institut Telecom / Telecom ParisTech, Paris, France
tamy.boubekeur@telecom-paristech.fr

Maher Ben Moussa
MIRALab, University of Geneva, Switzerland
benmoussa@miralab.ch

ABSTRACT

In this work, we describe a novel system that automatically evaluates dance performances against a gold-standard performance and provides visual feedback to the performer in a 3D virtual environment. The system acquires the motion of a performer via Kinect-based human skeleton tracking, making the approach viable for a large range of users, including home enthusiasts. Unlike traditional gaming scenarios, when the motion of a user must by kept in synch with a pre-recorded avatar that is displayed on screen, the technique described in this paper targets online interactive scenarios where dance choreographies can be set, altered, practiced and refined by users. In this work, we have addressed some areas of this application scenario. In particular, a set of appropriate signal processing and soft computing methodologies is proposed for temporally aligning dance movements from two different users and quantitatively evaluating one performance against another.

Categories and Subject Descriptors

I.4.8 [**Image Processing and Computer Vision**]: Scene Analysis—*Motion, Tracking*; I.5.A [**Image Processing and Computer Vision**]: Applications—*Signal processing*

General Terms

Algorithms, Experimentation

Keywords

Skeleton tracking, Microsoft Kinect, Signal Processing

1. INTRODUCTION

The future of social networking is gearing towards immersive, content-centric, collaborative environments that support real-time, realistic interaction between humans. The Huawei 3DLife/EMC^2 challenge [2] run as part of the ACM Multimedia Grand Challenge Series 2011 announced a call for demonstrations of relevant technologies that can support real-time online human interaction. The application scenario considers an online dance class provided by an expert Salsa dancer. In such a scenario, a dance teacher (for example) is free to illustrate to online users choreography steps of their choice. After viewing the sequence at a later date, another online user (a student, for example) can attempt to mimic the steps, and obtain feedback from the system to help refine his/her dance moves. At any time, the teacher can alter the choreography or introduce extra steps when the student has reached a certain level of competency. As such, there is real online interaction between users.

In this paper, we study some of the technical issues that would need to be addressed in this challenging scenario. In particular, we target the problem of real-time automatic alignment, evaluation and feedback of dance performances. More specifically, we present a system that can automatically align a student dance performance to that of a teacher, calculate an overall and an instantaneous score for his/her performance, and provide visual feedback on the performance compared to the teacher. In order to align and evaluate dance performances, Kinect depth-maps from the associated Grand Challenge dataset are considered. A set of signal processing methodologies, combined with human skeleton tracking from Kinect depth-maps, is proposed for evalaution. In addition, we provide visualization of the temporally aligned dance movement of both teacher and students, along with the associated evaluation scores, in a virtual 3D gaming environment. This visualization tool also provides functionality to slow down or change the orientation of the visualization, allowing users analyze their dance moves from multiple perspectives.

The paper is organized as follows: In section 2 we briefly describe the ACM Grand Challenge dataset. In section 3 we describe hoe the Kinect skeleton tracking module is used for the real-time tracking of the dancers. In section 4 we provide details on the proposed signal processing methodologies for dancer evaluation. Section 5 outlines the visualization tool and its operation. Finally, in section 6 we present some experimental results acquired using the developed software.

2. DATASET

In this work, we have utilized the dataset from the *Realistic Interaction in Online Virtual Environments* Huawei 3DLife/EMC^2 ACM Grand Challenge that includes recordings of Salsa dancers captured with a variety of modalites and equipment, including (among others) Microsoft Kinect sensors. The dataset includes recordings of two professional dancers (a male and a female), corresponding to teachers, and 13 amateur dancers (8 males and 5 females), corresponding to students, in six different Salsa choreographies. Although the dataset contains much more information, in this work we use solely the Kinect modality, as this may be all that is available for many home enthusiasts.

3. KINECT SKELETON TRACKING

The Kinect dataset recordings of dancer performances were captured using the OpenNI [3] drivers/SDK and are OpenNI-encoded (.ONI). The OpenNI SDK provides, among others, a high-level skeleton tracking module, which can be used for detecting the captured user and tracking his/her body joints. More specifically, the OpenNI tracking module produces the positions of 17 joints (Head, Neck, Torso, Left and Right Collar, L/R Shoulder, L/R Elbow, L/R Wrist, L/R Hip, L/R Knee and L/R Foot), along with the corresponding tracking confidence – see panel 7 in Figure 2.

The OpenNI tracking module requires a-priori user calibration in order to infer information about the user's height and body characteristics. More specifically, skeleton calibration requires the captured user to stay still in a specific "calibration pose" for a few seconds. However, this pose was not captured for the dancers and therefore custom skeleton tracking calibration for each dancer is not possible. Fortunately, our experiments show that skeleton tracking is quite effective even if non-exact calibration data is provided to the OpenNI tracking module. In this work, we created custom calibration results for each dancer by manually sourcing and calibrating persons with similar body characteristics to each dancer in the dataset. This tailored calibration data resulted in more robust skeletal tracking and consequently higher accuracy of the automatic evaluation methods.

4. AUTOMATIC DANCER EVALUATION

Based on the calibration procedure described in Section 3, we developed C++ OpenNI-based skeleton tracking software and a MATLAB wrapper to acquire the skeleton tracking output from the ONI recordings. The skeleton tracking module outputs the positions of the dancer's joints for each frame. These positions actually constitute a 3D vector signal. In addition, the dynamics of dancing movements can also be acquired from the outputs of the skeleton tracking module. In this work, these dynamic movements are acquired as the instantaneous 3D velocities of the joints and are calculated from the convolution of the (generally noisy) discrete-time position signals with a 1st order Derivative of Gaussian (DOG). In order to provide a score for each choreography we propose to compare the aligned position and velocity vector signals of an amateur dancer with the corresponding signals of a professional one. Note, that the Grand Challenge dataset signifies which dancers are amateurs and professionals.

4.1 Methodologies

In order to handle the three coordinate variables X, Y and Z in a holistic manner, the adopted signal processing techniques make use of hypercomplex numbers and specifically quaternions [5]. Quaternions, which are popular in the 3D graphics community, have recently been used for signal and image processing [5] and constitute a generalization of complex numbers, where instead of a scalar imaginary part, a 3D "vector" imaginary part is considered. As providing details on quaternion theory is beyond the scope of this paper, interested readers are referred to [5].

4.1.1 Dancer Alignment

Within the Grand Challenge dataset, all dancers align their dance routines with respect to the background music, however this audio is not available with the Kinect data, and the Kinect data stream is not synchronized with respect to the start/end of the background music. As such, the Kinect dance sequences are in effect non-synchronized with respect to the frame numbers. In addition, typically two distinct dancing sequences that we wish to compare are not of the same temporal length, i.e. number of frames. Additionally, the time-instance at which the skeletal tracking module detects the dancer and starts tracking is not common across all sequences. As such, in order to obtain more useful signals for comparison, preprocessing is required to align dance sequences. In this work, alignment is achieved by exploiting solely the Kinect data.

The adopted preprocessing scheme is as follows: 1) For each sequence, discard all the frames before the detection of the dancer, i.e. before the time-instance when at least one joint is detected; 2) Use a flag value, NaN (Not A Number), to represent an undetected/tracked joint; and 3) Pad the shortest sequences with NaN flag values, so that both sequences to be compared have the same temporal length. Note that NaN values are not considered in further calculations. In this work, dance alignment is achieved by exploiting only the Kinect data and using the quaternionic cross-covariance [5]. The time-shift between two dancing sequences is estimated by calculating the modulus of the quaternionic cross-covariance for all joints. An example is depicted in figure 1.

4.1.2 Dancer Evaluation

In this work three different scores are calculated for a dancer's performance, which are subsequently combined to produce an overall score. The proposed scores are calculated as follows:

Score #1 - Joint Positions
A score for each joint is calculated by considering the modulus of the quaternionic Correlation Coefficient (CC) for each pair of joint position signals. A total score S_1 is then computed as the weighted mean of the separate joint scores.

Score #2 - Joint Velocities
Similarly, an overall score S_2 is extracted based on the veloc-

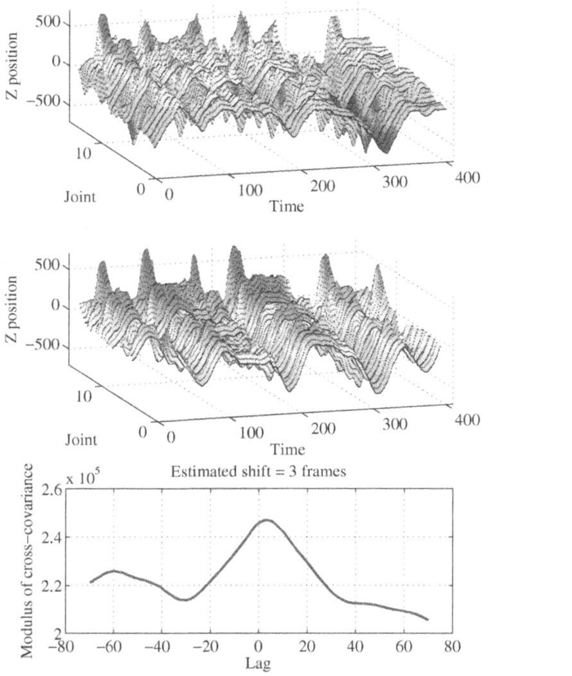

Figure 1: Two upper rows: The Z positions of all joints for the professional dancer (Betrand c3 t1) and an amateur dancer (Gabi c3 t1). Bottom row: The corresponding modulus of quaternionic cross-covariance. The estimated time-shift is 3 frames.

ities of the joints, instead of their positions, by considering the quaternionic CC for the joint velocity signals.

Score #3 - 3D Flow Error

For a given frame, the velocities of the joints are considered as 3D motion (flow) vectors. Inspired by the relevant 2D optical flow literature [4], we consider the normalized 3D velocity vectors in homogenous coordinates and calculate the vectors' inner product to obtain a score for each joint. An "all-joints" score is produced from the median of the separate inner products in order to reject outliers, i.e. very wrong estimates due to inaccurate skeleton tracking. A total score S_3 for the whole choreography is calculated from the median across time.

Combined score

Having computed three different scores S_1, S_2 and S_3, a combined score is calculated as the weighted mean of the three. The set of the three weights can be optimally selected using an optimization approach.

Relations with the ground-truth ratings

The calculated scores are produced by comparing the amateur's dance with the professional's one. Consequently, assuming that the ground-truth ratings for the reference dance is "excellent", the automatically extracted scores reflect more-or-less all five ground-truth criteria ("Upper" and "Lower Body Fluidity", "Musical Timing", "Body Balance" and "Choreography"). However, it is essential to consider that the calculated scores are mainly related to the "Choreography" (accuracy in executing a specific sequence of dance steps) and "musical timing" performance. This can be supported based on the fact that the scores S_1 and S_2 are correlation-based. Therefore, they constitute a measure of "similarity" of the "dancing signals" being compared and the degree to which they are time-aligned. Score S_3 presents also a similar behavior. The above arguments can be demonstrated by simple simulation scenarios experiments, the presentation of which is however beyond the scope of this paper.

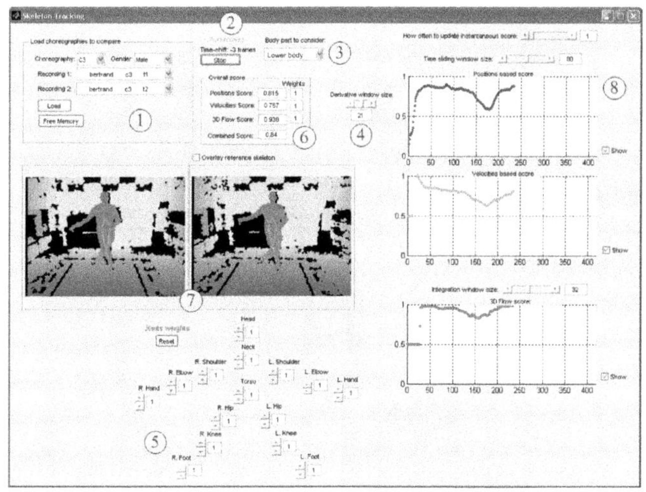

Figure 2: Data Acquisition Software GUI.

Instantaneous scores and separate scores for different body parts

If scoring is required for different sections the dance, rather than a single score for the entire recital, a straightforward methodology to produce instantaneous scoring can be adopted. In this case, instead of considering the vector's signals for the whole time interval, a time-sliding window is employed, whereby the instantaneous score for a time instance, t, is calculated by applying the described methodologies for the time-interval of length, L, around t.

Additionally, the described ideas can be extended in order to provide feedback to the amateur on how he/she can improve his/her performance. In such a scenario, separate scores can extracted for different body parts, for example the upper and the lower body parts, by separately considering the upper and lower body joints.

5. EVALUATION FRAMEWORK

The evaluation framework is split into two different parts; (A) Data acquisition and (B) Data visualization.

Data Acquisition Software.

A Graphical User Interface (GUI) was developed in Matlab, in order to integrate the developed methods, allow parameter selection and provide initial visualization of the results. The GUI is depicted in figure 2, where an evaluation example is presented. Among the possibilities provided by the GUI are (the enumeration is given with respect to figure 2): 1) Selection of two choreography recordings to compare, 2) Dancer alignment, 3) Selection of the body part to consider, 4) Methodologies' parameter selection, 5) Weights selection, 6) Calculation of three overall scores, 7) Visualization of the skeleton tracking results, 8) Visualization of the three scores over time. Using this GUI all parameters associated with the proposed system can be controlled.

Figure 3: Visualization results from multiple angles and time sequences, notice how images with similar poses have good scores, but the dances diverges in the bottom right and is assigned a low score.

Data Visualization Software.

Although the data acquisition software provides some basic 2D visualization of the dancers, we believe that users will benefit more from a virtual 3D gaming environment. In such an environment, users are free to view their dance (plus the aligned dance of the teacher) from any orientation they wish, allowing them to subjectively critique their movements from a variety of angles. In addition, a user can pause at a particular frame, step forward/backward, or continuously play back at a decreased framerate to facilitate users to accurately analyze their dance moves. For this visualization, we employed the Unity gaming development tool [1], mapping the human motions onto photo-realistic avatars and placing the avatars into a virtual dance studio. In addition, we provide feedback on their movements in terms of scoring their motion against a teacher's motion. Example images from the virtual environment can be seen in Figure 3.

6. EXPERIMENTAL RESULTS

Although it is of course extremely difficult to automatically evaluate something as subjective as dancer performance, according to our experiments, the adopted methodologies do produce meaningful results, in the following sense; (1) Considering the professional dancer (Bertand or Anne-Sophie-k) in two different captures for the same choreography, the calculated scores are high. For example, in figure 2, the professional male dancer Bertand is compared with himself with respect to choreography c3, considering two different captures, t1 and t2. Obtaining a high score in this case is essential for our system, since a professional dancer is able to perform almost identical dancing movements in two different captures; (2) All three scores produce more-or-less the same ranking of the amateur dancers; (3) The ranking does not deviate significantly from the ranking produced using the ground-truth ratings provided in the dataset; (4) The three instantaneous scores have similar behavior (e.g. they have minima or maxima at almost the same time instances, see figure 2); and (5) For not perfectly aligned dancers, the instantaneous scores are lower in time-intervals where synchronization of dance steps is lost.

Table 1: Teacher Ratings and Methodology Scores.

Choreography	BB	MT	CH	Score
thomas c2 t2	4	4	5	0.72
anne-sophie-k c2 t2	5	3	5	0.8
jacky c2 t1	5	3	5	0.71
habib c2 t1	5	5	4	0.70
habib c3 t2	5	3	4	0.33
jacky c3 t2	4	3	4	0.65
ming-li c2 t1	4	1	4	0.61
habib c3 t1	5	4	2	0.32
ming-li c3 t2	4	2	2	0.67
thomas c3 t1	3	2	2	0.59

Some experimental results are presented in table 1, where the overall score for the whole body calculated automatically is given in the last column ("Score") for choreographies c2 and c3. In these experiments, either Bertand or Anne-Sophie-k were used as the professional dancer (teacher), depending on the gender of the amateur dancer. In the same table, the ground-truth ratings assigned to the dancers by the teachers (i.e. a score between 1-5, the higher the better the performance) for "Choreography" (CH), "Musical Timing" (MT) and "Body Balance" (BB) are displayed. The rows of the table are sorted by CH, then by MT and finally by BB. It should be noted that in general there is strong correlation between the ground truth and the calculated scores, in the sense that the ground-truth-based ranking of the students is similar to the one obtained according to the calculated scores. Notice that the low scores of 0.33 and 0.32 for automatic evaluation are due to bad skeleton calibration and loss of the dancer during tracking.

7. CONCLUSIONS

Skeleton tracking from Kinect depth-maps can provide input to a set of appropriate signal processing methods that can support real-time evaluation of dancers in online interactive environments. In this paper, some relevant novel ideas were described and the implementation details of a working system were given. The experimental results were promising, demonstrating the appropriateness of the proposed approach for real-time interaction in an online dance class.

8. ACKNOWLEDGMENTS

This research was supported by the European Commission under contract FP7-247688 3DLife.

9. REFERENCES

[1] http://unity3d.com/.

[2] http://www.3dlife-noe.eu/3dlife/2011/04/3dlife-acm-grandchallenge-2011/.

[3] http://www.openni.org/.

[4] J. L. Barron, D. J. Fleet, and S. Beauchemin. Performance of optical flow techniques. *International Journal of Computer Vision*, 12:43–77, 1994.

[5] C. E. Moxey, S. J. Sangwine, and T. A. Ell. Hypercomplex correlation techniques for vector images. *IEEE Trans. on Signal Processing*, 51:1941–1953, 2003.

Dynamic Social Network for Narrative Video Analysis

Tsung-Hung Tsai, Wen-Huang Cheng, and Yung-Huan Hsieh
Research Center for Information Technology Innovation, Academia Sinica
Taipei 115, Taiwan, R.O.C.
{thtsai925,whcheng,yhhsieh}@citi.sinica.edu.tw

ABSTRACT

Narrative video analysis has attracted much research attention, for narrative scenes can provide meaningful representations of multimedia contents. To go beyond the limitations of content based appraoches, social network techniques was introduced in the literature to explore the high-level narrative structures by mining the relations between video characters. Taking into account the fact that such a social network is not static but changes over time as the video narrative evolves, in this work, we develop a novel social network model, namely dynamic social network, for capturing the spatiotemporal dynamics in the social network of video characters so as to enable the automatic segmentation of a video into a sequence of narrative scenes. The proposed approach is experimented with various genres of movies and the results demonstrate our effectiveness.

Categories and Subject Descriptors

H.3.1 [**Information Storage and Retrieval**]: Content Analysis and Indexing—*indexing methods*

General Terms

Algorithms, Experimentation, Human Factors

Keywords

social network, narrative analysis, video segmentation

1. INTRODUCTION

Narrative refers to the sequential structure of scenes (a.k.a story units) occurring in a cause-effect relationship [1, 2]. Two typical types of narrative videos are dramas and movies. The narrative structure is significant for the analysis of narrative videos because it is the foundation upon which all stories are built to develop the human's cinematic literacy [3]. The narrative video analysis has attracted much research attention, for narrative scenes can provide meaningful representations of multimedia contents [1, 2, 4, 5, 6].

Char.\Scene	#1	#2	#3	#4	#5	#6	#7
First Witch	√		√				
Second Witch	√		√				
Third Witch	√		√				
Duncan		√		√		√	
Malcolm		√		√			
Sergeant		√					
Lennox		√					
Ross		√	√				
Macbeth			√	√	√		√
Banqio			√	√		√	
Angus			√				
Lady Macbeth					√	√	√

Table 1: List of characters in the Act 1 (including seven scenes) of Shakespeare's tragedy "Macbeth". If a character sppears in a scene, the corresponding table entry is marked as "√".

In the literature, it has been showed that content based approaches, i.e. using audiovisual features alone, are not sufficient to compute the high-level semantics in a video [1, 2]. The semantic gap between low-level audiovisual features and high-level semantics is huge. In responding to this challenge, social network analysis has been introduced to explore video semantics by mining the relations between video characters [2, 7]. That is, given a narrative video, the social network (of video characters) is defined by a network graph with video characters as the nodes and the edge between two nodes represents the existence of an interaction between the two associated characters. Next, using network analysis tools in sociology, various social relations can be discovered and exploited to answer high-level semantic questions, such as "Which characters are the leading roles in this movie?" [2].

The task of narrative video analysis can take benefit from the social network based techniques. However, two major problems have not be addressed in the previous work [2, 7, 9]. First, the social network in a video is not static but changes over time as the narrative evolves. For example, Table 1 gives the list of characters appearing in the scenes of Act 1 in Shakespeare's tragedy "Macbeth" [10]. The appearance of characters between scenes are quite different. According to the drama theory [8], it is a narrative scheme for storytelling, namely "The Hero's Journey". That is, the main character will meet other people and various incidents will take place in different scenes and times. Obviously, such temporal dynamics of social networks can be important clue for story segmentation but this fact has long been ignored in

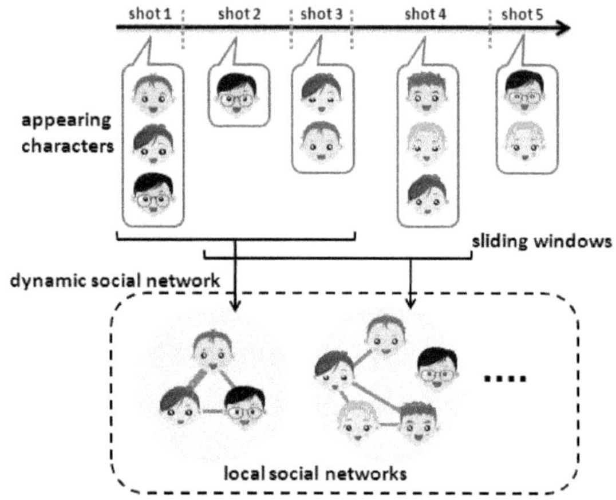

Figure 1: Constructing a dynamic social network

Figure 2: The plot synopsis of the movie "Catch Me If You Can" in the IMDB website, with the first five text paragraphs showed and marked.

the related research [2, 9]. Second, the interpretation of the narrative structures embedded in a video is subjective and can vary significantly among different people [1, 11]. For example, the number of narrative scenes and the locations of scene boundaries tend to be controversial. To reduce the ambiguity, text descriptions associated with videos are often used, e.g. film scripts [7]. However, text analysis is itself a challenging problem. Also, the assumption that a complete text description is always available is unpractical.

Observing the above difficulties, in this work, we develop a novel social network model, namely dynamic social network, for capturing the spatiotemporal dynamics in the social network of video characters so as to enable the automatic segmentation of a video into a sequence of narrative scenes. That is, inspired by the sliding-window filtering [12] in data mining research, instead of building a global social network for a single video, as shown in Figure 1 we employ overlapping sliding windows to construct a local social network for each temporal portion of the video to obtain a dynamic social network, i.e. a chain of local social networks. Next, based on our observations as shown in Table 1, the narrative scenes can be obtained from the proposed dynamic social network by grouping the local social networks into temporal clusters such that the local social networks in the same temporal cluster tend to be consistent. Without the need to analyze a full text script for determining the corresponding number of narrative scenes, we propose an easy alternative by simply counting the number of paragraph breaks in the plot synopsis from public knowledge websites, such as IMDB and Wikipedia. A real example is given in Figure 2.

The rest of this paper is organized as follows. Section 2 reviews the previous works. Our approach and the experiments are presented in Sections 3 and 4, respectively. The conclusions and future works are addressed in Section 5.

2. RELATED WORK

The analysis of semantic and narrative structures in videos has been an active research topic. Most of the prior work analyzed the videos using computable low-level features such as visual and audio clues. For example, Chen *et al.* [11] presented an action movie segmentation framework based on movie tempos. They adopted narrative methods such as film grammars to combine the visual and audio information for video analysis. Wang *et al.* [1] proposed an aesthetic model combining both visual and audio features and exploited the so-called expressive elements to detect video events.

In recent years, there are many studies adopting the social network analysis to summarize the multimedia contents and conduct advanced applications. Weng *et al.* [2] introduced a novel framework to analyze the community of characters in movies based on social network analysis. A specific social network called RoleNet is constructed according to the relationship of movie roles. Besides, Zhang *et al.* [7] constructed a name affinity network by video scripts and the face affinity networks by visual features so as to perform the face-name matching. In addition, Teixeira *et al.* [15] used three elements, i.e. story time, space, and character, to represent a user-selected video narrative.

3. DYNAMIC SOCIAL NETWORK BASED ANALYSIS

Given a narrative video v, the associated dynamic social network is defined as a chain of local social networks, i.e. $DNS_v = (SN_1, SN_2, \ldots, SN_N)$, where each SN_i is extracted locally from a temporal portion v_j of v, e.g. a set of successive video shots, as illustrated in Figure 1. Following the definition in [2], in a local social network, each graph node stands for a character and the edge between two nodes represent an interaction between the two characters, i.e. the two characters appear in the same shots of v_j and the corresponding edge weight is set to the frequence of their co-occurrence. The detailed extraction methods of our local social network are referred to [2].

After constructing a dynamic social network, we can observe that the narrative scene segmentation can be regarded as a change-point problem [13], i.e. grouping the local social networks into temporal clusters by locating a set of control points (scene boundaries) in the dynamic social network such that the local social networks in the same temporal cluster share a similar network structure. Therefore, in Section 3.1, we first define the similarity between social networks. Sections 3.2 and 3.3 describe our algorithms for the scene number determination and the scene segmentation.

3.1 Social Network Similarity

A (local) social network is to represent the relationship between characters. Hence, two social networks are considered to be similar if they contain almost the same characters and their relative interactions are going to be roughly the same. Therefore, we employ a social descriptor containing two different histograms, i.e. $\Omega = (\Psi, \Upsilon)$, to encode those information in a social network, where Ψ and Υ are co-occurrence and occurrence histograms of the characters, respectively. Let M be the total number of characters in a video. First, $\Psi = \sum_{i=1}^{M} \sum_{j=i+1}^{M} \Psi_{i,j}$ is a two dimensional histogram employed to record the interaction of characters, and each bin $\Psi_{i,j}$ stores the co-occurrence frequency of two different characters i and j. Second, based on our observations, some of the constructed social networks in a narrative video are purely consisted of isolated nodes without any connecting edge. It indicates that videos would have some sections of monologue. In such case, the co-occurrence histogram will contain all zero bins. One difficulty is that it can not distinguish whether the characters in continuous monologues are identical or not. In order to address this problem, a one dimensional occurrence histogram, $\Upsilon = \sum_{i=1}^{M} \Upsilon_i$, is also adopted, where each bin Υ_i stores a character's frequence of occurrence in the corresponding social network.

We then define the similarity S between two social networks, P and Q, by their social descriptors, Ω^P and Ω^Q, using the histogram intersection Θ as follows:

$$S^{P,Q} = \alpha\Theta(\Psi^P, \Psi^Q) + \beta\Theta(\Upsilon^P, \Upsilon^Q), \quad (1)$$

where $\alpha+\beta = 1$. It seems that both α and β can be set to 0.5 intuitively, but in some cases it will cause biased similarity values. For example, if two social networks both consist of only monologues with the same character, the resultant similarity will have 0.5 as the maximum value because the first term $\Theta(\Psi^P, \Psi^Q)$ becomes zero. In order to measure the social network similarity adequately, a dynamic weighting assignment scheme is adopted as follows:

$$\alpha = \frac{\min(\phi(\Psi^P), \phi(\Psi^Q))}{\min(\phi(\Psi^P), \phi(\Psi^Q)) + \min(\phi(\Upsilon^P), \phi(\Upsilon^Q))} \quad (2)$$

and $\beta = 1 - \alpha$. ϕ is a function returning the number of nonzero bins in the input histogram, e.g. $\phi(\Upsilon) = \sum_{i=1}^{M} I|_{\Upsilon_i > 0}$, where I is an indicator function. The proposed scheme is characterized by its prefering the character's interactions to the character's appearance. That is, in most cases, the number of nonzero bins would be much larger in a co-occurrence histogram Ψ than in the associated occurrence histogram Υ. Note that we have also experimented with other variants and the proposed scheme performs the best empirically.

3.2 Determining the Narrative Scene Number

When segmenting a video into scenes, it is often a very uneasy task to simultaneously estimate the number of scenes and the locations of scene boundaries due to its subjective nature [1, 2, 11]. In this work, we observe the problem can be alleviated by using web knowledge. Nowadays, people can easily find out a plot synopsis for almost all professionally produced narrative videos on public knowledge websites, such as IMDB and Wikipedia. For example, as showed in Figure 2, a movie synopsis is a brief summary of the movie plot. According to the writing theory, we know that a plot synopsis can be written in differnt styles but it always follows the basic writing rules, i.e. making a new paragraph when the themes change such that a paragraph is a self-contained unit. Therefore, it provides a feasible and reasonable way to set the narrative scene number to the same amount of paragraphs. The main advantage of the proposed scheme is its simplicity, i.e. the scene number can be quickly obtained by counting the number of paragraph breaks in a plot synopsis.

Input: A video v of T shots $SH = (SH_1, \ldots, SH_T)$ with M appearing characters $R = (R_1, \ldots, R_M)$; number of narrative scenes $K+1$; canonical model of homogeneity H

Output: Locations of K scene boundaries in v

1. Construct the dynamic social network of R in v from T, i.e. $DSN_v = (SN_1, \ldots, SN_N)$.
2. Transform DSN_v into the form of a similarity matrix $SM = [SM_{ij}]_{M\times M}$ with elements SM_{ij} assigned the similarity value between SN_i and SN_j.

for $j = 1; j \leq K;$ **do**

3. Traverse the diagonal of SM and, for each candidate dividing point, calculate the relative entropies, r_u and r_d, of the two sub-matrices, U and D, in the both sides using H, respectively.
4. Calculate the harmonic mean h for every pair of r_u and r_d:

$$h = \frac{2e^{-(r_u+r_d)}}{e^{-r_u} + e^{-r_d}} \quad (3)$$

5. Find the candidate dividing point with maximum h and take it as a scene boundary. Then replace SM with U if $r_u > r_d$, and vise versa.

end

Algorithm 1: Narrative Scene Segmentation

3.3 Segmentation Using Similarity Matrix

As mentioned above, our segmentation task can be formulated as a change-point problem with the known amount of change points, say K, the number of scene boundaries. Hence, a similarity matrix based approach is adopted [14]. First, we transform the dynamic social network DNS_v into a similarity matrix $SM = [SM_{ij}]_{M\times M}$ with elements $SM_{ij} = S^{SN_i,SN_j}$, i.e. the similarity between SN_i and SN_j. Next, along the diagonal of SM, our goal is to divide SM into $K+1$ square sub-matrices (blocks) such that the homogeneity of similarity values in each sub-matrix is maximized (i.e. the social networks tend to have a common graph structure). Then the resultant $K+1$ sub-matrices give the corresponding $K+1$ narrative scenes.

Note that we have an offline training stage beforehand to build a canonical model H for evaluating the homogeneity of a matrix. We collected a set of scenes from the ground truth (cf. Section 4), and computed a probability distribution of the similarity values in each of their corresponding similarity matrices. The H can then be regarded as an "average" of these training distributions. Therefore, we take a greedy method to search for the K dividing points along the diagonal of SM. In the first iteration, for example, we compute the relative entropy (Kullback Leibler divergence) to H for the both sides of a given candidate dividing point, respectively. Since a good dividing point should balance the homogeneity in the both sides, the one with the maximum harmonic mean of its two-side entropy values will be chosen. In the following iterations, the original similarity matrix will be replaced by the one with higher relative entropy from its two sub-matrices and the same computations will repeat until K dividing points are selected, c.f. Algorithm 1.

4. EXPERIMENTS

We conduct the experiments using eight Hollywood movies: "Casino Royale", "Catch Me If You Can", "Gladiator", "The Lake House", "The Devil Wears Prada", "Stranger Than Fictions", "Broken Flowers", and "You've Got Mail". For each video, we extracted two different versions of its plot synopsis from the IMDB and Wikipedia, respectively. We counted the paragraph number in the both versions so that each movie has two different ground truth values for the number of narrative scenes. Next, each video was partitioned into shots. According to each of the IMDB and Wikipedia plot synopsises, we then manually picked up a set of shot boundaries (the same number with the corresponding ground truth value) as the ground truth boundaries of narrative scenes.

We compared the resultant scene boundaries detected by our approach with two other previous works, i.e. a social network based RoleNet [2] and a content based Tempo [11]. Table 2 gives the results. Note that the "Broken Flowers" does not have a synopsis in IMDB and the parenthesized numbers after each movie title indicate the corresponding ground truth scene number. In addition, the table entries are in the form of a four-tuple of integers, i.e. (a, b, c, d). That is because even if the number of narrative scenes is given it is still hard to label the ground truth locations of scene boundaries exactly. In the experiments, we then claim if a detected boundary is a hit of the ground truth with four different tolerance ranges from 0 to 3. That is, a is the number of detected boundaries that exactly hit the ground truth, b is the detections that hit the ground truth within a 1-shot tolerance, and so forth. Hence, $a \leq b \leq c \leq d$. In Table 2(a) and (b), the best results of the three comparing approaches in different tolerance ranges are boldfaced, respectively.

We can observe our approach and RoleNet both outperform Tempo in the most cases. When the videos are action movies, e.g. "Casino Royale", Tempo can have better results. It is not a surprise because the narrative of an action movie is more correlated to the audiovisual tempo rather than the evolution of the character's social networks. In addition, when comparing our results with RoleNet, our approach is still the outperformer in general, especially in the case when movies have a single main character, such as "Gladiator". A reason is that RoleNet performs the scene segmentation simply according to the social network built by the whole movie but our approach consider the spatiotemporal dynamics of the character's social network. Another reason is the exploited measure of similarity between social networks such that RoleNet prefers to select the scene boundary where the main characters are switched. In contrast, our approach tend to claim a detection when the main structure of the character's social network is changing significantly.

(a) Movie (IMDB)	**Our Results**	**RoleNet[2]**	**Tempo[11]**
Casino Royale (8)	1;2;4;5	**4**;**5**;6;6	3;**5**;**7**;**7**
Catch Me If You Can (11)	2;**6**;**8**;**8**	**3**;5;5;5	1;**6**;7;7
Gladiator (8)	**2**;**2**;**2**;**2**	0;1;1;1	0;1;1;1
The Lake House (8)	**2**;2;2;3	1;1;3;5	**2**;**3**;**4**;**4**
The Devel Wears Prada (8)	2;**3**;**5**;**5**	**3**;**3**;4;4	2;2;3;4
Stranger Than Fictions (5)	**0**;1;**2**;2	**0**;**2**;**2**;**3**	**0**;**2**;**2**;**3**
Broken Flowers (N/A)	-	-	-
You've Got Mail (9)	2;5;**7**;**7**	2;4;**7**;**7**	**4**;**6**;**7**;**7**
(b) Movie (Wikipedia)	**Our Results**	**RoleNet[2]**	**Tempo[11]**
Casino Royale (5)	0;**2**;**3**;**3**	**1**;**2**;2;2	0;**2**;2;**3**
Catch Me If You Can (4)	**0**;**1**;**2**;**2**	**0**;0;0;0	**0**;**1**;1;1
Gladiator (7)	**4**;**4**;**4**;**5**	1;3;3;**5**	1;3;**4**;4
The Lake House (4)	**0**;**1**;1;1	**0**;**1**;**2**;**2**	**0**;0;0;1
The Devel Wears Prada (9)	**5**;**6**;**7**;**7**	1;4;4;5	4;4;6;6
Stranger Than Fictions (5)	**0**;1;**2**;2	**0**;**2**;**2**;**3**	**0**;**2**;**2**;**3**
Broken Flowers (5)	**1**;**3**;3;3	0;1;**4**;**4**	**1**;2;2;3
You've Got Mail (5)	**1**;**2**;**2**;**3**	**1**;**2**;**2**;**3**	0;0;**2**;2

Table 2: Segmentation Results

5. CONCLUSIONS

This paper presents a useful approach for narrative scene segmentation. We construct a dynamic social network according to the interaction and presence of characters in the movie and perform the segmentation by analyzing the social network similarity. The experiments demonstrate our approach can perform the scene segmentation effectively in different genres of movies. However, there is room for improvement. For example, we only used a synopsis to determine the scene number but it has richer information for analysis such as characters' name in each paragraph. In the future, we will extend our approach from movies to others, e.g. home and web videos. Moreover, we will try to exploit the social information on the web for advanced analysis, e.g. viewer reviews of movies can be taken into consideration for story segmentation and character identification.

6. REFERENCES

[1] C.-W. Wang *et al.* Film narrative exploration through the analysis of aesthetic elements. *MMM*, 2007.

[2] C.-Y. Weng *et al.* Rolenet: Movie analysis from the perspective of social networks. *IEEE TMM*, 2009.

[3] N. Abrams, I. Bell, and J. Udris *Studying Film.* Oxford University Press, 2001.

[4] B.-W. Chen *et al.* A novel video summarization based on mining the story-structure and semantic relations among concept entities. *IEEE TMM*, 2009.

[5] G. Irie *et al.* Automatic trailer generation. *ACM Multimedia Conf.*, 2010.

[6] X. Zhu and X. Wu. Sequential association mining for video summarization. *IEEE ICME*, 2003.

[7] Y.-F. Zhang *et al.* Character identification in feature-length films using global face-name matching. *IEEE TMM*, 2009.

[8] C. Vogler. *The Writers Journey: Mythic Structure for Writers.* Michael Wiese Productions, 1998.

[9] M. Xu *et al.* Cast2face: Character identification in movie with actor-character correspondence. *ACM Multimedia Conf.*, 2010.

[10] `http://www.shakespeare-navigators.com/macbeth/SceneTextIndex.html`

[11] H.-W. Chen, J.-H. Kuo, W.-T. Chu, and J.-L. Wu. Action movies segmentation and summarization based on tempo analysis. *ACM MIR*, 2004.

[12] C.-H. Lee *et al.* Sliding-window filtering: An efficient algorithm for incremental mining *ACM CIKM*, 2001.

[13] Y. Zhai and M. Shah. Automatic segmentation of home videos. *IEEE ICME*, 2005.

[14] M. Cooper *et al.* Temporal even clustering for digital photo collections. *ACM TOMCCA*, 2005.

[15] C. Teixeira *et al.* Representing and playing user selected video narrative domains. *ACM SRMC*, 2008.

Enhanced Visualisation of Dance Performance from Automatically Synchronised Multimodal Recordings

Marc Gowing[1]
Marc.gowing@gmail.com
Philip Kell[1]
kellyp@eeng.dcu.ie
Noel E. O'Connor[1]
Noel.OConnor@dcu.ie

Cyril Concolato[2]
cyril.concolato@telecom-paristech.fr
Slim Essid[2]
slim.essid@telecom-paristech.fr
Jean Lefeuvre[2]
jean.lefeuvre@telecom-paristech.fr
Robin Tournemenne[21]
robin.tournemenne@wanadoo.fr

Ebroul Izquierdo[3]
ebroul.izquierdo@elec.qmul.ac.uk
Vlado Kitanovski[3]
vlado.kitanovski@elec.qmul.ac.uk
Xinyu Lin[3]
xinyu.lin@eecs.qmul.ac.uk
Qianni Zhang[3]
qianni.zhang@elec.qmul.ac.uk

[1] CLARITY: Centre for Sensor Web Technologies
Dublin City University, Ireland

[2] Institut Telecom/Telecom ParisTech
CNRS/LTCI
75013 Paris

[3] Multimedia and Vision Group
School of Electronic Engineering and Computer Science
Queen Mary, University of London
London, E1 4NS

ABSTRACT
The Huawei/3DLife Grand Challenge Dataset provides multimodal recordings of Salsa dancing, consisting of audiovisual streams along with depth maps and inertial measurements. In this paper, we propose a system for augmented reality-based evaluations of Salsa dancer performances. An essential step for such a system is the automatic temporal synchronisation of the multiple modalities captured from different sensors, for which we propose efficient solutions. Furthermore, we contribute modules for the automatic analysis of dance performances and present an original software application, specifically designed for the evaluation scenario considered, which enables an enhanced dance visualisation experience, through the augmentation of the original media with the results of our automatic analyses.

Categories and Subject Descriptors
I.2.10 [**Vision and Scene Understanding**]: Video analysis.

General Terms
Algorithms

Keywords
Audio, video, synchronisation, multimodal processing.

1. INTRODUCTION
In this work, we address the Huawei/3DLife Grand challenge [1], which consists of multimodal recordings of Salsa dancers, including multi view videos from UniBrain cameras, Microsoft Kinect streams, data from Wireless Inertial Measurement Units (WIMU), and synchronised 16-channel audio capture of dancers' step sounds, voice and music. We focus on developing a system for the subjective evaluation of Salsa dancers. As dancers are captured with various recording equipment, it is essential to temporally synchronise all of the multimodal data when displaying/playing it to the evaluators. It is also essential to synchronise data between different dancers to allow an evaluator to compare the performances of two dancers, typically the tutor's performance, which is considered as a reference, and the student's performance. In this work, our primary concern is to propose efficient solutions to tackle these synchronisation problems. Furthermore, we contribute an original software application, specifically designed for this evaluation scenario, which enables an enhanced dance visualisation experience through the augmentation of the original media with the results of automatic analyses of the dance performances. In particular, we present a novel technique to achieve dancer step segmentation jointly using audio signals captured by the onfloor piezoelectric sensors and signals from the WIMU devices.

The outline of the paper is the following: The next section describes the methods used to address the synchronisation issues, before proceeding to the description of the automatic analysis components in Section 3. We present the software application design in Section 4, followed by conclusions in Section 5.

2. MULTIMODAL SYNCHRONISATION
Figure 1 gives an overview of our approach to synchronisation between the heterogeneous streams of data recorded.

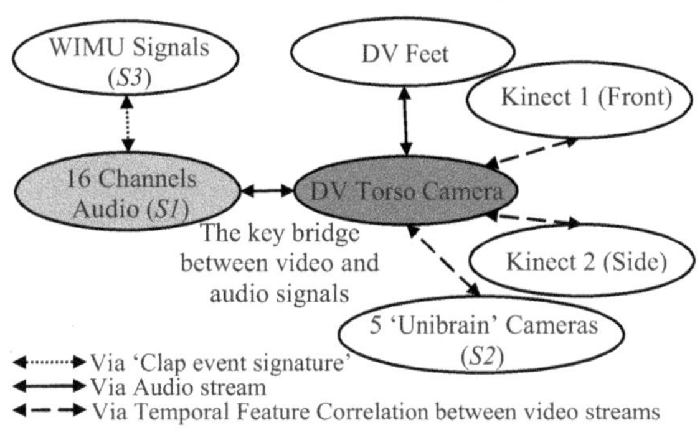

Figure 1 Overview of synchronisation strategy

The details of the different synchronisation components are given hereafter. To understand the rationale behind this synchronisation scheme it is important to keep in mind that some subsets of data streams are already synchronised via hardware [1], these include:

- Subset *S1* consisting of data from 16 audio channels
- Subset *S2* composed of video streams of 5 UniBrain cameras;
- Subset *S3* that is the different WIMU signals.

Therefore, it is sufficient to synchronise instances of each subset with the other data streams to achieve overall synchronisation.

2.1 Audio-based synchronisation

As illustrated in Figure 1, the audio modality is used as a bridge to synchronise other types of modalities. The procedure is as follows:

- Synchronise the videos taken by the feet and torso cameras using audio-to-audio synchronisation between the audio streams of these videos (as described in Section 2.1.1);
- Synchronise one of the audio channels of S1 with either audio streams of the feet or torso cameras, using the same audio-to-audio synchronisation method;
- Synchronise one of the audio channels of S1 with the WIMU signals in S3 as described in Section 2.2.

To complete overall synchronisation, one is left only with the problem of synchronising the videos of feet/torso cameras with the ones captured by the Kinects and UniBrain cameras, which is addressed in Section 2.3.

2.1.1 Audio-to-audio synchronisation method

Audio-to-audio synchronisation is achieved by first estimating the signals energy envelopes, then using a simple cross-correlation measure between these envelopes. The delay between the two signals is deduced as the time-lag that needs to be applied to one data stream in order to obtain maximum cross-correlation.

The audio envelopes are estimated by computing the energy values in 15-ms local audio frames with a 1-ms hop size. The sampling frequency of the envelopes is thus 1000 Hz, hence allowing us to speed-up the process compared to a situation where cross-correlation measures would be taken directly from the original audio signals whose sampling frequencies can be as high as 48 kHz. The other advantage of this approach is that it can cope with the fact that some audio streams are sampled at differing frequencies, for example the audio stream of the foot camera is at 32 kHz while signals from *S1* are sampled at 48 kHz.

Furthermore, it has been found unnecessary to consider the whole signal durations to achieve this synchronisation, rather only the first few seconds of each recording is taken, covering the initial clap event and the start of the music (on recordings with music).

2.1.2 Bridge between different dancer recordings

In the challenge scenario, all dancers are expected to execute the same choreographies and synchronise their movements to the same background music. Therefore synchronising the performances of two dancers is quite straightforward as it solely entails synchronising the recorded music signals relating to each dancer, that is channel 5/6 recordings of a dancer A with channels 5/6 recordings of dancer B. This is done using the previously described procedure.

2.2 Synchronisation of WIMUs

Synchronisation between audio and WIMUs is achieved by maximising the cross-correlation between a specific WIMU and audio features around the clap event. These features are designed to characterise the clap event signature.

The audio feature employed here is the output of an onset detection component [4] applied to the audio signal of channel 20, *i.e.* one of the overhead Shoeps microphones that clearly captures the sound of hands and feet claps.

The WIMU synchronisation feature exploits the accelerometer signal of the both wrist sensors (devices 1 and 2). A clap will appear as a large spike in the accelerometer signal of both wrist WIMU accelerometers simultaneously. To detect this event, all three axes are combined for each sensor. The average, maximum amplitude and its corresponding timestamp are calculated using 150-ms sliding window with 10-ms hops. The window with the largest variance for both WIMUs is identified as the clap signature.

As the sampling frequency of the audio feature is 360 Hz (due to the signal analysis parameters of the onset detection module) and the WIMU feature is 100 Hz, the WIMU frequency is upsampled to that of the audio stream before computing the cross-correlation.

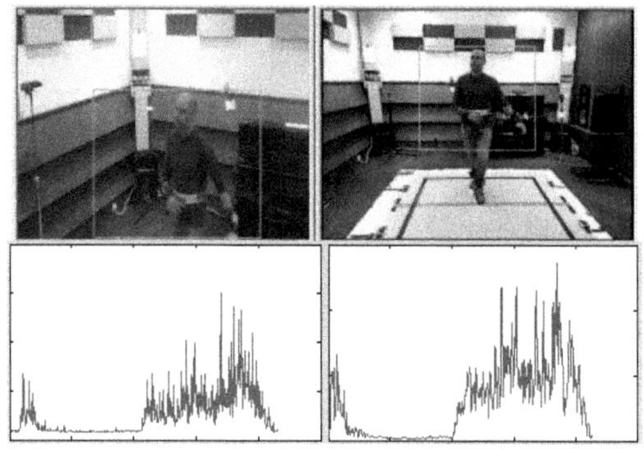

Figure 2: Top row: example for upped body detection; Bottom row: temporal features extracted from the two videos.

2.3 Multi-view video synchronisation

In this section, we describe the approach to uncover the time shift between two videos taken from unsynchronised cameras. The videos can be of different quality and frame rate. Temporal features are extracted for every video frame. Correlation-matching between features from two different videos is then used to obtain the offset between them. We also employed a method to detect the dancer's upper body to locate the area for feature extraction and improve the synchronisation accuracy.

2.3.1 Synchronisation based on co-occurrence appearances

The temporal features used for video temporal alignment are based on appearance changes [2]. This approach is suitable when cameras are static, and it does not require a high level of scene understanding. The total amount of appearance change between two successive frames is calculated by:

$$f_k[n] = \sum_{\Omega} (I_{n+1} - I_n)^2$$

where I_n is the luminance component of the nth frame, and the sum of squared differences is computed over the image region Ω. In order to achieve sub-frame accuracy, the vector f_k is interpolated on a 1-ms time grid. The time shift between two videos is obtained as the value that maximises the normalised correlation between the temporal features of each video. Region Ω should be chosen so that it contains only the moving objects (or part of moving objects) visible in both videos. As such, for the 3DLife dataset we use an upper-body detection method introduced in the next section to locate the dancer's upper-body movements, as some videos in the used dataset do not capture the whole body. Figure 2 shows temporal features for the DV torso camera and the Kinect camera respectively.

2.3.2 *Upper-body detection*

In order to improve the synchronisation accuracy, unexpected object movement in the video sequence should be excluded from the temporal features calculation. In the original work [2], this is achieved by splitting video frames into sub-regions of regular size and iteratively excluding sub-regions that have negative impact on the correlation between two video sequences. As this trial and error approach is inefficient in terms of computational cost, we employ a state of art upper-body detection algorithm [3] to facilitate adaptive selection of regions for temporal features calculation as opposed to searching sub-regions with negative impact iteratively. In this work, the algorithm uses trained part-based models combined with an optional face detector to improve the detection performance. Figure 2 (top row) shows the detection results applied to the videos captured using the Microsoft Kinect and the DV camcorder. By applying temporal features and correlation calculations only within detected region, the synchronisation accuracy is improved.

2.3.3 *Results*

We evaluated the described approach using videos from the dataset [1]. There are total 103 video sets included (each video set includes: 5 UniBrain videos, torsor video and feet video recorded by DV camcorders, and two videos recorded by Kinects). Table 1 shows the accuracy of synchronisation based on one video set performed by teacher dancer. UniBrain camera 1 was used as reference video. It can be seen that the error is mostly around one or two frames (corresponding to 30-80 ms in time).

Table 1: Errors were measured as the differences in number of frames between the ground-truth time shifts and the time shifts calculated using the proposed method. The first column is the videos being synchronised; columns 2-6 are the choreographies performed by teacher dancer

Camera:	CH 1	CH 2	CH 3	CH 4	CH 5
Torso	0	0	0	-1	0
Feet	0	0	0	0	0
Kinect	-1	1	-1	1	0

3. DANCE PERFORMANCE ANALYSIS FOR AUDIOVISUAL AUGMENTATION OF THE CAPTURED MEDIA

As described in the introduction, in this work we strive to provide an augmented-reality presentation of the captured dancer performances aimed to both facilitate the subjective evaluation of a dance recital and to enhance the viewing experience for a user. To this end, two types of analysis are proposed that are briefly described hereafter, namely automatic dance step detection and 3D dancer skeleton and joint extraction. The former is an audio-rendered augmentation, taking the form of beeps sounding every time a new dance step is detected, along with textual subtitles indicating the step classification. The latter is visually rendered additional video, taking the form of a skeleton overlaid onto a depth map of the scene.

3.1 Automatic dance steps detection

Step detection exploits both the audio and WIMU modalities that are first processed independently one from another before a heuristic fusion approach is used to reach a decision regarding step segmentation.

3.1.1 *Audio processing*

Audio-based step segmentation exploits the audio signals recorded by the on-floor piezoelectric sensors (channels 1, 2, 17 and 18). Step impacts on the dance floor are expected to give rise to energy bursts in the corresponding waveforms, which can be suitably characterised using onset detection [4] functions. Concatenating the coefficients of all onset detection functions for every time instant hence forms audio feature vectors, used for step detection. Next, a single-class Support Vector Machine (SVM) classifier [5] is applied to these feature vectors with the aim of achieving a fusion of the information conveyed by the different audio channels. The use of a single-class SVMs is motivated by the fact that they are able to detect extreme points of the feature vector sequence that are to be mapped with step impacts. These extreme points are found by looking at the sign of the SVM prediction values that are then negative.

This step detection strategy turns out to be very efficient as depicted in Figure 3 where it can be seen that the step impacts thus detected (represented by vertical dashed blue lines) accurately match the ground-truth (obtained by manual annotation of the impacts and represented with black vertical lines).

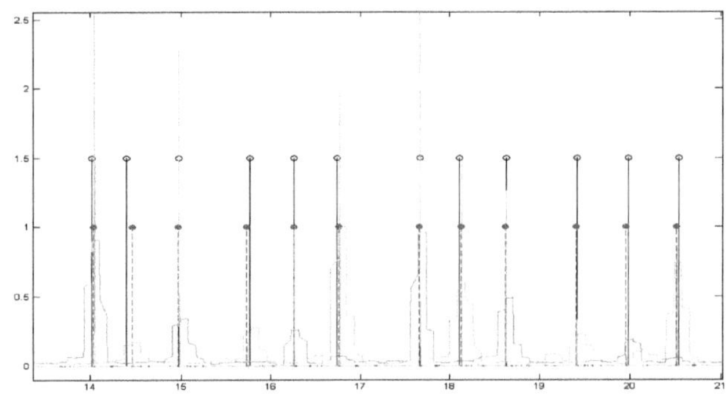

Figure 3: Step detection results on recording Bertrand_c1_t1. Negative SVM decision values across time (in green) along with detected steps (dashed blue), WIMU-based detection functions (in red and orange respectively for the left and right feet), and ground-truth annotations in black.

3.1.2 *WIMU processing*

WIMU based step detection is performed using the accelerometer signals of the ankle sensors (devices 5 and 6). As with the clap event, a large energy burst will occur on all three axes when the foot strikes the floor. However, the force of the impact can vary greatly, and the natural motion of the dancer's feet introduces noisy accelerations in the step detection process. In order to filter the signal, all three axes are combined and high passed to remove any acceleration values that are not the result of vibration. The signal is then normalized and integrated as shown in Figure 4, giving the probabilities of step impacts, as described in [6].

3.1.3 *Decision fusion and results*

Figure 3 illustrates the way in which audio-based and WIMU-based detectors play complementary roles in spotting the dancer's steps. The audio output allows us to locate the steps with a high temporal accuracy (thanks to a higher sampling frequency), while the WIMU output serves as a validation for the step occurrences thus detected (with the potential of eliminating possible false detections, as has been observed in other examples) and additionally permits the classification of steps as either *right* or *left* foot steps.

3.2 Dancer's skeleton and joints extraction

The OpenNI framework [7] includes standard tools for extracting the user's joint positions from the Kinect depth map and generating a skeleton overlay. Typically, a user will perform a calibration pose as shown in Figure 5, which allows OpenNI to detect joints positions. However, as none of the dancers in the dataset performed a calibration pose, we captured a user of similar height and build performing a calibration pose and applied it to the recordings. The output is shown in Figure 5 below.

4. DANCER EVALUATION APPLICATION

In this section we present the requirements for the design of a multimedia application designed to enable users to perform a subjective evaluation of dancer performance. Given the time-varying nature of the data, the application has to have a strong focus on synchronization. It has to be able to display various types of media data (audio, video, video with depth information, 2D graphics, 3D graphics, and text) and perhaps several media elements of each type, while keeping synchronization. In terms of layout, the ability to display mixed 2D/3D data, possibly in an augmented reality mode is also deemed important. And finally, in order to propose an interactive application to the evaluators, it has to incorporate some interactive capabilities. Finally we want to design the interaction logic in a flexible manner.

Based on these requirements, we decided to implement the application using declarative languages (with some scripting extensions using JavaScript) and to use the GPAC player [8] to render the application due to its capability to mix declarative languages and media elements of different types, and its streaming and synchronization features, which allows the possibility of streaming in the future. The declarative languages used are MPEG-4 BIFS for the 3D layout and 3D graphics objects, and SVG for the 2D layout and 2D graphics. The interactivity and application logic have been implemented using JavaScript.

Figure 6 shows a snapshot of the application GUI. The interface allows one to evaluate and compare the performances of two dancers, through a choice of viewpoints (displayed in the central columns of the interface). The user can play each dancer separately, or play dancers synchronously (by clicking the chain icon between the two players' controls). Central viewpoints can be dynamically changed during runtime, which is also true for the audio stream to be played. Some viewpoints and audio streams are augmented with overlays and effects, for instance dancer skeleton and joints displays or beeps signalling dance steps (detected automatically as previously explained).

5. CONCLUSIONS

In this work, we have presented a set of methods for the synchronisation of the multimodal recordings captured for the Huawei/3DLife Grand Challenge. The accurately synchronised data was further analysed and augmented for presentation in an original software application for an enhanced dance visualisation experience. The overall system serves as a comprehensive platform for evaluating Salsa dancers' performances.

6. ACKNOWLEDGEMENTS

This research was supported by the European Commission under contract "FP7-247688 3DLife". Affiliations and authors are listed in alphabetical order.

7. REFERENCES

[1] http://perso.telecom-paristech.fr/~essid/3dlife-gc-11/

[2] Ushizaki M., Okatani T. and Deguchi K., Video Synchronization Based on Co-Occurrence of Appearance Changes in Video Sequence, Proceedings of International Conference on Pattern Recognition, 2006

[3] Eichner M. Marin-Jimenez, A. Zisserman, V.Ferrari, Articulated Human Pose Estimation and Search in (Almost) Unconstrained Still Images, ETH Zurich, Technical Report No.272, 2010.

[4] M. Alonso, G. Richard, and B. David. Extracting note onsets from audio recordings. Proc. of IEEE-ICME, 2005.

[5] Shölkopf, B. and Smola, A. J. Learning with kernels, The MIT Press, Cambridge, MA, 2002.

[6] H. Ying, C. Silex, A. Schnitzer, S. Leonhardt, and M. Schiek, Automatic Step Detection in the Accelerometer Signal, International Workshop Body Sensor Networks, 2007.

[7] http://www.openni.org/

[8] Jean Le Feuvre, Cyril Concolato, and Jean-Claude Moissinac., GPAC: open source multimedia framework. In Proceedings of the 15th international conference on Multimedia '07. ACM, New York, USA, 2007

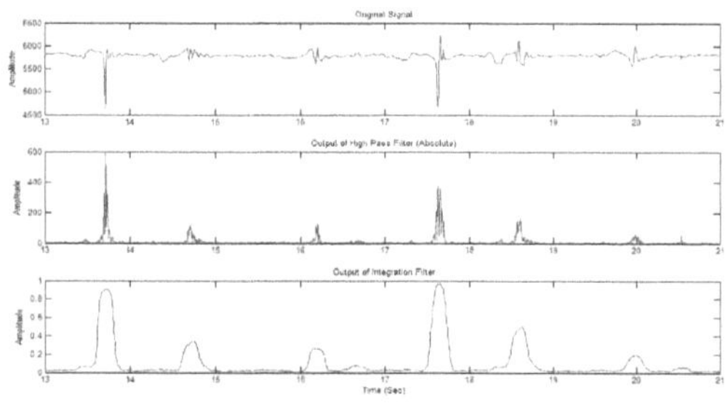

Figure 4: WIMU step detection process

Figure 5: Our Kinect calibration pose (left), applied to the pre-recorded depth map for Anne-c1-t1 (centre), giving a skeletal overlay (right).

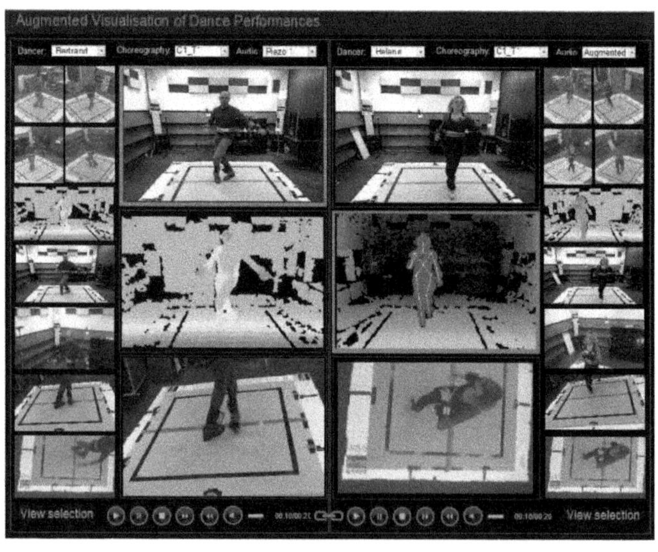

Figure 6: Snapshot of the application GUI

News Browsing System: Multimodal Analysis

Bruno do Nascimento Teixeira
bruno.teixeira@dcc.ufmg.br

Júlia Epischina Engrácia de Oliveira
julia@dcc.ufmg.br

Fillipe Dias Moreira de Souza
fdms@dcc.ufmg.br

Tiago Oliveira Cunha
tocunha@dcc.ufmg.br

Igor Calil Loures de Oliveira
igorcalil@gmail.com

Chrisitane Okamoto
chrisitane@dcc.ufmg.br

Lucas Figueiredo Gonçalves
lucas.figueiredo@hotmail.com

Vinícius de Oliveira Silva
vos3@ufmg.br

Arnaldo de Albuquerque Araújo
arnaldo@dcc.ufmg.br

Department of Computer Science
Federal University of Minas Gerais
Belo Horizonte, Brazil

ABSTRACT

This paper reports a system developed for video browsing based on multimodal analysis. Our multimodal approach performs audio transcription for shot categorization (sports, weather, politics and economy) combining audio and visual information for theme categorization. Its main features include static and dynamic summaries, segmentation using face detection, classification into Indoor and Outdoor scenes based on Support Vector Machine (SVM) and audio transcription for theme keyword search. Keywords are selected to represent the subjects, followed by a simple text search. We conduct a set of experiments for evaluating the effectiveness of the shot subject categorization using audio transcription information.

Categories and Subject Descriptors

H.3.1 [**Information Storage and Retrieval**]: Content Analysis and Indexing; H.5.1 [**Information Interfaces and Presentation**]: Multimedia Information Systems

General Terms

Algorithms, Experimentation.

Keywords

Multimodal analysis, multimedia user interfaces and interaction, static and dynamic summarizations, face detection, video segmentation, video browsing.

1. INTRODUCTION

A video sequence normally contains a large number of frames so as to ensure that humans do not perceive any discontinuity in a video stream. Typically, a frame rate of at least 25fps is required. However, the resulting volume of video data is a barrier to many practical applications and, therefore, there is a strong demand for a mechanism that allow the user to gain insight into video data without watching the entire video. This mechanism is called video summarization.

Video summarization is the process of extracting a summary of the content of a video, which aims to quickly provide concise information about the video content while preserving the original message. This concept can serve as a potential assistant to the automatic video retrieval approach, especially when content-based indexing and retrieval of video sequences have limited achievement. Video summaries are presented as a solution to enable early identification of video content in order to avoid the time spent in the task of manual analysis. The summary allows the user to judge whether the video is really relevant for the intended purpose, assisting him in making decisions [10].

Some works discuss the problem of turning video operation easier for the final user. For instance, Forlines [3] described a video presentation system prototype that takes into account the video content. The proposed prototype renders the frames of a video in various regions of the display, according to its content structure.

There are two types of video summaries: static and dynamic. The first one consists of a set of images that are considered most representative of the video, while the second one is comprised of a set of video segments arranged in temporal order. In general, the latter is more attractive once it incorporates elements of movement and audio.

The difficulty of some users to navigate in Web application interfaces is pointed by Komlodi et al. [5], specifically in history search systems. This raises the need for finding solutions that can help these users in the navigation, and their proposal was to identify design guidelines for these systems. Effective indexing requires a multimodal approach

[8] in which different modalities are used in collaborative fashion to the representation of videos. The problem of efficient retrieval and indexing in video databases is approached by Morand et al. [7]. Regarding video search, Su *et al.* [9] have presented a method for content-based video search that uses pattern-based indexing and combining techniques.

2. INTERFACE

System interface consists of three main areas: browsing, display, and editing which can enable users to search for a specific subject inside a video and organize its results effectively into a timeline. Browsing area corresponds to user first focal point and presents the results of the algorithms through images. These images can be clicked for player exhibition and also dragged to the editing area. The display area contains a player with simple reproduction buttons which can be resized without changing the video aspect ratio. Finally, the editing area presents a timeline that can be filled by dragging the available segments in the browsing area. When the play button is clicked, the segments are played sequentially and without gaps. Also, the segments can be easily rearranged on the timeline, forming a new edition for the video.

Besides these areas, there is a top menu on which the user can register himself, choose a new video to watch or send a new video to be processed.

The interface is a layer completely isolated from the video processing module. Both interact only through a database. The database used is MySQL[1] and data are manipulated by PHP, which is a language particularly suited for Web development, compound the server side of the application. The client-side is Flash based.

Web-based system was implemented, since this is the most effective way to allow real users to interact with the system. The internal architecture is based on the most common models of communication between the modules of a Web application.

At first, a video submitted by a user is processed using the algorithms available on the system. Next, users can navigate through this particular video or another one from the system database using the navigation mechanism. Figure 2 shows web interface for news video browsing which contains flash player, timeline (allows users to drag shots of interest) and frames of scenes.

3. METHODOLOGY

The specific methodologies for each proposed algorithm are presented together with the development of the interface.

3.1 Video Summarization

In this work we have used a method designed to be simple and effective in generating static abstracts [2]. Color histograms and line profiles are used to represent the video images, which accounts for the feature extraction phase.

After the extraction of the visual features, the images are grouped by the k-means algorithm [6]. First, each cluster is represented by its most representative frame, then, a set of key frames is obtained. In some cases, different key frames with very similar visual content can be selected, so, in order to create the static video summary, the key frames are filtered. With this filtering operation, the number of key frames is reduced while maintaining the quality of results. After that, the key frames are arranged in temporal order to facilitate the comprehension of the result.

Aiming to produce dynamic summaries, one additional step was incorporated to the static summary approach. At the end of the process of static summary generation, the shot boundary detection of the video is performed. The shots that have images presented in the static summary are selected to incorporate the dynamic summary and then presented as a short video.

3.2 Face Detection

The face detection is performed by the method of Viola-Jones [13], which is implemented in the OpenCV[2] library. This method, for detecting objects in images, is based on four concepts: simple rectangular features called Haar features, a complete picture for the early detection of features, the machine learning method Adaboost [4], and a cascade classifier to combine the characteristics efficiently.

3.3 Classification into Indoor/Outdoor Scenes

One feature of the application is the automated recognition of indoor and outdoor scenes in news videos. The goal of this task is to facilitate the search for the content of interest in voluminous video databases. Separating indoor scenes from outdoor scenes can be seen as a preprocessing step of a hierarchy-based search system. To illustrate, we can assume that it is easier to find clips of highlights of the Soccer World Cup matches if we just consider the search in the set of outdoor scenes than when using the whole dataset. That is, it suffices to work with only with a subset of the available data.

As outdoor scenes are separated, a set of static images representing the outdoor scenes of the news video is displayed in an independent tab of the system. This tab is intended to provide users with an alternative means to easily look for the content of interest. The user would be able to visually verify if any theme of interest is present in that particular news video.

3.3.1 Descriptor

In our particular case, we designate as indoor scenes those where the anchor reads the news inside the studio, whereas the outdoor scenes are those where interviews and presentations are performed in an outer setting. Naturally, color seems to be a distinguishable feature to differ inner from outer environments, even though shape description still plays its role. For this reason, we have chosen to use a color-shape based representation to characterize the video scenes. Sande et al. [11] have proposed many color-shape based descriptors, which have performed nicely to object and scene categorization, being one of them the HueSIFT. HueSIFT is a combination of the state-of-the-art local feature detector SIFT (to static images) with hue histograms. In this case, the neighborhood of each local feature is described in terms of hue (from the HSI color space) and its histogram is concatenated to histograms of oriented gradients (shape description).

3.3.2 Bag-of-Visual-Words Representation

Given a video clip, a higher level representation for its set of local features can be provided by the bag-of-feature ap-

[1]http://www.mysql.com/

[2]http://sourceforge.net/projects/opencvlibrary

proach. In this approach, a visual codebook is constructed by using a clustering algorithm (as k-means [6]) over a sample of the training dataset, and each cluster accounts for a visual word. Local features of an image are then assigned to the closest visual word (we used the Euclidean distance function). As a result, a histogram of visual word counts is built to represent the set of local features describing a certain image.

3.4 Classification and Performance

We have used supervised learning with Support Vector Machines (SVM) [12] to classify the videos. Since it is a binary problem, we decided to use linear kernels, as it have showed good results. The LibSVM [1] implementation was used to the experiments, which has been successfully applied to many applications in the literature.

To validate the employed scene classification method we tested the performance through a 5-fold cross-validation approach. In this scheme, a sample of frames is extracted from each video shot of both types. The whole set is uniformly split into 5 folds such that each fold is weighed in terms of the number of shots in the considered class. This way, each fold is tested having as the train set the union of the remaining folds, that is, if fold0 is the test set, then the training set is the concatenation of fold1, fold2, fold3, and fold4. Shots are distributed among the folds while represented by samples of frames. All frames are annotated and will serve as input to learn the classifiers for each fold testing. Once every frame of each fold is assigned a label (either indoor or outdoor), a majority voting scheme is applied to every shot's frame sample so as to compute the final label of each shot. Table 1 shows the performance evaluation in terms of shot, which is our final target, as we want to classify shots.

Table 1: Performance of the shot classification. *#inshot* and *#outshot* denote the number of indoor and outdoor shots, respectively. As follows, *inclass* and *outclass* correspond to the classification performance of the indoor and outdoor shot sets, respectively.

fold	*#inshot*	*#outshot*	*inclass*	*outclass*
fold0	46	40	86.96%	92.5%
fold1	46	40	97.83%	92.5%
fold2	46	40	89.13%	87.5%
fold3	46	40	91.3%	90%
fold4	45	40	73.33%	90%

The overall performance is given in Table 2, which demonstrates that the employed method is powerful to the intended application context.

Table 2: Confusion matrix table.

	outdoor	*indoor*
outdoor	**90%**	10%
indoor	11.11%	**88.89%**

3.5 Audio Transcription

In order to categorize scenes, audio transcription generates a description of each shot which represents the subjects presented in video. In news videos, it is very common that audio information describes the visual information. This observation suggests to convert audio in text information. We use julius (Open-Source Large Vocabulary CSR Engine Julius) speech recognition engine for audio transcription with acoustic and grammar models. A set of five keywords is defined to represent four themes: sports, politics, economy and weather. The rate of classified segments is approximately 5 %. With a video with 300 segments generated by visual features, only 15 will be classified, and 9 segments were classified correctly. The processing time is approximately 5 hours for all algorithms.

Figure 1: Scene interface with shots, indoor scenes, outdoor scenes, face and static summary tabs. The timeline enables users to visually organize video data in order to better analyze.

4. CONCLUSION

We have proposed a visual interface for video navigation to improve the effectiveness of information access in news videos. The interface consists of static and dynamic summarization, face detection, scene classification of (Indoor/Outdoor) and shot categorization (themes). Indoor and Outdoor classification based on supervised learning with SVM demonstrates to be powerful to the intended application context. It uses HueSIFT as local feature detector due the blue pattern observed in indoor scenes. The low rate of classification shot (audio analysis) is due to the few keywords used in theme description and to the segmentation based on visual features. This rate can be increased using text semantic and audio segmentation.

We are interested in several directions in the future. First, we seek an approach for semantic text analysis to improve the categorization using video descriptions created by an audio transcription engine. Also, we intend to combine audio and visual features using graph representation for video-video search.

5. ACKNOWLEDGMENTS

The authors would like to thank to CAPES, CNPQ and FAPEMIG for supporting this work.

6. REFERENCES

[1] C.-C. Chang and C.-J. Lin. LIBSVM: A library for support vector machines. *ACM Transactions on Intelligent Systems and Technology*, 2:27:1–27:27, 2011. Software available at http://www.csie.ntu.edu.tw/ cjlin/libsvm.

[2] S. de Avila, A. da Luz, A. de Araujo, and M. Cord. Vsumm: An approach for automatic video summarization and quantitative evaluation. In *Computer Graphics and Image Processing, 2008. SIBGRAPI '08. XXI Brazilian Symposium on Computer Graphics and Image Processing*, pages 103 –110, oct. 2008.

[3] C. Forlines. Content aware video presentation on high-resolution displays. In *Proceedings of the working conference on Advanced visual interfaces*, AVI '08, pages 57–64, New York, NY, USA, 2008. ACM.

[4] Y. Freund and R. E. Schapire. A decision-theoretic generalization of on-line learning and an application to boosting, 1997.

[5] A. Komlodi, G. Marchionini, and D. Soergel. Search history support for finding and using information: User interface design recommendations from a user study. *Information Processing & Management*, 43(1):10–29, Jan. 2007.

[6] J. B. Macqueen. Some methods of classification and analysis of multivariate observations. In *Proceedings of the Fifth Berkeley Symposium on Mathematical Statistics and Probability*, pages 281–297, 1967.

[7] C. Morand, J. Benois-Pineau, J. P. Domenger, J. Zepeda, E. Kijak, and C. Guillemot. Scalable object-based video retrieval in hd video databases. *Image Commun.*, 25:450–465, July 2010.

[8] C. G. Snoek and M. Worring. Multimodal video indexing: A review of the state-of-the-art. *Multimedia Tools and Applications*, 25:5–35, 2003.

[9] J.-H. Su, Y.-T. Huang, H.-H. Yeh, and V. S. Tseng. Effective content-based video retrieval using pattern-indexing and matching techniques. *Expert Syst. Appl.*, 37:5068–5085, July 2010.

[10] S. Uchihashi, J. Foote, A. Girgensohn, and J. Boreczky. Video manga: Generating semantically meaningful video summaries. pages 383–392. ACM Press, 1999.

[11] K. van de Sande, T. Gevers, and C. Snoek. Evaluating color descriptors for object and scene recognition. *Pattern Analysis and Machine Intelligence, IEEE Transactions on*, 32(9):1582 –1596, sept. 2010.

[12] V. N. Vapnik. *The nature of statistical learning theory.* Springer-Verlag New York, Inc., New York, NY, USA, 1995.

[13] P. Viola and M. Jones. Rapid object detection using a boosted cascade of simple features. pages 511–518, 2001.

An Audio-driven Virtual Dance-Teaching Assistant

Slim Essid*
Institut Telecom, Télécom ParisTech, CNRS-LTCI
Paris
France

Yves Grenier
Institut Telecom, Télécom ParisTech, CNRS-LTCI
Paris
France

Mounira Mazaaoui
Institut Telecom, Télécom ParisTech, CNRS-LTCI
Paris
France

Gaël Richard
Institut Telecom, Télécom ParisTech, CNRS-LTCI
Paris
France

Robin Tournemene
Institut Telecom, Télécom ParisTech, CNRS-LTCI
Paris
France

ABSTRACT

This work addresses the Huawei/3Dlife Grand challenge proposing a set of audio tools for a virtual dance-teaching assistant. These tools are meant to help the dance student develop a sense of rhythm to correctly synchronize his/her movements and steps to the musical timing of the choreographies to be executed. They consist of three main components, namely a music (beat) analysis module, a source separation and remastering module and a dance step segmentation module. These components enable to create augmented tutorial videos highlighting the rhythmic information using, for instance, a synthetic dance teacher voice, but also videos highlighting the steps executed by a student to help in the evaluation of his/her performance.

Categories and Subject Descriptors

H.4 [**Information Systems Applications**]: Miscellaneous

General Terms

Algorithms

Keywords

Grand Challenge, audio, 3DLife, music analysis, source separation, remastering.

*Authors are in alphabetical order

1. INTRODUCTION

The Huawei/3DLife grand challenge considers the scenario where online dance lessons are given by an expert Salsa-dance teacher through the Internet. In this scenario, both the teacher's and students' performances are to be automatically analyzed and rendered using their respective avatars in an online virtual dance room. One of the main originalities of this grand challenge is linked to the dance scenes acquisition which was done using a multitude of sensors, thus enabling novel means for multimedia scene analysis, interpretation and interaction. For instance, the recording set up includes a network of video cameras, multiple microphones (both overhead and onfloor microphones), inertial measurement units, etc.

In such a scenario, two main goals emerge, namely automatically enriching the teacher's performance or the music itself by appropriate metadata that will facilitate the learning and make it more lively; and automatically analyzing (and rating) the student's dance performance compared to the teacher's performance on the same choreography. For example, dancing in rhythm on Salsa music is known to be rather difficult for beginners mainly because it is not straightforward to locate the different beats in the music. However, the student will experience much less difficulty if the dance learning system integrates an automatic metronome or even better can synthesize the voice of the teacher counting in rhythm on the music.

Obviously, all sensors can be jointly exploited to reach the best possible analysis performance but it is also important to consider situations where only part of the sensors is available. Indeed, the capture devices available to a student joining the virtual dance lesson from his/her place may not be as sophisticated as the ones used by the teacher. In this work, we consider that only a subset of signals is available (namely all acoustic signals captured by the overhead and on-floor microphones) although all tools developed can be jointly used with other modalities for an enhanced system.

In this paper, we thus introduce a dance-teaching assistant system which exploits a number of tools that permit to enrich the student's learning experience and to help evaluate his/her performance.

The paper is organized as follows. An overview of the

complete system is given in next section. Then, the different components and modules are described in section 4 and 5 respectively for the music analysis and for the dance performance evaluation. Finally, some conclusions and future work directions are suggested in section 6.

2. ARCHITECTURE OF THE DANCE TEACHING ASSISTANT SYSTEM

An overview of the proposed system is provided in Figure 1. The system is organized around three main components, namely a *source separation* module, a *music analysis* module and a *dance performance analysis* module.

The source separation module relies on echo cancellation techniques (see section 3) to separate the teacher's voice and dance step sounds from the audio mixture consisting of all the overlapping audio signals that are captured by the overhead microphones. This then allows the student (joining the virtual dance room from a distant site) to re-create a new audio mix of the music, teacher's voice and step sounds using the mixing gains that best suit him/her, for example having the teacher's voice sound much louder than the music.

The music analysis module is built around a *musical beat extraction* block and a *beat controlled synthesis* block. The goal of the musical beat extraction is to provide an estimation of the quasi regular beat locations in the musical signal. This information is then used by the beat controlled synthesis component to generate a music track which is augmented with audio effects meant to explicitly provide musical timing information that is essential to help the dance students synchronize their movements to the rhythm of the music. These effects are here chosen to be either hand clapping in rhythm on the extracted musical beats or voice counting those beats using the teacher's voice templates. The latter is a particularly useful alternative to the previously mentioned teacher's voice enhancement component on recordings where the teacher is not actually giving rhythm-related voice instructions across the whole duration of the choreography (which is the case with a number of recordings of the grand challenge dataset).

The third component is dedicated to the evaluation of the student's dance performance. This analysis is achieved by comparing the timing of the dance steps executed by the students to the ideal step timing (given by the ground-truth annotations provided with the dataset). The students' steps timing is deduced after automatic step detection is performed using either the onfloor audio sensors or the enhanced versions of the overhead microphone signals to simulate a situation where only the latter recordings are available.

3. SOURCE SEPARATION AND AUDIO REMASTERING

We aim to separate the teacher's voice and dancers' step sounds from the audio mixture captured by the overhead microphones to be able to remaster the audio track in such a way to highlight the sound sources of interest.

To this end, we rely on an echo cancellation technique [5], to "cancel" the musical background, taking advantage of the fact that the original music that is played in the dance room is separately recorded on channels 5 and 6 of the audio setup.

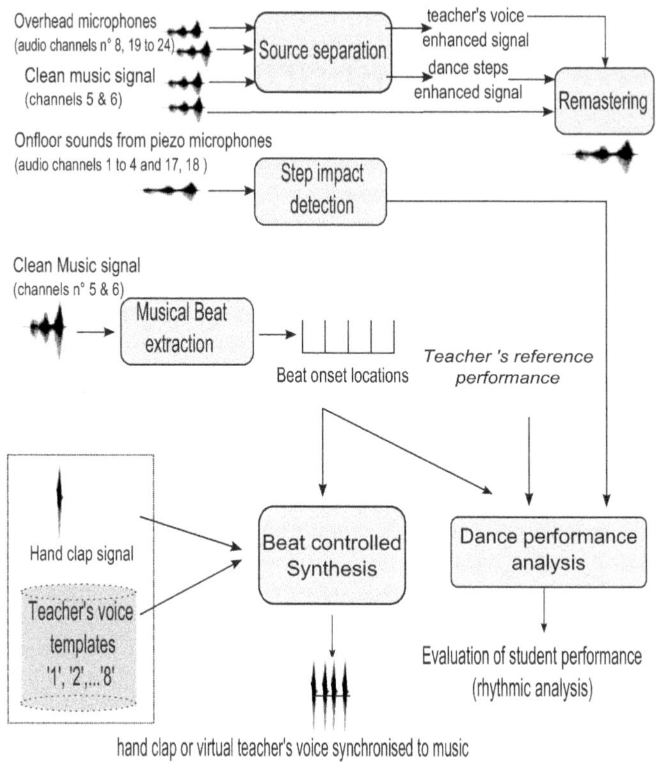

Figure 1: Overview of the 3Dlife Dance audio analysis system

The main challenge in real acoustic cancellation is to deal with the large impulse response present in this kind of application where thousands of FIR filter coefficients may be required to achieve the desired performance. We use an echo canceler based on a block frequency-domain adaptive filtering procedure which is the Generalized Multidelay Filter (GMDF) [5]. The key idea of this algorithm lies in the segmentation of the impulse response to be identified into small blocks and the introduction of a parameter that controls the overlap between the successive input blocks. The "echo" free signal, that is the music free signal, is reconstructed by a weighted overlap-and-add technique.

It is then possible to remix this signal with the "clean" music at a higher loudness level, thus realizing the desired remastering of the original audio. The reader is referred to [1] for some demonstrative examples.

4. MUSIC ANALYSIS AND AUDIO AUGMENTATION

4.1 Musical beat extraction

In many musical pieces, and especially in dance music, listeners can easily feel the *beat*, and tap their foot or clap their hands to the rhythm of the music. In most music, this tapping, or this beat sequence, is regular and this overall regularity is often summarized in the so-called *tempo*. Beat extraction from music signals or tempo estimation have been extensively studied in the past years and the interested reader is referred for the example to the following works [2],[4],[3],[7].

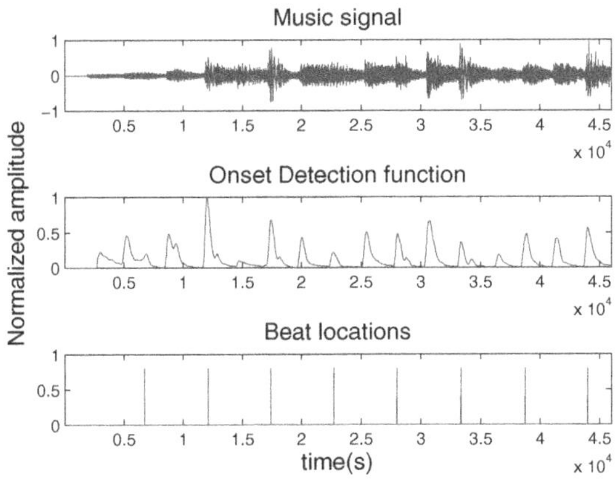

Figure 2: Illustration of the Musical beat extraction system: (top) the music signal; (middle) the corresponding onset detection function and (bottom) the beat positions.

Our approach is mainly based on [3] but integrates a specific module for the extraction of the beat locations. The first step of the musical beat extraction system is then computing an onset detection function (ODF). This ODF is obtained by summing over all frequencies the values of the spectral flux (*i.e.* a derivative of the signal spectrum amplitude) computed for each analysis window. The ODF is then further processed and an estimation of the tempo variations across the music excerpt is computed and smoothed using a Dynamic Programming approach (see [3] for more details). Then, based on this tempo curve the beat positions are estimated as a pseudo-periodic sequence (the period being given by the tempo at the corresponding time). To be well synchronized in time with the beats, the initial phase (or equivalently initial sequence delay) is also estimated.

The output of the module is illustrated in Figure 2.

4.2 Beat controlled synthesis

Once an estimation of the beat locations is obtained, it is possible to generate different types of signals that can enrich the original music signal and facilitate learning to the dance student. The simplest example is to generate a hand clap on each beat location, which can be regarded as the audio rendering of the scene corresponding to the teacher's virtual agent clapping his/her hands in rhythm to the music. A more sophisticated example would illustrate the situation where the virtual teacher is counting the beats by sequence of eight successive beats[1]. In this case, the synthesis is done by generating the successive teacher's speech templates on the beat locations. Note however, that for a fully automatic processing, it is necessary to automatically locate the downbeat, *i.e.* the strongest beat of the measure, (see for example [6]). However, on Salsa music, this is a particularly difficult task which is still today an open problem. In this work, one of the beat onset locations (found automatically) is supposed to be manually labeled by the teacher as a downbeat to improve the robustness of the system. Sound examples of beat controlled synthesis on the Huawei/3Dlife Grand challenge data are given on line [1].

[1]Western style music is, most often, rhythmically structured in segments that are built on a small number of measures, themselves containing a predefined number of beats. In Salsa music, a segment traditionally contains two measures of four beats each, which justifies a count between one to eight

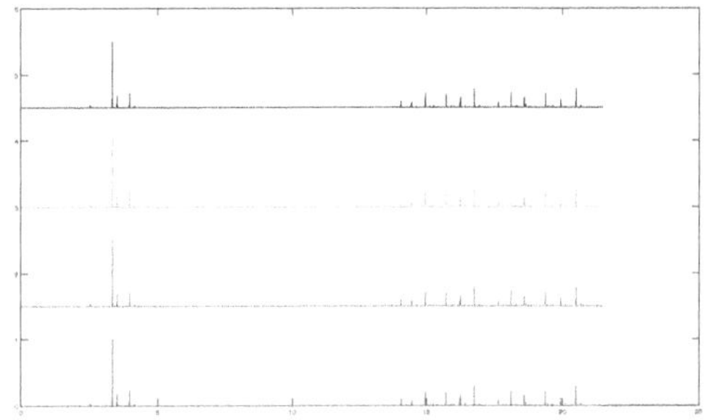

Figure 3: Audio ODF features extracted from signals captured by the onfloor Piezo sensors.

5. DANCE PERFORMANCE ANALYSIS

5.1 Step impact detection

Step impacts are detected using the signals captured by the onfloor piezoelectric transducers (audio channels 1, 2, 17 and 18). The impacts are located by:

- first, extracting onset detection functions $f_c(t)$ from every signal (as done in the beat extraction stage), where c is a channel number ($c \in \{1, 2, 17, 18\}$ or $c \in \{8, 19, 20, 21, 22, 23, 24\}$), and t is a time index;
- then forming feature vectors $\mathbf{x}_t$ which are, at every time instant t, merely the concatenation of the coefficients of every onset detection function, that is $\mathbf{x}_t = [f_1(t), f_2(t), f_{17}(t), f_{18}(t)]$;
- applying a one-class Support Vector Machine (SVM) [8] to those feature vectors (as a way of achieving a fusion of the onset detection functions) and taking the SVM output values which are below a negative threshold to be indicators of step impact instants.

To understand the rationale behind the one-class SVM approach let us examine Figure 3 depicting the onset detection functions $f_c(t)$ for a particular recording (identified as `bertrand_c1_t1` in the dataset). Most samples of these feature values are close to 0 except at a few time indices, expected to indicate the step impacts, where higher values are observed. The latter can then be considered as outliers[2] of the feature vectors distributions which motivates the use of the single-class SVM technique for its ability to robustly detect outliers [8]. These outliers are merely the feature vector $\mathbf{x}_t$ observations where the SVM output is negative.

[2]The reader should bear in mind that the word "outliers" is here used in a statistical sense, and that these extreme observations are actually the ones to be selected.

Step impacts are hence detected by thresholding the SVM decision function and applying a heuristic post-processing avoiding the detection of steps that would be too close in time based on the prior that two consecutive steps should be at least 0.25s away one from another.

Figure 4 shows the result of the automatic step impact detection on the same recording `bertrand_c1_t1` along with ground-truth annotations. It can be seen that the approach successfully detects all steps on this example.

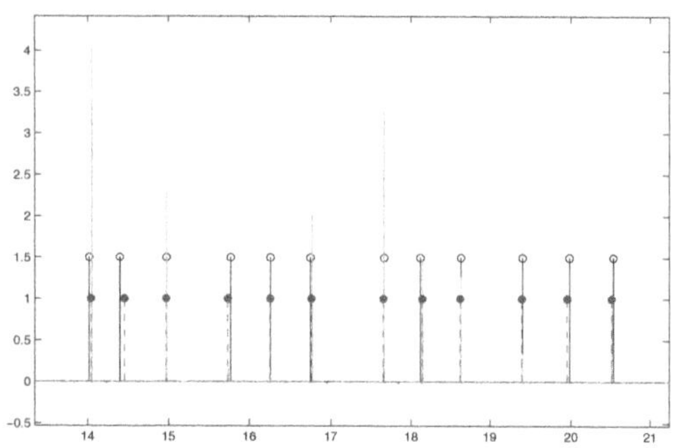

Figure 4: Step detection results on recording `Bertrand_c1_t1`. Negative SVM decision values across time (in green) along with detected steps (dashed blue), and ground-truth annotations in black.

5.2 Evaluation of students' performances

On the basis of the dance step segmentation previously exposed two types of evaluations of a student's performance are proposed:

- a means for a subjective evaluation of the dance performance timing that consists in the augmentation of the sound track of the feet video with audio effects under the form of synthetic beeps placed at time instants where steps are detected (see [1] for examples);
- an objective evaluation consisting in musical-timing ratings of the dance performance.

The automatic ratings aim to characterize two rhythmic aspects of each performance:

- the general timing precision of the dancer;
- the regularity of steps.

The first gives a general rating with respect to the ideal timing of the choreography (given by the automatic beat detection module or the ground-truth annotations in the dataset). The second assesses a dancer with respect to his/her own body rhythm, that is trying to determine whether he/she is arrhythmic or not. The two ratings refer to two different notions : an arrhythmic person may get an acceptable overall rating owing to the fact that he/she often steps at the right musical time instants, and yet be unable to be regular.

The general precision is computed as the arithmetic mean of the differences between step times and their nearest groundtruth counterparts. As for the regularity rating, we compute the standard deviation of the time-differences between every two consecutive steps (assuming a constant music tempo). We actually process only the first Salsa patterns of each choreography. Indeed, these patterns present the particularity of having a constant time interval between two consecutive steps : either 1 or 2 beats.

6. CONCLUSION

In this paper we have presented a set of audio tools composing a virtual dance-teaching assistant for the 3DLife/Huawei challenge centered on Salsa dance scenes. These tools are essential in teaching the dancers the sense of Salsa rhythm which is not easy to pick-up by beginners. Thanks to musical beat analysis, source separation and dancer's steps segmentation modules we are able to create videos of both tutorial and dance performance assessment content highlighting the rhythmic information of the music and the timing of the steps executed by the dancers.

Future work will look at improving the dance steps assessment component, in particular by tackling the problem of feet tracking using the onfloor sensors.

7. ACKNOWLEDGMENTS

This work was supported by the EU FP7 project 3DLife, ICT-247688.

8. REFERENCES

[1] http://huawei-3dlife-gc-submission.blogspot.com, Aug. 2011.

[2] M. Alonso, G. Richard, and B. David. Extracting note onsets from audio recordings. *Proc. of IEEE-ICME*, 2005.

[3] M. Alonso, G. Richard, and B. David. Accurate tempo estimation based on harmonic+noise decomposition. *Eurasip Journal on Advances in Signal Processing*, Jan. 2007.

[4] J. Bello, L. Daudet, and M. Sandler. Automatic piano transcription using frequency and time-domain information. *IEEE Transactions on Audio, Speech and Language Processing*, 14(6):2242–2251, aug 2010.

[5] E. Moulines, O. Ait Amrane, and Y. Grenier. The generalized multidelay adaptive filter: structure and convergence analysis. *Signal Processing, IEEE Transactions on*, 43(1):14 –28, jan 1995.

[6] H. Papadopoulos and G. Peeters. Joint estimation of chords and downbeats from an audio signal. *IEEE Transactions on Audio, Speech & Language Processing*, 19(1):138–152, 2011.

[7] G. Peeters. Beat-tracking using a probabilistic framework and linear discriminant analysis. *Proc. DAFX*, 2009.

[8] B. Shölkopf and A. J. Smola. *Learning with kernels*. The MIT Press, Cambridge, MA, 2002.

Understanding Images with Natural Sentences

Yoshitaka Ushiku
Grad. School of Information Science and Technology
The University of Tokyo
ushiku@isi.imi.i.u-tokyo.ac.jp

Tatsuya Harada
Grad. School of Information Science and Technology
The University of Tokyo / JST PRESTO
harada@isi.imi.i.u-tokyo.ac.jp

Yasuo Kuniyoshi
Grad. School of Information Science and Technology
The University of Tokyo
kuniyosh@isi.imi.i.u-tokyo.ac.jp

ABSTRACT

We propose a novel system which generates sentential captions for general images. For people to use numerous images effectively on the web, technologies must be able to explain image contents and must be capable of searching for data that users need. Moreover, images must be described with natural sentences based not only on the names of objects contained in an image but also on their mutual relations. The proposed system uses general images and captions available on the web as training data to generate captions for new images. Furthermore, because the learning cost is independent from the amount of data, the system has scalability, which makes it useful with large-scale data.

Categories and Subject Descriptors

I.2.10 [**Artificial Intelligence**]: Vision and Scene Understanding

General Terms

Algorithms, Theory

Keywords

Similarity measure, Probabilistic canonical correlation analysis, Multi-stack decoding

1. WHY SENTENCES?

A system by which a computer understands contents of multimedia automatically is indispensable for use with many multimedia web contents effectively. Existing methods of describing multimedia contents express contents with labels of objects, which is insufficient. Description with natural sentences including the objects' relations is important. For example, existing image search engines, which search for required images based on an example image or some words, cannot understand the objects' relations. Therefore, the engine cannot distinguish a sentence such as "A person bit a dog." or a picture in which a person bit a dog from data in which a dog bit a person because the engine can only understand independent words (Fig.1).

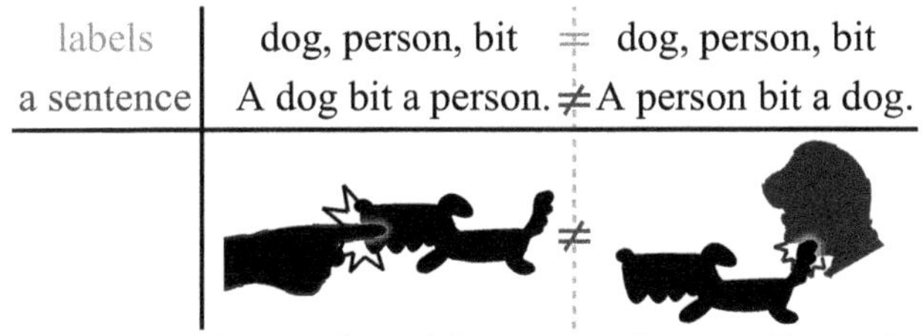

Figure 1: Examples of image understanding. Sentences can distinguish two images, but independent words cannot.

In other methods, the objects contained in each image are described using some labels to support searches and a user's understanding of images and videos in general web sites and sharing services. Although visual recognition, which has been studied actively, can perform this automatically, users cannot understand a story including relations between objects based on labels alone. Automatic generation of a multimedia caption enables users to search for data with a more flexible query and to understand the contents of each datum more easily.

2. DIFFICULTIES AND SOLUTION

Automated captioning of images is extremely difficult because it necessitates correct estimation not only of the objects in the images, but also correct estimation of those objects' mutual relations and expressions using correct grammar. For example, one-to-one relations of a thousand objects can run into the millions. Prior research of sentence outputs from a video, character recognition of subtitles, and speech recognition of conversation can be used instead of descriptions of the visual contents.

Moreover, the problem exists of what kinds of data are used for training to generate captions. Large quantities of training data are necessary to generate captions of general images. Therefore, using a vast quantity of web data, as is done for existing image recognition, presents the most realistic approach. However, only a single study [2] of caption generation uses triplets expressing ⟨object, action, scene⟩ for an image and a caption. It costs users dearly because it necessitates manual labeling.

In [8], we proposed caption generation for general images using data consisting only of images and texts. We devote

MM'11, November 28–December 1, 2011, Scottsdale, Arizona, USA.

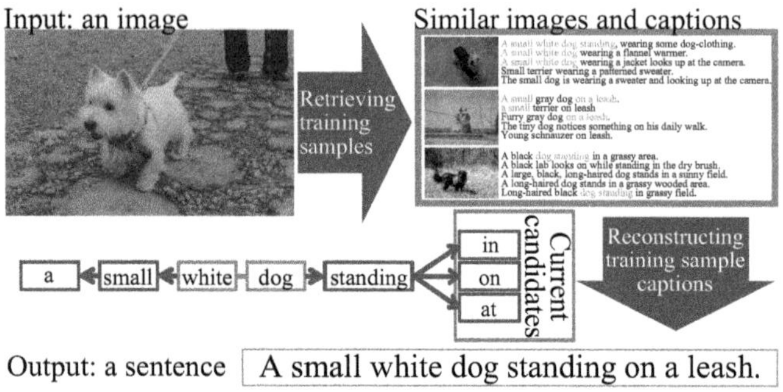

Figure 2: Methodology overview.

Figure 3: Demonstration of caption generation. Left: an inputted image and a generated caption. Right: referred pairs of an image and captions. They are considered similar to the inputted image.

attention to images, the contents of which resemble the contents of an inputted image, and persume as follows.

Assumption 1. In captions of similar images, some representations explain some parts of an inputted image. The objects in an image, their mutual relations and grammatical knowledge are already embedded there. Consequently, the image contents are explainable both grammatically and correctly by reconstructing these captions.

Therefore, captions are generated by (i) searching for similar training samples, and by then (ii) reconstructing the retrieved captions for an input image (Fig.2).

In searching for similar training samples, images with captions that partly explain the inputted image should be retrieved. Briefly, the objective is the acquisition of training samples with contents resembling the input image. Generally, however, a gap separates the similarity of image appearance and the similarity of contents. Therefore, we proposed the improvement of the gap by combining the similarity of an image and the similarity of a text [7]. In that study, a dataset consisting of pairs of an image and a text is constructed from web contents. Then the precision of searching for images with contents resembling the input image is superior to that obtained when using the similarity of visual appearance. Moreover, the approach is good for large-scale data because the computational cost for similarity learning is independent of the amount of data.

Judging which portion of each sentence explains the input is necessary for generation of a caption of an input image by reconstructing the captions of the searched images. Therefore, each sentence is divided into phrases of several words. Then phrases with following two properties are scored highly as discriminative, i.e. explainable phrases.

- It often appears in the captions of searched images.
- It seldom appears in the captions of other images.

A caption combining those phrases is generated to maximize the sum of the scores.

3. DEMO

This demonstration[1] is based on the technique proposed in [8]. Two functions are executable: (a) caption generation of an input image (Fig.3) and (b) image search from an input sentence. Users can search for images using a text query. The automatically generated caption is displayed on each image of search results. In this demonstration, learning is performed with the dataset consisting of images and texts offered in [2]. A caption is generated for new images.

First, (a) caption generation for an input image is described. The application has finished learning for similar image searches, according to results of our earlier study [8]. When a new image is inputted, similar images are sought, as in Sec. 2. The captions of the searched images are decomposed into arbitrary phrases, and a caption is reconstructed.

In [8], we do not perform (b) image search from an input sentence directly. Although it is necessary to assign a caption to an image beforehand for searching, variation occurs in vocabulary and word order when expressing an image in a natural sentence. In other words, even if the query sentence differs from the captions, some images have the same contents as those of the query. Then, the score is saved with a phrase that was not used at the time of caption generation, and the variation in expressions is absorbed by matching with the arbitrary phrases of an input query. The larger the scores of matched phrases become, the more highly the image is ranked among search results.

Because the dataset is small, the explainable contents are restricted. However, even in a larger dataset, caption accuracy is improved because similar images will accompany various sentences. The proposed technique can accept larger dataset because it is scalable, as described in Sec. 2.

4. CONCLUSION

As described in this paper, automatic caption generation for images is proposed as a new form of image understanding. The expressions in a sentence show not only the names of the objects; they also express their respective relations, which eases users' comprehension. Therefore, this method is effective for use with large-scale multimedia. Especially, this method is useful for seeking desired data more efficiently from many images, and for explaining the contents of each image automatically. Because of these benefits, the method is particularly useful for general websites and personal devices such as cameras and mobile phones. Furthermore, for data which require a long time for viewing such as videos and image folders, such caption generation is useful because users

[1] http://www.isi.imi.i.u-tokyo.ac.jp/~captionmultimedia/

can search for desired multimedia with natural sentences and experience the contents without playbacking. Therefore, caption generation for use with multimedia—not only for single images but also for groups of images and a video—is the subject of our future work.

5. REFERENCES

[1] G. Doddington. Automatic evaluation of machine translation quality using n-gram co-occurrence statistics. In *HLT*, pages 138–145, 2002.

[2] A. Farhadi, M. Hejrati, M. A. Sadeghi, P. Young, C. Rashtchian, J. Hockenmaier, and D. Forsyth. Every picture tells a story: Generating sentences from images. In *ECCV*, pages 15–28, 2010.

[3] H. Nakayama, T. Harada, and Y. Kuniyoshi. Evaluation of dimensionality reduction methods for image auto-annotation. In *BMVC*, pages 94.1–94.12, 2010.

[4] F. J. Och and H. Ney. Discriminative training and maximum entropy models for statistical machine translation. In *ACL*, pages 295–302, 2002.

[5] K. Papineni, S. Roukos, T. Ward, and W.-J. Zhu. Bleu: a method for automatic evaluation of machine translation. In *ACL*, number July, pages 311–318, 2002.

[6] G. Salton and C. S. Yang. On the specification of term values in automatic indexing. *Journal of documentation*, 29(4):351–372, 1973.

[7] Y. Ushiku, T. Harada, and Y. Kuniyoshi. Improving image similarity measures for image browsing and retrieval through latent space learning between images and long texts. In *ICIP*, pages 2365–2368, 2010.

[8] Y. Ushiku, T. Harada, and Y. Kuniyoshi. Automatic sentence generation from images. In *ACM MM*, 2011.

APPENDIX

In this section, we present the details of the proposed approach and evaluations. We describe them to make this paper self-contained though they are also described in [8].

A. SENTENTIAL CAPTION GENERATION

Sec. A.1 describes similarity learning used to search for similar training samples, and Sec. A.2 describes caption generation for an input image from the retrieved captions.

A.1 Retrieving training samples

Generally, a gap separates the similarity of image appearance and the similarity of contents. To search for training samples with contents resembling the input image from large data, scalable similarity learning must be done. Ushiku et al. [7] proposed the improvement of the gap by combining the similarity of an image and the similarity of a text. This method is an extension of the image annotation method Canonical Contextual Distance (CCD) [3] to images and texts. The algorithm can calculate the similarity between images as a distance of that context. Then we can search more precisely than when using the similarity of visual appearance. Moreover, the method is scalable because this similarity learning is independent of a data number.

We denote an image/text feature as $\boldsymbol{x}$ or $\boldsymbol{y}$, and the latent variable as $\boldsymbol{z}$. It is realized that $\boldsymbol{x}$ or $\boldsymbol{y}$ has appeared as a stochastic representation of an image or a text from $\boldsymbol{z}$ based on a certain contents. Then, a similar image retrieval turns into a nearest neighbor approach using the distance between probability distributions $p(\boldsymbol{z}|\boldsymbol{x})$ from an input image and $p(\boldsymbol{z}|\boldsymbol{x},\boldsymbol{y})$ from the training sample pair of an image and a text. These distributions are expressed as a normal distribution as $\boldsymbol{z}|\boldsymbol{x},\boldsymbol{y} \sim \mathcal{N}(\boldsymbol{\mu}_{xy}, \Phi_{xy})$ and $\boldsymbol{z}|\boldsymbol{x} \sim \mathcal{N}(\boldsymbol{\mu}_x, \Phi_x)$. For an exponential family such as a normal distribution, Kullback–Leibler Divergence (KLD) is used as a pseudo-distance. We denote i.i.d. $p(\boldsymbol{z}|\boldsymbol{x})$ with mean $\boldsymbol{\mu}_x$ and with variance Φ_x, and $p(\boldsymbol{z}|\boldsymbol{x},\boldsymbol{y})$ with mean $\boldsymbol{\mu}_{xy}$ and variance Φ_{xy}. Then CCD is defined by excepting constant terms from KLD from an input image $\boldsymbol{x}_q$ to a training sample $\{\boldsymbol{x}_t, \boldsymbol{y}_t\}$ as

$$\mathrm{CCD}(\boldsymbol{x}_t, \boldsymbol{y}_t|\boldsymbol{x}_q) = \left\| \Phi_{xy}^{-\frac{1}{2}} (\boldsymbol{\mu}_x - \boldsymbol{\mu}_{xy}) \right\|^2. \quad (1)$$

When we define latent variables $\boldsymbol{r}_t$ for a training sample and $\boldsymbol{r}_q$ for the input image, this is equivalent to a neighbor search using Euclidean distance with $\boldsymbol{r}$ defined as

$$\boldsymbol{r}_t = \Phi_{xw}^{-\frac{1}{2}} \boldsymbol{\mu}_{xy}, \boldsymbol{r}_q = \Phi_x^{-\frac{1}{2}} \boldsymbol{\mu}_x. \quad (2)$$

As described above, it is reduced to the estimation of $\boldsymbol{\mu}_{xy}$, $\boldsymbol{\mu}_x$ and Φ_{xy}. If maximum likelihood estimation is performed with training samples, then it is derived as

$$\boldsymbol{\mu}_x = M_x^T A^T (\boldsymbol{x} - \bar{\boldsymbol{x}}), \Phi_x = I - M_x M_x^T, \quad (3)$$

$$\boldsymbol{\mu}_{xy} = \begin{pmatrix} M_x \\ M_y \end{pmatrix}^T \begin{pmatrix} (I-\Lambda^2)^{-1} & -(I-\Lambda^2)^{-1}\Lambda \\ -(I-\Lambda^2)^{-1}\Lambda & (I-\Lambda^2)^{-1} \end{pmatrix} \begin{pmatrix} A^T(\boldsymbol{x}-\bar{\boldsymbol{x}}) \\ B^T(\boldsymbol{y}-\bar{\boldsymbol{y}}) \end{pmatrix}, \quad (4)$$

$$\Phi_{xy} = I - \begin{pmatrix} M_x \\ M_y \end{pmatrix}^T \begin{pmatrix} (I-\Lambda^2)^{-1} & -(I-\Lambda^2)^{-1}\Lambda \\ -(I-\Lambda^2)^{-1}\Lambda & (I-\Lambda^2)^{-1} \end{pmatrix} \begin{pmatrix} M_x \\ M_y \end{pmatrix}, \quad (5)$$

where $\bar{\boldsymbol{x}}$ and $\bar{\boldsymbol{y}}$ are feature averages, and where M_x and M_y are arbitrary matrices satisfying $M_x M_y^T = \Lambda$ and for which the spectrum norm of each matrix is less than 1. Here we denote them with $0 < \beta < 1$ as $M_x = \Lambda^\beta$ and $M_y = \Lambda^{1-\beta}$, which is exactly like probabilistic canonical correlation analysis (pCCA): a probabilistic interpretation of canonical correlation analysis (CCA). In fact, CCA maximizes the correlation between canonical variables $\boldsymbol{s} = A^T(\boldsymbol{x}-\bar{\boldsymbol{x}})$ and $\boldsymbol{t} = B^T(\boldsymbol{y}-\bar{\boldsymbol{y}})$. These are derived from the following generalized eigenvalue problem: $R_{XY}R_Y^{-1}R_{YX}A = R_X A\Lambda^2$, $R_{YX}R_X^{-1}R_{XY}B = R_Y B\Lambda^2$, where Λ^2 is a diagonal matrix of eigenvalues, $R_X = \sum_{i=1}^n (\boldsymbol{x}_i - \bar{\boldsymbol{x}})(\boldsymbol{x}_i - \bar{\boldsymbol{x}})^T$, $R_Y = \sum_{i=1}^n (\boldsymbol{y}_i - \bar{\boldsymbol{y}})(\boldsymbol{y}_i - \bar{\boldsymbol{y}})^T$, and $R_{XY} = \sum_{i=1}^n (\boldsymbol{x}_i - \bar{\boldsymbol{x}})(\boldsymbol{y}_i - \bar{\boldsymbol{y}})^T = R_{YX}^T$.

A.2 Reconstructing training sample captions

We define the training sample pair $\boldsymbol{s}_i$ of an image $\boldsymbol{x}_i$ and a caption $\boldsymbol{y}_i$, caption set of $\boldsymbol{s}_i$ as $\mathcal{W}_i$, and each caption as $\boldsymbol{w} = w_1^l = (w_1 w_2 \dots w_l)$, where l is the length and w_i represents the i-th word. Here, $\boldsymbol{s}_i$ is obtained using a neighborhood search with CCD described in the preceding section. Some phrases (word sequences) that explain the input image's own objects and those relations correctly and grammatically are expected in $\mathcal{W}_i$.

We generate captions of desired length l_{tar} to the input image. The scores of candidate captions are computed from the input image; then the caption having the highest score is output. Our objectives are 1) searching for explanatory phrases and 2) captioning for the desired length. Consequently, two feature functions are defined for each purpose. The first is a score $\phi(p_{hr}|\boldsymbol{x}_q)$ when phrase p_{hr} is selected for the input image $\boldsymbol{x}_q$. The second is a score for the current sentence length. Although other scores such as those of a grammar model with n-gram are usable, here we investigate the captioning ability accomplished solely by reconstruction of training sample captions.

We define the probability of retrieving $\boldsymbol{s}_i$ from an input image $\boldsymbol{x}_q$ as $p(\boldsymbol{s}_i|\boldsymbol{x}_q)$, and define the probability of selecting a phrase p_{hr} from the pair $\boldsymbol{x}_q$ as $p(p_{hr}|\boldsymbol{s}_i)$. The phrase score is defined as a logarithm with those probabilities as

$$\phi(p_{hr}|\boldsymbol{x}_q) = \left(1 - \frac{o(p_{hr})}{o_{max}(p_{hr})}\right) \log\left(\sum_i p(p_{hr}|\boldsymbol{s}_i) p(\boldsymbol{s}_i|\boldsymbol{x}_q)\right), \quad (6)$$

where $o_{max}(p_{hr})$ is the maximum occurrence of p_{hr} in one sentence, and $o(p_{hr})$ is the occurrence of p_{hr} in the currently generating sentence. The coefficient of the logarithm has a control for a specific dominant phrase so as not to produce meaningless repetition. The probability $p(\boldsymbol{s}_i|\boldsymbol{x}_q)$ of selecting a pair $\boldsymbol{s}_i$ is retrieved from the input image $\boldsymbol{x}_q$ is defined as $p(\boldsymbol{s}_i|\boldsymbol{x}_q) = \exp(-\mathrm{CCD}(\boldsymbol{s}_i|\boldsymbol{x}_q)) / \sum_i \exp(-\mathrm{CCD}(\boldsymbol{s}_i|\boldsymbol{x}_q))$. The probability $p(p_{hr}|\boldsymbol{s}_i)$ of selecting p_{hr} from each pair $\boldsymbol{s}_i$ is defined using tf-idf [6], the product of the frequency of each term in a document and the inverse of the appearance frequency of that term in all documents, as $p(p_{hr}|\boldsymbol{s}_i) = \text{tf-idf}(p_{hr})/\sum_{p_{hr}\in\mathcal{W}_i} \text{tf-idf}(p_{hr})$. Therein, Tf-idf represents how well each word distinguishes the text.

We denote the length score as a logarithm of the probability of current length $l \sim \mathcal{N}(l_{tar}, \sigma)$. Qualitatively, σ represents the tolerance level of caption length. In this paper, we define that $l_{tar} = 12$ and $\sigma = 1$.

Because generable captions increase exponentially with vocabularies, comparison of all captions is difficult. Consequently, output is determined with graph search. In a typical approach [4] to statistical machine translation, scores are first calculated using various feature functions from both languages. Then the translations are generated to maximize the sum of the scores using a graph search such as a multi-stack beam search.

Beam searching saves some high rank candidate sentences in one stack. The stack size can adjust the accuracy of graph search and the computational complexity. In a multi-stack beam search, a stack is divided according to the translated word amounts in the input sentence. The highest-ranked sentence in the last stack is output. In this paper, however, the input not as a sentence but as an image causes problems.

First, because there is nothing equivalent to word position correspondence of an input sentence and a translation, left-to-right expansion is impossible. Therefore, we take an approach to expand a sentence to both sides. We consider the l_s words' phrase which has the highest probability of explaining the input image as a seed. Then we expand a caption to both sides.

As another problem, because the judgment of *untranslated* portion of an image is difficult, neither the end of the translation and division of the stack based on the translated words' length is possible. Therefore, we divide a stack based on the sentence being generated. An index on which can be ended is given to the candidate captions in each stack. In the caption set $\mathcal{W}$, EDGE of Sentence (EOS) is added beforehand to the head and end of each caption. When the phrase that is connectable to EOS exists in $\mathcal{W}$, it is unrelated with the score when connected with EOS at the time, but the index and the score when connected to the EOS are memorized. When the expansion is finished, the word sequence that is inserted by EOS will be output as

$$\boldsymbol{w} = \underset{\boldsymbol{w}=(w_{i_s} w_{i_s+1} \cdots w_{i_e-1} w_{i_e})}{\arg\max} \sum_k \phi_k(w_{i_s}^{i_e}|\boldsymbol{x}_q), \quad (7)$$

where i is an index connectable to EOS. i_e and i_s are found in left-to-right and right-to-left expansion respectively.

B. EVALUATION

In [2], image captions themselves are manually evaluated, which makes fair comparison difficult. Therefore, we investigate automatic evaluation with which matching to the reference given to the input image in the dataset is quantified. Captions are evaluated with match of n-gram using BiLingual Evaluation Understudy (BLEU) [5] and NIST [1].

The CCD parameter used to search for a training sample is optimized by maximizing BLEU/NIST of the caption which originally accompanied the input image and the retrieved caption. Concurrently, Mean Average Precision (MAP) is also used as a typical retrieval evaluation. This calculates the match rate of the category of an input image and the retrieved sample. However, this evaluation can not be calculated without the category label to images and captions.

For caption generation from images and captions only, optimization without MAP, which needs labels, is desirable. Automatic evaluation was compared with evaluation by hands in advance of evaluating the proposed method. Six captions output to each image are shown to 10 subjects. The order of captions is random. For that reason, subjects cannot understand which system output which caption. Each caption is evaluated using a five-level rating according to how well it explains the image. The evaluations are standardized. The correlations between each of BLEU and NIST and hand evaluation are 0.63 and 0.82, respectively, showing that NIST especially is appropriate for evaluation of captions.

A Psychophysical Approach for Real-Time 3D Video Processing

Wanmin Wu, Ahsan Arefin, Gregorij Kurillo†, Pooja Agarwal, Klara Nahrstedt, Ruzena Bajcsy†
Department of Computer Science, University of Illinois at Urbana-Champaign, Urbana, IL, USA.
†Department of EECS, University of California at Berkeley, Berkeley, CA, USA.
{wwu23, marefin2, pagarwl, klara}@illinois.edu, †{gregorij, bajcsy}@eecs.berkeley.edu

ABSTRACT

This paper presents a psychophysical approach to control a new factor called Color-plus-Depth Level-of-Detail in polygon-based 3D tele-immersive video. Based on our psychophysical study that demonstrates the existence of perceptual thresholds on the factor, we present a real-time perception-based quality adaptor for 3D tele-immersive video. Our experimental results show that the adaptation scheme can reduce resource usage while considerably enhancing the overall perceived visual quality.

Categories and Subject Descriptors

H.1.2 [**Information Systems**]: Models and Principles—*human factors*; H.4.3 [**Information Systems Applications**]: Communications Applications—*Computer conferencing, teleconferencing, and videoconferencing*

General Terms

Design, Experiment, Human Factors, Measurement

Keywords

Tele-immersive Video, Perception, Psychophysics, Color-plus-Depth, Level-of-Detail, Adaptation

1. INTRODUCTION

Despite the great potentials, today's 3D tele-immersive systems still face significant challenges due to the high interactivity requirement and resource demand. Great research efforts have been devoted to making the systems more efficient [1][7], with notable improvement, but the focus has been primarily on system-centric, algorithmic optimizations, and the systems still struggle with heavy temporal and spatial overheads and complexities, limiting their broader deployment.

Since the ultimate goal of tele-immersion is to deliver satisfying experience to end users, we believe that taking a more human-centric perspective would be beneficial. It is known that Human Visual System (HVS) has perceptual limitations, so the research question is whether it is possible to exploit these limitations and reduce data load and/or rate without impairing much perceived quality. Similar questions have been studied in traditional video-conferencing systems for factors such as latency [3] and frame rate [5]. However, 3D tele-immersive video possesses unique characteristics whose perceptual impact is little understood.

Perhaps the most important trait that distinguishes 3D tele-immersion from the traditional video-conferencing is its color-plus-depth video format as the visual representations of users. Therefore, the density and accuracy of the texture and depth maps is a new and critical factor in tele-immersive video, which we combine and refer to as the *Color-Plus-Depth Level-of-Detail (CZLoD)*. We psychophysically study this factor in *polygon-based* 3D tele-immersive video. The results indicate that the threshold levels are actually fairly generous (i.e., a fair amount of degradation can be suffered).

We therefore design and implement a perception-based real-time adaptation scheme for CZLoD in 3D tele-immersion. Implemented as a closed feedback loop, the adaptor monitors various interdependent Quality-of-Service (QoS) parameters to determine the appropriate degradation ratio for CZLoD. The actual degradation, nevertheless, is achieved by controlling a *detailing parameter*, whose mapping to the degradation ratio is unpredictable as it varies with environments and activities. Thus a learning algorithm is used to learn the quantitative model of the relationship between the detailing parameter and the CZLoD degradation ratios. We evaluate the adaptation scheme in a real-world 3D tele-immersive testbed, and the experimental results demonstrate that the proposed scheme can achieve considerable improvement in frame rate without impairing perceived detailing quality. We also record the generated tele-immersive video with and without adaptation respectively and conduct a crowdsourcing subjective study to compare their overall quality. The collected responses show that over 90% of users thought the video with adaptation was better than the unimpaired video.

2. TELE-IMMERSIVE VIDEO

In this section, we describe the generation of color-plus-depth frames in greater detail. As Figure 1 illustrates, after the raw frames are fetched from the stereo camera, they are first preprocessed (e.g., resizing, rectification). Then one of the images is used as the "reference frame" (e.g., the image from the left eye of the camera as shown in Figure 1), where

MM'11, November 28–December 1, 2011, Scottsdale, Arizona, USA.

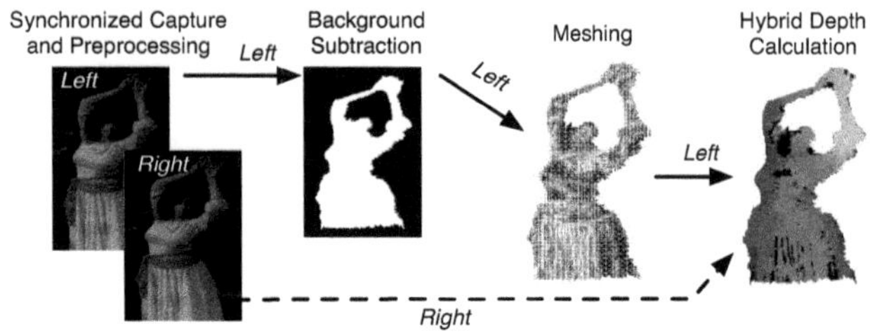

Figure 1: Depth mapping (adapted from [8]).

background subtraction is performed. The next major step would be to reconstruct the 3D information of the frame for each foreground pixel. However, obtaining an accurate, dense (per pixel) depth map on commodity hardware turns out to be very time-consuming. Several tele-immersive systems use the polygonal modeling approach [6][8], to alleviate both temporal and spatial overheads.

Specifically, after background subtraction the reference frame is decomposed into polygons (e.g., triangles) based on texture homogeneity. This is done by recursively refining bisection until the variance within every polygon is less than a threshold TH_{var}. Importantly, afterwards the expensive depth-correlation operation is only performed on mesh vertices [8]. The depth calculation for the other pixels can thus be largely simplified by linear interpolation. Similar subdivision can be applied for textures, too. Since now only the coordinates and textures of vertices need to be transmitted (and those of the remaining pixels to be approximated at the receiving/rendering side), such region-based representations (and the accompanying hybrid depth and texture mapping algorithms) lead to a reduction of frame size as well as data manipulation time in all stages of the tele-immersion pipeline, making them favorable for the resource-intensive tele-immersion applications. For its clear benefits compared to the conventional point cloud approach (with substantially less data to process and transmit), this polygon modeling approach is very likely to become more widely adopted in the future.

We can observe that the number of foreground vertices after meshing regulates the color-plus-depth granularity of the mesh. It also determines the density/accuracy of tele-immersive video due to the disparate treatment of vertices and non-vertices in 3D reconstruction and texture mapping. Hence, we refer to this metric as the *Color-plus-Depth Level-of-Detail (CZLoD)*, which characterizes the spatial (including z-axial) and textural richness and accuracy of polygon-based tele-immersive video. Clearly, it is largely impacted by the setting of the *variance threshold* $TH_{var}(\in \mathbb{Z})$. The smaller the variance threshold is, the finer the meshing is, the more dense/accurate the depth and texture maps will be. Therefore, the variance threshold TH_{var} is a *detailing parameter* for the CZLoD of tele-immersive video.

We are concerned about whether there are perceptual limits on the *degradation* of CZLoD for the purpose of data reduction. We employ the method of limits from psychophysics to examine two perceptual thresholds - Just Noticeable Degradation (JNDG) and Just Unacceptable Degradation (JUADG). We evaluate forty stimuli in four varied conditions with different contents and pixel resolution settings. JNDG is found to be 48%-70%, and JUADG is found to be 68%-90%. The details of the psychophysical study are omitted in this paper due to space limit.

3. ADAPTATION SCHEME

QoS parameters are characterized by spatial (intra-frame) and temporal (inter-frame) requirements. For tele-immersive video, the spatial parameter refers to the spatial (including z-axial) resolution, and the temporal parameter corresponds to the frame rate. Naive tele-immersive applications are often implemented without considering the temporal-spatial balance. The results from our psychophysical study suggest that CZLoD provides tele-immersion developers a powerful tool to control the detail complexity of the video, and in turn control the frame processing time or the frame rate. A major implication of our findings is that transparent degradation on spatial resolution (CZLoD) is possible to achieve "free" saving on resources without users being aware of it, i.e., by degrading CZLoD to a level where the distortion is just unnoticeable. In addition, when frame rate drops to a level that it hurts overall usability, the degradation on CZLoD can further increase (yet within acceptable ranges) to reduce data load and thereby elevate frame rate. Furthermore, past research has implied a curvilinear relationship between spatial quality and frame rate, e.g., improvements in frame rate become less noticeable above approximately 10 frames per second [5]. Therefore, when frame rates are found to be higher than necessary, the CZLoD degradation ratio can be lessened (if possible) to recover or promote the detailing quality thereby reducing frame rate. In a word, we can manipulate the CZLoD degradation ratio to achieve a balance between the temporal quality (frame rate) and the spatial quality (CZLoD).

Based on these principles, we propose a novel, human-centric, real-time adaptation scheme (at the sender side) for tele-immersive video. We design the adaptor as a closed feedback loop for the control of detailing quality in tele-immersive video. Figure 2 illustrates the schematic process of the adaptation. It has three major components: QoS Monitor, Decision Engine, and Variance Calculator. QoS Monitor collects and analyzes time series of QoS parameters (e.g., frame processing time, frame size, reconstruction time), and extracting meaningful information online to notify Decision Engine for triggering adaptation. Decision Engine computes an appropriate target CZLoD degradation ratio for the 3D reconstruction process. Since degradation ratio is actually controlled by manipulating the variance threshold, a Variance Calculator component is hence used to compute the correct variance threshold given a target degradation ratio from Decision Engine. Yet a challenge is that the mapping from a desired CZLoD degradation ratio to a variance threshold is unpredictable due to its dependency on scenes (e.g., clothing texture, skin colors, presence of objects, lighting illuminance). Therefore, Variance Calculator dynamically learns a quantitative model between the CZLoD degradation ratio and the appropriate variance threshold. Based on the model, it computes the proper variance threshold given a target degradation ratio, and feeds it into the 3D reconstruction pipeline for video quality adaptation.

QoS Monitor. Since providing real-time feedback in the control loop is a key, a simple yet efficient range checking approach is used for evaluating frame rate. Essentially, if the frame rate drops below a lower-limit threshold, Deci-

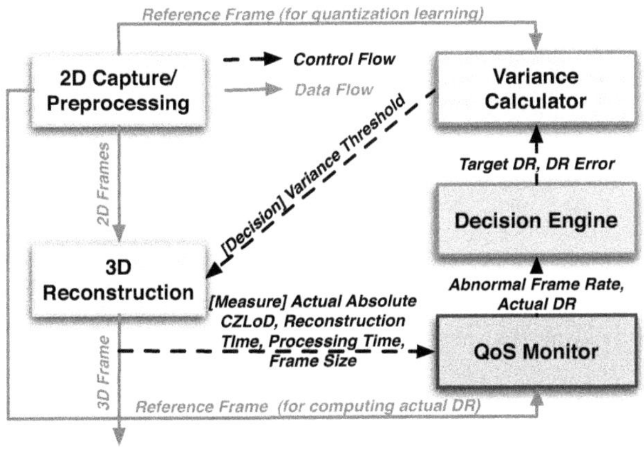

Figure 2: Adaptation Scheme Overview

sion Engine is notified for increasing degradation ratio (for lower CZLoD quality); if the frame rate increases beyond an upper-limit threshold, Decision Engine is notified for decreasing degradation ratio (for higher CZLoD quality). The thresholds should be set according to the perceptual characteristics of frame rate [5]. Apart from the frame rate reports, QoS Monitor also evaluates the actual degradation ratio of each frame, and reports it to Decision Engine for taking corrective measure. Degradation ratio needs to be measured because the sequence complexity and resource condition are constantly changing, meaning it is possible that a target degradation ratio would not be achieved exactly as desired.

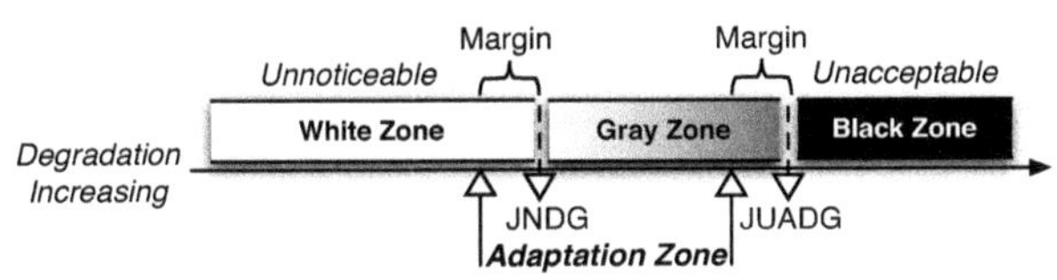

Figure 3: The Just Noticeable (JNDG) and Just Unacceptable (JUADG) thresholds decompose the range of CZLoD degradation to three zones.

Decision Engine. The foundation of the adaptation logic in Decision Engine is based on the perceptual thresholds (JNDG and JUADG) on the color-plus-depth spatial resolution of the video. The thresholds decompose the CZLoD quality of tele-immersive video into three zones: *white zone* where distortion is minimally noticeable, *gray zone* where the distortion gradually becomes noticeable yet still acceptable, and *black zone* where the degradation is unacceptable. The basic idea of Decision Engine is to dynamically adjust the target degradation ratio primarily in the gray zone, except with some margins (Figure 3). The margins are introduced to account for the step size in our psychophysical experiment as well as environmental and user dynamics.

As mentioned above, Decision Engine receives two types of information from QoS Monitor: (a) abnormal frame rate, and (b) actual degradation ratio ($DR^a(F_i)$) of every frame F_i. Upon receiving alarms of abnormal frame rate, Decision Engine computes an appropriate target degradation ratio. For this purpose, a linear control mechanism is used. Basically, an abnormally low frame rate means the need for lower CZLoD quality (or higher degradation ratio), thus the engine computes the target degradation ratio as $DR^t(F_i) = DR^a(F_{i-1}) + \Delta_d$ where $DR^t(F_i)$ denotes the target degradation ratio,Δ_d denotes the adjustment size for increasing DR. This ratio is then used for all frames until the next time adaptation is triggered. Similarly, an unnecessarily high frame rate ($FR_i > TH^h_{fr}$) triggers the engine to produce a desired degradation ratio as $DR^t(F_i) = DR^a(F_{i-1}) - \Delta_u$ whereΔ_u is the adjustment size for decreasing DR.

We utilize the measured thresholds to guide the adaptation zone (Figure 3). Simply, when frame rate is excessively low (i.e., to increase DR), if $DR^t(F_i)$ reaches the upper limit of the adaptation zone (close to the black zone in Figure 3), Δ_d is set to 0, i.e., no degradation is allowed any more otherwise the quality would become unacceptable. Likewise, when frame rate is excessively high (i.e., to decrease DR), if $DR^t(F_i)$ reaches the lower limit of the adaptation zone (close to white zone),Δ_u is set to 0, i.e., further improvement on the detailing quality would not be noticeable anyway thus unnecessary. Besides the calculation of target degradation ratio, Decision Engine also computes the adaptation error between the actual and target degradation which will be used for Variance Calculator (as explained below).

Variance Calculator. Given the target CZLoD degradation ratio DR^t, Variance Calculator is responsible for determining the proper value for the detailing parameter TH_{var} in the 3D reconstruction. However, the mapping $\mathcal{F}$ from DR^t to TH_{var} is nontrivial because it highly depends on external conditions such as scene complexities. Therefore, we dynamically learn a quantitative model in order to predict the correct TH_{var} value for a desired DR^t. The learning process is performed only when Decision Engine finds that the adaptation error $err = |DR^a(F_i) - DR^t(F_i)|$ is larger than some threshold $err > TH_{err}$, meaning that significant changes in scenes might have happened that make the previous model less applicable. To learn a new model, Variance Calculator repeatedly applies 3D reconstruction on the frame f_i with exponentially increased TH_{var} values, and the resultant $DR^a(F_i)$ values are logged. This process runs in parallel with the actual 3D tele-immersion pipeline and is thus unobtrusive. Then the used TH_{var} values and their resultant $DR^a(F_i)$ values are fed into a least-square regression module to develop an exponential model as follows [2]: $\mathcal{F} : TH_{var} = e^{a \cdot DR^t + b}$, where e is the Euler number, and a and b are constants. The choice of the above exponential model comes from our extensive curve-fitting experiments with extensive TI video, where their relationships are all a form of the above equation. With this simple model we are able to achieve a high accuracy (median residual of 0.022%) with as few as 10 training points (please refer to Section 3.1). With the model available, Variance Calculator is then able to set a proper variance threshold after 2D preprocessing and before 3D reconstruction for a desired degradation ratio.

3.1 Performance Evaluation

We evaluated the adaptation scheme in a real-world 3D tele-immersive system.

Figure 4(a) shows the frame rate comparison. In this case, the adaptation scheme achieved an average of 27% improvement on frame rate from about 8 fps to 10 fps. According to [5], any improvement below a frame rate of 10 fps is considerably noticeable to users. It is also worth noting that

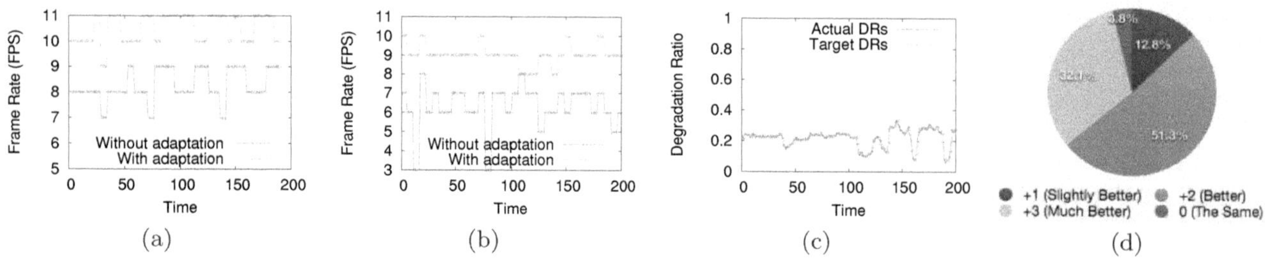

Figure 4: Experimental Results

even with the adaptation mechanisms added, the frame rate improves and real-time performance is guaranteed, meaning that the overhead of our algorithms is minimal. We also compared the frame rate with some CPU stress. For this, a process was run together with 3D tele-immersion that took at peak 16% of the CPU load. This could simulate the conditions where the CPU is less powerful or higher pixel resolution is configured. As Figure 4(b) shows, the frame rates without adaptation dropped to about 6-7 fps with several sudden dips to 3 fps. On the other hand, the frame rates achieved with adaptation (with the same conditions) remained relatively stable around 9 fps (with average improvement being 39.6%). Figure 4(c) shows the actual degradation ratios used with the projected target ratios. The prediction accuracy was high, with a median residual of 0.022%. The average degraded ratio was 22.7%, with a standard deviation of 0.063%. Considering that the JNDG is around 60% in our psychophysical study, there was still much room for more reduction if the frame rates were below desired thresholds.

We also conducted a user study to compare the visual quality of the recorded video. The crowdsourcing methodology was used due to the simplicity of the experiment. Following the ITU standard for double stimuli video comparison study [4], we made a short video with the following structure (in sequential order): (a) five seconds of text illustrating the purpose of the study, (b) two seconds of text indicating "Video 1" to be shown, (c) ten seconds of Video 1, (d) two seconds of text indicating "Video 2" to be shown, and (e) ten seconds of Video 2, and (f) ten seconds of text asking the rating question: "Compared to Video 1's quality, Video 2's quality is: [-3 (Much Worse), -2 (Worse), -1 (Slightly Worse), 0 (The Same), +1 (Slightly Better), +2 (Better), +3 (Much Better)]?" [4]. The video was uploaded to Youtube and was advertised to a mailing list (containing graduate students, staff, and professors in Department of Computer Science). The ranking data were collected anonymously through an online Google Doc Form. A total of 81 responses were collected. Three of them were discarded because respondents notified the experimenter that they submitted by mistake. Figure 4(d) shows the collected ratings. Among the 78 responses, 96.2% of the users thought the video with adaptation turned on had a better quality than the video with adaptation turned off, and 3.8% thought they were the same. 12.8% (of total) gave a "(+1) Slightly Better" ranking, 51.3% gave a "(+2) Better" ranking, and 32.1% gave a "(+3) Much Better" ranking. Clearly, our adaptation scheme not only saves system resource (i.e., CPU load), but also improves subjective video quality.

4. CONCLUDING REMARKS

This paper identifies a new critical quality factor called Color-plus-Depth Level-of-Detail (CZLoD) in 3D tele-immersive video. A psychophysical study of the perceptual thresholds of CZLoD is performed and presence of two perceptual thresholds - Just Noticeable Degradation (JNDG) and Just Unacceptable Degradation (JUADG) is demonstrated. Taking CZLoD as a guiding parameter, we design an online human-centric QoS adaptation scheme to dynamically adapt the video quality. Our experiments show that the adaptation scheme considerably reduces the resource demands while enhancing the perceived visual quality.

5. REFERENCES

[1] H. H. Baker, N. Bhatti, D. Tanguay, I. Sobel, D. Gelb, M. E. Goss, W. B. Culbertson, and T. Malzbender. Understanding performance in Coliseum, an immersive videoconferencing system. *ACM TOMCCAP*, 1(2):190–210, 2005.

[2] A. BjÄorc. *Numerical Methods for Least Squares Problems.* SIAM, 1996.

[3] S. Iai, T. Kurita, and N. Kitawaki. Quality requirements for multimedia communication services and terminals - interaction of speech and video delays. In *Proc. of GLOBECOM '93*, 1993.

[4] ITU. Methodology for the subjective assessment of the quality of television pictures. In *Rec. BT.500*, 2009.

[5] J. K. Kies. *Empirical methods for evaluating video-mediated collaborative work.* PhD thesis, Virginia Polytechnic Institute and State University, 1997.

[6] P. J. Narayanan, P. W. Rander, and T. Kanade. Constructing virtual worlds using dense stereo. In *Proc. of ICCV'98*, pages 3–10, 1998.

[7] D. E. Ott and K. Mayer-Patel. A mechanism for TCP-friendly transport-level protocol coordination. In *Proc. of USENIX'02*, pages 147–159, 2002.

[8] R. Vasudevan, G. Kurillo, E. Lobaton, T. Bernardin, O. Kreylos, R. Bajcsy, and K. Nahrstedt. High quality visualization for geographically distributed 3d teleimmersive applications. In *IEEE Transactions on Multimedia*, volume 13, pages 573–584, 2011.

Augmenting Mobile City-View Image Retrieval with Context-Rich User-Contributed Photos

Yin-Hsi Kuo[1,2], Wen-Yu Lee[1], Winston H. Hsu[1], and Wen-Huang Cheng[2]
[1]National Taiwan University and [2]Academia Sinica, Taipei, Taiwan
{kuonini, majorrei}@cmlab.csie.ntu.edu.tw,
winston@csie.ntu.edu.tw, whcheng@citi.sinica.edu.tw

ABSTRACT

With the growth of mobile devices, the needs for location-based services are emerging. Taking the advantage of the GPS information, we can roughly estimate a user's location. However, it is necessary to leverage extra information (e.g., photos) to precisely locate the object of interest through mobile devices for further applications such as mobile search. Users can simply take a picture (with GPS enabled) of an interesting target to retrieve the building information. Therefore, the raise of real-time building recognition or retrieval system becomes a challenging problem. The most recent approaches are to recognize buildings by the street-view images; however, the query photos from mobile devices usually contain different lighting conditions. In order to provide a more robust city-view image retrieval system, we propose to augment the visual diversity of database images by integrating the context-rich user-contributed photos from social media. Preliminary experimental results show that the street-view images can provide different angles of the target whereas the user-contributed photos can enhance the diversity of the target. Besides, for the real-time retrieval system, we also combine both visual and GPS constraints in the retrieval process on inverted indexing so that we can achieve a real-time retrieval system.

Categories and Subject Descriptors

H.3.3 [**Information Storage and Retrieval**]: Information Search and Retrieval— *etrieval models*

General Terms

Algorithms, Experimentation, Performance

1. INTRODUCTION

With the popularization of mobile internet devices such as smart phones and digital cameras, the dream of accessing the internet from anywhere is more of a reality than ever before. As a result, mobile online services become an emerging industry. In the last decades, most tourists have to follow their travel schedule to prevent getting lost in a new area. It is risky to break an expected tourist route but to explore further whenever they want. To remedy the deficiency, in this paper we study the city-view retrieval techniques on images from mobile internet devices to guide a tourist where he or she is in. Given a photo, i.e., a query image, the rationale behind the landmark retrieval techniques is to match the query image with images in datasets of online photo sharing websites, such as Flickr and Picasa, to determine the geographical location the photo reveals. By doing so, people can locate themselves almost anywhere by just taking and uploading a photo. However, city-view retrieval is more challenging than traditional image retrieval in that it contains richer messages behind an image such as user comments, geotags, and other textual tags. Essentially three problems have to be addressed: (1) the query images may be taken under various conditions and environments, e.g., daytime or night, (2) the targeted (or informative) object may only cover a small area of the query image, and (3) the query images may contain few discriminative visual features but many repetitive image patterns.

Nowadays we can easily obtain GPS (geotagging) information through mobile devices, which provides a great op-

Figure 1: Examples of mobile query images which are taken in different lighting conditions. The street-view images can provide different angles of the same building; however, it is a challenging problem to retrieve the correct target under different environments. Fortunately, we can utilize user-contributed photos from social media such as Flickr to enhance the diversity of the search target. If we can combine both kind of images, we can provide more complemental retrieval results.

portunity for recent researches [2][6]. For example, we may estimate the location or direction of images from geotagged image databases [3][8]. For a landmark identification system, [1] proposed to combine both facade-aligned and viewpoint-aligned images from street-view images, and adopted geometry verification to enhance the search results. In their experiments, most of the database and query images are taken from daytime; however, it is possible to recognize incorrect building when the query image is taken in different lighting conditions as show in Figure 1. And [5] proposed to suppress confusing features for each street-view image according to the GPS information. They further enhance a query image through query expansion by utilizing non-geotagged images from the photo-sharing website, Panoramio. In our work, we integrate both street-view and user-contributed photos in our database and further investigate the help from GPS information. We show a robust image retrieval approach for each mobile query from the city-scale database.

In summary, this paper has three main contributions: (1) we propose a scalable city-view retrieval approach (Section 2), (2) we unify both the GPS information and visual similarity with image retrieval process in inverted indexing, and (3) we investigate the help from both street-view and user-contributed photos (Section 4).

2. SCALABLE CITY-VIEW IMAGE RETRIEVAL SYSTEM

With the prevalence of mobile devices, large-scale image retrieval over mobiles becomes more and more important. It is also a challenging problem due to various lighting conditions, viewpoints, etc. An effective and efficient retrieval system for the mobile query is required especially when users want to obtain real-time information at hand. Although the state-of-the-art image retrieval system, the bag-of-words (BoW) model [10] is adopted to our system and those features are indexed by the inverted indexing structure, it is still time-consuming to calculate similarities of all the possible images in the inverted indexing structure. Therefore, we take the advantages of visual and GPS similarities to reduce the search time (Section 2.1). In tradition, building recognitions are usually based on the street-view images [1] which can provide different viewpoints of buildings. However, when photos taken in different lighting conditions, as shown in Figure 1, the retrieval system based on street-view images may fail. To address the problem, we propose to utilize both street-view and user-contributed images to improve the search results (Section 2.2).

2.1 Visual and GPS Constraints in Inverted Indexing Structure

Inverted file is a popular way to index large-scale data in the information retrieval community [11], and the BoW model is a robust feature representation for image retrieval [10]. The BoW representation quantizes high-dimensional local features into discrete visual words (VWs) so that we can index VWs in the inverted file. Following [11], we adopt similar approaches to our indexing structure. We apply index compression and remove stop list for those high frequency VWs.

Besides, we further consider the differences between the textual and visual domain. Conventional retrieval systems need to keep track of the scores of all images in the inverted lists. But in fact, it is observed that most of the scored images contain only a few matched VWs and most users prefer the top-ranked search results. Thus, we further propose to explore a small part of a large-scale database to reduce the online retrieval time. Because buildings usually contain repeated patterns, we first focus on those high frequency VWs shown in the query images. Second, we only calculate the similarity scores of those top-appeared candidate images (i.e., 1000). Finally, we remove non-salient VWs. By this way, we can reduce a large amount of computational time.

Moreover, we consider not only the visual constraint but also the GPS information in the retrieval process. We can directly modify the aforementioned steps to achieve this goal. In the second step of the retrieval process, similarity calculation is only applied in those candidate images within a predefined threshold from the query image, which are top-appeared images and GPS closed images. Note that the retrieval process can be achieved by utilizing inverted indexing structure without any further re-ranking process.

2.2 Combination of Street-View Images and User-Contributed Photos

Due to the large amount of buildings in a city, the difficulty of constructing an efficient retrieval system receives more attention. [1] proposed to identify buildings from street-view images. With the help of GPS information, the recall rate can achieve 65%. However, photos taken by users may contain different situations such as various lighting conditions as shown in Figure 1. As a result, visual appearances of mobile queries may be very different from street-view images which almost collected under similar conditions.

Although there are different kinds of visual appearances in the target building, we can utilize user-contributed photos from social media such as Flickr. We observe that street-view images contain different angles of the target whereas user-contributed photos contain different lighting conditions. The most intuitive way is to directly combine street-view images with user-contributed photos to construct a more diverse and large image database and further improve the search quality.

However, the combination of two databases will increase the memory and search time in the retrieval process. We attempt to retain informative VWs for database images. The main idea is to enhance the diversity of street-view images from user-contributed photos. We first associate two database images by their GPS information. We assume the closest GPS image can roughly estimate that the user-contributed image belongs to which street-view image (building), and we share VWs from user-contributed images to the closest street-view image. Based on our experiment (Section 4.1 and Table 1), it shows that we will have 25% probability to correctly estimate the target.

To mitigate the effect of incorrect images or VWs, we will select the most informative VWs from each image. We found that most of buildings contain repeated patterns such as similar windows. Therefore, we only retain those VWs with high frequency. Besides, the same buildings in different street-view images are partially similar to each other because they are taken under similar conditions. Hence, we first find similar street-view images (assuming the same building) which have similar visual appearances and GPS locations. Then we select those high frequency VWs based on those similar images.

3. EXPERIMENTAL SETUP

3.1 Dataset

In this paper, we combine street-view and user-contributed images as our dataset. For the street-view images, we use San Francisco (SF) dataset which is provided by [1]. The dataset was generated from 150K panoramic images of San Francisco and consisted of 14K buildings. Overall, the database contains more than 1.7 million images with precise ground truth labels and geotags. Note that we only use the perspective central images (PCIs) as our SF dataset (around one million images). For the user-contributed images, our data are collected from Flickr which is located at San Francisco (around one million images). Besides, [1] also provides 803 query images which are taken by cell phone to process city-scale landmark recognition.

3.2 Visual Feature

We applied two visual features: (1) visual words and (2) vector of locally aggregated descriptors (VLAD) [4]. Our retrieval system adopts the scale-invariant feature transform (SIFT) descriptor to capture local information and the BoW model to conduct the object matching.

The SIFT descriptors are quantized to VWs such that the well-developed indexing techniques in the text domain can be directly applied. The learned VW vocabulary directly affects the image object retrieval performance. We used one million VWs vocabulary which is suggested by [9] and further adopt hierarchical k-means (HKM) [7] to achieve efficient quantization. The similarity scores are calculated by the histogram intersection (i.e., L1 distance).

The VLAD feature [4] aggregates descriptors based on a locality criterion in feature space. For VLAD, first we learned the codebook $\mathcal{C} = \{c_1, ..., c_k\}$ of k VWs with HKM. Each feature vector x is associated to the nearest c_i VW. Thus, the VLAD is to accumulate, for each VW c_i, the differences of the vector x assigned to c_i (i.e., $x - c_i$). This characterizes the distribution of the vectors with respect to the center. Assuming the local descriptor to be d-dimensional, the dimension D of our representation is $D = k*d$. Following [4], we set $k = 64$ and use SIFT descriptor (i.e., $d = 128$) to generate VLAD feature with 8,192 dimensions. We choose L2 distance in the retrieval process.

3.3 Evaluation

Because all the SF database images are associated with one unique building ID, we can evaluate the retrieval accuracy. However, in reality, we do not know the exact building ID for each image so that we cannot calculate the total number of images related to this building. Therefore, we only evaluate recall at N (R@N) and precision at N (P@N) without providing mean average precision which is usually used in an image retrieval system. Since some query images have more than one correct building ID, we need to retrieval all correct building IDs (rather than images) to make the recall equal to one.

4. EXPERIMENTS AND DISCUSSIONS

4.1 The Impact of Different Features

We first show the fusion results by different features. As shown in Table 1, if we retrieve images by the GPS information, we can achieve a 0.252 precision (P@1), which means that building recognition systems highly rely on GPS information.[1] Based on the GPS ranking results, we can re-rank images by visual feature (i.e., GPS + R by VLAD, GPS + R by VW). For a real-time and scalable retrieval system, we do not adopt the geometry verification in our system. Although it may result in better retrieval results, it requires an additional query time and storage of those feature information, which is not affordable to a large-scale dataset.

Table 1: Comparison in retrieval accuracy of different features on San Francisco dataset. It shows that we can achieve the best result if we apply both visual and GPS constraints at the same time. 'R' represents re-ranking process.

	R@1	R@10	P@1	P@10
GPS	0.212	0.482	0.252	0.261
GPS + R by VLAD	0.329	0.513	0.384	0.355
GPS + R by VW	0.496	0.650	0.594	0.535
VW	0.272	0.387	0.324	0.236
VW + R by GPS	0.393	0.614	0.452	0.411
VW + GPS < 0.001	0.507	**0.657**	0.524	0.452

Adopting the state-of-the-art image representation (VW), we can get a 0.387 recall rate at 10. To further consider the GPS information (VW + R by GPS), we can have great improvement on recall rate. Those visually similar images with similar GPS information will have a higher probability to be the same building; hence, we can achieve a 0.614 recall rate. It is interesting that the recall rate and precision of the "VW + R by GPS" are slightly lower than those of the "GPS + R by VW." This phenomena is understandable because visually similar images may appear in different locations.

To further reduce the post-processing time, we consider both visual and GPS constraints in the retrieval process as mentioned in Section 2.1. The result shows in the bottom row of Table 1. We can achieve the best retrieval performance in 384 milliseconds (ms).[2] Moreover, we adopt index compression in inverted indexing so that we only need around 4G memory. We conduct another experiment on different thresholds of GPS constraint and find out that 0.001 (around 100 meter) has the best result. In a more careful examination, we found that some queries only retrieve a few (or zero) search results. It means that if the GPS information is not correctly labeled, then we may fail to retrieve related images unless we relax the constraint. It is also noticeable that the recall rate is similar to that in [1]. However, our method does not need to perform a geometry verification step, and considers only one kind of street-view images without extra efforts.

4.2 The Effect of User-Contributed Photos

In Table 2, we evaluate the effect of combining street-view (SF) and user-contributed (Flickr) images. It is impossible to label all the user-contributed photos. We assumed that the closest GPS image of San Francisco database will share the same building ID so that we can evaluate the retrieval

[1]Some query images have more than one ground truth building ID so that P@1 is not equal to R@1.

[2]The retrieval time does not include feature extraction. We evaluate on a Linux machine with C implementation.

Table 2: **Results for recall and precision by integrating user-contributed (Flickr) and San Francisco (SF) images. Because most of query images are taken under similar conditions, the result is still dominated by street-view images which can provide different angles of buildings. '*' denotes the results estimated by the closest street-view image which is associated with a building ID. Note that we adopt the same constraint for all methods (VW + GPS).**

	R@1	R@10	P@1	P@10
Flickr only*	0.165	0.382	0.184	0.161
SF + Flickr*	0.419	0.642	0.488	0.466
SF + Flickr	0.472	0.643	0.564	0.464
SF (shared VWs)	0.235	0.600	0.187	0.296
SF (selected VWs)	0.322	0.592	0.293	0.323

results, and the results are marked with a star label (i.e., Flickr only*, SF + Flickr*). Besides, we also manually labeled the results of "SF + Flickr." As shown in Table 2, the retrieval accuracy is similar to that of manual labeling. The combination of both datasets has similar results compared with using only one database (SF). This is mainly because street-view images contain multi-views of buildings whereas user-contributed photos usually contain some famous landmarks and lack all possible buildings. Most of the query images have similar lighting conditions (i.e., daytime); therefore, the retrieval results are still dominated by street-view images and the retrieval accuracy is similar. Hence, when we directly share VWs according to the closest GPS image, it will cause more noisy and incorrect VWs in SF database so that the result of "SF (shared VWs)" becomes worse. Although we further select those high frequency VWs (selected VWs), it only has small help to improve precision.

In reality, users may query different kinds of photos with different lighting conditions. We evaluated the effect on these cases and found under this situation the combination of both database images can provide better results as shown in Figure 2. The first two query results show that the lack of different visual appearances (upper results above the dotted line). The user-contributed photos will have a great help in these cases. In the bottom query result, because the query image is a little far from the target object, the original street-view images will only return near-by images. However, user-contributed photos can provide similar results. In summary, the street-view images can provide different angles of buildings whereas the user-contributed photos support more diverse photos of buildings. The results convince that both street-view and user-contributed images are very important for the retrieval system.

5. CONCLUSIONS AND FUTURE WORK

With popularization of the mobile devices, image-based landmark retrieval or recognition is becoming an important problem. When a user uploads the image, he/she wants to know where he/she is and more other information about the location. In this work, we use city-scale image database of San Francisco to find the buildings and landmarks. One of our main contribution in this work is providing preliminary experiments for combining street-view and user-contributed

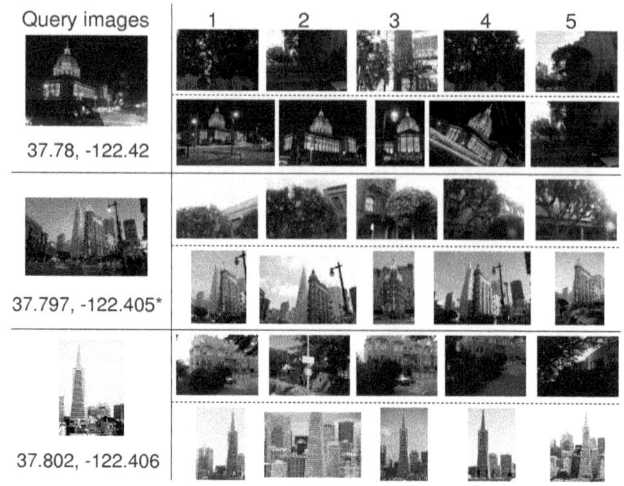

Figure 2: The search results of extra query images from Flickr. The results from the original San Francisco (street-view) dataset are shown above the dotted line. The other results are retrieved through both the San Francisco dataset and user-contributed images from Flickr. It shows that with the help of user-contributed images we can have better search results. The number below the query images are the GPS location, and the one with star mark (*) represents it is an estimated GPS.

photos. Moreover, we combine visual and GPS constraints in inverted indexing structure to achieve a 65.7% of the recall rate while the retrieval process only takes 384ms. In the future, we desire to find a better way to combine street-view and user-contributed photos and unify both characteristics to enhance the retrieval results.

6. REFERENCES

[1] D. Chen et al. City-scale landmark identification on mobile devices. In *I CV*, 2011.

[2] A.-J. Cheng et al. GPS, compass, or camera?: investigating effective mobile sensors for automatic search-based image annotation. In *ACM MM*, 2010.

[3] J. Hays et al. IM2GPS: estimating geographic information from a single image. In *CV*, 2008.

[4] H. Jégou et al. Aggregating local descriptors into a compact image representation. In *I CV*, 2010.

[5] J. Knopp et al. Avoding confusing features in place recognition. In *CCV*, 2010.

[6] J. Luo et al. Geotagging in multimedia and computer vision–a survey. *M A*, 2011.

[7] D. Nistér et al. Scalable recognition with a vocabulary tree. In *I CV*, 2006.

[8] M. Park et al. Beyond GPS: determining the camera viewing direction of a geotagged image. In *MM*, 2010.

[9] J. Philbin et al. Object retrieval with large vocabularies and fast spatial matching. In *CV*, 2007.

[10] J. Sivic et al. Video Google: A text retrieval approach to object matching in videos. In *ICCV*, 2003.

[11] J. Zobel et al. Inverted files for text search engines. *ACM Computing Surveys*, 2006.

OpenIMAJ and ImageTerrier: Java Libraries and Tools for Scalable Multimedia Analysis and Indexing of Images

Jonathon S. Hare
jsh2@ecs.soton.ac.uk

Sina Samangooei
ss@ecs.soton.ac.uk

David P. Dupplaw
dpd@ecs.soton.ac.uk

Electronics and Computer Science, University of Southampton
Southampton, United Kingdom

ABSTRACT

OpenIMAJ and ImageTerrier are recently released open-source libraries and tools for experimentation and development of multimedia applications using Java-compatible programming languages. OpenIMAJ (the Open toolkit for Intelligent Multimedia Analysis in Java) is a collection of libraries for multimedia analysis. The image libraries contain methods for processing images and extracting state-of-the-art features, including SIFT. The video and audio libraries support both cross-platform capture and processing. The clustering and nearest-neighbour libraries contain efficient, multi-threaded implementations of clustering algorithms. The clustering library makes it possible to easily create BoVW representations for images and videos. OpenIMAJ also incorporates a number of tools to enable extremely-large-scale multimedia analysis using distributed computing with Apache Hadoop.

ImageTerrier is a scalable, high-performance search engine platform for content-based image retrieval applications using features extracted with the OpenIMAJ library and tools. The ImageTerrier platform provides a comprehensive test-bed for experimenting with image retrieval techniques. The platform incorporates a state-of-the-art implementation of the single-pass indexing technique for constructing inverted indexes and is capable of producing highly compressed index data structures.

Categories and Subject Descriptors

D.2.13 [**Software Engineering**]: Reusable Software; I.4.0 [**Image Processing and Computer Vision**]: General; I.5.0 [**Pattern Recognition**]: General; H.3.3 [**Information Storage and Retrieval**]: Information Search and Retrieval; H.3.1 [**Information Storage and Retrieval**]: Content Analysis and Indexing

General Terms

Algorithms, Design, Experimentation

1. INTRODUCTION

OpenIMAJ and ImageTerrier are recently released, twinned open-source projects that contain software libraries and tools for experimenting with and developing multimedia analysis, classification and retrieval software. Whilst the codebase has only recently been publicly released, it is quite mature, having been under active development since around 2005 internally in the University of Southampton.

The OpenIMAJ project contains a number of tools and libraries for everything from state-of-the-art computer vision (i.e. SIFT descriptors [1] and salient region detection, face detection, etc.) and advanced data clustering, through to software that performs analysis on the layout and structure of web-pages. The ImageTerrier project implements a highly-scalable architecture for building and searching inverted-indexes of 'visual terms' extracted from images.

The majority[1] of the OpenIMAJ codebase has been released under the New BSD license which makes it freely available to both academic and commercial users. The ImageTerrier project is released under the same licensing terms as the Terrier project on which it is built — namely the Mozilla Public License. This license also allows both academic and commercial use of the code.

2. DESIGN AND PERFORMANCE

OpenIMAJ and ImageTerrier are primarily written in pure Java and, as such are completely platform independent. The video-capture and hardware libraries contain some native code but Linux, OSX and Windows are supported out of the box (under both 32 and 64 bit JVMs). It is possible to write programs that use the libraries in any JVM language that supports Java interoperability, for example Groovy[2 3]. OpenIMAJ can even be run on Android phones and tablets[4].

One of the main goals in the design and implementation of the two projects was to keep all components as modular as possible. For example, the OpenIMAJ difference-of-Gaussian SIFT implementation allows different parts of the algorithm to be replaced or modified at will. Implementations of commonly used algorithms are also made as generic as possible; for example, the OpenIMAJ RANSAC implementation works with generic `Model` objects and doesn't care

[1] Two non-core sub-projects have slightly different licensing conditions as they were originally derived from other open-source code, however all the licenses are business-friendly.
[2] Groovy: `http://groovy.codehaus.org`
[3] Groovy and OpenIMAJ: `http://bit.ly/OIMJGROOVY`
[4] Android and OpenIMAJ: `http://bit.ly/OIMJAND`

`openimaj`

- `core` — Submodule for modules containing functionality used across the library.
  - `core` — Core library functionality concerned with general programming problems rather than multimedia specific functionality. Includes I/O utilities, randomisation, hashing and type conversion.
  - `feature` — Core notion of features, usually denoted as arrays of data. Definitions of features for all primitive types, features with location and lists of features (both in memory and on disk).
  - `audio` — Core definitions of audio streams and samples/chunks. Also contains interfaces for processors for these basic types.
  - `image` — Core definitions of images, pixels and connected components. Also contains interfaces for processors for these basic types.
  - `video` — Core definitions of a video type, and functionality for displaying videos.
  - `video-capture` — Cross-platform video capture interface using a lightweight native interface. Supports 32 and 64 bit JVMs under Linux, OSX and Windows.
  - `math` — Mathematical implementations including geometric, matrix and statistical operators.
- `audio` — Submodule for audio related functionality.
  - `processing` — Implementations of various audio processors (e.g. multichannel conversion, volume change, ...).
- `image` — Submodule for image related functionality.
  - `processing` — Implementations of various image, pixel and connected component processors (resizing, convolution, edge detection, ...).
  - `feature-extraction` — Methods for the extraction of low-level image features, including global image features and pixel/patch classification models.
  - `local-features` — Methods for the extraction of local features. Local features are descriptions of regions of images (SIFT, ...) selected by detectors (Difference of Gaussian, Harris, ...).
  - `faces` — Implementation of a flexible face-recognition pipeline, including pluggable detectors, aligners, feature extractors and recognisers.
- `machine-learning` — Algorithms which aid the classification and search of data.
  - `nearest-neighbour` — Brute force and KD-Tree implementations of exact and approximate KNN.
  - `clustering` — Various clustering algorithm implementations for all primitive types including random, random forest [2], K-Means (Exact, Hierarchical [3] and Approximate [5]), ...
- `hadoop` — Extensions to enable interaction with the Apache Hadoop Map-Reduce implementation.
  - `core-hadoop` — Reusable wrappers to access and create sequence-files and map-reduce jobs.
- `hardware` — Various interfaces to hardware devices that we've used in projects built using OpenIMAJ.
  - `serial` — Interface to hardware devices that connect to serial or USB-serial ports.
  - `gps` — Interface to GPS devices that support the NMEA protocol.
  - `compass` — Interface to an OceanServer OS5000 digital compass.
- `web` — Support for analysing and processing web-pages.
  - `core-web` — Implementation of a programatic offscreen web browser and utility functions.
  - `analysis` — Utilities for analysing the content and visual layout of a web-page.

Figure 1: OpenIMAJ Library Modules as of July 2011

whether the specific model implementation is attempting to fit a homography to a set of point-pair matches or a straight line to samples in a space. ImageTerrier is equally as modular, and for example, it is possible to easily drop in different scoring implementations into the search engine.

The speed of individual algorithms in OpenIMAJ has not been a major development focus, however some decisions have been made during implementation to ensure efficiency (for example making fields public rather than using getters and setters). In order to give the reader some idea of the real-world performance of our Java code, we have compared the time taken to process an image by our SIFT implementation to Lowe's keypoint binary. For our test image, it takes 3.47 seconds to extract the features with Lowe's binary (averaged over 100 tests). If we count the time taken using our implementation and include the time taken to start the JVM, then we get times of around 10 seconds. However, if we discount the time to start the JVM, the averaged time over 100 iterations is just 3.94 seconds, which is agreeably close to the native version. See the OpenIMAJ wiki for a demo showing near-realtime SIFT extraction and matching in pure Java using OpenIMAJ[5]. Whilst the actual algorithm speed has not been a particular design focus, scalability of the algorithms to massive datasets has. Using the OpenIMAJ Hadoop tools on our small three-machine Hadoop cluster, we have extracted visual term features from datasets with sizes in excess of 10 million images. The OpenIMAJ clustering implementations are able to cluster larger-than-memory datasets by reading data from disk as necessary.

ImageTerrier is designed to be fast during searching and memory-efficient during indexing. The fundamental limit on ImageTerrier is the rate at which the inverted index can be accessed from disk. ImageTerrier uses heavy index compression to make the index smaller and thus faster to access. Experiments have shown that an ImageTerrier index of 1 million medium resolution images indexed with difference-of-Gaussian SIFT visual terms (with a one million term vocabulary) can be searched in under 400 milliseconds on a regular PC (i.e. Intel Core 2, 4GB ram, 7200 RPM disk).

[5] `http://bit.ly/OIMJVSIF`

3. OPENIMAJ

The OpenIMAJ library is structured into a number of modules. The modules can be used independently, so if for instance you were developing data clustering software using OpenIMAJ you wouldn't need the modules related to images. Figure 1 describes the modules and summarises the functionality in each component.

3.1 Tools

OpenIMAJ exposes key functionality through a set of a command-line tools. This allows more casual users to test the abilities of the library more easily as well as allowing use of OpenIMAJ in non-java projects. The main tools currently provided are outlined below.

GlobalFeatureTool. Allows extraction of low-level global features from images. For example: colourfulness, sharpness, number of faces and average brightness. Also allows comparison of extracted features.

LocalFeatureTool. Allows extraction of local features using internal implementations of various detectors and descriptors.

ClusterQuantiserTool. Provides methods for both creation and usage of clusters. Various kinds of clusters can be trained on various data sources and data sources can also be quantised using clusters. Currently random, random forest, RAC and KMeans (exact, approximate and hierarchical) clusters are supported. This tool can be used to create visual-term representations of images through SIFT features extracted with the LocalFeatureTool.

FlickrCrawler. A set of tools for the targeted downloading of images from Flickr in order to create experimental datasets.

3.2 Hadoop

OpenIMAJ was written with scalability in mind. Using the Hadoop framework a series of tools were written which implemented existing OpenIMAJ functionality as map-reduce tasks. This allows for scalability to large datasets limited only by the size of the Hadoop cluster. Together these tools form a tool chain which allows for the end to end construction of efficiently searchable indexes from images in a scalable way.

SequenceFileTool. Allows the easy creation, examination and extraction of Hadoop sequence-files. Sequence-files are a form of archive file containing many smaller files, used by the Hadoop framework. The tool may be used to construct a sequence-file containing a large number of images as a precursor step to extracting image features.

HadoopClusterQuantiserTool. Multithreaded map-reduce implementation of vector quantisation. Given an existing quantiser definition (usually created by the ClusterQuantiserTool), compute nodes read the quantiser into RAM and quantise data points in parallel.

HadoopFastKMeans. Iterative map-reduce implementation of the exact and approximate K-Means algorithms.

HadoopGlobalFeaturesTool and HadoopLocalFeaturesTool. Distributed feature extraction from large volumes of images.

HadoopImageDownload. Given a file containing a large number of URLs, download a the images in parallel. Used to download all the images from image-net for example.

SequenceFileIndexer. Construct ImageTerrier indexes using sequence-files as the source.

4. IMAGETERRIER

ImageTerrier is a platform for building efficient inverted indexes of visual-term information extracted from images. ImageTerrier is an extension of the Terrier text search platform [4]. ImageTerrier is capable of building compressed augmented inverted indexes using the highly efficient, state of the art, single-pass indexing technique. The index format supports term payloads which allows the optional specification of a given visual term's geometric information, such as a SIFT visual term's position, orientation and scale. The payload information is easily accessed when the index is being searched. ImageTerrier contains implementations of a number of geometric consistency algorithms that make use of this information in order to improve search precision. ImageTerrier is easily extended and it is possible to have complete control over both the payloads that get placed in the index and the operations involved in retrieval from the index.

4.1 Tools

ImageTerrier currently has two complete tools which wrap the entire process of building and querying an image database:

BasicIndexer. Generation of searchable inverted indexes from a directory of images. Allows specification of feature extraction, codebook generation and index options. The image-specific operations use the OpenIMAJ library.

BasicSearcher. Allows both one off and interactive querying of an index using images. Allows for the specification of searching scheme and consistency measures.

5. USAGE EXAMPLES

The tools implemented in OpenIMAJ and ImageTerrier and their applications are many; the reader is encouraged to experiment with the codebase and follow some of the many demos available on the websites[6]. In this section we attempt to give a taste of the capabilities of the two projects by showing two self contained examples, demonstrating some of the capabilities.

5.1 Example 1: Detecting interest points in an image

For OpenIMAJ we present a code example using the JVM language Groovy. Using Groovy's dynamic remote library loading technology, these demos can be directly copied into the `groovyConsole` and run without the need for OpenIMAJ installation. In Figure 2 we show an example of the capabilities of the OpenIMAJ library. In the example an image is loaded and converted to greyscale. At this point a few of the available interest point detectors are initiated and used to detect interest points in the greyscale version of the loaded image. Once detected, the interest points are drawn on the original colour image using the drawing functionality and finally the detected interest points are displayed.

5.2 Example 2: Building and searching an ImageTerrier Index

The ImageTerrier project comes with tools which use OpenIMAJ to allow the generation of a searchable index of image content from a directory of images. This includes extraction of image features, generation of a visual codebook, quantisation of image features and construction of an ImageTerrier index. Each of these stages supports a plethora of options,

[6] `http://openimaj.org` and `http://imageterrier.org`

```
@GrabResolver(name='octopussy-releases', root='http://octopussy.ecs.soton.ac.uk/m2/releases/')
@Grab('org.openimaj:core-image:1.0')
@Grab('org.openimaj:image-local-features:1.0')
import org.openimaj.io.*
import org.openimaj.image.*
import org.openimaj.image.colour.*
import org.openimaj.math.geometry.shape.*
import org.openimaj.image.feature.local.interest.*

img = ImageUtilities.readMBF(getClass().getResource("/org/openimaj/OpenIMAJ.png")) //Load an image
gimg = Transforms.calculateIntensityNTSC(img) //make a grey version
float intScale = 2.5f; float diffScale = 0.6f * intScale; //set the scales (std.dev of Gaussian)
float intScaleVar = intScale**2; float diffScaleVar = diffScale**2; //calculate the variance
ipds = [ //set up a list of detectors
    [ipd: new HarrisIPD(diffScaleVar, intScaleVar), colour:RGBColour.RED],
    [ipd: new HessianIPD(diffScaleVar, intScaleVar), colour:RGBColour.MAGENTA],
    [ipd: new LaplaceIPD(diffScaleVar, intScaleVar), colour:RGBColour.GREEN],
]
ipds.each{rec -> //loop through detectors and draw 100 best points found
    rec.ipd.findInterestPoints(gimg)
    img.drawPoints(rec.ipd.getInterestPoints(100), rec.colour, 3)
}
DisplayUtilities.display(img)//display the result
```

Figure 2: Interest point detectors working in OpenIMAJ

```
$> cat highfield.config
crawler {
    apikey="<key>",secret="<secret>"
    outputdir="highfield"
    queryparams {woeId="43761"}
    images {targetSize=["large", "original", "medium"]}
}
$> groovy FlickrCrawler.groovy highfield.config
$> BasicIndexer -o idx -qt RANDOM -k 100000 highfield
$> BasicSearcher -i idx -q query.jpg -dr
```

Figure 3: Example settings for the FlickrCrawler tool, highfield.config and the tools useage

here we present a basic example. Firstly, an image collection can be downloaded using the provided FlickrCrawler tool in OpenIMAJ. This tool is called using the command in Figure 3 which references a configuration file also shown in Figure 3. This configuration file supports various features including the specification of a Flickr query against which images are downloaded[7]. In this case we download images geo-tagged with coordinates with a specific Flickr Where On Earth ID (woe_id), which in the example is the id for Highfield, the location of the University of Southampton's main campus in the United Kingdom.

Once an appropriate directory of images is collected the indexer tool can be applied. This tool allows specification of: extracted feature type, generated codebook type and various ImageTerrier index options. In the example in Figure 3 we generate the default SIFT features and specify that a Random codebook of size 100000 be generated using all extracted features as training samples. Using the codebook, the features are quantised and used to construct an index. The image set is now searchable.

Once the index and codebook are generated the directory of images is now searchable. The `BasicSearcher` tool can be used to search indexes with images. The tool provides a useful command line interface for multiple queries, but in the example shown in Figure 3 a single query image is used. Elaborations and example query results using these tools can be found on the ImageTerrier Wiki[8]

[7] `http://bit.ly/OIMJFCR`

[8] `http://bit.ly/ITEREXMP`

6. APPLICATIONS IN EDUCATION

The codebase that makes up the core of OpenIMAJ has been used by undergraduate student projects in Southampton for around the last 5 years. Students have used the library in a range of projects, from performing road-sign recognition using local features through to experimenting with K-nearest-neighbour classification of city/landscape scenes using KD-Tree data-structures with large image collections crawled from Flickr. With the software now open-sourced, we expect that our future students will help contribute to the codebase in the coming years.

7. ACKNOWLEDGMENTS

Current development of the OpenIMAJ and ImageTerrier software is funded by the European Union Seventh Framework Programme (FP7/2007-2013) under grant agreement n° 270239 (ARCOMEM) and 231126 (LivingKnowledge) together with the LiveMemories project, graciously funded by the Autonomous Province of Trento (Italy). We are also grateful to the Arts and Humanities Research Council ('Bridging the Semantic Gap' - MRG-AN6770/APN17429) and Ordnance Survey, for earlier funding under which a number of the older OpenIMAJ classes were created.

References

[1] D. Lowe. Distinctive image features from scale-invariant keypoints. *IJCV*, 60(2):91–110, January 2004.

[2] F. Moosmann, E. Nowak, and F. Jurie. Randomized clustering forests for image classification. *IEEE PAMI*, 2008.

[3] D. Nistér and H. Stewénius. Scalable recognition with a vocabulary tree. In *CVPR*, pages 2161–2168, 2006.

[4] I. Ounis, G. Amati, V. Plachouras, B. He, C. Macdonald, and C. Lioma. Terrier: A High Performance and Scalable Information Retrieval Platform. In *Proc SIGIR*, 2006.

[5] J. Philbin, O. Chum, M. Isard, J. Sivic, and A. Zisserman. Object retrieval with large vocabularies and fast spatial matching. In *CVPR*, 2007.

From Images to 3D Models Made Easy

Isaac Esteban
TNO - University of Amsterdam
The Hague - Amsterdam, The Netherlands
isaac@nincompoop.es

Judith Dijk
TNO
The Hague, The Netherlands
judith.dijk@tno.nl

Frans Groen
University of Amsterdam
Science Park
Amsterdam, The Netherlands
f.c.a.groen@uva.nl

ABSTRACT

FIT3D is a Toolbox built for Matlab that aims at unifying and distributing a set of tools that will allow the researcher to obtain a complete 3D model from a set of calibrated images. In this paper we motivate and present the structure of the toolbox in a tutorial and example based approach. Given its flexibility and scope we believe that FIT3D represents an exciting opportunity for researchers that want to develop or test one particular method with real data without the need for extensive additional programming.

Categories and Subject Descriptors

I.2.10 [**Vision and Scene Understanding**]: Visions

General Terms

Algorithms, Standarization

Keywords

3d modeling, matlab, reconstruction, structure from motion, vision

1. INTRODUCTION

The process of reconstructing the scene depicted by a set of images is usually called Structure from Motion [2] (SFM). SFM does not rely on unnatural artifacts or markers, rather it makes use of the geometry of the camera and the scene itself in order to reconstruct the imaged world. However, the number of steps required to obtain a full 3D model and the complexity and method variety in each of those steps enforces a disjoint field. There are many publications and variations of methodologies that aim at solving a certain aspect of the process of reconstructing a scene. We characterize the complete process in 5 steps: *camera calibration*, *motion estimation*, *optimization*, *reconstruction* and *modeling*.

MM'11, November 28–December 1, 2011, Scottsdale, Arizona, USA.

Each step is a subfield in its own, which together with the complexity of the problem translates into a lack of unification and integration of the literature and more importantly of the available tools. This lack of global framework makes very difficult for researches to develop and test their specific techniques in a global context. For this reason we present the FIT3D Toolbox that aims at bridging the gap between the five independent subfields, providing a unifying framework. FIT3D is a highly flexible Toolbox built for Matlab. The functionality provided is either based on well founded research or exciting and promising novel approaches. A more comprehensible overview of the process is found in [4]. The toolbox consist of a large number of independent Matlab functions written in an educative and clear fashion and contain a large amount of inline comments. References to the original methods are provided within the code. In our spirit of integration and distribution, we provide example scripts and data sets for every of the five steps as well as the integration with related projects.

Section II relates and compares FIT3D to similar frameworks. The integration with related packages is also presented. In Section III we discuss in more detail each of the five steps of the FIT3D pipeline along with the conventions and definitions. In section IV we present some fo the results obtained with FIT3D in our daily research work. Finally in Section V we draw some conclusions and point out future work.

FIT3D is freely available for academics and university researchers at www.fit3d.info along with data sets and example scripts.

2. RELATED WORK

In recent years the literature on 3D reconstruction of a scene recorded in images has grown considerably. Along with this growth, a number of tools or software packages have been made available to the research community, and in some cases, to the general public. However, these packages are either very specific to the task at hand or are enclosed in a format that makes integration with novel techniques virtually impossible.

Photo Tourism is one of the most well known programs available. It provides a sparse 3D reconstruction from a set of unordered images of the same scene. The techniques used for estimating the relative motion between the images are well known and are also available in a more scientific package called Bundler [12]. Bundler is built in C++ for efficiency and it takes a collection of images, image features and image matches as input and produces a sparse 3D pointcloud. The optimization step is performed with a modified version of the Sparse Bundle Adjustment of Lourakis and Argyros [9]. FIT3D presents a number of advantages using novel motion estimation techniques and refinement procedures. It also provides a complete system where an ordered set of images needs to be provided and a complete model is obtained. Additionally, FIT3D is built as a set of independent functions and example scripts in Matlab, which makes the integration with novel techniques an easy task.

Hartley and Zisserman [7] is one of the most relevant references in the field of multiple view geometry and SFM. With the second edition they provide some Matlab code to perform a number of operations. However the number of functions is very limited with a scarce amount of inline comments and only a handful of example scripts. No full 3D models can be obtained from the raw material they provide. FIT3D is similar to these in that the functions perform very specific tasks and are coded in Matlab. FIT3D however is different in that we provide a larger amount of functions with more comprehensive inline comments and references. Data sets and example scripts are also provided.

Peter Kovesi [8] provides a number of Matlab functions for both image processing, multiple view geometry and model fitting. The inline code provided by Kovesi is very generous in the input/output/example but somewhat short in some of the inner workings of the functions. No examples scripts are provided. FIT3D overlaps with Kovesi's work in the area of model fitting and projective geometry. FIT3D extends Kovesi's work in that it is focussed on the full process of 3D reconstruction and provides full examples on the use of the Toolbox.

With respect to the integration to other packages, FIT3D is fully compatible with the Camera Calibration Toolbox of Bouguet [1]. We also provide integration with the SIFT implementation provided by Lowe [10] and the open source VLFeat [13], the 5-point algorithm from Nister [11] available online and provide interface tools for PMVS2 [6].

3. THE 3D RECONSTRUCTION PIPELINE

In this section we briefly describe each of the steps in the 3D modeling pipeline that is used and implemented in FIT3D (see Figure 1). A more complete article can be found in [3]. We divide the steps in two mayor blocks. The first one comprises the methods and techniques required to obtain an accurate and consistent estimation of the relative position between the consecutive images. The second entitles the required techniques for obtaining the final 3D model.

- **Calibration:** calibration is the process of obtaining the information, intrinsic parameters, that describes the camera. This includes parameters for radial distortion, focal length, skew parameters and center of projection.
- **Egomotion:** is the process of estimating the motion of the camera between frames based on the information that is depicted in the images (extrinsic parameters). In our work we only consider motion estimation between consecutive frames.
- **Refinement:** given that the images are recorded with noise and this noise is propagated to the motion estimation, an optimization step is desirable when computationally feasible in order to improve the estimates.

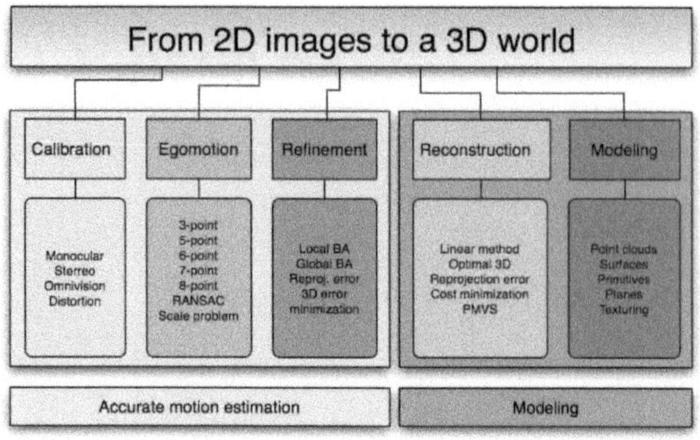

Figure 1: 3D modeling pipeline. Some well known alternatives for each step are pointed out.

- **Reconstruction:** given a set of camera positions, calibration parameters and recorded images, reconstruction is the process of obtaining the 3D representation of the scene as a set of 3D points.
- **Modeling:** it is desirable and sometimes necessary to obtain an economical description of the scene. Modeling is the process of converting a sparse 3D point cloud into a set of higher order primitives such as planes, surfaces or pre-calculated models.

4. RESULTS AND EXAMPLES

In this section we depict some examples of the use of FIT3D. We apply different functions for solving problems in camera motion estimation (homography and projective camera), triangulation and point cloud calculation and texture and modeling for the final 3D model.

Additionally, we present at the end of the section some larger 3D models obtained with FIT3D for urban areas.

4.1 Stitch two images using an Homography

The `stitchPano` function will stitch two images by selecting corresponding SIFT features and calculating the homography.

```
■ [panoramic,H] = stitchImages('ind1.jpg','ind2.jpg',0.4);
■ imshow(panoramic);
```

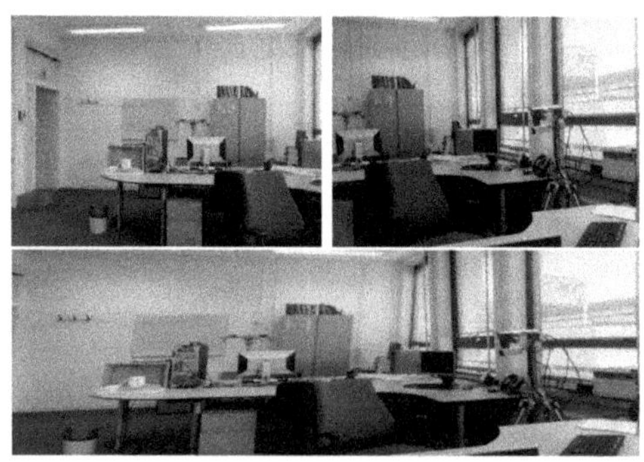

Figure 2: TOP: two input images. BOTTOM: stitched images.

4.2 8-point algorithm motion estimation using RANSAC

We assume we have a set of matching features $X1$ in image 1 and $X2$ in image 2. We obtain the fundamental matrix using RANSAC, then obtain the 4 possible solutions for the camera motion and obtain the true solution using a voting system.

Figure 3: TOP: Three views of a street. BOTTOM: calculated camera trajectory.

- `[F,inliers] = ransacF(X1,X2,K);`
- `Pall = getCameraMatrix(F);`
- `X1i = X1(inliers,:);`
- `X2i = X2(inliers,:);`
- `P = getCorrectCameraMatrix(X1i,X2i);`

4.3 Calculate scale linearly

For this example, we have 3 estimated camera poses $P1$, $P2$ and $P3$ along with 3-frame image feature correspondences $X1$, $X2$ and $X3$. The first camera is at the origin ($P1 = [I|0]$) and the other to cameras were calculated on a frame-to-frame basis. We triangulate the image features between cameras $P1$ and $P2$, resulting in the set of space points $X3D$. The scale of the third camera is computed linearly using [5].

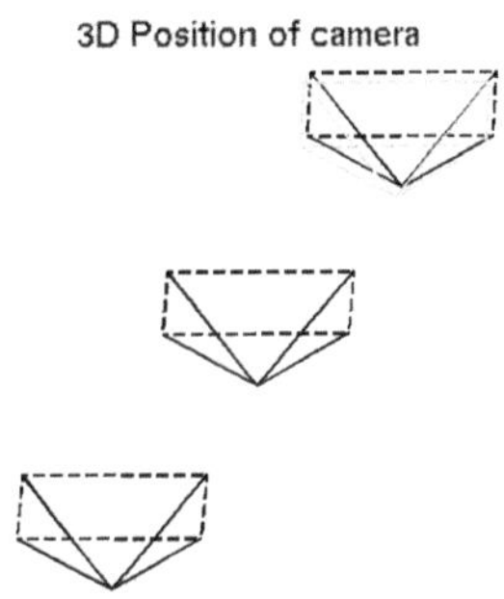

Figure 4: Black: camera before scale adjustment. Grey: camera after scale adjustment.

- `[x3d] = findTriangulationLM(X1, X2, P1, P2, K1, K2);`
- `[scale,P3scaled] = findScaleLinear(P3,x3d,X2,X3);`

4.4 Refine locally

In this example we iteratively refine the second camera pose and internal parameters to minimize the reprojection error in both the first and second camera. P1 is assumed to be at $[I|0]$.

- `[P2refined,K2refined] = bundleAdjust(P2,X1,X2,K2);`

4.5 Obtain 3D pointcloud

We use a linear triangulation method to obtain the set of 3D points corresponding to the selected image features.

- `[P2refined,K2refined] = findTriangulationLM(P2,X1,X2,K2);`

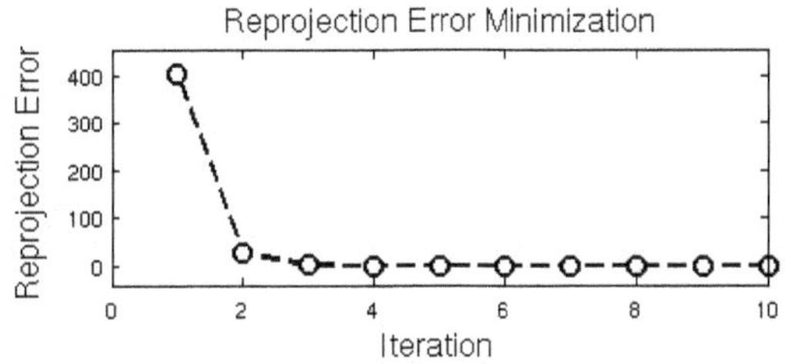

Figure 5: Reprojection error during local refinement.

4.6 Fit plane primitives

In this example we use the data set of the alley to find planar patches in the 3D point cloud (see Figure 6). Each planar patch is assigned a different color.

- `[planes] = fitPlanesRANSA( X3D, minPoints, maxPlanes, ransacThreshold, ransacIterations);`

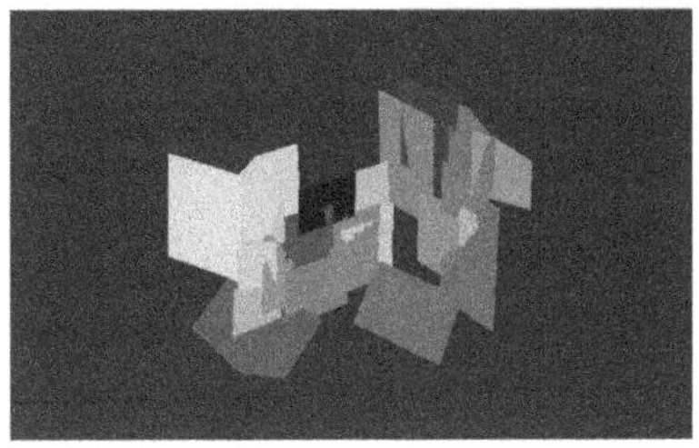

Figure 6: Colored planar patches.

4.7 Apply texture

Having obtained the set of planar patches, the most frontal view among the recorded images is used to reproject the texture (see Figure 7).

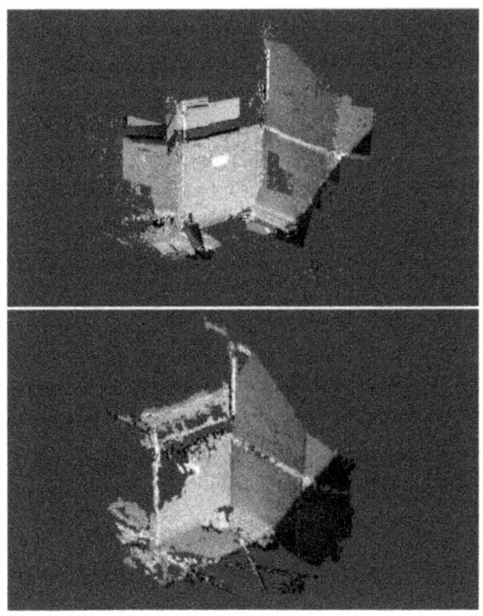

Figure 7: Top: Textured planar patches. Bottom: colored point cloud output using PMVS2.

4.8 Full 3D Models

Figures 8 and 9 show some larger scale 3D models. Figure 8 is reconstructed from the well known P11 Fountain dataset by EPFL. Figure 9 represents a fully form 3D reconstruction of an urban environment using planar textured patches.

5. CONCLUSION

Figure 8: 3D reconstruction obtained for the well known P11 dataset distributed by EPFL.

Figure 9: 3D model obtained for an urban area. No Bundle Adjustment was applied and only planar primitives used for modeling.

In this paper we have presented some of the functionality of our FIT3D Toolbox for 3D reconstruction from a set of ordered images. We believe that FIT3D fills a gap in the set of research tools that will help other scientist to develop and apply their methods and techniques in a more global context. FIT3D allows them to obtain a full 3D model with little effort in the integration. As compared to other relevant tools, FIT3D presents a set of novel approaches for both robust monocular visual motion estimation and refinement by point cloud distance minimization. Also, FIT3D is provided in an educative format where special care has been taken in building Matlab functions that are easy to use and understand. Along with the toolbox a set of example scripts and data sets are provided. In the future we plan to extend the Toolbox with error analysis methods and eliminate the constraint of ordered images using topological mapping techniques. An additional global interface can be added to allow a "one step" reconstruction approach where calibration and scene images are fed into the pipeline and a full 3D model is obtained.

Given the extent of FIT3D only a small portion of the functionality has been presented here. Additional functionality is provided for: mass feature extraction, feature matching, feature tracking, error measures, interfaces for PMVS2, motion sampling, simulators for ground truth generation and evaluation, and a long etcetera.

6. REFERENCES

[1] J. Bouguet. Camera calibration toolbox for matlab. http://www.vision.caltech.edu/bouguetj/.

[2] Frank Dellaert, Steven Seitz, Chuck Thorpe, and Sebastian Thrun. Structure from motion without correspondence. In *IEEE Computer Society Conference on Computer Vision and Pattern Recognition (CVPR'00)*, June 2000.

[3] I. Esteban, J. Dijk, and F.C.A. Groen. Fit3d toolbox: multiple view geometry and 3d reconstruction for matlab. In *International Symposium on Security and Defence Europe (SPIE)*, 2010.

[4] Isaac Esteban, Judith Dijk, and F.C.A. Groen. Automatic 3d reconstruction of the urban landscape. In *ICUMT*, 2010.

[5] Isaac Esteban, Leo Dorst, and Judith Dijk. Closed form solution for the scale ambiguity problem in monocular visual odometry. In *ICIRA*, 2010.

[6] Y. Furukawa and J. Ponce. Accurate, dense, and robust multi-view stereopsis. In *Computer Vision and Pattern Recognition, 2007. CVPR '07. IEEE Conference on*, pages 1–8, 2007.

[7] R. I. Hartley and A. Zisserman. *Multiple View Geometry in Computer Vision*. Cambridge University Press, ISBN: 0521623049, 2000.

[8] P. D. Kovesi. MATLAB and Octave functions for computer vision and image processing. School of Computer Science & Software Engineering, The University of Western Australia. Available from: <http://www.csse.uwa.edu.au/~pk/research/matlabfns

[9] M.I.A. Lourakis and A.A. Argyros. The design and implementation of a generic sparse bundle adjustment software package based on the levenberg-marquardt algorithm. Technical Report 340, Institute of Computer Science - FORTH, Heraklion, Crete, Greece, Aug. 2004. Available from `http://www.ics.forth.gr/~lourakis/sba`.

[10] D. Lowe. Distinctive image features from scale-invariant keypoints. In *Int. J. of Computer Vision*, 2004.

[11] D. Nister. An efficient solution to the five-point relative pose problem. In *CVPR*, 2003.

[12] Noah Snavely, Steven M. Seitz, and Richard Szeliski. Photo tourism: Exploring photo collections in 3d. In *SIGGRAPH Conference Proceedings*, pages 835–846, New York, NY, USA, 2006. ACM Press.

[13] A. Vedaldi. An open implementation of the SIFT detector and descriptor. Technical Report 070012, UCLA CSD, 2007.

Timesheets.js: Tools for Web Multimedia

Fabien Cazenave, Vincent Quint
INRIA
655 avenue de l'Europe
38334 Saint Ismier, France
{fabien.cazenave, vincent.quint}@inria.fr

Cécile Roisin
Grenoble University & INRIA
655 avenue de l'Europe
38334 Saint Ismier, France
cecile.roisin@inria.fr

ABSTRACT

Timesheets.js is a JavaScript library for publishing multimedia web documents that take advantage of the new features of HTML5 and CSS3. The library allows web developers to extend their skills to synchronized multimedia contents. This technology has been experimented in a class where students had to implement an XSLT transformation for converting OpenOffice Impress presentations into web formats. The resulting slideshows run in web browsers thanks to the timesheets.js library.

Categories and Subject Descriptors

I.7 [**Document and Text Processing**]: Document Preparation—*Languages and systems, Markup languages*

General Terms

Design, Experimentation

Keywords

Declarative languages, Multimedia web applications, SMIL, HTML5, Timesheets

1. INTRODUCTION

The SMIL language has been available for a while for publishing multimedia applications on the web, but the lack of widely deployed tools has limited its impact. Among its most attractive capabilities are its timing and synchronization features, but fortunately these features are not restricted to the SMIL language and can be added to other document languages.

With the advance of HTML5, and notably its new graphic, audio and video contents, it is now possible to develop multimedia standard-based applications that can run natively in web browsers. The only missing piece is the SMIL features, that are not currently supported by browsers, but this problem can be solved by implementing these features in JavaScript. This is what we have done with the timesheet.js library.

With this library, sophisticated multimedia applications can be developed in a completely declarative way, and based on languages that are widely known to web developers, such as HTML and CSS. This approach is also interesting for teaching. The timing and synchronization concepts on which SMIL is based are very convenient for introducing students to the multimedia domain. We were used to present these concepts to students with the SMIL language, separately from other web languages. They can now be taught in the same context and with a more consistent approach.

The rest of the paper is organized as follows: the next section presents the timesheets.js library. Section 3 gives an example of a media annotation application that runs in the browser with this library. Finally section 4 explains how these tools are used in a course on XML and multimedia.

2. THE TIMESHEETS.JS LIBRARY

SMIL has been thought as a full specification describing all aspects of a multimedia document: content, presentation, synchronization, and interaction. However, the SMIL 3.0 Timing and Synchronization module[1] (a.k.a. SMIL Timing) is also designed to be integrated into other host languages, thus bringing synchronization and user interaction features to otherwise a-temporal document languages. As specified in this module, timing can be inserted *inline* in the markup of a static document thanks to two attributes for timing integration: `timeContainer` and `timeAction`.[2]

SMIL Timimg is complemented by another W3C specification, SMIL Timesheets,[3] that allows the most significant SMIL timing features of a document to be gathered in external resources called *timesheets*, thus separating the timing and synchronization aspects from the host language, and allowing time behavior to be shared among several documents. To paraphrase the SMIL Timesheets specification, SMIL Timing and SMIL Timesheets can be seen as a temporal counterpart of inline style and external CSS stylesheets, respectively.

2.1 Using HTML5, CSS3 and SMIL Timing

The solution we propose [1] is to combine HTML5+CSS3 and SMIL Timing/Timesheets. We take advantage of the recent addition of new media objects such as audio and video

[1]http://www.w3.org/TR/smil/smil-timing.html
[2]http://www.w3.org/TR/SMIL3/smil-timing.html#q48
[3]http://www.w3.org/TR/timesheets/

MM'11, November 28–December 1, 2011, Scottsdale, Arizona, USA.

to HTML5, and new style properties such as animation and transition to CSS3. The addition of SMIL Timing extends these multimedia features significantly. It allows, for instance, some discrete parts (text, images) of a HTML page to be synchronized declaratively with the continuous parts or with other discrete parts. This also allows user interaction to be specified in a purely declarative way.

Our approach can be summed up in three points:

- use HTML5+CSS3 for structuring and styling the content and for rendering it natively in the browser with a clean content/presentation separation;
- rely on SMIL Timing/Timesheets to handle timing, media synchronization, and user interaction;
- do not redefine timing features that already exist in HTML, SVG and CSS (e.g. animations and transitions).

This approach applies to a very broad range of interactive synchronized multimedia web applications,[4] such as slide shows, captioned video clips, annotated audio recordings, graphic animations, augmented recorded conferences, interactive photo albums, web documentaries, and so on. All these applications can be developed using only declarative languages, thus making multimedia web authoring available to a broader audience. The declarative approach also provides advantages from an engineering point of view. It makes it easier to maintain and reuse content, as opposed to the purely scripting approach.

2.2 A Basic Example

As an example, here is the very simple case of a rotating banner.

```
<script type="text/javascript"
        src="timesheets.js"/>
<link href="banner.smil" rel="timesheet"
      type="application/smil+xml"/>
<div id="banner">
  <img src="image1.png"/>
  <img src="image2.png"/>
  <img src="image3.png"/>
</div>
```

where file `banner.smil` is a timesheet containing:

```
<?xml version="1.0" encoding="UTF-8"?>
<timesheet xmlns="http://www.w3.org/ns/SMIL">
  <seq repeatCount="indefinite">
    <item select="#banner img" dur="3s"/>
  </seq>
</timesheet>
```

The three images are turned by the timesheet into items displayed in a `sequence`, each one during 3 seconds, and this sequence is repeated indefinitely.

Like in CSS, selectors are used to associate elements from the HTML document with time behaviors defined in the external timesheet. For instance, the `select` attribute of element `item` performs a `querySelectorAll()` action: for each DOM node that is matched by the `#banner img` selector, a SMIL `item` is created. This allows the same timesheet to be reused for several HTML pages: the SMIL timesheet above always works whatever the number of images in the banner.

[4]see http://wam.inrialpes.fr/timesheets/

2.3 Timesheets Engine

As SMIL Timing and Timesheets are not supported natively by web browsers, a JavaScript implementation of these specifications is required to make them available widely. Therefore, we have developed timesheets.js which is an open-source, cross-browser, dependency-free library that supports the common subset of the SMIL Timing and Timesheets specifications.

This library parses the SMIL Timing data (both inline timing and timesheet files), finds all DOM elements that are targeted (for instance, the `img` elements that are selected by `item` nodes in the `banner.smil` example above), creates a `smil` attribute on each of them with the value "idle", and schedules the activation of each target DOM element.

This scheduler acts on these DOM elements when they are activated:

- the `smil` attribute is set to "active" (if web browsers supported SMIL Timing natively, this would be a CSS pseudo-class);
- if the `timeAction` attribute is set, a specific CSS style rule is applied (e.g. "display: none", "visibility: visible", or a class is added);
- the DOM element fires a '`begin` event.

When the target element has to be deactivated, its `smil` attribute is set to "done", the specific style rule (if any) is removed, and an "end" event is fired.

This implementation obviously relies on JavaScript, but as stated above, no specific JavaScript development is required from a web developer. When an application is running, some parts of it (HTML and CSS) are executed natively by the browser, some other parts are executed by the browser's JavaScript engine.

Timesheets.js is not the first SMIL Timesheets engine running in the browser. Vuorimaa [2], for instance, has developed a Timesheets JavaScript Engine, but it was before HTML5. Therefore, it can synchronize only discrete contents.

Our implementation is available in open source under the MIT license. It is rather compact (about 2000 lines of code), and the whole engine is less than 10 Kbytes in the minified/gzipped version. There is no need to install anything for using timesheets.js; a `script` link in the HTML page to the on-line library[5] is enough (see first line of the above example).

Technically speaking, the timesheet scheduler is very modular by design:

- Each time container node has its own clock, methods, properties and event handlers.
- Each time container parses its own descendants (time nodes) and pre-computes the begin/end times according to its temporal behavior: `seq`uential, `par`allel or `excl`usive.
- All time containers expose a significant part of the HTMLMediaElement API (which is exposed by the `audio` and `video` elements of HTML5): web developers can control SMIL time containers with the usual `.play() / .pause()` methods, check the time with

[5]http://wam.inrialpes.fr/timesheets/public/timesheets.js

the `.currentTime` property and register to standard `timeupdate` DOM events.

3. APPLICATION: INA WEBRADIO

We have worked with INA, the French national archive of audiovisual, to publish on the web archived radio programs enhanced with associated material.[6] A typical INA Webradio page involves (see Figure 1):

- a rich audio player, i.e. a segmented timeline displaying a specific HTML fragment for each section of the audio track (bottom of Figure 1);
- buttons that users can click to display complementary content – possibly involving other multimedia sources (top right corner of Figure 1).

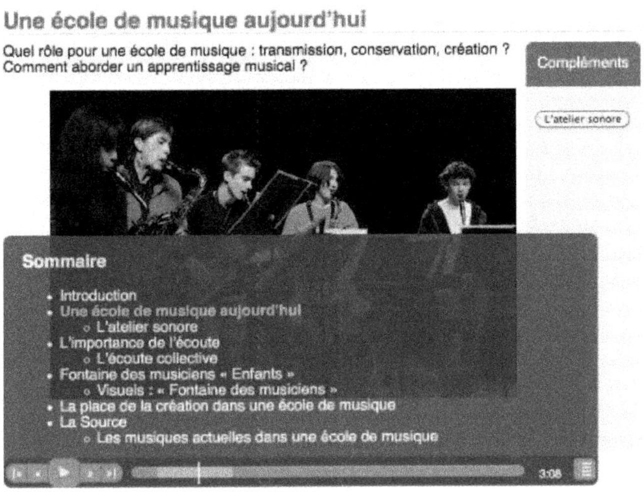

Figure 1: INA Webradio application

The idea is to propose a visually enhanced experience of a radio program, while allowing users to browse the content in a non-linear way, for instance with the table of contents (Sommaire) of Figure 1.

3.1 Document Processing Workflow

INA uses a SCENARI-based, XML publishing workflow to create multimedia documents. The SCENARI [7] authoring environment is used to divide a continuous media object (the recorded radio program) into several contiguous time segments, to associate an HTML fragment to each time segment, and finally to publish a dynamic multimedia document as a Flash object. One of the main limitations of this workflow, besides the usual Flash-related issues (accessibility, indexability, compatibility with mobile devices...), is that neither content authors nor web designers can control efficiently the presentation of resulting multimedia documents.

Our approach here is to keep the SCENARI content editor, but publish multimedia documents in HTML5 + CSS + SMIL Timesheets, in order to separate:

- content: every HTML fragment is defined in SCENARI;
- synchronization: SMIL Timesheets are used both to define time segments on the main audio track and to describe user interactions;
- presentation: generic CSS stylesheets can be defined by web designers for a consistent integration of these multimedia documents in the main website, and content authors can use specific style rules when necessary.

The idea here is to keep the efficiency of an XML publishing workflow and the benefits of CSS style sheets, while allowing multimedia documents to be modified in a way that is familiar to all web developers. The only specific part is the timesheet below:

```
<timesheet xmlns="http://www.w3.org/ns/SMIL">
  <!-- slide show / main section -->
  <excl timeAction="display" mediaSync="#main"
        controls="#timeController" dur="20:47">
    <item select="#section1" begin="00:00.000"/>
    <item select="#section2" begin="01:12.120"/>
    <item select="#section3" begin="04:41.742"/>
  </excl>
  <!-- extra material: multimedia pages -->
  <excl>
    <item select="#extra2"
          begin="open2.click; toc-extra2.click"
          end="close2.click; section2.end"/>
    <item select="#extra3"
          begin="open3.click; toc-extra3.click"
          end="close3.click; section3.end"/>
  </excl>
  <!-- extra material: audio -->
  <par mediaSync="#track2a" controls="#timeline2a"
       dur="2:24.039"/>
  <par mediaSync="#track2b" controls="#timeline2b"
       dur="3:59.928"/>
  <!-- extra material: rotating pictures -->
  <seq timeAction="display"
       repeatCount="indefinite">
    <item select="#extra4 img" dur="3s"/>
  </seq>
</timesheet>
```

3.2 Direct Editing

The goal of this modular approach is to enable "wysiwyg", fine-grain editing of the resulting multimedia documents.

With the initial document processing workflow, content editors could specify the semantic content for each audio section but had no easy way to refine the resulting document: that was a one-way, XML-to-Flash conversion. Every modification had to be done within the XML editor, then published in Flash to see how it looks like – and that only applied to semantic content. Now that the multimedia document is published in HTML5, it is possible to fine-tune all timing and presentation details, after conversion, directly in a Firefox extension.

Another benefit with the new workflow is that the workload can be shared efficiently between content authors and web designers: as presentation is entirely defined by CSS style sheets, web designers can work directly on the published multimedia documents to adapt the look to the website and to propose visual transitions between successive time segments, and content authors can see how all HTML fragments are displayed with these style sheets.

[6] http://wam.inrialpes.fr/timesheets/public/webRadio/
[7] http://scenari-platform.org/projects/scenari/en/pres/

As the content, presentation and synchronization data are defined in three separate resources (HTML5, CSS and SMIL Timesheets, respectively), all local modifications can be easily backported to the XML publishing chain.

3.3 Browser Support

These HTML5+SMIL Timesheets multimedia documents are supported natively by all modern desktop browsers implementing the `audio` and `video` tags. As a consequence, users of the HTML5 version of the INA Webradio pages get a better user experience with the native multimedia player of these browsers than with external players: better responsiveness, better CPU resource usage.

Unlike the Flash version, the HTML5 Webradio pages can be served to mobile devices: most smartphones support the `audio` and `video` tags natively and can play multimedia resources without draining the battery. As the layout is defined by style sheets, a specific touchscreen layout can be served to mobile devices with a simple declarative CSS media query.

3.4 Extensibility: DOM Events, JavaScript

Most of the synchronization logic and user interaction can be defined with SMIL Timesheets. However, there are cases where a more specific dynamic interaction should be implemented.

For this purpose, each node fires a `begin` and an `end` DOM event when it is activated and deactivated by the timesheet scheduler, respectively. This allows some specific JavaScript code to be triggered easily – either with an `onbegin` / `onend` attribute in the HTML document, or with event listeners in the JavaScript code.

Besides the APIs mentioned in section 2.3 that can be used to control time containers, timesheets.js also exposes an API that allows time containers to be created dynamically. This mechanism is used in the `timesheets-controls.js` companion library to display a segmented media timeline and to keep it synchronized with the main audio track.

4. TEACHING WEB MULTIMEDIA WITH TIMESHEETS.JS

We have experienced a first course with the timesheets.js library. This course was dedicated to XML technologies and addressed XML schema definitions, the XSLT language and multimedia documents. Basic web technologies such as HTML and CSS were already known to students through previous courses. A few classes were given and then most of the work was to realize a complete project in small groups.

The goal of the project was to implement a process that: 1) merges several OpenOffice Impress presentations, and 2) transforms the result into a web document that includes navigation and animation features.

The testbed source documents contain simple slides as well as animated text and graphics. It is worth noting that the name space used by OpenOffice documents for animations is the SMIL one. It was suggested to the students to generate HTML5 content with appropriate style sheets and to reuse the `slideshow` structures and styles available on-line.[8]

Most groups succeeded in producing an animated web slideshow and proved a good understanding of both XML transformation techniques and sound structuring of multimedia documents on the web. As an example, Figure 2 shows the architecture of a project along with the generated files.

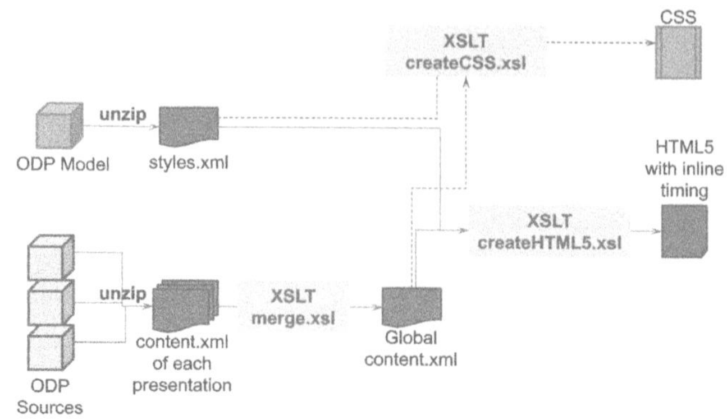

Figure 2: A student project

In the evaluation of the course, students have indicated that this project brought them a better perception of the role of the different languages of the web, including SMIL. The main difficulties they encountered were to master the XSLT language and to face the complexity of the OpenOffice style definitions.

5. CONCLUSION

We have presented the timesheets.js library and two use cases of this open technology for the web. The first one, Webradio, shows how it can be used for producing standard-based, high quality multimedia presentations, while the second one describes a teaching experience. The source code of the library and various examples are available on-line and developers are welcome to contribute on GitHub.[9]

We are currently working in two directions to 1) develop an authoring tool for media segmentation and annotation and 2) experiment microformats (such as HTML Slidy[10]) for rendering multimedia presentations with slideshow effects.

6. ACKNOWLEDGEMENTS

The work presented in this paper was done in the C2M project, funded by the French National Research Agency (ANR) under its CONTINT 2009 program. The authors are grateful to Dominique Saint-Martin from INA-GRM for providing the Webradio application.

The authors thank also Stéphane Bonhomme, the teacher of the XML course of LP SIL and the students of that class that have experimented with timesheets.js.

7. REFERENCES

[1] F. Cazenave, V. Quint, and C. Roisin. Timesheets.js: When SMIL meets HTML5 and CSS3. In *DocEng 2011: Proceedings of the Eleventh ACM Symposium on Document Engineering*. ACM, Sept. 2011.

[2] P. Vuorimaa. Timesheets JavaScript Engine, http://www.tml.tkk.fi/~pv/timesheets/, 2007.

[8] http://wam.inrialpes.fr/timesheets/

[9] https://github.com/fabi1cazenave/timesheets.js

[10] http://www.w3.org/Talks/Tools/Slidy2/

Opencast Matterhorn 1.1: Reaching New Heights

Christopher A. Brooks *
University of Saskatchewan
Saskatoon, SK, Canada
cab938@mail.usask.ca

Markus Ketterl *
Universität Osnabrück
Osnabrück, Germany
mketterl@uni-osnabrueck.de

Adam Hochman
University of California at Berkeley
Berkeley, CA, USA
adam@media.berkeley.edu

Josh Holtzman
University of California at Berkeley
Berkeley, CA, USA
jholtzman@berkeley.edu

Judy Stern
University of California at Berkeley
Berkeley, CA, USA
judy@media.berkeley.edu

Tobias Wunden
Eidgenössische Technische Hochschule Zürich
Zurich, Switzerland
tobias.wunden@id.ethz.ch

ABSTRACT

This paper gives a short overview of the Opencast Matterhorn system. Built by an open community of individuals and institutions, Matterhorn provides a lecture capture platform for both research and production environments. Matterhorn is comprehensive and scalable, and includes components for the acquisition, processing, and playback of content. Matterhorn is licensed under the liberal Educational Community License (ECL 2.0), a flexible OSI approved open source license, and the Opencast community is free for all institutions, corporations, or individuals to join.

Categories and Subject Descriptors

J.0 [**Computer Applications**]: General

General Terms

Design

Keywords

Human, Social, and Educational Aspects of Multimedia, Multimedia Systems and Middleware

1. INTRODUCTION

The Opencast community is a collaboration of higher education institutions, commercial partners, and individuals working together to explore, create, and document best practices and technologies with respect to rich media in higher education. The principal activity this community has undergone is the development of the Matterhorn product: an open source and enterprise strength platform for media acquisition, processing, and playback for lecture capture.

In 2009 a group of thirteen higher education institutions formed a team of designers, developers, and researchers charged with creating a reliable open source solution for lecture capture and content usage. Consisting of members from computer science research groups as well as institutional education and technology infrastructure support groups, the aim of this team was to take lessons learned from deployed home grown systems and build a scalable, accessible, open solution for higher education. Notably, the system was intended to be both a platform for research in multimedia, pedagogy, and education, as well as a production system intended to scale to the media processing needs of the institution, federations of institutions, and tens of thousands of students accessing and using lecture-created content.

Supported by a Mellon and Hewlett Foundation grant totalling $1.5M, and institutional matching funds of $2M, development has continued for two years and is currently maintained by over 17 committers from institutions and corporations from around the world. The Opencast community has over 650 members with more than 200 of them interested in the Matterhorn build project[1]. More information about Opencast Matterhorn can be found in [5] and by visiting the project webpage at www.opencastproject.org.

2. ARCHITECTURE & SYSTEM

Matterhorn is made up of three subsystems corresponding to content acquisition, processing, and playback, referred to within the project as capture agents, workflows, and engage respectively. In addition to these distinct systems, a variety of user interfaces and API's for administration and choreographing these subsystems are provided.

Matterhorn is built as a J2EE OSGI system, allowing for services to be swapped out dynamically at runtime as needed. API's are provided as REST endpoints, encouraging reuse outside of the Java domain. Matterhorn relies on other open source solutions (*gstreamer*, *ffmpeg*, and *apache*

*Corresponding authors. Other authors listed alphabetically. Corresponding authors are Ph.D. students at their institutions.

[1] As there are no membership fees or official membership process these numbers reflect subscriptions to our public mailing lists.

felix to name a few of the more significant frameworks used), and all contributed code is licensed under the OSI approved Educational Community License (ECL) 2.0. No proprietary code is part of Matterhorn, however, several hardware and software solutions (some open source, some proprietary) external to the project have been connected by interested third parties.

2.1 Content Acquisition (Capture Agents)

The principal method of content acquisition in Matterhorn is the *capture agent*; a hardware device connected to classroom audio/video infrastructure. The reference platform for this agent is based on commodity laptop-style x86 hardware and works with a number of different video capture devices including NTSC/PAL-based cards (such as the Hauppauge and bt787 chipsets), usb webcams, and specialized VGA capture devices (such as the Epiphan line of products). A fully capable agent with both VGA (5 FPS) capture and NTSC/PAL capture (30/25 FPS) costs roughly $1,500, and several vendors are beginning to offer embedded or value-added solutions to integrate with Matterhorn capture at a similar price point.

The agent polls a central service which provide iCalendar encoded schedules. Fault tolerance is provided through caching and retry timeouts, allowing capture agents to be deployed in environments with intermittent networking such as wireless or mobile cart situations. Schedules identify both the metadata associated with a capture (e.g. course call number, instructor name, etc.) as well as the inputs to capture from. Underlying the scheduling system the agent uses the *gstreamer* framework to acquire, transform, and encode video. The system allows for multiple specialized encoding pipelines to be run at once, and initial support for transforming video to still frames for confidence monitoring during capture is available.

Once captured, video and other artifacts are aggregated and packaged into an extensible structure called a *MediaPackage* and ingested into the Matterhorn workflow system. Integration with the video processing services of Matterhorn is purposefully limited to the *MediaPackage* declarative format; we wish to encourage maximum flexibility when choosing capture agents for different rooms or purposes (HD, research systems, live streaming, etc.), and using a media aggregation format instead of strong codec-specific contracts makes this more tractable.

2.2 Video Processing (Workflows)

The core of Matterhorn is the video processing workflow system. This system uses a service oriented architecture to dispatch jobs to worker nodes which may be specialized for particular services or provide a variety of different general purpose services. Workflows are linear compositions of these services (which may be synchronous or asynchronous) meant to be run in parallel depending upon the infrastructure topology. In this way Matterhorn can be scaled with more computing resources both to accommodate new services as well as to accommodate an increased load or responsiveness. It also holds out the opportunity to leverage the specialization of certain services to certain pieces of hardware; for instance, encoding services could be run across GPU-accelerated infrastructure while metadata services could be run on more general purpose machines.

Content is ingested into the system in one of three ways; through REST APIs as described previously, through an "inbox" metaphor to accommodate legacy applications (e.g. those that may use file share copying, FTP, etc.), or through end-user web interfaces. Once ingested, a workflow is started by the ingestion system which automatically distributes jobs across the platform depending on worker loads. Worker loads are calculated automatically, and new nodes can be enabled or disabled depending on demand .

Services included in the Matterhorn 1.1 distribution include video encoding (using *ffmpeg* or *gstreamer* as desired), metadata generation, scene detection, preview image generation, trimming and captioning (requiring user input from a web-based tools), and text analysis (using *tesseract*). A command line operation handler is also included allowing for end-user integration of other tools as services in a declarative manner.

Matterhorn publishing services for both progressive download and the open source *red5* streaming server are included, though out of the box Matterhorn will work with a variety of third party streaming services. A local search index service using *solr* is also available. Services for distribution to other popular portals such as YouTube.edu and iTunesU are highly requested and are under active development.

2.3 Media Playback (Engage)

Flexible media distribution is a built-in goal of the system, and standards-based aggregation solutions such as *rss* and *atom* feeds are generated by the system to group events. These feeds can further be filtered by search attributes, and enclose a variety of different media types and qualities specified by the workflow definition. This search feeds an ideal solution for integration to external platforms such as campus information systems and learning content management systems.

Accessibility has been a driving factor throughout the development of Matterhorn user interfaces. The media player, called *engage* was designed and developed to be accessible by supporting assistive technology across multiple platforms. The player can be used in different situations; as a standalone application, or embedded inside of other applications such as blogs, wikis or content management systems. The player enables features based on underlying Matterhorn services such as slide segmentation for previews and faster navigation based on video OCR and text analysis. The technology stack for *engage* is HTML and Javascript-based for navigation, and an AJAX bridge that forwards user interaction to an Adobe Flex-based video component is included. This hybrid approach allows to use the strength of plain standard based HTML regarding accessibility (e.g. tab order or keyboard navigation) extended with ARIA roles that describe functionality according to accessibility specifications while maintaining a quality user experience.

The video component provided with Matterhorn uses the *open source media framework (OSMF)* and supports a powerful, reliable, and platform independent video solution that can handle different distribution mechanisms such as progressive or streaming video. It allows for synchronization between different content sources, allowing the display of multiple videos (e.g. both the presentation and presenter video) in the browser at the same time. The video component can be easily replaced depending on client requirements (e.g. HTML 5 for mobile clients).

3. PRODUCTION SYSTEM

Matterhorn is used at institutions across the globe as a lecture capture solution for thousands of students. The open source nature of the product makes measurement of adoption difficult, however both corresponding authors of this document have overseen widespread local deployments of Matterhorn and offer a glimpse here of the effect it has had at their institution. More user testimonials can be found on the Opencast Matterhorn project website.

3.1 University of Saskatchewan

The University of Saskatchewan piloted Matterhorn 1.0 capture agents in 11 classrooms between September 2010 and April 2011. Custom Matterhorn workflows were created to connect to a legacy media player which had already been integrated into campus infrastructure.

Over this time period 944 events were captured with the majority of them being regular undergraduate lectures (between 1 hour and 4 hours long) along with some graduate lectures, special events, and meetings. A breadth first approach was taken to lecture capture deployment, and a variety of disciplines were recorded including the natural sciences, social sciences, humanities, and professional colleges.

During this two term deployment, 2,639 unique students watched over 1,543 days worth of video, an average of roughly 41 hours per student. Students were restricted to viewing videos from their enrolled classes only, though many students were enrolled in multiple classes at once.

In addition to this, several students at the university have been involved in the customization of Matterhorn through volunteering, summer research positions, professional internships, and graduate theses. The University of Saskatchewan was a mentoring institution in the Undergraduate Capstone Open Source projects (UCOSP)[2] where five senior undergraduate students from institutions across the country worked on various aspects of Matterhorn for completion of their bachelors degree. Some of these students became and committers on the project, and several of them continue to contribute to the system despite the conclusion of the program.

The University of Saskatchewan is increase its deployment with Matterhorn 1.1 over the summer of 2011 in preparation for the fall academic term.

3.2 Universität Osnabrück

The Universität Osnabrück migrated to Opencast Matterhorn 1.0 for the winter semester 2010/2011. The system was used to record 16 weekly lectures with Matterhorn capture agent hardware and a couple of additional events (e.g. workshops, conferences, talks) with traditional A/V equipment, subsequently ingested for further processing and distribution. In total, more than 300 (typically 1.5 hour long) recordings were processed and distributed using the Matterhorn ecosystem. Several of the recorded lectures were watched by more than 1,000 unique students over a small period of time on modest hardware infrastructure.

Running in full production with the first public 1.0 release in 2010 using a large scale distributed system unveiled the kinds of bugs that only longitudinal testing can identify. By being involved both in development and deployment of Matterhorn, the Universität Osnabrück acted as a sort of real-world litmus test as to the direction Matterhorn needed to be put in to achieve its scalability goals. While not a primary purpose, local experiences and knowledge have been leveraged to aid in undergraduate student learning as well. Several of the committers involved in the project have been instructing senior level software engineering courses focusing on the technologies, techniques, and solutions found in Matterhorn. Students in these courses are encouraged to get involved with the project and contribute to the open source world.

The Universität Osnabrück has since migrated to Matterhorn 1.1 for its current deployment.

[2]See http://ucosp.ca/

4. RESEARCH PLATFORM

One of the powerful aspects of a common platform for lecture capture in higher education is the ability to share not only research results but research innovations. Several institutions are actively developing, deploying, and validating systems based on Matterhorn, and the ease at which these institutions can share those results back with the broader community, allows for greater impact while reducing the costs of applying research in practice. Further, a collaborative production environment encourages a collaborative research program; many of the individuals involved with Matterhorn now have collaborative research agendas adding to the quality and impact of their results.

A sample of some of the research endeavours using Matterhorn that we are familiar with includes:

- **Student interaction modelling through clustering.** Using Matterhorn recorded lectures, clusters of students who share similar viewing patterns were discovered in [1]. Tying these clusters to pedagogical goals and educational strategies can allow for content recommendation or early warning of student problems. This research ties aspects of education and the social sciences to the use of rich media in the classroom.

- **Scene detection using Supervised Machine Learning.** The Matterhorn scene detection service was analysed in [2] against several other scene detection techniques. The workflow operation handler features of Matterhorn make both multiple detection techniques as well as supervised machine learning techniques feasible in large scale implementations if computational resources are available. This technique is being extended to add novel methods of trim point detection and pause detection to Matterhorn.

- **Social navigation support in web lectures.** User awareness has become one of the major features of today's Web 2.0 experience. Understanding how different people are using multimedia content opens up new possibilities for navigation and analysis [4]. Social footprints allow pedagogy and content researchers to track which parts of long video recordings have been watched more frequently by students. This information can then be used for machine learning or also for semantic based recommender systems [3].

- **Automated camera tracking.** A novel research spinoff of the Matterhorn project has been an undergraduate honours thesis work focusing on automated camera tracking. Written primarily by one of the Matterhorn committers, it will soon be released to the

Opencast community as an open source solution for tracking lecturers as they move about the classroom.

5. CONCLUSIONS

The Opencast Matterhorn platform is an open source and enterprise quality system for capturing, processing, and engaging with lecture content in higher education. It is a platform that marries the scalability and reliability demands of production environments with the possibilities made available by cutting edge research. Principle amongst its features is the service oriented approach which allows new image and audio recognition techniques to be plugged in dynamically as needed. Experimentation of new codecs, metadata analysis, and playback tools can all be added without the need for developers to understand (and potentially destabilize) other aspects of the system.

In addition to these services, the platform is built around three coarse grained components; capture agents (for content acquisition), workflows (for content processing), and engage tools (for content playback). Each of these components maintains low coupling with one another, allowing them to be swapped out as institutional or research requirements may dictate. This has been leveraged to quickly add new commercial capture devices to the system, to integrate with legacy processing engines, and to explore device-specific (e.g. mobile) playback systems.

Matterhorn began as an open source solution that was funded by 13 higher education institutions and the Mellon and Hewlett foundations. It is no longer grant funded, and is instead maintained by 17 committers representing various higher education institutions across the globe. Further, an ecosystem of solutions providers around the Matterhorn codebase is starting to emerge, including both hardware and service vendors. Matterhorn offers reduced costs and increased flexibility for service units in the academy, and provides a platform for rapid roll-out of novel research related to audio and video processing, recognition, and pedagogy.

6. ACKNOWLEDGMENTS

We would like to thank the Hewlett and Mellon foundations for their critical support that allowed us to coordinate, plan, execute, and sustain the vision we have for media in higher education.

In addition to the many committers who made this work possible, we would like to thank the following committers emeritus and contributors who played a pivotal role in bringing the product to fruition (in alphabetical order): Stefan Altevogt, Allison Bloodworth, Nils Birnbaum, Johannes Emden, Sebastian Ewert, Mara Hancock, Jamie Hodge, Andre Klassen, Bostjan Pajntar, Olaf Schulte, and Aaron Zeckoski.

7. ADDITIONAL AUTHORS

The cover page lists authors who are members of the product owner team and executed the vision for Matterhorn 1.0. Additional authors of this work include our numerous committers and designers (listed here alphabetically): Kristofor Amundson, Greg Logan, Kenneth Lui, Adam McKenzie, Denis Meyer, Markus Moormann, Matjaz Rihtar, Ruediger Rolf, Nejc Skofic, Micah Sutton, Rubén Pérez Vázquez, and Benjamin Wulff. Full citation of this work should acknowledge these persons as extended authors.

8. REFERENCES

[1] C. A. Brooks, C. Demmans Epp, G. Logan, and J. Greer. The Who, What, When, and Why of Lecture Capture. In *1st International Conference on Learning Analytics and Knowledge 2011 (LAK'11)*, 2010.

[2] G. S. Johnston, C. A. Brooks, C. Thompson, and J. Greer. Quantifying Accuracy of Algorithms Trained on Multiple Raters in Disagreement. In *In submission to the Conference on Educational Data Mining 2011*, 2011.

[3] M. Ketterl, J. Emden, and O. Vornberger. Using social navigation for multimedia content suggestion. In *Proceedings of the 2010 IEEE Fourth International Conference on Semantic Computing*, ICSC '10, pages 448–449, Washington, DC, USA, 2010. IEEE Computer Society.

[4] M. Ketterl, R. Mertens, and O. Vornberger. Bringing web 2.0 to web lectures. *International Journal of Interactive Technology and Smart Education*, 6(2):82–96, 2009.

[5] M. Ketterl, O. A. Schulte, and A. Hochman. Opencast matterhorn: A community-driven open source software project for producing, managing, and distributing academic video. *Interact. Techn. Smart Edu.*, 7(3):168–180, 2010.

The FCam API for Programmable Cameras

Sung Hee Park
Stanford University
shpark7@stanford.edu

Andrew Adams
Stanford University
abadams@stanford.edu

Eino-Ville Talvala
Stanford University, now at Google Inc.
etalvala@google.com

ABSTRACT

The FCam API is an open-source camera control library, enabling precise control over a camera's imaging pipeline. Intended for researchers and students in the field of computational photography, it allows easy implementation of novel algorithms and applications. Currently implemented on the Nokia N900 smartphone, and a custom-built "Frankencamera", it has been used in teaching at universities around the world, and is freely available for download for the N900.

This paper describes the architecture underlying the API, the design of the API itself, several applications built on top of it, and some examples of its use in education.

Categories and Subject Descriptors

I.4.1 [**Image Processing and Computer Vision**]: Digitization and Image Capture—*Digital Cameras*

General Terms

Experimentation

1. INTRODUCTION

The transition from film to digital cameras that has taken place over the last decade has opened new possibilities for photography. By incorporating computation into the process of creating a photograph we can extend the dynamic range, alter the depth of field, or reduce noise in dark environments. This field has come to be called computational photography. Many of these algorithms operate by acquiring a burst of images with precisely varying camera settings, and then fusing that burst into a single output photograph better than any of the inputs. One key requirement for high-quality results is that the burst must be captured in as short a time as possible.

However, the field has had limited impact to date, as current cameras are not programmable at all, and camera-equipped smartphones use APIs that are incapable of cleanly expressing these algorithms. Typical mobile imaging APIs do not give the programmer control over fundamental sensor parameters like exposure time, and even worse, act adversarily by running uncontrollable metering and focus algorithms.

These APIs typically operate the camera in either a streaming mode suitable for viewfinding, in which changes to camera parameters take effect an unknown number of frames in the future, or in a still capture mode which cannot quickly capture bursts of frames with varying settings. Neither mode is useful for much of computational photography.

To address this need, we developed the FCam API for programmable cameras. The goal for the API is to provide intuitive camera programming model that enables programmers to easily prototype new ideas for computational photography applications. The API makes it easy to precisely control all parameters of the camera, and facilitates capturing bursts of images with deterministically-varying settings at full sensor frame rate.

Such control enables many new applications such as HDR viewfinding, advanced low-light imaging, or synthetic aperture photography, in a straightforward way. The API currently runs on two platforms: The Nokia N900 smartphone, and the custom-built "Frankencamera" [2, 4]. It is written for C++, and was designed at Stanford University in collaboration with Nokia Research Center Palo Alto.

In this paper, we describe the software architecture behind the API, demonstrate use of the API with some code examples and sample applications, and describe the API's use in education. We have found FCam particularly useful in graduate-level classes teaching computer vision and computational photography, and it has been widely used for this purpose over the last year.

2. ARCHITECTURE

The Frankencamera architecture departs from the typical model of the camera sensor and imaging hardware exposed by mobile imaging APIs. Instead of viewing the imaging pipeline as a free-running source of image data, the Frankencamera architecture sees it as a pipeline that transforms requests into images. For each request fed into the pipeline, one output image is produced, in order. The stages of the imaging pipeline themselves store no state — everything needed to specify the image capture and post-processing parameters for a given frame is bundled into the requests, including a list of actions that need to be performed concurrently to sensor exposure by other parts of the camera hardware (e.g. firing a flash). Figure 1 illustrates the overall design.

MM'11, November 28–December 1, 2011, Scottsdale, Arizona, USA.

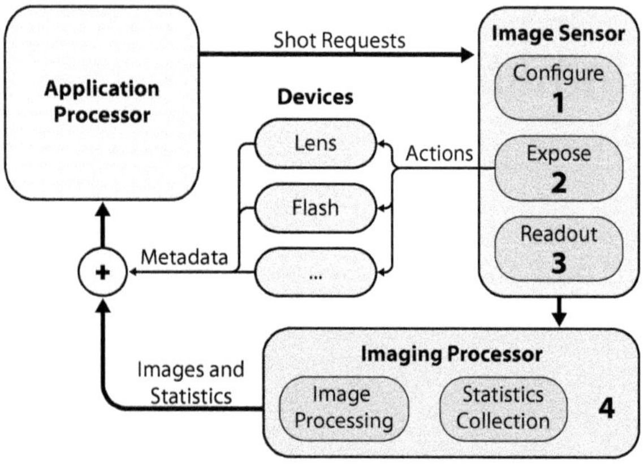

Figure 1: The Frankencamera architecture treats the image sensor as a pipeline, which converts requests for images into images and metadata on a one-for-one basis.

The Sensor.

The sensor simply converts requests into raw image data, matching the requested parameters as closely as possible. The images produced are bundled together with the actual parameters used into a "frame" that is passed down the imaging pipeline. The sensor also triggers device-specific actions at appropriate times during image capture.

Fixed-Function Imaging Processor.

Most cameras include dedicated fixed-function hardware for processing raw camera data efficiently. In the FCam architecture, such imaging processors can transform the raw image data into a form more suitable for display or later processing, but the raw data must always be available to the application if requested. In addition, the imaging processor produces various useful image statistics such as intensity histograms or sharpness maps. These are included in the final frame sent to the application to assist with control algorithms like metering and autofocus.

Other Devices.

A typical camera has many different pieces of hardware that must act in concert to capture a photograph, such as the lens and the flash. In addition, research systems may include novel hardware that must be synchronized with an exposure. These devices advertise a set of "actions" they can perform. Actions can be included in requests, and specify the time that they should take place relative to the start of the exposure.

Devices also produce additional metadata about their state during image capture (such as lens position, or whether the flash fired). This metadata is bundled into the frame sent to the application.

Control Algorithms.

All control algorithms run in the main application processor; there are no hidden daemons or hardware routines controlling metering or autofocus. This gives the camera applications full visibility into the imaging pipeline, and makes it simple for an application to write its own control algorithms. If standard control algorithms are desired, these are available as utility functions.

3. THE FCAM API

In this section we demonstrate use of the API with three brief examples. More examples and complete documentation can be found in [5], and implementation details and design rationale are covered in [4].

HDR Burst.

Our first example rapidly acquires three images at three different exposure times. This is the raw data necessary to make a high-dynamic-range photograph. First we allocate objects representing the image sensor, the three requests (called *Shots* in the API), and the three frames we expect to receive in return.

```
Sensor sensor;
Shot shortReq, midReq, longReq;
Frame short, mid, long;
```

Then we configure each shot to describe the all parameters necessary for its capture. In this example we merely configure exposure time, and allocate some storage for the returned image data. Other available parameters include gain, frame time, and white balance.

```
shortReq.exposure = 10000; // microseconds
midReq.exposure   = 40000;
longReq.exposure  = 160000;
shortReq.image = Image(sensor.maxImageSize(), RAW);
midReq.image   = Image(sensor.maxImageSize(), RAW);
longReq.image  = Image(sensor.maxImageSize(), RAW);
```

We then *capture* the three shots. This is a non-blocking call which enqueues the requests at the top of the pipeline in Figure 1.

```
sensor.capture(shortReq);
sensor.capture(midReq);
sensor.capture(longReq);
```

Finally, we call *getFrame* to retrieve the resulting images and metadata. This call blocks until the frames are produced. The API guarantees that we will receive one frame per shot requested, in the same order.

```
short = sensor.getFrame();
mid = sensor.getFrame();
long = sensor.getFrame();
```

HDR Viewfinding.

The above code captures a high-dynamic-range burst of images. We will now build this into a full HDR camera application by adding a high-dynamic-range viewfinder. Our viewfinding algorithm will instruct the sensor to alternate between two exposure times and fuse each returned pair of images for display (as in [3]). To accomplish this case we first create a vector of two shots with our two exposure times:

```
vector<Shot> hdr(2);
hdr[0].exposure = 40000;
hdr[1].exposure = 10000;
```

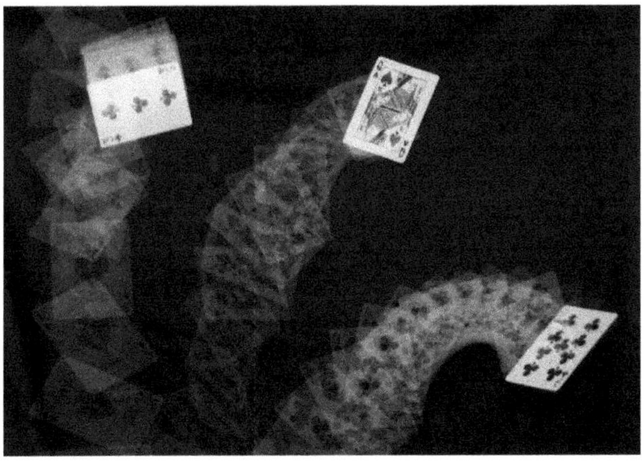

Figure 2: To capture this image, we attached two flash units to a Frankencamera. We use *actions* to direct one to strobe throughout the exposure, and the other to fire brightly once at the end of the exposure.

We then *stream* this pair of shots. This produces an endless stream of frames which alternates between the two shots in the vector. We *stream* instead of *capture* in order to keep the imaging pipeline full and run at video rate without dropping frames. This kind of alternating stream is almost impossible to achieve with conventional camera APIs.

```
sensor.stream(hdr);
```

We then enter a loop, retrieving each pair of frames in the same order as requested.

```
while(1) {
  Frame longExp = sensor.getFrame();
  Frame shortExp = sensor.getFrame();
```

Our high-dynamic range viewfinder will need to perform metering. The short exposure should meter to capture the highlights, and the long exposure should meter to capture the shadows. Fixed-function imaging processors compute histograms which we attach to each frame, so we need not inspect the image data itself in order to meter. We can compute a new exposure for each frame from the histogram and current exposure time alone. The *stream* call makes a copy of the shots passed to it, so after updating the exposure times we must call *stream* again to effect our change. After metering we fuse the two images for display and continue our loop.

```
  hdr[0].exposure = meterLong(longExp.histogram(),
                              longExp.exposure());
  hdr[1].exposure = meterShort(shortExp.histogram(),
                               shortExp.exposure());
  sensor.stream(hdr);
  overlayWidget.display( fuse(longExp, shortExp) );
}
```

Second-Curtain Sync Flash.

Our final example demonstrates the use of actions. This example fires a flash at the end of the exposure (this is known as second-curtain sync). First we create and configure our shot and the object that represents the flash.

Figure 3: Low-light imaging. The FCam API is used to create a low-light camera mode. A short-exposure noisy image (left), and a long-exposure blurry image (center) are captured, and combined into a high-quality result (right) directly on the camera.

```
Shot flashShot;
flashShot.exposure = 100000; // 0.1 seconds
Flash flash;
```

We then create and configure the *action* that represents firing the flash. We set it to trigger at the end of the exposure. On the N900 implementation, FCam can trigger actions with an accuracy of ± 30 microseconds, which is sufficient for photography.

```
Flash::FireAction fire(&flash);
fire.duration = 1000; // 1 ms
fire.brightness = flash.maxBrightness();
fire.time = flashShot.exposure - fire.duration;
```

Finally, we attach this action to the shot, and tell the sensor to *capture* this shot as in the previous examples. Using this kind of program, we produced the image in Figure 2.

```
flashShot.addActions(fire);
sensor.capture(flashShot);
Frame flashFrame = sensor.getFrame();
```

4. SAMPLE APPLICATIONS

To test the FCam API, we developed several sample applications. These were meant to demonstrate features of the API, and be representative of recent work in computational photography. Here, we'll discuss two examples.

Low-noise Viewfinding and Capture.

Taking high-quality photographs in low light is a challenging task. To achieve the desired image brightness, one must either increase gain, which increases noise, or increase exposure time, which introduces motion blur and lowers the frame rate of the viewfinder. In this application, the FCam API is used to implement a low-light camera mode, which augments viewfinding and image capture using the algorithms of Adams et al. [1] and Tico and Pulli [6], respectively. In brief, the application takes a burst of two images — one noisy, with short exposure time and high gain, and a second blurry image, with a long exposure time. These images are then combined into a high-quality result on the device.

Lucky Imaging.

Long-exposure photos taken without use of a tripod are usually blurry, due to natural hand shake. However, hand shake varies over time, and a photographer can get "lucky" and record a sharp photo if the exposure occurs during a period of stillness (Figure 4). Our lucky imaging application

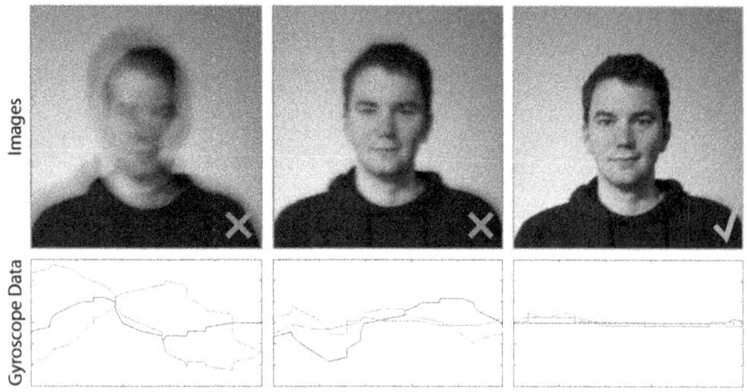

Figure 4: Lucky imaging. An image stream and 3-axis gyroscope data for a burst of three images with half-second exposure times. The Frankencamera API makes it easy to tag image frames with the corresponding gyroscope data.

uses an experimental 3-axis gyroscope affixed to the front of the N900 to detect hand shake. Newer smartphones, such as the Apple iPhone 4, have built-in gyroscopes of similar quality. By treating the gyroscope as a *device* in our API, we can easily attach a synchronized gyroscope trace to each returned frame. We then stream full-resolution images until we receive a frame with a trace indicating that there was little motion during that exposure.

5. EDUCATIONAL USE

With the assistance of Nokia, sets of Nokia N900s along with the FCam API have been distributed to universities around the world, to be used in teaching. Universities that have received devices include Brown University; Cornell; Carnegie Mellon; École Polytechnique Fédérale de Lausanne; ETH Zürich; Fachhochschule Brandenburg; Georgia Tech; IMPA (Brazil); Johannes Kepler University; National University of Ireland; MIT; Oregon State University; Rochester Institute of Technology; University of California, Santa Barbara; University of California, Santa Cruz; University of Catania; University of Hong Kong; University of New Mexico; University of Virginia; University of Zaragoza; and Stanford University.

As an example, at Stanford University FCam was used in a graduate-level course on computational photography. As a first assignment to learn the API, students were asked to write an auto-focus algorithm for the N900 in one week. The results were encouraging; the top students' methods were faster and more robust than the N900's built-in auto-focus routine.

After the initial assignment, the students had one month to complete a final project. Two of the resulting applications are shown in Figures 5 and 6.

6. CONCLUSION

FCam is an open-source API intended for researchers, developers, educators, and hobbyists interested in programming their camera. Since its release in mid-2010, the FCam source package has been downloaded over 7,000 times, and the compiled library has been downloaded over 100,000 times. The library is available under the BSD license.

In the future we intend to expand the reach of the API by porting it to other mobile platforms. Just as importantly, we hope the API demonstrates to camera and smartphone manufacturers the benefits of opening up the camera subsystem to third-party developers and the open-source community at large.

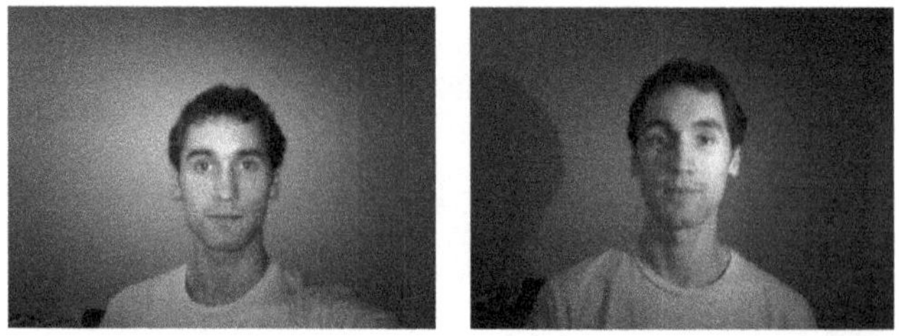

(a) On-camera flash. (b) Flash from helper N900.

Figure 5: Remote flash. In this project, the students synchronized two N900s so that the other smartphone fired its flash when the first took a picture. ***Images courtesy of D. Keeler and M. Barrientos, with post-processing for color balance and contrast.***

(a) A single captured frame. (b) 16 frames merged.

Figure 6: Painted aperture. By capturing a set of images from slightly different viewpoints, an image that appears to come from a camera with a much shallower depth-of-field can be created. ***Images courtesy of E. Luong.***

7. REFERENCES

[1] A. Adams, N. Gelfand, and K. Pulli. Viewfinder Alignment. *Computer Graphics Forum (Eurographics 2008)*, 27(2):597–606, 2008.

[2] A. Adams, E.-V. Talvala, S. H. Park, D. E. Jacobs, B. Ajdin, N. Gelfand, J. Dolson, D. Vaquero, J. Baek, M. Tico, H. P. A. Lensch, W. Matusik, K. Pulli, M. Horowitz, and M. Levoy. The Frankencamera: An experimental platform for computational photography. *ACM Transactions on Graphics (SIGGRAPH 2010)*, 29(4):29:1–29:12, 2010.

[3] N. Gelfand, A. Adams, S. H. Park, and K. Pulli. Multi-exposure imaging on mobile devices. In *Proceedings of the ACM International Conference on Multimedia*, pages 823–826, 2010.

[4] E.-V. Talvala. *The Frankencamera: Building a programmable camera for computational photography.* PhD thesis, Stanford University, 2011.

[5] E.-V. Talvala and A. Adams. The FCam API. http://fcam.garage.maemo.org, 2010.

[6] M. Tico and K. Pulli. Image enhancement method via blur and noisy image fusion. In *Proceedings of the 16th IEEE International Conference on Image Processing (ICIP)*, pages 1521–1524, 2009.

Just-In-Time Adaptive Decoder Engine: A Universal Video Decoder based on MPEG RVC

Jérôme Gorin
ARTEMIS, Institut Telecom/Telecom SudParis
UMR 8145, SudParis, France
jerome.gorin@etu.upmc.fr

Hervé Yviquel
IRISA, University of Rennes 1
6 rue de Kerampont
22300 Lannion, France
herve.yviquel@irisa.fr

Françoise Prêteux
MINES ParisTech
60 Boulevard Saint-Michel
75272 Paris, France
Francoise.Preteux@mines-paristech.fr

Mickaël Raulet
IETR, INSA Rennes
F-35000,
mickael.raulet@insa-rennes.fr

ABSTRACT

In this paper, we introduce the Just-In-Time Adaptive Decoder Engine (Jade) project, which is shipped as part of the Open RVC-CAL Compiler (Orcc) project. Orcc provides a set of open-source software tools for managing decoders standardized within MPEG by the Reconfigurable Video Coding (RVC) experts. In this framework, Jade acts as a Virtual Machine for any decoder description that uses the MPEG RVC paradigm. Jade dynamically generates a *native* decoder representation suitable for X86, ARM and CELL platforms with a possibility of exploiting multi-core CPUs. Thus, according to the MPEG RVC decoder description coupled with a video coded stream, Jade can create, configure and re-configure video decompression algorithms adapting to the video content.

Categories and Subject Descriptors

4 [**Multimedia systems and middleware**]: Miscellaneous; 3 [**Scalability in media processing, analysis, and applications**]: Miscellaneous

General Terms: Algorithms, Languages, Performance, Standardization.

Keywords: Adaptive decoding, multimedia application, dataflow programs, decoder reconfiguration, scalable execution, MPEG Reconfigurable Video Coding (RVC).

1. INTRODUCTION

MPEG Reconfigurable Video Coding (RVC) has been chosen by MPEG to be an alternative paradigm for codec deployment. The goal of MPEG RVC is to provide dataflow representations of existing reference software decoders at component level. Thus MPEG RVC enables arbitrary decoder representations of any combination of fundamental algorithms, without additional standardization steps. By adding the side-information of the decoder description alongside the video coded bitstream, MPEG RVC defines the new concept of an RVC decoder. As shown on Fig. 1, an RVC decoder can create and handle several decoder descriptions on-the-fly, either by using coding tools standardized in MPEG, or proprietary implementations of coding tools, or other hybrid versions composed from proprietary and standardized implementations.

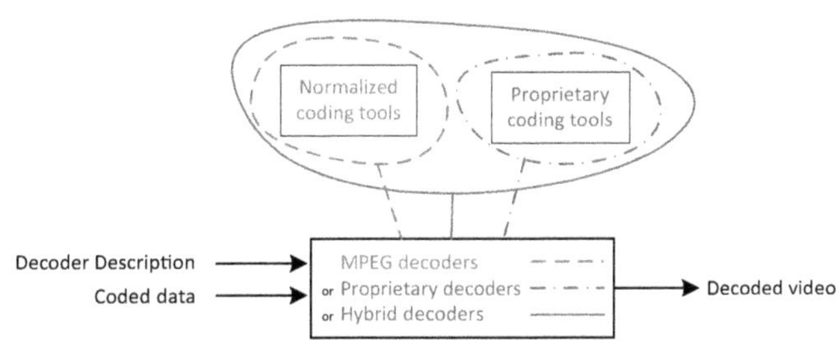

Figure 1: Representation of a dynamic MPEG RVC decoder.

In this paper, we introduce the Just-In-Time Adaptive Decoder Engine (Jade) as the first *portable* decoder engine capable of managing *on-the-fly* MPEG RVC decoder descriptions. The goal of Jade is to exploit the generic properties of a dataflow representation to produce an efficient *native* decoder representation suited to the architecture of the underlying platform. Jade can create, configure and re-configure the video decompression algorithms adaptively to the coded video bitstream, avoiding incompatibility issues between decoders and coded bitstreams. This concept has significant advantages compared to a "statically" compiled decoder: a Just-In-Time decoding platform does not need decoder software updates. Moreover, RVC descriptions are generic and provide sufficient information to produce an efficient implementation suited for a wide range of platforms.

In the following, section 2 gives an overview of the MPEG

RVC standard and the property of its description. In section 3, we provide a presentation of the main concept of Jade and its implemented features. Finally, we give use procedure in section 4.

2. MPEG RVC OVERVIEW

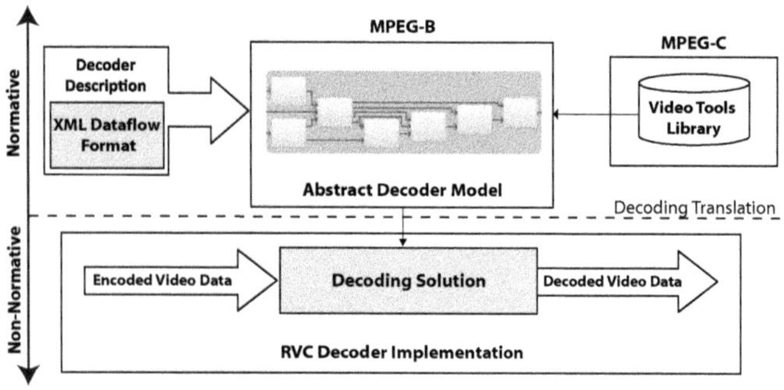

Figure 2: A typical use of the MPEG RVC Framework.

The MPEG Reconfigurable Video Coding (RVC) [16] framework is a new, still evolving ISO standard from MPEG. It aims at providing video codec specifications based on a high-level library of components. The main goal of MPEG RVC is to produce new *Abstract Decoder Model* (ADM) of already existing MPEG standard which will be suitable for both hardware and software implementation [16]. An ADM is a generic representation of a decoder, built as a dataflow diagram of coding tools encapsulated into Functional Units (FUs). Dataflow representations are expressed with the *XML Dataflow Format* (XDF), an XML dialect standardized in MPEG-B part 4 [16] (*Codec configuration representation*) that describes the connections between FUs. Each FU is described in RVC-CAL Actor Language (RVC-CAL) and defines a processing entity of a decoder.

Figure 2 shows a typical use of a normative ADM description to produce a non-normative decoding solution that can target either software or hardware platform. MPEG RVC provides both a normative standard library of FUs standardized in MPEG-C part 4 [16], the *Video Tools Library* (VTL), and a set of decoder descriptions/configurations expressed as networks of FUs. Such a representation is modular and helps the reconfiguration of a decoder by modifying the topology of the network. Adding new coding technologies in an existing standard is a particularly sensitive part of any standardization process. As a consequence, MPEG RVC mainly focuses on the reusability of the standardized coding tools by allowing different decoder descriptions to instantiate common FUs across standards.

3. JUST-IN-TIME ADAPTIVE DECODER ENGINE FEATURES

Jade [13, 12], represented in Fig. 3, extends a Virtual Machine to handle a RVC decoder description. Its configuration engine (Fig. 4) has two inputs, a decoder configuration and a representation of the Video Tools Library (VTL) [11] standardized in MPEG-C. It outputs a complete dataflow representation of the decoder as a set of interconnected functional processing units in byte code format. This decoder representation can then be compiled or interpreted by a specific

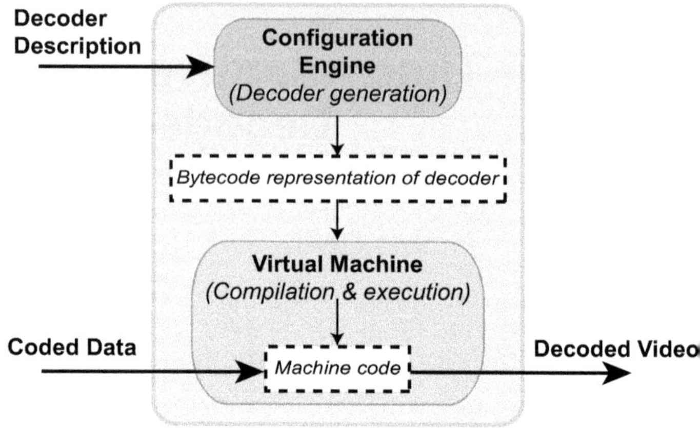

Figure 3: Structure of the Just-in-time Adaptive Decoder Engine.

Virtual Machine (VM). We chose to base Jade on the open source LLVM infrastructure [15]. This VM provides efficient Just-In-Time compilation and multicore execution for a wide range of platforms (X86, X86-64, PPC, ARM, etc.).

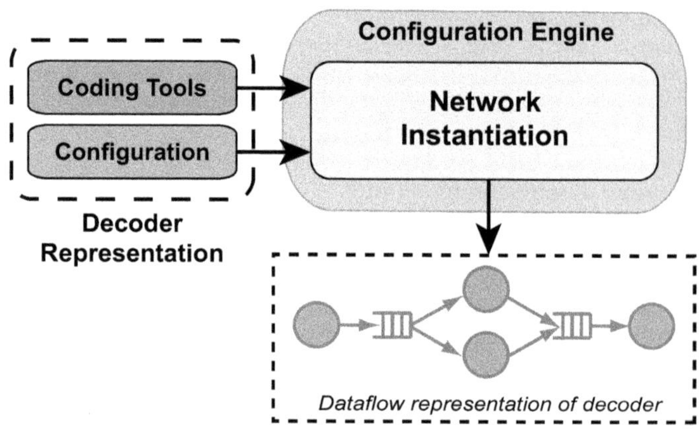

Figure 4: Configuration of an RVC description by the configuration engine.

3.1 On-the-fly reconfiguration of decoders

The configuration engine of Jade contains several mechanisms to switch between different decoder representations during the decoding process. The dataflow representation of the coding tools provided by MPEG RVC gives the ability to incrementally and partially re-program a decoder when receiving new configurations from a bitstream.

The configuration and the reconfiguration of decoder are illustrated in Table 1. Two representations of decoders are standardized by MPEG RVC; the *Simple Profile* (SP) [17, 14] from the MPEG-4 part 2 standards and the *Constrained Baseline Profile* (CBP) [10] of the Advanced Video Coding (AVC)/H.264 decoder from the MPEG-4 part 10. Reconfiguration is done by switching to a proprietary configuration of these decoders. The first configuration is an optimized configuration of the same decoder provided by Ericsson. The second reconfiguration is a configuration developed by the IETR laboratory which represents the *Fidelity Range Extensions* (FRExt) of MPEG-4 AVC. The benchmarks are realized on an Intel E6600 Core2 Duo processor at 2.40 GHz and the entire decoder configurations are available at *http://orc-apps.sourceforge.net.*

Table 1: Configuration and reconfiguration times between implementations of MPEG-4 part 2 *Simple Profile* (SP) and MPEG-4 part10 Advanced Video Coding.

Std.	Configurations	conf.	reconf.
SP	RVC -> Ericsson	1141 ms	380 ms
AVC	CBP -> FRExt	3313 ms	1610 ms

3.2 Clustering and spreading execution on processing units

Jade maximizes the use of the computing resources of any target platform by taking advantage of the inherent parallelism present in an MPEG RVC decoder. The *configuration* of a decoder gives information about the interconnection between coding tools (algorithms) that compose a decoder without carrying any implementation details for a specific platform. Therefore, Jade can execute the adaptive decoder according to the features (e.g. multiple cores) of the underlying platform.

Two optimizations algorithms based on execution models were incorporated in Jade to utilize the concurrency of a decoder configuration, depending on the number of cores in the underlying platforms. The first optimization analyzes a configuration and removes concurrency between tools to find an efficient execution on a same core. The second optimization applies an efficient distribution of independent coding tools onto separate cores. Table 2 shows the ability of Jade for exploiting multi-core CPUs. Each decoder configuration is executed on both cores of an Intel E6600 Core2 Duo processor at 2.40 GHz.

3.3 Easy edition and creation of decoders

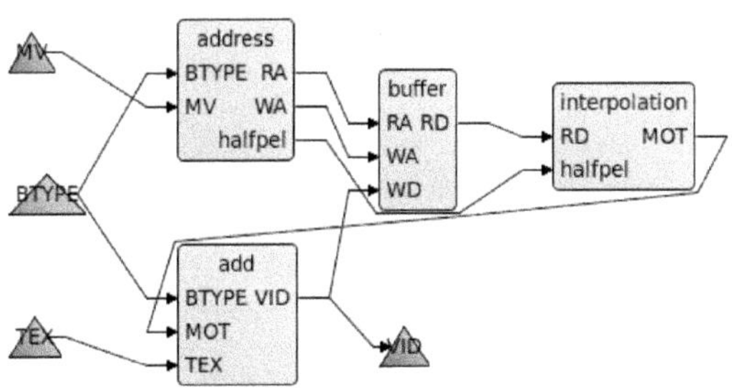

Figure 5: Graphiti edition of the motion compensation for the MPEG-4 part 2 decoder.

Jade is delivered with a complete framework, called Open RVC-CAL Compiler (Orcc), which permits exploring and editing decoder configurations. The configuration of a decoder is described using the XML Dataflow Format (XDF) and can be edited using Graphiti[1], a generic graph editor delivered as an Eclipse plug-in. Orcc also features a complete IDE based on XText for editing the Video Tool Library. It allows developers to add proprietary coding tools to VTLs and to enhance their decoder implementation with modified or completely new versions of decoder configuration.

Figure 5 shows a screenshot of the motion compensation part of the MPEG-4 part 2 *Simple Profile* decoder as a block diagram. The squares represent the coding tools of the configuration and the wires the communications between the coding tools. The triangles represent the inputs and outputs of the given network, allowing the use of a hierarchical description.

Table 2: Decoding performance of the two RVC implementations of MPEG-4 part 2 (SP) and MPEG-4 part 10 (AVC) running on 1 and 2 cores.

Decoder	One core	Two cores	Speedup
SP (RVC)	33 fps	61 fps	1.86
AVC (RVC)	36 fps	79 fps	2.19

4. USING JADE

The binaries and sources code of the first release version (1.0) of Jade can be downloaded at [3]. The source code package is organized in three different directories: the library sources (src), doxygen documentation (doc) and the VTL folder (VTL). Jade necessarily requires a version of the VTL as standardized in MPEG-C to be set in the VTL folder. One can be downloaded at [3] or be generated by the Orcc Framework. The installation documentation of the Orcc framework is available at [6]. The user can also find more open-source applications that are directly useable in Jade such as a JPEG encoder, a GZIP compressor and a cryptographic encoder (CTL) at [4].

The compilation of Jade also requires the use of three other open-source projects, selected with portability in mind. CMake [1] provides the ability of an easy cross-compilation onto multiple operating systems and multiple processor architectures. The SDL libraries [8] permit a portable display and LLVM [5] delivers the necessary libraries for an efficient Just-In-Time compilation for mixed platforms. For Windows users, a library of POSIX thread management [7] is necessary.

Jade provides several interfaces to test its different capabilities. It can be integrated into the Eclipse framework, used from the command line or directly in a player with GPAC [2]. The reader can refer to [6] to find more information about compilation, installation and use of Jade.

4.1 Interfaces of Jade

Jade provides a command line and a simulator interface to demonstrate its configurability. It also provides two other test interfaces : the *scenario* or *console* modes that provides dynamic interaction with the engine.

1. *Command line*: The simplest way to test Jade is to use the command line. The option *-help* gives a full list of all options available for tuning Jade performance depending on the underlying platform. The mandatory options to launch Jade are an XDF network (*-xdf*), an encoded video (*-i*), and the location of your Video Tool Library folder (*-L*).

2. *Console or scenario mode*: These interfaces enable testing the dynamic behavior of Jade. Series of commands can be applied to Jade manager for on-the-fly configuring and reconfiguring of multiple decoders.

[1]Graphiti is available at : http://graphiti-editor.sf.net

The list of commands is explained in detail in a README file provided with the project package.

3. *Orcc simulator*: Jade can be shipped as an eclipse plug-in for helping decoder developers to efficiently test their application. First, the Orcc development and the Graphiti editor must be correctly installed to the eclipse framework. [6] gives instructions to install the complete framework for creating and editing a decoder configuration. Once installed, Jade appears as a new simulator on the Orcc Framework.

4.2 Integration of Jade in a GPAC player

GPAC [2] is currently following ongoing standardization efforts such as HTTP streaming [18] or an MPEG-4 SVC decoder [9]. GPAC is also capable of encapsulating/de-encapsulating RVC decoder description into/from *mp4* video files. Jade is natively included in this project as a GPAC plug-in that allows the player to intantiate on-the-fly an RVC description from an mp4 files and to decode the associated embedded rawstream.

- Encapsulating RVC description: Use MP4Box -add *rawstream.264*:rvc=*config.xml* *rvc_video.mp4*. *rawstream.264* is an encoded bitstream filename, *config.xml* is an XDF network and *rvc_video.mp4* is the resulting mp4 files.
- De-encapsulating RVC description: Use MP4Client *rvc_video.mp4* as command line or Osmo4 as a GUI.

5. CONCLUSIONS

Orcc is a two year old framework now used by industry and research laboratories worldwide. In only one year, Jade has evolved from its experimental origins to become a real proof of concept of the MPEG RVC paradigm. It provides the first Virtual Machine which is able to dynamically instantiate RVC decoder descriptions avoiding inconsistency between a coded bitstream and a decoding platform. An interesting aspect of Jade and MPEG RVC is also its potential usage in the academic and research world. Students, developers and researchers can mix and modify on-the-fly video coding algorithms in a particular decoder to get the best trade-off between coding efficiency and computational cost.

Although the performance is lower than a manually optimized decoder on a single-core system, the property of the MPEG RVC decoder representation is suitable for the next generation of multi-core processor. Moreover, remembering that dataflow representation of decoder provides a considerable potential parallelism, we have already planned to integrate GPU management based on the OpenCL framework to the Jade's Virtual Machine.

6. ACKNOWLEDGMENTS

The authors would like to thank people having contributed directly or indirectly to the development of Jade. First, we cannot avoid offering our deepest respect to Matthieu Wipliez who has led the Orcc project to maturity and his genius for finding easy solutions to complex problems. We also would like to take this opportunity to extend warm thanks to Jean Lefeuvre and his team for their help and to Olivier Labois for his work on the integration of Jade to GPAC.

7. REFERENCES

[1] CMake. `http://www.cmake.org/`.

[2] GPAC. `http://gpac.wp.institut-telecom.fr`.

[3] Jade. `http://sourceforge.net/projects/orcc/files/Jade/`.

[4] Jade applications. `http://orc-apps.sourceforge.net/`.

[5] LLVM. `http://llvm.org`.

[6] Orcc. `http://orcc.sourceforge.net`.

[7] Pthreads-w32. `http://sourceware.org/pthreads-win32/`.

[8] Simple Direct Media Layer. `http://www.libsdl.org/`.

[9] M. Blestel and M. Raulet. Open SVC decoder: a flexible SVC library. In *Proceedings of the international conference on Multimedia*, MM '10, pages 1463–1466, New York, NY, USA, 2010. ACM.

[10] J. Gorin, M. Raulet, Y. L. Cheng, H. Y. Lin, N. Siret, K. Sugimoto, and G. G. Lee. An RVC dataflow description of the AVC Constrained Baseline Profile decoder. In *Image Processing (ICIP), 2009 16th IEEE International Conference on*, pages 753–756, 2010.

[11] J. Gorin, M. Wipliez, J. Piat, M. Raulet, and F. Preteux. A portable Video Tools Library for MPEG Reconfigurable Video Coding using LLVM representation. In *Design and Architectures for Signal and Image Processing (DASIP 2010)*, pages 281–286, 2008.

[12] J. Gorin, M. Wipliez, F. Preteux, and M. Raulet. LLVM-based and scalable MPEG-RVC decoder. *Journal of Real-Time Image Processing*, pages 1–12.

[13] J. Gorin, M. Wipliez, M. Raulet, and F. Preteux. An LLVM-based decoder for MPEG Reconfigurable Video Coding. In *IEEE Workshop on Signal Processing Systems (SiPS 2010), Washington, D.C., USA*, pages 281–286, 2008.

[14] J. W. Janneck, I. Miller, D. Parlour, G. Roquier, M. Wipliez, and M. Raulet. Synthesizing Hardware from Dataflow Programs: An MPEG-4 Simple Profile Decoder Case Study. *Journal of Signal Processing Systems*, 63(2):241–249, May 2011.

[15] C. Lattner and V. Adve. LLVM: A compilation framework for lifelong program analysis & transformation. In *Proceedings of the international symposium on Code generation and optimization: feedback-directed and runtime optimization*, page 75. IEEE Computer Society, 2004.

[16] M. Mattavelli, I. Amer, and M. Raulet. The Reconfigurable Video Coding Standard [Standards in a Nutshell]. *Signal Processing Magazine, IEEE*, 27(3):159 -167, May 2010.

[17] G. Roquier, M. Wipliez, M. Raulet, J. Janneck, I. Miller, and D. Parlour. Automatic software synthesis of dataflow program: An MPEG-4 simple profile decoder case study. In *Signal Processing Systems, 2008. SiPS 2008. IEEE Workshop on*, pages 281–286. IEEE, 2008.

[18] I. Sodagar. Overview of Dynamic Adaptive Streaming over HTTP (DASH). In *ISO/IEC JTC1/SC29/WG11 N11964*, March 2011, Geneva, Switzerland.

Experimenting with Multimedia Advances using GPAC

Jean Le Feuvre, Cyril Concolato, Jean-Claude Dufourd, Romain Bouqueau, Jean-Claude Moissinac
Multimedia Group, Telecom ParisTech, LTCI UMR 4141
Paris, France
{ lefeuvre, concolato, dufourd, bouqueau, moissinac }@telecom-paristech.fr

ABSTRACT

Multimedia applications are challenging software and require collaboration of very different components such as networking, rendering, or scripting to provide a nice user experience. GPAC is an open source multimedia framework that implements a vast number of components and helps experimenting with different types of multimedia applications. It provides a multimedia packager, some servers and a player for dynamic and interactive multimedia content. In this paper, we present the recent additions to the project which allow experimenting with new applications such as dynamic home networking or rich broadcasting of interactive content on the latest devices, including with 3D displays. Such experiments can be useful in research work and, as illustrated, in academic environment for educational purposes.

Categories and Subject Descriptors

H.5.1 [**Information Interfaces and Presentation**]: Multimedia Information Systems –*Animations, video;* H.5.2 [**Information Interfaces and Presentation**]: User Interfaces – *graphical user interfaces, standardization;* H.5.4 [**Information Interfaces and Presentation**]: Hypertext/Hypermedia – *Architectures.*

General Terms: Algorithms, Experimentation, Standardization, Languages.

Keywords: Multimedia, Interactivity, Broadcasting, Stereoscopy, Home Networking, MPEG, BIFS, SVG, Web3D, Streaming.

1. INTRODUCTION

GPAC [1] is a cross-platform open source multimedia framework distributed under the LGPL license. Since its creation the project has been known for its strong focus on standard technologies for the coding, delivery and playback of dynamic and interactive multimedia content, such as those developed within MPEG, W3C or Web3D standard bodies. More recently, the project has opened the way for experimenting with new multimedia technologies such as HTTP adaptive streaming, Home Networking (UPnP, DLNA) or stereoscopic multimedia, as will be described later on in this paper.

GPAC offers a collection of tools for interactive media packaging, distribution and playback, all built upon a single library, called libgpac; this library contains all core functionalities of the framework, enabling a simplified reuse of GPAC by third-party projects.

The main packaging application of GPAC is called MP4Box. Among its numerous functionalities, we can cite:

- Multiplexing many audio, video and text formats, multiplexed or not, in ISO Base Media Files (e.g. MP4),
- Encoding and decoding scene description formats such as MPEG-4 Binary Format for Scenes (BIFS) and Lightweight Application Scene Representation (LASeR),
- Preparing the content for HTTP download or streaming with the Real-Time Transport Protocol (RTP).

MP4Box has a large user base within the audio and video community (e.g. default MP4 packager for x264[1]), and is used by many academics[2]. GPAC also contains several servers for streaming with RTP and with MPEG-2 Transport Stream (MPEG-2 TS). These tools will be further detailed in the next section.

The main aspect of GPAC is however its multimedia player, MP4Client/Osmo4. With its focus on interactive content, the player differs from traditional media players in many ways, and is close to web browsers, as it enables playback of:

- Interactive, animated 2D vector graphics such as BIFS or W3C Scalable Vector Graphics (SVG),
- Interactive, animated 3D graphics such as MPEG-4 BIFS or Virtual Reality Modeling Language (VRML) or X3D, the XML successor of VRML,
- Multiple controllable video, sound or subtitles objects in 2D or 3D content,
- 2D content integrated in 3D content and vice-versa,
- Javascript for BIFS/SVG/VRML, including AJAX.

One particularity of the player is its extensibility through a large set of plug-ins covering media formats demultiplexing, media decoding, javascript extensions or user event filtering. The player already has support for a wide range of multimedia delivery protocols (HTTP including IceCast, ShoutCast, RTP streaming, MPEG-2 TS). This makes the player quite suitable for research experiments, as new functionality can be added without modifying the player code. The player can also be seen as a good candidate for testing new ideas for interactive multimedia. For instance, most (if not all) aspects of the upcoming HTML Media specification[3], such as buffer monitoring, media control or selection, are covered and demonstrated on the GPAC web site [1]. Advanced aspects such as integration of 3D content in Web content such as envisaged in [3]

---

[1] x264, http://www.videolan.org/developers/x264.html

[2] GPAC References, http://gpac.wp.institut-telecom.fr/about/references

[3] http://www.w3.org/TR/2011/WD-html5-20110405/video.html

can also be tested. Although quite versatile, one weakness of the project is its lack of support for HTML/CSS.

The GPAC project was already selected for the 2007 edition of the competition, and an in-depth overview of the software can be found in [2]. This paper presents, in Section 2, the major evolution of the platform in the recent years and in section 3, how it is used for educational purposes.

2. ADVANCED MULTIMEDIA USAGES

The field of multimedia applications is always evolving at a fast pace, with new technologies appearing every year or two. The GPAC projects tries to keep this pace and to integrate new software components in order to facilitate experimenting with these new technologies.

2.1 Home Networking

Among the foreseen new usages, the convergence between the internet world, the broadcast world and the home is seen as a promising source of new multimedia applications. Standards such as those developed by the Digital Living Network Alliance (DLNA) are being deployed, enabling devices in a home network to discover each other and to communicate. Connected TV sets are being shipped to propose Internet content in the home. Within this context, we have added the Universal Plug and Play (UPnP) support, through the Platinum library[4], and the ability for the GPAC player to act as a remote control for other DLNA media players on the network, selecting both target screens and source content.

Additionally, the scene description capabilities of the GPAC player have been leveraged to expose the information and control offered by DLNA within the scene. This work was done within the scope of the standardization of widget technologies. In the recent years, standard bodies such as MPEG or W3C have worked on Widgets, which are packaged (e.g. ZIP) multimedia presentations (HTML, SVG, BIFS) used as standalone applications. We have been particularly involved in this work at MPEG, especially on the following topics: communication between such widgets in a home network, and session mobility of such widgets between various devices (TV, laptop, smart phones).We have demonstrated interoperability of MPEG-U Widgets with UPnP-based services, especially DLNA media player and media server. MPEG-U is ISO/IEC 23007-1 and its GPAC implementation was released as the MPEG reference software; some videos demonstrations can be found on the GPAC web site[5]. GPAC is also a conformant implementation of W3C Widgets Packaging and Configuration[6] and The Widget Interface[7].

2.2 Media Transport

As part of its recent developments, new media transport methods, mostly related to broadcast or near-broadcast, were added to GPAC.

In the past few years, the French Government has been investigating the usage of the T-DMB standard [4] for Augmented Digital Radio, bringing high quality audio along with interactivity to the user. The GPAC player was used by many industrial during this phase, because of its native support for the T-DMB system. We have been working on enhancing this support in GPAC, and have introduced live BIFS encoding and live audio stream injection in our MP42TS tool to generate T-DMB compliant radio streams, as described in Figure 1. A video on GPAC web site demonstrates the result of this work[5], which is being integrated in the MPEG-2 Systems standard through a new amendment. Similar developments were made with the live injection of 3GPP DIMS content into MPEG-2 TS in the context of the DVB-H or ATSC-M/H standards were demonstrated at NAB2010.

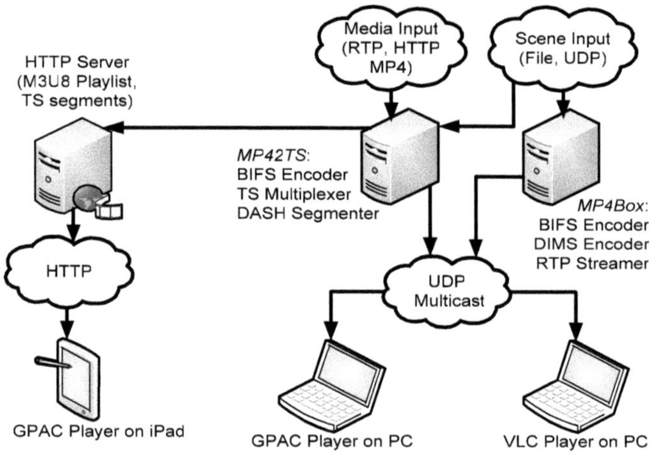

Figure 1 - GPAC Media Server Tools

Finally, GPAC has been extended towards HTTP streaming technologies. Solutions such as the proprietary Apple HTTP Live Streaming (HLS)[8] or standardized MPEG Dynamic Adaptive Streaming over HTTP (DASH) [5] have been added both in the player and in the content production tools. For instance the MP42TS application is now capable of truncating its MPEG-2 TS output in segments compatible with the DASH standard or with HLS, in live or offline mode, as described in Figure 1. The MP4Box tool can produce MP4 files compatible with the MPEG-DASH standard, and the player is capable of processing both types of content.

2.3 3D Screens

A recent trend in digital television industry is the deployment of 3D TV. We have started in 2007 a research activity around usage of auto-stereoscopic screens on mobile platforms, and demonstrated usage of video, slide shows and interactive contents for such devices. In order to test depth effects on other platforms, we have recently extended GPAC to be able to display multimedia content on many types of 3D screens [6]. GPAC now supports anaglyph rendering (stereo only), or any number of viewpoints rendered side-by-side, top-to-bottom, and columns- or row- interleaved output. Custom view interleaving is also possible through OpenGL shaders, and has been tested with a 5 views display built by SpatialView[9], as shown in Figure 2.

---

[4]Platinum UPnP SDK, http://www.plutinosoft.com/platinum

[5] http://gpac.wp.institut-telecom.fr/gpac-features/videos/

[6] http://www.w3.org/TR/2011/WD-widgets-20110322/

[7] http://www.w3.org/TR/2010/WD-widgets-apis-20100907/

[8] http://tools.ietf.org/html/draft-pantos-http-live-streaming-06

[9] http://www.spatialview.com/

Figure 2 - Depth-based rendering on 5 views 3D display

In multiview mode, the player currently handles 3D content (BIFS/VRML/X3D), 2D scalable content (BIFS/SVG) with some extensions to provide depth information (as explained in [2]), video with depth map as used in MPEG-C [7] and image with depth map. Although still in experimental stage, this makes GPAC the first open-source multimedia browser with support for many 3D displays, including multiview auto-stereoscopic display.

2.4 Scalable Video Coding

Among the new formats that have been developed recently, the MPEG Scalable Video Codec (SVC) [8] provides an interesting ability to represent video content as scalable layers. It is interesting for multimedia applications to adapt to the varying network conditions or display size. As said previously, the player functionalities can easily be extended with various plug-ins, in particular for media processing. To support SVC, the code of OpenSVC project[10] was integrated as a new plug-in and means to select a layer (quality, spatial resolution) from the scene was added. Additionally, the ability to manipulate SVC content within MP4 files was also added to MP4Box.

2.5 Platforms

Although most of the work on GPAC derives from research activities, the project tries to enable experimenting advanced multimedia applications on many platforms, even the latest ones.

For instance, a special effort has been made to produce installer packages for most desktop platforms (Linux-Debian, Windows, Mac OS X), enabling end-users or students to experiment GPAC without having to compile it.

Additionally to the existing Windows Mobile port, mobile versions of GPAC now exist for Apple's iOS and Google's Android. Videos of GPAC running in iPhone or Android devices are available on GPAC web site[5]. Figure 3 shows GPAC on an iPad playing an SVG electronic service guide transcoded from DVB-T broadcast with GPAC. Figure 4 shows GPAC on an ad-hoc digital radio device. The player has also been successfully ported on embedded SH4 platforms, typically set-top boxes.

Finally, one effort in GPAC was the design of a platform-independent graphical user interface based on GPAC-supported scene technologies such as BIFS or SVG and Javascript. This effort enables the deployment of applications on additional platforms more efficiently.

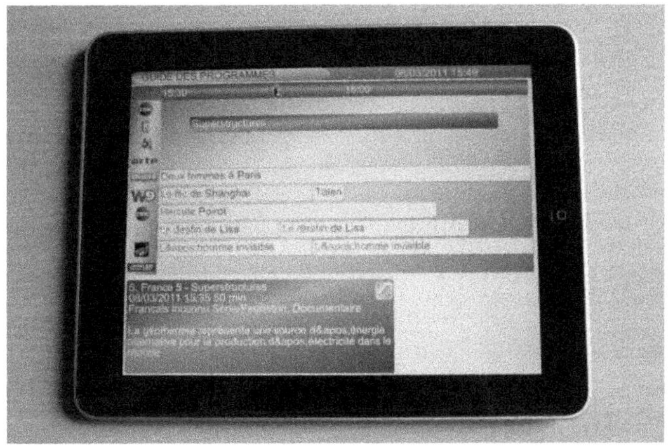

Figure 3 - GPAC on iPad showing an EPG application

Figure 4 - GPAC on a T-DMB kitchen-radio

3. EDUCATION

GPAC is a corner stone of our daily activities, and we use it in research projects as well as educational works. This section presents the effort made in this area.

3.1 Usage of GPAC in student projects

It is our very belief that programming projects play a very important part in the student's learning, as they help the student to acquire in-depth understanding f concepts seen in classes through practical cases. For a long time, we have been involving our students (master, PhD …) with GPAC, taking advantage of its plug-in and core-library based architecture to have them implement complex scenarios without having to program all the complexity of a full-featured multimedia player or delivery system. Depending on work quality and context, these projects may be released to the public.

We usually diversify the topics of our project. One recurrent topic is human-computer interaction modes in GPAC, and students have produced GPAC plug-ins for head-tracking based on OpenCV[11] (released as the *opencv_js* module), Wiimote control based on wiiuse[12] (released as the *wiis* module) or Voice recognition based on HTK[13].

Another recurrent topic is scene description technologies, usually based on BIFS or SVG. Some project only use GPAC tools such as

[10] http://opensvcdecoder.sourceforge.net

[11] http://opencv.willowgarage.com

[12] http://sourceforge.net/projects/wiiuse/

[13] http://htk.eng.cam.ac.uk/

Osmo4 or MP4Box in the content production or playback phase. Such projects include for example a DVD to BIFS transcoder or an Electronic Program Guide in BIFS. Other projects build on top of GPAC or extend it, as was done with a simple authoring tool based on GPAC (released as *V4Studio*) or with a plug-in building an SVG spectrogram out of an audio signal.

In parallel to our classes on multimedia transport, some students have realized an SVG streaming application, a DVB-H burst simulator or have included BIFS carouseling mechanism in some GPAC tools (MP42TS).

We have also proposed more programming-centric projects to our students, out of which we must cite the JPEG2000 decoder plug-in based on OpenJPEG[14] and the web-browser plug-ins for NPAPI-based browsers (Osmozilla) and ActiveX-enabled ones (GPAX). All these projects are now part of the public GPAC source.

Students in 2009 and 2010 used GPAC as a capture tool in projects comparing the playback of SVG files in any browser with a reference image. These results should soon appear in GPAC's upcoming automatic testing platform.

3.2 Other Academic Usages of GPAC

Apart from student projects, we use GPAC in several student classes. Students use MP4Box to construct, inspect and dump MP4 files, and based on box layout dumped by MP4Box, deduce media tracks interleaving properties. They use GPAC RTSP/RTP logging and RTP over RTSP tunneling capabilities to study the behavior of RTSP sessions, timing and network information exchanged and how they match values in RTP packet.

The player is also used in scene description classes, where students have to author simple SVG or BIFS (2D or 3D) content, progressively adding interactivity, scripting and AJAX support. The BIFS part of these classes has been extended into a tutorial in French and English publically available on [1].

We are also planning to use GPAC in an upcoming corporate training session on 3DTV to demonstrate auto-stereoscopic screens, and are proposing to our students subjects related to that topic, namely spatial view interpolation, where GPAC is used as the visualization tool for the generated frames.

Our collaborations with other academics have confirmed that GPAC is also used for lab sessions in other universities, such as Telecom SudParis or by master students in Klagenfurt University or Gent IBBT-MMLab.

Apart from student-related usage, GPAC is used in many of our research projects[15]. GPAC is also being used by academics throughout the world in many papers, and although it is quite hard to quantify due to lack of explicit references, we try to maintain a list of published work referring to GPAC on our web site.

4. CONCLUSION

In this paper, we have presented the GPAC multimedia framework and detailed the features added to the framework since the publication of [2].

We have also detailed how our students use GPAC for lab sessions or technical projects, and attempted to measure the impact of the framework on the academic community. Although GPAC is always in heavy development, we are pleased to see that the academic community is actively using it. Future directions of the project will include hybrid broadband/broadcast tools, stereoscopic enhancement, and advanced user interactions.

5. ACKNOWLEDGMENTS

Part of the work presented in this paper is financed by the following French-funded projects: HybRadio, Calder and EndT2End. The authors would like to thank all the other contributors to the project (from students, to developers and post-docs).

6. REFERENCES

[1] GPAC Web Site, http://gpac.sourceforge.net

[2] J. Le Feuvre, C. Concolato, J.C. Moissinac. "GPAC: open source multimedia framework". In *Proceedings of the 15th international Conference on Multimedia,* Augsburg, *Germany, September 25 - 29, 2007. MULTIMEDIA '07. ACM,* New York, NY, 1009-1012. DOI= 10.1145/1291233.1291452

[3] Johannes Behr, Peter Eschler, Yvonne Jung, and Michael Zöllner. 2009. X3DOM: a DOM-based HTML5/X3D integration model. In Proceedings of the 14th International Conference on 3D Web Technology (Web3D '09), Stephen N. Spencer (Ed.). ACM, New York, NY, USA, 127-135. DOI=10.1145/1559764.1559784

[4] G. Lee, S. Cho, K.-t. Yang, Y K. Hahm, and S. I. Lee, "Development of terrestrial DMB transmission system based on Eureka-147 DAB system", IEEE Trans. on Consum. Elec., vol. 51, no. 1, pp. 63-68, Feb. 2005. DOI=10.1109/TCE.2005.1405700

[5] Thomas Stockhammer. 2011. Dynamic adaptive streaming over HTTP : standards and design principles. In Proceedings of the second annual ACM conference on Multimedia systems (MMSys '11). ACM, New York, NY, USA, 133-144. DOI=10.1145/1943552.1943572

[6] N. A. Dodgson, "Autostereoscopic 3-D displays," IEEE Computer, vol. 38, no. 8, pp. 31–36, Aug. 2005. DOI=10.1109/MC.2005.252

[7] A. Bourge, J. Gobert and F. Bruls, "MPEG-C part 3: Enabling the introduction of video plus depth contents," in Proc. of IEEE Workshop on Content Generation and Coding for 3D-television, Eindhoven, The Netherlands, June 2006.

[8] Robert Kuschnig, Ingo Kofler, Michael Ransburg, and Hermann Hellwagner. 2008. Design options and comparison of in-network H.264/SVC adaptation. J. Vis. Comun. Image Represent. 19, 8 (December 2008), 529-542. DOI=10.1016/j.jvcir.2008.07.0

---

[14] http://www.openjpeg.org/

[15] http://gpac.wp.institut-telecom.fr/about/references/#rd

ClassX - An Open Source Interactive Lecture Streaming System

Sherif Halawa, Derek Pang, Ngai-Man Cheung, and Bernd Girod
Stanford University
Packard Bldg, Serra Mall
Stanford, CA 94305, USA
{halawa, dcypang, ncheung, bgirod}@stanford.edu

ABSTRACT

The ClassX open source project is a free experimental interactive video streaming platform designed for educators, researchers and software developers. With minimal infrastructure set-up, ClassX offers educational communities a cost-effective solution for online lecture delivery. Our goal is to encourage contributions from other researchers, developers and educators in building an open, cost-effective and state-of-the-art online education video viewing system for the general public.

Categories and Subject Descriptors

H.5.1 [**Multimedia Information Systems**]: Video

General Terms

Algorithm, Design

Keywords

Education, interactive region-of-interest video streaming, automatic lecturer tracking, electronic slide matching

1. INTRODUCTION

The advent of video streaming technology in the past decade has reshaped our educational systems significantly. More educators are making their lectures available online for students in their institutions or around the world to view. Nevertheless, the current status of lecture capture remains an obstacle that hinders many educators from recording and publishing their lectures. This is due to the special equipment and considerations that must be taken to ensure that important scene regions such as boards or projector screens are captured at sufficient quality.

Conventional lecture capture systems often rely on expensive recording and production equipment and require a camera operator. Some systems use multiple cameras to capture different views of the classroom. A human operator then selects one of the feeds at a time. Other systems use a single HD camera to capture the whole scene and manual or automatic tracking to crop out what is thought to be the student's region-of-interest (RoI). Prior work based on such systems includes [1, 8, 11].

The conventional video production model encounters a number of challenges when applied to lecture capturing. Professional recording and production equipment might be unaffordable. Camera operators tend to be unskilled, often students working a temporary part-time job. Nevertheless, wages for an extra person in the classroom might be prohibitive. Moreover, the camera operator might not have a deep understanding of the material presented and thus frame the shot incorrectly. A review of conventionally produced lecture videos reveals that this is a rather common problem. For example, the video might show a close-up of the instructor, when the attentive student wants to view the material on the blackboard that the instructor is referring to. Frequently, the camera operator lags behind a shift in focus by several seconds and might even appear "out of phase" if the focus shifts back and forth rapidly, say, between two wallboards. Note that it is not possible to correct for this in the conventional postproduction stage. Contents that is not recorded is lost.

ClassX efficiently addresses the abovementioned problems. A high-quality video is captured using a single consumer-grade HD camcorder. This makes it easy and cheap to record in any classroom. The camcorder is statically mounted to capture the front of the classroom in its entirety. This eliminates the need for a camera operator and the possibility of losing important scene content. The video is afterwards processed and transcoded to a special format which allows the student to choose his/her RoI. This RoI may be selected interactively in "interactive mode", or may be estimated by the system in the "automatic tracking mode". ClassX also synchronizes the video automatically with electronic slides, thus providing powerful video annotation with no human intervention.

ClassX was the idea and initiative of a group of graduate students at Stanford almost two years ago. The software has evolved through the contributions of numerous students since then, and we have learned tremendously from the practical deployment of the system from the very start. In March 2011, ClassX was released as an open source project under the GNU GPL in order to make it free for educators to use, and in order to attract researchers' and developers' inter-

MM'11, November 28–December 1, 2011, Scottsdale, Arizona, USA.

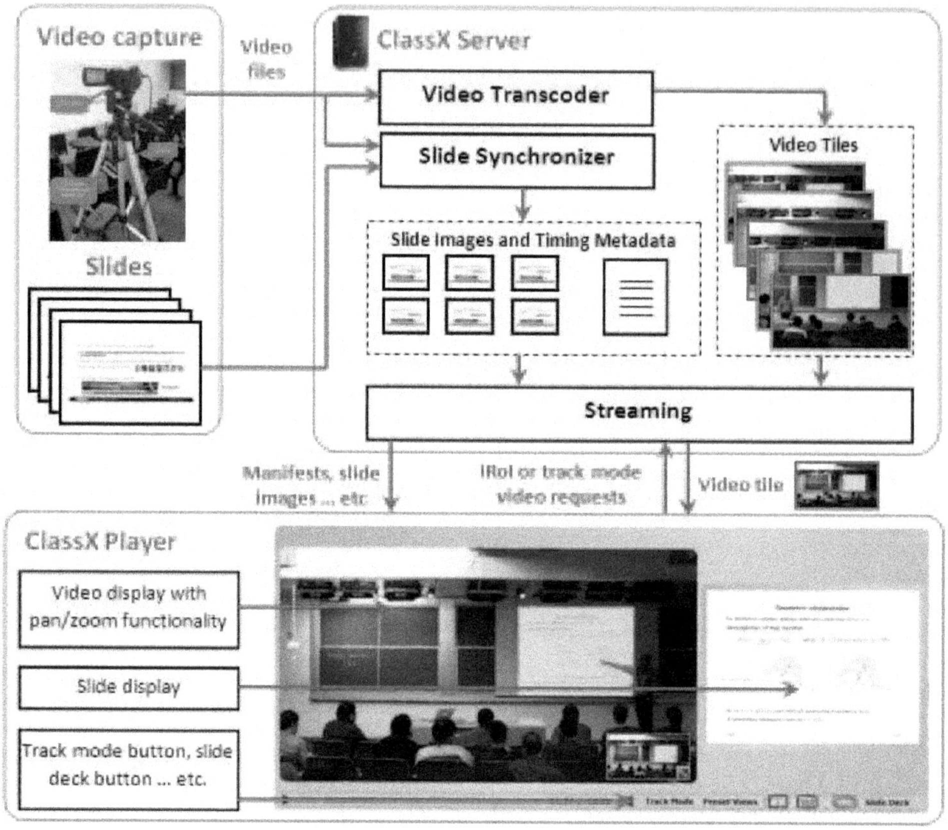

Figure 1: Overview of the ClassX System

est, who may then contribute to the project by adding new features that are useful to educators and students.

The rest of this paper is organized as follows. Section 2 provides a system overview of ClassX. Section 3 provides pointers to the locations of the resources needed to run or test ClassX. Section 4 provides usage statistics based on the deployment of ClassX as a lecture streaming system at Stanford University and as an open source project.

2. SYSTEM OVERVIEW

The ClassX system [4] is illustrated in Figure 1. It consists of the following components:

- A video transcoder
- A slide synchronizer
- Players to play the content to the user
- A web system that integrates the previous components and provides easy publishing and access interfaces

We will discuss each component in more details.

2.1 Video Transcoder

ClassX uses interactive region-of-interest (IRoI) to serve HD quality video at lower bit rates [5–7]. This is achieved as follows. When an input video is supplied to the ClassX video transcoder, it resamples the video, producing one or more representations of the video at different resolution levels. One or more tiles are then generated per resolution level, each of which is a differently cropped version of the video at that resolution level. The tiling scheme is designed such that any region of interest can be covered using one of the generated tiles. Figure 2 illustrates a scheme where an input video of resolution 1920×1080 pixels is transcoded into five tiles in two resolution levels. When the user zooms out, the ClassX server sends a tile of lower resolution. When the user zooms in on a specific RoI, the server sends a tile corresponding to that RoI generated from a higher resolution version of the video. This technique guarantees high video quality and saves 40% to 60% of the bandwidth compared to streaming the whole HD video.

In addition to the tiles, the transcoder also generates the tracking tile which automatically follows the lecturer. When the user activates tracking mode, there is no need to manually pan/zoom in the video.

2.2 Slide Synchronizer

When a slide deck is supplied, ClassX runs an automatic slide synchronizer that applies image matching techniques to determine when each slide is shown in the video and generate metadata that enables the ClassX player to automatically display the correct slide alongside the video. The synchronizer starts by locating keyframes (frames where slide transitions have occured). These keyframes are then input to a pairwise image matching stage using local features as described in [10]. The results of the image matching are used to generate a manifest listing the slides and their showtimes

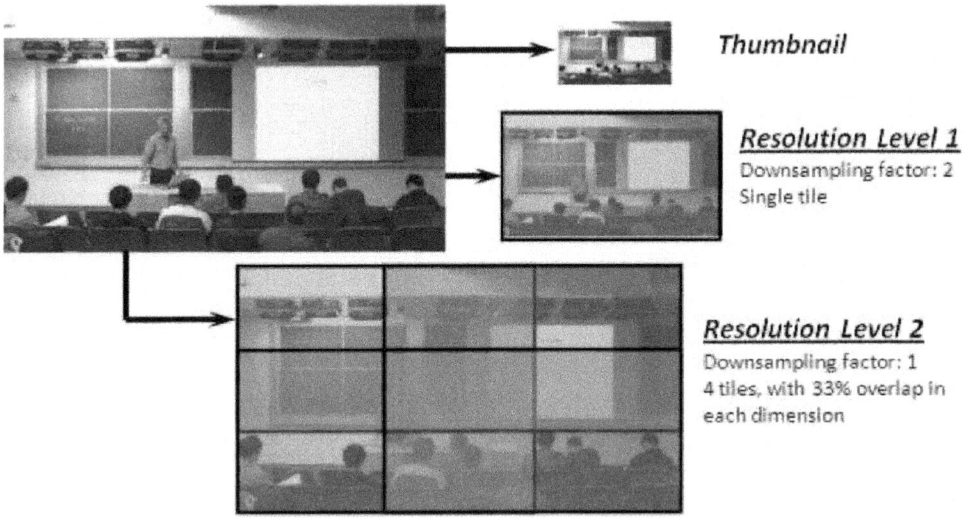

Figure 2: Tiling scheme with two resolution levels and five tiles

in the video. The ClassX player loads this manifest and uses it to show the correct slide in the slide display.

2.3 ClassX Players

The ClassX player, depicted in Figure 1, is the application which presents ClassX content to the user. It contains a video display through which the user views and interacts with the video. There is a track mode button that lets the user switch automatic lecturer tracking mode on or off.

When slides are synchronized with the video, the player also shows a slide display area and a button which can open or close a slide deck bar. This bar lists thumbnails of all available slides and lets the user seek to the point in the video when a selected slide is first shown.

Two versions of the ClassX player, running under the Microsoft Silverlight and Adobe Flash runtimes, have been released. These are currently optimized for desktop application only. A third version, built for Android, may run on any Android device with a multi-touch screen, including mobile phones and tablets [9]. This version will be released soon.

2.4 Web System

ClassX is provided as an integrated web system that is easy to install on any Unix-like server. The web system provides a publisher interface for easy publishing of ClassX presentations, as well as a user interface that the students may use to browse and view the published sessions.

3. INSTALLATION AND TEST

The ClassX open source page [2] provides links to useful resources for educators who want to use ClassX and developers who want to experiment with or contribute to the project. The web page at [3] contains a zipped file that contains all required packages and a list of instructions on how to build and test ClassX.

4. USAGE STATISTICS

ClassX was first deployed in Fall 2009 at Stanford university, and has been used since then to serve over 35 courses and events. The recordings covered a wide gamut of presentation styles, ranging from slide presentations to "chalk-and-talk" lectures to pre-recordings without an audience.. Different event types were also covered, ranging from group talks in small rooms to public events held in large auditoriums.

Users have been providing ratings for some of the aspects of ClassX, including video quality, streaming quality, and ease of use. The results are shown in figures 3, 4, and 5.

As of end of August 2011, the number of distinct IP addresses that have viewed one or more sessions on ClassX was approximately 6,390 and the total number of session views was approximately 14,830. The open source project page has been visited 447 times. The code has been downloaded approximately 108 times.

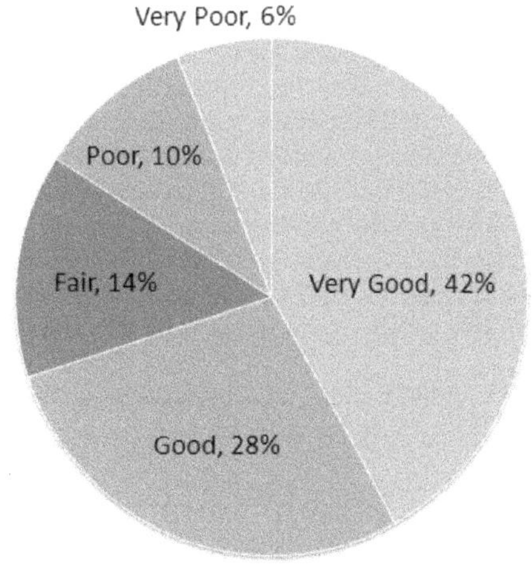

Figure 3: User feedback for video quality

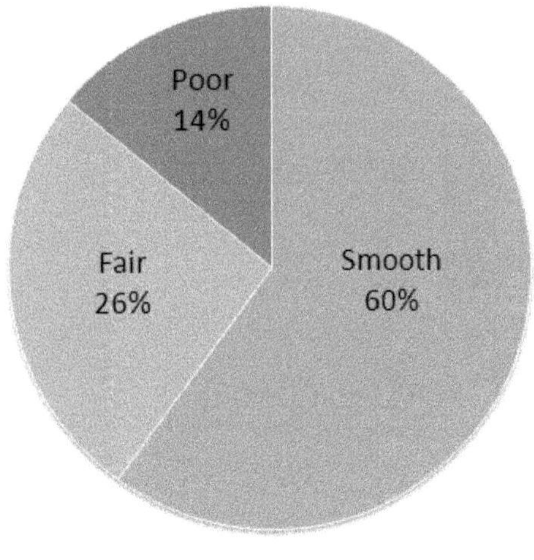

Figure 4: User feedback for streaming quality

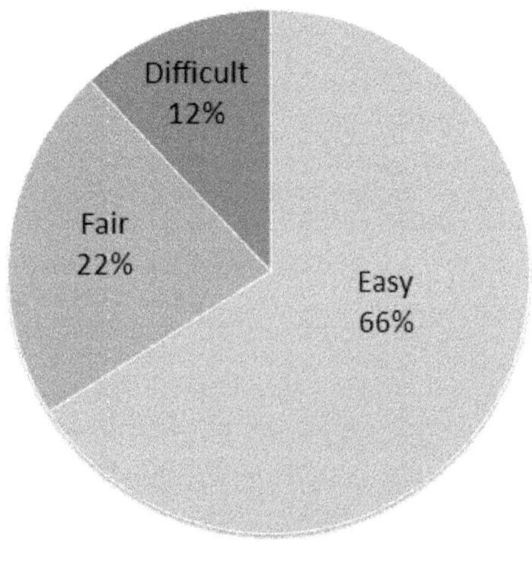

Figure 5: User feedback for system ease of use

5. CONCLUSIONS

We have presented the Class-X open source project. ClassX offers a low-cost solution for lecture capture, and has been used to cover many courses and events at Stanford University. ClassX also offers an interactive user experience through its IRoI video streaming and slide synchronization features. The viewer ratings of ClassX indicate their satisfaction with the video and streaming quality, and that they are finding the system in general easy to use.

Our user activity logs indicate that users often have different RoIs, and that the IRoI, automatic tracking, and slide synchronization features are actively being used by students. Publishers have also declared that they find the recording and publishing process easy. The system is built fully using open source tools to make it very easy to deploy and extend.

We have received many requests and suggestions to add content extraction features, such as board script and speech recognition, analytics, and accessibility features such as closed captioning and slide text-to-speech to the system. This was one of the motives behind the open source release. We aim to get more researchers and developers involved with the project to add these and other features that are useful to educators and students.

6. REFERENCES

[1] M. Bianchi. Automatic video production of lectures using an intelligent and aware environment. *Proc. 3rd Intl. Conf. on Mobile and ubiquitous multimedia (MUM'04), Maryland, USA*, pages 117–123, 2004.

[2] ClassX open source project homepage. `http://classx.sourceforge.net`.

[3] ClassX installer page. `http://classx.stanford.edu/Installer.html`.

[4] A. Mavlankar, P. Agrawal, D. Pang, S. Halawa, N. Cheung, and B. Girod. An interactive region-of-interest video streaming system for online lecture viewing. *Proc. of 18th International Packet Video Workshop*, pages 64 – 71, December 2010.

[5] A. Mavlankar, P. Baccichetand, D. Varodayan, and B. Girod. Optimal slice size for streaming regions of high resolution video with virtual pan/tilt/zoom functionality. *Proc. of 15th European Signal Processing Conference (EUSIPCO'07), Ponzan, Poland*, September 2007.

[6] A. Mavlankar and B. Girod. Background extraction and long-term memory motion-compensated prediction for spatial-random-access-enabled video coding. *in Proc. Picture Coding Symposium (PCS'09), USA*, May 2009.

[7] A. Mavlankar, J. Noh, P. Baccichet, and B. Girod. Peer-to-peer multicast live video streaming with interactive virtual pan/tilt/zoom functionality. *Proc. of IEEE Intl. Conf. on Image Processing (ICIP'08), USA*, pages 2296–2299, October 2008.

[8] S. Mukhopadhyay and B. Smith. Passive capture and structuring of lectures. *Proc. 7th ACM Intl. Conf. on Multimedia (Part 1) (MULTIMEDIA'99), FL, USA*, pages 477–487, 1999.

[9] D. Pang, S. Halawa, N.-M. Cheung, and B. Girod. ClassX mobile: An interactive video streaming system for mobile devices. Accepted for publication in Proc. ACM Intl. Conf. on Multimedia, AZ, USA, Nov. 2011.

[10] S. Tsai, D. Chen, J. Singh, and B. Girod. Rate-efficient, real-time CD cover recognition on a camera-phone. *Proc. ACM Intl. Conf. on Multimedia, Vancouver, BC, Canada*, Oct. 2008.

[11] C. Zhang, Y. Rui, J. Crawford, and L. He. An automated end-to-end lecture capture and broadcasting system. *ACM Trans. Multimedia Compt. Commun. Appl.*, 4(1):1–23, 2008.

A VLC Media Player Plugin enabling Dynamic Adaptive Streaming over HTTP

Christopher Müller and Christian Timmerer
Alpen-Adria-Universität Klagenfurt, Multimedia Communication
Universitätsstraße 65-67
9020 Klagenfurt am Wörthersee, Austria
+43 (0)463 2700 3600
{*firstname.lastname*}@itec.aau.at

ABSTRACT

This paper describes the implementation of a VLC media player plugin enabling Dynamic Adaptive Streaming over HTTP (DASH). DASH is an emerging ISO/IEC MPEG and 3GPP standard for HTTP streaming. It aims to standardize formats enabling segmented progressive download by exploiting existing Internet infrastructure as such. Our implementation of these formats as described in this paper is based on the well-known VLC. Hence, it is fully integrated into the VLC structure and has been also submitted to the VLC development team for consideration in future releases of VLC. Therefore, it is licensed under the GNU Lesser General Public License (LGPL). The plugin provides a very flexible structure that could be easily extended with respect to different adaptation logics or profiles of the DASH standard. As a consequence, the plugin enables the integration of a variety of adaptation logics and comparison thereof, making it attractive for the research community.

Categories and Subject Descriptors

H.5.1 [**Multimedia Information System**]: Video

General Terms

Documentation, Design, Standardization.

Keywords

Video, HTTP Streaming, DASH, Dynamic Adaptive Streaming over HTTP, MPEG, 3GPP.

1. INTRODUCTION

Video streaming is nowadays more and more provided over-the-top (OTT) using existing Internet infrastructures. This means that service providers do not build their own dedicated networks, they just use the Internet as it is. However, the Internet is not designed for real-time streaming, it is designed for best-effort delivery of files. Caches, proxies, and content distribution networks (CDN) are part of this infrastructure which support file transfer very well.

Existing streaming technologies like the real-time streaming protocol (RTP) could not take any advantage of this infrastructure due to their design and they also have other disadvantages, e.g., passing firewalls or network address translation (NAT) traversal. Bitrate variances are also very difficult to handle with RTP unless a video codec is used that supports a scalable transmission like Scalable Video Coding (SVC) [1]. RTP is a push protocol, i.e., the server pushes the data to the client. For that reason RTP is typically state full and the server has to keep track of all clients and the state of each session. An alternative way of streaming that is currently in heavy use on the Internet is called progressive download. As the name says it is not a "true" streaming but it is a kind of download. In comparison to RTP which is based on user datagram protocol (UDP) the progressive download is based on the hyper text transfer protocol (HTTP). Consequently, the session is stateless and the client pulls the data from the server. This has several advantages such as fully exploitation of existing Internet infrastructure (e.g., caches, proxies, CDNs) and no issues with firewalls or NAT traversals as the media data is encapsulated within HTTP. However, this approach has also some disadvantages. The HTTP protocol adds a significant overhead to the transmission which is approximately twice the media bitrate [2].

Some industry consortia try to address the drawback on how to handle varying bitrates. One of the first solutions has been specified within 3GPP as Adaptive HTTP Streaming (AHS) [3]. The basic idea is to chop the media file into segments which can be encoded at different bitrates or resolutions. The segments are provided on a Web server and can be downloaded through standard HTTP GET requests. The adaptation to the bitrate, resolution, etc. is done on the client side for each segment, e.g., the client can switch to a higher bitrate – if bandwidth permits – on a per segment basis. This has several advantages because the client knows its capabilities and its received throughput best. In order to describe the relationship between bitrates, segments, and the order of the segments AHS introduces the so-called Media Presentation Description (MPD). The MPD is a XML file that represents the different bitrates and HTTP uniform resource locators (URLs) of each individual segment. This structure

*Area Chair: Pablo Cesar, Wei-Tsang Ooi.

MM'11, November 28–December 1, 2011, Scottsdale, Arizona, USA.

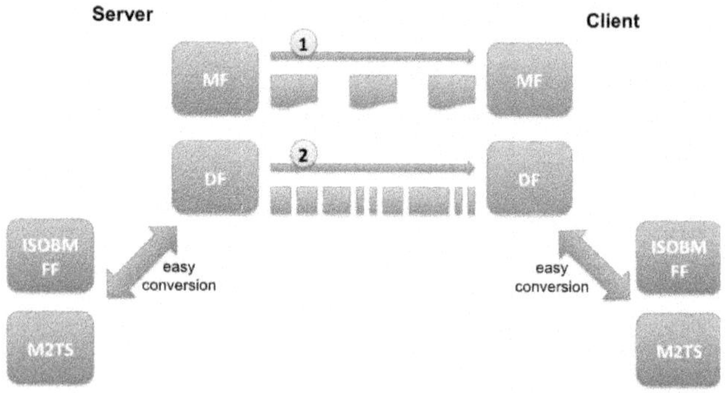

Figure 1. DASH System Architecture [7].

provides the binding of the segments to the bitrate (resolution, etc.) among others (e.g., start time, duration of segments). For example, a typical client would first request the MPD and with the information of the MPD it would then request the individual segments that fit best for its given bandwidth. If the bandwidth changes during the session the client could easily select a segment from another representation with a different bitrate that fulfills its bandwidth requirements best. This makes the progressive download method adaptive and dynamic in the same way. There are also other proprietary solutions from different companies like Microsoft's Smooth Streaming [4], Adobe's Dynamic HTTP Streaming [5] and Apple's HTTP Live Streaming [6] which more or less adopt the same approach. At the beginning of the session the client has to download a file that describes the URLs of the segments and the relation between the segments and a bitrate. After that the client could start with the download of the segments and eventually adapt dynamically to bandwidth fluctuations. The Dynamic Adaptive Streaming over HTTP (DASH) standard aims at combining the features of these proprietary solutions. The next section will give an overview of this standard.

2. Dynamic Adaptive Streaming over HTTP

During its 93rd meeting, MPEG evaluated 15 submissions from 20 organizations (including companies, research institutions and universities). The submissions provided technologies for the HTTP streaming of MPEG media in the following areas:

- Manifest File (MF), i.e., playlist, media presentation description, etc. which is mostly based on XML.
- Delivery Format (DF) as extensions/specializations of ISO Base Media File format (ISOBMFF) and MPEG-2 Transport Stream (TS).

The system architecture is depicted in Figure 1 [7] and based on that MPEG started a new work item called Dynamic Adaptive Streaming over HTTP (DASH).

On request, the manifest file will be provided to the client in order to initiate the session (cf. step-1 in Figure 1). The client will parse the manifest file and request individual segments compliant to the delivery format using HTTP and according to the information found in the manifest file (cf. step-2 in Figure 1). For the manifest file, DASH adopted the Media Presentation Description (MPD) as defined by 3GPP AHS [3] as a starting point. The MPD follows a data model comprising a sequence of one or more consecutive non-overlapping periods for which one or more representations may be available. A single representation refers to a specific media following certain characteristics such as bitrate, framerate, resolution, etc. Furthermore, each representation consists of one or more segments that actually describe the media and/or metadata to decode and present the included media content.

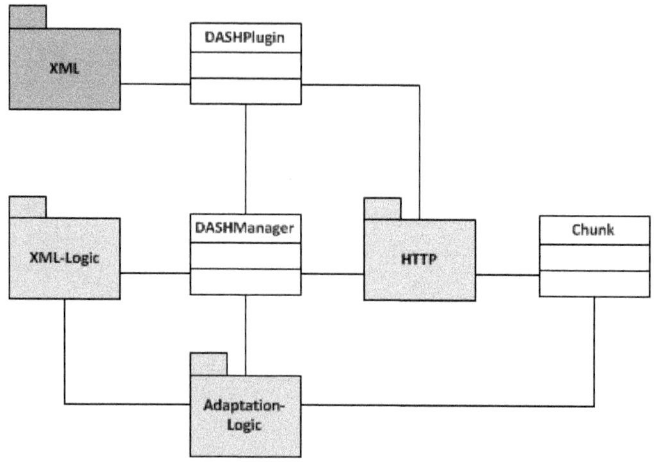

Figure 2. High-Level DASH Plugin Architecture.

The delivery format defines the format of the segments to be delivered to the client upon the HTTP requests based on the MPD. Finally, as the delivery format shall be compatible to existing MPEG formats (i.e. ISOBMFF and MPEG-2 TS), it shall be also possible to provide easy conversion from and to these formats. For example, easy conversion on the server would ease the usage of legacy content encoded in existing formats such as MP4 and its derivations. On the other hand, client-side easy conversion would facilitate repurposing of content received via DASH, e.g., in order to support legacy (decoding) infrastructures.

3. IMPLEMENTATION

This section provides information about the architecture of VLC media player and the DASH plugin which is fully integrated into VLC.

3.1 VLC Media Player

The VLC media player has a very clear and well defined layered architecture. Each layer is responsible for a concrete task and it could contain an undefined number of modules. Modules are representing a common action. The correct module for a given session will be chosen at runtime for each individual layer. This makes VLC very flexible. In the first version of the plugin it was located at the access layer because it is a kind of access. But at the newest version it has been moved one layer below because it is then independent from the access method. Due to the flexible structure of VLC and the reason that every module follows nearly the same structure this was not such a huge issue.

3.2 DASH Plugin

The DASH plugin is located at the stream filter layer of VLC and consists of four major components and two controller classes. Each of these components is depicted in Figure 2. The first component that is used at the startup of a DASH session is the *XML component* which is responsible for the XML parsing of the MPD and providing support to the other components. This component does neither provide means for the interpretation of the data nor the (adaptation) logic. The *HTTP component* handles all HTTP connections that have to be opened or closed during a DASH session. The current version of the plugin opens a HTTP connection for each individual segment. This will be improved in a future version of the plugin that will use persistent HTTP

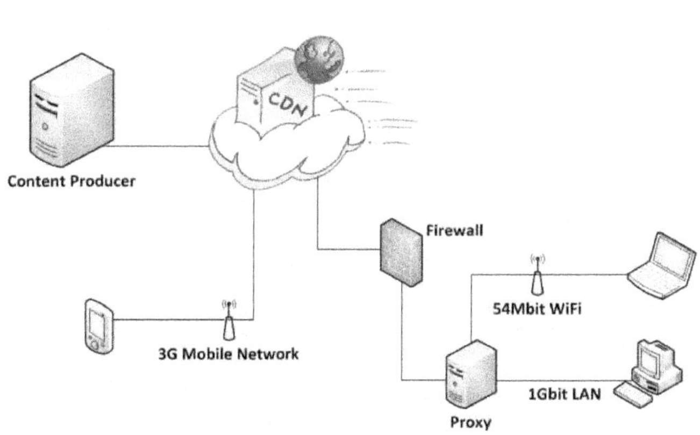

Figure 3. Example of DASH Deployment Architecture.

connections to reduce the HTTP overhead. The *XML-Logic component* adds the logic to the data representation that is provided though the XML component. As a consequence data and logic of the MPD are well separated. The plugin only supports a subset of the current DASH standard [8]. This is possible because the DASH standard defines profiles that describe such a subset. Currently the plugin only works with the *BasicCM* profile which is defined at [9]. Due to the structure it could easily be extended to support other profiles or even the full standard. The *Adaptation-Logic component* is responsible for the adaptation to the user preferences or device capabilities like bandwidth and resolution. The details of this component is also very flexible and is based on the well-known strategy pattern [10]. Thus, it is very easy to change the adaptation logic without affecting the other components. As a consequence, the plugin enables the integration of a variety of adaptation logics and comparison thereof, making it attractive for the research community.

4. DEPLOYMENT

Figure 3 shows an example of a DASH deployment. The three main components are the content producer the network and the clients. The content producer is responsible for the content production. This means that it provides the segments and the MPD to the CDN. Due to the flexible structure of DASH the content production could easily adopt to the needs of the CDN w.r.t. segment duration. Also legacy content could be reused, e.g., if there is a movie available in different bitrates, DASH could reuse these files because of the flexibility of the MPD. The content production could be done offline or online. Offline means that the video content in form of segments and the MPD will be created and then distributed over the CDN. This is the usual deployment strategy for on-demand content. DASH also supports live content preparation. Therefore, the content producer adds the segments online and updates the MPD accordingly. The MPD contains an update interval in order to inform the client that it must update the MPD during this period. On the network part nothing has to be changed because DASH uses the Internet as it is. As shown on Figure 3 the network may consist of CDNs that distribute the content. Due to the use of HTTP, DASH also passes firewalls and takes advantage of proxies. The flexible content preparation in case of different bitrates makes it possible that DASH could be used with nearly any connection as shown on Figure 3 where a mobile device is connected through a 3G network and a PC is connected through a 1Gbit connection. The actual streaming/adaptation logic is on the client side and, thus, the client decides which segments to download, the buffer size, and when the switch to another representation shall occur.

4.1 DASH Data Model

The DASH data model is hierarchical starting with the MPD. Each *MPD* could contain one or more Periods. The purpose of a *Period* is to separate the content, e.g., for ad insertion or for changing the camera angle in a live football game. Each Period could then contain one or more *Groups* which enables the grouping of different *Representations* that logically belong together. For example, representations with the same codec, language, resolution, etc. could be within the same group. This mechanism allows the client to eliminate a range of representations that does not fulfill its requirements. A period could also contain a *Subset* which enables the restriction of combinations of groups and expresses the intention of the creator of the MPD. Of course, the MPD also supports trivial cases just containing one or more representations of multiplexed content.

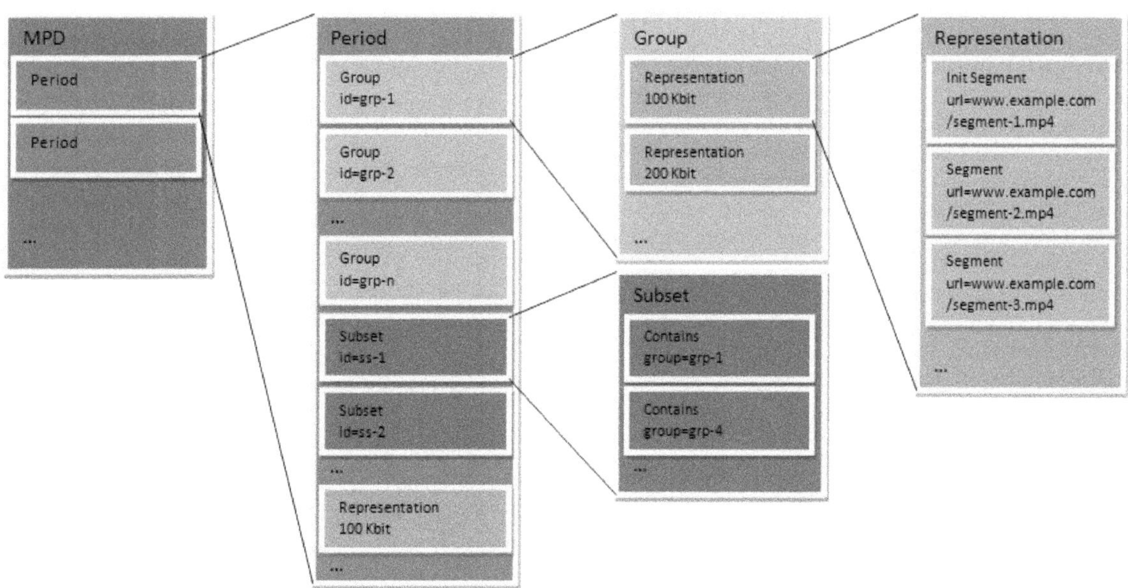

Figure 4. DASH Data Model.

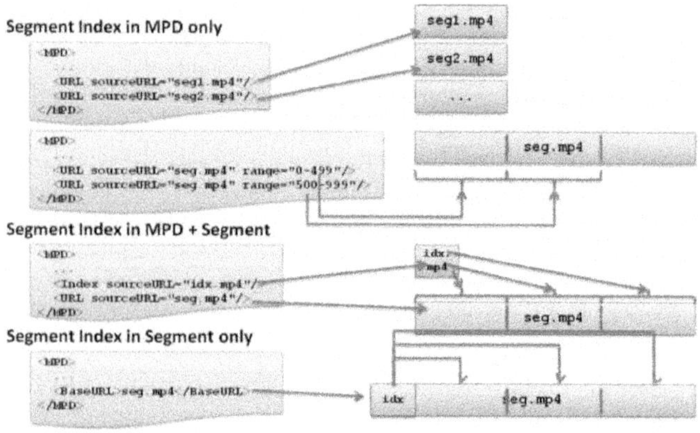

Figure 5. Segment Indexing.

The representations contain the actual *Segments*. Typically, the first segment of a representation is an initialization segment that contains only meta-information for the decoding process. The other segments contain the actual data (audio, video, text, etc.) and could be accessed from the client through the given URL.

4.2 Segment Indexing

DASH employs a very flexible segment indexing mechanism as depicted in Figure 5. In particular, there are three different methods how segments could be indexed. The first one is the MPD only mechanism where the index will be signaled within the MPD and not in the underlying data. However, there are two ways how to do that within the MPD. The first approach provides multiple segments on the server and the second approach provides only one file (i.e., one big segment). For the second one the MPD describes the byte ranges of the different segments. The second solution is a hybrid one where a part of the index is signaled in the MPD and the other one in the underlying data. This means that the MPD describes the location of a separate index file that contains the byte ranges of the segments. With this solution there are just two files located on the server. Finally, it is also possibly to include the whole index in the underlying data, i.e., at the beginning of file. All of these solutions could be used for on-demand use cases but only the first one is preferred for live sessions.

4.3 Deployment Remarks

As mentioned before, DASH is very flexible regarding the data model, indexing, segment duration, etc. which is intentionally as on-demand and live use case scenarios do have different requirements. For example, the segment duration may be as long as possible for on-demand sessions because segments are costly and unnecessary, byte range requests have much more caching efficiency, and on the server fewer files are needed. Typically there will be only one file on the server for each bitrate. However, for live sessions this is not a suitable approach as the session needs to be divided in multiple segments (i.e., the whole duration of the session is not known in advance). For live sessions also a high encoding performance is needed because several bitrates, languages, etc. must be encoded and packetized into segments in real time.

5. CONCLUSION AND FUTURE WORK

This paper describes an implementation of the emerging Dynamic Adaptive Streaming over HTTP (DASH) standard which is currently developed within MPEG and 3GPP. Our implementation is based on VLC and fully integrated into its structure as a plugin. Furthermore, our implementation provides a powerful extension mechanism with respect to adaptation logics and profiles. That is, it should be very easy to implement various adaptation logics and profiles. Future versions of the plugin will provide an update to the latest version of the standard (i.e., a lot of changes have been adopted recently, e.g., Group has changed to AdaptationSet), add support for persistent HTTP connections in order to reduce the overhead of HTTP streaming (e.g., compared to RTP), and seeking within a DASH stream. Finally, we will investigate adding support for live streaming. The plugin is available as open source at the DASH website of the Alpen-Adria-Universität Klagenfurt [11] which also provides a documentation describing how to build and use the plugin. Furthermore, test files and videos of the plugin are provided at this Web site.

6. ACKNOWLEDGMENTS

This work was supported in part by the EC in the context of the ALICANTE project (FP7-ICT-248652)

7. REFERENCES

[1] H. Schwarz, D. Marpe, T. Wiegland, "Overview of the scalable video coding extension of the H.264/AVC standard", *IEEE Transactions on Circuits and Systems for Video Technology*, vol 17, no. 9, Sep. 2007, pp. 1103-1120.

[2] B. Wang, J. Kurose, P. Shenoy, and D. Towsley, "Multimedia Streaming via TCP: An Analytic Performance Study", *ACM Transactions on Multimedia Computing, Communications and Applications*, vol. 4, no. 2, May 2008, pp. 16:1-16:22.

[3] 3GPP TS 26.234, "Transparent end-to-end packet switched streaming service (PSS)", Protocols and codecs, 2010.

[4] Microsoft Smooth Streaming, http://www.iis.net/download/smoothstreaming (last access: May, 2011).

[5] Adobe HTTP Dynamic Streaming, http://www.adobe.com/products/httpdynamicstreaming/ (last access: May, 2011).

[6] R. Pantos, W. May, "HTTP Live Streaming", IETF draft, March. 2011, http://tools.ietf.org/html/draft-pantos-http-live-streaming-06 (last access: May, 2011).

[7] C. Müller, C. Timmerer, "A Test-Bed for the Dynamic Adaptive Streaming over HTTP featuring Session Mobility", *ACM Multimedia Systems*, San Jose, California, USA, Feb. 2011, pp. 271-276.

[8] ISO/IEC CD 23001-6. 2010. Information technology – MPEG systems technologies – Part 6: Dynamic adaptive streaming over HTTP (DASH), Guangzhou, China, Oct. 2010.

[9] DASH BasicCM profile, http://www-itec.uni-klu.ac.at/dash/?page_id=10#SupportedProfile (last access: May, 2011).

[10] E. Freeman, E. Freeman, K. Sierra, B. Bates, *Head First Design Patterns*, O'Reilly Media, Oct. 2004.

[11] DASH at Alpen-Adria-Universität Klagenfurt, http://www-itec.uni-klu.ac.at/dash (last access: Jul. 2011).

GoalBit: A Free and Open Source Peer-to-Peer Streaming Network

Andrés Barrios
InCo., Facultad de Ingeniería
Universidad de la República
Montevideo, Uruguay

Matías Barrios
InCo., Facultad de Ingeniería
Universidad de la República
Montevideo, Uruguay

Daniel De Vera
InCo., Facultad de Ingeniería
Universidad de la República
Montevideo, Uruguay

Pablo Rodríguez-Bocca *
InCo., Facultad de Ingeniería
Universidad de la República
Montevideo, Uruguay
prbocca@fing.edu.uy

Claudia Rostagnol
InCo., Facultad de Ingeniería
Universidad de la República
Montevideo, Uruguay

ABSTRACT

This paper presents the GoalBit Starter platform. GoalBit is an open source peer-to-peer distribution system of real-time video streams over Internet. The main advantage of a P2P architecture is the possibility of using available upload bandwidth in the hosts connected. The main difficulty is that these hosts are typically highly dynamic, they continuously enter and leave the network. To deal with this problem a mesh connectivity approach is used (Bittorrent-like) where the stream is decomposed into several pieces and shared between different peers. Nowadays, the GoalBit platform is used by operators and by final users to broadcast their live contents. To illustrate its potential, we present some empirical results measured in an emulation of a GoalBit P2P streaming, with more than 300 peers concurrently connected.

Categories and Subject Descriptors

C.2.4 [**Computer-communication Networks**]: Distributed Systems

General Terms

Design, Performance, Measurement

Keywords

Video, Streaming, Peer-to-Peer

MM'11, November 28–December 1, 2011, Scotsdale, Arizona, USA.

1. INTRODUCTION

GoalBit is a free and open source peer-to-peer streaming network [4]. It provides the open source tools for broadcasting, distribute and watch live P2P video streamings. Live video P2P networks have to satisfy harder constraints than common P2P file–sharing system, mainly because video reproduction has real–time restrictions (file sharing do not) and because the nodes only remain connected to the network a few minutes [18]. Nowadays some commercial P2P networks for live video distribution are available. The most successful are PPlive [14] with more than 200,000 concurrent users on a single channel [16] (reaching an aggregate bit-rate of 100 Gbps), SopCast [17] with more than 100,000 concurrent users reported by its developers, CoolStreaming [6] with more than 25,000 concurrent users on a single channel [24], PPstream [15], TVAnts [20], and TVUnetwork [21].

PPLive [14] is the most popular P2PTV software, especially for Asian users. Born as a student project in the Huazhong University of Science and Technology of China, PPLive uses a proprietary protocol, and its source-code is not available. With reverse engineering, [11] and [2] show that it uses a Bittorrent-like approach, with a channel selection bootstrap from a Web tracker, and peer download/upload video in chunks from/to multiple peers. It uses two kinds of video encoding formats, Window Media Video (VC-1) and Real Video (RMVB), with average bit rates from 250 Kbps to 400 Kbps, and it uses the user native media player to display the video. The distribution engine (Bittorrent-like protocol) does not use the *rarest-first* download policy, because the streaming must satisfy real–time restrictions. Also the *tit-for-tat* upload policy is not applied: when a client joins a channel, the other peers in the swarm send chunks forcefully to minimize the playback startup delay.

SopCast [17], created at the Fudan University of China, is very similar to the PPLive project. Following the same reverse engineering procedure, [11, 2] show that SopCast uses a Bittorrent-like approach, with a proprietary protocol very close to the PPLive protocol. Read [16] for a complete performance study of this network.

CoolStreaming [6] (also known as DONet) is the predecessor of PPLive and SopCast, now forced to close down due to copyright issues. Also using a proprietary protocol, and closed source-code, as PPLive and SopCast, the CoolStreaming authors published information about its distribution engine [25, 23, 24]. The video stream is divided into chunks with equal size. A difference of CoolStreaming, with respect to PPLive and SopCast, is that the video stream is decomposed into six sub-streams by a rotating selection of video chunks. These commercial P2P networks implement a mesh–based distribution overlay, where there is not a defined topology and the list of peers connected is mantained through some method like the BitTorrent tracker [5] or Kademlia [12]. Its protocol applies more restrictions than a basic P2P sharing protocol for accomplishing natural requirements that live video reproduction has.

Another much more popular overlay in academic research is the tree–based one. In a P2P network with this overlay every peer is a node of a tree, receiving the stream from its parent and sending it to its child nodes. The possible childs every node can have influences the distance between the broadcaster (the first parent node) and the rest. The delay of the streaming is the most notorious undesired effect for the most far away nodes. This overlay also sensible to the disconnection of peers, un-providing its childs with the stream. Many systems are based in this overlay and have their own protocol for building and maintaining the multicast tree. For example, both NICE [3] and Zigzag [19] adopt hierarchical distribution trees and therefore scale to a large number of peers. SpreadIt [7] constructs a distribution tree rooted at the sender for a live media streaming session. A new receiver joins by traversing the tree starting at the root, until it reaches a node with sufficient remaining capacity. PeerCast [13] is a P2P network designed for live video and audio broadcast over Internet. Its protocol (based in the tree–based overlay) and source code is open–source and its usage is free for consumers and broadcasters.

In this paper we present the GoalBit platform. Its first difference with the previous mentioned commercial networks is that GoalBit is the first free and open source peer-to-peer platform with a mesh–based distribution overlay used by end-users on the Internet for real-time video streaming. Also, GoalBit is a complete suite for live media distribution, which implements the media generation, encapsulation, distribution and reproduction. For the generation, the live media can be captured using different kind of devices (such as a capture card, a webcam, another http/mms/rtp streaming, a file, etc.), it can be encoded to many different formats (MPEG2/4-AVC, VC-1, ACC, VORBIS, MPGA, WMA, etc.) and muxed into various containers (MPEG-TS, ASF, OGG, MP4, etc). The streaming encapsulation defined as GoalBit Packetized Stream (GBPS) takes the muxed stream and generates fixed size pieces (chunks), which are later distributed using the GoalBit Transport Protocol (GBTP). As we will explain later, the GBTP uses a Bittorrent-like approach. Finally (at the client side) the GoalBit player reproduces the video streaming consuming the pieces obtained through GBTP. For the reproduction we integrate the Videolan Media Player [22] into our source code, therefore the final users do not need to install an external media player software. Nowadays, GoalBit platform is used by operators (as ANTEL in their video portal AdinetTV [1] and by final users to broadcast their live contents.

The paper is organized as follows. Section 2 presents the global architecture of the GoalBit Starter platform, the software components needed and a description of their main functionalities. In Section 3 we introduce the GoalBit Transport Protocol. In Section 4 we show empirical results of an emulation of a GoalBit P2P streaming with more than 300 peers connected. Finally, the main contributions of this work are then summarized in Section 5.

2. SOFTWARE ARCHITECTURE

In a GoalBit P2P live video streaming three essential components must exist according to the GoalBit architecture, please read [10] for details. Firstly, the broadcaster, who creates the video streaming from some video source. Secondly, the tracker, who reports to the broadcaster and viewers the presence of the rest. Thirdly, the viewer, who receives the streaming and watches it. As of today, GoalBit provides the software for creating those three components.

Broadcasters and viewers must have the GoalBit Media Player installed in their hosts in order to send and receive video streams. GoalBit Media Player can be used embedded in a Web browser as a Web plugin (we also offer a small size GoalBit Media Player release with only the Web plugin interface). The Starter Suite is a Web server application that has a tracker incorporated and therefore enables viewers and broadcasters to make contact. Also, Starter Suite enables to configure a broadcaster via one of its web pages, and it easily shares the URL of the stream to viewers.

The main functionalities of the Starter Suite to the end-user are web broadcasting and channel management. When the user opens the Starter's Suite main page a list of the registered channels is shown, indicating the amount of viewers currently watching. A channel can be watched right there just by clicking its name. An URL for its sharing is given, along with HTML code for embedding it in another web page. If desired, a channel may be unregistered.

For web broadcasting and thus adding a new channel in the Starter Suite, the link named "Broadcast now!" at the top of the channel listing must be used. This opens a new web page where the channel and broadcaster are configured. The channel name must be specified, and then a playlist must be assembled for the broadcaster. It may contain video files, network streamings, CDs/DVDs, a webcam or a capture device as items of the playlist. Once the channel name and playlist are specified, the broadcast starts by clicking the button below the playlist. If the channel list is opened, the new channel is shown, along with the presence of the broadcaster. The creator sends then the channel's sharing URL to the viewers. They must open it using their web browsers with the Web Plugin previously installed. The channel name will be shown and also a play button to start displaying the video stream. The Web Plugin does not offer any other functionality than those offered indirectly through web pages, such as broadcasting and watching a GoalBit stream.

PHP, MySQL and JavaScript are the main technologies used for the Starter Suite. Its license is AGPL [8]. The Web Plugin is written in C and its source code is based on the VLC player's, plus the implementation of the GoalBit protocol and modifications for playing and broadcasting with it. Its license is GPLv2 [9].

3. GOALBIT PROTOCOL

As commented before the GoalBit Transport Protocol (GBTF is an extended version of the BitTorrent Protocol, optimized for live video transmissions. In this section we introduce some of its main characteristics and its specification, for a detailed information please read [4].

3.1 Basic Concepts

In GBTP (as in Bittorrent) each piece of the stream is identified by a unique number, called the piece ID. It is used to accomplish the exchange of pieces between peers. As GBTP is designed to distribute a continuous streaming and not a file, the piece numbering is cyclic in the $[0, MAX\_PIECE\_ID]$ interval[1].

Each peer has a sliding window (over previous interval of possible ID values) associated with it. The sliding window has a minimum value (called the *base*) and a length (which defines the maximum window value). Peers only can download or share pieces whose IDs are included in their respective windows

In order to reproduce the streaming, the peers have a player which consumes the pieces stored in their sliding windows in a sequential way. The *execution index* is defined as the next piece ID to be consumed by the player.

Other important concepts used in the protocol are the *active buffer* and the *active buffer index* (or ABI). The active buffer is defined as the consecutive sequence of pieces that a peer has, starting at the execution index. In other words, this corresponds to the downloaded video that the player will reproduce without interruption at a specific time. Finally, the active buffer index is the largest piece ID inside the active buffer.

3.2 Tracker-peer communication

There are two types of exchanges between tracker and peers: the initial one, and the exchanges that take place periodically during the sojourn of the peer in the network. These communications are carried out over the `HTTP/HTTPS` protocol and are based on a unique message called *announce*.

Initially, the peers contact the tracker in order to get a list of peers and an index from where to start asking for pieces. Normally, the peer sends an announce to the tracker with $numwant = 55$ and $ABI = MAX\_PIECE\_ID + 1$. In the answer, the peer gets a list of peers with at most *numwant* elements, the starting index and the peer type assigned.

Since the tracker needs to store status information for each peer, there must be a regular communication between them to allow this transfer of information. In the periodic communication (and leaving aside some particular cases), the peer sends an announce with $numwant = 0$, $ABI =$ the current ABI, and $QoE =$ the quality of experience measured by the peer in the last period. In this case, there is no relevant information in the tracker's answer. At those exchanges peers can also ask for more peers. These exchanges are regulated by the tracker, who defines the minimal time interval between two consecutive announces.

3.3 Peer-to-peer communication

Peers exchange messages using the TCP protocol. Two kinds of messages are exchanged. The first are used to inform about the contextual situation of each peer, i.e. which peer remains connected and which pieces already have been downloaded by every peer. To exchange contextual information five type of messages are used: HANDSHAKE, BITFIELD, HAVE, WINDOW UPDATE and KEEP-ALIVE.

[1]Currently the MAX_PIECE_ID parameter is set to 2^{31}.

The other group of messages are used to exchange pieces. The process to exchange a piece is non trivial, and eight types of messages are used: INTERESTED, NOT INTERESTED, CHOKE, UNCHOKE, REQUEST, CANCEL, PIECE and DONT HAVE.

4. TESTS AND RESULTS

An emulation of a GoalBit P2P network sharing a single video streaming was run on November, 2010. All the servers used were run inside a cloud computing service. The emulation lasted for two hours, reaching a peak of 300 simultaneous viewers (executed as computer processes). During the emulation eight human viewers and a total of 340 emulated viewers participated of the streaming.

Different type of servers participated, none of them was overloaded in RAM and CPU resources. One server ran the Starter Suite and the GoalBit Media Player as broadcaster. Two servers ran up to twenty viewers with special upload capacity, forty viewers in total. Seventeen servers ran viewers with normal upload capacity with a peak of twenty each. Eight personal computers ran just one viewer. The source of the streaming was a file that had an average bitrate of 2000 kbps. Each normal viewer had an upload bandwidth limit equal to the half of the video bitrate, being 1000 kbps.

The quality of experience of every viewer was measured according to the initial buffering time, rebuffering time (time spent waiting for video to start again), chunk loss rate (chunks lost vs chunks received), and general failure (were not able to watch even a frame of the video).

The results for the emulation were as follow. The average initial buffering time was 5.55 seconds, the average rebuffering time was 11.83 seconds, the amount of peers that rebuffered: 15.88% (they only rebuffered once), the average chunk loss rate was 0.0006% and the average failed peers was 2.9%.

Figure 1 shows the percentage of peers in function of the seconds that buffering lasted at most. 50% of the peers lasted at most 5 seconds to start showing the video. 80% of the peers lasted at most 7 seconds.

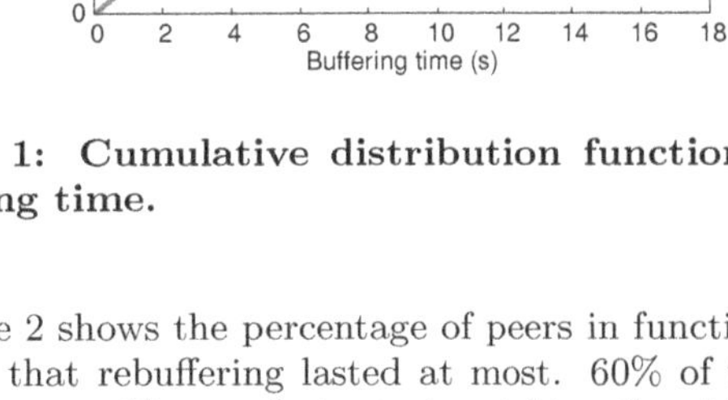

Figure 1: Cumulative distribution function of the buffering time.

Figure 2 shows the percentage of peers in function of the seconds that rebuffering lasted at most. 60% of the peers lasted at most 10 seconds to start watching the video again. 80% of the peers lasted at most 13 seconds.

None of the eight human viewers rebuffered and watched the video in its original conditions because no transcoding was applied to it.

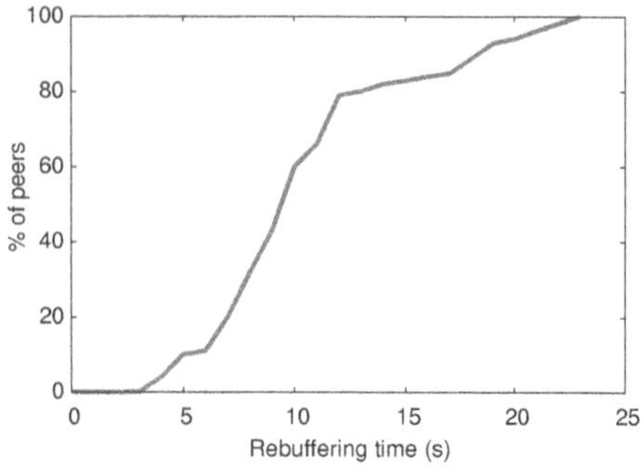

Figure 2: Cumulative distribution function of the rebuffering time.

The overhead is the extra amount of bit transference needed for the protocol. The global overhead was of 0.3293%. The average bandwidth saving was 59%. This means that viewers uploaded 59% of the total traffic.

5. CONCLUSIONS

This paper presents the GoalBit Starter platform, an open source peer-to-peer distribution system of real-time video streams over Internet. Nowadays, the GoalBit platform is used by operators and by final users to broadcast their live contents. Our empirical results, with more than 300 peers concurrently connected, showed a bandwidth saving of 59%, without lost of quality in the video playback and with an insignificant start-up delay.

People searching for a simple way of broadcasting using P2P technology should try this software. Organizations interested in sharing live video streamings in their LAN with a simple and easy to use starter platform will find this software useful. Organizations with live video streaming platforms over Internet trying to reduce bandwidth costs will find it useful too.

6. REFERENCES

[1] AdinetTV home page. http://www.adinettv.com.uy/, 2011.

[2] S. Ali, A. Mathur, and H. Zhang. Measurement of commercial peer-to-peer live video streaming. In *In Proc. of ICST Workshop on Recent Advances in Peer-to-Peer Streaming*, Weaterloo, Canadda, 2006.

[3] S. Banerjee, B. Bhattacharjee, and C. Kommareddy. Scalable application layer multicast. In *SIGCOMM '02: Proceedings of the 2002 conference on Applications, technologies, architectures, and protocols for computer communications*, pages 205–217, New York, NY, USA, 2002. ACM Press.

[4] M. E. Bertinat, D. D. Vera, D. Padula, F. Robledo, P. Rodríguez-Bocca, P. Romero, and G. Rubino. Goalbit: The first free and open source peer-to-peer streaming network. In *Proceedings of the 5th international IFIP/ACM Latin American conference on Networking (LANC'09)*, pages 83–93, New York, USA, September 2009. ACM.

[5] Bittorrent home page. http://www.bittorrent.org, 2007.

[6] CoolStreaming home page. http://www.coolstreaming.us, 2007.

[7] H. Deshpande, M. Bawa, and H. Garcia-Molina. Streaming live media over a peer-to-peer network. Technical Report 2001-30, Stanford InfoLab, April 2001.

[8] GNU Affero General Public License. Version 3. http://www.gnu.org/licenses/agpl-3.0.txt, 2007.

[9] GNU General Public License. Version 2. http://www.gnu.org/licenses/gpl-2.0.txt, 1991.

[10] GoalBit Architecture. http://goalbit.sourceforge.net/architecture.html, 2009.

[11] X. Hei, C. Liang, J. Liang, Y. Liu, and K. W. Ross. Insights into pplive: A measurement study of a large-scale p2p iptv system. In *In Proc. of IPTV Workshop, International World Wide Web Conference*, 2006.

[12] P. Maymounkov and D. Mazières. Kademlia: A peer-to-peer information system based on the xor metric. In *IPTPS '01: Revised Papers from the First International Workshop on Peer-to-Peer Systems*, pages 53–65, London, UK, 2002. Springer-Verlag.

[13] Peercast home page. http://www.peercast.org/, 2007.

[14] PPLive Home page. http://www.pplive.com, 2007.

[15] PPStream home page. http://www.ppstream.com/, 2007.

[16] A. Sentinelli, G. Marfia, M. Gerla, L. Kleinrock, and S. Tewari. Will iptv ride the peer-to-peer stream? *Communications Magazine, IEEE*, 45:86–92, 2007.

[17] SopCast - Free P2P internet TV. http://www.sopcast.org, 2007.

[18] K. Sripanidkulchai, B. Maggs, and H. Zhang. An analysis of live streaming workloads on the internet. In *IMC '04: Proceedings of the 4th ACM SIGCOMM conference on Internet measurement*, pages 41–54, New York, NY, USA, 2004. ACM Press.

[19] D. A. Tran, K. A. Hua, and T. T. Do. Zigzag: An efficient peer-to-peer scheme for media streaming. In *INFOCOM*, 2003.

[20] TVAnts home page. http://cache.tvants.com/, 2007.

[21] TVUnetworks home page. http://tvunetworks.com/, 2007.

[22] VideoLan home page. http://www.videolan.org, 2007.

[23] S. Xie, G. Y. Keung, and B. Li. A measurement of a large-scale peer-to-peer live video streaming system. In *ICPPW '07: Proceedings of the 2007 International Conference on Parallel Processing Workshops (ICPPW 2007)*, page 57, Washington, DC, USA, 2007. IEEE Computer Society.

[24] X. Zhang, J. Liu, and B. Li. On large scale peer-to-peer live video distribution: Coolstreaming and its preliminary experimental results. In *IEEE International Workshop on Multimedia Signal Processing (MMSP'05)*, Washington, DC, USA, 2005. IEEE Computer Society.

[25] X. Zhang, J. Liu, B. Li, and T.-S. P. Yum. Coolstreaming/donet: A data-driven overlay network for peer-to-peer live media streaming. In *IEEE Conference on Computer Communications (INFOCOM'05)*, Washington, DC, USA, 2005. IEEE Computer Society.

A C++ Library for Handling MPEG-7 Descriptions

Werner Bailer, Hermann Fürntratt, Peter Schallauer, Georg Thallinger, Werner Haas
JOANNEUM RESEARCH, DIGITAL – Institute for Information and Communication Technologies
Steyrergasse 17, 8010 Graz, Austria
mpeg7lib@joanneum.at

ABSTRACT
We present a C++ library implementing part 2, 3, 4 and 5 of the MPEG-7 multimedia content description standard, including the updated version finalized in 2004. The library supports handling of MPEG-7 descriptions as trees of typed objects, supporting (de)serialization from/to XML. It has convenient and powerful features such as creation of subtrees by XPath statements and is extensible at runtime. The library is available for Windows, Linux/Unix and Mac OS X. It has been provided under a free use license for several years, downloaded more than 5,200 times and used in a large number of projects. It has been published under GNU LGPL in 2009. This paper discusses the key functionalities of the library as well as some exemplary applications.

Categories and Subject Descriptors
E.2 [**Data Storage Representations**], H.3.7 [**Information Storage and Retrieval**]: Digital Libraries – *standards*, H.5.1 [**Information Interfaces and Presentation**]: Multimedia Information Systems.

General Terms
Management, Standardization.

Keywords
MPEG-7, metadata, description scheme, API, library, XPath.

1. INTRODUCTION
MPEG-7 [5] is a comprehensive standard for describing multimedia content in a diverse range of applications. The complexity of the standard and the lack of tools have hindered the wide adoption of the standard. Creating, modifying and navigating the structures of an MPEG-7 description is a key functionality needed in every application creating, modifying or consuming MPEG-7 documents. This has motivated us to develop an easy to use C++ class library for handling MPEG-7 descriptions.

The rest of this paper is organized as follows. The remainder of this section gives a short overview of the MPEG-7 standard and then introduces the MPEG-7 library. Section 2 describes the concept and key features of the library, and in Section 3 we present three applications of the library. Section 4 concludes the paper.

1.1 About MPEG-7
The ISO/IEC standard *Multimedia Content Description Interface* (MPEG-7) [5] has been defined as a format for the description of multimedia content in a wide range of applications. MPEG-7 defines a set of description tools, called description schemes (DS) and descriptors (D). Descriptors represent single properties of the content description, while description schemes are containers for descriptors and other description schemes. The definition of description schemes and descriptors uses the *Description Definition Language (DDL)*, which is an extension of XML Schema. MPEG-7 descriptions can be either represented as XML (textual format, TeM) or in a binary format (binary format, BiM).

A core part of MPEG-7 are the *Multimedia Description Schemes* (*MDS*, part 5), which provide support for the description of media information, creation and production information, content structure, usage of content, semantics, navigation and access, content organization and user interaction. Especially the structuring tools are very flexible and enable the description of content on different levels of granularity. In addition, the *Audio* (part 4) and *Visual* (part 3) parts define low- and mid-level descriptors for these modalities.

1.2 The MPEG-7 Library
We present a C++ library, which covers parts 2, 3, 4 and 5 of the MPEG-7 standard (ISO/IEC 15938:2001 – version 1 and ISO/IEC 15938:2004 – version 2). With this library application developers are able to create multimedia content descriptions, manipulate them, serialize to XML and de-serialize – with validation – from XML. Target operating systems are Windows, Linux/Unix and Mac OS X systems, supporting the 32 and 64 bit versions of the systems respectively.

The library is intended for application developers who want to handle MPEG-7 metadata, and who do not want to struggle with complex and not type-safe XML DOM [4] programming. MPEG-7 metadata, which is stored in a hierarchical XML representation, is made available to a developer in an object oriented hierarchical class tree. The MPEG-7 library avoids the time consuming task of implementing hundreds of necessary MPEG-7 classes before the implementation of MPEG-7 functionality can start. One major design goal is to simplify extending the implementation of classes to allow enrichment of interface functionality for certain descriptors.

Due to the lack of available implementations of the then new MPEG-7 standard, JOANNEUM RESEARCH has started the development of the library in 2002 as an API for handling MPEG-7 descriptions in own tools and projects. Realizing the need for such a library in the community of researchers and application developers, JOANNEUM RESEARCH has released the library in binary form under a free use license, first for Windows and in 2007 also for Linux and Mac OS X. In 2009 we have decided to release the library under the GNU LPGL. LGPL has been chosen over other open source licenses due to the compatibility with free software licenses on the one and commercial use of the library on the other side. The library has been downloaded by over 5,200 users as of April 2011.

The MPEG-7 library, including documentation and samples can be downloaded from [7] as source release and as binaries. Instructions how to build and use the library are included in the documentation. The web site of the MPEG-7 library also contains further MPEG-7 related resources and pointers to other MPEG-7 related web resources.

2. CONCEPT AND KEY FEATURES

The MPEG-7 library represents the MPEG-7 XML document as a tree structure. Each element or attribute, which has an XML type defined in the MPEG-7 schema, is represented by a node in this tree. Basically, each XML type is mapped to a class. This applies both for global types (those defined in the schema as a named simple or complex type) and local types (elements which do not have a named type but are defined where they are used). Sequences and choices with a maximum occurrence attribute larger than one and lists are mapped to collection classes. The inheritance hierarchy of the XML schema, i.e., extensions and restrictions of base types, are modeled as a class inheritance hierarchy. The implementation is separated by defining interfaces that model the XML types and classes implementing these interfaces.

There is one generic node type, which defines the common interface of all node classes. All classes that represent XML types are derived from the generic node type. The factory pattern is heavily used in the MPEG-7 library. For each class a factory class is generated, which handles creating and destroying instances of this class. This mechanism is especially useful due to the heavy use of type extensions in MPEG-7.

The factories return smart pointers to the nodes, which implement reference counting. Thus nodes or subtrees that are no longer referenced will be automatically destroyed.

Serialization and parsing is implemented based on Xerces C++ [2]. This XML library is licensed under the Apache License [1] and is available for a broad range of platforms. Parsing, serialization and validation are transparent to the user of the library.

2.1 Typed Access to Elements

In contrast to handling MPEG-7 documents with generic tools such as a DOM [4] API, the MPEG-7 library provides typed access to the elements in the document. For structured types, this provides a first level of conformance check as only certain types of elements and attributes may be added. For unstructured types, this enables access to numeric or enumeration types without string processing and ensures conformance of the value to the data type.

MPEG-7 uses a number of regular expression patterns to represent structured data as strings. For commonly used types, such as media time points and durations, the MPEG-7 library provides functionality to access fields using the appropriate (numeric) data type. This saves a lot of tedious string processing in the application.

2.2 XPath Support

The MPEG-7 library supports absolute and relative XPath statements to access nodes along the child axis. In the XPath statements, numeric indices and `xsi:type` attributes are supported.

There is also a powerful feature that combines the functionality of getting a node from an XPath statement with the option to create that fragment of the tree, if it is not yet there. This feature has been added based on our experience, that it is often necessary for users to add an element at a certain position in a tree, and most of the code is needed to check whether the elements on the path to this element are already there and to create them if needed. Doing this by XPath is a very efficient way that allows creating several hierarchy levels with correct node types within one statement. The sample code that comes with the library shows the saving in terms of lines of code between creating a subtree by XPath or node by node.

2.3 Extensibility

The MPEG-7 library can be easily extended by replacing the classes of the core library with other classes providing additional (application specific) functionality. This can be done at runtime (late binding). MPEG-7 part 7 specifies that MPEG-7 documents containing proprietary types which are extensions of MPEG-7 types do conform to the standard. The MPEG-7 library supports this concept by wrapping all unknown types it encounters during parsing into a special type of node. It can be handled like any other node in the tree and will contain the unknown subtree, which can be serialized again without modification.

Another type of extensions is to use other XML schemata together with MPEG-7. The library is prepared to handle this by managing namespace prefixes for the different schemata of a document. This is for example useful when defining schemata that extend MPEG-7 by descriptors for new features. This mechanism has been used to support novel visual descriptors in an application for visual quality analysis (the respective schema is published at [7]).

3. APPLICATIONS

The range of potential applications of the library is naturally as wide as that of MPEG-7 itself, i.e., including all areas dealing with production, analysis, modification and consumption of multimedia content. From the feedback we get from users it seems that analysis of audiovisual content, applications in audiovisual media production and surveillance applications are dominant. The majority of users come from academia, however, there is a significant share of users from industry.

The library has been used in a number of large research projects in content analysis and annotation tools, authoring tools, retrieval systems, summarization tools and much more. Some examples of these projects are listed at [7].

We discuss three application of the MPEG-7 library in more detail in the following.

3.1 Generic Metadata Engine

The Generic Metadata Engine [10] is a part of the emerging MPEG Extensible Middleware (MXM, MPEG-M) standard [8], which aims at providing APIs for parts of different MPEG standards, including MPEG-7. The Generic Metadata Engine is a read/write API for basic properties of media items, compatible with the set of core properties defined by the W3C Media Annotations WG [13]. The C++ reference implementation of the Generic Metadata Engine uses the MPEG-7 library. Source and binary distributions as well as build instructions for the Generic Metadata Engine are available at [10].

3.2 iPhoto MPEG-7 Exporter

iPhoto [3] is Apple's photo management software. It offers a plugin interface, among others for exporting photos to photo sharing sites, social networks, etc.

The MPEG-7 Exporter Plugin [9] uses this mechanism to export the photo metadata, which is kept in a proprietary file within iPhoto, as standardized MPEG-7 document. All the images selected when initiating the export are described in a single MPEG-7 document. Both metadata extracted from the EXIF information as well as metadata entered by the user are included in the exported document.

The plugin builds on the Mac OS X version of the MPEG-7 library and shows how the C++ code can be accessed from an application written in Objective C. Binaries as well as sources and an Xcode project can be downloaded from [9].

3.3 Semantic Video Annotation Suite

The Semantic Video Annotation Suite (SVAS) [11] is a suite of tools for analysis and annotation of video content by professional users, consisting of an automatic analysis tool and an interface for validation of analysis results and manual annotation.

The analysis tool automatically extracts metadata from video files for navigation and structuring (e.g., shot boundaries, key frames) and metadata which enables fast semi-automatic annotation, e.g., camera motion and face occurrences. Figure 1 shows the user interface for batch analysis.

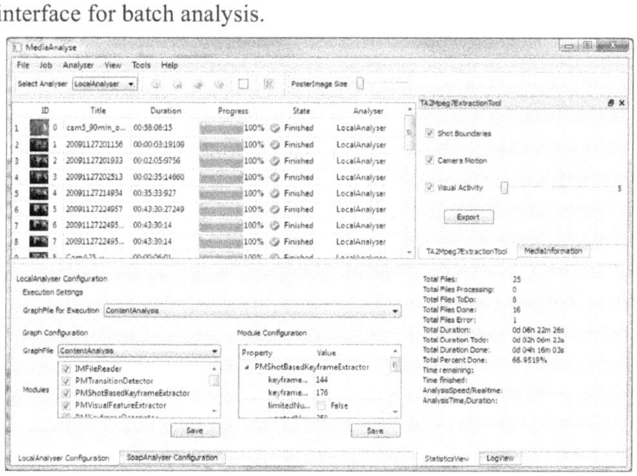

Figure 1: Interface of the analysis tool of SVAS.

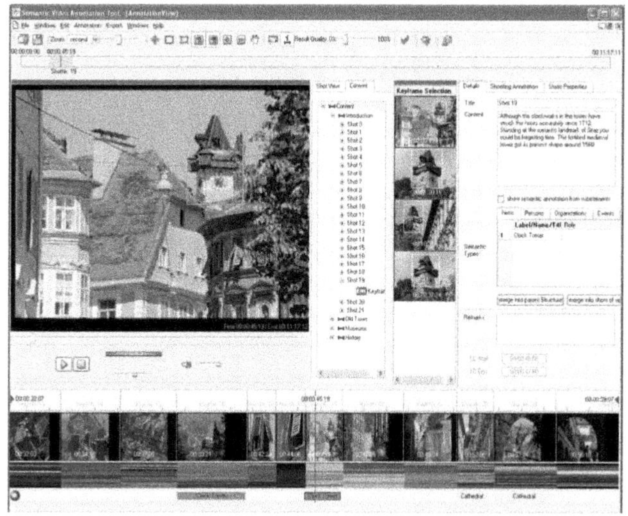

Figure 2: Interface of the interactive video annotation tool.

The following content analysis modules are included in the tool: shot boundary detection, detecting hard cuts and dissolves, key-frame extraction, camera motion estimation, face detection and extraction of global and local visual features for the key frames.

The interactive annotation tool allows viewing and editing the results of the automatic metadata extraction. Furthermore it supports to manually structure content, adding textual and semantic annotation, and the annotation of objects (image regions). As soon as content analysis results are available they can be displayed and modified.

Otherwise annotation can start from scratch, i.e. by creating a new MPEG-7 document for the content to be filled with manual annotation, including content structuring. A screenshot of the video annotation tool is shown in Figure 2.

All content structuring information, technical metadata, automatic analysis results and manual annotations are represented using MPEG-7. The MPEG-7 library is a core component of both applications and serves as internal representation of the underlying data model.

The Semantic Video Annotation Suite can be downloaded from [12].

4. CONCLUSION

We have developed a C++ class library for efficient handling of MPEG-7 documents, covering parts 2, 3, 4 and 5 of the standard. The standard has again gained more interest recently, by inclusion of parts of MPEG-7 into the MPEG MXM APIs and by specification of the Audiovisual Description Profile [6], an MPEG-7 profile targeting information extraction in audiovisual media production.

By providing typed access to the elements in the MPEG-7 document the MPEG-7 library simplifies handling documents and also facilitates conformance to the standard. The library also offers features that are not possible in generic DOM APIs, such as the efficient creation of subtrees by XPath statements. A number of quite diverse applications have been implemented using the library.

ACKNOWLEDGMENTS

The authors would like to thank their former colleagues at the Institute of Information Systems at JOANNEUM RESEARCH, who contributed to early versions of the library: Georg Mittendorfer, Rudolf Schlatte and Herwig Rehatschek. The research leading to these results has received funding from the European Union's Seventh Framework Programme under grant agreements no. FP6-027122, "SALERO" (http://www.salero.eu/), FP7-231161, "PrestoPRIME" (http://www.prestoprime.eu), and FP7-215475, "2020 3D Media" (http://www.20203dmedia.eu).

5. REFERENCES

[1] Apache License 2.0, http://www.apache.org/licenses/LICENSE-2.0 (accessed 2011-05-08)

[2] Apache Xerces C++. http://xerces.apache.org/ (accessed 2011-05-08)

[3] Apple iPhoto, http://www.apple.com/ilife/iphoto/ (accessed 2011-05-08)

[4] Document Object Model (DOM), http://www.w3.org/DOM/ (accessed 2011-05-08)

[5] Information Technology — Multimedia Content Description Interface, ISO/IEC standard 15938, 2001.

[6] Information technology — Multimedia content description interface — Part 9: Profiles and levels, AMENDMENT 1: Extensions to profiles and levels, ISO/IEC 15938-9:2005/PDAM 1, 2010.

[7] JOANNEUM RESEARCH MPEG-7 Resources, http://mpeg-7.joanneum.at (accessed 2011-05-08)

[8] MPEG Extensible Middleware (MXM), http://mxm.wg11.sc29.org/ (accessed 2011-05-08)

[9] MPEG-7 Export Plugin for Apple iPhoto, http://www.wbailer.com/work/mpeg7export (accessed 2011-05-08)

[10] MXM Generic Metadata Engine, http://mxm.wg11.sc29.org/2010/08/generic-metadata-engine/(accessed 2011-05-08)

[11] H. Rehatschek, W. Bailer, H. Neuschmied, S. Ober, and H. Bischof. A tool supporting annotation and analysis of video. In *Reconfigurations. Interdisciplinary Perspectives on Religion in a Post-Secular Society*, Vienna, pp. 253–268, 2007.

[12] Semantic Video Annotation, http://www.joanneum.at/en/digital/products-solutions/semantic-video-annotation.html (last accessed 2011-05-08)

[13] W3C Media Annotations WG (MAWG), http://www.w3.org/2008/WebVideo/Annotations/ (last accessed 2011-05-08)

Content Based Image Retrieval with LIRe

Mathias Lux
Klagenfurt University, Institute for Information Technology
Universitätsstrasse 65-67
Klagenfurt, Austria
mlux@itec.uni-klu.ac.at

ABSTRACT

LIRe (Lucene Image Retrieval) is an open source library for content based image retrieval. Besides providing multiple common and state of the art retrieval mechanisms it allows for easy use on multiple platforms. LIRe is actively used for research, teaching and commercial applications. Due to its modular nature it can be used on process level (e.g. index images and search) as well as on image feature level. Developers and researchers can easily extend and modify LIRe to adapt it to their needs.

Categories and Subject Descriptors

H.3.3 [**Information Storage and Retrieval**]: Information Search and Retrieval

General Terms

Documentation

Keywords

Image retrieval, image features, image search, image indexing

1. INTRODUCTION

Content based image retrieval has been around for some years. Commercial software like IBM QBIC or Cantos Cumulus did not result in a broad application of content based image retrieval. Also research has been consolidated and discussed on a general level several times [7, 21]. Different evaluation organisations and events provide playgrounds for researchers and practitioners to test new and consolidate current approaches [16, 20]. Many research groups and practitioners aim to build on existing tools to avoid re-implementation of existing approaches. LIRe satisfies this need by providing a library of basic and advanced functions needed in the field of visual information retrieval.

MM'11, November 28–December 1, 2011, Scottsdale, Arizona, USA.

2. ARCHITECTURE

LIRe is provided as Java library to be integrated in existing or yet to be built applications and code. Main approach of LIRe is to hide as much as possible of the underlying complexity of content based image retrieval. LIRe is based on Lucene [15], a text search engine providing inverted indexing, search and fast random access to text indexes.

At a first glance developers encounter in LIRe few parameters to be set and even fewer choices. *DocumentBuilder* classes provide easy access to different low level features and wrap the use of Lucene, which is used as index. *ImageSearcher* classes allow for search and retrieval based on single query images or already indexed documents (see Fig. 1).

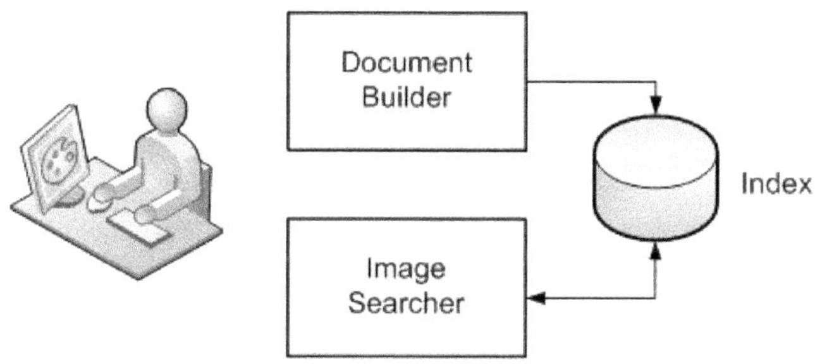

Figure 1: LIRe general architecture.

Developers can access parameters and modules at different levels. Low level features are organized in classes, which implement the LireFeature interface as shown in Fig. 2. Each of the different feature implementations provides means to extract the feature from an image, to compute the distance to a feature of the same class and to serialize and deserialize the histogram data for indexing and storage.

3. GLOBAL FEATURES

LIRe provides a broad range of common and state of the art global image features. Furthermore, extension of LIRe with new global features can be done short time by implementing the LireFeature interface. Indexing and search routines are provided by generalized classes. Features include but are not limited to

1. Color Histograms supporting different color spaces and quantization routines as well as different metrics for distance computation.

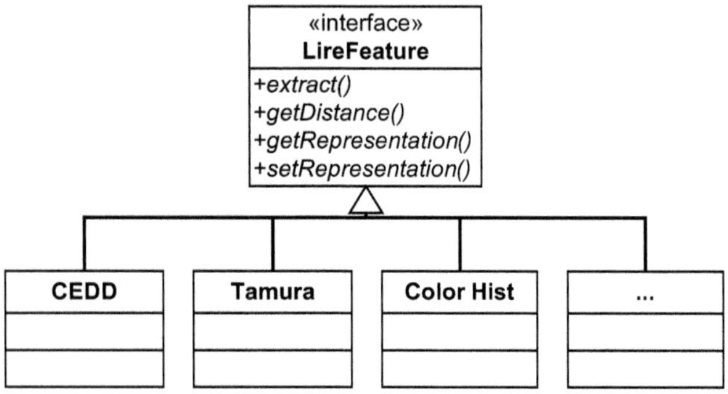

Figure 2: *LireFeature* interface and low level feature classes.

2. MPEG-7 descriptors scalable color, color layout and edge histogram, see [3].
3. The Tamura texture features coarseness, contrast and directionality, see [22]
4. Color and edge directivity descriptor, CEDD, see [4] and Fuzzy color and texture histogram, FCTH, see [5], which are joint histograms combining fuzzy color and edge histograms.
5. Auto color correlation feature defined by Huang et al. [10]

4. LOCAL FEATURES

Besides global features current research focuses also on local features and their application in visual information retrieval [19], the well known *bag of visual words* approach. It has been shown that for many tasks local feature histograms and visual words outperform global features [8]. In LIRe three types of local features are available.

1. Scale-Invariant Feature Transform, SIFT [13] based on the ImageJ[1] implementation,
2. Speeded Up Robust Feature, SURF [2] based on jopensurf[2] and
3. Maximally Stable Extremal Regions, MSER [14], based on the algorithm presented in [17].

All those local features are handled by LIRe like global features, but with a $1 : n$ relation of image to feature. Consequently local features are stored within the Lucene index just like global features. To employ the bag of visual words approach Lire provides *HistogramBuilder* classes. Those classes create a visual words vocabulary using k-means and (i) assign local feature histograms to images stored in the index and (ii) creates a *visual sentence*, like "v13 v522 v34 ...", from the set of visual words {v0, v1, v2, v3, ...}. This representation of visual words allows to utilize the fast text based retrieval mechanisms of Lucene for search. The corresponding searcher classes utilize an inverted list with a configurable similarity metric to search through all the visual sentences.

[1]http://rsbweb.nih.gov/ij/
[2]http://code.google.com/p/jopensurf/

5. INDEXING AND SEARCH

In general global as well as local features are stored as either text or byte payload in a Lucene based index. Basic search implementations then use linear search to find the most promising n candidates and return them in a ranked list. For local features a further indexing step allows for the use of an inverted index for the bag of visual words approach (see previous section). However, for several scenarios with millions of images and global features sub linear search in feature spaces is needed. In LIRe two basic mechanisms for faster search in feature spaces are included. *Fastmap* [9] is a rather aged but fast method that allows for dimensionality reduction. With the a reduced number of dimensions features can be organized in data structures for fast retrieval, like for instance R* trees. A newer and more promising approach is the *Metric Spaces* [1] method. This approach utilizes inverted lists to characterize data points in feature spaces by their distance to a set of reference data points. Utilizing a ranked list of nearest neighbours the footrule distance provides an approximation of the original pair wise distance. This approach has been shown to work well on sets of millions of images.

6. APPLICATIONS

Main showcase is the open source application LireDemo, which is provided in the LIRe SVN and on the LIRe web page. Fig. 3 shows the indexing screen of the demo UI. Features include indexing, search, index browsing, selection of different features and an image mosaic option, contributed by students.

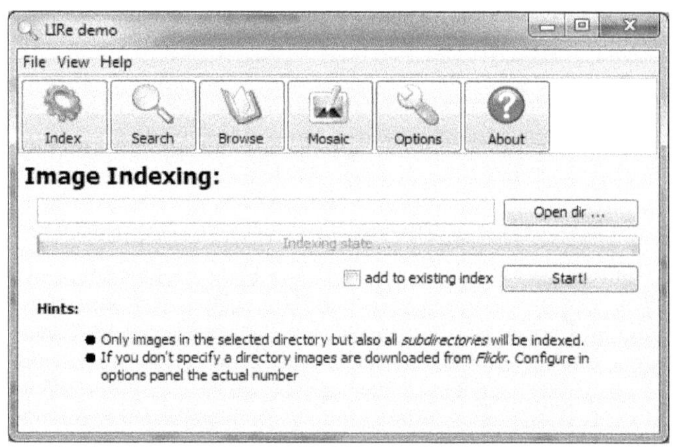

Figure 3: LireDemo user interface screenshot showing the indexing screen.

Within the lifetime of the project multiple uses have been reported. Usage ranges from teaching at university courses, integration in research and use in TRECVid and ImageCLEF, and multimedia retrieval tasks. Besides several others LIRe features are used in [18], [6], and [11]. LIRe has also for intance been integrated in other software like in ZoRa Photo Director[3] for duplicate detection, is used for finding similar photos in asset management application by

[3]http://www.photozora.de

Table 1: Performance of selected features tested on the Wang Simplicity data set [12] in terms of mean average precicion (map), precision at ten (p@10) and error rate (er).

Feature	map	p@10	er
Auto color correlogram	0.475	0.725	0.171
CEDD	0.506	0.710	0.178
Color histogram	0.484	0.704	0.205
FCTH	0.498	0.703	0.209
Gabor	0.233	0.248	0.707
JCD	0.510	0.719	0.177
JPEG coefficients histogram	0.446	0.669	0.215
MPEG-7 color layout	0.439	0.610	0.309
MPEG-7 scalable color	0.305	0.470	0.462
MPEG-7 edge histogram	0.333	0.500	0.401
SIFT BoVW	0.183	0.243	0.687
Tamura	0.253	0.359	0.601

mediamid[4] and has been employed for similarity search in mobile applications by R/GA[5].

In teaching LIRe allows for instance for easy construction of image search engines or analysis of image and video sets. Students can employ established methods on different data sets, extend existing methods or change parameters and learn about the impact.

7. PERFORMANCE

Retrieval performance is of course a matter of test data set and choice of parameters like number of bins, quantization routine and weighting scheme, but tests indicate that LIRe features performance similar to well known evaluations. Features tested include the standard RGB color histogram with 1024 bins and L1 distance function. The SIFT based bag of visual words implementation employs standard TF*IDF weighting from Lucene. Overall results are shown in Tab. 1. A closer look on the performance in different categories is presented in Fig. 4.

8. CONCLUSIONS

LIRe has been around for some time now after the inital release in 2006. It has been downloaded from sourceforge.net 18.521 times[6]. While this would not be an impressive number for an end user application it is a great success for a content based image retrieval software library, also in the light of the fact that this does not include downloads via SVN and beta releases not released on sourceforge.net. While LIRe has no regular stable release cycle its code base grows constantly. New features are added and tested and bugs are fixed as soon they are found and reported. All additions are submitted to the SVN and are available as open source for the public. All in all LIRe provides (i) a great base line for further research in content based image retrieval, (ii) a valuable resource for teaching the implementation of content based search, (iii) a robust and easy-to-use library for easy integratrion of standard content based image retrieval functions in applications.

[4]http://www.mediamid.com

[5]http://www.rga.com/

[6]as stated on May 9th, 2011, on the sourceforge.net homepage

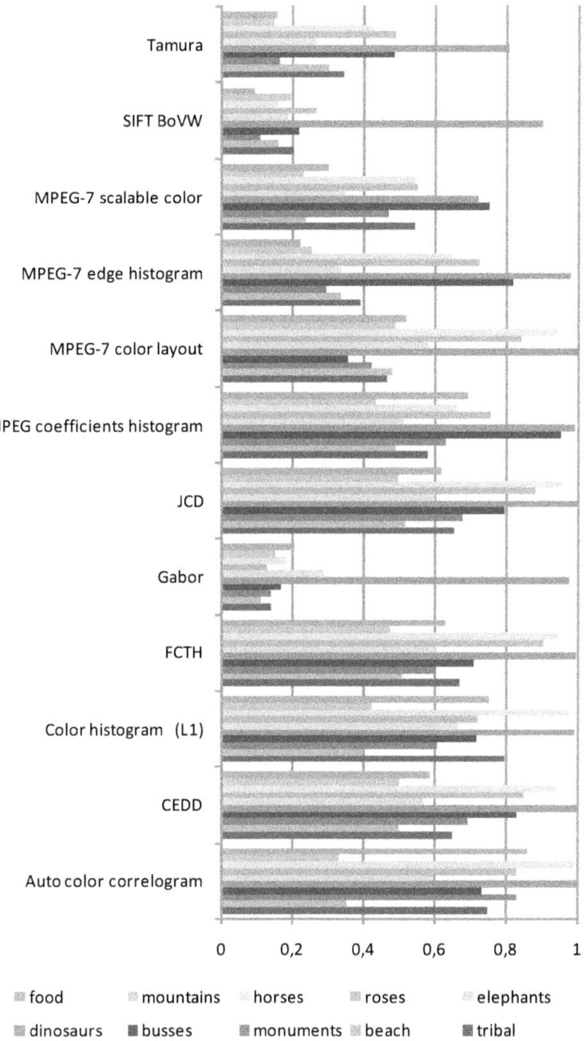

Figure 4: MAP per category in the Wang Simplicity data set.

9. ACKNOWLEDGMENTS

We'd like to thank at least some of the numerous people having contributed code and ideas to Lire or having published their work as open source allowing integration into LIRe: Anna-Maria Pasterk, Arthur Li, Arthur Pitman, Bastian Hösch, Benjamin Sznajder, Christian Penz, Christine Keim, Christoph Kofler, Dan Hanley, Daniel Pötzinger, Fabrizio Falchi, Giuseppe Amato, Janine Lachner, Katharina Tomanec, Lukas Esterle, Manuel Oraze, Marian Kogler, Marko Keuschnig, Rodrigo Carvalho Rezende, Roman Divotkey, Roman Kern and Savvas Chatzichristofis.

This work was partially supported by the Lakeside Labs GmbH, Klagenfurt, Austria and funding from the European Regional Development Fund and the Carinthian Economic Promotion Fund (KWF) under grant 20214/17097/24774.

10. REFERENCES

[1] G. Amato and P. Savino. Approximate similarity search in metric spaces using inverted files. In

Proceedings of the 3rd international conference on Scalable information systems, InfoScale '08, pages 28:1–28:10, ICST, Brussels, Belgium, Belgium, 2008. ICST (Institute for Computer Sciences, Social-Informatics and Telecommunications Engineering).

[2] H. Bay, T. Tuytelaars, and L. Van Gool. Surf: Speeded up robust features. In *Computer Vision - ECCV 2006*, volume 3951 of *Lecture Notes in Computer Science*, pages 404–417. Springer, 2006.

[3] S.-F. Chang, T. Sikora, and A. Puri. Overview of the mpeg-7 standard. *IEEE Transactions on Circuits and Systems for Video Technology*, 11(6):688–695, June 2001.

[4] S. A. Chatzichristofis and Y. S. Boutalis. CEDD: Color and Edge Directivity Descriptor. A Compact Descriptor for Image Indexing and Retrieval. In A. Gasteratos, M. Vincze, and J. Tsotsos, editors, *Proceedings of the 6th International Conference on Computer Vision Systems, ICVS 2008*, volume 5008 of *LNCS*, pages 312–322, Santorini, Greece, May 2008. Springer.

[5] S. A. Chatzichristofis and Y. S. Boutalis. FCTH: Fuzzy Color And Texture Histogram A Low Level Feature For Accurate Image Retrieval. In *Proceedings of the 9th International Workshop on Image Analysis for Multimedia Interactive Services, WIAMIS 2008*, pages 191–196, Klagenfurt, Austria, May 2008. IEEE.

[6] P. Daras, T. Semertzidis, L. Makris, and M. G. Strintzis. Similarity content search in content centric networks. In *Proceedings of the international conference on Multimedia*, MM '10, pages 775–778, New York, NY, USA, 2010. ACM.

[7] R. Datta, D. Joshi, J. Li, and J. Z. Wang. Image retrieval: Ideas, influences, and trends of the new age. *ACM Comput. Surv.*, 40(2):1–60, 2008.

[8] T. Deselaers, D. Keysers, and H. Ney. Features for image retrieval: an experimental comparison. *Inf. Retr.*, 11(2):77–107, 2008.

[9] C. Faloutsos and K.-I. Lin. Fastmap: A fast algorithm for indexing, data miningand visualization of traditional and multimedia datasets. In *ACM SIGMOG*, pages 163–174, CA, USA, 1995.

[10] J. Huang, S. R. Kumar, M. Mitra, W.-J. Zhu, and R. Zabih. Image indexing using color correlograms. In *Proceedings of the 1997 Conference on Computer Vision and Pattern Recognition, CVPR '97*, volume 00, pages 762–768, San Juan, Puerto Rico, June 1997. IEEE.

[11] D. Inkpen, M. Stogaitis, F. DeGuire, and M. Alzghool. Clustering for photo retrieval at image clef 2008. In *Proceedings of the 9th Cross-language evaluation forum conference on Evaluating systems for multilingual and multimodal information access*, CLEF'08, pages 685–690, Berlin, Heidelberg, 2009. Springer-Verlag.

[12] J. Li and J. Z. Wang. Automatic linguistic indexing of pictures by a statistical modeling approach. *IEEE Trans. Pattern Anal. Mach. Intell.*, 25:1075–1088, September 2003.

[13] D. Lowe. Object recognition from local scale-invariant features. In *Computer Vision, 1999. The Proceedings of the Seventh IEEE International Conference on*, volume 2, pages 1150 –1157 vol.2, 1999.

[14] J. Matas, O. Chum, M. Urban, and T. Pajdla. Robust wide-baseline stereo from maximally stable extremal regions. *Image and Vision Computing*, 22(10):761 – 767, 2004. British Machine Vision Computing 2002.

[15] M. McCandless, E. Hatcher, and O. Gospodnetic. *Lucene in Action, Second Edition.* Manning, 2010.

[16] H. MÃijller, P. Clough, T. Deselaers, and B. Caputo, editors. *ImageCLEF.* Springer, 2010.

[17] D. Nister and H. Stewenius. Linear time maximally stable extremal regions. In *Proceedings of the 10th European Conference on Computer Vision: Part II*, ECCV '08, pages 183–196, Berlin, Heidelberg, 2008. Springer-Verlag.

[18] M. Rahman, S. Antani, and G. Thoma. A biomedical image retrieval framework based on classification-driven image filtering and similarity fusion. In *Biomedical Imaging: From Nano to Macro, 2011 IEEE International Symposium on*, pages 1905 –1908, 30 2011-april 2 2011.

[19] J. Sivic and A. Zisserman. Video google: A text retrieval approach to object matching in videos. *Computer Vision, IEEE International Conference on*, 2:1470, 2003.

[20] A. F. Smeaton, P. Over, and W. Kraaij. Evaluation campaigns and trecvid. In *MIR '06: Proceedings of the 8th ACM International Workshop on Multimedia Information Retrieval*, pages 321–330, New York, NY, USA, 2006. ACM Press.

[21] A. Smeulders, M. Worring, S. Santini, A. Gupta, and R. Jain. Content-based image retrieval at the end of the early years. *Pattern Analysis and Machine Intelligence, IEEE Transactions on*, 22(12):1349–1380, December 2000.

[22] H. Tamura, S. Mori, and T. Yamawaki. Textural features corresponding to visual perception. *IEEE Transactions on Systems, Man, and Cybernetics*, 8(6):460–472, June 1978.

Tribler: P2P Media Search and Sharing

Niels Zeilemaker
Delft University of Technology
The Netherlands
niels@zeilemaker.nl

Mihai Capotă
Delft University of Technology
The Netherlands
mihai@mihaic.ro

Arno Bakker
Delft University of Technology
The Netherlands
arno@cs.vu.nl

Johan Pouwelse
Delft University of Technology
The Netherlands
peer2peer@gmail.com

ABSTRACT

Tribler is an open-source software project facilitating search, streaming and sharing content using P2P technology. Over 800 000 people have used Tribler since the project started in 2005. The Tribler P2P core supports BitTorrent-compatible downloading, video on demand and live streaming. Aside from a regular desktop GUI that runs on multiple OSes, it can be installed as a browser plug-in, currently used by Wikipedia. Aditionally, it runs on a 450 MHz processor, showcasing future TV support. We continuously work on extensions and test out novel research ideas within our user base, resulting in sub-second content search, a reputation system for rewarding upload, and channels for content publishing and spam prevention. Presently, 1200 channels have been created, enabling rich multimedia communities without requiring any server.

Categories and Subject Descriptors

C.2.2 [**Computer Communication Networks**]: Network Protocols—*applications*; C.4 [**Performance of Systems**]: Reliability, availability, and serviceability

General Terms

Algorithms, Design, Performance

Keywords

Tribler, BitTorrent, gossip, file sharing, video on demand

1. INTRODUCTION

As of 2001 BitTorrent has transformed the manner in which files are transfered over the Internet. While not the first P2P file-sharing application, it became the most successful because of its unprecedented efficiency. However, BitTorrent fails to properly address important issues, such as search, video on demand and long-term contribution incentives. In this paper, we introduce Tribler, our BitTorrent-based open-source project that adds missing features and new use-cases, while remaining fully backwards compatible.

BitTorrent introduced a new mechanism for transferring files that maximizes the resource contribution of peers. In BitTorrent, before the transfer begins, files are split into small *pieces* which can then be individually downloaded from different peers. This way, downloaders (called *leechers*) can upload completed pieces to other leechers, without the need to have the whole file first. Furthermore, this uploading is encouraged by the tit-for-tat incentive mechanism built into BitTorrent: a leecher will rank its peers by upload speed and will upload in return only to the fastest uploaders. Peers which have completed the file can help others by sending them pieces for free, these peers are called *seeders*.

To protect against transfer errors and malicious modifications, each file piece is accompanied by its SHA-1 cryptographic hash. The peer that initiates the transfer of a file will first record these hashes in a metadata file called a *torrent*. The torrent has to be distributed out-of-band to the users interested in downloading the file, e.g., through email or the Web. Only after getting hold of the torrent can a BitTorrent client start downloading the files. This is one of the problems of the original BitTorrent protocol. Searching for torrents is also not part of the BitTorrent protocol and is normally done through centralized websites.

The original BitTorrent protocol has another important design flaw. Peer discovery is done through centralized servers called *trackers*. The address of a tracker is recorded in the torrent and every interested peer will announce itself to the tracker. In turn, the tracker will provide the peer a list of other peers currently uploading or downloading the file. Whenever the tracker is offline, new peers cannot join the *swarm*—the group of peers sharing the file—because there is no other way to discover it.

Initiated in 2005, Tribler [1][1] is an open-source research project funded by multiple European research grants, which addresses the problems of the original BitTorrent protocol and extends it beyond file sharing to new areas such as video on demand and live streaming. The existence of Tribler was made possible by the open nature of BitTorrent. The protocol specification is freely available [4] and the original BitTorrent software used an open-source license [3]. After

[1]Sources and documentation can be found at `http://tribler.org/trac/wiki/TriblerForDevelopers`

MM'11, November 28–December 1, 2011, Scottsdale, Arizona, USA.

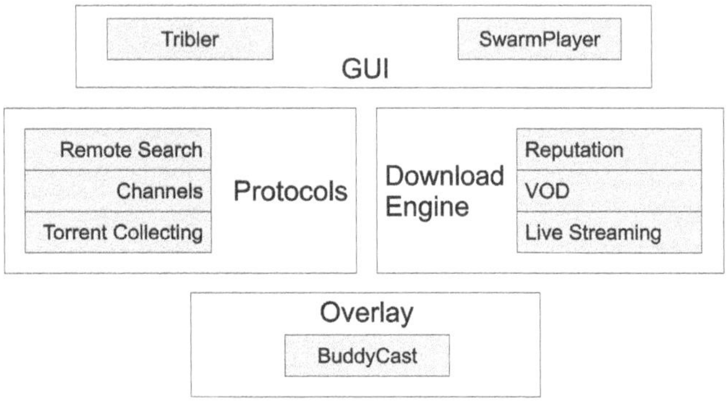

Figure 1: Tribler architecture

extensive research and numerous incremental improvements, Tribler has implemented and deployed fully decentralized remote search, channels, reputation, video on demand, and live streaming.

2. DESIGN AND FEATURES

Tribler consist of two base components, the *core* which implements all communication protocols, and the *GUI* which presents the features of the software to the user. As part of the project we have implemented a secondary GUI by repackaging the core as a browser plug-in called SwarmPlayer. This section first describes the overall structure of the core, then the Tribler GUI, and finally the SwarmPlayer.

2.1 Architecture

The core of Tribler can be further divided into three parts: (1) the *overlay* which allows for communication between Tribler peers, (2) the *protocols* implementing remote search, torrent collecting etc., and (3) the *download engine*, which allows users to download files in BitTorrent swarms.

One of the missing features of BitTorrent is cross-swarm identification of peers. Tribler addresses this by using public key cryptography to generate an identifier called *PermID* for each peer. This PermID is stored separately from the Tribler installation files, so that upgrading or reinstalling Tribler do not cause it to change. The PermID allows us to identify and authenticate messages from users, allowing for a secure method of communication.

A key feature of Tribler is its custom overlay network. Implemented as a BitTorrent swarm with a predefined identifier, it allows Tribler peers to exchange information using custom overlay communication protocols. At the same time, the overlay does not require more TCP sockets to be opened in addition to regular BitTorrent.

The *BuddyCast* protocol was implemented as one of the first overlay protocols. Using it, peers are exchanging preference lists containing the infohashes of downloaded torrents. Infohashes are a commonly used as an identifier for BitTorrent swarms. All the preference lists a peer receives are aggregated into an SQLite database which is then used to perform collaborative filtering. The embedded SQLite database, which we call the *MegaCache*, will store up to 2500 preference lists. By comparing a peer's own downloads to those of others, it can calculate a similarity between them. Peers with a high similarity, those which have downloaded the same torrents, are called *taste buddies*. During the BuddyCast handshake, in addition to the preference list, the currently connected taste buddies will be exchanged, as well as a number of random connected peers. This allows for peers to discover new taste buddies, both through exploitation of current taste buddies, and through exploration of random peers.

2.2 Torrent Collecting

After discovering new infohashes through BuddyCast, a peer will start collecting the associated torrents. An algorithm determines which torrents are the most interesting, form this list, and should be collected. It does so by sorting the torrents based on the similarity to the users which have downloaded them. A torrent downloaded by numerous taste buddies will thus be requested first. Requests for these are send back to the sending peer. While searching, a torrent is fetched when the user wants to see its details, e.g., file name, number of peers in the swarm. The first 25 torrents are prefetched to improve the speed of showing the user details of these highly relevant torrents. If no peer is willing to send the torrent, it is downloaded using the BitTorrent extension for sending torrents [7].

2.3 Remote Search

A Tribler peer will, by default, connect to 10 random peers and 10 taste buddies. By doing so, it will create a semantic overlay consisting of peers which are very similar it. Having a connection to similar peer allows us to implement *remote search* in a very efficient manner. By only using these connected peers, instead of flooding the network as is usually done, we can show very relevant results in less than a second. In addition, due to Tribler exchanging preference lists, the MegaCache of each peer can contain up to 50 000 relevant torrents. The local results can be shown to the user even quicker, resulting in a very responsive search.

2.4 Video on Demand

Another novel feature Tribler is our *video on demand* (VOD) implementation. BitTorrent, by default, uses a piece picking policy which downloads the rarest piece. As a result, a peer maximizes the demand for the pieces it downloads, allowing the peer to trade them with others. By modifying the piece picking policy of BitTorrent, we can allow users to start playing the video even before completing the download. With our VOD piece picking policies, a piece will be assigned one of three priorities: high, mid, and low. The high priority pieces are requested in order if playback has already started. Otherwise the rarest pieces is requested. If all high priority pieces are requested, then the rarest piece of the mid priority category is requested. If those are all requested, then the low priority pieces are requested, again rarest first. The pieces in the high and mid priority are defined by sliding windows, dependent on the current playback position. A peer decides whom to send the pieces to according to a metric which is called the forwarding rank. This metric will determine how well a peer is sending pieces to others and thus is cooperating in the system (for a detailed description we refer you to the paper by Mol et al. [9]).

2.5 Live Streaming

A slightly different technique, compared to VOD, is used to provide live streaming using BitTorrent. Since the pieces are not known in advance (the video content is generated live), it is impossible to record their hashes in the torrent.

The solution as implemented in Tribler is based on the same private/public key pair used for the PermID. We extend the specification of the torrent, so that it can hold the public key of the seeder. The seeder then signs all the pieces it generates with its private key. This way, all peers that receive the torrent can verify the authenticity of the pieces using the public key.

Live streaming can last an indefinitely long time. Hence, piece availability cannot be expected to be appropriate for old pieces. This is why our implementation currently discards pieces older than 15 minutes relative to the playback position. More details about live streaming are available in a technical report [2].

2.6 Reputation

Currently, we are experimenting with a global reputation system for Tribler peers. Having such a system will allow peers to identify others who are behaving well over a long time, not only in a single swarm, as is the case with normal BitTorrent. Lazy freeriders, peers who after downloading a torrent leave immediately, will have a lower reputation then peers who stay and seed. Cooperative behavior is thus encouraged, leading to better performance.

The system we implemented, called *BarterCast* [8], creates records stating how much data has been exchanged between two peers. By collecting these BarterCast records, each peer can create a subjective graph of the whole Tribler population, whose edges describe the data exchanged between peers. Using this graph, a peer can estimate the contribution another peer has made to the system. To protect from malicious peers that are misreporting data exchanges, a peer computes the actual reputation of other peers using a maximum flow algorithm starting from itself. This reputation can then be used to order the peers which are requesting pieces, or even decide to not send any pieces to peers with a low reputation.

2.7 Channels

Since the release of Tribler 5.2 we have implemented fully decentralized channels that each user can utilize to publish torrents they like. Other users can mark a channel as favorite, causing it to become more popular. Furthermore, channels can be marked as spam when users determine that the torrents provided are fake. Using both the total number of users marking a channel as a favorite or spam, a popularity metric is calculated and used to sort the channels. *ChannelCast*, the overlay protocol used to discover and update channels, exploits this popularity to ensure the right channels are discovered faster.

Currently more than 1200 channels have been created. The next version of ChannelCast we plan will allow for cooperation and communication. Moving away from a single injector publishing all content, users will be able to post comments and iteratively improve the metadata (title, description, etc.). A distributed permission system will allow for granting users specific permissions within a channel.

2.8 GUI

As part of the standalone Tribler client, we have implemented a GUI using the open-source wxPython toolkit, which allows us to implement a GUI once and run it on multiple platforms (Windows, Mac OS X, Linux).The Tribler GUI includes search, channels and a library view. VOD is available for torrents with video content; the embedded version of the open-source VLC media player is used for playback. We implemented some additional features, such as the "Network Buzz" which shows the user what popular content is currently available in the Tribler network. Furthermore, the GUI provides several hints to users suggesting a specific action or promoting the use of a feature of the program. In Figure 2, a screenshot of the search results view is shown. This view consists of a list of results, which expand after being selected by the user to show the torrent details. This view includes a short overview, but additionally provides specific information using tabs. Hiding these details was a design choice as we expect most users to be intimidated by them.

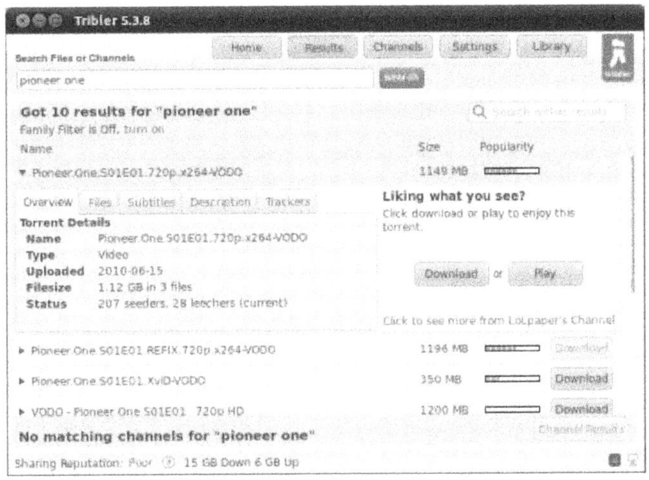

Figure 2: Tribler GUI showing search results

2.9 Other deployments: TV and Browser

As part of the European funded P2P-Next project, we developed two other deployments based on the same Tribler core. Being able to run Python, Pioneer has created a set-top box called NextShare TV which allows users to do BitTorrent live streaming and VOD on their TV. The set-top box is a 450 MHz machine, with a custom GUI designed to be used on TVs [10].

Another deployment of the Tribler core is called SwarmPlayer and provides users with the same functionality as NextShare TV, but is packaged as a browser plug-in. It uses the combination of the HTML 5 video tag and a custom `tribe://` protocol to download and stream the video data in the browser. After a torrent has been completely downloaded, it will be automatically seeded. Videos that have not been completely downloaded, due to the user browsing away from the Web page are considered unwanted videos and are removed. Seeding is supported through a limited cache which is normally transparent to the user. Manual control over the seeding is available using a separate HTML GUI, where users can stop and start torrents, as well as modify advanced settings like the upload speed limit.

The latest version of SwarmPlayer is experimenting with our new download engine called *Swift* [6], which radically simplifies the BitTorrent protocol by implementing it on top of UDP, stripping away the complexity of TCP and adding the benefit of easier NAT puncturing.

3. USAGE

Tribler serves two purposes; it is a BitTorrent client with additional features and, as such, it is used by people all over the world; on the other hand, it is also a tool for experimenting with and evaluating protocols and algorithms. In this section, we present both these use-cases.

3.1 Users

Since it's release in 2006, Tribler has been downloaded over 800 000 times. All big releases result in a temporary increase in usage. Tribler 5.3 was downloaded 10 000 times within a three day period. Temporary increases of usage are usually caused by articles on popular websites such as Slashdot, Ars Technica, and BBC News. After the dust settles, our loyal user base continues to use Tribler and participates in the forums to help us improve the client. In March 2011, we had more than 5000 unique Tribler users downloading more than 6500 torrents (of which 2500 using VOD).

SwarmPlayer, our other deployment of the Tribler core, has been incorporated into Wikipedia and VODO[2], where it has been downloaded by 6000 users and 13 000 users, respectively.

3.2 Scientists

Any researcher can use Tribler to experiment with and evaluate algorithms they are developing. Tribler is very well suited for this since it has both a stable user base, allowing for long experiments, and it gets downloaded by many users at every major release. These spikes in usage provide researchers with large amounts of data which have been used to conduct numerous experiments. There are three methods implemented to collect data, with user consent; the first is simply using a Tribler instance as an "ordinary" peer and keeping a log of all received responses. BuddyCast, for instance, allows us to record the profiles and taste/random buddy lists of peers, which can then be used to improve the similarity function building the semantic overlay.

Second, we can actively crawl the network. Tribler peers, by default, accept incoming crawl messages from a predefined list of crawlers. Users can, of course, disable this behavior. A crawler can extract many predefined statistics from a peer, and can even execute SQL statements. The third method is a periodic push to the server, in which every peer periodically sends a file to a server which is predefined.

After the initial release of our BarterCast reputation system, data collected using a crawler resulted in a clear understanding that simply using one-hop gossip was not sufficient. Simulations based on the data collected resulted in a complete redesign using BarterCast records signed by both peers that are involved in the data exchange. Signed BarterCast records will allow for full gossip, due to the records being immutable. Using this scheme and other modifications resulted in a large improvement in the error estimation and coverage of the reputation system [5].

4. CONCLUSION

With Tribler we have successfully deployed a BitTorrent client that pushes the boundaries of P2P technology. It allows a stable user base to benefit from a set of novel features, including remote search, VOD, live streaming, reputation, and channels. Testing research ideas with real users has always proven to be a significant challenge. Researchers therefore often rely on simulations instead of real systems with thousands of users. With Tribler we are providing scientists with an open platform to conduct experiments on.

All features have been implemented using open-source tools, readily available for all, while the Tribler source code is also available to be modified. Furthermore, SwarmPlayer and NextShare TV show how the implementation versatility of the Tribler core allows for different GUIs and use cases.

The overlay protocols have been designed with compatibility in mind and allow developers to incorporate them into other BitTorrent clients. In order to support this, a clear specification for each protocol is publicly available at the Tribler website [2]. Finally, due to indirect and direct support from European research programmes, the platform has been available for over five years with steady improvements; nine big releases have already been completed, with more scheduled in coming years.

[2]VODO is a website promoting and distributing free-to-share media `www.vodo.net`

5. ACKNOWLEDGMENTS

This work was partially supported by the European Community's Seventh Framework Programme through the P2P-Next, QLectives and PetaMedia projects (grant no. 216217, 231200, 216444).

6. REFERENCES

[1] Tribler website. `http://tribler.org`.

[2] A. Bakker et al. Tribler Protocol Specification. `http://svn.tribler.org/bt2-design/proto-spec-unified/trunk/proto-spec-current.pdf`, 1 2009.

[3] BitTorrent, Inc. BitTorrent downloads website. `http://download.bittorrent.com/dl/`.

[4] B. Cohen. The BitTorrent Protocol Specification. `http://www.bittorrent.org/beps/bep_0003.html`.

[5] R. Delaviz, N. Andrade, and J. Pouwelse. Improving accuracy and coverage in an internet-deployed reputation mechanism. In *Peer-to-Peer Computing (P2P), 2010 IEEE Tenth International Conference on*, pages 1 –9, aug. 2010.

[6] V. Grishchenko and J. Pouwelse. Swift, the multiparty transport protocol. `http://libswift.org/`.

[7] G. Hazel and A. Norberg. Extension for Peers to Send Metadata Files. `http://www.bittorrent.org/beps/bep_0009.html`.

[8] M. Meulpolder, J. Pouwelse, D. Epema, and H. Sips. Bartercast: A practical approach to prevent lazy freeriding in p2p networks. *Parallel and Distributed Processing Symposium, International*, 0:1–8, 2009.

[9] J. J. D. Mol, J. A. Pouwelse, M. Meulpolder, D. H. J. Epema, and H. J. Sips. Give-to-get: free-riding resilient video-on-demand in p2p systems. *Proceedings of SPIE*, pages 681804–681804–8, 2008.

[10] M. Stuart. P2P-Next. `http://www.dcia.info/activities/p2pmslv2009/1-7%20P2PMS%20P2P-Next.pdf`.

OpenMusic

Visual Programming Environment for Music Composition, Analysis and Research

Jean Bresson
STMS: IRCAM-CNRS-UPMC
1, place I. Stravinsky
75004 Paris, France
bresson@ircam.fr

Carlos Agon
STMS: IRCAM-CNRS-UPMC
1, place I. Stravinsky
75004 Paris, France
agon@ircam.fr

Gérard Assayag
STMS: IRCAM-CNRS-UPMC
1, place I. Stravinsky
75004 Paris, France
assayag@ircam.fr

ABSTRACT

OpenMusic is an open source environment dedicated to music composition. The core of this environment is a full-featured visual programming language based on Common Lisp and CLOS (Common Lisp Object System) allowing to design processes for the generation or manipulation of musical material. This language can also be used for general purpose visual programming and other (possibly extra-musical) applications.

Categories and Subject Descriptors

D.1.7 [**Software**]: Programming Techniques—*Visual Programming*; J.5 [**Computer Applications**]: Arts and Humanities—*Music*

General Terms

Design, Languages

Keywords

Visual Programming, Music, Computer-Aided Composition.

1. COMPUTER-AIDED COMPOSITION

OpenMusic (OM) is an environment designed for music composition in the tradition of what is conventionally called *computer-aided composition* in the contemporary music and computer music research communities [9]. The original purpose of computer-aided composition research was to provide composers with means to develop musical ideas and models using the computer: In this context, creating compositional tools in the form of standard applications, as is the case with most commercial music software, turned out to be too restrictive from a creative point of view. In order to better integrate the artistic thought and give musicians full access to the expressive and computational power of computer tools and formalisms, computer-aided composition environments needed to be more "programmable" and would actually better be *programming languages* than simple programs.

A number of computer music systems have therefore been developed during the past 20 years, with more or less explicit programming language features [22, 21, 29]. Some of them are open source and quite widely used software [27, 30].

While most "musical programming languages" principally deal with signal processing and sound synthesis, an original approach adopted by the IRCAM Music Representation team in the late 80s had the particularity to focus on symbolic musical structures and processes, that is, on compositional aspects traditionally ignored or carried out outside computer environments [11]. In this context and as far as they relate to formalisation and/or calculus, the design of compositional processes using programming languages and environments allows to better understand, explore and develop these processes than with other traditional or more specific media and applications. Fewer of such "symbolic" programming/computer-aided composition environments exist. Most of them are based on Common Lisp or other Lisp dialects (see for instance [33]).

OpenMusic [12] is one of the few visual programming environments existing to date for symbolic music processing (see also [26]). Initiated in 1997, this open source project derived from the PatchWork environment [25] and constitutes a complete visual language including powerful programming features, mostly inherited and adapted from Common Lisp, its underlying implementation language, and CLOS (Common Lisp Object System [24]).

2. BASIC DESCRIPTION

Visual programs in OpenMusic are created in *patch* editors, and are mainly compound of boxes and connections (see Figure 1). Each box represents a functional element in the program: generally, a function (e.g. *om-random*, *repeat-n*, *bpf-sample...* in Figure 1) or a class factory (boxes generating instances of a given class—e.g. the curve at the top or the score object at the bottom of Figure 1). The contents of the factory boxes can be edited thanks to specific graphical editors like score editors, sound editors, break-points function or 2D/3D editors etc., which leaves a significant freedom to the user regarding the algorithmic vs. manual/intuitive parts of his/her work.

The boxes in OpenMusic visual programs have inputs and outputs (represented by small round inlets and outlets respectively at the top and at the bottom of the box icons) which allow to connect them together: at *evaluation*, a box performs a call to its internal functional reference using the

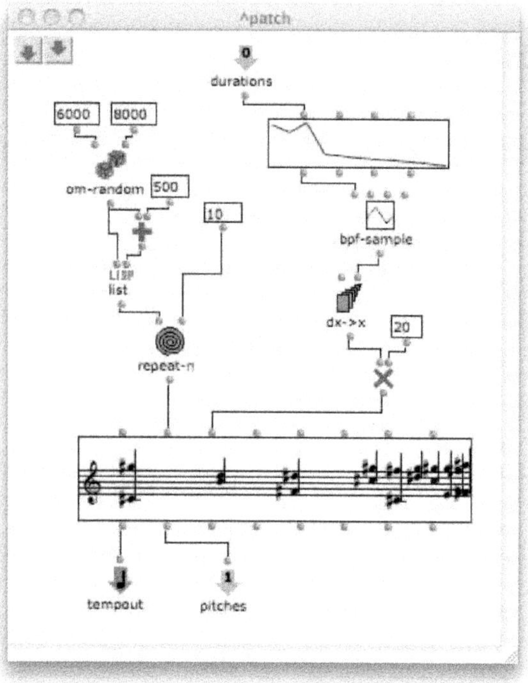

Figure 1: A *patch* or basic visual program editor in OpenMusic.

result of the boxes connected to its inputs as parameters (or arguments). A recursive "bottom-up" function call therefore occurs in the visual program graph, which corresponds to the execution of a program in a very similar way as would be interpreted and evaluated a Lisp expression.[1]

The boxes can actually refer either to in-built OpenMusic functions or classes, or to programming elements (functions, programs, classes) designed by the user graphically or in Lisp. A close and transparent relation exists between the visual and underlying text-based programming environments, which makes it possible to use together any kind of element in visual or Lisp programs.

The musical focus of the environment also led the authors to design advanced programming interfaces including a temporal dimension [1]. In the *maquette* (a "temporal" extension of the OpenMusic *patch*), time is considered as a structural dimension in both the visual program layout and execution, which allows to develop compositional processes integrated in an overall temporal context.

3. VISUAL PROGRAMMING FEATURES

OpenMusic provides a visual semantics implementing most functional and object-oriented features available in Common Lisp and CLOS. Abstraction, application, iterations and control structures are basics of most modern programming languages, although not always straightforward to represent in a visual language. Recursion, higher-level programming are examples of more advanced concepts also implemented in OpenMusic, which proved to be useful and pertinent in compositional situations and musical problems solving. Implementation details on these programming aspects are given in [19].

Visual object-oriented programming is another specificity of OpenMusic [1]. It is possible to define and instantiate classes graphically, but also to benefit from other CLOS features such as multiple inheritance or generic function and method definition, including multiple dispatch and standard method combination systems. The CLOS meta-object protocol (MOP) is another powerful feature making the basic language elements used in the Lisp program design (functions, methods, classes, etc.) instance of meta-object classes which can be manipulated, modified or extended at runtime by the same programs. The OpenMusic visual MOP described in [3] is an original extension of this system to the visual programming language.

The programming features and possibilities mentioned in this section often go far beyond the use of music composers, and extend the scope of the environment to a general new approach to programming using graphical interfaces.

4. A PLATFORM FOR COMPUTER MUSIC RESEARCH

Research in varied computer music areas have been carried out in or using OpenMusic, generally in the context of Master's or PhD theses, or in other types of institutional projects. Music notation and editors [17], quantification and representation of rhythmic structures [23, 5], style modeling and pattern recognition [10, 28], constraint programming and solving systems [31, 34] or sound synthesis and representation in music [6, 14] are example of such areas and projects. OpenMusic is also an important platform for computer-aided music analysis, allowing to carry out experiments and modeling processes leading to a new conception of "computational musicology" [8, 7, 2].

The output of these projects, as well as other more specific works carried out by composers, are generally integrated in the OpenMusic environment or made available to the user community as external, dynamically loadable libraries.

The latest developments in OpenMusic particularly aimed to extend the scope of its applications toward signal processing, for instance with a number of new libraries and tools dedicated to sound analysis, synthesis, and to the manipulation of audio and other low-level description data using the symbolic visual programming framework [16, 13, 18]. Spatial sound and the conception of new ways to represent and generate sound in space and/or using spatial rendering technologies is another currently active area of research and development in the environment [32, 20].

Different works have also been carried out using OpenMusic for extra-musical purposes. A recent example is the *Pixels* project, a library for the generation and processing of pixel arrays combined algorithmically to create pictures and graphics (see Figure 2).[2]

[1]The execution model in OpenMusic is called "demand-driven", as opposed to the "data-driven" model generally implemented in similar visual (graph-based) programming languages.

[2]*Pixels* has been developed and used for *Skyline*, by Shanta Rao (installation with computer-generated video, *Belleville Biennale / Nuit Blanche*, Paris, 2010).

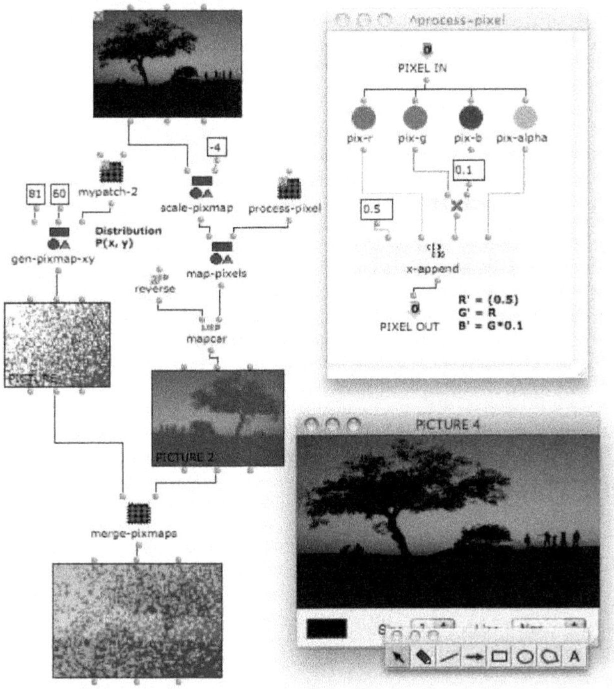

Figure 2: Algorithmic generation and processing of pixel arrays and in OpenMusic with the *Pixels* library (An example of extra-musical application).

5. APPLICATIONS AND USERS

The references provided in the previous section aim to illustrate the diversity of applications of OpenMusic in computer music research. The *OM Composer's Books* [4] can provide a relatively complete and rich overview of real musical applications of the visual programming environment by composers.

OpenMusic is taught in composition classes in many different institution around the world, such as the national conservatoires of Paris (CNSMDP) or Lyon in France, but also different Musikschulen in Germany (Stuttgart, Berlin) and universities in North America (Departments of Music in Columbia, Harvard, Stanford universities, UC San Diego, Université de Montréal, McGill University...) It is also used as a support in computer music or visual programming classes and workshops given at IRCAM or in several Master's program in French universities.

OpenMusic was also used as underlying kernel for the design and development of *Musique Lab 2* [15], an environment dedicated to music education now used and distributed by the French Ministry of Education.

6. REFERENCES

[1] C. Agon. *OpenMusic : Un langage visuel pour la composition musicale assistée par ordinateur.* PhD thesis, Université Pierre et Marie Curie, Paris, France, 1998.

[2] C. Agon, M. Andreatta, G. Assayag, and S. Schaub. Formal Aspects of Iannis Xenakis' "Symbolic Music": A Computer-Aided Exploration of Compositional Processes. *Journal of New Music Research*, 33(2), 2004.

[3] C. Agon and G. Assayag. OM: A Graphical Extension of CLOS using the MOP. In *Proceedings of ICL'03*, New York, USA, 2003.

[4] C. Agon, G. Assayag, and J. Bresson, editors. *The OM Composer's Book (2 volumes).* Editions Delatour / IRCAM, 2006-2008.

[5] C. Agon, K. Haddad, and G. Assayag. Representation and Rendering of Rhythmic Structures. In *WedelMusic*, Darmstadt, Germany, 2002.

[6] C. Agon, M. Stroppa, and G. Assayag. High Level Musical Control of Sound Synthesis in OpenMusic. In *Proceedings of the International Computer Music Conference*, Berlin, Germany, 2003.

[7] M. Andreatta and C. Agon. Implementing Algebraic Methods in OpenMusic. In *Proceedings of the International Computer Music Conference*, Singaphore, 2003.

[8] M. Andreatta, T. Noll, C. Agon, and G. Assayag. The Geometrical Groove: Rhythmic Canons between Theory, Implementation and Musical Experiments. In *Actes des Journées d'Informatique Musicale*, Bourges, France, 2001.

[9] G. Assayag. Computer Assisted Composition today. In *1st symposium on music and computers*, Corfu, Greece, 1998.

[10] G. Assayag, S. Dubnov, O. Lartillot, and G. Bejerano. Using Machine-Learning Methods for Musical Style Modeling. *Computer*, 36(10), 2003.

[11] G. Assayag and C. Rueda. The Music Representation Project at IRCAM. In *Proceedings of the International Computer Music Conference*, Tokyo, Japan, 1998.

[12] G. Assayag, C. Rueda, M. Laurson, C. Agon, and O. Delerue. Computer Assisted Composition at IRCAM: From PatchWork to OpenMusic. *Computer Music Journal*, 23(3), 1999.

[13] J. Bresson. Sound Processing in OpenMusic. In *Proceedings of the International Conference on Digital Audio Effects*, Montréal, QC, Canada, 2006.

[14] J. Bresson. *La synthèse sonore en composition musicale assistée par ordinateur : Modélisation et écriture du son.* PhD thesis, Université Pierre et Marie Curie, Paris, France, 2007.

[15] J. Bresson. ML-Maquette / Musique Lab 2. In *Proceedings of the International Computer Music Conference*, New York City / Stony Brook, USA, 2010.

[16] J. Bresson and C. Agon. Musical Representation of Sound in Computer-Aided Composition : A Visual Programming Framework. *Journal of New Music Research*, 36(4), 2007.

[17] J. Bresson and C. Agon. Scores, Programs and Time Representations: The Sheet Object in OpenMusic. *Computer Music Journal*, 32(4), 2008.

[18] J. Bresson and C. Agon. Processing Sound and Music Description Data Using OpenMusic. In *Proceedings of the International Computer Music Conference*, New York City / Stony Brook, USA, 2010.

[19] J. Bresson, C. Agon, and G. Assayag. Visual Lisp/CLOS Programming in OpenMusic. *Higher-Order and Symbolic Computation*, 22(1), 2009.

[20] J. Bresson and M. Schumacher. Representation and Interchange of Sound Spatialization Data for

Compositional Applications. In *Proceedings of the International Computer Music Conference*, Huddersfield, UK, 2011.

[21] R. B. Dannenberg, P. Desain, and H. Honing. Programming Language Design for Music. In C. Roads, S. T. Pope, A. Piccialli, and G. DePoli, editors, *Musical Signal Processing*. Swets and Zeitlinger, 1997.

[22] R. B. Dannenberg, P. McAvinney, and D. Rubine. Arctic : A Functional Language for Real-Time Systems. *Computer Music Journal*, 10(4), 1986.

[23] O. Delerue, G. Assayag, and C. Agon. Etude et réalisation d'opérateurs rythmiques dans OpenMusic, un environnement de programmation appliqué à la composition musicale. In *Actes des Journées d'Informatique Musicale*, La Londe les Maures, France, 1998.

[24] R. P. Gabriel, J. L. White, and D. G. Bobrow. CLOS: Integration Object-oriented and Functional Programming. *Communications of the ACM*, 34(9), 1991.

[25] M. Laurson and J. Duthen. Patchwork, a Graphic Language in PreForm. In *Proceedings of the International Computer Music Conference*, Ohio State University, USA, 1989.

[26] M. Laurson and M. Kuuskankare. PWGL: A Novel Visual Language Based on Common Lisp, CLOS, and OpenGL. In *Proceedings of the International Computer Music Conference*, Gothenburg, Sweden, 2002.

[27] J. McCartney. Rethinking the Computer Music Language: SuperCollider. *Computer Music Journal*, 26(4), 1996.

[28] B. Meudic. *Détermination automatique de la pulsation de la métrique et des motifs musicaux dans des interprétations à tempo variable d œuvres polyphoniques*. PhD thesis, Université Pierre et Marie Curie, Paris, France, 2004.

[29] M. Puckette. Combining Event and Signal Processing in the MAX Graphical Programming Environment. *Computer Music Journal*, 15(3), 1991.

[30] M. Puckette. Pure Data: Another Integrated Computer Music Environment. In *Proceedings of the Second Intercollege Computer Music Concerts*, Tachikawa, Japan, 1996.

[31] C. Rueda, M. Laurson, G. Bloch, and G. Assayag. Integrating Constraint Programming in Visual Musical Composition Languages. In *Proceedings of the European Conference on Artificial Intelligence*, Brighton, UK, 1998.

[32] M. Schumacher and J. Bresson. Spatial Sound Synthesis in Computer-Aided Composition. *Organised Sound*, 15(3), 2010.

[33] H. Taube. Common Music: A Music Composition Language in Common Lisp and CLOS. *Computer Music Journal*, 15(2), 1991.

[34] C. Truchet, G. Assayag, and P. Codognet. Visual and Adaptive Constraint Programming in Music. In *Proceedings of the International Computer Music Conference*, La Habana, Cuba, 2001.

APPENDIX

A. BUILD AND COMPILATION

OpenMusic is a Lisp-based system which requires an underlying runtime Lisp environment. It currently uses the *LispWorks*[3] Common Lisp implementation, which provides good graphical and GUI toolkits on which most of the low-level graphical aspects of the visual language rely.

The OpenMusic package therefore contains a pre-built executable running on MacOS X or Windows operating systems, *and* the Lisp sources of the software. These sources can easily be loaded in LispWorks (a free—limited—personal edition is available on the LispWorks website). All instructions are detailed in the OpenMusic webpage.[4]

This is generally not necessary, though, since OpenMusic itself embeds a Lisp interpreter and interface, so that is is possible to edit, (re)load and evaluate the sources or additional Lisp code and commands from within the running environment.

The limitations of using the OpenMusic in-built Lisp rather than LispWorks are the impossibility to generate and pack a new executable image, to compile Lisp files (they are only *evaluated*, hence the code is generally less efficient) and the absence of the LispWorks IDE tools. The OpenMusic executable, on the other hand, is easier to launch and to use for standard (non-programmer) users.

B. LICENCE AND DISTRIBUTION

OpenMusic is an open source project which sources are distributed under the GNU Public License (GPL). They can be downloaded from the OpenMusic website and are also distributed with the software itself. Making the sources available was for us an opportunity to raise collaborations and contributions, principally for the realization of specialized packages or libraries. As mentioned in this paper, OpenMusic modules are linked to the distributed sources so that it is possible to track and edit them and therefore to dynamically modify or extend the environment.

IRCAM owns professional LispWorks licenses, which allows us to build and distribute a compiled and packed application to the OpenMusic users. Since the beginning of this year, this released application is available for free and can also be downloaded from the website,[5] which we hope will consolidate and develop our user community.

IRCAM also commercially distributes a set of specialized external libraries for OpenMusic.

C. DOCUMENTATION

A set of documentation resources for OpenMusic is maintained and published online. This documentation features a user manual, a quick-start tutorial including a series of videos, tutorials and a number of additional resources. All pages and documents of interest are accessible from the OpenMusic website.[6]

A developer documentation also allows programmers to get into the OpenMusic architecture and provides the basics of programming in the environment.

[3] http://www.lispworks.com

[4] http://repmus.ircam.fr/openmusic/sources

[5] http://repmus.ircam.fr/openmusic/download

[6] http://repmus.ircam.fr/openmusic/documents

VOXALEAD: A Scalable Video Search Engine Based On Content

Julien Law-To
Exalead
75010 Paris
Julien.Lawto@3ds.com

Gregory Grefenstette
Exalead
75010 Paris
Gregory.Grefenstette@3ds.com

INTRODUCTION TO QUAERO PROJECT

Quaero, a research and innovation program addressing automatic processing of multimedia and multilingual content, fosters the development of new tools for navigation in large volumes of audiovisual content. Quaero projects (automatic information retrieval, analysis, segmentation and classification of text, speech, music, image and video) are supported by nearly 200 M€ of funding from Oséo Innovation, and involve 30 French and German partners. Data-centric application projects are led by industrial partners who share a research structure with universities. Each application area includes systematic use of technology evaluation. Entering its fourth year, Quaero very active eco-system has produced innovative applications, such as Voxalead presented here, that have been launched in large-scale deployments. A separate report can be found for each of the applications.

ABSTRACT

Most news organizations provide immediate access to topical news broadcasts through RSS streams or podcasts. Until recently, applications have not permitted a user to perform content based search within a longer spoken broadcast to find the segment that might interest them. Recent progress in both automatic speech recognition (ASR) and natural language processing (NLP) has produced robust tools that allow us to now provide users with quicker and more focused access to relevant segments of news broadcast videos. Our public online demonstrator of the Voxalead application currently indexes daily broadcast news content from 50 sources in English, French, Chinese, Arabic, Spanish, Dutch, Italian and Russian.

Categories and Subject Descriptors

H.3.1 [**Information Systems**]: Information storage and Retrieval – *Content Analysis and Indexing.*

General Terms

Management, Performance.

Keywords

content based search, podcast search engine

1. INTRODUCTION

Our new interface for browsing or searching news broadcasts exploits these new language processing tools to (i) provide immediate access to topical passages within news broadcasts, (ii) browse news broadcasts by *events* as well as by people, places and organizations, (iii) search for news through a geographic map interface, (iv) browse news by trending topics, and (v) see a brief, automatically-generated textual summary of news.

MM'11, November 28–December 1, 2011, Scottsdale, Arizona, USA.
ACM 978-1-4503-0616-4/11/11.

2. TECHNICAL DESCRIPTION

2.1 Automatic Speech Recognition

The core of the Voxalead application is its state-of-the art speech transcription system[1] for 8 languages: French, English, Spanish, Mandarin, Dutch, Russian, Italian and Arabic. The acoustic and language models and pronunciation dictionaries are language dependent and trained on large audio and text corpora. The system outputs an xml file containing the words identified in the audio document, along with their time codes and a confidence measure. Each language has recognition word lists containing from 50k to 300k words, providing and adequate to good coverage of the language. This technology has frequently achieved top performance in international benchmarks[2].

2.2 Indexing and enriching the transcriptions

Once speech is transcribed into text and segmented, standard natural language processing techniques are applied to each segment, each considered as a separate document in our Cloudview index, the search platform developed by Exalead. Documents are richly annotated using several semantic processors. Added tags used in this Voxalead application are:

- named entities: people, location, organization and events
- multi-word terms found in the documents

The segmented broadcast documents are then indexed by:

- video metadata (usually only title and date)
- the automatic textual transcription
- the semantically tagged entities extracted

2.3 Scalability issue

The system processes more than 150 new video and audio items each day on a single 6 core server, corresponding to roughly 3.5 Gb or 15 hours of new content each day. Potentially, this same underused server could absorb and process about 100 hours of videos per day. A separate dedicated server, which could also be parallelized, handles user queries. More than 140,000 podcasts are currently indexed and searchable. It can currently easily handle its 500 unique visits per day. Both sides are highly scalable, and similar to our public web search engine website (www.exalead.com/search which contains 16 billions of web pages). Voxaleadnews currently holds more than 70,000 podcasts.

3. USER INTERFACE

3.1 Search for relevant video

In response to a query, our interface provides multiple views on the results: thumbnails, timelines, and tag clouds views, a map view showing locations mentioned in the retrieved audio segments, and topic trends in retrieved segments. Maps and trends are calculated

[1] http://www.vocapia.com/voxsigma.html

[2] L Lamel and JL Gauvain, "Speech processing for audio indexing," GoTAL 2008, Advances in NLP, no.5221/2008 LNCS, pp. 4-15. Springer Verlag, 2008.

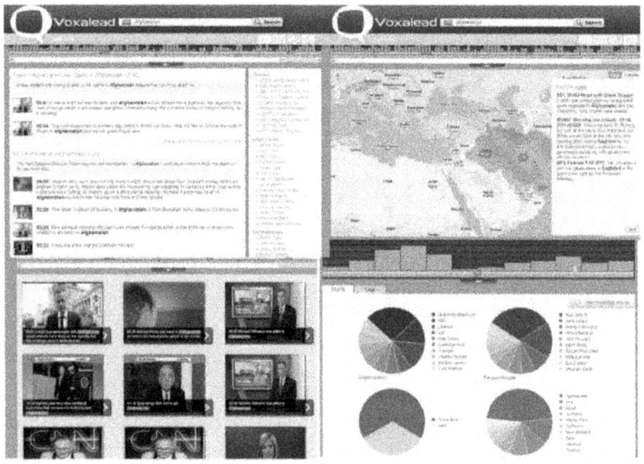

Figure 1. Different views for search results

from NLP over the ASR transcription of the audio streams of the broadcasts. Search is performed using a navigational look-and-feel familiar to search engine users. For all views, a histogram time-line allows users to restrict the search to a specific time period, which also allows the user to visualize the number of mentions of the query term over time.

3.2 Browsing videos

When a query result is clicked, the corresponding video is streamed starting directly from the segment relevant to the query. The timeline of the video player also displays markers with mouse-over snippets of 30 words containing the query-relevant keywords at every moment where the query words are mentioned. Topic segmentation allows us to display (on the right) mentioned named entities corresponding to each segment. Clicking on these named entities adds additional markers on the time line. Or the user can perform a further search in the displayed video and other markers will be added to the time line corresponding to the additional query words, along with mouse-over snippets that give the context of the word.

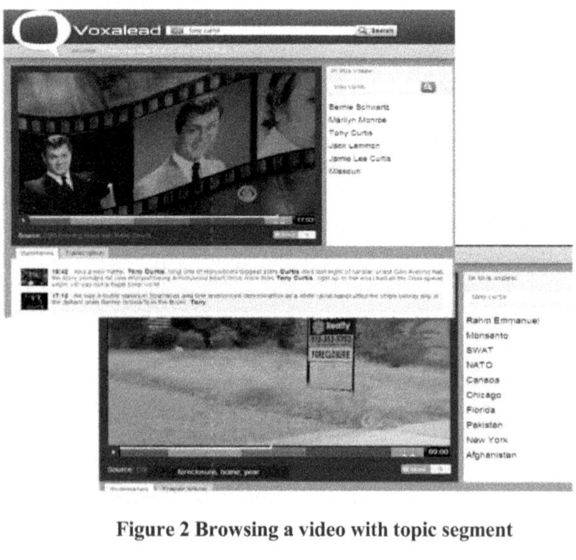

Figure 2 Browsing a video with topic segment

4. INDUSTRIAL USE CASES

The VoxaleadNews application focusses on one industrial use case: to make video and audio news podcast searchable by users with subsequent browsing, refinement on named entities and visualization of the transcription. Another use case is Education, for example, for the large sets of lectures now produced by schools and university. Figure 3 presents a prototype using lectures publicly available on the web. Here, the goal is first to find the lectures which deal with the targeted subject and then to navigate into the specific segments rather than listening to the entire hour long talk.

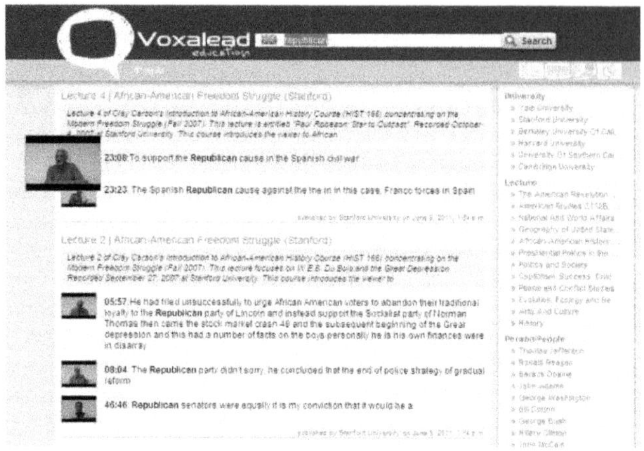

Figure 3 Voxalead Education

Some industrial use cases do not required the full transcription and in this case the system can be seen as a way to extract automatically keywords, tags or named entities for indexing audio and video content. Semantic tools included in Cloudview, the indexing system, can then be used to categorize these contents automatically following rules defined by the user.

Another further use case is the analysis of the trends based on the corpus indexed. For example, using the podcast news indexed over the last 3 months, the query "riot" displays the locations London, Tottenham, Syria (see Figure 4). The system can be used to monitor and explore trends in any given kind of field: videos for security, call centers, etc …

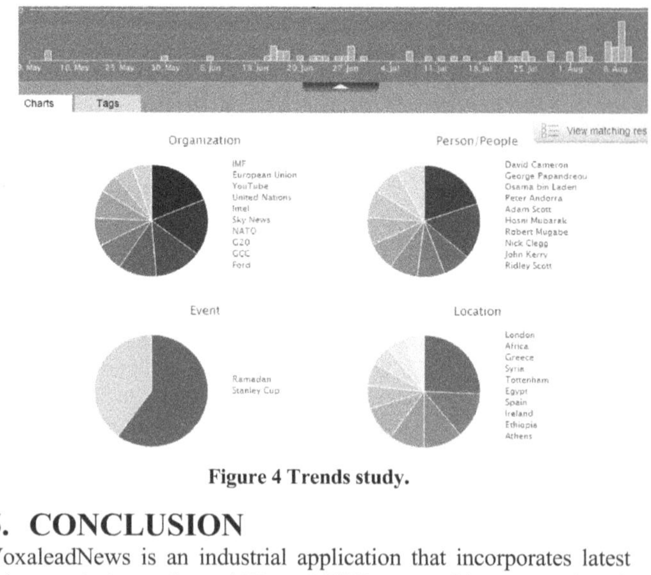

Figure 4 Trends study.

5. CONCLUSION

VoxaleadNews is an industrial application that incorporates latest robust techniques from ASR and NLP to provide content based, focused access to mentioned topics in video and audio streams. Exploiting implicit semantics and explicit metadata provides multiple paths into the results through timelines, maps, typed entities, and tag clouds.

MMSI Talk: An Applicative Use Case of Quaero Media Monitoring & Social Impact

Raphaël Blouet
Yacast R&D
4 rue Paul Valery
75016 Paris, France
rblouet@yacast.fr

Charlotte Juan
Yacast R&D
4 rue Paul Valery
75016 Paris, France
cjuan@yacast.fr

ABSTRACT

MMSI (Media Monitoring: Social impact) is an applicative project that is part of the European project Quaero. MMSI aims at developing a cross-media analysis and monitoring platform that enables to measure and understand information life-cycle within a set of radio, tv, newspaper and web sources. MMSI allows to quickly build *ad-hoc* web applications that implements study according to customers needs. We here present *MMSI Talk*, a platform for quantitative and qualitative analysis of political talks. *MMSI Talk* is a web interface that allows a global monitoring of broadcasted political content over a set of french radio. *MMSI Talk* allows intuitive search through queries by media, named entities, political party and/or politician. It includes access to talks, cumulative measure of speech duration at the politician or political party level. Moreover *MMSI Talk* provides a set of statistical and visualization tools that allow an advance understanding of political communication strategies. We first describe the context and motivation of the *MMSI Talk* talk platform. We then describe the global architecture of the platform before presenting the user interface through several concrete use cases.

Categories and Subject Descriptors: H.3[Information Storage and Retrieval]: Content Analysis and Indexing

General Terms: Legal Aspects, Design

Keywords: Media monitoring, speech transcription, information retrieval

1. INTRODUCTION

Quaero is a research and innovation program adressing automatic processing of multimedia and multilingual content. It fosters the development of new tools for navigation in large volumes of audiovisual content. The research and developments cover automatic information retrieval, analysis, segmentation and classification of text, speech, music, image and video. The nearly 200 M€ program, supported by Oséo Innovation, gathers 30 French and German partners around a data-centric collaboration between application projects led by industrials and a shared research structure, with a systematic use of technology evaluation. After three years of existence, Quaero is a very active eco-system leading to highly innovative demonstrators such as *Voxalead*, *MuMa* and *MMSI Talk*, that have been used already in large scale deployments. A separate file is submitted for each of the demonstrators, but all under the banner of the Quaero program.

Media Monitoring & Social Impact (MMSI) is an applicative project that is part of the Quaero collaborative research and development program. Quaero allows the realization of advanced demonstrators and prototypes that show feasibility of a set of innovative applications and services in the field of multimedia processing. MMSI aims at providing innovative tools to analyze and to understand how media information streams impact the opinion. Potential users of MMSI platform are: news agencies, public opinion trends analysts, marketing and communication agencies, media (Radio, TV, Print, Internet), content producers, governments...

MMSI Talk first comes with the obligation of all french media to declare the cumulative duration by political party of broadcasted content. It has then been enhanced and currently allows a full analysis of political communication on radio. 4200 politicians are currently registered and around 2 hours of audio are daily processed.

2. MMSI TALK

MMSI Talk is reachable at:

`http://viptdp.yacast.net/TalkQuaero/`

2.1 Back office

Figure 1 describes the back office architecture of the *MMSI Talk* platform. For each radio station of the panel, the platform continuously sends media chunks of 5 minutes to the `Speech Processing` module. This module is provided by `Vocapia` [1] and currently embedded two technologies: speaker turn detection and speech transcription. *MMSI Talk* then extracts names, places, event and organizations from transcribed speech thanks to a Named Entities detection module provided by Exalead [2]. This allows efficient content-based audio information retrieval from text queries. Speaker turn are manually corrected and annotated by manual operator. The add of a fully automatic workflow with a Speaker Verification step is in progress. Ones processed the content of each chunk is reachable by its media, the speaker and the name entities it contains.

MM'11, November 28–December 1, 2011, Scottsdale, Arizona, USA.
ACM 978-1-4503-0616-4/11/11.

[1] http://www.vocapia.com/
[2] www.exalead.com

2.2 User interface

MMSI Talk interface allows to visualize the amount of political talk for a given media / political party / politician during a given time period. It also offers to listen to each political talk. It is currently running on 3 radios from the group Radio France. The following running example shows the measure of political talk on France Inter broadcast news in September.
Talk Use Case consists in a web interface presenting the political speaker diarization. Talk homepage is presented in Figure 2.

For given radio channel, given types of programs, a period, the user visualizes in terms of duration or in percentage:

Speeches of politicians are also available. The user has to define a media, a politician or a political party, and a period, a day or eventually a time period. The audio player come with the written form of the speech; with words highlighted following the speech (see Figure 5). At present time, political speaker turn detection does not provide identity of politician. This capability is currently being integrated to the platform.

- The dashboard: speaking time according to political orientation, or political party (see Figure 3)
- Statistics : speaking time distribution according to political orientation, or political party (see Figure 4)

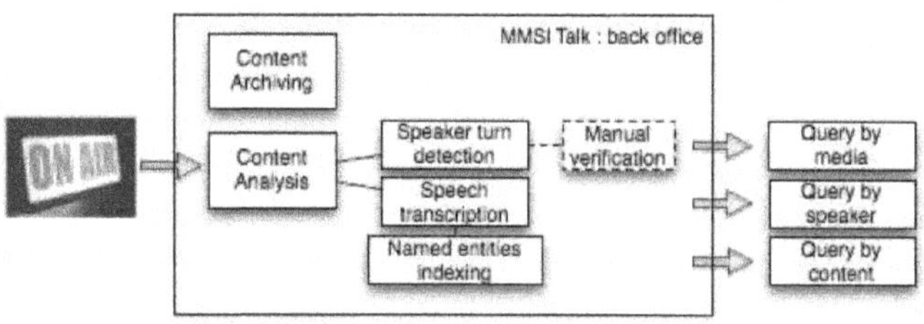

Figure 1: *MMSI Talk* back office.

3. CONCLUSION

MMSI Talk is one of the services of the MMSI applicative project, allowing a quantitative and qualitative analysis of political talks. Other services are also available, such as Infocast Lite, providing TV news show segmentation with corresponding metadata (title, theme, etc ...).
A new use case is currently under development based on both *MMSI Talk* and Infocast Lite : the news reporting tool MMSI Data Engine. The aim of MMSI Data Engine is to allow to create user-defined subject reports, based on cross-media data (radio, tv, newspapers, internet, ...). Each of them are processed to extract the relevant information (Speech-to-text, video segmentation, optical character recognition, ...), classified and ranked.

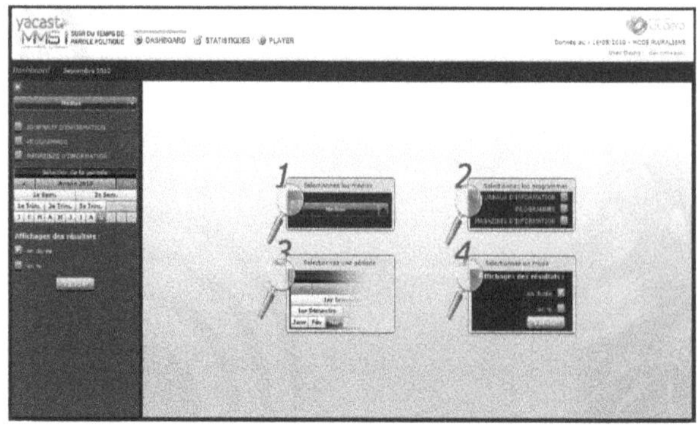

Figure 2: *MMSI Talk* Homepage.

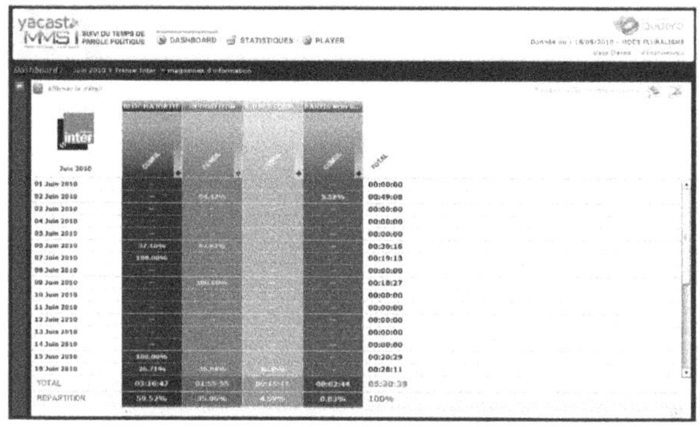

Figure 3: *MMSI Talk* Dashboard.

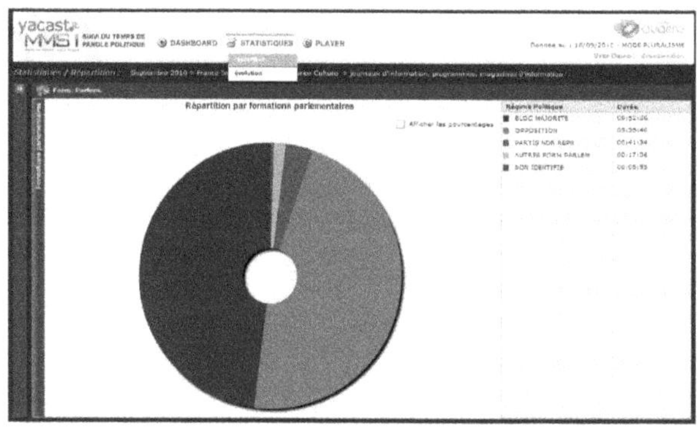

Figure 4: *MMSI Talk* Statistics.

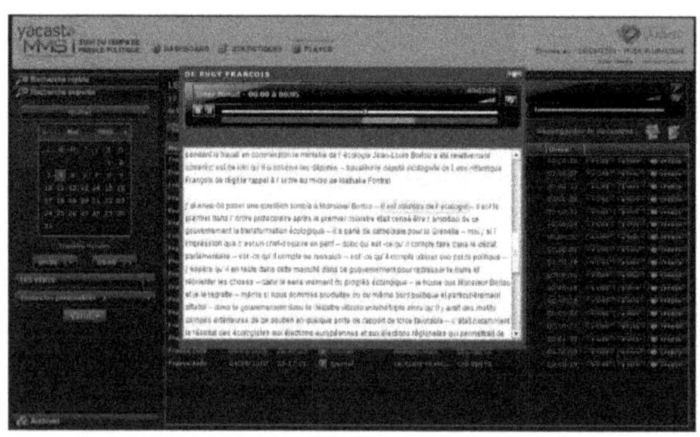

Figure 5: *MMSI Talk* Player with Highlighted Text.

Web-Scale Image Search by Color Sketch

Jingdong Wang[†] and Xian-Sheng Hua[‡]
[†]Microsoft Research Asia [‡]Microsoft Corporation
{jingdw, xshua}@microsoft.com

ABSTRACT

Most existing image search engines rely on the associated texts or tags with images to index and retrieval images, which results in limited ability on searching images with visual requirement. In this demonstration, we present an image search system, which enables consumers to find images on the requirement of how the colors are spatially distributed. It is a well-designed trade-off between scalability and feasibility. To the best knowledge, this system is the first one to scale up to Web-scale images. The interface is very intuitive and requires users to only scribble a few color strokes or drag an image and mask a few regions of interest, to express the search intent.

Categories and Subject Descriptors

H.3.3 [**Information Storage and Retrieval**]: Retrieval Models

General Terms

Algorithms, Experimentation

Keywords

Image search, web-scale, color sketch

Motivation Most existing image search engines rely on the tags or texts associated with images to index and search images. For example, Flickr image search allows users to type a textual query, and matches it with images in the database, in which images are organized through the tags annotated by human. Google/Bing/Yahoo image search alternatively explores the texts surrounding the images to index the images. However, those image search engines suffer from the lack of searching into image contents because the tags/texts are not sufficient or exact to describe image contents. Although a lot of research efforts on content-based image retrieval (CBIR), such as query by example, query by sketch, and so on, were made in last century, those techniques cannot scale up to Web-scale images.

System In this demonstrate, we present a novel image search system, image search by color sketch, which enhances text-based image search and enables end-users to intuitively sketch a color map to indicate how the colors are spatially distributed in the desired images for promoting images matching the specified color map. The proposed system is motivated by intuitive observations. For the text-based image search results with the query "Brooke Hogan" (an American singer, actress, model, and television personality), a color map, with the red color on the bottom, may mean to find Brooke Hogan walking on the red carpet.

MM'11, November 28–December 1, 2011, Scottsdale, Arizona, USA.
ACM 978-1-4503-0616-4/11/11.

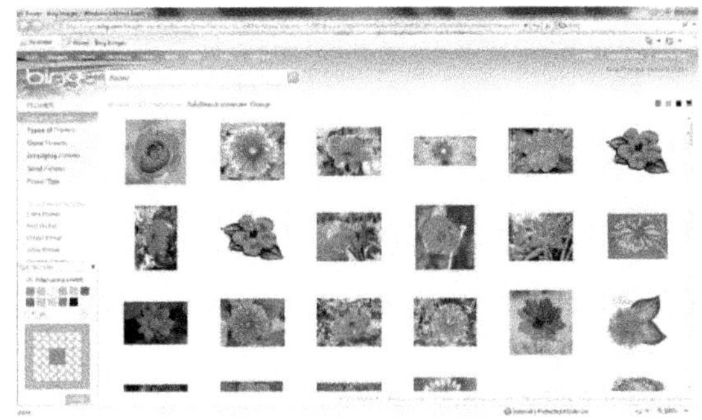

Figure 1: The snapshot of the interface.

This system presents two color-sketch modes. 1) Stroke scribbling. End-users merely scribble a few color strokes in a blank canvas; 2) Image dragging. Users may drag an image to the blank canvas and mask the color regions of interest, to show the desired spatial distribution of colors. Our system mines and formulates the search intent from the sketched color map, and reranks image search results to help users find desired images.

The snapshot of the system interface is shown in Fig. 1. Two example results are shown in Fig. 2 and Fig. 3. A user wants to find images that contain a red apple with green leaves on the top. The user may submit a target color map by drawing a few color strokes, shown in the bottom left image of Fig. 2(a), and then obtains the reordered results under the textual query *apple* as shown in Fig. 2(a). Fig. 2(b) shows another task searching for images that contain a red car on the green grass with the query *car*. As another interaction mode, the user may drag an image (e.g., an image with the query *sunset*) to find images with similar color map, shown in Fig. 3(a). Moreover, a user aims to find sunset images with the blue sky. She can draw blue strokes on the top. And the results are shown in Fig. 3(b). Furthermore, the user can erase the bottom part and gets the results shown in Fig. 3(c).

Techniques The flow chart of the online process is shown in Fig. 4. First, we process the target color map to extract

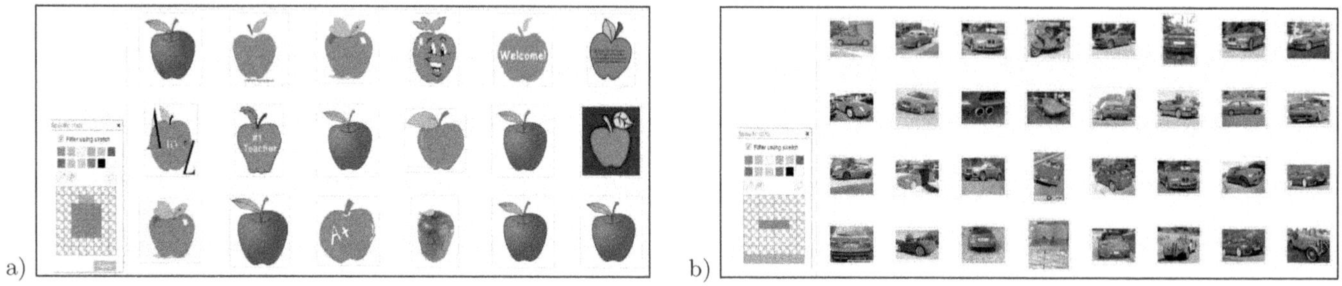

Figure 2: Two examples showing the search results using color sketches.

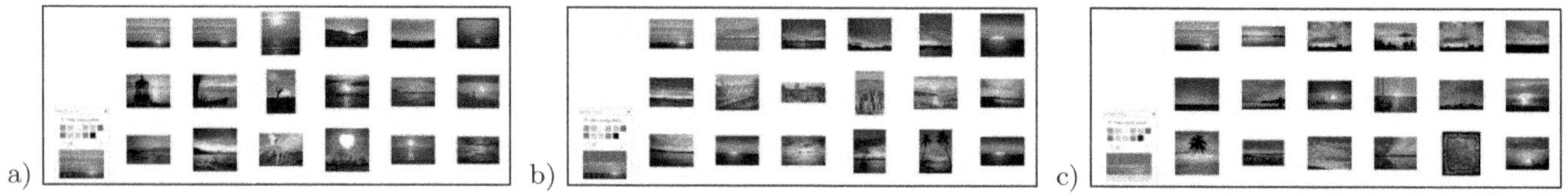

Figure 3: An example showing that our system can enable users to edit an image to illustrate the intent. (b) shows the results expecting a blue sky and (c) shows the results expecting the color pink at the top.

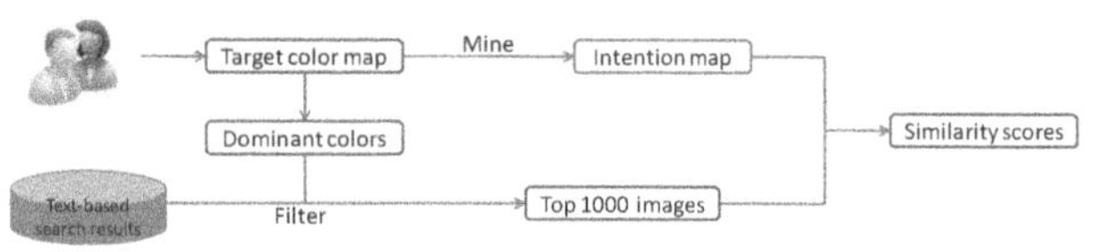

Figure 4: The flow chart of our approach.

the dominant colors and mine the intention map. Then, the dominant colors are used to filter the image search results associated with the text query. Next, we compute the similarity scores between the mined intention map and the top 1000 images that remain after dominant color filtering, and finally reorder those images.

The database images are preprocessed by extracting the dominant colors and the color map feature. The dominant colors are found from 11 colors: BLACK, BLUE, BROWN, GRAY, GREEN, ORANGE, PINK, PURPLE, RED, WHITE, and YELLOW. For each image, we compute the frequency of each color, and set the colors as dominant colors if their corresponding frequencies are larger than 10%.

To extract the color map, we divide the image uniformly into $g \times g$ grids. For each grid (x, y), we aim to find one or two representative colors by checking the frequencies for all the quantized colors. In our implementation, we find that $g = 8$ works well. In the preprocessing stage, we first transform the RGB (red, green, blue) color space into the HSV (hue, saturation, value) space, which is then quantized into $n_h \times n_s \times n_v$, where $n_h = 12$ $n_s = 4$, and $n_v = 4$.

The similarity between target color map and image color map is evaluated by mining the intention map and considering the intention consistency and propagation intention. Details can be found from [1].

User study We conducted user studies to compare our system with two Web image search engines, Google image search and Bing image search. In the following, we use engine A to represent one of the two engines, and engine B to represent the other one. We recruit 30 volunteers and collect 40 tasks for this study. To evaluate the performance, we consider two measures. The first is the degree of satisfaction (DoS) in the top 20 images. We do not check all

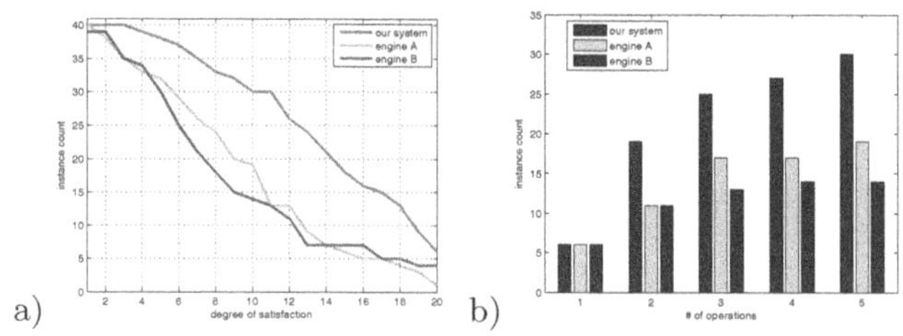

Figure 5: (a) shows performance comparison with the number of tasks (instances) against the degree of satisfaction. (b) shows the performance comparison of the number of tasks against the number of operations with the degree of satisfaction being 50%.

the search results since it is observed that users often check the images in the first several pages. The measure reflects whether users can successfully find their desired images using the search system. The second one is the number of units of operations required to get the satisfied result, which indicates the effort involved. The comparison is shown in Fig. 5.

Conclusions In this demo, we present a web-scale image search system, image search with color sketch, which enables users to find images with desired spatial distribution of colors. We have extended color map to concept map [2, 3]. Our ongoing work aims to design a more effective indexing algorithm to organize the color maps for efficiently searching for images with the target color maps in which there exist missing colors in cells.

1. REFERENCES

[1] J. Wang and X.-S. Hua. Interactive image search by color map. *ACM TIST*, 3(1):26, 2012.

[2] H. Xu, J. Wang, X.-S. Hua, and S. Li. Image search by concept map. In *SIGIR*, pages 275–282, 2010.

[3] H. Xu, J. Wang, X.-S. Hua, and S. Li. Interactive image search by 2d semantic map. In *WWW*, pages 1321–1324, 2010.

MuMa: A Scalable Music Search Engine Based On Content Analysis

Arthur Lenoir
Exalead
10, place de la Madeleine
75008 Paris, France
+33 1 55 35 26 78
arthur.lenoir@3ds.com

Rémi Landais
Exalead
10, place de la Madeleine
75008 Paris, France
+33 1 55 35 27 44
remi.landais@3ds.com

INTRODUCTION TO QUAERO PROJECT

Quaero is a research and innovation program addressing automatic processing of multimedia and multilingual content. It fosters the development of new tools for navigation in large volumes of audiovisual content. The research and developments cover automatic information retrieval, analysis, segmentation and classification of text, speech, music, image and video. The nearly 200 M€ program, supported by Oséo Innovation, gathers 30 French and German partners around a data-centric collaboration between application projects led by industrials and a shared research structure, with a systematic use of technology evaluation. After three years of existence, Quaero is a very active eco-system leading to highly innovative demonstrators such as Voxalead that have been used already in large scale deployments. A separate file is submitted for each of the demonstrators, but all under the banner of the Quaero program.

ABSTRACT

Existing music search engines process music as they would process text, ignoring the richness of this media. We introduce here MuMa[1] (MUsic MAshup), a web application which makes the most of audio contents (the signal itself) to provide the user with new ways of browsing music. MuMa allows the user to search for particular chords sequences, to generate smart playlists and to extend its musical universe.

Categories and Subject Descriptors

J.5 [**Arts and Humanities**]: *Categories: J.5* Music.

General Terms

Design, Experimentation, Performance

1. INTRODUCTION

MuMa is a web application designed to easily search and discover music. In this paper, we notably present the new improvements since its presentation at ICME 2011 [1].

2. TECHNICAL DESCRIPTION

Our framework relies on Cloudview[2] indexing product developed by Exalead. While Cloudview is initially designed to index texts, its structure is highly flexible and text analysis modules may in our case be replaced by modules focusing on audio analysis. MuMa takes also benefits from Cloudview object-oriented index and from its large-scale capacity.

2.1 Audio Analysis

Each indexed song is processed through different analysis modules:

---

[1] http://muma.labs.exalead.com

[2] http://www.exalead.com/software/products/cloudview/

MM'11, November 28–December 1, 2011, Scottsdale, Arizona, USA.
ACM 978-1-4503-0616-4/11/11.

2.1.1 Chords Extraction

All the chords are extracted from the song. The extracted chords are smoothed and only the most frequent chords sequences are indexed to avoid noise and false positives. These chords sequences are then indexed into a relative notation, allowing us to avoid transpositions.

2.1.2 Moods Detection

The songs are analyzed in order to extract a 12-dimensional weighted mood vector, one dimension per mood. Global moods for albums and artists are computed by averaging individual song moods vectors.

2.1.3 Fingerprinting for Similarity Search

A 16ko-fingerprint is calculated and indexed for each song. This fingerprint enables us to search for similar songs only based on acoustic features. It differs to application like Shazam since we are looking for similar songs, we don't search for a specific song.

2.1.4 Smart Summary Generation

Summaries are automatically produced with the most relevant segments in the song. These segments are concatenated into a summary using fade-outs between segments.

2.2 Indexed Data

2.2.1 A Structured Index

The structure of MuMa index is quite complex since artists may reference to each other through bands, albums contain tracks… An ontology of musical domain has then been designed and mapped onto a Cloudview index.

2.2.2 A Scalable Index

MuMa index contains more than 600,000 artists. For the moment over that 1100 of related discographies have been processed and

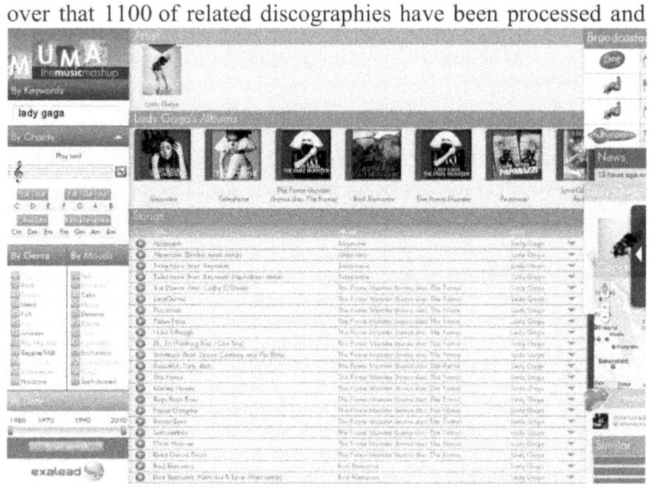

Figure 1: MuMa's interface overview

indexed leading to a total of 1.1 million objects on a single server. And this index is still growing since new discographies are indexed "on the fly" as artists are queried by some user

The query side of the application is also highly scalable and can be easily replicated on multiple servers.

2.3 User Interface

2.3.1 Global Overview

MuMa's user interface is divided in 3 parts as shown in Figure 1: the left part contains the search tools, the middle part presents search results and the right part shows further information about the selected artist (latest tweets, biography, coming concerts, photos, lyrics, etc.) that has been gathered from reference web sites such as LastFM.

2.3.2 Instant Search

Because performance is a feature, results are displayed while the user is typing its request. It improves both the user experience and the search efficiency.

2.3.3 Search by Chords

The user may enter a sequence of chords simply by clicking on the chord name, and then the chord is displayed on the HTML5 staff as in the Figure 4. The user may also input its chord sequence by using a MIDI USB keyboard.

2.3.4 HTML5 Player

MuMa includes an HTML5 audio player that enables the user to listen to the summaries of the songs. In the case of a search by chords, the user may also play the chords sequences that match to the query. The Figure 4 illustrates this feature with the chords sequence "Dm Am Bb F" chosen as the query: the song "Ode to my Family" contains a sequence of chords that has matched with the query and that is being played by the user (chord F# minor, which is chord that is being played is highlighted).

3. USE CASES

3.1 Music Discovering

Most of music recommendation systems are social based; they propose you songs that have been listened (LastFM), or bought (Amazon), by some persons who share some songs with your listen or purchase history. It generally works so well that the system recommends you songs you already know!

On the contrary, MuMa suggestions are based on acoustic similarity. It may thus lead to surprising (and so interesting) propositions: for instance, "Beautiful World" by Rage Against the Machine is similar to "I Will Always" by the Cranberries as shown in Figure 2.

3.2 Smart Playlists Generator

Smart playlists may be generated based on detected moods and/or the similarity feature. An example is shown in Figure 3 where the user selects one or several moods and the system gathers songs that convey selected moods. The playlist may then be extended by adding songs that are similar to the ones contained in the first list.

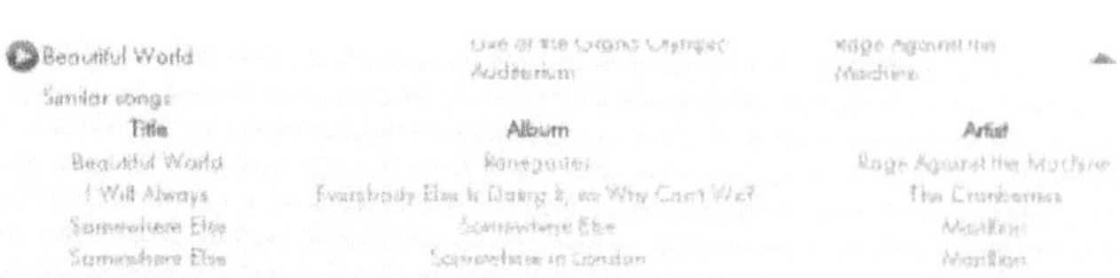

Figure 2: Similar Songs to "Beautiful World" by Rage Against the Machine

Figure 3: Playlist generation selecting songs being "romantic", "calm" and "enchanting" in the same time

3.3 Songwriter in Search of Inspiration

MuMa provides a simple user interface to input a chords sequence as presented in Figure 4 (one should here remind that the user may choose either to click on the chords or to select them with a MIDI/USB keyboard). This feature could be useful for a songwriter who wants to know how other songwriters use a particular chords sequence. In the example presented in Figure 4, we notice that 75% of the songs that use this sequence are considered as "romantic" by our moods classifier.

3.4 Pluggable to any Music Platform

MuMa is really flexible and may rely on any source of information. For instance spotify or google music members could sign up on MuMa using their account and then benefit from MuMa search facilities on their own remote library (similarity, playlist generation…).

4. FUTURE WORK

4.1 Genre, Moods, Instrumentation Detection

Figure 4: Search with the chords sequence "Dm Am Bb F"

The moods detection will be soon improved as the set of moods will be reduced to five more-understandable moods. A genre and an instrumentation classifier will enhance the playlists generator and the other search functionalities.

4.2 Album and Artist Similarity

The similarity song feature will be extended to the albums and the artists by aggregating the similarity information of the song on the albums and the artists.

5. REFERENCES

[1] Arthur Lenoir, Rémi Landais, Geoffroy Peeters, Laurent Oudre, Thomas Fillon. *MUMA: A Music Search Engine Based on Content Analysis*. ICME 2011.

[2] Geoffroy Peeters. *A Generic System for Audio Indexing: Application to Speech / Music Segmentation and Music Genre Recognition*. Proc. of the 10th Int. Conference on Digital Audio Effects (DAFx-07).

[3] Laurent Oudre, Yves Grenier, and Cédric Févotte. *Chord recognition using measures of fit, chord templates and filtering methods*. IEEE WASPAA, New York, 2009, pp. 9–12

Kooaba Interactive Posters

Christian Wengert, Tobias Jaeggli, Philippe Messmer
Peter Cech, Cristi Prodan, Tomas Carnecky
Franco Sebregondi, David Wisti, Till Quack

kooaba AG
Förrlibuckstrasse 178
8005 Zürich, Switzerland

lastname@kooaba.com

Categories and Subject Descriptors

I.4.10 [**Image processing and computer vision**]: Image representation; H.3.3 [**Information storage and retrieval**]: Information search and retrieval

General Terms

Algorithms

Keywords

Image Retrieval

1. INTRODUCTION

There is an ever increasing amount of digital visual information being produced. For instance, there are over 800 million mobile phones with integrated cameras. These cameras are increasingly used as a tool in order to remember and share things by just snapping pictures. Have a look at your digital photo collection today, and imagine how large it is going to be in 30 years.

The Kooaba Interactive Posters are built around our large-scale image recognition platform and provides a tool that enable you to share, explore and remember things visually. The image recognition allows for identifying objects in images. Once an image or object is identified, additional information about them is provided, e.g. related web-pages, description, tags etc which helps the user to better organize and remember these items.

In the context of an academic conference, the objects to be recognized are the conference posters, thus rendring them interactive by providing additional content such as the original paper, videos, source code etc.

2. SYSTEM OVERVIEW

The Kooaba Interactive Posters and the underlying image recognition and object retrieval engine was one of the first systems being deployed with several tens of millions images in an industrial context. The kooaba database currently includes book, cd and dvd covers, wine labels, newspapers, movie posters and advertisements.

The image retrieval problem requires to produce a description of the image, typically a fixed-size vector. This description must be discriminative, but sufficiently invariant to handle the transformations the image may have undergone (cropping, different viewpoints, rotation, etc). These transformations are especially difficult in the case of mobile search.

Most of the recent state-of-the-art large scale image search systems [3, 1] rely on local descriptors, in our case the SURF descriptor [2]. They are extracted from regions of interest using a scale-invariant detector [5, 2, 7, 6]. These descriptors are then used jointly with the bag-of-words (BOW) framework [4], which produces a single vector from a set of local descriptors.

For each image in the reference database, its BOW vector is computed and stored in an efficient inverted file system. The inverted file system can then be queried using the BOW vector of an incoming query image. This results in a ranked candidate list. The top candidates are then further verified in order to remove noise and false positives.

At this stage, the correspondance between the query and the reference database item is known, thus the associated content and metadata can be returned to the user. The user may then store, share and organize the results efficiently.

In the specific case of conference posters, the attendees can take a picture of a poster at the poster session with their mobile phones, the image will be recognized, and they will receive a result page, with direct links to the paper, and author's web site etc.

It is totally free for the organizer of the conference, all we need is a little support to e.g. send an email to all authors so they can upload a digital copy of their poster for the database.

The attendess only need to download a copy of our smartphone application (or use the web application). This application helps you remember things visually with a simple snap and is thus a perfect match for this use case (where attendess not only want to access additional content but also want to remember posters they were interested in). A simple interface and image recognition support you in organizing your visual memos. All images taken are first locally preprocessed and then sent to the cloud. There, each image is sent to the recognition server and matching results are sent back to the user.

The recognition usually takes less than one seconds and the recognition time is mainly determined by the network latency, which in case of bad signal quality over 3G can add several seconds.

Integration with other web services (such as Evernote, Twitter and Facebook) allow to share the information across different platforms and users.

MM'11, November 28–December 1, 2011, Scottsdale, Arizona, USA.
ACM 978-1-4503-0616-4/11/11.

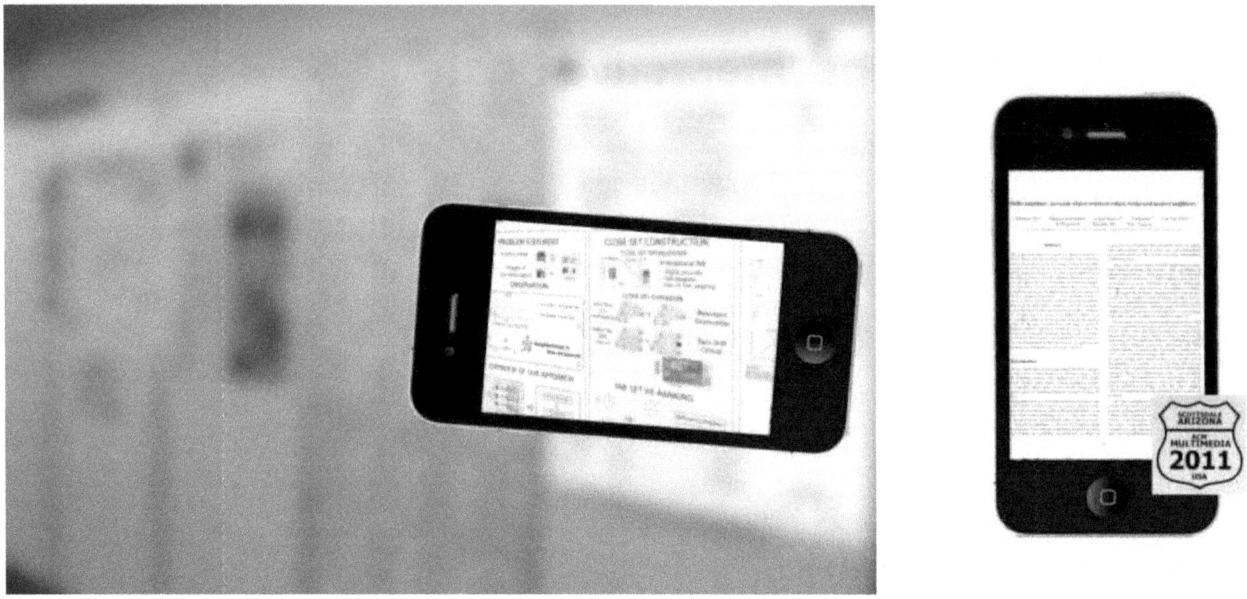

Figure 1: Example usage of the Kooaba Interactive Posters: It is sufficient to take a snapshot of a poster (left) in order to receive additional content such as the PDF (right).

3. ACKNOWLEDGMENT

We are grateful to the organizers for their support and for helping us getting this system up and running for ACM MM 2011.

4. REFERENCES

[1] H. Jégou, M. Douze, and C. Schmid. Improving bag-of-features for large scale image search. *IJCV*, 87(3):316–336, February 2010.

[2] H. Bay, A. Ess, T. Tuytelaars, L. Vangool Speeded-Up Robust Features (SURF) *CVIU*, 110(3):346–359, 2008.

[3] D. Nistér and H. Stewénius. Scalable recognition with a vocabulary tree. In *CVPR*, June 2006.

[4] J. Sivic and A. Zisserman. Video Google: A text retrieval approach to object matching in videos. In *ICCV*, October 2003.

[5] D. Lowe. Distinctive image features from scale-invariant keypoints. *IJCV*, 60(2):91–110, 2004.

[6] J. Matas, O. Chum, U. Martin, and T. Pajdla. Robust wide baseline stereo from maximally stable extremal regions. In *BMVC*, pages 384–393, September 2002.

[7] K. Mikolajczyk, T. Tuytelaars, C. Schmid, A. Zisserman, J. Matas, F. Schaffalitzky, T. Kadir, and L. V. Gool. A comparison of affine region detectors. *IJCV*, 65(1/2):43–72, 2005.

3D Object Retrieval with Semantic Attributes

Boqing Gong[1,3] Jianzhuang Liu[1,3] Xiaogang Wang[2,3] Xiaoou Tang[1,3]
[1]Department of Information Engineering, The Chinese University of Hong Kong
[2]Department of Electronic Engineering, The Chinese University of Hong Kong
[3]Shenzhen Key Laboratory for Computer Vision and Pattern Recognition,
Shenzhen Institutes of Advanced Technology, Chinese Academy of Sciences, China
{gbq008@ie, jzliu@ie, xgwang@ee, xtang@ie}.cuhk.edu.hk

ABSTRACT

Humans are capable of describing objects using attributes, such as "the object looks *circular* and is *man-made*". Motivated by these high-level descriptions, we build a user-friendly 3D object retrieval system, where the user can browse the database and search for targeted objects using semantic attributes. The main advantage of our system is that it does not require the user to find or sketch a 3D object as the query for 3D object retrieval. Besides, to the best of our knowledge, our system has obtained the best retrieval performance on three popular benchmarks.

Categories and Subject Descriptors

H.3.3 [**Information Search and Retrieval**]: Query formulation, Search process; H.5.2 [**User Interfaces**]: User-centered design

General Terms

Design, Experimentation, Human Factors

Keywords

3D object retrieval, attribute

1. INTRODUCTION

3D data have become more and more common in not only research and industry but also entertainment, such as computer vision, CAD, computer game, and digital city. As a result, 3D object retrieval draws more and more attention from researchers. Some experimental search engines have been developed [1], [2], [4]. Google 3D Warehouse [3], an online repository for sharing 3D models, also provides the functionality of allowing users to search for 3D models.

One key issue for a user-friendly search engine is how to deliver user search intention to the system. This problem is even more important in the 3D search scenario due to two facts: 1) Text-based query can only search for a small part of existing 3D objects because currently most 3D objects are pure shapes without well textual descriptions or tags. 2) Content-based retrieval, *i.e.*, using a 3D object as the query, causes great trouble for the user who does not have a 3D query that is similar to his/her targeted objects in the database. To circumvent this problem, some systems allow the user to form a query by sketching the object's silhouette or skeleton [4], [8]. The main drawback of these systems is that a 2D sketch has only a small part of shape information of a 3D object, leading to less retrieval accuracy.

In this paper, we develop an alternative solution. In our system, the user searches for targeted 3D objects in mind by simply clicking attribute bars (see Figure 1). This is a natural way of delivering search intentions to the system for common users, because humans tend to describe an object using high-level semantic attributes, such as "the object is man-made" and "the object is symmetric". Moreover, these semantic descriptions of 3D objects are good complement to low-level shape features, and thus can be used to improve existing 3D object retrieval algorithms. To the best of our knowledge, our system obtains the best retrieval accuracy on three popular benchmarks.

2. SYSTEM OVERVIEW

2.1 User Interface

As shown in Figure 1, the user interface (UI) of our system consists of two parts. On the left part, attributes are listed for the user to describe targeted objects in mind. Each attribute is accompanied with an input bar. The user clicks the bars to set the values of the attributes. Three values are used: 0 for having no this attribute, 1 for having this attribute, and 0.5 being the default value for not sure[1].

Search results are shown on the right part of the UI. The user can also trigger a new search by clicking the "Similar" button under an object. In this case, this object serves as the query. Besides viewing the images of the retrieved objects, the user can also observe the 3D models from different angles by clicking the "3D" button under each object.

The user can conveniently browse the database with the attributes. For example, if the user sets the value of "circular" to 1, the system will rank objects that look circular at top and display them on the UI. The most important application of the system is that the user can search for targeted objects naturally. Suppose that the user wants to find out object $\mathcal{O}$ in the database or objects similar to $\mathcal{O}$. Then he/she conducts the search in two steps:

Step 1: Set the values of some attributes to describe $\mathcal{O}$. After each input (a click on an attribute bar) by the user, the system returns top ranked objects on the right

[1]Since various symmetry exists on most objects, we use 0 for both rotational symmetry and no symmetry and 1 for reflectional symmetry to improve its distinguishing ability.

MM'11, November 28–December 1, 2011, Scottsdale, Arizona, USA.
ACM 978-1-4503-0616-4/11/11.

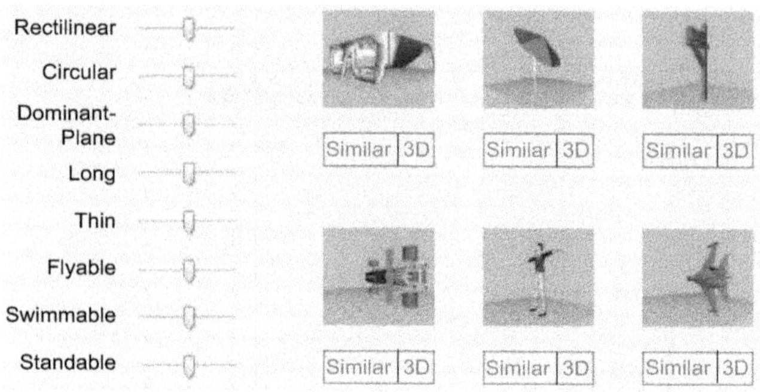

Figure 1: Part of the user interface of our 3D object retrieval system. On the left part, the user clicks the attribute bars to describe targeted objects in mind. After each click, a search is triggered and results are shown on the right. The user can also click the "Similar" button under an object to search for similar objects in the database. The "3D" button is for viewing the a 3D object from different angles.

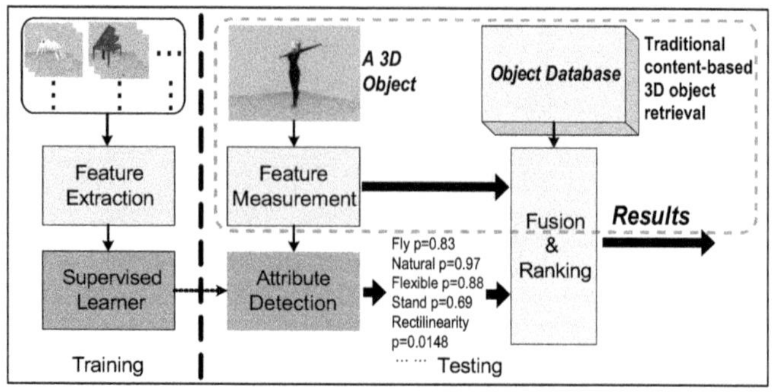

Figure 2: Framework of our system.

part of the UI in real time (the ranking procedure is explained in Section 2.2).

Step 2: Search the database by clicking the "Similar" button if $\mathcal{O}$ has not appeared yet. During the process in Step 1, some object(s) similar to $\mathcal{O}$, denoted as $\mathcal{O}^*$, may appear on the UI. Therefore, the user can stop setting the attributes and click the "Similar" button under $\mathcal{O}^*$ to find $\mathcal{O}$.

The two steps can be carried out multiple times to search for more similar objects. The user study of our system on a public testing database, Princeton shape benchmark (PSB) containing 907 3D objects [6], shows that most users can find out their targeted objects within 5 clicks, which includes 2 to 4 clicks on the attribute bars and 1 to 3 clicks on the "Similar" buttons.

2.2 Technical Details

We explain the technical details of our 3D object retrieval system in this section. The system so far provides eleven attributes for the user to describe 3D objects, including shape characteristics (symmetric, rectilinear, circular, planar, long, and thin), object functionalities (flyable, swimmable, and standable), and some semantic classifications (natural and flexible). The framework of the system is shown in Figure 2. At the training stage, we train a detector $\mathcal{D}$ for each attribute based on a public training set provided in PSB using a binary support vector machine. The detector $\mathcal{D}$ is then used at the testing stage to measure the corresponding attribute of a 3D object x with output $\mathcal{D}(x)$ representing the probability of x having this attribute. Besides the attribute measurements, we also extract traditional shape features from each object in the database. The retrieved objects are ranked according to their similarities to the user input. When the user describes the targeted object by clicking the attribute bars, the similarities are calculated using the attribute measurements only. When the user clicks a "Similar" button under an object, both the attribute measurements and the shape features are used to compute the similarities. The shape features and attribute measurements are mutually complementary. To the best of our knowledge, our system has obtained the best retrieval precision in terms of evaluation methods such as first tier and discounted cumulative gain [6] on three common benchmarks: PSB [6], watertight models used in SHREC'07 [7], and NTU 3D model benchmark [5].

3. CONCLUSION

We have built a user-friendly 3D object retrieval system. With this system, the user is able to search the database using semantic attributes to describe targeted objects, instead of finding or sketching a 3D object as the query. So far there are eleven attributes in our system. This set can be enriched in future work.

4. ACKNOWLEDGEMENTS

This work was supported by grants from Introduced Innovative R&D Team of Guangdong Province (Robot and Intelligent Information Technology), Natural Science Foundation of China (60975029, 61070148), Science, Industry, Trade, and Information Technology Commission of Shenzhen Municipality, China (JC200903180635A, JC201005270378A, ZYC201006130313A), and the Research Grants Council of the Hong Kong SAR, China (Project No. CUHK 415408).

5. REFERENCES

[1] *3D Model Retrieval System.* http://merkur01.inf.uni-konstanz.de/CCCC/.

[2] *3D Search Engine.* http://3d-search.iti.gr/3DSearch.

[3] *Google 3D Warehouse.* http://sketchup.google.com/3dwarehouse/.

[4] *Princeton 3D Model Search Engine.* http://shape.cs.princeton.edu/search.html.

[5] D. Chen, X. Tian, Y. Shen, and M. Ouhyoung. On Visual Similarity Based 3D Model Retrieval. *Computer Graphics Forum*, 22(3):223–232, 2003.

[6] P. Shilane, P. Min, M. Kazhdan, and T. Funkhouser. The Princeton Shape Benchmark. In *Proc. of Shape Modeling International*, 2004.

[7] R. Veltkamp and F. ter Haar. SHREC2007: 3D shape retrieval contest. *Dept of Info and Comp. Sci., Utrecht University, Technical Report*, 2007.

[8] S. Yoon, M. Scherer, T. Schreck, and A. Kuijper. Sketch-Based 3D Model Retrieval Using Diffusion Tensor Fields of Suggestive Contours. In *Proc. of ACM MM*, 2010.

Robust Hand Gesture Recognition with Kinect Sensor

Zhou Ren Jingjing Meng Junsong Yuan
Nanyang Technological University
50 Nanyang Avenue, Singapore 639798
{renzhou, jingjing.meng, jsyuan}@ntu.edu.sg

Zhengyou Zhang
Microsoft Research Redmond
Washington 98052-6399, USA
zhang@microsoft.com

ABSTRACT

Hand gesture based Human-Computer-Interaction (HCI) is one of the most natural and intuitive ways to communicate between people and machines, since it closely mimics how human interact with each other. In this demo, we present a hand gesture recognition system with Kinect sensor, which operates robustly in uncontrolled environments and is insensitive to hand variations and distortions. Our system consists of two major modules, namely, hand detection and gesture recognition. Different from traditional vision-based hand gesture recognition methods that use color-markers for hand detection, our system uses both the depth and color information from Kinect sensor to detect the hand shape, which ensures the robustness in cluttered environments. Besides, to guarantee its robustness to input variations or the distortions caused by the low resolution of Kinect sensor, we apply a novel shape distance metric called Finger-Earth Mover's Distance (FEMD) for hand gesture recognition. Consequently, our system operates accurately and efficiently. In this demo, we demonstrate the performance of our system in two real-life applications, arithmetic computation and rock-paper-scissors game.

Categories and Subject Descriptors

H.1.2 [**User/Machine Systems**]: Human information processing; I.4.8 [**Scene Analysis**]: Depth cues, Shape

General Terms

Experimentation

Keywords

Human-Computer-Interaction, Hand Gesture Recognition, Kinect Sensor, Finger-Earth Mover's Distance

1. INTRODUCTION

Hand gesture recognition is an important research issue in the field of Human-Computer-Interaction, because of its extensive applications in virtual reality, sign language recognition, and computer games [7]. Despite lots of previous work, building a robust hand gesture recognition system that is applicable for real-life applications remains a challenging problem. Existing vision-based approaches [1, 5, 6] are greatly limited by the quality of the input image from optical cameras. Variations in lighting and background clutters would only worsen the problem. Consequently, these systems have not been able to provide satisfactory results for hand gesture recognition.

MM'11, November 28–December 1, 2011, Scottsdale, Arizona, USA.
ACM 978-1-4503-0616-4/11/11.

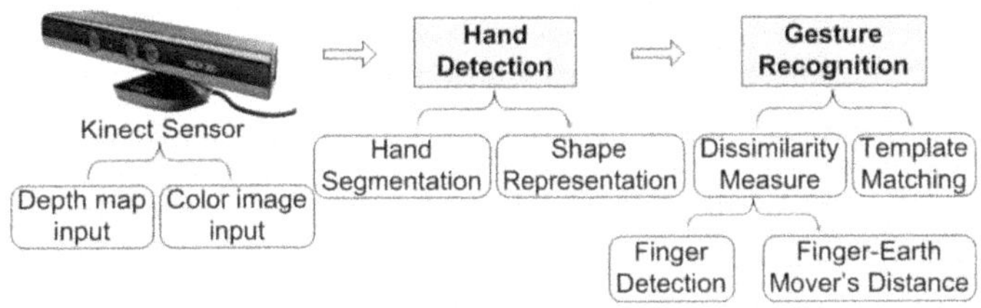

Figure 1: The framework of our robust hand gesture recognition system.

Hand gesture recognition concerns two challenging problems: *hand detection* and *gesture recognition*, namely how to robustly detect the hand and how to efficiently and accurately recognize the gesture of the hand.

The framework of our hand gesture recognition system is shown in Fig.1. As for hand detection, different from traditional methods that use color-markers for hand detection, our system uses both the depth map and color image obtained by Kinect sensor to detect the hand shapes. It ensures robustness to cluttered background. And the segmented hand shapes are represented as time-series curves [2].

As for the gesture recognition, even with the Kinect sensor, it is still a very challenging problem. Because typically, the resolution of a Kinect sensor is only 640×480. Although it works well to track a large object, e.g. the human body, it is difficult to detect and segment precisely a small object from an image at this resolution, e.g., a human hand that occupies a very small portion of the image. Therefore, we use a novel shape distance metric called Finger-Earth Mover's Distance (FEMD) to measure the dissimilarities between different hand shapes, which is proposed in [4]. FEMD metric is specifically designed for hand shape matching, which is robust to hand variations and distortions. FEMD represents a hand shape as a signature which considers each finger as a cluster, and the dissimilarity distance between two hand shapes is defined as the sum of the work needed to move the earth piles and the penalty on the unmatched fingers. In order to accurately detect the fingers, [4] also presents two novel finger detection algorithms, using thresholding decomposition and using a near-convex shape decomposition scheme presented in [3]. Finally, the input hand is recognized by template matching.

2. PERFORMANCE

The goal of this demo is to showcase two real-life applications built on top of our novel and robust hand gesture recognition system. Our technology performs robustly despite variations in hand orientation, scale or articulation. Moreover, it works well in uncontrolled environments with background clutters. As for the efficiency and accuracy, our system operates efficiently with a mean accuracy of 90.6% on the dataset of [4].

3. APPLICATIONS

We demonstrate our hand gesture recognition system using two real-life applications: arithmetic computation and rock-paper-scissors game.

3.1 Arithmetic computation

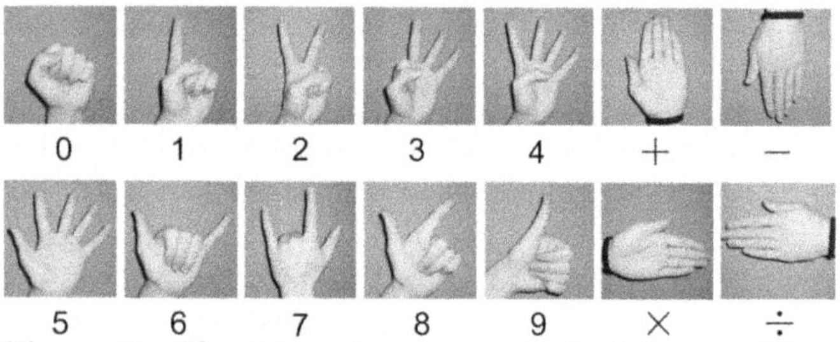

Figure 2: The 14 gesture commands in our arithmetic computation system.

Arithmetic computation is an interesting HCI application. Instead of interacting with the computer using the keyboard or mouse, we input arithmetic commands to the computer via hand gestures. As shown in Fig.2, 14 hand gestures are employed to represent 14 commands, namely number 0 – 9 and operator +, −, ×, ÷, respectively.

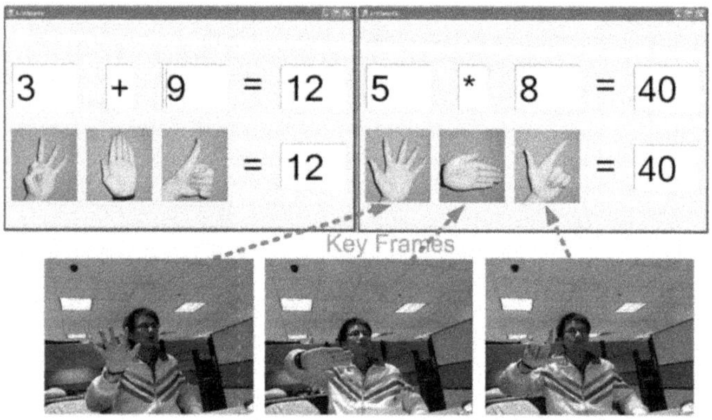

Figure 3: Arithmetic computation.

By recognizing each input gesture as a command, the computer can perform arithmetic computations instructed by the user. Two examples are shown in Fig.3. The key frames are shown as well.

3.2 Rock-paper-scissors game

Rock-paper-scissors is a traditional game. The rule is rock breaks scissors; scissors cut paper; and paper wraps rock. In this demo, we build a Rock-paper-scissors game system played between a human and a computer. Three hand gestures are defined as 3 different weapons in the game, as shown in Fig.4, which can be recognized by our system, and

Figure 4: Rock-paper-scissors game.

the computer just randomly chooses a weapon. Then, according to the game rule, our system can decide the winner between human and computer. Fig.5 shows two examples.

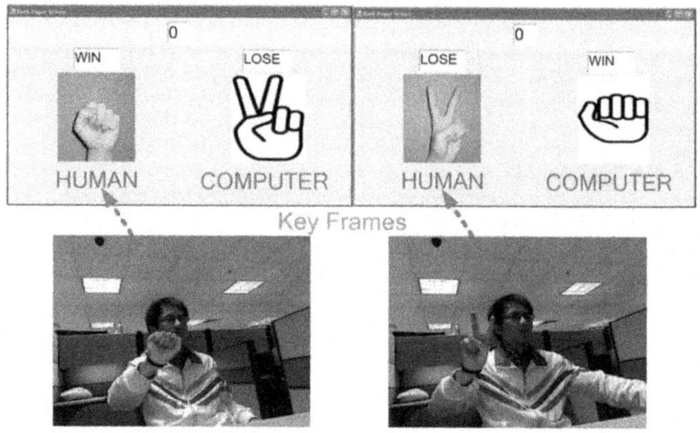

Figure 5: Rock-paper-scissors game.

4. CONCLUSION

In this demo, we present an efficient and accurate hand gesture recognition system using Kinect sensor as the input device. Both the depth and color information obtained from Kinect sensor are used for hand detection, which ensures the robustness of our system to cluttered environments. Besides, the Finger-Earth Mover's Distance metric employed in our gesture recognition module provides an effective mechanism for recognizing hand shapes with input variations and distortions. Such a hand gesture recognition system provides a robust solution in two real-life HCI applications, which can also be applied to many other hand gesture based HCIs.

5. ACKNOWLEDGEMENT

This work was supported in part by the Nanyang Assistant Professorship (SUG M58040015) to Dr. Junsong Yuan.

6. REFERENCES

[1] C. Chua, H. Guan, and Y. Ho. Model-based 3d hand posture estimation from a single 2d image. *Image and Vision Computing*, 20:191 – 202, 2002.

[2] E. Keogh, L. Wei, X. Xi, S. Lee, and M. Vlachos. Lb_keogh supports exact indexing of shapes under rotation invariance with arbitrary representations and distance measures. In *Proc. of 32th International Conf. on VLDB*, 2006.

[3] Z. Ren, J. Yuan, C. Li, and W. Liu. Minimum near-convex decomposition for robust shape representation. In *Proc. of ICCV*, 2011.

[4] Z. Ren, J. Yuan, and Z. Zhang. Robust hand gesture recognition based on finger-earth mover's distance with a commodity depth camera. In *Proc. of ACM MM*, 2011.

[5] N. Shimada, Y. Shirai, Y. Kuno, and J. Miura. Hand gesture estimation and model refinement using monocular camera-ambiguity limitation by inequality constraints. In *Proc. of Third IEEE International Conf. on Face and Gesture Recognition*, 1998.

[6] B. Stenger, A. Thayananthan, P. Torr, and R. Cipolla. Filtering using a tree-based estimator. In *Proc. of IEEE ICCV*, 2003.

[7] J. P. Wachs, M. Kölsch, H. Stern, and Y. Edan. Vision-based hand-gesture applications. *Communications of the ACM*, 54:60–71, 2011.

SRV-TAGS: An Automatic TAGging and Search System for Sensor-Rich Outdoor Videos

Zhijie Shen†, Sakire Arslan Ay†, Seon Ho Kim‡
†School of Computing, National University of Singapore, Singapore 117417
‡Integrated Media Systems Center, University of Southern California, Los Angeles, CA 90089
{z-shen, sakirear}@comp.nus.edu.sg, seonkim@usc.edu

ABSTRACT

Tagging facilitates video search in many social media and web applications. While manual tagging is time consuming, subjective and sometimes inaccurate, auto-tagging facilitated by content-based techniques is compute-intensive and challenging to apply across domains. We have developed a complementary system, named *SRV-TAGS*, to automatically generate tags for outdoor videos based on their geographic properties, to index the videos based on their generated tags and to provide textual search services. The system works with our geo-referenced video management web portal, enabling users to manage, search and watch videos.

Categories and Subject Descriptors

H.3.3 [**Information Storage and Retrieval**]: Information Search and Retrieval

General Terms

Algorithms, Design, Human Factors

Keywords

Video tags, location sensors, mobile video, geospatial

1. INTRODUCTION

Tagging is one of the most popular methods for users to index and search video corpora. While manual annotation is laborious and often subjective, auto-tagging through content-based methods is challenging for open domains and generally compute-intensive. Rapid developments in mobile phones and the availability of extensive geo-information sources make alternative solutions feasible. Here, we introduce a novel system, named *SRV-TAGS*, which automatically produces comprehensive tag sets based on the geographic properties of video scenes.

1.1 Architecture Overview

Recently we created geospatial video acquisition applications for both Android- and iOS-based mobile phones. These applications concurrently acquire location and orientation meta-data from multiple sensors in the phones while recording video. Subsequently, the collected meta-data is used to model the coverage areas of the video scenes as spatial extents, *i.e.*, a camera's set of field of views (FOVs) [1].

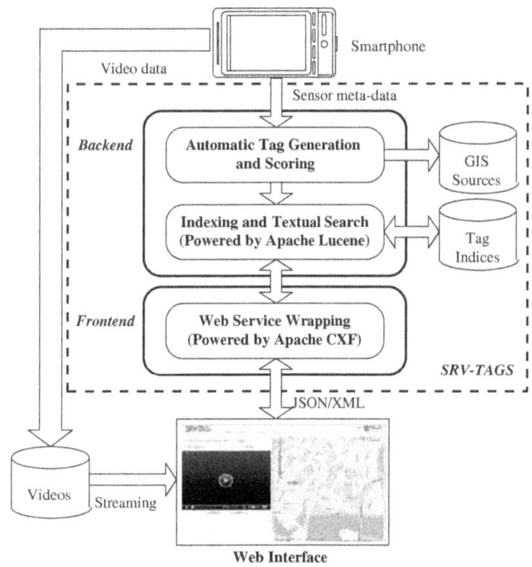

Figure 1: Architecture of the *SRV-TAGS* system.

The acquired sensor data sequences provide a rich source of information which is utilized in our *SRV-TAGS* system to query existing geo-information databases with the goal of identifying the geographical objects in the viewable region of the video (taking into account occlusions). Subsequently, it extracts textual descriptions of the visible objects to serve as tags, and scores them based on their relevance to the video and the hints provided by the geo-information databases. Notably, *SRV-TAGS* can accurately associate tags with not only whole video clips but also delimited sub-segments. The details are described in our full paper [3]. Then, *SRV-TAGS* ueses the tags to index the videos, leveraging Apache Lucene (http://lucene.apache.org/) to facilitate textual search, and integrating Apache CXF (http://cxf.apache.org/) to expose a programming interface for applications. Finally, our prototype *SRV-TAGS* system provides a client web interface, where users can search for videos and then watch the results and their coverage visualization on a map. Figure 1 illustrates the overall architecture. Unlike content-based methods, *SRV-TAGS* does not analyze video content throughout the procedures.

2. SYSTEM DETAILS

2.1 Automatic Tag Generation and Scoring

One of the key distinguishing features of *SRV-TAGS* is that it does not rely on analyzing the video content, but instead queries geo-information sources, presently GeoDec [2] and OpenStreetMap (http://www.openstreetmap.org/), in order to acquire the information of geographic objects within the FOVs of the video. Since not all the acquired objects are visible due to occlusions we devised a 3D visibility checking algorithm to filter out objects that are occluded. Subsequently, *SRV-TAGS* retrieves the names of the remaining objects to serve as tags.

As *SRV-TAGS* is prolific in generating multiple tags, it needs to rank them to enhance their utility. Thus, the system leverages multiple relevance criteria to score a tag's (or its corresponding object's) relevance to the video: the object's closeness to the scene center, the distance between the camera and the object location and the visible angle ranges/percentages of the object. Additionally, the scores of popular objects are promoted according to the hints provided by the geo-information sources. Furthermore, our system can determine the start and end timestamps between which the object remains visible. Therefore, *SRV-TAGS* provides users with answers of delimited video segments, which is especially useful for long videos.

2.2 Indexing and Textual Search Support

Given the tags and their relevance scores of the video clips/segments we can answer the textual queries from users. However, the queries may not exactly match the tags because of typos, incompletions, *etc.* For example, users may expect to retrieve videos showing either "the Fullerton Hotel" or "the One Fullerton" by entering the keyword "Fullerton." Hence we leverage Apache Lucene, a sophisticated full-text search engine, to judge the correspondence between the query text and the tags.

When a tag entry ⟨tag name, relevance score, video ID, segment boundaries⟩ is generated, it is fed into the Lucene indexing engine. *SRV-TAGS* maintains two separate indices: one at the granularity of whole clips and the other at the segment-level. As a query arrives, the tags similar to the query text will be retrieved and sorted according to their Lucene scores. Note that this score is calculated based on the similarity between the query and the tag, while our ranking score reflects the relevance between the tag and the video clip/segment. To calculate the most relevant results, *SRV-TAGS* first groups all the items by the tags, then sorts the groups by their Lucene score, and finally sorts the items in each group by our ranking score.

2.3 Web Service Integration and API

To be easily accessible, *SRV-TAGS* leverages Apache CXF, a web service framework, to wrap itself as a RESTful service. Three APIs are exposed to potential applications:

1. *Search*: Provides the basic functionality of the service. It takes in the query text and produces a list of matched tag entries.
2. *Get*: Acquires all the tags of a specific video, and their associated segment details. The input for this function is a video ID.
3. *Add*: Allows the adding of a new video into *SRV-TAGS*. It parses the sensor-data supplied by the recording apps, generates tags, and indexes them. Afterwards, the new video becomes immediately searchable through text queries.

The sensor-data input and the output of the API are organized in JSON or XML format.

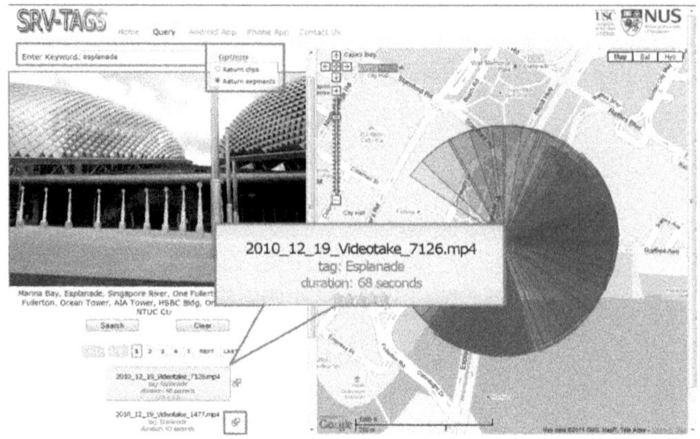

Figure 2: Snapshot of the web interface.

2.4 Demonstration

We developed a PHP-based web interface based on our geo-referenced video management web portal [1] to allow users to interact with *SRV-TAGS*, as illustrated in Figure 2. A text box and a drop-down menu on the left side of the query page allow users to input keywords and specify the result granularity. After calling the search API the results are listed in the bottom left area as a series of buttons, each of which displays the video ID, the tag name, the playback duration, and the rating (1 to 5 stars) derived from the relevance score. When a button is clicked, the video plays, the top related tags are shown below the player, and the viewable areas are visualized in terms of a series of field-of-view sectors on the map. Notably, when *segment* granularity is selected, only the specific segment will be played. Moreover, there is a link icon next to each result button which brings users to a web page that summarizes the tags and their associated segments of the video. Finally, one web page serves for video uploads. When a new video (the video content and the corresponding sensor-data in JSON format) is submitted, *SRV-TAGS* will be called to process its sensor-data. Afterwards, this video is available for textual search as well.

3. CONCLUSIONS

We introduced a novel video auto-tagging and search system, called *SRV-TAGS*. It processes the meta-data captured through smartphone sensors to automatically generate and score tags, and to particularly associate them with precisely delimited video segments. It incorporates Apache Lucene and CXF to be a complete textual search service. We demonstrate its functionality and usability through an integration with an end-user web portal.

4. REFERENCES

[1] S. Arslan Ay, R. Zimmermann, and S. H. Kim. Viewable Scene Modeling for Geospatial Video Search. In *ACM Multimedia*, 2008.

[2] C. Shahabi, F. Banaei-Kashani, A. Khoshgozaran, L. Nocera, and S. Xing. GeoDec: A Framework to Effectively Visualize and Query Geospatial Data for Decision-Making. *IEEE Multimedia*, 2010.

[3] Z. Shen, S. Arslan Ay, S. H. Kim, and R. Zimmermann. Automatic Tag Generation and Ranking for Sensor-rich Outdoor Videos. In *ACM Multimedia*, 2011.

A System for Reconstructing Multiparty Conversation Field based on Augmented Head Motion by Dynamic Projection

Kazuhiro Otsuka
NTT CSL*
3-1 Morinosato Wakamiya
Atsugi-shi, Japan
otsuka@ieee.org

Kamil Sebastian Mucha
NTT CSL
3-1 Morinosato Wakamiya
Atsugi-shi, Japan
kamil@cs.kecl.ntt.co.jp

Shiro Kumano
NTT CSL
3-1 Morinosato Wakamiya
Atsugi-shi, Japan
shiro.kumano@lab.ntt.co.jp

Dan Mikami
NTT CSL
3-1 Morinosato Wakamiya
Atsugi-shi, Japan
mikami.dan@lab.ntt.co.jp

Masafumi Matsuda
NTT CSL
3-1 Morinosato Wakamiya
Atsugi-shi, Japan
masafumi.matsuda@lab.ntt.co.jp

Junji Yamato
NTT CSL
3-1 Morinosato Wakamiya
Atsugi-shi, Japan
yamato@brl.ntt.co.jp

ABSTRACT

A novel system is presented for reconstructing, in the real world, multiparty face-to-face conversation scenes; it uses dynamics projection to augment human head motion. This system aims to display and playback pre-recorded conversations to the viewers as if the remote people were taking in front of them. This system consists of multiple projectors and transparent screens. Each screen separately displays the life-size face of one meeting participant, and are spatially arranged to recreate the actual scene. The main feature of this system is dynamics projection, screen pose is dynamically controlled to emulate the head motions of the participants, especially rotation around the vertical axis, that are typical of shifts in visual attention, i.e. turning gaze from one to another. This recreation of head motion by physical screen motion, in addition to image motion, aims to more clearly express the interactions involving visual attention among the participants. The minimal design, frameless-projector-screen, with augmented head motion is expected to create a feeling that the remote participants are actually present in the same room. This demo presents our initial system and discusses its potential impact on future visual communications.

Categories and Subject Descriptors

H1.2 [**Models and Principles**]: User/Machine System — Human Information Processing

General Terms

ALGORITHMS, DESIGN, HUMAN FACTORS

Keywords

face-to-face conversation, multimodal interaction, projector system, telepresence, visual attention, visual communication

*NTT Communication Science Laboratories, Nippon Telegraph and Telephone Corp.

MM'11, November 28–December 1, 2011, Scottsdale, Arizona, USA.
ACM 978-1-4503-0616-4/11/11.

1. INTRODUCTION

Face-to-face conversation is one of the most basic forms of communication in daily life and group meetings are used for conveying/sharing information, understanding others' intention/emotion, and making decisions. As a part of visual communication research, this study focuses on the essential problem of how people perceive and understand others' conversations, and how to design/built a system that allows outside people to re-experience the conversation by recreating the real face-to-face setting as closely as possible. We formulate the problem of *conversation field reconstruction* as the re-creation, in the real world, of multiparty face-to-face conversation scenes using novel devices with augmented expression modality.

2. DESIGN CONCEPT

Considering the importance of the nonverbal information exchanged in face-to-face conversations, such as facial expressions, eye-gaze, and head/body gestures, our system aims to reproduce it in an actual environment that closely mirrors the original one. Among the different forms of nonverbal information, this study focuses on the *visual attention* of conversation participants. Visual attention, also called *gaze*, can indicate "who is looking at whom"; it is particularly important in understanding the structure of a conversation, e.g. "who is talking to whom". To express visual attention to the viewers, we newly introduce a *dynamics projection* as an augmented modality that indicates the direction and shift of visual attention of the participants. Details of the design concept are as follows.

First, this system consists of multiple screens, where each screen corresponds to a different individual; they are spatially configured to recreate the original spatial arrangement of the participants. This arrangement is one requirement for intuitively understanding the visual attention shift during the conversation. Fig. 1 shows an overview of the proposed system.

Second, each screen displays the (near) frontal view of the life-sized face and upper body of one participant. Unlike avatar-based systems, we preserve the original image of the face itself, which gives viewers the full range of nonverbal messages including subtle facial expressions.

Third, our system employs flat transparent screens with back-projectors. Participant images are fused into the room background from the viewer's eye. The screen has no *frames*, *edges*, nor *margin*, unlike other display devices used for telecommunications. The frameless transparent screens create the impression that the people's faces are floating in the air.

Fourth, as the most notable feature, the screen dynamically changes its pose to emulate the head motion of each person. We place particular emphasis on head rotation around the vertical axis, i.e. head rotation when turning to one to another participant. This additional expression modality, augmented by physical screen motion, combines with original image details, aims to more clearly represent the changes in visual attention among the participants. This idea of head motion augmentation is based on the nature of human perception called *biological motion* and the *theory of mind*. These theories indicate that humans can anthropomorphize an object when it moves like a human. Also, the viewer's attention can be induced by screen motion in their peripheral vision, as in a real setting.

To summarize the above, our system features a *minimal design* approach, the simple and abstract display devices that are animated with realistic human motion. This tries to re-create the conversation scene 'as is', and allows the viewer to intuitively experience and understand the conversation.

3. SYSTEM CONFIGURATION

Fig. 1 overviews the proposed system [1]. Fig. 1(a) shows actual conversation scenes, and Fig. 1(b) shows the reconstructed conversation scenes. The sensing part (left in Fig. 1(a)) includes multiple cameras and microphones, which capture the face images and voice of each participant. One example of the sensing part can be found in [1]. The visualization part consists of multiple projectors and screens with actuators to control screen motion.

The projector screen is attached to an actuator, called Pan-Tilt Unit, which controls the pose of screen, here only rotation around the vertical axis, which represents head motion typically appeared when a person turns his/her eyes to another participant, is used. The head pose captured by visual face tracking from videos and/or motion capture devices. Fig. 2 (a) shows an example of the time series of head pose angles, including measured values and the values for PTU control, which is a simplified version of actual head motion.

Fig. 2 (b) shows an example of the projection images sent to the projectors. They cover the face and bust of each person and are centered on the face. The projection images are extracted from the captured images with cameras in Fig. 1(a), and are transformed so that the skew-correct images appear on the screen regardless of the screen pose, as shown in Fig. 1(b) Right. The transformation is synchronized with the screen pose as in Fig. 2 (a). The projectors are calibrated at system installation.

4. FUTURE PERSPECTIVE

This demo paper presents our initial system as a platform for investigating how conversations can be more clearly delivered to remote viewers. A comprehensive survey, a complete description of the system, and evaluation results will be described in another conference paper. So far, although there has been a lot of research effort in the field of visual communication, authors believe that this work can provide a new driving force in terms of introducing the idea of meeting analysis, i.e. extracting people's behavior and using it for enhanced understanding. We are now working to extend our system towards a commutation system that realizes multiparty-to-multiparty conversations across multi-locations.

[1]In this demo session, we plan to showcase the devices used in the system and/or a partial system, in addition to the demo movies. Demo movies are available on our website http://www.brl.ntt.co.jp/people/otsuka/.

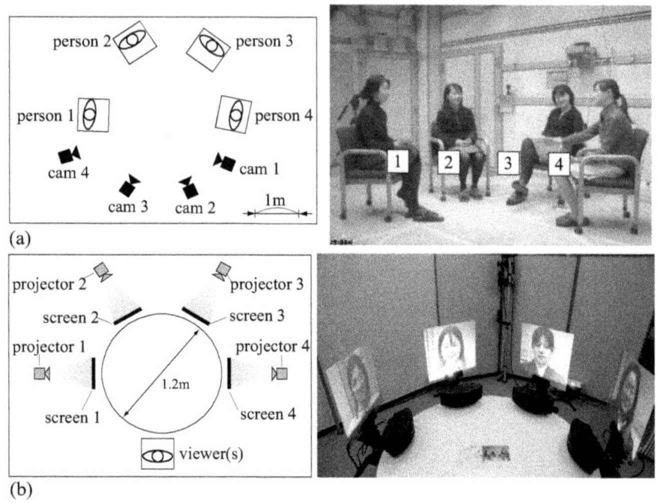

Figure 1: Overview of system. (a)Real conversation scenes, (b)reconstructed scenes

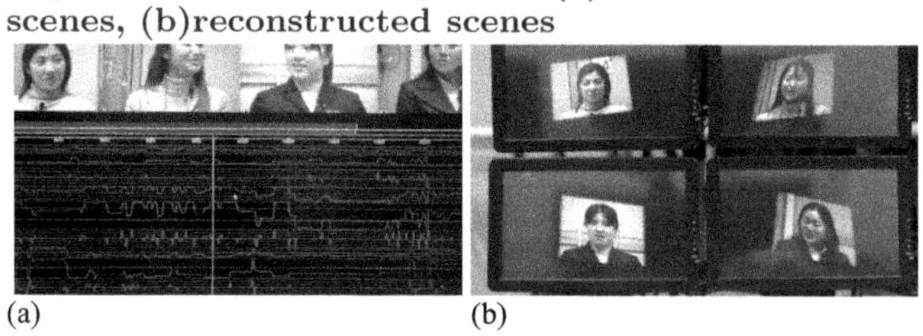

Figure 2: Screen shots of system console, (a)projection images, (b)time series of head rotation angle (measured and processed for PTU control)

5. REFERENCES

[1] K. Otsuka, S. Araki, K. Ishizuka, M. Fujimoto, M. Heinrich, and J. Yamato. A realtime multimodal system for analyzing group meetings by combining face pose tracking and speaker diarization. In *Proc. ACM ICMI'08*, pages 257–264, 2008.

Enabling the VJ as Performer with Rhythmic Wearable Interfaces

Andreas Zingerle M.A.
Kairus.org
andreas@kairus.org

Tyler Freeman M.A.
Odbol Productions
tyler@odbol.com

ABSTRACT
This paper proposes an experimental wearable controller for live video performances called the VJacket [15]. The VJacket can be worn by the performer or visual artist (VJ) to control video effects and transitions, trigger clips or scratch frames with the output of the integrated sensor system. The sensors detect body movements like bending, touching or hitting, and can send OpenSoundControl or MIDI messages wirelessly to the VJ program of your choice. The VJacket brings the rhythmic movement of dance to computer interaction, so the VJ won't have to fumble for knobs and buttons or look at the screen to be sure he's clicking on the right thing -he will be free to control the video using his body movements alone.

Categories and Subject Descriptors
J.5 [**ARTS AND HUMANITIES**]: Performing arts (e.g., dance, music) --- MIDI; H.5.2 [**INFORMATION INTERFACES AND PRESENTATION**]: User Interfaces --- Input devices and strategies; H.5.1 [**INFORMATION INTERFACES AND PRESENTATION**]: Multimedia Information Systems --- Video, Animations, Audio input/output

General Terms
Design, Experimentation, Human Factors, Standardization

Keywords
VJ, Wearable sensors, mobility, Entertainment Computing, Live video performance, Real-time image control.

1. INTRODUCTION
VJing is a rhythmic manipulation of moving video and animation. A mouse and keyboard are very rigid and unforgiving -not ideal rhythmic controllers. Anyone who's tried to scrub a video rhythmically with a mouse knows that the mouse is too precise in position and too slow in response for gestures of rhythm, which are innately imprecise in position but very precise in tempo and response. Knobs, sliders and touchpads are faster in response than a mouse, but still require tiny movements for grand rhythmic gestures, and require precise position and attention (most knobs can only be turned by two fingers at once: a precise movement). A more natural controller for such tempo-centric manipulation would mimic the movements of dancing, since dancing is the ultimate form of rhythmic expression. We see this concept in several new experimental VJ interfaces, including the Maraca-like interface Rhythmism [14], and the WiiJ Video interface which uses the Nintendo Wii remote to control video using sweeping, rhythmic hand gestures [16]. We sought to extend the gestural concept, past just the hands to all parts of the body, to enable a VJ to control video simply by dancing. We embedded sensors into clothing to insure minimal interference from the interface. The VJacket allows for wide, imprecise movements with a precise rhythmic response. The VJ will not have to fumble for knobs and buttons, will not have to look at the screen to be sure he's clicking on the right thing -he will be freed to control the video using his body movements alone.

MM'11, November 28–December 1, 2011, Scottsdale, Arizona, USA.
ACM 978-1-4503-0616-4/11/11.

Since it is wireless, the VJ will be free to interact with the audience and musicians -on stage or even walking through the crowd -something which most hermit-like VJs do not usually experience, since they are often delegated to the back corner of the club behind the video inputs and lighting controls. With a wireless system, a VJ becomes not just an engineer behind the curtain, but an actual live performer -one whose movements are directly connected to the video projections. The audience will be able to see the VJ's gestures in connection with the video, and thus will become more interested in the performance itself [2].

Reeves et al. explain the importance of "expressive latitude" in a performance: the stylistic gestures a performer makes "that are not directly sensed by the instrument" [12]. Wearing the VJacket, the performer transforms these superfluous gestures into *direct manipulations* of the instrument -indeed reducing the expressive latitude, yet simultaneously merging that expression into the movements of the video performance. The bend of the arm, the slap on the stomach, and the wave of the hand are no longer purely showmanship but are given meaning in the visual context provided by the on-screen projections, synthesizing the performance of the body with the performance of the technology. "Such gestures are an essential element of deliberately performing interactions for others to see and appreciate, expressing skill and control and introducing an aesthetic component to the use of technology" [12].

It is connecting the audience with the VJ that is our ultimate goal, since doing so will create a more legitimate space for VJing in the performance community, and hopefully encourage more people to try VJing themselves. With video and consumer production becoming more ubiquitous, projectors becoming cheaper and smaller -even integrated into our cell phones and cameras -soon every rock band, DJ, and karaoke bar will have their own VJ. If they don't, someone with a pocket projector and mobile VJ setup will guerrilla VJ anyway. This is the future we imagine, and we are trying to shape it with the VJacket.

2. FREE THE PEOPLE
We combined ideas from both percussion-based devices, such as the maracas-based 'rhythmism' [14], which transforms a simple percussion instrument into a VJ performance system, and more precise expressive instruments, such as the 'Djammer', a handheld device that can be used for 'air-scratching' -giving the DJ the possibility to leave his turntables and move around in the nightclub [13] -to give the VJ a wide range of control possibilities: traditional scratching and fading combined with

percussive elements for triggering effects or clips. The dutch performance artist 'Eboman' created the "SenSorSuit", a suit that he uses for staged body performances, mixing live video and a network of sensors spread over his body [1]. The SenSorSuit is full of bulky sensors and other equipment, which must be taped on the body. In contrast, we tried to make the VJacket as unobtrusive as possible, enabling the performer to just slip it on and switch it on with very little prep time, making spontaneous performance possible (not to mention more comfortable!) Unlike the sensor suit, which is a complete performance instrument, the VJacket is meant to be used in conjunction with other interfaces: it can provide basic functions that the VJ uses most often (e.g. global effects, clip loading, mixing and scratching) and keep them always in reach, leaving the more complicated, less-used functions to other controllers such as a piano keyboard, sequencer, or even the bane of live performance: the mouse/keyboard on the laptop [11].

3. CONSIDERATIONS

There are many projects out there that deal with converting Arduino sensor information into messages to control various software programs, including Maxuino [5], Funnel [3], NETLab Toolkit [7], among others. However, they are mostly libraries that require programming experience, expensive development tools (Max5 for Maxuino and Adobe Flash for NETLab Toolkit), and a good deal of development and testing time to use in a project. In consequence, many beginning users have a steep learning curve to climb before they can start creating.

In order to make Arudino projects easier and faster to realize, we designed the Arduino2OSC software to accept and process multiple types of sensor input, using live sensor readouts to adjust the behavior on-the-fly. The basics are there: scaling input and output values, adding cutoff thresholds, etc. and we also included filters to smooth errant sensor data and envelope triggers to automate gestures. Once you have configured all the sensor inputs to produce the desired data, you can route the output as Open Sound Control or MIDI messages, two standards which are supported almost universally by VJ and audio software, such as "Arkaos Grand VJ, Max/MSP/Jitter, Reaktor, Abelton Live, Propellerheads Reason, Supercollider, Kyma, Processing, OpenFrameworks, etc. Using OSC, you can even send the messages over the LAN for networked performances" [8].

Another important aspect of the software is to be able to adjust the sensor values on the fly, while preparing for or even during a performance. Sensor data can change slightly from performance to performance (variables include the strength of the battery, bend sensors slowly becoming permanently bent, the ambient light in a venue that effects light sensors, etc), or the behavior could change (the act could suddenly call for a "bleep" sound when there was a "bloop", a cut when there was a fade, etc.), so the performer needs a way to adjust for any unseen changes without having to open up the development environment and start changing code. We built the interface to be completely customizable while it's running, and to have customizable presets that you can load for different performance sections.

4. DEMO PROPOSAL

Our VJacket demo will be similar to the demo we proposed for the Maker Faire Bay Area [4]: a "VJ battle," where two participants each put on a VJacket and compete on the same screen. On the screen is a live 3D feed of each participant (created in real-time using a hacked XBox Kinect), and various visual effects are applied to the avatar *by his opponent's VJacket.* For instance, one VJ could bend his arm and make his opponent's avatar shrink and grow, and his opponent could counter by hitting a sensor on his own jacket to make the other VJ explode in a wash of colors. This VJ battle game, along with other codebendable games like *Miserable Pile of Secrets* and *savestate* [10], will be controlled completely by OSC messages sent from the VJackets. Depending on the allotted time for the demo, we will also showcase the live music performance possibilities by controlling Abelton Live and other MIDI instruments with the VJacket.

The demo will require a projector, sound system, and about 1-2 hours of setup time. We can supply all other equipment, and a projector if necessary. If that is too long or complicated there are simplified versions we can do as well, but an interactive installation that lets people try the VJacket for themselves is definitely the most fun and educational.

5. REFERENCES

[1] Eboman Website, http://wwwebomaninfo.wordpress.com/ (accessed Sep 1, 2011).

[2] Elsea, P., (2006). "The Role Of Virtuosity In A Technology-Enhanced Performance". Poster session presented at the Digital Artsand New Media Festival Symposia Proceedings, Santa Cruz, CA, U.S. (see http://danm.ucsc.edu/media/da_festival/advpr/) (last accessed Sep 1, 2011).

[3] Funnel, http://code.google.com/p/funnel/, (accessed Sep 1, 2011).

[4] Maker Faire, SF Bay Area, http://makerfaire.com/bayarea/2011/, (accessed Sep 1, 2011).

[5] Maxuino official Web Site, http://www.maxuino.org/, (accessed Sep 1, 2011).

[6] Negrillo, B., et. al. 'Wrist Brace VJ', http://www.mindness.net/ivrea/onthebody/index.html#video, (accessed Sep 1, 2011).

[7] NETLab Toolkit, http://www.netlabtoolkit.org, (accessed Sep 1, 2011).

[8] Nigten, A., et. al., (2010) "Real projects for real people", V2 Press.

[9] Paperkettle official Web Site, http://www.paperkettle.com/home/illucia/, (accessed Sep 1, 2011)

[10] Paperkettle codebending, http://www.paperkettle.com/codebending/, (accessed Sep 1, 2011).

[11] Quickswitches, http://blog.quickswitches.com/?page_id=2/, (accessed Sep 1, 2011).

[12] Reeves, S., et. al., (2005). "Designing the Spectator Experience". Proceedings of CHI 2005. ACM, 741-750.

[13] Slayden, A., et. al. "The DJammer: "Air-Scratching" and Freeing the DJ to Join the Party," *Proceedings of CHI 2005* (Portland, Oregon, July 2005).

[14] Tokuhisa, S., et. al. (2007). "Rhythmism: a VJ performance system with maracas based devices". *In Proceedings of the international conference on Advances in computer entertainment technology* (ACE '07). ACM, New York, NY, USA, 204-207. DOI=10.1145/1255047.1255089http://doi.acm.org/10.1145/1255047.1255089 (accessed Sep 1, 2011).

[15] Vjacket official Web Site, http://www.vjacket.com (accessed Sep 1, 2011).

[16] WiiJ Video official Web Site, http://www.wiivideo.com (accessed Sep 1, 2011).

InSPeCT: Integrated Surveillance for Port Container Traffic

David Sadlier*, Paul Ferguson, Dian Zhang, Noel E. O'Connor, Hyowon Lee
CLARITY: Centre for Sensor Web Technologies,
Dublin City University, Dublin 9, IRELAND.
david.sadlier@dcu.ie

ABSTRACT
This paper describes a fully-operational content-indexing and management system, designed for monitoring and profiling freight-based vehicular traffic in a seaport environment. The 'InSPeCT' system captures video footage of passing vehicles and uses tailored OCR to index the footage according to vehicle license plates and freight codes. In addition to real-time functionality such as alerting, the system provides advanced search techniques for the efficient retrieval of records, where each vehicle is profiled according to multi-angled video, context information, and links to external information sources. Currently being piloted at a busy national seaport, the feedback from port officials indicates the system to be extremely useful in supplementing their existing transportation-security structures.

Categories and Subject Descriptors
H.3.3 [**Information Storage and Retrieval**]: Information Search and Retrieval – *search process.*

General Terms
Algorithms, Design, Security, Human Factors.

Keywords
Content analysis, indexing, OCR, search and retrieval, HCI.

1. INTRODUCTION

1.1 Background
In the age of increased vigilance concerning homeland defense, transportation intelligence is a hot topic for authorities responsible for seaport security. Whilst, the policing and risk assessment of seaport bound vehicle traffic is clearly aided by CCTV monitoring, manual unaided review of these feeds is a highly inefficient task. Clearly, visual media that is indexed, and therefore index-retrievable, would go along way towards enhancing the efficiency of the risk assessment and evidence gathering abilities of traditional systems. In this demo we showcase InSPeCT: Integrated Surveillance for Port Container Traffic, a user-centric system that automatically indexes vehicular traffic flow using a number of complementary information sources.

1.2 Novelty
In vehicle monitoring systems, image-based technologies such as optical character recognition (OCR) have received significant attention, together with related sub-applications such as Automatic Number Plate Recognition (ANPR). Equally relevant in the context of seaport traffic surveillance, is Automatic Freight Code Recognition (AFCR), where the OCR methods are targeted towards interpreting the unique identifiers associated with the freight items that port bound vehicles may be transporting - see Figure 1. It should be noted that although ANPR/AFCR-based solutions are increasingly being deployed in real-world applications, the challenge of improving these technologies remains an active field of research: references to a variety of contributions to the state-of-the-art in ANPR/AFCR technologies may be found in [1]. Whilst there are already commercial products exploiting ANPR/AFCR in a seaport context, these systems exhibit limitations with respect to risk assessment, profiling, user-centricity, and overall level of functionality. The inherent value of the InSPeCT system is that it overcomes these deficiencies within an integrated platform.

2. SYSTEM DESCRIPTION
The InSPeCT system operates by capturing video snapshots of passing vehicles and then utilizing software-based ANPR/AFCR tools for indexing the transits according to vehicle license-plates and associated freight codes. The system is currently able to recognize Latin-character license plates (Europe, USA, etc.) as well as the ISO 'BIC codes' that uniquely identify inter-modal shipping containers. The indexed data is then processed and organized according to specially designed content management structures, such that it is efficiently primed for retrieval. At the front-end, the system is realized by a graphical user-interface (GUI), shown in Figure 2, that provides an efficient means for accessing transit profiles via advanced search facilities, various display options, etc.

2.1 Search and retrieval
Users can search through captured vehicle transits (termed 'events') based on a variety of criteria. The search options

Figure 1. Freight-transporting vehicle with corresponding license-plates and container codes highlighted.

MM'11, November 28–December 1, 2011, Scottsdale, Arizona, USA.
ACM 978-1-4503-0616-4/11/11.

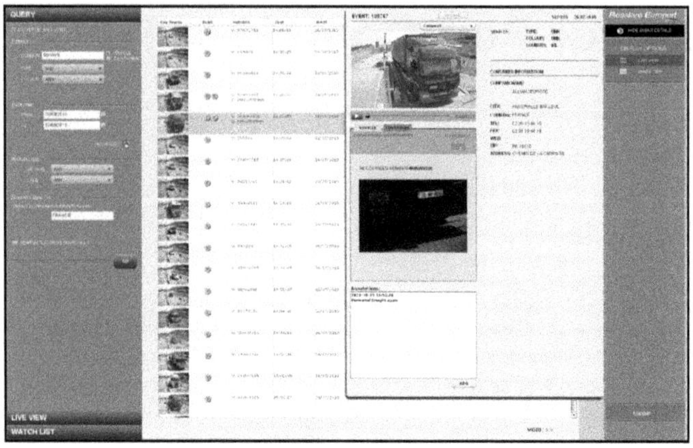

Figure 2. Graphical user-interface.

available relate to license-plate details (partial or complete), freight codes (partial or complete), calendar information (date/time range), geographical information (region/lane specification), and/or shipping company information. Initiating a search returns a results set, where each element corresponds to a unique event (captured and profiled by the system) that matches the search criteria entered.

2.2 Event details

Mouse-clicking on a particular result reveals a separate panel (see Figure 3) that displays detailed information relating to the selected event. Besides placeholders for context information (time/date, etc.), at the bottom-left of the panel is an annotation box, which can be used by the operator to tag the event item with text-based comments. Above this is another sub-panel, which is designed to provide feedback (capture details, confidence values, etc.) pertaining to the OCR capture(s) associated with the event. Above this again is an integrated video player, which provides the user with the ability to playback video of the transit from multiple angles of capture (selectable via drop-down menu). Finally, to the right of the video player is a placeholder dedicated to displaying information regarding the shipping company to which the identified freight is registered. This information is retrieved at query time from an online registry of shipping companies (and their respective identifiers).

2.3 Other Features

In addition to the retrieval of event profiles, the system supports real-time alerting functionality via email/SMS targeted towards alerting security officials to the arrival of specific vehicles/freight. This is achieved by maintaining an inventory of full/partial license-plate and freight-code patterns (a 'watchlist'), against which newly captured event data is compared. The GUI features comprehensive tools for managing watchlist entries. Finally, real-time event monitoring is supported, whereby the operator is afforded the ability to examine live video feeds whilst observing the real-time capture/processing of events.

3. DEMONSTRATION

The demonstration will show a fully interactive version of the InSPeCT system, which will illustrate the features of the system as described; multi-modal querying, retrieval and browsing of events (as captured from the deployed system in Rosslare Europort, Ireland), live video streaming, watchlist management (alerting), visualisation options, etc.

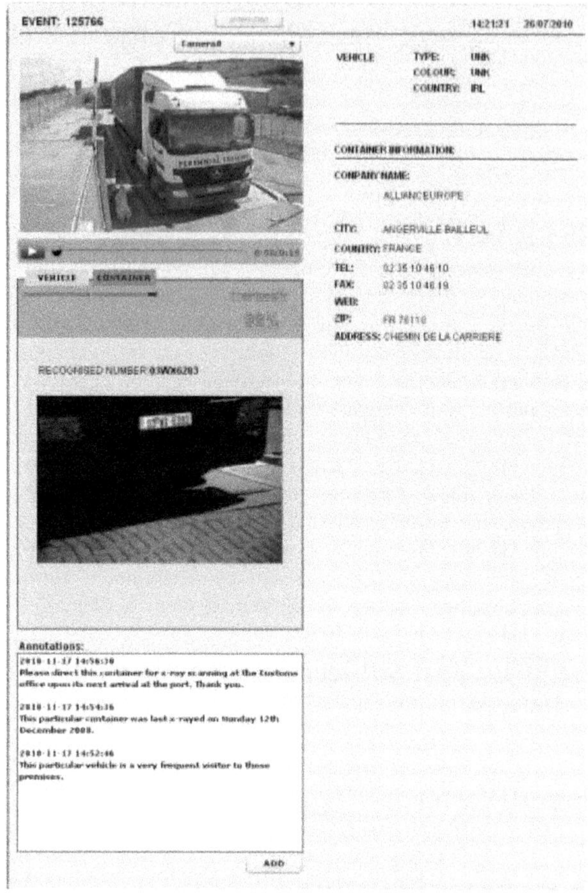

Figure 3. Event details panel.

4. CONCLUSIONS

Currently being piloted in a busy national seaport, the initial feedback indicates the system to be very useful in how it extends the port's existing security resources. Overall, the InSPeCT system represents an optimization of how technology can support the transportation-security remit of port authority officials, and thus exhibits genuine market potential for systems targeting such applications. Future work will involve extending the modality of the system to support the capture of different freight modes (e.g. trailers), incorporating more external resources linking in the system (e.g. to vehicle registry), and investigating interesting research areas such as automatic watchlist generation.

5. ACKNOWLEDGEMENTS

The support of Enterprise Ireland under Innovation Partnership IP/2009/010 is gratefully acknowledged. This work is supported by Science Foundation Ireland under grant 07/CE/I114.

6. REFERENCES

[1] Sadlier, D.A., Ferguson, P., O'Conáire, C., O'Connor, N.E., Doyle, K. Image-Based Vehicle Indexing for a Seaport Transport Surveillance System. In *Proceedings of 8th IEEE Int. Conf. on Advanced Video and Signal-Based Surveillance* (AVSS'11), Klagenfurt, Austria, Aug. 30th - Sep 2nd 2011.

Cognitive Intervention in Autism using Multimedia Stimulus

Svetha Venkatesh, Stewart Greenhill, Dinh Phung, Brett Adams
Department of Computing
Curtin University
GPO Box U1987, Perth, 6845, W. Australia
{s.venkatesh,s.greenhill,d.phung,b.adams}@curtin.edu.au

ABSTRACT

We demonstrate an open multimedia-based system for delivering early intervention therapy for autism. Using flexible multi-touch interfaces together with principled ways to access rich content and tasks, we show how a syllabus can be translated into stimulus sets for early intervention. Media stimuli are able to be presented agnostic to language and media modality due to a semantic network of concepts and relations that are fundamental to language and cognitive development, which enable stimulus complexity to be adjusted to child performance. Being open, the system is able to assemble enough media stimuli to avoid children over-learning, and is able to be customised to a specific child which aids with engagement. Computer-based delivery enables automation of session logging and reporting, a fundamental and time-consuming part of therapy.

Categories and Subject Descriptors

K.3.1 [**Computer Uses in Education**]; K.4.2 [**Social Issues, Assistive Technologies**]

General Terms

Algorithms, Experimentation, Human Factors

Keywords

Autism, assistive technology, therapy, multimedia stimulus

1. INTRODUCTION

Autism is a neurological disorder that disrupts early development in cognition and communication, leading to impairment in cognitive and social functions, and difficulty acquiring new adaptive behaviours. A staggering 1 in 150 children are diagnosed with Autism Spectrum Disorder (ASD). The cost of remediation is estimated at $3.2 million over the lifespan of someone with ASD;[1] the emotional cost to sufferers and carers in anxiety and depression is immeasurable.

Outcomes can be significantly improved if intervention is undertaken with children as young as two years. One such intervention is Applied Behavioural Therapy (ABA) [3], which aims to improve cognitive functions such as object labelling and categorisation. ABA involves the delivery of stimuli according to a program created by a therapist. A child will typically have 30 hours of therapy a week, often delivered by the parent, and requiring a similar additional amount of time in lesson preparation. For every lesson, media additional to that provided by the therapist must be manually sourced by the parent, printed and laminated for use as flashcards. This burden is exacerbated by lengthening waitlists for therapy, which leave parents conscious of the passing days in what is a crucial window of time for their children, but lacking the expertise and guidance to know how to help. In addition, paper-based delivery suffers from limited stimuli, which can lead to the child over learning, and being unable to generalise, and an inability to convey dynamic concepts such as verbs.

Commercial software exists to support early intervention, such as *Teachtown*, but their content is proprietary, and they lack flexibility. A host of iPad-based applications address specific skill shortages. Research has targeted affect recognition for ASD sufferers [1], and tools for early detection [2], but no attempt has been made to address automated early intervention.

In response, in collaboration with ASD experts, we have designed and implemented a web-based system to deliver early intervention therapy. It uses a database of media annotated with semantic concepts relevant to early language development to deliver therapy that adapts to the child's performance. Concepts are encoded in a language-agnostic way, so that therapy can be delivered in many languages, and across media types, making it modality-agnostic. Importantly, media resources can be extended via moderated community contributions. Our open data model avoids over-learning, and allows stimuli to be personalized (e.g., an image of concept "father" can be the child's father), which is an important feature for ASD sufferers. To our knowledge, this is the first framework created for the automatic and adaptive delivery of early intervention therapy for ASD.

2. MULTIMEDIA FOR AUTISM THERAPY

The framework has two parts: first, a database populated with multimedia content, which can grow with moderated, user-contributed content; second, metadata and logic for constructing a stimulus set to follow a syllabus, and a means to present the stimulus set to a child, record responses, and automatically adapt stimuli based on performance.

Intervention can begin with children as young as two years, so the delivery platform must support natural interactions,

[1]http://www.nationalautismcenter.org/

MM'11, November 28–December 1, 2011, Scottsdale, Arizona, USA.
ACM 978-1-4503-0616-4/11/11.

such as pointing and touching. Ideally, it must also be cheap, robust, and portable, so that it is not tied to specific locations. Our therapy client, termed *Playpad*, is implemented in Javascript and HTML5 and runs in a webkit-enabled browser. A specialized version runs on the iPad and is deployed as a native application, allowing media and data to be cached locally on the device so that it can be used offline.

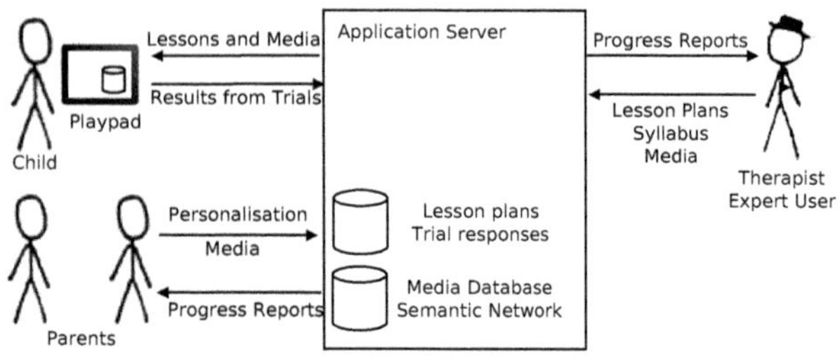

Figure 1: System Architecture

The Playpad client is served by a web application that hosts a database of media annotated with concepts that are fundamental to language development within and across cultures. Crucial concepts necessary for linguistic and congnitive development are: nouns, verbs, adjectives, functions, categories, prepositions and directions, pronouns, time and causation. Concepts include objects (e.g., spoon, dog, car), attributes (e.g., color, red, small), and actions (e.g., walking, eating). The database also contains semantic relations between these concepts, including taxonomical relationships (e.g., dog "is_a" animal), and functional relationships (e.g., spoon "used_for" eating). Together, concepts and relations comprise a semantic network that can be leveraged to assemble media stimuli of specified content and complexity.

The system can be used by a non-expert (parent) to deliver basic therapy. The curriculum includes activities that can be performed by the child using Playpad, either solo (eg. sensory matching) or with a partner (eg. two-person games, expressive language tasks). The system also includes activities done without the Playpad, which the parent can incorporate in the daily routine. These are presented in the daily lesson plan via instructional videos.

Therapists construct lessons by specifying sets of stimulus concepts (e.g., for color, [*green*, *red*]), and sets of dimensions of variation. The learner is shown how to attend to relevant aspects and ignore irrelevant aspects of the stimulus. Variation in *irrelevant dimensions* produces *variants* within a target concept; variations in *relevant dimensions* produce *distractors,* which are outside the target concept. Usually, few *variants* are introduced until the child has mastered the simpler stages. Multiple concepts may be taught simultaneously, in which case one stimulus concept serves as a *distractor* for another in the same set. Using the encoded semantic concepts and relationships, the system is able to automatically adjust stimulus complexity.

The curriculum includes a variety of matching tasks. E.g., *Symbolic Processing, Distinction of Categories*–where three exemplars of one category are presented along with one from another category. The system uses closeness in the semantic network to measure similarity. E.g., cat and dog are close because they are both sub-types of animal. Categories that are semantically closer are deemed to be more natural comparisons, but are correspondingly more difficult to discriminate. See Figure 2.

Figure 2: Example of symbolic processing task. The subject must identify which object (cat) is different from the others (dogs).

Other matching tasks include Visual or Auditory Sensory Matching, Symbolic Processing; Receptive Labelling (where the cue is a word rather than an image); Receptive Auditory, Visual Matching Sound; and Functional Matching–e.g., a broom (not a pencil or fork) is used for sweeping–which can be generalised to any semantic relation represented in the network, e.g., "found in location", and "is part of".

The ability to cue targets and exemplars in multimedia, using media potentially personalised to that child's affinities (e.g., matching colour using a favourite object, such as a train), or context (e.g., using audio spoken by the child's family or friends), increases the child's engagement with the therapy. The same platform can also provide rewards, such as games, for completing a target number of sessions. In addition, prompting and reinforcing the correct answer is an integral part of therapy, and again multimedia-based delivery accords an advantage over paper-based methods.

Computer-delivered therapy makes trivial logging and reporting, a fundamental and labour-intensive part of ABA. All of a given child's sessions are stored, which eases integration of therapy across locations (e.g., home to clinic), and when Playpad is deployed in the role of a wait-list program, enables the child to transition to professional therapy with a known performance history.

3. EVALUATION

Trials of the system using matching tasks have proved it effective at training both adults and autistic children. We are continuing to extend the curriculum by adding new tasks and concepts. Our framework for stimulus delivery can easily adapt to both the therapists goals and the child's needs.

4. REFERENCES

[1] K. Blocher and R.W. Picard. Affective social quest: emotion recognition therapy for autistic children. In *In Socially Intelligent Agents-Creating Relationships with Computers and Robots.* Kluwer Academic Pub., 2002.

[2] J.A. Kientz, G.R. Hayes, T.L. Westeyn, T. Starner, and G.D. Abowd. Pervasive computing and autism: Assisting caregivers of children with special needs. *IEEE Pervasive Computing*, pages 28–35, 2007.

[3] O.I. Lovaas. Behavioral treatment and normal educational and intellectual functioning in young autistic children. *Journal of consulting and clinical psychology*, 55(1):3–9, 1987.

iCabinet: Stand-alone Implementation of a Method for Preventing Illegal Recording of Displayed Content by Adding Invisible Noise Signals

Takayuki Yamada
Graduate University for Advanced Studies
2-1-2, Hitotsubashi, Chiyoda-ku, Tokyo, 101-8430, JAPAN
nii20081705@nii.ac.jp

Seiichi Gohshi
Kogakuin University
1-24-2, Nishi-Shinjuku, Shinjuku-ku, Tokyo, 163-8677, JAPAN
gohshi@cc.kogakuin.ac.jp

Isao Echizen
National Institute of Informatics
2-1-2, Hitotsubashi, Chiyoda-ku, Tokyo, 101-8430, JAPAN
iechizen@nii.ac.jp

ABSTRACT

A previously proposed method for preventing the illegal recording of displayed content by adding invisible noise signals to the recorded content during recording to make it unrecognizable has now been implemented in a stand-alone cabinet. Testing using the prototype stand-alone implementation demonstrated that it can effectively prevent illegal recording of displayed content by completely corrupting the recorded content. This illegal recording prevention method is applicable not only to content displayed on a screen but also to other things that should be protected against illegal recording such as confidential documents in a public office and art objects in a museum.

Categories and Subject Descriptors: H.4.0 General

General Terms: Design, Experimentation, Management, Security

Keywords: Copyright violation, Information leakage, Illegal recording, Content display, Infrared LED

1. INTRODUCTION

High-quality digital content, such as photos and videos shot by individuals, is now widely available due to the rapid growth of broadband networks and the popularity of high-performance consumer audio/video equipment. Anyone these days can easily shoot photos and videos by using a camera or camcorder and then share them over the Internet. A serious problem, however, is copyright violation and information leakage through recording of content shown on a display. Displayed content can easily be recorded using a camera or camcorder and then made available through the Internet or sold illegally on recording media such as DVDs. Content such as video data on commercial DVDs and confidential/personal data in enterprise databases is usually encrypted and can only be decrypted and displayed by users with the decryption key. However, when that content is shown on a display, it can be illegally recorded by using a digital camera or camcorder, thereby bypassing the protection offered by the encryption. Preventing the illegal recording of content shown on displays is thus essential for preventing copyright violation and information leakage. Digital watermarking technology can be used to trace the flow of illegally recorded content [1, 2], but it cannot be used to directly prevent a person from using a camcorder to record content being shown on a display.

MM'11, November 28-December 1, 2011, Scottsdale, Arizona, USA.
ACM 978-1-4503-0616-4/11/11.

We previously proposed a method for preventing the illegal recording of films at movie theaters that is based on the difference between human sensory perception and recording device characteristics and implemented it on a 100-inch cinema screen [3, 4]. It uses infrared (IR) rays to corrupt the recorded content with noise signals that are invisible to the naked eye but are picked up by the CCD or CMOS device in the camera. The IR emission units are mounted behind the screen. Since a cinema screen has many tiny holes (~1 mm in diameter) for letting sound from the back speakers pass through, the IR light output from these units can pass through the screen.

We have now developed an implementation of this method so that it can be used without modifying the display. Instead of mounting the components in the projection screen, they are mounted in a stand-alone cabinet comprising an IR emission unit, a half-silvered mirror, and a microlouver filter. Section 2 briefly reviews our illegal recording prevention method. Section 3 describes the prototype stand-alone implementation and the results of our experimental evaluation. Section 4 briefly summarizes the key points.

2. ILLEGAL RECORDING PREVENTION METHOD

As mentioned above, our proposed method for preventing the illegal recording of images and videos is based on the differences between human sensory perception and recording device characteristics. It uses IR rays to corrupt the recorded content by adding invisible noise signals generated by a CCD or a CMOS device during recording [3, 4]. According to the International Commission on Illumination (CIE), the wavelengths of visible light range from 380 to 780 nm [5]. In contrast, the wavelengths that can be picked up by the image sensor devices, such as CCDs and CMOS devices, used in digital cameras and camcorders range from 200 to 1100 nm. Because they can pick up wavelengths outside the visible range, digital camcorders have the high level of luminous sensitivity needed for shooting in the dark. Our proposed method prevents the recording of images and videos by adding a noise signal corresponding to the near IR rays between 800 and 1000 nm, which humans cannot see but to which sensor devices can react. The noise signal is added by devices implemented in the projection screen, so new functions do not need to be added to the camera user's equipment.

3. PROTOTYPE STAND-ALONE IMPLEMENTATION

3.1 Description

The prototype stand-alone implementation (iCabinet) is shown in Figs. 1 and 2. It was designed for use with a 4.2-inch liquid crystal display (LCD). It has an IR emission unit, a half-silvered mirror, and a microlouver filter. The IR emission unit is comprised of 174 infrared LEDs with a peak wavelength of 870 nm and a short-wavelength cut filter with a cut-on wavelength of 870 nm (cut ratio: 50%). The cut filter eliminates the LED emissions so that they do not degrade the displayed content [3, 4]. The half-silvered mirror (pass-through rate: 30%) reflects the IR light from the IR emission unit toward the viewing area and lets the displayed image pass through toward the viewing area. The microlouver filter (viewing angle: 30° to left and to right) is used to prevent recording from an oblique direction. The stand-alone cabinet is simply set in front of the display without any physical attachment to the display.

(a) Side (b) Front

Fig. 1. Prototype stand-alone implementation (iCabinet).

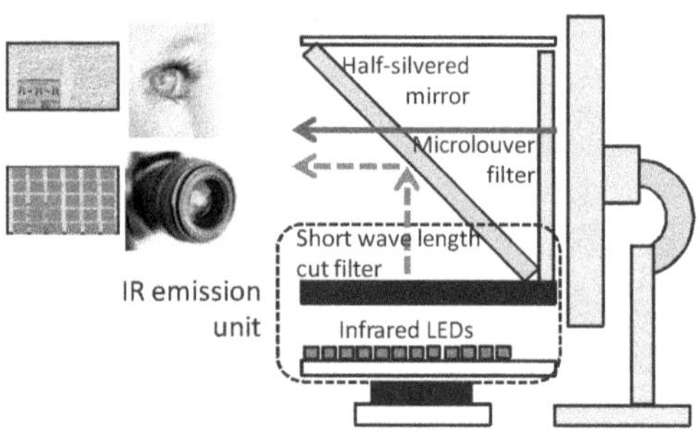

Fig. 2. System configuration.

3.2 Evaluation

We evaluated our stand-alone package using three samples for the displayed content (a journal article, a road map, and an aerial image). First, using a 1/2.3-inch CCD-based camera and a cell phone with a CMOS-based camera, we captured images of the samples when they were displayed on the 4.2-inch LCD without and with the prototype implementation. Next, ten people (seven men; three women; none an expert in image display technology) viewed the original samples when they were displayed on the 4.2-inch LCD with the prototype implementation. They then viewed the images captured of the displayed samples.

(a) Original samples viewed: All evaluators judged that the noise signal added by the prototype implementation was imperceptible for all samples. This confirmed that using the short-wavelength cut filter in the IR emission unit effectively prevents visual degradation of the displayed content.

(b) Recorded samples viewed: For both cameras, all evaluators were able to read or recognize the content for all images recorded without the prototype implementation but could not read or recognize it for any of the samples recorded with the prototype implementation.

Example content recorded using with the CCD-based digital camera with the prototype implementation is shown in Figure 3. As shown in Fig. 3(a), without IR emission, the content was clearly recorded. As shown in Fig. 3(b), IR emission completely corrupted the recorded content. The prototype implementation can thus prevent information leakage and copyright violation via displays.

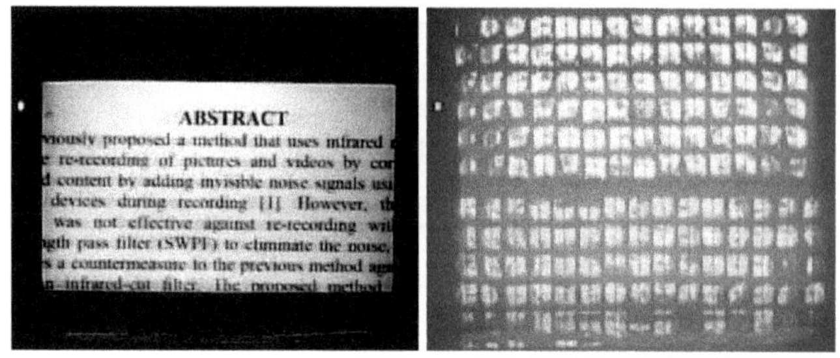

(a) Without IR emission (b) With IR emission

Fig. 3. Examples of displayed content.

4. CONCLUSION

Preventing people from illegally recording content shown on displays is essential for preventing information leakage and copyright violation. Digital watermarking technology cannot stop the recording of displayed content using cameras and camcorders. Our illegal recording prevention method corrupts the recorded content by adding invisible noise signals using a CCD or CMOS device during recording, making the recorded content unrecognizable. We have now implemented this method in a stand-alone cabinet. Testing using the prototype stand-alone implementation demonstrated that it can effectively prevent information leakage and copyright violation via display by completely corrupting the recorded content, which validates the feasibility of our illegal recording prevention method. Our illegal recording prevention method is applicable not only to content displayed on a screen but also to other things that should be protected against illegal recording such as confidential documents in a public office and art objects in a museum.

REFERENCES

[1] S. Gohshi et al., "A New Watermark Surviving After Re-shooting the Images Displayed on a Screen," *Proc. Knowledge-based Intelligent Information and Engineering Systems (KES 2005)*, LNAI 3682, pp. 1099–1107, 2005.

[2] J. Haitsma and T. Kalker, "A Watermarking Scheme for Digital Cinema," *Proc. 2001 International Conference on Image Processing (ICIP 2001)*, vol. 2, pp. 487–489, 2001.

[3] T. Yamada et al., "Preventing re-recording based on difference between sensory perceptions of humans and devices," *Proc. of the 17th International Conference on Image Processing (ICIP 2010)*, pp. 993–996, 2010.

[4] T. Yamada et al., "IR Hiding: A Method to Prevent Video Re-shooting by Exploiting Differences between Human Perceptions and Recording Device Characteristics," *Proc. of the 9th International Workshop on Digital Watermarking (IWDW 2010)*, LNCS 6526, pp. 280–292, Springer, 2010.

[5] J. Schanda (Ed.), "Colorimetry: Understanding the CIE System," Wiley-Interscience, 2007.

Purposive Hidden-Object Game (P-HOG) Towards Imperceptible Human Computation

Jian Dong, Yuzhao Ni, Jiashi Feng, and Shuicheng Yan
Dept. of Electrical and Computer Engineering, National University of Singapore, Singapore
{a0068947, dcsniy, a0066331, eleyans}@nus.edu.sg

ABSTRACT

This demonstration presents a novel purposive web game on iOS to collect object locations, named Purposive Hidden-Object-Game(P-HOG). Having su cient training images with known object locations is crucial for many multimedia tasks. P-HOG imperceptibly embeds localizing objects into the gaming process so that P-HOG preserves attractiveness to common players. During the game, players need to localize both automatically inserted known items and unknown objects (which are aimed to localize) to gain scores. The unknown objects are indicated by the re ned user-provided tags from photo sharing websites. The di culty mainly lies in how to insert known items naturally and thus preserve the game's playability. The P-HOG can be applied for constructing a large database, which contains located objects and may bene t general learning-based algorithms for multimedia tasks. The comprehensive experiments shows that P-HOG appeals to general players and can easily perform quality control, and hence e ective for collecting massive object locations with high accuracy.

Categories and Subject Descriptors

H.4 [**Information Systems Applications**]: Miscellaneous; D.2.8 [**Software Engineering**]: Metrics—*complexity measures, performance measures*

General Terms

Design

Keywords

Hidden Object Game, Human Computing, GWAP

1. INTRODUCTION

Many existing multimedia algorithms will bene t from a large-scale dataset with accurate object locations. Though the images with tags are available from many photo sharing websites, there are very few datasets with accurate object locations as the labeling is generally tedious and labor-intensive. Recently the emerging trend of games with a purpose (GWAP) has paved another way for more e ciently collecting such metadata [2]. GWAP aims at embedding the computational tasks in games and letting players implicitly solve the problem during game playing. However, the game mechanism used by most GWAPs are not attractive to common players, which hampers their e ectiveness.

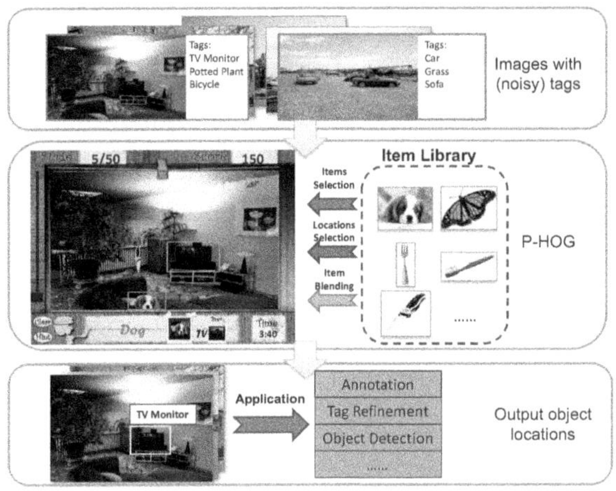

Figure 1: The system overview of the purposive hidden object game (P-HOG).

In this work, we develop a Purposive Hidden-Object-Game (P-HOG) based on the popular HOG games. Our system is able to hide known items into target image naturally by taking both the semantic and visual consistency into consideration. During the game, the players are required to nd those inserted items and original objects in the image, which are indicated by the re ned image tags. People play the game only for entertainment purpose and as a by-product we can collect large scale accurate object location information imperceptibly. Moreover, similar to the Captcha [1], inserted known items can be used to control the quality of the collected object locations.

2. SYSTEM ARCHITECTURE

Figure 1 illustrates the system architecture of P-HOG. (1) Images with noisy tags are obtained from the photo sharing websites and fed into the P-HOG system. (2) P-HOG automatically selects appropriate objects from the item library and inserts them naturally into the images. (3) After playing, the scores and annotations are sent back to the system. The re ned bounding boxes of the unknown objects are calculated based on the user annotations.

3. SYSTEM IMPLEMENTATION

We develop a three-step algorithm to insert objects naturally into images. First, given a target image, some appro-

MM'11, November 28–December 1, 2011, Scottsdale, Arizona, USA.
ACM 978-1-4503-0616-4/11/11.

priate items are selected to hide into it. The item selection is based on two criteria. The concept ltering is based on the Google distance between items and image tags, which helps remove items which are not likely to appear in the target image in the semantic sense. Then color ltering is performed to further remove the items with strong color contrast compared with the target image by calculating their color distribution di erence in LUV color space.

The second step involves selecting candidate locations to insert items. The selection criteria combine geometric and appearance consistencies. Patches of the over-segmented images are roughly categorized into three classes: ground, top(sky or ceiling) and other regions as in [3]. Items are inserted to the region with compatible geometric labels. For example, birds are placed in the sky. Among the regions with the same geometric label, the one with similar color to the selected item is preferred. Shape is also a useful cue for candidate location selection. Intuitively, it will be more natural for the object to be added into the region whose shape matches the item's. Shapes of the regions and items are roughly described by a tted ellipse. Then the system matches the patches with the items having similar shape features.

Once we have chosen the items and their target locations in the image, some image blending techniques are applied for seamlessly composing foreground items and the background images. In general, Alpha Matting [6] is used to conceal the artifacts long the item boundary. Besides, we utilize [4] to determine the correct size of the items in the image by considering the spatial layout of the background. Finally, we modify the color transfer method developed in [5] and impose the same color distribution on a item as that of its target region so that it appears more natural in the image.

4. DATA COLLECTION

The purpose of this work is to imperceptibly implant human computation into enjoyable game playing process. During game playing, the background program will record the bounding boxes provided by the users and automatically align them with the item tags. The gained scores of users annotation is calculated based on their accuracy on the known items. And the score further indicates the con dence of the bounding boxes of the unknown items provided by certain user. Thus bounding boxes with poor accuracy can be l-tered based on the con dence. The nal localization for each object is obtained by averaging of the collected bounding boxes from all users in a weighted manner.

5. EXPERIMENTS

To evaluate the e ectiveness of P-HOG, we compare it with two classical online HOG games [1] in three facets as indicated in the left panel of Figure 2. 30 volunteers are invited to play all the three games. The result shows that P-HOG is comparable to other two game in terms of interestingness, challenging, and naturalness. We also investigate whether users are more glad to label images using P-HOG than conventional image labeling tools. The right panel of Figure 2 shows that P-HOG is more attractive. Moreover, the object location accuracy via P-HOG is evaluated on the VOC2007 dataset. The results are shown in Figure 3. It can be seen that the nal bounding boxes returned by P-HOG are comparable in accuracy with the ground truth provided by the dataset.

[1]http://games-free-online.net/?a=game&id=558
http://games-free-online.net/?a=game&id=617

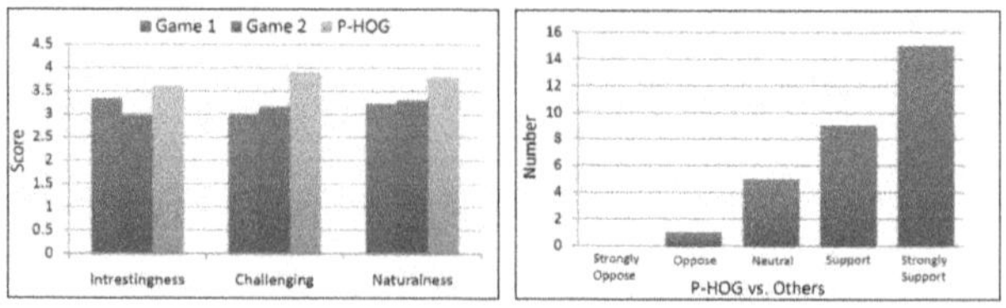

Figure 2: Result of user study. Left: Users ranking on the P-HOG compared with two other games. Right: Users voting on whether they prefer P-HOG than LabelMe and Peekaboom

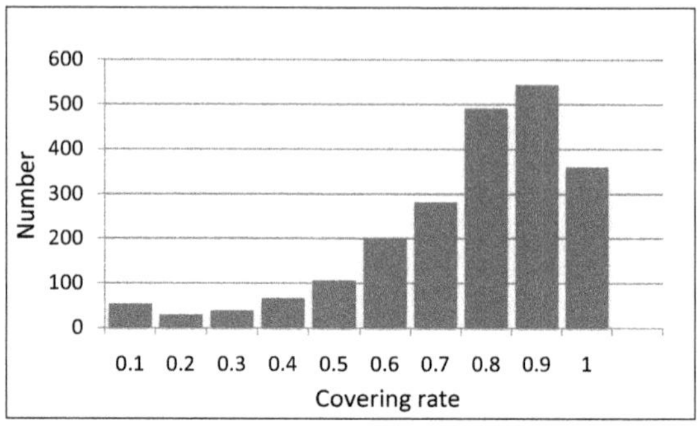

Figure 3: Covering rates of the bounding boxes obtained via P-HOG over the ground truths.

6. CONCLUSIONS AND FUTURE WORK

In this work, we propose the Purposive Hidden Object Game (P-HOG) to seamlessly embed localizing objects into the popular HOG game. Through the P-HOG, massive object location information can be imperceptively collected during game playing governed by a built-in data quality controlling mechanism. The work also points out that it is more reasonable to embed human computation to existing popular games than to design entirely new games. In the future, we may further investigate embedding human computations into other popular web games.

7. ACKNOWLEDGMENTS

This work is supported by the CSIDM Project No.CSIDM-200803 partially funded by a grant from the National Research Foundation (NRF) administered by the Media Development Authority (MDA) of Singapore.

8. REFERENCES

[1] L. Ahn, M. Blum, and J. Langford. Telling humans and computers apart automatically. *Commun. ACM*, 2004.
[2] L. Ahn and L. Dabbish. Labeling images with a computer game. In *CHI*, 2004.
[3] D. Hoiem, A. Efros, and M. Hebert. Recovering surface layout from an image. *I CV*, 2007.
[4] J. Lalonde, D. Hoiem, A. Efros, C. Rother, J. Winn, and A. Criminisi. Photo clip art. , 2007.
[5] E. Reinhard, M. Ashikhmin, B. Gooch, and P. Shirley. Color transfer between images. *C A*, 2001.
[6] J. Wang and M. Cohen. Image and video matting: A survey. *C V*, 2007.

StoryImaging: A Media-Rich Presentation System for Textual Stories

Genliang Guan
School of Information Technologies
University of Sydney, Australia
genliang.guan@sydney.edu.au

Zhiyong Wang
School of Information Technologies
University of Sydney, Australia
zhiyong.wang@sydney.edu.au

Xian-Sheng Hua
Microsoft
One Microsoft Way,Redmond, WA 98052
xshua@microsoft.com

Dagan Feng
School of Information Technologies
University of Sydney, Australia
feng@it.usyd.edu.au

ABSTRACT

In this demo, we develop the *StoryImaging* system to illustrate a textual story with both images harvested from the Web and synthesized speech. At the backend, a story is firstly processed to identify key terms such as named entities and to obtain the story summary. With the aid of commercial search engines, images are then collected from the Web for those key terms and re-ranked by taking the summary as context. At last, images are clustered to provide an overview of the story. At the web-based frontend, the user interface has been tailored to both improve information comprehension and provide engaging and explorative experiences for users by closely bridging textual and visual modalities.

Categories and Subject Descriptors

H.3.3 [**Information Storage and retrieval**]: Information Search and Retrieval; H.4 [**Information Systems Applications**]: Miscellaneous

General Terms

Algorithms, Experimentation

Keywords

Story imaging, story illustration, re-ranking, clustering, cross-media

1. INTRODUCTION

As said, one picture is worth a thousand words. The expressiveness of images makes comprehending information more effective and enjoyable. With the progress in image retrieval technologies and commercial image search engines nowadays, people have less troubles in finding relevant images for specific information need (e.g. place and person) with short queries consisting of a small number of keywords. However, in the scenario of comprehending some documents, such as news stories and biographies, users have to manually extract keywords from prior reading and understanding of each sentence, and query them by groups or one by one when being confronted with unknown information (e.g. the person of an unknown name). This process apparently has several issues. First of all, current commercial search engines often limit the text input to a small number of keywords. Users are forced to perform several, if not many, queries instead of one to obtain the most relevant images for a story, which often leads to interruption of reading experiences. Secondly, submitting multiple queries would significantly lose the contextual information and cohesion between sentences, which is critical in understanding the general idea of a story. Thirdly, it imposes extra burden to users in distilling a large number of results originated from a number of queries. Last but not least, the results may contain duplicates or near duplicates that causes information overloading.

Since traditional search engines are not able to address the above issues with rich content such as images, Story Picturing Engine (SPE) [1] made an attempt to this problem. It consists of three steps: 1) identifying semantic keywords from input texts; 2) searching a database of annotated images with those keywords for candidate images; and 3) selecting images from the candidate images with mutual-reinforcement-based rank. However, it worked only on a small closed database and semantic keywords were limited to objects such as flower and car. In addition, the global context of the story was not taken into account. Moreover, named entities such as persons and places, are the key elements of a story but were neglected.

Therefore, we propose a system, namely *StoryImaging*, to solve the aforementioned problems so as to bridge the gap between the textual and visual modalities with abundant web resources, whose interface also reinforce the cross-media linking between sentences and images. In order to further engage users in information comprehension by eliminating the dependence on text, synthesized speech is also generated for stories.

2. *STORYIMAGING* SYSTEM BACKEND

This paper briefly touches the technical ingredients in the backend and focuses on the frontend user interface. In general, our *StoryImaging* system automatically fetches images from the Web and chooses suitable ones for the visual illustration of a given text story. As shown in Figure 1, our system consists of five steps, text analysis, image search, search result reranking, near duplicate removal, and image clustering. Text analysis includes Part-of-Speech (POS)

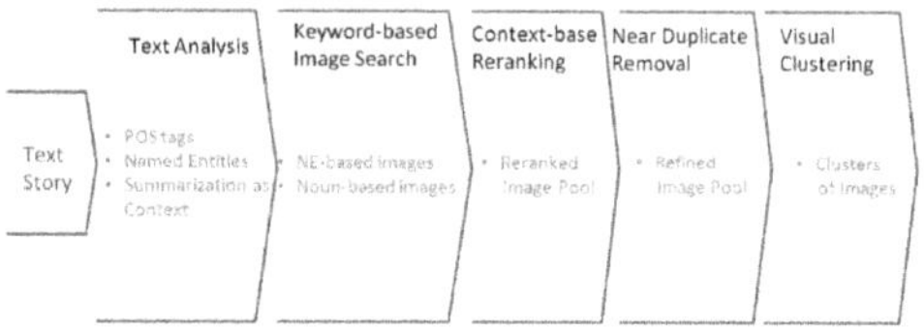

Figure 1: ***StoryImaging* System Backend**

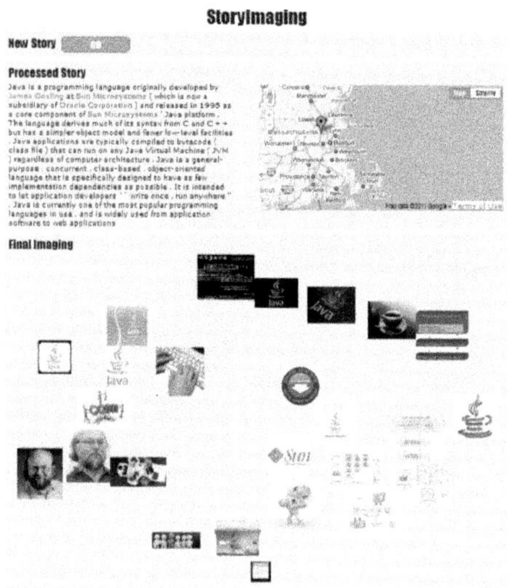

Figure 2: ***StoryImaging* System Frontend**

tagging for extracting noun words, identification of named entities (NE), and summarization of the text story for the following reranking process. Image search is to collect an initial set of images by issuing queries based on named entities and key terms in each sentence. The Reranking process measures the relatedness between a candidate image's web page and the text summary so as to find out the story-related images, followed by near duplicate removal. At the end visual clustering helps display the images into visual groups in order to provide an overview of the story and enable flexible exploration.

3. *STORYIMAGING* SYSTEM FRONTEND

StoryImaging utilizes a web-based frontend so it can be easily accessed through any browser. Currently it uses WebSocket, which is part of the latest HTML5 standard, to transfer the data successively from the backend. The frontend is divided into three parts, story input, processed story with a location map, and the final image clustering output. A screenshot of a the frontend is shown in Figure 2. Users input a story into the textarea and submit it, or use the bookmarklet to quickly illustrate the selected text in any website. Different from traditional image searching interfaces where images are listed in a flat list with relevant keywords highlighted for each, the frontend of *StoryImaging* system emphasizes the key terms within the story, the visual clusters of the resulting images, and the correspondence between sentences and images so as to improve both text and image comprehension. Showcases of two text story illustrations are included in the supplementary video.

Processed Story. After text analysis with natural language processing techniques at the backend, the processed output is displayed to the user with proper named entities highlighted. This helps user to quickly identify key subjects in the story. Locations and organizations are geocoded on the fly to provide geographic information. The map will also be collapsed if no location information is available.

Final Image Clustering. When it receives the clustering results, the frontend will render the images onto a canvas element using the Forced-Directed Graph algorithm. Visual groups are automatically formed, and users can easily capture the semantic meaning of each group instead of looking at a page of mixed images with different meanings (as being returned from different queries of keywords) and visual content. For instance, in the demo video for illustration of a story about Beijing (excerpted from Wikipedia), we can spot the maps, nightscapes and several groups of daylight scenery with ease. In regards to the demo for Java, logos and images describing the Java architecture are clearly separated as shown in Figure 2. In addition, by clicking each image thumbnail, the full-sized image flies out to show more details.

Cross-Media Linking. Sentences and images are interrelated. On the one hand, when the cursor hovers over a sentence, images not corresponding to this sentence become semi-transparent; hence users can easily find the relevant images and locate their visual groups. Clicking on a sentence triggers the slideshow of corresponding images with captions, and synthesized apeech is played to enhance the multimedia experience. On the other hand, hovering over an image will highlight the corresponding sentence within the processed text story, and keywords used for querying this image will also be floating on top of the image. As a result, the linking of text and images preserves their inherent relation by which images are collected, and users will not get lost when facing with a long text story and a pool of images.

Bookmarklet. A bookmarklet is a small Javascript application that can be triggered on any website. The *StoryImaging* bookmarklet launches the processing when a user highlights a piece of text story on a webpage, such as Wikipedia or news portals, and click the bookmarklet. A new window/tab will be opened to show the illustration result. Instead of tedious copy and paste, this simple yet useful technique enables one-click illustration to save efforts and delivers a smooth experience to users.

Speed. The near-realtime response is based on efficient near-duplicate removal and visual clustering. The processing time is mainly affected by image search through commercial search engines. On a Core2 E8600 machine, it roughly cost ten seconds for processing a text story of 200 words. Speed would be further improved by multi-thread downloading and feature extraction.

4. CONCLUSIONS AND FUTURE WORKS

In this technical demo, we present *StoryImaging* system which has a novel user interface backed by an image retrieval system proposed to address the task of story illustration. Our backend system generates the key terms highlighted text output and image clusters, and the frontend presents this information in a compact and organized way to facilitate within-text and within-images understanding, and reinforce the text-to-image and image-to-text correlation. In the future, other modalities such as video and audio will be integrated in augmenting textual information so as to eventually achieve multimedia story illustration.

5. ACKNOWLEDGMENT

The work presented in this paper is partially supported by ARC.

6. REFERENCES

[1] D. Joshi, J. Z. Wang, and J. Li. The story picturing engine—a system for automatic text illustration. *ACM Transactions on Multimedia Computing, Communications, and Applications*, 2:68–89, 2006.

TapTell: Understanding Visual Intents On-The-Go*

Ning Zhang †, Tao Mei ‡, Xian-Sheng Hua ‡, Ling Guan †, Shipeng Li ‡

† Ryerson Multimedia Research Laboratory, Ryerson University, Toronto, Ontario, Canada, M5B 2K3
‡ Microsoft Research Asia, Beijing 100080, P. R. China
† {n2zhang, lguan}@ee.ryerson.ca ‡ {tmei, xshua, spli}@microsoft.com

ABSTRACT

This demonstration presents a mobile-based visual recognition and recommendation application on Windows Phone 7 called TapTell. This is different from other mobile-based visual search mechanisms which merely focus on the search process. TapTell firstly discovers and understands users' visual intents via a circle based natural user interaction called "O" gestures. Following, a *Tap* action is operated to choose the "O" gestured regions. The context-aware visual search mechanism is utilized for recognizing the intents and associating them with indexed metadata. Finally, the *Tell* action recommends relevant entities utilizing contextual information. The TapTell system has been evaluated at different scenarios on million scale images.

Categories and Subject Descriptors

H.3.3 [**Information Storage and Retrieval**]: Information search and retrieval—*Search process*; H.5.2 [**Information Interfaces and Presentation**]: User interface—*User-centered design*

General Terms

Algorithms, Experiments, Human Factors

Keywords

Visual intent, mobile visual search, mobile recommendation.

1. INTRODUCTION

Mobile devices have played an important role in everyday life, much more powerful than their traditional telephony function. Due to its on-the-go characteristic, the mobile device is more versatile with a search function for providing useful information. However, conventional text and voice based search queries are not always operable due to the limitations of device input for keying text as well as often noisy environment which jeopardizes the voice input quality.

Alternatively, mobile based visual search has recently drawn attention from both academia and industry. Such visual based query is complementary to traditional text/voice queries. It performs better when users search intents are more precisely described in pictures than keywords. In industry, Google and Bing incorporate visual search in their mobile version of the search engines. In academia, researchers focus more on the compact feature expression for mobile transmission as well as contextual side information such as GPS location [2, 3]. However, both industry and research communities focus on the search and recognition tasks and pay less attention to the recommendation, which we believe are equally important. This is because the mobile device is highly personal with multi-sensors. By combining personal and local information, reasonable recommendation can be provided.

In this demonstration, we present a novel mobile based recognition and recommendation system called TapTell. This system involves a natural user interaction which seamlessly connects user intelligence to fill the semantic gap. Then recommendations are suggested based on the contextual entity and location information.

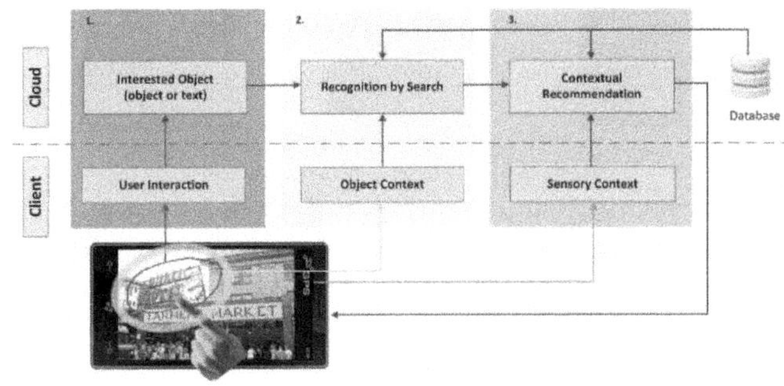

Figure 1: a flowchart of the TapTell, with a specified three-stage process: (1) intent expression; (2) intent prediction; and (3) entity recommendation.

2. SYSTEM ARCHITECTURE

The system consists of both a client and a cloud end, where the former is realized at the front-end mobile device and the latter is processed at the back-end server. A three-stage process is summarized and illustrated in Figure 1: (1) **intent expression** is achieved by a circle based user interaction called "O" gesture at the client and an interest object selection at the cloud; (2) **intent prediction** is realized as a recognition by search mechanism to identify either highlighted visual object or text region from users' specification, with the help of both selected object as well as the surrounding visual context; (3) **entity recommendation** as the final mission completion, is accomplished with the help of sensory context and associated metadata.

* This work was performed at Microsoft Research Asia.

MM'11, November 28–December 1, 2011, Scottsdale, Arizona, USA.
ACM 978-1-4503-0616-4/11/11.

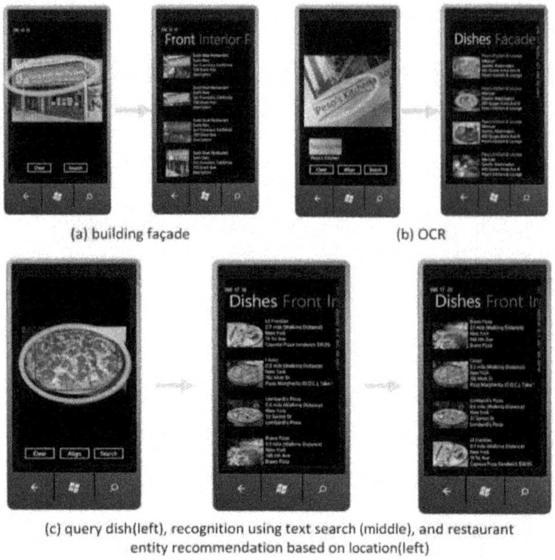

Figure 2: Snapshots of TapTell with three different scenarios. A user can take a photo, specify his/her interested object or text via "O" gestures, and then get the recognition and recommendation results through TapTell.

3. SYSTEM IMPLEMENTATION

3.1 User Intent Expression on the Client

A natural user interaction "O" gesture base on the mobile touch screen is proposed, such that users' intents are specified naturally and robustly. Therefore, object of interest (including either visual or textual intent) is selected from an image of multiple objects. As a result, accurate visual or textual intents are delivered via this user mobile interaction. Moreover, this "O" gesture requires no training and can be naturally engaged with the users. It also provides a robust interaction such that neither exact silhouette nor closed circle drawing is required.

3.2 Visual Intent Prediction on the Cloud

A recognition by search mechanism is adopted based on a scalable visual vocabulary tree method [4]. Database images are indexed based on the vocabulary tree and thus a very fast visual search can be realized on million scale image dataset. In image context-based search, a soft weighting scheme is proposed to combine the enclosed and the outside portions of the "O" gestured region. Therefore, image context also participates in searching for the query object and better performance is achieved than the usage of the "O" regions only.

Geo-location based context information collected by mobile sensors plays an important role in identifying the visual intent by filtering out the non-relevant images. This is due to the mobile nature of the smart devices as well as the on-the-go demands from the user intent. In our system, the Bing Maps Tile system is utilized and quadkey hashing method is used to quantize the GPS information to a computable representation, with the ground resolution of 305m as the effective regions in the filtering process [1].

Optical characteristic recognition (OCR) is useful in recognizing the textual intents from the visual input. However, most current OCR methods fail because of noisy background and tilted characters. Using "O" gesture, both the noise background is pruned and the tilted characters which were hard to recognize can be realigned for a better recognition. The realignment technique is based on a transform invariant low-rank textures approach [6].

3.3 Contextual Entity Recommendation

After recognizing the intent embedded in a visual input, we take the top return result which we hope is the duplicate of the input visual query. We then explore its metadata and extract the keywords from it in order to apply a text-based search. The Okapi BM25 ranking function is used by projecting these keywords to a pre-computed dictionary [5]. The text-based retrieval result is reranked using the contextual information in order to recommend contextual entity in certain criteria. In the application, we use the geolocation distance criterion to rerank the entities from the nearest to the furthest in distance.

4. SYSTEM DEMONSTRATION

Figure 2 shows the TapTell interface with the recognition and recommendation results. The system covers three scenarios of common mobile-based visual intents, i.e. the building façade; the OCR recognition with the tilted characters; and the dish recognition and restaurant entity recommendation based on the geolocation distance. We perform a mean average precision (MAP) metric on random selected 306 dish photos. The MAP at top 5 return positions of the contextual entity recommendation has an average of 73.3%. A subjective evaluation also demonstrates the merit of the proposed system, with the overall satisfactory of 4.1/5, based on a 13 users feedback.

5. CONCLUSIONS

We have demonstrated a visual intents recognition and recommendation system named TapTell on the mobile device that supports a visual input. This system complements the conventional text/voice query search on-the-go and presents its merit in certain scenarios of visual object search, OCR recognition, as well as interesting entity recommendation. Moreover, the TapTell system has potential to support more on-the-go situations, where visual input is more convenient to be captured than its counterparts in the text/voice domain.

6. ACKNOWLEDGMENTS

The authors would like to thank Mr. Xin Lin for his help in building the TapTell application.

7. REFERENCES

[1] http://msdn.microsoft.com/en-us/library/bb259689.aspx.

[2] V. Chandrasekhar *et al.* CHoG: Compressed histogram of gradients A low bit-rate feature descriptor. In *Proc. of IEEE CVPR*, pages 2504–2511, 2009.

[3] L.-Y. Duan and W. Gao. Side Discriminative Mobile Visual Search. In *Workshop on Mobile Visual Search*, 2011.

[4] D. Nister and H. Stewenius. Scalable recognition with a vocabulary tree. In *Proc. IEEE CVPR*, pages 2161–2168, 2006.

[5] S. Robertson and H. Zaragoza. The probabilistic relevance framework: BM25 and beyond. *Information Retrieval*, 3(4):333–389, 2009.

[6] Z. Zhang, X. Liang, A. Ganesh, and Y. Ma. TILT: transform invariant low-rank textures. *Proc. of ACCV*, pages 314–328, 2011.

A Mobile Player for Interactive Non-linear Video

Britta Meixner
Chair of Distributed Information Systems, University of Passau, Germany
meixner@fim.uni-passau.de

Johannes Köstler
University of Passau, Germany
koestler@fim.uni-passau.de

Harald Kosch
Chair of Distributed Information Systems, University of Passau, Germany
harald.kosch@uni-passau.de

ABSTRACT

With rapid improvements in available bandwidth and processing power of smart phones, the presentation of interactive non-linear video became possible. Web players for these form of video already exist, they usually have a video area and one or more annotation areas. Most of them can not be used for mobile phones because of their space consuming representation. This work presents a player to display interactive nonlinear videos on Android smart phones. The small display size and the possibility to switch between portrait and landscape mode have been taken into account. The player also provides functions to manage a library of downloaded interactive videos for off line use as well as bookmarks.

Categories and Subject Descriptors

H.5.2 [**Information Interfaces and Presentation**]: User Interfaces—*Interaction styles*; H.5.4 [**Information Interfaces and Presentation**]: Hypertext/Hypermedia—*Navigation, User issues*

General Terms

Human factors, Design

Keywords

Interactive Video, Non-linear Video, Video Annotations, Mobile Video Player

1. INTRODUCTION

Interactive videos are distributing more and more nowadays with increasing bandwidths to the Internet and cheaper end-user cameras. Many tools exist that allow an easy editing and annotation of videos (see [8]). Various web players are provided with these tools to display the output them. As smart phones become more and more popular and the bandwidths for these devices grow, interactive video can be played on these devices, too. But this leads to the problem of arranging the video and all information that have to be displayed with the video on a quite small display. Solutions have to be designed how the display can be split or how the viewer can be alerted if an annotation is available (if not displayed). Another problem is an intelligent download management and a library function for saved videos. This function allows the user to download the videos for displaying them, even if no connection to the Internet is available.

MM'11, November 28–December 1, 2011, Scottsdale, Arizona, USA.
ACM 978-1-4503-0616-4/11/11.

2. DEMONSTRATION

A mobile player for interactive non-linear video is proposed to be demonstrated at ACM Multimedia 2011. Viewers of the video are able to choose their own way through the video by clicking one of the buttons and selecting the next scene doing this. Each scene provides additional information containing details about the scene. During the presentation of the video, all functions of the player like the display of the video in two modes, the annotation observer or the table of contents are shown.

3. RELATED WORK

Browsing through a list of thumbnails representing the video content is introduced in the work of [6]. The size of thumbnails can be manipulated doing this. This work only deals with linear video where no additional information is displayed with the video content. The video is displayed at full size. [7] evaluated the size of static and dynamic video thumbnails. The results showed that even at small sizes, the content of dynamic thumbnails is still recognized by the viewers. This leads to the conclusion that it is possible to display the video at a smaller size than the full screen of a smart phone, which enables us to display additional information with the video. A similar form of interactivity and parallel courses of action like in interactive video can be found in [4]. Enhanced forms of content are represented in a mobile streaming environment. The viewer is able to zoom into the video, select one of the different provided streams or focus on regions of interest. No related work can be found in the area of displaying interactive non-linear video.

4. PLAYER

The mobile player for interactive non-linear video, called SIVID Player, has to fulfill the same requirements as the web player introduced in [8]. It reads the XML-file with the description of the order of the scenes and the points in time where annotations are displayed and hidden. Different actions are triggered to load new scenes, to display annotations, to show a button panel for the selection of the further course of the video or to end the video. A video control for play, pause and stop is shown as well as a table of contents as an additional form of navigation. A scheduler manages all elements that are displayed with the video in order to

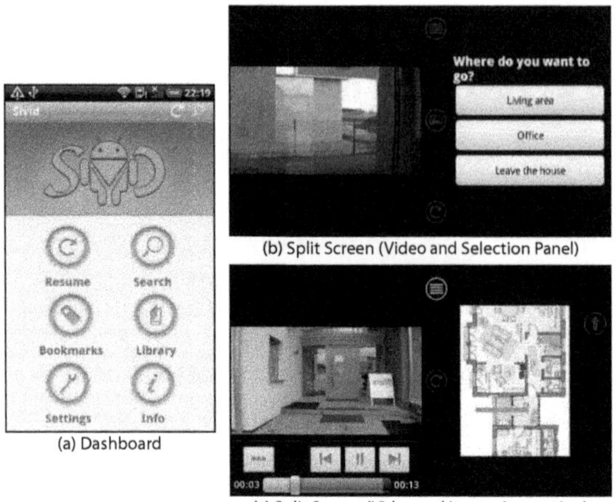

(a) Dashboard

(b) Split Screen (Video and Selection Panel)

(c) Split Screen (Video and Image Annotation)

Figure 1: Management and Video Player Screen of the SIVID Player

refresh the annotations displayed when fast-forward or fast-backward stops or the user jumps to a point in time in the scene. If different languages are defined in the XML-file, a control is provided to switch between them.

Beyond these functions, the SIVID Player has to fulfill further requirements. Additional contents can not be displayed in annotation areas arranged around the main video because of the lack of display space. An annotation observer at one side of the display indicates that one or more annotations of a certain type are available at a particular point in time. The viewer can chose if the annotation should be displayed by touching the annotation observer. The SIVID Player has three display modes. The full screen mode only shows the video and the annotation observer. A split screen mode (see figure 1, (a)) shows the video and a scrollable annotation stack. A long touch on the annotation pauses the main video and displays the annotation stack on the full screen. This is very useful if the scene is annotated with long texts or annotations the viewer wants to view in detail. The display modes are implemented for two orientations, the portrait and the landscape mode.

Annotations are downloaded or buffered up to a certain point in an application cache. The advantage of this cache is that the elements are kept in the cache if the application is interrupted, for example from a phone call. The home screen of the application is based on the dashboard-pattern [5] and shown in figure 1, (b). It provides six different functions. One is for resuming a video that was displayed before. A function for searching interactive videos on the Web or searching in the local library is implemented. Bookmarks that were set in videos which were displayed before can be shown in a list. A library provides an overview over videos that were downloaded before with an intelligent download function. The behavior of the application can be configured in a settings dialog. Information about the application is shown in an info panel. Wherever it is possible, GUI-patterns ([5] and [1]) are used for a better user experience.

The Android SDK is used for the development of the SIVID Player because of powerfulness and its range of functions. It also provides a high performance because no additional runtime environment is needed and code can be executed natively. Furthermore a wide range of codecs is supported. The code itself runs in a Dalvik Virtual Machine (DVM) based on the free Apache Harmony JVM (see [3] pp. 21). A message based MVC pattern as described in [9] is used as well as techniques for better code performance like the principle of simplicity, the avoidance of encapsulation, the waiver of getters and setters and the usage or the avoidance of certain structures or datatypes (see [2] and [3]).

5. CONCLUSION

A mobile player for interactive non-linear video is presented in this work. It allows users to display the video and all annotations provided with the video as well as enhanced forms of video navigation. Various player settings allow users with small bandwidth or smart phones with a low CPU power to watch the video anyway. Further work includes usability tests and improvements of the software as well as a quiz function that can be used for the assessment of training success in e-learning videos.

6. ACKNOWLEDGMENTS

This work was partially supported by European Social Fonds and the Bayrisches Staatsministerium für Wissenschaft, Forschung und Kunst (Bavarian State Ministry of Sciences, Research and the Arts) under project name "iVi-Pro 2.0".

7. REFERENCES

[1] Android ui design patterns (05/05/2011). http://www.androiduipatterns.com/p/android-ui-pattern-collection.html.

[2] Designing for performance (05/05/2011). http://developer.android.com/guide/practices/design/performance.html.

[3] A. Becker and M. Pant. *Android 2 - Grundlagen und Programmierung*. dpunkt.verlag, Heidelberg, 2. edition, May 2010.

[4] I. A. Fernandez, C. D. Vleeschouwer, F. Lavigne, and X. Desurmont. Worthy visual content on mobile through interactive video streaming. *IEEE Intl. Conf. on Multimedia and Expo*, pages 412–417, 2010.

[5] R. Fulcher, C. Nesladek, J. Palmer, and C. Robertson. Android ui design patterns (05/05/2011). http://dl.google.com/googleio/2010/android-android-ui-design-patterns.pdf.

[6] W. Hürst and P. Merkle. One-handed mobile video browsing. In *Proc. of the 1st intl. conf. on Designing interactive user experiences for TV and video*, UXTV '08, pages 169–178, New York, NY, USA, 2008. ACM.

[7] W. Hürst, C. G. Snoek, W.-J. Spoel, and M. Tomin. Keep moving!: revisiting thumbnails for mobile video retrieval. In *Proceedings of the international conference on Multimedia*, MM '10, pages 963–966, New York, NY, USA, 2010. ACM.

[8] B. Meixner, B. Siegel, G. Hölbling, F. Lehner, and H. Kosch. Siva suite: authoring system and player for interactive non-linear videos. In *Proc. of the intl. conf. on Multimedia*, MM '10, pages 1563–1566, New York, NY, USA, 2010. ACM.

[9] I. Memruk. Android architecture: Message-based mvc (05/05/2011). http://mindtherobot.com/blog/675/android-architecture-message-based-mvc/.

Real Time Extraction of Body Soft Biometric from 3D Videos

Carmelo Velardo and Jean-Luc Dugelay
Multimedia Department, EURECOM
2229 Route des Crêtes, 06560 Sophia Antipolis, France
velardo@eurecom.fr, dugelay@eurecom.fr

ABSTRACT

In this technical demonstration, we show the application of our research on body soft biometrics. Exploiting a 3D video sensor we are able to extract semantic information that describes subjects standing in front of a camera. Semantic analysis and tracking is performed, a series of anthropometric measures are extracted and used to compute subjects' height, weight, and gender information. Possible applications of such research fall in the medical domain for monitoring elderly people; in the gaming industry for automatic avatar creation, or in smart billboards which collects demographics of the public interested by the commercial. Our algorithm allows the estimation of all these parameters in real time without requiring the computational complexity of a 3D model fitting approach.

Categories and Subject Descriptors: H.5.2 [Information Interfaces and Presentation]: User Interfaces

General Terms: Experimentation, Verification.

Keywords: Soft biometrics, Kinect, user profiling, anthropometric measures.

1. INTRODUCTION

The explosion in the controller-free market of the gaming industry led to the proliferation of smart cameras that are able to extract more than just a 2D video. Sensors like Time of Flight cameras and Microsoft Kinect [1] allow to perceive the world by exploiting all the 4 dimensions. In our demonstration the Microsoft Kinect sensor, originally developed for gaming and natural user interaction, will be exploited to fill the gap between biometric theory and practice. Using off the shelves components and this new cheap sensor, we are able to extract semantic information from one or more users standing in front of the camera (see fig. 1). We convert this information into a soft biometric signature that profiles the user. In our case we will be able to extract the height, weight, and gender information of the user thanks to the application of our theoretical study based on anthropometric measures [2, 3].

In the following we will briefly describe the soft biometric characteristics that we are able to extract and the techniques that we developed to estimate the anthropometric measures from a RGBD video.

MM'11, November 28–December 1, 2011, Scottsdale, Arizona, USA.
ACM 978-1-4503-0616-4/11/11.

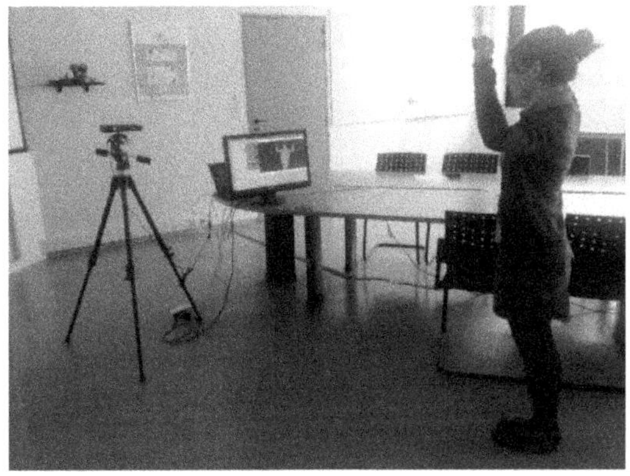

Figure 1: The setup of our demo. A person is standing in front of the sensor triggering the estimation phase by assuming the calibration pose.

2. BODY SOFT BIOMETRICS

Soft biometrics are traits that help to characterize people in predefined categories. Examples of soft biometric traits are the color of the hair or the eyes, the ethnicity, the stature, and the gait. They lack of the robustness which is necessary to discriminate among individuals. Nevertheless they can be extracted at a distance, they do not require users' cooperation, and they can enhance biometric systems' capabilities. We can identify three areas of interest: the soft biometrics related to the body, the ones extracted from the face, and the ones belonging to the accessories used in everyday life. To the first category belongs the height, the weight, and the gender, that are the principal targets of this study. Using such characteristics human are able to classify body into three main *phenotypes* (Ectomorph, Endomorph, and Mesomorph) which help them during the recognition process: for example, a physical description is of utmost importance in many cases of missing persons or for crimes investigations. In this work we introduce an automatic system that, by elaborating a 3D video stream, is able to extract semantic information related to one or more subjects facing the sensor. More precisely we extract the information about the height, the weight, and the gender of the person. Hereafter we will present a description of the soft biometric traits analyzed in this study.

2.1 Height

During his extensive study on how to apply projective geometry to computer vision, Criminisi was the first to explore the possibility of extracting geometrical information from 2D images. In [4] he gives details on how to reliably measure height of people standing in the field of view of a non calibrated camera. In our case we take advantage of the complexity of the Kinect capturing device that provides us with 3D information from the real world. The head and feet location of people facing the sensor are automatically extracted by our system so as to estimate user's stature.

2.2 Weight

Extracting weight information from images is not straightforward. Being an image a projective representation of the real world, it lacks measuring capabilities (it's a projection) and proportions can be lost (due to camera distortions). In [2] we already formulated a possible solution to the problem. A series of anthropometric measures is chosen to be representative of human's body. Combining this research outcome with the Kinect capabilities, we are able to extract anthropometric measures from a 3D video and apply our body mass estimator for each person that trigger our system.

2.3 Gender

Phenotypes refers to the *observable* characteristics which are embedded into our DNA (Genotype) and that define our human physical aspect. In the literature of gender classification many works concentrate their efforts for facial appearance analysis, others use gait sequences. Following our results in weight estimation, we use a trained Neural Network to classify the gender starting from the same set of anthropometric measures exploited to perform weight estimation.

3. ANTHROPOMEASURES EXTRACTION

Capturing the output of the Kinect with the OpenNI framework [5], and exploiting OpenCV [6] and PCL [7] open source libraries, we are able to extract the silhouette of people moving in front of the 3D sensor. A background subtraction and a blob tracking algorithm automatically segment and track each single user. Once a user is extracted, his/her bounding volume is extracted thanks to the cloud of points' coordinates. A sorting algorithm allow us to extract the information about the minima and the maxima in the 3D point cloud. To automatically measure height, we look for the head in the upper-central part of the bounding volume. Here we extract the 3D information for the outermost points of the silhouette. A similar approach is performed for the lower part were the feet are located. Height is then measured as distance between these two extrema (head and feet locations). In order to stabilize and filter out the outliers a moving median approach is used; this processing step is needed due to the noise produced around the edges of the silhouette by the 3D sensor.

We leverage the outcome of our previous theoretical work on weight estimation [2], to estimate the body mass from a series of anthropometric measures (height, arm and leg lengths, arm and leg circumferences, and waist circumference) extracted directly from the 3D silhouette. In order to locate the limbs of each user, we exploit the skeleton tracker embedded in the OpenNI framework that provides us with the location of joints of a stick figure.

The user has the possibility to trigger the automatic estimation assuming the calibration pose required by the skeleton tracker. Once the calibration pose is hold for few seconds, our system immediately trigger the mensuration step which computes lengths and estimates circumferences of the limbs required by our system. To filter out along time the outliers that may affect all the anthropometric measures we adopted a similar solution to the one employed for the height estimation.

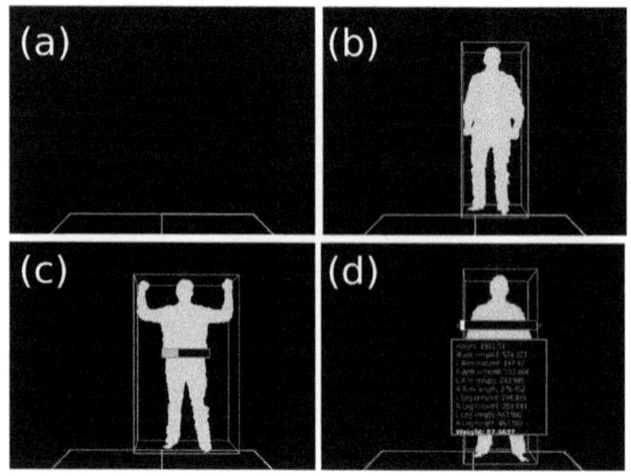

Figure 2: Processing steps breakdown. (a) Floor is estimated and initialized, (b) the person is detected and his/her silhouette segmented, (c) calibration phase, (d) as mensuration ends the measured and the estimated values of height, weight, and gender are shown.

Once all the measures are extracted both gender and weight are estimated. The weight is directly shown by its value, while the gender is extracted as probability measure of being part of one of the two classes (Male/Female) and is shown as a sliding bar on the system's interface (see figure 2).

4. CONCLUSIONS

We present a demo that extracts semantic information for user in front of a Kinect camera. Possible applications are in the medical domain, in the gaming industry, and in automatic demographic collection. Guests of ACM Multimedia that will volunteer will be welcome to come and challenge our system's reliability. Only people assuming the required pose will be able to trigger the demo that will display their anthropometric measures, height, weight, and gender information.

5. REFERENCES

[1] Microsoft. http://www.xbox.com/kinect. [08-05-2011].

[2] C. Velardo and J.-L. Dugelay. Weight estimation from visual body appearance. In *BTAS'10, September*, 2010.

[3] A. Dantcheva, C. Velardo, A. D'Angelo, and J.-L. Dugelay. Bag of soft biometrics for person identification. *Multimedia Tools and Applications*, 2011.

[4] A. Criminisi, I. Reid, and A. Zisserman. Single view metrology. Springer, 2000.

[5] PrimeSense Inc. http://www.openni.org/. [08-05-2011].

[6] Willow Garage. http://opencv.willowgarage.com/. [08-05-2011].

[7] Radu Bogdan Rusu and Steve Cousins. 3d is here: Point cloud library (pcl). In *IEEE International Conference on Robotics and Automation (ICRA)*, 2011.

Tele-immersive Gaming for Everybody*

Ahsan Arefin Zixia Huang Raoul Rivas Shu Shi Wanmin Wu Klara Nahrstedt
University of Illinois at Urbana-Champaign
Urbana, IL
{marefin2, huang21, trivas, shushi2, wwu23, klara}@illinois.edu

ABSTRACT

In this demonstration, we present two 3D tele-immersive games: *light-saber dual* and *block fencing* that merge 3D video representations of participants in real-time to enable remote interactions in a virtual world. The light-saber dual arranges participants in a symmetric setup where both participants interact with each other in a virtual world with similar goals. On the other hand, the block fencing creates an asymmetric setup where participants interact with virtual objects having different goals. Using these two setups, we address the challenges and novelty of our solutions in portable environment setup, data acquisition, multi-stream synchronization, multi-stream session management, mobile device rendering, and overlay communication in the design and implementation of advanced 3D tele-immersive systems.

Categories and Subject Descriptors

H.5.1 [**Multimedia Information Systems**]: [Video, Audio input/output]; C.2.4 [**Distributed Systems**]: [Distributed Applications]

General Terms

Algorithm, Design, Performance

Keywords

Tele-immersion, Gaming, Portability

1. INTRODUCTION

The last decade has witnessed the rising of multi-sensory, multi-modal distributed tele-immersive (TI) environments, which are much more advanced and media-enriched than traditional audio-visual interactive systems such as Skype, NetMeeting, Yahoo Messenger, QQ and others [3]. By capturing full-body human motion in 3D and exchanging the video data over the Internet, these systems can render 3D photo-realistic representations of remote users into a joint virtual space at interactive rates [4]. Technologies are now advancing towards collaborative interactive environments equipped with large number of correlated media sensors, multi-view displays, and advanced haptic-audio-visual user interfaces. They generate highly correlated multi-sensory contents (bundle of streams [1]) that require to be captured in a synchronous and real-time manner, distributed on a view base demand [5] and presented at output device(s) in a real-time and synchronous manner [3]. Current available single-stream based session management and synchronization protocols are not quite adequate to meet these requirements [3].

In this demonstration, we showcase our architecture, design and implementation towards building an advanced 3D tele-immersive environment meeting the real-time requirements. We present two real-time 3D interactive exer-gaming applications: *light-saber dual* and *block fencing* showing the novelty of our solutions in stream synchronization, mobile device rendering, and multi-stream session management, monitoring and adaptation. We introduce haptic sensors in the TI environment to provide game-specific sensing to the participants. In order to understand the performance of our solutions, we provide a visualization of the running session showing the QoS values at each part of the system. Furthermore, to support wider deployment of such 3DTI applications in open areas or home environments, we address the challenges in setting up a portable TI system.

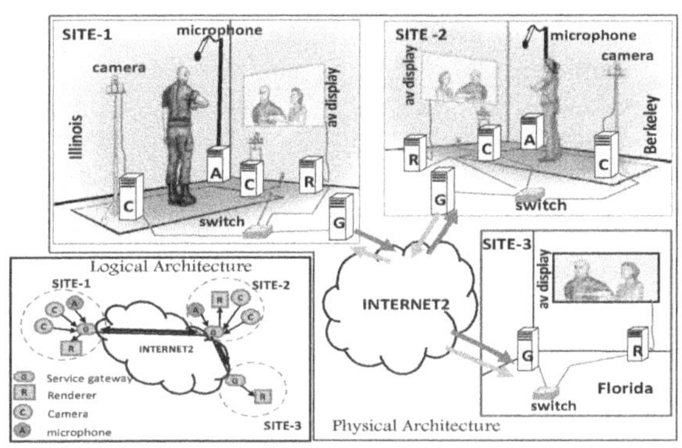

Figure 1: A 3D Tele-immersive Environment with Three Sites.

2. SYSTEM DESIGN

Figure 1 shows an architecture of our portable 3DTI environment with three tiers. In the capturing tier, several 3D cameras are used for capturing. Their host PCs grab the 2D video frames and perform 3D reconstruction in real time and then send the 3D video data to a Rendezvous Points (RP) called gateway node. All cameras are time synchronized by a trigger to capture images at the same time. In the transmission tier, the data is transmitted to/ from remote sites depending on user subscription to specific views. Remote communications are done via gateways. In the rendering tier, gateways send received streams to the local render to display. The inter-stream synchronization is done at the receiver-side gateway.

*First five authors are in alphabetical order

MM'11, November 28–December 1, 2011, Scottsdale, Arizona, USA.
ACM 978-1-4503-0616-4/11/11.

3D Video Acquisition. To improve portability, we use portable hardware and software components in 3D video acquisition. On the hardware side, we use the stereo camera BumbleBee2 from Point Grey Research Inc. They capture higher resolution images with one-time calibration. A new mesh based 3D video representation [2] is built based on the depth images generated by stereo cameras using point-cloud, which not only improves the image quality but also reduce the required transmission bandwidth to a few Mbps compared to other existing approaches.

Universal Gateway Architecture. The gateway architecture is uniquely designed as a distributed user-level kernel that features bundle of streams as first class object, provides a unified interface for end devices, provides separation of policy and mechanism, and allows dynamically loadable user-defined functions (such as compression, congestion control, encryption, and synchronization).

Inter-stream Synchronization. To achieve the inter-stream synchronization, we synchronize all the sensory devices in the capturing side periodically using NTP, and timestamp every produced media packets. At the rendering side, we develop a coordinated protocol across the received multi-stream from each site, and adapt the receiver buffer based on the media packet timestamp to achieve synchronization, which eventually satisfies 80msec skew threshold under Internet dynamics.

Mobile Rendering. Integrating mobile computing devices with 3DTI environments to receive and render 3D video streams in real-time are challenging due to their limited computation capability and low data rate of wireless networks. To support this, we have developed a remote rendering framework that converts 3D scene to 2D image frames based on user's current view and transmit them to mobile devices in real-time. To accommodate view change, it uses a 3D warping-based algorithm that responds to user control request locally on mobile devices to avoid the round-trip time of client-server communication.

Session Monitoring. To enable run-time session monitoring, we use an unobtrusive framework to capture and store system and application metadata (frame size, frame rate, reconstruction time, CPU load, etc.). The purpose of session monitoring is to allow applications as well as system administrators to ask run-time queries, understand system characteristics, metadata dependency, detect abnormal behaviors and adapt accordingly.

3. DEMONSTRATION

To show the novelty of our solutions, we present two interactive exer-gaming applications: *Light-saber Dual* and *Block fencing*.

Light-saber Dual. The light-saber duel game was designed to take full advantage of remote interaction. Figure 2 illustrates how the game is played. Participant 1 in Site-1 puts on a lab coat with red patches and takes a green light-saber, while Participant 2 in Site-2 puts on a coat with green patches and holds a red light-saber. Each participant then tries to use the light-saber to hit the opponent's color patches in the virtual space as much and as fast as possible in order to gain points. A collision detection module is developed in the renderer to automatically detect the hitting. Once a successful hit occurs, the sword and patches turn blueish for an electrifying effect; meanwhile, the game points, represented on a bar of the light-saber's color, get updated. Also the participant who is hit feels a haptic feedback (vibration) on his/her sword and the participant who hits see a lightning in his/her sword. Both players have identical goals and roles in the game (symmetric).

Block Fencing. This game is asymmetric, where the mobile device plays an important role. Figure 3 shows how the game is played.

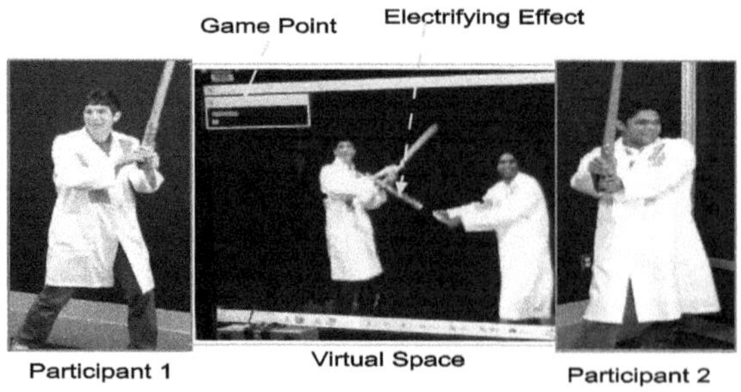

Figure 2: Virtual Light-saber Dual

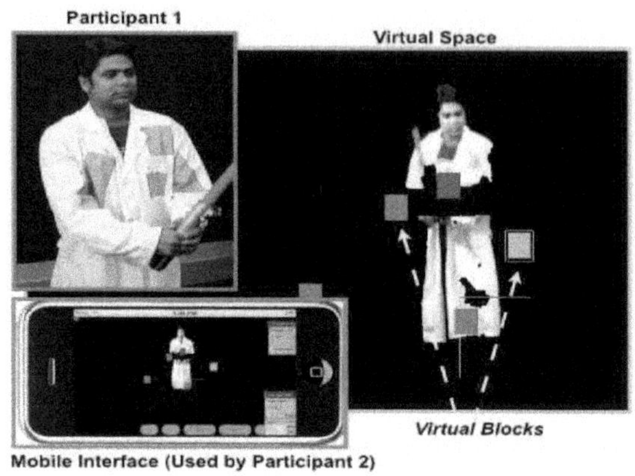

Figure 3: Virtual Block Fencing

Participant 1, captured by a 3D camera in Site-1, can see himself/herself in the virtual space together with a number of graphical red blocks when the game starts. The goal for him/her is to use a physical sword to "touch" all the blocks in the virtual space as fast as possible. As an additional challenge, the touching has to happen in a particular order - the next block to touch will turn from red to green as an indication for Participant 1. If the indicated block is successfully hit, it turns blue. Participant 2 (not shown in Figure 3) uses an iPhone (or iPod) to define the layout and touch-order of the blocks for participant 1. He/she can use a block controller to move the blocks in the virtual world before Participant 1 starts, as well as watch in real-time the actions of Participant 1 on a mobile 3D video viewer. An iPhone is used because of its intuitive touch screen interface. Buttons are design in the 3D video viewer for Participant 2 to change the number of blocks or reset the game.

4. REFERENCES

[1] P. Agarwal, R. Rivas, W. Wu, K. Nahrstedt, and A. Arefin. Bundle of streams: Concept and evaluation in distributed interactive multimedia environments. In *Proc. of ISM*, 2010.

[2] G. Kurillo, R. Vasudevan, E. Lobaton, and R. Bajcsy. A framework for collaborative real-time 3d teleimmersion in a geographically distributed environment. In *Proc. of ISM*, 2008.

[3] K. Nahrstedt, Z. Yang, W. Wu, A. Arefin, and R. Rivas. Next generation session management for 3D teleimmersive interactive environments. *MTAP*, 2011.

[4] W. Wu, R. Rivas, A. Arefin, S. Shi, and K. Nahrstedt. MobileTI: a portable tele-immersive systems. In *Proc. of ACM Multimedia*, 2009.

[5] W. Wu, Z. Yang, and K. Nahrstedt. Dynamic overlay multicast in 3D video collaborative systems. In *Proc. of Nossdav*, 2008.

A Home-based Adaptive Mixed Reality Rehabilitation System

Diana Siwiak, Nicole Lehrer, Michael Baran,
Yinpeng Chen, Margaret Duff, Todd Ingalls, Thanassis Rikakis
School of Arts, Media + Engineering at Arizona State University
{diana.siwiak, nicole.lehrer, michael.baran, yinpeng.chen, margaret.duff, todd.ingalls, thanassis.rikakis}@asu.edu

ABSTRACT

This paper presents an interactive home-based adaptive mixed reality system (HAMRR) for upper extremity stroke rehabilitation. This home-based system is an extension of a previously designed and currently implemented clinical system. The goal of HAMRR is to restore motor function to chronic stroke survivors by providing an engaging long-term reaching task therapy at home. The HAMMR system tracks movement of the wrist and torso, and provides real-time, post-trial, and post-set multimodal feedback to encourage the stroke survivor to self-assess his or her movement and engage in active learning of new movement strategies. This experiential media system uses a computational adaptation scheme to create a continuously challenging and unique multi-year therapy experience through the use of multiple, integrated audio and visual feedback streams. Novel design features include creating an over-arching story for the participant, the ability of the system to adapt the feedback over multiple time scales, and the ability for this system to integrate into any home.

Categories and Subject Descriptors

K.4.2 [**Computers and Society**]: Social Issues – *Assistive technologies for persons with disabilities.*

General Terms

Algorithms, Design, Experimentation, Human Factors.

Keywords

interactive, mixed reality, rehabilitation, adaptation, long-term usage, self-evaluation, affective multimedia, home healthcare

1. INTRODUCTION

Stroke is a leading cause of disability in the United States. On average, every 40 seconds, someone suffers a stroke in the US, leaving millions of people in the US with chronic upper-extremity impairments. The extent and severity of these impairments vary across stroke survivors, necessitating comprehensive rehabilitation systems that can provide meaningful experiences based on individual needs. However, repeated visits to receive clinical-based therapy can be costly to a stroke survivor, both financially and logistically [1]. Recent research has led to the development of telerehabilitation systems for home-based therapy [2]. Telerehabilitation systems generally lack automated real-time system adaptation of the tasks and feedback in response to user performance and progression, instead relying on constant therapist adjustment and telepresence. The optimal content and structure of task performance feedback are areas of ongoing research.

MM'11, November 28-December 1, 2011, Scottsdale, Arizona, USA.
ACM 978-1-4503-0616-4/11/11.

The Home-based Adaptive Mixed Reality Rehabilitation system (HAMRR) attempts to address the shortcomings of current home-based therapy systems. HAMRR is based on the design features and practical application of an Adaptive Mixed Reality Rehabilitation system (AMRR) [3] developed in our lab. The AMRR system provides an environment that integrates physical elements and interactive audio and visual feedback streams to train reach-and-grasp tasks and promote active motor learning. Preliminary results from the AMRR system show improvement in the stroke survivors' movement quality and Wolf Motor Function Test (WMFT) scores [4]. Also, improvements in movement quality are highly correlated to the associated media feedback [5].

Compared to AMRR, HAMMR provides three novel contributions: (a) a low-cost, home-integrated physical design that supports multimodal sensing, (b) an engaging and hierarchical multimedia feedback design, from real-time to summary feedback, where the experience of evolving feedback streams facilitates active learning by gradually reducing dependency on media feedback and facilitating new motor planning strategies, and (c) a semi-supervised adaptation framework that automatically customizes the therapy tasks based on the participant's progress and therapist's goals.

2. HAMRR SYSTEM

The mixed reality rehabilitation system integrates motion capture, kinematic analysis, interactive audio and visual feedback, and a semi-supervised adaptation scheme.

2.1 System Overview

The physical setup of our HAMRR system (Fig 1) includes a media center, a table, and a chair. The media center is an iMac computer, two speakers, and three infrared Opti-Track cameras. The table is lightweight and can be removed when not in use. There are three interchangeable tangible objects that can be inserted into the table [6]. The tangible objects feature pressure and touch sensing to detect participant manipulation. The chair is embedded with force sensing resistors to coarsely track the participant's torso movement. Compared to the AMRR system, the HAMRR system significantly reduces sensing cost and simplifies participant's setup. The participant need only wear a wristband adorned with a single reflective marker used for 3D hand tracking.

Figure 1 HAMMR Physical Setup

HAMMR architecture features six components (Fig 2). The sensing component collects 3D marker position of the wrist, force and contact data from the tangible objects, and force magnitude from the chair. These data streams provide the basis for feature extraction of hand position, velocity, and coarse torso position during the reaching tasks and are used to create feedback. This system creates an evaluation based on the participant's performance data, which can be reviewed by the therapist and used computationally to customize the adaptation framework [7]. HAMRR has a system dialog component to guide the participant through new feedback and task environments.

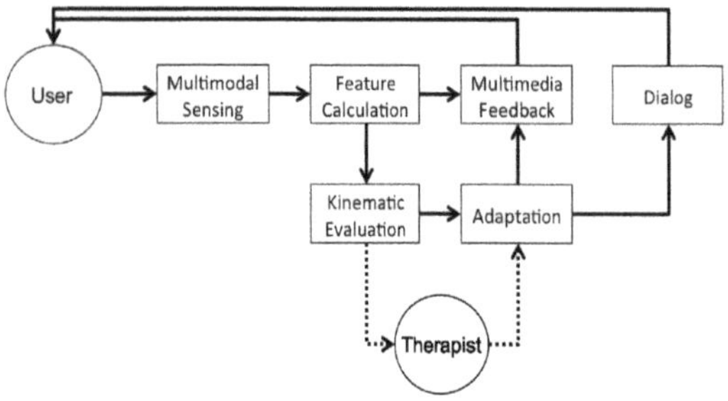

Figure 2 HAMMR Architecture Design

2.2 Multimodal Feedback

Our HAMRR system intuitively communicates levels of performance and direction for improvement to the participant by using three types of feedback – *tangible* feedback, *auditory* feedback, and *visual* feedback. The feedback is designed to provide a dynamic multimodal experience that evolves over time, incentivizes training, accommodates more complex tasks and facilitates active learning. The feedback is structured to provide movement information at three levels: (a) real time, (b) post-trial summary, and (c) post-set summary. For any training set (which includes several reaches), only one of these three levels is utilized.

Real-time feedback is coupled to the participant's hand trajectory and speed, which are key features for completing a reach. The LEDs embedded within the object change color based on the participant's trajectory. Green signifies minimal deviation from an efficient reference trajectory, yellow signifies moderate deviation, and red signifies large deviation. The objects also have embedded task completion indication lights to signify when the required interaction has been performed. Real-time auditory feedback communicates speed to the participant through note density. The sound is designed to encourage the participant to reach with a smooth, natural speed.

In post-trial summary, a visual representation of trajectory performance is communicated by the color and spatial distribution of stones in water (Figs. 3a & b). In post-set summary, visual and auditory feedback communicate affective tags. For example, changes in the boat's contour communicate a pattern of reaching without proper joint correlation (Fig. 3d). Visual tags include trajectory inaccuracy, tremor, segmented movement, and task incompletion. Sonic affective tags (or sonic images) are provided within the summary level to indicate movements that are too fast, too slow, or hesitant. Parameters such as harmonicity, timbre, reverberation time, note attack and decay, and note density are used to differentiate the sonic images.

Figure 3 HAMMR Visual Feedback
(a) efficient trial (b) trial trajectory error (c) efficient set (d) set of segmented trials

2.3 Adaptation

HAMMR is designed to provide unaided therapy. The type of tasks, tangible objects and locations, and feedback streams are designed to be adaptable, in order to offer a challenging and engaging personal experience. HAMMR employs a utility function to determine the adaptation decision (represented by a change in system parameters) based on (a) a prior established week-long sequence of tasks, (b) the history of foci and tasks for previous sets, and (c) the participant's performance [7].

The adaptation is structured as a semi-supervised framework, using a probabilistic graphical network representation. The adaptation framework customizes the system in the participant's daily training automatically and allows a therapist to review the rehabilitation progress weekly, and fine-tune the training strategy.

3. DEMONSTRATION SETUP

We will demonstrate how the participant will setup and interact with the system during a typical therapy session. The subject will wear a single reflective marker. The subject will interact with the system dialog to setup the table space with the appropriate tangible objects. Our demonstration will then show how the demo subject can interact with task and feedback tutorials. The demo subject will progress through the real-time, post-trial, and post-set feedback streams to demonstrate the components of the overall experience and how they scale in structure.

4. REFERENCES

[1] Centers for Disease Control and Prevention, "Outpatient rehabilitation among stroke survivors: 21 states and the District of Columbia," *MMWR Morb Wkly Rep*. vol. 56, pp. 504-507, 2001.

[2] W. Durfee, J. Carey, D. Nuckley, J. Deng, "Design and implementation of a home stroke telerehabilitation system," *IEEE EMBC 2009*. Sep. 3-6, 2009.

[3] J. W. Krakauer, "Motor learning: its relevance to stroke recovery and neurorehabilitation," *Curr Opin Neurol*, vol. 19, pp. 84-90, 2006.

[4] Y. Chen, et al, "A novel adaptive mixed reality system for stroke rehabilitation: principles, proof of concept and preliminary application in two patients," *Topics in Stroke Rehabilitation*, Accepted for publication, Nov. 2010.

[5] N. Lehrer, S. Attygalle, Y. Chen, S. Wolf, T. Rikakis, "Exploring the bases for a mixed reality stroke rehabilitation system, part II: application of principles for the design of interactive feedback of upper limb rehabilitation." *Journal of NeuroEngineering and Rehabilitation*. In review.

[6] M. Duff, T. Rikakis, "Interchangeable tangible object assembly for upper-extremity home-based stroke rehabilitation." Submitted to *IEEE EMBC 2011*.

[7] Y. Chen, M. Baran, H. Sundaram, T. Rikakis, "A low cost, adaptive mixed reality system for home-based stroke rehabilitation." Submitted to *IEEE EMBC 2011*.

ClassX Mobile: Region-of-Interest Video Streaming to Mobile Devices with Multi-Touch Interaction

Derek Pang, Sherif Halawa, Ngai-Man Cheung and Bernd Girod
Department of Electrical Engineering, Stanford University
Stanford, CA, USA 94305
{dcypang, halawa ,ncheung, bgirod}@stanford.edu

ABSTRACT

Small screen sizes, limited bandwidth, and low computational power often prohibit streaming of high-resolution videos to mobile devices over a wireless network. Recent advances in interactive region-of-interest (IRoI) video streaming technology enable users to interactively control pan/tilt/zoom, while provide bit-rate and complexity savings. One recent application of IRoI video streaming is *ClassX* developed at Stanford University. It offers an open-source experimental platform for interactive online lecture streaming. In this technical demonstration, we present *ClassX* Mobile, which extends the current *ClassX* system and delivers high-quality interactive video to smartphones and tablets with multi-touch screens.

Categories and Subject Descriptors

H.5.1 [**Information Interfaces and Presentation**]: Multimedia Information Systems - Video

General Terms

Design

Keywords

Mobile video, IRoI video streaming, online lecture delivery

1. INTRODUCTION

Mobile video data traffic is expected to grow by 35-fold to 4 exabytes per month in 2015 [2]. The need for video streaming systems to address the heterogeneities of mobile devices and networks becomes increasingly important. Although video content can now be recorded with high definition inexpensively, it entails high bandwidth cost for wireless streaming and is unsuitable for mobile devices with small displays. In this demo, we present *ClassX* Mobile, a novel online lecture video streaming system, that allows mobile viewers to interact with high-spatial-resolution videos on a small screen display over a wireless network.

ClassX is an online interactive lecture capturing and viewing system developed by Mavlankar et al. [4]. The system has been used in over 25 courses and dozens of seminars during its pilot deployment at Stanford University [1]. Unlike existing solutions that restrict users to watch only a predefined view, *ClassX* provides IRoI streaming that enables each user to independently choose an arbitrary region-of-interest (RoI) from a high-resolution video recorded by a static camera. *ClassX* Mobile builds upon this work and enables IRoI video streaming to mobile devices. Leveraging multi-touch displays, the user can control pan/tilt/zoom with simple finger gestures. To adapt to time-varying and bandwidth-constrained wireless networks, we use adaptive HTTP streaming to minimize playback interruptions. *ClassX* Mobile also offers an automatic tracking view of the lecturer, so users only have to exercise control over the region-of-interest when they desire.

MM'11, November 28–December 1, 2011, Scottsdale, Arizona, USA.
ACM 978-1-4503-0616-4/11/11.

Figure 1: Multi-touch interaction of *ClassX* Mobile for (left) zooming (right) panning/tilting. Double exposure illustrates how the image changes in response to user inputs.

We implemented *ClassX* Mobile on a Google Android-based smartphone and tablets. Our system demonstrates mobile users can view and interact with high-resolution videos according to their viewing preferences and experience high-resolution videos in a very compelling and engaging way. We are planning to release *ClassX* Mobile in near future as part of *ClassX* Open Source Project [3].

2. SYSTEM OVERVIEW

Fig. 2 shows an overview of *ClassX* Mobile system, which consists of the following three major components:

2.1 Pre-processing

To facilitate IRoI video streaming, *ClassX* Mobile uses a standard-compliant and spatial-random-access-enabled video coding scheme introduced by Mavlankar et al. [4]. An IRoI video encoder creates multiple resolution layers from a high-resolution video input and each layer is subdivided into tiles. Each tile is compressed independently using H.264/AVC and is stored on the server for streaming. We employ an overlapping tiling scheme such that only one tile is needed to satisfy to any RoI requests. To support different display sizes and rate-adaptive streaming, each tile is available at different spatial resolutions and quality. Using our tracking algorithm [4], the IRoI video encoder can also automatically generate a dedicated tile that provides the tracking view of the lecturer.

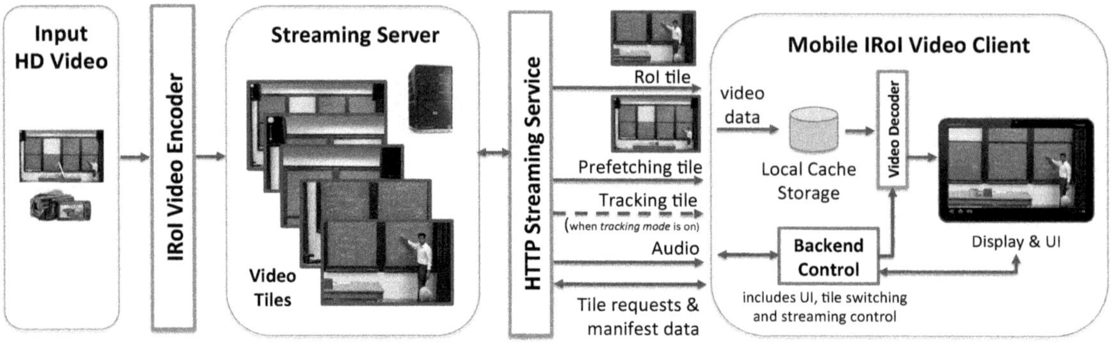

Figure 2: *ClassX* Mobile IRoI video streaming system

2.2 Rate-adaptive IRoI video streaming

Upon receiving a RoI request, the server determines and streams the corresponding tile to the mobile client. To avoid playback interruption, a prefetching tile is streamed to the client continuously. When a new tile is not readily available during a change in RoI, the prefetching tile is decoded and displayed on the client. In our implementation, the prefetching tile is set to be the entire view of the video encoded at the display resolution. When a user prefers to use the *tracking* mode, the tracking tile is streamed in the place of RoI tile. Audio is streamed separately from all the video tiles.

We adopt the stream-switching approach for adaptive HTTP streaming. This approach dynamically matches the best video representation from different bit-rate levels to the user's available bandwidth. When requesting a new RoI tile, our client adaptively determines the best starting position for playback based on past transmission delays and minimizes the probability of missing the playout deadline. To lower the delay of tile switching, our client also requests the first video segment to have a shorter duration and temporarily disables the transmission of the prefetching tile if possible.

2.3 Mobile client

All users interactions, streaming requests, rate adaptation, audio synchronization and tile playback control are handled by a backend control module in the mobile client. At the start of each streaming session, the server sends a manifest file to the client. This file generally contains tiling and layering information, available tile representations and other video information, such as duration and average bitrates. Video segments are downloaded and buffered for playback on the mobile device.

3. DEMONSTRATION

To realize *ClassX* Mobile, we developed an Android-based IRoI video streaming client. Using existing Android mobile phones and tablets, we will show our system's interactive functionalities, as well as its compatibility with devices of different display sizes and computational power. The demo videos comprises a collection of high-definition (1080p) lecture videos and will be streamed to our demo devices from our server [?] located at Stanford University over a WiFi network. In addition, we will also demonstrate IRoI video streaming of a 5016x1400 panoramic sport video taken at a soccer stadium and allow users to interact with very high-resolution content on a small display.

Table 1: Avg. total bit-rate & tile-switching delays

Display resolution	Total bit-rate	Switching delay
480x270	499 kbps	1.61 sec
640x360	910 kbps	1.66 sec
960x540	1160 kbps	1.75 sec

4. PERFORMANCE

Table 1 shows the average total bit-rate required for *ClassX* Mobile at different display resolutions. The average total bit-rate includes the bit-rates of the RoI tile, the prefetching tile and the audio. All of the video tiles are encoded using H.264 baseline profile with frame rate of 15 fps and keyframe interval of 1 second. Using the same encoding setting, the bit-rate of the original high-resolution demo videos exceeds 1.3 Mbps. Compared to streaming the original content, *ClassX* Mobile lowers the bandwidth as well as the computation required for decoding and display. We also include the tile-switching delay important for large RoI changes in Table 1, which shows that our system still maintains fast interaction response in a wireless environment. The above evaluation is based on a total of more than 350 minutes streaming sessions of our demo videos under different network conditions.

5. CONCLUSION

Our demonstration presents a new application of IRoI video streaming system for mobile devices over a wireless network. Our system overcomes the bandwidth, display size and computational power constraints to deliver high-resolution video for interactive display on mobile devices. By applying this technology in online lecture viewing, *ClassX* Mobile can provide very compelling user experience. By releasing our system as an open-source project, we encourage contributions from other researchers, developers, and educators in building an open, cost-effective, and advanced online lecture viewing system.

6. REFERENCES

[1] ClassX. `http://classx.stanford.edu`.

[2] Cisco Systems Inc. Cisco visual networking index: Global mobile data traffic forecast update, 2010 to 2015. Feb 2011.

[3] S. Halawa, D. Pang, N.-M. Cheung, and B. Girod. ClassX - An open source interactive lecture streaming system. In *Proc. of the International Conference on Multimedia*, MM '11.

[4] A. Mavlankar, P. Agrawal, D. Pang, S. Halawa, N.-M. Cheung, and B. Girod. An interactive region-of-interest video streaming system for online lecture viewing. In *Proc. International Packet Video Workshop*, pages 64 –71, Dec. 2010.

Sketch2Cartoon: Composing Cartoon Images by Sketching

Changhu Wang[1], Jun Zhang[2]*, Bruce Yang[1], Lei Zhang[1]
[1]Microsoft Research Asia, No. 5, Danling Streat, Beijing 100080, P.R.China
[2]Biological Intelligence and Information Lab, Shanghai Jiao Tong University, Shanghai 200240, P.R.China
{chw, v-junz, fany, leizhang}@microsoft.com

ABSTRACT

In this paper, we introduce the Sketch2Cartoon system, which is an automatic cartoon making system by leveraging a novel sketch-based clipart image search engine. Different from existing work, most of which either limited users to the pre-prepared characters or only used keyword queries to search materials, Sketch2Cartoon enables users to sketch major curves of characters and props in their mind, and real-time search results from millions of clipart images could be selected to compose the cartoon images. The selected components are vectorized and thus could be further edited. By enabling sketch-based input, the cartoon image making process becomes more natural, and even a child who is too young to read or write can draw whatever he/she imagines and get interesting cartoon images.

Categories and Subject Descriptors

H.3.3 [**Information Search and Retrieval**]: Query formulation, Search process

General Terms

Design, Experimentation

Keywords

Sketch2Cartoon, sketching, clipart, search

1. INTRODUCTION

Cartoon, which is famous for the ability of story telling and artistic expression, plays an important role in human's daily life, such as children education, comics in newspapers, and cartoon movies. However, to enrich artistic expression of cartoon images, it always needs artistic skills and the mastery of complicated softwares. This makes it too difficult to create beautiful cartoon images for common users, especially for children with unlimited imagination but limited software usage ability.

Most of existing cartoon making systems [3] limited users' imagination by only using pre-made clipart libraries. Although by leveraging Internet images, iClipart[1] has potential to provide unlimited categories of cartoon objects, the keyword-based inputs are not very natural, especially for children who are too young to read or write.

Figure 1: Illustration of Sketch2Cartoon system. The upper image is the input sketch, and the lower one is the resulting cartoon image.

As the popularity of devices with touch screens, input using a pen or a finger has become a very natural way to interact with computers. In [4], authors proposed to use Internet images to compose a realistic picture from a freehand sketch annotated with text labels. However, without an effective and efficient sketch-based image search technique, the text labels become a prerequisite in [4], and thus it costs minutes to compose one image, which makes the system far from practical. Moreover, the automatic montage technique for realistic images is still an open problem, which makes it more difficult.

Different from realistic images, characters and props from clipart images are much easier to extract, vectorize, and compose. Moreover, recently, we successfully built a sketch-based image search engine MindFinder [1, 2]. It supports real-time response on millions of images, and thus makes possible the sketch-based cartoon image composing system.

*Jun Zhang performed this work while being an intern at Microsoft Research Asia.

[1]iClipart is a research prototype in Microsoft Research Asia, leaded by Jian Sun and Ying-Qing Xu.

MM'11, November 28–December 1, 2011, Scottsdale, Arizona, USA.
ACM 978-1-4503-0616-4/11/11.

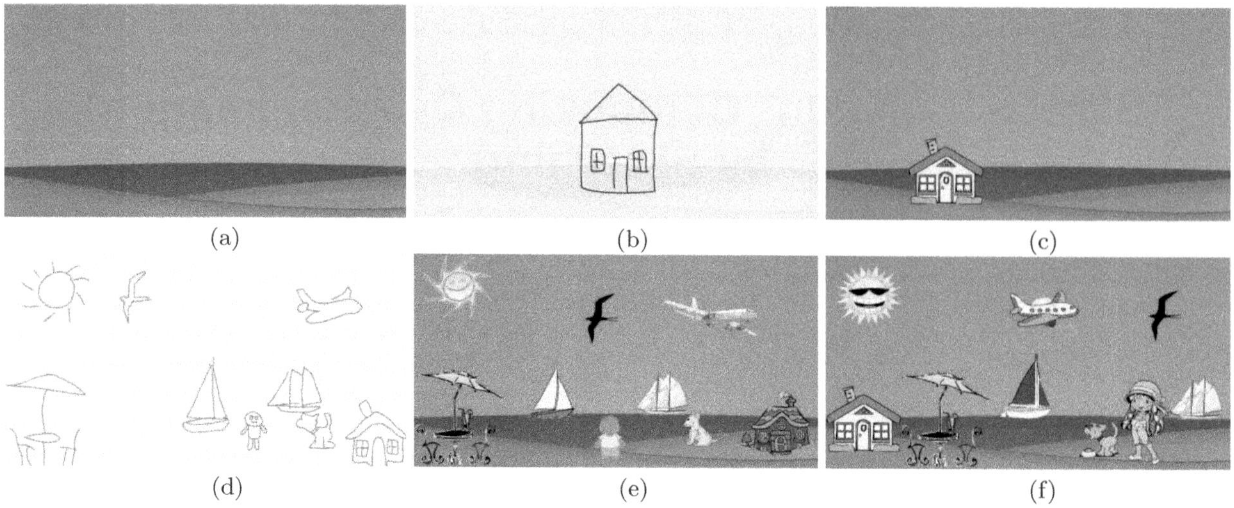

Figure 2: Illustration of the Sketch2Clipart system. (a) Select a backgroud image. (b) Draw a house. (c) Get a house from top results of ClipartFinder. (d) All sketches drawn by the user. (e) Resulting cartoon image. (f) Another cartoon image queried by the same sketches as in (d) but with different objects, scales and positions.

In this work, we present the Sketch2Cartoon system, which is a real-time cartoon making system that enables sketch-based input. In order to provide unlimited cartoon contents, we crawled about 1 million clipart images from the Internet, and built a novel clipart image search engine ClipartFinder [1] to support real-time keyword- and sketch-based search, as shown in Fig. 2. Different from MindFinder [1, 2] which requires that the objects in the resulting images have similar position as the sketch query, ClipartFinder is translation and scale invariant. Sketch2Cartoon enables users to sketch major curves of characters and props in their mind, and search each desired component by ClipartFinder. Each retrieved component has been vertorized and supports further editing. Sketch2Cartoon supports multi-touch control, and also enables users to write keywords on any position of the touch-screen using a finger or a pen, to trigger keyword-based search. Fig. 1 illustrates the input and output of Sketch2Cartoon.

2. SYSTEM OVERVIEW

In this section, we briefly introduce the main functions of Sketch2Cartoon step by step.

1. The user selects one image from the repository as the background. See Fig. 3(a)
2. The user can sketch a character/object or write a keyword on the canvas. The system will analyze the strokes, and then automatically extract keywords and sketches for further search. See Fig. 3(b)
3. After drawing, the system will fetch images through the ClipartFinder engine. Then the user can selected the most appropriate clipart to his/her imagination. The clipart will be automated scaled and moved to match with the sketches. See Fig. 3(c)
4. If needed, the user can edit the character/object, such as moving, scaling, rotating, and re-coloring. Multi-touch gestures such as pan, zoom and rotate are also enabled. The user can also replace current character/object by another one in the top results queried by current or modified sketch.

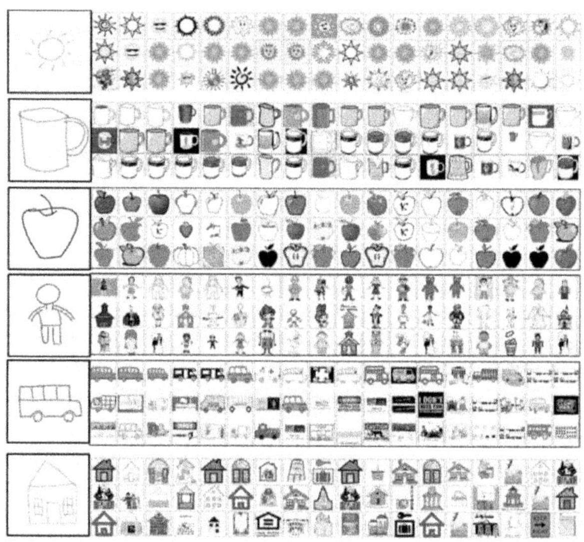

Figure 3: The queries and corresponding top results of ClipartFinder.

5. By repeating 2 to 4, the user can add more characters/objects. See Fig. 3(d-f)
6. If the user is satisfied with his/her work, he/she can save it to the gallery, or export to a SVG file, which is easy to share with others.

3. REFERENCES

[1] Y. Cao, C. Wang, L. Zhang, and L. Zhang. Edgel index for large-scale sketch-based image search. In *Proc. of CVPR*, 2011.

[2] Y. Cao, H. Wang, C. Wang, Z. Li, L. Zhang, and L. Zhang. Mindfinder: Interactive sketch-based image search on millions of images. In *ACM Multimedia*, 2010.

[3] S. Chen, Y. Tian, F. Wen, Y. Xu, and X. Tang. Easytoon: an easy and quick tool to personalize a cartoon storyboard using family photo album. In *Proc. of ACM Int'l Conf. Multimedia*, 2008.

[4] T. Chen, M. Cheng, P. Tan, A. Shamir, and S. Hu. Sketch2Photo: internet image montage. *TOG*, 2009.

Sensor-rich Video Exploration on a Map Interface

Beomjoo Seo, Jia Hao, Guanfeng Wang
School of Computing
National University of Singapore
Singapore 117417
[seobj,haojia,wanggf]@comp.nus.edu.sg

ABSTRACT

Result presentations from searches into video repositories is still a challenging problem. Current systems usually display a ranked list that shows the first frame of each video. Users then explore the videos one-by-one. In our recent work we have investigated the fusion of captured video with a continuous stream of sensor meta-data. These so-called *sensor-rich videos* can conveniently be captured with today's smartphones. Importantly, the recorded sensor-data streams enable processing and result presentation in novel and useful ways.

In this demonstration we present a system that provides an integrated solution to present videos based on keyframe extraction and interactive, map-based browsing. As a key feature, the system automatically computes popular places based on the collective information from all the available videos. For each video it then extracts keyframes and renders them at their proper location on the map synchronously with the video playback. All the processing is performed in real-time, which allows for an interactive exploration of all the videos in a geographic area.

Categories and Subject Descriptors

H.3.5 [**Information Storage and Retrieval**]: On-line Information Services—*Web-based services*; I.4.8 [**Image Processing and Computer Vision**]: Scene Analysis—*Sensor Fusion*

General Terms

Algorithms, Measurement, Performance

Keywords

Web services, hotspot estimation, keyframe extraction

1. INTRODUCTION

Due to the technological advancements and the popularity of smartphones it is now easy for users to capture, upload and share videos. A number of video hosting services cater to this popular trend. In fact, the explosive growth in mobile video services has already led to their significant contribution to the overall Internet traffic [2].

Some of these videos are associated with geographic locations (i.e., GPS coordinates) and existing hosting solutions make them available through map services for browsing and viewing. However, conventional approaches are limited in that videos are associated with just a single GPS location. Hence, in terms of presentation there exists only a minimal connection between the map interface and the videos that typically have been retrieved based on a user's query. To explore techniques that provide a more integrated and interactive experience, we have developed a video hosting system called *GeoVid* (`http://geovid.org`) [1]. In our novel and unconventional framework, videos and their corresponding meta-data streams are efficiently indexed and synchronously presented on a common map interface.

As a key feature of our demonstration we make use of our recently designed distance-aware video summarization algorithm. Different from existing keyframe extraction and summarization techniques [3, 4], our method processes and utilizes the video meta-data (specifically compass and GPS information) which makes it efficient and light-weight. In our methodology, we are conscious of the fact that the location of the most salient objects in a video are often times not at the position of the camera, but may in reality be quite a distance away (e.g., a video of the Niagara Falls). Clearly it would be very beneficial to place extracted keyframes in their correct geographic locations on a map. In the past, an automatic detection of popular points-of-interest was difficult to achieve[1]. Our approach provides a keyframe-distance computation and placement with no manual intervention and as such we believe it provides high utility for end-users.

2. SYSTEM ARCHITECTURE

Our **acquisition software** is implemented as smartphone applications available for both Android and iOS. The application software captures 720×480 resolution MPEG-4 videos and also records sensor measurements every 250 milliseconds. After a recording the user can upload the video through a network connection (either WiFi or 3G) to our demonstration server.

The **hotspot estimation and keyframe extraction** is performed on our demonstration server. After receiving a video and the corresponding sensor measurements (in JSON format) the server processes the GPS location and the view angle of every video frame and inserts them into a spatial database to make the information searchable. To enable efficient wide-area access we transcode the videos to a 768 kbps bitrate and 480×360 pixel resolution. A specific back-end process – depicted in a gray box in Fig. 1a – constructs the

[1]We do not use the term landmark since our technique is useful for a broad set of geographically related phenomena.

MM'11, November 28–December 1, 2011, Scottsdale, Arizona, USA.
ACM 978-1-4503-0616-4/11/11.

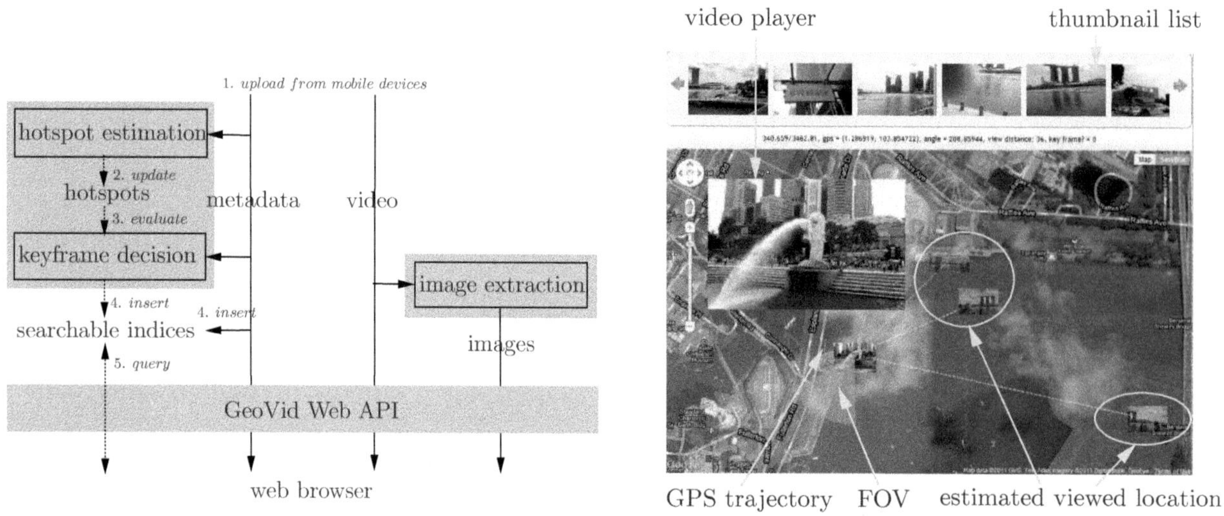

(a) Server-side processes and data flow.

(b) A sample screen-shot taken during playback.

Figure 1: Demonstration system processing modules and map-based user interface.

FOV (field of view) of every frame and updates the region that is affected on a map grid incrementally. Local maxima throughout the grid are selected as hotspots. Based on the set of hotspot locations the process computes the distances to the camera locations and determines the best-matching hotspot within each FOV as its *visible distance*. Subsequently, the estimated visible distance provides the input for the keyframe decision. Finally, the computed keyframes are actually retrieved via the image extraction module.

3. DEMONSTRATION

Our demonstration system allows users to experience sensor-rich videos based on the underlying key mechanisms described in the previous section. Fig. 1b illustrates the system interface. A list of video thumbnails are presented along the top and a Google Maps interface is shown in the lower part. The thumbnail list is automatically updated whenever a user navigates across the map. When the mouse pointer hovers over one of the thumbnails, the corresponding GPS trajectory and keyframe related information is asynchronously retrieved from the server and displayed on the map interface. When the user clicks a thumbnail, a map-overlaid player is launched and the video played at the designated starting location. During the playback of the video, the camera's current location and FOV are animated along the corresponding GPS trajectory, using the Raphaël[2] vector graphics engine. If a keyframe is encountered during playback, its thumbnail is positioned at its estimated location on the map along with a fade-out visual effect.

Our prototype system is also useful in identifying some interesting issues. For the keyframe extraction algorithm we observed that a few keyframes do not match well. We found that some popular places tend to have several distinct attractions which are challenging to distinguish. One possible enhancement would be to also leverage existing landmark information. An additional challenge is to provide correct distance estimations in the presence of obstructions such as large buildings. This issue can be reduced if 3D building models are available to check for occlusions.

[2]`http://raphaeljs.com`

4. CONCLUSIONS

We presented a novel and integrated video exploration approach where keyframes are positioned at an expected target location during playback on a map interface. Keyframes and their locations are computed in a fully automated manner. Thus, a number of visual cues are provided to the user to effectively navigate a large set of videos.

From our prototype system we have identified a number of areas for improvements and future work. First, there currently exists a slight asynchrony between the video and FOV renderings (typically less than one-second). This is caused by the difficulty of determining the exact time when the first video frame is recorded on the mobile device. Second, the GPS and compass signals are quite noisy and jittery, since we render the raw sensor data without any post-processing. To solve these issues, we plan to apply appropriate low-pass filtering mechanism combined with motion-vector analysis.

We plan to open our APIs for access to all sensor measurements and for users to submit their own keyframe extraction algorithms and hence visually evaluate their quality through our web browser.

5. REFERENCES

[1] S. Arslan Ay, L. Zhang, S. H. Kim, M. He, and R. Zimmermann. GRVS: a Georeferenced Video Search Engine. In *17th ACM Intl. Conference on Multimedia*, MM '09, pages 977–978. ACM, 2009.

[2] Cisco Systems, Inc. Cisco Visual Networking Index: Forecast and Methodology, 2009-2014. White Paper, 2010.

[3] H. Zhang, J. Wu, D. Zhong, and S. Smoliar. An Integrated System for Content-based Video Retrieval and Browsing. *Pattern Recognition*, 30(4):643–658, 1997.

[4] Y. Zhuang, Y. Rui, T. Huang, and S. Mehrotra. Adaptive Key Frame Extraction using Unsupervised Clustering. In *Intl. Conference on Image Processing (ICIP)*, volume 1, pages 866–870, 1998.

Ztitch: A Mobile Phone Application for 3D Scene Creation, Navigation, and Sharing

Andrew Au
Engineering Science
Simon Fraser University
Burnaby, BC, Canada
aau1@sfu.ca

Jie Liang
Engineering Science
Simon Fraser University
Burnaby, BC, Canada
jiel@sfu.ca

ABSTRACT

Modern smartphones provide an excellent platform for creating 3D scenes from photos. While there already exists many mobile applications that can stitch a set of photos to create a single, panoramic landscape photo, this paper proposes the creation of panoramic scenes where multiple photos are projected in a 3D space using the pinhole camera model, so that a realistic perspective of the scene is maintained. Our application allows users to automatically create a panoramic 3D scene in real-time using the live images from the phone's camera, and to manually fine-tune each photo's position via the touchscreen if the default position is inaccurate. The application enables scenes to be easily shared to other users, and was developed using the Silverlight framework so that it can run across multiple platforms.

Categories and Subject Descriptors

H.3.5 [**Online Information Services**]: Web-based services; I.3 [**Computer Graphics**]: Miscellaneous

General Terms

Algorithms, Design

1. INTRODUCTION

In recent years, Google Streetview and Microsoft Streetside have become useful tools for people to explore many streets in the world in a 360° panoramic setting. However, the images in these systems were generated using dedicated multiview cameras that have to be mounted on customized cars or tricycles.

Since most smart phones are equipped with high performance cameras and good computational resources, we have developed Ztitch, a mobile phone application for 3D scene creation, navigation and sharing.

Our application was released in November 2010. Months later, in April 2011, Microsoft released a mobile version of Photosynth [2] for iPhone/iPad2. Using algorithms of tracking and mapping found in augmented reality applications [5], the mobile Photosynth application also allows users to create panoramic scenes in real-time. Our approach is different in that we leverage sensors and allow a manual editing stage. It may be more robust in certain scenarios where the scene lacks features for finding keypoints (such as an empty wall sky), is poorly lit, or contains too many moving objects (as in a crowded place with moving people). An interesting future work would be to combine our approach with the one in Photosynth for a highly robust system.

Figure 1: Application screenshot

The application runs on the Windows Phone 7 OS. A screenshot is shown in Fig. 1. An accompanying Silverlight-based website is also developed to recreate the 3D scenes using the uploaded photos from Flickr/Facebook, so other mobile or desktop users can explore the same result to enable sharing. Note that our application differs from many existing photo stitching algorithms [4], where the output is simply a unfolded 2D static image without the 3D perception.

2. SCENE CREATION AND NAVIGATION

To create a 3D scene on the phone, each photo in our application is automatically placed by leveraging the directional sensors of the phone. These sensors include the compass, the accelerometer, and the gyroscope. All Windows Phone 7 devices come equipped with at least the compass and the accelerometer, although ideally, for the most accurate placement of each photo, all three sensors should be present. We also implemented a novel approach for the user to manually fine-tune the position of each photo in the 3D space via the touchscreen, in case the automatically sensed position is inaccurate.

2.1 Coordinate Pipeline

A key step in the 3D scene creation and navigation is to apply various perspective projection transforms to a photo. For this purpose, homogeneous coordinate is usually used in computer vision and 3D graphics. Our system uses the pinhole camera model. The corresponding graphics pipeline workflow consists of a sequence of transformations. Each transformation is represented by a 4×4 matrix. Specifically, a 3D point is first augmented to its projective equivalent $\mathbf{s}$, which then undergoes the following matrix multiplications

MM'11, November 28–December 1, 2011, Scottsdale, Arizona, USA.
ACM 978-1-4503-0616-4/11/11.

that yields a 2D Euclidean point $\mathbf{p}$ in the output device coordinates [1]:

$$\mathbf{M}_V \mathbf{C}_P \mathbf{T}_v \mathbf{M}_W \mathbf{s} \rightarrow \mathbf{p} \quad (1)$$

where $\mathbf{M}_W$ is the positioning transformation, $\mathbf{T}_v$ the viewing transformation, $\mathbf{C}_P$ the perspective projection transformation, and $\mathbf{M}_V$ the viewport transformation. These matrix transform operations are detailed in [1]. Finally, the right-hand side of the equation is projected as a 2D point.

In our implementation, we choose the recently released Windows Phone 7 operating system and the Microsoft Silverlight platform to implement our mobile application. Silverlight provides powerful APIs to implement various 3D projective transforms, which are essential to our application. Since our main objective is to render a panoramic environment in a 3D space, the spherical coordinate is very handy. All we need is to map the center of each photo to a point (x, y, z) on a sphere with radius r and certain orientation using the spherical coordinate system. The radius r is directly related to the focal length of the camera, which is a camera property equating to the image distance. In many cases, the focal length information can be extracted from the EXIF tags in the original photo file.

2.2 3D Scene Creation

Windows Phone 7 devices come equipped with at least a compass and an accelerometer. These two sensors collectively provide the data necessary to track the phone's 3-DOF orientation (the accelerometer provides the pitch and roll angles, while the compass provides the yaw angle). With the phone's instantaneous orientation acquired, the remaining task is to correlate the data with the live camera feed on the back of the phone to construct the scene in real time.

Currently, Ztitch only supports panoramic scenes. All photos are thus placed on the surface of a sphere. To manually edit a 3D scene, the user can use the touchscreen on the phone to manually position it in the 3D space by dragging it. To facilitate this process, each photo is displayed in a semi-transparent mode, so that all overlapped photos can be visible. Therefore, when users drag a photo, it is very easy for the users to identify and match its overlapped region with the adjacent photo.

To drag a photo to its best position in the 3D scene, we should adjust each coordinate of the center of the photo on a sphere. In our application, this is achieved by adjusting the rotation angles around the x, y, or z axis. In order to display the photo in the correct perspective when it is being dragged, we only need to update the photo's 3D matrix when the user moves his finger over the touchscreen.

2.3 Interactive 3D Scene Navigation

When users navigate the scene via the touchscreen, we detect the finger motion, and calculate the corresponding changes of the rotation angles, and update the viewing transform T_v. This matrix essentially transforms the world coordinates system into the coordinate system of the user's view (the pinhole). After applying the viewing transform, the coordinates of the photos will be relative to the user's view. By multiplying this viewing matrix by a rotation matrix and then plugging back to the pipeline equation (1), all the photos in the scene would appear rotated.

Our system also leverages the accelerometer to allow the users to navigate a scene by tilting the phone in different directions, giving the application a gaming flavour. The integration of the accelerometer is also achieved by adjusting the viewing transform T_v in (1), by multiplying it with rotation matrices.

We improve the rendering performance of our application by not rendering photos that are out of view from the user. This is done by constantly running a loop which finds the angle difference between T_v and each photo in the scene. If the difference is greater than the field of vision, then the rendering of that photo is skipped.

2.4 Photo Seamline Blending

After stitching photos in a 3D space, a seamline is usually visible at the intersection of two neighboring photos, due to their different brightnesses. In traditional photo stitching, various algorithms have been developed to remove this artifact [4]. In our system, since we need a real-time application, we can only use some simple algorithms. We achieve smooth transition by applying two linear gradients, one horizontal and one vertical. The gradients become transparent as they near the edge of the photo.

3. ONLINE SHARING AND WEB ACCESS

To increase the popularity of our system and to facilitate photo sharing via social networks, our application is integrated with email, Facebook, Flickr, and Bing Map services.

When the users upload the created 3D scenes in our system, each individual photo is stored separately on Facebook or Flickr. The URL of each uploaded photo is stored in a configuration file. To allow other people to access the 3D scenes created by our users from desktop computers, we develop an accompanying website, www.ztitch.com, which is also based on Silverlight. In this website, we only need to store the configuration file of each 3D scene. The required photos are still stored in Flickr or Facebook.

4. DEMO PLAN AT ACM MM'11

At the ACM Multimedia conference, we will show how to use our software on Windows 7 phone to create, navigate, upload 3D scenes, as well as viewing scenes uploaded by other users. In addition, we will access the Ztitch website from a laptop computer and browse the 3D scenes created by other users.

5. REFERENCES

[1] F. Nielsen. *Visual Computing: Geometry, Graphics, and Vision.* Charles River Media Inc, Massachusetts, 2005.

[2] N. Snavely, S. M. Seitz, and R. Szeliski. Photo tourism: Exploring image collections in 3D. *ACM Transactions on Graphics*, 25(3):835–846, 2006.

[3] B. Triggs, P. McLachlan, R. Hartley, and A. Fitzgibbon. Bundle adjustment - a modern synthesis. *Vision Algorithms: Theory and Practice*, Springer-Verlag, Berlin, Germany, 2000.

[4] Y. Xiong, and K. Pulli. Color matching for high-quality panoramic images on mobile phones. *IEEE Trans. Consumer Electronics*, 56(4):2592–2600, 2010.

[5] G. Klein, and D.Murray. Parallel Tracking and Mapping on a Camera Phone. *Proc. International Symposium on Mixed and Augmented Reality*

Automatic Comic-like Image Layout System Preserving Image Order and Important Regions

Emi Myodo, Satoshi Ueno, Koichi Takagi, and Shigeyuki Sakazawa
KDDI R&D Laboratories Inc., 2-1-15 Ohara Fujimino-shi Saitama 356-8502 Japan
{em-myoudou, sa-ueno, ko-takagi, sakazawa}@kddilabs.jp

ABSTRACT

In this paper, we present a practical and automatic comic-like image layout system for event photos or event movies. We focus on the comic-like layout with cropping. The comic-like layouts allow viewers to track events in time sequential order like comic books, in which event images are cropped and arranged in panels from top left to bottom right on a screen so that the resultant layout has variety of image shapes and gives a pleasant impression. The main drawback of the conventional method is that an important region such as a face or a salient object area is sometimes cropped. In order to avoid excessive cropping of important regions while maintaining the image order, our system achieves adaptive layout to input images by generating all possible templates suitable for comic and deciding appropriate templates based on our proposed layout evaluation. In the demo, we will show that our full automatic system generates comic-like layouts immediately. Furthermore, the system allows a user to select his/her favorite layout from the multiple ones with different looks.

Categories and Subject Descriptors

H.5.2 **[User Interfaces]**

General Terms: Algorithms, Design

Keywords: image layout, viewing system, comic, tree enumeration, cropping

1. INTRODUCTION

As the popularity of digital cameras increase, more and more event photo and movie collections are stored on our storage devices or on the Web, and there is a strong demand for an intuitive and attractive viewing system. Various automatic image layout services are released, which lay out multiple images on a screen with and without image cropping. Considering event image viewing, maintaining the time sequence of images is required for an intuitive understanding. The variety of image shapes on a screen is also a preferable feature to look attractive though it sometimes causes excessive image cropping. Some methods for (semi) automatic image layout methods [1]-[3] have been proposed. Although Atkins et al. [1] generate attractive layouts having shape variety, the image order is not maintained. Calic et al. [2] preserve the image order as in comic books, but the image shape has no variety. Hong et al. [3] solve such problems, but the important regions of the images are likely cropped since they only manually prepare the small number of templates. Here, a template consists of blank panels in a specific order, and the images are forced to be cropped according to the shape of the corresponding panels on the templates. If a variation of templates is not enough, important regions of the images are likely to be removed in the cropping process.

MM'11, November 28-December 1, 2011, Scottsdale, Arizona, USA.
ACM 978-1-4503-0616-4/11/11.

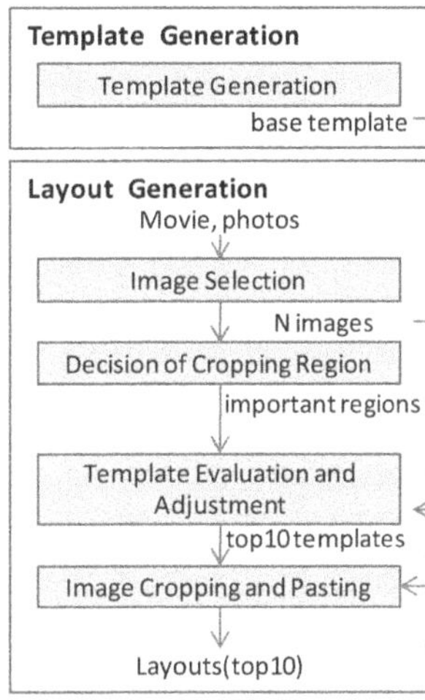

Figure 1.System architecture.

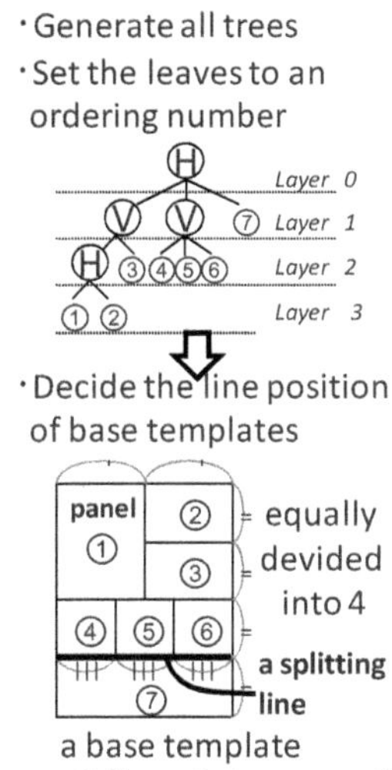

Figure 2.Template generation.

Since the key issue is difficulty in providing a variety of templates, we propose a method of automatically generating all possible templates for adaptive layout to input images. We also propose an automatic decision of cropping regions and the evaluation of templates in terms of the cropping penalty.

2. PROPOSED METHOD

2.1 General Framework

The general framework of our system is illustrated in Figure 1 with the following processes: (1) automatic templates generation by our new method (subsection 2.2); (2) selection of N images per page from input photo collections or movie files, and conventional image selection or key frame extraction techniques can be used; (3) decision of the cropping regions (subsection 2.3); (4) evaluation of templates and adjustment of splitting lines of layouts to alleviate crop-off of important regions (subsection 2.4); and (5) output of image layout based on the best template.

2.2 Template Generation

We adopt a tree structure to describe the structure of splitting lines on a screen as in [4]. In order to generate all possible but not duplicated trees for comic layouts, we enhance the enumeration method of rooted ordered trees [5]. The original method [5] is effective for data mining, but it generates many useless or unattractive trees for the image layout. In our modified method, we incorporate the following five restrictions in the tree pruning process. In order to prune useless trees, we force this following 1) and 2) restrictions: 1) the number of child vertices has to be two or more than two or zero, because trees with one child vertex cannot express layout and 2) the number of leaves N, which corresponds with the number of images. To prune unattractive trees, we apply the following restrictions: 3) the maximum number of layer I; 4) the maximum number of child vertices $b[i]$ (i=0,1, ⋯, I) for layer i, and we denote (b[0],b[1], ⋯, b[I]) as 3)-4) restrictions; 5) the direction of splitting lines that first divide the screen [4]. The direction is horizontal or vertical. Then, all trees that satisfy the above restrictions are generated.

The proposed method sets the leaves to an ordering number from left to right as shown in Figure 2. The number corresponds to the image order to read. Then, the positions of splitting lines are set to divide the panels in the same length of lines as shown in Figure 2. Thus, all base templates are derived based on the generated trees.

2.3 Decision of Cropping Region

Our method automatically determines an important region *R* to be preserved for each image. As shown in Figure 3(a), the *R* surrounds all detected important objects such as face or head areas and salient areas [6]. If an important object is not detected, the center region of the image is determined for as the *R*. In addition, images with intentional camera framing are prioritized. If the number of portrait style images is much fewer than that of landscape style images, then it is regarded as intentional, and we allocate the large important region *R* as shown in Figure 3(b).

2.4 Template Evaluation

In our approach, we choose the best template with the minimum penalty from all possible templates. An image *Ij* is cropped so that the shape of cropped image *Rp* is geometrically similar to the shape of the corresponding panel *Lj*. Then, the image size of *Rp* is adjusted so that *Rp* fits the panel *Lj* without blank space. In order to fully utilize the pixels in the original image, *Rp* should be an inscribed rectangle of the image *Ij*. Here, as shown in Figure 3(c)(d), we define the vertically extended region *Rv* and the horizontally extended region *Rh* including the whole *R*. They show the upper limit for cropping without penalty in each direction. For instance, the important region *R* is cropped when the shape of *Rp* is horizontally thinner than *Rh* or vertically thinner than *Rv*. We employ the logarithm of the cropped area of *R* as a penalty for each *Rp*, and the whole penalty *P* for a template is defined as follows. Here, *A* is area of each region.

$$P = \sum_{j=1}^{j=N} \max(\log(A(Rhj)/A(Rpj)), \log(A(Rpj)/A(Rvj)), 0)$$

All templates are evaluated, sorted and the top 200 templates are selected. The positions of the splitting lines of those templates are automatically adjusted, evaluated and sorted again in order to reduce the penalty. Thus, the shapes of panels are adapted to the important regions *R*. The length of adjusted lines is limited to be more than half of the original panel in order to avoid small panels. Then, the top 10 templates are selected for display. Then, effects such as slanted lines can be inserted. As another enhancement, when a user chooses a specific image *Ij* manually, our system only displays the layout where the designated image is in a large panel.

3. DEMONSTRATION

We describe the demonstration set up. Let set *N* per page as seven and the number of pages is two. The restrictions (3)(4) described in 2.2 are set to (4,3,3,2) and (5) is horizontal. These restrictions cover the almost all the real comic tree structures.

An example of the generated best layout with the lowest penalty is shown in Figure 4(a). This wedding event can be traced from top left to bottom right as in comic books. The image order is perfectly maintained. Users can select the favorite layout as shown in Figure 4(b) among the generated different layouts. In this case, we select the layout with kissing scene (7) and the group photo (14) in the big panels.

Figure3. Important region *R* and expanded region *Rh and Rv*.

1: church, 2-3: entrance with father, 4: entrance with groom, 5-6: praying, 7: kiss, 8-9: marriage vow, 10-12: exit, 13: flower shower, 14: group photo

(a) Best layout with the lowest penalty

(b) Layout variation with low penalty

Figure 4. Examples of generated comic-like layouts.

4. ACKNOWLEDGMENTS

Our thanks to Zeno Jonke for his support.

5. REFERENCES

[1] C.B.Atkins, "Blocked Recursive Image Composition", ACMMM'08, pp.821-824, 2008.

[2] J.Calic et al., "Efficient Layout of Comic-like Video Summaries", IEEE Trans. on CSVT, Vol.17, No.7, pp.931-936, 2007.

[3] R. Hong et al., "Movie2Comics: A Feast of Multimedia Artwork", ACM MM'10, pp.611-614, 2010.

[4] T. Tanaka et al., "Layout Analysis of Tree-structured Scene Frames in Comic Images", IJCAI-07, pp.2885-pp.2890, 2007.

[5] M.J. Zaki, "Efficiently mining frequent trees in a forest", ACM SIGKDD'02, pp.71-80, 2002.

[6] X. Hou et al., "Saliency Detection: A Spectral Residual Approach", CVPR, 2007.

Towards A Real Time Public Transport Awareness System: Case Study In Dublin *

Eric Bouillet, Luca Gasparini, Olivier Verscheure
IBM Research, Mulhuddart, Ireland
{bouillet,luca.gasparini,verscheure}@ie.ibm.com

ABSTRACT

In this paper we discuss our experience with the design of a public transport awareness application developed for the city of Dublin. The application is capable to ingest, analyze and visualize in real-time high volumes of traffic data coming from a variety of sources. We address the challenges encountered during the design of the application and propose novel solutions to tackle those challenges.

Categories and Subject Descriptors

H.4.2 [**Information Systems Applications**]: Decision Support

General Terms

Management

Keywords

Transport

1. INTRODUCTION

The rapid growth of demand for transportation and high levels of car dependency has resulted in severe traffic congestion in many cities worldwide. The general consensus is that congestion reduction efforts are best invested in Intelligence Transportation Systems (ITS) that leverage sensor networks, communications and computing technologies to manage existing infrastructure and transportation systems more efficiently. A recent development within ITS is the emergence and installation of sensor technologies such as Automated Vehicle Location (AVL) systems for collecting data on the state of the transport systems. ITS systems can make use of such data collected from a variety of sources to gain a more accurate insight about the performances of the transport infrastructure and enable real time traffic monitoring and management. There are, however, major challenges in building systems that are flexible and powerful enough to handle diverse demands from a large user base. The first challenge is one of scalability. As various kinds of sensor technologies become ubiquitous, the massive amount of data they produce must be analyzed in real-time. A second challenge is the quality of the data. As the sensor technologies grow larger so does the risk of receiving invalid data from faulty sensors, or noisy data from less accurate sensors. Data sparsity is another challenge. Even though the volume of data can be extremely large, because of the equally large dimension space of the system, the volume is usually insufficient for deriving accurate traffic models. A final challenge is different kinds of end-users have different needs for the traffic-data. These users not only pose large numbers of simultaneous analysis requests, but also require analyses of significantly different natures, the result of which must be displayed in near real time in the respective clients.

In this presentation, we discuss an ITS framework that tackles the challenge mentioned above. The framework is based on the IBM InfoSphere Streams platform[1], a scalable data stream processing platform. We describe a case study demonstrating the use of our framework and InfoSphere Streams with an actual application, called Public Transport Awareness (PTA), implemented for the road administration authority at the Dublin City Council to monitor the public transport infrastructure.

2. DESCRIPTION OF THE PUBLIC TRANSPORT AWARENESS APPLICATION

The application ingests live Service Interface for Real time Information (SIRI) Vehicle Monitoring[3] data from the main bus operators in Dublin. Although the data feed currently consists of the bus transit network only, the SIRI protocol is applicable to other ground transport modalities, such as tramways or trains, and these transport modalities are supported as well should they become available. The information contained in the feed consists of time stamps, vehicle ID, route ID, and GPS positions, among others, of the bus vehicle fleet. The fleet consists of about 1000 vehicles, each sending their positions at 20 seconds intervals on average, thus a resulting rate of about 50 bus position updates per seconds. Upon receiving the bus GPS positions, the application performs a number of analytics, such as:

- Locate the buses along their respective routes, or identify buses that do not follow their assigned route,
- Measure the average speed of individual vehicles and aggregate the speeds measured within a given time window on shared sections of route,
- Deduct from the aggregated average speeds the travel time between sequences of bus stops.

*Area chair: Dr Deepak Turaga

MM'11, November 28–December 1, 2011, Scottsdale, Arizona, USA.
ACM 978-1-4503-0616-4/11/11.

- Estimate the time of arrivals of the buses at their next stops along their route.
- Infer statistical models from the observed data, such as dynamic histograms of service delays, speeds, busses in congestion etc. from the real-time data, as well probability distribution of delays at stops or travel times at stops at different time of the day or different days of the week from historical data.
- Transcode the above derived data streams (bus speeds, estimated time of arrival, etc) into a standard format and export to other services, such as a Traffic Management Data Dictionary (TMDD)[2] gateway allowing the integration with other services like the IBM Intelligent Operation Center.

The list of possibilities is not exhaustive. The platform is open and if desired it can easily be extended to support additional data sources and analytics as new ones become available. The application includes a visualization interface, which allows multiple users to individually query and visualize the results of the analytics mentioned above. The visualization consists of an interactive dashboard showing the main key performance indicators such as delay histograms, speed histograms aggregated along the streets, number of buses in congestion, and system indicators such as rate of updates per seconds. Each user is presented with an individual view of the dashboard for the length of the user session, and each session is associated with a Keyhole Markup Language (KML) update stream allowing the user to view the results of their interaction with the dashboard in a KML compliant GIS viewer such as Google Earth. Figure 1. Illustrates the dashboard with the resulting GIS view in Google Earth Pro.

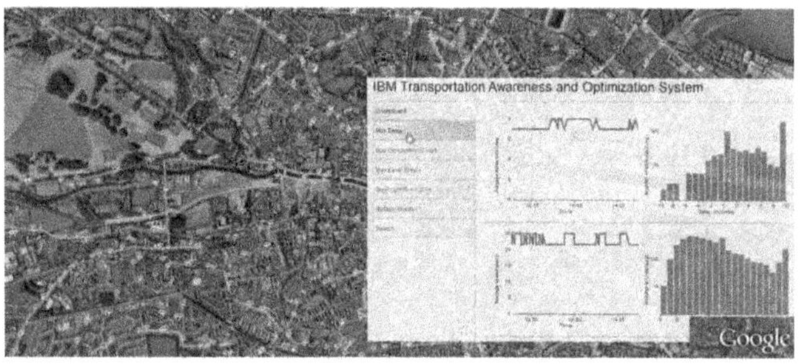

Figure 1: Public Transport Awareness Visualization interface, dashboard (foreground) and GIS view (background).

Example of visualizations include:

- Position and description (vehicle id, speed, route, direction) of all the vehicles, or a subset of the vehicles matching a user selection, e.g. all vehicles with a given delay selected by the user from the delay histogram in the dashboard.
- Color map of speed along the different road sections covered by the public transport network, or from a user selection of road sections matching a given speed, selected from a histogram.
- Estimated time of arrivals of buses at their next stops, calculated from the latest known bus positions, and recent history of measured travel times between the stops.

In addition the dashboard offers an autofill search feature allowing the user to search for stop or route names, vehicle IDs, etc. and to subscribe or unsubscribe to events related to the selected entities only. For instance a user can select a subset of the bus routes and visualize only buses and average speeds on the segments of the selected routes.

An important feature of the application is its ability to provide the operator with a detailed representation of the public transit status, including the results of analytics mentioned above, which is less than 10 seconds old on the average (half interval between two GPS observations). This estimation of the lag is validated in practice through a side-by-side comparison of the visualization of the vehicle position in our GIS viewer with a ground truth observed from CCTV cameras.

3. PUBLIC TRANSPORT AWARENESS APPLICATION ARCHITECTURE

The application is comprised of two main components. The first component is a data streams application built on the IBM InfoSphere Streams platform. It is responsible for the processing of the vehicle position and the computation of the analytics described in the previous section. InfoSphere Streams was selected here because of its ability to execute complex analytics with very low latency requirements on massive amount of data with a minimum hardware footprint. Also the data streams programming paradigm provides a platform on which scalable solutions can be built to address the challenges of data quality, data sparsity, and diversity of data sources and user requests. The result of the processing performed by the InfoSphere Streams application are sent in the form of updates to the second component, a web service that maintains a global state of the public transport network infrastructure. Each user who accesses this web-service is associated with a user-session that provides the user with an individual view of the global state. When the users start a new session they first receive a KML file, which contains URLs to KML updates corresponding to their session settings. In this effect, the users are presented with two screens, the web-client containing a dashboard through which the users can interact with the web-service to modify their view of the global state of the public transport infrastructure, and the KML client, such as Google Earth, where the result of this interaction is displayed. Both components run in production environment on a single RHEL 5.3 vmware deployed on a single server with 8 Intel Xeonl 2.27GHz CPU cores, and 6GBytes RAM, with a total of less than 10% CPU utilization.

4. REFERENCES

[1] Biem A., Bouillet E., Ranganathan A., Riabov A., Verscheure O., Koutsopoulos H.N., and Moran C. Ibm infosphere streams for scalable, real-time, intelligent transportation services. In *SIGMOD Conference*, 2010.

[2] Traffic Management Data Dictionary. www.ite.org/standards/tmdd.

[3] Service Interface for Real Time Information. www.siri.org.uk.

ARA: The Active Reading Application

Gene Golovchinsky, Scott Carter, Anthony Dunnigan
FX Palo Alto Laboratory, Inc.
3174 Porter Drive
Palo Alto, CA 94304
gene,carter,tonyd@fxpal.com

ABSTRACT

The Active Reading Application (ARA) brings the familiar experience of writing on paper to the tablet. The application augments paper-based practices with audio, the ability to review annotations, and sharing. It is designed to make it easier to review, annotate, and comment on documents by individuals and groups. ARA incorporates several patented technologies and draws on several years of research and experimentation.

Categories and Subject Descriptors

H.4 [**Information Systems Applications**]: Miscellaneous

General Terms

Design, Human Factors

Keywords

Mobile, Reading, Annotation

1. INTRODUCTION

> "The linear, continuous reading of single documents by people on their own is an unrealistic characterization of how people read in the course of their daily work." [1]

Work-related reading is a misnomer. Most "reading" involves an array of activities, often driven by some well-defined goal, and can include skimming, searching, cross-referencing, or annotating. For example, a lawyer might browse a collection of discovery documents in order to find where a defendant was on the night of October 3, 1999, annotate that document, and cross-reference it with another document describing conflicting information from a witness.

More than that, reading can be collaborative and can involve multiple displays. For example, a designer might skim documents on a phone to find a graphic that supports an idea in a collaborative brainstorming session and send it to a colleague's tablet for review.

There are many examples of passive reading applications on mobile devices, such as Adobe's *Acrobat Reader*, but most are designed for the linear, continuous reading model that

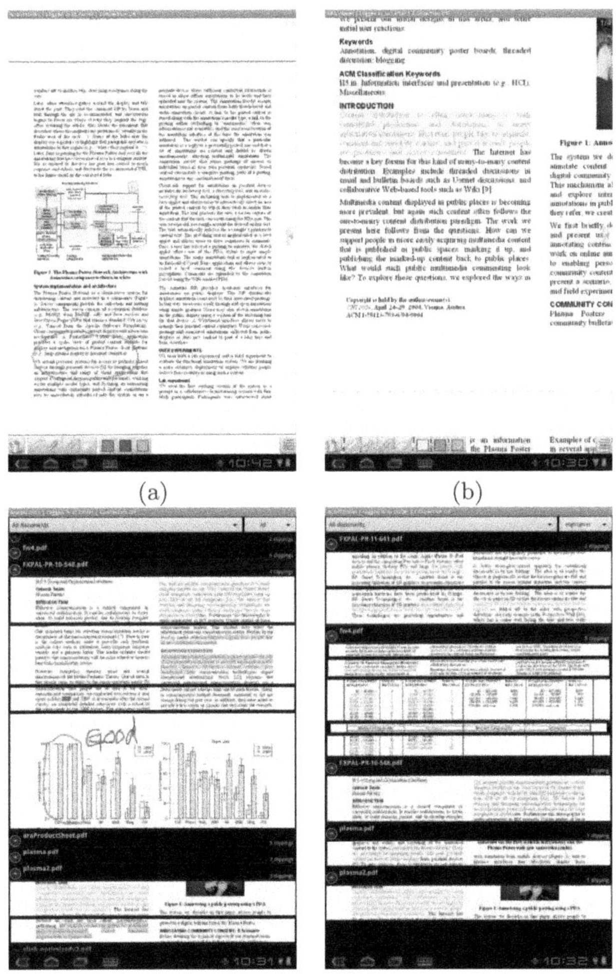

Figure 1: ARA supports document annotation. Users can ink directly on the document (a) or highlight text in the document (b). An annotation overview screen shows regions annotated across all documents (c). A variety of filters can be applied to the overview screen, for example to show only highlighted areas (d).

MM'11, November 28–December 1, 2011, Scottsdale, Arizona, USA.
ACM 978-1-4503-0616-4/11/11.

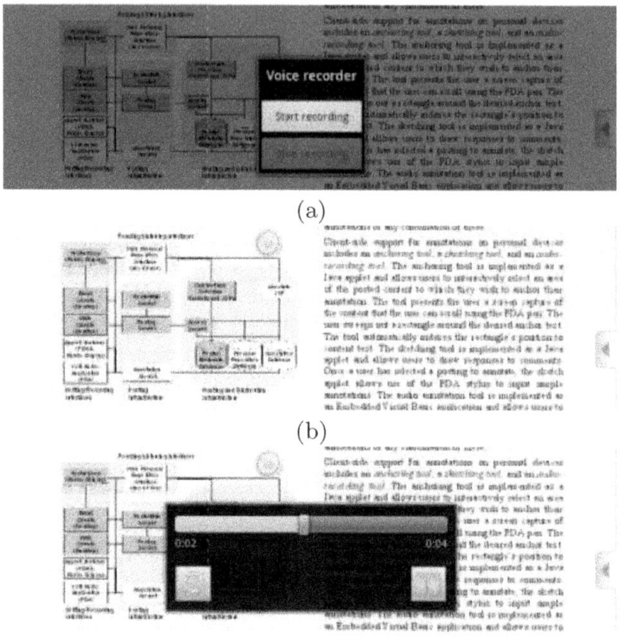

(a)

(b)

(c)

Figure 2: When mobile it can be difficult or impossible to sketch directly on the tablet. For these situations ARA supports audio-based annotations. Like sketches, audio clips are linked directly to the document and are synchronized with a remote server. After the user clicks an area to annotate, and records their message (a), an audio icon appears on the page and the annotation is uploaded (b). When a user clicks the icon (c) the audio starts playing immediately and an interface appears allowing the user to control playback.

tends not to apply to most work-related reading. Other projects, such as *XLibris* [2] , support a richer variety of annotation and cross-referencing features. The Active Reading Application (ARA) borrows heavily from this work while translating concepts from the early, relatively slow and memory constrained platforms for which XLibris was designed to modern touch displays.

2. ARA

ARA builds on the strengths of the paper but augments it with computation. Rather than simply emulating paper, it evolves paper-like interaction to the next level. With ARA, students and knowledge workers can highlight, mark, and comment on documents, just as they might on paper (Figures 1, 2). But they can also go beyond paper: They can read and annotate a wide variety of documents, and refer to these over time. Doing this on paper would involve carrying large numbers of documents, which can get heavy.

An annotation overview screen allows users to see only those passages of documents that they found interesting, compelling, controversial, or otherwise important based on the presence of annotation marks (Figure 1 (c,d)). This technique makes it easy to find the important passages in a large document even after considerable time has passed.

Knowledge work is seldom solitary, which is why ARA

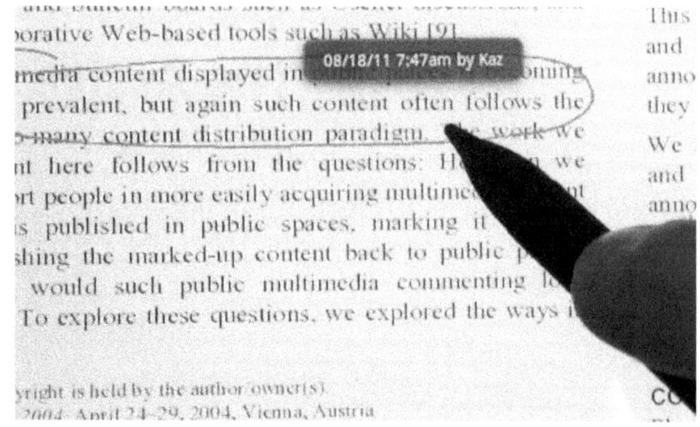

Figure 3: ARA can take advantage of the extra affordances of digital styluses. Here, a user hovers the pen over an annotation, causing ARA to display the annotation's creation time and owner.

also supports seamless sharing of annotations on documents. Collaborators can see each other's annotations and hear audio notes almost instantaneously. ARA can improve the effectiveness of teleconferencing by augmenting conversations with shared views of the documents being discussed. Furthermore, users can continue to add shared annotations even when the tablet loses its connection to the server – annotations will be stored locally and synchronized when the connection returns. This ability allows distributed teams to work together in ways not possible with paper.

ARA supports both touch- and stylus-based annotations, enabling users to easily switch between gross and fine-grained markup. The stylus also supports other types of input not possible with touch-only displays, such as hover (Figure 3). However sometimes marking up a document with a pen or finger can be difficult, in particular when a user is mobile and does not have both hands free. To support users on-the-go ARA also supports audio annotations (Figure 2). Crucially, behind-the-scenes these annotations behave the same as inks or highlights – all annotations are stored, integrated into the overview screen, uploaded, and potentially shared.

3. FUTURE WORK

ARA is a work-in-progress. We are currently experimenting with a variety of extensions, including more sophisticated sharing techniques and multi-touch and simultaneous pen- and touch-interaction. We are also exploring the integration of other types of multimedia content.

4. REFERENCES

[1] A. Adler, A. Gujar, B. L. Harrison, K. O'Hara, and A. Sellen. A diary study of work-related reading: design implications for digital reading devices. In *CHI '98*, pages 241–248, ACM.

[2] M. N. Price, B. N. Schilit, and G. Golovchinsky. Xlibris: the active reading machine. In *CHI '98*, pages 22–23, ACM.

myUnity: A New Platform to Support Communication in the Modern Workplace

Jacob T. Biehl, Thea Turner, William van Melle, and Andreas Girgensohn
FX Palo Alto Laboratory, Inc.
3174 Porter Drive
Palo Alto, CA 94304
650-842-4800
{biehl, turner, billvm, andreasg}@fxpal.com

ABSTRACT
Modern office work practices increasingly breach traditional boundaries of time and place, making it difficult to interact with colleagues. To address these problems, we developed myUnity, a software and sensor platform that enables rich workplace awareness and coordination. myUnity is an integrated platform that collects information from a set of independent sensors and external data aggregators to report user location, availability, tasks, and communication channels. myUnity's sensing architecture is component-based, allowing channels of awareness information to be added, updated, or removed at any time. Our current system includes a variety of sensor and data input, including camera-based activity classification, wireless location trilateration, and network activity monitoring. These and other input channels are combined and composited into a single, high-level presence state. Early studies of a myUnity deployment have demonstrated that use of the platform allows quick access to core awareness information and show its utility in supporting communication and collaboration in the modern workplace.

Categories and Subject Descriptors
H5.m Information interfaces and presentation (e.g., HCI): Miscellaneous.

General Terms
Human Factors

Keywords
Awareness, workplace studies, mobile communication

1. INTRODUCTION
A shift is taking place in the modern office: being "at work" no longer implies being physically at a desk in an office building. Workers are increasingly mobile, on both a small and large scale. Work is more frequently conducted outside the conventional "9-to-5" Monday through Friday work schedule. This shift is a result of factors such as pressures from globalization, soaring transportation costs, environmental concerns, technological advancement, and desire for a healthy work-life balance. At the same time, the volume of peer-to-peer interactions necessary to successfully perform work tasks remains high in most professional domains. With assumptions about a colleague's location and availability more uncertain than ever, breakdowns are becoming more frequent and costly.

*Area Chairs: A. Divakaran, D. Ponceleon, and D.S. Turaga

MM'11, November 28–December 1, 2011, Scottsdale, Arizona, USA.
ACM 978-1-4503-0616-4/11/11.

While there has been work in building systems to address this challenge, much of the existing work addresses a previous generation of technology and work practices. New design challenges have emerged; the critical importance of mobile devices in the day-to-day lives of workers and the explosion of communication tools used in the office are just a few examples.

myUnity is a new communication platform to address the challenges of this new landscape. In particular, myUnity seeks to provide an ongoing, easy-to-understand awareness of workers' presence and availability. It is the first system that supports both information collection and dissemination across multiple platforms (desktop and mobile), aggregating data from automatic sensors and existing systems (e.g., calendars, IM). Below we describe the components of the myUnity platform and discuss the value each component provides to the modern worker.

2. THE MYUNITY PLATFORM
myUnity's major platform components include client applications, sensor and data aggregators, and a central server.

2.1 Client Applications
The clients provide users with quick access to awareness information. myUnity can provide a user's presence information, approximate location, current status message, and links to phone numbers, IM, and email (see Figure 1). Users can independently select which information is reported on their behalf. In addition, myUnity provides facilities that assist in coordinating communication with peers. For example, clicking on a link launches the application to communicate over that channel.

Figure 1 shows the dashboard (the main visual display) for the desktop and mobile clients. It features an array of tiles, each representing an individual in the organization. The tile's border and/or background color reflects the individual's current state:

Green	physically in office, alone
Purple	in office with at least one other person
Yellow	in office building, but not in office
Blue	using computer from remote location (not office)
Orange	not in office building (if person is using mobile client)
Grey	system has no current information

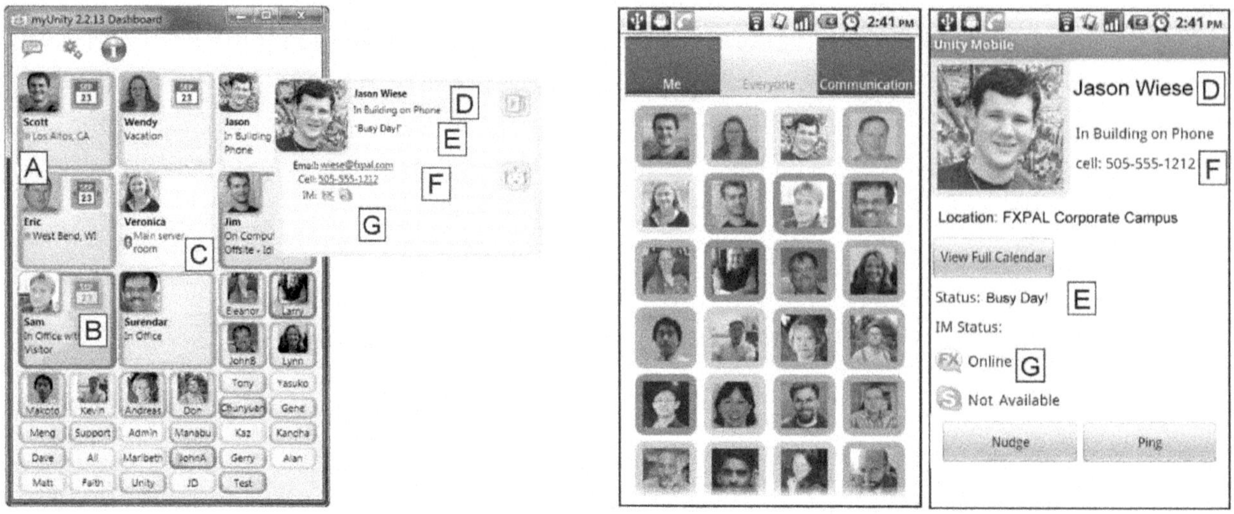

Figure 1. The desktop (left) and mobile (middle) dashboards. In addition to presence state, the desktop dashboard displays location from phone (A) or Bluetooth/Wi-Fi (C) as well as calendar information (B). The detail views for the mobile client (far right) and desktop (popup over dashboard) show presence data (D), status messages (E), contact information (F), and IM client status (G).

The desktop dashboard (Figure 1) is configurable. As the application window is enlarged, the tile size expands and can include additional information (e.g., full name, a description of presence state, and calendar data). Users can choose to represent individual tiles in one of three sizes, allowing users to customize the visual representation to maximize the awareness details about specific individuals while minimizing details of others.

The dashboard allows users to determine the presence state of their colleagues at a glance. With quick access to presence states, users can efficiently acquire information useful in determining a channel and time to communicate with a colleague. For instance, one could quickly confirm that a peer is alone in his office before initiating a phone call or walking to his office.

Mobile clients provide the same awareness and communication options as the desktop client. This enables our users to stay in touch with co-workers while they are away from the office. At the same time, the mobile clients can provide information about the user's location and, in the Android client, the call status. The mobile clients use a background service to periodically determine location and then upload it to the server.

2.2 Sensors and External Data Aggregators

myUnity collects information from a bank of independent sensors and external data aggregators for presentation in the clients. Our aggregator architecture is component-based, allowing channels of awareness information to be added, updated, or removed at any time. We implemented six aggregators for the platform:

- *Vision-based office activity.* Using a video feed from a small wide-angle camera (mounted in the corner of personal offices), users can specify the physical space of their office that they typically occupy and the space occupied by visitors. When motion is detected in these spaces, the corresponding state is reported. Raw video is not shared.
- *Mobile phone location.* In addition to the mobile clients' reported location, Bluetooth and Wi-Fi access points installed throughout the office building can trilaterate the signal of a user's phone or other wireless device to provide a user's approximate physical location within the building.
- *Computer and network location software client.* The desktop client can report when a user is actively using the computer by detecting mouse and keyboard activity. It also uses the type of network connection (on a fixed or mobile computer inside a corporate network, remotely on VPN, or external).
- *Calendar.* Users can link information from various calendaring systems. This includes information from corporate calendars (e.g., vacation, sick, or travel day) and personal calendars (e.g., personal and professional meetings).
- *IM presence.* Users can report their status from IM protocols (e.g., Jabber, Google Talk, Skype, and Windows Live Messenger) by supplying their connection information.
- *Phone call status.* The Android mobile client and the IP-based office phones can report whether a person is in a call.

An important design characteristic of the myUnity aggregators is that users can independently select which ones report information on their behalf. Thus, people can customize data collection to conform to their own privacy concerns and requirements. This aspect of the architecture is different from most existing systems that control how data are *disseminated*, not *collected*.

2.3 Central Server

The central server is responsible for collecting information provided by the aggregators, fusing and summarizing this information, and streaming the result to client instances. myUnity takes a slightly different approach to fusion and summarization in that it does not infer or predict state (as is done by other systems), but rather degrades the data's resolution to convey only what it knows to be true. For example, if it receives data that a user is present in the building and is logged on to several IM protocols but no evidence from her office activity sensors, it will not infer that she is in her office, only that she is in the building. While degrading the state may produce less useful results, it avoids situations where the system is incorrect.

Galaxy Browser: Exploratory Search of Web Videos

Lei Pang§ Song Tan§ Hung-Khoon Tan† Chong-Wah Ngo§
leipang3@student.cityu.edu.hk songtan@student.cityu.edu.hk
thkhoon@utar.edu.my cwngo@cs.cityu.edu.hk

Department of Computer Science§
City University of Hong Kong
Kowloon, Hong Kong

Faculty of Information & Communication Technology†
University Tunku Abdul Rahman
Perak, Malaysia

ABSTRACT

Most search engines return a ranked list of items in response to a query. The list however tells very little about the relationship among items. For videos especially, users often read to spend significant amount of time to navigate the search result. Exploratory search presents a new paradigm for browsing where the browser takes up the role of information exploring and presents a well-organized browsing structure for users to navigate. The proposed interface Galaxy Browser adopts the recent advances in near-duplicate detection and then synchronizes the detected near-duplicate information with comprehensive background knowledge derived from online external resources. The result is a topic structure on which users can easily browse and explore.

Categories and Subject Descriptors

H.3.3 [**Information Search and Retrieval**]: Retrieval models

General Terms

Algorithms Performance Experimentation

Keywords

Video browsing, information visualization, summarization

1. INTRODUCTION

Existing video search engines typically provide a *flat* list in response to a user query on a particular topic-of-interest. They are designed mainly to cater for *targeted search* where users have a certain degree of idea and knowledge of the topic-of-interest. However, more often than not, this is not the case. A user may not be familiar with the topic and indeed does not have a clear search goal. Instead, the search goal is changed and refined when more information is revealed. As indicated in a recent survey [1], 37% of the users were found to browse casually without any specific video in mind. Therefore, a more appealing paradigm for browse-and-search is by providing functionalities that expose different patches of visual information for efficient navigation, namely *exploratory search*. This demo will show our search engine which organizes and visualizes videos in a manner that enables users to grasp the gist of a search topic and interact with various information facets mined from videos and external resources.

To facilitate exploratory search, our system consolidates multi-faceted information to facilitate the switch of search goal and navigation path. First, the videos are linked based on overlapping content and this allows users to view the redundancy between the videos. Furthermore, when partially overlapping videos are linked, users may gain insight into how a topic evolves in content over time. Second,reliable milestone events are extracted. They constitute the high-level semantic organization of the topic which gives users a bird-eye's view of how critical a particular video and event is with respect to the whole topic. Basically, the system encompasses the *what*, *when* and *how* aspects of the topic and thus forms a very informative basis for exploratory search. Guided by the resultant structure of the topic, users can browse for videos intelligently without having to go through blindly all the videos in a flat list.

MM'11, November 28–December 1, 2011, Scottsdale, Arizona, USA.
ACM 978-1-4503-0616-4/11/11.

2. TECHNOLOGY

The metadata associated with web videos are often sparse and not informative which is difficult for users to find important videos. Our system addresses this challenge by exploiting visual redundancy among videos and authoring the search results with rich media information. The first part is achieved by hyperlinking hundreds to thousands of videos under a search topic to form and visualize different islands of visual content. The second part is to augment the islands with events extracted from multiple knowledge sources through media synchronization.

Given a set of somewhat correlated but diverse videos, a scene that are broadly found across different videos and in addition uploaded by different users, is usually related to an important event based on the fact that it triggers significant user interest. The set of videos associated to a common scene through near-duplicate links forms a *visual snippet.* To mine visual snippets, we employ the near-duplicate algorithm in [3] for its capability to match two partially near-duplicate videos. A video is represented using sparse keyframe representation and each keyframe is represented using Bag-Of-Words (BoW). Near-duplicate (ND) keyframe pairs are then extracted by BoW matching and Hamming Embedding [2] verification. The ND pairs are then aligned using temporal network [3] by imposing temporal constraints. The links detected by partial near-duplicate detection is used to hyperlink the videos, forming constellations of videos or visual snippets to present a galaxy view of the topic.

To infuse the visual snippets with semantic connotations,

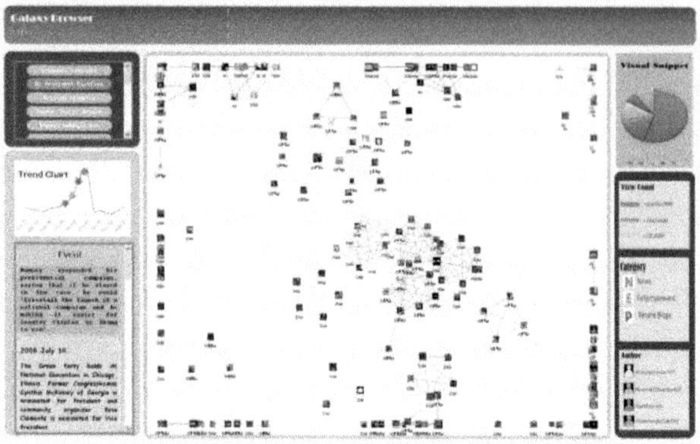

Figure 1: The main interface of the Galaxy Browser.

we rely on external resources to supplement the visual information. Directing the search using the original queries to *Wikipedia*, *Google News* and *Google Trend* retrieves useful patches of information related to the topic. Wikipedia articles provides a very concise and complete summary of the event while online news articles further offer the details of these events if they are present. Google Trend provides user browsing history where spikes in the query frequency hints the important time when milestone events occur. Hence, one major component of the system is to synchronize the visual snippets with these auxiliary modalities with respect to time. The similarity is based on textual information resulting in a heterogeneous network. Performing time-constraint alignment [4] on the network produces the milestone events, each defined by a visual snippet, atomic event and news article. With the milestone events, the Galaxy Browser can organize the video in a manner that is conducive towards exploratory video browsing.

3. BROWSING

Figure 1 shows the main interface of Galaxy Browser which comprises 3 panels. The left panel is the *key-info panel* which summarizes the topic structure mined by the system. Given a topic of interest selected from top left panel, it presents to the users the set of all milestone events in the *event list* sub-panel in the bottom of the panel. Another important feature is the trend chart grabbed from Google Trend which informs the user of the fluctuations in interest among the online community on the topic. Thus, user can acquire a certain degree of understanding on *what* happens through the milestone events, *when* it happens and *how crucial* these events are through the trend chard. In practice, the panel acts as a filtering tool. Users can rapidly grab all videos associated to a specific event (spatial filtering) in the event list or a hot time (temporal filtering) from the trend chart and the associated visual snippet will be highlighted in the middle panel, i.e., the *Galaxy Window*.

The *Galaxy Window* illustrates the set of all visual snippets which depicts how the videos are linked to each other topically. For example, a fully connected structure indicates high redundancy among the videos. Conversely. a sparsely connected graph expose the evolving nature of the particular event. This allows users to select and go through a bare minimum number of videos and yet acquire the most information within the shortest time span. More importantly, each snippet is annotated with the description from the associated Wikipedia atomic event. This gives users an in-depth textual prelude of the snippet content. An interested user can choose to venture deeper into the topic by exploring the details of the visual snippet or read the associated news article.

The right panel is the *info panel* which lists the details of a selected visual snippet or video. In this panel, detailed information for the visual snippets is given, including *category*, *author* and *view counts* of the videos. These auxiliary data is displayed in the Galaxy window as well. Indeed, though not directly describing videos' content, they tell a great deal about a snippet. For example, a snippet with mostly entertainment category videos or with very low view count is most likely unimportant. On the other hand, when videos in a snippet are uploaded by the same user with back-to-back partial links, the individual videos are likely separate parts derived from the same video and are equally important.

Another interesting feature is the *snippet window* which is activated when a user clicks a video in a certain snippet. The videos belonging to the snippet are visualized as a series of thumbnail keyframes aligned horizontally which allows user to have a first-hand preview of the video content itself without having to play them. The overlapping near-duplicate segments will also be highlighted and users will know directly how these videos are related. The users can choose a specific video for viewing.

In summary, Galaxy Browser is a new generation browser system which adopts the exploratory search paradigm. Different facets of information offered by search results are visualized by mining visual snippets. Search exploration is further facilitated by augmenting the snippets with knowledge such as the time duration of the topic, milestone events, the hot degree or intensity of each event, which provide navigational guidance. These features result in an engine that goes beyond traditional fact-finding browsers such as storyboard and video skimming for more interactive visual information seeking. Interested readers can find our demo video at http://vireo.cs.cityu.edu.hk/demovideo.wmv.

ACKNOWLEDGEMENT

The work described in this paper was fully supported by a grant from the Research Grants Council of the Hong Kong Special Administrative Region, China (CityU 119610).

4. REFERENCES

[1] R. D.Oliveira, M. Cherubinia, and N. Oliver. Understanding near-duplicate videos: A human-centric approach. In *ACM Multimedia*, 2009.

[2] H. Jégou, M. Douze, and C. Schmid. Hamming embedding and weak geometric consistency for large scale image search. In *European Conference on Computer Vision*, 2008.

[3] H. K. Tan, C. W. Ngo, R. C. Hong, and T. S. Chua. Scalable detection of partial near-duplicate videos by visual-temporal consistency. In *ACM Multimedia*, 2009.

[4] S. Tan, H. K. Tan, and C. W. Ngo. Topical summarization of web videos by visual-text time-dependent alignment. In *ACM Multimedia*, 2010.

A Mobile Location Search System with Active Query Sensing

Felix X. Yu, Rongrong Ji, Tongtao Zhang, and Shih-Fu Chang
Department of Electrical Engineering, Columbia University
{yuxinnan,rrji,ttzhang, sfchang}@ee.columbia.edu

ABSTRACT

How should the second query be taken once the first query fails in mobile location search based on visual recognition? In this demo, we describe a mobile search system with a unique Active Query Sensing (AQS) function to intelligently guide the mobile user to take a successful second query. This suggestion is built upon a scalable visual matching system covering over 0.3 million street view reference images in New York City, where each location is associated with multiple surrounding views and panorama. In online search, once the initial search result fails, the system will perform online analysis and suggest the mobile user to turn to the most discriminative viewing angle to take the second visual query, from which the search performance is expected to greatly improve. The AQS suggestion is based on both offline salient view discovery and online viewing angle prediction and intelligent turning decision. Our experiments show our AQS can improve the mobile location search with a performance gain as high as 100%, reducing the failure rate to only 12% after taking the second visual query.

Categories and Subject Descriptors

H.4.3 [**Information Systems Applications**]

General Terms

Algorithms, System, Measurement

Keywords

Mobile Visual Search, Mobile Location Recognition

1. APPLICATION SCENARIOS

With the popularity of mobile handheld devices, we are seeing increasing demand and promising progresses in mobile location search using visual recognition techniques. The mobile user takes a photograph of his/her surrounding view and sends the captured image over the wireless link to the server, which matches the reference images of the candidate locations stored in the server to identify the true location of the mobile user. Such visual matching capabilities can be found in several commercial systems such as snaptell [1], Nokia point and find [1], kooaba [1], as well as research prototypes [2–4]. Complementary GPS or network based localization techniques, mobile location search provides more precise localization plus indication of orientation. For instance, GPS information is typically in the range of 20-100 feet without orientation; but using visual search, improvement to about 10 feet plus orientation information is feasible. Furthermore, visual based localization can still be used if GPS signals are not available, as the case of urban jungles.

MM'11, November 28–December 1, 2011, Scottsdale, Arizona, USA.
ACM 978-1-4503-0616-4/11/11.

Figure 1: Top: Location coverage of 0.3 million reference images in our system; Bottom: six views of an example location in New York City.

However, current visual-based localization systems still lack robust performance deemed acceptable in practice. In a preliminary trial we conducted, only less than 50% of the visual location queries were successful. This is consistent with the moderate accuracy (0.4-0.7 average precision) reported in the literature so far. Often the failure cases can be attributed to false alarms caused by the confusing locations with high visual similarities.

Distinct from prior works, we focus on a novel system [5] to improve the mobile visual search experience in subsequent user interaction, namely how to guide users to find the right queries that are more likely to work. We develop the system based on the observations that there exist certain unique salient views for each target location. For instance, certain views of a location are more discriminative since they contain unique "signatures" such as distinctive landmarks or skylines. In contrast, other views are less useful in distinguishing the given location from others because they contain common and confusing objects (trees, walls, *etc.*).

We demonstrate a mobile location search system with Active Query Sensing (AQS) capabilities to guide a user in turning the camera to capture the best views for subsequent queries. Our current prototype includes 0.3 million geographical reference images[1] of Manhattan, New York City,

[1]We thank NAVTEQ for providing the NYC image data set, Dr. Xin Chen and Dr. Jeff Bach for their generous help.

Figure 2: Our system finds and plot the top matched location (indicated by the geo tag) and associated surrounding views and points of interest in response to the given query. The user may verify the correctness of the result by comparing the surrounding views and the points of interest returned by the system.

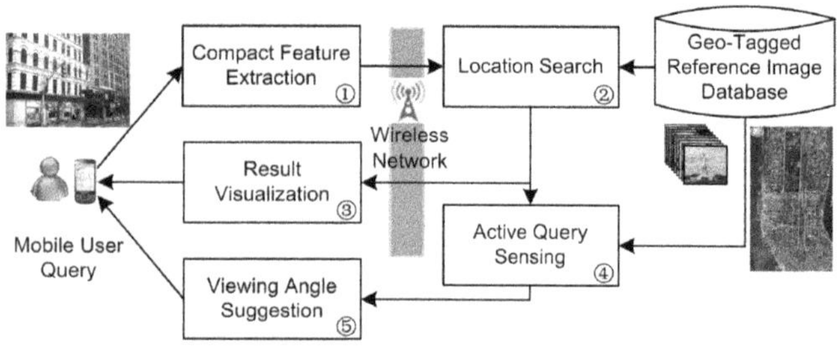

Figure 3: Workflow of the active query sensing system

covering about 50,000 locations each with six surrounding views (see Figure 1).

2. SYSTEM WORKFLOW

The procedure of our proposed AQS system is as follows (shown in Figure 3):

Step 1: First, user captures a query image of his surrounding using the camera phone. And the image (or alternatively the extracted compact descriptor [4]) is sent to the server through the wireless link.

Step 2: The location search system receives the visual query, searches matched images, and returns the top matched location (Figure 2).

Step 3: After checking and comparing the surrounding views and points of interest (as shown in Figure 2), if the user determines the predicted location is wrong, he may trigger active query sensing function to ask for the suggestion of the best query view.

Step 4: Upon user's request, our system calls the active query sensing module to come up with the best view for the next query. It sends specific instructions to the user (*e.g.*, turn to the right about 30 degrees, turn up about 30 degrees etc.). Figure 4 shows a sample interface, indicating how the user is guided to follow the suggested view change.

Step 5: User follows the suggestion to turn the camera and take the next query image and send it for another location search, as shown in Figure 4.

Figure 4: Our AQS interface guides users to the best view that is predicted to have a better chance of successful location search. (upper left subwindow: the previous query image, upper right arrows: the view angles of previous query, current and suggested viewing angles; the main window: the current camera view). User follows the suggestion by trying to align the green arrow with the target arrow (red).

3. SYSTEM IMPLEMENTATIONS

Our current prototype includes a search server and client applications using both the actual mobile phones (either iPhone or Android) and desktop simulations. The demos on mobile phones may use pre-loaded street images or live street image captures as queries. The mobile applications communicate with the server through Wi-Fi or cellular services. The desktop simulation uses online street map services on which users can roam to any location in Manhattan and crop any view from the interface to simulate mobile search. Our search system implemented a codebook of one-million visual words using hierarchical k-means clustering [2] of SIFT descriptors, with inverted indexing to facilitate real-time search over 0.3 million reference images. Based on the implementation on a regular workstation, each query takes about 1.2 seconds.

Our AQS system implemented several unique ideas [5] - (1) an offline process for analyzing the saliency of each view associated with each location in the database (2) an online process to estimate the likely view of the current query, and determine the optimal view change in order to disambiguate the uncertainty of the top confusing locations. Details can be found in [5].

4. REFERENCES

[1] snaptell.com, pointandfind.nokia.com, kooaba.com.

[2] D. Nister and H. Stewenius. Scalable recognition with a vocabulary tree. In *CV*, 2006.

[3] B. Kaneva, J. Sivic, A. Torralba, S Avidan, and W. Freeman. Matching and predicting street level images. In *or shop on Vision for Cognitive as s, CCV*, 2010.

[4] B. Girod *et al.* Mobile visual search. In *I Signal rocessing Magazine*, July, 2011.

[5] F. Yu, R. Ji, and S-F. Chang. Active query sensing for mobile location search. In *ACM Multimedia*, 2011.

Collaborative Authoring of Serious Games for Health

Florian Mehm, Sandro Hardy, Stefan Göbel, Ralf Steinmetz
TU Darmstadt, Multimedia Communications Lab - KOM
Rundeturmstraße 10
64283 Darmstadt, Germany
+49 6151 16 {Florian Mehm: 6885, Sandro Hardy: 75164, Stefan Göbel: 6149, Ralf Steinmetz: 6150}
{florian.mehm, sandro.hardy, stefan.goebel, ralf.steinmetz}@kom.tu-darmstadt.de

ABSTRACT
The efficient production of Serious Games typically requires the collaboration of technical and game development experts, i.e. game developers and domain experts such as pedagogues or sports experts. For the use case of exergames with educational aspects, we demonstrate how an authoring tool for Serious Games can be specialized for collaborative authoring by defining roles of users and providing different views on the created game to each user group carrying out different tasks in the production of the game.

Categories and Subject Descriptors
H.5.3 [**Group and Organization Interfaces**]: Computer-supported cooperative work

General Terms
Design

Keywords
Serious Games, Exergame, Authoring Tool, Collaborative Authoring, Multi-User Software

1. INTRODUCTION
Serious Games, i.e. games not only intended to entertain but to fulfill another primary purpose, can be differentiated from regular digital games by the increased need of collaboration of technical experts with experts in the target domain of the game. We have previously presented the authoring tool "StoryTec" [1,3] for non-programmers as a possible software solution to this process. In the present work, we expand upon the collaborative aspect of StoryTec by providing specialized views (comprising different tasks to be carried out in the authoring tool) to different user groups of the authoring tool. Note that in the context of this paper, we are not using the term "collaborative authoring" as indicating real-time interaction.

The research project Motivotion60+, into which the presented concept was integrated, targets at incorporating a motivational way of being active in the daily life of older persons. Sensors, web-technologies and communications technologies are combined with a game-based multimedia system. The resulting exergame combines physical exercises in the form of small games with an educational part involving multimedia presentation of information and associated quiz elements.

MM'11, November 28–December 1, 2011, Scottsdale, Arizona, USA.
ACM 978-1-4503-0616-4/11/11.

2. RELATED WORK
In the field of authoring tools for games or similar multimedia applications, few tools offer collaborative features. Among those are the TLTCS system [2], which is comprised of a set of different tools for different author groups and a version control system or the Narratoria system [4], which introduces collaboration by breaking storytelling applications down into small parts which authors can work on simultaneously.

The need for authoring tools for exergames which allow collaboration between different groups of experts can be observed by the growing interest in the field, exemplified by the submissions to the Game Days 2010 conference which was centered on exergames [5].

3. COLLABORATIVE AUTHORING
3.1 Basic Approach
The basic approach to authoring in StoryTec is discussed in detail in [3]. For an impression of the user interface see Figure 1. Authors define the overall structure of the game by decomposing it into scenes and transitions between these secenes, which are visualized in the Story Editor component of StoryTec. Authors define the actual gameplay for a specific scene (i.e. what the player will experience in this scene, including the game type, rules and parameters) by choosing what we refer to as interaction templates. Authors can choose from various templates and fill the scene with content, using the WYSIWYG Stage Editor. More advanced possibilities such as player modeling are covered in detail in [1].

3.2 Involved User Groups
In the following the user groups found in the production of an exergame such as the motivotion 60+ game are described with the roles they have in the authoring process. Note that this list extends the one provided in [3] and that not all groups are necessary for the creation of a Serious Game for Health.

Domain experts, in a first step, formulate the requirements for the games, e.g. the training effects to be achieved.

Game designers formulate ideas and designs for configurable, re-usable interaction templates for games based on these requirements.

Programmers: Game programmers are only indirectly involved in the authoring process, since they are tasked with implementing the game designs which includes the implementation of interaction templates which are run on the target platform of the game. **Authoring tool programmers** are responsible for creating implementations of the interaction templates inside the authoring tool, which support the WYSIWYG authoring approach. This group as well as the previous one is supported by a component-based software engineering approach in StoryTec, which is outside the scope of this paper.

Expert authoring tool users are able to control the authoring tool and configure the domain-specific views for the domain experts by specifying which parts of the game they will be able to change and which parameters are displayed to them.

Domain experts in a final step become active again to fill the game with content according to their expertise. These experts do not require the same level of knowledge of the authoring tool as the previous group; they are only able to make changes in those areas designated to them which require their specific expertise. In the example of Motivotion 60+ these could be content providers tasked with entering the quizzes and the associated information such as texts or images.

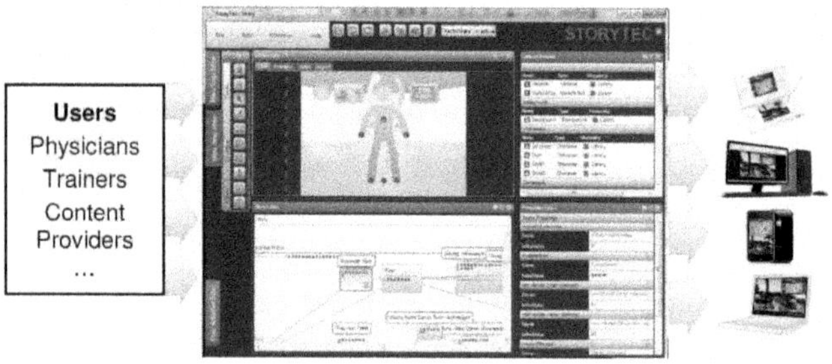

Figure 1. The authoring tool StoryTec in the version used to collaboratively author the motivation 60+ game. The Stage Editor (upper part) shows the parameters to be set for the exercise in the specified scene. Games can be exported in various formats.

3.3 Interaction Template Creation

A player application is required to interpret the data entered by the authors into an interaction template and realize the gameplay of the template. This can mean interpreting user input, rendering graphics, playing sounds and other multimedia aspects. This implementation of an interaction template is carried out by game programmers, since they are familiar with the target machine/environment and the implementation of games.

For the visualization of the interaction template in the authoring tool we implemented to variants. The first is a specialized view, which is provided by authoring tool programmers and allows very specific WYSIWYG editing of the interaction template. The alternative requires no programmers but an advanced user of the authoring tool. This user can create new interaction templates by specifying the parameters that are used to configure the interaction template and build a visual representation of the interaction template from basic multimedia objects found in StoryTec such as images or text labels. The implementation of this interaction template then uses these parameters as input. This is especially useful for rapid prototyping when no full implementation of an interaction template yet exists.

In the described use case, a specialized authoring view could use a modifiable 3D character for setting the correct poses of the player directly in the authoring tool. On the other hand, an advanced user could create an interaction template in the authoring tool, specifying fields for parameters such as the angles between the joints of the player.

3.4 Domain-Specific Mode

A user who is tasked with creating a serious game using StoryTec is provided with the interaction templates described above as well as structural templates which provide useful structures to be inserted into a game, for example a structure for branching between different story paths in the game.

This user can enter the basic structure of the game as he or she sees fit. After this structure and the interaction templates have been assigned, the user can specify user groups which are responsible for subsequent tasks.

The game in the basic form is then distributed to each of the user groups. Upon opening StoryTec, they are only able to change those parameters that they require for their work. For example they might be not able to add new scenes or transitions to the game. When opening a scene containing a physical exercise, the physicians are only presented with the parameters for configuring this exercise. The content providers are only able to change the content of scenes which are marked as quizzes, adding content such as images or the questions and answers for multiple choice quizzes.

4. CONCLUSION

We have shown how an authoring tool specifically designed for the creation of games can be augmented with mechanisms which allow collaboration between different user groups, supporting the domain-specific workflows of each of these groups. While the work presented here shows the technical feasibility of this approach and previous studies have investigated the usability of StoryTec, the extensions supporting collaboration presented herein have to be evaluated in detail, including acceptance tests which will be carried out in the context of the described project.

5. ACKNOWLEDGMENT

The research and development introduced in this work is funded by the German Federal Ministry of Education and Research in the project motivation 60+ in the field of Ambient Assisted Living (www.motivotion.org).

6. REFERENCES

[1] Göbel, S., Hardy, S., Wendel, V., Mehm F., and Steinmetz, R. 2010. Serious Games for Health - Personalized Exergames. *Proceedings of ACM Multimedia 2010*. ACM, New York

[2] Johnson, W.L., and Valente, A. 2008. Collaborative Authoring Of Serious Games For Language And Culture. *Proceedings of SimTecT 2008*

[3] Mehm, F., Göbel, S., Radke, S., and Steinmetz, R. . 2009. Authoring Environment for Story-based Digital Educational Games. *Proceedings of the 1st International Open Workshop on Intelligent Personalization and Adaptation in Digital Educational Games*, 113-124

[4] Velsen, M.V. 2008. Towards Real-time Authoring of Believable Agents in Interactive Narrative. *Proceedings of the 8th International Conference on Intelligent Virtual Agents*. Springer-Verlag Berlin, Heidelberg

[5] Wiemeyer, J., Göbel, S. (eds.). 2010. Serious games for sports and health. *Proceedings - Game Days 2010*. Technische Universität Darmstadt / Institut für Sportwissenschaft, Darmstadt

Capturing a Great Photo via Learning from Community-Contributed Photo Collections

Haojie Li
School of Software,Dalian University of Technology
Road 8,KaiFaQu
Dalian, China
hjli@dlut.edu.cn

Lei Yi
School of Software,Dalian University of Technology
Road 8,KaiFaQu
Dalian, China
yilei@mail.dlut.edu.cn

Jinhui Tang
School of Computer Science, Nanjing University of Science and Technology
200 Xiao Ling Wei Street
Nanjing, China
tangjh1981@acm.org

ABSTRACT

We present a novel system, named *PhotoReference*, to help users, especially amateur photographers, to interactively learn to improve photograph skills by leveraging the available web image collections. The idea behind is based on the observation that the quality of a photo is mainly determined with the important camera parameters set by users when the photo is taken. In the proposed system, given a user-provided photo and its associated metadata, the system first retrieves sets of high-quality community-contributed photos with similar visual content and shoot settings to the input photo. Then users are allowed to interactively explore the returned photos as per different camera parameters, such that they can easily share and learn the photograph experiences of other people; and more importantly, users are able to get intuitive knowledge on the relationship between camera parameters and the resulted shooting effects and thus can use it to guide their future photograph activities.

Categories and Subject Descriptors

H.4 [**Information Systems Applications**]: Multimedia application

General Terms

Algorithms, Design, Experimentation

Keywords

Photography, EXIF, View Categorization

1. INTRODUCTION

As digital cameras are becoming more and more affordable and powerful, photography has become a popular hobby among people and they are keen to record their enjoyable experience or things of interests by taking photos. However, taking a great photo with camera usually needs professional training and years of experiences, thus it is a rather challenging task for most beginners or amateurs. Though many photography references are available, such as digital camera handbooks or photography technical exchange websites (like *www.photography.com*), users cannot directly get intuitive knowledge on the relationship between the quality of taken photos and important camera parameters. Guidance got from such resources is static and is not closely related to what users are capturing.

Recent years have witnessed the great development of social network services and there have emerged lots of photo sharing websites. Flickr (*www.flickr.com*) is one example which allows people to upload and share the high-quality photos they have taken, accompanying with the metadata and EXIF information of photos. While the huge amount of user-contributed photos have initiated many novel multimedia applications [1] and research [2], they also pave a possible way to enhance people's photograph skills by sharing others' experiences and mining the influences of important camera settings on photos quality. But, how to find similar photos with user given photos in terms of visual content and capturing conditions, and how to further leverage them for referencing is not easy, and remain less investigation before. It is evident that current image search engines or photo sharing web services cannot fulfill such tasks.

In this demo, we will show a novel system for 1) photograph experiences sharing and learning and 2) illustrating the meaning of parameters of digital camera by mining from large-scale social photos, aimed at improving users' photograph skills. To take a desired photo, many factors are involved and among them camera parameter settings, i.e., camera metadata, are most critical. For example, to shoot a close-up photo of a flower of interests, the photographer should intentionally adjust longer *focus length* and larger *aperture* to blur the foreground and the background so that the interesting object can vividly stand out [3]. Oppositely, to capture a far-view photo of scene, *focus length* and *aperture* needs be adjusted to be smaller to produce deeper field of view. Though it is well known that through adjusting the camera metadata, photographers can acquire great photos of objects or scenes, how to control the values for such parameters is rather difficult for beginners or amateurs. It is highly desirable for them to learn what parameters are appropriate to obtain specific effects with their cameras on specific object/scene; or what effects can be produced when changing parameter settings of their cameras.

2. SYSTEM OVERVIEW

As depicted in Figure 1, the proposed system works as follows. Given a user input photo and keywords describing

MM'11, November 28–December 1, 2011, Scottsdale, Arizona, USA.
ACM 978-1-4503-0616-4/11/11.

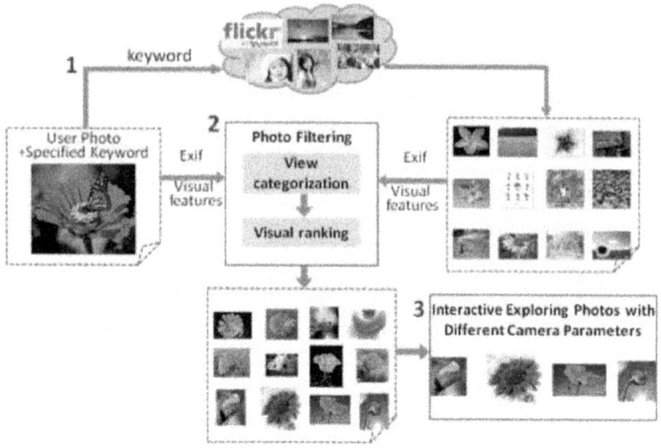

Figure 1: System pipeline of *PhotoReference*

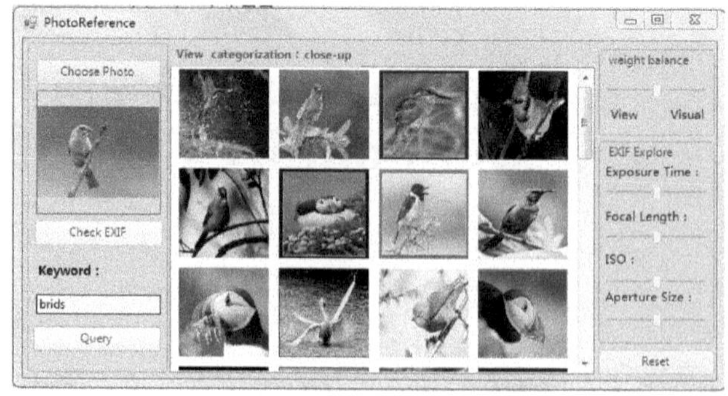

Figure 2: User Interface

its content, we first retrieve a set of high-quality photos (i.e., photos with enough positive comments) shot with same camera model as the input photo from *Flickr*. Then we combine the metadata and visual saliency features of input photo to classify it into one of three view categories using the trained SVM classifiers. The retrieved photos are also categorized and those of different categories are filtered and the rest are ranked according to their visual similarities to the input photo. Finally, users can interactively explore these photos using different camera parameters to visually perceive the influences of camera metadata on the quality of photos. Since the retrieved photos are closely related to the input photo, the perception users obtained is more impressed than that got from traditional photography references.

We consider four metadata in current work: *focus length, aperture, exposure time* and *ISO* due to their importance in configuring the capturing conditions of photos [4]. Comparing two conditions directly using metadata matching is not practical because there are not enough strictly matched photos available. Instead, we use three view categories, namely, close-up, mid-view and far-view to identify the capturing conditions based on the observations that each category has own characteristic settings of metadata combination, and most photos can be classified into one of these categories.

3. TECHNOLOGIES

We briefly introduce the main techniques used in *PhotoReference*: the view categorization and visual ranking.

3.1 View Categorization

The view categorization problem has been studied extensively before, relying exclusively on features derived from image content. Recent work began to use EXIF data to tackle this issue [3]. We propose combining both EXIF and visual features for view categorization in this work and the results have demonstrated its superior performance than methods using either single feature. The EXIF features used are *focus length* and *aperture* and the saliency region features are used as visual cues. The whole features used are photos' *focus length*, *aperture*, the position and relative size of the salient area.

3.2 Visual Ranking

Color and texture features are used to measure the visual similarity between each retrieved photo and the input photo and accordingly to rank the retrieved photo. Cosine similarity is used to compare two feature vectors. These two kinds of similarities are equally weighted in our system. In the implementation, we also rank the retrieved photos using the view categorization score for photos that passed the filtering. We balance the visual weight and view categorization weight equally. However, an option is also provided to users to allow them to manually adjust the weight through a sliding bar, as illustrated in Figure 2.

4. DEMONSTRATION INTERFACE

Figure 2 shows the screenshot of user interface of *PhotoReference*. The left part of the interface is the query panel. Users can load in a photo which contains the object or scene that they want to know what metadata can produce a great photo on such content; or when they want to know what effects can be generated with approximately similar metadata to the input photo. The metadata of input photo can also be displayed using the *Check EXIF* button. The middle panel shows the ranked photos with specified parameters. The EXIF information and the original URL of each photo (which contains more information, such as description, other users' comments) can be shown or accessed from the right-click menu of the photo. The right part is the control panel. The weight between visual and view categorization and four camera metadata can be adjusted using the respective sliding bars. When change the value of parameter, photos captured with corresponding settings are displayed in the middle panel, such that users can get intuitive impression on the shooting effects produced by the parameter.

5. ACKNOWLEDGMENTS

This work was supported by NSFC (61033012), Doctor Startup Fund of Liaoning Province, China (042003) and NUST Research Fund (2011ZDJH09).

6. REFERENCES

[1] Z. Luo, H. Li, J. Tang, R. Hong, T.-S. Chua, ViewFocus: explore places of interests on Google maps using photos with view direction filtering, *ACM Multimedia*, 2009

[2] J. Tang, S. Yan, G. Qi, R. Hong, and T.-S. Chua, Inferring Semantic Concepts from Community-Contributed Images and Noisy Tags, *ACM Multimedia*, 2009

[3] Z. Li, H. Luo, J. Fan, Incorporating camera metadata for attended region detection and consumer photo classification, *ACM Multimedia*, 2009

[4] R. Jain, P. Sinha, Content without context is meaningless, *ACM Multimedia*, 2010

Changing Video Arrangement for Constructing Alternative Stories

Alberto Piacenza, Fabrizio Guerrini, Nicola Adami, Riccardo Leonardi
Department of Information Engineering, University of Brescia, Italy
{firstname.lastname}@ing.unibs.it

Jonathan Teutenberg, Julie Porteous, Marc Cavazza
School Of Computing, Teesside University, Middlesbrough, UK
{J.Teutenberg,J.Porteous, M.O.Cavazza}@tees.ac.uk

ABSTRACT

Currently, automatic generation of filmic variants faces a number of key technical issues and thus it usually resorts to the shooting of multiple versions of alternative scenes. However, recent advancements in video analysis has made this objective feasible, though semantic consistency must be somehow preserved. This demo presents a video-based storytelling (VBS) system that successfully integrates video processing with narrative generation by means of a shared semantic description. The novel filmic variants are constructed through a flexible video recombination process that takes advantage of the polysemy of baseline video segments. The short output video clips shown in this demo prove how the generated narratives are semantically consistent while keeping generative power intact.

Categories and Subject Descriptors

I.2.10 [**Artificial Intelligence**]: Vision and Scene Understanding—*Video Analysis*

General Terms

Algorithms

Keywords

Interactive Storytelling, Narrative Modeling

1. INTRODUCTION

Current interactive movie systems rely on the shooting of multiple versions of alternative scenes due to the inability to automatically generate video content in real-time [1]. In contrast, a number of narrative generation systems have opted to use 3D computer graphics [2], whose visual quality however is not comparable to that of video imagery. A key technical challenge for the automatic generation of video content in real-time is the need to generate multiple instances of novel narrative actions from the same baseline video. The video-based storytelling (VBS) system presented in this demo exploits advances in content and semantic analysis of videos to generate multiple instances of new narrative actions from any baseline movie. In particular the system features a novel approach based on the conceptual integration of video processing and narrative generation.

MM'11, November 28–December 1, 2011, Scottsdale, Arizona, USA.
ACM 978-1-4503-0616-4/11/11.

Our technical solution recombines video segments to generate short (by filmic standards), completely novel filmic variants of a movie, given an expected plot goal and characters set provided by the user. In this demo, we illustrate the VBS system by showing some alternative narratives of Michael Radford's *The Merchant of Venice* [4].

The paper is organized as follows: Section 2 glances briefly at the technical aspects of the VBS system, with particular emphasis on its inputs and outputs, Section 3 describes what will be actually shown during the demo and Section 4 concludes the paper.

2. SYSTEM DESCRIPTION

The VBS system is schematized in Fig. 1. The core of the VBS system integrates video analysis on the one hand and the generation of narrative variants on the other. The narrative generation module outputs story variants (sequences of narrative actions) in response to user input (see Section 3). When a new plot variant is constructed its consistency cannot be preserved by means of low-level video analysis alone, hence our approach features high level reasoning through a Planning AI.

The integration of video analysis and narrative generation is achieved via the use of a shared semantic representation to enable communication between low-level video content and the model of the narrative domain. In particular, a video is first segmented into shots. They are annotated by the video system with several semantic tags that describe intermedi-

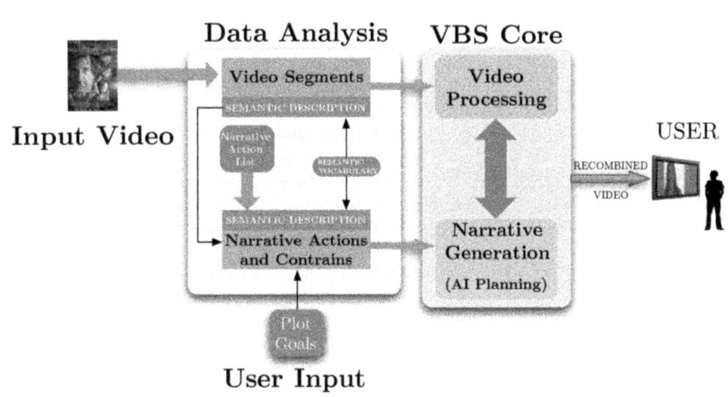

Figure 1: VBS system overview: at its core, it integrates video processing and narrative generation by allowing the exchange of semantic information drawn from a common vocabulary.

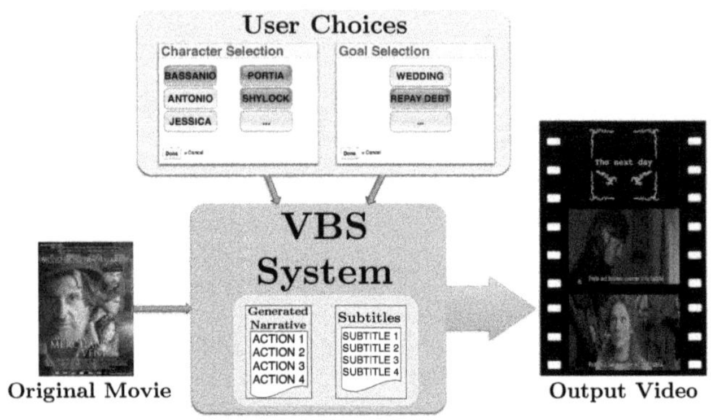

Figure 2: Typical demo workflow: the user inputs its narrative choices; the VBS system recombines the shots of the baseline movie and adds subtitles and panels to reflect those choices in the output video.

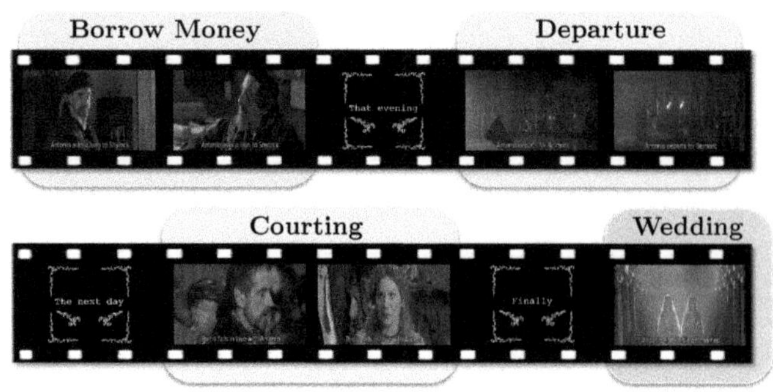

Figure 3: Excerpt of a recombined video output for the case of a wedding goal between Antonio and Portia: in this case, Antonio asks Shylock for a loan in order to make the trip and adequately court Portia and later they are eventually married.

ate level concepts as specified by an agreed vocabulary, and the planner provides the bridge between them and the narrative actions through an appropriate mapping as part of its domain model. Shot semantic tagging is commonly adopted for a variety of tasks, e.g. for emotional categorization. The tags extracted in this work are: the characters' name and mood (positive, negative or neutral), the field of vision of the camera (a ternary value) and a triplet of environmental binary descriptors: time of the day, crowd presence and location (indoor or outdoor). For more details, refer to [3].

Individual narrative actions are then described by a recombination of shots appropriately selected according to their semantic description. This is a powerful result since it provides a complete decoupling of the narrative model and the baseline video content, which is only described by its semantics. Another innovative feature of the system is that the output of video processing is able to constrain the narrative generation process by preventing the creation of narrative variants that feature individual actions that can't be presented given the content of the baseline video.

Last, to attach a different high-level meaning to a given narrative action (a sequence of shots), the video is stripped of its audio portion and an appropriate subtitle is added for each action. Moreover, to further improve the overall narrative understanding by the user, a text panel detailing the change of context is interposed between a narrative action and the next when any of the environmental tags changes.

3. DEMO DESCRIPTION

This section describes the functionality of the proposed VBS system demo, how the user can drive its flow and what output is expected. At the beginning of a standard demo session, the user is presented with a list of choices that allows him to influence the generation of the filmic variants. In particular, the user can select the characters who wants to be involved in the narration, chosen among the main characters of the original movie, and the goals of the new plot. Some plot goals may be unavailable for certain characters selection, e.g. for insufficient video content resources. The user input forces the narrative generation module to build a narrative path that satisfies the input requirements and then the user is presented with the actual output of the system, i.e. a recombination of video segments taken from the baseline video. The demo workflow is depicted in Fig. 2. Fig. 3 shows an excerpt of a recombined video output.

Another feature of our VBS system is that, at any time during the playback, the user can revisit the choices that he has made, thus changing dynamically the evolution of the story. This can be performed at run-time, forcing the AI Planning to take into account what has already been shown in the playback and changing only the future actions. However, dynamic radical changes of the narrative or characters are not allowed. In those cases, as an alternative the planner can be rewinded and asked to construct a whole new narrative back from scratch.

4. CONCLUSIONS

This demo shows the functionalities of the video content-based storytelling system for the automatic generation of novel filmic variants. To better highlight the good performance in terms of both visual presentation and narrative generation power, actual video output is generated and then shown to the audience. As soon as the user provides a new set of input parameters, the system can generate and playback the requested narrative almost in real-time.

5. ACKNOWLEDGEMENTS

This work has been founded (in part) by the European Commission under grant agreement IRIS (FP7-ICT-231824).

6. REFERENCES

[1] P. Cesar, D. Bulterman, and L. Soares. Human-centered television: directions in interactive television research. *ACM Trans. on Multimedia Computing, Communication and Applications*, 4(4), 2008.

[2] M. Mateas and A. Stern. Structuring Content in the Façade Interactive Drama Architecture. In *Proc. 1st Conf on AI and Interactive Digital Entertainment (AIIDE)*, Marina Del Rey, USA, 2005.

[3] A. Piacenza, F. Guerrini, N. Adami, R. Leonardi, J. Porteous, J. Teutenberg, and M. Cavazza. Generating story variants with constrained video recombination. In *Proc. ACM Multimedia Conf.*, Scottsdale, AZ, USA, 2011.

[4] M. Radford. MGM Home Ent. (Europe) Ltd., 2004. The Merchant of Venice (film adaptation).

Visual-based Plant Species Identification from Crowdsourced Data

Hervé Goëau
INRIA, IMEDIA Team
Rocquencourt, France
herve.goeau@inria.fr

Alexis Joly
INRIA, IMEDIA Team
Rocquencourt, France
alexis.joly@inria.fr

Souheil Selmi
INRIA, IMEDIA Team
Rocquencourt, France
souheil.selmi@inria.fr

Pierre Bonnet
INRA, UMR AMAP
Montpellier, France
pierre.bonnet@cirad.fr

Elise Mouysset
Tela Botanica Association
Montpellier, France
elise@tela-botanica.org

Laurent Joyeux
INRIA, IMEDIA Team
Rocquencourt, France
laurent.joyeux@inria.fr

ABSTRACT

This demo presents a crowdsourcing web application dedicated to the access of botanical knowledge through automated identification of plant species by visual content. Inspired by citizen sciences, our aim is to speed up the collection and integration of raw botanical observation data, while providing to potential users an easy and efficient access to this botanical knowledge. The result presented during the demo is an enjoying application where anyone can play to shoot fresh cut leaves and observe the relevance of species suggested in spite of various visual difficult queries.

Categories and Subject Descriptors: H.5.1 [Information systems]: Information interfaces and presentation I.5 [Pattern Recognition]Applications

General Terms: Human Factors.

Keywords: Collaborative Data Collection, Plant Species Identification, Educational aspects of multimedia.

1. INTRODUCTION

If agricultural development is to be successful and biodiversity is to be conserved, then accurate knowledge of the identity, geographic distribution and uses of plants is essential. Unfortunately, such basic information is often only partially available for professional stakeholders, scientists, teachers and citizens, and often incomplete for ecosystems that possess the highest plant diversity. A noticeable consequence, expressed as the *taxonomic gap*, is that identifying plant species is usually impossible for the general public, and often a difficult task for professionals, such as farmers or wood exploiters and even for botanists themselves. The only way to overcome this problem is to speed up the collection and integration of raw observation data, while simultaneously providing to potential users an easy and efficient access to this botanical knowledge. In this context, content-based visual identification of plant's images can be considered as one of the most promising solution to help bridging the taxonomic gap. Building effective computer vision and machine learning techniques is clearly one side of the problem. But building a real-world collaborative system allowing any user to enrich the visual botanical knowledge is an even more critical one.

We developed a citizen science project around the identification of common woody species covering the Metropolitan French territory with the support of the Tela Botanica[1] association, a large social botany network. Tela Botanica with both researchers and engineers involved in this collaborative project, animates and promotes consistently to a larger public this educational project about trees identification.

2. MATCHING-BASED IDENTIFICATION

Technically, the first side of our application deals with content-based identification of plant leaves. State-of-the-art methods addressing this objective are mostly based on leaf segmentation and boundary shape features [1, 5, 2]. Segmentation-based approaches have however several strong limitations including the presence of clutter and background information as well as other acquisition shortcomings (shadows, leaflets occlusion, holes, cropping, etc.). These issues are particularly critical in a crowdsourcing environment where we do not control accurately the acquisition protocol. Alternatively, our system is based on local features and large-scale matching. Indeed, we realized that large-scale object retrieval methods [6, 4], usually aimed at retrieving rigid objects (buildings, logos, etc.), do work surprisingly well on leaves. This can be explained by the fact that even if a small fraction of the leaf remains affine invariant, this is sufficient to discriminate it from other species. Concretely, our system is based on the following steps: (i) Local features extraction (local shape & texture features computed around Harris points) (ii) Local features nearest neighbors search with an efficient hashing-based indexing scheme (AMP-LSH [3]) (iii) Spatially consistent matches filtering with a RANSAC algorithm using an affine model (see e.g. [4]) (iv) Basic top-K decision rule as classifier: for each species, the number of occurrences in the top-K images returned is used as its score.

Besides clutter robustness, the method has several advantages: it does not require any complex training phase allowing fast dynamic insertion of new crowdsourced training data, and it is weakly affected by unbalanced class distribution thanks to the selectivity of the spatial consistency filtering.

[1] http://www.tela-botanica.org/

MM'11, November 28–December 1, 2011, Scottsdale, Arizona, USA.
ACM 978-1-4503-0616-4/11/11.

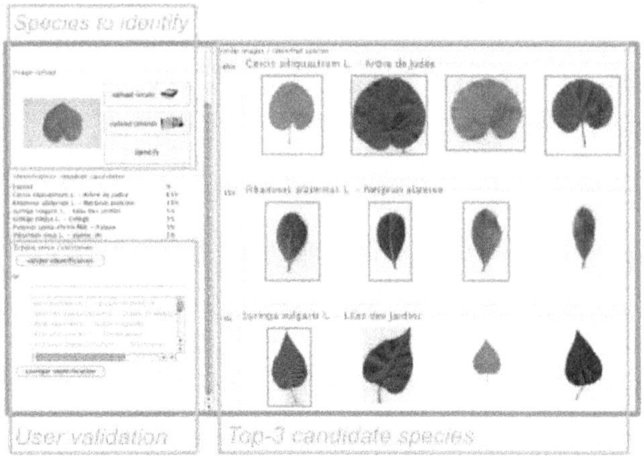

Figure 1: GUI of the web application.

3. WEB APPLICATION & TAG POOLING

Figure 1 presents the Graphical User Interface of the web application. On the left, the user choose to load a scan or a photograph, and then, the system returns and displays on the right the top-3 species with the most similar pictures. On the bottom left part, the user can then either select and validate the top-1 suggested species, or he can choose an other species in the list, or even enter a new species name if it is not available. The uploaded image used as query is temporary stored with its associated species name. Then other users might interact with these new pictures later. So far, this last step is done offline, after that some professional botanists involved in the project validate the images and theirs species names. But, the aggregation to the visual knowledge of these uploaded images will be integrated automatically in further versions. The species names and pictures are clickable and bring the user to online taxon descriptions from the Tela Botanica web site. In this way, beyond the visual content-based recognition process, the species identification is considered as one way to access richer botanical information like species distribution, complementary pictures, textual descriptions, etc.

4. COLLABORATIVE DATA COLLECTED

The current data was built by several cycles of collaborative data collections and taxonomical validations. Scans of leaves were collected over two seasons, between June and September, in 2009 and 2010, thanks to the work of active contributors from Tela Botanica social networks. The idea of collecting only scans during this first period was to initialize the training data with limited noisy background, so that the online identification tool works sufficiently well to atract new users. Notice that this did not prevent users to submit unconstrained pictures, since our matching-based approach is relatively robust to such asymetry between training and query images. The first online application did contain 457 validated scans over 27 species and the link was mostly disseminated through Tela Botanica. It finally allowed to collect 2228 scans over 55 species. A public version of the application[2] was opened in October 2010[3]. At the time of writing, 858 images were uploaded and tested by about 25 new users. These images are either scans or photographs with uniform background, or free photographs with natural background, and involve 15 new species from the previous set of 55 species. Note that the collected data will be used within ImageCLEF2011 plant retrieval task[4].

[2]http://combraille.cirad.fr:8080/demo_plantscan/

[3]http://www.tela-botanica.org/actu/article3856.html

5. EVALUATION

Performances, basically in terms of species identification rates, will be actually shown during the demo, with an offline version connected to a digital camera. It will consists in an enjoying demo where anyone can play to shoot fresh cut leaves. Users would notice short response times for identification (around 2 seconds), and observe relevance of species suggested in spite of the intra-species visual variability, or cases with occlusions or with non-uniform backgrounds. As a rough guide, a leave one out cross-validation (i.e. each scan used one by one as external query), gives an average precision around 0.7 over the 20 first most similar images, and gives basically the correct species as the first rank 9 times out of 10 with the knn basic rule of decision.

6. CONCLUSIONS

This demo represents a first step to a large scale crowdsourcing application promoting collaborative enrichment of botanical visual knowledge and its exploitation for helping users to identify biodiversity. The next version will consider a full autonomous and dynamical application integrating collaborative taxonomical validation. If the application focuses here on an educational subject, the performances obtained and the emulation created during this project are encouraging for addressing others floras and more narrow studies.

7. ACKNOWLEDGMENTS

This research has been conducted with the support of the Agropolis Fondation. Great thanks to all users of Tela Botanica social networks who spent hours to cut, scan and test fresh leaves on our system.

8. ADDITIONAL AUTHORS

Jean-François Molino (IRD, UMR AMAP, Montpellier, France), Philippe Birnbaum (CIRAD, UMR AMAP), Daniel Barthelemy (CIRAD, BIOS, Direction and INRA, UMR AMAP, F-34398) and Nozha Boujemaa (INRIA, Saclay, France).

9. REFERENCES

[1] P. Belhumeur, D. Chen, S. Feiner, D. Jacobs, W. Kress, H. Ling, I. Lopez, R. Ramamoorthi, S. Sheorey, S. White, and L. Zhang. Searching the world's herbaria: A system for visual identification of plant species. In *ECCV*. 2008.

[2] O. M. Bruno, R. de Oliveira Plotze, M. Falvo, and M. de Castro. Fractal dimension applied to plant identification. *Information Sciences*, 2008.

[3] A. Joly and O. Buisson. A posteriori multi-probe locality sensitive hashing. In *Proceeding of the 16th ACM international conference on Multimedia*, 2008.

[4] A. Joly and O. Buisson. Logo retrieval with a contrario visual query expansion. In *Proceedings of the seventeen ACM international conference on Multimedia*, 2009.

[5] J. C. Neto, G. E. Meyer, D. D. Jones, and A. K. Samal. Plant species identification using elliptic fourier leaf shape analysis. *Computers and Electronics in Agriculture*, 2006.

[6] J. Philbin, O. Chum, M. Isard, J. Sivic, and A. Zisserman. Object retrieval with large vocabularies and fast spatial matching. In *Proceedings of the IEEE Conference on Computer Vision and Pattern Recognition*, 2007.

[4]http://www.imageclef.org/2011/plants

Dynamic Media Show Drivable by Semantics

Vivek K. Singh[1*], Jiebo Luo[2], Dhiraj Joshi[2], Madirakshi Das[2], Phoury Lei[2], Peter Stubler[2]

[1] University of California, Irvine, California, USA [2] Eastman Kodak Company, Rochester, New York, USA

singhv@uci.edu, {jiebo.luo, dhiraj.joshi, madirakshi.das, phoury.lei, peter.stubler}@kodak.com

ABSTRACT

We demonstrate a system to generate *dynamic* media shows that are significantly richer than *static* slide shows, which are currently the most popular form of photo playback. The goal is to enable media reliving experiences that are aesthetically pleasing, interactive, and semantically drivable as they center on people, locations, time, and events discovered in a media collection. Dynamic shows allow for better *sharing* of one's media collections in diverse social networks because people have different time availabilities and perspectives, and hence may want to interact, customize, and reroute the media flow per their individual needs.

Categories and Subject Descriptors

H.5.2 [INFORMATION INTERFACES AND PRESENTATION]: User Interfaces - Interaction styles. H.5.4 [INFORMATION INTERFACES AND PRESENTATION]: Hypertext/Hypermedia-Navigation

General Terms

Design, Human Factors.

Keywords

Reliving, sharing, semantic, interaction, slide-show

1. INTRODUCTION

Widespread proliferation of cameras has allowed mass chronicling of human lives through photos and videos. We surmise that this is done for two reasons: so the participants can (1) *relive* the events of their lives later; and (2) *share* their experiences with friends and family, who were not present at the events but still want to know the event's details (e.g., the vacation, the wedding, or trip). The importance of sharing is underscored by the *billions* of image uploads performed per month on social media sites such as Facebook, Flickr®, and Picasa™.

The primary purpose of the proposed demonstration system is digital *re-living* of events captured on photos and videos by the protagonists, their family, and friends. The most commonly used tools to achieve this are static slide-shows that usually follow timelines and focus primarily on visual effects rather than the semantics of the media assets. As far as we know, the concept of a viewer-driven experience is virtually unknown in the media-sharing world. Sharing across different users requires accommodating people who have different time availabilities, motivations, interests, and perspectives. These factors of difference need to be explored in both research and commercial applications. While sophisticated tools are being created to bridge the *semantic gap* on the organizer or the producer side of media collections, little effort is put into bridging the *intent gap* on the *recipient* side of the media sharing equation.

MM'11, November 28 - December 1, 2011, Scottsdale, Arizona, USA.
ACM 978-1-4503-0616-4/11/11.

We present a novel system for digital *reliving* and *sharing*. We do not consider the recipient to be a passive consumer, but rather someone who can interact with and redirect the flow of the presented media stream based on different semantic facets, interjecting their preferences as and when they choose. This redirection should occur in an aesthetically pleasing manner and "on-the-fly" (i.e., without the need to restart the show or recompile the data collection). Users can interact with the show in a variety of ways (e.g., by clicking "Hotspots," i.e., on any of the faces displayed) without sensing a disruption in the media flow itself. Media reliving is different from both media search and media browsing. Media search involves clear user intent, while the intent is significantly weaker in media browsing [3]. Our media reliving system provides a valuable middle ground for user interaction and clarity of intent, and does so in an aesthetically pleasing manner.

A number of commercial products (e.g., iPhoto, Picasa, Flickr, and Facebook) provide ways to upload and share personal media collections. However, the slide shows they support are basic, with little to no user interaction present at run time, thus keeping the *intent gap* unaddressed. Tiling slide shows [1] create dynamic (simultaneous, multiple tiles of images) slide shows with synchronous (matching beat) music to improve user experience. iSlideshow [2] aims to understand the "content" of the images and creates collages of images based on concepts; iSlideshow supports transitions that dissolve at face ROIs (regions of interest). These works show an increased research trend toward understanding the semantics of media to provide better quality slide shows. Our system takes media sharing one step further by providing mechanisms that capture and react to user intent in several ways, yet it preserves the aesthetics of the experience.

2. PROPOSED APPROACH

2.1 System Overview

Fig. 1 provides an overview of our media reliving system. The system preprocesses the media collection so that each user can extract different event and geographical clusters, and obtain their corresponding metadata (location, time, and people). At run-time, the system presents to the viewer a default media flow plus the capability to interact with the system. The presentation dynamically adapts to match the user intent each time they provide an intent cue. Specifically, the presentation's order of events and the relative screen presence devoted to each photo within the event is recomputed according to user input. We also maintain a log of user interactions that can potentially be analyzed to identify different user interaction patterns.

* Work was done when the author was interning at Kodak Research Laboratories, Eastman Kodak Company, Rochester, NY, USA.

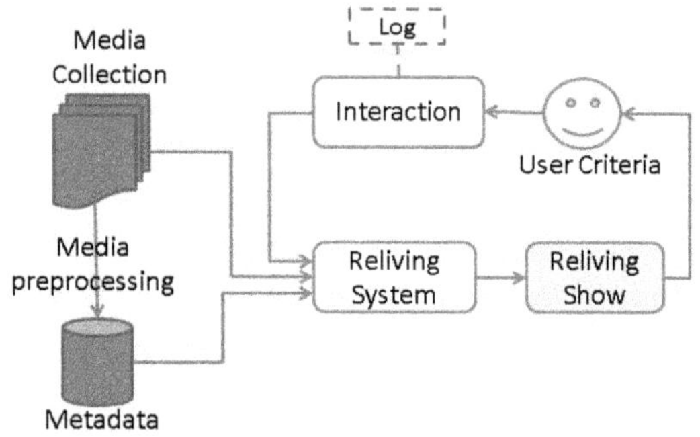

Figure 1: The high-level design of our reliving system.

Figure 2: A screenshot of the media reliving interface showing all the features.

A screenshot of the developed system is shown in Fig 2. As can be seen, the user can opt to passively view the default media show, or actively control the flow through the semantic axes of ***places***, ***people***, and ***time***. The actual icons in the different axes are populated based on their relevance to the displayed event. For example, the people most closely associated with the displayed event populate the people axis. The user can click any of them, or look for other people using the "more" option. At any given event, the user also can opt to preview the following few events and advance forward or backwards. The user can also control the pace of the slide show and pause to view important images if desired. Last, the system can automatically go into "full-screen" mode and back to show/hide the controlling toolbars depending upon whether the user is interacting with the system.

2.2 Media Reliving Flow

The steps required for dynamic re-ordering and presentation reconfiguration are shown in Fig. 3. The system performs preprocessing to cluster the media collection into events and extracts the corresponding metadata. The system chooses "time" as the default criterion to generate the media show. Reordering based on user clicks on "places," "time," or "people" criteria is determined by geographic proximity, time gap (in increasing temporal direction only), and the ratio of the chosen persons' images in the event media collection, respectively. Next, based on the user criterion, the system determines the suitability of each image inside the event media sub-collection. Suitability scores of the images are computed based on both semantic attributes (e.g., whether or not the chosen person is present, face position, etc.) as well as image aesthetics. Depending upon the number of relevant images that are found to be suitable, a presentation layout is selected. Similarly, based on the criterion, the transition method across images and the background music are selected. The image set is shown in temporal order and the show continues until a new criterion is selected by the user (in our current version, the show loops back to the beginning when all of the pictures corresponding to a user criterion have been displayed).

3. DEMONSTRATION

We have preprocessed 11 different family collections and invited the contributors, their families, and friends to share their reliving experiences. Further technical details as well as findings from the user interaction logs are presented in a companion submission [4].

At the conference, we will invite all interested attendees to interact with our system. They can view the system-created presentations, interact, and experience the system in person. We would also request permission to use the collected anonymous data for later analysis in an effort to improve our system. We look forward to valuable user-feedback by multimedia experts at the conference.

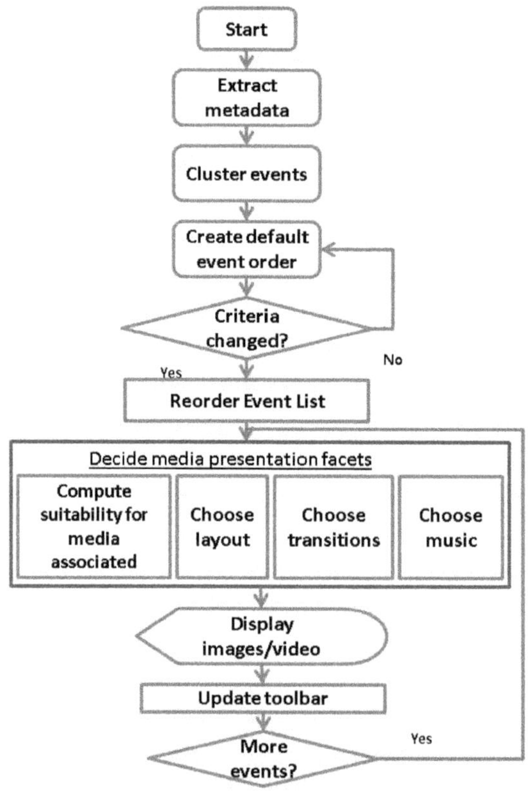

Figure 3: A flow diagram of the reliving system.

4. REFERENCES

[1] J.-C. Chen, W.-T. Chu, J.-H. Kuo, C.-Y. Weng, and J.-L. Wu. Tiling Slideshow. *ACM Int. Conf. on Multimedia*, 2006.

[2] J. Chen, J. Xiao, and Y. Gao. iSlideShow: A Content-aware Slideshow System. *Int. Conf. on Intelligent User Interfaces*, 2010.

[3] R. Datta D. Joshi, J. Li, and J.Z. Wang. Image Retrieval: Ideas, Influences, and Trends of the New Age. *ACM Computing Surveys*, 40(2), 2008.

[4] V. Singh, J. Luo, D. Joshi, P. Lei, M. Das, and P. Stubler. Reliving On Demand: A Total Viewer Experience. *ACM Int. Conf. on Multimedia*, 2011.

SIRE: A Social Image Retrieval Engine

Steven C.H. Hoi and Pengcheng Wu
School of Computer Engineering, Nanyang Technological University, Singapore 639798
{chhoi,wupe0003}@ntu.edu.sg

ABSTRACT

With the explosive growth of social media applications on the internet, billions of social images have been made available in many social media web sites nowadays. This has presented an open challenge of web-scale social image search. Unlike existing commercial web search engines that often adopt text based retrieval, in this demo, we present a novel web-based multimodal paradigm for large-scale social image retrieval, termed "Social Image Retrieval Engine" (SIRE), which effectively exploits both textual and visual contents to narrow down the semantic gap between high-level concepts and low-level visual features. A relevance feedback mechanism is also equipped to learn with user's feedback to refine the search results interactively. Our live demo is available at `http://msm.cais.ntu.edu.sg/SIRE`, and a video is available at `http://www.youtube.com/user/msmntu`.

Categories and Subject Descriptors

H.4 [**Information Systems Applications**]: Miscellaneous

General Terms

Experimentation

Keywords

social media, social images, text-based image retrieval, content-based image retrieval, multi-modal search

1. INTRODUCTION

Nowadays one can easily capture a photo and share it with friends or public through the internet anywhere and anytime owing to the advances of low-cost digital camera devices and powerful smartphones and the popularity of various user-centric social media applications on the internet. Today, online social networks and social web sites, such as Flickr, Facebook, and PicasaWeb, host billions of social images, which have been shared and tagged among friends, or published in groups that cover some specific topic of interest. This has raised an open and critical challenge of building an effective social image search engine to retrieve images over the massive collections of social images on the internet.

Unlike existing web image search engines that adopt text-based retrieval for image search, in this demo, we propose a novel multimodal paradigm for large-scale social image search, termed "Social Image Retrieval Engine" (SIRE), which has indexed over 1 million social images from Flickr by exploiting both textual and visual contents of social images to narrow down the semantic gap between high-level concepts and low-level visual features. Figure 1 shows the web user interface of SIRE. In particular, SIRE allows to search social images by either a text-based query or an image-based query or a multimodal search. It is also equipped with a relevance feedback mechanism to refine the retrieval results by learning with user's feedbacks.

For the rest of this paper, we first discuss the difference between SIRE and existing work, then overview the key innovations of SIRE, and finally show some major functions.

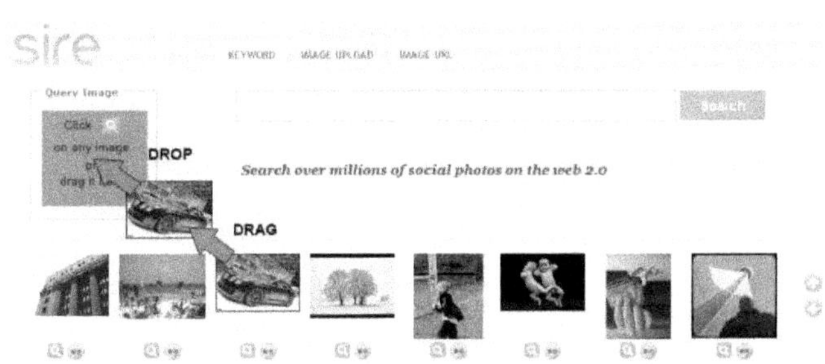

Figure 1: Web-based user interface of SIRE.

2. RELATED SYSTEMS

Image search has been extensively studied in literature, which in general can be categorized into two major groups: (i) text-based web image search, and (ii) content-based image retrieval (CBIR) [6]. On one hand, SIRE differs from most existing text-based commercial search engines on the web (e.g., Google [2][1], Flickr search[2], etc.) in that SIRE not only allows a user to search by text, but also provides visual search functions for retrieving social images based on visual contents. On the other hand, SIRE also differs from conventional pure CBIR systems (e.g., QBIC [1]) which retrieve images purely based on visual contents of images and have been extensively studied for years [6]. SIRE is alike to some existing work that combines both text and visual contents for WWW image search [7], but differs in that SIRE focuses on social images. To the best of our knowledge, there is no such a real social image retrieval system on the internet that implemented all the functions of SIRE.

[1]http://www.google.com
[2]http://www.flickr.com

MM'11, November 28–December 1, 2011, Scottsdale, Arizona, USA.
ACM 978-1-4503-0616-4/11/11.

3. SYSTEM OVERVIEW

SIRE is a web-based social image retrieval engine, which has indexed 1 million social images crawled from Flickr.com. Figure 1 illustrates the user-friendly web user interface for SIRE, where a new Drag-and-Drop search (DnDs) approach has been implemented to facilitate the search. The client of SIRE has been carefully designed and implemented by web 2.0 techniques. SIRE enables users to perform flexible social image search by several different ways, including (i) text search by typing keywords, (ii) visual search by uploading an image example, (iii) visual search by providing a URL of a web image, and (iv) multimodal search by combining both text and visual contents. Besides, it is also equipped with a relevance feedback mechanism using machine learning techniques to help users refine the retrieval results through an interactive retrieval process. Figure 2 shows the system architecture of SIRE. Due to limited space, below we briefly overview some key innovations and implementations.

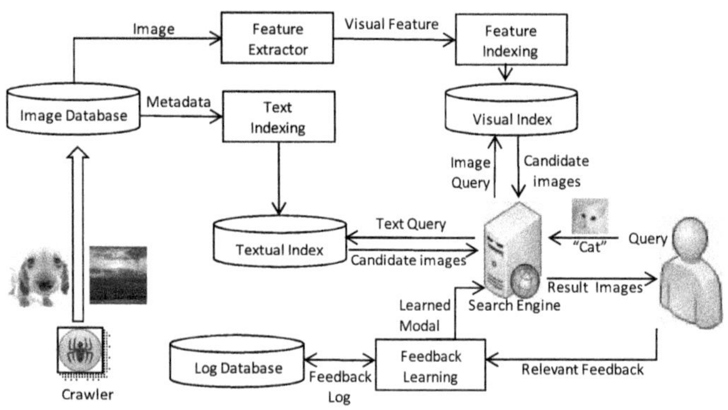

Figure 2: The system architecture of SIRE.

Text-based Search. We apply some existing text-based retrieval techniques to implement text-based social image search functions in SIRE. In our implementation, only image titles and user-annotated tags of social images are used to index the textual contents of social images, although other textual contents, such as descriptions and comments, might also be explored to further enhance the performance.

Visual Search. Three issues are critical to implement visual search (i.e., CBIR) functions. The first issue is about low-level feature extraction. In SIRE, we extract several kinds of effective and compact low-level features from images, including Grid Color Moment, Local Binary Pattern, Gabor, and Edge features [3, 8]. The second issue is about the indexing of large-scale high-dimensional image features. In SIRE, we employ some emerging efficient approximate nearest neighbor search techniques [8] to index high dimensional low-level features of social images. Besides, we also deploy a parallel and distributed indexing scheme, making the visual search solution scalable to millions or even billions of social images. The third issue about distance measure of images based on low-level features. Instead of using a rigid Euclidean distance, we have investigated the application of distance metric learning techniques [9] to optimize the metric for distance measure of visual contents between images.

Multimodal Search. SIRE provides multimodal search to exploit both textual and visual contents of social images for the retrieval task. Specifically, the multimodal search is conducted by a two-step approach. A user can first type keywords as text-based query to search all social images with related text. The user can further refine the search results by selecting some relevant/similar image from the text search results pool as a query image for visual search, which can be operated smoothly through the proposed DnDs function. We have investigated a graph-based multimodal ranking technique [4] to combine both visual and textual contents in the multimodal re-ranking task.

Relevance Feedback. Last but not least, SIRE provides a relevance feedback mechanism to help users refine their retrieval results in an interactive way. We have applied a state-of-the-art semisupervised active learning technique [3] to identify the informative image examples for labeling, and employed the semi-supervised SVM to re-rank the retrieval results based on both labeled and unlabeled social image examples. The user feedback history data are also saved in server, which could be explored to improve the performance of SIRE for a long-term learning purpose [5].

Figure 3: interface of relevance feedback in SIRE.

4. DEMONSTRATION

In this demo, we present a novel Social Image Retrieval Engine (SIRE), as a prototype system for web-scale social image retrieval. In the demo session, we will demonstrate several key functions of SIRE, including (i) text search, (ii) visual search by uploading an image example, (iii) visual search by a URL of a web image, (iv) multimodal search by combining both text and visual clues and (v) interactive search by relevance feedback. We hope our demo would inspire future research and development efforts of next generation social image search engines.

5. REFERENCES

[1] J. Ashley, M. Flickner, J. L. Hafner, D. Lee, W. Niblack, and D. Petkovic. The query by image content (qbic) system. In *SIGMOD Conference*, page 475, 1995.

[2] S. Brin and L. Page. The anatomy of a large-scale hypertextual web search engine. *Computer Networks*, 30(1-7):107–117, 1998.

[3] S. C. H. Hoi, R. Jin, J. Zhu, and M. R. Lyu. Semisupervised svm batch mode active learning with applications to image retrieval. *ACM Trans. Inf. Syst.*, 27(3), 2009.

[4] S. C. H. Hoi and M. R. Lyu. A multimodal and multilevel ranking scheme for large-scale video retrieval. *IEEE Transactions on Multimedia*, 10(4):607–619, 2008.

[5] S. C. H. Hoi, M. R. Lyu, and R. Jin. A unified log-based relevance feedback scheme for image retrieval. *IEEE Trans. Knowl. Data Eng.*, 18(4):509–524, 2006.

[6] M. S. Lew, N. Sebe, C. Djeraba, and R. Jain. Content-based multimedia information retrieval: State of the art and challenges. *ACM Trans. Multimedia Comput. Commun. Appl.*, 2(1):1–19, 2006.

[7] S. Sclaroff, M. L. Cascia, S. Sethi, and L. Taycher. Unifying textual and visual cues for content-based image retrieval on the world wide web. *Computer Vision and Image Understanding*, 75(1-2):86–98, 1999.

[8] P. Wu, S. C. H. Hoi, D. D. Nguyen, and Y. He. Randomly projected kd-trees with distance metric learning for image retrieval. In *MMM (2)*, pages 371–382, 2011.

[9] P. Wu, S. C. H. Hoi, P. Zhao, and Y. He. Mining social images with distance metric learning for automated image tagging. In *WSDM*, pages 197–206, 2011.

Processing of Multimedia Data using the P2G Framework

Paul B. Beskow, Håkon K. Stensland, Håvard Espeland, Espen A. Kristiansen, Preben N. Olsen, Ståle Kristoffersen, Carsten Griwodz, Pål Halvorsen
Simula Research Laboratory, Norway
Department of Informatics, University of Oslo, Norway
{paulbb, haakonks, haavares, prebenno, espeak, staalebk, griff, paalh}@ifi.uio.no

ABSTRACT

In this demo, we present the *P2G* framework designed for processing distributed real-time multimedia data. P2G supports arbitrarily complex dependency graphs with cycles, branches and deadlines. P2G is implemented to scale transparently with available resources, i.e., a concept familiar from the cloud computing paradigm. Additionally, P2G supports heterogeneous computing resources, such as x86 and GPU processing cores. We have implemented an interchangeable P2G *kernel language* which is meant to expose fundamental concepts of the P2G programming model and ease the application development. Here, we demonstrate the P2G execution node using a MJPEG encoder as an example workload when dynamically adding and removing processing cores.

Categories and Subject Descriptors

D.1.3 [**PROGRAMMING TECHNIQUE**]: Concurrent Programming—*Parallel programming*

General Terms

Languages, Performance

1. INTRODUCTION

As the number of multimedia services grows, so do the computational demand of multimedia data processing. New multi-core hardware architectures provide the required resources, but parallel, distributed applications are much harder to write than sequential programs. Large processing frameworks like Google's MapReduce [1] and Microsoft's Dryad [3] are steps in the right direction, but they are targeted towards batch processing. As such, we present *P2G* [2], a framework designed to integrate concepts from modern batch processing frameworks into the world of real-time multimedia processing. We seek to scale transparently with the available resources (following the cloud computing paradigm) and to support heterogeneous computing resources, such as GPU processing cores. The idea is to encourage the application developer to express the application as fine granular as possible along two axes, i.e., both data and functional parallelism. In this respect, many of the existing systems sacrifice flexibility in one axis to accommodate for the other, e.g., MapReduce has no flexibility in the functional domain, but allows for fine-grained parallelism in the data domain. In P2G, functional blocks called kernels operate on slices of multi-dimensional fields. We use fields to store multimedia data and implicitly express data decomposition. A write-once semantics of the fields provides the needed boundaries and barriers for functional decomposition to exist in our run-time and ensures deterministic output. P2G has intrinsic support for deadlines. Moreover, the compiler and run-time analyze dependencies dynamically and then merge or split kernels based on resource availability and performance monitoring.

We have implemented a prototype of a P2G execution node. Here, we demonstrate an operating execution node of P2G using MJPEG as an example. We are able to show that P2G scales dynamically with the number of available x86 processing cores.

MM'11, November 28–December 1, 2011, Scottsdale, Arizona, USA.
ACM 978-1-4503-0616-4/11/11.

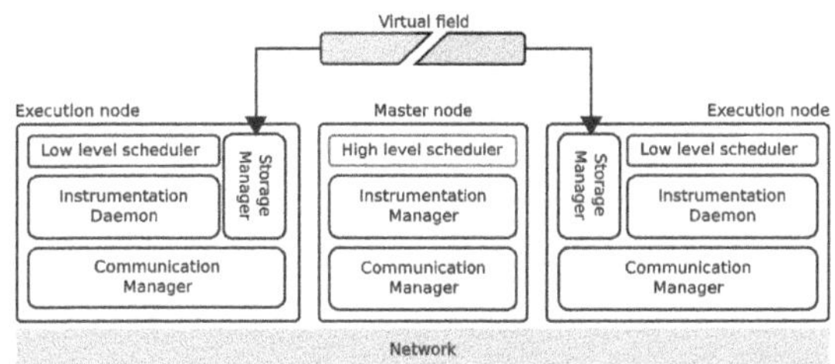

Figure 1: Overview of nodes in the P2G system.

2. THE P2G ARCHITECTURE

As shown in figure 1, P2G consists of a *master node* and an arbitrary number of *execution nodes*. Each execution node reports its local topology (i.e., multi-core, GPU, etc) to the master node, which combines this information to form a global topology of available resources. As such, the global topology can change during run-time as execution nodes can be dynamically added and removed to accommodate for changes in the global load.

As the master node receives workloads, it uses its high-level scheduler to determine which execution nodes to delegate partial or complete parts of the workload to. This process can be achieved in a number of ways. However, as a workload in P2G forms an implicit dependency graph based on its *store* and *fetch* operations, the high-level scheduler can utilize graph partitioning algorithms, or similar, to map such an implicit dependency graph to the global topology. The utilization of available resources can thus be maximized.

P2G uses a low-level scheduler at each execution node to maximize the local scheduling decisions, i.e., the low-level scheduler can decide to combine functional and data decomposition to minimize overhead. During run-time, the master node will collect statistics on resource usage from all execution nodes, which all run an instrumentation daemon to acquire this information. The master node can then combine this run-time instrumentation data with the implicit dependency graph derived from the source code and the global topology to make continuous refinements to the high-level scheduling decisions. As such, P2G relies on its combination of a high-level scheduler, low-level schedulers, instrumentation data and the global topology to make best use of the performance of several (possibly heterogeneous) cores in a distributed system.

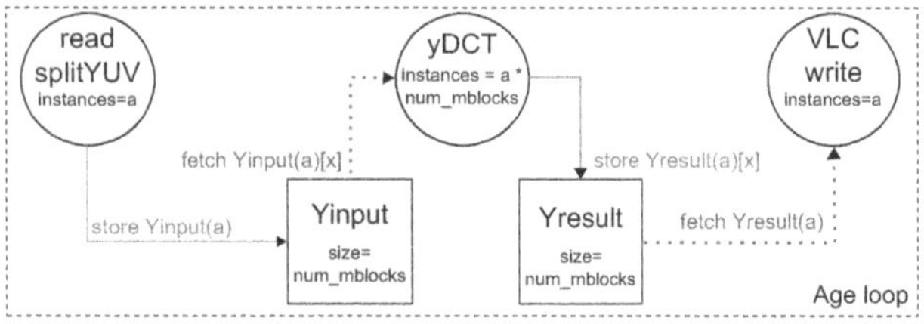

(a) Implicit dependency graph for the Y-component

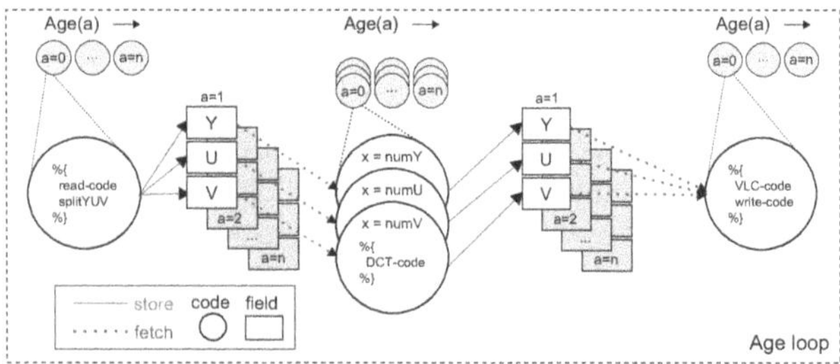

(b) Kernel and field instances

Figure 2: Programming model (MJPEG example)

P2G provides a kernel language for the programmer to write their application in, which they do by writing isolated, sequential pieces of code (kernels). Kernels operate on slices of *fields* through *fetch* and *store* operations and have native code embedded within them. In this model, we encourage the programmer to specify the inherent parallelism in their application in as fine a granularity as possible in the domains of both functional and data decomposition.

The multi-dimensional fields offer a natural way to express multimedia data, and provide a direct way for kernels to *fetch* fine granular data slices. A write-once semantics of the fields provides deterministic output, though not necessarily deterministic execution of individual kernels. Given write-once semantics, iteration is supported in P2G by introducing the concept of aging, as seen in figure 2(a), where storing and fetching to the same field position, at different ages, makes it possible to form loops. The write-once semantics also provides natural boundaries and barriers for functional decomposition, as the low-level scheduler can analyze the dependencies of a kernel instance to determine if it is ready for execution. Furthermore, the compiler and the run-time can analyze dependencies dynamically and merge or split kernels based on resource availability and performance monitoring.

Given a workload specified using the P2G kernel language, P2G is designed to compile the source code for a number of heterogeneous architectures. At the time of writing, P2G consists of what we call an execution node, which is capable of executing workloads on a single x86 multi-core node. As such, the implementation of a high-level scheduler, support

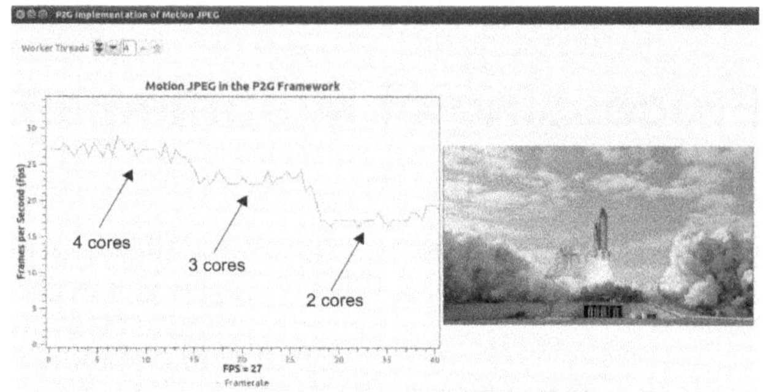

Figure 3: Screenshot of the MJPEG demo.

for heterogeneous architectures and distribution mechanisms are ongoing work.

3. WORKLOAD

We have implemented several simple workloads used in multimedia processing, such as matrix multiplication, k-means clustering to test the prototype implementation of P2G. In this demo, we will focus on our implementation of the MJPEG encoder.

Figure 2(b) shows how the MJPEG encoding process is split into kernels and their running instances. YUV-input video are read into 8x8 macro-blocks and stored in three global fields, by the *read + splitYUV* kernel. For example, given the CIF resolution of 352x288 pixels per frame used in our tests, this generates 1584 macro-blocks of Y (luminance) data, each with 64 pixel values. This makes it possible to create 1584 instances per age of the *DCT* kernel transforming the luminance component of the picture. Each of these kernel instances stores the DCT'ed macro-block into global result fields. Finally, the *VLC + write* kernel does variable length coding and stores the MJPEG bit-stream to disk.

4. DEMONSTRATION

In this demo, we will explain and discuss the P2G ideas for multimedia processing. A screenshot of the MJPEG encoder running in the P2G framework is shown in figure 3. We are able to dynamically add and remove processing cores available to the framework. To show the performance, we live plot the achieved frame-rate from the encoder (left) and show a preview of the encoded video stream (right) as seen in the screenshot.

Acknowledgements

This work has been performed in the context of the *iAD* centre for Research-based Innovation (project number 174867) funded by the Norwegian Research Council.

5. REFERENCES

[1] Dean, J., and Ghemawat, S. Mapreduce: simplified data processing on large clusters. In *Proc. of USENIX OSDI* (2004), pp. 10–10.

[2] Espeland, H., Beskow, P. B., Stensland, H. K., Olsen, P. N., Kristoffersen, S., Griwodz, C., and Halvorsen, P. P2G: A framework for distributed real-time processing of multimedia data. In *Proc. of SRMPDS 2011* (2011), IEEE.

[3] Isard, M., Budiu, M., Yu, Y., Birrell, A., and Fetterly, D. Dryad: distributed data-parallel programs from sequential building blocks. In *Proc. of ACM EuroSys* (2007), ACM, pp. 59–72.

PositionIt – An Image-based Remote Target Localization System on Smartphones

Qia Wang, Alex Lobzhanidze, Suman D. Roy, Wenjun Zeng and Yi Shang
Dept. of Computer Science, University of Missouri, Columbia MO 65201, USA
{qwch9, agl7dd, debs}@mail.mizzou.edu, {zengw, shangy}@missouri.edu

ABSTRACT
We present *PositionIt*, a novel, low-cost, image-based remote target localization system using commodity smartphones. By leveraging smartphones' built-in sensors such as camera, digital compass, GPS, etc., the system can estimate the distance/position of remote targets. The system also takes advantage of the user-friendly interface of the smartphones to facilitate low complexity implementation (e.g., to locate target of interest and restrict the search area for matching).The feasibility of both single-image and two-image based systems are demonstrated.

Categories and Subject Descriptors
I.4.9 [**Image Processing and Computer Vision**]: Application; J.7. [**Computers in other systems**]: Consumer Products.

General Terms: Algorithms, Design, Experimentation

Keywords
Android Application, Position Estimation, Remote Target, Multi-View Geometry

I. INTRODUCTION
Smartphones are becoming a powerful computing, sensing, and communication platform. In this demo, we present *PositionIt*, a novel remote target localization system using commodity smartphones that integrates efficient image based sensor fusion algorithms with digital compass and GPS readings of the smartphones.

In order to find a target's position with smartphones, we collect phone's GPS location, direction through digital compass, and use image processing and computer vision techniques. With our system, a single smartphone can determine the target position/distance with pre-estimated camera intrinsic parameters and physical size of the remote object. Furthermore, target position/distance estimation can be obtained using multiple views of the same target, using multi-view triangulation [5]. Thus, with multiple networked smartphones, their sensor data can be fused together to derive more accurate and robust position estimations.

Such positioning system on commodity smartphones would be very useful in a number of scenarios. For example, on the battlefield, enemy vehicle's position estimation is required for missile attack, while laser range finder only tells distance. On the golf course, players often would like to estimate the distance to the hole. People interested in hunting need to know how far the target is. The military and commercial value of such positioning systems is very significant.

MM'11, November 28–December 1, 2011, Scottsdale, Arizona, USA.
ACM 978-1-4503-0616-4/11/11.

To our best knowledge, *PositionIt* is the first of its kind and no similar systems are commercially available on smartphones.

II. SYSTEM OVERVIEW
Our system is implemented using JAVA and C++ native package on the smartphone. For image processing purposes we integrate OpenCV [6] into our smartphone application.

In order to position the remote object, we need to collect the compass reading and the GPS coordinates of the phone. We then take images of the remote object to calculate the distance/position of the remote object. Under the circumstances where no GPS coordinates and/or digital compass readings are available on the phone, we can still estimate the distance (but not position) based on the image.

Before running the position estimation application, the smartphone camera needs to be calibrated. We provide tools integrated in the application package for users to easily calibrate the camera. In the following, we present the single image based system, and the two images based system, respectively.

A. Single Image based Position Estimation
In the case of single image, we are aiming at the objects with regular shape, such as car, monument, road sign, etc. When estimating position/distance based on a single image, user is expected to know the object height and width. For example, if the target object is a car, its precise size can be found on the web. After user input of the bounding rectangular around the target object in the image, our application will estimate the distance between the camera and the target object. Putting together the GPS location and the angle of the phone, we can estimate the GPS coordinate of the object, as illustrated in Fig. 1(a).

B. Two images based Position Estimation
In case we don't have the object size information, we can still estimate the object position given two images of the remote object. Photo can be taken with two different phones or with one phone from two different positions. User does not need to know the target object size, however GPS location of the phone for both images taken is required. In case only the remote target's distance is of interest, then it is sufficient to estimate the distance between the two phones, e.g., using the single image based system. When user collects the two images, she/he can choose to identify the remote target using a bounding box on both photos, after which our application will perform image feature matching, camera relative position estimation, and remote target position estimation based on two view triangulation. If the two images are taken on different phones, we utilize Android phone's Bluetooth or WiFi network capabilities to send image from one to the other.

Performing image feature matching is computationally expensive and our application generates results approximately within 25 seconds. Please refer to Fig. 1(b) for an illustration on how two images are used for target localization.

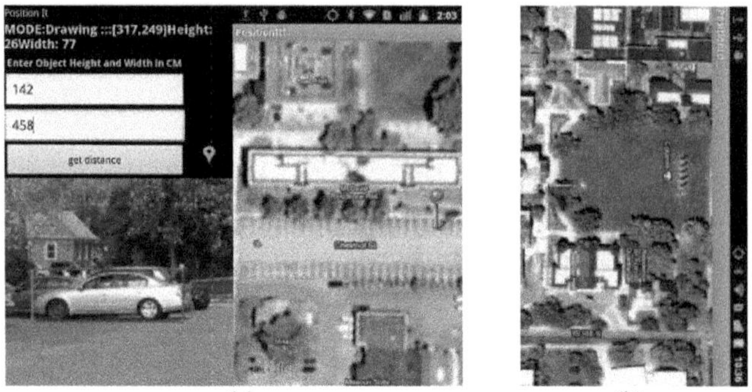

(a) (b)

Figure 1. (a) Left: user inputs the bounding rectangular of the object, as well as object's height and width; Right: Blue dot indicates user's position; Red Pin indicates the estimated object's position; (b) Blue dots are the two places where the images are taken; Red Pin is the estimated position of the remote object.

III. ALGORITHM DESCRIPTION

A. The Single Image Case

POSIT [2] is the algorithm we apply with variation for single image based position estimation. It uses at least four image features of the object and their corresponding 3-D coordinates. In our application, we treat the object as planar. The four corners of the bounding rectangular drawn by the user around the object make up the above mentioned four 3-D points. The system generates a translation vector, the L-2 norm of which is treated as the distance of the object. It should be noted that, the user input of the bounding rectangular is an important step for accurate distance estimation; the tighter the bounding rectangular of the target object, the better the estimate result will be produced. Given the distance, we can compute the target object's location with the help of the phone's GPS coordinates and compass reading.

B. The Two Images Case

In this case, to estimate the distances between the target object and the cameras, we perform triangulation between two image views. First, we perform SURF [4] feature matching between two sub-images surrounding the user selected area, given that these two image areas are more likely to be overlapping. Here, user's selected area will help image matching in two aspects: one is to lower computational burden, since we are only interested in feature matching of the overlapping area; another one is to reduce the potential mis-matches, making feature matching results more robust. We select the best feature matches and use them to calculate the fundamental matrix and essential matrix based on the 8 Point Algorithm [1]. Following the procedure outlined in [5], we obtain the camera's relative pose, Rotation matrix R, and Translation Vector T with the L-2 norm equaling one. After T's norm is scaled based on the true distance, we perform Two-View Triangulation to estimate the target's position and the distances from the target to the two camera positions.

IV. PERFORMANCE

Google Nexus One with 1GHz processor and 512 MB memory is chosen as our test phone. The performance of our distance estimation system for the single image and two images cases are listed in Table 1 and Table 2 respectively. The ground truth distances are obtained from a Laser Range Finder. As mentioned earlier, it takes less than a second for the single-image case with any image resolution and 20-25 seconds for the two-image case with image size 1024x768 to run our application.

Table1. Single Image based Distance Estimation (Unit: Yards)

Ground Truth	11	14	21	32	41	80
Estimated	12.26	15.71	22.10	33.68	41.94	76

Table2. Two Images based Distance Estimation (Unit: Yards)

Ground Truth	7	40	49	50	96
Estimated	5	34	45	42	111

It can be observed from Table 1 and Table2, our single image based approach can achieve an accuracy up to 94% and two image based can get 83%. Performance of the two images based algorithm looks slightly worse for a couple of reasons: first the distance between the two cameras is an estimated value based on the Single Image Method, so the error will propagate during two images based estimation. Second, if the object is far away and its image is very small, the feature detection and matching accuracy becomes a constraint. Third, the highest resolution image (2592x1944) is not chosen due to smartphone's computing limitation. We can achieve accuracy up to 89% on the two image based with image size (2592x1944) on PC simulation. In order to improve the two images based distance estimation, camera pose estimation optimization will be incorporated in the future work.

V. CONCLUSION AND FUTUREWORK

We demonstrate that remote target position estimation using widely available smartphone is feasible, utilizing image processing and computer vision techniques combined with Android phone sensors. Such application could be very handy for a number of scenarios. Future work will include accuracy improvement and video based moving trajectory estimation of remote targets on smartphones.

VI. ACKNOWLEDGEMENT

This research is supported by the Leonard Wood Institute / Army Research Lab (award #: W911NF-07-2-0062 and sub-award No.: 400-120). The authors also would like to thank Hyun Ik Jang for his help to our final application.

VII. REFERENCES

[1] Richard I. Hartley, "In Defense of the Eight-Point Algorithm", *IEEE Transaction on Pattern Recognition and Machine Intelligence,* vol.19, pp. 580–593, 1997.

[2] D. F. Dementhon and L. S. Davis, "Model-based object pose in 25 lines of code," *Inter. Journal of Computer Vision*, vol. 15, pp. 123-141, 1995.

[3] Z. Zhang, "A flexible new technique for camera calibration", *IEEE Transactions on Pattern Analysis and Machine Intelligence*, vol. 22, pp. 1330-1334, 2000.

[4] H. Bay, A. Ess, T. Tuytelaars, L. V. Gool, "SURF: Speeded Up Robust Features", *Computer Vision and Image Understanding (CVIU)*, vol. 110, No. 3, pp. 346-359, 2008.

[5] R. Hartley and A. Zisserman. *Multiple View Geometry in Computer Vision*. Cambridge University Press. ISBN 978-0-521-54051-3, 2003.

[6] http://sourceforge.net/projects/opencvlibrary/files/opencv-android/2.3.1

Low-cost Creation of a 3D Interactive Museum Exhibition

David Monaghan
CLARITY: Centre for Sensor Web Technologies
Dublin City University, Ireland

James O'Sullivan
CLARITY: Centre for Sensor Web Technologies
Dublin City University, Ireland

Noel E. O'Connor
CLARITY: Centre for Sensor Web Technologies
Dublin City University, Ireland

Bridget Kelly
CLARITY: Centre for Sensor Web Technologies
University College Dublin, Ireland

Olivier Kazmierczak
National Museum of Ireland
Decorative Arts & History
Collins Barracks, Ireland

Lorraine Comer
National Museum of Ireland
Decorative Arts & History
Collins Barracks, Ireland

ABSTRACT

We present a demonstration of a multi-sensory virtual experience that accurately reflects the experience of a real visit to a museum. We have developed a 3D interactive digital museum exhibition corresponding to a photo-realistic 3D reconstruction of the Iconic Treasures exhibition at the National Museum of Ireland's archaeology building. Users can explore the 3D virtual environment and interact with the displays by accessing high resolution photographs and historical descriptions of the artefacts. This demo will showcase the experience on a 3D laptop with the use of active shutter LCD glasses to create an immersive experience. A key aspect of the demonstration is that it was developed using low-cost or freely available OTS tools wherever possible putting the creation of such digital exhibitions within reach of even modest budgets.

Categories and Subject Descriptors

I.4.5 [**Computing Methodologies**]: Image Processing and Computer Vision—*Reconstruction*

General Terms

Design, Measurement, Experimentation

Keywords

3D Reconstruction, Museum Exhibition, 3D Vision

1. INTRODUCTION

The archaeology building of the National Museum of Ireland[1] (NMI), originally designed by Thomas Newenham Deane in the late 19th century, is a magnificent example of Victorian Palladian architecture and a stunningly beautiful building. The building spans two floors connected by a grand staircase and several compact spiral stair cases. It is a historically "listed building" and is protected against alterations under Irish law. An unfortunate side-effect of these protective measures is that the NMI is unable to have an elevator installed in the building and thus the upper floors of the archaeology museum are not accessible to visitors of limited mobility.

This provided our motivation to create a virtual museum exhibition that reflects as accurately as possible the experience of actually visiting the museum in person. An ancillary motivation is that if provided in-class, this virtual museum experience could also provide a platform to enthuse school children, to foster learning and to encourage visits to the museum. With the ever increasing popularity of 3D and augmented reality technology, many museums around the world have moved to provide a digital experience for visitors. The Louvre in Paris, for example, has an online interactive tour with photographs of the exhibits superimposed on a virtual recreation of the museum. To the best of our knowledge, however, our demo is the first time that a photo-realistic virtual museum exhibition has been demonstrated that utilises cheap laser scanning technology combined with interactive audio and visual content.

A key novelty of our demo is the cost to achieve the final results. Given the budget-constrained conditions under which most museums operate, it was imperative that our goals be achievable in a cost-effective manner. To this end, we used off the shelf (OTS) low-cost or free tools wherever possible, putting the creation of such digital exhibitions within reach of even modest budgets. Our demo was completed by a single graduate student with no prior experience of 3D tools over a period of 3 months.

2. SYSTEM DESCRIPTION

We decided to approach the 3D reconstruction of the exhibition from two perspectives. From the macro perspective, we performed 3D modeling of the entire room based on wire mesh drawing. To do this, we captured 50 photographs taken at random locations throughout the exhibition and utilised Autodesk's Imagemodeller[2] to enable us to draw the wire mesh. The wire mesh represents an accurate scale model of the entire room in which the exhibition is housed. Next, an open source game engine called Unity[3] was

[1]http://www.museum.ie/

[2]http://usa.autodesk.com/

[3]http://unity3d.com/

MM'11, November 28–December 1, 2011, Scottsdale, Arizona, USA.
ACM 978-1-4503-0616-4/11/11.

Figure 1: The Iconic Treasures Exhibition, National Museum of Ireland

employed to allow us to create the 3D interactive environment. Texturing of the mesh was performing using the same 50 photos, and then pre-existing museum content, such as audio and text descriptions of the artefacts, were integrated into the virtual exhibition. Finally, realistic lighting conditions were added.

From the micro perspective we used a NextEngine[4] desktop 3D laser scanner to scan various artefacts, which produced high definition, textured, wire-mesh scans of selected exhibits. This allows a user to interact with a given artefact by rotating and moving the virtual artefact so it can be viewed from any angle providing a more comprehensive experience than simply viewing an artefact behind a glass display case. The laser scans of the artefacts were then imported into the virtual exhibition, resized and displayed in a virtual display case.

Finally, to complete the visual experience the Nvidia[5] 3D vision system was used to provide the stereoscopic images that produce the 3D effect. This creates images for both the left and right eye and displays them sequentially on the screen in an interlaced format. It works with LCD active shutter glasses that open and close 120 times a second and isolate the appropriate image for each eye resulting in a virtual 3D image. These glasses are currently expensive, however, the system can also be configured to produce content for ultra-cheap red/cyan passive 3D glasses with only a small reduction in terms of the quality of the immersive experience.

3. DEMONSTRATION

The demonstration will consist of a laptop with a special 3D screen coupled with active shutter glasses. The 3D digital museum exhibition with be show cased on the laptop and users can explore the virtual museum exhibition and interact with the displays. Users will need to wear the 3D glasses in order to experience the 3D effect produced by the laptop. A poster detailing the project and showing graphically the steps involved will also be displayed.

[4]https://www.nextengine.com/

[5]https://www.nvidia.com

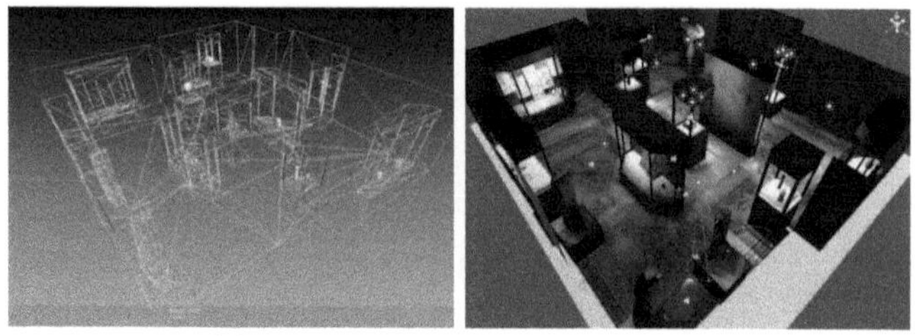

(a) (b)

Figure 2: Wire mesh reconstruction of the exhibition space

(a) (b)

Figure 3: (a) The Aghaboe artefact and (b) the laser scan after texturing is applied

Figure 4: A 3D display showing the virtual exhibition

Acknowledgments

This work is supported by Science Foundation Ireland under grant 07/CE/I114.

Interactive Rich Reading: Enhanced Book Reading Experience with a Conversational Agent

Koichi Mori[1], Rafael Ballagas[1], Glenda Revelle[2], Hayes Raffle[1], Hiroshi Horii[1], Mirjana Spasojevic[1]

[1] Nokia Research Center
955 Page Mill Rd, Palo Alto CA 94306
koichi.mori | tico.ballagas | hayes.raffle | hiroshi.horii | mirjana.spasojevic @nokia.com

[2] Human Environmental Sciences
University of Arkansas
Fayetteville, AR 72701
grevelle@uark.edu

ABSTRACT
In this work, we introduce Interactive Rich Reading, a new enhanced book experience designed to run on smartphones and a tablet device. Interactive Rich Reading is characterized by a video-based conversational agent that asks questions or makes comments about the current page and is specifically designed to promote engagement with the contents of children's books. We use video compositing techniques to overlay the conversational agent directly over the book contents, creating a magical experience for children by bringing the book to life. We describe technical issues related to enabling this experience on mobile platforms for easier adoption of this technique by other researchers and practitioners.

Categories and Subject Descriptors
H.5.2 User Interfaces

General Terms
Design, Experimentation, Human Factors

Keywords
Interactive e-book, mobile application, conversational agent

1. INTRODUCTION
Tablets and mobile phones are changing the way we consume books. High-resolution, color, touch-enabled screens enable books with integrated multimedia including narration, music, animation, video, and mini-games. Digital book publishing is a growing industry, with electronic books (e-books) being targeted at a wide range of platforms including tablets and smartphones. There are already millions of digital book titles available at major digital bookstores. According to Mobclix, the number of books surpasses number of games in a popular App Stores[1].

A majority of e-books are published using the EPUB standard. While good for text-centric books, current version of EPUB may be unsuitable for publications which require precise layout or specialized formatting, such as with children's illustrated books[2].

A growing number of e-books are embedding book contents into native applications to enable multimedia integration, especially for children books and educational books (e.g. *Jack and Beanstalk* by Aryars Animation, *Toy Story* by Disney, *Cat in the Hat* by Oceanhouse Media, *Curious George* by Iceberg Reader, and *Our Choice* by Push Pop Press). These interactive e-books typically provide features like animated images or sounds triggered by the user's input, zooming, embedded video, and embedded activities or mini-games. These features make the book significantly more interactive and engaging when compared to static e-books or printed books. These activities enable deeper exploration of the topics of the book.

Figure 1 (Top) Interactive Rich Reading running on a smartphone. (Bottom) Screenshot of Interactive Rich Reading with text zooming

2. DESIGN AND CONCEPT
Interactive Rich Reading is different than most interactive book experiences in that it leverages a conversational agent to get readers (especially children) to talk about the book. Research on dialogic reading has shown that the more children talk about the book during the reading experience, the better their vocabulary development [3]. Furthermore, educational media that engages children socially has demonstrated learning benefits [2]. The agent character is placed in front of the book giving impression that it is part of the book contents, and brings the book to life.

[1] http://blog.mobclix.com/2010/03/01/books-outnumber-games-in-the-app-store/

[2] This issue may be addressed in future versions of the standard (http://idpf.org/epub/30/wg-charter)

MM'11, November 28–December 1, 2011, Scottsdale, Arizona, USA.
ACM 978-1-4503-0616-4/11/11.

This experience was initially designed and built as a part of a web-based solution, called Story Visit [1], to help grandparents read books to children over the Internet. Based on the positive response from our Story Visit deployment, we were inspired to try and adapt parts of the experience for mobile devices.

Error! Reference source not found. shows a screenshot from Interactive Rich Reading running on a Nokia N8 smartphone. The user can turn the page by swiping the screen. Elmo from Sesame Street (our conversational agent in this title) stays in the same position at the center bottom of the screen throughout the reading experience. Touching Elmo triggers him to ask the child questions related to the story. If Elmo is touched again, he will ask another question, wave his hand, laugh, or dance. The book content itself is a digital copy of the larger form factor printed book, and hence most of the text is too small to read on mobile devices. To compensate, users can tap on the text to enlarge the font size (see Figure 1). If narration audio is available and enabled, it is played when zoomed text is displayed. However, we found in our preliminary tests that the best dialogic reading occurs with the parents read the book together with their child, using Elmo to promote more discussion around the book contents.

3. IMPLEMENTATION

Each title of Interactive Rich Reading is implemented as an application using Qt Quick[3], a cross-platform application framework that allows rapid development of fluid and natural user interfaces using a declarative scripting language. We have tested our cross-platform experience on Maemo smartphones, Meego tablets, and Symbian smartphones so far. An Interactive Rich Reading title contains cross-platform Qt Quick code, book images, video files of the conversational agent, optional narration audio files, and text from the book if the title needs text zooming. The diagram in Figure 2 illustrates necessary resources to create one book title and how those are used on the mobile device.

Compositing the video on top of the book content was a significant technical challenge. There was no video codec supporting alpha channel commonly available on the target mobile platforms. Also, H.264 decoding is typically hardware accelerated on mobile platforms, making it more desirable from both a performance and power consumption perspective. Although the H.264 standard[4] officially supports color spaces with alpha transparency, most implementations of H.264 do not. We used an alternative technique to spatially encode both the video and alpha mask together in the same video frame (see Figure 2). When rendering this video, the application simply needs to convert each frame back into an image buffer with alpha channel by merging the color region and the alpha region. This workaround is a known technique to realize video with alpha layer on the platform that does not support it[5], but we are the first to demonstrate its feasibility on mobile platforms. Due to extra buffer processing, this technique has some performance impact in the application, but we found a video with 320x240 pixel dimension at 15 fps can spare enough CPU/GPU resource for Qt Quick to process smooth graphical animation and the agent character looks acceptable on the mobile devices with smooth scaling.

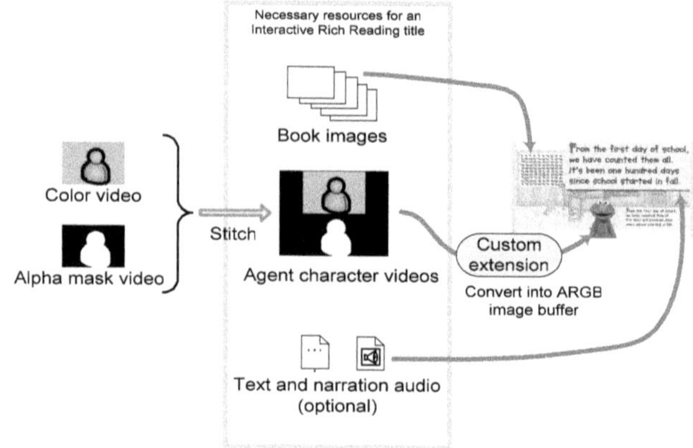

Figure 2 Elements of Interactive Rich Reading title

Making conversational agent character videos is one of the time consuming effort in creating an Interactive Rich Reading title, assuming the book content itself is already available (e.g. as a printed book). There should be at least two different comments or questions on each page, which means a 15 page book needs about 30-40 videos. That is a lot of work writing scripts, shooting and editing videos, and testing on the devices. One possible way to reduce this effort is to re-use some videos from other titles, once several titles are made. We indeed made one title with the videos from five other titles. This title was a sequel of one of the five, and the result was quite acceptable. A series of books could potentially share many conversational agent character videos.

4. SUMMARY

Interactive Rich Reading is a new approach to interactive e-books. The conversational agent character overlaid on top of the page asks questions or talks about the page to help children engage more with the contents of the book.

Video with alpha layer is a key enabler for Interactive Rich Reading to make the agent character most engaging to the users, but we faced many technical difficulties because of poor alpha channel support in the video codec on the mobile platforms. We believe video with alpha layer is useful for many other digital contents, and hope mobile platform vendors will consider adding alpha channel support in their video codecs.

5. REFERENCES

[1] Raffle, H., Revelle, G., Mori, K., Ballagas, R., Buza, K., Horii, H., Kaye, J., Cook, K., Freed, N., Go, J., Spasojevic, M. "Hello, is Grandma there? Let's Read! StoryVisit: Family Video Chat and Connected E-Books." *Proc. CHI 2011*, 1195-1204.

[2] Richter, R. A., Robb, M. B., and Smith, E. I. Media as social partners: The social nature of young children's learning from social media. *Child Development*, 82(1):82–95, Jan/Feb 2011.

[3] Whitehurst, G. J., Falco, F. L., Lonigan, C. J., Fischel, J. E., DeBaryshe, B. D., Valdez-Menchaca, M. C., et al. (1988). "Accelerating language development through picture book reading." *Developmental Psychology*, 24(4), 552-559.

---

[3] http://qt.nokia.com/qtquick/

[4] http://www.itu.int/rec/T-REC-H.264

[5] http://jakearchibald.com/scratch/alphavid/

Hierarchical Video Browsing with a 3D Carousel

Klaus Schoeffmann
Institute of Information Technology
Klagenfurt University, Klagenfurt, Austria
ks@itec.aau.at

Manfred del Fabro
Institute of Information Technology
Klagenfurt University, Klagenfurt, Austria
manfred@itec.aau.at

ABSTRACT

We present a video browsing tool that combines advantages of the hierarchical browsing concept with 3D projection and multi-threaded programming in order to provide a convenient and efficient interface. The tool allows for instantaneous hierarchical browsing of video and uses a dynamic approach (i.e. tree of playable video segments instead of static key frames) that also supports parallel playback.

Categories and Subject Descriptors

H.5.2 [**Information Interfaces and Presentation**]: User Interfaces

General Terms

Design, Experimentation, Human Factors.

Keywords

Video Browsing, Video Navigation, Video Exploration

1. INTRODUCTION

Hierarchical browsing is a simple method for video content exploration that was introduced almost two decades ago[6]. A hierarchical video browser decomposes a video into segments that may be decomposed again until a specific level of detail is reached. For example, the top level could show semantic scenes while the second level may show subsegments of a selected scene. Furthermore, the third level could show all shots of a selected subsegment. This hierarchical navigation should facilitate interactive search in videos. However, as already mentioned by Jansen et al. [4] the most challenging part of hierarchical browsing is the visualization that should allow a user to inspect every detail without getting lost. The user study of their *2D VideoTree* approach revealed that it is too confusing for novice users, which they lead back to the fact that users weren't able to see the duration of one node in their tree. I.e. every node was visualized with a static image of the same size regardless of the duration of the corresponding video segment.

We propose a more flexible approach for hierarchical video browsing that takes advantage of 3D graphics and multi-threaded programming in order to provide a novel and flexible interface that allows for both good screen estate utilization and navigation context preservation.

MM'11, November 28–December 1, 2011, Scottsdale, Arizona, USA.
ACM 978-1-4503-0616-4/11/11.

2. RELATED WORK

Many approaches for video browsing have been proposed in the literature, a recent review is given in [7]. However, only a few of them concentrate on hierarchical browsing. Most of them are static approaches that visualize a tree of static images. For example, Guillemot et al. [3] and Jansen et al. [4] propose a key frame based video browser that allows for browsing on three levels (scenes, shots and key frames). A cone-tree representation of key frames has been proposed by Manske [5]. This approach provides already a simple 3D interface for navigation through a hierarchy of key frames. A more dynamic video browsing tool is described in [2]. On each level of the browsing hierarchy a RSVP carousel interface [8] can be used to scroll through the key frames. Another tree-based dynamic video browsing tool is presented in [1], which also supports parallel playback of tree nodes. However, so far no one has concentrated on hierarchical video browsing with 3D graphics support that provides a flexible and intuitive way of content navigation in a video.

3. INTERFACE

The proposed tool uses a 3D visualization for hierarchical video browsing, where every node is represented as a *3D carousel* that can be rotated by user interaction with the mouse-wheel. The 3D carousel allows a good utilization of screen estate through 3D projection and provides a flexible and intuitive way of interaction and navigation, which conveniently preserves the navigation context. The position and the radius of the ring is selected according to its parent. Each ring consists of a specific number of entries that contain linear sampled segments of its parent ring. We have chosen linear sampling instead of decomposition into scenes, subscenes, and shots for several reasons: (i) it overcomes the duration-problem mentioned in [4], (ii) it allows for instantaneous use with any video file (i.e. without preprocessing), (iii) it supports browsing of single-shot videos that are common in non-professional areas. The user starts browsing with a top level view that shows all available videos in a row. The user can navigate forward and backward in this street-like view (see Fig. 1) with the mouse-wheel and start playback for a specific file with a left mouse click.

A right mouse-click will open the first hierarchy level and show a 3D carousel directly below the selected video, consisting of k linearly sampled segments of equal duration (see

Figure 1: Top level – shows all videos in collection

Fig. 2; the missing segment indicates begin/end of the samples). The mouse-wheel can be used to rotate the carousel in either direction in order to focus on a specific segment. A left mouse click starts playback for a segment, whereas parallel playback is also supported. Any further right mouse click on a tree node/segment will open another sub-tree and increase the level of detail until frame level granularity is reached. Moreover, the user may switch between different levels/sub-trees or close a sub-tree. It is also possible to switch to an outer view that provides a good overview of the currently created tree (Fig. 4).

Figure 2: First hierarchy level of selected video ($k = 12$), each node represents 140 secs. of the video

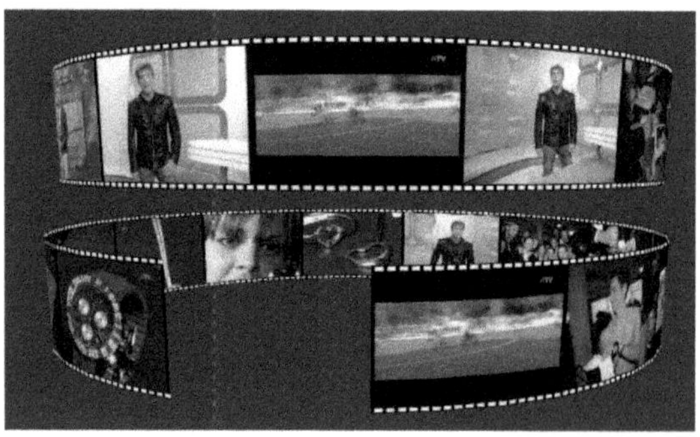

Figure 3: below: second hierarchy level of selected segment ($k = 12$), each node represents approx. 12 secs. of the segment

4. CONCLUSIONS

We have presented a tool that combines advantages of hierarchical content browsing and 3D graphics in order to provide a novel and flexible user interface that is expected to efficiently support users at the task of interactive search in video. In further work we will evaluate its usefulness through several user studies and compare it with other approaches.

Figure 4: Outer view of current tree

5. REFERENCES

[1] M. Del Fabro, K. Schoeffmann, and L. Böszörmenyi. Instant video browsing: a tool for fast non-sequential hierarchical video browsing. In *Proceedings of the 6th international conference on HCI in work and learning, life and leisure: workgroup human-computer interaction and usability engineering*, USAB'10, pages 443–446, Berlin, Heidelberg, 2010. Springer-Verlag.

[2] A. Girgensohn, F. Shipman, and L. Wilcox. Adaptive Clustering and Interactive Visual. to Support the Selection of Video Clips. In *Proc. of the 2011 ACM Int. Conf. on Multimedia Retrieval (ICMR11)*. ACM, 2011.

[3] M. Guillemot, P. Wellner, D. Gatica-Perez, and J.-M. Odobez. A hierarchical keyframe user interface for browsing video over the internet. 2003.

[4] M. Jansen, W. Heeren, and B. van Dijk. Videotrees: Improving video surrogate presentation using hierarchy. In *Content-Based Multimedia Indexing, 2008. CBMI 2008. Int. Workshop on*, pages 560 –567, June 2008.

[5] K. Manske. Video browsing using 3d video content trees. In *Proc. of the 1998 WS on New paradigms in information visualization and manipulation*, NPIV '98, pages 20–24, New York, NY, USA, 1998. ACM.

[6] M. Mills, J. Cohen, and Y. Y. Wong. A magnifier tool for video data. In *Proceedings of the SIGCHI conference on Human factors in computing systems*, CHI '92, pages 93–98, New York, NY, USA, 1992. ACM.

[7] K. Schoeffmann, F. Hopfgartner, O. Marques, L. Boeszoermenyi, and J. M. Jose. Video browsing interfaces and applications: a review. *SPIE Reviews*, 1(1):018004, 2010.

[8] K. Wittenburg, C. Forlines, T. Lanning, A. Esenther, S. Harada, and T. Miyachi. Rapid serial visual presentation techniques for consumer digital video devices. In *Proc. of the 16th annual ACM symposium on User interface software and technology*, UIST '03, pages 115–124, New York, NY, USA, 2003. ACM.

COZI: Crowdsourced and Content-based Zoomable Video Player

Axel Carlier
IRIT-ENSEEIHT
University of Toulouse
carlier.axel@gmail.com

Arash Shafiei
IRIT-ENSEEIHT
University of Toulouse
arash.shafiei@gmail.com

Julien Badie
IRIT-ENSEEIHT
University of Toulouse
julien.badie@gmail.com

Salim Bensiali
IRIT-ENSEEIHT
University of Toulouse
salim.bensiali@gmail.com

Wei Tsang Ooi
Dept. of Computer Science
Nat. Univ. of Singapore
ooiwt@comp.nus.edu.sg

ABSTRACT

We present a new user interface designed to allow easy yet effective zooming and panning into high-definition videos for playback on low resolution displays. Our system first applies state-of-the-art video analysis algorithms to detect salient regions of interest and recommends them to users. These recommendations help users to quickly identify important regions in the video and zoom into the regions with a single mouse click. The salient regions may moves according to the movement of track objects, further reducing the need for users to manually pan to track an object of interests. To further improve the relevance of the recommended regions, users' interactions are logged and analyzed. The actual regions selected and viewed by users serve as a feedback and is integrated into the system to improve the recommendations. We have implemented a Web-based version of the user interface, running on modern browsers supporting HTML5. We describe the algorithms and optimizations used to implement and improve the system.

Categories and Subject Descriptors: H.5.1 [Multimedia Information Systems]: Video

General Terms: Human Factors, Design

Keywords: Interaction Techniques, Zoomable Video, Content Analysis, Crowdsourcing

1. INTRODUCTION

Resolution of videos are getting higher and higher (up to $7,680\times 4,320$ pixels) while the display size of electronic devices such as laptops or smartphones remains limited. This observation motivated the study of new paradigms of interaction such as zoomable video, first presented in [2]. In this work, Ngo et al. propose different compression algorithms to adapt to this new form of interaction and present an interface that includes functionalities such as zooming in and out the video, and moving the selected viewport by dragging with the mouse (panning).

Although the work by Ngo et al. provides some insight into the ways users interact with zoomable video (studied in [1]), this interface can be tedious and sometimes confusing to use. Indeed, when zooming in a moving object, a user might be disoriented because the object leaves the viewport. The action of panning needed to follow the object is not very intuitive, and must sometimes be repeated several times in order to track the object along its entire movement.

Figure 1: Our zoomable video interface

Motivated by that problem, we decided to develop a new zoomable video interface in which we recommend viewports to users. We call our new interface *COZI*, short for COntent-aware Zoomable Interface. Figure 1 shows an example of such a recommendation in COZI: when the mouse cursor hovers over a region of interest (ROI), i.e., a region we detected as potentially interesting, the recommended viewport appear as a semi-transparent white rectangle. After left clicking inside the recommended viewport, the user zooms in and views the corresponding ROI at a higher resolution. The detected ROIs might be moving. In that case, the recommended viewport automatically tracks the object, which considerably reduces the number of interactions needed from the user. The user may left click outside the recommended viewports. In which case, the interface would zoom in by one zoom level, centered around the click position. Users can right click to zoom out by one zoom level. As in the interface proposed by Ngo et al., users can drag with a mouse to pan while zoomed into the video.

In this paper, we describe the architecture of our web-based zoomable video interface, as well as the content analysis algorithms we implemented to detect ROIs and generate the recommended viewports. We also show how users' interactions can be added as an input to improve the quality of the recommendations.

2. SYSTEM IMPLEMENTATION

The overview of COZI is presented in Figure 2. There are two parts for this system: an off-line content analysis process and a web application.

The web application was developed using new features of HTML5 such as canvas and video tags. We handle users' interactions with Javascript, allowing us to collect those interactions into

MM'11, November 28–December 1, 2011, Scottsdale, Arizona, USA.
ACM 978-1-4503-0616-4/11/11.

a remote MySQL database. The interface takes a JSON (JavaScrip Object Notation) file as an input, which is downloaded along with the video. This JSON file is generated during a video analysis offline process and contains the information (time, position and size) of the recommended viewports.

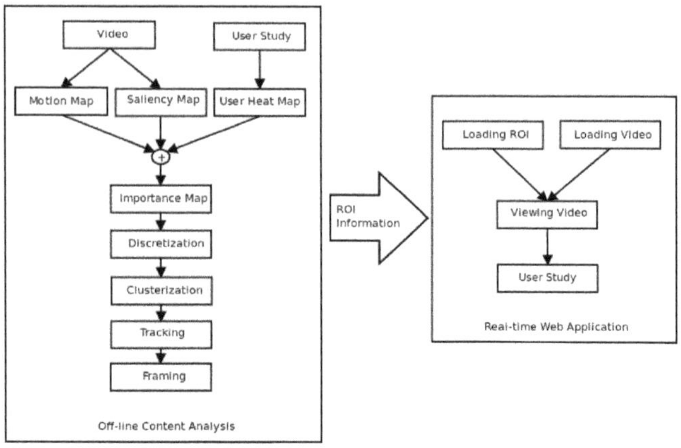

Figure 2: System Overview

2.1 Importance Map Generation

We now describe the three main steps of our content analysis. The first step to detect ROIs on the video is to apply some content analysis algorithms. We compute a saliency map (Figure 3(b)) based on color gradients and strong luminosity variations. Motion is also detected by comparing color maps from successive frames (Figure 3(a)). Finally, we generate an importance maps by summing and normalizing the saliency and motion maps (Figure 3(c)). Brightest regions of this importance maps are likely to be ROIs, and therefore they are recommended as viewports in our interface.

(a) Motion (b) Saliency (c) Importance

Figure 3: (a) Motion map (b) Saliency map (c) Importance map

2.2 Viewport Optimization

We now briefly describe how we get viewports out of this importance map. We first discretize the importance map by generating a set of points following the probability distribution described by the importance map. We then clusterize this set of points using a Mean-shift algorithm. At this point we have clusters of points in every frame. Our next step is to track clusters over time, by looking for the closest clusters in successive frames.

The last step, which we call *framing*, consists in positioning optimally the viewports on the frames. We allow in our interface three different levels of zooming, which means the viewports can be of three different sizes (see Figure 4). Framing is therefore an optimization algorithm where we aim at placing viewports at the best position regarding several criterias, such as maximizing the number of points contained in a viewport, or minimizing the cuts of clusters. Figure 4 shows the output of our framing algorithm. We can see that in this example the viewports are focused on the different characters of the scene.

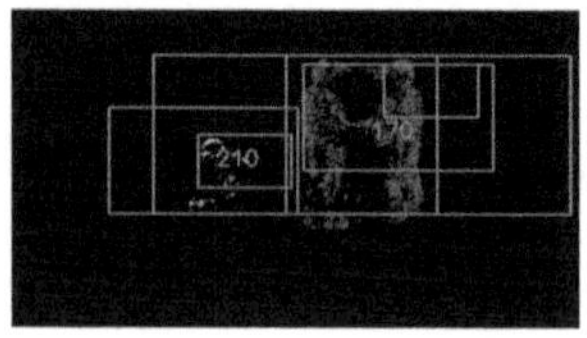

Figure 4: Output of our *Framing* algorithm

2.3 Combining User Feedback with Content Analysis

In the following section we describe how we take users' interations in account to recommend better viewports.

On every frame, we know which viewports have been visualized by the users. We decide to model the attention of a user as a gaussian centered in the viewport he visualized. By adding the gaussians obtained from every users on a single frame, we compute a *user map*, as shown in Figure 5(a). We then reapply our entire algorithm on a new importance map that includes the user map. The new importance map is shown as Figure 5(b), along with the new framing results (Figure 5(c)). The viewports are now focusing on an object laying on the table between the two characters, which is indeed a ROI of the scene that is neither salient nor moving, making it almost impossible for a classic content analysis algorithm to detect.

(a) User Map (b) New Importance Map (c) New Framing results

Figure 5: (a) User heat map (b) Importance map containing user heat map

3. CONCLUSION

In this demo, we briefly present COZI, a novel interface for zoomable video based both on content analysis and crowdsourcing. This interface provides recommendations to users, by indicating to them the regions that are likely to be interesting. We conducted a user study (we can not present it here because of the lack of space), and results show our interface not only provides better viewing experience with fewer interactions, but also enhances users' understanding of the videos by showing them where to look.

4. REFERENCES

[1] A. Carlier, R. Guntur, and W. T. Ooi. Towards characterizing users' interaction with zoomable video. In *Proceedings of the 2010 ACM workshop on Social, adaptive and personalized multimedia interaction and access*, pages 21–24, Florence, Italy, 2010.

[2] K. Q. M. Ngo, R. Guntur, A. Carlier, and W. T. Ooi. Supporting zoomable video streams via dynamic region-of-interest cropping. In *Proceedings of MMSys'10*, pages 259–270, Scottsdale, AZ, USA, 2010.

A Smart Assistant for Shooting Virtual Cinematography with Motion-Tracked Cameras

Christophe Lino
IRISA/INRIA Rennes
Campus de Beaulieu
35042, Rennes Cedex, France
christophe.lino@inria.fr

Marc Christie
IRISA/INRIA Rennes
Campus de Beaulieu
35042, Rennes Cedex, France
marc.christie@irisa.fr

Roberto Ranon
HCI Lab, University of Udine
via delle Scienze 206
33100, Udine, Italy
roberto.ranon@uniud.it

William Bares
Millsaps College
1701 North State St Jackson
MS 39210
bareswh@millsaps.edu

ABSTRACT

This demonstration shows how an automated assistant encoded with knowledge of cinematography practice can offer suggested viewpoints to a filmmaker operating a hand-held motion-tracked virtual camera device. Our system, called *Director's Lens*, uses an intelligent cinematography engine to compute, at the request of the filmmaker, a set of suitable camera placements for starting a shot that represent semantically and cinematically distinct choices for visualizing the current narrative. Editing decisions and hand-held camera compositions made by the user in turn influence the system's suggestions for subsequent shots. The result is a novel virtual cinematography workflow that enhances the filmmaker's creative potential by enabling efficient exploration of a wide range of computer-suggested cinematographic possibilities.

Categories and Subject Descriptors

H.5.1 [**Multimedia Information Systems**]: Animations, Video

General Terms

Algorithms, Human Factors

Keywords

Virtual Cinematography, Motion-Tracked Virtual Cameras, Virtual Camera Planning

1. INTRODUCTION

Creating camera edits and movements for computer generated animation remains a time-consuming and largely manual endeavor requiring cinematographic skill and experience with 3D animation packages. Some technically-savvy filmmakers are now using motion-sensing devices to capture complex virtual camera movements rather than key-framing the camera [1]. However, these existing devices operate as plugins to animation packages such as Maya that can rapidly create an infinity of variations in visual effects, but offer no similar ability to create variations in virtual cinematography.

Researchers in automated virtual cinematography systems have produced increasingly sophisticated algorithms that can generate virtual 3D camera work to mimic textbook guidelines [2]. But in succeeding to reduce human effort, they fail to harness the input of creative human filmmakers and as a result produce cinematography of little creative value. Our *Director's Lens* system introduces a novel workflow that combines creative human intelligence with the computational power of an automated cinematography system, to enable a filmmaker to explore a variety of automatically suggested virtual camera compositions (see Figure 2). Camera compositions represent cinematically distinct ways one might film a given shot and which are consistent in user-specified continuity properties with the previous shot. For computing its suggestions, the system exploits an annotated screenplay which provides the narrative context in the form of text descriptions of locations, subjects, and time-stamped actions, with links to the 3D models employed in the scene. Moreover, the system tries also to mimic users' composition from previous shots. With the help of a motion-tracked virtual camera (see Figure 1), the cinematographer can easily refine a suggestion to use it as a starting point to craft a shot.

2. THE DIRECTOR'S LENS

In this interactive demonstration of our Director's Lens system, a user operates a small hand-held touchscreen LCD screen equipped with motion sensors and custom-built button and joystick controls (see Figure 1) to record virtual camera movements (i.e., shots) to visualize a recreation of a scene from Michael Radford's film version of Orwell's 1984. The application runs on a notebook PC with a USB cable to communicate with the device's buttons, joysticks, and touchscreen, and an HDMI cable to mirror the PC's display on the handheld LCD. Optical motion capture cameras mounted on tripods track the position and orientation of a rigid body marker cluster affixed to the device, which in turn map to the position and orientation of the virtual cam-

MM'11, November 28–December 1, 2011, Scottsdale, Arizona, USA.
ACM 978-1-4503-0616-4/11/11.

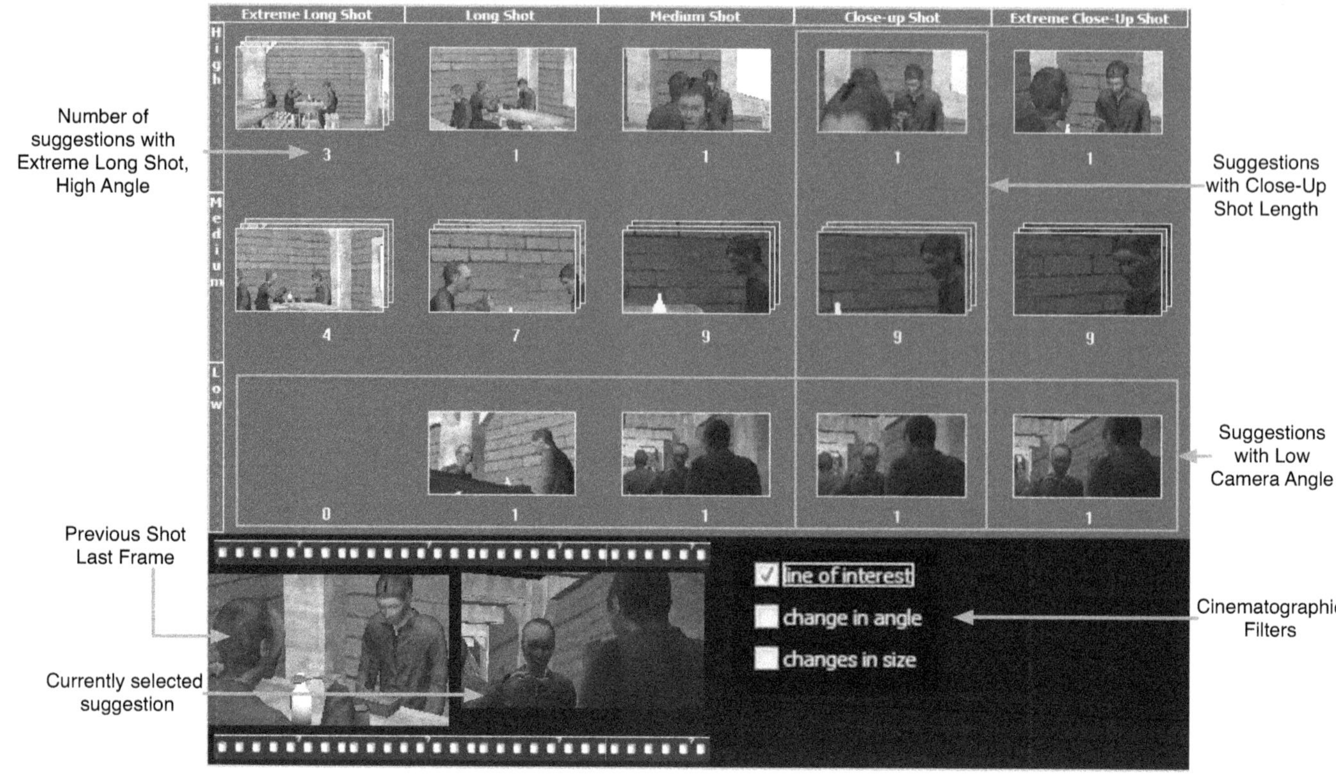

Figure 2: Screenshot of the interface in Explore Suggestions mode. User selects *Line of Interest* visual filter requesting only those suggestions that respect the line of interest relative to the previous shot's last frame (pictured in the bottom left).

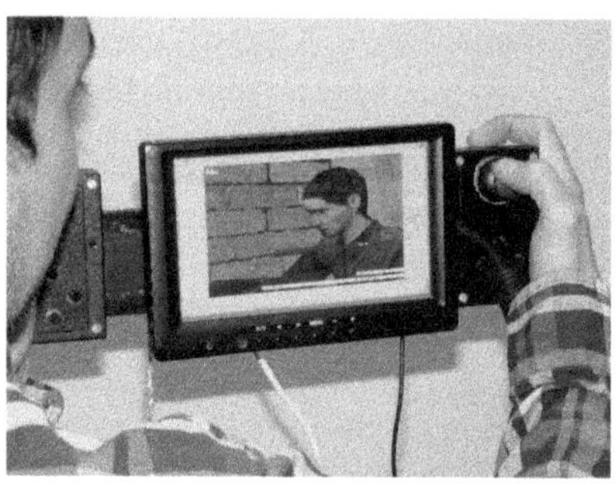

Figure 1: Our custom-built hand-held virtual camera device with dual handgrip thumbsticks, buttons, and 7-inch LCD touch-screen.

era. Other versions were built from a Microsoft XBOX 360 gamepad and the same type of LCD touchscreen, but with a gyroscope sensor to drive camera orientation and gamepad thumbsticks to drive camera position.

A user can record a movie by iterating the following workflow: (i) identify the instant in the movie produced so far where a cut should be introduced (initially, at the beginning of the animation); (ii) ask the system to compute suggestions to start a new shot; (iii) browse the suggestions by their cinematic properties (see Figure 2); (iv) choose the one that is closest to what the user likes; (v) possibly move or turn the virtual camera device to refine the composition, and start shooting by moving the device like a real camera.

An alternative, simpler workflow can very rapidly produce a sequence of static shots by simply exploring and selecting suggestions, without using motion tracking.

When browsing suggestions users explore variations in shot distance, height, and angle in addition to whether or not suggestions conform to or differ from the previous shot in continuity, size, and angle. In this way the user rapidly explores many different possible ways to film a given sequence and assume manual control to improve upon the system's compositions and movements.

3. CONCLUSION

This demonstration[1] represents the very first coupling of motion-tracked virtual camera devices and automated computation of suggested viewpoints to support a filmmaker's creative choices. The demonstration highlights both the tool's creative potential to play and explore distinct cinematic possibilities for a scenario and to rapidly compose cinematography that follows desired continuity and editing conventions.

4. REFERENCES

[1] Autodesk. The new art of virtual moviemaking. Autodesk whitepaper, 2009.

[2] M. Christie, P. Olivier, and J.-M. Normand. Camera Control in Computer Graphics. *Computer Graphics Forum*, 27(8):2197–2218, Dec. 2008.

[1]This work has been funded in part by the European Commission under grant agreement IRIS (FP7-ICT-231824)

Video2GPS: A Demo of Multimodal Location Estimation on Flickr Videos

Gerald Friedland
International Computer Science Institute
1947 Center Street, Suite 600
Berkeley, CA 94704-1198
fractor@icsi.berkeley.edu

Jaeyoung Choi
International Computer Science Institute
1947 Center Street, Suite 600
Berkeley, CA 94704-1198
jaeyoung@icsi.berkeley.edu

Adam Janin
International Computer Science Institute
1947 Center Street, Suite 600
Berkeley, CA 94704-1198
janin@icsi.berkeley.edu

ABSTRACT

The following article describes our demo of an approach to determine the geo-coordinates of the recording place of Flickr videos based on both textual metadata and visual cues. The underlying system has been tested on the MediaEval 2010 Placing Task evaluation data, which consists of 5091 unfiltered test videos is able to classify 14 % of the videos to within an accuracy of 10 m.

Categories and Subject Descriptors

H3.1 [**Information Storage and Retrieval**]: Indexing methods; I4.8 [**Image Processing and Computer Vision**]: Scene Analysis—*Sensor Fusion*

General Terms

Experimentation

Keywords

Video, Tagging, Multimodal, Location Estimation, Content Analysis

1. INTRODUCTION

A multimedia content analysis task that has only recently become tractable to research is estimating the location of origin of a video recording that lacks geo-location metadata. The task is sometimes called "multimodal location estimation" or "placing". Just as a human analyst uses multiple sources of information and context to determine geo-location, it seems obvious that for location estimation, the investigation of clues across different modalities and combination with diverse knowledge sources from the web can lead to better results than investigating only one stream of sensor input.

This article describes an approach to determining the geo-coordinates of the place where Flickr videos were recorded based on textual metadata and visual cues. The system was tested on the MediaEval 2010 Placing Task evaluation data and is able to classify 14 % of the videos to within 10 m or less.

MM'11, November 28–December 1, 2011, Scottsdale, Arizona, USA.
ACM 978-1-4503-0616-4/11/11.

2. RELATED WORK

In earlier articles [7, 8, 3], the location estimation task is reduced to a retrieval problem on self-produced, location-tagged image databases. The idea is that if the image is the same then the location must be the same too. Previous work that has been carried out in the area of automatic geo-tagging of multimedia based on tags, has also been mostly carried out on Flickr images. The approach in [2] reports on combining visual content with user tags. However, the accuracy is only reported with a minimum granularity of 200 km. Multimodal location estimation on videos has been first defined and attempted in [1] where the authors match ambulance videos from different cities, even without using textual tags. The first evaluation on multimodal location estimation on randomly selected consumer-produced videos has been performed in the 2010 MediaEval Placing task [4]. Several notable systems participated in the evaluation, including the predecessor of the system described herein. We have made significant strides in accuracy since the Placing Task evaluation in August 2010, while at the same time using less training data and reducing the complexity of the system.

3. ALGORITHM

Our approach to location estimation is a data-driven multimodal method that uses both the textual tags as well as visual features. The input is a test video with metadata. From the metadata, we only use the user-annotated tags (not the title, or descriptions) that are included in the metadata record for each Flickr video or photo. The algorithm is described as follows.

First we process the tags. For each given tag in the test video record, we determine the spatial variance by searching the training data for an exact match of the tag and creating a list of the geo-locations of the matches. If only one location is found, the spatial variance is trivially small. We pick the centroid location of the top-3 tags with the smallest spatial variance. This results in 0 to 3 coordinates. In the case of 0 coordinates (e.g. because the video is not tagged or no tags match), we assume the most likely geo-coordinate based on the prior distribution of the MediaEval training set, which is the point with latitude and longitude (40.71257011, -74.10224). A place close to New York City. For example, if a test video's metadata contains the tags "Campanile", "Berkeley", and "California", the system would match all training videos that contain any of those tags. We then plot the GPS coordinates of the training videos containing the

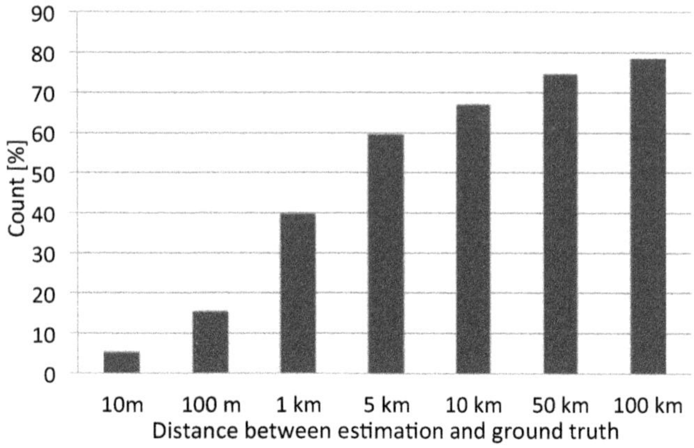

Figure 1: The resulting accuracy of the algorithm as described in Section 3.

tags "Campanile", "Berkeley", and "California" and select the centroid of the tag with the smallest spacial extent (in this case, "Campanile").

For the visual processing step, the input is the median frame of the test video and the 1 to 3 coordinates of the previous stop. We resize the frame to 256×256 pixels and extract GIST [5] features and color histogram. The GIST descriptor is based on a 5×5 spatial resolution with each bin containing responses to 6 orientation and 4 scales. The color histograms were created based on the CIELAB transformed pixels for the frame, like in [3]. The histogram has 4 bins for L, and 14 bins for A and B, respectively. We then also adopt the matching methodology from [3]. We used Euclidean distance to compare GIST descriptors and chi-square distance for color histograms. Weighted linear combination of distances was used as the final distance between the training and test frames. The scaling of the weights was learned by using a small sample of the training set and normalizing the individual distance distributions so that each the standard deviation of each of them would be similar. We use 1-nearest neighbor matching between the test frame and the all the images in a 100 km radius around the 1 to 3 coordinates from the tag-processing step. We pick the match with the smallest distance and output its coordinates as a final result.

4. RESULTS

The MediaEval 2010 Placing Task, organized by [6], is to automatically guess the location of the video, i.e., assign geo-coordinates (latitude and longitude) to videos using one or more of: video metadata (tags, titles), visual content, audio content, social information. The data set consists of Creative Common-licensed videos that were manually crawled from Flickr divided into training data (5091 videos) and test data (5125 videos). The evaluation of our results is performed by applying the same rules and using the same metric as in the MediaEval 2010 evaluation, i.e. by calculating the geographical distance from the actual geo-location of the video (assigned by a Flickr user, creator of the video) to the predicted geo-location (assigned by the system). While it was important to minimize the distances over all test videos, runs were compared by finding how many videos were placed within a threshold distance of 1 km, 5 km, 10 km, 50 km and 100 km. For analyzing the algorithm in greater detail, here we also show distances of below 100 m and below 10 m. The lowest distance category is about the accuracy of a typical GPS localization system in a camera or smartphone. The results are visualized in Figure 1. The results shown are superior in accuracy than any system presented in MediaEval 2010. At the same time, our approach relies on less data and its implementation seems to be the least complex compared to related work.

5. CONCLUSION

In this article we described a system for the estimation of the recording location of Flickr videos. The system uses tags as well as video content and achieves significant accuracy improvements due to the integration of the two media. The demo is a web interface to the system. It allows a user to specify the URL of a Flickr video and the system shows the results step by step, including the tags that contributed most to the estimation. Further information about the project can be found at `http://mmle.icsi.berkeley.edu`.

Acknowledgments

This research is supported by an NGA NURI grant #HM11582-10-1-0008.

6. REFERENCES

[1] G. Friedland, O. Vinyals, and T. Darrell. Multimodal Location Estimation. In *Proceedings of ACM Multimedia*, pages 1245–1251, 2010.

[2] A. Gallagher, D. Joshi, J. Yu, and J. Luo. Geo-location inference from image content and user tags. In *Proceedings of IEEE CVPR*. IEEE, 2009.

[3] J. Hays and A. Efros. IM2GPS: estimating geographic information from a single image. In *IEEE Conference on Computer Vision and Pattern Recognition, 2008. CVPR 2008*, pages 1–8, 2008.

[4] M. Larson, M. Soleymani, P. Serdyukov, S. Rudinac, C. Wartena, V. Murdock, G. Friedland, R. Ordelman, and G. J. Jones. Automatic Tagging and Geo-Tagging in Video Collections and Communities. In *ACM International Conference on Multimedia Retrieval (ICMR 2011)*, page to appear, April 2011.

[5] A. Oliva and A. Torralba. Building the gist of a scene: The role of global image features in recognition. *Progress in brain research*, 155:23–36, 2006.

[6] Petamedia. Mediaeval web site. *http://www.multimediaeval.org*, 2010.

[7] G. Schindler, M. Brown, and R. Szeliski. City-scale location recognition. In *IEEE Conference on Computer Vision and Pattern Recognition, 2007. CVPR'07*, pages 1–7, 2007.

[8] W. Zhang and J. Kosecka. Image based localization in urban environments. In *3D Data Processing, Visualization, and Transmission, Third International Symposium on*, pages 33–40, 2006.

Towards a Privacy Preserving Personal Photo Album Manager with Semantic Classification, Indexing and Querying Capabilities

Alexis Fesnin
CNAM/CEDRIC
292, rue Saint-Martin
F75141 Paris Cedex 3, France
afesnin@yahoo.fr

Valérie Gouet-Brunet
CNAM/CEDRIC
292, rue Saint-Martin
F75141 Paris Cedex 3, France
valerie.gouet@cnam.fr

Scott Kominen
New Jersey Institute of Technology
Newark, NJ, USA
skominek@optonline.net

Vincent Oria
New Jersey Institute of Technology
Newark, NJ, USA
vincent.oria@njit.edu

Jichao Sun
New Jersey Institute of Technology
Newark, NJ, USA
js87@njit.edu

ABSTRACT

This paper presents the prototype of a personal photo album manager that we build over three years. It integrates state of the art techniques of both database systems and computer vision to propose to publishers a privacy preserving sharable photo album manager where the publisher decides what each user is allowed to see. In addition, the photo album manager provides tools for an easy semantic annotation, classification and querying of the images.

Categories and Subject Descriptors

H.2.4 [**Systems**]: Multimedia databases; H.2.8 [**Database Applications**]: Image databases

General Terms

Algorithms, Experimentation, Management, Performance

Keywords

Personal Photo Album, Privacy, CBIR

1. INTRODUCTION

The best way of getting semantic annotations for images remains manual tagging which is a tedious task. On the other hand, content-based retrieval based on visual features is known to be limited. It is also true that no computer system will be able to come up with the name of a person in an image unless the name has been previously entered into the system. We are sure that nobody will mind entering some semantic information of a limited number of people of interest (e.g. family members) once. In this project, we would like the owner of a photo album (a publisher) to provide semantic annotations of some people of interest once and have the system propagate this knowledge to other pictures as soon as the same publisher uploads them. In addition, the owner can decide which pictures a user is allowed to see. The prototype combines recent progress in computer vision with database concepts such as dynamic views to provide: 1) a privacy preserving photo album management system based on dynamic views; 2) easy semantic annotations using a propagation algorithm; and 3) scene classification based on image background matching. The aim of the demonstration is to present the functionalities of the prototype and show how current technologies can be combined to obtain a fully functional image database system that allows semantic querying with little human intervention. The rest of the paper is organized as follows: Section 2 presents the functionalities of the photo album manager and Section 3 discusses the tools that help the publisher annotate and organize the pictures.

MM'11, November 28–December 1, 2011, Scottsdale, Arizona, USA.
ACM 978-1-4503-0616-4/11/11.

2. A SELECTIVE SHARABLE WEB-BASED PERSONAL PHOTO ALBUM MANAGER

The prototype provides a Web interface where people (publishers) can create and share personal photos. The publisher organizes the photos in an album hierarchy with a root album. Similarly, the users are organized into classes (called *user groups* or simply *groups*) with *veryone* as the root class. Each publisher defines her own albums, the user groups and manages the user group permissions.

Every album has three options for security: *ublic*: anyone visiting the web site can view the album; *Inherit ermissions*: the album inherits security permissions from its parent album (option is not available for the root albums); *Selected roups*: only selected groups and their child groups can view the album. The user group hierarchy follows the iceberg visibility model [5] and the most trusted users are put towards the leave nodes of the user group hierarchy. The Iceberg model defines a partial order among classes of objects of the same type according to a visibility scheme where objects in the uppermost class are also part of all the classes whilst the objects in the leave node classes are restricted to their native classes.

In the Iceberg model, the more you go towards the leaf nodes, the more objects you see. If a group is granted permission an album, every child group is automatically given permission to that album. But the permission inheritance on the photo album hierarchy is not automatic and depends on the security setup. Since each user class is granted permission on one or more albums and a user can belong to more than one class, a virtual album is dynamically generated for every user at query time.

3. EXPLOITING IMAGE CONTENT ANALYSIS FOR IMAGE CLASSIFICATION AND ANNOTATION

This section presents two powerful and intuitive functionalities that we provide to the personal photo album managing: The face detection and annotation propagation (Section 3.1) and image classification (Section 3.2). The tools aim at easing the annotations of images.

3.1 Face detection and label propagation

Several approaches have been developed for face detection in images [8]. Among them, we have employed the well-known approach of Viola and Jones [7], improved in [4] and made available in the open source library OpenCV. Once a face is detected, the user can label it by assigning it a name (label) and other useful information. The detected faces can be viewed in bounding rectangles in original photos, and users have control to add, remove and label some of them in a user-friendly way. The labels are then propagated to faces which are detected from the photos being uploaded through an influence graph, which links face nodes based on some predefined similarity function. To improve the precision of the propagation, for each detected face, the corresponding clothing region is also detected as in [1]. The matching a person's face with visual clothing information can be done during idle time according to certain weighting and combination rules. Matching faces and visual features can help propagate the labels through a different influence graph built on visual features.

Following the *rop* approach [3], each unlabeled face iteratively weights opinions collected from its neighbors, decides its own status, and when the system stabilizes, is assigned the label with the highest score. The whole process is performed as efficient matrix computations and requires no human intervention besides the original labeling. Notice that the propagation tools is to help the publisher provide semantic annotation more easily. The publisher has to validate the labels and sometimes correct improperly labeled faces, which in future will act as new knowledge sources for label propagation. The knowledge propagation is limited to the albums of one and only one publisher who initiates it and validates it.

3.2 Scene retrieval and classification

The scene in an image represents the location shown in the image. It can be a landscape taken in picture during a trip as well a living-room with a Christmas tree and people in a picture taken at Christmas. To capture the scene visual content, we focus on the image background, areas of the image which are connected to its borders, as we make the assumption that people or regions of interest are usually found around the center or the upper tier of the image. The areas thought to be part of the background are extracted after performing a segmentation in regions, and only the border regions are kept. After testing several approaches, we have selected the one based on the clustering of local distributions of quantized colors proposed in [2], which integrates the diversity of colors in large pixel neighborhoods. For describing the regions, we have employed a bag of visual word representation [6] structured in inverted files, because of its robustness to occlusion and to cluttering as well as its efficiency against large datasets. This description enables scene retrieval and classification through region similarity.

The classification of images can be done automatically (*offline*), while similar images retrieval can be performed *online* on demand in a user-friendly way. The photos to be analyzed for classification can be picked among one or several albums, or subsets of albums. The publisher can tune the result by integrating some of the metadata (e.g. time, camera information). The classified/retrieved photos can then constitute new albums, e.g. "Christmas events at home since 2002", or can initiate label propagation to similar scene images. The image background based classification is a way to help the publisher define homogeneous albums.

4. CONCLUSION

This project shows that with current technology combined with little human intervention, it is possible to have a functional image database system that allows semantic querying. A scene classification technique based on image background similarity together with the image metadata provided along with the pictures by most cameras such as time, camera model help group the images and suggest photo albums. In addition, a label propagation technique is used to help the publisher easily annotate the pictures by providing the labels once. We have also implemented a selective publication technique that allows the publisher to decide which pictures a given user is allowed to see. All these modules will be part of the system prototype demonstration.

5. REFERENCES

[1] M. Everingham, J. Sivic, and A. Zisserman. "Hello! My name is... Buffy" – automatic naming of characters in TV video. In *roceedings of the British Machine Vision Conference*, 2006.

[2] J. Fauqueur and N. Boujemaa. Coarse detection and fine color description for region-based image queries. In *International Conference on attern ecognition*, pages 1027–1034, 2002.

[3] M. E. Houle, V. Oria, S. Satoh, and J. Sun. Knowledge propagation in large image databases using neighborhood information. In *roceeding of ACM Multimedia*, 2011.

[4] R. Lienhart and J. Maydt. An extended set of haar-like features for rapid object detection. In *I International Conference on Image rocessing*, pages 900–903, 2002.

[5] V. Oria, T.-T. Phan-Quang, and J.-M. Saglio. A selective publication model for the web: the webograph approach. *International ournal of eb Based Community(I BC)*, 7(1):98–115, 2011.

[6] J. Sivic and A. Zisserman. Video Google: A text retrieval approach to object matching in videos. In *I ICCV*, pages 1470–1477, 2003.

[7] P. Viola and M. Jones. Rapid object detection using boosted cascade of simple features. In *I Computer Vision and attern ecognition*, pages 1511–1518, 2001.

[8] M. H. Yang, D. J. Kriegman, and N. Ahuja. Detecting faces in images: A survey. *I ransactions on attern Analysis and Machine Intelligence*, 24(1):34 – 58, Jan. 2002.

Million-scale Near-duplicate Video Retrieval System*

Yang Cai[†‡], Linjun Yang[‡], Wei Ping[§‡], Fei Wang[+], Tao Mei[‡], Xian-Sheng Hua[+], Shipeng Li[‡]
[†]Zhejiang University [‡]Microsoft Research Asia [+]Microsoft Bing [§]Tsinghua University
yangcai1988@gmail.com,{linjuny,feiw,tmei,xshua,spli}@microsoft.com,weiping.thu@gmail.com

ABSTRACT

In this paper, we present a novel near-duplicate video retrieval system serving one million web videos. To achieve both the effectiveness and efficiency, a visual word based approach is proposed, which quantizes each video frame into a word and represents the whole video as a bag of words. The system can respond to a query in 41ms with 78.4% MAP on average.

Categories and Subject Descriptors

H.3.3 [**Information Storage and Retrieval**]: Information Search and Retrieval tenance—*Search process, Selection process, Information filtering.*

General Terms

Algorithms, Experimentation, Performance

Keywords

Near-duplicate, video retrieval, large scale

1. INTRODUCTION

Near-duplicate video retrieval has been a hot research topic for the past decades, since it is highly useful for automatic video indexing, management, retrieval, rights protection, copy detection, etc. The recent rapid growth of the web videos, evidenced by the fact that on YouTube there are over 35 hours videos being uploaded every minute, imposes an urgent need for a practical large-scale near-duplicate video retrieval system, to facilitate users' consumption of the ever-increasing web videos.

While the decades' research on near-duplicate video retrieval witnessed a large amount of achievements, the practical large-scale near-duplicate video retrieval system is still not mature enough. Most of the existing methods require several seconds to minutes to respond to a normal video query on a database comprising tens of thousands of videos. The approach based on a compact video representation and an improved inverted file index, requires 17ms to query against a 50K video database [4]. However its scalability remains unknown when applied to a web-scale system, which comprises millions or even billions of web videos. The multiple feature hashing method [5] which costs 553ms to retrieve a dataset of 133K videos may still not meet the web search requirement.

*This work was performed when Yang Cai and Wei Ping were visiting Microsoft Research Asia as research interns.

MM'11, November 28–December 1, 2011, Scottsdale, Arizona, USA.
ACM 978-1-4503-0616-4/11/11.

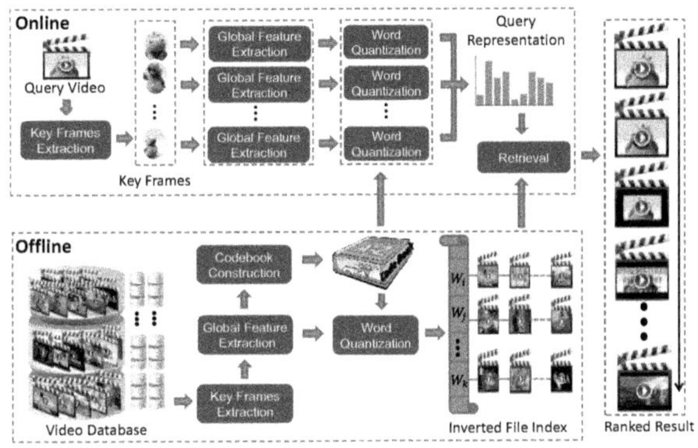

Figure 1: The framework of our proposed system.

To make a further step towards the large-scale near-duplicate web video retrieval, we construct a one million video database by crawling from the web, and based on that, propose a million-scale near-duplicate video retrieval system. To the best of our knowledge, this is the first near-duplicate video retrieval system, serving one million web videos.

The increasing scale imposes a big challenge to the retrieval system in order to achieve a reasonably high precision with a low time cost. To this end, we propose a visual word based approach by generalizing the video signature in [4]. Different from previous methods which construct visual words on each interest points detected in frames, we quantize each frame into a word, to achieve a fast and compact video representation. Specifically, the global features are extracted from each frame and then quantized into a so-called "word". Then the inverted file index is naturally adopted to index these words. While simple, our system demonstrates that it is both effective and efficient for most web video near-duplicates. The system can respond to a query in 41ms on average with a MAP(Mean Average Precision) of 78.4%.

2. THE PROPOSED APPROACH

To develop a scalable near-duplicate video retrieval system, we first need to design a compact video representation, also called video fingerprint. As suggested by [4], representing a video by a bag of visual words extracted from key frames seems to be a promising approach and can achieve a reasonable performance in a moderate scale. We implemented this method and applied it on our collected one

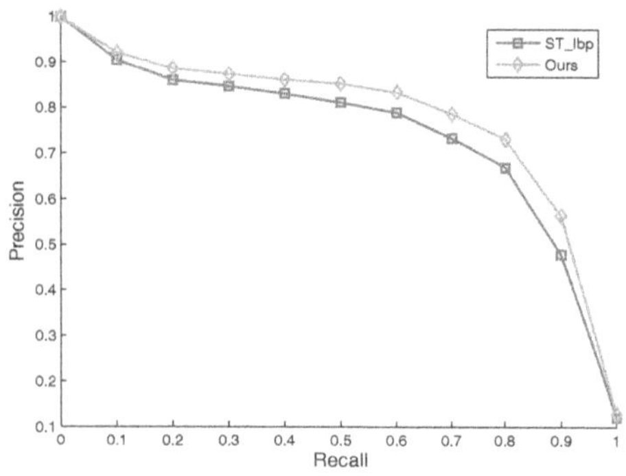

Figure 2: The performance comparison of ST_lbp [4] and ours in terms of precision-recall.

million video database. However, the retrieval time for one query is still more than 300ms and a lot of false alarm videos are included in the retrieval results for some queries. There are two-fold reasons. First, the ordinal feature based video representation lacks discrimination and will lead to more false alarms in the large-scale setting. Second, due to the heuristics inherent in the quantization method in [4], the words distribute non-evenly and a small portion of words appear frequently in a large amount of videos. Hence, the inverted file index cannot speed up the retrieval too much and the retrieval time is nearly linear to the size of the database.

In this demo, we extend the visual word based approach in [4] by incorporating more complex and discriminative frame features. Instead of extracting ordinal relations from frames and encoding the ordinal relations based on heuristic, we extract more discriminative global features based on proven image processing techniques, e.g., color correlogram [1]. Then the high-dimensional frame features are quantized into words using Kmeans clustering algorithm. In this demo, a scalable Kmeans clustering algorithm [2] and the Kmeans tree search algorithm [3] are used to speed up the codebook construction and quantization. Compared to the previous methods, especially the bag of visual words on local features, the proposed approach is easier to scale up. Due to the content redundancy across frames, even though the frame representation is simple, aggregating them for an entire video will greatly improve the discrimination. Compared to [4], the application of color correlogram and Kmeans quantization can lead to a more discriminative video representation. Besides, with a large codebook being constructed, the induced video fingerprint can be made sparse and can therefore make the inverted file index more efficient.

Fig.1 illustrates the flowchart of our proposed system. Uniform sampling is employed to extract key frames every second from videos. After extracting the color correlogram features from the extracted key frames for all the one million videos in our database, we constructed 100K visual vocabulary by clustering on 1M randomly sampled key frames. The inverted file index is adopted to index the visual words and the *cosine* retrieval model with *tf-idf* weighting is employed to compute the relevance score between the query video and videos in the database.

3. SYSTEM DESCRIPTION

The system is implemented in a client-server architecture.

Figure 3: A snapshot of our proposed system.

The client is implemented using Silverlight 3.0 and the server side is implemented using Asp.Net 3.5 and C++.

In our system, a text-based video search engine is implemented based on Lemur[1]. Users can first input a text query and then select one of the returned videos in the text-based search results as query to retrieve near-duplicates. Fig.3 shows a snapshot of our demo system.

The video database comprises about one million videos crawled from the Web as well as 12K videos from CC_WEB_VIDEO dataset[2], which finally leads to 1,148,050 videos in our database.

4. EXPERIMENTAL RESULTS

We compared our method with LBP-based Spatiotemporal (ST_lbp) method [4], using the query sets in CC_WEB_VIDEO and the extended ground-truth. As shown in Fig.2, our proposed method outperforms ST_lbp in terms of precision-recall. Moreover, the retrieval time for one query is only 41ms, which is 9.4 times faster than ST_lbp (386ms). This demonstrates that our proposed approach is highly applicable for web-scale near-duplicate video retrieval, in terms of both precision and time cost.

5. CONCLUSION

In this demo we proposed a million-scale near-duplicate video retrieval system, which achieves both satisfactory precision and high efficiency by incorporating discriminative low-level frame features with visual word quantization techniques. Specifically, one query can be responded in only 41ms and the MAP can arrive at 78.4%, on average.

6. REFERENCES

[1] J. Huang, S. Ravi Kumar, M. Mitra, W.-J. Zhu, and R. Zabih. Spatial color indexing and applications. *IJCV*, 1999.

[2] D. Li, L. Yang, X.-S. Hua, and H.-J. Zhang. Large-scale robust visual codebook construction. In *ACM MM*, 2010.

[3] M. Muja and D. G. Lowe. Fast approximate nearest neighbors with automatic algorithm configuration. In *VISSAPP*, 2009.

[4] L. Shang, L. Yang, F. Wang, K.-P. Chan, and X.-S. Hua. Real-time large scale near-duplicate video retrieval. In *ACM MM*, 2010.

[5] J. Song, Y. Yang, Z. Huang, H. T. Shen, and R. Hong. Multiple feature hashing for real-time large scale near-duplicate video retrieval. In *ACM MM*, 2011.

[1] http://www.lemurproject.org/

[2] http://vireo.cs.cityu.edu.hk/webvideo/

Mobile Product Search with Bag of Hash Bits

Junfeng He, Tai-Hsu Lin, Jinyuan Feng, Shih-Fu Chang
Electrical Engineering Department, Columbia University
jh2700@columbia.edu, lord.lth@gmail.com, {jf2651, sfchang}@ee.columbia.edu

ABSTRACT

The advent of smart phones has provided an excellent platform for mobile visual search. Most of previous mobile visual search systems adopt the framework of "bag of words",in which words indicate quantized codes of visual features. In this work, we propose a novel mobile visual search system based on "bag of hash bits". Using new ideas for hash bit selection, multi-hash table generation, and hamming-distance soft scoring, we overcome the problem of bit inefficiency affecting the traditional hashing approaches, and achieve promising accuracy outperforming state of the art. The framework is also general in that general feature type can be used for generating the hash bits. Demos and experiments over a large scale product image set demonstrate the effectiveness of our approach.

Categories and Subject Descriptors

H.3 [INFORMATION STORAGE AND RETRIEVAL]: Information Search and Retrieval

General Terms

Algorithms

Keywords

Mobile Visual Search, Image Search and Retrieval

1. INTRODUCTION

The advent of smartphones provides a perfect platform for mobile visual search, in which many interesting applications have been developed, such as mobile product search (Google Goggles, Amazon Snaptell), location search or augmented reality,etc. For mobile visual search, local feature(LF) like SIFT or SURF etc., is a popular choice, since global features usually can not support object-level partial search or match, which is crucial in applications like product search.

One unique challenge of mobile visual search is to reduce the amount of data sent from the mobile to the server because of limited bandwidth of networks such as 3G. Many mobile visual systems extract features in the mobile side. However, such local features need to be compressed before transmission; Since sending the raw local features may cost more than sending the image. Typical ways for compressing local features is to quantize them to visual words, or apply novel coding like CHoG[1]. On the server side, most systems adopt the model of "bag of words" (BoW), which represents one image as histograms of visual words contained in the image. Usually a subset of candidate images would be chosen from the database , according to some kinds of distance (e.g., L_2) between the query BoW histogram and the histgorams of database images. Then some geometric reranking/verification such as RANSAC, will be applied to rerank the candidates.

MM'11, November 28–December 1, 2011, Scottsdale, Arizona, USA.
ACM 978-1-4503-0616-4/11/11.

2. PROPOSED SYSTEM

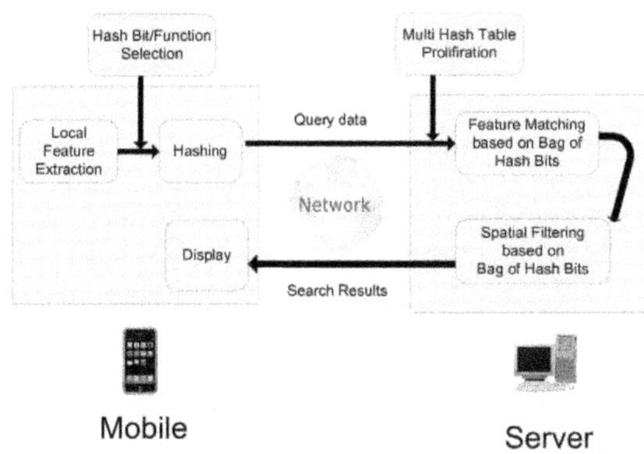

Figure 1: Architecture of the Proposed Bag of Bits Mobile Search System.

We have developed new algorithms and a visual search system based on bag of hash bits instead of conventional bag of words. Figure 1 shows the overall workflow of the system. First, on the client (mobile) side, we compress local features to tens of bits by hashing, which meet the bandwidth requirements in practical mobile networks. On the server side, after receiving hash bits of each local feature, we can represent the whole image as bag of hash bits. To some extend, the hash bits of each local feature can also be viewed as visual word index, however, the advantage of using hash bits are: the hamming distance between "word index" of hash bits, can be used to approximate the feature distance, and moreover, the hash bits allows us to create indexing structure in a very flexible manner. These advantages are important in developing successful search systems that minimize the transmission delay and maintain high retrieval accuracy. With matched local features, we then apply an image-level spatial filtering to re-rank the images and choose the top returned results. The spatial filtering utilizes both the hash bits and the location of local features in one image.

Some previous works have reported that hashing may not

be a good choice for mobile visual search, since a large number of bits are needed for each local feature, hence causing high much transmission cost. In this work, however, we introduce several novel ideas (summarized below with details in the next section).

1. Reducing the number of required hash bits on the mobile side by balancing and selecting hash bits[3].
2. Generating multiple hash tables on the server side by re-using a compact pool of hash bits.
3. Leveraging the hamming distance provided by hash bits in the spatial verification/filtering step.

Our system will have similar bit budgets (and hence transmission cost) as the state-of-art works like CHoG [1], but a higher search accuracy.

3. DESCRIPTIONS

3.1 Mobile side–Hash Local Feature into Bits

In the current implementation, we choose SURF as the local feature, of its proven performance in accuracy and speed in several existing systems.. We apply the Locality Sensitive Hahsing(LSH)method [2] to compress the SURF features. Following the considerations in [1], constrained by transmission speed, we limit to 80 hash bits for each local feature, so the hash bits must be very compact. We balance each hash bit so that half of bits produced by each hashing function are +1, and the other -1. To further improve the efficiency and compactness of the hash bits, we applied a bit selection algorithm as described [3], which chooses 80 most compact bits from an initial candidate set of 1024 LSH bits. As shown in [3, 4], bit balancing and selection can greatly reduce the number of hash bits needed. More details about the hash bit selection algorithm can be found in [3].

3.2 Server Side–Search with Bag of Bits

3.2.1 Matching Local Features with Hash Bits

For one local feature in the query image, we need to find out its nearest neighbors from all local features stored in the database. One popular technique in improving the hashing performance (especially the recall rate) is to use multiple hash tables. We adopt the same idea, but instead of sending multiple sets of hash bits over the mobile network, we randomly select multiple subsets of bits from a single pool of hash bits (80 bits in the current implementation) and use each subset to construct a table. We can thus construct multiple tables without increasing the total amount of bits needed to be transmitted. We search each table by checking the buckets within a hamming radius to the query, instead of checking only the same bucket of the query, which can further reduce the number of tables needed. Matched images retrieved from each table are combined to form the candidate set for subsequent verification. In our system, we choose to use 12 tables, each indexed with 36 bits randomly drawn from the 80 bits pool aforementioned, with hamming radius $r = 1$ to 3, according to different tradeoffs between accuracy and time.

3.2.2 Spatial Filtering

Given the set of features in the database that were matched to features in the query image, one would like to check if these matches are geometrically consistent, i.e., whether a valid geometric transformation can be established between the feature positions on the query image and the positions in the database image. Considering the popular geometric verification method, RANSAC, is too slow, recently, a method based on length ratios [1] has been proposed to efficiently verify geometric correspondences without actually computing the transformation. Intuitively, it estimates the portion of matched features between query and reference images that share a consistent scale change. The higher value this is, the higher score the candidate reference image receives. Leveraging the hamming distance enabled by the hash bits, we further modify this step by placing higher weights on matched feature pairs with smaller hamming distances when computing the dominant scale change between query and reference images. This is in contrast to the previous method that only counts the frequency of match pairs. Our experiments confirmed clear performance improvement by this modification step incorporating the hamming distance of the hash bits.

4. PROTOTYPE AND EXPERIMENTS

Figure 2: Example user interfaces on iphone. Users may select the whole image, or a subwindow as query input, which can further be refined by interactive object segmentation tools like Grabcut. Matched products are shown on the right.

We have collected a product set with around 360K images crawled from Amazon.com. It contains diverse categories such as DVD/book covers, shoes, furnitures, groceries, kitchen supplies, etc. Each image contains about 100 SURF features on average, and hence we have about 36M local features in the database.

We have created a test set of more than 100 query images, which are separated from the reference database. The speed of our system is comparable to the state-of-the-art mobile visual search system, such as the one based on CHoG [1]. More specifically, the speed for the SURF feature extraction (1-1.5s), transmission of query hash bits(1-2s), search (1-3sec), result download/display (1-2s). However, our method can perform significantly better, with at least 20% improvement on precision of the top 100 search results, than the CHoG method [1] (i.e., compressing local features with CHoG in mobile side, and then applying BoW with a vocabulary tree of 1M codewords, and reranking with the spatial filtering in the server side).

5. REFERENCES

[1] V. Chandrasekhar, et.al. Mobile Product Recognition. *In Proceedings of ACM MM*, 2010.

[2] M. Charikar. Similarity estimation techniques from rounding algorithms. *In Proceedings of STOC*, 2002.

[3] J. He, T.-H. Lin, and S.-F. Chang. Hash Bit Selection for Large Scale Similarity Search. *Technical Report, Columbia University*, Sept., 2011.

[4] J. He, R. Radhakrishnan, S.-F. Chang, C. Bauer. Compact Hashing with Joint Optimization of Search Accuracy and Time. In Proceedings of CVPR, 2011.

From Local Features To Local Regions

Stefan Romberg
Multimedia Computing Lab
University of Augsburg
Augsburg, Germany
romberg@informatik.uni-augsburg.de

ABSTRACT

Local features are omnipresent in computer vision applications and an important building block for applications like object recognition and image retrieval. Such applications often involve feature matching or use an inverted index to efficiently retrieve similar local features for a given query.

In such cases it is commonly known that local features are often not informative yielding mismatches and false positives when used for feature matching (see Figure 1) or retrieval. As a result retrieval systems employ expensive post-retrieval verification steps. These observations underline the importance of embedding spatial information of a local image region directly within the index to decrease the number of false positives upon retrieval.

We present our latest method for embedding spatial information into an index by bundling local feature triples for logo recognition. We give an overview of our feature representation, describe currently ongoing research and pose open questions for discussion.

Categories and Subject Descriptors

I.4.10 [**Image Processing and Computer Vision**]: Image Representation

General Terms

Algorithms

Keywords

local features, region representation, feature bundling

MM'11, November 28–December 1, 2011, Scottsdale, Arizona, USA.

Figure 1: Local feature correspondences (colored lines) between image pairs showing the FedEx logo. The upper example shows mostly correct correspondences, the lower example illustrates the common case of many false feature matches.

1. INTRODUCTION

The decade of 2000-2010 has been the decade of local features. Starting with Lowe's publication on SIFT features [10] in 1999, a vast number of different features were proposed. Local features describe local image patches around keypoints which are either determined by an interest point detector or by a regular grid. The description of that image patch is chosen to be invariant against a certain set of transformations. These vital properties allow to derive a robust representation of the image patch around the keypoint. Subsequent operations are thereby provided with coordinates, scale, orientation and a visual description of each patch.

Each image contains multiple local features, thus any local feature-based approach implicitly deals with occlusion or partial appearances of an object/region. A change in lighting conditions or the perspective viewpoint may change the image patch around a certain keypoint significantly. The performance of any local feature therefore largely depends on the robust detection of keypoints and the invariance of the descriptor. Thus, both interest point detectors as well as descriptors are optimized for repeatability. Repeatability commonly measures how many identical interests points with similar descriptor remain whenever a test image is changed by perspective, lighting or other imaging artifacts.

However, due to the optimization for repeatability local features are often not informative [21]. This can easily be observed when local features are used to determine similar subregions in images. Figure 1 shows two examples where the similarities between visual descriptors have been used to match local features of image pairs. The upper image shows the computed feature correspondences with the majority of them being correct. The same technique produces many incorrect matches for a different image pair with bigger difference of perspective. That is, a single local feature describes only a small image patch which is often not sufficient to describe an object or a part of it in a precise and discriminative way.

These small sizes of local feature patches allow high repeatability of the descriptors among different images but the visual descriptions are not discriminable even if their immediate surroundings are substantially different.

These observations clearly indicate that an embedding of any spatial information like relative positions or orientations into a high-level region representation that can be compared and indexed efficiently is desirable. As local features are among the most robust and powerful visual features, we consider them as low-level visual representations that are then aggregated into a high-level region representation. In this relatively new research field we plan to contribute by exploring the following points:

- Development of a region description that is robust yet highly discriminative and suited for efficient indexing.
- Exploration and adaption of data mining techniques that allow to index the region representations efficiently in large-scale indexes.
- Evaluation of the region representations in object retrieval, object recognition and image retrieval tasks.

2. RELATED WORK

The related work on local features and their application is vast. In this section we highlight the related work on local features and indexing methods that are relevant in the context of our approach.

Much research has been dedicated to both the actual visual descriptors and the interest point detectors [11][12][2][16]. Research has also focused on improving speed [2] or invariance against perspective changes [12]. Commonly local feature are extracted from gray-scale images but color descriptors also have been explored [17].

A turning point in scalable image/object retrieval has been the introduction of the bag-of-words approach [15]. At the core of the visual bag-of-words approach is the quantization of local features for efficient indexing instead of matching the raw descriptors directly. The descriptors are quantized to discrete visual words from a vocabulary derived by clustering the descriptors. This data reduction makes it possible to use classical text retrieval and data mining techniques for the indexing and retrieval of visual words [13].

However, for such an approach to be successful, a post-retrieval verification step is needed to employ a spatial consistency check of the retrieved images. The gold standard for this task is the estimation of the homography with a reference image or class model with RANSAC [4]. However, this full spatial verification is computationally expensive, especially if the raw retrieval yields results that require the verification of many classes.

By embedding spatial information about local features into the index, one can significantly reduce the number of false positives. Several approaches use regular structures that partition the whole image to encode the locality of local features, e.g. a grid of regular partitions [9], spatial pyramids of partitions [8], random partitions [20] or random projections into spatial histograms [3].

In contrast several approaches that bundle features within a small local neighborhood have been proposed. Recently, global geometry was incorporated into an index by means of feature map hashing [1]. In general there are two ways of feature bundling: The bundling of spatially close features into a single description [19][21][3] or the bundling of features of different types [5].

In our recent work we developed a new feature bundling approach and index spatial structure of local features for logo recognition [14]. In the following section we will give a brief outline of this approach.

3. SPATIAL FEATURE TRIPLES

In this section we present our latest approach that encodes the spatial layout of local features into a compact signature for efficient multi-class logo recognition. Essentially different to other existing approaches is the encoding of spatial structure with a hash function. We briefly describe this approach here, further details are found in [14].

In short, similar regions in two images can be determined by indexing geometric layout of local features in hash tables. Our work in this area is similar to geometric hashing [18], however we do not have a single model image but create a model for each logo-class out of several training images. The result of the training is a set of local feature triples, which consistently appear across the different training images.

Our logo recognition system is inspired by the bag of visual words approach, but through embedding spatial knowledge into the index, we demonstrate that we can get rid of the expansive post-retrieval processing step during which existing image object retrieval systems have to validate the existence of the query object. The system is explicitly designed to scale with a large number of classes.

At the core of our approach lays a method for encoding and indexing spatial structure that is derived from local features detected in the logo images. In this work we used hessian-affine SIFT features as local features but the presented approach is not limited to a specific feature type.

Similar to [7] a highly discriminative feature is constructed by bundling local feature triples and encoding both their visual appearance as well as their relative positions. This discriminative representation is then hashed and the hash key allows to detect logos with high precision by performing index lookups. It is important to note that the proposed representation is highly discriminative even without extremely specific visual descriptions. This explicitly allows the usage of small visual vocabularies of only a few thousands words. This has been a major design goal and is in contrast to the large vocabularies of several tens of thousands up to millions of different visual words commonly used for near-duplicate detection tasks [13][6]. These huge vocabularies lead to extremely specific visual words. In other words, the quantized visual description is highly discriminative. However, once

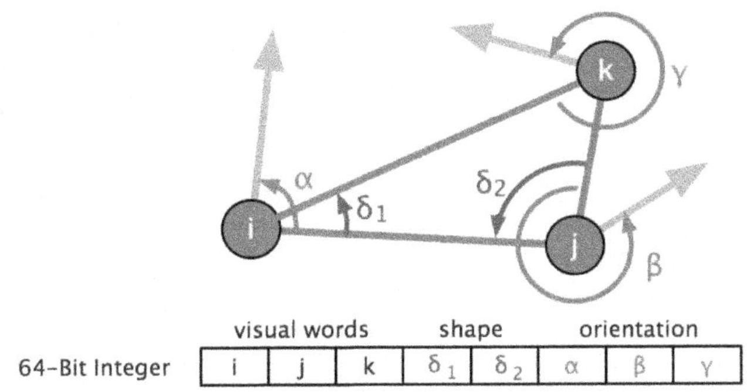

Figure 2: Our representation of local feature triples

Figure 3: Example of feature triples that match across images. The three points span the triangle (blue) used as representation. Green lines denote the orientation of the SIFT features.

perspective of an image changes it is likely that the quantization of previously matching features will be different.

Feature triples in our approach are represented as triangles (see Figure 2) as this allows to encode both visual and spatial information into a single representation. A local feature triple is then represented by three corresponding visual words labels derived from the quantized visual descriptor of each feature. In addition the relative spatial layout of the points is described by two additional angles δ_1 and δ_2. Finally the representation also includes the relative orientations of the SIFT features α, β, γ. As all angles and orientations are relative to each other, the whole representation is both scale and rotation invariant. The resulting 8-tuple is quantized and encoded into a 64-bit integer that is then stored within a hash table. This compressed signature allows memory-efficient storage and fast lookup of items even with a huge number of items within the hash table.

We use an automatic method for constructing a model for each logo-class out of multiple training images, which significantly extends our ability to detect logos under varying conditions. For all pairs of training images of a given class the feature correspondences across each image pair are determined. Given these feature correspondences of an image pair the triangle signatures of the first image are compared to those of the second image. All the triangles that have identical features and also a matching triangle signature are stored. Figure 3 shows such a feature triple for a pair of training images of the class "Ford". The training then aggregates all the triangles that were determined for each of the classes into a single hash table. This hash table acts as index whereby each signature is associated with its corresponding class.

The hashing of these triangle signatures within a hash table is a major benefit of our approach: Instead of testing each signature against all others in the database and instead of testing an unknown image explicitly for every class in the database, each query directly yields a response. A quick hash table lookup is sufficient to determine if a query signature of the test image is contained in the index.

As each signature in the hash table is associated with a class, the detection of any feature triple contained in the index yields a vote for that class. In other words, each lookup acts as a weak multi-class classification.

The logo recognition itself is therefore performed as follows: The given image is scanned for logos by selecting feature triples that are then used to determine if their representation is included in the index. If the representation is included, a triangle of a certain class has been detected. This detection can be counted as a single vote for the presence of that class. While we require several votes and therefore detections for the decision whether a logo is present or not, a small number of these highly discriminative detections are sufficient to rule out false positives. Once the number of detections for a certain class is larger than a corresponding class-specific threshold the logo is considered to be depicted in the image. To adapt to varying visual complexity and difficulty of logo classes we optimize all the class-specific decision thresholds on a validation set and use these thresholds for decision on the test set.

For recognition, random feature triples are selected and tested if these are included in the index. Given n features, there are n^3 possibilities to select a feature triple. To cut the number of possibilities down, constraints on both locality of feature points and shape of the triangle are employed.

We further address this problem by a data structure that allows an efficient search for feature triples. The proposed cascaded index consists of two linked indexes. Its structure is motivated by the way test images are scanned for the presence of logos: An edge index stores the representations of feature pairs (edges) and a triangle index stores the representations of the actual feature triples. As each triangle consists of three edges, the edge index stores the corresponding three edge representations. Thus, the edge index contains only edges that are part of the triangle index. This dependency allows to scan the sparsely populated high-dimensional space of feature triples by determining feature pairs which are part of a subspace first. Once these feature pairs are detected, these pairs plus an additional point are taken for constructing a query to the triangle index.

We evaluated our logo recognition approach on a dataset of 32 logo classes[1]. Both test and validation set contain 30 images per class and 3000 non-logo images. On this dataset the best performance obtained was a precision of 0.95 with a recall of 0.60 (See [14] for further details). These results show that the proposed approach for feature bundling is highly discriminative and allows to perform multi-class logo recognition with high precision.

4. OPEN ISSUES / CURRENT RESEARCH

While the approach presented is highly discriminative and has excellent precision, experiments show that recall is bounded by the training and the perspective views that were covered by the given training images. To improve this, the training could e.g. use additional synthetic training images that

[1]The dataset is available at
http://www.multimedia-computing.de/flickrlogos

are generated by applying random perspective transformation to the original image. This should greatly increase the coverage of perspective views that are stored in the index and it also increases the number of training data available. Furthermore it also allows the detection of features that are stable across several views.

Current work also includes the exploration of other robust feature bundling techniques. Specifically I work on encoding local histograms of spatial feature positions into a high-level description that is then stored within a large index. The detection of such a histogram within an image leads to similar behavior and capabilities as in the case of triangles. To date the question of which spatial tiling is beneficial is still open.

Future implementations will also have to deal with memory requirements of large-scale hash-based indexes. Hashing usually involves redundancy to increase recall. To keep the amount of data stored in hash tables as small as possible the hashed data should be noise free. With increasing index sizes feature selection techniques might have to be employed before bundles are selected for further processing.

5. ISSUES FOR DISCUSSION

- There are contrary philosophies to define a region. A region may be defined as the neighborhood of each local feature and be aligned to its position, scale and orientation. Alternatively an image can also be divided into regular partitions. The number and size of the regions and therefore the encoding of spatial relationship heavily depends on that definition.
- The description of a region may be coarse e.g. for scene classification or very specific as desired in the case of logo recognition. When measuring similarity of region representations a smooth transition between a coarse similarity and a strict similarity is desirable.
- One important issue regarding feature bundling that has not been addressed yet is how commonly high-dimensional and sparse bundle representations can be used for tasks like image classification or (whole) image retrieval. These tasks often require a single global feature representation of an image which is not directly available in such cases.

6. REFERENCES

[1] Y. Avrithis, G. Tolias, and Y. Kalantidis. Feature map hashing: sub-linear indexing of appearance and global geometry. In *ACM Multimedia*, 2010.

[2] H. Bay, A. Ess, T. Tuytelaars, and L. Van Gool. Speeded-up robust features (SURF). *Computer Vision and Image Understanding (CVIU)*, 110(3):346–359, 2008.

[3] Y. Cao, C. Wang, Z. Li, and L. Zhang. Spatial-Bag-of-Features. *csr.bu.edu*, 2010.

[4] O. Chum, J. Matas, and J. Kittler. Locally Optimized RANSAC. *Lecture Notes in Computer Science, Pattern Recognition, Springer*, 2003.

[5] O. Chum, M. Perdoch, and J. Matas. Geometric min-Hashing: Finding a (thick) needle in a haystack. In *IEEE Conference on Computer Vision and Pattern Recognition (CVPR)*, June 2009.

[6] O. Chum, J. Philbin, and M. Isard. Scalable near identical image and shot detection. *ACM International Conference on Image and Video Retrieval (CIVR)*, 2007.

[7] N. Hoàng, V. Gouet-Brunet, M. Rukoz, and M. Manouvrier. Embedding spatial information into image content description for scene retrieval. *Pattern Recognition*, 43(9):3013–3024, Sept. 2010.

[8] S. Lazebnik, C. Schmid, and J. Ponce. Beyond bags of features: Spatial pyramid matching for recognizing natural scene categories. In *IEEE Conference on Computer Vision and Pattern Recognition (CVPR)*, 2006.

[9] D. Lee, Q. Ke, and M. Isard. Partition Min-Hash for Partial Duplicate Image Discovery. *Proceedings of the European Conference on Computer Vision (ECCV)*, 2010.

[10] D. Lowe. Object recognition from local scale-invariant features. *International Conference on Computer Vision (ICCV)*, pages 1150–1157 vol.2, 1999.

[11] J. Matas. Robust wide-baseline stereo from maximally stable extremal regions. *Image and Vision Computing*, 22(10):761–767, Sept. 2004.

[12] K. Mikolajczyk, T. Tuytelaars, C. Schmid, A. Zisserman, J. Matas, F. Schaffalitzky, T. Kadir, and L. V. Gool. A Comparison of Affine Region Detectors. *International Journal of Computer Vision (IJCV)*, 65(1-2), 2005.

[13] D. Nistér and H. Stewénius. Scalable Recognition with a Vocabulary Tree. In *IEEE Conference on Computer Vision and Pattern Recognition (CVPR)*, 2006.

[14] S. Romberg, L. Garcia Pueyo, R. Lienhart, and R. van Zwol. Scalable Logo Recognition in Real-World Images. In *ACM International Conference on Multimedia Retrieval (ICMR)*, 2011.

[15] J. Sivic and A. Zisserman. Video Google: a text retrieval approach to object matching in videos. *International Conference on Computer Vision (ICCV)*, 2003.

[16] T. Tuytelaars. Dense interest points. *IEEE Conference on Computer Vision and Pattern Recognition (CVPR)*, 2010.

[17] K. van de Sande, T. Gevers, and C. Snoek. Evaluating Color Descriptors for Object and Scene Recognition. *IEEE Transactions on Pattern Analysis and Machine Intelligence (PAMI)*, X(X):1–33, 2009.

[18] H. Wolfson and I. Rigoutsos. Geometric hashing: An overview. *IEEE Computational Science & Engineering*, 4(4), 1997.

[19] Z. Wu, Q. Ke, M. Isard, and J. Sun. Bundling features for large scale partial-duplicate web image search. In *IEEE Conference on Computer Vision and Pattern Recognition (CVPR)*, 2009.

[20] J. Yuan and Y. Wu. Spatial Random Partition for Common Visual Pattern Discovery. In *International Conference on Computer Vision (ICCV)*. Ieee, Oct. 2007.

[21] S. Zhang, Q. Huang, G. Hua, S. Jiang, W. Gao, and Q. Tian. Building Contextual Visual Vocabulary for Large-scale Image Applications. In *ACM Multimedia*, 2010.

Synchronized Dissemination Framework for Supporting High-Quality Tele-Immersive Shared Activity

Zixia Huang
Department of Computer Science
University of Illinois at Urbana-Champaign
zhuang21@illinois.edu

ABSTRACT

My Ph.D. thesis aims to develop a synchronized dissemination framework for supporting high-quality *tele-immersive shared activity* (TISA). Synchronization in TISA is complicated by (a) the multi-modal, bandwidth-savvy and timing-dependent media streaming over shared network resources, and (b) the delay-sensitive and interaction-critical nature of TISA in the real two-site and multi-site applications. This paper provides an outline of my thesis which includes four major contributions: (1) proposing a generalized layered framework for multi-stream synchronization sourced at one or multiple sites, (2) presenting an adaptive media packet scheduling scheme based on multi-stream timing correlations under Internet dynamics, (3) proposing a synchronized multicast topology based on diverse user interests, and (4) studying human subjective satisfactions to guide the system adaptation. This study is expected to output research results significant for next-generation systems, where timing-dependent media multi-modality is critical.

Categories and Subject Descriptors

H.4.3 [**Information Systems Applications**]: Communications Applications

General Terms

Design, Performance, Experimentation

Keywords

Tele-Immersive Shared Activity, Synchronization

1. INTRODUCTION

A tele-immersive (TI) system can offer a joint virtual space for distributed users to conduct meaningful shared activities. To achieve a realistic user experience, each TI site is configured with media devices with different functionalities, including multiple 3D cameras, microphones and haptic devices outputting timing-dependent 3D video, audio and haptic sensory streams respectively. A gateway at each site aggregates these local media streams and communicates with the remote sites who are then responsible for media rendering at the output devices (Fig. 1).

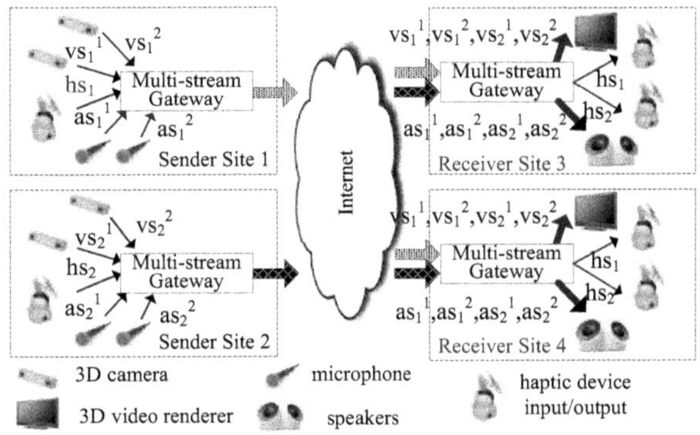

Figure 1: TI multi-stream configurations. vs: 3D video stream, as: audio stream, hs: haptic stream.

To provide seamless collaboration similar to a face-to-face interaction, an ideal TI system should disseminate the media signals with minimal latency, while preserving their rendering quality and timing synchronization. However, current best-effort network can delay the media delivery and introduce packet jitters and losses which will inevitably downgrade the user subjective satisfactions. This motivates me to design a synchronized dissemination and adaptation framework for supporting high-quality *tele-immersive shared activity* (TISA) over the Internet.

In the two-site TI system, three factors complicate the synchronized dissemination of the timing-dependent media streams. (a) *Shared network resources.* Because multiple bandwidth-savvy TI media streams share and compete the same network resources, packets can be dropped when bandwidth is not abundant. This can degrade the media rendering, and may lose the synchronization information which is important at the receiver. (b) *Heterogeneous characteristics.* Media with different traffic characteristics usually demand diverse streaming QoS, so they can employ their own transport protocols and adaptation algorithms in response to the Internet dynamics. This can lead to the end-to-end delay (EED) heterogeneity of different media streams between the two sites, and create synchronization skews across the media (*inter-media*) and among the streams within each *media bundle* (*inter-stream*). (c) *Interactivity.* While the receiver buffer can be used to smooth packet jitters (for rendering quality and *inter-frame synchronization*) and remedy the

EED differences (for *inter-stream* and *inter-media synchronization*), the tradeoff is that the buffer size can be added to the EED which will degrade the TISA interactivity.

A multi-site TI system can further complicate the inter-stream and inter-media synchronization, because the media streams from a same sender to a same receiver can follow multiple paths by relaying through different intermediate sites. In addition, two new problems arise in the multi-site support. (a) *Inter-site synchronization.* Because of the diverse network conditions, different streams from multiple senders can experience heterogeneous EED to a same receiver (*inter-sender skew*). Streams from a sender can also arrive at multiple receivers at different time (*inter-receiver skew*). Depending on activities, a TI system can demand different constraints on inter-site synchronization skews according to the user satisfactions. (b) *User interest diversity.* Multiple receivers may request different subsets of the multi-stream from each sender because of their diverse interests. For example, not all 3D video streams from a sender has visual contributions to the user view at a receiver, and thus only those useful streams need to be delivered.

Synchronization, interactivity and media rendering are three integral attributes combinedly impacting the user experience in TISA. Existing adaptation algorithms, however, usually focus on optimizing objective metrics which are either irrelevant or partially relevant to the real human perceptions [7, 14]. To realize high-quality TISA, subjective evaluations are needed to find the user preferences. The drawback is that subjective tests are expensive and can only be conducted off-line. Therefore, a good design should be able to generalize the offline subjective findings to guide the online system adaptations.

2. RESEARCH CONTRIBUTIONS

Based on the motivation and problems stated above, I present an outline of my research contributions in this section. The goal of my study is to design a dissemination, adaptation and synchronization framework which can maximize the user perceptions in both two-site and multi-site TISA.

1. My study first answers what are the *synchronization quality* and synchronization skew for multi-modal media multi-stream bundle sourced at one or multiple sites in the interactive multimedia. The definitions are missing in the previous related literature where the prevalent studies are on the audio-visual synchronization of 2D videos. In my thesis, a generalized layered architecture is proposed to describe and simplify the complications. Specifically, the four *sync layers* from bottom to top are: inter-frame, inter-stream, inter-media and inter-site synchronization. My study formulates the synchronization skew at each layer, and model the interrelations of synchronization quality across different layers. The *dominance* of each layer is also prescribed for synchronization references.

2. An adaptive dissemination scheme is proposed for in-time delivery of media streams under Internet dynamics. Specifically, because 3D video streams demand a much larger bandwidth overhead compared to audios and haptic sensory streams, my study presents a cooperative frame rate allocation scheme at the sender for the videos based on online bandwidth estimation. This can either be sender-driven (by source localization of 3D spatial audios [11]) or receiver-driven (based on the user interests of the 3D videos [14]). The TI system also improves the rendering and synchronization quality by adapting the media packet scheduling with receiver buffering control according to network conditions.

3. In a multi-site TISA scenario, I extend the previous ViewCast study [14], and build a multicast topology based upon the diversity of user interests and the prioritization of dissemination path options. The new scheme is able to (a) satisfy the inter-site synchronization demand, (b) minimize the EED of dissemination paths between senders and receivers, and (c) maximize the network resource utilization and reduce the number of undelivered *victim* streams because of bandwidth inadequacy.

4. User-observable objective and subjective metrics affecting the human perceptions are identified for both two-site and multi-site TISA. The objective metrics are able to capture the effects of synchronization, interactivity and media rendering quality, while the subjective counterparts can describe the overall user satisfactions. My research investigates the interrelations and trade-offs among these metrics at different TI activities. It also finds a mapping from objective metrics to subjective findings, and generalizes the offline subjective results. All these efforts can contribute to the online perception-driven system adaptation for achieving high-quality TISA under Internet dynamics.

5. The prerequisite of the above studies is that we are able to obtain accurate synchronized timestamps across multiple distributed sites, and among different input/output media devices within a single site. For practical considerations, I study the clock synchronization among/across different devices/sites, as an integral part of the synchronized dissemination framework. My thesis is intended to answer the following two questions. (a) *How often do we need to synchronize clocks* ? (b) *How do we minimize the impact of clock skews in our framework* ? Because [15] has discussed the problems of delay predictions errors on several network applications, my plan is to extend their approaches for this TI synchronization study.

3. RELATED WORK

Previous studies are unable to model the timing correlations of media multi-modality, and to identify the impact of real human subjective preferences in TISA. Therefore, there work cannot be directly applied to our TI system design.

Media synchronization. Although approaches and techniques have been heavily studied in the past for synchronization in one or multiple sync layers [1, 6, 8], no literature has systematically modeled the synchronization problem of all layers and investigated the interrelations across the layers. In addition, none of existing work manages to study the impact of network resource inadequacy over the synchronization quality, and to formulate the resulting synchronization skews at the presence of multi-source multi-modal media streams, which are expected to be prevalent in the next-generation media system. A new generalized layered synchronization architecture is, thus, imperative in the design.

Synchronized multicast topology. Existing studies on multicast topology for multi-site interactive multimedia aim to minimize the delay and delay variation with or without bandwidth constraints [12, 13, 16]. They oversimplify the problem by assuming the homogeneity of the media data requested at different receiver sites. The ViewCast algorithm [14], proposed specifically for multi-site TI system, can disseminate multiple video streams and allow cross-tree

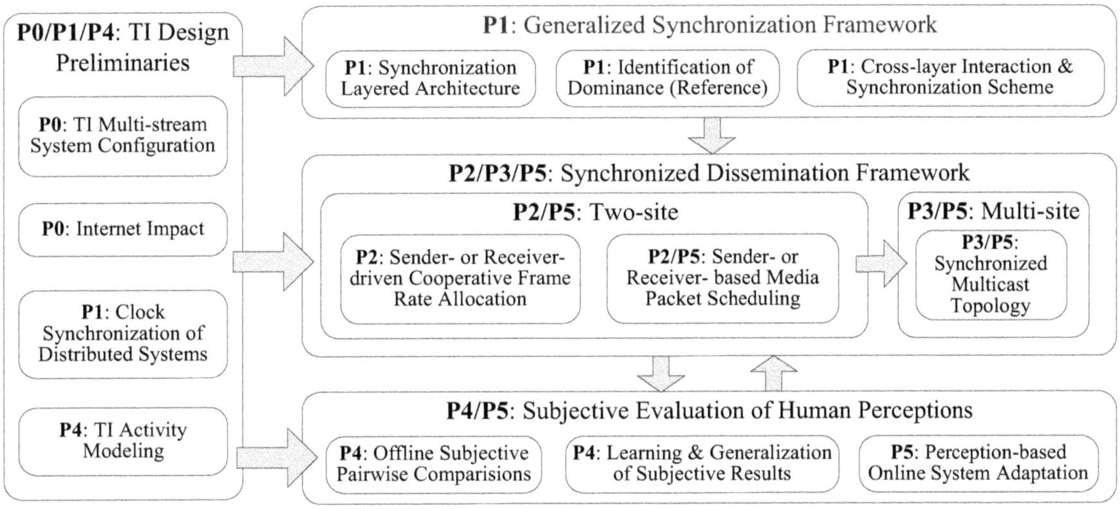

Figure 2: An overview diagram of research study

adjustment under bandwidth constraints and user interest heterogeneity. But ViewCast does not take into account the interactivity and synchronization aspects of the dissemination problem. In addition, the algorithm only studies the video streams, and does not identify the impact of audio or haptic sensory streams. A new multicast algorithm is needed to address these issues.

Impact of human perceptions. ITU G.1070 [5] estimates the synchronization, interactivity and media rendering quality in a closed multiplicative form for 2D video conferencing. But its assumption is that the three quality attributes can be computed independently. In addition, the standard only studies the conversational task and ignores the impact of TI activity heterogeneity on human perceptions. [10] concludes that people are unable to notice a maximum audio-visual skew of 80 ms, but only for best-quality on-demand videos. In our previous study, we have developed a VoIP algorithm that is able to adapt the audio buffer based upon the subjective perceptions of the audio quality and the conversational interactivity [2, 9]. But in TISA, the huge bandwidth overhead and the multi-modal stream correlations can complicate the design.

4. RESEARCH APPROACH DETAILS

In this section, I will show the detailed six-stage research approaches solving the whole problem. Fig. 2 presents an overview diagram of my study.

P0: I configure the TI system with multiple 3D video, audio and haptic streams. To evaluate its performance in different network conditions, I emulate a real TISA setting in PlanetLab, prerecord these sensory streams, and replay them using UDP. Media streams are sent based on their real frame size and arrival time at the sender gateway. To study the sole Internet impact, I do not impose any sender- or receiver-based system adaptation. Bandwidth is not limited at both sides. I study the TI streaming behaviors, and classify Internet traces into different categories based on the network delay, jitter and loss statistics. Repeatable experiments can be conducted and analyzed in each category.

P1: I identify the overall synchronization problem using a four-layer architecture. Each sync layer is self-contained so that the system configuration changes within a layer can create minimal impacts on other layers. I present systematic rules to decide the application- (or activity-) specific dominant frame, stream, media or site based upon the user interests. I propose metrics to compute the synchronization skew from the dominance at each layer, and present methodology to model the interrelations of synchronization quality across layers. To investigate the impact of the clock drift for computers all over the world, I plan to synchronize these computers to the local NTP servers periodically. At a span of 24-hour period, I measure the clock skews of the distributed computers, and examine whether they will affect the real applications. An automated clock skew detection and repair scheme is expected to be part of our framework.

P2: I start with two-site dissemination which includes the design of (a) the cooperative resource allocation and (b) the media packet scheduling. In (a), I allocate the available bandwidth to different 3D video streams (from multiple 3D cameras) based on the ordering of their visual contributions. The corresponding frame rate is then computed by estimating future frame sizes. I use two methods to determine the video stream with the largest contribution. The first method is sender-driven, meaning that it picks the camera that is closest to the sender speaker whose location can be obtained by the microphone array. The second one is receiver-driven similar to [14] in which the algorithm decides the camera whose orientation is closest to the receiver user view. The quality of audio and haptic sensory streams is not changed due to their low bandwidth demand. For (b), I intend to propose an adaptation algorithm which schedules media packet buffering and delivery at both sender and receiver based on the network conditions. The algorithm can be further extended in P5 by taking into account the human preferences.

P3: I extend the research findings in P2 for multi-site support. In addition, a synchronized multicast tree topology is expected for inter-site synchronization. The prolonged EED as a result of the multi-hop dissemination should be minimized for preserving the TISA interactivity. To maximize the bandwidth utilization, I intend to propose rules to prioritize media streams and dissemination path candidates. Note that users can impose different expectations on inter-site synchronization quality at different TI activities. Therefore, the upper bounds of both inter-sender and inter-receiver synchronization skews can only be decided by subjective evaluations (P5).

Table 1: SyncCast [4] vs ViewCast [14]

	SyncCast	ViewCast
Delay	Minimize delay	Delay-bounded
Bandwidth	Bandwidth-bound	Bandwidth-bound
Path Prioritization	Yes	No
Stream Prioritization	Yes	Yes
Inter-stream Sync	Yes	No
Inter-media Sync	Yes	No
Inter-site Sync	Yes	No

P4: TI activities are modeled according to their functionalities. Some activities attach more importance to the uninterrupted audio conversation, while people in other activities may prefer smooth video rendering. Multiple user-observable objective metrics are also identified to describe the human perceptions of synchronization, interactivity and media rendering quality. In each activity, I generate test samples characterizing these metrics at different values. Pairwise comparisons are expected in the subjective test for the purpose of computing the degradation score of a sample to the other. Similar to my previous VoIP study [2], I use regression to generalize the subjective results in this thesis.

P5: By employing the learned regression model at run time, I propose perception-driven algorithm which can dynamically and consistently select the operating point for media packet scheduling (P2) that leads to the best user experience, even under unseen conditions. The upper bounds of the inter-site synchronization skews are also empirically obtained from the subjective tests at different activities, as a critical factor in the multicast tree construction (P3).

5. CURRENT PROGRESS & NEXT STEPS

Current Progress. Most of my accomplished studies up to date are focusing on the dissemination of multiple 3D video streams and one single audio stream from each site. I have evaluated the multi-stream characteristics in PlanetLab (P0). The results demonstrate strong correlations of delay and loss distributions of the two media over the Internet. I have proposed receiver-driven video cooperative frame rate allocation scheme (P2) in [3] based on the dominance of the audio and video streams (P1). I have also presented synchronized multicast algorithm (P3) in [4] which have two new features: synchronization functionality and bandwidth utilization optimization, as compared to the previous ViewCast study [14] (Table 1). I have identified four user-observable objective metrics that respectively describe the subjective 3D video quality, audio quality, interactivity and synchronization (P4). I have also presented the subjective results of the pairwise comparisons for samples characterizing different values of the four metrics (P4). I have shown that G.1070 [5] is unable to describe the complications and tradeoffs of different quality attributes, and to identify the TI activity heterogeneity on user perceptions. I have generalized the offline subjective findings to guide the online media packet scheduling. The study is only limited to two-site scenario at this stage.

Next Steps. I will extend the current study to the TI system configuration with the support of multiple multi-source video, audio, and haptic sensory streams. I will propose the generalized synchronization framework and identify the dominance at each sync layer (P1). I will study the microphone array characteristics and investigate how it will help guide the network resource allocation (P2). I will also identify the impact of user subjective perceptions in multi-site TISA (P4) and achieve optimal perception-driven system adaptations (P5). All these work are expected to be done within the next 15 months.

6. IMPACTS ON COMMUNITY

The impact of our study on the research community is expected to be twofold. First, the generalized synchronization and dissemination framework can be applied to next-generation distributed systems or virtual gaming environment where multi-modal sensory streams with strong timing correlations are becoming prevalent. Second, the perception-driven streaming adaptation scheme can also be extended to any two-site or multi-site real-time 2D or 3D (stereoscopic) video conferencing for enhancing the user satisfactions.

7. REFERENCES

[1] F. Boronat, M. Montagud, and J. C. Guerri. Multimedia group synchronization approach for one-way cluster-to-cluster applications. In *Proc. IEEE Conference on Local Computer Networks*, pages 177–184, 2009.

[2] Z. Huang, B. Sat, and B. W. Wah. Automated learning of play-out scheduling algorithms for improving the perceptual conversational quality in multi-party VoIP. In *Proc. IEEE ICME*, pages 493–496, July 2008.

[3] Z. Huang, W. Wu, K. Nahrstedt, A. Arefin, and R. Rivas. Tsync: A new synchronization framework for multi-site 3d tele-immersion. In *Proc. ACM NOSSDAV*, June 2010.

[4] Z. Huang, W. Wu, K. Nahrstedt, R. Rivas, and A. Arefin. Synccast: synchronized dissemination in multi-site interactive 3D tele-immersion. In *ACM MMSys*, 2011.

[5] ITU-G.1070. Opinion model for video-telephony applications, 2007.

[6] K. Nahrstedt and L. Qiao. Stability and adaptation control for lip synchronization skews. Tchnical report, University of Illinois, USA, 1997.

[7] D. Ott and K. Mayer-Patel. Coordinated multi-streaming for 3D tele-immersion. In *ACM MM*, 2004.

[8] T. Peng and K. Du. Requirements and strategy for presentation stage synchronization of multi-object multimedia applications. In *Int'l Conference on Advanced Information Networking and Applications*, 2009.

[9] B. Sat and B. W. Wah. Playout scheduling and loss-concealments in VoIP for optimizing conversational voice communication quality. In *ACM MM*, 2007.

[10] R. Steinmetz. Human perception of jitter and media synchronization. *IEEE Journal on Selected Areas in Communications*, 14(1):61–72, 1996.

[11] J.-M. Valin, F. Michaud, J. Rouat, and D. Letourneau. Robust sound source localization using a microphone array on a mobile robot. In *Proc. IEEE Int'l Conference on Intelligent Robots and Systems*, pages 1228–1233, 2003.

[12] K.-H. Vik, P. Halvorsen, and C. Griwodz. Multicast tree diameter for dynamic distributed interactive applications. In *IEEE INFOCOM*, 2008.

[13] Z. Yang. Multi-stream synchronization for 3D tele-immersive and collaborative environment. In *Proc. of ICST Conference on Immersive Telecommunications*, 2009.

[14] Z. Yang, W. Wu, K. Nahrstedt, G. Kurillo, and R. Bajcsy. Enabling multi-party 3d tele-immersive environments with viewcast. *ACM Transactions on Multimedia Computing, Communications, and Applications*, 6(2), 2010.

[15] R. Zhang, C. Tang, Y. C. Hu, S. Fahmy, and X. Lin. Impact of the inaccuracy of distance prediction algorithms on internet applications: an analytical and comparative study. In *IEEE INFOCOM*, 2006.

[16] R. Zimmermann and K. Liang. Spatialized audio streaming for networked virtual environments. In *ACM MM*, 2008.

Session Management of Correlated Multi-stream 3D Tele-immersive Environments

Ahsan Arefin
University of Illinois at Urbana-Champaign
IL, USA
marefin2@illinois.edu

ABSTRACT

Quality control and resource optimization are challenging problems in 3D tele-immersive (3DTI) environments due to their large scale, multi-stream dependencies and dynamic peer (viewer) behavior. Such systems are also prone to performance degradation due to undesired behavior in the event of drastic demand changes, such as view change and large-scale simultaneous viewer arrivals or departures. Therefore, it is crucial to localize undesired behavior inside the system and re-organize the streaming overlay structures accordingly. Doing this accurately for a large scale is even more challenging and it requires to capture all *events* effecting the data plan and control plan of the system. Moreover, to do this, we need to understand the desired behavior of the application first, which is defined by the dependency patterns of performance and configuration metadata at each participating peers. To assist that, we propose a learning framework that discovers metadata dependency patterns from the time series metadata and uses an online profiler to detect undesired behavior of the system during run-time. Such universal protocol also enables the prediction of large scale performance degradation due to irregular dependencies. Finally an adaptation is proposed that reallocates the resources and rearranges overlay structures to overcome the undesired behavior. In summary, our goal is to provide a universal session monitoring and management framework for complex multi-stream 3DTI environments to support large number of concurrent viewers. We consider the difficulty in overlay construction, collecting metadata, answering queries, learning patterns, detecting undesired behavior at the participating peers and finally overlay adaptation considering multi-stream dependencies.

Categories and Subject Descriptors: C.4 [Performance of Systems]: Measurement Techniques; Modeling Techniques; C.2.3 [Network Operations]: Network Monitoring; Network Management

General Terms: Design, Algorithms, Measurement, Performance, Reliability, Management

Keywords: Monitoring, Streaming, Learning, Resource Allocation, Adaptation

1. INTRODUCTION

3D tele-immersive (3DTI) systems allow real-time remote collaborations in a shared virtual environment providing a platform for various exciting activities such as online gaming, collaborative learning and performing arts for a large number of remotely distributed participants. Due to such large scale and their unique nature of multi-stream dependencies and dynamic peer (viewer) behavior, quality control and resource optimization are extremely challenging problems in 3DTI environments. Examples include 3DTI at Illinois, Berkeley, UNC, UPenn and other research laboratories [32, 13, 9], and 2D tele-presence rooms from HP and Cisco [8, 16]. Technologies has now advanced towards collaborative interactive environments with large number of geographically distributed sites equipped with large number of correlated media sensors, multi-view displays, and/ or advanced haptic-audio-visual user interfaces [21]. They generate highly correlated multi-sensory contents called bundle of streams [24]). Depending on the view request, such bundles are distributed among the participating peers in real-time and synchronous manners. Even traditional QoS (Quality of Service) metrics fail to measure the true QoS in such multi-streaming environments [24].

Figure 1 shows an example of our 3DTI environment (TEEVE [32]) with 4 geographically distributed sites. Site-1 and Site-2 both represent active participants where users actively participate to generate media contents (called producers). However, Site-3 and Site-4 are passive in nature, which are used for only viewing purpose (called viewers). In practice, there can be limited number of content producers (due to the space limitation in virtual world), but hundreds-to-thousands of content viewers with different *view* requirements. A view is defined as the field of interest or a viewing perspective that the users prefer to observe in the environment and it is usually composed of multiple camera streams [33]. Examples of multi-view applications are synchronized dancing [29] and Tai-chi learning [18]. Participating streams are strongly correlated both locally (inside a site) and globally (across sites). The skew between these correlated streams are called local and global inter-stream skews respectively and the value must be low to represent a synchronized and consistent view. Therefore, supporting such multi-site and multi-view participation is challenging in time-critical and bandwidth-demanding large scale TI environments.

To leverage the burden of streaming among content producers, some of the previous works [33, 30] focused on constructing p2p trees considering the user subscriptions to specific views. However with large number of viewers and their dynamic view requirements, the number and structure of streaming trees are getting very large and dynamic in practice, which make the proper session management very hard. A recent study shows that most of the current Internet traffics are produced by distributed multimedia applica-

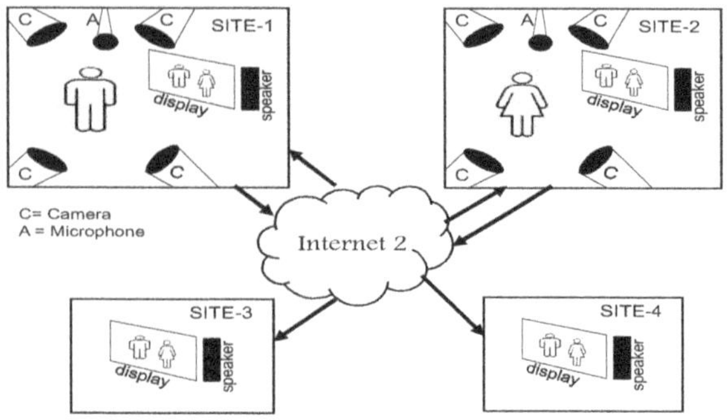

Figure 1: A 3D Tele-immersive environment with four sites.

tions. Therefore, we need an Internet scale management solution for 3DTI environments. Due to the heterogeneity of paths taken by correlated streams and dynamic requirement of CPU and network resources along the path, it is not always possible to get real-time and synchronization guarantee in a static setup. Many session management protocols are currently available [19, 20, 15] to support real-time session management. But they suffer from two major drawbacks. Firstly, they are designed for single stream protocols and do not consider dependencies across streams; hence have little use in Distributed Interactive Multimedia Environments (DIMEs). Secondly, they degrade media quality (image resolution, depth resolution, frame rate, audio-video codec, quantization, number of streams in view etc.) to adapt in case of QoS violation rather than identifying the true reasons of violation and troubleshooting them accordingly (e.g., by re-arranging the overlay) without degrading the media quality.

We first propose a view-based hybrid streaming architecture using both CDN and p2p communication techniques to support large number of concurrent viewers. Using CDN servers alone are very expensive in terms of deployment and maintenance. On the other hand, a p2p based architecture requires sufficient number of seed supplying peers to *jumpstart* the distribution process and offers less out-bound streaming rate compared to a CDN server [10, 6]. Hence a hybrid approach provides large streaming rate with cost-effective manner. In addition, we provide a cooperative resource allocation framework that aims for optimized allocation of network bandwidth and CPU/ memory loads of the participating peers while constructing the overlay. Our work is different from previous works in the way that we consider stream dependencies while providing such adaptations. Streams originated from a single site are correlated (locally) to represent a consistent local view whereas streams across sites are also correlated (globally) to represent a consistent global view. It is a wastage of resource to transmit a single stream without its correlated streams. In case of large skew, we need to localize the peers causing large delay and the reasons of the delay. To accomplish that, a learning framework is used that discovers the behavior of the application at participating viewers. In case of QoS (such as inter-stream skew or end-to-end delay) violation at the receiver, the learner localizes the reasons of violation by detecting outliers from the expected behavior of peers on the path. The adaptation framework then tries to resolve it by re-allocation the resources and re-balancing the streaming tree without degrading the media quality (if possible).

However, an important step in modeling network and application behavior, analyzing its performance, and troubleshooting problems in real-time when things go wrong, involve *monitoring* its operations in real-time. Real-time monitoring is a highly challenging problem in DIMEs because of large number of metadata that needs to be logged from large number of devices. Some haptic sensors work at the frequency of 10-100 Hz [27] and some cameras generate frames at 30-50 fps [30]. In practice, a large number of such cameras and sensors are used at each 3DTI site. For example, to cover 360^0 view, TEEVE [30] uses 10 cameras. To understand application behavior, it is necessary to monitor metadata of these multimedia data (video data, sensor data, audio data) and their behaviors along the streaming paths. However, monitoring media metadata (such as frame size, reconstruction time, resolution, frame rate, arrival time, arrival order) and system metadata (such as CPU load, memory load, bandwidth) at different nodes in the streaming tree at a high rate causes horizontal and vertical burst of information. To handle this, an unobtrusive monitoring framework is required.

In summary, the purpose of our work is to provide a session management and monitoring framework for 3D multi-stream TI environments. It includes constructing streaming overlay, monitoring configuration and performance metadata, resolving queries, learning application behavior at participating peers, detecting and localizing undesired behavior in run-time and finally adapting using cooperative resource provisioning. Each step in learning, detection, localization and adaptation considers multi-stream dependencies defined by the application configuration parameters.

2. GOALS AND TAXONOMY

Our high level goal is to support large number of concurrent viewers in real-time 3DTI streaming. To accomplish this, we observe the stream behavior in as much detail as possible in real-time and predict underlying environment using a learning framework for proper resource provisioning. The stream behavior includes: 1) subscription information of users, 2) structures (path information) of streaming trees, 3) time and ordering information of frames at overlay nodes, and 4) frame metadata. While 3DTI sessions are running, such behavioral information are stored in a Configuration Management Database (CMDB). The concept of CMDB is itself a novel technique used widely in large scale distributed system management specially in industry [23]. It serves as a Management Information Base (MIB) of the system and stores a complete life-cycle (or history) of participating streams. Furthermore, maintaining a stream CMDB removes the necessity of other monitoring tasks in the application that eventually impacts the performance. In addition we maintain a Performance Management Database (PMDB) storing the system performance of underlying nodes participating in applications. The goal is to correlated the stream CMDB and PMDB for efficient construction of streaming trees.

Logged metadata are used to identify the events effecting data plane and events affecting control plane in TI environments. Therefore, the logged information should preserve the *signature* of the original event (the way the event manifests itself on operation). In particular, there are three key cases: events may manifest themselves in the *data plane* (affecting how data frames are forwarded), in the *control plane* (affecting how forwarding routes are computed), or both. Many kinds of events trigger undesired data-plane behavior, including failures of links or nodes, congestion, and misconfiguration. The underlying cause of these events may vary widely: a node/link may fail due to hardware and software errors, overload, configuration errors or peer leave. However, all these events cause one or more data frames to be handled in a manner differently than the desired behavior (e.g., they are dropped, or they oscillate back and forth between paths, or loop between nodes). Hence a mechanism that can log frame forwarding behavior at the data plane would be sufficient to collect signatures of a number of such events. However, many events can harm the correctness of tree route computations within the network: route advertisements or stream subscription requests may flap due to internal or external instability (which can overload nodes), misconfiguration, or gateway software implementation errors. Even though the tree routes are computed correctly, the path delay among dependent streams may cause large skew (local or global skew) violating the consistent real-time view. However, in any of these cases, there can only be two kinds of effects on the system: either streaming tree becomes logically incorrect, or it becomes inconsistent with the values of the data plane. In either case, maintaining a log of control-plane information, and correlating them with data-plane logs, is sufficient to contain the signatures of these events.

However, doing fine-grained logging of stream behavior in large scales seems extremely challenging. We need to log vast volumes of state for storing timing and ordering information of frames and metadata of frames at each nodes, need to retain that state over long periods, and keep it up-to-date over time [3]. In general, monitoring architectures in such cases are composed of two levels. Level one uses fast indexing to collect statistics to allow faster query response, and the second level is used to store long-term logs. Compression is important at both levels for real-time and unobtrusive analyses and query responses.

The final goal is to provide human-centric adaptations (via overlay restructuring) in case of local and global skew in the system that could happen due to node/ link failures, or improper allocation of resources. Following the taxonomy in [22], we define three resource states at each participating peers: *surplus*, *normal* or *deficit*. When a system is running, it is not obvious to identify these states. To address this, we propose a learning framework by analyzing CMDB and PMDB. Stream dependencies are considered while reassigning resources to the system.

3. RELATED WORK

Recently, we have seen a lot of works in applying inference, learning and statistical tools to detect, localize, diagnose and improve the reliability of large scale networking systems. Bahl et al. [25] propose Sherlock that explores the dependencies among services, software and physical components in a large enterprise network based on network traffic, and uses such dependencies to identify and localize problems. A further study by Chen et al. [31] shows the performance and limitations of automated dependency discovery from network traffic. They propose Orion to discover dependencies in an enterprise network using the delay information between every pair of network flows. Mahimkar et al. [4] characterize performance issues in a large-scale IPTV network. They propose Giza to localize regions and physical components in the IPTV distribution hierarchy that are experiencing performance problems. In contrast to these application domains, TI streaming overlays are designed to be resilient by dynamically changing the set of views and sites. As a result, the flow or service level dependencies of DIMEs change from time to time. Recently, Niu et al. [22] propose a learning framework that attempts to characterize performance statistics inside p2p streaming to discover bandwidth states in media channels. Their work requires previous knowledge about applications to understand which metrics to consider for learning. This paper tries to learn this by conditional independence learning approach. The learned dependencies then can be leveraged to optimize system operation and forecast performance issues due to irregular demand patterns.

Peterson et al. [28] propose Antfarm, a BitTorrent-like P2P learning system based on managed swarms. When multiple swarms coexist, Antfarm gathers information on swarm dynamics and directs bandwidth allocation to each peer so as to minimize the overall download latencies. Wu et al. [7] also propose a server capacity provisioning algorithm for P2P live streaming systems, which proactively adjusts the server bandwidth allocated to concurrent channels, based on the demand and performance prediction. But they do not consider multi-stream dependency and hence p2p streaming trees are configured and adapted independently for each stream. Cohen *et al.* [17] used a tree-augmented naive (TAN) bayesian network to learn the probabilistic relationship between SLA violations and system resource usages. They further used this learned bayesian network to identify performance bottlenecks during SLA violations. Bodik *et al.* [26] proposed a "Fingerprint" approach, which identifies the problem with performance fingerprinting. The authors proposed a method to correlate key performance indicators (KPIs) with system SLA. Several other papers [5, 11] took similar statistical analysis approaches to diagnose problems from system monitoring data. Jiang *et al.* [14] developed an invariant-based approach to profile large systems for system management. But none of these works require real-time guarantee in diagnosis. Our goal is to leverage the knowledge of system characteristics to aid efficient allocation of resources in case of correlated multi-stream environment by using an unobtrusive and real-time logging framework. Moreover, our framework for learning channel operating rules have advanced the state of the art, as they focus on relationships between more detailed performance and configuration metrics in the system on a fine-grain time scale.

4. PROPOSED GUIDELINE

Considering our goals, we divide this work into several modules; metadata collection and answering queries, metadata analysis, learning, constructing streaming overlay and their adaptation. To collect metadata in an unobtrusive manner, multi-level compressions are used (as mentioned earlier). We propose a scalable and reliable architecture [3] that uses aggregation-based "compression" techniques to reduce the amount of storage required (at both levels) to analyze application behavior. The application is originally proposed to monitor Internet scale traffic inside ISP (Internet Service Provider) routers, but the solution is also applicable to DIMEs containing large number of gateways and components (such as cameras, microphones, sensors, etc.). The main idea is to exploit common properties across logs and compress the log by removing them. Experimental results show that our compression scheme in system nodes as well as in the central storage reduce the log size by an order of magnitude yet achieves 99% accuracy in capturing events.

Our earlier results in [1] show that instead of storing metadata in a particular location, the query latency can be improved by distributing them using an index structure for faster lookup. The purpose of the index structure is to localize the metadata to be searched to answer the query. We build a range based indexing tree for querying purpose while a TI session is running. Only one tree is created for all metadata. Queries such as "cameras who are running with frame rate between 15 to 20 fps","How many number of cameras are ON at Site-2?" "How many viewers are requesting stream 128.174.247.97?", "How many streams Viewer-2 requests?", "What is the average frame size of the system" etc. can be answered within a second using this query architecture.

To explore linear dependencies among metadata we proposed DIAMOND [2]. It tries to detect undesired behavior of the system by identifying the violation in correlations of collected metadata in a compressed form. It works very well in some cases. For example, in our tele-immersive setup, we observed a violation of expected positive correlation between sending and receiving stream rate at the application level between two distance sites while using DCCP communication protocol even though we observed sufficient network bandwidth. These observations localized the possible errors in the underlying system-level and we identified bounded queue lengths in our LINUX kernel that caused the frame loss. As DCCP allows frame drop, violation of dependency equations at any single point in time is not significant. Without detecting the existence of linear correlations, it is hard to localize such unwanted behavior alone while the system is running. Experiments show that DIAMOND is very lightweight and efficient for exploring linear dependencies. Similar dependencies can be found in camera streams of the same view, camera streams participating in synchronized activities, sending and receiving frame size and so on.

However having linear dependency is not always a practical assumption in a general setup. Therefore, to understand both linear and non-linear dependency relations among metadata, our goal is to use a learning framework. The objective of this framework is to provide a Grainger mixed graph [12] of all metadata. Once we know the graph, we can build a multi-dimensional online profiler considering the learned dependencies. The undesired behavior can be detected in two ways; by analyzing data and control plan events and by identifying outliers in the profiler, which implies violation of dependencies. The solution needs to define separate regions representing surplus, deficit and normal state of resource variables on different parts of the system for reallocation purpose.

Finally we propose a hybrid (CDN-p2p) overlay architecture for supporting large number of concurrent viewers by efficient allocation of network and host resources. To allow consistency in views while supporting large number of viewers, 3DTI requires cooperative resource provisioning considering CMDB, PMDB and the dependencies learned in the learning phase.

5. CONCLUSION

My thesis goal is to provide a learning based session monitoring and management for large scale tele-immersive environments. We consider scalability in terms of number of metadata and number of participating sites (and number of components per site). A hybrid structure and multi-stream dependencies are considered in the construction of overlay structure with efficient resource provisioning. We introduce the notion of "stream CMDB" that works as a MIB for managing TI applications. Further investigations need to be done to understand the learned dependencies and their applicability in resource provisioning of TI applications.

6. REFERENCES

[1] A. Arefin *et al.* Q-tree: A multi-attribute based range query solution for tele-immersive framework. In *Proc. of ICDCS*, 2009.

[2] A. Arefin *et al.* Diamond: A correlation-based anomaly monitoring daemon for dimes. In *Proc. of ISM*, 2010.

[3] A. Arefin *et al.* Scaling data-plan logging for large scale networks. In *Proc. of MILCOM*, 2011.

[4] A. Mahimkar *et al.* Towards automated performance diagnosis in a large iptv network. In *Proc. of SIGCOMM*, 2009.

[5] B. Cook *et al.* Toward self-healing multitier services. In *Proc. of ICDEW*, 2007.

[6] C. Huang *et al.* Understanding hybrid cdn-p2p: Why limelight needs its own red swoosh. 2008.

[7] C. Wu *et al.* Multi-channel live p2p streaming: Refocusing on servers. In *Proc. of INFOCOM*, 2008.

[8] Cisco Telepresence. , http://www.cisco.com/telepresence.

[9] O. De and K. Patel. Coordinated multi-streaming for 3d teleimmersion. In *Proc. of MM*, 2004.

[10] Dongyan Xu *et al.* A cdn-p2p hybrid architecture for cost-effective streaming media distribution. In *Computer Networks*, 2004.

[11] S. Duan and S. Babu. Guided problem diagnosis through active learning. In *Proc. of ICAC*, 2008.

[12] M. Eichler. Granger causality and path diagrams for multivariate time series. 137(2):334–353, 2007.

[13] F. Daniilidis *et al.* Towards the holodeck: an initial testbed for real-time 3d teleimmersion. In *Proc. of SIGGRAPH*, 1999.

[14] G. Jiang *et al.* Ranking the importance of alerts for problem determination in large computer systems. In *Proc. of ICAC*, 2009.

[15] H. Schulzrinne *et al.* Real time streaming protocol (RFC 2326). 1998.

[16] Hp Halo. , http://www.hphalo.org.

[17] I. Cohen *et al.* Correlating instrumentation data to system states: A building block for automated diagnosis and control. In *Proc. of OSDI*, 2004.

[18] J. Bailenson *et al.* The effect of interactivity on learning physical actions in virtual reality. *Journal of Media Psychology*, 2008.

[19] J. Rosenberg *et al.* SIP: session initiation protocol (RFC 3261). 2002.

[20] J. Schulzrinne *et al.* RTP: a transport protocol for real-time applications (RFC 3550). 2003.

[21] K. Nahrstedt *et al.* Next generation session management for 3D teleimmersive interactive environments. *Journal of MTAP*, 2011.

[22] M. Niu *et al.* Self-diagnostic peer-assisted video streaming through a learning framework. In *Proc. of ACM MM*, 2010.

[23] ONE CMDB. http://www.onecmdb.org.

[24] P. Agarwal *et al.* Bundle of streams: Concept and evaluation in distributed interactive multimedia environments. In *Proc. of ISM*, 2010.

[25] P. Bahl *et al.* Towards highly reliable enterprise network services via inference of multi-level dependencies. In *Proc. of SIGCOMM*, 2007.

[26] P. Bodik *et. al.* Fingerprinting the datacenter: automated classification of performance crises. In *Proc. of EuroSys*, 2010.

[27] R. Jafari *et al.* Customed: A power optimized customizable and mobile medical monitoring and analysis system. In *Proc. of CHI*, 2005.

[28] R. S. Peterson *et al.* Antfarm: Efficient content distribution with managed swarms. In *Proc. of NSDI*, 2009.

[29] R. Sheppard *et al.* Advancing interactive collaborative mediums through tele-immersive dance (TED): A symbiotic creativity and design environment for art and computer science. In *Proc. of ACM MM Interactive Arts Program*, 2008.

[30] W. Wu *et al.* Towards multi-site collaboration in tele-immersive environments. In *Proc. of ACM MM*, 2007.

[31] X. Chen *et al.* Automating network application dependency discovery: Experiences, limitations, and new solutions. In *Proc. of OSDI*, 2008.

[32] Z. Yang *et al.* TEEVE: The next generation architecture for tele-immersive environments. In *ISM*, 2005.

[33] Z. Yang *et al.* Viewcast: View dissemination and management for multi-party 3d tele-immersive environments. In *Proc. of ACM MM*, 2007.

Local Features for Partial Shape Matching and Retrieval

Ivan Sipiran
Department of Computer Science, University of Chile
Santiago, Chile
isipiran@dcc.uchile.cl

ABSTRACT

This PhD thesis proposal is focused on proposing solutions to the problem of Partial Shape Retrieval which is part of the Three-Dimensional Object Retrieval problem and represents a very challenging problem. Given a shape (or a part of a shape) as query, one wants to retrieve from a collection of 3D models those objects which contain parts visually similar to the query. Difficulties can arise due to the need of representing a model in a compact way with local information, where the extent of the locality is unknown a priori. In addition, the matching becomes an expensive task because of the large amount of possible memberships of the partial query in the shapes. Typically, assumptions are made to constrain the problem in order to solve it effectively. Therefore, partial shape retrieval is a challenging and open problem. In this document, we provide proposals to address this problem and furthermore, we discuss the open problems and the important issues that should be tackled in order to solve the problem of Partial Shape Matching and Retrieval.

Categories and Subject Descriptors

H.3.3 [**Information Storage and Retrieval**]: Information Search and Retrieval—*Retrieval models; selection process*; I.2.10 [**Computing Methodologies**]: Vision and Scene Understanding—*Shape*; I.3.5 [**Computer Graphics**]: Computational Geometry and Object Modeling—*Curve, surface, solid, and object representations; geometric algorithms, languages, and systems; object hierarchies*; I.3.7 [**Computer Graphics**]: Three-Dimensional Graphics and Realism; I.3.8 [**Computer Graphics**]: Applications

General Terms

Algorithms, Desing, Performance

Keywords

3D Local Feautures, Shape Matching, Shape Retrieval

1. INTRODUCTION

There is a growing interest in providing capacities to understand visual information to a computer. Coupled with this, the production of this kind of information has considerably increased due to the proliferation of cheap capture devices such as digital cameras. The same effect has occurred with 3D information due to the potential applications involving them in fields such as engineering, security, medicine, and so forth. A concern is how to manipulate and analyze this information based on its content. Unfortunately, it is difficult to compare the visual information directly and therefore we require techniques to handle it effectively.

Recently, there is an interest of the research communities on 3D information as an alternative to face some problems involving multimedia data. For instance, 3D shape retrieval and recognition may be used to support high level computer vision tasks such as human activity recognition and disease recognition. In addition, several applications have been presented such as geometric 3D comparison for shoe industry, 3D hippocampi retrieval, just to name a few.

We are interested in content-based 3D shape matching and retrieval, where the aim is to retrieve visually similar objects from a collection of 3D models given a 3D object as query. Most techniques presented for shape retrieval rely on the entire shape information. Therefore, they are not suitable to address retrieval tasks when the queried object is just a part of an object. This is commonly called **partial retrieval** and differs from classic **global** 3D shape retrieval in the way how the query is provided. In partial retrieval, one wants to retrieve objects from the collection which contain substructures visually similar to the query. Therefore, taking into account the potential applications, this is an interesting and challenging open problem.

This problem is interesting to address because it represents a generalization of the shape retrieval problem as studied so far, in addition to support more complex operations on 3D shapes. Furthermore, it is challenging because a partial similarity model implies that we can retrieve objects with parts similar to a given query regardless their tessellation, level of detail, or even whether the mesh is well-formed.

The main contribution in this research work will be to develop robust approaches for partial shape matching and retrieval using local features, with special interest in the feature detection and description step. We hypothesize that by detecting robust local features, the matching process can be performed effectively. In addition, with only a few robust features, less information needs to be considered for the feature description and the subsequent matching step, thus making the whole process fast and effective. By robust, we mean that, as much as possible, our methods will not require strong assumptions about the meshes such as manifoldness and regularity (tesselations, level of detail, noise, etc.).

This document is organized as follows. Section 2 presents some previous works about local features, shape matching and retrieval. Section 3 describes our approach to face the problem of partial shape retrieval. Section 4 provides details about obtained results and the ongoing work. Finally, Section 5 presents our concluding remarks.

2. RELATED WORK

Many methods have been proposed to retrieve 3D objects by global similarity. Bustos et al. [3] described a methodology for representing and comparing 3D shapes. The authors surveyed a plethora of methods and presented experimental results comparing several representations where the Depth Buffer descriptor showed the best results. Iyer et al. [11] and Tangelder et al. [18] also discussed techniques for 3D object retrieval, identifying future trends and important issues to be addressed.

For partial shape retrieval, some attempts have also been presented so far. Gal and Cohen-Or [9] proposed to represent a 3D object as a set of salient geometric features. The method involved to cluster vertices with high curvature subject to an empirical measure. The set of clusters constitutes the Salient Geometric Features. These features were organized in a geometric hash table and the matching was intended to find the best geometric transformation between features from query objects and stored objects. Toldo et al. [19] proposed to segment a given mesh and build a descriptor for each segment. Subsequently, a Bag-of-Features approach combined all the descriptors into a descriptor for each mesh.

Hu and Hua [10] detected and described interest points using a eigen-decomposition of the Laplace-Beltrami operator. The mathing was modeled as an Integer Quadratic Problem where two set of local features were involved. Similarly, Bronstein et al. [14] recently proposed the Shape Google method. It calculates robust descriptors (Heat Kernel Signatures - HKS) for each vertex in a mesh. Subsequently, the method applies a Bag-of-Features approach to compute a mesh descriptor. The matching is performed by measuring the distance between two Bag-of-Features descriptors.

Obviously, the use of local features is important to perform a robust partial shape matching. In addition, due to their importance, local features methods have been extensively studied, independently to the matching task. Thus, several approaches have been proposed in order to detect and describe local features on meshes.

On the one hand, local feature detection methods are intended to select relevant local information which is uncommon on the mesh. Several methods have trying to adapt feature detection methods from images such as DoG [4, 21, 20]. Differently, methods based on an eigen-decomposition of the Laplace-Beltrami operator have showed to be robust [10, 17]. Recently, Bronstein et al. [2] presented a benchmark for feature detection with evaluations of some aforementioned methods.

On the other hand, local feature description methods try to find a representation which encodes the locality of a feature. Early efforts to accomplish this task were the point signature [5], spin images [12], and 3D shape contexts [8]. More recently, Zaharescu et al. [20] proposed an extension of HOG descriptor to 3D. Differently, Heat Kernel Signatures [17] and local Laplace-Beltrami spectrum [10] have also proposed.

3. THE PROPOSAL

Although there are some proposed methods to deal with local features and partial matching, these work in restricted situations (for example, few vertices and manifold meshes). By using information of curvature or the Laplace-Beltrami operator, shapes need to be well-formed (manifolds) in order to use them robustly for matching. Generally,we need to preprocess the meshes which fall into an extra time. In order to maintain the efficiency in matching tasks, it should not be necesssary to make any assumption about well-formed meshes.

In this regard, our work is focused on extracting local features from meshes, as much as possible, without any assumption about them. Furthermore, we also are interested in efficiency, so there is a non-trivial challenge to address.

To address the problem of Partial Shape Retrieval, we plan to proceed in three stages which we describe following. Figure 1 shows the pipeline of the proposal.

- **Local Features Detection:** Two main issues are the support to multi-scale and non-manifoldness. Our work will be focused on proposing new robust feature detection techniques. A first attempt will be consider a smooth auto-correlation geometric function in a multi-scale way. We plan to compare our method against techniques from the state of the art such as Heat Kernel Signatures.

- **Local Features Description:** With detected multi-scale information from meshes, in this stage we plan to investigate appearance-based local descriptors. This is because we are interested in maintaining the robustsness against the lack of regularity on meshes. In addition, we hypothesize that local appearance is a possible way to deal with shapes in a robust manner. Because the geometry can be altered due to noise, change of tessellation, and other transformations, it is not reliable for describing any shape. The insight behind our proposal is based on the success obtained with descriptors such as Depth Buffer in global retrieval We plan to compare the proposed methods with techniques from the state of the art such as Heat Kernel Signatures, 3D shape context, spin images, etc.

- **Matching:** In this stage, we plan to adapt known matching methods within our framework. Particularly, matching by optimization and the effective application of the signature quadratic form distance will be investigated.

3.1 Methodology

In order to perform the evaluation, we plan to proceed in a stage-wise manner. It is worth noting that performing an evaluation in this way, we can evaluate the robustness of each stage. Our hypothesis is that robust detection and description methods will lead to an effective matching.

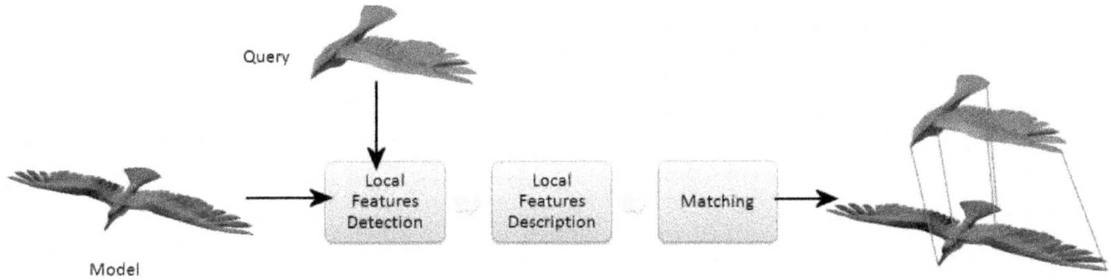

Figure 1: Processes involved in our proposal.

3.1.1 *Feature Detection*

For the evaluation of the proposed methods, we will consider three standard benchmarks:

- SHREC'2010 and SHREC'2011 [2, 1] - robust feature detection and description benchmark: based on the repeatability criterion under several transformations such as noise, sampling, tesselations, etc.

  These collections contain a set of shapes with different transformations depending of some issues to be evaluated such as different levels of detail, topology changes, scale, noise, and so on. On the other hand, the measure commonly used to evaluate feature selection tasks is the *repeatability criterion* [2]. Given two shapes X and Y, there will be a set of correspondences $C(X,Y)$ such that for each point $x \in X$ (untransformed shape), there is a corresponding point $y \in Y$ (transformed shape). The benchmark will provide the information about correspondences. For a set of feature points $F(Y)$, the repeatability with respect to the shape X is defined as:

  $$R(Y,X) = \frac{|F_{R,X}(Y)|}{|F(Y)|} \tag{1}$$

  where

  $$F_{R,X}(Y) = \{y_k \in F(Y) : F(X) \cap B_R(x_k) \neq \emptyset, (x_k, y_k) \in C(X,Y)\} \tag{2}$$

  and $B_R(x_k) = \{x \in X : geodesic(x, x_k) \leq R\}$. The parameter R defines how large is the neighborhood around the corresponding point in order to find an equivalent interest point. Therefore, the quality of feature detection is evaluated between an untransformed shape X and a transformed shape Y as $(R(X,Y) + R(Y,X))/2$.

- Dutagaci et al. [6]: based on measuring the localization error of interest points based on user information.

3.1.2 *Feature Description*

For the evaluation of the proposed methods, we will consider the following benchmark:

- SHREC'2010 [2] - robust feature detection and description benchmark: based on average distance between descriptors of corresponding points.

  In order to measure the quality of local descriptors, we will use an average normalized L_2 distance between the descriptors in corresponding points, as follows:

  $$Q(X,Y) = \frac{1}{|F(X)|} \sum_{k=1}^{|F(X)|} \frac{\|f(y_k) - g(x_j)\|_2}{\|f(y_k)\|_2 + \|g(x_j)\|_2} \tag{3}$$

  where $(x_j, y_k) \in C(X,Y)$, $f(.)$ and $g(.)$ are local descriptors.

3.1.3 *Matching*

For the evaluation of this stage, we will consider the following dataset:

- SHREC'2009 Partial Shape Retrieval Benchmark [7]: dataset with partial queries extracted from objects in the collection.

In addition, we will create a standard dataset to evaluate partial similarity retrieval methods. The idea is to provide a benchmark with a considerable size in both the test set and the query set.

To evaluate shape retrieval methods, it is commonly accepted by the community to use *information retrieval measures* such as *precision* vs *recall* graphs, R-Precision, and so forth.

4. RESULTS AND PROGRESS

To date, we have presented important advances in local feature detection. We have proposed the **Harris3D** method, which has shown to be very robust taking into account two aspects: repeatability and localization of local features. A list of contributions follows:

- A method for 3D interest points detection. A description has been presented in a paper in *3DOR'2010 (Eurographics Workshop on 3D Object Retrieval)* [15] and a complete evaluation has been submitted to The Visual Computer Journal which is under minor revision [16]. The method selects interest points based on the application of an auto-correlation function to local patches centered on a vertex. The advantage of our method is that it works with any kind of meshes and it supports severe transformations such as noise and topological changes.

- Evaluations have been presented in *SHREC'2010 and SHREC'2011 feature detection and description bechmarks* [2, 1].

- Application of Harris 3D for matching of non-rigid shapes has been presented in *SHREC'2011 shape retrieval on Non-Rigid 3D Watertight Meshes* [13].

Currently, we are working on proposing a multi-scale extension for Harris 3D interest points. In addition, we are investigating the extraction of region of interest based on Harris responses. Furthermore, we are investigating the extraction of local views from interest points in order to describe them robustly.

5. CONCLUDING REMARKS

From the state of the art shown in this document, it is clear that the partial shape matching and retrieval is still an open problem which requires attention owing to the potential applications that might arise. Certainly, the problem is challenging and difficult, however, we believe that by properly using local information on shapes, good results can be expected. In addition, as this problem represents a generalization of shape retrieval, we expect that our results can generate new interests in the research community.

Acknowledgements

This research project is partially funded by FONDECYT (Chile) Project 1110111, and CONICYT (Chile) through a Doctoral Scholarship.

6. REFERENCES

[1] E. Boyer, A. M. Bronstein, M. M. Bronstein, B. Bustos, and et al. SHREC 2011: robust feature detection and description benchmark. In *Proc. Eurographics 2011 Workshop on 3D Object Retrieval (3DOR'11)*. Eurographics Association, 2011.

[2] A. Bronstein, M. Bronstein, B. Bustos, U. Castellani, and et al. SHREC 2010: robust feature detection and description benchmark. In *Proc. Eurographics 2010 Workshop on 3D Object Retrieval (3DOR'10)*, pages 79–86. Eurographics Association, 2010.

[3] B. Bustos, D. A. Keim, D. Saupe, T. Schreck, and D. V. Vranic. Feature-based similarity search in 3D object databases. *ACM Comput. Surv.*, 37(4):345–387, 2005.

[4] U. Castellani, M. Cristani, S. Fantoni, and V. Murino. Sparse points matching by combining 3D mesh saliency with statistical descriptors. *Computer Graphics Forum*, 27(2):643–652, 2008.

[5] C. S. Chua and R. Jarvis. Point signatures: A new representation for 3D object recognition. *Int. J. Comput. Vision*, 25(1):63–85, 1997.

[6] H. Dutagaci, C. Cheung, and A. Godil. Evaluation of 3D interest point detection techniques. In *Proc. Eurographics 2011 Workshop on 3D Object Retrieval (3DOR'11)*. Eurographics Association, 2011.

[7] H. Dutagaci, A. Godil, A. Axenopoulos, P. Daras, T. Furuya, and R. Ohbuchi. SHREC'09 Track : Querying with Partial Models. In *Eurographics Workshop on 3D Object Retrieval*, 2009.

[8] A. Frome, D. Huber, R. Kolluri, T. Bülow, and J. Malik. Recognizing objects in range data using regional point descriptors. In T. Pajdla and J. Matas, editors, *Proc. Eur. Conf. Comput. Vis.(ECCV)*, volume 3023 of *Lecture Notes in Computer Science*, pages 224–237. Springer, 2004.

[9] R. Gal and D. Cohen-Or. Salient geometric features for partial shape matching and similarity. *ACM Trans. Graph.*, 25(1):130–150, 2006.

[10] J. Hu and J. Hua. Salient spectral geometric features for shape matching and retrieval. *Vis. Comput.*, 25(5-7):667–675, 2009.

[11] N. Iyer, S. Jayanti, K. Lou, Y. Kalyanaraman, and K. Ramani. Three-dimensional shape searching: state-of-the-art review and future trends. *Computer-Aided Des.*, 37(5):509–530, 2005.

[12] A. E. Johnson and M. Hebert. Using spin images for efficient object recognition in cluttered 3D scenes. *IEEE Trans. Pattern Anal. Mach. Intell.*, 21(5):433–449, 1999.

[13] Z. Lian, A. Godil, B. Bustos, M. Daoudi, J. Hermans, S. Kawamura, Y. Kurita, G. Lavoue, H. Nguyen, R. Ohbuchi, Y. Ohishi, F. Porikli, M. Reuter, I. Sipiran, D. Smeets, P. Suetens, H. Tabia, and D. Vandermeulen. SHREC'11 track: Shape retrieval on non-rigid 3d watertight meshes. In *Proc. Workshop on 3D Object Retrieval (3DOR'11)*. Eurographics Association, 2011. To appear.

[14] M. Ovsjanikov, A. M. Bronstein, L. J. Guibas, and M. M. Bronstein. Shape google: a computer vision approach to invariant shape retrieval. In *Proc. Workshop on Non-Rigid Shape Anal. and Deform. Image Alignment(NORDIA)*, 2009.

[15] I. Sipiran and B. Bustos. A robust 3D interest points detector based on harris operator. In *Proc. Eurographics 2010 Workshop on 3D Object Retrieval (3DOR'10)*, pages 7–14. Eurographics Association, 2010.

[16] I. Sipiran and B. Bustos. Harris 3D: A robust extension of the harris operator for interest point detection on 3D meshes. *The Visual Computer Journal. In review process.*, 2011.

[17] J. Sun, M. Ovsjanikov, and L. J. Guibas. A concise and provably informative multi-scale signature based on heat diffusion. *Comput. Graph. Forum*, 28(5), 2009.

[18] J. W. H. Tangelder and R. C. Veltkamp. A survey of content based 3D shape retrieval methods. *Multimedia Tools Appl.*, 39(3):441–471, 2008.

[19] R. Toldo, U. Castellani, and A. Fusiello. Visual vocabulary signature for 3D object retrieval and partial matching. In M. Spagnuolo, I. Pratikakis, R. C. Veltkamp, and T. Theoharis, editors, *Proc. Workshop on 3D Object Retr. (3DOR)*, pages 21–28. Eurographics Association, 2009.

[20] A. Zaharescu, E. Boyer, K. Varanasi, and R. Horaud. Surface feature detection and description with applications to mesh matching. In *Proc. IEEE Conf. Comput. Vision and Pattern Recognit.(CVPR)*, pages 373–380. IEEE, 2009.

[21] G. Zou, J. Hua, M. Dong, and H. Qin. Surface matching with salient keypoints in geodesic scale space. *Computer Animation and Virtual Worlds*, 19(3-4):399–410, 2008.

Recognizing Clothes Patterns for Blind People by Confidence Margin based Feature Combination

Xiaodong Yang
Department of Electrical Engineering
The City College of New York, CUNY
New York, NY, USA
xyang02@ccny.cuny.edu

Abstract

Clothes pattern recognition is a challenging task for blind or visually impaired people. Automatic clothes pattern recognition is also a challenging problem in computer vision due to the large pattern variations. In this paper, we present a new method to classify clothes patterns into 4 categories: stripe, lattice, special, and patternless. While existing texture analysis methods mainly focused on textures varying with distinctive pattern changes, they cannot achieve the same level of accuracy for clothes pattern recognition because of the large intra-class variations in each clothes pattern category. To solve this problem, we extract both structural feature and statistical feature from image wavelet subbands. Furthermore, we develop a new feature combination scheme based on the confidence margin of a classifier to combine the two types of features to form a novel local image descriptor in a compact and discriminative format. The recognition experiment is conducted on a database with 627 clothes images of 4 categories of patterns. Experimental results demonstrate that the proposed method significantly outperforms the state-of-the-art texture analysis methods in the context of clothes pattern recognition.

Categories & Subject Descriptors

I. 4. 8 [**Scene Analysis**]: Object Recognition

General Terms

Algorithms, Design.

Bio

The speaker is a Ph.D. student advised by Prof. YingLi Tian, in the Media Lab of Electrical Engineering Department at The City College of New York, CUNY. He received his B. E. from Huazhong University of Science and Technology, Wuhan, China. His current research focuses on recognition of object, texture, and scene categories, as well as the development of computer vision-based techniques to assist visually impaired or blind people. His research interest also includes image processing, object detection, and developing effective image representations for recognition. His website is http://media-lab.engr.ccny.cuny.edu/PersonalHomepage/xiaodongYang/XYang.html

MM'11, November 28–December 1, 2011, Scottsdale, Arizona, USA.
ACM 978-1-4503-0616-4/11/11.

Building Low-Latency Remote Rendering Systems for Interactive 3D Graphics Rendering on Mobile Devices

Shu Shi
Department of Computer Science
University of Illinois at Urbana-Champaign
201 N Goodwin Ave., Urbana, IL 61801, USA
shushi2@illinois.edu

ABSTRACT

The recent explosion of mobile devices is changing people's computing behaviors and more and more applications are ported to mobile platforms. However, some applications, such as 3D video tele-immersion and 3D video gaming that require intensive computation or network bandwidth are not capable of running on mobile devices yet. Remote rendering is a simple but effective solution. A workstation with enough computation and network bandwidth resources (e.g., cloud server) is served as the rendering server. It receives and renders the source contents (e.g., 3D graphics or 3D video), and sends the rendering results (2D images) to one or multiple clients. The client simply receives and displays the result images. Using remote rendering for 3D game or 3D video rendering on mobile devices can solve both computation and bandwidth problems.

However, there are some issues with remote rendering 3D video/3D games for mobile devices: (1) *Interaction Latency*: The interaction latency is defined as the time from the generation of user interaction request till the appearance of the first updated rendering frame on the mobile client. In our application scenario, the interaction latency is mainly determined by the round trip time of wireless networks. (2) *Bandwidth*: Since we are considering the mobile devices using wireless mobile networks as the client in our remote rendering system, the available network bandwidth is very limited compared with the wired networks. The system design should consider the bandwidth limitation and try to minimize the network bandwidth usage. (3) *Real Time*: There are real-time requirements in our system design. The rendering rate of 3D video is determined by the recording 3D camera and the frame rate of 3D gaming depends on the game motion. The processing operations of every frame should be completed before the start of next frame.

My researches propose novel remote rendering designs to enhance the interactive experience of 3D graphics rendering on mobile devices by reducing the interaction latency. Different from conventional approaches, the proposed system applies no restriction on the network latency to provide low latency rendering services. Instead, the rendering server sends an image-based representation of the current 3D scene/model to the client. Once any viewpoint change interaction happens, the mobile client can directly synthesize the appropriate image using image-based rendering techniques.

The research problems can be summarized as the follows:

1. What image-based representation of the 3D scene/model should the rendering server generate in order to reduce interaction latency?
2. Given the real-time requirement, how does the rendering server generate the image-based representation of every frame efficiently?
3. What encoding scheme can be applied to compress the generated image-based representation to meet the limited wireless bandwidth requirement?
4. How can the remote rendering system with latency reduction enhancements be evaluated effectively?

This research started in 2009 and progresses of all topics have been made. For problem (1), our full paper in MM'09[1] proposed to generate two depth images as the image-based representation and use 3D image warping algorithm to synthesize the view at the new rendering viewpoint on the mobile client. For problem (2), our full paper in MM'10 introduced several computation efficient algorithms in how to select reference frames for 3D image warping. For problem (3), we have studied a novel video coding method by integrating H.264/AVC together with 3D image warping algorithm and this new coding method can potentially beat the state of art x264 in terms of compression efficiency in the scenario of real-time 3D game video encoding. The full paper with the latest research results has been accepted by MM'11. For the last problem, we developed a new metric: DOL (Distortion Over Latency) to evaluate the interactive performance of remote rendering systems by combining both latency and rendering quality in one score and the paper has been presented in ICME'11.

Categories and Subject Descriptors

H.5.1 [**Multimedia Information System**]: Video

General Terms

Design, Human Factors, Measurement, Performance

Keywords

Interaction Latency, Remote Rendering

MM'11, November 28–December 1, 2011, Scottsdale, Arizona, USA.
ACM 978-1-4503-0616-4/11/11.

[1]Please refer to my CV at http://www.cs.illinois.edu/homes/shushi2/ for publication details

Intelligent Query Formulation for Mobile Visual Search

Felix X. Yu
Department of Electrical Engineering
Columbia University, New York, NY 10027
yuxinnan@ee.columbia.edu

ABSTRACT

While much progress is being made in mobile visual search, most efforts are on how to improve search performance (precision, recall, speed) given queries. How to help the user form a good query has generally left unexplored. Successful mobile search should keep users in the loop and have the machine and user work closely as a team to solve the difficult problem - user provide fast feedback on the fly and machine does the data intensive analysis. Therefore, helping the user to form a good query has a great potential in improving the search performance. We describe a novel framework, Active Query Sensing, to provide interactive query formulation solutions for mobile location search. We also discuss new research directions addressing the important open issues of interactive query formulation for mobile visual search.

Categories and Subject Descriptors

H.4 [**Information Systems Applications**]: Miscellaneous; I.4 [**Image Processing and Computer Vision**]: Scene Analysis, Object recognition

General Terms

Algorithms, Human Factors, Measurement

Keywords

Mobile Visual Search, Query Formulation, Mobile Location Recognition, Content-based Image Retrieval

1. MOTIVATION

Mobile visual search is to search the target of interest like products, locations, landmarks *etc.*, by matching a photo captured by the mobile device against the reference database. Due to the content variance among reference images of the same target, and distortion added to the query image during the imaging process, in practice the search accuracy is still far from being satisfactory. Intelligent query formulation can potentially improve the performance of mobile visual search. For example, while searching a specific product, user and machine may work together to get the proper photography condition, and to select the most discriminative aspect of the object as query in order to find correct results .

MM'11, November 28–December 1, 2011, Scottsdale, Arizona, USA.
ACM 978-1-4503-0616-4/11/11.

2. APPROACHES

Part of my thesis work has focused on the development of a novel framework, Active Query Sensing [1,2], to address the optimal query formulation for mobile location search. Distinct from prior works, my research focuses on a novel aspect of improving the mobile visual search experience. We hypothesize that there exist unique preferred views for successful recognition of each target location. For example, some views of a location consist of unique "signatures" that are distinctively different from others. Other views may contain common objects like trees, walls, *etc.*, that are much less distinctive. When searching for specific targets, queries using preferred views will lead to much better results.

In Active Query Sensing, the first query, if unsuccessful (meaning the true target is not ranked as the first result), can be used as a probe to narrow down the solution space. This assumption is valid because searching one image will cost time and money: User will unlikely take junk image with no hope for finding the true target. Then a second query is selected by maximizing the discriminability across candidate locations in term of additional views. Two major components, offline salient view learning and online active query sensing are developed in [1]. Using a scalable visual search system implemented over a NYC street view data set (close to 0.3 million images), we show a performance gain as high as in two folds, reducing the failure rate of mobile location search to only 12% after the second query. This work may open up an exciting new direction for developing interactive mobile media search applications through innovative exploitation of query formulation.

3. FUTURE WORKS

Similar ideas and approaches can be applied to other visual search scenarios, such as product and object search. Another direction ongoing is to predict the query difficulty, which can be well incorporated into a new formulation of Active Query Sensing. In addition, imaging process causing distortion to the query image can be seen as a domain transformation process. Approaches of cross-domain image retrieval will be investigated to further address the problem.

4. REFERENCES

[1] F. Yu, R. Ji, and S.-F. Chang. Active query sensing for mobile location search. In *ACM MM*, oral, 2011.

[2] F. Yu, R. Ji, and S.-F. Chang. A mobile location search system with active query sensing. In *ACM MM*, demo, 2011.

Robust Image Representation for Efficient Recognition and Retrieval

Xia Li
Department of Computer Science
University of Texas at San Antonio
xial@cs.utsa.edu

ABSTRACT

Image representation plays an essential role in image categorization and retrieval applications. Images span on visual and spatial space. Encoding both visual and spatial information for effective and efficient image matching remains a fundamental problem in computer vision. The objective of my research is to construct a robust image representation for efficient recognition and retrieval.

Categories and Subject Descriptors

I.4.8 [Scene Analysis]: Object recognition.

General Terms

Algorithms, Experimentation, and Verification.

Keywords

Visual Codebook, Spatial Transformation, and Object Classification.

1. INTRODUCTION

Recently Bag-of-Word model (BoW) has drawn much attention, due to its compactness and the easy indexing. In BoW, visual words are desired to perform like the textual words to describe the image. Traditional visual words may suffer from large quantization error which has a significant negative effect on image representation [1]. The classical clustering method has to increase codebook size to reduce quantization error which however cannot ensure improved matching performance. Soft quantization [2], which implicitly reduces the quantization error by representing a local feature with multiple weighted visual words is good solution for this issue. However, the computation complexity of soft-quantization methods is expensive, especially for visual codebook with tens of thousands visual words. It has been shown that residual information contains extra discriminative power [3, 4]. But encoding residual often results in high dimensional representation which imposes heavy burden on the matching process.

Furthermore, BoW model discards the spatial order of local features, which limits its descriptive power for image matching. To make it robust against various transformations, noises, and occlusion, the image representation needs to capture both global and local information so that big intra class variance can be overcome to some extent. The previously proposed "subdivide and reorder" strategy reserves the finer level spatial information to achieve more accurate matching [5]. Although it greatly improves the matching performance, it cannot handle object transformations, such as rotation, flipping or translation. Matching on finer levels performs even worse than global matching.

MM'11, November 28–December 1, 2011, Scottsdale, Arizona, USA.
ACM 978-1-4503-0616-4/11/11.

2. METHODOLOGY

We propose a novel multi-layer codebook generation algorithm. The basic idea is to generate multiple codebooks by incorporating information from the residual space that is complementary to the one spanned by the existing codebook. It explicitly compensates the quantization error. The residual codebook can be constructed globally to be more general, or locally to be more image specifically. The proposed multi-layer codebook based image representation may benefit from: 1) simple clustering scheme, 2) explicit minimization of quantization error, and 3) efficient feature quantization. Experimental results on several benchmark datasets show that the proposed approach achieves better performance on both effectiveness and efficiency over the state-of-the-art methods.

Besides, we propose multiple spatial layouts to address different transformations. Experimental results show that our proposed spatial pyramid ring pooling works best for rotation and flipping variance. A refined version of spatial pyramid matching (Relative Re-ordered SPM) can improve the classification accuracy with large translation variance. Furthermore, the simplicity of the proposed representation makes it a promising potential for real time applications.

3. REFERENCES

[1] O. Boiman, E. Shechtman and M. Irani, "In defense of nearest-neighbor based image classification," *In Proc. CVPR*, 2008.

[2] J. Gemert, J. Geusebroek, C. Veenman, and A. Smeulders, "Kernel codebooks for scene categorization," *In proc. ECCV*, 2008.

[3] H. Jegou, M. Douze, C. Schmid, and P. Perez, "Aggregating local descriptors into a compact image representation," *In Proc. CVPR*, 2010.

[4] X. Zhou, K. Yu, T. Zhang, and T. S. Huang, "Image classification using Super-Vector coding of local image descriptors," *In Proc. ECCV*, 2010.

[5] S. Lazebnik, C. Schmid, and J. Ponce, "Beyond bags of features: Spatial pyramid matching for recognizing natural scene categories," *In proc. CVPR*, 2006.

Modeling Tagged Photos for Automatic Image Annotation

Neela Sawant
The Pennsylvania State University, University Park, PA, USA
nks125@ist.psu.edu

A semantic concept can be a physical object (e.g., 'car', 'zebra-fish'), an activity (e.g., 'demonstration', 'running') or an obscure category (e.g., 'historical', 'autumn'). In automatic image annotation, machines are taught to infer such semantic concepts by training with hundreds of manually selected images that contain those concepts. So far, remarkable progress has been made in the areas of visual feature extraction and machine learning algorithms that relate features to concepts. Now the new challenge is to scale the inference and annotation capacity to thousands of semantic concepts in the real world.

The key to large-scale machine annotation lies in automatic training data selection from user-tagged photos shared on social websites. To learn an annotation model for a concept such as 'car', one can exploit the fact that 'car' is also a common tag associated with photos of day-to-day activities. We may consider the concept to be illustrated by the collection of all photos thus annotated. The photos can be retrieved through a text-search interface and readily used to train the annotation model. While this seems like a straightforward idea, a few ramifications have to be considered:

- **Substandard images**: Tagging is an uncontrolled activity not geared towards scientific computation, but guided by personal motivations and communal influences. Tags may be incorrect or incomplete and some images may be poor examples of the target concept. Such substandard training images may hamper the annotation performance.
- **Modeling constraints:** As tags as well as visual features determine the quality of training data, a joint analysis of visual-textual features is necessary. Additionally, a diverse set of features need to be effectively combined even if some features are incapable of modeling specific concepts in the large annotation vocabulary. Efficient computing techniques and infrastructure is necessary to maintain scalability and adaptability to new concepts and training data.

We recently surveyed the application of tagged photographs for image annotation [2]. The literature was organized to address four main annotation types: (a) general-purpose concepts, (b) names of people, (c) names of locations, and (d) events. An important observation was that a majority of studies resorted to semi-supervised learning to annotate an unlabeled (or partially labeled) image. Specifically, content based retrieval techniques were used to identify similar images and a tag-ranking model was developed to transfer the annotations of the retrieved results on to the query image. Such data-driven techniques can potentially access an arbitrarily large annotation vocabulary. However, they do not conform to the idea of model-based vision and only work if large labeled image sets can be analyzed at run-time.

We adopted a supervised learning approach to large-scale image annotation where training data was selected from Flickr images [3]. The selection process was designed to reject substandard images. Annotation models were trained and stored for 1000 words, so that only pixel information of test images needed to be analyzed at run-time. The time required to select training data for a single concept from 10,000 images (634-dimensional feature) using a single CPU of 2.66 GHz speed and 24.4 GB memory was under 5 minutes. Also, the results as compared to a state-of-the-art annotation system showed marked diversity and accuracy.

The supervised annotation approach can only predict the concepts used in its training. In this sense, the approach does not cater to the preferred vocabularies of users. To address this issue, we developed a personalized tagging extension [1]. We proposed a transfer learning model to translate the set of machine annotations to a user's vocabulary using a Naïve Bayes formulation. The highlight of the technique was the computation of the translation model from the collective tagging behavior of the user's local social network.

In conclusion, the proposed research harnesses user-tagged images and social interactions on photo sharing websites to develop a practical image annotation system.

Categories and Subject Descriptors: H.3.1 [Information Search and Retrieval]: Selection process; I.4.8 [Learning]: Concept Learning; H.2.8 [Database Applications]: Image databases

General Terms: Algorithms, Design, Experimentation

Keywords: image annotation, automatic training data selection, user-tagged photos, social interactions

MM'11, November 28–December 1, 2011, Scottsdale, Arizona, USA.
ACM 978-1-4503-0616-4/11/11.

REFERENCES

[1] N. Sawant, R. Datta, J. Li, and J. Z. Wang. Quest for relevant tags using local interaction networks and visual content. In *Proc. ACM Multimedia Information Retrieval*, pages 231–240, 2010.

[2] N. Sawant, J. Li, and J. Z. Wang. Automatic image semantic interpretation using social action and tagging data. *Multimedia Tools and Applications*, 51:213–246, 2011.

[3] N. Sawant, J. Z. Wang, and J. Li. Large-scale image annotation using machine-selected tagged pictures. *under submission*, 2011.

Acropolis: Operating System for Real-Time Multi-Streaming Systems

Raoul Rivas
University of Illinois at Urbana-Champaign
Champaign, Illinois, USA
trivas@illinois.edu

Categories and Subject Descriptors

D.4.1 [**Operating Systems**]: Process Management—*scheduling, synchronization*

General Terms

Algorithms, Design, Performance

1. INTRODUCTION

In the recent years, Real-Time Multi-Streaming Systems (RTMSS) have become ubiquitous and examples are Distributed Interactive Multimedia Environments (DIMEs) like Halo, Tele-prescence, Teeve, Cave; Multi-view Peer-to-Peer (P2P) systems and Video on Demand (VoD) systems.

A RTMSS is composed of multiple capturing devices (e.g camera arrays), rendering devices and Content Delivery Gateways (CDGs). Each one of these gateways is responsible of processing, aggregating and disseminating multiple codependent and correlated streams, called bundle of streams, from the capturing devices in the RTMSS. The real-time nature of data streams imposes tight Quality of Service (QoS) requirements in terms of delay, bandwidth, jitter that require the use of specialized soft real-time support.

2. CHALLENGES

The multi-stream and multi-source nature of RTMSS requires extended synchronization and concurrent scheduling of each stream produced at capturing devices to minimize the skew between streams. For example, in a DIME, multiple cameras and sensors capture video, audio and sensory data from the local site, creating a bundle of streams. The bundle of streams is then distributed across multiple sites. Each of the streams in the bundle are correlated in time and must be synchronized and delivered with minimal skew between each other

In a RTMSS, different activities yield different data frame sizes and different data frame rates on each stream. Our stream based Operating System (OS) should be able to properly handle the elastic demand of computational processing in terms of job period and utilization.

Also as multiprocessor and multi core architectures become ubiquitous, our Operating System should be able to exploit the parallel nature found in RTMSS. Therefore our Operating System should provide mechanisms that allow soft real-time scheduling for these multi core systems.

Scalability is very important in RTMSS as the number of streams and data sizes of these applications increases considerably fast. For example, as the prices of capturing devices and sensors decrease and data dissemination algorithms improve, the number of capturing devices and physical sites within a DIME system will increase considerably. Our OS should be able to assign and multiplex system resources in theses multi core architectures efficiently with minimal impact from the number of streams or the number of cores in the system.

Finally, in a multi core architecture, some components might be underutilized depending on the specific use of the RTMSS. This can cause a significant waste of energy. Advanced power management techniques will be required to coordinate with the resource manager of the Operating System to ensure optimal resource allocation under power management constraints. Our Operating System will provide a coordinated resource-power schedule for all the tasks in the system.

3. APPROACH AND PROGRESS

Our approach to the problem is through th development of new algorithms, data structures, abstractions and interfaces not available in current Operating Systems. These include architecture redesign of the Operating System and replacement of some of the components with specialized entities on these Operating Systems.

We are finalizing a design of Zeus, a soft real-time CPU scheduling architecture for Content Delivery Gateways to support bundle of streams on multi-core architectures. Zeus allows CDG to obtain reservation-based CPU guarantees for each bundle based on its streams' QoS requirement. It supports scheduling of group of streams with dependencies and concurrency constraints.

Our future work involves a coordinator and I/O scheduler that allows reservation-based bandwidth allocation and coordinated I/O scheduling of each of the group of streams scheduled by Zeus.Our solution includes a Stream based Power Manager that globally decides power management policies for each of the components in the system. This modules use group streams as first class objects.

MM'11, November 28–December 1, 2011, Scottsdale, Arizona, USA.
ACM 978-1-4503-0616-4/11/11.

Human-centric Control of Video Functions and Underlying Resources in 3D Tele-immersive Systems

Wanmin Wu, Klara Nahrstedt
Department of Computer Science
University of Illinois at Urbana-Champaign, Urbana, IL, USA.
{wwu23, klara}@illinois.edu

ABSTRACT

3D tele-immersion (3DTI) has the potential of enabling virtual reality interaction among remote people with real-time 3D video. However, today's 3DTI systems still suffer from various performance issues, limiting their broader deployment, due to the enormous demand on temporal (computing) and spatial (networking) resources. Past research focused on system-centric approaches for technical optimization, without taking human users into the loop. We argue that human factors (including user preferences, semantics, limitations, etc.) are an important and integral part of the cyber-physical 3DTI systems, and should not be neglected. This thesis proposes a comprehensive, human-centric framework for managing video data and functions across the 3DTI pipeline. Our approach is comprehensive because it involves all components of the video function pipeline. It is also comprehensive in the sense that both temporal and spatial resource challenges are considered and tackled.

Categories and Subject Descriptors

H.1.2 [**Information Systems**]: Models and Principles—*human factors*; H.4.3 [**Information Systems Applications**]: Communications Applications—*Computer conferencing, teleconferencing, and videoconferencing*

General Terms

Design, Experiment, Measurement

Keywords

Tele-immersion, video, adaptation, resources

1. INTRODUCTION

1.1 Problems

This pipeline of 3DTI is severely resource demanding. Temporally, the one-way latency (or end-to-end delay from the capturing site to the rendering site) for interactive applications needs to be small (e.g., no more than 150 milliseconds), and the frame rate needs to be reasonable, preferably over 10 frames per second (fps), meaning that each frame has to be processed within 100 milliseconds. This is non-trivial because the operations that need to be applied on every frame (such as 3D reconstruction, rendering) are very expensive. We refer that as the **temporal challenge** in the environment. Spatially, the use of 3D representation and multi-view capturing leads to a high demand on network bandwidth, because within a stream not only color but also depth information is encoded and multiple streams need to be sent from each site for different views. With 10 cameras running at a pixel resolution of 320x240, a frame rate of 10 fps, 5 bytes for each pixel (3 bytes for RGB color and 2 bytes for depth), for example, the outgoing traffic alone could require $10 \times 320 \times 240 \times 10 \times 5 \times 8 = 307$ Mbps of bandwidth. Obviously, the resource demand directly depends on the amount of video data to process and/or disseminate. We refer to that as the **spatial challenge** in this thesis.

Great research efforts have been devoted to making the systems more resource-efficient (e.g., [1][2][4][5]), but the focus has been primarily on *system-centric*, algorithmic optimizations of the video functions or data reductions that leave end users out of the loop. Therein, resource allocation runs without considering the user inputs, preferences, or semantics. Data are not prioritized according to user needs but rather treated equally for resource competition. Trade-offs among different Quality-of-Service (QoS) metrics are not carefully examined in terms of their impact on the overall perceived quality or Quality-of-Experience (QoE) of users. Such approaches are inherently limited because the human factors - an important and integral part of cyber-physical tele-immersive environments - are neglected.

Without more intelligent data adaptation and accompanying algorithms for controlling video functions, immersive 3DTI communication would not be possible with today's hardware and communication infrastructure. The immense amount of data generated from multi-view cameras in each site causes long computing delay, hurdling the interactivity (e.g., frame rate) of the systems. It also causes network congestion that in turn causes packet loss (flickering or freezing effect on the display), prolonged network delay (inconsistency across sites), and decreased or unstable frame rate, all of which negatively impact user experience. In order to promote the overall system performance and eventually the overall perceived quality, we must develop intelligent and efficient adaptation schemes on tele-immersive video data.

However, this is a grand challenge with three main unanswered research questions. First, how do we reduce/adapt data to address the temporal and spatial challenges aforementioned in a way that does not hurt perceived visual quality but actually improves it? Eliminating data is beneficial for lessening resource load, but it intuitively comes

MM'11, November 28–December 1, 2011, Scottsdale, Arizona, USA.
ACM 978-1-4503-0616-4/11/11.

at the cost of sacrificing visual quality as e.g., details are removed, resolutions are down-sampled. How do we intelligently reduce/adapt data to achieve better perceived quality for users? Second, how do we improve performance of the systems given the stringent resource constraint? Efforts to improve qualities in 3DTI are largely complicated by the dire demand on temporal and spatial resources even with data reduced. For example, in a work we show how resource constraints render the data dissemination problem to be NP-complete. Then how do we efficiently improve qualities subject to the constraints? Third, how do we quantify user experience, and how does it relate to system performance? What is user experience? Does it simply refer to user satisfaction? Or is it equivalent to the perceived quality of video? How do technical metrics (e.g., frame rate, delay) impact user experience? How do we measure their relationships? We refer to this as the **quality challenge** in the thesis.

1.2 Our Approaches

Human-centric-ness. In this thesis, we take the paradigm shift towards the Human-Centric Computing (HCC) model in addressing the above research challenges. HCC represents a set of principles and strategies that "bear the human focus from the beginning to the end" [3]. Since the ultimate goal of tele-immersion is to deliver compelling experience to end users, we believe that taking a more human-centric perspective is crucial. We argue that human factors (such as user inputs, preferences, semantics, and limitations etc.) are an essential part of the cyber-physical tele-immersive systems, and should be carefully taken into consideration throughout the design, development, and evaluation process of 3D tele-immersion.

The HCC model empowers us to center our thinking around users, and make according design choices throughout the development and implementation of the systems. The instillation of human-awareness allows us to develop new approaches for managing the daunting resource demand in the complex cyber-physical tele-immersive systems. In the thesis, we demonstrate that by taking human into our control loop, we can have better understanding in various aspects of the 3DTI systems, such as (1) which image details are actually imperceptible to human eyes, thus unnecessary, (2) with the same resources, whether one should rather want lower frame rate with higher spatial resolution, or higher frame rate with lower spatial resolution, (3) which streams are semantically more important to users at a given point of time, and (4) which is more important: increasing the number of views, or reducing end-to-end latency (in terms of improving perceived usefulness of the systems).

This thesis proposes a novel, comprehensive, human-centric framework for improving the qualities of 3DTI throughout its video function pipeline. We make three major contributions at different phases of the pipeline.

Addressing the temporal challenge. At the sending side, we develop an intra-stream data adaptation scheme that reduces level-of-details within each stream without users being aware of it. It effectively alleviates the data load for computation-intensive operations, thus improves the temporal efficiency of the systems.

Addressing the spatial challenge. Yet even with intra-stream data reduced, spatial efficiency is still a problem due to the multi-stream/multi-site nature of 3DTI collaboration. We thus develop an inter-stream data adaptation scheme at the networking phase to reduce the number of streams with minimal disruption to the visual quality. It considerably reduces the data load for networking, and thus enhances the spatial resource efficiency.

Addressing the quality challenge. Finally, at the receiving side, we take a holistic approach to study the "quality" concept in 3DTI environments. Our human-centric quality framework focuses on the Quality-of-Experience (QoE) concept that models user's perceptions, emotions, performances, etc. It investigates how the traditional Quality-of-Service (QoS) impacts QoE, and reveals how QoS should be improved for the best user experience. This thesis essentially demonstrates the importance of bringing human-awareness into the design, execution, and evaluation of the complex resource-constrained 3DTI environments.

2. CONCLUSION

Despite great potential, the existing 3DTI environments are crippled due to a huge demand for computing and networking resources that are needed to maintain high interactivity (e.g., in end-to-end delay, video frame rate) and rich vividness (e.g., in video spatial resolution, depth accuracy) of collaboration. The main focus of this thesis is to improve qualities of 3DTI environments under stringent resource constraints. To achieve this goal, we follow the human-centric principle and focus on those perceptually important qualities, i.e., interactivity and vividness, for the users. Our methodology is human-centric as we leverage the semantics and constraints at the user level for the purpose of quality improvement.

3. REFERENCES

[1] H. H. Baker, N. Bhatti, D. Tanguay, I. Sobel, D. Gelb, M. E. Goss, W. B. Culbertson, and T. Malzbender. Understanding performance in Coliseum, an immersive videoconferencing system. *ACM Transaction on Multimedia Computing, Communications, and Applications*, 1(2):190–210, May 2005.

[2] M. Gross, S. Würmlin, M. Naef, E. Lamboray, C. Spagno, A. Kunz, E. Koller-Meier, T. Svoboda, L. V. Gool, S. Lang, K. Strehlke, A. V. Moere, and O. Staadt. blue-c: a spatially immersive display and 3D video portal for telepresence. In *Proceedings of ACM SIGGRAPH'03*, pages 819–827, 2003.

[3] A. Jaimes, N. Sebe, and D. Gatica-Perez. Human-centered computing: a multimedia perspective. In *Proceedings of the 14th annual ACM international conference on Multimedia*, MULTIMEDIA '06, pages 855–864. ACM, 2006.

[4] N. Kelshikar, X. Zabulis, J. Mulligan, K. Daniilidis, V. Sawant, S. Sinha, T. Sparks, S. Larsen, H. Towles, K. Mayer-Patel, H. Fuchs, J. Urbanic, K. Benninger, R. Reddy, and G. Huntoon. Real-time terascale implementation of tele-immersion. In *Proceedings of the 2003 international conference on Computational science*, ICCS '03, pages 33–42. Springer-Verlag, 2003.

[5] D. E. Ott and K. Mayer-Patel. A mechanism for TCP-friendly transport-level protocol coordination. In *Proceedings of the General Track of the annual conference on USENIX Annual Technical Conference*, pages 147–159. USENIX Association, 2002.

Analysis, Indexing and Visualization of Presentation Videos

Michele Merler
Department of Computer Science,Columbia University, New York
mmerler@cs.columbia.edu

ABSTRACT

The exponential diffusion of unstructured multimedia content on sites such as YouTube has lately fostered a rapid growth of interest in the multimedia community toward a new line of systems to recognize visual content "in the wild", that is, in less structured, unconstrained and more realistic domains. Due to the lack of structure and to the low quality of the data, algorithms and paradigms designed for professional content often cannot directly be applied to the aforementioned domains, thus presenting a new challenge.

One instance of such "wild videos" is represented by unstructured presentation videos, which are tools nowadays employed in a large variety of systems for different purposes, spanning from distance or e-learning to generation of conference proceedings, from corporate talks to student presentations.

We are interested in helping users efficiently and effectively access visual information, in particular technical information, and learn from such online multimedia sources. Our proposed system aims at summarizing, indexing, cross-referencing and browsing unstructured ("wild") presentation videos, with a focus on the quality of the produced indexes as perceived by the end users.

Categories and Subject Descriptors H.3 [Information Storage and Retrieval]: H.3.1 Content Analysis and Indexing
General Terms Experimentation, Human Factors
Keywords Presentation Video, Multi-modal Indexing

1. PROPOSED SOLUTION

We propose to index presentation videos based on four major cues: text (integrated with audio transcripts), speaker faces, graphics and mosaics.

Our system segments a video into semantically separated shots (each of which contains a different slide or blackboard image), automatically extracts the text from the content in the video (without any reference or electronic copies of the slides), builds a semantic index based on the obtained vocabulary of words, enriches such index with other visual cues such as diagrams and speaker faces, and finally represents the shot under the form of a mosaic image where the semantically relevant objects (text and graphics) are enhanced by highlighting and/or enlargement. In short, we want to situate emphasized content in enhanced context.

MM'11, November 28–December 1, 2011, Scottsdale, Arizona, USA.
ACM 978-1-4503-0616-4/11/11.

Figure 1: Examples of speakers face index automatically generated by the system.

We extract and recognize the text of the slides directly from the presentation videos in which they appear [2]. Experiments on 8 presentation videos showed that adopting our novel binarization algorithm, Local Adaptive Otsu (LOA), before applying the open source Tesseract OCR engine helped to deal with the low quality of the detected video scene text and doubled performances, achieving 0.534 Precision and 0.744 Recall Character recognition rates.

We employ an optimal combination of 3 user preference measures (skin ratio, 3/4 pose and resolution) to maximize matching accuracy between face tracks (extracted with standard face detection and a new steady-state Kalman filter augmented tracking) and to select humanly preferred face icons as representative images for each speaker[3]. Our system achieved track matching accuracy of 94.22% on 3 presentation videos, building face summaries containing 54 out of 58 speakers from 795 detected tracks.

Finally, we will assert through user studies the performances of our system in an interactive environment, the relevance of our enhanced representation of semantic shots and the utility of the controls exposed to the user. For example a user study confirmed that humans prefer the head and shoulders, 3/4 view speaker indexes automatically produced by our system (detail in Figure 1) over frontal, face-only ones. We will use the VAST Multimedia Browser [1] as a testbed for our experiments, since it provides a powerful tool where our contributions can be easily integrated.

Our system will allow users to search for a presentation of professor X on topic Y, containing graph Z, and interact with an enhanced representation of the retrieved video shot.

2. REFERENCES

[1] A. Haubold and J. R. Kender. VAST MM: multimedia browser for presentation video. In *CIVR*, pages 41–48, 2007.

[2] M. Merler and J. Kender. Semantic keyword extraction via adaptive text binarization of unstructured unsourced video. In *ICIP09*, pages 261–264, 2009.

[3] M. Merler and J. Kender. Selecting the best faces to index presentation videos. In *ACM MM*, 2011.

Towards Efficient Resource Utilization in Internet Mobile Streaming

Yao Liu
Department of Computer Science
George Mason University
yliud@cs.gmu.edu

ABSTRACT

Internet video streaming to mobile devices is challenging because of device heterogeneity, resource constraints, and limited battery power supply of mobile devices. From mobile users' perspective, we examine the power efficiency of existing streaming protocols, and propose to reduce the power consumed by data transmission. Moreover, from the service provider's perspective, we propose to efficiently utilize resources at server side to better serve mobile users.

Categories and Subject Descriptors

C.2.4 [**Distributed Systems**]: Distributed applications

General Terms

Measurement, Design, Experimentation

Keywords

Internet Mobile Streaming, Power Saving

1. MOTIVATION

Internet video streaming applications are very popular today. It has been estimated that video traffic will account for more than 90% total Internet traffic in a few years. In tandem with the increasing demand for videos, video access from mobile devices is also increasing. However, compared to their counterpart of streaming to desktop computers, Internet streaming to mobile device is more challenging.

First, mobile devices are very heterogeneous. On one hand, they have different screen sizes, varying from small-sized smartphones to large-sized tablets. On the other hand, mobile devices run on different mobile operating systems, and have different support for video and audio codecs. The heterogeneity in terms of both hardware and software requires videos to be customized to play on mobile devices. However, such customization process, also referred to as video transcoding, is computing intensive.

Second, mobile devices have limited resource compared to desktop computers, including slower CPU, slower and less reliable wireless connection, and limited battery supply. Among them, the limited battery supply brings an unique challenge for Internet mobile streaming. For example, if computing-intensive video transcoding is done at the mobile device's side, it will drain the battery very quickly. Moreover, continuously receiving video streaming data at the wireless network interface card (WNIC) would also consume a significant amount of battery power.

The objective of my research is to examine how to provide and receive video streaming services in a way that efficiently deals with device heterogeneity and resource constraints of mobile devices.

MM'11, November 28–December 1, 2011, Scottsdale, Arizona, USA.
ACM 978-1-4503-0616-4/11/11.

2. PROBLEM DESCRIPTION

Motivated by the inherent challenges of Internet mobile streaming, I propose to examine two problems for my PhD research:

- For a mobile device to receive streaming service, a large amount of power is consumed by WNIC for streaming data transmission. In order to reduce battery power consumption and increase battery lifetime, how should streaming data be transmitted?
- Since transcoding at mobile device's side would drain out the battery very quickly, now it is mostly done at the server side. In order to best serve mobile users, how should the resources at server side be efficiently used?

3. PROGRESS TO DATE

We present our initial study of state-of-the-art of mobile streaming in [1]. In this work, we have studied various deployed Internet mobile streaming services, focusing on the streaming quality and resource utilization including CPU usage for transcoding/decoding and battery power consumption. Focusing on the battery power consumed by streaming data transmission, we empirically examined four different streaming protocols that are currently being used in Internet mobile streaming systems [2]. Our measurement results show that streaming data transmission using peer-to-peer (P2P) protocol is among the least power efficient streaming protocols. Motivated by the measurement results, we design and implement power efficient P2P streaming to mobile devices in [3].

4. REFERENCES

[1] Y. Liu, F. Li, L. Guo, and S. Chen, "A Measurement Study of Resource Utilization in Internet Mobile Streaming," in *Proc. of ACM NOSSDAV*, 2011.

[2] Y. Liu, L.Guo, F. Li, and S. Chen, "An Empirical Evaluation of Battery Power Consumption for Streaming Data Transmission to Mobile Devices," in *Proc. of ACM Multimedia*, 2011.

[3] Y. Liu, F. Li, L. Guo, Y.Guo, and S. Chen, "BlueStreaming: Towards Power-Efficient Internet P2P Streaming to Mobile Devices," in *Proc. of ACM Multimedia*, 2011.

From Multimedia Data to Situation Detection

Vivek K. Singh*
University of California, Irvine
singhv@uci.edu

Categories and Subject Descriptors
H.5.1 [**Multimedia Information Systems**]:

General Terms
Design, Measurement

Keywords
Events, Situation Modeling, Detection, Social Networks

EXTENDED ABSTRACT

We are witnessing a phenomenal increase in multimodal human and device sensing to measure and report parameters such as temperature, vehicle speed, visual experiences, flu cases, and people happiness. Soon we expect these *heterogeneous* datasets (e.g. images, videos, weather sensors, check-ins and tweets) to become available in *real-time* in the *Cloud* for reasoning and decision making.

Important human decisions however cannot be undertaken by piecemeal treatment of these individual data points. Rather we need computational tools to ***integrate*** and ***abstract*** these data points into higher level actionable representations.

This underscores the need for computational tools to model and detect ***situations*** from large heterogeneous spatio-temporal data sets. In this thesis, we computationally define the notion of *situations* and propose a methodology to bridge the semantic gap between the widely available low level *spatio-temporal* data and actionable situation inference needed for decision making.

We define a situation as:

"An actionable abstraction of observed spatio-temporal descriptors"

This definition underscores our viewpoint of computationally defining situations based on statistical ***descriptors*** (as opposed to say situation-calculus or recognition-by-parts), a focus on ***spatio-temporal*** data (which is indeed the most common connotation associated with situations), scoping of problem only to ***observable*** (via human/device sensors) data, and a focus on ***actionable abstractions*** (as defined explicitly by human domain experts).

The problem of modeling and detecting situations from ***(STT) i.e. spatio-temporal-thematic*** data is relevant in multiple domains like traffic, weather, healthcare, business analysis, emergency response, and political decision making.

Situation Modeling
STT data spreads across very disparate application domains as well as data types. However, focusing on the commonalities and not the differences, we realize that there is a core set of operations which is central to defining spatio-temporal *situations* across different applications. Once a domain expert defines a situation of interest (e.g. a 'flu pandemic', 'hurricane advise') based on data sources, core operations, and user parameters, the same situation model can act as a standing query on realtime data streams and provide 'mass-personalization' to billions of end-users.

Just like E/R modeling, or UML we merely provide the basic building blocks. It is each domain expert's responsibility to define actionable situations by combining these building blocks. These building blocks are designed to be *computable, modular* and *explicit* and hence translatable into executable code once the modeling is complete.

Approach
Our approach for integrating and characterizing heterogeneous spatio-temporal data is based on the concept of ***social pixels***. We simply organize spatio-temporal values related to any theme on a two dimensional data grid. Such a grid provides heat-map like intuitive visualization, and also an *image* like computational data structure. Hence multiple spatio-temporal situational descriptors can be implemented as off-the-shelf image and video processing operations (Refer Fig 1).

(a) (c)

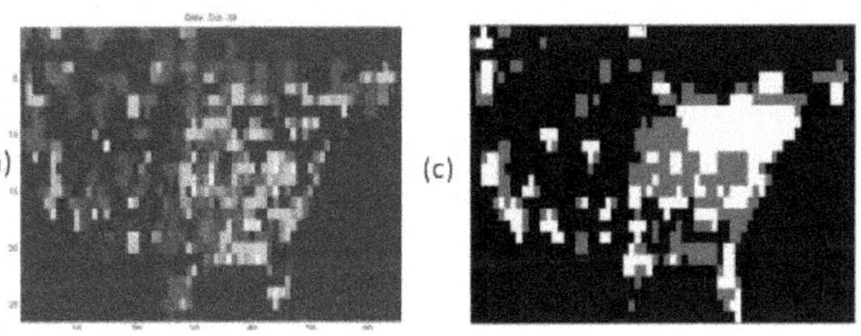

Figure 1(a) A representation for number of 'flu' reports on Twitter across continental USA (b) Data *segmentation* into high, mid, low activity zones

Current status
We have made progress in terms of identifying the generic set of situation detection operations [1]. We have run multiple experiments with STT data sets to answer situational queries like 'what recommendation to give to user indicating flu-like symptoms' [2] and 'where to open a new iphone store'[1]. We are currently implementing the core STT analysis engine which will allow modeling and detection of multiple situation queries across applications. We are also finalizing a methodology to guide domain experts when they model situations in terms of building blocks like data sources, characterizations operators, and user parameters.

* Advised by Professor Ramesh Jain.

REFERENCES

[1] V.K. Singh, M. Gao, and R. Jain, "Social pixels: genesis and evaluation", in Proc. ACM Multimedia, 2010, pp.481-490.

[2] Singh, V.K., Gao, M., Jain, R.: From microblogs to social images: event analytics for situation assessment. In Multimedia Information Retrieval(2010) 433-436.

The Building Blocks of Somatic Information Delivery

Troy McDaniel, Sethuraman Panchanathan
Center for Cognitive Ubiquitous Computing
School of Computing, Informatics and Decision Systems Engineering
Arizona State University
Tempe, Arizona, USA 85281
{troy.mcdaniel, panch}@asu.edu

ABSTRACT
With each technological breakthrough, our visual and auditory modalities are becoming increasingly overloaded with information. In this work, we explore the sense of touch as an alternative channel for communication for multimedia applications. We propose a novel theoretical framework, inspired by natural language, for the design of *somatic information delivery systems*, and validate this framework in applications of motor learning and accessible movies for individuals who are blind.

Categories and Subject Descriptors
H.5.2 [User Interfaces]: Haptic I/O.

General Terms
Design, Experimentation, Human Factors, Theory.

Keywords
Haptics, communication, somatic phonemes, somatemes.

1. MOTIVATION & PROBLEM
Our lives are inundated with digital information given its ease of access, particularly in recent years, due to advances in smart phone technology and wireless networks. Today's computerized devices and interfaces largely engage our visual and auditory modalities when delivering information. In this respect, our sense of touch is underutilized as an information receiver. By assuming that vision and/or hearing provide an optimal channel for information delivery, we have overloaded these senses, increasing distractions, cognitive load and even life threatening situations (e.g., reading a text while driving). Touch presents a unique challenge as a channel for information delivery: touch lacks the high spatial acuity of vision and the high temporal acuity of hearing. Therefore, a useful design framework is needed to ensure a low learning curve as well as low cognitive load. While related approaches in haptic communication, such as tactile icons [1] and haptic icons [2], have shown some promise and work well for certain applications, achieving a rich, expressive language through these frameworks presents a difficultly due to the use of arbitrary associations of meaning and lack of contextual cues, respectively.

MM'11, November 28–December 1, 2011, Scottsdale, Arizona, USA.
ACM 978-1-4503-0616-4/11/11.

2. APPROACH & PROGRESS
Our proposed approach is motivated by fundamental inspirations from natural language to improve versatility, scalability, efficiency and richness of somatic language. Our theory is independent of the type of somatic stimulation, which could be kinesthetic or tactile. Metaphorically, phonemes are the building blocks of spoken language, but languages may have different sets of phonemes. Similarly, there is no single set of somatic building blocks (which we call somatic phonemes or *somatemes*) for every application. Therefore, each application may have a different *somatic language*, composed of a very small set of *somatemes*, and another larger, but still relatively small set of *somatic words*. Somatic words are formed from somatemes, and designed such that they are distinct and intuitive based on the application. Unlike words of natural language, somatic words naturally convey their intended meaning, but are similar in that they convey a general concept that may be made more *expressive* with the use of context and "tone". Here, *context* refers to the environment in which the signal is delivered including the body site of the stimulation; and just as we have tonal variations in speech, *stimulation variations* provide a method for changing the meaning of somatic words by varying the signal at the word level. Lastly, somatic words may be combined, *temporally* and/or *spatially*, to create *somatic sentences*.

Thus far, the proposed theoretical framework has been successfully applied to add vibrotactile stimulation to two applications: motor learning and audio-described movies. In the former application, the framework was used to design distinct and natural vibrotactile saltation patterns targeting fundamental movements. In the latter application, vibrotactile cues were added to audio-described movies to improve their accessibility for individuals who are blind by conveying positions of actors across the screen and their distance from the camera. As part of future work, we are exploring motor rehabilitation and conveying facial expressions to individuals who are blind during social interactions.

3. REFERENCES
[1] S. Brewster and L. M. Brown. 2004. "Tactons: structured tactile messages for non-visual information display," *Proceedings of the Fifth Conference on Australasian User Interface*, 28, 15-23.

[2] M. Enriquez, K. MacLean, and C. Chita. 2006. "Haptic phonemes: basic building blocks of haptic communication," *Proceedings of the Eighth International Conference on Multimodal Interfaces*, 302-309.

Video Genre Detection Using a Multimodality Approach

Richa Tiwari
Department of Computer and Information Sciences
The University of Alabama at Birmingham
Birmingham, Alabama, USA
(001) 205-934-8669
rtiwari@cis.uab.edu

Chengcui Zhang
Department of Computer and Information Sciences
The University of Alabama at Birmingham
Birmingham, Alabama, USA
(001) 205-934-8606
zhang@cis.uab.edu

ABSTRACT
In this abstract, we introduce the idea of our new multimodality approach towards video genre detection. The two novelties of this algorithm are that firstly it is based on identifying relationships between semantic concepts and genres in videos, which can later help in distinguishing videos in different genres. Secondly, we apply topic level genre detection such as a 'talk show' genre can be further categorized as 'political talk show' or 'economic talk show', etc., which is a more precise categorization.

Categories and Subject Descriptors
H.5.1 [**Information Interfaces and Presentation**]: Multimedia Information Systems - Audio input/output, Evaluation/methodology, Video.

General Terms
Algorithms, Reliability, Languages, Verification.

Keywords
Video genre detection, video classification, multimodality approach, machine learning.

1. INTRODUCTION
With the advancement in video technology, the utilization of videos as a means of communication has increased. Oftentimes, it is much simpler to describe an event or procedure with a video rather than to write it down. And with the Internet being readily accessible and websites like YouTube becoming freely available for uploading videos, it has become much easier to communicate using videos. As the amount of video media grows on the web, the problems connected with any kind of large data set or media storage and retrieval also get associated with it. If we want people to view and communicate with us through our videos, it is important that those videos are visible to them or are easily searchable on the Internet. To make videos easily searchable, it is important that the video indexing is correct and precise. Genre based indexing of videos can aid viewers in choosing the videos to watch, in a more refined way. Genres help in deciding the content of the videos as well as the purpose of the video. Genres provide an important frame of reference, which helps viewers to identify, select and interpret videos. Videos annotated with concepts as well as genres can help users choose what to watch more effortlessly. Most of the work being done towards automatic annotation of videos is towards identifying the semantic concepts and content in the videos for annotation. In this work we propose to provide an algorithm that can help in annotating videos with their genres. This algorithm learns the relationship between the semantic concepts, content, and genres and then automatically identifies the genre for any particular video. Hence, our proposed solution can be divided into two tasks:

1) To identify relationship between concepts, contents, and genres.

2) To automatically assign genres to new videos based on the relationship established in the previous step.

We would like to undertake this task of automatic genre detection using a multimodality approach. Our approach will include all the three modalities, *Visual, Audio* and *Textual*, for learning genres and concepts in videos. A video can consist of multiple concepts and multiple genres. We would like to identify multiple concepts and multiple genres in the videos (although preferably a closed set of genres and concepts).

Once we have the concepts and genres identified in the videos, the next step would be identifying relationship between them. A video genre is a classification of videos such that the videos belonging to same genre share similar style, which is chosen by the director of the program, and a video concept represents semantics of the video content. A concept can be specific to one genre, i.e., it never occurs in other genres, e.g., *Anchors* appear only in *News Broadcast* genre. In a second case, one concept might occur in several genres. For example, *Indoor* or *Outdoor* can be in the *Home Video* and *Sports* genres. We can also say that some concepts are specific to one genre, whereas other concepts can occur in several genres.

We would apply a probabilistic model to find the relationship between concepts and genres (in the training set) and, given this model, we propose to automatically assign genres to any new given video (test set) based on the identified concepts in them. The model we will employ should take into consideration that there is more than one observation variable (the semantic concepts) which can lead to an output variable (the video genres). Usually most of the machine learning probabilistic models calculates conditional or joint probability of obtaining an output variable given one particular observation variable. In that case we can first find individual concept-genre relationships (probabilities) and then perform a fusion of those results. Or, we could also advance towards this problem by forming "association rules" between concepts and genre. Hence in this abstract we suggest a new approach towards multimodality based genre detection using the relationship between semantic concepts and genres in videos.

MM'11, November 28–December 1, 2011, Scottsdale, Arizona, USA.
ACM 978-1-4503-0616-4/11/11

Multiple Object Retrieval in Image Databases Using Hierarchical Segmentation Tree

Wei-Bang Chen
Department of Computer and Information Sciences
The University of Alabama at Birmingham
Birmingham, Alabama, USA
wbc0522@cis.uab.edu

Chengcui Zhang
Department of Computer and Information Sciences
The University of Alabama at Birmingham
Birmingham, Alabama, USA
zhang@cis.uab.edu

ABSTRACT
With the rapid growth of information, efficient and robust information retrieval techniques have become increasingly more important. Multiple object retrieval remains challenging due to the complex nature of this problem. The proposed research, unlike most existing works that are designed for single object retrieval or adopt heuristic multiple object matching scheme, aims at contributing to this field through the development of an image retrieval system that adopts a hierarchical region-tree representation of image, and enables effective and efficient multiple object retrieval and automatic discovery of the objects of interest through users' relevance feedback. We believe this is the first systematic attempt to formulate a comprehensive, intelligent, and interactive framework for multiple object retrieval in image databases that makes use of a hierarchical region-tree representation.

Categories and Subject Descriptors
H.3.3 [**Information Storage and Retrieval**]: Information Search and Retrieval – *relevance feedback, retrieval models, search process.*

General Terms
Algorithms, Performance, Design, Experimentation.

Keywords
Content-based image retrieval, multi-object retrieval, hierarchical region-tree, multi-resolution image segmentation

1. INTRODUCTION
With the rapid growth of information, efficient and robust information retrieval techniques have become increasingly more important. One of the challenges in this context is the ability to process, extract and discover semantically relevant information that may be embedded in visual data. The purpose of the proposed research is to develop a new visual information analysis, representation, and retrieval framework for automatic discovery of salient objects that are likely to be the user's query interest in image databases. This abstract will describe a content-based image retrieval framework which supports multiple object retrieval.

MM'11, November 28–December 1, 2011, Scottsdale, Arizona, USA.
ACM 978-1-4503-0616-4/11/11.

Multiple object retrieval remains challenging due to the complex nature of this problem. The proposed research, unlike most existing works that are designed for single object retrieval or adopt heuristic multiple object matching scheme, aims at contributing to this field through the development of an image retrieval system that enables effective and efficient multiple object retrieval and automatic discovery of the objects of interest through users' relevance feedback.

We believe the key to achieving the above goal is a new systematic and hierarchical representation of visual information, and a related analysis and retrieval framework that make it possible for a machine to interpret an image in terms of its containing regions and their relationships. In the proposed research, an efficient and accurate hierarchical image segmentation algorithm based on multi-resolution analysis will be developed to alleviate the over- and/or under-segmentation problems through the preservation of associative relationships between image regions as a hierarchical region-tree. This algorithm will be designed in a way to simultaneously produce image segmentation results and hierarchical region-tree representations, which are typically obtained through two separate processes in existing approaches, so as to reduce the time complexity. The proposed framework uses the query-by-example approach which allows users to search image database given a query image. With hierarchical region-tree representations, the relevance of an image to the query image is thus measured according to the proper sub-tree comparison. As a full comparison of all sub-trees is unlikely to be feasible, we will design and develop an efficient strategy for selecting and comparing proper sub-trees. One possible selection strategy is based on the assumption that nodes at a higher level usually reflect the dominant objects which are often users' interest, while nodes at a lower level often provide local details for the objects at higher levels and are more likely to be over-segmented regions. Based on these heuristics, the proposed approach will perform proper sub-tree comparison in a top-down manner and stop searching further down the tree when a certain matching criteria is met. Another key contribution of the proposed research is the integration of relevance feedback into the proposed multiple object retrieval system, which allows automatic discovery of the objects of users' interest and is expected to improve the retrieval accuracy through feedback-retrieval loops. While there is a clear indication of needs for such interactive learning capabilities, we believe this is the first systematic attempt to formulate a comprehensive, intelligent, and interactive framework for multiple object retrieval in image databases that makes use of a hierarchical region-tree representation.

Bilinear Deep Learning for Image Classification

Sheng-hua Zhong
Department of Computing
The Hong Kong Polytechnic University
Hung Hom, Kowloon
999077 Hong Kong, P. R. China
csshzhong@comp.polyu.edu.hk

Yan Liu
Department of Computing
The Hong Kong Polytechnic University
Hung Hom, Kowloon
999077 Hong Kong, P. R. China
csyliu@comp.polyu.edu.hk

Yang Liu
Department of Computing
The Hong Kong Polytechnic University
Hung Hom, Kowloon
999077 Hong Kong, P. R. China
csygliu@comp.polyu.edu.hk

Categories and Subject Descriptors
I.2.0 [**Artificial Intelligence**]: General *–cognitive simulation*; I.2.6 [**Artificial Intelligence**]: Learning *–connection and neural nets*

General Terms
Algorithm

Keywords
Deep learning, bilinear discriminant projection, image classification.

Despite more than fifteen years of extensive research, image classification for real-world applications remains a well-known challenge in multimedia area. But humans, even children, do not have difficulty with classifying images. Motivated by this fact, researchers in the fields of cognitive science and neuroscience have conducted pioneering work on modeling human brain using computational architectures. Among these architectures, deep architecture composed of multiple layers of parameterized nonlinear modules is a representative paradigm that has achieved notable success in modeling the human visual system.

This paper proposes a novel deep learning model called bilinear deep belief network (BDBN) for image classification. Unlike previous image classification models, BDBN aims to provide human-like judgment by referencing the architecture of the human visual system and the procedure of intelligent perception. Inherited from deep belief network (DBN), the architecture of BDBN is identical to the multi-layer physical structure of the human visual cortex. Moreover, in the primary visual cortex, all the way through the optic tract to a nerve position is a direct correspondence from an angular position in the field of view of the eye, just like a matrix. Therefore, the input layer and all hidden layers in BDBN are constructed by a set of second-order planes. Based on this new deep architecture, we propose a novel deep learning algorithm with three stages: bilinear discriminant initialization, greedy layer-wise reconstruction, and global fine-turning. The rationale for three-stage learning comes from the phenomenon of two peaks of activation in the visual cortex areas. The early peak is related to the activation of an "initial guess" based on the discriminative knowledge that has been acquired, while the late peak reflects the post-recognition activation of conceptual knowledge related to the recognized object. The greedy layer-wise reconstruction is a good simulation of the information propagation in the visual cortex, in which top-down connections can be used to generate low-level features of images from high-level representations, and bottom-up connections can be used to infer the high-level representations that would have generated an observed set of low-level features. Last but not least, we develop our deep model under a semi-supervised learning framework because of the insufficiency of the labeled images in real-world applications. The learning procedure is listed below:

1. The initial weighted connections are constructed between adjacent layers based on the discriminant information.
2. The size of the next layer is determined based on the optimum dimension to retain discriminant information.
3. The parameter space is refined by the greedy layer-wise information reconstruction.
4. Repeat first to third stages until the parameter space in all layers is constructed.
5. The whole model is fine-tuned to minimize the classification error based on backpropagation.

In the empirical validation section, three standard datasets, including Caltech101, the Urban and Natural Scene, and CMU PIE, are utilized to compare the performance of BDBN with other representative classifiers. The comparison classifiers include k-nearest neighbor (KNN), support vector machines (SVM), transductive SVM (TSVM), neural network (NN), EmbedNN, Semi-DBN, DBN-rNCA, DDBN, and deep convolutional network (DCNN).

In every dataset, BDBN shows the distinguishing classification ability with an insufficient number of labeled data. To Caltech101, we compare the convergence curve of BDBN with other deep networks. To the Urban and Natural Scene, we provide the real running time. To CMU PIE, we demonstrate the layer-wise information reconstructions of BDBN, which are useful to remove the noise in input images and lead to better classification ability. In summary, experiments on three real-world image classification tasks not only show the distinguishing classification ability of BDBN but also demonstrate our intention of providing a human-like image analysis by referencing the human visual system and perception procedure.

In conclusion, BDBN has demonstrated its effectiveness and efficiency in image classification with several attractive characters. First, the novel deep architecture simulates the multi-layer physical structure of the visual cortex and enables the preservation of the natural tensor structure of the input image in the information propagation. Second, the three-stage learning of BDBN faithfully realizes the procedure of object recognition by human beings, especially for the "initial guess" part. Third, the bilinear discriminant initialization of BDBN not only prevents the propagation of information from falling into a bad local optimum but also provides a more meaningful setting for deep architecture.

MM'11, November 28–December 1, 2011, Scottsdale, Arizona, USA.
ACM 978-1-4503-0616-4/11/11.

Beyond Video Searching: Summarization and Exploration

Song Tan
City University of Hong Kong
Kowloon, Hong Kong
songtan@student.cityu.edu.hk

Categories and Subject Descriptors: H.3.3 Information Search and Retrieval: Retrieval models

General Terms: Algorithms Performance Experimentation

Keywords: Video browsing, media content synchronization, event extraction, visual summarization

1. MOTIVATION

Nowadays, video sharing web sites are getting more and more popular. However, being mixed with large portion of noisy, duplicate, and irrelevant videos, it is difficult for users to reach the content-of-interest especially when the search intention is fuzzy. Commercial search engines, which emphasize the focus search of relevant videos, are incapable of dealing with this problem. This brings out two practical difficulties for general web users: 1) how to navigate the search results and quickly digest the key information from massive pool of returned videos; 2) how to mine the relationship among videos and come out with a topic structure that facilitates exploratory search. My research works address these challenges by seeking solutions that allow efficient authoring of search results for large-scale exploratory search. Specifically, the focus of research is on the organization and visualization of multimedia data by leveraging heterogeneous online knowledge sources. The ultimate goal is to develop a search system which goes beyond traditional fact-finding and presents search results that facilitate rapid exploration of information and easy switch of search focus.

2. PROBLEM DESCRIPTION

Organizing web videos faces a common obstacle - semantic gap. Unlike a book with subject heading catalogues which are arranged manually with suitable keywords by trained experts, the meta data of web videos provided by users are sparse and noisy. Furthermore, a video can comprise a lot more than thousands words. The textual descriptions from different users tend to subjective and each of them may present different views of a topic. Although recent advance in face-name association and concept detection allow more objective way of content annotation, these techniques are often limited and fail in producing satisfactory description.

With the rapid growth of social media, there are plenty of information sources freely available online for use. I address the problem of search exploration through hyperlinking the search results with multiple online knowledge sources. We consider two issues: uncovering the semantic themes of a query topic, and mining the essential content of short clips for matching the topic themes. The technical challenges include how to synchronize the diverse forms of information for hyperlinking, and how to leverage them to avoid conflict and information overload.

MM'11, November 28–December 1, 2011, Scottsdale, Arizona, USA.
ACM 978-1-4503-0616-4/11/11.

3. CONTENT SELECTION AND SYNCHRONIZATION

The proposed solution is composed of three parts: content selection, media synchronization, information visualization and interaction. First, given thousands of returned web videos, important segments of videos are mined by proposing techniques for rapid localization of partial near-duplicate videos. Second, the extracted segments are synchronized with online knowledge sources based on space-time alignment. In temporal alignment, important segments are picked out according to milestone events, and hyperlinked with timeline information available online. In spatial alignment, snippets are matched with a free-style wiki page at the sentence level. The important videos are then hyperlinked to the corresponding wiki page for cross-reference browsing. Third, different browsing systems that author search results with rich media information are proposed. They provide visualization in exploring information landscapes of a topic.

4. RESEARCH PROGRESS

I have proposed solutions for the content selection and synchronization of web videos. Three types of interfaces: (a) timeline based visualization, (b) wiki add-ons, and (c) galaxy browsing have also been developed for search exploration. Both objective and subjective evaluations have been conducted on a large video dataset for performance evaluation. I will present this work in ACM Multimedia 2011.

For content synchronization, currently only YouTube videos, Wikipedia and Google news are considered. More heterogeneous sources such as Yahoo! Answers will be incorporated in the future. Potential issues such as information extraction from diverse formats and content contradictory will be studied. In addition, more in-depth study will be conducted for information exploration and user interaction. In particular, we will investigate how to build latent topic structures from multiple knowledge sources, as well as devise effective question and answering techniques to facilitate user interaction.

Image Search 2.0

Xirong Li
Intelligent Systems Lab Amsterdam, Informatics Institute, University of Amsterdam
Science Park 904, 1098XH Amsterdam, The Netherlands
x.li@uva.nl

ABSTRACT

This abstract sketches my PhD research towards establishing a generic mechanism for exploiting social intelligence for next-generation image search.

Categories and Subject Descriptors: H.3.3 Information Storage and Retrieval: Information Search and Retrieval
General Terms: Algorithms, Experimentation, Performance

Keywords: Image search, big social data

1. PROBLEM STATEMENT

Image search is crucial for users with varying sorts of information needs. Applications of image search include personalized information delivery, cultural heritage preservation, knowledge representation, and forensic intelligence, to name just a few. The problem is scientifically challenging due to the famous semantic gap problem.

Traditionally, research on image search focuses on ingredients ranging from robust representation of visual content, semantic-sensitive visual rankers, to user-friendly visualization of search results. In this tradition, which we term *Image Search 1.0*, the image data itself is seldom recognized as the source of innovation. However, the world has started to collect massive amounts of user-generated data online. Social image tagging is making a profound impact on the way people manage and access visual content. We hypothesize the proliferation of social data will reshape research on image retrieval. After all, it is not just a matter of big data. Intellectual approaches are essential to conquer the ambiguity, unreliability, and sparseness of social tagging, and to aggregate the immense miscellaneous information scattered in the social web.

The main goal of my PhD research is to study the value of big data on the social web, to gain insight into their visual nature, and to obtain universal knowledge from the data for semantic understanding of visual content, for free. We term this *Image Search 2.0*.

2. APPROACHES AND PROGRESS

Given the subjective nature of social tagging, interpreting the relevance of a social tag with respect to the visual content is crucial for the effective exploration of social data. We propose a neighbor voting algorithm which accurately and efficiently learns tag relevance by accumulating votes from visual neighbors [3, 5]. In our best paper awarded work [6], we extend the algorithm to fuse multiple tag relevance estimates driven by diverse features. We clean up social data by tag relevance learning, and leverage them for tagging unlabeled images [4].

To bridge the semantic gap for retrieving unlabeled images, we need both positive examples and negative examples for obtaining visual classifiers. Along with our tag relevance learning approach to harvesting positive examples [5, 6], we study how to harvest negative examples from the social web [2, 8]. We show the potential of data-mining informative negative examples without the need of extra manual annotation [8].

Grounded on the above work, we initiate an image search engine which searches for the co-occurrence of multiple visual concepts in unlabeled images, fully driven by social data [7]. We study personalizing image annotation with respect to a user's multimedia tagging history [1]. We consider these two pieces of work as important steps towards answering complex queries for personalized image search.

In sum, this research aims to reveal the value of social multimedia, providing a generic mechanism to exploit social intelligence for image search.

Acknowledgements. This research was sponsored by the EC-FP6 VIDI-Video and the STW SEARCHER projects.

3. REFERENCES

[1] X. Li, E. Gavves, C. Snoek, M. Worring, and A. Smeulders. Personalizing automated image annotation using cross-entropy. In *ACM MM*, 2011.
[2] X. Li and C. Snoek. Visual categorization with negative examples for free. In *ACM MM*, 2009.
[3] X. Li, C. Snoek, and M. Worring. Learning tag relevance by neighbor voting for social image retrieval. In *MIR*, 2008.
[4] X. Li, C. Snoek, and M. Worring. Annotating images by harnessing worldwide user-tagged photos. In *ICASSP*, 2009.
[5] X. Li, C. Snoek, and M. Worring. Learning social tag relevance by neighbor voting. *IEEE Trans. MM*, 11(7):1310–1322, 2009.
[6] X. Li, C. Snoek, and M. Worring. Unsupervised multi-feature tag relevance learning for social image retrieval. In *CIVR*, 2010.
[7] X. Li, C. Snoek, M. Worring, and A. Smeulders. Harvesting social images for bi-concept search. *IEEE Trans. MM*. submitted.
[8] X. Li, C. Snoek, M. Worring, and A. Smeulders. Social negative bootstrapping for visual categorization. In *ICMR*, 2011.

MM'11, November 28–December 1, 2011, Scottsdale, Arizona, USA.
ACM 978-1-4503-0616-4/11/11.

Author Index

www.ingramcontent.com/pod-product-compliance
Ingram Content Group UK Ltd.
Pitfield, Milton Keynes, MK11 3LW, UK
UKHW051454290926
15471UKWH00008B/1201

9 781450 313605